Linda Paalanne

The **Rough Guide** to

Southeast Asia

written and researched by

Jeremy Atiyah, Stephen Backshall, Russell Briggs, Jeff Cranmer, David Dalton, Jan Dodd, Ron Emmons, Paul Gray, Charles de Ledesma, David Leffman, Mark Lewis, Simon Lewis, Jeroen van Marle, Steven Martin, Lesley Reader, Lucy Ridout, Henry Stedman, Andrew Stone and Carl Thompson

NEW YORK • LONDON • DELHI

www.roughguides.com

Contents

◄◄ Boracay, The Philippines ◄ Angkor Wat, Cambodia

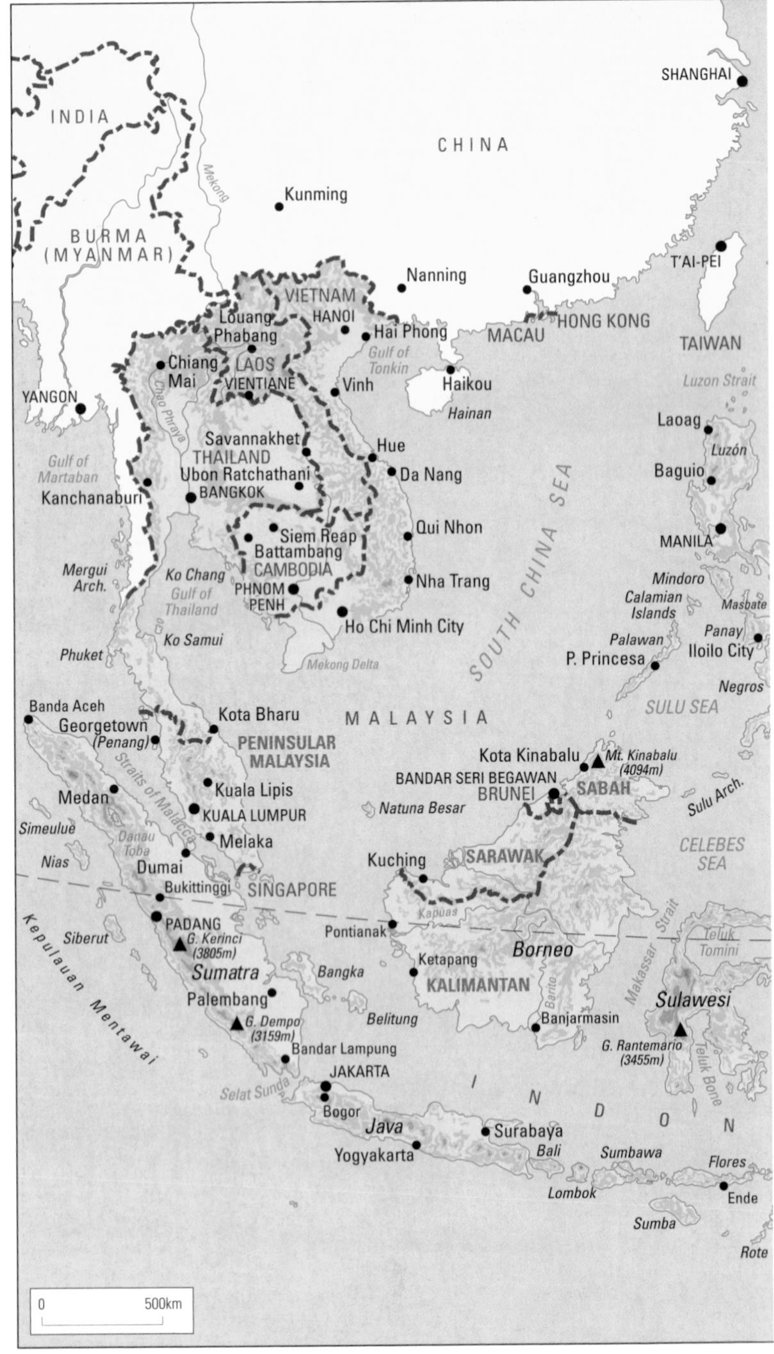
INDIA
CHINA
SHANGHAI
Mekong
Kunming
BURMA (MYANMAR)
T'AI-PEI
Nanning
Guangzhou
VIETNAM
HANOI
Louang Phabang
Hai Phong
MACAU
HONG KONG
TAIWAN
Gulf of Tonkin
Chiang Mai
LAOS
VIENTIANE
Vinh
Haikou
Hainan
Luzon Strait
YANGON
Chao Phraya
Laoag
Luzón
Savannakhet
Hue
THAILAND
Gulf of Martaban
Ubon Ratchathani
Da Nang
Baguio
BANGKOK
Kanchanaburi
SOUTH CHINA SEA
Siem Reap
Qui Nhon
Battambang
MANILA
CAMBODIA
Mergui Arch.
Ko Chang
Nha Trang
Mindoro
Gulf of Thailand
PHNOM PENH
Calamian Islands
Masbate
Ho Chi Minh City
Panay
Ko Samui
Palawan
Iloilo City
Phuket
Mekong Delta
P. Princesa
Negros
SULU SEA
Banda Aceh
Kota Bharu
MALAYSIA
Georgetown (Penang)
PENINSULAR MALAYSIA
Kota Kinabalu
Mt. Kinabalu (4094m)
Straits of Malacca
BANDAR SERI BEGAWAN
Kuala Lipis
SABAH
Medan
BRUNEI
Sulu Arch.
KUALA LUMPUR
Natuna Besar
Simeulue
Melaka
Danau Toba
CELEBES SEA
Nias
Dumai
Kuching
SARAWAK
SINGAPORE
Bukittinggi
Kapuas
Kepulauan Mentawai
PADANG
Pontianak
Strait
Teluk Tomini
Siberut
G. Kerinci (3805m)
Borneo
Ketapang
Sumatra
Bangka
KALIMANTAN
Makassar
Barito
Palembang
Sulawesi
G. Dempo (3159m)
Belitung
Banjarmasin
G. Rantemario (3455m)
Bandar Lampung
Teluk Bone
JAKARTA
I
Selat Sunda
N
D
O
N
Bogor
Java
Surabaya
Yogyakarta
Bali
Sumbawa
Flores
Lombok
Ende
Sumba
Rote
0 500km

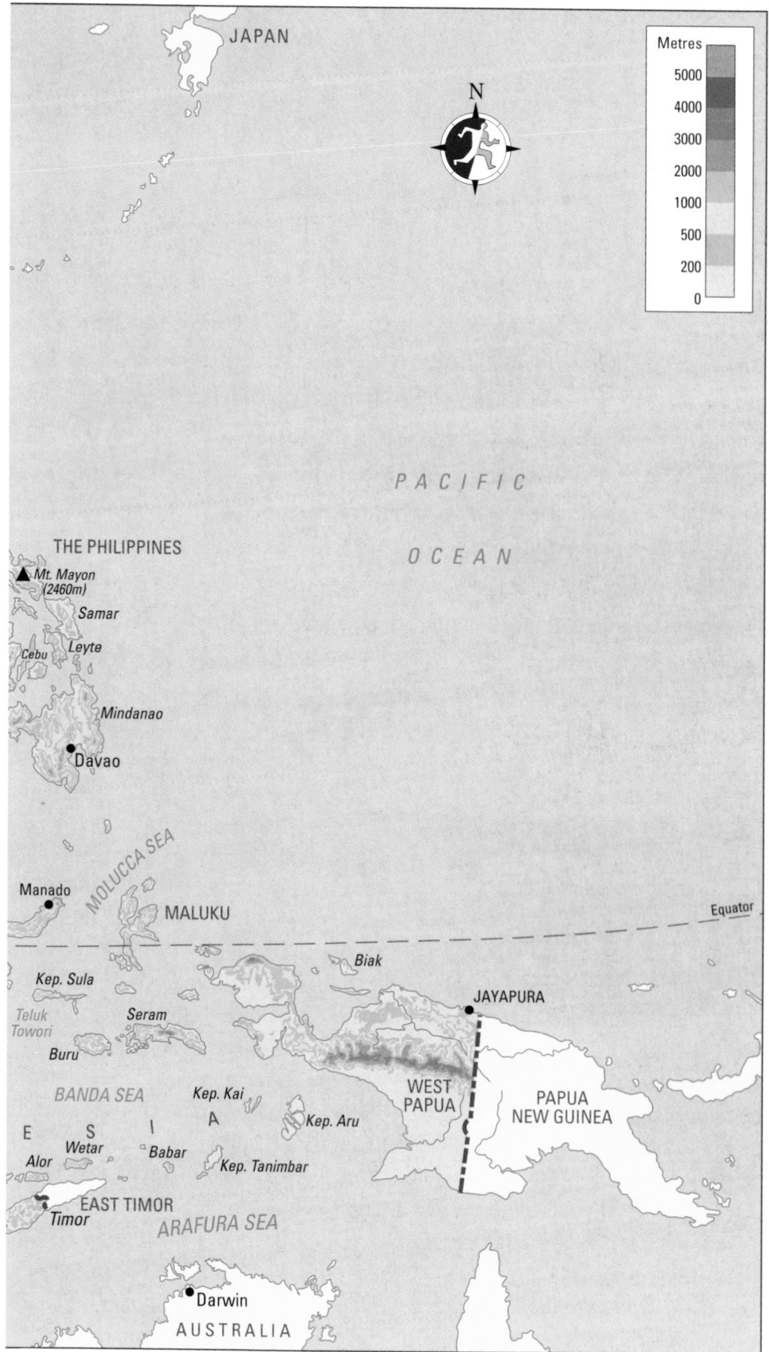
JAPAN
Metres
5000
4000
3000
2000
1000
500
200
0
N
PACIFIC
OCEAN
THE PHILIPPINES
Mt. Mayon
(2460m)
Samar
Cebu
Leyte
Mindanao
Davao
MOLUCCA SEA
Manado
MALUKU
Equator
Biak
Kep. Sula
JAYAPURA
Teluk
Towori
Seram
Buru
BANDA SEA
Kep. Kai
WEST
PAPUA
PAPUA
NEW GUINEA
E S I A
Kep. Aru
Wetar
Alor
Babar
Kep. Tanimbar
EAST TIMOR
Timor
ARAFURA SEA
Darwin
AUSTRALIA

Introduction to

Southeast Asia

Bordered by the Indian subcontinent to the west, and by China and Japan to the north and east, Southeast Asia is a tropical region of volcanoes, rainforest, ricefields and coral reefs, whose constituent countries – Brunei, Cambodia, Indonesia, Laos, Malaysia, the Philippines, Singapore, Thailand and Vietnam – together make one of the most stimulating and accessible regions for independent travel in the world. Here you can spend the day exploring thousand-year-old Hindu ruins, and the night at a rave on the beach; attend a Buddhist alms-giving ceremony at dawn and go white-water rafting in the afternoon; chill out in a bamboo beach hut for a fortnight or hike through the jungle looking for orang-utans.

In short, there is enough diversity here to keep anyone hooked for months, and the average cost of living is so low that many Western travellers find they can actually afford to be here for months. In addition, the tourist infrastructure is sufficiently developed to make travel reasonably comfortable and straightforward, and there are recognizable tourist trails that span the region. We have also included in this Guide sections on Southeast Asian neighbours **Hong Kong and Macau**, which are useful gateways to the region; we have excluded Burma (Myanmar), respecting the boycott on tourism requested by Aung San Suu Kyi, the democratically elected leader of the country.

The most popular destination in Southeast Asia is **Thailand**, and the vast majority of travellers begin their journey through the region in Bangkok, tempted both by the number of cheap flights from the West, and by the well-established backpackers' scene there. Thailand offers some of the best beaches in the world, as well as plenty of cultural stimulation, and has fast, inexpensive road and rail links to neighbouring Malaysia and Laos. Conveniently, Bangkok is also the easiest place in the world to get hold of visas for Laos, Vietnam and Cambodia. The prime trans-Southeast Asia route takes travellers down to one of the beaches in south Thailand, and then on into Malaysia by train or bus. Considered less exciting than Thailand, but a similarly straightforward place to get around, **Malaysia** boasts equally nice beaches, particularly on the east coast, good diving, and some rewarding national-park hikes. East Malaysia, which shares the large island of Borneo with Indonesia's Kalimantan province and the little kingdom of Brunei, is much more off the beaten track and offers adventurous (if costly) travel by river through the jungle and nights in tribal longhouses. Marooned in the middle of Malaysian Borneo, the tiny independent kingdom of **Brunei** is expensive and dull, so most people stop here only when obliged to by plane schedules. Overland travellers with plenty of time might stop off for a couple of days in hi-tech **Singapore**, which sits at the southern tip of Peninsular Malaysia, but as it's relatively pricey and has no unmissable sights, Singapore's main appeal is the boat service across to Sumatra, the northernmost island of Indonesia. (Alternatively, you can opt for the boats from Melaka or Penang to Sumatra.) **Indonesia** vies with Thailand as the region's most visited destination, with fantastic volcanic landscapes, an unparalleled diversity of tribal cultures, decent beaches and diving, and lots of arts and crafts. It could take you a lifetime to explore the whole archipelago, but the classic itinerary

Cambodia now figures on an increasing number of itineraries, mainly because of the fabulous temple ruins at Angkor

▲ Gunung Batukau, Bali

Diving and snorkelling

The tropical waters of the Indian and Pacific oceans support a phenomenal population of reef- and open-water fish, plus a host of bizarre invertebrates, a (dwindling) number of turtles, and myriad species of hard and soft corals. Indonesia, Malaysia, the Philippines and Thailand all have outstanding, world-class dive sites with exceptionally good visibility, where you're as likely to spot a barracuda or a manta ray as a moorish idol or a parrot fish, and may even sight a whale shark. Dive excursions are extremely good value – from $30/£16 for a day-trip with two tanks – and novices can learn the ropes for as little as $190/£100. For more details on the best underwater sites, see individual chapter introductions.

takes you through Sumatra, across to Java and then on to Bali and Lombok. With extra time, you could continue east as far as Flores, from where it's just a few hours' flight to northern Australia.

The less common route out of Thailand heads northeastwards, across the Mekong River and into Laos, with the possibility of continuing overland into Vietnam and Cambodia. For many, **Laos**'s main appeal lies in the fact that it's a lot less developed than Thailand. Accommodation here is generally basic, and road transport can be tiresome, but there are memorable long-distance boat journeys, some fine old temples, and the chance to experience traditional rural culture. Neighbouring **Vietnam** offers some impressive old Chinese towns and plenty of sobering memorials from the American (Vietnam) War. Until quite recently a dangerous and rarely visited country owing to bandits, guerrillas and mines, **Cambodia** now figures on an increasing number of itineraries, mainly because of the fabulous temple ruins at Angkor. Cambodia has several legal border crossings with Thailand, which makes it possible to complete the entire circuit overland.

Stuck way out beyond both Thailand loops, the **Philippines** is often omitted from Southeast Asia trips because it has no overland access – most people fly there via Hong Kong. However, the Philippines archipelago boasts some of the best beaches and most dramatic diving in the whole region, along with good volcano hikes, plus some exceptionally exuberant festivals.

Parts of Southeast Asia were hit extremely hard by the Indian Ocean **tsunami** of December 2004, which caused massive loss of life and extensive damage to properties and livelihoods in areas of northwest Indonesia and southwest Thailand. Although some villages and beach resorts were able to rebuild almost immediately, other places will take longer to recover: see the relevant chapters for details.

▲ Travelling by rickshaw, Thailand

Where to go

The **beaches** of Southeast Asia are some of the finest in the world, and you'll find the cream of the crop in Thailand, the Philippines and Malaysia, all of which boast postcard-pretty, white-sand bays, complete with azure waters and wooden beach shacks dotted along their palm-fringed shores. The clear tropical waters also offer supreme **diving** opportunities, with particularly rich reefs off Puerto Galera, Moalboal, Malapascua Island and Palawan in the Philippines, off Pulau Tioman and Pulau Sipadan in Malaysia, near Phuket and Ko Tao in Thailand, and at Pulau Bunaken, Pulau Menjangan and Tulamben in Indonesia.

Almost every visitor to Indonesia makes an effort to get up before dawn and climb Java's spectacular volcano **Mount Bromo** in time for sunrise; further east, on the more remote Indonesian island of Flores, the famous three-coloured crater lakes of **Kelimutu** are another must-see. East Malaysia (Borneo) is also off the main trail, but here you get the chance to explore parts of the largest cave system in the world, in **Gunung Mulu National Park**, and to climb the 4101-metre-high **Mount Kinabalu**. Similarly challenging mountains await in the Philippines, most popularly at **Mount Mayon**, an active volcano, and **Mount Apo**, which takes four days to conquer. The much shorter hikes around **Banaue** in the Philippines are classics of a different order, drawing you through breathtakingly beautiful amphitheatres of sculpted rice terraces.

Tribal culture is a highlight of visits to many less explored areas, and among the most approachable communities are the **Iban longhouses of Sarawak**, which can only be reached by taking a boat along the river systems of East Malaysia; the **Torajans of Sulawesi** in Indonesia, known for their intriguing architecture and ghoulish burial rituals;

The beaches of Southeast Asia are some of the finest in the world, and you'll find the cream of the crop in Thailand, the Philippines and Malaysia

The Buddhist stupa

Nearly every Buddhist temple in Southeast Asia contains a stupa (*chedi* or *that*) built to hold the ashes of a revered or important person. The most sacred stupas enshrine relics of the Buddha himself, as at Wat Ounalom in Cambodia (see p.132), which is dedicated to one of his eyebrows, but these days stupas are usually commissioned as memorials to wealthy patrons.

Legend has it that the Buddha came up with the prototype stupa, to evoke his philosophy. Famously lacking in material possessions, he assembled his worldly goods – a teaching stick, a begging bowl and a length of cloth – and constructed a stupa shape using the folded cloth as a three-tiered base (representing hell, earth, and heaven), the inverted bowl as the dome (meditation), and the stick as the spire, graded into rings for each of the Buddhist heavens. Stupa symbolism has become much more complex since then, as illustrated by the magnificent Borobudur temple in Indonesia (see p.294).

▲ Borobudur, Java, Indonesia

and the **Igorot of Sagada** in the Philippines, famous for their hanging coffins and burial caves. The **hilltribe villages of northern Thailand** are now such a major feature on the tourist trail that the experience can feel akin to visiting a human zoo – you'll have more rewarding encounters with other branches of these same tribal groups at **Muang Sing** in Laos and around **Sa Pa** in Vietnam.

The dominant threads of mainstream **Southeast Asian culture** came originally from India and China, and since the start of the first millennium, Hindu and Buddhist practices have had a lasting impact. The Hindu Khmers of Cambodia left a string of magnificent temple complexes, the finest of which can still be seen today at **Angkor** in Cambodia, with smaller-scale versions at **Wat Phou** in Laos and at **Phanom Rung** in Thailand. The Buddhists' most impressive legacy is the colossal ninth-century stupa of **Borobudur** in Indonesia, but there are plenty more modern Buddhist temples to admire, particularly in **Louang Phabang**, the Lao city of golden spires. In Vietnam, the eighteenth-century Imperial City and seven Royal Mausoleums of **Hue** rate as some of the finest examples of traditional Chinese architecture in the world. However, it's often not just the monuments to faith that fascinate, but the daily devotions still practised – be it Thai Buddhist monks collecting food at their neighbours' doors every morning, or Balinese housewives setting out daily offerings for the spirits.

▲ Thanon Khao San, Bangkok, Thailand

With the exception of Thailand, every Southeast Asian nation has lived under Western **colonial rule** for a significant span of recent history, and there are particularly well-preserved relics from the region's colonial past in **Georgetown**, Malaysia, a former British trading post, on the cobbled streets of the old Spanish town of **Vigan** in the Philippines, and in the grand French facades of civic buildings across **Phnom Penh** and **Hanoi**. Vietnam, Cambodia and Laos are also littered with reminders of more recent encounters with the West – the war between America and the communists of Indochina that dominated the 1960s and 70s has left thousands of bomb craters and unexploded mines and a large population of amputees. Many visitors are curious to descend into the 250-kilometre network of **Cu Chi tunnels**, where the Vietcong guerrillas lived for many years, and to see for themselves a chunk of the legendary **Ho Chi Minh Trail**.

If you just want somewhere nice to **hang out** for a week or more – on a beach, at the foot of a mountain, in the heart of a happening city – there are scores of options: on the beach at **Cherating** in Malaysia, **Ko Pha Ngan** in Thailand (site of the famous monthly full-moon raves), and the **Gili Islands**, off Lombok in Indonesia; or inland in the Minang tribal village of **Bukittinggi** on Sumatra, at riverside **Vang Viang** in Laos, and in the Thai city of **Chiang Mai**.

With religion and tradition playing such overt roles in everyday life, it's easy to over-emphasize the picturesque and the quaint. In reality, the region has its share of banal fast-food outlets and standard-issue urban sprawl, and there are pockets of extreme poverty, too. Inevitably, this book focuses on the most rewarding and most visited destinations in Southeast Asia. Because of their overwhelming popularity, some of the more developed tourist **hot spots**, like Ko Samui in Thailand, Boracay in the Philippines or Bali's Kuta can isolate travellers almost completely from authentic local culture. If you confine yourself to these places, it's quite possible never to take a local bus, eat a typical meal, or utter so much as a greeting in the local language. Generally, the most memorable encounters with local people happen away from the beach resorts and tourist restaurants, and for most visitors it is these meetings that stand out as the greatest highlights of a Southeast Asian trip.

When to go

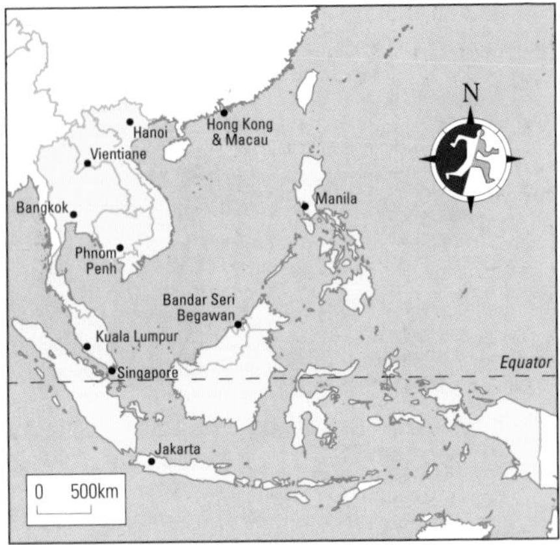

Southeast Asia sits entirely within the tropics and so is broadly characterized by a hot and humid climate that varies little throughout the year, except during the two annual monsoons ("seasonal winds"). The **southwest monsoon** arrives in west-coast regions at around the end of May and brings daily rainfall to most of Southeast Asia by mid-July (excepting certain east-coast areas, explained below). From then on you can expect overcast skies and regular downpours across the region till October or November. This is not a great time to travel in Southeast Asia, as west-coast seas are often too rough for swimming, some islands become inaccessible and less well-maintained roads may get washed out. However, rain showers often last just a couple of hours a day and many airlines and guesthouses offer decent discounts. The **northeast monsoon** brings drier, slightly cooler weather to most of Southeast Asia (east-coast areas excepted) between November and February, making this period the best overall time to travel in the region. The main exceptions to the above pattern are the east-coast regions of Vietnam, Peninsular Thailand and Peninsular Malaysia, which get rain when the rest of tropical Asia is having its driest period, but stay dry during the southwest monsoon. If you're planning a long trip to Southeast Asia, this means you can often escape the worst weather by hopping across to the other coast. Indonesia and Singapore are hit by both monsoons, attracting the west-coast rains from May through October, and the east-coast rains from November to February.

The **climate chart** below lists average maximum daily temperatures and average monthly rainfall for the capital cities of Southeast Asia. Bear in mind, however, that each country has myriad micro-climates, determined by altitude and proximity to the east or west coast amongst other factors; for more detail, consult the introduction to each chapter.

Average temperatures and rainfall

	Jan	Feb	Mar	Apr	May	June	July	Aug	Sept	Oct	Nov	Dec
Bandar Seri Begawan, Brunei												
Av daily max (°C)	30	30	31	32	32.5	32	31.5	32	31.5	31.5	31	31
Av daily max (°F)	86	86	88	89.5	90.5	89.5	89	89.5	89	89	88	88
Rainfall (mm)	133	63	71	124	218	311	277	256	314	334	296	241
Bangkok, Thailand												
Av daily max (°C)	28	28	29	30	31	31	30	31	31	30	29	28
Av daily max (°F)	82.5	82.5	84	86	88	88	86	88	88	86	84	82.5
Rainfall (mm)	66	28	33	36	58	112	147	147	170	178	206	97
Hanoi, Vietnam												
Av daily max (°C)	17	18	20	24	28	30	30	29	28	26	22	19
Av daily max (°F)	62.5	64.5	68	75	82.5	86	86	84	82.5	79	71.5	66
Rainfall (mm)	18	28	38	81	196	239	323	343	254	99	43	20
Hong Kong & Macau												
Av daily max (°C)	18	17	19	24	28	2	31	31	29	27	23	20
Av daily max (°F)	64.5	62.5	66	75	82.5	84	88	88	84	80.5	73.5	68
Rainfall (mm)	33	46	74	137	292	394	381	367	257	114	43	31
Jakarta, Indonesia												
Av daily max (°C)	29	29	30	31	31	31	31	31	31	31	30	29
Av daily max (°F)	84	84	86	88	88	88	88	88	88	88	86	84
Rainfall (mm)	300	300	211	147	114	97	64	43	66	112	142	203
Kuala Lumpur, Malaysia												
Av daily max (°C)	32	33	33	33	33	32	32	32	32	32	31	31
Av daily max (°F)	89.5	91.5	91.5	91.5	91.5	89.5	89.5	89.5	89.5	89.5	88	88
Rainfall (mm)	159	154	223	276	182	119	120	133	173	258	263	223
Manila, the Philippines												
Av daily max (°C)	28	28	30	31	32	30	29	29	29	29	29	28
Av daily max (°F)	82.5	82.5	86	88	89.5	86	84	84	84	84	84	82.5
Rainfall (mm)	35	25	25	35	130	260	415	415	340	210	145	80
Phnom Penh, Cambodia												
Av daily max (°C)	25	27	28	29	29	29	29	29	29	28	27	26
Av daily max (°F)	77	80.5	82.5	84	84	84	84	84	84	82.5	80.5	79
Rainfall (mm)	10	10	45	80	120	150	165	160	215	240	135	55
Singapore												
Av daily max (°C)	31	32	32	32	32	32	31	31	31	31	31	30
Av daily max (°F)	88	89.5	89.5	89.5	89.5	89.5	88	88	88	88	88	86
Rainfall (mm)	146	155	182	223	228	151	170	163	200	199	255	258
Vientiane, Laos												
Av daily max (°C)	28	30	33	34	32	32	31	31	31	31	29	28
Av daily max (°F)	82.5	86	91.5	93	89.5	89.5	88	88	88	88	84	82.5
Rainfall (mm)	5	15	38	99	267	302	267	292	302	109	15	3

35 things not to miss

It's not possible to see everything Southeast Asia has to offer in one trip – and we don't suggest you try. What follows is a selective and subjective taste of the region's highlights: magnificent temples, incredible beaches, spectacular landscapes and atmospheric towns. They're arranged in five colour-coded categories, so you can browse through to find the very best things to see, do, buy and experience. All highlights have a page reference to take you straight into the Guide, where you can find out more.

01 Royal Palace and Silver Pagoda, Cambodia Page **129** • Step away from the hectic streets and enjoy the serene gardens and refined architecture of Phnom Penh's royal compound.

02 Trekking in Banaue, The Philippines Page **825** • For the best view of Banaue's impressive rice terraces, trek through them to the isolated tribal barrio of Batad.

03 Taman Negara National Park, Malaysia Page **670** • Enjoy a different perspective on one of the world's oldest rainforests from the forty-metre-high canopy walkway.

04 Climbing Mount Kinabalu, Malaysia Page **737** • A challenging but straightforward two-day hike will get you up to the summit and back.

05 City skyline, Hong Kong Page **199** • Viewed from the cross-harbour ferry, this is one of the most eye-popping urban vistas on earth.

06 Hotel Lisboa's casinos, Macau Page **606** • Experience Macau the way weekending locals do – from the inside of one of its countless casinos.

07 Ubud, Indonesia Page **373** • Immerse yourself in Balinese culture at this most charming and sophisticated of arty villages.

08 Surfing in Indonesia Page **312** • G-Land, host of the annual Quiksilver Pro, is just one of many legendary Indonesian surf spots.

09 Orang-utans, Indonesia Page **323** • Observe the antics of these engaging creatures at the Bukit Lawang Orang-Utan Rehabilitation Centre in North Sumatra.

10 Hoi An, Vietnam Page **1180** • A charming, picturesque town with some fine old residences and a tempting line in hand-tailored silk outfits.

11 Ko Tao, Thailand Page **1067** • Learn to dive on this diminutive island, or just go swimming in one of its secluded coves.

12 Torajan funeral ceremonies, Indonesia

Page **477** • Visitors are welcome to attend Sulawesi's dramatic funeral ceremonies, which are far from sombre affairs.

13 Angkor Wat, Cambodia

Page **148** • Cambodia's immense twelfth-century Hindu temple complex is nothing short of magnificent.

14 Hawker centres, Singapore

Page **926** • Singapore's ubiquitous food courts are fun places to sample the country's multi-ethnic cuisines.

15 Malapascua Island, The Philippines

Page **848** • Swim amongst turtles, thresher sharks and manta rays at one of Southeast Asia's top dive spots.

16 Sea-kayaking in the Krabi region, Thailand Page **1082** • A great way to find your own lonely bays and mysterious lagoons.

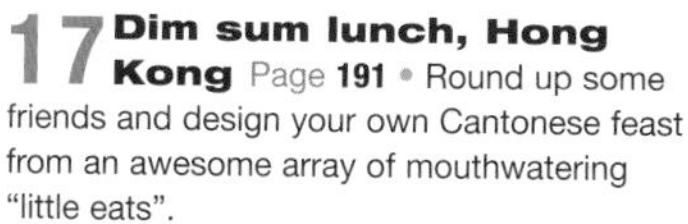

17 Dim sum lunch, Hong Kong Page **191** • Round up some friends and design your own Cantonese feast from an awesome array of mouthwatering "little eats".

18 Pulau Tioman, Malaysia Page **696** • A popular but undeniably beautiful resort island, graced with fine beaches and excellent diving.

19 Climbing Gunung Rinjani, Indonesia Page **430** • Trek up Lombok's highest volcano to discover its awesome crater lake.

20 Ha Long Bay, Vietnam Page **1219** • A famously dramatic landscape of weird rock formations, hidden bays and gloomy caves.

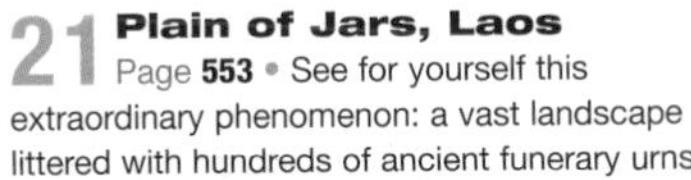

21 Plain of Jars, Laos Page **553** • See for yourself this extraordinary phenomenon: a vast landscape littered with hundreds of ancient funerary urns.

22 Louang Phabang, Laos Page **536** • Wat Xiang Thong is just one of many graceful temples in this enchanting and beautifully preserved city.

23 Sa Pa, Vietnam Page **1225** • Base yourself in the upland town of Sa Pa for invigorating day hikes and easy access to ethnic minority villages.

24

Hanoi's Old Quarter, Vietnam Page **1206** • Browse and bargain your way through Hanoi's buzzing merchant's district, where some streets have specialized in the same wares for five hundred years.

25

The Gili Islands, Indonesia Page **421** • Pure white sand and crystal-clear turquoise waters fringe these laid-back islands off Lombok's northwest coast .

26

Ride the Reunification Express, Vietnam Page **1106** • Sit back and relax as the train chugs past paddy-fields on its way between Ho Chi Minh City and Hanoi.

27

Boracay, The Philippines Page **856** • Powder-white beaches, first-class diving and lively nightlife – this is the most famous holiday island in the Philippines.

28 Cameron Highlands, Malaysia Page **650** • A quaint colonial-era hill station, surrounded by tea plantations and criss-crossed by trails.

29 Royal City of Hue, Vietnam Page **1189** • Take a boat down the Perfume River to visit the magnificent mausoleums and pleasure gardens of the Nguyen emperors.

30 Prambanan, Indonesia Page **297** • The facades of Java's majestic ninth-century Hindu temple-complex are covered with exquisite carvings.

31 Khao Sok National Park, Thailand Page **1073** • Hike through humid jungle overshadowed by limestone crags, then spend the night in a treehouse.

32 Vang Viang, Laos Page **532** • Float down the river, investigate local caves, or just enjoy the scenery at this relaxed backpackers' haven.

33 The Grand Palace, Thailand Page **974** • Exuberant murals, a highly revered Buddha image, and Thailand's holiest temple, Wat Phra Kaeo, make this palace compound Bangkok's top sight.

34 Slow boat on the Mekong, Laos Page **562** • The perfect way to absorb Lao life and landscapes.

35 Kanchanaburi, Thailand Page **988** • Chill out on a rafthouse, explore the temples and waterfalls of the River Kwai valley, and ride the historic Death Railway.

Basics

Basics

Getting there

The quickest and easiest way to get to Southeast Asia is by air. One of the cheapest options is to buy a one-way flight to one of the region's gateway cities, such as Singapore or Bangkok, and make onward travel arrangements from there – the recent explosion of low-cost, no-frills airlines has made for some real bargains, and air travel within Southeast Asia is cheaper than ever. If you're keen to combine your trip with a visit to India or China, you could consider a stopover or open-jaw ticket, which flies you into one country and out of another, allowing you to explore overland in between. If you're planning a multi-stop trip, then a Round-the-World or Circle Asia/Pacific ticket offers good value. As an alternative to air travel, you could consider taking one of the world's classic overland trips, the Trans-Siberian railway, through Russia and Mongolia to China, and from there to Indochina.

The next cheapest airfares are often available through a **specialist flight agent** – either a consolidator, who buys up blocks of tickets from the airlines and sells them at a discount, or a **discount agent**, who, in addition to dealing with discounted flights, may also offer special student and youth fares and a range of other travel-related services, such as travel insurance, rail passes, car rentals, tours and the like. Some agents specialize in **charter flights**, which may be cheaper than anything available on a scheduled flight, but departure dates are fixed and withdrawal penalties are high.

Package tours can offer an excellent opportunity to take in regions you might not have access to as an independent traveller. While these do take care of a lot of the legwork, they can also take away some of the spontaneity of travelling on your own. Most operators give you the option of buying your own flights and joining the tour on the ground.

A further possibility is to see if you can arrange a **courier flight**, although you'll need a flexible schedule, and preferably be travelling alone with very little luggage. In return for shepherding a parcel through customs, you can expect to get a deeply discounted ticket. You'll probably also be restricted in the duration of your stay.

Booking flights online

Many airlines and discount travel websites offer you the opportunity to book your tickets online, cutting out the costs of agents and middlemen. Good deals can often be found through discount or auction sites, as well as through the airlines' own websites.

Online booking agents and general travel sites

Ⓦ **www.etn.nl** A hub of consolidator and discount-agent web links, maintained by the non-profit European Travel Network.
Ⓦ **www.deckchair.com** Claims to have the Net's biggest single screen selection of flights.
Ⓦ **www.geocities.com/Thavery2000** Has an extensive list of airline toll-free numbers and websites.
Ⓦ **www.flynow.com** Online air travel info and reservations site.
Ⓦ **www.smilinjack.com/airlines.htm** Lists an up-to-date compilation of airline website addresses.
Ⓦ **http://travel.yahoo.com** Incorporates a lot of Rough Guide material in its coverage of destination countries and cities across the world, with information about places to sleep, eat, drink, etc.
Ⓦ **www.cheaptickets.com** Discount flight specialists.
Ⓦ **www.cheapflights.com** Flight deals, travel agents, plus links to other travel sites.
Ⓦ **www.lastminute.com** Bookings from the UK only. Offers good last-minute holiday-package and flight-only deals.
Ⓦ **www.expedia.com** Discount airfares, all-airline search engine and daily deals.
Ⓦ **www.travelocity.com** Destination guides, hot web fares and best deals for car rental, accommodation and lodging as well as fares.

Provides access to the travel agent system SABRE, the most comprehensive central reservations system in the US.

www.hotwire.com Bookings from the US only. Last-minute savings of up to forty percent on regular published fares. Travellers must be at least 18 and there are no refunds, transfers or changes allowed. Log-in required.

www.priceline.com Name-your-own-price website that has deals at around forty percent off standard fares. You cannot specify flight times (although you do specify dates) and the tickets are non-refundable, non-transferable and non-changeable.

www.skyauction.com Bookings from the US only. Auctions tickets and travel packages using a "second bid" scheme. The best strategy is to bid the maximum you're willing to pay, since if you win you'll pay just enough to beat the runner-up regardless of your maximum bid.

www.travelshop.com.au Australian website offering discounted flights, packages, insurance, online bookings.

www.gaytravel.com Gay online travel agent, concentrating mostly on accommodation.

Getting there from the UK and Ireland

The cheapest way of getting to Southeast Asia **from the UK and Ireland** is to buy a **one-way flight** to one of the region's major gateways – Bangkok, Singapore, Bali, Kuala Lumpur or Hong Kong – and make onward travel arrangements from there, by air, road, rail or sea. If you want to visit India and China en route to Southeast Asia, you should consider a **stopover** or an **open-jaw ticket**. Popular alternatives to this are the air tickets that take you via two or more Asian cities en route; these are generally known as **Circle Asia** tickets, or **Round-the-World** (RTW) tickets if they include Australia, and are offered by all long-haul travel agents. There's also the possibility of following one of the world's great overland trips, the **Trans-Siberian Railway**, through Russia and Mongolia to China, and from there continuing by road or rail into Indochina.

Booking a scheduled ticket direct with the airline is the most expensive way to fly. Generally, you're best off booking through an established **discount agent**, who can usually undercut airline prices by a significant amount. See the list of recommended agents on p.31 and the websites listed on pp.27–28, or check the adverts in national Sunday papers and major regional newspapers and listings magazines.

The biggest factor affecting the price of a ticket is the time of year you wish to travel. **High season** for many Asian destinations is over Christmas, when much of Asia is experiencing its driest period of the year, and during the UK summer holidays, when many people want to travel. It's best to book well in advance for a ticket in high season. Some airlines charge more than others, as do some travel agents, so it's always good to shop around. It's usually more expensive to fly non-stop than to change planes in Europe or Asia en route. If you're a **student** or **under 26**, you may be able to get special discounts on flights, especially through agents like STA Travel. Some European airlines offer competitive fares to Asia from **regional airports** such as Glasgow, Manchester, Dublin and Belfast, otherwise you'll need to go via London, adding the relevant return fare.

Gateway cities

Flying into Southeast Asia on a one-way ticket is fairly inexpensive and gives you plenty of options for onward travel, but it can cause **problems at Immigration**. Many officials like to see proof of onward or return transport, fearing that you may stay illegally in their country. Some will be happy if you show proof of sufficient funds to keep you going (about £1350), others will be more satisfied if you can give details of a convincing onward route, with dates. Some travellers get round all this by buying the cheapest return flight available and then cashing in the return sector, but read the small print before going for this option.

In some countries, you may have to apply for a **visa** in advance if arriving on a one-way ticket, rather than being granted one automatically at Immigration, so always check with the relevant embassy before you leave. If you are continuing overland, you need to research visa requirements at the border crossings before leaving home (see p.44). Details on **overland transport from neighbouring Southeast Asian countries** are given in the introduction to each chapter. One of the cheapest and most useful gateways to Southeast Asia is **Bangkok**. London–Bangkok flights start at about £250 one-way, £400 return, rising to at least £300/£480 during peak times (July, Aug, Dec), and take a minimum of twelve hours. Once in Bangkok, you can choose to travel overland to Laos or Cambodia, or head south by road or rail into Malaysia and Singapore and then across to Sumatra in Indonesia. Or, you can buy one of the good-value flights to Southeast Asian destinations offered by many Bangkok travel agents, eg Bangkok–Bali for about £150, or Bangkok–Phnom Penh for £65. Visit the websites ⓦwww.thaiairline.com and ⓦwww.orient-thai.com for a fuller list of current fares from Bangkok to destinations in Southeast Asia. If you're planning to fly direct from London to either Vientiane or Phnom Penh, you will have to change planes in Bangkok or Singapore anyway, as there are currently no long-haul flights to these destinations. It's also much faster and easier to get visas for Laos, Vietnam and Cambodia in Bangkok than in London (see "Entry requirements and visa extensions" in the introduction to each country), so it's worth building in a stopover just for that.

Another inexpensive and popular gateway city is **Singapore**. London–Singapore flights start at £260 one-way, £450 return, or £300/£500 during peak times (mid-July to Sept), and take at least thirteen hours. Locally bought flights from Singapore are generally a little more expensive than from Bangkok (eg Singapore–Bali £100), but good deals can sometimes be found with low-cost airlines Tiger Airways (ⓦwww.tigerairways.com) and ValuAir (ⓦwww.valuair.com), and you can fly direct from Singapore to Lombok or Sulawesi for about £100. Few travellers stay long in Singapore itself, but it's just half an hour's bus ride into Malaysia, from where you could continue north to Thailand and Indochina, or a short ferry ride across to Sumatra, and then island-hop across the Indonesian archipelago. It's also possible to get a ferry direct from Singapore to Indonesia.

If you're keen to see China as well as Southeast Asia, consider buying a flight to **Hong Kong**. London–Hong Kong flights start at about £250 one-way, £350 return or £300/£500 during peak times (mid-June to Sept, Christmas, Chinese New Year, and Easter), and take at least twelve hours. Hong Kong gives you easy and inexpensive local transport options into Guangdong province, from where you could continue west into Vietnam, and on into Laos, then Thailand and down to Malaysia and Indonesia. It's also a good place from where to buy a cheap local flight: eg from Hong Kong to Vietnam on Cathay Pacific costs around £200, to the Philippines £150.

Sample low-season fares from London to other Southeast Asian cities include: **Bali** £300 one-way, £500 return; **Ho Chi Minh City** £350/£550; **Kuala Lumpur** £300/£425; **Manila** £315/£500; and **Phnom Penh** £350/£600. For high-season fares, add at least an extra 35 percent.

If you do decide to buy a single or return flight to a gateway city, ask your travel agent about the **Asean Air Passes** offered as a joint package by the national airlines of Brunei, Indonesia, Malaysia, the Philippines, Singapore, Thailand and Vietnam. You choose which of the above countries you would like to start from and then buy a return ticket, with stopovers in any two, three, four, five or six of the other countries. There's a minimum stay of three nights and a maximum of three months for each stopover. Prices vary according to your departure point, and how many stopovers you require: an Asean Air Pass beginning and ending in Vietnam or Indonesia costs about £315 with two stopovers, £385 with three stopovers and £455 with four, five or six stopovers; if you begin and end your tour in the Philippines you're looking at £350/£420/£450.

Airlines

Air China UK ⓣ020/7630 0919 or 7630 7678, ⓦwww.air-china.co.uk.
Air India UK ⓣ020/8560 9996, ⓦwww.airindia.com.
Air New Zealand UK ⓣ0800/028 4149, ⓦwww.airnz.co.uk.
British Airways UK ⓣ0870/850 3377, Republic of Ireland ⓣ1890/626 747, ⓦwww.britishairways.com.
Cathay Pacific UK ⓣ020/8834 8888, ⓦwww.cathaypacific.com.

China Airlines UK ⓣ020/7434 0707, ⓦwww.china-airlines.com.
Continental UK ⓣ0800/776 464, Republic of Ireland ⓣ1890/925 252, ⓦwww.continental.com.
Emirates Airlines UK ⓣ0870/243 2222, ⓦwww.emirates.com.
Eva Airways UK ⓣ020/7380 8300, ⓦwww.evaair.com.
Garuda Indonesia UK ⓣ020/7467 8600, ⓦwww.garuda-indonesia.co.uk.
Gulf Air UK ⓣ0870/777 1717, ⓦwww.gulfairco.com.
Japan Airlines UK ⓣ0845/774 7700, ⓦwww.jal.co.jp/en.
KLM UK ⓣ0870/507 4074, ⓦwww.klmuk.com.
Korean Air UK ⓣ0800/0656 2001, Republic of Ireland ⓣ01/799 7990, ⓦwww.koreanair.com.
Lufthansa UK ⓣ0845/773 7747, Republic of Ireland ⓣ01/844 5544, ⓦwww.lufthansa.com.
Malaysia Airlines (MAS) UK ⓣ0870/607 9090, Republic of Ireland ⓣ01/676 1561 or 676 2131, ⓦwww.mas.com.my.
Qantas UK ⓣ0845/774 7767, ⓦwww.qantas.com.au.
Royal Brunei Airlines UK ⓣ020/7584 6660, ⓦwww.bruneiair.com.
Singapore Airlines UK ⓣ0870/608 8886, Republic of Ireland ⓣ01/671 0722, ⓦwww.singaporeair.com.
Thai Airways International UK ⓣ0870/606 0911, ⓦwww.thaiair.com.
United Airlines UK ⓣ0845/844 4777, ⓦwww.united.com.
Virgin Atlantic Airways UK ⓣ0870/3802007, ⓦwww.virgin-atlantic.com.

Stopover returns and open-jaw tickets

If you're only visiting a couple of countries in Asia, buying a ticket with a **stopover** option may be your best deal. As an example, you can fly London–Singapore return with a stopover in Bangkok (of up to three months) for about £450.

On some airlines, it's possible to buy an **open-jaw** ticket that flies you into one country (eg Thailand) and out of another (eg Singapore). A more challenging itinerary might take in India and Pakistan en route to China and Indochina: you might buy an open-jaw plane ticket from London that flies you into **Delhi** and then takes you out of Bangkok or Singapore a few months later, giving yourself the option of buying some internal flights en route if necessary. From India, you can either cross into **Pakistan** overland (via Amritsar) or, provided the political situation allows, fly to Karachi from Delhi or Bombay, or to Lahore from Delhi. From Pakistan, buses run along the spectacularly scenic Karakoram Highway into northwest **China**, and you can then continue into Vietnam and on into Laos, Thailand, Malaysia and Singapore. Another variation would be to exit China via Hong Kong and fly on to the Philippines, then take a cargo boat to Indonesia, from where you could overland to Thailand and on into Indochina. Open-jaws are usually more expensive than standard or stopover returns: prices are generally calculated by halving the return fares to each destination and then adding the two figures together.

Circle Asia and RTW tickets

Multi-stop **Circle Asia and RTW (Round-the-World)** tickets are good value, and with all your major travel expenses sorted out in advance, you can budget realistically for your trip, and don't have to waste time organizing onward travel when you're there. It also eliminates the hassle that Immigration officials sometimes give travellers with no onward or return tickets. Circle Asia and RTW tickets are in fact a whole series of tickets, generally put together by a travel agent using the cheapest flights they can find to construct a trans-Asia route via a series of key cities chosen by you. Once you've bought your ticket, dates can be altered at any point along the way (with Circle Asia tickets the itinerary cannot be changed; with RTW tickets it can, for a small fee); tickets are generally valid for one year.

The cheapest and most popular Circle Asia and RTW routes include one or more "surface sectors" where you have to make your way between point A and point B by road, rail or sea or by a locally bought flight. A typical **Circle Asia** from London to Bali and back, for example, would include a flight from London to Bangkok, then a surface sector from Bangkok to Singapore, followed by flights from Singapore to Bali, then Bali to London; total cost from £580. Similarly, you could fly from London to Hong Kong and on to Manila, then go overland to Cebu, from where you fly to Singapore and finally back to London; total cost from £750. For help with planning surface sectors, see the sections on overland travel in the introductions to each chapter.

An **RTW** ticket is similar, but includes stops in Australia and the Pacific, North America or South Africa. For example, a one-year open RTW ticket from London taking in Bangkok, Singapore, Perth, Sydney, Auckland and Los Angeles starts at as little as £820, rising to around £1220 if you add stops in India or China and the South Pacific. The cheapest time to begin your RTW trip is usually April to June.

Discount flight and travel agents in the UK

Aossa Travel UK ⓣ01273/202 641, ⓦwww.aossa-travel.co.uk. Excellent service and a comprehensive range of budget fares and RTW options.
Austravel UK ⓣ020/7734 7755, ⓦwww.austravel.com. Very good deals on flights to Australia and New Zealand via Indonesia, also on RTW tickets.
Bridge the World UK ⓣ0870/814 4400, ⓦwww.bridgetheworld.com. Specializing in RTW tickets, with good deals aimed at the backpacker market.
Co-op Travel Care Belfast ⓣ028/9047 1717. Budget fares agent.
Destination Group UK ⓣ020/7400 7045, ⓦwww.destination-group.com. Good discount airfares, as well as Far East inclusive packages.
Faraway Traveller ⓣ01435/873 666, ⓦwww.farawaytraveller.co.uk. Good service, low fares found, RTW itineraries painstakingly researched.
Flightbookers UK ⓣ0870/010 7000, ⓦwww.ebookers.com. Low fares on an extensive selection of scheduled flights.
Flight Centre UK ⓣ0870/499 0040, ⓦwww.flightcentre.co.uk. Friendly service with competitive discounts on airfares plus a wide range of package holidays.
Flynow UK ⓣ0870/444 0045, ⓦwww.flynow.com. Large range of discounted tickets.
North South Travel UK ⓣ01245/608 291, ⓦwww.northsouthtravel.co.uk. Travel agency that supports projects in the developing world, especially sustainable tourism.
Quest Travel UK ⓣ0870/442 2699 or 020/8547 3322, ⓦwww.questtravel.com. Specialists in RTW and Australasian discount fares.
Rosetta Travel Belfast ⓣ028/9064 4996, ⓦwww.rosettatravel.com. Flight and holiday agent.
STA Travel UK ⓣ0870/1600 599, ⓦwww.statravel.co.uk. Worldwide specialists in low-cost flights and tours for students and under-26s, though other customers welcome.
Top Deck UK ⓣ020/7370 4555, ⓦwww.topdecktravel.co.uk. Long-established agent dealing in discount flights.
Trailfinders UK ⓣ020/7628 7628, ⓦwww.trailfinders.com. One of the best-informed and most efficient agents for independent travellers; produces a very useful quarterly magazine worth scrutinizing for RTW routes.
Travel Bag UK ⓣ0870/900 1350, ⓦwww.travelbag.co.uk. Discount flights to Australia, New Zealand, USA and the Far East; official Qantas agent.
Travel Cuts UK ⓣ020/7255 2082, ⓦwww.travelcuts.co.uk. Canadian company specializing in budget, student and youth travel, and RTW tickets.

Discount flight and travel agents in Ireland

Apex Travel Dublin ⓣ01/241 8000, ⓦwww.apextravel.ie. Flights to Australia and the Far East.
Aran Travel International Galway ⓣ091/562 595, ⓦhomepages.iol.ie/~arantvl/aranmain.htm. Good-value flights to all parts of the world.
CIE Tours International Dublin ⓣ01/703 1888, ⓦwww.cietours.ie. General flight and tour agent.
Joe Walsh Tours Dublin ⓣ01/676 0991, ⓦwww.joewalshtours.ie. Budget fares agent.
Lee Travel Cork ⓣ021/277 111, ⓦwww.irelandwide.com/travel/leetrav. Flights and holidays worldwide.
Trailfinders Dublin ⓣ01/677 7888, ⓦwww.trailfinders.ie. One of the best-informed and most efficient agents for independent travellers; produces a very useful quarterly magazine worth scrutinizing for round-the-world routes.

Overland to Hong Kong via the Trans-Siberian

The **Trans-Siberian Railway** is the classic overland route into Asia. All trains begin in Moscow (you can take the train from London to Moscow as well if you want), and there are two possible routes into Asia. The Trans-Mongolian route and the Trans-Manchurian route both end up in **Beijing**, take about six days to get there (if you don't break your journey on the way), and start at £266 from Moscow; it's then another 24 hours by rail to **Hong Kong**, or about five days by train to **Hanoi**. Providing you arrange relevant visas, you can stop off anywhere en route. The cheapest tickets are for intolerably uncomfortable four-berth hard-sleeper compartments, so it's well worth upgrading to a two-berth cabin for an extra £140. For a full rundown of everything you need to know about visas, life on the train and ideas for stopoffs, see the *Trans-Siberian Handbook*, published by Trailblazer. Alternatively, talk to an experienced agent like Regent Holidays (☎0117/921 1711, Ⓦwww.regent-holidays.co.uk) or China Travel Service (☎020/7836 9911), who can organize all tickets, visas and stopovers.

Courier flights

A number of **courier** companies offer heavily discounted international flights to travellers willing to accompany documents and/or freight to the destination for them. These flights can be more than fifty percent cheaper than advertised rates, but are only available to certain destinations (chiefly Hong Kong, Singapore and Malaysia). Most have considerable restrictions attached: you will probably have to come back within a month, you will have to travel alone, and you might only be allowed to take carry-on luggage. Courier deals are advertised in the press and sold through special agents; see below.

International Association of Air Travel Couriers UK ☎0800/0746 481 or 01305/216 920, Ⓦwww.aircourier.co.uk. Agent for lots of companies.

Organized tours and package holidays

Dozens of tour operators organize trips to Southeast Asia, offering **packages** that cover the whole range of options, from beach holidays to cultural tours, from city breaks to overland expeditions through several countries. A selection of specialist operators are listed below, but any travel agent will be able to furnish you with a bigger selection of brochures.

Tour operators in the UK and Ireland

Unless otherwise stated, the prices below generally refer to the land tour only, so you'll need to factor in extra for flights from the UK and Ireland.

Audley Travel UK ☎01869/276 200, Ⓦwww.audleytravel.com. Tailor-made travel for individuals rather than group tours, with prices starting at around £1500.

Bales Worldwide UK ☎0870/252 0780, Ⓦwww.balesworldwide.com. Family-owned company offering high-quality escorted tours to the Far East, the Indian sub-continent and Southeast Asia, as well as tailor-made itineraries.

Destinations Worldwide Holidays Dublin ☎01/677 1029, Ⓦwww.destinations.ie. Specialists in Far Eastern and exotic destinations.

Earthwatch Institute UK ☎01865/318 831, Ⓦwww.earthwatch.org. Volunteer work on projects in Southeast Asia and throughout the world. A wide range of opportunities to assist archeologists, biologists and community workers, staying with local people. Around £1000 for two weeks.

Exodus UK ☎020/8675 5550, Ⓦwww.exodus.co.uk. Overland trips aimed at 18–45-year olds, including "Indochina Overland", which goes from Hong Kong to China, Laos, Thailand, Malaysia and Singapore in six weeks (£1210); and "Ultimate Asia" (30 weeks; £5900), an epic trip through the Middle East, India and Nepal into China, Laos and Thailand.

Explore Worldwide UK ☎01252/760 000, Dublin ☎01/677 9479, Ⓦwww.explore.co.uk. Heaps of options throughout Southeast Asia, including tours that explore the Angkor ruins in Cambodia and the jungles of Borneo.

Guerba Expeditions UK ☎01373/826 611, Ⓦwww.guerba.com. Small-group, walking, trekking and discovery holidays throughout the region, including the fourteen-day "Thailand, Laos & Cambodia" tour.

Imaginative Traveller UK ☎020/8742 8612, Ⓦwww.imaginative-traveller.com. Broad selection of tours to less-travelled parts of Asia, including walking, cycling, camping, cooking and snorkelling. There's a fifteen-day "Journey through Laos" tour as well as the 22-day "Bangkok to Ho Chi Minh City by bike" tour.

Silverbird UK ☎020/8875 9191, Ⓦwww.silverbirduk.com. Established Far East and Australasia specialist catering to the upper end of the market. Arranges a wealth of tailor-made itineraries around the region.

Symbiosis UK ☎020/7924 5906, Ⓦwww.symbiosis-travel.com. Environmentally aware outfit that offers specialist interest holidays in Southeast Asia, including an island-hopping trip through the Philippines, and trekking through jungles and longhouse communities of Sarawak and Sabah.

Getting there from the USA and Canada

There's no way around it, **flights from North America** to Southeast Asia are long. With the exception of non-stop services to

Singapore, Bangkok and Hong Kong from the US West Coast, all flights, including so-called "direct flights", will require a stop somewhere along the way. This, however, offers a good chance for travellers to take advantage of the **stopovers** offered by many airlines. **Open-jaw** tickets, where you fly into one country and out of another, also give you some flexibility. Popular alternatives to this are **Round-the-World** tickets (RTW) or **Circle Pacific** tickets, which will take you to a series of destinations, pre-determined before you leave American or Canadian soil. There's also the possibility of following one of the world's classic overland trips, the **Trans-Siberian Railway**, through Russia and Mongolia to China, and from there continuing on by road or rail into Indochina.

You'll find the cheapest flights are not through the airlines themselves, but with a **discount flight agent**. See p.35 for a list of recommended agents, or check the adverts in national Sunday papers. The **Internet** is also a useful resource. Try one of the websites listed on pp.27–28, such as Ⓦ www.cheaptickets.com or Ⓦ www.lastminute.com, for deals or just to compare prices quoted to you by agents. In addition to offering discounted flights, discount travel agents may also offer a range of other travel-related services, such as travel insurance, rail passes, car rentals, tours and the like. Bear in mind, though, that penalties for changing your plans can be stiff. Remember, too, that these companies make their money by dealing in bulk – don't expect them to answer lots of questions. If you travel a lot, it is worth getting in contact with discount travel clubs, where, for an annual fee, they will offer a number of savings on air tickets and car rental.

What will most affect the price of your ticket is the time of year you choose to travel. Air fares from the US and Canada to Southeast Asia are highest between June and August, and then again over the Christmas period (early Dec to early Jan). The **price difference between high and low season** is about US$300/CAN$450 on a typical round-trip fare. It is also worth noting that reservations in high season should be made further in advance, as tickets get booked up quickly.

You can also get good deals if you are a **student or youth** under 26 with discount agents such as Council Travel, STA and Travel CUTS (a passport or driving licence is sufficient proof of age), though these tickets are subject to availability and can have eccentric booking conditions.

Gateway cities

If you're keen to see China as well as Southeast Asia, consider flying to **Hong Kong**. The cheapest low-season fare from the US West Coast is around US$600 round-trip and the flight takes at least fourteen hours. From the East Coast it's a different story, with most flights to Hong Kong stretching to 22 hours, and all including a connection, most commonly in Vancouver, Tokyo, or Taipei. The cheapest published fares from New York are around US$700. The best options for flights **from Canada** to Hong Kong include non-stop flights from Vancouver (13hr) and direct flights from Toronto and Montréal (21hr). Fares from Canada's West Coast start at around CAN$1410. Hong Kong gives you easy and inexpensive local transport options into Guangdong province in China, from where you could continue west into Vietnam, and on into Laos, then Thailand and down to Malaysia and Indonesia. Alternatively, you could buy a flight from Hong Kong itself: eg from Hong Kong to Vietnam on Cathay Pacific costs around US$350, to the Philippines US$275.

Singapore is another popular gateway city, with flights from New York, Los Angeles, and San Francisco. Flying eastbound is more direct and a fraction faster at about 21 hours' travelling time. Consolidators consistently offer the best deals on tickets, with prices starting at around US$750 from New York. If you're travelling from Washington, Miami, or Chicago expect to pay from US$780; from Houston US$700; from Los Angeles, San Francisco or Seattle $600. From Toronto or Montréal, prices start at CAN$1275 and from Vancouver CAN$1200. From Singapore, you can fly direct to Lombok or Sulawesi for US$215. Locally bought flights from Singapore are generally a little more expensive than from Bangkok (eg Singapore–Bali US$175), but good deals can sometimes be found with low-cost airlines Tiger Airways

(Ⓦ www.tigerairways.com) and ValuAir (Ⓦ www.valuair.com), and you can fly direct from Singapore to Lombok or Sulawesi for about US$175. Few travellers stay long in Singapore itself, but it's just half an hour's bus ride into Malaysia, from where you could continue north to Thailand and Indochina, or make a short ferry ride across to Sumatra, and then island-hop across the Indonesia archipelago. It's also possible to get a ferry direct from Singapore to Indonesia.

Plenty of airlines run daily flights to **Bangkok** from major East-and West-coast cities, usually making only one stop. Flying time from the West Coast via Asia is approximately eighteen hours, and from New York via Europe it's around nineteen hours. From Canada, if you are travelling via Japan, you can expect the flight to take something like sixteen hours from Vancouver or 21 from Toronto. From the US West Coast, expect to pay from US$600. From the East Coast, prices start at about US$750. For Canadians coming from Toronto, you'll most likely have stops in Vancouver and Osaka, although at certain times of the year there are non-stop flights from Toronto to Osaka. Barring special promotions you can expect to pay from around CAN$1400 from Vancouver, and CAN$1600 from Toronto. Once in Bangkok, you can choose to travel overland to Laos or Cambodia, or head south by road or rail into Malaysia and Singapore and then across to Sumatra in Indonesia. Or, you can buy one of the good-value flights to Southeast Asian destinations offered by many Bangkok travel agents, eg Bangkok–Bali for about US$275, or Bangkok–Phnom Penh for US$105. Visit the websites Ⓦ www.thaiairline.com and Ⓦ www.orient-thai.com for a fuller list of current fares from Bangkok to destinations in Southeast Asia.

Airlines

Air China East Coast Ⓣ 1-800/982-8802, West Coast Ⓣ 1-800/986-1985, Toronto Ⓣ 416/581-8833, Ⓦ www.airchina.com.cn/en/index.jsp.
Air New Zealand US Ⓣ 1-800/262-1234, Canada Ⓣ 1-800/663-5494, Ⓦ www.airnewzealand.com.
All Nippon Airways Ⓣ 1-800/235-9262, Ⓦ www.anaskyweb.com.
Aloha Airlines Ⓣ 1-800/367-5250, Ⓦ www.alohaair.com.
America West Airlines Ⓣ 1-800/235-9292, Ⓦ www.americawest.com.
American Airlines Ⓣ 1-800/433-7300, Ⓦ www.aa.com.
American Trans Air Ⓣ 1-800/435-9282, Ⓦ www.ata.com.
Asiana Airlines Ⓣ 1-800/227-4262, Ⓦ www.flyasiana.com.
British Airways Ⓣ 1-800/247-9297, Ⓦ www.britishairways.com.
Cathay Pacific Ⓣ 1-800/233-2742, Ⓦ www.cathaypacific.com.
China Airlines Ⓣ 1-800/227-5118, Ⓦ www.china-airlines.com.
Continental Airlines domestic Ⓣ 1-800/523-3273, international Ⓣ 1-800/231-0856, Ⓦ www.continental.com.
Delta Air Lines domestic Ⓣ 1-800/221-1212, international Ⓣ 1-800/241-4141, Ⓦ www.delta.com.
Emirates Air Ⓣ 1-800/777-3999, Ⓦ www.emirates.com.
EVA Airways Ⓣ 1-800/695-1188, Ⓦ www.evaair.com. Flights from the US and Canada to Taiwan.
Japan Air Lines Ⓣ 1-800/525-3663, Ⓦ www.jal.co.jp/en.
KLM/Northwest US domestic Ⓣ 1-800/225-2525, US international Ⓣ 1-800/447-4747, Ⓦ www.klmuk.com.
Korean Airlines Ⓣ 1-800/438-5000, Ⓦ www.koreanair.com.
Lufthansa US Ⓣ 1-800/645-3880, Canada Ⓣ 1-800/563-5954, Ⓦ www.lufthansa.com.
Malaysia Airlines Ⓣ 1-800/552-9264, Ⓦ www.mas.com.my.
Qantas Airways Ⓣ 1-800/227-4500, Ⓦ www.qantas.com.au
Royal Nepal Airlines Ⓣ 1-800/266-3725, Ⓦ www.royalnepal.com.
Singapore Airlines Ⓣ 1-800/742-3333, Ⓦ www.singaporeair.com.
Thai Airways International Ⓣ 1-800/426-5204, Ⓦ www.thaiair.com.
United Airlines domestic Ⓣ 1-800/241-6522, international Ⓣ 1-800/538-2929, Ⓦ www.united.com.
US Airways domestic Ⓣ 1-800/428-4322, international Ⓣ 1-800/622-1015, Ⓦ www.usairways.com.
Virgin Atlantic Airways Ⓣ 1-800/862-8621, Ⓦ www.virgin-atlantic.com.

Stopover returns and open-jaw tickets

If you're only visiting a couple of countries in Asia, buying a ticket with a **stopover** option may be your best deal. For example, a return ticket from New York to Singapore with a stopover in Hong Kong (of up to three months) would only be an extra US$100.

To give yourself some freedom, you might consider buying an **open-jaw** ticket, offered by most major airlines. This allows you to fly into one country and out of another. You might choose to fly into Bangkok and out of Jakarta a few months later, allowing you to decide how you want to make your travel arrangements once inside Asia. Open-jaws are usually more expensive than standard round-trip flights: prices are generally calculated by halving the round-trip fares to each destination and then adding the two figures together.

RTW and Circle Pacific tickets

Round-the-World (RTW) tickets or **Circle Pacific** tickets can be very good value if you are planning a multi-stop trip. An example of an RTW itinerary is San Francisco–Bali–Singapore surface to Bangkok–Cairo–Athens surface to London–San Francisco for US$1850. A typical Circle Pacific ticket might be New York–Hong Kong–Bangkok–Jakarta–Bali–Los Angeles–New York for US$1200.

Another option is Cathay Pacific's **All-Asia Pass**, which allows you to fly into Hong Kong and then gives you 21 days of flights to a choice of seventeen different cities with prices starting from just US$999.

Discount flight and travel agents

Air Brokers International ⓣ 1-800/883-3273, ⓦ www.airbrokers.com. Consolidator and specialist in RTW and Circle Pacific tickets.

Educational Travel Center ⓣ 1-800/747-5551 or 608/256-5551, ⓦ www.edtrav.com. Student/youth and consolidator fares.

High Adventure Travel ⓣ 1-800/350-0612 or 415/912-5600, ⓦ www.airtreks.com. RTW and Circle Pacific tickets. The extensive website features an interactive database called "Farebuilder" that lets you build and price your own RTW itinerary.

STA Travel ⓣ 1-800/777-0112 or 781-4040, ⓦ www.statravel.com. Worldwide specialists in independent travel; also student IDs, travel insurance, car rental, rail passes, etc.

Travel Avenue ⓣ 1-800/333-3335, ⓦ www.travelavenue.com. Full-service travel agent that offers discounts in the form of rebates.

Travel CUTS Canada ⓣ 1-800/667-2887, US ⓣ 1-866/246-9762, ⓦ www.travelcuts.com. Canadian student-travel organization.

Worldtek Travel ⓣ 1-800/243-1723, ⓦ www.worldtek.com. Discount travel agency for worldwide travel.

Courier flights

If you're prepared to forgo a few creature comforts for a cheaper airfare, then you might consider **courier flights**. In exchange for an inexpensive airline ticket you will most likely be expected to take a package through customs and/or give up your luggage allowance entirely. Courier flights to Hong Kong, Malaysia, and Singapore are the easiest to come by, and from there you might be able to arrange another courier flight. To arrange a flight, contact one of the organizations listed below.

Air Courier Association ⓣ 1-800/282-1202, ⓦ www.aircourier.org or ⓦ www.cheaptrips.com. Courier flight broker. Membership (1yr $39, 3yr $59, 5yr $89, lifetime $99) also entitles you to twenty percent discount on travel insurance and name-your-own-price non-courier flights.

International Association of Air Travel Couriers ⓣ 561/582-8320, ⓦ www.courier.org. Courier flight broker with membership fee of $45 a year or $80 for two years.

Now Voyager ⓣ 212/431-1616, ⓦ www.nowvoyagertravel.com. Courier flight broker and consolidator.

Packages and organized tours

The scope of **packages and tours** that are available in Southeast Asia is vast. It won't be hard to find something that suits your needs, be it trekking, eco-tourism, or a five-star hotel on the beaches of Bali. The listings below will give you ideas of what's on offer.

Another option to bear in mind is a trip on the incredible **Trans-Siberian Express** from Moscow to Beijing, then on to Hong Kong. Train tickets can be purchased from agents in the US, and package tours including overnight stays in Beijing and Moscow are available. Mir Corp in Seattle (see p.36) offers a wide range of packages – a fifteen-night trip from Moscow to Beijing, for example, costs $1575. See "Getting there from the UK and Ireland", p.31, for more information on the route.

Tour operators

Unless otherwise stated, the prices below generally refer to the land tour only; flights are extra.

Abercrombie & Kent ⓣ1-800/323-7308 or 630/954-2944, ⓦwww.abercrombiekent.com. Offers, among others, "Images of Indochina", a sixteen-day tour of Vietnam and Cambodia. It departs from Bangkok, and visits Hanoi (with a helicopter ride over Ha Long Bay), Hue, Da Nang and Ho Chi Minh City (basic tour $6390 – land only – plus $965 internal air fares).

Adventure Center ⓣ1-800/228-8747, ⓦwww.adventure-center.com. Offering extremely affordable Southeast Asian tours. "Hanoi to Singapore" is a 43-day trip taking in well-known and off-the-beaten-track destinations, and includes the limestone landscapes of Ha Long Bay and the temples at Angkor (from $2155). You can also do a 22-day bicycle tour from Bangkok to Ho Chi Minh City for $1650.

Adventures Abroad ⓣ1-800/665-3998 or 604/303-1099, ⓦwww.adventures-abroad.com. Specializing in small-group tours, such as a nineteen-day tour of Cambodia and Vietnam for $2589. A 45-day tour of Thailand, Burma, Laos, Vietnam and Cambodia costs $7538. Other combinations include Burma, Laos, Vietnam and Cambodia for $5960.

Geographic Expeditions ⓣ1-800/777-8183 or 415/922-0448, ⓦwww.geoex.com. Specialists in "responsible tourism" with a range of customized tours and/or set packages. Their trips are perhaps a bit more demanding of the traveller than the average specialist, although each tour is rated from easy to rigorous. The "Mekong Pansea" tour is based around the Mekong River and features a boat journey from Ho Chi Minh City to Angkor (from $3585).

Mir Corp ⓣ1-800/424-7289, ⓦwww.mircorp.com. Specialists in Trans-Siberian Express trips. Moscow to Vladivostok in seventeen days costs $4495.

Mountain Travel-Sobek ⓣ1-888/687-6235, ⓦwww.mtsobek.com. Tours to Laos, Vietnam, Thailand and Cambodia.

Pacific Holidays ⓣ212/629-3888, ⓦwww.pacificholidaysinc.com. Inexpensive tour group. Trips include a fifteen-day "Best of Southeast Asia" sightseeing tour of Bangkok, Bali, Singapore, Hong Kong from $1995.

TEI Tours ⓣ925/825-6104, ⓦwww.teiglobal.com/travel.html. Trans-Siberian-Express packages and customized tours.

Getting there from Australia and New Zealand

The fastest and most reliable way to get to Southeast Asia **from Australia or New Zealand** is to fly, and the cheapest is to buy a one-way flight to one of the region's gateways such as Kupang, Denpasar, Jakarta, Singapore, Kuala Lumpur, Bangkok or Hong Kong, and carry on from there by air, sea or overland. There's no shortage of direct flights to major Southeast Asia gateways, although it's well worth taking advantage of a **stopover** en route or considering an **open-jaw** ticket that allows you to fly into one country and out of another and travel overland in between. Other options are **Circle Asia** tickets – which can be a little complicated, as each sector needs to be costed separately – and **Asean Air Passes**, which take you via two or more Asian cities en route, or **Round-the-World (RTW)** tickets if you're taking in Southeast Asia as part of a wider trip.

Tickets purchased direct from the airlines are usually expensive – more than likely you'll be quoted the published rate. You'll get a much better deal with a **discount travel agent**. Fares are very competitive, so whatever kind of ticket you're after it's best to shop around. The travel agents listed on p.38 can fill you in on all the latest deals and any special limited offers. If you're a student or under 26, you may be able to get a discounted fare; STA is a good place to start. Fares are seasonally rated, with prices for flights usually higher during Christmas and New Year and mid-year periods; generally, high season is mid-May to end-August and December to mid-January. Airfares from east-coast **Australian gateways** are all pretty much the same. Perth and Darwin are around AUS$100–200 cheaper. **From New Zealand**, you can expect to pay about NZ$150–300 more from Christchurch and Wellington than from Auckland. Published fares to Indonesia, Malaysia, the Philippines and Brunei start at roughly AUS$900/NZ$1090 for a single and AUS$1300/NZ$1570 for a return, while to Thailand, Indochina and Hong Kong you can expect to pay from AUS$1200/NZ$1290 single and AUS$1680/NZ$2030 return.

See "Getting there from the UK and Ireland", p.28, for information on flying to **gateway cities**.

Airlines

Air Canada Australia ⓣ1300/655 767 or 02/9286 8900, New Zealand ⓣ09/379 3371, ⓦwww.aircanada.com.
Air China Australia ⓣ02/9232 7277, New Zealand ⓣ09/379 7696, ⓦwww.airchina.com.cn/en/index.jsp.
Air India Australia ⓣ02/9299 9202, New Zealand ⓣ09/303 1301, ⓦwww.airindia.com.
Air New Zealand Australia ⓣ13 24 76, New Zealand ⓣ0800/737 000, ⓦwww.airnewzealand.com.au.
Air Pacific Australia ⓣ1800/230 150, New Zealand ⓣ0800/800 178, ⓦwww.airpacific.com.
All Nippon Airways Australia ⓣ1800/251 015 or 02/9367 6711, ⓦwww.ana.co.jp/eng.
American Airlines Australia ⓣ1300/650 747, New Zealand ⓣ09/309 0735 or 0800/887 997, ⓦwww.aa.com.
British Airways Australia ⓣ02/8904 8800, New Zealand ⓣ0800/274 847, ⓦwww.britishairways.com.
Cathay Pacific Australia ⓣ13 17 47, New Zealand ⓣ09/379 0861 or 0508/800 454, ⓦwww.cathaypacific.com.
China Airlines Australia ⓣ02/9244 2121, New Zealand ⓣ09/308 3364, ⓦwww.china-airlines.com.
China Eastern Airlines Australia ⓣ02/9290 1148, ⓦwww.ce-air.com.
Continental Airlines Australia ⓣ02/9244 2242, New Zealand ⓣ09/308 3350, ⓦwww.continental.com.
Emirates Australia ⓣ02/9290 9700 or 1300/303 777, New Zealand ⓣ09/377 6004, ⓦwww.emirates.com.
Eva Air Australia ⓣ02/9221 0407, New Zealand ⓣ09/358 8300, ⓦwww.evaair.com.
Garuda Australia ⓣ02/9334 9970, New Zealand ⓣ09/366 1862, ⓦwww.garuda-indonesia.com.
Japan Airlines Australia ⓣ02/9272 1111, New Zealand ⓣ09/379 9906, ⓦwww.jal.co.jp/en.
KLM Australia ⓣ1300/303 747, New Zealand ⓣ09/309 1782, ⓦwww.klmuk.com.
Korean Air Australia ⓣ02/9262 6000, New Zealand ⓣ09/914 2000, ⓦwww.koreanair.com.
Lufthansa Australia ⓣ1300/655 727 or 02/9367 3887, New Zealand ⓣ09/303 1529 or 008/945 220, ⓦwww.lufthansa.com.
Malaysia Airlines Australia ⓣ13 26 27, New Zealand ⓣ09/373 2741, ⓦwww.mas.com.my.
Northwest Airlines Australia ⓣ1300/303 747, New Zealand ⓣ09/302 1452, ⓦwww.nwa.com.
Qantas Australia ⓣ13 13 13, New Zealand ⓣ09/661 901, ⓦwww.qantas.com.au.
Royal Brunei Airlines Australia ⓣ07/3017 5000, ⓦwww.bruneiair.com.
Royal Nepal Airlines Australia ⓣ02/9285 6855, New Zealand ⓣ09/309 8094, ⓦwww.royalnepal.com.
Singapore Airlines Australia ⓣ13 10 11, New Zealand ⓣ09/303 2129 or 0800/808 909, ⓦwww.singaporeair.com.
Thai Airways Australia ⓣ1300/651 960, New Zealand ⓣ09/377 3886, ⓦwww.thaiair.com.
United Airlines Australia ⓣ13 17 77, New Zealand ⓣ09/379 3800 or 0800/508 648, ⓦwww.united.com.
Vietnam Airlines Australia ⓣ02/9283 1355, ⓦwww.vietnamairlines.com.vn.
Virgin Atlantic Airways Australia ⓣ02/9244 2747, New Zealand ⓣ09/308 3377, ⓦwww.virgin-atlantic.com.

Stopover returns and open-jaw tickets

In a region the size of Southeast Asia, it's well worth taking advantage of a **stopover** en route, often a little cheaper than flying non-stop. All Asian airlines fly via their home base, giving you a perfect opportunity to explore a bit more of the area. You can stopover in a city for up to three months. Alternatively, **open-jaw** tickets are a good idea if you want to travel overland between gateways; for example, Darwin to Kuala Lumpur on the outward leg and Bangkok to Darwin on the return costs around AUS$800 in low season when travelling via Brunei.

Circle Asia and RTW tickets

If you intend to visit the region as part of a wider trip then tickets that are put together by an alliance of airlines such as **Circle Asia**, that allow you to travel via two or more Asian cities en route, and **Round-the-World (RTW)** tickets offer greater flexibility than a straightforward return flight. For example, an RTW ticket from Sydney to Singapore, taking in London, New York, Los Angeles and Auckland, starts at around AUS$2400/NZ$3000; a round-trip to Brunei from Singapore or Kuala Lumpur will add an extra AUS$450/NZ$500 to the basic price. Another good-value option is an **Asean Air Pass**, which is put together by the national airlines of Brunei, Indonesia, Malaysia, the Philippines, Singapore, Thailand and Vietnam. Prices depend on which country you choose to start from and the number of stopovers you want to make. Stopovers are allowed in any two to six of the other countries with a minimum stay of three nights and a maximum of three months for each one: an Asean Air Pass beginning and ending in Malaysia or Brunei costs from around AUS$650/NZ$800 for three coupons, AUS$900/NZ$1000 for four coupons, AUS$1100/NZ$1400 for five coupons or AUS$1300/NZ$1500 for six coupons. For more information on Asean Air Passes and RTW tickets, see "Getting there from the UK and Ireland", p.30.

Discount flight agents

Budget Travel New Zealand ⓣ09/366 0061 or 0800/808 040, ⓦwww.budgettravel.co.nz. Discount/budget fares and holidays.
Destinations Unlimited New Zealand ⓣ09/414 1680, ⓦwww.etravelnz.com. Worldwide fare discounts, plus a good selection of tours and holiday packages.
Flight Centre Australia ⓣ13 31 33 or 02/9235 3522, New Zealand ⓣ09/358 4310, ⓦwww.flightcentre.com.au. Friendly service with competitive discounts on airfares plus a wide range of package holidays.
Northern Gateway Australia ⓣ08/8941 1394, ⓦwww.northerngateway.com.au. Specialists in discount fares to Southeast Asia.
STA Travel Australia ⓣ1300/733 035, ⓦwww.statravel.com.au, New Zealand ⓣ0508/782 872, ⓦwww.statravel.co.nz. Fare discounts for students and under 26s, plus visa, student cards and travel insurance.
Student Uni Travel Australia ⓣ02/9232 8444, ⓦaustralia@backpackers.net. Student/youth discounts and travel advice.
Thomas Cook Australia ⓣ02/9231 2877, New Zealand ⓣ09/379 3920, ⓦwww.thomascook.com. Discounts on fares, travellers' cheques, bus and rail passes.
Trailfinders Australia ⓣ02/9247 7666, ⓦwww.trailfinders.com.au. Independent travel advice, good discounts on fares.
Travel.com.au Australia ⓣ02/9262 3555, ⓦwww.travel.com.au. Online worldwide fare discounter.

Overland routes

Many travellers from Australia and New Zealand fly to **Indonesia** and overland from there. The main onward routes are from Bali to Bangkok via Java, Sumatra and the Malaysian Peninsula (of course, this can be extended to Indochina), and Bali to the Philippines via Java, and either Borneo or Sulawesi.

There are regular direct **flights to Denpasar** on Qantas and Garuda from eastern Australian gateway cities (published fares from AUS$900 one-way, AUS$1300 return). Garuda flies from Auckland to Jakarta with a Denpasar stopover. If you're thinking of entering Indonesia on a one-way fare, make sure you have a valid onward ticket (air or ferry) out of the country. From Bali, you can either pick up a flight to another gateway at Denpasar, a ferry to Makassar in Sulawesi, or carry on through Java to either Malaysia and Thailand, or to Surabaya in Java, where there are flights and ferries to Banjarmasin in Kalimantan and Makassar. From Banjarmasin, you can bus it through Kalimantan to Sarawak or Sabah and then island-hop through the Philippines to Manila. Alternatively, fly or take the ferry from Surabaya to Makassar, then bus it to the ferry port of Bitung in the north of the island where there's a regular ferry service to Davao on the southern Philippine island of Mindanao. Make sure you plan your route well, allowing at least two weeks longer than you think your trip will take, as local transport doesn't always leave at the time or on the day specified.

Another possibility is to fly into **Singapore** and make your way upland from there: a one-way fare from Auckland to Singapore on Air New Zealand costs about NZ$1900.

Organized tours and package holidays

Package holidays to Southeast Asian destinations are numerous and generally good value. As well as flights and accommodation, most companies also offer a range of itineraries that take in the major sights and activities. Bookings are usually made through travel agents who carry a wide selection of brochures for you to choose from. An organized tour is worth considering if you're after a more energetic holiday, have ambitious sightseeing plans and limited time, are uneasy with the language and customs, or just don't like travelling alone. The specialists listed below can also help you get to more remote areas and organize activities that may be difficult to arrange yourself, such as extended overland tours that take in several countries, white-water rafting, diving, cycling and trekking. Most organized tours don't include airfares from Australasia.

Tour operators

Unless otherwise stated, the prices below generally refer to the land tour only; flights are extra.

The Adventure Travel Company New Zealand ⓣ09/379 9755, ⓦwww.adventuretravel.co.nz. NZ's one-stop shop for adventure travel are agents for Intrepid, Peregrine, Guerba Expeditions and a host of others.
Adventure World Australia ⓣ02/8913 0755, ⓦwww.adventureworld.com.au, New Zealand ⓣ09/524 5118, ⓦwww.adventureworld.co.nz. Agents for a vast array of international adventure travel companies.
Allways Dive Expeditions Australia ⓣ1800/338 239, ⓦwww.allwaysdive.com.au. All-inclusive dive packages to prime locations through Southeast Asia.
Earthwatch ⓣ03/9682 6828, ⓦwww.earthwatch.org/australia. Volunteer work on projects in Indonesia and Thailand.
Intrepid Adventure Travel Australia ⓣ1300/360 667, ⓦwww.intrepidtravel.com. Small-group tours to China and Southeast Asia with an emphasis on cross-cultural contact and low-impact tourism.
Peregrine Adventures Australia ⓣ03/9662 2700, ⓦwww.peregrine.net.au. Affordable small-group adventure travel company and agent offering a range of graded trips.
Pro Dive Travel Australia ⓣ02/9281 5066 or 1800/820 820, ⓦwww.prodive.com.au. Dive packages to Southeast Asia.
San Michele Travel Australia ⓣ02/9299 1111 or 1800/22 22 44, ⓦwww.asiatravel.com.au. Customized rail tours throughout Southeast Asia.
Silke's Travel Australia ⓣ1800/807 860 or 02/8347 2000, ⓔsilke@silkes.com.au. Specially tailored packages for gay and lesbian travellers.
The Surf Travel Co Australia ⓣ02/9527 4722 or 1800/687 873, New Zealand ⓣ09/473 8388, ⓦwww.surftravel.com.au. A well-established surf travel company that can arrange airfares, accommodation and yacht charter in Indonesia, as well as give the low-down on the best surf beaches in the region.
Travel Indochina Australia ⓣ1300/365 355, ⓦwww.travelindochina.com.au. Offers low-impact tour packages, using mid- to top-range hotels.

Getting around

Local transport across Southeast Asia is uniformly good value compared to public transport in the West, and is often one of the highlights of a trip, not least because of the chance to fraternize with local travellers. Overland transport between neighbouring Southeast Asian countries is also fairly straightforward – a variety of trains, buses, share taxis and ferries shuttle across most of the region's international borders and are available to foreigners, so long as they have the right paperwork; full details on cross-border transport options are given in the introduction to each chapter.

Local transport

Not surprisingly, the ultra-modern enclaves of Singapore and Hong Kong boast the fastest, sleekest and most efficient transport systems in the region. Elsewhere, **trains** are generally the most comfortable way to travel any distance, if not always the fastest or most frequent. Thailand and Malaysia both have decent train networks and rolling stock, while Indonesia's is a notch below them. Vietnam's train system is fairly hardscrabble, while Cambodia's is downright dilapidated. Faster and more frequent, but often a lot more

The Mekong River

The **Mekong** is one of the great rivers of the world, the third longest in Asia, after the Yangtse and the Yellow rivers. From its source, 4920m up on the east Tibetan Plateau, it roars down through China's Yunnan province, where it's known as Lancang Jiang, the "Turbulent River", then snakes its way more peacefully through Laos, by way of the so-called Golden Triangle, where Burma, Thailand and Laos touch. From Laos, it crosses Cambodia and continues south to Vietnam, where it splinters into the many arms of the Mekong Delta before flowing into the South China Sea, 4184km from where its journey began.

For the adventurous traveller, it may be possible to travel almost the entire length of this great waterway by boat, though the uppermost reaches are characterized by steep descents and fierce rapids, and the Yunnan stretch is only served by the occasional barge from Jinghong. Once in **Laos**, however, river transport becomes more of a possibility, and the two-day trip by cargo boat from Houayxai to Louang Phabang (see p.536) is one of the highlights of Southeast Asia. Laos was once truly a country of the Mekong: the river was its lifeline, its highway and its rice basket, and for 750km it also defines the Lao–Thai border. Laos's two most important cities were built on the banks of the Mekong: both the ancient royal city of **Louang Phabang** and the modern capital **Vientiane** make the most of their riverside settings. The country's other big Mekong draw is the riverine archipelago in the far south known as **Si Phan Don**, or "Four Thousand Islands", where the fourteen-kilometre-wide Mekong is dotted with tiny islands inhabited by fishing communities, and there is even a rapidly vanishing pod of rare freshwater dolphins.

Across in **Thailand**, the Mekong attractions are more low-key, with a string of laid-back guesthouses, such as those at Chiang Khan and Sri Chiangmai, offering short trips up or downriver to see local caves and waterfalls. Here, too, lives the endangered giant catfish, found only in the Mekong and, at up to 3m long, the world's largest freshwater fish. **Chiang Khong** is one of the most popular Mekong-side stops in Thailand, chiefly because of its shuttle boats to Houayxai on the Lao bank of the river, where you can pick up a boat down to Louang Phabang. **Nong Khai** is the main transport hub on the Thai side of the Mekong, linked to Laos by the Friendship Bridge that spans the great river close to Vientiane.

As in Laos, **Cambodia**'s greatest cities have also been shaped by the Mekong. The Cambodian capital, **Phnom Penh**, is one of the most important ports along the whole course of the river, at the confluence of the Mekong and the Tonle Sap River. The 100-kilometre-long **Tonle Sap River** is quite extraordinary, as it changes direction according to the level of the Mekong. During the rainy season, the Mekong forces the waters of the Tonle Sap River to back up, sending them northwards to fill the enormous lake at its head. By the climax of the rainy season, this very shallow lake covers 8000 square kilometres, spawning hundreds of tonnes of freshwater fish and irrigating vast plains of rice. It was this natural bounty that fuelled the ancient Khmer Empire, enabling it to prosper, to expand its territories across Southeast Asia, and to construct the magnificent temples at nearby Angkor. When the Mekong waters subside, in early November, the Tonle Sap River changes direction and drains once more into the Mekong. During most of the year, it is possible to take a series of boats from Phnom Penh all the way into southern Laos.

The Mekong saves its most spectacular dramas for its final act, when it separates into the many tributaries known as **Cuu Long** or "Nine Dragons" to water the vast alluvial plains of **Vietnam's Mekong Delta**. This agricultural powerhouse near Ho Chi Minh City is one of the greatest rice-growing areas of the world and has always been crucial to Vietnam's economy; it is also densely populated, and was the scene of some of the most intense fighting of the Vietnam War. These days, however, the region is more tranquil and there are boats and sampans aplenty to ferry travellers to the floating markets at Can Tho and the delta villages of My Tho and Ben Tre, where the views of emerald paddies, coconut palms and conical-hatted farmers make a fitting climax to any Southeast Asian journey.

nerve-wracking, **long-distance buses** are the chief mode of travel in Southeast Asia. Drivers tend to race at dangerous speeds and are sometimes high on amphetamines to keep them going through the night. Seats are usually cramped and the whole experience is often uncomfortable, so wherever possible, try to book a pricier but more comfortable air-con bus for overnight journeys – or take the train. Shorter bus journeys can be very enjoyable, however, and are often the only way to get between places. Buses come in various shapes, many of them quite novel to Western eyes. In small towns and rural areas in particular, **local buses** are often either minivans or even small pick-up trucks fitted with bench seats, while in parts of east Malaysia and Laos, riverboats function as buses; full details of all these idiosyncrasies are given in each chapter. On many buses, you just shout out when you want to get off, though the larger government-run buses tend to have conductors who issue tickets and tell the driver where you're going.

Taxis also come in many unrecognizable forms, including the infamous tuk-tuk (three-wheeled buggies with deafening two-stroke engines), elegant rickshaws powered by a man on a bicycle, or simply a bloke on a motorbike (usually wearing a numbered vest); none of these have meters, so all prices must be bargained for and fixed before you set off. In many riverine towns and regions, it's also common to travel by taxi boat. Regular **ferries** connect all major tourist islands with the mainland, and often depart several times a day, though some islands become inaccessible during the monsoon. In some areas, **flying** may be the only practical way to get around. Tickets are reasonably priced considering the distances involved, especially if the route is covered by one of the region's growing number of low-cost airlines – as of writing, the best bets for these were Singapore's Tiger Airways (Ⓦ www.tigerairways.com) and ValuAir (Ⓦ www.valuair.com), Malaysia's Air Asia (Ⓦ www.airasia.com), and Thailand's Orient Thai (Ⓦ www.orient-thai.com).

In most countries, **timetables** for any transport other than trains and planes are vague at best and sometimes don't exist at all; the vehicle simply leaves when there are enough passengers to make the journey profitable for the driver. The best strategy is to turn up early in the morning when most local people begin their journeys. For an idea of frequency and duration of transport services between the main towns, check the "**Travel details**" at the end of each chapter. **Security** is an important consideration on public transport. On buses, never fall asleep with your bag by your side, and never leave belongings unattended at a food-stop. On trains, be especially vigilant when the train stops at stations and takes on hawkers, ensure your money belt is safely tucked under your clothes before going to sleep and that your luggage is safely stowed (preferably padlocked to an immovable object). See "Crime and personal safety" on p.66 for more advice.

Throughout Southeast Asia it's possible to rent your own transport. **Cars** are available in all major tourist centres, and range from flimsy Jimnys to air-con 4x4s; you will need your international driver's licence. If you can't face the traffic yourself, you can often hire a **car with driver** for a small extra fee. One of the best ways to explore the countryside is to rent a **motorbike**. They vary from small 100cc Yamahas to more robust trail bikes and can be rented from guesthouses, shops or tour agencies. Check the small print on your insurance policy, and buy extra cover locally if necessary. **Bicycles** are also a good way to travel, and can be rented from guesthouses or larger-scale rental places.

Transport between Southeast Asian countries

All countries in Southeast Asia open some of their land borders to travellers with the right **visa**, which means you can explore the region without backtracking. Most countries demand that you specify the exact land border when applying – see the section on "Entry requirements and visa extension", in the introduction to each chapter, for more advice on this. Travelling between countries by bus, train or boat is obviously more time-

Overland routes and inter-Asia flights

The following information provides an overview of those **land and sea crossings** that are both legal and straightforward ways for tourists to travel between the countries of Southeast Asia. The information is fleshed out in the accounts of relevant border towns within the Guide. There are so many **flights** between Southeast Asian countries that we have only singled out the most exceptional (outstanding routes or prices); you can make inter-Asia flights to and from every capital city in Southeast Asia, and from many other major airports besides. A new option for flights within the region are the so-called low-cost airlines. These have some great savings, but there are also restrictions to contend with.

To Brunei

From Malaysia Boats to Brunei depart daily from Lawas and Limbang in northern Sarawak, and from Pulau Labuan, itself connected by boat to Kota Kinabalu in Sabah. From Miri in Sarawak, several **buses** travel daily to Kuala Belait, in the far western corner of Brunei. The overland route from Sabah to Brunei necessitates taking a bus to the Temburong district, from where it's only a short boat trip to Bandar Seri Begawan.

To Cambodia

From Vietnam By **bus** from Ho Chi Minh City via Moc Bai to Phnom Penh. There are also two crossings just north of Chau Doc on the Bassac River.
From Thailand By **bus and boat** from Trat to Sihanoukville, via Hat Lek and Koh Kong. By **bus and/or train** from Aranyaprathet to Sisophon, Siem Reap (for Angkor) and Phnom Penh, via Poipet. By **bus** across the two border crossings near Pailin (at Phsa Prom and Daung Lem) and the more recently opened crossings in northeast Thailand – the Chong Chom–O'Smach border pass and the little-used Sa Ngam–Choam crossing. Daily Bangkok Airways **flights** from Bangkok to Phnom Penh and Siem Reap.
From Laos It's possible to cross from Laos on the Mekong at the "unofficial" border Voen Kham to Stung Treng and take **boats and buses** down to Phnom Penh.

To Hong Kong and Macau

From China By **train** from Beijing to Hong Kong (via Guangzhou in Canton).

To Indonesia

From Malaysia and Singapore By **ferry** or **speedboat** from Penang to Medan in northern Sumatra; from Melaka to Dumai in northern Sumatra; from Johor Bahru in far southern Malaysia to Pulau Batam and Pulau Bintan; from Singapore to Pulau Batam, Pulau Bintan and Pulau Karimun, in Indonesia's Riau Archipelago; and from Kuala Lumpur to Tanjung Balai in Sumatra. By **bus** from Kuching (Sarawak) via Entikong to Pontianak (Kalimantan). By **ferry** from Tewau (Sabah) to Pulau Nunukan in northeastern Kalimantan. There are direct **flights** from Kuala Lumpur to Makassar in southern Sulawesi, and from Singapore to Mataram on Lombok and Manado in northern Sulawesi.

To Laos

From Thailand Five legal border crossings (by various combinations of **road, rail and river** transport): Chiang Khong to Houayxai; Nong Khai to Vientiane; Nakhon Phanom to Thakhek; Mukdahan to Savannakhet; and Chong Mek to Pakxe. Many travellers also **fly** from Bangkok or Chiang Mai to Vientiane or Louang Phabang.
From Vietnam There are four border points. The Lao Bao Pass, 80km southwest of Dong Ha, is about 240km from Savannakhet, and there's also an international **bus** link between Da Nang and Savannakhet. The Kaew Nua Pass (known as Nam Phao in Lao), links Vinh with Lak Xao, and is reasonably convenient for Vientiane and Thakhek, while the Nam Can to Nong Het crossing gives you access to Phonsavan. A new crossing was opened in 2004 at Nameo, just east of Xam Nua in northeastern Loas. Both Vietnam Airlines and Lao Airlines **fly** from Hanoi to Vientiane (1hr).
From China By **bus** from Kunming in China's southwestern Yunnan province to Vientiane; from Jinghong to Oudomxai or Louang Namtha; from Mengla via Mo Han to Boten, northeast of Louang Namtha. Lao Airlines operates **flights** from Kunming to Vientiane, via Louang Phabang.
From Cambodia It's possible to take **boats and buses** from Phnom Penh, via Anlong Veng, to Stung

consuming than flying, but it's also cheaper and can be more satisfying. The permutations for overland travel are endless, and worth investigating before you buy your initial flight from home, but by far the most common place to start is Bangkok, as it

Treng on the Mekong at the "unofficial" border Voen Kham and take **boats and buses** down to Phnom Penh. Lao Airlines operates **flights** between Phnom Penh and Vientiane via Pakxe.

To Malaysia and Singapore

From Thailand By direct **train** from Bangkok to: Penang, Kuala Lumpur via Hat Yai, or Singapore via Penang. By **bus** or **share taxi** from the southern Thai town of Hat Yai to Alor Setar, via Dan Nok, and to Penang, KL or Singapore. By road from Sungai Kolok and Ban Taba to Kota Bharu. By **boat** from Satun to Kuala Perlis and Pulau Langkawi. From Phuket, you can **fly** to Penang, KL and Singapore; while from Hat Yai, there are services to KL and Singapore.

From Indonesia By **ferry** from Medan in northern Sumatra to Penang; from Dumai (northern Sumatra) to Melaka; from Pulau Batam in the Riau Archipelago to either Johor Bahru or Singapore; and from Tanjung Balaito Kukup, just to the southwest of JB. From Kalimantan, you can take a **bus** from Pontianak to Kuching in Sarawak, or walk across the border at Nanga Badau then take a bus to Kuching. Alternatively, you can cross into Sabah on a two-hour ferry from Pulau Nunukan to Tawau, two days' bus ride southeast of Kota Kinabalu.

From Brunei Direct **boats** from Bandar Seri Begawan to Lawas (for Sabah), Limbang, and Pulau Labuan (just off Sabah). Also, **buses** from Bandar Seri Begawan to Miri in Sarawak (via Seria and Kuala Berait) and Kota Kinabalu in Sabah.

To the Philippines

From Hong Kong Both Cathay Pacific and Philippine Airlines have **flights** to Manila. British Airways, Emirates and Gulf Air all fly to Manila through Hong Kong, and it's possible to get good fares because they are keen to fill seats for the last leg of the journey.

From Malaysia and Singapore Malaysia Airlines **flies** from Kuala Lumpur to Manila and Cebu City. From Singapore, there are **flights** to Manila.

To Thailand

From Malaysia and Singapore By **train** to Hat Yai and Bangkok from Singapore, Kuala Lumpur and Penang. By **bus** to the southern Thai town of Hat Yai from Singapore, KL, Penang and Alor Setar, via Dan Nok. Also, long-distance buses and minibuses to Bangkok, Krabi, Phuket and Surat Thani from KL, Penang and Singapore. By **boat** from Kuala Perlis and Pulau Langkawi to Satun. Bangkok Airways operates daily **flights** between Singapore and Ko Samui.

From Laos By **bus and/or boat** from Houayxai to Chiang Kong; Vientiane to Nong Khai; Thakhek to Nakhon Phanom; Savannakhet to Mukdahan; and Pakxe to Chong Mek. Lao Airlines operates a handy **flight** between Vientiane and Chiang Mai.

From Cambodia By **bus and/or train** from Sisophon, Siem Reap and Phnom Penh to Bangkok, via Poipet and Aranyaprathet. By **bus and boat** from Sihanoukville via Koh Kong and Hat Lek to Trat in east Thailand. By **bus** across the two border crossings northeast of Chanthaburi (at Phsa Prom and Daung Lem) to Pailin, and the more recently opened crossings in northeast Thailand, at the Chong Chom–O'Smach border pass and the little-used Sa Ngam–Choam crossing. Daily Bangkok Airways **flights** between Phnom Penh and Bangkok and Siem Reap and Bangkok.

To Vietnam

From Laos There are now four border crossings: the Lao Bao Pass, some 80km southwest of Dong Ha; the Kaew Nua Pass, 100km west of Vinh; at Nam Can, east of Phonsavan; and at Nameo, east of Xam Nua. All four are accessible by **bus**. Both Vietnam Airlines and Lao Airlines **fly** from Vientiane to Hanoi (1hr).

From Cambodia By **bus** from Phnom Penh to Moc Bai, and from there on to Ho Chi Minh City. There are also two crossings just north of Chau Doc on the Bassac River.

From China The Beijing–Nanning–Hanoi **train** enters Vietnam at Dong Dang, north of Lang Son, where there's also a road crossing known as Huu Nghi. By **bus** from Kunming to Lao Cai, and then by **train** on to Hanoi.

gives easy access to Cambodia, Laos (and then on into Vietnam), as well as to Malaysia and by extension Singapore and Indonesia. From Australia, however, it makes sense to begin in eastern Indonesia.

Red tape and visas

Country-specific advice about visas, entry requirements, border formalities and visa extensions is given in the introduction at the beginning of each chapter. As a broad guide, the only countries in Southeast Asia for which citizens of the EU, USA, Canada, Australia and New Zealand need to buy a visa in advance if arriving by air and staying less than thirty days are: Laos (15 days maximum on arrival), the Philippines (21 days maximum on arrival) and Vietnam (no entry without advance visa). However, as all visa requirements, prices and processing times are subject to change, it's always worth double-checking with embassies. Also, different rules usually apply if you're staying more than thirty days or arriving overland. Nearly every country requires that your passport be valid for at least six months from your date of entry. Some also demand proof of onward travel (such as an air ticket) or sufficient funds to buy a ticket.

Southeast Asian embassies and consulates abroad

It's usually straightforward to get visas for your next port of call while you're on the road in Southeast Asia. Details of **neighbouring Southeast Asian embassies** are given in the "Listings" section of each capital city within the Guide.

Brunei

ⓦwww.brunet.bn/gov/mfa/abroad.htm
Australia 16 Bulwarra Close, O'Mally ACT 2606, Canberra ⓣ02/6290 1801.
Canada 395 Laurier Avenue East, Ottawa, Ontario K1N 6R4.
New Zealand Contact the embassy in Canberra (see above).
UK and Ireland 19–20 Belgrave Square, London SW1X 8PG ⓣ020/7581 0521.
USA Watergate Hotel, Suite 300, 2600 Virginia Avenue, Washington DC 20037 ⓣ202/342-0159.

Cambodia

ⓦwww.cambodia.gov.kh/unisql1/egov/english/country.embassy.html
Australia 5 Canterbury Crescent, Deakin, ACT 2600 ⓣ02/6237 1259.
Canada Contact the embassy in Washington (see below).
France 4 Rue Adolphe Yvon, 75116 Paris ⓣ01/45 03 47 20.
New Zealand Contact the embassy in Canberra (see above).
UK and Ireland Contact the embassy in France (see above).
USA 4500 16th St, Washington DC 20011 ⓣ202/726-7742; 866 UN Plaza, Suite 420, New York 10017 ⓣ212/223-0676; 422 Ord St, Los Angeles, California 90112 ⓣ213/625-7766.

Hong Kong

Contact your nearest Chinese embassy.
ⓦwww.fmprc.gov.cn/eng/wjb/zwjg/default.htm
Australia 15 Coronation Drive, Yarralumla, ACT 2600 ⓣ02/6273 4783; 539 Elizabeth St, Surry Hills, Sydney ⓣ02/9698 7929; plus offices in Melbourne ⓣ03/9822 0607/4 and Perth ⓣ08/9321 8193.
Canada 515 St Patrick's St, Ottawa, Ontario K1N 5H3 ⓣ613/791-0511.
Ireland 40 Ailesbury Rd, Dublin 4 ⓣ01/269 1707.
New Zealand 2-6 Glenmore Street, Wellington, ⓣ04/472 1382.
UK 31 Portland Place, London W1; visa line ⓣ0900/188 0808.
USA 2300 Connecticut Ave NW, Washington DC 20008 ⓣ202/328-2500.

Indonesia

ⓦwww.indonesianembassy.org.uk/link_indo_embassy.html
Australia 8 Darwin Ave, Yarralumla, Canberra, ACT 2600 ⓣ02/6250 8600; 20 Harry Chan Ave, Darwin, NT 5784 ⓣ089/41 0048; 72 Queen Rd, Melbourne, VIC 3004 ⓣ03/9525 2755; 134 Adelaide Terrace, East Perth, WA 6004 ⓣ08/9221

5858; 236–238 Maroubra Rd, Maroubra, NSW 2035 ⓣ02/9344 9933.
Canada 287 Maclaren Street, Ottawa, Ontario K2P OL9 ⓣ613/236-7403.
New Zealand 70 Glen Rd, Kelburn, Wellington, PO Box 3543 ⓣ04/475 8697.
UK and Ireland 38 Grosvenor Square, London W1X 9AD; visa line ⓣ0906/550 8962.
USA 2020 Massachusetts Avenue, NW, Washington DC 20036 ⓣ202/775-5200.

Laos

It's much easier to apply for a visa in Bangkok (takes less than a week) than in the West (about two months), as all visa applications must be sent to Laos for approval.
ⓦwww.laoembassy.com
Australia 1 Dalman Crescent, O'Malley, Canberra, ACT ⓣ02/6286 4595.
Canada Contact embassy in Washington (see below).
France 74 Ave Raymond Poincaré, Paris ⓣ01/45 53 02 98.
New Zealand Contact embassy in Canberra (see above).
UK and Ireland Contact embassy in France (see above) or Thailand.
USA 2222 S Street NW, Washington DC 20008 ⓣ202/332-6416.

Macau

Contact your nearest Chinese embassy, listed under "Hong Kong", on p.44.

Malaysia

ⓦwww.kln.gov.my/english/Fr-missionworldwide.html
Australia 7 Perth Ave, Yarralumla, Canberra, ACT 2600 ⓣ02/6273 1543.
Canada 60 Boteler St, Ottawa, Ontario K1N 8Y7 ⓣ613/241-5182.
New Zealand 10 Washington Ave, Brooklyn, Wellington ⓣ04/385 2439.
UK and Ireland 45 Belgrave Square, London SW1X 8QT ⓣ020/7235 8033.
USA 2401 Massachusetts Ave NW, Washington DC 20008 ⓣ202/328-2700.

The Philippines

ⓦwww.dfa.gov.ph/posts/pemb.htm
Australia 1 Moonah Place, Yarralumla, Canberra, ACT 2600 ⓣ02/6273 2535; Philippine Centre, Level 1 27–33 Wentworth Ave, Sydney, NSW 2000 ⓣ02/9262 7377.
Canada 130 Albert St, Suite 606–608, Ottawa, Ontario K1P 5G4 ⓣ613/233-1121.
New Zealand 50 Hobson St, Thorndon, Wellington ⓣ04/4729 848; 8th Floor, 121 Beach Rd, Auckland 1 ⓣ09/303 2423.
UK and Ireland 9a Palace Green, London W8; visa line ⓣ020/7937 1600.
USA 1600 Massachusetts Ave NW, Washington DC 20036 ⓣ202/467-9300.

Singapore

ⓦnotesapp.internet.gov.sg/mfa/dipcon/dipcon.nsf/Smagent
Australia 17 Forster Crescent, Yarralumla, Canberra, ACT 2600 ⓣ02/6273 3944.
Canada 999 West Hastings St, Suite 1820, Vancouver, BC V6C 2W2 ⓣ604/669-5115.
New Zealand 17 Kabul St, Khandallah, Wellington, PO Box 13-140 ⓣ04/479 2076. Visas on entry.
UK and Ireland 9 Wilton Crescent, London SW1X 8SA ⓣ020/7235 9852.
USA 3501 International Place NW, Washington DC 20008 ⓣ202/537-3100.

Thailand

ⓦwww.thaiembassy.org
Australia 111 Empire Circuit, Yarralumla, Canberra ACT 2600 ⓣ02/6273 1149; consulates in Adelaide, Brisbane, Melbourne, Perth and Sydney.
Canada 180 Island Park Drive, Ottawa, Ontario K1Y 0A2 ⓣ613/722-4444.
New Zealand 2 Cook St, PO Box 17-226, Karori, Wellington ⓣ04/4768 618.
UK and Ireland 30 Queens Gate, London SW7; visa line ⓣ09003/405 456, ⓦthailand.embassyhomepage.com.
USA 1024 Wisconsin Ave NW, Suite 401, Washington DC 20007 ⓣ202/944-3600, ⓦwww.thaiembdc.org.

Vietnam

ⓦwww.vietnamembassy-usa.org
Australia 6 Timbarra Crescent, O'Malley, Canberra, ACT 2606 ⓣ02/6286 6059; 489 New South Head Rd, Double Bay, NSW 2025 ⓣ02/9327 1912.
Canada 470 Wilbrod St, Ottawa, Ontario K1M 6M8 ⓣ613/236-0772.
New Zealand Contact embassy in Canberra (see above).
UK and Ireland 12–14 Victoria Rd, London W8 5RD ⓣ020/7937 1912.
USA 1233 20th St NW, Suite 400, Washington DC 20037, ⓣ202/861-0737.

Information, websites and maps

Although some Southeast Asian countries have no dedicated tourist information offices abroad, there's plenty of information available on the Internet, as well as in guidebooks and travelogues.

Tourist offices abroad

Local **tourist information** services are described in the introduction to each chapter.

Brunei

Contact your nearest Bruneian embassy or consulate (see p.44).

Cambodia

No tourist offices abroad. The most useful information is to be found online; see pp.47–48.

Hong Kong

ⓦwww.discoverhongkong.com/eng
Australia Level 4, 80 Druitt St, Sydney, NSW 2000 ⓣ02/9283 3083.
Canada 3rd Floor, 9 Temperance St, Toronto, ON M5H 1Y6 ⓣ416/599-6636.
New Zealand contact Sydney office (see above).
UK and Ireland 6 Grafton St, London W1S 4EA ⓣ020/7533 7100.
USA 115 East 54th Street, 2/F, New York, NY 10022 ⓣ212/412-3382; 10940 Wilshire Blvd, Suite 1220, Los Angeles, CA 90024 ⓣ310/208-4582, ⓦwww.discoverhongkong.com/usa.

Indonesia

ⓦwww.tourismindonesia.com
Australia and New Zealand Contact the Indonesian Consulate General, 236–238 Maroubra Rd, Maroubra, NSW 2035, Australia ⓣ02/9344 9933.
UK and Ireland Contact the embassy (see p.45).
USA and Canada Contact the embassy (see p.45).

Laos

No tourist offices abroad. Attempting to contact and extract information from Lao embassies often results in frustration. The most useful information is to be found online; see pp.47–48.

Macau

ⓦwww.macautourism.gov.mo
If your country has no representation, contact the relevant Portuguese National Tourist Office (ⓦwww.portugal.org) for information.
Australia Level 17, 456 Kent St, Sydney, NSW 2000 ⓣ02/9264 1488.
New Zealand 101 Customs Street, Ballantyne House, Auckland ⓣ09/308 5206.
UK and Ireland 121 Deodar Rd, London SW15 2NU ⓣ020/8877 4517.

Malaysia

ⓦwww.tourism.gov.my
Australia 171 Clarence St, Sydney, NSW 2000 ⓣ02/9299 4441; 56 William St, Perth, WA 6000 ⓣ09/481 0400.
Canada 1590 West Gerogia Street, Vancouver, BC V6E 4M3 ⓣ604/689-8899.
New Zealand Contact the embassy (see p.45).
UK and Ireland 57 Trafalgar Square, London WC2 ⓣ020/7930 7932.
USA 818 West 7th St, Suit 970, Los Angeles, CA 90017 ⓣ323/689-9702; 120 E 56th St, Suite 810, New York, NY 10022 ⓣ212/754-1113.

The Philippines

ⓦwww.wowphilippines.com.ph
Australia Level 1, Philippine Centre, 27–33 Wentworth Ave, Sydney, NSW, 2000 ⓣ02/9283 0711.
Canada 151 Bloor St West, Suite 1120, Toronto, Ontario M5S 1S4 ⓣ416/924-3569.
New Zealand Contact the Sydney office (see above) or the consulate in Auckland (see p.45).
UK and Ireland 146 Cromwell Rd, London SW7 ⓣ020/7835 1100.
USA 30 North Michigan Ave #913, Chicago, IL 60602 ⓣ312/782-2475; 556 Fifth Ave, New York, NY 10036 ⓣ212/575-7915; 447 Sutter St, Suite 507, San Francisco, CA 94108 ⓣ415/956-4060.

Singapore

ⓦwww.visitsingapore.com
Australia 47 York St, Sydney, NSW 2000 ⓣ02/9290 2888.
Canada Contact nearest office in the USA (see below).
New Zealand 18 Ronwood Ave, Manukau, Auckland ⓣ09/262 3393.
UK and Ireland 1st Floor, Carrington House, 126–130 Regent St, London W1R 5FE ⓣ020/7437 0033.
USA 4929 Wilshire Blvd #510, Los Angeles, CA 90010 ⓣ323/677-0808; 1156 Avenue of the Americas, Suit 702, New York, NY 10036 ⓣ212/302-4861.

Thailand

ⓦwww.tourismthailand.org
Australia 75 Pitt Street, Sydney NSW 2000 ⓣ02/9247 7549.
Canada Contact nearest office in the USA (see below).
New Zealand 3rd Floor, 43 High St, Auckland ⓣ09/358 1191.
UK and Ireland 49 Albemarle St, London W1 ⓣ020/7499 7679; recorded information available on ⓣ0870/900 2007.
USA 611 N Larchnont Blvd, 1st Floor, Los Angeles, CA 90004 ⓣ323/382-2353, 61 Broadway, Suit 2810, New York, NY, 10006 ⓣ212/432-0433.

Vietnam

ⓦwww.vietnamtourism.com
Australia and New Zealand Contact the embassy (see p.45).
UK and Ireland Contact the embassy (see p.45).
USA and Canada Contact the embassy (see p.45).

Useful websites

There's plenty of **online information** about Southeast Asia. For details of Internet access within the region, see p.63.

General Southeast Asian travel

1000 Travel Tips ⓦwww.1000traveltips.org. Useful site that gathers travellers' practical reports on fairly recent trips through Indonesia, Singapore, Vietnam, Thailand, Laos and Cambodia.
Accommodating Asia ⓦwww.accomasia.com. Heaps of good traveller-oriented stuff on nearly all parts of Southeast Asia, with especially interesting links to travellers' homepages, under "Travellers notes".
AsianDiver ⓦwww.asiandiver.com/magazine/current.htm. Online version of the divers' magazine, with good coverage of Southeast Asia's diving sites, including recommendations and firsthand diving stories.
Excite Travel's City Net ⓦwww1.excite.com/travel/travelguide. Features geopolitical and tourist information for every country in Southeast Asia, with detailed links plus hotel bookings, sightseeing and weather forecasts.
Internet Travel Information Service ⓦwww.itisnet.com. Specifically aimed at budget travellers, this site is a really useful resource of current info on many Southeast Asian countries, regularly updated by travellers and researchers. Up-to-the-minute info on airfares, border crossings, visa requirements and hotels.
Online tourist information ⓦwww.efn.org/~rick/tour. Exhaustive online travel resource, with links for more than 150 other countries to both official websites and travellers' homepages.
Open Directory Project ⓦwww.dmoz.org/Recreation/Travel. Scores of backpacker-oriented links, including a lot of Asia-specific ones, plus travelogues, web rings and message boards.
Travel-Library.com ⓦwww.travel-library.com. Highly recommended site, which has lively pieces on dozens of travel topics, from the budget travellers' guide to sleeping in airports to how to travel light. Good links too.
Tourism Concern ⓦwww.tourismconcern.org.uk. Website of the British organization that campaigns for responsible tourism. Plenty of useful links to politically and environmentally aware organizations across the world, and a particularly good section on the politics of tourism in Burma.
Weather ⓦwww.usatoday.com/weather/forecast/wglobe.htm. Five-day forecasts from capital cities across the world.

Travellers' forums

Fielding's adventure forum ⓦwww.fieldingtravel.com. Travellers' forum on adventurous and "dangerous" places to travel. Especially useful on the less-travelled routes across borders.
Lonely Planet Thorn Tree ⓦthorntree.lonelyplanet.com. Very popular travellers' bulletin boards, divided into regions (eg islands of Southeast Asia). Ideal for exchanging information with other travellers and for starting a debate, though it does attract an annoying number of regular posters just itching for an argument.
Rough Guides ⓦwww.roughguides.com.

Interactive site for independent travellers, with forums, bulletin boards, travel tips and features, plus online travel guides.
Virtual Tourist ⓦwww.virtualtourist.com. Interactive site that allows travellers to post reviews and photos of destinations, accommodation, restaurants, and travel-related advice.

Country-specific sites

BRUNEI: Brunei Net ⓦwww.tourismbrunei.com This is about the best of a limited but growing number of sites about Brunei.
CAMBODIA: Tales of Asia ⓦwww.talesofasia.com. Mainly Cambodia but lots of information on other Asian countries too, this site has reliable advice on Cambodia's border crossings and overland options.
HONG KONG: Hong Kong Tourist Association ⓦwww.hkta.org. Provides one of the most detailed and up-to-date sites, featuring festivals, weekly events, shopping, food and entertainment listings, plus full visa and visitor information.
INDONESIA: Indonesia and Bali Tourism ⓦwww.indonesia-tourism.com. This is the best of many Indonesia sites, with a little bit of everything on offer as well as links to more in-depth sites.
LAOS: Visit Laos ⓦwww.visit-laos.com. An excellent overview of the country and travel options, from boats on the Mekong to domestic flights.
MACAU: Macau Government Tourist Office ⓦwww.macautourism.gov.mo. Lively general site, including useful links to three-, four-, and five-star hotels, plus a roundup of sights and special events.
MALAYSIA: Virtual Malaysia ⓦwww.virtualmalaysia.com. A comprehensive site to all the states of Malaysia – just click on the flags.
PHILIPPINES: Wow Philippines ⓦwww.tourism.gov.ph. The Philippine Department of Tourism's official site offers a detailed list of festivals and special events.
THAILAND: Amazing Thailand ⓦwww.thailand-travelsearch.com. Lots of links to destinations, places of accommodation and transportation options.
VIETNAM: Vietnam Adventures Online ⓦwww.gocvietnam.com. This general site looks at customs and culture, as well as featuring tourist destinations around the country.

Books and maps

Recommended **maps** of individual countries are detailed in the introduction to each chapter, but the clearest and most detailed map of the whole region is the *Southeast Asia* 1:4,000 000, published by GeoCenter. For **books** specific to each country, see the relevant chapter; only general introductions to the region and books that cover more than one country are reviewed below. The abbreviation o/p means out-of-print. Where a book is published in the UK and the US, the UK publisher is given first, followed by the US one.

Books about Southeast Asia

Nigel Barley (ed.) *The Golden Sword: Stanford Raffles and the East* (British Museum Press, UK). An excellent, well-illustrated introduction to the man, his life, work and the full extent of his fascination with all the countries he explored.
Hans-Ulrich Bernard with Marcus Brooke *Insight Guide to Southeast Asian Wildlife* (APA). Adequate introduction to the flora and fauna of the region, full of gorgeous photos, but not very useful for identifying species in the field.
Russell Braddon *The Naked Island* (Penguin/Simon & Schuster, o/p). Southeast Asia under the Japanese: Braddon's disturbing yet moving first-hand account of the POW camps of Malaya, Singapore and Siam displays courage in the face of appalling conditions; worth scouring secondhand stores for.
Michael Carrithers *The Buddha* (Oxford University Press). Clear, accessible account of the life of the Buddha, and the development and significance of his thought.
Joseph Conrad *Lord Jim* (Penguin). Southeast Asia provides the backdrop to the story of Jim's desertion of an apparently sinking ship and subsequent efforts to redeem himself; modelled upon the sailor, AP Williams, Jim's character also yields echoes of Rajah Brooke of Sarawak.
Harry Foster *A Beachcomber in the Orient* (Dodd, Mead & Company, o/p). A hilarious first-person account of a proto-backpacker who travelled the region in the 1920s. Well worth the effort to find a copy – online sources are your best bet.
Henri Mouhot *Travels in Siam, Cambodia, and Laos* (White Lotus, Bangkok). The account of the final journey of the legendary "discoverer of Angkor Wat", filled with characteristically blunt observations.
George Orwell *Burmese Days* (Penguin). This novel of Burma during British colonial times is reminiscent of all colonised countries in Southeast Asia and wonderfully illustrates the hardships experienced by European empire builders in the early 20th century.
Philip Rawson *The Art of Southeast Asia* (Thames & Hudson, UK). Attractive glossy volume, crammed with colour plates.
Lucy Ridout & Lesley Reader *First-Time Asia: A Rough Guide Special* (Rough Guides).

Easy-to-digest book aimed at backpackers planning their first-ever trip to Asia. It fills in the gaps that guidebooks don't cover, addressing common pre-departure fears, advising on which countries to avoid, and giving heaps of practical tips. Also includes anecdotes from other travellers.

Stan Sesser *The Lands of Charm and Cruelty: Travels in Southeast Asia* (Picador/Vintage Departures). Superb book of insightful essays and well-observed accounts based on articles Stesser originally wrote for *The New Yorker.*

Liesbeth Sluiter *The Mekong Currency* (International Books). An excellent, earthy account of green issues along the Mekong corridor, in Laos, Cambodia and Thailand.

John Tenhula *Voices from Southeast Asia: The Refugee Experience in the United States* (Holmes & Meier). A moving collection of oral histories of Indochinese refugees, many of whom have relocated to the USA.

Map outlets in the UK and Ireland

Blackwell's Map and Travel Shop 50 Broad St, Oxford OX1 3BQ ⓣ01865/793 550, ⓦmaps.blackwell.co.uk/index.html.

Easons Bookshop 40 O'Connell St, Dublin 1 ⓣ01/858 3881, ⓦwww.buy4now.ie/eason.

Hodges Figgis Bookshop 56–58 Dawson St, Dublin 2 ⓣ01/677 4754, ⓦwww.hodgesfiggis.com.

The Map Shop 30a Belvoir St, Leicester LE1 6QH ⓣ0116/247 1400, ⓦwww.mapshopleicester.co.uk.

National Map Centre 22–24 Caxton St, London SW1H 0QU ⓣ020/7222 2466, ⓦwww.mapsnmc.co.uk.

Newcastle Map Centre 55 Grey St, Newcastle-upon-Tyne NE1 6EF ⓣ0191/261 5622.

Ordnance Survey Ireland Phoenix Park, Dublin 8 ⓣ01/802 5349, ⓦwww.osi.ie.

Ordnance Survey of Northern Ireland Colby House, Stranmillis Ct, Belfast BT9 5BJ ⓣ028/9025 5761, ⓦwww.osni.gov.uk.

Stanfords 12–14 Long Acre, London WC2E 9LP ⓣ020/7836 1321, ⓦwww.stanfords.co.uk. Maps available by mail, phone order, or email. Other branches within British Airways offices at 156 Regent St, London W1R 5TA ⓣ020/7434 4744, and 29 Corn St, Bristol BS1 1HT ⓣ0117/929 9966.

The Travel Bookshop 13–15 Blenheim Cres, London, W11 2EE ⓣ020/7229 5260, ⓦwww.thetravelbookshop.co.uk.

Map outlets in the USA and Canada

Adventurous Traveler Bookstore 102 Lake Street, Burlington, VT 05401 ⓣ1-800/282-3963, ⓦwww.adventuroustravel.com.

Book Passage 51 Tamal Vista Blvd, Corte Madera, CA 94925 ⓣ1-800/999-7909, ⓦwww.bookpassage.com.

Distant Lands 56 S Raymond Ave, Pasadena, CA 91105 ⓣ1-800/310-3220, ⓦwww.distantlands.com.

Elliot Bay Book Company 101 S Main St, Seattle, WA 98104 ⓣ1-800/962-5311, ⓦwww.elliotbaybook.com.

Forsyth Travel Library 226 Westchester Ave, White Plains, NY 10604 ⓣ1-800/367-7984, ⓦwww.forsyth.com.

Get Lost Books 1825 Market St, San Francisco, CA 94103 ⓣ415/437-0529, ⓦwww.getlostbooks.com.

Globe Corner Bookstore 28 Church St, Cambridge, MA 02138 ⓣ1-800/358-6013, ⓦwww.globecorner.com.

Map Link 30 S La Patera Lane, Unit 5, Santa Barbara, CA 93117 ⓣ805/692-6777, ⓦwww.maplink.com.

Rand McNally ⓣ1-800/333-0136, ⓦwww.randmcnally.com. Around thirty stores across the US; dial ext 2111 or check the website for the nearest location.

The Travel Bug Bookstore 2667 W Broadway, Vancouver V6K 2G2 ⓣ604/737-1122, ⓦwww.swifty.com/tbug.

World of Maps 1235 Wellington St, Ottawa, Ontario K1Y 3A3 ⓣ1-800/214-8524, ⓦwww.worldofmaps.com.

Map outlets in Australia and New Zealand

The Map Shop 6–10 Peel St, Adelaide, SA 5000 ⓣ08/8231 2033, ⓦwww.mapshop.net.au.

Mapland 372 Little Bourke St, Melbourne, VIC 3000 ⓣ03/9670 4383, ⓦwww.mapland.com.au.

MapWorld 173 Gloucester St, Christchurch, New Zealand ⓣ0800/627 967 or 03/374 5399, ⓦwww.mapworld.co.nz.

Perth Map Centre 900 Hay St, Perth, WA 6000 ⓣ08/9322 5733.

Specialty Maps 46 Albert St, Auckland 1001 ⓣ09/307 2217.

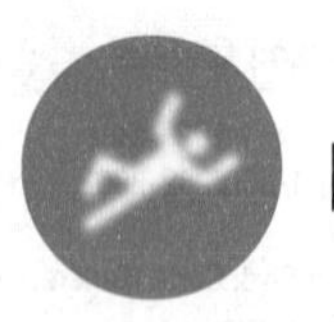

Insurance

If you're unlucky enough to require hospital treatment in Southeast Asia, you'll have to foot the bill, so make sure you have adequate travel insurance before you leave. A typical travel insurance policy should also provide cover for the loss of baggage, tickets and – up to a certain limit – cash or cheques, as well as cancellation or curtailment of your journey. Most policies exclude so-called dangerous sports unless an extra premium is paid: in Southeast Asia, this can mean scuba diving, white-water rafting and bungee jumping, though probably not trekking. Read the small print and benefits tables of prospective policies carefully; coverage can vary wildly for roughly similar premiums.

Many policies can be chopped and changed to exclude coverage you don't need, but for Southeast Asia you should definitely take **medical coverage** that includes both hospital treatment and medical evacuation; be sure to ask for the 24-hour medical emergency number. Keep all medical bills and, if possible, contact the insurance company before making any major outlay. Very few insurers will arrange on-the-spot payments in the event of a major expense – you will usually be reimbursed only after going home, so a credit/debit card could be useful to tide you over.

When securing **baggage cover**, make sure that the per-article limit – typically under £500 – will cover your most valuable possession. If you have anything stolen, get a copy of the police report, otherwise you won't be able to claim. Always make a note of the policy details and leave them with someone at home in case you lose the original.

Before buying a policy, check that you're not already covered. Your home insurance policy may cover your possessions against loss or theft even when overseas, or may be able to extend your cover through your household contents insurer. Many bank and charge accounts include some form of travel cover, and insurance is also sometimes included if you pay for your trip with a credit card (though it usually only provides medical or accident cover).

Rough Guides Travel Insurance

Rough Guides has teamed up with Columbus Direct to offer you travel insurance that can be tailored to suit your needs.

Readers can choose from many different travel insurance products, including a **low-cost backpacker option** for long stays; a **short-break option** for city getaways; a typical **holiday package option**; and many others. There are also **annual multi-trip** policies for those who travel regularly, with variable levels of cover available. Different sports and activities (trekking, skiing, etc) can be covered if required on most policies.

Rough Guides travel insurance is available to the residents of 36 different countries with different language options to choose from via our website – ⓦwww.roughguides.com – where you can also purchase the insurance.

Alternatively, UK residents should call ⓣ0800 083 9507; US citizens should call ⓣ1-800 749-4922; Australians should call ⓣ1 300 669 999. All other nationalities should call ⓣ+44 870 890 2843.

Health

The vast majority of travellers to Southeast Asia suffer nothing more than an upset stomach, so long as they observe basic precautions about food and water hygiene, and research pre-trip vaccination and malaria prophylactic requirements.

The standard of **local healthcare** varies across the region, with Laos having the least advanced system (best to get across the border and go to a Thai hospital) and Singapore boasting world-class medical care. If you have a minor ailment, it's usually best to head for a pharmacy – most have a decent idea of how to treat common ailments and can provide many medicines without prescription. Otherwise, ask for the nearest doctor or hospital. Details of major hospitals are given throughout the Guide and there's an overview of local healthcare under "Medical care and emergencies" in the introduction to each country. If you have a serious accident or illness, you may need to be evacuated home or to Singapore, so it's vital to arrange **health insurance** before you leave home (see opposite).

When planning your trip, **visit a doctor** at least two months before you leave, to allow time to complete any recommended courses of vaccinations. Most general practitioners in the UK can give advice and certain vaccines on prescription, though they may not administer some of the less common immunizations. For up-to-the-minute **information**, call the Travellers' Health phone lines or visit a travel clinic (listed on pp.57–58), although immunizations at these clinics can be costly. In the UK, pick up the Department of Health's free publication, *Health Advice for Travellers*, available at the post office, or by calling ⓣ0800/555 777. The content of the booklet, which contains immunization advice, is available at ⓦwww.direct.gov.uk. It's also advisable to have a trouble-shooting dental check-up before you leave – and remember that if you're visiting a malarial country (see p.53) you generally need to start taking **anti-malarial tablets** one week before your departure.

Inoculations

There are no compulsory vaccinations required for entry into any part of Southeast Asia, but health professionals strongly recommend that travellers to all Southeast Asian destinations get **inoculations** against the following common and debilitating diseases: typhoid, hepatitis A, tetanus and polio (you may be up-to-date with polio and tetanus anyway). In addition, you may be advised to have some of the following vaccinations, for example, if travelling during the rainy season or if planning to stay in remote rural areas: rabies, hepatitis B, Japanese encephalitis, diphtheria, meningitis and TB. If you're only going to Hong Kong and Macau, you may not have to get any inoculations. All shots should be recorded on an **International Certificate of Vaccination** and carried with your passport when travelling abroad; some immigration officials levy "fines" for those without a certificate, in particular at the Thai/Cambodian border in Poipet (see pp.160 & 1035). If you've been in an area infected with yellow fever during the fourteen days before your arrival in Southeast Asia, you will need a certificate of vaccination against the disease.

General precautions

Bacteria thrive in the tropics, and the best way to combat them is to keep up stand-

Some of the **illnesses** you can pick up in Southeast Asia may not show themselves immediately. If you become ill within a year of returning home, tell your doctor where you have been.

ards of personal hygiene. Frequent **bathing** is essential and hands should be washed before eating, especially in countries where food is traditionally eaten with the hands. Cuts or scratches can become infected very easily and should be thoroughly cleaned, disinfected and bandaged to keep dirt out.

Many countries in Southeast Asia have significant **AIDS** problems. Using latex condoms during sex reduces the risks. Bring a supply of them with you, take special care with expiry dates and bear in mind that condoms don't last as long when kept in the heat. Blood transfusions, intravenous drug use, acupuncture, dentistry, tattooing and body piercing are high-risk. Get a dental check-up before you leave home, and carry a sterile needles kit for medical emergencies.

Ask locally before **swimming** in freshwater lakes and rivers, including the Mekong River, as tiny worms carrying diseases such as bilharzia infect some tracts of freshwater in Southeast Asia. The worm enters through the skin and may cause a high fever after some weeks, but the recognizable symptoms of stomach pain and blood in the urine only appear after the disease is established, which may take months or even years. At this point, some damage to internal organs may have occurred.

Malaria and dengue fever

The whole of Southeast Asia lies within a **malarial zone**, although in many urban and developed tourist areas there is little risk (see opposite). Most health professionals advise that travellers on a multi-country trip through Southeast Asia should take full precautions against malaria – it's essential to take medical advice on this as malaria can be fatal and comes in a variety of strains, some of which are resistant to the most common anti-malarial drugs (prophylactics). Information regarding malaria is constantly being updated, and pregnant women and children should seek specialist advice.

Malaria is caused by a parasite in the saliva of the anopheles mosquito that is passed into the human when bitten by the mosquito. There are various prophylactic drug regimes available, depending on your destination, all of which must be taken according to a strict timetable, beginning one week before you go and continuing for four weeks after leaving the area. If you don't do this, you are in danger of developing the illness once you have returned home. One drug, Mefloquine (sold as Larium) has received some very critical media coverage; in some people it appears to produce disorientation, depression and sleep disturbance, although it suits other people very well. If you're intending to use Larium, you should begin to take it two weeks before you depart to see whether it will agree with your metabolism. Anyone planning to **scuba dive** should discuss the use of Larium very carefully with their medical advisers, as there has been some indication of an increased risk of the "bends".

None of the drugs is one hundred percent effective, and it is equally important to the **prevention of malaria** to stop the mosquitoes biting you. Malarial mosquitoes are active from dusk until dawn, and during this time you should wear trousers, long-sleeved shirts and socks and smother yourself and your clothes in mosquito repellent containing the chemical compound DEET: shops all over Southeast Asia stock it. DEET is strong stuff, and if you have sensitive skin a natural alternative is citronella (sold as Mosi-guard in the UK), made from a blend of eucalyptus oils. At night, you should either sleep under a mosquito net sprayed with DEET or in a room with screens across the windows. Accommodation in tourist spots nearly always provides screens or a net (check both for holes), but if you're planning to go way off the beaten track, you can either take a net with you or buy one locally from department stores in capital cities. Mosquito coils – widely available in Southeast Asia – also help keep the insects at bay.

The **symptoms** of malaria are fever, headache and shivering, similar to a severe dose of flu and often coming in cycles, but a lot of people have additional symptoms. Don't delay in seeking help fast: malaria can be fatal. You will need a blood test to confirm the illness, and the doctor will prescribe the most effective treatment locally. If you develop flu-like symptoms any time up to a year after returning home, you should inform a doctor and ask for a blood test.

Malarial or not?

Brunei – Not malarial.
Cambodia – Malarial in all forested and hilly rural areas, but Phnom Penh, Sihanoukville and Battambang are malaria-free, and transmission is very low in Siem Reap.
Hong Kong – Not malarial.
Indonesia – Malarial, except on Bali.
Laos – Very malarial.
Macau – Not malarial.
Malaysia – Malarial, but low risk on the Peninsula.
Philippines – Malarial only in the southern tip of Palawan and in the Sulu Archipelago.
Singapore – Not malarial.
Thailand – Malarial, but only high-risk along the Burma and Cambodia borders, including northern Kanchanaburi province, and parts of Trat province, including Ko Chang.
Vietnam – Very malarial in the highlands and rural areas, but low risk in Hanoi, Ho Chi Minh City, northern Red River delta and coastal regions of the south and centre.

Dengue fever

Another important reason to avoid getting bitten is **dengue fever**, a virus carried by a different species of mosquito, which bites during the day. There is no vaccine or tablet available to prevent the illness, which causes fever, headache and joint and muscle pains, as well as possible internal bleeding and circulatory-system failure. There is no specific drug to cure it, and the only treatment is lots of rest, liquids and Panadol (or any other acetaminophen painkiller, not aspirin), though more serious cases may require hospitalization. Reports indicate that the disease is on the increase across Asia, and it can be fatal. It is vital to get an early medical diagnosis and get treatment.

Food and water

Most health problems experienced by travellers are a direct result of **food** they've eaten. Avoid eating uncooked vegetables and fruits that cannot be peeled, and be warned that you risk ingesting worms and other parasites from dishes containing raw meat or fish. Cooked food that has been sitting out for an undetermined period of time should also be treated with suspicion. Avoid sharing glasses and utensils. The amount of money you pay

Medical kit

Some of the items listed below can be purchased more easily and cheaply in local pharmacies; Imodium and dental/sterile surgical kits will need to be bought before you leave home. Condoms are available at pharmacies throughout Southeast Asia, though quality is not always reliable; oral contraceptives are only available at pharmacies in Brunei, Malaysia and Singapore. Tampons are available only in the major cities, so it's advisable to bring your own supplies.

- ❒ Antiseptic cream
- ❒ Insect repellent
- ❒ Antihistamine cream
- ❒ Plasters/band aids
- ❒ Water sterilization tablets or water purifier
- ❒ Sunscreen
- ❒ Lint and sealed bandages
- ❒ A course of flagyl antibiotics
- ❒ Anti-fungal/athletes-foot cream
- ❒ Imodium (Lomotil) for emergency diarrhoea treatment
- ❒ Paracetamol/aspirin
- ❒ Anti-inflammatory/ibuprofen
- ❒ Multivitamin and mineral tablets
- ❒ Rehydration salts
- ❒ Emergency dental kit with temporary fillings
- ❒ Hypodermic and intravenous needles, sutures and sterilized skin wipes
- ❒ Condoms and other contraceptives

for a meal is no guarantee of its safety; in fact, food in top hotels has often been hanging around longer than food cooked at roadside stalls. Use your common sense – eat in places that look clean, avoid reheated food and be wary of shellfish.

Most **water** that comes out of taps in Southeast Asia has had very little treatment, and can contain a whole range of bacteria and viruses (local water conditions are described in the "Food and drink" section in the introduction to each chapter). These micro-organisms cause diseases such as diarrhoea, gastroenteritis, typhus, cholera, dysentery, poliomyelitis, hepatitis A and giardia, and can be present even when water looks clean and safe to drink. Therefore, you should stick to bottled, boiled or sterilized water; fortunately, except in the furthest-flung corners of Southeast Asia, **bottled water** is on sale everywhere. Be wary of salads and vegetables that have been washed in tap water, and bear in mind that **ice** is not always made from sterilized water.

The only time you're likely to be out of reach of bottled water is trekking into remote areas when you'll be relying on **boiled water**. Boiling for ten minutes gets rid of most bacteria in water but at least twenty minutes is needed to kill amoebic cysts, a cause of dysentery. To be safe, you may wish to use some kind of **chemical sterilization**. Iodine purification tablets or solutions are more effective than chlorine compounds, though still leave a nasty aftertaste – using a filter afterwards makes the water slightly more palatable. Note that iodine products are unsuitable for pregnant women, babies and people with thyroid problems. **Purification**, a two-stage process involving both filtration and sterilization, gives the most complete treatment. Consider taking a portable purifier with you, such as the ones made by Pre-Mac (ⓦwww.pre-mac.com).

Heat problems

Travellers who are unused to tropical climates regularly suffer from **sunburn** and **dehydration**. Limit your exposure to the sun in the hours around midday, use high-factor sunscreen and wear dark glasses and a sunhat. You'll be sweating a great deal in the heat, so the important thing is to make sure that you drink enough. If you are urinating very little or your urine turns dark (this can also indicate hepatitis), increase your fluid intake. When you sweat you lose salt, so you may want to add some extra to your food. A more serious result of the heat is **heatstroke**, indicated by high temperature, dry red skin and a fast, erratic pulse. As an emergency measure, try to cool the patient off by covering them in sheets or sarongs soaked in cold water and turn the fan on them; they may need to go to hospital, though. **Heat rashes**, **prickly heat**, and **fungal infections** are also common: wear loose cotton clothing, dry yourself carefully after bathing and use medicated talcum powder.

Stomach problems and viruses

If you travel in Asia for an extended period of time, you are likely to come down with some kind of stomach bug. For most, this is just a case of **diarrhoea**, caught through bad hygiene, or unfamiliar or affected food, and is generally over in a couple of days if treated properly; **dehydration** is one of the main concerns if you have diarrhoea, so rehydration salts dissolved in clean water provide the best treatment. **Gastroenteritis** is a more extreme version, but can still be cured with the same blend of rest and rehydration. You should be able to find a local brand of **rehydration salts** in pharmacies in most Southeast Asian towns, but you can also make up your own by mixing three teaspoons of sugar and one of salt to a litre of water. You will need to drink as much as three litres a day to stave off dehydration. Eat non-spicy, non-greasy **foods**, such as young coconut, unbuttered toast, rice, bananas and noodles, and steer away from alcohol, coffee, milk and most fruits. Since diarrhoea purges the body of the bugs, taking blocking **medicines** such as Lomotil and Imodium, or charcoal tablets, is not recommended unless you have to travel. Antibiotics are a worse idea, as they can wipe out friendly bacteria in the bowel and render you far more susceptible to future attacks.

The next step up from gastroenteritis is **dysentery**, diagnosable from blood and mucus in the (often blackened) stool. Dysentery is either amoebic or bacillary, with the latter characterized by high fever and vomiting. Serious attacks will require antibiotics, and therefore must always be treated, preferably in hospital.

Giardia can be diagnosed by foul-smelling farts and burps, abdominal distension, evil-smelling stools that float, and diarrhoea without blood or pus. Don't be over-eager with your diagnosis though, and treat it as normal diarrhoea for at least 24 hours before

Tropical fruits of Southeast Asia

One of the most refreshing snacks in Southeast Asia is **fruit**, and you'll find it offered everywhere – neatly sliced in glass boxes on hawker carts, blended into delicious shakes at night-market stalls, and served as dessert in restaurants. The fruits described below can be found in all parts of Southeast Asia, though some are seasonal. The region's more familiar fruits are not listed here, but include forty varieties of banana, dozens of different mangoes, three types of pineapple, coconuts, and watermelons. To avoid stomach trouble, peel all fruit before eating it, and use common sense when buying it pre-peeled on the street, avoiding anything that looks fly-blown or has been sitting in the sun for hours.

Custard apple (soursop) Inside the knobbly, grey-green skin you'll find creamy, almond-coloured blancmange-like flesh and many seeds. Described by Margaret Brooke, wife of Sarawak's second Rajah, Charles, as "tasting like cotton wool dipped in vinegar and sugar".

Durian Southeast Asia's most prized, and expensive, fruit has a greeny-yellow, spiky exterior and grows to the size of a football. Inside, it divides into segments of thick, yellow-white flesh that give off a disgustingly strong stink that's been compared to a mixture of mature cheese and caramel. Not surprisingly, many airlines and hotels ban the eating of this smelly delicacy on their premises. Most Southeast Asians consider it the king of fruits, while most foreigners find it utterly foul in both taste and smell.

Guava The apple of the tropics has green, textured skin and sweet, crisp flesh that can be pink or white and is studded with tiny edible seeds. Has five times the vitamin C content of orange juice and is sometimes eaten cut into strips and sprinkled with sugar and chilli.

Jackfruit This large, pear-shaped fruit can weigh up to 20kg and has a thick, bobbly, greeny-yellow shell protecting sweet, yellow flesh. Green, unripe jackfruit is sometimes cooked as a vegetable in curries.

Mangosteen The size of a small apple, with smooth, purple skin and a fleshy inside that divides into succulent, white segments that are sweet though slightly acidic.

Papaya (paw-paw) Similar in size and shape to a large melon, with smooth, green skin and yellowy-orange flesh that's a rich source of vitamins A and C. It's a favourite in fruit salads and shakes, and sometimes appears in its green, unripe form in vegetable salads.

Pomelo The pomelo is the largest of all the citrus fruits and looks rather like a grapefruit, though it is slightly drier and sweeter and has less flavour.

Rambutan The bright-red rambutan's soft, spiny exterior has given it its name – *rambut* means "hair" in Malay. Usually about the size of a golf ball, it has a white, opaque fruit of delicate flavour, similar to a lychee.

Salak (snakefruit) Teardrop-shaped, the *salak* has a brown, scaly skin like a snake's and a bitter taste.

Sapodilla (sapota) These small, brown, rough-skinned ovals look a bit like kiwi fruit and conceal a grainy, yellowish pulp that tastes almost honey-sweet.

Star fruit (carambola) A waxy, pale-green fruit with a fluted, almost star-like shape. It resembles a watery, crunchy apple and is said to be good for high blood pressure. The yellower the fruit, the sweeter its flesh.

resorting to flagyl antibiotics.

Hepatitis A or **E** is a waterborne viral infection spread through water and food. It causes jaundice, loss of appetite, and nausea and can leave you feeling wiped out for months. Seek immediate medical help if you think you may have contracted hepatitis. The Havrix vaccination lasts for several years, provided you have a booster the year after your first jabs. **Hepatitis B** is transmitted by bodily fluids, during unprotected sex or by intravenous drug use.

Cholera and typhoid are infectious diseases, generally spread when communities rely on sparse water supplies. The initial symptoms of **cholera** are a sudden onset of watery, but painless diarrhoea. Later, nausea, vomiting and muscle cramps set in. Cholera can be fatal if adequate fluid intake is not maintained. Copious amounts of liquids, including oral rehydration solution, should be consumed and medical treatment should be sought immediately. Although there is a vaccine against cholera, few medical professionals recommend it, as it is only about fifty percent effective. Like cholera, **typhoid** is also spread in small, localized epidemics. Symptoms can vary widely, but generally include headaches, fever and constipation, followed by diarrhoea. Vaccination against typhoid is recommended for all travellers to Southeast Asia.

Things that bite or sting

The most common irritations for travellers come from tiny pests whose most serious evil is the danger of infection to or through the bitten area, so keep bites clean and wash with antiseptic soap. **Fleas**, **lice** and **bed bugs** adore grimy sheets, so examine your bedding carefully, air and beat the offending articles and then coat yourself liberally in insect repellent. Visitors who spend the night in hilltribe villages where hygiene is poor, risk being infected by **scabies**, which cause severe itching by burrowing under the skin and laying eggs.

Ticks are nasty pea-shaped bloodsuckers that usually attach themselves to you if you walk through long grass. A dab of petrol, alcohol, tiger balm or insect repellent, or a lit cigarette, should make them let loose and drop off; if not, it's not a good idea to pull them off as they will leave their head embedded under your skin and the wound may become infected. Bloodsucking **leeches** can be a problem in the jungle and in fresh water. The best way to get rid of them is to rub them with salt, though all the anti-tick treatments also work. **DEET** is also an effective deterrent, and applying it at the tops of your boots and around the lace-holes is a good idea.

Southeast Asia has many species of both land and sea **snakes**, so wear boots and socks when hiking. Most snakes will get out of your way long before you know they are there, but if you're confronted, back off. If **bitten**, the number one rule is not to panic. Try to stay still in order to slow the venom's entry into the bloodstream. Wash and disinfect the wound, apply a pressure bandage as tightly as you would for a sprain, splint the affected limb, keep it below the level of the heart and get to hospital as soon as possible. Tourniquets, cutting open the bite, and trying to suck out the venom cause more harm than good. **Scorpion** stings are very painful but not fatal; swelling usually disappears after a few hours.

If stung by a **jellyfish**, the priority treatment is to remove the fragments of tentacles from the skin – without causing further discharge of poison – which is easiest done by applying vinegar to deactivate the stinging capsules. The best way to minimize the risk of stepping on the **toxic spines** of sea urchins, sting rays and stone fish is to wear thick-soled shoes, though these cannot provide total protection; sea-urchin spikes should be removed after softening the skin with a special ointment (likely to be Tiger Balm), though some people recommend applying urine to help dissolve the spines; for sting-ray and stone-fish stings, alleviate the pain by immersing the wound in very hot water – just under 50°C – while waiting for help.

Rabies is transmitted to humans by the bite of carrier animals, who have the disease in their saliva; **tetanus** is an additional danger from such bites. All animals should be treated with caution, but particularly monkeys, cats and dogs. Be extremely cautious with wild animals that seem inexplicably tame, as this can be a symptom. If you do get bitten, scrub the wound with a strong antiseptic and then alcohol and get to a hospital as soon as possible. Do not attempt to close the wound. The incubation period for the disease can be as much as a year or as little as a few days; once the disease has taken hold, it will be fatal.

Medical resources for travellers

Websites

Ⓦ**health.yahoo.com** Information on specific diseases and conditions, drugs and herbal remedies, as well as advice from health experts.
Ⓦ**www.tmvc.com.au** Contains a list of all Travellers' Medical and Vaccination Centres throughout Australia, New Zealand and Southeast Asia, plus general information on travel health.
Ⓦ**www.istm.org** The website of the International Society for Travel Medicine, with a full list of clinics specializing in international travel health.
Ⓦ**www.tripprep.com** Travel Health Online provides an online-only comprehensive database of necessary vaccinations for most countries, as well as destination and medical service provider information.
Ⓦ**www.fitfortravel.scot.nhs.uk** UK NHS website carrying information about travel-related diseases and how to avoid them.

Travel clinics in the UK and Ireland

British Airways Travel Clinics 28 regional clinics (call Ⓣ01276/685 040 for the nearest, or consult Ⓦwww.britishairways.com/travel/healthclinintro), with several in London (Mon–Fri 9.30am–5.15pm, Sat 10am–4pm), including 156 Regent St, London W1 7RA Ⓣ020/7439 9584, no appointment necessary. There are appointment-only branches at 101 Cheapside, London EC2 Ⓣ020/7606 2977; and at the BA terminal in London's Victoria Station Ⓣ020/7233 6661. All clinics offer vaccinations, tailored advice from an online database, and a complete range of travel healthcare products.
Communicable Diseases Unit Brownlee Centre, Glasgow G12 0YN Ⓣ0141/211 1074. Travel vaccinations, including yellow fever.
Dun Laoghaire Medical Centre 5 Northumberland Ave, Dun Laoghaire Co, Dublin Ⓣ01/280 4996, Ⓕ280 5603. Advice on medical matters abroad.
Hospital for Tropical Diseases Travel Clinic 26 Danbury St, London N1 8JU (Mon–Fri 9am–5pm by appointment only; Ⓣ076/6133 7729; a consultation costs £15, which is waived if you have your injections here). A recorded Health Line (Ⓣ09061/337 733; 50p per min) gives hints on hygiene and illness prevention as well as listing appropriate immunizations.
Liverpool School of Tropical Medicine Pembroke Place, Liverpool L3 5QA Ⓣ0151/708 9393, Ⓦwww.liv.ac.uk/lstm. Walk-in clinic Mon–Fri 1–4pm; appointment required for yellow fever, but not for other jabs.
Malaria Helpline 24-hour recorded message Ⓣ0891/600 350; 60p per minute.
MASTA (Medical Advisory Service for Travellers Abroad) London School of Hygiene and Tropical Medicine, Ⓦwww.masta.org. Operates a pre-recorded 24-hour Travellers' Health Line (UK Ⓣ0906/822 4100, 60p per min; Republic of Ireland Ⓣ01560/147 000, 75p per minute), giving written information tailored to your journey by return of post.
Nomad Pharmacy Surgeries 40 Bernard St, London WC1N; and 3–4 Wellington Terrace, Turnpike Lane, London N8 0PX (Mon–Fri 9.30am–6pm, Ⓣ020/7833 4114 to book vaccination appointment). They give advice free if you go in person, or their telephone helpline is Ⓣ09068/633 414 (60p per minute). They can give information tailored to your travel needs.
Trailfinders Immunization clinics (no appointments necessary) at 194 Kensington High St, London W8 7RG (Mon–Fri 9am–7pm Sat-Sun 10am–6pm; Ⓣ020/7938 3939, Ⓦwww.trailfinders.com/london.htm).
Travel Health Centre Department of International Health and Tropical Medicine, Royal College of Surgeons in Ireland, Mercers Medical Centre, Stephen's St Lower, Dublin Ⓣ01/402 2337. Expert pre-trip advice and inoculations.
Travel Medicine Services PO Box 254, 16 College St, Belfast 1 Ⓣ028/9031 5220. Offers medical advice before a trip and help afterwards in the event of a tropical disease.
Tropical Medical Bureau Grafton Buildings, 34 Grafton St, Dublin 2 Ⓣ01/671 9200, Ⓦwww.tmb.ie.

Travel clinics in the USA and Canada

Canadian Society for International Health 1 Nicholas St, Suite 1105, Ottawa, ON K1N 7B7 Ⓣ613/241-5785, Ⓦwww.csih.org. Distributes a free pamphlet, *Health Information for Canadian Travellers*, containing an extensive list of travel health centres in Canada.
Centers for Disease Control 1600 Clifton Rd NE, Atlanta, GA 30333 Ⓣ1-800/311-3435 or 404/639-3534, Ⓕ1-888/232-3299, Ⓦwww.cdc.gov. Publishes outbreak warnings, suggested inoculations,

precautions and other background information for travellers. Useful website plus International Travelers Hotline on ⓣ1-877/FYI-TRIP.

International Association for Medical Assistance to Travellers (IAMAT) 417 Center St, Lewiston, NY 14092 ⓣ716/754-4883, , and 40 Regal Rd, Guelph, ON N1K 1B5 ⓣ519/836-0102, ⓦwww.iamat.org. A non-profit organization supported by donations, it can provide a list of English-speaking doctors in the countries you're visiting, climate charts and leaflets on various diseases and inoculations.

International SOS Assistance Eight Neshaminy Interplex Suite 207, Trevose, PA 19053-6956 ⓣ1-800/523-8930, ⓦwww.intsos.com. Members receive pre-trip medical referral info, as well as overseas emergency services designed to complement travel insurance coverage.

Travel Medicine ⓣ1-800/872-8633, ⓕ1-413/584-6656, ⓦwww.travmed.com. Sells first-aid kits, mosquito netting, water filters, reference books and other health-related travel products.

Travelers Medical Center 31 Washington Square West, New York, NY 10011 ⓣ212/982-1600. Consultation service on immunizations and treatment of diseases for people travelling to developing countries.

Travel clinics in Australia and New Zealand

Travellers' Medical and Vaccination Centres Branches include: 27–29 Gilbert Place, Adelaide, SA 5000 ⓣ08/8212 7522; 1/170 Queen St, Auckland ⓣ09/373 3531; 5/8–10 Hobart Place, Canberra, ACT 2600 ⓣ02/6257 7156; 147 Armagh St, Christchurch ⓣ03/379 4000; 5 Mill St, Perth, WA 6000 ⓣ08/9321 1977; 7/428 George St, Sydney, NSW 2000 ⓣ02/9221 7133; Shop 15, Grand Arcade, 14–16 Willis St, Wellington ⓣ04/473 0991; ⓦwww.tmvc.com.au.

Costs, money and banks

Western tourists have always found Southeast Asia an extremely cheap place to travel, with accommodation, food and transport costing a fraction of what it does in the West. Since 1997, the region has become even more of a bargain for Western travellers as a result of a financial crisis which hit the whole of Southeast Asia very hard, sending local currencies into freefall against the US dollar, and giving foreigners a lot more for their money. Local people suffered horribly, however, with prices for daily necessities such as rice and fuel shooting up, but no corresponding hike in wages. At the time of writing, most Southeast Asian economies seem to have stabilized, but the dollar has yet to fetch as good a rate as it did before (and especially during) the crisis.

Average costs

Your **daily budget** in Southeast Asia depends both on where you're travelling and on how comfortable you want to be. You can survive on £6/US$10 a day in most parts of Cambodia, Laos, Indonesia, Thailand and Vietnam, on around £12/US$20 a day in Malaysia, Singapore and the Philippines, and about £24/$US40 in Hong Kong and Brunei, but for this money you'll be sleeping only in the most basic accommodation, eating every meal at simple food stalls, and travelling only on local non-air-con buses. You should carry extra funds to cover more expensive places such as capital cities and major tourist resorts, as well as for other occasional outlays like tourist buses, air-con rooms, the odd taxi or hire car, a few classier meals and the occasional beer. Fairly regular indulgence in all these small luxuries cranks up the daily budget to £12/US$20 and £20/US$35 respectively. In some countries, prices for tourist accommodation and foreigners' restaurants are quoted in **US dollars**, though the local equivalent is always acceptable.

More specific budgets for different styles of travel are given in the "Money and costs" section in the introduction to each chapter.

Travellers soon get so used to the low cost of living in Southeast Asia that they start **bargaining** at every available opportunity, much as local people do. Pretty much everything is negotiable, from cigarettes and woodcarvings to taxi-hire and accommodation rates. Most buyers start their counterbid at about 25 percent of the vendor's opening price, and the bartering continues from there. If your price is way out of line, the vendor's vehement refusal should be enough to make you increase your offer: never forget that the few pennies you're making such a fuss over will go a lot further in a local person's hands than in your own.

Price tiering also exists in some parts of Southeast Asia, with foreigners paying more than locals for services such as public transport, hotels, and entry fees to museums and historical sites. Be cautious about causing a scene until you've established the cost of things, and remember prices vary within individual countries, especially when you enter more remote areas.

Very few **student discounts** are offered on entry prices, tours and airfares in Southeast Asia, but if you have an **International Student ID Card (ISIC)** it's worth bringing it just in case. Full-time students are eligible for this card, but it's very easy to buy fake versions in Bangkok, which is one of the reasons why they're rarely accepted in the region. Most tourist sights give discounts for **children** under 14 years old, and many hotels don't charge for children sharing their parents' room. **Tipping** isn't a Southeast Asian custom, although some upmarket restaurants expect a gratuity, and most expensive hotels add service taxes.

Cash, travellers' cheques and exchange

In Laos and Cambodia, it's easier if you carry a reasonable amount of US dollars cash, especially if you are going to get off the beaten track. Throughout the rest of the region, the safest way to carry the bulk of your money is in **travellers' cheques**, which can be cashed at banks, exchange booths and upmarket hotels in most sizeable Southeast Asian towns, and are refundable if stolen. The best cheques to take are those issued by the most familiar names, particularly American Express and Visa, ideally in US dollars, though pounds sterling are widely accepted and many other currencies are fine in the largest resorts. Note that dollar travellers' cheques are the only ones commonly accepted in Cambodia; when they are exchanged you will be given US dollars and not local currency. Small-denomination cheques are generally less economical than larger ones as you get a lower rate per cheque, though it might be advisable to take a few for exchange in smaller banks that don't keep large stocks of cash. Some outlets offer better rates for cheques than for straight cash and most charge commission, either per cheque or per transaction. Hold on to the **receipt** (or proof of purchase) that you get when you buy your travellers' cheques, as some exchange places require seeing it before cashing your cheques.

Most **international airports** have exchange counters that open for arriving passengers, which is useful, as you can't always buy Southeast Asian currencies before leaving home. Wherever you change your money, ask for a mix of denominations, as in some backwaters bigger bills can be hard to split. Refuse really dog-eared banknotes, as you'll have difficulty getting anyone else to accept them. If you're staying in a developed tourist centre, you'll probably find that the money **exchange counters** are the most convenient places to cash your cheques. Many of these open daily from around 8am to 8pm, and rates generally compare favourably with those offered by the banks, but always establish any **commission** before signing cheques – the places that display promising rates may charge a hefty fee. Always count your money carefully, as it's not uncommon for moneychangers to short-change tourists in a variety of ways, including by miscalculating amounts (especially when there are lots of zeros involved), using a rigged calculator, folding over notes to make the amount look twice as great, and invisibly removing a pile of notes after the money's been counted. In some **banks**, the foreign-exchange counter only opens for a few hours, and in some small towns, banks won't accept travellers' cheques at all, so get into the habit of carrying **a few dollars cash** with you to allow for unforeseen circumstances. Banking hours and other local idiosyncrasies are described in the "Opening hours" section in the introduction to each country. Details of **local currencies** and **exchange rates** are also given in the introduction to each chapter, but for the up-to-the-minute exchange rate, visit the Oanda online currency converter (Ⓦ www.oanda.com/convert/classic), which gives you the day's Interbank rate for 164 currencies.

Keep a record of cheque serial numbers safe and separate from the cheques themselves. All travellers' cheque issuers give you a list of numbers to call in the case of **lost or stolen cheques** and will refund you if you can produce the original receipts and a note of your cheque numbers. Instructions in cases of loss or theft vary, but you'll usually have to notify the police first and then call the issuing company collect, who will arrange a refund, usually within 24 hours.

Credit and debit cards

American Express, Visa, MasterCard and Diners Club **credit cards** and **charge cards** are accepted at top hotels and by a growing number of posh restaurants, department stores, tourist shops and travel agents, but surcharging of up to five percent is rife, and theft and forgery are major industries – always demand the carbon copies and destroy them immediately, and never leave cards in baggage storage.

Except in Cambodia and Laos, many of the biggest tourist centres and cities have a useful number of **ATMs** that accept international debit and credit cards such as MasterCard, Cirrus and Visa; see individual accounts for details. For an up-to-date list of ATM locations in Southeast Asia, check the relevant websites (Ⓦ www.mastercard.com and Ⓦ www.visa.com). All banks charge a handling fee of about 1.5 percent per transaction when you use your debit card at overseas ATMs. Don't rely on plastic alone, however, which is more tempting to thieves and less easy to replace than the trusty travellers' cheque. In countries without ATMs (such as Laos), you can obtain **cash advances** on Visa cards, and less frequently MasterCard, in major urban centres, but you will most likely be required to withdraw a minimum of $100 at a rate of 2.5 to 3 percent commission.

A compromise between travellers' cheques and plastic is **Visa TravelMoney**, a disposable pre-paid debit card with a PIN that works in all ATMs that take Visa cards. You load up your account with funds before leaving home, and when they run out, you simply throw the card away. You can buy up to nine cards to access the same funds – useful for couples or families travelling together – and it's a good idea to buy at least one extra as a back-up in case of loss or theft. The card is available in most countries from branches of Thomas Cook and Citicorp. For more information, check the Visa TravelMoney website at Ⓦ usa.visa.com/personal/cards/prepaid/visa_travel_money.html.

Wiring money

Wiring money through a specialist agent (see opposite) is a fast but expensive way to send and receive money abroad. The money wired should be available for collection, usually in local currency, from the company's local agent within twenty minutes of being sent via Western Union or MoneyGram; both charge on a sliding scale, so sending larger amounts of cash is better value.

It's also possible to have money wired **directly from a bank in your home country** to a bank in Southeast Asia, although this is somewhat less reliable because it involves two separate institutions. Most banks will allow account holders to nominate almost any branch of any bank as a collection point, though if this is not the central bank that they usually deal with, it will take longer than normal. It's therefore a good idea to check with your bank before travelling to see which branch of which bank they have reciprocal arrangements with. Your home bank will need the address of the branch where you want to pick up the money and the address and telex number of the head office, which will act as the clearing house; money wired this way will take at least two working days to arrive, and costs around £25/US$40 per transaction.

Money-wiring companies

American Express MoneyGram UK and Republic of Ireland ☎0800/6663 9472, US and Canada ☎1-800/926-9400, Australia ☎1800/230 100, New Zealand ☎09/379 8243 or 0800/262 263, ⓦwww.moneygram.com.
Thomas Cook UK ☎01733/318 922, Belfast ☎028/9055 0030, Dublin ☎01/677 1721, US ☎1-800/287-7362, Canada ☎1-888/823-4732, ⓦwww.thomascook.com.
Western Union UK ☎0800/833 833, Republic of Ireland ☎1800/395 395, US and Canada ☎1-800/325-6000, Australia ☎1800/649 565, New Zealand ☎09/270 0050, ⓦwww.westernunion.com.

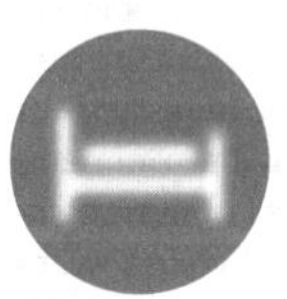

Accommodation

You'll rarely have a problem finding inexpensive accommodation in Southeast Asia, particularly if you stick to the main tourist areas. In most parts of the region, electricity is supplied at 220 volts, though socket type varies from country to country, so you should bring a travel plug with several adapters. Specific details are given in the "Accommodation" section in the introduction to each chapter. Power cuts are common, so bring a torch. There are hardly any coin-operated laundries in Southeast Asia, but nearly every guesthouse and hotel will wash your clothes for a reasonable price. Every guesthouse and hotel will store luggage for you, though sometimes only if you make a reservation for your anticipated return; major train stations and airports also have left-luggage facilities.

Guesthouses and hotels

The mainstay of the travellers' scene in Southeast Asia are the **guesthouses** (also known as bungalows, homestays or backpackers'), which provide inexpensive, basic accommodation specifically aimed at Western travellers and are usually good places to meet other people and pick up information. They are found in all major tourist centres and can be anything from a bamboo hut to a three-storey concrete block. A standard guesthouse room will be a simple place with one or two beds, hard mattresses, thin walls and a fan – some, but not all, have a window (usually screened against mosquitoes), and the cheapest ones share a bathroom. Always ask to see several rooms before opting for one, as standards can vary widely within the same establishment. For a **basic double room** with shared bathroom in a guesthouse that's in a capital city or tourist centre, rates start at about US$3 in Indonesia, US$5 in Laos, US$6 in Thailand, Cambodia and the Philippines, US$7 in Malaysia and Vietnam; the highest prices are in Singapore (from US$15 a

Accommodation price codes

All accommodation reviewed in this guide has been graded according to the following **price codes**, in US dollars, which represent the cost of the cheapest double room available in high season. Where a price range is indicated, this means that the establishment offers rooms with varying facilities – as explained in the write-up. In cases where an establishment charges per bed, the actual price is given.

❶ under $5	❹ $15–20	❼ $40–60
❷ $5–10	❺ $20–25	❽ $60–80
❸ $10–15	❻ $25–40	❾ $80 and over

double) and Hong Kong (from US$25). In smaller towns and beach resorts, rates can be significantly lower, and prices everywhere are usually negotiable during low season. **Single rooms** tend to cost about two-thirds the price of a double, but many guesthouses also offer dormitory beds, which can cost as little as US$2 a night. More specific costings for accommodation are given in the introduction to each chapter. Some guesthouses also offer more comfortable rooms, with private bathroom, extra furnishings and even air con. In addition, the most clued-up places provide useful **facilities**, such as restaurants, travellers' noticeboards, safes for valuables, baggage-keeps, tour-operator desks and their own poste restantes. At most guesthouses, **check-out time** is noon, which means that during high season you should arrive to check in at about 11.30am to ensure you get a room: few places will draw up a "waiting list", and they rarely take advance bookings unless they know you already.

If you venture to towns that are completely off the tourist circuit, the cheapest accommodation is usually the bland and sometimes seedy **cheap urban hotels** located near bus and train stations. These places are designed for local businesspeople rather than tourists and often double as brothels; they tend to be rather soulless, but are usually inexpensive and clean enough.

For around US$15–30 almost anywhere in Southeast Asia except Singapore and Hong Kong, you can get yourself a comfortable room in an upmarket guesthouse or small **mid-range hotel**. These are often very good value, offering pleasantly furnished rooms, with private hot-water bathroom, and quite possibly air con, a fridge and a TV as well. Some of these also have a swimming pool. And for $60, you'll get the kind of **luxury** you'd be paying well over $100 for in the West.

Bathrooms

Many budget guesthouses and cheap hotels, and all mid-range accommodation in Southeast Asia, will provide bathrooms with Western-style facilities such as sit-down toilets and showers (only the more expensive rooms have hot water and bathtubs). But in rural areas, on some beaches, and in some of the cheapest accommodation, you'll be using a **traditional Asian bathroom**, where you wash using the scoop-and-slosh method, known in Malay-speaking countries as a **mandi**, after the Malay word for "bath". This entails dipping a plastic scoop or bucket into a huge vat or basin of water (often built into the bathroom wall) and then sloshing the water over yourself. The basin functions as a water supply only and not a bath, so never get in it; all washing is done outside it and the basin should not be contaminated by soap or shampoo. If you're really far off the beaten track, you may have to pump your own water from a well or even bathe in a stream. **Toilets** in these places will be Asian-style squat affairs, flushed manually with water scooped from the pail that stands alongside. Keep in mind that **toilet paper** tends to clog these things up so if you want to avoid an embarrassing situation, learn to wash yourself like the locals do.

Village accommodation

In the more remote and rural parts of Southeast Asia, you may get the chance to stay in **village accommodation**, be it the headman's house, a family home, or a traditional longhouse. Accommodation in these places usually consists of a mattress on the floor in a communal room, perhaps with a blanket and mosquito net, but it's often advisable to take your own net and blanket or sleeping bag. As a sign of appreciation, your hosts will welcome gifts, and a donation may be in order, too. Actually, the chance of encountering this kind of arrangement is quite rare. Some countries such as Laos forbid tourists from sleeping in homes that aren't approved by the government as tourist accommodation. In most towns, however, there is either a basic guesthouse or government rest house in which you can stay.

Hostels

As a rule, it's not worth becoming an HI member just for your trip to Southeast Asia, as there are so few **youth hostels** in the region, and prices don't necessarily compare favourably with other budget options. The one exception is Hong Kong, whose seven youth hostels offer the cheapest accommodation in the territory.

Camping

Because accommodation is so inexpensive in Southeast Asia, few travellers bother to take a tent with them, and anyway, there are hardly any campsites. The only times when you may need to **camp** are in the national parks or when trekking, and you may be able to rent gear locally – check the Guide for details. In theory, you could also camp on most beaches, though nearby guesthouse or bungalow owners usually take a dim view of this. Beaches, especially in heavily touristed areas, are often unsafe at night. This is especially true for solo women travellers – in most Southeast Asian countries, the idea of a lone woman spending the night on the beach will be taken by local men to be a sign of sexual availability. It is almost always worth spending the money to get some secure walls around you.

Communications

Country-specific information on phone, mail and Internet facilities is given in the introduction to each chapter. What follows is general advice about communications across the region.

Poste restante

Travellers can receive mail in any country in Southeast Asia via **poste restante**. The system is universally fairly efficient, but tends only to be available at the main post office in cities and backpackers' centres, not in small towns and villages. Of course, it's much easier to send email (see p.65), so unless you're a confirmed Luddite or enjoy clawing through stacks of dead letters, you'll simply find yourself an Internet café. Most post offices hold letters for a maximum of one month, though some hold them for up to three, and others seem to hold them forever. Mail should be addressed: Name (family name underlined or capitalized), Poste Restante, GPO, Town or City, Country. It will be filed by family name, though it's always wise to check under your first initial as well. To collect mail, you'll need to show your passport and may have to pay a tiny fee per item received. The poste restante system works best if you have given friends and relatives an outline of your itinerary, so that they can send mail in time for your anticipated arrival. Mail takes three to fourteen days to get from Europe, North America or Australia to Southeast Asia, depending on the destination. For a small fee, you can arrange for poste restante mail to be forwarded from one GPO to another, though you usually have to apply for this service in person.

In certain major cities and upmarket resorts, holders of Amex credit cards or travellers' cheques can also make use of the **American Express** poste restante facility, which holds mail for up to sixty days: see individual city "Listings" in the Guide for details.

Phones

You should be able to **phone** home from any city or large town in Southeast Asia. The cheapest method is to make an **IDD call** (International Direct Dialling) from the national telecommunications office or post office, some of which are open 24 hours. You can also make IDD calls from private telephone offices and guesthouses – these places charge higher rates than the public phone offices, but are often more conveniently located. IDD calls from rooms in expensive hotels are usually subject to huge surcharges. In some countries, it's also possible to

IDD codes

To phone abroad from the following countries, you must first dial the international access code, then the IDD country code, then the area code (usually without the first zero), then the subscriber number:

International access codes when dialling from:

Australia ⓣ0011	Ireland ⓣ010	Singapore ⓣ001
Brunei ⓣ01	Laos ⓣ00	Thailand ⓣ001
Cambodia ⓣ00	Macau ⓣ00	UK ⓣ00
Canada ⓣ011	Malaysia ⓣ007	USA ⓣ011
Hong Kong ⓣ001	New Zealand ⓣ00	Vietnam ⓣ00
Indonesia ⓣ00	Philippines ⓣ00	

IDD country codes

Australia ⓣ61	Ireland ⓣ353	Singapore ⓣ65
Brunei ⓣ673	Laos ⓣ856	Thailand ⓣ66
Cambodia ⓣ855	Macau ⓣ853	UK ⓣ44
Canada ⓣ1	Malaysia ⓣ60	USA ⓣ1
Hong Kong ⓣ852	New Zealand ⓣ64	Vietnam ⓣ84
Indonesia ⓣ62	The Philippines ⓣ63	

make IDD calls from public phone boxes, using high-value phonecards.

In phone centres where there's no facility for reverse-charge calls, you can almost always get a "**call-back**". Ask the operator for a minimum (one-minute) call abroad and get the phone number of the place you're calling from; you can then be called back directly at the phone centre.

In addition to IDD, some big hotels, national telephone offices and airports also have **home-country direct** phones. With these, you simply press the appropriate button for the country you're ringing, and you'll be put through to the international switchboard of that country. You can **call collect** (reverse-charge calls), or the operator will debit you and you can settle with the cashier. Home-country direct phones are also useful if you have a chargecard. They do, however, cost more than using IDD phones.

One of the most convenient ways of phoning home from abroad is via a **telephone chargecard** from your phone company back home. Using a PIN number, you can make calls from most hotel, public and private phones that will be charged to your account. Since most major chargecards are free to obtain, it's certainly worth getting one at least for emergencies; enquire first, though, whether your destination is covered, and bear in mind that rates aren't necessarily cheaper than calling from a public phone.

In the **UK and Ireland**, British Telecom (ⓣ 0800/345 144, ⓦ www.payphones.bt.com/callingcards) will issue free to all BT customers the BT Charge Card, which can be used in 116 countries; AT&T (Dial ⓣ0800/890 011, then 888/641-6123 when you hear the AT&T prompt to be transferred to the Florida Call Centre, free 24 hours) has the Global Calling Card; while NTL (ⓣ 0500/100 505) issues its own Global Calling Card, which can be used in more than sixty countries abroad, though the fees cannot be charged to a normal phone bill.

In the **USA and Canada**, AT&T, MCI, Sprint, Canada Direct and other North American long-distance companies all enable their customers to make credit-card calls while overseas, billed to your home number. Call your company's customer service line to find out if they provide service from your location, and if so, what the toll-free access code is.

To call **Australia and New Zealand** from Southeast Asia, telephone chargecards such as Telstra Telecard or Optus Calling Card in Australia, and Telecom NZ's Calling Card can be used to make calls abroad, which are charged back to a domestic account or credit card. Apply to Telstra (ⓣ1800/038 000), Optus (ⓣ1300/300 937), or Telecom NZ (ⓣ04/801 9000).

Mobile phones

If you want to use your **mobile phone** in Southeast Asia, you'll need to check with your phone provider whether it will work abroad, and what the call charges are. Generally speaking, UK, Australian and New Zealand mobiles should work fine in Southeast Asia, as they use GSM, which gives access to most places worldwide, except the US. However, US mobiles, apart from tri-band models, are unlikely to work outside the States.

In the **UK**, for all but the very top-of-the-range packages, you'll have to inform your phone provider before leaving home to get international access switched on. You may get charged extra for this depending on your existing package and where you are travelling to. You are also likely to be charged extra for incoming calls when abroad, as the people calling you will be paying the usual rate. If you want to retrieve messages while you're away, you'll have to ask your provider for a new access code, as your home one is unlikely to work in Southeast Asia. For further information about using your phone abroad, check out ⓦwww.telecomsadvice.org.uk/features/using_your_mobile_abroad.htm.

Email

Email can make a good alternative to post office poste restantes, as Internet access has become widespread in Southeast Asia, and there are now cybercafés in even the poorest nations such as Cambodia and Laos, while backpackers' areas such as Thanon Khao San in Bangkok and Kuta in Bali have dozens of them. Fees are nearly always very low. Most travellers use the **free web-based email accounts** offered by Hotmail (ⓦwww.hotmail.com) or Yahoo (ⓦwww.yahoo.com), and all Internet cafés have these bookmarked. This is easy enough as all you have to do is log on to the sites and they basically hold your hand from there; don't forget to log off again, though. You are very unlikely to be able to access your own home-based email account owing to the difficulty in getting an international line to your local ISP; even if you can get a line, the cost will be phenomenal. Some international ISPs, such as AOL and IBM, do have local numbers in Asian capital cities so you may get lucky if you're at a cybercafé in Bangkok or Singapore for example, but it's far less complicated and more efficient to organize a forwarding service from your home email account to your Hotmail or Yahoo account for the duration of your trip.

ⓦwww.kropla.com is a useful website giving details of how to plug your lap-top in when abroad, phone country codes around the world, and information about electrical systems in different countries. For a list of other useful websites, see p.46.

Faxes

Most telephone centres, major post offices and clued-up guesthouses and hotels offer a domestic and international **fax service**. Many of these places also do "fax restante". As with phone calls, the post offices usually offer the cheapest rates.

Short-wave radios

With a shortwave radio, you can pick up the **BBC World Service**, **Radio Australia**, **Voice of America** and various other international stations on a variety of bands (depending on the time) right across the region. Times and wavelengths change frequently, so get hold of a recent schedule just before you travel. The BBC World Service website (ⓦwww.bbc.co.uk/worldservice) carries current frequency details in a useful format that's designed to be printed out and carried with you.

Crime and personal safety

For the most part, travelling in Southeast Asia is safe and unthreatening, though, as in any unfamiliar environment, you should keep your wits about you. The most common hazard is opportunistic theft, which can easily be avoided with a few sensible precautions. Occasionally, political trouble flares in the region, as it has done recently in parts of Indonesia, so before you travel you may want to check the official government advice on international troublespots (see box below). Most experienced travellers find this official advice less helpful than that offered by other travellers – the online travellers' forums listed on pp.47–48 are a particularly useful resource. In some countries, there are specific year-round dangers such as banditry (parts of Laos), kidnapping (southern Philippines), and unexploded ordnance (Laos, Cambodia, Vietnam); details of these and how to avoid them are described in the introduction to the relevant country.

Theft and how to avoid it

As a tourist, you are an obvious target for opportunistic **thieves** (who may include your fellow travellers), so don't flash expensive cameras or watches around. Most people carry travellers' cheques, the bulk of their cash and important documents (airline tickets, credit cards and passport) under their clothing in a **money belt** – the all-too-obvious bum-bags are easy to cut off in a crowd. It's a good idea to keep $100 cash, photocopies of the relevant pages of your passport, insurance details and travellers' cheque receipts separate from the rest of your valuables.

Ensure that **luggage** is lockable (you can buy gadgets to lock backpacks), and never keep anything important in outer pockets. A **padlock** and chain, or a cable lock, is useful for doors and windows at inexpensive guesthouses and beach bungalows, and for securing your pack on **buses**, where you're often separated from your belongings. If your pack is on the top of the bus, make sure it is attached securely, and keep an eye on it whenever the bus pulls into a bus station. Be especially aware of pickpockets on buses, who usually operate in pairs: one will distract you while another does the job. On **trains**, either cable lock your pack or put it under the bottom bench-seat, out of public view. Be wary of accepting food and drink from strangers on long overnight bus or train journeys: it may be drugged so as to knock you out while your bags are stolen.

Don't hesitate to check that doors and windows – including those in the bathroom – are secure before accepting **accom-**

Official advice on international troublespots

The following sites provide useful advice on travelling in countries that are considered unstable or unsafe for foreigners.

Australian Department of Foreign Affairs
www.dfat.gov.au. Advice and reports on unstable countries and regions.

British Foreign and Commonwealth Office
www.fco.gov.uk. Constantly updated advice for travellers on circumstances affecting safety in over 130 countries.

Canadian Foreign Affairs Department
www.fac-aec.gc.ca/menu-en.asp. Country-by-country travel advisories.

US State Department Travel Advisories
travel.state.gov/travel/warnings.html. Website providing "consular information sheets" detailing the dangers of travelling in most countries of the world.

modation. Some guesthouses and hotels have **safe-deposit boxes** or lockers, which solve the problem of what to do with your valuables while you go swimming. The safest lockers are those that require your own padlock, as valuables sometimes get lifted by hotel staff. Padlock your luggage when leaving it in hotel or guesthouse rooms.

Other hazards

Violent crime against tourists is not common in Southeast Asia, but it does occur. If you're unlucky enough to get **mugged**, never resist and, if you disturb a thief, raise the alarm rather than try to take them on – they're unlikely to harm you if you don't get in their way. Obvious precautions for travellers of either sex include locking accessible windows and doors at night, preferably with your own padlock, and not travelling alone at night in an unlicensed taxi, tuk-tuk or rickshaw. Think carefully about motorbiking alone in sparsely inhabited and politically sensitive border regions. If you're going hiking on your own for a day, inform hotel staff of your route, so they can look for you if you don't return when planned.

Con-artists try their luck with tourists all over Southeast Asia, but are usually fairly easy to spot. Always treat **touts** with suspicion – if they offer to take you to a great guesthouse/jewellery shop/untouristed village, you can be sure there'll be a huge commission in it for them, and you may end up being taken somewhere against your will. A variation on this theme involves taxi drivers assuring you that a major sight is closed for the day, so encouraging you to go with them on their own special tour.

Some, but by no means all, **travel agencies** in the backpackers' centres of Southeast Asia are fly-by-night operations. Although it's not necessarily incriminating if a travel agent's office seems to be the proverbial hole in the wall, it may be a good idea to pass on those that look too temporary in favour of something obviously permanent and thriving.

Reporting a crime

If you are a victim of theft or violent crime, you'll need a **police report** for insurance purposes. Try to take someone along with you to the police station to translate, though police will generally do their best to find an English speaker. Allow plenty of time for any involvement with the police, whose offices often wallow in bureaucracy; you may also be charged "administration fees" for enlisting their help, the cost of which is open to sensitive negotiations. You may also want to contact your **embassy** – see the "Listings" section of the nearest capital city for contact numbers. In the case of a medical emergency, you will also need to alert your **insurance company**: see p.50 for more details on this.

Drugs

Drugs penalties are tough throughout the region – in many countries there's even the possibility of being sentenced to death – and you won't get any sympathy from consular officials. Beware of drug scams: either being shopped by a dealer or having substances slipped into your luggage – simple enough to perpetrate unless all fastenings are secured with padlocks. Drug enforcement squads in some countries are said to receive 25 percent of the market value of seized drugs, so are liable to exaggerate the amounts involved. If you are arrested, or end up on the wrong side of the law for whatever reason, you should ring the consular officer at your embassy immediately: see the "Listings" section of the nearest capital city for details.

Cultural hints

Although the peoples of Southeast Asia come from a huge variety of ethnic backgrounds and practise a spread of religions, they share many social practices and taboos, most of which are unfamiliar to Westerners. You are unlikely to get into serious trouble if you flout local mores, though you will get a much friendlier reception if you do your best to be sensitive, particularly when it comes to dress. Social and religious customs specific to each country are dealt with in the relevant chapters.

Dress

Appearance is very important in Southeast Asian society, and dressing neatly is akin to showing respect. Clothing – or the lack of it – is what bothers Southeast Asians most about tourist behaviour. You need to **dress modestly** whenever you are outside a tourist resort, and in particular when entering temples, mosques, churches, important buildings and people's homes, and when dealing with people in authority, especially when applying for visa extensions. For women, that means below-knee-length skirts or trousers, a bra and sleeved tops; for men, long trousers. "Immodest" clothing includes thongs, shorts, vests, and anything that leaves you with bare shoulders. Always take your **shoes** off when entering temples, pagodas, mosques and private homes. Most Southeast Asian people find **topless** and nude bathing extremely unpalatable. True, villagers often bathe publicly in rivers and pools, but there's an unspoken rule of invisibility under these circumstances; women wear sarongs, and men shorts or underwear, often using segregated areas. If you bathe alongside them, do as they do. If you wash your own clothes, hang out your **underwear** discreetly. Women should take particular care to hang underwear low to the ground, as women's undergarments are believed by some to have the power to render talismanic tattoos and amulets powerless if a man passes under them.

Visiting temples, mosques and shrines

Besides dressing conservatively there are other conventions that must be followed when visiting **Buddhist temples**. Theoretically, **monks** are forbidden to have any close contact with women, which means, as a female, you mustn't sit or stand next to a monk, even on a bus, nor brush against his robes, or hand objects directly to him. When giving something to a monk, the object should be placed on a nearby table or passed to a layman who will then hand it to the monk. All **Buddha images** are sacred, and should never be clambered over. When sitting on the floor of a monastery building that has a Buddha image, never point your feet in the direction of the image.

When visiting a **mosque**, women should definitely cover their shoulders and may also be asked to cover their heads as well (bring a scarf or shawl).

Many religions prohibit **women** from engaging in certain activities – or even entering a place of worship – during menstruation. If attending a **religious festival**, find out beforehand whether a dress code applies.

Social practices and taboos

In Buddhist, Islamic and Hindu cultures, various parts of the body are accorded a particular status. The **head** is considered the most sacred part of the body and the **feet** the most unclean. This means that it's very rude to touch another person's head – even to affectionately ruffle a child's hair – or to point your feet either at a human being or at a sacred image. Be careful not to step over any part of people who are sitting or lying on the floor (or the deck of a boat), as this is also considered rude. If you do accidentally kick or brush someone with your feet, apologize immediately and smile as you do so. That way, even if the words aren't understood, your intent will be. On a more practical note, the **left hand** is used for washing after defecating, so Southeast Asians never use it to put food in their mouth, pass things or shake hands.

Public displays of sexual affection like kissing or cuddling are frowned upon across the region, though friends (rather than lovers) of the same sex often hold hands or hug in public. Most Asians dislike **confrontational behaviour**, and will rarely show irritation of any kind. Arguing, raising one's voice and showing anger are all considered extremely bad form. However bad things become, try to keep your temper, as tourists who get visibly rattled for whatever reason will be derided, and even baited further, rather than feared.

Religion

Religion pervades every aspect of life in most Southeast Asian communities, dictating social practices to a much greater extent than in the West. All the world's major faiths are represented in the region, but characteristic across much of Southeast Asia is the syncretic nature of belief, so that many Buddhists, Hindus and Muslims incorporate animist rituals into their daily devotions as well as occasional elements of other major faiths.

Buddhism

Buddhists follow the teachings of Gautama Buddha who, in his five-hundredth incarnation, was born in present-day Nepal as **Prince Gautama Siddhartha**, to a wealthy family some time during the sixth century BC. At an early age, Siddhartha renounced his life of luxury to seek the ultimate deliverance from worldly suffering and strive to reach **Nirvana**, an indefinable, blissful state. After several years he attained enlightenment and then devoted the rest of his life to teaching the Middle Way that leads to Nirvana.

His **philosophy** built on the Hindu theory of perpetual reincarnation in the pursuit of perfection, introducing the notion that desire is the root cause of all suffering and can be extinguished only by following the eightfold path or Middle Way. This **Middle Way** is a highly moral mode of life that encourages compassion and moderation and eschews self-indulgence and anti-social behaviour. But the key is an acknowledgement that the physical world is impermanent and ever-changing, and that all things – including the self – are therefore not worth craving. Only by pursuing a condition of complete detachment can human beings transcend earthly suffering.

In practice, most Buddhists aim only to be **reborn** higher up the incarnation scale rather than set their sights on Nirvana. Each reincarnation marks a move up a kind of ladder, with animals at the bottom, women figuring lower down than men, and monks coming at the top. The rank of the reincarnation is directly related to the good and bad actions performed in the previous life, which accumulate to determine one's **karma** or destiny – hence the obsession with "**making merit**". Merit-making can be done in all sorts of ways, including giving alms to a monk or, for a man, becoming a monk for a short period.

Schools of Buddhism

After the Buddha passed into Nirvana in 543 BC, his doctrine spread relatively quickly across India. His teachings, the Tripitaka, were written down in the Pali language and became known as the **Theravada School of Buddhism** or "The Doctrine of the Elders". Theravada is an ascetic form of Buddhism, based on the principle that each individual is wholly responsible for his or her own accumulation of merit or sin and subsequent enlightenment; it is prevalent in **Thailand**, **Laos** and **Cambodia** as well as in Sri Lanka and Burma.

The other main school of Buddhism practised in Southeast Asia is **Mahayana Buddhism**, which is current in **Vietnam**, and in **ethnic Chinese communities** throughout the region, as well as in China itself, and in Japan and Korea. The ideological rift between the Theravada and Mahayana Buddhists is as vast as the one that divides Catholicism and Protestantism. Mahayana Buddhism attempts to make Buddhism more accessible to the average devotee, easing the struggle towards enlightenment with a pantheon of Buddhist saints or bodhisattva who have postponed their own entry into Nirvana in order to work for the salvation of all humanity.

Chinese religions

The **Chinese communities** of Singapore, Hong Kong, Macau, Malaysia Vietnam and Thailand generally adhere to a system of belief that fuses Mahayana Buddhist, Taoist and Confucianist tenets, alongside the all-important ancestor worship.

Ancestor worship

One of the oldest cults practised among both city dwellers and hilltribespeople who migrated into Southeast Asia from China is that of **ancestor worship**, based on the fundamental principles of filial piety and of obligation to the past, present and future generations. Practices vary, but all believe that the spirits of deceased ancestors have the ability to affect the lives of their living descendants, rewarding those who remember them with offerings, but causing upset if neglected. At funerals and subsequent anniversaries, paper money and other **votive offerings** are burnt, and special food is regularly placed on the ancestral altar.

Confucianism

The teachings of **Confucius** provide a guiding set of moral principles based on piety, loyalty, humanitarianism and familial devotion, which permeate every aspect of Chinese life. Confucius is the Latinized name of K'ung-Fu-Tzu, who was born into a minor aristocratic family in China in 551 BC and worked for many years as a court official. At the age of 50, he set off around the country to spread his ideas on social and political reform. His central tenet was the importance of **correct behaviour**, namely selflessness, respectfulness and non-violence, and loyal service, reinforced by ceremonial rites and frequent offerings to heaven and to the ancestors.

After the death of Confucius in 478 BC, the doctrine was developed by his disciples, and by the first century AD, Confucianism had absorbed elements of Taoism and evolved into a **state ideology** whereby kings ruled under the Mandate of Heaven. Social stability was maintained through a fixed hierarchy of relationships encapsulated in the notion of filial piety. Thus children must obey their parents without question, wives their husbands, students their teacher, and subjects their ruler.

Taosim

Taoism is based on the **Tao-te-ching**, the "Book of the Way", traditionally attributed to **Lao Tzu** ("Old Master"), who is thought to have lived in China in the sixth century BC. A philosophical movement, it advocates that people follow a central path or truth, known as Tao or "The Way", and cultivate an understanding of the nature of things. The Tao emphasizes effortless action, intuition and spontaneity; it cannot be taught, nor can it be expressed in words, but can be embraced by virtuous behaviour. Central to the Tao is the duality inherent in nature, a tension of complimentary opposites defined as **yin** and **yang**, the female and male principles. Harmony is the balance between the two, and experiencing that harmony is the Tao.

In its pure form Taoism has no gods, but in the first century AD it corrupted into an organized religion venerating a deified Lao Tzu, and developed highly complex rituals. The vast, eclectic pantheon of Taoist **gods** is presided over by the Jade Emperor, who is assisted by the southern star, the north star, and the God of the Hearth. Then there is a collection of immortals, genies and guardian deities, including legendary and historic warriors, statesmen, scholars. Confucius is also honoured as a Taoist saint.

Islam

Islam is the youngest of all the major religions, and in Southeast Asia is practised mainly in **Indonesia**, **Malaysia**, **Singapore**

and **Brunei**. It all started with **Mohammed** (570–630AD), an illiterate semi-recluse from Mecca in Arabia, who began, at the age of 40, to receive messages from Allah (God). On these revelations Mohammed began to build a new religion: Islam or "Submission", as the faith required people to submit to God's will. Islam quickly gained in popularity not least because its revolutionary concepts of equality in subordination to Allah freed people from the feudal Hindu caste system that had previously dominated parts of the region.

The Islamic religion is founded on the **Five Pillars**, the essential tenets revealed by Allah to Mohammed and collected in the **Koran**, the holy book that Mohammed dictated before he died. The first is that all Muslims should profess their faith in Allah with the phrase "There is no God but Allah and Mohammed is his prophet". It is this sentence that is intoned by the muezzin five times a day when calling the faithful to prayer. The act of praying is the second pillar. Praying can be done anywhere, though Muslims should always face Mecca when praying, cover the head, and ritually wash feet and hands. The third pillar demands that the faithful should always give a percentage of their income to charity, whilst the fourth states that all Muslims must observe the fasting month of **Ramadan**. This is the ninth month of the Muslim lunar calendar, when the majority of Muslims fast from the break of dawn to dusk, and also abstain from drinking and smoking. The reason for the fast is to intensify awareness of the plight of the poor. The fifth pillar demands that every Muslim should make a pilgrimage to Mecca at least once in their lifetime.

Hinduism

Hinduism was introduced to Southeast Asia by Indian traders more than a thousand years ago, and spread across the region by the Khmers of Cambodia who left a string of magnificent castle-temples throughout northeast Thailand, Laos and most strikingly at Angkor in Cambodia. The most active contemporary Hindu communities live in **Singapore** and **Malaysia**, and the Indonesian island of **Bali** is also a very vibrant, if idiosyncratic, Hindu enclave.

Central to Hinduism is the belief that life is a series of reincarnations that eventually leads to spiritual release. The aim of every Hindu is to attain **enlightenment** (moksa), which brings with it the union of the individual and the divine, and liberation from the painful cycle of death and rebirth. Moksa is only attainable by pure souls, and can take hundreds of lifetimes to achieve. Hindus believe that everybody is reincarnated according to their **karma**, this being a kind of account book that registers all the good and bad deeds performed in the past lives of a soul. Karma is closely bound up with caste and the notion that an individual should accept rather than challenge their destiny.

A whole variety of **deities** are worshipped, the most ubiquitous being Brahma, Vishnu and Shiva. **Brahma** is the Creator, represented by the colour red and often depicted riding on a bull. As the Preserver, **Vishnu** is associated with life-giving waters; he rides the garuda (half-man, half-bird) and is honoured by the colour black. Vishnu also has several avatars, including Buddha – a neat way of incorporating Buddhist elements into the Hindu faith – and Rama, hero of the Ramayana story. **Siwa**, the Destroyer or, more accurately, the Dissolver, is associated with death and rebirth, and with the colour white. He is sometimes represented as a phallic pillar or lingam. He is the father of the elephant-headed deity **Ganesh**, generally worshipped as the remover of obstacles.

Animism

Animism is the belief that all living things – including plants and trees – and some non-living natural features, such as rocks and waterfalls, have **spirits**. It is practised right across Southeast Asia, by everyone from the Dayaks of Sarawak and the hilltribes of Laos, to the citydwellers of Bangkok and Singapore, though rituals and beliefs vary significantly. As with Hinduism, the animistic faiths teach that it is necessary to live in harmony with the spirits; disturb this harmonious balance, by upsetting a spirit for example, and you risk bringing misfortune upon yourself, your household or your village. For this reason, animists consult, or at least consider the spirits before almost everything they do, and you'll often see small **offerings** of flowers or food left by a tree or river to appease the spirits that live within.

Work and study

As Southeast Asia is such an inexpensive region to travel through, most travellers on longish trips save enough money to get them as far as Australia, where temporary jobs are both more plentiful and more lucrative. Casual work in Southeast Asia tends to be thin on the ground, though it is possible to earn enough to keep yourself ticking over for a few extra weeks. Depending on the job, you might get away with working on your tourist visa for a month or two; to work any longer entails regular "visa runs" across the nearest border. For more official employment you'll need a working visa – contact the relevant embassy, listed on p.44.

It's quite popular to do short, **traveller-oriented courses** in local arts, crafts and cuisines, in particular in traditional music and dance (Indonesia); batik (Indonesia and Malaysia); cookery (Thailand and Indonesia); massage (Thailand); and meditation (Thailand and Indonesia). Most capital cities also offer language courses. Details of all these are given in the relevant chapters of the Guide.

For a roundup of longer, more serious **study programmes** in Asia, visit ⓦ www.studyabroad.com. For a guide to the wealth of short-term **voluntary-work projects** available in Southeast Asia, see ⓦ www.volunteerabroad.com.

Teaching English

Teaching English is the most common and most lucrative type of short-term work available in Southeast Asia. It's easier to get work if you have an English-teaching qualification, but not every job requires that. You can get a CELTA (Certificate in English Language Teaching to Adults) qualification at home or on the road: International House (ⓦ www.ihlondon.com) has branches in many countries that offer the course. They also recruit teachers for posts worldwide, as does the British Council (ⓣ 016/1957 7755, ⓦ www.britishcouncil.org).

Other work options

Aside from English-teaching, the jobs that you're most likely to be offered are: **bar and restaurant work** (in Hong Kong and Singapore), though pay and conditions are generally poor; **modelling** (in Hong Kong), where it helps if you have a portfolio with you – and if you're exceptionally attractive; and work as a **dive instructor** (in Indonesia, Malaysia, the Philippines and Thailand), for which you will need relevant experience and certificates, though you could also take your dive instructor course while you're in Southeast Asia.

Travellers with disabilities

Most Southeast Asian countries make few provisions for their own disabled citizens, which clearly affects travellers with disabilities. Pavements are usually high, uneven, and lacking dropped kerbs, and public transport is not wheelchair-friendly. On the positive side, however, most disabled travellers report that help is never in short supply, and wheelchair users with collapsible chairs may be able to take cycle rickshaws and tuk-tuks, balancing their chair in front of them. Also, services in much of Southeast Asia are very inexpensive for Western travellers,

so you should be able to afford to hire a car or minibus with driver for a few days, stay at better-equipped hotels, and even take some internal flights. You might also consider hiring a local tour guide to accompany you on sightseeing trips – a native speaker can facilitate access to temples and museums. Or perhaps book a package holiday – see below for useful contacts.

The two most-clued up destinations in Southeast Asia are **Hong Kong** and **Singapore**, both of which have some wheelchair-accessible public transport. Both countries publish brochures listing all amenities for people with disabilities: *A Guide for Physically Handicapped Visitors to Hong Kong* is distributed by the Hong Kong Tourist Association (see p.46); and *Access Singapore* is produced by the Singapore Council of Social Service, 11 Penang Lane, Singapore.

Before you travel, read your **insurance** small print carefully to make sure that people with an existing medical condition are not excluded. And use your travel agent to make your journey simpler: airlines can provide a wheelchair at the airport, for example. A **medical certificate** of your fitness to travel, provided by your doctor, is also extremely useful; some airlines or insurance companies may insist on it. Take a backup prescription including the generic name of any drugs in case of emergency, and carry spares of any equipment that might be hard to find.

Make sure that you take sufficient supplies of any **medications**, and – if they're essential – carry the complete supply with you whenever you travel (including on buses and planes), in case of loss or theft. Carry a doctor's letter about your drug prescriptions with you when passing through airport customs, as this will ensure you don't get hauled up for narcotics transgressions. If your medication has to be kept cool, buy a thermal insulation bag and a couple of freezer blocks before you leave home. That way you can refreeze one of the two blocks every day while the other is in use; staff in most hotels, restaurants and bars should be happy to let you use their freezer compartment for a few hours. You may also be able to store your medication in hotel and guesthouse refrigerators.

Contacts for travellers with disabilities

In the UK and Ireland

Access Travel 6 The Hillock, Astley, Lancashire M29 7GW ⓣ01942/888 844, ⓦwww.access-travel.co.uk. Flights, transfer and accommodation.

Disability Action Group 2 Annadale Ave, Belfast BT7 3JH, ⓣ028/9049 1011. Provides information for disabled travellers abroad.

Holiday Care 2nd floor, Imperial Building, Victoria Rd, Horley, Surrey RH6 7PZ ⓣ01293/774 535, Minicom ⓣ01293/776 943, ⓦwww.holidaycare.org.uk. Provides free lists of accessible accommodation abroad.

Irish Wheelchair Association Blackheath Drive, Clontarf, Dublin 3 ⓣ01/833 8241, ⓕ833 3873, ⓦwww.iwa.ie. Useful information provided about travelling abroad with a wheelchair.

Tripscope Alexandra House, Albany Rd, Brentford, Middlesex TW8 0NE ⓣ08457/585 641, ⓦwww.justmobility.co.uk. Free advice on international travel for those with a mobility problem.

In the USA and Canada

Access-Able ⓦwww.access-able.com. Online resource for travellers with disabilities.

Directions Unlimited 123 Green Lane, Bedford Hills, NY 10507 ⓣ1-800/533-5343 or 914/241-1700. Tour operator specializing in custom tours for people with disabilities.

Mobility International USA 451 Broadway, Eugene, OR 97401, voice and TDD ⓣ541/343-1284, ⓦwww.miusa.org. Information, guides and tours.

Society for the Advancement of Travelers with Handicaps (SATH) 347 5th Ave, New York, NY 10016 ⓣ212/447-7284, ⓦwww.sath.org. Organization that actively represents travellers with disabilities.

Twin Peaks Press Box 129, Vancouver, WA 98661 ⓣ360/694-2462 or 1-800/637-2256, ⓔtwinpeak@pacifier.com. Publishes several guides on travel for the disabled.

Wheels Up! ⓣ1-888/389-4335, ⓦwww.wheelsup.com. Discounted airfares and tours for disabled travellers.

In Australia and New Zealand

ACROD (Australian Council for Rehabilitation of the Disabled) PO Box 60, Curtin ACT 2605 ⓣ02/6282 4333; 24 Cabarita Rd, Cabarita NSW 2137 ⓣ02/9743 2699, ⓦwww.acrod.org.au. Keeps lists of travel agents and tour operators for people with disabilities.

Disabled Persons Assembly 4/173–175 Victoria St, Wellington, New Zealand ⓣ04/801 9100, ⓦwww.dpa.org.nz. Resource centre with lists of travel agencies and tour operators for people with disabilities.

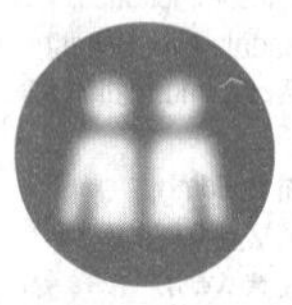

Gay and lesbian travellers

Homosexuality is broadly tolerated in Southeast Asia, if not exactly accepted. Most gay Asian men and women are private and discreet about being gay, generally pursuing a "don't ask, don't tell" understanding with their family. But, as it's more acceptable in Asia to show a modest amount of physical affection to friends of the same sex than to lovers of the opposite sex, gay couples generally encounter less hassle about being seen together than they might in the West.

Thailand and the Philippines have the most public and developed **gay scene** in Southeast Asia, and gay travellers are generally made to feel welcome in both places. Indonesia, Cambodia, Laos and Vietnam all have less obvious gay communities, but they do exist and homosexuality is not illegal in any of them. The situation is less rosy in Malaysia, where Islamic laws can be used to punish gay sexual activity and travellers should be especially discreet – despite this, there are gay bars and meeting places in Kuala Lumpur and Penang. In Singapore, where the government follows a repressive line on homosexuals, sodomy is illegal. In practice, however, enforcement of such laws seems to be less rigid than in the past.

A lot of gay visitors and expats have affairs with Asian men, and these **liaisons** tend to fall somewhere between holiday romances and paid sex. Few gay Asians in these circumstances would classify themselves as rent boys – they wouldn't sleep with someone they didn't like and most wouldn't admit to having sex for money – but they usually expect to be financially cared for by the richer man (food, drinks and entertainment expenses, for example), and some do make their living this way. The tourist-oriented gay sex industry is a tiny but highly visible part of Southeast Asia's gay scene, and is most obvious in Thailand where gay venues are often nothing more than brothels. Studies have shown that a significant percentage of male sex workers in Thailand are not even gay, and are often addicted to drugs or from broken families.

For detailed **information** on the gay scene in Southeast Asia, check out the **website** created by Bangkok's Utopia gay and lesbian centre (ⓦwww.utopia-asia.com), which is an excellent resource for gay travellers to all regions of Asia and has travellers' reports on gay scenes across the region.

Contacts for gay and lesbian travellers

In the UK

ⓦ**www.gaytravel.co.uk** Online gay and lesbian travel agent.

Dream Waves Redcot High St, Child Okeford, Blandford, DT22 8ET ⓣ01258/861 149, ⓦwww.gayholidaysdirect.com. Specializes in exclusively gay holidays.

Madison Travel 118 Western Rd, Hove, East Sussex NN3 1DB ⓣ01273/202 532, ⓦwww.madisontravel.co.uk. Packages to gay- and lesbian-friendly destinations.

In the USA and Canada

Damron Company PO Box 422458, San Francisco CA 94142 ⓣ1-800/462-6654 or 415/255-0404, ⓦwww.damron.com. Publisher of *Damron Accommodations*, which lists 1000 accommodations for gays and lesbians worldwide.

Ferrari Publications PO Box 37887, Phoenix, AZ 85069 ⓣ1-800/962-2912 or 602/863-2408, ⓦwww.ferrariguides.com. Publishes several worldwide gay and lesbian guides.

International Gay & Lesbian Travel Association 4331 N Federal Hwy, Suite 304, Ft Lauderdale, FL 33308 ⓣ1-800/448-8550, ⓦwww.iglta.org. Keeps a list of gay- and lesbian-friendly travel agents and accommodation.

In Australia and New Zealand

Gay and Lesbian Travel ⓦwww.galta.com.au. Directory for gay and lesbian travel worldwide.

Gay Travel ⓦwww.gaytravel.com. Trip planning and bookings.

Parkside Travel 70 Glen Osmond Rd, Parkside, SA 5063 ⓣ08/8274 1222 or 1800/888 501, ⓔhwtravel@senet.com.au. All aspects of gay and lesbian travel worldwide.

Silke's Travel 263 Oxford St, Darlinghurst, NSW 2010 ⓣ02/9380 6244 or 1800/807 860, ⓔsilba@magna.com.au. Long-established gay and lesbian specialist.

Tearaway Travel 52 Porter St, Prahan, VIC 3181 ⓣ03/9510 6344, ⓦwww.tearaway.com. Gay-specific travel agent.

Women travellers

Southeast Asia is generally a safe region for women to travel around alone. Most people will simply be curious as to why you are on your own and the chances of encountering any threatening behaviour are rare. That said, it pays to take the normal precautions, especially late at night when there are few people around on the streets; after dark, take licensed taxis rather than cycle rickshaws and tuk-tuks.

It's as well to be aware that the Asian perception of Western female travellers is of sexual availability and promiscuity. This is particularly the case in the traditional Muslim areas of Indonesia and Malaysia, as well as southern Thailand and the southern Philippines, where lone foreign women can get treated contemptuously however decently attired. However, even in the majority Buddhist countries it pays to keep your wits about you. Most Southeast Asian women **dress modestly** and it usually helps to do the same, avoiding skimpy shorts and vests, which are considered offensive (see also p.68). Some Asian women travelling with white men have reported cases of serious harassment, from verbal abuse to rock throwing – something attributed to the tendency of Southeast Asian men to automatically label all such women as prostitutes. These incidents are most common in Vietnam. Be wary of invitations to drink with a man or group of men if there are no other women present. To many Southeast Asian men, simply accepting such an invitation will be perceived as tacit agreement to have sex, and some Southeast Asian men will see it as their right to rape a woman who has "led them on" by accepting such an invitation and then refused to follow through. Women should also take care around Buddhist monks. It should go without saying that monks who touch women (an act that is strictly against the Buddhist precepts) or who suggest showing you around some isolated site – such as a cave – should be politely but firmly rebuffed. The key is to stay aware without being paranoid: A good rule of thumb is to simply avoid doing anything you wouldn't do at home.

Guide

Guide

Brunei

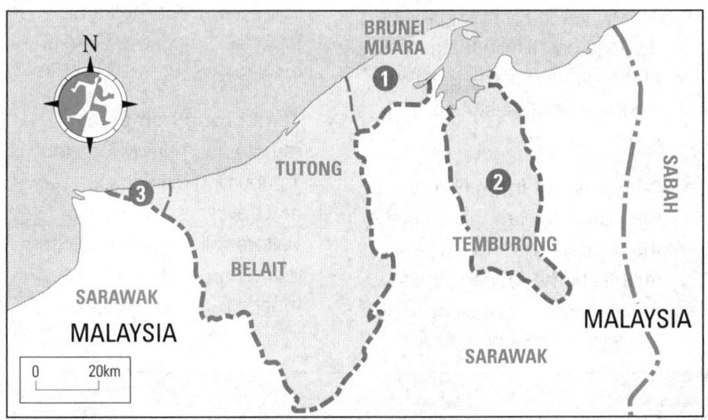
N
BRUNEI MUARA
TUTONG
BELAIT
TEMBURONG
SABAH
SARAWAK
MALAYSIA
MALAYSIA
SARAWAK
0 20km

Brunei highlights

* **Omar Ali Saifuddien Mosque** Take off your shoes and step into the magnificent Omar Ali Saifuddien Mosque, in Bandar Seri Begawan, whose golden dome is mirrored in the surrounding lagoon. See p.91

* **Kampung Ayer, Bandar Seri Begawan** Thirty thousand people live in Kampung Ayer, a village on stilts in the middle of a river. One of the great sights of Southeast Asia. See p.91

* **Istana Nurul Iman** Bigger than Buckingham Palace or the Vatican, the Istana Nurul Iman is home to the world's richest man and opulent beyond description. For a good look, take a boat ride along the neighbouring Sungei Brunei. See p.92

* **Boat ride, Sungei Temburong** Known as "flying coffins" because of their shape, these passenger boats scream past the mangrove-lined riverbanks of Sungei Temburong. If you're lucky, you'll see crocodiles and proboscis monkeys along the way. See p.95

* **Temburong homestays** The remote and heavily forested Temburong district sees very few travellers. Courteous visitors will be made welcome in the house of one of the tribal chiefs. See p.95

△Omar Ali Saifuddien Mosque

Introduction and basics

The tiny, but thriving, Islamic Sultanate of Brunei perches on the northwestern coast of Borneo, completely encircled by the East Malaysian state of Sarawak, which divides it in two. It has a population of 365,000, nearly seventy percent of which is made up of Malays and indigenes from the larger ethnic groups such as the Murut and Dusun; the rest are Chinese, Indians, smaller indigenous tribes and expats. They enjoy a quality of life that is quite unparalleled in Southeast Asia, with the literacy rate a staggering 93.9 percent of the population. Education and healthcare are free; houses, cars and even pilgrimages to Mecca are subsidized; taxation on personal income is unheard of; and the average per capita salary is around US$19,000. The explanation is simple: oil, first discovered in 1903 at the site of what is now the town of Seria. That said, the problem remains that Brunei is more expensive than neighbouring Malaysia or even Singapore – hotel prices in the capital are at least double those in nearby Kota Kinabalu or Miri. Most travellers still end up in Brunei either because of an enforced stopover on a Royal Brunei Airlines flight, or as a stepping-stone to either Sabah or Sarawak. In the latter case, however, it can work out cheaper to take an internal MAS flight between Miri and Labuan or Kota Kinabalu, rather than bussing it through Brunei. Brunei's climate, like that of neighbouring Sabah and Sarawak, is hot and humid, with average temperatures in the high twenties throughout the year. Lying 440km north of the equator, Brunei has a tropical weather system so, even if you visit outside the wet season (usually November to February), there's every chance that you'll see some rain.

Overland and sea routes into Brunei

Boats to Brunei depart daily from Lawas (see p.725) and Limbang (see p.725) in northern Sarawak, and from Pulau Labuan (see p.734), itself connected by boat to Kota Kinabalu in Sabah. From Miri (see p.734) in Sarawak, several **buses** travel daily to Kuala Belait, in the far western corner of Brunei. The overland route from Sabah to Brunei necessitates taking a bus to Lawas and on to Bangar in the Temburong District, from where it's only a short boat trip to Bandar Seri Begawan.

Entry requirements and visa extension

The passports of British nationals, New Zealanders, Singaporeans and Malaysians are stamped upon arrival with a thirty-day **visa**; US citizens can stay up to three months; Australian, Canadian, French, Dutch, German, Swedish, Norwegian, Swiss and Belgian citizens can stay for fourteen days; and all other visitors must apply for visas at local Brunei diplomatic missions (see p.44) or, failing that, at a British consulate. Visas are normally valid for two weeks, but renewable in Brunei. Officials may ask to see either an onward ticket, or proof of sufficient funds to cover your stay, though it's unlikely if you look reasonably smart.

Although Brunei is a **dry state**, all non-Muslim travellers are permitted to bring in twelve cans of beer or two bottles of liquor (wine or spirits), but make sure to declare them in customs.

Airport departure tax

Bruneian **airport departure tax** is B$5 for flights to East Malaysia and B$12 to West Malaysia and Singapore and all other destinations.

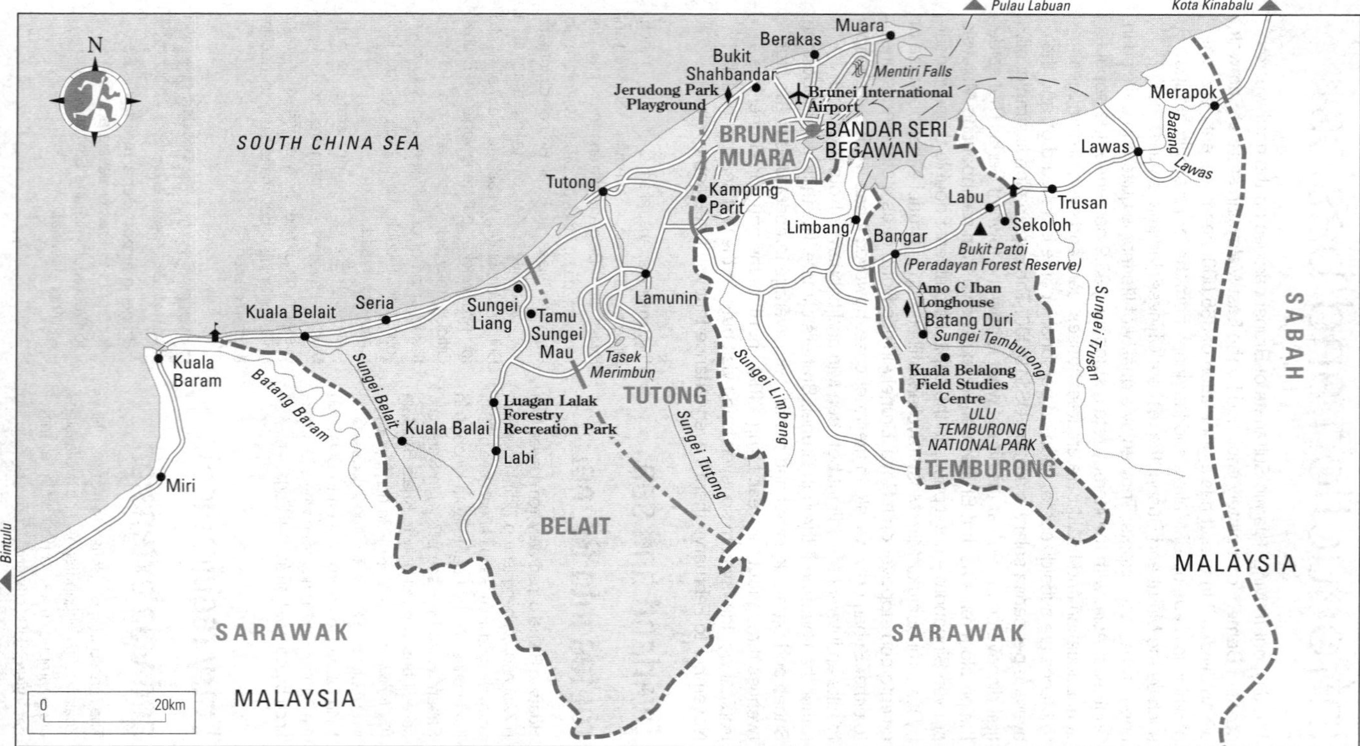
Kota Kinabalu
Pulau Labuan
Bintulu
N
SOUTH CHINA SEA
SABAH
MALAYSIA
SARAWAK
SARAWAK
MALAYSIA
BRUNEI MUARA
TUTONG
BELAIT
TEMBURONG
BANDAR SERI BEGAWAN
Muara
Berakas
Bukit Shahbandar
Jerudong Park Playground
Brunei International Airport
Mentiri Falls
Merapok
Batang Lawas
Lawas
Trusan
Labu
Sekoloh
Limbang
Bangar
Bukit Patoi
(Peradayan Forest Reserve)
Amo C Iban Longhouse
Batang Duri
Sungei Temburong
Kuala Belalong Field Studies Centre
ULU TEMBURONG NATIONAL PARK
Sungei Trusan
Sungei Limbang
Kampung Parit
Tutong
Lamunin
Tasek Merimbun
Sungei Tutong
Sungei Liang
Tamu Sungei Mau
Luagan Lalak Forestry Recreation Park
Labi
Kuala Balai
Sungei Belait
Seria
Kuala Belait
Kuala Baram
Batang Baram
Miri
0
20km

Money and costs

Brunei's **currency** is the Bruneian dollar, which is divided into 100 cents; you'll see it written as B$, or simply as $. The Bruneian dollar has parity with the Singapore dollar, and both are legal tender in either country. Notes come in B$1, B$5, B$10, B$50, B$100, B$500, B$1000 and B$10,000 denominations; coins are in denominations of 1, 5, 10, 20 and 50 cents. At the time of writing, the **exchange rate** was B$3 to the pound or B$1.65 to the US dollar. There were 2.3 Malaysian ringgit to one Bruneian dollar.

Sterling and US dollar **travellers' cheques** can be cashed at banks, licensed moneychangers and some hotels. Major **credit cards** are accepted in most hotels and large shops. Banks will **advance cash** against major credit cards, and with MasterCard, Visa, American Express or any bank card bearing a Maestro, Plus or Cirrus logo, you can withdraw money from most automatic teller machines (ATMs). You can get **money wired** to you (see "Wiring money", p.60) via any of the major banks in Kuala Belait or the capital.

There's only one budget place to stay in the capital and, if you can't get in there, you're looking at around £20/US$38 minimum per night in a hotel, which means an average **daily budget** in Brunei is likely to start at around £25–30/US$48–58.

Information and maps

Brunei still doesn't have a Ministry for Tourism, but there is now a tourism department (☎02/382831) under the Ministry of Industry and Primary Resources. Bandar has two **tourist offices**, a small information booth at the airport and a large walk-in centre on Jalan Elizabeth Dua in the city itself. In addition, you'll find the excellent *Explore Brunei* and *Places of Interest* leaflets and a city map at most hotels. **Local tour operators** are another source of information. Sunshine Borneo Tours and Travel, 2nd Floor, Unit 1, Block C, Abdul Razak Complex, Gadong, Bandar (☎02/441791), has dozens of leaflets on attractions in the city and around the state. They also run numerous tours, including a three-day excursion to Brunei's Temburong district (B$200). Owner Anthony Chieng can offer good insights into travelling in the state. Borneo Outdoors, 3b Kiarong Apts, Simpang, Bandar (☎02/454764), also organizes trips.

Nelles East Malaysia **map** includes the best country map of Brunei, while the Bruneian government publication, *Explore Brunei*, includes a reasonable map of Bandar city centre.

Getting around

If you intend to explore Brunei in some depth, you've got little option but to **rent a car**. South of the main coastal roads, bus services are non-existent, while taxis are expensive. Apart from short hops across Sungei Brunei in Bandar's water taxis, the only time you're likely to use a boat is to get to Temburong district (see p.95), which is cut off from the rest of Brunei by the Limbang corridor of Sarawak. For an idea of journey times between major destinations, see "**Travel details**", p.97.

Accommodation

Accommodation in Brunei is much more expensive than in Sabah and Sarawak. On the whole, you can expect to pay double what you would pay in Malaysia. Accommodation outside Bandar is limited, although recently the government has launched a **homestay programme**, whereby travellers stay in Malay and Murut villages and Iban longhouses. Electricity in Brunei is supplied at 220 volts.

Food and drink

The **food** in Brunei is very similar to that of Malaysia, though unlike Sabah and Sarawak you'll find a good deal of Indian and Bangladeshi dishes here; see the Malaysia "Food and drink" section for further details. It is illegal to buy alcoholic **drink** in Brunei.

Communications

Postcards to anywhere in the world cost 50c; aerogrammes 45c; and overseas **letters** 90c for every 10g. Local calls cost 10c flat fee from phone boxes and are free from private **phones**. International (IDD) calls can be made through hotels, in booths at Bandar's Telekom office (see p.94) or from card phones. Phonecards (B$5, B$10, B$20 or B$50) can be bought from the Telekom office and post offices. To **phone abroad** from Brunei, dial ☎00 + IDD country code (see p.64) + area code minus first 0 + subscriber number. There are a number of **cybercafés** around Bandar, charging around B$4 per hour.

Time differences

Brunei is eight hours ahead of London (GMT), sixteen hours ahead of Los Angeles, thirteen hours ahead of New York, two hours behind Sydney and four hours behind Auckland.

Opening hours and festivals

Government offices in Brunei open Mon–Thurs & Sat 7.45am–12.15pm & 1.30–4.30pm; **shopping centres** daily 10am–10pm. **Banking hours** are Mon–Fri 9am–3pm and Sat 9–11am. **Post offices** are open Mon to Thurs & Sat 7.45am–4.30pm; see p.94 for details of the GPO in Bandar.

Most of Brunei's **festivals** have no fixed dates, but change annually according to the lunar calendar, so check with the tourist office. During **Ramadan**, Muslims spend the ninth month of the Islamic calendar (Jan–April) fasting in the daytime; during this time it is culturally sensitive for tourists not to eat or smoke blatantly in public during daylight hours. The festival celebrations of most interest to tourists include **Brunei National Day** (Feb 23), when the sultan and 35,000 other Bruneians watch parades and fireworks at the Sultan Hassanal Bolkiah National Stadium, just outside Bandar; **Hari Raya Idul Fitri**, the end of the Ramadan fasting period (March/April), which is marked by the annual opening of the Istana Nurul Iman, Brunei's royal palace, to the public; **Brunei Armed Forces' Day** (May 31), when Bandar's square hosts parades and displays; and His Majesty the **Sultan of Brunei's Birthday Celebrations** (July 15), which kicks off a fortnight of parades, lantern processions, traditional sports competitions and fireworks.

Public holidays

January 1: New Year's Day
January/February: Chinese New Year
February/March: Hari Raya Haji
February 23: National Day
March/April: First Day of Hijrah
May/June: Birthday of the Prophet Mohammed
May 31: Armed Forces' Day
July 15: Sultan's Birthday
October: Israk Mikraj
November/December: First day of Ramadan
November/December: Anniversary of Revelation of the Koran
December: Hari Raya Idul Fitri
December 25: Christmas Day

Cultural hints

Brunei broadly shares the **same attitudes to dress and social taboos** as other Southeast Asian cultures, though it's a little more conservatively Islamic than neighbouring Malaysia; see "Cultural hints", p.68 for details.

Crime and safety

Brunei has very **little crime** and travellers rarely experience any trouble. Note that the possession of **drugs** – whether hard or soft – carries a hefty prison sentence, and trafficking is punishable by the death penalty. If you are caught smuggling drugs into or out of the country, at the very best you will face a long stretch in a foreign prison; at worst, you could be hanged.

Medical care and emergencies

Medical services in Brunei are excellent; staff speak good English and use up-to-date techniques. See p.94 for details of hospitals in Bandar. Oral **contraceptives** and condoms are available at pharmacies.

Emergency phone numbers

Ambulance ☎991
Fire brigade ☎995
Police ☎993

History

Contemporary Brunei's modest size belies its pivotal role in the formative centuries of Bornean history. China was probably trading with Brunei as long ago as the seventh century, and Brunei later benefited from its strategic position on the trade route between India, Melaka and China, exercising a lucrative control over merchant traffic in the South China Sea. It became a staging post, where traders could stock up on local supplies such as beeswax, camphor, rattan and brasswork, which were traded for ceramics, spices, woods and fabrics. For a brief period in the fourteenth century, the region was taken over by the Majapahit Empire but, by the end of the century, it had become independent and was governed by the first of a long line of sultans.

By the mid-fifteenth century, as the sultanate courted foreign Muslim merchants' business, **Islam** began to make inroads into Bruneian society. This process was accelerated by the decamping to Brunei of wealthy Muslim merchant families after the fall of Melaka to the Portuguese in 1511. In the first half of the sixteenth century, Brunei was Borneo's foremost kingdom, its influence stretching along the island's northern and western coasts, and even as far as territory belonging to the modern-day Philippines. Such was the extent of Bruneian authority that Western visitors found the sultanate and the island interchangeable: the word "Borneo" is thought to be no more than a European corruption of Brunei. But by the close of the sixteenth century, things were beginning to turn sour. Trouble with **Catholic Spain**, now sniffing around the South China and Sulu seas with a view to colonization, led to a sea battle off the coast at Muara in 1578; the battle was won by Spain, whose forces took Brunei Town, only to be chased out days later by a cholera epidemic. The threat of piracy caused more problems, scaring off passing trade. Worse still, at home the sultans began to lose control of the noblemen, as factional struggles ruptured the court.

Western entrepreneurs arrived in this self-destructive climate, keen to take advantage of gaps in the trade market left by Brunei's decline. One such fortune-seeker was **James Brooke**, whose arrival off the coast of Kuching in August 1839 was to change the face of Borneo for ever. For helping the sultan to quell a Dyak uprising, Brooke demanded and was given the governorship of Sarawak; Brunei's contraction had begun. Over subsequent decades, the state was to shrink steadily, as Brooke and his successors used the suppression of piracy as the excuse they needed to siphon off more and more territory into the familial fiefdom. This trend culminated in the cession of the Limbang region in 1890 – a move that literally split Brunei in two.

Elsewhere, more Bruneian land was being lost to other powers. In January 1846, a court faction unsympathetic to foreign land-grabbing seized power in Brunei and the chief minister was murdered. British gunboats quelled the coup and Pulau Labuan was ceded to the British crown. A treaty signed the following year, forbidding the sultanate from ceding any of its territories without the British Crown's consent, underlined the **decline of Brunei's power**. Shortly afterwards, in 1865, American consul Charles Lee Moses negotiated a treaty granting a ten-year lease to the **American Trading Company** of the portion of northeast Borneo that was later to become Sabah. By 1888, the British had declared Brunei a protected state, which meant the responsibility for its foreign affairs lay with London. The turn of the twentieth century was marked by the discovery of **oil**: given what little remained of Bruneian territory, it could hardly have been altruism that spurred the British to set up a Residency here in 1906. By 1938, oil exports, engineered by the British Malayan Petroleum Company, had topped M$5 million.

The **Japanese invasion** of December 1941 temporarily halted Brunei's path to recovery. While Sabah, Sarawak and Pulau Labuan became Crown Colonies in the early postwar years, Brunei remained a **British Protectorate** and retained its British Resident. Only in 1959 was the Residency finally withdrawn and a new constitution established, with provisions for a democratically elected legislative council. At the same time, Sultan Omar Ali Saifuddien (the present sultan's father) was careful to retain British involvement in matters of defence and foreign affairs – a move whose sagacity was made apparent when, in 1962, an **armed coup** was crushed by British Army Gurkhas. The coup was led by Sheik Azahari's pro-democratic Brunei People's Party (PRB) in response to Sultan Omar's refusal to convene the first sitting of the legislative council. Despite showing interest in joining the planned Malaysian Federation in 1963, Brunei suffered a last-minute attack of cold feet, choosing to opt out rather than risk losing its new-found oil wealth and compromising the pre-eminence of its monarchy.

Brunei remained a British Protectorate until January 1, 1984, when it attained full **independence**. Ever since the 1962 coup, Brunei has been ruled by the decree of the sultan, who fulfils the roles of (non-elected) prime minister, finance minister and defence minister, while the post of minister of foreign affairs is held by his brother Prince Mohamed. The sultan's other brother, Jefri, was the previous finance minister but was famously sued in 1998 for embezzling B$3bn of state funds: the court cut his living expenses down to a meagre US$300,000 a month. Seven other ministerial advisors have a hand in government but the sultan's say is final. Political parties were countenanced for three years in the mid-1980s, but outlawed again in 1988 – the sultan is quoted in Lord Chalfont's biography, *By God's Will*, as saying, "When I see some genuine interest among the citizenry, we may move towards elections." The government's emergency powers have also remained in place since 1962, which include provisions for the detention, without trial, of citizens.

Meanwhile, oil reserves have fulfilled all expectations, particularly in the 1970s, the decade that saw oil prices shoot through the roof, when money really began to roll in. Oil has made Bruneians rich, none more so than Brunei's twenty-ninth sultan, **Hassanal Bolkiah** (his full title is 31 words long). The *Guinness Book of Records* and *Fortune Magazine* have both credited the present sultan as the richest man in the world, with assets estimated to be as high as US$37 billion. The sultan himself disputes such claims, asserting that he doesn't have unlimited access to state funds. Nevertheless, he has managed to acquire hotels in Singapore, London and Beverly Hills; a magnificent residence, the US$350-million Istana Nurul Iman;

a collection of three hundred cars and a private fleet of aircraft; and over two hundred fine polo horses, kept at his personal country club.

Although Brunei can only grow richer with its oil reserves and massive global investments, in recent years the sultan has decided that the economy should **diversify** into hi-tech industries, the service sector and ecotourism – evidence of a less isolationist and self-contained outlook. Bruneians themselves want to feel part of a larger world – many pop over to Miri in Sarawak on the weekends, where they see the benefits of a tourist infrastructure, such as cheaper goods, and where they encounter less restrictive traditions.

Ecotourism is viewed as appropriate for a religiously conformist state like Brunei. It certainly plays to the state's strengths – with logging almost nonexistent, the southern parts of the country consist mostly of pristine rainforest and are a delight to travel in, now that a basic infrastructure has been put in place.

Religion

The overwhelming majority of Bruneians are Muslim, though there are significant Christian minorities amongst tribes peoples. See "Religion", p.69, for an introduction to Islam.

Books

James Bartholomew *The Richest Man in the World* (Penguin, UK). Despite an obvious (and admitted) lack of sources, Bartholomew's study of the Sultan of Brunei makes fairly engaging reading – particularly the mind-bending facts used to illustrate his wealth.

C. Mary Turnbull *A Short History of Malaysia, Singapore & Brunei* (Graham Brash, Singapore). Decent, informed introduction to the region.

Language

The national language of Brunei is Bahasa Malaysia, as spoken in Malaysia; see p.634 for an introductory vocabulary. English is also widely spoken.

1.1

Bandar Seri Begawan

BANDAR SERI BEGAWAN, also known as BSB or simply Bandar, is the capital of Brunei and the sultanate's only settlement of any real size. Straddling the northern bank of a twist in the Sungei Brunei, the city is characterized by its unlikely juxtaposition of striking modern buildings (the latest and most impressive being the twin malls of the Yayasan Sultan Haji Hassanal Bolkiah shopping complex) and traditional stilt houses. These stilt houses make up the water village, or **Kampung Ayer**, Brunei's original seat of power and still home to half the city's population. Indeed, as recently as the middle of the nineteenth century, Brunei's capital was little more than a sleepy water village, but with the discovery of oil came its evolution into the attractive, clean and modern waterfront city of today. Large-scale urbanization took place north of the Sungei Brunei, resulting in housing schemes, shopping centres and, more obviously, the magnificent **Omar Ali Saifuddien Mosque**, which dominates the skyline of Bandar. First-time visitors are pleasantly surprised by a sense of space that's rare in Southeast Asian cities. Although Bandar isn't somewhere you're likely to stay for long – most of its sights can be seen in a day or two – you might end up staying a bit longer if you use it as a base to explore outlying attractions such as Temburong and Tutong. Tourism in Brunei is still in its infancy and is not yet seen as a moneyspinner, so you'll find that many sites in the capital have no entrance charge.

Arrival

Flying into Bandar, you'll arrive at plush **Brunei International Airport** (Lapangan Terbang Antarabangsa; ☎02/331747). If you need to book a room on arrival, there are free public phones to your right beyond passport control. To the left, as you walk out of the arrivals concourse and into the car park, is a **tourist information** booth. If you are here on a long stopover (as on flights between the UK and Australia), half-day tours of the city are surprisingly easy to arrange. Taking a **taxi** to cover the 11km into Bandar costs B$15–20, but if you bear right as you exit arrivals, into the free parking zone, you can catch a **bus** (every 15min; 8am–8pm; B$1) into town. You can get change for the fare at the airport branch of the **Islamic Bank of Brunei** (Mon–Thurs 9am–noon & 2–3pm, Fri 8–11am & 2.30–3.30pm, Sat 9–11am) or from the HSBC ATM.

Boats from Limbang dock centrally, beside the Customs and Immigration Station at the junction of Jalan Roberts and Jalan McArthur. Boats from Pulau Labuan and Lawas dock at Serasa Wharf in **Muara**, 25km northeast of the city; regular buses run from here to Bandar. Services from Miri in Sarawak (via Seria and Kuala Belait) arrive at the **bus station** below Jalan Cator.

City transport

With as much as half of Bandar's population living in the villages that make up Kampung Ayer, the most common form of city transport are **water taxis**, nicknamed "flying coffins" because of their shape and speed; they charge B$2 for a short hop. The

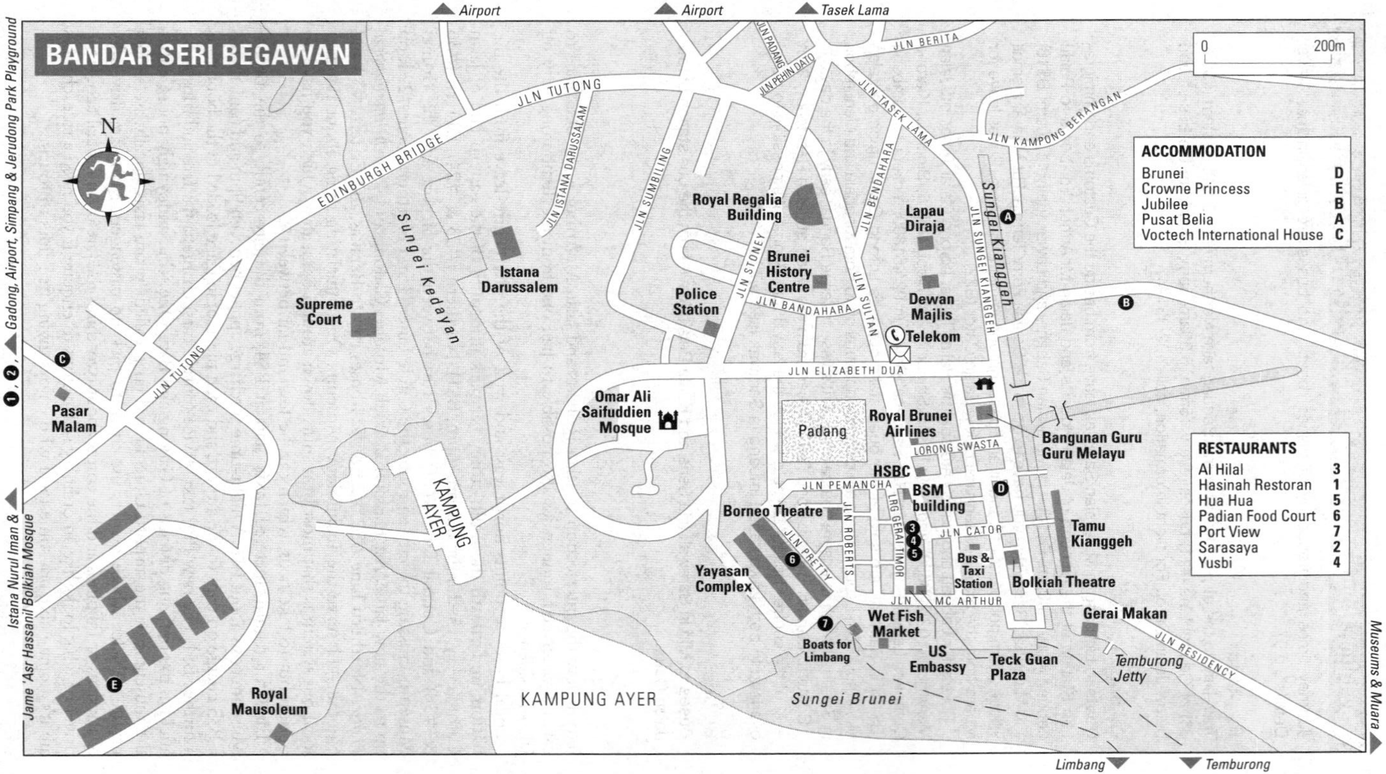

BANDAR SERI BEGAWAN

ACCOMMODATION

Brunei	D
Crowne Princess	E
Jubilee	B
Pusat Belia	A
Voctech International House	C

RESTAURANTS

Al Hilal	3
Hasinah Restoran	1
Hua Hua	5
Padian Food Court	6
Port View	7
Sarasaya	2
Yusbi	4

0 200m
N
Airport
Airport
Tasek Lama
1, 2, Gadong, Airport, Simpang & Jerudong Park Playground
Istana Nurul Iman & Jame 'Asr Hassanil Bolkiah Mosque
Museums & Muara
Limbang
Temburong
JLN TUTONG
EDINBURGH BRIDGE
JLN ISTANA DARUSSALAM
JLN SUMBILING
JLN PADANG
JLN PEHIN DATO
JLN BERITA
JLN TASEK LAMA
JLN KAMPONG BERANGAN
JLN STONEY
JLN BENDAHARA
JLN BANDAHARA
JLN SULTAN
JLN SUNGEI KIANGGEH
Sungei Kianggeh
JLN ELIZABETH DUA
LORONG SWASTA
JLN PEMANCHA
LRG GERAI TIMOR
JLN CATOR
JLN ROBERTS
JLN PRETTY
JLN MC ARTHUR
JLN RESIDENCY
Sungei Kedayan
Sungei Brunei
KAMPUNG AYER
KAMPUNG AYER
Royal Regalia Building
Lapau Diraja
Brunei History Centre
Dewan Majlis
Telekom
Police Station
Istana Darussalem
Supreme Court
Pasar Malam
Omar Ali Saifuddien Mosque
Padang
Royal Brunei Airlines
HSBC
BSM building
Bangunan Guru Guru Melayu
Borneo Theatre
Tamu Kianggeh
Bus & Taxi Station
Bolkiah Theatre
Yayasan Complex
Wet Fish Market
Gerai Makan
Boats for Limbang
US Embassy
Teck Guan Plaza
Temburong Jetty
Royal Mausoleum

Moving on from Bandar Seri Begawan

Journey times and frequency of planes, boats and buses are given in the "Travel Details", p.97.

By plane

Travelling to the **airport** from central Bandar, take Northern (#23 & 24), Eastern (#36 & 38) or Central Line (#11) buses (every 15min; 6.30am–6pm; B$1) from the bus station below Jalan Cator. For flight information, call ☎02/331747.

By boat

Boats to Limbang in Malaysian Sarawak leave from beside the Customs and Immigration Station at the junction of Jalan Roberts and Jalan McArthur. For boats to Pulau Labuan (daily 4.40pm; B$16) – in Malaysian Sabah – and Lawas (daily 11.30am; B$16) – in Malaysian Sarawak – you have to go to the Serasa Ferry Terminal at Muara, a small village 25km northeast of Bandar, and pass through immigration there. Buses leave for Muara from the main bus terminal below Jalan Cator (B$2).

Tickets for Labuan and Lawas are sold by Halim Tours, Lorong Gerai Timor, off Jalan McArthur (☎02/226688) and New Island Shipping, 1st Floor, Unit 5, Block C, Kiarong Complex, Lebuh Raya Sultan Haji Hassanal Bolkia (☎02/451800); tickets for Limbang (B$10) in Sarawak are sold at the open stalls opposite Lorong Gerai Timor, on Jalan McArthur. From Labuan, there are daily connections on to Kota Kinabalu and Menumbok in Sabah, though to ensure you catch one, it's wise to leave Bandar early in the day.

Boats to Bangar in Temburong (B$7) depart from the wharf at Jalan Residency, 2km east of the centre. Tickets are sold beside the jetty. From Bangar, it's possible to travel overland to both Lawas and Limbang in Sarawak (see p.725).

By bus

Buses to Miri in Sarawak (via Seria and Kuala Belait) leave from the bus station below Jalan Cator.

jetty below the intersection of Jalan Roberts and Jalan McArthur is the best place to catch a water taxi, though it's also possible to hail one from the Temburong jetty off Jalan Residency.

Local buses to points north, east and west of the city centre leave from the bus station, underneath the multi-storey car park just south of the eastern end of Jalan Cator (every 15–20min; 6.30am–6pm; B$1). Northern (#23 & #24), Eastern (#36 & #38) and Central Line (#11) buses run between the airport and the Brunei Museum, crossing the city en route; the Circle Line #1 and Northern Line #22 loop up to the new Jame 'Asr Hassanil Bolkiah Mosque, Gadong and *Voctech International House*. Northern Line #22, #23 & #24 buses run to Berakas, and Eastern #39 and Central #11 serve the Technology Museum. One infuriating thing about Bandar's local bus system is that most of it shuts down around 6pm, after which you have no option but to take taxis, which can be few and far between.

Fares for regular, metered **taxis** start at B$4; from the city centre to the Brunei Museum costs about B$6. A night-time surcharge applies between 9pm and 6am, there's a B$5 charge on trips to the airport, and each piece of luggage loaded in the boot costs a further B$1. The new PPP taxi service (purple cars) charges a flat fare and runs as far afield as the outlying districts of Gadong and Batu One – but annoyingly not to either the museums or the airport. Unregistered taxis, called "pirate taxis" locally, are simply private vehicles whose owners use them to pick up passengers. Many are driven by Malaysians or Filipinos and the cost is about two-thirds the fare of an official taxi. If the driver of what looks like an ordinary sedan stops to enquire if you need a ride, chances are it's a pirate taxi, not some local who enjoys giving free rides to tourists.

Accommodation

Brunei is almost bereft of budget **accommodation**, with the *Pusat Belia* (youth hostel) being the only real option. Some visitors have resorted to taking a bus to the coast and sleeping on the beach, though this is hardly advisable. Otherwise, most double rooms start at B$70.

Brunei 95 Jalan Pemancha ☎02/242372. Comfortable and fully equipped, this is Bandar's most central commercial hotel. ❼
Crowne Princess Jalan Tutong ☎02/241128. Featuring 117 well-appointed rooms, and situated a little way out of town over the Edinburgh Bridge, this place is connected to the city centre by regular shuttle bus. ❻
Jubilee Jubilee Plaza, Jalan Kampung Kianggeh ☎02/228070. East of Sungei Kianggeh, a smart, mid-range hotel with complimentary breakfast set opposite a patch of traditional kampung houses. ❻
Pusat Belia Jalan Sungai Kianggeh ☎02/222423. Brunei's youth hostel, and by far the cheapest option in town; there's a very small chance you'll need an ISIC or IH card to get in. Rooms are shared with three others, and there's a pool (B$1) downstairs. B$10 per person per night the first three nights, and B$5 for each further night. ❷
Voctech International House Jalan Pasar Baharu, Gadong ☎02/447992. A short drive from the centre (bus #1 & #22 from the station) on the way to Gadong and opposite the excellent pasar malam, this massive, comfortable place has large en-suite rooms, a well-priced café, cooking facilities and a library with Internet access. ❻

The City

Downtown Bandar is hemmed in by water. To the east is Sungei Kianggeh; to the south, the wide Sungei Brunei; and to the west, Sungei Kedayan, which runs up to the Edinburgh Bridge. The classical Omar Ali Saifuddien Mosque is Bandar's most obvious point of reference, cradled by the floating village of Kampung Ayer.

The Omar Ali Saifuddien Mosque

At the very heart of both the city and the sultanate's Muslim faith is the magnificent **Omar Ali Saifuddien Mosque** (Mon–Wed, Sat & Sun 8am–noon, 1–3.30pm & 4.30–5.30pm, Thurs closed to non-Muslims, Fri 4.30–5.30pm). Built in classical Islamic style, it was commissioned by and named after the father of the present sultan, and completed in 1958 at a cost of US$5 million. Because the mosque is something of a national showcase, non-Muslims are made to feel more welcome here than at most mosques in the region. The mosque makes splendid use of opulent yet tasteful fittings – Italian marble, granite from Shanghai, Arabian and Belgian carpets, and English chandeliers and stained glass. Topping the cream-coloured building is a 52-metre-high golden dome, whose curved surface is adorned with a mosaic comprising over three million pieces of Venetian glass. It is sometimes possible to obtain permission to ride the elevator up the 44-metre-high minaret, and look out over the water village below. The usual dress codes – modest attire, and shoes to be left at the entrance – apply when entering the mosque.

Kampung Ayer

From the mosque, it's no distance to Bandar's **Kampung Ayer**, or water village, whose sheer scale makes it one of the great sights of Southeast Asia. Stilt villages have occupied this stretch of the Sungei Brunei for hundreds of years, and today an estimated thirty thousand people live in the scores of sprawling villages that comprise Kampung Ayer, their dwellings connected by a maze of wooden promenades. These villages have their own clinics, mosques, schools, a fire brigade and a police station; the homes have piped water, electricity and TV. The waters, however, are distinctly unsanitary, and the houses susceptible to fire. Even so, a strong sense of community has meant that attempts to move the inhabitants onto dry land and into housing more in keeping with a state that has the highest per capita income in the world have met with little success.

The meandering pathways of Kampung Ayer make it an intriguing place to explore on foot. For a real impression of its dimensions though, it's best to charter a water taxi, which can seat up to nine people. A half-hour round trip will cost B$20 per person. A handful of traditional cottage industries continue to turn out copperware and brassware (at Kampung Ujong Bukit) and exquisite sarongs and boats (Kampung Saba Darat); the boatmen should know the whereabouts of some of them.

The Brunei Museum and Malay Technology Museum

The **Brunei Museum** (Tues–Thurs, Sat & Sun 9am–5pm, Fri 9.30–11.30am & 2.30–5pm; free), about 5km east of Sungei Kianggeh on Jalan Residency (Central Line bus #11 & Eastern Line #39), has several outstanding galleries. The undoubted highlight is its superb **Islamic Art Gallery** where, among the riches on display, are beautifully illuminated antique Korans from India, Iran, Egypt and Turkey, exquisite prayer mats, and quirkier items like a pair of ungainly wooden slippers. In the inevitable **Oil and Gas Gallery**, exhibits, graphics and captions recount the story of Brunei's oil reserves, from the drilling of the first well in 1928, to current extraction and refining techniques. Also interesting, though tantalizingly sketchy, is the **Muslim Life Gallery**, whose dioramas allow glimpses of social traditions, such as the sweetening of a new-born baby's mouth with honey or dates, and the disposal of its placenta in a *bayung*, a palm-leaf basket which is either hung on a tree or floated downriver. At the back of the gallery, a small collection of early photographs shows riverine hawkers trading from their boats in Kampung Ayer.

Steps around the back of the museum drop down to the riverside **Malay Technology Museum** (Mon, Wed, Thurs, Sat & Sun 9am–5pm, Fri 9–11.30am & 2.30–5pm; free), whose three galleries provide a mildly engaging insight into traditional Malay life, including examples of Kedayan, Murut and Dusun dwellings.

The Jame 'Asr Hassanil Bolkiah Mosque

Many people reckon that the **Jame 'Asr Hassanil Bolkiah (State) Mosque** (Mon–Wed, Sat & Sun 8am–noon, 1–3.30pm & 4.30–5.30pm, Thurs & Fri closed to non-Muslims), set in harmonious gardens in the commercial suburb of Gadong, has a distinct edge over the Omar Ali Saifuddien Mosque both in style and grandeur. With its sea-blue roof, golden domes and slender minarets, this is Brunei's largest mosque, constructed to commemorate the silver jubilee of the sultan's reign in 1992. It's also referred to as the Kiarong Mosque. Circle Line buses skirt the grounds of the mosque en route to Gadong.

The Istana Nurul Iman

The **Istana Nurul Iman**, the official residence of the sultan, is sited at a superb riverside spot 4km west of the capital. Bigger than either Buckingham Palace or the Vatican, the istana is a monument to self-indulgence. Its design, by Filipino architect Leandro Locsin, is a sinuous blend of traditional and modern, with Islamic motifs such as arches and domes, and sloping roofs fashioned on traditional longhouse designs, combined with all the mod cons you'd expect of a house whose owner earns an estimated US$5 million a day.

James Bartholomew's book, *The Richest Man in the World*, lists some of the mind-boggling figures relating to the palace. Over half a kilometre long, it contains a grand total of 1778 rooms, including 257 toilets. Illuminating these rooms requires 51,000 light bulbs, and simply getting around the building involves 18 lifts and 44 staircases. The throne room is said to be particularly sumptuous: twelve one-tonne chandeliers hang from its ceiling, while its four grand thrones stand against the backdrop of an eighteen-metre arch, tiled in 22-carat gold. In addition to the throne room, there's a royal banquet hall that seats 4000 diners, a prayer hall where 1500 people can worship at any one time, an underground car park for the sultan's hundreds of vehicles, a state-of-the-art sports complex, and a helipad. Unfortunately, the palace is rarely open to the general public, though the sultan does declare open house every year during Hari Raya. Otherwise, nearby Taman Persiaran Damuan, a kilometre-long park sandwiched between Jalan Tutong and Sungei Brunei, offers the best view, or you can fork out for a boat trip (B$15 for 30min) and see the palace lit up at night from the water. All westbound buses travel along Jalan Tutong, over the Edinburgh Bridge and past the istana.

Eating

Fortunately, Bandar's **restaurants** are more reasonably priced than its hotels. If you're on a tight budget, head for the night stalls situated in the car park of the main market across the road from *Voctech* on the way to Gadong. Here, Malay favourites are laid out buffet-style, though there are no tables and chairs. Gadong, with its numerous Malay cafés, is a very good place to eat in the day. Unfortunately, there is no public transport to the suburb after 6pm, and the area closes down quite early anyway. Another cheap, more accessible option is the cluster of stalls behind the Temburong jetty on Jalan Residency, serving good and cheap *soto ayam*, nasi campur and other Malay staples.

Al Hilal Jl Sultan. Indian food heaven and good for vegetarians. If you ask for it, they've probably got it here; don't miss the pakoras, jalebi, dosais and rotis, to name but a few.

Hasinah Restoran Unit 9, Block 1, Abdul Razak Complex, Gadong. Quite fabulous and inexpensive Malay and South Indian daytime café. Serves nine types of dosai and a mouth-watering nasi campur spread.

Hua Hua 48 Jl Sultan. Steamed chicken with sausage is one of the highlights in this hole-in-the-wall Chinese establishment, where B$15 feeds two people. Daily 7am–9pm.

Padian Food Court 1st Floor, Yayasan Complex, Jl Kumbang Pasang. A/c food court whose stalls serve Thai, Arabic, Japanese, Indian and other regional cuisines. Daily 9am–10pm.

Port View The jetty, western end of Jl McArthur. Western and Malay food in relaxing setting overlooking the harbour and Kampung Ayer. Main courses are around B$15. Bands play at weekends 10pm–2am. Midweek 6pm–midnight.

Sarasaya Block C, Abdul Razak Complex, Gadong. Excellent Japanese restaurant. Reckon on around B$30 a head. Daily 6–11pm.

Yusbi Jl Sultan. Possibly the cheapest restaurant in the whole country, this Indian eatery attracts a lunchtime working-class crowd with its roti chanai and tea, which cost just under B$2 per person.

Listings

Airlines MAS, 144 Jl Pemancha ☎02/224141; Philippine Airlines, 1st Floor, Wisma Haji Fatimah, Jl Sultan ☎02/244075; Royal Brunei Airlines, RBA Plaza, Jl Sultan ☎02/242222; Singapore Airlines, 49–50 Jl Sultan ☎02/244901; Thai Airways, 4th Floor, Kompleks Jalan Sultan, 51–55 Jl Sultan ☎02/242991.

Bookshops English-language books at Best Eastern Books, G4 Teck Guan Plaza, Jl Sultan, and Paul & Elizabeth Book Services, 2nd Floor, Yayasan Complex.

Car rental Sukma, Avis, Lot 16, Ground Floor, Hj Duad Complex (☎02/426345); Budget, 5th Floor Dangerek Service Apartments (☎02/345573).

Embassies and consulates Australia, 4th Floor, Teck Guan Plaza, Jl Sultan ☎02/229435; Indonesia, Simpang 528, Lot 4498, Sungei Hanching Baru, Jl Muara ☎02/330180; Malaysia, Lot 27

& 29, Simpang 396–397, Kampong Sungai Akar, Jl Kebangsaan ☎02/3456520; Philippines, no. 17, Simpang 126, Km 2, Jl Tutong ☎02/241465; Singapore, 5th Floor, RBA Plaza, Jl Sultan ☎02/262741; Thailand, no. 2, Simpang 682, Kampung Bunut, Jl Tutong BF 1320 ☎02/653108; UK, Unit 2.01, Block D, Complex Yayasan Sultan Hassanal Bolkiah ☎02/222231; USA, 3rd Floor, Teck Guan Plaza, Jl Sultan ☎02/229670.

Exchange There are many cash-only money-changers on Jl McArthur, and a variety of banks with ATMs on Jl Sultan.

Hospital The Raja Isteri Pengiran Anak Saleha Hospital (RIPAS) is across Edinburgh Bridge on Jl Putera Al-Muhtadee Billah (☎02/242424); or there's the private Hart Medical Clinic at 47 Jl Sultan (☎02/225531).

Immigration The Immigration Office is on Jl Menteri Besar (Mon–Thurs & Sat 7.45am–12.15pm & 1.35–4.30pm; ☎02/383106). Take Circle Line bus #1 to get there.

Internet access FS School of Computing, Unit 1, 1st Floor, Block C, Abdul Razak Complex, Gadong; LA Cyber Café, Floor 2, Yayasan Complex.

Laundry Superkleen, opposite *Brunei Hotel*, Jl Pemancha.

Pharmacies Khong Lin Dispensary, G3A, Wisma Jaya, Jl Pemancha; Teck Onn Dispensary, 29 Jl Sultan.

Police Central Police Station, Jl Stoney ☎02/222333.

Post office The GPO (Mon–Sat 8am–4.30pm) is at the intersection of Jl Elizabeth Dua and Jl Sultan. Poste restante/general delivery is at the Money Order counter.

Taxis ☎02/222214/226/853.

Telephone services IDD calls at Telekom (daily 8am–midnight), next to the GPO on Jl Sultan. You can also use public phones if you get a phone card.

Tour operators Sunshine Borneo Tours and Travel, 2nd Floor, Unit 1, Block C, Abdul Razak Complex, Gadong (☎02/441791), runs numerous tours, including a three-day excursion to Brunei's Temburong district (B$200), and offers good advice on travelling in the state. Borneo Outdoors, 3b Kiarong Apts, Simpang (☎02/454764).

Jerudong Park Playground

An evening spent enjoying the funfair rides at **Jerudong Park Playground** (grounds daily 2pm–2am; games and rides Mon & Wed 5pm–midnight, Thurs & Sat 5pm–2am, Fri & Sun 2pm–midnight; during Ramadan daily 8pm–2am; B$15 entry and all rides; Western Line bus #55 and #57), 20km northwest of Bandar on the road to Tutong, is the only activity close to the capital worth considering. The park is a funfair/adventure park with scores of rides, conceived as a lasting testimony to His Majesty's generosity to his *rakyat* ("people"). Though daily gates average two thousand, there's very little queuing for rides, which include a rollercoaster, a giant drop, supakarts, shooting galleries, boat rides, space-ride simulators, bumper cars and carousels. Jerudong Park Playground is tricky to get back from once buses have stopped in the early evening, so taking a taxi (B$25) is your best bet.

1.2

Bangar and the Temburong district

Brunei's main ecotourism effort is focused on the **Temburong district**, a sparsely populated part of the state that is only accessible by boat from Bandar. It has been isolated from the rest of Brunei since 1890, when the strip of land to the west was ceded to Sarawak. The area's chief attractions are the superb **Ulu Temburong National Park** and the chance to stay in **Malay and Murut kampungs** or an **Iban longhouse**. The majority of visitors come to the park on an organized tour from Bandar (see opposite); otherwise, the starting point is the district's only town of any size, Bangar.

BANGAR stands on the Sungei Temburong in the hilly Temburong district. Bangar can only by reached by a hair-raising speedboat journey from Bandar (B$7). Boats scream through narrow mangrove estuaries that are home to crocodiles and proboscis monkeys, swooping around corners and narrowly missing vessels travelling the opposite way, before shooting off down Sungei Temburong. After such a lead-up, the town of Bangar is something of a disappointment; its main street, which runs west from the jetty to the town mosque, is lined only with a handful of coffee shops and provision stores. Across the bridge is Bangar's grandest building, its new District Office, whose waterfront café is the town's best place to eat. There are no places to stay in Bangar.

From Bangar, it's a twenty-minute drive south to the jetty at the small kampung, **Batang Duri**. There's no public transport to this spot; either hitch a lift (quite a safe practice in Brunei) or take a taxi (B$15). From here you'll have to charter a longboat (1hr 30min; B$50) to Ulu Temburong Park Headquarters. This upstream stretch of Sungei Temburong is very shallow, and when the water level is low you may have to get out and help pull the boat over rocks. Dense jungle cloaks the hills on either side, and birds and monkeys abound in the trees. At the headquarters it is possible to stay in cabins (❹), and a canteen serves food from 7am until 7pm.

The main attraction of the park, one hour's walk over a hanging bridge and along a wooden pathway, is the **canopy walkway**, a near-vertical aluminium structure, a climb that tests your nerves to the limit. It is the highest of its type in Borneo, and the view from the top is breathtaking: you can see Brunei Bay to the north and Gunung Mulu Park in Sarawak to the south. Other activities in the park include chartering a small longboat (around B$50 for 2hr) to go further upstream to a tree house, passing the Kuala Belalong Field Studies Centre along the way. The centre is the site of a scientific research project examining the unique fauna of the park.

Iban homestays

Besides being a good base for exploring the park, staying in an Iban longhouse is also an excellent opportunity to absorb the local culture. Iban homestays are also the only accommodation bargain to be found in the whole country. From Bangar, take a taxi (20min; B$15) to Amo C, a five-door **Iban longhouse** on the Batang Duri road (no telephone, just turn up), where the people offer their longhouse as a "homestay" for independent travellers. There are always people around to welcome you and invite you in; many of them speak some English. It's always best to take some small gifts for the children – not expected but you'll make friends. Guests sleep on the veranda. You will have to pay for the meals and give something for your stay, but this doesn't amount to much – the Iban are very hospitable and rather embarrassed to ask for money, since traditionally they invite people to stay for free. A rough framework is B$3 for breakfast, B$6 for lunch and dinner and B$5 for staying the night. Being generous will keep this longhouse from posting prices, as has happened at several in Malaysia, where foreign tourists were staying weeks and then skipping off without paying any kind of remuneration. Around the longhouse there are some pleasant trails into the forest that the Ibans use for hunting. You will need a guide, which you can arrange from a travel agent in Bandar (B$20–30 per person for a day-trip; B$50 overnight). If you choose an overnight trip, take your own gear and ask the people at the longhouse to take food for you, too.

Malay and Murut homestays

Twenty kilometres east of Bangar on the road to Lawas is the Labu region of Temburong. Again, the only way to get here is by taxi from Bangar. Rice paddies line the road on one side, while thick forest lines the other – this used to be largely rubber plantations until the bottom dropped out of the rubber market in the Fifties. Fifteen kilometres further along this road you come to the **Peradayan Forest Reserve**. There are no facilities here, but the small park includes a strenuous three-hour trek on a wooden pathway up Bukit Patoi. From the top of the hill there are great views across Brunei's spectacular, largely undisturbed rainforests south towards Sarawak. Five kilometres further on, take a road to the right. This leads to **SEKOLOH**, a Malay and Murut village comprising a few dozen elevated dwellings (see pp.629–631 for more on the Malay and Murut peoples). Visitors are welcome here – just ask around to find out which is the house you can stay in. The villagers take turns putting people up, thereby sharing the "fun" of having foreigners in their isolated kampung; prices are about the same as at the Iban longhouse (see above). Besides walking around the kampung, meeting people, eating and relaxing, there's little to do. Nevertheless, a visit to a **homestay** like this one gives you a rare insight into the lifestyle of traditional, rural Bruneians, and it's well worth making the effort to go for that alone.

Crossing the Malaysian border to Limbang and Lawas

If you're planning to **cross into Sarawak** – either to Limbang or to Lawas – you'll first have to make for the immigration post beside the turning for Kampung Puni, 5km west of Bangar. **Limbang** is easiest and cheapest to reach: after a B$5–10 taxi ride from Bangar, take a ferry (B$1) across the river at Kampung Puni, which marks the border with Malaysia, and then catch one of the connecting buses (B$2) that run into Limbang until 5pm. The only way to get to **Lawas** is to catch the Lawas express, which starts in Limbang at 8am, reaches Bangar around 9am and pulls into Lawas at 1pm. Coming the other way towards Limbang, it arrives at Bangar around 3pm, terminating in Limbang about an hour later.

1.3

Kuala Belait

It's a little under 85km from Bandar to Brunei's second biggest town, **KUALA BELAIT**. There's nothing very enticing here, but it's the main transit point for buses to and from **Miri** in **Sarawak**. Buses to Sarawak leave from the **bus station** on the intersection of Jalan Bunga Raya and Jalan McKerron (B$10.20); the fare includes the ferry across Sungei Belait and the connecting Sarawakian bus over the border. The town's taxi stand is across the road from the bus station: drivers charge around B$100 for a full car to Miri, though you should be able to haggle them down substantially. To get to Kuala Belait from Bandar, you have to go via Seria, 20km east (see "Travel details" below).

Jalan McKerron houses several good **restaurants** – the best of which are the *Buccaneer Steakhouse* at no. 94, whose mid-priced international food is aimed squarely at the expat market, and the *New Akhbar Restaurant*, at no. 99a, with a Malay and North Indian menu. Next door to the *Buccaneer Steakhouse*, at no. 93, *Hotel Sentosa* (☎03/331345; ❼) offers well-appointed and welcoming **rooms**. You can **change money** at the HSBC, diagonally opposite the bus station, and there's an Internet café, Netcom Internet café, on Jalan Pretty – a minute's walk from the bus terminal.

Brunei travel details

Buses

Bandar Seri Begawan to: Muara (every 30min; 30min); Seria (hourly until 2pm; 1hr 45min).
Kuala Belait to: Miri (5 daily 7.30am–3.30pm; 1hr 30min); Seria (every 35min until 8pm; 45min).
Seria to: Bandar Seri Begawan (every 35min until 3.30pm; 1hr 45min); Kuala Belait (every 30 min; 45min).

Boats

Bandar Seri Begawan to: Bangar (every 45min 6.30am–4.30pm; 50min); Limbang (at least 8 daily; 30min).
Muara to: Lawas (daily at 11.30am; 2hr); Pulau Labuan (daily at 4.40pm; 1hr 30min).

Flights

Bandar Seri Begawan to: Bangkok, Thailand (3 weekly; 2hr); Kota Kinabalu, Sabah (daily; 40min); Kuala Lumpur, Malaysia (daily; 2hr 20min); Kuching, Sarawak (3 weekly; 1hr 10min); Singapore (2 daily; 2hr).

Cambodia

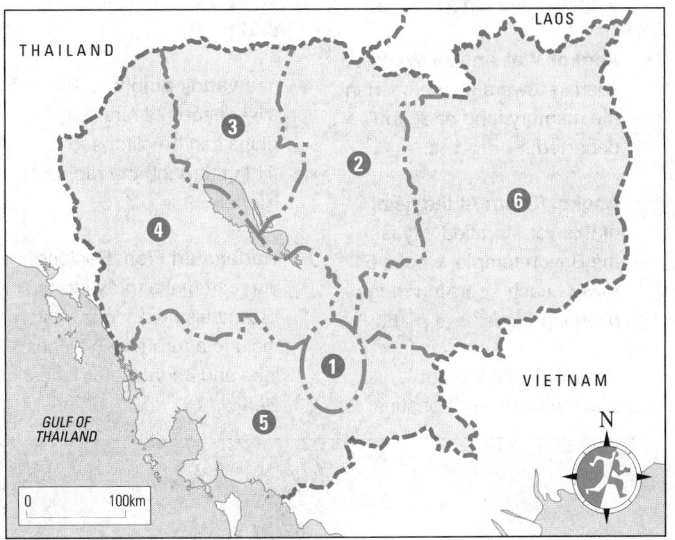

Cambodia highlights

* **Royal Palace and Silver Pagoda** Gleaming golden spires and vivid Ramayana murals make for a stunning sight. See p.129

* **National Museum** Showcases prized statuary from Cambodia's Angkorian temples. See p.130

* **Angkor Wat** Angkor Wat's soaring towers stay etched in the memory long after you've departed. See p.148

* **Angkor Thom** At the heart of this vast fortified city is the Bayon temple, whose 54 towers each sport four huge beaming faces. See p.150

* **Sihanoukville** Vibrant seaside resort with pristine white-sand beaches, succulent seafood and a party atmosphere. See p.161

* **Bokor National Park** Cloud washes over the deserted hill station, while the stunning mountain countryside offers the possibility of spotting some scarce wildlife. See p.171

* **Irrawaddy dolphins** The silver heads of rare dolphins can be glimpsed flitting through the rapids at Kampie. See p.175

* **Rattanakiri** From Banlung, you can make forays to the province's attractions, which include a turquoise volcanic lake and chunchiet villages. See p.176

△ Beach hawker at Sihanoukville

Introduction and basics

Cambodia was largely out of bounds to tourists until recently, but now areas that were unsafe because of Khmer Rouge guerrillas and bandit groups have been returned to the control of the Cambodian army, and virtually the whole of the country has become accessible. For many travellers, lured by the prospect of little explored and unspoilt regions, Cambodia has become a top destination on Southeast Asia's otherwise well-trodden tourist trail.

The Kingdom of Cambodia, with a population of ten million, occupies a modest wedge of land, almost completely hemmed in by its neighbours, Vietnam, Laos and Thailand. Its glory days began in the early ninth century, when the rival Indian-influenced Chenla kingdoms united under King Jayavarman II to form the **Khmer Empire**, a powerful and visionary dynasty, which, at its peak, stretched from Vietnam in the east to China in the north and Burma in the west.

Recent history has been less kind to the country. French colonization was followed by an extended period of turbulence and instability, culminating in the devastating Kampuchean holocaust instigated by Pol Pot's Khmer Rouge in 1975. The brutal regime lasted four years before invading Vietnamese forces reached the capital in 1979 and overthrew the Khmer Rouge. Pol Pot and his supporters fled to the jungle bordering Thailand, from where they continued to wage war on successive governments in Phnom Penh. Pol Pot's death in 1998 finally signalled the demise of the Khmer Rouge, and their subsequent surrender has given Cambodia a real chance for peace for the first time in thirty years. There are indeed many signs that Cambodia is at last shaking off the shadows of its past and looking to the future with a cautious confidence. International investors are beginning to back business ventures, there is increasing evidence of development and modernization in urban areas, and foreign aid is flowing in.

Most visitors to Cambodia head for the stunning **Angkor** ruins, a collection of over one hundred temples dating back to the ninth century. Once the seat of power of the Khmer Empire, Angkor is royal extravagance on a grand scale, its imposing features enhanced by the dramatic setting of lush jungle greenery and verdant fields. The complex is acknowledged as the most exquisite example of ancient architecture in Southeast Asia, and has been declared a World Heritage Site by UNESCO.

The flat, sprawling capital of **Phnom Penh** is also an alluring attraction in its own right. Wide, sweeping boulevards and elegant, if neglected, French colonial-style facades lend the city a romantic appeal. However, there's also stark evidence of great poverty, a reminder that you're visiting one of the world's poorest countries.

Those enterprising travellers who look beyond the standard itinerary of Angkor and Phnom Penh will be rewarded with a rich variety of experiences. Its worth stopping off for a day halfway between Angkor and Phnom Penh, at **Kompong Thom**, to make a side trip to the **pre-Angkor ruins** of Sambor Prei Kuk; here, you can explore several groups of early brick-built towers with scarcely another tourist in sight.

Miles of unspoilt beaches and remote islands offer sandy seclusion along the **southern coastline**. Although **Sihanoukville** is the main port of call, it's easy enough to commandeer transport to nearby hidden coves and offshore islands, with only the odd fisherman or smuggler to interrupt your solitude. **Rattanakiri** province in the northeastern corner of the country, with its hilltribes and volcanic scenery, is also becoming increasingly popular with visitors. Neighbouring **Mondulkiri** is less well known, but equally impressive, offering dramatic alpinesque woodlands, villages and mountains. In the central plains, **Battambang**, Cambodia's second city, is a sleepy provincial capital, and the gateway to the old Khmer Rouge stronghold of **Pailin**.

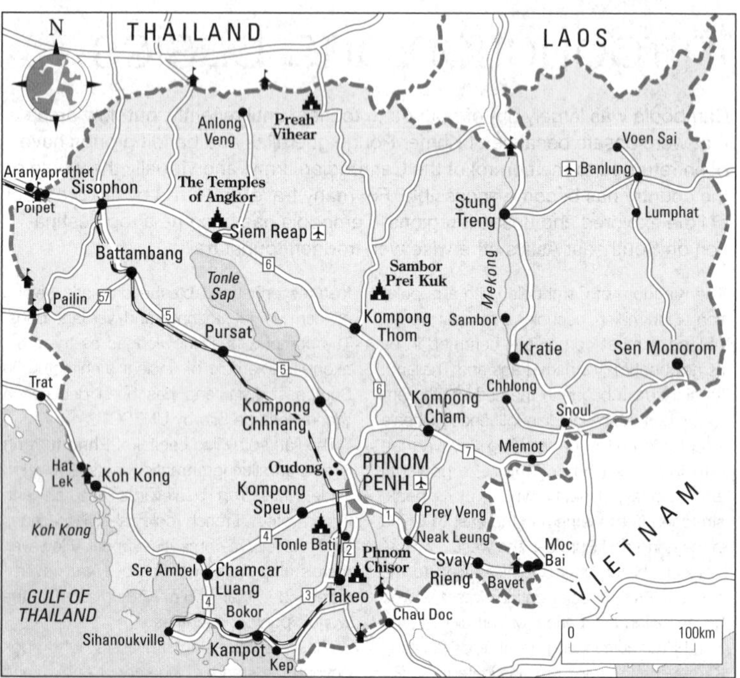

Getting around Cambodia is really no problem, although it's often a less-than-comfortable exercise; the road system still leaves a lot to be desired, and **travel** outside the main tourist routes can be slow and punishing.

Cambodia's **monsoon climate** creates two distinct seasons. The southwesterly monsoon from May to October brings heavy rain, humidity and strong winds, while the northeasterly monsoon from November to April produces dry, hot weather, with average temperatures rising from 25°C in November to around 32°C in April. The best months to visit are December and January, as it's dry and relatively cool, though Angkor is at its most stunning during the lush rainy season.

Overland routes into Cambodia

Travelling overland into Cambodia is now possible from the neighbouring countries – Thailand, Vietnam and Laos. From **Thailand**, there are six entry points: the border crossing at Aranyaprathet, east of Bangkok, near Poipet (see p.160); two crossings at Pailin (see p.158); the coastal border at Hat Lek, near Trat, to Cham Yeam, west of Koh Kong (see p.167); and the more recently opened crossings in northeast Thailand, at the Chong Chom–O'Smach border pass, near Kap Choeng in Thailand's Surin province (see p.1044), and the little-used Sa Ngam–Choam border in Si Saket province. From **Vietnam**, three crossings are open to foreigners: northwest of Ho Chi Minh City at Moc Bai to Bavet, southeast of Phnom Penh (see p.1131); and two near Chau Doc, northwest of Can Tho on the Bassac River (see p.1152). From **Laos**, the only crossing open is in the far south on the Mekong island of Voen Kham, to the north of Stung Treng.

Entry requirements and visa extension

All foreign nationals, except Malaysians, need a **visa** to enter Cambodia. Tourist visas are valid for thirty days and cost $20. Tourist visas are issued on arrival at Pochentong Airport in Phnom Penh and at the airport at Siem Reap; one passport photo is required. It's also possible to obtain a visa on arrival at the Thai overland border crossings of Cham Yeam, at Poipet and Pailin, but not as yet at the other overland crossings – Bavet and Chau Doc, the border crossings with Vietnam, or at Voen Kham, north of Stung Treng into Laos. For these border points, you'll need to obtain a visa beforehand. You can either organize this before you leave home (see p.44 for a list of Cambodian embassy addresses) or obtain one at a Cambodian embassy in one of the respective neighbouring countries. In **Bangkok** (see p.984), you'll need a passport photo, and the visa takes up to two working days to process; if you don't want the hassle of queuing at the embassy yourself, **travel agencies** on Thanon Khao San will organize the visa for you for an additional charge of $5. **In Vietnam**, you can get visas from the Cambodian Embassy in Hanoi (see p.1210) or from the consulate in Ho Chi Minh City (see p.1140), but note that the latter charges $30 instead of the standard $20. **In Laos**, the Cambodian Embassy is in Vientiane near That Khao, on Thadua Road (see p.531).

Extending a tourist visa is a painless process in Phnom Penh, but impossible elsewhere in Cambodia, so if you're planning a long trip into the provinces think about whether you'll need an extension before you go. Extensions are issued at the Department of Immigration, Pochentong Road, opposite the airport in Phnom Penh (Mon–Fri 8–10.30am & 2.30–4.30pm); you'll need two passport photos. Next-day service costs $40 for a one-month extension or $75 for three months. Given the location of the offices, it's easier to take advantage of the extension services offered by travel agents and guesthouses; they can do the running around for you and charge just a couple of dollars' commission.

Airport departure tax

Cambodian **airport tax** is currently $20 for international departures, and $10 for domestic departures from Pochentong; from Siem Reap, it's $25 and $6 respectively.

A tourist visa can only be extended once, for one month; you are charged $5 per day for overstaying your visa.

Money and costs

Cambodia's unit of currency is the **riel**, abbreviated to "r". **Notes** come in denominations of 50, 100, 200, 500, 1000, 2000, 5000, 10,000, 20,000, 50,000 and 100,000, although the bigger notes are seldom seen, as dollars tend to be used for larger transactions. **US dollars** are accepted everywhere; you'll be expected to pay in dollars rather than riel at guesthouses, restaurants and for most entrance fees to tourist sites. In fact, it's possible to get by in Cambodia without actually changing any foreign currency into riel, but there are times when riel notes are useful – lower-priced items such as street food and motos are normally paid for in riel, and bargaining in riel for crafts at a market, for example, gives you more room for manoeuvre. Changing up to say $10 worth will give you a chunky pile of riel, enough to last you a few days. **Thai baht**, abbreviated to "B", are also widely used in the border areas, and on the main trade routes from Thailand.

It's best to change your currency into dollars before you enter Cambodia, although banks in Phnom Penh and Siem Reap will exchange most currencies. Travellers' cheques can be changed at most banks for a small commission, normally two percent. **Credit-card cash advances** are available in Phnom Penh, Siem Reap, Sihanoukville and Battambang, but don't rely on them as a source of cash, as systems are unreliable. Branches of the Canadia Bank give commission-free cash advances on MasterCard. ATMs have yet to arrive in Cambodia.

To **exchange** dollars into riel, don't bother with the banks – they issue riel at a low rate, if at all. Head instead for the nearest market, where moneychangers display bundles of riel in their glass cabinets. The exchange rate usually fluctuates between 4000r to 4100r to the dollar.

On the whole, food and accommodation is slightly more expensive in Cambodia than in its neighbouring countries. However, it's possible to live quite **cheaply**: if you stay in the cheapest guesthouses, eat only at the markets and street stalls and travel in the back of pick-ups, you'll be able to scrape by on £7/$13 a day, not including entrance fees to museums and other sights. However, eating a few guesthouse or restaurant meals and staying in en-suite accommodation will quickly increase daily costs to around £10/$18. For decent air-con accommodation, three good meals a day and a bit of nightlife, reckon on spending around £20/$37. A **two-tier pricing system** is beginning to develop and tourists are being asked to pay a hefty premium for some transport and entrance fees, though unlike neighbouring Vietnam you're unlikely to be ripped off for local services, with motos, pick-ups, accommodation and food charged at the Cambodian price.

The easiest way to get money **wired** to you in Cambodia (see "Wiring money", p.60) is via the branches of the Acleda Bank, agents for Western Union in Cambodia, or via MoneyGram handled by Canadia Bank; both have branches in major towns. See the "Listings" sections of these towns for details.

Information and maps

Cambodia is beginning to recognize the importance of tourism to its economy, and is establishing a network of basic **tourist offices**. These offices, however, are desperately starved of resources and generally don't have much information, so it's better to ask at local guesthouses.

Websites that specialize in Cambodia information are a good place to begin research before arriving. Of the many, two stand out: ⓦwww.talesofasia.com and ⓦwww.bayonpearnik.com.

International Travel Maps publishes a useful 1:800,000 **map**. If you're travelling around the region, you could try the 1:2,000,000 regional map of Vietnam, Cambodia and Laos published by UBD or Bartholomew. Bear in mind, however, that all these maps are based on dated surveys. The existence of a road is no guarantee as to condition; many of the older roads featured no longer exist, and new roads are not shown.

Getting around

Transport in Cambodia is all part of the adventure. The roads are in a terrible state, although this is slowly changing; boats can only operate when the water is high enough, and the packed trains travel at walking speed. Fortunately, Cambodia is not a big country and there is a ready supply of aged pick-ups, the workhorse of the local transport system, that get to most parts of the country. For an idea of journey times between major destinations, see "Travel details", p.180.

By train

Travel by **train** is cheap but the routes are limited. It's popular with budget travellers, and while it can be fun for an hour, after a while it becomes tedious and pretty uncomfortable – the only seating is on hard wooden benches. There are no reservations, so you'll need to turn up early to stand a chance of a seat, though don't expect the train to leave on time. Some trains consist only of cargo carriages, so a hammock can be useful. Men usually sit on the roof of busy trains.

There are just two narrow-gauge **railway lines** in Cambodia: one from Phnom Penh to Sihanoukville; the other from Phnom Penh to Battambang. Trains are a good place to meet and talk to locals, and you'll probably be the centre of attention, as foreigners on trains are still very much a novelty. It's a good idea to take food and water, although hawkers sell food along the way.

By road

Buses and coaches of the conventional sort are a rarity in Cambodia, the exceptions being on the routes from Phnom Penh to

Sihanoukville and Kompong Cham, which are in a state of good repair. Elsewhere, the roads vary from dodgy to impassable, but they are improving year by year. The usual mode of public transport is a share taxi or a **pick-up truck** – often scarcely adequate two-wheel-drive Toyotas. Journeys are long and uncomfortable, but reasonably cheap. **Prices** vary, depending on how far you're going, and with pick-ups they vary as to whether you sit in the cab or out in the open in the back. Many travellers prefer sitting **in the back**, as it's cheaper and there's generally more space to get comfortable. You'll need to protect yourself from the sun, though there's little you can do about the dust. For half a seat in the cab, you'll pay up to twice the price of a seat in the back; for the luxury of a whole seat you'll pay double again. Prices given in the Guide refer to travel in the back. **Timetables** don't exist for shared transport: they leave as soon as they're full, from early in the morning normally through to about noon, but for long-distance destinations the majority move off first thing around 6 or 7am.

By boat

Boats are an easy way to travel to areas on the Tonle Sap, Mekong River and south coast. On the whole, Malaysian-made express boats are used – a cross between an old school bus and a torpedo. The ride is more comfortable (and much faster) than pick-ups or trains, but conditions are still fairly cramped, so don't expect the luxury that the foreigner prices imply. Many tourists opt to sit on the roof for the views. Having said all that, it should be noted that some boat routes along the Mekong have recently been dropped due to the improvement of the road system that parallels the river. Also, some routes may not be navigable in the dry season, when the water level falls.

By plane

There are three domestic **airlines** in Cambodia: Siem Reap Airways flies only the prestigious Phnom Penh to Siem Reap route, while President Airlines and Royal Phnom Penh Airways cover the Phnom Penh to Banlung route as well; all other routes are currently suspended.

Vehicle rental

Renting a **motorbike** is the most practical self-drive option for Cambodia's poor provincial roads. At the rental shops in Phnom Penh, you can pick up a fairly good 250cc trials bike ($6 per day), which should be able to handle most terrain. **Cars** tend to come with a driver. They're almost exclusively white Toyota Camrys, and cost a reasonable $20–30 per day.

If you do intend to **self-drive** any vehicle in Cambodia, bear in mind that road conditions are unpredictable. Your journey may take much longer than you anticipate, you should never travel alone, and it's a good idea to carry food and water. Really, it's only practical if you've had extensive experience with driving in Southeast Asia already.

Officially, vehicles drive on the right, but **traffic regulations** in Cambodia are flexible and you may encounter people driving on the left. Driving on the roads to Sihanoukville and Kompong Cham can be dangerous, as the traffic is heavy and hectic, but elsewhere, traffic is much lighter.

Bicycles are available to rent cheaply. Although in Phnom Penh the traffic is intimidating, especially at rush hour, most other towns in Cambodia can be pleasantly explored on two wheels.

Local transport

Motorcycle taxis, commonly called **motos**, are the most convenient way of getting around town and are inexpensive – short journeys cost between 500r and 2000r. Their baseball-capped drivers are highly skilled at spotting customers before they even realize they need a moto. English-speaking drivers can usually be found outside hotels, guesthouses and other tourist spots, though they may well charge a small premium for being able to communicate. Non-English-speaking drivers will often nod enthusiastically in a show of understanding, only to proceed to the nearest guesthouse or tourist site. You can hire a moto for the day to visit sights in and around towns all over the country: for a journey of a twenty-kilometre radius, $6 is a pretty good deal for both sides; over that, around $10 is the norm.

Three-wheeled **cyclos** are a more relaxing way to trundle around Phnom Penh, but are only practical for shorter trips. Cyclo fares are subject to negotiation, usually a little more than motos ($2–3), and a little more in the midday heat or pouring rain. With both motos and cyclos, it's best to agree a fare in advance.

Taxis aren't really used for short hops around town. There is one metered taxi service in Phnom Penh, which you must book in advance. Otherwise, cars are booked by the day, or by the journey.

Accommodation

There are **guesthouses** or basic **hotels** in every provincial town, with a wide range of styles from traditional wooden houses to modern concrete blocks. In general, expect to have an en-suite cold-water shower, with towel and toilet paper. The cheapest hotel rooms go for a bargain $5 and almost always have cable TV – a Cambodian necessity.

Tourist-oriented **budget guesthouses** are found only in the main tourist areas of Phnom Penh, Siem Reap and Sihanoukville. It's possible to get a bed for $2, or even $1 if you don't mind basic facilities. Most establishments offer a range of rooms; the cheapest usually have one bed – although it is often a double, *graiy thom* – and a fan. A dollar or so more expensive are those with attached bathrooms and two beds. Throughout the country, you'll pay $5 more per night for air conditioning. You'll also find a number of **mid-range guesthouses** in the main towns, offering better-appointed accommodation with hot water, for $7–15. It's always worth negotiating at these, especially in low season (May–Oct). At the other end of the scale, **luxury international hotels** can be found in Phnom Penh and Siem Reap, charging upwards of $120.

Electricity is usually supplied at 220 volts. Plugs are the two-flat-pin variety. Power cuts and power surges are common, and hotels and guesthouses often have back-up generators.

Addresses

Many roads in Cambodia have no names, and those that do are often known by a number rather than a name, so for example, 50 Street 125 means building number 50 on Street 125. Throughout the chapter, where street names are non-existent, we have located places by describing their location or giving a nearby landmark.

Camping is theoretically illegal in Cambodia, but is a possibility in some places – for example, on the beaches and islands of the south coast. In the dry season, all you need is a mosquito net and hammock for a comfortable night's sleep.

Food and drink

Cambodian **food** is heavily influenced by China, with stir-fries featuring on most menus. Some dishes are similar to Thai cuisine, but with herbs being used for flavouring rather than spices. Chilli is usually served on the side rather than blended into the dish. Even curry dishes, such as the delicious coconut milk and fish *amok*, tend to be served very mild. Rice is the staple food for mealtimes, while noodles are more for breakfast – when they're served as a soup – and as a snack. Hygiene standards may not match what you're used to, but Cambodians are surprisingly fussy over food, and produce is always fresh. At street stalls though, given the lack of refrigeration it's as well to make sure the food is piping hot. If you have a choice, always pick somewhere that's really busy.

Where to eat

The cheapest Khmer cuisine is to be found at **street stalls** and **markets**, which is where you'll find dishes more like the locals eat at home. There are usually one or two dishes on offer at each stall, perhaps pigs' organ soup, fried noodles or a tasty filled baguette. If you're ordering soup, you can pick and choose the ingredients to taste. These stalls are dirt cheap – you can certainly get a meal

Food and drink glossary

See the language section on p.120 for pronunciation guide.

General terms and requests

How much is it?	*t'lai bpon maan?*
Cheers!	*lerk gai-o*
Only vegetables, please	*dtai bon-lai soam*
I don't eat meat or fish	*k'nyom niam sait dtey, sait dt'ray*
I'd like...	*k'nyom chong...*
Could I have the bill?	*ket-loi?*

Rice and noodles

geautiev	noodle soup
mee sOOp sait goa	noodle soup with beef
mee chaa	fried noodles
mee leung	yellow noodles
bai	cooked rice
bai chaa	fried rice
bor bor	rice porridge

Fish, meat and vegetables

bong-kong	shrimp/prawn
bon-lai	vegetables
bpayng boh	tomato
bpoat	corn
chaa bon-lai	stir-fried vegetables
dom-loang barang	potato
dt'ray chaa	fried fish
dt'ray	fish
dtee-a	duck
dtray-meuk	squid
g'daam	crab
moa-un	chicken
saa-lut	lettuce
sait goa	beef
sait j'rook	pork
sait	meat
spay-ee k'daop	cabbage

Basics

ber	butter
bpong moa-un	chicken egg
om-ma-let	omelette
bpong moa-un chien	fried eggs
dtao-oo	tofu
m'tayh	chilli
nOOm	cake
nOOm-bpung	bread
om-beul	salt
plai cher	fruit
s'gor	sugar
bpong dtee-a	duck egg

Drinks

bee-yair	beer
dteuk dtai	tea
dteuk groatch-grobaight	orange juice
dteuk groatch ch'maa	lemon juice
dteuk doang	coconut milk
dteuk t'naout choo	palm wine
dteuk sot moi dorb	bottle of water
dteuk om bpow	sugar-cane juice
dteuk sot	drinking water
ka-fei dteuk doh goa	coffee with milk
gdao	hot coffee
gaa-fay khmao	coffee (black)
ot dak dteuk goa	no milk
ot dak dteuk kork	no ice

for less than 2000r – though the portions tend to be on the small side.

Khmer restaurants are the next step up, recognizable by their beer signs outside. In the evenings, the better ones fill up early on, and most places close soon after 9pm. Buying a selection of dishes to share is the norm: each dish costs 5000–10,000r and there's also a small cover charge. In these restaurants, as in beer gardens, drinks are purchased from "beer girls" (see "Drinks" on p.108).

Western restaurants are plentiful in Phnom Penh, Siem Reap and Sihanoukville, though standards vary enormously. Most places cost more than eating at a Khmer restaurant, with meals at $3–5, although the more upmarket restaurants charge $5–10.

Many **guesthouses** also do meals – typically noodles, rice and pasta – for about the same price as Khmer restaurants. It's easy to make do with guesthouse food after a hard day's sightseeing, but for authentic Cambodian culinary colour, you'll need to be more adventurous.

Khmer food

A standard **meal** in Cambodia consists of rice, plus two or three other dishes, either a fish or meat dish, and a steaming bowl of soup. Flavours are dominated by fish sauce, herbs – especially lemongrass (particularly in soup) – coconut milk and tamarind.

If you only try one Khmer dish, it should be *amok dt'ray*, a delightful fish curry with a rich coconut-milk sauce baked in banana leaves – you'll stand the best chance of finding it in Siem Reap. Most fish served in Cambodia is freshwater, and close to the Tonle Sap it is particularly abundant. Fish turns up on every menu, in popular dishes such as *dt'ray chorm hoy* (steamed fish), *dt'ray aing* (grilled fish) and *sumlar mjew groueng dt'ray* (Cambodian fish soup with herbs).

For **snacks**, try *noam enseum j'rook* (sticky rice, soy beans and pork served in a bamboo tube) or *noam enseum jake* (sticky rice and banana). Baguettes (*noam pang*) are always a handy snack food, especially when travelling. Vendors have a selection of fillings, normally pork pâté, sardines, pickled vegetables and salad.

There are some surprisingly tasty **desserts** to be found at street stalls, markets and some restaurants, many of them made from rice and coconut milk. They're very cheap, so you could try a selection. Succulent **fruits** are widely available at the markets. Rambutan, papaya, pineapple, mangosteen and dragonfruit are all delicious, and bananas incredibly cheap. Durians grow in abundance in Kampot, and are, according to Cambodians, the world's finest; they're in season from late March.

Drinks

If you want to reduce the chance of stomach problems, don't drink the **water** and don't take **ice** out on the streets, although it's generally safe in Western bars and restaurants. Bottled, sealed water is available everywhere. Other thirst-quenchers are the standard international **soft drinks** brands, available in bottles or cans, and a few local variants. Freshly squeezed sugar-cane juice is another healthy roadside favourite, although the tastiest Khmer beverage has to be *dteuk krolok*, a sweet, milky fruit shake, to which locals add an egg for extra nutrition.

Coffee is often served iced and black, with heaps of sugar; if you have it white, it comes with a slug of condensed milk already in the glass. Chinese-style tea is commonly drunk with meals, and is served free in most restaurants. You'll only find Western **tea** in tourist restaurants.

The **local brew** is Angkor beer, a fairly good drop, owing in part to the use of Australian technology at the Sihanoukville brewery. International brands, such as Tiger, Fosters and Heineken, are also on offer at restaurants and beer gardens and are purchased from so-called **beer girls**. Each brand has its own beer girls, so if you want a particular brand you have to order from the corresponding beer girl. Once you've ordered, a tray of cans is brought to your table and a beer girl will keep coming back to open the cans and top up your glass.

Communications

To send anything by **mail** it's best to use the main post office in Phnom Penh, as all mail from the provinces is consolidated here anyway. International post is often delivered in around a week, but can take up to a month, depending on the destination. Post offices are open every day from 7am until at least 5pm, sometimes later. **Poste restante** is also available at the Phnom Penh, Siem Reap and Sihanoukville post offices.

Domestic and **international calls** (IDD) can be made from guesthouses, hotels, post offices and public phone booths. Phonecards are usually on sale at the shop nearest to the phone booth. Making a phone call in Cambodia, however, is expensive, about double the amount you'd pay in Bangkok, for example. International calls cost from $3 per minute in Phnom Penh, while calls from the provinces are generally more expensive. To **phone abroad** from Cambodia, dial ⓣ001 + IDD country code (see p.64) + area code minus first 0 + subscriber number. For international directory enquiries, call ⓣ1201. Some Internet cafés can do cheap international calls via the Internet.

The cost of **Internet access** in Phnom Penh and Siem Reap has been sent tumbling by an improved telephone system and an influx of Internet cafés. Surfing the net costs $1 an hour on average. Internet access is available in most major cities, although it can

Time differences

Cambodia is seven hours ahead of London (GMT), twelve hours ahead of New York, fifteen hours ahead of Los Angeles, three hours behind Sydney and five hours behind Auckland.

cost up to three times as much as in Phnom Penh and is unreliable.

Opening hours and festivals

Opening hours vary. Even when "official" opening times are posted, these tend to be flexible, as many people juggle more than one job. In theory, **office hours** are Monday to Saturday, 7.30am to 5.30pm, with a siesta of at least two hours from around 11.30am. **Banking hours** are generally Mon–Fri 8.30am–3.30pm, and many banks are also open on Saturday morning. **Post offices** (7am–5pm, or later), markets, shops (7am–8pm, or later), travel agents and many tourist offices open every day.

Festivals

Bonn P'chum Ben, "Ancestors' Day", in late September, marks the beginning of **festival** season, which continues through until Khmer New Year in April. In between, the highlight is **Bonn Om Tuk**, the "Water Festival"– celebrated every year when the current of the Tonle Sap returns to normal after the rainy season and flows down into the Mekong River. The centre of festivities is Phnom Penh's riverbank, where everyone, including the royal family, gathers to watch boat racing, an illuminated boat parade and fireworks. At this time, Phnom Penh's population swells massively, as thousands of country workers head to the capital for the occasion. Festivals tend to be fixed by the lunar calendar, so dates vary from year to year. Offices may shut on national holidays, but everything else continues much as normal.

Cultural hints

Cambodia shares many of the same attitudes to **dress** and **social taboos** as other Southeast Asian cultures; see "Cultural hints", p.68, for details. Cambodians are extremely conservative, and regardless of their means do their very best to keep clean; you'll gain more respect if you're well turned out and modest in your dress. Men should wear tops and women avoid skimpy tops and tight shorts. But particularly offensive to Cambodians is any display of public affection between men and women: even seeing foreigners holding hands is a source of acute embarrassment to them.

Public holidays

January 1: International New Year's Day
January 7: Victory Day over the Genocidal Regime. Celebrates the liberation of Phnom Penh in 1979 from the Khmer Rouge
March 8: International Women's Day
April 13–16: Bonn Chaul Chhnam. Khmer New Year
May 1: Labour Day
May (variable): Bonn Chroat Preah Nongkoal, the "Royal Ploughing Ceremony"
May (variable): Visakha Bochea. Commemorates the birth of Buddha
June 1: International Children's Day
June 18: Her Majesty the Queen's Birthday
September 24: Constitution and Coronation Day
Late September: Bonn P'chum Ben, "Ancestors' Day" (offerings made to deceased relatives)
September 24: Constitution and Coronation Day
October 23: Anniversary of the Paris Peace Accord. Commemorates the 1991 Paris conference on Cambodia
October 30–November 1: King Sihanouk's Birthday
November 9: Independence Day
Early November: Bonn Om Tuk, "Water Festival"
December 10: UN Human Rights' Day

Crime and safety

The **security situation** in Cambodia has improved significantly over the last few years. Areas that were once plagued with bandit activity or by the threat of unpredictable Khmer Rouge factions, are now safe to travel in. In spite of recent crackdowns, there is still a culture of guns in Cambodia, and there have been incidents of armed robbery against locals and tourists alike. All areas covered in this book are safe to travel to overland, but you should remain alert to the fact that Cambodia, as well as being one of the most mined countries in the world, also has a terrible legacy of unexploded ordinances (UXO). When travelling in the countryside, stick to well-trodden paths and don't pick up or kick anything that you can't identify.

Gun crime is actually more frequent in Phnom Penh than anywhere else in the country, and reaches a peak at festival times, most notably Khmer New Year. Even so, the threat is small, so it shouldn't stop you enjoying the nightlife. Taking a few simple precautions can reduce the risk further:

- Do not carry your passport or other valuable items; lock them in your hotel safe.
- Carry only a small amount of cash.
- Use a moto or taxi rather than walk.
- Use a trustworthy moto-driver, preferably someone recommended by your hotel or guesthouse.
- If you are robbed, do not resist and do not run.

There are plenty of civilian and military **police** hanging around, whose main function appears to be imposing arbitrary fines or tolls for motoring "offences". Of the two, the **civilian police**, who wear blue or khaki uniforms, are more helpful. Military police wear black-and-white armbands.

Landmines

The war has ended, but the killing continues. Years of guerrilla conflict have left Cambodia the most densely mined country in the world. The statistics are horrendous – up to eight million **landmines** in the country; 50,000 amputees; a further 2000 mine victims every year. The worst affected areas are the province of Battambang and the border regions adjacent to Thailand in the northwest, namely Banteay Meanchey, Pailin and Preah Vihear provinces.

Slow progress is being made by mine-clearance organizations, such as the British-based Mine Action Group (MAG) and The Halo Trust, but resources are extremely limited compared to the scale of the problem.

Although the risk is very real for those who work in the fields, the threat to tourists is minimal. The main **tourist areas** are clear of mines, and even in the heavily mined areas, towns and roads are safe. The main danger occurs when striking off into fields or forests, so the simple solution is to stick to known safe paths. If you must cross a dubious area, try to use a local guide, or at least ask the locals "*mian min dtay*?" ("Are there mines here?"). Look out for the red mine-warning signs, and on no account touch anything suspicious-looking.

Medical care and emergencies

For serious **medical emergencies**, consider flying to Bangkok, although clinics and hospitals in Phnom Penh are equipped to deal with most ailments (see "Listings", p.135, for addresses). Sihanoukville and Siem Reap have limited facilities, but generally medical facilities outside Phnom Penh are poor. If you're stuck in the provinces and require emergency evacuation to Phnom Penh, contact International SOS on ⓣ023/216911. General emergency telephone numbers are listed in the box opposite, but whatever the emergency, it's probably best to contact the English-speaking operators, available 24 hours.

Street-corner **pharmacies** throughout Cambodia are well stocked with basic supplies, and money rather than a prescription gives easy access to anything available, though beware of out-of-date medication. Standard shop hours (7am–8pm, or later) apply at most of these places, but some stay open in the evening. More reputable operations with English- and French-speaking pharmacists can be found in Phnom Penh, where a wider variety of specialized drugs are available. Some even offer 24-hour service (see "Listings", p.135).

Emergency phone numbers

Police ☎117
Fire ☎118
Ambulance ☎119
Police assistance (English, French and Italian spoken) ☎023/724793 or 012/942484

History

Little is known about the early history of Cambodia. Archeological evidence suggests that the area was occupied and cultivated from at least 4000 BC. These early dwellers lived in buildings similar to those inhabited by today's Khmers, indicating that they may be direct ancestors, but the origin of these first settlers and the date of their arrival in Cambodia is unknown. It wasn't until the first century AD that the indigenous population began to adopt advanced concepts of rice cultivation, religious beliefs and social structure and to establish themselves as a civilization worthy of note. This transformation owes much to the visiting Indian traders, en route to China, who brought ideas as well as goods to the region. Thus, the area to the west of the Mekong Delta began establishing itself as an important commercial settlement centred around the port of Oc Eo (now in Vietnam). The civilization became known by the Chinese as Funan.

The Indianized **Funan** port community enjoyed prosperity for several centuries, but gradually declined in importance from the sixth century, as farmers began to move away and cultivate the fertile areas around the Mekong and Tonle Sap. From this time, the Chinese referred to the inhabitants as the **Chenla**. Although this term implies a cohesive culture, the Chenla actually consisted of small, disparate fiefdoms operating independently. It took the foresight and inspirational guidance of King Jayavarman II, recently returned from Indonesia, to guide these rival factions towards a prosperous unification.

Angkorian period

Cambodia's heyday, the Angkorian period, started in the early ninth century when the rival Chenla kingdoms united under Jayavarman II as their universal monarch. Forging alliances through marriages and offerings of land, and gaining territory through military campaigns, he created the beginnings of the mighty Khmer Empire. Jayavarman II also introduced the religious cult of Devaraja god-king, a belief system that continued with his successors. In total, 39 successive kings reigned over the Angkor Empire (known at the time as Kambuja-desa) from various capitals to the northeast of the Tonle Sap; the temples of Angkor remain as a legacy of these cities. The last major king, Jayavarman VII, embarked on a massive programme of construction, culminating in the creation of the magnificent walled city of Angkor Thom.

For most of the Angkorian period, the biggest military threat came from the **Champa Kingdom**, located in central Vietnam. It was at the hands of the Cham that the Khmers suffered their worst defeat: sailing their fleet up the Mekong Delta and into the Tonle Sap, the Cham devastated the capital and occupied Cambodia for four years. It was Jayavarman VII who eventually pushed them out, annexing Champa in the process.

Thailand was a further threat to the supremacy of the Khmer Empire, and by the fourteenth century the Thai army had become a formidable force, mounting raids on Cambodian territory and virtually destroying Angkor Thom. It was probably due to the proximity of Angkor to the hostile Thai-occupied areas that the capital was abandoned in favour of more southerly locations by the middle of the fifteenth century. By this time, repeated wars had taken their toll, in both human and financial terms, and Jayavarman VII's royal excesses had further depleted the coffers. The Khmer Empire was in irreversible decline.

From empire to protectorate

The **Thai** army continued to grow in strength during the fifteenth century. Conversely, the Khmers were in a state of disarray and could not mount an effective defence. In 1594, their capital fell to the Thais. From that point on, Cambodian fortunes looked decidedly bleak. As different factions of the Cambodian royal family looked to either Thailand or Vietnam for military and financial assistance, vast swathes of land were lost in tribute payments to both nations. Had the French not arrived in the 1860s, Cambodia may have been entirely swallowed up by Thailand and Vietnam.

French control

By 1863, the **French** already had a strong foothold in the area, with the Mekong Delta in Vietnam under their control, and missionaries already in residence in Cambodia. The then-monarch King Norodom saw an opportunity to use the French as a way of reducing Thai control, and securing his own position against other claims to the throne. In August 1863, he exchanged timber concessions and mineral exploitation rights for military protection, ushering in an era of French control that would last until 1941. When the French pushed for more control in Cambodian affairs, a vicious rebellion erupted across the country that ended only when the French agreed to revert to the older agreement. Despite the insurrection and subsequent agreement, French control tightened, and after King Norodom's death in 1904, the following three kings were selected by the French. In 1941, 18-year old Prince Norodom Sihanouk was chosen to succeed King Monivong, but before the French had a chance to manipulate the impressionable young monarch, the Japanese marched into Cambodia, and World War II interrupted French control.

Independence

Following the Japanese surrender in 1945, King Sihanouk stunned the French by campaigning for **independence**. As international support for Sihanouk grew, and conflict in Vietnam occupied French troops and resources, France was left with no option but to grant independence. This was formally recognized by the Geneva Conference in May 1954, with a stipulation that elections should follow. As communism was gaining popular support across Southeast Asia, King Sihanouk embarked on a drastic course of action to retain control of Cambodia. He abdicated from the throne, installing his father Norodom Suramarit as king, and formed a political party to fight in the 1955 elections. Capitalizing on his recent success at gaining independence, his party, The People's Socialist Community, won every seat in the newly formed parliament, and 99 percent of the vote in the subsequent 1958 elections. But the power-crazed monarch-turned-politician ruled with an iron hand, and political opposition was ruthlessly smothered. Communist elements, termed "Khmers Rouges" by Sihanouk, fled to the countryside to avoid arrest. When, in 1960, his father died, he appointed himself Chief of

State, in a further gesture of despotic power.

The Vietnamese factor

Meanwhile, things were beginning to heat up in **Vietnam**, and Sihanouk was being pressured into taking sides in the conflict. Despite publicly declaring neutrality, he signed an alliance with the North Vietnamese government that allowed them to use Cambodian soil for supplying South Vietnamese guerrillas, the Vietcong, and tolerated deliveries of arms and supplies through the port of Sihanoukville to Vietcong encampments. In 1969, the Americans began covert bombings of Cambodia's eastern provinces, where they believed **Vietcong** guerrillas were hiding. Hundreds of Cambodian civilians were killed or maimed in these raids (which continued until 1973 and are widely acknowledged to have led to the rise of the Khmer Rouge). Left-wing disquiet began to grow, and General Lon Nol and Prince Sisowath Matak seized an opportunity to depose Sihanouk while he was away in France in 1970. The Vietnamese were ordered to leave Cambodian soil, but instead they pushed deeper into Cambodia, pursued by US and Southern Vietnamese troops, transforming the country into a savage battlefield. Thousands of war refugees fled the fighting and headed to Phnom Penh. With the country in complete disarray under a weak and ineffective leadership, the communist Khmer Rouge regrouped, and began taking control of large areas of the provinces.

The Khmer Rouge regime

Khmer Rouge forces marched into Phnom Penh on April 17, 1975 to the cheers of the Cambodian people. The war was over, and peace would prevail, they assumed. Unfortunately, this was not to be. From the very day that the Khmer Rouge arrived in Phnom Penh, a systematic process of communist re-engineering was ordered, presumably by Communist Party leader Saloth Sar, or **Pol Pot** as he was subsequently known. The deranged attempt to transform the country into an agrarian collective, inspired by Maoist ideology, proved a monumental human disaster and caused international outrage, but little action. The entire population of Phnom Penh and other provincial capitals was forcibly removed to the countryside to begin their new lives as peasants working on the land. They were the lucky ones. Pol Pot ordered the mass extermination of intellectuals, teachers, writers, educated people, and their families. Even wearing glasses was an indication of intelligence, a "crime" punishable by death. The brutal regime lasted four years before invading **Vietnamese forces** reached the capital in 1978; by this time, at least one million, perhaps three million, Khmers had died as a result of the Khmer Rouge genocide. Pol Pot and his supporters fled to the jungle bordering Thailand, from where they continued to wage civil war on successive governments in Phnom Penh.

Vietnamese occupation

The **Vietnamese-backed government** installed in Phnom Penh was led by Hun Sen and Heng Samrin, both Cambodians who had served in the Khmer Rouge, but defected to Vietnam. Meanwhile, a Chinese-backed coalition government-in-exile was being created to unify opposition to the Vietnamese government. It was dominated by the Khmer Rouge, and headed by Sihanouk. For Cambodian people, Vietnamese occupation was by no means the perfect solution, but compared to the suffering and death of the previous four years, it was a welcome change. The international community, however, came down on the side of a Khmer Rouge-dominated coalition, and refused to recognize the new government. After all, the new Vietnamese occupation could be the start of communist expansionism, whereas the Khmer Rouge, despite being communists, only killed their own and didn't pose a threat to the capitalist world. So Thailand, Britain and the US colluded to train the genocidal rebels, shelter them on Thai soil, provide money, arms and food, and offered them the Cambodian seat in the United Nations.

However, in 1985, there was a transformation in the international communist landscape. Mikhail Gorbachev rose to power in the Soviet Union, and in the face of harsh economic pressures, cancelled aid to Vietnam. Vietnam in turn could no longer support the Cambodian occupation, and in 1987, negotiations began between the Hun Sen government and the coalition led by Sihanouk. Finally, after intense fighting between rival factions of the coalition in Cambodia, the Paris Peace Accords were signed in 1991.

UNTAC

Under the Paris Peace Accords, sweeping powers were granted to the **United Nations Transitional Authority in Cambodia (UNTAC)**, who were to implement and oversee free and fair elections in 1993, at that point the largest UN operation in history. But the demobilization and disarmament that was essential for free and fair elections never occurred. Hun Sen's troops remained in charge, able to intimidate voters, so the Khmer Rouge refused to participate in the election process. The elections took place amid assassinations, intimidation tactics, bribery, corruption and the shelling of some polling stations. Despite this, a huge turnout of voters supported the royalist FUNCINPEC party, led by Prince Norodom Ranariddh, who won 58 seats. The Cambodian People's Party (CPP) led by Hun Sen gained 51 seats, and eventually a fragile coalition was agreed. Prince Ranariddh was named First Prime Minister and Hun Sen was named Second Prime Minister. Sihanouk was reinstated as constitutional monarch in August 1993.

The end of the Khmer Rouge

Khmer Rouge guerrilla activity intensified after the 1993 elections. An amnesty for Khmer Rouge soldiers had already begun to attract some defections to the Royal Cambodian Armed Forces (RCAF), and in 1996 the government scored a coup; Ieng Sary, Pol Pot's trusted Number Two, defected with 3000 troops. This signalled a major split in the Khmer Rouge ranks, and isolated the ageing Pol Pot. Further defections looked likely, and a paranoid Pol Pot ordered the murder of his defence minister and his entire family. Another senior Khmer Rouge military commander, the notorious Ta Mok, turned on his former master. He arrested Pol Pot, and sentenced him to life imprisonment. More defections followed, and as the RCAF troops began a final push into the last Khmer Rouge stronghold of Anlong Veng in April 1998, the infamous Pol Pot died, possibly of a heart attack, although it may be that he was executed by his own cadre.

Recent history

Hun Sen has been consolidating his powerful position since UNTAC left. In 1997, he accused Prince Ranariddh of planning a military coup after arms apparently bound for Ranariddh's private army were found at Sihanoukville port. Ranariddh fled in fear of his life, but was arrested, tried and eventually pardoned, to participate in another round of elections in July 1998. This time, Hun Sen's CPP came out on top, gaining 64 of the 122 seats. FUNCINPEC won fifteen seats, and the newly formed Sam Rainsy Party also won fifteen. Again, an alliance was negotiated, this time with Hun Sen as sole prime minister. Hun Sen continues to be the most powerful man in Cambodia. Although he stands accused of nepotism, corruption and human rights violations, he remains popular, particularly among those benefiting financially from the current economic climate. The first-ever local council elections were held in 2002, with accompanying intimidation and murder of opposition candidates, and resulted in a landslide victory for Hun Sen's CPP. Having won office once again in 2003, Hun Sen is as powerful as ever. In 2004, King Sihanouk engineered his own abdication by inviting one of his sons to replace him as king. Norodom Sihamoni, who was living in Paris, returned to take the throne, and in October that year Phnom Penh was the site of grand and ancient royal ceremonies that hadn't been performed since Sihanouk was crowned in 1941.

Religion

The state religion in Cambodia is Theravada Buddhism, but Hinduism, the dominant religion at the time of Angkor, still has an influence, as seen in the Ramayana classic dances. Animism and ancestor worship are not only practised by the minority chunchiet, but affect the everyday life of most Buddhist Cambodians. Cambodian Muslims, often referred to as Cham, comprise five percent of the population. For an introduction to all these faiths, see "Religion", pp.69–71.

The **Cham** were the medieval inhabitants of the Hindu Champa kingdom, on the coast of what is now Vietnam. In the fifteenth century, as the Vietnamese began to extend their territory, the Cham were forced to flee south seeking refuge amongst the Buddhist Khmers and settling in fertile areas north of Phnom Penh, primarily in the area known today as Kompong Cham. Soon after, the Cham converted to Sunni Islam as the religion swept through the region. Khmer Muslims tend to live in their own villages or in small neighbourhoods within the larger cities. Marriage outside the Muslim community is prohibited, so the community has retained a strong identity over the years. There are thought to be more than 300,000 Cambodian Muslims in Cambodia.

All religions suffered **persecution** from 1975 to 1979: monks and priests were murdered and wats and mosques destroyed. Buddhism has still not fully recovered, and you'll notice that Buddhism is less strict in Cambodia than in other Southeast Asian nations.

The architecture of ancient Cambodia

While its form is unmistakably rooted in India, the wealth of architecture that the ancient Khmer left scattered across Southeast Asia has no Indian parallel. This is largely due to the uniquely Khmer cult known as devaraja, literally "god-king". Founded on the belief that Khmer kings were earthly incarnations of Shiva, Vishnu or the Buddha, the cult inspired dizzying heights of architectural megalomania as each successive king endeavoured to construct a temple to his own greatness that would eclipse the efforts of all his predecessors.

The monuments from Cambodia's glorious past rival those of ancient Egypt and Mesoamerica in size and grandeur, and like their counterparts on far-off continents, the ancient Khmer suffused their imposing stone architecture with religious symbolism.

Many **Khmer temples** are actually scale models of the Hindu–Buddhist universe. Moats and walls symbolize oceans and mountain ranges that encircled the five-peaked Mount Meru, the lofty home of the gods. The majority of these temples face east to catch the rays of the rising sun, symbolic of life. The exception is **Angkor Wat**, which faces west, the direction of the setting sun and death. While the mathematical equations that dictated the dimensions of Khmer temples are no longer understood, it is known that the ancient Khmer placed great stock in the auspiciousness of such precise measurements. This can be discerned in the layout of Khmer temples, most of which possess a severe symmetry.

The building materials used by the ancient Khmer changed over time. **Early Angkor-period temples** were constructed of brick. Using a now-forgotten technique to cement the bricks together, the Khmer built towers that were similar in style to those built by the Cham in what is present-day central Vietnam. Examples of these early towers can be seen at Roluos, but the most impressive brick temple is Angkor's **Prasat Kravan**, the interior of which has bas-reliefs carved right into the brick. A type of stucco made from such esoteric ingredients as pounded tamarind and the soft earth of termite mounds was used as a medium to sculpt ornamentation for the brick structures. Laterite, a porous stone that resembles lava rock, was utilized for foundations and walls. The use of **sandstone** was, of course, what set Khmer temples apart from religious architecture constructed by the ancient Cham, Thai and Burmese, all of whom worked almost exclusively in brick and stucco. As a medium for decoration, sandstone also allowed the wondrous talent of Khmer sculptors to shine through.

While the extent of **sculpted motifs** varies from temple to temple, two portions of Khmer edifices were always lavishly decorated: lintels and pediments. The lintel, a rectangular stone block fixed over doorways, became an important element in Khmer architecture when the Khmer began carving ornate designs into them several centuries before the Angkor period. Early prototypes have been found dating back to the seventh century and indicate that the designs were influenced by pre-Angkor kingdoms such as Funan. As the styles and motifs have evolved over the centuries, experts on Khmer art are able to date lintels by comparing them to known works. A motif commonly found on **lintels** is Kala, an ogre-like temple guardian usually depicted with two stylized garlands spewing from the corners of his mouth. Often a deity or divinity is perched atop Kala's head. **Pediments**, the triangular space just above doorways and lintels, were also favourite spots for lavish adornment. Often, these depict elaborate scenes from Hindu or Buddhist legends – the pediments at Angkor Wat and Banteay Srei being particularly fine examples. Framing the pediments are usually the undulating forms of **nagas**, long, multi-headed water serpents, issuing forth from the gaping mouths of **makaras**, another type of water beast. So popular was this particular architectural detail that it has survived to this day, and cobra-like nagas can be seen framing the pediments of modern temples in Cambodia as well as in neighbouring Thailand and Laos. Other images found in the vicinity of doorways are **dvarapalas**, standing male guardians usually depicted wielding a club or spear, and **devatas**, guardian female divinities. The realistically portrayed guardian images at Banteay Srei are thought by experts to be pinnacles of Khmer art. To many modern visitors, the most easily admired of the mythical representations are the

apsaras, the celestial nymphs who seem to dance upon the smooth sandstone walls. Angkor Wat has by far the most sensitively rendered collection of apsaras, and it is readily apparent that the artisans who sculpted these sublime images spent much time ensuring that no two were alike.

Apart from the images carved in bas-relief described above, **"story telling" bas-reliefs** were used to striking effect by the Khmer. Illustrating historical events, mythology (such as the Ramayana and Mahabharata) and exploits of the kings who had them commissioned, they cover over a thousand square metres of gallery walls in Angkor Wat alone. Depending on how they were executed, the bas-reliefs could be "read" like pages from a giant comic book, from panel to panel. Sometimes the bas-reliefs on a wall were divided into several levels, such as the depiction of the levels of heaven and hell found at Angkor Wat. Often though, a story or event was illustrated in a single large panel. As in Egyptian art, an image's importance is illustrated by its size in relation to the images around it. Thus, the bas-reliefs at Angkor Wat depict grand images of the Hindu god Vishnu, his vehicle Garuda, and Vishnu's incarnations as Krishna, Rama and Kurma – evidence that Suryavarman II, the devaraja who had Angkor Wat commissioned, believed himself to be an incarnation of Vishnu on earth.

To Suryavarman II goes the credit for erecting ancient Cambodia's greatest architectural masterpiece, the silhouette of which graces the Cambodian national flag. Yet not long after his death, the Cham sacked Angkor and the empire fell into disarray. Not until a young prince, Jayavarman VII, took the throne and drove out the invaders was building to begin again in earnest. But major changes came with Jayavarman VII's reign that would affect Khmer architecture. The king's embrace of Buddhism caused the ascendancy of **Mahayana Buddhism** over Hinduism as the official religion. This is most readily seen in the mixed Buddhist and Hindu iconography of temples such as Ta Phrom and Preah Khan, where bas-reliefs depicting meditating Buddhas are found alongside the usual Hindu deities and demigods. At least, this would have been more apparent before Jayavarman VII's death. Following the Buddhist king's demise, there was a backlash against Buddhism, and many of the carvings of meditating Buddhas at Ta Phrom and Preah Khan were defaced or recarved to resemble meditating Hindu ascetics.

Jayavarman VII's reign was also a time of vast territorial gains. Owing mainly to Jayavarman VII's rush to plant monuments across his newly expanded empire, the artisans and architects of the **Bayon period** have been accused by modern art historians of producing crude, hurried works. **Laterite blocks** were used in place of sandstone in the construction of many of Jayavarman VII's temples outside of the Angkor region. Because it was more easily quarried, laterite made it possible for Jayavarman VII to erect edifices in the more far-flung corners of his empire in a relatively short time. Unfortunately, the rough surface of laterite makes it impossible to carve reliefs upon. **Stucco** was used to decorate some of these laterite temples, but the effect could never match the intricate bas-reliefs of carved sandstone. In the same vein, the bas-reliefs at the Bayon, Jayavarman VII's grandest monument, seem rather primitive when compared to the delicate intricacies of those at Angkor Wat. Despite the inferior quality of Jayavarman VII's works, there is one unique design innovation from his reign that many agree is the Khmers' most striking contribution to architecture: the **colossal stone faces** that gaze with blissful detachment from the towers of the Bayon and the gates of Angkor Thom. Thought to depict the Bodhisattva Lokeshvara, the Mahayana Buddhist "Lord of Compassion", the faces can also be seen adorning gates at Banteay Kdei and Ta Phrom, as well as the towers of Banteay Chmar in western Cambodia. Not surprisingly, this powerful visual theme – stone visages smiling enigmatically as the roots of mammoth banyan trees threaten to topple them into jumbled heaps – has been used extensively by modern artists, including several Hollywood film makers, to symbolize ancient civilizations lost to the ravages of time.

While the architecture of the ancient Khmer manages to inspire awe even in its ruined state, it is important to remember that when we look at the monuments today, we see only what did not perish with the centuries – stone, brick and stucco. What we don't see are the ornately carved pavilions of golden teak that housed troupes of court dancers, minstrels, high priests and the god-kings themselves. Gone are the decorative embellishments that would have brought the monuments to life: the sheets of gilded copper that covered unadorned stone walls and towers, the parasols, banners and tapestries of delicate silk that gave colour to dimly lighted galleries and antechambers, the finely woven mats of aromatic grasses that covered rough stone causeways. Important elements which, when combined with the grandeur of bold stones rising up to dominate the jungle canopy, would surely have evoked paradise on earth.

Books

Most books about Cambodia concentrate either on Angkor or the Khmer Rouge atrocities. Travelogues are hard to come by, most date to the 1920s and 1930s. If you can't find the following books before you leave home, you should be able to get them in Bangkok or Cambodia itself. Where a book is published in the UK and the US, the UK publisher is given first, followed by the US one. The abbreviation o/p means "out of print", and these are best ordered online through Amazon (®www.amazon.co.uk).

David Chandler *A History of Cambodia; Brother Number One* (both Westview Press). In *A History of Cambodia*, Chandler, the acknowledged authority on Cambodian history, examines the changing fortunes of the country during the two thousand years of its existence. His considered biography, *Brother Number One*, serves to shed some light on the enigma of Pol Pot, a man with apparently mild manners, but a genocidal bent.

Harry Foster *A Beachcomber in the Orient* (Dodd, Mead & Company, o/p). A hilarious first-person account of a proto-backpacker who travelled the region in the 1920s. Well worth the effort to find a copy – online sources are your best bet.

Amit Gilboa *Off the Rails in Phnom Penh – Into the Dark Heart of Guns, Girls and Ganja* (Asia Books, Bangkok). A shallow, seedy, sensational account of expat life in Phnom Penh. Gilboa sets out to shock rather than to create a literary masterpiece.

Harry Hervey *King Cobra* (Cosmopolitan Book Corporation, o/p). This travelogue by an American writer who visited French Indochina in the 1920s is something of a fantasy but the poetic prose is a joy to read.

Claude Jacques *Angkor* (Konemann). One for the library rather than the suitcase, this generous volume tracks the rise and fall of the great Khmer civilization. Bright, readable history and thorough technical descriptions of the temples are interspersed with stunning photographs and detailed temple plans.

Henry Kamm *Cambodia – Report from a Stricken Land* (Arcade). The truth of contemporary Cambodian history laid bare – an informed and authoritative narrative of the complex international manoeuvres that destroyed Cambodia's chances of an early recovery.

Norman Lewis *A Dragon Apparent* (Picador/Transatlantic-Publications Inc). Now only available as part of the *Norman Lewis Omnibus: A Dragon Apparent; Golden Earth; A Goddess in the Stones*, Lewis's colourful travelogue describes his journey through Indochina during the last years of French rule.

Carol Livingstone *Gecko Tales* (Phoenix). A light-hearted yarn concerning Cambodia's free-rolling UNTAC era – a touch of politics, some human interest and a pinch of history.

Harish and Judith Mehta *Hun Sen – Strongman of Cambodia* (Graham Brash, Singapore). Insight into how a military commander in the Khmer Rouge became the long-standing prime minister of Cambodia.

Chris Moon *One Step Beyond* (Macmillan). Working in Cambodia as a de-miner, Moon and Cambodian colleagues were kidnapped by Khmer Rouge, and only released as a result of his negotiations. Moon was later disabled by a mine in Mozambique, but tells his story with humour and no hint of self-pity.

Henri Mouhot *Travels in Siam, Cambodia, Laos and Annam* (o/p). The original travelogue on Cambodia, an easy read and a fascinating account of the "discovery" of Angkor Wat.

Milton Osborne *Sihanouk, Prince of Light, Prince of Darkness* (Silkworm Books, Chiang Mai). Biography of the prevaricating king who has been on and off the throne of Cambodia for over sixty years.

Milton Osborne *Mekong* (Allen & Unwin) An engaging mix of historical details concerning the river's exploration and personal anecdotes, highlighting many of the environmental issues that threaten the river today.

Dith Pran *Children of Cambodia's Killing Fields* (Yale University Press). A moving compilation of memoirs from those who experienced the Cambodian holocaust first-hand.

Vittorio Roveda *Khmer Mythology* (Thames and Hudson/Weatherhill). Roveda explains the legends and histories behind Angkor's incredible carvings, bringing numerous reliefs to life.

David Smyth *Colloquial Cambodian* (Routledge). An easy-to-use introduction to written and spoken Cambodian.

Lucretia Stewart *Tiger Balm – Travels in Laos, Vietnam and Cambodia* (Chatto & Windus). A rare account of travel in the poverty-stricken and oppressed Cambodia of 1989 makes an engaging read, and has parallels with Lewis's *A Dragon Apparent*.

Chou Ta-Kuan *The Customs of Cambodia* (Siam Society, Bangkok). A translation of the intriguing accounts of thirteenth-century Chinese Mandarin Chou Ta-Kuan. His detailed chronicles offer an amazing insight into daily life at Angkor, at the peak of the Khmer Empire.

Usha Welaratna *Beyond the Killing Fields* (Stanford University Press). As fearful Cambodians fled the country in 1979, thousands of refugees were left without homes. Welaratna's perceptive book examines the experiences of nine Cambodian refugees who settled in the United States to rebuild their lives.

Ray Zepp *The Cambodia Less Traveled* (o/p). Part travelogue, part dated guidebook, this rare edition is worthy of a read if a copy can be found. Reveals the wonders, limitations and frustrations of travelling through Cambodia in the mid-1990s.

Language

Khmer is the national language of Cambodia. Unusually for this region, it is not a tonal language, which theoretically makes it easier to master. However, the difficulty lies with pronunciation, as there are both vowels and consonant clusters that are pronounced unlike any sounds in English. That makes it difficult to represent accurately in romanized form, and what follows here is a phonetic approximation widely used for teaching Khmer. (People and places throughout this chapter follow the commonly used romanized spellings rather than the phonetic system used below.)

Consonants

Most consonants follow English pronunciation, except the following;

bp a sharp "p" sound, between the English "b" and "p"
dt a sharp "t" sound, between the English "d" and "t"
hs soft "h"
n'y/ñ as in "canyon"

Vowels

a as in "ago"
aa as in "bar"
ai as in "Thai"
ao as in "Lao"
ay as in "pay"
ee as in "see"
eu as in the expression of disgust "uugh"
i as in "fin"
o as in "long"
oa as in "moan"
oo as in "shoot"
ou similar to "cow"
OO as in "look"
u as in "fun"

Greetings and basic phrases

Hello	soo-a s'day
How are you?	sok sa- bai jee-a dtay?
Fine, thanks	sok sa-bai jee-a dtay
Goodbye	lee-a hou-ee
Good night	ree-a-dtree soo-a s'day sewesedai
Excuse me	soam dtoah
Please	soam
Thank you	or-gOOn
What's your name?	nee'ak ch'moo-ah ay?
My name is…	k'nyom ch'moo-ah…
Can you speak English?	nee'ak jeh ni-yee-ay pee-a-saa ong-klayh reu dtay?
I don't understand	k'nyom s'dup meun baan dtay
Yes (male)	baht
Yes (female)	jahs
No	dtay

Getting around

Where is the?	… noo-ee-naa?
How many kilometres is it to…?	dtou… bpon-maan gee-loa-mait?
How long does it take?	joom-nai bpayl brohaily bpon-maan?
I'd like to go to…	k'nyom jong dtou…
Ticket	som-bot
Aeroplane	yoo-un hoh
Airport	jom nort yoo-un hoh/aa-gaah-sa-yee-un-taan
Boat (no engine)	dtook
Boat (with engine)	karnowt
Bus/coach	laan tom /laan krong
Train station	staa-nee roteh pleung
Taxi	dtak-see
Car	laan toit
Petrol station	gar-ahs sang
Bicycle	gong
Bank	tor-nee-a-gee- a
Post office	bprai-sa-nee
Passport	li-keut ch'lorng dain
Hotel	son-ta-gee-a
Motorbike taxi	moto/motodub
Cyclo	see-klo
Pick-up	laan ch'noo-ul
Restaurant	poa-cha-nee-ya-taan
Please stop here	soam chOOp tee neeh
Left/right	ch'wayng/ s'dam
North	kaang jerng
South	kaang t'boang

East	kaang gart
West	kaang leuch

Accommodation

Do you have any rooms?	nee'ak mee-un bon-dtOOp dtay?
How much is it?	t'lai bpon maan?
Can I have a look?	soam merl baan dtay?
Do you have…	mee-un…
Room with bathroom	bon-dtOOp mee-un bon-dtOOp dteuk
Cheap/expensive	taok/t'lai
Single room (one bed)	bon-dtOOp graiy moo-ay
Room for two people	bon-dtOOp som-rabp bpee nee-ak
Air conditioner	maa-seen dtro-chey-at
Electric fan	dong-harl
Mosquito net	mOOng
Toilet paper	gra-daah
Telephone	dtoo-ra-sup
Laundry	boak-cow-ow
Blanket	poo-ay
Open/closed	bark/but

Numbers

1	moi
2	bpee
3	bai
4	bpoo-oun
5	bprahm
6	bprahm-moi
7	bprahm bpee/bprahm bpeul
8	bprahm-bai
9	bprahm- bpoo-oun
10	dop
11, 12, 13, etc	dop moi/moi don dop, dop bpee/bpee don dop, dop bai/bai don-dop
20	m'pay
21, 22, 23, etc	m'pay moi, m'pay bpee, m'pay bai
30, 40, 50, etc	saam seup, sai seup, haa seup
100	moi roy
101	moi roy moi
200, 300, 400, etc	bpee roy, bai roy, bpoo-oun roy
1000	moi bpoa-un
10,000	moi meun
100,000	dop meun/moi sain
1,000,000	moi lee-un

Days of the week and time

Monday	th'ngay jan
Tuesday	th'ngay angkia
Wednesday	th'ngay pot
Thursday	th'ngay prohoa
Friday	th'ngay sok
Saturday	th'ngay sav
Sunday	th'ngay ahtut
Today	t'ngai nih
Tomorrow	t'ngai sa-ait
Yesterday	m'serl meun~
What's the time?	maong bpon-maan?
Morning	bpreuk
Afternoon	ro-see-ul
Evening	l'ngee-ich
Night	yOOp
Noon	t'ngai dtrong
Midnight	aa-tree-ut
Minute	nee-a-dtee
Hour	maong
Day	t'ngai
Week	aa-dtut
Month	kai
Year	chnam
Now	ay-lou nih

Emergencies

Help!	choo-ee!
Are there any mines here?	mee-un meen dtay?
Can you help me?	joo-ay k'nyom baan dtay?
Accident	kroo-ah t'nak
Please call a doctor	soam hao kroo bphet moak
Please call an ambulance	soam hao laan bphet-laan moak
Hospital	moo-un dtee bphet
Police station	bpohs bpoli

2.1

Phnom Penh and around

Cambodia's capital, **PHNOM PENH**, sprawls west from the confluence of the Mekong and Tonle Sap rivers. When approaching from the airport, the city is a confusing mess with no obvious landmarks. The main boulevards are choked with motos and other traffic and lined with generic low-rise, concrete blocks. Despite initial impressions, however, the heart of Phnom Penh, immediately west of the rivers, has a strong appeal. The French influence is evident in the colonial shop-houses lining the boulevards, with here and there a majestic monument or public building animating the cityscape. The Phnom Penhois are open and friendly, and the city itself is small enough to get to know quickly. Phnom Penh may not have much in the way of tourist attractions – the majority of sights can be covered in a day or two – but many visitors end up lingering, if only to soak up the unique indolent atmosphere of this neglected city.

Phnom Penh's **history** began in 1372, when a local widow, Lady Penh, stumbled across a floating trunk containing four bronze Buddha statues and another in stone, washed up by the Mekong River. She saw them as bearers of good fortune and had a small temple built for them high above the water level to guard against flooding. This hill became known as Penh's hill – Phnom Penh – a name adopted by the town that grew up around the site. Phnom Penh was briefly made the capital in the fifteenth century, sacked and destroyed by the invading Thais in 1834, then reinstated as capital again in 1866 under the French. The city flourished during the Indochina years, but the departure of the French signalled the beginnings of political in-fighting in Cambodia, with Phnom Penh at the centre. Then came the Khmer Rouge whose experimental ideology rejected an urban existence, and the city was completely emptied, many of its buildings destroyed. It wasn't until 1979 and the Vietnamese victory over the Khmer Rouge that people began drifting back to the devastated capital. From a low of around fifteen thousand during the Pol Pot era, the population now stands at around one million. Prosperity has also been slowly returning, and mobile phones, Land Cruisers and glitzy karaoke joints are much in evidence. Although not a modern, developed capital by any means, it still provides a huge contrast to the rest of the country.

Arrival and information

Pochentong Airport, Cambodia's international gateway, lies 6km west of the city centre. The terminal has a tourist information desk (opening hours variable), with a list of hotels and travel agents. There's a post office, where you can make domestic and international calls and send faxes, and a foreign-exchange kiosk (Mon–Fri 8.30am–3.30pm). Licensed taxis operate from a counter directly outside the terminal building; these charge a flat fee of $7 for the journey into the city centre. If you want to get straight down to some haggling, head out to Pochentong Boulevard, outside the airport, where you can negotiate your own fare for the moto ride to town – reckon on $1–2 (there are no taxis outside the airport).

Trains pull into Phnom Penh station, a crumbling Art Deco delight situated centrally at the corner of Pochentong and Monivong boulevards. Most **buses** draw up near the southwest corner of the central market, Psar Thmei. Share **taxis** and **pick-ups** will either draw up at the transport stop just northwest of the central market or will drop you off along the way into town. Express **boats** dock at the terminal just east of the post office on Sisowath Quay.

Pick up a copy of the free *Phnom Penh Visitors' Guide*, which has a wealth of information on activities and sights around the city plus a useful map; you'll find it in restaurants, Internet shops and bars. Extracts of the guide are available online at ⓦwww.canbypublications.com. Most guesthouses and hotels have reliable information; *Capitol Guesthouse* (see p.126) has set itself up as the tourist guru in the absence of official information, though, naturally, they will try and peddle their own tours.

City transport

Motorcycle taxis, or **motos**, are the most convenient way of getting around the city and are inexpensive. Expect to pay $2 for a short hop, or up to $3 for a longer journey. Prices go up after dark and in the rain – $5 is usual. You can also hire a moto-driver for a day – explain to the driver exactly where you want to go and negotiate a price beforehand. A good English-speaker will charge around $6–7 per day for his services as driver and guide. If you're not in a hurry, **cyclos** are handy for short trips. Fares are subject to negotiation – usually $2-3. Phnom Penh has no public bus service; a trial on two routes in the city met with considerable scepticism from a population used to being collected from the kerbside and dropped off at their destination.

Taxis are not hailed on the street – you can either book them over the phone (see "Listings", p.135, for numbers) or pick one up at Monivong Boulevard near the central market, where they tend to gather. Negotiate the fare in advance. Taxis are also available for hire for the day: expect to pay around $20. Most hotels and guesthouses also have cars with driver available.

Accommodation

Phnom Penh has plenty of rooms in all price ranges, and the competition has led to some of the lowest **accommodation** prices in Cambodia. There is a cluster of budget guesthouses around Boeung Kak offering beds for as little as $2. Other budget options are scattered throughout town, the most popular being *Capitol Guesthouse* and *Narin*, recently joined by newer alternatives. Many of these budget places also have cheap single rooms. Mid-range hotels are plentiful, and more are being opened, so it's worth negotiating on price, particularly in the low season. In addition to those mentioned here, there is a concentration of mid-range hotels on Monivong Boulevard running south from the train station. This is a good place to shop around for a bargain if you have the time and energy. Phnom Penh also has its share of international hotels, with the refurbished *Hotel Le Royal* setting the standard.

The Riverfront

Cambodiana 313 Sisowath Quay ⓣ023/426288. Huge, international-class hotel overlooking the river. Features restaurants, bars, a swimming pool, tennis courts and business/conference facilities. ⓽

Foreign Correspondents' Club (FCC) 363 Sisowath Quay ⓣ023/724014. Each of the three spacious and individually decorated rooms is just downstairs from the famous restaurant. Rooms with river views are best. Booking essential. ⓻

Indochine 351 Sisowath Quay ⓣ023/211525. Friendly Khmer-owned hotel right on the river, offering spacious, good-value, en-suite rooms. ⓸

River Star 185 Sisowath Quay ⓣ023/990501. Corner building with five floors of rooms, some with balconies and view of the river. Newish rooms have TV and a/c. ⓷

River View 33 Sothearos Blvd ⓣ&ⓕ 023/555788. In a superb location near the National Museum and Royal Palace, this modern hotel offers clean if sparsely furnished rooms. All have TV, a/c, and hot water. Breakfast – included

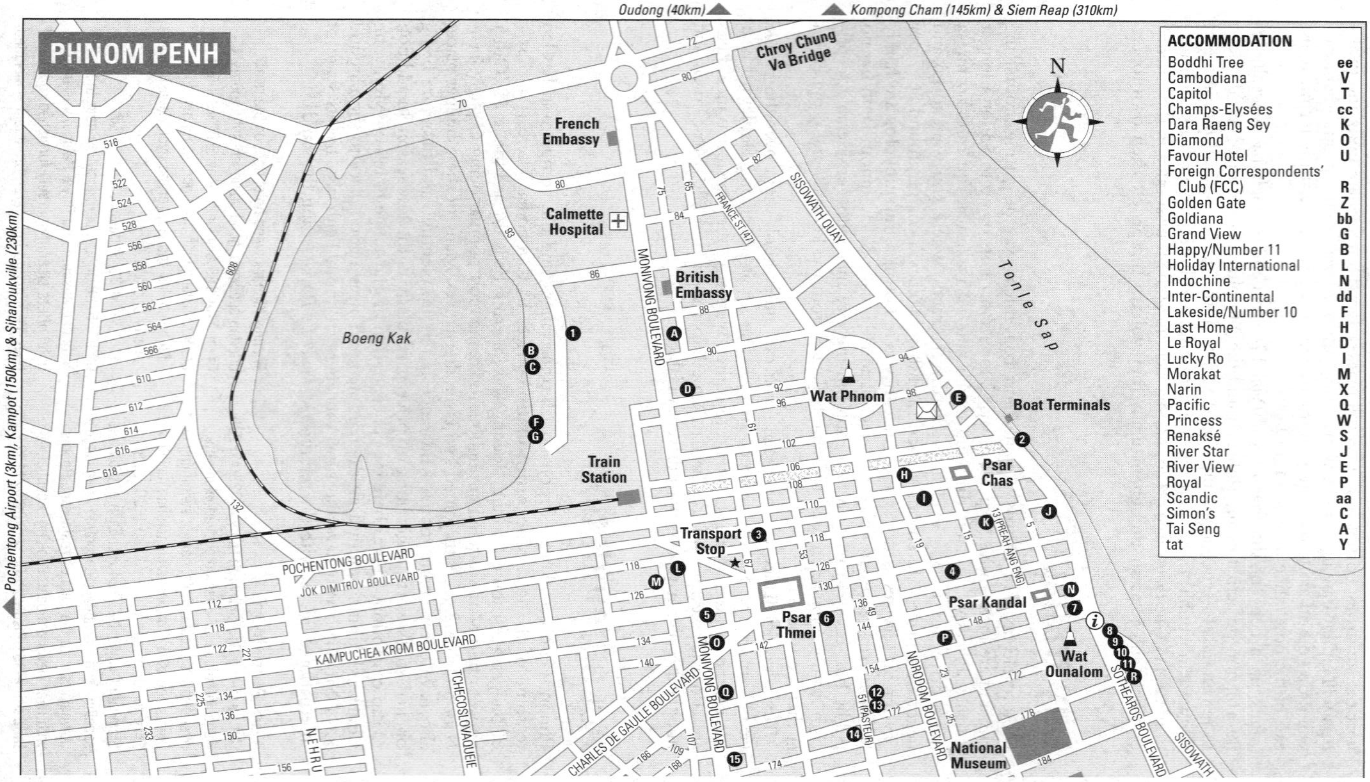

PHNOM PENH

Oudong (40km)

Kompong Cham (145km) & Siem Reap (310km)

Pochentong Airport (3km), Kampot (150km) & Sihanoukville (230km)

ACCOMMODATION

Boddhi Tree	ee
Cambodiana	V
Capitol	T
Champs-Elysées	cc
Dara Raeng Sey	K
Diamond	O
Favour Hotel	U
Foreign Correspondents' Club (FCC)	R
Golden Gate	Z
Goldiana	bb
Grand View	G
Happy/Number 11	B
Holiday International	L
Indochine	N
Inter-Continental	dd
Lakeside/Number 10	F
Last Home	H
Le Royal	D
Lucky Ro	I
Morakat	M
Narin	X
Pacific	Q
Princess	W
Renaksé	S
River Star	J
River View	E
Royal	P
Scandic	aa
Simon's	C
Tai Seng	A
tat	Y

Chroy Chung Va Bridge

Tonle Sap

Boeng Kak

French Embassy

Calmette Hospital

British Embassy

Train Station

Transport Stop

Wat Phnom

Boat Terminals

Psar Chas

Psar Kandal

Psar Thmei

Wat Ounalom

National Museum

SISOWATH QUAY

FRANCE ST (47)

MONIVONG BOULEVARD

POCHENTONG BOULEVARD

JOK DIMITROV BOULEVARD

KAMPUCHEA KROM BOULEVARD

TCHECOSLOVAQUEIE

CHARLES DE GAULLE BOULEVARD

NORODOM BOULEVARD

51 (PASTEUR)

13 (PREAH ANG ENG)

SOTHEAROS BOULEVARD

SISOWATH

NEHRU

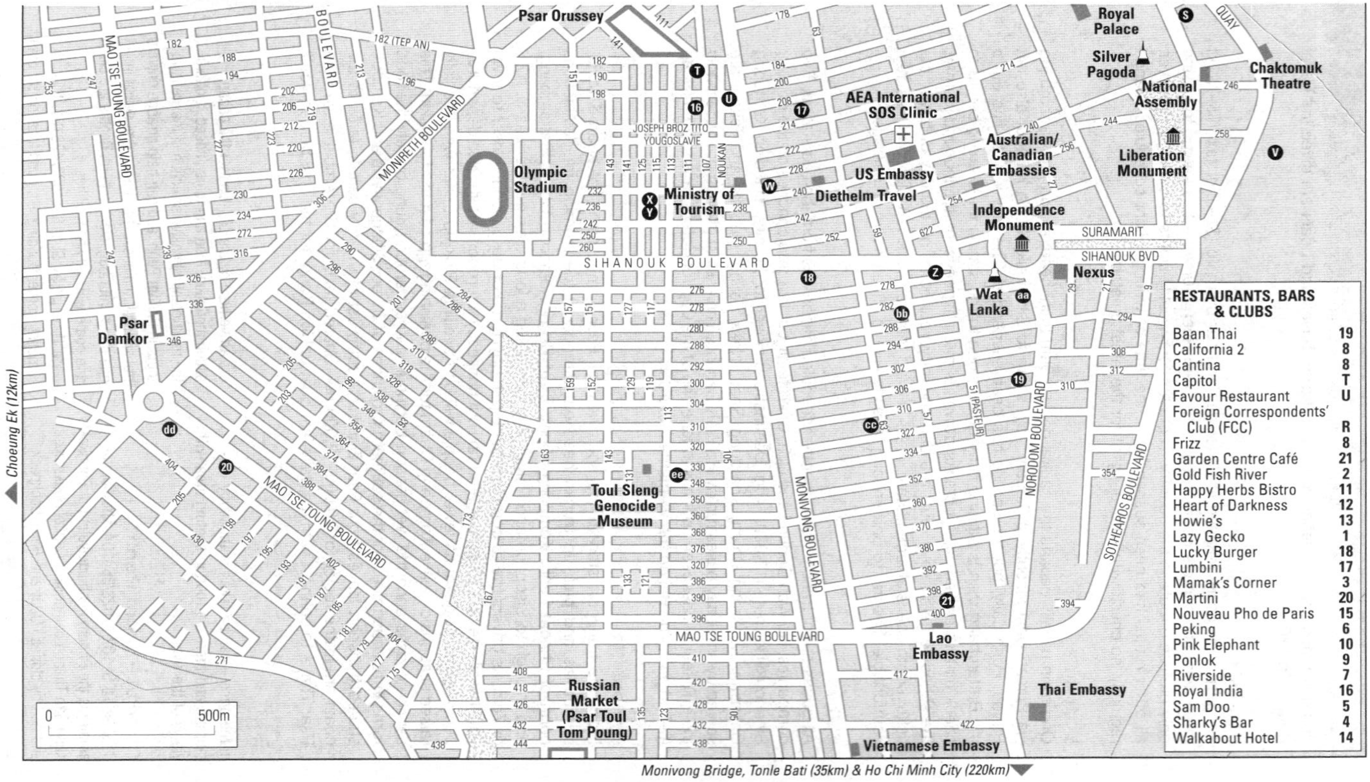

Psar Orussey
Royal Palace
Silver Pagoda
National Assembly
Chaktomuk Theatre
Liberation Monument
AEA International SOS Clinic
Australian/ Canadian Embassies
US Embassy
Diethelm Travel
Ministry of Tourism
Olympic Stadium
Independence Monument
Nexus
Wat Lanka
Psar Damkor
Toul Sleng Genocide Museum
Russian Market (Psar Toul Tom Poung)
Lao Embassy
Thai Embassy
Vietnamese Embassy
SIHANOUK BOULEVARD
MONIVONG BOULEVARD
NORODOM BOULEVARD
MAO TSE TOUNG BOULEVARD
MONIRETH BOULEVARD
SOTHEAROS BOULEVARD
JOSEPH BROZ TITO YOUGOSLAVIE
SURAMARIT
SIHANOUK BVD
51 (PASTEUR)
182 (TEP AN)
NOUKAN
QUAY
Choeung Ek (12km)
Monivong Bridge, Tonle Bati (35km) & Ho Chi Minh City (220km)
0 500m

RESTAURANTS, BARS & CLUBS

Baan Thai	19
California 2	8
Cantina	8
Capitol	T
Favour Restaurant	U
Foreign Correspondents' Club (FCC)	R
Frizz	8
Garden Centre Café	21
Gold Fish River	2
Happy Herbs Bistro	11
Heart of Darkness	12
Howie's	13
Lazy Gecko	1
Lucky Burger	18
Lumbini	17
Mamak's Corner	3
Martini	20
Nouveau Pho de Paris	15
Peking	6
Pink Elephant	10
Ponlok	9
Riverside	7
Royal India	16
Sam Doo	5
Sharky's Bar	4
Walkabout Hotel	14

Moving on from Phnom Penh

Journey times and frequency of planes, trains, buses and boats are given in "Travel details", p.180.

By plane

The **airport** is easily reached in under half an hour by moto ($2–3) or taxi ($5–7). All three domestic carriers operate flights to Siem Reap (40min) – this seems to be the only profitable route in the country. There are four weekly flights to Banlung; however, all other routes had been suspended at the time of writing. Flight schedules change regularly, so check with a travel agent for the latest timetable.

By train

One **train** usually departs the capital daily: a 6am train, heading north to Battambang via Pursat. Until recently, a 6.30am train south to Sihanoukville via Kampot also left Phnom Penh daily, but the service has been suspended. The only way to find out if the Battambang train is running is by going along to the station the evening before to check that it's arrived as, if it breaks down (as often happens) on the inbound journey, the schedule gets thrown out. You can only buy your ticket on the day of travel; the ticket booth opens at around 5am. Keep in mind that trains are very slow and less than comfortable. The trip to Battambang takes twelve to fifteen hours on average.

By bus

All **buses** out of Phnom Penh operate scheduled departures from the bus station. Two companies, Ho Wah Genting and GST, operate air-con express coaches on the popular Sihanoukville route (12,000r; 4hr). Destinations closer to the city, including Kompong Chhnang, Kompong Cham, Kompong Speu, Neak Leung, Oudong and Takeo, are served by small city buses run by Ho Wah Genting. The easiest (though not necessarily the quickest or cheapest) option is to take one of the *Capitol Hotel*'s vans to Siem Reap (6–8hr) and Moc Bai on the Vietnamese border.

By share taxi, minibus and pick-up

From the transport stop at the southwest of Psar Thmei, plenty of **shared taxis**, **minibuses** and **pick-up trucks** head out throughout the morning for destinations north of Phnom Penh: Kompong Thom, Siem Reap, Kompong Cham, Battambang, and through to Sisophon and Poipet. If you're going a long way, get there early, by 6 or 7am, as drivers like to complete the trip in daylight. For destinations closer to town you'll easily be able to get a shared taxi out until early afternoon, after which departures become less frequent as fewer people will be travelling. Pick-up trucks with specially raised suspension leave Kompong Cham for the punishing trip east to Mondulkiri. This service ceases once the wet season begins in earnest around June or July the road turns into a quagmire. For the southern provinces of Takeo, Sihanoukville and Kampot, shared transport leaves from Psar Damkor, southwest of the city centre; fares to the coast are in the region of 10,000–12,000 riel. Shared taxis for Sre Ambel leave from Psar Thmei to connect with the daily fast boat to Koh Kong, for the Thai border; you'll

in the price – can be taken in the lobby restaurant, and there's a rooftop seating area with views of the river. ❸

Central Phnom Penh

Capitol 14 St 182 ⓣ023/364104. The *Capitol* empire is the Phnom Penh equivalent of Bangkok's Khao San Thanon comprising *Capitol Guesthouse* and nearby clones *Happy* and *Hello*. Backpackers arrive here by the bus-load for the cheap accommodation, food and tours. Indeed, it offers the most comprehensive selection of inexpensive tours in Phnom Penh, and can help arrange onward transport. If minibussing all the central sights in one day is your bag, sign up here. Rooms are clean and come with varying facilities. ❶

Dara Raeng Sey St 118. ⓣ023/428181. This rambling corner building is a good location for both

need to leave Phnom Penh by 8am to make the connection. More flexibly, you can get a shared taxi to Chamcar Luang, 6km south of Sre Ambel on National Route 4, then another shared taxi up National Route 18 to Koh Kong.

By boat

From the new passenger boat terminal (aka the tourist docks) on the river near the main post office, **express boats** take around five hours to power up the Tonle Sap River to Siem Reap, subject to variations in the river's flow (tickets cost $25 for foreigners, though some guesthouses sell tickets for a few dollars less). Boats leave at 7am and have allocated seating; you can buy your ticket at the dock the day before or on the morning of departure. Boats heading up the Mekong to Kompong Cham and Kratie have been discontinued due to dwindling passenger numbers in the wake of better roads. This short-circuits the boat trip up the Mekong to Laos, but it can still be done with a combination of road and river travel, starting your journey on the Mekong at Kratie instead.

Organized tours

If the trials of the public transport system prove too much, you could opt for the easy life with an **organized tour**; call into any travel agent. Tours are, however, limited to the major tourist spots.

Crossing the border into Vietnam

Two border crossings are open to foreigners between Cambodia and Vietnam: at **Bavet** to Moc Bai, 160km from Phnom Penh; and at **Chau Doc** on the Bassac River. The popular 245-kilometre trip from Phnom Penh to HCMC has become easier and cheaper over the last few years, as guesthouses in these cities are teaming up to offer hassle-free **public transport all the way**. It's now possible to get a minibus for $12. Check the prices at *Capitol* and *Narin* (see pp.126 & 128), not the cheapest way to get there, but certainly less hassle – on this trip, you'll have to walk 500m or so across the border, complete the necessary formalities and change to transport from the guesthouse's associate in HCMC. The alternative is to get yourself a place in a share taxi ($4) or take a pick-up to the border, and then minibus it to HCMC (US$4) after crossing the border; there are plenty of touts at Bavet to help you out. For extra comfort, Ho Wah Genting operates air-con coaches through to HCMC from the bus station (Tues, Thurs & Sat; $14).

However you get to the border, allow plenty of time to clear **immigration**: it can take two hours or more. The border closes at 5pm. The city-to-city trip takes about eight or nine hours, including immigration formalities. Visas are available from the Vietnamese Embassy at the southern end of Monivong Boulevard in Phnom Penh (Mon–Fri 8–11am & 2–4pm) for $50, but guesthouses can usually organize this for slightly less.

The newly opened route through **Chau Doc** is more complicated than crossing at Bavet; you'll have to get to Neak Leung and then take a boat down the Mekong to the border, where you can pick up a moto for the short ride to the immigration point on the Bassac River. Again, you'll need to be in possession of a valid visa.

the riverfront and the old French Quarter. Rooms have either fan or a/c as well as TV. Staff are very friendly and helpful. ③

Diamond 172–184 Monivong Blvd ⓣ023/217221–2. Established hotel with large, modern, well-appointed en-suite rooms offering plenty of polished wood, TV, mini-bar, a/c and in-room safe. ⑥

Favour Hotel 429 Monivong Blvd ⓣ023/219336. Chinese-style hotel, heavy on the white tiling, with a very popular Khmer/Chinese restaurant downstairs. ③

Holiday International 89 Monivong Blvd ⓣ016/817333. A relaxing four-star hotel, its luxurious rooms equipped to international standards with a choice of suites available. For dining, there's a choice of restaurants including the *La Marina*, an Italian restaurant. Breakfast is included in the rate. ⑧

Last Home 47 St 108 ⓣ023/724917. Quirky little guesthouse near the main post office. Rooms come in all shapes and sizes, including a large room with balcony and glimpses of Wat Phnom and the river. ❶

Lucky Ro 122 St 110 ⓣ023/986559. Small, friendly hotel with good-sized, clean and tidy rooms, all with TV and en suite; those with a/c have hot water. ❷

Morakat 33 St 107 ⓣ023/880180. Just off the main thoroughfare, a welcoming hotel with clean, presentable rooms, all with en-suite bathrooms, a/c, TV and fridge. ❸

Narin 50 St 125 ⓣ023/820873. One of the long-standing budget guesthouses in Phnom Penh. Rooms are clean and quite adequate; the best part is the pleasant terrace restaurant, which is a good place to meet up with other travellers. ❶–❷

Pacific 234 Monivong Blvd ⓣ023/218592. Recently refurbished, this hotel has a pleasant reception area with seating and a lobby bar; rooms are large, bright and nicely furnished, with sturdy Cambodian wood furniture. The room rate includes breakfast in the downstairs restaurant. ❻

Princess 302 Monivong Blvd ⓣ023/801089. A stylish and efficient modern hotel. Rooms are large, light and well equipped. Rate includes breakfast, and there are often special deals. ❻

Renaksé 40 Sothearos Blvd ⓣ023/215701. This old colonial gem commands a superb location between the Royal Palace and the river. The rate is worth it for the free terrace breakfast buffet alone, which is just as well, because the standard rooms are small and dark, though cable TV, mini-bar, a/c and bathroom make them tolerable. ❻

Royal 91 St 154 ⓣ023/218026. Family-run, bustling guesthouse in the centre of town with average rooms with cable TV, fridge and en-suite facilities plus optional a/c. ❶–❷

tat 52 St 125 ⓣ023/986620. Decently sized, bright rooms in this cheerful guesthouse mostly come with en-suite facilities. Boasts Internet access, communal TV and video, and the rooftop restaurant serves cheap Cambodian and Chinese food. ❶

South of Sihanouk Road

Boddhi Tree 50 St 113 ⓣ016/865445. You'll feel more like a friend of the family than a tourist at this new, well-decked-out little guesthouse opposite Toul Sleng Genocide Museum. Immaculate, homely rooms have shared bath, and decent meals are served in the leafy courtyard. ❷

Champs-Elysées 185 St 63 ⓣ023/721080. Behind the imposing glass facade is a friendly, modern hotel with comfortable, good-sized rooms, all with hot water, fridge, TV and a/c. The restaurant serves Khmer and Chinese food. ❹

Golden Gate 9 St 278 ⓣ023/721161. A variety of rooms available in two buildings, but the impressive lobby outclasses the rooms themselves. Similar rooms are available next door at the smaller *Golden Bridge* and *Golden Sun* hotels. ❺

Goldiana 10–12 St 282 ⓣ&ⓕ023/219558. Well-regarded hotel with its own restaurant, plus fitness centre and swimming pool. Though the decor is a bit dated, the rooms are comfy and come with en-suite facilities, satellite TV, mini-bar, a/c and a spare phone line for Internet access. ❻

Inter-Continental 296 Mao Tse Toung Blvd ⓣ023/424888. Business-class hotel with international restaurants, bars, gym and swimming pool. ❾

Scandic 4 Street 282 ⓣ023/214498. Good-value, small hotel with swimming pool, restaurant and bar. Rooms are clean and have TV and a/c. Located just up the street from the *Goldiana*. ❹

Boeng Kak and around

Grand View Off St 93 ⓣ023/430776. The rooftop restaurant, which affords views of the lake, is what makes this place stand out. Rooms are smallish but clean and have a choice of fan or a/c. Located south of the mosque. ❶–❷

Happy/Number 11 Off St 93 ⓣ012/884506. Homely and scrupulously clean lakeside guesthouse, full of potted plants. The simple rooms have immaculate communal bathrooms and the great terrace restaurant dishes up Cambodian and Vietnamese fare. Shared stereo and TV, and a free pool table. ❶

Lakeside/Number 10 Off St 93 ⓣ012/552901. A guesthouse offering budget rooms in a spectacular spot, with a large terrace overlooking Boeng Kak. Free pool table, plus videos, hammocks and sunset views. ❶

Le Royal Corner of Monivong Blvd and St 92 ⓣ023/981888. Fully restored to colonial glory by the Raffles group, and now the most luxurious hotel in Phnom Penh. Fine dining, cocktail bars, conference facilities, spa and swimming pool. ❾

Simon's Off St 93 ⓣ012/608892. Friendly, helpful and immaculately kept guesthouse; the cheapest rooms have shared bathrooms. Pleasant terrace restaurant with pool table and TV. ❶

Tai Seng 56 Monivong Blvd ⓣ023/427220. Well-established, clean mid-range hotel, though rooms fronting the boulevard are very noisy. ❺

The City

Phnom Penh **city centre** can be loosely defined as the area between Monivong Boulevard and the Tonle Sap River, stretching as far north as Chroy Chung Va Bridge, and as far south as Sihanouk Boulevard. Its tourist hub is the scenic Sisowath Quay, from where most of the sights and monuments are easily accessible.

Sisowath Quay and around

The heart of Phnom Penh life is a small, fairly nondescript square of land at the junction of **Sisowath Quay** and Street 184, in front of the Royal Palace. It's here that Cambodians used to congregate to listen to declarations and speeches from the monarch, and where Khmer families still gather in the evenings and at weekends. Picnics, games, kite-flying and perhaps a cup of *dteuk k'nai choo* are the order of the day. Running to the north and south of here is Sisowath Quay, lined with tall palms on one side, and bars, cafés and restaurants on the other. In the middle of the day the area is deserted, save for the odd tourist, but as evening draws in, the quay is transformed into a popular and lively social centre – the people of Phnom Penh enjoy the simple pleasures of the fine river views from the riverbank, the expats, tourists and well-to-do locals do the same from the luxury of the bars across the road.

The Royal Palace and Silver Pagoda

Behind the park, set back from the riverbank on Sothearos Boulevard, stand the **Royal Palace** and adjacent **Silver Pagoda** (daily 7.30–11am, 2.30–5pm; $3, additional $2 charge for cameras, $5 for videocams; entrance at Silver Pagoda). These are Phnom Penh's principal tourist sights and its finest examples of twentieth-century Khmer-influenced architecture. Both are one-storey structures – until the Europeans arrived, standing above another's head (the most sacred part of the body) was strictly prohibited.

You'll catch glimpses of the glistening, golden Royal Palace buildings behind the high daffodil-yellow perimeter walls with their white-painted castellations. The buildings are at once simple and ornate – the main building structures follow uncomplicated geometry, but are crowned with highly decorative roofs. Naga finials ripple and curl towards the heavens and the multi-gabled golden-yellow roofs, finished with wide green borders, draw the eye to the central wedding-cake spires, which in turn climb skywards to the hot Cambodian sun.

The **palace** itself is strictly off-limits, but it's possible to visit several buildings within the compound, even when the king is around – a blue flag flies when he is in residence. The original palace on this site was built in 1866 during the reign of King Norodom, great-grandfather to the present king. Norodom decided to move his residence from the then capital, Udong, to Phnom Penh, presumably on the advice of his colonial masters. In 1913, work began to replace the deteriorating wood-and-brick structures with the current concrete buildings, remaining faithful to the original designs.

Visitors enter via the Silver Pagoda and are directed to the palace compound first, an oasis of order and calm, its perfect gardens and well-maintained buildings strangely at odds with the chaos of the city outside. Head straight for the main building in the centre of the compound, the exquisite **Throne Hall**, guarded on either side by statues of naga. The cambered ornamental curves that adorn the tiered roof are also likenesses of naga, their flowing tails peeling upwards into the air, as if trying to prise open the layered roof. The hall is crowned by a spire with four heads carved around its base, a modern-day rendering of the ancient carved faces at the Bayon (see p.117). Inside, the ceiling is adorned with colourful murals recounting the Hindu legend of Ramayana. The throne itself, watched over by busts of past monarchs, only sees action at coronations.

Leaving the Throne Hall via the main stairs, on your left you'll see the **Elephant Pavilion** where the king waited on coronation day and mounted his elephant for the ceremonial procession. A similar building on the right, the **Royal Treasury**, houses the crown jewels, royal regalia and other valuable items. In front and to the left, bordering Sothearos Boulevard, is the **Dancing Pavilion**, from where the king used to address his subjects. Classical dancing also used to be a regular event at this podium, but it's little used nowadays.

Back towards the Silver Pagoda stands the quaint, grey **Pavilion of Napoleon III**, originally erected at the residence of Empress Eugénie in Egypt, then packed up and transported to Cambodia as a gift to King Norodom. It was reassembled on this site in 1876, and now contains royal portraits, dresses for the royal ballet, and other royal paraphernalia. From the balcony, it's possible to view the ornate detail of the roof of the neighbouring Royal Offices.

The internal wall of the **Silver Pagoda courtyard** is decorated with a fabulous, richly coloured and detailed mural of the Ramayana myth, painted in 1903–4 by forty Khmer artists. A Polish project to restore the fresco ran out of money, so it remains in a state of disrepair. The Silver Pagoda takes its name from the floor of the temple, completely covered with silver tiles – 5329 to be exact. The temple is also known as Preah Vihear Keo Morakot ("Temple of the Emerald Buddha"), after the famous **Emerald Buddha** image kept here. Made from baccarat crystal, the Buddha image was a gift from France in 1885. Near the central dais stands another Buddha, a solid-gold life-size statue, decorated with over 2000 diamonds and precious stones.

Returning to the stupa-filled courtyard, seek out the artificial Mount Kailassa to see one of the Buddha's extremely large footprints. Notice also the statue of King Norodom in front of the pagoda, a gift from France in 1875. The body and horse actually belonged to a statue of Napoleon that was surplus to requirements; the French simply knocked up a Norodom head and stuck it on Napoleon's shoulders.

National Museum

Just north of the Royal Palace on Sothearos Boulevard, the grand, red-painted structure that houses the **National Museum** (Tues–Sun 8–11am & 2.30–5pm; $3) is a collaboration of French design and Cambodian craftsmanship. Opened in 1920, the museum houses the country's most important collections of ancient Cambodian culture. Its four galleries, set around a tranquil courtyard, shelter an impressive array of ancient relics, art and sculpture, and general craftsmanship covering Cambodian history from the sixth century to the present day. Angkor buffs will not be disappointed – in addition to numerous Angkor relics and sculptures, some of the sculpted heads from the bridge at Angkor Thom are exhibited, as is the original statue of Yama God of the Underworld from the Terrace of the Leper King in Angkor. The catalogue of exhibits continues to grow as treasures hidden from the Khmer Rouge are rediscovered. Some ten thousand pieces of art found in the basement are currently being cleaned and restored. The statues and images are arranged chronologically, becoming fatter and happier with the increasing prosperity of the Angkor kingdom. An interesting exhibit from more recent history is the king's boat cabin, a portable wooden room used by the king for travelling on the Tonle Sap. Closer inspection of the intricate wooden carvings reveals images of birds, dogs, monkeys, crocodiles and dragons.

If you have time, it's worth exploring Street 178 that runs beside the museum, dotted with art-and-craft shops, selling paintings, woodcarvings and silverware; if you're here on a week day, you could also pop into the School of Fine Arts behind the museum to check out the work being undertaken by students (Tues–Fri 8–11am & 2.30–5pm; visitors are welcome).

The National Assembly and around

Back on Sothearos Boulevard, just south of the Royal Palace, you'll come to the **National Assembly**. You'll know if the Assembly is in session by the excessive police presence and a row of black limousines. Just beyond, on the other side of the road, there's a park, in the middle of which stands the **Liberation Monument**, sometimes called the Cambodia–Vietnamese Friendship Monument, commemorating the defeat of the Khmer Rouge in 1979. Designed by the Vietnamese and crafted by Phnom Penh's own School of Fine Arts, it was erected in 1979. The southern tip of the park is crossed by Sihanouk Boulevard, lined with colonial-era buildings. Following Sihanouk Boulevard west brings you to **Independence Monument**, at the roundabout at the junction of Norodom Boulevard. Built in 1958 to celebrate Cambodian independence from France, the curious muddy-brown tower now serves as a war memorial.

Toul Sleng Genocide Museum (S21)

As the Khmer Rouge were commencing their reign of terror, Toul Svay Prey Secondary School, in a quiet Phnom Penh neighbourhood, was transformed into a primitive prison and interrogation centre. Corrugated iron and barbed wire were installed around the perimeter, and classrooms were divided into individual cells, or housed rows of prisoners secured by shackles. From 1975 to 1979, an estimated twenty thousand victims were imprisoned in **Security Prison 21**, or S21 as it became known. Teachers, students, doctors, monks and peasants suspected of anti-revolutionary behaviour were brought here, often with their spouses and children. They were subjected to horrific tortures, and then killed or taken to extermination camps outside the city.

The prison is now a **museum** (daily 7.30–11.30am & 2–5pm; $2) and a monument to the thousands of Khmers who suffered at the hands of the Khmer Rouge. It's been left almost exactly as it was found by the liberating Vietnamese forces – the fourteen victims found hideously disfigured in the individual cells have been buried in the school playground. It's a thoroughly depressing sight, and it's not until you see the pictures of the victims, blood stains on the walls and instruments of torture that you get any idea of the scale of suffering endured by the Cambodian people.

Wat Phnom

The most popular of Phnom Penh's temples, **Wat Phnom** (dawn–dusk; $1), atop the city's only hill, was originally founded by Lady Penh in 1372 (see p.122). The current construction, dating from 1927, sees hundreds of Cambodians converge daily for elephant rides, photos and perhaps a prayer or two. Weekends and holidays are especially busy.

At the eastern entrance, lions and naga images beckon the visitor to the top of the staircase, where a gold-painted bas-relief depicts the victory of King Jayavarman VII over the Cham army in the twelfth century. Apsara images flank the mural. Inside the temple, a resplendent Maitreya Buddha ("Buddha of the Future") looks down from the central dais. Some of the paintings adorning the walls and ceiling are barely visible – years of incense burning have taken their toll – but you can just about make out tales of the Buddha's life and the Ramayana. Behind the main sanctuary, King Ponhea Yat's stupa remains the highest point in Phnom Penh, a fact not lost on the French, who commandeered the shrine as a watchtower. Rumour has it that Lady Penh's original Buddhas are entombed here and there's a small shrine to her between the temple and the stupa.

On the northern side of the hill nestles a temple to the spirit **Preah Chau**, popular among the Chinese and Vietnamese communities. Gifts of raw meat and eggs are offered to the stone lions outside in return for protection from enemies. The empty, half-finished construction on the western side of the hill was intended to house the Buddha relics currently enshrined in the small blue stupa outside Phnom Penh train station. However, financial and engineering problems have caused the project to be abandoned.

Wat Ounalom

Set back slightly from the river at the northern junction of Sothearos Boulevard and Sisowath Quay, **Wat Ounalom** ("Eyebrow Temple") is the centre of modern-day Khmer Buddhist teaching, led by Supreme Patriarch Taep Vong, respectfully referred to by the novices as "The King of Monks". The main temple building, built in 1952, is a modern reincarnation of the original, built in the fifteenth century. The building to the right is the main residence for the monks, and the five-hundred-year-old stupa behind the temple encases one of the Buddha's eyebrows, after which the temple is named. Just in front stands a monument to those killed during the Pol Pot regime. It's pleasant to stroll around the complex – many of the monks are learning English, and are happy to tell you what they know about the temple and its history. The best time to visit is at 6pm, when the monks congregate in the main sanctuary to chant their prayers.

Eating

Street stalls will keep shoestring travellers happily fed on noodle dishes or filled baguettes for 2000r or less. Stalls spring up in different places at various times of day: markets are a good place for a daytime selection, and the riverside in the early evening. Next up in the price range, guesthouses tend to serve a standard selection of local and Western dishes for $1–3. Khmer street-corner **restaurants**, with plastic garden chairs, charge around the same for standard local fare. Eating out is the fulcrum of evening social activity for moderately well-off Khmers, so it's often difficult to find a table in the more popular restaurants. The more fashionable options are concentrated just south of the junction of Sihanouk and Monivong boulevards. For a slightly more upmarket variation on the same theme, make for the cluster of popular Khmer joints on the other side of Chroy Chung Va Bridge. Finally, there are innumerable reasonably priced restaurants aimed at expats and tourists; expect to pay $3–5 per dish. Most restaurants open from around 7am until 9pm, although places catering to a mainly Western clientele stay open until 11pm.

Cafés and restaurants

Baan Thai St 306. Classy, upmarket Thai restaurant in a charming wooden house, with seating on cushions on the floor. Extensive menu with plenty of choices for meat eaters and vegetarians.

California 2 317 Sisowath Quay. This guesthouse restaurant has the best Baja fish tacos in town, possibly the whole region.

Capitol 14 St 182. Cheap and cheerful travellers' fare at this much-improved busy street-corner café.

Favour Restaurant 429 Monivong Blvd. One of the most popular of the early-evening Monivong Khmer/Chinese restaurants. Get here early for a table.

Foreign Correspondents' Club (FCC) 363 Sisowath Quay ⓣ023/724014. Fine dining in this famous riverside colonial building. Bar snacks also available, or just pop in for a soothing ale.

Frizz Sisowath Quay. Small but excellent restaurant with charcoal braziers, similar to a Korean barbecue, that allow you to cook your own Cambodian meat and vegetable dishes.

Garden Centre Café Southern end of St 57 ⓣ023/363002. Moderately priced food from the MSG-free menu includes homemade bread, granola breakfasts, burgers, and baked goods; on weekends, the special features a generous helping of a roast and a veggie option, plus choice of salads. Tues–Sun 7am–10pm.

Gold Fish River Sisowath Quay, at the junction with St 106. In a lovely location out over the Tonle Sap, with a menu of Khmer food that's consistently good. Curried frog and stir-fried squid are just two tasty options, and they can rustle up French fries, too.

Happy Herbs Bistro 345 Sisowath Quay. Cheap pizza and pasta. A large "Special" pizza will get you nicely full or have it to share between two.

Lazy Gecko 23 St 93, near Boeng Kak. This friendly place is an inexpensive travellers' eatery featuring all the old favourites, from banana pancakes to French fries, plus some Khmer dishes.

Lucky Burger 160 Sihanouk Blvd. Phnom Penh's attempt at American burgers and fries.

Lumbini 51 St 214, near the intersection with St 63. Good ambience and friendly service at this North Indian place. Besides curries, the extensive menu includes a selection of tandoori dishes, bhajis and vegetarian options. Moderately priced and definitely worth a visit.

Mamak's Corner 18 St 114. Nasi goreng, roti pratha, satay and other Malaysian delights for $2 a plate, tasting as good as anything you'd buy at a KL street stall.

Nouveau Pho de Paris 258 Monivong Blvd. Busy Chinese, Cambodian and Vietnamese restaurant, with plenty of vegetarian options and a picture menu to help you choose. Huge steaming bowls of *pho* are popular and the crispy fried duck mouth-watering.

Peking St 136. Modest, inexpensive Chinese restaurant, with welcoming staff and divine food; hard to beat for price and quality are the beef with green peppers and steamed spring rolls, all washed down with glasses of iced tea.

Ponlok 319 Sisowath Quay. Illustrated menus in English and French make ordering good Khmer food here easy. Attentive service and a busy, breezy balcony.

Riverside 273 Sisowath Quay. Pavement terrace partially shielded from the passing shoe-shine boys by a jungle of potted plants. Reasonably priced European, Khmer and Russian dishes, plus Cuban cigars and a pool table.

Royal India 15b St 107, just south of *Capitol Guesthouse*. The most consistently good Indian food in town, all at economical prices and served with a smile at this simple restaurant. The menu is comprehensive and halal, including chicken and mutton curries which come with rice or nan bread. Freshly made vegetarian samosas, and tasty sweet lassis.

Sam Doo 56–58 Kampuchea Krom Blvd. The basic surroundings belie the delicious fare: juicy Sichuan prawns come with a spicy dressing and dim sum, for which *Sam Doo* is especially reputed.

Entertainment and nightlife

Unfortunately, cultural events in Phnom Penh are few and far between. The ancient tradition of Cambodian **classical dance**, which originated in the twelfth century, was all but wiped out in the 1970s. It is slowly beginning to resurface, but lack of funding means that performances at the Chaktomuk Theatre on Sisowath Quay are infrequent – check the listings in the Friday edition of the *Cambodia Daily*. The theatre is also the venue for occasional Khmer **plays** and **musical shows**. If you're in Phnom Penh during one of the big festivals, there may be a live free Khmer **pop music** concert at the podium south of the Liberation Monument.

A popular Phnom Penh Sunday-afternoon outing used to be a trip to the **kick-boxing**, but now the stadium has been closed there's no set venue. If you want to watch a bout, and it's sometimes as much fun to watch the crowd as the competitors, ask at your guesthouse for details. Otherwise, do as many Cambodians do and watch it on TV.

Your chance to watch **films** in Phnom Penh is pretty limited, with just a few options: the French Cultural Centre (St 184, just east of Monivong; free) screens French films with English subtitles: check local listings for details. *Nexus*, on Sihanouk Boulevard, just east of the Independence Monument, screens the latest blockbuster on Sunday evenings (showings at 6pm & 8pm). Otherwise, select your own laser-disc movie at Movie Street Video Centre, 116 Sihanouk Blvd, and watch it in their comfortable screening rooms ($5 per person).

For most Khmers, **nightlife** centres around an early evening meal out, followed by a tuneful burst of karaoke. The southern end of Monivong Boulevard has a particular concentration of the larger, glitzy joints, but karaoke can be found all over town: just follow your ears. Western nightlife tastes are more than catered for, and an oversupply of bars and clubs means that many are less than full, especially during the low season. However, you'll always find a crowd in established favourites such as the *FCC*, *Heart of Darkness*, *Sharky* and *Martini*.

Bars and clubs

Cantina Sisowath Quay. Operated by long-time Phnom Penh icon Hurley Scroggins, this no-frills place on the riverfront is distinctive from its immediate neighbours due to its cheerful staff. The sidewalk seating here feels like a party on Friday and Saturday evenings.

Foreign Correspondants' Club (FCC) Sisowath Quay ⓣ023/210142. No, it's not really a foreign correspondents' club, but a Southeast Asian version of Bogart's bar in the film *Casablanca*. The balmy air, whirring ceiling fans and spacious armchairs invite one to spend a hot afternoon getting slowly, purposefully smashed. Prices are relatively high but worth it.

Heart of Darkness 26 St 51. Overrated, but it's been here for ages and is one of those places everybody has to visit once. Buy a T-shirt, but wait until you get home to wear it. Nightly from 7pm.

Howie's 32 St 51. Located near the *Heart of Darkness*, *Howie's* is the place to go after the former invariably disappoints. It's worth arriving early to stake out a table on the sidewalk outside.

Martini 402 Mao Tse Toung Blvd. Western-style disco and girly bar, with movies on the big screen, inexpensive food on the menu and plenty of company available. 7pm–5am.

Pink Elephant 343 Sisowath Quay. Relaxed, backpacker-oriented bar on the river, with cheap drinks, free pool and board games. Popular after a *Happy Herbs* pizza next door. 9am–late.

Sharky's Bar 126 St 130. Busy nightspot, with large bar and balcony and plenty of "taxi girls". Happy-hour deals (5–7pm), pool tables and sports TV. Open until 2am.

Walkabout Hotel Corner of 51 & 174 sts. A 24hr bar with pool table, restaurant and sports TV. Popular with ageing long-termers, probably because of its proximity to nearby bordellos.

Markets

Phnom Penh may not be world-renowned as a shopping destination, but there are certainly bargains to be had. A trip to one of the capital's numerous **markets** is essential, if only to buy the red-checked *krama* (traditional chequered Khmer scarf), popular with Khmers and visitors alike. The markets all open early and are liveliest in the morning; many vendors have a snooze at midday for a couple of hours and things wind down by 5pm.

Although the drugs, guns and ammunition are no longer available, a stroll around the **Russian Market** (Psar Toul Tom Poung) remains a colourful experience. Situated in the southern end of town at the junction of 163 and 440 streets, it's a good balance of tourist-oriented curios and stalls for locals. Jewellery, gems, CDs, food stalls, souvenirs, furniture and motorbike parts are all grouped in their own sections. Don't expect an easy bargain – you'll have to work hard to pay the locals' price.

Vendors at **Psar Thmei** are also wise to the limitless funds that all *barangs* (Westerners) apparently possess, and will price their wares accordingly. Electronic goods, T-shirts, shoes and wigs are all in abundance here. Confusingly, it's usually known as the central market (its name in Khmer means "new market"), but generally even if you just ask for "psar" most moto drivers will correctly assume you want this Art Deco market at the eastern end of Kampuchea Krom.

The other markets around town are less tourist-friendly, but are good places to pick up cheap toiletries, clothes and food. For convenience of location, you might try Psar Damkor, Psar Chas, near the Tonle Sap boat terminals, or Psar Orussey, 1km west of the National Museum (see map on pp.124–125).

Listings

Airlines Bangkok Airways, 61 Street 214 ⓣ023/426624; China Southern Airlines, A3 Regency Square, 168 Monireth Blvd ⓣ023/424588, ⓕ424082; Dragon Air, A4–A5 Regency Square, 168 Monireth Blvd ⓣ023/424300, ⓕ217652; Lao Airlines, 58C Sihanouk Blvd ⓣ&ⓕ023/216563; Malaysia Airlines, 1st Floor, *Diamond Hotel*, 172–184 Monivong Blvd ⓣ023/218923,

Ⓕ426665; President Airlines, 50 Norodom Blvd Ⓣ023/993089, Ⓕ212992; Royal Phnom Penh Airways, 209 Street 19 Ⓣ023/217419; Siem Reap Airways, 61 Street 214 Ⓣ023/720022; Silk Air, 219B Monivong Blvd, inside *Mi Casa Hotel* Ⓣ023/426808; Thai Airways, A15–A16 Regency Square, Mao Tse Toung Blvd Ⓣ023/214359-61; Vietnam Airlines, 41 Street 214, Ⓣ023/363396.

Banks and exchange Travellers' cheques can be cashed at virtually any bank around town for a commission of two percent. For credit-card cash advances, either the Cambodian Commercial Bank (just up 120 St from the transport stop) or the Foreign Trade Bank of Cambodia can assist. Most banks are open Mon–Fri 8.30am–3.30pm, and a few are open until 11.30am on Saturday. The best rates for changing dollars into riel can be found at the moneychangers in and around Psar Thmei. Western Union Money transfer is available at the Acleda Bank, 28 Mao Tse Toung Blvd; Cambodian Commercial Bank, 26 Monivong Blvd; Canadia Bank, 265–269 Ang Duong St; Foreign Trade Bank of Cambodia, 3 Kramoun Sar St; Singapore Bank, Street 214.

Bicycle rental *Capitol Guesthouse* (see p.126); $1 per day.

Bookshops The *FCC* stocks a wide range of English and French books, including novels, as well as books on Cambodia and Angkor. Monument Books (111 Norodom Blvd; Ⓣ023/217617) has a large collection of new books. Secondhand books are sold at The London Book Centre (51 St 240; Ⓣ023/214258), which has over 5000 titles in English, French and German.

Dentists International SOS Dental Clinic, 161 Street 51 (Ⓣ023/216911) has English-speaking staff.

Embassies and consulates Australia, 11 Street 254 Ⓣ023/213470, Ⓕ213413; Canada,11 Street 254 Ⓣ023/213470, Ⓕ211389; Laos, 15–17 Mao Tse Toung Blvd Ⓣ023/982632, Ⓕ720907; Thailand, 196 Norodom Blvd Ⓣ023/726306; UK, 29 Street 75 Ⓣ023/427124, Ⓕ427124; USA, 27 Street 240 Ⓣ023/216436, Ⓕ216437; Vietnam, 426 Monivong Blvd Ⓣ023/362531, Ⓕ427385.

Hospitals and clinics For any travel-related illness, tests or vaccinations, head for AEA International SOS Clinic at 161 St 51 (Ⓣ023/216911) or the Tropical & Travellers' Medical Clinic, 88 St 108 (Ⓣ023/366802). The Naga Medical Centre at 108 Sothearos Blvd (Ⓣ011/811175) also has English- and French-speaking doctors. The main hospital is Calmette Hospital, 3 Monivong Blvd (Ⓣ023/426948).

Immigration department For visa extensions, it's easier to go to one of the travel agents in town or to your guesthouse – they'll charge a couple of dollars. The Department of Immigration (Ⓣ012/581558) is now well out of town on Pochentong Rd opposite the airport, although you'll need to go there for other immigration queries. The office is open Mon–Fri 8–10.30am & 2.30–4.30pm.

Internet access Prices for Internet access have dropped dramatically and you can get deals below $2 per hour; there are outlets all over town and you're seldom far away from one.

Motorbike rental Lucky! Lucky!, 413 Monivong Blvd (Ⓣ023/212788), charges $5 per day for a 110cc moped, $9 per day for a 250cc off-road bike, with discounts on rentals of a week or longer. Helmets are provided but no insurance. It's worth paying the 500r to park in the many moto compounds around the city – thieves are rather partial to unattended Hondas.

Newspapers and magazines The best selection of international newspapers and magazines can be found at the *FCC* or *Le Royal*.

Pharmacies Drug stores are literally everywhere. Trained English-speaking pharmacists are available at Pharmacie de la Gare, cnr of Monivong and Pochentong boulevards (daily 8.30am–6pm). It's arguably the best in Cambodia, stocking a good selection of Western pharmaceuticals. Credit cards are accepted.

Post office The main post office is east of Wat Phnom, on St 13 between sts 98 and 102 (daily 6.30am–9pm. Poste restante pick-up is at the far left-hand counter (300r per item).

Sports The *Inter-Continental*, *Cambodiana*, and *Goldiana* hotels have pools that non-guests can use for around $5 per visit. The Phnom Penh Water Park on the Airport road has water slides and swimming pools.

Supermarkets Bayon Supermarket, 135 Monivong Blvd (7am–8pm); Lucky Supermarket, 160 Sihanouk Blvd (8am–9pm); Pencil Supermarket, 15 St 214 (7am–9pm); Big A on Monivong between 178 & 184 sts (8am–9pm). There are also minimarts, which stock a remarkable variety of imported goods, attached to some petrol filling stations of Caltex Star Mart and Total La Boutique.

Taxis Baileys Taxi Service (Ⓣ012/890000) offers a 24hr taxi service with experienced, reliable English-speaking drivers.

Telephone services International phone and fax services are available at the main post office or any sizeable hotel. Public phones can only be used with a pre-paid phonecard, available at shops everywhere. Some Internet cafes offer cheap long-distance connections via the Internet.

Tourist police Ⓣ023/724793 or 012/942484.

Travel agencies The following established firms

employ English-speaking staff and act both as travel agents and domestic tour operators. Diethelm Travel, 65 Street 240 ⓣ023/219151, ⓕ023/219150, ⓔdtc@dtc.com.kh; Exotissimo Travel Cambodia Ltd, above Monument Books at 46 Norodom Blvd ⓣ023/218948, ⓕ023/426586, ⓦwww.exotissimo.com; KU Travel & Tours, cnr of streets 240 and 19 ⓣ023/723456, ⓕ023/427425, ⓔinfo@kucambodia.com.

Around Phnom Penh

Escaping into Phnom Penh's surrounding **countryside** for some peace and fresh air is very easy – it doesn't take long to get out past the shanty-town suburbs, and the majority of roads that extend from the capital are in fairly good condition, making the excursions listed here an easy day- or even half-day trip.

Choeung Ek (The Killing Fields)

A visit to **CHOEUNG EK** (daily 7am–5pm; $2), 15km southwest of Phnom Penh, signposted from Monireth Boulevard, is a sobering experience. It was here in 1980 that the bodies of 8985 people, victims of Pol Pot and his Khmer Rouge comrades, were exhumed from 86 mass graves. A further 43 graves have been left untouched. Many of those buried here had suffered prolonged torture at S21 prison in Phnom Penh, before being led to their deaths at Choeung Ek. Men, women and children were beaten to death, shot, beheaded, or tied up and buried alive.

The site is dominated by a tall, white, hollow stupa that commemorates all those who died from 1975 to 1979, displaying thousands of unearthed skulls, demographically arranged on glass shelves. A pile of the victims' ragged clothing lies scattered underneath. A pavilion has a small display of the excavation of the burial pits and a hand-written sign nearby (in Khmer and English) outlines the Khmer Rouge atrocities, a period described as "a desert of great destruction which overturned Kampuchean society and drove it back to the stone age". Although Choeung Ek is by far the most notorious of the killing fields, scores of similar plots can be found all over Cambodia, many with no more than a pile of skulls and bones as a memorial. **Transport** to Choeung Ek can be arranged at *Capitol Guesthouse* (see p.126), or take a moto for $5 return.

Royal Tombs of Oudong

The ancient capital of **OUDONG**, 40km to the northwest of Phnom Penh, served for over two hundred years as the seat of power for successive Cambodian kings until, in 1866, it was sacked by King Norodom, who transferred his court to Phnom Penh. Nowadays, visitors come to see the hill of Phnom Oudong, dotted with stupas harbouring the ashes and spirits of bygone royalty along its east–west ridge. A long line of food and drink stalls marks your arrival. Continue to the end of the road, where a staircase will lead you up to the larger of two ridges. You can then descend via the staircase at the eastern end of the ridge to complete the circuit.

At the top of the staircase at the western edge of the hill, sits what's left of Vihear Preah Atharas, also known as **Wat Preah Thom**, built by the Chinese in around the thirteenth century to house a giant stone Buddha. The buildings and Buddha were badly damaged by the Khmer Rouge in the 1970s. Continuing eastwards along the ridge, you come to a series of viharas containing statues of the sacred bull Preah Ko, his younger brother Preah Keo, a naga-guarded Preah Prak Neak and the strong and powerful Preah Boun Dai. The **royal stupas** themselves are higher on the ridge to the northeast. The first you'll see is the decorative, yellow stupa that houses the ashes of King Sisowath Monivong, who died in 1941. Elephants, garudas and lotus-flower motifs make this the most interesting of the stupas. The adjacent Tray Troeng chedi, said to house the ashes of King Ang Duong and his wife, is weather-beaten and neglected, but bright-painted tiles can still be seen. The third stupa, Damrei Sam Poan, now rather overgrown, was built by King Chey Chetar II for the former King Soriyopor. At the end of the ridge, a further stupa is just being completed, designed to house Buddha relics currently contained in Preah Sack Kyack Moni chedi, outside Phnom Penh train station.

From the Royal Stupas, the eastern staircase descends to a small, dusty monument in memory of those killed at a nearby **Khmer Rouge detention centre**. Bones and skulls of the victims were exhumed from mass graves in the early 1980s, and are displayed here.

To get to Oudong by rented Honda or bicycle, follow Route 5 northwards from Phnom Penh for about 37km, turn left at a large Angkor Beer-sponsored picture of Oudong and follow the road for a few kilometres to the western staircase. Guesthouses and hotels in Phnom Penh organize tours for $5. A taxi here and back costs $20, a moto around $10.

Tonle Bati

If, for some reason, you can't make it to Angkor, you might consider a trip to **TONLE BATI** (daily 8am–4pm; $2), some 40km south of Phnom Penh and the nearest Angkorian site to the capital. The site consists of two temples located near Tonle Bati's lake, Ta Prohm and Yeah Peau. The temples are small by ancient Cambodian temple standards, but impressive nonetheless. Many legends surround their construction, but it is thought King Ta Prohm had them built in the twelfth century. **Ta Prohm** is set in a garden of palms and tamarind trees. Approaching from the eastern entrance, don't miss the carved stones either side of the path, one depicting The Churning of The Ocean of Milk, the other an episode from the Ramayana. Inside, there is only one intact Buddha image, the Khmer Rouge having destroyed most of the other artefacts. You'll need to take a torch to examine the bas-reliefs in the smoky darkness, and to find the upright lingam phallic symbol in the central chamber. In the southern chamber, a headless Vishnu statue presides over a local fortune-teller who will tell you what you want to hear for a few thousand riel.

The smaller temple of **Yeah Peau** is to the north of Ta Prohm, dwarfed by the new, colourful buildings of Wat Tonle Bati. Inside, a headless Madame Peau (Ta Prohm's mother) stands next to a seated Buddha. The **lakeside** to the northwest of the temples is a popular spot for lunch and a swim. You can rent a platform (*p'deh tdeuk*) for the whole day for 3000r (or 2000r just for lunchtime), and inflatable tyres are available for splashing around in the lake for 500r each. There's a restaurant and food stalls nearby.

To get to Tonle Bati by **moto** ($10) take the smooth National Route 2, and after about 32km turn right onto a bumpy track, then right again for the temples. A **taxi** for the day will cost about $25. **Buses** from Psar Thmei cost 2500r each way, and *Capitol Guesthouse* (see p.126) organizes a day tour for $5. It's quite feasible to combine the trip with a visit to Phnom Chisor, further south on Route 2.

Phnom Chisor

Originally known as Suryaparvata in honour of the monarch Suryavarman I, the eleventh-century temple of **Phnom Chisor**, around 17km south of Tonle Bati just off National Route 2, looks east from its hilltop vantage point, across the green palm and paddy plains of Takeo province. There are two routes to the top of the hill, both of which are best climbed in the cooler early-morning temperatures. The track that skirts around the hill is an easier climb and gets you to the top in about twenty minutes.

The modern pagodas and shrines that surround Phnom Chisor are of little interest, so make straight for the main courtyard of the ancient temple. Eight edifices surround the main sanctuary tower dedicated to Shiva. Although the buildings were badly damaged by American bombing raids in the 1970s, you can still see some of the sculptural reliefs. The most impressive of these is to be found in the former library, where there is a pediment carved with a dancing Shiva figure set above a lintel, showing Indra riding a three-headed elephant. Looking down from the eastern edge of the complex, you'll see a long causeway, interrupted by temple ruins, stretching to the lake of Tonle Om, the former gateway to Phnom Chisor.

The site lies off National Route 2 – a few kilometres along a dirt track that bears left at Prasat Neang Khmau. You can **hire a moto** for around $10 in Phnom Penh, or a **taxi** for about $25 – a side-trip to Tonle Bati should be included in the price. *Capitol Guesthouse* (see p.126) runs a **tour** to both destinations for $8.

2.2

Central Cambodia

Central Cambodia is a forgotten territory stretching from north of Phnom Penh through sparsely populated countryside right up to the Thai border. The region is hardly a popular tourist destination: the most that visitors usually see of it is the rice paddies that stretch either side of National Route 6, the major trunk road between the capital and Siem Reap, which cuts across the southern part of the area. But for those prepared to venture into obscure backwaters, central Cambodia has a few ancient temple sites worth visiting. The starting point is invariably **Kompong Thom**, the only town of any size hereabouts, and thus your last taste of comforts or luxuries for a few days if you're planning an intrepid foray into the interior. Thankfully, it's no major expedition if you want to see **Sambor Prei Kuk**, where there are three groups of well-preserved brick-built temples.

Kompong Thom

KOMPONG THOM, just about midway between Phnom Penh and Siem Reap on National Route 6, is the starting place for a trip to the pre-Angkor temple ruins of **Sambor Prei Kuk**, 30km northeast. The town itself is little more than a busy transport stop, but it's incredibly friendly and has a good choice of decent accommodation and several respectable restaurants. The main features are a double-bridge – where the old one has been left alongside the new, over the Sen River – and gaudy Wat Kompong Thom, the local **pagoda** with massive leopard and rhino statues standing guard outside.

Practicalities

The **transport stop** is in the square behind the Department of Arts and Culture, east of the main road. Taxis from Phnom Penh (10,000r) arrive at the south side of the square, while transport from Siem Reap (12,000r) comes in at the north. You won't have to walk more than 500m from here to reach a hotel or guesthouse, but there are plenty of moto drivers around if you need one. The friendly **tourist office** is in the wooden building just off the southeast corner of the transport stop. The post office and **Camintel** office, for international calls, are in the same building next door to the seven-storey *Arunras Hotel* on the main road. The **hospital** is on Pracheathepatay, west of the *Arunras Hotel*. You can **change money** in the market, which is on the main road just south of the bridge, or at the Acleda Bank, about half a kilometre south of the market on the opposite side of the road. There is a shop with a single terminal available for **Internet access** (at $4 per hour) on the main road just north of the market.

The best **hotel** in town is the *Stung Sen Royal Garden* (☎062/961228; ❹), on the main road overlooking the river; comfy rooms all have TV, air-con and hot water. Just acoss the river, also on the main road, the friendly *Sambor Prey Kuh Hotel* (☎012/960300; ❷), boasts en-suite rooms with TV, and one of the best restaurants in town. The best budget accommodation is east of the transport stop on Pracheathepatay. The *Santepheap Guesthouse* (❶) is a traditional wooden house with a shady courtyard and simply furnished fan rooms, some with shared facilities. All Kompong Thom's restaurants serve Cambodian and Chinese fare. The **restaurant** in the *Arunras Hotel* is one of the most popular, with some great soups and stir-fries, but can occasionally get rowdy. Its sister restaurant next door is the best place in town for breakfast, serving up excellent rice and noodle soups. Just south of the *Stung Sen Royal Garden Hotel*, the huge *Stung Sen Restaurant* dishes up succulent sweet-and-sour fish and generous portions of stir-fried pork with vegetables, but you can feel a bit lost here when it's quiet. Across the river, the restaurant at the *Sambor Prey Koh* can rustle up a delicious *sumlar mjew vietnam* (a fishless version for vegetarians can be prepared without fuss), though it's not on the menu. If you're pining for cookies or cakes, there's a small bakery on the main road just north of the market.

Inexpensive **food stalls** at the market open from early morning to mid-afternoon, and you can enjoy your fill of fruit shakes and desserts at the night market, which sets up outside the east entrance to the market from late afternoon. There is no nightlife to speak of in Kompong Thom, unless you enjoy listening to locals croaking through Cambodian tunes in seedy karaoke bars.

Sambor Prei Kuk

Sambor Prei Kuk is the site of a Chenla-era capital, the seventh-century Ishanapura, and once boasted hundreds of temples; built of brick, most have crumbled or been smothered by the encroaching forest, but three fine sets of towers have been cleared and are worth the excursion.

The site is about 15km east of **National Route 64** and is easily reached by moto ($5 round trip) from Kompong Thom; the road is good and the journey takes around an hour. You'll have to sign in at the entrance booth and pay a donation, though an official fee of $2 is likely to be introduced soon.

The site

The site is divided into the north (closest to the entrance booth), central (more recent than the other two, being ninth century) and south groups. If you've come with a driver, he may well know of temples that have recently been uncovered, as new sites are being cleared all the time. The north group is also called **Prasat Sambor Prei Kuk**. It's the reliefs of the central sanctuary tower that are the main feature here: they depict **flying palaces**, and are the home of the gods who look after the temples. In spite of their age, you can make out figures and the floors of the palace. Other things to look out for are the rather cute reliefs of winged horses and tiny human faces. The rubble piles around the site are ruins of the numerous other towers that once stood here.

Only the main sanctuary tower, **Prasat Tor**, still remains of the central group, and it's particularly photogenic with its sprouting vegetation and reproduction lions flanking the entrance steps. Carvings of intricate foliage patterns – for which Sambor Prei Kuk is highly regarded – are still visible on the south lintel.

The south group, also called **Prasat Neak Pean**, was the most important temple at Ishanapura. Inside the brick-walled enclosure, you'll be able to spot flying palaces on the octagonal towers and – in the building east of the central tower – large medallion-shaped reliefs.

2.3

Angkor

The world-renowned temples of **Angkor**, in northwest Cambodia, stand as an impressive monument to the greatest ancient civilization in Southeast Asia. Spiritually, politically and geographically, Angkor was at the heart of the great Khmer Empire. During the Angkorian period, the ruling god-kings (*devarajas*) built imposing temples as a way of asserting their divinity. As successive kings came and went, so new temples were built, and cities were created around them. What remains today are the stone-built monuments of that period – a legacy of more than one hundred temples built between the ninth and fifteenth centuries.

The nearest town to the temples is **Siem Reap**, which has established itself as the base from which to make your way round Angkor, a tradition begun by American Frank Vincent Jr, who borrowed three elephants from the governor of Siem Reap in 1872 to explore the ruins. These days, there are plenty of motos, tuk-tuks and taxis on hand for the journey.

Siem Reap

SIEM REAP is Cambodia's most touristy town, and has sacrificed some of its charm and authenticity as a result. However, Western luxuries are freely available, and there are plenty of English-speaking locals. **Arriving** in Siem Reap by share taxi or **pick-up**, you'll probably be dropped at the smart new market, Psar Leu, to the east of the city, a hectic, noisy transport hub. **Boats** cruise into the port, around 12km south of Siem Reap (the distance varies with the level of the lake) – the approach is a tranquil introduction to the area, passing hundreds of floating houses, children splashing about in the water, and families going about their daily chores. At the port, guesthouse reps will be keen to offer a free ride into town, so it's a good idea to decide beforehand where you want to stay; otherwise, there are motos ($2) and taxis ($5). Guesthouse touts also meet the planes at the **airport**, 8km west of town; or you can take a registered taxi from the booth in the airport ($5).

There is a **tourist information office** (daily 7–9.30am & 2.30–4pm; ⓣ063/964347), opposite the *Grand Hôtel d'Angkor*, on Tosamut Boulevard, but you'll find they're only interested in selling you a tour. You'll do better to check out the couple of free town guides: *Siem Reap Visitors Guide* can be found at shops, bars and guesthouses. **Transport** around town is limited to motos ($1) or to a motorbike-drawn carriage, which the locals call a tuk-tuk ($1-2).

Accommodation

Guesthouse **accommodation** is largely concentrated in three areas: just east of the river, off National Route 6 (also known as Airport Road); on the sidestreets west of Sivatha Street; and around the junction of National Route Route 6 and Sivatha Street. Most accommodation in these areas is aimed at budget travellers. There's not much to choose between these places, though an increasing number of guesthouses are adding newer annexes with mid-range facilities. Mid-range establishments with TV, air-con and en-suite facilities charge $15–20 and are concentrated on Sivatha

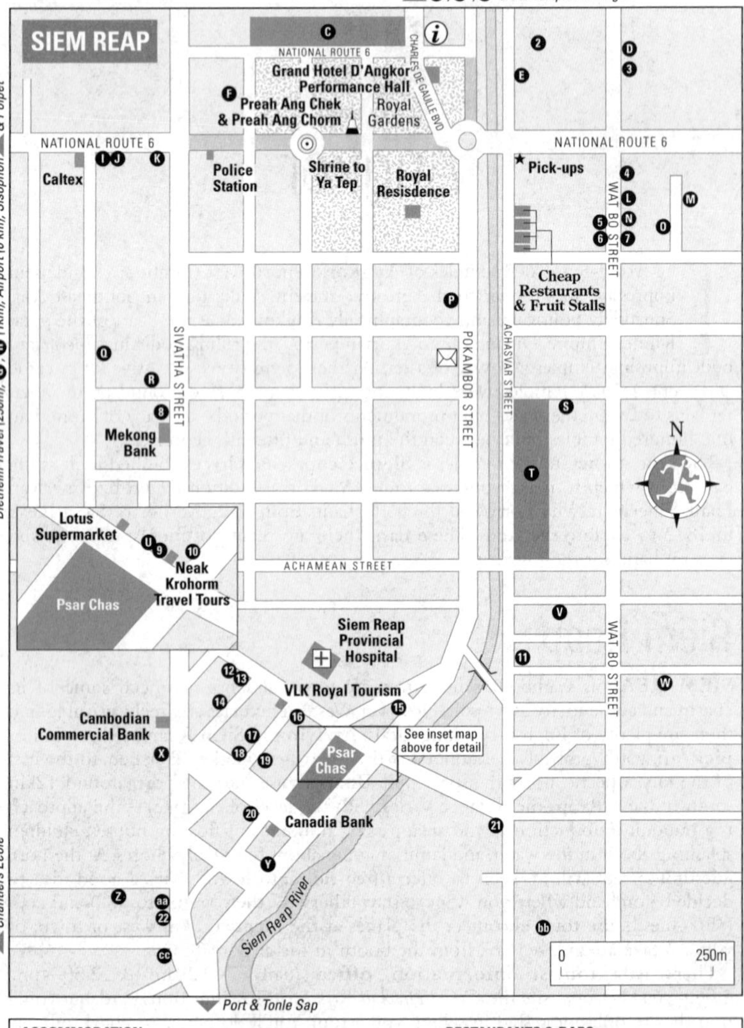

ACCOMMODATION			
Angkor Village	W	Mahogany	N
Angkor Wat	Q	Mandalay Inn	aa
Big Lyna Villa	V	Mom's	L
Chao Say	U	Pansea La Residence d'Angkor	T
Chenla	I	Ponloue Angkor Siem Reap	cc
Dead Fish Tower	X	Red Piano	Z
Earthwalkers	H	Secrets of Elephants	G
European	M	Sofitel Royal Angkor	A
FCC Angkor Suites	P	Sovan Angkor	K
Golden Banana	bb	Sweet Dreams	O
Grand Hotel d'Angkor	C	Ta Phrom	Y
Green Garden Home	R	Takeo	J
Green Park	S	Victoria Angkor Wat	F
La Noria	E	Yaklom Angkor Lodge	D
La Villa Loti	B		

RESTAURANTS & BARS			
Angkor What?	19	Ivy	20
Arun	2	Kampucino Pizza	10
Bayon	4	Khmer Kitchen	14
Blue Pumpkin	13	Martini Dancing	21
Café Indochine	8	Moloppor	11
Chao Praya	1	New Delhi	12
Chivit Thai	5	Only One	9
Continental Café	15	Red Piano	18
Dead Fish Tower	X	Sawasdee Food Garden	3
Elephant Bar	C	Soup Dragon	16
FCC	P	Temple Bar	17
Forest Hut	6	Zanzibar	22
Hawaii Pizza	7		

Moving on from Siem Reap

By plane

Besides **flights** to Phnom Penh, there are an increasing number of international departures to Bangkok, HCMC and Vientiane, and further afield to Kuala Lumpur, Singapore and Hong Kong. You can buy plane tickets from the airline offices or from travel agents in town. If you're staying at a hotel, they'll generally drive you to the airport free of charge. The domestic departure tax is $6; the international departure tax is $25. If you overstay your visa, you'll be charged $5 per day.

By bus

No public **buses** run out of Siem Reap, though guesthouses in town operate their own small coaches to Phnom Penh ($9) and, via Poipet – where they link up with onward transport operated by their Thai associate – to Bangkok ($12–15). Travel agents in Siem Reap (see p.146) can also get you tickets for private buses bound for Phnom Penh and Bangkok. For the latter destination in particular, it pays to shop around as competition can lead to the fare halving at times. Note that on the Bangkok route, the buses tend to arrive at Poipet at around 1pm, convenient if you're hooking up with onward road transport, but leaving little time to catch the train from Aranyaprathet; to do the latter, you'd be advised to get an early ride on shared transport out to the Thai border.

By boat

Boats leave from the port daily at 7am for Phnom Penh ($25) and for Battambang ($12). When the water level is really low (Feb–May) the express boats for Phnom Penh moor some way out, and you'll be taken out to them on smaller craft; Battambang boats are scarcely larger than speedboats and so are usually able to get into port. You'll need to **book your ticket at least a day ahead** – two days ahead between March and November when often just one boat runs on each route. If you get your ticket at a travel agent or from the boat company offices (they have several premises around the centre, each displaying a large sign of a boat), you'll need to find your own transport to the port ($2 by moto; allow at least 30min on the truly dreadful road), but if you buy from a guesthouse or hotel, a minibus will collect you, which may mean setting out as early as 5.30am, as the vehicle will pick up passengers from various locations before heading down to the port.

Street. The town now has a number of international-standard hotels, but for colonial charm the *Grand Hotel d'Angkor* is still tops.

The Old City

Chao Say Psar Chas ☎063/964032. Immaculate, good-value rooms, including en-suite bathrooms, cable TV and optional a/c. ❸

FCC Angkor Suites Pokambor Street ☎063/760280. A branch of the famous *Foreign Correspondents Club* (*FCC*) in Phnom Penh, the rooms (as well as adjacent restaurant) are more modern but just as stylish as the original. The picturesque riverfront location and easy access to the restaurant and adjoining galleries make it a great place to come back to after touring the temples. ❻

Grand Hotel d'Angkor Opposite tourist information, 1 Charles de Gaulle Blvd ☎063/963888. Colonial splendour fit for upmarket tourists and visiting dignitaries. Superior international-standard accommodation; facilities include spa, swimming pool and tennis court. ❾

La Villa Loti North of Old City near the Angkor Conservatory ☎063/964242. Just north of the town centre, this traditional Khmer wooden house has been nicely furnished and is surrounded by trees. Rooms have en-suite baths, a/c or fan. Bicycles are provided to guests free of charge. ❹

Sofitel Royal Angkor Angkor Wat Rd, 1500m north of the Royal Gardens ☎063/964600. Modern, low-rise affair with Art Deco touches. The rooms, set in blocks around the colourful gardens, feel like home from home with their own lounges and satellite TV. A swimming pool, fitness centre, shop and a range of restaurants and bars complete the picture. ❾

Ta Phrom South of the Psar Chas ☎063/380117. Very nice rooms with all the usual refinements of a top-end hotel. Favoured by tour groups. Breakfast included. ❽
Victoria Angkor Wat Western edge of the Royal Gardens, ☎063/760428. A newly built five-star hotel with all the mod cons; restaurants, boutique, spa, etc. Though for these prices, why not stay at the *Grand Hotel d'Angkor* and absorb some real history? ❾

East of the River

Angkor Village One block east of Wat Bo St. ☎063/963563. Luxurious wooden bungalow-style eco-accommodation in a jungle setting. Includes telephone, a/c, en-suite bathroom and fridge. $75 per bungalow. ❽
Big Lyna Villa 659 Wat Bo Village, off Achasvar St ☎0063/964807. The most delightful rooms in this old wooden house are the large wood-panelled affairs upstairs, though their attached bathrooms don't have hot water, which you can only get if you stay in the less atmospheric downstairs rooms. Big balcony and a garden for lazing about. ❹
European Near junction of National Route 6 and Wat Bo St ☎012/582237. Large and extremely clean rooms at this new guesthouse, tucked away in a quiet street. Good-value evening set-menu available. ❶
Golden Banana East of Psar Chas ☎012/888366. A five-minute walk over the bridge next to the Psar Chas ("Old Market") leads to this gay-friendly place in a quiet neighbourhood. Bungalows in a pleasant garden feature a/c and TV. Breakfast is included. ❸
Green Park 182 Wat Bo Village, between Wat Bo and Achasvar sts ☎063/380352 or 012/890358. Range of rooms from basic with shared facilities to well-appointed ones with en-suite bathrooms and a/c. Also features a restaurant, a booking service for transport tickets, plus a communal TV. ❶
La Noria East bank of the river, north of National Route 6 ☎063/964242. Mid-range, villa-style accommodation frequented mainly by French guests. All rooms are en suite, with either fan or a/c. ❻
Mahogany Wat Bo Street ☎063/963417. The hospitable "Mr. Prune" is still running his guesthouse, one of the first in Siem Reap to open in the early 1990s. It hasn't changed much since then, offering basic rooms in a traditional wooden building. Though it may not be as flashy as the newer establishments, the friendly atmosphere is hard to beat. ❷
Mom's Wat Bo Street ☎063/964037. An old favourite, especially popular with French visitors. Basic rooms in the characterful old wooden house are reasonable, but the new building with en-suite rooms for $20–40 is overpriced. ❷–❻
Pansea La Residence d'Angkor Achasvar St ☎063/963390. Top-shelf establishment, part of a chain specializing in sympathetically designed accommodation in heritage sites worldwide. Luxuriously appointed rooms with teak furniture, Khmer cotton and silk furnishings, and bamboo screens to mask the enormous baths. Unsurprisingly, there's an à la carte restaurant, bar and souvenir shop, and swimming pool fed with water bubbling from a lion and a linga. ❾
Sweet Dreams Off Wat Bo St ☎063/963245. Smart modern guesthouse; rooms feature attached bathrooms and some have a/c, and there's also a small restaurant dishing up reasonably priced Khmer food. ❷
Yaklom Angkor Lodge 100m north of National Route 6 ☎012/983510. Spacious accommodation in a cottage around the restaurant's gardens; all rooms feature en-suite bathrooms, TV and a/c. The decor makes tasteful use of chunchiet fabrics, water gourds and khapas. ❺

West of Sivath Street

Angkor Wat South off Airport Rd ☎063/963531 or 012/630329. Modern family-run guesthouse with spacious rooms, some en suite, and a small restaurant serving Khmer/Chinese food and Western breakfasts. ❷
Chenla Junction of National Route 6 and Sivatha St ☎063/963233. A popular guesthouse, recently extended with a brand-new building, including deluxe rooms with all facilities. Older rooms ❶, deluxe ❺
Dead Fish Tower Sivatha Street ☎063/963060. Lower mid-range place with comfortable rooms and an excellent restaurant and bar attached. A fun place for families with kids. ❸
Earthwalkers Down a side road south off Airport Rd ☎012/967901. Scandinavian managed, this newly built guesthouse gets good reviews for being well run and friendly. Breakfast is included in the rates. ❷
Green Garden Home Just off Sivatha St ☎012/890363. Friendly guesthouse with a variety of ample-sized rooms, run by a budding photographer. Pleasant terrace area. ❸
Mandalay Inn Southwest of Psar Chas ☎063/963960. A good value mid-range place, rooms feature a/c, hot water, TV and fridge. If you're tiring of Cambodian cuisine, the restaurant here also does up a number of Burmese dishes. ❸
Ponloue Angkor Siem Reap 3 Sivatha St ☎063/963371. A friendly, modern hotel exuding

an air of calm; rooms are well appointed and feature TV, fridge, a/c and en-suite facilities with hot showers. ❹

Red Piano Southwest of Psar Chas ☎063/963240. Under the same management and around the corner from the restaurant of the same name, this newly opened guesthouse is tastefully decorated and comfortable. ❹

Secrets of Elephants Airport Rd ☎063/964328. Elegantly furnished rooms in a traditional wooden house each have a unique theme, based on a different Southeast Asian country. Set in lush gardens, it's a terrific place to unwind. ❻

Sovan Angkor Near the Airport Rd/Sivatha St intersection ☎063/964039. Hotel rooms at guesthouse prices; though far from lavish, rooms at this friendly place have hot showers, TV, fridge and a/c. ❹

Takeo Junction of Sivatha St and National Route 6 ☎063/922674. Small, cheap hole-in-the-wall guesthouse, popular with Japanese tourists. One-dollar dinners are a bargain. ❶

Eating

Siem Reap boasts a huge selection of **restaurants** catering to tourist tastes, but if you want to try something more authentic, head for the markets and the cheap fruit stalls on the eastern side of the river, near National Route 6. In the evenings, more impromptu stalls set up all over town, with the culinary epicentre being the market. Out at the temples, you're never far from food, and although the choice is a bit limited the prices are only marginally dearer than in town. Restaurants in Siem Reap tend to open for breakfast and stay open until around 11pm.

Arun East bank of the river, just north of National Route 6. Excellent food, huge portions and great service; also a handy spot to listen to Khmer music wafting across the river from the nightly traditional dancing at the nearby *Grand Hotel d'Angkor. Amok*, their Cambodian coconut and fish curry – served in a coconut – is so delicious it'll have you coming back for more.

Bayon One block east of the river, south of National Route 6 ☎012/855219. It's a good idea to book a table during peak season at this popular, atmospheric garden restaurant. Good-value Khmer and Western dishes are priced around $3, and there's an extensive wine list.

Café Indochine Sivatha St. This French-run restaurant in a traditional wooden house has some excellent Khmer dishes on offer. Ask about the daily specials.

Chao Praya Angkor Wat Rd ☎063/964666. You can eat your fill at their buffet lunches and dinners, featuring hot and cold Thai, Japanese and Chinese dishes. Booking is recommended for the evening, when they stage open-air cultural performances.

Chivit Thai Opposite *Bayon*. More than just the usual Thai and Khmer menu at a reasonable $2–4. Relaxed veranda and Thai-style seating.

Continental Café Pokambor St, just north of Psar Chas. Sophisticated European chic at sophisticated European prices. Good selection of Western meals and drinks. Happy hour 5–8pm includes Tiger draught for $1.

FCC Pokambor Street ☎063/760280. Many of your favourite dishes on the menu at the *Foreign Correspondents Club* (*FCC*) in Phnom Penh can be had here, too. Relaxed seating will ensure that you linger long after your meal is finished.

Forest Hut Wat Bo St, 50m south of National Route 6. Both Khmer and western food are on offer here, but the Khmer food stands out. Be sure to have a look at the special of the day before ordering.

Hawaii Pizza Wat Bo St. Fantastic food at a good price; Cambodian food, Italian and salads are all on the menu, plus great sandwiches. Turns into a popular bar in the late evening.

Kampucino Pizza By Psar Chas. The riverside location sells this newly expanded place, which is more a restaurant than a pizza parlour despite its name. They do brunch breakfasts until 11am, following which the menu switches to a wide range of pastas, grills and salads.

Khmer Kitchen Off Hospital Rd. Family-run restaurant formerly a cluster of tables in an alley, their popular food has allowed them to move into the ground floor of a nearby shop-house. The move has not affected the winning recipes – they still do up great Khmer home cooking with the odd modern twist.

Moloppor Achesvar St. Every dish is a dollar at this hugely popular Japanese-run eatery. Chinese stir-fry, dim sum and some delightful noodle dishes are just a few of the things on offer.

New Delhi Opposite Siem Reap Provincial Hospital. Vegetarian and non-veg Indian dishes in a converted shop-house. There is other Indian food to be had in Siem Reap, but this is the best of the lot.

Only One Psar Chas. This restaurant serving Western food used to be the only one in Siem Reap. Main courses cost $5–6.

Sawasdee Food Garden One block east of the river, north of National Route 6. Fantastic Thai food in a relaxed garden setting. Dishes around $1–4.
Soup Dragon Hospital Rd. Fantastic Vietnamese, Cambodian and Western food, including a good selection for veggies. Fish barbecue and salad is highly recommended. Moderately priced, friendly staff and nicely decorated.

Entertainment and nightlife

Siem Reap is a bustling place with **bars** targeted at foreigners opening up all over town, but especially around Psar Chas: you can easily while away a week or so visiting a different venue each evening. Plenty of the bars stay open until the last customer leaves. Siem Reap is also a good place to take in a cultural performance of **traditional dance** and **music** packaged with dinner by several of the hotels. The most popular is the nightly event staged by the *Grand Hotel d'Angkor*, incorporating dinner and a show for $22.

Angkor What? One block northwest of Psar Chas. Quiet, chilled-out bar, good for a relaxing drink. 2pm–late.
Blue Pumpkin Near the Siem Reap Provincial Hospital. Rattan furniture and plenty of potted plants cheer up this cocktail bar; beer and food available too.
Dead Fish Tower Sivatha St. Whacky decor featuring meandering stairways to multi-levels as well as a crocodile pit make this place a world-class challenge to navigate while drunk. Live music and excellent food will ensure that you come back a second time.
Elephant Bar At the *Grand Hotel d'Angkor*. Start your evening off in style in the luxurious cellar bar, with happy-hour cocktails (daily 4–8pm); a ready supply of free popcorn may mean you won't need dinner.
Ivy By Psar Chas. Very much an expat hangout, with free use of the pool table.
Martini Dancing Across the river from Psar Chas. The beer garden is the place to be seen for an evening drink, and to enjoy some live Khmer music. The disco is a bit racier than the others in town.
Red Piano Northwest of Psar Chas. Attractive bar-restaurant with quirky touches, such as massive tables and chairs that make you feel like Alice after she went through the looking glass. You can also sample a *Tomb Raider* cocktail or two.
Temple Bar Nourthwest of Psar Chas. This is one of Siem Reap's more popular watering holes, in part due to the $2 cocktails and $1 beers, with a DJ, and a sports bar upstairs. Stays open very late.
Zanzibar Sivatha St, near the night market. Small, popular expat bar with $1.50 beers and free pool table.

Listings

Airlines Bangkok Airways, 571 Airport Rd ⓣ063/380191–2, ⓕ380191; Lao Airlines, 114 Airport Rd ⓣ063/963283; President Airlines, 468 Airport Rd ⓣ063/964887; Siem Reap Airways, 571 Airport Rd ⓣ063/380191; Vietnam Airlines, 342 Airport Rd ⓣ063/964488.
Banks and exchange Acleda Bank, next to *Angkor Hotel*, Airport Rd; Cambodian Commercial Bank, Sivatha St; Canadia Bank, southwest of Psar Chas; UCB, west of Psar Chas; Mekong Bank, Sivatha St (with an exchange booth operating outside the bank Mon–Fri 6.30–8.30am & 4–6pm, Sat 6.30–8.30am); Krung Thai Bank, northern end of Sivatha St.
Hospital and clinics International SOS (c/o their Phnom Penh clinic on ⓣ023/216911) has a doctor on call in Siem Reap and can arrange emergency evacuations. The Naga Medical Centre, 593 Airport Rd (ⓣ016/964500) has English- and French-speaking staff. The government-run Siem Reap Provincial Hospital is 500m north of Psar Chas (ⓣ063/963111). The provincial hospital is very basic and really should be approached only as a last resort.
Internet access Expect to pay around $1-2/hr to get online at one of the many Internet cafés around town. Hotels generally charge their guests a bit more.
Post office At the post office, on Pokambor St (daily 7am–5.30pm), they sell stamps and offer facilities for poste restante and making domestic and international calls. Cheap international calls via the Internet can be made at many of Siem Reap's Internet cafés.
Supermarkets Stock up on bottles of spirits, Rizlas and a scattering of Western luxuries at Lotus Market, opposite Psar Chas.
Tourist police Junction of Sivatha St and National Route 6 ⓣ012/893297–8.
Travel agents Diethelm Travel 4 Airport Rd ⓣ063/963524; Neak Krorhorm Travel & Tours 3 Psar Chas ⓣ063/964924; VLK Royal Tourism, opposite the Siem Reap Provincial Hospital ⓣ063/760071.

The temples of Angkor

In 802, Jayavarman II united the warring Chenla factions and worked towards building a magnificent and prosperous kingdom. He declared himself universal god-king, and became the first of a succession of 39 kings to reign over the most powerful kingdom in Southeast Asia at that time. So the **Angkor era** was born, a period marked by imaginative building projects, the design and construction of inspirational **temples** and palaces, the creation of complex irrigation systems and the development of magnificent walled cities. However, as more resources were channelled into ever more ambitious construction projects, Angkor became a target for attack from neighbouring **Siam**. Successive invasions by the Siamese army culminated in the sacking of Angkor in the fifteenth century and the city was abandoned to the jungle. Although Khmers knew of the lost city, it wasn't until the West's "discovery" of Angkor in the nineteenth century that international interest was aroused. A French missionary, Father Bouillevaux, first reported on the "pagoda of Angcor and the ruins of Angcor-Thom", overgrown and camouflaged with jungle greenery. Soon after, in 1858, the famous botanist **Henri Mouhot** led a journey of exploration that began years of continuing archeological work to restore the temples.

More than one hundred Angkorian monuments are spread over some 3000 square kilometres. The best-known monuments are the vast Hindu temple of **Angkor Wat** and the walled city of **Angkor Thom**. Jungle-ravaged **Ta Phrom** and exquisitely decorated **Banteay Srei** are also popular sites. The **Roluos** ruins are significant as the site of the empire's first capital city and as a point of comparison with the later architectural styles of **Banteay Kdei** and Ta Keo. A visit to Angkor wouldn't be complete without the compulsory late-afternoon sunset trip to **Phnom Bakheng**, with its stunning views of Angkor Wat and the surrounding countryside. For more background on the art and architecture of Khmer temples, see pp.115–118.

Many of the artefacts on display at the temples of Angkor are not originals. **Thefts** of the valuable treasures have been common since the 1970s, but have accelerated since the peace process began in 1993, when access to the temples became easier. Attempts have been made to protect the most valuable artefacts by moving them to the National Museum in Phnom Penh, or to the Angkor Conservation Office in Siem Reap, and replacing them with copies.

Practicalities

The temples are officially open daily from 5am till 6.30pm. Exceptions are Banteay Srei (closes 5pm) and Kbal Spean (closes 3pm). Entry passes are required to enter the Angkor area, and must also be shown at several of the temples. Although passes are not required to visit Phnom Kulen or Beng Mealea, entrance fees of $20 and $5 respectively are collected at these more-distant temples. At the main entrance, on the Siem Reap–Angkor Wat road, three categories of pass are available, valid for one day ($20), three days ($40) or seven days ($60); additionally, one-day passes only can be bought at Angkor Wat and at Bakong (Roluos). The week pass allows you to dwell a little over the key sites, perhaps returning at different times of the day to your favourite spots, but most people find it adequate to buy the three-day pass, which gives enough time to see all the temples in the central area and to visit the outlying temples at Roluos, Banteay Srei and Banteay Samre. If you're short on time, you can just about cover Angkor Wat, the Bayon, Ta Prohm and Banteay Srei in one full day. For three- and seven-day tickets, you'll need to furnish a passport photograph of yourself to be laminated into your ticket. Photos can be taken for free at the main entrance but the long line means you'll waste precious time if you don't come with one. Children under 12 are admitted free, but you must take their passport with you as proof of age. Keep in mind that entry passes must be used on consecutive days. For example, a three-day pass that is first used on a Monday will only be good for the following Tuesday and Wednesday.

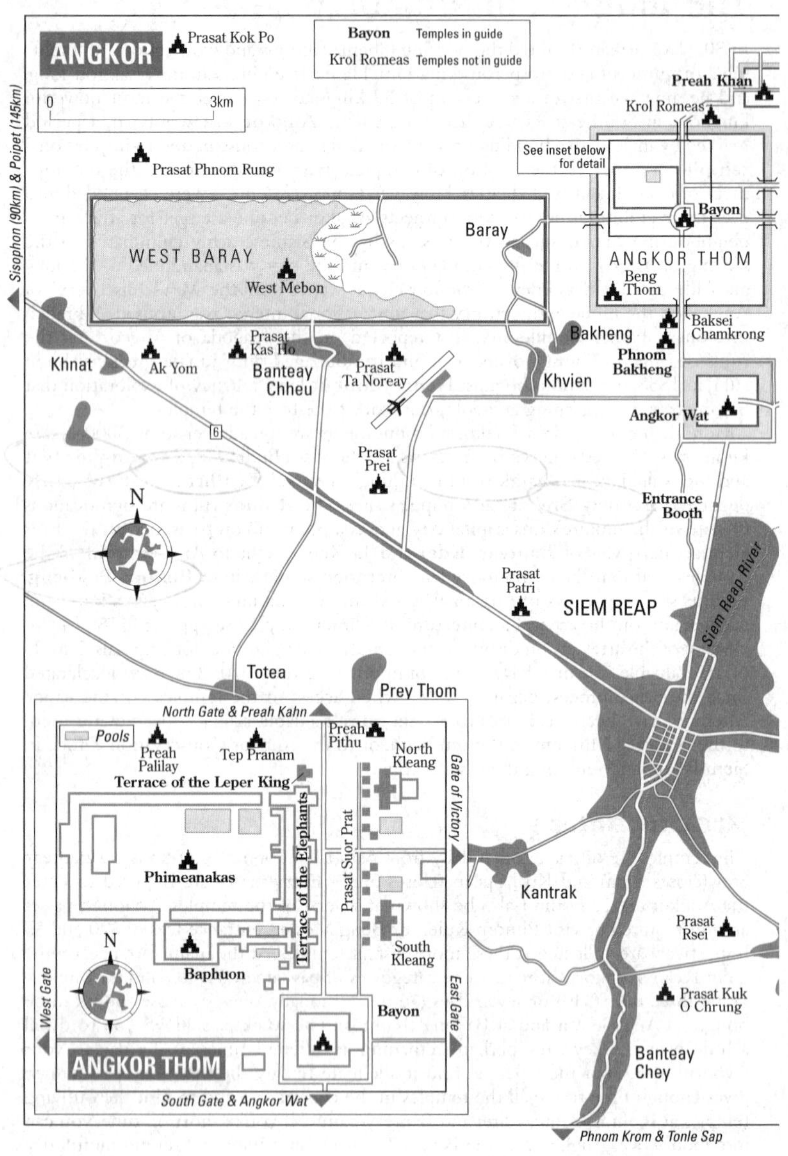

Angkor Wat

Built in the twelfth century as a mausoleum and temple for King Suryavarman II, **Angkor Wat** represents the height of inspiration and perfection in Khmer art, combining architectural harmony, grand proportions and detailed artistry. Your first close-up view of Angkor Wat is likely to be a memorable sight. Approaching along the sandstone causeway across a broad moat and through the western gate, you're

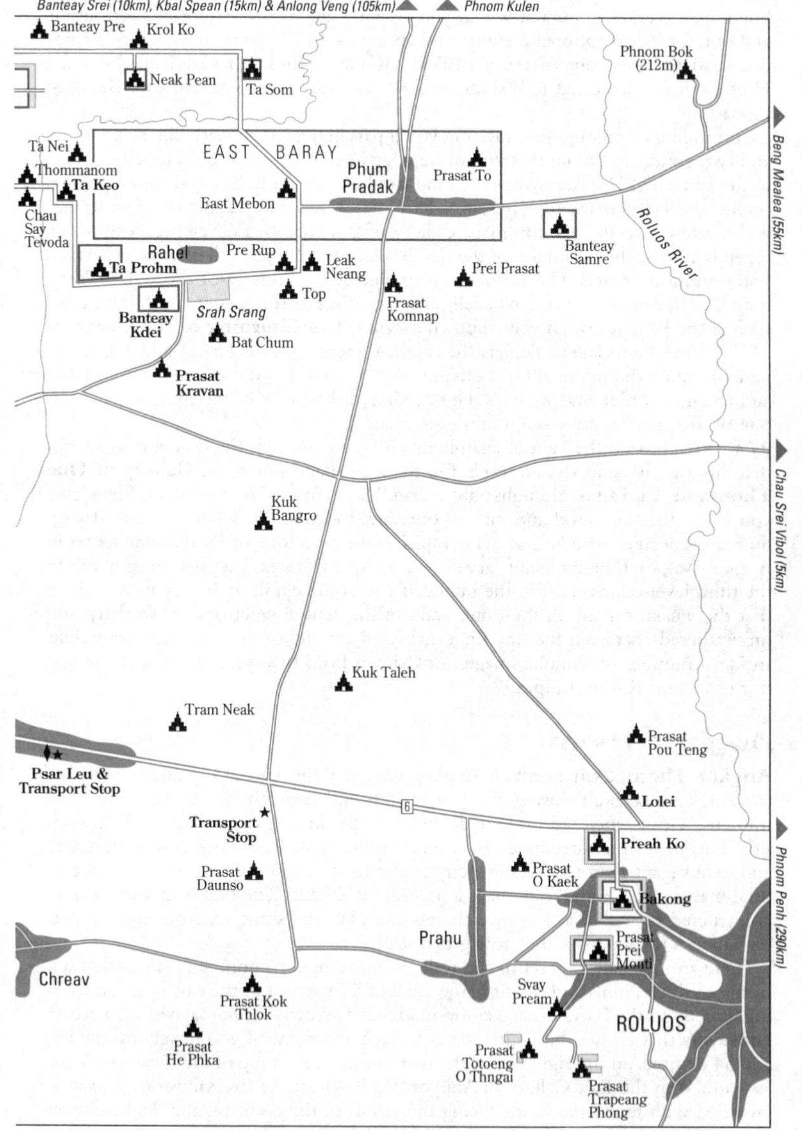

teased with glimpses of the central towers, but it's not until you're through the gate that the full magnificence of the temple comes into view. At once, its size and scale becomes apparent – a truly stunning sight. The causeway, extending 300m across the flat, open compound, directs the eye to the proud temple and its most memorable feature, the distinctive conical-shaped towers, designed to look like lotus buds. Four smaller towers surround a taller central one. The temple is made up of three platforms, linked by stairways, and long, columned galleries extend outwards from the central gopura. If you can resist the urge to head straight for the main temple building, the entry gopura at which you're standing is worth exploring, both inside and out, for its exceptional carvings and an eight-armed Vishnu image with a Buddha head, an interesting marriage of Buddhism and Hinduism. Originally built as a Hindu temple dedicated to Vishnu, Angkor Wat was later converted to a Buddhist monastery.

Continuing east along the causeway, you'll pass between the wat's library buildings and two ponds, and mount a flight of steps, guarded by a set of four crouching lions, to the Terrace of Honour, where the king would no doubt have stood, looking down on his subjects, perhaps enjoying some festivities or receiving dignitaries. The terrace is the gateway to the extraordinary Gallery of Bas Reliefs, a covered gallery which extends around the perimeter of the first level, and the inner wall of which is carved with sandstone reliefs. The carvings cover almost the entirety of the wall – 700m long, 2m in height – and depict religious narratives, battle scenes and Hindu epics such as the Ramayana. The best-known carving, **The Churning of the Ocean of Milk**, in the East Gallery, depicts the myth of creation: gods (*devas*) and evil spirits (*asuras*) churn the ocean for a thousand years to produce the elixir of immortality, and to create order out of chaos. The detail and sharpness of the images make this one of the greatest stone sculptures ever created.

As you approach the central chamber, you'll pass through the cruciform galleries that link the first and second levels. On the right-hand side is the **Gallery of One Thousand Buddhas**, though only a handful of figures now remain. Steps take you up to the next level and into a courtyard, the walls of which are carved with numerous detailed *apsaras*, celestial nymphs. There are a total of 1850 *apsara* figures in Angkor Wat, each individually carved with unique features. The final steep climb to the third level is closed off to the public. If you could climb up here, you would see that the *apsaras* carved on the outer walls of the central sanctuary are so sharp and unweathered, that even the tiny fingernails and cuticles of the nymphets are visible. Inside, a number of Buddha images look down from this vantage point at the seat of the ancient Khmer Empire.

Angkor Thom

Angkor Thom, 2km north of Angkor Wat, was the last and greatest capital of the Angkor era, built during the late twelfth and early thirteenth centuries. The immense city is enclosed by four defensive walls, 8m high and 3km long on each side. This in turn is surrounded by a moat, 100m wide. Certainly more spectacular and extravagant than any Western city at the time, Angkor Thom was an architectural masterpiece, home to perhaps a million inhabitants. The buildings were mainly constructed of wood, so have weathered away, but the stone religious monuments remain as a testament to the city's grand scale.

There are five gateways set in the walls around Angkor Thom, four covering each of the cardinal points and the fifth, the Gate of Victory, set in the east wall and leading directly to the Royal Palace compound. Each gateway is approached via a **stone causeway** that crosses the wide moat. On each causeway, 54 god images on the left and 54 demons on the right depict the myth of the Churning of the Ocean of Milk, as featured in the East Gallery of Angkor Wat. Each of the five sandstone *gopuras* is crowned with four large heads, facing the points of the compass, and flanked by an image of the Hindu god Indra riding a three-headed elephant.

If you're approaching from Angkor Wat, your entrance to Angkor Thom will probably be through the South Gate. Continuing directly northwards will bring you to the **Bayon**, at the centre of Angkor Thom. Despite its poor workmanship and haphazard sculpting, this is one of Angkor's most endearing temples, its unusual personality created by large carved faces that adorn the sides of its 54 towers; each tower has four heads, each facing one of the points of the compass. The celebrated Bayon heads have been subject to much scholarly conjecture, one theory has it that

△ Angkor Thom

they are images of Jayavarman VII. These smiling guardians have aged over time, so that now each face is unique with weathering, war damage and weeds.

The temple is pyramid-shaped, the towers rising successively to the highest central tower. Although small, it's actually a confusing temple to navigate, owing in large part to its complex history. It was built on top of an earlier monument, follows an experimental layout, and was added to at various times. It is thought to have been completed in the early thirteenth century, but its chaotic plan was further complicated by damage from the Siamese invasion in 1431. Although originally a Buddhist temple, it has a Hindu history too, and themes of both religions can be found in the reliefs adorning the galleries. The inner gallery displays religious and mythological themes, while the outer gallery, added later, is decorated with historical motifs, including the fight with the Chams in 1181.

Lying 200m to the northwest, the neighbouring temple of **Baphuon**, though now no more than a pile of rubble, was, at its peak, even more impressive than the Bayon. Baphuon's tower was originally covered in bronze, and writings of the era testify to its magnificence. Restoration work is being carried out and access is restricted until completion.

Just beyond the gate to Baphuon is the **Terrace of the Elephants**, extending 300m to the north. Three-headed elephants guard the stairway at the southern end, but before ascending, be sure to view the terrace from the road, where a sculpted frieze of hunting and fighting elephants adorns the facade. The terrace, which originally housed wooden pavilions, would have been used by the king to address his public and as a viewing platform on ceremonial occasions.

Immediately north of here is the **Terrace of The Leper King**, named after the statue of a naked figure that was originally discovered here. The original has been transferred to Phnom Penh's National Museum and a copy now stands on the platform; it's uncertain who the Leper King was or even where the name originates from. An inscription on the statue suggests that it may represent Yama, the god of the underworld and judge of the dead. This would also bear out the theory that the terrace was used as a royal crematorium. Superb sculptures of a variety of figures and sea creatures grace the sides of the terrace. The existing outer wall is in fact a later extension to the terrace. The original wall, also adorned with beautiful carvings, can be accessed via a viewing passageway. You'll need a torch to see the detail.

The two terraces mark what would have been the western edge of the Royal Palace. The timber buildings have since disintegrated, leaving just the temple mountain of **Phimeanakas** and the king's and queen's **bathing pools**. Now little more than a pyramid of stones, Phimeanakas was the palace chapel, crowned with a golden tower and probably completed in the early eleventh century. The western staircase has a handrail to aid the short, steep climb to the upper terrace. From the top, there's a good view of Baphuon to the south through the trees, and to the north, the royal baths.

Phnom Bakheng

The hilltop temple of **Phnom Bakheng**, south of Angkor Thom, is the earliest building in this area, following Yasorvarman's move westwards from Roluos. The state temple was built from the rock of the hill on which it stands. Upon its completion in the early tenth century it boasted 108 magnificent towers, set on a spectacular pyramid. Only part of the central tower now remains. The five diminishing terraces rise to the central sanctuary, adorned with female divinities, and once housing the lingam of the god Yashodhareshvara. Bakheng, however, is visited less for its temple than for the view from the hilltop – Angkor Wat soars upwards from its jungle hideout to the east. At sunset, the best time to visit for great views of Angkor, it becomes a circus crowded with tourists and vendors, with elephant rides on offer and one-dollar drinks and souvenir T-shirts piled up on the ancient stones.

Preah Khan

Just beyond the northeast corner of the perimeter wall around Angkor Thom stands **Preah Khan**, a tranquil, jungle-ravaged temple, surrounded by dense foliage on all sides. The twelfth-century temple served as the temporary residence of King Jayavarman VII while he was rebuilding Angkor Thom, damaged in an attack by the Siamese. A systematic tour of the temple is impossible, as routes are blocked with piles of fallen stones, trees or archeological excavation. Most people enter from the western entrance, but it's worth continuing all the way to the eastern edge of the temple. Here you'll find an unusual two-storey structure, with circular columns supporting the second floor of square columns and windows, unique in Khmer architecture. Not far from here, at the southern end of the east gopura, a photogenic battle of wood and stone is being fought as an encroaching tree grows through the ruins: the tree appears to be winning. Preah Khan can be visited in the hotter hours of the day, as it's largely in shade.

Ta Keo

About 2km east of the Bayon, this towering replica of Mount Meru scores well on the height points, but is awarded nothing for decoration. **Ta Keo** is bereft of the usual Angkor refineries; perhaps they were to be added later, as the temple was never finished. It's commonly believed that it was struck by lightning, a truly bad omen. The sandstone pyramid, although imposing and architecturally significant, is hard to get really excited about, especially as there's so much else on offer at Angkor.

Ta Phrom

The stunning twelfth-century temple-monastery of **Ta Phrom**, 1km southeast of Ta Keo, has a magical appeal. Rather than being cleared and restored like most of the other Angkor monuments, it's been left to the ravages of the jungle and appears roughly as it did to the Europeans who rediscovered these ruins in the nineteenth century. Roots and trunks intermingle with the stones and seem almost part of the structure. The temple's cramped corridors reveal half-hidden reliefs, while valuable carvings litter the floor.

Jayavarman VII originally built Ta Phrom as a Buddhist monastery, although Hindu purists have since defaced the Buddhist imagery. The temple was once surrounded by an enclosed city. An inscription found at the site testifies to the importance of Ta Phrom: it records that there were over 12,000 people at the monastery, maintained by almost 80,000 people in the surrounding villages.

Banteay Kdei

Southeast of Ta Phrom and one of the quieter sites in this area, **Banteay Kdei** is a huge twelfth-century Buddhist temple, constructed under Jayavarman VII. It's in a pretty poor state of repair, but the crumbling stones create an interesting architecture of their own. Highlights are the carvings of female divinities and other figures in the niches of the second enclosure, and a frieze of Buddhas in the interior court. Opposite the east entrance to Banteay Kdei are the **Srah Srang** or "Royal Bath", a large lake, which was probably used for ritual ablutions, and its landing stage, decorated with lions and nagas.

Roluos group

Not far from the small town of **Roluos** are three of Angkor's oldest temples: **Bakong**, **Preah Ko** and **Lolei**. Signposts mark the route from National Route 6, about 13km east of Siem Reap; Lolei is 1km to the north of the road, while Preah Ko and Bakong lie to the south, a couple of kilometres down the track. The relics date from the late ninth century, the dawn of the Angkorian era. With the emphasis on detail rather than size, the period is characterized by innovative construction methods, architecture and ornamentation, evident in all three temples.

South of National Route 6, the first temple you come to is **Preah Ko**, built by Indravarman I as a funerary temple for his ancestors. It's in poor condition, but is charming; the highlights are the six brick towers of the central sanctuary, which sit on a low platform at the centre of the inner enclosure. Before the central sanctuaries are three ruined sculptures of the sacred bull Nandin, the mount of Shiva. Up on the platform you can see a few patches of stucco – a lime plaster that would have coated the temples. Male figures are carved into the three eastern towers, while those on the smaller western towers are female.

Cambodia's earliest temple-mountain, **Bakong**, a kilometre or so south of Preah Ko, is made up of five tiers of solid sandstone surrounded by brick towers. Entering from the east across the balustraded causeway you'll come into the inner enclosure through a ruined gopura; originally eight brick towers surrounded the central sanctuary, but only five remain standing today. In the heart of the enclosure is a five-tiered pyramid, which you can climb on any of the four sides. Twelve small sanctuaries are arranged symmetrically around the fourth tier, and above you on the summit is the well-preserved central sanctuary. If you're wondering why it's in such good nick, it was rebuilt in 1941.

Return to the main road for the sanctuary of **Lolei**, built by Yashovarman I on an artificial island. Its collapsing four brick-and-sandstone towers are only worth visiting for the Sanskrit inscriptions in the door jambs that detail the work rosters of the temple "slaves"; a few carvings remain but are badly eroded.

Banteay Srei

The pretty tenth-century temple of **Banteay Srei** is unique amongst its Angkorian peers. Its miniature proportions, unusual pinkish colour and intricate ornamentation create a surreal effect, enhanced by its astonishing state of preservation. The journey to the site, about 30km northeast of Angkor Wat, takes about an hour. Tour groups start arriving en masse from 8.30am, and because of its small size, it gets crowded quickly. Hiring a car or a moto from Siem Reap, you could arrive here an hour or so beforehand, when you'll have the temple to yourself.

The sharp and detailed carving above the doorway of the east gopura is a prelude to the delights within. The roseate tones here and throughout the temple are caused by the quartz arenite sandstone used in construction. A paved causeway flanked by rows of sandstone markers takes you to the entry tower. From here, across the moat, the tops of the three intricate central towers and two libraries are visible over the low enclosure wall. The reddish sandstone against the green backdrop of the jungle is a magnificent sight, as if you've stumbled across a fairytale city. Inside the enclosure wall, there's a riot of intricate decoration and architecture with elegant pillars and exquisite frontons; walls are covered with carved foliage and guardian divinities, and panels are extravagantly decorated with scenes from Hindu mythology. It's a magical, miniature fantasyland; the central towers have midget doors barely a metre tall, though getting in is academic now, as they're roped off prohibiting entry – not so much to preserve the site, but to prevent a tourist jam inside.

2.4

Western Cambodia

The flat stretch of land that fans out from Phnom Penh to the border with Thailand is sandwiched between the **Cardamom Mountains** in the southwestern corner of the country, and the **Dangrek Range** in the north. A perfect hideout, these frontier hills were home to the Khmer Rouge guerrillas for nearly twenty years from 1979. Until the defections of the late 1990s, the Khmer Rouge had a tight grip over these upland regions. However, government control has now been officially restored, and travellers are returning to areas that were previously off-limits. The towns within the former occupied territories, such as the remote frontier outpost of **Pailin**, are not attractive places, as you might expect after twenty years of war and isolation, but the countryside is stunning in places and has a Wild West appeal. Many of the residents are ex-soldiers who have spent most of their lives living in the jungle; sticking to the roads and paths is essential, as this is the most densely mined area in the country. Stretching across the vast central plain is Southeast Asia's largest lake, the **Tonle Sap**, which swells to over 8000 square kilometres during the rainy season, and is the region's primary focus of transport, livelihood and leisure. The area's commercial hub is **Battambang**, an agreeable town, bearing traces of its French colonial days. Its northern neighbour, **Sisophon**, makes a convenient stopping-off point on the route into Thailand.

Battambang

BATTAMBANG, 71km south of Sisophon, is one of Cambodia's biggest cities, but it's a world apart from Phnom Penh's urban bustle, enjoying an unhurried, pedestrian pace and a reputation for friendliness and pleasant atmosphere. The city, however, is keen not to get left behind in the country's recent surge of development and modernization. French-colonial-era terraces on the riverside are rapidly filling with private English-language schools and mobile-phone shops. The busiest Battambang gets, however, is at the central market, Psar Nat, where gemstones from the town of Pailin, southwest of the city, are cut and traded. Don't expect to pick up a bargain unless you know what to look for – the better stones are shipped straight to Thailand. The local museum (Mon–Fri 8–11am & 2–5pm; US$1) is well worth a visit, as are two temples near the town centre – Wat Phephittham and Wat Dhum Rey Sor.

Trains from Phnom Penh trundle into the station at the western edge of town in the early evening, from where it's just a 500-metre walk into the town centre. Shared taxis and **pick-ups** arrive at the transport stop in the northwest of town just off National Route 5; arriving from the south, they'll drop you at Psar Nat, if you ask. On the river, just opposite the hospital, is the boat dock; hotel reps and English-speaking moto drivers meet the boats, so you'll have no trouble getting to your accommodation speedily.

When you're ready to **move on**, buses leave from the riverfront by the market or pick you up at your hotel if you arrange it beforehand with the staff (Phnom Penh 16,000r; Siam Reap 20,000r; Poipet 12,000r). Shared taxis and pick-ups leave from the transport stop. For Pailin, join a pick-up in the south of town, near the start of Route 10 at Psar Leu (20,000r). **Boats** depart daily at 7am for Siem Reap; the foreigner price is $15 for the three- to four-hour trip.

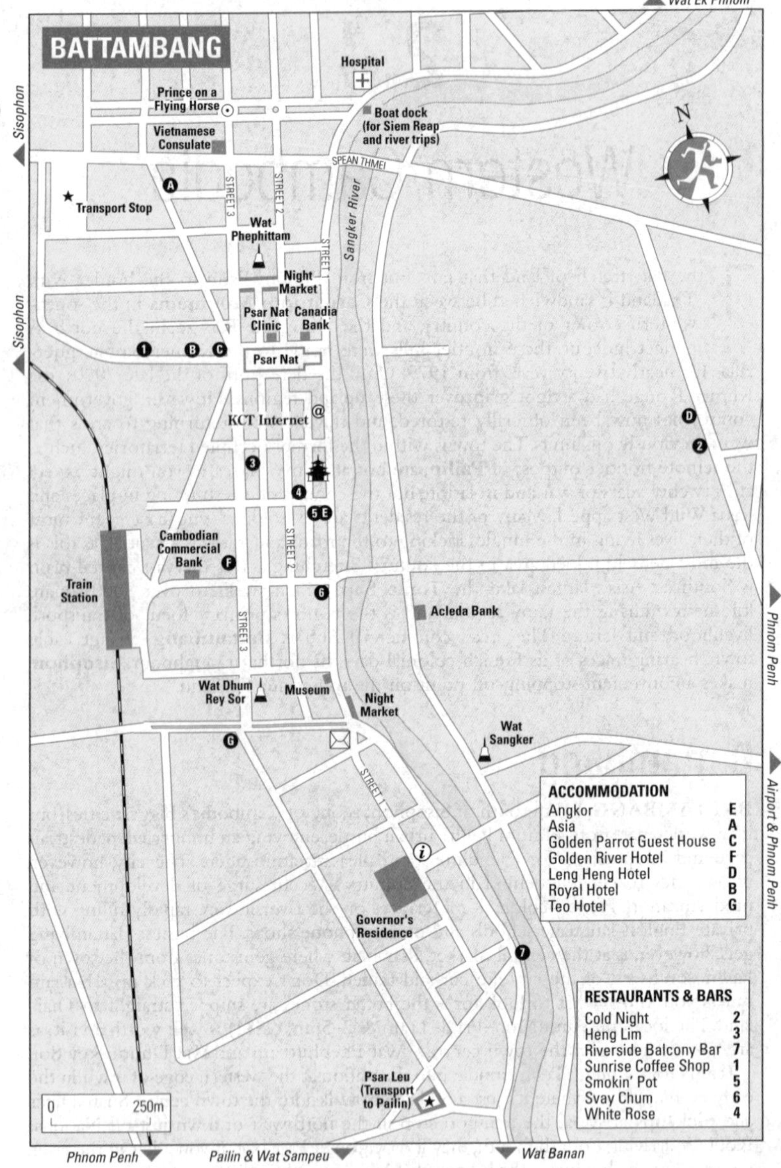

The **post office** on the riverside has stamps and a national telephone facility. **Internet access** is available at KCT Internet and several other places on the riverfront south of the market; prices at the time of writing were $1.50 per hour and dropping fast. Canadia Bank, near Psar Nat, and the Cambodian Commercial Bank, near the train station, cash travellers' cheques and provide credit card advances; both change money. The **provincial hospital** is at the northern end of the riverside, but has limited facilities. The Psar Nat Clinic just north of the market is convenient for minor problems.

Accommodation

An abundance of **hotels** and guesthouses makes for competitively priced accommodation in Battambang, with decent rooms available for $3–5 per night, all with cable TV, en-suite bathroom, and fan, unless otherwise stated.

Angkor St 1 ☎053/952310. Overlooking the river, this hotel has one of the nicest situations in Battambang, so it's a shame the rooms don't quite live up to the location: though clean and en suite, with a/c, TV and fridge, they're a bit run-down, and you'll need to pay slightly more if you want a room with hot water. ❸

Asia North of the market, towards the transport stop ☎016/944955. A modern hotel, where the rooms have cold-water en-suite facilities, fan and TV. Some a/c rooms available. ❶

Golden Parrot Guest House Just west of Psar Nat ☎015/530201. Basic guesthouse, with a central location beside the market and some of the cheapest rates in town. ❶

Golden River Hotel St 3, south of the market ☎053/952158. This friendly, helpful place, run by an Australian/Khmer family, enjoys a good location. Some of the single rooms are a bit small. ❶

Leng Heng Hotel East of the river on National Route 5 ☎053/370088. Modern, friendly hotel set in a cheerful courtyard with plenty of flowering plants; rooms are light and airy, with a/c, fridge and hot shower. ❷

Royal Hotel Western end of the market ☎015/912034. This smart hotel is probably now the best value in Battambang, offering huge modern rooms with cable TV, fridge and en-suite facilities. Cheap singles are also available, and some rooms have balconies. ❶

Teo Hotel St 3, on the southern edge of town ☎053/952288. The top-end hotel in Battambang, not as expensive as it looks from the outside and a bit of a distance from the town-centre action. Double rooms include a telephone in addition to the usual facilities. ❸

Eating, drinking and entertainment

One of the best **places to eat** is a little way out of town to the east: *Cold Night* (aka *T's*) serves fabulous steaks, grills and fries accompanied by home-made creamy coleslaw all for less than $5; they also have Cambodian and Thai food and the draft Angkor beer's cheap at 60c a mug. *Cold Night* is next door to the *Leng Heng Hotel*; you may want to take a moto from town. For good Western breakfasts, sandwiches and tea or coffee, head for *Sunrise Coffee Shop* just west of the *Royal Hotel*. Despite its name, *Smokin' Pot*, behind the *Angkor Hotel*, serves nothing more than good Khmer and Thai food; it does, however, also offer cookery classes at around $7 a day. For economical **Khmer** dishes, the *White Rose* on Street 2 is hard to beat, with *Heng Lim* on Street 3 a close runner-up; both have English-language menus and serve up tasty fare from early morning until around 9pm.

In the evening, a buzzing **night market** opens up on the street south of Wat Phephittam; here, you'll find all the dishes that are normally eaten in Cambodian homes and not found in restaurants. For desserts and fruit shakes, though, you'll need to head down to the riverfront opposite the post office, where stalls set up late in the afternoon, and you can sit and enjoy the music from *Svay Chum*, a karaoke bar on the riverfront in the grounds of the Department of Provincial Land. In an idyllic spot overlooking the river, south on Street 1 near Psar Leu, the Swiss-run *Riverside Balcony Bar* (Tues–Sun 4-11pm) serves a range of beers and cocktails as well as some Western snacks on a tastefully designed terrace. They have a pool table, too.

Around Battambang

Two popular places to visit near Battambang are **Phnom Sampeu** and **Wat Banan**. Since they are both located to the southwest of the city, they can be combined conveniently into a day-trip by moto (about $5). The entrance ticket is $2 for both places.

Phnom Sampeu

Around 15km along the road that heads west from Battambang, you'll see two lop-sided hills rising from the plain. They supposedly resemble a sinking boat, **Phnom Sampeu** being the broken hull, and Phnom G'daong the broken sail bobbing around in the water. An unshaded ten-minute climb up the northeast side of Phnom Sampeau takes you to **Wat Sampeau**, where you can explore various temple buildings and big caves. The site was used to great advantage by the government forces in their skirmishes with the Khmer Rouge. Across the ridge are the temple of Prasat Brang, built in 1964, and a small decorative stupa.

If your moto-driver doesn't know it, ask children in the area to show you the complex of **caves**, known as Laang Lacaun ("Theatre Cave"), nearby. The caves were the site of atrocities committed by the Khmer Rouge – smashed skulls are collected in a small metal cage - the victims were thrown into the deep cave from a hole above. An adjacent cave, trailing eerily downwards into the darkness, is apparently still full of the scattered bones of victims. It's thought that more than 10,000 people died in these caves at the hands of the Khmer Rouge. A smaller cave nearby houses a primitive cage full of more bones and skulls, with victims' clothes hanging from the vines. This was allegedly the torture chamber. In previous times, these caves had a pleasanter role: the larger cave was used for plays and theatrical productions, its approaching slope providing the seats for the audience. The smaller caves off to the side were used as dressing rooms and props storage.

Wat Banan

The best preserved of the temples around Battambang, **Wat Banan** can be reached from Wat Sampeu by a pleasant back-country road. If your moto driver doesn't know the way, offer one of the local kids a dollar to show you – it's just a few kilometres. As you approach, you'll see some distinctive Angkor Wat-like towers; the temple lies immediately at the top of a steep laterite stairway, which ascends a seventy-metre-high hill.

It's known that Wat Banan was consecrated as a Buddhist temple, but scholars are uncertain who built the temple or exactly when it was completed – estimates put this between the tenth and thirteenth centuries. Five corn-on-the-cob towers remain, all in a somewhat collapsed state, and several of the carvings have lost their heads to vandalism, though there are a few still in reasonable condition. You'll likely be accompanied on the climb by young kids hoping for a tip by telling you a bit about the temple. It's certainly worth the steep clamber up to see the detailed lintels, beheaded apsaras, and views out over endless paddies, with Phnom Sampeu clearly visible to the north.

Pailin

Some 80km southwest of Battambang, **PAILIN** may not appeal to everyone; remote and isolated, it's a down and dirty **frontier town**, the heart of old **Khmer Rouge** Cambodia, and a fading **gem-mining** outpost. The only link to the rest of the country is the atrocious National Route 57 from Battambang. Once you finally arrive at Pailin, there's really no reason to be here unless you're crossing the border into Thailand. Though it's set among some pretty countryside, this was one of the most heavily mined regions of the country; not all of the mines have been cleared yet, so don't stray from the path.

The town has a wild and edgy atmosphere: high up and surrounded by jungle, it was long a Khmer Rouge stronghold, supplied with food and weapons from the nearby Thai border. The highly organized, well-disciplined group of guerrilla soldiers was led by **Ieng Sary**, who created a prosperous town, gutting the countryside of gems and logs for miles around and selling them to Thailand for an estimated $10m a month, until in a surprise move he defected – with over 3000 of his soldiers

– to the government side in 1996. Granted immunity, he now lives comfortably in Phnom Penh; his move, though, precipitated the demise of the Khmer Rouge, which finally disappeared when Brother Number 2, Nuon Chea, surrendered in 1998; he still lives in a house in town. You might not be surprised to learn that Pailin has the lowest crime rate in Cambodia: in a hangover from the Khmer Rouge tradition, criminals are executed without trial, often on the spot.

Forget French terraces and colonial mansions; Pailin is a worn and shabby collection of timber shacks and concrete blocks. The area became famous for its **gem mining**, though the land is now pretty much mined out, and all you're likely to see today are a few dealers in the market, ready to hand over cash for rough, uncut stones pulled from the ground. Rubies are occasionally found, but sapphires are now very rare.

The carving of the legend The Churning of The Ocean of Milk that covers the outer wall of **Wat Ratanasaoporn** on the way into town is the pagoda's only feature; its claim to fame is that most of the monks were defrocked in 2000 for entertaining local taxi girls. The adjacent hill of **Phnom Yat** houses a small pagoda, its outer wall decorated with startling images of people being tortured in hell – tongues are pulled out with pliers, women drowned, people stabbed with forks and heads chopped off. The main buildings have been repaired and restored, but its strategic hilltop position meant that the pagoda took a beating, and there are bullet holes everywhere. Large artillery shells are painted yellow and are used to house incense sticks and offerings to Ta Dom Don Dai. From the hill, there's a great view of Pailin and the mountains around.

To **Thailand**, the easier of the two border crossings near Pailin is at Phsa Prom (7am–8pm), 20km from Pailin and reached in about half an hour by shared taxi (B40) or moto (B50–100, depending on your bargaining skills). The road passes deforested hillsides and small farming plots along the way. At the border itself is a small market and two rather incongruous **casinos**, Caesar's and Flamengo, which entertain an almost exclusively Thai clientele. If you're crossing the border here, take a minibus to Chanthaburi (B130; see p.1034), then another bus to Bangkok, or Trat (for Ko Chang).

Practicalities

The only way to **get to Pailin** is by pick-up from Battambang, a tiring trip that can take anywhere between three and seven hours; they leave from Psar Leu from early morning until midday (20,000r). In Pailin, you arrive at the market in the centre of town, which is where you come to get transport back to Battambang.

The best **hotel** in town is the *Hang Meas* (☎012/787546; ❸), a little west of the centre, towards the border. Rooms here are clean and pleasant, with chunky wood furniture, hot-water en-suite bathrooms, air conditioning and TV. The *Kim Young Heng Guest House* (☎016/939841; ❶), located a few steps up the hill from the market behind the restaurant of the same name, has a range of fan and air-con rooms, some bright and appealing, others windowless cells. Opposite the market, the *Lao Lao Kang Guest House* (☎012/712316; ❶) and the *Punleu Pich Guest House* (☎016/958611; ❶) both offer basic facilities and the cheapest rates in town.

Eating in Pailin is no gastronomic delight, but there are plenty of stalls in the market and cheap restaurants nearby. The best **restaurants** in town are at the *Hang Meas Hotel*, which has an English-language menu and does a selection of Khmer, Thai and Western dishes, as well as eggs and bread for breakfast, and the *Kim Young*, just up from the market, which turns out tasty Khmer food and also has an English menu. At the latter, try the sweet-and-sour fish and morning glory with garlic.

Sisophon

SISOPHON has emerged from the shadows of the Khmer Rouge to become an increasingly important staging post for Thai–Cambodian trade. Thai goods are

Overland into Thailand via the Poipet border crossing

From Sisophon, it's a one-hour pick-up ride to the border crossing at Poipet (daily 7am–8pm). Thai visas are arranged on the spot. From the border, take a tuk-tuk to Aranyaprathet (see p.1035), from where you can head on to Bangkok by train (daily 1.30pm; 7hr) or bus (4 daily, last one 5pm; 4hr 30min).

Coming **into Cambodia**, thirty-day visas are issued on arrival at the Poipet border crossing (US$20 and two photos). The border officials will also ask to see a medical card to check your vaccinations. It's a scam, of course, but if you don't have your card, you'll be asked to pay a B100 "fine"; you can decline to pay without repercussions.

Another scam is to get new arrivals to change dollars into riel – at poor rates. It's not necessary to change money at all, as dollars and baht are accepted everywhere in Sisophon. Many people travelling from Bangkok opt for an all-in trip to Siem Reap organized by guesthouses on the Thanon Khao San, but bear in mind this doesn't give you the flexibility, and regardless of what the travel companies say, you're in for plenty of hanging about as it takes quite a while to process a bus-load of people at immigration; you're unlikely to arrive in Siem Reap until early evening and will be strongly encouraged to stay where they want you to.

trucked into the town and transferred to trains for the slow journey to Phnom Penh. Travellers, too, are passing through in increasing numbers from the Poipet border crossing (see above), though they don't tend to hang around – Sisophon is a pretty nondescript town, but it's a handy place to break your journey, especially if you're not going to make the border before it closes or if you've crossed late and can't get on to Battambang or Siem Reap.

Shared taxis and pick-ups stop either at the northern edge of town (from Phnom Penh) or at the transport stop near the market in the centre (from everywhere else); motos (1000r) will be on hand to ferry you to a guesthouse or hotel. **Accommodation** in Sisophon is nothing to write home about. One of the most convenient places to stay is the *Phnom Svay Hotel* (☎012/656565; ❷) up on the Poipet to Siem Reap road, offering a variety of rooms, all with bathroom and TV. Another centrally located place is the *Neak Meas Hotel* (☎012/971287; ❸), where all rooms have air-con, hot water, TV and fridge; be warned, though, that it also functions as an "entertainment centre", with girls hovering outside the VIP karaoke rooms at the hotel entrance in the evening. A cheaper alternative is the *Rong Roeung Hotel* (☎054/958823; ❷), where there is a choice of air-con or fan rooms but no hot water. The cheapest place in town is the *Sarat Tong Guest House* (❶) located on the north side of the main road heading east out of town (look out for the "Quest House" sign). Some of the small rooms have attached bathrooms while others share. Sisophon has a surprisingly good, inexpensive **restaurant**, *Phkay Proek* (daily 6am–9pm), just downhill from the *Phnom Svay Hotel*, serving Western breakfasts, fabulous pancakes and good Chinese/Khmer food. Apart from this, the only place with an English-language menu is the restaurant at the *Neak Meas Hotel*, which serves up a good range of Khmer, Chinese and Thai dishes. In the late afternoon and early evening, stalls selling basic Khmer food, desserts and fruit juices open on the south side of Independence Park, a block north of the transport stop.

While US dollars and riel are accepted in Sisophon, many transactions are in **baht**.

2.5

The southwest

To the southwest of Phnom Penh, a series of mountain ranges, known as the Cardamom and Elephant mountains, rise up imposingly from the plains, as if shielding Cambodia's only stretch of coast from the world. Indeed, only a few places along the coast are accessible by road. The most popular destination is the beach resort of **Sihanoukville**, whose sandy shores are the launching point for trips to **Ream National Park** or remote and sparsely populated islands in the Gulf of Thailand. Further east along the coast, the city of **Kampot** makes a good base for exploring the ghost-town hill station of **Bokor** and the quaint coastal village of **Kep**. On Cambodia's western border, **Koh Kong** serves as a transit point for visitors arriving from or leaving for Thailand.

The accessible areas of the southwest are well served by public **transport**. National Routes 3 and 4 are in a fairly good state of repair, while comfortable Malaysian-made speed express boats ply the sea routes.

Sihanoukville

The closest that Cambodia gets to a full-blown beach resort, **SIHANOUKVILLE** is overrun with locals on weekends and holidays, enjoying the sandy beaches, well-stocked seafood stalls and slow-paced ambience. It's a friendly, prosperous town, thanks to the soothing influence of the sea and the healthy local economy, based on port trade, fishing and tourism. It may not be able to compete with the best of the **beaches** in neighbouring countries – the vistas are pleasant rather than stunning, and facilities, though improving, are not exactly up to international standards – but the town does have a certain charm and is proving a popular stop with travellers, not just those en route to or from Thailand, but also Phnom Penh visitors looking for an easy excursion. The resort is certainly a good place to relax and unwind, especially if you've been travelling hard on the provincial Cambodian roads. Moreover, lazy days on the beach can be complemented by an evening of partying at one of the town's vibrant nightspots.

Sihanoukville came into being just after the dissolution of Indochina. The French-occupied Mekong Delta reverted to Vietnamese possession, depriving Cambodia of a maritime port. The Cambodians decided to build a new one at Kompong Som, as Sihanoukville was then known, with work beginning in 1955. Sihanoukville has since been used to supply arms to Vietcong guerrillas, Nationalist troops and Khmer Rouge soldiers, depending on prevailing political conditions. In 1998, containers of illegal arms heading for Prince Ranarridh's soldiers were discovered here, allegedly evidence of a proposed coup against Hun Sen. These days though, the port is the centre for imports of petroleum and for the export of garments and shoes, many made in sweat shops and destined for the European and American markets.

Arrival, orientation, information and city transport

Buses arrive in the centre of Sihanoukville, on Ekareach Street, not far from the market, Psar Leu. **Pick-ups** and **taxis** usually terminate at the transport stop on

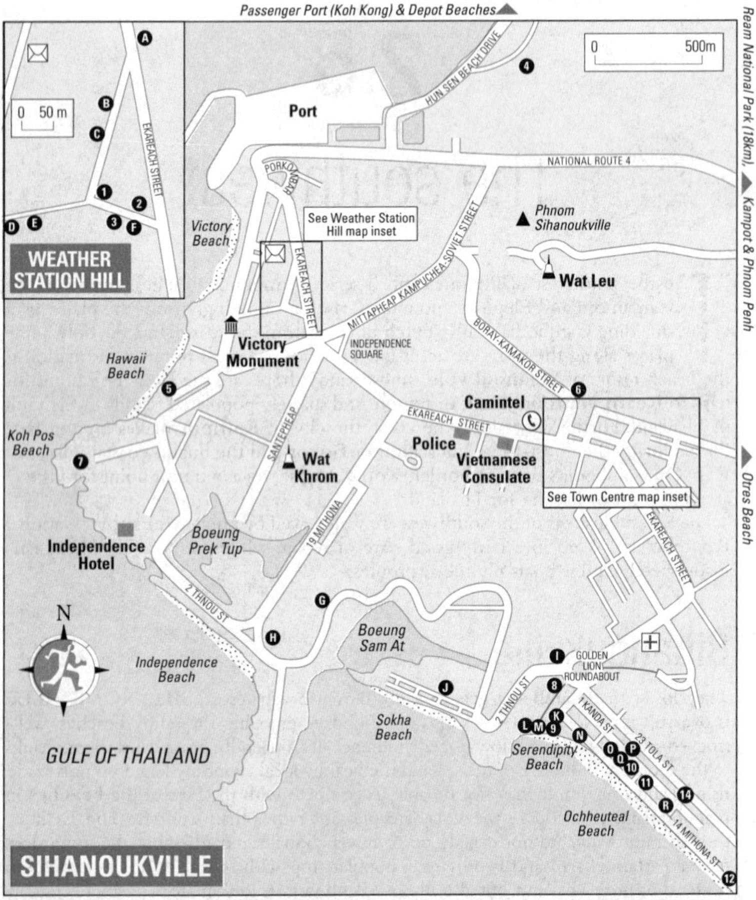

Passenger Port (Koh Kong) & Depot Beaches
Ream National Park (18km), Kampot & Phnom Penh
Otres Beach
0 500m
WEATHER STATION HILL
0 50 m
EKAREACH STREET
Port
HUN SEN BEACH DRIVE
NATIONAL ROUTE 4
PORK MBAR
See Weather Station Hill map inset
Victory Beach
Phnom Sihanoukville
Wat Leu
MITTAPHEAP KAMPUCHEA-SOVIET STREET
BORAY-KAMAKOR STREET
Victory Monument
INDEPENDENCE SQUARE
Hawaii Beach
Camintel
EKAREACH STREET
Police
Vietnamese Consulate
See Town Centre map inset
Koh Pos Beach
SANTEPHEAP
Wat Khrom
19 MITHONA
Boeung Prek Tup
Independence Hotel
2 THNOU ST
Boeung Sam At
GOLDEN LION ROUNDABOUT
Independence Beach
N
Sokha Beach
2 THNOU ST
1 KANDA ST
23 TOLA ST
Serendipity Beach
Ochheuteal Beach
14 MITHONA ST
GULF OF THAILAND
SIHANOUKVILLE

TOWN CENTRE
PSAR PINCHECOM
BORAY KAMAKOR
Nightmarket
SOPHEAKMONGKOL NORTH
OMUI STREET
STREET 109
Transport Stop
STREET 108
Cambodian Commercial Bank
SOPHEAKMONGKOL WEST
SOPHEAKMONGKOL EAST
Psar Leu
ABC Computer
EKAREACH STREET
Transport Stop
GST Bus Station
Caltex
DH Cambodia
Ho Wah Genting Bus Station
7 MAKARA
Samudera
EKAREACH STREET
Canadia Bank
0 200m

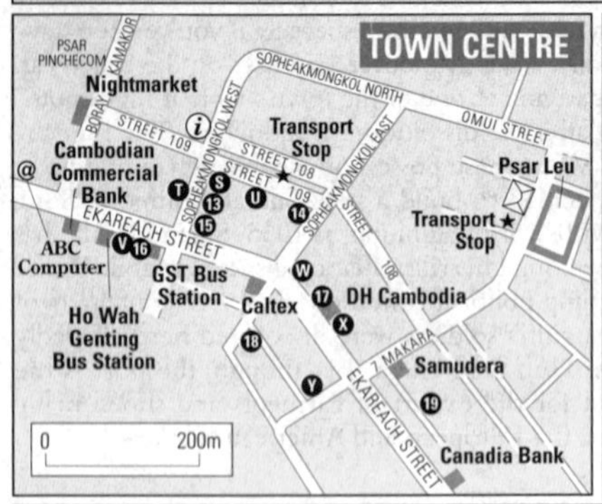

RESTAURANTS, BARS & CLUBS

Angkor Arms	15	Hawaii Seaview	5
Angkor Beer	6	Les Feuilles	11
Apsara	14	Melting Pot	3
Bamboo Light Café	17	Mick and Craig's	8
Biba	4	Sam's	2
Blue Storm	16	Sea Dragon	10
Chiva's Shack	12	Starfish Bakery	19
Corner Bar	1	Treasure Island Seafood	7
Dusk Till Dawn	13	Unkle Bob's	9
Fishermans Den	18		

ACCOMMODATION

Angkor Inn	T	Coasters	L	Golden Castle	I	Oasis	X	Royal Hotel	Y
Bungalow Village	D	Crystal	Q	Marlin	W	Ochheuteal Beachside Bungalows	N	Sea Breeze	H
Chez Claude	G	Da Da	B	MASH	F	Orchidee	P	Sea View Villa	K
Chez Mari-yan	E	Eden	M	Mealy Chenda	C	Princess	V	Seaside Hotel	O
Chhe Nin	A	Freedom Hotel	S	Mohasal	U			Sokha Beach Resort	J
								Susaday	R

Street 108 near the tourist office or opposite the market, and most town-centre accommodation is within walking distance. But if you're heading to any of the beach suburbs or Weather Station Hill, you'll need to invest around 2000–3000r in a moto. **Boat** arrivals from Koh Kong speed into the passenger port 4km to the northwest of the town centre on Hun Sen Beach Drive around midday; guesthouse reps meet the boats and will give you a free ride if you're going to stay with them.

The town itself is inland, with its centre around the market; sprawling over a large **peninsula**, it's ringed by beaches with many of the mid-range hotels, a selection of guesthouses and plenty of restaurants and bars. Towards the port is the **backpacker area** up on Weather Station Hill (2km from the town centre); here, you'll find plenty of guesthouses, cheap Western-oriented restaurants and a smattering of bars. If you want to stay at the beach, you can expect to pay a bit more for the privilege, but some of the places at **Ochheuteal beach**, where most of the sea-view accommodation is located, are still moderately priced; at its northwest end is Serendipity beach, with a few budget rooms right on the sand.

Motos are the principal form of **local transport** in Sihanoukville, with journey fares reflecting the distances involved. Reckon on 2000–3000r from town to the beaches, and to avoid misunderstandings negotiate the fare beforehand. If lazing on the beach doesn't provide enough excitement, and you want to explore Sihanoukville and the area, the best option is to rent a **motorcycle**. Most guesthouses can provide this service; a 100cc bike goes for about $3 per day and a 250cc for $4 to $5. You'll probably need to leave your passport as security, and make sure you lock your moto when you leave it – thefts are common. A **car** with driver can be arranged for around $20 through most hotels and guesthouses or at the taxi stand. Many guesthouses also offer day-trips out to nearby islands or to Ream National Park.

For the latest **tourist information**, track down a copy of *The Sihanoukville Visitors' Guide*, a comprehensive, regularly updated tourist guide available from guesthouses and bars around town.

Accommodation

Sihanoukville is not short of **accommodation**, although hotels tend to fill up quickly at weekends and holidays. Midweek, it's fairly easy to haggle down the price at all types of accommodation. Budget accommodation is available all over town with a concentration on Weather Station Hill above the Victory beach; in addition to the list below, many local families with a spare room or two will put up a "Guesthouse" sign to attract the tourist over-spill at peak times; there are plenty along Ekareach Street, and their prices are a pretty consistent $5.

The town centre

Angkor Inn Sopheakmongkol West, just off Ekareach St. ☎016/896204. Well-regarded budget guesthouse offering plain, but cool and tidy rooms with en-suite facilities; the quietest rooms are at the back. ❶

Freedom Hotel Sopheakmongkol West. Western-run place with good-value fan and a/c rooms (monthly rates available) and one of the town's best bars on the ground floor. ❷

Marlin Ekareach Street. ☎034/320169. Conveniently located, Western-run place, where all rooms have a/c and hot-water bathrooms. Popular bar/restaurant downstairs and Internet access, too. ❷

Mohasal St 109 ☎034/ 933 488. Impressively clean modern city-centre hotel: good-sized rooms, all with TV, a/c and hot water. ❸

Oasis Ekareach Street. ☎034/933487. This new place is trying to be bigger and better than the rest, with massive rooms and a range of facilities, plus a big bar and restaurant and a three-metre-wide TV screen. ❷

Princess Ekareach St ☎034/934789. Smart hotel in the town centre, kitted out with plenty of wood and marble. Rooms have the usual facilities with the added treat of actual bathtubs. Secure parking at the back if you need it. ❻

Royal Hotel 7 Makara St ☎012/899797. Nice clean rooms with all the facilities. ❸

Weather Station Hill

Bungalow Village Weather Station Hill, towards Victory beach. ☎034/933875. Rustic bungalows set in tropical gardens, all with attached cold-water en-suite bathrooms. Fabulous sea views from the restaurant. 1

Chez Mari-yan Weather Station Hill ⓣ034/933709. Mid-range bungalows overlooking Victory beach, with tasty food on the classy restaurant deck. 2

Chhe Nin Ekareach St, near Weather Station Hill ⓣ034/933611. Don't be put off by the tacky green-and-gold facade: this well-maintained guesthouse beats the average town-centre hotels on price, homeliness and cleanliness. Offers the usual mid-range luxuries and is close to budget restaurants. 2

Da Da Weather Station Hill ⓣ012/879527. Friendly, family-run place, with ocean views, offering six large, clean en-suite rooms. Close to budget eateries. 1

MASH Weather Station Hill ⓣ012/913714. Zany guesthouse with a choice of rooms from $3. A good place to get local information and meet other travellers. The restaurant serves up generous portions of Indian and European food from Western fry-ups to tasty casseroles, and the Dutch owner organizes regular boat trips and camping expeditions to the offshore islands. 1

Mealy Chenda West of Ekareach St, above Victory beach ⓣ034/933472. Legendary on the budget circuit, and still popular despite increasing competition. Accommodation is en-suite, and there's a $2 dorm. A limited number of rooms have sea views, and there's a travellers' restaurant, too. 1

Sokha, Serendipity and Ochheutal beaches

Chez Claude On the hill between Independence and Sokha beaches ⓣ012/824870. Individually designed timber bungalow suites on the hill overlooking the bay; all are en suite and boast private balconies looking out to sea. There's a French restaurant, and the owners arrange diving trips. 4

Coasters Serendipity beach ⓣ012/964170 or 012/979625. Idyllic rooms in bungalows overlooking the beach; all rooms with en-suite facilities, fans and balconies. The bar-restaurant serves breakfast, drinks and fantastic food. Booking advised. 3

Crystal Ochheuteal beach ⓣ034/933880. Futuristic glass- and mirror-tiled hotel, a short distance from the beach, which has pleasant, airy rooms, all with their own tea- and coffee-making facilities. The room rate includes a buffet breakfast in the *Sea Breeze* restaurant. 6

Eden Serendipity Beach. ⓣ034/933585; ⓔserendipityeden@yahoo.com. Just five rooms that are often full at this popular beachside bar, all with a/c and hot water. 2

Golden Castle On the Golden Lions roundabout ⓣ034/933919. Massive, modern hotel 5min from the beach; don't be put off by the outside, as the rooms are stylish and comfy. All rooms have a bathtub and larger ones have sofas. 4

Ochheuteal Beachside Bungalows Behind Ochheuteal Beach.ⓣ016/953896. Not exactly beachside, but only 70m away. Attractive thatched rooms with veranda, all with a/c, some with hot water. A big plus about this place is its excellent restaurant. 3

Orchidee One block back from Ochheuteal beach ⓣ015/933639. Fully equipped, spacious rooms, with pleasant breakfast terrace. 3

Sea Breeze Independence beach ⓣ034/320217. The only accommodation option on Independence beach. Enormous, slightly rundown but clean rooms with chunky wooden double beds. All facilities, with a terrace overlooking the sea. 4

Sea View Villa Just back from Serendipity Beach. ⓣ034/935555. A range of big, clean rooms that are better value than most of those on the beach just 20m away. Internet access, too. 2

Seaside Hotel Ochheuteal beach ⓣ034/933641. At the upper end of the Sihanoukville accommodation spectrum, popular with conferences and expats. 6

Sokha Beach Resort Sokha Beach. ⓣ034/935999, ⓦwww.sokhahotels.com. The city's most luxurious (and most expensive) hotel features nearly 200 rooms in a huge complex occupying almost all of Sokha Beach. Rooms have all the facilities and some have great views. Beautiful swimming pool, spa, fitness centre, tennis courts, watersports equipment, three restaurants and three bars. 6

Susaday Ochheuteal beach ⓣ034/933907. Within a towel's throw of the beach, this French-owned guesthouse offers smallish but spotless, secure rooms, all with fan and bathroom. 2

The City

Sihanoukville's main attraction is its beaches. **Victory beach** is the nearest to Weather Station Hill, but its small size and proximity to the port, about 3km north of the downtown area, render it the least attractive. You're more likely to find a few fishermen working on their boats than tourists soaking up the sun on this quiet beach and, after a ten-minute stroll southwest, you can be on the almost-completely undeveloped Hawaii beach. However, it's worth making the trip to **Sokha** and **Ochheuteal beaches**, the most impressive of Sihanoukville's seaside offerings. Ochheuteal, about 2km south of the town centre, is the most popular and has the most facilities and accommodation, all concentrated at the western end of the three-kilometre strand. At the far west, a mini-resort – the aptly named Serendipity beach – has sprung up, with a mixture of mid-range and budget accommodation, restaurants and bars Sokha, west of Ochheuteal, is dominated by the new *Sokha Beach Resort*, but there's still public access, and it's one of the town's most attractive stretches of sand, with rockpools to explore. **Independence beach**, the next beach along, is named after a seven-storey 1960s monolith, the *Independence Hotel* at the western end of the beach, now renovated and, at the time of writing, about to open as a new hotel. The beach itself is on a gently curved bay, with a line of drinks stalls and shaded huts. As the beach sweeps round, rocks and small, secluded bays allow some privacy. As at the other beaches, deckchairs and inner tubes are available for 1000r.

The town's sights are limited; the main pagoda, **Wat Leu**, atop Phnom Sihanoukville, north of the town, is a worthy excursion for the panoramic views and the colourful vihara interior. To get there, take the turning off from National Route 4 at the brewery. **Wat Krom**, on Santepheap Street, is set in a tranquil spot among Bodhi trees, with views across the sea and surrounding countryside.

Boat trips to Sihanoukville's offshore islands are organized by most guesthouses. A day-trip, including barbecue, costs around $15 – snorkelling equipment provided – and camping trips for two to three days are also arranged ($50 per head). For **diving trips**, contact *Chez Claude* (see opposite) or EcoSea Dive (see p.166) on Sopheakmongkol West, which offers snorkeling and scuba diving trips to offshore islands, including a one-day "Discover Scuba Diving" trip for $50.

Eating, drinking and entertainment

Sihanoukville has a good selection of Western-oriented **restaurants** and **bars**, so it's worth leaving behind the comfort of Weather Station Hill and exploring some of the options. In town, most places are clustered along Ekareach Street at the junction with Sopheakmongkol East – which, incidentally, is where you'll find the night market. Other than those mentioned below, new places are opening up all the time and you're sure to find something to suit. Most of the Western places stay open beyond midnight, and a couple only shut when the last person leaves. Other **entertainment** options include a few karaoke bars and the casinos.

Restaurants and cafés

Angkor Arms Cnr of Sopheapmongkol West and Ekareach. Real English-pub atmosphere, with friendly staff and a wide range of Khmer and Western food, including fish and chips and pork chops. Draft beer, cocktails and sports on cable TV. 9am–late.

Apsara Cnr of St 109 and Sopheakmongkol East. Locals swear by this town-centre restaurant, specializing in Khmer and Chinese food, but their double-pricing system makes it expensive for foreigners. Open for lunch and dinner.

Bamboo Light Café Ekareach St. Popular place serving generous portions of Sri Lankan and Indian dishes. Buffet on Tuesdays and Fridays, all-day "happy hour". 8am–late.

Corner Bar Weather Station Hill. Popular bar/restaurant serving sandwiches, great pizzas and other Western dishes. Delivery service, too. 2pm–late.

Hawaii Seaview Seafood restaurant right on Hawaii beach. Open all day, but popular early evening for sunset views of Koh Pos Island.

Les Feuilles One block back from Ochheuteal beach. Excellent French/Khmer menu at this bar-restaurant, especially popular with weekending French expats. The steaks are the pick of the extensive menu, and come with a choice of sauces, including a creamy blue-cheese dressing. 7am–late.

Melting Pot Weather Station Hill. Atmospheric candlelit Indian restaurant, with some interesting Western dishes, too. Great food (and music), with plenty of veggie options. On Sunday, there's roast pork with apple sauce.

Mick and Craig's Between the Golden Lion Roundabout and Serendipity beach. Choice Western grub for the discerning budget traveller. Serves sandwiches, quiches and grills. Open all day and bar open till late.

Sam's Weather Station Hill. Excellent, inexpensive food (Thai a speciality) from these well-established Sihanoukville veterans, who know everything there is to know about the area. Open all day.

Sea Dragon Nice spot on Ochheuteal beach, with very reasonably priced seafood specials. Serves breakfast, lunch and dinner.

Starfish Bakery Off Sopheakmongkol East, behind Samudera Supermarket. Delicious Western breads, cakes, scones and other goodies to eat in a garden setting, or take away. Daily 7am–6pm.

Treasure Island Seafood Between Hawaii and Independence beaches. A gem of a restaurant serving succulent Chinese food with the emphasis on seafood and fish, set on its own small, secluded beach, ideal for watching the sunset. Moderately priced and friendly. Open for lunch and dinner.

Bars and clubs

All **bars** and **clubs** are open daily and some stay open 24 hours.

Angkor Beer Discotheque Boray Kamakor St. Teenage Khmers giving it large to techno and Euro pop.

Biba Nightclub Hun Sen Beach Drive, Dom Thmei Village. Popular Khmer disco, a little way out of town.

Blue Storm Ekareach St. The nightclub for *really* loud Khmer, Thai and other Asian music.

Chiva's Shack South end of Ochheuteal Beach. Happening beach bar, with parties every Tuesday and Friday.

Dusk Till Dawn Sopheakmongkol West, just around the corner from the *Angkor Arms*. One of the best late-night places in town – a pleasant rooftop bar with eclectic music. Opens 9pm.

Fishermans Den Sopheakmongkol East, off Ekareach St, near Caltex. Bustling rooftop girly bar, with satellite TV. Closes when the last punter leaves.

Unkle Bob's Serendipity beach. A 24hr beach bar with beers, fruit shakes, and Western and Asian food.

Listings

Banks and exchange Canadia Bank, Ekareach St, east of 7 Makara St for cash on MasterCard and MoneyGram; Cambodian Commercial Bank, Ekareach St, junction of Boray-Kamakor St; First Overseas Bank, Ekareach St, west of 7 Makara St; Union Commercial Bank, on the corner of Ekareach and Sopheakmongkol sts.

Diving To arrange a trip, contact Claude at *Chez Claude* (☎012/824870) or EcoSea Dive (☎012/654104; www.EcoSea.com), on Sopheakmongkol West.

Hospitals and clinics Sihanoukville Public Hospital (☎034/933111) is on Ekareach St, between the town centre and Golden Lion roundabout; it has very limited facilities. Dr Kav Sokhan is English-speaking and can be contacted on ☎034/ 933842.

Internet access Internet access in Sihanoukville is easy to find, with outlets all over town and rates of around $1.50/hr. Two options are ABC Computer and the Camintel office, both on Ekareach St west of the town centre.

Police On Ekareach St between Independence Square and the town centre (☎034/933222 or 016/889776).

Post office The main post office is one block behind Krong St, off Victory beach; post restante is available. You can get stamps and post items at the smaller branch office opposite the market.

Supermarkets Samudera Supermarket, 7 Makara St, 50m from Ekareach St.

Telephone services International calls cost around $3.50 from Sihanoukville and can be made from hotels and the Camintel office on Ekareach St just west of Boray-Kamakor St. Domestic calls are best made from the cheap-rate booths around the market.

Ream National Park

Ream National Park, also known as Preah Sihanouk National Park, located 18km east of Sihanoukville, is one of the most accessible national parks in Cambodia. Its 21,000 hectares include evergreen and mangrove forests, sandy beaches, coral reefs, offshore islands and a rich diversity of flora and fauna. It's a great place to explore some of Cambodia's unique, unspoilt natural environment. To get to the **park headquarters** you'll need to join a group from a guesthouse, or take a taxi or moto (about $10 per person depending on number in the group) from Sihanoukville along National Route 4 to Ream village and then turn right down the track next to the airport. The rangers at the park headquarters (☎012/875096) are extremely helpful, and can arrange boat trips (about $30 for the boat, or $5 per person for large groups) along the Prek Toek Sap estuary, to the fishing village of Thmor Tom, and perhaps on to the islands of Koh Thmei and Koh Ses. The river is bordered by mangroves, and you're likely to see kingfishers, sea eagles and maybe monkeys along the way.

Koh S'dach

The small island of **KOH S'DACH** is the fishing capital of Cambodian waters, just off Koh Kong province in the Gulf of Thailand. If you're rushing between Sihanoukville and Thailand, there's little here to warrant an overnight stop, but with time on your hands, the area is worth exploring. Koh S'dach ("King's Island") takes its name from the legend of a visiting monarch who sheltered here with his soldiers in ancient times. Searching for fresh water, they came upon a miraculous spring bubbling up from the rocks; the **royal spring** can still be found near the passenger boat port.

The real reason for stopping here is to get out in a boat to explore the coast – just off the north shore of Koh S'dach you'll find brilliantly coloured coral within paddling distance. A cluster of **islands** nearby – Koh Samai, Koh Samot, Koh Chan and Koh Totang – are all within a boat's row. A fishing boat to the islands is open to negotiation: $20 a day seems the going rate. Alternatively, you can hop in one of the small, fibreglass boats that go across to the mainland (around 4000r) where there are also some fine, deserted beaches.

Accommodation can be found on Koh S'dach, although it's possible to camp on any of the beaches if you have a hammock, mosquito net, food and water – make it clear to the fisherman when you want to be picked up. The island's guesthouse is within easy walking distance of the jetty. As you leave the pier, go along to the left to the *Koh S'Dach* (❶), marked only by a sign with white Khmer writing; it's a charming wooden family house with small, clean rooms, mosquito nets and shared bathroom.

Note that all transactions on the island are in **baht**. The pathway from the port to the small market area is the centre of activity on the island. Fishermen gather to gamble at streetside games of cards, dice, or playing-card pool. You can buy simple **food** here, and at the stalls around the port. A well-stocked village store sells beer, snacks and sundries.

The only way **to get** to Koh S'Dach is by the express boat, which stops briefly as it surges between Koh Kong and Sihanoukville. The fare is a flat B300 to or from any of these destinations and takes about two hours.

Koh Kong

Boat schedules and border opening times used to conspire to make an overnight stop in **KOH KONG** more of a necessity than a choice. Since the border post extended its hours to 8pm, it's no longer necessary to stay, though a few days exploring the surrounding area is well rewarded. One option is to hire a small boat and head to the waterfalls at **Tatai**, a fifty-minute trip upstream under the cliffs of the Cardamom Mountains. Several **islands** lie near to the town, the largest of which is **Koh Kong** itself, which has pristine stretches of sand on the seaward side. However, an easier excursion is to **Koh Kapi**, where you'll find some of the nicest beaches in the district. A small speedboat will cost around B200 each way for the thirty-minute trip.

The town of Koh Kong is not on an island as is commonly assumed, but on the mainland in the province of the same name. Situated on the eastern bank of the Kah Bpow River, where it empties into the Gulf of Thailand, the town was historically a remote and insular outpost, its prosperity based on fishing, logging and smuggling. The logging has long gone and smuggling is no longer overt, and now it's the border that brings in the trade. A new bridge, nearly 2km long, crosses the river, and a left turn shortly after the bridge takes you to Beach 2000, a popular weekend spot for locals. The biggest local attraction is the **Koh Kong Safari World** (☎016/800811; open 9am-5pm; admission $12, kids $8), out by the Thai border, which presents shows featuring dolphins, orang-utangs, crocodiles, sea lions and parrots, in a Disney-like setting. Despite the fact that much of the rich sandalwood forest has been transported to Thailand, the area around the town remains beautiful and unspoilt. This remote outpost owes its identity more to **Thai** influences than Khmer culture: most people speak Thai, **baht** is the favoured currency and Beer Chang is the drink of choice. Even the governor of the province sends his children to school in Thailand.

Practicalities

Arriving by **road** along National Route 48 from Sre Ambel (155km), you can stop off in town or head straight through to the border. If you're stopping in Koh Kong, get out at the market or the port, from where you can easily walk to guesthouse accommodation. From the dock, it's a five-minute walk to the market in the town centre. When it comes to **moving on**, an express boat leaves at 8am for **Sihanoukville** every day (B600); it takes four hours and goes via Koh S'dach. Be warned, however, that this can be an unpleasant experience in stormy weather. Alternatively, shared taxis ($10) or minibuses ($15) cover the long road journey to either Sihanoukville or Phnom Penh.

Koh Kong also has an airport to the northeast of town, but no flights were operating at the time of writing. Koh Kong town is not a large place, so you can get around **on foot**, but motos are not expensive at just 500r a trip. There's an Acleda Bank on the north side of the market, or you can change baht and dollars at the market itself.

Accommodation

Accommodation options have improved remarkably in recent years with the opening of two smart yet inexpensive hotels on the riverfront.

Asean Just north of the jetty, set back from the river ☎035/936667. The town's newest (and currently, best-value) hotel has spotlessly clean rooms, many of them with views over the river. ❷–❹

Koh Kong Guest House South of the jetty, ☎035/936034. Clean fan rooms with shared bathrooms, some with river views. ❶

Koh Kong International Resort Club Beside the Thai border, ☎016/700970. This hotel and casino complex is the most luxurious place around, with a choice of deluxe rooms and bungalow suites, set in tropical gardens running down to an attractive beach. ❺

Otto's On a side road south of the jetty ☎012/924249. The most popular budget hotel in town. Rooms here are pretty simple, with shared bathrooms, and there's an upstairs terrace that acts as a combination of lounge, bar and inexpensive restaurant. ❶

Phoumint Koh Kong Just north of the jetty on the riverbank, ☎011/948255. Some rooms here have fine river views. The best ones are large and comfy with a/c and hot-water bathrooms, but the cheapest fan rooms are also very good value. ❷–❹.

Rasmey Buntham Guest House Southeast of the market, ☎016/719449 Features good-sized rooms set around a central lobby, with a pleasant patio. Staff can help with travel arrangements, and offer a free pick-up from the border if you phone ahead. ❶

Eating

Both the *Phoumint Koh Kong* and the *Asean* hotels have good **restaurants**, the former with great river views, the latter with a useful picture menu. All the guest-houses listed above have attached restaurants and turn out reasonable Khmer food,

Overland into Thailand via the Koh Kong–Hat Lek border crossing

From Koh Kong, it's a twelve-kilometre shared taxi or moto ride (B100) to the border crossing at Cham Yeam (daily 7am–8pm). Thai visas are arranged on the spot. From Hat Lek, minibuses leave for **Trat** (see p.1034), 91km northwest, roughly every 45 minutes between 6am and 5pm (1hr–1hr 30min; B100); Trat has regular connections on to Ko Chang and Bangkok.

Coming **into Cambodia**, thirty-day visas are issued on arrival at the border crossing (US$20 and two photos). If you want to reach **Sihanoukville** in one day, you'll need to catch the 6am minibus from Trat, which should give you just enough time to connect with the daily 8am boat to Sihanoukville from Koh Kong (see above).

while *Otto's* also offers some Western dishes. The nicest ambience in town is at the *Baan Peakmai*, on the road that runs past the east side of the market, three blocks to the north. This place has a covered terrace around a garden and serves good Khmer, Thai and Western food, including many vegetarian dishes, all at reasonable prices. On this same road but nearer the market are the *Number One Bar* and the *Moto Bar*. Both are run by Westerners, the former being a chill-out bar offering some snacks, and the latter serving a wide range of Khmer and Western food, including big breakfasts. *Moto Bar* also has a range of rooms for rent (❷–❺).

Kampot

KAMPOT, with its riverside location, backdrop of misty Bokor Mountains and terraces of French shop-houses, is one of the most attractive of Cambodia's provincial towns. It's also the staging post for side trips to Bokor and Kep, and a pleasant place to spend an afternoon, browsing round the market, strolling along the Teuk Chhou River, or heading out to nearby Teuk Chhou Zoo and rapids. The river marks the western boundary of the town, with the new market to the north and the roundabout in the centre.

Taxis and **pick-ups** will drop you either at the market or at the transport stop in the southeast of town, off the road to Kep. Taxis to Phnom Penh and Sihanoukville cost 12,000r, and a place on the back of a pick-up half this. Most places around Kampot are walkable, but **motos** are readily available to take the weight off tired feet for 500 to 1000r.

The main **hotel** in town is the *Borey Bokor Hotel* (☎016/960700; ❸), between the roundabout and the river, with brand-new en-suite rooms, equipped with cable TV and air conditioning. *Borey Bokor II* (☎012/820826; ❷), on the north side of the roundabout, is almost identical, but has no hot water. *Mealy Chenda* (☎012/831559; ❷) operates a guesthouse a block south of the roundabout with a range of bright cheerful rooms and a dorm ($2), as well as a travellers' restaurant. Another good budget alternative is *Blissful Guesthouse*, located on a quiet side street about 1km south of the traffic circle (☎012/513024 or 012/679607; ❷). It's a Western-run place with very competitive rates. Rooms are well-kept and all beds have mosquito nets. There's also a dorm ($2), a chill-out room upstairs and a travellers' restaurant downstairs. Another friendly option is *Ta Eng Guesthouse* (☎012/330058; ❶) on the road towards Kep, where the comfy rooms have en-suite showers; there are also cheaper no-frills rooms and another $2 dorm. To spoil yourself, consider staying in the lovely colonial *Bokor Mountain Club* on the riverfront (☎033/932314; ❺), which boasts stylish rooms upstairs and an extravagant Italian restaurant downstairs. They also organize excursions by four-wheel drive and boat.

The best **restaurant** in town is the *Ta Eou* on the east bank of the river near the market; the delicious seafood is inexpensive and the setting overlooking the river is peaceful for a late afternoon beer or two. On the roundabout in town, the *Phnom Kamchay Thmey* is a hugely popular place serving excellent Khmer food, including delicious rice and noodle soups for breakfast. For Western options, there's the *Little Garden Bar* on the riverfront north of the bridge, which has tasty and filling daily specials, or the *Mealy Chenda* or *Blissful* guesthouses, both of which serve up cheap travellers' fare. If you feel like splashing out, head for the pricey *Bokor Mountain Club*'s Italian restaurant down on the river. A cheaper riverside option, just north of the *Bokor Mountain Club*, is the *Bamboo Light Café*, which serves Western breakfasts and sandwiches, as well as some tempting Sri Lankan and Indian dishes.

Nightlife in Kampot is very low-key and mostly involves sitting around in the guesthouse restaurants exchanging travellers' tales. Both the *Little Garden Bar* and *Bokor Mountain Club* include a range of cocktails on their drinks menu. Otherwise, you're limited to the usual karaoke places, the most popular of which are across the river towards the railway bridge.

Kep

Some 25km southeast of Kampot, **KEP** itself is rather a disappointment for its narrow, grubby beach, though it does have a laid-back atmosphere, which you can soak up on palm-shaded walks and whilst eating delicious, inexpensive seafood freshly plucked from the clean waters. The main attraction of coming here, however, is to take a boat trip to one of the pretty **islands** just offshore. Kep is really no more than a fishing village during the week, but at weekends hordes descend on it from the capital, and the pace picks up a notch. Approaching Kep from Kampot, you'll see the remains of magnificent **colonial villas** and holiday homes half-hidden in the shrubs along the three-kilometre seafront. Once an exclusive coastal resort, many of the town's houses were destroyed by the Khmer Rouge and now most are lived in by squatters, although one or two have been renovated.

The old **Royal Palace** occupies a fine sunset vantage point atop the cliff as you run into Kep; past the food stalls, you'll round the headland and see the large Vietnamese island of **Phu Quoc** rising offshore in the Gulf of Thailand. The sovereignty of the island has long been in dispute, however, and the white statue of a woman at Kep beach looks out towards the island, yearning for the day when it will be returned to Cambodia.

One of the highlights of a trip to Kep is a boat tour to one of the nearby islands, such as quaint **Koh Tonsay** ("Rabbit Island"), with its three good beaches and five welcoming families. Nicer still is the beautiful **Koh Poh** ("Coral Island"), with blue water and white beaches, and great coral for snorkelling. Boat trips can be arranged at any of the guesthouses in Kep or Kampot, or down on the beach in Kep. A boat to Koh Tonsay costs about $15, or $40 to Koh Poh.

Practicalities

To get to Kep from Kampot, take a moto (12,000r one way) or negotiate a **share taxi** from the Kampot stand. **Accommodation** in Kep is expanding fast, but seldom fills up, as most Cambodians only visit for the day from Phnom Penh – when they go, the *barangs* have it to themselves. Most places only have electricity from dusk till dawn, if that, so check before choosing a place. On the main road into town, just before the start of the one-way system, a side road on the right leads to the *Kep Seaside Guesthouse* (⊕012/684241; ❷), right on the beach and offering rooms with en-suite facilities; they also have a small restaurant serving Western and Khmer food. The owners are friendly, and speak a little English. For spectacular views and nature at your fingertips though, the *Veranda* (⊕012/888619; ❶) takes some beating. Located on the hill behind the town (to reach it, turn inland at the Aspeca orphanage and follow the track up for about a kilometre), this funky and well-run complex of thatched bungalows connected by wooden walkways above the ground offers a range of rooms from simple to sophisticated, as well as a good restaurant and atmospheric bar. The fanciest (and priciest) place by far in Kep is the *Champey Inn* (Ⓣ012/501742, Ⓦwww.artsuriyatravel.com; ❺), on the west coast near the start of the one-way system. It has a swimming pool, a French/Khmer restaurant, and the small (but overpriced) rooms are stylish. Some of the best-value rooms in town can be found at the new *Raksmey Guest House* (Ⓣ012/685769; ❷), where all rooms are big and comfortable and have attached bathrooms. It's located back from the beach, just behind the **tourist office**. Kep is heaven for the **seafood** connoisseur. The Crab Market on the first stretch of seafront on the way in from Kampot is the place for crab bisque; further on, the stalls around the centre cook up grilled fish, chicken, and other delights, but only during the day. Apart from the *Raksmey*, all the guesthouses have restaurants, and the one at the *Veranda* is recommended for its fresh veggies straight from the garden.

Bokor

Unable to cope with the Cambodian heat during the hottest months of the year, the French searched for cool relief among the higher elevations of the Elephant Mountains. Thus, the hill station of **BOKOR**, 40km northwest of Kampot, was born, combining the requirements of a milder climate at its elevation of just over 1000m, with magnificent views across the Gulf of Thailand. As in Kep, the villas, King Sihanouk's former royal palace and casino were abandoned in the 1970s, but here the buildings, while still derelict, remain somewhat more intact. It's a ghost town that feels as if its former inhabitants might re-appear around any corner at any moment.

Bokor has been given a new lease of life as **Bokor National Park** (daily; 20,000r), nearly 350,000 acres of prime forest. This is a vast wildlife sanctuary with tigers, leopards, pythons and elephants believed still to be at large; they keep well away from the touristy areas, however, so your most exciting brush with nature is likely to be a dive-bomb attack by exotic butterflies or a sighting of the great hornbill – they stand over a metre tall.

Popokvil Waterfall is a magnificent sight after a spot of rain – an easy twenty-minute walk on a well-marked path through the jungle brings you to the top of the falls, where four streams converge just before the rocks to push the discoloured jungle water over two giant steps of more than 10m each, flanked on both sides by dense vegetation. In the dry season, however, the torrent dwindles to a trickle.

Bokor's real attraction, though, is the deserted hill station with its church, casino and hotel, the **Bokor Palace**. In 1979, the Vietnamese were holed up in the hotel shooting at the Khmer Rouge sheltering in the church; more recently, it was the scene of a different kind of shooting when Matt Dillon and crew arrived to use the buildings as a backdrop for the feature film *City of Ghosts*. It's safe to explore the buildings, which are all smothered with an unusual orange lichen, and the hotel especially is atmospheric as mist wafts across the hills and in through the broken windows. It's worth walking to the edge of the terrace, and looking over the sheer drop into the dense jungle as a concert of jungle calls rises up from the foliage. Legend has it that high-rollers who lost big at the casino would throw themselves over this steep ledge in despair.

Practicalities

Bokor can be reached on a guesthouse **tour** from Kampot or Sihanoukville (the former is nearer and therefore cheaper at about $6 per person), or by rented motorbike if you are an experienced off-road biker. The turning to the park is signposted to the right off National Route 3, towards Sihanoukville. The track that twists up the mountain through banana and pineapple plantations, followed by lush, green jungle-scape, varies in condition from adequate to poor, and the trip to the top takes two hours on a good day. About 15km up the hill, the strange-shaped rock that juts out from the left is known locally as Kabal Barang (the "French Head"). The trees begin to thin out as you approach the summit, and once you're on the plateau it's a marshy scrub; look out for the carnivorous pitcher plants, as well as ground orchids and other wild flowers in the rainy season. The first house and gardens you'll come across are part of King Sihanouk's old palace. At the first junction, Bokor is to the left, while Popokvil Waterfall is to the right – beyond here, you'll see the church, standing on an isolated hillock. Just before the church, a road forks left for the casino and ranger's office and right to the church, hotel and other deserted buildings.

The large green-roofed building sitting proudly in the centre of Bokor is the National Park Research and Training Centre, where you can **stay** in large, comfy bunk beds for $5 per person. If you're planning on staying, though, bring your own **food** as none is available.

2.6

Eastern Cambodia

The further east you travel from the Mekong River to the Vietnamese border, the poorer the people and the more basic the infrastructure. The Mekong is the overland gateway to this region, punctuated by the three very different towns of **Kompong Cham**, **Kratie** and **Stung Treng**. Travellers are beginning to make the journey here and beyond to the remote hilly provinces of **Rattanakiri** and Mondulkiri, populated by chunchiet, Cambodia's indigenous minority people, and dotted with spectacular waterfalls. Others travel on the Mekong River en route to and from Laos.

During the **American War**, the eastern provinces were heavily bombed by the Americans in their attempt to flush out the Vietcong from the Ho Chi Minh Trail. These attempts proved largely unsuccessful, however, and thousands of Cambodian civilians were killed, wounded or left homeless by the attacks. It was during this period that the Khmer Rouge began gathering strength and momentum in the area. Pol Pot was using the remote northeastern provinces to hide from Sihanouk's troops, while receiving support from his communist brothers in the Viet Minh. Recruiting countrymen for the cause was not difficult – they were happy to join the fight against the systematic destruction of the region.

Nowadays, the Mekong towns, Kompong Cham in particular, are forward-looking and relatively prosperous, having integrated well with modern-day Cambodia. But striking off eastwards, you'll see a different picture, as the remote uplands remain stuck in their own isolated world, largely untouched by the march of modernization and development.

Kompong Cham

The northeast's largest city and capital of the province of the same name, **KOMPONG CHAM**, 120km northeast of Phnom Penh, is a busy transport hub, though with a very relaxed atmosphere. It has become even more laid-back since the huge Japanese-funded bridge across the Mekong was completed, rendering ferry services obsolete. Improved roads in the region also mean that it's no longer necessary to stop over here, though it's a shame to pass it by, as the city has a distinctive charm.

It's well worth taking a casual stroll around the town centre near the market and along the banks of the massive Mekong, which is about 1.5km wide here, to look at the delightful but crumbling colonial buildings that line the streets. **Wat Pra Tohm Nah Day Doh**, a modern temple located on the riverbank about a kilometre south of the bridge, also merits a view; fronted by a huge standing Buddha, its grounds are scattered with intriguing statues of people and animals, and a forest of miniature stupas that stab up into the sky.

The most important (and most interesting) sight around town is **Wat Nokor**, about 2km north of town just off Route 7, an unusual fusion of ancient and modern Khmer religious architecture, with a new temple built in and around the eleventh-century ruins. Approaching the main vihara through the darkness of the crumbling east gate highlights the juxtaposition of old and new: luminous blues, pinks, oranges and greens from the paintings on the walls, columns and ceilings framed by the ancient laterite walls, still painted black from the days of Khmer Rouge occupation. The unusual combination makes for some striking sights, such as bright pink Buddha images sitting in recesses in the monochrome sandstone stupa.

About 12km further out of town past Wat Nokor rise the twin temple hills of **Phnom Bpros** and **Phnom Srei**, "Man and Woman Mountains". The legend goes that, in ancient times, it was the women who had to ask the men to marry them. Getting fed up with this, the women invited the men to compete against them to see who could build the best temple by daybreak – the winners would also win the right to be proposed to in future. They set to work, building their temples on adjacent hills. The women, realizing that they were lagging behind their male counterparts, built a huge fire, which the men took to be the rising sun. Exhausted, they headed for bed, while the women carried on building; they produced a magnificent temple, thereby winning the right to receive marriage proposals. Both Phnom Bpros and Phnom Srei afford fine views – of Lake Boeng Tom to the west, and Kompong Cham town and the Mekong River in the east. To get there, rent a motorbike in town or negotiate with a moto driver.

There are several other interesting places within the vicinity of Kompong Cham that can be reached **by boat** and make for a rewarding day out. One such trip is along the winding Tonle Tuok, a tributary of the Mekong, to the **Maha Leap Pagoda**, an old wooden structure with gilt-adorned teak columns that was somehow spared by the Khmer Rouge, and is now surrounded by modern temple buildings. From here, you can continue to **Proek Changkran**, a weaving village where silk is woven on traditional handlooms, located just upstream from Maha Leap Pagoda. Silk traders from around the country come here to purchase the fine, detailed cloth. You can approach local boatmen (found either in front of the *Mekong Hotel* or by the boat jetty just south of the bridge) to arrange such a day out (expect to pay about $20), or ask at the *Mekong Crossing Restaurant* for more details of this and other outings. If you're travelling alone, most of these sites can be reached more cheaply by moto.

Practicalities

Boats from Kratie stop at the jetty just south of the new bridge, and the express boat to Kratie (28,000r) leaves at 7.30am every day. **Pick-ups** serve Kratie (20,000r), but it's a roundabout (and even longer) journey. **Buses** from Phnom Penh (8000r) – an easy two-hour trip – arrive at the depot northwest of the market, while taxis (10,000r) and minibuses (7000r) arrive at the market. The best-value **accommodation** can be found at the *Mekong Hotel* (☎042/941536, ❷), located on the riverfront a short way north of the bridge, boasting spotless, sizeable rooms with TV, some with air-con. Another smart option is the *Mittapheap Hotel*, north of the market (☎042/941565; ❷), which has comfortable en-suite rooms with TV and fridge for very reasonable prices. The best of the guesthouses is the *Bophear Thmey* (☎012/796803; ❶), one block back from the river behind the *Mekong Hotel*. Clean fan rooms with attached bathrooms go for just $3, and they have bicycles for rent as well. Also worth considering, the *Nava* (☎042/941742; ❶), near the market, offers clean, smallish twin-bed rooms, with bathroom and TV.

Given its size, **eating** options are rather limited in Kompong Cham, and some places close by around 9pm so don't leave it too late to eat. For Western breakfasts, the *Mekong Crossing Restaurant*, just round the corner from the *Mekong Hotel*, serves a huge plate of eggs, bacon, chips and baked beans for a very reasonable price. They also have a short menu of Khmer and Western dishes available throughout the day and evening. The *Hao An Restaurant* at the corner of Pasteur and Monivong has a vast selection of delicious food from 8000r, and easy ordering from the full-colour picture menu. West of town beside the lake, the *Boeng Kan Seng Restaurant* has over 100 Khmer and Chinese dishes on its menu, and is a pleasant, relaxing spot. Around the market, you'll find some decent food stalls and noodle shops, with drink stalls along the riverfront.

Kratie

Life ticks by slowly in **KRATIE** (pronounced "Kracheh"). This tiny town on the Mekong is an unexpected delight, with a relaxing, indolent atmosphere. Away from the blemish of the modern market, Kratie is a wonderful hotchpotch of colonial terraces and traditional old Khmer buildings – sturdy wooden structures, with dark-red roof tiles and often a decorative flourish. There's not much for visitors to do in the town itself, but it makes a good base for exploring the surrounding countryside. About 11km north of Kratie following the river road, **Phnom Sambok** is set in a grotto of lush-green vegetation on a twin-peaked hill. The dense trees hide a meditation commune on the first level, and a small temple on the higher summit. Around 10km further north on the same road, a sign marks your arrival at **Kampie**, the only riverside vantage point from which to view the rare freshwater **Irrawaddy dolphins**. A small group of dolphins live in this area of rapids, and can usually be seen at any time of day, being particularly evident when the water is low. It's thought that no more than a hundred of these snub-nosed dolphins remain in the Mekong. The only way to visit these places is to hire a moto from Kratie (about $3). If you can spare a full day, you could also include a visit to **Sambor**, some 35km north of Kratie, the site of an ancient pre-Angkorian capital.

Practicalities

The 7.30am express **boat** from Kompong Cham to Kratie takes around three hours and costs 28,000r. It then continues on to Stung Treng (32,000r) during the rainy season, leaving at noon and arriving there around 4pm. There's little point getting a pick-up here from Kompong Cham (20,000r), as it's a circuitous journey that takes even longer. Between Kratie and Stung Treng, the road is appalling and the journey by shared taxi (25,000r) takes around five hours on a good day. However, the road will shortly be sealed and times will decrease. There are two buses that leave directly to Phnom Penh each morning at around 7.30am (18,000r). For **accommodation**, the plushest place in town is the *Oudom Sambath Hotel* (☎012/965944; ❶–❹), situated a short way north of the boat dock, which has some large rooms with fancy furnishings and all facilities, as well as particularly good-value fan rooms with en-suite bathrooms Opposite the boat dock is the *Santepheap Hotel* (☎012/971537; ❷–❸); rooms here are well appointed and feature en-suite bathrooms and TV, with some also boasting hot water and air conditioning. The *Heng Heng I* and *II* (☎072/971405; ❶), almost next door to each other on the riverfront and just south of the dock, both have pleasant rooms with en-suite bathrooms and TV, and there is a good restaurant on the ground floor of *Heng Heng I*. Opposite the southwest corner of the market is the long-standing, family-run *Star Guesthouse* (☎012/753401; ❶). The cheapest rooms have neither windows nor frills, but others are spacious affairs with en-suite bathroom and cable TV. The owners speak good English, can arrange motos and run a small restaurant serving some Western food.

The first **restaurant** likely to catch your eye is the *Red Sun Falling*, a Western-run place just south of the boat dock that has a short menu of Khmer dishes chalked up on a blackboard, a range of beers and cocktails and a cosy ambience. For a wider choice of food, head for the *Heng Heng Hotel I*, open from early morning to mid-evening. They do a good range of fish and Khmer/Chinese dishes, including a pretty good sweet-and-sour vegetables. The *Mekong Restaurant*, just round the corner from *Red Sun Falling*, offers competent, if unexciting, renditions of the standard range of Khmer dishes, with an English-language menu. The *Star Guesthouse* serves a good Western breakfast, great shakes and other backpacker staples such as pancakes. Snack and drink **stalls** also set up every evening by the riverside.

Stung Treng

For most people, **STUNG TRENG** is just a staging post on the overland trek to Rattanakiri or on the way to Laos, but the surrounding countryside is beautiful and can be explored by boat, moto or bicycle. Hotel and guesthouse owners can arrange visits to a silk weaving centre, fruit orchards, lakes and waterfalls, and boat trips to remote villages, so more and more travellers are hanging around here a few days. One of the most popular outings is a **Mekong trip to the Laos border** (the Sekong joins the Mekong 2km west of town), offering the possibility of some dolphin-spotting and a glimpse at the waterfalls that make the river impassable here. Back in town, the charm of Stung Treng is in seeking out your own entertainment – supping a cool drink at the riverfront, or wandering around the market with its chunchiet products.

Practicalities

Boats only come up from Kratie when the river is high enough (32,000r), generally July to late October, when they dock on the river in front of the town. At other times, the usual way to get here is by share taxi or **pick-up** from Kratie (25,000r) or Banlung (30,000r). All road transport arrives and leaves from the transport stop on the riverfront.

Moving on to Rattanakiri, shared taxis and pick-ups leave at around 7.30am and then intermittently through the day, depending on demand. Prepare for a cramped and bumpy trip of about four hours. For Kratie, just turn up at the transport stop, while for the Laos border, hotel and guesthouse owners will help fix you up with a boat ($25 for the boat, or $5 per person). Opt for an ordinary boat; in a speedboat, there's little chance of enjoying the scenery as you hurtle by, legs cramped up and clinging on for dear life. If you plan to cross the border, you'll need to be in possession of a Laos (or coming the other way Cambodian) visa. Immigration officials on both sides ask for a $2–3 fee to stamp your passport, just one of many scams that operate at all land borders into Cambodia. If you ask for the official's name and demand a receipt, you may find they back down on this request.

Virtually opposite the boat terminal and taxi stand is the most convenient **place to stay** in town, the *Riverside Guest House* (☎012/439454; ❶), where the few simple but adequate rooms are often full. Its owner, Mr T, also happens to be the best fixer in town and can arrange trips to a range of interesting destinations in the local area. A notch up in price is the *Sekong Hotel* (☎074/973762; ❶–❷), a five-minute walk west along the riverside, where the best rooms are bright and spacious but its cheapest rooms look rather neglected. If it's comfort you're after to recover from a long journey, head for the *Sok Sambath Hotel* (☎012/327677; ❷–❸) at the eastern end of the market.

The market in Stung Treng is exceptional for serving delicious Khmer **food** of the type people cook at home: throughout the day and into the evening, you can fill up easily for less than a $1. Other than that, the *Riverside Guest House* includes Western breakfast, spaghetti and pancakes among its offerings, which you can enjoy downstairs or in the neat rooftop restaurant and bar. The restaurant at the *Sekong Hotel* does good Chinese/Cambodian dishes and has a menu in English.

Rattanakiri

Tucked away in the remote northeastern corner of Cambodia is hilly **Rattanakiri** province, bordered by Vietnam to the east and Laos to the north. If you like nature and wildlife, this is the place to be. The rainy season leaves the area dripping with greenery and alive with exotic animals and rushing waterfalls. The rich and fertile lands are covered with plantations: rubber, coffee, sugar cane, bananas, cashew nuts and pineapples all grow in abundance. The upland forests are also home to around twelve distinct groups of **chunchiets**, who comprise over eighty percent of the province's population. Despite forgoing traditional dress for modern clothing, they remain among the most deprived people in Cambodia, with poor education and health care, and practically no way of making a living other than their traditional slash and burn farming. Banlung only became the provincial capital in 1979, when it was chosen as the site to replace the Khmer Rouge capital of Voen Sai (Voen Sai having replaced Lumphat, which was devastated by American bombs). Banlung is a good base for trips into the surrounding area to see chunchiet villages and unspoilt countryside. Particularly scenic is **Voen Sai**, one of the most accessible villages in the region, and the gateway to the **Virachey National Park**, where it is now possible to go on an organized trek.

Banlung and around

The sprawling town of **BANLUNG**, approximately 600km northeast of Phnom Penh, may be the provincial capital, but not a lot happens here. At its heart is the **market**, especially lively in the early morning when the chunchiet come in to sell fresh produce and forest foods on the scruffy patch of land nearby.

Chunchiets aside, Banlung is chiefly known for **Yeak Laom Lake** 4km east of town (daily; 4000r), created by a volcanic eruption many thousands of years ago and the centrepiece of a government Protected Area project, covering around 12,000 acres. The lake's three-kilometre circumference is lined with stands of bamboo and dense green forest, its remarkable tranquillity interrupted only by the occasional birdcall. A swim in the clean, turquoise waters is a good way to cleanse yourself of the penetrating dust from Banlung's unsealed red dirt roads. The committee responsible for managing the lake and surrounds is comprised of Tampoun villagers, the indigenous inhabitants of the area. Along the banks of the lake is the Chunchiet Cultural Centre; built in traditional Tampoun style, it houses a collection of memorabilia and examples of craft work.

About 14km from Banlung is a bizarre clearing in the forest covered by an almost circular area of flat stone – the remains of a cooled lava flow. The area is known in English as Field of Stone, and in Khmer as **Veal Rum Plan**. Rum Plan, so the legend goes, was a young boy who fell to his death from a tree onto the black volcanic rock while trying to retrieve his kite. His spirit is believed to live on, protecting the plateau and surrounding trees.

There are a number of **waterfalls** around Banlung, the most impressive of which are Ka Chhang and Chha Ong; at Chha Ong, water sprays from a rock overhang into a small jungle clearing. It lacks a decent pool for a swim, but brave visitors shower under the smaller column of water – be careful, though, as it's slippery. To get there, follow the Stung Treng road past the airport and continue for about 2km. A small road to the right leads to Chhaa Ong, and the one on the left goes to Ka Chhang. On the western fringe of Banlung, before the turning for the waterfalls, an easy ten-minute climb up **Eisey Patamak Mountain**, behind the temple of the same name, is well worth it for the glorious views of the O Traw Mountains. Locals even claim it's possible to see the mountains of Laos to the north, and Vietnam to the east. All this is lost on the five-metre-long Reclining Buddha, which lies at the summit, its eyes closed. If you've time to spare, you could ask about elephant rides at your guesthouse. Nearby villagers are only too happy to give these animals a break from hard work and let them stroll around for a while with tourists on board. Expect to pay $10 for a ride of an hour or two.

Practicalities

The airport, in the centre of Banlung, is currently served by four **flights** a week ($65; Mon, Wed, Fri & Sun) to and from Phnom Penh. Planes are met by moto-drivers and guesthouse reps. Shared taxis and pick-ups from Stung Treng to Banlung cost 30,000r. All road transport arrives at the transport stop near the market; National Route 78 is passable year round but in wet weather it becomes incredibly slippery and gets churned up, causing delays. Banlung is small enough to walk around, but **motos** are available at 500r a go if the heat gets too much.

To **move on from Banlung**, you can either fly to Phnom Penh or go by road to Stung Treng (30,000r) and then on to Kratie (25,000 r) There is a trail to Sen Monorom from Lumphat, but it's virtually impassable and locals who've done it swear "never again". Hotel and guesthouse owners can help to sort out onward transport, including getting tickets for the plane. If you'd rather do it your self, the airline offices are near the market.

There's nowhere to change travellers' cheques in town, so come with enough **cash** in small dollar bills to get you through and note that you can only buy a plane ticket with cash. Telephone, fax and postal facilities are available at the **post office**, on the right-hand side of the road out towards the lake. Internet access is also available at the post office, and at the Tribal Hotel, but rates are an expensive $5 per hour.

Accommodation and eating

Accommodation choices are getting better as the town attracts more visitors. As well as functional and reasonably priced concrete blocks in the centre, there are some stylish wooden bungalows surrounded by greenery on the outskirts of town. Most of the hotels and guesthouses have decent **restaurants**, so you shouldn't go hungry. The *Ratanak Hotel* is particularly good (try the grilled mountain beef and Chinese soup with seaweed and minced pork) and does delicious fruit shakes, too. For a special treat, make a reservation to eat at *Terre Rouge Lodge*, where you'll feast on French or Khmer fare. The only restaurant worth mentioning that isn't in a hotel or guesthouse is the *American Restaurant*, just west of the airport on the main road, which does a good line in hamburgers, calzone pizza and salads, plus Cambodian food.

Mountain Guesthouse At the crossroads northwest of the airport, ☎075/974047. This long-established wooden building has a balcony overlooking the airport's landing strip and fan rooms, some with attached bathroom and others sharing facilities. ❶

Ratanak Hotel Just east of Independence Monument, ☎075/974033. This popular place is run by a fabulous family who go out of their way to please. Rooms are spacious, with en-suite bathrooms; even if you don't stay, you should come to eat as it has one of the best restaurants in town. ❷–❸

Ratanak 2 Directly opposite the *Ratanak Hotel*, ☎075/974177. One of the newest hotels in town, this place offers some stylish rooms with heavy furnishings and wood panelling, some a/c and some with fan, set well back from the road. It also happens to have the best bar in town. ❷–❸

Terres Rouge Lodge Overlooking Boeung Kansaign to the north of town, ☎075/974051. An idyllic wooden house where rooms are luxuriously appointed using chunchiet and Cambodian fabrics and bric-a-brac. ❺

Tribal Hotel One block south of the post office and just over two blocks east of the market, ☎075/974074. An attractive addition to Banlung's accommodation scene, catering for all budgets in an attractive compound just away from the town centre. ❶–❸

Yak Lom Hill Lodge Six kilometres east of town, beyond the Hill Tribe Monument, ☎012/644240, Ⓦwww.yaklom.com. This is a cheaper place for a rural idyll, albeit further out of town. A dozen sturdily built wooden bungalows on stilts with ample verandas are surrounded by dense greenery. The simple but stylish rooms all have attached bathroom, and breakfast in the restaurant is included in the price. ❷–❹.

Voen Sai and Virachey National Park

The road north of Banlung winds its way past numerous chunchiet villages until, after around 38km, it reaches the village of **VOEN SAI**, located on the San River, the headquarters of **Virachey National Park**. Covering over 800,000 acres, the park is a haven for a variety of endangered species, including tigers, deer, rare hornbills, and kouprey, the almost-extinct jungle cow. Rangers have made real progress in the reduction of logging and poaching of rare animals, but face a continuing struggle – the price commanded by a tiger on the open market could feed a whole family for a generation. The park headquarters are on the left as you enter Voen Sai, and overnight treks in the park (including a visit to a chunchiet village, a night in a hammock and a ride downriver on a bamboo raft) can be organized through *Mountain Guesthouse* in Banlung. Prices vary from $15–25 per person per day, depending on group size.

Voen Sai itself is home to an unusual mix of **ethnic minorities**, predominantly Lao and Chinese, but also Kreung. A small boat (200r) connects Voen Sai with villages on the opposite bank – to the right, there is a small Lao settlement, and to the left a Chinese community. It's best to visit these places with a local guide, as you'll need someone to act as an interpreter and smooth the way. Ask at the river about boats ($20) to the chunchiet village of **Oh Lalay**, or further on to **Chort Preas**, inhabited by Kavet chunchiets and home to a high waterfall. The easiest way to **get to Voen Sai** is to rent a moto from Banlung ($10); a rickety bus (2000r) makes the trip between Voen Sai and Banlung daily. It's also possible to get to Voen Sai via boat from Stung Treng, but it takes two days and costs in the region of $100.

Mondulkiri

The province of **Mondulkiri** is Rattanakiri's forgotten southern neighbour, in the far east of the country and bordering Vietnam. It's less visited but can claim similar attractions: a high proportion of chunchiet, waterfalls and beautiful landscapes – its forested highlands are interrupted occasionally by grassy fields and gentle hills that would look more at home in rural England. Indeed, the climate is not dissimilar either: the temperature is a mere 18°C on average in the dry season, with chilly nights. The provincial capital, **Sen Monorom** is the only place to stay and is the base for excursions into the countryside.

Sen Monorom and around

Provincial capitals don't get more remote or inaccessible than **SEN MONOROM**, 420km from Phnom Penh. The town extends for a short way down either side of a low hill, atop which is an airstrip, now disused. It's not a very appealing place, but makes a good base from which to explore the surrounding countryside and chunchiet villages.

Locals will direct you to the **Monorom Falls** (aka Sihanouk Falls), a peaceful nook on the edge of the jungle, where a ten-metre-high cascade of water drops into a swirling plunge pool. You can either walk the few kilometres here or hire a moto for the easy road. The path ends at the top of the waterfall, where brave souls hurl themselves into the deep water during the rainy season. The less brave scramble down through the foliage for a refreshing swim. The more distant but spectacular **Bou Sraa Falls**, about 40km northeast from Sen Monorom, are reached by a exciting, some would say hair-raising, ride, along a stunningly beautiful forest trail. The falls themselves are a dramatic two-tiered affair, with more than thirty metres of water gushing into a jungle-clad gorge.

There are hundreds of chunchiet villages around Sen Monorom, but the shy chunchiet like to keep themselves to themselves and some villages are not keen on foreign visitors, so it's best to take a local to act as a guide and interpreter. One of the largest and easiest villages to access is **Phulung**, inhabited by Phnong, the majority chunchiet group in Mondulkiri. The curious huts have woven wooden walls and thatched roofs almost to the floor. Three or more families often live in just one hut, but you'll be lucky to see more than a handful of people during daytime, as they're all out working in the fields. Phulung is also the starting point for half- or full-day elephant treks in the area ($15-30), which you can arrange through guesthouses in Sen Monorom.

Practicalities

The only way to Sen Monorom is overland by shared taxi or pick-up, either direct from Phnom Penh (40,000r), a bone-rattling eight- to ten-hour marathon, or from the Mekong at Kompong Cham (7hr) or Kratie (7hr). The road is pretty good in parts but terrible in others. Returning to Phnom Penh, it's possible to get a shared taxi or pick-up all the way (40,000r). It is sometimes necessary to change transport in Snuol, about midway between Sen Monorom and Kompong Cham, though there's nowhere decent to stay there.

To see most sights, you'll need to employ the help of a **guide**, either at your guesthouse or the **tourist office**, behind the post office (the white building just off the airstrip), but they don't come cheap at a starting price of $20 per day. Motos are also pricey here: expect to pay up to $20 to get to Bou Sraa, but you're unlikely to complain once you see the road, which is virtually non-existent.

There are only a few **places to stay** in Sen Monorom, the most convenient being the well-maintained *Pich Kiri Hotel* (☎012/932102, ❶), on the left as you enter the town. It has a choice of rooms, either in the main house or in bungalows around the verdant gardens. Terrific food is served at the restaurant, and you can hang out with a beer or two while it's cooked; the generator is noisy but at least you'll have power in the evening – the rest of town only gets electricity until 9pm. A little further out of town on the same road, the *Holiday Guesthouse* (☎012/936606; ❷) is a newer place with single and double rooms, all of which have attached bathroom. Even further out of town on the same road (about 1.5km), the *Arun Reah 2 Guesthouse* (☎012/856667; ❷) has some secluded bungalows with good views, plus a choice of single or double rooms and cold or hot water.

Eating options in Sen Monorom are limited: a no-name restaurant on the corner of the main road by the airstrip serves up good soups and chicken dishes, while the restaurant at the *Pich Kiri* has a wider selection of fare. Rice and noodle soup can be had for breakfast at the market, or at a couple of noodle shops near the transport stop.

Cambodia travel details

Shared taxis, pick-ups and buses

For more information on **share taxis**, **pick-ups** and **buses** in Cambodia, see "Getting around", p.105. Share taxis and pick-ups leave when full on a frequent basis until at least midday, unless otherwise stated.

Banlung to: Kratie (8hr); Stung Treng (4hr).
Battambang to: Kompong Chhnang (4hr); Pailin (4–5hr); Phnom Penh (6hr); Poipet (3hr); Siem Reap (daily; 3hr), Sisophon (2hr).
Kampot to: Phnom Penh (3hr); Sihanoukville (2hr).
Koh Kong to: Sihanoukville (6 daily; 6hr); Phnom Penh (6 daily; 6hr).
Kompong Cham to: Kratie (5hr); Phnom Penh (2hr 30min); Sen Monorom (1 daily; 6hr).
Kratie to: Banlung (8hr); Kompong Cham (5hr); Phnom Penh (2 daily; 7hr); Stung Treng (6hr).
Pailin to: Battambang (4–5hr).
Phnom Penh to: Battambang (6hr); Bavet (for Vietnam; 5hr); Ho Chi Minh City, Vietnam (daily; 8hr); Kampot (3hr); Kompong Cham (2hr 30min); Kompong Thom (3hr); Kratie (2 daily; 7hr); Poipet (8hr): Sen Monorom (daily; at least 8hr); Siem Reap (daily; 6–8hr); Sihanoukville (3hr 30min); Sisophon (7hr); Sre Ambel (2hr 30min).
Poipet to: Battambang (3hr); Phnom Penh (8hr); Siem Reap (4hr); Sisophon (20 daily; 1hr).
Sen Monorom to: Kompong Cham (daily; 6hr); Phnom Penh (daily; at least 8hr).
Siem Reap to: Battambang (daily; 3hr); Kompong Thom (3hr); Phnom Penh (daily; 6–8hr); Poipet (4hr); Sisophon (2hr).
Sihanoukville to: Kampot (2hr); Koh Kong (6hr); Phnom Penh (3hr 30min).
Sisophon to: Battambang (2hr); Phnom Penh (7hr); Poipet (1hr); Siem Reap (2hr).

Sre Ambel to: Phnom Penh (2hr 30min).
Stung Treng to: Banlung (4hr); Kratie (6hr).

Trains

A **train** departs every other day from Phnom Penh to Battambang – see p.126 for details of the schedule.
Battambang to: Phnom Penh (1 every other day; at least 12hr).
Phnom Penh to: Battambang (1 every other day; at least 12hr).

Boats

Boats between Kratie and Stung Treng may not run in April and May if the water level is too low.
Battambang to: Siem Reap (2 daily; 3hr 30min).
Koh Kong to: Sihanoukville via Koh S'dach (daily; 4hr).
Kompong Cham to: Kratie (daily; 4hr); Stung Treng (July–Oct daily; 8hr).
Kratie to: Kompong Cham (daily; 3hr); Stung Treng (July–Oct daily; 4hr; Nov–May daily; 6hr).
Phnom Penh to: Siem Reap (1–2 daily; 5hr).
Siem Reap to: Battambang (2 daily; 3hr 30min); Phnom Penh (1–2 daily; 5hr).
Sihanoukville to: Koh Kong via Koh S'dach (daily; 4hr).
Stung Treng to: Kompong Cham (July–Oct daily; 7hr 30min); Kratie (July–Oct daily; 3hr; Nov–May daily; 6hr).

Flights

Banlung to: Phnom Penh (4 weekly; 1hr).
Phnom Penh to: Siem Reap (6 daily; 45min); Banlung (4 weekly; 1hr).
Siem Reap to: Phnom Penh (6 daily; 45min).

3

Hong Kong

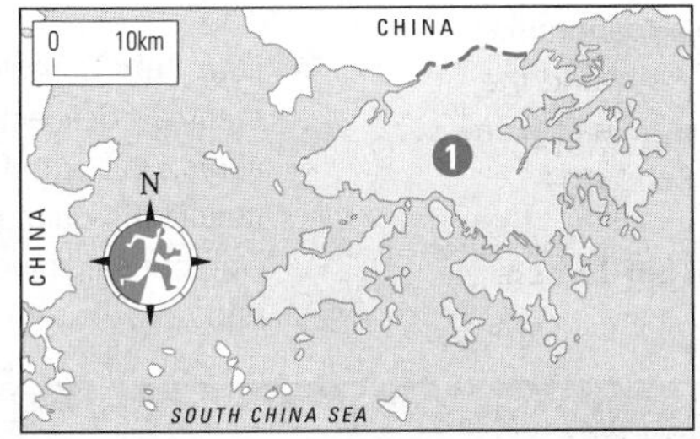

Hong Kong highlights

* **City Skyline** Gaze across the harbour from the tip of Tsim Sha Tsui promenade or crane your neck from a Central-bound Star Ferry at one of the world's great city vistas. See p.217

* **The Peak** Every bit as breathtaking as the views from the bottom, the Peak's summit offers spectacular panoramas across the city and the South China Sea by day or night. See p.214

* **Wong Tai Sin Temple** Among swirling incense and the clatter of bamboo fortune sticks you'll get an absorbing glimpse of modern-day Taoist worship and, perhaps, your future foretold. See p.219

* **Weekend bar-hopping** Party down with corporate fat cats in teeming Lan Kwai Fong and Soho. See p.227

* **Dim Sum** Sampling steamed delicacies served in bamboo baskets is the quintessential Cantonese dining experience. See p.226

△ Char Siu steamed buns

Introduction and basics

A staging post between Southeast Asia, China and the rest of the world, Hong Kong all too often serves merely as a transit point for long-haul air passengers heading to other lands, but it's a beguiling place to visit in itself. One of the great world city-states, Hong Kong New York with an Asian heart, or Shanghai on a less daunting scale, and with all the ease and accessibility of any wealthy Western city – an extraordinary, complex and crowded territory of seven million people; a repository of traditional Chinese culture; a recently relinquished British outpost; and one of the key economies of the Pacific Rim. The view of sky-scrapered Hong Kong Island, across the harbour from Kowloon, is one of the most stunning urban panoramas on earth, but Hong Kong also holds some surprises for the traveller: alongside the myriad shopping possibilities are a surprising number of inviting beaches, rewarding hiking trails and some surviving bastions of Chinese village life, most of them in the New Territories. An excellent infrastructure, an efficient underground system and all the other facilities of an international city make this an extremely soft entry into the Chinese world.

Some visitors dislike the speed, the obsessive materialism and the addiction to shopping, money and brand names in Hong Kong. Downtown is certainly not a place to recover from a headache, but it's hard not to enjoy the sheer energy of its street and commercial life. Hong Kong's per capita **GNP** has doubled in a decade, overtaking that of the former imperial power, and the territory is currently the largest trading partner and largest source of foreign investment for the People's Republic of China, a country of 1.3 billion people. Yet the inequality of incomes is staggering: the conspicuous consumption of the few hundred super-rich (all Cantonese), for which Hong Kong is famous, tends to mask the fact that most people work long hours and live in crowded, tiny apartments, many of them still getting over the buffeting Hong Kong's economy suffered after the 1997 Asian financial crisis.

Since the **handover** to China earlier that year, the people of Hong Kong have found themselves in a unique position: subject to the ultimate rule of Beijing, they live in a semi-democratic capitalist enclave – a "Special Administrative Region (SAR) of China" – under the control of an unaccountable communist state, but given (in theory) greater freedom of expression and a (very limited) say in how things are run. This is not to say that the people of Hong Kong weren't glad to see the end of colonialism – an overwhelming majority supported the transfer of power, and a huge majority speak only the Cantonese dialect, eat only Cantonese food, pray in Chinese temples and enjoy close cultural and blood relations with the Cantonese population that lives just over the border, in the southern provinces of mainland China.

Indeed, it's hard to overstate the symbolic importance that the handover had for the entire Chinese population, marking the end of the era of foreign domination. However, worrying questions remain, notably whether the One Country/Two Systems policy created by Deng Xiaoping will work in the longer term, especially if China's own economic progress begins to falter, and whether recent attempts from above to stifle dissent are a sign of things to come.

Hong Kong's **climate** is subtropical. The best time to visit is between October and April, when the weather is cooler, humidity and pollution levels drop, and the flowers are in bloom. In January and February, it can get quite rainy and cold – you'll need a light jacket and sweater. The temperature and humidity start to pick up in mid-April, and between late June and early September readings of 30°C and 95 percent humidity or more are the norm. Walking and other physical activities become unpleasant and sleeping without air-con difficult. May to September is also the peak typhoon season, when ferry and airline timetables are often disrupted by bad weather.

Overland and sea routes into Hong Kong

The main land route into Hong Kong is by **train**. Both express trains and cheaper local trains leave daily from Guangzhou on the Chinese mainland. There are also regular daily **bus** services from Guangzhou. **Sea routes** from China include ferries from Guangzhou, Zhuhai, Zhaoqing, Zhongshan and Xiamen. Frequent ferries also run from Macau. For details on all these routes, see the "Moving on to China and Macau" box, p.201.

Entry requirements and visa extension

Most nationalities need only a valid passport to enter Hong Kong, although the length of time you can stay varies. Citizens of the United Kingdom get six months, whereas most European nationalities (including Irish citizens), along with travellers from Canada, Australia, New Zealand and the United States, can stay for up to three months.

The easiest way to **extend your stay** is to go to Macau or China for a day or so (for which you'll need to get a visa in advance, see p.44) and come back, getting another period stamped in your passport. For a longer stay, though, you'll need to apply for a visa in advance of your visit from the **Immigration Department**, Immigration Tower, 7 Gloucester Rd, Wan Chai, Hong Kong (Ⓣ2824 6111), as you will if you're intending to work in the territory; allow at least six weeks for most visa applications.

Airport departure tax

Airport **departure tax** in Hong Kong is HK$120.

Money and costs

Hong Kong's unit of **currency** is the Hong Kong dollar (HK$), divided into one hundred cents. Bank notes are issued by the Hong Kong and Shanghai Banking Corporation (HSBC), the Standard Chartered Bank and the Bank of China, and are of slightly different design and size, but they're all interchangeable.

Notes come in denominations of HK$20, HK$50, HK$100, HK$500 and HK$1000; there's a nickel-and-bronze HK$10 coin; silver coins come as HK$1, HK$2 and HK$5; and bronze coins as 10c, 20c and 50c. At the time of writing, the exchange rate was around HK$14 to the **pound sterling**, and it's pegged at HK$7.78 to the US dollar. There's no black market, and money, in any amount, can be

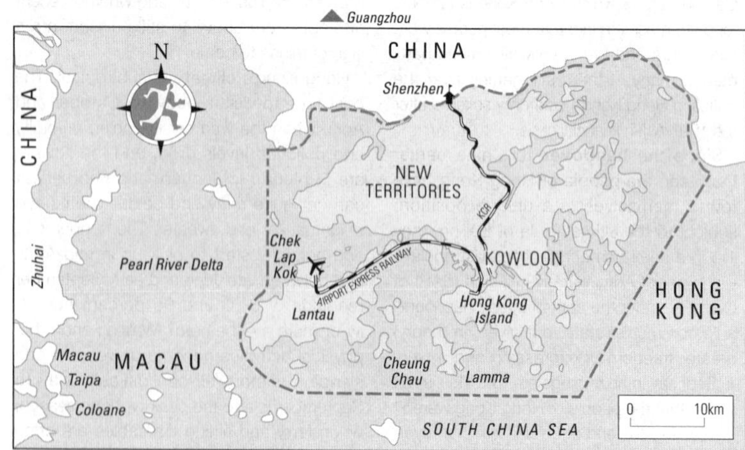

freely taken in and out of the SAR.

All major **credit cards** are accepted in Hong Kong, but watch out for the three- to five-percent commission that lots of travel agencies and shops try to add to the price. Many **ATM machines** will take American Express, MasterCard and Visa.

Wiring money to Hong Kong is no problem. Any of the major international banks here can organize a transfer from your home bank to a specific branch in Hong Kong. It will take the best part of a day, though, and you'll be charged a handling fee. International companies, such as Western Union Money Transfer, can also handle the transaction for you and charge a percentage of the sum transferred. See "Wiring money", p.60 for more details.

Costs

Food and accommodation are more expensive in Hong Kong than most other Southeast Asian destinations, so you'll need to give yourself a bigger **daily budget** here. The cheapest dorm beds will set you back £6/US$11 a night, while it's hard to come by a decent double room for under £35/US$60. Staying at cheap lodgings and eating simply from noodle stalls will cost you about £22/US$40 a day, up to £33/US$60 with a mid-range restaurant meal thrown in. For more comfort and classier food, budget from £60/US$115 and up.

Information and maps

The **Hong Kong Tourism Board** (HKTB; ⓦ www.discoverhongkong.com) has an office in the arrivals area of the airport (daily 7am–11pm, information and cyberlink available 24 hours), at the Star Ferry Pier in Tsim Sha Tsui (daily 8am–6pm) and on the ground floor of The Centre, 99 Queen's Rd, Central (daily 8am–6pm). There's also an HKTB multilingual **telephone service** (Mon–Fri 8am–6pm, Sat & Sun 9am–5pm; ⓣ 2508 1234). The HKTB's website is packed with information but is hard to navigate and apt to break down.

HKTB **maps** and the maps in this guide should be enough for most purposes, though more detailed versions such as the paperback *Hong Kong Guide*, which includes all major bus routes, can be bought from English-language bookstores (see "Listings", p.229).

Accommodation

Hong Kong boasts some of the most luxurious **hotels** in Asia – if not the world – as well as some of the seediest guesthouses. **At the top end** of the spectrum, a suite or room with the classic harbour view will set you back thousands of dollars a night. For that, guests – mostly business people – get considerable luxury in the room, plus five-star service and all the other facilities of international hotels. These hotels also function as meeting and dining places for the local business and social elite, and it can be worth hanging out in their lobbies to see the world go by, or taking a drink in one of their bars to enjoy the uniformly spectacular views for the price of an (albeit expensive) cocktail.

All these hotels – the *Mandarin,* the *Grand Hyatt* and the *Inter-Continental* among others – will be packed when a big trade fair or conference is on, as will the three- and four-star places. However, when business is quieter, for example, in the rainy summer season, **mid-range hotels** can offer some interesting bargains, particularly those in areas like north Kowloon, away from the main business districts. They usually charge by the room rather than the person, and include breakfast in the rate as well as extras such as free airport transfers, but beware of service charges and taxes, which can add another thirteen percent to the bill. If you're interested, check travel agents' offers before you get to Hong Kong, or ask the Tourism Board at the airport. If you're looking for bargains, it's worth remembering that travel agents can usually wangle discounts of up to half of the regular tariff on mid-and upper-range hotels. The hotels' own websites can also be a source of good deals.

Sky-high property prices mean that cheaper accommodation is not nearly as plentiful as in other Asian cities, or generally as good value. **Guesthouses** are almost all in Tsim Sha Tsui and Causeway Bay, and the majority are crammed into a couple of huge, warren-like and frankly rather filthy blocks, *Mirador Mansions* and *Chungking Man-*

sions. Both have poor fire safety standards. Inside, quality and cleanliness varies greatly from guesthouse to guesthouse, but all the rooms will be small, and some will have no windows. Often, very little English is spoken. These two blocks are also crammed with shops, travel agents and restaurants, and the noticeboards are focal points for travellers' information. If you want something a bit better, try heading north up the Kowloon peninsula or to the **new towns** such as Shatin, where land prices, and so room rates, are lower. An alternative is to stay at a **youth hostel**, where rates are as low as HK$35 for members or HK$65 for non-members. These are usually packed out at weekends but empty during the week, although as most are some way out of town you should ring to check availability first. Expect to bring your own food. Another budget option is to stay on one of **the islands**, like Lamma or Lantau. During the week, hotel rates are around HK$300–500 for a double – half the weekend price. Guesthouses are less, around HK$200 mid-week, but the rooms can be very basic, as most are used by local couples for getaway weekends. **Electricity** throughout the territory is usually supplied at 220 volts.

Food and drink

As one of the great culinary capitals of the world, Hong Kong can boast not only a superb native cuisine – Cantonese – but also perhaps the widest range of international restaurants of any city outside Europe or North America. This is due in part to the cosmopolitan nature of the population, but perhaps more importantly, to the incredible seriousness attached to dining by the local Chinese.

As well as the joys of *dim sum* – another Hong Kong speciality – the city offers the full gamut of Chinese restaurants, from Beijing to Shanghai to Szechuan (Sichuan), and many smaller localities. It also offers excellent curry houses from the Indian subcontinent, surprisingly reasonable Japanese sushi bars, British pub-style food and numerous cheap **street stalls** (*dai pai dongs*), which are often the best value for money of all – although these are becoming rarer as the government cracks down on outdoor canteens, refusing to issue or renew licences. You'll also find the local Chinese fast-food chains, *Café de Coral* and *Maxim's*, alongside *McDonald's*, *Pizza Hut* and *KFC*. The choice is seemingly limitless, and all budgets are catered for. English **menus** are widely available. Nearly all non-fast food restaurants will add a ten percent **service charge** to your bill, and if there are nuts and pickles on your table you'll often pay a small cover charge, too.

What to eat

The kind of **snacks** you'll find at the *dai pai dongs*, or street stalls, and many indoor food halls and canteens (called *cha chan tengs*), include fish, beef and pork balls, stuffed buns, grilled chicken wings, spiced noodles, fresh and dried squid, spring rolls, *congee* (rice gruel served with an oily, doughnut-type stick), cooked intestines, tofu pudding and various sweets. Some *dai pai dongs* have simple tables and chairs and serve slightly more elaborate food, such as seafood, mixed rice and noodle dishes, stews and soups, and bottled beer. A meal here will cost around HK$55–65.

The most common Chinese food in Hong Kong is **Cantonese**, from China's southern Guangdong province. Dishes consist of extremely fresh food, quickly cooked and only lightly seasoned. Popular ingredients are fruit and vegetables, fish and shellfish, though the cuisine is also known for its more unusual ingredients – things like fish maw, snake liver, jellyfish, dog and guinea pig – which most Westerners would baulk at eating. Cantonese restaurants also have the best selection of **dim sum** ("little eats"), a late breakfast or midday meal consisting of small flavoured buns, dumplings and pancakes, washed down with copious amounts of tea (see p.191 for a list of the most common dishes). In the more traditional *dim sum* restaurants the food is wheeled in trolleys through the restaurant: they'll come to your table and you select what you want. Most things cost the same, around HK$25–45 each, and you'll find it hard to spend more than HK$120 a head. Restaurants that specialize in *dim sum* open early in the morning, from around 7am, and serve right through lunch up until around 5pm; many regular Cantonese restaurants also serve *dim sum*, usually 10–11am until

Food and drink glossary

The following lists should help out where you can't make yourself understood – and, if they're written clearly, in deciphering the characters on a **Chinese menu**. If you know what you're after, try sifting through the staples and cooking methods to create your order, or sample one of the everyday or regional suggestions. Don't forget to tailor your demands to the capabilities of where you're ordering, however – a street cook with a wok isn't going to be able to whip up anything much more complicated than a basic stir-fry. Remember to note whether dishes are priced per order or per hundred grams – common for seafood. See p.198 in "Language" for a guide to pronunciation.

Ordering food

Bill/cheque	賣單	*Mai daan*
Chopsticks	筷子	*Fai tzee*
House speciality	拿手好菜	*La sow ho choy*
How much is that?	幾多錢	*Gay dor cheen?*
I'm a Buddhist/vegetarian	我係佛教徒/我只食素	*Ngor hi fut gow toe/ngor tzee sik soe*
I would like...	我想要..........	*Ngor serng yew...*
Main/set menu/English menu	菜單/頭菜/英文菜單	*Choy daan/toe choy/Ying man choy daan*
Small portion	少量	*Sew lerng*
Spoon	匙羹	*Chee gung*
Waiter/waitress	服務生/小姐	*Fook mo yeen/sew jye*

Drinks

Beer	啤酒	*Beh tsow*
Coffee	咖啡	*Ga fay*
Tea	茶	*Char*
Mineral water	礦泉水	*Kong tuen soy*
Wine	葡萄酒	*Poe toe tsow*

Staple foods

Bamboo shoots	荀尖	*Sun jeem*
Beans	豆	*Dow*
Bean sprouts	豆芽	*Dow ah*
Beef	牛肉	*Ow yok*
Black bean sauce	黑豆豉	*Hat dow see*
Buns (plain)	饅頭	*Man tow*
Buns (filled)	包子	*Bow tzee*
Cashew nuts	腰果	*Yew gaw*
Chicken	雞	*Gai*
Chilli	辣椒	*Lar jew*
Crab	蟹	*Hi*
Duck	鴨	*Aap*
Eel	鱔魚	*Suen yue*
Fish	魚	*Yue*
Garlic	大蒜	*Dai suen*
Ginger	薑	*Gerng*
Green vegetables	綠葉蔬菜	*Lok yip soe choy*
Lotus root	蓮心	*Leen sum*

MSG	味精	*Mei jing*
Mushrooms	蘑菇	*Mor goo*
Noodles	麵條	*Meen tew*
Pancake	攤餅	*Taan beng*
Peanut	花生	*Far sun*
Pork	豬肉	*Jew yok*
Potato	土豆	*Toe dow*
Prawns	蝦	*Ha*
Preserved egg	皮蛋	*Pey daan*
Rice (boiled)	白飯	*Bak faan*
Rice (fried)	炒飯	*Chow faan*
Rice porridge congee	粥	*Jook*
Salt	鹽	*Yeem*
Snake	蛇肉	*Seh yok*
Tofu	豆腐	*Dow foo*

Cooking methods

Boiled	煮	*Joo*
Casseroled	炆	*Mun*
Fried	炒	*Chow*
Poached	白煮	*Bak joo*
Roast	烤	*How*
Steamed	蒸	*Jing*
Stir-fried	清炒	*Ching chow*

Everyday dishes

Braised duck with vegetables	燉鴨素菜	*Dun aap soe choy*
Chicken and sweetcorn soup	粟米雞絲湯	*Sook mai gai see tong*
Chicken with cashew nuts	腰果雞片	*Yew gaw gai peen*
Crispy aromatic duck	香酥鴨	*Herng sow aap*
Egg fried rice	蛋炒飯	*Daan chow faan*
Fish ball soup with white radish	蘿蔔魚蛋湯	*Law bat yue daan tong*
Fish casserole	炆魚	*Mun yue*
Fried shredded pork with garlic and chilli	大蒜辣椒炒肉片	*Dai suen lar jew chow yok peen*
Hotpot	火鍋	*For war*
Kebab	肉串	*Yok choon*
Noodle soup	湯麵	*Tong meen*
Prawn with garlic sauce	大蒜炒蝦	*Dai suen chow ha*
Roast duck	烤鴨	*How aap*
Sliced pork with yellow bean sauce	黃豆肉片	*Wong dow yok peen*
Steamed eel with black beans	豆豉蒸鱔	*Dow see jing suen*
Stewed pork belly with vegetables	回鍋肉	*Wooy war yok*
Sweet and sour spare ribs	糖醋排骨	*Tong choe pai gwut*
Sweet bean paste pancakes	赤豆攤餅	*Chek dow taan beng*
Wonton soup	餛飩湯	*Wun dung tong*

Vegetables and eggs

Aubergine with chilli and garlic sauce	大蒜辣椒炒茄子	*Dai suen lar jew chow ke tzee*
Braised mountain fungus	燉香菇	*Dun herng goo*
Fried beancurd with vegetables	豆腐素菜	*Dow foo soe choy*
Fried bean sprouts	炒豆芽	*Chow dow ah*

Spicy braised aubergine	香辣茄子條	*Herng la ke tzee tew*
Stir-fried bamboo shoots	炒冬筍	*Chow dong sun*
Stir-fried mushrooms	炒鮮菇	*Chow seen goo*
Vegetable soup	素菜湯	*Soe choy tong*
Regional dishes		
Northern Mongolian hotpot	蒙古火鍋	*Mong goo for war*
Peking duck	北京烤鴨	*But ging how aap*
Shark fin soup	魚翅湯	*Yue chee tong*
Crab soup	蟹肉湯	*Hai yok tong*
Drunken prawns steamed in wine	醉蝦	*Joy ha*
Shark fin and crab meat soup	蟹肉魚翅湯	*Hai yok yue chee tong*
Steamed sea bass	清蒸鱸魚	*Ching jing loe yue*
Sichuan and western China		
Deep-fried green beans with garlic	大蒜刀豆	*Dai suen doe dow gongbao*
Gongbai chicken with chillis and peanuts	宮爆雞丁	*Gong bow gai ding*
Green peppers with spring onion and black bean sauce	豆豉青椒	*Dow see cheng jew*
Hot and sour soup	酸辣湯	*Suen lar tong*
Ham	火腿	*For toy*
Stuffed aubergine slices	餡茄子	*Harm ke tzee*
Southern Chinese/Cantonese		
Braised crab with chilli and black beans	辣椒豆豉炆蟹	*Lar jew dow see mun hai*
Casseroled beancurd stuffed with pork mince	豆腐煲	*Dow foo boe*
Crisp-skinned pork on rice	脆皮肉飯	*Choy pey yok faan*
Fish-head casserole	炆魚頭	*Mun yue tow*
Fish steamed with ginger and spring onion	清蒸魚	*Ching jing yue*
Fried chicken with yam	芋頭炒雞片	*Woo tow chow gai peen*
Barbecued pork	叉燒	*Char sew*
Dim Sum (Yum Cha)		
Barbecue pork bun	叉燒包	*Char sew bao*
Crab and coriander dumpling	蟹肉蝦餃	*Hai yok ha gow*
Custard tart	蛋撻	*Daan tat*
Doughnut	炸麵餅圈	*Zar meen beng goon*
Fried taro and mince dumpling	蕃薯糊餃	*Faan sue woo gow*
Joazi steamed pork dumplings	餃子	*Gow tzee*
Lotus paste bun	蓮蓉糕	*Leen yong goe*
Moon cake sweet bean paste in flaky pastry	月餅	*Yuet beng*
Pork and prawn dumpling in ornate wrapping	燒賣	*Sew mai*
Prawn crackers	蝦片	*Ha peen*
Prawn dumpling	蝦餃	*Ha gow*
Prawn paste on fried toast	芝麻蝦	*Tzee ma ha*
Shanghai fried and vegetable dumpling	鍋帖	*Wo teet*
Spring roll	春卷	*Chun goon*

3pm. It's best to go in a group so that you can order a number of items to share.

Beijing food is heavier than Cantonese cooking, based around a solid diet of wheat and millet buns, noodles, pancakes and dumplings, accompanied by the savoury tastes of dark soy sauce and bean paste, white onions and cabbage. The north's cooking has also been influenced by neighbours and invaders: Mongols brought their hotpots and grilled roast meats, and Muslims a taste for mutton and chicken. Combined with exotic items imported by foreign merchants, these rather rough ingredients were turned into sophisticated marvels such as Peking duck and bird's nest soup.

Shanghainese cuisine delights in seasonal fresh seafood and river fish. Dried and salted ingredients feature, too, pepping up a background of rice noodles and dumplings. The cuisine is characterized by little, delicate forms and light, fresh, sweet flavours, sometimes to the point of becoming precious – tiny meatballs are steamed in a rice coating and called "pearls" for example.

Sichuan food is the antithesis of Shanghainese cuisine. Here, there's a heavy use of chillies and pungent, constructed flavours – vegetables are concealed with "fish-flavoured" sauce, and even normally bland tofu is given enough spices to lift the top off your head. Yet there are still subtleties to enjoy in a cuisine that uses dried orange peel, aniseed, ginger and spring onions, and the cooking methods themselves – such as dry frying and smoking – are refreshingly unusual.

In most Chinese restaurants, the usual **drink** with your meal is **jasmine tea**, often brought to your table as a matter of course. **Beer** and **wine** are also popular. The **water** is fit for drinking everywhere in Hong Kong, though the bottled water tastes nicer.

Communications

Airmail takes three days to a week to reach Britain or North America. Letters sent **poste restante** will arrive at the GPO building in Central (see p.230 for details). To send parcels, turn up at the post office with the goods you want to send and the staff will help you pack them. You can either bring your own paper and tape or buy boxes at the post office. You'll also need to fill out a customs declaration form. Parcels go by surface mail unless you specify otherwise.

Local calls from private phones are free; most shops and restaurants will let you use theirs for nothing. There are no area codes. Public **phones** usually cost HK$1 for five minutes, and every pay- and cardphone has instructions in English. **Phone cards** come in units of HK$50, HK$100, HK$200 and HK$300, and are available from PCCW Service Centres, tourist offices and convenience stores such as 7-11 and Circle K.

Time differences

Hong Kong is eight hours ahead of London (GMT), thirteen hours ahead of New York, sixteen hours ahead of Los Angeles, two hours behind Sydney and four hours behind Auckland.

You can make **international calls** from International Direct Dialling (IDD) phones or one of the several **PCCW Service Centres** in the territory. Collect or reverse-charge calls and home-direct calls can be made free of charge from these centres. They also have fax services. To phone abroad from Hong Kong, dial ⓣ001 + IDD country code (see p.64) + area code minus first 0 + subscriber number. For directory enquiries in English, call ⓣ1081.

Internet and **email access** are available at the Hong Kong Central Library; inside the convention centre; at most branches of the *Pacific Coffee Company* and other cybercafés (see "Listings", p.229); or in the business centres of major hotels. There's also limited Internet access at terminals dotted around many of the large shopping centres, such as Times Square in Wanchai.

Opening hours and festivals

Generally, **offices** are open Monday–Friday 9am–5pm, and some open Saturday 9am–1pm; **shops**, daily 10am–7/8pm, though later in tourist areas. **Banks** are open Monday–Friday 9am–4.30pm, Saturday 9am–12.30pm. **Post office** opening hours are Monday–Friday 9.30am–5pm, Saturday 9.30am–1pm (the main post offices in Central and Tsim Sha Tsui are also open 8am–6pm on Saturday and 9am–2pm on Sunday). All government offices close on public holidays and some religious festivals. As the Chinese use the **lunar calendar** and not the Gregorian calendar, many of the festivals fall on different days, even different months, from year to year; for exact details, contact the Hong Kong Tourist Board (HKTB; see p.202).

With roots going back hundreds (even thousands) of years, many of Hong Kong's **festivals** are highly symbolic and are often a mixture of secular and religious displays and devotions. On these occasions, there are dances and Chinese opera displays at the temples, plenty of noise, and a series of **offerings** left in the temples – food and paper goods that are burned as offerings to the dead. The most important is **Chinese New Year** (Jan/Feb), when the entire population takes time out to celebrate and there are spectacular firework displays over the harbour. The **Mid-Autumn Festival** in September is almost as popular, and celebrations are more public. Festivals particular to Hong Kong rather than the whole of China include the **Tin Hau Festival** (late April or May), in honour of the Goddess of Fishermen, when large seaborne festivities take place at Joss House Bay on Sai Kung Peninsula (see p.221); the **Tai Chiu (Bun) Festival**, which is held on Cheung Chau island in May; and the **Tuen Ng (Dragon Boat) Festival** in early June, with races in various places around the SAR in long, narrow boats.

Cultural hints

Generally speaking, Hong Kong people are not as worried as other Southeast Asian cultures about covering the skin – girls often wear skirts as short as those in the West. Having said that, however, don't think of **bathing topless** on any of Hong Kong's beaches: you'll draw a lot of attention to yourself, offend some people and, in any case, it's illegal. In general, Hong Kong residents are markedly less friendly and polite than other Asian cultures and indeed than most Western cultures. They also talk more openly about money – it's quite common for people to ask you what you paid for things, or your salary back home.

Crime and safety

You're very unlikely to encounter any trouble in Hong Kong. The main thing to look out for is **pickpockets**: it's best to keep money and wallets in inside pockets, carry handbags around your neck and be careful when getting on and off packed buses and trains. The only other problems you might encounter are in bars where the emphasis is on buying very expensive drinks for the "girls": if you get drunk and refuse or are unable to pay, the bar heavies will soon make sure you find your wallet.

There is a fairly heavy **police** street presence – they are on the look out for illegal immigrants largely from the mainland – but everyone is required to carry some form of **identification** at all times: your driving licence will do, or anything with your photograph. Most officers can speak some English, and

Public holidays

Hong Kong's **public holidays** are changing as China jettisons the old colonial holidays in favour of its own celebrations. For now, the following public holidays are observed. Sundays are also classed as public holidays.

January 1: New Year
January/February: Chinese New Year (three days' holiday)
March/April: Easter (holidays on Good Friday, Easter Saturday and Easter Monday)
April: Ching Ming Festival
May 1: Labour Day
May: Buddha's Birthday
June: Tuen Ng (Dragon Boat) Festival
July 1: HKSAR Establishment Day
September: Mid-Autumn Festival
October 1: Chinese National Day
October: Chung Yeung Festival
December 25 and 26: Christmas Day and the next working day

will quickly radio help for you if they can't understand and you have a major problem.

Medical care and emergencies

Pharmacies (daily 9am–6pm) can help with minor injuries or ailments and will prescribe basic medicines. Contraceptives and antibiotics are also available over the counter. All pharmacies are registered and are usually staffed by English-speakers.

For a **doctor**, look in the local phone directories' *Yellow Pages* under "Physicians and Surgeons". Large hotels also have a clinic for guests offering diagnosis, advice and prescriptions. You'll have to pay for a consultation and any medicines that are prescribed; be sure to get a receipt so that you can make an insurance claim when you get home.

Hospital treatment is very expensive, making it important to have some form of medical insurance (see "Insurance", p.50). Casualty visits are free, however, and public hospitals have 24-hour casualty departments. See p.229 for hospital addresses. Note that both doctors and **dentists** are known as "doctor" in Hong Kong.

Emergency phone numbers

Dial ☎999 for fire, police and ambulance.

History

While the Chinese argue that Hong Kong has always been Chinese territory, the development of the city only began with the arrival of the British in Guangzhou in the eighteenth century. The Portuguese had already been based at Macau, on the other side of the Pearl River Delta, since the mid-sixteenth century, and as Britain's sea power grew, so its merchants, too, began casting covetous eyes over the Portuguese trade in tea and silk. The initial difficulty was in persuading the Chinese authorities there was any reason to deal with them, though a few traders did manage to get permission to set up their warehouses in Guangzhou – a remote southern outpost, from the perspective of Beijing – and slowly trade began to grow. In 1757, a local Guangzhou merchants' guild called the Co Hong, won the exclusive rights to sell Chinese products to foreign traders, who were now permitted to live in Guangzhou for about six months each year.

In the meantime, it had not escaped the attention of the foreigners that the trade was one-way only, and they soon began thinking up possible products the Chinese might want to buy in exchange. It didn't take long to find one – **opium** from India. In 1773, the first British shipload of opium arrived, and an explosion of demand for the drug quickly followed, despite an edict from Beijing banning the trade in 1796. Co Hong, which received commission on everything bought or sold, had no qualms about distributing opium to its fellow citizens and before long the balance of trade had been reversed very much in favour of the British.

The scene for the famous **Opium Wars** was now set. Alarmed at the outflow of silver and the rising incidence of drug addiction among his population, the emperor appointed Lin Zexu as Commissioner of Guangzhou to destroy the opium trade. Lin, later hailed by the Chinese communists as a patriot and hero, forced the British in Guangzhou to surrender their opium, before ceremonially burning it. Such an affront to British dignity could not be tolerated, however, and in 1840, a naval expeditionary force was dispatched from London to sort the matter out once and for all. After a year of gunboat diplomacy – blockading ports and seizing assets up and down the Chinese coast – the expeditionary force finally achieved one of their main objectives, through the **Treaty of Nanking** (1842), namely the ceding to Britain "in perpetuity" of a small offshore island. The island was called Hong Kong. This was followed eighteen years later, after more blockades and a forced march on Peking, by the **Treaty of Peking**, which granted Britain the Kowloon peninsula, too. Finally, in 1898, as the Qing dynasty was entering its terminal phase, Britain secured a 99-year lease on an additional one thousand square kilometres of land to the north of Kowloon, which came to be known as the New Territories.

During the twentieth century, Hong Kong grew from a seedy merchants' colony to a huge international city, but progress has not always been smooth. The drug trade was voluntarily dropped in 1907 as the Hong Kong merchants began to make the transfer from pure trade to manufacturing. Up until World War II, Hong Kong prospered, as the growing threat of both civil war and Japanese aggression in mainland China increasingly began to drive money south into the apparently safe confines of the British colony. This glaringly misplaced confidence was exposed in 1941 when **Japanese forces** seized Hong Kong along with the rest of eastern China, though after the Japanese defeat in 1945, Hong Kong once again began attracting money from the mainland, which was in the process of falling to the communists. Many of Hong Kong's biggest tycoons today are people who escaped from mainland China, particularly from Shanghai, in 1949.

Since the beginning of the **communist era**, Hong Kong has led a precarious existence, quietly making money while taking care not to antagonize Beijing. Had China wished to do so, it could have rendered the existence of Hong Kong unviable at any moment, by a naval blockade, by cutting off water supplies, by a military invasion – or by simply opening its border and inviting the Chinese masses to stream across in search of wealth. That it has never wholeheartedly pursued any of these options, even at the height of the Cultural Revolution, is an indication of the huge **financial benefits** that Hong Kong brings to mainland China in the form of its international trade links, direct investment and technology transfers.

In 1982, negotiations on the future of the colony began, although during the entire process that led to the **Sino-British Joint Declaration** nerves were kept on edge by the public posturings of both sides. The eventual deal, signed in 1984, paved the way for Britain to hand back sovereignty of the territory – something the Chinese would argue they never lost – in return for Hong Kong maintaining its capitalist system for at least fifty years.

Almost immediately the deal sparked controversy, in part over concerns that the lack of democratic institutions in Hong Kong – a status that had suited the British – would in future mean the Chinese could do what they liked. Fears grew that repression and the erosion of freedoms such as travel and speech would follow the handover. The **Basic Law**, which was published by the government in 1988, in theory answered some of those fears. It served as the constitutional framework, setting out how the One Country/Two Systems policy would work in practice. However, it failed to restore confidence in Hong Kong, and a brain-drain of educated, professional people to other countries began to gather pace.

The **1989 crackdown in Tiananmen Square** seemed to confirm the Hong Kong population's worst fears. In the biggest demonstration seen in Hong Kong in modern times, a million people took to the streets to protest at what had happened. Business confidence was equally shaken, and the Hang Seng Index, the performance indicator of the Stock Exchange, dropped 22 percent in a single day.

The 1990s were a roller-coaster ride of domestic policy dramas: the arrival of tens of thousands of Vietnamese boat people (ironically, refugees from communism), the rise of the **democracy movement** and arguments about whether Britain would give passports to the local population. When Chris Patten arrived in 1992 to become the last Governor, he walked into a delicate and highly charged political situation. Much to the fury of Beijing, Patten quickly introduced a series of reforms, including measures that broadened the voting franchise for the 1995 **Legislative Council elections** (Legco) from around 200,000 to 2.7 million people. Even though these and other changes he introduced guaranteed that the run-up to the 1997 handover would be a bumpy ride, they won the Governor significant popularity among ordinary Hong Kong people, although the tycoons and business community had far more mixed feelings.

After the build-up, the **handover** itself was something of an anticlimax. The British sailed away on HMS *Britannia*, Beijing carried out its threat to disband the elected Legco and reduce the enfranchised population, and Tung Chee Hwa, a shipping billionaire, became the first Chief Executive of the Hong Kong Special Administrative Region (SAR) of the People's Republic of China. But if local people had thought that they would be able to get on with "business as usual" post-handover, they were wrong. Within days, the **Asian Financial Crisis** had begun, and within months Hong Kong was once again in the eye of a storm. While the administration beat off attempts to force a devaluation of its currency, the stock and property markets suffered dramatic falls, tourism collapsed, unemployment rose to its highest levels for fifteen years, and the economy officially went into recession. While the administration characterized these as temporary setbacks – part of a global economic downturn – there was undoubted dismay amongst official circles in both Hong Kong and Beijing at the increasing – and unprecedented – level of criticism of officials and their policies in newspapers, on radio phone-ins and among ordinary people. Just as alarming to the powers-that-be has been the enduring and not unrelated popularity of the democratic parties.

Political activism is not something usually associated with Hong Kong's politically agnostic and commercially minded citizens but an anti-subversion bill, proposed and then dropped by the government in 2003, provoked 500,000 protestors on to the streets and added to the general unease at the more authoritarian direction Hong Kong seemed to be heading in.

Yet there's little sign that democracy is just around the corner in Hong Kong. The resignation of chief executive Tung Chee Hwa in March, 2005 may have marked the territory's first leadership change since it returned to Chinese rule in 1997 but, with the government having already ruled out direct elections for the post in 2007, his exit may only succeed in allowing Beijing to tighten its control over Hong Kong.

Religion

The most prevalent religions in Hong Kong are Taoism, Confucianism and Buddhism; for an introduction to all these faiths, see "Religion", p.69–71. Importance is also attached to superstition and ancestor worship, and things are further complicated by the way in which deities from various religions are worshipped in each other's temples – it's common for Buddhist deities to be worshipped in Taoist temples, for example. The Catholic community is also prominent – because of their schooling many leading government and business figures are Catholic, as of course are the tens of thousands of Filipina amahs.

Books

In the selection of books below, where a book is published in the UK and the US, the UK publisher is given first, followed by the US one; o/p signifies out of print.

Martin Booth *Gweilo: Memories of a Hong Kong Childhood* (Doubleday). Powerful and poignant childhood reminiscences from celebrated novelist Martin Booth offer some vivid insights into expat life in the Hong Kong of yesteryear.

Jonathan Dimbleby *The Last Governor* (Little Brown, UK & US). Charts Chris Patten's struggle to introduce more democracy and the run-up to the handover. The author was given unprecedented access to Government House, though critics say that the book – a TV tie-in – does a poor job of fully recording what went on in the last crucial years of Britain's rule.

John Le Carré *The Honourable Schoolboy* (Coronet/Bantam). Perhaps not Le Carré's best novel, but the usual George Smiley mix of spooks, moles and traitors is a good, racy read. The Hong Kong scenes capture the atmosphere of the dying years of colonialism well – paranoia, money, drink and politics mixed together.

Jan Morris *Hong Kong: Epilogue to an Empire* (Penguin/Vintage). A great introduction to Hong Kong by one of travel writing's most incisive observers. Morris mixes history, storytelling and colour in an easy-to-read style that ignites one's curiosity to visit.

Christopher Patten *East and West* (Random House, UK & US). The last British Governor's views not just of his controversial years in Hong Kong, but more broadly of the Asian "miracle", democracy, and the region's future. Thoughtful, with as much relevance to Asia's future as its most recent past.

Edward Stokes *Exploring Hong Kong's Countryside, a visitor's companion* (Hong Kong Tourist Authority). This guide contains all you need to investigate Hong Kong's most popular country-park walks and hikes, and see another – green – side to the city, which most visitors never discover. Stokes has been photographing and writing about Hong Kong's countryside for years, and few know more about this subject.

Language

Cantonese is the national language, with Mandarin a fast-growing second. English is widely spoken among the well-educated and many in the tourist trade (although not many taxi drivers). Otherwise, people speak only basic English; the standard has dropped noticeably since the 1997 handover when English was scrapped as the medium of instruction in most schools.

Cantonese is a **tonal language**, which means that the tone a speaker gives to a word will determine its meaning. As a simple two-letter word can have up to nine different, completely unrelated meanings depending on the pitch of the voice, the romanized word is really only an approximation of the Chinese sound.

Pronunciation

oy as in **boy**
ai as in **fine**
i as in **see**
er as in **urn**
o as in **pot**
ow as in **now**
oe as in **oh**
or as in **law**

Words and phrases in Cantonese

Greetings and basic phrases

Good morning	joe sun
Hello/how are you?	lay hoe ma?
Thank you/excuse me	m goy
Goodnight	joe tow
Goodbye	joy geen
I'm sorry	doy m joot
Can you speak English?	lay sik m sik gong ying man?
Yes	yow
No	mo
I'm sorry, I can't speak Cantonese	doy m joot, ngor m sik gong gong dong wa
I don't understand	ngor m ming bat
What is your name?	lay gew mut yeh meng?
My name is...	ngor gew...
I am from England/ America	ngor hai ying/may gwok yan
What time is it?	ching mun, gay dim ah?

Getting around

Where is this place? (while pointing to the place name or map)	ching mun, leedi day fong hai been do ah?
Where is the train station?	for chair tsam hai been do ah?
Where is the bus stop?	ba-see tsam hai been doe ah?
Where is the ferry pier?	ma-tow hai been doe ah?
Train	for chair
Bus	ba-see
Ferry	do lun schoon
Taxi	dik-see
Airport	fay gay cherng
Hotel	jow deem
Hostel	loy gwun
Restaurant	charn Teng
Toilets	chee saw
Where is the toilet?	chee saw hai been doe ah?
Police	ging chat
I want to go to...	ngor serng hoy...

Numbers

Note that the number two changes when asking for two of something – *lerng wei* (a table for two) – or stating something other than counting – *lerng mun* (two dollars).

1	yat
2	yee
3	saam
4	say
5	mm
6	lok
7	chat
8	bat
9	gow
10	sap
11, 12, 13, etc	sap yat, sap yee, sap saam
20, 21, 22, 23, etc	yee sap, yee sap yee, yee sap saam
30, 40, 50, etc	saam sap, say sap, mm sap
100	yat bat
1000	yat cheen

3.1

Hong Kong

The territory of **HONG KONG** comprises an irregularly shaped peninsula abutting the Pearl River Delta to the west, and a number of offshore islands, which cover more than a thousand square kilometres in total. The bulk of this area, namely the land in the north of the peninsula, as well as most of the islands, is semi-rural and is known as the **New Territories** – this was the land leased to Britain for 99 years in 1898. The southern part of the peninsula, known as **Kowloon**, and the island immediately south of here, **Hong Kong Island**, are the principal urban areas of Hong Kong. They were ceded to Britain "in perpetuity", but were returned to China at midnight on June 30, 1997, since when it has been the **Hong Kong Special Administrative Region** (SAR) of the People's Republic of China.

The island of Hong Kong offers not only traces of the old colony – from English place names to ancient trams trundling along the shore – but also superb modern architecture and bizarre cityscapes, as well as unexpected opportunities for **hiking** and even bathing on the **beaches** of its southern shore. Kowloon, in particular its southernmost tip, **Tsim Sha Tsui**, boasts a countless number of shops, offering a greater variety of goods per square kilometre than anywhere in the world, and is also the budget accommodation centre of Hong Kong. North of Tsim Sha Tsui, Kowloon stretches away into the **New Territories**, an area of so-called New Towns as well as ancient villages, secluded beaches and rural tranquillity. In addition, there are the **offshore islands**, including **Lamma** and **Lantau**, which are well worth a visit for their fresh fish restaurants, scenery and, if nothing else, for the experience of chugging about on the inter-island ferries.

Hong Kong phone numbers have no area codes. From outside the SAR, dial the normal international access code + ☎852 (country code) + the number. However, from Macau you need only dial ☎01 + the number.

Orientation

Orientation for new arrivals in the main urban areas is relatively easy: if you are "**Hong Kong-side**" – on the northern shore of Hong Kong Island – **Victoria Harbour** lies to your north, while to your south the land slopes upwards steeply to **The Peak**. The heart of this built-up area on Hong Kong Island is known, rather mundanely, as **Central**. Just across the harbour, in the area known as **Tsim Sha Tsui**, you are "**Kowloon-side**", and here all you really need to recognize is the colossal north–south artery, **Nathan Road**, full of shops and budget hotels, that leads down to the harbour, and to the phenomenal view south over Hong Kong Island. Two more useful points for orientation on both sides of Victoria Harbour are the **Star Ferry piers** where the popular cross-harbour ferries dock, in Tsim Sha Tsui (a short walk west of the south end of Nathan Road) and in Central.

Arrival

Public **transport** is so convenient and efficient that even first-time arrivals are unlikely to face any particular problems in reaching their destination within the city – apart from the difficulty of communicating with taxi drivers or reading the destinations on minibuses.

By plane

Hong Kong's new **Chek Lap Kok Airport** (known officially as Hong Kong International Airport; ☎2181 0000) is some way from downtown areas, 34km west of Central, on the north coast of Lantau Island, but it's connected to the urban areas by excellent rail and road links. The high-speed **Airport Express** rail service (AEL; ☎2881 8888) can be accessed directly from arrivals (every 10min; 5.50am–12.48am), whisking you to Central on Hong Kong Island in 23 minutes (HK$100), via Tsing Yi (12min; HK$60) and Kowloon (20min; HK$90). There are taxi ranks, bus stops and hotel-shuttle bus stops at the AEL stations, plus a left-luggage service at Hong Kong AEL Station (5.30am–1.30am) in Central.

There are six **Airbus** routes from the airport (frequent; 6am–midnight); the airport customer-service counters sell tickets (exact money only if you pay on the bus). The #A11 and #A12 go to Causeway Bay on Hong Kong Island via Sheung Wan, Central, Admiralty and Wan Chai; the #A12 continues to Fortress Hill, North Point, Quarry Bay, Tai Koo and Shau Kei Wan. Bus #A21 goes to Hung Hom KCR Station via Tsim Sha Tsui, Jordan, Yau Ma Tei and Mongkok; #A22 to Kowloon and Lam Tin MTR Station via Kwun Tong, Ngau Tau Kok, Kowloon Bay, Kowloon City, Hung Hom and Jordan; #A31 and #A41 go to the New Territories, with #A31 calling at Tsuen Wan MTR Station, Kwai Chung Road, Kwai Fong, Tsing Yi Road, and #A41 going to Sha Tin.

Taxis into the city are metered and reliable, but get the tourist office in the Buffer Hall, in the arrivals area of the airport, to write down the name of your destination in Chinese characters, so that you can show it to the taxi driver. It costs roughly HK$280 to get to Tsim Sha Tsui (20–30min), and about HK$340 for Hong Kong Island (30–50min). There may be extra charges for luggage and for tunnel tolls – on some tunnel trips the passenger pays the return charge too. Rush-hour traffic can slow down journey times considerably.

By train

The main land route into Hong Kong is by **train**. Express trains from Guangzhou (7 daily; 2hr) arrive at **Hung Hom KCR Station**, also known as the **Kowloon–Canton East Railway Station**, or **KCR Station** (☎2947 7888), east of Tsim Sha Tsui. You can transfer to the East Rail KCR line for one stop to East Tsim Sha Tsui Station, a short walk from Nathan Road and the heart of Tsim Sha Tsui. Alternatively, signposted walkways lead from here to an adjacent bus terminal, taxi rank and – a few minutes' walk west around the harbour – the pier for high-speed ferries to Central. For Tsim Sha Tsui, take bus #5C to the Star Ferry Pier; for Hong Kong Island, take the fast ferry to Central.

A cheaper alternative is to take a **local train** from Guangzhou to the Chinese border city of Shenzhen, from where you walk across the border to Lo Wu on the Hong Kong side and pick up the regular KCR trains to Kowloon (50min). There are now regular daily **bus** services from Guangzhou and Shenzhen operated by CTS; these take about one hour longer than the direct train and drop you off at CTS branches in Mongkok and Wan Chai.

Moving on to China and Macau

To enter China, you'll need a **visa** – easily obtainable in Hong Kong. Any travel agency and most hotels, even the cheapest hostels, offer this service. A single-entry visa costs about HK$150 with a three-day wait, HK$300 if you want it the next day or HK$400 for the express same-day service. You can also get more expensive multiple-entry visas. Depending on your nationality and passport, it's now also possible to make brief trips to Shenzhen only without a pre-arranged visa (you get a temporary one at the border), but check with the Ministry of Foreign Affairs 5th Floor, Lower Block, China Resources Building, 26 Harbour Rd, Wan Chai (Mon–Fri 9am–noon & 2–5pm; ⓣ2827 1881 or 2585 1794) as to whether you qualify – British passport-holders don't.

By train and bus

The simplest route into China is by **direct train to Guangzhou** (7 daily; 2hr–2hr 40min; HK$190–230). Tickets are obtainable in advance from CTS offices (see "Listings", p.230), or on the same day from the Hung Hom KCR Station. For more information, call ⓣ2947 7888. As a cheaper alternative, ride the KCR from East Tsim Sha Tsui up to Lo Wu (frequent; 50min; HK$36.50), walk into Shenzhen and pick up one of the hourly trains to Guangzhou – tickets can be easily purchased in Hong Kong dollars and cost about HK$100. Alternatively, hop on one of the CTS Guangzhou-bound buses that you can pick up from outside their offices in Mongkok or Wan Chai (7 daily; 2–3hr; HK$100).

By boat

By **boat**, you can travel to several Chinese cities, the majority from the China Ferry Terminal in Tsim Sha Tsui, where tickets can be bought in advance from a branch of CTS or directly from the booths in the terminal itself. There are services to **Shenzhen Airport** (8 daily; around 1hr; HK$180) and **Zhuhai** (12 daily; 1hr 10min; HK$180 depending on departure time). Turbojets and catamarans to **Macau** (24hr service every 15min, 7am–8pm, at least every hour thereafter; HK$141–176, depending on departure time and service) leave from the Macau Ferry Terminal on Hong Kong Island (nearest MTR is Sheung Wan). Ferry services to several Chinese destinations (as well as Macau) also operate from Chek Lap Kok Airport. Using this service, it's possible to transfer direct to China without passing through Hong Kong immigration (although you'll need a China visa for all destinations).

By plane

Finally, you can **fly** from Hong Kong into virtually all major Chinese cities on regional Chinese carriers such as China Southern and China Northwest, or to a more restricted number on the Hong Kong-based Dragonair. It's always worth shopping around since prices can vary sharply, and even on the major airlines special seasonal deals and discounts are often attractively priced. Destinations include Beijing (16 daily; 4hr); Chengdu (1–2 daily; 2hr 30min); Fuzhou (4–5 daily; 1hr 30min); Guangzhou (5 daily; 50min); Guilin (2 daily; 1hr 10min); Haikou (1–2 daily; 1hr 10min); Hangzhou (4–5 daily; 2hr); Kunming (2 daily; 2hr 30min); Nanjing (3 daily; 2hr); Ningbo (2-3 daily; 2hr); Shanghai (20–27 daily; 2hr); Shengyang (daily; 3hr 40min); Tianjin (daily; 3hr); Wuhan (1–2 daily; 1hr 40min); Xiamen (3–4 daily; 1hr); and Xi'an (5 weekly; 2hr 45min). You'll save substantially on ticket prices if you opt to fly from the nearby airports of Macau, Shenzhen or Guangzhou inside China. Macau airport in particular is becoming a mini-hub for budget airlines operating routes to Southeast Asia and Australia (see "Air and sea routes into Macau" in the Macau chapter, p.589, for more details).

By ferry

Arriving by sea is probably the most dramatic and picturesque way to approach Hong Kong for the first time. There are two important long-distance **ferry terminals**, one for Macau ferries and one for ferries from other Chinese ports. The

Macau Ferry Terminal is in the Shun Tak Centre, on Hong Kong Island, from where the Sheung Wan MTR Station is directly accessible; Macau ferries run frequently throughout the day and take an hour. The China Ferry Terminal, where ferries from Xiamen (20hr), Guangzhou (2–3hr), Shekou (45min) and Zhuhai (1hr 10min), plus a few from Macau, dock, is in the west of Tsim Sha Tsui, just ten minutes' walk from Nathan Road. There is also a berth for international cruise liners at Ocean Terminal in Tsim Sha Tsui.

Information

Countless leaflets on what to do including *Where* magazine and *Hong Kong: A Traveller's Guide* can be picked up at **Hong Kong Tourism Board** (HKTB) outlets (see p.187 for locations). Among the unofficial listings magazines (which you can pick up from most bars and some cafés and restaurants), the free *HK Magazine*, published every Friday, contains excellent up-to-date information on restaurants, bars, clubs, concerts and exhibitions, as does the fortnightly *BC* magazine.

City transport

Hong Kong's **public transport** system is efficient, comfortable, extensive and cheap, although it can be extremely crowded during rush hours. The MTR system and the main bus routes are easy to use and most signs are in English as well as Chinese, although don't expect staff to speak much English. The same is true with the drivers of taxis and minibuses. It's a good idea to get someone to write down your destination (and where you've come from for the return) in Chinese characters. If you get stuck, tourist maps also print the Chinese characters for the main tourist places.

Trains and trams

The **MTR** (Mass Transit Railway) is Hong Kong's **underground train system**, comprising four lines, which operate from 6am to 1am. The Island Line (marked blue on maps) runs along the north shore of Hong Kong Island, from Sheung Wan in the west to Chai Wan in the east, taking in important stops such as Central, Wan Chai and Causeway Bay. The Tsuen Wan Line (red) runs from Central, under the harbour, through Tsim Sha Tsui, and then northwest to the new town of Tsuen Wan. The Kwun Tong Line (green) connects with the Tsuen Wan Line at Yau Ma Tei in Kowloon, and then runs east in a circular direction, eventually coming back down south under the harbour to join the Island Line at Quarry Bay. Finally, the Tung Chung Line (yellow) follows much of the same route as the Airport Express, linking Central and Tung Chung. You can buy single-journey **tickets** (HK$4.50–36.50) from machines in the stations, or a rechargeable (and slightly better value) stored-value **Octopus Card** (☎2266 2266 for information) for travel on the MTR, KCR, LR (see p.204), the Airport Express, the tram and most ferries, buses, minibuses and maxicabs. You pay a deposit of HK$50 to get the plastic card, then add value to it by feeding it and your money into machines in the MTR. Your fare is electronically deducted each time you use the ticket – just swipe it over the yellow sensor pad on the top of the entry barrier. You can also buy one-day tourist MRT passes for $50.

The **KCR** (Kowloon–Canton East and West railways) are Hong Kong's main **overground train lines**, the former – and far more useful – running from East Tsim Sha Tsui Station, north through the New Territories to the border with China at Lo Wu, the latter running from Nam Cheong Station, through the western New Territories to Tuen Mun. Apart from the direct trains running through to Guangzhou, there are frequent local trains running between Kowloon and Lo Wu,

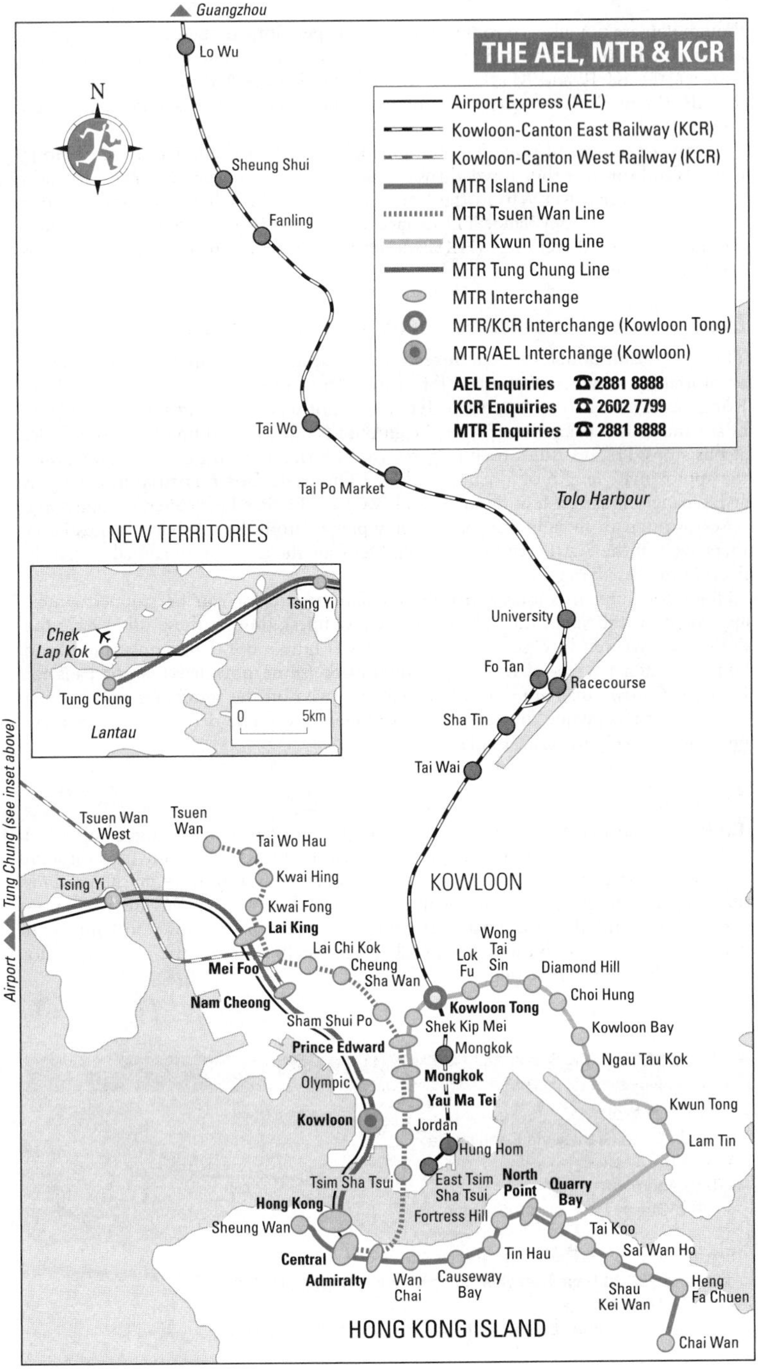

THE AEL, MTR & KCR

Airport Express (AEL)
Kowloon-Canton East Railway (KCR)
Kowloon-Canton West Railway (KCR)
MTR Island Line
MTR Tsuen Wan Line
MTR Kwun Tong Line
MTR Tung Chung Line
MTR Interchange
MTR/KCR Interchange (Kowloon Tong)
MTR/AEL Interchange (Kowloon)

AEL Enquiries ☎ 2881 8888
KCR Enquiries ☎ 2602 7799
MTR Enquiries ☎ 2881 8888

Guangzhou
Lo Wu
N
Sheung Shui
Fanling
Tai Wo
Tai Po Market
Tolo Harbour
NEW TERRITORIES
Tsing Yi
Chek Lap Kok
Tung Chung
Lantau
0 5km
University
Fo Tan
Racecourse
Sha Tin
Tai Wai
Airport
Tung Chung (see inset above)
Tsuen Wan West
Tsuen Wan
Tai Wo Hau
Kwai Hing
Tsing Yi
Kwai Fong
Lai King
KOWLOON
Mei Foo
Lai Chi Kok
Cheung Sha Wan
Lok Fu
Wong Tai Sin
Diamond Hill
Choi Hung
Nam Cheong
Kowloon Tong
Sham Shui Po
Shek Kip Mei
Kowloon Bay
Prince Edward
Mongkok
Ngau Tau Kok
Mongkok
Olympic
Yau Ma Tei
Kwun Tong
Kowloon
Jordan
Lam Tin
Hung Hom
Tsim Sha Tsui
East Tsim Sha Tsui
North Point
Quarry Bay
Hong Kong
Fortress Hill
Tai Koo
Sheung Wan
Tin Hau
Sai Wan Ho
Central
Admiralty
Wan Chai
Causeway Bay
Shau Kei Wan
Heng Fa Chuen
HONG KONG ISLAND
Chai Wan

though you are not allowed to travel beyond the penultimate station of Sheung Shui unless you have documentation for crossing into China. There is an interchange between the KCR and MTR at Kowloon Tong Station. A third transport system, the **LR** (Light Rail) runs between towns in the western New Territories, though tourists rarely use it.

Trams are a great (if non-air-conditioned) way to tour the north shore of Hong Kong Island (outside the crowded rush hour). They run between Kennedy Town in the west and Shau Kei Wan in the east, via Central, Wan Chai and Causeway Bay (some going via Happy Valley and its racecourse). You board at the back, and drop the money in the driver's box (HK$2; no change given) when you get off (Octopus Cards are accepted).

Buses, minibuses and maxicabs

The single- and double-decker **buses** that run around town aren't fast, but they're comfortable enough, and essential for many destinations, such as the south of Hong Kong Island and parts of the New Territories not served by trains. You pay as you board and exact change is required; the amount is often posted up on the timetables at bus stops. HKTB issues useful up-to-date information on bus routes, including the approximate length of journeys and cost. The **main bus terminal** in Central is at Exchange Square, a few minutes' walk west of the Star Ferry Pier, though some buses also start from right outside the ferry pier, or from the Outlying Islands Ferry Piers, west of the Star Ferry Pier. In Tsim Sha Tsui, the main bus terminal is right in front of the Star Ferry Pier.

Ubiquitous cream-coloured **minibuses** and **maxicabs** can be stopped almost anywhere on the street (not on double yellow lines), though these often have the destination written in Chinese only. They cost a little more than regular buses, and you can often pay the driver as you disembark (some now have sensor pads for Octopus Cards); small amounts of change are given on the minibuses only (which have a red stripe, while the maxicabs have green ones). The drivers of any of these buses are unlikely to speak English.

Taxis

Taxis in Hong Kong are not expensive, though they can be hard to get hold of in rush hours. Note that there is a toll to be paid (around HK$10) on any trips through a tunnel, and drivers often double this – as they are allowed to do – on the grounds that they have to get back again. Many taxi drivers do not speak English, so be prepared to show the driver the name of your destination written down in Chinese. If you get stuck, gesture to the driver to call the dispatch centre on the two-way radio; someone there will speak English.

A few important local bus routes

From Central:

#6 and #6A to Stanley via Repulse Bay
#15 to The Peak
#70 to Aberdeen
#629 to Ocean Park (also Admiralty)

From Tsim Sha Tsui Star Ferry Pier:

#8A and #5C to East Tsim Sha Tsui and Hung Hom KCR stations
#1 and #1A to Mongkok
#1, #1A, #2, #6, #6A, #7 and #9 to Temple Street Night Market

Ferries

One of the most enjoyable things to do in Hong Kong is to ride the **Star Ferry** between Kowloon and Hong Kong Island. The views of the island are superb, particularly at dusk. You'll also get a feel for the frenetic pace of life on Hong Kong's waterways, with ferries, junks, hydrofoils and larger ships looming up from all directions. You can ride upper deck (HK$2.20) or lower deck (HK$1.70). Ferries run every few minutes between Tsim Sha Tsui and Central (daily 6.30am–11.30pm; 8min), and between Tsim Sha Tsui and Wan Chai (daily 7.30am–10.50pm). There are also similarly cheap and fun ferry crossings from Hung Hom to Central and Wan Chai (daily 7am–7pm). For ferries to the **outlying islands**, see p.222.

Accommodation

Hong Kong boasts a colossal range of **hotels and guesthouses**, particularly in the Tsim Sha Tsui area of Kowloon. A fast-growing number of mainland visitors is pushing up occupancy levels and during large exhibitions the better hotels tend to fill up. Despite this, it's always worth checking for good package deals in mid-market hotels before you arrive. At the lower end, most of the options are squeezed into one or two giant, grimy blocks on Nathan Road, principally *Chungking Mansions* and the barely more salubrious *Mirador Mansions*. Even budget hotel accommodation is not that cheap, however – you'll be lucky to find a room for less than HK$150, and dorm beds cost HK$70–80 a night. Among the cheapest options are Hong Kong's seven official **youth hostels**, all of which offer very reasonable dormitory accommodation at around HK$30–65 if you've got an IYHF membership card, slightly more if you don't.

Kowloon

Most of the accommodation listed below is within fifteen minutes' walk of the Star Ferry Pier – conveniently central, though very touristy.

Accellerators International Hotel 182 Nathan Rd ☎3119 0397. Small, oddly named and catering largely to mainland visitors (so English is spoken haltingly), but well worth considering for its central location and realistically priced, large, clean rooms that are a cut above most guesthouses and cheaper than most hotels. ❼

Dadol Hotel 1st Floor, Champagne Court, 16–20 Kimberley Rd ☎2369 8882. A non-sleazy "love" hotel that's very welcoming, with English spoken. Comprises forty well-kept rooms with carpet, sparkling bathroom, TV, telephone and a/c. ❼

Golden Crown Guest House 5th Floor, Golden Crown Court, 66–70 Nathan Rd ☎2369 1782. A very friendly and clean if rather cramped place in one of the better Nathan Road blocks. Bathrooms are mostly communal. Dorm HK$150, double ❺

Lee Garden Guest House 8th Floor, 36 Cameron Rd ☎2367 2284. Friendly owner Charlie Chan offers a comfortable range of clean, small singles, doubles and triples with carpets, clean beds, bathrooms and reasonably sized windows. ❻

Rooms for Tourist 6th Floor, Lyton House Building, 36 Mody Rd ☎2721 8309. Basic, small, clean and quiet rooms with en-suite bathrooms throughout. ❻

Salisbury YMCA 41 Salisbury Rd, Tsim Sha Tsui ☎2368 7888. Occupying an unbeatable waterside location overlooking Hong Kong Island, this place offers the facilities (including swimming pool and a fitness centre) and comfort of hotels twice its price. Book early. Terrific four-bed dorms (HK$200) with attached shower are also available, but cannot be reserved in advance. Add a ten-percent service charge to all room rates. ❾

Yangcheng (Guangzhou) Hotel 7th Floor, Pak On Building, 1A Tak Shing St ☎2376 0263. The rooms are smart, bright, clean and inexpensive at this brand new, and hard-to-find hotel (head into the minimall behind the Chung Kee Supermarket and take the lift on the right-hand side). This is another mainlander-oriented place, so English is hardly spoken. Haggling is possible, though. ❻

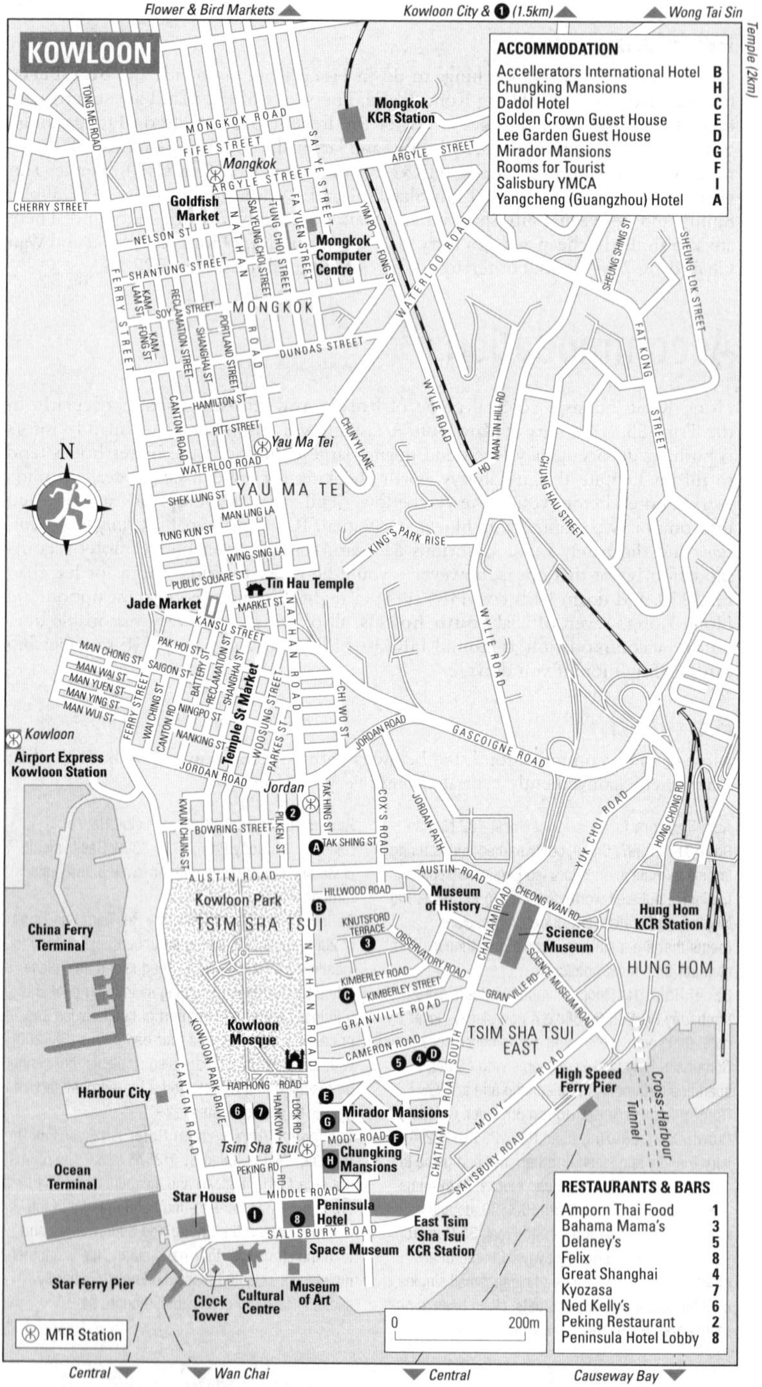

KOWLOON

Flower & Bird Markets ▲ Kowloon City & 1 (1.5km) ▲ Wong Tai Sin Temple (2km) ▲

ACCOMMODATION

Accellerators International Hotel	B
Chungking Mansions	H
Dadol Hotel	C
Golden Crown Guest House	E
Lee Garden Guest House	D
Mirador Mansions	G
Rooms for Tourist	F
Salisbury YMCA	I
Yangcheng (Guangzhou) Hotel	A

RESTAURANTS & BARS

Amporn Thai Food	1
Bahama Mama's	3
Delaney's	5
Felix	8
Great Shanghai	4
Kyozasa	7
Ned Kelly's	6
Peking Restaurant	2
Peninsula Hotel Lobby	8

MTR Station

0 200m

▼ Central ▼ Wan Chai ▼ Central Causeway Bay ▼

Chungking Mansions

A stay at **Chungking Mansions** is a badge of honour for some budget travellers, an unpleasant memory for others. Occupying one of the prime sites towards the southern end of Nathan Road, the whole block looks fit for demolition. The arcades on the lowest two floors are a warren of tiny shops and restaurants, while the remaining sixteen floors are crammed with budget guesthouses and various dodgy goings-on regularly resulting in regular police raids. Above the second floor, the building is divided into five blocks, lettered A to E, each served by two tiny, stuffy lifts, usually attended by long queues. Most of the guesthouses inside are pleasant enough but the whole building is a dirty, smelly, cluttered fire and safety hazard.

Dragon Inn 3rd Floor, B Block ☎2368 2007. Well-organized, friendly and secure hostel-cum-travel agent with 21 clean and basic singles, doubles and triples, some with shared bathroom, some en suite. ❻

Double Seven Guest House 7th & 8th Floor, A9, Block A ☎2367 1406/ 9310 0347. Opposite *Tom's Guesthouse* (and also part of the floor below), the appeal of this place is that the rooms are large and clean and the guesthouse is a (comparative) haven of calm and quiet. ❺

Happy Guest House Flat 3, 10th Floor, B Block ☎2368 0318; reception at Flat 3, 9th Floor. As the name suggests, this is a popular and welcoming guesthouse with singles and doubles, some shared, some en suite. There's a $10 surcharge for a/c use. ❹

Peking (and New Peking) Guest House Flat 2, 12th Floor, Block A ☎2723 8320. The new block boasts brand new rooms featuring tiled floors, fridges and big windows, with space for four people; the old block has cheaper, smaller, scruffier rooms. ❻

Tom's Guesthouse Flat 5, 8th Floor, Block A ☎2722 4956. Run by friendly management, the double and triple rooms here are reasonably bright and very good value. *Tom's* has another branch at Flat 1, 16th Floor, C Block (☎2722 6035), where the rooms are positively salubrious. ❹

Travellers' Hostel 16th Floor, Block A ☎2368 7710. A time-worn, shabby retreat for backpackers with mixed six-bed dorms (HK$90) and some singles, with or without a/c. Shared bathrooms. ❸

Welcome Guest House 7th Floor, Block A ☎2721 7793. A recommended first choice, offering a/c doubles, with and without shower. Nice clean rooms, luggage storage, laundry service, t'ai chi lessons and China visas available. ❹

Mirador Mansions

This is the big block at 54–64 Nathan Rd, on the east side, in between Carnarvon Road and Mody Road, right opposite the Tsim Sha Tsui MTR Station. Dotted around in among the residential apartments are large numbers of guesthouses. The advantage of the **Mirador Mansions** over the *Chungking Mansions* is that the stairwells and corridors are a lot cleaner and quieter, and the central section is open to the sky and so it doesn't smell as bad.

Cosmic Guest House Flat A1, 12th Floor ☎ 2739 1223/2366 8588. Traveller-savvy, English-speaking staff with everything from grubby dorms (HK$160) to deluxe doubles. ❺

Garden Hostel Flat F4, 3rd Floor ☎2311 1183. *Mirador's* finest: friendly and laid back with free washing machines, Kung Fu lessons, lockers and even a patio garden. Mixed and women-only dorms (HK$60); discounts for long stays. ❺

Kowloon Hotel Flat F1, 13th Floor ☎2311 2523. Not to be confused with the ritzy hotel of the same name across the road, this guesthouse offers a range of clean singles and doubles, but a gruesome fourteen-bed dorm. Discounts for long stays. ❻

Hong Kong Island

The budget rooms on Hong Kong Island are all in Causeway Bay, largely concentrated in Paterson Street and the Central Building, while the rest of the accommodation on offer is nearly all upmarket, though you may be able to get a good package deal in advance.

Garden View International House 1 Macdonnell Rd, Central ☎2877 3737. This YWCA-run place is just off Garden Road, south of the Zoological and Botanical Gardens. Take the Airbus to Central's

Exchange Square Bus Terminal and then green maxicab 1A from just outside the Star Ferry Pier or a taxi (about $30). Very salubrious, and the cheapest place in this area of Central. ⑨

Harbour View International House 4 Harbour Rd, Wan Chai ☎2802 0111. Very close to the Wan Chai Ferry Pier, and next door to the Arts Centre, this is an excellent place to stay, with recently refurbished, good-value doubles. Big discounts apply when business is slow. ⑨

Mount Davis Youth Hostel (Ma Wui Hall) Mt Davis Path, Mt Davis ☎2817 5715. Perched on top of a mountain, this place has superb views over the harbour and is unbelievably peaceful. Conditions are excellent, though all guests have to do one small chore daily. YHA members pay less. Getting here is a major expedition: take bus #47A from Admiralty, or minibus #54 from the Outlying Islands Ferry Piers in Central and get off near the junction of Victoria Road and Mt Davis Path; walk back 100m from the bus stop and you'll see Mt Davis Path branching off up the hill – a long, hot 45min walk. Otherwise, get off the bus in Kennedy Town and catch a taxi (around HK$50 plus HK$5 per item of luggage). A hostel shuttle bus (HK$10) departs from the bus terminal next to the Shun Tak Centre at the Macau Ferry Terminal at 9.30am, 7pm, 9pm & 10.30pm; the return service leaves Ma Wui Hall at 7.30am, 9am, 10.30am & 8.30pm. Dorms from HK$40. ⑤–⑥

Noble Hostel Flat A3, 17th Floor, Great George Building, 27 Paterson St, Causeway Bay ☎2576 6148. Friendly Mrs Lin runs her 45-room hostel efficiently and tailors to all budgets with a range of singles, twins and triples, all light, clean and equipped with TV and a/c (plus a choice of en-suite bathroom or shared facilities). One of the best-run guesthouses in town and right in the middle of Causeway Bay. ⑦

The Wesley 22 Hennessy Rd ☎2866 6688. A quiet and comfortable modern hotel with glimmers of a harbour view if you crane your neck; very cheap for the location. ⑨

Central Building

Causeway Bay's equivalent to *Mirador* and *Chungking* in miniature, the **Central Building** holds about six guesthouses in various states of cleanliness, and is just around the corner from Causeway Bay MTR Station at 531 Jaffe Rd.

Bin Man Hotel Room F, 1st Floor ☎2838 5651. Fantastic name for this small and friendly guesthouse with tiny, clean rooms most with a/c, TV and attached bathroom. ⑥

Clean Guest House Room N, 1st Floor ☎2833 2063. *Bin Man*'s welcoming sister guesthouse lives up to its name, providing spotless rooms with towels, slippers and soap thrown in. ⑥

The New Territories and outlying islands

These tranquil outer regions are a good place to stay if you want to escape the noise and bustle. The best time to visit is during the week, when rooms may be discounted by forty percent or more. At weekends, many will be booked solid, so advanced planning is essential. Six of Hong Kong's seven official **youth hostels** are here, two on Lantau Island, and four in the New Territories. Don't imagine, however, that you can use them as a base for exploring the rest of Hong Kong – they are far too remote, and you're even advised to take your own food with you. If you're not an IYHA member you'll have to buy a HK$30 welcome stamp for each night's stay; after you've collected six of them you become a member.

Bradbury Lodge Tai Mei Tuk, Tai Po, New Territories ☎2662 5123. Of all the hostels this is about the easiest to get to. Take the KCR train to Tai Po, then bus #75K to Tai Mei Tuk Terminal. Walk south a few minutes, with the sea on your right. Lots of boating, walking and cycling opportunities right by the scenic Plover Cove Reservoir. Dorms are HK$40.

Concerto Inn Hung Shing Ye Beach, Lamma Island ☎2982 1668. Lamma's best (and actually only proper) hotel – all rooms have a TV and fridge, and some have a kitchen and balconies overlooking the beach. ⑨

Pak Sha O Hostel Pak Sha O, Hoi Ha Road, Sai Kung, New Territories ☎2328 2327. Take bus #94 from Sai Kung (see p.221). Get off at Ko Tong, walk 100m farther on and take Hoi Ha Road on the left – from here it's a 40min walk. Close to Hong Kong's cleanest, most secluded beaches. Dorms are HK$40.

S G Davis Hostel Ngong Ping, Lantau Island ☎2985 5610. From Mui Wo (see p.224), take bus

#2 to the Ngong Ping Terminal and follow the paved footpath south, away from the Tian Tan Buddha and past the public toilets (10min). A great base for hill-walking on Lantau, and you can eat at the nearby Po Lin Monastery. It's cold on winter nights, though – bring a sleeping bag. Dorms are HK$40.

Hong Kong Island

As the oldest colonized part of Hong Kong, its administrative and business centre, and site of some of the most expensive real estate in the world, **Hong Kong Island** is, in every sense, the heart of the whole territory. Despite its size, just 15km from east to west and 11km from north to south, the island encompasses the best the territory has to offer in one heady hit: lavish temples to consumer excess, the vivid sights and smells of a Chinese wet market and (away from the North shore's steel and concrete mountains) surprising expanses of sandy beach and forested nature reserves.

Central

On the northern shore of Hong Kong Island, overlooking Victoria Harbour and Kowloon on the mainland opposite, lies the territory's major financial and commercial quarter, known as **Central**. The area takes in the core of the old city, which was originally called Victoria, after the queen, and in the last two decades has sprouted several of Asia's tallest and most interesting skyscrapers (the tallest to date is the unmistakable new **Two IFC** tower, which looms – all 420m of it – just west of the Star Ferry Pier). Central extends out from the Star Ferry Pier a few hundred metres in all directions, east to the Admiralty MTR, west to the Central Market and south, up the hill, to the Zoological and Botanical Gardens.

Inland from the shore, the main west–east roads are Connaught Road, Des Voeux Road and Queen's Road respectively (affixed by either "East", "Central" or "West", depending on which area they're winding through), though pedestrians are better off concentrating on the extensive system of **elevated walkways**. To get to this system from the Star Ferry Pier, climb the stairs to the west (beside **Jardine House**, the porthole-covered skyscraper nearby). Before reaching the entrance to the International Finance Centre (on the ground floor of which is the Airport Express Station), you take the walkway to the left and follow it inland. Alternatively, head right for the neck-crickingly tall Two IFC tower and **Exchange Square**; the three gloriously opulent marble-and-tinted-glass towers here house the Hong Kong Stock Exchange. The Exchange Square Bus Station is located underneath the square. A further branch of the elevated walkway runs northwest from here, parallel with the shore and along the northern edge of Connaught Road, past Exchange Square and all the way to the Macau Ferry Terminal and Sheung Wan MTR. Otherwise, continue across Connaught Road into the heart of an extremely upmarket shopping area, around Des Voeux Road.

Easily recognizable from the tramlines that run up and down here, **Des Voeux Road** used to mark Hong Kong's seafront before the days of reclamation, hence the name of the smartest shopping mall in the area, the **Landmark**, on the corner with Pedder Street. In addition to all the top Western designer outlets here, you'll find **Shanghai Tang**, across Pedder Street from the Landmark, which sells kitschy communist memorabilia, *cheongsams* and other colourful designer garments influenced by traditional Chinese wear.

The stretch of Des Voeux Road running west from the Landmark is connected by a series of lanes running south to the parallel Queen's Road. Leading uphill from Queen's Road Central, is **Graham Street**, one of the great fruit-and-vegetable

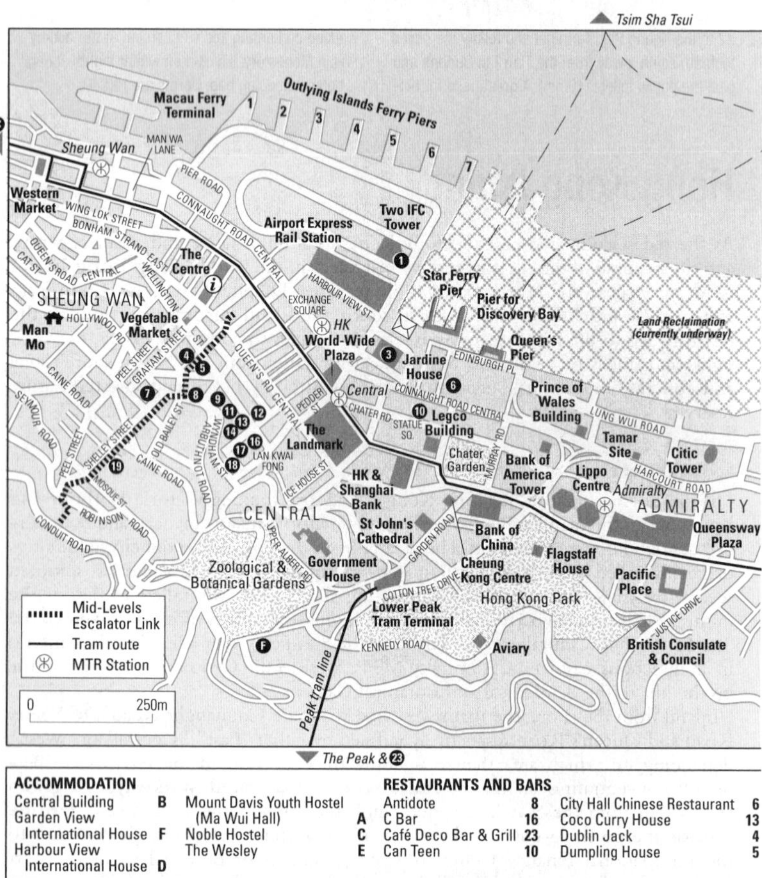

markets that still manage to survive in downtown Hong Kong. Also leading uphill from Queen's Road, immediately south of Central Market, is the fantastic **Mid-Levels Escalator Link**, basically a giant series of escalators that runs 800m straight up the hill as far as Conduit Road, servicing the expensive **Mid-Levels** residential area, as well as the thriving restaurant district of **SoHo** (short for south of Hollywood Road). During the morning rush hour (6am–10am), when people are setting out to work, the escalators run downwards only; from 10.20am to midnight they run up, offering a convenient way to explore some of Central's most interesting and historic streets.

In the opposite direction from the Landmark, east along Des Voeux Road, you'll find Statue Square on your left towards the shore, and, immediately south, the magnificently hi-tech, "inside-out" **Hong Kong and Shanghai Bank** building, designed by Norman Foster and guarded by two huge, haughty bronze lions. At the time of construction it was one of the most expensive office blocks ever built. The whole structure is supported on giant pillars, and it's possible to walk right under it and come out on the other side – a necessity stipulated by the old *feng shui* belief that the centre of power on the island, Government House, which lies directly to the north of the bank, should be accessible in a straight line by foot from the main

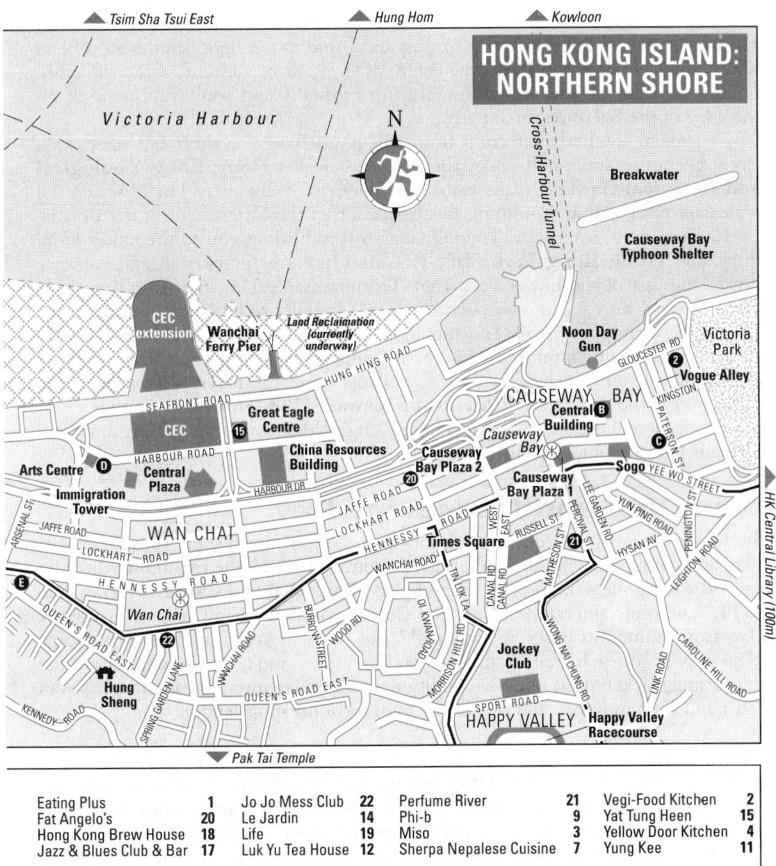

point of arrival on the island, the Star Ferry. From under the bank the building's insides are transparent, and you can look up, through the colossal glass atrium, into the heart of the building.

A couple of hundred metres east of the Hong Kong and Shanghai Bank is the three-hundred-metre-high blue glass geometric shard of the **Bank of China** tower, designed by the internationally renowned architect I.M. Pei, who was also responsible for the National Gallery of Art in Washington, DC, and the pyramid in the forecourt of the Louvre in Paris. Although under instructions from Beijing, the designers of this bank had no hesitation in by-passing all the normal *feng shui* sensitivities, and this knife-like structure is accordingly feared and disliked in Hong Kong.

South of Queen's Road

South of Queen's Road the land begins to slope seriously upwards, and walking can become extremely laborious in hot weather. Head south up D'Aguilar Street (just west of Pedder Street) from Queen's Road, and you'll enter the **Lan Kwai Fong** area, the main focus for eating and, particularly, drinking in Central. One of the most interesting places here for visitors is the traditional Chinese **Luk Yu Tea**

House on Stanley Street (see p.226). Just above and to the right (southwest) of Lan Kwai Fong is Hollywood Road, the centre of Hong Kong's antique and curio trade. Follow the road west to where the escalator crosses it, and you'll find yourself on the edge of the SoHo restaurant area.

In a general southerly direction from Lan Kwai Fong – a short but steep walk along Glenealy Street and under the flyover – are the **Hong Kong Zoological and Botanical Gardens** (daily 6am–7pm; free), originally opened in 1864 and still a pleasant refuge, though nothing spectacular. From the eastern exit of the Botanical Gardens, a ten-minute walk along Garden Road brings you to the rather more impressive **Hong Kong Park** (daily 6.30am–11pm; free); there's also an entrance just to the east of the Lower Peak Tram Terminal (see p.214), and from the north, on Supreme Court Road – follow signs from Admiralty MTR Station, through the Pacific Place shopping mall. The highlight here is the excellent **Edward Youde Aviary** (daily 9am–5pm; free), where you find yourself in a cool, shady rainforest setting, surrounded by rare birds as you negotiate the raised walkways. At the north end of the park is the **Museum of Teaware** (Tues–Sun 10am–5pm; free), an unremarkable collection housed in Hong Kong's oldest surviving colonial building, Flagstaff House, completed in 1846.

Wan Chai and Causeway Bay

Stretching away east of Central, the built-up area on the north shore runs for at least 6km and comprises a number of localized centres, of which the two most visited by tourists for nightlife, dining and shopping are **Wan Chai** and **Causeway Bay**. The MTR train route and tramline connects Central with both Wan Chai and Causeway Bay, as do numerous buses, including #2 and #111. If you're in Tsim Sha Tsui, a pleasant way to reach Wan Chai is by Star Ferry or, if you're in Central, aboard the endearingly rickety (but non-air-conditioned) trams. Hennessy Road connects Wan Chai and Causeway Bay and carries the tram for some of its length.

Wan Chai

In the 1950s and 1960s, **Wan Chai** was known throughout east Asia as a thriving red-light district, catering in particular for US soldiers on leave from Korea and Vietnam. Hong Kong's most famous fictional character, Suzy Wong, a prostitute from Richard Mason's novel *The World of Suzy Wong*, resided and worked here. Wan Chai has since lost most of its raunchy air, but the **restaurants** and **bars** are still certainly worth a visit.

In the far west of the area, just north of Gloucester Road on the corner of Fenwick Street and Harbour Road, is the **Hong Kong Arts Centre** (ten minutes' walk from Wan Chai MTR), which is worth dropping in on for its art galleries, films and other cultural events. You can pick up a free copy here of the monthly magazine *Artslink*, which has a detailed diary and reviews of what's happening on the art scene in Hong Kong. There are also two good cafés, both with harbour views.

Immediately to the east of the Arts Centre stands a vast set of gleaming modern buildings that have changed the face of Wan Chai beyond all recognition. The **Hong Kong Convention and Exhibition Centre** (**CEC**) on the seafront is probably the biggest and best of its kind in Asia. When there are no events going on, you can visit the centre's extraordinary interior. There's also a cybercafé in the foyer. You can reach the CEC by following raised walkways from Wan Chai MTR Station, or from the ferry terminal immediately in front.

On Queen's Road East, south of the tramlines on Johnston Road, is the little **Hung Sheng Temple**, built into the hillside. This old brick building, smoke-blackened and hung with ancient draperies, was once a shrine by the sea, but has long since been marooned far inland by reclamation. A short walk east on Stone Nullah Lane is the **Pak Tai Temple**, where you can see craftsmen making fantastic burial offerings out of bamboo and coloured paper, including cars, houses and aeroplanes.

Causeway Bay

Causeway Bay is a lively district packed with shops, restaurants and, on weekends, seemingly most of Hong Kong's seven million citizens. It's centred between the eastern end of Lockhart Road and the western edge of Victoria Park. Trams run just to the south of here along Yee Wo Street, a continuation of Hennessy Road from Wan Chai. Causeway Bay has an MTR station and is also the point of arrival of the original **cross-harbour tunnel**, which carries vehicle traffic over from Kowloon.

The main activity in Causeway Bay is shopping. Within a few minutes of the MTR station you'll find a couple of ultra-modern Japanese department stores and Jardine's Crescent, a narrow alleyway packed with market stalls selling cheap clothes, jewellery and knick-knacks. On the shore, in front of the *Excelsior Hotel* on Gloucester Road, stands the **Noon Day Gun** – immortalized in Noel Coward's song *Mad Dogs and Englishmen* – which is fired every day at noon. The eastern part of Causeway Bay is dominated by **Victoria Park**, which contains a swimming pool and other sports facilities. In recent years, this has become the location for the annual candle-lit vigil held on June 4 to commemorate the victims of Tiananmen Square.

Heading inland from Hennessy Road, on the corner of Matheson and Russell streets is Causeway Bay's most famous shopping plaza, the half-moon shaped **Times Square**, fronted by a huge video screen, a packed courtyard, thirteen floors of themed shops and restaurants and a cinema. Just to the west of Times Square lies **Bowrington Road Market** and the streets of market stalls surrounding it, worth dropping in on in the morning (if you're not squeamish) to see poultry, fish and meat being hacked about on a huge scale.

Happy Valley

The low-lying area extending inland from the shore south of Wan Chai and Causeway Bay and known as Happy Valley means only one thing for the people of Hong Kong: horseracing, or more precisely, gambling. The **Happy Valley Racecourse**, which dates back to 1846, was for most of Hong Kong's history the only one in the territory, until a second course was built at Shatin in the New Territories. A night at the races is a quintessential, and extremely cheap, Hong Kong experience. Gambling fever hits during the racing season, which runs from September until June, with meetings once or twice a week at Happy Valley. Entrance to the public enclosure is just HK$20 and the beer inside is cheap. There's a racing museum (Tues–Sun 10am–5pm, race days 10am–12.30pm; free), and HKTB (see p.187) runs a "Come Horse-racing Tour" (HK$490), which includes transport to and from the track, entry to the Members' Enclosure and a buffet meal at the official Jockey Club – plus tips on how to pick a winner. Happy Valley can be reached from Central or Causeway Bay on a spur of the tramline, or on bus #1 from Central.

Western District

West of Central lies a district rather older and more traditional in character than other parts of Hong Kong. An almost entirely Chinese-inhabited area, its crowded residential streets and traditional shops form a striking contrast to Central.

Sheung Wan, immediately adjacent to Central, spreads south up the hill from the seafront at the modern Shun Tak Centre, which houses the Macau Ferry Terminal and the Sheung Wan MTR Station, the last stop on the Island line. The Shun Tak Centre is a pleasant fifteen-minute walk along the elevated walkway from Exchange Square in Central, though you'll get more flavour of the district by following the tramlines along Des Voeux Road, west from Central Market towards **Western Market** (daily 10am–7pm), a brick Edwardian building, where you'll find shops selling fabric and kitsch, plus a couple of cafés. Head south to **Bonham Strand East** for an intriguing range of peculiar specialist shops such as seafood wholesalers, piled high, rather pathetically, with mounds of dried seahorses and shark fins. You'll also find Chinese herbalist wholesalers offering some gruesome and bizarre ingredients (ground deer horn and dinosaur-tooth health tonic anyone?).

If that's not enough of a grisly assortment, you'll also find shop windows displaying snakes (alive and dead), snake-bile wine, birds' nests, shark fins, antlers, crushed pearls, as well as industrial quantities of expensive ginseng root. You'll find medicinal shops scattered along an east–west line extending from Bonham Strand to the small **Ko Shing Street** – the heart of the trade – which is adjacent to, and just south of, Des Voeux Road West. This section of Des Voeux Road specializes in every kind of dried food, including sea slugs, starfish, snakes and flattened ducks.

A short but stiff walk uphill from Bonham Strand leads to **Hollywood Road**, running west from Wyndham Street in Central (immediately southwest of Lan Kwai Fong; see p.211) as far as the small Hollywood Park in Sheung Wan, where it runs into Queen's Road West. Bus #26 takes a circular route from Des Voeux Road in Central to the western end of Hollywood Road, then east again along the whole length of the road. The big interest here is the array of **antique and curio shops**, and you can pick up all sorts of oddities, from tiny embroidered women's shoes to full-size traditional coffins. The antique shops extend into the small alley, Upper Lascar Row, commonly known as **Cat Street**, which is immediately north of the western end of Hollywood Road and due south of the Sheung Wan MTR. Here you'll find wall-to-wall curiosity stalls with coins, ornaments, jewellery and chops (Chinese character name stamps carved from stone or wood) all on sale. If you want to buy, healthy scepticism and hard bargaining are useful tools but it's a good hunting ground for portable, kitschy Chinese keepsakes.

Another attraction in the Cat Street area is **Ladder Street**, which runs north–south across Hollywood Road and is, almost literally, as steep as a ladder. This is a relic from the nineteenth century when a number of such stepped streets existed to help sedan-chair carriers get their loads up the steep hillsides. On Hollywood Road, adjacent to Ladder Street, the 150-year-old **Man Mo Temple** (daily 7am–5pm) is notable for its great hanging coils of incense suspended from the ceiling. The two figures on the main altar are the Taoist gods of Literature (Man) and the Martial Arts (Mo). Located as it is in a deeply traditional area, this is one of the most atmospheric small temples in Hong Kong.

The Peak

The uppermost levels of the 552-metre hill that towers over Central and Victoria Harbour have always been known as **Victoria Peak** (or simply "**The Peak**"), and, in colonial days, the area was populated by upper-class expats. Meanwhile, most of the population lived down below, where the climate was hotter and less healthy. The story of the colonization of what was originally a barren, treeless rock is an extraordinary one. Before 1859, when the first path up to The Peak was carved out, it was barely possible to get up here at all, let alone put houses on it. And yet, within twenty years, a number of summer homes had been built, with everything – from human beings to building materials – carried laboriously up the hill by bearers. In 1888, the opening of a hair-raisingly steep **funicular railway**, known as the Peak Tram, allowed speedy and regular connections to the harbour. By 1924, when the first road to The Peak was built, permanent homes had begun to appear on it. Aside from its exclusive residential area, The Peak is still a cool, peaceful retreat and a vantage point offering some extraordinary panoramic views over the city and harbour below.

Ascending The Peak is half the fun, assuming you plan to ride the **Peak Tram**, which climbs 373 vertical metres to the terminus in eight minutes. To find the Lower Peak Tram Terminal in Central, catch the free shuttle bus (daily 9am–7pm) from outside the Star Ferry Pier or take bus #15C (HK$3.20). On foot, it's on Garden Road a little way up the hill from St John's Cathedral. The Peak Tram itself (daily 7am–midnight; HK$20 single, HK$30 return) runs every ten to fifteen minutes, and you can also use the shuttle bus back to the Star Ferry afterwards. You can also catch bus #15 to The Peak from just in front of the Star Ferry, which is a slower but still scenic route.

On and around The Peak

The Peak Tram drops you at the terminal in the **Peak Tower**. This building and the **Peak Galleria** across the road are full of souvenir shops and pricey bars and restaurants, some with spectacular views. From the Peak Tower Tram Terminal area, Mount Austin Road leads up to the very top of The Peak, where you'll find the Victoria Peak Garden, formerly the site of the Governor's residence. But it's more interesting to follow Harlech Road, due west of the terminal area, for a delightful rural stroll through trees; after half an hour the road runs into Lugard Road, which heads back towards the terminal around the northern rim of The Peak, giving magnificent views over Central and Kowloon. The fourth road from the Peak Tower Terminal area, Old Peak Road, leads down to the May Road Tram Station.

An excellent way to descend The Peak is to walk, the simplest route being to follow the sign pointing to Hatton Road, from opposite the picnic area on Harlech Road. The **walk** is along a very clear path all the way through trees, eventually emerging after about 45 minutes in Mid-Levels, near the junction between Kotewall Road and Conduit Road. Catch bus #13 or minibus #3 from Kotewall Road to Central, or you can walk east for about 1km along Conduit Road until you reach the top end of the Mid-Levels Escalator (see p.211), which will also take you down into Central. Another good route down is to take a road leading from Peak Road, not far from the Peak Tower Tram Terminal, signposted to **Pokfulam Reservoir**, a very pleasant spot in the hills. Beyond the reservoir, heading downhill, you'll eventually come out on Pokfulam Road, from where there are plenty of buses to Central, or south to Aberdeen.

Hong Kong Island: the southern and eastern shores

On its south side, Hong Kong Island straggles into the sea in a series of dangling peninsulas and inlets. The atmosphere is far quieter here than on the north shore, and the climate reputedly sunnier. You'll find not only separate towns such as **Aberdeen** and **Stanley** with a flavour of their own, but also beaches, such as that at **Repulse Bay**, and much farther east, at the remote and pretty village of **Shek O**. Buses are plentiful to all destinations on the southern shore, and Aberdeen is linked to Central by a tunnel under The Peak. Nowhere is more than an hour from Central.

Aberdeen

Aberdeen is the largest separate town on Hong Kong Island, with a population of more than sixty thousand, a dwindling minority of whom still live on **sampans and junks** in the narrow harbour that lies between the main island and the offshore island of Ap Lei Chau. The boat people who live here are following a tradition that certainly preceded the arrival of the British in Hong Kong, although their ancient way of life is now facing extinction. In the meantime, a time-honoured and enjoyable tourist activity in Aberdeen is to take a **sampan tour** around the harbour. From the bus stop, just head towards the ornamental park by the waterfront until you reach a sign advertising "Water Tours" (around HK$50 per head for a thirty-minute ride). The trip offers great photo opportunities of the old houseboats jammed together, complete with dogs, drying laundry and outdoor kitchens. Along the way you'll also pass boat yards and the floating restaurants, which are especially spectacular when lit up at night. To reach Aberdeen, catch **bus** #7 or #70 from Central, or #72 from Causeway Bay (30min). There's also a **boat** connection between here and nearby Lamma Island (see p.222).

Ocean Park

Ocean Park, a gigantic theme and adventure park (daily 10am–6pm; HK$185, children HK$93 including all rides), covers an entire peninsula to the east of Aberdeen. You could easily spend the best part of a day here, though make sure you arrive early in summer to avoid queues (likely to shorten somewhat when the New Disneyland opens on Lantau Island in 2006). The park's rarest living attraction is a pair of Giant Pandas, An-An and Jia-Jia, for whom a special complex has been created, complete with fake slopes, bamboo groves and misting machines. Other highlights include one of the fastest and longest roller coasters in the world, the Abyss Turbo Drop ride; an aquarium with sharks, dolphins and whales; and the Middle Kingdom, which aims to re-create five thousand years of Chinese history through architecture, crafts, theatre and opera. A special **bus** service, the #629 Citybus Tour, runs from Central Star Ferry Pier and from Admiralty MTR to Ocean Park (every 15min, 9am–6.30pm); the ticket includes the entrance fee. Otherwise, a number of regular services cover the route, including the #6 minibus (Mon–Sat) from the car park in front of the Star Ferry Pier, and buses #70, #75, #90, #97 and #590 from Central; #72, #92, #96 and #592 from Causeway Bay. Get off immediately after the Aberdeen Tunnel and follow the signs. On Sundays, bus #72A from Central stops right by the park.

Repulse Bay and beyond

Popular with locals, but rather packed and polluted, are the beaches of Deep Water Bay and **Repulse Bay** just east of Ocean Park. Repulse Bay has a **Tin Hau Temple** (dedicated to the goddess of the sea), with a longevity bridge, the crossing of which is said to add three days to your life. South of Repulse Bay, you'll find the more secluded but narrower beaches of **Middle Bay** and **South Bay**, fifteen and thirty minutes' walk respectively farther along the coast. You can reach Repulse Bay on **buses** #6, #61 or #260 from Central. Between Aberdeen (to the west) and Stanley (to the east) there are frequent buses that pass all of the bays mentioned above.

Stanley

Straddling the neck of Hong Kong's southernmost peninsula, **Stanley** is a moderately attractive, tiny residential village, of which the main draw is the number of pubs and restaurants catering to expatriates. A little way to the north of the bus stop is **Stanley Beach**. Walk downhill from the bus stop and you'll soon find **Stanley Market** (selling a mish-mash of cheap clothes and tourist souvenirs). To the west, on Stanley Main Road, there are some great seafront restaurants and bars. If you continue walking beyond the restaurants, you'll come to another **Tin Hau Temple**, built in 1767, on the western side of the peninsula. Inside, there's a large tiger skin, the remains of an animal shot near here in 1942 – a poignant symbol of how the area has changed. In a direct *feng shui*-friendly line from the temple to the shore is **Murray House**, built in 1843 for the British Army and originally sited in Central. It was recently painstakingly rebuilt in Stanley (having been knocked down to make way for the Bank of China) using salvaged stonework and elements from other historical buildings, such as twelve stone columns covered in calligraphy from Shanghai Street in Yau Ma Tei. Today, it houses a few decent restaurants offering that Hong Kong rarity: al fresco dining (with pleasant sea views thrown in for free). Stanley is accessible on **buses** #6 and #260 from Central, or #73 from Aberdeen or Repulse Bay.

Shek O

In the far east of the island, **Shek O** is Hong Kong's most remote settlement and still has an "undiscovered" feel about it, if such a thing is possible in Hong Kong. There's a strong surf beating on the wide, white **beach** and, during the week, it's more or less deserted. Come for sunbathing and lunch at one of the cheap local restaurants. The beach is just a few minutes' walk east from the bus stop, beyond a small roundabout. For a small detour through the village, however, stop at the excellent Thai restaurant with outdoor tables that you see on your left just before the roundabout. If you take the small lane on the left that runs right through the restaurant area, you'll pass first the local temple and then a variety of shops and stalls.

Reaching Shek O in the first place is one of the best things about it. First, you need to get to **Shau Kei Wan** on the northeastern shore of Hong Kong Island, either by tram or MTR. From the bus terminal outside the MTR station, catch bus #9 to Shek O, a great journey over hills (30min) during which you'll be able to spot first the sparkling waters of the Tai Tam Reservoir, then Stanley (far to the southwest) and finally Shek O itself, appearing down below like a Mediterranean village on the shore.

Kowloon

A four-kilometre strip of the mainland grabbed by the British in 1860 to add to their offshore island, **Kowloon** was part of the territory ceded to Britain "in perpetuity" and was accordingly developed with gusto and confidence. With the help of land reclamation and the diminishing significance of the border between Kowloon and the New Territories at Boundary Street, Kowloon has, over the years, just about managed to accommodate the vast numbers of people who have squeezed into it. Today, areas such as Mongkok, jammed with soaring tenements, are among the most densely populated urban areas in the world (in places shoehorning 100,000 people into each square kilometre).

While Hong Kong Island has mountains and beaches to palliate the effects of urban claustrophobia, Kowloon has just more shops, more restaurants and more hotels. It's hard to imagine that such a relentlessly built-up, crowded and commercial place as this could possibly have any cachet among the travelling public – and yet it does. The **view** across the harbour to Hong Kong Island, wall-to-wall with skyscrapers, is one of the most unforgettable city panoramas you'll see anywhere, especially at night.

Tsim Sha Tsui and beyond

The tourist heart of Hong Kong, **Tsim Sha Tsui**, is an easy place to find your way around. The **Star Ferry Pier**, for ferries to Hong Kong Island, is right on the southwestern tip of the peninsula. East of here, along the southern shore, facing Hong Kong Island, are a number of hi-tech, modern museums and galleries built on reclaimed land, while **Salisbury Road**, just to the north, is dominated by the magnificently traditional *Peninsula Hotel*. Running south to north right through the middle of Tsim Sha Tsui, and on through the rest of Kowloon, is Hong Kong's most famous street, Nathan Road, jammed with shoppers at all hours of the day and night.

The distinctive ski-slope roofline of the **Hong Kong Cultural Centre**, which occupies the former site of the Kowloon Railway Station, about 100m east of the Star Ferry Pier, is unmissable. Inside, there are concert halls, theatres and galleries, including, in an adjacent wing, the **Museum of Art** (daily except Thurs; HK$10, free Wed), which is worth a visit. As well as calligraphy, scrolls and an intriguing selection of paintings covering the history of Hong Kong, the museum has a good Chinese antiquities section. Immediately to the east of the Cultural Centre, the domed **Hong Kong Space Museum** (Mon & Wed–Fri 1–9pm, Sat & Sun 10am–9pm; HK$10, free Wed) houses some highly user-friendly exhibition halls on astronomy and space exploration. The **Space Theatre** next door presents wide-screen space shows for an additional fee (HK$32, concessions HK$16; call ®2721 0226 for show times).

Immediately east of the *Peninsula Hotel*, running north from Salisbury Road, neon-lit **Nathan Road** dominates the commercial hub of Kowloon and boasts Hong Kong's most concentrated collection of electronics shops, tailors, jewellery stores and fashion boutiques. The variety of goods on offer is staggering, but the southern section of Nathan Road, known as **the Golden Mile** for its commercial potential, is by no means a cheap place to shop these days, and tourist rip-offs are all too common. One of the least salubrious, but most exotic, corners of Nathan Road is the gigantic *Chungking Mansions*, 200m north of the junction with Salisbury Road. The shopping arcades here on the two lowest floors are a steaming jungle of ethnic shops, curry houses and dark corners, which seem to stretch away into the impenetrable heart of the building, making an interesting contrast with the antiseptic, air-conditioned shopping malls that fill the rest of Hong Kong. The upstairs floors are packed with guesthouses (see p.205) – the mainstay of Hong Kong's backpacker accommodation.

A few hundred metres north of *Chungking Mansions*, **Kowloon Park** (daily 6am–midnight) is marked at its southeastern corner by the white-domed Kowloon Mosque (not open to tourists). There's also an indoor and outdoor swimming-pool complex in the park, with Olympic-size facilities (daily 6.30am–9.30pm; ®2724 3577).

Over on Chatham Road South, east of Nathan Road, are two hulking museums that are worth a browse. The first, the **Hong Kong Science Museum** at 2 Science Museum Rd (Tues–Fri 1–9pm, Sat & Sun 10am–9pm; $25, Wed free) has three floors of terrific hands-on science exhibits especially designed for children. Just opposite is the new $390 million **Hong Kong Museum of History** (daily except Tues 10am–6pm; $10, Wed free), where you can walk through four million years of the territory's history in a couple of hours in the ambitious permanent exhibit called "The Story of Hong Kong". The exhibition has been put together in a blaze of colour, and is supplemented by video screenings, light shows, computer interactive software and life-size reproductions of everything from patches of prehistoric jungle to a mocked up pre-colonial coastal village complete with bat-winged junks.

Yau Ma Tei and Mongkok

The part of Kowloon north of the tourist ghetto of Tsim Sha Tsui is more rewarding to walk around, with more authentic Chinese neighbourhoods and interesting markets. **Yau Ma Tei** is jammed with high-rise tenements and busy streets and begins north of Jordan Road, with most of the interest lying in the streets to the west of Nathan Road. You can walk here from Tsim Sha Tsui in about twenty minutes – otherwise take the MTR.

Temple Street, running north off Jordan Road, a couple of blocks west of Nathan Road, becomes a packed **night market** after around 7pm every day, although the market actually opens in the early afternoon. As well as buying cheap clothing, watches, souvenirs and all sorts of tack, you can get your fortune told here, eat some great seafood from street stalls, and sometimes listen in on impromptu performances of Chinese opera. Just to the north of here is the local **Tin Hau Temple**, off Nathan Road, tucked away between Public Square Street and Market Street, a couple of minutes' walk south of Yau Ma Tei MTR. Surrounded by urban hubbub, this little old temple, devoted to the sea, sits in a small concreted park, usually teeming with old men gambling on card games under the banyan trees. A couple of minutes' walk west of the Tin Hau Temple, just under the Gascoigne Road flyover, the **Jade Market** (daily 10am–3.30pm) has hundreds of stalls in two different sections offering an amazing variety of items from trinkets to family heirlooms in jade, crystal and quartz.

To the east of Nathan Road, at the corner of Nelson Street and Fa Yuen Street, is a specialist market of a rather different flavour, the **Mongkok Computer Centre**, where some incredibly cheap hardware and bargain software can be picked up; though, as much of this is pirated and, strictly speaking, illegal, you should exercise caution when importing such material into your own country. Around the corner, the electronics shops on Sai Yeung Choi Street are also worth checking out. A few hundred metres north of here in the direction of Prince Edward MTR are three delightful markets. The Goldfish Market (daily 10am–6pm) is on Tung Choi Street, and just to the north of Prince Edward Road are the **Flower Market** (daily 7am–8pm), in Flower Market Road, and the **Bird Market** (daily 7am–8pm), at the eastern end of the same street, where it meets the KCR flyover. The flower market is at its best on Sundays and in the run-up to Chinese New Year, when many people come to buy narcissi, orange trees and plum blossom to decorate their apartments for good luck. The bird market is set in a Chinese-style garden, with trees, seats and elegant carved marble panels. As well as the hundreds of birds on sale here, along with their intricately designed bamboo cages, there are live crickets – whose fate is bird-feed. Many local men bring their own songbirds here for an airing, and the place gives a real glimpse into a traditional area of Chinese life.

Outer Kowloon

Head a few hundred metres north of Mongkok and you reach **Boundary Street**, which marks the border between Kowloon and the New Territories – though these days this distinction is pretty meaningless.

By far the busiest tourist attraction in this area is well to the northeast of Boundary Street. The **Wong Tai Sin Temple** (daily 7am–5.30pm; small donation), a huge thriving place packed with more worshippers than any other temple in Hong Kong (especially during Chinese New Year). Big, bright and colourful, it's interesting for a glimpse into the practices of modern Chinese religion: solemn devotees kneel and pray, burn incense, rattle fortune-telling sticks in jars, and present food and drink to the Taoist deities. Large numbers of fortune-tellers, some of whom speak English, have stands to the right of the entrance and charge around HK$200 for palm-reading, and about half that for a face-reading. The temple can be reached directly from the Wong Tai Sin MTR Station.

One stop east of here on the MTR at Diamond Hill is the new **Chi Lin Nunnery** (daily except Wed 9am–4pm; free), a modern complex of beautiful multi-tiered Tang-dynasty-style buildings in dark timber. It's a short signposted walk from the MTR station. Craftsmen from as far away as Anhui province in mainland China employed styles and skills dating from the seventh century AD, and not a single nail, bolt or screw was used. The nunnery is home to a few nuns who run religious, educational and social-service projects, though you can wander around inside its wooden halls and admire the statues of Buddha and deities in gold and precious wood. Access to the nunnery is through the **Western Lotus Pond Garden** (daily 6.30am–7pm), beautifully tended landscaped grounds with rocks, tea plants, bonsai and fig trees and, of course, lotus ponds.

The New Territories

Comprising some 750 square kilometres of land abutting the southern part of China's Guangdong province, the **New Territories** include some of the most scenic and traditionally Chinese areas of Hong Kong – complete with country roads, water buffalo, ancient walled villages, valleys and mountains – as well as booming New Towns. The highlights are the designated country parks, offering excellent **hiking trails** and secluded beaches. Frequent **buses** connect all towns in the New Territories, while the MTR reaches as far as Tsuen Wan and the KCR runs north through Sha Tin, the Chinese University and Tai Po. Tuen Mun is the terminus of the LR line that runs north to Yuen Long. By public transport, a satisfying do-it-yourself **tour** can be made in a few hours along the following route, starting from the Jordan Road bus terminus in Kowloon (accessible by bus #8 from Tsim Sha Tsui): take bus #60X to Tuen Mun bus terminal, then from here ride the LR north to its terminus at Yuen Long. From Yuen Long, take bus #76K to Sheung Shui KCR Station in the north. Finally, ride the KCR train south back to Kowloon. If you're coming from Hong Kong Island, you can take the #960 or #961 from Des Voeux Road in Central directly to Tuen Mun.

The west

Tsuen Wan in the west of the New Territories is one of Hong Kong's **New Towns**, built from scratch in the last 25 years, and easily reached by MTR. Virtually in the middle of Tsuen Wan is the **Sam Tung Uk Museum** (daily except Tues 9am–5pm; free), a restored two-hundred-year-old walled village of a type typical of this part of southern China. The village was founded in 1786 by a Hakka clan named Chan, who continued to live here until the 1970s. Now the houses have been restored with their original furnishings, and there are various exhibitions on aspects of the lives of the Hakka people. Follow signs out of Tsuen Wan MTR Station – it's about a five-minute walk.

From the bus terminal opposite the Tsuen Wan MTR, catch bus #51 north to Kam Tin. The ride is spectacular, running right past Hong Kong's highest peak, **Tai Mo Shan**, which at 957m is nearly twice the height of Victoria Peak. If you want to climb up to the top, there's a bus stop on a pass right under the peak – get off here and follow a signposted path up to the top. The excellent **Maclehose Trail** runs right through here, and this is as good a place as any to join it. Every autumn there's a charity race along the mountainous one-hundred-kilometre trail – the record time is an astonishing 13 hours 18 minutes. For detailed information on the trail, which runs across the New Territories from Tuen Mun in the west to the Sai Kung Peninsula in the east, contact the HKTB (see p.187), who publish a guide for walkers, *Exploring Hong Kong's Countryside* (HK$80), or the Country and Marine Parks Branch on the 14th Floor, 393 Canton Rd, Tsim Sha Tsui, Kowloon (Mon–Fri 9am–5pm, Sat 9am–noon; ☎2733 2211).

The small town of Kam Tin is famous as the site of **Kat Hing Wai**, one of Hong Kong's last inhabited walled villages. Dating back to the late seventeenth century when a clan named Tang settled here, this atmospheric village (HK$1 donation) still comprises thick six-metre-high walls and guard towers, although most traces of the moat have gone. Inside the walls, there's a wide lane running down the middle of the village, with tiny alleys leading off it. The village is on your left, a few minutes' walk from the Kam Tin bus stop.

North: the KCR route

Several possible excursions present themselves from the stops dotted along the **Kowloon–Canton East Railway** as it wends its way north from Kowloon to the border with mainland China. The first important stop is at the booming New Town of **Sha Tin**, best known to Hong Kongers as the site of the territory's second racecourse, but also the location of the forty-year-old **Ten Thousand Buddhas Monastery** (daily 9am–5pm; free), which is probably the single most interesting temple in the whole of the New Territories, if not in all Hong Kong. To reach it from the KCR station, follow the signs saying "buses", and exit the station on the side facing the green hilly area – it's a few minutes' walk north along the road from here. Head towards the larger white-and-green complex of Chinese buildings, which house the **Po** (or Bo) **Fook Ancestral Worship Halls** (9am–5pm; free). Turn right just before the Halls entrance and the path will take you up the side of that complex – a stiff climb of around 400 steps – until you emerge on the terrace of the monastery. The "Ten Thousand Buddhas" – actually more like thirteen thousand – are stacked on shelves filling the inside walls of the main temple hall, surrounding the central Buddha. The terrace outside, which commands some great views, also contains a quite bizarre array of giant statues, including an elephant and a dragon. Overall, the mixture of jungle, panoramic views and colourful statuary makes this an excellent spot. From the monastery, you can also follow a path farther up the mountain to another terrace containing some smaller temples.

Back in Sha Tin, you can take a ten-minute stroll through the riverside park to the unique **Heritage Museum** (Tues–Sun 10am–6pm, Fri 10am–9pm; $10, Wed free), an enormous orange-roofed structure built around the traditional design of Si He Yuan, a compound with houses laid out around a central courtyard. The highlight here is the fantastic **Cantonese Opera Heritage Hall**, which richly documents this local art with glittering displays of costumes, embroidered shoes, lustrous stage props, and artists' dressing rooms complete with their grease-paint-filled make-up chests.

The east

The eastern part of the New Territories, and in particular the **Sai Kung Peninsula**, is where you'll find the most secluded beaches and walks in Hong Kong. Go at the right time and you may have an entire beach to yourself, although at weekends they do begin to fill up. The starting point for buses into both areas is Choi Hung MTR Station.

Sai Kung Peninsula

The jagged **Sai Kung Peninsula**, with headlands, bluffs and tiny offshore islands, is one of the least developed areas in the whole of Hong Kong, and a haven for hikers and beach-lovers. The only sizeable town in the area, **Sai Kung Town**, accessible on minibus #1A and bus #92 from Choi Hung MTR, is the jumping-off point for explorations of Sai Kung.

Sai Kung's highlights are the **country parks** that cover the peninsula with virgin forest and grassland leading to perfect sandy beaches. Although it's possible to see something of these on a day-trip, the best way to really appreciate them is to bring a tent and stay overnight or consider staying at the youth hostel in Sai Kung. Access to the parks is by hourly bus #94 from Sai Kung Town and #96R (Sundays only) from Diamond Hill MTR to **Pak Tam Chung Visitors' Centre** (daily except Tues 9.30am–4.30pm; ⓣ2792 7365), which supplies hikers with maps and trail information. Of the many possible hikes, the Maclehose Trail, liberally dotted with campsites, heads east from here, circumventing the **High Island Reservoir** before heading west into the rest of the New Territories. If you want to follow the trail just part of the way, the **beaches** at Long Ke, south of the reservoir, and Tai Long, to the northeast, are Hong Kong's finest, though to walk out to them and back from Pak Tam Chung takes several hours. The last bus back from Pak Tam Chung is at 9pm.

The outlying islands

Officially part of the New Territories, the **outlying islands** of Hong Kong offer a delightful combination of seascape, old fishing villages and relative rural calm, almost entirely free of motor vehicles, except for the taxis and buses on Lantau Island. The

Ferries to the islands

The following is a selection of the most useful island **ferry services**. Schedules differ slightly on Saturdays and Sundays (services generally start later in the morning), when prices also rise:

To Cheung Chau

From Outlying Islands Ferry Piers (Pier 5): first boat out 5.10am, last boat back 1.30am (at least hourly; 1hr).

To Sok Kwu Wan, Lamma Island

From Outlying Islands Ferry Piers (Pier 4): first boat out 7.20am, last boat back 10.40pm (11 daily; 50min).

From Aberdeen (via Mo Tat Wan): first boat out 6.50am, last boat back 9.45pm (12 daily; 30min).

To Yung Shue Wan, Lamma Island

From Outlying Islands Ferry Piers (Pier 4): first boat out 6.30am, last boat back 11.30pm (roughly every 20–30min; 40min).

From Aberdeen (via Pak Kok Tsuen): first boat out 6.30am, last boat back 7.30pm (9 daily; 30min).

To Mui Wo (Silvermine Bay), Lantau Island

From Outlying Islands Ferry Piers (Pier 6): first boat out 6.10am, last boat back 11.30pm (at least hourly; 30–50min). Some sailings go via Peng Chau.

From Peng Chau: first boat out 5.40am, last boat back 11.20am (roughly every 2hr 30min; 25min).

To Peng Chau

From Outlying Islands Ferry Piers (Pier 6): first boat out 7am, last boat back 11.30pm (roughly hourly; 50min).

islands are conveniently connected to Central by frequent ferries and other boats. By comparison with other areas, development has been relatively restrained, although the advent of Chek Lap Kok Airport and the development of a Disneyland on the largest island, Lantau, means this is likely to change. Although most tourists come on day-trips, there is some accommodation on the islands (see p.208).

Lamma Island

Lying just to the southwest of Aberdeen, **Lamma** is the closest island to Hong Kong Island, with a population of less than ten thousand, no cars, a spine of greenery-clad hills, a few sandy beaches, and lots of cheap, interesting restaurants. There are two possible **ferry** crossing points, from Central or Aberdeen to either Yung Shue Wan or Sok Kwu Wan. By far the best way to appreciate the island is to take a boat to either Yung Shue Wan or Sok Kwu Wan, then walk to the other side and catch the boat back from there.

Yung Shue Wan is a pretty, little tree-shaded village, with one or two hotels and a cluster of small grocery stores, bars and eating places. There's a very relaxed feel to the place in the evening, when people sit out under the banyan trees. To walk to Sok Kwu Wan from here (1hr), follow the easy-to-find cement path that branches away from the shore by the *Light House Pub*, shortly before the Tin Hau Temple. Make your way through the rather grotty apartment buildings on the outskirts of the village and you'll soon find yourself walking amid butterflies, long grass and trees. After about fifteen minutes, you'll arrive at **Hung Shing Yeh Beach**, nicest in its northern half. The *Han Lok Yuen Restaurant* here is well known for its roast pigeon. On from the beach, the path climbs quite sharply up to a little summit, with a pavilion commanding views over the island. Thirty minutes' walk further on will take you to **Sok Kwu Wan**, which comprises a row of seafood restaurants with terraces built out over the water. The food and the atmosphere are good, and consequently the restaurants are often full of large parties. Some of the larger places also operate their own boat services for customers. Many people get the ferry over to Sok Kwu Wan in the evening for dinner but, if you're not taking a restaurant service, make sure you don't miss the last scheduled boat back at 10.40pm. If you get stuck, there are a few holiday apartments to rent here (ask at some of the restaurants), or you'll have to hire a sampan back to Aberdeen (likely to be at least HK$400).

Cheung Chau Island

Another great little island where you can spend a couple of hours strolling around and then have dinner, **Cheung Chau** is just south of Lantau and an hour from Hong Kong by ferry. Despite its minuscule size of 2.5 square kilometres, Cheung Chau is nevertheless the most crowded of all the outer islands, with a population of some twenty thousand. The island is one of the oldest settled parts of Hong Kong, being notorious as a base for pirates who waylaid the ships that ran between Guangzhou and the Portuguese enclave of Macau. Today, it still gives the impression of being an economically independent little unit, with the narrow strip between its two headlands jam-packed with tiny shops, markets and seafront restaurants. As well as romantic dinners and late-night ferry rides home, the island offers some relaxed **walks** around the old fishing port, past traditional junk and fishing boat chandleries. It also features some interesting temples, the most important being the two-hundred-year-old **Pak Tai Temple**, a few hundred metres northwest of the ferry pier, along Pak She Street, which is lined with old herbalists and shops selling religious trinkets. Fishermen come to the temple to pray for protection; beside the statue of Pak Tai (the god of the sea) is an ancient iron sword, discovered by fishermen and supposedly symbolizing good luck. For a few days in late April or early May the temple is the site of one of Hong Kong's liveliest and most spectacular festivals, the so-called **Tai Chiu (Bun) Festival**.

The main beach on the island, the scenic but crowded **Tung Wan Beach**, is due west of the ferry pier. Windsurfers are available for rent at the southern end of the beach from a centre run by the family of Hong Kong's Olympic medal-winning windsurf champion, Lee Lai Shan, who won a gold at the 1996 Atlanta games. If you catch a small sampan from the ferry pier across the bay to the small pier of **Sai Wan** – a five-minute ride – you can then follow marked trails to the nearby **Tin Hau Temple** and on to the tiny (and not particularly atmospheric) **Cheung Po Tsai Cave**, supposedly used as a pirates' hide-out in the early nineteenth century. The walk back from the cave area to the beach on the eastern side of the island is an attractive one that takes about an hour.

Lantau Island

With wild countryside, monasteries, old fishing villages and seriously secluded beaches, **Lantau Island** – twice the size of Hong Kong Island – offers the best quick escape from the city; more than half the island is designated as a "country park". However, this tranquillity is unlikely to last, at least along the northern and northeastern shores, as Hong Kong's airport at Chek Lap Kok and its associated transport links are spawning a range of new commercial and residential developments, and the building work for the new Hong Kong Disneyland – scheduled to open in 2006 – gets underway.

The tranquillity of other parts of the island are unlikely to be fatally disturbed though, and serious hikers might want to take advantage of the seventy-kilometre

Lantau Trail, which links up the popular scenic spots on the island and is dotted along its length by campsites and youth hostels. The main point of arrival for visitors to Lantau Island is **Mui Wo**, otherwise known as **Silvermine Bay**, thirty or so minutes' ferry ride from Central. Some of the Mui Wo boats stop at the small island of Peng Chau en route. There are also a few daily ferries that connect Mui Wo with Cheung Chau. Mui Wo itself is not much to speak of, and having disembarked at the ferry pier, most people head straight for the attractions in the west of the island, reached by regular services from the bus station right outside.

Western Lantau

The road west from Mui Wo passes along the southern shore, which is where Lantau's best beaches are located. **Cheung Sha Beach**, with a couple of cafés and a hotel, is the most appealing, and buses #1, #2, and #4 all pass by here.

Beyond the beaches, there are a couple of more interesting sights in the western part of the island that can also be reached by direct bus from Mui Wo. The first of these is the **Po Lin Monastery** (daily 10am–5.30pm; free), which is by far the largest temple in the whole territory of Hong Kong. Located high up on the Ngong Ping Plateau, this is not an ancient site; indeed, it was only established in 1927. Nevertheless, it is very much a living, breathing temple, and busloads of tourists arrive here by the hour, in particular to pay their respects to the bronze **Tian Tan Buddha** or Big Buddha, the largest seated bronze outdoor Buddha in the world, and to eat in the huge vegetarian **restaurant** (11.30am–5pm); it costs HK$60 for a filling multi-course meal, while the "deluxe" version served in an air-con annexe costs HK$100 – meal tickets are available from the office at the bottom of the steps to the Buddha. The Po Lin Monastery is often referred to in bus schedules as Ngong Ping and is reached by bus #2 from Mui Wo; it's a spectacular forty-minute ride through the hills (the last bus back to Mui Wo leaves at 7.20pm). Plans to build a cable-car connection between Tung Chung near the airport to the site have horrified locals, who fear the area may be overwhelmed by the commercial bustle found on The Peak.

Right on the far northwestern shore of Lantau is the interesting little fishing village of **Tai O**. This remote place, constructed over salt flats and a tiny offshore island, has become a popular tourist spot particularly at weekends, but still retains much of its old character (the government has plans for further development, but plans have consistently stalled in the worsening economic climate). There are some interesting local temples, wooden houses built partially on stilts and a big trade in dried fish. You can reach it by bus #1 from Mui Wo (last bus back 12.10am) and also by the relatively infrequent bus #21 from the Po Lin Monastery (last service out to Tai O is at 5pm).

Eating

Hong Kong has it all, from cheap steaming canteens and bargain burger joints to world-class haute cuisine. Menus in all but the cheapest restaurants should be in English as well as Chinese. The busiest, brightest restaurants of all are often those serving inexpensive **dim sum** for breakfast or lunch (see p.191, for an introduction to *dim sum*). The streets around D'Aguilar Street in Central, just a couple of minutes' walk south from the MTR, are particularly popular with young people and western expats. Known as **Lan Kwai Fong**, after the small lane branching off D'Aguilar Street to the east, this area is chock-a-block with bars and restaurants. Five minutes' walk away is the newest restaurant area, known as **SoHo**, which, with its traditional streets and shop-houses, has a less frenetic character. Generally, **prices** are comparable to those in the West: a full dinner without drinks is unlikely to cost less than HK$150 per head, although set-price lunches can offer a good-value alternative.

△ The Big Buddha, Lantau Island

Central

Café Deco Bar & Grill Level 1 & 2, Peak Galleria, 118 Peak Rd, The Peak ☎2849 5111. Superbly located, with unrivalled views and a stylish Art Deco interior. The menu includes gourmet pizzas, curries, Thai noodles, grilled meats, as well as afternoon tea, and the chefs carry off such a diverse menu better than you might expect. Prices aren't outrageous, given the location, and they don't mind if you just go for a drink, plus there's live jazz in the evening. Closes around 11pm (1am on Fri & Sat).

Can Teen M20-28, Prince's Building, Chater Rd, Central ☎ 2524 6792. A smart, modern and very cheap lunch stop (up the escalator from the posh designer boutiques), serving a range of tasty dishes including sushi, Chinese rice- and noodle-based fare, sweet pastries and fresh juices.

City Hall Chinese Restaurant 2nd Floor, City Hall Lower Block, Central ☎2521 1303. A short walk east of the Star Ferry Pier. Some of the best *dim sum* in Hong Kong with great harbour views. Come for breakfast around 10am.

Coco Curry House 8 Wing Wah Lane, Central ☎ 2523 6911. Casual and very good-value al fresco dining yards from Lan Kwai Fong's drinking holes. The tasty curries are best enjoyed with the superb Malay roti that the chef prepares with great theatre out front.

Dumpling House 26 Cochrane St (facing the escalator), Central ☎2815 5520. Inexpensive steamed Beijing dumplings with veggie options are served almost before you've ordered them. A local favourite is pork dumplings in hot and sour soup. There's no obvious signage in English, but you'll find the restaurant next to the sign reading "Between Wu Yue".

Eating Plus 1009, 1st Floor, International Finance Centre, Central ☎2868 0599. A lively, modern, minimalist noodle joint with bench seating, funky music and tall plate-glass windows, serving fresh, light, reasonably priced dishes.

Life 10 Shelley St, SoHo, Central ☎2810 9777. Head to this modest but welcoming café for whole-foods, fresh juices, vegetarian and organic fare.

Luk Yu Tea House 24–26 Stanley St, just west of D'Aguilar St ☎2523 5464. A living museum with spittoons, sixty-year-old furniture and authentically rude staff, this is possibly the most atmospheric restaurant in Hong Kong. Tea and *dim sum*, as well as full meals, are available, though the prices are inflated for tourists.

Miso Basement, Jardine House, Central ☎2845 8773. Eat some of the best sushi set-meals in town for around HK$200, just a tuna roll's throw from the Star Ferry Pier. Try the Kobe Beef sushi.

Sherpa Nepalese Cuisine 11 Staunton St, SoHo ☎2973 6886. Friendly restaurant with an interesting range of tasty dishes and beers to go with them. Food is good for veggies, too. The *Nepal* opposite is under the same management.

Yellow Door Kitchen 6th Floor, 37 Cochrane St, Central ☎2858 6555. Entrance on Lyndhurst Terrace next to the *Dublin Jack* bar. The *Yellow Door* is a refreshing and friendly place offering two evening sittings with a fixed menu at HK$220 per person. Great Shanghai cuisine (the chef is related to former Taiwan leader, Chiang Kai Shek), and the lunchtime menu has a few inexpensive Sichuan options, which can be as hot as you like.

Yung Kee 32–40 Wellington St, on the corner with D'Aguilar St ☎2522 1624. An enormous place with bright lights, scurrying staff and seating for a thousand, this is one of Hong Kong's institutions. Roast meats (often served cold) are a speciality, and the *dim sum* is also good.

Wan Chai and Causeway Bay

Fat Angelo's 414 Jaffe Rd ☎2574 6263. Homely Italian-American place serving vast portions of pasta and rich, sinful desserts. Popular and well priced.

Jo Jo Mess Club 1st Floor, 86–90 Johnston Rd, Wan Chai ☎2527 3776. Entrance on Lee Tung St. Deservedly popular spot for tandoori dishes and street views.

Perfume River 89 Percival St, Causeway Bay ☎2576 2240. Tasty Vietnamese dishes, cold Vietnamese beer, bemused staff and green tables. The fried curried crab is recommended.

Vegi-Food Kitchen 13 Cleveland St, Causeway Bay ☎2890 6660. A couple of blocks east of Paterson Street at its northern end. Classy, strictly vegetarian Chinese food.

Yat Tung Heen 2nd Floor, Great Eagle Centre, 23 Harbour Rd, Wan Chai ☎2878 1212. Busy, large, inexpensive restaurant, popular with local office workers. The noodles are excellent.

Chungking Mansions

Delhi Club 3rd Floor, C Block ☎23681682. A curry house par excellence; the ludicrously cheap set-meal would feed an army.

Khyber Pass 7th Floor, E Block ☎2721 2786. Consistently good food, with lukewarm but efficient service. One of the best in *Chungking Mansions*.

Sher-E-Punjab 3rd Floor, B Block ☎2368 0859. Excellent food with friendly service in clean surroundings. Slightly more expensive than its neighbours.

Kowloon

Amporn Thai Food 3rd Floor, Cooked Food Hall, Kowloon City Market, 100 Nga Tsin Wai Rd,

Kowloon City ☎2716 3689. The big market is hard to miss – just head for the third floor. A noisy place with industrial yellow ventilation pipes snaking across the ceiling. Dishes up excellent cheap Thai food cooked and served by Thais – hotpot and fresh prawns are their best sellers. There's no English menu, but the staff are friendly and can speak a little English.

Great Shanghai 26 Prat Ave, Tsim Sha Tsui ☎2366 8158. One of the most reliable of Hong Kong's Shanghai restaurants, with especially fine fish and seafood; a good choice for a first Shanghai meal.

Kyozasa 20 Ashley Rd, Tsim Sha Tsui ☎2376 1888. Homely Japanese country food in relaxing and unpretentious surroundings.

Peking Restaurant 227 Nathan Rd, Tsim Sha Tsui ☎2730 1315. Despite its glum decor, this place serves some of the best Beijing food in Hong Kong. The Beijing Duck is particularly good.

Peninsula Hotel Lobby *Peninsula Hotel*. The set-tea served in the lobby comes to around HK$165 plus ten-percent service. As well as a lot of food, you also get a chance to sit in Hong Kong's most beautiful lobby, serenaded by a string quartet. Get there just before 2pm or be prepared to queue.

Bars, pubs and clubs

The most concentrated collection of bars is in Central, spreading from the long-standing popular **Lan Kwai Fong** to the network of streets leading into and including the new and upmarket **SoHo** area. Rubbing shoulders with the "girly bars" in Jaffe and Lockhart Roads in **Wan Chai** are a dozen or more earthier clubs and bars where beer-swilling antics are more en vogue. **Tsim Sha Tsui's** smaller nightlife scene is rather sparse. The best places to head for are Knutsford Terrace (just off Kimberely Road), Hart Avenue and Prat Avenue, west from Chatham Road South. For up-to-the-minute listings, consult the latest issues of *HK Magazine* (weekly) and *BC Magazine* (fortnightly).

Hong Kong Island

Antidote "Ezra Lane", Lower Ground Floor, 15–19 Hollywood Rd, Central ☎2526 6559. A spacey funky bar with white padded walls, sinkable sofas and relaxing trip-hop beats. Cool atmosphere but expensive drinks.

C Bar Shop A, Ground Floor, California Tower, 30–32 D'Aguilar St, Lan Kwai Fong, Central ☎ 2530 3695. Tiny corner bar, whose big draw is frozen cocktails dispensed with a giant syringe. The associated *C Club* downstairs pulls in hip and very young crowds with Ibiza-hailed DJs playing house music.

Dublin Jack 37 Cochrane St, SoHo, Central ☎2543 0081. Reliable Irish-style pub, just under the escalator exit for Lyndhurst Terrace. Draught Guinness, Irish food, reasonable prices, and well over a hundred different varieties of whiskey.

Hong Kong Brew House 33 Wyndham St, Lan Kwai Fong, Central ☎2522 559. Quaff down the decent premises-brewed ale while you take in Lan Kwai Fong's neon-lit hubbub beneath you. A great spot from which to people watch as you plan your evening out.

Le Jardin 10 Wing Wah Lane, Lan Kwai Fong, Central ☎2526 2717. One of the few places where you can sit and drink al fresco, this friendly bar is on a small raised terrace at the end of the lane. Watch out for "Melvis", the Cantonese Elvis impersonator.

Jazz & Blues Club & Bar 2nd Floor, 34–36 D'Aguilar St, Lan Kwai Fong, Central ☎2845 8477. The narrow bar is open to non-members. Live jazz on Friday and Saturday nights (entrance around HK$100).

Phi-b Lower Basement, Hariela House, 79 Wyndham St, Central ☎2869 4469. Made famous by its resident DJs spinning everything from funk, house, soul, rare groove and breakbeat. Come on a weekday when you can find a seat and chill out.

Kowloon

Bahama Mama's 4–5 Knutsford Terrace, just north of Kimberly Rd, Tsim Sha Tsui ☎2368 2121. A good atmosphere with plenty of space for pavement drinking. There's a beach-bar theme and outdoor terrace that prompts party crowd antics.

Delaney's 3–7A Prat Ave, Tsim Sha Tsui ☎2301 3980. Friendly Irish pub with draught beers, Guinness and Irish pub food; features Irish folk music most nights. Also at 2nd Floor, 18 Luard Rd, Wan Chai (☎2804 2880).

Felix 28th Floor, *Peninsula Hotel*, Sailsbury Rd, Tsim Sha Tsui ☎2920 2888. Cocktails here cost much the same as in any regular bar in Hong Kong; it's worth supping one just for the experience of the imposing surroundings and the opportunity to slip into the men's toilets, the urinals of which look down onto the back of Tsim Sha Tsui.

Ned Kelly's Last Stand 11A Ashley Rd, Tsim Sha Tsui ☎2376 0562. Very popular with both travellers and expats. Features excellent nightly ragtime jazz.

Shopping

Visitors are still coming to Hong Kong to go **shopping** despite the fact that the cost of living in the territory has risen above that of most other countries in the world. The famed **electronic goods** of Nathan Road, for example, are by no means cheap any more but you can find some good deals at some of the electronics malls further along the road. Tsim Sha Tsui is also good for second-hand camera shops, such as those in Stanley Street, if you know what you're after. Some goods are undoubtedly cheap, particularly **clothes**, **silk**, **jewellery**, **Chinese arts and crafts**, some **computer accessories** and **pirated goods**. In Tsim Sha Tsui, Causeway Bay and Wan Chai, opening hours are generally 10am–9.30pm; in Central, it's 10am–7pm.

Arts and crafts

For Chinese **arts and crafts**, including fabrics, porcelain and clothes, visit Chinese Arts and Crafts, which has branches at the China Resources Building, 26 Harbour Rd, Wan Chai; 230 The Mall, One Pacific Place; 88 Queensway, Admiralty; and Star House, 3 Salisbury Rd, Tsim Sha Tsui. Other good outlets include Mountain Folkcraft, 12 Wo On Lane (off D'Aguilar Street), Central, which has beautiful folk crafts from Southeast Asia; Shanghai Tang, Pedder Building, Pedder Street, Central, which does upmarket gifts and clothes, including the ever-popular Mao watches; and Wah Tung China Ltd, 59 Hollywood Rd, Central, which offers high-quality ceramics and can ship and make to order.

Clothes

Clothes can be good value in Hong Kong, particularly the local casual wear chain stores including Giordano, Wanko and Bossini, which have branches all over the city, but big-name foreign designer clothes are often more expensive than back home. For local fashion designs and cheap and unusual togs, head for Granville Road in Tsim Sha Tsui; the Beverley Commercial Building, 87–105 Chatham Rd, two blocks north of Granville Road; the boutiques behind SOGO in Causeway Bay; the Pedder Building on Pedder Street in Central; and just round the corner, Wyndham Street and D'Aguillar Street. Beware of size labels – they're often way out.

Tailor-made clothes are a traditional speciality of the Hong Kong tourist trade, and wherever you go in Tsim Sha Tsui you'll be accosted by Indian tailors. However, you may find better work elsewhere – in residential areas and locations like hotels or shopping arcades, where the tailors rely on regular clients. Don't ask for something to be made in 24 hours – it won't fit, will fall apart, or both. The best-known tailor in town is probably Sam's Tailors, at 94 Nathan Rd, Tsim Sha Tsui. Sam is famous as much for his talent for self-publicity as for his clothes. Others include the well-established ladies' tailors, Linva Tailor, 38 Cochrane St, Central; Margaret Court Tailoress, 8th Floor, Winner Building, 27 D'Aguilar St, Central; and Shanghai Tang, 12 Pedder St, Central, which does glamorous Chinese-style garments for men and women. All tailors can supply fabric, though if you want more choice go to the Western Market near Sheun Wan MTR. For **shoes and leather goods**, try Wong Nai Chung Road in Happy Valley. For **clothing repairs**, there are many shops in World-Wide Plaza, Des Voeux Road, Central, including Perfect Fashion Alteration on the 3rd Floor.

Computers

Both hardware and software can work out very cheap in Hong Kong, though you'll need to make sure you get an international warranty. Check special offers in Tuesday's *South China Morning Post*. **Pirated computer software** is also big business, though these days it's more discreet. Some recommended outlets include Asia

Computer Plaza, 2nd Floor, Star House, Salisbury Road, Tsim Sha Tsui; Computer Zone, 298 Hennessy Rd, Wan Chai; Golden Shopping Arcade, 156 Fuk Wah St, Sham Shui Po, Kowloon; and Mongkok Computer Centre, at the corner of Nelson and Fa Yuen streets, Mongkok.

Department stores

Some of Hong Kong's longest-established **department stores** include the typically Chinese CRC Department Store, Chiao Shang Building, 92 Queen's Rd, Central; the Lok Sing Centre, 488 Hennessy Rd, Causeway Bay; Wing On, 111 Connaught Rd, Central (and other branches); Yue Hwa Chinese Products Emporium, 39 Queen's Rd, Central, plus 301–309 Nathan Rd, Yau Ma Tei (and other locations). For an upmarket Western-style store, check out Lane Crawford, 70 Queen's Rd, Central; Levels 1–3, The Mall, One Pacific Place, 88 Queensway, Admiralty.

Jewellery

There are literally thousands of **jewellers** in Hong Kong, and prices are relatively low. Some places to start include Gallery One, 31–33 Hollywood Rd, Central, which has a huge selection of semi-precious stones and beads. For precious stones and gold, try Johnson & Co, 44 Hankow Rd, Kowloon; New Universal or 10 Ice House St, Central. Finally, if you're looking for **jade**, there's a special Jade Market in Kansu Street, Yau Ma Tei (see p.218).

Listings

Airlines Air India ☎2522 1176; British Airways ☎2822 9000; Cathay Pacific ☎2747 1888; Dragonair ☎3193 3888; JAL ☎2523 0081; Korean Air ☎2368 6221; Malaysia Airlines ☎2521 8181; Qantas ☎2822 9000; Singapore Airlines ☎2520 2233; Thai International ☎2876 6888; United Airlines ☎2810 4888; Virgin Atlantic Airways ☎2532 6060.

American Express Unit C, 1/F China Insurance Building, 48 Cameron Rd, Tsim Sha Tsui (Mon–Fri 9am–5pm, Sat 9am–12.30pm; ☎3121 3900; report stolen cheques on ☎3002 1276).

Bookshops Dymock's bookshop at the Star Ferry Pier, Central and 1st Floor, Prince's Building, Central, is good for paperbacks and travel guides. The SAR's largest is Page One in Festival Walk, Kowloon Tong, and Times Square, Causeway Bay. For cheap second-hand books, try either Collectables at 1st Floor, Winning House, 26 Hollywood Rd or Flows at 40 Lyndhurst Terrace, both in Central.

Embassies and consulates Australia, 23rd Floor, Harbour Centre, 25 Harbour Rd, Wan Chai ☎2827 8881; Britain, 1 Supreme Court Rd, Admiralty ☎2901 3000; Canada, 14th Floor, 1 Exchange Square, Central ☎2810 4321; China, 7th Floor, China Resources Bldg, Lower Block, 26 Harbour Rd, Wan Chai ☎3413 2300; India, 16th Floor, United Centre, Tower One, 95 Queensway, Admiralty ☎2529 1289; Japan, 46th Floor, One Exchange Square, Central ☎2522 1184; Korea, 5th Floor, Far East Financial Centre, 16 Harcourt Rd, Central ☎2529 4141; New Zealand, Rm 6501, Central Plaza, 18 Harbour Rd, Wan Chai ☎ 2525 5044; The Philippines, 6th Floor, United Centre, 95 Queensway, Admiralty ☎2823 8544; Taiwan (for visas) Chung Hwa Travel Service, 4th Floor, East Tower, Lippo Centre, 89 Queensway, Admiralty ☎ 2525 8315; Thailand, 8th Floor, Fairmont House, 8 Cotton Tree Drive, Central ☎2521 6481; US, 26 Garden Rd, Central ☎2523 9011; Vietnam, 15th Floor, Great Smart Tower, 230 Wan Chai Rd, Wan Chai ☎2591 4510.

Hospitals Government hospitals have 24hr casualty wards, where treatment is free except for overnight stays, which cost $3100 per day. These include the Princess Margaret Hospital, Lai King Hill Rd, Lai Chi Kok, Kowloon (☎2990 1111) and the Queen Mary Hospital, Pokfulam Rd, Hong Kong Island (☎2855 3838). For an ambulance, dial ☎999.

Internet access Free Internet access at most branches of *Pacific Coffee Company* cafés: Ground Floor, Bank of America Tower (Mon–Sat 7.30am–6pm); Shop C3-4, Queensway Plaza, Admiralty (Mon–Sat 7.30am–10pm, Sun 8am–9pm). Hong Kong Central Library also offers access (Mon–Fri

10am–7pm), as does the British Council, 3 Supreme Court Rd, Admiralty and all public libraries (need to book in advance). Try the Central Library at 66 Causeway Rd, Causeway Bay (Mon, Tues, Thurs & Fri 10am–9pm, Wed 1–9pm, Sat & Sun 10am–6pm) or City Hall library on the 9th Floor, City Hall High Block, Central, just opposite the Star Ferry Pier (Mon–Thurs 10am–7pm, Fri 10am–9pm, Sat & Sun 10am–5pm). There's also limited free Internet access in many central shopping malls, including Star Computer City, Harbour City and Times Square.

Laundry On the ground floor of Golden Crown Court, Nathan Rd (one block north of *Mirador Mansions*; red entrance). Also at *Mirador Mansions*, 13th Floor. Dry cleaners are everywhere; if you get stuck try in the concourse of an MTR station. Some also do laundry.

Left luggage In the departure lounge at the airport (daily 6.30am–1am), at Hong Kong MTR Station (Central's stop on the Airport Express) and in the China Ferry Terminal in Tsim Sha Tsui.

Police Crime hotline and taxi complaints ☎2527 7177. For general police enquiries, call ☎2860 2000.

Post office The general post office is at 2 Connaught Place, Central (Mon–Sat 8am–6pm and Sun 8am–2pm; ☎2921 2222), just west of the Star Ferry Pier and north of Jardine House. Poste restante mail is delivered here (you can pick it up Mon–Sat 8am–6pm), unless specifically addressed to "Kowloon". The Kowloon main post office is at 10 Middle Rd, Tsim Sha Tsui (☎2366 4111).

Telephone services For IDD calls, use a payphone (which take coins or stored-value cards). You can buy IDD call cards from convenience stores such as 7-11s.

Travel agents Hong Kong is full of budget travel agents including: Shoestring Travel Ltd, Flat A, 4th Floor, Alpha House, 27–33 Nathan Rd, Tsim Sha Tsui ☎2723 2306; China Touring Centre (HK), 703 Stag Building, 148–150 Queen's Rd, Central ☎2545 0767; and Hong Kong Student Travel Ltd, 608, Hang Lung Centre, Paterson St, Causeway Bay ☎2833 9909. For train tickets, tours, flights and visas to mainland China, try the Japan Travel Agency, Room 507–513, East Ocean Centre, 98 Granville Rd, Tsim Sha Tsui East (☎2368 9151), which does the best deals on visas, or the State-run CTS, whose main office is on the Ground Floor, CTS House, 78–83 Connaught Rd, Central (☎2851 1700). The classifieds section of the *South China Morning Post* carries flight agency telephone numbers and current ticket deals.

4

Indonesia

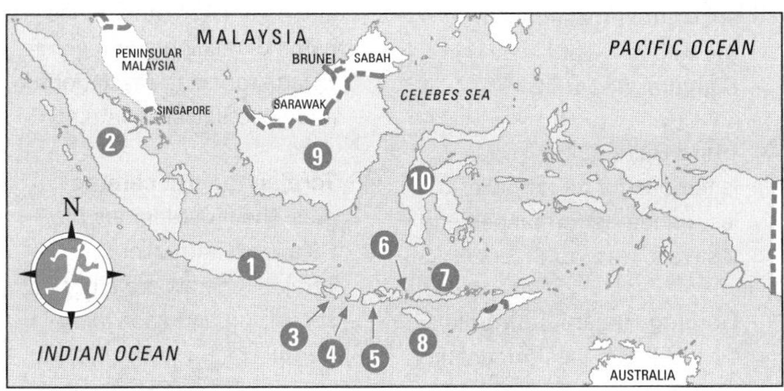
MALAYSIA
PENINSULAR MALAYSIA
BRUNEI
SABAH
SARAWAK
SINGAPORE
CELEBES SEA
PACIFIC OCEAN
INDIAN OCEAN
AUSTRALIA
N
1
2
3
4
5
6
7
8
9
10

Indonesia highlights

* **Borobudur and Prambanan, Java** The former is the biggest Buddhist stupa in the world; the latter is the Hindu faith's spectacular response. See p.294 & p.297

* **Surfing** The best waves in Southeast Asia break off east Java's G-Land. See p.313

* **Orang-utans** See these enchanting creatures in the wild at Bukit Lawang in Sumatra. See p.323

* **Ubud** Bali's cultural capital is famous for its art galleries, dance performances and festivals. See pp.373–382

* **Gunung Rinjani, Lombok** One of the highest mountains in Indonesia, with a stunning crater lake. See pp.429–431

* **Komodo and Rinca** While Komodo gave its name to the world's largest lizard, uninhabited Rinca Island, the dragon's other home, is more atmospheric. See p.439

* **The pasola festival, Sumba** Men on horseback throwing spears at each other in the name of religion and revenge. Bizarre, ancient, mysterious and spectacular. See p.454

* **Torajan funeral ceremonies** The most famous of Sulawesi's attractions, Torajan funerals are a riot of socializing and sacrificing. See p.477

△ Komodo Dragon, Komodo Island

Introduction and basics

The Indonesian archipelago spreads over 5200km between the Asian mainland and Australia, all of it within the tropics, and comprises between 13,000 and 17,000 islands. Its ethnic, cultural and linguistic diversity is correspondingly great – around 500 languages and dialects are spoken by its 200 million people, whose fascinating customs and lifestyles are a major attraction. And while travelling around Indonesia is often arduous and occasionally dangerous – to the extent that many tourists have been put off coming to the archipelago because of the country's recent negative press – those who do visit will experience a dynamic, colourful country with a huge range of sights and experiences that cannot be matched in Southeast Asia.

Because Indonesia encompasses such a diversity of cultures, it can be very difficult to decide where to go. There is a well-worn overland travellers' route across the archipelago, however, which begins by taking a boat from Penang in Malaysia to **Medan** on **Sumatra**'s northeast coast. From here, the classic itinerary runs to the **orang-utan sanctuary** at Bukit Lawang, the hill resort of **Berastagi**, the lakeside resorts of **Danau Toba** and the surfers' mecca of **Pulau Nias**. Further south, the area around **Bukittinggi** appeals because of its flamboyant Minangkabau architecture and dances. Many travellers then hurtle through the southern half of Sumatra in their headlong rush to **Java**, probably bypassing the exhaustingly overpopulated capital **Jakarta**, but perhaps pausing at the relaxed beach resort of **Pangandaran** in West Java. Next stop is always the ancient capital of **Yogyakarta**, a cultural centre that hosts daily performances of traditional dance and music and offers batik courses for curious travellers. Yogya also makes a good base for exploring the huge **Borobudur** (Buddhist) and **Prambanan** (Hindu) temples. Java's biggest natural attractions are its volcanoes: the **Dieng Plateau**, with its coloured lakes and ancient Hindu temples and, most famously, **Gunung Bromo**, where most travellers brave a sunrise climb to the summit.

Just across the water from East Java sits **Bali**, the long-time jewel in the crown of Indonesian tourism, a tiny island of elegant temples, verdant landscape and fine surf. The biggest resorts are the party towns of **Kuta** and adjacent **Legian**, with the more subdued beaches at **Lovina** and **Candi Dasa** appealing to travellers not hell-bent on nightlife. Most visitors also spend time in Bali's cultural centre of **Ubud**, whose lifeblood continues to be painting, carving, dancing and music-making. The islands east of Bali – collectively known as Nusa Tenggara – are now attracting bigger crowds, particularly neighbouring **Lombok**, with its beautiful beaches and temples. East again, the chance of seeing the world's largest lizards, the **Komodo dragons**, draws travellers to **Komodo** and **Rinca**, and then it's an easy hop across to **Flores**, which has great surfing and the unforgettable coloured crater lakes of **Kelimutu**. South of Flores, **Sumba** is famous for its intricate fabrics, grand funeral ceremonies and extraordinary annual ritual war, the pasola.

North of Flores, **Sulawesi** is renowned for the intriguing culture of the highland Torajans, whose idiosyncratic architecture and impressively ghoulish burial rituals are astonishing. West of Sulawesi, the island of Borneo is divided into the East Malaysian districts of Sabah and Sarawak, the independent kingdom of Brunei, and the Indonesian state of **Kalimantan**. For the overland traveller short on time, there's not much here that can't be experienced more rewardingly across the border in Sarawak, but there are opportunities for river travel in remote jungle.

Much of the **recent news** about Indonesia has emphasized the fragility of the state. The Bali bomb of 2002, which left over 200 dead and the country's entire tourist industry in tatters, was preceded by the horrifying chaos of the East Timor elections in 1999. What's more, riots in many parts of the archipelago have pitched Muslims against their Christian neighbours, while locals in other provinces, inspired by the success of East Timor in winning its independence, have begun to fight for the secession of their own province from the state. With all this upheaval, it's little wonder that the Indonesian economy has, for the past few years, continually teetered on the point of collapse, though signs of some sort of economic recovery are now beginning to appear.

One area that continues to suffer more than any other is the **Maluku Islands**, which since 1999 has been devastated by an internecine war that has left thousands dead; while a few travellers are trickling back to the Banda Islands, and one or two are even going further afield to Ambon and Halmahera, it's still considered unsafe to travel here, and for that reason the Maluku Islands have been omitted from this edition. The unpredictable security situation of other "troublespots" such as **Aceh** in northern Sumatra and the Poso region of **central Sulawesi** (see p.467 for more) mean that they, too, have been omitted from this edition. We also do not cover remote and little-visited **West Papua** (formerly known as Irian Jaya), whose ongoing separatist struggle has in the past resulted in violence against foreigners, or East Timor's neighbour, **West Timor**. If you insist on visiting Indonesia's more unsettled areas, make sure you are fully aware of the latest situation, and heed any warnings given out by your foreign office, as well as the local people who, along with your fellow travellers,

are usually the best source of up-to-date information.

Climate-wise, the whole archipelago is tropical, with **temperatures** at sea level always between 21°C and 33°C, although cooler in the mountains. In theory, the year divides into a wet and dry season, though it's often hard to tell the difference. Very roughly, in much of the country, November to April are the wet months (Jan and Feb the wettest) and May through to October are dry. However, in northern Sumatra, this pattern is effectively reversed. The **peak tourist season** is between mid-June and mid-September and again over the Christmas and New Year season. This is particularly relevant in the major resorts, where prices rocket and rooms can be fully booked for days, and sometimes weeks, on end.

Sea routes into Indonesia

Indonesia has good ferry connections with Malaysia and Singapore, and there are occasional cargo boats from the Philippines.

From Malaysia and Singapore

A variety of ferries and speedboats depart from Penang (see p.660), on the west coast of Peninsular Malaysia, to **Medan** and from Melaka (see p.691) in southern Malaysia to **Dumai** or Pekanbaru. You can also take ferries from Johor Bahru (see p.695), in far southern Malaysia and Singapore to the Sumatran islands of **Batam** and **Bintan**;

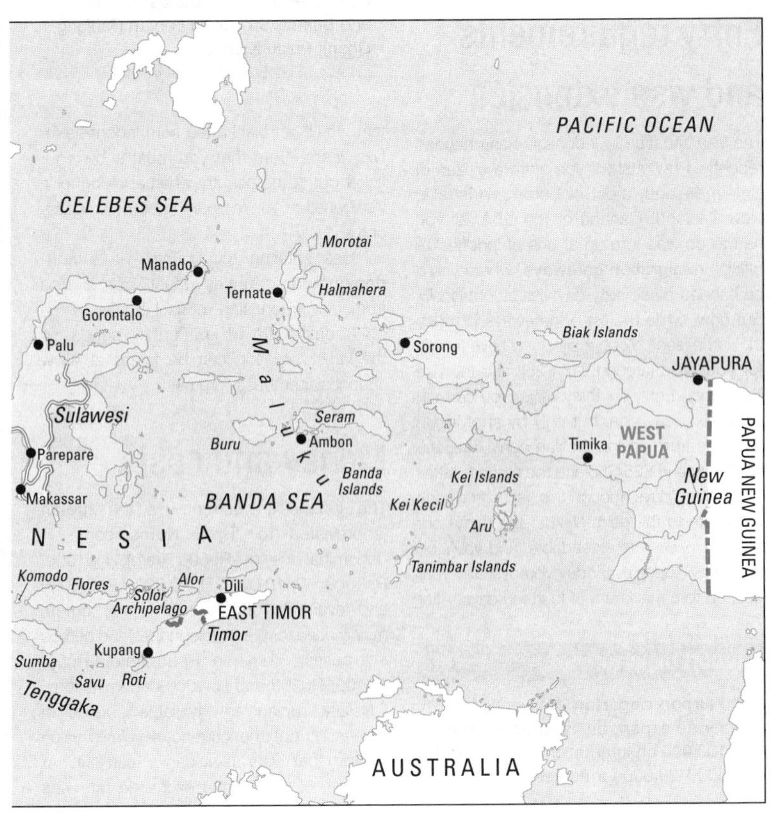

and from Port Klang (see p.649), near Kuala Lumpur, to **Tanjung Balai** in Sumatra.

There are two entry points between **East Malaysia and Kalimantan**. You can catch a bus between the capital of Malaysian **Sarawak** at Kuching (see p.703) to West Kalimantan's capital, Pontianak; alternatively, you can cross from the East Malaysian state of **Sabah** by catching a two or three-hour ferry (see p.726) to **Pulau Nunukan** or **Tarakan** from Tawau, two days' bus ride southeast of Kota Kinabalu.

From the Philippines

There is still the occasional cargo boat from General Santos in the Philippines to Bitung in Northern **Sulawesi**. It's a rough ride shorn of any sort of comfort, but at around US$30 one-way (US$40 return), it's a lot cheaper than flying. See p.879 for details.

Entry requirements and visa extension

The visa situation in Indonesia has changed recently. Previously, if you were a citizen of Britain, Ireland, most of Europe, Australia, New Zealand, Canada or the USA, all you had to do was turn up at one of Indonesia's official **immigration gateways**, where you'd be handed a free sixty-day visa automatically. But now, while the list of gateways is much the same (see box opposite), you have to **pay for your visa** (around £15/$25), and the visa itself is valid only for thirty days. You *can* still get a sixty-day visa, but only by applying in advance from an Indonesian consulate; the cost is around £35/$55 and the process takes about three days, though this varies from one consulate to the next. Neither the thirty- nor sixty-day visas are extendable, and you'll be **fined** US$20 for every day you overstay your visa, up to a maximum of fourteen days. After that, you'll get blacklisted from Indonesia for two years. Note that you must show your ticket out of the country when applying for a visa, whether you're applying at the embassy or the port.

Those entering the country via a **non-designated gateway** must get a visa from an Indonesian consulate (listed on p.44) before travelling. Further details on the latest situation can be found at www.indonesianembassy.org.uk.

Airport departure tax

The **airport departure tax** varies from airport to airport, but is approximately Rp100,000 on international flights, and Rp5000–20,000 for domestic flights.

Official immigration gateways into Indonesia

The following airports and seaports have facilities for issuing visas to tourists on arrival:

Airports

Bali Ngurah Rai, Denpasar
Java Soekarno-Hatta, Jakarta; Juanda, Surabaya
Sumatra Polonia, Medan; Sultan Syarif Kasim II, Pekanbaru; Tabing, Padang
Sulawesi Sam Ratulangi, Manado

Seaports

Bali Padang Bai
Java Tanjung Priok
Sumatra Belawan, Medan; Sibolga; Dumai; Teluk Bayur, Padang
Riau Islands Batam: Batu Ampar, Nongsa, Sekupang, Teluk Senimba; Bintan: Telani Lagoi, Bandar Bintan, and Bandar Sri Udana Lobam (Tanjung Uban); Pulau Karimun.

Money and costs

The Indonesian currency is the **rupiah** (abbreviated to "Rp"). **Notes** come in denominations of Rp500 (rare), Rp1000, Rp5000, Rp10,000, Rp20,000, Rp50,000 and even Rp100,000 (also rare); **coins**, mainly used for public telephones and bemos (minibuses), come in Rp25 (rare), Rp50, Rp100, Rp500 and Rp1000 denominations. Officially, rupiah are available outside of Indonesia, but the currency's volatile value means that very few banks carry it. At the time of writing, the exchange rate was

Rp17,000 to £1 and Rp9500 to US$1.

You'll find **banks** capable of handling foreign exchange in provincial capitals and bigger cities throughout Indonesia, with privately run **moneychangers** (who sometimes offer better rates) in major tourist centres. You may be asked to supply a **photocopy** of your passport, or the **receipt** (or proof of purchase) that you get when you buy your travellers' cheques. Always count your money carefully, as unscrupulous dealers can rip you off, either by folding notes over to make it look as if you're getting twice as much, or by distracting you and then whipping away a few notes from your pile. Moneychangers in Kuta, Bali are notorious for this.

In less-travelled regions, provincial banks won't cash travellers' cheques, but will take **US dollar notes**. Over-the-counter **cash advances** on Visa can be used for obtaining the full international rate. Even more conveniently, most islands now have at least one **ATM** (major islands that still don't include the Alor and Solor islands to the east of Flores). These **ATMs** take at least one from Visa, MasterCard, or Cirrus-Maestro. For details on getting **money wired** to you, see "Wiring money" p.60.

Costs

It's difficult to say exactly how much Indonesia **costs** on a daily basis. However, you'll keep all costs to a minimum if you concentrate on Java, Sumatra (the cheapest place), Bali and Nusa Tenggara, where it's possible to travel cheaply. In Kalimantan and Sulawesi, flying or cruising between places is often the only option for travel, while the cost of importing goods makes everything more expensive. Taking all this into account, if you're happy to eat where the locals do, use public transport and stay in simple accommodation, you could manage on a **daily budget** of £7.50–10/US$13–18 per person. For around £15/US$27 a day (less if you share a room), you'll get hot water and air conditioning in your room, bigger meals and a few beers.

Information and maps

There's a range of **tourist offices** in Indonesia, including government-run organizations, normally called **Dinas (or Kantor) Pariwisata** (Diparda). Though they can lack hard information, staff often speak some English, usually have a map of the town or district, and may advise about local transport options or arrange guides. Many **private tour operators** are also excellent, if sometimes partisan, sources of information. In remote locations, you can try asking the local **police**.

Good all-round **maps** include GeoCentre's 1:2,000,000 series and the Nelles Indonesia series. In the same league is Periplus' range of user-friendly city and provincial maps.

Getting around

Delays are common to all forms of **transport** – including major flights – caused by weather, mechanical failure, or simply not enough passengers turning up, so you'll save yourself a good deal of stress if you keep your schedule as flexible as possible. For an idea of the duration and frequency of journeys between major destinations, see "**Travel Details**" on p.486.

Planes

In some areas, **flying** may be the only practical way to get around. State-operated **Garuda** handles international flights (though you might also use them for transport within Indonesia), while **Merpati** is the domestic operator. Provincial services are supplemented by **Mandala** and **Bouraq**, who have recently been joined by a huge number of new airlines, including Lion Air and Adam Air amongst others. Many of these smaller airlines serve a handful of destinations only. The quantity and quality of services is very uncertain at present, however, and some marginal routes have closed. It's essential to **reconfirm** your seat, as waiting lists can be huge and being bumped off is a regular occurrence; get a computer printout of the reconfirmation if possible. Arrive at the airport **early**, as seats on overbooked flights are allocated on a first-come, first-served basis. At other times, "fully booked" planes can be almost empty, so if you really have to get somewhere it's always worth going to the airport to check.

Buses and minibuses

Buses are cheap, easy to book and leave roughly on time. But they're also slow, cramped and often plain terrifying: accidents can be devastating. Where there's a choice of operators on any particular route, ask local people which bus company they recommend. **Tickets** are sold a day or more in advance from the point of departure or bus company offices – which are not necessarily near the relevant **bus station** (*terminal*). Where services are infrequent it's a good idea to buy tickets as early as possible. Tell the driver your exact destination, as it may be possible to get delivered right to the door of your hotel. The average **long-distance** bus has padded seats but little leg- or head-room; it's worth forking out for a luxury bus, if available, which costs twice as much but will have reclining seats. You'll get regular meal stops at roadhouses along the way. On shorter routes, you'll use minibuses, widely known by their Balinese tag, **bemo**, along with **kijang**, a jeep look-a-like. Once on their way, they're faster than buses and cheaper; fares are handed over on board, and rarely advertised. You may also have to pay for any space your luggage occupies. In resort areas such as Bali, a more pleasant option are **tourist shuttle buses** – though far more expensive than local services, these will take you between points as quickly as possible. The longest-established firm on Bali and Lombok is **Perama**. They have offices in most major tourist destinations and produce a useful leaflet outlining their routes.

Boats and ferries

Most Indonesians choose to travel between islands by boat, either on the state shipping line, Pelni, or on anything from cargo freighters to tiny fishing vessels. **Pelni** currently operates more than twenty **passenger liners**, most of which run on two-week or monthly circuits and link Java with ports on all the main island groups between Sumatra and Papua; see pp.240–241 for a chart of the Pelni routes covered in this chapter.

The vessels carry 500 to 1600 passengers each, are well maintained, as safe and punctual as any form of transport in Indonesia can be, and the only widespread form of public transport that offers any luxury. Comprehensive timetables for the whole country can be picked up from their head office in Jakarta; provincial offices should have complete timetables of all the ferries serving their ports, which you can copy or take away. **Tickets** are available from Pelni offices two or three days before departure, but as there's a big demand for cabin berths it's best to pay an agent to reserve you these as early as possible. You can only buy tickets for services that depart locally.

Accommodation on board is usually divided into two or four classes. All are good value, and include **meals**; cabins also have large **lockers** to store your luggage. **First class** consists of a private cabin with a double bed, washroom, TV and air conditioning – about US$30 a day is standard. **Second class** is similar, but with four bunks and no TV (US$20); **third class** is a six-bunk cabin without the washroom (US$15); and **fourth class**, more commonly called **economy** or **deck class**, is just a bed in a dorm (US$10). If the fourth class is full, which it usually is, then the only option is to sleep in the corridors, stairwells or on deck; if you plan to travel in this class, it's a good idea to buy a rattan mat before boarding to sit/lie on, and get to the port early to stake out your spot on the floor. Lock luggage shut and chain it to something immovable. Fourth-class food is edible at best, so stock up in advance with instant noodles and biscuits. It's always possible to upgrade after boarding, if space is available.

A new and very welcome introduction has been the arrival of the three **ASDP fast ferries**, two of which connect Surabaya on Java with Bali and Nusa Tenggara, and one of which sails north from Surabaya to Kalimantan. While not cheap (a seven-hour journey costs about Rp175,000 in the cheapest, "Bisnis" class) the service is very good, and they take less than a third of the time of Pelni vessels. In addition to these, there are numerous local craft plying various routes between the islands, including many run by the cargo company Perintis. While these are always willing to rent deck space to passengers for next to nothing – say US$5 for 24 hours – comfort and privacy aboard will be nonexistent. Bring your own sleeping mat, drinking water and snacks, though you may be able to buy rice and fish heads on board. Guard your gear and don't flash anything around. Schedules for these services are posted at ports.

Rental vehicles

Car-rental agencies abound in tourist hot spots such as Bali. Local operators offer a range of **cars**, most frequently 800cc Suzuki Jimneys (US$40 per day), and larger, more comfortable jeep-like 1600cc Toyota Kijangs (US$50). The rates drop if you rent for a week or more; one day means twelve hours, and the above prices exclude fuel. You'll need to produce an **international drivers' licence** before you rent. Rental **motorbikes** vary from small 100cc Yamahas to trail bikes. Prices start at US$5 per day without insurance. If you don't have a valid international motorbike **licence**, you may be able to get one by taking a test (Rp100,000). Conditions are not suitable for inexperienced drivers, with heavy traffic on major routes; there are increasing numbers of accidents involving tourists, so don't take risks. A few rental outfits offer **insurance** for an extra US$5 a day for a car and US$3 for a motorbike. Before you take a vehicle, check it thoroughly, and get something in writing about any existing damage.

Traffic in Indonesia **drives on the left** and there is a maximum speed limit of 70kph. Drivers must always carry an international driving licence and the vehicle registration documents. All motorcyclists must wear a **helmet**. In some places, certain roads change from two-way to one-way during the day, not publicized in any way that is comprehensible to foreigners. The **police** carry out regular spot checks, and you'll be **fined** for any infringements.

Urban transport

In cities, colour-coded or numbered minibus **bemos** might run fixed circuits, or adapt their routes according to their customers. Rides usually cost a few hundred rupiah, but fares are never displayed, and you'll get overcharged at first. Other standbys include **ojek** (single-passenger motorbikes) and **becak** (cycle-rickshaws), which take two passengers. Jakarta also has motorized becak, called **bajaj**. Negotiating **fares** for these vehicles requires a balance of firmness and tact; try for around Rp3000 for ojek for a trip around town, and Rp1500 a kilometre for becak, though you'll have to pay more for the latter if there are any hills along the way. They are also notoriously tough negotiators – never lose your temper with one unless you want a serious fight.

Accommodation

Prices for the simplest double room start at around US$2, and in all categories are at their **most expensive** from mid-June through August, and in December and January. Single rooms are a rarity, so lone travellers will get put in a double at about 75 percent of the full price. Check-out time is usually noon. The cheapest accommodation has shared **bathrooms**, where you wash using a mandi (see "Bathrooms", p.62). **Toilets** in these places will be squat affairs, flushed manually with water scooped from the pail that stands alongside, so you'll have to provide toilet paper yourself.

The bottom end of Indonesia's accommodation market is provided by homestays and hostels. *Penginapan*, or **homestays**, are most often simply spare bedrooms in the family home, though there's often not much difference between these and losmen, *pondok* and *wisma*, which are also family-run operations. Rooms vary from whitewashed concrete cubes to artful bamboo structures – some are even set in their own walled gardens. Hard beds and bolsters are the norm, and you may be provided with a light blanket. Most losmen rooms have fans and cold-water bathrooms.

Almost any place calling itself a **hotel** in Indonesia will include at least a basic breakfast in the price of a room. Most of the middle and top-end places add a service-and-tax surcharge of between 10 and 22 percent to your bill, and upmarket establishments quote prices – and prefer foreigners to pay – in dollars, though they accept plastic or a rupiah equivalent. In popular areas such as Bali and Tanah Toraja, it's worth booking ahead during the peak seasons; some hotels will also provide transport to and

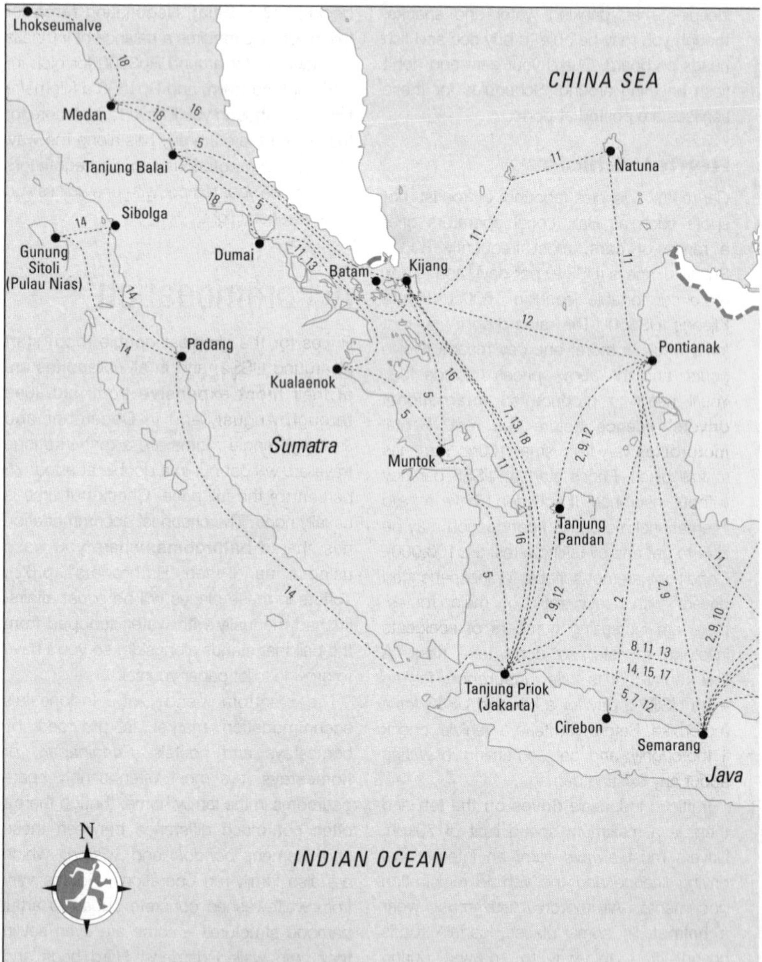

USEFUL PELNI ROUTES

	Name of Ferry	Main ports of call	Frequency
1	*KM Kelimutu*	Balikpapan, Flores	monthly
2	*KM Lawit*	Tanjung Priok, Pontianak, W. Java, Padang, Pulau Nias	monthly
3	*KM Tidar*	Balikpapan, W. Sulawesi, Makassar, Surabaya	fortnightly
4	*KM Tatamailau*	Surabaya, Sumbawa, Flores, S. Papua, Bali	monthly
5	*KM Sirimau*	Flores, Makassar, N. Java, Tanjung Priok	fortnightly
6	*KM Awu*	Denpasar, Sumba, Flores, W. Timor, Makassar, W. Sulawesi, Nunakan	fortnightly
7	*KM Ciremai*	Kijang, Tanjung Priok, Surabaya, Makassar, Sulawesi	fortnightly
8	*KM Dobonsolo*	Kijang, W. Sulawesi, E. Kalimantan	fortnightly
9	*KM Leuser*	Tanjung Priok, N. Java, W/S. Kalimantan	fortnightly
10	*KM Binaiya*	Surabaya, W. Sulawesi, S/E. Kalimantan	fortnightly
11	*KM Bukit Raya*	Tanjung Priok, S. Kalimantan, Natuna, Pontianak	fortnightly

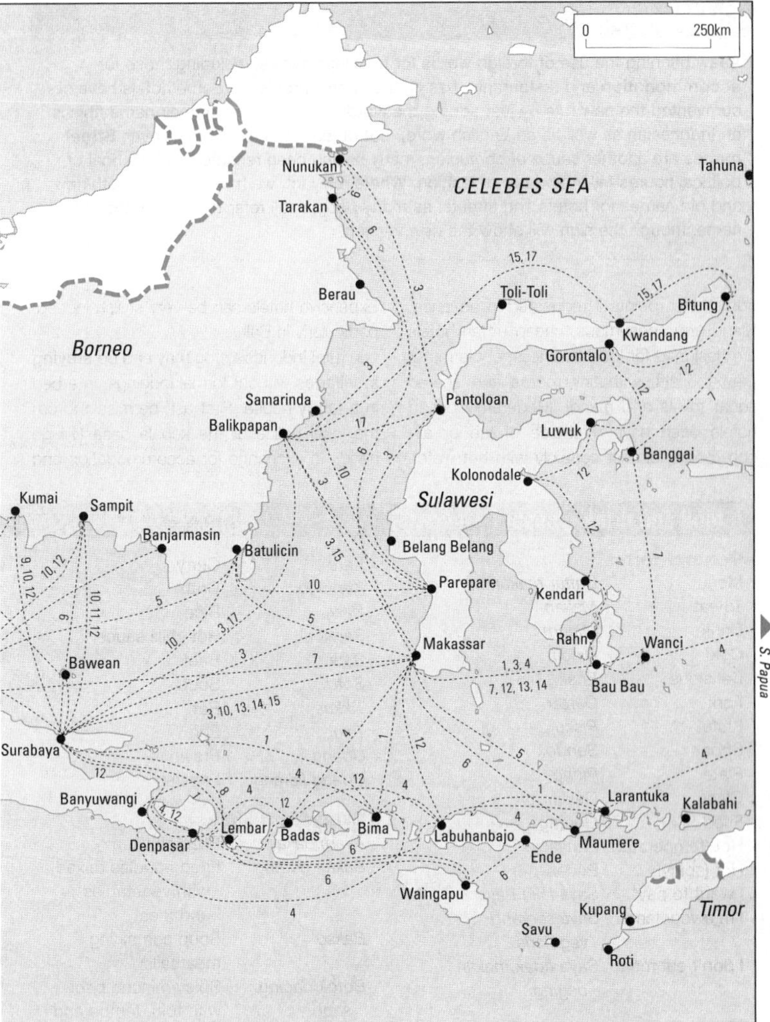

	Name of Ferry	Main ports of call	Frequency
12	*KM Tilongkabila*	Denpasar, W. Flores, Sumbawa, Sulawesi	fortnightly
13	*KM Bukit Siguntang*	Tanjung Priok, Makassar	fortnightly
14	*KM Lambelu*	Bitung, Makassar, Surabaya, Tanjung Priok, Padang, Kijang	fortnightly
15	*KM Sinabung*	Tanjung Priok, Makassar, N.Sulawesi	fortnightly
16	*KM Kelud*	Tanjung Priok, Batam, Medan	every four days
17	*KM Doro Londa*	Tanjung Priok, Surabaya, Makassar	fortnightly
18	*KM Pangrango*	Samarinda, Makassar, Pantoloan, Toli Toli, E. Sulawesi	fortnightly
19	*KM Sangiang*	Surabaya, Bima, Waingapu, Ende	fortnightly
20	*KM Fudi*	Balikpapan, Surabaya/Tanjung Priok	every four days
21	*KM Ganda Dewata*	Surabaya/Jakarta	every two/four days
22	*KM Egon*	Semarang/Surabaya	every two days

Addresses

A law banning the use of foreign words for business names, including those for **accommodation** and restaurants, has caused a few problems. Some hotels have circumvented the new rule by just adding the word "Hotel" in front of their name (this is an Indonesian as well as an English word), but others have had to start over. **Street names** are another cause of confusion, many having been renamed as historical or political figures fall in and out of fashion. Where relevant, we have included both new and old names for hotels and streets, as many people still refer to them by the old name, though the sign will show the new version.

from transit points if requested in advance. Bland and anonymous, cheap urban hotels are designed for local businesspeople rather than tourists, with tiny rooms and shared squat toilets and mandi. Moderately priced hotels often have a choice of fan or air-con rooms, almost certainly with hot water. Expensive hotels can be very stylish indeed, particularly in Bali.

In rural Indonesia, you may end up **staying in villages** without formal lodgings, in a bed in a family house. First ask permission from the local police or the kepala desa (village head). In exchange for accommodation and

A food and drink glossary

General terms

Menu	*Daftar makanan*
To eat	*Makan*
Drink	*Minum*
Cold	*Dingin*
Delicious	*Enak*
Fork	*Garpu*
Knife	*Pisau*
Spoon	*Sendok*
Plate	*Piring*
Glass	*Gelas*
Fried	*Goreng*
Hot (temperature)	*Panas*
Hot (spicy)	Pedas
I want to pay	*Saya injin bayar*
I'm a vegetarian	*Saya seorang vegetaris*
I don't eat meat	*Saya tidak makan daging*

Meat, fish and basic foods

Anjing	Dog
Ayam	Chicken
Babi	Pork
Bakmi	Noodles
Buiah	Fruit
Es	Ice
Garam	Salt
Gula	Sugar
Ikan	Fish
Itik	Duck
Jaja	Rice cakes
Kambing	Goat
Kare	Curry
Kepiting	Crab
Nasi	Rice
Samibal	Hot chilli sauce
Sapi	Beef
Soto	Soup
Tikkus	Rat
Telur	Egg
Udang	Prawn
Udang karang	Lobster

Everyday dishes

Ayam bakar	Fried chicken
Bakmi goreng	Fried noodles mixed with vegetables and meat
Bakso	Soup containing meatballs
Botok daging sapi	Spicy minced beef with tofu, *tempe* and coconut milk
Cap cay	Mixed fried vegetables
Es campur	Fruit salad and shredded ice
Fu yung hai	Seafood omelette
Gado-gado	Steamed vegetables served with a spicy peanut sauce
Ikan bakar	Grilled fish
Krupuk	Rice or cassava crackers
Kue tiaw	Singaporean stir-fry of flat rice noodles

meals, you should offer cash or useful gifts, such as rice, salt, cigarettes or food, to the value of about US$1.50. The only bathroom might be the nearest river, with all bodily functions performed in the open. With such readily available and inexpensive alternatives, **camping** is only necessary when trekking.

Usually, **electricity** is supplied at 220–240 volts AC, but outlying areas may still use 110 volts. Most outlets take plugs with two rounded pins.

Food and drink

Compared to other Southeast Asian **cuisines**, Indonesian meals lack variety. Coconut milk and aromatic spices at first add intriguing tastes to the meats, vegetables and fruits, but after a while everything starts to taste the same – spiced, fried and served with rice. Be particularly careful about food **hygiene** in rural Indonesia, avoiding poorly cooked fish, pork or beef, which can give you flukes or worms.

Rice (*nasi*) is the favoured staple across much of the country, an essential, three-times-a-day fuel. Noodles are also widely popular. The seafood is often superb, and chicken, goat and beef are the main meats in this predominantly Muslim country. **Vegetarians** can eat well in Indonesia, though restaurant selections can be limited to *cap cay* – fried mixed vegetables. There's also plenty of tofu and the popular *tempe*, a fermented soya-bean cake.

	and meat
Lalapan	Raw vegetables and *sambal*
Lawar	Balinese raw meat paste
Lontong	Steamed rice in a banana-leaf packet
Lumpia	Spring rolls
Murtabak	Thick, dough pancake, often filled with meat
Nasi ayam	Boiled rice with chicken
Nasi campur	Boiled rice served with small amounts of vegetable, meat, fish and sometimes egg
Nasi goreng	Fried rice
Nasi gudeg	Rice with jackfruit and coconut-milk curry
Nasi putih	Plain boiled rice
Nasi soto ayam	Chicken-and-rice soup
Pisang goreng	Fried bananas
Rendang	Dry-fried beef and coconut-milk curry
Rijsttaffel	Dutch/Indonesian buffet made up of six to ten different meat, fish and vegetable dishes with rice
Rujak	Hot spiced fruit salad
Rujak petis	Vegetables and fruit in spicy peanut and shrimp sauce
Tahu goring telur	Tofu omelette
Sate	Meat or fish kebabs served with a spicy peanut sauce
Soto ayam	Chicken soup
Sayur bening	Soup with spinach and corn
Sayur lodeh	Vegetable and coconut-milk soup
Urap-urap/urap timum	Vegetables with coconut and chilli
Drinks	
Air jeruk	Orange juice
Air jeruk nipis	Lemon juice
Air minum	Drinking water
Arak	Palm or rice spirit
Bir	Beer
Brem	Local rice beer
Kopi	Coffee
Kopi susu	White coffee
Sopi	Palm spirit
Susu	Milk
Teh	Tea
Tolong tanpa es	Without ice, please
Tolong tanpa gula	Without sugar, please
Tuak	Palm wine

Indonesian food

The backbone of all Indonesian cooking, **spices** are ground and chopped together, then fried to form a paste, which is either used as the flavour-base for curries, or rubbed over ingredients prior to frying or grilling. **Chillies** always feature, along with *terasi* (also known as *belacan*), a fermented shrimp paste. Meals are often served with *sambal*, a blisteringly hot blend of chillies and spices.

Light meals and snacks include various rice dishes such as **nasi goreng**, a plate of fried rice with shreds of meat and vegetables and topped with a fried egg, and **nasi campur**, boiled rice served with a small range of side dishes. Noodle equivalents are also commonly available, as are **gado-gado**, steamed vegetables dressed in a peanut sauce, and **sate**, small kebabs of meat or fish, barbecued over a fire and again served with spicy peanut sauce. Indonesian **bread** (*roti*) is made from sweetened dough, and usually accompanies a morning cup of coffee.

Sumatran **Padang restaurants** are found right across Indonesia, the typically fiery food pre-cooked – not the healthiest way to eat – and displayed cold on platters piled up in a pyramid shape inside a glass-fronted cabinet. There are no menus; you either select your composite meal by pointing, or wait for the staff to bring you a selection and pay just for what you consume. You may encounter boiled *kangkung* (water spinach); *tempe*; egg, vegetable, meat or seafood curry; fried whole fish; potato cakes; and fried cow's lung.

Where to eat

The cheapest places to eat in Indonesia are at the **mobile stalls** (*kaki lima*, or "five legs"), which ply their wares around the streets and bus stations during the day, and congregate at night markets after dark. You simply place your order and they cook it up on the spot. **Warung** are the bottom line in Indonesian restaurants, usually just a few tables, and offering much the same food as *kaki lima* for as little as 50c a dish. **Rumah makan** are bigger, offer a wider range of dishes and comfort, and may even have a menu. Anything labelled as a **restaurant** will probably be catering to foreigners, with fully fledged service and possibly international food; many close by 8 or 9pm. Tourist restaurants will charge at least three times as much for the same dish you'd get in a warung. In addition, many of the moderate and all of the expensive establishments will add up to 21 percent service tax to the bill.

Drinks

Most **water** that comes out of taps in Indonesia has had very little treatment, and can contain a whole range of bacteria and viruses (see p.54). Drink only bottled, boiled or sterilized water. Boiled water (*air putih*) can be requested at accommodation and restaurants, and dozens of brands of **bottled water** (*air minum*) are sold throughout the islands. Indonesian **coffee** is amongst the best in the world, and drunk with copious amounts of sugar and, occasionally, condensed milk.

Alcohol can be a touchy subject in parts of Indonesia, where public drunkenness may incur serious trouble. There's no need to be overly paranoid about this in cities, however, and the locally produced **beers**, Anker and Bintang Pilsners, are good, and widely available at Chinese restaurants and bigger hotels. In non-Islamic regions, even small warung sell beer. **Spirits** are less publicly consumed, and may be technically illegal, so indulge with caution. Nonetheless, home-produced brews are often sold openly in villages. *Tuak* (also known as *balok*) or palm wine is made by tapping a suitable tree for its sap, comes in plain milky white or pale red varieties, and varies in strength. Far more potent are rice wine (variously known as *arak* or *brem*), and *sopi*, a distillation of *tuak*, either of which can leave you incapacitated after a heavy session.

Communications

Aside from the usual services, many **post offices** (*kantor pos*) now offer email and fax facilities. Indonesia's **poste restante** system is fairly efficient, but only in the cities; poste restante is officially held for a maximum of one month. See p.63 for general advice on poste restante. **Overseas letters** to Western

Time differences

The islands of the Indonesian archipelago covered in this Guide are divided into **two time zones**. Sumatra, Java, Kalimantan Barat and Kalimantan Tengah are on **Western Indonesian Time** (7hr ahead of London GMT, 12hr ahead of New York, 15hr ahead of Los Angeles, 3hr behind Sydney and 5hr behind Auckland); Bali, Lombok, the Nusa Tenggara islands, Sulawesi and South and East Kalimantan are on **Central Indonesian Time** (8hr ahead of London GMT, 13hr ahead of New York, 16hr ahead of Los Angeles, 2hr behind Sydney and 4hr behind Auckland). Note that Bali is one hour ahead of Java.

Europe and America take between seven and ten days to arrive.

In larger post offices, the **parcels** section is usually in a separate part of the building, and sending one is expensive and time-consuming. The cheapest way of sending mail home is by surface (under 10kg only). Don't seal the parcel before staff at the post office have checked what's inside it; in the larger towns, there's usually a parcel-wrapping service near the post office.

There are two types of **telephone** office in Indonesia: the ubiquitous government-run **Telkom** offices (often called Yantel, which are open 24hr), and privately owned **wartels** (usually 7am–midnight), which tend to be slightly more expensive, but are often conveniently located. Both also offer fax services, though the wartels rarely have a collect-call service.

Public **payphones** are useful for local calls and take Rp100 and Rp500 coins. Put the coins in only after someone picks up the phone and starts speaking. Many payphones now take telephone cards only (*kartu telefon*), available in various denominations from 20 units (Rp5000) to 680 units (Rp78,000). Cards can be bought from most local corner stores. In the big cities, there are also *kartu cip* phones that take the new microchip cards. Long-distance **domestic calls** (*panggilan inter-lokal*) are charged according to a zone system, with different rates; it's cheaper between 9pm and 6am. **Mobile phone coverage** is good across most of Java, Sumatra and Bali, but elsewhere is confined largely to the main cities and populated areas only.

Rates for **international calls** are fixed, though the premium charged by the private wartels varies. All calls at weekends and on national holidays are discounted by 25 percent. IDD rates are as follows, per minute: Australia Rp8300 (plus 20 percent 9am–noon, minus 25 percent 10pm–6am); New Zealand, USA and Canada Rp8300 (plus 20 percent 9am–noon, minus 25 percent 11pm–7am); UK Rp9700 and Ireland Rp7150 (both plus 20 percent 2–5pm, minus 25 percent 3–11am). To **call abroad** from Indonesia, dial ☎001 or ☎008 + country code + area code (minus the first 0) + number. For international directory enquiries call ☎102; the international operator is ☎101. Some Telkom offices and airports also have home-country direct phones, from which you can call collect (reverse-charge calls), or settle up after the call; they cost more than IDD phones.

Internet access is becoming increasingly widespread in Indonesia, and there are now tourist-friendly internet offices and cybercafés in many towns and cities; prices vary widely from Rp4000 to Rp20,000 per hour. **Email** can make a good alternative to post office postes restantes – even if you're not on the Internet at home; see "Communications" p.65 for details.

Opening hours and festivals

As a rough outline, **businesses** such as airline offices open Monday to Friday 8am–4pm & Sat 8am–noon. **Banking hours** are Monday to Friday 8am–3pm & Sat 8am–1pm, but banks may not handle foreign exchange in the afternoons or at weekends. Moneychangers usually keep shop rather than bank hours. **Post offices** operate roughly Monday to Thursday 8am–2pm, Friday 8–11am and Saturday 8am–1pm,though in the larger cities the hours are much longer. Muslim businesses, including **government offices**, may also close at 11.30am on Fridays, the main day of prayer, and **national public holidays** see all commerce compulsorily curtailed.

Ramadan, a month of fasting during daylight hours, falls during the ninth Muslim month (starting in November/December/January). Even in non-Islamic areas, Muslim restaurants and businesses shut down during the day, and in staunchly Islamic parts of rural Lombok, Sumatra and Kalimantan's Banjarmasin, you should not eat, drink or smoke in public at this time. **Idul Fitri**, also called *Hari Raya* or *Lebaran*, marks the end of Ramadan and is a two-day national holiday of noisy celebrations.

Local festivals

In addition to national public holidays, there are frequent **religious festivals** throughout Indonesia's Muslim, Hindu, Chinese and indigenous communities. Each of Bali's 20,000 temples has an anniversary celebration, for instance, and other ethnic groups may host elaborate marriages or funerals, along with more secular holidays. Many of these festivals change annually against the Western **calendar**. The *Calendar of Events* booklet, produced annually by the Directorate General of Tourism, should be available in tourist offices in Indonesia and overseas.

Erau Festival Tenggarong, Kalimantan. September. A big display of indigenous Dayak skills and dancing.

Funerals Tanah Toraja, Sulawesi. Mostly May to September. With buffalo slaughter, bullfights, and *sisemba* kick-boxing tournaments.

Galungun Bali. Takes place for ten days every 210 days to celebrate the victory of good over evil.

Kasada Bromo, East Java. Offerings are made to the gods and thrown into the crater. Held on the 14th day of Kasada, the twelfth month in the Tenggerese calendar year (Dec).

Nyepi throughout Bali. End of March or beginning of April. The major purification ritual of the year. In the lead-up, religious objects are paraded from temples to sacred springs or the sea for purification. The night before *nyepi*, the spirits are frightened away with drums, cymbals, firecrackers and huge papier-mâché monsters. On the day itself, everyone sits quietly at home to persuade any remaining evil spirits that Bali is completely deserted.

Pasola West Sumba. Held four times in February and March, the exact dates being determined by local priests, this festival to balance the upper sphere of the heavens culminates with a frenetic pitched battle between two villages of spear-wielding horsemen.

Public holidays

Most of the **national public holidays** fall on different dates of the Western calendar each year, as they are calculated according to Muslim or local calendars.

December/January *Idul Fitri*, the celebration of the end of Ramadan
January 1 New Year's Day (*Tahun Baru*)
March/April *Nyepi*, Balinese saka New Year
March/April Good Friday and Easter Sunday
May *Idul Adha* (*Hajh*), Muslim Day of Sacrifice
May *Waisak* Day, anniversary of the birth, death and enlightenment of Buddha
May/June Ascension Day
June/July *Muharam*, Muslim New Year
July/August *Maulud Nabi Muhammad*, the anniversary of the birth of Mohammed
August 17 Independence Day (*Hari Proklamasi Kemerdekaan*) celebrates the proclamation of Indonesian Independence in 1945 by Dr Sukarno
December Ascension Day of Mohammed
December 25 Christmas Day

Sekaten Central Java. July or August The celebration of the birthday of the prophet Mohammed, held in the royal courts of Central Java, includes a month-long festival of fairs, gamelan recitals, *wayang kulit* (Javanese shadow puppet performances) and *wayang orang* (a form of Javanese ballet) performances, culminating in a procession.

Cultural hints

Indonesia shares the same **attitudes to dress and social taboos** as other Southeast Asian cultures, described in "Cultural hints" on p.68. In addition, Indonesians are generally very sociable, and dislike doing anything alone. It's normal for complete strangers engaged in some common enterprise – catching a bus, for instance – to introduce themselves and start up a friendship. **Sharing cigarettes** between men is in these circumstances a way of establishing a bond, and Westerners who don't smoke should be genuinely apologetic about refusing; it's well worth carrying a packet to share around even if you save your own "for later".

Diving, surfing and trekking

Indonesia has many of the world's best **diving sites**, one of the finest of which is Pulau Bunaken off **Sulawesi**, where the vast diversity of tropical fish and coral is complemented by visibility that can reach over 30m. **Bali** has many good sites, including the famous Liberty wreck, and reputable tour operators at all major beach resorts; **Lombok**'s operators are limited to Senggigi and the Gili Islands.The best time for diving is between April and October. Most major beach resorts have dive centres, but once you get further afield you'll probably have to rely on live-aboard cruises or even on having your own gear. A day's diving with two tanks, lunch and basic equipment costs anything from $30 to $100. Be sure to enquire about the reputation of the dive operators before signing up, check their PADI or equivalent accreditation and, if possible, get first-hand recommendations from other divers. Be aware that it is down to you to **check your equipment**, and that the purity of an air tank can be suspect, and could cause serious injury. Also check your guide's credentials carefully, and bear in mind that you may be a long way from a decompression chamber.

Surfing

Indonesia is also one of the world's premier **surfing** destinations, with an enormous variety of class waves and perfect, uncrowded breaks. The best-known waves are found on **Bali**, **G-Land** (Grajagan) on Java, and **Pulau Nias** off Sumatra, but **Sumba** and the **Mentawai Islands** are the destinations of the future. In June and July, during the best and most consistent surf, you can expect waves to be crowded, especially in Java and Bali. For all-in **surf safaris** on luxury yachts, try STC (@ surftrav@ozemail.com.au), who have boat trips around all major destinations. Try to bring your own **board**, and a padded board-bag; though in the popular surf spots (Pulau Nias in North Sumatra and Kuta in Bali, for example) you can hire some decent boards on the beach, which saves all the hassle and extra cost of bringing one from home. Most public transport charges extra for boards. Also pack high-strength sun block; plenty of iodine (to treat cuts from coral), a helmet and thin suit are advisable, too.

Trekking

There are endless **trekking** opportunities in Indonesia. The most popular volcano treks include **Gunung Batur** on Bali and **Gunung Bromo** on Java; more taxing favourites include **Gunung Rinjani** on Lombok and **Gunung Semeru** on Java. In Sumatra, the **Gunung Leuser National Park** is Southeast Asia's largest, and includes the famous Bukit Lawang orang-utan sanctuary. Many routes need **guides**, and not just to find the paths: turning up at a remote village unannounced can cause trouble, as people may mistrust outsiders, let alone Westerners. Guides are always available from local villages and tourist centres.

Emergency phone numbers

Police ☎110
Ambulance ☎118
Fire ☎113

Crime and safety

The bombing of a nightclub in the tourist centre of Kuta on Bali in 2002, which left over 200 (mostly foreigners) dead, as well as foreign fatalities resulting from the suppression of independence movements in West Papua and Timor, and the urban violence that surrounded the political and religious upheavals of the last couple of years, all undermine the idea that Indonesia is a safe place to travel. However, it's also true that serious incidents involving Westerners are rare. **Petty theft**, however, is a fact of life, so don't flash around expensive jewellery or watches. Don't hesitate to check that doors and windows – including those in the bathroom – are secure before accepting **accommodation**; if the management seems offended by this, you probably don't want to stay there anyway. Some guesthouses and hotels have safe-deposit boxes.

If you're unlucky enough to get **mugged**, never resist and, if you disturb a thief, raise the alarm rather than try to take them on. Be especially aware of **pickpockets** on buses or bemos, who usually operate in pairs: one will distract you while another does the job. Afterwards, you'll need a **police report** for insurance purposes. In smaller villages where police are absent, ask for assistance from the headman. Try to take along someone to translate, though police will generally do their best to find an English speaker. You may also be charged "administration fees", the cost of which is open to sensitive negotiations. Have nothing to do with **drugs** in Indonesia. The penalties are tough, and you won't get any sympathy from consular officials. If arrested, ring your embassy immediately.

Medical care and emergencies

If you have a minor ailment, head to a pharmacy (*apotik*), which can provide many medicines without prescription. Condoms (*kondom*) are available from pharmacists. Only in the main tourist areas will assistants speak English; in the village health posts, staff are generally ill-equipped to cope with serious illness. If you need an English-speaking **doctor** (*doktor*) or dentist (*doktor gigi*), seek advice at your hotel (some of the luxury ones have an in-house doctor) or at the local tourist office. You'll find a public **hospital** (*rumah sakit*) in major cities and towns, and in some places these are supplemented by private hospitals, many of which operate an accident and emergency department. If you have a serious accident or illness, you will need to be evacuated home or to Singapore, which has the best medical provision in Asia. It is, therefore, vital to arrange health insurance before you leave home (see "Insurance", p.50).

History

Until the late nineteenth century when the Dutch subsumed most of the islands under the title the "Dutch East Indies", the Indonesian archipelago was little more than a series of unrelated kingdoms, sultanates and private fiefdoms with distinct histories.

Beginnings

Hominids first arrived in Indonesia about eight hundred thousand years ago. Excavations uncovered parts of the skull of *Pithecanthropus erectus*, since renamed *Homo erectus erectus* – or **Java Man** – in Sangiran near Solo.

Homo sapiens first made an appearance in about 40,000 BC, having crossed over to the Indonesian archipelago from the Philippines, Thailand and Burma, using land bridges exposed during the Ice Ages. Later migrants brought knowledge of rice irrigation and animal husbandry, sea navigation and weaving techniques, and from the seventh or eighth centuries BC, the **Bronze Age** began to spread south from southern China.

Early traders and kingdoms

One of the methods of rice growing brought by the early migrants was wet-field cultivation, which required substantial inter-village co-operation and so gave rise to the first **kingdoms** in the archipelago.

Merchants from India brought **Hinduism** with them, which spread quickly, and by the fifth century AD, a myriad small Hindu kingdoms peppered the islands, the most successful being the **Srivijaya** kingdom, based in Palembang in South Sumatra. For approximately four hundred years, beginning in the seventh century AD, Srivijaya controlled the Melaka Straits – and the accompanying lucrative trade in spices, wood, camphor, tortoise shell and precious stones – and extended its empire as far north as Thailand and as far east as West Borneo. Srivijaya was also a seat of learning and religion, with over a thousand **Buddhist** monks living and studying within the city.

Whilst the Srivijayans enjoyed supremacy around the coasts of Indonesia, small kingdoms began to flourish inland. In particular, the rival **Saliendra** and **Sanjaya** kingdoms began to wield considerable influence on the volcanic plains of Central Java, constructing spectacular monuments such as the magnificent temple at **Borobudur**, built by the Buddhist Saliendras, and the manifold temples of **Prambanan**, built, in response, by the Hindu Sanjayas. But by the twelfth century things had begun to change: the Cholas of southern India destroyed the Srivijayan Empire, and the influence of the Saliendras and Sanjayas was declining in the face of new empires emerging in the east of Java.

The Majapahit Empire and the arrival of Islam

The **Majapahit Empire**, a Hindu kingdom based in East Java, enjoyed unrivalled success from 1292 to 1389, boasting at least partial control over a vast area covering Java, Bali, Sumatra, Borneo, Sulawesi, Lombok and Timor. This was the first time the major islands of the Indonesian archipelago had been united under one command. As well as economic prosperity, the Majapahit Empire also saw the first flowering of Indonesian culture, in particular certain courtly traditions still extant. However, the arrival of Islam on Java and a massive revolt in the north of the island eventually left the empire weak and in disarray, although it managed to survive for over a hundred years longer on its new home in Bali.

Islam first gained a toehold in the archipelago during the rule of the Srivijaya Empire. Merchants from Gujarat in India who called in at Aceh in northern Sumatra were the first to bring the message of Mohammed, followed soon after by traders from Arabia. From Sumatra, Islam spread eastwards, first along the coast and then into the interior of Java and the rest of Indonesia (Bali, Flores and West Papua excepted), where it syncretized with the Hindu, Buddhist and animist faiths that were already practised throughout the archipelago. The first Islamic kingdoms emerged on Java, where small coastal sultanates grew in the vacuum left by the Majapahit.

The spice trade and the Dutch conquest

Portuguese ships began appearing in the region in the early sixteenth century and soon established a virtual monopoly over the lucrative spice trade. They took control of the Moluccas (Maluku), which became known as the **Spice Islands**, because of their wealth of pepper, nutmeg, cloves, mace, ginger and cinnamon.

Dutch forays into the Indonesian archipelago only began at the very end of the sixteenth century, but by 1600 they had become the supreme European trading power in the region. In 1602, they founded the **Dutch East India Company** (Verenigde Oostindische Compagnie or VOC), with monopoly control over trade with the Moluccas. They then invaded and occupied the Banda Islands, part of the Moluccas, in 1603 – the first overtly aggressive act by the Dutch against their Indonesian hosts. Two years later, the VOC successfully chased the Portuguese from their remaining strongholds on Tidore and Ambon, and the Dutch annexation of Indonesia began in earnest. Trading vessels were now being replaced by warships, and the battle for the archipelago commenced.

By the end of the first decade of the seventeenth century, the VOC had begun to build a loose but lucrative **empire**, becoming the Dutch government's official representatives in the archipelago. At the helm of the VOC was the ruthless Jan Pieterzoon Coen, who set about raising the prices of nutmeg and clove artificially high by destroying vast plantations on the island, thus devastating the livelihood of Banda's already decimated population.

Coen then turned his attention to Java, and in particular Jayakarta (now Jakarta), which he wanted to become the capital of the ever-expanding VOC territories. When he built a fortress there, the local population responded angrily, upon which the Dutch retaliated by razing the city and renaming it **Batavia**. Further strategically important territories were acquired soon after, including Melaka (in modern-day Malaysia) and Makassar.

The plains of Central Java and the northern shores were by this time in the grip of the influential Islamic **Mataram Empire**, whose rulers were treated almost as deities by their subjects. However, the royal house was often riven with squabbles, and during the early years of the eighteenth century the region was paralysed by the **Three Wars of Succession**. The last of these (1746–57) brought about the division of the empire into three separate sultanates, two at Solo and one at Yogyakarta, aided and abetted by the politically astute Dutch who then subjugated the entire territory.

Though they were now the first rulers of a united Java, the VOC began to see their fortunes dwindle in the face of huge competition from the British and French. In 1795, the Dutch government, investigating the affairs of the company, found mismanagement and corruption on a grand scale. The VOC was bankrupt, and eventually expired in 1799. The Netherlands government took possession of all VOC territories, and thus all of the islands we regard as Indonesia today formally became part of the **Dutch colonial empire**.

The arrival of the British

In 1795, the French, under Napoleon, invaded and occupied Holland, and Herman Willem Daendels was made governor-general of the East Indies. He ruled for just three years, but was unable to fend off attacks by the **British** who, under the leadership of Sir Thomas Stamford Raffles, picked off the islands one by one, eventually landing at Batavia in 1811.

Raffles' tenure lasted for just five years before he was forced to hand back the territories to the Dutch. But he left a lasting impact, having ordered surveys of every historical building, and conducted extensive research into the country's flora and fauna.

The return of the Dutch

With the end of the Napoleonic Wars in Europe, the **Dutch** returned to Indonesia in 1816 and were soon embroiled in a couple of bloody disputes against opponents of their rule. But, having finally regained control over their old colonies, the rest of the nineteenth century and the beginning of the twentieth saw the Dutch attempting to expand into previously independent territories. Their early efforts met with limited success: the **Balinese** only surrendered in 1906, a full sixty years after the Dutch had first invaded, whilst the war in Aceh, which the Dutch had first tried to annex in 1873, dragged on until 1908, costing thousands of lives on both sides. By 1910, however, following the fall of **Banjarmasin** in 1864, **Lombok** in 1894 and **Sulawesi** in 1905, the Dutch had conquered nearly all of what we today call Indonesia; the only major exception, **West Papua**, finally accepted colonial rule in 1920.

Following debilitating battles in Java and Sumatra and facing bankruptcy, the Dutch devised the **Cultural System** in 1830, under which Javanese farmers had to give up a significant portion of their land to grow lucrative cash crops that could be sold in Europe for a huge profit. Java became one giant plantation and Indonesia evolved into a major world exporter of indigo, coffee and sugar, to the detriment of indigenous farmers who suffered hugely, some even starving to death.

The **Liberal System** (1870–1900) aimed to rectify the injustices of the Cultural System and end the exploitation of the local population, but unfortunately coincided with some devastating natural and economic disasters, including widespread coffee-leaf disease and a sugar blight. A vocal, altruistic minority in the Dutch parliament began pressing for more drastic policies to end the injustices in Indonesia, giving rise to what is now called the **Ethical Period**. During this time, radical irrigation, healthcare, education, drainage and flood control programmes were started, and **transmigration** policies, from Java to the outlying islands, were introduced. But transmigration, as is still seen today, while temporarily alleviating over-population on Java, brought its own set of problems, with the displaced often ending up as the victims of ethnic violence in their new homelands.

The Independence movement

Though education amongst Indonesians was still the preserve of a rich minority, it was from this minority that the leaders of the **Independence movement** would emerge. The Partai Nasional Indonesia (PNI), founded in 1927 by Achmed Sukarno, grew to become the biggest of the independence organizations. It aimed to achieve independence through non-co-operation and mass action, and quickly became a major threat to Dutch domination, so much so that the Dutch outlawed the party four years after its foundation, throwing its leaders, Sukarno included, in prison, and later exiling them. But when Hitler invaded Holland on May 10, 1940, the Dutch government fled to London, and the issue of Indonesia's independence was put on hold.

The Japanese made no secret of their intention to "liberate" Indonesia and when they finally invaded, in January 1942, most Indonesians did see them as liberators, rather than just another occupying force. On March 8, 1942, the Dutch on Java surrendered, and a three-and-a-half-year **Japanese occupation** began. Though every bit as ruthless as the Dutch, the Japanese did at least encourage the nationalist movement, and by 1945 were negotiating with Sukarno and others. Sukarno came up with his constitutional doctrine of **Pancasila**, the "five principles" by which an independent Indonesia would be governed: belief in God, nationalism, democracy, social justice and humanitarianism.

On August 17, 1945, two days after the Japanese surrender to the Allied forces, Sukarno read a simple, unemotional **Declaration of Independence** to a small group of people outside his house in Menteng. The Republic of Indonesia was born, with Achmed Sukarno as its first president.

The birth of the Republic

However, under the terms of the surrender agreed with the Allies, the Japanese actually had no right to hand over Indonesia to the Indonesian people. Lord Louis Mountbatten arrived in mid-1945 with several thousand **British** troops to accept the surrender of the Japanese occupying force. The Japanese tried to retake towns that they'd previously handed over to the local people and some intense, short-lived battles occurred. The British tried to remain neutral, withdrawing only when the Dutch were in a position to resume control in November 1946.

The **war with the Dutch** continued for the next three years, but the occupiers finally withdrew in December 1949, and sovereignty was handed over to the new **Republic of Indonesia**.

The Sukarno years

Sukarno introduced the concept of **guided democracy**, an attempt to create a wholly Indonesian political system based on the traditional hierarchical organization of Indonesian villages. Decisions were to be made with the consent of everyone, and not simply the majority; the various political factions would all have their say, though Sukarno would now play the part of village chief, with all the power that entailed.

In reality, guided democracy was the first step on the road to **authoritarian rule**, removing power from the elected cabinet and investing it instead with the presidency and a non-elected cabinet. Unsurprisingly, many people, both within and outside government, were suspicious of Sukarno's real motives, and lengthy protests in Sulawesi and Sumatra marred the early years of guided democracy.

Meanwhile, Sukarno began to forge strong ties with the **Soviet Union**, who appreciated his Marxist leanings and anti-Western foreign policy. They began financing the **Konfrontasi** ("Confrontation"), Sukarno's bid to wrest the northern Borneo states of Sabah, Sarawak and Brunei from neo-colonial Malaysia, which he saw as a puppet of the British. However, Sukarno was unwilling to commit too many troops to the jungles of Kalimantan, and his ambition to bring Sabah, Sarawak and Brunei into the Indonesian republic failed.

Sukarno's ties with the Soviet Union made him more sympathetic towards the views of Indonesia's **communist party**, the PKI, and he openly sided with them against the increasingly powerful **Indonesian army**. This led to the polarization of the entire parliament, with Sukarno and the communists on one side, and the army and its unlikely allies – including the Islamic NU and nationalist PNI – on the other. The political fighting in parliament was mirrored by pitched battles between the various factions on the streets of the capital, and law and order began to break down.

The Communist coup, 1965

Sukarno's political demise was accelerated by the still-not-completely-explained events of September 30, 1965, when a number of leading generals were taken from their homes at gunpoint to Halim Airport; their bodies were later discovered down a nearby well. Their abductors were a group of **communist** and other leftist sympathizers, who later claimed that they were only preventing an army-led coup. Of more significance, however, was the presence of President Sukarno at Halim. Although the rebels claimed he was only taken there for his own safety, it was hard not to see Sukarno as being in cahoots with them, fabricating the idea of an army coup as an excuse for getting rid of senior army personnel.

The communist rebels managed to occupy **Medan Merdeka** in the middle of Jakarta, controlling the telecommunications centre and the presidential palace situated nearby. Their success was shortlived, however. General Suharto, a senior member of the Indonesian army, rounded up those generals who weren't kidnapped and eventually took control of Medan Merdeka.

Suharto takes control, 1965–67

Though he lived until 1970, Sukarno's grip on power had almost completely slipped by the end of 1965, and for the remaining year of his presidency he ruled in name only, as **General Suharto** manoeuvred himself to the top of the political ladder. Communists throughout the archipelago became the victims of a massive Suharto-led purge, with the **slaughter of communist sympathizers** continuing until the early months of 1966. It was the bloodiest episode in Indonesia's history: most experts today reckon that at least 500,000 people lost their lives, although the official figure was a more modest 160,000. The army was now the dominant force in Indonesian politics. Struggling to keep a hold on power, tried desperately to weaken the might and authority of the armed forces but Suharto's response was to encourage a renewed outbreak of violence. On March 11, 1966, Sukarno was informed that unidentified troops were surrounding his palace, and in panic he fled to Bogor. Once there, Sukarno was persuaded to give Suharto full authority to restore order and protect the president by whatever means necessary.

The following year, pro-Suharto Adam Malik was made minister for foreign affairs, and quickly set about restoring **relations with the West** and loosening existing ties with communist China. Soon, aid began pouring back into Indonesia, rescuing the ailing economy and providing essential relief to thousands of the poorest in Indonesian society. Suharto now had popular support to go with his burgeoning political power and, in the new bourgeoisie, he found a powerful and secure foundation for his regime. On March 12, 1967, Sukarno was stripped of all his powers and Suharto was named **acting president**.

The New Order

Suharto dubbed his new regime the **New Order**. His first few years in power were seen as a brave new dawn, as the economy improved beyond all recognition and he managed to create a pluralistic society where religious intolerance had no place – providing people belonged to one of the five main faiths.

But this was not matched by political tolerance, and people were forced to live under a suffocating **dictatorial regime**, taking part in the charade of the so-called "festivals of democracy", the "elections" that took place every five years. Where beforehand there had been a multitude of **political parties**, Suharto reduced them to just three: the PPP (United Development Party) made up of the old Islamic parties; the PDI (Indonesian Democratic Party) made up largely of the old nationalist party, the PNI; and the government's own political vehicle, Golkar. The re-election of Suharto was a foregone conclusion, and critics were jailed and tortured. A huge underclass developed in rural areas and in slum districts on the outskirts of large cities. There was also widespread corruption throughout society, from the president down.

East Timor, independent since a revolution in Portugal had emancipated the tiny former colony in 1974, collapsed into civil war the following year as various factions failed to agree on whether the territory should become part of Indonesia. In the event, the decision was taken out of their hands by the Indonesians themselves, who invaded on Suharto's orders in December 1975. Despite strong condemnation from the United Nations, and regular Amnesty International reports of human rights abuses in East Timor, the US and Europe were unwilling to upset their new Southeast Asian ally. East Timor was incorporated into the Republic of Indonesia the following year.

The oil crisis of the 1970s raised the price of oil, then Indonesia's most lucrative export, significantly. This windfall lasted until 1983, allowing the government to use the **oil revenue** to create a sound industrial base founded on steel and natural gas production, oil refining and aluminium industries. Welfare measures were introduced, with 100,000 new schools built, and the 1980s also saw an increase of fifty percent in agricultural production. Yet the beneficiaries of Suharto's economic miracle were a small minority who lived in air-conditioned luxury in the big cities, while the majority continued to eke out a meagre existence in the rural areas of the country.

Suharto's downfall

Resentment against Suharto's regime grew throughout the 1990s, but he would probably have survived for a few more years if it hadn't been for the **currency crisis** that hit the region in the latter part of 1997, a crisis triggered by a run on the Thai baht. In a few dramatic months, the rupiah slipped in value from Rp2500 to the US dollar to nearly Rp9000. Prices of even the most basic of goods, such as fuel and food, rose five hundred percent.

The International Monetary Fund (**IMF**) promised to help Indonesia out of the crisis only after certain conditions had been met, including the removal of Suharto's family and friends from a number of senior and lucrative posts. Foreign investors lost all confidence in Suharto, and the rupiah went into freefall.

Pressure on the president was also growing from his own people, as many took to the streets to protest against his incompetence and demand greater political freedom. These **demonstrations**, initially fairly peaceful, grew more violent as the people's frustration increased, until a state of lawlessness ensued. For over a week, riots took place in all the main cities, buildings were set on fire and shops looted. The **Chinese community**, long resented in Indonesia for their domination of the economy and success in business, were targeted by the rioters for special persecution. Over 1200 people died in the mayhem that followed the May elections, until, on May 21, 1998, Suharto stepped down and his vice-president, BJ Habibie, took over.

Democracy

Despite promises to introduce sweeping reforms, many believed Habibie was dragging his feet over a number of issues, and, in early November 1998, more rioting occurred. The cry for "*Reformasi*" grew more voluble by the day as the rioters demanded the removal of the army from parliament, an end to corruption within government, the bringing to trial of Suharto on charges of mismanagement and corruption, and a return to democracy.

Despite the widespread mistrust of Habibie, he did lay the ground for the first **free and democratic elections** ever to be held in Indonesia, in which the Indonesian Democratic Party of Struggle, led by Megawati Sukarnoputri, the daughter of the country's first president, Sukarno, scored an easy victory. However, Indonesia's parliament decided she couldn't be trusted to lead – a decision that led to widespread rioting – and in the vote that followed, chose Abdurrahman Wahid, leader of the third-placed Islamic National Awakening Party, to be the country's first democratically elected president. To placate the rioters, Megawati was installed as vice-president.

Gus Dur – a president impeached

Though Gus Dur, as Abdurrahman Wahid was affectionately known, had an administration riddled with controversy, his achievements should not be overlooked. Perhaps the most important of these was the removal from his cabinet – and therefore from political power – of the army, but he also did much to reform the political process in Indonesia, nurturing the country's newly won democracy, making government much more accountable (as he would later find out to his cost), and giving the press greater freedoms.

However, his rather erratic leadership style and inability to make an impact on the problems that beset Indonesia soon lost him the support of the people. In particular, it was his failure to do anything about the rising tide of regional conflict that secured his downfall. With East Timor showing the way in 1999, other far-flung Indonesian provinces began to become more vocal – and violent – in their own **struggle for sovereignty**. Gus Dur's offers of greater autonomy were rejected by independence leaders, and the unrest continues to this day, with fighting in several areas having claimed thousands of lives.

Foreign jaunts in his vain quest to find foreign investors earned Gus Dur a reputation as a leader who holidayed while his country burned. His failure to bring Suharto to account for the massive corruption and human rights abuses that took place during his rule and the fact that the economy showed little signs of recovery from the collapse of 1998, meant dissatisfaction with the president's effectiveness began to be voiced. Corruption charges were levied against him in late 2000 (and subsequently dropped) and he was **impeached** in July 2001.

A few low-key protests followed, but Gus Dur refused to mobilize militias from his homeland of East Java, winning him praise from observers worldwide. His unwillingness, however, to step down following his impeachment, smacked of childish petulance, while his declaration on July 23 of a state of emergency (which parliament quickly rejected) and his plea to the army to support him against his impeachment, almost undid his good work by bringing the armed forces back into the political arena.

Megawati

While Gus Dur remained in the palace, his vice-president, Megawati Sukarnoputri, wasted little time in setting up her own administration, counting on a huge groundswell of support. At the start of her presidency there was considerable hope that Megawati, thanks largely to the popularity of her late father, would be able to heal the divisions in the country. A well-liked leader who enjoyed widespread support among the many different sections of society, including both Muslims and Christians, it was hoped she could heal Indonesia's wounds, unite the country and make real progress on social and economic issues, her popular mandate carrying her through any difficulties she would encounter.

Unfortunately, things didn't turn out quite like that. While some progress was made in economic and legal spheres, overall her rule was characterized by procrastination and ineffectiveness. She failed to make any great inroads in the separatist problems of Papua and Aceh and, perhaps more worryingly, she presided over a rise in **Islamic terrorism**, culminating in the Bali bombing of 2002, when twin bombs in a nightclub and an Irish bar in Kuta left 202 dead and scores more injured. Further bombings in Jakarta, at a hotel in August 2004 that killed twelve people, and at the Australian Embassy in September of that year that left nine dead, both believed to be the work of Jemaah Islamiyah, the group allegedly behind the Bali bombing, have confirmed, at least in many Indonesians' minds, that this Islamic terrorist organization are able to cause devastation and mayhem at will, with the government powerless to prevent further tragedies. Their activities remain one of the major problems still besetting the country to this day.

Ironically, however, perhaps Megawati's greatest achievement was also instrumental in her downfall. The foundations she lay for Indonesia's first ever direct presidential election meant that, despite the logistical problems of having 150 million registered voters (of which a massive 114 million voted) spread across 14,000 islands, they passed off peacefully and were hailed as a great success by European election monitors. At the end, however, Megawati lost the vote, polling just 39 percent – 22 percent less than her rival, Susilo Bambang Yudhoyono.

Susilo Bambang Yudhoyono and the future

Susilo Bambang Yudhoyono, or SBY as he is more commonly known among Indonesians, is a retired general and had already served as a minister in both Gus Dur's cabinet – where he lost his job after refusing to declare a state of emergency following calls for Dur's impeachment – and Megawati's, where he again lost his job, this time stepping down as security minister following a public spat with the president.

Fortunately for SBY, his actions on both occasions led the Indonesian people to view him not as a quitter, but as a man of principle. Furthermore, as a leading figure in the fight against terror in the wake of the Bali bombing, his reputation is that of a decisive and proactive leader, and thus as a welcome breath of fresh air after the hesitant and ineffective tenure of Megawati.

But as with his predecessor, he comes to the head of a country that is beset by problems, and though it is clear from his early speeches that he talks a good fight – with promises to "roll up his sleeves" and tackle the triple evils of corruption, nepotism and terrorism that so hamper his country – it is hard to overestimate the challenges he faces. The devastating **tsunami** (see p.315) that hit his country just one hundred days into his presidency has only added to these challenges. With more than sixteen percent of his population still living below the poverty line, and the separatist wars in Aceh and Papua still far from being resolved, the "Thinking General" will need to utilize every ounce of his talents, not to mention a huge slice of luck, if his tenure is to be a success.

Religion

Indonesia has a predominantly Muslim population, though with significant Buddhist (the Chinese populations in the large cities and in West Kalimantan), Hindu and animist minorities (in Bali, West Papua, Sumatra, Kalimantan and other remote outposts). There are pockets of Christianity all over the archipelago, from the Batak people of North Sumatra to the tribes of West Papua, though their numbers are growing. For an introduction to all these faiths, see "Religion", p.69–71. Yet the major faiths in the archipelago bear striking differences to their counterparts in other parts of the world because religion in Indonesia is dynamic, not dogmatic, adapted over the centuries to incorporate rituals and beliefs of existing faiths, in particular indigenous animism.

Indonesia is the largest **Islamic** nation in the world. The northernmost province of Aceh, which received Islam directly from India, is still the most orthodox area, whereas Muslims in the rest of the archipelago follow a style of Islam that has been syncretized with animism, Buddhism and Hinduism. Nearly all Indonesian Muslims are followers of the Sunni sect. Women in veils or full *purdah* are a rare sight in Indonesia, and men are only allowed two wives, as opposed to four in Arabian countries, though just one wife is the norm.

Animism is still the predominant faith in some of the villages of the outlying islands, particularly Sumatra, Kalimantan and West Papua. The rituals and beliefs vary significantly between each of these islands. Many of these ancient animist beliefs permeate each of the major religions, and many Indonesian people, no matter what faith they profess, still perform animist rituals.

Despite certain obvious similarities, Balinese **Agama Hinduism** differs dramatically from Indian and Nepalese Hinduism. At its root lies the understanding that the natural and supernatural world is composed of opposing forces. Positive forces, or *dharma*, are represented by the gods and need to be honoured with offerings, dances, paintings and sculptures, fine earthly abodes (temples) and rituals. The malevolent forces, *adharma*, which manifest themselves as earth demons and cause sickness, death and volcanic eruptions, need to be neutralized with elaborate rituals and special offerings. All Balinese gods are manifestations of the Supreme Being, Sanghyang Widi Wasa, a deity who is only ever represented by an empty throne-shrine, which stands in the holiest corner of every temple. Sanghyang Widi Wasa's three main aspects manifest themselves as the Hindu trinity: Brahma, Vishnu and Shiva. Siwa's consort is the terrifying goddess Durga, whose Balinese personality is the gruesome widow-witch Rangda, queen of the demons.

Traditional dance and music

Given the enormous cultural and ethnic mix that makes up Indonesia, it's hardly surprising that the range of traditional music and dance across the archipelago is so vast. Best-known are the highly stylized and mannered classical dance performances in Java and Bali, accompanied by the gamelan orchestra.

Every step of these dances is minutely orchestrated, and the merest wink of an eye, arch of an eyebrow and angle of a finger has meaning and significance. The tradition remains vibrant, passed down by experts to often very young pupils. Ubud on Bali and Yogyakarta on Java are the centres for these dances, with shortened performances staged in several venues every night for Western visitors. Yogya is also the main place in Indonesia to catch a performance of **wayang kulit**, shadow puppet plays.

Gamelan

A **gamelan** is an ensemble of tuned percussion, consisting mainly of gongs, metallophones and drums. Gamelan instruments may be made of bronze, iron, brass, wood or bamboo, with wooden frames, which are often intricately carved and painted.

The largest bronze gamelans in Indonesia are found in **Central Java**. A complete Javanese gamelan is made up of two sets of instruments, one in each of two scales – the five-note *laras slendro* and the seven-note *laras pelog*. The two sets are laid out with the corresponding instruments at right angles to each other. Various hanging and mounted gongs are arranged at the back and provide the structure and form of the music. In the middle, the metallophones play the central melody. At the front are the more complex instruments, which lead and elaborate the melody. These include metallophones, a wooden xylophone, spike fiddle, bamboo flute and zither. The full ensemble also includes vocalists – a male chorus and female solo singers – and is led by the drummer in the centre of the gamelan. Although a large gamelan may be played by as many as thirty **musicians**, there is neither a conductor nor any visual cues, as the players all sit facing the same way. Gamelan musicians learn all the instruments and so develop a deep understanding of the music plus great flexibility in ensemble playing. It is a communal form of music-making – there are no soloists or virtuosos. Most village halls and neighbourhoods in Central Java have a gamelan for use by the local community, and the majority of schoolchildren learn basic gamelan pieces.

Villages in Bali boast several gamelans owned by the local music club. The club members meet in the evenings to rehearse, after earning their living as farmers, craftsmen or civil servants. Gamelan playing is traditionally considered a part of every man's education, as important as the art of rice growing or cooking ceremonial food. When the Dutch took control of Bali in the early twentieth century, the island's courts all but disappeared. The court gamelans were sold or taken to the villages, where they were melted down to make new gamelans for the latest style that was taking Bali by storm: **kebyar**, a fast, dynamic music, full of dramatic contrasts, changes of tempo and sudden loud outbursts. It is this dynamic new virtuoso style that makes much Balinese gamelan music today sound so different from the Javanese form.

The sound of Sundanese (West Javanese) **degung** is arguably the most accessible of all gamelan music to Western ears. Its musical structures are clear and well defined, and the timbres of the instruments blend delicately with one another without losing any of their integrity or individuality. The ensemble is small, consisting only of a few instruments, but includes the usual range of gongs and metallophones found in all gamelan.

By Jenny Heaton and Simon Steptoe

Books

In the selection of books below, where a book is published in the UK and the US, the UK publisher is given first, followed by the US one; the abbreviation "o/p" means "out of print".

Nigel Barley *Not a Hazardous Sport* (Penguin). Humourous, double-sided culture-shock tale, as the anthropologist author persuades craftsmen from Sulawesi to return to London with him and build a traditional Torajan rice barn for the British Museum.

Lawrence and Lorne Blair *Ring of Fire* (Bantam). Possibly the definitive account of a tour around the Indonesian archipelago. The photos are great, the tales are occasionally tall and certainly not lacking in genuine passion for the country and its inhabitants.

Guy Buckles *Dive Sites of Indonesia* (New Holland). Exhaustively researched, attractive, up-to-date guide with strong practical details.

Vern Cook (ed.) *Bali Behind the Seen: Recent Fiction from Bali* (Darma Printing, Australia). Interesting collection of short stories by contemporary Balinese and Javanese writers.

Cubitt & Whitten *Wild Indonesia* (New Holland). Plenty of good pictures and text in this overview of Indonesia's natural history, including coverage of national parks.

Jacques Dumarcay *The Temples of Java* (OUP Asia). Slim but entertaining rundown of all the major historical temple complexes in Java.

Fred B. Eisemann Jr *Bali: Sekala and Niskala Vols 1 and 2* (Periplus, Singapore). The fascinating and admirably wide-ranging cultural and anthropological essays of a contemporary American, thirty years resident in Bali.

Anna Forbes *Unbeaten Tracks in Islands of the Far East* (OUP Asia). Island life in remote corners of Maluku and Nusa Tenggara as observed by the resourceful wife of nineteenth-century naturalist Henry Forbes.

John Gillow and Barry Dawson *Traditional Indonesian Textiles* (Thames & Hudson). Beautifully photographed and accessible introduction to the *ikat* and batik fabrics of the archipelago.

Rio Helmi and Barbara Walker *Bali Style* (Thames & Hudson). Sumptuously photographed, glossy volume celebrating all things Balinese, from the humblest bamboo craftwork to the island's most fabulous buildings.

Paul Jepson and Rosie Ounsted *Birding Indonesia: A Bird-watcher's Guide to the World's Largest Archipelago* (Periplus, Singapore). Excellent introduction to the subject, with plenty of photographs and practical detail.

Garret Kam *Perceptions of Paradise: Images of Bali in the Arts* (Yayasan Dharma Seni Neka Museum, Bali). One of the best introductions to Balinese art, with helpful sections on traditions and practices, and plenty of full-colour plates.

Hugh Mabbett *The Balinese* (January Books, New Zealand). Accessible collection of anecdotal essays on contemporary Balinese life, from the role of women to the impact of tourism.

Anna Matthews *Night of Purnama* (o/p). Evocative and moving description of village life and characters of the early 1960s, focusing on events in Iseh and the surrounding villages, from the first eruption of Gunung Agung until 1963.

Jean McKinnon *Vessels of Life: Lombok Earthenware* (Saritaksu, Indonesia). Fabulously photographed and exhaustive book about Sasak life, pottery techniques and the lives of the women potters.

George Monbiot *Poisoned Arrows: An Investigative Journey Through Indonesia* (Joseph). The author travels through some of the less well-known areas of West Papua, researching the effects of the Indonesian government's transmigration policy.

Kal Muller *Underwater Indonesia: A Guide to the World's Best Diving* (Periplus, Singapore). This is the must-have handbook for anybody planning to dive in Indonesia. Exquisitely photographed, with useful maps.

Sri Owen *Indonesian Regional Cooking* (St Martin's Press). Relatively few recipes, but plenty of background.

Christopher VV Parnell *Hell's Prisoner: The Shocking True Story of an Innocent Man Jailed for Eleven Years in Indonesia's Most Notorious Prisons* (Mainstream). Doing pretty much exactly what it says on the tin, this is *Midnight Express* Indonesia-style.

MC Ricklefs *A History of Modern Indonesia Since c.1300* (Macmillan). The most thorough study of Indonesian history, Ricklefs' three-hundred-page account is written in a rather dry and scholarly style and, with its comprehensive index, is probably best used as a textbook to dip into rather than as a work to be read from start to finish.

Neville Shulman *Zen Explorations in Remotest New Guinea: Adventures in the Jungles and Mountains of Irian Jaya* (Summersdale). Not a drop of rain escapes without some obscure explanatory proverb or quotation, but even if you find his determination to find the zen in everything irritating, you can't escape the author's genuine enthusiasm for his journey.

Tara Sosrowardoyo, Peter Schoppert and Soedarmadji Damais *Java Style* (Thames and Hudson). Sumptuous volume, evocatively photographed, with illuminating descriptions of buildings and design all across the island.

John G Taylor *Indonesia's Forgotten War: The Hidden History of East Timor* (Zed Books/Humanities Press). Clear and incisive account of the disastrous events in East Timor, from the fifteenth century to the present.

Adrian Vickers *Bali: A Paradise Created* (Periplus, Singapore). Detailed, intelligent and highly readable account of the outside world's perception of Bali, the development of tourism and how events inside and outside the country have shaped the Balinese view of themselves.

Alfred Russell Wallace *The Malay Archipelago* (o/p). A thoroughly readable account of the eight years that British naturalist Wallace spent in Indonesia collecting and studying wildlife during the mid-nineteenth century.

Simon Winchester *Krakatoa: The Day the World Exploded* (Penguin). Analysis of the huge volcanic eruption of 1883, and its effects on Indonesia and the wider world.

Language

The national language of Indonesia is Bahasa Indonesia, although there are also over 250 native languages spoken throughout the archipelago. Bahasa Indonesia is a form of Bahasa Malay and, because it's written in Roman script, has no tones and uses a fairly straightforward grammar, it's relatively easy to learn. If you need more help, try ***Indonesian: A Rough Guide Phrasebook***.

Pronunciation

a as in a cross between **fa**ther and **cu**p
e sometimes as in **a**long; or as in p**ay**; or as in g**e**t; or sometimes omitted (**selamat** pronounced "slamat")
i either as in bout**i**que; or as in p**i**t
o either as in h**o**t; or as in c**o**ld
u as in b**oo**t
ai as in f**i**ne
au as in h**ow**
Most consonants are pronounced as in English, with the following exceptions:
c as in **ch**eap
g always hard as in **g**irl
k hard, as in English, except at the end of the word, when you should stop just short of pronouncing it.

Greetings and basic phrases

If addressing a **married woman**, it's polite to use the respectful term *Ibu* or *Nyonya*; if addressing a **married man** use *Bapak*. *Mau ke mana*? (literally "want to where") is the usual opening gambit in any conversation, and means "**where are you going**?" The proper reply is *mau ke...* (want to go to...) followed by your intended destination. Other good answers are **saya jalan jalan** (I'm just walking) or *saya makan angin* (literally "I'm eating the wind"). When asked **if you can speak Indonesian**, *bisa berbicara bahasa Indonesia*?, the usual response is *saya belum lancar* (I'm not yet fluent) or *sedikit sedikit* (just a little); the less confident should go for *ma'af tidak bisa* (sorry not at all).

Good morning (5–11am)	Selamat pagi
Good day (11am–3pm)	Selamat siang
Good afternoon (3–7pm)	Selamat sore
Good evening (after 7pm)	Selamat malam
Good night	Selamat tidur
Goodbye	Selamat tinggal
See you later	Sampai jumpa lagi
Have a good trip	Selamat jalan
Enjoy your meal	Selamat makan
Cheers/Enjoy your drink	Selamat minum
How are you?	Apa kabar?
I'm fine	Bagus/Kabar baik
Please (requesting)	Tolong
Please (offering)	Silakan
Thank you (very much)	Terima kasih (banyak)
You're welcome	Sama sama
Sorry/Excuse me	Ma'af
No worries/Never mind	Tidak apa apa
Yes	Ya
No (with noun)	Bukan
Not (with verb)	Tidak (sometimes pronounced "tak")
What is your name?	Siapa nama anda?
My name is...	Nama saya...
Where are you from?	Dari mana?
I come from...	Saya dari...
Do you speak English?	Bisa bicara bahasa Inggris?
I don't understand	Saya tidak mengerti
Do you have...?	Ada...?
I want/would like...	Saya mau...
I don't want it/No thanks	Tidak mau
What is this/that?	Apa ini/itu?
When?	Kapan?
Where?	Dimana?
Boyfriend or girlfriend	Pacar
Foreigner	Turis
Friend	Teman
Men/women	Laki-laki/perempuan or wanita

Adjectives

Another	Satu lagi
Beautiful	Cantik
Big/small	Besar/kecil
Clean/dirty	Bersih/kotor
Cold	Dingin

Expensive/ inexpensive	Mahal/murah
Good/bad	Bagus/buruk
Unwell	Sakit
Married/single	Kawin/bujang
Open/closed	Buka/tutup
Very much/a lot	Banyak

Getting around

Where is the...?	dimana...?
I would like to go to the...	Saya mau pergi ke...
...airport	...lapangan terbang
...bank	...bank
...beach	...pantai
...bemo/bus station	...terminal
...city/city centre	...kota
...hospital	...sakit
...hotel	...losmen
...market	...pasar
...pharmacy	...apotik
...police station	...kantor polisi
...post office	...kantor pos
...shop	...toko
...telephone office	...wartel/kantor telkom
Bicycle	Sepeda
Bus	Bis
Car	Mobil
Entrance/exit	Masuk/keluar
Ferry	Ferry
Motorbike	Sepeda motor
Taxi	Taksi
Ticket	Karcis
To come/go	Datang/pergi
How far?	Berapa kilometre?
How much is the fare to...?	Berapa harga karcis ke...?
Where is this bemo going?	Kemana bemo pergi?
Stop!	Estop!
Here	Disini
Right	Kanan
Left	Kiri
Straight on	Terus

Accommodation

How much is...?	Berapa harga...?
...single room	...kamar untuk satu orang
...double room	...kamar untuk dua orang
Can I look at the room?	Boleh saya lihat kamar?
Is there...?	Apakah ada...?
...air conditioning	...AC
...bathroom	...kamar mandi
...breakfast	...makan pagi
...fan	...kipas
...hot water	...air panas
...mosquito net	...kelambu nyamuk
...toilet	...kamar kecil/wc (pronounced "way say")

Numbers

Zero	Nol/kosong
1	Satu
2	Dua
3	Tiga
4	Empat
5	Lima
6	Enam
7	Tujuh
8	Delapan
9	Sembilan
10	Sepuluh
11, 12, 13, etc	Sebelas, duabelas, tigabelas
20	Duapuluh
21, 22, 23, etc	Duapuluh satu, duapuluh dua, duapuluh, tiga
30, 40, 50, etc	Tigapuluh, Empatpuluh, Limapuluh
100	Seratus
200	Duaratus
1000	Seribu
2000	Duaribu
10,000	Sepuluhribu
20,000	Duapuluhribu
100, 000	Seratusribu
1,000,000	Sejuta
2,000,000	Dua juta

Time and days of the week

What time is it?	Jam berapa?
It's three o'clock	jam tiga
...ten past four	jam empat lewat sepuluh
...quarter to five	jam lima kurang seperempat
...six-thirty	jam setengah tujuh (literally "half to seven")
...in the morning	...pagi
...in the afternoon	...sore
...pm/in the evening	...malam
Today/tomorrow	Hari ini/besok
Yesterday	Kemarin

Monday	Hari Senin	**Friday**	Hari Jumat
Tuesday	Hari Selasa	**Saturday**	Hari Sabtu
Wednesday	Hari Rabu	**Sunday**	Hari Minggu
Thursday	Hari Kamis		

4.1

Java

One of the most populous places in all of Asia, **Java** is characterized by great natural beauty. Its central spine is dominated by hundreds of volcanoes, many of which are still very evidently active, their fertile slopes supporting a landscape of glimmering ricefields spotted with countless small villages. To the south of this mountainous backbone is the homeland of the ethnic Javanese and the epicentre of their arts, culture and language, epitomized by the royal courts of **Yogyakarta** and **Solo**. Still steeped in traditional dance, music and art, these two cities are the mainstay of Java's tourist industry and offer first-rate facilities for travellers. They also provide excellent bases from which to explore the giant ninth-century Buddhist temple **Borobudur**, and the equally fascinating **Prambanan** complex, a contemporary Hindu site. To the east, the huge volcanic massif of **Gunung Bromo** is the other major stop on most travellers' itineraries, not least for the sunrise walk to its summit. But there are plenty more volcanic landscapes to explore, including the coloured lakes of the windswept **Dieng Plateau**, and the world's most famous – and destructive – volcano, **Krakatau**, off the west coast of Java. Less visited but very worthwhile destinations abound in the mountains around the West Java capital of **Bandung**. Aside from Yogyakarta (often refered to as "Yogya"), Java's cities are not that enticing, but **Jakarta**, the chaotic sprawl that is Indonesia's capital, does boast several worthwhile museums. And once you've exhausted the pleasures of Java you can move easily on to neighbouring islands – Sumatra is just ninety minutes' ferry ride from Merak in the west; Bali a mere half hour from Banyuwangi in the east.

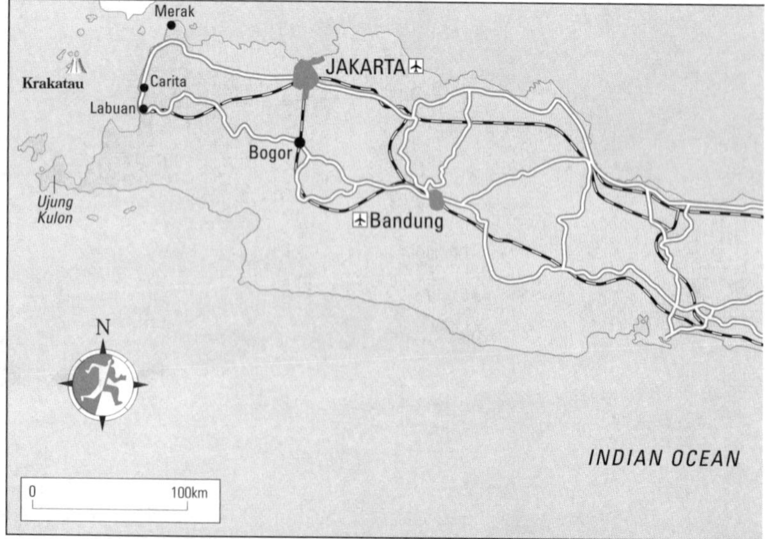

Jakarta

Bounded to the north by the Java Sea and the south by the low Bogor Hills, Indonesia's overwhelming capital, **JAKARTA**, is one of the fastest-growing cities in the world. From a mere 900,000 inhabitants in 1945, the population is well over thirteen million (and nearer twenty million if you take into account the greater urban region known as Jabotabek) and continues to grow at a rate of 200,000 every year. The capital sprawls over 656 square kilometres of northern Java. Unfortunately, few foreign visitors find the city as alluring as the local population, and down the years Jakarta has been much derided. Yet the suburb of **Kota** in the north, the former heart of the old Dutch city, still retains a number of beautiful historic buildings, as does the neighbouring port of **Sunda Kelapa**. The capital also has some of the country's finest museums, including the **Maritime Museum**, the **Wayang Museum** and the **National Museum**.

The site of modern-day Jakarta first entered the history books in the twelfth century, when the Pajajarans, a Sundanese kingdom based in West Java, established a major trading port at Sunda Kelapa and held on to it for over three hundred years. In the early sixteenth century, the Islamic Sultanate of Banten, 50km to the west, invaded the city and renamed it **Jayakarta**, "City of Victory"; the date of their invasion, June 22, 1527, is still celebrated as the city's birthday today. By 1619, the Dutch had won control of the city, and the newly named **Batavia** became the administrative centre of their vast trading empire; it was also given a facelift, with a new network of canals and a host of imposing civic buildings. When the Japanese invaded Batavia on March 5, 1942, the city was once again re-titled Jayakarta, or **Jakarta** for short. Immediately after World War II, a British force engaged the new Republic of Indonesia. Dutch power declined, and many of their buildings were pulled down. In 1949, Sukarno entered Jakarta, amid scenes of wild jubilation, to become the first president of the Republic. In the following two decades, ugly, Soviet-style monuments sprouted like warts on the face of the city and huge shantytowns emerged on the fringes to house economic migrants from across the archipelago, a population shift that continues to this day. Since then, Jakarta has continued to be the focus of Indonesia's changing political face, most dramatically in recent times with the **demonstrations** against Suharto in May 1998, during which time the city was

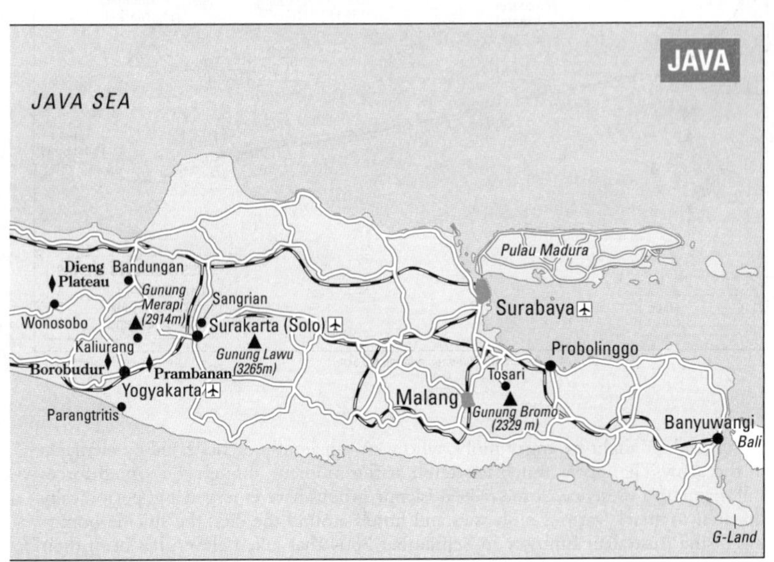

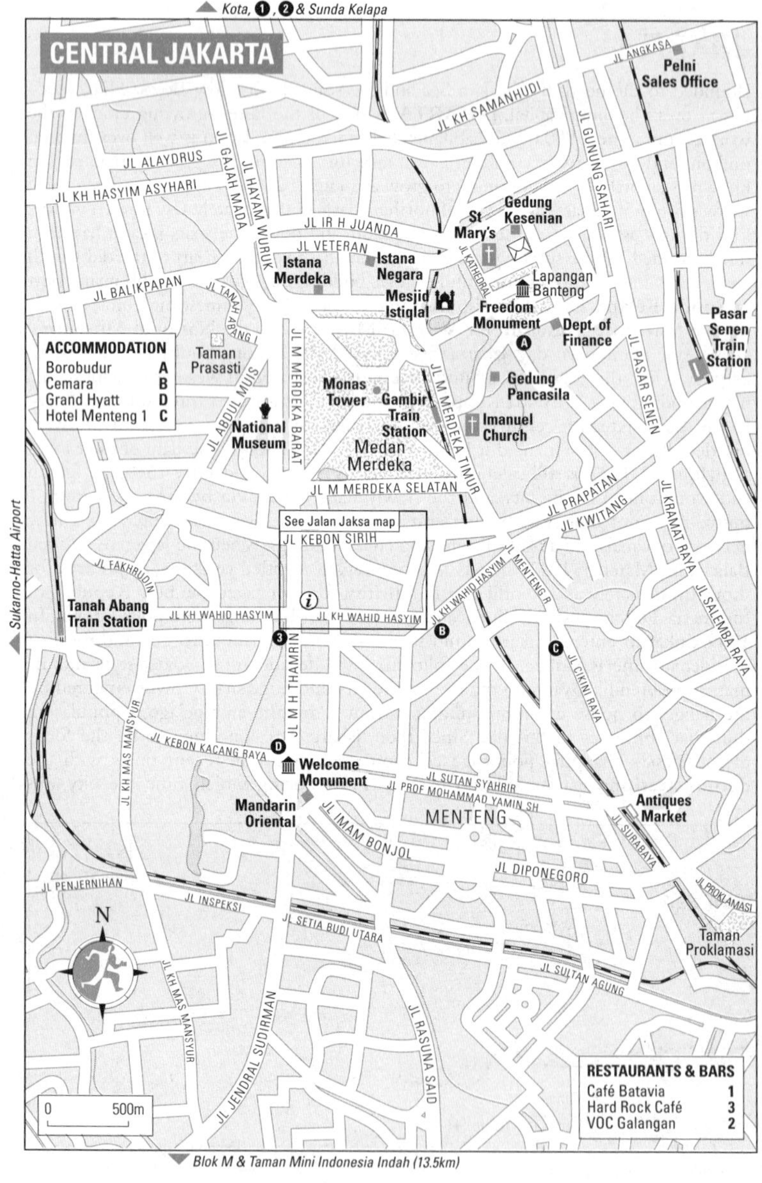

looted and set alight by angry mobs, who were apparently orchestrated by elements in the army. The city is much less tense at the moment, though the armed forces still maintain a presence. Some radical Islamic groups have emerged and periodically threaten to attack various embassies and hotels around the city; the suicide bombing of the Australian Embassy in September 2004 that killed eleven has been their greatest success so far. That said, most of the city remains stoically unperturbed by their presence, and indeed the city is progressing forward on many fronts, not least in regards to its huge congestion problem. The recent installation of the Busway, an express busline running north to south through the Jakarta, is a welcome introduction and the first of many planned improvements, including eventually, perhaps, the long-talked about MRT system.

Arrival

By air

Both international and domestic flights into Jakarta land at **Sukarno-Hatta Airport**, 13km west of the city centre. The baggage reclamation area has currency exchange booths and hotel booking desks. Through customs, there's a small **tourist office** and more exchange booths, most of which close at 10pm; rates are 25 percent lower than in the city centre. If you need a **hotel** at the airport, head for the *Aspac* (☎021/5590008; ⑤) at terminal 2E.

DAMRI buses run from the airport every thirty minutes from 6am to 9.30pm (45min; Rp10,000) to the central Gambir train station – a fifteen-minute walk from the backpackers' enclave of Jalan Jaksa – and also to Blok M in the south, Rawamangun (east) and Kemayoram (north), with the occasional one heading straight to Bogor (Rp14,000). To find these, turn left out of Arrivals and walk about 200m to the bus stand. With **taxis**, in addition to the metered fare, passengers must also pay the toll fees (about Rp7000) plus another Rp2500 guaranteed service fee; all of which means a taxi ride from the airport to Jalan Jaksa costs approximately Rp70,000. Recommended taxi firms include Steady Safe, Kosti, Blue Bird Group and Citra.

By train

There are four central train stations (and dozens of minor suburban ones), of which **Gambir** station is the most popular and convenient, being just a fifteen-minute walk from Jalan Jaksa or Rp5000 by bajaj (motorized rickshaw). To reach Jalan Jaksa on foot (15min), exit the station facing the National Monument and turn left. Follow the overhead railway line as far as Jalan Kebon Sirih where the traffic's coming from your right. Turn right and proceed for 300m or so until you see the arch reading "Kawasan Wisata Malam" at the north end of Jaksa.

Of the other stations, **Kota**, near old Batavia, is the busiest. Although Kota is on the same line as Gambir, some of the trains departing from Kota do not stop at Gambir, and vice versa. To reach Jalan Jaksa from Kota, catch the Busway (which leaves from outside the station) to Sarinah (Rp2500), about a five-minute walk away from Jalan Jaksa along Jalan KH Wahid Hasyim. From there, the Busway continues south to the Welcome Monument and Blok M.

By ferry

All Pelni ferries dock at **Tanjung Priok harbour**, 500m from the bus station of the same name. For Jalan Jaksa, catch **bus** #P145 from the harbour bus station and alight at the junction of Jalan Kebon Sirih and Jalan MH Thamrin. A taxi to Jalan Jaksa should cost Rp30,000 or so. Travelling by ferry from Borneo, the majority of vessels dock at the Sunda Kelapa harbour, near the Kota district. Walk for twenty minutes or catch one of the light blue minivans (Rp1000) to the Kota bus station, then take the Busway down to the Sarinah stop, a five-minute walk away from Jalan Jaksa along Jalan Wahid Hasyim.

By bus

Jakarta's three major **bus stations** are all inconveniently situated. Each serves different destinations, although there are overlaps: buses to and from Sumatra, for example, arrive at both Kalideres and Pulo Gadung stations.

Moving on from Jakarta

For addresses and telephone numbers of airlines, embassies and travel agents in Jakarta, see "Listings", p.274. For details of transport from the capital, see "Travel details", p.486.

By plane

All scheduled **flights**, both domestic and international, use **Sukarno-Hatta Airport** (☎021/5505000). DAMRI buses depart for the airport from Gambir station every thirty minutes from 6am to 6pm (45min; Rp10,000). A taxi from town to the airport costs from Rp50,000.

By train

Most of the **trains** travelling to West and Central Java destinations begin their journeys at **Gambir** station, including those to Yogya, Surakarta (Solo), Bogor and Bandung. There are two special offices (daily 7.30am–7pm) selling tickets for the luxury trains, such as the Parahiyangan Express to Bandung and the Argolawu Express to Yogya and Solo.

Of the other stations, **Kota**, near old Batavia, is the busiest. Although Kota is on the same line as Gambir, some of the trains departing from Kota do not stop at Gambir, and vice versa. To reach Kota from Jalan Jaksa, catch the Busway (Rp2500) to Sarinah, about a five-minute walk away. From there, buses continue south to the Welcome Monument. The other two train stations, Tanah Abang and Pasar Senen, are further out of town, have fewer services and rarely see tourists.

By ferry

Pelni ferries sail from **Tanjung Priok harbour**. Bus #P125 runs from opposite the Sari Pan Pacific to Tanjung Priok bus station, 500m from the harbour. Allow at least 75 minutes for your journey from Jalan Jaksa. Tanjung Priok is on the circuits of Pelni boats *KM Bukit Raya*, *KM Bukit Siguntang*, *KM Dobonsolo*, *KM Labobar*, *KM Kelud*, *KM Lambelu*, *KM Lawit*, *KM Sirimau*, *KM Sinabung*, *KM Nogapulu*, *KM Leuser* and *KM Ciremai*. For details, see "Getting around", p.237 and "Travel details", p.486. For the latest timetable, call in at the fifth floor of the Pelni head office at Jl Gajah Mada 14. The Pelni booking office is at Jl Angkasa 18 (Mon–Thurs 8am–noon & 1–2.30pm, Fri 8–11.30am & 1–2.30pm); catch bus #15 or #P15 to Pasar Senen station, then bus #10 to Angkasa.

The **Kapuas Express ferry** runs from Godown 2 at the **Sunda Kelapa harbour** to Pontianak in Kalimantan. Tickets can be bought from PT Egel Tripelti, Rajawali Condominium Edelweiss Tower, Jl Rajawali Selatan 1/1b (☎021/6409288). The harbourmaster's office is on the second floor of the Departemen Perhubungan at the end of Baruna III in Sunda Kelapa.

By bus

The capital has good **bus** connections to all points in Java, and many cities on neighbouring islands, too. There's usually a range of prices for every destination, depending on the type of bus you're travelling in. Tickets bought from an agency in town are more expensive, but as some of the buses leave from right outside the agency, you're saved a trip to the bus station, all of which are inconveniently located. If your bus does depart from the station, leave at least an hour and a half to get from the city centre to your terminal. It's advisable not to try to travel by bus at the end of Ramadan.

Most buses to Central Java, East Java and Bali depart from Pulo Gadung station. Buses to West Java, including Bogor and Bandung, use Rambutan Kampung station, 18km south of the city centre near Taman Mini. As an alternative means of reaching Bogor, catch #AC10 southbound to Universitas Kristen Indonesia (UKI) at Cawang and from there a local bus to the Bogor terminal. Buses to Carita (for Krakatau) and Labuan leave from the Kalideres station, 15km west of the city centre; buses #78 and #64 run between Jalan MH Thamrin and Kalideres.

Most buses from Central Java, East Java and Bali pull into **Pulo Gadung** station, 12km to the east of the city. To get to the centre of town, catch bus #AC08, which passes the western end of Jalan Cokroaminoto in Menteng, from where you can take a bajaj from the Batak church to the south end of Jalan Jaksa (ask for **Ujung Jalan Jaksa**). Buses from West Java use **Kampung Rambutan** station, 18km south of the city centre near Taman Mini. Buses #P10, #P11, #P16 and #AC10 all ply the route between Rambutan and the stop opposite the *Sari Pan Pacific Hotel* on Jalan Thamrin (1hr 30min). Buses from the west of Sumatra arrive at a third station, **Kalideres**, 15km west of the city centre. Buses #78 and #64 run from here to Jalan Thamrin.

City transport and information

The new **Busway** system is the only bus service in Jakarta with designated stops. It runs between the sightseeing heart of the city at Kota and the nightlife centre of Blok M, and as such is the easiest and most useful service for tourists in the city. With its own designated bus lane, it's also far quicker than other transport services. You buy your ticket (Rp2500 regardless of distance travelled) before boarding from the ticket office at one of the stations. Other useful stations include Sarinah (for Jalan Jaksa) and Monumen (for the Monas Tower and National Museum).

Other **buses** serving the city operate a set-fare system, regardless of distance, but prices depend on the type of bus. The cheapest are the small, **pale-blue minivans**, which operate out of Kota bus station (their numbers are always preceded by the letter "M") and the **large coaches** found all over the city; they all charge Rp1000. Air-con buses cost Rp3500. To alight from the bus, hail the driver or conductor with "*kiri*!" (left) or rap the overhead rail with a coin.

Now that the traditional cycle-rickshaws, or becak, have been banned from Jakarta, the two-stroke motorized rickshaws, or **bajaj** (pronounced "ba-jais"), have monopolized the city's backstreets. Be sure to bargain very, very hard and remember that bajaj are banned from major thoroughfares such as Jalan Thamrin, so you might get dropped off a long way from your destination. A sample fare, from Jalan Jaksa to the post office, would be Rp4000.

Jakarta's **taxis** are numerous and, providing you know your way around the city, inexpensive. There are two types of fare being charged: *tarif lama* (old fare) and *tarif baru* (new fare), the latter with a standard flag-fall of Rp4000. **Tourist information** can be found in the Jakarta Theatre building, opposite Sarinah's department store on Jalan Wahid Hasyim (Mon–Fri 10am–7pm; ☎021/3142067).

Accommodation

Jakarta has relatively few budget hotels, so they fill up fast and should be booked ahead – prices start at Rp20,000 for a dorm bed. Nearly all budget places are located on or around **Jalan Jaksa**, the city's travellers' enclave to the south of Medan Merdeka in the heart of Jakarta. **Jalan Wahid Hasyim**, at the southern end of Jalan Jaksa, plays host to a number of mid-priced places, while the best and most expensive hotels in the city huddle around the Welcome Monument on **Jalan Thamrin**, to the southwest of Sarinah's department store.

Jalan Jaksa and around

Bloemsteen Jl Kebon Sirih Timur I/174 ☎021/325389. One of the cleaner hostels around Jaksa, with spacious rooms, good bathrooms, and a pleasant, sunny balcony. ❶

Borneo Jl Kebon Sirih Barat 35–37 ☎021/3140095. Large, ramshackle and friendly hostel. ❶–❷

Bumi Johar Jl Johar 17–19 (☎021/3145746). Two minutes' walk from Jl Jaksa, this small hotel affords comfortable rooms with a/c and TV. ❻–❼

Cipta Jl Wahid Hasyim 53 ☎021/3904701. Reasonable mid-priced hotel facing the south end of Jl Jaksa; every room is en suite, with a/c. ❻

Delima Jl Jaksa 5 ☎021/337026. The oldest of the city's hostels, though looking tired now and some rooms could be cleaner. Dorms Rp20,000. ❶

Djody Hotel Jl Jaksa 35 ☎021/3151404. Fair but unexceptional hostel in a central position on Jl Jaksa. ❶–❸

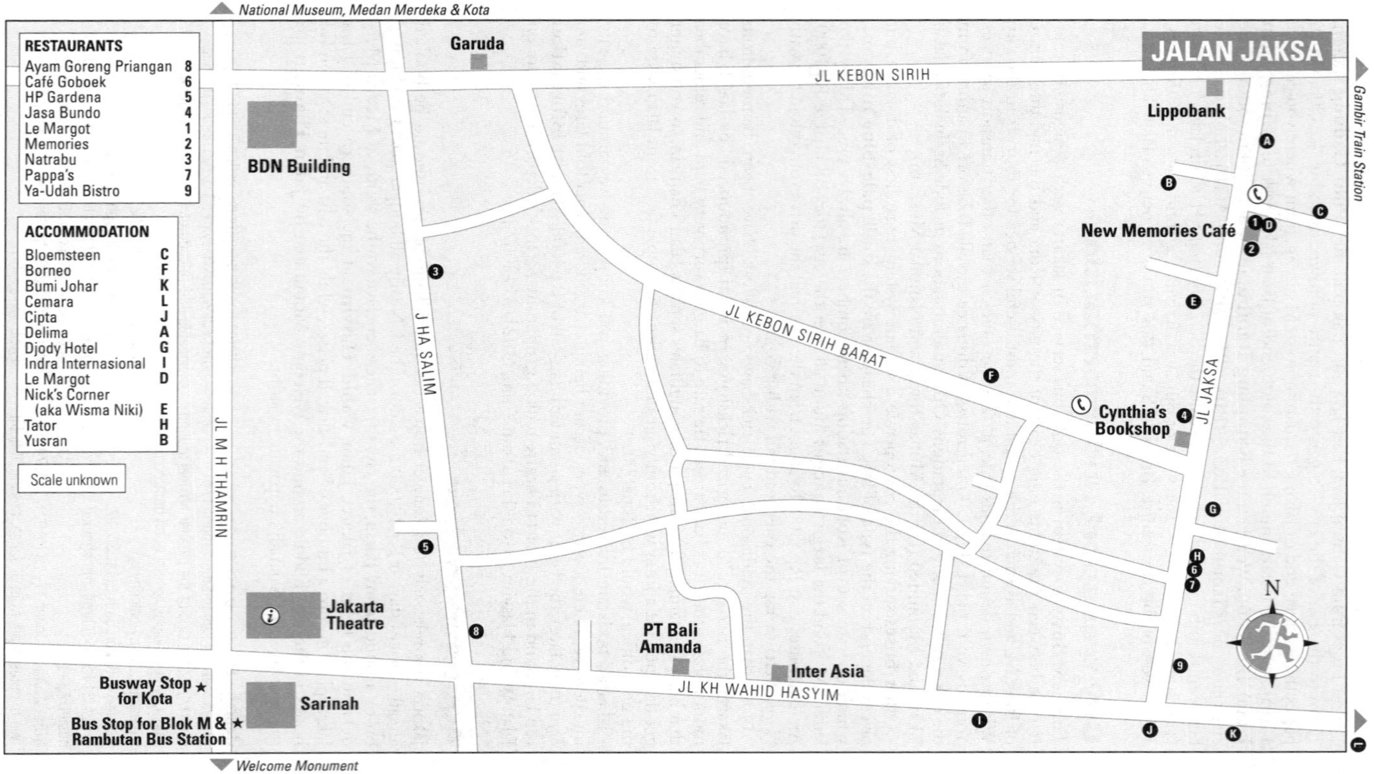

JALAN JAKSA

RESTAURANTS

Ayam Goreng Priangan	8
Café Goboek	6
HP Gardena	5
Jasa Bundo	4
Le Margot	1
Memories	2
Natrabu	3
Pappa's	7
Ya-Udah Bistro	9

ACCOMMODATION

Bloemsteen	C
Borneo	F
Bumi Johar	K
Cemara	L
Cipta	J
Delima	A
Djody Hotel	G
Indra Internasional	I
Le Margot	D
Nick's Corner (aka Wisma Niki)	E
Tator	H
Yusran	B

Scale unknown

National Museum, Medan Merdeka & Kota

Gambir Train Station

Welcome Monument

Garuda

JL KEBON SIRIH

Lippobank

BDN Building

New Memories Café

JL KEBON SIRIH BARAT

J HA SALIM

JL JAKSA

Cynthia's Bookshop

JL M H THAMRIN

Jakarta Theatre

PT Bali Amanda

Inter Asia

JL KH WAHID HASYIM

Busway Stop for Kota

Bus Stop for Blok M & Rambutan Bus Station

Sarinah

N

Indra Internasional Jl Wahid Hasyim 63 ⓣ021/3152858. Light, airy hotel, with clean a/c rooms (all with TV) and friendly service. ❺–❻
Le Margot Jl Jaksa 15 ⓣ021/3913830. Average, mid-priced hotel offering reasonable rooms with a/c, TV, room safe and hot water, and a popular attached restaurant. ❸–❹
Nick's Corner (aka Wisma Niki) Jl Jaksa 16 ⓣ021/3107814. Large, popular hostel offering a variety of budget and not-so-budget rooms. The two mixed-sex dormitories (Rp20,000 for a dorm bed) are reasonable, though they have no windows. ❷
Tator Jl Jaksa 37 ⓣ021/323940. Many people's favourite, this spotless hotel has friendly staff, hot water and breakfast is included in the price. ❸
Yusran Jl Kebon Sirih Barat Dalam VI/9 ⓣ021/3140373. Perhaps Jaksa's best-kept secret, this pleasant budget hotel lies at the end of Gang 6 to the west of Jl Jaksa. Doubles are spotless and comfortable; try bargaining. ❶–❷

The rest of the city

Borobudur Jl Lapangan Banteng Selatan ⓣ021/3805555. Once the best in the city, this grand hotel is set in lovely gardens with a pool and has sumptuous rooms. ❾
Cemara Jl Cemara 1 ⓣ021/3908215, ⓔcemara@centrim.net.id. Two minutes' east of Jl Jaksa, a medium-range hotel featuring its own pool and a comfortable restaurant. ❻–❼
Grand Hyatt Jl MH Thamrin ⓣ021/3901234, ⓦwww.jakarta.grand.hyatt.com. Massive complex in the centre of town with luxurious rooms, a pool and several restaurants. ❾
Hotel Menteng 1 Jl Gondangdia 28, Menteng ⓣ021/3144150. Very reasonable, mid-priced hotel popular for attached disco; rooms have a/c, phone, hot water and TV. ❹–❺

The City

To head from north to south through the centre of Jakarta is to go forward in time, from the pretty, old Dutch city of Batavia, **Kota**, in the north, to the modern golf courses and amusement parks in the south. **Medan Merdeka**, a giant, threadbare patch of grass, marks the spiritual centre of Jakarta, if not exactly its geographical one, bordered to the west by the city's major north–south thoroughfare. The main commercial district and the budget accommodation enclave of **Jalan Jaksa** lie just a short distance to the south of Medan Merdeka.

Kota (Old Batavia)

Located in the north of the city, the quaint old district of Kota was once known as **Batavia** and used to serve as the administrative centre of the great Dutch trading empire that stretched from South Africa all the way to Japan. The easiest way to reach Kota is to take the Busway (Rp2500), which drives north along Jalan Gajah Mada, terminating in front of the impressive facade of **Kota train station**, a good place to begin your tour of the area. Head north from Kota station along Jalan Lada, past the Politeknik Swadharma, and enter the boundaries of what was once the walled city of Batavia. The centre of Batavia, **Taman Fatahillah**, lies 300m to the north of the train station, an attractive cobbled square hemmed in on all four sides by museums and historical monuments. On the south side is the largely disappointing **Jakarta History Museum** (Tues–Sun 9am–3pm; Rp2000), which sets out to describe (in Indonesian only) the history of the city from the Stone Age to the present day, but unfortunately only really gets as far as the seventeenth century. Upstairs is more interesting, with many of the rooms furnished as they would have been two hundred years ago. Perhaps the finest exhibit is the ornate **Cannon Si Jagur**, which until recently stood on the north side of the square and was built by the Portuguese to defend the city of Melaka. On the side is the Latin inscription *Ex me ipsa renata sum* – "Out of myself I was reborn" – and the whole thing is emblazoned with sexual imagery, from the clenched fist (a suggestive gesture in Southeast Asia) to the barrel itself, a potent phallic symbol in Indonesia.

The more entertaining **Wayang Museum** (Tues–Sun 9am–3pm; Rp2000), to the west of the square, is dedicated to the Javanese art of puppetry and is housed in one of the oldest buildings in the city. Exhibits display puppets from right across the archipelago, and every Sunday between 10am and 2pm some of them perform in a free **wayang show**. Continuing clockwise around the Taman Fatahillah, don't miss the chance to luxuriate in the stylish surroundings of the historic *Café Batavia*, on the northwestern corner of the square. To the east of the square, the **Balai Seni Rupa** (Tues–Sun 9am–3pm; Rp2000), Jakarta's fine arts museum, and accompanying **Ceramics Museum** house some works by Indonesia's most illustrious artists, including portraits by Affandi and sketches of the capital by Raden Saleh.

Sunda Kelapa

About 1km north of Taman Fatahillah lies the historic harbour of **Sunda Kelapa** (Rp1000) that, established during Pajajaran times, grew to become the most important in the Dutch Empire. Although the bulk of the sea traffic docks at Tanjung Priok these days, a few of the smaller vessels, particularly some picturesque wooden schooners, still call in at this eight-hundred–year-old port. You can either walk here from Taman Fatahillah (about 20min) or hail an ojek (Rp1000).

From the port, cross over the bridge to the west of the harbour and turn right at the nineteenth-century watchtower, the **Uitkijk**, originally built to direct shipping traffic to the port. Here, buried in the chaotic Pasar Ikan (fish market) that occupies this promontory, you'll find the entrance to the excellent **Museum Bahari**, or **Maritime Museum** (Tues–Sun 9am–3pm; Rp2000), housed in a warehouse that was built in 1652 for spice, pepper, tea, coffee and cotton. The highly informative museum charts the relationship between the Indonesian archipelago and the sea that both divides and surrounds it, beginning with the simple, early fishing vessels and continuing through the colonial years to the modern age. All kinds of sea craft, from the Buginese *pinisi* to the *kora-kora* war boat from the Moluccas can be seen here.

Heading south, across the busy road is yet another former seventeenth-century building turned restaurant, the *VOC Galangan*, yet another great place to take five minutes out with a cold drink. From here, keep the Kali Besar canal on your left until you come to the ornate two-hundred–year-old wooden drawbridge, **Jembatan Pasar Ayam**. The streets south of here were once the smartest addresses in Batavia, and the grand Dutch terrace houses still stand, the most famous being the Chinese-style **Toko Merah** (Red Shop) at no. 11 Jalan Kali Besar Barat – the former home of the Dutch governor general Van Imhoff. The Batavia bus station lies on the eastern side of the canal, from where you can catch a pale-blue minivan (Rp1000) back to Kota and the Busway.

Medan Merdeka

The heart and lungs of Jakarta, **Medan Merdeka** is a square kilometre of sun-scorched grass in the centre of the city. It was here in the 1940s that Sukarno whipped his supporters up into a revolutionary frenzy, and here that the biggest demonstration of the May 1998 riots took place. At the centre of the square stands the **Monas Tower**, a soaring 137-metre marble, bronze and gold torch, commissioned by Sukarno in 1962 to symbolize the indomitable spirit of the Indonesian people, and known to expats and locals as "Sukarno's last erection" in recognition of his world-famous philandering. You can take a lift up to its top for a city view (daily except last Mon of every month, 8.30am–5pm; Rp3500, students Rp2600); the ticket includes entry to the **National History Museum** or Goblet Yard in Monas' basement, a series of 48 dioramas that depict the history of Jakarta.

The **National Museum** (Tues–Thurs & Sun 8.30am–2.30pm, Fri 8.30–11.30am, Sat 8.30am–1.30pm; Rp750), on the western side of Medan Merdeka, is a fabulous place and a great introduction to Indonesia; the Indonesian Heritage Society conducts tours in English (Tues–Thurs 9.30am). The eclectic range of items from all over the archipelago are grouped together into categories such as musical instruments, costumes and so on. Many of the country's top ruins have been plundered for their statues, which now sit, unmarked, in the museum courtyard. Other highlights include huge Dongson kettledrums, the skull and thighbone of Java Man, found near Solo in 1936, and the cache of golden artefacts discovered at the foot of Mount Merapi in 1990. There are sometimes cultural performances such as dance and theatre here.

The dazzling white, if rather unprepossessing, **Mesjid Istiqlal** looms over the northeastern corner of Medan Merdeka. Completed in 1978, it is the largest mosque in Southeast Asia and can hold up to 250,000 people. For a donation, and providing you're conservatively dressed, the security guards will take you on an informal tour. At the foot of the minaret sits a 2.5-tonne wooden drum from east Kalimantan, the only traditional feature in this otherwise state-of-the-art mosque.

The outskirts

Eighteen kilometres south of Medan Merdeka, the **Taman Mini Indonesia Indah** (Sun–Tues 8am–5pm; Rp5000) is a huge theme park celebrating the rich ethnic and cultural diversity of the archipelago. At its centre is a man-made lake, around which are 27 houses, each built in the traditional style of Indonesia's 27 provinces. The park also contains several **museums** (Rp2000 each), including the Science Museum; the Asmat Museum, housing woodcarvings from West Papua; and the Museum of Indonesia, with displays on the country's people, geography, flora and fauna. Neighbouring **Museum Purna Bhakti Pertiwi** (daily 9am–4pm; Rp5000) displays a fabulously opulent collection of stunning gifts presented to President Suharto. Highlights include a whole gamelan orchestra made of old Balinese coins, a series of carved wooden panels depicting Suharto's life story, and an enormous rubber-tree root decorated with the nine gods of Balinese Hinduism. To get to all these attractions, catch **bus** #P10, #P11 or #P16 to Rambutan bus station, then minibus #T19 or #M55 to the Taman Mini entrance (1hr total).

Eating

Food is more expensive in the capital than anywhere else in Indonesia: nasi goreng can cost twice as much here. Local **street food** thrives in the city, particularly along Jalan HA Salim (also known as Jalan Sabang).

Jalan Jaksa and Jalan HA Salim (Jalan Sabang)

Ayam Goreng Priangan Jl HA Salim 55a. Fairly inexpensive Indonesian fried-chicken restaurant. Try *ayam bakar*, chicken cooked in coconut milk and grilled in a sweet soya sauce, for Rp7700.

Café Goboek Jl Jaksa. Some of the cheapest food on the street, and pretty decent fare it is, too. Has a grill during the daytime only (10am–4pm), but cooks some great curries in the evening, and the beer's only Rp13,000.

HP Gardena Jl HA Salim 32a. Unusual hot-pot restaurant, where you choose the ingredients – ranging from fish cakes (Rp4500) to meatballs (Rp4500), salads and spicy sauce dips.

Jasa Bundo Jl Jaksa 20. The better Padang restaurant on the street – but prizes should be given for anyone making the waiters smile.

Le Margot Jl Jaksa 15. The service can be somewhat slow, but this is a reasonable spot for simple breakfasts such as fried egg, toast and jam with tea or coffee, and it has satellite TV.

Memories Jl Jaksa 17. A popular café on two floors with a small bookshop built into one corner of the ground floor and a pool table upstairs. The large menu of Western and local dishes is somewhat overpriced – though some of the dishes, including the fiery Sichuan chicken (Rp16,000), are terrific, and this place remains one of the most popular on the street.

Natrabu Jl HA Salim 29a. Flashy but excellent mid-priced Minang restaurant serving Padang-style food from West Sumatra and live Minang music every evening (7–9.30pm).

Pappa's Jl Jaksa 41. A good place for lunch at the quieter southern end of Jalan Jaksa, *Pappa's* specializes in Indian-style curries (Rp16,000–20,000).

Ya-Udah Bistro Jl Jaksa 49. By far the best-value place to eat on Jalan Jaksa, Swiss-run *Ya-Udah*'s lengthy menu includes excellent Hungarian goulash (Rp17,500), mussels and spinach cream soup (Rp17,500), and an unbeatable Chef's Salad (Rp13,500). The American breakfasts are also very popular (Rp23,500), and a large beer costs Rp20,000. The waitress service puts many other emporia to shame.

Jalan Wahid Hasyim and elsewhere

Akbar Palace Plaza Senayan, Jl Asia-Afrika. Excellent north Indian restaurant, which serves some wonderful tandoori dishes.

Café Batavia Taman Fatahillah, Kota. One of the city's most stylish and popular places, serving delicious Chinese, Indonesian and Western dishes, and over sixty cocktails. Nightly live jazz and soul. Pricey – but worth it. Open 24hr.

Eastern Promise Jl Kemang Raya 5. British-style pub and Indian restaurant serving the best pies for hundreds of miles as well as balti-style curries.

Oasis Jl Raden Saleh 47 ☎021/3150646. Jakarta's finest, this historic restaurant is housed in a 1920s Dutch villa in Cikini, complete with crystal chandeliers and enormous stained-glass window. The menu ranges from steak tartare to rijsttaffel and is expensive but worth the splurge.

Raden Kuring Jl Raden Saleh Raya 63, Cikini. Best of the Sundanese kuring restaurants. Try *ikan mas pepes*, the spicy baked fish.

VOC Galangan Jl Kakap 1. One of a new breed of restaurants in the Kota and Sunda Kelapa area, the mid-range *VOC Galangan*, set in a seventeenth-century edifice, serves a variety of Western and Indonesian dishes It's a great place to stop for lunch or a cold drink while sightseeing, has considerable charm… and is a fair bit cheaper than the *Café Batavia*. Often has live music at nights.

Nightlife and entertainment

Most travellers don't even leave Jalan Jaksa in the evening, preferring to hang out in one of the many **bars** that are strung along the road: *Ya-Udah* is currently the most popular. There's also a pool hall on the street, Tatto Bilyard, charging Rp2000 per game, and only ten minutes away the Jakarta Theatre has a cinema (Rp30,000). The expensive *Hard Rock Café* has just opened a new **live-music** venue virtually opposite its old location of the Sarinah department store, on Jalan Thamrin. It's the nearest club to Jalan Jaksa and remains popular, particularly with Jakarta's teenyboppers. If you're after a big night out, head for **Blok M**, which has a wealth of bars. A good place to start a crawl is the *Top Gun Bar*, just opposite the *Sportsman's* (best for televised football)) as well as *The Stanford Arms* in *Hotel Ambhara* and *Orleans*, a quiet veteran expat hangout upstairs at Jl Adityawarman 67 just two minutes' walk away. The most interesting place to rave is the *Tanamur Disco* (Rp15,000), at Jl Tanah Abang Timur 14, where the music is a fairly mainstream mix of European and American house, and the lively clientele includes expats, pimps, prostitutes, ladyboys, junkies and the occasional traveller; up to 1500 revellers on Friday and Saturday nights, though some say it's now had its heyday. Goths (yes, Indonesia does have them!) should head to *The Gate*, Wisma GKBI, Jl Sudirman 28, a basement club that's popular with a young crowd, while the *Stadium*, Jl Hayam Wuruk 111, is a full-on club and perhaps Jakarta's most popular venue.

Shopping

While Jakarta has no particular indigenous craft of its own, the capital isn't a bad place to go **souvenir shopping**. The antiques market on Jalan Surabaya, one block west of Cikini station in Jakarta's Menteng district, sells fine silver jewellery, and traditional Javanese wooden trunks and other pieces of furniture, as well as old records. The entire third floor of the Sarinah department store is given over to souvenirs, with wayang kulit and wayang golek puppets, leather bags and woodcarvings a speciality.

For new **books**, there are a couple of places in the basement of the smart Indonesia Plaza, including a branch of the excellent Periplus chain. For secondhand books, visit Cynthia's bookshop on Jalan Jaksa, or the small store in the corner of *New Memories Café*.

Listings

Airlines AdamAir, Jl Thamrin 8-9 ☎021/39836312; Air Canada, Jl Mega Kuningan Lot 5.1 Menara Rajawali 8th Floor ☎ 021/5761629; Air China, Jl Jend Sudirman Kav 25 Plaza Lippo Lt 15, Suite 1502, ☎021/5203910; Air France, Summitmas Tower, 9th Floor, Jl Jend Sudirman ☎021/5202262; Bouraq, Jl Angkasa 1–3, Kemayoran ☎021/6288815; British Airways, Menara Bank, Jl Thamrin 5 ☎021/2300277; Cathay Pacific, Gedung Bursa Efek, Jl Jend

Sudirman Kav 52–53 ☎021/5151747; China Airlines, Wisma Dharmala Sakti, Jl Jend Sudirman 32 ☎021/2510788; Emirates, *Hotel Sahid Jaya*, 2nd Floor, Jl Jend Sudirman 86 ☎021/5205363; Eva Air, Price Waterhouse Centre, 10th Floor, Jl Rasuna Said Kav C3 ☎021/5205363; Garuda, Jl Merdeka Selatan 13 ☎021/2310082, and at the BDN Building, Jl Thamrin 5; Gulf Air, Jl Jend Sudirman Kav 45–46, Wisma Danamon Aetna Life Lt 25 ☎021/5770789; Japan Airlines, Jl Jend Sudirman Kav 3–4 Wisma Kyoei Prince Indonesia Lt 1–2 ☎021/5723211; Jatayu, Jl Batu Tulis Raya 19B ☎021/3458666; Kartika Airlines, Jalan Medan Merdeka Timur 7 ☎021/3452947; KLM, Summitmas II, 17th Floor, Jl Jend Sudirman Kav 61–62 ☎021/2526740; Korean Airlines, Jl Jend Sudirman Kav 28, Mayapada Tower 9th floor, ☎021/5212175; Kuwait Airways, Jl Sudirman 28 ☎021/5714488; Lion Air, Lion Air Tower, Jl Gajah Mada 7 ☎021/6337272; Lufthansa, Panin Centre Building, 2nd Floor, Jl Jend Sudirman 1 ☎021/5702005; Malaysian Airlines, World Trade Centre, Jl Jend Sudirman Kav 29 ☎021/5229682; Mandala, Jl Garuda 76 ☎021/4246100, also Jl Veteran I 34 ☎021/3811057; Merpati, Jl Angkasa 7, Blok B15 Kav 2 & 3 ☎021/6548888; Pelita, Jl Abdul Muis 52-56A ☎021/2312222; Philippine Airlines, 15th Floor, World Trade Center Building, Jl Jend Sudirman Kav 29-31 ☎021/5268668; Qantas Airways, Menara Bank, Jl Thamrin 5 ☎021/2300277; Royal Brunei Airlines, World Trade Centre, 11th Floor, Jl Jend Sudirman Kav 29–31 ☎021/5211842; Saudi Arabian Airlines, Jl Rasuna Said Kav 1 Menara Imperium 11th floor ☎021/8356201; Singapore Airlines, Menara Kadin Indonesia, 8th Floor, Jl HR Rasuna Said Blok X-5, Kav 2&3, ☎021/57903747; Sri Lankan Airlines, Mayapada Tower, 16th Floor, Jl Jend Sudirman Kav 28, ☎021/5212009; Thai International, BDN Building, Ground Floor, Jl Thamrin 5 ☎021/2302552.

Banks and exchange Many of the banks, Sarinah, the post office and Gambir train station have their own ATM machines, which offer a better rate than any bank or moneychanger. Otherwise, Lippobank, just west of the northern end of Jl Jaksa on Jl Kebon Siri, offers the best rates in town, as well as credit-card advances. The AMEX representative is the Suman Leisure Group, Jl Tanah Abang III / 28E, ☎021/344 6235; or PT Dwidaya Tour and Travel, Jalan KH Samanhudi, No.22 A–B. The InterAsia moneychanger at Jl Wahid Hasyim 96a is reasonable for cash exchanges, but offers poor rates for travellers' cheques. PT Ayu in Toko Gunung Agung, Jl Kwitang Raya (Rp3000 bajaj from Jl Jaksa) gives consistently good rates for notes.

Embassies and consulates Australia, Jl H Rasuna Said Kav 15-16, ☎021/25505555; Britain, Jl Thamrin 75 ☎021/3156254; Canada, Metropolitan Building 1, Jl Jend Sudirman Kav 29 ☎021/25507800; Germany, Jl Thamrin 1 ☎021/3901750; India, Jl Rasuna Said S-1, Kuningan ☎021/5204150; Japan, Jl Thamrin Kav 3 ☎021/31925076; Malaysia, Jl Rasuna Said 1–3, Kuningan ☎021/5224947; Netherlands, Jl Rasuna Said S-3, Kuningan ☎021/5251515; New Zealand, Jl Diponegoro 41 ☎021/330680; Singapore, Jl Rasuna Said 2, Kuningan ☎021/5201489; South Africa, Wisma GKBI Jl Sudirman ☎021/7193304; Thailand, Jl Imam Bonjol 74 ☎021/3904055; US, Jl Medan Merdeka Selatan 5 ☎021/360360.

Hospitals and clinics The MMC hospital on Jl Rasuna Said in Kuningan is the best in town (☎021/5203435). The private SMI (Sentra Medika International) clinic at Jl Cokroaminoto 16 in Menteng (☎021/3157747), is run by Australian and Indonesian doctors. Any *Praktek Umum* (public clinic) will treat foreigners cheaply.

Internet access Perhaps the best, and certainly the best-value, Internet café in the Jaksa area is Mnet, next to *Pappa's*, which charges just Rp5,000 per hour.

Post office The GPO lies to the north of Lapangan Benteng (Mon–Sat 8am–8pm, Sun 9am–5pm), northeast of Medan Merdeka (catch bus #15 or #P15 from Jl Kebon Siri, to the north of Jl Jaksa). Poste restante is at counter no. 55. The *Sari Pan Pacific* will also handle mail.

Telephone services There is no main government-run communications centre in the city. The Indosat building at 21 Jl Medan Merdeka Barat has IDD and HCD on its ground floor (cash only), as do the RTQ warpostel at Jl Jaksa 17 (8am–midnight) and the wartel on Jl Kebon Siri Barat. IDD calls can be made from the lobby of *Hotel Cipta* at any time as well as *Pappa's*, Jl Jaksa, during opening hours.

Travel agents Good travel agencies on or near Jl Jaksa include the highly respected Global at no. 49 and PT Robertur Kencana at no. 20b, Lipta Marsada Pertala at no. 11 (☎021/326291), and PT Bali Amanda at Jl Wahid Hasyim 110a, which can book Pelni ferry tickets on the Internet.

Merak and ferries to Sumatra

At the extreme northwestern tip of Java, **MERAK** is the port for ferries across the Sunda Straits to Bakauheni on Sumatra. **Ferries** to **Sumatra** leave about every thirty minutes and take about two hours and thirty minutes; crowds of buses connect with the ferries to take you on to Bandar Lampung, Palembang or destinations further north in Sumatra. If you get stuck at Merak, the *Hotel Anda* at Jl Florida 4 has basic rooms with fan and mandi (☎0254/71041; ❶).

Krakatau

At 10am on August 27, 1883, an explosion equivalent to 10,000 Hiroshima atomic bombs rent **Krakatau** Island; the boom was heard as far away as Sri Lanka and Reunion. As the eruption column towered 40km into the atmosphere, a thick mud rain began to fall over the area, and the temperature plunged by 5°C. Tremors were detected as far away as the English Channel and off the coast of Alaska. One single **tsunami** (pressure wave) as tall as a seven-storey building, raced outwards, erasing 300 towns and villages and killing 36,417 people; a government gunboat was carried 3km inland and deposited up a hill 10m above sea level. Once into the open sea, the waves travelled at up to 700kph, reaching South Africa and scuttling ships in Auckland harbour. Two-thirds of Krakatau had vanished for good, and on those parts that remained not so much as a seed or an insect survived.

Today, the crumbled caldera is clearly visible west of the beaches near Merak and Carita, its sheer northern cliff face soaring straight out of the sea to nearly 800m. But it is the glassy black cone of **Anak Krakatau**, the child of Krakatau volcano, that most visitors want to see, a barren wasteland that's still growing and still very much active. It first reared its head from the seas in 1930, and now sits angrily smoking amongst the remains of the older peaks. To get here requires a **motorboat trip** (4–6hr) from Labuan or Carita, then a half-hour walk up to the crater, from where you can see black lava flows, sulphurous fumaroles and smoke. The easiest way to visit Krakatau is with the Black Rhino **tour** company in **Carita** (see below) or through the *Beringin Hotel* in Kalianda on Sumatra (see p.350). If you have your own group, inquire at the PHPA parks office in **Labuan** (see below) and see if they can fix you up with a boat, which should cost around Rp500,000 for the day. Bring lots of water and some food (including emergency supplies).

Carita and Labuan

Most people organize their trips to **Krakatau** from the west coast towns of **CARITA** and **LABUAN**: the former – boasting one of the most sheltered stretches of sea in Java – is the best spot to arrange **tours** (day-trips $50); the latter – a dull and dirty port town – is the best place to arrange **independent trips**. In Carita, tours run by Black Rhino (☎0253/81072), across from the marina, are recommended, but don't fall for the unqualified guides who approach you on spec. The **PHPA parks office** in Labuan will provide park permits (Rp5000) for independent visitors; their office is quite far out along Jalan Perintis Kemerdekaan, heading towards Carita, almost opposite the *Rawayan* hotel.

Practicalities

Buses to Lubuan run from the Kalideres bus station in Jakarta (3hr). You can pick up a **colt** for the onward journey to Carita at the Labuan terminal; don't get conned into taking transport round to the stop for colts, which is just two minutes' walk towards the seafront and round to the right.

All **accommodation** in Carita is on or close to the main seaside road, known as Jalan Carita Raya or Jalan Pantai Carita. Prices shoot up at the weekend, when the town is invaded by jetskiers. Friendly staff, clean rooms and interesting decor make *Sunset View* (☎0253/81075; ❶) one of the best-value places on the west coast. *Carita Krakatau* (☎0253/83027; ❶–❷), behind the restaurant of the same name, is also recommended and offers spotless rooms with mandi, fan and breakfast. *Lucia Cottages* (☎0253/81262; ❷) has bungalows and rooms around a pool and some of the comfiest beds in Carita. The best budget place in Labuan is *Telaga Biru*, just off Jalan Carita Raya, about 2km from Labuan, across the road from the sea (❷); all the quiet rooms have mandi inside. The more central *Hotel Citra Ayu*, Jl Perintis Kemerdekaan 27 (☎0253/81229; ❶), is basic but clean. The nicest place in the area is *Rawayan*, out on the road towards Carita, at Jl Raya Carita 41 (☎0253/81386; ❹), with quaint bungalows and private rooms, all en suite.

The public parts of the beach in Carita are lined with **food** carts selling *murtabak*, sate and soto. *Carita Krakatau*, 30m towards Anyer from the marina, cooks a good fish steak for Rp35,000, while *Diminati*, opposite the entrance to the marina, boasts the cheapest cold beer in town (Rp12,000), and does an excellent *kakap* fish steak meal for Rp28,000.

Bogor

Located 300m above sea level and just an hour's train journey south of Jakarta, **BOGOR** enjoys a cool, wet climate – the *Guinness Book of Records* notes the city for the "most days per year with thunder" – and famously lush Kebun Raya Bogor or **Botanical Gardens** (daily 7am–5pm; Rp5000, plus Rp1000 for the orchid house; catch bus #2 from the train station), which were founded by Sir Stamford Raffles in 1811. In the gardens, pathways wind between towering bamboo stands, climbing bougainvillea, a small tropical rainforest, and ponds full of water lilies and fountains. Perhaps the garden's best-known occupants are the giant rafflesia and *bungu bangkai*, two of the world's hugest (and smelliest) flowers. Near the gardens' main entrance, the rather dilapidated **Zoological Museum** (daily 8am–4pm; Rp1000) houses some 30,000 specimens, including a complete skeleton of a blue whale, a stuffed Javan rhino and, most impressively, the remains of a huge coconut crab. **Wayang golek puppets** are made at a workshop to the northeast of the gardens; ask for Pak Dase's place. If you're interested in **gamelan** and Javanese gongs, visit Pak Sukarna's factory on Jalan Pancasan to the southwest of the gardens. Here the instruments are forged using traditional methods, and are also for sale.

Practicalities

The **train station**, which is prone to rainy-season flooding, is about 500m northwest of the Botanical Gardens and close to some of the town's budget accommodation; trains from Jakarta's Gambir Station take either 55 minutes (Pakuan Express) or one hour and five minutes. Buses from Jakarta's UKI at Cawang arrive at the **bus terminal** about 500m southeast of the gardens. There are also buses every fifteen minutes or so to and from Bandung, four hours or so away. The main bemo stop is behind the bus terminal, but the best place to pick up bemos is by the train station. Bemo #2 runs between the station and the botanical gardens; #3 runs between the station and bus terminal. There's a small **tourist information** centre (Mon–Fri 9am–4pm) at the southern entrance to the gardens, and a second by the train station (8am–5pm).

With excessively friendly staff, river views and excellent breakfasts, *Abu Pensione*, Jl Mayor Oking 15 (☎0251/322893; ❷–❸), is probably the best budget **place to stay** in Bogor, though it's twice the price of other losmen; the pricier rooms here have hot water and air-con. Turn right out of the station, then right again a few hundred metres later down Jl Mayor Oking. *Pensione Firman*, Jl Paledang 48 (☎0251/323246; ❶) has long been the budget travellers' favourite accommodation and has neat and basic rooms; the price includes breakfast. To reach it from the station, walk for 1km along Jalan Paledang or catch #2 and jump out at the junction of Jalan Juanda and Jalan Paledang. *Wisma Karunia*, Jl Sempur 35–37 (☎0251/323411; ❷) is friendly and quiet, with a range of rooms and breakfast included. *Hotel Mirah*, Jl Pangrango 9a (☎0251/328044; ❻–❾) has an inviting pool (open to non-guests for Rp15,000) and air-con en-suite rooms; from the station, catch bemo #3 and jump out by the hotel's sign on Jalan Salak.

One of the best places to try genuine Sundanese **food** is in the garden at *Restoran Si Kabayan*, Jl Bina Marga I 2, where *ikan mas* is a speciality. *Bogor Permai*, on the corner of Jalan Jend Sudirman and Jalan Sawojajar, is a small food complex housing a fine delicatessen, the best bakery in Bogor and a stand selling tasty pizza slices (Rp2000). The *Bogor Permai* restaurant in the back of the building serves quality seafood and steaks from Rp25,000. The *Salak Sunset Café*, 50m down from the *Pensione Firman* on Jalan Paledang, is the only traveller-oriented place in Bogor. Hidden behind a beauty salon, it overlooks the river and serves great pizzas as well as ice-cold beer. Along Jalan Pengadillan, near the Telkom and train station, are bunches of **night stalls**, which set up after 6pm.

Bandung and around

Set 750m above sea level, and protected by a fortress of watchful volcanoes 190km southeast of Jakarta, **BANDUNG** is the third largest city in Indonesia and a centre of industry and traditional Sundanese arts – with plenty of cultural performances for tourists – though it suffers from incredible traffic pollution and uninteresting modern developments. Sundanese culture has remained intact here since the fifth century when the first Hindu Sundanese settled in this part of West Java. Modern Bandung's main tourist attraction is nearby **Tangkbuhan Prahu volcano**, from where there's a very pleasant two-hour forest walk down to the city, too.

The Dutch spotted the potential of this lush, cool plateau and its fertile volcanic slopes in the mid-seventeenth century, and set about cultivating coffee and rice here. But it wasn't until the early nineteenth century that the planters decided to settle in the area, at Bandung, rather than commute from Batavia. Several relics from the city's colonial era remain, including some of the elegant shops along Jalan Braga, and some fine buildings on Jalan Asia-Afrika.

Arrival and city transport

Bandung's civilized **train station** is located within walking distance of most budget accommodation, fairly close to the centre of town. **Bus** services to Bandung run from every major town in Java, including Jakarta. The main Leuwi Panjang **bus terminal** for buses from the west is 5km south of the city; the Cicaheum bus terminal for those from the east is at the far eastern edge of town. Local DAMRI buses serve both stations. The **airport** is 3km northwest of the train station, served by plenty of taxis.

Bandung's white-and-blue **DAMRI buses** cost Rp2000 a journey, and ply routes between the bus terminals through the centre of town. Red **angkots** (minibuses) also run a useful circular route, via the train station and the alun-alun (town square), to the Kebun Kelapa bus terminal, which services Cicaheum bus terminal, Dago, Ledeng and Lembang.

Information

The **tourist information** office (Mon–Sat 9am–5pm; ☎022/4206644) is on the alun-alun, though with all the building works going on around it, it may not be there for much longer. There is another office at the train station, and a regional office at Jl A Yani 227 (☎022/7210768). The two Golden Megacorp moneychangers, at Jl Juanda 89 opposite the Telkom building and at Jl Otista 180, have excellent rates. The main post office is at Jl Asia-Afrika 49 at the corner of Jalan Banceuy (Mon–Sat 8am–9pm). Internet cafés are surprisingly sparse in such a big town, though there is a small warung Internet next to the Bandung Indah Plaza on Jalan Merdeka (Rp4000 per hour). The main Telkom office is on Jalan Lembang (24hr). Garuda's airline office is inside the *Hotel Preangher Aerowisata* Jl Asia-Afrika 81

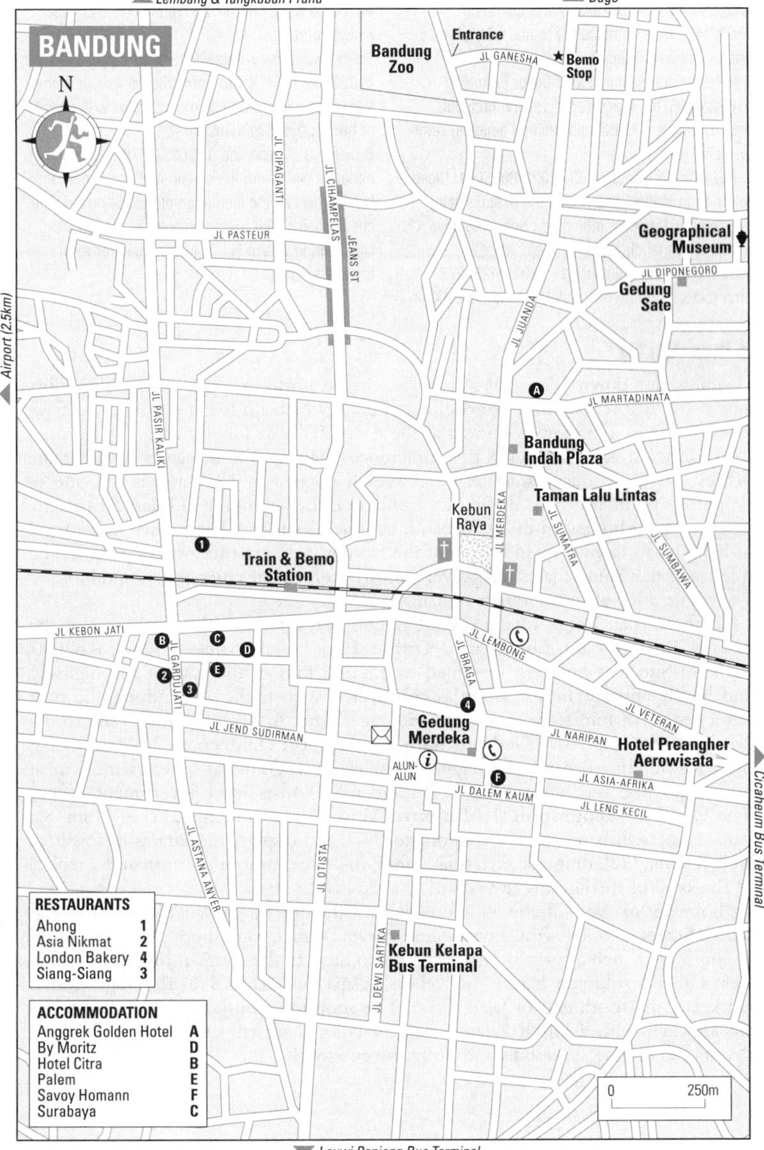

(☎022/4209468); Merpati is at Jl Kebonjali Kav A-1 62 (☎022/7302746), Lion Air at Jl Dr Djundjunan 155B (☎022/6020333) and the Bouraq office is at Jl Naripan 44 (☎022/4236436).

Accommodation

Coming into town from the airport or bus terminals, it's best to get dropped off at the train station, which is close to all the cheap **hostels**.

Anggrek Golden Hotel Jl Martadinata 15 ☎022/4205537. Immaculate rooms with a/c, phone and hot water. 6
By Moritz Jl Belakang Pasar/Luxor Permai 35 ☎022/4205788. A popular travellers' hangout, with dorms (Rp27,500), singles and doubles, some en-suite. 1
Hotel Citra Jl Gardujati 93 ☎022/6005061. Close to the train station, and one of the best bargains in Bandung, though a little noisy. Sparkling new rooms with mandi, TV, fan and a/c. 1–2
Palem Jl Belakang Pasar 117 ☎022/4236277. Smart, clean and friendly hotel in central location. All rooms come with TV and bathroom, and rates include breakfast. 2–3
Savoy Homann Jl Asia-Afrika 112 ☎022/4232244. If you want colonial flavour then this is the place. Sizeable rooms, some with views of the courtyard gardens. 8–9
Surabaya Jl Kebonjati 5 ☎022/4216791. Two minutes' walk from the station and popular with locals, this has the look of an old coaching inn with cheap rooms with balconies outside, though the olde-worlde charm is a little *too* faded for most travellers. 1–2

The City

Heading east down Jalan Asia-Afrika, along the northern edge of the alun-alun, you come to the **Gedung Merdeka** building, which hosted the first Asia-Afrika Conference in 1955 and is known as the Asia-Afrika or Liberty building. Inside, a small museum commemorates the conference. Many of the delegates stayed at the nearby Art Deco *Savoy Homann* hotel, which opened in 1939 and is still one of Bandung's premier hotels. Slightly west of here is the beginning of **Jalan Braga**, the chic shopping boulevard of 1920s Bandung. There's still one bakery here that's tried to hang on to its history, and a few of the facades maintain their stylish designs. The sidestreets that run off Jalan Braga were notorious for their raucous bars and brothels – at night, a lot of the seediness remains.

North of Jalan Braga, to the east of Kebun Raya park, off Jalan Sumatra, is the bizarre **Taman Lalu Lintas**, the "**Traffic Park**" (daily 8am—3.30pm; Rp2000, Rp3000 Sun and holiday). Designed to educate kids in the way of the highway, and highly appropriate for a city as constipated with traffic as Bandung, the park has a system of miniature cars, roads and street signs. A twenty-minute walk to the northeast, the impressive **Gedung Sate** building at Jl Diponegoro 22, is known as the Sate Building because the regular globules on its gold-leaf spire resemble meat on a skewer. It was built in the 1920s and now houses local government offices. The excellent **Geographical Museum** (Mon–Thurs 9am–2pm, Fri 9–11am, Sat 9am–1pm; free) is nearby at Jl Diponegoro 57, and displays mountains of fossils, as well as several full dinosaur skeletons, a four-metre mammoth skeleton and a replica of the skull of the famous Java Man.

About 750m west of the museum, Jalan Cihampelas, known to Westerners as **Jeans Street**, is lined with shops selling cheap T-shirts, bags, shoes and jeans. These are no longer such a bargain, and it's better to head to the shops at the south end of Jalan Dewi Sartika just before the Kebon Kelapa bus terminal, or the huge clothes market at the south end of Jalan Otista. The shopfronts on Jeans Street themselves are adorned with a kitsch kaleidoscope of colossal plaster superheroes, including Rambo, straddling spaceships and fluffy stucco clouds.

Eating

There are **food** courts in the numerous shopping centres, and sidestreets near the square serve some of the best warung **food**.

Ahong Jl Kebon Kawang. Chinese place serving *kangkung* (water spinach) and *sapi* (beef) hotplate (R25,000).
Asia Nikmat Jl Gardujati 45. Similar Chinese restaurant to the nearby *Siang-Siang*, with slightly inferior food at slightly higher prices, though it does serve beer.

London Bakery Jl Braga. Specializing in a range of coffees and teas, this is a modern European-type place with newspapers and books in English.
Siang-Siang Jl Gardujati 34. Brassy Chinese restaurant that does reasonably priced dishes in typically large portions – but no beer.

Nightlife

On weekdays, you're best off heading for the **bars** like *Fame Station*, 11th Floor, Lippo Building, Jalan Gatot Subroto 2 (11am–2am; Rp25,000), which draws a young crowd and often features live music. Expats tend to gravitate towards *Laga Pub*, Jl Junjungan 164, which has live music, cheapish beer (Rp11000) and a Rp5000 cover charge; *North Sea*, Jalan Braga 82, a Dutch-owned emporium with a good reputation for food; or the seedier *Duta Pub* at Jl Dalem Kaum 85.

Cultural performances

Bandung is the capital of Sundanese culture; pick up the *Jakarta and Java Kini* magazine from the tourist information office to find out about special performances. The *Panghegar* hotel, Jl Merdeka 2, stages Sundanese cultural performances in its restaurant (Wed & Sat). On Sunday mornings there are often shows at Bandung Zoo in the north of town, usually either the Indonesian martial art *pencak silat*, or **puppet shows**. The most spectacular local event is the **ram fighting** (*adu domba*), held every other Sunday at 10am near the Sari Ater hot spring, 30km from the city. Take a minibus from the train station to Lembang terminal, then a second minibus to Ciater (Rp5000). To the sound of Sundanese flutes and drums, the magnificently presented rams lunge at each other until one of them fades; there's no blood, just flying wool and clouds of dust.

Tangkuban Prahu volcano and the Dago Tea House walk

The mountainous region to the north of Bandung is the heart of the Parahyangan Highlands – the "Home of the Gods" – a highly volcanic area considered by the Sundanese to be the nucleus of their spiritual world. A very pleasant day out from Bandung on public transport takes you first to the 1830–metre-high **Tangkuban Prahu volcano**, the most visited volcano in West Java, 29km north of Bandung. Although it hasn't had a serious eruption for many years, the volcano still spews out vast quantities of sulphurous gases and at least one of its ten craters is still considered to be active. To get there from Bandung, take a Subang **minibus** from the train station (30min; Rp1500) and ask to be put down at the turn-off for the volcano, where there's a Rp1250 entrance fee. From here you can either charter an ojek or minibus up the asphalt road to the summit (10min; Rp5000) or walk up – it's about 4km up the road, or there's a good footpath via the Domas Crater, which starts just over 1km up the road from the guard post, to the right by the first car park. The **information booth** at the summit car park has details about crater walks; lots of guides will offer their services, but it's pretty obvious where you should and shouldn't go – just be sure to wear strong hiking boots. The main crater is called **Kawah Ratu** and is the one you can see down into from the end of the summit road, a huge, dull, grey cauldron with a few coloured lakes. From the summit you can trek down to **Domas Crater**, site of a small working sulphur mine.

On the return journey from Tangkuban Prahu to Bandung you'll pass through Lembang, where you should change on to a minibus for the resort of **MARIBAYA** (4km; Rp500). There are waterfalls near the entrance gate and hot springs, which have been tapped into a public pool. Further down is the largest **waterfall**, which you have to pay extra to see. An ugly iron bridge has been built right across the lip of the falls, and this is the starting point for a wonderful **walk down to the Dago Teahouse** on the edge of Bandung (6km; 2hr). The path winds downhill through a gorge and forests – just before the teahouse are tunnels used by the Japanese in World War II and the Dago waterfall, which lies amongst bamboo thickets. At the end of your walk is the teahouse, with private tables under their own thatched roofs, and superb views over Bandung city. From here, plenty of minibuses head back into the centre of town (15min; Rp500).

The Dieng Plateau

The **Dieng Plateau** lies in a volcanic caldera 2093m above sea level and holds a rewarding mix of multicoloured sulphurous **lakes**, craters that spew pungent gases, and some of the oldest **Hindu temples** in Java. The volcano is still active – in 1979, over 150 people died after a cloud of poisonous gas bled into the atmosphere – and the landscape up on this misty, windswept plain is sparse, denuded and terraced. Recently, the authorities have given the temple complex and surroundings a makeover, which has succeeded in increasing the number of local tourists, but has had a detrimental effect on the plateau's formerly isolated atmosphere. Indeed, many travellers are now turning their backs on Dieng, considering its flagging charms a poor return for the effort it takes to get here. Nevertheless, the temples are interesting, as are the other sights up here, and the plateau is still a worthy destination for those seeking a different, chillier side to Java.

Although travel agents run day-trips from Yogya, these involve eight hours' travelling for just one hour on the plateau, so it's better to spend a night up here, in the damp and isolated village of **DIENG**, just across the road from the plateau's main temple complex; bring warm clothes and waterproofs. To get to Dieng **from Yogya** you need to change **buses** twice, going first to **MAGELANG** from the Jombor terminal (Rp6000 – infrequent bus #5 in Yogya takes you from the western end of Jalan Sosro to the terminal), then to Wonosobo (Rp6000), and then to Dieng itself (Rp5000). The total journey time is around four to five hours.

The tiny village of Dieng lines Jalan Raya Dieng, the road that runs along the plateau's eastern edge, and hosts the limited choice of some fairly grim **accommodation**. The *Dieng Homestay*, on the junction with the road to Wonosobo at Jl Raya Dieng 16 (Ⓣ0286/92823; ❶), has basic, cell-like rooms, and the mandi are excruciatingly cold; this is, however, the best of the budget bunch. *Bu Djono*, next door (Ⓣ0286/322755; ❷), has shabbier rooms but superior **food** – eat here.

The temples and other sights

It is believed that the Dieng Plateau was once a completely self-contained **retreat** for priests and pilgrims. Unfortunately, it soon became completely waterlogged, and the entire plateau was eventually abandoned in the thirteenth century, only to be rediscovered, drained and restored some six hundred years later. The eight temples left on Dieng today are a tiny fraction of what was once a huge complex built by the Sanjayas in the seventh and eighth centuries.

Of these temples, the five that make up the **Arjuna complex** (daily 6.15am–5.15pm; Rp12,000), standing in fields opposite Dieng village, are believed to be the oldest. They have been named after heroes from the Mahabharata tales, although these are not the original names. Three of the five were built to the same blueprint: square, with two storeys and a fearsome kala head above the main entrance. The northernmost of these two-storey temples, the **Arjuna Temple**, is the oldest on Java (c680 AD). Dedicated to Shiva, the temple once held a giant lingam (phallic-shaped stone), which was washed by worshippers several times a day; the water would then drain through a spout in the temple's north wall. Next to Arjuna stands **Candi Srikandi**, the exterior of which is adorned with reliefs of Vishnu (on the north wall), Shiva (east) and Brahma (south). **Candi Gatutkaca** overlooks the Arjuna complex 300m to the southwest, and twenty minutes' walk (1km) south of here stands the peculiar-looking **Candi Bima**, named after the brother of Arjuna. Rows of faces stare impassively back at passers-by from the temple walls, a design based on the temples of southern India.

From Candi Bima, you can continue down the road for a kilometre or so to **Telaga Warna** (Coloured Lake; Rp6000), the best example of Dieng's coloured lakes, where sulphurous deposits shade the water blue, from turquoise to azure. The lake laps against the shore of a small peninsula that holds a number of meditational caves. It was in one of these caves, **Gua Semar**, that Suharto and Australian Prime Minister Gough Whitlam decided the future of Timor in 1974.

Of the other lakes on the plateau, **Telaga Nila** and **Telaga Dringo**, 12km west of Dieng village, are the prettiest and can be combined with seeing **Sumur Jalatunda**, a vast, vine-clad well just off the main road – for a small fee, small boys will show you a little-used path from the well to the two lakes. Just 250m further along the road is the turn-off to **Kawah Candradimuka**, one of a number of *kawah* (mini-craters) dotted around the plateau. The crater is a twenty-minute walk up the hill from the road; five minutes along its length a small path on the left heads west to Telaga Nila. The sulphurous smell can be nauseating, and the steaming vents may obscure your view of the bubbling mud pools below. Further east along the road, an extremely overgrown path leads up to **Gua Jimat**, where the sulphurous emissions are fatal to anything (and anyone) that stands too close. To get to all these lakes and caves involves a fairly tortuous route by public transport, so you might prefer to hire an **ojek** from Dieng village (50,000 per day) or join a **tour** from *Dieng Homestay* (Rp25,000). Otherwise, take a Batur-bound **bus** from Dieng to **Pasurenan** (7km; Rp1000), and then an ojek (Rp2000) up the hill to the Sumur Jalatunda. Note that place-name spellings change frequently on the signposts, but Dieng and Tieng really are two different places.

Yogyakarta

YOGYAKARTA (pronounced "Jogjakarta" and often just shortened to "Jogja") ranks as one of the best-preserved and most attractive cities in Java, and is a major centre for the classical **Javanese arts** of batik, ballet, drama, music, poetry and puppet shows. At its heart is Yogya's first family, the Hamengkubuwonos, whose elegant palace lies at the centre of Yogya's quaint old city, the **Kraton**, itself concealed behind high castellated walls. Tourists flock here, attracted not only by the city's courtly splendour but also by the nearby temples of **Prambanan** and **Borobudur**, so there are more hotels in Yogya than anywhere else in Java and, unfortunately, a correspondingly high number of touts, pickpockets and con artists.

Yogyakarta grew out of the dying embers of the once-great Mataram dynasty. In 1752, the Mataram Empire, then based in nearby Solo, was in the throes of the Third Javanese War of Succession. The reigning susuhunan, **Pakubuwono II**, had been steadily losing power in the face of a rebellion by his brothers, Singasari and Mangkubumi, and the sultan's nephew, Mas Said. To try to turn the tide, Pakubuwono II persuaded Mangkubumi to swap sides and defend the court, offering him control over three thousand households within the city in return. Mangkubumi agreed, but the sultan later reneged on the deal. In fury, Mangkubumi headed off to establish his own court. Thus Yogyakarta was born, and Mangkubumi crowned himself **Sultan Hamengkubuwono I**. He spent the next 37 years building the new capital, with the Kraton as the centrepiece and the court at Solo as the blueprint. By the time he died in 1792, his territory exceeded Solo's. After his death, however, the Yogya sultanate went into freefall and spent most of the nineteenth century concentrating on artistic pursuits rather than warmongering. In 1946, the capital of the newly declared Republic of Indonesia was moved to Yogya from Jakarta, and the Kraton became the unofficial headquarters for the republican movement. With the financial and military support of **Sultan Hamengkubuwono IX**, Yogya became the nerve centre for the native forces. Today, over fifty years on from the War of Independence, the royal household of Yogya continues to enjoy almost slavish devotion from its subjects and the current sultan, Hamengkubuwono X, is one of the most influential politicians in the country.

Arrival

Arriving at **Adisucipto Airport**, 10km east of the city centre, walk 200m south of the terminal on to Jalan Adisucipto, where you can flag down any **bus** (Rp2000) heading west to Yogya. A taxi costs Rp25,000. **Tugu train station** lies just one block north of Jalan Sosrowijayan, on Jalan Pasar Kembang. A becak to Jalan Prawirotaman costs Rp5000, a taxi, Rp10,000; or catch southbound bus #2 (Rp1000) from Jalan Mataram, one block east of Jalan Malioboro. All inter-city buses arrive at the **Giwangan station**, just inside the city ring road a few kilometres southeast of the city centre. If you're arriving in Yogya from Borobudur or elsewhere in the north, you can alight at **Jombor terminal**, around 3km north of the city centre, from where you can catch infrequent bus #5 (Rp1000) to the main post office. From near Giwangan, there are regular services into town, including bus #2 (Rp1000), which travels via Jalan Prawirotaman, and #5, which travels via the western end of Jalan Sosrowijayan.

Orientation and information

Most of the interest for visitors is focused on the two-kilometre-wide strip of land between the two westernmost rivers, Kali Winongo and Kali Code – this is the site of the **Kraton**, the historic heart of the city. A kilometre north of the Kraton walls, the budget travellers' mecca of **Jalan Sosrowijayan** (known as Jalan Sosro) runs west off Jalan Malioboro to the south of Tugu train station. There's a second, more upmarket cluster of tourist hotels and restaurants on **Jalan Prawirotaman**, in the suburbs to the southeast of the Kraton.

The **tourist office** is at Jl Malioboro 14–16 (Mon–Sat 8am–7pm; ☎0274/566000) and keeps plenty of information on local events, language and meditation courses.

City transport

All **city buses** charge a set Rp1000 and begin and end their journeys at the Giwangan bus station. Most buses stop running at about 6pm, although the #15 runs to the main post office until 8pm. The most useful buses for travellers are the #4, which runs south down Jalan Malioboro before heading to Kota Gede and the Giwangan bus station; and the #5, which runs between Giwangan and Jombor stations via Jalan Sosro (when heading north) and the main post office (when returning to Giwangan).

There are literally thousands of **becak** in Yogya, and they are the most convenient form of transport. It should cost no more than Rp2000 from Jalan Sosro to the main post office (Rp5000 from Jalan Prawirotaman), although hard bargaining is required. The horse-drawn carriages, known as **andong**, which tend to queue up along Jalan Malioboro, are a little cheaper. **Taxis** are good value (Rp4,000 minimum). You can usually find them hanging around the main post office, or ring Setia Kawan (☎0274/522333) or Sumber Rejo (☎0274/514786). Yogya is a flat city, so you might want to rent a **bicycle**: try Bike 33 in Jl Sosro Gang I (Rp5000 per day); motorbikes

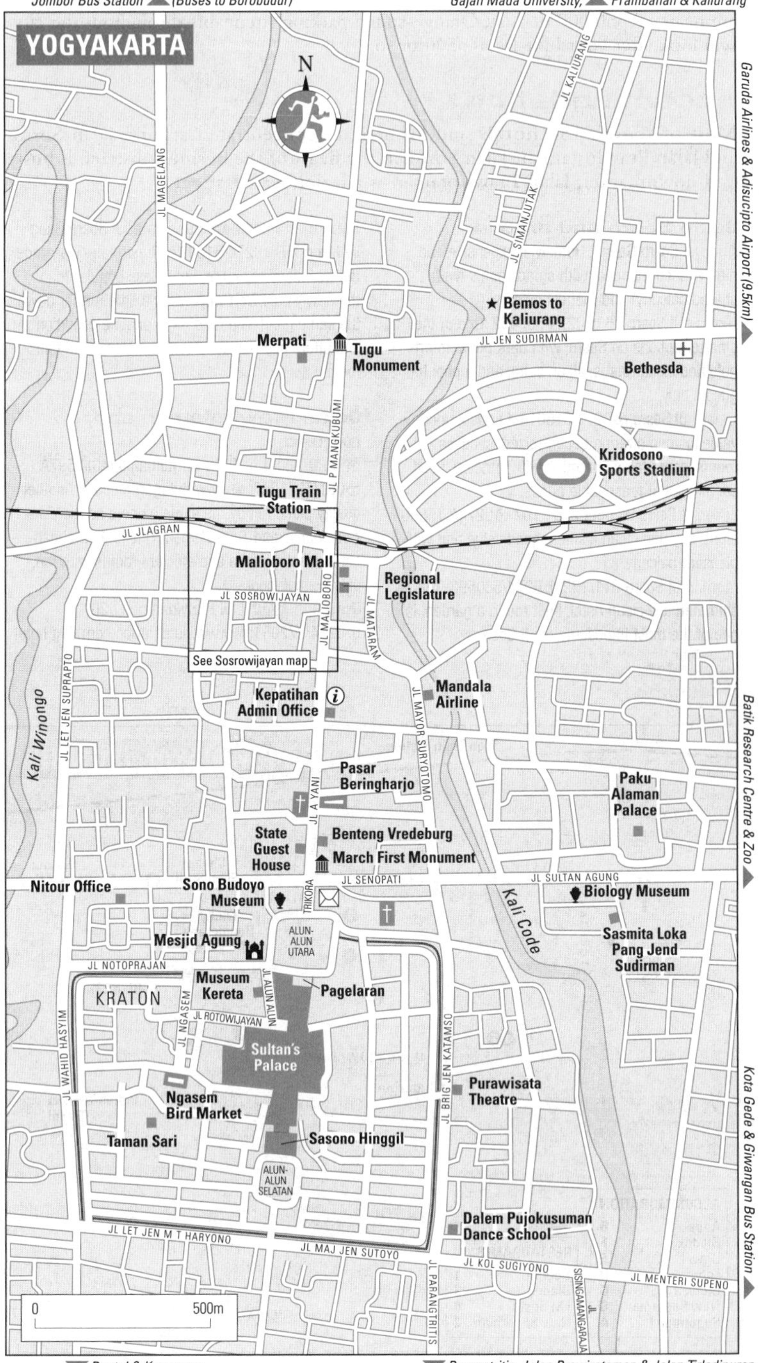
Jombor Bus Station (Buses to Borobudur)
Gajah Mada University, Prambanan & Kaliurang
YOGYAKARTA
N
Garuda Airlines & Adisucipto Airport (9.5km)
Batik Research Centre & Zoo
Kota Gede & Giwangan Bus Station
Bantul & Kasongan
Parangtritis, Jalan Prawirotaman & Jalan Tirlodipuran
JL MAGELANG
JL KALIURANG
JL SIMANJUNTAK
Bemos to Kaliurang
Merpati
Tugu Monument
JL JEN SUDIRMAN
Bethesda
JL P MANGKUBUMI
Kridosono Sports Stadium
Tugu Train Station
JL JLAGRAN
Malioboro Mall
Regional Legislature
JL SOSROWIJAYAN
JL MALIOBORO
JL MATARAM
See Sosrowijayan map
JL LET JEN SUPRAPTO
Kali Winongo
Kepatihan Admin Office
Mandala Airline
JL MAYOR SURYOTOMO
Pasar Beringharjo
JL A YANI
Paku Alaman Palace
State Guest House
Benteng Vredeburg
March First Monument
Nitour Office
Sono Budoyo Museum
TRIKORA
JL SENOPATI
JL SULTAN AGUNG
Biology Museum
Kali Code
ALUN-ALUN UTARA
Mesjid Agung
Sasmita Loka Pang Jend Sudirman
JL NOTOPRAJAN
Museum Kereta
Pagelaran
KRATON
JL NGASEM
JL ALUN ALUN
JL ROTOWIJAYAN
JL WAHID HASYIM
Sultan's Palace
JL BRIG JEN KATAMSO
Purawisata Theatre
Ngasem Bird Market
Taman Sari
Sasono Hinggil
ALUN-ALUN SELATAN
Dalem Pujokusuman Dance School
JL LET JEN M T HARYONO
JL MAJ JEN SUTOYO
JL KOL SUGIYONO
JL MENTERI SUPENO
JL PARANGTRITIS
JL SISINGAMANGARAJA
0
500m

are nearer Rp50,000 per day. Orange-suited parking attendants throughout the city will look after your bike for Rp500 or so.

Accommodation

Most of Yogya's 150 **hotels** and losmen are concentrated around Jalan Sosro and Jalan Prawirotaman. Jalan Sosro, in the heart of the business district, is busy and downmarket; Jalan Prawirotaman is a lazier, leafier street.

Jalan Sosro and around

Anda Jl Sosro Gang I. Homely, inexpensive and highly recommended, with smart rooms (with shared balcony) and friendly owners. 1

Bladok Jl Sosro 76 ☎0274/560452. One of the smarter options on Sosro, with dark but comfortable and clean rooms, all en suite, and a pool for guests only. 2–3

Dewi I Jl Sosro ☎0274/516014. Largish, good-value losmen offering decent-sized, spotless rooms, some fairly charming with intricate wood carving, all at reasonable prices. 1

Lotus Jl Sosro Wetan Gang I 167 ☎0274/515090. Light, airy and clean losmen, good value and with a pleasant balcony. 1

Monica Jl Sosro GT1/192 ☎0274/580598. This shimmeringly clean hotel, built round a garden, is one of the most handsome on Jl Sosro. 2–3

Superman I and **New Superman** Jl Sosro Gang I/71 and 79 ☎0274/515007. *Superman I* was once the travellers' favourite, but is less popular than the newly built *New Superman* a little further down the same gang. The latter is in pristine condition and offers good-value accommodation, with fine rooms. 1

Jalan Prawirotaman and around

Delta Homestay Jl Prawirotaman II MGIII/597A ☎081/7271047, @www.dutagarden.com. Another quality place run by the same owners as the *Duta Guesthouse* and *Duta Garden*. This is their cheapest homestay, clean and efficient rooms with fan, plus a small pool. 2

Duta Guesthouse Jl Prawirotaman I 26 ☎0274/372064, @www.dutagarden.com. Big hotel

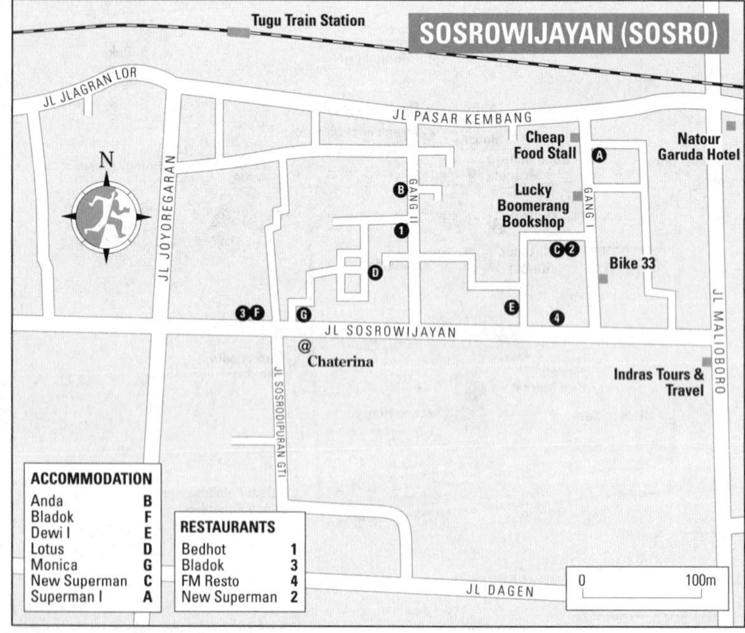

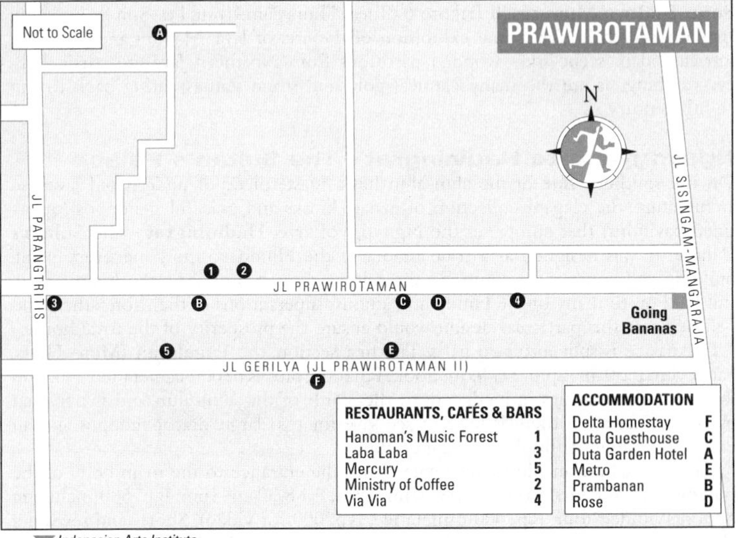

that comes highly recommended by all who stay here and which is popular with tour groups; it has a good pool and does huge breakfasts. ②–⑤

Duta Garden Hotel Jl Timuran MGIII/103 ☎0274/373482, Ⓦwww.dutagarden.com. Exceptionally beautiful cottage-style hotel smothered in a thick blanket of bougainvillea and roses, sister of *Duta Guesthouse* (above). Rooms are equally exquisite; bargain hard in the low season for a discount. ⑤–⑥

Metro Jl Prawirotaman II 71 ☎0274/372364, Ⓔcafeyg2@idola.net.id. A big hotel with a pool and restaurant, and a fairly grotty economy section in a different building at the end of the street. ②–④

Prambanan Jl Prawirotaman I 14 ☎0274/376167, Ⓦwww.prambananguesthouse.info. A quiet hotel with bamboo-walled rooms, swimming pool and eager-to-please staff. Breakfast and afternoon tea included. ①–②

Rose Jl Prawirotaman I 28 ☎0274/377991. The best value in Prawirotaman. Hearty breakfasts, a swimming pool and very cheap rooms. Bargain in the low season for an even better deal. ③

The Kraton

The layout of Yogya reflects its character: modern and brash on the outside, but with a very ancient and traditional heart in the **Kraton**, the walled city designed by Yogya's first sultan, Mangkubumi. Kraton means "royal residence" and originally referred just to the Sultan's Palace, but today it denotes the whole of the walled city (plus Jalan Malioboro), which includes not only the palace but also an entire town of some ten thousand people. The Kraton has changed little in the two hundred years since Mangkubumi's time; both the palace, and the 5km of crenellated icing-sugar walls that surround the Kraton, date from his reign.

Alun-alun Utara

Most people enter the Kraton through the northern gates by the main post office, beyond which lies the busy town square, Alun-alun Utara. As is usual in Java, the city's grand mosque, **Mesjid Agung** (visit outside of prayer times), built in 1773 by Mangkubumi, stands on the western side of the alun-alun. It's designed along traditional Javanese lines, with a multi-tiered roof on top of an airy, open-sided prayer hall. A little to the north of the mosque, just by the main gates, stands the

Sono Budoyo Museum, Jl Trikoro 6 (Tues–Thurs 8am–1pm, Fri–Sun 8–11.30am; Rp750), which houses a fine exhibition of the arts of Java, Madura and Bali. The intricate, damascene-style wooden partitions from Northern Java are particularly eye-catching, as are the many classical gold and stone statues dating back to the eighth century.

Ngayogyokarto Hadiningrat - The Sultan's Palace

On the southern side of the alun-alun lies a masterpiece of understated Javanese architecture, the elegant collection of ornate kiosks and graceful pendopos (open-sided pavilions) that comprises the **Ngayogyokarto Hadiningrat** – the **Sultan's Palace**. It was designed as a scale model of the Hindu cosmos, and every plant, building and courtyard is symbolic; the sultans, though professing the Islamic faith, still held on to many of the Hindu and animist superstitions of their forefathers and believed that this particular design would ensure the prosperity of the royal house.

The palace is split into two parts. The first section, the **Pagelaran** (Mon–Thurs, Sat & Sun 8.30am–2pm, Fri 8.30–noon; Rp2000, plus Rp1000 camera fee, Rp2000 for video camera) lies immediately to the south of the alun-alun and is bypassed by most tourists, as there is little to see save for two large, drab pendopos and an extremely mediocre display of regal costumes.

Further down Jalan Alun-alun Utara stands the entrance to the main body of the **palace** (Mon–Thurs, Sat & Sun 8.30am–2pm, Fri 8.30am–1pm; Rp7500 including optional guided tour, Rp1000 camera fee, Rp2000 for video). Shorts and revealing clothes are frowned upon here, so you may have to rent a batik shirt from the ticket office. The palace has been the home of the sultans ever since Mangkubumi arrived here from Solo in 1755, and little has changed. The hushed courtyards, the faint stirrings of the gamelan drifting on the breeze and the elderly palace retainers, still dressed in the traditional style with a kris (traditional dagger) tucked by the small of their back, all contribute to a remarkable sense of timelessness. You enter the complex through the palace's outer courtyard or **Keben**, where the sultan used to sit on a stone throne and pass sentence on lawbreakers. Two pendopos stand on either side of a central path in the next courtyard, each sheltering an antique gamelan orchestra; the eastern pendopo also houses royal curios including an early royal playpen.

Two silver-painted *raksasa* (temple guardian statues) guard the entrance to the largest and most important palace courtyard, the Pelataran Kedaton. On your right, the ornate **Gedung Kuning** contains the offices and living quarters of the sultan. This part of the palace is out of bounds to tourists, as the current sultan (Hamengkubuwono X), his wife and five daughters still spend much of their time here. A covered corridor joins the Gedung Kuning with the Golden Throne Pavilion, or **Bangsal Kencono**, the centrepiece of the Pelataran Kedaton. In the imagery of the Hindu cosmos, the pavilion represents Mount Meru, the sacred mountain at the very centre of the universe. Its intricately carved roof is held aloft by hefty teak pillars, whose carvings neatly sum up the syncretism of the three main religions of Indonesia, with the lotus leaf of Buddhism supporting a red-and-gold diamond pattern of Hindu origin, while around the pillar's circumference runs the opening line of the Koran: "There is no God but Allah and Mohammed is his prophet." In the eastern wall, a large, arched gateway flanked by two huge drums connects the Pelataran Kedaton with the **Kesatrian** courtyard, home to both another gamelan orchestra and a collection of royal portraits, while to the south is a display dedicated to Hamengkubuwono IX.

The Taman Sari

A five-minute walk to the west of the palace, along Jalan Rotowijayan and down Jalan Ngasem and Jalan Taman, is the **Taman Sari** (Water Garden) of Mangkubumi (daily 9am–3pm; Rp5000 including tour). This giant complex was designed in the eighteenth century as an amusement park for the royal house, and features a series of swimming pools and fountains, an underground mosque and a large boating lake. Unfortunately, it fell into disrepair and most of what you see today is a concrete reconstruction, financed by UNESCO. While the renovation gives a better idea of what the complex used to look like, it's been rather over-reconstructed and there isn't much atmosphere to be gained.

Jalan Malioboro

The two-kilometre stretch of road heading north from the alun-alun is as replete with history as it is with batik shops and becak. Originally this was designed as a **ceremonial boulevard** by Mangkubumi, along which the royal cavalcade would proceed on its way to Mount Merapi. The road changes name three times along its length, beginning as Jalan A Yani in the south before continuing as Jalan Malioboro, and then finally Jalan Mangkubumi. At the southern end of the street, near the junction of Jalan A Yani and Jalan Senopati, stands the **Benteng Vredeburg**, Jl A Yani 6 (Tues–Thurs 8.30am–1 pm, Fri 8.30–11am, Sat & Sun 8.30am–noon; Rp750) a fort ordered by the Dutch, and built by Mangkubumi in the mid-eighteenth century. This relic of Dutch imperialism has been restored to its former glory, and now houses a series of well-made and informative dioramas that recount the end of colonialism in Indonesia. Nearby, the raucous, multi-level market complex **Pasar Beringharjo** buzzes noisily throughout the day, selling mass-produced batik (with a small, quality selection in the southeastern corner on the ground floor).

The rest of the city

Yogyakarta's second court, **Paku Alaman Palace** (Tues, Thurs & Sun 9.30am–1.30pm; free) lies 50m to the northeast of the Biology Museum on the north side of Jalan Sultan Agung. As is traditional, the minor court of the city faces south as a mark of subservience to the main palace. The royal household of Paku Alam was created in 1812 by the British in a deliberate divide-and-rule tactic. The current prince, the octogenarian Paku Alam VIII, is by far the longest-reigning ruler of all Central Java's royal courts, having been in place for over sixty years. The part that is open to general view – by the southeastern corner of the courtyard – houses a motley collection of royal artefacts, including a room filled with the prince's chariots, which unfortunately appear to be permanently shrouded in dust sheets.

Eating and drinking

Yogya's specialities are *ayam goreng* and *nasi gudeg* (rice and jackfruit), and many foodstalls serve nothing else. Every evening a **food market** sets up on Jalan Malioboro, and by 8pm the entire street is thronged with diners. Beware of being overcharged, and note that in many of the larger *lesehan* places (where you sit on the floor by low tables), particularly those by the end of Jalan Sosro, diners pay restaurant prices. The stalls by Tugu train station and on the top floor of the Malioboro Mall are cheaper. Jalans Sosro and Prawirotaman are chock-full of good-quality **restaurants** asking reasonable prices (about Rp7000 for nasi goreng). Most of these open from midday until about 10pm.

Yogya's **nightlife** is really an early-evening life; very few places stay open beyond midnight, and most of the action happens between 7 and 10pm, when the city's **cultural entertainment** is in full swing. A few of the **bars** are worth checking out. *Laba Laba*, Jl Prawirotaman II, is an over-priced restaurant and bar, with weird cocktails a speciality: try the "Laba Laba Special", a potent mixture of Guinness, whisky and shandy. Not far from the Sultan's Palace in Jalan Brigen Katamso is the new *Etnik Kafe* (Ⓣ0274/375705, Ⓔetnikkafe@etnikkafe.every1.net) combining a café and outdoor nightclub. Bands from Yogya and other cities regularly perform from 9.30pm–1am. Also try *Java Kafe*, Jl Magelang 163 (Ⓣ0274/624190). This has live music, a well-stocked bar and an international menu. Best of all, however, is the *Djogja Kafe* at Jl Kyai Mojo 57, a favoured nightspot with al fresco drinking and live music.

Jalan Sosro

Bedhot Jl Sosro Gang I Laid-back place serving some decent interpretations of Western and Indonesian food, including some tasty *tempe* burgers.
Bladok Jl Sosro 76. Part of a hotel, this open-air mid-priced restaurant serving mainly Indonesian dishes is a little more expensive than the Sosro norm, but definitely worth it.
FM Resto Jl Sosro 10. Great atmosphere with live music; the most popular travellers' place in Yogya. The food is good, varied but quite expensive.
New Superman JL Sosro Gang I/99. Popular restaurant in Sosro, with delicious pancakes, ice-cold beer, regular screenings of European football, and Internet facilities.

Jalan Prawirotaman

Hanoman's Music Forest Jl Prawirotaman. Now under new (Dutch) management, the main reason for visiting this restauraunt is to catch one of its live shows – traditional wayang on Sun and Monday (Rp15,000; see below), live acoustic sets for the rest of the week.
Mercury Jl Parawirotaman II MG3/595. Beautiful, colonial-style restaurant serving surprisingly affordable mid-priced Indonesian and Western dishes.
Ministry of Coffee Jl Prawirotaman. The sort of café that wouldn't look out of place on one of the smarter high streets of Europe. Great coffee, fine snacks and cakes, and a wonderful escape from the hubbub outside. Treat yourself.
Via Via Jl Prawirotaman 24b ☎0274/386557. A foreign-run and popular travellers' hangout. Good European and Indonesian food. Also a good place to get information on what there is to do in Yogya.

Traditional cultural performances

Wayang kulit is the epitome of Javanese culture, and visitors should really try to catch at least a part of one of these shows, although **wayang golek**, where wooden puppets are used, tends to be easier to follow, as the figures are more dynamic and expressive. For a preview of both forms, head to the Sultan's Palace – on Saturday mornings (9am–1pm), there's a practice-cum-performance of wayang kulit in the Sriminganti courtyard, and every Wednesday (9am–noon) a free wayang golek show. On Monday and Wednesday mornings between 10.30am and noon, free **gamelan** performances are given. The *Natour Garuda Hotel* on Jalian Malioboro also holds regular gamelan recitals every evening at 8pm.

With one honourable exception, all of the wayang performances listed below are designed with tourists' attention span in mind, being only two hours long. Hardcore wayang kulit fans, however, may wish to check out the all-nighter at the Alun-alun Selatan (see Sasono Hinggil below). For the latest timings and schedules, ask at the tourist office or your hotel.

Ambarrukmo Palace Hotel Jl Adisucipto 66. A free wayang golek show in the hotel's restaurant is put on as an accompaniment to the food (Mon 8pm).
Hanoman's Music Forest Jl Prawirotaman. Every Sunday and Monday, this restaurant presents a two-hour wayang (kulit or golek) show from 7 to 9pm (Rp15,000).
Nitour Jl KHA Dalan 71 ☎0274/376450. This centre, outside of the northern walls of the Kraton, puts on a wayang golek performance of the Ramayana tales. Daily except holidays 11am–1pm; Rp5000.
Sasono Hinggil Alun-alun Selatan. Yogya's only full-length wayang kulit performance runs from 9pm to 5.30am on the second Saturday of every month, and on alternate fourth Saturdays (Rp5000).
Sono Budoyo Museum Jl Trikora 1. The most professional and popular wayang kulit show, performed daily for 2hr (8pm; Rp7500).

Javanese dancing

The **Ramayana** dance drama is a modern extension of the court dances of the nineteenth century, which tended to use that other Indian epic, the Mahabharata, as the source of their story lines. The biggest crowd-pulling spectacle around Yogya has to be the moonlit performance of the Ramayana ballet, which takes place every summer in the open-air theatre at Prambanan Temple, and can be booked in Yogya (see p.297 for details).
Ndalem Pujokusuman Jl Brig Jen Katamso 45. A two-hour performance of classical Javanese dance at this, one of the most illustrious dance schools in Yogya (Mon, Wed & Fri 8pm; Rp15,000).
Purawisata Theatre Jl Brig Jen Katamso

(☎0274/374089). Every night for the last two decades, the Puriwisata Theatre has put on a 90min performance of the Ramayana. The story is split into two episodes, with each episode performed on alternate nights. On the last day of every month, the whole story is performed.

Sultan's Palace Every Sunday and Thursday, the Kraton Classical Dance School holds public rehearsals (10am–noon). No cover fee once you've paid to get into the palace. Well worthwhile.

Shopping

Yogya is Java's souvenir centre, with keepsakes and mementoes from all over the archipelago finding their way into the city's shops and street stalls. **Jalan Malioboro** is the main shopping area for inexpensive souvenirs (batik pictures, leather bags, woodcarvings and silver rings). A recent development on the shopping scene is the establishment of a number of upmarket **souvenir emporiums** that steer clear of the usual mass-produced offerings, selling tasteful, individual local craft items instead: Going Bananas in Prawirotaman is one such place. Batik Keris, Jl A Yani 104 (☎0274/512492) and Batik Mirota, Jl A Yani 9 (☎0274/588524) are both reputable shops offering a huge array of souvenirs from Yogya and elsewhere in Indonesia.

Silver

The suburb of Kota Gede is the home of the **silver industry** in Central Java, famous for its fine **filigree** work. If you can't find exactly what you want, it's possible to commission the workshops to produce it for you. Some workshops, such as the huge Tom's Silver at Jl Ngeksi Gondo 60 (daily 8.30am–7.30pm) and MD Silver, Jl Pesegah KG 8/44 (just off Jalan Ngeksi Gondo), which is cheaper than Tom's, allow you to wander around and watch the smiths at work.

If your budget is limited, then the many stallholders along Jalan Malioboro sell perfectly reasonable silver jewellery, much of it from East Java or Bali. Expect to pay Rp10,000 for a ring, and Rp15,000–20,000 for earrings.

Batik

With the huge influx of tourists over the last twenty years, Yogya has evolved a **batik** style that increasingly panders to Western tastes. However, there is still plenty of the traditional indigo-and-brown batik clothing – sarongs, shirts and dresses – for sale, especially on Jalan Malioboro and in Pasar Beringharjo. **The Batik Research Centre** Jl Dr Sutomo 13 (☎0274/515953) will help you to put the craft in an historical context and provides examples of the several techniques and styles.

There are a gaggle of **galleries** in the Kraton, most of them tucked away in the kampung that occupies the grounds of the old Taman Sari. For the best-quality – and most expensive – batiks in town, head to **Jalan Tirtodipuran**, west of Jalan Prawirotaman, home of the renowned artists Tulus Warsito (at 19a) and Slamet Riyanto (61a), as well as a galaxy of good-quality galleries. If you still haven't found a piece of batik that you like, you could try and make one yourself by signing up for one of the many batik courses held in Yogya; see p.292 for details.

Leather and pottery

All around Yogya, and particularly in the markets along Jalan Malioboro, hand-stitched, good-quality **leather** bags, suitcases, belts and shoes can be bought extremely cheaply. A number of Maliobro's shops also sell leather goods. Many of these leather products originate from the village of **Manding**, 12km south of Yogya. To see them being made and get a better deal than you would in town, catch a white Jahayu bus to Manding from Jalan Parangtritis (25min; Rp3000).

Javanese pottery is widely available throughout Yogya. Again, the markets along Jalan Malioboro sell ochre pottery, with huge Chinese urns, decorative bowls, erotic statues, whistles, flutes and other pottery instruments.

Antiques, puppets and curios

In the vicinity of Jalan Prawirotaman there are a number of cavernous antique shops dealing mainly in **teak furniture** from Jepara and the north. Much of it is very fine quality, but the cost of sending these bulky items home may be prohibitive. Many of these outlets sell traditional Javanese wooden trunks, the exteriors beautifully carved with detailed patterns, for which you can expect to pay at least US$50. Harto is a large company with a number of outlets around Jalan Tirtodipuran, each specializing in a particular sort of souvenir. One shop sells **woodcarvings**, for instance, and another deals in **wayang kulit puppets**; expect to pay at least Rp75,000 for a reasonable-quality thirty-centimetre puppet. There are also a couple of puppet shops on Jalan Prawirotaman, and two at the northern end of Malioboro. Check out Moesson Antik, too, on Jalan Prawirotaman near the *Ministry of Coffee*; the shop's collection ranges from simple tat to genuine antiques – great for a rummage even if you have no intention of buying.

Other popular souvenirs include personalized **rubber stamps**, made while you wait for about Rp15,000 a stamp on the pavements of Jalan Malioboro, and the traditional Yogyan batik **headdresses** (*blangkon*), distinguishable from the Solo variety by the large pre-tied knot at the back, costing about Rp5000. Samudra Raya at Jl Sosro GT1/32, specializes in selling good-quality models of traditional Indonesian ships. Prices start at about Rp250,000.

Listings

Airlines Batavia, Jl Urip Sumoharjo ☎0274/547373; Bouraq, Jl Menteri Supeno 58 ☎0274/383414; Garuda, *Ambarrukmo Palace Hotel* ☎0274/487983, and at the airport ☎0274/560108; Lion Air, *Hotel Melia Purosani*, Jl Mayor Suryotomo 31 ☎0274/555028; Merpati, Jl Diponegoro 31 ☎0274/514272; Mandala, *Hotel Melia Purosani*, Jl Mayor Suryotomo 573 ☎0274/520603. All have the same opening hours: Mon–Fri 7.30am–5pm, Sat & Sun 9am–1pm.

Banks and exchange Yogya is one of the few places where the moneychangers offer a better deal than the banks, at least for cash. In particular, PT Gajahmas Mulyosakti, Jl A Yani 86a, and PT Dua Sisi Jogya Indah, at the southern corner of the Malioboro Mall, offer very competitive rates. PT Baruman Abadi in the *Natour Garuda Hotel*, Jl Malioboro 60, offers good rates and stays open longer (Mon–Fri 7am–7pm, Sat 7am–3pm). In Prawirotaman, the Agung moneychanger at Jl Prawirotaman 68 and Kresna at no. 18 offers the best rates. Of the banks, go for the BNI, Jl Trikora 1, just in front of the post office or BCA Jl Mangkubumi, both of which accept Visa and MasterCard at their ATMs. Banks are closed on Saturdays and Sundays.

Batik courses Right by the entrance to the Taman Sari is the workshop of Dr Hadjir (☎0274/377835), who runs a three- to five-day course (US$25 for three days, plus US$5 for materials). His course is one of the most extensive and includes tutoring on the history of batik and the preparation of both chemical and natural dyes. Gapura Batik, Jl Taman KP III/177 (☎0274/377835) runs a three- or five-day course. The Puriwisata School, on Jl Brig Jen Katamso, features a rather expensive but comprehensive batik course (Rp50,000 per session). The Batik Research Centre at Jl Kusumanegara 2, has intensive three-day courses for US$55. For the truly committed, they also run a three-month course. Booking is often required for courses.

Bookshops The Lucky Boomerang at Jl Sosro Gang I/67 has the best selection of English-language novels, guidebooks and other books on Indonesia. The Gramedia Bookshop in the Malioboro Shopping Centre also has a fair selection of English-language books on Indonesia.

Car and motorbike rental A Honda Astrea motorbike can be rented for Rp35,000 per day from various places around Jl Sosro.

Cookery courses The *Via Via* café, Jl Prawirotaman 24b, runs afternoon courses (Rp50,000), where they teach you to make their wonderful version of gado-gado as well as other Indonesian staples. They also hold one-week courses for US$150.

Dance and gamelan courses Several places offer courses in gamelan – the traditional orchestra of Java. The following offer introductions and tuition: Gajah Mada University, Faculty of Cultural Sciences, Jl Nusantara 1, Bulaksumur ☎0274/901137 or 513096 ext 217; Indonesian Arts Institute, Faculty of Performing Arts, Gamelan Studies, Jl Parangtritis Km 5.6 ☎0274/384108 or 375380; and Santa Dharma University, ILCIC, Mrican Tromol pos 29, Yogyakarta ☎0274/515352 ext 534. Mrs Tia of the Ndalem Pujokusirman dance school at Jl Brig Jen Katamso 45 (☎0274/371271) invites

foreigners to join her two-hour group lessons beginning at 4pm. At the northern end of the same street is the Puriwisata (☎0274/374089), an open-air theatre and mini-theme park which holds Javanese dance courses for Rp50,000 per 3hr session. They also run a school for gamelan (Rp50,000 per session). The *Via Via Café* on Jl Prawirotaman has intensive one-week courses for US$150.
Hospitals and clinics The Gading Clinic, south of the Alun-alun Selatan at Jl Maj Jen Panjaitan 25, has English-speaking doctors (☎0274/375396). The main hospital in Yogya is the Bethesda, Jl Jen Sudirman 70 ☎0274/566300. Also Ludira Husada Tama Hospital, Jl Wiratama 4 ☎0274/620091.
Internet access A proliferation of Internet places have recently opened in Yogya. For Sosro, Chaterina's, on the main street (Rp8000 per hour), continues to be popular and reliable, while the Metro Internet in the *Metro* guesthouse, Jl Prawitotaman II/71, performs the same service down in Prawirotaman.
Post office Jl Senopati 2, at the southern end of Jl Malioboro (Mon–Sat 6am–10pm, Sun 6am–8pm). The parcel office is on Jl Mayor Suryotomo (Mon–Sat 8am–3pm, Sun 9am–2pm). Parcel-wrappers loiter outside the office during these times.
Swimming The *Hotel Batik Yogyakarta*, south of Jl Sosro, allows non-guests to use their pool for Rp7000 (daily 9am–9pm). In Prawirotaman, you can use the *Rose Guesthouse*'s pool for Rp7000.
Telephone The main Telkom office at Jl Yos Sudarso 9 is open 24hr and has Home Direct phones, too. There's a wartel office at no. 30 Jl Sosro and another on Jl Parangtritis, south of Jl Prawirotaman Gang II.
Tour operators Yogya is full of tour companies offering trips to the nearby temples (Rp45,000 for a tour of both Prambanan and Borobudur), as well as further afield. The price generally doesn't include entrance fees, and the only advantage of taking a tour is convenience. Jaya, based on Jl Sosro Gang II ☎0274/586735), but with agents all over the city, is one of the largest and most experienced. However, a couple of companies offer something a little different, including *Via Via Café*, the travellers' café on Jl Prawirotaman, which organizes bicycle and hiking tours around the local area.
Travel agents Probably the most respected of Yogya's travel agents, and certainly one of the more reliable, is Indras Tours and Travel at Jl Malioboro 131 (☎0274/561972), just a few metres south of the eastern end of Jl Sosro.

Gunung Merapi and Kaliurang

Marking the northern limit of the Daerah Istimewa Yogyakarta, symmetrical, smoke-plumed **Gunung Merapi** (Giving Fire) is an awesome 2914-metre presence in the centre of Java, visible from Yogyakarta, 25km away. This is Indonesia's most volatile volcano, and the sixth most active in the world. The Javanese worship the mountain as a life-giver, its lava enriching the soil and providing Central Java with its agricultural fecundity. Down the centuries its ability to annihilate has frequently been demonstrated. Thirteen hundred people died following a particularly vicious eruption in 1930, and as recently as 1994 an entire mountain village was incinerated by lava, which killed 64 people.

Kaliurang

Nearly a kilometre up on Merapi's southern slopes is the village of **KALIURANG**, a tatty, downmarket but tranquil hill station and an extremely popular weekend retreat for Yogyakartans. A bus from Yogya's Giwangan station costs Rp2000; it's Rp3000 by bemo from behind the Terban terminal on Jalan Simanjutak. In Kaliurang, you can join a trekking group to the summit, a fairly arduous five-hour scramble through the snake- and spider-infested forest that beards Merapi's lower slopes. The tigers, which terrorized this forest as recently as the 1960s, have now all been killed off. During Merapi's dormant months (usually March to Oct) it's possible to climb all the way to the top, but at other times, when the volcano is active, you may have to settle for a distant view from the observation platform. All treks begin in the dark at 3am, when the lava, spilling over the top and tracing a searing path down the mountainside, can be seen most clearly. Bring warm clothes, a torch and sturdy boots (not sandals, which offer little protection against poisonous snakes).

Treks (Rp15,000 including breakfast) are organized by *Vogel's Hostel* in Kaliurang, Jl Astya Mulya 76 (☎0274/895208; ❶–❷), which also happens to be one of the best budget **hostels** in Java. The hostel is split into two parts: the rooms in the new extension are beautiful and good value, while those in the old building (a former holiday home for one of Yogya's lesser nobility) are spartan but inexpensive ranging from Rp20,000 in the dormitory to Rp50,000 for a bungalow. The **food**, including Indonesian staples and Western snacks, is truly delicious, and there's a large travellers' library. The owner is a veritable encyclopedia of volcano knowledge, and is the head of the rescue team in Kaliurang. If you're looking for somewhere plusher, try the *Village Taman Eden*, Jalan Astya Mulya (☎0274/895442; ❸–❺), a collection of reasonably luxurious villas of varying quality and price built round a central swimming pool. *Wisma Gadja Mada*, Jl Wreksa 447 (☎0274/895225; ❸–❹), is a colonial-period guesthouse with villa-style accommodation.

Borobudur and around

Forty kilometres west of Yogya, surrounded on three sides by volcanoes and on the fourth by jagged limestone cliffs, is the largest monument in the southern hemisphere. This is the temple of **Borobudur**, the number one tourist attraction in Java and the greatest single piece of classical architecture in the entire archipelago. The temple is actually a colossal multi-tiered Buddhist stupa lying at the western end of a four-kilometre-long chain of temples (one of which, the nearby **Candi Mendut**, is also worth visiting), built in the ninth century by the Saliendra dynasty. At 34.5m tall, however, and covering an area of some 200 square metres, Borobudur is on a different scale altogether, dwarfing all the other *candi* in the chain.

The world's largest Buddhist stupa was actually built on Hindu **foundations**, which began life in 775 AD as a large step pyramid. Just fifteen years later, however, the construction was abandoned as the Buddhist Saliendras drove the Sanjayas eastwards. The Saliendras then appropriated the pyramid as the foundation for their own temple, beginning in around 790 AD and completing the work approximately seventy years later. Over 1.6 million blocks of a local volcanic rock (called andesite) were used in Borobudur's construction, joined together without mortar. Sculpted reliefs adorned the lower galleries, covered with stucco and painted. Unfortunately, the pyramid foundation proved to be inherently unstable, cracks appeared, and the hill became totally waterlogged. After about a century, the Saliendras abandoned the site and for almost a thousand years Borobudur lay neglected. The English "rediscovered" it in 1815, but nothing much was done until 1973, when UNESCO began to take the temple apart, block by block, in order to replace the waterlogged hill with a concrete substitute. The project took eleven years and cost US$21million.

Practicalities

Most people choose to see the **site** (daily 6am–5.30pm; US$10, Rp40,000 for guided tour, Rp3000 for the tourist train around the site plus Rp3000 for the rather poor museum; Ⓦwww.borobudurpark.com) on a day-trip from Yogya. Plenty of agencies offer **all-inclusive tours**, or you can go independently by catching one of the regular buses from Yogya's Giwangan station, which calls in at Jombor bus station (handy for Jalan Sosro; irregular bus #5) before heading off to Borobudur village bus station (1hr 30min; Rp6000-8000), though you may have to change one more time in Muntilan. The entrance to the temple lies 500m southwest of the bus stop.

A number of **hotels** have sprouted up in the village in recent years. The most popular budget choice is the *Lotus Guesthouse* at Jl Medang Kamulan 2 (☎0293/788281; ❷–❹) on the northern side of the park, with good views of the temple from the rooftop. The *Manohara* (☎0293/788131; ❻) is actually in the temple grounds, just

100m or so south of the main entrance. It's expensive, but when you consider that entry into the temple is included, and it means staying in the smartest rooms around, the hotel seems very fair value. To the south, the quiet, unassuming *Rajasa* at Jl Badrawati 2 (☎0293/788276; ❸–❹) has beautiful views over the ricefields and some smart rooms, the most expensive having hot water, air-con and a bathtub.

Most people who stay in Borobudur overnight choose **to eat** in their hotel, though there are a couple of inexpensive Padang places opposite the entrance to the temple grounds.

The ruins

Borobudur is pregnant with symbolism, and precisely oriented so that its four sides face the four points of the compass; the **entrance** lies to the north. Unlike most temples, it was not built as a dwelling for the gods, but rather as a representation of the Buddhist cosmic mountain, Meru. Accordingly, at the base is the real, earthly world, a world of desires and passions, and at the summit is nirvana. Thus, as you make your way around the temple passages and slowly spiral to the summit, you are symbolically following the path to enlightenment.

Every journey to enlightenment begins in the squalor of the real world, and at Borobudur the first five levels – the square terraces – are covered with three thousand **reliefs** representing man's earthly existence. As you might expect, the lowest, subterranean level has carvings depicting the basest desires, best seen at the southeast corner. The reliefs on the **first four levels above ground** cover the beginning of man's path to enlightenment. Each of the ten series (one on each level on the outer wall and one on the inner wall) tells a story, beginning by the eastern stairway and continuing in a clockwise direction. Follow all the stories, and you will have circled the temple ten times – a distance of almost 5km. Buddha's own path to enlightenment is told in the upper panels on the inner wall of the first gallery. As you enter the **fifth level**, the walls fall away to reveal a breathtaking view of the surrounding fields and volcanoes. You are now in the Sphere of Formlessness, the realm of enlightenment: below is the chaos of the world, above is nirvana, represented by a huge empty stupa almost 10m in diameter. Surrounding this stupa are 72 smaller ones, each occupied by a statue of Buddha.

Candi Mendut

Originally Borobudur was part of a chain of four temples joined by a sacred path. Two of the other three temples have been restored and at least one, **Candi Mendut** (daily 6.15am–5.15pm; Rp1000), 3km east of Borobudur, is worth visiting. Buses between Yogya and Borobudur drive right past Mendut (Rp5000 from Yogya for the 1hr 20min journey, Rp1000 for the 10min trip from Borobudur). Built in 800 AD, Mendut was restored at the end of the nineteenth century. The exterior is unremarkable, but the three giant **statues** sitting inside – of Buddha and the Bodhisattvas Avalokitesvara and Vajrapani – are exquisitely carved and startling in their intricacy.

The Prambanan Plain

Nourished by the volcanic detritus of Mount Merapi and washed by innumerable small rivers, the verdant **Prambanan Plain** lies 18km east of Yogya, a patchwork blanket of sun-spangled paddy-fields and vast plantations sweeping down from the southern slopes of the volcano. As well as being one of the most fertile regions in Java, the plain is home to the largest concentration of ancient ruins on the island. Over thirty **temples** and **palaces**, dating mainly from the eighth and ninth centuries, lie scattered over a thirty-square-kilometre area. The temples, a number of which have been fully restored, were built at a time when two rival kingdoms, the

△ Prambanan

Ramayana ballet performances

The highlights of the dancing year in Central Java are the phenomenal Ramayana ballets held during the summer months at the **Prambanan Open-Air Theatre**, to the west of the complex. The Ramayana story is performed just twice monthly from May to October, spread over the two weekends closest to the full moon. The story is split into four episodes, each evening from Friday to Monday (7.30–9.30pm). The second night is the best, with most of the characters making an appearance, and the action is intense. Tickets cost Rp30,000–150,000, depending on where you sit; plenty of agents in Yogya organize packages including entrance fees and transport. Yogya's tourist office also organizes taxis to and from the theatre for around Rp25,000.

Throughout the year, Prambanan's **Trimurti Theatre** (☎0274/496408), an indoor venue to the north of the open-air arena, performs the Ramayana ballet (Tues–Thurs 7.30–9.30pm; Rp30,000–100,000 in Jan to April and Nov to Dec). Tickets are available on the door or from the tourist office in Yogya.

Buddhist Saliendra and the Hindu Sanjaya dynasties, both occupied Central Java. In 832 AD, the Hindu Sanjayas gained the upper hand and soon the great Hindu Prambanan temple complex was built, perhaps in commemoration of their return to power. It seems that some sort of truce followed, with temples of both faiths being constructed on the plain in equal numbers.

Practicalities

Most people visit the Prambanan temples on a **day-trip** from Yogya. Although many tour companies in Yogya offer all-inclusive packages to Prambanan, it's easy enough to get there by local **bus** from Yogya's Giwangan bus station or Solo. Public buses drop passengers off in **Prambanan village**, a tiny huddle on the southern side of Jalan Adisucipto, a five-minute walk from the eastern entrance to the temple complex. The only disadvantage to coming by bus is that you can't then get to the other ruins on the plain, which is why several visitors choose to **cycle** here from Yogya. Fume-choked Jalan Adisucipto is the most straightforward route, but there's a quieter alternative that begins by heading north along Yogya's Jalan Simanjutak and Jalan Kaliurang until you reach the Mataram Canal, just past the main Gajah Mada University compound. Follow the canal path east for 12km (1hr), and you'll come out eventually near Candi Sari on Jalan Adisucipto. Prambanan village is 4km east of Candi Sari, along Jalan Adisucipto. You can **stay** in the village at one of the rudimentary losmen (❶). To the north of the open-air theatre, the *Prambanan Village Hotel* (☎0274/496435; ❻) provides more salubrious accommodation and houses a fine Japanese restaurant.

The Prambanan complex

As you drive east along Jalan Adisucipto from Yogya, your eye will be caught by three giant, rocket-shaped temples, each smothered in intricate narrative carvings, that suddenly loom up by the side of the highway. This is the **Prambanan complex** (daily 6am–5pm; US$10, Rp40,000 for guided tour), the largest Hindu complex in Java and a worthy rival to the Buddhist masterpiece at Borobudur.

The Sanjayas began work on the three giants around 832 AD, finishing them 24 years later. Their choice of location, just a few hundred metres south of the once mighty Buddhist **Candi Sewu**, is of great significance. Not only was it a reminder to the Saliendras that the Hindus were now in charge but, by leaving Sewu unharmed, it also gave a clear message to the Buddhists that the Sanjayas intended to be tolerant of their faith. The three Prambanan temples were in service for just fifty years before they were abandoned. Restoration work finally began in the 1930s.

The complex itself consists of six temples in a raised **inner courtyard**, surrounded by **224 minor temples**, which now lie in ruins. The three biggest temples in the courtyard are dedicated to the three main Hindu deities: Shiva, whose 47-metre temple is the tallest of the three, Brahma (to the south of the Shiva temple) and Vishnu (north). Facing these are three smaller temples housing the animal statues – or "chariots" – that would always accompany the gods: Hamsa the swan, Nandi the bull and Garuda the sunbird respectively.

The **Shiva Temple** is decorated with exceptional carvings, including a series along the inner wall of the first terrace walkway, beginning at the eastern steps and continuing clockwise around the temple, that recounts the first half of the Ramayana epic. At the top of the steps is the inner sanctuary of the temple, whose eastern chamber contains a statue of Shiva himself, while in the west chamber is Shiva's elephant-headed son, Ganesh, and in the northern chamber there's Durga. A beautiful sculpture of Nandi the Bull stands inside the temple of Shiva's chariot. Though smaller than the Shiva Temple, the other two temples are just as painstakingly decorated. The first terrace of the **Brahma Temple** takes up the Ramayana epic where the Shiva Temple left off, whilst the carvings on the terrace of Vishnu's temple recounts stories of **Krishna**, the eighth of Vishnu's nine earthly incarnations.

Other temples on the Prambanan Plain

The other ancient sites on the Prambanan Plain (dawn–dusk; free) are not as spectacular as the Shiva Temple, but you are almost certain to be the only person on site. Only the three temples immediately to the **north of Prambanan** are within easy walking distance of the Shiva Temple, reached via the children's park next to the museum. All three date from the late eighth century, just predating Borobudur. **Candi Lumbung** consists of sixteen small, crumbling temples surrounding a larger, but equally dilapidated, central temple. Separated from Lumbung by the unimpressive pile of rubble that is Candi Bubrah, Buddhist **Sewu** once consisted of 240 small shrines surrounding a large, central temple but has been severely looted. A ten-minute bike ride or thirty-minute walk to the east of Candi Sewu, **Candi Plaosan** is also surrounded by building debris, but the two-storey building still houses two stone Bodhisattvas.

The other worthwhile ruins lie to the **south of Prambanan** and are best tackled by bicycle. From the village, cycle down the path that begins by the small graveyard to a small village school on the left-hand side (10min). Turn left, and after five minutes you reach **Candi Sojiwan**, a plain, square temple, sparingly decorated with Jataka scenes. Return to the main path and head south towards the foot of the Shiva Plateau. The path to the summit of the plateau and **Kraton Ratu Boko** (US$5) is unsuitable for bicycles, so ask to leave them at the house at the bottom. The ruins are in two parts: a series of bathing pools and, 400m to the west, the ceremonial gate that adorns many tourist posters. The views from the kraton are wonderful, as they are from **Candi Barong**, to the south – to get there, head west towards the main road, Jalan Raya Piyungan, where you turn left (south) and cycle for 1.5km until a signpost on your left points to Barong, 1km to the east. This *candi* is actually two hillside Buddhist temples mounted on a raised platform on the southern slopes of the plateau. A little way back along this path and to the south is **Banyunibo**, a pretty Buddhist shrine dedicated to Tara. From there, head back onto the main road and turn right; Prambanan village lies 2km away.

Surakarta (Solo)

Sixty-five kilometres northeast of Yogya stands quiet, leafy low-rise **SURAKARTA**, or, as it's more commonly known, **SOLO**. This is the older of the two royal cities in Central Java, and its ruling family can lay claim to being the rightful heirs to the Mataram dynasty. Like Yogya, Solo has two **royal palaces** and a number of muse-

ACCOMMODATION	
Cakra Homestay	G
Cakra Hotel	E
Dana	H
Istana Griya	D
Novotel	F
Sahid Jaya	C
Sahid Kusuma	B
Trihadhi	A

RESTAURANTS	
Bima	3
Kafé Solo	6
Kusuma Sari	2
Lumba Lumba	5
O Solo Mio	4
Warung Baru	1

ums, yet its tourist industry is nowhere near as developed. The city's main source of income is from textiles, and Solo has the biggest **batik market** on Java. Solo also makes an ideal base from which to visit the home of Java Man at Sangiran, as well as the intriguing temples Candi Ceto and Candi Sukuh.

Up until 1744, Solo was little more than a quiet backwater village, 10km east of Kartasura, the contemporary capital of the Mataram kingdom. But in that year the Mataram susuhunan (king), **Pakubuwono II**, backed the Chinese against the Dutch, and the court at Kartasura was sacked as a result. Pakubuwono II searched for a more auspicious spot to rebuild his capital, and in 1745 the entire court was dismantled and transported in a great procession to Surakarta, on the banks of the Kali Solo. However, the decline continued, and in 1757 a rival **royal house of Mangkunegoro** was established right in the centre of Solo. Thereafter, Solo's royal houses wisely avoided fighting and instead threw their energies into the arts, developing a highly sophisticated and graceful court culture. The gamelan pavilions became the new theatres of war, with each city competing to produce the more refined court culture – a situation that continues to this day.

Arrival, information and city transport

Adisumaryno Airport, Central Java's only international airport, occupies a square of former farmland 10km to the west of Solo and just 2km north of Kartasura. There is no public transport direct to Solo from the airport, although a half-hourly **minibus** to Kartasura (Rp2000) goes along the main road alongside the runway, and from Kartasura you can catch a bus to Solo (Rp2000). A **taxi** from the airport to Solo will cost approximately Rp25,000, slightly less in the opposite direction.

All buses to Solo terminate at the **Tirtonadi bus station** in the north of the city. Just across the crossroads by the northeastern corner of Tirtonadi is the **minibus terminal**, Gilingan. From the front of the *Hotel Surya*, overlooking Tirtonadi, orange angkuta #6 departs for the town centre, stopping at **Ngapeman**, the junction of Jalan Gajah Mada and Jalan Brig Jen Slamet Riyadi. Heading to the bus station from the town centre, catch a BERSERI bus (Rp1000) from the bus stop on Jalan Brig Jen Slamet Riyadi, 100m east of Jalan Dahlan. A becak from the bus station to Jalan Dahlan costs approximately Rp4000. You'll pay the same fare from the **Balapan train station**, 300m south of Tirtonadi.

Solo boasts three **tourist offices**, located at the airport, at Tirtonadi bus station and behind the Radya Pustaka Museum at Jl Brig Jen Slamet Riyadi 275. Only the latter (Mon–Sat 8am–6pm; ⓣ0271/711435) is of any real use, however, with a reasonable range of brochures and a couple of staff who speak a little English.

The main **taxi** stand is situated by the Matahari department store; are metered. The **becak** are more reasonable: unlike the ones in Yogya, Solo's becak do not charge a higher rate if there is more than one person in the carriage. As ever, remember to bargain hard. Being flat and, for a Javanese city, relatively free of traffic, **cycling** is an excellent way to get round the city. Bikes can be rented from many of the homestays for Rp10,000 per day.

Accommodation

Some of the **budget hotels** are hidden in the kampung to the south of Jalan Brig Jen Slamet Riyadi, and can be difficult to find. The simplest solution is to hire a becak to take you there, although, as usual, the driver's commission will result in a higher room rate.

Cakra Hotel Jl Brig Jen Slamet Riyadi 201 ⓣ0271/645847. With its swimming pool, billiard room, batik shop, parking facilities and a/c rooms, this is one of the best-value hotels in this category, and in a great location, too. ❻–❾

Cakra Homestay Jl Cakra II/15, Kauman ⓣ0271/634743. Not to be confused with the hotel above, this place is a bit of a secret delight, with its own pool, Javanese charm and furnishings, and even a gamelan orchestra – all tucked away behind high walls. Popular with those staying for a long time in Solo, and would be popular with everyone else too, if only it was easier to find. ❷

Dana Jl Brig Jen Slamet Riyadi 286 ☎0271/711976; danasolo@indo.net.id. Large hotel with 49 a/c rooms, conveniently situated opposite the tourist office and museum. ❺

Istana Griya Jl Dahlan 22 ☎0271/ 632667. New and highly efficient homestay tucked away down a quiet little *gang* behind the *Steak House*, with the smartest and best-value rooms in this price range. ❶–❸

Novotel Jl Brig Jen Slamet Riyadi 272 ☎0271/724555 or 716800; reservation@novotelsolo.com. Luxury hotel with its own pool; gym; Indonesian, Japanese and Chinese restaurants and plush a/c rooms. ❼–❽

Sahid Kusuma Jl Sugiopranoto 20 ☎0271/646356. Once the royal court of Susuhunan Pakubuwono X's son, this place is undoubtedly the most stylish in central Solo. Set in five landscaped acres with a swimming pool at the back and pendopo reception, complete with gamelan orchestra, at the front. A/c, TV and fridge come as standard in all rooms. ❼–❾

Sahid Jaya Jl Gajah Mada 82 ☎0271/644144; ⓦwww.sahidhotels.com. Four stars and 160 rooms. Facilities include a swimming pool, pub, café, and rooms with a/c, fridge and TV. ❽–❾

Trihadhi Jl Monginsidi 97 ☎0271/637557. One of the better options by the train station, and one of the cheapest in town; a sparkling-new place that is professionally run but homely. Rooms are large and cool. ❶–❸

The City

Brought from Kartasura by Pakubuwono II in one huge day-long procession in 1745, the **Kasunanan Palace** (Mon–Thurs 9am–2pm, Sat & Sun 9am–3pm; Rp8000, plus Rp2000 camera fee) is Solo's largest and most important royal house. It stands within the kraton, just south of the alun-alun; guides are available free of charge and are definitely worth taking. Non-royals must enter the main body of the palace by the eastern entrance. This opens out into a large courtyard whose surrounding buildings house the palace's **kris collection**, as well as a number of chariots, silver ornaments and other royal knick-knacks. An archway to the west leads into the susuhunan's living quarters; the current sultan, the septuagenarian Pakubuwono XII, is still in residence, along with a few of his 35 children and two of his six wives. Many of the buildings in this courtyard are modern copies, the originals having burnt down in 1985. By the southwest corner of the town's main alun-alun, the three-storey Pasar Klewer (daily 9am–4pm), claims to be Java's largest **batik market**, and designs from all over Java can be found here.

The second royal house in Solo, the **Puro Mangkunegoro** (guided tours only Mon–Sat 8.30am–2pm, Sun 8.30am–1pm; Rp10,000 includes guided tour) stands 1km west of the kraton and, like Yogya's court of Paku Alam, faces south towards the Kasunanan Palace as a mark of respect. With its fine collection of antiques and curios, in many ways the Puro Mangkunegoro is more interesting than the Kasunanan Palace. It was built in 1757 to placate the rebellious Prince Mas Said (Mangkunegoro I), a nephew of Pakubuwono II, whose relations with Mangkubumi deteriorated after the latter founded Yogya and was recognized as its sultan. Exhausted by fighting wars on three fronts, Mas Said eventually accepted a peace deal that gave him a royal title, a court in Solo and rulership over four thousand of Solo's households. The palace hides behind a high white wall, entered through the gateway to the south. The vast **pendopo** (the largest in Indonesia) that fronts the palace shields four gamelan orchestras underneath its rafters, three of which can only be played on very special occasions. Be sure to look up at the vibrantly painted roof of the pendopo, with Javanese zodiac figures surrounding the main batik centrepiece that took three years to complete. A portrait of the current resident, Mangkunegoro IX, hangs by the entrance to the **Dalam Agung**, or living quarters, whose reception room has been turned into an extremely good museum, displaying ancient coins, ballet masks and chastity preservers.

A kilometre west along Jalan Brig Jen Slamet Riyadi brings you to the **Radya Pustaka Museum** (Mon–Thurs & Sun 8am–1pm, Fri & Sat 8–11am; Rp1000). Built by the Dutch in 1890, this is one of the oldest and largest museums in Java, housing a large Dutch and Javanese library as well as collections of wayang kulit puppets, kris, and scale models of the mosque at Demak and the cemetery at Imogiri.

Eating and drinking

Solo's warung are renowned for local **specialities** such as *nasi liwet* – chicken or vegetables and rice drenched in coconut milk and served on a banana leaf – and *nasi gudeg*, a variation on Yogya's recipe. For dessert, try *kue putu* (coconut cakes) or *srabi*, a combination of pancake and sweet rice served with a variety of fruit toppings. Most of these delicacies can be purchased along Jalan Teuku Umar, one block west of Jalan Dahlan, and around the Sriwedari Park at night.

Bima Jl Brig Jen Slamet Riyadi 128. Large and swish ice-cream parlour serving a reasonable selection of Indonesian and European dishes at surprisingly low prices, plus a decent choice of ice creams. Open 11am–9.30pm.

Kafé Solo Jl Secoyadan 201. Stylish mid-priced restaurant with an excellent selection of beef and chicken steaks, salads and other Western dishes. Great if you fancy a change from rice, although they offer that, too.

Kusuma Sari Jl Brig Jen Slamet Riyadi. 111. Serving ice cream and grilled dishes, with, unusually for Indonesia, a no-smoking policy. Popular local hangout.

Lumba Lumba Pasar Pujosari, Jl Riyadi 275. One of a large number of restaurants/warung to the east of Sriwedari Park, most of which offer a similar, small menu. A shady, welcoming retreat serving standard Indonesian snacks and lunches.

O Solo Mio Jl Brig Jen Slamet Riyadi 253. A smart Italian restaurant with top-rate service, a great selection of wines, pizzas (Rp23,000) and other Italian dishes, including steaks. Great for a splurge.

Warung Baru Jl Dahlan 8. The most popular travellers' restaurant in Solo. Good and very inexpensive food, with delicious homemade bread. Also organizes tours and batik courses.

Performing arts

For the last two centuries, the royal houses of Solo have developed highly individual styles for the traditional Javanese arts of gamelan and wayang. The Puro Mangkunegoro's performances of **wayang orang** (Wed 10am–noon) are more rumbustious and aggressive than the graceful, fluid style of the Kasunanan Palace (Sun 9–11am). Another option is the three-hour performance at Sriwedari Park (Mon–Sat 8–11pm). **Gamelan** is also something of a Solonese speciality. The *Sahid Kusuma* gamelan orchestra plays every afternoon and evening in the hotel's reception hall, and the Puro Mangkunegoro stages a ninety-minute performance on Saturday evening (9pm).

The **radio station** Radio Republik Indonesia (RRI), Jl Marconi 55, just to the south of the Balapan train station, regularly records performances of Solo's traditional arts, including wayang orang (every first and third Tuesday of the month); gamelan (every second and fourth Thursday of the month), and wayang kulit (third Tuesday and Saturday of every month); performances generally start around 9pm and tickets should be bought in advance from the RRI Building just to the south of the Balapan train station.

Listings

Airlines Bouraq, Jl Gaja Madah 86 ☎0271/634376; Garuda, *Cakra Hotel*; also Bank Lippo Building, Jl Brig Jen Slamet Riyadi 328 ☎0271/630082; Lion Air, Jl Yosodipuro 111B ☎0271/722599; Silk Air, *Novotel*, Jl Brig Jen Slamet Riyadi 272 ☎0271/724604.

Banks and exchange The Bank BCA, in the vast BCA building at the eastern end of Jl Riyadi, currently offers the best rates in town. The exchange offices are on the second floor (10am–noon). The Golden Money Changer at the northern end of Jl Yos Sudarso, and PT Desmonda, next to the *Bima* restaurant at Jl Brig Jen Slamet Riyadi 128, are both open throughout the day, though their rates are inferior to the banks. Most of the banks, which can be found at and around the eastern end of Jl Riyadi, have ATMs, as does the *Novotel* hotel at Jl Brig Jen Slamet Riyadi 272.

Batik courses For all the hype of Yogya, the best place to try your hand at batik is Solo. Homestays and restaurants organize a number of courses costing Rp10,000–20,000: the *Warung Baru* restaurant on Jl Dahlan runs an extremely popular course.
Ferries On Jl Veteran, there are a couple of kiosks that have details of the Pelni ferries.
Hospital Rumah Sakit Kasih Ibu, Jl Brig Jen Slamet Riyadi 404, Rumah Sakit Panti Kosala (aka Rumah Sakit Dr Oen), Jl Brig Jen Katamso 55. Both have English-speaking doctors.
Internet access Aloha Café in the *Kusuma Sahid* hotel charges Rp300 per minute.
Post office Jl Jend Sudirman (daily 6am–10pm). The poste restante closes in the evening.
Telephones Just behind the Telkom offices on Jl Sumoharjo, Jl Mayor Kusmanto 3, there's a 24hr wartel office. There's also a wartel on Jl Brig Jen Slamet Riyadi to the west of Jl Yos Sudarso.
Tours The cycling tours organized by *Warung Baru*, Jl Dahlan 8, are very rewarding and usually includes a visit to a gamelan factory, bakery, tofu factory and even an *arak* manufacturer.
Travel agents Inta Tours & Travel Jl Brig Jen Slamet Riyadi 96 (☎0271/751142), comes recommended.

Surabaya

Polluted, noisy and sprawling, **SURABAYA** is the second-largest city in Indonesia, and the major port of East Java. With time and effort the city is comprehensible and even somewhat enjoyable, but for most tourists Surabaya is nothing more than a transport hub. If you do want to linger, the **Chinese** and **Arab quarters** to the north of the city centre, the fascinating **Kalimas harbour**, and the **zoo** and **museum** to the south are the most interesting sights.

Arrival and information

Surabaya is a visa-free entry point for international arrivals **by air**; all flights arrive at **Juanda International Airport** (☎031/8667642), 18km south of the city, where there's a tourist office. No public bus service connects with the town centre, but there's a rank for fixed-price **taxis** (Rp30,000). Arriving **by sea**, probably by Pelni ferry, you'll dock at **Tanjung Perak** in the far north of the city, served by C, P and PAC buses. Surabaya has three main **train stations**. **Gubeng station** is in the east of town it has a hotel reservation desk (daily 8am–8pm), but only for expensive places. **Kota station** is towards the north of the city centre, while **Pasar Turi station** is in the west of the city centre. The main **bus station** is Bungusarih (also known as Purabaya), 6km south of the city. All long-distance and inter-island buses start and finish here, plus many of the city buses and bemos. **Local buses** into the city leave from the far end of the Bungusarih terminal: follow the signs for "Kota". Many of the C (Rp1000), P (Rp2000) and both PAC (Rp3500) buses serve Bungusarih. There's also a huge **taxi rank** here: expect to pay about Rp20,000 to anywhere in town. **Crossing the road** in Surabaya is so hair-raising that there are special long poles with red dots on them at some traffic lights – you hold them high towards the traffic to let drivers know you're there.

The most useful **tourist office** is at Jl Jend Basuki Rachmat 119–121 opposite the *Hyatt* (Mon–Fri 7am–2pm; ☎031/5344710). One of the best places to get **information** is the losmen *Bamboe Denn* (see below), which gives guests up-to-date transport timetables.

Accommodation

Much of the cheaper **accommodation** is slightly out of the centre, in the area north of Kota station, which isn't good either for buses (you'll need to figure out the bemos around here) or the central sights.

Moving on from Surabaya

Surabaya is the main air, sea, rail and road hub for East Java and has excellent connections across Indonesia and internationally. Some international **flight** destinations are reached direct, while others have connections via Jakarta or Denpasar; see "Listings", p.307, for airline offices in Surabaya, and p.486 for flight details. There are numerous domestic flights. Taxis from Gubeng train station taxi rank to the airport are fixed at Rp30,000.

Tanjung Perak is the major port in East Java, and no fewer than fifteen of **Pelni's ferry** fleet call here on their routes through the archipelago: *KM Binaiya*, *KM Bukit Raya*, *KM Bukit Siguntang*, *KM Dobonsolo*, *KM Ciremai*, *KM Lambelu*, *KM Dorolonda*, *KM Leuser*, *KM Tidar*, *KM Tatamailau*, *KM Lawit*, *KM Egon* and *KM Sangiang*. For details, see "Getting around", p.237 and "Travel details", p.486. The main Pelni office is at Jl Pahlawan 112 (Mon–Thurs 9am–noon & 1–3pm, Fri–Sat 9am–noon; ☎031/3539048).

Trains from Gubeng station go to Banyuwangi, Malang, Yogyakarta, Solo and Jakarta via the southern route across Java – some, but not all of these trains, also pass through Kota station, which is towards the north of the city centre. The entrance to Kota is at the junction of Jalan Semut Kali and Jalan Stasiun Kota. Pasar Turi station serves destinations along the northern route across the island to Jakarta via Semarang.

For **bus** journeys **within East Java** (including Probolinggo for Gunung Bromo), just buy your ticket on the bus, but be wary of overcharging. You will pay Rp200 to get into the departure area at Bungusarih station – the bays are clearly labelled. **Long-distance journeys** are completed by night buses (departing 2–6pm) from Bay 8 – the ticket offices for all the night-bus companies are in the bus station; book ahead. If you can't bear the slog out to Bungusarih station, central **minibus** companies run more expensive daily trips to the main Javan destinations, leaving from their offices.

Bamboe Denn Jl Ketabang Kali 6a ☎031/5340333. The main backpacker accommodation in the city, it isn't easy to find – about 30min walk from Gubeng train station (Rp5000 by becak) – but local people will point you in the right direction. Accommodation is very basic in tiny singles, doubles and dorms (Rp20,000), all with shared bathrooms, but there's a pleasant sitting room and simple, inexpensive meals and snacks are available. The real plus is the excellent information available – everyone gets a sketch map of the city and staff are always keen to help. ❶

Hotel Irian Jl Samudra 16 ☎031/3520953. A pleasant old-style bungalow, cool and with a choice of rooms. There are shared bathrooms and fan at the lower end and attached bathrooms in the more expensive rooms. ❶–❸

Hotel Paviljoen Jl Genteng Besar 94–98 ☎031/5343449. Spotlessly clean rooms in an old colonial bungalow; the ones at the back have excellent verandas around a courtyard and all have attached cold-water mandi, while top-end rooms have a/c. This is an excellent choice if you want to be fairly central and have a bit of comfort. Southbound buses P1 and P2 stop just at the end of the street on Jl Tunjungan, and guests get a small sketch map of the city. ❷–❸

Hotel Semut Jl Samudra 9–15 ☎031/24578. All rooms have a/c and attached bathroom: cold water in the less expensive rooms and hot water in the pricier ones. There are deep, cool verandas looking into the garden, as well as a coffee shop and restaurant. ❹

Hotel Weta Jl Genteng Kali 3–11 ☎031/5319494. With a small but attractive lobby area; friendly and helpful staff; and clean, attractive rooms with a/c and hot-water bathrooms; this is a central, good-value choice in this price range. Staff will always discuss discounts. ❹–❼

The City

Surabaya's **Chinese quarter** hums with activity, an abundance of traditional two-storey shop-houses lining narrow streets, and minuscule red-and-gold altars glinting in shops and houses. The area centres on Jalan Slompretan, Jalan Bongkaran and the part of Jalan Samudra southwest of the three-hundred–year-old **Hok Teck Hian Temple** on Jalan Dukuh. The temple itself is a vibrant place with several tiny shrines

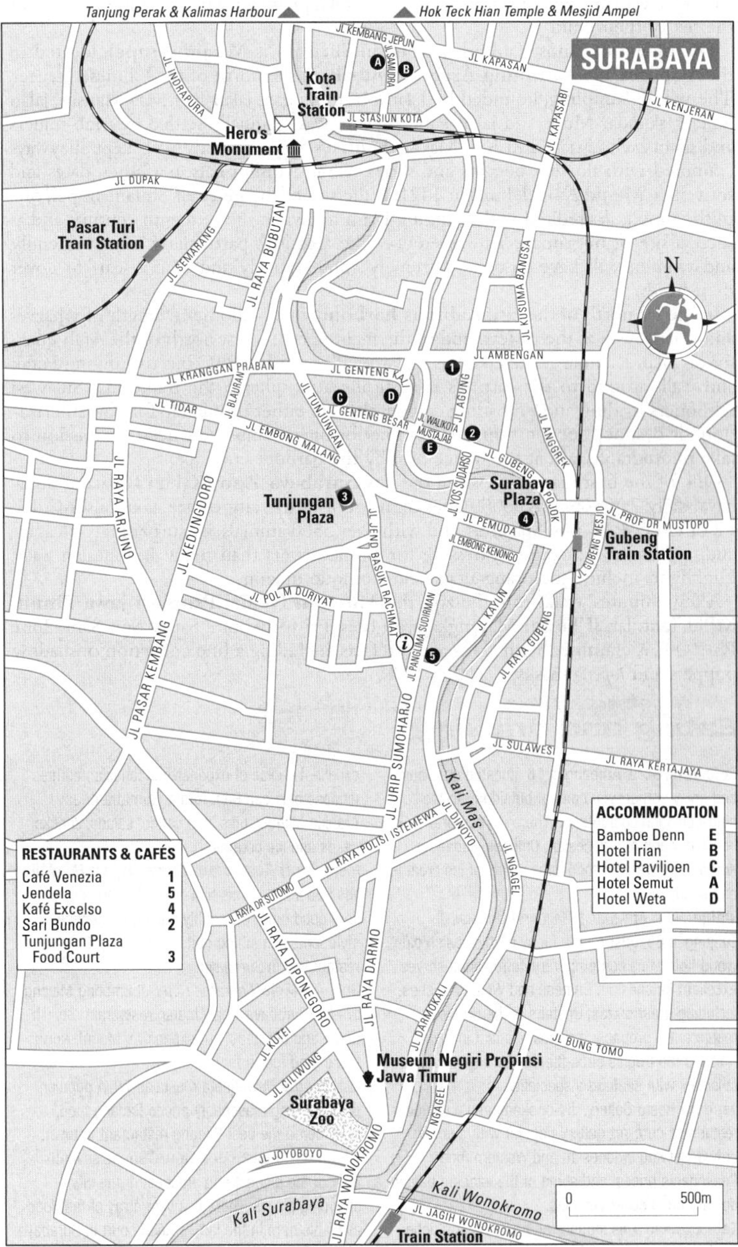

SURABAYA
Tanjung Perak & Kalimas Harbour
Hok Teck Hian Temple & Mesjid Ampel
Kota Train Station
Hero's Monument
Pasar Turi Train Station
Tunjungan Plaza
Surabaya Plaza
Gubeng Train Station
Kali Mas
Museum Negiri Propinsi Jawa Timur
Surabaya Zoo
Kali Surabaya
Kali Wonokromo
Train Station
Bungusarih Bus Station & Juanda International Airport (17km)
JL KEMBANG JEPUN
JL KAPASAN
JL KENJERAN
JL INDRAPURA
JL SAMUDRA
JL STASIUN KOTA
JL KAPASARI
JL DUPAK
JL SEMARANG
JL RAYA BUBUTAN
JL KUSUMA BANGSA
JL AMBENGAN
JL KRANGGAN PRABAN
JL GENTENG KALI
JL TIDAR
JL BLAURAN
JL TUNJUNGAN
JL GENTENG BESAR
JL WALIKOTA MUSTAJAB
JL AGUNG
JL EMBONG MALANG
JL GUBENG POJOK
JL ANGGREK
JL RAYA ARJUNO
JL KEDUNGDORO
JL YOS SUDARSO
JL PEMUDA
JL PROF DR MUSTOPO
JL GUBENG MESJID
JL EMBONG KENONGO
JL JEND BASUKI RACHMAT
JL POL M DURIYAT
JL KAYUN
JL PANGLIMA SUDIRMAN
JL RAYA GUBENG
JL PASAR KEMBANG
JL URIP SUMOHARJO
JL SULAWESI
JL RAYA KERTAJAYA
JL DINOYO
JL RAYA POLISI ISTEMEWA
JL NGAGEL
JL RAYA DR SUTOMO
JL RAYA DIPONEGORO
JL RAYA DARMO
JL DARMOKALI
JL BUNG TOMO
JL KUTEI
JL CILIWUNG
JL JOYOBOYO
JL RAYA WONOKROMO
JL JAGIH WONOKROMO
0
500m
RESTAURANTS & CAFÉS
Café Venezia 1
Jendela 5
Kafé Excelso 4
Sari Bundo 2
Tunjungan Plaza Food Court 3
ACCOMMODATION
Bamboe Denn E
Hotel Irian B
Hotel Paviljoen C
Hotel Semut A
Hotel Weta D

spread over two floors, and Buddhist, Confucian and Hindu effigies. Upstairs, at the altar to Kwan Im Poosat, the "Valentine Angel", pregnant women come to pray for the sex of their child.

The oldest and most famous mosque in Surabaya is **Mesjid Ampel**, located in the Arab area, the **kampung Arab** or **Qubah**, to the north of the Chinese quarter. The whole kampung, bounded by Jalan Nyanplungan, Jalan KH Mas Mansur, Jalan Sultan Iskandar Muda and Jalan Pabean Pasar, was originally settled by Arab traders and sailors who arrived in Kali Mas harbour. It's a maze of tidy, well-kept alleyways crammed with flowers, beggars and shops selling Muslim hats, perfumes, dates and souvenirs. Mesjid Ampel, built in 1421, is the site of the grave of Sunan Ampel, one of the nine *wali* credited with bringing Islam to Java in the sixteenth century, and as such, a site of pilgrimage and reverence. The area isn't particularly tourist-friendly, and women will have to dress extremely conservatively and take a scarf to cover their heads.

In the far north of the city, **Kalimas harbour**, a two-kilometre length of wharves and warehouses at the eastern end of the main port, lies just north of the Arab quarter on Jalan Kalimas Baru; take bus C, P1 or P2 or either PAC bus to Tanjung Perak and walk around to the east. It's fantastically atmospheric, the traditional Sulawesi schooners loading and unloading cargoes that are either unsuitable for containerization, or destined for locations too remote for bigger ships. You need permission to take photographs; ask at the police post by the harbour entrance.

One of the best places to visit in the city, **Surabaya Zoo** (Kebun Binatang Surabaya; daily 7am–6pm; Rp5000), lies 3km south of the city centre; take buses C, P1, P2 or either PAC bus. Spacious, and with over 3500 animals, it's surprisingly pleasant and, at least in parts, less distressing for animal-lovers than many Indonesian zoos. Highlights include the orang-utans and Komodo dragon.

A few minutes' walk from the zoo, the **Museum Negiri Propinsi Jawa Timur**, MPU Tantular, Jl Taman Mayangkara 6 (Tues–Fri 8am–3pm, Sat & Sun 8am–2pm; Rp1000), is crammed with crafts and artefacts, including a fine collection of shadow puppets and *topeng* masks.

Eating and drinking

Café Venezia Jl Ambengan 16. Located on a busy and noisy corner; you can eat outside or in the high-ceilinged cool interior. There's a comprehensive menu of Indonesian, Chinese, Japanese, Korean and Western food, plus plenty of ice creams and sundaes.

Indigo *Hotel Majapahit Mandarin Oriental*, Jl Tunjungan 65. Just off the lobby of this stylish old-world hotel, this contemporary coffee shop serves excellent Indonesian, Chinese and Western dishes, including great pizzas. Upstairs is the *Sarkies* restaurant – probably the most elegant in town – styled the tropics circa the 1920s, serving Asian cuisines, with seafood a speciality.

Jendela Resto Gallery, Jl Sonokembang 4. Outdoor restaurant-cum-art gallery popular with a young crowd, serving Indonesian and Western food. Reasonable prices, and some of the evening bands do very good cover versions.

Kafé Excelso This Indonesian chain has branches on the ground floor of Surabaya Plaza and a couple in Tunjungan Plaza, and is very popular with well-heeled Indonesians and expatriates. They have an excellent choice of expensive Indonesian coffees (choose between Bali, Toraja, Sumatra or Java Arabica blends), plus iced coffee, salads, snacks, cakes and ice creams.

Ming Court Restaurant *Garden Palace Hotel*, Jl Yos Sudarso 11. This first-floor restaurant offers very good (and reasonably priced) Cantonese-style food, something quite rare among Chinese restaurants in Surabaya.

Queen's Mela *Sheraton Hotel*, Jl Embong Malang 25–31. Surabaya's only Indian restaurant. Stylish decor and delicious, but expensive, Mogul, North Indian and fusion food.

Sari Bundo Jl Walikota Mustajab 70. A popular place serving reasonably priced Padang food. Considered the best Padang restaurant in town.

Tunjungan Plaza Food Court On the seventh floor of the biggest and brashest of the city's shopping plazas. There is a vast array of fast food available here in the largest food court in Surabaya: *KFC*, *McDonald's*, Singaporean noodles, Cajun grills, New Zealand ice cream, crepes and kebabs.

Entertainment

There's no shortage of **entertainment** in Surabaya, although it's a lot easier to find a disco or cinema in the city than a wayang kulit show. The **discos** (daily 10pm–2am) listed here alternate recorded music with live, and are generally fairly expensive. Popular discos include *Desperadoes* at the *Shangri-La Hotel*, Jl Mayjen Sungkono 120 and the *Qemi Club Discotheque* at the *Elmi Hotel*, Jalan Panglima Sudirman 42-44, which is good for golden oldies With a large student population in the city there are plenty of **live-music** venues (bands start playing from 9.30pm): *Colors* at Jalan Sumatera 81; the *Tavern Pub* at the *Hyatt Regency*, Jl Jen Basuki Rachmat 106–128; and *Jendela* at Jl Sonokembang 4.

More traditional entertainment is available at RRI Surabaya, Jl Pemuda 82–90, where every Saturday evening there are free **wayang kulit** shows (10pm). At Taman Hiburan Rakyat (locally called Tay Ha Air), on Jalan Kusuma Bangsa, regular folk **comedy** performances are held (6pm–11pm; ask the tourist office for performance schedules).

Listings

Airline offices The following airlines are found in the Hyatt Graha Bumi Modern (next to the *Hyatt Hotel*), Jl Jen Basuki Rachmat 106–128: British Airways, 5th Floor ⓣ031/5471508; Cathay Pacific, 1st Floor ⓣ031/5317421; Eva Air, 5th Floor ⓣ031/5465123; Garuda, Level 4 ⓣ031/5326321; Malaysia, 1st Floor ⓣ & ⓕ031/5318632; Northwest, 5th Floor ⓣ031/5317086; Qantas, 5th Floor ⓣ031/5452322; Thai, 5th Floor ⓣ031/5340861. Elsewhere are: Batavia, Jl Raya Gubeng 68E ⓣ031/5049666; Bouraq, Jl P Sudirman 70–72 ⓣ031/5452918, and Jl Genteng Kali 63 ⓣ031/5344940; Emirates, Lt Dasar, *Hyatt Regency*, Jl Jend Basuki Rachmat 106–128 ⓣ031/5460000; Jatayu, Jl Diponegoro 54E ⓣ031/560018; KLM, World Trade Centre, Jl Pemuda 27–31 ⓣ031/5315096; Lion Air, Jl Sulawesi 75 ⓣ031/5036111; Mandala, Jl Diponegoro 91D ⓣ031/5610777; Merpati, Jl Raya Darmo 111 ⓣ031/568111; Pelita, Juanda Airport ⓣ031/8667584; Singapore Airlines, 10th Floor, Menara BBD Tower, Jl Jend Basuki Rachmat 2–6 ⓣ031/5319217; Trans Asia Airways Regency, Jl Jend Basuki Rachmat 106–128 ⓣ031/5463181.

Airport information ⓣ031/8667642 or 8667513.

Banks and exchange All of the main Indonesian banks have huge branches in Surabaya, with exchange facilities.

Consulates Australia (actually a Western Australia trade office, not a consulate, but they'll help where possible), World Trade Centre, Jl Pemuda 27–31 ⓣ031/5319123; Belgium, Jl Raya Kupang Indah III/24 ⓣ031/716423; Britain, c/o Hong Kong and Shanghai Bank, 3rd Floor, Graha Bumi Modern, Jl Jend Basuki Rachmat 106–128 ⓣ031/5326381; Denmark, Jl Sambas 7 ⓣ031/5675047; France, Jl Darmokali 10–12 ⓣ031/5678639; Germany, Jl TAIS Nasution 15 ⓣ031/5343735; India, Jl Pahlawan 17 ⓣ031/5341565; Japan, Jl Sumatra 93 ⓣ031/5344677; the Netherlands, Jl Pemuda 54 ⓣ031/5311612 ext 558; USA, Jl Dr Sutomo 33 ⓣ031/5676880.

Ferries The Pelni office is at Jl Pahlawan 112 (Mon–Thurs 9am–noon & 1–3pm, Fri–Sat 9am–noon; ⓣ031/339048).

Hospitals The following are respected and have staff and doctors who speak English and Dutch: Rumah Sakit Darmo, Jl Raya Darmo 90 ⓣ031/5676253; Rumah Sakit Katolik St. Vincentius A Paulo (known as "RKZ"), Jl Diponegoro 51 ⓣ031/5677562.

Immigration office Jl Jend S. Parman 58a ⓣ031/8531785, and see "Post office" below.

Internet access All the big plazas have at least one Internet café (Rp3000–8000 per hour).

Post office The main post office (Mon–Thurs 8am–3pm, Fri & Sat 8am–1pm), is at Jl Kebonrojo 10. To get there from the city centre, take a C, P1, P2, PAC1 or PAC2 bus from outside Tunjungan Plaza to the junction of Jl Kebonrojo and Jl Bubutan; to get back to the city, go along to the other end of Jl Kebonrojo and pick up the same buses on Jl Pahlawan. Poste restante is at the philatelic counter in the centre of the post office; get mail addressed to you at Poste Restante, Post Office, Jl Kebonrojo 10, Surabaya 60175, Java Timur. The parcel office (Mon–Thurs 8am–3pm, Fri 8–11am & 12.30–3pm, Sat 8am–1pm) is to the right of the main building. If you're just sending letters, a more central post office is at Jl Taman Apsaril 1 (Mon–Thurs 8am–12.30pm, Fri 8–11am, Sat 8am–noon), just off Jl Pemuda in the city centre.

Souvenirs Shopping for souvenirs in Surabaya doesn't give you the number or range of shops or choice of goods that you'll get in Bali or Yogyakarta, but don't despair if you arrive here with things still to buy. Batik Keris, in the Tunjungan Plaza and Mal Galaxi, is a well-known chain of textile and souvenir shops that has an extensive range, from tiny batik purses to pure-silk sarong and scarf sets. Mirota, Jl Sulawesi 24, is a brilliant souvenir shop with plenty of items from across the islands: carvings in modern and classical style, basketware, leatherwork, furniture, paintings, ready-made batik items and material, T-shirts, silk textiles and silver. There is also a good secondhand book selection, one of very few in the city. Finally, Oleh Oeh, Jl Kupang Indah III/22 ⓣ031/7311941, features an excellent range of Indonesian furniture, souvenirs and gifts. Expat-run, with reasonable set prices.

Telephone and fax The warpostel at Jl Genteng Besar 49 (daily 5am–11pm) has telephone, fax and letter services. One of the most convenient wartels (daily 24hr) is the one on the ground floor of Tunjungan Plaza. It's a bit tucked away, under the main steps leading down into Tunjungan 2, just behind *Kafé Excelso*. There's another 24hr wartel at Jl Walikota Mustajab 2–4.

Travel agents The following is a selection of the largest, best-established set-ups. Many agents in Surabaya offer all-inclusive tours to the sights of the region, either day-trips or longer, plus international bookings. Haryono Tours and Travel, Jl Sulawesi 27–29 ⓣ031/5033000 or 5034000; Orient Express, Jl Panglima Sudirman 62 ⓣ031/5456666; Pacto, *Hyatt Regency Hotel*, Jl Jend Basuki Rakhmat 106–128 ⓣ031/5460628.

The Bromo region

The **Bromo region** is best known for its awesome scenery; at its heart is a vast, ancient volcanic crater with sheer walls over 300m high. Within this crater, a host of picturesque mountains, including the dramatic, still-smoking Gunung Bromo (2329m), rises up from the Sea of Sand, the sandy plain at the crater's base. Hundreds of thousands of visitors come here each year to climb Bromo for the sunrise – a stunning sight, and less strenuous than many other Indonesian peaks.

One hypothesis for the formation of the area is that Gunung Tengger, then the highest mountain in Java at over 4000m, erupted to form a caldera of between 8km and 10km in diameter and crater walls between 200m and 700m high. This is now the main outer crater rim with the Sea of Sand in the bottom. However, eruptions continued to occur, forming the smaller inner peaks such as Bromo, Batok and Kursi that rise up from the Sea of Sand.

This unique landscape now comprises the Bromo-Tengger-Semeru National Park, whose highlights are the dramatic smoking crater of **Gunung Bromo**, **Gunung Penanjakan** – on the outside crater's edge and one of the favourite sunrise spots – and **Cemoro Lawang**, with its brilliant panoramic view of the crater. The park also contains the highest mountain in Java, **Gunung Semeru**, which can be climbed by experienced trekkers. Views are best in the dry season but, whatever time of year, you should bring warm clothes.

There are two main approaches to the Bromo region. The most popular is to head inland from **Probolinggo**, on the north coast, to the crater's edge at Cemoro Lawang, where most people stay in order to make the dawn trip to Gunung Bromo as easy as possible. Alternative access is from **Pasuruan**, also on the north coast, inland to the villages of Tosari and Wonokitri. These villages are linked by road to Gunung Penanjakan, so they offer an excellent approach for the sunrise from there.

Gunung Bromo, Gunung Penanjakan and Gunung Semeru

There are a variety of excursions possible from Cemoro Lawang, the most popular being the climb to the top of **Gunung Bromo** (2392m); if you're lucky with the clouds, there may be an absolutely spellbinding sunrise. There's a Rp4000 per person entry fee for the park. To get to the base of Gunung Bromo, you can walk (1hr; bring

△ Bromo-Tengger-Semeru National Park

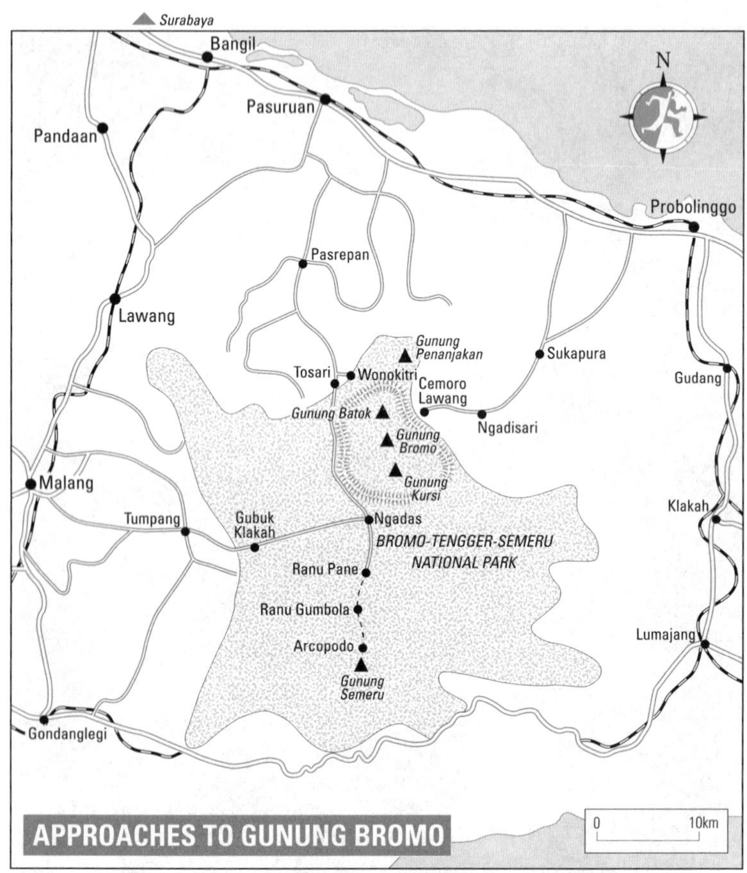

a torch and follow the white pillars through the Sea of Sand), get a horse (Rp10,000 from Cemoro Lawang), or hire a car or ojek. However you get there, you'll still have to manage the 249 concrete stairs (10min) up to the crater rim, from where there are great views down into the smoking crater and back across the Sea of Sand.

The best spot for the sunrise across the entire Bromo area is **Gunung Penanjakan** (2770m). Leave Tosari or Wonokitri at around 4.30am to get to the lookout in time. The whole crater area lies below, Bromo smoking and Semeru puffing up regular plumes while the sun rises dramatically in the east. You can **camp** up here if you wish, but you'll be invaded before dawn by the hordes. To see the sunrise, either organize return transport from Wonokitri or Tosari (Rp100,000 per jeep, Rp40,000 motorcycle); do a loop to Penanjakan for the sunrise, across the Sea of Sand to Bromo and then back to Wonokitri or Tosari after you've climbed to the top; or (less popular) go to Penanjakan and Bromo and then on to Cemoro Lawang.

Essentially a dry-season expedition (from June to September or possibly October), the climb up **Gunung Semeru** (3676m), Java's highest mountain, is for fit, experienced trekkers only and requires good preparation and equipment. It takes at least three full days. The volcano is still active, with over 20,000 seismic events recorded in a typical year; in 1997, two climbers were killed by a big eruption that sent boulders flying out of the crater, so it's vital to take a guide (ask at the PHPA office or your hotel) and heed local advice. The path starts at the village of **RANU PANE**, to the north of the mountain, accessible via a path across the Sea of Sand. In the village, you need to check in at the **PHPA office** and get your **permit** (Rp5000). The PHPA office will also recommend porters (one per person at Rp50,000 each). Bring your own sleeping bag and tent, and rent a cooking stove in Ranu Pane. In the village, trekkers can stay in the *Forest Guest House* (Rp40,000), where you'll need to cook for yourself, or there's a **campsite** near the PHPA office.

Probolinggo

PROBOLINGGO is 100km southeast of Surabaya. The **train station** is on the northern side of the alun-alun. The **bus terminal** is 6km southwest of town; yellow microlets run to the town centre. **Minibuses** for Cemoro Lawang leave from the terminal, and there are two buses daily – they are labelled "Sukapura" and "Ngadisari" on the front but also serve Cemoro Lawang.

The best **accommodation** is *Hotel Bromo Permai*, Jl Raya P Sudirman 237 (☎0335/427451; ❷–❹), where staff can arrange chartered transport to Cemoro Lawang and have train information. To get here from the bus station, take a G or F yellow microlet and, from here to the terminal or station, a G. For **eating**, *Restaurant Malang*, Jl Raya P Sudirman 48, has an extensive menu of reasonably priced well-cooked Indonesian and Chinese dishes, plus plenty of drinks.

Cemoro Lawang

The small village of **CEMORO LAWANG**, 46km from Probolinggo, is perched on the crater's edge and is the easiest place from which to set off on the pre-dawn excursion to Gunung Bromo itself. From the crater's edge in Cemoro Lawang, there are brilliant views of the entire area – best at the end of the road from the north coast and in front of *Lava View Lodge*. **Minibuses** (Rp10,000) from Probolinggo run up to the crater rim from 6am to 5.30pm; they do the return journey from 8am till 4pm. Several places advertise minibus and express-bus tickets, which are more expensive but more convenient.

The **national park office** (Kantor Taman Nasional Bromo Tengger Semeru; daily 7.30am–4pm) in Cemoro Lawang has displays about the area. *Hotel Yoschi* is the best place for local information, especially if you want to trek. The postal agent at the *Hotel Bromo Permai* charges a lot, so bring stamps with you. There's a wartel (daily 3am–10pm) on the left as you reach the top of the road, and a **health centre** in Ngadisari, Jl Raya Bromo 6, just by the checkpost.

Accommodation in and around Cemoro Lawang

There's plenty of **accommodation** in Cemoro Lawang, Ngadisari (3km from the rim), Wonokerto (5km) and Sukapura (18km). You can **camp** anywhere: Penanjakan is popular, although you will get disturbed at sunrise, and there's a good site 200m along the rim from the *Lava View Lodge*. There are plenty of **places to eat** in the vicinity of Cemoro Lawang, and many of the hotels have restaurants.

Café Lava Hostel ☎0335/541020. A justly popular travellers' choice, close to the crater rim, on the main road into Cemoro Lawang. There are two standards of room, the less expensive ones being basic with shared cold-water mandi (often a long walk away) and the more expensive ones, which are spotless, with lovely sitting areas in an attractive garden. ❷

Cemoro Indah ☎0335/541197. On the crater's rim around to the right from the *Hotel Bromo Permai*. The main road into Cemoro Lawang forks about 200m before it reaches the crater rim; the left fork goes to the centre of the village, and the right fork to the *Cemoro Indah*. There's a big choice of rooms, from basic ones with cold-water shared mandi to stunningly positioned bungalows with hot water. The attached restaurant is equally well located. ❶–❻

Lava View Lodge ☎0335/541009. About 500m left along the crater's edge from the centre of Cemoro Lawang; go through the concrete area between the row of shops and *Hotel Bromo Permai* and follow the main track. This is a very popular choice, offering comfortable rooms – all have attached bathrooms, very good Indonesian buffet, live music and the views are brilliant, especially from the more expensive rooms and the restaurant. ❸–❻

Hotel Yoschi Jl Wonokerto 1, Wonokerto ☎0335/541014. A great place with many options: the cheaper rooms have shared bathroom, while the top-priced ones are actually cottages. The decor is attractive and the garden a delight. Staff provide plenty of good information on the area and sell maps of local hikes. You can also use the book exchange, book bus tickets, arrange local guides, charter transport and rent warm jackets. ❸

Pasuruan

Located 60km southeast of Surabaya, the port town of **PASURUAN** is a convenient stopping-off spot close to Bromo on the way to or from Tosari and Wonokitri; buses run every few minutes throughout the day between Surabaya and Pasuruan (1–2hr), and there are daily trains (1hr 30min) from Gubeng station in Surabaya. The main north-coast road is Jalan Raya, with the **bus terminal** at its eastern end, about 1.5km from the alun-alun. **Microlets** run direct to Tosari, although there is no sign at the terminal. The **train station** is just north of Jalan Raya, on Jalan Stasiun.

Hotel Pasuruan, Jl Nusantara 46 (☎0343/424494; ❸–❹), has three standards of room, from cold-water bathroom and fan rooms up to those with air-con and hot water bathrooms. *Wisma Karya*, Jl Raya 160 (☎0343/426655; ❷), has a range of rooms behind an old colonial bungalow, although the cheaper ones are often full. The top-end rooms have air-con, but the cheaper ones with fan and attached cold-water mandi are adequate.

You can **eat** at the small night market around the alun-alun, or try the inexpensive Indonesian and Chinese food at *Rumah Makan Savera*, on Jl Raya 92a. The **tourist office**, Jl Hayam Wuruk 14 (☎0343/429075), is in the district government offices, Kantor Kapeputan Pasuran. The post office (Mon–Thurs 7.30am–2pm & 3–8pm, Fri 7.30–11.30am & 1–8pm, Sat 7.30am–1pm & 2–8pm), Jl Alun-alun Utara 1, provides **Internet** access (Rp3000 for 15min). There's a 24hr **wartel** at Jl Stasiun 11 and **exchange** facilities at BNI, Jl A Yani 21 and BCA, Jl Periwa 200, 200m west of the bus terminal.

Tosari and Wonokitri

Just over 40km south from Pasuruan, the small villages of Tosari and Wonokitri sit 2km apart on neighbouring ridges of the Bromo massif foothills. These are excellent choices for early access to **Gunung Penanjakan** and are less tourist-oriented than Cemoro Lawang. Microlets that go to one also go to the other, and both villages have accommodation. The road from Pasuruan divides 500m before Tosari: the right fork leads up to the market area of that village, and the left fork twists up to the next ridge and Wonokitri. Wonokitri is a compact, shabby town with good views, while Tosari is more spread out, with an attractive ridge to the northeast that leads to the *Hotel Bromo Cottages*. It's better to take a minibus direct from Pasuruan, rather than changing at **Pasrepan**, though that's also possible.

In **TOSARI**, *Penginapan Wulun Aya*, Jl Bromo Cottage 25 (☎0343/57011; ❶–❷), is small and clean with good views. *Mekar Sari*, Jl Raya 1 (❶), is a small rumah makan and has a few simple rooms and a good roof terrace.

WONOKITRI features several places to stay. The best choices are *Kartiki Sari* (❶–❷) with simple rooms, and *Bromo Surya Indah* (☎0343/571049; ❷), which is just before the Balinese-style village meeting hall, about 300m before the national park checkpost at the far end of the village; rooms have attached bathroom, clean bedding and good views. At the **national park checkpost** and information centre at the southern end of Wonokitri you pay the **admission fee** to the park (Rp5000, Rp7500per car, Rp5000 per motorcycle).

Banyuwangi and ferries to Bali

The town of **BANYUWANGI** has excellent transport links and is 8km south of **KETAPANG**, from where ferries run to Gilimanuk in **Bali** (every 30min, 24hr a day; Rp3300). A helpful East Java **tourist office** (daily 8am–7pm) is located inside the terminal building. You'll find convenient **Pelni** agents on the main road opposite the Ketapang ferry terminal. The Pelni office is at Jalan Raya Situbondo at Pelabuhan Tanjung Wangi (☎0333/510325), though at the time of writing Pelni ferries had removed Banyuwangi from their routes.

There are several **bus terminals** serving Banyuwangi. The main long-distance terminal is **Sri Tanjung**, 2km north of Ketapang. If you're heading to Surabaya, you can either go around the north coast via Situbondo, or via Jember (further but more scenic); travel time on both routes is similar, at five to seven hours.

For **exchange**, go to BCA at Jl Jend Sudirman 85–87 or BNI at Jl Banetrang 46. The **post office**, Jl Diponegoro 1 (Mon–Thurs 8am–3pm, Fri 8–11am, Sat 8am–1pm, Sun & hols 8am–noon), is on the west side of the sports field and has public **Internet** access. Just around the corner, off the southwest corner of the sports field, the 24hr **Telkom office** is at Jl Dr Sutomo 63, and there are plenty of wartels around town, including Jl Jaksa Agung Suprapto 130.

For **accommodation**, *Hotel Baru*, Jl MT Hariyono 82–84 (☎0333/421369; ❸–❹) is popular with travellers and sits in a quiet, central location ten minutes' walk from the post office. All rooms have attached mandi, and the more expensive ones have air-con. On the south side of the square, about 100m from the post office, *Hotel Blambangan*, Jl Dr Wahidin 4 (☎0333/421598; ❶–❹), is in an old colonial bungalow with a two-storey building behind. All rooms are large with high ceilings, and those upstairs have balconies. Foodwise, many of the hotels have attached **restaurants** and there is a night market along Jalan Pattimura offering warung food.

Grajagan: G-Land

In the far southeastern corner of Java, the fishing village of **GRAJAGAN** has become famous for the world-class surf in Grajagan Bay, whose awesomely long left-handers, promising endless tubes and walls are known as **G-LAND**. The surf is so clean and consistent that G-Land plays host to the annual Quksilver Pro (Ⓦwww.quiksilver.com)The beach, Pantai Coko, is signed from the village: it's 300m to the gate (admission Rp2000, car Rp500, motorcycle Rp300) and then another 2km through the forest to the black-sand beach. Due to the surf, take local advice from the forestry office about safe swimming spots, and never swim near the rocks. There is accommodation at *Wisma Perhutani* (❶) in basic rooms (bring your own sheet sleeping bag). To get to Grajagan, take a minibus from Banyuwangi's Brawijaya terminal to **PURWOHARJO**, and then a microlet for the final 14km to Grajagan. To get to **PLENGKUNG**, 15km east across the bay, where a surf camp caters for surfers from April to October, you can charter boats from Grajagan – you'll start bargaining at US$200 for a boat for ten people. Book Plengkung accommodation through Waasari Wisata in Kuta, Bali (see p.358), or Plengkung Indah Wisata, Andika Plaza Blok A 22/23, Jl Simpang Dutah 38–40, Surabaya (☎031/5315320). Several tour operators on Bali and Lombok run all-inclusive surfaris that feature G-Land in their itineraries.

4.2

Sumatra

North Sumatra now receives more tourists than any other place in Indonesia except Bali and Yogyakarta, and the main interest lies in the rugged central highlands, the homelands of the **Batak** who arrived over four thousand years ago and evolved almost completely in isolation from the rest of the island, developing languages and cultures that owe little to any outside influences. The Batak are divided into six distinctive ethnolinguistic groups, each with its own rituals, architectural style, mode of dress and religious beliefs. Many Batak have been exposed to Western education since Dutch missionaries arrived in the early 1800s, and as a result, the Toba Batak people, in particular, are amongst the most educated, powerful and richest minorities in the country today.

The hill station of **Berastagi**, part of the Karo Batak territory, and the many waterside resorts around beautiful **Danau Toba** – Southeast Asia's largest lake and the spiritual home of the Toba Batak – throng with tourists every summer. The province also features the hugely popular Orang-utan Rehabilitation Centre at **Bukit Lawang** – just a couple of hours' drive from the provincial capital of **Medan**, an entry point from Malaysia – as well as the surfer's mecca of **Pulau Nias**. Bukit Lawang, Berastagi, Danau Toba and Pulau Nias form such a perfect diagonal route across the centre of Sumatra that most tourists bypass the troubled province of Aceh to the north (see box on p.316).

Major gateways into Indonesia are also provided by the west coast port of **Padang** and the islands of **Batam** and **Bintan** in the Riau archipelago, between the Sumatran mainland and Singapore. Travellers entering Sumatra through the Riau Islands can transit in the prosperous city of **Pekanbaru** before heading north to Medan and Danau Toba, south to Bandar Lampung, or west to picturesquely located **Bukittinggi**, the heartland of Minang culture and a major tourist destination with a thriving travellers' scene. Nearby, **Danau Maninjau** is developing plenty of low-key lakeside guesthouses. Most travellers rush between Bukittinggi and Java, with perhaps an overnight stop in the city of **Bandar Lampung** or, better, in smaller, quieter **Kalianda** nearby, but in between lie the isolated **Mentawai Islands**, 100km off the west coast of Sumatra and home to some very traditional groups of people.

Getting around Sumatra on **public transport** can be gruelling – distances are huge, the roads tortuous and the driving hair-raising. There are plenty of road connections on to Java from even the smallest towns, but if you intend going by sea or air to make your trip less stressful, you'll need to plan carefully as only the large cities have airports, and ferry connections are generally irregular. For all major Pelni ferry connections and inter-city flights, see "Travel details", p.486.

Medan

MEDAN, Indonesia's fourth-largest city, occupies a strategic point on Sumatra's northeast coast and is a major entry point for boats and flights from Malaysia. It has acquired a reputation for being filthy and chaotic, but also holds some glorious examples of nineteenth-century colonial architecture, built by the Dutch gentry,

The tsunami disaster in Aceh and North Sumatra

On **December 26, 2004**, a devastating underwater **earthquake** measuring 9.0 on the Richter Scale struck off the coast of Sumatra, causing a giant tsunami that smashed into the northern and western coastlines of Aceh – Indonesia's troubled Sumatran province – as well as the coastlines of Sri Lanka, Thailand, Malaysia, and even East Africa.

The sheer scale of the disaster was slow to emerge, but the final "official" death toll provided by the government a month after the disaster was 166,000. The provincial capital, **Banda Aceh**, suffered almost unimaginable devastation, but this was nothing compared to some of the towns and villages on **Aceh's west coast**, which had borne the brunt of the tsunami. When the tidal wave struck, entire villages were all but washed away, and the UN Office for Coordinating Humanitarian Affairs estimated that in some areas the fatality rate was more than 75 percent.

Even before the disaster, Aceh had been a province plagued by problems. A thirty-year **civil war** between the government and members of the **Free Aceh Movement**, or GAM, who had been seeking independence for the oil-rich state, had escalated over the past two years to a point where the province had come under military rule, and foreigners had been banned. As a result, Aceh had suffered from a lack of investment, and communications were minimal – factors that would hamper the subsequent relief effort following the tsunami.

As the number of refugees displaced by the tsunami topped one million, President Yudhoyono described it as the worst disaster to hit his country since the eruption of Krakatoa over a century before. In terms of the number of people dead and displaced, even this seemed an underestimate. Kofi Annan, the general secretary of the UN, estimated that it would take at least ten years for the affected areas to recover.

The world was quick to mobilise as the terrifying scale of the disaster emerged. Billions of dollars of **aid** were collected around the world, and despite accusations of incompetence on behalf of the Indonesian authorities in distributing the aid, overall the relief effort has, thus far at least, been progressing well.

There may even be something positive to emerge from the Aceh disaster. Urged on by the international community, and encouraged by the **ceasefire** agreed upon by both sides in the wake of the disaster, the Indonesian government and the leaders of GAM – many of whom live in exile in Sweden – met in Helsinki in January 2005 to discuss a possible **peace settlement**. Although the summit finished early with nothing concrete emerging, further meetings scheduled for later in 2005 could see an end to three decades of strife in Aceh.

Advice for travellers

Even before the tsunami struck, the separatist struggle in **Aceh** had rendered the province out-of-bounds to tourists, and for this reason Aceh is not covered in this Guide.

The province of **North Sumatra** thankfully escaped the worst of the tsunami's destruction. However, a second earthquake struck **Pulau Nias** (see p.332) on 28 March 2005, destroying its capital, Gunung Sitoli, and killing over 1000 people. At the time of writing (May 2005), the island is still devastated. If you do intend to visit Nias, ask locals and other travellers on the mainland what the latest situation is on the island, and whether it is both safe and appropriate to visit at this time. And if you do decide to go, do be considerate, for a lot of locals lost relatives, friends and their livelihoods as a result of the earthquake, and relief and construction work will be continuing for some time.

who grew rich on the back of the vast plantations that stretch up the slopes of the Bukit Barisan to the west of the city. The boom was started by the entrepreneurial Jacob Nienhuys, who saw the potential for tobacco plantations, prompting even the local royalty to migrate to the city to be nearer the action.

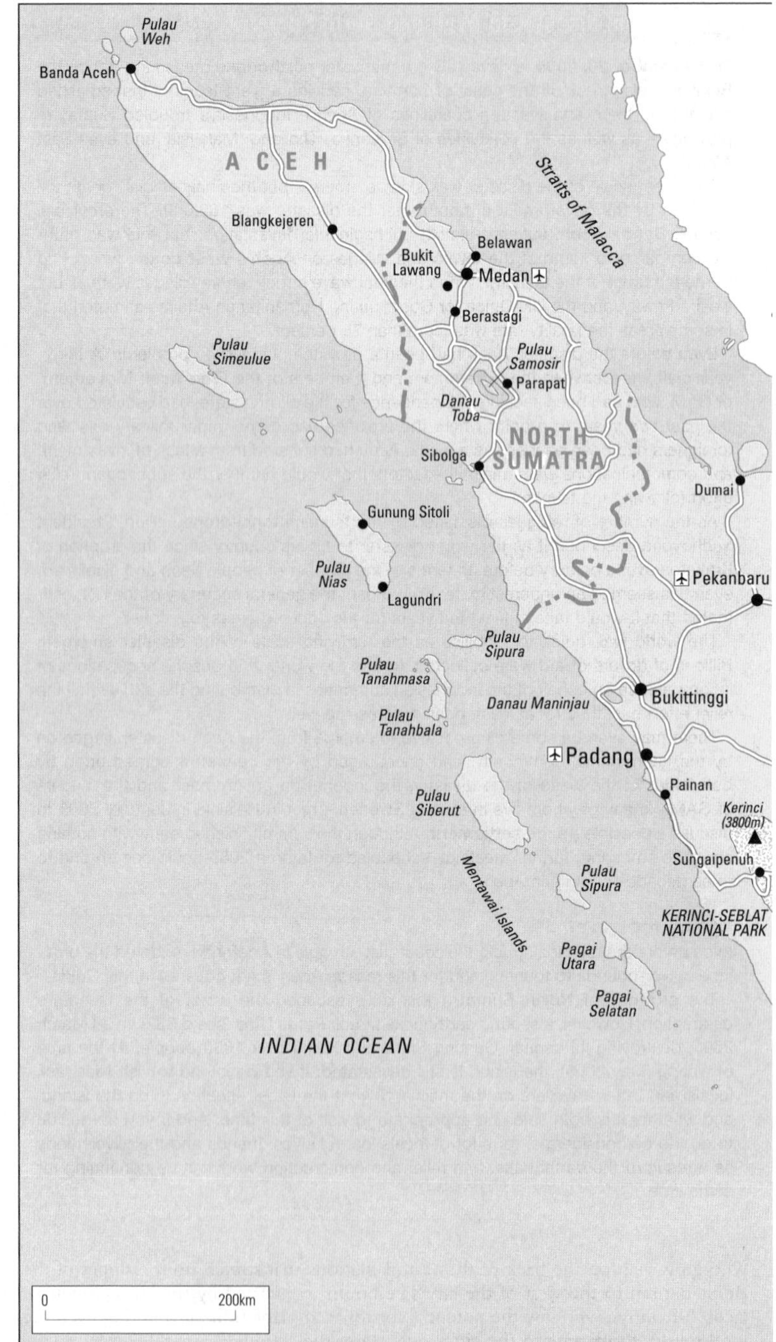
Pulau Weh
Banda Aceh
ACEH
Straits of Malacca
Blangkejeren
Belawan
Bukit Lawang
Medan
Berastagi
Pulau Simeulue
Pulau Samosir
Parapat
Danau Toba
NORTH SUMATRA
Sibolga
Dumai
Gunung Sitoli
Pulau Nias
Lagundri
Pekanbaru
Pulau Sipura
Pulau Tanahmasa
Pulau Tanahbala
Danau Maninjau
Bukittinggi
Padang
Painan
Pulau Siberut
Kerinci (3800m)
Sungaipenuh
Mentawai Islands
Pulau Sipura
KERINCI-SEBLAT NATIONAL PARK
Pagai Utara
Pagai Selatan
INDIAN OCEAN
0
200km

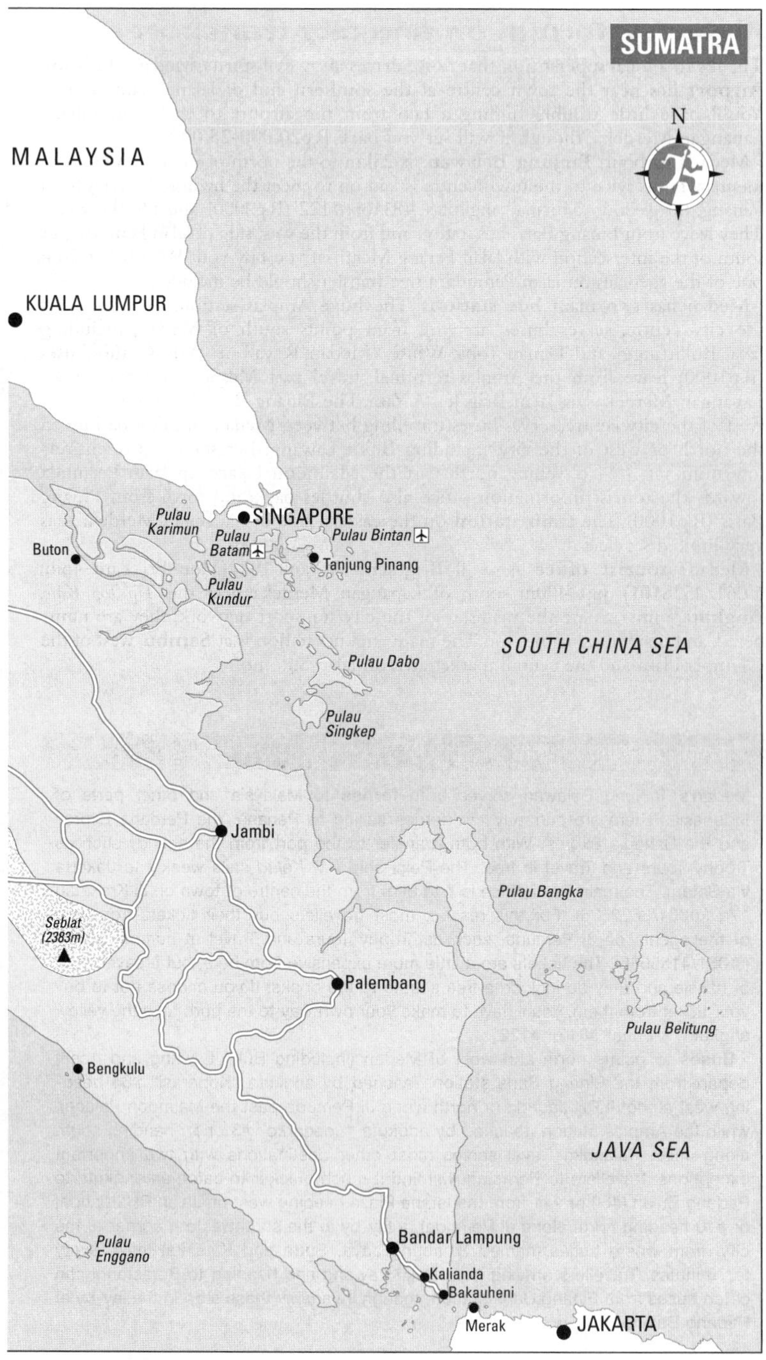
SUMATRA
N
MALAYSIA
KUALA LUMPUR
Pulau Karimun
SINGAPORE
Pulau Batam
Pulau Bintan
Buton
Tanjung Pinang
Pulau Kundur
SOUTH CHINA SEA
Pulau Dabo
Pulau Singkep
Jambi
Pulau Bangka
Seblat (2383m)
Palembang
Pulau Belitung
Bengkulu
JAVA SEA
Bandar Lampung
Pulau Enggano
Kalianda
Bakauheni
Merak
JAKARTA

Arrival, information and city transport

Thanks to a local superstition that noise drives away evil spirits, Medan's **Polonia Airport** lies near the town centre at the southern end of Jalan Imam Bonjol. You'll have little trouble finding a taxi from the airport to the main square, Lapangan Merdeka, though it will set you back Rp20,000–25,000.

Medan's harbour, **Tanjung Belawan**, is 25km to the north of the city. A complimentary bus service to the town centre is laid on to meet the hydrofoil ferries from Penang; the yellow "Morina" angkutas #81 or #122 (Rp2000) also ply the route. They leave from Pinang Baris bus station and from the west side of Jalan Pemuda, just south of the intersection with Jalan Perang Merah. If you buy your Pelni ticket from one of the agencies on Jalan Pemuda, a free transfer should be included.

Medan has two main **bus stations**. The huge Amplas station, 5km south of the city centre, serves buses arriving from points south of Medan, including Java, Bukittinggi and Danau Toba. White "Medan Raya" or "MRX" minibuses (Rp1000) leave from the Amplas terminal, travel past Mesjid Raya and on to Lapangan Merdeka via Jalan Brig Jen A Yani. The Pinang Baris bus station, 10km west of the city centre, serves buses travelling between Medan and destinations to the north or west of the city, including Bukit Lawang, Berastagi and Aceh. Yellow mini-van #64 travelling north past the Maimoon Palace up Jalan Permuda towards the tourist information office also shuttles back and forth from Pinang Baris (Rp1000). The **train station** on the eastern side of Lapangan Merdeka, has very limited services.

Medan's **tourist office** is at Jl Brig Jend A Yani 107 (Mon–Fri 8am–4pm; ⓣ061/4538101), just 400m south of Lapangan Merdeka near the *Tip Top Kafé*. **Angkuta** minivans are the mainstay of the city transport network; they are numbered, and many have names too. The main angkuta station is at **Sambu**, west of the Olympia Plaza and the central market area on Jalan Sutomo.

Moving on from Medan

Medan's Tanjung Belawan serves both **ferries** to Malaysia and other parts of Indonesia. There are currently two ferries sailing to Penang: the Perdana Expres and the Bahagia Expres. With both, transfer to the port from the agency such as Trophy Tours and Travel is free. The Pelni ship *KM Kelud* sails weekly to Jakarta via Batam. The main Pelni office is 7 to 8km from the centre of town on Jl Krakatau 17a (ⓣ061/6622526). For this reason, most travellers buy their tickets from one of the agents on Jl Pemuda, such as Trophy Tours and Travel at number 33d–e (ⓣ061/4155666). The tickets are a little more expensive from here, but it saves a lot of hassle and they do include a free shuttle to the docks; if you choose not to buy your ticket from them, you'll have to make your own way to the port: take the yellow angkuta "Morina" #81 or #122.

Buses to points north and west of Medan (including Bukit Lawang and Aceh) depart from the Pinang Baris station (reached by angkuta "Koperasi" #64 heading west along Jl RH Jaunda or north along Jl Pemuda past the Maimoon Palace), while the Amplas station (reached by angkuta "Soedarko" #3 or #4 heading south along Jalan Palangka Raya) serves most other destinations with two important exceptions: travellers to Berastagi will find it much quicker to catch an angkuta to Padang Bulan (#60 or #41 from the Istana Plaza heading west on Jalan RH Juanda, or #10 heading north along Jl Pemuda), a lay-by in the southwestern corner of the city, from where buses (named Sinabung Jaya, Sutra and Karsima) leave every ten minutes. Travellers arriving from Bukit Lawang and heading to Berastangi can catch buses from Pinang Baris station, though invariably these stop in the lay-by at Padang Bulan, too.

Accommodation

Medan has no distinct travellers' centre, although some cheap **hotels** cluster around Mesjid Raya.

Danau Toba Jl Imam Bonjol 17 ☎061/4157000. The liveliest of the luxury hotels, with first-class facilities including a health centre and an excellent outdoor pool. ④

Deli Raya Jl Sisingamangaraja 53 ☎061/736 7208. A noticeable step up from the bottom end, all rooms are clean and come with TVs and nice bathrooms. ①

Ibunda Jl Sisingamangaraja 33 ☎061/7345555. One of the smaller, cheaper and friendlier hotels along Jl Sisingamangaraja and one of the best mid-range options – a family-run place where all the rooms come with TV, a/c (temperamental), solar hot showers and telephone. ②

Tamara Jl Sisingamangaraja, Gg Pagaruyung 1 ☎061/7322484. The third of three budget hotels to the east of the Mesjid Raya and, like the others, basic, cheap and friendly but offering little else. ①

Zakia Jl Sipisopiso 10–12 ☎061/722413. The best of the budgets, with fine views of the mosque and rooftops and clean, basic dorms (Rp8000), plus rooms with or without plumbing. ①

The City

The large, informative **Museum of North Sumatra** (Tues–Thurs 8am–4pm, Fri–Sun 8am–3.30pm; Rp750), at Jl Joni 51, 500m east of Jalan Sisingamangaraja on the southern side of the Bukit Barisan cemetery near the stadium, tells the history of North Sumatra, and includes a couple of Arabic gravestones from 8 AD and some ancient stone Buddhist sculptures. Eight hundred metres north of the museum, on Jalan Sisingamangaraja, the black-domed **Mesjid Raya** (daily 9am–5pm, except prayer times; donation) is one the most recognizable buildings in Sumatra. Designed by a Dutch architect in 1906, it has North African-style arched windows, blue-tiled walls and vivid stained-glass windows. The mosque was commissioned by Sultan Makmun Al-Rasyid of the royal house of Deli and, 200m further west, opposite the end of Jalan Mesjid Raya, stands their **Maimoon Palace** (daily 8am–5pm; donation), built in 1888, with yellow walls (the traditional Malay colour of royalty), black crescent-surmounted roofs and Moorish archways. Relatives of the current sultan still lives here so only two rooms are open to the public, but they are dull and don't justify the entrance fee.

At the northern end of Jalan Pemuda, Jalan Brig Jend A Yani was the centre of colonial Medan, and a few early twentieth-century buildings still remain. The weathered **Mansion of Tjong A Fie** at no. 105 is a beautiful, green-shuttered, two-storey house that was built for the head of the Chinese community in Medan. It's closed to the public, but the dragon-topped gateway is magnificent, with the inner walls featuring some (very faded) portraits of Chinese gods. The fine 1920s **Harrison-Crossfield Building** (now labelled "London, Sumatra, Indonesia TBK"), at Jalan Brig Jend A Yani's northern end, was the former headquarters of a rubber exporter. Continuing north along Jalan Balai Kota and taking a left, you reach the grand, dazzlingly white headquarters of **PT Perkebunan IX** (a government-run tobacco company), which was commissioned by Jacob Nienhuys in 1869; it's on narrow Jalan Tembakau Deli, 200m north of the *Natour Dharma Deli* hotel.

In the west of the city, on Jalan H Zainul Arifin, the **Sri Mariamman Temple** is Medan's oldest and most venerated Hindu shrine. It was built in 1884 and is devoted to the goddess Kali. The temple marks the beginning of the Indian quarter, the **Kampung Keling**, the largest of its kind in Indonesia. Curiously, this quarter also houses the largest Chinese temple in Sumatra, the Taoist **Vihara Gunung Timur** (Temple of the Eastern Mountain), which, with its multitude of dragons, wizards, warriors and lotus petals, is tucked away on tiny Jalan Hang Tuah, 500m south of Sri Mariamman.

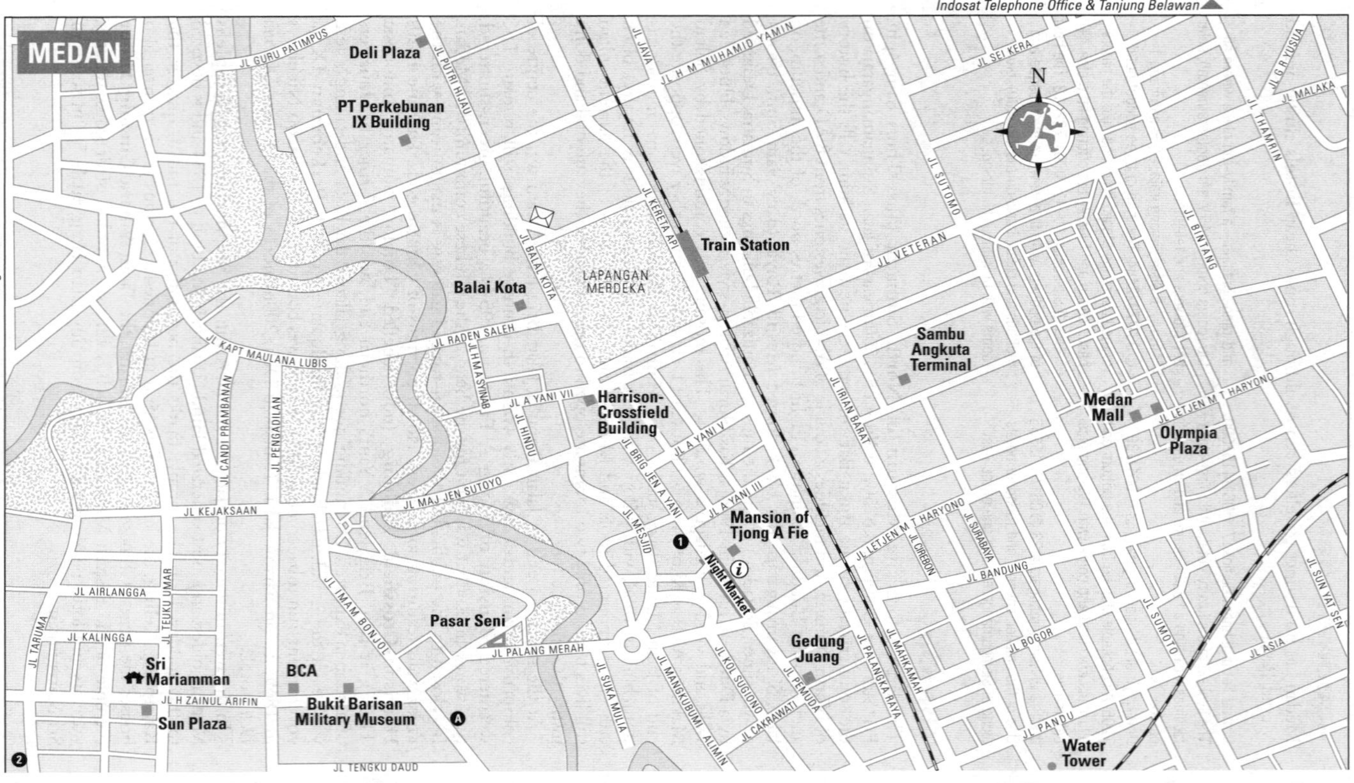
MEDAN
Indosat Telephone Office & Tanjung Belawan
Pinang Baris Bus Station
N
Deli Plaza
PT Perkebunan IX Building
Balai Kota
Train Station
LAPANGAN MERDEKA
Sambu Angkuta Terminal
Medan Mall
Olympia Plaza
Harrison-Crossfield Building
Mansion of Tjong A Fie
Night Market
Pasar Seni
Gedung Juang
Sri Mariamman
BCA
Bukit Barisan Military Museum
Sun Plaza
Water Tower
JL GURU PATIMPUS
JL PUTRI HIJAU
JL JAVA
JL H M MUHAMID YAMIN
JL SEI KERA
JL G R YUSUA
JL MALAKA
JL THAMRIN
JL SUTOMO
JL BINTANG
JL VETERAN
JL KERETA API
JL BALAI KOTA
JL RADEN SALEH
JL KAPT MAULANA LUBIS
JL H M A SYINAB
JL A YANI VII
JL HINDU
JL A YANI V
JL A YANI III
JL BRIG JEN A YANI
JL MESJID
JL IRIAN BARAT
JL LETJEN M T HARYONO
JL CIREBON
JL SURABAYA
JL BANDUNG
JL SUMOTO
JL SUN YAT SEN
JL ASIA
JL BOGOR
JL PANDU
JL MAHKAMAH
JL PALANGKA RAYA
JL PEMUDA
JL CAKRAWATI
JL KOL SUGIONO
JL MANGKUBUMI
ALIMIN
JL SUKA MULIA
JL PALANG MERAH
JL IMAM BONJOL
JL MAJ JEN SUTOYO
JL KEJAKSAAN
JL PENGADILAN
JL CANDI PRAMBANAN
JL AIRLANGGA
JL KALINGGA
JL TARUMA
JL TEUKU UMAR
JL H ZAINUL ARIFIN
JL TENGKU DAUD

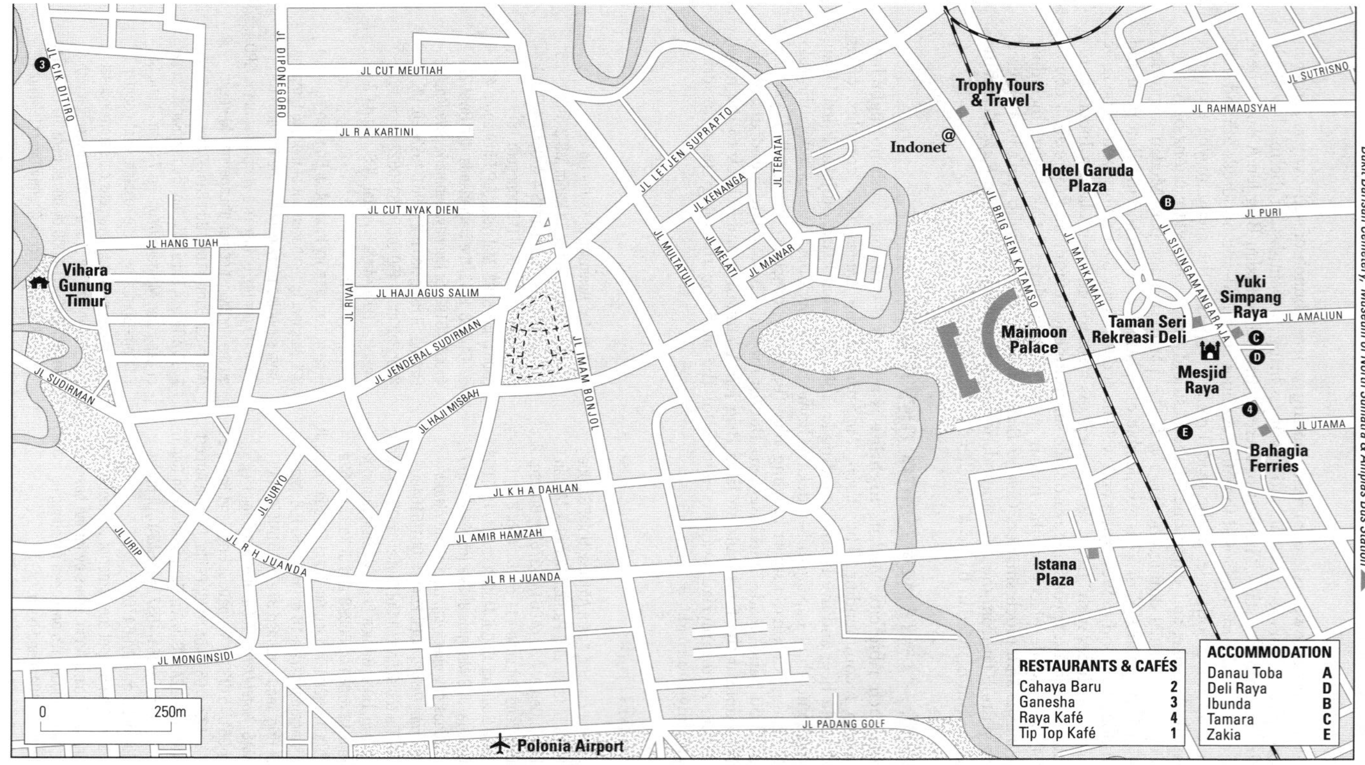
Bukit Barisan Cemetery, Museum of North Sumatra & Amplas Bus Station
JL CIK DITIRO
JL DIPONEGORO
JL CUT MEUTIAH
JL R A KARTINI
JL CUT NYAK DIEN
JL HANG TUAH
Vihara Gunung Timur
JL RIVAI
JL HAJI AGUS SALIM
JL SUDIRMAN
JL JENDERAL SUDIRMAN
JL HAJI MISBAH
JL IMAM BONJOL
JL LETJEN SUPRAPTO
JL KENANGA
JL TERATAI
JL MULTATULI
JL MELATI
JL MAWAR
Trophy Tours & Travel
Indonet
JL BRIG JEN KATAMSO
Maimoon Palace
JL MAHKAMAH
Hotel Garuda Plaza
Taman Seri Rekreasi Deli
JL SISINGAMANGARAJA
Yuki Simpang Raya
Mesjid Raya
Bahagia Ferries
JL SUTRISNO
JL RAHMADSYAH
JL PURI
JL AMALIUN
JL UTAMA
JL SURYO
JL URIP
JL R H JUANDA
JL K H A DAHLAN
JL AMIR HAMZAH
Istana Plaza
JL MONGINSIDI
JL PADANG GOLF
Polonia Airport
0
250m
RESTAURANTS & CAFÉS
Cahaya Baru 2
Ganesha 3
Raya Kafé 4
Tip Top Kafé 1
ACCOMMODATION
Danau Toba A
Deli Raya D
Ibunda B
Tamara C
Zakia E

Eating

Medan has its own style of al fresco **eating**, where a bunch of stall-owners gather in one place, chairs are put out, and a waitress brings a menu listing the food available from each of the stalls. The best of these is currently on Jalan Brig Jen A Yani where, from 6pm, the road is closed to traffic, awnings are raised, and hundreds of food stalls line up along both sides of the road. Take a seat, peruse the menu, maybe even join in the karaoke, and enjoy one of the best and most unique attractions of Medan. For more formal dining, the *Tip Top Kafé* – part restaurant, part Medan institution – at Jl Brig Jen A Yani 92 is a venerable old place that's been serving European and Indonesian food to Westerners and well-heeled locals for over eighty years. The large menu includes such "treats" as frog's legs. As hosts to Indonesia's largest Indian community, you'd expect some reasonable subcontinental cuisine and there are a couple of worthwhile places on the Indian quarter's main drag, Jl Cik Ditiro, including *Ganesha* and, much smarter, *Cahaya Baru*. Finally, for those who can't be bothered to venture far from their accommodation near the Mesjid Raya, the *Raya Kafé* is the closest thing Medan has to a travellers' café and is open 24 hours.

Entertainment and nightlife

For such a big city, Medan's **nightlife** is a bit of a wash-out, with no nightclubs worth recommending. The *Tavern Pub*, part of the *Danau Toba* complex, offers draught beer and live music including karaoke. The Deli Plaza, on Jalan Putri Hijau, to the north of Lapangan Merdeka, is home to the city's best cinema, while the Yuki Simpang Raya has a smart bowling alley (Rp5000 per game), pool hall (Rp20,000 per hour) and arcade in its basement. But for most, the best way to spend an evening is to dine at the food stalls on Jalan Brig Jen A Yani, then amble back to the hotel, gazing at the myriad swallows resting for the night on the telegraph wires criss-crossing the road.

Listings

Airline offices Adam Airlines, Hotel Garuda Plaza Batavia, Jl S Parman Komplek Medan Bisnis Center A20 ☎061/4537620; Bouraq, Jl Brig Jend Katamso 411 ☎061/4552333; Cathay, Tiara Building, Jl Cut Mutiah ☎061/4537008; Garuda, Jl S Monginsidi 34a (☎061/4556777; includes city check-in), also at the *Natour Dharma Deli*, Jl Balai Kota (☎061/516400), and the Tiara building, Jl Cut Mutiah ☎061/538527; Jatayu, Hotel Garuda Plaza, Jl Sisingamangaraja 18 ☎061/7360888 and Jl Katamso 62a ☎061/4528988; Lion Air, Hotel Garuda Plaza, Jl Sisingamangaraja 18 ☎061/7351168; Mandala, Jl Brig Jend Katamso 37e ☎061/4579100; MAS, *Hotel Danau Toba*, Jl Imam Bonjol 17 ☎061/4519333; Merpati, Jl Brig Jend Katamso 72–122 ☎061/4551888; Pelita, Polonia Airport ☎061/562241; Silk Air, Tiara Convention Centre, Jl Meutiah, ☎061/4537744; SMAC, Jl Imam Bonjol 59 ☎061/564760.

Banks The BCA, at the corner of Jl Diponegoro and Jl H Zainul Arifin, offers by far the best rates in town, though it's only open for changing money between 10am and noon.

Consulates Australia, Jl Kartini No 32 ☎061/455780; France, Jl Karim MS 2 ☎061/456 6100; Germany, Jl Karim MS 4 ☎061/5437108; Japan, Wisma BII 5, Jl P Diponegoro 18 ☎061/457 5193; Malaysia, Jl P Diponegoro 43 ☎061/453 1342; the Netherlands, Jl A Rivai 22 ☎061/4519025; Norway, Denmark, Sweden, Finland, Jl Hang Jebat 2 ☎061/4553020; UK, Jl Kapt Pattimura 450 ☎061/82105259.

Hospital Dewi Maya Hospital, Jl Surakarta 2 ☎061/4574279.

Internet access Try Indonet, Jl Brig Jen Katamso 32I, Nusanet in the basement of the Yuki Simpang Raya shopping plaza opposite the Mesjid Raya (Rp4000 per hr), or there's a Warposnet at the GPO on the northwest corner of Lapangan Merdeka (Mon–Sat 8am–11pm, Sun 8am–7pm).

Post office Jl Balai Kota, on the northwest corner of Lapangan Merdeka (Mon–Fri 7.30am–8pm, Sat 7.30am–3pm). The poste restante is at counter 11.

Telephone services Overseas calls from Indosat (7am–midnight), on Jl Jati at the intersection with Jl Thamrin (Rp2000–3000 by becak from the GPO). The *Tip Top Kafé* has a Home Country Direct telephone.

Bukit Lawang

On November 2, 2003, a flash-flood ripped through the heart of the popular tourist resort of **BUKIT LAWANG**, tucked away on the easternmost fringes of the Bukit Barisan range, 78km north of Medan. The village, which sits on the easternmost fringes of the Gunung Leuser National Park, was home to the **Orang-Utan Rehabilitation Centre** as well as a string of hotels and restaurants. In just fifteen minutes, the Sungai Bohorok rose seven metres, knocking down many hotels that lined its eastern bank, and leaving over 200 dead, including five tourists.

In earlier editions of this guide, Bukit Lawang was described as "one of the most enjoyable places in North Sumatra", and despite obvious signs of devastation – and the resulting absence of tourists – it's an opinion we still maintain. After closing for three months, the resort is now open again, and with new rules forbidding the building of hotels within 100m of the water and a promotional drive planned for the near future, it's hoped that tourists will return in large numbers once more. And so they should: Bukit Lawang's setting, on the eastern banks of the Sungai Bohorok, opposite the forest-clad slopes of Gunung Leuser, is idyllic, while a trip to see the orang-utans being fed at the rehab centre is never less than magical.

The Orang-Utan Rehabilitation Centre

The reason for the existence of the tourist resort is the **Bukit Lawang Orang-Utan Rehabilitation Centre**, founded in 1973 by two Swiss women, Monica Borner and Regina Frey, with the aim of returning captive and orphaned orang-utans into the wild. The wild orang-utan population had been pushed to the verge of extinction by the destruction of their natural habitat, and the apes themselves had become extremely popular as pets, fetching up to US$40,000. Here, apes that have spent most of their lives in captivity are retaught the art of tree climbing and nest building before being freed into the nearby forest. Still under threat, the orang-utans should never be touched or fed by the public as this could spread disease and discourage their return to the wild. For more information, take a look at Ⓦwww.orangutans-sos.org.

Since the flooding, the rehabilitation programme has been suspended. Despite this, and though the rehab centre is normally closed to the public, visitors are allowed to watch the twice-daily (8.30am & 3.30pm), hour-long **feeding sessions** that take place on the hill behind the centre. All visitors must have a permit from the PHPA office (see opposite). The centre is reached by a small pulley-powered canoe that begins operating approximately one hour before feeding begins. All being well, you should see at least one orang-utan during the session, and to witness their gymnastics is to enjoy one of the most memorable experiences in Indonesia.

Trekking

Bukit Lawang is the most popular base for organizing **treks** into the Gunung Leuser National Park, with plenty of guides based here. If you want only a short day-trek, a walk in the forest around Bukit Lawang is fine, and your chance of seeing monkeys, gibbons, macaques and, of course, orang-utans is very high. If you do decide to do a **long trek** from Bukit Lawang, the five- to seven-day walk to Ketambe is pleasant and passes through some excellent tracts of primary forest. Do check on the latest situation in Aceh, however, before attempting any trek of more than a couple of days. The three-day hike to Berastagi (see p.324) is also possible.

In order to trek, you must have a **permit** (see below), for every day that you plan to spend in the park. You must also have a **guide**, and should also be careful when choosing him. Their daily fee is set at approximately US$15 (US$10 for a half day), which includes lunch and permit for a one-day trek. Whoever you decide to hire, they should never feed or touch the orang-utans. Make this clear before you set out.

There are a couple of **minor walks** around Bukit Lawang that don't actually cross into the park, so permits and guides are unnecessary. The short, twenty-minute (one-way) walk to the **Gua Kampret** (Black Cave; more commonly called Bat Cave, though you'll see very few of them in the cave itself) is the simplest. It begins behind the *Ecolodge Bukit Lawang Cottages* and heads west through the rubber plantations, and though it's easy you'll still need good walking shoes and a torch if you're going to scramble over the rocks and explore the single-chamber cave. Officially, there's an Rp2000 entrance fee, though there's often nobody around to collect it.

By contrast, the path to the **Panorama Point**, in the hills to the east of Bukit Lawang, is difficult to follow. Most people take the path that begins south of the *Jungle Inn*, though this heads off through secondary forest and it's very easy to lose your way. A slightly easier route to follow – though much longer – is the path behind the Poliklinik near the visitor centre. It passes through cocoa and rubber plantations, and if you're successful, ninety minutes after setting out you should be able to gaze upon the valley of Bohorok.

Tubing

Tubing – the art of sitting in the inflated inner tube of a tyre as it hurtles downstream, battered by the wild currents of the Bohorok – is popular though not without risk. The tubes can be rented from almost anywhere in Bukit Lawang for about Rp5000 per day, or your losmen may supply them for free. There is a bridge 12km downstream of the village, from where you can catch a bus back. If you're not a strong swimmer, consider tubing on a Sunday, when lifeguards are dotted along the more dangerous stretches of the river around Bukit Lawang.

Practicalities

Buses from Medan's Pinang Baris bus station stop at the terminal, 1km from the Bohorok Visitor Centre and the tourist heart of Bukit Lawang. Motorized becaks travel the distance for Rp2000.

You'll need a **permit** (Rp20,500 per day) to watch the feeding sessions at the rehab centre, which are available from the **PHPA Permit Office** (daily 7am–4pm) that overlooks the square to the east, by the visitor centre. Separate trekking permits (Rp4000 per day) are also available here. The permit office is part of the excellent **Bohorok Visitor Centre** (daily 8am–3pm), which is packed with information about the park. The present lack of tourists has resulted in the cancellation of the 8.30am bus service to Berastagi, so you'll currently have to catch a bus back to Medan and head out from there. The Medan buses start around 5am and are more or less half-hourly.

Accommodation

Since the flood, the long string of **hotels** on Bohorok's eastern banks has largely disappeared and the two that remain open, the *Jungle Inn* (❶–❷) and neighbouring *Garden Inn* (❶), near the crossing to the rehab centre, are in violation of the law forbidding hotels within 100m of the river and may soon be forced to close, or at least moved downstream. Nevertheless, these two lodges, the last of the old-style laid-back rough-and-ready places, are charming in a rustic sort of way. These apart, the tourist centre has now relocated to the western side of the river, across the bridge from the permit office. The pick of these is the *Ecolodge Bukit Lawang Cottages* (❷), with large clean rooms with mandi and pleasant gardens. It's more expensive than the others but one of the few to maintain high standards, and it does offer discounts of about fifty percent with a little haggling. North of here is the *Wisma Leuser Sibayak* (❶), by the bridge, which is now looking very tired and was undergoing refurnishment at the time of research. For roughly the same price, and equally shabby, is neighbouring *Bukit Lawang Indah* (❶), while in between is the *Yusman* (❶), possibly the best value of them all at just Rp20,000 for a smart room with mandi.

The Karo Highlands

Covering an area of almost five thousand square kilometres, from the northern tip of Danau Toba to the border of Aceh, the **Karo Highlands** comprise an extremely fertile volcanic plateau at the heart of the Bukit Barisan mountains. The plateau is home to over two hundred farming villages and two main towns: the regional capital, Kabanjahe, and the popular market town and tourist resort of **Berastagi**.

According to local legend, the Karo people were the first of the Batak groups to settle in the highlands of North Sumatra and, as with all Batak groups, the strongly patrilineal Karo have their own language, customs and rituals, most of which have survived, at least in a modified form, to this day. These include convoluted wedding and funeral ceremonies, both of which can go on for days, and the **reburial ceremony**, held every few years, where deceased relatives are exhumed and their bones are washed with a mixture of water and orange juice.

When the Dutch arrived at the beginning of the twentieth century they assumed, mistakenly, that the Karo were cannibals. The now-defunct Karonese tradition of filing teeth, combined with a fondness for chewing betel nut that stained their mouths a deep red, gave the Karo a truly fearsome and bloodthirsty appearance. In fact, the Karo, alone amongst the Batak tribes, abhorred cannibalism, though their traditional **animist religion** was as rich and complex as any of the other Batak faiths. Today, over seventy percent of the Karo are Christian, fifteen percent Muslim and the rest adhere to the traditional Karo religion. Every member of Karonese society is bound by obligations to their clan, which are seen as more important than any religious duties.

Berastagi

Lying 1330m above sea level, 70km southwest of Medan and 25km due north of the shores of Danau Toba, **BERASTAGI** is a cold, compact little hill station in the centre of the Karo Highlands. It was founded by the Dutch in the 1920s as a retreat from the sweltering heat of Medan, and has been popular with tourists ever since. The town is set in a gorgeous bucolic landscape bookended by two huge but climbable **volcanoes**, Gunung Sibayak and Gunung Sinabung, and provides a perfect base for **trekking**. It's little more than a one-street town, with nearly all accommodation running north of the bus station on Jalan Veteran.

There are a number of attractions in the town itself, including three markets: the photogenic **general market**, which takes place five times a week (not Wed or Sun) behind the bus station; the daily **fruit market**, which also sells souvenirs, to the west of the roundabout, and the **Sunday market**, which takes place every other week on top of Gundaling Hill and attracts such novelty acts as the teeth-pulling man (Rp1000 per tooth) and the snake charmer.

The **post office** (Mon–Thurs 7.30am–3pm, Fri 7.30–noon, Sat 7.30am–1pm) and Telkom office stand together by the war memorial, just off Jalan Veteran. The **tourist office** (Mon–Sat 8am–5pm) is just over the road, but the information at the losmen is better. The BNI **bank**, with ATM, is on Jalan Veteran, and you can change US dollars and travellers' cheques at *Losmen Sibayak*. Buses to Medan leave from the bus station at the southern end of Jalan Veteran, while minibuses to the Karo villages leave from outside the *Wisma Sibayak* heading south down Jalan Udara. To **get to Danau Toba**, either take the *Losmen Sibayak*'s direct tourist bus – if you are a large enough group to make it worth their while – or three minivans (starting at 8am) from the road next to and just east of the *Wisma Sibayak*. The first van gets you to Kabenjahe (15min; Rp1000), the second – called either "Simas" or "Sepedan" – to Pematangsiantar, usually just called Siantar (3hr; Rp6000) and the third to the jetty at Parapat (1hr, Rp5000). A direct bus from Medan costs Rp5000.

Accommodation

Ginsata Jl Veteran 27 ⓣ0628/91441. Quiet, unfussy hotel overlooking the main roundabout that's good if you want solitude. Rooms are basic and rather expensive, though there's cheaper accommodation available in the cottage behind the hotel. ❶

Losmen Sibayak Jl Veteran 119 ⓣ0628/91122 or 91104. Younger sister of the *Wisma Sibayak*, under the same management but with a few added features such as a book exchange, Pelni ticket office, numerous tours, and a pizza restaurant that shows videos every evening. ❶

Wisma Sibayak Jl Udara 1 ⓣ0628/91104. One of Sumatra's best and longest-established hostels: the walls are smothered with good information (though some is a little dated), the travellers' comments books are very useful, and the beds are clean. ❶

Sibayak Internasional Jl Merdeka ⓣ0628/91301, ⓦwww.hotelsibayak.com. The oldest of Berastagi's luxury hotels, with 73 rooms and 30 cottages. Facilities include squash and tennis courts, a heated swimming pool, a billiards table and even a small cinema. ❽

Sibayak Multinational Guest House Jl Pendidikan 93 ⓣ0628/91031. Yet another branch of the Sibayak chain, set in its own gardens to the north of town on the way to Sibayak. Even the cheapest rooms come with their own terrace and a hot shower; rooms in the old 1930s Dutch section of the house are larger and cost more. ❶–❷

Eating

There are several no-nonsense Chinese **restaurants** on Jalan Veteran, the pick being the *Eropa* on the western side of the street (to your left if walking up from *Wisma Sibayak*). Both the Sibayak guesthouses in town have restaurants with extensive menus including pizza, though a lack of guests means that many of the dishes (and in the case of the *Losmen Sibayak*, beer as well) are currently unavailable. The best travellers' café is *Raymond's*, north of *Losmen Sibayak*, with huge portions of delicious, cheap food.

The Karo villages

During the Dutch invasion of 1904, most of the larger villages and towns in the Karo Highlands were razed by the Karonese themselves to prevent the Dutch from appropriating them. But there are villages where you can still see the **traditional wooden houses**, built on thick, metre-high stilts and home to eight to ten families. Their most striking features are the palm-frond gables, woven into intricate patterns and topped by a set of buffalo horns. Inside, there are no partitions, save for the sleeping quarters, and family life is carried out in full view of the neighbours.

The most accessible of the Karo villages is **PECEREN** (Rp1000 entrance fee), just 2km northeast of Berastagi. Coming from the town, take the road to Medan and turn down the lane on your right after the *Rose Garden* hotel. There are six traditional houses here, but although some are in good condition, the village itself is probably the least picturesque in the region.

There are three more villages to the south of Berastagi that, when combined, make a pleasant – but very long – day-trek from town: it takes about three hours to cover all three. Be warned, however, that many of these houses are now slipping into a terrible state of repair, as the inhabitants move into the ghastly bathroom-tile-and-concrete affairs, complete with satellite dishes, that have become the new vernacular architecture for Berastagi. As a result, the villages no longer have that charmingly rustic air about them. Note too, that the villages tend to be extremely muddy, and many of the villagers, especially the women, are very shy, so always ask before pointing your camera at them. Nevertheless, if you fancy a walk in Berastagi's verdant countryside, past fields embellished with family graves and worked by friendly locals, it's not a bad walk. The first village, **GURUSINGA**, lies about an hour due south of Berastagi. From the southern end of Jalan Veteran, take the road running southwest alongside the *Wisma Sibayak*. After about twenty minutes you'll come to a path by the "Expedisi C.V. Lakona" site. This path heads off through fields dotted with family graves to Gurusinga, home to several huge, traditional thatched longhouses. The path continues along the western edge of Gurusinga to the village of **LINGGA TULU**, before passing through a bamboo forest. At the road at the end of the path, you can turn left and walk the 2km to the next village, **LINGGA**, though it's a hot and sweaty trek on a busy road, so flagging down a bemo is a better option. Three hundred metres before Lingga is the one-room Karo Lingga Museum (daily 7am–5pm; donation). The village itself has some of the best traditional houses in the area, many of which are over 150 years old, though many are suffering from the same level of neglect as the other villages. Finding a bemo heading back to Kabanjahe can be tricky, so it might be quicker to walk back to the main road and catch a **minibus** from there (last bus 5pm; Rp1000). From Kabanjahe, you can catch a bemo back to Berastagi (last bus 7pm; Rp1200).

Volcanoes around Berastagi

There are two active **volcanoes** more than 2000m high in the immediate vicinity around Berastagi: **Sibayak**, to the north of town, is possibly the most accessible volcano in the whole of Indonesia, and takes just four hours to climb up and three hours down, while the hike up **Sinabung**, to the southwest of town, is longer and tougher and involves an hour by car to the trailhead. The lists of missing trekkers plastered all around Berastagi prove that these climbs are not as straightforward as they may at first seem. The tourist office urges climbers always to take a guide – which you can hire from them or from your losmen – though for Sibayak a guide is unnecessary providing you're climbing with someone else. For both volcanoes, set off early in the morning. It's a good idea to take some food, too, particularly bananas and chocolate for energy, and warm clothing, and if you're looking to take advantage of the hot springs at the foot of Sibayak, your swimming costume and a towel, too. *Losmen Sibayak* offers various guided treks to both peaks.

Gunung Sibayak

Before attempting your assault of **Sibayak** (2094m), pick up one of the *Wisma Sibayak*'s free maps and read their information books, too. Walk up the left fork after the monument (but keep the fruit market on your left) and continue under the arch to the *Sibayak International*. Turn right just before the hotel itself and, keeping the hotel to your left, carry on along the road for a kilometre or so beyond the *Sibayak Multinational Guest House* until you reach a signpost by a large arch with the words "Mejuah-Juah" written on them. Next to and below this arch is a café where you pay the hiking fee of Rp1500 and (importantly) register your name. From here, walk past the bemo station on the tarmac lane and you'll begin the series of up-and-down dips that leads to the summit. Near the top, look out for some rough bamboo steps cut into the embankment on your left. If you reach the end of the tarmac, you've gone too far, and will need to head back 150m or so to the steps, which lead up to a concrete path up to the crater. You'll see steam roaring out of yellow, sulphurous fissures near the summit.

Finding the path back down to the hot springs is the hardest part of the walk. Indeed, if you've got less than three hours' daylight left and you're not certain of the way down, walk back down the way you came up. For those who wish to visit the hot springs, however, upon arriving at the crater rim you'll see the lake below you, and ahead of you a cluster of antennae high up on a pinnacle. Facing the antennae, walk anticlockwise to about 3 o'clock and head up to your right from there – there is a rough path, but it's not easy to discern. At the top you'll see a path running along the rim. Turn right, and after about 50m you'll come to the first couple of broken steps – little more than concrete strips in the ground at this stage though they do increase in quality and quantity further down. As you continue following both the path and these steps, you'll enter into a forest, pass through a grove of bamboo before emerging at a geothermal plant. Below this is a series of **hot springs** (Rp2000) – a great reward for a hard trek. Afterwards, bemos leave occasionally from the junction, charging Rp2500 for the trip back to Berastagi; otherwise, you'll have to continue along the road for several kilometres to the junction with the main road and pick one up from there.

Gunung Sinabung

Take a taxi to tiny **Danau Kawar** (1hr), where the path begins by the side of a restaurant to the north of the water, and continues through cabbage fields for approximately an hour, before entering fairly thick jungle. The walk becomes relentlessly tough soon after; having left the jungle you soon find yourself scrambling up some steep and treacherous rocky gullies. A couple of hours later, you'll be standing on the edge of a cliff looking down into **Gunung Sinabung**'s two craters. Take care when walking around up here, as the paths are crumbling and it's a long way down.

Danau Toba

Lying right in the middle of the province, jewel-like **Danau Toba** is Southeast Asia's largest freshwater lake, and at 525m possibly the world's deepest, too. It was formed about 80,000 years ago by a colossal volcanic eruption: the caldera that was created eventually buckled under the pressure and collapsed in on itself, the high-sided basin that remained filling with water to form the lake. A second, smaller volcanic

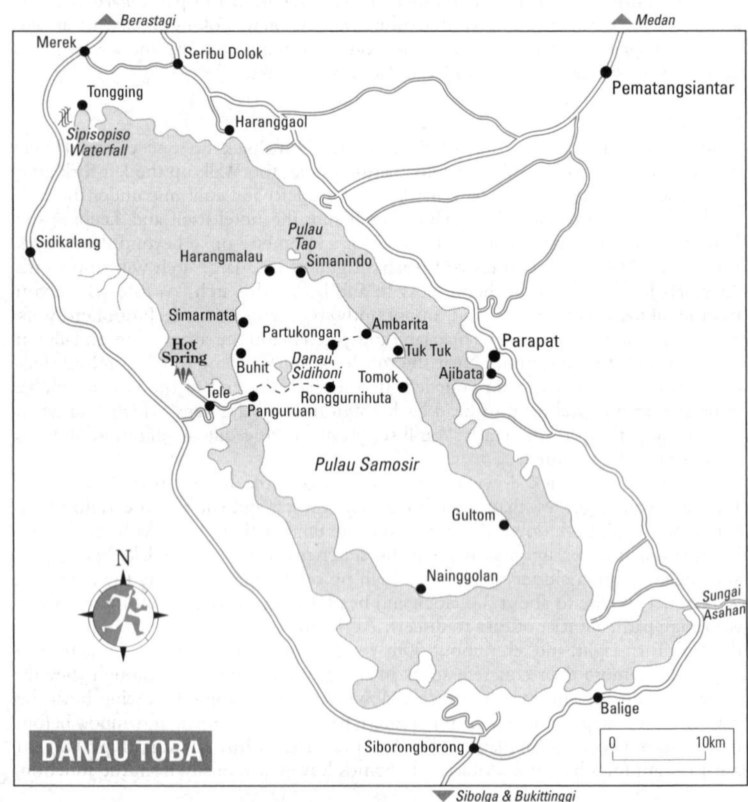

eruption, 50,000 years after the first, created an island the size of Singapore in the middle of the lake. This island, **Samosir**, is the cultural and spiritual heartland of the **Toba Batak** and the favoured destination for foreign travellers. Ferries leave regularly from **Parapat** – the largest and most convenient gateway for Samosir – and other lakeside towns for the tiny east coast peninsula of **Tuk Tuk** and neighbouring **Ambarita**, the most popular resorts on Samosir. The **resorts**, with their bookshops, bars and magic mushroom omelettes (illegal but ubiquitous), make Danau Toba the perfect spot to chill out after the rigours of travel in Sumatra. From these resorts you can go trekking in the deforested hills in the centre of Samosir, or cycle around the coastline, calling in at the tiny Batak villages with their flamboyant tombs and distinctive concave-roofed houses.

Getting there

Most tourists catch a ferry (ask to be dropped at your specific guesthouse) from the Tigaraja harbour in the resort of **Parapat**; there are ferries every hour during the day to Tuk Tuk, with the last at around 7.30pm. If you have your own transport, **Ajibata**, the next cove south of Parapat, operates five car ferries per day to Tomok, the main town on Samosir's east coast.

Less conveniently, the market town of **Haranggaol**, 40km north of Parapat, has just two weekly ferries to Samosir, while **Tongging** has just one (Mon 9am). With the decline in tourism, these services are no longer as reliable. Tongging is ideally located on Toba's northern shore near the 120-metre **Sipisopiso waterfall**; you can stay at the *Wisma Sibayak Guesthouse* (❶), but check that it's open before you arrive by contacting the *Losmen Sibayak* in Berastagi (see p.325), which is run by the same family. Buses from the Pakpak Batak town of Sidikalang travel to the east coast of Samosir via the **bridge** that connects the western shores of the island with the mainland.

Parapat

Situated at the point where the Trans-Sumatran Highway touches the eastern shore of Toba, **PARAPAT** is a town split in two. There's the rather tawdry **resort**, crammed with hotels and souvenir shops and, set on the hills away from the lake, the bus station, bank and telephone office. Buses arriving in Parapat drive through the resort to Tigaraja harbour before heading back to the bus station. You can get a minivan to and from the bus station at any time for Rp1000.

The town does have its financial advantages over the island of Samosir. The rates at Parapat's **Bank BNI**, for example, on Jalan Sisingamangaraja, are far superior to anything offered on the island, and there's an ATM here, too. Furthermore, the cost of calling home from one of the wartels or Parapat's **Telkom office**, on the back road between the bus station and the quay, is fifty percent cheaper than from Samosir. But apart from the lively and diverting twice-weekly (Wed & Sat) **food markets** by the Tigaraja harbour, there's little reason to linger in town.

With over sixty hotels in Parapat, there's plenty of **accommodation** to choose from, though only a few places at the budget end of the market. Of these, *Charley's*, right by the ferry terminal and next to the market at Jl Pekan Tiga Raja 7 (☎0625/41277; ❶), is by far the best. In the mid-range, *Hotel Wisata Bahari*, Jl Pulau Samosir 3–6 (☎0625/41302; ❸–❻), does the job; otherwise, try *Natour Parapat*, Jl Marihat 1 (☎0625/41012; ❻).

Pulau Samosir

Pulau Samosir is the spiritual heartland of the Toba Batak people, and one of the most fascinating, pleasant and laid-back spots in Indonesia. Most tourists make for the eastern shores of Toba where there's a string of enjoyable resorts, from **Tomok**, to **Tuk Tuk**, **Ambarita** and the island's cultural centre, **Simanindo**, on Samosir's northern shore.

There's no official **tourist office**, though many of the guesthouses, in particular *Bagus Bay Homestay* and *Tabo*, have their own travel agencies, which can book transport and tours. *Samosir Cottages*' useful printed guide to the island – with some of it taken from this guide – was stopped at the end of 2004, but maybe as the tourists return, so will the guide. None of the **banks** change money, but guesthouses and a handful of moneychanging shops often will. There are many **wartels** where you can make (expensive) international calls, and many places offer **Internet**, though at hugely inflated prices (usually Rp20,000-25,000 per hour); the quickest connection by far is *Carolina's*. The waters that lap the shores of Tuk Tuk are safe for **swimming**; the roped-off section of the lake by *Carolina's*, complete with pontoons, canoes and a diving board, is the most popular place. There are also a few activities on offer in Tuk Tuk, including cruises around Samosir (Rp80,000), speedboat trips (Rp700,000 for half a day, or Rp210,000 per hour). You can also rent **bicycles** (Rp15,000–20,000 per day) and **motorbikes** (Rp50,000 per day), should you want to visit the more far-flung reaches of the island, which will allow you to visit Simalungun and the **hot springs** at Tele on the western side. The Sunshine Beauty and Wellness Studio at Tuk Tuk (Ⓣ0625/451108) includes massage (Rp40,000) amongst its range of services. Many of the hotels also have sports facilities, including table tennis at *Libertas* and badminton, pool and volleyball at *Bagus Bay*. The latter also show videos nightly at 5pm and 8pm, except on Wednesday and Saturday when they host exhibitions of traditional Batak dancing. Finally, the *Tumba Disco* lies on the southern side of Tuk Tuk, about 300m inland.

Tuk Tuk

Over thirty losmen and hotels, numerous restaurants, bars, bookshops, travel agents and souvenir stalls stand cheek-by-jowl on the **Tuk Tuk** peninsula. If you plan to stay here, tell the ferryman which hotel you're going to and he'll drop you off at the nearest quay. In general, the cheapest accommodation is on the northern side of the peninsula, the more popular budget options lie on the southern side nearest the main "harbour", and the more luxurious hotels stretch down the long eastern shoreline.

Bagus Bay Homestay Ⓣ0625/451287, Ⓦwww.bagusbay.com. One of the finer budget options on Tuk Tuk, with excellent facilities, including a pool table, Internet café, bike rental, badminton court, board games, bar, videos three times a night and a twice-weekly Batak dancing display. The food has improved recently and the menu is large. Also has one of the few dormitories (Rp10,000) on Tuk Tuk. ❶–❷

Carolina's Ⓣ0625/41520, Ⓔcarolina@psiantar.wasantara.net.id. Classy and huge Batak-style bungalows, each with a lakeside view and their own little section of beach. The Rp120,000 luxury rooms with fridge, hot water and TV are amongst the best on the island. ❶–❸

Libertas Ⓣ0625/451035. Currently the most popular budget homestay, and understandably so: six smart, traditional-style bungalows, good facilities and a limited but varied menu of superb and enormous food, all cooked by the likeable and honest manager, Mr Moon. Recommended. ❶/❷

Romlan's Ⓣ0625/41557. Excellent value – if slightly scruffy – little guesthouse with some of the cheapest traditional bungalows on the island, many overlooking the water to Parapat. It's hard to find: turn down the track signposted to the *Sumber Pulomas* hotel, then take a right on the small grassy path leading to the reception. ❶

Samosir Cottages Ⓣ0625/41050. Once the best mid-range accommodation on the peninsula and still OK, with rooms ranging from the basic to luxury bungalows (complete with hot water and a bathtub) overlooking the lake. Has a good restaurant and Internet access. ❷/❸

Tabo Cottages Ⓣ0625/451318,Ⓦwww.tabo-cottages.com. The best mid-range option on the peninsular by far, attractive and efficiently run with a wide range of facilities. Rooms range from the comfy to the exquisite, with the best of them coming with a veranda and hammock; the food conjured up in the restaurant and bakery is terrific, too. ❶–❺

Timbul Peninsula Ⓣ0625/41374. A welcome new addition to the northern side of Tuk Tuk that's suffered even more than the rest of the peninsula from the lack of tourists. The bungalows, some in traditional Batak style, are all at the water's edge and are set in a pleasant and quiet garden. Ask to be dropped of at *Sony's Guesthouse* and walk for ten minutes northwards along the road from there. ❶

Ambarita

Guesthouses in Ambarita have been hit even harder than the rest of the island by the fall in the number of tourists visiting Sumatra, and the closure of Ambarita Harbour hardly helps matters. Nevertheless, the places *are* all still open, and even if you don't stay they provide a nice place to drop into for lunch and enjoy the kingfishers skimming the lake. *Barbara's* (☎0625/41230; ❶) is the most popular thanks to its friendly service and comfortable rooms; neighbouring *Thyesza* (☎0625/41443; ❶) is similarly priced and with simple neo-Batak rooms.

Around the island

TOMOK, 2km south of Tuk Tuk, is the most southerly of the resorts on the east coast; dozens of virtually identical souvenir stalls line the main street. Tomok's most famous sight is the early nineteenth-century stone **sarcophagus of Raja Sidabutar**, the chief of the first tribe to migrate to the island. The coffin has a Singa face – a part-elephant, part-buffalo creature of Toban legend – carved into one end, and a small stone effigy of the king's wife on top of the lid. On the way to Ambarita from Tomok, due west of Tuk Tuk, is the tiny village of **Garoga**, from where you can hike to the waterfall of the same name (after rainfall). Ask the locals for directions.

In **AMBARITA** there is a curious collection of stone chairs (daily 7am–5pm; Rp2000), one of which is mysteriously occupied by a stone statue. Most of the villagers will tell you that these chairs acted as the local law courts two hundred years ago, others say that the chairs are actually less than fifty years old, and the work of a local mason who copied drawings of the original.

SIMANINDO lies at the northern end of the island, 15km beyond the town of Ambarita. The **Simanindo Museum** (daily 12.30–5pm; Rp3000) is housed in the former house of Raja Simalungun, and has some mildly diverting household implements, including spears, magical charms and a wooden *guri guri* (ashes urn). The large *adat* houses in the **traditional village**, through the stone archway, are unexceptional save for their thatched roofs – a rarity on Samosir. The museum and village also hold traditional Batak dancing performances every morning (10.30–11.10am at the museum, 11.45am–12.30pm in the village).

Continuing round to the western side of the island, **Simarmata**, halfway between Simanindo and Pangururan, is one of the best-preserved Batak villages on Samosir. There's little to see in **Pangururan** itself, though there's a **hot spring** (Rp2000) across the bridge in the village of **Tele**.

Trekking across Samosir

The hills in the centre of Samosir tower 700m above the lake, and at the heart of the island is a large plateau and **Danau Sidihoni**, a body of water about the size of a large village pond. It's a ten-hour walk from one side of the island to the other, but a stopover in one of the villages on the plateau is usually necessary.

The climb from the eastern shore is very steep, but from the western shore the incline is far more gradual, so some trekkers start by catching the first bus to Pangururan (leaving at 7.30am from Tomok), arriving at about 10am. Most, however, begin in Ambarita on the eastern shore, on the uphill path, from where it's two to three hours' climb to the tiny hilltop village of **Partukongan** – aka Dolok or "summit" – the highest point on Samosir. There are two homestays here, *John's* and *Jenny's*, and three losmen in the next village on the trail, **Ronggurnihuta**. The villagers can be a bit vague when giving directions, so take care and check frequently with passers-by that you're on the right trail. Ronggurnihuta is a three- or four-hour walk away, with **Panguruan** three to fours hours further on at the end of a torturously long downhill track (18km) that passes **Danau Sidihoni** on the way. Arrive in Pangururan before 5pm and you should be in time to catch the last bus back to the eastern shore; otherwise, stay at the *Wartel Wisata* (☎0626/20558; ❶) at Jl Dr TB Simatupang 42 by the bus stop.

Moving on from Danau Toba

Ferries leave every hour on the hour from Tuk Tuk (8am–5pm; Rp4000) to Parapat, often – but not always – calling in at the other ferry ports on the peninsula before they do so. There's also the occasional ferry to Tongging (from Tuk Tuk) and Haranggaol, though with the decline in tourism these services have become less regular and reliable; ask at your hotel on Samosir for details. There is still the five-times-a-day car ferry service from Tomok to Ajibata.

The trip to **Berastagi** (see p.325) is a complex one: firstly, you'll have to catch a bus to Pematangsiantar from Parapat (1hr; Rp5000), and then a bus to Kabanjahe (3hr; Rp6000), and finally a bemo to Berastagi (15min; Rp1000). An alternative is to catch the daily tourist bus (Rp350,000 for up to six passengers), a four-hour ride that takes in the Sipisopiso waterfall and the small Pematangpurba King's Palace on the way.Unfortunately, this bus runs only if there are enough passengers to make it worth their while – and with the dwindling number of people visiting Toba, there seldom is. There are also a number of public buses to Sibolga (6hr), the grimy port town for Pulau Nias. For **Bukittinggi**, there are numerous buses from Parapat, particularly in the morning, taking anything from ten to fourteen hours; and there are plenty going in the other direction, for **Medan** (4–6hr), too.

Pulau Nias

Though the journey is long and arduous, and involves passing through the unlovely town of **Sibolga**, most visitors agree that any effort expended to get to Pulau Nias is worth it. An island the size of Bali, with a rich tribal culture, wonderful beaches and some of the best surfing in the country, **Pulau Nias** is a microcosm of almost everything that's exciting about Indonesia. The north of Nias is largely swampland and unappealing save for the capital, **Gunung Sitoli**. The south, however, plays host to a number of fascinating hilltop villages, such as Orahili, Bawomataluo and the spiritual heartland of Gomo, where the last few remnants of Nias's famed megalithic culture survive. The south also has the best and most popular beaches, such as the surfer's paradise at **Lagundri Bay**. The island is **malarial**, and chloroquine-resistant strains have been reported. Take the correct prophylactics and bring repellent and a mosquito net.

Lying 125km southwest of Sibolga, the island's reputation as a land of malarial swamps and bloodthirsty natives succeeded in keeping visitors at bay for centuries, leading to the development of a culture free from the influences of India, Arabia, Europe and, indeed, the rest of Indonesia. The 600,000 **Niasans** speak a distinct language, one that has more in common with Polynesian than any Indonesian tongue, and their sculptures resemble closely those of the Nagas in the eastern Himalayas. Their traditional class system depended on slaves – usually people captured from nearby villages in raids – which eventually attracted slave-traders from as far afield as Europe, including the Dutch, who arrived in 1665 and remained on the island for most of the next 250 years. During this time, nearly all the animistic totems and megaliths were either destroyed or shipped to Europe. Today, over 95 percent of Nias is, nominally at least, Christian, and the last recorded instance of headhunting, an essential component of Niha animism, occurred way back in 1935.

This section on **Pulau Nias** was researched prior to the **March 28 earthquake**, which left the island's capital, **Gunung Sitoli**, in ruins and killed over 1000 people. Whilst it is still possible to visit Nias, pleas heed the advice given in the box on p.315 and bear in mind that much of what is written here will now be out of date.

Approaching Pulau Nias: Sibolga

With its series of pitch-black tunnels cut into the jungle-clad cliffs, roadside waterfalls and heart-stopping hairpin bends, the last, vertiginous five kilometres of the six-hour drive down to **SIBOLGA** from Parapat is breathtakingly dramatic. Unfortunately, Sibolga itself is a small, drab place with a chronic lack of anything worth seeing. It is, however, the main port for ferries to Pulau Nias. Recently, there have been reports of a few **scams** involving tourists and fake-uniformed "narcotics police" looking for a bribe; be on your guard.

All **buses** and bemos use the terminus on Jalan Sisingamangaraja, at the back of the town away from the coast, though some long-distance tourist minivans (for Medan and Bukittinggi) leave in the morning from just east of the jetty. The **port** for ferries to Nias – as well as the occasional Pelni boat from Padang – is about 1.5km south of here, at the end of Jalan Horas. **Tickets** for all ferries to Nias (both to Gunung Sitoli and Teluk Dalam), as well as the Pelni ferries to Padang, can be bought from the harbour. A large steel car ferry leaves for Gunung Sitoli (8–10hr; Rp25,000) every night at 8pm except Sunday. Tickets for the small wooden ferry, which runs on Monday, Wednesday and Friday at 8pm, are a little cheaper, though the ride is rougher. Currently, there's also an even smaller wooden boat to Teluk Dalam, in the south of Nias near Lagundri and Sorake (convenient for the southern beaches) that leaves on Tuesday, Thursday and Saturday. If you're going to Nias, it's advisable to **change money** before you go, unless you're using plastic (there's an ATM in Gunung Sitoli). The BNI bank with ATM at Jl S Parman 3 (Mon–Fri 8am–4.15pm) is your last chance. Travellers forced to stay in Sibolga overnight should head to one of the Chinese-run **hotels**, such as the friendly and efficient *Pasar Baru*, on the junction of Jalan Raja Djunjungan and Jalan Imam Bonjol (ⓣ0631/22167; ❸–❹) or the more upmarket *Prima Indah* at Jl Brig Jend Katamso 45 (ⓣ0631/22872; ❸–❺). Just down the road, the stately *Wisata Indah* at Jl Brig Jend Katamso 51 (ⓣ0631/23688; ❻–❾) is the swishest option.

The best **restaurants** are on Imam Bonjol. *Hebat Baru* at no. 79 and the slightly cheaper *Restoran Restu* opposite at no. 58c both serve excellent Chinese food and are very popular with the locals. If Chinese food isn't your thing, surgically clean *Hidangan Saudara Kita* at Jl Raja Djunjungan 55 serves some excellent Padang dishes.

Gunung Sitoli

The capital of Nias, **GUNUNG SITOLI**, isn't the sort of place you'd want to spend much time in – and most travellers scoot straight through to the beaches in the south – but if you want to send a letter, make a phone call or change money, this is the best place to do it.

Ferries arrive in the **harbour**, approximately 2km north of the town; minivans (Rp1000) connect the two, terminating at the **bus station** on Jalan Diponegoro near the southern end of town. Those who take advantage of SMAC airlines' reasonably priced flights between Medan and Gunung Sitoli (Mon, Wed, Fri), arrive at the tiny **airstrip** to the southeast of town; the twenty-kilometre jeep ride to the town centre is included in the flight price.

Tickets for the **Sibolga ferries** can be bought from a number of agencies on the main road by the harbour. The **Pelni** office also lies on this street, about 200m to the south of the Nias museum; currently, the *KM Lawit* calls in monthly from Padang, heading to Sibolga and back to Padang before continuing on to Jakarta. The **post office** stands on the corner of the green at Jl Hatta 1, next to the **Telkom office**. One block further south, at Jl Imam Bonjol 40, is the **Bank BNI**; the rates (US dollar cash and travellers' cheques only) are pretty poor, but it's got an international ATM. Sitoli is also the only place on the island with **Internet** access, so the Laser Computer Café 150m south of the bus station will be your last chance for a while.

There's a paucity of decent **accommodation**, and most foreigners avoid the fleapits in the town centre altogether in favour of the *Wisma Soliga* (ⓣ0639/21815; ❶–❸), 4km to the south on the main road to Teluk Dalam. It's overpriced, but is comfy and, if seeing Gunung Sitoli is not a priority, is a pleasant enough place to while away a day, writing postcards in the garden or eating at their restaurant. Those who want to brave a trip into town will find Sitoli's most popular **restaurant**, the excellent Padang-food specialist *Rumah Makan Nasional*, is at Jl Sirao 87.

If you do decide to stay, you might visit the **Nias museum** (Tues–Sun 8.30am–5pm; US$5), halfway between the town and the harbour. On display are some twentieth-century leather shields and tunics. The centre also offers visitors the chance to watch videos of the traditional dances of Nias.

Lagundri and Sorake

The horseshoe bay of **Lagundri** and its neighbour **Sorake** lie 12km west of Teluk Dalam. Buses run in the morning between the two (Rp3000); Sorake is also the place to wait for buses out of Lagundri. A motorbike ride from the losmen costs Rp8000. In July and August, the waves can reach 5m and travel for up to 150m – fantastic for experienced surfers. In the small-wave season (Christmas), beginners can try out the one-metre waves. There are lots of other breaks around, including the islands of **Bawa** and **Asu**, which you can reach by boat (Rp80,000 for a maximum of 8 people). Board rental is Rp20,000 a day, or less if you're going to use it all week. Lagundri Bay (Sandy Lagundri) is the place to swim. Tales of pickpockets and robbers are numerous, and you should ask for a mosquito net as this is a malaria hot-spot.

Losmen on both beaches are virtually identical and cost around Rp10,000-15,000 per night. Be careful, however: most losmen serve food, but don't tell you the prices until it's time to leave – and the prices can be extortionate. In addition to the losmen, there's also the luxurious air-con *Sorake Beach Resort* (ⓣ0630/21195; ④) at the western end of Sorake, though this was closed for business at the time of research. The **food** in Lagundri is slightly more expensive than elsewhere in Sumatra; *ToHo*, on the road running along the back of Sorake, has an extensive menu of Western food and some ice-cold beer. The only other alternative in Sorake is *Dolyn Café* on Sorake beach by the judges' tower. Just up the road from the *Dolyn* is a **wartel** from where you can make international calls; this is also the best place to find out about Pelni ferries.

Hilltop villages

The villages of southern Pulau Nias are one of the best attractions in Sumatra – and one ignored by most travellers to the island. To get a taster, the closest village to Sorake is **Botohili**, a mere ten minutes' walk from the beach: take the tarmac path leading up the hill from near the wartel, which heads past the church. Though not as charming as some of the more remoter places, the basic village layout is there, with thatched houses running along a wide, main street decorated with stone chairs and benches, interesting designs carved into the pavements and walls and, of course, a **jumping stone** (*fahombe*), which once would have been topped by sharp sticks and thorns. The custom was for teenage boys to jump over this stone to show their bravery and agility.

The most impressive of the hilltop villages, however, is **Bawomataluo** (Sun Hill), an hour's walk uphill from the turn-off on the Teluk Dalam–Lagundri road; taxis from Lagundri to the turn-off charge Rp2000, and ojek cost Rp3000 (or Rp5000 all the way to Bawomataluo). Bawomataluo has been exposed to tourism for too many years now, and touts are persistent. The old village consists of an east–west road and a wide cul-de-sac that branches off due south from opposite the Chief's House. In the centre of the village you'll find the two-metre-tall *fahombe*. This quality of craftsmanship is continued inside the nineteenth-century **Chief's House** (daily 9am–5pm; donation), where the walls are decorated with carvings of lizards, monkeys, and a depiction of an early European ship. A pair of carved royal seats for the chief and his wife share the same wall. Other notable features of the house are the plethora of pig's jaws hanging from the rafters, and the huge hearth at the back of the room. The stonework on the tables and chairs outside the Chief's House is exceptional. These chairs once held the corpses of the recently deceased, who were simply left to decay in the street before being buried.

Trekking around the villages

For those who wish to explore the villages in more detail, there is a pleasant, if lengthy and tiring, trek that can be done around all the villages in the immediate vicinity of Bawomataluo (including Bawamataluo itself), a fifteen-kilometre loop that a fairly fast walker should be able to complete in five hours (not counting stops). When trekking, always take waterproof clothing, plenty of food (there aren't many shops en route) and a torch, and aim to reach a main road by mid-afternoon at the latest in order to catch a bus back. Buses from Teluk Dalam to Lagundri along the south coast road cease running at about 4pm, and along the Trans-Nias Highway to Lagundri they stop at about 5pm. The trek begins one hour uphill from the Bawomataluo turn-off at the pleasant but plain village of **Orahili**, home to a couple of small and unimpressive stone carvings and a number of traditional houses, most of which have swapped the thatch on their roofs for more practical corrugated metal. You can take a minivan here from Lagundri (ask at your losmen). At the far end of Orahili, at the end of the cul-de-sac on your left, a series of steps heads uphill to **Bawomataluo**.

Behind the Chief's House in Bawomataluo, a scenic path leads to **Siwalawa**, one hour away. The village stretches along the path for at least 500m, though the oldest part actually lies at the very end, up some steps to the left of the main path. At the end of this old quarter a path heads downhill and divides: turn right along the obvious path and you eventually arrive at Hilifalago; turn left and you pass through the rather unexciting village of Onohondro and, twenty minutes further on, the large village of **Hilinawalofau**. The old part of the village features some good examples of traditional housing and the former chief's house has been converted into a guesthouse, the *Ormoda*.

After Onohondro the path descends to a large stream (which can be waist-high in the rainy season) and continues for an hour, via Hilinawalofau, to **Bawogosali**, a small village with some recent stone carvings lining the path. The village is dominated by the large church, behind which a path leads up to the crest of a hill and along to **Lahuna**. This village lies at an important crossroads: continue past the end of the village and you'll reach, 45 minutes later, Bawomataluo, or turn right, and after a steep descent you arrive at **Hilisimaetano** with its impressive chief's house. For many visitors, Hilisimaetano is their favourite spot on Nias: the village is in an excellent state of preservation and, unusually, many of the paving stones have been carved with reliefs of lizards, ships and signs of the zodiac. At the very end of the path, twenty minutes beyond Hilisimaetano, the Trans-Nias Highway thunders by, from where you can catch an ojek back to Lagundri (Rp8000).

Padang

A bustling port and university town, attractive **PADANG** is an important transport hub and famed throughout Indonesia for its spicy local cuisine, **Makanan Padang** (Padang food). Its climate is equally extreme: hot and humid and with the highest rainfall in Indonesia at 4508mm a year (in the top ten of rainiest inhabited spots in the world). Most tourists pause only briefly here, before aiming for the nearby hill town of Bukittinggi or the Mentawai Islands. The city's main sight is the very pleasant **Adityawarman Museum** (Tues–Sun 8.30am–4pm; Rp5000), housed in a traditional Minang house on Jalan Bundo Kandung and specializing in Minangkabau culture, with textiles, kris and finely worked basketware. For a good local shopping experience, ignore the large new shopping centres and head instead for Pasar Raya in the city centre, a terrific general **market**.

Practicalities

Padang is a **visa-free entry point** to Indonesia. All flights land at **Tabing Airport**, 9km north of the city centre. The bank and moneychangers are located at the front

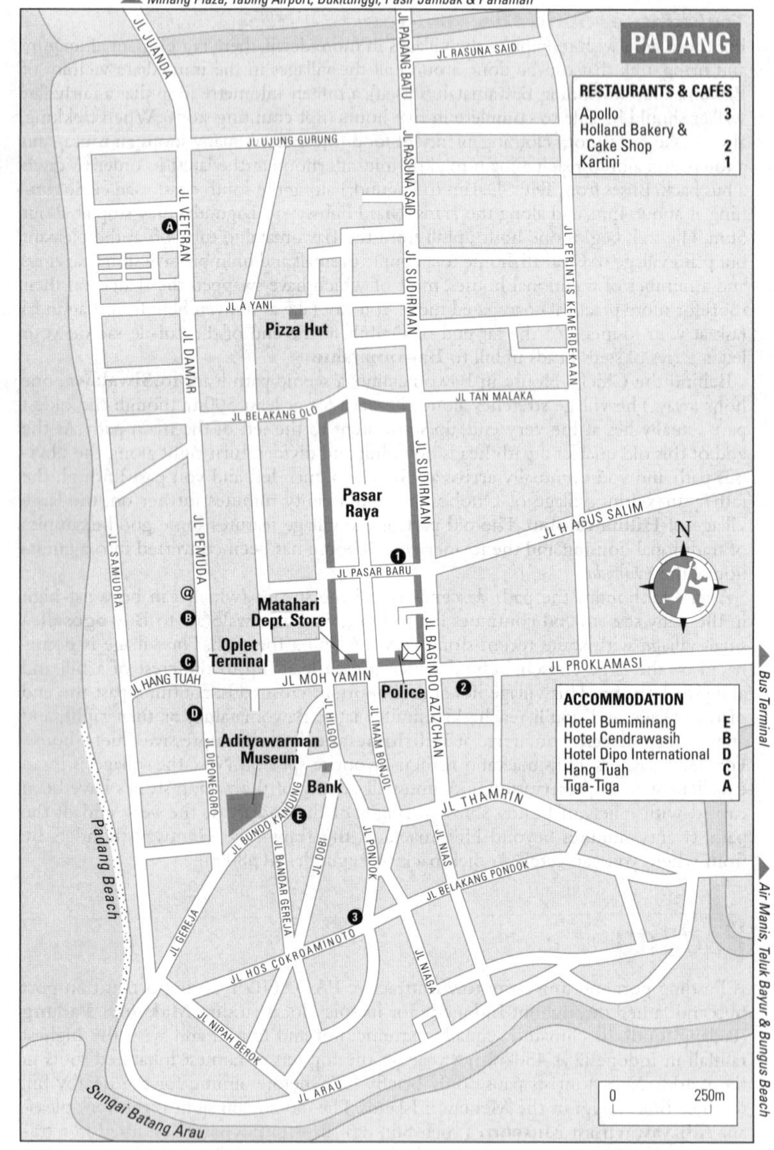

of the international arrivals building, and there's a taxi ticket office – collect the fixed-price ticket from the office and pay the driver on arrival (prices within the city are around Rp20,000). Out on the main road (200m walk from the terminal), buses #14a and #14b (Rp1000) stop just outside the airport gates: those heading to the left go into the city. Small white bemos (called "oplets" in Padang) also stop here bound for the oplet terminal in town for Rp1000. Pelni **boats** arrive at the port of

Teluk Bayur, 7km south of town, from where you can take a oplet to the city centre. Pelni currently connect Padang with Pulau Nias and Jakarta; their ticket office is at Jl Tanjung Priok 32 in Teluk Bayur (☎0751/61624).

Padang is quite compact and easy to negotiate by public transport, the exception being Pelabuhan Muara (for boats to the Mentawai Islands; see p.344) in the district of Batau Arau, for which you'll have to walk or grab a taxi. The main road in the central area of the city is Jalan Moh Yamin, within easy reach of which are the oplet terminal, banks and exchange facilities, a post office, police station and a fair range of hotels. Two main roads head north from the centre: Jalan Pemuda in the west and Jalan Bagindo Azizchan in the east, eventually (after a few name changes) joining Jalan Prof Hamka, which heads north past Tabing Airport.

The local bus terminal has now moved to a new location ten kilometres east of the city. Unfortunately, few of the bus firms have actually adopted the new terminal as their home, leading to a rather confusing situation regarding transport, and where exactly the buses depart from. For this reason, it's quicker and easier for travellers heading to Bukittinggi to catch a white oplet heading north along Jalan Pemuda to the Minang Plaza, opposite from which you can catch a Kijang jeep – or "Travel" in the local parlance – to Bukittinggi (Rp10,0000). Similarly, those heading south should also, at the present time, head to the Minang Plaza, from where the Jakarta buses also leave. Note that the situation is very fluid and likely to change over the coming months, so ask your hotel for the latest details. The oplet terminal is on Jalan Moh Yamin, in the market area. If you're using oplets to get around the city and surrounding area, look out for the route number and destination signs suspended high above the oplet waiting area. White oplets run north from Jalan Pemuda out to Minang Plaza and towards the airport; blue #437, signed "Tl Kabung Bungus", travels to Bungus beach; white #423 heads north to Pasir Jambak; while blue #402 leads to Air Manis and blue #432, #433 and #434 run to the harbour of Teluk Bayur. Local buses (flat fare Rp750) and oplets (Rp1000) run from 6am to 10pm.

Accommodation

As with most Sumatran cities, **accommodation** in Padang is aimed predominantly at domestic business travellers.

Hotel Bumiminang Jl Bundo Kandung 20–28 ☎0751/37555, ⓦwww.bumiminang.com. The most luxurious and expensive hotel in Padang, with pool, tennis courts, business centre and tasteful communal areas, in a central location. ❼–❾

Hotel Cendrawasih Jl Pemuda 27 ☎0751/22894. A local's place – with all the noise and scruffiness that entails – but one of the cheapest, too. Avoid the economy rooms (no fan) and opt for the standard or deluxe rooms instead. ❷

Hotel Dipo International Jl Diponegoro 13 ☎0751/34261. One of Padang's smarter, and yet good-value, hotels, all the *Dipo*'s rooms come with a/c, TV, bath and hot-water shower. ❻

Hang Tuah Jl Pemuda 1 ☎0751/26556. One of the better and more popular of the hotels on Jl Pemuda. Facilities range from fan and attached cold-water mandi up to hot water, a/c and satellite TV. ❷–❺

Tiga-Tiga Jl Veteran 33 ☎0751/22173. Once a travellers' favourite, *Tiga-Tiga* stills has some light, airier rooms on the upper floors, but no tourists with which to fill them. The budget rooms have no fan and feature outside mandi, while the most expensive have attached bathrooms and a/c. ❷–❸

Eating

It makes little sense to come to the homeland of **Padang food** without visiting at least one of the city's **restaurants**. There's no menu: you simply tell staff you want to eat and up to a dozen small plates are placed in front of you. Generally, the redder the sauce, the more explosive it is to the taste buds: the yellow, creamy dishes are often less aggressive but there's a volcanic but innocent-looking green sauce, too.

At the southern end of Jalan Pondok, due south of the market area towards the river, you'll find a small **night market** of satay stalls: this street, and nearby Jalan Niaga, has a range of good places. Another night market operates on Jalan Imam Bonjol, a few hundred metres south of the junction with Jalan Moh Yamin. More convenient for the hotels, the small restaurants on Jalan Moh Yamin, near the junction with Jalan Pemuda, serve cheap and filling *martabaks* and sweet *roti canai*.

Apollo Jl Hos Cokroaminoto. Busy Chinese seafood place, which fills up fast with locals at night, so come early.

Holland Bakery and Cake Shop Jl Proklamasi 61b. With a good choice of cakes and sweet breads, this is especially popular at weekends with local people.

Kartini Jl Pasar Baru 24. The most popular of the many Padang-style restaurants along this street. They are unfazed by tourists, and the food is fresh and well cooked, with all the usual Padang specialities on offer.

Listings

Airline offices Batavia, Jl Damar 36a ☎0751/28383; Garuda, Jl Jend Sudirman 2 ☎0751/30737; Jatayu, *Hotel Pangeran Beach*, Jl Juanda79 ☎0751/446890; Malaysian, in *Hotel Bumiminang* ☎0751/35888; Lion Air, *Hotel Pangeran Beach*, Jl Juanda 97 ☎0751/55555; Mandala, Jl Veteran 20C ☎0751/39737; Merpati, Jl Gereja, in *Natour Muara Hotel* ☎0751/31852; Pelangi, Jl Gereja 34, in the grounds of the *Natour Muara Hotel* ☎0751/38103; Silk Air, in *Hotel Bumiminang* ☎0751/38120.

Banks and exchange Bank of Central Asia, Jl H Agus Salim 10a; Bank Dagang Negara, Jl Bagindo Azizchan 21; Bank Negara Indonesia, Jl Dobi 1. There are several moneychangers along Jl Pemuda offering slightly poorer rates but longer hours and less paperwork. ATMs are everywhere.

Hospitals Rumah Sakit Umum Padang, Jl Perentis Kemerdekan ☎0751/26585; Rumah Sakit Selasih, Jl Khatib Sulaiman 72 ☎0751/51405.

Immigration office Jl Khatib Sulaiman ☎0751/55113.

Internet There are plenty of warnets posted around town, though the service continues to be slow in most of them. The Warnet by the post office continues to be one of the cheapest (Rp4000) though the speed is appallingly lethargic at times.

Post office The main post office is conveniently located at Jl Bagindo Azizchan 7, just north of the junction with Jl Moh Yamin. Poste restante here is reasonably efficient.

Telephone and fax The main Telkom office lies several kilometres north of the city centre on Jl Khatib Sulaiman, at the junction with Jl K Ahmad Dahlan. More convenient 24hr wartels are everywhere in the city.

The Minang Highlands

The gorgeous mountainous landscape, soaring rice terraces and easily accessible traditional culture make the Minang Highlands a justly popular stop on any trip through Sumatra. The highlands consist of three large valleys, with **BUKITTINGGI**, a bustling hill town, the administrative and commercial centre of the whole district. The surrounding area holds plenty of attractions, including craft villages, the rafflesia reserve at **Batang Paluh**, the beautiful Harau Canyon, and some fine examples of Minang culture. Located to the west of the main highland area, **Danau Maninjau** is rapidly developing as an appealing travellers' destination.

The highlands around Bukittinggi are the cultural heartland of the **Minangkabau** (Minang) people. The Minang are staunchly matrilineal, one of the largest such societies extant, and Muslim. The most visible aspect of their culture is the distinctive architecture of their homes, with massive roofs soaring skywards at either end (to represent the horns of a buffalo). Typically, three or four generations of one family would live in one large house built on stilts, the *rumah gadang* (big house) or *rumah adat* (traditional house), a wood-and-thatch structure often decorated with fabulous wooden carvings. In front of the line of sleeping rooms, a large meeting room is the focus of the social life of the house. Outside the big house, small rice barns, also of traditional design, hold the family stores.

Bukittinggi

Situated on the eastern edge of the Ngarai Sianok Canyon and with the mountains of Merapi and Singgalang rising to the south, **Bukittinggi** spreads for several kilometres in each direction. However, the central part of town, which is of most interest to visitors, is relatively compact and easy to negotiate. The most useful **landmark** is the clock tower at the junction of Jalan A Yani (the main thoroughfare) and Jalan Sudirman (the main road leading out of town to the south). Due north of the tower is the enormous **market**, the biggest in Sumatra, which swells to bursting point on Wednesdays and Saturdays. Jalan A Yani, 1km from north to south, is the tourist hub of Bukittinggi, and most of the sights, hotels, restaurants and shops that serve the tourist trade are on this street or close by.

Arrival, information and city transport

A few tourist services may drop you at your hotel of choice (check at the time of booking), but other **long-distance buses** terminate at the Aur Kuning terminal, 3km southeast of the town centre. Buses from Padang stop on the southern outskirts of town on Jalan Sudirman before turning off for the terminal; you can get a red #14 or #19 bemo into the town centre from this junction, and all but one of the accommodation choices are within an easy walk of the route.

The **tourist office** is by the clock tower (Mon–Sat 8am–4pm, closed Fri prayers). **Bemos** scurry around town in a circular route, with a flat fare of Rp1000. To get to the bus terminal, stop any red bemo heading north on Jalan A Yani, which will circle to the east of town and pass the main post office before turning for Aur Kuning.

Accommodation

D'Enam Jl Yos Sudarso ⓣ0752/32240. Rooms in an airy bungalow. All are good value – some of the cheapest in Bukittinggi – with hot water in the most expensive rooms; there's also a lounge for residents and a laundry service next door. ❶

Merdeka Jl Dr Rivai 20 ⓣ0752/23937. A small guesthouse in and around a colonial bungalow set in a good-sized garden – the large, cool rooms have high ceilings and cold-water mandi (though there's hot water in the most expensive rooms). Clean and pleasant. ❷

Novotel Jl Laras Datuk Bandaro ⓣ0752/35000, ⓦwww.accorhotels.com/asia. Top of the pile, with a heated swimming pool and classy ambience. ❼–❾

Orchid Jl Teuku Umar 11 ⓣ0752/32634. Clean, presentable rooms, many with balconies, and currently the most popular choice of travellers. The price includes breakfast, and the more expensive rooms have TVs and hot water. Fair value. ❷–❸

Singgalang Indah Jl A Yani 130 ⓣ0752/21576. Central though soulless, it's a good place for enquiring about silat classes. Only the top rooms (Rp100,000 and above) come with hot water. ❷–❸

Sumatera Jl Dr Setia Budhi 16e ⓣ0752/21309. Centrally located on a quiet road, the rooms have attached bathroom with hot water. The accommodation is adequate for this price but the real bonus is the balcony with its stunning views. ❷

Moving on from Bukittinggi

Local buses (7am–5pm) for Bukit Paluh, Danau Maninjau, Batusangkar, Payakumbuh and Padang leave from the Aur Kuning terminal, where you'll also find the ticket offices. **Long-distance buses** (book ahead) also use Aur Kuning; destinations include Sibolga, Parapat, Medan, Pekanbaru, Palembang, Lubuklinggau (for the South Sumatra train service), Jakarta and Bandung. **Tourist buses** to Danau Toba are also on offer, through the travel agents in town (see p.342). Travel agents in Bukittinggi can also arrange Pelni and airline tickets from Padang, which is the closest port and airport.

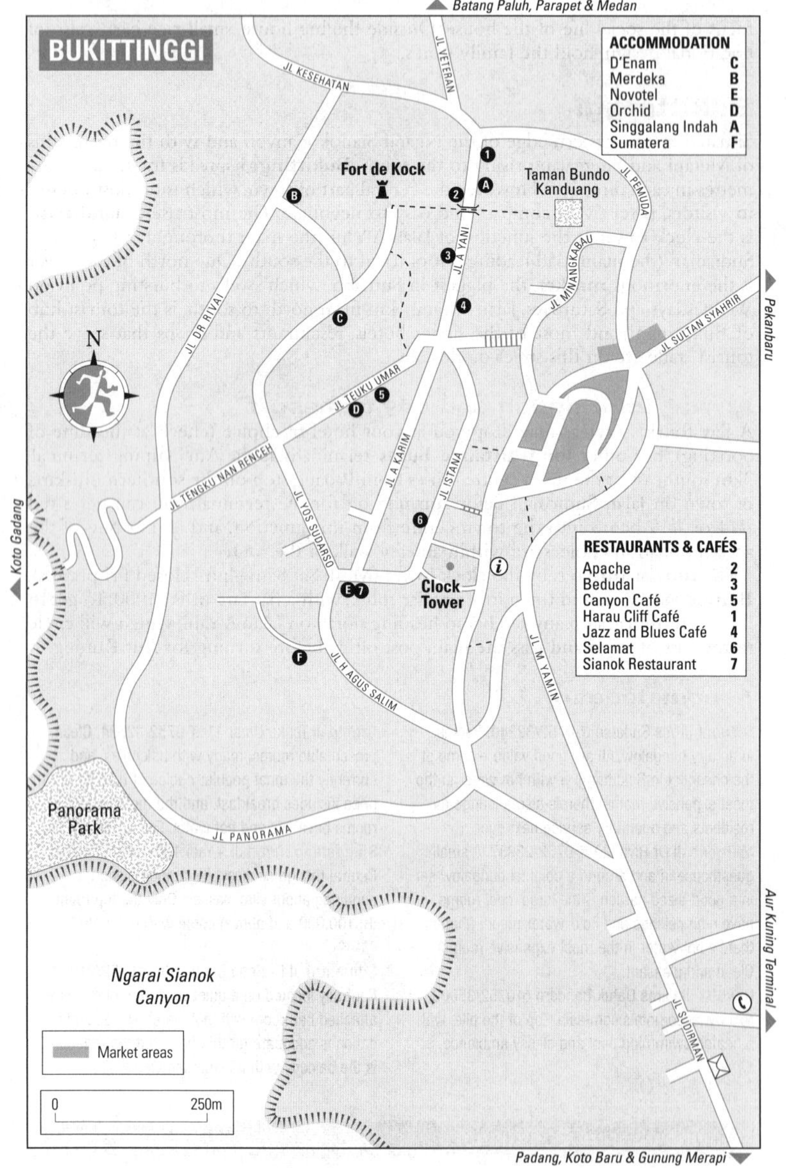

The Town

A few hundred metres to the north of the clock tower, **Fort de Kock** (daily 8am–5pm; Rp5000, including entry to museum, zoo and bridge) was built by the Dutch in 1825 and is linked by a footbridge to the park, Taman Bundo Kanduang, on the hill on the other side of Jalan A Yani; there's little left of the original fort but some old cannons and parts of the moats. From here you can see Gunung Merapi, on the left, and the much more dramatic cone-shaped Gunung Singgalang to the right. The park's **museum** is housed in a traditional *rumah gadang*, and features clothing, musical instruments, textiles, models of traditional houses, and stuffed freaks of nature, including a two-headed buffalo and an eight-legged goat. Surrounding it is the abysmally inhumane zoo – depressing, despite the new facelift.

Much more pleasant is a trip to **Panorama Park** (daily 7am–7pm; Rp2000), perched on a lip of land overlooking the sheer cliff walls down into Ngarai Sianok Canyon, the best Bukittinggi sight by far. Beneath the park stretch 1400m of Japanese **tunnels** and rooms built with local slave labour during World War II as a potential fortress. You can venture down into these dank, miserable depths, although there's nothing really to see. The **Ngarai Sianok Canyon** is part of a rift valley that runs the full length of Sumatra – the canyon here is 15km long and around 100m deep, with a glistening river wending its way along the bottom.

Eating

A small **night market** sets up near the Jalan A Yani/Jalan Teuku Umar junction.

Apache Jl A Yani. Travellers' fare at reasonable prices. Good for people-watching and potato salad.

Bedudal Jl A Yani. A pleasant place with an extensive, good-quality menu of Western fare including steaks, the speciality being pizzas and calzone.

Canyon Café Jl Teuku Umar. The most popular restaurant in Bukittinggi, with good Western food and a few local dishes, including *rendang*.

Harau Cliff Café Jl A Yani. Good value (steak is Rp10,000 and satay, gado-gado and *cap cay* under Rp6000), with attractive furnishings and a relaxed atmosphere and an Internet café attached.

Jazz and Blues Café Jl A Yani. Somewhere between a bar and a restaurant, this is where the local rastas – a very friendly lot – hang out. The Western and local food is fair, and there's always a tune on the stereo.

Selamat Jl Istana. One of the best Padang restaurants in town, they usually have eggs in coconut sauce, especially good for vegetarians, and are used to Westerners.

Sianok Restaurant *Novotel Hotel*, Jl Laras Datuk Bandaro. Expensive joint with Italian, Chinese, Indonesian, Minang and Western barbecue nights, special Minang lunches and daily afternoon tea.

Listings

Banks and exchange Bank Rakyat Indonesia, Jl A Yani 3; Bank Negara Indonesia, Jl A Yani (with international ATM). There's also an ATM by the clock tower. Several travel agents including PT Tigo Balai, Jl A Yani 100 (daily 8am–8pm; ☎0752/31996), change travellers' cheques and offer cash advances against Visa and MasterCard.

Bookshops Anyone heading into central and southern Sumatra, an English-language book desert, should stock up in the new and secondhand bookshops on Jl Teuku Umar and Jl A Yani.

Car and motorbike rental Enquire at your

Traditional entertainment

Local dance troupes stage recommended **Minangkabau dance shows** (8.30pm; Rp20,000) nightly in a hall just behind Hotel Jogya on Jalan Moh Yamin; head up the small road on the left of the hotel and the hall is on the right. The dancing is accompanied by talempong pacik, traditional Minang music performed by a gamelan orchestra similar to those of Java and Bali, with gongs, drums and flutes. Most shows also include a demonstration of silek, the Minang martial art taught to both young men and women, and the tari piriang, a dance that originated in the ricefields after harvest time when young people danced with the plates they had just eaten from: piles of crockery shards are trodden and even rolled in by the dancers.

Animal-lovers may balk at the idea of watching **buffalo fights**, a popular local event, but the reality is rarely gory and usually good fun. Regular contests take place in Koto Baru on Tuesday and Saturday at around 4pm. A bemo there costs around Rp2000, and it's another Rp4000 or so to enter.

accommodation or any of the travel agents in town. Typical prices are Rp35,000 for a 12hr motorbike rental.

Hospital Rumah Sakit Dr Achmad Mochtar is on Jl Dr Rivai (☎0752/21013 or 33825). The tourist information offices will advise on English-speaking doctors in Bukittinggi.

Internet Fifals, on Jl Teuku Umar, currently has the fastest connection, though they charge a little more, too, at Rp15,000 per hour. Those on Jl A Yani, such as Harau, are slightly more reasonable at around Rp12,000 per hour.

Post office The main post office is inconveniently far from the town centre on Jl Sudirman.

Telephone The main telephone office is on Jl M Syafei towards the southern end of town, around the corner from the post office. There are also many wartels in town.

Travel agents Try Jogja Wisata Travel, Jl Yani 85 ☎0752/33507; PT Tigo Balai, Jl A Yani 100 ☎0752/31996; and Travina Tours and Travel Service, Jl A Yani 105 ☎0752/21281 – this is a good place to enquire about the many tours of the area on offer.

Koto Gadang

KOTO GADANG is a small, attractive village situated on the western edge of the Ngarai Sianok Canyon, an hour or so from Bukittinggi, with plenty of small silver workshops and shops. Though you can get local transport to the village, many people try to find the route from Bukittinggi by foot that starts off down Jalan Tengku Nan Renceh, and then heads along a footpath to the footbridge across the river and up the steps on the other side of the canyon. Be aware that there's a well-orchestrated scam, with local people refusing to point the way and hapless tourists being led by young lads on a two-hour rough trek through the canyon, for which they expect payment.

Batang Paluh

Rafflesia arnoldi is the largest flower in the world – up to 90cm across – has remarkable red-and-white colouring, and an appalling smell like rotting meat. One of the most accessible places in Sumatra to see this rare and extraordinary flower is at **BATANG PALUH**, 13km north of Bukittinggi; take a local bus (Rp2000) and ask in the village. Enquire at the tourist office in Bukittinggi first as it generally flowers for a couple of weeks between August and December – but even in bud the plant is quite something.

Climbing Gunung Merapi

Access to 2890-metre **Gunung Merapi** (Fire Mountain) is from Koto Baru, 12km south of Bukittinggi. Typically, the climb, which is strenuous rather than gruelling if you're reasonably fit, takes five hours up and four down; most people climb at night to arrive at the top for the sunrise. The first four hours or so are through the forest and then across bare rocks leading to the summit. The top is actually a plateau area with the still-smoking crater in the middle. You may spot bats, gibbons and squirrels in the forest, but the main reason to go is the view across to Gunung Singgalang. Engage an experienced local guide through your losmen (around Rp100,000 per person) and take enough water and energy food, plus sturdy footwear and warm clothes for the top.

Danau Maninjau

A very pleasant and hassle-free area for rest and relaxation on the way to or from Danau Toba, **Danau Maninjau** (Lake Maninjau) is situated 15km due west of Bukittinggi, although public transport on the road takes a long-winded 37km (1hr 30min) to get there. At an altitude of 500m, the lake is 17km long and 8km wide and set 600m below the rim of an ancient volcanic crater, with jungle-covered walls, almost sheer in places, providing a picturesque backdrop. The area of interest for tourists, and with all the facilities, centres on the village of **MANINJAU**, just where the road from Bukittinggi reaches the lakeside road, and becoming increasingly popular, the village of **Bayur** 4km to the north. There's not that much to do here apart from relax and frolic in the lake, though you may like to try to track down a rafflesia in the jungle-clad hills behind the village, or visit the nearby waterfall. For either trip, Pak Juney, often found at the *Parantha Café*, is an excellent guide, very knowledgeable and fluent in English. Or you can go pig-hunting with dogs, a traditional local activity, on Wednesdays and Sundays; contact one of the little agents in town for details. Cycling around the lake is also popular: bikes can be rented for Rp30,000 per day from *Kafe Kawa*. Motorbikes (just about essential if you want to circumnavigate the entire lake) cost around Rp75,000 per day.

There is no official **tourist information office** but Indo Wisata Travel (☎0752/61418) just north of the main junction next to *Bagoes Café* is a helpful spot. This is also the best place for **Internet** and changing travellers' cheques (but not plastic). The **post office** isn't far from the main junction on Jalan Telaga Biru Tanjung Raya; the 24hr **Telkom office** is on the main street by the junction; the nearby bank sadly won't change money. There are a couple of secondhand **bookshops**: Bacho Bookshop is the best. **Moving on**, there are regular **buses** back to Bukittinggi. If you want to go to Padang, either head back to Bukittinggi or take a minivan travelling to Lubukbasung, from where you can pick up Padang buses during the day.

Accommodation

Accommodation is ranged along the east side of the lake, from about 500m south of the junction of the lakeside road with the road from Bukittinggi, to just north of the five-kilometre marker. Buses from Bukittinggi drive along this road, so tell the conductor where you want to stay and he may let you out on the hotel's doorstep. The following places go from south to north, from the hotels in Maninjau village itself to those in Bayur.

44 ☎0752/61238. Very inexpensive shoreside bungalows with attached mandi and a small restaurant. Rooms are simple – consisting of a mattress on the floor – though the family are very welcoming, and it's good value. ❶

Arlen ☎0815/358685. Far away from the "action" of Maninjau village, this is a great place to get away from it all, and has some of the smartest lakeside bungalows around. ❷

Beach Guest House ☎0752/61082. Bustling and popular place in a great location on the lakeside, with a small beach and hammocks. Offers two sorts of simple concrete rooms, some with attached mandi and a small veranda. ❶

Lili's. Very attractive option with fine, shared-mandi bungalows and a tree house. Lili, a New Zealander, runs the outfit with her husband, and they can both be convinced to sing and strum the guitar at night; currently a popular hangout for the local teenage boys. ❶

Rizals ☎0752/61404. Scruffy bungalows in a poor state of repair (though renovations are promised) with mosquito nets, set back from their own little beach in a coconut grove just over 4km north of Maninjau village. Good views of the lake, friendly staff, and there's a restaurant with an area on stilts over the water. ❶

Tan Dirih ☎0752/61263. Small, tiled, spotless place with sunloungers on a terrace overlooking the lake. It's the best mid-range choice, and all rooms have hot water and tubs. ❸

Eating and drinking

Bagoes Café Good-quality Western and Indonesian restaurant specializing in fish from the lake. Has the best Internet access in town.

Kafe Kawa Serving tasty and cheap food, this unassuming place lies just to the north of the village centre; also offers bike hire.

Parantha Situated on the northern edge of the village, this place serves good, cheap and large portions of Indonesian and Western food.

Simple Café Situated close to the road but with good views across the rooftops down to the lake. A vast, inexpensive menu offering all the usual Western and Indo-Chinese favourites.

Srikandi Café This place at the southern end of Maninjau village has a large and varied menu of soups (pumpkin, curried apple, Thai tom yam), and main courses including stir-fries, sate, fish, steak, pizzas and burgers.

Batusangkar and Pagaruyung

Accessed via Padangpanjang, the largest town in the Tanah Datar Valley is **BATUSANGKAR**, 39km southeast of Bukittinggi and served by frequent buses (1hr 30min). The Minang court of the fourteenth to nineteenth centuries was based in the valley, the gold and iron mines of ancient times the source of its riches. The entire area is awash with cultural relics, megaliths and places of interest, and to explore it fully takes more than the limited time available on the one-day Minangkabau tours from Bukittinggi. The most worthwhile tourist destination in the area is **Pagaruyung** (daily 7am–6pm; Rp1500), the reconstructed palace of the last Raja Alam of the Minangkabau, Sultan Arifin Muning Alam Syah. The palace was reconstructed using traditional techniques some twenty years ago, the woodcarving alone taking two years to complete. The building comprises the traditional three storeys – the first for official visitors, the second for unmarried daughters and the third for meetings; the rice barn at the front would traditionally have held food to help the poor, and the palace mosque is in the garden, with the kitchen at the back.

In Batusangkar, the **tourist office** is at Jl Pemuda 1 (☎0752/71300), and the **accommodation** all clustered fairly close together on the same street: *Pagaruyung*, Jl Prof Hamka 4 (☎0752/71533; ❷); *Yoherma*, Jl Prof Hamka 15 (☎0752/71130; ❷); and *Parma*, Jalan Hamka (☎0752/71330; ❶–❷), all have a range of basic but adequate rooms and **restaurants** attached.

The Mentawai Islands

The enticing rainforest-clad **Mentawai Islands**, 100km off the west Sumatran coast, are home to an ethnic group who are struggling to retain their identity in the modern world. There are over forty islands in the chain, of which the four main ones are Pulaus Siberut, Sipora, North Pagi and South Pagi. Only **Pulau Siberut**, the largest, at 110km long by 50km wide, is accessible to tourists; all visitors must be registered by the authorities. The islanders' **traditional culture** is based on communal dwelling in longhouses (*uma*) and subsistence agriculture, their religious beliefs centring on the importance of coexisting with the invisible spirits that inhabit the world. With the advent of Christian missionaries and the colonial administration in the early twentieth century, many of the islanders' religious practices were banned, but plenty of beliefs and rituals have survived and some villages have built new *uma*. However, the islanders are still under threat, not least from an Indonesian government seeking to integrate them into mainstream life.

Pulau Siberut

The island of **Siberut** is the best-known, largest and most northerly of the Mentawai chain and the only one with anything approaching a tourist industry. Access to the island is by overnight ferry from Padang and, whilst it's possible, still, to visit the island independently, the vast majority of visitors go on tours arranged from Bukittinggi by young men from West Sumatra rather than Mentawai people. Malaria is endemic on the island, so take your own net or borrow one from the tour company.

The main town of **MUARASIBERUT** is in reality a sleepy little shanty-style village on the coast and around the mouth of the river. Small, unstable "speedboats" ferry passengers and cargo around. The only **accommodation** in Muarasiberut is *Syahruddin's Homestay* (☎0759/21014; ❶) on the coast at the mouth of the river. It's light and airy, but at low tide looks straight onto stinking mud flats; rooms have no mosquito nets, and unattached mandi. There's an excellent coffee shop across the road. The post office and Telkom offices are just behind the mosque, but there are no exchange facilities on the island.

Taking a tour

The **tours** of Mentawai are loudly marketed in Bukittinggi as a trip to see the "primitive" people and "stone-age" culture. Generally, Mentawai people welcome tourism as a way of validating and preserving their own culture, although they get little financial benefit from it. Be sure to read and obey guidelines about behaviour that are given to you, as the people have a complex system of taboo behaviour. Be aware that on a five-day trip, Day One usually means a 3pm departure from Bukittinggi and Day Five may well end at 10am when you get back to Bukittinggi. Most tours centre on the southeast of the island, where you'll be able to watch and join in with people going about their everyday activities, such as farming, fishing and hunting. The ceremonies of Siberut are something of a draw for tourists, but many are actually staged for them.

Visiting independently

To visit Siberut **independently**, you may need to get a **permit** in Padang depending on the current situation. These are available from Pelabuhan Muara, the harbour in Padang from where boats to Pulau Siberut leave. Go to the office at least a day in advance of when you want to travel (for travel on Monday, apply on Friday), with a photocopy of your passport, including the Indonesian entry stamp, and the immigration card you got on arrival in the country.

Sailing days are currently Monday and Wednesday to Pulau Siberut, with return trips on Tuesday and Thursday, though the exact days change frequently. You can try to secure a guide in Padang or Bukittinggi before you go, or you can run the gauntlet of touts in Siberut itself. One person staying in the southeast area will be looking at about Rp600,000 for five days, to include transport, accommodation, food, porters and a guide, whilst three people will pay about Rp350,000 each.

Dumai and into Malaysia

Sumatra's major east-coast port is **Dumai**, 189km north of Pekanbaru and just across the Straits of Malacca from the Malaysian city of Melaka. Dumai recently became a **visa-free entry point**, and a fast ferry runs daily to and from Melaka (2hr 30min). Regular **buses** run between Dumai and Pekanbaru, but if you get stranded you can stay at the *City Hotel*, Jl Sudirman 445 (☎0765/21550; ❷); Pelita Air have an office at the **airport** (☎0765/31121).

Pekanbaru

The booming oil town of **PEKANBARU** is a major gateway into Indonesia from Singapore, via Pulau Batam and Pulau Bintan. Most travellers head straight through but it's worth considering a journey break here – it's six hours west to Bukittinggi and another nine or ten hours east to Singapore. Pekanbaru's main street is Jalan Sudirman, which runs north–south from the river through the centre of town to the airport. Most hotels, restaurants and shops are within easy reach of this thoroughfare. However, the **tourist information office** is inconveniently sited at Jl Diponegoro 24 (Mon–Thurs 8am–2pm, Fri 8–11am, Sat 8am–12.30pm; ☎0761/31562). Pekanbaru's **markets** are fun: Pasar Pusat is the food and household-goods market, and Pasar Bawah and Pasar Tengeh in the port area have an excellent range of Chinese goods, including ceramics and carpets.

Practicalities

All domestic and international **flights** (Singapore, KL, Melaka) touch down at Simpang Tiga Airport, 9km south of the city centre. Fixed-price taxis into town charge Rp25,000.

Moving on from Pekanbaru

Pekanbaru has extremely good sea, land and air connections with the rest of island, as well as the rest of the archipelago. **Long-distance buses** to destinations throughout **Sumatra** and in **Java** depart from the station on Jalan Nangka. Many of the bus offices are in the station itself but others are spread along Jalan Nangka, up to about 500m west of the station and also at the very start of Jalan Taskurun. Shop around and book ahead.

High-speed **ferry** services for **Pulau Batam** and **Pulau Bintan** leave from the ticket offices at the northern end of Jalan Sudirman. Although located near the river and with adverts conspicuously picturing speedboats, most services actually involve a three-hour bus journey to Buton, where you transfer to the high-speed ferry for the trip to the islands. Prices are Rp190,000 to Pulau Batam and Rp215,000 to Pulau Bintan, and there are typically two departures a day, one at around 7.30am and another at 5pm. Ticket sellers make all sorts of dramatic claims for the length of the trip from Pekanbaru, but it will take six to eight hours travelling time, plus up to a two-hour wait for a ferry at Buton. Some companies also sell tickets straight through to Tanjung Pinang on Pulau Bintan, but check whether you have to change boats in Pulau Batam. If you're planning to go straight through to **Singapore**, take the earliest departure from Pekanbaru. You can also sail directly to Melaka from Pelabuhan Duku, beyond the eastern end of Jalan Datuk. The ferry leaves at about 9am and the crossing takes about seven hours. Tickets (Rp165,000) are available from PT Jasa Sarana Citra Bestari, Jl Tanjung Datuk 153 (☎0761/858777) or, more expensively, from agencies around town. A taxi from the bus station to the harbour is Rp25,000.

Long-distance buses arrive at the terminal on Jalan Nangka, about 5km south of the river. Most **express ferry** services from Pulau Batam and Pulau Bintan dock at **BUTON**, connected to Pekanbaru by a three-hour bus journey; buses arrive at the express-ferry offices at the northern end of Jalan Sudirman or at the bus terminal. **Slow ferries** come into the main port area at the northern end of Jalan Saleh Abbas in the Pasar Bawah market area, a couple of hundred metres west of Jalan Sudirman.

Accommodation and eating

Accommodation in Pekanbaru is a dire subject: there's little charm or hospitality to most hotels.You can usually divide the rates by two before they seem value for money, especially at the lower end of the scale, which bottoms out at Rp35,000. Steer clear of the basic, noisy and poor-value places on Jalan Nangka right by the bus station – the only exception to this rule being *Hotel Linda*, Jl Nangka 145 (☎0761/36915; ❷–❹), which lies opposite the bus station and is a better bet than any of the more obvious places on the main road; *Penginapan Linda* – a cheaper version – is nearby (☎0761/22375; ❷). Elsewhere, *Anom*, Jl Gatot Subroto 1–3 (☎0761/36083; ❸–❹), is located centrally, about 100m from Jl Sudirman, and has spotlessly clean rooms opening off a central courtyard, some with hot water. For something a little more upmarket, *Hotel Pangeran Pekanbaru*, Jl Sudirman 371—373 (☎0761/853636; ❾) has rooms with air-con and minibar, and boasts the best pool in the city.

Even if you stayed in the city for a month, you could have every meal at the brilliant Pasar Pusat **night market** (located in the market area near Jalan Bonjol) and not eat the same thing twice. *Sederhana*, Jl Nangka 121–123, is one of many Padang-style **restaurants** that offer good-value but spicy eating in the area near the bus station.

Listings

Airline offices Batavia, Jl Jend Sudirman 312 ☎0761/856031; Garuda, in *Hotel Pangeran Pekanbaru*, Jl Sudirman 371—373 ☎0761/45063; Jatayu, in *Hotel Mutiara Merdeka*, Jl Yos Sudarso 12a ☎0761/855775; Lion Air, in *Hotel Mutiara Merdeka*, Jl Yos Sudarso 12 ☎0761/40670; Mandala,

Jl Sudirman 3485 ☎0761/34777; Merpati, Jl Jend Sudirman 343 ☎0761/41555; Pelangi, Jl Pepaya 64c ☎0761/28896.

Banks and exchange All the main banks have branches in the city, including BCA, Jl Sudirman 448, and BNI 1946, Jl Sudirman 63.

Post office The main post office is at Jl Sudirman 229, but there's a more convenient post office for sending mail at Jl Sudirman 78, close to its northern end.

Telephone and fax The Telkom office is at Jl Sudirman 117, and there are wartel all over town, including Jl Gatot Subroto 6.

Pulau Karimun and ferries to Malaysia

Pulau Karimun, at the southern end of the Straits of Malacca is of most interest to travellers as a gateway to **Malaysia**. The busy port of **TANJUNG BALAI** lies on the south coast, and its ferry terminal is at the eastern end of town; boats leave from here for Kukup at the south of the Malaysian peninsula. All the ferry ticket offices are located just inside the gates. The Pelni agent, PT Barelang Surya, is at counter jetty 3 (☎0777/23157), though you can also buy Pelni tickets from the travel agents on Jalan Trikora in town. Pelni's *KM Kelud* sails via Tanjung Balai on its way to Medan or Jakarta. **Guesthouses** include the slightly ramshackle, though characterful, *Wisma Gloria*, Jl Yos Sudarto 46 (☎0777/21133; ❶–❷), at the far eastern end of Tanjung Balai; to get here, come out of the ferry terminal car park, turn right along the coast past *Wisma Karimun* and it's about 100m up on the hill at the end of the road. For a big jump in quality, try the *Paragon Hotel*, Jalan Trikora and Jl Nusantara 38d (☎0777/21688; ❹–❻): it's situated 200m from the ferry terminal in the heart of the town.

Pulau Batam and on to Singapore

Apart from its proximity to Singapore, just 20km at the closest point, and usefulness as a major staging post on to Indonesia, there's little to recommend **Pulau Batam** to travellers, and nothing to make staying overnight worthwhile. Most travellers arrive at the port of **SEKUPANG**, in a bay at the northwest of the island, from where boats run to Singapore (see below).The international terminal at Sekupang runs boats every thirty minutes to and from **Singapore**'s World Trade Centre (7.30am–7pm; to 8pm on Mon & Wed), and the domestic terminal (200m away) operates services to and from Sumatran destinations such as **Pekanbaru** and Dumai, as well as running boats to Tanjung Pinang on Pulau Bintan. There are several other ferry terminals on the island. The bayside **Waterfront ferry terminal**, Teluk Senimba, has fourteen daily ferries to the World Trade Centre in Singapore (8.45am–8.30pm); services in the other direction operate 7.40am–7.40pm.

Including Sekupang, there are four main ferry terminals on Pulau Batam. Two of the other three are on peninsulas on the north of the island; all three are a fair taxi ride from the main town. **Batu Ampar**, east of Sekupang, has departures to Singapore (World Trade Centre) with nine crossings daily 7.30am to 9pm. **Nongsa**, further east again operates six crossings a day (8am–7pm) to and from Tanah Merah terminal in Singapore. The fourth, **Telaga Punggur**, lies on the east coast and also serves Tanjung Pinang; ferries run every fifteen minutes from 8am to 5pm. No bus service serves Telaga Punggur, so you'll need to use taxis: expect to pay Rp50,000 between the terminal and Nongsa, Rp35,000 into the town of Nagoya and Rp45,000 to Sekupang.

The **Pelni boat**, *KM Kelud*, operates from Sekupang to Jakarta and Medan, while the *KM Labobar* sails to Jakarta. You can book at the Sekupang terminal, any travel agent or from the Pelni office at Jl Dr Cipto Mangunkusumo 4, Sekupang

(☎0778/321070). For **flights**, Lion Air are based at the *Planet Holiday Hotel*, Jalan Raja Ali Haji, Sei Jodoh (☎0778/432801); Bouraq are at Jalan Imam Bonjol Komp. Bumi Ayu Lestari blok A/3, Nagoya (☎0778/421830); Jatayu are at Komp. Penuin Centre Blok E 3 (☎0778/421800); Garuda are at the *Mandarin Regency*, Jl Imam Bonjol 1 (☎0778/458620); Mandala are at Komplek Lumbung Rezeki Blok G No.5 Lubuk Baja, Nagoya (☎0778/ 4032000); and Merpati are at Jodoh Square Blok A 1 (☎0778/427745).

If you get stuck on Pulau Batam, you can **stay** in the island's main town, **NAGOYA** (also known as Lubuk Baja), on the northeast coast of the island, though it's inconvenient for all transport points and the room charges are extortionate – anywhere below Rp40,000 is probably a brothel. *Hotel Bahari*, Kompleks Nagoya Business Centre Block D, No 100 (☎0778/421911; ❸) is the closest you'll get to a decent mid-range place in Nagoya. If you're not on a budget, stay at the *Mandarin Regency*, Jl Imam Bonjol 1 (☎0778/458899; ❹–❽). This is the classiest hotel in Nagoya, with a grand yet relaxed look and feel, extremely comfortable rooms, all the facilities and eating options to be expected at this end of the range, and a good-sized pool in the central courtyard.

Bandar Lampung

Occupying a stunning location in the hills overlooking Lampung Bay, from where you can see as far as Krakatau, **BANDAR LAMPUNG** is an amalgamation of Teluk Betung, the traditional port, and Tanjung Karang, the administrative centre on the hills behind. Local people continue to talk about Teluk Betung and Tanjung Karang, and when you're coming here from other parts of Sumatra your destination will usually be referred to as Rajabasa, the name of the bus terminal.

Arrival

Buses from the north arrive at the **Rajabasa terminal**, 7km north of the city: follow the signs towards the main road for "microlet" – the local name for bemos – and you can either get a light blue bemo into Pasar Bawah in town (24hr), or catch the bus (services finish at about 6pm) that goes to Pasar Bawah but then continues its circular route down Jalan Raden Intan, along Jalan A Yani and up Jalan Kartini before going out to Rajabasa again.

Coming to the city from Bakauheni or Kalianda, buses arrive at the **Panjang terminal**, about 1km east of Pasar Panjang to the east of the city on the coast. Some terminate there, while others go on to the Rajabasa terminal. Orange bemos run between Panjang terminal and Sukaraja terminal in the heart of Teluk Betung; from here, you can get a purple bemo into the city (Rp1000; until 10pm) as far as Pasar Bawah, or a large orange bus direct to Rajabasa via the eastern ring-road.

Bandar Lampung is part of the triangular **rail network** that extends between Bandar Lampung, Palembang and Lubuklinggau. The train station is on Jalan Kotoraja, about 100m from Pasar Bawah. The local **high-speed ferry terminal** from Jakarta is at Sukaraja, just next to the bemo and bus terminal.

Branti Airport is 25km north of the city; walk 200m onto the main road and catch a Branti–Rajabasa bus to Rajabasa terminal (Rp250) and take connections to the city from there. Fixed-price taxis from the airport into town will cost Rp30,000.

City transport

DAMRI **bus services** (6am–6pm) operate between the two major terminals or up and down Jalan Randen Intan and Jalan Diponegoro. The **Rajabasa–Karang** bus runs from the Rajabasa terminal along Jalan Teuku Umar into the city and along Jalan

Useful bemos

Dark purple Between Tanjung Karang and the Sukaraja bus terminal via Jalan Diponegoro, Jalan Salim Batubara, the southern end of Jalan KHA Dahlan and Jalan Yos Sudarso. Coming back up, they run along Jalan Yos Sudarso, Jalan Malahayat, up Jalan Ikan Tenggiri, Jalan Pattimura, Jalan Diponegoro, Jalan A Yani, Jalan Kartini and around to Pasar Bawah.

Light blue Between the Rajabasa bus terminal and Tanjung Karang.

Orange Sukaraja and Panjang bus terminals.

Green Tanjung Karang and Garuntang (Jalan Gatot Subroto) via Jalan Sudirman and Jalan KHA Dahlan, which is useful for the post office.

Dark red Tanjung Karang and Kemiling (Langka Pura) on the western edge of the city.

Grey Tanjung Karang and Sukarame on the eastern edge of the city.

Kotoraja to Pasar Bawah, where it terminates. Its return route to Rajabasa is down Jalan Raden Intan, along Jalan A Yani and up Jalan Kartini to Rajabasa. The **Karang–Betung** bus operates from Pasar Bawah, down Jalan Raden Intan, Jalan Diponegoro and Jalan Salim Batubara, the southern end of Jalan KHA Dahlan and Jalan Yos Sudarso to Sukaraja terminal. Coming back up, they run along Jalan Yos Sudarso, Jalan Ikan Kakap, up Jalan Ikan Tenggiri, Jalan Pattimura, Jalan Diponegoro, Jalan A Yani, Jalan Kartini and around to Pasar Bawah. There's also an orange bus (not the orange bemo), which runs from the Sukaraja terminal direct to Rajabasa terminal via the eastern ringroad.

Bemo routes are less fixed than buses: tell them your destination as you enter. Most stop at about 9pm, though purple ones run until 10 or 11pm, and the light blue service runs 24 hours a day. **Taxis** meters start at Rp1350 and a fare across the city is under Rp15,000. Be firm with drivers about using the meter before you get in.

Information

There's a useful **tourist office** in town: Dinas Investasi Kebudayaan Dan Parwisata (or you could just ask for the *Kantor Parwisata*), Jl Jend Sudirman 29 (☎0721/261430). The **post office** is at Jl KHA Dahlan 21; the main Telkom office is at Jl Kartini 1, and there's also a 24hr wartel at Jl Majapahit 14 – one of many in town. The **immigration office** is at Jl Diponegoro 24 (☎0721/482607 or 481697). Local **hospitals** include Rumah Sakit Bumi Waras, Jalan Wolter Moginsidi (☎0721/255032); Rumah Sakit Immanuel Way Halim, Jalan Sukarno Hatta B (☎0721/704900); and Rumah Sakit Abdul Muluk, Jalan Kapten Rivai (☎0721/703312). Merpati has an office at Jl Diponegoro 189 (☎0721/268486) and there's **Internet** at the post office (open until 6pm).

Accommodation

Whilst Bandar Lampung has a good range of mid- to top-range hotels, offering pleasant and good-value **accommodation**, if you're on a very tight budget the situation is grim. In particular, the area around Pasar Bawah, while simply noisy during the day, gets unpleasant at night.

Gading Jl Kartini 72 ☎0721/255512. Offering a variety of rooms, conveniently located near the market area, it's a short walk from the bus route from Rajabasa terminal and is a large setup on a quiet alleyway in a busy area. ❷

Lusy Jl Diponegoro 186 (Karang–Betung buses and purple bemos pass the door) ☎0721/485695. The accommodation is very basic but clean, and all rooms have attached mandi. Some have fans and some a/c. ❶–❷

Rarem Jl Way Rarem 23 ☎261241. Tucked away behind Jl KHA Dahlan and on the green bemo route; super-clean rooms with shared mandi or private bath and a/c. The small garden is a haven of peace in the bustling city. ❷–❸

The Town

Other than the views down onto Lampung Bay, there are few sights in town. The **Krakatau monument**, set in a small park on Jalan Veteran, is a huge metal buoy that was washed up here from Lampung Bay in 1883 in the tidal waves that followed the eruption of Krakatau, killing over 35,000 people on both sides of the straits (see p.276). The **Museum Negeri Propinsi Lampung**, 1km south of the Rajabasa terminal at Jl Abdin Pagar Alam 64 (Tues–Thurs 8am–1.30pm, Fri 8–10.30am, Sat & Sun 8am–noon; Rp500), houses a good collection of artefacts, including drums, kris, statues, jewellery and masks, plus some megalithic figures, unfortunately not labelled in English.

Eating

There's a great range of places to eat in Bandar Lampung, the highlight being a visit to Pasar Mambo, the **night market**, at the southern end of Jalan Hassanudin, which operates from dusk until about 11pm. The range of food on sale is huge and each stall has its own set of tables. Chinese and seafood stalls are a speciality, and the more exotic stuff such as prawns and crabs can be pricey. There are plenty of stalls selling sweets and ices: *Es John Lenon* is one.

Bukit Randu Perched on top of the hill of the same name with panoramic views of the city and Lampung Bay. The menu is so extensive that there's an information booth at the entrance.

East Garden Jl Diponegoro 106. Excellent and very wide-ranging Chinese/Indonesian place with lots of *tauhu* (tofu) and *tempe* dishes as well as soup, noodles, seafood and many iced fruit juices. Clean, inexpensive and excellent value – they've even got a take-away.

Gembira Jl Pangkhal Pinang 20. Next door to *KFC* in a street with plenty of good *mie ayam* places, *Gembira* offers a huge range of local dishes including *pempek*, soups, chicken dishes and ice confections. Inexpensive and popular.

Marcopolo Restaurant At the *Marcopolo Hotel*. The outside terrace, with a fantastic view over the entire city and out into Lampung Bay, makes this a great place for Western, Chinese and Indonesian food, which ranges from rice and noodle dishes at Rp6000, up to pepper steak at Rp20,000.

Moro Seneng Jl Diponegoro 38. Easy to get to on public transport. You can eat in basic style at the front or in the garden at the back; they offer good-value Indonesian and Chinese food such as nasi and *mie* dishes at Rp2500–3000, up to shrimp, *gurame* and squid at Rp8000–10,000.

Pemplek 56 Jl Salim Batubara 56. Just one of a huge range of *pempek* places along this road; they are named by the number on the street, and all serve inexpensive *pempek*, the grilled or fried Palembang speciality of balls made from sago, fish and flavourings, which are dished up with a variety of sauces.

Kalianda

Situated just under 60km south of Bandar Lampung, the small coastal town of **KALIANDA** is a great alternative to the hassles and expenses of the city, and an excellent stopping-off point whether you're entering or leaving Sumatra. It's served by public transport from the Bakauheni ferry terminal and from the Panjang and Rajabasa bus terminals in Bandar Lampung. Public transport in Kalianda arrives at Terminal Pasar Impress in front of the main market; wander the alleyways here to enjoy the sights, sounds and smells.

The best travellers' **accommodation** is in the *Beringin Hotel*, Jl Kesuma Bangsa 75 (☎0727/2008; ❶–❷), in a large, colonial-style bungalow with big rooms, an airy lounge and a garden. To get here from the terminal, go back onto the road, turn right for about 400m to a junction where a large road joins from the right; head down here past the local school and the hotel is at the far end on the left. Alternatively, hire an ojek. The hotel organizes local trips, including excursions to Krakatau (see p.276). The **post office** is at Jalan Pratu M Yusuf and the **telephone office** on the main street is open 7am to midnight. The main shopping street is Jalan Serma Ibnu Hasyim, a short walk from the *Beringin Hotel.*

Bakauheni and ferries to Java

Around 30km south of Kalianda, lies **Bakauheni**, the departure point for **ferries** to Merak, on Java's northwest tip. There's no reason to stay in Bakauheni itself. The town is served by regular **buses** from the Rajabasa and Panjang terminals in Bandar Lampung, and by bemos from Kalianda. There's also a 24hr wartel and a couple of shops. Ferries from Bakauheni operate round the clock for the two-and-a-half-hour crossing to Merak, leaving every thirty minutes during the day and less frequently at night. High-speed ferries (40min) also depart hourly from 7.40am to 5pm.

4.3

Bali

With its fine beaches, pounding surf, emerald-green rice terraces and exceptionally artistic culture, the small volcanic island of **Bali** – the only Hindu society in Southeast Asia – has long been Indonesia's premier tourist destination. Although it suffers the predictable problems of congestion and commercialization, Bali's original charm is still much in evidence, its stunning temples and spectacular festivals set off by the gorgeously lush landscape of the interior.

Bali's most famous and crowded resort is **Kuta**, an eight-kilometre sweep of golden sand, with plenty of accommodation, shops and nightlife. Nearby **Sanur** is much quieter, but most backpackers prefer the beaches of peaceful east-coast **Amed**, **Candi Dasa** and **Padang Bai**, **Lovina** on the north coast or tranquil **Nusa Lembongan**, easily accessible from Sanur. The island's other major destination is the cultural centre of **Ubud**, where traditional dances are staged every night of the week and the streets are full of juice bars and arts-and-crafts galleries. In addition, there are numerous elegant Hindu temples to visit, particularly at **Tanah Lot**, **Batukau** and **Besakih**, and a good number of volcano hikes, the most popular being the route up **Gunung Batur**, with **Gunung Agung** only for the very fit. **Transport** to and from Bali is extremely efficient: the island is served by scores of international and domestic flights, which all land at **Ngurah Rai Airport** just south of Kuta beach, as well as round-the-clock ferries to Java, thirty minutes' west across the sea from **Gilimanuk**, and to Lombok, four hours' east of **Padang Bai**. Several Pelni ferries also call at Benoa Harbour; see "Getting around", pp.42–43 and "Travel Details", p.486. Prices throughout Bali rocket during the **peak tourist seasons** from mid-June to mid-September and over Christmas, when rooms can be fully booked for days, if not weeks, in advance.

Bali was a more or less independent society of Buddhists and Hindus until the fourteenth century, when it was colonized by the strictly **Hindu** Majapahits from neighbouring Java. Despite the subsequent Islamicization of nearly all her neighbours, Bali has remained firmly Hindu ever since. In 1849, the Dutch started to take an interest in Bali, and by January 1909 had wrested control of the whole island. Following a short-lived Japanese occupation in World War II, and Indonesia's subsequent declaration of independence in 1945, Bali became an autonomous state within the Republic in 1948. But tensions with Java are ongoing and there is concern about wealthy entrepreneurs from Jakarta (and the West) monopolizing the benefits from Bali's considerable attractions, with the Balinese fearing they may lose control of their own homeland. These tensions were horrifically highlighted when Muslim extremists from Java bombed Kuta's two most popular nightclubs on October 12, 2002, killing over two hundred people and sending Bali's tourist-dependant economy into severe decline. Reprisals and religious conflict have not ensued, however, due in part to Bali's impressively equanimous Hindu leadership; by the beginning of 2005, tourist numbers were as healthy as ever, though it will take a lot longer to redress the hardships caused by the attack.

Denpasar

Bali's capital city, **DENPASAR** (sometimes known by its old name, Badung), is dogged by the roaring motorbikes and major traffic congestion common to much of south Bali, but remains a fairly pleasant small-town city at heart, dominated by family compounds grouped into traditional *banjar* (village association) districts, with just a few major shopping streets crisscrossing the centre. It feels nowhere near as hectic as Kuta but, as there's no nightlife (and no beach), few tourists spend long here.

Puputan Square marks the heart of the downtown area. It commemorates the ritual fight to the death (*puputan*) on September 20, 1906 when the raja of Badung and hundreds of his subjects – all dressed in holy white – stabbed themselves to death rather than submit to the Dutch invaders. Overlooking the square's eastern edge on Jalan Mayor Wisnu, the **Bali Museum** (Mon–Thurs & Sun 8am–3pm, Fri 8am–1pm; Rp2000, children Rp1000; on the turquoise Kereneng–Ubung bemo route) is Denpasar's most significant attraction, prettily set in a series of traditional courtyards. The Gedung Timur, at the back of the entrance courtyard, houses items from Bali's prehistory. The compact Gedung BuluIeng displays Balinese textiles; the Gedung Karangasem, which resembles an eighteenth-century Karangasem-style palace, contains the most interesting exhibits, detailing the spiritual and ceremonial life of the Balinese; and the Gedung Tabanan exhibits theatrical masks and puppets. Just over the north wall of the Bali Museum stands the modern state temple of **Pura Agung Jagatnata**, built in 1953.

The biggest and best of Denpasar's markets is **Pasar Badung**, which trades 24 hours a day from the traditional three-storey covered stone-and-brick *pasar* (market) beside the Badung River, just off Jalan Gajah Mada. The most browsable section is the art market on the top floor, which is crammed with sarongs, batik cloth, ceremonial gear and the like. You may get landed with one of the market's self-appointed guides, who hang out around the entrances and try to steer you towards particular stalls. Across on the west bank of the river, also just south off Jalan Gajah Mada, the four-storey **Pasar Kumbasari** is dedicated to handicrafts, souvenirs and clothes, many of them much cheaper than in the shops of Kuta and Ubud.

Practicalities

If you're **arriving** in Bali by air, you'll land at **Ngurah Rai Airport**, which is not in Denpasar as sometimes implied, but just south of Kuta (all information on the airport is given on p.361). Similarly, Denpasar's port, **Benoa Harbour** (Pelabuhan Benoa), located about 10km southeast of the capital, is where all Pelni ships to and from the rest of Indonesia dock. Bemos meet the ships and ferry passengers into Denpasar, terminating near Sanglah hospital, or a taxi-ride to Kuta will cost about Rp25,000. Tickets can be bought at Pelni offices at Benoa Harbour (Mon–Fri 8am–4pm, Sat 8am–12.30pm; ☎0361/723689) or in Kuta (see p.361); see "Getting around", p.238 for Pelni information.

Arriving in Denpasar by bemo or public bus from another part of the island, you'll be dropped at one of the four main **bus and bemo terminals** on the outskirts, from where trans-city bemos beetle into the town centre – and out to the other bemo stations, if you need to make connections (see opposite). Destinations south of Denpasar, including Kuta, Ngurah Rai Airport and Sanur, are served by **Tegal** bemo station. **Kereneng** bemo station runs services to Sanur. **Batubulan** station runs bemos to and from Ubud, Padang Bai and Candi Dasa, and buses to Klungkung (also known as Semarapura), Kintamani and Singaraja. **Ubung** bemos run to and from the north and west of the island, including Medewi, Gilimanuk, Bedugul and Singaraja. Buses to Java also use Ubung. No tourist **shuttle buses** serve Denpasar.

Denpasar's **city transport** system relies on the fleet of colour-coded public bemos that shuttle between the city's bemo terminals; see the "City bemo routes" box opposite. Prices are fixed, but tourists are often obliged to pay more – generally

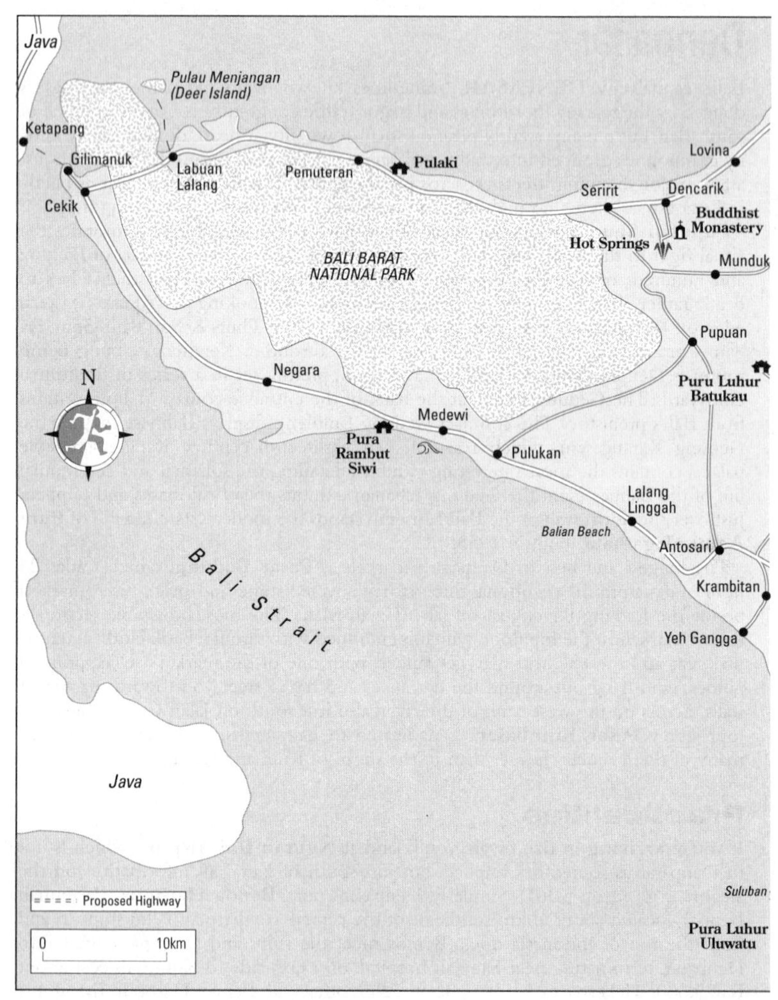

Rp2000 for a cross-city ride. Metered **taxis** also circulate around the city.

The **tourist office** is just off Puputan Square, at Jl Surapati 7 (Mon–Thurs 7.30am–3.30pm, Fri 8am–1pm; ⓣ0361/234569).

Accommodation and eating

Very few backpackers **stay** in Denpasar, but those who do usually head for *Adi Yasa*, Jl Nakula 23 (ⓣ0361/222679; ❶), a family-operated losmen that's slightly run-down and not all that secure. Yellow/turquoise Tegal–Kereneng bemos pass the front door; from Kereneng, take an Ubung-bound bemo to the Pasar Seni market at the Jalan Abimanyu/Jalan Veteran junction. Across the road is the much nicer *Nakula Familiar Inn*, Jl Nakula 4 (ⓣ0361/226446, ⓔnakula_familiar_inn@yahoo.com; ❷), which has clean, modern, en-suite rooms (bemo access as above).

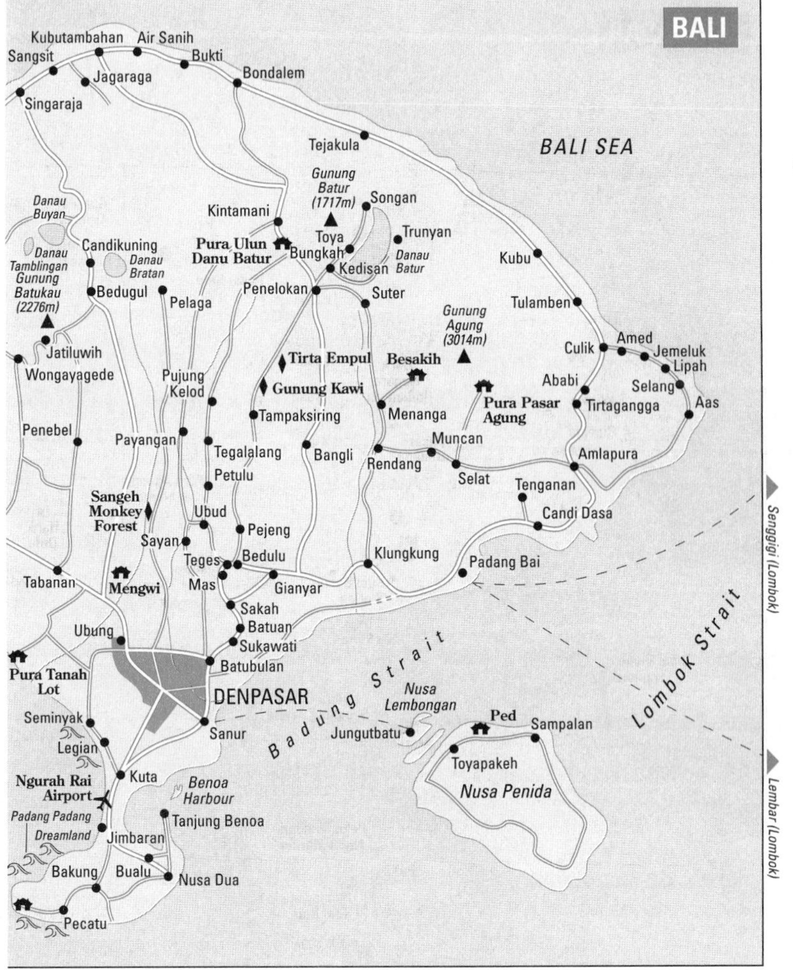

One of the best **places to eat** in Denpasar is *Betty*, Jl Sumatra 56, whose long, cheap Indonesian menu includes an imaginative vegetarian selection. *Warung Satriya* on Jalan Kedongdong is a cheap neighbourhood warung convenient for the Jalan Nakula losmen. After dark, the huge Kereneng Night Market sets up just off Jalan Hayam Wuruk and adjacent to Kereneng bemo.

Listings

ATMs, banks and exchange Most central Denpasar banks have exchange counters. There are ATMs every few blocks on the main shopping streets.
Cinema Five screens at Wisata 21, Jl Thamrin 29 ⓣ0361/424023; seats cost Rp12,500. Programmes are listed in the free tourist newspapers *Bali Travel News* and *What's Up Bali*. Soundtracks are usually original and shown with Indonesian subtitles.
Department stores Ramayana Mal Bali, Jl Diponegoro 103 (Kereneng–Tegal and Tegal–Sanur

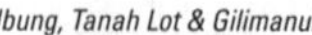

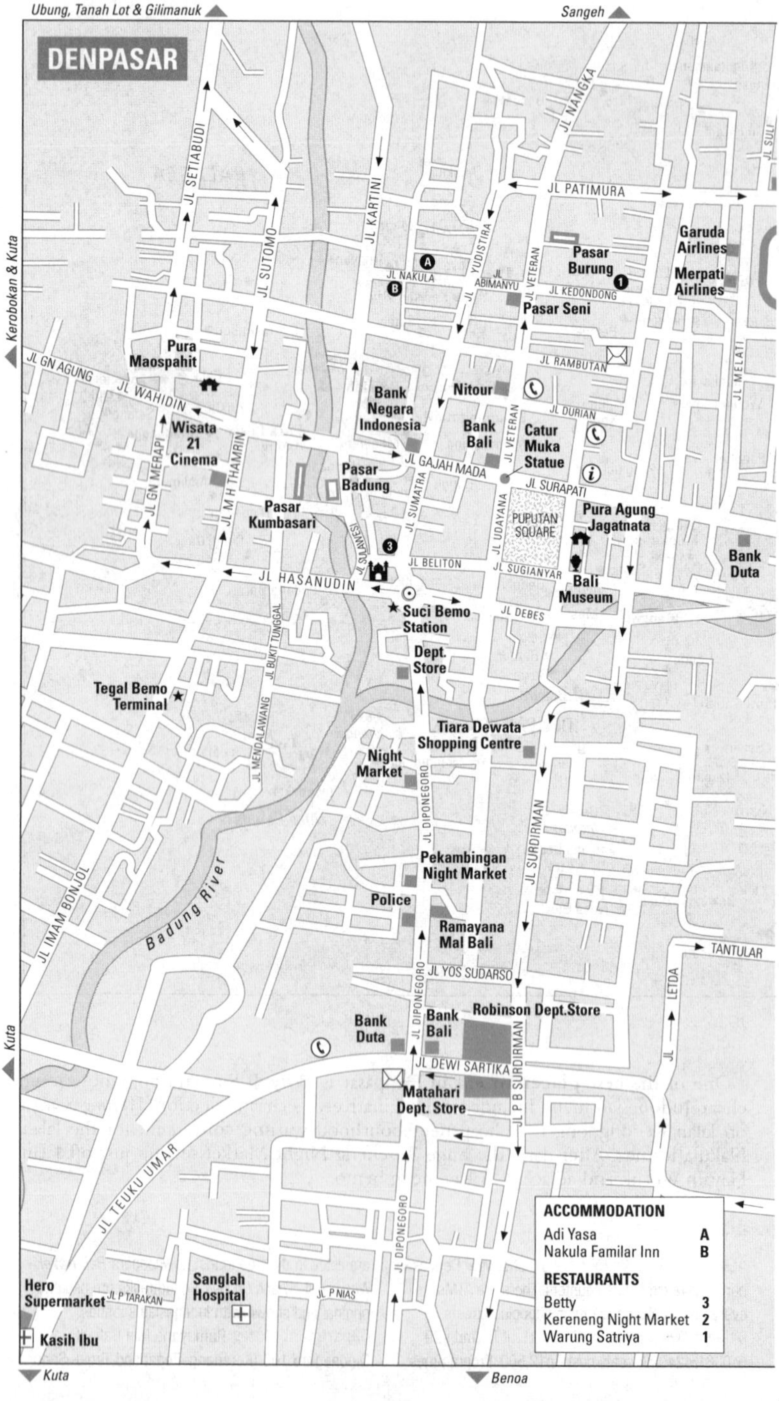
DENPASAR
Ubung, Tanah Lot & Gilimanuk
Sangeh
Kerobokan & Kuta
Kuta
Kuta
Benoa
JL SETIABUDI
JL SUTOMO
JL KARTINI
JL NANGKA
JL PATIMURA
JL SULI
JL YUDISTIRA
JL NAKULA
JL ABIMANYU
JL VETERAN
JL KEDONDONG
JL RAMBUTAN
JL MELATI
JL DURIAN
JL GN AGUNG
JL WAHIDIN
JL GN MERAPI
JL M H THAMRIN
JL GAJAH MADA
JL SUMATRA
JL SURAPATI
JL UDAYANA
JL SULAWESI
JL BELITON
JL SUGIANYAR
JL HASANUDIN
JL DEBES
JL BUKIT TUNGGAL
JL MENDALAWANG
JL DIPONEGORO
JL SURDIRMAN
JL IMAM BONJOL
Badung River
TANTULAR
JL YOS SUDARSO
JL LETDA
JL DEWI SARTIKA
JL P B SURDIRMAN
JL TEUKU UMAR
JL P TARAKAN
JL P NIAS
Garuda Airlines
Merpati Airlines
Pasar Burung
Pasar Seni
Pura Maospahit
Bank Negara Indonesia
Nitour
Bank Bali
Catur Muka Statue
Wisata 21 Cinema
Pasar Badung
Pasar Kumbasari
PUPUTAN SQUARE
Pura Agung Jagatnata
Bank Duta
Bali Museum
Suci Bemo Station
Dept. Store
Tegal Bemo Terminal
Tiara Dewata Shopping Centre
Night Market
Pekambingan Night Market
Police
Ramayana Mal Bali
Robinson Dept.Store
Bank Duta
Bank Bali
Matahari Dept. Store
Hero Supermarket
Sanglah Hospital
Kasih Ibu
ACCOMMODATION
Adi Yasa A
Nakula Familar Inn B
RESTAURANTS
Betty 3
Kereneng Night Market 2
Warung Satriya 1

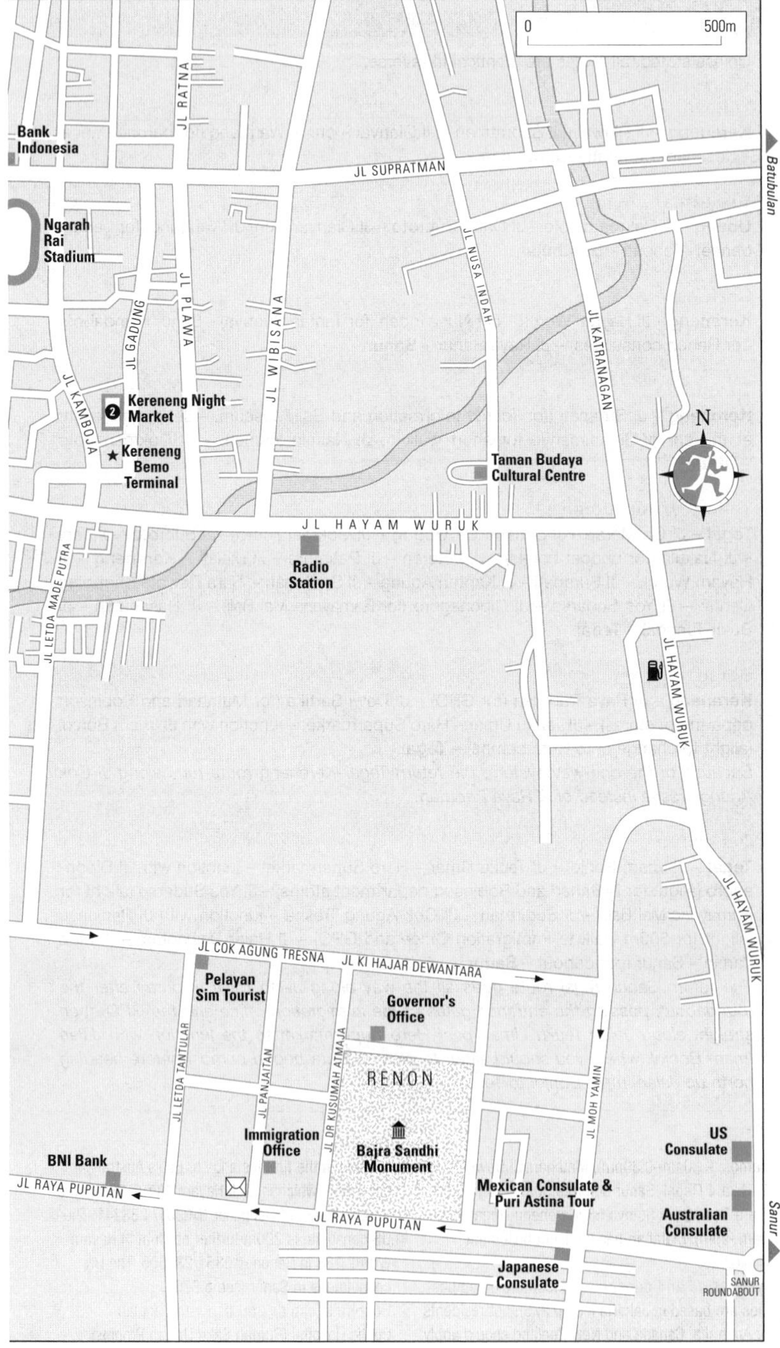

0
500m
Bank Indonesia
JL RATNA
JL SUPRATMAN
Batubulan
Ngarah Rai Stadium
JL NUSA INDAH
JL GADUNG
JL PLAWA
JL WIBISANA
JL KATRANAGAN
JL KAMBOJA
Kereneng Night Market
Kereneng Bemo Terminal
N
Taman Budaya Cultural Centre
JL HAYAM WURUK
Radio Station
JL LETDA MADE PUTRA
JL HAYAM WURUK
JL HAYAM WURUK
JL COK AGUNG TRESNA
JL KI HAJAR DEWANTARA
Pelayan Sim Tourist
Governor's Office
RENON
JL LETDA TANTULAR
JL PANJAITAN
JL DR KUSUMAH ATMAJA
JL MOH YAMIN
Immigration Office
Bajra Sandhi Monument
US Consulate
BNI Bank
JL RAYA PUPUTAN
Mexican Consulate & Puri Astina Tour
JL RAYA PUPUTAN
Australian Consulate
Sanur
Japanese Consulate
SANUR ROUNDABOUT

City bemo routes

Unless stated, all routes are identical in reverse.

Yellow

Kereneng – Jl Plawa – Jl Supratman – Jl Gianyar – cnr Jl Waribang (for barong dance) – Kesiman – Tohpati – **Batubulan**.

Grey-blue

Ubung – Jl Cokroaminoto – Jl Gatot Subroto – Jl Gianyar – cnr Jl Waribang (for barong dance) –Tohpati – **Batubulan**.

Dark green

Kereneng – Jl Hayam Wuruk – cnr Nusa Indah (for Taman Budaya) – Sanur roundabout (for Renon consulates) – Jl Raya Sanur – **Sanur**.

Turquoise

Kereneng – Jl Surapati (for Tourist Information and Bali Museum) – Jl Veteran (alight at the cnr of Jl Abimanyu for short walk to Jl Nakula losmen) – Jl Cokroaminoto – **Ubung**.

Yellow or turquoise

Tegal – Jl Gn Merapi– Jl Setiabudi – **Ubung** – Jl Cokroaminoto – Jl Subroto – Jl Yani – Jl Nakula (for budget hotels) – Jl Veteran – Jl Patimura – Jl Melati – **Kereneng** – Jl Hayam Wuruk – Jl Surapati – Jl Kapten Agung – Jl Sudirman – Tiara Dewata Shopping Centre – Jl Yos Sudarso – Jl Diponegoro (for Ramayana Mal Bali) – Jl Hasanudin – Jl Bukit Tunggal – **Tegal**.

Beige

Kereneng – Jl Raya Puputan (for GPO) – Jl Dewi Sartika (for Matahari and Robinson department stores) – Jl Teuku Umar – Hero Supermarket – junction with Jl Imam Bonjol (alight to change onto Kuta bemos) – **Tegal**.

Because of the one-way system, the return Tegal–Kereneng route runs along Jl Cok Agung Tresna instead of Jl Raya Puputan.

Dark blue

Tegal – Jl Imam Bonjol – Jl Teuku Umar – Hero Supermarket – junction with Jl Diponegoro (alight for Matahari and Robinson department stores) – Jl Yos Sudarso (alight for Ramayana Mal Bali) – Jl Sudirman – Jl Cok Agung Tresna – junction with Jl Panjaitan (alight for 500m walk to Immigration Office and GPO) – Jl Hajar Dewantara – Jl Moh Yamin – Sanur roundabout – **Sanur**.

The return Sanur–Tegal route goes all the way along Jalan Raya Puputan after the roundabout, passing the entrance gates of the immigration office and the GPO, then straight along Jalan Teuku Umar, past Hero Supermarket to the junction with Jalan Imam Bonjol (where you should alight to pick up Kuta-bound bemos) before heading north up Jalan Imam Bonjol to Tegal.

bemos; 9.30am–9.30pm); Matahari, Jl Dewi Sartika 4 (Tegal–Sanur bemo; 9.30am–9pm); and Tiara Dewata, Jl Sutoyo 55 (Kereneng–Tegal bemo; 9am–9pm). Matahari has a decent basement bookstore.

Embassies and consulates Most foreign embassies are based in Jakarta (see p.275), but residents of Australia, Canada and New Zealand should apply for help in the first instance to Bali's Australian consulate, which is at Jl Hayam Wuruk 88B in the Renon district of Denpasar ☎0361/ 283241. The US consulate is 200m further north at Jl Hayam Wuruk 188 in Renon ☎0361/233605. The UK consulate is in Sanur (see p.370).

Hospitals, clinics and dentists Sanglah Public Hospital (Rumah Sakit Umum Propinsi

Sanglah) at Jl Kesehatan Selatan 1, Sanglah (five lines ⓣ0361/227911–227915; public bemo from Kereneng) is the main provincial public hospital, with an emergency ward and some English-speaking staff. It also has Bali's only divers' decompression chamber. Kasih Ibu, next to Hero Supermarket at Jl Teuku Umar 120 ⓣ0361/223036, is a 24hr private hospital that is fine for minor ailments, but not equipped for emergencies; most expats use BIMC or International SOS, both near Kuta, instead (see p.366). For dental problems, contact Dr Indra Guizot, Jl Patimura 19, Denpasar, ⓣ0361/222445.

Immigration office At the corner of Jl Panjaitan and Jl Raya Puputan, Renon (Mon–Thurs 8am–3pm, Fri 8–11am, Sat 8am–2pm; ⓣ0361/227828; Sanur–Tegal bemo).

Internet access At Hello Internet on the top floor of the Ramayana Mal Bali on Jl Diponegoro.

Pharmacies Inside Tiara Dewata, Matahari and Ramayana Mal Bali department stores; inside Hero Supermarket on Jl Teuku Umar, and at Apotik Kimia Farma, Jl Diponegoro 125.

Police There are police stations on Jl Patimura and Jl Diponegoro; the main police station is in the far west of the city on Jl Gunung Sanghiang (ⓣ0361/424346).

Post offices Denpasar's poste restante (Mon–Fri 8am–7pm, Sat 8am–6pm; Sanur–Tegal bemo) is at the GPO on Jl Raya Puputan in Renon. The Jl Rambutan PO, near Puputan Square, is more central.

Telephone services Telkom offices at Jl Teuku Umar 6, and on Jl Durian. IDD phones in the Tiara Dewata Department Store on Jl Sutoyo; Home Country Direct phone at the Bali Museum.

Tourist driving licence Available for cars or motorbikes (Rp150,000) in 20min from Pelayan Sim Tourist (Mon–Fri 8am–3pm, Sat 8am–1pm; ⓣ0361/243939) inside the Kantor Bersama Samsat on Jl Cok Agung Tresna in Renon. Take a passport and home driving licence.

Travel agents Domestic airline tickets from Nitour, Jl Veteran 5 ⓣ0361/234742, ⓔnitourbali@denpasar.wasantara.net.id. International and domestic airline tickets from Puri Astina Tour, Jl Moh Yamin 1A, Renon ⓣ0361/223552, ⓔastina@denpasar.wasantara.net.id, next to the Mexican consulate. Pelni boat tickets from Jl Diponegoro 165 ⓣ0361/234680. Train tickets (for Java) from Jl Diponegoro 150 Blok B4 ⓣ0361/227131.

Kuta-Legian-Seminyak

The **KUTA-LEGIAN-SEMINYAK** conurbation, 10km southwest of Denpasar, is the biggest, brashest, least traditional beach resort in Bali. It's packed with hundreds of hotels, restaurants, bars, clubs and shops and yet, for all its hustle, remains a good-humoured place and surprisingly unsleazy. Although the resort's party atmosphere was shattered in late 2002, when Islamic extremists from Java bombed Kuta's two most popular clubs, the old vibe has since re-emerged and the nightlife rages on. A Monument of Human Tragedy now occupies the "Ground Zero" site.

Kuta beach is quite possibly the most beautiful in Bali, with its gentle curve of golden sand stretching for 8km, lashed by huge breakers. These waves make Kuta a great beach for surfers, but less pleasant for swimming, with a strong undertow: always swim between the red- and yellow-striped flags. Poppies 1, Poppies 2 and Jalan Benesari form the heart of Kuta's **surf scene**, and are the best areas to buy boards or get them repaired; you can also rent boards on the beach (about Rp25,000). Monthly tide charts are available at *Tubes* bar on Poppies 2 and most surfwear shops; you can learn to surf at the Rip Curl School of Surf, based at the *Blue Ocean* hotel, Jl Pantai Kuta Arjuna, Legian (ⓣ0361/735858, ⓦwww.schoolofsurf.com; US$39/half-day). Wanasari Wisata, Jl Pantai 8b Kuta (ⓣ0361/755588, ⓦwww.grajagan.com) and *Tubes* bar on Poppies 2 (ⓣ0361/751620, ⓦwww.g-land.com) organize surfing tours to the mega-waves off Sumbawa and East Java, including the awesome G-Land (see p.312). Most of south Bali's **dive centres** are based in Sanur (see p.368), but in Kuta there's the UK-run AquaMarine Diving, Jl Raya Seminyak 2A (ⓣ0361/730107, ⓦwww.aquamarinediving.com). Waterbom Park on Jl Dewi Sartika, Tuban (9am–6pm; adults $18.50, 3- to 12-year-olds $9.50) is an enjoyable **aquatic adventure park** with water slides and helter-skelters as well as trampolines

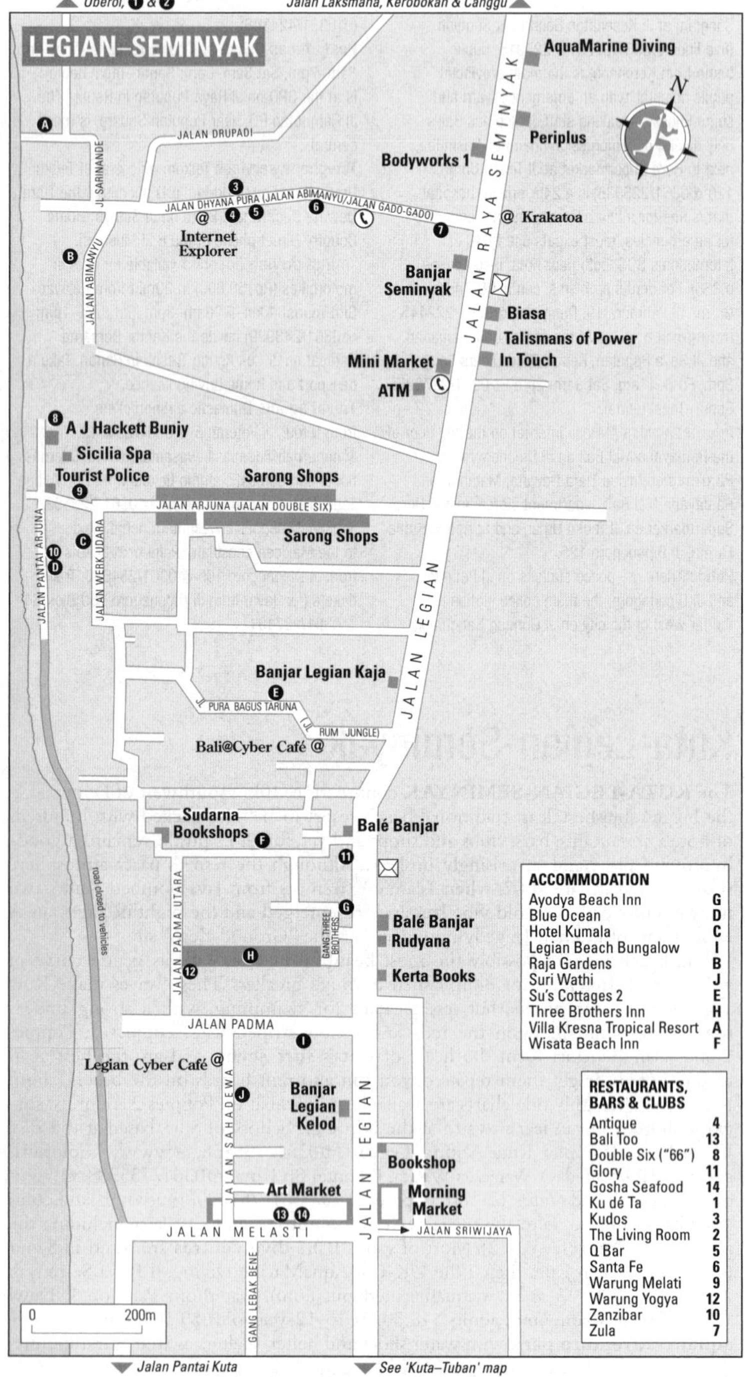

LEGIAN–SEMINYAK
Oberoi, 1 & 2
Jalan Laksmana, Kerobokan & Canggu
Jalan Pantai Kuta
See 'Kuta–Tuban' map
JALAN RAYA SEMINYAK
JALAN DRUPADI
JL SARINANDE
JALAN DHYANA PURA (JALAN ABIMANYU/JALAN GADO-GADO)
JALAN ABIMANYU
JALAN ARJUNA (JALAN DOUBLE SIX)
JALAN PANTAI ARJUNA
JALAN WERK UDARA
JALAN LEGIAN
JL PURA BAGUS TARUNA
JL RUM JUNGLE
JALAN PADMA UTARA
GANG THREE BROTHERS
JALAN PADMA
JALAN SAHADEWA
JALAN MELASTI
JALAN SRIWIJAYA
GANG LEBAK BENE
road closed to vehicles
AquaMarine Diving
Periplus
Bodyworks 1
Internet Explorer
Krakatoa
Banjar Seminyak
Biasa
Talismans of Power
In Touch
Mini Market
ATM
A J Hackett Bunjy
Sicilia Spa
Tourist Police
Sarong Shops
Sarong Shops
Banjar Legian Kaja
Bali@Cyber Café
Sudarna Bookshops
Balé Banjar
Balé Banjar
Rudyana
Kerta Books
Legian Cyber Café
Banjar Legian Kelod
Bookshop
Art Market
Morning Market
0 200m
ACCOMMODATION
Ayodya Beach Inn G
Blue Ocean D
Hotel Kumala C
Legian Beach Bungalow I
Raja Gardens B
Suri Wathi J
Su's Cottages 2 E
Three Brothers Inn H
Villa Kresna Tropical Resort A
Wisata Beach Inn F
RESTAURANTS, BARS & CLUBS
Antique 4
Bali Too 13
Double Six ("66") 8
Glory 11
Gosha Seafood 14
Ku dé Ta 1
Kudos 3
The Living Room 2
Q Bar 5
Santa Fe 6
Warung Melati 9
Warung Yogya 12
Zanzibar 10
Zula 7

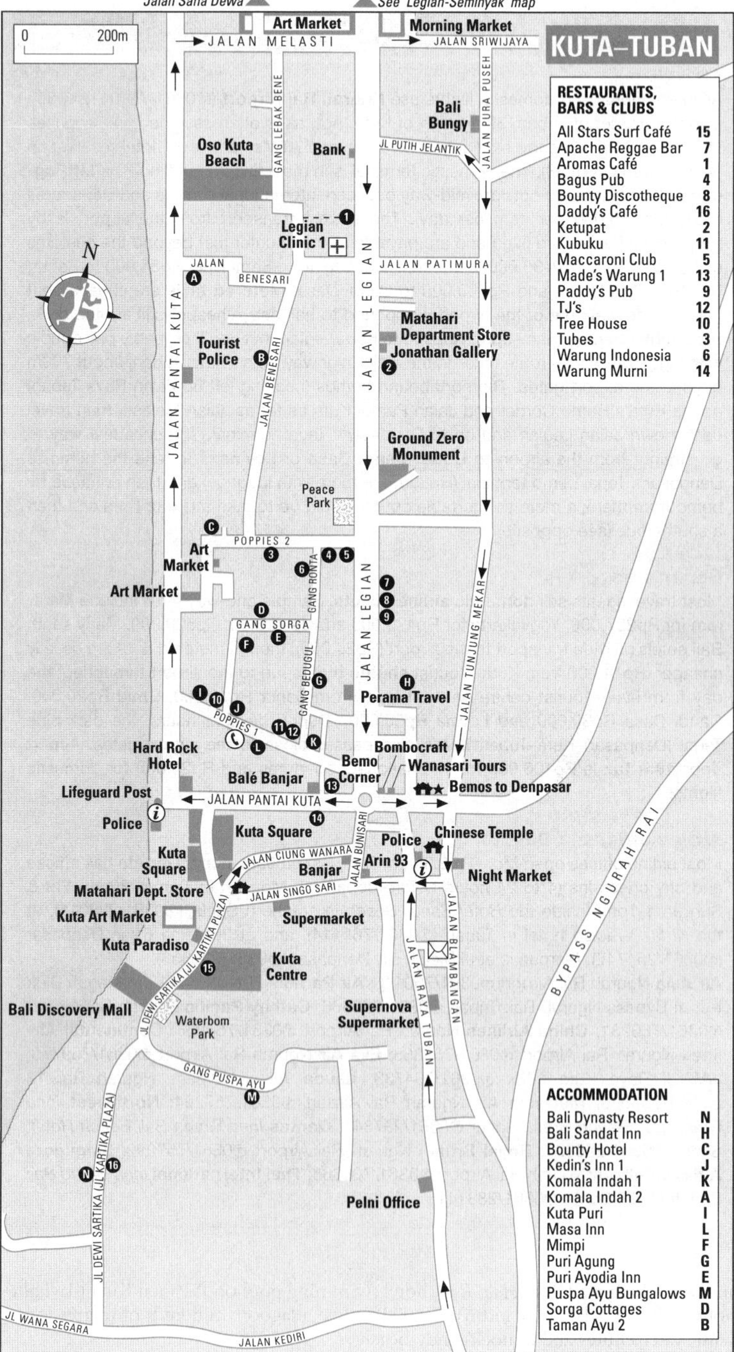

RESTAURANTS, BARS & CLUBS

All Stars Surf Café	15
Apache Reggae Bar	7
Aromas Café	1
Bagus Pub	4
Bounty Discotheque	8
Daddy's Café	16
Ketupat	2
Kubuku	11
Maccaroni Club	5
Made's Warung 1	13
Paddy's Pub	9
TJ's	12
Tree House	10
Tubes	3
Warung Indonesia	6
Warung Murni	14

ACCOMMODATION

Bali Dynasty Resort	N
Bali Sandat Inn	H
Bounty Hotel	C
Kedin's Inn 1	J
Komala Indah 1	K
Komala Indah 2	A
Kuta Puri	I
Masa Inn	L
Mimpi	F
Puri Agung	G
Puri Ayodia Inn	E
Puspa Ayu Bungalows	M
Sorga Cottages	D
Taman Ayu 2	B

Ngurah Rai Airport

Arrivals

All international and domestic flights use **Ngurah Rai Airport** (☎0361/751011), which is in the district of Tuban, 3km south of Kuta, not, as is often assumed, in Denpasar. There are 24hr currency exchanges here, several **ATMs**, and two hotel-reservation desks (rooms from $8). The domestic terminal is in the adjacent building. The **left-luggage** office is located outside, mid-way between International Arrivals and Departures (Rp10,000–15,000 per item per day). The easiest transport from the airport is by **prepaid taxi**: rates are fixed and are payable at the counter just beyond the customs exit doors: Rp20,000–35,000 to Tuban, Kuta, Legian or Seminyak; Rp55,000 to Sanur; Rp115,000 to Ubud; and Rp200,000 to Candi Dasa. **Metered taxis** are cheaper, but you have to walk out of the airport compound to hail one. Cheaper still are the dark-blue **public bemos** (5am–6pm; Rp2000 to Kuta/Legian, but you'll probably pay double with luggage), whose route takes in the major highway, Jalan Raya Tuban, about 700m beyond the airport gates. The northbound bemos (heading left up Jalan Raya Tuban) go via Kuta's Bemo Corner and Jalan Pantai Kuta as far as Jalan Melasti, then travel back down Jalan Legian and on to Denpasar's Tegal terminal. The cheapest way to go straight from the airport to **Ubud**, **Candi Dasa** or **Lovina** is to take the bemo to Denpasar's Tegal bemo terminal (Rp3000, or more with luggage) and then continue by bemo from there; a more comfortable option would be to take a taxi to Kuta and then a shuttle bus (see opposite).

Departures

Most travel agents sell **domestic airline tickets**. Sample one-way fares include Mataram for Rp237,000, Yogyakarta for Rp473,000 and Jakarta for Rp529,000. Many south Bali hotels provide transport to the airport (Rp20,000), though metered taxis are usually cheaper (Rp14,000 from Kuta). Tourist **shuttle buses** run to the airport throughout the day from every tourist centre on the island (from Sanur Rp10,000, Ubud Rp20,000, Candi Dasa Rp30,000 and Lovina Rp50,000). During daylight hours, the dark-blue Tegal (Denpasar)–Kuta–Tuban **bemo** also passes close to the airport gates. Airport **departure tax** is Rp100,000 for international departures and Rp20,000 for domestic flights.

Airline offices in Bali

Most airline offices open Mon–Fri 8.30am–5pm, Sat 8.30am–noon. **Garuda** has offices and city check-ins (4 to 24 hours before departure; Mon–Fri 7.30am–4.30pm, Sat & Sun 9am–1pm) inside the *Hotel Sanur Beach* in southern Sanur (☎0361/288011), at the *Kuta Paradiso* hotel in Tuban (☎0361/761414), and at Jl Melati 61 in Denpasar (☎0361/254747). Merpati is at Jl Melati 51, Denpasar (☎0361/235358).

Air Asia Ngurah Rai Airport ☎0361/760116; **Air Paradise** Pertokoan Kuta Megah Blok I-J, Jl Bypass Ngurah Rai, Tuban ☎0361/756666; **Cathay Pacific** Ngurah Rai Airport ☎0361/766931; **China Airlines** Ngurah Rai Airport ☎0361/754856; **Continental Airlines** Ngurah Rai Airport ☎0361/768358; **Eva Air** Ngurah Rai Airport ☎0361/759773; **JAL** Jl Raya Kuta 100x ☎0361/764733; **Lauda Air** Jl Bypass Ngurah Rai 12 ☎0361/758686; **Malaysia Air** Ngurah Rai Airport ☎0361/757294; **Northwest** *Inna Grand Bali Beach Hotel*, Sanur ☎0361/287841; **Qantas** *Inna Grand Bali Beach Hotel*, Sanur ☎0361/288331; **Royal Brunei** Ngurah Rai Airport ☎0361/757292; **Singapore Airlines/Silk Air** Ngurah Rai Airport ☎0361/768388; **Thai International** *Inna Grand Bali Beach Hotel*, Sanur ☎0361/288141.

and a climbing wall. The *Hard Rock* hotel swimming pool on Jl Pantai Kuta (daylight hours; adults Rp100,000, kids Rp50,000) is like a lagoon: hundreds of metres long, with water chutes and a mock sandy beach.

Arrival

Arriving in Kuta by **tourist shuttle bus**, you could be dropped almost anywhere, depending on your shuttle-bus operator. Drivers for the biggest shuttle bus operator, Perama, drop passengers at their office on Jalan Legian, about 100m north of Bemo Corner, but will sometimes stop at spots en route if asked.

Coming by **public bemo** from Denpasar's Tegal terminal, you can get off at any point on their round-Kuta loop, which runs via Bemo Corner, west and then north along Jalan Pantai Kuta, east along Jalan Melasti before heading north up Jalan Legian only as far as Jalan Padma before turning round and continuing south down Jalan Legian as far as Bemo Corner.

Orientation and information

Although Kuta, Legian and Seminyak all started out as separate villages, they've now merged together so completely that it's impossible to recognize the borders. **Kuta** stretches north from the Matahari department store in Kuta Square to Jalan Melasti, while its southern fringes, extending south from Matahari to the airport, are defined as **Tuban**; **Legian** runs from Jalan Melasti as far as Jalan Arjuna (aka Jalan Double Six); and **Seminyak** goes from Jalan Arjuna up to the *Oberoi* hotel in the north. The resort's main road, Jalan Legian, runs north–south through all three districts, a total distance of 6km, and a lot of businesses give their address as nothing more than "Jalan Legian". Kuta's other main landmark is Bemo Corner, the tiny roundabout at the southern end of Kuta that stands at the Jalan Legian–Jalan Pantai Kuta intersection.

The official but pretty unhelpful **Badung Tourist Office**, Jl Raya Kuta 2 (Mon–Thurs 8am–3pm, Fri 8am–12 noon; ⓣ0361/756175), also has a counter beside the lifeguard post on the beach off Jalan Pantai Kuta (Mon–Fri 9am–12 noon; ⓣ0361/755660).

Moving on from Kuta

Shuttle buses and transport to other islands

If you're going from Kuta to anywhere beyond Denpasar, it's always quicker – although more expensive – to take a tourist **shuttle bus** rather than public transport. All tour agencies offer "shuttle bus services" to tourist destinations on Bali, and some feature Lombok as well. **Perama Travel** (daily 7am–10pm, ⓣ0361/751551, ⓦwww.peramatour.com), located 100m north of Bemo Corner at Jl Legian 39, is the biggest operator and does several daily runs to Sanur, Ubud, Lovina, Bedugul, Padang Bai and Candi Dasa, as well as to Nusa Lembongan, the Gili Islands and Lombok. Prices are reasonable, for example Rp20,000 to Ubud, Rp70,000 to Lovina and Rp120,000 to the Gilis. Perama buses leave from their office, but you can buy tickets on the phone and through other agents and can arrange a pick-up from your hotel for an extra Rp5000.

Many Kuta travel agents sell express **boat tickets** to Lombok (see p.384 for operators) and Nusa Lembongan. Tickets for Pelni long-distance boats to other parts of Indonesia are sold at the Pelni office (see "Listings", p.384). For airport information, see p.362.

Bemos

To get from Kuta to most other destinations in Bali by **bemo** almost always entails going via Denpasar. Dark-blue bemos to Denpasar from Kuta run throughout the day and terminate at Denpasar's Tegal terminal (25min; Rp3000). The easiest place to catch them is at the Jalan Pantai Kuta/Jalan Raya Tuban intersection, about 15m east of Bemo Corner. For destinations further afield, you'll need to get a cross-city bemo from Tegal to another bemo terminal (see p.358).

You'll get a lot more tourist information and details of forthcoming events from the free **tourist newspapers and magazines** available at hotels, shops and restaurants; the best include the fortnightly magazine *the beat* (nightlife and restaurant listings), the weekly fold-out pamphlet *What's Up Bali* (tourist attractions, festivals, nightlife and cinema) and the fortnightly glossy newspaper *Bali Travel News* (temple festivals and cinema schedules).

Be extremely careful when **changing money** at currency exchange counters in Kuta as many places short-change tourists by using well-known **rip-offs** including rigged calculators and folded notes. One chain of recommended moneychangers is PT Central Kuta, which has several branches on Jalan Legian plus one on Jalan Melasti, many of them inside Kodak film shops.

City transport

Public transport in Kuta-Legian-Seminyak is less than ideal, as the dark-blue Tegal-Kuta-Legian **bemos** (every 5–10min; 5am–8.30pm) only cover a clockwise loop around Kuta, leaving out most of Legian and all of Seminyak (see "Arrival", opposite). You can flag them down at any point along this route; the standard fare for any distance within this area is Rp2000, but tourists are sometimes obliged to pay more. The easiest alternative is the resort's **metered taxis**, such as the light-blue Blue Bird Taxis (Ⓣ0361/701111), which charge Rp4000 flagfall and Rp2000/km, day and night. The informal taxi service offered by the ubiquitous transport touts involves tiresome bargaining and is rarely cheaper.

Every major road in the resort is packed with tour agents renting **cars, motorbikes and bicycles**: see "Getting around", p.238 for price guidelines and advice. A recommended freelance English-speaking guide and **driver** is Wayan Artana (Ⓣ0812/396 1296, Ⓔiartana@hotmail.com), who charges Rp250,000/day inclusive.

Accommodation

The cheapest **accommodation** is mainly concentrated in the Kuta area, particularly along Poppies 1 and the *gang* (alleys) running off it, and along Poppies 2 and Jalan Benesari. Legian has good-value places with pools and air-con.

Kuta and Tuban

Kuta is the most congested and hectic part of the resort, with the bulk of the bars, restaurants, clubs and shops. Its beach gets crowded, but has clean, fine sand. The southern, **Tuban**, end of the beach is a bit quieter but some distance from most shops, bars and restaurants.

Bali Dynasty Resort Jl Dewi Sartika Ⓣ0361/752403, Ⓦwww.balidynasty.com. Big, family-friendly, package-tourist-oriented hotel right on the beach. Two pools, a playground and a kids' club. 9

Bali Sandat Inn Jl Legian 120 Ⓣ0361/753491. Clean, well-maintained fan and a/c rooms right in the heart of the action. 2–3

Bounty Hotel Poppies 2 Ⓣ0361/753030, Ⓦwww.balihotels.com/kuta/bounty.php. Large, very good-value terraced bungalows set in a garden, with two pools and a games room. 7

Kedin's Inn 1 Poppies 1 Ⓣ0361/756771. Twenty-four big, fairly basic, fan-cooled losmen rooms, crammed into a small compound. 2

Komala Indah 1 Poppies 1 #20 Ⓣ0361/751422. Compact square of seven clean, well-priced terraced bungalows set around a courtyard garden. 2

Komala Indah 2 Jl Benesari Ⓣ0361/754258. Good, simple rooms in a nice garden near the beach. 2

Kuta Puri Poppies 1 Ⓣ0361/751903, Ⓔkuta_puri@hotmail.com. Terraced a/c rooms and more luxurious bungalows in a very spacious garden with a large pool. 6–7

Masa Inn Poppies 1 #27 Ⓣ0361/758507, Ⓦwww.masainn.com. Well-priced hotel with a good pool, sociable garden area and plain but fine a/c rooms. 4

Mimpi Gang Sorga, off Poppies 1 Ⓣ0361/751848, Ⓔkumimpi@yahoo.com.sg. Just seven characterful, thatched, fan-cooled Balinese cottages in a shady garden with pool. ❸–❻

Puri Agung Gang Bedugul, off Poppies 1 ☎0361/750054. Welcoming little losmen with cheap, sprucely kept rooms packed into two storeys around a minuscule courtyard. ❶

Puri Ayodia Inn Gang Sorga ☎0361/754245. Exceptionally cheap, quite funky little pastel-painted place with fairly primitive rooms and bungalows. ❶

Puspa Ayu Bungalows Gang Puspa Ayu ☎0361/756721. Quiet, pleasant spot with sixteen typical fan and a/c rooms and bungalows arranged round a garden. ❸–❹

Sorga Cottages Gang Sorga ☎0361/751897, ⓦwww.angelfire.com/nb/sorgacott. Good-value fan and a/c rooms in a three-storey block set round a small pool and a restaurant. ❸–❺

Taman Ayu 2 Jl Benesari ☎0361/754376, ⓕ754640. Very reasonably priced and well-maintained bamboo-walled, fan and a/c rooms, plus some bungalows. ❷–❸

Legian and Seminyak

Slightly calmer than Kuta, **Legian** attracts fewer backpackers and more Australian families and package tourists. Upmarket **Seminyak** is quiet and sophisticated and tends to appeal to tourists who've been to Bali before.

Ayodya Beach Inn Gang Three Brothers ☎0361/752169, ⓔayodyabeachinn@yahoo.com. Cheap and friendly if rather dilapidated losmen with fifteen terraced fan rooms. ❷

Blue Ocean Jl Pantai Arjuna (Blue Ocean beach) ☎0361/730289, ⓕ730590. Simply furnished fan rooms (some with kitchens) in a prime spot on the beachfront road. Surf school on the premises. ❸

Hotel Kumala Jl Werk Udara ☎0361/732186, ⓦwww.hotelkumala.com. Great-value place close to shore, with appealing a/c rooms and cottages, plus two pools. ❹–❻

Legian Beach Bungalow Jl Padma ☎0361/751087, ⓔgadinglbb@yahoo.com. Inviting place with simple but pleasant fan and a/c rooms and bungalows set in a spacious garden with pool. ❷–❹

Raja Gardens Jl Abimanyu ☎0361/730494, ⓔjdw@eksadata.com. Six unusual, nicely furnished fan-cooled bungalows and a big pool one minute's walk from the beach. ❻

Suri Wathi Jl Sahadewa 12 ☎0361/753162, ⓔsuriwati@yahoo.com. Quiet, family-run losmen with well-priced fan and a/c rooms and bungalows, plus a decent pool. ❷–❺

Su's Cottages 2 Jl Pura Bagus Taruna ☎0361/752127, ⓕ750372. Spotless, nicely furnished fan and a/c rooms plus pool in a lively location. ❸–❹

Three Brothers Inn Jl Three Brothers ☎0361/751566. Rambling garden complex that holds dozens of characterful, differently styled bungalows and a pool. Upstairs fan rooms are especially attractive. ❺–❼

Villa Kresna Tropical Resort Jl Sarinande 19 ☎0361/730317, ⓦwww.villa-kresna.com. A tiny compound of charming colonial-style suites, villas and rooms just one minute's walk from the beach and 5min from Jl Dhyana Pura. ❼–❾

Wisata Beach Inn Off Jl Padma Utara ☎0361/755987. Quiet little place with just four split-level fan bungalows (each sleeps four) and balconies on both floors. ❸

Eating

In general, the most sophisticated, interesting – and expensive – **restaurants** are located in Seminyak, while Kuta and Legian are dominated by unexceptional tourist cafés and fast-food joints. The main **night market** sets up on Jalan Blambangan at the southern edge of Kuta. For a memorable, reasonably priced dining experience, take a taxi to **Jimbaran beach**, 4km south of Kuta, for the candlelit seafood barbecues prepared by the countless beachfront warung there.

Kuta and Tuban

Aromas Café Jl Legian. Delicious Lebanese, Indian and Indonesian vegetarian food – including good nasi campur for Rp25,000 – served in huge portions.

Daddy's Café Jl Dewi Sartika. Reasonably priced and very authentic Greek restaurant with an unrivalled selection of medzes, seafood platters and kebabs.

Ketupat Behind the Jonathan Gallery jewellery shop at Jl Legian 109. Superb fairly pricey menu of

exquisite Indonesian dishes based around fish, goat and chicken, plus some vegetarian options.
Kubuku Poppies 1. Big, rowdy and unfailingly popular restaurant serving a wide-ranging, well-priced menu including fried fish with basil, and beef fillet in Bali spices.
Maccaroni Club Jl Legian 52. Lounge-style dining with mellow DJ sounds, comfy armchair seating, twenty different Absolut cocktails and predominantly Italian food (pizzas from Rp60,000).
Made's Warung 1 Jl Pantai Kuta. Long-standing, quite pricey Kuta favourite whose table-sharing policy encourages sociability. Serves Indonesian and Balinese fare, including multi-dish *rijsttafels* at Rp80,000, plus cappuccino and cakes.
TJ's Poppies 1. Popular Californian/Mexican restaurant with tables set around a water garden. Mid-priced menu of fajitas, buffalo wings and enchiladas (around Rp40,000), plus margaritas and strawberry daiquiris.
Tree House Poppies 1. Cheap and tasty travellers' fare, including good fruit salads with yoghurt, filling *tempeh* burgers, juices and plenty of cocktails.
Warung Indonesia Gang Ronta. Welcoming, surfer-friendly warung (you can book G-Land tours here) where nasi campur costs just Rp5000.
Warung Murni Jl Pantai Kuta. Exceptionally cheap, old-style travellers' warung where the nasi goreng costs a bargain Rp7500 and there are just six formica tables.

Legian and Seminyak

Antique Jl Dhyana Pura. Dinner only; closed Mon. Creative but not overpriced modern-Asian cuisine, including a tasty chicken, prawn and *urap* combo for Rp28,000.
Bali Too Jl Melasti. Popular cheapie that's famous for its good-value breakfast buffets: all you can eat for Rp15,000 (daily 7.30–11.30am).
Glory Jl Legian 445. Long-running mid-priced tourists' favourite that's known for its huge Rp27,500 "outback breakfasts".
Gosha Seafood Jl Melasti 7. The most popular seafood restaurant in Legian and reasonably priced; lobster a speciality.
Ku dé Ta next to the *Oberoi* on Jl Laksmana ☎0361/736969. Bali's most talked-about restaurant has sea views that are as breathtaking as its prices (Rp135,000 for a plate of gnocchi, Rp210,000 for Australian pork ribs) and its variable modern-European food.
The Living Room About 700m beyond the *Oberoi* at Jl Petitenget 2000xx ☎0361/735735; nightly from 7pm; reservations advisable. Exquisite, upmarket, expensive pan-Asian menu (swordfish with red capiscum coulis, baby squid marinated in lemongrass), served in a romantic setting.
Warung Melati Jl Arjuna. Bargain-priced Padang-style place with a good range of ready-cooked foods (deep-fried *tahu*, curried eggs, *tempeh* chips) from which to assemble your meal.
Warung Yogya Jl Padma Utara 79. Another unpretentious Indonesian eatery serving cheap nasi campur (Rp11,000), *nasi pecel* and fried chicken.
Zanzibar Jl Pantai Arjuna (Blue Ocean beach). Good sandwiches and cakes plus fifteen different pizzas and calzones (about Rp40,000), all served with uninterrupted sea views.
Zula Jl Dhyana Pura 5. Good, mid-priced organic vegetarian fare, with macrobiotic nasi campur (Rp38,000), daily grain specials and booster juices.

Bars and clubs

Kuta-Legian-Seminyak boasts the liveliest and most diverse nightlife on the island, with many **bars and clubs** staying open till 6am. The cheapest, most traveller-friendly bars are concentrated in Kuta, with the more sophisticated expat-oriented clubs up in Legian and Seminyak, particularly around Jalan Dhyana Pura, which is the main area for gay nightlife.

All Stars Surf Café Kuta Centre, Jl Dewi Sartika 8, Tuban. Popular surf bar where bands and DJs play Top 40 hits nightly (8pm–midnight). Also has pool tables, and stages regular sumo competitions.
Apache Reggae Bar Jl Legian 146, Kuta. Dark, mellow dive where bands and DJs only play reggae. Upstairs, the *Apache Surfers' Bar* sticks to more mainstream pop. Nightly from 11pm.
Bagus Pub Poppies 2, Kuta. Large and loud tourist restaurant and video bar, popular with Australians and surfers.
Bounty Discotheque Jl Legian, just south of Poppies 2 intersection, Kuta. Infamous hub of Australian excess, housed in a replica of Captain Bligh's eighteenth-century galleon. There are videoscreens and an R&B dancefloor on the top deck, pool tables and hard-house below deck, plus a courtyard bar out front. "Arak-attack" jam jars are the signature drink (get wasted for Rp30,000), happy hour runs from 9pm–midnight, and the place

stays open 24hr.

Double Six ("66") Off the beachfront end of Jl Arjuna, Legian. Huge, lively, very popular open-fronted club that heaves to current club sounds. Nightly 11pm–6am; free before midnight, after which it's Rp30,000 including one free drink. Bungee jumping on Fri & Sat nights. Free transport from *Paddy's Pub* every Wed & Sat at 2am.

Kudos Jl Dhyana Pura, Seminyak. DJ-lounge and dance-bar that's popular with gay sophisticates, though mixed crowds are welcome. Stages regular drag, cabaret and go-go shows. Nightly from 10pm.

Paddy's Pub Jl Legian 66, just south of Poppies 2 intersection, Kuta. Part of the *Bounty* complex and just as popular, this open-walled place gets crammed with Australian drinkers and hosts frequent drinking competitions and foam parties. Daily 11am–4am; happy hour 9–11pm.

Q Bar Jl Dhyana Pura, Seminyak. Seminyak's main gay venue stages different events every night, including drag shows, cabarets and retro theme nights. Nightly 6pm till 1.30am.

Santa Fe Jl Dhyana Pura, Seminyak. Very popular bar and restaurant that gets lively quite soon after dark and has live music from cover bands several nights a week. Open 24hr.

Tubes Poppies 2, Kuta. Kuta's number one surfers' hangout serves cheap food and drink (happy hour daily 3–6pm) in its mainly open-plan, open-air space. Closes around 2am.

Listings

Airline offices See box on p.361.

ATMs There are ATMs every few hundred metres and a Moneygram agent at Bank BII in Kuta Square.

Batik classes Batik artist Heru gives three-day workshops (Rp400,000) at his Arin 93 studio at Jl Singo Sari 20, Tuban ⓣ0361/763091, ⓔarin93batik@hotmail.com.

Bookshops Several secondhand bookstores on Jl Legian and along Poppies 1, Poppies 2, Jl Benesari and Jl Padma Utara. New books from branches of Periplus inside Matahari Department Store, Kuta Square and in the *Made's Warung 2* complex, Jl Raya Seminyak.

Cinema Galleria 21 Cineplex at the Mal Bali Galeria/Planet Hollywood Complex on Jl Bypass, near the road to Sanur (ⓣ0361/767021); tickets cost Rp20,000 and most films are shown in their original language with Indonesian subtitles.

Hospitals and clinics The nearest hospitals are in Denpasar; see p.357. Most expats go to one of two reputable places on the outskirts of Kuta, both of which have English-speaking staff, A&E facilities, ambulance and medivac services: Bali International Medical Centre (BIMC) at Jl Bypass Ngurah Rai 100x ⓣ0361/761263, ⓦwww.bimcbali.com; and International SOS at Jl Bypass Ngurah Rai 24 ⓣ0361/710505, ⓦwww.sos-bali.com. Alternatively, there's the tourist-oriented Legian Clinic 1 on Jl Benesari, Kuta ⓣ0361/758503, which also offers dental services.

Internet access Available every few hundred metres, but the best include: Bali @ Cyber Café and Restaurant, Jl Pura Bagus Taruna 4, Legian; Legian Cyber Café, Jl Sahadewa 21, Legian; and Internet Explorer, Jl Dhyana Pura, Seminyak.

Pharmacies On every major shopping street, as well as next to Legian Clinic 1, Jl Benesari, Kuta; next to Bemo Corner on Jl Legian; inside Matahari Department Store, Kuta Square; and on Jl Singo Sari, Tuban.

Police The English-speaking community police, Satgas Pantai Desa Adat Kuta have a 24hr office on the beach in front of *Inna Kuta Beach Hotel* ⓣ0361/762871. The government police station is at the Jl Raya Tuban/Jl Singo Sari intersection ⓣ0361/752110.

Post office Kuta's GPO and poste restante is on indistinct, unsignposted Gang Selamat, between Jl Raya Tuban and Jl Blambangan (Mon–Thurs 8am–2pm, Fri 8am–11, Sat 8am–1pm). There are many small postal agents elsewhere in the resort, including: on the ground floor of Matahari Department Store in Kuta Square, Kuta; on Gang Ronta off Poppies 2, Kuta; and opposite *Glory* restaurant on Jl Legian, Legian.

Shopping Generally, browse the southern (Kuta) end of Jl Legian for cheaper crafts, souvenirs and surfwear, and the northern (Legian/Seminyak) end of Jl Legian for designer clothes and homewares. Matahari Department store, Kuta Square (daily 10am–10pm) for necessities, groceries, clothes, etc (the branch on Jl Legian is closed except for its games arcade). Cheap clothes, sarongs and souvenirs at Kuta "Art Market", beach end of Jl Singo Sari; along Poppies 1; and at the beach end of Poppies 2. Cheek-by-jowl sarong outlets along Jl Arjuna, Seminyak.

Spas and massage Bodyworks 1, Jl Raya Seminyak 63 ⓣ0361/730454; Sicilia Spa, Jl Arjuna ⓣ0361/736292, ⓦwww.siciliaspa.com; and Putri Bali beauty salon, next to *Wisata Beach Inn*, Jl

Padma Utara ⓣ0361/755987.

Telephone services The government wartel is inconveniently sited down at the airport, but there are dozens of private wartels in the resort, most of them open 8am–midnight.

Travel agents Lila Tours, inside *Inna Kuta Beach Hotel*, Jl Pantai Kuta ⓣ0361/761827; Perama Travel, Jl Legian 39 ⓣ0361/751551, ⓦwww.peramatour.com; and KCB Tours, Jl Raya Kuta 127 (the main road to Denpasar, on the eastern outskirts) ⓣ0361/751517 ⓦwww.kcbtours.com. Pelni boat tickets from the Pelni office, about 500m south of Supernova Supermarket at Jl Raya Tuban 299 ⓣ0361/763963.

Bukit surf beaches and Uluwatu

Just south of Kuta, southern Bali narrows to a sliver before bulging out again into the **Bukit** ("hill"), a harsh, infertile limestone plateau whose craggy coastline challenges surfers with its world-class breaks, most famously at Uluwatu and Padang Padang. There's almost no public transport round here, so you'll need to rent a car or bike from Kuta; to get to the beaches, simply follow signs for the temple, Pura Luhur Uluwatu, at Bali's southwesternmost point, until directed otherwise.

The first of the main surf beaches is **DREAMLAND**, a long stretch of stunning coast with great surf, wide, white sands and breathtakingly aquamarine waters that are fine for swimming. Access is via a signed, four-kilometre side road and dirt track, then down a long flight of steep steps. There are several warung down on the sands and a couple, including *Warung Wayan* (❷), also offer basic overnight accommodation.

Back on the main Uluwatu road, a couple of kilometres south of the Dreamland turn-off, follow signs for **PADANG PADANG**, whose surf break is considered to be one of the most exciting in Indonesia. There's roadside accommodation here, all within a few minutes' walk of the breaks, at the cheap and fairly basic *Sunny* (❷) and at the *lumbung*-style bungalows of *Ayu Guna Inn*, Jl Melasti 39 (ⓣ0815/575 6294, ⓔayugunabali@yahoo.com; ❷).

SULUBAN, location of the famous **Uluwatu surf breaks**, is signed off the Uluwatu road about 2km south of Padang Padang. Access to these breaks is either down the steep steps beside the ultra-posh *Blue Point* villas or from near *Uluwatu Resort*. There's plenty of accommodation on the clifftop above the breaks and along the roadside nearby: *Uluwatu Resort* (ⓣ0361/742 2689, ⓦwww.uluwaturesort.com; ❾) occupies a prime spot and offers beautiful rooms; the comfortable fan rooms at *Rocky Bungalows* (ⓣ081/734 6209; ❸) are just a short bike-ride from the surf; and further south towards Pura Luhur Uluwatu *The Gong* (ⓣ0815/578 4754, ⓔthegongacc@yahoo.com; ❷) surf shop and board repair has fan-cooled losmen rooms.

Pura Luhur Uluwatu

Revered since the tenth century as one of Bali's holiest and most important temples, **Pura Luhur Uluwatu** (daylight hours; Rp3000) commands a superb position on a rocky promontory 70m above the foaming surf, at the far southwestern tip of Bali, 18km south of Kuta. As a directional temple, or *kayangan jagat*, Pura Luhur Uluwatu is the guardian of the southwest and is dedicated to the spirits of the sea; it's also a state rather than a village temple and so has influence over all the people of Bali, not just the local villagers or ancestors. Despite all this, the temple structure itself lacks magnificence, being relatively small, and its greyish-white coral bricks for the most part unadorned. Most tourists come to Pura Luhur at **sunset**, when the setting is at its most dramatic and there's a performance of the *kecak* and fire dance (daily 6–7pm; Rp35,000).

Sanur

Stretching down the southeast coast just 18km northeast of Ngurah Rai Airport, **SANUR** is an appealing, more peaceful alternative to Kuta, with a long, fairly decent white-sand beach, lots of attractive accommodation in all price brackets and a distinct village atmosphere. There are plenty of restaurants and some bars, but the nightlife is pretty tame. A huge expanse of shore gets exposed at low tide and the reef lies only about 1km offshore at high tide. The currents beyond the reef are dangerously strong, which makes it almost impossible to swim here at low tide, but at other times swimming is fine and watersports are popular. An esplanade runs the length of Sanur's five-kilometre shoreline: the busiest stretch of beach is in the north, between the *Inna Grand Bali Beach* and the *Gazebo Hotel*, while the southern areas are quieter but still pleasant.

Sanur's two biggest **water sports** operators are the Jeladi Wilis Boat Co-operative (ⓣ0361/284206) in front of the *Inna Grand Bali Beach* in north Sanur, and the Blue Oasis Beach Club at *Hotel Sanur Beach* in the south (ⓣ0361/288011). They both rent out kayaks, windsurfers and jet skis, and do parasailing. Sanur is quite a good place to learn to **dive**, as the local diving sites are close by, if unexciting. All Sanur dive centres, including Bali International Diving Professionals at Jl Danau Poso 26, southern Sanur (ⓣ0361/285065 ⓦwww.bidp-balidiving.com), and Crystal Divers at Jl Duyung 25, south-central Sanur (ⓣ0361/286737, ⓦwww.crystal-divers.com), run certificated diving courses (US$300–380) and one-day diving excursions (including tanks and weights only) for US$70–120.

Practicalities

The fastest and most direct way of getting to Sanur is by **tourist shuttle bus**. Perama (ⓦwww.peramatour.com) runs several shuttle buses a day between Sanur and major destinations on Bali and Lombok (see "Travel details", p.486); their main agent in Sanur, and their drop-off and pick-up point, is Warung Pojok minimarket, Jl Hang Tuah 31, north Sanur (ⓣ0361/285592): bemos run from here to Jalan Danau Tamblingan. Other Perama ticket outlets include Nagasari Tours (ⓣ0361/288096) opposite *Griya Santrian* hotel, Jl Danau Tamblingan 102, and Tunas Tour, next to *Resto Ming* on the southern stretch of the same road at Jl Danau Tamblingan 105 (ⓣ0361/288581).

The only direct **bemos** to Sanur leave from Denpasar. Dark-green bemos from Denpasar's Kereneng terminal run to north Sanur (15min; Rp3000), where they will drop passengers just outside the *Inna Grand Bali Beach* compound at the Ngurah Rai Bypass/Jalan Hang Tuah junction if asked; otherwise, they usually head down Jalan Danau Beratan and Jalan Danau Buyan, before continuing down Jalan Danau Tamblingan to the *Trophy Pub Centre* in south Sanur. Direct dark-blue bemos from Denpasar's Tegal terminal run via Jalan Teuku Umar and Renon (30min; Rp3000) and then follow the same route as the green Kereneng ones, depending on passenger requests. To travel between **Kuta** and Sanur by bemo, you need to change at Tegal terminal; transport to and from **Ubud** involves changing bemos twice in Denpasar, at Kereneng and Batubulan terminals (see p.357).

Sanur is the main departure point for **boats** to **Nusa Lembongan**, which leave from a jetty at the eastern end of Jalan Hang Tuah in north Sanur. There are currently two public services a day, for which tickets are sold from the beachfront office near the *Ananda Hotel*; these depart daily at 8am (Rp33,000) and 10.30am (Rp43,000); and take one hour thirty minutes. There is also one Perama shuttle boat, which should be booked a day ahead (daily 10.30am; 1hr 30min; Rp50,000). See p.386 for full details.

The Sanur–Tegal and Sanur–Kereneng public bemos are also useful for **getting around** Sanur and cost Rp2000 for short hops. Otherwise, flag down a metered **taxi** (Rp4000 flagfall, then Rp2000/km), or bargain hard with a transport tout; a ride to

Kuta in a metered taxi costs about Rp30,000. The touts also **rent cars** and motorbikes (see "Getting around", p.238 for price guides), and some hotels rent bicycles.

Accommodation

There's a surprisingly decent amount of low-budget homestay **accommodation** in Sanur, and many of the mid-range hotels are also small, personable places

Agung & Sue Watering Hole 1 Jl Hang Tuah 37, north Sanur ⓣ0361/288289, ⓔwatering-hole_sanurbali@yahoo.com. Traveller-friendly place with good-quality fan and a/c rooms only 250m from the beach. Very handy for boats to Nusa Lembongan. ❷–❸

Enny's Homestay Jl Danau Tamblingan 172, south-central Sanur ⓣ0361/287363. Seven immaculate modern losmen rooms (some a/c) behind the family shop. ❷–❸

Jambu Inn Jl Hang Tuah 57, north Sanur ⓣ0361/286501, ⓔjbadwkbl@denpasar.wasantara.net.id. Tiny, quiet place with just seven fan and a/c bungalows, many with a separate living area, set round a cute garden with pool and gazebo. ❸–❹

Keke Homestay Gang Keke 3, off Jl Danau Tamblingan 96, central Sanur ⓣ0361/287282. Tiny losmen that's basic but good and offers five simple fan rooms. ❷

Luisa Homestay Jl Danau Tamblingan 40, central Sanur ⓣ0361/289673. Elementary but cheerful accommodation, some with hot water, that's among the cheapest in Sanur. ❷

Respati Bali Jl Danau Tamblingan 33, central Sanur ⓣ0361/288427, ⓔbrespati@indo.net.id. Large, well-kept, good-value a/c bungalows in a narrow compound, with pool, that runs down to the sea. ❼

Hotel Segara Agung Jl Duyung 43, south Sanur ⓣ0361/288446, ⓦwww.segaraagung.com. Nice fan and a/c bungalows and a spacious garden with pool in a very quiet, residential spot just two minutes' walk from the beach. ❺–❼

Swastika Jl Danau Tamblingan 128, central Sanur ⓣ0361/288693, ⓦwww.swastika-bungalows.com. Deservedly popular, variously styled, fan and a/c bungalows set around a delightful garden with two big pools. Named after the ancient Buddhist symbol, not the Nazi emblem. ❻–❼

Yulia Homestay 1 Jl Danau Tamblingan 38, central Sanur ⓣ0361/288089. Attractive, terraced, fan-cooled bungalows at the largest, longest-running and best of the three similar losmen in this cluster. ❷

Eating

Many **restaurants** offer free transport for diners within the Sanur area: for these places, we've listed the phone number. Several restaurants on Jalan Danau Tamblingan stage free **traditional dance** shows for diners, including *Penjor* near Hardy's supermarket; *Swastika Garden 2* in central Sanur; and *Legong* in south Sanur. The **night market** sets up at the Jalan Danau Tamblingan/Jalan Sindhu intersection in north Sanur.

Bonsai Café Beachfront walkway just north of *La Taverna* hotel, access off Jl Danau Tamblingan, central Sanur. Breezy seafront restaurant and bar (open till late) that serves standard nasi goreng, pizza, pasta and seafood (Rp25,000–45,000), plus cocktails.

Resto Ming Jl Danau Tamblingan 105, south Sanur ⓣ0361/281948. Deservedly popular place that's known for its French cuisine (most dishes Rp30,000–65,000) and seafood.

Sari Bundo Jl Danau Poso, Blanjong. Typical, very cheap *masakan Padang* place serving spicy Sumatran dishes 24 hours a day.

Segara Agung Beachfront next to *Desa Segara*, central Sanur ⓣ0361/288574. Tree-shaded tables on the sand make this a great spot for lunch, and on Saturday nights there's a kids' dance performance. Serves everything from lobster and *babi guling* to seafood and Chinese standards (Rp20,000–45,000). All profits go to local schools and clinics.

The Village Opposite *La Taverna* hotel, Jl Danau Tamblingan, central Sanur. Classy menu of unusual, mid-priced dishes (Rp25,000–45,000) including spicy chicken, macadamia nut ice cream and European breads.

Warung Agung Jl Danau Tamblingan 97, south Sanur ⓣ0361/288029. Cheerful little place serving well-priced tourist fare (Rp14,000–37,000), including Balinese grilled chicken, plenty of seafood, and a *rijsttafel*-style Balinese platter.

Warung Blanjong Jl Danau Poso 78, south Sanur. Good, cheap Balinese dishes (Rp15,000–30,000), including lots of vegetarian options.

Bars and live music

There are several **bar-restaurants** in Sanur, some of which stage live music, but for clubs you'll need to head to Kuta.

The Cat and the Fiddle Opposite *Hotel Sanur Beach*, Jl Cemara, south Sanur. Inviting, expat-oriented bar-restaurant serving draught Guinness, and hosting live Irish music nights every Tuesday from 8pm.
Jazz Bar & Grille Komplek Pertokoan Sanur Raya 15, next to *KFC* at the Jl Ngurah Rai Bypass/Jl Hang Tuah crossroads, north Sanur. Some of Bali's best jazz, blues and pop bands play here every night from 9.30pm (8pm on Sundays); food is served upstairs. Daily 8am–1am.
Lazer Sports Bar Opposite *Gazebo Hotel* at Jl Danau Tamblingan 68, central Sanur. Rowdy bar dominated by big-screen TV sports coverage. Has pool tables and occasional live music.
Matahari Beach Bar Beachfront end of Jl Sindhu, north-central Sanur. Beachfront bar-restaurant, with a pool table. Stages live music and occasional dance performances from 7pm. Closes around 1am.
The Trophy In the *Trophy Pub Centre*, Jl Danau Tamblingan 49, south Sanur. Typical expat pub with a darts board, pool table and satellite TV. Live music (Wed, Fri & Sat) and Western bar food.

Listings

Airline offices See p.361.
Banks and exchange There are ATMs and exchange facilities all over the resort.
Bookshops New books for sale inside the arcades at the *Inna Grand Bali Beach* and the *Hotel Sanur Beach*, at the Gazebo Piazza's Internet centre and in Hardy's supermarket on central Jl Danau Tamblingan.
Embassies and consulates Most embassies are in Jakarta (see p.275), but there's a UK consulate at Jl Tirta Nadi 20A, Sanur ⓣ0361/270601, ⓔbcbali@dps.centrin.net.id, and US and Australian consulates in Denpasar (see p.357).
Hospitals and clinics The 24hr tourist-oriented Sanur Clinic at Jl Danau Tamblingan 27, central Sanur ⓣ0361/282678 has English-speaking staff and a dental service and will respond to emergency call-outs. Or try the doctor at the *Inna Grand Bali Beach* ⓣ0361/288511, or the *Bali Hyatt* ⓣ0361/288271. Expats tend to use the two international clinics on the edge of Kuta (see p.366); the nearest hospitals are all in Denpasar (see p.357).
Internet access At Go, opposite *Besakih* hotel at Jl Danau Tamblingan 84, central Sanur; and in the nearby Gazebo Piazza.
Pharmacies Several on Jl Danau Tamblingan, plus one inside Hardy's Supermarket on central Jl Danau Tamblingan.
Police The police station is on the Ngurah Rai Bypass in north Sanur, just south of the *Paradise Plaza* hotel ⓣ0361/288597.
Post office Sanur's main post office is on Jl Danau Buyan, north-central Sanur. There are additional postal agents inside the Trophy Centre on Jl Cemara in south Sanur, and opposite *Respati* hotel at Jl Danau Tamblingan 66, central Sanur (poste restante here c/o Agen Pos, Jl Danau Tamblingan 66, Sanur 80228; Mon–Fri 8.30am–5.30pm, Sat 8.30am–1pm).
Telephone services Direct-dial public telephones in the basement shopping arcade of the *Inna Grand Bali Beach* in north Sanur.
Travel agents International and domestic flights, plus day-trips, from Sumanindo Tour, Jl Danau Tamblingan 22, central Sanur ⓣ0361/288570 JBA, inside the compound of the *Diwangkara Hotel*, Jl Hang Tuah 54, north Sanur ⓣ0361/286501, ⓔjbadwkbl@denpasar.wasantara.net.id; Nagasari Tours, Jl Danau Tamblingan 102, central Sanur ⓣ0361/288096, ⓔnagasari@mega.net.id; and Tunas Tour, next to *Resto Ming*, Jl Danau Tamblingan 107, south Sanur ⓣ0361/288581, ⓔtunas@denpasar.wasantara.net.id.

Pura Tanah Lot and around

Dramatically marooned on a craggy, wave-lashed rock sitting just off the coast about 30km northwest of Kuta, **Pura Tanah Lot** (Rp3300, kids Rp1800) really does deserve its reputation as one of Bali's top sights. Framed by frothing white surf and glistening black sand, its elegant multi-tiered shrines have become the unofficial symbol of Bali, appearing on a vast range of tourist souvenirs and attracting huge crowds of visitors every day, particularly around sunset. The temple is said to have been founded in the sixteenth century by the wandering Hindu priest Nirartha and is one of the most holy places on Bali. Only bona fide devotees are allowed to climb the stairway carved out of the rock face and enter the compounds; everyone else is confined to the base of the rock.

Although there are occasional bright-blue **bemos** from Denpasar's Ubung terminal direct to Tanah Lot, you'll probably have to go via **Kediri**, 12km east of the temple on the main Denpasar–Tabanan road. All Ubung (Denpasar)–Gilimanuk bemos drop passengers at Kediri bemo terminal (about R3000; 30min), where you should change on to a Kediri–Tanah Lot bemo (more frequent in the morning; about Rp5000; 25min). Alternatively, join one of the numerous tours to Tanah Lot that operate out of all major tourist resorts.

If you get stuck between bemos, you can **stay** at the rudimentary but prettily located *Pondok Wisata Astiti Graha* (ⓣ0361/812955; ❷), about 500m up the road from the Tanah Lot car park. With your own transport – or time to negotiate several bemo changes – the very spacious, laid-back *Bali Wisata Bungalows* (ⓣ0361/7443561, ⓦwww.baliwisatabungalows.com; ❹–❻) on wild and remote **YEH GANGGA** beach make a much more enjoyable place to spend a few days. Yeh Gangga is less than two hours' walk northwest along the coast from Tanah Lot (easier in reverse), or about 14km southwest of Kediri by road: take a bemo from Kediri to nearby Tabanan's Pesiapan terminal, then connect on to the (infrequent) Yeh Gangga service, or charter one for about Rp15,000.

Gunung Batukau and Jatiluwih

With your own transport, it's well worth making a day-trip to the lower slopes of Bali's second-highest mountain, **Gunung Batukau** (2276m), site of an atmospheric and important garden temple, and close to some spectacular rice-terraces. The 21-kilometre approach road begins in the city of **TABANAN**, about 25km northwest of Denpasar, from where you should follow signs for Pura Luhur Batukau, via Penatahan and Wongayagede. Usually silent except for its resident orchestra of cicadas, frogs and prolific bird-life, **Pura Luhur Batukau** (donation requested) is a charming complex of grassy courtyards planted with flowering shrubs and surrounded by the montane forest that carpets Gunung Batukau. It is Bali's directional temple for the west and the focus of many pilgrimages. The large square pond to the east of the main compound honours the gods of Lake Tamblingan, and its tiny island shrine is only accessible to priests.

If accompanied by a guide from Pura Luhur Batukau, it is possible to **climb Gunung Batukau** from the trailhead near the temple, but only from April through October. It takes four to six hours to reach the summit and three to five hours to return; guides charge Rp700,000 per small group for a day hike or Rp1,000,000 if camping overnight: trekkers must bring all their own food, water and sleeping bags.

The tiny village of **WONGAYAGEDE**, about 2km south of the temple car park, makes a cool and enjoyable **place to stay**, with awesome morning views of the mountain and lots of tracks through surrounding ricefields to explore. You'll get a genuine homestay welcome and a rustic cabin at *Warung Kaja* (ⓣ0811/398052, ⓔpkaler@dps.centrin.net.id; ❸), about 750m east along the Wongayagede–Jatiluwih road, or more sophisticated accommodation at the inspirational, eco-minded *Prana Dewi* (ⓣ08133/866 0154, ⓦwww.balipranaresort.com; ❻–❼) on the temple road.

The road to **JATILUWIH** branches east from Wongayagede about 2.5km south of Pura Luhur Batukau and takes you through some of the most famous rice-paddy vistas on Bali, offering expansive panoramas over the gently sloping terraces and several perfectly positioned restaurants from which to soak it all up. About 11km from Wongayagede, you reach the **SENGANAN** junction, where the northeast (left) fork brings you to the main Denpasar–Bedugul–Singaraja artery at **PACUNG** 7.5km away.

Southwest surf beaches

West of Tabanan, the Denpasar–Gilimanuk coast road passes a couple of appealingly low-key black-sand **surf beaches**, both of them served by Denpasar (Ubung)–Gilimanuk bemos. The current can be severe all along this coast, so check locally before swimming.

About 26km west of Tabanan, the village of **LALANG LINGGAH** gives access to **Balian beach**, where welcoming little *Pondok Pisces* (ⓣ08133/879 7722, ⓦwww.pondokpisces.com; ❸–❻), has five idiosyncratic bungalows just 300m from the sea (follow signs for nearby *Gajah Mina* from the main road).

Twenty-five kilometres further west, **MEDEWI** beach (about 2hr by bemo from Ubung) is known for its light current and fairly benign waves, making it a popular spot for novice surfers. The most popular accommodation here is *Homestay G'de* (ⓣ0812/397 6668; 1), whose exceptionally cheap warung sits right on the shore and gives access to eight primitive but perfectly acceptable en-suite rooms.

Ubud and around

Ever since the German artist Walter Spies arrived here in 1928, **UBUD** has been a magnet for any tourist with the slightest curiosity about Balinese arts. The people of Ubud and adjacent villages really do still paint, carve, dance and make music, and hardly a day goes by without there being a festival in the area. However, although it's fashionable to characterize Ubud as the real Bali, especially in contrast with Kuta, it actually bears little resemblance to a typical Balinese village. Cappuccino cafés, riverside bungalows and craft shops crowd its central marketplace, chic expat homes occupy some of the most panoramic locations, and side streets are dotted with spas and alternative treatment centres. There is major (mostly tasteful) development along the central Jalan Monkey Forest (now officially known as Jalan Wanara Wana), and the peripheries of the village have merged so completely into its neighbouring hamlets that Ubud also now encompasses Campuhan, Sanggingan, Penestanan, Nyuhkuning, Peliatan, Pengosekan and Padang Tegal.

Arrival

Perama runs several **shuttle bus** services a day to Ubud from the major tourist centres on Bali and Lombok; all services terminate at the Perama office at the southern end of Jalan Hanoman in Padang Tegal, about 750m from the bottom of Jalan Monkey Forest and 2.5km from the central market. There are no local bemos or metered taxis from this inconvenient spot, so you'll either have to pay Rp5000 extra for the Perama drop-off service, negotiate a ride with a transport tout, or walk. If you travel to Ubud with an independent shuttle bus operator (from Kuta or Lovina for example), you may get dropped off more centrally.

Arriving in Ubud by **public bemo**, you'll stop at the central market, on the junction of Jalan Raya (the main road) and Jalan Monkey Forest (signed as "Jalan Wanara Wana").

Information and getting around

Ubud **Tourist Information** on Jalan Raya (daily 8am–8pm; ⓣ0361/973285) posts dance-performance schedules and details of upcoming festivals. If you're planning to do any local walks or cycle rides, buy the annually updated *Bali Pathfinder* **map** from any bookstore.

Keep Walking Tours, alongside Tegun Galeri, Jl Hanoman 44 (ⓣ0361/970992, ⓦwww.balispirit.com/tours/bali_tour_keep_walking.html), runs guided cultural and ecological **walks** as well as sunrise treks up Gunung Agung ($99) and Gunung

Moving on from Ubud

The easiest way to get **to the airport** from Ubud is by shuttle bus (Rp20,000 per person); transport touts charge about Rp100,000 per car. Airport information is on p.362.

By shuttle bus

Tickets for Perama **shuttle buses** to Bali's main tourist destinations, as well as to Lombok (see "Travel details", p.486), are sold by most tour operators. Perama do pick-ups from central Ubud and from their office on southern Jalan Hanoman (☎0361/973316, ⓦwww.peramatour.com). If travelling to northwest Bali, take a shuttle bus to Lovina and then change on to the bemo system.

By bemo

All **bemos** depart from central Jalan Raya: the east- and southbound bemos leave from the central marketplace, and the north- and westbound ones from in front of the tourist information office. There's a regular service between Ubud and Kintamani (brown bemos usually; 1hr), and frequent turquoise and orange bemos go to Gianyar (20min) via Goa Gajah (10min), where you can make connections to Padang Bai (for Lombok), Candi Dasa, Singaraja and Lovina. Any journey south, to Kuta or Sanur, involves an initial bemo ride to Denpasar's Batubulan terminal (50min), plus at least one cross-city connection (see p.358). To reach western Bali and Java by bemo, you'll need to take an equally convoluted route via Batubulan.

Batur ($49). Numerous places on Jalan Monkey Forest rent out **motorbikes** and **cars**, including Three Brothers (☎0361/973240), which has two outlets; or try Ary's Business and Travel Service (☎0361/973130) on Jalan Raya.

There are no metered taxis in Ubud, so you need to negotiate with the ubiquitous **transport touts**: expect to pay around Rp8000 for a ride from the Perama office to Jalan Bisma, or around Rp200,000 for a day-trip to Kintamani. You can use the **public bemos** for short hops around the area (Rp2000): for Campuhan/Sanggingan, just flag down any bemo heading west, such as the turquoise ones going to Payangan.

Accommodation

Jalan Monkey Forest is the most central **place to stay**, and also the most congested, but accommodation on the tiny adjacent roads (Jalan Karna, Jalan Maruti, Jalan Gautama, Jalan Kajeng and Jalan Bisma) is more traditional and more peaceful. Staying in **Peliatan** or **Penestanan** will be more of a village experience, and Penestanan's ridgetop bungalows also offer great high-level views (note, however, that some are inaccessible to cars). **Campuhan/Sanggingan** is a bit of a hike from the main restaurants and shops, while **Nyuhkuning** is a good in-between option, with fine paddy-field views and only a ten-minute walk from Jalan Monkey Forest (though you need to walk or cycle through the forest itself after dark).

Central Ubud and Padang Tegal

Except where stated, all the losmen listed here are marked on the Central Ubud map (see p.375).

Artja Inn Jl Kajeng 9 ☎0361/974425. Classic, peaceful losmen offering six simple but pleasant bamboo-walled cottages with open-roofed, cold-water mandi. ❷

Donald Jl Gautama 9 ☎0361/977156. Tiny, well-run and very cheap sparsely furnished bungalows (two with hot water) in a secluded garden compound. ❶–❷

Gusti's Garden Bungalows Jl Kajeng 27 ☎0361/973311, ⓔgustigarden@yahoo.com; see map on pp.374–375. Fifteen pleasant, better-than-average losmen rooms, all with hot water, set

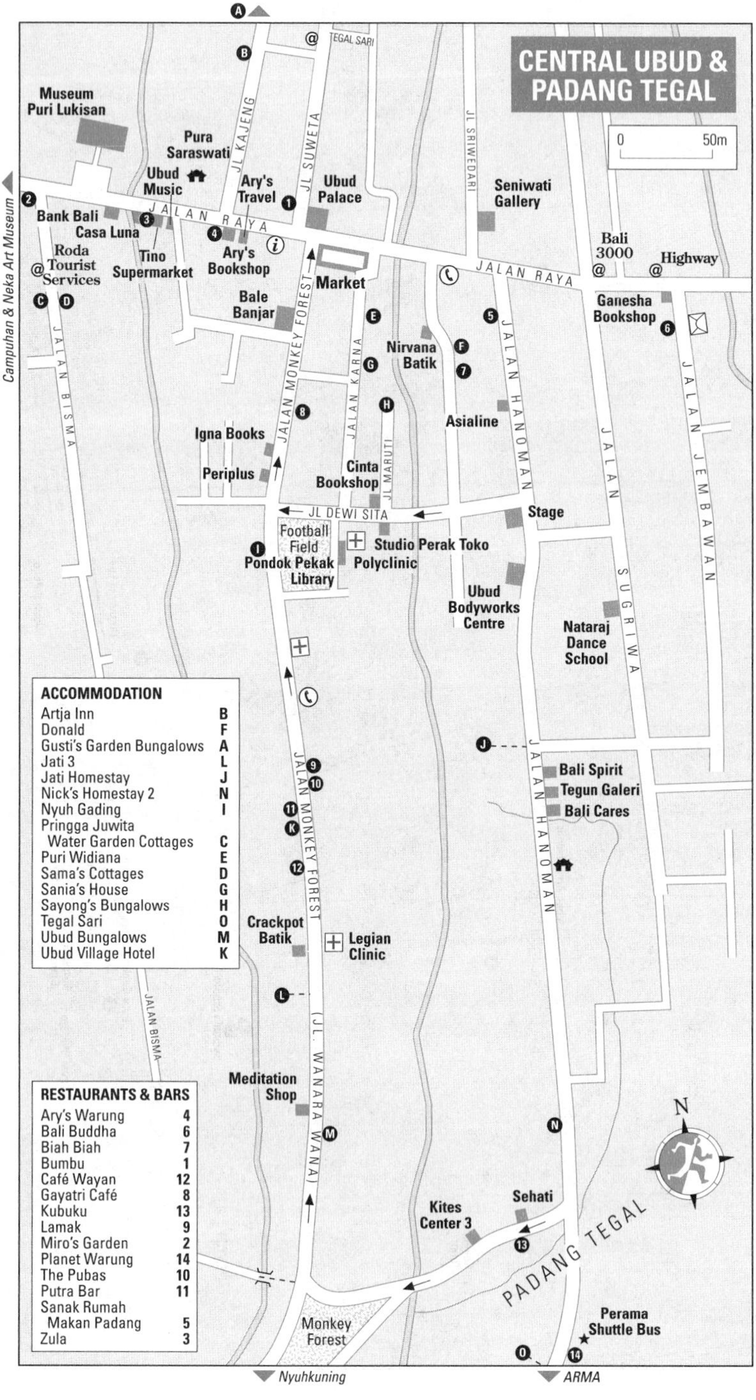

CENTRAL UBUD & PADANG TEGAL

0 50m

Museum Puri Lukisan
Pura Saraswati
Ubud Music
JL KAJENG
Ary's Travel
JL SUWETA
Ubud Palace
TEGAL SARI
JL SRIWEDARI
Seniwati Gallery
Bank Bali
Casa Luna
JALAN RAYA
Tino Supermarket
Roda Tourist Services
Ary's Bookshop
Market
Bale Banjar
Bali 3000
Highway
Ganesha Bookshop
Campuhan & Neka Art Museum
Peliatan
JALAN BISMA
JALAN MONKEY FOREST
JALAN KARNA
Nirvana Batik
JALAN HANOMAN
JALAN JEMBAWAN
JL MARUTI
Asialine
Igna Books
Periplus
Cinta Bookshop
JALAN SUGRIWA
JL DEWI SITA
Stage
Football Field
Studio Perak Toko
Polyclinic
Pondok Pekak Library
Ubud Bodyworks Centre
Nataraj Dance School
Bali Spirit
Tegun Galeri
Bali Cares
Crackpot Batik
Legian Clinic
(JL. WANARA WANA)
Meditation Shop
Kites Center 3
Sehati
PADANG TEGAL
Monkey Forest
Perama Shuttle Bus
Nyuhkuning
ARMA
N

ACCOMMODATION

Artja Inn	B
Donald	F
Gusti's Garden Bungalows	A
Jati 3	L
Jati Homestay	J
Nick's Homestay 2	N
Nyuh Gading	I
Pringga Juwita Water Garden Cottages	C
Puri Widiana	E
Sama's Cottages	D
Sania's House	G
Sayong's Bungalows	H
Tegal Sari	O
Ubud Bungalows	M
Ubud Village Hotel	K

RESTAURANTS & BARS

Ary's Warung	4
Bali Buddha	6
Biah Biah	7
Bumbu	1
Café Wayan	12
Gayatri Café	8
Kubuku	13
Lamak	9
Miro's Garden	2
Planet Warung	14
The Pubas	10
Putra Bar	11
Sanak Rumah Makan Padang	5
Zula	3

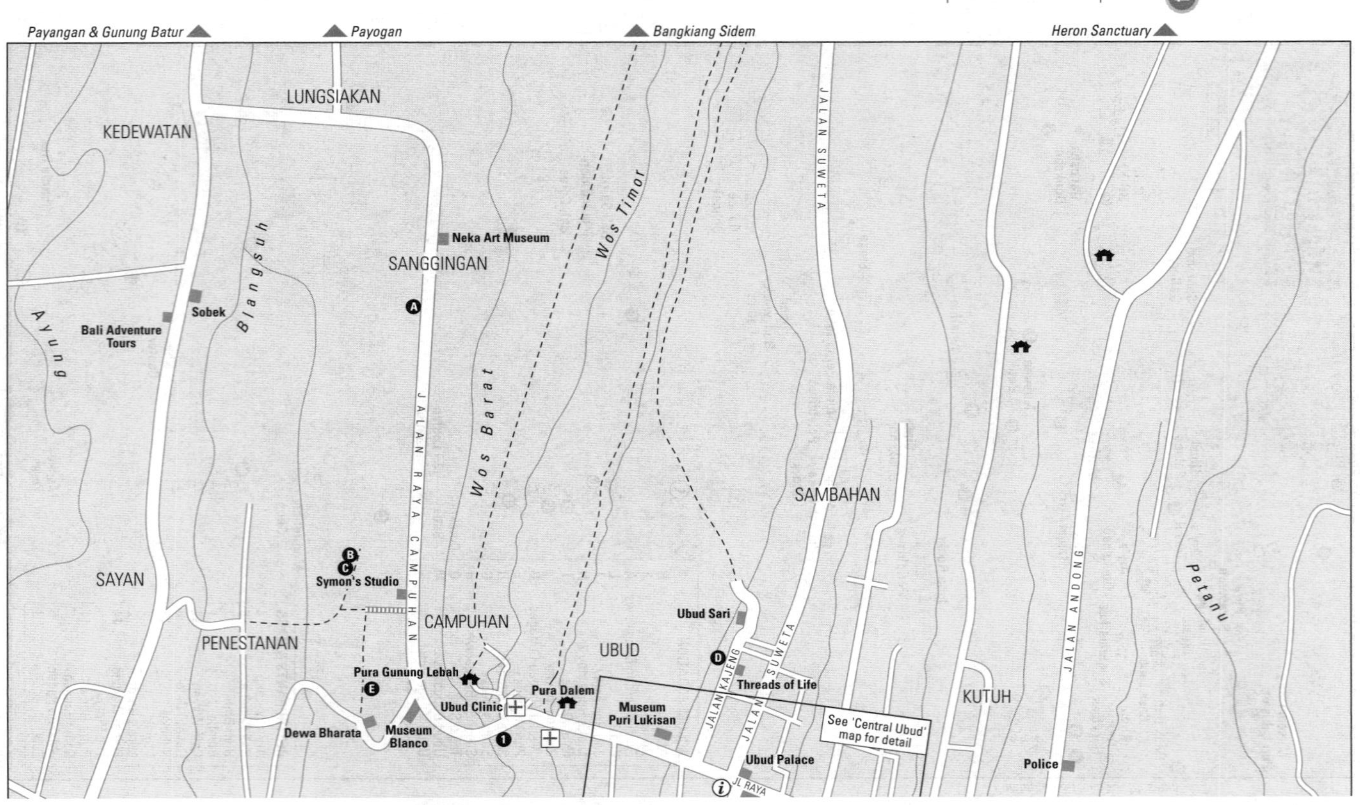
Payangan & Gunung Batur
Payogan
Bangkiang Sidem
Heron Sanctuary
LUNGSIAKAN
KEDEWATAN
SANGGINGAN
Neka Art Museum
Wos Timor
Wos Barat
JALAN SUWETA
Sobek
Bali Adventure Tours
Blangsuh
Ayung
JALAN RAYA CAMPUHAN
SAMBAHAN
SAYAN
Symon's Studio
CAMPUHAN
PENESTANAN
UBUD
Ubud Sari
JALAN KAJENG
JALAN SUWETA
Threads of Life
Pura Gunung Lebah
Pura Dalem
Ubud Clinic
Museum Puri Lukisan
See 'Central Ubud' map for detail
Dewa Bharata
Museum Blanco
Ubud Palace
JL RAYA
KUTUH
Police
JALAN ANDONG
Petanu

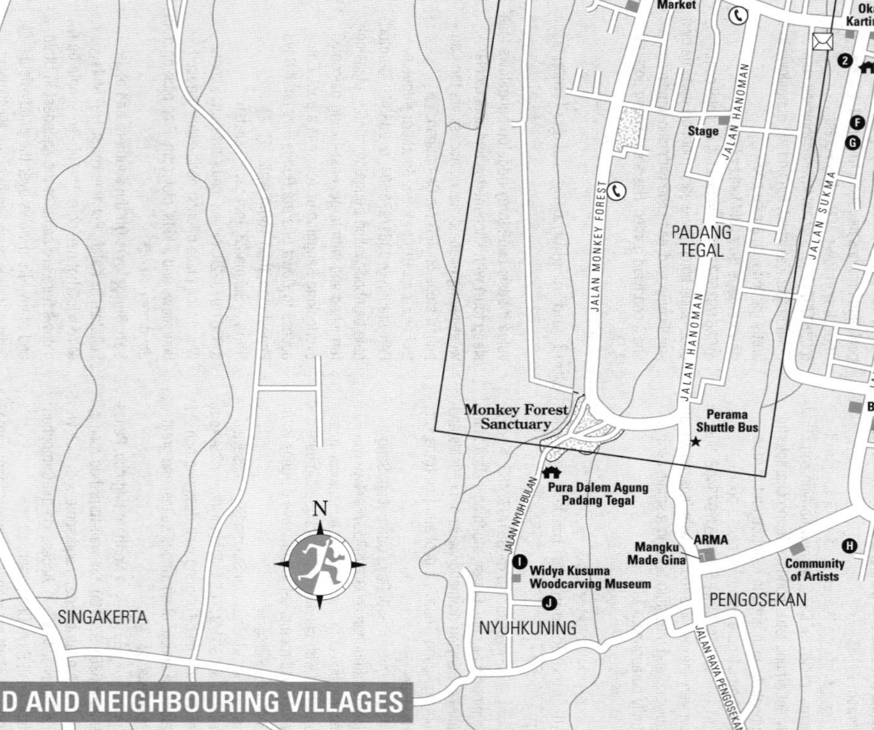
UBUD AND NEIGHBOURING VILLAGES
Pejeng
Gianyar & Goa Gajah
Lodtunduh
Batuan & Denpasar
RESTAURANTS & BARS
Jazz Café 2
Murni's Warung 1
ACCOMMODATION
Alam Jiwa J
Ananda Cottages A
Family Guest House G
Gusti's Garden Bungalows D
Kori Agung Bungalow C
Londo 2 B
Penestanan Bungalows E
Rona F
Sari Bungalows H
Swasti 2 Hideaway
Nyuhkuning I
Balé Banjar
Market
Oka Kartini's
Pharmacy
Bank Danamon
Stage
Pura Dalem
JALAN HANOMAN
JALAN SUKMA
JALAN PELIATAN
JALAN MONKEY FOREST
PADANG TEGAL
PELIATAN
Puri Agung Stage
Pura Agung
Agung Rai Gallery
Monkey Forest Sanctuary
Perama Shuttle Bus
Pura Dalem Agung Padang Tegal
JALAN NYUH BULAN
The Duck Man
TEGES
Mangku Made Gina
ARMA
Community of Artists
Widya Kusuma Woodcarving Museum
PENGOSEKAN
NYUHKUNING
SINGAKERTA
JALAN RAYA PENGOSEKAN
Museum Rudana
N
0
1km

around a swimming pool. ❹

Jati 3 Off Jl Monkey Forest ⓣ & ⓕ0361/973249. Good-quality losmen-style bungalows in a courtyard, plus four huge, split-level, riverside bungalows with big windows. ❸–❹

Jati Homestay Jl Hanoman ⓣ0361/977701, ⓔasa_dewa2000@yahoo.com. Comfortable bungalows facing the rice paddies. Run by a family of painters. ❷–❹

Nick's Homestay 2 Jl Hanoman 57 ⓣ0361/975526, ⓔnicksp@indosat.net.id. Seven clean, very good-value rooms in a tidy, losmen-style garden compound. Guests can use the pool at *Nick's 1* on Jl Monkey Forest. ❷

Nyuh Gading Jl Monkey Forest ⓣ0361/973410. Seven standard bungalows set in a pretty garden behind a restaurant, plus one family house with kitchen. ❷–❹

Pringga Juwita Water Garden Cottages Jl Bisma ⓣ0361/978274, ⓦwww.fibrainn.com. Prettily set among lotus ponds, offering characterful bungalows with antique furniture and garden bathrooms (some with a/c), plus a pool. ❼–❽

Puri Widiana Jl Karna 5 ⓣ0361/973406. Just four very inexpensive rooms, with fans, cold-water showers, and mosquito nets, in a small, central family compound. ❷

Sama's Cottages Jl Bisma ⓣ0361/973481, ⓦwww.balilife.com/sama's. Lovely, ultra-typical Ubud hideaway of eight fan-cooled brick and thatch cottages built on steep tiers in a river gully. Also has a tiny pool. ❺

Sania's House Jl Karna 7 ⓣ0361/975535. Efficiently run if rather congested place with good, clean bungalows (some a/c) and a small pool. ❷–❻

Sayong's Bungalows Jl Maruti ⓣ0361/973305. Seven simply furnished bungalows with hot water, set in a typical losmen garden, with a swimming pool across the lane. ❷–❸

Tegal Sari Jl Hanoman ⓣ0361/973318, ⓦwww.tegalsari-ubud.com. Exceptionally appealing, tastefully furnished rooms, all with both fan and a/c, strung out alongside the paddy-fields. Also has a pool, and provides free local transport. ❻–❼

Ubud Bungalows Jl Monkey Forest ⓣ0361/971298, ⓔw_widnyana@hotmail.com. Comfortable, detached, fan and a/c bungalows in a pretty garden with a nice pool. ❻

Ubud Village Hotel Jl Monkey Forest ⓣ0361/975571, ⓦwww.ubudvillagehotel.com. Good-value hotel where each room occupies its own small compound, complete with chic furnishings, a/c and a courtyard garden. Has a swimming pool. ❾

The outskirts

All listed losmen are marked on the "Ubud and neighbouring villages" map (see pp.376–377).

Alam Jiwa Nyuhkuning ⓣ0361/977463, ⓦwww.alamindahbali.com. Classy, stunningly sited bungalows, enjoying dramatic views of ricefields and Gunung Agung. There's a pool and free transport into Ubud. ❽–❾

Ananda Cottages Jl Raya Campuhan, Sanggingan/Campuhan ⓣ0361/975376, ⓦwww.anandaubud.com. Fan and a/c bungalows, most furnished with carved doors, antique furniture and garden bathrooms, set in attractive gardens with a pool. ❼–❽

Family Guest House Jl Sukma 39, Tebesaya, Peliatan ⓣ0361/974054, ⓔfamilyhouse@telkom.net. Friendly place offering well-designed bungalows, a couple of enormous suites, and great breakfasts. ❷–❻

Kori Agung Bungalow Northern ridgetop, Penestanan ⓣ0361/973100. Six well-furnished rooms, each with a large terrace and some with nice westerly paddy-field views. Access via the Campuhan steps on Jl Raya Campuhan. ❸–❹

Londo 2 Northern ridgetop, Penestanan; same contact details as for the less scenic *Londo Ricefield* so specify *Londo 2* ⓣ0361/976548, ⓦwww.londobungalows.bigstep.com. Amazingly good-value if basic two-storey ridgetop bungalows (can sleep four) with kitchenettes and spectacular west-facing ricefield views. Access via the Campuhan steps on Jl Raya Campuhan. ❷

Penestanan Bungalows Southern ridgetop, Penestanan ⓣ0361/975604, ⓕ288341. Comfortable bamboo-walled bungalow rooms, pleasingly furnished and with large, east-facing balconies overlooking Sanggingan. Also has a pool. Car access to *Dewa Bharata Bungalows* on Jl Raya Penestanan, then 100m walk. ❹–❺

Rona Jl Sukma 23, Tebesaya, Peliatan ⓣ0361/973229, ⓔrona_chicken@yahoo.com. Welcoming place offering good-value terraced bungalows and a kids' playroom. Free pick-up from Ubud area. ❷–❹

Sari Bungalows Off the southern end of Jl Peliatan, Br Kalah, Peliatan ⓣ0361/975541, ⓔironkic@hotmail.com. The fifteen simple bungalows here are some of the cheapest in Ubud and many afford views over the paddy-fields. ❶

Swasti 2 Hideaway Nyuhkuning Nyuhkuning ⓣ0361/974079, ⓔswasti2@hotmail.com. Six large, comfortably furnished rooms (some a/c), all with hot water and ricefield views. There's a pool too. ❻–❼

Central Ubud and adjacent villages

The major attractions of Ubud and adjacent villages are their art museums, galleries and craft workshops. The oldest and most central art collection is the **Museum Puri Lukisan** on Jalan Raya (daily 9am–5pm; Rp20,000; ⓦwww.mpl-ubud.com), which, though set in prettily landscaped grounds, suffers from dim lighting and poor labelling and is outshone by the Neka Art Museum in nearby Campuhan. In central Ubud, the well-curated **Seniwati Gallery of Art by Women**, Jl Sriwedari 2B (Tues–Sun 9am–5pm; free; ⓦwww.seniwatigallery.com), is more rewarding. Established to redress the absence of works by women artists in nearly all Bali's major exhibition spaces, it displays, explains and sells pictures by over seventy local women painters, including the famously provocative Murni.

The temple complex of **Pura Saraswati** is set in an atmospheric water garden behind central Ubud's *Café Lotus* – enter either via the gateway on Jalan Raya, or through the restaurant. A forest of metre-high lotus plants leads you to the red-brick entrance gate, through which you'll find a pavilion housing the two huge *barong* costumes used by villagers for exorcizing rituals: the lion-like Barong Ket and the wild boar Barong Bangkal.

Ritual textiles from Bali, Sumba, Flores, Lembata and Sulawesi are beautifully displayed and elucidated at the **Threads of Life Textile Arts Center and Gallery**, Jl Kajeng 24 (Mon–Sat 10am–6pm, ⓦwww.threadsoflife.com). The centre is run by a foundation that's trying to halt the decline in traditional weaving by commissioning modern-day weavers to recreate the ceremonial textiles of their grandmothers.

Campuhan and Penestanan

Extending west from central Ubud, the hamlet of **CAMPUHAN** is famous as the home of several charismatic expatriate painters, including the late Antonio Blanco, a flamboyant Catalan whose house and gallery on Jalan Raya Campuhan has been turned into the enjoyably camp **Museum Blanco** (daily 9am–5pm; Rp20,000; ⓦwww.blancobali.com).

Across the road from Museum Blanco, the track that extends north along the grassy spine behind Pura Gunung Lebah forms part of a very pleasant ninety-minute circular **Campuhan Ridge walk**, taking you around the outskirts of Campuhan via the beautiful elevated spur between the Wos Barat and Wos Timor river valleys. You leave the ridge at the northern end of the village of Bangkiang Sidem, taking a sealed road that forks left and continues through Payogan and Lungsiakan before hitting the main road about 1.5km northwest of the Neka Art Museum.

The side road that turns off southwest beside Museum Blanco leads to the old-fashioned village of **PENESTANAN**, known in the 1960s as the birthplace of the Young Artists' style of naive painting and more recently as a centre for beadwork. The most dramatic approach to the village is via the steep flight of steps a few hundred metres further north along the Campuhan road from Museum Blanco, just south of the refreshingly exuberant **Symon's Studio** gallery (daylight hours; free). The steps climb the hillside to a narrow west-bound track, which passes several arterial paths to panoramic hilltop accommodation before dropping down into the next valley and reaching a crossroads with Penestanan's main street. Turn left for the 1500-metre walk through the village and back to Museum Blanco.

The Neka Art Museum

About 1500m further north up the road from Museum Blanco, the **Neka Art Museum** (daily 9am–5pm; Rp20,000; ⓦwww.museumneka.com) boasts the most comprehensive collection of traditional and modern Balinese paintings on the island and is housed in a series of pavilions set high on a hill, about 2.5km from Ubud central market; any westbound bemo from the market (Rp2000) will pass the entrance. The first pavilion gives an overview of the major schools of Balinese painting from the seventeenth century to the present day and includes the lovely Ubud-style painting

The Bumblebee Dance by Anak Agung Gede Sobrat, and the typically modern Batuan-style *Busy Bali* by I Wayan Bendi, which takes a wry look at the effects of tourism on the island. The second pavilion exhibits naive, expressionistic works in the Young Artists' style as well as paintings by their mentor, Arie Smit; the third pavilion houses an interesting archive of black-and-white photographs from Bali in the 1930s and 1940s; and the small fourth pavilion is dedicated to local Renaissance man, I Gusti Nyoman Lempad, who produced scores of cartoon-like line drawings inspired by religious mythology and secular folklore. The fifth pavilion focuses on contemporary works by artists from other parts of Indonesia, and the sixth pavilion features the Javanese artist Affandi's bold expressionist portrait of fighting cocks, *Fight to the Finish*, and the *Temptation of Arjuna* by the influential Dutch painter Rudolf Bonnet.

The Monkey Forest Sanctuary and Nyuhkuning

Ubud's best-known tourist attraction is its **Monkey Forest Sanctuary** (8am–6pm; Rp10,000, kids Rp5000), which occupies the land between the southern end of Jalan Monkey Forest (ten minutes' walk south from Ubud's central market) and the northern edge of Nyuhkuning. The focus of numerous day-trips because of its resident troupe of monkeys, the forest itself is actually small and disappointing, traversed by a concrete pathway. Five minutes into the forest, you'll come to **Pura Dalem Agung Padang Tegal**, the temple of the dead for the Padang Tegal neighbourhood. *Pura dalem* are traditionally places of extremely strong magical power and the preserve of evil spirits; in this temple you'll find half a dozen stone-carved images of the witch-widow Rangda, immediately recognizable by her hideous fanged face, unkempt hair, lolling metre-long tongue and pendulous breasts. South from the temple, the track enters the tiny settlement of **NYUHKUNING**, whose villagers are renowned for their woodcarvings; you can buy carvings and take inexpensive lessons at several workshops here, and there's a small display of outstanding pieces at the makeshift Widya Kusuma Woodcarving Museum, which keeps random hours.

The Agung Rai Museum of Art (ARMA)

Ubud's other major art museum is the **Agung Rai Museum of Art**, usually referred to as **ARMA** (daily 9am–6pm; Rp20,000; ⓦwww.armamuseum.com). It's in Pengosekan, on the southern fringes of Ubud, with entrances on Jalan Hanoman and next to the *Kokokan Club* restaurant on the Pengosekan–Peliatan road. Here, in the upstairs gallery of the large Balé Daja pavilion, you get a brief survey of the development of Balinese art, with highlights including Anak A Sobrat's *Baris Dance* (in typical Ubud style), and the contemporary Batuan-style piece by I Wayan Bendi, *Life in Bali*, which is crammed with classic Balinese scenes and laced with satirical observations, such as the figures of long-nosed tourists. Across the garden, the middle gallery of the Balé Dauh reads like a directory of Bali's most famous expats, displaying works by Rudolf Bonnet, Antonio Blanco and Arie Smit and, the highlight, *Calonnarang* by the German artist Walter Spies, a dark portrait of a demonic apparition being watched by a bunch of petrified villagers.

Eating, drinking and entertainment

Ubud is packed full of **places to eat**, many with a higher proportion of vegetarian and organic dishes than anywhere else on the island. Most restaurants shut at about 10pm.

Restaurants and cafés

Ary's Warung Jl Raya. Fashionable local landmark where the contemporary Asian menu includes veal cutlets with wasabi sauce (Rp130,000), slowly roasted duck in Balinese spices, and over a hundred imported wines (but not much of a vegetarian selection).

Bali Buddha Jl Jembawan 1, opposite the GPO. The perfect place to chill out: floor cushions, organic juices, filled bagels, chocolate mud pie, and brown-bread sandwiches (from Rp15,000). Plus a noticeboard with details of yoga and language classes.

Biah Biah Jl Gautama 13. Authentic, well-priced Balinese fare such as vegetarian and fish nasi campur (Rp13,000).

Bumbu Jl Suweta 1. Indian and Balinese dishes – chilli-fried fish, vegetarian thalis (from Rp25,000) – and plenty of veggie options, served in a pleasant water-garden setting. Also runs cookery classes (see below).

Café Wayan Jl Monkey Forest. Long-established place that's known for its fairly pricey breads and cakes (eat in and take-away), which include the signature temptation, Death by Chocolate. Also does Indonesian, Thai and European dishes (from Rp20,000).

Gayatri Café Jl Monkey Forest 67. Cheap and cheerful place whose menu (from Rp15,000) includes chilli (vegetarian or meat), pizza, salads and nasi campur.

Kubuku Off south end of Jl Monkey Forest. Laid-back café with partial ricefield view, an orchestra of wind-chimes and a fairly cheap all-vegetarian menu (from Rp20,000).

Lamak Jl Monkey Forest. Outstanding, exceptionally creative modern-Asian food is the hallmark of this large, fashionable restaurant, whose menu includes medallions of butterfish with risotto (Rp55,000), caramelized apple with chocolate mousse, and lots of vegetarian dishes. Well worth the money.

Miro's Garden Jl Bisma. An especially atmospheric place at night, when the garden is illuminated by oil lamps. Specializes in Indian and Balinese dishes, including various *dosa*-style filled pancakes (Rp35,000), plus a decent vegetarian selection, and *babi guling* (at lunch only).

Murni's Warung Jl Raya Campuhan; see map on pp.374–375. Multi-tiered restaurant built into the wall of the steep-sided Wos River valley and serving curries, homemade soups and Indonesian specialities, as well as strawberry cheesecake and banana and caramel cake (Rp12,500).

Sanak Rumah Makan Padang Jl Hanoman 7. Authentic, very cheap Sumatran fare. Assemble your own meal from the selection of cold platters in the window display (from Rp6000).

Zula Jl Raya 24. Small, innovative, organic veggie restaurant that does macrobiotic nasi campur and wholesome platter sets (from Rp28,000).

Bars and nightlife

Jazz Café Jl Sukma 2, Peliatan ⓣ0361/976594; see map on pp.374–375. Lively bar-restaurant that stages quality live jazz from Tuesday to Saturday from about 7.30pm. Phone for free local transport.

Planet Warung Southern end of Jl Hanoman. Stages live music twice a week – rock (Wed) and reggae (Sat) – and occasional video shows on other nights.

The Pubas Jl Monkey Forest. Bar-lounge that serves wine, beer and cocktails till late and hosts occasional special events.

Putra Bar Jl Monkey Forest. Backpacker-oriented bar-restaurant that runs a weekly schedule of theme nights, including frequent reggae evenings, shows live international sports on the TV, and has a faintly Kuta-ish atmosphere.

Traditional dance performances

The Ubud region boasts dozens of outstanding traditional **dance and music** groups, and there are up to five different shows performed every night in the area; the tourist office gives details of the regular weekly schedule (also available at ⓦwww.whatsup-bali.com/dance.html) and arranges free transport to outlying venues. Tickets cost Rp50,000 and can be bought at the tourist office, from touts, or at the door. If you have only one evening to catch a show, then either choose the lively *kecak* (monkey dance), or go for whatever is playing at the Ubud Palace (Puri Saren Agung), opposite the market in central Ubud. The setting of this former raja's home (now a hotel) is breathtaking, with the torchlit courtyard gateways furnishing the perfect backdrop.

Listings

Banks and exchange There are plenty of ATMs on Ubud's Jl Raya, a couple on Jl Monkey Forest, and one just north of Perama on Jl Hanoman in Padang Tegal; there are currency exchange facilities but no ATMs in Campuhan or Penestanan. Numerous tour agents on Jl Raya and Jl Monkey Forest offer exchange services.

Bookshops New English-language books and maps at Ary's Bookshop, Jl Raya; Ganesha Bookshop, Jl Raya, cnr Jl Jembawan; and Periplus, Jl Monkey Forest. Secondhand books at Cinta Bookshop, Jl Dewi Sita; Pondok Pekak, Jl Dewi Sita; and Rona Bookshop, Jl Sukma 23, Peliatan.

Cultural courses Balinese cooking at *Casa Luna*

restaurant, Jl Raya ⓣ0361/973282, ⓦwww.casalunabali.com; and *Bumbu* restaurant, Jl Suweta 1 ⓣ0361/974217, ⓔbumbu_bali@plasa.com. Balinese music and dance lessons at Sehati, Jl Monkey Forest ⓣ0361/976341, ⓔhanaubud@indo.net.id; and Nataraja Dance School, Jl Sugriwa 20 ⓣ0361/975916, ⓔgauranataraja@yahoo.com. Batik courses at Crackpot Batik, Jl Monkey Forest; and Nirvana Batik, Jl Gautama 10 ⓣ0361/975415, ⓔrodanet@denpasar.wasantara.net.id. Indonesian language courses at Pondok Pekak Library, Jl Dewi Sita ⓣ0361/976194, ⓔpondok@indo.net.id. Silversmithing at Studio Perak, Jl Gautama ⓣ0812/365 1809, ⓦwww.studioperak.com. Classes in woodcarving, beadwork, painting, batik, basketry, kite-making, mask-painting and shadow-puppet making at Museum Puri Lukisan, Jl Raya ⓣ0361/971159, ⓦwww.mpl-ubud.com.

Hospitals and clinics For minor casualties go to the Legian Clinic, Jl Monkey Forest ⓣ0361/970805, or to the Ubud Clinic, which also has a dental service, at Jl Raya Campuhan 36 ⓣ0361/974911. Both are open 24hr, are staffed by English-speakers, and will respond to emergency call-outs. For anything serious, the nearest hospitals are in Denpasar (p.357).

Internet access Highway on Jl Raya (high-speed connection and personal laptop hookups; open 24hr); Bali 3000 on Jl Raya; Roda Tourist Services, Jl Bisma 3; and Ary's Business and Travel Service on Jl Raya.

Pharmacies Two on Jl Monkey Forest.

Police The main police station is on the eastern edge of town, on Jl Andong, but there's a more central police booth beside the market at the Jl Raya/Jl Monkey Forest crossroads.

Post office Poste restante (daily 8am–6pm) at the GPO on Jl Jembawan.

Shopping Souvenirs, mass-market handicrafts, sarongs etc at the central market, Jl Raya. Silver jewellery at Studio Perak Toko, Jl Dewi Sita. Handicrafts at Asialine, Jl Hanoman 8; Tegun Galeri, Jl Hanoman 44; and Mangku Made Gina near ARMA on Jl Hanoman. Kites at Kites Center 3, off southern Jl Monkey Forest. CDs and DVDs at Ubud Music, Jl Raya.

Spas and massage At Nur Salon, Jl Hanoman 28 ⓣ0361/975352, ⓔnursalonubud@yahoo.com; Ubud Bodyworks Centre, Jl Hanoman 25 ⓣ0361/975720, ⓦwww.ubudbodyworkscentre.com; and Zen Bali Spa, Jl Hanoman ⓣ0361/970976 ⓦwww.zenbalispa.com.

Telephone services The Kantor Telcom is at the eastern end of Jl Raya. Slightly higher rates at all the above-listed Internet centres.

Travel agents Ary's Business and Travel Service, just west of the market on Jl Raya ⓣ0361/973130, ⓔary_s2000@yahoo.com.

Yoga and meditation Daily yoga at Bali Spirit, Jl Hanoman 44B ⓣ0361/970992, ⓦwww.balispirit.com. Daily meditation at the Meditation Shop, Jl Monkey Forest ⓣ0361/976206.

Around Ubud

Thought to be a former hermitage for eleventh-century Hindu priests, the moderately interesting **Goa Gajah** (Elephant Cave; 8am–5.30pm; Rp4100, children Rp2100), displays impressive carvings around its entranceway and used to serve as meditation cells or living quarters for priests. To get there, either walk, cycle or drive the 3km east from Ubud's Jalan Peliatan, or take an Ubud–Gianyar bemo, which goes past the entrance gate.

Chipped away from the sheer rock face, the 25-metre-long series of fourteenth-century rock-cut carvings at **Yeh Pulu** (6am–6pm; Rp4100, kids Rp2100) are more interesting but less visited. The story of the carvings is uncertain, but scenes include a man carrying two jars of water, and three stages of a boar hunt. The small holy spring after which the site is named rises close by the statue of Ganesh at the end of the panel. To reach Yeh Pulu, get off the Ubud–Gianyar bemo at the signs just east of Goa Gajah or west of the **BEDULU** crossroads, and then walk 1km south through the hamlet of Batulumbang. You can also walk (with one of the ever-present guides) through the ricefields from Goa Gajah; guides also lead two-hour treks from Yeh Pulu through nearby countryside (prices for both routes are Rp50,000 for up to two people, or Rp100,000 for larger groups).

Balinese people consider **Pura Penataran Sasih** (donation required), in the village of **PEJENG**, to be a particularly sacred temple, because this is the home of the so-called Moon of Pejeng – hence the English epithet, **Moon Temple**. The moon in question is a large hourglass-shaped bronze gong that probably dates from the 3rd century BC, and at almost 2m long is thought to be the largest such ket-

△ Terraced ricefields near Ubud

tledrum ever cast. Etched into its green patina are a chain of striking heart-shaped faces punctured by huge round eyes. From Ubud, take a Gianyar-bound bemo to the Bedulu crossroads and then either wait for a Tampaksiring-bound one, or walk 1km to the temple.

A few hundred metres north of **TAMPAKSIRING'S** bemo terminus (served by Gianyar–Bedulu–Tampaksiring bemos), a sign points east off the main road to **Gunung Kawi** (daylight hours; Rp4100, kids Rp2100), the site of a series of eleventh-century royal tombs hewn from the rock face. It's a lovely, impressive spot, enclosed in the lush valley of the sacred Pakrisan River.

Balinese from every corner of the island make pilgrimages to the nearby holy springs at **Tirta Empul** (daylight hours; Rp4100, kids Rp2100), where they bathe in the traditional red-brick bathing pools. It's a very commercialized spot, signposted off the main Tampaksiring–Penelokan road, about 500m north of the turn-off to Gunung Kawi.

Besakih

The major tourist draw in the east of Bali, attracting hundreds of thousands of tourists a year, is undoubtedly the **Besakih** temple complex (daily 8am–5pm; Rp7500, camera Rp1000, video camera Rp2500, parking Rp1000), the most venerated site in Bali, situated on the slopes of **Gunung Agung**, the holiest and highest mountain on the island. Tours start arriving around 10.30am, after which the sheer volume of tourists, traders and guides make the place pretty unbearable – it's well worth coming early in the morning to get the best of the atmosphere.

Besakih is totally schizophrenic. On the one hand it is the most sacred spot on Bali for Balinese Hindus, who believe that the gods occasionally descend to earth and reside in the temple, during which times they don their finery and bring them elaborate offerings. The complex's sheer scale is impressive, and on a clear day, with ceremonies in full swing, it is a wonderful place. On the other hand, Besakih is a jumble of buildings, unremarkable in many ways, around which has evolved the habit of separating foreign tourists from as much money as possible. Even the stark grandeur of Besakih's location is often shrouded in mist, leaving Gunung Agung towering behind in all-enveloping cloud and the splendid panorama back south to the coast an imaginary delight.

Unless you're praying or making offerings, you're **forbidden to enter** any of the temples, and most remain locked unless there's a ceremony in progress. However, a lot is visible through the gateways and over walls. The rule about wearing a sarong and sash appears to be inconsistently applied but you'll definitely need them if you're in skimpy clothing; **sarong rental** is available, with negotiable prices from Rp2000, but it's much easier to take your own.

There are huge numbers of local **guides** at Besakih hoping to be engaged by visitors, but you don't need one to explore the complex; stick to the paths running along the walls outside the temples, wear a sarong and sash, and you'll be in no danger of causing religious offence. If you do hire a guide, the official advice is only to use one who has an official guide badge and is wearing an *endek* shirt as uniform. You should also always establish the **fee** beforehand; Rp20,000 is reasonable and you can always add extra if you feel you've received a good service. Be aware that if you're escorted into one of the temples to receive a blessing from a priest you'll be expected to make a "donation" to the priest, the amount negotiable through your guide.

The complex consists of more than twenty separate temples spread over a site stretching for more than 3km. The central temple is **Pura Penataran Agung**, the largest on the island, built on seven ascending terraces, and comprising more than fifty structures and plentiful carved figures. Start here, and then wander at will: the *meru* (multi-tiered shrine roofs) of **Pura Batu Madeg**, rising among the trees in the north of the complex, are particularly enticing; if you feel like a longer walk, **Pura Pengubengan**, the most far-flung of the temples, is a couple of kilometres through the forest.

Without your own transport, the easiest way of getting to Besakih is to take an organized **tour**, but anything offering less than an hour at the temple is hardly worth it. By **public transport**, one way is to approach from Klungkung: bemos pass through Jalan Gunung Rinjani just north of the main road in the town centre, although you may have to change at Rendang or Menanga, the turn-offs for Besakih. Green bemos also run from Amlapura via Selat and Muncan to Rendang, with some going on to Menanga and Besakih. Bemos dry up in both directions on both routes in the afternoon: after 1 or 2pm, you'll have trouble getting back. There are no public bemos north of Menanga to Penelokan, or between Rendang and Bangli.

Accommodation near Besakih is limited. The *Lembah Arca* hotel (☎0366/23076; ❷–❸) on the road between Menanga and Besakih, a couple of kilometres before the temple complex, has a few rooms if you get stranded. There are also a few basic, unsigned and unauthorized lodgings (❷–❸) behind the shops lining the road from the car park up to the temple; ask at the **tourist office** (daily 8am–7pm), on the right as you head through the main gate beyond the car park. These places are useful if you're climbing Gunung Agung, or want to explore the site early or late.

Climbing Gunung Agung

According to legend, **Gunung Agung** was created by the god Pasupati when he split Mount Meru (the centre of the Hindu universe), forming both Gunung Agung and Gunung Batur. At 3014m, the superb conical-shaped Agung is the highest Balinese peak. The spiritual centre of Bali, it is believed that the spirits of the ancestors of the Balinese people dwell on Gunung Agung. Villages and house compounds are laid out in relation to the mountain, and many Balinese people prefer to sleep with their heads towards it. Directions on Bali are always given with reference to Agung, *kaja* meaning "towards the mountain" and *kelod* meaning "away from the mountain".

If you want to **climb** Gunung Agung, there are two main **routes**, both involving a long, hard climb. One path leaves from Besakih and the other from Pura Pasar Agung on the southern slope of the mountain, near Selat. You'll need to set out very early in the morning if you want to be at the top to see the spectacular **sunrise** around 7am. It's essential to take a **guide** with you, as the lower slopes are densely forested and it's easy to get lost. You'll also need strong footwear, a flashlight that you can attach to some part of yourself (leaving both hands free for climbing), water and snacks to keep you going, and for the descent, a stout stick is handy.

This is an extremely sacred peak for the Balinese, and climbing is forbidden at many times of the year because of **religious festivals**: March and April are generally impossible from the Besakih side because of ceremonies. **Weather**-wise, the dry season (April to mid-October) is the best time; don't even contemplate it during January and February, the wettest months. At other times during the rainy season, you may get a few dry days if you're very lucky.

From Pura Pasar Agung, it's at least a three-hour climb with an ascent of almost 2000m, so you'll need to set out at 3am or earlier. The track initially passes through forest, ascending onto bare, steep rock. It doesn't go to the actual summit, but ends at a point on the rim, which is about 100m lower. From here, the summit masks views of part of the island, and between April and September, the sunrise on the horizon, but you'll be able to see Gunung Rinjani, the south of Bali and Gunung Batukau, and look down into the five-hundred-metre crater.

From Besakih, the climb is longer (5–7hr) and much more challenging; you'll need to leave between 10pm and midnight. This path starts from Pura Pengubengan, the most distant of the Besakih temples, and leads to the summit of Gunung Agung, with views in all directions. You climb initially through forest but the path gets very steep, very quickly even before it gets out onto the bare rock, and you'll soon need your hands as well as your feet to haul yourself upwards. The descent is particularly taxing from this side and feels very precarious when you're already exhausted; allow at least five hours to get down.

A route from the north side, **from Dukuh Bujangga Sakti**, inland from Kubu on the north coast, is offered by just one company, M & G Trekking (see below). You start out at an altitude of 300m, so the climb is greater but not as steep as the other routes. It's also less strenuous, as you start climbing in the afternoon, camp on the mountain at 1750m and complete the three hours to the summit pre-dawn. The north of Bali is generally drier so this side is less often shrouded in cloud, and you can see the sunrise on the horizon all year round from here.

Practicalities

There are many established **guiding** operations leading climbs up Agung from bases throughout Bali. Talk to potential guides carefully and satisfy yourself that they have the necessary experience and knowledge.

Closest to **Pura Pasar Agung**, you'll find guides at Muncan, 4km east of Rendang, at Selat and up at the temple itself. I Ketut Uriada (ⓣ0812/364 6426) is a part-time teacher and an enormously experienced guide who has trained several local guides. His house is marked by a sign advertising guides on the left as you enter Muncan from the east. Expect to pay around US$30 for a guide for one person, US$40 for two, US$50 for three. Larger groups may need more than one guide. He'll help you arrange a bemo charter between Muncan and Pura Pasar Agung (about US$10). He will also quote for climbs from Besakih. If you go directly to Pura Pasar Agung you'll find guides hanging around at the temple who'll charge about Rp350,000 (negotiable) to take up to four people but you'll need to take all your own food and water. There's **accommodation** at *Pondok Wisata Puri Agung* (ⓣ&ⓕ366/23037; 3) in Selat, 4km east of Muncan on the Amlapura road. They can arrange a guide for the climb (Rp350,000 for two people, not including accommodation or transport to and from Pura Pasar Agung). Gung Bawa, Jl Sri Jaya Pangus 33 in Selat (ⓣ366/24379 or 0812/384 0752, ⓔgbtrekk@yahoo.com), offers packages from Selat from US$40 for two people making the climb from Pura Pasar Agung and from US$60 for two people climbing from Besakih, both including resting time in a local guesthouse, transport to and from the start of the climb, snacks and mineral water on the way. Transport to and from Selat can also be arranged, check the price at the time of booking.

If you're at **Besakih**, guides can be arranged at the tourist office in the temple complex (see p.383); they can also help with nearby lodgings. The going rate for a guide from this side is Rp700,000 for two people.

Inevitably, prices are higher if you arrange the trek from further afield. An established established guide in **Tirtagangga** is Komang Gede Sutama (ⓣ081338/770893, or contact him through *Good Karma* restaurant), who leads climbs from Pura Pasar Agung (Rp500,000 for one person, Rp750,000 for two people, Rp900,000 for three people; prices include transport and breakfast), and from Besakih (from Rp650,000 for one person). The *Pondok Lembah Dukuh* and *Geria Semalung* losmen in the nearby village of **Ababi** (see p.393) also arrange Agung climbs. M & G Trekking (ⓣ363/41464 or 0812/361 9625, ⓔmgtrekking@hotmail.com) has an office in Balina, **Candi Dasa** (see p.387). It costs Rp890,000 per person for a minimum of two people for their climb from Dukuh, including transport, equipment and food. Bali Sunrise 2001 in **Ubud** (ⓣ0361/980470 or 0818/552669, ⓦwww.balisunrise2001.com) will arrange pick-ups from pretty much anywhere on Bali for the climb, charging from U$100 per person depending on where you start from. The guiding operations in **Toya Bungkah** in the area of Gunung Batur (see p.398) charge from $80 per person (minimum numbers apply). The Perama tour company also organizes the trip (from U$100 per person); enquire at any of their offices.

Nusa Lembongan

Circled by a mixture of white beaches and mangrove swamps, the tiny island of **NUSA LEMBONGAN** (4km by 3km) is sheltered by coral reefs that provide excellent snorkelling and create the perfect conditions for seaweed farming. It is a major draw for surfers and anyone seeking some relaxation away from the resorts of southern Bali. Accommodation is in **Jungutbatu** on the west coast, to the southwest in **Coconut Beach**, **Chelegimbai** and **Mushroom Bay**, where the more expensive places are situated, and at **Dream Beach**, around on the south coast.

There's no post office, and electricity is produced by a generator from 3pm to 8am (all day Sun), though some hotels supplement this with their own generators. The **surf breaks** are all accessible from Jungutbatu, and you can charter boats to take you **snorkelling** (ask at your losmen); one of the best spots is off Mushroom Bay with others at Mangrove Corner (also known as Jet Point) to the north, and Sunfish nearby. Boats will also take you to Nusa Penida, where Crystal Bay, is renowned for its clear waters. Prices depend on distance; start negotiating at around Rp100,000 per hour for a boat holding up to four people, including equipment.

The most established **dive operator** is World Diving Lembongan (Ⓣ0812/390 0686, Ⓦwww.world-diving.com), based next to *Pondok Baruna* in Jungutbatu, who dive the more frequented sites less often and use areas where the coral is in better condition and the larger marine life more abundant. They offer dives for certified divers (US$30 each, including equipment, for the first two dives), PADI courses up to Divemaster level (Open Water US$345; Advanced US$260), a Scuba Review (US$35) if you have a certificate but haven't dived for some time, and Discover Scuba (US$60) for those new to the sport. World Diving also take snorkellers along on day-trips for Rp60,000 per person, including equipment.

You can **walk** around Nusa Lembongan in three to four hours and there are **bikes** (from Rp20,000 per day) and **motorbikes** (Rp25,000–30,000 per hour) for rent in Jungutbatu, ask at your losmen or check out the places advertising on the beach.

There are two **public boats** daily from Sanur to Nusa Lembongan (Jungutbatu) taking about two hours. Boats leave at 8am (Rp33,000) and 10am (Rp43,000), returning at 8am (Rp35,000). Buy tickets from the office at the beach end of Jalan Hang Tuah near the *Ananda Hotel* and from the beachfront office in Jungutbatu. Perama operates a daily **tourist boat** (Rp50,000) at 10.30am, returning at 8.30am; book one day in advance.

Jungutbatu

Ranged along the west coast for well over 1km, the attractive village of **JUNGUTBATU** is a low-key place, with plenty of losmen and restaurants and a few shops. You can **change money** at the moneychangers along the beach or at Bank Pembangunan Daerah Bali (Mon–Fri 10am–1pm). There's a **wartel** at *Mainski Inn*; you can access the **Internet** here and further down the beach at *Bunga Bungalows*, both open during the hours of electricity. The Perama office (daily 7.30am–6pm) is situated between *Pondok Baruna* and *Nusa Indah* bungalows; there is one daily departure serving all the main tourist destinations on Bali and Lombok, but many of them require a stopover on the way.

Accommodation and eating

All the **accommodation** has attached **restaurants** offering the usual travellers' fare. On the beachfront, *Sukanusa* serves up imaginative options, impressively cooked. *Ketut's Warung* is a bit tucked away; access is via the land to the north of *Agung's*, but it's worth searching out for its well-cooked, cheap local food. *Full Moon Warung* on the road through the village has a purely Indonesian menu with fresh food in a peaceful setting.

Agung ⓣ0366/24483. Some rooms in a concrete building, but the two-storey thatched places have most character; ones at the front have the best views, and there's a good sunbathing area. ❶–❸

Bunga Bungalows ⓣ0366/24529. At the southern end of the beach about 400m south of *Pondok Baruna* with several standards of simple rooms in two-storey buildings. ❷–❸

Bungalo No. 7 ⓣ0366/24497. Justifiably popular, extremely good-value rooms at the far southern end of the beach, all with balconies or verandas. There's a sunbathing area overlooking the beach. ❷–❸

Ketut's ⓣ0366/24487. Well-built, attractive accommodation, some of it with excellent sea views, set in pleasant grounds. A/c and hot water are available. ❷–❻

Linda Bungalows t0812/360 0867. Rooms are in well-built two-storey buildings, with good quality furnishings. The owners pride themselves on Aussie cleanliness. ❷

Nusa Indah ⓣ0366/24480. Set back slightly from the beach behind the *Surfer's Beach Café* and offering a choice of older, cheaper rooms, or better quality, newer ones at the front. ❶–❷

Pondok Baruna ⓣ0812/390 0686, ⓦwww.world-diving.com. A few hundred metres south of the main accommodation area, with clean, tiled rooms looking straight onto the beach. World Diving Lembongan is based here. ❷–❸

Puri Nusa ⓣ&ⓕ0361/298613. Reasonable rooms with good verandas or balconies in an attractive garden. One of the most northerly places. so a bit away from the main tourist action. ❶–❷

Around the coast

Southwest of Jungutbatu, the glorious white-sand bays of **Coconut Beach** (Pantai Songlambung), **Chelegimbai** and **Mushroom Bay** (Tanjung Sanghyang) and the footpaths linking them offer attractive moderate and top-end accommodation. This area is the destination for day-trippers from the mainland, which can disturb the peace in the middle of the day but does little to detract from the idyllic beaches and turquoise waters. Slightly further afield, **Dream Beach** is around on the south coast of the island. You can **charter a boat** to all these beaches from Jungutbatu.

Most of the accommodation at Chelegimbai and Mushroom Bay is pricey and best booked as an add-on to the luxury day-trips. However, there are a couple of affordable but excellent places here: *Tamarind Beach Bungalows* (ⓣ0812/398 4234; ❹–❺) have huge bungalows with fans and attached cold-water bathrooms plus great views along Chelegimbai Beach from their location at the far eastern end, and *Dream Beach Bungalows* (ⓣ0812/367 1123; ❹) occupies a secluded setting in the far south of the island just above a fantastic white-sand beach. Accommodation here is in large rooms with fans and cold-water bathrooms. Both places will collect you from the boat in Jungutbatu if you let them know when you'll be arriving.

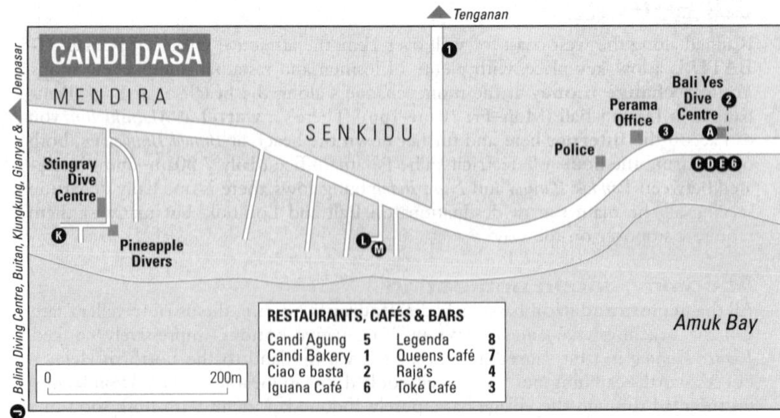

If you're in the market for a **luxury day-trip** to the island, Bali Hai (ⓣ0361/720331, ⓦwww.balihaicruises.com), Bounty (ⓣ0361/726666, ⓦwww.bountycruises.com), Island Explorer (ⓣ0361/728088, ⓦwww.bali-cruise.com) and Lembongan Island Cruise (ⓣ0361/271212, ⓔvillawayan@dps.centrin.net.id) are good choices among the many that advertise widely in the southern resorts. Prices range upwards from US$45 a day.

Candi Dasa

At the eastern end of Amuk Bay, **CANDI DASA** is a relaxed resort that makes a good centre for snorkelling and diving. There's a wide choice of accommodation and restaurants, and it's a convenient base from which to explore the east of Bali, with easy road access to the main sights. Following the destruction of the offshore reef in the 1980s to produce lime for cement to fuel the building boom for tourist facilities, the beach in the centre of Candi Dasa was left so exposed that it simply washed away. Large sea walls now protrude into the sea in the hope, largely justified, that the beach will build up again behind them. So far, the signs are good: there are now many pockets of pretty, white sand, while the beaches to the west and east of the centre are a respectable size. Tourist developments extend west around the bay, through the villages of **Senkidu**, **Mendira**, **Buitan** and **Manggis**.

Candi Dasa is an ideal base from which to arrange **diving trips** – either to the group of small islands lying just off the coast (Gili Tepekong, Gili Biaha and Gili Mimpang), which offer excellent diving for experienced divers (currents can be strong), including walls, a pinnacle and the dramatic Tepekong Canyon, or further afield to Padang Bai, Nusa Penida, Nusa Lembongan, Amed, Gili Selang and Tulamben. There are many dive operators; established ones include Balina Diving Center at *Balina Beach Resort* (ⓣ0363/41725, ⓦwww.balinadivingcenter.com); Bali Yes Dive Centre (ⓣ0363/41604, ⓔbali_yesdive@hotmail.com); Baruna, in the centre of town (ⓣ0363/41185) and at *Puri Bagus Candidasa* (ⓣ0363/41217); Divelite (ⓣ0363/41660, ⓦwww.divelite.com); Maoka Dive Centre (ⓣ0363/41563); Pineapple Divers at *Candi Beach Cottage* (ⓣ0363/41760, ⓦwww.bali-pineapple-divers.com); Stingray Dive Centre at Mendira (ⓣ0363/41268, ⓕ1062). Candi Dasa is also a good place to take a diving course (PADI Open Water US$300–380 and Advanced US$250–300; Divemaster can be arranged), as hotel swimming pools

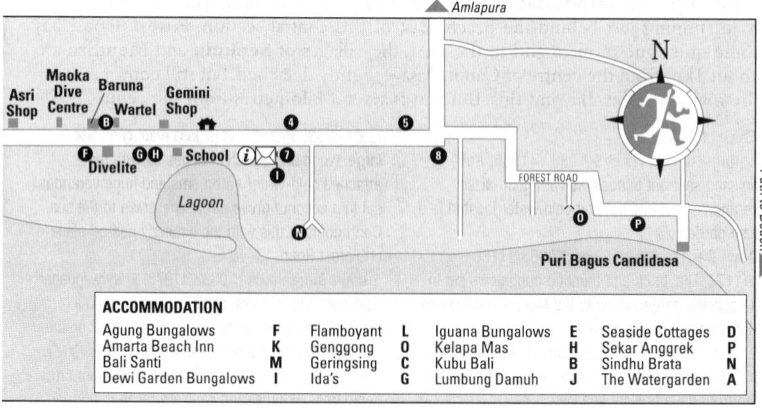

are available for initial tuition. Trips for experienced divers are US$50–70 for the Candi Dasa, Padang Bai, Tulamben and Amed areas; US$75–85 for Nusa Lembongan and Nusa Penida; and US$70 for Pulau Menjangan (see p.407). Most places in Candi Dasa quote equipment rental on top of this (approx US$15 per set per day) so check at the time of booking. See "Diving, surfing and trekking", p.247, for guidelines on choosing a dive operator.

The reef along the coastline in Candi Dasa is gradually rejuvenating and there is now some decent **snorkelling** just offshore, stretching for about 1km westwards from the area in front of *Puri Bagus Candidasa*. Take care not to venture too far out and always keep an awareness of your position, the currents can be hazardous. Not all of the dive spots offer great snorkelling: the best places are off Gili Mimpang and Blue Lagoon on the western side of Amuk Bay, closer to Padang Bai (see p.391). Local boat owners will approach you to fix up snorkelling trips; the going rate is around Rp100,000-150,000, including equipment, for a boat taking up to three people out for a couple of hours. Many dive operators take snorkellers along on trips; prices vary from US$25 to US$39 so it pays to shop around. Always be clear whether or not equipment is included in the price. It's also possible to arrange **fishing trips** with the local boats, either pre-dawn or after sun-up; prices are similar to snorkelling.

Long-distance Denpasar (Batubulan)–Amlapura **buses** and **mini-buses** serve Candi Dasa. **Tourist shuttle buses** serve Candi Dasa, and Perama (Ⓣ0363/41114; daily 8am–9pm) has an office in central Candi Dasa. There's a **tourist office** in the main street close to the lagoon, but it has erratic opening hours. There are **moneychangers** every few metres along the main street and an **ATM** at the BNI bank opposite Asri Shop. The **post office** (Mon-Thurs & Sat 8am-noon, Fri 8-11am) provides poste restante. Mail should be addressed to you, c/o Post Restan, Kantor Pos, Candi Dasa, Amlapura, Bali 80851. There's a **wartel** (daily 7am–10.30pm) next to the *Kubu Bali Restaurant*, and **Internet** access is widely available (Rp300/min) but unreliable. **Car rental** is easy to arrange (Rp80,000–100,000 for a Suzuki Jimney for one day, Rp150,000 for a Kijang). A **motorbike** costs Rp30,000–50,000. Well-established companies are Safari (Ⓣ0363/41707) and Amarta (Ⓣ0363/41260) in the centre of town; and Candidasa Rent Car (Ⓣ0363/41225), just at the start of Forest Road. The insurance included varies considerably. If you want to charter transport, Ketut Lagun (Ⓣ0812/362 2076) and I Nengah Parni (Ⓣ0812/399 4975) are both recommended drivers.

Accommodation

Most of the **accommodation** in Candi Dasa is spread about 1km along the main road running just behind the beach. East of this central section, **Forest Road** has some quiet guesthouses, and to the west, the villages of **Senkidu** and **Mendira** are about 1km from the centre of Candi Dasa – slightly detached, but still convenient for the main facilities. Beyond this, Buitban is several kilometres from the centre.

Candi Dasa

Agung Bungalows Ⓣ&Ⓕ0363/41535. Well-finished seafront bungalows with good-sized verandas, fans and hot and cold water located in a lush garden. ❸

Dewi Garden Bungalows Ⓣ0363/41166, Ⓕ1177. Tile, brick and bamboo bungalows set in a spacious garden close to the lagoon and the sea. Hot water is available. ❷

Geringsing Ⓣ0363/41084. Smart stone and tile bungalows all with a/c and hot water. The ones at the front have brilliant sea views. ❻

Ida's Ⓣ0363/41096, Ⓔjsidas1@aol.com. Six large, wood and thatch cottages all with fan, attached cold-water bathrooms and huge verandas set in a coconut grove stretching down to the sea. Don't confuse this with the similarly named place on Forest Road. ❸–❺

Iguana Bungalows Ⓣ0363/41973, Ⓦwww.iguana-bali.com. Clean, comfortable bungalows with a choice of fan or a/c and cold or hot water set on the seafront. There's a pool just above the beach. ❹–❻

Kelapa Mas Ⓣ0363/41369, Ⓦwww.welcome.to/kelapamas. Popular and centrally located, offering a range of clean bungalows set in a lovely garden on the seafront. The more expensive options have hot water and a/c. 4–6

Kubu Bali ⓣ0363/41532, ⓕ1531. Excellent, well-furnished bungalows. All have fan, a/c and hot water, and are widely spaced up the hillside. There's also a great swimming pool. 7–8

Seaside Cottages ⓣ363/41629, ⓦwww.bali-seafront-bungalows.com. Small, central place that offers several standards of clean, fan-cooled accommodation, from basic bungalows to ones on the seafront with picture windows and hot water. 1–5

Sindhu Brata ⓣ0363/41825, ⓕ1954. Tiled, well-kept bungalows fronting onto the sea in a quiet spot near the lagoon. Hot water and a/c is available. 3–5

The Watergarden ⓣ0363/41540, ⓦwww.watergardenhotel.com. Superb, characterful hotel. Accommodation is in excellently furnished bungalows, each overlooking a lotus pond set in an atmospheric garden. All have a/c and hot water. There's a pretty, secluded swimming pool, and the service is excellent. 9

Forest Road

Genggong ⓣ0363/41105. Bungalows and rooms with a choice of fan or a/c, and there's hot water available. There's a large garden and a white-sand beach just over the wall. 2–3

Sekar Anggrek ⓣ0363/41086, wwww.sekar-orchid.com. Great little place offering excellent value with seven clean bungalows with fan, hot water and mosquito screens at the windows, in a quiet seafront garden. 3

Senkidu, Mendira and Buitan

Amarta Beach Inn, Mendira ⓣ0363/41230. Large bungalows, all with fan, in a pretty, spacious garden facing the ocean. The more expensive ones have hot water. 3

Bali Santi, Senkidu t0363/41611, ⓦwww.balisanti.com. Good-quality accommodation just above the beach in a lovely garden. One room has a/c, the others have fan. 2–4

Flamboyant, Senkidu ⓣ0363/41886, ⓔflamboyant_bali@tiscali.co.uk. Next door to *Bali Santi*. Spotless bungalows in a gorgeous garden beside the sea, with great coastal views. There's a restaurant with DVD player for guests' use. 2–3

Lumbung Damuh ⓣ0363/41553, ⓦwww.damuhbali.com. Three *lumbung*-style cottages in a garden on the coast at Balina Beach. Spread over two floors, with the bedrooms upstairs and the bathroom and sitting areas below. Look out for the sign to *Royal Bali Beach Club* to identify the turning from the main road. 4–6

Eating, drinking and nightlife

Candi Dasa offers a great variety of **restaurants**. Several have set menus for Rp20,000 and upwards and others feature Balinese dancing, mostly *legong*, to accompany your meal – look out for local adverts. All the places listed below offer inexpensive to moderately priced food. **Nightlife** is low-key in Candi Dasa: there's no club scene and live music currently alternates between *Legenda* and *Iguana Café*. Videos are the main entertainment at *Raja's* and *Ciao e basta*, and are advertised on flyers around town.

Candi Agung A big food and drink menu with well-cooked main courses and set menus at Rp29,000 and upwards for three courses. *Legong* dances held nightly.

Candi Bakery About 300m up the road to Tenganan from the main road. Produces an appetizing selection of bread and cakes plus moderately priced lunches and dinners.

Ciao e basta Slightly hidden away off the main street, this two-storey place has an extensive menu of pasta, pizza (recommended), salads, homemade ice cream and desserts, plus a good selection of drinks and coffees.

Legenda Situated close to the junction of Forest Rd with the main road. One of the live-music venues, *Legenda* also has a wide-ranging menu, with plenty of Western dishes (including spaghetti, pizza and steak), alongside Indonesian food.

Queens Café There's a good buzz here, aided by the fact that diners get a free welcome drink. Set-menus are Rp18,000–22,000; the choices aren't vast but the food is cheap and cheerful.

Raja's Almost opposite the lagoon in central Candi Dasa. Lots of people come here for the nightly videos, but there's also a vast drinks list and plenty of Indonesian and Western dishes, including sausage and mash. Pizzas are worth the 30min wait: they're thin and crispy with a generous topping.

Toké Café This long-term Candi Dasa favourite offers gamelan music three times a week, diners get a free welcome drink, and there's a vast menu of seafood, pasta, pizza, Indian, Indo-Chinese and International dishes. Set menus at Rp35,000–55,000 are real feasts and the more expensive ones include a glass of wine.

Tenganan

Rejecting the Javanization of their land, and the caste system and the religious reforms that followed the Majapahit conquest of the island in 1343, the Bali Aga ("original Balinese") withdrew to their village enclaves to live a life based around ritual and ceremony. The village of **TENGANAN** (admission by donation), near Candi Dasa, is unique among the Bali Aga communities in its strong adherence to traditional ways, and is the only place in Indonesia that produces *geringsing* or double *ikat*, a ceremonial cloth in brown, deep red, blue-black and tan that can take five years to make. Most of the complex round of daily rituals and ceremonies observed by the villagers are not open to the public, but there are plenty of festival days (see wwww.baliplus.com for specific dates), of which the month-long Usaba Sambah (May/June) is one of the most colourful. The road up to Tenganan is a pleasant three-kilometre **walk** from the centre of Candi Dasa or **ojek** (Rp5000) wait at the bottom to transport you up to the village. It is a shoppers' paradise with textiles, baskets produced from *ata* grass and intricate pictures inscribed on lontar palms amongst a host of other crafts. Tenganan is a stop on the tour-bus circuit, so it's best to avoid the 11am to 2pm rush.

Padang Bai

PADANG BAI, the port for Lombok (ferries run to Lembar every 1hr 30min), nestles in a small white-sand cove lined with fishing boats. The jetty, ferry offices and car park are all at the western end of the bay, and everything is within easy walking distance from here. Many travellers stay a night or two in Padang Bai, and the village has developed into a small laid-back resort. If you find the main beach a bit busy, the bay of **Biastugal**, to the west, is smaller and quieter. Follow the road past the post office and, just as it begins to climb, take the track to the left. Alternatively, over the headland in the other direction, take the path from Pura Silayukti, to another small white cove known as **Blue Lagoon**, where you can snorkel off the beach or charter a boat for a couple of hours (about Rp100-150,000; check whether equipment is included); ask at the beach, at *Celagi* restaurant or your guesthouse. Several places in Padang Bai rent snorkelling equipment (Rp20,000 per day).

There are many dive operations, the most established of which are Geko Dive (Ⓣ0363/41516, Ⓦwww.gekodive.com), a large set-up on the seafront, Water Worxx (Ⓣ0363/41220, Ⓦwww.waterworxbali.com) almost next door and Diving Groove (Ⓣ0812/398 9746, Ⓦwww.divinggroove.com) just up the hill. All these companies can arrange airport transfers and offer advice on accommodation. Expect to pay about US$45 for two dives in the Padang Bai area (including equipment rental), US$55 in Amed, Tulamben or Candi Dasa, and US$60 at Nusa Lembongan, Nusa Penida, Pulau Menjangan or Gili Selang. Of the courses on offer, Discover Scuba is US$55-65, the PADI Open Water is US$280, and the Advanced Open Water is US$200.

Bemos and minibuses arrive at, and depart from, the port entrance; orange bemos from Amlapura via Candi Dasa, blue or white bemos from Klungkung and pale-brown minibuses for Amlapura or Batubulan terminal in Denpasar. The nearest government **tourist office** is in Candi Dasa (see p.389). Perama **tourist shuttle buses** operate from their office near the jetty (daily 7am–7pm; Ⓣ0363/41419). There's a **post office** near the port entrance and **wartels** on the seafront (daily 7am–10pm). **Internet** services are available throughout the resort (Rp300/min) but connection can be slow. Many seafront restaurants **change money** and there is a BRI bank with an ATM. **Car rental** (Rp125,000 per day for a Suzuki Jimney, Rp200,000 for a Kijang) and **motorbike rental** (Rp40,000 daily) are widely available.

Accommodation, eating and nightlife

A wide choice of **accommodation** is available in the village and along the road behind the beach. Upstairs rooms in the village places, especially up on the hill, catch the breeze and have fine views. Padang Bai **restaurants** feature good-priced seafood and the usual travellers' fare. There are two clusters of warung along the beach; the main one starts with *Dharma* to the west through to *Marina* and includes *Celagi*. Then there's a break, after which there's a row from *Babylon Reggae Bar* through to *Dewi Café*. In the village, it's worth checking out *Ozone* for its slightly wacky decor, and *Omang Omang* up on the hill has good food and decor a cut above the rest. Padang Bai's **nightlife** revolves around the reggae bars towards the eastern end of the beach, which offer live music most evenings in high season, getting going around 10pm and staying open as long as there are customers, and *Omang Omang*, also a regular venue for live music.

Bagus Inn ⓣ0363/41398. A good budget choice in the village, with small rooms in a friendly family compound. ❶

Darma ⓣ0363/41394. A clean, family set-up in the village; upstairs rooms are big and have good sitting areas outside. ❷

Kembar Inn ⓣ&ⓕ0363/41364. Pleasant tiled place in the village. Pricier rooms have a/c and hot water, and there's a pleasant sitting area upstairs. ❷–❸

Kerti Beach Inn ⓣ0363/41391. Near the beach; some accommodation is in bungalows, some in two-storey *lumbung*-style bamboo and thatch barns. ❷

Made Homestay ⓣ0363/41441, ⓔmades_padangbai@hotmail.com. Clean, tiled rooms in a two-storey block in a small compound convenient for both the beach and the village. ❷

Padang Bai Beach Homestay ⓣ0812/360 7946. Set in an attractive location near the seafront, newer rooms are worth considering. ❷–❸

Parta ⓣ0363/41475. Pleasant, clean village place. Some rooms have hot water and a/c, but the real gem is the room perched way up on the top floor, where there's also a great sitting area. ❶–❸

Serangan Inn II ⓣ0363/41425. Spotless place built high up, which catches the breeze and boasts good rooms. If they're full, *Serangan Homestay I* in the village has the same owners, and *Pantai Ayu* (ⓣ0363/41396) is next door on the hillside. ❷

Tirtagangga

TIRTAGANGGA's main draw is its Water Palace, but the town is refreshingly cool and surrounded by paddy-fields offering pleasant walks and glorious views of Gunung Agung and Gunung Lempuyang, on whose slopes lies the temple of **Pura Lempuyang Luhur**. It's an energetic climb but the views from the temple and the summit of the mountain are stunning. The **Water Palace** (daily 7am–6pm; Rp3100, Rp1000 for camera, Rp2500 for video camera; ⓦwww.tirtagangga.nl) was built in 1946 by Anak Agung Anglurah, the last rajah of Karangasem, and is an impressive terraced area of pools, water channels and fountains set in a garden. You can swim in an upper, deeper pool (Rp6000) or a lower, shallower pool (Rp4000).

An established **guide** for local and longer treks is Komang Gede Sutama (ⓣ081338/770893 or contact him through *Good Karma* restaurant just near the main parking area). At Nyoman Budiarsa's small shop (ⓣ0363/22436), next to *Genta Bali Warung* on the main road you can buy a printed **map** of walks to local villages and temples. There's a **moneychanger** and **wartel** next to *Rijasa* on the main road and a postal agent on the track to the Water Palace from the main road. Tirtagangga is served by **minibuses** and **buses** plying the route between Amlapura and Singaraja. If you are coming from the direction of Candi Dasa get off on the outskirts of Amlapura at the junction with the Singaraja road - the turning is marked by a huge black and white pinnacle, a monument to the fight for independence, which is adorned with a *garuda*. Bemos and minibuses wait here for passengers to the north. Charter transport is available to Tirtagangga from Candi Dasa through Perama for

Rp50,000 per person for a minimum of two people - keep an eye on their website (Ⓦwww.peramatour.com) or check in their office whether they re-establish their bus service to Tirtagangga in the future.

Accommodation and eating

There is plenty of **accommodation** in and around Tirtagangga. *Rijasa* (Ⓣ0363/21873; ❷–❸), across the main road from the track leading to the Water Palace, has a neat row of bungalows in an attractive garden. *Good Karma* (Ⓣ0363/22445; ❷) has clean, tiled rooms set in a small garden in the paddy-fields; enquire at the restaurant of the same name close to the main parking area. *Kusumajaya Inn* (Ⓣ0363/21250; ❷) is about 300m north of the Water Palace; it's a climb of about 100 steps from the road but all the bungalows have verandas that make the most of the splendid views.

ABABI, a lovely rural spot just north of Tirtagangga, is also worth considering for its accommodation, all of which can be reached along a left-hand turn signed from the main road just over a kilometre north of Tirtagangga or via footpaths from Tirtagangga itself. *Pondok Lembah Dukuh* (❷) has five simple rooms with cold-water bathrooms and fine views, just five minutes' walk from Tirtagangga along footpaths. Staff can arrange trekking both locally (Rp20,000/hr per person) or further afield to climb Gunung Agung Rp700,000 for two people including transport).

Pondok Batur Indah (Ⓣ0363/22342; ❷), offers four clean, tiled rooms with hot water in a small family compound with fine views, about fifteen minutes' walk down to Tirtagangga and *Geria Semalung* (Ⓣ&Ⓕ0363/22116; ❹), with four clean, tiled bungalows with hot water in a pretty garden with stunning views, has a small vegetarian restaurant attached and is about thirty minutes' walk from Tirtagangga. Its staff can arrange a **guide** for local treks (Rp35,000 per person per hour) and for climbing Gunung Agung (US$60 for one person; negotiable for more). For **food**, try the tourist menu at *Good Karma*, close to the main parking area, and the *Rice Terrace Coffee Shop*, in a lovely location in the fields, just 100m beyond the Water Palace, on a track heading left from a sharp turn in the main road.

Amed, Jemeluk and the far east coast

The stretch of coast in the far east of Bali from Culik to Aas has acquired the name of **AMED** in traveller-speak, although this is actually just one village in an area of peaceful bays, calm waters and stunning coastal views. Accommodation extends 11km from Amed to Aas, with Lipah Beach and Bunutan the most developed areas (but even they remain quiet and low-key). Transport is slim: all minibuses heading north through Tirtangangga go through Culik (from Candi Dasa, change on the outskirts of Amlapura for north-bound transport), from where **bemos** ply the Amed–Aas route in the morning (hard bargaining should get a fare of around Rp5000 to Lipah Beach); after that, though, you'll need to charter one yourself or use an ojek (Rp10,000 by ojek to Lipah Beach). A Perama charter service runs from Candi Dasa (Rp50,000 per person, minimum two people). Staff at your accommodation will help arrange transport for your return.

The Amed coast is an excellent place to arrange dives. The main **diving area** is around the rocky headland in Jemeluk: a sloping terrace of coral leads to a wall dropping to a depth of more than 40m. The density of fish is high and the current is generally slow. There are plenty of diving operators in the area, all of which offer trips for certified divers; expect to pay US$40-50 for two dives in Jemeluk. Introductory dives are US$50-90, while courses include the PADI Open Water (US$290–320) and the PADI Advanced Open Water (US$240–250). Eco-Dive (Ⓣ0363/23482, Ⓦwww.ecodivebali.com) in Jemeluk and Euro-Dive (Ⓣ0363/23469, Ⓦwww.eurodivebali.com) in Congkang are two of the most established. See "Diving, trekking and surfing", p.247, for guidelines on choosing a dive operator. There are also some excellent **snorkelling** spots, including Lipah Beach and a Japanese wreck not far off the coast at Banyuning.

There's no post office in the area, but there are several **moneychangers** and **wartels** at Amed and Lipah Beach, both of which also have **Internet** access.

Access to Amed is from the small junction village of **Culik** just over 9km north of Tirtagangga on the Amlapura–Singaraja road. From Culik, it's 3km east to the picturesque, sleepy fishing village of **AMED** with a long black-sand beach and hills rising up behind. Just beyond the village, the new *Baliyogi Cottages* (Ⓣ0363/23459, Ⓔgedenyeneng@yahoo.com; ❷) has eight tiled cottages with fan and cold water around a small pool, Another kilometre further east, in the area between Amed and Jemeluk known as **CONGKANG**, *Three Brothers* (Ⓣ0363/23472; ❸), almost next door to Euro-Dive, offers clean, tiled bungalows right beside the beach. A hundred metres further east, across the road from the beach, *Pondok Kebun Wayan* (Ⓣ0363/23473, wwww.amedcafe.com; ❸–❻) is a big set-up offering several standards of room, with most near a small pool. There's air-con and hot water at the top-end rooms and Internet access, a supermarket and dive shop here as well. Just next door on the beach side of the road, *Jukung Bali* (Ⓣ0363/23479; ❸) is a great little place with two tiled bungalows just a few feet from the beach in a pretty garden.

Some 200m further east, at the beginning of **JEMELUK**, *Bamboo Bali* (Ⓣ0363/23478; ❷) is a good budget choice, across the road from the beach, with clean, fan-cooled bungalows in a pretty garden on the hillside. A couple of hundred metres further on, just before the centre of the village, *Diver's Café and Bungalows* (Ⓣ0363/23479, Ⓦwww.balidiverscafe.com; ❷–❸) is across the road from the beach with ten bungalows, hot water and air-con in the more expensive, and a beachside café. A hundred metres further east, *Galang Kangin* (Ⓣ0363/23480; ❷) offers rooms in a two-storey block on the beach side of the road and cottages in a garden across the road. Another hundred metres or so brings you to the car park at Jemeluk, where all the visiting divers congregate. Across the road, just behind Eco-Dive (Ⓣ0363/23482, Ⓦwww.ecodivebali.com: ❶) there are basic bamboo and thatch rooms with attached bathroom. Hardened backpackers will relish the bamboo doors, lack of windows and limited comfort.

Over a headland, the next village to the east, about 600m from the centre of Jemeluk, is **BUNUTAN**, about 8km from Culik. *Deddy's* (Ⓣ0363/23510, Ⓔwarung_deddys@hotmail.com; ❸) has three bungalows set on the hillside. It's a short walk to the beach, and hot water (but no air-con) is available. Another five hundred metres east, the fan or air-con bungalows at *Kusuma Jaya Indah* (Ⓣ0363/23488, ❺) are spacious and set in a lush garden ranging down the hillside from the road to the beach, where there's a good beachside pool. Across the road, *Prema Liong* (Ⓣ0363/23486, Ⓦwww.bali-amed.com; ❹) has bungalows way up on the hillside with stunning views. On the climb up out of the village look out for *Waeni's Warung* (Ⓣ0363/23515; ❷), right on the headland with fabulous views west and just three tiled bungalows. Down the other side of the headland, tucked away down a track off the main road, *Wawa Wewe II* (Ⓣ0363/23522, Ⓔwawawewevillas@yahoo.com; ❹) has bungalows in a garden overlooking the coast with a choice of fan or air-con, hot or cold water. A pool is under construction, so prices may rise.

The next bay east, **LIPAH BEACH**, located around 10km from Culik, is the most developed beach in the area although still very peaceful. The best budget choice is across the road from the beach and *Tresna Yoga* (Ⓣ08180/556 2960, Ⓔigedejiwa@yahoo.com; ❷) has clean, tiled rooms in two-storey buildings.

Over the next two headlands and into the bay at **SELANG**, almost 12km from Culik, the long-standing, ever-popular *Good Karma* (Ⓣ0817/471 3352; ❸–❺) is located right on the black-sand beach, with two standards of accommodation in wood, bamboo and thatch bungalows, all with fan and cold-water. About 500m further on, *Blue Moon Villas* (Ⓣ0812/362 2597, Ⓦwww.bluemoonvilla.com; ❼–❽) is up on the headland as the road climbs out of Selang bay. Their excellent rooms have air con and hot water, there's a great little pool and some superb views.

A kilometre beyond, on the way down into the long bay of **BANYUNING**, *Eka Purnama* (ⓣ086812/121685, ⓦwww.eka-purnama.com; ❸) has four bamboo bungalows with tiled roofs perched on the hillside. All have large verandas looking seawards, fan and attached cold-water bathroom. There's a Japanese wreck not far off the coast here, which is visible to snorkellers.

The village of **AAS** is 1500m beyond *Eka Purnama*, almost 15km from Culik. *Meditasi* (ⓦwww.meditasibungalowsbali.biz; ❸) is just behind the beach in a lovely garden, offering three bamboo bungalows with garden bathrooms and entire walls that open to reveal a fine seaward view for the sunrise. The attached *Kick Back Café* offers inexpensive travellers' fare. Accommodation doesn't come much more isolated than this in modern Bali.

If you have your **own transport**, it's a picturesque 27km from Aas to Amlapura via Seraya but allow at least ninety minutes for the trip. Take local advice on the condition of the road before setting off; rivers cross the road, which may become impassable in the rainy season. There's no public transport between Aas and Seraya.

Tulamben

The small village of **TULAMBEN**, about 10km west of Culik, is the site of the most famous and most popular dive in Bali, the **Liberty wreck**, which lies just offshore, and is completely encrusted with coral, providing a habitat for over 400 species of fish. Parts of the wreck are shallow, making this a good **snorkelling** site, too. Up to a hundred divers a day now visit, so it's worth avoiding the rush hours (11.30am–4pm); night dives are especially good. Most divers come here on day-trips but staying in the village enables you to avoid the crowds and see a few more of the many other local dive sites. There are plenty of local **dive operators**; Tauch Terminal and Tulamben Wreck Divers (see below) are among the most respected. Expect to pay around US$55 for two dives at Tulamben. Courses and excursions to other dive sites on Bali can also be arranged. See "Diving, trekking and surfing, p.247, for guidelines on choosing a dive operator.

Tulamben is easily accessible from Singaraja or Amlapura by public **bus**. Charters are available from Perama in Candi Dasa for Rp50,000 per person for a minimum of two people. There's a **wartel** at the eastern end of the village, and **Internet** access is available at Tulamben Wreck Divers (Rp500 per min), but it isn't easy to **change money** here, and there's no post office – don't trust the post box on the main road.

Accommodation

All the **accommodation** is quite close together making it fairly easy to check out a few places.

Bali Coral Bungalows ⓣ&ⓕ0363/22909. On the track leading to *Tauch Terminal Resort*. Set in a small area; hot water and a/c are available. ❸–❹

Matahari Resort ⓣ0363/22907, ⓔmatahari.tulamben@hotmail.com. Near the sea at the eastern end of the village. There are two standards of rooms, fan and cold-water or a/c and hot water, and there's a small pool. ❷–❹

Paradise Palm Beach Bungalows ⓣ0363/22910, ⓔdive@bali.net. Long-established bungalows with several standards of accommodation – the most expensive have a/c and hot water – and a small restaurant overlooking the sea. ❷–❻

Puri Aries ⓣ0363/23402 Eight budget bungalows above the main road. They are fine if you don't need to be next to the sea. ❶

Puri Madha ⓣ0363/22921. The most westerly place, about 400m beyond the village and very near the *Liberty* wreck. Rooms have fan and cold-water bathrooms, and there's a beachside restaurant. ❷

Tauch Terminal Resort ⓣ0363/22911 or 0361/774504, ⓦwww.divebali.com. Large, gleaming establishment with landscaped gardens, an attractive pool and a busy dive centre. All rooms, the best in the area, have a/c and hot water. ❻–❼

Tulamben Wreck Divers ⓣ0363/23400, ⓦwww.tulambenwreckdivers.com. Just above the main road with three standards of tiled, spacious rooms all with a/c, plus a good pool. ❺–❻

Gunung Batur and Danau Batur

The centre of Bali is occupied by the awesome volcanic masses of the Batur and Bedugul areas, where dramatic mountains shelter crater lakes, and tiny villages line their shores. The entire Batur area is sometimes referred to as **Kintamani**, although this is just one of several villages dotted along the rim of an ancient crater. More villages are situated around **Danau Batur** (Lake Batur) at the bottom of the crater: **Toya Bungkah** is the start of the main route up Gunung Batur and the chief accommodation centre, although **Kedisan** offers some options. The highest points on the rim are **Gunung Abang** (2153m) on the eastern side, and **Gunung Penulisan** (1745m), on the southwest corner, with Pura Puncak Penulisan, also known as Pura Tegeh Koripan, perched on its summit. Rising from the floor of the main crater, **Gunung Batur** (1717m) is an active volcano with four craters of its own.

The main reason that most visitors come to the area is to **climb Gunung Batur**, usually for the sunrise. Anyone who wants to climb is under intense pressure to engage a local guide. These are organized into the **Association of Mount Batur Trekking Guides** (ⓣ0366/52362, ⓔvolcanotrekk@hotmail.com), known locally as "the Organization", which has an office in Toya Bungkah and another at Pura Jati where prices are displayed. The price for the short climb up Batur to see the sunrise is fixed at Rp300,000 per guide for a maximum of four people, Rp450,000 for a five- to six-hour trek around the main crater and Rp600,000 for a seven-hour exploration trek. You can also get **information** about the Gunung Batur area and organized **trekking services** from three companies in Toya Bungkah: Roijaya Wisata (ⓣ0366/51249, ⓔjero_wijaya@hotmail.com), which has an office at *Lakeside Cottages*; Bali Sunrise 2001, at the *Volcano Breeze Café* (ⓣ0366/51824, ⓦwww.balisunrise2001.com); and Arlina's (ⓣ0366/51165). They all use guides from the Association of Mount Batur Trekking Guides, but are more used to working with tourists.

The crater rim

Spread out along the rim of the crater for 11km, the villages of **Penelokan**, **Batur** and **Kintamani** almost merge with each other. If you're planning to stay up here, beware that the mist (and sometimes rain) that obscures the view in late afternoon carries with it a creeping dampness, and the nights are extremely chilly, so bring warm clothes. There's an **admission charge** for visiting the crater area of Rp3100 per person (Rp2000 for a car, Rp1000 for a motorbike). The ticket offices are just south of Penelokan on the road from Bangli and at the junction of the road from Ubud and the rim road.

The views from **PENELOKAN** (1450m) are majestic. Danau Batur lies far below, while Gunung Batur and Gunung Abang tower on either side of the lake. The hoardes of day-trippers who pass through Penelokan attract an entourage of **hawkers** selling all sorts of goods. The only way to avoid the circus is to come early or late, or stay overnight (see below).

Four kilometres north of Penelokan, there are four temples in a row along the crater's rim. The most northerly and the most imposing is **Pura Ulun Danu Batur** (admission by donation; sarong and scarf rental available) the second most important temple on the island after Besakih and one of the highly venerated directional temples or *kayangan jagat*; this one protects Bali from the north. It's a fascinating place to visit at any time as there are usually pilgrims making offerings and praying, and the mist that frequently shrouds the area adds to the atmosphere.

Practicalities

Getting to the rim is straightforward, with **buses** running about every half-hour until mid-afternoon between Singaraja (Penarukan terminal) and Denpasar (Batubulan terminal), via Gianyar and Bangli. Coming from Air Sanih, you can pick up the bus from Singaraja at the junction of the Kintamani road at Kubutambahan, from where Kintamani is 40km away. The route from Ubud is served by brown (Kintamani) **bemos**, and the roads via Suter, Tampaksiring and Payangan are good-quality and easy to drive. At the time of writing Perama omits Kintamani from its regular **tourist shuttle bus** schedule, but charters (Rp50,000 per person, minimum two people) are available from Ubud. Once in the area, it's about Rp2000 for all short bemo hops along the rim.

Yayasan Bintang Danu, a local organization, runs the **tourist office** (daily 9am–3pm; ⓣ0366/51730) in Penelokan, almost opposite the turning down to Kedisan; they can provide information about accommodation, charter rates, and routes up the volcano, and may be able to rustle up some leaflets and maps. The **post office** and **phone office** are close together just off the main road 2km north of Penelokan. It's difficult to **change money** in the area, so bring plenty of cash.

Most people opt **to stay** down at the lake but, if your budget will run to it, go for the *Lakeview Hotel* (ⓣ0366/51394, ⓦwww.indo.com/hotels/lakeview; ❻–❼), located in Penelokan on the edge of the crater rim, with hot water, thick quilts and stunning views. A couple of hundred feet below, on the road down to Kedisan, *Windu Sari* (ⓣ0366/52467, ⓕ52468; ❻) is smaller but has similar views and facilities. The only budget accommodation on the rim is *Miranda* (ⓣ0366/52022; ❶) about 100m north of the market in **KINTAMANI**; all public transport along the rim passes the door. The rooms are very basic with attached mandi and squat toilet. The owner, Made Senter, also works as a **tour guide**.

The crater rim is packed with plush **restaurants**, but cheaper meals are available at *Ramana* – about 300m towards Kintamani from Penelokan, right on the crater's rim. Closer to Penelokan, on the opposite side of the road, *Wibisana* is also good value.

Climbing Gunung Batur

There are several ways to conquer **Gunung Batur** (1717m). With your own transport, the easiest way to get to the top is to drive to **SERONGGA**, west of Songan on the lakeside. From the car park, it's a climb of between thirty minutes and one hour to the largest and highest crater, **Batur I**.

Climbing Batur is best as a dry-season expedition (April–Oct) as paths are unpleasant in the wet season and there are no views. If you're reasonably fit and don't have your own transport, the most common route is to climb up to Batur I from either **Toya Bungkah** or the road near **Pura Jati**. Allow two to three hours to get to the top and about half that time to get back down. **In daylight**, you shouldn't really need a guide for this route, but fewer people climb during the day because of the possibility of clouds obscuring the view. From Toya Bungkah, numerous paths head up through the forest – one starts just south of the car park near *Arlina's* (see p.398) – and after about an hour you'll come out onto the bare slope of the mountain. From here, follow the paths that head up to the tiny warung perched way up on the crater rim. Local people could easily point you in the right direction, although whether they will do so is another matter as all visitors are under intense pressure to use local guides. Most people climb **in the dark** to get to the top for the fabulous dawn view over Gunung Abang and Lombok's Gunung Rinjani. You'll need to leave early (4–5am), and you should take a **guide** as it's easy to get lost in the forest. There are also longer routes on the mountain exploring the other craters, for which you'll need a guide. The Association of Mount Batur Trekking Guides and Trekking Services in Toya Bungkah (see p.398) offer guides for all the climbs.

Danau Batur

Home of Dewi Danu, the goddess of the crater lake, **Danau Batur** is especially sacred to the Balinese, and the waters from the lake are believed to percolate through the earth and reappear as springs in other parts of the island. Situated 500m below the crater rim, Danau Batur is the largest lake in Bali, 8km long and 3km wide, and one of the most glorious. The road to the lakeside, served by **public bemos**, leaves the crater rim at Penelokan. The fare from Penelokan to any of the accommodation places around the lake is Rp5000, as long as you bargain.

Toya Bungkah

TOYA BUNGKAH, 8km from Penelokan, is the accommodation centre of the lakeside area and the main starting point for climbs up Gunung Batur. Toya Bungkah's **Natural Hot Springs** (daily 8am–5pm; US$5) are clean and attractive with cold- and hot-water pools but expensive. **Changing money** can be difficult, so it's best to bring cash. There's a 24-hour **wartel** at the start of Toya Bungkah with **Internet** access.

Places to stay line the road in Toya Bungkah, with a few more down by the lakeside. *Arlina's* (ⓣ0366/51165; ❹–❺) is a friendly, popular set-up at the southern end of the village, with some hot-water rooms; *Nyoman Mawar (Under the Volcano;* ⓣ0366/51166; ❶) is in the village, offering clean rooms with cold-water bathrooms; *Nyoman Mawar III (Under the Volcano III;* ⓣ0366/51166; ❶) has simple, clean cold-water bungalows close to the lake with fabulous views; *Pualam* (❶) is a quiet place on the main road, close to the hot springs, with rooms set around a pleasant garden. For something more comfortable, *Lakeside Cottages* (ⓣ0366/51249, ⓕ51250; ❸–❻) has a range of accommodation, from large cottages with good verandas, lake views, hot water and TV, down to cheaper, cold-water rooms further from the lake. It also has a swimming pool. Several losmen have inexpensive **restaurants** serving a good range of Western and Indo-Chinese options and freshwater fish from the lake at decent prices. *Volcano Breeze Café* on the track from the main road to the lake also serves good-value food in relaxed surroundings.

Kedisan, Trunyan and Buahan

At the bottom of the steep descent, 3km from Penelokan, the road splits in the lakeside village of **KEDISAN**; the right fork leads to the jetty for boats to Trunyan before continuing on to the villages of Buahan and Abang; the left fork leads to Toya Bungkah.

Kedisan is convenient for visits to the Bali Aga village of Trunyan across the lake but further from the start of the Gunung Batur climb. A few hundred metres from the junction, towards Toya Bungkah, *Hotel Segara* (ⓣ0366/51136, ⓔhotelsegara@plasa.com; ❷–❹) has three standards of accommodation, with hot water and TV in the most expensive. The hotel offers pick-ups from throughout Bali; check the transport cost when you phone to arrange it. Next door, *Hotel Surya* (ⓣ0366/51139; ❷–❸) also has good rooms, some with hot water. Many of the balconies here have lovely views. They offer a free and discounted pick-up service; again, check the details when you phone. A couple of hundred metres further on, *Hotel Astra Dana* (ⓣ0366/52091, ⓔdizzymade@yahoo.com; ❶–❷) has new rooms by the lakeside, the most expensive of which have hot water and lake views.

Turning right at the bottom of the road from Penelokan brings you to the jetty for boats to Trunyan and a quiet section of road with picturesque views that hugs the lakeside for several kilometres.

Candikuning and Danau Bratan

Neither as big nor as dramatic as the Batur region, the **Danau Bratan** (Lake Bratan) area, sometimes just known as Bedugul, has impressive mountains, beautiful lakes, quiet walks and attractive and important temples. There is no direct route between the two regions: Bedugul and Danau Bratan lie on a busy parallel road, 53km from Denpasar and 30km from Singaraja, nestling in the lee of Gunung Catur, with the smaller, quieter lakes Buyan and Tamblingan about 5km to the northwest, both worth exploring if you have time.

The small village of **CANDIKUNING**, situated above the southern shores of Danau Bratan, is the location of the highly recommended **Bali Botanical Gardens** (Kebun Raya Eka Karya Bali; daily 8am–6pm; Rp3500; parking for cars Rp1500, for motorbikes Rp500; entry for cars Rp6000; motorbikes prohibited). The gardens host hundreds of species of plants, including bamboo and orchids, and is a rich area for birdwatching. The entrance is a short walk from the market area, along a small side road marked by a giant corn-on-the-cob statue. Candikuning's daily **market**, Bukit Mungsu, is small but offers a vast range of fruit, spices and plants, including orchids.

Situated at 1200m above sea level and thought to be 35m deep in places, **Danau Bratan** is surrounded by forested hills and, like Danau Batur, revered by Balinese farmers as the source of freshwater springs across a wide area of the island. The lake (and its goddess) are worshipped in the temple of **Pura Ulun Danu Bratan** (daily 7am–5pm; Rp3300, cars Rp1500), one of the most photographed temples in Bali, which consists of several shrines, some dramatically situated on small islands that appear to float on the surface of the lake.

Practicalities

Situated north of Candikuning's market, *Sari Artha Inn* (☎0368/21011; ❶–❷) has a choice of **rooms** with or without hot water, all with verandas, set in a pretty garden. It's also the location for the Perama office, so is especially convenient if you're using them. *Cempaka* (☎0368/21402; ❷) is a quiet budget place just off the road to the Botanical Gardens, and the pricier rooms have hot water; nearby *Permata Firdaus* ☎0368/21531; ❷) is also a good-value possibility. *Ashram Guesthouse* (☎0368/21450; ❷–❹) occupies lovely grounds on the lakeside and offers a range of rooms.

For inexpensive **food**, a row of stalls lines the road where it runs along the lakeside south of Pura Ulun Danu Braton and the warung in the temple car park are worth a try. *As Siddiq*, about 100m north of the car park on the opposite side of the road, is a popular, good-value place serving Taliwang and Sasak food. In Candikuning, *Ananda* and *Anda* just across the road from the turning to the Botanical Gardens both offer a range of inexpensive Indonesian and Chinese food.

There are **bus** services to and from Denpasar (Ubung terminal; 1hr 30min) and Singaraja (Sukasada terminal; 1hr 30min). For **tourist shuttle bus** tickets the Perama office (☎0368/21011) is at the *Sari Artha*, just below the market on the main road in Candikuning. There's one daily service to the north of the island and one to the south. There's a **wartel** (daily 8am–9.30pm) in the market, and you can **change money** at the moneychangers in the car park at Pura Ulun Danu Bratan or in Bukit Mungsu.

Singaraja and around

The second-largest Balinese city after Denpasar, **SINGARAJA** has an airy spaciousness created by its broad avenues, impressive monuments and colonial bungalows set in attractive gardens. It's of most interest to tourists for its transport connections: if you're exploring the north you'll probably pass through at some point. There are three bemo and bus **terminals** in Singaraja. **Sukasada** (locally called Sangket), to the south of the town, serves Bedugul and Denpasar; **Banyuasri**, on the western edge of town, serves the west, including Lovina, Seririt and Gilimanuk; and **Penarukan** is for services eastwards along the north coast via Tulamben to Amlapura and along the Kintamani/Penelokan road for the Batur area and on to Bangli. Small bemos (flat rate Rp2000) ferry passengers between the terminals.

The **tourist office** is south of the town centre at Jl Veteran 23 (Mon–Thurs 8.30am–2pm, Fri & Sat 8.30am–1pm; ⓣ0362/25141). As Lovina is just 6km west of Singaraja, there's little reason to stay, but if you want to *Wijaya*, Jl Sudirman 74 (ⓣ0362/21915, ⓕ25817; ❷–❹), has the widest range of rooms and is conveniently close to Banyuasri terminal. The night market is in the Jalan Durian area. The most central place to **change money** is Bank Central Asia on Jl Dr Sutomo, which has an ATM. Singaraja has several **hospitals**, including the public hospital, Rumah Sakit Umum, on Jalan Ngurah Rai (ⓣ0362/41046). **Long-distance bus** tickets to Surabaya, Yogyakarta and Jakarta are available at bus offices along Jalan Jen Achmad Yani, The main **post office** is at Jl Gajah Made 156 (Mon–Thurs 8am–4pm, Fri 8am–2pm, Sat 8am-12noon), which also has **Internet** access.

East of Singaraja

To the east of Singaraja lies a string of interesting temples with unusual, sometimes humorous, carvings. They can all be reached by **bemo** from Singaraja's Penarukan terminal. Eight kilometres east of Singaraja, a small road north takes you 200m to the pink sandstone **Pura Beji** of **SANGSIT**, famous for the sheer exuberance of its carvings. About 400m to the northeast across the fields from Pura Beji, carvings at the **Pura Dalem** cover the whole range of heavenly rewards and hellish punishments, including a lot of soft pornography that could count as either.

Back on the main road, 500m east of the Sangsit turning, you come to the road that leads 4km to **JAGARAGA** and the famous carvings at **Pura Dalem Jagaraga** temple, which depict life before and after the Dutch invasion in 1848. On the right-hand front wall is the much-photographed carving of two Dutch men driving a Model T Ford, being held up by bandits.

The most spectacular of the temples in the area is **Pura Meduwe Karang** at **KUBUTAMBAHAN**, 12km east of Singaraja and 300m east of the junction with the Kintamani road. It's built on a huge scale and features numerous **carvings** of Balinese villagers. In the inner courtyard, you'll find one of the most famous carvings on Bali: a cyclist (possibly the Dutch artist WOJ Nieuwenkamp, who first visited Bali in 1904), wearing floral shorts, with a rat about to go under the back wheel, apparently being chased by a dog.

Further east, 6km from Kubutambahan, **AIR SANIH**, also known as Yeh Sanih, is a beach resort based around the freshwater springs on the coast, although the accommodation is spread out along the coast between Air Sanih and the small village of Bukti 3km to the east. All **public transport** between Singaraja and Amlapura passes through Air Sanih. The freezing cold **springs** are set in attractive gardens on the coast with changing rooms (daily 7am–7pm; Rp2000).

Just next door, *Hotel Puri Sanih* (❷) is the most convenient **place to stay**; all rooms have fan and cold water. About 1500m west of the springs on the south side of the road, *Cleopatra* (ⓣ0812/362 2232; ❷) with new fan and cold water bungalows set in a huge garden.

Lovina

LOVINA stretches along 8km of black-sand beach, the largest resort in Bali outside the Kuta-Legian-Seminyak conurbation. Beginning 6km west of Singaraja, the resort encompasses six villages: Pemaron, Anturan, Tukad Mungga, Kalibukbuk, Kaliasem and Temukus. **Kalibukbuk** is the centre of Lovina, with the greatest concentration of accommodation and restaurants.

Arrival, information and getting around

All inter-island **buses** from Java to Singaraja pass through Lovina, as do Gilimanuk–Singaraja and Amlapura–Gilimanuk services and all buses from the west of the island. You can also come directly on Denpasar (Ubung)–Singaraja services via Pupuan, or on minibuses to Seirit before swapping onto local services. From the east of Bali, you'll come via Singaraja. As the accommodation is so spread out, it's worth knowing where you want to be dropped off. **Tourist shuttle buses** also serve the resort from other parts of Bali as well as Lombok; the Perama office (daily 8am–10pm; ⓣ0362/41161) is in Anturan, a short walk from the Anturan accommodation. They charge an additional Rp5000 to be dropped off elsewhere. Check with other shuttle bus operators whether they will drop you off more centrally. Lovina's **tourist office** (Mon–Sat 8am–8pm) is on the main road at Kalibukbuk. To **get around** the resort, you can pick up the frequent bemos (4am–6pm) that zip between Singaraja and Seririt.

Accommodation

Generally, it's better to go for **accommodation** away from the noisy main road. Access to restaurants and other facilities is easiest from places in Kalibukbuk and Banyualit, especially as public transport closes down after dark, after which you'll have to negotiate with transport touts if you're staying outside walking distance.

Tukad Mungga

Most accommodation in **TUKAD MUNGGA** is on side roads leading to the beach (known as Pantai Happy). It's quiet but there are no amenities nearby and the nightlife of Kalibukbuk and Banyualit is several kilometres away.

Happy Beach Inn (*Bahagia*) ⓣ0362/41017. Four basic, rooms with attached cold-water bathrooms close to Pantai Happy beach. There's a small garden and a beachside restaurant. ❷

Kubu Lalang ⓣ0362/42207, ⓦhttp//kubu.balihotelguide.com. Traditional bungalows in a garden just behind the beach midway between Pantai Happy and Anturan (5–10min walk in either direction). ❸–❹

Hotel Permai ⓣ0362/41471. A large set-up with rooms in two-storey buildings around the pool. Most have fans but a couple have a/c. Permai dive centre is here. ❷

Puri Bedahulu ⓣ0362/41731. Next to the beach at Pantai Happy with a restaurant looking across the sand. All the bungalows have hot water and the most expensive have a/c. ❷

Anturan

The main turning to the accommodation at **ANTURAN** is almost opposite the petrol station and Anturan health centre (*Puskesmas*). Coming from the east, look out for big signs for *Bali Taman Lovina*, *Yudha* (*Simon Seaside Cottages*) and *Villa Agung*. The Perama office is just west of the turning, and all the accommodation below is within ten minutes' walk of the office.

Bayu Mantra ⓣ0362/41930. Clean, tiled fan bungalows in a large garden set back from the beach. Hot water available. ❷

Gede Homestay ⓣ0362/41526. Simple bungalows in a small garden near the beach. More expensive rooms have a/c and hot water. ❷

Mandhara Chico ⓣ0362/41271. Close to the beach with a range of rooms, some with hot water and a/c. ❷–❸

Puspa Rama ⓣ0362/42070, ⓔagungdayu@yahoo.com. A small row of six, clean rooms all with fan and some with hot water on the lane leading to the beach from the main road. ❶

Sri Homestay ⓣ0362/41135, ⓔsrihomstay@yahoo.com. In a beachfront location with all the bungalows (fan and cold water only), facing seawards. Reached via a track from the main road or via the beach. ❷
Villa Agung ⓣ0362/41527, ⓦwww.agungvilla.com. Rooms, all with hot water, some with a/c, are set back from the sea behind the small swimming pool. There are also cottages sleeping four or five people. The real bonus is the seafront restaurant, lounge, sunbathing area and bar. ❸
Yudha (formerly *Simon Seaside Cottages*) ⓣ0362/41183, ⓕ1160. Beside the beach with a pool and a choice of a/c or fan rooms and hot water is available. Look at several rooms, they vary a lot. ❸

Banyualit

The **BANYUALIT** side road marks the beginning of the most developed part of Lovina, about 1.5km east of Kalibukbuk, with plenty of accommodation and a few restaurants. The *Volcano Club*, Lovina's main nightlife, is in this area.

Indra Pura ⓣ0362/41560. Budget choice at the main road end of the main Banyualit turning. ❷
Juni Arta ⓣ0362/41885, ⓔevyrs_luvy@hotmail.com. Reached via a path behind *Hotel Kalibukbuk*, and offering good-value bungalows with cold water and a choice of fan or a/c. ❷
Mas ⓣ0362/41773. Behind an impressive gateway, rooms with hot water, some with fan and some with a/c. ❸
Ray ⓣ0362/41088. Tiled rooms in a two-storey block with balcony or veranda. All have cold water and fan. ❷
Sartaya ⓣ0362/42240. Good-quality. clean, tiled bungalows all with cold-water and a choice of fan or a/c. ❷
Suma ⓣ&ⓕ362/41566. Clean, well-maintained rooms in a two-storey block a short walk from the beach. There are lots of options, a/c and hot water are available. ❷–❹

Kalibukbuk

Centred around two side roads, Jalan Mawar, also known as Jalan Ketapang or Jalan Rambutan, and Jalan Bina Ria, **KALIBUKBUK** has most of the tourist facilities. The narrow entrance to Jalan Mawar is across from *Khi Khi Restaurant*.

Astina Jl Mawar ⓣ0362/41187, ⓔselisakadek@hotmail.com. Several standards of accommodation in a quiet spot a short walk from the beach. ❶–❹
Harris Homestay ⓣ0362/41152. A popular budget gem tucked away in the backstreets off Jalan Bina Ria. Good-value budget rooms. ❶
Padang Lovina ⓣ0362/41302, ⓔpadanglovina@yahoo.com. Accommodation in a two-storey block just off Jalan Bina Ria. Some rooms have hot water. Guests can use the pool at *Pulestis*. ❷
Pondok Elsa ⓣ0362/41186. Just off Jalan Bina Ria. There's good-quality accommodation with a choice of fan or a/c and more expensive rooms have hot water. ❷
Pulestis Jl Bina Ria ⓣ0362/41035, ⓔjokoartawan@hotmail.com. A short walk from the beach, with a choice of hot- or cold-water rooms with fan or a/c, and a pool. ❸
Puri Bali Jl Mawar ⓣ0362/41485, ⓦwww.puribalilovina.com. A variety of rooms, in a quiet location, not far from the beach. There's an excellent pool. ❷–❹
Puri Manik Sari ⓣ0362/41089. Accessible from the main road and Jalan Bina Ria, there are several standards of bungalows, with a/c and hot water at the top end. ❶–❸
Rini Jl Mewar ⓣ0362/41386, ⓔrinihotel@telkom.net. Several standards of extremely clean accommodation, a short walk to the beach. More expensive rooms have a/c and hot water, and there's a pool. ❸–❺
Taman Lily's Jl Mewar ⓣ&ⓕ0362/41307. A row of excellent-value spotless bungalows, with fans or a/c and hot water. ❷

Kaliasem and Temukus

West of Kalibukbuk, restaurants and accommodation line the roadside in the villages of **KALIASEM** and **TEMUKUS**. Road noise is the enemy here; the places below are set far enough back to block the noise out.

Agus Homestay ⓣ&ⓕ0362/41202. At the far western end of Lovina. Clean, tiled rooms, with verandas that face the ocean. All have a/c and hot water. ❸
Bagus Homestay ⓣ0362/93407, ⓕ93406. Situated 1.5km west of its sister operation, *Agus Home-*

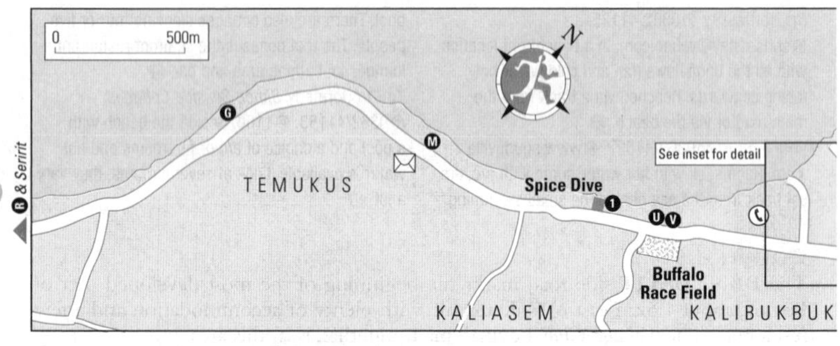

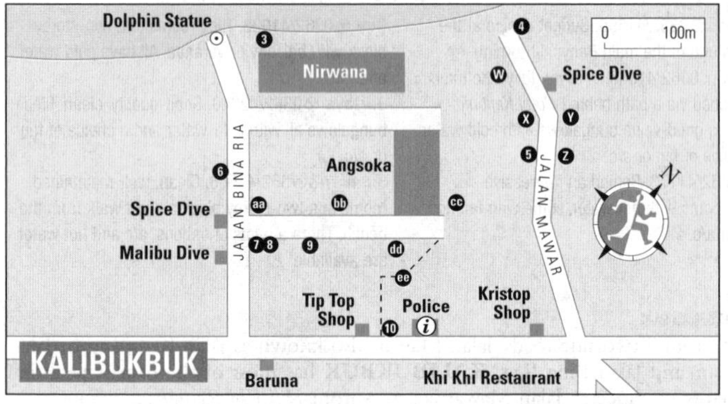

stay. Bungalows beside the beach with a swimming pool. All are clean, with a/c and hot water. 3–5

Billibo ⓣ0362/42020, ⓕ1355. Tiled bungalows close to the beachfront; a/c and hot water are available. 2

Mutiara ⓣ0362/41132. Family-run place offering simple rooms in a two-storey building all with fan and cold water. It's a short walk to the beach. 1

Puri Manggala ⓣ0362/41371. Simple rooms in a family compound tucked between the beach and the road. There's hot water and a/c in the most expensive rooms. 2–3

The resort

Many people consider the early-morning **dolphin trips** from Lovina to be the highlight of their stay, but others find them grossly overrated. Boats leave at 6am and cost Rp30,000 per person for the two-hour trip; book directly with the skippers on the beach. The skippers also know the best spots for **snorkelling** and will take you out for Rp30,000 per person for a one-and-a-half to two-hour trip. Situated between the main diving areas on the north coast of Bali – Pulau Menjangan to the west (see p.407), and Tulamben (p.396) and Amed (p.394) to the east – Lovina is a good place to base yourself for **diving**. There are plenty of dive operators in the resort, offering introductory dives, dive trips and courses. Two dives in the Lovina area cost US$40–50, Pulau Menjangan US$50-65, Tulamben US$50-55 and Amed US$50-75. Introductory dives and refresher sessions are about US$75 and a PADI Open Water course US$250-285. The most established operator is Spice Dive at Spice Beach in Kaliasem (ⓣ0362/41509, ⓦwww.balispicedive.com), with additional shops on Jalan Bina Ria and one on Jalan Mawar. Others include Permai at *Hotel Permai*, Pantai Happy (ⓣ0362/41223), and Malibu Dive next to *Malibu* restaurant (ⓣ&ⓕ0362/41225) and on Jalan Bina Ria (ⓣ0362/41061).

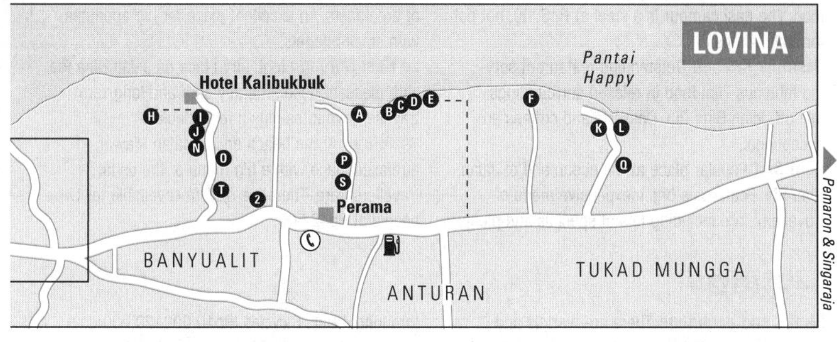

ACCOMMODATION						RESTAURANTS & CLUBS	
Agus Homestay	G	Mandhara Chico	B	Puspa Rama	S	Bali Apik	9
Astina	W	Mas	O	Ray	N	Barakuda	5
Bagus Homestay	R	Mutiara	U	Rini	Y	Bu Warung	10
Bayu Mantra	P	Padang Lovina	dd	Sartaya	J	Café Spice	1
Billibo	M	Hotel Permai	Q	Sri Homestay	E	Funky Monkey	3
Gede Homestay	A	Pondok Elsa	bb	Suma	I	Jasmine Kitchen	8
Happy Beach Inn	K	Pulestis	aa	Taman Lily's	X	Kopi Bali	6
Harris Homestay	cc	Puri Bali	Z	Villa Agung	D	Le Nasi Goreng	7
Indra Pura	T	Puri Bedahulu	L	Yudha	C	Volcano Club	2
Juni Arta	H	Puri Manggala	V			Waru Bali	4
Kubu Lalang	F	Puri Manik Sari	ee				

Watersports are currently in their infancy in Lovina, but Spice Dive offers parasailing, wakeboarding, kneeboarding and water-skiing while sailing, fishing and spearfishing can be arranged at *Kubu Lalang* restaurant (☎0362/42207). If water-based action palls, Lovina stages **buffalo races** (*sapi gerumbungan*) in the late afternoon in a field in Kaliasem (Rp40,000) in the high season, supplemented by cooking, rice-pounding and martial arts displays. Look out for local flyers advertising the races.

Eating and entertainment

There's a good range of **restaurants** in Lovina, and several of the places on Jalan Bina Ria offer live music with dinner. The club scene centres on the *Volcano Club* on the main road a couple of kilometres east of Kalibukbuk. In the high season, there are occasional **parties** at *Café Spice* lasting until the early hours of the morning; look out for flyers.

Bali Apik Tucked away off Jalan Bina Ria and serving an excellent choice of breakfasts as well as a large Indo-Chinese, seafood and Western menu.

Barakuda On Jalan Mawar, specializing in well-cooked, good-value seafood. Your choice is served with one of eleven Balinese or Chinese sauces. There are plenty of vegetarian, pork and chicken options as well.

Bu Warung Probably the best-value food in Kalibukbuk, this tiny place on the main road has a small menu of around a dozen well-cooked main courses (Rp7500–8500). There are also sandwiches, pancakes and fried bananas and pineapples on offer.

Funky Monkey Shady chill-out spot at the beach end of Jalan Bina Ria. Drinks are cheap, and there's a tiny menu of Indonesian and Western

food. The nasi campur is a steal at Rp5000, but not for chilli wimps.
Jasmine Kitchen Outstanding restaurant serving fabulous Thai food in relaxed surroundings just off Jalan Bina Ria. Desserts and coffees are exceptional.
Kopi Bali Popular place at the ocean end of Jalan Bina Ria. Features a big, inexpensive menu of travellers' fare including lots of specials and plenty of breakfasts. An excellent place for big appetites with small budgets.
Le Nasi Goreng Light, airy place on Jalan Bina Ria with pleasant decor, friendly staff and long-term traveller favourites plus a few specials.
Waru Bali At the beach end of Jalan Mawar, a relaxed place with a big menu of the usual travellers' fare. There's a *rijstaffel* available for two people at Rp42,500.

Listings

Banks and exchange There are wartels and moneychangers throughout the resort, and there's a BCA ATM on the main road in Kalibukbuk and another on Jl Bina Ria.
Car, bike motorbike rental Prices start at Rp90,000 a day for a Suzuki Jimney and Rp125,000 for a Kijang. Insurance deals vary and are only available with established companies, which include Yuli Transport, at Yuli Shop not far from *Barakuda* restaurant on Jalan Mawar (☎0362/41184), and Dupa (☎0362/41397) next to Baruna on the main road, where Made Wijana (☎08133/856 3027) is a recommended driver. If you want to charter a vehicle plus driver, it's about Rp250,000 per day, including petrol. It's also possible to arrange one-way drops to destinations throughout Bali. Bicycles (Rp10,000–20,000/day) are also widely available, as are motorbikes (Rp30,000–40,000/day).
Hospitals The closest are in Singaraja, although for anything serious you'll have to go to Denpasar (p.355).
Internet access Widely available; prices are Rp350–400 per minute.
Police The police station is in the same building as the tourist office, on the main road at Kalibukbuk.
Post The post office (Mon–Thurs 7.30am–3pm, Fri 7.30am–1pm, Sat 7.30am–11.30am) is 1km west of Kalibukbuk. For poste restante, have mail addressed to you at the Post Office, Jalan Raya Singaraja, Lovina, Singaraja 81152, Bali. Several postal agents in Kalibukbuk sell stamps.

Around Lovina

One popular outing from Lovina is to Bali's only Buddhist monastery, the **Brahma Vihara Ashrama**, 10km southwest of Lovina, which can be combined with a visit to the hot springs at Banjar Tega. Catch any westbound bemo to **DENCARIK**, where a sign points inland to the monastery, and ojek wait to take you the last steep 5km. From the temple you can walk to the **hot springs** (daily 8am–6pm; Rp3000, parking Rp1000). To reach them, head back downhill from the monastery and take the first major left turn. After a few hundred metres you'll reach a major crossroads and marketplace at the village of **BANJAR TEGA**. Turn left and a *kulkul* tower will now be on your right. After about 200m you'll see a sign for the "Holy Hot Springs, Air Panas" (1km).

Bali Barat National Park

Nearly the whole of west Bali's mountain ridge, 20km west of Lovina, is conserved as **Bali Barat National Park** (**Taman Nasional Bali Barat**), a 760–square kilometre area of savannah, rainforest, monsoon forest and reef, which supports some 160 species of bird, including the endangered **Bali starling**, Bali's one true endemic creature. Only a few trails are open to the public, but most visitors come for the spectacular diving and snorkelling off the **Pulau Menjangan** reefs. Anyone who enters Bali Barat has to go with a guide and must also have a permit, both of which need to be arranged either through the **National Park headquarters** (daily 7am–5pm) in **CEKIK**, at the Denpasar–Gilimanuk–Singaraja T-junction, 3km south of Gilimanuk, or at their office at the Labuan Lalang jetty (departure point for Pulau Menjangan; see p.407). **Guides** charge Rp150,000 for a two-hour hike for up to two people or Rp400,000 for seven hours. Permits costs Rp2500 per person per day. All dark-green Ubung (Denpasar)–Gilimanuk **bemos** pass the park headquarters, as do all dark-red Singaraja–Gilimanuk bemos.

There are three major **trails** through the park. If your main interest is birdspotting, opt for the Tegal Bunder trek (1–2hr), which takes in the Bali Starling Pre-Release Centre, or the Teluk Terima trail (2hr); possible sightings include the rufous-backed kingfisher, the black drongo, and the olive-backed sunbird. The Gunung Klatakan–Gunung Bakingan trail (7hr) is strenuous and features some steep inclines, passing through moderately interesting rainforest, though you're unlikely to spot much wildlife.

If student groups are not in residence you can usually pitch your own **tent** at the Cekik national park headquarters, though there are no facilities except for a noodle cart that sets up outside the gate every day. The nearest **hotel** and restaurant is *Pondok Wisata Lestari*, about 1.5km north of the headquarters on the road into Gilimanuk (see p.407 for details). Or you could head for the lovely little beach in **PEMUTERAN**, 28km east of Cekik (or just 15km from Labuan Lalang), where, in among the pricey but very appealing accommodation, *Jubawa Homestay* (☎0362/94745; ④–⑤) offers eight immaculate fan and air-con bungalows set back from the road, about 300m from the beach, and *Pondok Sari* (☎0362/94738, ⓦwww.pondoksari.com; ⑥–⑦) has delightful bungalows on the shore. Both places are easily reached on the Gilimanuk–Singaraja bemos, and Pemuteran has several operators running snorkelling and dive trips to Pulau Menjangan.

Pulau Menjangan (Deer Island)

By far the most popular part of Bali Barat is **Pulau Menjangan** (**Deer Island**), a tiny uninhabited island just 8km off the north coast, whose shoreline is encircled by some of the most spectacular **coral reefs** in Bali, perfect for snorkelling and diving, with drop-offs of up to 60m, first-class wall dives and superb visibility. There's also an old shipwreck that is frequented by sharks and rays.

As the island is part of the national park, you're obliged to go with a guide and must also have a permit. Guides, permits and boat transport should be arranged at the jetty in **LABUAN LALANG**, 13km east of Cekik, on the Gilimanuk–Singaraja bemo route (25 min from Gilimanuk or 2hr from Lovina). There's a small national park office here (daily except national holidays 8am–3pm), as well as several warung. **Boats** to Pulau Menjangan can be hired any time up to 3pm; they hold ten people and cost Rp250,000 for a four-hour snorkelling tour – it's thirty minutes to the island. You'll also have to pay Rp60,000 for your guide (one per boat), plus Rp2500 per person for the national park permit. You can rent snorkelling equipment at the jetty for Rp40,000 a set. There are occasional reports of thefts from the boats while snorkellers are underwater, so leave your valuables elsewhere. Pulau Menjangan also features on day- and overnight tours for snorkellers (from US$30) and divers (from US$70) who are based in Pemuteran, Lovina, Kuta, Sanur or Candi Dasa.

Gilimanuk and ferries to Java

Situated on the westernmost tip of Bali, less than 3km from East Java and about 17km west of Labuan Lalang, the small, ribbon-like town of **GILIMANUK** is used by visitors mainly as a transit point for boats to and from Java. **Ferries** shuttle constantly between Gilimanuk and Ketapang (every 20min, day and night; 30min; Rp3300), near **Banyuwangi** (see p.313). If you're travelling quite a way into Java, to Probolinggo or Yogyakarta for example, consider buying an all-inclusive ticket from your starting point in Bali. The cheapest **long-distance buses** travel out of Denpasar's Ubung bemo terminal, but more convenient tourist bus-and-train combinations can be booked through travel agents in major tourist centres across Bali.

Getting to Gilimanuk by **bus or bemo** from almost any major town in north, south and west Bali is straightforward. Gilimanuk's main bus depot is behind the ferry terminal, while bemos run from in front of the market, near the mosque on Jalan Raya Gilimanuk, about ten minutes' walk from the ferries. From Denpasar (128km southwest) and the southern beaches, take a bus or dark-green bemo from Ubung terminal. From Lovina and Singaraja (88km northeast), dark-red bemos run to Gilimanuk, as do a few buses. Buses also run here from Padang Bai. You can change money at the bank near the market.

Accommodation in Gilimanuk is grim. One of the better options is *Hotel Sampurna* (❷), which has half a dozen fan and air-con rooms opposite the mosque on Jalan Raya Gilimanuk, about 900m south of the ferry terminal. Otherwise, head 2km south of the port along the road to Cekik, where you'll find slightly more tourist-friendly rooms and a restaurant at *Pondok Wisata Lestari* (☎0365/61504; ❶–❸).

4.4

Lombok and the Gili Islands

Thirty-five kilometres east of Bali at its closest point, Islamic **Lombok** (80km by 70km) is populated by Sasak people. It differs considerably from its Hindu neighbour, with lots of wide-open spaces and unspoilt beaches, and much less traffic and pollution. Tourist facilities are less widespread and public transport sparser. The island's northern area is dominated by the awesome bulk of **Gunung Rinjani**. Trekking at least part of the way up Rinjani is the reason many tourists come to Lombok and most base themselves in the nearby villages of **Senaru** and **Batu Koq** or head for **Sembalun Lawang** on the eastern flanks. Other visitors enjoy the cool foothills at tiny **Tetebatu** and **Sapit**. The other big draw are the beaches: the resort of **Senggigi** on the northwest coast, the trio of **Gili Islands**, just offshore, and south-coast **Kuta**, a popular surfing spot. Lombok's capital and main city area **Ampenan-Mataram-Cakranegara-Sweta** has excellent transport connections and is a user-friendly Indonesian city.

Ampenan-Mataram-Cakranegara-Sweta

The **AMPENAN-MATARAM-CAKRANEGARA-SWETA** conurbation comprises four towns and stretches over 8km from west to east, but there's a fairly straightforward local transport system that makes it easy to get around. The westernmost part of the city is the old port town of **Ampenan**, the jumping-off point for Senggigi a few kilometres up the coast. Merging into Ampenan to the east, **Mataram** is the capital of West Nusa Tenggara province as well as the district of West Lombok and full of offices and government buildings. East again, **Cakranegara**, usually known as just Cakra (pronounced "Chakra"), is the commercial capital of the island, with shops, markets, workshops and hotels all aimed at Indonesian trade but welcoming to tourists as well. Furthest west is **Sweta**, the location of the island's main bus station and a huge market.

Arrival, information and city transport

Planes land at **Selaparang Airport**, a couple of kilometres north of Mataram and Ampenan. There is an exchange counter, open for all international arrivals, and a taxi counter with fixed-price fares (to Mataram Rp15,000; central Senggigi Rp30,000; north Senggigi Rp40,000; Bangsal Rp60,000; Sekotong Rp75,000–110,000; Tetebatu Rp105,000; Labuhan Lombok Rp135,000; Senaru Rp175,000; Sembalun Rp200,000; maximum four people). There's a wartel here (7am–9pm). To get to Bangsal (for the Gili Islands) on public transport, turn left on the main road at the front of the airport, head straight on across the roundabout and 500m further on there's a set of traffic lights on a crossroads; turn left and catch any bus heading north; they will all drop you at Pemenang, a cidomo (horse-drawn cart) ride or a 1.5-kilometre walk away from Bangsal.

If you're arriving in the city by bus or bemo from pretty much anywhere other than Senggigi and Pemenang, you'll come into the main **bus station** on the island on the eastern edge of the conurbation, known variously as Bertais, Mandalika or Sweta, and if you're heading on to anywhere otherthan Senggigi you can pick up a

Getting to Lombok

By plane

Mataram's Selaparang Airport is the only one on the island, and the only direct international flights are from Singapore on Silk Air (Mon, Thurs & Sat). Regular internal flights with Garuda, Citilink, Merpati and Lion Air link Lombok with other points in Indonesia (see "Getting around", p.237, for more details).

By boat

From Bali

Padang Bai to Lembar
Ferry: every 90min; 4hr–4hr 30min. Tickets cost Rp15,000. An extra charge is made for bicycles (Rp17,600), motorbikes (Rp36,400), and cars (from Rp225,000).

Padang Bai to Senggigi and the Gili Islands Perama boat: Daily; Senggigi (3–4hr; Rp100,000) and Gili Islands (5–6hr; Rp150,000).

Amed to the Gili Islands
Increasing numbers of skippers are willing to arrange charters direct to the Gili Islands (Rp750,000 plus per boat). Be aware that the boats are often small with single engines, they don't carry radios, and mobile phones may well be out of range in the middle of the Lombok Strait. If you're still interested, contact I Nengah Suande through the *Diver's Café* at Bungalows Amed. For the return trip, Din (Ⓣ081339/509859) is one of the boat captains on Gili Meno; he's often in front of the Blue Marlin dive shop.

From Sumbawa

Poto Tano to Kayangan, Labuhan Lombok Every hour; (1hr 30min; Rp9000). An extra charge for bicycles (Rp7500), motorbikes (Rp15,000) and cars (from Rp114,000).

From other islands

The Indonesian passenger line, Pelni (Ⓦwww.pelni.co.id) operates services between the islands of the archipelago, calling at Lembar on Lombok. See the map on p.240 for details of routes, and p.415 for details of the Pelni office on Lombok.

By bus

Java, Bali, Sumbawa and Flores to Bertais/Mandalika/Sweta terminal, Sweta. Several services daily. Sample fares include Rp275,000 for air-con and reclining seats from Jakarta to Lombok (32hr), Rp200,000 from Yogyakarta (22hr). Other fares include Denpasar (6–8hr; Rp85,000); Surabaya (20hr; Rp135,000); Sumbawa Besar (6hr; Rp55,000); Bima (12hr; Rp85,000); Sape (14hr; Rp95,000); and Labuhan Bajo (24hr; Rp125,000).

Tourist shuttle buses operate from Bali to the main tourist destinations on Lombok: Mataram, Senggigi, the Gili Islands (via Bangsal) and Kuta, Lombok. Perama are the most established company, with offices in all major tourist areas.

connection here. **Long-distance bus** tickets are available from the numerous ticket counters here both east as far as Flores and west to Java and Sumatra. Arriving from Senggigi, and on some of the bemos from Pemenang, you'll come into the Kebon Roek terminal in **Ampenan**. These two bus terminals are linked by the frequent yellow bemos that zip around the city.

If you intend to stay in the city, it's best to head to Cakranegara, where there's good accommodation not far from the main bemo routes. The **tourist office** is the Provincial Tourist Service for West Nusa Tenggara, which is rather out of the way off Jalan Majapahit in the south of the city, at Jl Singosari 2 (Mon–Thurs 7.30am–2pm,

Fri 7.30–11.30am, Sat 7.30am–1pm; ⓣ0370/634800, ⓕ637233). There are shorter opening hours during Ramadan (see p.71).

Yellow **bemos** (flat fare Rp1300) ferry between Kebon Roek terminal in Ampenan and Bertais/Mandalika/Sweta terminal in Sweta from early morning until late evening. Most follow Jalan Langko–Jalan Pejanggik–Jalan Selaparang heading west to east, and Jalan Tumpang Sari–Jalan Panca Usaha–Jalan Pancawarga–Jalan Pendidikan heading east to west, although there are numerous less-frequently served variations. Yellow bemos heading via "Kekalik" pass by the end of Jalan Singosari as they head along Jalan Majapahit from Bertais/Mandalika/Sweta terminal or Kebon Roek in Ampenan. There are plenty of easily identifiable official metered **taxis**. Flagfall is Rp3000 for the first kilometre, then Rp1250 per kilometre thereafter; a trip across the entire city area is unlikely to be more than Rp12,000. The horse-drawn carts here, unlike the ones on Bali, have small pneumatic tyres and are called **cidomo**; they aren't allowed on the main streets, instead covering the back routes that bemos don't work. Always negotiate a fare beforehand.

Accommodation and eating

Few tourists stay in the city as Senggigi is only just up the road. However, there's a clutch of **losmen** in Cakranegara, where *Shanta Puri*, Jl Maktal 15 (ⓣ0370/632649; ❶–❸) is the most popular travellers' place, offering a wide range of rooms. Other good Cakra options are *Adiguna*, Jl Nursiwan 9 (ⓣ0370/625946; ❶), *Ayu*, Jl Nursiwan 20 (ⓣ0370/621761; ❶) and *Oka*, Jl Repatmaja 5 (ⓣ0370/622406; ❶) all situated in quiet, convenient streets near the bemo routes and featuring reasonable rooms in small gardens.

There's a wide range of **places to eat**. If you're really watching the rupiah, head for the food stalls in the Kebon Roek terminal, which sell cheap local food. In Cakra, the top floor of the gleaming Mataram Mall on Jalan Pejanggik offers a great range of well-cooked local food, while across the road *Kristal*, Jl Pejanggik 22A, serves a huge Chinese and Indonesian menu in air-con comfort. On Jalan Maktal, *Suharti Sate House* is inexpensive, and for good-value Padang food try *Simpang Raya*, Jl Pejangik 107. For a sugar fix, *Mirasa Modern Bakery* on Jalan AA Gede Ngurah has as much as you can need but is only take-away.

It's worth noting that although Lombok is predominantly Muslim, visiting **during Ramadan** does not mean hours of daylight fasting. Most of the places above remain open during the day at this time, although a curtain at the window discreetly hides diners from the streets outside.

The City

There aren't that many sights in the city area but the local **markets** are well worth a visit for their vibrancy and a chance to see local life. The Kebon Roek market at the bemo terminal in Ampenan is hectic, as is the Cakranegara market that centres on Jalan Gede Ngurah just south of the crossroads with Jalan Pejanggik and Jalan Selaparang. The huge covered market near the Bertais/Mandalika/Sweta bus terminal at Sweta is also worth wandering around. You may find some crafts scattered amongst the vegetables, fish, meat and household goods here – if you're thinking of buying anything, take a flashlight with you, as details are hard to see in the gloom. If you feel like venturing further afield, the daily market at Gunung Sari around 5km north of the city on the road to Pemenang is another fascinating destination, with the exotic amidst the mundane.

There's a craft shopper's paradise at the **Lombok Handicraft Centre** (also known as Sayang Sayang; daily; 9am–6pm), which is just beyond the Jangkok River about 2km north of Cakranegara along Jalan Hasanudin at Rungkang Jangkok. It has dozens of shops both small and large selling every type of craftwork imaginable, and you can see some of them being made.

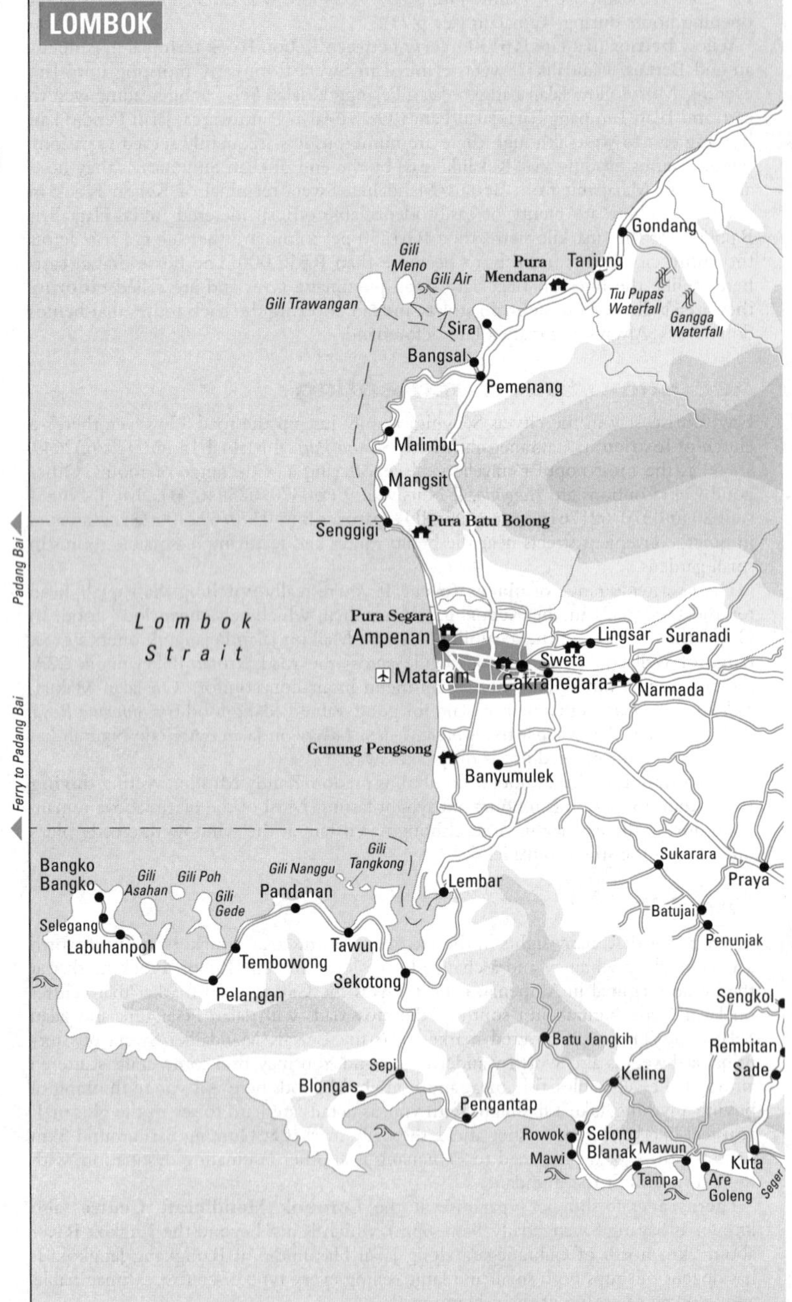
LOMBOK
Gili Meno
Gili Air
Pura Mendana
Tanjung
Gondang
Gili Trawangan
Sira
Tiu Pupas Waterfall
Gangga Waterfall
Bangsal
Pemenang
Malimbu
Mangsit
Senggigi
Pura Batu Bolong
Padang Bai
Lombok Strait
Pura Segara
Ampenan
Mataram
Lingsar
Suranadi
Sweta
Cakranegara
Narmada
Ferry to Padang Bai
Gunung Pengsong
Banyumulek
Gili Tangkong
Gili Nanggu
Bangko Bangko
Gili Asahan
Gili Poh
Gili Gede
Pandanan
Lembar
Sukarara
Praya
Batujai
Penunjak
Selegang
Labuhanpoh
Tembowong
Tawun
Sekotong
Pelangan
Sengkol
Batu Jangkih
Rembitan
Sade
Sepi
Blongas
Keling
Pengantap
Rowok
Selong Blanak
Mawun
Mawi
Tampa
Are Goleng
Kuta
Seger

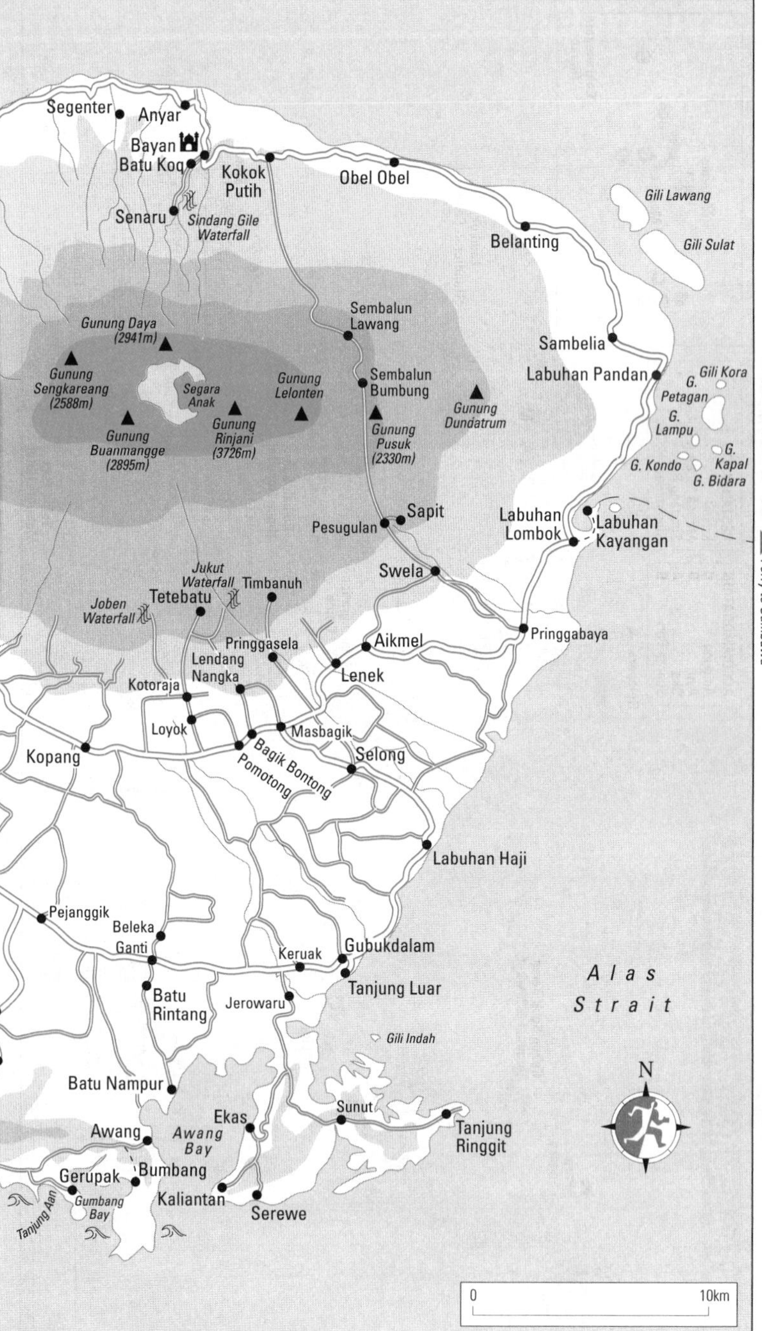
Segenter
Anyar
Bayan
Batu Koq
Kokok Putih
Obel Obel
Senaru
Sindang Gile Waterfall
Gili Lawang
Gili Sulat
Belanting
Sembalun Lawang
Sambelia
Gunung Daya (2941m)
Gunung Sengkareang (2588m)
Segara Anak
Gunung Lelonten
Sembalun Bumbung
Labuhan Pandan
Gili Kora
G. Petagan
G. Lampu
Gunung Dundatrum
Gunung Buanmangge (2895m)
Gunung Rinjani (3726m)
Gunung Pusuk (2330m)
G. Kondo
G. Kapal
G. Bidara
Sapit
Pesugulan
Labuhan Lombok
Labuhan Kayangan
Ferry to Sumbawa
Jukut Waterfall
Timbanuh
Swela
Joben Waterfall
Tetebatu
Pringgabaya
Pringgasela
Aikmel
Lendang Nangka
Lenek
Kotoraja
Loyok
Masbagik
Kopang
Bagik Bontong
Pomotong
Selong
Labuhan Haji
Pejanggik
Beleka
Ganti
Keruak
Gubukdalam
Tanjung Luar
Batu Rintang
Jerowaru
Alas Strait
Gili Indah
N
Batu Nampur
Sunut
Ekas
Tanjung Ringgit
Awang
Awang Bay
Gerupak
Bumbang
Gumbang Bay
Tanjung Aan
Kaliantan
Serewe
0
10km

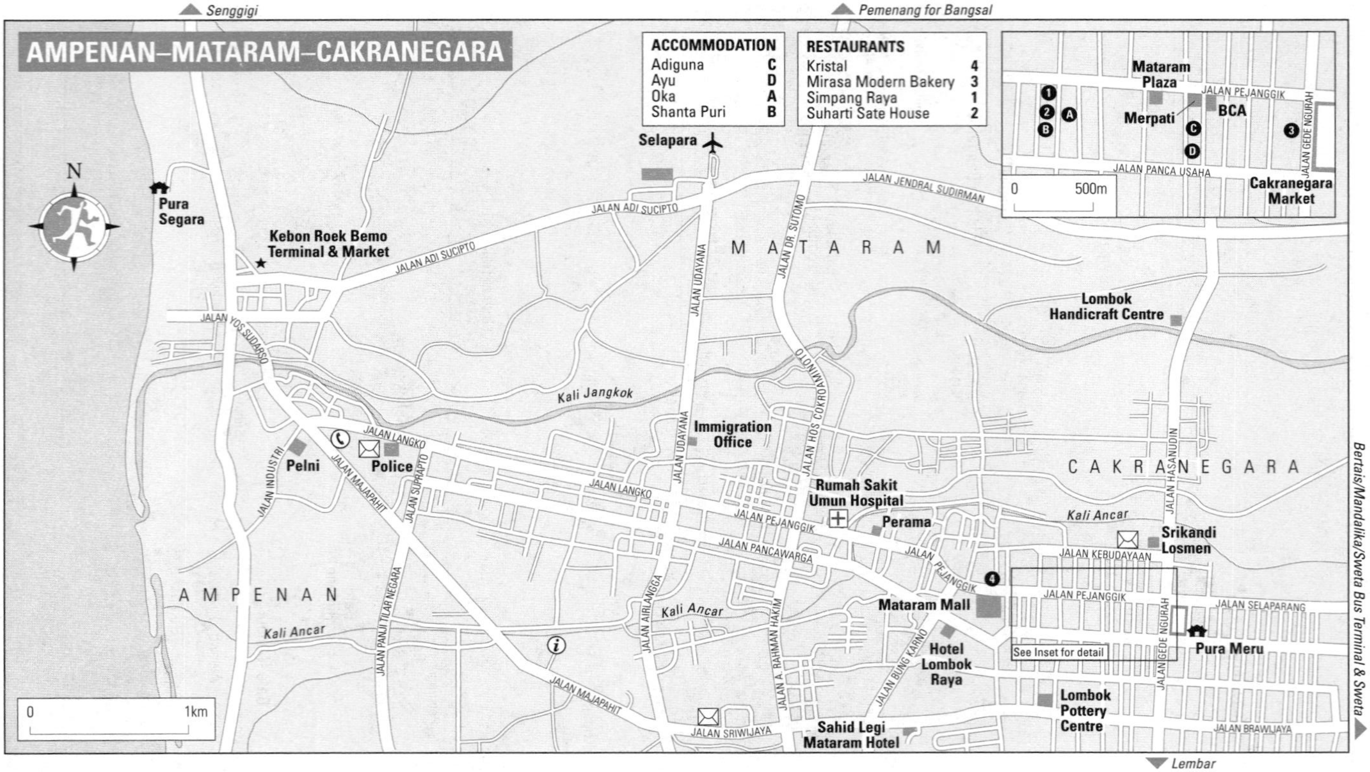

AMPENAN–MATARAM–CAKRANEGARA

ACCOMMODATION	
Adiguna	C
Ayu	D
Oka	A
Shanta Puri	B

RESTAURANTS	
Kristal	4
Mirasa Modern Bakery	3
Simpang Raya	1
Suharti Sate House	2

Senggigi
Pemenang for Bangsal
Bertais/Mandalika/Sweta Bus Terminal & Sweta
Lembar
N
0 1km
AMPENAN
MATARAM
CAKRANEGARA
Pura Segara
Kebon Roek Bemo Terminal & Market
Selapara
Lombok Handicraft Centre
Immigration Office
Pelni
Police
Rumah Sakit Umun Hospital
Perama
Srikandi Losmen
Mataram Mall
Hotel Lombok Raya
Pura Meru
Lombok Pottery Centre
Sahid Legi Mataram Hotel
See Inset for detail
Kali Jangkok
Kali Ancar
Jalan Yos Sudarso
Jalan Adi Sucipto
Jalan Jendral Sudirman
Jalan Udayana
Jalan Dr. Sutomo
Jalan Hos Cokroaminoto
Jalan Langko
Jalan Industri
Jalan Majapahit
Jalan Suprapto
Jalan Panji Tilar Negara
Jalan Airlangga
Jalan A. Rahman Hakim
Jalan Bung Karno
Jalan Pejanggik
Jalan Pancawarga
Jalan Sriwijaya
Jalan Hasanudin
Jalan Kebudayaan
Jalan Selaparang
Jalan Gede Ngurah
Jalan Brawijaya

Mataram Plaza
Merpati
BCA
Jalan Pejanggik
Jalan Panca Usaha
Jalan Gede Ngurah
Cakranegara Market
0 500m

Lombok **pottery** has an international reputation for style and beauty, and it's possible to buy it in the city; **Lombok Pottery Centre**, Jl Sriwijaya 111a, Ampenan (Ⓣ0370/640351, Ⓕ640350, Ⓦwww.lombokpottery.com; Mon–Fri 8am–5pm, Sat noon–4pm) is the shop and showroom of the Lombok Craft Project and stocks a range of products from and information about the three main pottery centres on the island: Banyumulek to the south of the city, Penujak in southern Lombok, and Penakak close to Masbajik in the east.

Listings

Airlines Most of the airlines serving Lombok have ticket counters at the airport and offices in the city area. Citilink, Selaparang Airport Ⓣ0370/622987 ext246, and at *Hotel Lombok Raya*, Jl Panca Usaha 11, Cakranegara Ⓣ0370/649999; Garuda, Selaparang Airport Ⓣ&Ⓕ0370/6646846 and at *Hotel Lombok Raya*, Jl Panca Usaha 11, Cakranegara t0370/638259 (Mon-Fri 8am–5pm, Sat, Sun & hols 9am–1pm), Indonesia-wide call centre Ⓣ08071/427832; Lion Air at *Sahid Legi Mataram* hotel Ⓣ0370 629111, Ⓕ636213 (Mon–Sat 8.30am–5pm, Sun 9am–2pm); Merpati, Jl Pejanggik 69, Ⓣ0370/621111(Mon–Sat 8am–5.30pm, Sun 9am–3pm), 24hr information line Ⓣ0800/101 2345, Ⓦwww.merpati.co.id; Silk Air – the only international airline with offices on Lombok – *Hotel Lombok Raya*, Jl Panca Usaha 11, Cakranegara Ⓣ0370/628254, Ⓕ628292, Ⓔsilkair-lombok@mataram.wasantara.net.id. For details of international airline offices in Bali, see box on p.362.

Banks and exchange All the large Mataram and Cakra banks change money and travellers' cheques. The most convenient are the Bank of Central Asia, Jl Pejanggik 67 Ⓣ0370/622587; BNI, Jl Langko 64, Ⓣ0370/622788; Bank Danamon, Jl Pejanggik Ⓣ0370/622408; Bank Internasional Indonesia (BII), Jl Gede Ngurah 46b, Ⓣ0370/635027. All have Visa, MasterCard and Cirrus ATMs, and there's a row of ATMs outside the back entrance to Mataram Mall. For getting money wired from overseas (see "Wiring money", p.60), the main post office is a Western Union agent.

Boats Pelni, Jl Industri 1, Ampenan, Ⓣ0370/637212, Ⓕ631604, (Mon–Fri 8am–3pm, Sat 8am–2pm).

Buses You'll get the best choice of inter-island departures at the Bertais/Mandalika/Sweta terminal at Sweta. Perama can advise on fares and timings and book tickets for you.

Dentist Dr Darmono, Jl Kebudayan 108, Mataram, Ⓣ081/836 7749, speaks good English. Speak directly to him to make an appointment. If you can't get through on his mobile you can contact him from 8am–4pm on Ⓣ0370/636852 and from 4pm–9pm on Ⓣ0370/643483. Clinic Opening times are daily 8am–noon & 5pm–9pm.

Hospital The public hospital, Rumah Sakit Umum, Jl Pejanggik 6, Mataram Ⓣ0370/623498 has an English-speaking "Tourist doctor", Dr Felix.

Immigration office *Kantor Imigrasi*, Jl Udayana 2, Mataram Ⓣ0370/632520.

Internet access The main concentration of places is on Jalan Panca Usaha along the back of Mataram Mall. Also convenient is Wartel Jenny, Jl Penjanggik 69 (8am–midnight). All are significantly cheaper than in Senggigi.

Motorbike rental If you know a bit about bikes and don't feel the need for insurance, the main rental place is at the roadside at Jl Gelantik 21, Cakranegara, a couple of hundred metres west of the *Srikandi* losmen on Jl Kebudayaan. See "Rental vehicles" p.239 for general advice on hiring vehicles.

Phones The main phone office is at Jl Langko 23, Ampenan (daily 24hr). There are plenty of wartels in town, including Wartel Jenny, Jl Penjanggik 69 (6am–midnight), which is convenient for the Cakra losmen.

Police Jalan Langko, Ampenan Ⓣ0370/631225.

Post office Lombok's main office is at Jl Sriwijaya 21, Mataram (Mon–Sat 8am–7pm, Sun 8am–noon). Offices at Jl Langko 21, Ampenan (Mon–Sat 8am–7pm) and on Jalan Kebudayaan in Cakranegara (same hours) are more accessible. For poste restante, the Senggigi post office is more used to dealing with tourists.

Lembar and boats to Bali

Boats to and from Bali dock at **LEMBAR**, 22km south of Mataram (for details of boat services, see box on p.415). Pelni ferries also dock here (see map on p.238). **Bemos** run between Sweta's Bertais/Mandalika/Sweta terminal and Lembar. If you're arriving in Lembar and need transport, you'll find the Lembar bemo drivers hard bargainers; the fare should be about Rp5000 to the Ampenan-Mataram-Cakranegara-Sweta area, but you'll do well to bargain them down to anything respectable. This is one good reason to book through to Mataram or Senggigi with Perama or another tourist shuttle company. Alternatively, **metered taxis** are available at the terminal or just outside the gates all day and all night. Typical fares are Rp25,000 to Cakranegara, Rp40,000–45,000 to Sengiggi. There's little **accommodation** here and no advantage in staying. If you do get stranded, *Tidar* (☎0370/681444; ①–②) has five rooms with fan and attached bathrooms, and a restaurant with a small menu of inexpensive Indonesian food. It's about 300m along the road to the port from the junction with the main road from the city.

The southwest peninsula

With enticing offshore islands, wonderful beaches and bays and a totally rural atmosphere, the **southwest peninsula** is an alluring proposition if you want to get off the beaten track. If you arrive in Lombok by ferry, you may glimpse the peninsula and islands as you approach the turn into Lembar harbour. Even if you only follow part of the fifty-kilometre road that leads from Lembar to Bangko Bangko, almost at the western tip of Lombok, you'll get a feel for this arid land, with only a few villages, whose sparse populations make their living from the sea. Accommodation is limited, and although you can get around on bemos having your own transport is a far better option. Public bemos to the southwest peninsula leave from the large terminal 500m north of the port, at the junction of the main road and the turning to Bangko Bangko via Sekotong (this turn is marked with hotel signs, including notices for "*Hotel Bola Bola Paradis*" and "*Hotel Sekotong Indah*"). Bemos operate from Lembar to Selegang during daylight hours, although you may need to change on the way. A metered **taxi** from Lembar port to Tawun will cost about Rp40,000.

Nineteen kilometres from Lembar, **TAWUN** is a white-sand, sweeping bay with brilliant views to the islands of Gili Sudak, Gili Tangkong and Gili Nanggu. You can charter boats (there's no public boat service) to **Gili Nanggu** (20min; Rp60,000 each way), while snorkelling trips to several of the islands (Rp160,000–170,000) are also possible; boat captains rent out **snorkelling** gear (Rp40,000 per set). The only **accommodation** on the islands is at *Gili Nanggu Cottages* (☎0370/623783, Ⓦwww.gilinanggu.com; ③–⑥) with a choice of fan or air-con, and there's a moderately priced **restaurant** attached. They can arrange a boat between the island and Tawun or Lembar. There's nothing else on Gili Nanggu so it's ideal for total relaxation or trips to nearby islands; Gili Tangkong closest to the east and Gili Poh, the minuscule desert-island look-a-like to the west.

Just 2km west around the coast from Tawun, in the village of **LABU**, *Hotel Sekotong Indah* (☎0818/362326; ②) has bungalows in a pleasant garden just across the road from the beach. Rooms have fan (one has air con) and attached cold-water bathroom.

At the village of **TEMBOWONG**, 10km from Tawun, *Putri Duyung Homestay* (☎0812/375 2459; ①) is a family-run place owned by Pak Gede Patra. Rooms are extremely simple with attached mandi and squat toilet. This is an ideal base from which to explore **Gili Gede**, the largest offshore island visible from here, and the surrounding six, smaller islands; the family rent out a **boat** at Rp200,000 per day.

A further 2km west, **PELANGAN** is the largest village in this part of the peninsula. *Hotel Bola Bola Paradis* (☎0370/623783, Ⓔbatuapi99@hotmail.com; ④) boasts a great coastal location 2km beyond Pelangan. All rooms have fan, and hot water is available. Book between April and September, when they get packed out, and ring at other, quieter, times to let them know you are coming. **Boat** trips are available (Rp200,000 for 3hr).

The end of the black-topped road is at the small hamlet of **SELEGANG**, from where it's 3km on sandy tracks to the beach at **BANGKO BANGKO**, which from mid-May to September and again in December, draws hundreds of surfers from across the globe in search of Desert Point, an awesome break just off the coast here. The landscape is harsh but the views are fine – Bali appears incredibly close, Nusa Penida is about an hour's sail away, and stretches of the Lombok coast way to the north are also visible. From here, there's no choice but to turn around and head back.

Senggigi

Covering a huge stretch of coastline, **SENGGIGI**, with sweeping bays separated by towering headlands, is an attractive and laid-back beach resort, offering a wide range of accommodation and restaurants, and low-key nightlife. Parts of the area are packed wall-to-wall with hotels, but it's perfectly possible to have an inexpensive and relaxing stay here, and proximity to the airport makes it an ideal first- or last-night destination. There are, however, plenty of hawkers in the central areas – keeping your cool and getting to know them is the best approach.

Plenty of operators cater for people who want to **dive** in the Gili Islands, but stay in the comfort of Senggigi. Qualified divers will pay US$45-65 for two dives, while PADI courses range from Scuba Review (US$50) and Discover Scuba (US$70), to Open Water ($300) and Advanced Water (US$225). Check whether equipment rental is included in the price. Most operators run **snorkelling** trips to the Gili Islands; you go along with the divers but have to be fairly self-reliant in the water. Expect to pay US$15–25, including equipment and lunch. Contact Blue Coral Dive (Ⓣ0370/693441, Ⓕ634765); Blue Marlin Dive (Ⓣ0370/692003, Ⓦwww.diveindo.com); Dive Indonesia (Ⓣ0370/693521, Ⓦwww.diveindonesiaonline.com); Dream Divers (Ⓣ0370/692047, Ⓦwww.dreamdivers.com); all have booking offices in central Senggigi. Most of them also have offices in the Gili islands if you're heading that way.

Easily accessible by public transport, Senggigi is served by **bemos** from Ampenan throughout the day (every 15–20min), pick them up on Jalan Saleh Sungkar just north of the turn-off to the Kebon Roek bemo terminal. Metered taxis zip between the city and the resort at all hours. From the **airport**, fixed-price taxis charge Rp30,000 to central Senggigi, Rp40,000 to the north. Perama, Gora and Anjani amongst others operate **tourist shuttle buses** to Senggigi from all the main Bali and Lombok tourist destinations, and Perama have a daily **boat service** to Senggigi from Bali (Rp100,000) that runs on to the Gili Islands (Rp150,000). The resort is very spread out, so it's useful to have an idea of where you're heading; the southern end of Senggigi is just 5km north of Ampenan, and there are a few places spread out along the next 4km until the main concentration of hotels that stretches for roughly 1km from the *Graha Senggigi Beach* to the *Sheraton*. Low-density development continues for another 8km to the most northerly development, *Bulan Baru* at

Trips to Sumbawa, Komodo and Flores

Various travel agencies on Lombok run boat trips via **Sumbawa** and **Komodo** to **Flores**, with the highlight being a visit to see **Komodo dragons**. Typically, trips take four days and four nights to reach Labuanbajo and are not especially luxurious; it's best to go by personal recommendation if possible. Prices vary enormously, starting at about Rp600,000 per person for a four-day-boat/overland trip in one direction. Air transport out of Labuanbajo can be difficult to arrange, so allow plenty of time if you book a one-way journey – it's a very long slog back by bus. The following organize trips: Perama – contact any office; Citra Lombok Indah, Senggigi (Ⓣ0370/693921), Gora Tour & Travel, Senggigi (Ⓣ0370/693477).

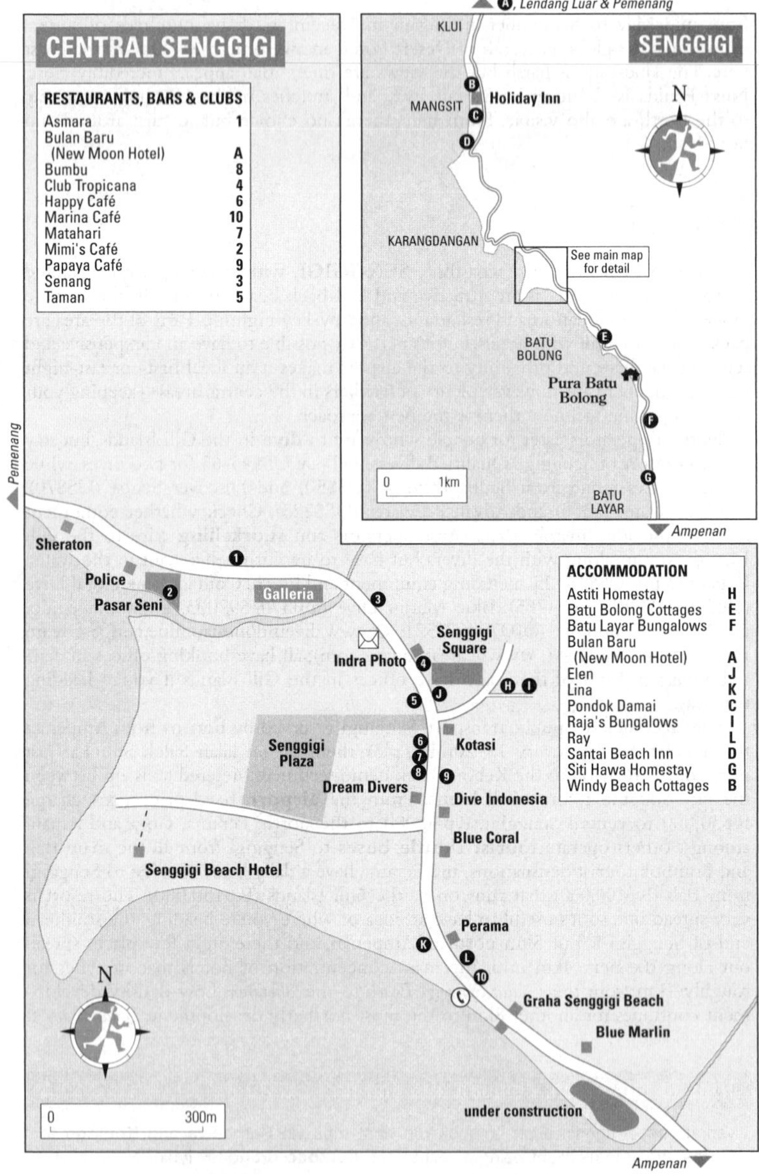

Lendang Luar. **Bemos** ply this entire stretch of coast during the day and metered **taxis** operate throughout the area from early morning to late at night; a ride from central Senggigi to Lendang Luar costs about Rp11,000. Perama can also provide **information** and book **long-distance bus tickets**, and they, Anjani and Gora, operate tourist shuttles to Bali and Lombok.

Accommodation

There's a reasonable range of budget **accommodation** in the resort, although you'll get more choice the more you can spend. The most attractive part of the coast is **north Senggigi**, with great views across to Bali. In **central Senggigi**, there's plenty happening, with bars, restaurants and good shopping on offer. **South Senggigi** has the advantage of being closer to the city area and airport.

South Senggigi

Batu Bolong Cottages Ⓣ&Ⓕ0370/693198. Just north of Pura Batu Bolong, these are attractive, clean cottages in pleasant gardens, on both sides of the road; the more expensive ones have a/c and hot water, and the deluxe seafront rooms have fabulous coastal views. ❸–❺

Batu Layar Bungalows Ⓣ0370/692235, Ⓦhttp://lombokbg.hp.infoseek.co.jp. Clean, tiled bungalows with fan and hot water, in an attractive garden. It's a 200m walk through a coconut grove to the beach, and there's free transport to central Senggigi. ❷

Siti Hawa Homestay Ⓣ0370/693414, Ⓔpondok_sitihawa@hotmail.com. Small, basic rooms, some with attached bathroom, all with mosquito net in a simple, family compound about 4km south of central Senggigi. ❶

Central Senggigi

Elen Ⓣ0370/693077. Tucked away up an alleyway opposite *Taman* restaurant, a reasonable central budget choice. All rooms have cold water, and a/c is available. ❶–❷

Lina Ⓣ0370/693237. On the seafront in central Senggigi just opposite the Perama office. All the rooms in this tiny compound have a/c but only the more expensive ones have hot water. This long-standing Senggigi favourite is justifiably popular and highly recommended in this price bracket. ❶–❷

Raja's Bungalows Ⓣ0812/377 0138, ⒺRajas22@yahoo.com. Tucked away off the road to the mosque, four excellent clean, tiled budget bungalows with fan and attached cold-water bathrooms set in a lush garden. If this is full, then *Astiti Homestay* (Ⓣ0370/693041) on the same track is a slightly cheaper alternative. ❷

Ray Ⓣ0370/6605599. Ranged up the hillside in central Senggigi, close to the Perama office, a short walk from the beach. Rooms are good value (the more expensive ones have a/c), but be aware that it's right next door to the *Marina Café*, which has loud music until late. ❷

North Senggigi

Bulan Baru (New Moon Hotel) Ⓣ0370/693785, Ⓕ693786, Ⓔbulanbaru@hotmail.com. Situated at Lendang Luar, 7km north of central Senggigi. It has a "no children" policy. Spotless bungalows with a/c and hot water situated in a pretty garden with a pool. It's fabulously peaceful up here and just a short walk to nearby Setangi Beach, over a kilometre long and with decent snorkelling off the coast. There's an excellent restaurant attached. ❸

Pondok Damai Ⓣ&Ⓕ0370/693019. On the coast 4km north of central Senggigi, this is a quiet spot with good-value accommodation in bamboo and thatch bungalows built on a tiled base in a lovely garden. Hot water is available. ❸

Santai Beach Inn Ⓣ0370/693038, Ⓦwww.santaibeachinn.com. On the coast at Mangsit, these popular thatched bungalows are set in a wonderful garden. All rooms have fan and cold water, but there are a couple of larger family rooms with hot water. Bookings are only accepted for the large rooms but ring before coming out here, as they do get full. Meals can be provided (booking needed) and are eaten communally; the menu is ideal for fish-eating vegetarians, but they can also cater for vegans. Carnivorous guests dine separately. ❷–❹

Windy Beach Cottages Ⓣ0370/693191, Ⓔlidya@mataram.wasantara.net.id. Simple bamboo, wood and thatch bungalows 5km north of central Senggigi, on the coast at Mangsit. All rooms have hot water and the more expensive ones have a/c. You can book shuttle-bus tickets and tours here, and rent snorkelling equipment; there are a couple of good spots off the beach. ❷–❸

Eating, drinking and nightlife

There's a good choice of **restaurants** and cuisines in Senggigi with something for every taste and budget. If you want local food and aren't concerned about ambience, small street carts congregate on the main stretch in central Senggigi after dark, and there's a row of sellers along the road as it climbs up beyond the *Sheraton*. These are the only places in Senggigi that shut for the hours of daylight fasting during the month of Ramadan: all tourist places remain open. Several restaurants offer **live music** while you eat - the standard is incredibly high, with some remarkable musicians playing regularly.

The **nightlife** in Senggigi is low key, in-keeping with the Muslim sensibilities on the island. *Marina Café* close to the Perama office offers regular live music, sometimes with big-name bands from Jakarta. There's a mix of local people, tourists and expats, a good dance floor plus balcony and garden areas and bars, and excellent pizzas straight from a wood-burning oven. *Club Tropicana* at the front of Senggigi Square is also open nightly and has some live music, with Friday and Saturday the main nights. There's a cover charge of Rp10,000–25,000, which includes a drink, and there's often a large Indonesian crowd here.

Asmara ☎0370/693619. Set back from the main road in central Senggigi, this tasteful restaurant serves a huge menu of excellent Western, Indonesian and seafood dishes and has a massive drinks list. There's good homemade bread for breakfast (from 7am), and also baby and children's meals. Free pick-up throughout Senggigi. Booking recommended.

Bulan Baru (New Moon Hotel) At Lendang Luar, 7km north of central Senggigi. Well-cooked, moderately priced Indonesian, Thai and Western food, all described on the menu in mouth-watering detail. For homesick travellers, there's bangers and mash. There's a big drinks list, including Australian wines. This is a good spot for lunch, with lots of soups, salads, sandwiches and rolls on the menu, and with Setangi Beach a short walk away.

Bumbu Small, popular place in central Senggigi. Thai food is the speciality and the best choice, but there are plenty of other options including steaks and sandwiches. Tell the waiters if you can't cope with industrial quantities of chilli in your curry.

Happy Café Offering the most accomplished live music in Senggigi, with a friendly and relaxed atmosphere. There's a gigantic bar that reflects the vast drinks list and an excellent menu of moderately priced Indonesian, Thai, Chinese and Western food.

Matahari One of a row of places in central Senggigi selling the usual travellers' fare at moderate prices.

Mimi's Café A relaxed spot in the Pasar Seni (Art Market), with good Indonesian and Western meals at moderate prices, although they do have some expensive options, up to barbecued lobster at Rp339,500.

Papaya Café Opposite *Bumbu*. Excellent live music in a welcoming atmosphere. There's an Indonesian, Western and Chinese menu – the Chinese dishes in small, medium or large servings. There's a lot of seafood, especially if you plump for the King of Seafood for two for Rp220,000. Thin and crispy pizzas are a speciality.

Senang Set slightly back from the main road in central Senggigi, this small place is lacking in frills but has well-cooked main courses from Rp7000.

Taman Imposing two-storey restaurant with an eclectic Western and Indonesian seafood menu presented in attractive, relaxed surroundings. There's an attached deli/bakery where you can put together a gourmet beach picnic.

Listings

Airlines See p.362 for details of airlines that serve Lombok. Information on international airline offices in Bali is on p.362.

Banks and exchange BCA and BNI banks both have central ATMs. There are exchange counters (daily 10am–10pm) on the main street.

Boats Perama (☎0370/693007, ℱ693009) operate a daily boat to the Gili Islands at 1.30pm (1hr 30min; Rp50,000) and a daily boat to Padang Bai at 9am (Rp100,000). If you're interested in chartering a boat to the Gili Islands or for local fishing or sightseeing up the coast, head down to the beach and negotiate with the owners. You'll be looking at about Rp250,000–300,000 per day.

Buses Perama (☎0370/693007, ℱ693009), Anjani (☎0370/693587) and Gora (☎0370/693477) are among the companies that offer tourist shuttles to destinations on Bali and Lombok, and prices are comparable; they advertise along the main street. They each have a daily departure but serve smaller destinations by charter. Perama can advise on inter-island bus journeys and book tickets.

Car and bike rental Plenty of places rent vehicles with and without drivers. Kotasi is the local transport co-operative. Currently, car rental includes insurance (the maximum you'll pay in case of an accident is US$100), but check the deal at the time of renting. Suzuki Jimneys (Rp150,000/

day), Kijangs (Rp200,000–225,000), motorbikes (Rp30,000–35,000 without insurance) and bicycles (Rp15,000–20,000). Expect to pay around Rp50,000/day for a driver. Chartering a vehicle, driver and fuel (from Kotasi, travel agents or street touts) costs about Rp250,000–300,000/day all-in, depending on where you want to go. One highly recommended local driver is Hasan Nur (Ⓣ081/854 8227, Ⓔ Hsn_y@yahoo.com) who can also be contacted through *Bulan Baru* (see above).

Doctor Some of the luxury hotels have in-house clinics, including the *Sheraton* Ⓣ0370/693333 (3–11pm with a paramedic and a doctor on call 24hr), *Senggigi Beach Hotel* Ⓣ0370/693210 (24hr service) and *Holiday Inn* Ⓣ0370/693444 (9am–5pm daily except Friday). See p.415 for hospitals in Ampenan-Mataram-Cakranegara-Sweta.

Internet access Several Internet cafés along the main street (daily 8am–10pm; Rp300/min).

Left luggage Perama, Rp10,000 per item per day, maximum one week or most accommodation will store stuff if you're coming back to them.

Phones A couple of wartels are in the centre; the one above Indah Photo is as good as any (daily 8am–11pm).

Post office In the centre of Senggigi (Mon–Thurs 7.30am–5pm, Fri & Sat 7.30am–4pm). Poste restante is available here, get mail addressed to yourself at Post Office, Senggigi, Lombok 83355, West Nusa Tenggara.

The Gili Islands

Strikingly beautiful, with glorious white-sand beaches lapped by warm, brilliant-blue waters, the trio of **Gili Islands** just off the northwest coast of Lombok are a magnet for visitors. Of the three, **Gili Trawangan** best fits the image of "party island", with heaps of accommodation, restaurants and nightlife. The smallest of the islands, **Gili Meno**, has absolutely no nightlife and a more limited choice of accommodation and, closest to the mainland, **Gili Air** offers a mix of the two, with plenty of facilities in the south, and more peace elsewhere.

Prices vary dramatically depending on the season and are probably more fluid than anywhere else on Bali or Lombok, being totally dependent on what the market will bear. A bungalow costing Rp50,000 in February will rise to Rp100,000 or even more in the frantic months of July, August and December. None of the islands has a particular **crime** problem, although take reasonable precautions against theft (see "Crime and safety", p.248). Women should take care during and after the Gili Trawangan parties - don't leave on your own, even to go to the toilet. There are no police on the Gilis, so in the event of trouble it is the role of the kepala desa, the head man who looks after Gili Air (where he lives) and Gili Meno, and the kepala kampung on Gili Trawangan, to deal with the situation and take you to police at Tanjung or Ampenan to make a report.

The **access port** for the Gili Islands is **BANGSAL**, 25km north of Senggigi. If you need to stay here, the losmen *Taman Sari* (Ⓣ0370/646934; ❶–❷), just by the gate where vehicles stop on the way to the harbour, has two standards of accommodation opening onto a small, quiet garden. All rooms have an attached bathroom, the cheaper ones with squat toilet.

Bangsal is a short cidomo (horse-drawn cart) ride or a shadeless 1.5-kilometre walk from **PEMENANG**, 26km beyond the Ampenan-Mataram-Cakranegara-Sweta area and served by **bemos or buses** from Bertais/Mandalika/Sweta terminal in Sweta. All transport between this terminal and points around the north coast passes through Pemenang. There is no public bemo service along the coastal road north from Senggigi to Pemenang. Perama by-passes Bangsal on the way to the Gili Islands as their boat goes directly from Senggigi. On the way back, you'll transfer from the boat from the islands to a bus at Bangsal.

It's **useful to know** that, despite anything you might be told at Bangsal, everything on sale in Bangsal is also on sale on the Gili Islands, including water, mosquito coils and return boat tickets. The **ticket office** for boats to the islands is right on the sea front at the end of the road where there's a printed price list covering public boats, shuttles and charters. You should go directly there and buy your ticket. Ideally, travel light enough to get your own bag onto and off the boats

– if you need to use one, negotiate with the porters before you let them touch the bags and be clear whether you are talking about rupiah, dollars, for one bag or for the whole lot. **Boats** take between twenty and forty-five minutes to the islands. Public boats serve Gili Air (Rp3500), Gili Meno (Rp4000) and Gili Trawangan (Rp4500) from 7.30am until 4.30pm, leaving when full. **Shuttle boats** are more expensive and depart at 4.30pm from Bangsal; Gili Air (Rp10,000), Gili Meno (Rp11,000) and Gili Trawangan (Rp12,000), with an additional shuttle at 2pm from Bangsal to Gili Meno (Rp8000). Charters are also available with p rices posted at the ticket office (one-way from Rp68,000). From **Senggigi**, you can take the Perama shuttle boat to the islands (Rp50,000). At both ends of all boat trips you'll get your feet wet, as the boats anchor in the shallows and you have to wade to and fro.

Once on the islands, the "**hopping island**" boat service is extremely handy. It does one circuit – Air–Meno–Trawangan–Meno–Air – in the morning, and one in the afternoon. It's conveniently timetabled and fast, and makes a day-trip to another island a feasible option. Prices and times are posted in ticket offices on the islands.

Returning to the mainland, the times, frequencies and fares on the public boats are the same as for getting to the islands. Shuttle boats leave the islands at 10am. Several operators on the islands offer shuttle tickets direct to Lombok or Bali destinations. Whichever operator you use, whatever your destination, there is one departure daily, and you'll walk from the port at Bangsal to the gate on the road where you'll be collected by the tour operator. Perama currently have a counter on

Snorkelling and diving

The **snorkelling and diving** around the Gili Islands is some of the best and most accessible in Lombok and, despite a lot of visitors, the reefs remain in reasonable condition. All the islands are fringed by **coral reefs** and visibility is generally around 15m. The **fish** life here is the main attraction and includes white-tip and black-tip reef sharks, sea turtles, manta rays, Napoleon wrasse and bumphead parrotfish.

There are good **snorkelling spots** just off the beaches of all the islands. Snorkel gear is widely available for Rp15,000–20,000 per day, but the condition does vary. You can buy good-quality gear on the islands in many of the dive shops. Dive companies take snorkellers further afield; it'll cost about US$10. It's worth noting that the **offshore currents** around the island are strong and can be hazardous. Dive operators are aware of this and on the alert; however, if you're snorkelling or swimming off the beach, you're potentially at risk – it's easy to lose awareness of your distance from the shore, get carried out further than you intend and then be unable to get back to land. There has been at least one drowning in recent years.

Most of the best **dive sites** involve short boat trips.There are plenty of **dive operators** on the islands with overseas instructors offering tuition and dive-guiding in a variety of European languages, plus dive shops with PADI materials in several languages (see below). There's a price agreement, with operators charging identical rates; however, they vary significantly in approach and atmosphere and you should choose one carefully. See "Diving, surfing and trekking", p.247, for general advice on choosing a dive operator. Check at the time of booking whether the price includes equipment rental. If you're a qualified diver, expect to pay US$25 per dive and US$35 per night dive. PADI course include Discover Scuba and Scuba Review (both US$50), Open Water (US$300), and Advanced Open Water (US$200–235). Some operators are qualified to take people on the Instructor Development Course, which costs US$900–1000.

All divers off the Gili islands pay a one-off **reef tax** of Rp30,000 (snorkellers pay Rp10,000) to the Gili Eco Trust, which works to protect the reefs around the islands.

Dive operators

Big Bubble Gili Trawangan ⊕0370/625020, ⊛www.bigbubblediving.com. Small, friendly

Gili Trawangan and one on Gili Air; on Gili Meno, you should telephone the Senggigi office and book through them (see p.417).

Gili Trawangan

Furthest from the mainland, the largest of the islands, with a local population of 700, **GILI TRAWANGAN** attracts the greatest number of visitors. The southeast of the island is wall-to-wall bungalows, restaurants and dive shops, although it still manages to be pretty low-key and relaxed, especially outside the high season. For quieter surroundings, head to the laid-back northeast, northwest or southwest coasts.

Island transport is by cidomo, or you can rent bicycles, though the tracks around the island are very sandy in parts. A **walk around the island**, less than 3km long by 2km at its widest part, takes four hours or less. Inland, the hundred-metre **hill** is the compulsory expedition at sunset – follow any of the tracks from the southern end of the island, for views of gunungs Agung, Abang and Batur on Bali. The area towards the northern end of the east coast of the island is very popular for **snorkelling**, and most people hang out here during the day; see the box below for a list of **dive** operators on the island.

The art market has a **postal agent**. **Moneychangers** all along the main strip change cash and travellers' cheques. You can make international calls from the **wartel** (8am–11pm). The Perama office (daily 7am–10pm) is close to the jetty. Several places offer **Internet access** (about Rp400/min; minimum 5min), including the wartel, which has the advantage of air-con.

place owned by two British women; they keep groups small and dive at times to suit guests or when the sites are quiet.

Blue Marlin Gili Trawangan ⓣ0370/632424, Gili Meno ⓣ0370/639979, Gili Air ⓣ0370/634387, ⓦwww.diveindo.com. The Trawangan centre is a PADI Five Star IDC Dive Centre. There's a full range of courses, including PADI Instructor Development Courses (IDC) as well as International Association of Nitrox and Technical Divers (IANTD) Technical Diving International courses and Trimix instruction, up to the IANTD Instructor Training course. There are diver propulsion vehicles for hire at $25 per dive. Their 65-foot Indonesian *pinisi* boat, the *Ikan Biru*, equipped with all mod-cons, departs weekly for a five-day live-aboard trip, and is available for private charter.

Dive Indonesia Gili Trawangan ⓣ0370/644174, ⓦwww.diveindonesiaonline.com; courses up to PADI IDC level, and all divers are loaned dive computers to use. They also feature live-aboards.

Dream Divers Gili Trawangan ⓣ0370/634496, Gili Air ⓣ0370/634547, ⓦwww.dreamdivers.com; For those with more than fifty dives, who can cope with currents and surge, they offer a two-day diving trip to southern Lombok, to intact coral that attracts plenty of big fish, including schools of barracuda and hammerhead sharks. This is one of very few places in the world where it's possible to see schools of 100 or more hammerhead sharks (April–Oct). IANTD runs dives and courses as well.

Manta Dive Gili Trawangan ⓣ0370/643649, ⓦwww.manta-dive.com. Under British ownership but with highly respected local dive-guides who have thousands of dives on the local reefs. They offer courses up to PADI Divemaster level and there are always lots of Divemaster trainees around who give the place a good buzz. Two-day trips to east Lombok are on offer diving in the channel between Gili Lawang and Gili Sulat.

Vila Ombak Diving Academy Gili Trawangan ⓣ0370/638531, ⓦwww.scubali.com. Don't be deterred by the location in one of the smartest hotels on the island – prices here are similar to those elsewhere. All divers are provided with a computer attached to their regulator. There are also very good value "Dive and Stay" packages on offer with *Vila Ombak* hotel.

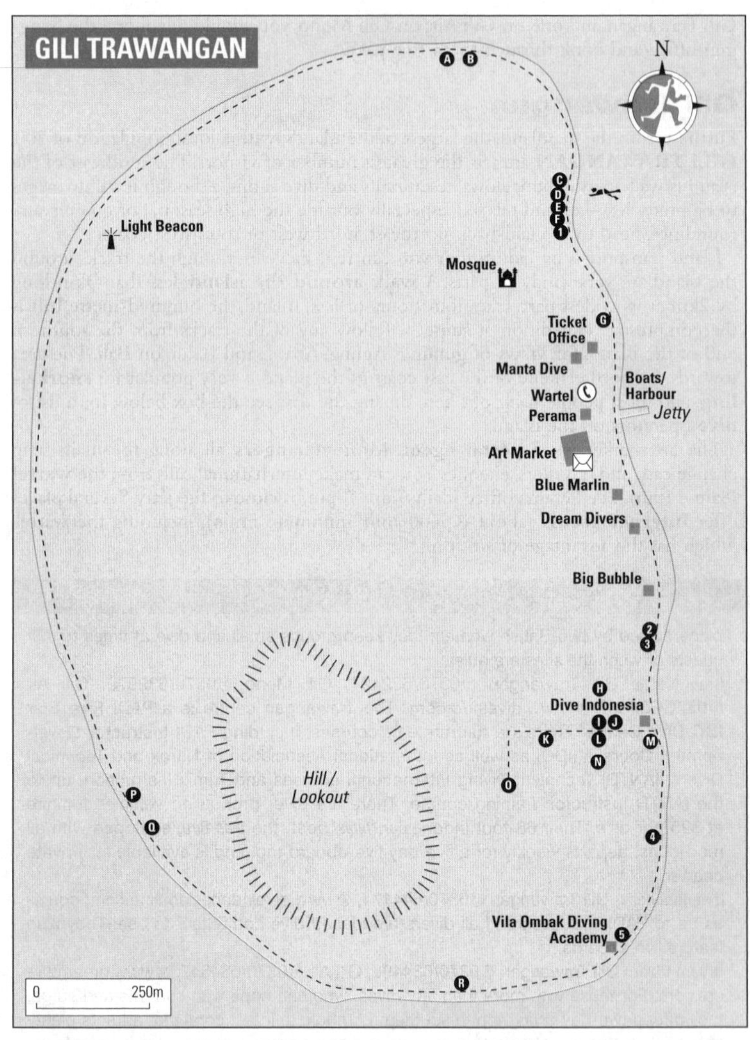

ACCOMMODATION								RESTAURANTS & BARS	
Aldi	I	Flush	F	Pondok Funny	L	Trawangan		Paradise	2
Beach Winds	G	Marta's	J	Pondok Lita	H	Cottages	M	Recchi Living Room	1
Coral Beach 2	C	Nusa Tiga	A	Pondok Santi	R	Trawangan Dive	E	Rudy's	3
Dewi Sri	P	Ozzy Homestay	D	Rumah Kita		Sunset	Q	Tír Na Nóg	4
Edy	K	Pandan Wangi	N	Sanctuary	O	Windy	B	Vila Ombak	5

Most of the east coast of the island is lined with **restaurants** and **warung**. In the northeastern part, simple warung provide plenty of cold drinks and inexpensive Indo–Chinese options in basic surroundings, while the places from the jetty southwards, are more upmarket. Wherever you eat, the quality and variety of the food is good and prices are reasonable, with **seafood** the best option. *Recchi Living Room* just north of the ticket office offers possibly the best food on the island, in simple surroundings, and *Vila Ombak* has the most upmarket dining experience. Gili Trawangan is renowned for its regular high-season **parties**, which get going at about 11pm and last until they finish. Venues are advertised on flyers around the island; currently, Monday is Blue Marlin, Wednesday *Tir Na Nog*, Friday *Rudy's*, Saturday Dive Indonesia and Sunday *Paradise*. Monday and Wednesday are the biggest nights and likely to draw revellers from the other islands and Lombok. *Tír Na Nóg* closes late, and apart from the parties is the late-night venue of choice. Please note that, for reasons of **personal safety**, women should not leave late-night venues alone, even to go to the bathroom.

Accommodation

Accommodation includes simple bamboo bungalows, comfortable concrete bungalows, and more upmarket places with hot water, air-con and ambience. The southern tip, west coast and north end of the island are relatively quiet, while the eastern side, especially at the southern end, is more lively and closer to restaurants and parties. For simple, good-value accommodation, slightly away from the hustle and bustle, there are several places behind the warung on the northeast coast and in the village. It's always worth keeping your eyes open for **new places**: they spring up fast and are often sparkling clean and good value.

Beach Winds ⓣ0812/376 4347. Good-value fan or a/c bungalows in the northeast. Prices include breakfast, and party-goers may appreciate being able to get breakfast at any time of day. ③

Coral Beach 2 ⓣ0812/376 8534. A fair option in the northeast with simple, straightforward fan bungalows just behind the beach. ②

Dewi Sri ⓔsliehchelet@hotmail.com. On the west coast, thirty minutes' walk from the main restaurant area. Some accommodation is in basic wood, bamboo and thatch bungalows with squat toilet, but the newer, tiled rooms are the best ones in the area. Nearby *Sunset* (ⓣ0812/3785 290, ⓔlily_karyani@hotmail.com) is also worth a look. ①–②

Marta's ⓣ0812/372 2777, ⓔmartas_trawangan@yahoo.com. Good-quality, two-storey accommodation in the village, all with a/c and hot water and lovely verandas looking out into an atractive garden. ⑤

Nusa Tiga ⓣ0370/643249. On the north coast, with basic tiled bungalows. *Windy* next door (②) is also worth a look. ②

Ozzy Homestay ⓣ0812/371 8039. Small place with good-quality fan rooms. Next door *Trawangan Dive* is similar, while *Flush* (both ③), further south has a two storey, traditional place. ③

Pondok Lita ⓣ0370/648607. An excellent, clean budget choice – tucked away in the village, about five minutes' walk from the beach (follow the track between Dive Indonesia and *Trawangan Cottages*). Rooms have fan and cold-water attached bathroom, set around a small garden. *Aldi*, *Pondok Funny*, *Edy* and *Pandan Wangi* (all ②) are all close by, in the same vein. ②

Pondok Santi ⓔnans95_5@hotmail.com. Well-built traditional bungalows with attached mandi, in a coconut grove in the south. A popular option, as the bungalows have large verandas, and it's only a 5–10min walk to the main restaurant area. ②

Rumah Kita Sanctuary ⓔrumahkita99@hotmail.com. Three bamboo and thatch bungalows in the village. They have fans and attached cold-water bathrooms, plus a more spacious garden than many places in this area. ②

Trawangan Cottages ⓣ0370/639282. Two rows of clean, tiled simple cottages in the southeast corner, close to the action. One set is further away from the beach along a track. A/c and hot water in the more expensive. ④

Gili Meno

A similar oval shape to Gili Trawangan, **GILI MENO** is much smaller, about 2km long and just over 1km wide. This is the most tranquil island of the three, with a small local population and no nightlife. The only "sight" is **Gili Meno Bird Park** (daily 9am–5pm; Rp30,000; ⓦwww.balipvbgroup.com) in the middle of the island; it has a collection of hornbills, orioles, cockatoos and parrots, plus a wallaby, deer and Komodo dragon, but animal and bird lovers may end up rather depressed.

The **snorkelling** is good along the east coast; start at Royal Reef and drift down to Kontiki in the south. Take care – there may well be boats coming in and out to the harbour along here. The other option is to start at the yellow lighthouse in the north of the island, turn left and the current will take you round to the west coast over the Meno Wall and you can get out at the Bounty jetty part of the way down the west coast. Keep your fins on until you're in very shallow water, as there can often be quite an undertow; see p.422 for a warning about **offshore currents**. A boat allows you to venture further afield; ask on the beach (Rp160,000 per boat, for four people). Equipment is available on the island but a lot has seen (far) better days. Blue Marlin (see box on p.422) has some decent sets (Rp30,000 a day), and is also the place to go for **diving**. If a **boat trip** is more your style, search out Din (☎081339/509859) one of the boat captains; he's often in front of the Blue Marlin dive shop. He'll take you out on fishing trips, to see dolphins (best in Nov and March–Aug), to a shipwreck off the Lombok coast and to see spring water in the sea off the north coast of Lombok. Prices are generally from Rp200,000 for the boat (2-4 people). You can charter him to Amed in eastern Bali, but see the warning in the box on p.314.

All boats arrive at the **harbour** on the east coast. You can **change money** at two kiosks, one south of *Mallia's Child* and one just north of the harbour. There's a **wartel** (daily 8am–10pm) near the harbour, with **Internet** access, but phone lines aren't totally reliable. There's no Perama office, although you can book by ringing the Senggigi office (☎0370/693007), and shuttle bus tickets with *Gora* are widely advertised to destinations on Lombok and Bali.

Accommodation and eating

The range of **accommodation** on Gili Meno is wide, from budget through to luxury available. Most is spread along the east coast. There's no island-wide electricity generator; most places have their own, but operate them part-time only.

There are plenty of **places to eat**. For local food, *Balenta* and *Ya Ya* to the north of the east coast are both good choices, while *Rust* restaurant near the harbour is excellent for fresh fish, and *Bibi's Café*, attached to *Vila Nautilus*, serves the best pizzas on the island - but is good for pretty much everything. The location of *Jali* – looking out onto the harbour, with Gili Air and the Lombok mountains rising behind – is excellent, and over the west side of Gili Meno *Good Heart* and *Café Lumba Lumba* make ideal spots for drinks on the way round the island or at sunset. In the **evening**, the *Jungle Bar* at *Tao' Kombo'* is the place to hang out, with cool music and plenty of drinks.

Amber House ☎0370/643676, ⓔamber_house02pm@hotmail.com. Traditional, thatch and bamboo bungalows in a shady garden, set slightly back from the beach towards the north of the island. ❶–❷

Biru Meno ☎081/736 1915. In a great location at the southern end of the island, ten minutes' walk from the harbour, with good-quality bamboo and thatch bungalows on a tile base, plus attached cold-water bathrooms. Fans can be rented from the village for Rp5000 a night. ❷

Cafe Lumba-Lumba Book through *Casablanca*. Three tiled bungalows on the west coast, with the two at the front having fine views to the sea. A great spot for the sunset. ❷

Casablanca ☎0370/633847, ⓔlidyblanca@mataram.wasantara.net.id. Offering four standards of room set about 100m back from the beach on the east side of the island with a pretty garden. Accommodation ranges from basic fan and cold-water rooms to large a/c ones with hot water. There's a tiny pool (check its condition if it is important to you) and a restaurant. ❸–❻

Fantastic Cottages ☎081339/509859. Wood, thatch and bamboo bungalows with attached mandi, set back from the beach near the harbour. There are large verandas for relaxing. The similar *Rawa Indah* is nearby. ❶

Jali Bungalows ☎0370/639800 Just behind the restaurant near the harbour, simple bungalows with attached bathrooms. Very convenient for the harbour. ❷

Karang Biru (Blue Coral) ☎0812/378 2030. In an isolated location in the north of the island. This is a row of traditional bungalows with attached bathrooms facing seawards. *Good Heart* further west and *Pondok Santai* to the southeast both offer similar accommodation and equal isolation. ❶

Kontiki ☎0370/632824. Close to a good beach in the south of the island. Bungalows are tiled, with fans and attached cold-water bathrooms, though there is one with a/c. 4–6

Mallia's Child ☎0370/622007, Ⓦwww.gilimeno-mallias.com. Well-built bungalows in a good location near a fine beach just south of the harbour, with fine sea views from the verandas. 4

Royal Reef Resort ☎0370/ 642340. Very close to the harbour, these good-quality wood, bamboo and thatch bungalows, set in a large garden, have fans and good verandas. 3–4

Rust Bungalows ☎0370/642324 Traditional wood and thatch bungalows with attached bathrooms behind the restaurant of the same name just near the harbour. 2

Tao' Kombo' ☎0812/372 2174, Ⓔtao_kombo@yahoo.com. Set in a shady spot about 200m behind the beach in the south, with a large bar and communal area. Three good bungalows have bathroom, fan and a fresh-water shower. There are also four *brugak* (open-sided sleeping platforms; 1) with lockable cupboards, mattress, screen, mosquito net and shared bathrooms. 2

Gili Air

Closest to the mainland, with the largest local population (1000) of the three islands, **GILI AIR** stretches about 1.5km in each direction and takes a couple of hours to walk round. It sits somewhere between lively, social Gili Trawangan and peaceful Gili Meno. Although **accommodation** is spread around most of the coast, it's concentration on the southeast corner and the **beach** here is the most popular, with good **snorkelling**.

Snorkelling gear is available for rent; try Ozzy's Shop on the east coast (Rp15,000 per day), while, for snorkelling further afield, **glass-bottomed boat trips** are advertised pretty much everywhere, or ask at Ozzy's Shop or on the beach, (Rp40,000 per person, six people min; 9.30am–3pm, taking in sites off all three islands). See the box on p.422 for a list of **dive** operators on the island. Yan's Bookshop and Ozzy's Shop rent **bicycles** (Rp15,000 for 24hr).

There are plenty of **moneychangers** around the island. There's a **wartel** (daily 8am–10pm) behind *Hotel Gili Indah* and another at Ozzy's Shop, where there is also **Internet** access (Rp400/min, min Rp4000). The Perama office (8am–10pm; ☎0370/637816) is near the harbour, where tourist shuttle tickets to destinations throughout Bali and Lombok can be booked. Postcards and stamps are available from the shops; mail gets taken to the mainland regularly by Perama.

The most popular places to hang out in the day are the **bars** and **restaurants** that line the southeast coast, from *Dream Divers* in the south up to *Warung Munchies* (afternoon specials with cake are excellent). All have fine views across to the mainland – *Sunrise Restaurant* is as pleasant as any. It's worth moving inland to *Gecko Café* (closed Fri) for its small but excellently cooked menu of Western and Indonesian food including homemade bread and cakes. The most imaginative dining is at *Coconut Cottages*, with seating in the main restaurant or in *brugak* in the garden. It has a menu of appetizing and well-presented Western and local cuisine including Sasak dishes. *Harry's Blues Bar*, attached to *Salabose* on the west coast is an excellent spot for a sunset drink. At the time of writing, **parties** were only permitted twice a week; *Legend* warung on Wednesday and *Gogo* on Saturday. During the high season, **Full Moon parties** arranged by bars in the southeast of the island are also popular. Enquire at your guesthouse about the current situation.

Accommodation

There's a selection of good-value **accommodation** spread around the island; the quietest spots are the north and west coasts. It makes sense to engage a cidomo to reach the more far-flung spots when you arrive with your bags.

Abdi Fantastik ☎0370/636421. In a great location looking seawards on the east coast; bungalows are simple but clean, have fans and mosquito nets, and there are sitting areas overlooking the water. 2

Coconut Cottages ☎0370/635365, Ⓦwww.coconuts-giliair.com. Widely-spaced bungalows in a great garden set back from the east coast, about a 25min walk from the harbour. There are several standards of room, all attractive and clean, some with hot water. 2–4

Gili Air Santay ☎0370/641022, ⓔgiliair-santay@yahoo.com. Popular, good-quality traditional cottages set 100m back from the east coast in a shady garden. *Brugak* on the beach for relaxing. 4

Gita Gili ☎0812/372 4813. In a good location near the coast and convenient for the harbour, with thatch, wood and bamboo bungalows facing the sea. 4

Gusung Indah ☎0812/378 9054. Close to the east coast, with two standards of bungalows facing seaward, some with squat toilets. *Sandi Cottages*, just north, is also worth a look. 2–3

Hotel Gili Indah ☎0370/637328, ⓔgili_indah@mataram.wasantara.net.id. With a big compound near the harbour and several standards of bungalows (from fan and cold water to a/c and hot water). All are reasonably furnished, and the ones at the front have sea views. 3–6

Legend ☎0812/376 4552. Relaxed, popular spot on the northeast coast with *brugak* near the beach. The bungalows are traditional; smaller ones have squat toilets. The attached warung holds weekly parties. 2–3

Lombok Indah ☎0812/373 6746. Budget place on the northeast coast, set just behind the beach (nearby *Legend* has weekly parties). There are older, basic rooms and larger, better-quality ones. 1–3

Lucky's ☎0812/378 2156. A good choice over on this side of the island (5–10min walk from the harbour). Rooms are simple but OK and there are many *brugak*. Both nearby *Salabose* and *Safari* (both 2–3) have some rooms worth considering. 2–3

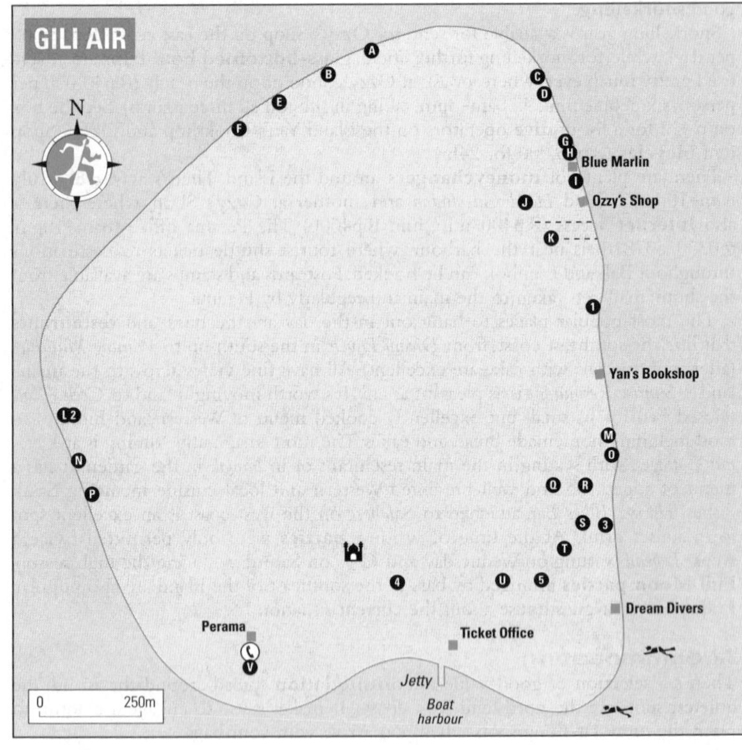

ACCOMMODATION										RESTAURANTS & BARS	
Abdi Fantastik	I	Gita Gili	M	Matahari	B	Resota	U	Coconut Cottages	I
Bunga	A	Gusung Indah	H	Nina	Q	Safari	P	Gecko Café	4
Coconut Cottages	J	Island View	F	Nusa Tiga	T	Salabose	L	Gogo	5
Corner Bungalows	R	Legend	C	Pino	O	Sandi Cottages	G	Harry's Blues Bar	2
Gili Air Santay	K	Lombok Indah	D	Pondok		Sunrise	S	Sunrise Restaurant	3
Hotel Gili Indah	V	Lucky's	N	Pantai	E			Warung Munchies	1

Matahari Decent choice on the far northwest coast. The bungalows are slightly better quality than the ones nearby – but things can change. Nearby options are *Bunga*, *Pondok Pantai* and *Island View* (all ❶–❷). ❶–❷

Nina ⓣ08180/362 2893. Popular cottages reached by walking through *Corner Bungalows* (❷–❸), which is also worth considering, in the southeast of the island. Bungalows are simple but good quality, with attached bathroom with Western toilet. ❷–❸

Nusa Tiga Traditionally built bungalows with Western toilets in the attached bathrooms and deep verandas. A reasonable budget choice in this area, set back from the coast in the south of the island. The nearby *Resota* (❷) is similar. ❷

Pino Good bamboo, thatch and wood cottages in a neat garden just on the edge of the island's southeast corner. There are sitting places on the beach with brilliant views, and there's snorkelling off the beach here. ❷

Sunrise ⓣ&ⓕ0370/642370. On the southeast corner. Accommodation is in two-storey *lumbung* barns with sitting areas upstairs and down. The ones at the front have excellent sea views. All have cold-water attached bathrooms and fans. ❸–❻

Gunung Rinjani and around

From a distance, **Gunung Rinjani** (3726m) appears to rise in solitary glory from the plains, but in fact the entire area is a throng of bare summits, wreathed in dense forest. The most breathtaking feature of the range is **Segara Anak**, the magnificent crater lake, measuring 8km by 6km.

Most visitors come to the area to **trek** at least part of the way up Rinjani. This is the most energetic and rewarding trek on either Bali or Lombok; access points and places to arrange treks are **Batu Koq** and **Senaru**, to the north of the mountain, and **Sembalun Lawang**, in a high valley on the eastern flanks.

Batu Koq and Senaru

Buses from Bertais/Mandalika/Sweta terminal in Sweta terminate at **ANYAR**, from where bemos and ojek run to the neighbouring villages of **BATU KOQ** and **SENARU** (about 86km from Mataram) via Bayan. Alternatively, buses from Labuhan Lombok in the east run to Bayan. Just to the south of *Pondok Senaru* losmen, a small path heads east to the river and **Sindang Gile waterfall** with Tiu Kelep, another waterfall, where the water pours down in a double-horseshoe shape, a further hour's scramble beyond the first. You can also swim at Tiu Kelep and probably should – local belief is that you become a year younger every time you swim behind the falls here.

The **traditional village** at Senaru, a fenced compound with houses of bamboo and thatch set out in rows, next to the *Bale Bayan Senaru*, is also worth visiting. Someone will appear to show you around, and you'll be expected to make a donation and sign the visitors' book. You can arrange at the Rinjani Trek Centre (in the far south of the village, just at the start of the track up Gunung Rinjani) to go on the **Senaru Panorama Walk** (4hr; Rp45,000 per person; two people min) or **Rice Terraces and Waterfalls Walk** (1hr; Rp35,000 per person; two people min) through the immediate area, guided by local women.

Accommodation

The **accommodation** in Batu Koq and Senaru is spread out for several kilometres along the road: *Segara Anak* is the most northerly (furthest from the mountain), while *Bale Bayan Senaru* lies at the end of the road, where the path up the mountain begins. Most are basic concrete and tile with attached cold-water bathrooms. Breakfast is usually included in the price. Places on the east of the road generally have the best views towards the mountain. They will store your stuff while you climb, and many have small **restaurants** attached, serving simple Indonesian and Sasak meals.

Achita Bayan ☎0817/577 3878. Concrete-floored bungalows with verandas both back and front for mountain and garden views. Some squat and some Western toilets. ❶

Bale Bayan Senaru ☎0817/579 2943. At the top of the road. Tiled, basic bungalows in a small garden with attached mandi and squat toilet. ❶

Bukit Senaru ☎086812/104252. Well-spaced bungalows in a pleasant garden with good verandas. They're bigger than many in the area, and have Western toilets. ❶

Gunung Baru ☎0817/572 4863. Small set-up, not far from the start of the trail, with a few basic bungalows. ❶

Guru Bakti ☎08180/362 8240. Ignore the tumble-down places visible from the road, there's a good row of places further back with great views of the waterfall from the verandas. ❶

Pondok Indah ☎08180/363 6058. Clean bungalows and fine north-coast views in the more expensive ones. ❶

Pondok Senaru ☎086812/104141. The biggest set-up, offering good quality accommodation, all with great verandas, in a pretty garden. The huge restaurant has fine views from the *bale* at the far end. Hot water in a bucket on request. ❷–❸

Puri Jaya Wijaya Small place with verandas overlooking the garden, rather than the great views behind. ❶

Rinjani ☎0817/575 0889. Doesn't take advantage of the views, but the four bungalows are clean and tiled and better quality than many. ❶

Segara Anak ☎0817/575 4551. The first place on the road from Bayan. There are fine panoramas from the verandas of the more expensive bungalows. ❶

Sembalun Lawang

A steep road twists 16km south from Kokok Putih to **SEMBALUN LAWANG**, set in countryside that is unique in Lombok – a high, flat-bottomed mountain valley virtually surrounded by hills. There are several **places to stay** in the area. Just 200m up the track at the start of the Rinjani trek, just behind the Rinjani Information Centre, *Lembah Rinjani* (☎08180/362 0918; ❷–❹) has a choice of rooms; basic ones with shared mandi, or large tiled rooms with attached showers and Western toilet plus verandas facing the mountain. *Bale Geleng* (☎086812/109271; ❶) is on the main road 600m beyond the entrance to the trek. They offer wood, thatch and bamboo *lumbungs* on stilts with outside bathrooms, all set in a pretty garden.

Some 4km south of Sembalun Lawang is **SEMBALUN BUMBUNG**, an attractive village. From Sembalun Bumbung, the mountain road winds for 15km across Gunung Pusuk to Pesugulan, the turn-off for Sapit (see p.432), and on to Pringgabaya or Aik Mel on the cross-island road. This road is prone to closure due to landslides; check on its status before heading off. There's daily **public transport** on this route and also via Kokok Putih from Anyar and from Labuhan Lombok to the valley. It's possible to arrange one-way drops from the valley (Rp200,000-250,000 to most Lombok destinations) at *Lembah Rinjani*.

Climbing Gunung Rinjani

The **summit of Rinjani** is reached by relatively few trekkers; the majority are satisfied with a shorter, less arduous trip to the crater rim and down to the crater lake. From **the rim**, you can see the beautiful turquoise lake, **Segara Anak** inside the massive crater, with the small perfect cone of Gunung Baru rising on the far side. There are three main **climbs**: to the crater rim from Senaru (2 days); to the rim and then down to the lake from Senaru (3 days); and, the hardest of all, to the summit – the shortest summit trips (3 days) start and finish in Sembalun Lawang; the longer version (4 days) heads up from Sembalun Lawang and then back down via the lake and crater rim to Senaru. **Trekking** on Rinjani is not for the frail or unfit and shouldn't be attempted alone or without adequate food and water. **Information** about the timing and altitude gain on the different routes is available at the Rinjani Trek Centre in Senaru and the Rinjani Information Centre in Sembalun Lawang.

Arranging the trek

If you're climbing up from Senaru to the rim or down to the lake you don't need a **guide**, although a porter who will carry your gear, cook your food and pitch your tent is a great advantage. The path leaves to the left just beyond *Bale Bayan Senaru* in Senaru and is difficult to lose. For the longer treks, you'll definitely need a guide. Each of the losmen in the area has a local trek organizer who should have printed information about the different treks and prices – which, in theory, are fixed. Alternatively, contact John's Adventures in Senaru (Ⓣ0817/578 8018; Ⓦwww.rinjanimaster.com), who also arrange lengthier explorations of the entire area, including to caves, hot springs and Gunung Baru. Prices depend on which trek you want to do and the number of people climbing but should be quoted to include guide, porters, all equipment (including sleeping bags) and all meals. As a price-guide, a three-day trip to the lake in a group of two climbers currently costs Rp840,000 per person, a four-day trip to the summit in a group of two people is Rp1,092,000 per person.

Rinjani treks are advertised in tourist centres around Lombok. If your time is extremely short, you may want to consider them – prices quoted from further afield should include accommodation, equipment and transport to and from Senaru or Sembalun Lawang, which can save some time but is significantly more expensive than arranging treks closer to the mountain. Contact Perama; Gora Tour & Travel, Senggigi (Ⓣ0370/693477); Citra Lombok Indah, Senggigi (Ⓣ0370/693921, Ⓦwww.citralombokindah.blogspot.com); or Rinjani Trekking Club, Senggigi (Ⓣ0817/573 0415; Ⓔimronrosadi@hotmail.com).

Tetebatu

Set amidst picturesque scenery on the southern slopes of Gunung Rinjani, 50km east of Sweta, the small village of **TETEBATU** is a cool, quiet spot for a few days of relaxation.

On public transport, get off the **bemo** or **bus** at Pomotong on the main cross-island road and either take an ojek straight up to Tetebatu or a bemo to Kotaraja and then an ojek on to Tetebatu. Alternatively, you can reach Tetebatu by Perama charter from Senggigi (Rp60,000 per person, two people min).

From Tetebatu, you can explore nearby **waterfalls** and **craft villages**: the *Green Orry* and *Pondok Tetebatu* (see below) rent motorcycles (Rp30,000-45,000 per day) or vehicle charters (Rp150,000-200,000 per day including driver and petrol), and *Green Orry* can arrange a cidomo charter (Rp50,000 per day). These places can also arrange guides for local treks (Rp30,000-50,000 for 4hr) and supply charter transport to other Lombok destinations: sample prices are Rp150,000 to Senggigi, Rp125,000 to Labuhan Lombok, Rp175,000 to Kuta, Lombok or Bangsal, Rp300,000 to Senaru.

It's not easy to change money locally. There's a **wartel**, just above the *Salabuse* restaurant on the road up to *Wisma Soedjono* but no Internet access.

Accommodation and eating

Accommodation is on the main road up to the *Wisma Soedjono* from Kotoraja and the road off to the east, Waterfall Street. At the time of writing, a lot of it was looking rather sad – the area has suffered badly in the tourist downturn of the last couple of years so it pays to look at a few places first. Most have **restaurants** attached, although a few simple restaurants have also sprung up, all serving the usual Indo-Chinese and travellers' fare, plus some Sasak options. *Warung Harmony* and *Salabuse* on the main road are both worth a try.

Cendrawasih Accommodation on Waterfall Street, in four two-storey traditional *lumbung*-style barns, is charming, and there's a thatched restaurant with fine views. ❶

Green Orry Ⓣ0376/632255, Ⓕ632233. Tiled, clean bungalows in a pleasant compound, plus a restaurant on Waterfall Street. ❷

Hakiki Set in the middle of paddy-fields at the eastern end of Waterfall Street, accommodation is in basic two-storey traditional *lumbung* with excellent verandas and attached mandi and squat toilet. There's a fine view of Gunung Rinjani from here. ❶–❷

Nirwana Cottages Some 200m off Waterfall Street: two basic brick and thatch cottages, which have verandas benefiting from brilliant views of Rinjani. ❶

Pondok Bulan Ⓣ0376/632581. Located on Waterfall Street, with good views south. Traditional bamboo and thatch *lumbung*-style bungalows as well as bigger, less traditional family rooms. ❶–❷

Pondok Tetebatu Ⓣ0376/632572, Ⓕ632622. Good-quality, clean, tiled rooms in two rows facing across a small garden on the main road up to *Wisma Soedjono*. ❶

Wisma Soedjono Ⓣ&Ⓕ0376/21309. This used to be the home of Dr Soedjono, the first doctor in eastern Lombok, and is still owned by his family. It offers a range of accommodation set in great grounds at the far north end of the village and is the most upmarket option in the area and the only place offering hot water. There's also a swimming pool. ❶–❷

Lendang Nangka

Developed as a tourist destination by local teacher Haji Radiah, **LENDANG NANGKA** is a small farming community 2km north of the main cross-island road, and served by cidomo and ojek from Bagik Bontong. Although the scenery is not as picturesque as Tetebatu, the atmosphere in the village is more welcoming, and this is a great place to experience village life and to practise your Indonesian or Sasak. There's a wealth of walks through the rice-fields around the village, and the local people are used to strangers wandering around.

Established in 1983, *H.Radiah's* (Ⓣ0376/631463, Ⓔsoul-lenka@hotmail.com; ❶ full board) is a **homestay** in the real sense of the word. It's in the middle of the village, but tucked away behind the school, so ask for directions. There are rooms in the family compound or in a house in the local fields. Bathrooms are shared or attached, with either squat or Western toilets. It's great to be part of a household and many visitors enjoy an afternoon walk in the area with Radiah. Sannah, Radiah's wife, cooks traditional Sasak food and is used to guests in the kitchen learning recipes. There's a great *bale* in the garden where you can while away a few hours, and visitors get a map with suggestions for local excursions. There's a **wartel** with **Internet** access across the road.

Sapit

Situated at 1400m on the southern slopes of Gunung Pusuk, the small village of **SAPIT** is a quiet retreat with wonderful views. It's 15km from Sembalun Lawang (2hr by bus) but the road is prone to landslides and blocking – check in Sembalun or Sapit on its condition before setting off. It's the same distance from the cross-island road, either via Aik Mel or Pringgabaya. For **accommodation**, try *Hati Suci* (Ⓣ0818/545655, Ⓦwww.hatisuci.tk; ❷) or nearby *Balelangga* (same contact; ❷). *Balelangga* is the simpler of the two, with outside toilet, while *Hati Suci* has bungalows with attached bathrooms, some with squat toilets. Both have lovely gardens and great views across the paddy-fields to Sumbawa. Each has a small **restaurant** offering a basic menu, and staff here will point you in the right direction for local walks and, for the hardy, the fifteen-kilometre trek across to Sembalun Bumbung and on the Sembalun Lawang (see p.430).

Labuhan Lombok and on to Sumbawa

The port town of **LABUHAN LOMBOK** runs **ferries to Sumbawa** (every hour; Rp9000) from the ferry terminal, Labuhan Kayangan, at the far end of the promontory, 3km around the south side of the bay (Rp1000 by local bemo). **Buses** run regularly along the cross-island road between Labuhan Lombok and the Bertais/Mandalika/Sweta terminal at Sweta with some continuing on to the ferry terminal. Buses also run between Labuhan Lombok and Sembalun Lawang; change at Kokok Puitih for Batu Koq or Senaru. Travelling between Kuta and Labuhan Lombok involves changing at Praya and then Kopang, on the main road. A decent **place to stay** is *Hotel Melati Lima Tiga*, Jl Kayangan 14 (☎0376/23316; ❷), about 150m from the town centre on the road to the ferry terminal.

If you want to linger on the northeast coast, head up to the village of **LABUHAN PANDAN**, 13km from Labuhan Lombok; all public transport heading north from Labuhan Lombok passes through here. *Pondok Matahari* (☎0812/374 9915; ❷) is an attractive place with a choice of bungalows on the seafront or larger rooms set further back in a two-storey block, with an attached **restaurant**. There's **snorkelling** off the beach here and you can rent snorkelling gear (Rp15,000-20,000). You can also arrange fishing, snorkelling and boating trips to the offshore islands (from Rp180,000).

Kuta and around

The peaceful south-coast fishing village of **KUTA**, 54km from Mataram, has a wide, white-sand beach and is a favourite choice of Lombok travellers. The big swell makes the sea good for **surfing** and there are lovely beaches within walking or cycling distance. Prabu Bagus (☎0370/655207) in the village arranges four- to five-hour fishing and sightseeing **boat trips** along the coast, a fabulous way to see the coastline (Rp400,000, 4 people max).

Coming from the west, **buses** and **bemos** run to Praya from Bertais/Mandalika/Sweta terminal in Sweta. From Praya, bemos either go as far Sengkol, where you can change, or right through to Kuta. From the east of Lombok, bemos run to Praya from Kopang on the main cross-island road. Perama offer **tourist charters** to Kuta (Rp60,000 per person, 2 people min) from Mataram (see p.409) and Senggigi (see p.417).

You can **change money** at *Kuta Indah* and *Segare Anak* bungalows. **Internet** access is available in *Segare Anak* and *Alam Anda*. There's a **wartel** in the village (daily 7am–10pm) and one at *Segare Anak* (7am–9pm). *Segare Anak* is also a **postal agent** and the Perama agent.

If you want to **charter transport** to some of the south-coast beaches, ask at your accommodation or at *Segare Anak*. It costs around Rp250,000 per day for a car (including driver and fuel). Motorcycles are available at *Mimpi Manis* at Rp30,000 per day but there's no insurance in Kuta. Decent bicycles cost Rp20,000 per day from *Mimpi Manis* or *Segara Anak*.

Around Kuta

The glorious beaches of Seger and Tanjung Aan to the **east of Kuta** are easily accessible and, at a push, walkable, though bicycles are a good idea. Past Tanjung Aan, the small fishing village of **GERUPAK**, just under 8km from Kuta, perches on the western shores of Gumbang Bay. From Gerupak, there are fine views across the bay to **BUMBANG** on the eastern shore, and you can rent a canoe or motorboat to take you across. The thriving fishing village of **AWANG**, 16km east of Kuta, is well worth the trip for the stunning views of **Awang Bay**, a massive inlet whose beach spreads magnificently north and south from the village.

Along the coast **west of Kuta** you can explore half a dozen or more of the prettiest beaches on the island, but you'll need your own transport. The closest is **Are Goleng** a couple of kilometres out of Kuta, and heading west you come to **Mawun**, **Tampa**, **Mawi** and **Rowok** before reaching the small coastal village of **Selong Blanak**, 15km from Kuta. Take a decent road map if you're exploring any further west from here and be aware that the road deteriorates badly the further west you go. There's an eighteen-kilometre inland road to the pretty coastal village of **Pengangtap**, from where you can access the bays of **Sepi** and **Blongas** further west. From Sepi, you can head 11km north through the coastal hills to **Sekotong**, where you can head west to Bangko Bangko or north to Lembar.

Accommodation, eating and drinking

The **accommodation** here is mostly simple losmen-style, but there are a few upmarket options. In Kuta itself, the road runs about 50m inland from the beach and there's accommodation spread out along the coast for about 500m on the far side, so don't expect cottages on the beach itself. All Kuta's losmen have **restaurants** attached, offering inexpensive or moderately priced travellers' fare; seafood is the speciality. *Puri Rinjani* has well-cooked food and *Segare Anak* a vast menu, while *Warung Melati* and *Biota* at the eastern end of the beach strip offer the best beach views. In the village, *Lizard Lounge* is a cute, friendly little place near *Kuta Indah*. For stunning views, *Ashtari* at the top of the hill on the road west from Kuta is unbeatable.

Anda ⓣ0370/654836. A good budget choice; the rooms – clean and tiled with fans and mosquito nets – are set in a shady garden on the road along the beach. ❶

G'day Inn ⓣ0370/655342. Five well-kept rooms with attached bathrooms in a friendly family compound in the village. ❶

Kuta Indah ⓣ0370/653781, ⓕ654628. Located at the western end of the bay, with fan rooms at the bottom end and hot water and a/c at the top. There's a good garden and excellent pool. Depending which room you're in, there's free or discounted transport to Tanjung Aan and Mawun beaches. ❻

Lamancha Homestay ⓣ&ⓕ0370/655186. Little family place in the village, a short walk from the beach comprising three rooms with attached mandi and squat toilet. ❶

Mimpi Manis ⓣ081/836 9950, ⓦwww.mimpi-manis.com. Just over 1.5km north of the village on the way to Sengkol, this spotless place is run by a Balinese-English family. Choose between a/c or fan rooms or a two-storey house; bathrooms have cold-water shower and Western toilet. ❷–❸

Puri Rinjani ⓣ0370/654849, ⓕ654852. Six rooms (one with a/c) in a big garden; all are clean and tiled with cold water. ❷–❸

Segare Anak ⓣ0370/654846, ⓔsegaranakcottage@hotmail.com. Set in the middle of the accommodation strip along the beach road, this long-standing favourite has a big choice of rooms set in a lovely garden. Safe deposit boxes are available. ❶–❷

Sekar Kuning ⓣ0370/654856. There are a few very cheap, very basic rooms. However, with new building going on in the compound, quality and prices may well rise. ❶

Surfer's Inn ⓣ0370/655582, ⓔlombok_hotel@yahoo.com. Surrounded by an unmissable pink wall, this new place has rooms ranged around a pretty pool. All have cold water, and there's a choice of fan or a/c. ❷–❻

4.5

Sumbawa

East of Lombok, the scorched, mountainous island of **Sumbawa** is often perceived as an inconvenient but necessary bridge between Lombok and Flores, but it does hold some fine west-coast **beaches**. Sumbawa is a strictly Muslim enclave and both male and female travellers should dress conservatively.

Historically, the Sumbawan people in the western half of the island have always been influenced by the Balinese and the Sasaks of Lombok, while the Bimans in the east share linguistic and cultural similarities with the Makarese of Sulawesi and the peoples of Flores and Sumba. Up until the end of the sixteenth century, Bima Region was still mostly animist, ostensibly ruled by a succession of Hindu rajahs with Javanese origins, but when the Makarese of Sulawesi took control in the early seventeenth century they converted the people to **Islam**. The Dutch only really controlled the area at the beginning of the twentieth century, and were ousted by the Japanese in World War II. Soon after, Sumbawa became a part of the modern republic of Indonesia. **Transmigration** and the wholesale reaping of the sappanwood and sandalwood forests have put huge pressure on the little land that is useable and Bima's once illustrious bay is now filling with silt as a result.

Ferries to and **from Lombok** (90min) dock at Poto Tano, at the extreme western end of Sumbawa; buses meet all incoming ferries and run south from the harbour to **Taliwang** (1hr; Rp7500), and north to **Alas** (45min; Rp4000), **Sumbawa Besar** (2hr; Rp10,000), and sometimes all the way to Bima (9hr; Rp30,000), but it's easy to change at Sumbawa Besar if not. **Ferries** to and **from Flores** (6–9hr) and **Sumba** (6-9hr) use the port at Sape (see p.438). **Pelni** ferries dock at Bima (see p.438).

Sumbawa Besar

SUMBAWA BESAR's open streets are lined with crumbling white plaster buildings, bright-blue and green wooden doors adorning its many shopfronts. It's now the largest town on the island, and visitors looking to break up the bus-run across the island could do worse than stop here for a night. (It's a sprawling city without a real centre), but you'll find several places to stay and eat on Jalan Hasanuddin near the river.

All buses arrive at and leave from the **Sumer Payong bus terminal**, just off the Trans-Sumbawa highway, about 3km along Jalan Garuda, past the airport. Buses leave for Bima (7hr; Rp25,000), Dompu (5hr; Rp20,000), Taliwang (3hr; Rp10,500) and places en route at regular intervals between 6am and 1pm. The larger buses that run between Jakarta, Surabaya and Bima stop at the terminal almost hourly, day and night. The yellow **bemos**, *bemo kota*, do round-trips of the town, and most head out to the bus terminal. They can be flagged down on the street or picked up at the **Seketeng market terminal** on Jalan Setiabudi; there is a flat rate of Rp1000. There are also plenty of **dokars** that gather outside the market, which are fun for short trips (Rp1000). The **Barang Barat bus terminal** on Jl Kaharuddin by the river is now used for local services to nearby towns and villages. The **airport** is a

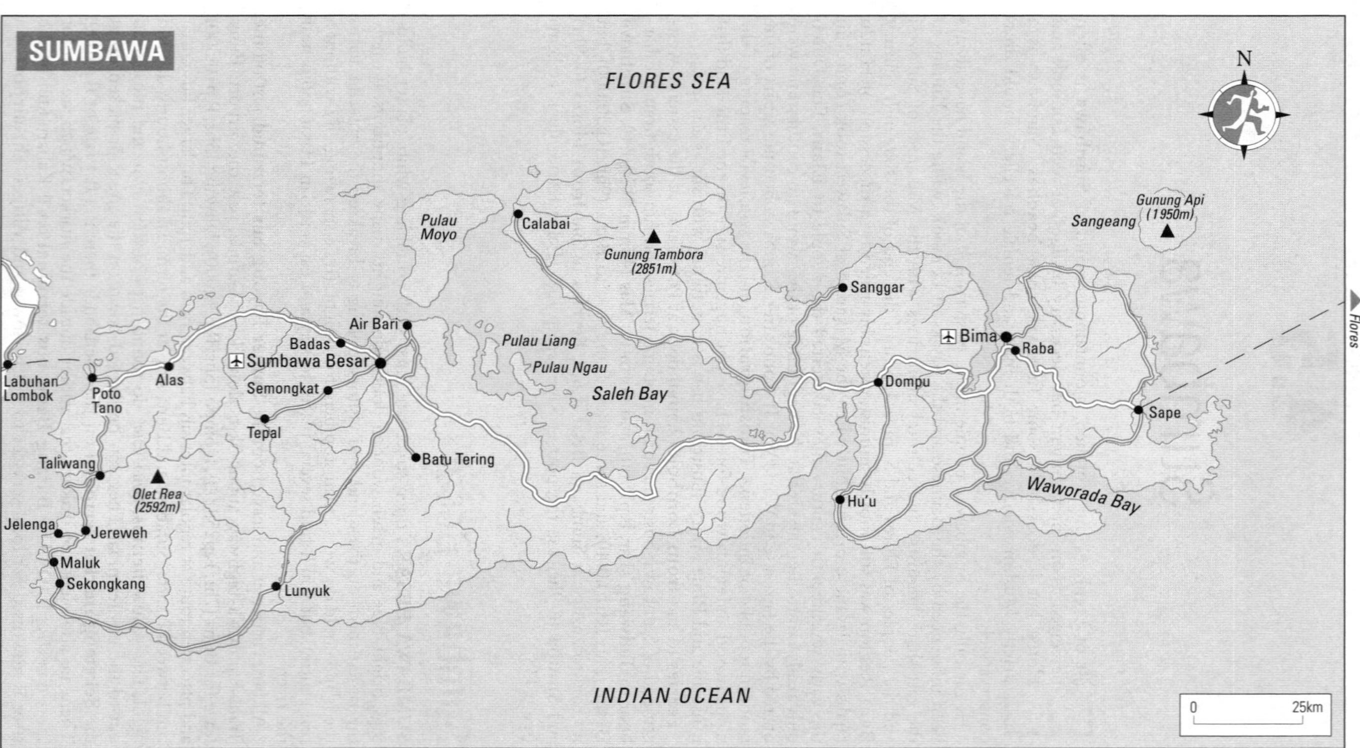
SUMBAWA
FLORES SEA
INDIAN OCEAN
N
Flores
Gunung Api (1950m)
Sangeang
Pulau Moyo
Calabai
Gunung Tambora (2851m)
Sanggar
Bima
Raba
Sape
Dompu
Hu'u
Waworada Bay
Air Bari
Badas
Sumbawa Besar
Semongkat
Tepal
Batu Tering
Pulau Liang
Pulau Ngau
Saleh Bay
Labuhan Lombok
Poto Tano
Alas
Taliwang
Olet Rea (2592m)
Jelenga
Jereweh
Maluk
Sekongkang
Lunyuk
0
25km

short dokar ride into town or a five-minute walk to the *Tambora Hotel.* Merpati fly four times a week to Mataram; their office is on Jalan Yos Sudarso by the post office, and the *Tambora Hotel* is also an agent.

The **BNI bank** on Jalan Kartini is the best place to change foreign currency or travellers' cheques; indeed, it offers better rates than most banks further east in Nusa Tenggara. The bank has an **ATM**, and there are also a couple of others around town, including one outside the *Hotel Tambora*. The **post office** is on Jalan Yos Sudarso, and the **Telkom** opposite has international telephone, telex, telegram and fax. One hundred metres to the east, Gaul **Internet Café** offers food and drink and **Internet** access (Rp10,000 for 1hr). The regional **tourist office** (Mon–Thurs 7am–2pm, Fri 7–11am, Sat 7am–12.30pm; ☎0371/23714) is about the best you'll find in Nusa Tenggara: it's 2km out of town at Jl Bungur 1 – take a yellow bemo from Jalan Hasanuddin heading west (Rp1000) and get off at the roundabout past the airport. The office is just off the left turn-off. The **PHPA parks office** (Mon–Sat 8am–3pm; ☎0371/23941) lies in the village of Nijang, about 4km from the town centre – an ojek there should cost no more than Rp3000.

Accommodation and eating

Although there's not a great selection of **places to stay In Sumbawa Besar**, there's something to suit all budgets, but do check your room before making a decision as many can be damp and bug ridden. At the cheaper end, *Losmen Harapan*, Jl Dr Cipto 7 (☎0371/21629; ❶) is friendly and has fan rooms clustered around a lovely old timber house. The best of those to be found on Jalan Hasanuddin is the *Dewi Hotel*, at no. 60 (☎0371/21170; ❶–❸); which has 31 rooms ranging from basic ekonomi to large doubles with minibar, TV, bathtub and air-con. The more upmarket *Hotel Tambora*, Jl Kebayan (☎0371/21555; ❶–❻) has everything from simple four-bed rooms to (reasonably priced) luxury.

While the majority of **eating places** in Sumbawa Besar are the usual local warung serving goat stews and sate, two options stand out: the *Aneka Rasa Jaya*, at Jl Hasanuddin no. 14, for its selection of seafood and the *Sadi Dadi* at Jl Dr Wahidi no. 7, close to the main BNI bank, which also has a good range of food and friendly staff. At each, a full meal washed down with a cold beer will set you back around Rp30,000.

Bima

The rather sleepy port town of **BIMA** is a useful place to break up the otherwise agonizing overland trip to Flores, but little remains from the days when it served as the most important port in Nusa Tenggara. The town is centred around the market on Jalan Flores; most of the accommodation lies to the west of the **Sultan's Palace**, whose museum (Mon–Sat 8am–2pm; Rp3000) houses a rather shabby collection of traditional costumes. Next to the *Hotel Parewa* on Jalan Sukarno Hatta is the **Merpati office** (☎0374/42897); also on Jalan Sukarno Hatta but further out of town is the **Telkom office,** for international telephone and fax. The **tourist office** lies just 50m further on, on the other side of the road. A yellow bemo (Rp1000) runs along Jalan Sukarno Hatta from the market. The **BRI bank** by the sports field is the best place to change foreign currency, while the **BNI** on Jalan Hasanuddin has the only ATM in town that will accept foreign cards.

The best **place to stay** by far is the *Hotel La'mbitu*, facing the market at Jl Sumbawa 4 (☎0371/42222; ❷-❹), which has great-value standard rooms, with TV and hot water. If it's full, you could try the *Lila Graha* a few doors down at Jl Sumbawa 19 (☎0371/42740; ❷-❹), which has a lot of dark, tatty, overpriced rooms. The rooms in the new block are much better but the staff are remarkably unfriendly. If you're really on a budget, the *Losmen Komodo*, Jl Sultan Ibrahim (☎0371/42070; ❶), is passable. For **eating,** there are lots of warung and restaurants, the best being the *Pemuda* on Jalan Sulawesi, which has decent seafood. *Café DC* on Jalan Sumbawa is a small, friendly place and very handy for the hotels.

Most travellers arriving in Bima from the west or the airport end up at the **bus terminal** just south of town, a short dokar or bemo ride to the centre. There are several **night-bus agents** on Jalan Pasar that offer air-con and standard buses to all major destinations, including Mataram and Sumbawa Besar. Kumbe terminal for **buses to Sape** (2hr; Rp5000) is in Raba, about 5km out of town and served by yellow bemos (Rp1000). If you need to catch one of the early-morning ferries from Sape to Labuanbajo, tell your hotel the night before and the bus to Sape should pick you up at 4am. Nearly all **buses from Sape** continue into town and stop outside the BNI bank on Jalan Hasanuddin. **Pelni ferries** dock at the harbour, 2km west of Bima and served by dokar. The **Pelni office** is about 1.5km out of the centre at Jl Kesatria 2 (☎0374/42046); yellow bemos can drop you there to arrange tickets for the *KM Tilongkabila, KM Wilis* and *KM Tatamailau* (see "Getting around" p.237 and "Travel details" p.486). The **airport** is 20km away on the main road to Sumbawa Besar. Buses stop in both directions; otherwise, taxis are on hand to meet arrivals.

Sape and on to Flores

SAPE and the port of Bugis are seeing a few more travellers who choose to stay here rather than Bima, though it remains a quiet, dusty town where livestock wander the streets. Most of the town's facilities, including the **post office** and a **BNI Bank** with an ATM, are on the main road down to the port. Just past these on the left is the *Friendship Losmen* (☎0374 71006; ❶), whose friendly English-speaking owner will happily help you organize a three-day trip to the offshore active volcanic island of Sangeang, if you've a few days to spare. Down in the port area, *Losmen Mutiara* (☎0374/71337; ❶–❷) offers good-value standard rooms in a new annexe. Nearby **Gili Banta** is a good day-trip should you get stuck, with nice beaches and a burgeoning turtle population. The best **place to eat** and stock up for the long ferry ride is the *Arema* restaurant, just up from the *Mutiara*, near the port entrance.

There is one daily direct **ferry** service to **Labuanbajo** on Flores (6–9hr; Rp26,000; Mon & Wed 8am; Tues, Thurs-Sat & Sun 4pm) and one weekly service to **Waikelo** on Sumba (6–9hr; Rp25,000; Mon 8pm). Neither is particularly comfortable, but on the Waikelo ferry it's worth trying to sneak upstairs to the much quieter crew area, where you could ask to kip down on one of the wooden benches, out of range of the livestock noises from the car deck below.

4.6

Komodo and Rinca

Off the east coast of Sumbawa lies **Komodo National Park**, a group of parched but majestic islands that have achieved fame as the home of the Komodo dragon, or *ora* as it is known locally, which lives nowhere else but here and on a few neighbouring islands. The south coast of the main island is lined with impressive, mostly dormant volcanoes, the north with mainly dusty plains, irrigated to create rice paddies around the major settlements.

Varanus komodoensis, the **Komodo dragon**, is the largest extant lizard in the world, and there is no evidence that such creatures have existed anywhere other than the Komodo area for well over a million years. Unlike many rare species, the dragon is actually steadily increasing in numbers. The largest recorded specimen was well in excess of 3m long and weighed a mammoth 150kg, but most fully grown males are a more manageable 2m and around 60kg. The dragon usually strikes down prey with its immensely powerful tail or slices the leg tendons with scalpel-sharp fangs. Once the animal is incapacitated, the dragon eviscerates it, feeding on its intestines while it slowly dies. Contrary to popular belief, the dragon has neither poisonous breath nor bite, but its prey usually die of infected wounds.

The two most visited islands in the national park are **Komodo** and **Rinca**; the best way to reach them is by organizing a **trip from Labuhanbajo** (see p.441), although private (and more expensive) trips can be arranged in Sape. There are a host of agencies competing for tourists, so it's worth shopping around or asking others for recommendations. A full-day trip to Komodo from Labuanbajo costs around Rp500,000 per boat, whilst Rinca can be seen in half a day for about Rp300,000. Multi-day trips are also popular, which include nights on either Komodo or Rinca, or on the boat itself.

Around the islands

The PHPA charges Rp20,000 for **entry** to the park (which includes Rinca too, and is valid for three days); in addition, there are guide fees (Rp10,000 per person), insurance (Rp2000 per person) and dock fees (Rp2000 for a small boat, up to Rp10,000 for a large one) to pay as well. Note that these fees are rarely included in the price negotiated with the boat owner/travel agent, so be sure to bring enough money and plenty of small change, hard to come by on the islands. On all excursions around the islands a guide is a necessity: they have sharp eyes and excellent knowledge of the area. Treks around the national park should reward you with sightings of wild horses, deer, wild pigs and, on Rinca, macaques, but remember: trekking on both islands can be hot and tiring, so make sure you also bring decent footwear with you and take plenty of water. The **accommodation** on Komodo and Rinca (❶) comprises wooden cabins, which are pretty basic. Many people bring their own food (which the cafés will happily cook for you) but the island's **restaurants** serve noodles, omelettes and pancakes. Don't be surprised to see several dragons sleeping near the cabins, drawn by the chance of leftovers.

Most visitors to **Komodo Island** offload at the PHPA camp at **LOH LIANG,** where you'll find all the facilities. Although the practice of feeding live goats to the dragons stopped a long time ago, you may still feel like you've stepped straight into

Treks and excursions on Komodo Island

The full day's walk to the top of **Gunung Ara**, the highest point on the island, from the PHPA camp doesn't promise dragon sightings, but is absolutely extraordinary. It's an arduous, excruciatingly hot march, but you'll see scores of unusual plants, animals and birdlife, such as sulphur-crested cockatoos, brush turkeys, and the **megapode bird**, which builds huge ground nests where its eggs are incubated in warm dung. Bring water and wear decent boots.

There are also regular guided walks from the PHPA camp to **Banunggulung**, the river bed where the dragons used to be fed fresh goats daily, and to **Sebita**, one of the mangrove forests that are vital for providing shelter and food for the island's populations of bats, birds, crabs and fish.

The seas around Komodo, though home to spectacular coral reefs and an abundance of fish, are a far cry from the Gili Islands or Bali, and riptides, whirlpools, sea snakes, sea-wasp jellyfish and a healthy shark population make these waters potentially dangerous, so stick to recommended snorkelling locations such as the excellent **Pantai Merah**. Many boat operators will include at least one snorkelling stop on visits to the island. If you come during the summer, you may even be lucky enough to catch sight of migratory whales that pass through these waters between October and January.

Jurassic Park if your visit coincides with big tour groups. That said, the longer treks around the island, especially out of high season, should guarantee you some peace and quiet, and with a good guide you should have an excellent chance of enjoying the full primordial experience.

With its proximity to Labuanbajo, **Rinca** is now receiving as many visitors as Komodo, if not more; and given that the dragon populations are denser here and there's less cover, you're much more likely to catch sight of them here. Rinca consists mostly of parched grassland covering steep slopes, drought-resistant lontar palms and huge patches of flowering cacti and other hardy shrubs. The PHPA camp at **LOH BUAYA** has just eight cabins and a small café. There are a couple of well-marked treks and at the right time (mornings and late afternoons) you shouldn't have any problems spotting dragons, monkeys, buffalo, deer and wild pigs.

4.7

Flores

A fertile, mountainous barrier between the Savu and Flores seas, **Flores** comprises one of the most alluring landscapes in the archipelago. The volcanic spine of the island soars to 2500m, and torrential wet seasons result in a lushness that marks Flores apart from its scorched neighbours. It also differs in its religious orientation – 95 percent of islanders are Catholic. The most spectacular natural sight in Flores is magnificent **Kelimutu**, unique volcano near Moni, northeast of **Ende**. The three craters of this extinct peak each contain a lake, of vibrantly different and gradually changing colours. In the east of Flores, high-quality **ikat weaving** is still thriving. At the extreme west end of the island, **Labuanbajo** has some fine **coral gardens** nearby and is also the port for ferries to and **from Sumbawa**.

Labuanbajo and around

The sleepy little port town of **LABUANBAJO** is experiencing a boom in tourism, serving as the gateway to Flores and as the main departure point for trips to **Komodo National Park** (see p.439). **Ferries from Sumbawa** pass myriad beautiful green islands before docking at the port, where there's no shortage of touts and tour operators waiting to take passengers to losmen or further afield. You can choose to stay in town or at one of the beach hotels within an hour's boat trip – a pleasant option, as most of these places offer a quiet getaway with unspoilt beaches and decent snorkelling. You can also easily organize dive trips from one of the dive shops in town; prices start at around $45 for two dives.

Practicalities

The harbour of Labuanbajo marks the extreme northern end of the main street, on which almost all of the town's losmen and restaurants are situated. The **airport** is about 2km out and you'll probably have to charter a bemo. Merpati fly five times a week to Denpasar via Bima or Mataram; their office (☎0385/41177) is on the way to the airport on Jalan Lantoro. As demand exceeds supply, you may well find other airlines starting services in the next few months but there are no guarantees; either way, book well in advance. **Bank BNI** at the south end of town and the **BRI bank** next to the **post office** change most common currencies but only the BNI takes travellers' cheques or provides credit card advances. The **Telkom** office is quite a hike out of town, just past the Komodo national park conservation office; walk south from the harbour, passing most of the hotels, and take the second left up the hill past the market. For most phone calls, the **wartels** in town are just as good a bet.

Buses heading east to **Ruteng** (4–5hr; Rp20,000) leave at 6.30am and 1pm, and tickets can be bought from all the hotels, or you can just hail them from the street; there are also regular services to **Bajawa** (11hr; Rp30,000)while buses meet the ferry for the fourteen-hour trip to **Ende** (Rp50,000). There is a daily **ferry** to Sape on Sumbawa (8.30am; Rp26,000) as well as fortnightly **Pelni** services to Makassar and Bima. Other ferries also operate, sometimes to Waikelo on Sumba (10-12hr), so it's worth asking at the port office for routes other than those mentioned.

Of the pretty decent selection of **accommodation** in town, *Gardena Hotel*, Jalan Sokarno (☎0385/41258; ❷-❸), remains popular, with nineteen bamboo bungalows providing great views over the bay. The better ones are those higher up. *Chez Felix* (☎0385/41032; ❷) also has great views from its restaurant and has twelve clean and spacious rooms set around a neat garden, but it's quite a trek uphill from the main road; take the turning opposite the market area. About 1km north of the harbour, the Dutch-run *Golo Hilltop* (☎0385/41337; ⓦwww.golohilltop.com ❷-❸) has lovely, smartly furnished rooms overlooking the bay. They also run the nearby *Paradise Bar*, a romantic spot with intimate tables spread across the slope below the main bar. The best **restaurants** in Labuanbajo are the *Sunset*, which has fresh seafood daily, the *Nirwana*, which serves excellent hot plates, and the *Dewata Ayu*, all located on the road near the port. The restaurant at the *Gardena* is usually quite busy, but lacks a little atmosphere.

All **beach accommodation places** offer regular free boats or bemos to and from the harbour; if you're leaving first thing in the morning, you shouldn't have any problem connecting with the ferries west or the second bus to Ruteng. Just twenty minutes south of Labuanbajo is the *New Bajo Hotel* (☎0385/41075; ❸-❹) with sixteen new, large air-con rooms and a beach to itself. If you want even more seclusion, try the *Seraya Bungalows* (❷), or the *Kawana Hotel* (❷), on their own islands just north of Labuanbajo (45mins–1hr by boat). Both have reasonable huts set back from the beach, and the price includes meals; be aware, however, that running water and electricity may not always be available.

Ruteng

The first large town near Labuanbajo is **RUTENG**, 140km to the east. Surrounded by stark, forested volcanic hills and rolling rice-paddy plains, it's an archetypal hill town and a cool, relaxing place. The market just to the south is the central meeting point for the local **Manggarai** people, as Ruteng is their district capital. They speak their own language and have a distinctive culture that's most in evidence in villages on the south coast. Their traditional houses are conical and arranged in concentric circles around a circular sacrificial arena; even the rice paddies are round, divided up

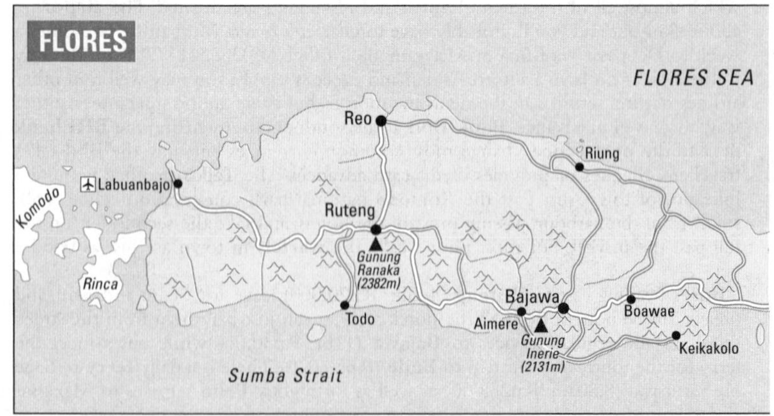

like spiders webs, with each clan receiving a slice. Most of these formations are no longer used, but a good example can still be seen at **GOLO CARA**, thirty minutes by bemo (Rp3000) from the central bus station.

Buses from Labuanbajo arrive at the **Central bus terminal**. Buses from the east will drop you at the **Puspasari terminal,** from where it's a three-kilometre bemo ride into town (Rp2000); the driver will stop where you ask. Moving on, buses for Bajawa (4-5hr; Rp20,000) leave every couple of hours from about 7.30am until around 1.30pm; your hotel can arrange for the bus to pick you up to save you the hassle of getting back out to the terminal. Buses for Labuanbajo (4-5hr; Rp20,000) use the central bus terminal; there are services throughout the day from 7am. You will also find bigger buses running to Ende (8–10hr), Moni (12hr) and Maumere (15hr) in the early morning. Again, arrange a pick-up from your hotel. The **airport** is 2km from the centre, served by bemo from the Central bus terminal (Rp2000). **Merpati's** office is on the way to the airport. The main **Bank Rakyat Indonesia** is on Jalan Yos Sudarso opposite the *Sindha Hotel*, and the BNI is up near the cathedral on Jalan Kartini, next to the 24-hr **Telkom** office. Both banks have ATMs. The **post office** is at Jl Baruk 6.

By far and away the nicest **accommodation** is at the chalet-style *Rima Hotel*, Jl A Yani 14 (☎0385 22196; ❶), with helpful staff, comfortable rooms and an upstairs restaurant with a nice balcony looking out over the town. More central is the *Hotel Sindha* on Jl Yos Sudarso 26 (☎0385/21197; ❶–❸). Their standard rooms out the back offer the best value for money. The most upmarket in town is the *Hotel Dahlia* at Jl Bhayangkara 18 (☎0385 21377; ❶–❸), though most of its forty-plus rooms are rather overpriced, housed in a brand new block and lacking showers. For **food**, there are a few Indonesian-Chinese places near the *Dahlia*. The *Lestari* on Jalan Komodo, probably has the edge in terms of variety and comfort, and serves plenty of fresh seafood. On the road up to the cathedral, just past the sports field, the *Pemuda* specializes in fried chicken. Otherwise, you're limited to the handful of rumah makan on Jalan Montangrua.

Bajawa and the Ngada district

The hill town of **BAJAWA** is one of the most popular tourist destinations in Flores, surrounded by lush slopes and striking volcanoes. **Gunung Inerie** is just one of the active volcanoes near Bajawa: it's an arduous but rewarding hike, and you can

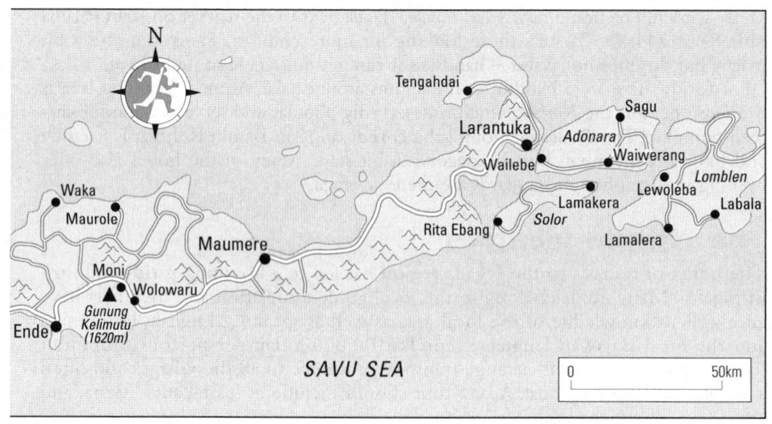

see all the way to Sumba from the summit if it's clear. Not for the faint-hearted are the local specialities of **moke**, a type of wine that tastes like methylated spirits, and **raerate** or **'rw'** (pronounced 'air-vay'), dog meat marinated in coconut milk and then boiled in its own blood.

Bajawa is the largest town in the **Ngada district**, an area that maintains its status as the spiritual heartland of Flores. Here, despite the growing encroachment of curious travellers, indigenous animist religions flourish and the villages maintain fascinating houses, megalithic stones and interesting totemic structures. Up to 60,000 people in the Ngada district speak the distinct Ngada language, and a good proportion of the older generation don't understand basic Bahasa Indonesian.

In the centre of most villages in this district stand several **ceremonial edifices**, which represent the ancestral protection of, and presence in, the village. These include the **Ngadhu**, which resembles a man in a huge hula skirt, the thatched skirt sitting atop a crudely carved, phallic forked tree-trunk, which is imbued with the power of a male ancestor. The female part of the pairing, the Bhaga, is a symbol of the womb, a miniature house. The symbolic coupling is supplemented by a carved stake called a Peo, to which animals are tied before being sacrificed.

Practicalities

The **bus terminal** is 2km out of town at **Watujaji**. Regular bemos from the terminal to the town cost Rp1000. When it comes to **moving on**, most buses come into town to look for passengers, but it's best to be on the safe side and go to them. Buses east to Ende (4hr; Rp20,000) run hourly from 6.30am till about 4pm. There's also one direct bus to Moni daily at 6.30am (Rp25,000); otherwise, change at Ende. There are regular services to Ruteng (4-5hr; Rp20,000); the direct bus for Labuanbajo leaves at 7am (11hr; Rp30,000).

The **BNI** on the street west of the *Barubudur* restaurant and **BRI** on Jalan Sukarno-Hatta both have ATMs and the BNI changes dollars and dollar travellers' cheques. The **Telkom** office on Jalan Sukarno Hatta is open 24hr, and the main **post office** is further north, at the crossroads.

Accommodation in Bajawa is centred either around Jalan Ahmed Yani as you come into town, or up just past the main market. The *Edelweiss* at Jl Ahmed Yani 76 (☎0384/21345; ❷) and the *Korina* opposite at 81 (☎0384/21162; ❷) are often busy; the former offers quiet, clean and comfortable rooms, whilst the latter has very helpful and friendly staff with en-suite rooms set around a spacious lounge. Whilst both offer good breakfasts and a daytime menu, they're also handy for the town's main **restaurants**. Up in the centre, the most popular place to stay is the *Hotel Kembang* on Jl Datadimata 18 (☎0384/21072; ❷), which has eight good-sized rooms set around a pretty garden. The brand new *Hotel Bintang Wisata* next to the market on Jalan Palalpa (☎0384/21744; ❸–❺) suits those looking for more comfort. The rooms are a bit pricey but do offer hot water – handy, as it can get quite cold at night here.

For **food**, there are a handful of restaurants around Jalan Ahmed Yani. The best is the *Lukas* next to the *Korina*, which is deservedly popular and serves wonderful sautéed pumpkin. The *Barubudur* around the corner on Jalan Basuki Rahmat is friendly and has a decent menu but the decor is a bit stark. Many of the hotels also offer evening meals, although standards are pretty average.

The Ngada villages

The influx of tourists to the Ngada region has led to a booming **guide** industry in Bajawa. Many guides belong to the local guide association and members have an excellent knowledge of the local area as well as speaking English, Indonesian and the local Bajawan language. For Rp100,000 a day per person (minimum four people), a guide will arrange transport, entrance to all the villages and often a traditional Bajawan meal. A day-tour should include at least Langa, Bena, and

Wogo, as well as the hot springs at Soa, but many guides now include a trip up to **Wawo Muda**, one of Indonesia's newest volcanoes. Most guides visit the hotels and restaurants looking for custom, so arranging an organized trip shouldn't pose a problem.

Although a guided trip is the best way to see all the sites in one day, it's also possible to make your own way to some of the more popular places. From Bajawa, the easiest Ngada village to visit is **LANGA**, which sits under the dramatic shadow of **Gunung Inerie**. Tourists pass through here every day, and you'll be asked to sign a visitors' book and pay at least Rp1000 to take photographs, though you're advised to save your film for Bena. If you want to scale Inerie, you'll have to set out very early from Bajawa. Bear in mind this is quite a stiff climb and you'll need a decent pair of boots or other sturdy footwear. Expect to pay an additional Rp50,000 per person, which should include transport from Bajawa to Langa.

From Langa, it's about 10km, mostly downhill, to **BENA** (Rp2500), another village that's very popular with tourists. You'll probably have to walk, though occasional trucks ply the route. Here they have nine different clans, in a village built on nine levels with nine Ngadhu/Bhaga couplings. It's the central village for the local area's religions and traditions, and one of the best places to see **festivals** such as weddings, planting and harvest celebrations.

Some of the finest megaliths and Ngadhu can be found at the twin villages of **WOGO**. To get here, take one of the regular bemos from Bajawa to **Mataloko** (30min; Rp1000), then walk south along the road for about 1km to Wogo Baru. There are some distinctly eerie megaliths set in a clearing about 1.5km further down the road in Wogo Lama; local kids will lead you to them. On Saturdays, Mataloko has a decent market selling sarongs and Bajawan knives.

The most popular destination near Bajawa is the **hot springs** at **SOA**. The springs are set in magnificent surroundings and are a joy, especially in the chilly late afternoon. Buses and **bemos** from Bajawa bemo station run to Soa village (Rp2500), from where it's a two-kilometre walk to the springs.

In the first few months of 2001 a new **volcano** erupted above the small village of Ngoranale, about 10km to the north of Bajawa. What had previously been just a large hill covered with pasture – one among many in this part of the world – suddenly burst its top, incinerating the vegetation in the newly formed crater and turning the trees into spindly blackened sticks. There are currently five small red lakes in the bottom of the crater. To visit Wawo Muda, catch a bemo to Ngoranale from the market (Rp1000) or the main road to the west of the *Hotel Anggrek*, then ask a villager to show you the start of the wide and easy-to-follow trail, which takes about an hour and a half to meander up to the summit.

Ende

Situated on a narrow peninsula with flat-topped Gunung Meja and the active volcano Gunung Ipi at its sea end, the port of **ENDE** is the largest town on Flores and provides access for Kelimutu and Moni. Ende suffered severe damage in the 1992 earthquake that razed Maumere and killed several hundred people here. The town still seems shaken by the whole thing – ramshackle, battered and with little to attract the tourist other than banks and **ferries** to other destinations – but there are signs that the place is getting back on its feet as tourism on Flores increases. Black-sand **beaches** stretch down both east and west coasts: the Bajawa road runs right along the seafront, so just catch a bemo out to Ndao bus terminal and the beach begins right there. The town is also an ideal starting point for exploring villages that specialize in **ikat** weaving. **NGELLA** is a weaving village about 30km east from Wolowana bus terminal in Ende, near the coast: take a bemo or truck (Rp3000).

Practicalities

The **airport** is just north of the town, close to Ipi harbour, on Jalan Jenderal Ahmad Yani. Both **Pelita** (Jl Gatot Subroto 11; ☎0381/21016) and **Merpati** (Jl Nangka; ☎0381/21355) offer regular flights from Ende; the former flying four times a week to Denpasar via Waingapu or Bima, the latter twice a week to Surabaya and Kupang. Buses from the east arrive 4km further on at the **Wolowana bus terminal**, served by bemo or ojek from the town centre. Buses from the west into **Ndao bus terminal**, which is on the beach about 2km west of the centre of town; bemos are in plentiful supply.

Buses for Moni (Rp6000) and Maumere (Rp25,000) leave the Wolowana terminal from around 7am, and there are hourly services till mid-afternoon. Buses for Bajawa (Rp20,000) and Ruteng (Rp30,000) run from Ndao terminal from 7am till mid-afternoon. One bus a day serves Labuanbajo (Rp50,000), leaving Ndao **terminal** around 7am.

Ipi harbour on the southeastern coast of the peninsula is used for all long-distance **boats**: the ferry and harbour master's offices are on the road that leads down to the harbour. The **Pelni ferries** *KM Awu* and *KM Wilis* stop here on their route around the islands (see "Getting around", p.237, and "Travel details", p.486), and there's also an ASDP ferry serving Sumba on a continuous loop (via Timor) once a week. Two private ferries, the *KM Titian* and *KM Kirana II,* run to Surabaya (Sat midnight and Tues 2.30pm respectively). The Pelni office at Jl Kathedral 2 (☎0381/21043) can help with Pelni and ASDP tickets, whilst the private ferries can be booked through some of the losmen on the way to the airport.

The cheaper losmen, some restaurants and the **BNI bank** are spread out along Jl A Yani and around the airport roundabout, whilst the rest are down in the old town; travelling between the two areas is easily done by bemo or ojek. Although the BNI is the only place that changes dollars and travellers' cheques, the BRI and Danamon **banks** – two blocks up from the sea on Jl Hatta – have ATMs. The main **post office** is way out up the hill on Jl Basuki Rahmat (☎0381/86318).

Accommodation and eating

Most people use Ende as a simple overnight stop, in which case the losmen near the airport on Jalan A Yani are fine; in fact, the *Losmen Ikhlas* at Jl A Yani 65 (☎0381/21695; ❶) offers what may be the best value in Nusa Tenggara. Their superior rooms are a bargain and it is deservedly popular, so book ahead. Close by, the *Hotel Merpati* on Jl A Yani (☎0381/25535; ❷) has ten newish en-suite rooms, some doubles, around a cosy reception area, and next to the *Ikhlas* the *Safari*, also Jl A Yani 65 (☎0381/21997; ❶–❸) offers a bit more choice with air-con VIP and superior rooms with showers and TV. If you prefer to stay in the town itself, try the *Dwi Putra* on Jl Sudarso, which has fairly decent standard rooms (☎0381/21685; ❷–❹). The staff at its makeshift reception on the first floor may be indifferent but the hotel is much better value than the nearby over-priced *Mentari* up on Jl Pahlawi (☎0381/21802; ❸–❹). However, the latter does have a good first-floor restaurant with fantastic views over the bay.

The best option in the town centre for **food** is *Istana Bambu* at Jl Kemakmuran 30a, serving a good range of Chinese dishes and delicious fresh juices. The *Minang Baru* on Jl Sukarno opposite the football pitch is a friendly Padang restaurant with a decent, if limited, menu and nice cold beer. Up near the airport roundabout, the *Simpang Raya Baru* and *Bangkalan II* both offer cheap and good helpings of Padang food.

Kelimutu and Moni

Stunning **Kelimutu** volcano, with its three strangely coloured crater lakes, is without doubt one of the most startling natural phenomena in Indonesia. The picturesque village of **Moni**, 40km northeast of Ende, stretches along the road from the lower slopes of the volcano down to the valley floor, and makes a great base from which to take a hike up to Kelimutu and around.

Kelimutu

The summit of **Kelimutu** (1620m) is a startling lunar landscape with, to the east, two vast pools separated by a narrow ridge. The waters of one are a luminescent green that changes to a milky jade in the sun; the other is the colour of coca-cola. A few hundred metres to the west, in a deep depression, is a huge brown lake that resembles a big bowl of chocolate. The colours of the lakes are due partly to the levels of certain **minerals** that dissolve in them. As the waters erode the caldera they lie in, they uncover bands of different compounds and, as the levels of these compounds are in constant flux, so are the colours. Just as important, however, is the level of oxygen dissolved in the water. When their supply is low, the lakes look green. Conversely, when they are rich in oxygen, they range between deep red to black. In the 1960s, the lakes were red, white and blue, and locals predict that within years they will have returned to these hues.

Every morning at around 4am, bemos will pick you up from your hotel in Moni and take you up to Kelimutu (Rp15,000 one way, plus Rp1000 park fee); make sure you organize this the night before. They return at 7am sharp, so tell the driver to wait if you're not intending to walk back. The best view is from the south crater rim, looking north over the two sister lakes; the trails that run around other rims are extremely dangerous – tourists have disappeared up here. The **walk** back down to Moni, which takes about three hours, with rolling grassy meadows flanking extinct volcanic hills, and views all the way to the sea, is a joy, especially in fine weather. Practically the whole walk is downhill, but always bring water and wear good boots. A shortcut by the PHPA post cuts off a good 4km from the road route, takes you through some charming local villages and past the **waterfall** (air terjun) less than 1km from central Moni, which is a great spot for a dip after what can be a very hot walk. A little further down is a hot spring, the perfect place to soak weary feet.

Moni

Nestling among scores of lush rice paddies, the village of **MONI** exudes a definite lazy charm. Full of cheap places to stay and home to several decent restaurants, it's a relaxed place to spend a few days, with great walking in the surrounding hills. Evening local music (*kalo*) and dance performances are held near the *Arwanti bungalows*, and you will often find traders here trying to sell *ikat*. Prices are better at the market further down the hill, where Tuesday seems to be the best trading day. There is no bank, post office, Internet or Telkom in Moni, despite the increasing number of tourists, but you can make phone calls at the **wartel** between the *Maria* and *John homestays*.

Buses from Ende (1hr 30min; Rp6000) and Maumere (4hr; Rp15,000) stop here regularly throughout the day, and there's one bus daily to Ruteng; ask at the losmen. For such a small isolated village, the **cuisine** in Moni is impressive. The *Chentry* and *Bintang* restaurants both offer very tasty and filling potato cakes and have great views across the valley. Further down the hill, the *Nusa Bunga* has an all you can eat buffet for Rp25,000, but you need to give them a bit of notice before you indulge.

Accommodation

All the **accommodation** is laid out along the hill at the top of the village, with most concentrated around the two main bends in the road. Many of the cheap homestays offer the same rates and have very similar rooms, but do take your time to look around as some rooms are much worse than others.

Arwanti With three huge bungalows, each with a double bed, en-suite shower, rest area and balcony, this is the nicest place to stay in Moni. Also has a good restaurant. ❷

Hidayah Bungalows The last place you'll find on the road in the direction of Ende, *Hidayah*'s six rickety bamboo huts are set in a pretty little garden. Very cheap, and a decent breakfast is included in the price. ❶

Maria Homestay Don't be put off by the approach, or the three semi-derelict bungalows at the front. There are four decent-sized, clean rooms out the back, all en suite. ❷

Watugona Bungalows Opposite the *Chantry* and *Bintang* restaurants, the friendly *Watugona* has five clean rooms, all with mosquito nets. Rooms range in size but all include a good breakfast. ❷

Maumere and around

On the north coast of Flores, roughly equidistant between Ende and Larantuka, **MAUMERE** was once the visitor centre and best diving resort on the island. In 1992, a devastating earthquake and tsunami destroyed most of the town, and it's only just getting itself back together. However, improved transport links and regular air services are steadily making it one of the main stops on trips around the Nusa Tenggara; from here, you can even organize tours that take in all of Flores' attractions. Diving is also improving and there are now a number of dive centres offering divers the chance to see fresh coral emerging from the seabed after its destruction. Maumere is the capital of the Sikka district, which stretches all the way to the east coast. It's especially renowned for its **weaving**, which characteristically has maroon, white and blue geometric patterns, in horizontal rows on a black or dark-blue background.

Practicalities

The main square and market are just up from the seafront but don't expect a massive amount of activity. Buses to and from Ende, Moni and other destinations in the west are served by the **Ende bus terminal**, a couple of kilometres down Jalan Gajah Mada southwest of town. Lots of bemos go here but most buses meander around the town centre for at least an hour before heading off to make absolutely sure there's no one left in town who might be thinking of leaving. When it comes to moving on, most long-distance buses circle town several times before leaving, so ask locally before taking a bemo to the bus terminal. There are regular services to Moni (3hr; Rp15,000) and Ende (4–5hr; Rp25,000), but Bajawa (Rp45,000) and Ruteng (Rp65,000) services set off around 7am. Arriving by **air**, most accommodation will offer you a lift if you decide to stay with them, otherwise shared taxis or minibuses from the airport into town are around Rp20,000. **Merpati** at Jl Don Thomas 18 (☎0382/21342) have daily flights to Denpasar. **Pelita** fly to Waingapu on Sumba three times a week, but you'll have to go to the airport for tickets unless you can get your hotel to arrange them. Two fortnightly **Pelni ferries** stop at Maumere: the *Km Awu* (which goes to Makassar) and the *Km Tatamailau* (to Bima). Tickets can be obtained at the Pelni office next to the *Lareska Hotel* on Jl Mgr Sugyopranoto (☎0382/21013).

The two biggest **banks** are the BRI on Jalan A Yani and the BNI on Jalan Sukarno Hatta; both change money. You will also find **ATMs** here, as well as at a couple of other smaller banks in the town centre. The **Telkom** office is opposite the BNI bank, whilst the **post office** is on Jalan A Yani near the sports field. Maumere also has the only **Internet** place in Flores – the Comtel Internet café is down near the seafront on Jalan Bandeng, and offers a surprisingly reliable service for Rp10,000 per hour.

Accommodation and eating

Many travellers bypass the **accommodation** on offer in Maumere and instead opt for the out-of-town beachside establishments, especially if they've come here for the diving or snorkelling. However, some of these resorts are now adopting pretty heavy-handed tactics to lure their clientele away from Maumere and other dive centres, so be prepared. There are places to stay both east and west of town, and many offer a full day's diving with food for between $60 and $80. For **places to eat**, there's a selection of restaurants on Jalan Raja Centis near the market, the best being the *Sarinah,* which has a good range of fish and seafood, as well as cold beer. The *Sumber Inda* opposite has made a token gesture to tourism by providing an English menu, but the service is pretty miserable. For really fresh seafood and great views over the bay, you should try the *Golden Fish* restaurant on Jalan Hasanuddin near the Internet café.

Hotel Gardena Jl Patirangga 28 ⓣ0382/22644. By far the best of all the budget options – many of which are well overdue for an overhaul – a warm welcome from the staff, and clean rooms, ensure this is still the travellers' favourite. Includes a decent breakfast. ❷

Hotel Maiwali Jl Don Thomas 6 ⓣ0382/21220. Offers a wide range of rooms – from simple ekonomis to gorgeous superiors in a new annexe at the back – but the cheaper rooms inside the building are a bit grim. ❷–❻

Hotel Wini Rai I Jl Gajah Mada 50 ⓣ0382/21388. Handy for the bus terminal, this hotel has some big, clean and very comfortable rooms towards the top end. Surprisingly, some of the better rooms are those set around the lobby. ❷–❻

Sao Wisata Jl Sawista, Waiara ⓣ0382/21555, ⓦwww.saowisata.com. Definitely one of the smartest outfits on the coast, this dive resort has a/c or fan cottages and cabins, all with private shower, and a swimming pool on the beachfront. ❹–❻

Sea-World Club ⓣ0382/21570, ⓦwww.sea-world-club.com. Another smart beachside dive resort, this one German-run, offering thatched wooden bungalows with a sense of privacy. ❹–❻

4.8

Sumba

Sumba has a genuine reputation in Indonesia for the excesses of its funerals, the wealth of its *ikat* fabrics and the thrill of the **pasola**, an annual ritual war fought on horseback. One of the main reasons to visit Sumba is to experience first-hand the extraordinary agrarian **animist cultures** in the villages. These villages comprise huge clan houses set on fortified hills, centred around megalithic graves and topped by a totem made from a petrified tree, from which villagers would hang the heads of conquered enemies. The national government insisted that all totems be removed back in the 1970s, and though some do remain, many have disappeared. The most important part of life for the Sumbanese is death, when the mortal soul makes the journey into the spirit world. Sumbanese **funerals** can be extremely impressive spectacles, particularly if the deceased is a person with prestige, inspiring several days' worth of slaughter and feasting, the corpse wrapped in hundreds of exquisite *ikat* cloths.

The difficulty for **Western visitors** to Sumba is that traditions and taboos in Sumbanese village life are still very powerful and sit ill at ease with the demands of modern tourism. A visitor to a Sumbanese village must first take the time to share *cirih pinang* (**betel nut**) with both the kepala desa (village headman) and his hosts. Bringing betel nut is seen as a peace offering (enemies would rarely turn up

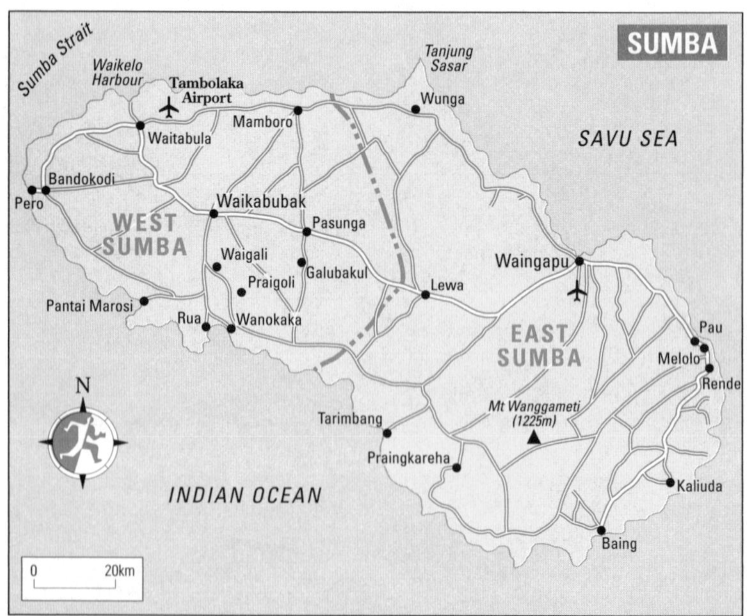

brandishing gifts), while its use is a sign of unity; Sumbanese ritual culture sets great store by returning blood to the earth, and the bright-red gobs of saliva produced by chewing *cirih* represent this. Many villages that are on the regular trail for group tours have supplanted the tradition of sharing betel with a simple request for money, but if you come with gifts (betel nuts, cigarettes) you'll be far more welcome.

The east of the island is rocky, parched and fairly mountainous; the west is contrastingly fertile and green, with rolling hills and a long rainy season. **Waingapu** is well known for producing the finest *ikat* in the whole of Indonesia. A little further out at **Rende** and **Melolo** are stone tombs with bizarre carvings, and other villages right out on the east coast offer the chance to see quality weaving and traditional structures near some deserted beaches. On the south coast, **Tarimbang** is an up-and-coming surfers' Mecca with a few waterfalls inland. The main town in the west is **Waikabubak**, where characteristic houses with thatched roofs soar to an apex over 15m above the ground.

Access to Sumba is either by **ferry** from Ende in Flores to Waingapu or from Sape in Sumbawa to Waikelo, or by **air** to either Waingapu or Waikabubak (the airport is at Tambolaka). Most people choose to fly out of **Waingapu** rather than Waikabubak, which has a very chequered record for reliability and cancellations.

Waingapu

It may be the largest port and town on Sumba, but **WAINGAPU** is far from a modern metropolis. Pigs and chickens roam the backstreets and locals still walk around barefoot, with *ikat* tied around their heads and waists. The older half of the hourglass-shaped town is centred around the port, and the newer part around the bus terminal and market, where the government has channelled development in recent years. It's only a fifteen-minute walk between the two, but an endless army of bemos do the circular trip (Rp1000). The bay to the west of town has a harbour at the extreme point of either shore; all ASDP, Pelni and the car ferries dock at the **western harbour**, requiring an eight-kilometre journey around the bay to town (Rp1000 by bemo). The eastern harbour in the old town is now just used for fishing boats. It's also worth taking a trip 15km up to the **huge pasola statues** on the main road to the southwest from where there are some spectacular views over the bay and surrounding countryside.

PRAILU is the most visited of the local **ikat-weaving villages**, just a ten-minute bemo hop away. After signing in at the large, traditional house (Rp2000), you can inspect weavings that weren't good enough to be bought by the traders. The **ikat** blankets of East Sumba are ablaze with symbolic dragons, animals, gods and head-hunting images. The cloth worn by men is called the **hinggi**, and is made from two identical panels sewn together into a symmetrical blanket. One is worn around the waist and another draped across one shoulder. These are the most popular souvenirs, as they make great wall hangings. Small blankets of medium quality usually retail for under $50 but will mainly use only chemical dye. Most pieces retailing at up to US$100 will use a *campur* (mix) of traditional vegetable **dyes** and manufactured chemical dyes. For larger, high-quality pieces, you can pay anything from $100 to $1000; some of the more expensive pieces are in demand all over the world. A tight weave, clean precise motifs and sharp edges between different colours are all signs of a good piece. Dealers in the towns will often give you better prices than those in the villages.

Practicalities

Passengers arriving at the main western harbour can get any **bemo** to drop them at the hotel of their choice (Rp1000). The **Pelni** office is down at the bottom of the hill near the old harbour; the *Km Awu* and *Km Wilis* run between Flores and Lombok, and Sumbawa and Flores respectively, stopping in Waingapu every fortnight. The **ASDP** office is at Jalan Wanggameti (☎0387/61533), 4km out of town on the main road to Waikabubak; they have twice weekly services to Flores (Ende and Aimere). The travel agent PT Andrew Jonathan at Jl A Yani 81 (☎0387/61363) will provide tickets for Pelni ferry services, as well as for **Pelita**, who fly to Ende and Maumere. The **Merpati office** is on Jalan Sukarno (☎0387/61232) near the sports field; their flights to Denpasar stop here and at Waikabubak in western Sumba. The **airport** is about 10km to the southeast on the road to Rende. Representatives from the main hotels are usually on hand to ferry tourists into town – as long as you agree to look at their hotel first; if they're not there, head out to the main road and flag a bus down or take a cab (Rp10,000).

Two **bus** terminals serve Waingapu. Buses to Waikabubak (Rp15,000) and the west leave from the terminal five kilometres to the west of town; bemos will take you there for around Rp2000. The bus terminal near the market in the new town serves the rest of east Sumba, with buses to Melolo, Rende and Baing. There are several **banks** in the new part of town, but the BRI on Jalan A Yani has the only ATM that accepts foreign cards. The main **post office** is in the old town at Jl Dr Sutomo 21 while the **Telkom** office is on Jalan Cut Nyak Dien.

Accommodation and eating

The majority of the accommodation is in the newer part of town near the bus terminal and market, despite the older part having more character. All the hotels can offer transport to the airport if required. You're almost spoilt for choice for **food,** with warung lining the main road linking the old and new towns. The popular *Nazareth* restaurant opposite *Losmen Kaliuda* has a fairly good choice of food but is not too friendly. Just off to the left at the top of the hill towards the old town, the *Rindu Alam* has a lovely setting but they often don't have much to choose from. Just a few metres further down the road the *Restu Ibu* has a better selection and even does "cappuccino".

Hotel Elvin Jl A Yani ☎0387/62097. The owner is indulging in a two-year renovation project but still has a few clean en-suite rooms, and the hotel boasts its own multi-gym. ❷

Hotel Merlin Jl Dil Panjaitan 25 ☎ 0387/61300. Looks like it ought to be more expensive than it is, but the staff's experience with large tour groups can make them indifferent to the independent traveller. ❷–❹

Hotel Sandle Wood Jl Dil Panjaitan 23 ☎ 0386/61887. One of the two more expensive options in town; nevertheless, it offers good value for money, and you'll receive a warm welcome from the helpful staff. ❷–❸

Losmen Kaliuda Jl Lalamentik 3 ☎ 0387/61264. Ten decent rooms with mandi and fan, and conveniently close to the eastern bus station. ❶–❷

Permata Jl Kartini ☎ 0387/61265. One of the only places to stay in the old town, and run by the genial Pak Ali, now a national senator, the accommodation is currently undergoing a redevelopment with twenty-three large budget rooms in a brand new building due to open early 2005. You'll also find one of the best restaurants in town here, with views over the harbour from a huge terrace. ❶

The east Sumban villages

The villages of eastern Sumba have made small concessions to modernity, some now sporting rusty metal roofs on their houses and using concrete to build their tombs. Most of these villages are used to visitors and will request around Rp1000 as a "signing-in fee". East of Waingapu, and just before the larger town of Melolo, are **PAU** and **UMBARA**. Pau, though tiny, is actually an independent kingdom with its own rajah, an interesting character who is very knowledgeable about Sumba and its traditions. Umbara has a few thatched-roof houses. Buses from Waingapu to

Melolo (Rp5000) run until late afternoon, and you can ask the driver to stop at Pau or Umbara.

MELOLO, 62km from Waingapu, has three high-roofed houses and a few crudely carved tombs as well as a friendly **losmen** (❶). The next major settlement as you head east is **RENDE**. Here, the house roofs are all made from tin, but are nevertheless spectacular, and doorways are adorned with huge buffalo horns. Rende is also the site of the finest **tombs** in East Sumba, huge flat slabs topped by animal carvings. There are buses every couple of hours direct to Rende from Waingapu (2hr), and occasional trucks; otherwise, catch a bus to Melolo (Rp5000) and one of the regular bemos, buses or trucks from there. Down the coast, **Kalala beach** at Baing (3hr from Waingapu) is becoming a popular place for surfers. *Mr Davids* (☎0387/61333; ⓦwww.eastsumba.com; ❺) offers all-inclusive accommodation on the beach and they have another resort in the nearby, uninhabited island of **Manggudu**. If you want to stay here, it's worth ringing ahead to check transport arrangements. About 40km out of Waingapu on the road west to Waikabubak, a turn-off leads down to **TARIMBANG** on the south coast. Here, the *Marthen's Homestay* (❷ full board), with its simple bamboo huts with roofs fashioned to resemble Sumbanese houses, caters for surfers and those looking for quiet beaches and a bit of relaxation. You'll either have to hire a driver to get here or take the lorry that runs every second day from Waingapu (5hr; Rp10,000).

Waikabubak

Surrounded by lush green meadows and forested hills, tiny **WAIKABUBAK** is a small town enclosing several small kampung with slanting thatched roofs and megalithic **stone graves**, where life proceeds according to the laws of the spirits. Kampung **Tarung**, on a hilltop just west of the main street, has some excellent megalithic graves and is regarded as one of the most significant spiritual centres on the island. The **ratu** (king) of Tarung is responsible for the annual **wula padu** ceremony, which lasts for a month at the beginning of the Merapu New Year in November. The ceremony commemorates the visiting spirits of important ancestors, who are honoured with the sacrifice of many animals and entertained by singing and dancing. Kampung **Praijiang**, a five-tiered village on a hilltop surrounded by rice paddies, is another fine kampung, several kilometres east of town. You can catch a bemo (Rp1500) to the bottom of the hill. Waikabubak enjoys an extended rainy season that lasts way into May, when the countryside can be drenched by daily downpours and it can get chilly at night.

Practicalities

The **bus terminal** is in the southeast of the town and serves Waingapu (Rp15,000) as well as all areas of western Sumba including Bandokodi and Pero; trucks and bemos also stop here. Services start around 8am and dry up around 2pm. **Waikabubak Airport** at Tambolaka is a good ninety-minute drive from the north of town towards Waikelo harbour; buses (Rp5000) and taxis (Rp20,000) meet arriving planes. Merpati fly twice a week to Denpasar via Bima, but be warned that flights are often cancelled in the rainy season. In **pasola** season (see box opposite), flights are more reliable but are often booked for months in advance, so if you're coming at this time make sure you have a reservation. The **Merpati office**, which often has no one in attendance, is on Jalan Ahmad Yani sharing the ground floor with a dusty general store (☎0387/21051). The weekly ferry to Sape in Sumbawa operates from **Waikelo harbour**, served by buses from the main terminal (Rp5000).

Most things that you will need in Waikabubak are either on the main street of Jalan Ahmad Yani, or within several minutes' walk of it. At the southern end, the market and bus terminal are sandwiched together, with the **Telkom** office a few hundred metres further south. Opposite the bus-station turn-off is an interesting family-run **art shop** full of old carvings, jewellery and **ikat**. The **BNI bank** at the junction of Jalan A Yani and Jalan Sudirman and the **BRI bank** on Jalan Gajah Mada both change money, and the latter has an ATM. You'll find the **post office** on Jalan Sudirman, just west of the BNI bank.

Accommodation and eating

For such a small town, the choice of **places to stay** in Waikabubak is pretty good. At the cheaper end are the *Tarung Wisata*, Jl Pisang 26 (☎0387/21332; ❶) near the market and the *Pelita*, Jl A Yani 2 (☎0387/21104; ❶-❷). They're both pretty tatty and run down but the latter does have some decent, if slightly overpriced, standard rooms upstairs at the back. Much better value for money is the *Hotel Artha* on Jalan Veteran (☎0387/21112; ❷–❹), which has big, clean rooms with fans, set around a garden courtyard, and very helpful and friendly staff. Competing with the Artha in terms of price and accommodation standards is the nearby new *Hotel Karanu*, Jl Sudirman 43 (☎0387/21645; ❷–❸). It has 24 en-suite rooms from ekonomi to VIP and a decent restaurant. The smartest place in town is the *Hotel Manandang*, Jl Pemuda 4, (☎0387/21634; ❷–❺) with a variety of huge rooms around a well-kept garden. Their restaurant is a bit pricey by local standards but has a decent selection of food and cold beer; a bit pricey by local standards but clean and efficient.

Other than the restaurants at the hotels and the handful of warung scattered around town, there are not really many **places to eat**. However, it's worth the 1km walk along the main road west out of town to the *Gloria* restaurant opposite the petrol station. It's always busy and they have a reasonable choice of curries, which you can wash down with cold beer or fresh juice.

Kodi and Pero

In the extreme west of Sumba lie the increasingly popular areas of **Kodi** and **Pero**. The Kodi district, with its centre in the village of **Bandokodi**, is particularly well known for the towering roofs that top the traditional houses. It is also one of the main **pasola** venues in West Sumba. There is one direct bus a day from Waikabubak to Bandokodi (Rp5000); otherwise, you'll have to take a bus to **Waitabula** in the north and then wait for a bus to fill up for the trip around the coast. As the trip between Bandokodi and Waikabubak takes approximately four hours, and the last bus back to Waitabula is at 2pm, a stopover in Pero is in order.

The pasola

By far the best-known and most dazzling festival in Nusa Tenggara, the **pasola** is one of those rare spectacles that actually surpasses all expectations. It takes place in Kodi and Lamboya in February and in Wanokaka and Gaura in March; most hotels can give you a rough idea of the date. This brilliant pageant of several hundred colourfully attired, spear-wielding horsemen in a frenetic and lethal pitched battle is truly unforgettable. It occurs within the first two moons of the year, and is set off by the mass appearance of a type of sea worm which, for two days a year, turn the shores into a maelstrom of luminous red, yellow and blue. The event is a rite to balance the upper sphere of the heavens and the lower sphere of the seas. The pasola places the men of each village as two teams in direct opposition; the spilling of their blood placates the spirits and restores balance between the two spheres. The proceedings begin several weeks before the main event, with villages hurling abuse and insults at their neighbours in order to get their blood up. The actual fighting takes place on the special pasola fields where the battle has been fought for centuries.

Pero

The Waikabubak bus will usually take you all the way to **PERO**, a seaside village with a solitary losmen. The village is not constructed in traditional Sumbanese style, but its rough, cobbled street flanked by colourful wooden houses has a certain charm. Numerous kampung with teetering high roofs and mossy stone tombs dot the surrounding countryside, only a short walk away. The *Homestay Story* (full-board only; ❷), about half way towards the sea on the right, offers basic but clean rooms and massive portions of really tasty food. There are a lot of mosquitoes and no nets are provided, so come prepared. The main surfers' beach, a desolate long stretch where high waves all the way from Antarctica crash onto the steeply sloping sand, is down to the right, but the currents and undertow are ferocious. There's a more sheltered beach down to the left over the river.

4.9 Kalimantan

Cupped in the palm of an island arc between the Malay peninsula and Sulawesi, **Kalimantan** comprises the southern Indonesian two-thirds of the vast island of Borneo, whose northern reaches are split between the independent sultanate of Brunei and the Malaysian states of Sabah and Sarawak. Borneo has conjured up sensational images in the outside world ever since Europeans first visited in the sixteenth century and found coastal city-states governed by wealthy sultans and a jungle-cloaked land inhabited by the infamous headhunting Dayak.

Modern Kalimantan has a tough time living up to its romantic tradition, however. In all Kalimantan's 500,000-square-kilometre spread, there are few obvious destinations, and even the provincial capitals of **Pontianak**, **Palangkaraya** and **Samarinda** offer little aside from their services. However, despite increasingly rapacious logging and regular catastrophic forest fires, sizeable tracts of the forested interior remain, sporting ancient **longhouses**. With few roads, Kalimantan's waterways are the interior's highways, and cruising up the mighty **Sungai Mahakam** is one of the world's great river journeys.

Kalimantan is well connected to the outside world, with **flights from Brunei** to Balikpapan, and **from Kuala Lumpur and Singapore** to Pontianak, and **boats from Tawau in Sabah** to northeastern Pulau Nunukan. From elsewhere in Indonesia, there are direct flights from Java, with a half-dozen Pelni vessels stopping off in Kalimantan on their Java–Sulawesi–Maluku runs.

Crossed by the equator, Kalimantan has no real **seasons**. April through to July is the optimum time for a visit: at the height of the rains (Jan–March) you'll find towns isolated by flooding, and planes grounded for weeks on end, while the driest months (Aug–Oct) see boats stranded by low river levels. With only fragmentary infrastructure, Kalimantan's **costs** are higher than in most of the rest of the country, especially for transport in remote areas. **Accommodation** is pricey, too: even simple country losmen charge US$3 a night, and it's rare in cities to find anything under US$10. West and Central Kalimantan operate on Western time, but the south and eastern provinces run on Eastern time.

Pontianak

The capital of West Kalimantan, or Kalbar (short for "Kalimantan Barat"), **PONTIANAK** is a sprawling, grey industrial city of over half a million lying right on the equator on the confluence of the Landak and Kapuas Kecil rivers. It is hot and noisy, often smoky from the vast forest fires that recurrently rage inland, and most travellers stay just long enough to stock up on supplies before flying on to Balipapan, or heading up the Kapuas Kecil or straight on to Kuching (see p.704).

Arrival and information

On the western side of Sungai Kapuas Kecil you'll find the Chinese quarter, the commercial heart of the city where most of the hotels, restaurants and travel agents are located. The majority of the buses that serve Pontianak arrive at and leave from

the **Kapuas Indah terminal**, perched on the water's edge in the centre of this quarter. Here, an army of agents can supply you with tickets for Kuching in Sarawak (Rp120,000–150,000), or for interior towns such as Sintang and Putussibau. Alternatively, you can catch one of the regular ferries that cross the river (Rp600) to the **Siantan bus terminal,** where you'll find another cluster of agents and buses across from the market. Buses to Sarawak tend to run either in the morning or late at night.

Supadio Airport lies 20km south of the city centre. Bemos (Rp3000) run to the Kapuas Indah terminal, or you can catch a cab (Rp35,000). The main **ferry port** is a few hundred metres west of the Kapuas Indah bemo terminal along Jalan Rahadi Usman. There are lots of agents on Jalans Gajah Mada and Diponegoro who can organize tickets for the express boats to Jakarta, Surabaya. PT Indo Pacific Jasaprataura at Jl Gajah Mada 2a is one of the better ones. For **Pelni** ferries, you can buy tickets at their office at Jl Sultan Abdur Rahman 12 (Mon–Thurs 8.30am-3pm, Fri & Sat 8.30am–noon; ☎0561/748124). The place may look closed but the ticket office is round to the right-hand side on the ground floor. The *KM Leuser, KM Bukit Raya* and *KM Lawit* all call in at Pontianak fortnightly; their routes include various places in Sumatra and Java as well as the Sunda islands; (see "Getting around" p.237 and "Travel details" p.486).

The Dayak

Dayak is an umbrella name for all of Borneo's indigenous peoples, who arrived here from mainland Southeast Asia around 2500 years ago and have since divided into scores of interrelated groups. In Dayak religions, evil is kept at bay by attracting the presence of helpful spirits, or scared away by protective tattoos, carved spirit posts (*patong*), and lavish funerals. Shamans also intercede with spirits on behalf of the living but, formerly, the most powerful way to ensure good luck was by headhunting, which forced the victim's soul into the service of its captor. Although these days you'll often find ostensibly Christian communities whose inhabitants dress in shorts and T-shirts, the Dayak are still feared for their jungle skills, abilities with magic, and the way they violently take the law into their own hands if provoked – in 1997, West Kalimantan's Dayak exacted fearsome revenge against Madurese transmigrants, reviving the practice of headhunting, and killing an estimated 300 to 2000. Similar violence has since occurred between the Malays and the Madurese but the general situation in Kalimantan is peaceful. It's interesting to note that the ethnic Chinese are not usually a target as, sad to say, they are elsewhere in Indonesia. There's a resurgence in the more acceptable side of tradition, too: communal houses, once banned by the government, are being restored, and public festivals like the annual **Erau Festival**, a massive assembly of Kalimantan's eastern Dayak groups on Sungai Mahakam, provide an assurance that Dayak culture is still very much alive, if being redefined.

Accommodation

Accommodation in Pontianak is spread out across the city, so where you stay will depend mostly on how long you plan spending here. Sadly, most of the budget places, especially those near the river, are way past their best. However, it's worth checking out some of the mid-price hotels, as most offer big discounts.

Hotel Gajah Mada Jl Gajah Mada 177–183 ⓣ0561/761598, ⓔhotel-gajahmada@ptk.centrin.net.id. The best value of the handful of mid-price hotels on Jl Gajah Mada. Rooms are bright and comfortable, and the staff are very helpful. ❹–❼

Kapuas Palace Jl Gajah Mada 889 ⓦwww.hotelkapuas.com. Luxury-class establishment but rates are exceptional for the facilities it offers. Avoid the cheaper poolside rooms, as they can get a bit damp and musty. ❹–❼

Patria Jl Hos Cokroaminoto 497 ⓣ0561/736063. Not an ideal location but it definitely has the edge over its competitors, with some enormous ekonomi rooms, as well as good-value standard rooms with a/c and TV; all rooms are en suite. ❶–❷

Hotel Tanaputra Jl Gajah Mada 141–143 ⓣ0561/767232. Closer to the centre than the *Patria*, this new hotel has excellent-value a/c rooms, although most have shared bathrooms. ❷

The Town

Signs of an economic upturn are in evidence throughout Pontianak – the new Ayani Megamall on Jalan A Yani, is typical of the region's growth – but there are still several old buildings of interest. The eye-catching **Istana Kadriyah**, built in 1771, and the traditional Javanese four-tiered roof of **Mesjid Jami** stand near each other on the eastern side of the Kapuas Kecil, just to the south of its confluence with the Landak. Small passenger boats from next to the Kapuas Indah terminal cost a few hundred rupiah or you can walk over the bridge just to the east if you're feeling energetic. But Pontianak's most entertaining attraction is the **Museum Negeri Pontianak** (Mon–Thurs & Sat 8am–1pm, Fri 8–11.30am, Sun 9am–noon; Rp750), a comprehensive collection of Dayak tribal masks, weapons and musical instruments. The museum lies 1.5km south of the town centre on Jalan Jend A Yani, Rp1000 by bemo or Rp3000 by becak from town. Just round the corner from the museum, on Jalan Sutoyo, is an impressive replica of a **Dayak longhouse**, over 50m long and 15m

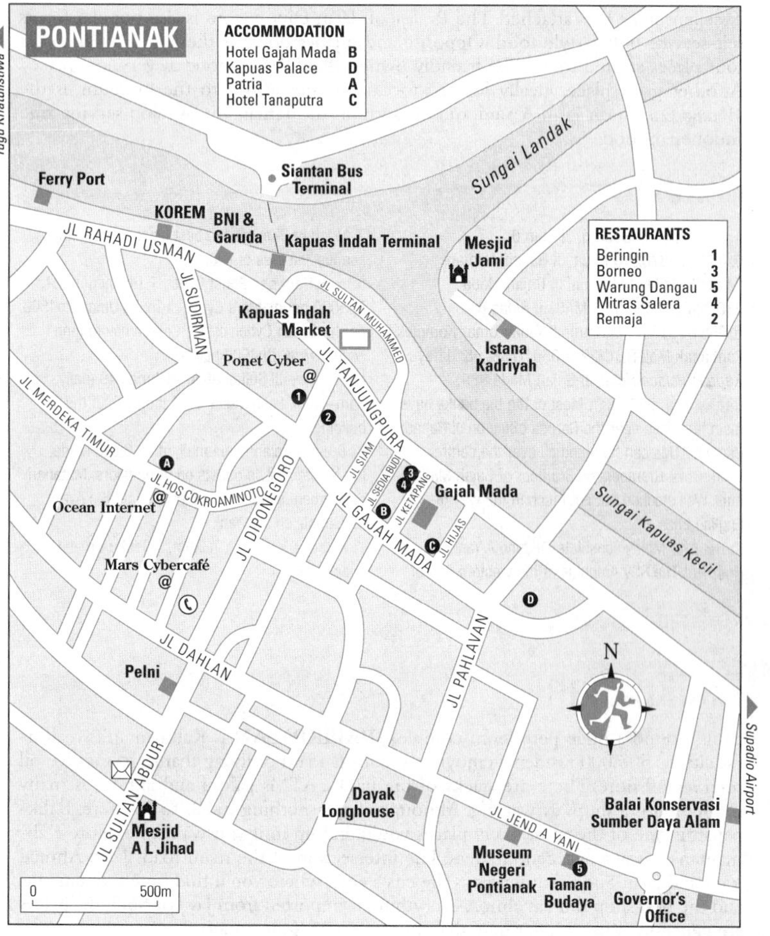

high, where you're free to wander around. Pontianak's twelve-metre-high **equator monument** (Tugu Khatulistiwa) is 2km west of the Siantan bus terminal. Catch any bemo (Rp1000) but ask if they're heading that far. The monument is on the left after the Pertamina petroleum depot. The enclosed exhibit is not much to look at but it's interesting to see the equator line turning into a drainage ditch on the western side of the visitor centre. You can amuse yourself here by stepping in and out of either hemisphere to your heart's content.

Eating

There are plenty of **street stalls** down near the market (KOREM) and ferry dock, as well as a blooming population of **bakeries** and **coffee houses** (local coffee is a speciality). At the north end of Jalan Sedia Budi are a couple of wonderful rumah makan; the *Borneo* sees a constant turnover of Chinese families eating good seafood and shark-fin soup, whilst the *Mitras Salera* specializes in spicy beef soup. Both have excellent juice bars attached. The *Remaja* on Jalan Diponegoro is also popular for its self-service buffet-style food. Opposite and further down is the largest of *Beringin*'s four places around town. The friendly owner offers Padang food at very low prices. Another great place, ideally located for lunch after a visit to the museum, is the *Warung Dangau* on Jalan A Yani, tucked away in the Taman Budaya and serving fine Indonesian food.

Listings

Airline offices Bouraq, Jl Irian 6 ⓣ0561/738702; Garuda, Jl Rahadi Usman 8a ⓣ0561/741441; Lion, Jl Gajah Mada 210, ⓣ0561/736378; MAS, Jl Sidas 8 ⓣ0561/737327; Merpati, Jl Teuku Umar Komplek Pontianak Mall Bl. C/29 ⓣ0561/768768; Jatayu, *Kapuas Palace Hotel*, Jl Gajah Mada 889.
Banks and exchange Most of the big banks have main branches near the Garuda office on Jl Rahadi Usman. ATMs can be found all over the centre.
Bookstore Gramedia on 3rd floor of Gajah Mada mall. Well stocked but not much in the way of English titles.
Consulate Malay consulate, Jl Jend A Yani 42.
Hospital The RSV Antonius at the western end of Jl Merduka Timur is the best place to treat any serious illnesses or injuries.
Internet access Ponet Cyber, Jl Diponegoro 81, Rp5000 per hr. Mars Cyber, Jl Teuku Umar, Rp4500 per hr. Ocean Cyber, Jl Hos Cokroaminoto (opp. *Hotel Patria*), Rp4000 per hr.
Post office Jl Sultan Abdur Rahman 49 (daily 8am–7pm). Poste restante at the back of the building.
Shopping Gajah Mada mall, off Jl Gajah Mada, has western-style outlets on three floors. Matahari department store, Jl Nusa Indahi, and the Ayani Megamall, on Jl A Yani.
Telephone services Telkom, Jl Teuku Umar 15, is open 24hr.

Balikpapan

Built around a huge petroleum complex, **BALIKPAPAN** is Kalimantan's wealthiest city, its 500,000 residents enjoying a high standard of living thanks to massive oil reserves offshore. There are stacks of big banks, ATMs galore and almost as many mobile phone shops as warung. Although there's nothing much to see here, Balikpapan is one of the most likely places you'll end up in if you want to explore Kalimantan's eastern and central areas. The intersection of the main roads Jalan Ahmed Yani and Jalan Sudirman serves as the city's core, where you'll find hotels, restaurants and the best shops but, as almost everything is imported from Java or Sumatra, prices are generally much higher here than in the rest of Kalimantan.

Arrival and information

Sepinggan Airport is 8km east of the city (15min by taxi, Rp24,000, or walk to the airport gates, get a green #7 bemo to Damai terminal, then either the #5 or #6 bus into town). **Buses to and** from Samarinda (3hr; Rp11,000-25,000) use **Terminal Batu Ampar**, 6km north from the centre and served by bemo #3 (Rp2000 into town). Tell the driver you want to go to Batu Ampar as not all travel that far out.

Boats from Java, Sumatra and Sulawesi berth at the **Pelni docks**, 2.5km west of the centre on Jalan Sudirman. Bemos #3 and #6 both go here. Several Pelni ferries call here between Sulawesi, Java and Sumatra; see "Getting around", p.237, and "Travel details", p.486 for details. Tickets are available from the Pelni office at the harbour or from one of the many travel agents in the centre. There are also non-Pelni ferries to Surabaya and Sulawesi. The helpful Agung Sedayu agency next to the Bouraq and Merpati airline offices on Jalan Sudirman can assist with details for all the ferry operators.

City bemos charge a flat fee of Rp1500 arround town (Rp2000 out to the terminals); three useful ones are the sky-blue #3, which runs from the Batu Ampar bus terminal through the centre, then turns right onto Jalan Sudirman before terminating at the Pelni harbour; the yellow #5, which runs from Kampung Baru ferry dock (for west Balikpapan across the bay) through the centre and terminates at Damai terminal east of town; and the dark blue #6, which runs along the coast from the Damai terminal up to the Kampung Baru dock via the Pelni harbour.

Accommodation and eating

Balikpapan's **accommodation** is mainly clustered into two groups: one at the central intersection of Jalan A Yani and Jalan Sudirman, the other a few kilometres north up Jalan A Yani.

There are some cheap **warung** along the coast road, at the Pelni harbour and next to the post office west on Jalan Sudirman. *Terminal Rasa*, a massive food court near the Gelora cinema on Jalan Sudirman, is worth a look for its huge choice. The best **place to eat**, though, is the *Bondy* on Jalan A Yani, a gorgeous, tiered open-air restaurant that serves great food at pretty decent prices. Those with a taste for adventure can try pigeon or frog at the Chinese *Atomik*, round the corner from the police station on Jalan Sudirman, and very popular with big families.

Hotel Aida Jl A Yani 12 ⓣ0542/421006. A sprawling place north up Jalan A Yani, with clean, decent-sized rooms. ❷–❹

Hotel Ayu Jl Antasari 18 ⓣ0542/425290. Similar in style to the nearby *Aida*, but its newer rooms are extremely cramped. ❷–❸

Dusit East on Jl Sudirman, towards the airport ⓣ0542/420155 ⓦwww.dusit.com. The best in town, offering all the luxuries and facilities you'd expect of a world-class hotel, with rooms to match. Popular with visiting professionals; discounts sometimes available on its website. ❾

Hotel Gajah Mada Jl Sudirman 14 ⓣ0542/734634. By far the best value of the hotels at the main intersection. Good-sized rooms, and a really handy location. ❸–❻

Hotel Mirama Jl APT Pranoto 16 ⓣ0542/412442. ⓔmirama@indo.net.id. Worth a look if you can't get into the *Gajah Mada*. It has clean, decent rooms catering mainly for corporate clients and it even has its own pub and music lounge across the road. ❺–❼

Hotel Murni Jl Antasari 1 ⓣ0542/738692. Just down thre road from the *Ayu*, this is the only real budget place in town, though rooms are basic and the en suites a bit grim. ❷–❸

Listings

Airline offices Almost all airlines have regular flights to Jakarta and Surubaya. In addition, Batavia, Jl Sudirman (ⓣ0542/739225) fly to Manado; Bouraq, Jl Sudirman (ⓣ0542/731475) fly to Yogyakarta, Tarakan, Makassar and Denpasar; Garuda, at the *Adika Bahtera Hotel* on Jl Sudirman (ⓣ0542/422301) fly to many other places in Java and Sumatra and operate many international flights from here. Merpati, Jl Sudirman 22 (ⓣ0542/424452) fly to Banjarmasin, Makassar, Pontianak and Tarakan and Star Air at the *Hotel Benakutai* (ⓣ0542/737222) fly to Denpasar. Other airlines include Lion Air Jl Sudirman 271 (ⓣ0542/441006), Mandala, Jl Sudirman at Komplek Permai (ⓣ0542/410708) and Silk Air, also at the Hotel Benakutai on Jl A Yani (ⓣ0542/419555).

Banks and exchange There are scores of ATMs and big branches of BNI, BCA and BRI can be found along Jl Sudirman.

Bookshops Gramedia, 2nd Floor, Balikpapan Plaza, is Kalimantan's best-stocked bookshop but don't expect much English reading material unless you're an oil worker or botanist.

Hospital Public Hospital (Rumah Sakit Umum) is halfway up Jl Yani ⓣ0542/434181.

Internet access There's a good Internet café beneath the main BRI building on Jl Sudirman (Rp8000/hr) and a reasonable one in the *Hotel Budiman* (Rp8000/hr). The post office also has access (Rp6000/hr) but only from 8am to 5pm. Other smaller places are easy to find.

Pharmacies The Kimia Farma has two 24hr pharmacies with consultation services. One is on Jl Sudirman near the Terminal Rasa, the other on Jl A Yani, no.95.

Police Jl Wiluyo ⓣ0542/421110.

Post The main post office with poste restante and EMS counters is at Jl Sudirman 31.

Telephone services The main Telkom office is up Jl Yani near the hospital but wartels are scattered all over town.

Samarinda

Some 120km north of Balikpapan, the tropical port town of **SAMARINDA** is 50km upstream from the sea, where the Sungai Mahakam is 1km wide and deep enough to be navigable by ocean-going ships. It has become increasingly prosperous since large-scale logging of Kalimantan Timur's interior began in the 1970s, its western riverfront abuzz with mills. There's not much to see here; indeed, the town remains a rather sprawling smelly mess, with open sewers, and while it does serve as a convenient place to stock up for trips into Kalimantan's wilds, Tenggarong is a nicer, more relaxed place to start your journey upriver.

Hemmed in by hills, the bulk of Samarinda occupies the north bank of the Mahakam. Most services are near the river in the vicinity of Pasar Pagi, along Jalan Khalid and Jalan Panglima Batur. For an insight into what Samarinda once looked like, head north to **Pasar Sigiri** and Jalan Pernia Gaan, where the canal behind the market remains crowded with rickety wooden housing and boats pulled up on the muddy banks. **Pasar Pagi** is the standard Indonesian maze of overflowing stalls and tight spaces; shops nearby are strangely divided between gold stores and chandlers. The liveliest place is the **Mesra Indah** department store, just up the road on Jalan Khalid, outside which scores of stalls set up for the day. East between Jalan Gajah Mada and Jalan Panglima Batur, **Citra Niaga** is a purpose-built bazaar for cheap clothing and souvenir stalls. For some peace and quiet, meander around the lanes just north west of the Mesra Indah store, where low-rise communities seem to inhabit a different world.

Arrival and information

The **airport** is 2km north of the centre, Rp10,000 by taxi, Rp3000 by ojek. The helpful Borneo Kersik Luwai travel agent on Jalan Abul Hasan can help arrange flights if you don't want to deal with the airlines direct. **Buses** from the north terminate 5km northeast of the city at **Terminal Bontang**, from where you catch a brown bemo to the centre; moving on, you can get here by brown bemo from Jalan Bhayangkara. **Taksis** (minibuses) to and from **Tenggarong** (1hr–1hr 30min; Rp7000) use **Terminal Banjarmasin** on the south bank of the Mahakam; cross over the road to the pier and catch a boat directly across to Pasar Pagi (Rp1000). However, larger buses to Tenggarong and **Kota Bangun** (3hr; Rp11,000), further up the Mahakam, use **Terminal Sungai Kunjang,** on the north side of the river and 5km west of the centre. There are regular departures till mid-afternoon. Buses from Balikpapan (Rp11,000–25,000) also pull into Terminal Sungai Kunjang. Green "A" bemos run between here and Jalan Gajah Mada, outside Pasar Pagi (Rp2000).

The **Mahakam river ferries** use the Sungai Kunjang docks (green bemo into town). All **ocean-going vessels** use the docks east of the centre along Jalan Sudarso: Pelni's *KM Binaiya* runs twice monthly from here to Surabaya via Sulawesi. You can get tickets at their office at Jl Yos Sudarso 76 (☎0541/741402). (See "Getting around" p.237 and "Travel details" p.486).

Samarinda's colour-coded **bemos** cost Rp1500 a ride and run between particular areas rather than following strict routes – tell the driver your destination. Jalan Awang Long is a good place to find one heading north, while either side of Pasar Pagi on Jalan Sudirman or Jalan Gajah Mada is where to hail westbound traffic. **Ojek** wait around Pasar Pagi and the Mesra store; **taxis** can be found west of Pasar Pagi on Jalan Veteran, or at the rank on Jalan Pangalima Batur.

The Dinas Pariwisata, or provincial **tourist office,** is on the corner of Jalan Awang Long and Jalan Sudirman. The service, though, doesn't live up to the grandeur of the building itself.

Accommodation and eating

As you're only likely to stop here for a night or two before heading up the Sanghai Mahakam, you're better off staying near the centre, within easy reach of all Samarinda's services. Unfortunately, there's little decent budget **accommodation** in town. The *Hotel Latansa* on Jalan Sudirman (☎0541/746312; ❶–❷) has some cheap rooms but they're pretty shabby. Better is the *Hidayah 2*, Jl KH Khalid 25 (☎0541/741712; ❷–❸), whose eighteen decent fan rooms are fine for a night or two. They can also help organize river trips. Slightly pricier but offering better value for money, the *Hotel Pirus*, Jl Pirus 30 (☎0541/741873; ❸–❹) has good-sized rooms with shower, air-con and TV, and has pretty friendly staff.

Other than the bounty of cheap **warung** around Jalan Awang Long and the Mesra Indah store, Samarinda doesn't offer a great deal of interesting **places to eat**. The *Tepian* on Jalan Awang Long near the *Pirus Hotel* is a large seafood restaurant where you may be invited to sing along with the other diners. The *Hadayani* on Jalan Abul Hasan, just north of the Mesra Indah store, can't decide whether it's a florist or a restaurant; they have a big enough menu (and one with pictures for the tourists) but service is decidedly indifferent. The best food can be found at the unpretentious *Lezat Baru* Chinese restaurant on Jalan Mulawarman, near the Ramayana shopping mall, where they have some delicious king prawn dishes.

Listings

Airline offices Bouraq, Jl Mulawarman 24 (☎0541/732532); DAS, Jl Gatot Subroto 92 (☎0541/735250); Jatayu, Jl Sudirman (☎0541/394466); KAL Star, Jl Sudirman 86 (☎0541/731350); Star Air in *Hotel MJ*, Jl KH Khalid 1 (☎0541/410337).

Banks and exchange The BCA on Jl Sudirman has fair rates. ATMs are everywhere.

Guides You'll need to find a guide in Samarinda if you're heading further upstream than Long Bagun on the Mahakam. The best are accredited by the Dinas Pariwisata, so ask there or try at *Hotel Pirus* or the *Hotel Hidayah 2*. Prices vary enormously, so check the details of what you're paying for; expect to pay between Rp100,000 and Rp150,000 per day just for a guide.

Internet access Kaltimnet on the ground floor of the *MJ Hotel* is open 24 hours (Rp10,000/hr). There's also Cybercafe in the Mesra Indah mall.

Pharmacies Rumah Sakit Bhakti Nugraha on Jl Basuki Rachmat ☎0541/741363.

Police Jl Bhayangkara, ☎0541/741340.

Post office Corner of Jl Gajah Mada and Jl Awang Long, near the tourist office.

Telephone services Wartels can be found all over town. Good rates are given at the Wartel Palapa Sakti on Jl Dermaga. They also double up as a money changer.

Travel agents Borneo Kersik Luwai Tour & Travel, Jl Hasan 3 (☎0541/741486) can arrange most airline tickets and private Mahakam cruises. Also good is Duta Miramar, Jl Sudirman 20 (☎0541/743385).

Sungai Mahakam

Borneo's second-longest river, the **Mahakam**, winds southeast for over 900km from its source far inside the central ranges on the Malaysia border, before emptying into the Makassar Straits through a multi-channelled delta. Closest to Samarinda, the Lower Mahakam is the most touristy area, and there's an established three-day circuit taking in the historic town of **Tenggarong** and the Benuaq Dayak settlements at **Tanjung Issuy** and adjacent **Mancong**. With a week to spare, scanty forest and less cosmetic communities inland from the Middle Mahakam townships of **Melak** and **Long Iram** are within range; ten days is enough to include a host of Kenyah and Benuaq villages between Long Iram and **Long Bagun**, where the Upper Mahakam begins. Whatever your plans, bring as little as possible with you. A change of clothes, wet-weather gear, decent footwear, a torch and first-aid kit are adequate for the Lower and Middle Mahakam, as there are accommodation and stores along the way. Don't bother with a tent or cooking gear. After Tenggarong, there are **no banks** on the Mahakam capable of changing money. **Guides** are essential beyond Long Bagun if you can't speak the language. Samarinda is a good place to hire a guide, though there are a few opportunities to pick one up along the way.

Mahakam transport

Crowded **public ferries** are the cheapest way to tackle the Lower and Middle reaches of the Mahakam. Passengers sit on the floor, though night services provide a bedroll on an upper, enclosed level. Toilets are a simple bucket-and-hole affair at the back; some ferries also serve basic snacks, though hawkers are the main source of food. If you plan to disembark before the boat's ultimate destination, make sure that the pilot, not the ticket collector, knows.

Ferries leave Samarinda's **Terminal Sungai Kunjang** every morning for towns as far upstream as Long Iram but, unless you're a real boat enthusiast, Tenggarong, or better still **Kota Bangun,** make shrewder starting points for Mahakam's middle or upper reaches – both are served by regular buses from Samarinda, and have places to stay. As all ferries depart at roughly the same time, if you get out at any stage you'll have to stop over for 24 hours until the next batch arrive. The following **schedule** from Samarinda is a guide only and varies according to the weather and number of stops: Tenggarong (3hr; Rp20,000); Kota Bangun (10hr; Rp50,000); Muara Muntai (14hr; Rp70,000); Melak (24hr; Rp100,000); Long Iram (30hr; Rp120,000); and Long Bagun (40hr; Rp150,000). To catch a ferry from smaller settlements, stand on the jetty and hail passing traffic.

A more luxurious option for seeing the Mahakam are **private houseboats**, which can be rented for upwards of US$150 a day (with discounts of up to fifty percent in the low season) through agencies in Samarinda and Balikpapan, and come complete with guides, cooks and private cabins.

Tenggarong

On from Samarinda, the river is broad and slow, with sawmills and villages peppering the banks. **TENGGARONG** is 45km and three hours upstream – or just an hour by road. This small, neat and very prosperous country town was, until 1959, the seat of the Kutai Sultanate, whose territory encompassed the entire Mahakam basin and adjacent coastline. The former palace, just opposite the **ferry dock**, is now **Museum Negeri Mulawarman** (Tues–Thurs, Sat & Sun 9am–4pm; Rp2500) on Jalan Diponegoro, and includes statuary from Mahakam's Hindu period (pre-fifteenth century), and replicas of fourth-century conical stone *yupa***,** which are Indonesia's oldest written records. Dayak pieces include Benuaq weaving, Kenyah beadwork and Bahau *hudoq* masks. The plastic monkeys and dolphins in the flora and fauna display are rather ironically placed opposite reconstructions of the major industrial processes that are destroying so much of their habitat.

Tenggarong is a far more relaxed – and cheaper – place to stay than Samarinda, and it's worth visiting the Kalimantan theme park on nearby **Pulau Kumara** (ferry Rp3000; entrance fee Rp2000). Although it's all rather Disney-esque, the longhouse and temple reconstructions provide an interesting insight into Kalimantan life, while a ride on Indonesia's only **Alpine ski lift** gives great views over the river and town.

Taksis run around Tenggarong and out to the **bus terminal**, 5km south of town beyond the huge road bridge, for Rp1500. Minibuses to Samarinda run fairly regularly (Rp7000), but if you're going straight on to Balikpapan by bus, ask them to drop you off at the junction with the main Balikpapan road in Loa Janan, just before you get to Samarinda; are rarely full so will stop if you flag them down. For buses to Kota Bangun (Rp10,000), you'll need to wait (probably a long time) by the junction beyond the bus terminal – check at the terminal first. There's an **ATM** at the Lippobank on Jalan Sudirman, north of the docks. The **tourist information** centre is at the back of the marketplace. For **accommodation,** the *Penginapan Anda II*, near the canal at Jl Sudirman 129 (☎0541/661409; ❶–❷), is welcoming and has decent rooms, though the ekonomis only have electricity after dark. About 100m up from the Pulau Kumara pier on Jl Sudirman the *Hotel Fatma*, Jl KH Ahmed Muksin 39 (☎0541/661356; ❷–❹) has good ekonomi rooms and a balcony overlooking the river – it will probably insist that it's full, but do persevere. For **eating**, you'll find the usual collection of average warung strung out along the riverfront between the Lippobank and the main dock. The *Tepian Pandan* opposite the museum is about the only proper restaurant, with a great location right on the river and offering excellent Chinese food; fresh grilled prawns are a speciality. For sate lovers, there's the *Sate Madura Pamekasan* next to the canal, where you can choose from chicken, goat and liver. It's also one of the few places that serves beer, though you'll need to ask for some ice as they come straight from the shelf on the back wall.

Kota Bangun and Muara Muntai

The river narrows perceptibly as it continues to **KOTA BANGUN**, a largish, well-supplied town, three hours from Samarinda by bus (Rp11,000). A single short stretch of tarmac marks the centre of the town's commercial area. Market stalls and warung line the street either side of the main pier where all the river ferries stop. The only **place to stay** is the *Penginapan Mukjizat* (❶), 100m west of the pier, though Kota Bangun's increasing popularity as a stopover may well see other places opening soon. Buses arrive at the road junction just up from the pier. There are plenty of opportunities to charter private boats from the town to explore villages upstream, but if you do, make sure you know exactly what you're getting for your money.

Beyond Kota Bangun, there's a definite thickening of the forest along the banks as the river enters the marshy lakelands, and you might see big black hornbills, symbols of the Dayak people. Around four hours from Kota Bangun and fourteen from Samarinda, **MUARA MUNTAI** sits due north of Danau Jempang, the town raised over the swamps on piles and boardwalks. Unfortunately, a massive fire in July 2004 destroyed over 250 homes, so if you are intending to stay the night check what's available with a local guide. From here, you can visit **Benuaq** settlements across the lake by *ces* speedboat (Rp85,000).

Tanjung Issuy and Mancong

Taking the morning river taxi to Tanjung Issuy from Muara Muntai (Rp20,000), watch for the slate-grey backs of *pesut* (freshwater dolphins) and, in the woods, proboscis monkeys, as you pass through the channels into Danau Jempang's hundred square kilometres of reed beds, waterfowl and fishermen. It takes about an hour to reach **TANJUNG ISSUY**, a small township of gravel lanes, timber houses and fruit trees. Turn right off the jetty, past a couple of lumber yards, stores and workshops, and follow the street around to **Losmen Wisata**, a restored Dayak *lamin* (traditional house) maintained as tourist accommodation (❶). It's not that authentic, but the place is surrounded by carved wooden *patong* posts (spirit posts), and tour groups get Benuaq dances performed for them. Out the back is a six–tier mausoleum where Tanjung Issuy's founder was laid to rest in 1984, decorated with carvings of dragons, hornbills and scenes from reburial ceremonies. The unnamed one-table rumah makan right by the dock does a reasonable fish curry. There's also an unrestored *lamin* with bigger *patong* to check out near Tanjung Issuy's mosque, or you can spend the day at **MANCONG**, a pretty Benuaq village built on boardwalks like Muara Muntai, whose own two-storey *lamin* can house two hundred people. You can walk to Mancong in a couple of hours, though it's a hot and unpleasant tramp along a wide road through farmland, while ojek usually drive like maniacs, so your best option is to charter a *ces* (Rp100,000 return). Continuing your journey **up the**

Mahakam from Tanjung Issuy, you could either return to Muara Muntai, or hire a *ces* to take you across the forested northwest corner of Danau Jempang and back to the Mahakam west at Muara Pahu (Rp150,000).

Tarakan, Nunukan and into Malaysia

A twenty-four-kilometre spread of low hills just off the coast northeast of Tanjung Selor, Pulau Tarakan floats above extensive oil reserves: offshore rigs dot the horizon, while the west-coast town of **TARAKAN** is surrounded by smaller-scale "nodding donkey" pumps. It's a surprisingly brisk, busy place, just a stone's throw from **Pulau Nunukan** and the open **border with Malaysia**.

The junction at Jalans Sudarso and Sudirman, 2km north of the port, marks the town centre. The **airport** is 2km north of town, Rp15,000 by taxi, and there are regular flights to Balikpapan with Bouraq and Merpati. Wisma Murni Travel (☎0551/21697) at the *Hotel Wisata* can book these as well as flights to Nunukan and Samarinda. All marine traffic docks at the southern end of Jalan Yos Sudarso: **ferries** to and from Berau and Nunukan use the Tengkayu jetty about 1.5km south of the intersection. The Mulundung harbour, 500m further down, is served by **Pelni**'s *KM Agoa Mas, KM Kerinci, KM Tidar* and *KM Awu* to Balikpapan, Nunukan, Sulawesi and Java; see "Getting around" p.237 and "Travel details" p.486. The Pelni office is here too. Bemos around town are plentiful and cost Rp1500 a ride.

There are numerous **places to stay**, mostly east down Jalan Sudirman within 150m of the centre. If you're arriving by one of the Pelni ships, it's essential that you reserve a room before you arrive; otherwise, the grotty but friendly *Hotel Wisata,* Jl Sudirman 46 (☎0551/21245; ❷) is the place most likely to have rooms. Further along, the tidy *Barito,* Jl Sudirman 133 (☎0551/21212; ❸) and its more expensive brother *Barito Timur* down the road at number 129 (☎0551/21181; ❸–❺) are acceptable, but the latter, like most things in Tarakan, is ridiculously overpriced. For the same money, you're better off at the *Tarakan Plaza*, Jl Yos Sudarso 1 (☎0551/21870; ❸–❺). Straight across from the *Hotel Wisata*, the *Depot* is a fine and popular Chinese **restaurant** with *lesehan* seating upstairs, serving large portions. Good exchange rates and ATMs can be found at the BNI **bank** just south of the intersection and across from the police station on Jalan Sudarso.

Crossing into Malaysia

The visa-free border-crossing between Indonesia and the Malaysian town of **Tewau** in Sabah is open every day except Sunday. From Tarakan, the *Indomaya Express* fast ferry departs Mulundung harbour daily (except Sunday) at 7.30am, taking three hours to reach Tewau (Rp150,000), leaving for the return journey at 11am. Their main agents in Tarakan are Tanjung Harapan Mulia, Jl Yos Sudarso 38 (☎0551/21272), or you can usually pick up a ticket at the harbour an hour before departure. Border formalities are completed without fuss at both the Mulundung and Tewau harbours. Return tickets to Indonesia can be bought at *Indomaya*'s office at Tewau's harbour (☎089/762583).

A slightly cheaper if more complex option is to travel via **NUNUKAN**, a busy, sleazy town on an island of the same name 100km north of Tarakan, right up against Malaysian **Sabah**. Crossing is straightforward: Nunukan's **Immigration Department** (Kantor Imigrasi), is about 200m from the port on the main road into town, and opens at 8am; it can take a little while to sort out the paperwork, so if you get stuck overnight catch a bemo to the downmarket *Losmen Nunukan* (❶) or, slightly better, the *Monaco* (❶). Once exit formalities are complete, *Saturia I* and *Saturia Utama* leave Nunukan in the morning and putter along the coast for a couple of hours to **Tewau** in Sabah. Return tickets can once again be bought at the harbour (RM20), with the boats back to Indonesia leaving at 2pm and 4pm.

4.10

Sulawesi

Sulawesi sprawls in the centre of the Indonesian archipelago, its bizarre outline resembling a 1000-kilometre letter "K", a foretaste of the many peculiarities that make this one of the country's most compelling regions. Nowhere in Sulawesi is much more than 100km from the sea, though an almost complete covering of mountains not only isolated its four separate peninsulas from one another, but also made them difficult to penetrate individually. Invaders were hard pushed to colonize beyond the coast and, despite echoes of external forces, a unique blend of cultures and habitats developed. By the time the Portuguese first marked Sulawesi as the "Celebes" on their maps during the sixteenth century, the island was ethnically divided much as it is today, with the south split between the highland **Torajans** and the lowland **Bugis**, various isolated tribes in the central highlands, and the Filipino-descended **Minahasans** in the far north. And it wasn't until the late nineteenth century that the Dutch decided to bring the whole island under their thumb.

The most settled part of the island, the south, is home to most of Sulawesi's fifteen million inhabitants, and the energetic capital, the port of **Makassar**. Rich in history, the southern plains rise to the mountain vastness of **Tanah Toraja**, whose beautiful scenery and unusual architecture and festivals are the island's chief tourist attraction. Those after a more languid experience can soak up sun and scenery on the **Togian Islands**, and there's fabulous diving at **Pulau Bunaken**, out from the northern city of **Manado**. In many areas, Sulawesi's roads are well covered by **public transport**, though freelance Kijang (pick-up trucks) and minibuses are often faster and cheaper than scheduled buses. Where these fail you'll find ferries, even if services are unreliable. Crossed by the equator, Sulawesi shares its **weather** patterns with western Indonesia, with August through to November the driest time of year, and December to April the wettest. Tourism peaks with the European summer holidays (June–Sept) and Christmas, so April is the best time to see things at their greenest and least crowded.

Makassar

Set down at Sulawesi's southwestern corner and facing Java and Kalimantan, **MAKASSAR** (also known as Ujung Pandang) is a large, hot and crowded port

Trouble in Sulawesi

Between 2001 and 2003, violent unrest and bloody fighting between Christians and Muslims in and around the town of **Poso** claimed over a thousand lives, and although people have been travelling through the area for the past couple of years, the situation is still far from stable – there have been clashes as recently as December 2004. If you insist on travelling through Poso, make sure you check the local situation first: contact your foreign office for up-to-date advice and try to find out if any other travellers have made the trip recently. Military checkpoints in almost every village in and around Poso stop public buses and travel through this region can take a long time.

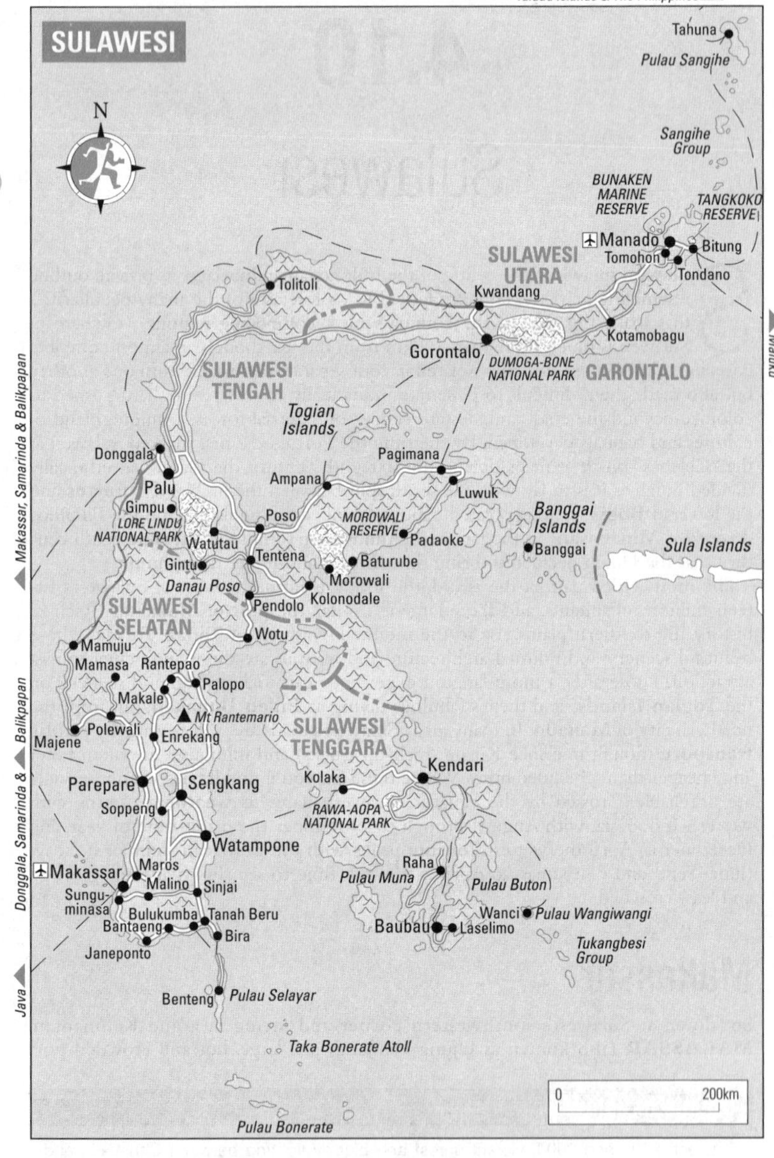

city with good transport links between eastern and western Indonesia, and several attractions. More than anything, Makassar offers an introduction to Sulawesi's largest ethnic group, the **Bugis**, who continue to export their goods and presence well beyond Sulawesi in prahu, distinctive vessels with steep, upcurved prows. The city has a long and distinguished history as a crucial trading port and coastal defence.

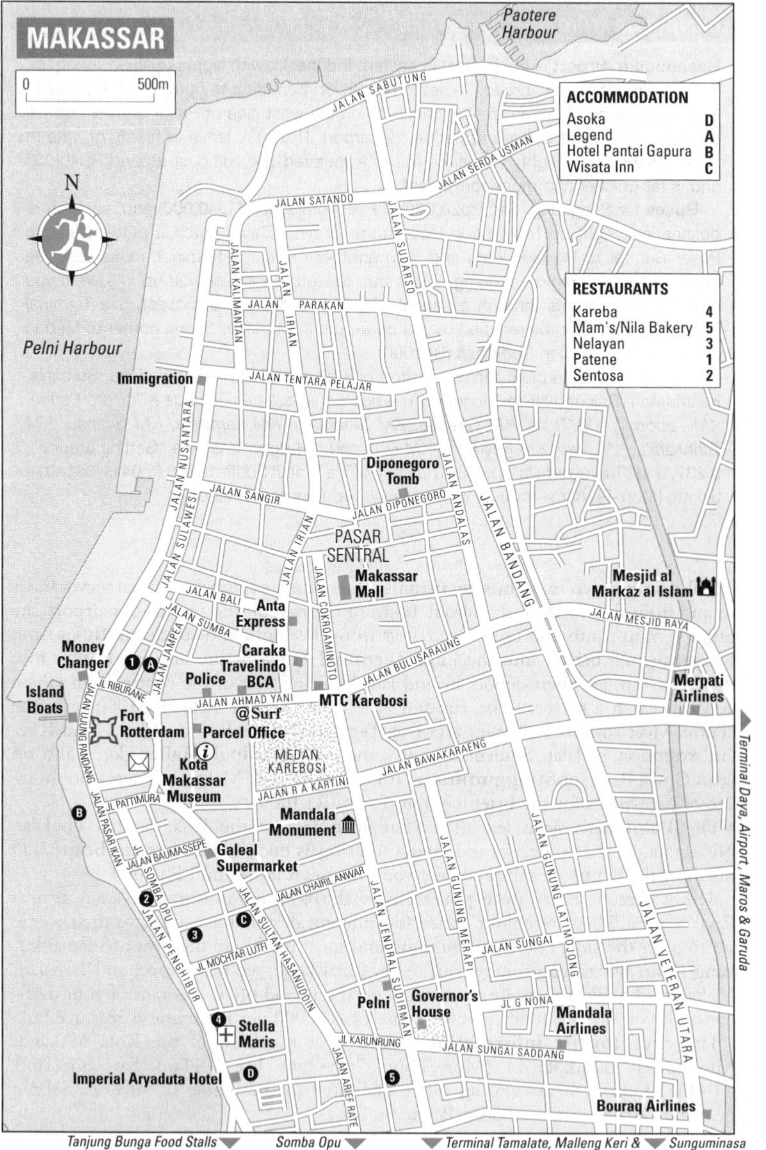

Arrival, city transport and information

Flights arrive at **Hasanuddin Airport**, 25km northeast of the city. Taxis to the town centre take forty minutes and cost a fixed fare of Rp45,000 (pay at the booth on the left of the exit hall). From 6.30am to 6.30pm, you can also opt for a pete-pete (bemo; Rp1000) or bus (Rp2000) from just beyond the terminal car park to Pasar Sentral.

Moving on from Makassar

Hasanuddin Airport is the busiest in eastern Indonesia, with flights to Nusa Tenggara, Java, Kalimantan and abroad. To get to the airport from 6am to 6pm, catch the thrice-hourly Maros bus from Jalan Cokroaminoto on the west side of Pasar Sentral and tell the driver you want to be dropped at the airport (Rp2000); leave in plenty of time to allow for the bus's highly circuitous route. A metered taxi will cost around Rp40,000 and is far quicker and more convenient.

Buses for Sengkang (6hr; Rp20,000), Tanah Toraja (8hr; Rp40,000) and many other destinations right up to Manado leave from Terminal Daya; catch a pete-pete from Pasar Sentral to Panakkukang and then another on to the terminal; make sure the driver knows where you're going. Some bus operators will pick you up in town if you organize your tickets through an agent. For Bira and the south coast, use Terminal Tamalate, which can be reached by red pete-pete from the northeast corner of Medan Karebosi on Jalan Jen Sudirman (Rp1000).

From the Pelni harbour, **ferries** run to ports all over Sulawesi, plus Java, Sumatra, Kalimantan, Bali and Nusa Tenggara. The boats that call here include *KM Doro Londa*, *KM Labobar*, *KM Tidar*, *KM Ciremai*, *KM Sinabung*, *KM Lambelu*, *KM Sirimau*, *KM Tilonkabila*, *KM Awu*, *KM Kelimutu*, *KM Fudi* and *KM Agoa Mas*; see "Getting around", p.237, and "Travel details", p.486. The Pelni office is at Jl Sudirman 38 (☎0411/331401); tickets (Mon–Fri 8am–4pm) on ground level; top floor for timetables.

Makassar has two main **bus terminals**. The massive regional terminal serves buses to and from the north, and is about 16km to the east on the way to the airport; the other is 5km south and used for arrivals from the south and southeast. Buses from Rantepao pull briefly into the huge **Terminal Daya** before heading further into the city to stop at their depots around Panakkukang, east of the centre, from where you can catch a metered taxi (around Rp20,000) or pete-pete (Rp1000) into the centre. Most south-coast buses arrive at **Terminal Tamalate** on Jalan Gowa Raya (an extension of Jalan Sudirman), but some use **Terminal Mallengkeri**, also on Jalan Gowa Raya, or **Sungguminasa**, 10km southeast of Makassar. There's no shortage of pete-petes for the brief trip into town (Rp1000).

The **Pelni** harbour is less than 1km northwest of the Pasar Sentral on Jalan Nusantara, served by becaks and taxis. Other boats dock at **Paotere harbour**, 3km north of the centre; becaks will take you into town for around Rp3000.

Bemos here are called **pete-petes**, charge Rp1000, and most terminate at or near Pasar Sentral. They are colour coded for different destinations and have their routes written on the side. The most common and most useful are those out to Panakkukang (from where you can get out to Terminal Daya, see box above) and Tamalate. Makassar's **becak** drivers are annoyingly persistent and often ignorant of your destination if you do eventually give in; a fare of Rp2000 per kilometre is reasonable.

The city's **tourist information office** is at the back of the Kota Makassar Museum, Jl Balaikota 11 (Mon–Thurs 7am–2pm, Fri 7–11am, Sat 7am–1pm; ☎0411/333357); there's also an office dedicated to the whole of Sulawesi Selatan near the Garuda office on Jalan Pettarani.

Accommodation

There are very few cheap **places to stay** in Makassar, but mid-range hotels (Rp140–160,000 for a double) are decent value.

Asoka Jl Latumahina 21/38 ☎0411/873476. Four gorgeous rooms and one suite in a huge house just around the corner from the *Imperial Aryaduta Hotel*. ④–⑥

Legend Jl Jampea 5g ☎0411/328203. The city's backpacker favourite, with cheap rooms and a small dorm (Rp15,000). The staff fall over themselves to be helpful but the noticeboard doesn't seem to have been updated since the 90s. ❶–❷

Hotel Pantai Gapura Jl Pasar Ikan 10 ⓣ0411/325791; ⓦwww.pantaigapura.com. A real away-from-it-all kind of place, with beautiful wooden bungalows on stilts over the sea. For the more affluent, the VIP suite has two bedrooms, gazebo, terrace, jacuzzi, dining room, kitchen, lounge and its own security staff. Check the website for special offers. ❻–❾

Wisata Inn Jl Sultan Hasanuddin 36–38 ⓣ0411/324344. A nicely placed, very welcoming and well-run hotel. Older rooms with fans, and doubles in the new wing with a/c. ❹–❻

The City

A monument to Sulawesi's colonial era, **Fort Rotterdam** on Jalan Ujung Pandang (daily 8am–4pm; free – ignore the guard asking for "donations"; La Galigo museum same times; Rp1700) was established as a defensive position in 1545 and enlarged a century later when the Dutch commander Cornelius Speelman rechristened it in memory of his home town. It remained the regional Dutch military and governmental headquarters until the 1930s. The fort's high, thick walls are its most impressive feature and worth climbing to get a look at the tall, white buildings inside. On the northwest side, Speelman's House – actually dating from after his death in 1686 – is the oldest surviving building, and nestles next to one half of the museum, whose most interesting item is a prehistoric megalith from Watampone. Other displays include local silk weaving, agriculture and boatbuilding.

Five hundred metres **west of Medan Karebosi**, and one block east of the **post office**, is the **Museum Kota Makassar** (Tues–Thurs 8am–2pm, Fri 8–11am, Sat & Sun 9am–2pm; free) a run-through of the history of the city with a number of mildly diverting old photos, maps and official documents. The upstairs seems to be more like a shrine to the ex-Mayor Patompo. Northwest from here, and bordered by north-oriented Jalan Nusantara and Jalan Irian, the **Chinese quarter** is worth a look for its half-dozen temples, decked in dragons and brightly coloured decor, which cluster along the lower reaches of Jalan Sulawesi.

From Pasar Sentral, catch a pete-pete heading 3km north up Jalan Sudarso to where Bugis prahu from all over Indonesia unload and embark cargo at **Paotere harbour** (Rp1000 admission). Though the smell and lack of sanitation can be a bit much on a hot day, it's quite a spectacle when the harbour is crowded, the red, white and green prahu lined up along the dock wall with much shifting of bales, boxes, barrels and jerry cans on backs and carts.

Eating and drinking

For a taste of local colour head down the coast road past the *Imperial Aryaduta Hotel* towards the huge ornate gatehouses that mark the start of Jl Metro and the **Tanjung Bunga food stalls**. On either side of the parade for about 1km are dozens of bars, cafés and warung selling a mouthwatering variety of cheap snacks and drinks.

Kareba Jl Penghibur 12. On the seafront next to the *Losari Hotel*, this fairly atmospheric restaurant specializes in seafood, though the music and traffic on the main road can be a bit distracting.

Mam's/Nila Bakery Jl Layaligo 31A, just off Jl Sudirman. This mid-price "cakery" is great for mid-morning iced coffee or afternoon tea, and serves exquisite black forest gateaux and some quintessentially European dishes from bruschetta to fish and chips.

Nelayan Jl Ali Malaka 25. A busy but brilliant fish restaurant combining Manado and Makassar cooking styles. Choosing which fish to have from the icebox outside is infinitely easier than selecting from the vast array of sauces and extras that immediately fill your entire table.

Patene Jl Sulawesi 48. In the centre of the Chinese quarter, this restaurant is open all day, and despite its shabby appearance offers excellent (and inexpensive) noodles, soups and fish.

Sentosa Jl Penghibur 26. The number 1 Bakso restaurant in Makassar is a must. Rice comes wrapped in banana leaves (*burasa*) and you're encouraged to try their *es pisang ijo* (banana milk shake) for which they are famous. It's open from 10am to 10pm; you'll struggle to get a table in the evening but it's worth the wait.

Listings

Airline offices Bouraq, Jl Veteran Selatan 1 ☎0411/452506 to Balikpapan; Garuda, Jl Andi Pangeran Pettarani 18 ☎0411/437676; Kartika, Jl Vetaran Selatan 61 ☎0411/452447 to Denpasar, Manado and Yogyakarta; Lion Air, Jl Balaikota 11 ☎0411/3227038 to Manado, Denpasar, Ambon and Yogyakarta; Mandala, Komplex Latanette Plaza, Jl Sungai Saddang ☎0411/314888 to Manado; Merpati, Jl Gunung Bawakaraeng 109 ☎0411/442471 to Manado, Yogyakarta and Gorontalo; Pelita Air, Jl Bandara Hasanuddin ☎0411/553294 to Yogyakarta; Xpressair (Celebes), Jl Andi Pangeran Pettarani ☎0411/425555 to Jayapura, Manado and Gorontalo. In addition, most airlines fly to Surubaya and Jakarta.
Banks and exchange Most banks in Makassar have ATMs, with many located along the northern side of Medan Karebosi. BCA has the best rates for cash exchange, whilst BNI has the best for travellers' cheques. The best moneychanger in town is Haji La Tunrung, in the building by the seafront at the southern end of Jl Nusantara.
Diving Marlin Dive Centre, Jl Bangkau 14 (Ⓦwww.marlindive.co; ☎0411/858762) is a Belgian operation that specializes in dives around the Speermonde archipelago and Bira. Rates start at US$45 for two dives, including weights, tank, boat, dive guide and food.
Hospitals Stella Maris, Jl Penghibur ☎0411/854341. Your best chance in southern Sulawesi for correct diagnosis and treatment by English-speaking staff.
Immigration Jl Tentara Pelajar 2 8–12 ☎0411/831531. Officials here can be obstructive, and it's not the easiest place in Indonesia to get a visa extended.
Internet access By far the most pleasant and efficient of Makassar's many Internet places is the Surf@Cybercafe, above the *Pizza Ria* on Jl Yani (Rp6000 per hour). Also good is the Neocorner Internet café next to the *Wisata Inn* (Rp4000 per hour).
Police Main office is on Jl Ahmad Yani.
Post office Jl Slamet Riyadi near Fort Rotterdam.
Shopping The huge MTC Karebosi on the north east corner of Karebosi Square is a good place to cool off and shop for bargains.
Telephone services International wartel booths on the western side of Medan Karebosi on Jl Kajaolaliddo, and also on Jl Bali, west of Pasar Sentral.
Travel agents Caraka Travelindo, Jl Samalona 12 (☎0411/318877), is splendid, with English speakers; Limbunan Tour and Travel (☎0411/333555) on Jl Bawakaraeng is also good for flight tickets and buses north. Though if it's obvious you're not buying anything, they can be less helpful.

Bira Beach

About 190km southeast from Makassar, tiny Bira is an unassuming group of wooden homes 4km north of **BIRA BEACH**, also known as Paloppalakaya Bay, where the blindingly white sand is fringed by heaps of tourist accommodation. Shallow water off the beach is safe for swimming, ending in a coral wall dropping into the depths about 150m from shore. Snorkellers can see turtles and manta rays here, with exciting diving deeper down featuring strong currents, cold water and big sharks. All accommodation rents out snorkels and fins, and both *Bira Beach Hotel* and *Anda Bungalows* have scuba gear and packages for qualified divers starting at US$35. The pick of the cheaper **places to stay** includes *Riswan Guest House* (❶), a nice traditional Bugis house on a breezy hilltop with all meals included, and the cabins run by *Riswan Bungalows* (❶) and *Anda Bungalows* (☎0413/82125; ❶). More upmarket are *Bira Beach Hotel* (☎0413/81515; ❷–❹), chic cabins with sea views, with a travel agent and the only international public **telephone** in the area; and *Bira View Inn* (☎0413/82043; ❸–❻), which has bungalows with ocean views. From Makassar's Terminal Mallengkeri, **Kijangs** to Bulukumba (5hr; Rp15,000) leave early in the morning, from where you can catch a bemo to Bira (Rp5000); although you may have to travel from Bulukumba via Tanah Beru (Rp2500 to Tanah Beru; Rp2000 to Bira). There are **no banks** capable of exchanging foreign currency in the region.

Mamasa and around

Cocooned in a cool, isolated valley 1200m up in the mountains above Polewali, the **Mamasa region** – also known as **Western Toraja** – occupies a landscape of terraced hills with fairly easy hiking to numerous traditional villages, most of which feature extraordinary architecture and noticeably friendly people. Though culturally similar to their eastern neighbours in Tanah Toraja (whose homes are less elaborately carved), Western Toraja's heritage is much lower key; consequently, the hordes of foreigners are absent, and the area is welcoming without overly catering to mass tourism.

The only settlement of any size in the valley is **Mamasa**, reached either along a two- to four-day hiking trail from Tanah Toraja (see p.475) or **by road** from the coast via Polewali, covered by buses from Makassar and Rantepao. Vehicles also originate in **Polewali** itself in the morning (usually between 8 and 9am), leaving whenever full; try to do the five-hour journey by bus if possible, as minibuses are very cramped and on their last legs. If you need to stay in Polewali, the delightful *Hotel Melati* (☎0428/21075; ❷–❸) is at Jl Ahmad Yani 71, 500m east of where transport departs for Mamasa. Their restaurant opposite is also about the best place to eat.

Mamasa

MAMASA is a spacious village of wooden houses beside Sungai Mamasa, where electricity and telephones are still very much recent arrivals. The marketplace and most amenities are on Jalan Ahmad Yani, with everything else scattered around the perimeter of a large football field. A mosque sits in the shadows between the market and river, but Mamasa is predominantly Christian, and a white stone church dominates the slope above town. The market (which, like most in the Torajan region, is held every six days) attracts people from distant hamlets often dragging their wares – including the heavy, boldly coloured **sambu blankets** (Rp70,000–100,000) for which Mamasa is famed – into town on horseback.

As if by decree, all **accommodation** in town charges Rp30,000 for a room. However, if you want something a bit smarter, head for the popular *Matana Lodge* (❷), around the corner from the market on Jalan Emy Salean. For those who prefer a more homely option, the *Losmen Mini* (❶) offers cosy rooms in an old wooden house near the market on Jalan Ahmad Yani. **Leaving**, there's transport back to Polewali every day (with the last one departing at around 2.30pm), a daily service to Makassar, and a thrice-weekly service straight to Rantepao (12hr; contact the Heryanto agency in Mamasa for details). There's also a daily service to Makale, from where you can easily go on to Rantepao. Your accommodation can find out departure times and arrange a pick-up, or organize **horses and guides** for the trail to Tanah Toraja.

Mamasa trails

Walking trails surround Mamasa, allowing for hikes of anything from two hours to three days or more. Scenery aside, one of the big attractions here are traditional houses, covered in carvings and adorned with buffalo horns like those in Tanah Toraja. Homemade **maps** available from your losmen in Mamasa show paths between villages, but don't distinguish between easily discernible tracks and those completely invisible without local knowledge. Some trails return to Mamasa, others terminate south of town at various points along the Polewali road, such as the very dirty open-air hot springs 3km south of town at **Mese Kada**. Bemos run in both directions along the Polewali road (not all go as far as Polewali) at least until mid-afternoon. Wear shoes with a good grip, and take a torch, rainwear, food and drink, and a packet of cigarettes to share around.

The Loko circuit

There's a great four- or five-hour **circuit from Mamasa** via **Loko**, involving much cross-country tracking. From Mamasa, aim across the river for **Tusan**, about fifteen minutes from Mamasa's market. Past here are some newish graves and two churches, before **TONDOK BAKARU**, whose wobbly houses are said to be the oldest in the valley. The most interesting is towards the far end of the village, a much-patched home under a twenty-metre roof covered in ironwood shingles – a sign of status – with elaborate carved panels of buffalo, geometric patterns and birds. Bearing left into a creaking bamboo grove after Tondok Bakaru, follow a path downhill, across a covered bridge, then uphill again to **Rantebonko**. At this point the Loko trail simply vanishes into the fields, and you'll need continual help to know which of the instep-wide tracks to follow. But it's worth the effort: **LOKO** perches like an island on a hilltop, with fields dropping straight off the eastern side into the valley, sacrificial stones fronting its heavily carved houses, buffalo horns adorning their front posts. Continue south to Taupe, but the track is in no way clear and sometimes steep; **TAUPE** itself is not that engrossing. From here, there's a further 5km of cross-paddy weaving to the Polewali road via **Osango**, situated on the Polewali road 2km south of Mamasa, or a direct trail **back to Mamasa** which fizzles out midway, leaving you to choose your own path down the river, and into town behind the market.

Around Ranteballakalua

Mamasa's most-celebrated *sambu* weavers live southwest of town around the village of Ranteballakalua. Start by taking a bemo 9km down the Polewali road to **RANTE SEPANG**; cross Sungai Mamasa over a small suspension bridge and follow the path uphill for ten minutes to simply ornamented homes at **Sumua**. A kilometre further on, past **Tumangke**, eight house-graves face west towards the hills. At this point the path bears right (ignore left fork) to **RANTEBALLAKALUA**, a large village of fifty homes surrounded by tall trees at the upper end of a small valley; among thatched dwellings is a row of three fine old houses and accompanying rice barns adorned with buffalo horns, pig-jaws stacks, and drums. Weavers or their agents will find you, invite you to sit down and start bargaining. A short walk downhill leads to more of the same at **BATARIRAK**, where you can stay in one impressive old building with dozens of ancestor carvings and horns. At this point there are two alternatives to backtracking to Rante Sepang: either spend ninety minutes following the usual obscure rice-field course northeast to **Lumbatu**, where a further hour will take you across to the Polewali road at Osango; or take a similar length of time to cover a nice trail southeast of Batarirak, via more graves and buffalo-horn-bedecked houses at **Buntu Balla**, and get back to the Polewali road some 14km from Mamasa at **Pana**, where you can easily get a bemo back down to Mamasa.

Rambu Saratu

Mamasa's easiest trek follows the vehicle road for 3km north from town to alternative accommodation and a splendid traditional house at Rambu Saratu, past postcard-pretty scenery of vivid green fields and mountain slopes. After about half an hour you'll see a turning west across the river to **Kole** and *Mamasa Cottages* (5), the best accommodation in the valley with its own hot-springs. Back on the main road, another ten minutes and you're at **RAMBU SARATU** (also known as **Rante Buda**), a name meaning something like "a hundred possibilities", referring to the number of interconnected families in this village. The main building here is magnificent, easily the finest traditional house in the whole Mamasa district: the body is 25m long and the roof extends this considerably, with every possible space on the front wall intricately carved. Visitors are often encouraged to spend the night here by the caretaker and his wife, who speak some English.

Beyond Rambu Saratu, there's a **hiking trail** 70km east **to Bittuang** in **Tanah Toraja**, possible either simply on foot or using ponies to help carry your gear. The walk spreads comfortably over three days, with regularly spaced kampung along the way; the homestays charge around Rp30,000 for room and board. There has been an ongoing engineering project to build a road between Bittuang and Mamasa (expected to be finished by the end of 2006), so your pleasant rural trek may be marred in places by the noise from heavy industrial machinery.

Tanah Toraja

Some 250km north of Makassar, a steep wall of mountains marks the limits of Bugis territory and the entrance into the highlands of **Tanah Toraja**, a gorgeous spread of hills and valleys where fat buffalo wallow beside lush green paddy-fields and where the people enjoy one of Indonesia's most confident and vivid cultures. Anthropologists place Torajan **origins** as part of the Bronze Age exodus from Vietnam; Torajans say that their ancestors descended from heaven by way of a stone staircase, which was later angrily smashed by the creator Puang Matua after his laws were broken. These laws became the root of *aluk todolo*, the way of the ancestors, which, at its most basic, divides the world into opposites associated with directions: north for gods, south for humanity, east for life, and west for death. Only a fraction of Torajans now follow the old religion, the strict practice of which was prohibited after headhunting and raunchy life-rites proved unacceptable to colonial and nationalist administrations. But its trappings are still an integral part of Torajan life: everywhere

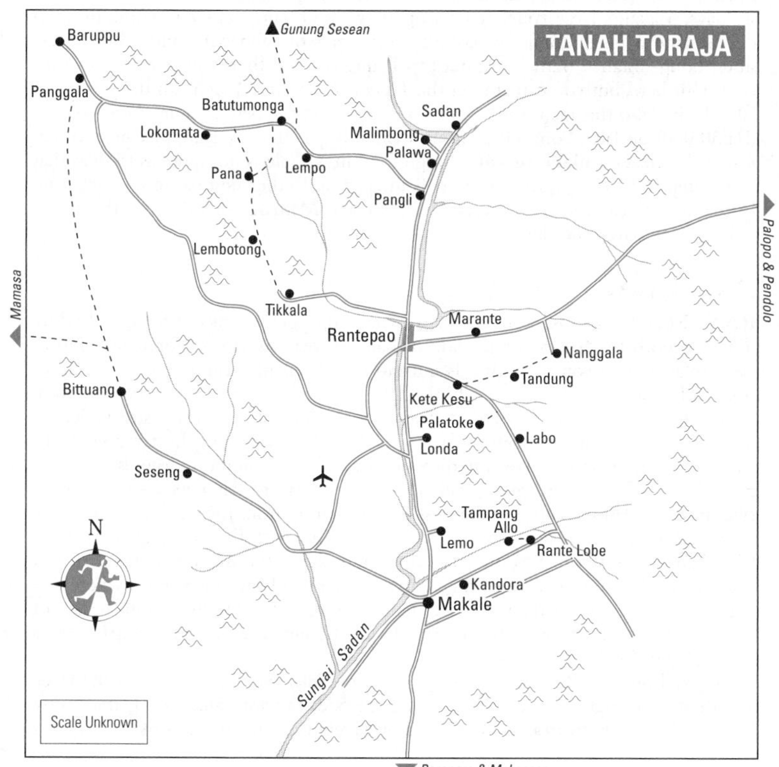

you'll see extraordinary **tongkonan** and **alang**, traditional houses and rice-barns, while the Torajan social calendar remains ringed with exuberant ceremonies involving pig and buffalo sacrifices. Torajans are masters at promoting their culture, positively encouraging outsiders to experience their way of life on its own terms. With easy access, Tanah Toraja is planted firmly on the agenda of every visitor to Sulawesi. Tour groups tend to concentrate on key sites, though it's not hard to find more secluded corners.

Tanah Toraja's main towns are the district capital of **Makale** and larger **Rantepao**, 18km further north along the Sungai Sadan Valley. Rantepao's range of services makes it the favoured base for tourists, the bulk of whom descend for the major **festival season** between July and September, though the only really quiet time is from February to perhaps May. Expect hot days and cool nights; there is a "dry" season between April and October, but this is relative only to the amount of rain at other times, so bring non-slip walking boots and rainwear.

Tanah Toraja is known as **Tator** in the local idiom, and you should look for this on transport timetables. At the time of writing, the only way to Tanah Toraja was by **bus**, with Makale and Rantepao connected to points all over Sulawesi. From Makassar, buses leave day and night from Terminal Daya. Flights into the airport near Rantepao may resume in the near future.

Makale

MAKALE is a small town studded with churches and administrative offices set around a large pond and public square. Jalan Merdeka enters from the south into the square, while Jalan Pong Tiku exits north from the pond towards Rantepao. Every six days, Makale's large **market** fires up after about 9am, drawing people from all over southern Tanah Toraja to buy pigs, jerry cans of palm wine and other necessities. Long-distance traffic continues to Rantepao, and there's little reason to stop overnight here, but you can **stay** at the *Losmen Litha* (❶–❷) right on the square on Jalan Pelita (also the agent for buses back south), and the better-value *Wisma Bungin* (Rp50,000) on Jalan Pong Tiku; up near the mosque, the nasi campur-oriented *Idaman* is the cleanest **place to eat**, though food in Makale is not quite as fresh as that in Rantepao. Moving on, **bemos** to Rantepao and other destinations – including Bittuang, trailhead for the three-day walk west to Mamasa – leave the square when full between dawn and dusk.

Rantepao

RANTEPAO is a prosperous market town on the rocky banks of **Sungai Sadan**, home to both the Sadan Toraja and, for half the year, swarms of foreigners. However unfavourably you view this, Rantepao has excellent facilities and a couple of sites within walking distance. Sadly though, its popularity has yet to spur the local administration into a long-overdue cleanup – the dusty, litter-strewn streets detract from the town's gorgeous setting between the mountains, and the river seems to take the brunt of large-scale waste disposal. West of the exhibition grounds and away from the couple of main streets, stalls supply locals' day-to-day needs – heavy stone rice mortars, plastic chairs, noodles, fish (couriered up from the coast by motorbike every morning), fresh noodles and *tempe*, and chillies, with a warung or two for fried bananas and coffee. Rantepao's main **market** – the biggest in Tanah Toraja and located 2.5km northeast of the centre at Terminal Bolu – is a must: where else could you pick up a bargain buffalo then celebrate your purchase with a litre or two of palm wine? It operates on a six-day cycle, and an entry fee of Rp10,000 is demanded of foreigners.

An easy hour's **walk from Rantepao** follows Jalan Singki west across the river, and then bears right into the fields along the Sadan's west bank. Across the paddy, hamlets such as **Pa'bontang** are marked by stately tongkonan, but look for where a

Torajan festivals

Although **festivals** have been largely stripped of their religious meaning to become social events, witnessing a traditional ceremony is what draws most visitors to Tanah Toraja, particularly during the "peak festival season" in the agriculturally quiet period from June to September. Take a **gift** for your hosts – a carton of cigarettes, or a jerry can of balok (palm wine) – and hand it over when they invite you to sit down with them. Gift-giving is an integral part of Torajan ceremonies, an expression of the reciprocal obligations binding families and friends. Do not sit down uninvited, or take photos without asking; dress modestly, and wear **dark clothing** for funerals – a black T-shirt with blue jeans is perfectly acceptable, as are thong sandals. Most importantly, spend time at any ceremony you attend, drinking coffee and *balok* with your hosts, as too many tourists just breeze in and out.

Ceremonies are divided into rambu tuka, or smoke ascending (associated with the east and life), and rambu solo, smoke descending (west and death); all rambu tuka events begin in the morning, while the sun is rising, and rambu solo start after noon, when the sun is falling westwards. A typical rambu tuka ceremony is the **dedication of a new tongkonan**. Tongkonan design is credited to Puang Matua, the upcurving roof symbolizing the shape of the sky. They face north, so the front door is a gate between human and divine worlds, and are aligned north–south, defining a borderline between life and death.

The biggest of all Torajan ceremonies are **funerals**, the epitome of a rambu solo occasion. The ceremony is held over several days in a special field and starts with the parading of the oval coffin. At the end of the first afternoon you'll see **buffalo fights**. The following day – or days, if it's a big funeral – is spent welcoming guests, who troop village by village into the ceremonial field, led by a noblewoman dressed in orange and gold, bearing gifts of *balok*, pigs trussed on poles, and buffalo. The day after all the guests have arrived, the **major sacrifice** takes place: the nobility must sacrifice at least 24 buffalo, with one hundred needed to see a high-ranking chieftain on his way. Horns decorated with gold braid and ribbons, the buffalo are tied one by one to a post and their throats slit, the blood caught in bamboo tubes and used in cooking. Finally, the coffin is laid to rest in a west-oriented house-grave or rockface mausoleum, with a **tau-tau**, a life-sized wooden effigy of the deceased, positioned in a nearby gallery facing outwards, and – for the highest-ranking nobles only – a megalith raised in the village rante ground.

white mausoleum at **TAMBOLANG** stands below a cliff-side niche sporting rows of tau-tau and coffins. A path leads briefly south from here and then climbs through woodland to the summit of **Bukit Singki** and a fine view over Rantepao.

Orientation, arrival and information

Rantepao stretches for 1km along the eastern bank of the Sadan. The central **crossroads** is marked by a miniature tongkonan on a pedestal: north from here, Jalan Mappanyuki is a short run of souvenir shops, bus agents and restaurants; Jalan Ahmad Yani points south towards Makale past more of the same before becoming Jalan Pong Tiku; east is Jalan Diponegoro and the Palopo road; while westerly Jalan Landorundun heads over to the riverside along the bottom edge of a large exhibition ground.

Long-distance **buses** will either drop you off at accommodation or in the vicinity of the exhibition ground or crossroads. **Bemos** from northern and northwestern parts of Toraja, as well as some southern locations and Palopo, however, may terminate either on Jalan Suloara, immediately north of town across the Sadan, or at **Terminal Bolu**, 2.5km northeast from the centre. It's an easy Rp1000 bemo ride into town from here.

Moving on, for Makassar, use Litha bus agent, across from the Abadi supermarket on Jalan Andi Mappanyuki, who run basic, comfortable and luxury buses (daily 7.30am–9pm; 8hr; Rp40,000-60,000). Departures north to Pendolo, Tentena and Palu also leave from here. Agents along Jalan Andi Mappanyuki can arrange tickets. Bemos leave Jalan Ahmad Yani every few minutes for Makale, and just as often from riverside Jalan Mongsidi for Terminal Bolu.

Many tour agents, restaurants and hotels will try to set you up with a **guide,** which is pretty essential if you intend to do some serious trekking and want to get the best from the villages you visit. Prices start at around Rp100,000 a day depending on how many people there are, where you want to go and for how long. Competition is fierce and most agents are experienced and reliable, but it's worth taking some time to ask around, especially amongst fellow travellers.

Accommodation

Accommodation in Rantepao is scattered across town, and there's a good variety of places offering excellent value for money, though some aren't that easy to find.

Duta 88 Jl Sawerigading 12 ⓣ0423/23477. Seven beautiful, tightly packed traditional-style bungalows in a pretty garden set around a rice barn. Good value and a brilliant location. ❷

Hotel Indra Toraja 1 and 2 Jl Landorundun 63 and Jl Sam Ratulangi 26 ⓣ0423/21163; ⓔindrahotel63@yahoo.com. Chain hotels that maintain pretty good standards and are always busy. The rooms in the *Toraja 2* nearer the river are slightly more comfortable and a bit pricier, though both hotels could be considered overpriced given the other choices in Rantepao. The *Toraja 2* also has a library, massage service and beauty salon. All rooms come with TV and hot water. ❸–❻

Wisma Malita Jl Suloara 110 ⓣ0423/21011. Extremely tidy, well-run wisma but a bit out of town, which accounts for the permanent vacancies. The standard rooms with hot showers are excellent value. ❶–❷

Wisma Maria I Jl Sam Ratulangi 23 ⓣ0423/21165. Quiet, interesting medium-sized hotel with pretensions of grandeur built around a central courtyard. However, the cheapest rooms are pretty tatty and the hot-water rooms overpriced given the alternatives. ❶–❷

Wisma Monton Jl Abdul Gani 14 ⓣ0423/21675. Lovely clean rooms in a Torajan-motifed wisma located in a quiet lane west of the main street. There are great views from the slightly more expensive 3rd-floor rooms. All rooms come with hot water and a breakfast of homemade bread and jam. ❷–❸

Pia's Poppies Jl Pong Tiku 27 ⓣ0423/21121. Each of the attractive rooms here has an individually designed rock-pool bathroom, and you'll receive a very warm welcome from the owner, Paul, who hails from Toraja. Worth the walk south out of town. ❷

Pison Jl Pongtiku 8 ⓣ0423/21344. Across from *Pia*'s but without the charm. Pretty ordinary rooms, but all with hot water, and many with balconies and views across the river. ❷

Pondok Pelangi Homestay Jl Penbangunan 11 ⓣ0423/21753. Pleasant, central, backstreet homestay, a little bit cramped but fair value, with an attached restaurant is also here. ❷

Wisma Surya Jl Mongsidi 36 ⓣ0423/21312. Very similar to the *Pondok Pelangi*, with half a dozen basic rooms, but in dire need of a facelift. ❷

Eating and drinking

All **restaurants**, including Chinese and Wetsern-style places, offer local Torajan dishes such as *Piong* (chicken, fish, pork or buffalo cooked over an open fire in bamboo shoots with coconut, herbs and spices) and *Pamarassan* (again chicken, fish, pork or buffalo cooked in black Torajan spice), though most will ask for at least two hours' notice.

Gazebo Jl Andi Mappanyuki 96. Western, Indonesian and Chinese dishes in a very pleasant setting with some outside tables. The portraits on the walls are all for sale.

Mambo Jl Sam Ratulangi. A very popular place near the river, with good food, a huge Western/Chinese/Indonesian menu to choose from, and beer in frosted glasses, though the lights are a bit bright.

Mart's Café Jl Sam Ratulangi. Another popular choice, with a lovely candlelit setting. If you're lucky, you may even be serenaded with some local folk songs.

Riman Jl Andi Mappanyuki 113. Opposite the *Gazebo*, and you might be forgiven for thinking they've studied each other's menus. Not much atmosphere, but friendly enough staff.

Setia Karam Jl Andi Mappanyuki 32. Great location in the centre of town, and done out with the traditional Torajan colours of red, white, black and yellow.

Listings

Banks and exchange The BRI, BNI and Danamon banks on Jl Ahmad Yani all have ATMs, and the BNI offers reasonable rates on currency and travellers' cheques.

Hospital The best doctors are at Elim Hospital, Jl Ahmad Yani.

Internet Service is available at Warnet on Jl Mappanyuki opposite the Litha bus agent (Rp8000 per hour).

Maps Travel Treasure Maps' "Tanah Toraja" sheet shows distances, villages, important sites and heaps of local information. Cheapest at Abadi supermarket and *Setia Karam* restaurant.

Post office Jl Ahmad Yani 111 just south of the main crossroads.

Telephone services At Jl Ahmad Yani (8am–late). Toraja Permai Tours and Travel, next to the Abadi supermarket on Jl Andi Mappanyuki, have good international phone rates.

Touring Tanah Toraja

There's a morbid attraction to many of Tanah Toraja's sights, which feature ceremonial animal slaughter, decaying coffins and dank mausoleums spilling bones. Fortunately, the people and landscape are very much alive, and there's nothing depressing about spending time here. **Entry fees** of around Rp10,000 are becoming common at sites around Rantepao. If you speak a little Indonesian, **guides** are seldom necessary for hiking or visiting villages, though outsiders should really have an **invitation** to visit a ceremony, which guides can provide. As more participants means greater honour, however, it's also possible to turn up at an event and hang around the sidelines until somebody offers to act as your host.

Bemos to just about everywhere originate at Rantepao's Terminal Bolu, though those heading south can be hailed on Jalan Ahmad Yani; the further you're going, the earlier you should start looking for transport. Accommodation and tour agents also rent out **motorbikes** (Rp60,000 a day), or **minibus/car and drivers** (Rp150,000). Hikers heading off to villages should carry cigarettes, if only to initiate conversations. A far better gift is a pig, for which you can barter at the market if it's on at the time of your visit.

Rantepao to Makale

Tanah Toraja's most famous sites lie off the eighteen-kilometre Rantepao–Makale road. Just south of Rantepao, a concrete statue of a pied buffalo marks the four-kilometre road east to four much-restored tongkonan at **KETE KESU** (Rp10,000). The central one is said to be the oldest in the district. An adjacent rante ground sports a dozen megaliths, the tallest about 3m high, with a path leading up the hill past hanging and no-longer-hanging coffins mortised into the side of the truncated peak.

Back on the Makale road, a signpost at 5km prompts you east towards **Londa** (Rp10,000), a twenty-minute walk from the highway. A shaded green well underneath tall cliffs, overhung with a few coffins and a fantastic collection of very lifelike tau-tau, Londa boasts two **caves** whose entrances are piled high with more coffins and bones, all strewn with offerings of tobacco and booze. **Guides** with pressure lamps (Rp15,000) are a necessity for venturing inside the labyrinth.

Around 8km south of Rantepao, a trail heads up to a **swimming hole** in the forest at **Tilangnga**. One kilometre further on, another road runs 1km east to **LEMO** (Rp10,000), past a church curiously designed in the shape of a boat. Lemo is famous for the sheer number of its much-photographed tau-tau, set 30m up on a flat cliff-face; they're not as sophisticated as those at Londa but more expressive, mutely staring over the fields with arms outstretched. There are also several dozen square-doored mausoleums bored straight into the rock face. The best time to see the tau-tau is between 8 and 9am, when clarity of light is at its peak.

East to Nanggala, and north to Sadan

If you're pushed for time, you can see almost all the main features of Tanah Toraja at **MARANTE**, a spread-out village 6km east from Rantepao on the Palopo road. Close to the road is a fine row of tongkonan; behind, a path leads to where tau-tau and weathered coffins face out over a river. **NANGGALA**, about 11km along the Palopo road and then 2km south, is a stately village with a dozen brilliantly finished tongkonan; sadly, most of them have had their traditional roofs replaced with tin. There's a very pleasant five-hour walk due west to Kete Kesu from here, via **Tandung** village and a couple of small lakes, and if you're lucky you may even see one of the region's only flying fox population.

For something a bit different, spend a day making the slow haul from Rantepao's bemo terminal **north to Sadan**. Seven kilometres along the way you pass **PANGLI**, famed for its *balok*. Not much further, a rante ground with thirty upright stones marks the short track to **PALAWA**, whose tongkonan are embellished with scores of buffalo horns stacked up their tall front posts, while in the hills beyond the village are babies' graves, wooden platforms in the trees. Five kilometres more brings you to a fork in the road: east is **SADAN** itself, with another market every six days; west is riverside **MALIMBONG**, famous for its *ikat*.

Northwest to Batutumonga

The area northwest of Rantepao surrounding Gunung Sesean, the region's highest peak, is quite accessible but not overly explored. There's a smattering of morning traffic about 17km to **LEMPO**, which has a great series of moss-ridden tongkonan. **Accommodation** in the area provides the perfect rural base: before Batutumonga, a sign points to basic bamboo rooms at friendly *Mama Siska's* (❶); *Mentirotiku* a little further along, is a smart, pretentious affair with cosy accommodation in tongkonan (Rp40,000 per person) or cabins (Rp150,000). Around the corner is **BATUTUMONGA** itself, where you'll find the excellent-value *Betania's* (also known as *Mama Rina's*; ❶).

Gunung Sesean's 2328-metre **summit** can be reached in about three hours from Batutumonga; your accommodation place can point you to the nearest trails. Another fine walk from Batutumonga can take you **back to Rantepao** in under four hours; take the road through Batutumonga until you see a sign to your right pointing down a broad stone trail to **PANA**. Towards the end of the village, concrete steps to the left of the path lead up the site of some very old **graves** set into the side of a huge rock, with baby graves located in a nearby tree; back on the main track, the next left after the graves brings you to a rante ground with four-metre-high **megaliths**. From here, the track continues; along this stretch you may even find bemo to Rantepao, but it's worth walking at least as far as **Lembotong**, a kampung famed for its blacksmiths. The remainder of the walk down to the flat fields below is less interesting, and you end up at **TIKKALA**, where you'll find bemos for the seven-kilometre ride back to Rantepao.

Ampana

If you're **arriving** in **Ampana** from **the south** and heading **to the Togian Islands**, then the chances are you'll have to spend the night in the dusty and ramshackle port of **AMPANA**, whose only sign of life seems to be a few dokars and the odd manic motorcyclist. However, you can hide away in the excellent *Oasis Hotel*, Jl Kartini 5 (☎0464/21058; ❷–❸), perfectly placed on the seafront near the port. Run by the same family that own *Paradise Bungalows* on **Kadidiri**, the *Oasis* has sixteen en-suite fan and air-con rooms set around a lovely garden. The next best place is the *Family Hotel*, Jl Moh Hatta 37 (☎0464/21034; ❷), followed by the *Irama*, just up from the *Oasis* at Jl Kartini 11 (☎0464/21055; ❶–❷). Both have fairly basic rooms with mandi, though the *Irama* does have one with air-con. For **food**, the huge and beautiful *Green Garden Café* at the *Oasis* has a delightful upstairs terrace where you can watch the sunset and prepare for your five-hour stint on the morning ferry. Arriving **from the Togian islands,** you're better off catching a bus south through Poso, to Palopo (for Rantepao; Rp125,000) or even Makassar (Rp150,000). Staff at the *Oasis* can arrange for a pick-up from the café (and it's a pleasant place to while away the time) or you can make your own way to the main petrol station just west of town where most buses from Luwuk stop to refuel; however, there's never a guarantee with either that there'll be seats available and the buses can be very cramped and smelly. **Ferries** run almost daily to **Wakai** (for Kadidiri) and **Bomba,** and there are weekly services to **Gorontalo**, the latter stopping at Wakai and other Togian islands en route.

The Togian Islands

The **Togian Islands** form a fragmented, 120-kilometre-long crescent across the shallow blue waters of Tomini Bay, their steep grey sides weathered into sharp ridges capped by coconut palms and hardwoods. The exceptional **snorkelling and diving** around the islands features turtles, sharks, octopus, garden eels, and a mixed bag of reef and pelagic fish species. On the down side, there are also nine depots in the Togians dealing in the live export of seafood to restaurants in Asia; many of these operations employ cyanide sprays, which stun large fish but kill everything else – including coral.

From west to east, **Batu Daka**, **Togian** and **Talata Koh** are the Togians' three main islands, with **Walea Kodi** and **Walea Bahi** further east. The main settlements here are **Bomba** and **Wakai** on Batu Daka, and **Katupat** on Togian. Wakai is something of a regional hub, with transport out to smaller islands. There are no vehicle roads or widespread electricity in the Togians and, with all travel by boat, you'll find it pays not to be on too tight a schedule; most accommodation places offer day-trips and shared transfers. Tourism in the islands is budget-oriented but good, and prices usually include meals. July through to September are the coolest months, when winds can interrupt ferries. Diving is usually good all year round, though visibility in December can be variable.

There are **ferries** to the islands from both Ampana (4-5hr; almost daily at 10am; Rp20,000) and Gorontalo (15hr; Wed 10pm; Rp50,000). The Gorontalo ferry stops at most of the major islands before leaving Wakai for Ampana; it's worth trying to book a cabin (Rp50,000 per person) from Gorontalo for a good nights' sleep. There are also ferries every second day from Gorontalo to **Pagimana** (5hr; Rp15,000), from where you can get a bus to Ampana. In addition, a **fast boat** from Ampana serves Bomba (3hr; Rp50,000).

On the Togians themselves, a ferry runs from Wakai to **Dolong** (Walea Kodi) twice a week via Katupat and **Malenge** (off Talata Koh), then back again. Other ferries do operate to other islands from Wakai, but schedules are unpredictable. For resorts in Kadidiri, the main diving resort island near Wakai, the owners usually run small boats to their accommodation from Wakai for free if you plan to stay there. Elsewhere, there's bound to be something along eventually if you can afford to wait, or you can **charter** a motorized outrigger at about Rp125,000 an hour.

Around the islands

Three hours from Ampana and at the western end of Batu Daka, **BOMBA** comprises two dozen houses and a mosque facing north across a pleasant bay. There's a long beach 5km west of town, but it's the sea that warrants a visit here, with the Togians' best snorkelling an hour distant at **Catherine reef**. The coast roundabout is interesting, too, with the possibility of seeing crocodiles in remote inlets, and some islets east of Bomba completely covered by villages, their sides reinforced with hand-cut coral ramparts. In Bomba itself, dockside *Losmen Poya Lisa* (❶) is a fine **place to stay** with excellent food; but just a little way to the south of Bomba, the American-run *Island Retreat* (Ⓦwww.togian-island-retreat.com; ❹–❻) is a fair bit smarter and just that little bit better. They also run a diving operation (US$50 for two dives). Bomba can only be reached from Wakai by chartering a boat. If you want to stay at the *Island Retreat*, you should contact them at least two weeks in advance to arrange for them to pick you up.

At the eastern end of Batu Daka, about five hours from Ampana and two from Bomba, **WAKAI** is similar to the dock area at Ampana. There are only a couple of basic **places to stay** if you're stuck for the night: the *Penginapan Sederhana* and the *Losmen Suria* (both ❶). Half an hour by motorized outrigger from Wakai, Kadidiri is one of the nicest of the islands, 3km long and with fine beaches and ample lodges. Of the two all-inclusive resorts on the island, the *Paradise Bungalows* (❸–❻, meals included) is undoubtedly the least pretentious, with something to suit all budgets, from basic wooden cabins to enormous, beautiful bungalows with private garden showers and loo. The *Black Marlin* (Ⓣ0435/831869; Ⓦwww.blackmarlindive.com; ❹–❻, meals included) next door has several smart cabins set back from the beach but is not quite as welcoming or social. Both have attached dive centres and can organize all manner of dive courses and diving and snorkelling trips, as well as shuttles to and from Wakai. Just offshore, there are secluded cabins on *Pulau Taipi* (Rp100,000 per person), run by *Paradise Bungalows*. Again, all meals are included, as well as transport to and from the island.

Gorontalo

GORONTALO, since 2001 the capital of its own province, is a pleasant, sleepy Muslim city with useful ferry links to the Togian Islands, Pagimana and Ampana, and buses to Manado. It's centred on the Mesjid Baitur Rahim, which stands at a wide crossroads. Many streets have been renamed and, though the streets themselves carry the new names, many shops and offices display the old ones. The two main north–south streets are Jalan A Yani, on which you'll find most banks and accommodation and some restaurants, and Jalan Sutoyo, which runs south from the delicious food stalls that make up the busy evening market.

The **harbour** is twenty minutes from the centre by *bentur* (motorized rickshaw), which have sadly replaced the more sedate dokars and compete with each other for the loudest on-board sound system. The boat to Pagimana runs every second day at around 8pm; the *Puspita Sari,* which serves the Togian Islands and then Ampana, departs every Wednesday at around 10pm. The **Pelni** office is on the corner of Jalan Sutoyo and Jalan 23 Januari and the *KM Tilongkabila* calls in to Gorontalo twice a month on its way to Luwuk from Bitung (though check at the office, as this isn't always the case). **Buses** to and from Manado, Palu and Makassar use **Terminal Andalas**, 3km and a short microlet ride north of the centre (Rp1000), or, if you're unlucky, at the very remote **Terminal Isimu,** a full 30km from the town centre but linked by plenty of transport. There are also regular **flights** from Gorontalo to Makassar (operated by XpressAir and Pelita), while Merpati and Bouraq have flights to Manado. The Tiki travel agent at the top of Jalan A Yani or Mitra Line Travel next to the Danamon bank can book all of these.

The best **place to stay** is without doubt the popular *Melati Hotel*, Jl Mongin-sidi 33 (Ⓣ0435/822934; Ⓔavelberg@hotmail.com; ❷–❸) run by the extraordinarily helpful Alex. The older ekonomi rooms have bags of character. The

Mini Saronde at Jl Kalengkongan 17 (☎0435/822677; ②–③), across the sports field, also has decent air-con rooms and friendly staff. The BNI and Danamon **banks** on Jalan A Yani both have ATMs. The **post office** is on the corner of Jalan A Yani and Jalan 23 Januari but the **Telkom** office is 5km out of town; however, the **Internet** café at the *Hotel Melati* (Rp5000/hr) has several phone booths for international calls. There's also another good Internet café, the Waroeng@Cyber (Rp4000/hr) next to the uninviting *Regina Bakery*. Better is the *Toko Brantas* opposite the mosque, which has some delicious pastries. For a more filling **meal**, try the Chinese *Agung* restaurant a couple of blocks down from the *Melati*, or for something a lot more local, go to *Cikia* on the corner of Jalan 23 Januari and Jalan Tribrata, where they do wonderful *milu siram* (corn soup) with chillies, onions, garlic and fish.

Manado

Capital of Sulawesi Utara, **MANADO** is mainly seen as the major stopping-off point for spectacular **diving and snorkelling** at the Bunaken Marine reserve. You can either base yourself in Manado and do day-trips to the reefs, base yourself just outside Manado at one of the dive resorts that offer all-inclusive packages, or, the cheapest but least reliable option, base yourself on Pulau Bunaken itself (see p.486). Day-trips from the mainland start at around US$65 for two dives, plus US$30 for full equipment. Blue Banter, on the second floor of the *Ritzy Hotel* on the seafront, is a well-established and professional outfit.

The town itself is enjoying a bit of a boom – the entire seafront south of the harbour is being given over to huge new malls, shops and office complexes that stretch a good couple of kilometres – and makes an agreeable enough place to spend a couple of days. The centre of town consists of the blocks of markets, alleys, shops and fish stalls that surround the tiny **harbour** and **Pasar 45**, a busy square constantly jammed with hundreds of light-blue **microlets** that seem to converge on it all at once.

Manado was flattened in 1844 by a devastating **earthquake**, and tremors measuring up to 5.0 on the Richter scale continue to rattle the town for a few seconds every three months or so.

Practicalities

Sam Ratulangi Airport is 12km northeast of the centre. Taxis will take you into town for around Rp25,000, or you can arrange a pick-up from your hotel. Some of the bigger dive centres also have representatives on hand. The numerous long-distance **buses** that serve Gorontalo (8hr; Rp45,000), Palu (13hr; Rp100,000) and Makassar (two days; Rp190,000) use the **Terminal Malalayang** about 6km south along the coast. Buses for Gorontalo leave about 6am; those to further afield leave around lunchtime. For the Minahasa highlands, use **Terminal Karombasan**, served by microlet from Jalan Sam Ratulangi. The regional **Pelni ferry** port is actually in **Bitung** on the opposite coast. You'll need to get a microlet to **Terminal Paal Dua**, from where there are regular buses. All microlets have their route and destination displayed on the roof or painted on the outside. Fares around town and to the terminals are fixed at Rp1000.

The travel agent at the *Hotel Manado Bersaharti* (see opposite) can provide excellent information on flights and ferries, and on Manado itself. The **Pelni** office is on Jalan Sam Ratulangi, near the Telkom office. They also have an office in Bitung (☎0438/835818).

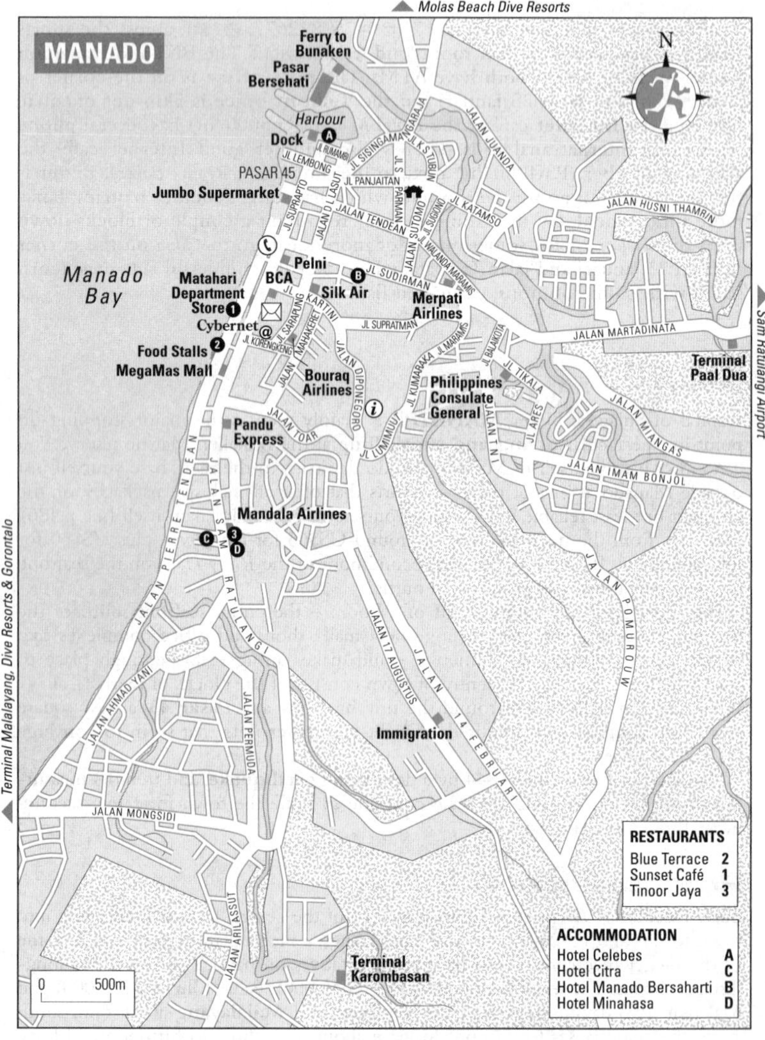

Accommodation

Hotel Celebes Jl Rumambi 8a ☎0431/870425. This expansive hotel (the *Celebes* incorporates the old *Smiling Hostel*) has everything from tiny singles to luxurious rooms with views over the harbour. Good location, with incredibly helpful and friendly staff. ②–⑥

Hotel Citra Jl Sam Ratulangi, lane 8, 12 ☎0431/863812. Down a quiet lane almost opposite the *Minahasa*, this secluded hotel offers cheap rooms. Handy for early-morning buses. ①–②

Hotel Manado Bersaharti Jl Sudirman 20 ☎0431/855022. The best value in the centre, with cheap singles (shared mandi) through to a/c doubles with TV and hot showers. The hotel also has an excellent travel agent and its own wartel. ①–③

Hotel Minahasa Jl Sam Ratulangi 199 ☎0431/862559. 1.5km south of the centre. All the rooms in this lovely hotel have showers and hot water. The ones right at the top also have great views. ③–④

Eating

Minahasan cooking features dog (*rintek wuuk* in Minahasan, usually shortened to *rw*, or "airvay"), rat (*tikkus*) and fruit bat (*paniki*), generally unceremoniously stewed with blistering quantities of chillies. Try it at *Tinoor Jaya*, Jl Sam Ratulangi 169, or at the cheap warung around Pasar 45 and Jalan Sudirman. For something more conventional, the seafront *Sunset Café* opposite the Matahari department store serves pizzas, burgers, pasta and some Indonesian dishes. It may not be particularly inspiring (or cheap), but it has a great location and good cocktails. Bring some mosquito repellent, though.

For a feel of how Manado is changing, head out to the long row of cafés and restaurants set further along from the *Sunset Café* behind the MegaMas centre on Jalan Pierre Tendean. Tables are placed as close to the edge of the sea wall as you can get without falling in. The *Blue Terrace* is probably one of the coolest hangouts, with a decent range of food in a candlelit setting. Many places seem to be trying to outdo each other in the loudest-sound-system stakes, but don't let this put you off.

Listings

Airline offices Batavia, P Tendean Komplek, Kawasan MegaMas B1A-1/20 ☎0431/855878 for Jakarta via Balikpapan; Bouraq, Jl Sarapung 27B ☎0431/841470 for Gorontalo, Jakarta and Surabaya; Garuda, Jl P. Tendean Komplek ☎0431/852154 for Makassar, Jakarta, Semarang, Surabaya and Yogyakarta; Lion Air, Jl Sam Ratulangi (*Grand Puri Hotel*) ☎0431/827260 for Makassar, Jakarta and Surabaya; Mandala Airlines, Jl Sam Ratulangi 175 ☎0431/859333 for Makassar, Jakarta and Surabaya; Merpati, Jl Sudirman 111 ☎0431/853200 for Makassar, Gorontalo, Jakarta and Surubaya; Silk Air, Jl Sarapung 5 ☎0431/863744 for Singapore.

American Express agents Pula Pelita Express, tucked away on the driveway to the *Ritzy Hotel* (☎0431/852231).

Banks and exchange There are lots of ATMs around town. The best place to change cash and travellers' cheques is BCA on Jl Sam Ratulangi.

Hospital Public hospital 6km south of the city near Terminal Malalayang (☎0431/853191); microlets to the bus terminal pull in here.

Immigration Jl 17 Augustus ☎0431/863491.

Internet access CyberNet (daily 8am–9pm; Rp6000 per hour) next to the post office is the best place in town.

National Park Office Jl Santo Joseph 39 ☎0431/827387.

Post office Jl Sam Ratulangi 21. Also has wartel for international calls.

Swimming pool At the *Swahid Kawanua Hotel*, Jl Sudirman 30 (Rp7000 to non-residents).

Telephone services The main Yantel office is at Jl Sam Ratulangi 4.

Tour Guides Monal at Indag souvenir shop (Jl Sam Ratulangi 12A ☎0812/4404882) can help with organizing tours around Sulawesi, and has a wealth of local information.

Bunaken Marine Reserve

Northwest of Manado, a 75-square-kilometre patch of sea is sectioned off as **Bunaken Marine Reserve** and promoted as Indonesia's official scuba centre, where **coral reefs** around the reserve's four major islands drop to a forty-metre shelf before falling into depths of 200m and more, creating stupendous reef walls abounding with Napoleon (maori) wrasse, barracuda, trevally, tuna, turtles, manta rays, whales and dolphin. Set aside concerns about snakes and sharks and avoid instead the metre-long Titan triggerfish, sharp beaked and notoriously pugnacious when guarding its nest; and small, fluorescent-red anemone fish, which are prone to giving divers a painful nip.

You can visit the reserve in two ways, either on day-trips from Manado, which can be arranged privately, or through dive operations, or by staying at budget accommodation within the reserve on Pulau Bunaken. As regards what type of **dive operation** to go for, if you need any training or qualified assistance you might be better off opting for one of the pricier, professional operators in Manado itself, or with one of the larger operators – such as Froggies or Two Fish (see below for details) – on Pulau Bunaken. If you're already certified, however, you'll save money by shopping around the budget operators on the island, though you must check the **reliability** of rental gear and **air quality**, the two biggest causes for concern here.

The best **weather conditions** are between June and November, with light breezes, calm seas and visibility underwater averaging 25m and peaking beyond 50m. Try to avoid the westerly storms between December and February and less severe, easterly winds from March until June.

Pulau Bunaken and around

About an hour by ferry out from Manado, **Pulau Bunaken** is a low-backed, five-kilometre-long comma covered in coconut trees and ringed by sand and mangroves. Entry into the national park currently costs Rp150,000, which buys a tag valid for one year. Bunaken's homestays usually arrange free transport to and from the island for its guests; if you haven't already organized this in Manado, there are **public ferries** (Rp15,000) from the harbour behind the *Hotel Celebes* daily at 2pm (get there 30min early; return 7.30am), and plenty of private boat owners (Rp50,000). Either way, you end up at **Bunaken village** on the island's southeastern tip.

There is plenty of **accommodation** on the island, either close to the main village on the east side, or west along the beach. Recommended places on the eastern **Pangalisang** beach are *Two Fish Divers* (Ⓣ0811/432805; Ⓦwww.twofishdivers.com; ❹–❻), run by a UK couple, and *Living Colour* (Ⓣ0812/4306063; Ⓦwww.livingcoloursdiving.com; ❺). Both places offer wooden bungalows on the beach, three meals a day and day trips with two dives for between $35 and $50. If your budget doesn't stretch that far, then *Lorenso's* have some basic accommodation nearby (Ⓔlorenso@sulawesi-info.com; ❷–❸). On the more popular western **Liang** beach, *Froggies* (Ⓣ0431/850210; Ⓦwww.divefroggies.com; ❻–❼) and *Bastianos* (Ⓣ0431/853566; Ⓦwww.bastianos.com; full-board ❻–❼) offer similar bungalow accommodation, though *Froggies* only include evening meals and breakfast in their prices. The most upmarket place is *ChaCha Dive Lodge* (Ⓦwww.bunakenchacha.com; ❼–❽; all inclusive), where there are six beautiful wooden bungalows with fans and mosquito nets. They also offer discounts for long stays, and dive packages that include accommodation. Check their website for details. Budget travellers should head for the *Nelson Homestay* (❷) near the *Nyiur Melambai* restaurant, or the *Panorama Cottages* (❷) up the hill.

Froggies and Two Fish Divers are amongst the more popular outfits for dive courses and trips, and both have good instructors; do check the state of the equipment, though, as some is in pretty poor repair. Off the west beach between Bunaken village and Liang beach, **Lekuan** 1, 2 and 3 are exceptionally steep, deep walls, and the place to find everything from gobies and eels to deep-water sharks. Further around on the far western end of the island, there are giant clams and stingrays at **Fukui**, while **Mandolin** is good for turtles and occasional mantas, and **Mike's Point** attracts sharks and sea snakes.

Indonesia travel details

Java buses

Where the bus frequency is not given, buses depart at least once an hour.

Bandung to: Banyuwangi (daily; 24hr); Bogor (4hr 30min); Jakarta (from Leuwi Panjang terminal; 4hr 30min–5hr 30min); Pangandaran (2 daily; 5hr); Yogya (9hr 30min).

Banyuwangi to: Bandung (daily; 24hr); Jakarta (daily; 20–24hr); Madura (Sumenep, hourly; 12hr); Malang (hourly; 7hr); Pasuruan (5 hourly; 6hr); Probolinggo (5 hourly; 5hr); Situbondo (every

20min; 2–3hr); Solo (hourly; 11–13hr); Yogyakarta (hourly; 12–14hr).
Jakarta (Pulo Gadung station unless stated otherwise) to: Banda Aceh (60hr); Bandung (from Kampung Rambutan station; 4hr 30min); Bogor (from Kampung Rambutan station; every 15min; 1–2hr); Bukittinggi (30hr); Carita (from Kalideres; 3hr 30min); Denpasar (24hr); Medan (from Pulo Gadung or Kalideres; 2 days); Labuan (from Kalideres; 3hr); Merak (from Kalideres; 3hr); Padang (from Pulo Gadung or Kalideres; 32hr); Pangandaran (12hr); Solo (13hr); Surabaya (15hr); Yogya (12hr).
Magelang to: Wonosobo (2hr).
Pasuruan to: Banyuwangi (5 hourly; 6hr); Denpasar (daily; 12hr); Jember (hourly; 3hr); Malang (hourly; 2–3hr); Probolinggo (5 hourly; 1hr); Surabaya (5 hourly; 1–2 hr).
Probolinggo to: Banyuwangi (5 hourly; 5hr); Bondowoso (1–2 hourly; 2–3hr); Denpasar (hourly; 11hr); Jakarta (hourly; 24hr); Jember (4 hourly; 2–3hr); Malang (hourly; 2–3hr); Mataram (Lombok, hourly; 16hr); Pasuruan (5 hourly; 1hr); Situbondo (5 hourly; 2–3hr); Solo (hourly; 7hr); Yogyakarta (hourly; 8–9hr).
Surabaya to: Banyuwangi (every 30min; 5–7hr); Bondowoso (hourly; 4hr); Bukittinggi (daily; 48hr); Denpasar (5 daily; 11hr); Jakarta (20 daily; 14hr); Madura (Sumenep; hourly; 5hr); Mataram (2 daily; 20hr); Medan (daily; 3 days); Padang (daily; 48hr); Pekanbaru (daily; 48hr); Probolinggo (every 30min; 2hr); Solo (every 30min; 5hr); Sumbawa Besar (daily; 26hr); Yogyakarta (every 30min; 7hr).
Wonosobo to: Dieng (1hr).
Yogyakarta to: Bandung (9hr 30min); Bogor (10hr 30min); Borobudur (2hr); Cilacap (5hr); Denpasar (15hr); Jakarta (11hr 30min); Magelang (1hr 30min); Prambanan (45min); Probolinggo (9hr); Solo (2hr); Surabaya (7hr 30min).

Java trains

Bandung to: Banjar (hourly; 4hr); Jakarta (hourly; 2hr 20min); Yogyakarta (8 daily; at least 9hr).
Bondowoso to: Jember (2 daily; 2hr); Panarukan (2 daily; 2hr); Situbondo (2 daily; 1hr 30min).
Jakarta (Gambir station) to: Bandung (hourly; 2hr 20min); Bogor (every 20min; 1hr 30min); Cilacap (1 daily; 6hr 13min); Cirebon (18 daily; 5hr); Malang (1 daily; 18hr 5min); Solobapan, Solo (4 daily; 7hr–10hr 25min); Surabaya (5 daily; 9hr–14hr 30min); Yogyakarta (6 daily; 6hr 50min–8hr 40min).
Pasuruan to: Banyuwangi (4 daily; 5hr); Malang (daily; 1hr 40min); Surabaya (daily; 1hr 30min); Yogyakarta (daily; 10hr).
Probolinggo to: Banyuwangi via Jember (4 daily; 5–6hr); Kediri via Malang and Blitar (daily; 5–6hr); Surabaya (3 daily; 2–4 hr).
Solo to: Bandung (5 daily; 8hr 50min); Jakarta (6 daily; 10hr 30min); Malang (1 daily; 6hr 25min); Purworketo (6 daily; 3hr 15min); Surabaya (6 daily; 3hr 20min); Yogya (14 daily; 1hr 30min).
Solobapan to: Jakarta Gambir (3 daily; 7hr 30min); Surabaya (3 daily; 6hr); Yogyakarta (14 daily; 1hr 30min).
Surabaya/Kota station to: Bandung (2 daily; 16–18hr); Banyuwangi (3 daily; 6–7hr); Malang (7 daily; 3hr); Jakarta (3 daily; 14–16hr); Yogyakarta (3 daily; 5–6hr).
Surabaya (Pasar Turi station) to: Jakarta (6 daily; 12–16hr).
Surabaya (Gubeng station) to: Bandung (3 daily; 16–18hr); Banyuwangi (2 daily; 6–7hr); Jakarta (3 daily; 14hr); Pasuruan (daily; 1hr 30min); Probolinggo (3 daily; 2–4 hr); Yogyakarta (daily; 5hr 10min).
Yogyakarta to: Bandung (6 daily; 6hr 30min); Banjar (2 daily; 4–5hr); Jakarta (14 daily; 8hr 45min); Solo (14 daily; 1hr 30min); Surabaya (11 daily; 4hr 50min).

Java Pelni ferries

For further details, see the map of Pelni routes on pp.240–241.
Banyuwangi monthly to: Bima (20hr); Denpasar (7hr); Kaimana (6 days); Labuanbajo (26hr); Larantuka (48hr); Makassar (48hr).
Jakarta (Tanjung Priok) fortnightly (except where stated) to: Balikpapan (3 days); Banda (4 days); Pulau Batam (every 4 days; 24hr); Belawan, Medan (every 4 days; 48hr); Denpasar (39hr); Jayapura (7 days); Kijang (24–39hr); Kumai (3–4 days); Kupang (5 days); Larantuka (4 days); Nias (48hr); Nunukan (5 days); Padang (29hr); Makassar (48hr); Nias (48hr); Padang (27hr); Pontianak (every 3 days; 11–31hr); Surabaya (24hr); Tarakan (5 days); Ternate (4 days).
Surabaya fortnightly (except where stated) to: Banda (3 days); Banjarmasin (5 times fortnightly; 24hr); Batulicin (23hr); Denpasar (16hr); Dumai (3 days); Ende (3 days); Jayapura (6–7 days); Kaimana (monthly; 4 days); Ketapang (3 days); Kijang (48hr); Kumai (22hr); Kupang (44hr); Labuanbajo (48hr); Makassar (24hr); Nias (3 days); Nunukan (3 days); Padang (30–42hr); Pontianak (39hr); Rote (3 days); Sabu (3 days); Samarinda (3 days); Sibolga (3 days); Tanjung Priok (16–21hr); Tarakan (weekly; 3 days); Waingapu (48hr).

Java other ferries

Jakarta (Sunda Kelapa) to: Pontianak (2 weekly; 19hr).

Java flights

Bandung to: Mataram (daily; 8hr 25min); Singapore (daily; 3hr); Solo (3 weekly; 1hr 30min); Surabaya (3 daily; 1hr 20min); Makassar (daily; 4hr 20min); Yogyakarta (4 weekly; 1hr 20min).
Jakarta to: Banda Aceh (daily; 3hr 45min); Bandung (10 daily; 40min); Banjarmasin (5 daily; 1hr 40min); Denpasar (16 daily; 1hr 50min); Jayapura; (2 daily; 8hr); Makassar (12 daily; 2hr 20min); Manado (4 daily; 4hr 45min); Mataram (6 weekly; 3hr 15min); Medan (16 daily; 2hr 10min); Padang (7 daily; 1hr 40min); Pekanbaru (7 daily; 1hr 40min); Pontianak (9 daily; 1hr 30min); Pulau Batam (8 daily; 1hr 35min); Surabaya (33 daily; 1hr 20min); Solo/Surakarta (4 daily; 1hr 5min); Yogyakarta (14 daily; 1hr 5min).
Solo to: Jakarta (6 daily; 1hr 5min); Singapore (2 weekly; 2hr 20min); Surabaya (2 daily; 1hr 5min).
Surabaya to: Banda Aceh (daily; 10hr); Bandung (4 daily; 1hr–2hr 30min); Banjarmasin (2 daily; 2hr); Denpasar (12 daily; 1hr 10min); Gorontalo (4 weekly; 5hr); Jakarta (22 daily; 1hr 20min); Jayapura (5 daily; 9hr); Kendari (2 daily; 5hr); Kupang (3 daily; 6hr 35min); Makassar (11 daily; 1hr 30min); Manado (daily; 4hr); Mataram (5 daily; 1hr 30min); Medan (5 daily; 7hr); Palangkarya (daily; 5hr); Palu (2 daily; 6hr); Pekanbaru (daily; 6hr); Pontianak (4 daily via Jakarta; 6hr); Pulau Batam (3 daily; 3hr 25min); Samarinda (daily; 7hr); Solo (daily; 1hr 10min); Ternate (daily; 8hr 15min); Waingapu (3 weekly; 3hr 20min–5hr 35min); Yogya (8 daily; 50min).
Yogyakarta to: Bandung (4 weekly; 1hr 15min); Denpasar (6 daily; 2hr 15min); Jakarta (13 daily; 1hr 5min); Surabaya (6 daily; 1hr).

Sumatra buses

Where the bus frequency is not given, buses depart at least once an hour.
Bakauheni to: Bandar Lampung (2–3hr).
Bandar Lampung to: Bakauheni (every 30min; 2–3hr); Banda Aceh (3 daily; 3 days); Bukittinggi (6 daily; 24hr); Denpasar (4 daily; 3 days); Dumai (4 daily; 48hr); Jakarta (20 daily; 8hr); Kalianda (every 30min; 1–2hr); Medan (10 daily; 2 days); Padang (6 daily; 24hr); Parapat (10 daily; 2 days); Pekanbaru (6 daily; 24hr); Yogyakarta (20 daily; 24hr).
Bukittinggi to: Aceh (3 daily; 25hr); Bandar Lampung (5 daily; 24hr); Bandung (5 daily; 34hr); Batusangkar (hourly; 1hr 30min); Bengkulu (4 daily; 16hr); Jakarta (5 daily; 35hr); Maninjau (hourly; 1hr 30min); Medan (5 daily; 18hr); Palembang (4 daily; 15hr); Pekanbaru (6 daily; 6hr); Prapat (5 daily; 14hr); Pulau Batam (daily; 24hr); Sibolga (2 daily; 12hr).
Gunung Sitoli to: Teluk Dalam (every 30min, last at 4pm; 4hr).
Kalianda to: Bandar Lampung (1–2hr).
Maninjau to: Bukittinggi (1hr 30min); Padang (2 daily; 3hr); Pekanbaru (daily; 8hr).
Medan (Amplas terminal) to: Bukittinggi (hourly; 18hr); Jakarta (hourly; 48hr); Padang (hourly; 20hr); Parapat (hourly, last at 6pm; 3hr); Sibolga (daily; 12hr).
Medan (Padang Bulan terminal) to: Berastagi (every 20min; 2hr).
Medan (Pinang Baris terminal) to: Banda Aceh (10hr); Bukit Lawang (every 20min until 6pm; 3hr); Kutacane (12 daily; 8hr).
Padang to: Banda Aceh (4 daily; 30hr); Bandar Lampung (10 daily; 25hr); Bukittinggi (every 20min; 2hr 30min); Jakarta (10 daily; 30–35hr); Medan (10 daily; 20hr); Pekanbaru (10 daily; 8hr); Prapat (10 daily; 18hr); Sibolga (4 daily; 18hr).
Parapat to: Berastagi, via Kabanjahe and Pematangsiantar (daily; 6hr); Bukittinggi (14hr); Jakarta (3 daily; 43hr); Medan (10 daily; 3hr); Padang (3 daily; 16hr); Sibolga (daily; 6hr).
Pekanbaru to: Bandar Lampung (10 daily; 24hr); Bukittinggi (10 daily; 6hr); Denpasar (daily; 4 days); Dumai (10 daily; 3hr); Jakarta (10 daily; 34hr); Maninjau (daily; 8hr); Mataram (Lombok, daily; 4 days); Medan (daily; 25–35hr); Padang (10 daily; 8hr); Prapat (daily; 22–30hr); Yogyakarta (4 daily; 42hr).

Sumatra trains

Bandar Lampung to: Palembang (3 daily; 6–8hr).
Palembang to: Bandar Lampung (3 daily; 6–8hr).

Sumatra Pelni ferries

For further details, see the map of Pelni routes on pp.240–241.
Medan (Tanjung Belawan) every 4 days to: Pulau Batam (18hr) and Jakarta (42hr); daily to Penang (4hr).
Padang fortnightly to: Balikpapan (4 days); Makassar (3 days); Nias (9–20hr); Sibolga (13hr–16hr); Surabaya (48hr); Tanjung Priok (30hr).
Parapat to: Ambarita (hourly 8.45am–6.45pm; 45min); Tuk Tuk (hourly 9.30am–7.30pm; 30min).
Pulau Batam every four days to: Belawan (20hr); Tanjung Priok (28hr).
Pulau Bintan (Kijang) fortnightly (except where stated) to: Balikpapan (4 days); Banda (5 days);

Banjarmasin (4 days); Dobo (monthly; 6 days); Dumai (15hr); Kaimana (monthly; 6 days); Kupang (7 days); Larantuka (7 days); Makassar (3 days); Nunukan (6 days); Pontianak (3 days); Pulau Batam (7hr); Semarang (3 days); Surabaya (3 days); Tanjung Priok (26–38hr); Tarakan (6 days).

Sumatra other ferries

Ambarita to: Haranggaol (Mon 6.30am; 3hr); Parapat (hourly 6.45am–4.45pm; 45min); Tongging (Tues 9am; 3hr 30min).
Bakauheni to: Meraka (every 20min; 40min–2hr).
Bandar Lampung to: Kalianda (every 30min; 1–2hr).
Haranggaol to: Ambarita (Mon 1pm; 3hr); Simanindo (Mon 1pm, Thurs 7pm; 1hr 10min).
Pekanbaru to: Pulau Batam (9–12hr); Pulau Bintan (daily; 12hr).
Pulau Batam to: Dumai (daily; 6–8hr); Pekanbaru (daily; 18hr); Singapore's World Trade Centre (frequent departures daily; 1–2hr); Tanah Merah, Singapore (6 daily 8am–6pm; 1–2hr); Tanjung Pinang, Pulau Bintan (every 15min 8am–5pm; 45min).
Pulau Bintan (Tanjung Pinang) to: Jakarta (Tanjung Priok: daily; 24hr); Johor Bahru (daily; 6hr); Pulau Batam (every 15min; 45min); Pekanbaru (daily; 12hr); Singapore (Tanah Merah; 3 daily; 1hr 30min); Tanjung Balai on Pulau Karimun (2 daily; 2–3hr).
Pulau Karimun (Tanjung Balai) to: Johor Bahru (4 daily; 4–6hr); Pekanbaru (2 daily; 6–7hr); Sekupang on Pulau Batam (8 daily; 3hr); Singapore (9 daily; 1hr 30min); Tanjung Pinang on Pulau Bintan (4 daily; 3hr).
Sibolga to: Gunung Sitoli (Jambo Jet, daily except Sun 8.30am; 4hr/*KM Cucit*/Poncan Moale, daily except Sun 8pm; 8hr/Sumber Rezeki, daily except Sun 6pm; 10hr).
Tongging to: Tuk Tuk via Ambarita (Mon 9am; 3hr 45min).

Sumatra flights

Gunung Sitoli to: Padang (weekly; 1hr).
Medan to: Banda Aceh (2 daily; 55min); Dumai (weekly; 1hr 25min); Gunung Sitoli (6 weekly; 1hr 10min); Jakarta (15 daily; 2hr 15min); Kuala Lumpur (17 daily; 1hr); Padang (3 daily; 1hr 10min); Pekanbaru (daily; 2hr); Penang (11 weekly; 40min); Pulau Batam (3 daily; 1hr 15min); Sibolga (6 weekly; 1hr); Singapore (2 daily; 1hr 30min).
Padang to: Bandung (daily; 2hr–3hr 30min); Jakarta (4 daily; 45min); Medan (1–2 daily; 1hr 10min); Pekanbaru (3 weekly; 50min); Pulau Batam (daily; 1hr).
Pekanbaru to: Jakarta (6 daily; 1hr–1hr 40min); Kuala Lumpur (4 weekly; 1hr); Melaka (4 weekly; 40min); Medan (daily; 1hr 20min); Padang (3 weekly; 40min); Pulau Batam (3–4 daily; 45min); Tanjung Pinang (4 weekly; 50min).
Pulau Batam to: Balikpapan (9 weekly; 4hr 25min); Bandung (2 daily; 3hr 20min); Banjarmasin (daily; 6hr); Denpasar (daily; 4hr 20min); Jakarta (5 daily; 1hr 35min); Makassar (9 weekly; 6hr 30min); Manado (daily; 7hr 40min); Mataram (2 weekly; 3hr 55min); Medan (daily; 1hr 20min); Padang (daily; 1hr); Pekanbaru (daily; 45min); Pontianak (5 weekly; 3–4hr); Semarang (daily; 3hr 10min); Surabaya (3 daily; 3hr 30min); Yogyakarta (2 daily; 2hr 5min).
Pulau Bintan (Kijang) to: Jakarta (6 weekly; 1hr 45min); Pekanbaru (6 weekly; 55min).

Bali public bemos and buses

Air Sanih to: Culik (1hr 30min); Gilimanuk (3hr); Lovina 1hr); Singaraja (Penarukan terminal; 30min); Tirtagangga (2hr); Tulamben (1hr).
Bedugul to: Denpasar (Ubung terminal; 1hr 30min); Singaraja (Sukasada terminal; 1hr 30min).
Candi Dasa to: Amlapura (30min); Denpasar (Batubulan terminal; 2hr); Klungkung (40min); Padang Bai (20min).
Culik to: Aas (1hr 30min); Air Sanih (1hr 30min); Amed (20min); Bunutan (45min); Jemeluk (30min); Lipah beach (1hr); Lovina (2hr 30min); Selang (1hr 15min); Singaraja (Penarukan terminal; 2hr 30min).
Denpasar (Batubulan terminal) to: Candi Dasa (2hr); Kintamani (1hr 30min); Klungkung (1hr 20min); Padang Bai (1hr 40min); Singaraja (Penarukan terminal; 3hr); Ubud (50min).
Denpasar (Kereneng terminal) to: Sanur (15–25min).
Denpasar (Tegal terminal) to: Kuta (25min); Ngurah Rai Airport (35min); Sanur (25min).
Denpasar (Ubung terminal) to: Bedugul (1hr 30min); Cekik (3hr); Gilimanuk (3hr 15min); Jakarta (24hr); Kediri (30min); Lalang Linggah (1hr 15min); Medewi (1hr 30min); Singaraja (Sukasada terminal; 3hr); Solo (15hr); Surabaya (10hr); Tabanan (35min); Yogyakarta (15hr).
Gilimanuk to: Cekik (10min); Denpasar (Ubung terminal; 3hr 15min); Kediri (2hr 45min); Labuan Lalang (25min); Lalang Linggah (2hr 15min); Lovina (2hr 15min); Medewi (1hr 45min); Pemuteran (1hr); Singaraja (Banyuasri terminal; 2hr 30min); Tabanan (2hr 30min).
Kintamani to: Denpasar (Batubulan terminal; 1hr 30min); Singaraja (Penarukan terminal; 1hr 30min); Ubud (40min).

Klungkung to: Besakih (45min); Candi Dasa (40min); Denpasar (Batubulan terminal; 1hr 20min); Padang Bai (20min).
Kuta to: Denpasar (Tegal terminal; 25min).
Lovina to: Gilimanuk (2hr 30min); Jakarta (24hr); Pemuteran (1hr 15min); Probolingo – for Bromo (7hr); Seririt (20min); Singaraja (Banyuasri terminal; 20min); Surabaya (10–12hr); Yogyakarta (17hr).
Padang Bai to: Amlapura (1hr); Candi Dasa (20min); Denpasar (Batubulan terminal; 1hr 40min); Klungkung (20min).
Penelokan to: Buahan (30min); Denpasar (Batubulan terminal; 1hr 30min); Singaraja (Penarukan terminal; 1hr 30min); Songan (45min); Toya Bungkah (30min).
Sanur to: Denpasar (Kereneng terminal; 15–25min); Denpasar (Tegal terminal; 25min).
Singaraja (Banyuasri terminal) to: Gilimanuk (2hr 30min); Jakarta (24hr); Lovina (20min); Seririt (40min); Surabaya (8hr); Yogyakarta (12hr).
Singaraja (Penarukan terminal) to: Culik (2hr 30min); Denpasar (Batubulan terminal; 3hr); Penelokan (1hr 30min); Kubutambahan (20min); Tirtagangga (2hr 30min); Tulamben (1hr).
Singaraja (Sukasada terminal) to: Bedugul (1hr 30min); Denpasar (Ubung terminal; 3hr).
Tirtagangga to: Air Sanih (2hr); Amlapura (20min); Culik (30min); Singaraja (2hr 30min); Tulamben (1hr).
Tulamben to: Air Sanih (1hr); Culik (30min); Lovina (2hr 30min); Singaraja (2hr); Tulamben (1hr).
Ubud to: Campuhan/Sanggingan (5–10min); Denpasar (Batubulan terminal; 50min); Gianyar (20min); Kintamani (1hr).

Bali Perama shuttle buses

STO – overnight stopover is sometimes needed
Bedugul to: Candi Dasa (daily; STO); Kuta, Bali/Ngurah Rai Airport (daily; 2hr 30min–3hr); Kuta, Lombok (daily; STO); Lovina (daily; 1hr 30min); Mataram (daily; STO); Padang Bai (daily; STO); Sanur (daily; 2hr–2hr 30min); Sengiggi (daily; STO); Ubud (daily; 1hr 30min).
Candi Dasa to: Bedugul (daily; STO); Kuta, Bali/Ngurah Rai Airport (3 daily; 3hr); Lovina (2 daily; 3hr–3hr 30min); Mataram (2 daily; 5hr–5hr30min); Nusa Lembongan (daily; STO); Padang Bai (3 daily; 30min); Sanur (3 daily; 2hr–2hr 30min); Sengiggi (2 daily; 5hr 30min–6hr); Ubud (3 daily; 1hr 30min–2hr).
Kuta to: Bedugul (daily; 2hr 30min–3hr); Candi Dasa (3 daily; 3hr); Gili Islands (daily; 9hr 30min); Kuta, Lombok (1 daily; STO); Lovina (daily; 4hr); Mataram (2 daily; 8hr 30min); Ngurah Rai Airport (3 daily; 30min): Nusa Lembongan (daily; 2hr 30min); Padang Bai (3 daily; 2hr 30min); Sanur (4 daily; 30min); Senggigi (2 daily; 9hr); Ubud (4 daily; 1hr–1hr 30min).
Lovina to: Bedugul (daily; 1hr 30min); Candi Dasa (2 daily; 3hr–3hr 30min); Kuta, Bali/Ngurah Rai Airport (daily; 3hr); Mataram (daily; 7–8hr); Padang Bai (daily; 2hr 45min); Sanur (daily; 2hr 30min–3hr); Sengiggi (daily; 7hr 30min–8hr 30min); Ubud (daily; 3hr 30min–4hr).
Nusa Lembongan to: Bedugul (daily; STO); Candi Dasa (daily; 3hr); Kuta, Bali/Ngurah Rai Airport (daily; 2hr 30min–3hr); Kuta, Lombok (daily; STO); Lovina (daily; 5hr); Mataram (daily; 9hr); Padang Bai (daily; 3hr 30min); Senggigi (daily; 9hr); Ubud (daily; 3hr 30min).
Padang Bai to: Bedugul (2 daily; STO); Candi Dasa (3 daily; 30min); Kuta, Bali/Ngurah Rai Airport (3 daily; 2hr 30min); Lovina (2 daily; 2hr 30min–3hr); Mataram (2 daily; 4hr 30min–5hr); Nusa Lembongan (daily; STO); Sanur (3 daily; 1hr 30min–2hr); Sengiggi (2 daily; 5hr–5hr 30min); Ubud (3 daily; 1hr–1hr 30min).
Sanur to: Bedugul (1 daily; 2hr–2hr 30min); Candi Dasa (3 daily; 2hr–2hr 30min); Gili Islands (1 daily; 9hr); Kuta/Ngurah Rai Airport (5 daily; 30min–1hr); Kuta, Lombok (2 daily; STO); Lovina (1 daily; 2hr 30min–3hr); Mataram (2 daily; 8hr); Padang Bai (3 daily; 1hr 30min–2hr); Senggigi (2 daily; 8hr 30min); Ubud (4 daily; 30min–1hr).
Ubud to: Bedugul (1 daily; 1hr 30min); Candi Dasa (3 daily; 1hr 30min–2hr); Gili Islands (1 daily; 8hr); Kuta/Ngurah Rai Airport (5 daily; 1hr–1hr 30min); Kuta, Lombok (2 daily; STO); Lovina (1 daily; 1hr 30min–2hr); Mataram (2 daily; 7hr); Nusa Lembongan (1 daily; 2hr 30min); Padang Bai (3 daily; 1hr–1hr 30min); Sanur (5 daily; 30min–1hr); Senggigi (2 daily; 7hr 30min).

Bali Pelni ferries

For further details, see the map of Pelni routes on pp.240–241.
Denpasar (Benoa harbour) except where indicated, fortnightly services to: Bima (3 times a fortnight; 21–31hr); Bitung (twice a fortnight; 5 days); Ende (2 days); Kupang (3 times a month; 26hr); Labuhanbajo (30hr); Makassar (3 times a fortnight; 2–4 days); Maumere (3 times a month; 3 days); Surabaya (monthly; 23hr); Waingapu (26hr).

Bali other ferries

Benoa harbour to: Bima (1–2 weekly by Barito Express; 7hr); Kupang (weekly by Barito Express; 20hr); Maumere (weekly by Barito Express; 12hr); Surabaya (weekly by Barito Express; 7hr); Waingapu (weekly by Barito Express; 13hr).

Gilimanuk to: Ketapang (every 20min; 30min).
Jungutbatu (Nusa Lembongan) to: Kusamba (daily; 1–2hr); Sanur (daily; 1–2hr).
Kusamba to: Nusa Lembongan (daily; 1–2hr).
Padang Bai to: Benoa harbour (daily; 1hr); Lembar (Lombok; every 90min, 4–5hr).
Sanur to: Jungutbatu (Nusa Lembongan; 3 daily; 1hr 30min).

Bali flights

Denpasar Ngurah Rai Airport to: Bima (1–2 daily; 1hr 15min); Dili (4 weekly; 1hr 50min); Ende (daily; 2hr); Jakarta (15 daily; 1hr 40min); Jayapura (4 weekly; 5hr 10min); Kupang (3–4 daily; 1hr 35min); Labuhanbajo (4 weekly; 2hr 20min); Makassar (1 daily; 1hr 10min); Mataram (8 daily; 30min); Maumere (6 weekly; 2hr 20min); Medan (5 daily; 4hr 30min); Surabaya (3 daily; 45min); Waingapu (4 weekly; 1hr 50min); Yogyakarta (3 daily; 1hr 10min).

Lombok bemos and buses

Ampenan to: Senggigi (20min).
Labuhan Lombok to: Bayan (2hr); Kopang (for Praya; 1hr); Sembalun Lawang (2hr 30min); Sweta (Bertais/Mandalika/Sweta terminal; 2hr).
Lembar to: Sekotong (1hr); Selegang (3hr); Sweta (Bertais/Mandalika/Sweta terminal; 30min); Tawun (2hr); Tembowong (2hr 30min).
Praya to: Kuta (1hr); Sweta (Bertais/Mandalika/Sweta terminal; 30min).
Sapit to: Aik Mel (1hr); Sembalun Lawang (2hr); Pringabaya (1hr).
Sembalun Lawang to: Obel Obel (2hr); Sapit (2hr).
Senggigi to: Ampenan (20min).
Sweta (Bertais/Mandalika/Sweta terminal) to: Bayan (for Rinjani; 2hr 30min); Bima (Sumbawa; 12hr); Jakarta (Java; 32hr); Labuanbajo (Flores; 24hr); Labuhan Lombok (2hr); Lembar (30min); Pemenang (50min); Pomotong (for Tetebatu; 1hr 15min); Praya (for Kuta; 30min); Sape (Flores; 14hr); Sumbawa Besar (Sumbawa; 6hr); Surabaya (20hr); Yogyakarta (22hr).

Lombok Perama shuttle buses

Mataram to: Bedugul (daily; STO); Candi Dasa (daily; 5hr–5hr 30min); Kuta, Bali/Ngurah Rai Airport (daily; 8hr 30min); Kuta, Lombok (daily; 2hr 30min); Lovina (daily; 7hr–8hr); Padang Bai (2 daily; 4hr 30min–5hr); Sanur (2 daily; 8hr); Sengiggi (daily; 30min); Tetebatu (daily; 2hr 15min); Tirtagangga (daily; 6hr–6hr 30min); Tulamben (daily; 7–8hr); Ubud (daily; 8hr).
Senggigi to: Air Sanih (daily; STO); Bangsal (daily; 45min); Bedugul (daily; STO); Candi Dasa (two daily; 5hr 30min–6hr); Kintamani (daily; STO); Kuta, Bali/Ngurah Rai Airport (2 daily; 9hr); Kuta, Lombok (daily; 3hr); Lovina (daily; 7hr 30min–8hr 30min); Mataram (daily; 30min); Padang Bai (2 daily; 4hr 30min–5hr); Sanur (2 daily; 8hr); Tetebatu (daily; 2hr 45min); Tirtagangga (daily; 6hr 30min–7hr); Tulamben (daily; 7hr 30min–8hr 30min); Ubud (daily; 7hr 30min).
Tetebatu to: to: Air Sanih (daily; STO); Bangsal (daily; 3hr); Bedugul (daily; STO); Candi Dasa (daily; 8hr); Kintamani (daily; STO); Kuta, Bali/Ngurah Rai Airport (2 daily; 10hr–11hr); Lovina (daily; STO); Mataram (daily; 2hr 30min); Padang Bai (daily; 7hr 30min); Sanur (daily; 10hr); Senggigi (daily; 3hr); Tirtagangga (daily; STO); Tulamben (daily; STO); Ubud (daily; 9hr).

Lombok Pelni ferries

For further details, see the map of Pelni routes on pp.240–241.
Lembar except where indicated, fortnightly services.
KM Awu: Ende (34hr); Kalabahi (59hr); Larantuka (7 days); Maumere (72hr); Nunukan (7 days); Tarakan (6 days); Ujung Pandang (95hr); Waingapu (24hr).
KM Tilongkabila: Bau-Bau (61hr); Benoa harbour (4hr); Bima (15hr); Bitung (5 days); Kendari (3 days); Kolonedale (4 days); Labuan Bajo (24hr); Luwuk (4 days); Raha (42hr); Ujung Pandang (37hr).

Lombok other ferries

Bangsal to: Gili Islands (several daily; 20–45min).
Labuhan Lombok to: Poto Tano (Sumbawa; every hour; 1hr 30min).
Lembar to: Padang Bai (every 90min; 4hr–4hr 30min).
Senggigi to: Gili Islands (2 daily; 2hr).

Lombok flights

Mataram Selaparang Airport to: Denpasar (12 daily; 30min); Jakarta (daily; 3hr); Singapore (6 weekly; 2hr 30min); Surabaya (4 daily; 50min); Yogyakarta (daily; 1hr 15min).

Sumbawa buses

Bima to: Mataram via Sumbawa Besar (Bima terminal; 11hr); Sape (Kumbe terminal; 2hr); Sumbawa Besar (Bima terminal; 7hr).
Sumbawa Besar to: Bima (regular; 7hr); Dompu (regular; 5hr); Taliwang (regular; 3hr).

Sumbawa Pelni ferries

For further details, see the map of Pelni routes on pp.240–241.
Bima to: Denpasar (*KM Tatamailau*, monthly; 18hr/ *KM Tilongkabila*, fortnightly; 24hr); Labuanbajo (*KM Tilongkabila*, fortnightly; 12hr); Makassar (*KM Tilongkabila*, fortnightly; 27hr); Surabaya (*KM Wilis*, fortnightly; 34hr); Waingapu (*KM Wilis*, fortnightly; 13hr).

Sumbawa other ferries

Sape to: Labuanbajo (daily; 6–9hr); Waikelo (weekly; 6–9hr).

Sumbawa flights

Bima to: Denpasar (daily; 1hr 15min); Mataram (4 weekly; 1hr 10min).
Sumbawa Besar to: Mataram (4 weekly; 45min).

Flores buses

Bajawa to: Ende (several daily; 4hr); Labuanbajo (2 daily; 11hr); Moni (daily; 6hr); Ruteng (several daily; 4–5hr).
Ende to: Bajawa (several daily; 4hr); Labuanbajo (daily; 18hr); Maumere (several daily; 6hr); Moni (several daily; 1hr 30min); Ruteng (several daily; 10hr).
Labuanbajo to: Bajawa (2 daily; 11hr); Ende (daily, 14hr); Ruteng (2 daily, 4–5hr).
Maumere to: Bajawa (daily; 10hr); Ende (several daily; 6hr); Moni (several daily; 3hr); Ruteng (daily; 15hr).
Ruteng to: Bajawa (several daily; 4–5hr); Labuanbajo (several daily; 4–5hr); Ende (daily; 8–10hr); Maumere (daily; 15hr); Moni (daily; 12hr).

Flores Pelni ferries

For further details, see the map of Pelni routes on pp.240–241.
Ende to: Denpasar (*KM Wilis*, fortnightly; 44hr); Labuanbajo (*KM Wilis*, fortnightly; 20hr); Makassar (*KM Wilis*, fortnightly; 64hr); Maumere (*KM Wilis*, fortnightly; 40hr); Surabaya (*KM Wilis*, fortnightly; 58hr); Waingapu (*KM Wilis*, fortnightly; 8hr/*KM Wilis*, fortnightly; 8hr).
Labuanbajo to: Bima (*KM Tilongkabila*, fortnightly; 12hr); Makassar (*KM Tilongkabila*, fortnightly; 20hr); Surabaya (*KM Wilis*, fortnightly; 40hr); Waingapu (*KM Wilis*, fortnightly; 10 hr).
Maumere to: Bima (*KM Tatamailau*, monthly; 24hr); Kalabahi (*KM Wilis*, fortnightly; 15hr); Makassar (*KM Wilis*, fortnightly; 24hr).

Flores other ferries

Ende to: Surabaya (2 weekly; 2 days); Waingapu (weekly; 8hr).
Labuanbajo to: Sape (daily; 6–9hr).

Flores flights

Ende to: Bima (2 weekly; 1hr 30min); Denpasar (4 weekly; 1hr 30min); Kupang (2 weekly; 1hr 10min); Surubaya (2 weekly; 3hr 10min); Waingapu (2 weekly; 45min).
Labuanbajo to: Bima (2 weekly; 45min); Mataram (2 weekly; 1hr 15min); Denpasar (5 weekly; 1hr 40min).
Maumere to: Denpasar (daily; 2hr 10min); Kupang (8 weekly; 55min); Waingapu (3 weekly; 1hr).

Sumba buses

Waikabubak to: Bandokodi and Pero (daily; 4hr); Waingapu (several daily; 4hr 30min).
Waingapu to: Melolo and Rende (several daily; 2hr); Waikabubak (several daily; 4hr 30min).

Sumba Pelni ferries

For further details, see the map of Pelni routes on pp.240–241.
Waingapu to: Bima (*KM Wilis*, fortnightly; 13hr); Denpasar (*KM Wilis*, fortnightly; 30hr); Ende (*KM Wilis*, fortnightly; 10hr/*KM Wilis*, fortnightly; 10hr).

Sumba other ferries

Waikelo to: Sape (weekly; 7hr).
Waingapu to: Aimere (weekly; 10hr); Ende (weekly; 10hr).

Sumba flights

Waikabubak to: Denpasar via Bima (2 weekly; 2hr 30min).
Waingapu to: Denpasar via Waikabubak (3 weekly; 2hr 20min); Ende (weekly; 40min); Maumere (3 weekly; 1hr).

Kalimantan buses

Balikpapan to: Samarinda (several daily; 2hr 30min).
Pontianak to: Kuching (several daily; 12hr).
Samarinda to: Balikpapan (several daily; 2hr 30min); Kota Bangun (several daily; 3hr); Tenggarong (several daily; 1hr 30min).

Kalimantan Pelni ferries

For further details, see the map of Pelni routes on

pp.240–241.
Balikpapan to: Makassar (*KM Awu*, weekly; 26hr/*KM Agoa Mas*, fortnightly; 28hr/*KM Kelimutu*, monthly; 30hr); Nunukan (*KM DB Solo*, fortnightly; 52hr); Pantoloan (*KM Kerinci*, fortnightly; 17hr/*KM Nggapulu*, fortnightly; 12hr); Surabaya (*KM Kerinci*, fortnightly; 46hr/KM Ganda Dewata, weekly; 38hr/*KM Tidar*, fortnightly; 27hr/*KM Nggapulu*, fortnightly; 27hr/*KM DB Solo*, fortnightly; 46hr); Tanjung Priok (*KM Agoa Mas*, fortnightly; 69hr); Tarakan (*KM Tidar*, fortnightly; 24hr/*KM DB Solo*, fortnightly; 42hr); Tolitoli (*KM Kerinci*, fortnightly; 27hr).
Nunukan to: Balikpapan (*KM Tidar*, fortnightly; 31hr)/*KM Kerinci*, fortnightly; 40hr); Makassar (*KM Awu*, fortnightly; 60hr/*KM Wilis*, fortnightly; 46hr); Surubaya (*KM Kerinci*, fortnightly; 90hr/*KM Tidar*, fortnightly; 77hr); Tolitoli (*KM Kerinci*, fortnightly; 17hr).
Pontianak to: Semarang (*KM Leuser*, fortnightly; 38hr/*KM Lawit*, fortnightly; 37hr); Surubaya (*KM Bukit Raya*, fortnightly; 42hr); Tanjung Priok (*KM Leuser*, fortnightly; 38hr/*KM Lawit*, fortnightly; 35hr).
Samarinda to: Surabaya (KM Binaiya, fortnightly; 3 days).
Tarakan to: Balikpapan (*KM Kerinci*, fortnightly; 48hr/*KM Tidar*, fortnightly; 24hr); Makassar (*KM Tidar*, fortnightly; 38hr/*KM Wilis*, fortnightly; 60hr); Tolitoli (*KM Kerinci*, fortnightly; 24hr).

Kalimantan other ferries

Balikpapan to: Makassar (4 weekly; 18hr); Surubaya (4 weekly; 10hr).
Nunukan to: Tarakan (about 2 daily; 6–12hr).
Pontianak to: Jakarta (KM Farina, 3 weekly; 19hr); Surubaya (3 weekly; 20hr).
Samarinda to: Kota Bangun (morning only; 10hr); Long Bagun (seasonally; 2 daily, 40hr–4 days); Long Iram (1–2 daily; 30hr); Melak (daily; 24hr); Muara Muntai (daily; 14hr); Tenggarong (daily; 3hr).
Tarakan to: Berau (3 weekly; 10hr); Nunukan (4 daily; 6–12hr); Tanjung Selor (14 daily; 1–2hr); Tewau, Malaysia (Indomaya Expres, daily except Sunday; 3hr).

Kalimantan flights

Balikpapan to: Jakarta (many daily with Bouraq, Lion, Star Air, Mandala, Batavia, Jatayu and Garuda; 2hr); Makassar (3 weekly with Merpati; 1hr 10min); Manado (daily with Batavia; 2hr 30min); Pontianak (daily with Merpati; 1hr 25min); Surabaya (many daily with Bouraq, Garuda, Lion, Merpati, Star Air, Mandala and Batavia; 1hr 25min); Tarakan (daily with Bouraq and Merpati; 2hr).
Pontianak to: Balikpapan (daily with Merpati; 1hr 25min); Jakarta (many daily with Merpati, Garuda, Batavia and Adam Air; 1hr 30min); Kuching (3 weekly; 1hr 45min); Medan (3 weekly; 3hr 35min).
Samarinda to: Berau (several each week with KAL Star and Doraya; 45min); Tarakan (2 daily with KAL Star; 2hr).
Tarakan to: Nunukan (4 weekly with DAS; 30min).

Sulawesi buses

Regular daily departures.
Ampana to: Luwuk (6hr); Makassar (26hr); Pagimana (5hr); Palu (15hr); Palopo (18hr).
Gorontalo to: Makassar (2 days); Manado (8hr).
Makassar to: Ampana (28hr); Bira (5hr); Mamasa (15hr); Manado (2–3 days); Palu (29hr); Polewali (7hr); Rantepao (8hr); Tentena (19hr).
Manado to: Gorontalo (8hr); Makassar (2–3 days); Palu (24hr).
Rantepao to: Makassar (8hr); Palu (21hr); Pendolo (9hr); Tentena (11hr).

Sulawesi Pelni ferries

For further details, see the map of Pelni routes on pp.240–241.
Bitung to: Balikpapan (*KM Nggapulu*, fortnightly; 36hr); Banggai (KM Sinabung, fortnightly; 15hr); Luwuk (*KM Tilongkabila*, fortnightly; 17hr); Pantoloan (*KM Nggapulu*, fortnightly; 24hr).
Gorontalo to: Bitung (*KM Tilongkabila*, fortnightly; 10hr); Luwuk (*KM Tilongkabila*, fortnightly; 10hr).
Makassar to: Balikpapan (*KM Tidar*, fortnightly; 20hr/*KM Kelimutu*, monthly; 31hr/*KM Agoa Mas*, fortnightly; 37hr); Bima (*KM Tilongkabila*, fortnightly; 27hr); Denpasar (*KM Tilongkabila*, fortnightly; 48hr); (*KM Tilongkabila*, fortnightly; 20hr); Maumere (*KM Wilis*, fortnightly; 31hr); Larantuka (*KM Sirimau*, fortnightly; 27hr); Nunukan (*KM Awu*, weekly; 72hr/*KM Wilis*, fortnightly; 69hr); Surabaya (*KM Doro Londa*, fortnightly; 26hr/*KM Labobar*, fortnightly; 24hr/*KM Tidar*, fortnightly; 26hr/*KM Ciremai*, fortnightly; 27hr/*KM Lambelu*, fortnightly; 26hr); Tanjung Priok (*KM Ciremai*, fortnightly; 51hr/*KM Sinabung*, fortnightly; 45hr/*KM Sirimau*, fortnightly; 78hr); Tarakan (*KM Tidar*, fortnightly; 40hr/*KM Wilis*, fortnightly; 60hr).

Sulawesi other ferries

Ampana to: Bomba (daily; 4hr); Gorontalo (weekly; 20hr); Wakai (daily; 5hr).
Gorontalo to: Pagimana (every second day; 10–12hr); weekly to Togian Islands (15hr) then Ampana (20hr).
Manado to: Bunaken (daily; 1hr).

Sulawesi flights

Gorontalo to: Manado (several weekly with Merpati and Bouraq; 1hr 15min); Makassar (several weekly with XpressAir and Pelita; 1hr 30min).

Makassar to: Ambon (several weekly with Merpati; 2hr 45min); Balikpapan (several weekly with Bouraq; 1hr 10min); Denpasar (daily with Garuda and Lion Air; 1hr 20min); Jakarta (several daily with Garuda, Bouraq, Lion Air, Mandala, Merpati, Pelita and Xpressair; 2hr 10min); Manado (daily with Garuda, Mandala, Merpati and Lion Air; 1hr 35min); Palu (several weekly with Bouraq, Lion and Merpati; 55min); Surabaya (several daily with Bouraq, Garuda, Lion Air, Mandala, Merpati, Pelita and Xpressair; 1hr 20min); Yogyakarta (several weekly with Lion, Merpati and Pelita; 2hr 50min).

Manado to: Balikpapan (daily with Batavia; 2hr 30min); Gorontalo (several weekly with Bouraq and Merpati; 1hr 15min); Jakarta (several daily with Bouraq, Garuda, Lion Air, Merpati and Mandala; 2hr 10min); Makassar (several daily with Garuda, Lion, Mandala and Merpati; 1hr 35min); Palu (several weekly with Bouraq and Merpati; 1hr 20min); Singapore (3 weekly with Silk Air; 3hr 30min); Surabaya (several daily with Bouraq, Garuda, Lion, Mandala and Merpati; 1hr 35min).

5

Laos

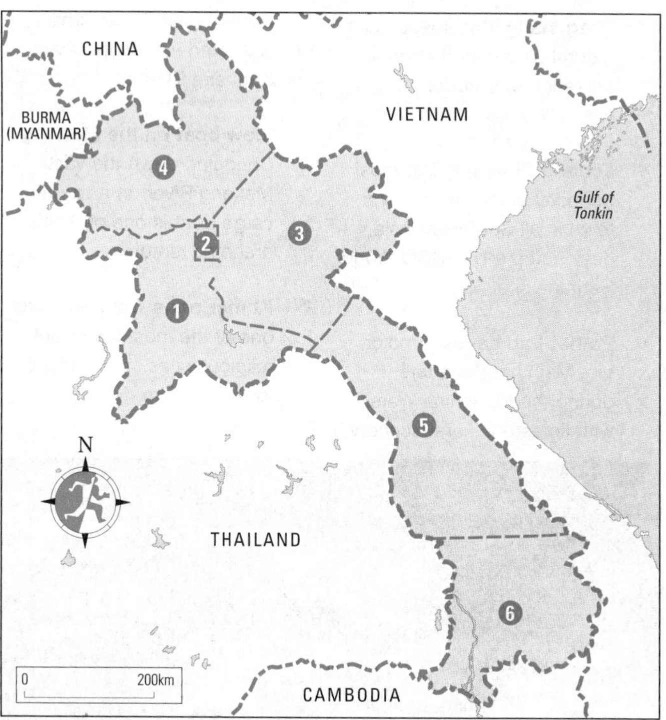
CHINA
BURMA (MYANMAR)
VIETNAM
Gulf of Tonkin
THAILAND
CAMBODIA
0 200km
N
1
2
3
4
5
6

Laos highlights

* **Wat Sisaket, Vientiane** An historic monastery, the only temple spared in the catastrophic sack of the city in 1828. See p.528

* **Vang Viang** This spectacular natural playground offers a full range of outdoor activities. See p.532

* **Louang Phabang** The most perfectly preserved historic town in all Southeast Asia, designated a UNESCO World Heritage site. See p.536

* **Pathet Lao caves** A major Viet Minh headquarters during the Indochina Wars, with limestone karst scenery reminiscent of Chinese paintings. See p.551

* **Plain of Jars** One of the world's great archeological mysteries: hundreds of ancient giant stone urns scattered across the Xiang Khouang Plateau. See p.553

* **Slow boat on the Mekong** Chugging down the vast Mekong River on a wooden cargo boat is one of Asia's grand adventures. See p.562

* **Khmer ruins** Wat Phou was one of the most important religious sites of the mighty Khmer Empire. See p.577

△ Pak Ou Caves

Introduction and basics

Only a decade ago, Laos (population 5.25 million) was largely unknown to Western travellers. Other than a brief period during the 1960s, when the former French colony became a player in the Vietnam War, it has been largely ignored by the West – a situation that only intensified after the 1975 revolution and the years of xenophobic communist rule that ensued. However, since the Lao People's Democratic Republic (PDR) reluctantly reopened its doors in the 1990s, a steady flow of visitors has trickled into this poverty-stricken, old-fashioned country, and a few traveller-oriented services have begun to emerge. For many, a journey through Laos consists of a whistle-stop tour through the two main towns of Vientiane and Louang Phabang, with perhaps a brief detour to the mysterious Plain of Jars or ancient Wat Phou. However, those willing to explore further and brave difficult roads and basic, candlelit accommodation will be rewarded with a rugged natural landscape and an ethnically diverse people not much changed from those that greeted French explorers more than a century ago.

Laos's lifeline is the **Mekong River**, which runs the length of the landlocked country and in places serves as a boundary with Thailand. Set on a broad curve of the Mekong, **Vientiane** is perhaps Southeast Asia's most modest capital city, and provides a smooth introduction to Laos, offering a string of cosmopolitan cafés to compensate for a relative lack of sights. From here, most tourists dash north, usually by plane, to tiny, cultured **Louang Phabang**, once the heart and soul of the ancient kingdom of **Lane Xang** and now the country's most enticing destination, with a spellbinding panoply of gilded temples and weathered shop-houses. However, it's worth taking more time and doing the journey by bus, stopping off en route at the town of **Vang Viang**, set in a spectacular landscape of rice paddies and karsts.

The wild highlands of the **far north** aren't the easiest to get around, but the prospect of trekking to nearby hilltribe villages has put easy-going **Muang Sing** on the map. From here, you can travel to the Burmese border at **Xiang Kok**, and then down the Mekong River to **Houayxai**, an entry point popular with travellers arriving from Thailand in search of a slow boat for the picturesque journey south to Louang Phabang. Lost in the misty mountains of the far northeast, the provincial capital of **Xam Nua** gives access to **Viang Xai**, where the Pathet Lao directed their resistance from deep within a vast cave complex. Following Routes 6 and 7 south brings you to the bustling town of **Phonsavan**, set beside the **Plain of Jars**, a moonscape of bomb craters dotted with ancient funerary urns. In the south, the vast majority of travellers zip down Route 13, stopping off in the three major southern towns: **Thakhek**, genial and cultural **Savannakhet** – also a handy border crossing with Thailand, and offering buses to Vietnam, too – and the important transport hub of **Pakxe**. Further south, near the former royal seat of **Champasak**, lie the ruins of **Wat Phou**, one of the most important Khmer temples outside Cambodia. South again, the countless river islands of **Si Phan Don** lie scattered across the Mekong, boasting scores of traditional fishing communities and the chance to spot the rare Irrawaddy dolphin.

November to February are the most pleasant months to travel in lowland Laos, when daytime **temperatures** are agreeably warm and evenings slightly chilly; at higher elevations, temperatures can drop to freezing point. In March, temperatures begin to climb, reaching a peak in April, when the lowlands are baking hot and humid. Generally, the rains begin in May and last until September, rendering many of Laos's unsealed roads impassable.

Overland routes into Laos

Laos has borders with Thailand, Vietnam, Cambodia, China and Burma.

From Burma

Western tourists are not permitted to cross between Burma and Laos at Muangmom or Xiang Kok, the two main border points between the two countries.

From Cambodia

Although the border crossing between Cambodia and Laos at Voen Kham is not "officially" open, a steady stream of Western travellers continue to get through in both directions without incident.

From China

From the town of Jinghong in China's southwestern Yunnan province, daily buses travel to and from Muang Sing, Oudomxai and Louang Namtha. The last town on the Chinese side is the village of Mo Han and the first Lao village you come to is Boten. The river route from China to Laos is currently only open to cargo boats but there is talk of allowing foreign tourists to use this route in the near future.

From Thailand

There are currently five points along the Thai border where Westerners are permitted to cross into Laos: Chiang Khong (see p.1029) to Houayxai; Nong Khai (p.1051) to Vientiane; Nakhon Phanom (p.1053) to Thakhek; Mukdahan (p.1053) to Savannakhet; and Chong Mek (p.575) to Pakxe. For visa information, see below.

From Vietnam

There are now four border crossings open to foreigners between Vietnam and Laos: Highway #8 across the Kaew Nua Pass, from Cau Treo (see p.1196) to Lak Xao; Highway #9 across the Lao Bao Pass, from Lao Bao (see p.572) to Daen Sawan and Savannakhet; and Highway #7 Nam Can to Nong Het, east of Phonsavan. The latest crossing, Namsoi to Nameo (due east of Xam Nua) was officially opened to third-country nationals in mid-2004.

Entry requirements and visa extension

Visas are required for all foreign visitors to Laos except Thais. A fifteen-day visa-on-arrival is available for $30 (US dollars – cash only – plus one photo) to travellers flying into Vientiane's Wattay Airport or Louang Phabang Airport. The fifteen-day visa-on-arrival is also available to travellers crossing the Mekong from Thailand at the five points mentioned in "From Thailand" above. As at the airports, the fee is $30 and one to two photos are required, depending on the border crossing point.

If you want a longer visa, you will have to apply for it in advance at a Lao embassy (see "Red tape and visas", p.45) or through a travel agency. Many visitors do this while staying in Bangkok or Hanoi. In **Bangkok**, you can apply for a fifteen- or thirty-day tourist visa directly from the Lao embassy (see p.45); for B1000–1600 (depending on your nationality), fifteen-day visas are not significantly cheaper. You will need two passport photos, and if you apply before noon, it may be ready the same afternoon. An alternative option is to apply through a travel agent in Bangkok; they charge B750 for a fifteen-day tourist visa, and B1200–1800 for a thirty-day tourist visa; allow three working days for processing. There is a Lao consulate in Khon Kaen in northeastern Thailand (see p.1047) that can also issue visas, though fees and processing times are variable.

Travellers from Vietnam can get visas for Laos at the Lao embassy in **Hanoi** or at the consulates in **Ho Chi Minh City** and **Da Nang**. It's important to note that the conditions and fees for Lao visas issued in Vietnam vary from place to place and change constantly. The Lao Embassy in Hanoi does one-month visitor visas ($50–70; three working days) and five-day transit visas ($25–40; three working days), the latter of which may only be valid for one province. The one-day express service costs an extra $20. In Ho Chi Minh City, you can get a thirty-day visitor visa ($50; same-day service), but in Da Nang, you can only get a fifteen-day tourist visa ($50; two working days) or a five-day transit visa ($30; two working days), which will allow you to take Route #9 over to Mukdahan, Thailand.

Although the border with Cambodia at Voen Kam is not "officially" open (see above), travellers who do make the crossing here must obtain a Laos visa from the Lao embassy in **Phnom Penh**.

Non-extendible, five-day transit visas ($25–30; three working days) are also offered at the Lao embassy in Hanoi and the consulate in Kunming, China, for travellers flying to Bangkok who wish to make a stopover in Vientiane.

Visa extensions can be applied for at the immigration office in Vientiane on Hatsady Road. The extension charge is $2 per day; the maximum length of your visa extension is fifteen days but this is up to the official

Airport departure tax

When leaving Laos by air or via the Friendship Bridge, you have to pay a **departure tax** equivalent to $10, payable in US dollars, Thai baht or kip. There is also a domestic airport tax of 20,000 kip per flight.

on duty. Officially, only the immigration office in Vientiane can issue visa extensions, but it's always worth trying in other towns. Both airport and border immigration offices generally charge $10 per day for overstays.

Money and costs

Lao currency is the **kip** and is available in 20,000K, 10,000K, 5000K, 2000K, 1000K and 500K notes. There are no coins in circulation. In addition, the Thai baht and US dollar operate parallel to the kip. Although a 1990 law technically forbids the use of foreign currencies to pay for local goods and services, many hotels, restaurants and tour operators actually quote their prices in dollars, and accept payment in either **baht** or **dollars**. The government-owned airline, Lao Airlines, only accepts payment in US dollars cash.

The **Asian financial crisis** in 1997 badly affected the kip. Between June 1997 and early 1999, the kip, which is not freely convertible, fell more than eighty percent against the dollar and inflation was running at over a hundred percent a year. Although inflation has settled to 35 percent per annum, many Lao are suffering real hardship, as prices continue to rise while salaries remain the same.

The difference between the official and black-market rate is now so small that the once thriving black market (*talat meut*) in foreign currencies hardly exists. The government urges tourists to use banks and official exchange kiosks but just about every business in Laos is happy to change your currency at a favourable rate. At the time of writing, the official **exchange rate** was 10,500 kip to the US dollar, 265 kip to the Thai baht.

Travellers' cheques are a safe way to carry your money, but it's a good idea to have a decent supply of US dollars or Thai baht in **cash** if you intend to spend time in the remoter parts of the country. Before travelling to smaller towns, change enough money to use until the next major town. Major **credit cards** are accepted at many hotels, upmarket restaurants and shops in Vientiane and Louang Phabang. **Cash advances** on Visa cards and, less frequently, MasterCard are possible in most major towns. At present, it still isn't possible to withdraw cash from ATMs in Laos. Bear in mind that you cannot change kip back into dollars or baht when leaving the country – and that duty-free shops only accept dollars and baht.

Costs

Given the volatility of the kip, **prices** for accommodation, river travel and car rental in this chapter have been given in their more stable dollar equivalents. Indeed, many hotels and guesthouses have opted to fix their rates to the dollar. The prices quoted in kip for transport, museum entrance fees and so on were correct at the time of research and have been retained to give a relative idea of costs, though in practice many of these prices will be higher.

By eating at noodle stalls and cheap restaurants, taking local transport and opting for basic accommodation, you can travel in Laos on a **daily budget** of less than £12/$20. Food and accommodation tend to be more expensive in Vientiane.

While restaurants and some shops have fixed prices, you should always **bargain** in markets and when chartering transport (fares on passenger vehicles are fixed). Room rates can be bargained for in low season. As the Lao in general – with the exception of some tourist businesses in Vientiane and Louang Phabang – are less out to rip off tourists than their counterparts in Thailand and Vietnam, they start off the haggling by quoting a fairly realistic price and expect to come down only a little. **Price tiering** does exist in Laos, with foreigners paying more than locals for airfares, bus fares, speedboat tickets and entry to museums and famous sites. Tipping isn't a Lao custom, although upmarket restaurants in Vientiane expect a gratuity of around ten percent.

Information and maps

The **National Tourism Authority of Laos** (NATL) operates offices in a few major towns, but the staff are generally untrained and speak little English. Sodetour and Diethelm, two privately owned companies with offices in most major towns, can provide more reliable data. Word-of-mouth information from other travellers is often the best source, as conditions in Laos change with astonishing rapidity.

Good **maps** for Laos are difficult to find. The best road map of Laos is the *Laos 2002 Guide Map* published by Golden Triangle Rider and available at bookstores in Thailand. The latest edition of Nelles 1:1,500,000 map of Vietnam, Laos and Cambodia is adequate for orientation but not very good for pin-pointing towns or villages. Likewise, the Bartholomew 1: 2,000,000 Vietnam, Cambodia and Laos map is attractive but not always reliable.

Getting around

Boats, the traditional means of **travel**, still regularly ply the Mekong and its tributaries, Laos's ancient highways, but as the roads are gradually surfaced, buses have begun displacing river boats as the main mode of transportation. Already on rivers like the Nam Ou, most of the boat services are for foreigners, locals preferring the bus. However, many roads are still potholed and there are plenty of opportunities for adventure. Regardless of whether you go by road or river, you only need to travel for a week or two in Laos before realizing that timetables are irrelevant, and estimated times of arrival pointless. For an idea guide of journeys between major destinations, see "Travel details", p.586.

Planes

The government-owned **Lao Airlines**, formerly Lao Aviation, is the country's only domestic carrier. Along with the name change came a supposed increase in maintenance of aircraft on certain domestic routes; namely the flights between Vientiane and Louang Phabang, and Vientiane and Phonsavan. At any rate, domestic routes were cut by almost half as the airline downsized in the last couple of years. Most Western embassies still have travel advisories warning against flying Lao Airlines. For some travellers, flying with Lao Airlines demonstrates bravado, but it's not really something you want to do if you don't absolutely have to.

Lao Airlines only accepts **US dollars cash**, and the foreigner fare is significantly more than for locals. In the event you're stuck out in the provinces without dollars, it should be possible to pay by credit card. Alternatively, you could get a letter from Lao Airlines informing the local bank that you need to exchange a travellers' cheque for dollars or get a cash advance on Visa in dollars. Sample one-way **fares** are: Vientiane–Phonsavan $50; Vientiane–Xam Nua $72; Louang Phabang–Vientiane $57; and Vientiane–Pakxe $87.

Boats

With roughly 4600km of navigable waterways, rivers are the traditional highways of Laos. Today, the main routes along the Mekong River link Houayxai to Louang Phabang, and Pakxe to Champasak and Si Phan Don. Smaller passenger **boats** also cruise up the Nam Ou River, linking Louang Phabang to Phongsali, and vessels still travel the remote Louang Phabang–Vientiane route, a journey that takes four days to a week.

The diesel-chugging **slow boats** (*heua sa*) that ply the Mekong routes are built to carry cargo and don't have seats, leaving passengers to grab any spot they can find on the floor. Along the Houayxai to Louang Phabang route, boats for foreign passengers have been fitted out with seats, and there is an overnight stop at Pakbeng, the town that marks the halfway point. The stops on this route are few and far between, so it's a good idea to bring extra water and food.

Along many of the Mekong's tributaries, long, motorized passenger boats, also known as "slow-boats" still carry passengers between villages. As road conditions gradually improve, many of these services are dying out. Such boats still ply the Nam Ou and the Nam Tha in Northern Laos, provided water levels are high enough (normally July–Feb).

On the Mekong, **speedboats** (*heua wai*)

are a more costly but faster alternative to the plodding cargo boats. Connecting towns along the river from Vientiane all the way to the Chinese border, these five-metre terrors accommodate up to eight passengers and can shave hours off a river journey. Fares for speedboats cost two to three times the slow-boat fare. Crash helmets are handed out before journeys and life-jackets are occasionally available. Speedboats are by no means safe, though; the Mekong has some particularly tricky stretches, with narrow channels threading through rapids and past whirlpools, and can be particularly rough late in the rainy season. Although the drivers swear by their navigational skills, fatal accidents occur with an alarming frequency. Think twice about taking a speedboat. If you do, insist on a life-jacket and helmet, and be sure to bring earplugs.

On the northern routes, ports are overseen and tickets sold by government officials. The **fares** are posted but foreigners pay significantly more than locals. Southern routes are more haphazard: fares are not posted and you just bargain for and buy your ticket on the spot.

Buses

Buses in Laos range from the new, air-con tourist coaches on the Vientiane–Louang Phabang route to the rattling wrecks that serve the outlying provinces. Cramped, overloaded and extremely slow, the latter can be profound tests of endurance and patience. Flat tyres and breakdowns are frequent and, during the rainy season, unpaved roads dissolve into rivers of mud, slowing buses to a crawl.

As there are no public toilets in Laos, passengers relieve themselves by the road during breaks on long journeys – Lao women usually go further into the bushes on such occasions. Keep in mind that some areas still have unexploded ordnance about (see p.509), so it's not a good idea to go too far off the road.

Ordinary buses run between major towns, and occasionally link provincial hubs with their surrounding areas. In Vientiane, for instance, a fleet of blue, **government-owned buses** serves the capital's outlying districts. Buses plying long-distance routes tend to be in poor shape and can be either regular buses or souped-up tourist vans. In a few remote areas, converted Russian flat-bed trucks, once the mainstay of travel in Laos, still operate.

Except for buses out of major towns – where you buy a ticket from the bus station before boarding – it's common practice to pay on board. **Timetables** exist but it's always safer to get to the bus station well before your scheduled departure, especially if you want a decent seat.

Where there's no fixed departure time, you should get to the bus station between 6 and 7am, as that is when most Lao passengers travel. There are generally few departures after midday. Occasionally, buses won't even depart if there aren't enough passengers. It's also possible to flag down a bus from the side of the road, provided it's not full.

Sawngthaews

In most provinces, the lack of a bus network is made up for by **sawngthaews** – converted flat-bed trucks – into which drivers cram as many passengers as they can get onto two benches in the back. Smaller sawngthaews also ply routes between larger towns and their satellite villages, charging roughly the same as buses. They usually depart from the regular bus station, and only leave when there are enough passengers to make the trip worthwhile. If there aren't enough passengers, the driver may try to cajole extra kip out of passengers in order to get things going. The fare is paid at the end of the ride (but agreed at the beginning) and foreigners are routinely over-charged. To catch a sawngthaew in remote areas simply flag it down from the side of the road and tell the driver where you're headed. In some situations, it's better to simply hire the entire sawngthaew and driver to take you wherever it is you want to go.

Jumbos and tuk-tuks

Transport within Lao towns is by motorized *samlaw* (literally "three wheels") which function as share taxis for four or five passengers. There are two types of *samlaw*: **jumbos** and **tuk-tuks**. Jumbos are homemade three-wheelers consisting of a two-wheeled carriage soldered to the front half of a motorcycle. Tuk-tuks are just bigger, sturdier jumbos, and Lao tend to refer to these vehicles interchangeably. To catch one, flag it down and tell the driver where you're going. You pay at the end of the ride, but again, agree the fare upfront. Payment is according to the number of passengers, the distance travelled and your bargaining skills. Rates vary depending on a number of circumstances, but figure on around 5000K per kilometre. In some towns, tuk-tuks leave from a stand and run fixed routes to surrounding villages.

Vehicle rental

Self-drive car rental is possible in Laos, but unless you're experienced with local driving habits, it's easier to hire a **car and driver**. In most major towns tour agencies have air-conditioned vans and 4WD pick-up trucks, and can provide drivers as well. Prices can be as much as $80–100 per day. Always clarify who pays for fuel and repairs and the driver's food and lodging, and be sure to ask what happens in case of a major breakdown or accident. A much cheaper alternative for short distances or day-trips is to simply charter a tuk-tuk or sawngthaew. If you do have experience with driving in the region and want to do it yourself, you'll find car and pick-up truck rental service in Vientiane.

Renting a **motorbike** ($6–10 per day) is currently only an option in Vientiane, Vang Viang, Louang Phabang, Thakhek and Pakxe. Except for Vientiane – where 250cc dirt bikes are available – you'll be limited to 100cc step-throughs such as the Honda Dream. A licence is not required and insurance is not available, so it's a good idea to make sure your travel insurance covers you for any potential accidents. Before zooming off, check the bike thoroughly for any damage and take it for a test run. Few rental places will have a helmet on offer, but it doesn't hurt to ask. If you plan on touring Laos on a motorbike, consider buying a helmet in Thailand before you arrive, where they are much cheaper. **Bicycles** can also be rented from guesthouses and tourist-oriented shops for around $1 per day. Sunglasses are essential and proper shoes, long trousers and a long-sleeved shirt will provide some protection if you take a spill.

Accommodation

Inexpensive **accommodation** can be found all over Laos. For a basic double room, prices start at around $2 in the provinces and $8 in Vientiane. Moving up the scale, $25 lands you a cosy room in a restored French villa. The higher standards of accommodation are in the larger Mekong towns, particularly Vientiane and Louang Phabang. Remote towns and villages lag far behind.

Standards and **room types** can vary widely within the same establishment so always ask to see several rooms before choosing one. In the north, many towns only have **electricity** for a few hours in the evening, so you should weigh the added cost of air-con against the number of hours you'll have power to use it. Electrical wiring in budget guesthouses is usually an accident waiting to happen; even turning on the light can sometimes require caution. Electricity is supplied at 220 volts AC. Two-pin sockets are the norm.

En-suite showers and flush toilets are now found in most tourist-quality hotels. At local hotels, showers and toilets are communal and will probably be Asian-style (see "Bathrooms", p.62).

The distinction between a **guesthouse** and a **hotel** is blurred in Laos. Either can denote anything ranging from a bamboo-and-thatch hut to a multi-storey concrete building. As rooms are so cheap, few guesthouses offer dorm accommodation. Guesthouses and budget hotels don't take advance bookings unless they know you already. In order to secure a good room, it helps to check-in mid-morning, just after people begin checking out.

New, **mid-range hotels** have been opening up in medium-sized towns all over Laos for the last few years, greatly improving the accommodation situation. Most of these hotels are four or five storey and offer large rooms with tiled floors and en-suite bathrooms from $5. The beds are usually hard but the sheets and quilts are consistently clean. Bathroom fittings in such hotels are usually brand new but they don't all have hot water. Because the construction is poor and there is no concept of maintaining buildings, they tend to age very quickly.

Addresses

Lao **addresses** can be terribly confusing because property is usually numbered twice – when numbered at all – to show firstly which lot it stands in, and then to signify where it is on that lot. In addition, some cities have several conflicting address systems. To avoid unnecessary confusion, numbers have been omitted from addresses given in the guide text, and locations are described as far as possible using landmarks. Only a handful of cities in Laos actually have street names, signs are rare, and many roads change names from block to block. Use street names to find a hotel on a map in the guide text, but when asking directions or telling a tuk-tuk driver where to go, refer to a landmark, monastery or prominent hotel.

Once you cross the $20 threshold, you enter a whole new level of comfort. In the former French outposts on the Mekong, this translates into an atmospheric room in a restored **colonial villa** or recently built accommodation with cable TV, fridge, air conditioning and a hot-water shower. Colonial-era hotels usually only have a limited number of rooms, so book ahead if you plan to visit during the peak months (Dec–Jan).

If you find yourself stuck in a remote town or village overnight, someone will usually put you up in the absence of a guesthouse. In such situations you should fix the price for your food and lodging ahead of time – around 10,000K ($1) per person, or twice that if they feed you is a fair rate.

Food and drink

Fiery and fragrant, with a touch of sour, **Lao food** owes its distinctive taste to fermented fish sauces, lemon grass, coriander leaves, chillies and lime juice and is closely related to Thai cuisine. Eaten with the hands along with the staple sticky rice, much of Lao cuisine is roasted over an open fire and served with fresh herbs and vegetables. Pork, chicken, duck and water buffalo all end up in the kitchen, but freshwater fish is the main source of protein. An ingredient in many recipes is *nâm pa*, or fish sauce, which is used like salt. Most Lao cooking calls for fish sauce so you may want to order "*baw sai nâm pa*" ("without fish sauce").

Vientiane and Louang Phabang boast the country's best food, with excellent Lao food and international cuisine, but in remote towns you'll often only find noodles. Although Laos is a Buddhist country, very few Lao are **vegetarian**. It's fairly easy, however, to get a vegetable dish or a vegetable fried rice.

Hygiene is always an important consideration when eating out in Southeast Asia. All over Laos, the kitchen is often just a shack without proper lighting or even running water. Furthermore, in many northern towns, there is no electricity to run refrigeration. As a rule, sticking to tourist-class restaurants is the safest bet but it is by no means a guarantee of not getting an upset stomach.

In smaller towns and villages, there may not be any sit-down restaurants as so few people can afford to eat out. Street stalls and food shacks that do a brisk business are the safest bets but cooked food that has been left standing should be treated with suspicion. Dishes containing raw meat or raw fish are considered a delicacy in Laos, but people who eat them risk parasites.

Where to eat

The **cheapest** places for food are markets, street stalls and noodle shops. Found in most towns throughout Laos, **morning markets** (*talat sâo*) remain open all day despite their name and provide a focal point for noodle shops (*hân khãi fõe*), coffee vendors, fruit stands and sellers of crusty French loaves. In Louang Phabang and Vientiane, vendors hawking pre-made dishes gather in **evening markets** known as *talat láeng* towards late afternoon. Takeaways such as grilled chicken (*pîng kai*), spicy papaya salad (*tam màk hung*) and minced pork salad (*làp mu*) are commonly available.

Some **noodle shops** and street stalls feature a makeshift kitchen surrounded by a handful of tables and stools, inhabiting a permanent patch of pavement or even an open-air shop-house. Most stalls will specialize in only one general food type, or even only one dish, for example a stall with a mortar and pestle, unripe papayas and plastic bags full of pork rinds will only offer spicy papaya salads. Similarly, a noodle shop will generally only prepare noodles with or without broth – they won't have meat or fish dishes that are usually eaten with rice. A step up from street stalls and noodle shops are *hân kin deum*, literally "eat-drink shops", where you'll find a somewhat greater variety of dishes, as well as beer and whisky. Outside of Vientiane, street stalls and noodle shops rarely stay open beyond 8pm.

Most proper **restaurants** (*hân ahãn*) are run by ethnic Vietnamese and Chinese. Since the Lao seldom eat Lao food outside the home, there are few Lao-food restaurants. Many local eateries don't have menus – in Lao or English – so it's a good idea to memorize a few stock dishes such as fried rice (*khao phat*). Restaurants catering more to foreigners usually have an English menu and offer fried noodles and fried rice as well as a variety of Lao, Chinese and Thai dishes. Vientiane has a range of more expensive Lao restaurants, as well as good international food. A meal in one of these places won't cost more than $15.

Lao food

Most Lao meals feature **sticky rice** (*khào niaw*), which is served in a lidded wicker basket (*típ khào)* and eaten with the hands. Typically, the rice will be accompanied by a fish or meat dish and soup, with a plate of fresh vegetables, such as string beans, lettuce, basil and mint, served on the side. Grab a small chunk of rice from the basket, squeeze it into a firm wad and then dip it into one of the dishes. At the end of your meal, it's thought to be bad luck not to replace the lid. Plain, steamed, white rice (*khào jâo*) is eaten with a fork and spoon; chopsticks (*mâi thu*) are reserved for noodles.

So that a variety of tastes can be enjoyed during the course of a meal, Lao meals are eaten **communally**, with each dish, including the soup, being served at once, rather than in courses. If you're eating a meal with steamed white rice, only put a small amount of one dish onto your rice at a time; when the meal is accompanied by sticky rice, it's normal to simply dip a ball of rice into the main servings. For two of you, it's common to order two or three dishes, plus your own rice.

If Laos were to nominate a **national dish**, a strong contender would be *làp*, a "salad" of minced meat mixed with garlic, chillies, shallots, aubergine, galingale and fish sauce. *Làp* is either eaten raw (*díp*) – a culinary experience you may want to avoid – or *súk* (cooked). Another quintessentially Lao dish is *tam màk hung* (or *tam sòm*), a spicy salad made with shredded green papaya, garlic, chillies, lime juice, fish paste (*pa dàek)* and, sometimes, dried shrimp and crab. Each vendor will have their own particular recipe, but it's also acceptable to pick out which ingredients – and how many chilli peppers – you'd like. Usually not too far away from any *tam màk hung* vendor, you'll find someone selling *pîng kai*, basted grilled chicken. Fish, *pîng pa*, is another grilled favourite, with whole fish skewered and barbecued.

When the Lao aren't filling up on glutinous rice, they're busy eating *fõe*, the ubiquitous **noodle soup** that takes its name from the Vietnamese soup *pho*. Although primarily eaten for breakfast, *fõe* can be enjoyed at any time of day, and, outside of towns, may well be the mainstay of your diet. The basic bowl of *fõe* consists of a light broth, to which is added thin rice noodles and slices of meat (usually beef, water buffalo or grilled chicken) and is served with a plate of lettuce, mint and coriander leaves and bean sprouts. Also on offer at many noodle shops is *mi*, a yellow wheat noodle served in broth with slices of meat and a few vegetables. It's also common to eat *fõe* and *mi* without broth (*hàeng*), and at times fried (*khùa*).

The best way to round off a meal is with **fresh fruit** (*màk mâi*), as the country offers a wide variety, including guavas, lychees, rambutans, mangosteen and pomelos. Sweets don't figure on many restaurant menus, although some offer desserts such as banana in coconut milk (*nâm wãn màk kûay*). Markets often have a food stall specializing in inexpensive **coconut-milk desserts**, generally called *nâm wãn*. Look for a stall displaying a dozen bowls,

Food and drink glossary

Useful words and phrases

Do you have a menu?	*mi laikan ahãn baw?*
Do you have...?	*mi...baw?*
Not spicy...	*baw phét*
I am vegetarian	*khói kin te phák*
I would like...	*khói ao...*
Can I have the bill?	*khãw sek dae*
Without fish sauce	*baw sai nâm pa*
I can't eat meat	*khói kin sîn baw dâi*
No sugar	*baw sai nâm tan*
No ice	*baw sai nâm kâwn*
Bon appétit	*soen sàep*
Delicious	*sàep*
Fork	*sawm*
Spoon	*buang*
Noodle shop	*hãn kãi fõe*
Restaurant	*hân ahãn*

Staples

jeun khai	omelette
kai	chicken
khai dao	egg, fried
khào jâo	rice, steamed
khào ji	bread
khào niaw	rice, sticky
kûng	shrimp
màk kûay	banana
màk len	tomato
màk mo	watermelon
màk muang	mango
màk náo	lime/lemon
màk nat	pineapple
màk phét	chilli
mu	pork
nâm pa	fish sauce
nâm tan	sugar
nóm sòm	yoghurt
pa	fish
pa dàek	fish paste
pét	duck
phák	vegetables
phõng sú lot	MSG
pu	crab
sìn ngúa	beef
tâo hû	bean curd

Noodles

fõe	rice noodle soup
fõe hàeng	rice noodle soup without broth
fõe khùa	fried rice noodles
khào piak sèn	rice noodle soup, served in chicken broth

containing everything from water chestnuts to fluorescent green and pink jellies, from which one or two items are selected and then added to a sweet mixture of crushed ice, slabs of young coconut meat and coconut milk.

Drinks

The Lao don't drink **water** straight from the tap and nor should you; contaminated water is a major cause of sickness (see "Food and water", p.54). Plastic bottles of drinking water (*nâm deum*) are sold countrywide for around 2000K, even in smaller towns. Noodle shops and inexpensive restaurants generally serve free pitchers of weak tea or boiled water (*nâm tóm*), which is fine, although perhaps not as foolproof. Most **ice** in Laos is produced in large blocks under hygienic conditions, but it can become less pure in transit or storage, so be wary. Brand-name soft drinks are widely available for around 6000K per bottle or 10,000K per can. More refreshing are the **fruit shakes** (*màk mâi pan*) available in larger towns, which consist of your choice of fruit blended with ice, liquid sugar and sweetened condensed milk. Freshly squeezed fruit juices, such as lemon (*nâm màk nao*) and coconut juice (*nâm màk phao*) are a popular alternative, as is sugar-cane juice (*nâm oi*).

Twenty thousand tonnes of **coffee** are produced in Laos annually, nearly all of it grown on the Bolaven Plateau, outside Pakxong in southern Laos. The Lao drink very strong coffee, or *kafeh hâwn*, which is served with sweetened condensed milk and sugar. If you prefer your coffee black, and without sugar, ask for *kafeh dam baw sai nâm tan*. Black **tea** is available at most coffee vendors and is what you get, mixed with sweetened condensed milk, when you request *sá hâwn*.

Just about everybody agrees that **Beer Lao** (*Bia Lao*) is a very enjoyable brew and

khào pûn	flour noodles with sauce
mi hàeng	yellow wheat noodles without broth
mi nâm	yellow wheat noodle soup

Everyday dishes

khào ji pateh	bread with Lao-style pâté and vegetables
khào ji sai boe	bread with butter
khào khùa or khào phát	fried rice
khào khùa sai kai	fried rice with chicken
khùa khing kai	chicken with ginger
khùa phák baw sai sìn	stir-fried vegetables
làp mu	minced pork
man falang jeun	chips
mu phát bai hólapha	pork with basil over rice
pîng kai	grilled chicken
pîng pa or jeun pa	grilled fish
tam màk hung	spicy papaya salad
tôm yam pa	spicy fish soup with lemon grass
yam sìn ngúa	spicy beef salad
yáw díp	spring rolls, fresh
yáw jeun	spring rolls, fried

Drinks

bia	beer
bia sót	beer, draught
kafeh	coffee
kafeh dam	black coffee
kafeh nóm hawn	hot Lao coffee (with milk and sugar)
kafeh nóm yén	iced coffee (with milk and sugar)
lào-láo	rice whisky
màk kuay pan	banana shake
màk mai pan	fruit shake
nâm deum	water
nâm kâwn	ice
nâm màk phâo	coconut juice
nâm sá	tea
nâm soda	soda water
nâm yén	water, cold
nóm	milk
sá jin	tea, Chinese

very cheap as well. Some foreign beers are also available but Beer Lao is far more popular and the cheapest at 6000k a bottle. In Vientiane and Louang Phabang, draft Beer Lao known as *bia sót*, is available at bargain prices by the litre. There are dozens of *bia sót* outlets in the capital, most of which are outdoor beer gardens with thatch roofs. Drunk with equal gusto is *lào-láo*, a clear **rice alcohol** with the fire of a blinding Mississippi moonshine. Although the government distils its own brand, Sticky Rice, which is sold nationally, most people indulge in local brews. *Lào-láo* is usually sold in whatever bottle the distiller had around at the time (look twice before you buy that bottle of Fanta) and is sold at drink shops and general stores for around 5000K per 750ml. Drunk from a large earthenware jar with thin bamboo straws, the rice alcohol *lào hái* is fermented by households in the countryside and is weaker *than lào-láo*, closer to a wine in taste. Drinking *lào hái*, however, can be a bit risky, as unboiled water is sometimes added during fermentation. Several brand-name rice whiskies, with a lower alcohol content than *lào-láo*, are available for around $1 per bottle at local general stores.

Communications

Mail takes one to two weeks in or out of Laos. Express Mail Service operates to most Western countries and certain destinations within Laos; the service cuts down on delivery time and automatically registers your letter. When sending parcels, leave the package open for inspection. However, it's not advisable to ship anything of value home from Laos; if you're going to Thailand, wait and send it from there. Incoming **parcels** are also subject to inspection.

Poste restante services are available in

Vientiane and Louang Phabang; always address mail using the country's official name, "Lao PDR", rather than "Laos". See "Poste restante", p.63 for further information on poste restante.

The best place to make **overseas telephone calls** is the local Telecom Office (8am–9pm); elsewhere, international calls can sometimes be placed at the post office. To **call abroad** from Laos, dial ⓣ00 + IDD country code (see "IDD codes" box, p.64) + area code minus first 0 + subscriber number. Calls cost approximately $3 per minute to the UK and North America, $1.50 to New Zealand and less than $1 to Australia. There's no facility for collect or reverse-charge calls, but you can often get a "call back" for a small fee: ask the operator for the minimum call abroad and then get the person you're calling to ring you back. International **fax** services are available at upmarket hotels in Vientiane and Louang Phabang and at most provincial post offices.

Public **card-phones** are wired for both domestic and international calls. Phone booths are usually stationed outside post offices in provincial capitals, and occasionally elsewhere in larger towns. Phonecards (*bat tholasap*; $2.50–6) are sold at shops and post and telephone offices in several denominations of time "units"; these are units of time rather than money. Because of high charges for overseas calls and the low amount of time units available, it's difficult to make an overseas call that lasts for more than a few minutes before you're cut off. Local calls can be made at hotels and guesthouses for a small fee. **Regional codes** are given throughout the chapter: the "0" must be dialled before all long-distance calls.

The emergence of an Internet Service Provider (ISP) in Laos has drastically reduced the price and increased the availability of access to the Web. Currently, you'll find email and **Internet** services at cybercafés and computer shops in Vientiane, Louang Phabang, Vang Viang, Oudomxai, Houayxai, Thakhek, Savannakhet and Pakxe, although it won't be long before these services spring up in other parts of the country. **Charges** range from 100K to 200K per minute, or 10,000K per hour. For details on using email as an alternative to poste restante, see p.65.

Time differences

Laos is seven hours ahead of London (GMT), twelve hours ahead of New York, fifteen hours ahead of San Francisco, three hours behind Sydney and five hours behind Auckland.

Opening hours and festivals

In 1998, the official **working hours** of all government offices were adjusted. The two-hour lunch break was shortened to one, and government workers were given Saturday off. Old habits die hard though, which means that while official hours for **government offices** are 8am–noon and 1–5pm Monday to Friday, very little gets done between 11am and 2pm. **Post offices** are generally open 8am–5pm Monday to Friday, 8am–4pm on Saturday and 8am–noon on Sunday. **Banking hours** are usually 8.30am–noon and 1–4pm, Monday to Friday nationwide; exchange kiosks keep longer hours but are rare. The hours of private **businesses** vary, but almost all are closed on Sunday. During the heat of the day many shop owners will partly close their doors and snooze, but it is perfectly acceptable to wake them up. All government businesses close on public holidays, though some shops and restaurants should stay open. The only time when many private businesses do close – for three to seven days – is during Chinese New Year (new moon in late Jan to mid-Feb), when the ethnic-Vietnamese and Chinese populations of Vientiane, Thakhek, Savannakhet and Pakxe celebrate with parties and temple visits.

Festivals

All major **festivals**, whether Buddhist or animist, feature parades, music and dancing, not to mention the copious consumption of *lào-láo*. Because the Lao calendar is dictated by both solar and lunar rhythms, the

Public holidays

January 1: New Year's Day
January 6: Pathet Lao Day
January 20: Army Day
March 8: Women's Day
March 22: Lao People's Party Day
April 13–16: Lao New Year
May 1: International Labour Day
June 1: Children's Day
August 13: Lao Isara
August 23: Liberation Day
October 12: Freedom from France Day
December 2: National Day

dates of festivals change from year to year. Tourists are usually welcome to participate in the more public Buddhist festivals, but at hilltribe festivals, you should only watch from a distance.

Festivals of most interest to tourists include **Lao New Year**, *pi mai lao* (April 13–16), which is most stunningly observed in Louang Phabang, where there's a big procession, and sand stupas are erected in monastery grounds. In Vientiane and most everywhere else in the country, you'll be ambushed by young people carrying pails of water and armed with squirt guns. Also known as the "Rocket Festival", **Bun Bang Fai** (May) is a rainmaking ritual that predates Buddhism in Laos, and involves launching crude rockets, accompanied by plenty of bawdy jokes and props. **Lai Heua Fai** (full moon in October) is a festival of lights, again most magically celebrated in Louang Phabang, where each neighbourhood builds a large float, festoons it with lights, and parades it first through the streets and then on the Mekong. In the days leading up to the **That Louang Festival** (full moon in November), Vientiane's great stupa becomes the centrepiece of a fairground, where vendors, musicians and other performers gather for the annual celebrations.

Cultural hints

Laos by and large shares the same attitudes to dress and **social taboos** as other Theravada Buddhist Southeast Asian cultures; see "Cultural hints", p.68, for details. The lowland Lao traditionally **greet** each other with a *nop* – bringing their hands together in a prayer-like gesture. The status of the persons giving and returning the *nop* determines how they will execute it, so most Lao prefer to shake hands with Westerners. If you do receive a *nop* as a gesture of greeting or thank you, it is best to reply with a smile and nod of the head, the customary way for strangers to show that they mean well.

Crime and safety

Laos is a relatively **safe country** for travellers. For the most part, if you keep your wits about you, you shouldn't have any problems. In Vientiane, avoid walking alone on dark streets late at night. If you do have anything stolen, you'll need to get the police to write up a report for your insurance: bring along a translator if you can. Women should be wary of Lao monks and novices who try to lure them into an isolated part of the monastery. There have been incidents, especially in Louang Phabang, where monks or novices have attempted to rape foreign women.

Banditry

The section of **Route 13** between Kasi and Vang Viang continues to be the target of Hmong bandits and insurgents. Although the risk is very small, it's a good idea to ask around before taking a bus that traverses this route. South of Route 7 lies the **Xaisomboun Special Zone**, an administrative district carved out of parts of Xiang Khouang and Bolikhamxai provinces and controlled by the army. It is considered unsafe and is currently closed to tourists. **Route 6** from Muang Khoun to Pakxan in the eastern part of the Special Zone should be avoided. Likewise, take extra precautions and ask around before setting out on Route 7 between Phonsavan and Phou Khoun.

Unexploded ordnance

The Second Indochina War left Laos with a legacy of **bombs**, **land mines** and **mortar shells** that will haunt the country for decades to come, despite the efforts of de-mining organizations. Round, tennis-ball sized anti-personnel bomblets, known as "bombi", are the most common type of **unexploded ordnance** (UXO), and large bombs, ranging in size from 100kg to 1000kg, also proliferate. Ten provinces have one or more districts severely contaminated with UXO. Listed in descending order of contamination they are: Savannakhet, Xiang Khouang, Salavan, Khammouan, Xekong, Champasak, Saisomboun, Houa Phan, Attapu and Louang Phabang. Another five provinces have at least one district with significant contamination: Louang Namtha, Phongsali, Bolikhamxai, Vientiane province and Vientiane prefecture.

Although most towns and tourist sites are free of UXO, 25 percent of villages remain contaminated and accidents continue at a rate of two hundred per year. As accidents often occur while people are tending their fields, the risk faced by the average visitor is extremely limited. Nonetheless, the number-one rule is: don't be a trailblazer. When in rural areas, always stay on well-worn paths, even when passing through a village, and don't pick up or kick at anything if you don't know what it is. Take special care in areas known to be heavily contaminated, such as the districts surrounding the former Ho Chi Minh Trail.

Drugs

It is **illegal** to smoke ganja and opium in Laos although it continues to be available in some places. Tourists who use illegal drugs risk substantial "fines" if caught by police, who do not need a warrant to search you or your room. Since 2001, there have been wide-scale government crack-downs on drug tourism, and opium dens in tourist centres such as Vang Viang and Muang Sing have been shut down.

Emergency numbers

In **Vientiane** dial the following numbers: fire ☎190, ambulance ☎195, police ☎191. There are no emergency numbers for the rest of the country.

Medical care and emergencies

You'll find **pharmacies** in all the major towns and cities. Pharmacists in Vientiane and Louang Phabang are quite knowledgeable and have a decent supply of medicines.

Healthcare in Laos is so poor as to be virtually non-existent. The nearest **medical care** of any competence is in neighbouring Thailand, and if you find yourself afflicted by anything more serious than travellers' diarrhoea, it's best to head for the closest Thai border crossing and check into a hospital. A clinic attached to the Australian embassy in Vientiane is mainly for embassy personnel, but can be relied upon in extreme emergencies.

History

Laos as a unified state within its present geographical boundaries has only existed for little more than one hundred years. Its national history stretches back six centuries to the legendary kingdom of Lane Xang, once a rival to the powerful empires of mainland Southeast Asia.

The beginnings

The earliest known **indigenous culture** in Laos was an iron-age megalithic people that lived on the Plain of Jars, at the centre of trade routes to China, Vietnam and points south. The early inhabitants of Laos and the surrounding parts of central and southern Indochina spoke Austroasiatic languages such as Mon and Khmer, while the ancestors of the lowland Lao spoke proto-Tai languages, and were still living in the river valleys of southeastern China.

With the lowlands to the east and northeast densely settled by Vietnamese and Chinese populations, the **Tai** peoples slowly migrated west and southwest into northern Laos and southern Yunnan, displacing the sparse indigenous population of Austronesian and Austroasiatic groups and forcing them into the less desirable upland areas – where their descendants still live today. This migration of the Tai is reflected in the Lao legend of **Khoun Borom**, the heavenly first ancestor, a version of which dates this event in 698 AD.

Early influences

The cultural roots of the present-day Lao lie in **Indian civilization**, not Chinese. From the first century AD, Indian traders began introducing Buddhism to Southeast Asia, and between the sixth and ninth centuries, upper Laos, along with central and northeastern Thailand, was dominated by the Theravada Buddhist culture of the Mon people, known as **Dvaravati**.

As the ninth century drew to a close, Dvaravati's influence was rapidly being eclipsed by the **Khmer Empire** of Angkor. At its height, the mostly Hindu Khmer Empire extended from its core of Cambodia and lower northeastern Thailand into Vietnam, central Thailand and Laos, where it built dozens of Angkor-style temple complexes.

The rise of Lane Xang

By the thirteenth century, Louang Phabang had emerged as one of the chief Tai centres of the Upper Mekong, an area settled by people who called themselves **Lao**. A century later, though still significant, Louang Phabang, then known as Xiang Dong Xiang Thong, had become but one of many small Lao principalities on the fringes of two larger Tai states: Lan Na, centred on Chiang Mai, and Sukhothai.

Lao legends tell of a young prince called **Fa Ngum** who was cast out of Xiang Dong Xiang Thong principality, only to be taken in by the Khmer court at Angkor, where he married a Khmer princess. Provided with an army by the Khmer king, Fa Ngum fought his way up the Mekong valley in 1351 – subduing the principalities of the lower Mekong valley, capturing Muang Phuan, the capital of Xiang Khouang principality, and then ascending the throne in Xiang Dong Xiang Thong in 1353. Fa Ngum called his new kingdom **Lan Xang Hom Khao** – the "Kingdom of a Million Elephants and the White Parasol" – and during his reign expanded its borders south into northeastern Thailand and north into present-day Xishuangbanna in China.

Fa Ngum's son, Oun Heuan (1373–1417), ruled peacefully for 43 years, but there then followed a turbulent period culminating in a major Vietnamese invasion in 1479, which destroyed Xiang Dong Xiang Thong. But Lane Xang recovered quickly, coalescing in particular under Visoun (1500–1520), who reinforced the role of Buddhism in Laos by bringing the golden Buddha image, the **Pha Bang**, to Xiang Dong Xiang Thong from Vientiane in 1512 and establishing it as the symbol of a unified kingdom.

The Burmese invasions

By the time Visoun's grandson, Setthathilat (1548–1571), came to power, Burma was becoming an increasing threat to Lane Xang, so he officially moved his capital to the more strategically sited **Vientiane** in 1563; the revered Pha Bang was left in Xiang Dong Xiang Thong, and the city renamed after it. Despite the relocation, Burmese warrior-kings still managed to reduce Lane Xang (along with Lan Na and Ayutthaya) to vassalage within a decade.

The division of Lane Xang

The decisive character who returned stability to the kingdom and eventually ushered in the **Golden Age** of Lane Xang was Sourinyavongsa (1637–1694). He aligned Lane Xang through marriage with neighbouring powers, invaded Xiang Khouang, forged a border treaty with Vietnam, and confirmed the watershed line between the Mekong and the Chao Phraya rivers as the frontier with Ayutthaya.

Following Sourinyavongsa's death in 1694, however, the three regions of the country went their separate ways. Sourinyavongsa's grandson Kingkitsalat became the first ruler of an **independent Louang Phabang kingdom**, while another prince, who called himself Setthathilat II, ruled over Vientiane.

Meanwhile, the kingdom was further divided by the emergence of a new ruling house in the south, at **Champasak**, under a long lost son of Sourinyavongsa, King Soi Sisamut. Rivalry between Louang Phabang and Vientiane was bitter, however, and when a second wave of Burmese invasions swept across the Tai world in the 1760s, forces from Vientiane aligned with the invaders and helped sack Louang Phabang.

The rise of Siam

In 1767, the Burmese also razed Ayutthaya, but the **Siamese** quickly rebuilt their kingdom downriver from the city, near Bangkok, and within a decade had retaken its territory, and were preparing to expand eastwards. Twenty thousand Siamese soldiers set out for Vientiane in 1778, devastating the city and dragging hundreds of prisoners back to Thailand, as well as the kingdom's precious Pha Bang image. Champasak and Vientiane were reduced to vassal states and Louang Phabang brought into an unequal alliance.

Over the next century, Siam and Vietnam jockeyed for control over the fragmented Lao muang, or principalities, with the Lao territories eventually forming a buffer zone between the two powers. This balancing act was upset, however, by the arrival of the French.

French rule

France's initial interest in Laos stemmed from a belief that the Mekong River would provide a backdoor route to China and the resource-rich Yunnan region. Although the Mekong Exploration Commission of 1867–1868 soon discovered that significant stretches of the river were unnavigable, enthusiasm for Laos was rekindled by explorer **Auguste Pavie**, who conducted a "conquest of hearts" in the name of France in the 1880s and 1890s. As vice-consul in Louang Phabang, Pavie persuaded the northern kingdom to pay tribute to France instead of Siam, and by 1893, Siam had relinquished its claim to all territory east of the Mekong River.

For half a century, Laos was ruled as a French colony, with Vientiane as the administrative capital, a period during which the country's present-day borders began to take shape. But the French interest was half-hearted and Laos was in reality a neglected backwater of France's other Southeast Asian acquisitions.

World War II

The fall of France to Germany in 1940 suddenly changed the political landscape. The Japanese occupied Laos, and Siam, renamed Thailand in 1939, seized the west-bank territories of Xainyabouli and Champasak. In April 1945, the Japanese forced Sisavang Vong, the pro-French Lao king, to declare independence. Prince Phetsarath, viceroy of the royal house of Louang Phabang, became prime minister and an independent-minded Lao elite formed a government that became known as the **Lao Issara**, literally "Free Laos". Phetsarath wanted the Kingdom of Louang Phabang and the territory of Champasak to be a single, independent Kingdom of Laos, and King Sisavang Vong was deposed.

The **Potsdam Agreement**, which marked the end of World War II, failed to recognize the Lao Issara government. In March 1946, French reoccupation forces, along with their Lao allies, recaptured Vientiane and Louang Phabang. Thousands of Lao Issara supporters fled to Thailand, where Phetsarath established a government-in-exile in Bangkok, as the French reasserted their control over Laos.

The Kingdom of Laos

By early 1947, the Kingdom of Laos had begun to take shape as Laos – under French political, military and economic control – became unified under the royal house of Louang Phabang.

The French, however, were increasingly bogged down in their struggle with Vietnam's nationalist Viet Minh, which had erupted in December 1946 and was to become known as the First Indochina War. The **Viet Minh** were also active in Laos, participating in Lao Issara guerrilla raids on French convoys and garrisons. In July 1949, France appealed to the more moderate elements of the Lao Issara by conceding greater authority and independence to the Vientiane government. The Lao Issara announced its dissolution.

While the moderate members of the dissolved Lao Issara joined the new Royal Lao Government (RLG) in 1950, Souphanouvong (younger brother of Phetsarath) founded the resistance group **Pathet Lao**, literally "the Land of the Lao", which called for a truly independent Laos to be governed by a coalition government with the RLG. The group pledged to co-operate with the Vietnamese and Khmer in the struggle against the French, and set about recruiting for the Lao People's Party and the Liberation Army.

The First Indochina War

By the early 1950s, the **First Indochina War** had engulfed the region. Chinese military aid flowed to the Viet Minh, while the United States supported France. For the Viet Minh, Laos was an extension of their battle against the French. Twice in 1953 they staged major invasions of Laos, seizing large areas of the country and turning them over to the Pathet Lao. By the time full independence was granted in October 1953, Laos was a divided country, with large areas controlled by the Pathet Lao and the rest of the country under the Royal Lao Government. Eventually, the French surrendered on May 7, 1954.

At the **Geneva Conference**, which convened on May 8, Laos was reaffirmed as a unitary, independent state with a single government. The Royal Lao Government agreed not to pursue a policy of aggression or to allow a foreign power to use its soil for hostile purposes. And the Pathet Lao were allotted the provinces of Phongsali and Houa Phan in which to regroup.

America intervenes

After the 1954 Geneva Accords (which the US did not sign), the administration of US President Dwight Eisenhower made it a priority to strengthen Indochina's anti-communist governments. US policy was motivated by the fear of a chain reaction that could follow in Southeast Asia if Indochina was overrun by communism – the so-called **Domino Effect**.

As of 1955, the US was **bankrolling** the Royal Lao Army, countering the Viet Minh, which was financing the Pathet Lao's army. For the next eight years, the US spent more on foreign aid to Laos per capita than it did on any other Southeast Asian country, including South Vietnam.

When the **elections** of May 1958 gave leftist candidates 21 seats in the National Assembly, a concerned United States got worried and engineered the collapse of the government led by the moderate Prince Souvannaphouma (Phetsarath's younger brother) and the arrest of Pathet Lao leaders, including Souphanouvong. Power in Vientiane had shifted to the American Embassy, and civil war in Laos seemed inevitable.

With help from the US-backed Committee for the Defence of National Interests (CDNI), Minister of Defence Phoumi Nosavan, a ruthless and powerful general, staged a coup in December, and when new elections were held, a rigged ballot left the leftists without a seat. As a result, national support for the **Pathet Lao** increased, and by 1960, roughly twenty percent of the population was no longer under government control. Meanwhile, all fifteen Pathet Lao prisoners, including Souphanouvong, escaped from jail.

The Laotian crisis

In August 1960, self-proclaimed "neutralist" Kong Le seized control of Vientiane, and invited Souvannaphouma to lead a new government. Phoumi, who refused to join Souvannaphouma's government, gained the backing of the CIA and in November began marching forces on Vientiane. The Soviet Union responded by airlifting supplies to Kong Le's neutralist forces. Laos was now at the centre of a **Cold War** showdown. By the time Phoumi's troops reached Vientiane in December, the neutralists had allied themselves with the Pathet Lao and the Viet Minh. With both sides reluctant to spill Lao blood, a sloppy battle ensued that was won by the rightists.

By March 1961, however, the Americans had decided Laos wasn't worth fighting over after all, and President Kennedy announced support for a political settlement. A draw was preferable to losing Laos. A second conference was convened at Geneva, resulting in a new coalition government and an agreement that all foreign military personnel would leave Laos. For the US, Laos was now seen, in the words of Secretary of State Dean Rusk, as little more than "the wart on the hog of Vietnam."

Meanwhile, the CIA recruited a clandestine army of ethnic **Hmong**, under the command of Vang Pao, a brilliant Hmong lieutenant-colonel. The Hmong were naturals as guerrilla soldiers: determined to defend their homeland and masters of their terrain. But by 1968, Vang Pao's forces were no longer fighting for their homeland, they were fighting for the United States, pawns of the war in Vietnam.

The Second Indochina War

Despite the 1962 accords of a second Geneva conference, Laos was being drawn increasingly into the **Second Indochina War**, as North Vietnam and the United States undermined the country's neutrality in the pursuit of their agendas in Vietnam.

Lao territory was a crucial part of the North Vietnamese war effort. They could not risk allowing the US to use northern Laos to threaten North Vietnam and they needed to control the mountainous eastern corridor of southern Laos in order to move soldiers and supplies to South Vietnam along the **Ho Chi Minh Trail**. The US saw no option but to challenge North Vietnam's strategy. So the right-wing Lao, the Americans and the Thais on the one side and the Pathet Lao, the North Vietnamese and their Chinese and Soviet backers on the other all tacitly agreed to pretend to abide by the accords, "guaranteeing Laos's neutrality" while in reality keeping the country at war.

In 1964, a new phase of the war in Laos began. With the US pushing hard for an escalation of the **bombing**, Souvannaphouma (kept in power with help from the US) gave the go-ahead for so-called "armed reconnaissance" flights over Laos, which essentially meant the US could bomb wherever it pleased.

The war took place in **total secrecy**. US ground troops were kept out and military planes had to take off outside the country. As journalist Christopher Robbins wrote, "There was another war even nastier than the one in Vietnam, and so secret that the location of the country in which it was being fought was classified." From 1964 until the ceasefire of February 1973, United States planes flew 580,944 sorties – or 177 a day – over Laos and dropped 2,093,100 tons of **bombs** – equivalent to one planeload of bombs every eight minutes around the clock for nine years – making Laos the most heavily bombed country per capita in the history of warfare.

The Lao People's Democratic Republic

The US, North Vietnam, South Vietnam and the Viet Cong at last signed the **Paris Accords** on January 27, 1973, and a ceasefire was established. In April 1974, a coalition government was formed, with Souvannaphouma as prime minister and Souphanouvong heading the National Political Consultative Council.

When Phnom Penh and then Saigon fell to communist forces in April 1975, a complete communist takeover in Laos appeared inevitable. "Liberating" towns as they went, Pathet Lao forces reached Vientiane on August 23. On December 2, 1975, the **Lao People's Democratic Republic** (PDR) was proclaimed and the abdication of King Sisavang Vatthana accepted. Kaysone Phomvihane, the party secretary-general, was named prime minister, and Souphanouvong president.

Although the Pathet Lao took power in a bloodless coup, they sent as many as fifty thousand royalists to **re-education camps**, which turned out to be malaria-ridden labour camps. (On their release, many lowland Lao left the country, and by the mid-1980s Laos had lost ten percent of its population – including an overwhelming majority of its educated class.) The communist government, fearful that the populace would rally around the figure of the king, arrested the royal family in 1977 and exiled them to Houa Phan province, where the king, queen and crown prince died – effectively extinguishing the centuries-old Lao monarchy.

The new government took over a country stripped of resources, and with an economy in a shambles. Intent on ushering in a socialist state, the Pathet Lao followed **Eastern bloc models**, collectivizing farms, centralizing control of prices, and nationalizing what little industry there was. Long-haired teenagers were obliged to get haircuts, women had to wear traditional skirts, and prostitutes and petty thieves were shipped off to re-education camps. Gradually, a less rigid form of socialism was adopted, but Laos remained one of the world's poorest countries, with a per capita income of $100.

The new thinking

In November 1986, Kaysone implemented the **New Economic Mechanism**, essentially a market economy. Political changes did not accompany the economic reforms, however, and dissenters were still arrested. But by the late 1980s, Lao refugees were returning from Thailand, and Western tourists began to visit the country. The government improved ties with Thailand, ambassadorial relations were re-established with the US in 1992, and in 1997, Laos became a member of the Association of Southeast Asian Nations.

Unfortunately, the 1997 **Asian economic crisis** proved a major setback for Laos. The Lao currency lost eighty percent of its value between June 1997 and early 1999, inflation soared to a hundred percent, direct investment plummeted and infrastructure projects were put on hold. The crisis has brought many of the weaknesses of the Lao economy to the surface, including the country's heavy reliance on foreign aid, which accounts for fifteen percent of GDP. The Lao People's Revolutionary Party (LPRP), which strictly forbids any opposing political parties within Laos, appears to have few answers for the current economic dilemma.

On October 26, 1999, a number of

students and teachers attempted to hold a **demonstration** in front of the Presidential Palace in Vientiane to protest against the desperate state of the Lao nation. In a rare show of defiance against the government, the protesters passed out a list of reforms and urged their leaders to loosen their grip on the economy and to institute more freedoms. Predictably, the government cracked down hard on the demonstrators and several were arrested and imprisoned. The Lao government was successful in suppressing news of this event and reports that did reach the outside world were brief and vague.

On January 1, 2000, the Lao government held an **exorcism ceremony** at the former royal palace in Louang Phabang in an attempt to placate the spirits of the dead royals that, the old communists believe, are avenging their own murders by ruining the Lao economy. Nearly thirty years after the Revolution, the government is still attempting to blame the monarchy for its woes.

Today, Laos remains one of Asia's poorest nations, its human rights record has yet to show signs of improvement, and the government, led by President Khamtai Siphandon, appears entrenched. However, Vientiane's long days of isolation at least appear to have passed for good; in 2004, ASEAN members flocked to the Lao capital as the country played host to its first major summit – a sign, hopefully, that the government will someday follow in the footsteps of regional powerhouses Thailand, Indonesia and Singapore and ease toward a more open society.

Religion

Theravada Buddhism is the majority religion in Laos, practised by approximately two-thirds of the population, followed by animism and ancestor worship. The remainder practise Mahayana Buddhism and Taoism, and a small percentage follow Christianity or Islam. As with many Buddhists of Southeast Asia, most Lao also make offerings to animist spirits and certain Hindu deities. For an introduction to all these faiths, see "Religion", pp.69–71.

Lao-style **Theravada Buddhism** is a blend of indigenous and borrowed beliefs and rituals that owes much to the practices of neighbouring Thailand. In particular, the Hindu deities Brahma and Indra (who were adopted by Siam after the sacking of Angkor) have become icons in the Theravada Buddhist pantheon. Chinese and Vietnamese immigrants brought Mahayana Buddhism with them, and today you may well see alongside images of the Buddha a representation of a Hindu god, such as Ganesh, or a Mahayana Buddhist deity, such as Kuan Yin.

Following the Revolution, the communists banned alms-giving, effectively making it impossible to live as a monk, as it's against Buddhist precepts for monks to cultivate plants or raise animals for food. But popular outcry forced the government to rescind these measures, and Lao Buddhism has made a strong comeback.

The Buddhist Lao still harbour vestiges of **animist beliefs**, building "spirit houses" (miniature dolls-house- or temple-style buildings on a pedestal) on their property to provide a dwelling for the spirits who have been displaced from the land by humans. Some midland and highland tribal peoples in Laos are exclusively animist, and ancestor worship in different forms is also practised by many of the highland tribes that emigrated from China, including the Akha, Hmong and Mien.

People

Laos is a country whose minorities have not been totally assimilated into the culture of the majority. The Lao government officially divides the population into three brackets, according to the elevation at which they live, though there is often no link between peoples in these brackets, as many unrelated ethnic groups may reside at any one elevation.

The lowland Lao

The so-called **Lao Loum** (or lowland Lao) live at the lowest elevations and on the land best suited for cultivation. For the most part, they are the ethnic Lao, a people related to the Thai of Thailand and the Shan of Burma. The lowland Lao make up the majority in Laos: between fifty percent and sixty percent of the population. They prefer to inhabit river valleys and practise Theravada Buddhism as well as some animist rituals. Of all the ethnicities found in Laos, the culture of the lowland Lao is dominant, mainly because it is they who hold political power. Their language is the official language, their religion is the state religion and their holy days are the official holidays.

Akin to the ethnic Lao are the **Tai Leu**, **Phuan** and **Phu Tai**, found in the northwest, the northeast and mid-south respectively. They are all Theravada Buddhists and, like the Lao, also placate animist spirits. Most have assimilated into Lao culture.

Other Tai peoples related to the Lao are the so-called **tribal Tai**, who are mostly animists. These include the Tai Daeng (Red Tai), Tai Khao (White Tai) and Tai Dam (Black Tai). Tai Dam women wear long-sleeved, tight-fitting blouses in bright colours with a row of butterfly-shaped silver buttons down the front, plus a long, indigo-coloured skirt and an indigo bonnet.

Mon-Khmer groups

The ethnic Lao believe themselves to have originally inhabited an area that is present-day Dien Bien Phu in Vietnam. As they moved southwards they displaced the original inhabitants of the region, forcing them to resettle at higher elevations. The **Khamu** of northern Laos, speakers of a Mon-Khmer language, are the most numerous of the indigenes, but have assimilated to a high degree. A large spirit house located outside the village gates attests to the Khamu belief in animism.

Another Mon-Khmer-speaking group that inhabits the north, particularly Xainyabouli province, are the **Htin**. Owing to a partial cultural ban on the use of any kind of metal, the Htin excel at fashioning bamboo baskets and fish traps.

The Bolaven Plateau in southern Laos is named for the **Laven** people, yet another Mon-Khmer-speaking group whose presence predates that of the Lao. The Laven were very quick to assimilate the ways of the southern Lao. Other Mon-Khmer-speaking minorities found in the south, particularly in Savannakhet and Salavan, include the **Bru**, who are skilled builders of animal traps; the **Gie-Trieng**, who are expert basket weavers; the **Nge**, who produce textiles featuring stylized bombs and fighter planes; and the **Katu**, a very warlike people.

Highland groups

The **Lao Soung** (literally the "high Lao") live at the highest elevations, having migrated from China at the beginning of the nineteenth century. This group includes the Hmong, Mien, Lahu and Akha.

Of these the **Hmong** are the most numerous, with a population of approximately 200,000. They migrated from China to escape persecution, and found relative freedom in Laos until the arrival of the French, who sought to tax them. This led to a number of bloody revolts. Later, a schism between two Hmong clans saw the French back one side, while the other allied itself with the fledgling Lao communist movement. The communists promised the Hmong their own independent state if they were victorious. After the French defeat, their Hmong allies were recruited by the CIA to form a "secret army" against the communists. With the communist victory in 1975, the promise of an independent homeland was conveniently forgotten and many Hmong were severely persecuted. Tens of thousands of Hmong fled to refugee camps in Thailand for eventual resettlement in the United States and France. Today, Hmong bandits (or patriots, depending on whom you talk to) continue to make some roads in northeastern Laos dangerous. Hmong apparel is among the most colourful to be found in Laos and their silver jewellery is prized by collectors. Their written language uses Roman letters and was devised by Western missionaries.

The **Mien** are linguistically related to the Hmong and also emigrated from China, but they write in Chinese characters and worship Taoist deities. Like the Hmong, they cultivate opium, which they trade for salt and other necessities. Mien women wear intricately embroidered pantaloons with a coat and turban of indigo blue and a woolly red boa. It is estimated that nearly half the population of Mien fled Laos after the communist victory.

Speakers of a Tibeto-Burman language, the **Akha** began migrating south from China's Yunnan province in the mid-nineteenth century. In Laos, they are found mainly in Phongsali and Louang Namtha provinces. Their villages are easily distinguished by the elaborate "spirit gate" hung with woven bamboo "stars" that block spirits, as well as talismanic carvings of helicopters, aeroplanes and even grenades, and crude male and female effigies. The Akha are animists and rely on a village shaman to help solve problems of health, fertility or protection against malevolent spirits. They use opium to soothe aches and pains. The Akha women's distinctive headgear is covered with rows of silver baubles and coins.

The **Lahu** inhabit areas of northwestern Laos, as well as Thailand and Burma. A branch of the Lahu tribe known as the Lahu Na, or Black Lahu, are renowned first and foremost for their hunting skills. Formerly, they used crossbows but now manufacture their own muzzle-loading rifles, which they use to hunt birds and rodents.

Books

As Laos is one of the least-known countries in the world, it should come as no surprise to find that books on Laos are hard to come by. With demand very limited, you might have more luck searching for many of the titles listed below at an online bookstore such as www.amazon.com than you would wandering the aisles of your local bookstore. The best place to buy books on Laos over the counter is at any of the major English-language bookstore chains in Thailand.

Area Handbook Series *Laos: A Country Study* (Federal Research Division, Washington DC). This comprehensive (though somewhat outdated) study provides in-depth background and analysis of Laos's economic, social and political institutions, as well as the cultural and historical factors that shape them. Also available online.

Marthe Bassenne *In Laos and Siam* (White Lotus, Bangkok). The beautifully evocative account of a French woman's 1909 journey up the Mekong River to Louang Phabang.

Tom Butcher and Dawn Ellis *Laos* (Pallas Athene). A rambling wrap-up of the country's customs, religion and history.

Sucheng Chan (ed) *Hmong Means Free* (Temple University Press). Fascinating personal narratives by three generations of Hmong refugees from five different families, which describe their lives as farmers on the hilltops of Laos, as refugees in the camps of Thailand and as immigrants in the United States.

Patricia Cheesman Naenna *Costume and Culture: Vanishing Textiles of some of the Tai Groups in Lao PDR* (published by the author). A breakdown of the myriad textiles to be found in Laos, including detailed descriptions of Lao weaving and dyeing techniques.

Grant Evans *The Politics of Ritual and Remembrance: Laos Since 1975* (University of Hawaii Press). A provocative collection of anthropological essays focusing on the rituals and social structures of Laos yesterday and today and the attempts by the post-1975 government to reinvent "Laos".

Betty Gosling *Old Luang Prabang* (Oxford University Press). Describing the history, geography and culture of the former royal capital.

Jane Hamilton-Merritt *Tragic Mountains: the Hmong, the Americans, and the Secret Wars for Laos, 1942–1992* (Indiana University Press). This impressive account, written by a correspondent during the Second Indochina War, follows the Hmong from the battlefields to life after the war.

F.J. Harmand *Laos and the Hilltribes of Indochina* (White Lotus, Bangkok). A cultural barbarian by today's standards, the French explorer's report on his late-nineteenth-century journey through southern Laos is liberally sprinkled with amusing anecdotes.

Christopher Kremmer *Stalking the Elephant Kings: In Search of Laos* (University of Hawaii Press). A journalist's search for the monarch who went missing shortly after the communists assumed power in 1975. Aside from its main theme of the fate of the Lao royals, this book contains many interesting anecdotes and a good overview of Lao politics since the revolution.

Alfred W. McCoy, with Cathleen B. Read and Leonard P. Adams II *The Politics of Heroin in Southeast Asia* (Harper & Row). This classic work lays bare the mechanics of the international opium and heroin trade and the governmental corruption behind it at the time of the Second Indochina War.

Dervla Murphy *One Foot in Laos* (Overlook Press). An Irish travel writer's impressions and opinions of Laos as it opened to independent travellers in the late 1990s.

Auguste Pavie *The Pavie Mission Indochina Papers 1879–1895* (Volume 1–6) (White Lotus, Bangkok). Published in six volumes with the original illustrations, this is the classic explorer's description of the Land of a Million Elephants on the eve of the intrusion of the modern world.

Christopher Robbins *The Ravens: Pilots of the Secret War of Laos* (Asia Books, Bangkok). Many of the details of America's secretive Laos operations during the Second Indochina War didn't come out until this gripping work by a British journalist was published in 1987. Based on interviews with American pilots who fought in Laos, this book makes exciting reading.

Martin Stuart-Fox *A History of Laos* (Cambridge University Press). Written by an Australian scholar who covered the Second Indochina War as a foreign correspondent, this is the best available overview of Laos's history.

Roger Warner *Shooting at the Moon: The Story of America's Clandestine War in Laos* (Steerforth Press). This prize-winning, thoroughly researched and crisply written account of American involvement reads like an adventure novel.

Charles Weldon MD *Tragedy in Paradise* (Asia Books, Bangkok). This book offers an eye-witness, anecdotal account of Laos during the Secret War from the first-hand perspective of a USAID field doctor in Laos at the height of the Second Indochina War from 1963 to 1974.

Language

The main language of Laos is Lao, which belongs to the Tai family of languages, which includes Thai; Shan (Tai Yai), spoken in Burma; Phuan, spoken in Laos and parts of Thailand; and Tai Leu, spoken by the Dai minority of southern China's Yunnan province. The spoken Thai of Bangkok and the spoken Lao of Vientiane are very similar, as akin as Spanish is to Portuguese, though there are pockets of Laos where no dialect of Lao, much less the Vientiane version, will be heard. Since economic liberalization, English has become the preferred foreign tongue, and it's quite possible to get by without Lao in the towns. But once out in the countryside, you will need some Lao phrases.

The **Lao script** was based on an early version of written Thai. Official government maps of Laos use a modified form of the old French transliteration system. This can create problems for English speakers, but if you keep in mind, for example, that the Lao "ou" rhymes with the French "vous" not the English "noun", reading Lao place names shouldn't be a problem. The transliteration of place names in this book follows the modified French system used by the Lao National Geographic Service. For the transliteration of Lao words in the following section, a simplified version of the same system is used. However, the Lao are quite cavalier when it comes to consistency in transliteration. In Vientiane, for instance, it is possible to see the Arch of Victory monument transliterated as "Patouxai", "Patousai", "Patuxai" and "Patusai".

Tones and markers

Lao is a **tonal language**, which means that the tone a speaker gives to a word will determine its meaning. The dialect of Lao spoken in Vientiane, which has been deemed the official language of Laos, has six tones. Thus, depending on its tone, the word "*sang*" can mean either "elephant", "craftsman", "granary", "laryngitis", a species of bamboo, or "to build". Since it's impossible to learn the six tones properly without actually hearing them, try getting a speaker of Vientiane Lao to recite numbers one to nine in Lao to you, since all six tones feature in these numbers (see p.522). "One" is a mid tone (unmarked) and since the mid and low tones are so similar, the beginner may pronounce these two tones identically. "Two" is a rising tone (~), "five" is a low-falling tone (`), "six" is a high tone (´), and "nine" is a high-falling tone (^).

Key to pronunciation

Vowels

a as the "ah" as in "autobahn"
ae as the "a" in "cat"
ai as in "Thai"
aw as in "jaw"

ao as in "Lao"
e as in "pen"
eu as in French "fleur"
i as in "mimi"
ia as in "India"
o as in "flow"
oe as in "Goethe"
u (or ou) as the "ou" in "you"
ua (or oua) as the "ua" in "truant"

Consonants

b as in "big"
d as in "dog"
f as in "fun"
h as in "hello"
j (or CH) as in "jar"
k as in "skin" (unaspirated)
kh as the "k" in "kiss"
l as in "luck"
m as in "more"
n as in "now"
ng as in "singer" (this combination sometimes appears at the beginning of a word)
ny as in the Russian "nyet"
p as in "speak" (unaspirated)
ph as the "p" in "pill"
s (or x) as in "same"
t as in "stop" (unaspirated)
th as the "t" in "tin"
w (or v) as in "wish"
y as in "yes"

Words and phrases in Lao

Questions in Lao are not normally answered with a yes or no. Instead the verb used in the question is repeated for the answer. For example: "Do you have a room?" ("*mí hàwng wàng baw*"), would be answered "Have" ("*mí*") in the affirmative or "No have" ("*baw mí*") in the negative.

Greetings and basic phrases

Hello	sabai di
How are you?	sabai di baw
I'm fine	sabai di
Can you speak English?	jâo wâo phasã angkit dâi baw
Yes	lâew
No	baw
Please	kaluna (rarely used)
Thank you	khop jai
I only speak a little Lao	khói wâo phasã láo dâi nói neung
Do you understand?	jâo khào jai baw
I don't understand	khói baw khào jai
Where are you from?	jâo má tae sãi
I'm from England/America/Australia/New Zealand	khói má tae angkit/amelika/awsteli/nyu silaen
What's your name?	jâo seu nyãng
My name is...	khói seu...
Are you married yet?	jâo taeng ngan léu baw
Yes, I'm married	taeng ngan lâew
No, I'm not married	yáng baw taeng ngan
Goodbye	lá kawn
Goodbye (in reply)	sok di

Common answers to questions

I don't know	baw hû
There isn't/aren't any	baw mí
It cannot be done	baw dâi
It's uncertain	baw nàe

Getting around

Where are you going?	pai sãi (often used as a familiar greeting)
To the market	pai talat
To the guesthouse	pai bân phak
One thousand kip per person	phù la phán kip
Where is the...?	...yu sãi
Where is the guesthouse?	bân phak yu sãi
Where is the boat launch/pier?	thà heuá yu sãi
Pharmacy	hân kãi ya
Police station	sathani tamluat
Post office	paisani
Thai embassy	sathanthut thai
Vietnamese embassy	sathanthut wiatnam
Go straight	pai sêu sêu
Turn right	lîaw khwã
Turn left	lîaw sâi
Does this vehicle go to...?	lot nî pai...baw
How much is it to go to...?	pai...thao dai
How many hours will it take?	sai wela ják sua móng
What time will the bus depart?	lot si awk ják móng
What time will we arrive?	si hâwt ják móng
How much to hire the vehicle/boat outright?	mão lot/héua thao dai

Do you agree to the price?	tók lóng lakha baw
I agree	tók lóng
I don't agree	baw tók lóng
Please stop here	jàwt nî dae
Please stop so I can urinate	jàwt thai bao dae

Accommodation

Do you have a double room?	mí hàwng sãwng tiang baw
Does the room have a fan?	hàwng mí phat lóm baw
Mosquito net	mûng
Bathroom	hàwng nâm
Toilet	suam
Air conditioning	ae yen
Blankets	phà hom
Hot water	nâm hâwn
Can I see the room?	khãw beung hàwng kawn dâi baw
How much per night?	khéun la thao dai
Can you discount the price?	lút lakha dâi baw
Where is the toilet?	hàwng suam yu sãi
I will stay two nights	si phak sãwng khéun
Do you have a laundry service?	mí bawlikan sak phà baw
Do you have bicycles for rent?	mí lot thip hâi sao baw

Shopping

How much is this?	an nî thao dai
I'd like to buy...	khói yak sêu...
Medicine	ya
Do you have...?	mí...baw
Do you have soap?	mí sabu baw
Toothpaste	yã si khâew
Washing powder	sabu fun
Toilet paper	jîa hàwng nâm
Candles	thian
Mosquito coils	ya kan nyung baep jút
I only have kip	khói mí tae ngóen kip

Numbers

0	sun
1	neung
2	sãwng
3	sãm
4	si
5	hà
6	hók
7	jét
8	pàet
9	kâo
10	síp
11, 12, 13, etc	síp ét, síp sãwng, síp sãm
20	sao
21, 22, 23, etc	sao ét, sao sãwng, sao sãm
30, 40, 50, etc	sãm síp, si síp, hà síp
100	hôi
200, 300, 400, etc	sãwng hôi, sãm hôi, si hôi
1000	phán
2000, 300, 400, etc	sãwng phán, sãm phán, si phán
10,000	síp phán
100,000	sãen
1,000,000	lân

Days of the week and time

Monday	wán jan
Tuesday	wán angkhán
Wednesday	wán phut
Thursday	wan phahát
Friday	wán súk
Saturday	wán são
Sunday	wán thít
Today	mêu nî
Yesterday	mêu wan nî
Tomorrow	mêu eun
Morning	tawn sâo
Noon	thiang wán
Afternoon	tawn bai
Early evening	tawn láeng
Late evening	tawn khám
Midnight	thiang khéun
Next week	athit nà
Now	tawn nî
Later	theua nà

Emergencies and health

Help!	suay dae
There's been an accident	mí ubatihet
I need a doctor	khói tâwng kan hã mãw
I'm not well	khói baw sabai
I have a fever	khói pen khai
I have diarrhoea	thâwng khói baw di
Please take me to the hospital	song khói pai hong mãw dae
I lost my passport	pâm doen thang khãwng khói siã hãi
My pack is missing	kheuang khãwng khói siã hãi

5.1

Vientiane and around

Hugging a bend of the Mekong River, the low-rise capital of Laos is a quaint and easygoing place compared to Southeast Asia's other frenetic capitals, looking more like a rambling collection of villages than a city. However, in the mere decade and a half since Laos reopened its doors to foreign visitors, **VIENTIANE** has changed with dizzying rapidity. Happily, most of the changes have been for the better: there's an excellent selection of restaurants and accommodation to chose from, and the city still retains much of its placid charm. Vientiane's **history** has been a turbulent one, as its meagre collection of structures from the past suggests. It had been occupied and subsequently abandoned by the Mon and then the Khmer long before the Lao king Setthathilat moved his capital here from Louang Phabang in 1560. After that, the city was overrun or occupied several times by the Burmese, Chinese and, most spectacularly, by the Siamese, who levelled the entire place in 1828. By the end of the nineteenth century, the French controlled most of what is now Laos, Cambodia and Vietnam, and had rebuilt Vientiane as an administrative capital. As with other urban centres in the region, the majority of modern Vientiane's merchant class are ethnic Chinese and Vietnamese, whose forefathers immigrated to Laos during the French era. Though the city was left relatively unscathed by the Second Indochina War, a large percentage of Vientiane's population found it necessary to escape across the Mekong after the formation of the Lao People's Democratic Republic; they were replaced by immigrants from the former "liberated zone" in northeastern Laos, further changing Vientiane's ethnic make-up. Not until the collapse of the Soviet Union in 1991 was the government forced to rethink its opinions of capitalism, paving the way for the explosion of new ventures and businesses.

Two days is sufficient to see Vientiane's sights, of which the museum of Lao art, housed at the **Haw Pha Kaew** should be high on your list. The placid Buddhist monastery known as **Wat Sisaket** offers a good half-day diversion, and you should take a ride out to **That Louang**, Laos's most important religious building, to admire the effects of a sunset on its golden surface. If the weather isn't too steamy, many visitors opt for a soak in one of Vientiane's **herbal saunas**, and then top it off with a traditional massage. A popular day-trip destination is **Xiang Khouan** or the "**Buddha Park**", a Hindu-Buddhist fantasy in ferro-concrete on the banks of the Mekong, while a couple of hours north of the capital, the laid-back town of **Vang Viang**, set amid spectacular scenery on the road to Louang Phabang, has become a travellers' favourite.

Arrival

Vientiane, located at the centre of Laos, is the main hub for all domestic travel and also has a very convenient land crossing into Thailand. Vientiane taxi drivers will accept Thai baht and American dollars as well as Lao kip.

Wattay International Airport is 6km west of downtown Vientiane. Airport facilities include **visa-on-arrival** ($30 plus one photo; see p.498 for details) and exchange services. The cheapest way of getting into town is to take a tuk-tuk or

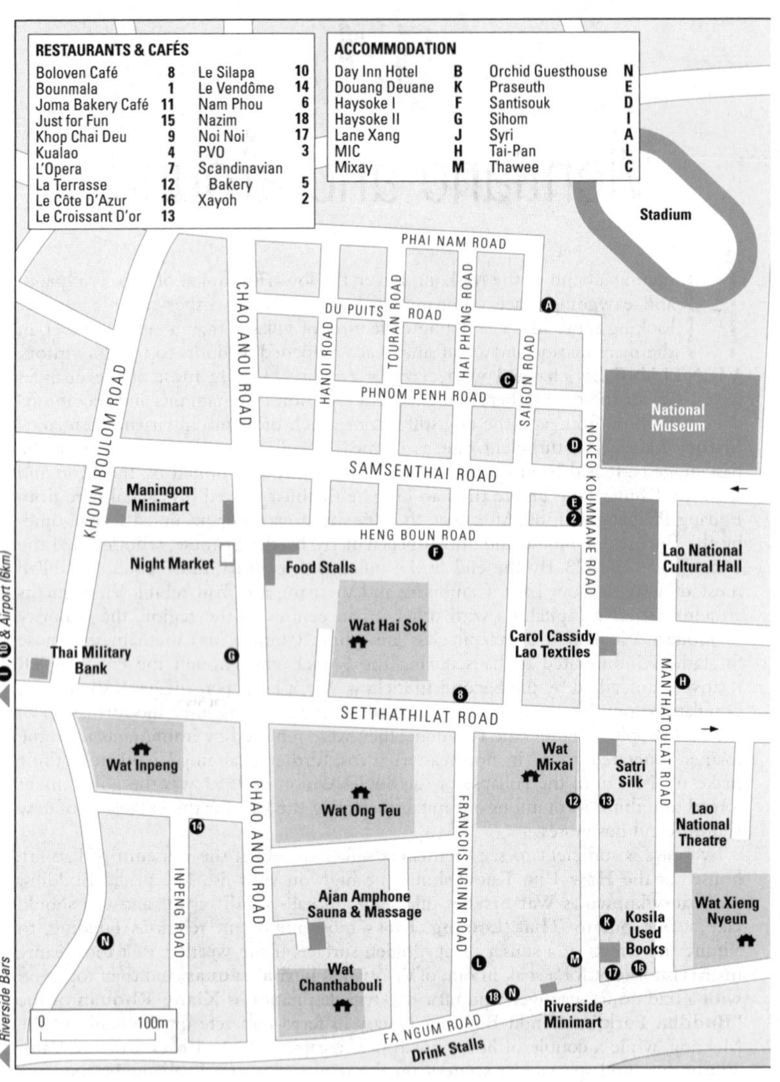

jumbo, a three-wheeled motorized taxi ($1), or a taxi ($3). Alternatively, walk out to Louang Phabang Avenue, a few hundred metres from the terminal, and hail an east-bound sawngthaew (5000K), which will drop you off anywhere along the route to the main bus station next to the Morning Market.

The major land crossing into Laos is the **Thai–Lao Friendship Bridge**, which spans the Mekong River at a point 5km west of Nong Khai in Thailand, and 20km east of Vientiane. There are two daily buses from both Nong Khai and Udon Thani in Thailand, but these are used primarily by Lao making shopping trips to Thailand. For travellers arriving in Nong Khai by bus or train from Bangkok, catch a tuk-tuk to the bridge and clear Thai immigration formalities before boarding one of the

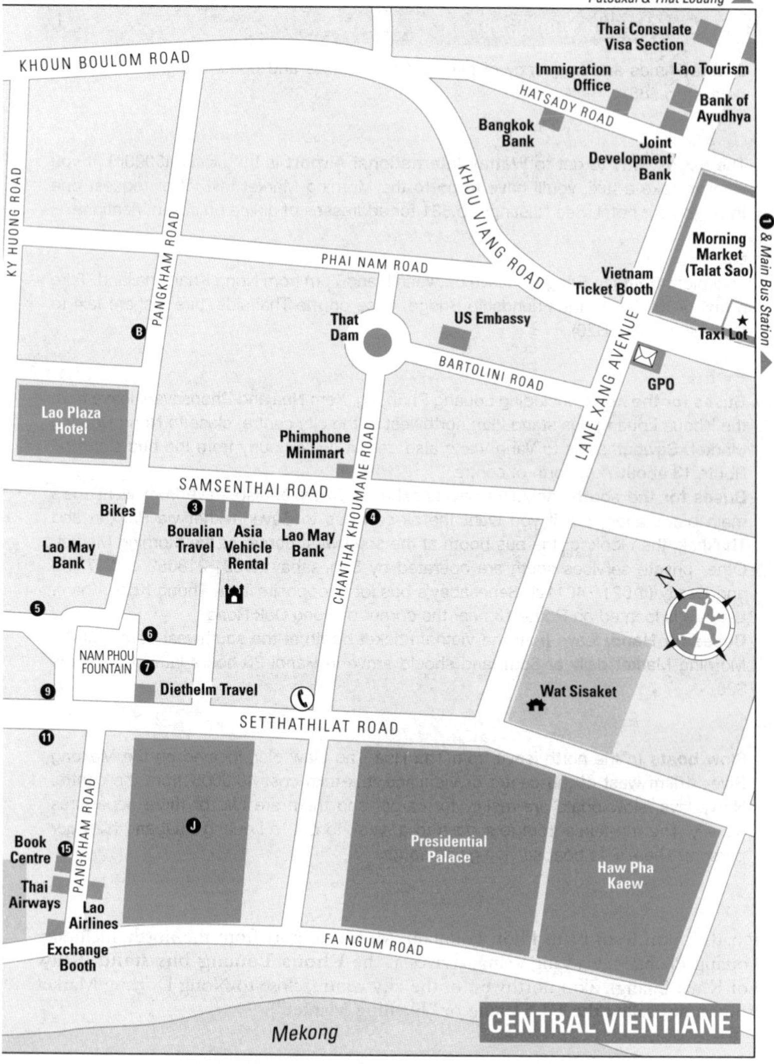

minibuses that shuttle passengers across the bridge (every 15min 8am–7.30pm; B10), stopping at **Lao immigration** on the opposite side of the river. At the Lao terminal, you can get a fifteen-day visa-on-arrival ($30 plus one photo; see p.498 for details), and change money. Tuk-tuks ($1) and car taxis ($4) run from here into the city centre (30min). The public bus is no longer allowed to pick up passengers at the bridge; if you were to hike out on the road to town and wait to catch it, chances are this overcrowded vehicle would not stop for foreigners toting backpacks. The cheapest option is to share a tuk-tuk ride with other passengers.

Most buses from the south, including Savannakhet and Pakxe, arrive at Vientiane's compact main **bus station**, next to the Morning Market (Talat Sao) on Khou Viang

Moving on from Vientiane

Journey times and frequency of planes, trains, buses and boats are given in "Travel details", p.586.

By plane

The easiest way to get to **Wattay International Airport** is by tuk-tuk (5000K); if you want to take a taxi, you'll have to go to the Morning Market taxi lot or request one through your hotel. See "Listings" p.531 for addresses of airline offices in Vientiane.

By train

Overnight **trains** to Bangkok leave between 5 and 7pm from Nong Khai, Thailand. Take a taxi or tuk-tuk to the Friendship Bridge; once on the Thai side, hire a share taxi to the train station (B20).

By bus

Buses for the north, including Louang Phabang, Xam Nua and Phonsavan, leave from the Khoua Louang bus stand 2km northwest of the city centre, close to Nong Douang Market. Sawngthaews to Vang Viang also depart twice hourly from the bus stand on Route 13 about 7km north of centre.

Buses for the south, including Savannakhet and Pakxe, also leave from Vientiane's main bus station, but if you want the air-con bus to Savannakhet via Pakxan and Thakhek, then look for the bus booth at the southwest corner of the Morning Market. Other private services south are operated by Senesabay (☎021/218052 or 217318) and Laody (☎021/740112). Senesabay's bus lot is opposite Talat Thong Khan Kham. Laody's is located on Route 13 near the corner of Dong Dok Road.

Buses for Hanoi leave from the Vietnam ticket booth at the southwest corner of the Morning Market daily at 6pm, and should arrive in Hanoi 20 hours later. The fare is $25.

By boat

Slow **boats** to the north leave from Tha Hua Kao Liaw pier, located on the Mekong River, 10km west of the centre of Vientiane; tuk-tuks cost 40,000K from the centre. Nowadays, slow boats are mainly for cargo, and there are two or three departures weekly. The trip takes from four days to a week to get to Louang Phabang ($20 per person). There's no boat service going south.

Road, 1.5km from Nam Phou Fountain. Most transport from the north, including Louang Phabang, via Vang Viang, arrives at the **Khoua Louang bus stand** (Khiw Lot Khua Luang), 2km northwest of the city centre, close to Nong Douang Market (sometimes called the Talat Laeng or "Evening Market").

Information and orientation

The fairly helpful **Lao National Tourism Authority** (NTAL; Mon–Fri 8am–5pm; ☎021/212248 or 212356) operates out of an imposing building on Lane Xang Avenue, near the Morning. Phimphone minimarkets, *Scandinavian Bakery* and *Le Croissant d'Or* (see "Eating", p.529) maintain more useful noticeboards, displaying information on everything from language classes to motorbikes for sale. Two widely available free city **maps** are the *NTAL Guide 2004*, and the slightly better LAO-ITECC *Vientiane Map*, which has large- and small-scale maps of the city.

Finding an **address** in Vientiane can be something of a challenge, as street signs are confined to the centre, road names can bleed into one another and house numbers are generally useless. As elsewhere in Laos, local inhabitants often use monasteries as landmarks to identify parts of town: for example, Ban Wat Phaxai ("Wat Phaxai village") refers to the area around Wat Phaxai. When showing addresses in this chapter, we have given the road name, but have omitted the house number, using landmarks instead.

City transport

Vientiane is a very walkable city, but **bicycles** are also handy and can be rented for $1 per day at many guesthouses and shops. Motorbikes are also easy to find ($6–10 per day) and easy to ride in Vientiane's bucolic traffic; the longest established rental shops are next door to each other on Samsenthai Road, near Pangkham Road – PVO (☎021/214444) and Boualian Travel (☎021/213061). A selection of cars and pick-up trucks can be rented for self-drive trips into the provinces at Asia Vehicle Rental (☎021/217493) on Samsenthai Road. Rates are approximately $55 per day, or you can hire a car with driver for $10 a day extra.

Otherwise, shared **tuk-tuks** and **jumbos** operate as a bus system within the city (picking up people heading in vaguely the same direction), and charge about 5000K per person around the town centre, adding about two thousand kip per kilometre beyond that. Shared tuk-tuks generally ply frequently travelled routes, such as Lane Xang Avenue between the Morning Market and That Louang and along Louang Phabang Avenue heading out from the city centre, and charge a flat fee of 2000K. There are usually a few tuk-tuks parked and waiting for foreign passengers near Nam Phou. A fleet of unmetered taxis, none with air-con, gathers outside the Morning Market, in the car park on the Khou Viang Road side of the market. Prices are negotiable.

Accommodation

The majority of Vientiane's **accommodation** is found in the central vicinity around Nam Phou within the general area formed by Khoun Boulom Road and Lang Xang Avenue. Although there are plenty of other options outside of this area, all the hotels below are within walking distance of the city centre and Nam Phou.

Day Inn Hotel Pangkham Rd ☎021/223847. A consistently well-run, mid-range hotel combining all the mod cons with a real tropical Fifties ambience. One of the best value-for-money hotels in the city, so book in advance. The restaurant downstairs does good Thai food. ⑤

Douang Deuane Nokeo Koummane Rd, near Wat Mixai ☎021/222301–3. A newish gloss and location near the Mekong make this standard mid-range hotel a worthy option. All rooms en suite with a/c, TV and phone. Offers motorbike and bicycle rental, as well as airport pick-up. ④–⑤

Haysoke I Heng Boun St ☎021/219711. Chinese-run place with good-value, fairly priced rooms. ②–③

Haysoke II Near *Haysoke I*, on Chao Anou Rd ☎021/240888. Similar good value to its namesake but more geared towards budget travellers and more atmospheric – it's the only budget option in a colonial-era building. ①–②

Lane Xang Fa Ngum Rd ☎021/214102. Once Laos's premier hotel, this place has a retro Fifties feel, a pool, spacious grounds along the quay, and 109 tremendously good-value rooms. The downside is noise on weekends – the Lane Xang is a popular venue for wedding receptions. ⑤

MIC (Ministry of Information and Culture) Manthatoulat Rd, near Setthathilat Rd ☎021/212362. This backpacker's favourite has very cheap dorms and en-suite rooms. Fills up quickly because of its rock-bottom rates. ②

Mixay Nokeo Koummane Rd, near Wat Mixai ☎021/217023. One of the cheapest places in town, with spartan but super-cheap rooms ranging from $2 dorms to fan doubles with bath ($6). ①–②

Orchid Guesthouse Fa Ngum Rd ☎021/252825. Given its location right on the main restaurant strip and facing the Mekong, the prices here are extremely reasonable. ③

Praseuth Samsenthai Rd, near the National Museum ⓣ021/217932. A friendly establishment offering large, very basic rooms with shared facilities. ❷

Santisouk Nokeo Koummane Rd, near the National Museum ⓣ021/215303. Situated above the *Santisouk Restaurant*, with nine budget a/c rooms – all recently refurbished – and an upstairs balcony. ❷

Sihom Sihom Rd, along the dirt alley to the west of *Le Silapa Restaurant* ⓣ021/214562. Eleven tastefully decorated rooms, some with a/c and satellite TV. The a/c rooms are only $1 more than fan. ❷

Syri Saigon Rd ⓣ021/212682. A large house on a quiet lane in the Chao Anou residential district, with spacious double and triple a/c rooms and a nice balcony. Motorbikes and bikes for rent. ❸

Tai-Pan François Nginn Rd, near the Mekong ⓣ021/216906–9; Bangkok bookings ⓣ02/260 9888. Vientiane's best-value business hotel, with all mod cons including Internet access and gym. Popular, so best to book in advance. ❽–❾

Thawee 64 Phnom Penh Rd ⓣ021/217903. Comfortable, well-decorated rooms for less money than a lot of the older, rundown places charge. Almost always full, so book in advance. ❶–❸

The City

A plaza surrounding **Nam Phou Fountain** marks the heart of downtown Vientiane, where you'll find the greatest concentration of accommodation, restaurants and shops catering to visitors. Once the centre of a roundabout, the fountain was recently renovated and half the roundabout blocked off, creating a pleasant public space in which both locals and visitors congregate to cool off after the sun goes down. North of Nam Phou, on Samsenthai Road, the **National Museum** (daily 8am–noon & 1–4pm; 3000K) was closed for renovation at the time of writing but when open deals primarily with the events, both ancient and recent, that led to the "inevitable victory" of the proletariat in 1975. Inside, scenes portray Lao patriots liberating the motherland from Thai and Burmese feudalists, and French colonialists bullwhipping villagers. Black-and-white photographs tell the story of the struggle against "the Japanese fascists" and "American imperialists".

Towards the eastern end of Setthathilat Road, the attractive street that runs parallel to and just south of Samsenthai Road, stands **Wat Sisaket** (daily 8am–noon & 1–4pm; 2000K), the oldest wat in Vientiane. Constructed by King Anouvong (Chao Anou) in 1818, it was the only monastery to survive the Siamese sacking ten years later. Surrounded by a tile-roofed cloister, the *sim* (building housing the main Buddha image) contains some charming, though badly deteriorating, murals. A splendidly ornate candle holder of carved wood situated before the altar is a fine example of nineteenth-century Lao woodcarving. Outside, the cloister holds countless niches from which peer diminutive Buddhas.

Opposite Wat Sisaket stands the **Presidential Palace**, an impressive French Beaux Arts-style building, built to house the French colonial governor, and nowadays used mainly for government ceremonies. Just east of the palace, the **Haw Pha Kaew** (daily 8am–noon & 1–4pm; 2000K), once the king's personal Buddhist temple, now functions as a **museum of art and antiquities**. The temple is named for the Emerald Buddha, or Pha Kaew, which was pilfered by the Siamese in 1779 and carried off to their capital, where it remains today. The museum houses the finest collection of Lao art in the country, one of the most striking works being a Buddha in the "Beckoning Rain" pose (standing with arms to the sides and fingers pointing to the ground) and sporting a jewel-encrusted navel. Also of note are a pair of eighteenth-century terracotta *apsara*, or celestial dancers, and a highly detailed "naga throne" from Xiang Khouang that once served as a pedestal for a Buddha image. Sheltered under an adjacent pavilion is a rather poor-quality sample stone urn from the Plain of Jars.

It has been said that, along with coffee and baguettes, the Lao inherited a taste for pompous town-planning from the French. Seedy **Lane Xang Avenue**, leading off north from Setthathilat Road, was to be Vientiane's Champs Elysées and **Patouxai** its Arc de Triomphe. Popularly known as *anusawali* (Lao for "monument"), this massive ferro-concrete Arch of Victory (daily 8am–noon & 1–4pm; 2000K), 1km from the Presidential Palace, was built in the late 1950s to commemorate casualties of war on the side of the Royal Lao Government. Said to have been completed with concrete donated by the US government for the construction of an airport, the structure has been jokingly referred to as "the vertical runway". The view of Vientiane from the top is worth the climb. A handful of hawkers are sheltered by a ceiling adorned with reliefs of the Hindu deities; the walls depict characters from the Ramayana, the epic Hindu story of battles between good and evil.

One-and-a-half kilometres east of Patouxai stands the Buddhist stupa, **That Louang** (daily except Mon & public holidays 8am–noon & 1–4pm; 3000K), Laos's most important religious building and its national symbol. The original That Louang is thought to have been built in the mid-sixteenth century by King Setthathilat, whose statue stands in front, and was reported to have looked like a gold-covered "pyramid". Today's structure dates from the 1930s: the tapering golden spire of the main stupa is 45m tall and rests on a plinth of stylized lotus petals; it's surrounded on all sides by thirty short, spiky stupas. Within the cloisters are kept a collection of very worn Buddha images, some of which may have been enshrined in the original Khmer temple that once occupied the site.

Eating

The influx of tourists and a growing foreign community have given rise to **restaurants** catering to virtually every taste, from sauerkraut to Korean BBQ. Aside from tourist restaurants, there are a number of cheap travellers' cafés along Fa Ngum Road as well as riverside food stalls offering Lao staples such as *tam màk hung* (spicy papaya salad), *pîng kai* (grilled chicken) and fruit shakes. A **night market** sets up on Khoun Boulom Road and along Heng Boun Road in the early evening, and there's a more extensive version at Dong Palane Market on Ban Fai Road near Wat Ban Fai. Most of Vientiane's restaurants open for lunch and then again for dinner; no-frills eateries are usually open throughout the day, closing around 9pm. In most restaurants you'll pay on average $3 for a meal, and even in more upmarket Western restaurants you'll rarely spend more than $15.

Breakfast, bakeries and cafés

Joma Bakery Café Setthathilat Rd, just west of Nam Phou Fountain. Does the best sandwiches in town, great desserts, and good quiches and coffee. Canadian-managed with fast, friendly service. The breakfast sets here are particularly good.

Le Croissant D'or Nokeo Koummane Rd, just around the corner from *Joma Bakery Café*. The pastries and croissants here are as good as the other big two bakeries, and you can always get a seat.

Scandinavian Bakery Nam Phou. Vientiane's most popular bakery offers sandwiches and a wide selection of pastries and cookies. Usually completely overrun with tourists.

Lao food

Bounmala Khou Viang Rd, near Wat Phaxai. Classic, inexpensive Lao-beer-and-roast-chicken joint under a tin roof. Also worth sampling is the roast beef, served with *khào pun* (flour noodles in a sauce), star fruit and lettuce.

Kualao Samsenthai Rd. Lao food with traditional music and dance performances in a restored colonial-era house. Tends to cater mostly to large tour groups. Definitely overpriced but worth it if you're looking for some music and entertainment.

Noi Noi Fa Ngum Rd. Very cheap Lao, Thai and Western dishes: this is the best one of the row of five popular travellers' cafés facing the river here.

Vietnamese and Indian

Nazim Fa Ngum Rd. Indian restaurant facing the Mekong with inside and sidewalk seating. Strong on vegetarian dishes, and immensely popular with backpackers.

PVO Samsenthai Rd. Highly recommended, great-value eatery, serving fantastic submarine sandwiches, spring rolls, *nâm neuang* and *baw bun* on the spot or to go.

Western food

Boloven Café Setthathilat Rd, opposite Francois

Nginn Rd. Features European fare and coffee from the plateau for which it is named. The picture windows afford a pleasant view of a particularly leafy stretch of Setthathilat Road.

La Terrasse Nokeo Koummane Rd, near Wat Mixai. Outstanding steaks, pizza, a fair approximation of Mexican food and salads at prices lower than most of the other Western joints. Nightly BBQ from 7.30pm. Closed Sun.

Le Côte D'Azur Fa Ngum Rd, near Nokeo Koummane Rd. One of Vientiane's better restaurants, boasting terrific service and a great menu of Provençal-style seafood and pasta, plus a large selection of excellent pizzas. Closed Sun lunchtime.

Le Silapa Sihom Rd, west of the Thai Military Bank. French food served in a beautifully restored colonial shop-house. The food here is not cheap but they do feature a good-value $5 set lunch.

Le Vendôme Inpeng Rd, near Wat Inpeng. Cosy restaurant in an old house serving French and Thai food, good pizzas and very tasty calzone. Closed Sat & Sun lunchtime.

L'Opera Nam Phou, on the southern edge of the plaza, Vientiane's longest-running Italian restaurant is not as expensive as the atmosphere might suggest. The vegetarian lasagne is a winner.

Nam Phou Restaurant Nam Phou, on edge of the plaza. Offers Continental cuisine, with outdoor seating that makes the most of the new incarnation of Vientiane's old fountain. Moderately expensive for Vientiane but worth a splurge for the charming alfresco dining.

Xayoh Corner of Samsenthai and Nokeo Koummane, facing the Lao National Cultural Hall. This is Vientiane's latest, greatest yuppie-style bistro serving burgers and salads as well as coffees and desserts.

Vegetarian

Just for Fun Pangkham Rd. Time your meal at this tiny, clean vegetarian-friendly restaurant to avoid the lunchtime crowds, as the tasty over-rice dishes are very good value. Also does some of the best chocolate cake in town and a great selection of herbal teas. Closed Sun.

Nightlife and entertainment

Vientiane's location along an east–west stretch of the Mekong positions it for spectacular sunsets, and makeshift **stalls** selling bottles of Beer Lao and fruit shakes set up on the riverfront sidewalk every afternoon. Heading west upriver along Fa Ngum Road, a score of **beer gardens** with wooden terraces over the riverbank continues well past the *Riverview Hotel*. These places seem to go through a couple of name changes each year, but a stroll down the river road is the best way to ascertain which is the most popular at any given time – just look for the rows of motorbikes parked out front.

Many of Vientiane's **nightclubs** feature live music, $2 cans of beer, dim lighting, deep couches and absurdly overdressed hostesses; the nightclub at the *Lane Xang Hotel* is a good option for checking out this scene. A newer set of dance clubs playing Thai pop and international dance mixes, catering to well-heeled teenagers, has cropped up along Louang Phabang Avenue, just beyond the *Novotel*. They don't usually get going until after 9pm, and are unplugged by 2am at the latest. There's normally no cover charge, but if there is it will include a $2-a-bottle Beer Lao. Sadly, Vientiane's live music scene is largely derivative, popular taste being overwhelmed by a flood of Made-in-Thailand pop. Late nights in Vientiane are not always guaranteed. For the last couple of years there has been an on-again off-again 11pm curfew.

Performances at the **National Theatre** (℗021/242978) located on Manthatoulat Road near Wat Xieng Nyeun, feature lowland Lao music, dance and even a mock wedding ceremony. Equally colourful are lowland renditions of the music and dance of the hilltribe peoples. While the costumes and numbers aren't always strictly traditional, the enthusiasm of the performers makes up for any liberties taken in the authenticity department. Shows are nightly at 8.30pm, except the third Sunday of every month, and cost $7 for adults and $4 for children under 12.

Bars and clubs

Chess Café Sakkalin Rd. Something of a pick-up bar, with deafening Thai pop, where Lao youths come to shake their post-communist booties.

Gecko Club *Royal Dokmaideng Hotel*, Lane Xang Ave. An interesting place to get a cocktail and people-watch. Popular hangout for the twenty-something expat crowd and the children of the new elite.

Khop Chai Deu Nam Phou Fountain. Popular outdoor café with cheap pitchers of draft beer and passable Lao, Indian, and falang food. Full of tourists, yes, but still the most fun place in town.
Marina Louang Phabang Ave, 3km west of the centre. The best of a number of big discos on the edge of town for Lao teenagers, with a good dance floor and a separate bar.
Sala Sunset Khounta Fa Ngum Rd. Known to some simply as "*The End of the World*" and others as "*The Sunset Bar*", the original spot for sundowners in Vientiane was expanded owing to its immense popularity with expats and tour groups, but it still ends up crowded at sunset. Get here early to sample the *tam kûay tani*, a spicy salad of green bananas, eggplant and chillies.

Shopping

On the whole, **silverwork** and **textiles** are more expensive in Vientiane than in Louang Phabang, where they're produced, and Vientiane is no bargain-hunters' paradise. However, the **Morning Market** (Talat Sao) has some good bargains in homespun cotton clothing ($2–5) and handicrafts: shoulder bags (*nyam*) are cheap and functional while hand-woven *pha biang*, a long, scarf-like textile, are good buys. Shops specializing in traditional textiles and authentic **silk** include Satri Silk (☎021/219295), Carol Cassidy Lao Textiles (☎021/212123) and the Lao Women's Union's The Art of Silk, located on Manthatoulat Road near Wat Xieng Nyeun.

Besides the Morning Market, most textile, souvenir and antique shops are found on Samsenthai and Setthathilat roads and along the lanes running between them. These days, however, the vast majority of the "antiques" on offer in Laos are cheap imitations produced in neighbouring Vietnam and China. Keep in mind, too, that a lot of the "silk" and "silver" items to be found here are neither silk nor silver. If you're heading north, it's best to save your shopping for Louang Phabang.

Vientiane is, however, an excellent place to have men's tailor-made clothes fitted. Although the selection of fabrics is sometimes limited, the tailors along Pangkham Road, just north of Nam Phou, are amazingly cheap and fast. Saigon Tailleur (look for the "Atomic" building) and Udom just opposite are recommended. If you find some silk or cotton fabric in the Morning Market, you can bring it here and have a shirt made in a day or two for about $10.

The Book Centre on Pangkham Road, south of Nam Phou, has the biggest selection of **English-language books** in the city. On Nokeo Koummane, near the river, Kosila Used Books (☎021/241352) has a very good selection of secondhand titles.

Listings

Airline offices Lao Airlines, Pangkham Rd ☎021/212053 or at Wattay International Airport, Louang Phabang Ave ☎021/512028; Thai Airways International, Pangkham Rd ☎021/216143; Vietnam Airlines, Samsenthai Rd, mezzanine floor of the *Lao Hotel Plaza* ☎021/217562.
American Express The representative agent in Laos is Diethelm Travel, on the corner of Setthathilat Rd and Nam Phou Fountain (☎021/213833).
Banks and exchange Lao and Thai banks, many of which are located on Lane Xang Ave, exchange travellers' cheques and do cash advances on Visa and MasterCard; a few local banks also maintain exchange booths around the city centre.
Embassies and consulates Australia, Nehru Rd ☎021/413600 or 413805; Cambodia, near That Khao, Thadua Rd ☎021/315251; China, near Wat Nak Noi, Wat Nak Rd ☎021/315100 or 315103; France, Setthathilat Rd ☎021/215253 or 215257–9; Germany, Sok Pa Louang Rd ☎021/312110–1; India, near Wat Phaxai, That Louang Rd ☎021/413802; Indonesia, Phon Kheng Rd, Ban Phon Sa-at ☎021/413908-10; Malaysia, near Wat Phaxai, That Louang Rd ☎021/414205–6; Philippines, near Wat Nak, Salakoktane Rd ☎021/215826; Sweden, near Wat Nak, Sok Pa Louang Rd ☎021/315018; Thailand (visa section), across from the NTAL building, Lane Xang Ave ☎021/214582; United States, near That Dam,

Bartholonie Rd ☎021/212580–1; Vietnam, near Wat Phaxai, That Louang Rd ☎021/413400–2.
Emergencies Dial ☎190 in case of fire, ☎195 for an ambulance, or ☎191 for police. In the event of an accident, dial ☎021/413363 for the Friendship Hospital Trauma Centre.
Hospitals and clinics Australian Clinic, Nehru Rd (☎021/413603), by appointment only, with vaccinations on Thursdays; International Clinic, Mahosot Hospital Compound, Fa Ngum Rd (☎021/214022), open 24hr; Mahosot Hospital, Mahosot Rd ☎021/214018; Setthathilat Hospital, Phon Sa-at Rd ☎021/450197; Swedish Clinic, near Swedish Embassy, near Wat Nak, Sok Pa Louang Rd (☎021/315015).
Immigration department Hatsady Rd, near the junction with Lane Xang Ave ☎021/212520; open Mon–Fri 8am–noon & 1–4pm.
Internet access There are dozens of small Internet centres scattered all around city centre that charge 100K per minute and close at about 10pm.
Language courses Centre de Langue Française, Lane Xang Ave ☎021/215764; Lao-American Language Center, Phon Kheng Rd, Ban Phon Sa-at ☎021/414321.
Massage and herbal sauna A massage costs about $3 per hour and saunas $1 at: Ajan Amphone, next to Wat Chanthabouli, Chao Anou Rd (Mon–Fri 2–5pm, Sat & Sun 10am–7pm); Hôspital de Médicine Traditionnelle, near Wat Si Amphon; Wat Sok Pa Louang, Wat Sok Pa Louang Rd.
Pharmacies The best pharmacies are on Mahosot Rd in the vicinity of the Morning Market.
Post office The GPO is on the corner of Khou Viang Rd and Lane Xang Ave. Poste restante is held for up to three months (Mon–Fri 8am–5pm, Sat 8am–4pm, Sun 8am–noon).
Telephone services International calls and faxes at Telecom, Setthathilat Rd (daily 7am–10pm).
Tour agencies Diethlem Travel, Nam Phou Fountain ☎021/215920; Inter-Lao Tourisme, Setthathilat Rd ☎021/214832; Lane Xang, Pangkham Rd ☎021/213198; Lao Tourism, Lane Xang Ave ☎021/216671; Lao Travel Service, Lane Xang Ave ☎021/216603 or 216604; Phudoi Travel, Phonxai Rd ☎021/413888; Sodetour, Fa Ngum Rd ☎021/216314.

Buddha Park

Located on the Mekong River 27km from downtown Vientiane, **Xiang Khouan** or the "**Buddha Park**" (daily 8am–5pm; 5000K), is surely Laos's quirkiest attraction. This collection of massive ferro-concrete sculptures, which lie dotted around a wide riverside meadow, was created under the direction of Luang Phu Boonlua Surirat, a self-styled holy man who claimed to have been the disciple of a cave-dwelling Hindu hermit in Vietnam. Upon returning to Laos, Boonlua began the sculpture garden in the late 1950s as a means of spreading his philosophy of life and his ideas about the cosmos. Besides the brontosaurian reclining Buddha that dominates the park, there are concrete statues of every conceivable deity in the Hindu-Buddhist pantheon. After the revolution, Boonlua was forced to flee across the Mekong to Nong Khai in Thailand, where he established an even more elaborate version of his philosophy in concrete at Sala Kaeo Kou, also known as Wat Khaek (see p.1052). To **get to the park**, either take bus #14 from Vientiane's main bus station (every 40min), or hire a tuk-tuk to do the round trip, including a wait of an hour or so, for $5.

Vang Viang and around

Just 155km north of the capital lies the spectacular limestone karst valley of **VANG VIANG**, which, with its beautiful **caves** and nearby ethnic minority villages, makes an ideal stopover on the way to or from Louang Phabang. This friendly town lies on the east bank of the Nam Xong River, and offers a huge range of backpacker-oriented guesthouses and services, including Internet cafés, corner bars, massage, laundry services, video movies and pizzerias. Beyond the town, there are many outdoor activities, one of the most popular of which is floating down the Nam Xong on huge tractor inner **tubes**. It's a great way to take in the view, with just enough rapids and tiny islands to keep things interesting. Some people stop for shots of *lào-láo* while floating down the river, but be warned that alcohol and tubing don't mix; there have been a number of drownings on tube trips in recent years. The most popular launching point is the village of Pakpok, about 4km north of Vang Viang, which makes for a two- to three-hour trip. Longer (10km) tube trips start from Ban Pha Thao off Route 13. Tubes (10,000K

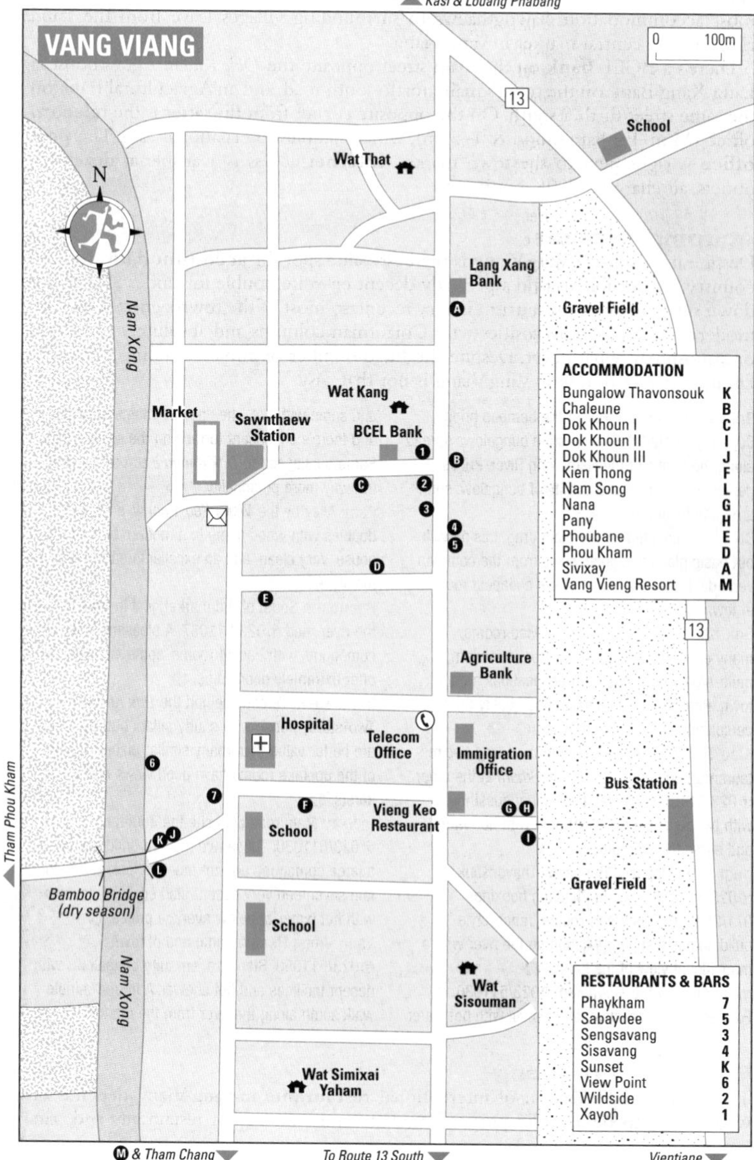

per day), **bicycles** (15,000K per day) and **motorcycles** ($7 per day) can be rented at many places around town. A number of restaurants and guesthouses advertise tubing and caves as an organized tour but the groups can be uncomfortably large so ask if there's a maximum limit.

Practicalities

Pick-ups and buses to and from Vientiane and Louang Phabang arrive at the **bus station** on Route 13 just to the east of town, which is within walking distance of most accommodation. Sawngthaews to surrounding villages leave from the stand right off the central market in Vang Viang.

There's a BCEL **bank** on the main street opposite the *Dok Khoun I* guesthouse, a Lang Xang Bank on the town's main north–south road, and an Agricultural Bank on the same street further south. On the opposite corner from the latter is the **telecom** office (Mon–Fri 8am–noon & 1–5pm), which handles international calls. The **post office** is right next to the town market. **Internet** access is available at dozens of outlets, all charging 200K per minute.

Accommodation

Despite its small size, Vang Viang is the best-value spot for **accommodation** in the country; it's possible to find a perfectly decent en-suite double for under $4. On the down side, the boom in tourism is very recent, so most of the town's guesthouses are modern, concrete monstrosities with Corinthian columns and absolutely no charm or atmosphere whatsoever. Despite the huge number of choices, finding a friendly, family-run guesthouse in Vang Viang is not that easy.

Bungalow Thavonsouk At the bamboo bridge. Superbly located deluxe en-suite bungalows spread along the banks of the Nam Xong River. Prices depend on the size and quality of bungalow: some are quite luxurious. 4–6

Chaleune Located on the main drag, this newish but basic place has good views from the common veranda. It also has some of the cheapest rooms in town. 1

Dok Khoun I, II, and III Clean, tiled rooms, many en suite and with hot water, in modern, multi-storey buildings at three locations around town. Reasonably good value and quality but no personality or atmosphere at all. 1–2

Kien Thong On the street with the *Vieng Keo* restaurant at one end and the *Phaykham* at the other ☎023/511069. Popular, two-storey guesthouse with twenty clean doubles, most with hot-water and en-suite bathrooms. 1–2

Nam Song Opposite Bungalow Thavonsouk ☎023/511016; Louang Phabang bookings 071/252400. This green-roofed, ranch-style building has a superb location on the river with a magnificent view of the karsts. 6

Nana Alley by the *Vieng Keo* ☎023/511036. Fourteen clean, en-suite doubles, all with hot water and some with a/c. The upstairs rooms are best, and there's a pleasant terrace on the second floor. Same quality as the *Dok Khoun II* across the road but way more personality. 1–2

Pany Alley by the *Vieng Keo*. Roomy, en-suite doubles with wood floors in a modern two-storey house. Very clean, and an excellent deal for the money. 1

Phoubane South of the market, just in from the river road ☎023/511037. A pleasant, leafy compound, with decent rooms, some en suite, that offer extremely good value. 1

Phou Kham Directly behind the *Dok Khoun I*. Two-storey house with gaudy pillars but the rooms are better value than many similar places. Several of the upstairs rooms have good views of the karsts. 1

Sivixay Main road opposite the Bountang ☎023/511030. These two modern buildings set in a large compound are not much to look at but contain seventeen very decent tiled en-suite doubles with hot water at below average prices. 1

Vang Vieng Resort South end of town ☎023/511050. Standard, en-suite bungalows with decent facilities and hot shower. A fifteen-minute walk south along the river from the market. 5–6

Eating and drinking

The quality and selection of international **restaurants** in Vang Viang depends on what seems to be a cyclic purge: foreigners come and open restaurants and bars, and prosper for a year or two, before resentful locals begin looking for a reason to shut them all down (or take them over). If your timing is right, Vang Viang will have restaurants and bars to rival those of Vientiane. If not, you may find there's a lot of mediocre pizza on offer.

Budget travellers tend to gravitate to the main north–south road, where there's a whole strip of cheap eateries (many of which show DVD movies) offering a choice of Western-style seating or reclining on cushions at low tables. Three of the most popular are the *Sengsavang*, *Sisavang* and *Sabaydee*, but the food at these, like the other places along here, almost invariably takes a back seat to the action on the screen.

The best place for a **sun-downer** is the riverfront *Sunset Restaurant* at *Bungalow Thavonsouk*, which boasts a million-dollar view and also serves good Western and Lao food. Just to the north of this, and similar in food and layout, is the *View Point Restaurant*. Just three houses north of the turn-off to the *Sunset*, *Phaykham* also has a big deck which boasts spectacular views over the river and the majestic peaks beyond. The two most popular **bars** in town are the *Wildside* and the *Xayoh*, opposite each other on the town's main corner.

The caves

If you decide to visit the **caves** on your own, you can find hand-drawn maps at most restaurants and guesthouses. You'll also find that locals are more than happy to point you in the right direction. There is usually someone posted at each cave to collect a small entrance fee. Likewise, there is normally someone collecting a toll from foreigners who cross the bamboo footbridge heading west towards the caves.

Six kilometres west of Vang Viang, **Tham Phou Kham** makes a rewarding half-day trip that takes in some fine scenery. Cross the river by the bamboo footbridge near the *Nam Song* and follow the road to Na Thong, 4km west. Follow the signs along the trail until it forks off through the rice fields towards the cliff-face, 1km away. It's a short, steep climb to the entrance. In the main cavern reclines a bronze Buddha; bring a torch if you want to explore the tunnels branching off the main gallery. Outside the cave, the perfectly blue stream is a great spot for a swim; you can buy cool drinks and fruit nearby.

Another good day-trip is to **Tham Pha Thao**, 10km north of Vang Viang. Stretching for more than 2km, the tunnel-like cave is pitch-black, filled with huge stalactites and stalagmites, and is the most satisfying caving trip you can make from Vang Viang. It's best visited near the end of the rainy season, when the water level is perfect for a swim in the subterranean swimming pool 800m into the cave. Bear in mind that you'll be up to your chest in water at times, so travel light and don't bring anything valuable. In the height of the dry season, it's possible to go beyond the pool and explore the full length of the cave. The cave is near the Hmong village of **Pha Thao**, which lies 13km north of Vang Viang. Turn left after the bridge just beyond the Km10 marker on Route 13 – a road sign points the way to the "Nam Xong-Pha Thao Irrigation Project" – and either ford the river or hail a boat for a few thousand kip. Once across, head for the village at the base of the cliff, where you'll find a few simple restaurants. The villagers will point the way to the cave mouth.

5.2

Louang Phabang and around

Nestling in a slim valley shaped by lofty, green mountains and cut by the swift Mekong and Khan rivers, **LOUANG PHABANG** exudes tranquillity and grandeur. A tiny mountain kingdom for more than a thousand years and designated a World Heritage site in 1995, it is endowed with a legacy of ancient, red-roofed temples and French-Indochinese architecture, not to mention some of the country's most refined cuisine, its richest culture and most sacred Buddha image. The very name Louang Phabang conjures up the classic image of Laos – streets of ochre colonial houses and swaying palms, lines of saffron-robed monks gliding through the morning mist, and, of course, longtail boats racing down the Mekong. This is where the first proto-Lao nation took root. It's the most Lao city in Laos, the only one where ethnic Lao are in the majority and where the back streets and cobblestoned lanes have a distinctly village-like feel. It's the birthplace of countless Lao rituals and the origin of a line of rulers. Conveniently, Louang Phabang is also the **transport hub** of northern Laos, with road, river and air links – both domestic and international – all leading to the city.

The earliest Lao settlers made their way down the Nam Ou Valley, sometime after the tenth century, absorbing the territory on which the city lies and naming it **Xiang Dong Xiang Thong**. But it wasn't until legendary Lao warrior Fa Ngum captured the town in 1353 that it emerged as the heart of a thriving, independent kingdom in its own right. He founded the kingdom of **Lane Xang Hom Khao** – the "Land of a Million Elephants and the White Parasol" – and established the line of kings that was to rule Laos for six centuries. With Fa Ngum came monks, artisans and learned men from the Khmer court, a legal code, and Theravada Buddhism. Striking temples were built, epic poems composed and sacred texts copied, and in 1512, King Visoun brought the very holy Pha Bang Buddha image to the city, a hugely significant event. Lane Xang was, for the moment, a major power on the Indochinese peninsula, but by 1563 the fear of encroaching Burmese led to the capital being moved to Vientiane. The Pha Bang was left behind and the city renamed after the revered image. From then on, Louang Phabang had a roller-coaster ride, invaded first by the Burmese and then by the Siamese, until King Oun Kham finally agreed to co-operate with France, and the city's French period began. During the two Indochina wars, Louang Phabang fared better than most towns in Laos. However, the Second Indochina War ultimately took its toll on the city's ceremonial life, which lost its regal heart when the Pathet Lao ended the royal line by forcing King Sisavang Vatthana to abdicate in 1975.

Arrival

Louang Phabang Airport is 2km northeast of the city. If you're arriving on an international flight, you can get a fifteen-day **visa on arrival** here (see p.498). There

Moving on from Louang Phabang

By plane

The easiest way to get to the **airport** is by tuk-tuk ($1 per person). Lao Airlines' office is on Visounalat Road (☎071/212172), opposite Jaliya Guesthouse.

By bus or sawngthaew

Buses heading to Vientiane and Vang Viang and points south along Route 13 use the **Southern bus station**, 3km south of the centre, best reached by tuk-tuk (5000K). There are ten buses a day to Vientiane, with the final departure at 5pm. Tickets are sold at the bus station. There is also a three-times-a-month air-con tourist coach to Vientiane ($10), which can be booked through most guesthouses. Buses and sawngthaews to all points north use the **Northern bus station**, 6km north of town. Almost all northbound buses depart in the morning, but there's no need to buy your ticket in advance. Tuk-tuks to the station cost around 5000K.

By boat

Slow boats set off from the Navigation Office: departures down to Vientiane (occasional) or up to Houayxai, as well as up the Nam Ou, are all posted on a chalk board here, but arrive at the pier early. Speedboats leave from a separate landing in the village of Ban Don, 7km north of the city (20,000K by tuk-tuk). The eight-seat **speedboats** travel to points north and south along the Mekong River, as well as for destinations along the Nam Ou River. Passengers sign up for their destinations, and the boats leave when full. Arrive early to get a seat, although there's no guarantee that every destination is served every day. Alternatively, you can charter a speedboat. In fact, the boatmen will practically insist that you do just that.

are also exchange facilities. Arrivals on domestic flights don't need to pass immigration. Tuk-tuks (10,000K) will ferry you into town.

Louang Phabang has three **bus stations**, all served by shared tuk-tuks into town (5000K). Buses from Vientiane, Vang Viang and other points south along Route 13 stop at the Southern bus station, 3km south of the centre. Buses and sawngthaews from the north arrive at the Northern bus station, 6km north of town, while buses from Xainyabouli terminate at the Pakkhon depot near the Southern bus station.

Slow boats dock at the Navigation Office landing behind the former Royal Palace in the old city, an easy walk from most guesthouses. **Speedboats** dock at a separate landing in the village of Ban Don, 7km north of the city (20,000K by tuk-tuk).

Information, orientation and city transport

The new Louang Phabang **Tourism Information Centre** (Mon–Fri 8am–5pm; ☎071/212487) is on 3 Visounalat Road, next to the Red Cross Sauna. Their new, free **Map of Louang Phabang** is extremely useful. For local ads and info, check the bulletin board at the *Scandinavian Bakery*, Xiang Thong Road.

Beyond having very long **street names** (eg Maha Ouphalathphetsalat Road), often with multiple spellings, some roads in Louang Phabang switch names four or five times as they cross the city. For clarity's sake, we've chosen one street name and stuck with it. But, as elsewhere in Laos, locals prefer to use landmarks, such as monasteries, to identify parts of town: thus Ban Wat That ("Wat That village"), refers to the area south of Setthathilat Road, between Wat That and the Mekong River.

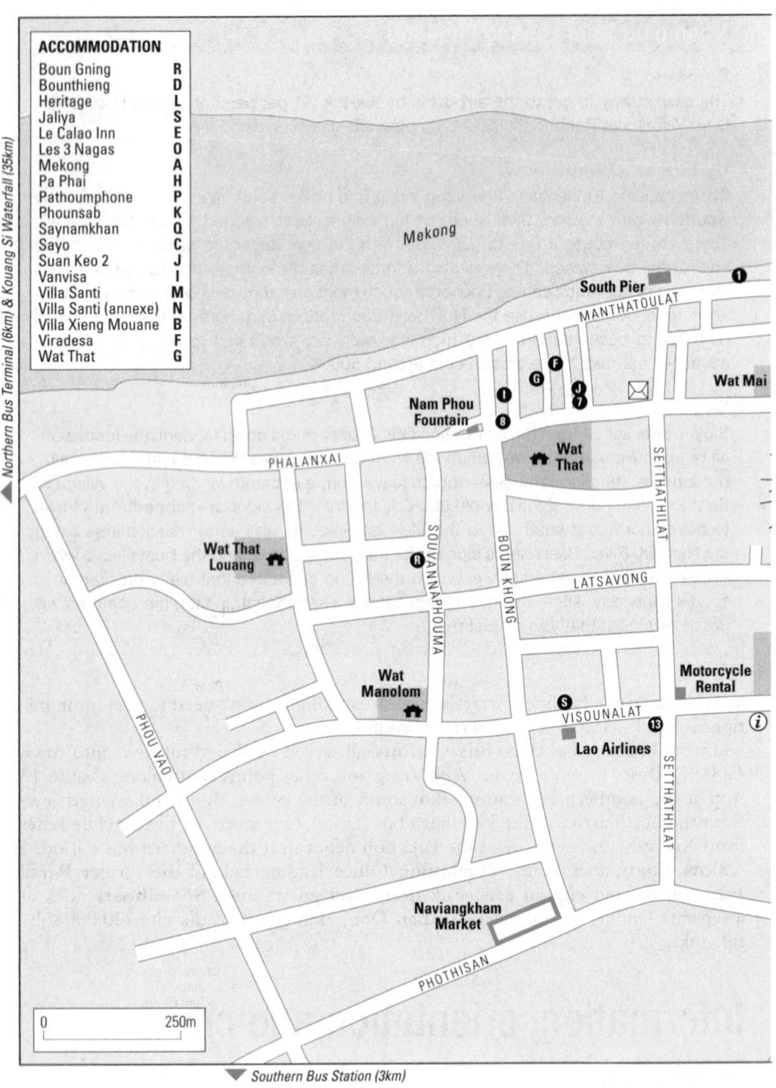

Although you can comfortably walk everywhere in the old city, **bicycles** are a great way of getting around town at large. They're available at most guesthouses and at tourist shops on Xiang Thong Road ($1 per day). Motorbikes are available to rent for $7 a day but must be returned before dark. To get out to the bus stations or airport, you'll have to rely on the town's small fleet of **tuk-tuks**, which can be flagged down easily on most busy streets. Typically, a ride anywhere in town is 5000K per person, although some drivers will refuse to take a falang for less than 10,000K.

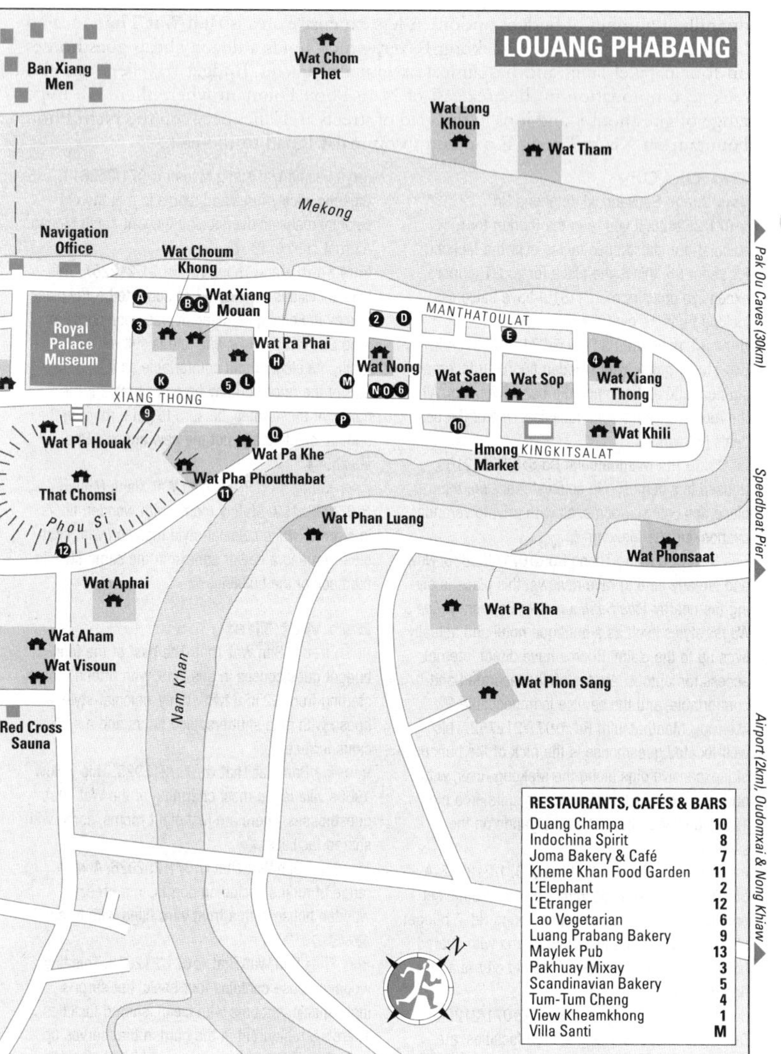

Accommodation

Louang Phabang has a wide range of **accommodation**, from unfussy rooms in characterful, inexpensive guesthouses to five-star, luxury resorts. Prices tend to rise around December but you can get good discounts in **low season** (May–Oct). It's an early-to-bed-early-to-rise town, so always ask what time guesthouse doors are locked at night. To make the most of the town's tropical daydream atmosphere, seek out accommodation among the gilded temples of the **old city**, still home to a dwindling number of budget options. A less expensive area is **Ban Wat That**, located between Wat That and the Mekong River, which holds a dozen cheap guesthouses on four parallel lanes and has almost as much character. Budget travellers can also seek accommodation in the area east of Nam Phou Fountain where there is a huge range of guesthouses and inns in the grid of streets and lanes between the Nam Phou Fountain on Xiang Thong Road and Visounnalat Road to the east.

The Old City

Bounthieng Souvannakhamphong Rd ⓣ071/252488. If you're in the market for a colonial-era guesthouse facing over the Mekong for under $5, this is the place for you. The more expensive upstairs rooms ($10) have balconies looking right out over the river. ❶–❷

Heritage near Wat Pa Phai ⓣ071/252537. A lovely two-storey house with wooden floorboards, green shutters and a charming little bar downstairs. All the rooms have en-suite facilities. One of the best deals in town. ❷

Le Calao Inn Manthatoulat Rd ⓣ071/212100. Housed in a century-old colonial mansion, this place has only six rooms, all with private veranda overlooking the Mekong. ❽

Les 3 Nagas Xiang Thong Rd ⓣ071/253888. New and already getting rave reviews, this place is giving the nearby *Villa Santi* a run for its money. *Les 3 Nagas* styles itself as a boutique hotel and actually lives up to the claim. Rooms have direct Internet access for laptops, are tastefully decorated and comfortable, and the service is impeccable. ❽

Mekong Manthatoulat Rd ⓣ071/212752. This well-located guesthouse is the pick of the bunch of inexpensive digs along the Mekong River, with budget rooms, including some en suite, in a big 1960s building. Great shared veranda on the second floor. ❶

Pa Phai Opposite Wat Pa Phai ⓣ071/212752. A quirky little guesthouse with a pleasant patio set on a quiet street right off Xiang Thong Rd. A budget place like this, offering simple rooms with shared facilities right in the heart of the old city, is a rare find indeed. ❶–❷

Pathoumphone Kingkitsalat Rd ⓣ071/212946. Decent rooms, some with shared facilities, are spread out across three houses and offer views of the Nam Khan River and the mountains. ❷

Phounsab Xiang Thong Rd ⓣ071/212595. In a prime location on the old city's restaurant and souvenir strip, this hotel has high-ceilinged rooms, with or without en-suite facilities. Excellent if you want a budget place right in the heart of the café-land. ❶–❷

Saynamkhan Kingkitsalat Rd ⓣ071/212976. This marvellous, restyled 1939 shop-house next to the Nam Kham River and just 40m from the main tourist strip is a great mid-range option. Rooms come with a/c and TV. ❺

Sayo Facing Wat Xiang Mouan ⓣ071/252614. Gigantic, nicely furnished rooms in a grand old colonial mansion overlooking the Wat Xiang Mouan. A great choice. ❸–❺

Villa Santi Xiang Thong Rd ⓣ071/212267. This colonial villa is considered by some to be *the* place to stay in Louang Phabang: it was once home to King Sisavang Vong's wife and is still run by her family. As elegant and comfortable as it is, a huge part of the price you pay here is simply for the name. At these rates, be sure to get a room in the original building and not the new annexe. Book ahead. ❾

Villa Xieng Mouane Facing Wat Xiang Mouan ⓣ071/252152. Stately rooms with wooden floors in a pretty white colonial-style mansion with light-blue trim and a newer annexe in the same style in the back of the building. ❺

Ban Wat That

Suan Keo 2 Ban Wat That. The best of the four budget guesthouses in this lane, with fifteen rooms starting from $2 in a two-storey, colonial-style house with blue shutters, tiled floors and a spacious terrace. ❶

Vanvisa Ban Wat That ⓣ071/212925. This yellow 1960s villa is the most charming of the Wat That guesthouses. There are just eight rooms, some with shared facilities. ❷

Viradesa Ban Wat That ⓣ071/252026. A wide range of rooms, including dorms, in a breezy wooden house with a front yard filled with trees. ❶–❷

Wat That Ban Wat That ⓣ071/212913. This tiny wooden house contains four basic, but surprisingly spacious rooms with clean, shared facilities. There's a restaurant in the garden that serves up pancakes, sandwiches and great fruit shakes. ❶

East of Nam Phou Fountain

Boun Gning Souvannaphouma Rd ⓣ071/212274. This budget backpacker's place in a two-storey wooden house on a quiet street is in need of some renovations. The rooms are cheap, though and the management somehow keeps things limping along. ❶

Jaliya Visounalat Rd ⓣ071/252154. Across from Lao Airlines, the dozen en-suite rooms tucked away behind this shop-house travel agency are clean and comfortable, and all face onto a private garden. ❶

The Old City

Louang Phabang's **old city** is largely concentrated on a tongue of land, approximately 1km long and 0.25km wide, with the confluence of the Mekong and Nam Khan rivers at its tip. This peninsula is dominated by a steep and forested hill, **Phou Si** ("Sacred Hill"), crowned with a Buddhist stupa that can be seen for miles around. Most of Louang Phabang's architecture of merit – monasteries and French-influenced mansions – is to be found on the main thoroughfare, **Xiang Thong**, between the tip of the peninsula and Setthathilat Road. Beyond Setthathilat Road, near the Mekong, lies the old silversmithing district, **Ban Wat That**, centred on its monastery, Wat That.

A good place to start your tour of the old city is the dry-goods market, **Dala Market**, on Setthathilat Road. Wild chicken calls, resembling tin whistles, are on display beside bags of saltpetre and sulphur which, when mixed with ground charcoal, produce homemade gunpowder. Stalls selling gold and silver jewellery double as pawn shops and usually display royalist regalia — brass buttons, badges and medals decorated with the Hindu iconography of the old kingdom. This is also a popular haunt of black-market currency dealers. Near Dala Market, a small **Hmong Market** occupies a vacant lot on the corner of Setthathilat and Xiang Thong roads, selling traditional hats, bags and clothes.

Further along Xiang Thong, Wat Mai Suwannaphumaham, or **Wat Mai**, dates from the late eighteenth or early nineteenth century, but it is the *sim*'s relatively modern facade with its gilt stucco reliefs that is the main focus of attention. Depicting the second-to-last incarnation of the Buddha set amidst traditional Lao scenes, the facade was created in the 1960s and recently restored, but is already starting to deteriorate.

The Royal Palace Museum

Centrally located between Phou Si and the Mekong River, the former **Royal Palace** (Mon–Fri 8.30am–noon & 1–4pm; 10,000K) is now a museum preserving the paraphernalia of Laos's recently extinguished monarchy. It was constructed in 1904 by the French, and displays a tasteful fusion of European and Lao design. The pediment over the main entrance is decorated with the symbol of the Lao monarchy: Airavata, the three-headed elephant, being sheltered by the sacred white parasol. This is surrounded by the intertwining bodies of the fifteen guardian naga of Louang Phabang; the naga is a sacred water serpent, both a symbol of water and its life-giving properties and a protector of the Lao people.

At the far end of the gallery to the right of the main entrance is a small, barred room that once served as the king's personal shrine room. It is here that the **Pha Bang**, the most sacred Buddha image in Laos, is being kept until the completion of the Haw Pha Bang – the temple in the eastern corner of the palace compound. The Pha Bang is believed to possess miraculous powers that safeguard the country. According to legend, it was crafted in the heavens and then delivered, via Sri Lanka and Cambodia, to the city of Xiang Dong Xiang Thong, later renamed Louang Phabang (the Great Pha Bang) in its honour. In the early eighteenth century, the Pha Bang was moved to Vientiane, whence it was stolen twice by the Siamese (who always returned it, believing it to be bad luck); since 1867, the Pha Bang has been kept in Louang Phabang.

The most impressive room inside the palace is the dazzling **Throne Hall**, its high walls spangled with mosaics of multicoloured mirrors. On display here are rare articles of royal regalia: swords of hammered silver and gold, an elaborately decorated fly-whisk and even the king's own *howdah* (elephant saddle). Also on exhibit is a cache of small crystal, silver and bronze Buddha images taken from the inner chamber of the "Watermelon Stupa" at Wat Visoun. Other rooms show theatrical masks and musical instruments used by the royal dance troupe in their performances of the Ramayana, diplomatic gifts presented to the people of Laos by a handful of nations, and larger-than-life portraits of King Sisavang Vattana, his wife and their son, painted by a Soviet artist.

Wat Pa Phai and Wat Saen

The neighbourhood encompassing the section of Xiang Thong Road just north of the Royal Palace Museum is known to locals as "Ban Jek" or **Chinatown**, and contains some fine examples of Louang Phabang shop-house architecture, a hybrid of French and Lao features superimposed on the South Chinese style that was once prevalent throughout urban Southeast Asia. A left turn at the end of the row of shop-houses will take you to **Wat Pa Phai**, the "Bamboo Forest Monastery", whose *sim* is painted and lavishly embellished with stylized naga and peacocks.

Doubling back up to the corner, turn left to continue down Xiang Thong Road as far as **Wat Saen**, where an ornate boatshed houses the monastery's two **longboats**, used in the annual boat race festival. Held at the end of the rainy season, the boat races are believed to lure Louang Phabang's guardian naga back into the rivers after high waters and flooded rice paddies have allowed them to escape. The boathouse is decorated with carved wooden images of these mythical serpents.

Wat Xiang Thong

Probably the most historic and enchanting Buddhist monastery in the entire country, **Wat Xiang Thong**, the "Golden City Monastery" (daily 8am to dusk; 5000K), near the northernmost tip of the peninsula, should not be missed. The wonderfully graceful main temple or *sim* was built in 1560 by King Setthathilat and, unlike nearly every other temple in Louang Phabang, was neither razed by Chinese marauders nor over-enthusiastically restored. You'll need to stand at a distance to get a view of the roof, the temple's most outstanding feature. Elegant lines curve and overlap, sweeping nearly to the ground, and evoke a bird with outstretched wings or, as the locals say, a mother hen sheltering her brood.

The **walls** of the *sim* are decorated inside and out with stencilled gold motifs. Many of these depict a variety of tales, including the Lao version of the Ramayana – the *Pha Lak Pha Lam* – and scenes from the *jataka* (stories about the lives of the Buddha), as well as graphic scenes of punishments doled out in the many levels of Buddhist hell. Such depictions were meant to give a basic education in religion to illiterate laypeople. In one of these punishment scenes, on the wall to the right of the main entrance, an adulterous couple is being forced to flee a pack of rabid dogs by climbing a tree studded with wicked thorns. In the branches above perch a flock of crows, awaiting the chance to peck out the sinners' eyes. Other unfortunate souls are being cooked in a copper cauldron of boiling oil (for committing murder) or are suspended by a hook through their tongues (guilty of telling lies).

In the rafters above and to the right of the main entrance runs a long wooden **aqueduct** in the shape of a mythical serpent. During Lao New Year, lustral water is poured into a receptacle in the serpent's tail and spouts from its mouth, bathing a Buddha image housed in a wooden pagoda-like structure situated near the altar. A drain channels the water under the floor of the pagoda and out of the mouth of a mirror-spangled elephant's head on the exterior wall. The water is considered to be highly sacred; the faithful will use it to anoint themselves or to ritually bathe household Buddhas. To the left of the *sim*, as you face it, is a small brick-and-stucco shrine containing a standing Buddha image. The intricate purple- and gold-mirrored mosaics on the pediments are probably the country's finest example of this kind of ornamentation, which is thought to have originated in Thailand and spread to Burma as well. Directly behind the shrine, the Red Chapel enshrines a sixteenth-century reclining Buddha image, one of Laos's greatest sculptures in bronze.

On the other side of the monastery grounds is the **Funerary Carriage Hall** (daily 8am to dusk) or *haw latsalot*. Built in 1962, the hall's wide teakwood panels are deeply carved with depictions of Rama, Sita, Ravana and Hanuman, characters from the Lao version of the Ramayana. Check out the carved window shutters on the building's left side where Hanuman, the King of the Monkeys, is depicted in pursuit of the fairer sex. Inside, the principal article on display is the *latsalot*, the royal funerary carriage, used to transport the mortal remains of King Sisavong Vong to cremation. The vehicle is built in the form of several bodies of parallel naga, whose jagged fangs and dripping tongues heralded the king's final passage through Louang Phabang. Atop the carriage are three gilded urns in which the royal corpse was kept in foetal position until the cremation.

Phou Si – the Sacred Hill

Phou Si ("Sacred Hill") is both the geographical and spiritual centre of the city, a miniature Mount Meru, the Mount Olympus of Hindu-Buddhist cosmology. The hill's peak affords a stunning panorama of the city, and can be reached by three different routes. The first and most straightforward is via the stairway directly opposite the main gate of the Royal Palace Museum. An 8000K fee must be paid before ascending and this is when you should ask to be let into the adjacent *sim*, which is sometimes padlocked shut. Known as **Wat Pa Houak**, this fine little temple contains the city's most fascinating murals, which depict Lao, Chinese, Persian and European inhabitants of Louang Phabang. From the *sim*, it's a steep but shady climb to the peak. There is a second approach, on the other side of the hill, up a zigzag stairway flanked by whitewashed naga and a third, rambling but more atmospheric, approach via **Wat Pha Phoutthabat** near Phou Si's northern foot (across from *Saynamkhan Guest House*). There are actually three monasteries in this compound, and the most interesting structure is the *sim* of **Wat Pa Khe**, a tall, imposing building with an unusual inward-leaning facade. Most noteworthy here is a pair of carved shutters to the left of the main entrance, said to depict seventeenth-century Dutch traders. Behind and to the left of the *sim* is a stairway leading to the "**Buddha's footprint**", a larger-than-life stylized footprint complete with the 108 auspicious marks after which Wat Pha Phoutthabat was named. The shrine housing the footprint is usually locked. The path meanders up past monks' stone quarters and the remains of an old anti-aircraft gun, to the summit, crowned by the stupa **That Chomsi**.

Outside the Old City

The older parts of the city may have a higher concentration of monasteries and old buildings, but there is plenty to see beyond Setthathilat Road. **Wat That**, officially known as Wat Pha Mahathat, is situated on a rise next to the *Phou Si Hotel* and is reached via a stairway flanked by some impressive seven-headed naga. At the top of the stairs is perhaps the most photographed window in all of Louang Phabang. Framed in ornately carved teak, it's a blend of Lao, Chinese and Khmer design. Other elements of the wat suggest influence from northern Thailand, namely the gold-topped *that* for which the monastery was named.

Wat Visoun and Wat Aham share a parcel of land on the opposite side of Phou Si from the Royal Palace Museum. The *sim* of the former was once lavishly decorated but was razed in 1887, and the bulbous, finial-topped stupa, known as *That Makmo* – the "Watermelon Stupa" – was destroyed as well. The looters made off with many treasures stored within, but what they left behind is now on display in the throne room of the Royal Palace Museum. Wat Visoun's reconstructed *sim* is an unremarkable mix of Louang Phabang and Vientiane styles, but the Watermelon Stupa is still quite unique. Neighbouring **Wat Aham** features a delightfully diminutive *sim* and a couple of mould-blackened *that*. A small fee is sometimes collected from foreign visitors for access to these monasteries.

Eating and drinking

Louang Phabang prides itself on its **food**, and the city boasts more restaurants than anywhere in the country outside of Vientiane. Despite the high availability of international cuisine here, visitors shouldn't miss out on having a traditional Lao meal. At the top of your list should be *aw lam*, a bitter-sweet soup, heavy on aubergines and mushrooms. Other local specialities include *jaew bong*, a condiment of red chillies, shallots, garlic and dried buffalo skin, and *phak nâm*, a type of watercress particular to the area and widely used in salads.

Most of the city's tourist **cafés** are located along a 500-metre strip of Xiang Thong Road that expats sarcastically call "Thang Falang" or "White Man's Way", and tend to be fairly pricey by Lao standards. It's quite easy to spend as much on a meal here as on your guesthouse room. Having said that, with the exception of upmarket restaurants at five-star hotels like the *Pan Sea Phou Vao* (western end of Phou Vao Rd; ⓣ071/212194) or *Souvannaphoum* (Phalanxai Rd; ⓣ071/212200), a two-course meal in Louang Phabang usually only costs $6 and seldom will you spend more than $12. Much cheaper meals can be found at the delightful **riverside restaurants** along Ounkham Road. Generally, the further you get from "Thang Falang", the cheaper things get. Restaurants open daily for lunch and stop serving food by 9pm.

Cafés

Joma Bakery & Café Xiang Thong Rd. Formerly the *Healthy & Fresh Bakery*, and recently relocated, this is still one of the best places in town for breakfast.

Luang Prabang Bakery Xiang Thong Rd. Very tasty "tea-bread" sandwiches and good fruit shakes are available here but the hot food is very hit-and-miss, and the service is slow and extremely disorganized.

Scandinavian Bakery Xiang Thong Rd. A bit too popular, but a handy spot to catch up on the Bangkok newspapers and watch the news on satellite TV.

Restaurants

Indochina Spirit Xiang Thong Rd, near the Nam Phou Fountain. Perhaps the best restaurant in Louang Phabang and maybe even Laos, this absolutely charming antique house with a lovely al fresco patio and traditional music should be right at the top of anyone's dining list.

Kheme Khan Food Garden Kingkitsalat Rd. High on the bank of the Nam Khan River behind Phou Si, this is a great venue for traditional Lao food, with lovely views of the Nam Kham. The *keng kai màk nao*, a soup served with chicken, and the *sai-ua Louang Phabang*, or Lao-style sausages, are standouts.

L'Elephant Straight towards the Mekong from the *Villa Santi*. A cross between Southern California and Casablanca, this has a great atmosphere, as well as some of the best vegetarian food in town.

Lao Vegetarian Xiang Thong Rd. Formerly the *Lamach*, this is an inexpensive vegetarian restaurant with outdoor tables and a variety of tasty tofu and vegetable dishes. The mango shake is fabulous.

Pakhuay Mixay Near Wat Xiang Mouan. The main draw is the garden atmosphere, in a quiet residential corner of the old city, away from the bustle of Xiang Thong Rd, but the Lao cuisine served here is worth seeking out on its own merits.

Tum-Tum Cheng Sisaleumsak Rd, near Wat Xiang Thong. This guesthouse restaurant serves tasty Lao food in a cool, old colonial building.

View Kheamkhong Ounkham Rd. Lovely outdoor restaurant right on the banks of the Mekong River with inexpensive, delicious food. The Gong Bao-style cashew chicken is to die for.

Villa Santi Xiang Thong Rd. One of the classy places in town to sample Lao cuisine, with recipes by the daughter of the legendary Phia Sing, the last chef to cook for the Lao royal family. A drink at the garden bar of this former royal residence is also something of a Louang Phabang tradition.

Nightlife and entertainment

If you're looking for some lively **nightlife**, head over to the *Duang Champa*, on Kingkitsalat Road, with a DJ and live bands on some nights. Another cool bar is the *Maylek Pub*, which tends to stay open later at the weekend than other spots in town. If you're looking for the laid-back literary scene, check out *L'Etranger* at the junction of Chao Sisouphan and Phommathat roads for books, coffee and tea.

Demonstrations of classical Lao dance are given three times a week (Mon, Wed & Fri 6.30pm) at the **Royal Ballet Theatre**, located at the Royal Palace Museum (☎071/212200). Performances include excerpts of the Lao version of the Ramayana (the *Pha Lak Pha Lam*) and cost $5 per person.

Shopping

As the royal capital of Laos, Louang Phabang was traditionally a centre for skilled **artisans** from around the kingdom and today the traditional arts have been experiencing a revival thanks to the tourism boom. Many of the town's souvenir shops are on **Xiang Thong Road**, especially in the neighbourhood known as "Ban Jek", near the Royal Palace Museum. Other good places to look are the Hmong Market (6–9pm) on Kingkitsalat Road, and on Siphouthabath Road on the northern side of Phou Si.

Although Thai antique dealers have made off with quite a bit of old Lao silver, items still worth looking out for are paraphernalia for betel chewing: round or oval boxes for storing white lime, cone-shaped containers for betel leaves and miniature mortars used to pound areca nuts. Hilltribe silver jewellery is usually bold and heavy – the better to show off one's wealth – and most is the handiwork of the Hmong. The antique brass weights known as "**opium weights**" are also well represented in the silver shops. Weights cast as stylized birds, elephants and lions are an established collectable and can command high prices, but simpler designs are more reasonably priced. New silver of superior quality should be bought directly from Louang Phabang's expert **silversmiths**. The best known of these is Thithpeng Maniphone, whose workshop is located just down the small lane opposite Wat That. Other silversmiths are located near the Royal Palace Museum and opposite Wat Aham. Gold jewellery shops can be found on Chao Sisouphan Road.

There are now many upmarket boutiques specializing in high-quality Lao **textiles**. Ock Pop Tok Textiles, next to *L'Elephant*, is typical of the kind of chic shops popping up around this end of town. Also see the Lao Antique Textiles Collection (☎071/212775) on Xiang Thong Road next to the *Naunenapha Restaurant*. More basic Lao textile products are cheapest at the Hmong Market and at Talat Dala where *nyam* – shoulder bags – and the all-purpose *pha khao ma*, a chequered, wrap-around sarong used by Lao men, are all very inexpensive. Lao **woodcarving** is traditionally religious in nature, and Buddha images can be found everywhere, but these are now supplemented by souvenirs such as carved wooden hangers for displaying textiles. Ban Khili (opposite Wat Sop) offers a good selection of originally designed traditional mulberry **paper lanterns**, including collapsible models.

Listings

Banks and exchange There are several exchange places along Xiang Thong Rd, including the main branch of Lane Xang Bank opposite the Hmong Market, which changes travellers' cheques and can do cash advances on Visa; Lane Xang Bank also maintains an exchange bureau (daily 8.30am–4pm) on Latsavong Rd; cash and travellers' cheques only.

Hospitals and clinics The main hospital is on Setthathilat Rd; an International Clinic (☎071/252049) is around the corner on the hospital's western side.

In case of a serious illness, you should fly direct to Thailand, where there are many good hospitals.

Internet access A high concentration of businesses and cafés with Internet access can be found along Xiang Thong Rd east of the Royal Palace Museum, as well as on Setthathilat Rd. Most places charge 200K per minute and will stay open as late as midnight as long as there are customers at the terminals.

Massage and herbal sauna The Red Cross Sauna (daily 5–9pm) on Visounalat Rd (☎071/252856) has traditional Lao massage at $3 per hour (reserve ahead) and an excellent sauna for $1 (bring a sarong).

Post office The GPO (Mon–Fri 8am–noon & 1–5pm, Sat 8am–noon) is located on the corner of Xiang Thong and Setthathilat roads. Poste restante is kept for three months.

Telephone services International calls and faxes at Telecom (daily 8am–9pm), behind the GPO. No collect calls, but a callback service is available. International direct dial phones are located outside the GPO, and phonecards are available at many convenience stores.

Tour agencies Sodetour, Manthatoulat Rd ☎071/212092; Lane Xang, Visounalat Rd ☎071/212793; Lao Travel Service, Xiang Thong Rd ☎071/212725; Diethlem, Xiang Thong Rd ☎071/212277; Inter-Lao Tourisme, Setthathilat Rd ☎071/212034.

Around Louang Phabang

You haven't seen Louang Phabang until you **cross the Mekong** to Xiang Men and climb up to Wat Chom Phet, a hilltop monastery that offers superior views of the city's gilded temples at sunset. The popular **Pak Ou Caves** excursion gets you out on the water, and is a wonderful day-trip, especially if you haven't had a chance to travel the Mekong by boat before. Another good day-trip is nearby **Kouang Si waterfall** – a good spot for a picnic and splashing around in turquoise waters.

Xiang Men

Surprisingly few tourists bother to cross the Mekong and explore the sleepy village of **XIANG MEN**, but it makes a good half-day trip and gives you a chance to view Louang Phabang from across the river. A passenger ferry operates between Louang Phabang and Xiang Men and leaves from the landing west of the Royal Palace Museum. You could also strike a deal with one of the many boats to be found along the riverbank: the short journey should cost around 5000K per person and you can ask to be let off at **Wat Long Khoun**, once used by Louang Phabang's kings as a pre-coronation retreat, which involved ritual baths, meditation and reflection. Of note are the two Chinese door guardians painted either side of the main entrance to the *sim* and the murals within. An easy climb to the top of the hill behind Wat Long Khoun brings you to the *sim* and stupas of **Wat Chom Phet**, a disused monastery best visited at dusk, when the views of the sunset are spectacular.

Kouang Si

The best day-trip from Louang Phabang is the picturesque, multi-level **Kouang Si waterfall** (entry 15,000K), which tumbles 60m before spilling through a series of crystal-blue pools – a great spot for a picnic and a swim. A large landslide has altered the setting somewhat but it shouldn't be long before nature sets things right again. Vendors near the lower pool sell *tam màk hung*, fruit and drinks. The steep path on the opposite side of the falls leads to a grassy meadow filled with brilliantly coloured butterflies. The path can get quite slippery, and several barefoot trampers have broken a leg here.

There are several options for reaching the waterfall, which is situated 35km southwest of Louang Phabang. The easiest is to rent a **motorcycle** in Louang Phabang, but the most scenic is by **boat** down the Mekong River – many of the same boat drivers running trips to the Pak Ou caves will also offer to take you to the falls. This entails taking a tuk-tuk for the last portion of the journey, something that is handled by the boat driver and usually worked into his fee: check when negotiating your fare. Boatmen hang out along the Mekong riverside and charge $10 for a boat that can accommodate up to ten people and a further $2 for the tuk-tuk. You can also do the whole journey by **tuk-tuk**; if you can assemble a group, this works out quite cheap ($8 return). Drivers, who can be found at the Hmong Market, will wait for you while you visit the falls.

The Pak Ou Caves and Whisky Village

A popular river excursion, some 25km out of Louang Phabang, is centred around the confluence of the Mekong and Nam Ou rivers, known as Pak Ou. Numerous caves punctuate the limestone cliffs here, the best known of which are the "**Buddha Caves**", Tham Ting and Tham Phoum. These caves have been used for centuries as a repository for old and unwanted Buddha images that can no longer be venerated on an altar, and the hundreds upon hundreds of serenely smiling images covered in dust and cobwebs make an eerie scene. **Tham Ting**, the lower cave, just above the water's surface, is more of a large grotto and is light enough to explore without artificial light. The upper cave is unlit, so bring a torch, or better still, a handful of candles to enhance the spooky effect. An 8000K entrance fee is collected at the lower cave (50,000K if you plan to take photographs).

On the opposite bank of the river is a village that for thousands of years produced stoneware jars but has now found that distilling liquor is more lucrative. The inhabitants of Ban Xang Hai, referred to by English-speaking boatmen as the **Whisky Village**, are quite used to thirsty visitors stopping by for a pull on the bamboo straw. The liquor is made from fermented sticky rice, and pots filled with hooch are lined up on the beach awaiting transport up or down the river. Both sites can be seen in a couple of hours, and boatmen hired in Louang Phabang usually treat it as a package, assuming that after you've seen a cave-full of Buddhas you'll be ready for a good, stiff drink. Boats are easily arranged at the slow-boat landing in Louang Phabang and cost $10 for up to five people to hire for the trip there and back. The ride upriver takes less than an hour.

5.3
The northeast

Difficult to reach and short on proper tourist sites, the remote **northeast** is one of the least-visited parts of Laos. This area was heavily bombed during the Second Indochina War, and much of the bombing was directed at the strategic **Plain of Jars**, which takes its name from the fields of ancient, giant funerary urns that are the northeast's main tourist draw. Indeed, for most visitors a trip to the northeast means a flying visit to the town of Phonsavan to see the nearby Jar sites. The region's other significant sight are the dozens of **caves** at **Viang Xai**, close to the Vietnam border, that served as the homes and headquarters for the Pathet Lao during their Thirty Year Struggle; very few travellers make it here, however, though since the opening to foreigners of the Vietnamese border crossings at Nam Can-Nong Het and Namsoi-Nameo (due east of **Xam Nua**), those who do can now continue their journey into Vietnam.

At present, the only way to get to the region is to bus in along one of the difficult **overland routes** (Route 1 and Route 7) from Louang Phabang province, or to **fly** into Xam Nua or Phonsavan and begin exploring the region from there.

To get from Louang Phabang to Xam Nua by Route 1 takes a day by private vehicle or two to three days by public transport. Travelling in this part of Laos is still something of an adventure so leave on the earliest possible vehicles, bring some food and bottled water, and be prepared to overnight in Viang Thong, Viang Kham or Nam Neun.

To get from Vientiane to Phonsavan takes eight to nine hours by public bus since the 140-kilometre stretch of Route 7 from Phou Khoun to Phonsavan has been rebuilt. Route 7 is open to foreigners, but buses traversing this section were ambushed by bandits or insurgents in 2003 and 2004; in some cases, tourists were killed. Check the current situation with your embassy before making this journey. There is a very basic guesthouse (❶) at the Phou Khoun junction if you get stuck overnight here.

Nong Khiaw

Resting at the foot of a striking red-faced cliff, amid towering blue-green limestone escarpments, the dusty town of **NONG KHIAW** on the banks of the Nam Ou River lies smack in the middle of some of the most dramatic scenery in Indochina. Local entrepreneurs are gradually realizing that there's money to be made from the backpackers who use the town as a hub, and it's well on its way to becoming a popular tourist destination. Part of Nong Khiaw's attraction lies in reaching the town itself – taking a slow boat up the picturesque Nam Ou from Louang Phabang is one of the best **river journeys** in Laos.

Although the old town stretches a kilometre along a dirt road parallel to Route 1, all of Nong Khiaw's **tourist facilities** are located by the big bridge over the Nam Ou. Here, at the western end of the bridge, you'll find the boat mooring, the bus lot, and most of the guesthouses and restaurants. At the eastern end of the bridge on the opposite bank is the village of **Ban Lao**, which also has a couple of guesthouses (both ❶) and a very popular restaurant.

Practicalities

There are two ways to reach Nong Khiaw from Louang Phabang. The fastest is the road route, which takes under three hours up Route 13. Many buses from Louang Phabang drop passengers at the junction town of **PAKMONG**, where Route 1 and Route 13 meet and from where you can take a connecting sawngthaew the rest of the way. However, the most scenic route to Nong Khiaw is the six-hour **boat trip** up the Nam Ou, a stunning journey through rural Laos. Approximately four hours into the trip, the scenery turns spectacular, with jungle-clad limestone peaks and miniature beaches of pristine white sand along the river's banks. Since most locals now prefer to travel to Nong Khiaw by road, catching a passenger boat on the Nam Ou isn't as easy as it used to be. The best method is get a group of fellow travellers together and hire a passenger boat ($50 for 10 people).

There are now over a dozen **guesthouses** in Nong Khiaw. *Philasouk* (❶), next to the bridge opposite the bus stop, has a dozen rooms in a big old wooden house. This was Nong Khiaw's first place of accommodation, but there are now far better options. Also on Route 1, a short walk to the west, is *Phayboun* (❶), which has twenty rooms in two buildings. Built for tour groups, the rooms here are a cut above the rest, especially those in the new wing that all feature en-suite bathrooms. At the top of the main street, near the bridge, the good-value *Manypoon* (❶) features seven simple rooms in a lovely house with a small garden. The upstairs rooms are the best and there's a small balcony with a nice view east. Across the river, *Sunset* (❶) is the "in" place with backpackers largely because of its excellent **restaurant** and lovely sun-deck overlooking the river. The guesthouse itself is clean and well run, and the owner is quite friendly and generous with information about the surrounding area.

Nong Khiaw to Nam Neun

The journey from Nong Khiaw to Nam Neun across Route 1 is one of northern Laos's great **road journeys**, crossing numerous mountain ranges and valleys. It's a very tough trip but the scenery more than makes up for the discomfort. From Nong Khiaw to **Viang Thong** the road is paved, but beyond the town of Sop Heuang, it becomes progressively worse until finally hitting pavement again at Nam Neun Junction, where paved Route 6 links Xam Nua to Phonsavan and the Plain of Jars.

Although it's possible to cover the entire route from Nong Khiaw to Xam Nua or Phonsavan by hired vehicle in a day, the same trip by public transport usually requires two or even three days. If you're travelling by local sawngthaews, you'll probably have to change vehicles at both Viang Kham, and again at Viang Thong (sometimes known as Muang Hiam), the first major town of Houa Phan province. Travellers going east often have to overnight in **Viang Thong**, while those travelling west may have to break the trip in **Viang Kham**.

In Viang Kham, sawngthaews will drop you at the bus stop 3km out on the northeast edge of town. If you're staying overnight, you'll have to hike into town or flag down a passing motorcycle. Both the town's two basic guesthouses (❶) are located close to the river bridge. In Viang Thong, there are three very basic **guesthouses**. The best choices for people transiting through are the *Santisouk* (❶) or the *Souksakhone* (❶), both near the bus lot; neither has a phone. There's very little to choose from among the handful of **food shacks** clustered at the heart of town.

Moving east from Viang Thong, buses depart as early as 6am. If you miss the onward bus, you have to get a truck or sawngthaew over the mountains to Nam Neun, a gruelling three hours to the east, where there are connections to Phonsavan and Xam Nua. If you arrive in Nam Neun late in the morning, you may wind-up stuck there overnight as well, since vehicles travelling Route 6 leave early.

Nam Neun

From Viang Thong, Route 1 crosses the mountains down to the tiny settlement of **Houa Phou** (the actual junction of Route 1 and Route 6) before winding a further 6km down into a deep river valley to the village of **NAM NEUN**, which functions as the practical hub for travel along Routes 1 and 6. The steep valley walls and churning river make Nam Neun a diamond in the rough, and for many it's a very welcome spot to break the long journey from Nong Khiaw. Travellers moving along Route 6 between Xam Nua and Phonsavan can also break up their 240-kilometre haul by overnighting here before making the final 140-kilometre run to Phonsavan. Basic *Nam Neun Guesthouse* (➊) at the bus lot has the cheapest **accommodation**, but the best place is *Phouchomkub* (➊), which has a terrific location right on the river and next door to the town wat.

Xam Nua

You could be forgiven for thinking that you'd crossed into Vietnam on descending into **XAM NUA**, the only sizeable Lao town east of the Annamite Mountains. Unlike the rest of Laos, which drains west into the Mekong, all of Houa Phan province's rivers flow southeast to the Gulf of Tonkin. Sitting in the narrow Nam Xam River valley, the provincial capital of Xam Nua is currently undergoing a construction boom, with new multi-storey buildings going up everywhere. Although there's little to see in town itself, it serves as a comfortable base for the **Viang Xai Caves**, forests and hilltribe villages, and trips along the Vietnamese frontier. Now that the border is open for Westerners, travellers will be able to pass through Xam Nua on the way to and from Hanoi.

Transport from Nam Nuen and Vieng Thong offloads at the **bus station** on Phathy Road, the town's main street. Across the big bridge over the Nam Xam, Route 6 continues to the airport, 3km away. If you've arrived at the **airport**, taxis (5000K) will be on hand to shuttle you to a hotel. There's a **tourist office** (Mon–Fri 8am–noon & 1–4pm) in the small building at the front of the *Lao Houng Hotel* but the official only speaks Lao and Vietnamese. Better information can be obtained at the Houaphanh Tourism Company (211 Phathy Rd; ⓣ064/312190), which can organize tours and has rental vehicles. Exchange services are available at Lang Xang Bank's Xam Nua branch, on the Phathy Road towards Wat Xaysanalam.

Xam Nua's best-value hotel is the *Khaem Xam* (ⓣ064/312111; ➊) located around the corner from the bus station, near the bridge over the Nam Xam River. This four-storey hotel overlooking the Nam Xam has eighteen clean rooms, many en suite, and all with hot water, as well as rooms with shared facilities that are also spotless. Of a similar quality, but slightly more expensive and further from the centre, is the *That Meuang Guesthouse* (ⓣ064/312141; ➋) off Phathy Road, behind the *Phanxay Guesthouse*. Travellers on a tight budget should head for *Long Ma* (ⓣ064/312230; ➊) just behind the bus station, which has perfectly good, tiled rooms with shared facilities and hot water.

Xam Nua boasts several tourist-class **restaurants**. *Chitthavanh*, facing the river a few doors down from *Khaem Xam*, is widely considered the best restaurant in town, with a range of reasonably priced dishes and an English-language menu. Right next door, *Yiensingchien* is similar and does a good beef noodle soup. *Houaphan Restaurant*, at 211 Phathy Road, dishes up exceptionally good Western food, including chicken kiev, and fish with white sauce.

Viang Xai

Sprawled across a valley surrounded by the cave-riddled karst formations used by the Pathet Lao as their wartime headquarters, **VIANG XAI** was cobbled together by comrades from Russia, North Korea and Vietnam as well as labourers from Houa Phan's notorious re-education camps. In 1973, at the end of the war, there were plans to make Viang Xai the heart of a new socialist nation, but in the end, the Pathet Lao leadership moved out and decided to keep Vientiane as the country's capital. Today, a victory arch made of oil drums is the gateway to this wax museum of empty kerbed streets, lined with broken, sci-fi street lamps.

Aside from the **noodle stalls** in the bare-bones market, satisfying meals are hard to come by in Viang Xai. If you're planning to stay for more than one night, you may want to bring supplies from Xam Nua, 30km to the west. A little less than 2km from the market, on the northwestern edge of town, the deserted *Viang Xai Guesthouse* (❶), surrounded by marvellous karsts and pine trees, is the only **place to stay**, but quite acceptable and great value.

Sawngthaews from Xam Nua (30min; 5000K) leave every hour until mid-afternoon and stop in front of the market. Alternatively, you could charter a sawngthaew for $5 from Xam Nua. You must register and pay a 3000K entrance fee at the Viang Xai **tourist office** (daily 8am–noon & 1–4pm) before you can **tour the caves**. From the market, bear left at the big stupa, and the tourist office is in the middle of the second block on the right. A guide will be assigned to you here for no extra charge.

The Pathet Lao caves

Like Vang Viang in central Laos and Mahaxai in the south, the limestone karst formations in the valleys east of Xam Nua are pockmarked with **caves** and crevices – a perfect hideout for the Pathet Lao's parallel government (see "History", p.513). Viet Minh army units began using the caves in the early 1950s and were soon joined by Lao leftists, so that by the mid-1960s, the Viang Xai area had become a troglodyte city of thousands. The inhabitants of the more than one hundred caves would sleep by day and work at night in the fields or in the caves themselves: caverns held weaving mills, printing presses and workshops where American bombs and worn-out trucks were upgraded into farming tools and appliances. On Saturdays, adults would take a break and attend professional, cultural and political courses. After the Paris peace accords were signed in 1973, a few of the cave-dwelling Pathet Lao leaders built houses outside their caves, where they lived until moving to Vientiane in 1975 to take up government office. After 1975, the caves became a "re-education camp" for the soldiers of the Royal Lao government.

Viang Xai has long been regarded as a national treasure and a symbol of revolutionary resolve along the lines of Mao's Long March, and recently five caves have been opened up to foreigners. Each of these caves, named after the Pathet Lao leaders who lived there, had multiple exits, an office and sleeping quarters, as well as an emergency chamber for use in case of chemical weapons attacks, kitted out with a Soviet oxygen machine and a metal door. The two-hour **tours** of the caves usually begin with **Tham Than Kaysone**, the cave of Kaysone Phomvihane, who led the Lao communist movement from its formation in 1955, and remained head of the Lao People's Democratic Republic from 1975 until his death in 1992. It's around the corner from the tourist office and now has a large brown house and a meeting hall in front of it. Northwest of the tourist office, **Tham Than Souphanouvong** was Prince Souphanouvong's cave, with a garage grotto for his car and an outdoor kitchen on a natural patio. Considered for years by the West to be the Pathet Lao's most important leader, the Red Prince lived here with his wife and ten children from 1963 to 1973; in 1975, he became president of the new government. Beyond the decrepit grandstand on the north side of town, you'll come to **Tham Than**

Safety in Xiang Khouang province

Occasional attacks by bandits or insurgents have given **Xiang Khouang** province an uncertain reputation. Buses have been strafed by machine-gun fire, and at least a dozen passengers were killed in separate incidents in the first half of 2004. Because the Lao government is so intent on controlling information, news of these attacks rarely reaches the international media unless a foreigner is killed. That said, hundreds of tourists visit the area each month without incident. Of more immediate danger are the **mines, bombis and bombs** littering the province. The three main Jar sites have been cleared of unexploded ordnance (UXO), but it's advisable to stick to the paths. The usual precautions apply: see "Crime and safety", p.509, for details.

Khamtay, the cave of Khamtay Siphandone, now prime minister of Laos. It features a kilometre-long secret tunnel – now shoulder-deep in water – that leads to a cavernous chamber, formerly used as a meeting hall and bizarrely, for the odd circus performance; the Soviets allegedly brought in a dancing bear for a subterranean May Day celebration in 1970.

Phonsavan

Faced with the prospect of a long (and potentially dangerous) road trip via Route 7 or Routes 1 and 6, many visitors opt for a flight into **PHONSAVAN**, which also gives an unforgettable view of the treeless flatlands and crater-ridden landscape of the Plain of Jars. The capital of **Xiang Khouang province**, Phonsavan has gradually emerged as the most important town on the Plain of Jars since the total devastation of the region in the Second Indochina War. The bomb-casing collections in many guesthouse lobbies are a grim reminder of the area's tragic past, when possession of the strategic plain was seen as the key to control of Laos. Hastily rebuilt in the aftermath of decades of fighting, Phonsavan is only now, thirty years after the conflict, just beginning to recover economically, thanks in a large part to international interest in the world-famous **jar sites** scattered around the perimeter of the plain. Despite the dreadful destruction rained upon the province and its people, the region's future prospects for tourism look bright. Although most visitors come only to see the jar sites, the Xiang Khouang Plateau is a place of great natural beauty and its backroads are well worth exploring.

Practicalities

Flying into Phonsavan, you'll need a **tuk-tuk** (10,000K per person) for the four-kilometre ride from the airport into town. Alternatively, you can get a free lift with one of the hotel reps. Arriving by bus, you'll be dropped at the bus lot opposite the dry-goods market and the GPO, an easy walk to most guesthouses. Vehicles towards Vientiane and Xam Nua all leave from here. Vehicles for Muang Khoun and other points south leave from the Talat Nam Ngum bus station, 3km to the southwest of town, on the road to the jar sites. The tuk-tuk stand is on the main road just opposite the *Daophouan Guesthouse*. For journeys further afield, four-wheel-drives can be hired through most hotels and travel agencies; Lao Airlines' office is located at the airport but most guesthouses can handle bookings. There are as many as four **flights** a week between Phonsavan and Vientiane, though during the low season this may drop to one flight per week. Lane Xang Bank is on the main road, at the south end of town across from the *Phudoi Hotel*, and can **exchange** US dollars travellers' cheques. You'll also find an exchange kiosk at the airport. An **Internet centre** is located next to the *Phonekeo Restaurant*; the Telcom is next to the GPO.

Accommodation

Phonsavan boasts many **guesthouses** and **hotels**, most of which line Route 7, east of the dry-goods market. Since the opening of Route 7 to foreigners, the food and accommodation situation has gradually improved, and Phonsavan is slowly losing its edge-of-the-world feel. There is now 24-hour electricity, and no longer is it necessary to bathe in freezing water.

Auberge de Plaine de Jarres ☎061/312044. On a hill southeast of town, this very classy lodge has deluxe two-room cabins with fireplaces, and private bathrooms that overlook the town. Spectacular views from the French restaurant. ⑥

Daophouan Across from the GPO ☎061/312171. The eleven rooms in this three-storey building are a notch above others in the same category and all are en suite with hot water. Good quality but a bit pricey. ②

Dokkhoun Route 7, east of the dry-goods market ☎061/312189. Two separate buildings with clean, tiled en-suite doubles with hot water. The mid-range rooms here are better value than the budget ones. ①–②

Kong Keo Off Route 7, next to the old airstrip ☎061/211354. Whether you're looking for an inexpensive room with clean, shared facilities or a deluxe bungalow with en-suite bathroom and hot water, *Kong*'s is simply the best value in town. ①–②

Maly Located 1km south of the market, on the road to Jar Site 1 ☎061/312031. This newish place has comfortable rooms with en-suite bathroom and hot water. The attached restaurant is one of the best in town. After a day of hiking around the jars, try the house speciality – medicinal mushroom liquor. ④

Vanearoun Route 7, next to the *Phonekeo Restaurant* ☎061/312070. Old and basic but better value than a lot of other places in the same price range. The bathrooms are tiled and clean but without hot water. ①

Vinhtong Route 7, another block further east of the *Dokkhoun* ☎061/212622. Basic but clean with tiled floors and en-suite bathrooms with hot water. There are also some bigger units out back for slightly more. ①–②

Eating

Phonsavan is still not a great town for **eating** out. If you're a true fan of *fŏe*, you're in luck – Phonsavan seems to thrive on it. Typical is *Nang Sila*, 600m west of the dry-goods market, a two-storey grey house on the left. Stay at the *Maly Hotel* and you probably won't find the need to eat elsewhere. The food at *Kong Keo Guesthouse* is also worth trying: they've been getting cooking lessons from all the falangs, and have now added mashed potatoes, fresh fruit salad and homemade peanut butter to their menu. For a splurge, the views from the French restaurant up at the *Auberge de Plaine de Jarres* are outstanding, but you'll need to phone and place your order a few hours in advance (☎061/312044).

The Plain of Jars

The fifteen-kilometre-wide stretch of grassy meadows and low rolling hills around Phonsavan takes its name from the clusters of chest-high funerary urns found there. Scattered across the **Plain of Jars** and on the hills beyond, the ancient jars, which are thought to be around two thousand years old, testify to the fact that Xiang Khouang province, with its access to key regional trade routes, its wide, flat spaces and temperate climate, has been considered prime real estate in Southeast Asia for centuries. The largest jars measure 2m in height and weigh as much as ten tonnes. Little is known about the iron-age megalithic civilization that created them, but in the 1930s, bronze and iron tools as well as coloured glass beads, bronze bracelets and cowrie shells were found at the sites, leading to the theory that the jars were funerary urns, originally holding cremated remains. More recent discoveries have also revealed underground burial chambers. During the **Second Indochina War**, the region was bombed extensively. American planes levelled towns and forced villagers to take to the forest, as the two sides waged a bitter battle for control of the Plain of

Jars, which represented a back door to northern Vietnam. The plain was transformed into a wasteland, the treeless flatlands and low rolling brown hills pockmarked with craters which leave a lasting impression on those who fly over it on their way into Phonsavan.

Exploring the jar sites

Of the dozens of jar sites that give the Plain of Jars its name, three groups have become tourist attractions, largely because they are accessible and have a greater concentration of jars. All three of these jar sites and old **Xiang Khouang** (see below) can be seen in a day, with hotels and tour companies pitching the four spots as a **package**. As such, local tour agencies mainly deal with package tourists, but will hire a van and driver to walk-in customers, charging as much as $100 for a tour of the sites. A far cheaper option is to book a vehicle and guide through one of the local guesthouses ($30–40 for a van). Hiring a vehicle for a do-it-yourself tour is impossible since tuk-tuks aren't allowed to go and private taxis and vehicles must be registered for "safety" and have a special permit to serve the jar sites, a system introduced by the big tourist hotels and travel agencies.

Of the three main groups, the closest one, **Thong Hai Hin** ("Stone Jar Plain") – known as Site 1 – is just 2km southwest of town, has over two hundred jars and is the most visited. There's a 4000K entrance fee at the pavilion. From here, a path leads up to **Hai Cheaum** ("Cheaum Jar"), a massive 2m-high jar named after a Tai-Lao hero. Nearby is another group of jars, one of which has a crude human shape carved onto it. In the hill off to the left is a large cave that the Pathet Lao used during the war – and which, according to local legend, was used as a kiln to cast the jars. Erosion has carved two holes in the roof of the cave – natural chimneys that add weight to the kiln theory. It may also have been used as a crematorium.

Sites 2 and 3 are much more scenic than Site 1 and are located about 10km southwest of the village of Lat Houang, which is on the road to Muang Khoun. There is a 4000K entry charge per site at Sites 2 and 3 as well. Site 2 is located on two adjacent hills called Phou Salato. Nearly a hundred jars are scattered across the twin hills here, lending the site the name **Hai Hin Phou Salato** ("Salato Hill Stone Jar"). Site 3, the most atmospheric of the three sites, lies 4km up the road, just beyond the village of Ban Xiang Di. Here you'll see Wat Xiang Di, a simple wooden monastery that holds a bomb-damaged Buddha. A path at the back of the monastery leads up a hill through several fields to Site 3, **Hai Hin Lat Khai**, where there are more than a hundred jars on a hillside with sweeping views of the plain below.

Muang Khoun (Xiang Khouang)

A ghost of its former self, **MUANG KHOUN**, old Xiang Khouang, 35km southeast of Phonsavan, was once the royal seat of the minor kingdom of Xiang Khouang, renowned in the sixteenth century for its 62 opulent stupas, whose sides were said to be covered in treasure. Years of bloody invasions, pillaging and a monsoon of bombs that lasted nearly a decade during the Second Indochina War taxed this town so heavily that, by the time the air raids stopped, next to nothing was left of its exquisite temples. Although the town has been rebuilt and renamed, all that remains of the kingdom's former glory are a few evocative ruins, usually visited as part of a day-trip to the jar sites. A path alongside the market leads up to the blackened hilltop stupa of **That Dam**, the base of which has been tunnelled straight through by treasure-seekers. Continuing on the main road beyond the market, you'll pass the ruins of a villa, the only reminder that this town was once a temperate French outpost of ochre colonial villas and shop-houses, and arrive at the ruins of sixteenth-century Wat Phia Wat. Brick columns reach skywards around a seated Buddha of impressive size, a mere hint at the temple architecture for which the city was renowned.

5.4

The far north

Decades of war and neglect have done their part to keep this isolated region in far northern Laos from developing and have unwittingly preserved a way of life that has virtually vanished in neighbouring countries. The hills and mountains up here have long been the domain of a scattering of **animist tribal peoples**, including the Hmong, Mien and Akha, and it is largely the chance to experience first-hand these near-pristine cultures that draws visitors to the region today.

By far the most popular route out of Louang Phabang is the road through **Oudomxai** and **Louang Namtha** to **Muang Sing**, a laid-back Tai Leu town that lies within the borders of the Golden Triangle, the world's most notorious opium-producing zone. Of late, Muang Sing has become a popular base for trekking, owing to its decent accommodation and easy access to Akha, Mien and Tai Dam villages. Travellers en route to **China** are allowed to cross at **Boten**, reached by bus from Louang Namtha or Oudomxai. From Muang Sing, the road leads southwest to the village of **Xiang Kok** on the Mekong, the launching point for speedboats to Houayxai, an official border crossing with **Thailand**. Many travellers exit Laos here after completing their trip around the north, but it's also possible to come full circle and return to Louang Phabang via a memorable **Mekong boat journey**. The usual direction of the loop is counter-clockwise (Louang Phabang–Oudomxai–Muang Sing–Xiang Kok–Houayxai–Louang Phabang), but a clockwise route, heading north up the Mekong to Xiang Kok first, avoids the crowds on the Mekong slow boat and means you don't constantly run into the same travellers at every stop.

Oudomxai

Most travellers heading north to Muang Sing and Louang Namtha begin their journey in Louang Phabang and head up Route 13 to **OUDOMXAI** (Muang Xai), an important transport hub at the junction of Route 1 and Route 4. Although there's no reason to visit Oudomxai, if you travel around the north, chances are you'll end up having to stop-over here at some point, like it or not. From Oudomxai, **public transport** runs in all directions – see "Travel details", p.586. Most vehicles leave early morning (8–10am), but there are some afternoon departures.

Oudomxai is a popular springboard into Laos for Chinese tourists and traders, and the town's hotels and karaoke lounges readily accept Chinese yuan. Oudomxai itself has a Chinese border-town feel about it, but without the exciting intensity of actually being on the border. Few stay longer than a night here, but with 24-hour electricity, laundry service, hot water and Internet cafés, it does have its uses. You'll find a Lane Xang **bank** 500m north of the market just past the *Misay Restaurant*, and a BCEL west of the bus station, opposite the Konica Express lab. Both exchange foreign currency and travellers' cheques, and accept Visa. Several **Internet cafés** are located on the main street.

Oudomxai's position as a transportation hub means the town gets its share of Chinese truckers, who treat the town as a last-chance saloon – hence, many of the its hotels are involved in the sex trade. All the newer **guesthouses** are on the east side of the river, on or just off the main road. Although there are a dozen places here, most of them are noisy, badly built and poorly maintained. Of the slim choice of backpacker-oriented accommodation, the ugly but well-maintained *Phouxay Hotel* (☎081/312140; ❶) is probably the best value, offering clean rooms with fan or air-con, en-suite bathroom, and hot water; more importantly, everything seems to work. Around the corner, the cheaper *Linda Guesthouse* (☎081/312147; ❶) also has a choice of fan or air-con, but if you choose the latter, make sure it works – the top floor rooms tend to get hot in the afternoons. Twenty metres north, up the first alley east of the *Linda*, the *Kongchai Guesthouse* (☎081/211141; ❶) features simple but clean and reasonably priced rooms with en-suite bathrooms and hot water. The rooms at the front of the building overlook the football field and have views of the mountains.

There are plenty of **restaurants** in Oudomxai, particularly Chinese-run places, so few of the guesthouses have an attached restaurant. *Si Moang Restaurant* is one of the town's better-organized establishments; to find it, take the first alley on the right, east of the bridge, then turn right at the T-junction and it's on the first corner. *Misay*, about 400m north past the *Fu Shan Hotel*, is one of Oudomxai's longest running eateries and worth the short hike.

Louang Namtha

Straddling Route 3, four hours' drive northwest of Oudomxai, **LOUANG NAMTHA** was heavily contested during Laos's civil war, which is to say that it was razed to the ground. Once the fighting stopped, the surrounding hills were stripped of their trees and the mammoth logs were trucked away to China. Today, the once-devastated and depopulated valley is making a comeback as a booming tourist area with rafting, kayaking and trekking activities.

In the town itself there's little to do except drop by the **Louang Namtha Provincial Museum** (Mon–Fri 8.30am–noon & 1–3.30pm; 1000K), housed in a green-roofed building behind the Kaysone Monument, where you'll find displays of traditional hilltribe costumes and artefacts, a model depicting battles that took place in the area during the civil war, and a rusty collection of weaponry. The real reason to come to Louang Namtha though is to visit the Namha NBCA (National Biodiversity Conservation Area), walk or cycle to nearby Hmong and Leten villages, take a trek in the hills, or go kayaking or rafting on the Nam Tha and Nam Ha rivers. Louang Namtha is also a launch base for passenger boat trips down the Nam Tha River to Houayxai.

Although Louang Namtha only has electricity from 6pm to 10pm, there is quite a good range of **tourist facilities**, including colour photo labs, bicycle rental shops, two Lao herbal saunas, Internet cafes, two banks and a travel agency. All of the above are located on or just off the main street. For currency exchange, head to the BCEL service unit at the bus station, which accepts cash, travellers' cheques and Visa; there's also a Lane Xang Bank on the main street just north of Lao Airlines which can exchange foreign currency and travellers' cheques, and a BCEL branch on the main street almost opposite the Lao Telcom.

Accommodation and eating

Louang Namtha has the best selection of accommodation and restaurants north of Louang Phabang, with over twenty **guesthouses** and hotels. The best **food** in the area is at the *Boat Landing Restaurant*, located at the hotel of the same name 6km south of town. This is a great place to sample quality Lao food and there's a wide choice of northern specialities – the spicy Lao purees are particularly worth trying. In town, the flashiest option is the *House Lao Restaurant* on the main street, at the north end of town opposite the *Sinsavanh Guesthouse*. This marvellous

Lao-style restaurant, completely built of wood, is far too nice for its poor location, but the Lao specialities make it a must. Decent, inexpensive travellers' cafés can be found at *Many Chan*, *Dalasavath* and *Saikhonglongsak* guesthouses, all on the main street. Also worth checking out is the highly popular *Panda Restaurant* (☎086/211304) just north of the bus station, which does very cheap Western dishes and stir-fries.

The Boat Landing 6km south of the centre on the banks of the Nam Tha River ☎086/312398. Northern Laos' most famous eco-style resort and good value at $17–45 a room. Treks and rafting can also be arranged here. ❻

Bus Station Guesthouse ☎086/211090. Entrance facing the bus field on its eastern side. Despite the name and location, this ten-room guesthouse is actually one of the best deals in town. The attractive, well-constructed building is inside a walled compound, so it's quite peaceful. The rooms are clean and have en-suite bathrooms. ❶–❷

Khammanivong Main road 50m south of Lao Airlines. Ten simple but clean rooms with shared bathrooms in an attractive wooden house. All the rooms have wood floors, large windows, and Lao textile quilts. There are hot showers and the rear balcony has mountain views. One of the best-value places in town at $2.50 per room. ❶

Luang Namtha Guesthouse North up the road running along the west side of the bus field ☎086/312087. This varied place has several types of accommodation, including large rooms in a huge modern house, nicely built thatched bungalows out back, and another concrete hotel-style building. The latter's rooms are the cheapest, but the bungalows overlooking the pond and the main house are good value for money. ❶–❷

Many Chan Main street opposite the dry market ☎086/312209. Eight rooms on the second floor of a wooden house, with toilets and hot shower below. The rooms are spartan but very clean. This is the favourite backpacker hotel in town so it fills up very quickly. ❶

Palanh Main street, directly opposite the *Saikhonglongsak* ☎086/312439. The rooms here, some with shared bath, are about standard quality but the place is starting to show wear. Prices tend to start high, but discounts are readily given on request. ❶–❷

Soulivong On the corner one block east of the GPO ☎086/312253. This large, new three-storey house with a peaked blue roof has clean rooms with tile floors and en-suite bathrooms with hot water. The rooms on the 2nd and 3rd floors are the best. ❶

Trekking, rafting and kayaking around Louang Namtha

Trekking in the Namha NBCA must be booked through a licensed agent or through the Louang Namtha Guide Services Office (GSO; daily 8am–noon & 1–5pm); they offer a full range of one- two- and three-day guided treks. The GSO is located opposite the south side of the Kaysone Monument, just in off the main street. Groups have a four-person minimum and a six- to eight-person maximum limit and generally work out about $10 per person per day. Not all the tours leave daily, so the GSO should be your first stop after checking into your hotel. The GSO also has a wall display showing the villages that can be visited and which tribal peoples inhabit them, as well as a big topographical map of the NBCA, and plenty of pamphlets.

For **kayaking** and **rafting** trips, see the Wildside Outdoor Adventures office on the main street. Wildside has a number of river packages on the Nam Tha and Nam Ha, ranging from one to four days and with stays in tribal villages en route. Prices vary and are significantly cheaper when there are more people joining the tour, but you're generally looking at about $20 a day. Programmes vary, too, so see Wildside for information on tours, departures and group sizes as soon as you get to town.

Moving on from Louang Namtha

Sawngthaews for Muang Sing and Oudomxai leave from Louang Namtha's bus station, next to the morning market. Travellers with a valid visa for China can take a Chinese-operated bus in the morning from Louang Namtha bus station to the border crossing at Boten and on to Jinghong in China. Sawngthaews only go as far as the border. The road trip down to Houayxai is one of those dusty Lao journeys that are fast disappearing with the ongoing road-paving programme. This particular road has been under construction since the mid-1990s and is still quite bad. The route is plied by sawngthaews, taking between eight and ten hours ($6). During dry season, passengers eat a lot of dust; during the monsoon season, you get wet and the mire is sometimes barely passable. If the ride gets too much, there's a basic guesthouse in the village of Vieng Phou Kha, 66km south of Louang Namtha. Once the upgrading of the road has been completed, the journey should take under six hours.

During the wet season, travellers heading for Houayxai have the option of going by **boat**. The Nam Tha is navigable from about July until January. Since the locals no longer rely on the river for transportation, you must hire a boat outright ($100 for a boat that holds up to ten people). If water levels are high, it's a one-day trip but if the water is low it takes one-and-a-half days, with an overnight stop in Na Lae. Boatmen usually only go as far as Paktha, where the Nam Tha meets the Mekong. From there, you get a speedboat for the last 36-kilometre stretch along the Mekong to Houayxai (1hr; B200 per person). It's very important to strike a clear deal with the boatman, as they have been known to want to re-negotiate the fare once en route.

Muang Sing and around

In a short space of time, **MUANG SING**, located some 60km northwest of Louang Namtha, has progressed from a quaint, middle-of-nowhere Tai Leu village to a full-on backpacker haven. Ten years ago, barely a trickle of travellers made it to Muang Sing, but since then its residents have opened dozens of guesthouses and restaurants to cater to tourists and trekkers in search of exotic **hilltribes** in traditional garb.

However, it's still an agreeable and friendly little town where great, sway-backed sows drag their teats down the main road and young novice monks play *kataw* and ride bicycles around the monastery grounds. The ancient-looking **Wat Sing Jai**, hidden behind the *Muangsing Guest House*, has a wonderfully rustic *sim*, painted in festive bright hues with a huge Buddha image inside.

Muang Sing's morning **market** was famous for its colourfully dressed vendors and shoppers, though nowadays camera-toting tourists almost outnumber the locals, who these days are more likely to be wearing track suits and Nike knock-offs. If you want to take a photo of a vendor, it's only polite to buy something first and try to have a little conversation. The market convenes very early, just after sunrise, and winds down by noon, though goods are on sale all day long. To get a look at lifestyles beyond the town limits, you can join a one-, two- or three-day **trek** through the surrounding mountains to remote and unspoilt hilltribe villages where daily life has barely changed in centuries.

Practicalities

Pick-ups to Muang Long (2hr), Xiang Kok (2hr 30min) and Louang Namtha (2hr) wait in the station in front of the market and leave when full. Most vehicles depart in the morning but it's still possible to find one leaving at around 2pm. The Chinese border north of Muang Sing is not open to Westerners. There is a visitor **information booth** on the northwest corner of the market, and you can **exchange** cash and travellers' cheques at BCEL opposite the *Vieng Xai* guesthouse or the Lane Xang Bank service unit on the south side of the market square. The **post office** is directly opposite the market, and the telecom office is located west of the main road, on the street running parallel to the stream. **Trekking** must be booked through the Muang Sing Guide Services Office (GSO) near the market. **Bicycles** are available from the Mountain Tour postcard shop on the main road, a little further north of the stream. A traditional Lao massage place and herbal **sauna** (10,000K) is located on the main road, 100m south of the market.

Accommodation and eating

Viengxay and *Vieng Phone*, right next to each other on the main street, are the most popular tourist **restaurants** in town. The *Phou Iu Guesthouse* has the nicest restaurant and serves fresh fish brought in from fish-farms in nearby China. The *Muang Sing View Restaurant* attached to the Lao sauna place at the south end of the main street has a very nice covered deck with a superb view over the rice fields.

Although Muang Sing is still pretty rustic, the town now has a fair range of **hotel** options, from basic rooms in old wooden buildings to comfortable rooms with en-suite bathrooms in modern houses. However, electricity is still only available from 6pm to 10pm and none of the hotels has hot running water.

Adima 8km north of town, on the road to the Chinese frontier ☎086/212372. Muang Sing's first eco-tourist resort, featuring bamboo architecture in a rural setting. There's a choice of rooms in two big thatched bungalows with grass roofs or in A-frame cabins. The nice bamboo restaurant with a deck overlooking the fields is worth visiting even if you stay in town. ❶–❷

Charmpadeang Northeast corner of the market ☎086/212374. The best of the four budget hotels facing the market. Rooms on the second floor have terrific views over the rice fields towards the mountains. ❶–❷

Danneua Main road just north of the *Muangsing*

A brief history of opium

In the first half of the twentieth century, Muang Sing was a weigh station and market for the French government's **opium** monopoly, Opium Régie, which suppressed cultivation of the poppy among local Hmong and Mien tribals in order to tax and control the supply of opium to the licensed dens of Indochina. By the beginning of World War II, taxes on the sale of opium throughout French Indochina made up fifteen percent of the colonial government's revenues. When global war disrupted the traditional maritime route of opium into Indochina, Opium Régie started to encourage local Hmong farmers, resulting in an 800 percent increase in Hmong opium production within four years.

Two decades later, America's CIA operatives trained the Hmong guerrillas that had previously sided with the French, using their cash crop to fund their operations. A Byzantine alliance between the Royal Lao Government, opium warlords and the CIA was formed. The CIA co-ordinated the collection of opium, which was transported to refineries in the **Golden Triangle**, the resulting heroin eventually finding its way to markets all over the globe. By the war's end, the production of opium in the Golden Triangle, which overlaps into Burma and Thailand (see p.1028), had reached epic proportions. Eradication programmes in Thailand have been largely successful, and opium cultivation in Burma and Laos seems to be decreasing as traffickers are now focusing their efforts on the much more lucrative methamphetamine trade, which is cheaper and less conspicuous to produce. The Deutsche Gesellschaft für Technische Zusammenarbeit or GTZ, a German federal corporation that helps run opium prevention, reduction and rehabilitation programmes, has a project office on the western edge of town. A small but informative free exhibition there (Mon–Fri 9am–4pm) documents their work. Cultivating, trafficking and using opium is illegal in Laos. You may be offered opium in Muang Sing, but if you indulge, you should be aware that by partaking you are also encouraging a vice that creates poverty and shortens lives.

Guesthouse ☎086/212369. Typical of the newer places, this is an unsightly concrete building, but the eight upstairs rooms are clean and modern and have en-suite bathrooms. There's a nice wide balcony overlooking the main drag. ❶

Muangsing Guesthouse Main street near Wat Sing Jai. This very friendly, family-run place is the backpacker favourite. One- and two-bed rooms with shared bath, and a nice coffee shop downstairs. The sitting area on the roof is also good for sunsets. ❶

Phou lu Main road south of market ☎086/212348. This newish hotel has clean rooms with tile floors and en-suite bathrooms. There are also bungalow-style rooms of wood and bamboo with small verandas. ❷

Saengdeuang Main road, 100m north of the Exhibition building ☎086/212376. This large, well-built, two-storey building has eight rooms and a clean restaurant downstairs. But the real draw are the thatched bungalows with shake roofs out back. The bungalow rooms have wooden floors, big windows and en-suite bathrooms. ❶–❷

Singcharean West off the main road from the *Phou lu*. Muang Sing's biggest tourist hotel with 22 rooms aimed at package-tour groups from France. Institutional and devoid of atmosphere, but if you need something clean and modern with an en-suite bathroom, this fits the bill. ❷

Villages and trekking around Muang Sing

Muang Sing is located in the centre of a flat, triangular plain surrounded on all three sides by high mountains. There are scores of **hilltribe settlements** both in the valley and all through the surrounding mountains populated by Tai Leu, Tai Dam, Akha, Mien and Hmong people. Until recently, trekking here was a do-it-yourself venture using local youths as guides and hoping for the best. In 2003, however, the Tourist Authority opened a GSO (Guide Services Office) in Muang Sing to ensure that foreign trekkers would hire a licensed guide. Visitors are no longer allowed to wander in and out of hilltribe villages unescorted, and locals are fined if caught guiding foreigners on unauthorized treks. This is not necessarily a negative development, as the townspeople had done very little towards developing a local trekking industry; there has even been resentment among some villagers who came to realize that they were the attraction yet were receiving no financial gain from the daily parade of gawkers. The GSO-organized tours are supposed to rectify that situation, as well as be more professional and environmentally friendly.

Muang Sing to Xiang Kok

The road between Muang Sing and Xiang Kok passes through one of Laos's most remote regions. While the peaceful scenery of forest-covered hills belies it, the history of this region is tied to the production of illicit drugs: opium, heroin and, more recently, methamphetamine. Travellers are unlikely to see any indication of this activ-

Trekking etiquette

If you decide to do a **trek**, always trek in groups, as there have been assaults on Western tourists in rural areas. If you are approached by armed men and robbery is clearly their intent, do NOT resist. Most hilltribe peoples are animists. Offerings to the spirits, often bits of food, left in what may seem like an odd place, should never be touched or tampered with. The Akha are known for the elaborate gates that they construct at the entrances to their villages. These gates have special meaning to the Akha and should also be left alone. Many hill folk are willing to be photographed, but old women, particularly of the Hmong and Mien tribes, are not always keen, so ask first. Passing out sweets to village kids is a sure way to generate mobs of young beggars. Likewise, the indiscriminate handing out of medicine, particularly antibiotics, does more harm than good. Unless you are a trained doctor, you should never attempt to administer medical care.

ity from the road though. While the Lao government has mundanely designated this 75-kilometre stretch of road Route 322, a more apt designation might be the **Akha Road**, given the high density of Akha villages through which it passes. This is one of the few areas in Laos where you will see Akha men still wearing their traditional headgear: disk-shaped red turbans or tall hats festooned with seed-beads. The road is now paved all the way, and sawngthaews run in both directions in the early morning. The main stop between Muang Sing and Xiang Kok is **Muang Long**, where there are guesthouses and good independent trekking.

Xiang Kok

A sleepy frontier town on a remote stretch of the Mekong, **XIANG KOK**, some two-and-a-half hours southwest of Muang Sing, is currently the last river-town stop before China. The Upper Mekong scenery is fantastic, with great views up and down the river and Akha villages dotted along the road. At this point, the river is narrow and studded with islets of craggy stone, and the region's remoteness gives it a wilderness feel. Plans are already underway to open the river road from Jinghong in China to Chiang Khong in Thailand to tourists, which should give the town a major boost. Meanwhile, the local economy seems to be based on trade between Thailand and China, and smuggling. The town itself is ramshackle: there's a customs post, half a dozen guesthouses, a few shops and a brothel. Chinese cargo trucks transfer loads at the boat landing before heading back to China.

Most budget travellers stay at the *Khem Khong Guesthouse and Restaurant* (❶) near the customs office above the boat landing. The rooms here are clean and there are some with en-suite bathrooms and cold water shower. The veranda overlooking the river is a pleasant place to spend a couple of hours. Even if you don't stay here, you'll probably end up eating at the restaurant downstairs. More comfortable is the *Xieng Kok Resort* (❷) on the embankment. Built by a Thai investor, the resort has twelve comfortable, self-contained bungalows with en-suite bathrooms and charming balconies over-looking the Mekong. There's also a basic restaurant on the grounds. Electricity in Xiang Kok is by private generators and generally runs from dusk until 9.30pm. None of these places has a phone.

From Xiang Kok, you can only **travel downriver**. The Xiang Kok boatmen have a bad reputation for extorting money from tourists. They know well that Xiang Kok is the end of the line and many travellers need to get down to Houayxai and exit into Thailand before their visas expire. What should be a $12-per-person ride can cost $30 or more and no amount of haggling will bring the price down. Some frustrated travellers simply return to Muang Sing. The best bargaining technique is to pretend you don't want to go downriver at all. Spend some time chatting with the boatmen, share some cigarettes, and then rhetorically ask how much it might cost if you did want to go downriver.

Houayxai

The town of **HOUAYXAI**, situated on a hilly stretch of the Mekong River, is a favourite border crossing for people moving between Laos and Thailand. Travellers arriving in Houayxai can strike up or down the Mekong by boat, or bus overland up Route 3 to Louang Namtha. Those exiting Laos here can obtain a thirty-day **visa-on-arrival** from Thai immigration in Chiang Khong (daily 8am–5.30pm; see p.498) on the Thai side. Once in Chiang Khong, there are direct buses on to Chiang Rai or Chiang Mai.

Houayxai's main sight is the hilltop **Wat Chom Khao Manilat**, boasting a tall, Shan-style building of picturesquely weathered teakwood, now used as a classroom for novice monks. There's also a traditional Lao herbal **sauna** run by the Red Cross in Bokeo (daily 5–9pm; sauna 8000K; massage 25,000K for 1hr), located just past the wooden bridge as you go north up the main road.

There are a dozen choices of **accommodation** in Houayxai, all on the main road just up-hill from the ferry landing. Since the older hotels haven't lowered their prices, the newer places are actually better value for money. *Thaweesinh Hotel* (☎021/211502; ❶–❷) is a four-storey concrete building with a nice rooftop patio. It's clean and modern and therefore popular with group tours. Rooms range from windowless singles ($2) to air-con doubles with TV ($8). Thirty metres south, on the same side of the street, is the *Friendship Guesthouse* (☎084/211219; ❶–❷), which is almost identical to the *Thaweesinh Hotel* in price and standard. North of the *Thaweesinh*, *Savanh Bokeo* (❶) offers about the cheapest deal in town, with its large two-, three- and four-bed rooms and shared facilities in a nice, old wooden house. A little further along on the west side of the road, the newish *Sabaydee Guesthouse* (❶) offers the top value in town with spotless rooms with tiled, en-suite bathrooms. The four corner units give terrific views of the Mekong. Just opposite and slightly to the north is the *Thanormsub Guesthouse* (☎084/211095; ❶), a blue-roofed house with fourteen very clean, tiled rooms with en-suite bathrooms and hot water. Some rooms are available with air-con.

Mouang Neua **restaurant** opposite the *Thaweesinh Hotel* has an English menu and specializes in tourist fare – the vegetable omelette is a must. The basic *River View* does stir-fry dishes, cold beer and fruit smoothies under a big, old mango tree on the banks of the Mekong. *Arimid Guest House* restaurant, opposite the bank, is quite good and a comfortable place to sit and relax. There are also riverside restaurants overlooking both the ferry landing and the slow-boat pier.

Down the Mekong to Louang Phabang

Slow boats take two days to complete the journey from Houayxai to **Louang Phabang**, stopping overnight at the village of **Pakbeng** (see opposite). You can also do the trip by speedboats in just over six hours, but this is potentially dangerous as they seem to crash into rocks with an alarming frequency.

Despite the general lack of comfort, most travellers agree that the two-day journey by **slow boat** (*heua sa*) to the old royal capital is one of those once-in-a-lifetime experiences. Every morning, slow boats leave from the slow-boat pier, 1km upriver from the Chiang Khong ferry landing, and arrive at Pakbeng in the late afternoon. The following morning the boat continues on to Louang Phabang, arriving around dusk. Fares ($8 to Pakbeng, $15 to Louang Phabeng) are payable in Thai baht, dollars or kip. A few years back, all the slow boats plying this route were cargo boats. Once the cargo had been loaded, passengers sat wherever they could find space. Nowadays, some of the boats have been converted to take only foreign passengers. While the level of comfort has increased, these new boats are lacking in the romance department. There are still genuine cargo boats doing the run, however, so it just depends on which boat is making the trip the day you want to depart. Bring along food and bottled water, as none is available on board. A closed-in area on the stern serves as the toilet. During high season it's not unusual for the boatmen to pack as many as eighty tourists into a single vessel. If this isn't your cup of tea, simply do the trip in reverse, upriver from Louang Phabang to Houayxai, where the same boat is virtually empty.

Speedboats (*heua wai*) also make the journey from Houayxai to Pakbeng ($15) and Louang Phabang ($30); crash helmets and life-vests are supposed to be provided, and don't forget to bring earplugs. The speedboat landing is located 2km downriver for boats going south. Speedboats going upriver to Xiang Kok now leave from the Nam Keng landing, a ridiculous 27km north of town. The road to Nam Keng is paved and the fare is B100. It's important to arrive at the landings as early as possible in order to get a boat – if there are no other passengers, it may be necessary to hire the boat outright. The speedboats are fast but the bottom of the boat pounds the river and the noise from the huge engine is truly deafening. Keep in mind that they also crash on occasion. Provided you have sunglasses, sunblock, and good earplugs, you might find the ride is quite fun – at least for the first hour or so.

Pakbeng and around

A single-lane dirt road winding up the side of a mountain makes up the bustling, frontier riverport of **PAKBENG**, the halfway point between Houayxai and Louang Phabang and the only sizeable town along the 300-kilometre stretch of river between them. As slow boats don't travel the Mekong after dark, a night here is unavoidable if you're travelling this way – a taste of backcountry Laos complete with hilltribes and rustic accommodation. Stumbling off the slow boat at the end of a long day, the ramshackle settlement of wood-scrap, corrugated tin and hand-painted signs that constitutes the port area can be a bit of a culture shock. Since Pakbeng is many travellers' first night in Laos, the expression on a lot of faces is "What have I got myself into?" Don't worry; Pakbeng is only typical of the northern backwoods. You'll be sipping lattés in Louang Phabang in no time.

Accommodation and eating

Once the boat pulls in, don't waste any time securing a room. From the landing, the majority of **guesthouses** are just up the hill, well before you reach the actual town of Pakbeng itself. The largest is the three-storey, concrete building right above the landing, the *Sarika* (☎081/212306; ❸). This fifteen-room guesthouse – all rooms have en-suite bathrooms – is aimed at package groups and is the most expensive on the street. Further up the road you'll find another half-dozen guesthouses – all in the $2 range. They are all pretty much the same, comprising very basic wooden rooms with beds, mosquito nets and fans, with shared cold-water washrooms out back. The best of these are the *Phanh Thavong* (❶) and the *Donevilasak* (❶) almost at the top of the hill. If you want something fancier, turn left from the boat landing and walk about 200m to the newly rebuilt *Bunmy Guesthouse* (☎081/212294 ❶–❷), which has rooms with or without private bath, in three concrete houses next to the Mekong. Another 800m down the road is the luxurious *Pakbeng Resort* (❾) with eighteen luxury bungalows with all mod cons and its own boat pier and fancy restaurant.

All the town's guesthouses have **restaurants** of about the same quality. The ones on the eastern side of the street have Mekong views provided the sun hasn't set before you get round to eating. *Dokkhoune*, *Pinekham* and *Souksakkhong* are all pleasant, and *Bounmy* across the street has a bit of candlelit atmosphere. In the morning, takeaway submarine sandwich-makers line the road down to the boat landing. Electricity seems to be seasonal: reliable in the rainy season, not so reliable in the dry. Most guesthouses in Pakbeng have a generator on standby just in case.

Moving on from Pakbeng

Trucks up Route 2 from Pakbeng to Oudomxai leave from the foot of the hill between 8am and 9am. The 150-kilometre-long road passes through Hmong and Tai Leu villages, and takes about four hours. There are two very basic guesthouses in Muang Houn, a small town 52km north of Pakbeng.

If you're continuing **to Louang Phabang on the boat**, you should be down at the landing before 8am to avoid being left behind. Some captains stop briefly at the caves at Pak Ou (see p.547) before Louang Phabang, charging each passenger who disembarks for a look a couple of thousand kip extra. If you're up for it, this does work out cheaper than chartering a boat from Louang Phabang, but leaves little time for exploring.

5.5

South central Laos

Many travellers see very little of **south central Laos**, spending just a night or two in the town of Savannakhet before pressing on to the far south or **crossing the border** into Vietnam. The two principal settlements of south central Laos – Thakhek and Savannakhet – both lie on the Mekong River, and both offer straightforward border crossings into Thailand. Route 8 between Vientiane and **Thakhek** is the best and easiest overland route to Vietnam, the newly paved road snaking through mountains, rainforests and the Phu Pha Man "stone forest" before winding down to the city of Vinh on the Gulf of Tonkin. The riverside town of Thakhek lies within day-tripping distance of the awesome limestone tunnels and caverns of the Khammouane Limestone NBCA, and north-east of Thakhek, between Routes 8 and 12, is the largest of all Laos's NBCAs, the massive, 3700-square-kilometre Nakay-Nam Theun NBCA. **Savannakhet** has been described as southern Laos's Louang Phabang, its inhabitants living comfortably among the architectural heirlooms handed down by the French, and is certainly a pleasant enough place. East from Savannakhet, Route 9 climbs steadily until it eventually bisects another route of more recent vintage: the **Ho Chi Minh Trail**. Actually a series of parallel roads and paths, the trail was used by the North Vietnamese Army to infiltrate and finally subdue its southern neighbour. The area is still littered with lots of war junk, some of it highly dangerous. The safest way to view these rusting relics is to use the town of **Xepon** as a base. Journeying further east leads to the **Vietnam border crossing** at Daen Sawan, popularly known as "Lao Bao".

Route 8: Lak Xao and the Vietnamese border

Halfway between Pakxan and Thakhek, at the junction town of **BAN VIANG KHAM**, 88km south of Pakxan, Route 8 heads across central Laos to the Kaew Nua Pass, which marks the border with Vietnam, before switchbacking down to the city of Vinh on the coast of Vietnam. Most travellers pass through here on direct, air-con buses running the Vientiane/Vinh route, but the newly paved road traces a centuries' old trading route to Vietnam zigzagging through ruggedly beautiful countryside, and the frontier town of Lak Xao can be used as a base for trips into the Nakay-Nam Theun NBCA.

Lak Xao

One hundred kilometres east of Ban Viang Kham, Route 8 passes through the sprawling boom town of **LAK XAO**, which was carved out of the hills by the logging company, Phudoi, in the 1980s to facilitate border trade with Vietnam. For the handful of overland travellers doing this route by local transport, Lak Xao is little more than a stop on the way to Kaew Nua Pass 35km to the east. The market does have some interesting gold and silver stalls selling ethnic jewellery, and it's also possible to see villagers from remote hilltribes, dressed in their finest traditional clothes.

Trips can also be arranged into the nearby Nakay-Nam Theun NBCA.

The rag-tag **buses** that make the trip to Lak Xao from Thakhek and Vientiane stop at the market, 3km from the town's main **hotel**, the *Phudoi* (❶). Much newer is the *Souriya Guesthouse* (❶) near the market, which has clean rooms with en-suite bathrooms. Tuk-tuks (5000K) are on hand to ferry you down the main road to the hotel complex. Across from the market, the *Only One* **restaurant** serves steamboats while the *Thiphavongsay* nearby has a range of traditional Lao dishes. The **bank** next door can exchange dollars and Vietnamese dong.

Kaew Nua Pass

The **Vietnamese border**, known as **Kaew Nua Pass** (or Nam Phao in Lao), is 35km from Lak Xao and best reached by hiring a tuk-tuk (50,000K) from the market. Shared tuk-tuks (5000K) can be had, but are often overcrowded and leave infrequently – except when the border market's open (from the 15th to the 20th of each month). For those crossing into Laos from Vietnam, there's usually a tuk-tuk on hand for hire into Lak Xao.

Crossing the border (daily 7.30am–5pm) is generally hassle-free, but start your journey early to ensure you don't end up stuck at the border: transport on both sides is sparse and neither immigration office is near a town of any size. A small exchange kiosk sits in the Lao terminal, but don't expect to get a decent rate. The settlement on the Vietnamese side of the border is **Cau Treo**, 105km west of Vinh on Highway 8; see p.1196 for details.

Thakhek and around

The least-visited of the major Mekong towns, **THAKHEK**, 360km south of Vientiane, is gradually gaining popularity as the best base from which to explore the massive Khammouane NBCAs and nearby **Mahaxai Caves** and karst formations. Thakhek is also an entry point into Laos from Nakhon Phanom in Thailand, and a good place to break up the long journey down Route 13 to Savannakhet.

A wander round the streets leading out from the tiny town square reveals French villas and shop-houses crumbling into overgrown gardens, and wide streets. This tranquil air of neglect is shattered nightly by club-hopping teenagers who buzz about town on brand-new motorcycles, the inheritors of a tradition half buried by the revolution in 1975. During the Second Indochina War, Thakhek was a sort of Havana on the Mekong, with visiting Thais flocking to its riverbank casino. These days, it's Nakhon Phanom on the opposite bank that's the big metropolis while sleepy Thakhek slumbers.

Practicalities

Bus passengers disembark either at the Km2 Market (2km from the riverbank), or at the main **bus station**, located near Souksomboun Market. There are plenty of tuk-tuks on hand at both markets. The town **tourist office** (Mon–Fri 8–11am & 2–4pm) is in the *Phudoi Hotel*, but the best place for useful local information is the *Thakhek Travel Lodge* (see p.565). For Visa cash advances and exchange of travellers' cheques, head for BCEL on Vientiane Road, or the Lao May Bank next to the *Phudoi Hotel* at the Km2 Market traffic circle. Thakhek has a handful of **Internet** shops, which charge 200K a minute. **Motorbikes** for exploring the Mahaxai Caves and karst formations can be rented at all the guesthouses listed below for about $8 a day. *Travel Lodge* and *Southida* also have vans for rent. Bicycles ($2 a day) are also available for getting around town. The ferry to Nakhon Phanom in Thailand (see p.1053) leaves from the ramp near the immigration office and runs daily during daylight hours (B50), making crossings every half hour or so. From Nakhon Phanom bus terminal, 2km west of the centre, buses leave for Ubon Ratchathani, Mukdahan, Khon Kaen and Nong Khai.

Accommodation and eating

There are several good **accommodation** choices in Thakhek. The most popular budget place is the new *Thakhek Travel Lodge* (☎020/515137; ❶–❷), located up a side road halfway between the Km2 and Km3 markers. Most backpackers head here as there are dormitories and fan rooms with shared facilities as well as air-con rooms with en-suite bathrooms, all reasonably priced. Perennial favourite, the extremely ugly *Khammuan Hotel* on Setthathilat Road (☎051/212216; ❶–❷), is supposedly slated for demolition, or perhaps renovation. At any rate, it was closed when we visited but may have reopened by the time you read this. Thakhek's best value accommodation can be found around the corner at the *Southida* (☎051/212568; ❷) on Chao Anou Road, which has eight clean, tiled-floored, air-con rooms with en-suite bathrooms and hot water in a new three-storey building. On the riverfront, the *Souksomboun* (☎051/212225; ❸) is housed in a colonial-era police station. The rooms, high ceilings and all, look as though they were given a makeover circa 1974. Smoked mirrors and lots of synthetic leather give this place a surreal retro feel.

Many of Thakhek's local **restaurants** are far out on the outskirts of town. Closer to the centre, most of the eateries are located on or near the town square. The most popular place with local expats is the humble *Seng Houn Hun* (no English sign) under the huge tree at the west side of the town square. Nearby, at the southwest corner of the square, sits *Phawilai*, which serves up noodles, grilled chicken and *mu yáw*, a local sausage, all washed down with cold beer. For a proper sit-down meal, the restaurant at the *Southida* in the old quarter is the best bet: it specializes in "suki" steamboats.

The Mahaxai Caves

East of Thakhek, Route 12 is swallowed up by a surreal landscape of karst formations. Hidden among the sea of jagged limestone hills are scores of caves, known as the **Mahaxai Caves**, a handful of which are popular tourist spots. The easiest way to get to them is by renting a motorbike ($8 per day) or tuk-tuk from Thakhek, but some visitors prefer to catch a Mahaxai-bound bus to the caves and then explore on foot. Public transport can be tricky, however: though pick-ups and buses travel the road frequently enough in the morning, you can't count on catching one back late in the afternoon. A good point to start an exploration of the caves is Tham Ban Tham, 7km from Thakhek, on the road to Mahaxai. From here you can walk to Tham En, taking in other caves en route, a twelve-kilometre walk in all. Even if you're not that interested in caves, the scenery provides a stunning backdrop for a walk.

To find the first cave, after getting off the bus, turn right down the dirt road that peels off Route 12 towards **BAN THAM**, a small village at the base of the first limestone escarpment. Cut through the village to find the concrete stairs leading up to **Tham Ban Tham**, which contains a shrine centred round a sizeable Buddha image. From Ban Tham, follow the road cutting north to get back on the main road. A few hundred metres after the second wooden bridge along this road, roughly 17km from Thakhek, drink vendors set up shop in the recesses of two cliffs, signposting the path leading to **Tham Sa Pha In**, which is the best of the caves and only a short walk from the main road. Look for the bamboo gate to find the cave entrance. The cave was renamed for the Hindu god Indra after the Second Indochina War, when villagers claimed to see the Hindu deity's image reflected in the pool. Illuminated by an inaccessible opening in the ceiling of the cave, the sacred pool glows emerald green, the colour of Indra's skin.

The most visited of Mahaxai's caves, **Tham En** (entry 1000K) is named for the large number of sparrows that are said to inhabit it and lies another 1.5km up the road. It's crowded at weekends. A concrete stairway takes you deep into the tunnel mouth, but there is still plenty of room to clamber on the rocks and climb up to one of the several cave mouths that offer commanding views of the forest outside.

Savannakhet

The town of **SAVANNAKHET**, known locally as "Sawan", is southern Laos's most-visited provincial capital. Its popularity is due in part to its central location on the overland routes between Vientiane and Pakxe, and Thailand and Vietnam. Travellers doing the "Indochina loop" – through Cambodia, Vietnam, Laos and Thailand – have the option of taking the 240-kilometre-long Route 9 on their way between Laos's two neighbours, hence the presence of both a **Thai** and a **Vietnamese consulate**. But Savannakhet also has its own appeal, with impressive architecture inherited from the French colonial period and narrow streets and shop-houses of ochre-coloured stucco that are reminiscent of parts of Hanoi. A large percentage of the town's population is ethnic Vietnamese, though most have been living here for generations and consider themselves to be Lao in habit and temperament.

Arrival and information

Most **buses** offload at the station on the north side of Savannakhet. Air-con buses from Vientiane drop passengers at a separate stand nearby, known locally as *khiw Sensabay*. Tuk-tuks make the two-kilometre run from the bus stations into the city centre (5000K), while the **airport** is on the southeastern side of the town, not far from the centre. At the time of writing, there were no flights to Savannakhet. Similarly, there is no longer a slow-boat service between Savannakhet and Vientiane.

As Savannakhet is incredibly spread out, you'll find that **tuk-tuks** are a better idea than trying to walk the long blocks outside the old quarter. **Bicycles** ($1 per day) can be rented at *Sensabay* restaurant and some guesthouses. Both the *Savanbanhao* and the *Nanhai Hotel*, a block north of the Lao May Bank, have vans with drivers for hire. Self-drive at either place is not an option, though you can rent **motorcycles** for $5 a day at the Canon Internet shop on the town square. There is a Tourism Authority (☎041/212755) on Latsaphanit Road, just south of the square.

Accommodation

Savannakhet has a very good choice and range of **accommodation**. It's more convenient and atmospheric to stay in the Old French Quarter. Many hotels in Savannakhet have their own travel agencies that can organize tours of the Ho Chi Minh Trail (see p.570).

Leena Guesthouse Chao Kim Rd, 200m east off Latsavongseuk Rd ☎041/212404. Huge two-storey building in a quiet residential area with twelve clean, en-suite rooms, some with a/c. ❶–❷

Nong Soda Guesthouse Tha He Rd. This new

Overland into Thailand: Savannakhet to Mukdahan

The **passenger ferry** that runs across the Mekong between Savannakhet and Mukdahan in Thailand (B50) docks at the immigration office on Tha He Road; the ferry departs six times a day on weekdays, and three times a day on weekends. There is an exchange kiosk in the ferry terminal. On the Thai side, frequent buses leave for That Phanom and Ubon Ratchathani. When crossing after 6pm or on Sundays, immigration on both sides sometimes charges extra.

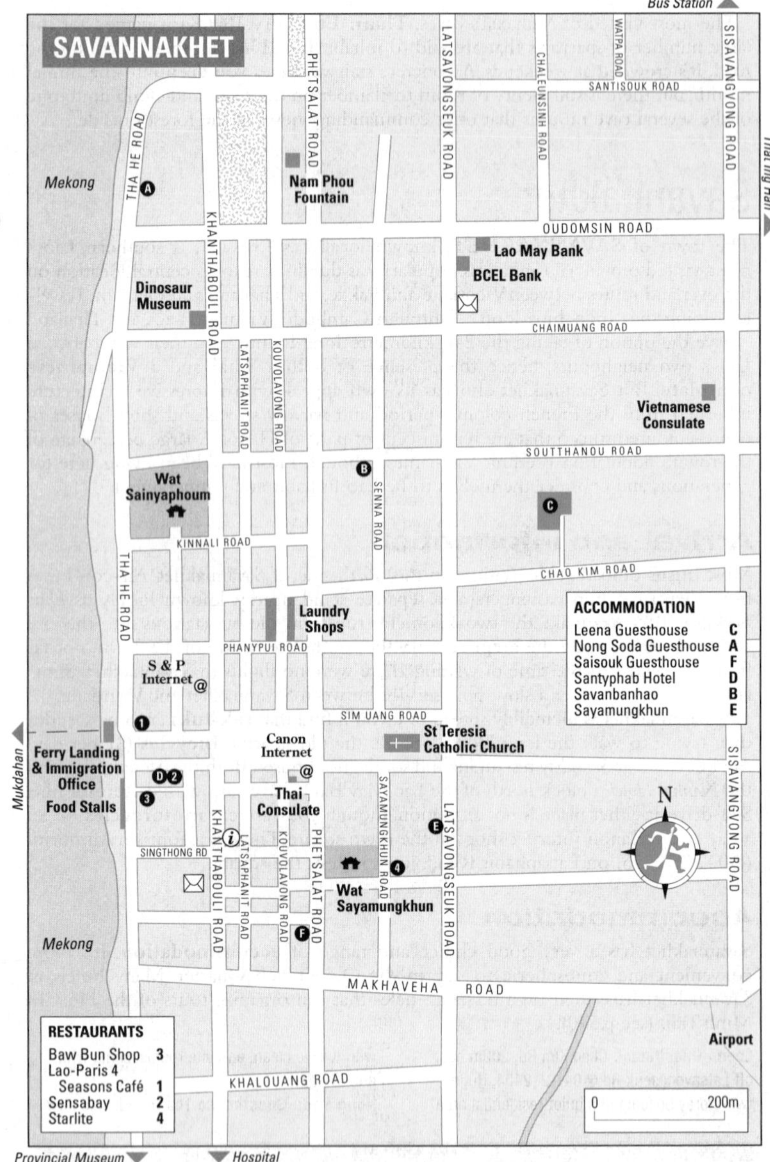

place is a short walk north from the customs pier. Good-value rooms with a/c and hot water. ❶–❷

Saisouk Guesthouse Phetsalat Rd, a block south of Wat Sayamungkhun ☎041/212207. Homestay-style guesthouse in a lovely wooden house in a quiet area. Shared facilities and no hot water, but if you're looking for a friendly, relaxed atmosphere with genuinely nice people, this is the place for you. ❶

Santyphab Hotel Between the square and the river ☎041/212277. Dingy rooms that are strictly for those on a tight budget, with especially inexpensive a/c rooms. Cheap and central but not really good value for money. ❶

Savanbanhao Senna Rd, four blocks north of the church ☎041/212202. Six large houses set in a big walled compound. Unfriendly service and no atmosphere at all, but a wide range of good-value rooms with en-suite bathrooms and hot water. ❶–❷

Sayamungkhun Latsavongseuk Rd ☎041/212426. A large house on the main street close to the old quarter, with sixteen spacious, en-suite, a/c rooms. Excellent value, and one of the few guesthouses in a heritage building. ❶–❷

The Town and around

Heading inland from the ferry landing, you soon come to the town square, dominated by the octagonal spire of **St Teresia Catholic Church**, which was built in 1930. Objects of interest include an old teakwood confessional and, high up on the walls, a set of hardwood plaques, with Vietnamese mother-of-pearl inlay work, depicting the fourteen Stations of the Cross. Not surprisingly, the biblical characters have distinctly Asian faces: Christ resembles a Confucian sage, while the Roman soldiers look more like turban-wearing Mongols.

Roads laid out on a neat grid surrounding the square constitute the **Old French Quarter**, and are lined with some fine examples of European-inspired architecture. Aside from wandering about admiring the crumbling buildings and the town's pleasant wats and Chinese temples, there's really nothing to do in Savannakhet but watch the sun set over the Mekong. Neither of the town's museums offers much in the way of enticement: housed in a peeling colonial-era mansion on Tha He Road, about 1km south of the ferry landing, the unswept, rundown **provincial museum** (daily 8am–noon & 2–4pm; 5000K) mostly contains dusty photographs of former communist party leader Kaysone Phomvihane (1920–92), Savannakhet's most revered native son but is almost always closed; the newly opened **Dinosaur Museum** on Khanthabouli Road isn't really very interesting except for the opportunity to chat with the friendly curators.

Outside of town is a much-revered Buddhist stupa, the **That Ing Hang**, which can be reached by bicycle. Follow Route 13 north for 13km until you see a sign on the right and follow this road for a further 3km. The stucco work that covers the stupa is crude yet appealing, especially the whimsical rosettes which dot the uppermost spire. Off to one side of the stupa stands an amusing sandstone sculpture of a lion, grinning like a Cheshire cat, which could only have been hauled here from one of the Khmer ruins downriver. The stupa is best visited during its annual festival in February when thousands make the pilgrimage here; it can be a bit of a letdown during the rest of the year.

Eating and drinking

The food and service at all of Savannakhet's traveller's cafés is notably poor, but the town does have some good **restaurants** if you know where to look. One local noodle dish worth seeking out is *baw bun* (Vietnamese rice noodles served with chopped-up spring rolls and beef). In the evening, shops selling soft drinks and a few *tam màk hung* vendors crop up on the riverbank in front of Wat Sainyaphoum, a pleasant spot to catch the sunset over Thailand and mingle with the locals. The fruit shakes are in a class of their own – look for the blenders.

Baw Bun Shop Fourth shop-house from the river, in the alley behind *Santyphab Hotel*. If it's *baw bun* you're after, this is the place, but it's only open in the morning.

Lao-Paris 4 Seasons Café Tha He Rd, near the immigration office. All the travellers seem to end up at this Vietnamese shop-house near the river. Alright for sandwiches and coffee, but the service is slow and unfriendly. At the time of writing, the whole operation was for sale, so hopefully things will change for the better.

Sensabay Next to *Santyphab Hotel*. Popular backpacker spot with quite tasty Western and Asian food but slow service. The fried chicken is well worth trying.

Starlite Restaurant Sayamungkhun Rd behind Wat Sayamungkhun. Very good Korean BBQ steamboat with a choice of beef or fish, and lots of fresh veggies and glass noodles.

Listings

Airlines If flights ever resume, Lao Airlines (☎041/212140), at the airport, southeast of the city centre.
Banks and exchange There are two banks near the intersection of Latsavongseuk and Oudomsin roads. The Lao May Bank faces Oudomsin Rd, and the BCEL faces Latsavongseuk Rd.
Consulates Thai: on Kouvolavong Rd on block south of the square (Mon–Fri 8.30am–noon & 2–3.30pm; ☎041/212373); tourist visas costs $7 and require two photos. Provided you apply before noon, the visa will be ready the next afternoon. Vietnamese: on Sisavangvong Rd (Mon–Fri 7.30–11am & 1.30–4.30pm; ☎041/212418); visas cost $50, require two photos and take five working days.
Hospitals and clinics The biggest hospital is located on Khanthabouli Rd, near the provincial museum; a 24hr clinic operates on Phetsalat Rd, a block south of the *Hoongthip Hotel.* The biggest pharmacy is on the corner of Oudomsin and Senna roads.
Internet access Canon Internet on the southeast corner of the town square (daily 1–9pm; 20,000K per hr); a second Internet shop (daily 9am–8pm) with cheaper prices is on Khanthabouli Rd, 200m north of the GPO, in the S&P furniture store.
Laundry Fast and cheap at the laundry shops along Kouvolavong Rd, north of the town square.
Post and telephone The GPO is on Khanthabouli Rd, a few blocks south of the town square (Mon–Fri 8am–noon & 1–5pm, Sat & Sun 8–11am). The Telcom building with overseas phone and fax service (daily 8am–10pm) is just behind it. There is a post office branch near the BCEL Bank, on the corner of Chaimuang and Latsavongseuk roads.

Route 9: the Ho Chi Minh Trail and the Vietnamese border

Newly paved Route 9 weaves east through a series of drab towns from Savannakhet to the **Lao Bao border crossing** into Vietnam. The road ends its Lao journey at the Lao Bao Pass before heading on to Dong Ha, where it connects with Vietnam's Highway 1. While most travellers barrel through on the direct buses, the frontier is not without sites of interest. Muang Phin can be used as a base for the Dong Phou Viang NBCA and there are **Ho Chi Minh Trail** sites open for tourism on both sides of the border.

Xepon

A picturesque village in the foothills of the Annamite Mountains, 40km from the Vietnamese border, **XEPON** is a pleasant rural stopover between Vietnam and Savannakhet. The old town of Xepon was obliterated during the Second Indochina War – along with every house in the district's two hundred villages – and was later rebuilt here 6km west of its original location, on the opposite bank of the Xe Banghiang River. The old city had been captured by communist forces in 1960 and became an important outpost on the Ho Chi Minh Trail. As such, it was the target of a joint South Vietnamese and American invasion in 1971, Operation Lam Son 719 (see box opposite), aimed at disrupting the flow of troops and supplies headed for communist forces in South Vietnam.

Buses arriving from Savannakhet or the Lao Bao border stop at the market, from where it's a short walk uphill to the government **guesthouse** ($1 per bed), which offers dormitory-style accommodation. If you don't mind the 1.5-kilometre walk, the forestry department runs a somewhat nicer dorm-style guesthouse ($1 per bed) at the edge of town. To get here, take a left at the second road west of the market and follow the road to the foot of the hill. A small **restaurant** across from the market offers noodles, omelettes and stir-fries. There are no **official exchange** services in Xepon, but cash can always be exchanged. Sawngthaews run up to Ban Dong as well as the border-town of Daen Sawan, where you can continue by motorcycle taxi to the Lao Bao border post.

Operation Lam Son 719

In 1971, US President Richard Nixon ordered an attack on the **Ho Chi Minh Trail** to cut off supplies to communist forces. Although US ground troops were prohibited by law from crossing the border from Vietnam into Laos and Cambodia, the US command saw this as a chance to test the strengths of Vietnamization, the policy of turning the ground war over to the South Vietnamese. For the operation, code-named **Lam Son 719**, it was decided that ARVN (Army of the Republic of Vietnam) troops were to invade Laos and block the trail with US air support. The objective was **Xepon**, a town straddled by the Trail, which was 30–40km wide at this point. In early February 1971, ARVN troops and tanks pushed across the border at Lao Bao and followed Route 9 into Laos. Like a caterpillar trying to ford a column of red ants, the South Vietnamese troops were soon engulfed by superior numbers of North Vietnamese (NVA) regulars. ARVN officers stopped halfway to Xepon and engaged the NVA in a **series of battles** that lasted over a month. US air support proved ineffectual, and by mid-March, scenes of frightened ARVN troops retreating were being broadcast around the world. In an official Lao account of the battle, a list of "units of Saigon puppet troops wiped out on Highway 9" include four regiments of armoured cavalry destroyed between the Vietnam border and Ban Dong.

The most tangible relics of Operation Lam Son 719 are two rusting **American tanks** that sit on the outskirts of Ban Dong, on Route 9. The tank that's easiest to find lies five minutes' walk off the road that cuts south out of town towards Taoy, and which was once a crucial artery of the Ho Chi Minh Trail. Shaded by a grove of jack-fruit trees, it rests atop a small hill east of the road, partially dismantled for its valuable steel. As of 1998, UXO-Lao (the Lao National Unexploded Ordnance Programme) has cleared Ban Dong of unexploded war debris, but it's still a good idea to ask a villager to show you the way, as you should always take extra care when leaving a well-worn path.

The Ho Chi Minh Trail at Ban Dong

Halfway between Xepon and the Vietnam border is the town of **BAN DONG**, the site of one of America's most ignominious defeats during the war, and a popular stop on tours of the **Ho Chi Minh Trail**. Situated in the foothills of the Annamite Mountains, bomb craters and spent ordnance still litter the landscape more than a quarter of a century after the war. If you're travelling by public transport, it's best to visit Ban Dong in the morning, as few late-afternoon sawngthaews ply this stretch of Route 9 and Ban Dong has no guesthouses, although there are some bamboo-and-thatch drink shops. It's common to see women squatting by the road selling bamboo shoots – a local speciality. The area's abundant bamboo crop is in fact partially a by-product of the spraying of defoliants by American forces who hoped to expose the arteries of the Ho Chi Minh Trail: hardy bamboo is quick to take root in areas of deforestation.

Daen Sawan

Route 9 ends its journey through Laos in the village of **DAEN SAWAN**, 1km from the Lao immigration office. For a remote border town, Daen Sawan is quite tourist-friendly, with food, accommodation and exchange services. The *Friendly* **guesthouse** (❶) has basic rooms with shared bathrooms and a helpful owner. Attached to the guesthouse is the popular *Loung Aloune* **restaurant**. There's a Lao May Bank in town as well as a branch at the Lao immigration office on the border. The rates are not good, so only change what you need: $20 is more than enough to get you to Savannakhet, via Xepon. From Daen Sawan, you can hire a motorcycle taxi for the final one-kilometre ride to the Lao immigration office. If you've entered Laos from Vietnam, there are four buses a day to Savannakhet from Daen Sawan, the last leaving at 2pm.

Lao Bao border crossing

A short distance from the Lao immigration office is the **Lao Bao border crossing** (daily 7am–9pm) into Vietnam. Travellers to Vietnam must have a valid visa, and the crossing is not always hassle-free. Vietnamese officials may send you back if your visa is not stamped for "Lao Bao". Motorcyclists have also reported problems, with officials sometimes unwilling to allow larger bikes to enter. On the Vietnamese side, there are motorcycle taxis to take you down the hill to Lao Bao town (see p.1196) where buses leave for the twenty-kilometre journey to Khe Sanh every thirty minutes, with some going straight through to Dong Ha on Route 1, where bus or train connections can be made to Hanoi and Hue; see p.1193 for details. Accommodation is available in Lao Bao town.

5.6

The far south

Bordered by Thailand, Cambodia and Vietnam, the far south conveniently divides into two regions, with **Pakxe**, the most important market town and the access point for the Chong Mek **border crossing** into Thailand, as the hub. In the west, the Mekong River corridor is scattered with dozens of ancient Khmer temples, including **Wat Phou**, one of the most important Angkorian ruins outside Cambodia, and the main tourist attraction in southern Laos. From the nearby town of **Champasak**, it makes sense to go with the flow of the river south to **Si Phan Don**, where the Mekong's 1993-kilometre journey through Laos rushes to a thundering conclusion in a series of tiny riverine islands at the Cambodian border; the waters here are home to a dwindling number of very rare Irrawaddy **dolphins**. The border with Cambodia is now open and a growing stream of intrepid backpackers are using it. In the east of the region, the fertile highlands of the **Bolaven Plateau** separate the Mekong corridor from the Annamite Mountains that form Laos's border with Vietnam. Much of the area east of the Mekong lies off the beaten track and involves hard journeys on bumpy roads. One city well worth making the effort for is **Attapu**, known as the garden city for its pleasant atmosphere and undemanding pace.

Pakxe

Capitalizing on its location at the confluence of the Xe Don and the Mekong rivers, roughly halfway between the Thai border and the fertile Bolaven Plateau, **PAKXE** is the far south's biggest city, and its commercial and transport hub. For travellers, it is a necessary stopover en route to Si Phan Don and Cambodia, and makes a more comfortable base than Pakxong for exploration of the Bolaven Plateau and nearby NBCAs. There is also a border crossing to Thailand just west of Pakxe at Chong Mek, making it a logical entry or exit point for travellers doing a north–south tour of Laos.

The City

Very few travellers spend two consecutive nights in Pakxe. The city only has two real tourist attractions, both just east of the town centre on Route 13 and easily reached by tuk-tuk. The first is the **Champasak Palace Hotel**, a majestic eyesore resembling a giant cement wedding cake. Legend has it that the late Prince Boun Oum na Champasak, a colourful character who was the heir to the Champasak kingdom and one of the most influential southerners of the twentieth century, needed a palace this size so that he could accommodate his many concubines. The palace, left incomplete after the one-time prime minister wound up on the wrong side of history and left for France in the 1970s, is now a hotel. The second attraction, 500m further along Route 13, is the **Champasak Provincial Museum** (Mon–Fri 8–11.30am & 2–4pm; 1000K), which houses some fine examples of ornately carved pre-Angkorian sandstone lintels taken from sites around the province. Upstairs is a selection of local tribes' costumes and jewellery. The very large and lively **East Market** along No. 38 Road is also well worth a visit.

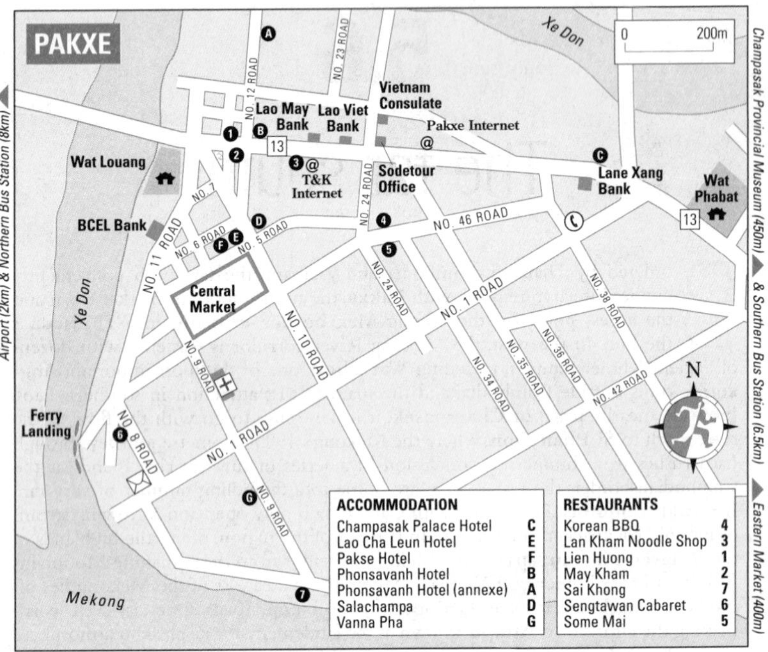

Arrival

Pakxe has a lot of transport options and is served by an **airport**, two bus stations, a sawngthaew station and a boat landing. The airport lies 2km northeast of the city on Route 13, from where tuk-tuks run into town. The Lao Airlines office (ⓣ031/212252) is on No. 11 Road, near BCEL bank.

There are two separate **bus stations**, both of which are served by **tuk-tuks** to hotels (5000K). Buses to and from Savannakhet and the north use the Northern bus

Moving On

Most towns in the far south are only served by one or two buses a day, from the Southern bus station, which tend to leave early in the morning. Buses for towns to the east, including Tad Lo, Xekong and Attapu also depart from Pakxe's southern station. An express van departs for Attapu from the Southern bus station daily in the early afternoon – arrive early, as seating is limited.

There is also a huge **sawngthaew** lot located on the eastern side of the East Market. Here you'll find sawngthaews heading in all directions, including Champasak and the Thai border, so if you miss a bus, you can always come here and try for a sawngthaew. Just to confuse matters even more, there are also northbound buses from the sawngthaew lot, although these also pull into the Northern bus station before leaving town.

Passenger boats to Si Phan Don as well as ferries to Ban Muang Kao, on the opposite bank, depart from the Xe Don landing off No.11 Road. Boats to Si Phan Don ($4) via Champasak ($1) leave daily in the mornings and arrive late afternoon.

Overland into Thailand via the Chong Mek border crossing

To get to the **Lao–Thai border crossing** at Chong Mek, go to the East Market and catch a sawngthaew for the forty-kilometre trip to the border crossing (daily 8.30am–4pm), which takes around one hour. The fare is 10,000K or B50 per person if the vehicle is full, more if not. The expansive market that straddles the border thrives on weekends. After crossing into Thailand, sawngthaews will be waiting to shuttle you to **Ubon Ratchathani**, which has plentiful road and rail links (see p.1045). There are also two direct Chong Mek-to-**Bangkok** air-con buses that leave from the market at 4pm and 5pm respectively.

station, 7km north of the city on Route 13. Buses to and from points south and east use the Southern bus station, 8km southeast of town on Route 13. Tuk-tuks to either station cost 5000K and can be flagged down in town or taken from the stand near the boat landing.

Passenger boats from Si Phan Don dock at the Xe Don landing off No.11 Road, an easy walk from most hotels.

Accommodation

Most of the **hotels** are north of the Central Market, along Route 13. Budget travellers should head for *Phonsavanh Hotel*, on the corner of Route 13 and No. 12 Road (☎031/202842; ❶). It's a dump, but the staff are friendly, the location's good and it has a certain seedy charm. Ask about the *Phonsavanh*'s annexe a short walk down No. 12 Road, which has newer rooms for the same low price. If you're looking for a colonial-era hotel, the *Salachampa* on No. 10 Road, near the market (☎031/212273; ❷), has spacious rooms with high ceilings in an elegant restored French villa, with teak floors and breezy verandas. If the *Salachampa* is full, try the newish *Lao Cha Leun Hotel* (☎031/251333; ❷) directly opposite, which features clean air-con rooms with en-suite bathrooms with hot water for the same price. A bit of a walk south of centre, but one of the best-value options in town, is the *Vanna Pha*, No. 9 Road (☎031/212502; ❶–❷), set in a quiet compound and boasting clean, air-con rooms with wood floors and en-suite, hot-water bathrooms. The recently renovated *Pakse Hotel*, No. 5 Road (☎031/212131; ❷–❸), is clean and well run, with comfortable rooms boasting all the modcons. The top hotel in Pakxe, though, is the ninety-room *Champasak Palace Hotel* on Route 13 (☎031/212263; ❺), which was obviously fit for a prince, and is great value at $25 for a double.

Eating

Pakxe has the best range of **restaurants** south of Savannakhet. Most of the town's better restaurants are found either on Route 13 between No. 12 and No. 24 roads, or on No. 46 Road, just east of the latter. *May Kham*, on the corner of Route 13 and No. 12 Road, offers an extensive array of Chinese dishes in a proper sit-down setting. Directly across the street is *Lien Huong*, a small Vietnamese place dishing up cheap spring rolls and *fõe*. Further east, *Lan Kham Noodle Shop*, below the hotel of the same name, is immensely popular but closes by early afternoon. For a more lively atmosphere, Pakxe's two most popular restaurants are *Korean BBQ* on No. 46 Road and *Some Mai*, almost opposite, which serve very tasty, inexpensive BBQ-meat steamboats, and are always crowded to capacity. There are two **bars** in the town proper – *Sai Khong*, on No. 9 Road near the Mekong River, and *Sengtawan Cabaret*, above the boat landing – both featuring bad bands and taxi dancers. A more peaceful spot for a cold beer is the stall under the shady trees directly above the boat landing, where you can look out over the Mekong River.

Listings

Banks and exchange BCEL, on No. 11 Rd; Lao May Bank and Lao Viet Bank on Route 13, just past the Sodetour office; and Lane Xang Bank on Route 13, opposite the *Champasak Palace Hotel*.
Consulates Vietnamese: on No. 24 Rd (Mon–Fri 8–11am & 2–4.30pm; ⓣ031/212058); visas cost $50, require two photos and take five working days.
Internet access Lan Kham Internet ⓣ031/213314, T&K Internet ⓣ031/214542, and Pakxe Internet ⓣ031/213435, all on Route 13 between No. 12 and No. 35 roads.
Post office At the corner of No. 8 Rd and No. 1 Rd (daily 7.30am–9pm).
Telephone services International calls and faxes at Telecom, on the corner of No. 1 and No. 38 roads (daily 8am–9pm).
Tour agencies Sodetour, corner of Route 13 and No. 24 Rd ⓣ031/212122; Lane Xang Travel, Route 13, below the *Phonesavanh Hotel* ⓣ031/212002; Inter-Lao Tourisme, in the lobby of the *Champasak Palace Hotel* ⓣ031/212778.

Champasak

From Pakxe, daily passenger boats ply the forty-kilometre stretch of the Mekong south, past misty green mountains and riverbanks loaded with palm trees, to the charming riverside town of **CHAMPASAK**. An up-and-coming backpacker resort, Champasak also serves as the gateway to **Wat Phou** and the **Khmer** ruins, although it is also possible to do Wat Phou as a day-trip from Pakxe. Meandering for 4km along the right bank of the Mekong, Champasak is now an unassuming town, but was once the capital of a Lao kingdom, whose territory stretched from the Annamite Mountains into present-day Thailand. A former **palace of Prince Boun Oum na Champasak**, the scion of the royal family of Champasak and a one-time prime minister, can be seen below Wat Phou.

Practicalities

Buses and **sawngthaews** (7000K) will let you off at Champasak's tiny roundabout, where you'll find almost everything you need, including a post office (open until 9pm weekdays for phone calls), and a tiny wooden bank, which can **exchange** cash and travellers' cheques. The boat and ferry **dock** lies about 2km north off the roundabout; **tuk-tuks** are available at the dock. In town, just south of the roundabout, the *Saythong* (❶) has basic rooms with shared facilities in an old wooden house, above a restaurant overlooking the Mekong. Across the street, *Kham Phou* (❶) has roomy doubles and triples and wooden, en-suite bungalows in the garden. Fifty metres south, just opposite the stunning colonial mansion, is the *Souchittra Guesthouse* (❶) with basic rooms in the old house with a clean, shared bath or self-contained bungalows on the lawn overlooking the Mekong. The *Kham Khong* (❶), 2km south of the roundabout, features rather tatty bungalows and a restaurant with a deck overlooking the Mekong. *Dok Champa GH & Restaurant*, on the roundabout, offers the best selection of **Lao dishes** in Champasak and also rents bicycles ($1 per day). For a splurge, the *Sala Vat Phou Hotel* (ⓣ031/213280; ❺–❻), near the roundabout, has spacious, nicely decorated rooms in a vintage 1960s building with a rather retro feel. The restaurant here does the finest food in town.

Tuk-tuks can be hired for the eight-kilometre journey to Wat Phou. The drivers charge $6 for up to six passengers, and wait for you while you visit the ruins. When it comes to moving on, three **buses** pass through Champasak each morning en route to Pakxe (1hr 30min) and can be hailed from the town's main road. For bus connections to Si Phan Don, you'll have to cross the river to Ban Muang and wait for a bus heading south on Route 13, or wait for the **boat** from Pakxe which calls at around 9am at the Ban Phapin ferry landing, located at the northernmost end of Champasak.

Wat Phou

Easily the most evocative Khmer ruin outside Cambodian borders, **Wat Phou** (daily 8.30am–4.30pm; 5000K), 8km southwest of Champasak, should be at the top of your southern Laos must-see list. A romantic and rambling complex of pre-Angkorian temples dating from the sixth to the twelfth centuries, Wat Phou occupies a setting of unparalleled beauty in a lush river valley dominated by an imposing mountain. Unlike ancient Khmer sites of equal size or importance found in neighbouring Thailand, Wat Phou has yet to be over-enthusiastically restored, so walking among the half-buried pieces of sculpted sandstone gives an idea of what these sites once looked like. The pristine state of the environment was a major factor in UNESCO's decision to award the area its World Heritage site status in 2001.

Wat Phou, which in Lao means "Mountain Monastery", is actually a series of ruined temples and shrines at the foot of Lingaparvata Mountain. Although the site is now associated with Theravada Buddhism, sandstone reliefs indicate that the ruins were once a **Hindu place of worship**. When viewed from the Mekong, it's clear why the site was chosen. A phallic stone outcropping is easily seen among the range's line of forested peaks: this would have made the site especially auspicious to worshipers of Shiva, a Hindu god often symbolized by a phallus.

Some history

Archeologists tend to disagree on who the original founders of the site were and when it was first consecrated. The oldest parts of the ruins are thought to date back to the sixth century and were most likely built by the ancient Khmer, although some experts claim to see a connection to Champa, a Hinduized kingdom once centred in what is now south-central Vietnam. Whatever the case, the site is still considered highly sacred to the ethnic Lao and is the focus of an annual festival (Jan or Feb) that attracts thousands of pilgrims.

The **Khmer**, ancestors of modern-day Cambodians, were the founders of a highly sophisticated culture, whose influence stretched north to Vientiane in Laos and as far west as the present-day border between Thailand and Burma. From its capital, located at Angkor in what is now northwestern Cambodia, a long line of kings reigned with absolute authority, each striving to build a monument to his own greatness that would outdo all previous monarchs. With cultural trappings inherited from earlier Khmer kingdoms, which in turn had borrowed heavily from India, the Khmer rulers at Angkor venerated deities from the **Hindu** and **Buddhist** pantheons. Eventually, a new and uniquely Khmer cult was born, the devaraja or god-king, which propagated the belief that a Khmer king was actually an incarnation of a certain Hindu deity on earth.

In 1177, armies from the rival kingdom of **Champa**, taking advantage of a period of political instability, were able to sack Angkor, leaving the empire in disarray. Convinced that the old state religion had somehow failed to protect the kingdom from misfortune, the new Khmer leader Jayavarman VII embraced Mahayana Buddhism and went on to expand his empire to include much of present-day Thailand, Vietnam and Laos. But after his death, the empire began to decline and by 1432 was so weak that the **Siamese** were also able to give Angkor a thorough sacking. They pillaged the great stone temples of the Angkorian god-kings and force-marched members of the royal Khmer court, including classical dancers, musicians, artisans and astrologers, back to Ayutthaya, then the capital of Siam. To this day, much of what Thais perceive as Thai culture, from the sinuous moves of classical dancers to the flowery language of the royal Thai court, was actually acquired from the Khmer. Much of the Khmer culture absorbed by the Siamese was passed on to the Lao, including the gracefully curving lines of written Lao.

Exploring the site

Approaching from the east, a **stone causeway** – once lined with low stone pillars – leads up to the first set of ruins. On either side of the causeway there would have been reservoirs, which probably represented the oceans that surrounded the mythical Mount Meru, home of the gods of the Hindu pantheon. Just beyond the causeway, on either side of the path, stand two megalithic structures of sandstone and laterite, which may have served as segregated **palaces**, one for men and the other for women. The structure to the right displays a carved relief of Shiva and his consort Uma riding the sacred bull Nandi.

Continuing up the stairs, you come upon a ruined temple containing the finest examples of decorative **stone lintels** in Laos. Although much has been damaged or is missing, sketches done at the end of the nineteenth century show the temple to have changed little since then. The Khmer artisans' depictions of deities, divinities, characters and events from Hindu and Buddhist mythology are some of the most exquisite art ever created; the earliest examples date from around the twelfth century. Some of the most significant include a depiction of the god **Krishna** defeating the naga Kaliya, to the left of the main entrance; the god **Vishnu** riding the bird-man Garuda, on the right of the main entrance; two versions of the god **Indra** riding the three-headed elephant Airavata; seven different images of the temple guardian **Kala**, usually depicted with two stylized garlands spewing from the corners of his mouth, each time supporting a different deity, including Shiva and Vishnu; and a gruesome depiction of Krishna tearing his uncle Kamsa in half, on the west wall. On the altar, inside the sanctuary, stand four Buddha images, looking like a congress of benevolent space aliens. Originally, this altar would have supported a Shivalinga, or phallic stone, representing Shiva.

Just behind the temple is a relief carved into a half-buried slab of stone depicting the Hindu trinity. A multi-armed, multi-headed Shiva (standing) is flanked by Brahma (left) and Vishnu (right). Continuing up the hill behind the temple you'll come to a **shallow cave**, the floor of which is muddy from the constant drip of water that collects on its ceiling. This water is considered highly sacred, as it has trickled down from the peak of Lingaparvata. In former times, a system of stone pipes directed the run-off to the temple, where it bathed the enshrined Shivalinga. Even today, Lao pilgrims will dip their fingers into a cistern located in the cave and ritually anoint themselves. Foreign visitors should resist the temptation to wash with this water, which would be akin to having a clean-up in the baptismal font.

If you follow the base of the cliff in a northerly direction, a bit of sleuthing will lead you to the enigmatic **crocodile stone**, which may or may not have been used as an altar for pre-Angkor-period human sacrifices. A few metres away to the north is the elephant stone, a huge, moss-covered boulder carved with the face of an elephant, probably dating from the nineteenth century.

Si Phan Don

In Laos's deepest south, just above the border with Cambodia, the muddy stream of the Mekong is carved into a fourteen-kilometre-wide web of rivulets, creating a landlocked archipelago. Known as **Si Phan Don**, or "Four Thousand Islands", this labyrinth of islets, rocks and sandbars has acted as a kind of bell jar, preserving traditional southern lowland Lao culture from outside influences. Island villages were largely unaffected by the French or American wars and the islanders' folk ways have been passed down uninterrupted since ancient times. The archipelago is also home to rare flora and fauna, including a species of **freshwater dolphin**. Southeast Asia's largest, and what many consider to be most impressive, **waterfalls** are also located here.

Don Khong

The largest of the Four Thousand Islands group, **Don Khong** draws a steady stream of visitors, most of whom use it as a base to explore other attractions in Si Phan Don. It boasts a venerable collection of Buddhist temples, some dating back to the sixth or seventh century, good-value accommodation and interesting fresh-fish cuisine.

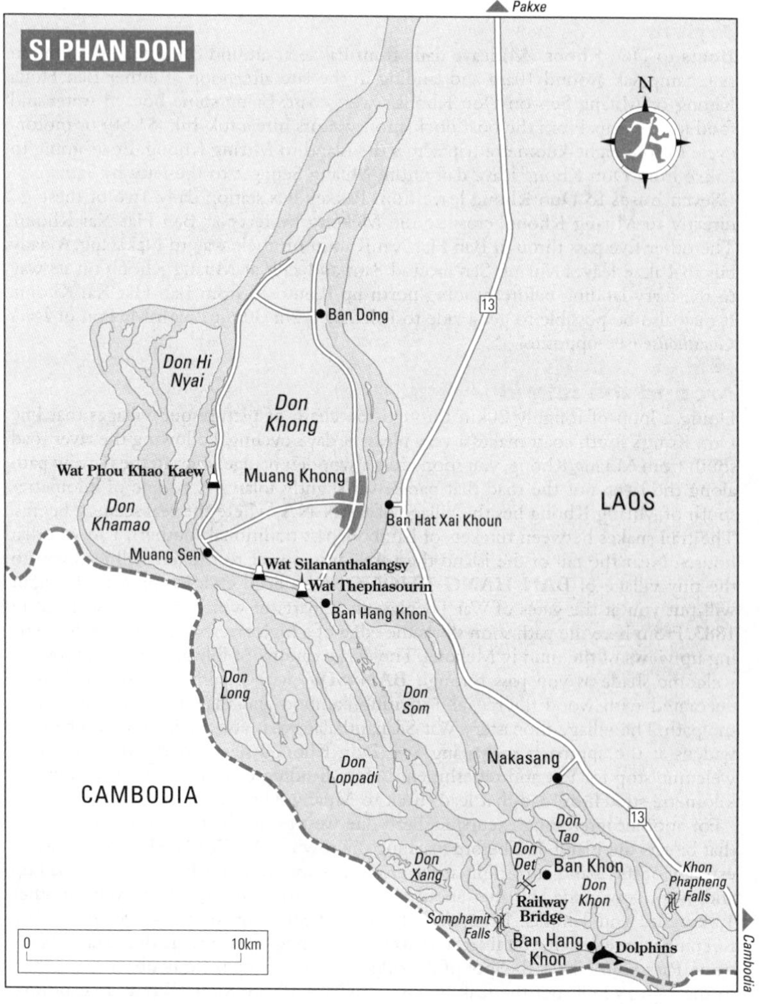

Don Khong has only two settlements of any size, the port town of **Muang Sen** on the island's west coast, and the east-coast town of **Muang Khong**, where most of the accommodation and cafés are. Like all Si Phan Don settlements, both Muang Sen's and Muang Khong's homes and shops cling to the bank of the Mekong for kilometres, but barely penetrate the interior, which is reserved for rice fields. The best way to explore the island is to rent a **bicycle** and set off along the road that circles it – the flat terrain and almost complete absence of motor vehicles make for ideal cycling conditions.

In Muang Khong you'll find the island's only **post office**, just south of the bridge, and a **Telecom** office, about 200m west of the ferry landing, where international calls can be made (Mon–Fri 8am–noon & 1–4pm, Sat 8am–noon). Several of the guesthouses and shops facing the Mekong offer bicycles (10,000K per day) for rent. Don Khong has 24-hour electricity.

Arrival

Boats to Don Khong ($4) leave daily from Pakxe at around 8am, usually calling in at Champasak around 10am and landing in the late afternoon at either Ban Houa Khong or Muang Sen on Don Khong's west coast. Bring some bottled water and food for the trip. From the boat dock, most visitors hire a tuk-tuk ($1.50) or motorcycle for the eight-kilometre trip across the island to Muang Khong. Boats going to Pakxe from Don Khong leave daily from Muang Sen; get to the jetty by 7am.

Seven **buses** to Don Khong leave from Pakxe's bus station daily. Two of these go directly to Muang Khong, crossing the Mekong by ferry at Ban Hat Xai Khoun. The other five pass through Ban Hat Xai Khoun on their way to Nakasang. A daily bus to Pakxe leaves Muang Sen around 8am and calls at Muang Khong on its way to the ferry landing before heading north up Route 13 from Ban Hat Xai Khoun. It may also be possible to get a ride to Pakxe ($1; 2hr 30min) with Mr Pon of *Pon's Guesthouse* (see opposite).

Around the island

Doing a loop of roughly 20km through the chain of picturesque villages that line Don Kong's south coast makes a very pleasant day's cycling. Following the river road south from Muang Khong, you soon cross a wooden bridge: stick to the narrow path along the river, not the road that parallels it slightly inland. A couple of kilometres south of Muang Khong lies the village of **BAN NA**, where the real scenery begins. The trail snakes between thickets of bamboo, past traditional southern Lao wooden houses. Near the tail of the island the path forks: a veer to the left will lead you to the tiny village of **BAN HANG KHONG** and a dead end. Keeping to the right will put you at the gates of Wat Thephasourin, parts of which were constructed in 1883. From here the path soon skirts the edge of a high riverbank, at intervals opening up views of the muddy Mekong. The dense canopy of foliage overhead provides welcome shade as you pass through **BAN SIW**, with quaint gingerbread houses, decorated with wood filigree, and inviting bamboo-and-thatch drink shops lining the path. The village monastery, Wat Silananthalangsy, is also worth a look. The path widens at the approach to Muang Sen, Don Khong's sleepy port, which makes a welcome stop for rest and refreshment before heading east via the unshaded eight-kilometre stretch of road that leads back to Muang Khong.

For another interesting excursion, head due west from Muang Khong, on the road that bisects the island. Just before reaching the town of **MUANG SEN** on the western side of the island, turn right at the crossroads and head north. Follow this road up and over a low grade and after about 4km you'll cross a bridge. Keep going another 1.5km and you'll notice large black boulders beginning to appear off to the left. Keeping your eyes left, you'll see a narrow trail leading up to a ridge of the same black stone. Park your bike at the foot of the ridge, and, following the trail up another 200m to the right, you'll spot the teak buildings of **Wat Phou Khao Kaew**, an evocative little forest monastery situated atop a stone bluff overlooking the Mekong. A fractured pre-Angkorian stone lintel lies at the base of its central stupa, which possibly dates the whole structure to the middle of the seventh century. Nearby sits a charming miniature *sim*, flanked by plumeria trees. A curious collection of carved wooden deities that somehow found their way downriver from Burma decorate the ledges.

Accommodation

Most of the **accommodation** is concentrated in **Muang Khong**, which is on the quieter side of the island and provides a good launching point for excursions around the Si Phan Don area. Highly recommended is *Villa Kang Khong* (☎031/213539; ❶), 100m west of the Muang Khong ferry landing, which offers great service at bargain prices in a colonial-era teak house. *Done Khong II* (❶–❷), 300m from the ferry landing on the road to Muang Sen, is a good alternative. Set in an airy teak house with verandas offering commanding views of the countryside, its accommodation ranges from dorm beds to comfortable en-suite doubles. Along the waterfront, *Mr*

Pon's Guesthouse has recently expanded and has a decent restaurant, while *Done Khong Guest House* (☎031/214010; ❷), adjacent to the ferry landing, is similar, offering basic rooms with shared facilities, and a popular restaurant. For a smarter option, try *Auberge Sala Done Khong* (☎031/212077; ❻), south of the ferry landing, whose nicely restored French-era villa has air-con and hot water, catering largely to a package-tour clientele.

Over in **Muang Sen** there are only two guesthouses. *Say Khong* (❷), directly above the boat dock, has spacious fan doubles and triples, and a balcony, excellent for viewing Mekong sunsets. A little further east, on the road to Muang Khong, you'll find *Muong Sene Guest House* (❶), whose roomy doubles are the cheapest on the island. Since Muang Sen has the island's main pier, it tends to be a bit noisier than Muang Khong.

Eating and drinking

All of Don Khong's guesthouses serve **food** and as you might expect, fish is a staple. The islanders have dozens of good recipes – from the traditional *làp pa* (a Lao-style salad of minced fish mixed with garlic, chillies, shallots and fish sauce) to tropical fish steamed in coconut milk. Be sure to try the island speciality *mók pa*, fish steamed in banana leaves, which has the consistency of custard and takes an hour to prepare. For this and just about anything else, *Mr Pon's* stands out as the best **restaurant** in Muang Khong, serving tasty, plentiful dishes at the guesthouse of the same name, 200m north of the ferry landing. If it's Chinese food and a perfect river view you're after, head for *Souksan's* restaurant, which stands on stilts above the Mekong.

The people of Si Phan Don are very proud of their *lào-láo*, which has gained a reputation nationally as one of the best **rice whiskies** in Laos. For those who haven't taken a shine to Lao white lightning, Muang Khong has devised a gentler blend known as the "Lao cocktail", a mix of wild honey and *lào-láo* served over ice.

Don Khon and Don Det

Tropical islands in the classic sense, **Don Khon** and **Don Det**, 15km downstream from Don Khong, are fringed with swaying coconut palms and planted with jade- and emerald-coloured rice paddies. Besides being a picturesque little haven, they also offer some leisurely trekking. Linked by a bridge and traversed by a trail, Don Khon and Don Det can be easily explored on foot. The fee is 5000K for a day pass or 9000K for ten days; there's a ticket booth at the southern end of the railway bridge near the trail-heads for the falls and dolphin pools.

A delightfully sleepy place with a timeless feel about it, **BAN KHON**, located on Don Khon east of the bridge, is the islands' largest settlement. If you're interested in exploring the remnants of Laos's old French railway, head to the southern side of the foot of the bridge back behind some houses, where you'll find the rusty remains of the locomotive that once hauled French goods and passengers between piers on Don Khon and Don Det, bypassing the rapids that block this stretch of the river.

A short walk west of the bridge stands the village monastery, Wat Khon Tai. Taking the southerly path behind the wat for 1.5km, you'll come to a low cliff overlooking **Somphamit Falls**, a series of high rapids that crashes through a jagged gorge.

Another good walk is from Don Khon to Don Det across the bridge and along the three-kilometre elevated trail to the small village at the northern end of the island. A Stonehenge-like structure that was used for hoisting cargo from the train onto awaiting boats is all that remains of the railway's northern terminus.

Ban Hang Khon

From Ban Khon, follow the easterly former railway trail adjacent to the high school through rice paddies and thick forest and eventually, after 4km, you'll reach the village of **BAN HANG KHON**, the jumping-off point for **dolphin-spotting** excursions. The April–May dry season, when the Mekong is at its lowest, is the optimum time of year to catch a glimpse of this highly endangered species (early mornings and late afternoons are said to be best), and boats can be hired out from the village to see them. During the rest of the year, chances of seeing the dolphins decrease, as deeper water allows them more range. Visitors should also bear in mind that the security situation on the Cambodian side of the river is variable. If boatmen refuse to shuttle you out to see the dolphins, don't insist: they will know what the current situation is. Boats cost $5 and you're obliged to pay for the boat regardless of whether you see any dolphins.

The bluish-grey freshwater **Irrawaddy dolphin** (*Orcaella brevirostris*) known as *pa kha* in Lao, grows to a length of 2.5m and lives in coastal waters stretching from the Bay of Bengal to the northern Australian coast, and inhabits the Irrawaddy River in Burma, the Mahakam in Kalimantan and the Ganges in India. The dolphins are rare in Lao waters, as most are unable to swim beyond the Khon Phapheng Falls near the Lao–Cambodian border. Over the past century their numbers in the Mekong have dwindled dramatically, from thousands to little more than one hundred today. The present dolphin population off Ban Hang Khon is only ten, down from thirty in 1993. Gill-net fishing and, across the border, the use of poison, electricity and explosives are to blame. In the past, fishermen were reluctant to cut costly nets to free entangled dolphins, but Lao villagers are now compensated for their nets – part of an initiative begun by the Lao Community Fisheries and Dolphin Protection Project.

Khon Phapheng Falls

Despite technically being the largest waterfall in Southeast Asia, **Khon Phapheng**, to the east of Don Khon, is not all that spectacular. Indeed, it's best described as a low but wide cliff that just happens to have a huge volume of water running over it. The vertical drop is highest during the March–May dry season and becomes much less spectacular when the river level rises during the rainy season. Still, the sight of all that water crashing down on its way to Cambodia is quite mesmerizing and a tourist pavilion above the falls provides an ideal place to sit and enjoy the view. There's also no shortage of food shacks serving *som tom*. Most tourists do the falls as a package from Don Khong (see p.578) but it is also possible to get there by sawngthaew from Ban Hat Xai Khoun (opposite Muang Khong) or Nakasang (4000K). An admission charge of 10,000K is made for foreigners.

Practicalities

It's possible to do Don Khon–Don Det–Khon Phapheng as a **day-trip** from Don Khong, although ideally Don Khon on its own is worth a few days' visit. ask at any of the guesthouses or restaurants. The boat for the day-trip costs 10,000K per person, and you can see both waterfalls and the defunct railway≠ in one day. The boat can't go directly to Khon Phapheng Falls, so the boatman will take you to the right bank, where a tuk-tuk (another 10,000K per person) will be waiting to take the passengers on the thirty-kilometre round-trip to the falls (10,000K admission). Afterwards, your boatman will take you back to Don Khong.

If you intend to stay on Don Khon or Don Det, the cheapest option from Muang Khong is to take the ferry (1000K) across the river to Ban Hat Xai Khoun and then get a bus to **Nakasang**, where you can get a boat to Don Khon or Don Det ($1–2). The boats depart from the landing a short walk from the market. Alternatively, you can join a Don Khon day-trip and negotiate a one-way, discounted price for the boat trip to Don Khon. The asking price is $4 for up to three passengers.

Although Don Khon was the first island to take off with travellers, Don Det has already surpassed its larger neighbour in popularity. On **Don Khon**, most of the bungalows are located near the village of Ban Khon on the north end of the island. On **Don Det**, there are now bungalow places scattered all the way around the island, but the largest concentration is at the northern end. The truth is, there's not a huge difference in the two islands, and where you stay is largely a matter of finding a bungalow to suit your taste and budget. If you're arriving by boat you should specify

Overland into Cambodia via the Voen Kam border crossing

To get to the **Cambodian border** at Voen Kam, you need to hire a boat at the southern end of Don Khon to take you down the Mekong. Although the crossing at Voen Kam is not "officially" open, as long as you're in possession of a Cambodian **visa** – available at the Cambodian Embassy in Vientiane (see p.531) – you should have no problems getting through. Immigration officials on both sides ask for a $2–3 fee to stamp your passport, just one of many scams that operate at all land borders into Cambodia. If you ask for the official's name and demand a receipt, you may find they back down on this request.

if you want to disembark at Don Khon or Don Det.

Many travellers who come to Don Det and Don Khon stay for an extended period. With so many similar places to choose from, the best option is to shop around for your own ideal piece of paradise (none of the accommodation places have phones). Typically, you can expect a bamboo and wood hut with a small veranda and hammock overlooking the river. Bathing facilities are usually shared. Candles are used for lighting at places without generators. It should go without saying, but be sure to snuff out your candles before going to bed. Every year, a couple of bungalows burn down due to tourists. Regardless of where you stay, never leave any valuables unattended in your bungalow.

On Don Khon, moving upstream from the bridge, is *Pon's River Resort* (❶), a collection of stilted **bamboo huts** with shared facilities and a decent restaurant. *Mr Bounh's* (❶) offers simple bungalows with clean, shared facilities in a quiet compound close to the river. Next door is the upscale *Sala Don Khone* (❸–❺) where the beautifully built wooden bungalows in the garden, with fan and attached cold-water bath, are the best value. On Don Det, *Santiphab* (❶), next to the railway bridge, is popular, with views of the bridge from the bungalow verandas. About 2km further up the trail from the bridge, *Mr Tho's Bungalows* (❶) has basic bamboo-and-thatch huts and hammocks from which you can idly watch river life passing by. If they're full, try *Souksan Bungalow* (❶), on the northern tip of the island.

Every bungalow place on the islands has a **restaurant** serving Lao food and the usual travellers' fare. Remember that food, not accommodation, is the real money-earner here, so do take at least some meals at the bungalow you stay at.

The Bolaven Plateau and Tad Lo Falls

High above the hot Mekong River Valley stands the natural citadel of the **Bolaven Plateau** dominating eastern Champasak province and overlooking the provinces of Salavan, Xekong and Attapu to the east. Hilly, roughly circular in shape, and with an average altitude of 600m, rivers flow off the high plateau in all directions and then plunge out of lush forests along the Bolaven's edges in a series of spectacular waterfalls, some more than 100m high, before eventually finding their way to the Mekong. The provincial capitals of Pakxe, Salavan, Xekong and Attapu surround the Bolaven, but the main settlement on the plateau itself is the town of **Pakxong**. South of Route 23 between Pakxe and Pakxong is the Dong Hua Sao NBCA.

Tad Lo Falls

The ten-metre-high **Tad Lo Falls**, on the banks of the Xe Set River, draw a steady stream of foreign visitors, providing the perfect setting for a few days' relaxation and the opportunity to ride an elephant along the breezy western flank of the fertile Bolaven Plateau. In the hot season, the pools surrounding Tad Hang, the lower falls, are a refreshing escape from the heat; be sure to clear the water before 8pm, however, when the floodgates of a dam upstream unleash a torrent of water without warning. Elephant treks ($4 for 2hr) through the forested hills around Tad Lo are easy to arrange through any of the guesthouses in Tad Hang.

The Tad Lo Falls are just two hours northeast of Pakxe by bus and about 30km southwest of Salavan; the road is mostly dirt but is flat and in good condition. The turn-off for Tad Lo is 88km northeast of Pakxe, just beyond the village of Lao Ngam; buses will drop you at the turn-off, from where it's a 1.5-kilometre tuk-tuk ride (2000K per person) along a dirt road to Tad Hang. When leaving, find a driver to take you back to the highway, where you can pick up a morning bus to Salavan or Pakxe. High on a hill overlooking Tad Hang perches *Tad Lo Resort* (☎031/212105 ext 3325; ❺–❻), the best accommodation in the area, with thirteen rooms in an assortment of bungalows. Across the river, *Saise* guesthouse has a handful of cheaper rooms with shared facilities in a raised house (❷), plus some very pleasant en-suite ones in a "green house", a few hundred metres upstream (❷). Beds fill up quickly at both establishments, so reserve ahead; the Sodetour office in Pakxe can do this. *Tad Lo Resort* has a relaxed open-air **restaurant**, with commanding views and a range of moderately priced French and Lao dishes. For cheaper fare, head down the hill to the *Little Shop*.

The Xe Kong River Valley

The **Xe Kong** is one of Laos' great rivers, starting high in the Annamite Mountains from the eastern flanks of 2500m-high Mount Atouat and flowing southwestward around the southern edge of the Bolaven Plateau and then across the plains of Cambodia to join the Mekong at Stung Treng. The main towns along the Xe Kong in Laos are **Xekong** and **Attapu**, which are linked by a paved road. Roads into the vast forest interior are still extremely poor but various tributaries link the Xe Kong to no less than four of Laos's most pristine NBCAs, and organized kayaking tours are starting to take off.

Xekong

In 1984, a wide expanse of jungle was cleared of trees and graded flat and the town of **XEKONG** was born. Founded partly because nearby Ban Phon was deemed no longer habitable owing to unexploded ordnance (UXO), Xekong has something of a frontier feel about it, but it is the departure point for a very scenic journey downriver to Attapu. Three major branches of the Ho Chi Minh Trail snaked through the jungle surrounding Xekong, making this area one of the most heavily bombed in Laos, and an astonishing amount of UXO still blankets this province, so you shouldn't go off exploring here. In addition, there is a disturbing beasty lurking in Xekong's waterways: the *pa pao* is a **blowfish** with a piranha-like appetite and, according to locals, a particular fondness for lopping off the tip of the male member.

Practicalities

Buses to and from Pakxe operate from the dirt lot outside the morning market, about 1km from the main market (2000K by tuk-tuk). Heading into town, you'll pass a branch of the Lao May Bank, where you can exchange cash and travellers' cheques, and the **post office** and the Telecom building, where international calls can be made. A daily **bus** plies the paved route that follows the Xe Kong River south to Attapu; it leaves the morning market at 7am, arriving in Attapu about two hours later, and departs for the trip back to Xekong at noon. A pleasant alternative is to hire a boat to Attapu (see opposite).

Sekong Souksamlane (☎031/212022; ❷–❸), is located 500m downriver from the market and has decent, if somewhat over-priced **rooms**. Cheap **restaurants** surround the hotel, but the hotel restaurant cooks up rather good Thai food, too.

Down the Xe Kong River

If you've made it as far as Xekong, the scenic **Xe Kong River**, which meanders through little-visited countryside, provides a strong incentive to hire a boat for the journey south to Attapu. Emerging from high in the Annamite Mountains, the Xe Kong meanders south by southwest until it eventually joins the Mekong River north of Stung Treng in Cambodia. Motorized pirogues make the four-hour journey through gentle rapids and past lushly forested riverbanks. At around $40 per boat, it's expensive, but well worth it. Late in the dry season, the trip can take seven hours, and the shallow waters require passengers to walk some short stretches – at this time of year, captains will only take two passengers, thereby increasing the price per person. To find a captain, follow the road from the *Sekong Souksamlane* hotel south for 1km until you reach a boat landing.

Attapu

A cosy settlement of almost 20,000 people, most of whom are Vietnamese, Chinese or Lao, remote **ATTAPU** occupies a bend in the Xe Kong River. Coconut palms and banana trees shade spacious wooden houses with generous balconies, high on stilts, and the town is known throughout southern Laos as the "garden city". Although it was near this distant outpost that the Ho Chi Minh Trail diverged, with one artery running south towards Cambodia and the other into South Vietnam, Attapu somehow eluded the grave effects of war and remains an easygoing place that's ideal for leisurely wandering. This region of Laos has the country's highest rate of malaria, so heed the advice on p.52.

Practicalities

Arriving in Attapu by **bus**, you'll wind up in a dirt field on the southwestern outskirts of the city, a two-kilometre walk or tuk-tuk ride from the centre. If you're on the express bus from Pakxe, don't automatically get off here, as the bus may continue into town. Arriving by **boat** from Xekong, walk up the ramp and follow the road into town to the Lao May Bank, which is a good point of orientation.

Attapu has two **guesthouses**, the better of which is *Souksomphone* (☎036/211046; ❶–❷), a modern building opposite the bank, with seven clean, spacious rooms. Near the post office, the *Tawiwan* (❶) has rooms with shared bathrooms in a cluster of two-storey houses set back from the road. There is also a newish hotel, *Yingchokchai* (☎036/211031; ❸), opposite the *Tawiwan*. Clean rooms with TV and air-con are only a couple of dollars more than what you'll pay at the *Souksomphone*. There's also an attached restaurant, and breakfast is included in the room price. At the eastern end of the *Tawiwan* compound is the town's most popular **restaurant**, where you'll find good, moderately priced noodle and rice dishes; service, however, is terribly slow. The main area for food stalls lies along the same east–west road that the *Souksomphone* is on, with hawkers setting up between the bank and the wat.

Moving on from Attapu, the **bus** to Xekong leaves at noon, arriving at the town's morning market at around 2pm. The **express bus** to Pakxe leaves Attapu at 6am, taking just four hours. Otherwise, you're stuck with the gruelling regular bus, which can take twice as long. Route 18 to Si Phan Don via Route 13 is still unpaved and there is no public transport across, although there are plans to eventually upgrade this road as far as Vietnam. **Boats** up the Xe Kong River to Xekong ($40) can be arranged through the *Souksomphone*.

Laos travel details

Buses and sawngthaews

Daen Sawan/Lao Bao to: Savannakhet (4 daily; 3hr); Xepon (4 daily; 1hr).
Lak Xao to: Thakhek (3 daily; 4hr); Vientiane (daily; 8hr).
Louang Namtha to: Boten (4 daily; 2 hr); Houayxai (8hr); Jinghong, China, via Boten (daily; 11hr); Muang Sing (4 daily; 2hr 30min); Oudomxai (4 daily; 4hr).
Louang Phabang to: Muang Nan (3 daily; 3hr); Nam Bak (2 daily; 2hr); Nong Khiaw (3 daily; 3hr); Oudomxai (5 daily; 4hr); Pakmong (5 daily; 2hr); Vang Viang (8 daily; 6–7hr); Viang Kham (daily; 4hr); Vientiane (10 daily; 10–12hr).
Muang Sing to: Louang Namtha (4 daily; 2hr 30min); Xiang Kok (2 daily; 2hr 30min).
Nam Neun to: Phonsavan (1–2 daily; 6hr); Viang Thong (daily; 3hr) and Xam Nua (daily; 3hr 30 min).
Nong Khiaw to: Louang Phabang (2 daily; 3hr).
Oudomxai to: Boten (4hr); Jinghong, China, via Boten (12hr); Louang Namtha (5 daily; 4hr); Louang Phabang (5 daily; 4hr); Muang Sing (6hr); Pakbeng (2 daily; 4hr); Phongsali (daily; 9-11hr); Vientiane (daily; 19hr).
Pakxe to: Attapu (2 daily; 4–7hr); Champasak (3 daily; 1hr 30min); Chong Mek (hourly; 45min); Muang Sen (2 daily; 5hr 30min); Nakasang (5 daily; 3hr); Pakxong (hourly; 2hr); Salavan (5 daily; 3hr); Savannakhet (5 daily; 4hr); Tad Lo (3 daily; 2–3hr); Thakhek (4 daily; 6hr); Vientiane (4 daily; 12hr); Xekong (2 daily; 4–5hr).
Phonsavan to: Muang Kham (4–5 daily; 1hr 30min); Muang Khoun (2–3 daily; 1hr); (1–2 daily; 3hr); Nam Neun (1–2 daily; 6hr); Nong Het (daily; 4hr).
Savannakhet to: Daen Sawan/Lao Bao (4 daily; 3hr); Da Nang, Vietnam (6 weekly; 10hr); Dong Ha, Vietnam (daily; 8hr); Hanoi, Vietnam (weekly; 20hr); Hue, Vietnam (6 weekly; 8hr); Pakxe (5 daily; 4hr); Thakhek (8 daily; 2hr); Vientiane (16 daily; 8hr); Xepon (4 daily; 2hr).
Thakhek to: Hanoi, Vietnam (weekly; 24 hr); Lak Xao (5 daily; 4hr); Mahaxai (5 daily; 2hr 30min); Pakxe (3 daily; 6hr); Savannakhet (8 daily; 2hr); Vientiane (10 daily; 6hr).
Vang Viang to: Louang Phabang (9 daily; 8–10hr); Vientiane (10 daily; 3hr).
Viang Kham to: Louang Phabang (daily; 4h); Nong Khiaw (2–3 daily; 2hr); Viang Thong (1–2 daily; 4hr).
Viang Thong to: Nam Neun (daily; 3hr); Viang Kham (1–2 daily; 4hr); Xam Nua (daily; 6–7hr).
Vientiane to: Lak Xao (3 daily; 8hr); Ban Pako (3 daily; 1hr); Louang Phabang (9 daily; 10–12hr); Oudomxai (daily; 19hr); Pakxan (12 daily; 2hr); Pakxe (6 daily; 12hr); Savannakhet (8 daily; 8hr); Somsamai (3 daily; 1hr); Thakhek (10 daily; 6hr); Vang Viang (10 daily; 3hr); Xam Nua (daily; 24hr).
Xam Nua to: Nam Neun (1–2 daily; 3hr 30min); Viang Thong (1 daily; 6–7hr); Viang Xai (7 daily; 30min); Vientiane (daily; 24hr).
Xepon to: Daen Sawan/Lao Bao (4 daily; 1hr); Savannakhet (4 daily; 3hr).

Boats

Houayxai to: Louang Namtha (passenger boat: 1–2 days); Louang Phabang (slow boat: 2 days; speedboat: 6hr); Pakbeng (slow boat: 1 day; speedboat: 3hr); Xiang Kok (speedboat: 4hr).
Louang Namtha to: Houayxai (passenger boat: 1–2 days).
Louang Phabang to: Houayxai (slow boat: 2–3 days; speedboat: 6hr); Nong Khiaw (passenger boat; 8hr); Pakbeng (slow boat: 1–2 days; speedboat: 3hr).
Pakxe to: Champasak (1hr 30min); Don Khong (8–10hr).
Vientiane to: Louang Phabang (2–3 weekly; 4 days).

Flights

Houayxai to: Vientiane (3 weekly; 1hr 20min).
Louang Phabang to: Chiang Mai, Thailand (6 weekly; 2hr); Vientiane (2–3 daily; 40min).
Pakxe to: Phnom Penh, Cambodia (weekly; 1hr 20min); Siem Reap, Cambodia (2 weekly; 1hr); Vientiane (5 weekly; 1hr 20min).
Phongsali to: Vientiane (2 weekly; 1hr 40min).
Phonsavan to: Vientiane (10 weekly; 40min).
Vientiane to: Bangkok, Thailand (2 daily; 1hr); Chiang Mai, Thailand (6 weekly; 2hr); Hanoi, Vietnam (10 weekly; 1hr 10min); Houayxai (3 weekly; 1hr 20min); Kunming, China (2 weekly; 3hr); Louang Namtha (4 weekly; 1hr 10min); Louang Phabang (2-3 daily; 40min); Oudomxai (6 weekly; 50min); Pakxe (5 weekly; 1hr 20min); Phnom Penh, Cambodia (8 weekly; 2hr 30min); Phonsavan (10 weekly; 40min); Siem Reap, Cambodia (2 weekly; 2 hr 30min); Xam Nua (4 weekly; 1hr 10min).

6

Macau

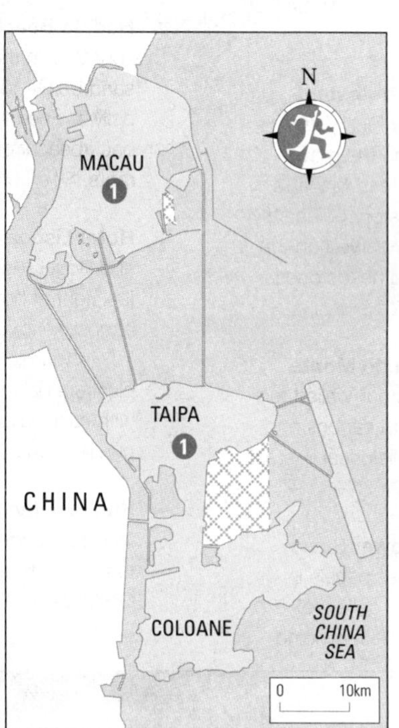

Macau highlights

✱ **Macanese cuisine** Discover Portuguese classics with a Chinese twist, served, often as not, in charmingly old-fashioned colonial surroundings. See pp.591 & 605

✱ **The Old Protestant Cemetery** Pick your way among the grave plots and read Macau's colonial history poignantly and vividly carved on the tombs and headstones. See p.602

✱ **Fortaleza do Monte** Macau's stout-walled fort bristles with canons and plenty of historical interest. See p.602

✱ **Macau Tower** Stand on the glass panels in the viewing gallery of Macau's tallest building and set your heart aflutter by looking. If that's not scary enough, rope up and clamber around the outside. See p.604

✱ **Hac Sa Beach** Wiggle your toes in the black sand before filling your belly at one of the laid-back beachfront restaurants. See p.605

✱ **Hotel Lisboa** Tony Curtis and Roger Moore would feel right at home in this atmospheric, over-the-top 1970s marble and neon pleasure palace, packed with casinos and eager punters. See p.599

✱ **Kun Iam Temple** A beautiful four-hundred-year-old temple dedicated to the Goddess of Mercy. See p.603

△ Fortaleza do Monte

Introduction and basics

Things are changing fast in Macau, a tiny former Portuguese trading enclave that lies sixty kilometres west across the Pearl River Delta from Hong Kong. A mere sliver of mainland and a couple of islands covering about twenty-four square kilometres, it may seem a geographic and economic midget compared to its high-rise cousin across the water but it's catching up quickly.

Macau is booming like never before – thanks largely to a recent, rapid and vast expansion of gambling in the territory. Indeed, the millions (literally) of gambling fanatics that now pour over the borders into Macau every year see it as little more than one giant **casino**. To meet the demands of this sudden gambling gold rush, land is being vigorously reclaimed from the sea: a huge waterfront dining and entertainment area, **Fisherman's Wharf**, is emerging on reclaimed land at the Porto Exterior (scheduled for completion by mid-2005), while a giant sports stadium (part of a massive building programme for the 2005 Asian Games) has been built between what used to be the islands of Taipa and Coloane.

Rapid development has already changed the character of this formerly sleepy colonial backwater beyond recognition (and ambitious plans for a road bridge to Hong Kong are still in the pipeline), but old Macau is still very much in evidence if you look in the right places. With a colonial past predating that of Hong Kong by nearly three hundred years, Macau's **historic buildings** – from old fortresses to Baroque churches to faded mansion houses – are plentiful, while the crumbling backstreets behind the port are reminiscent of Hong Kong as it might have been fifty years ago.

The cheap Portuguese wine and Macanese cooking – an interesting marriage of Chinese and Mediterranean influences – are further reminders of Macau's colonial heritage and reason alone for a visit. South of the main city, on **Taipa** and **Coloane**, are beaches and quiet villages where, bar the odd mainland tour group, you can dine in relative peace.

If you're already in Hong Kong, considering the lower costs in Macau and the ease of travel between Guangzhou, Hong Kong and Macau, it's a great pity not to drop in on the territory. A day-trip from Hong Kong is very easy, though you need a couple of nights really to do the place justice. With the development of Macau's **airport** into a hub for cheap regional flights, it can work out cheaper doing the trip in reverse. If you're visiting Hong Kong from other Asian destinations, it's worth checking out the price of flying into Macau and then getting the ferry to Hong Kong, as there are often bargains to be had.

In addition to sharing a common language with its larger neighbour (the majority of Macau's population of 463,000 are Cantonese-speaking Chinese), Macau's **climate** is also the same as Hong Kong's. Between June and September conditions are hot and humid – above 30°C – with frequent rainstorms, as well as a danger of typhoons. Between October and April conditions are cooler and much pleasanter, and while it can rain a lot in January and February, the temperature rarely falls below 14°C.

Air and sea routes into Macau

Access to Macau is chiefly by **boat from Hong Kong**: see p.201 for details. There are also plenty of **flights** from major Chinese cities and a handful of Southeast Asian capitals, from where an increasing number of budget carriers have also begun serving Macau.

Entry requirements and visa extension

Citizens of Britain, Ireland, Australia, New Zealand, Canada, the US and most Western European countries need only a valid

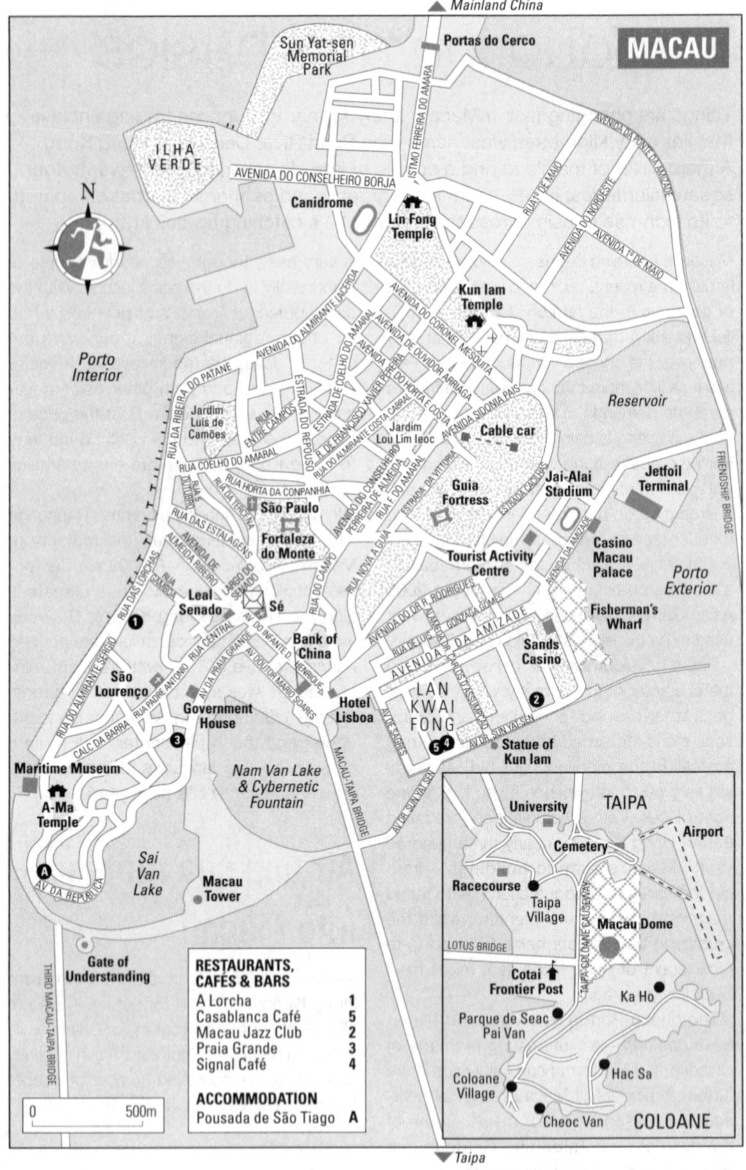

passport to enter Macau, and can stay up to thirty days (Europeans get ninety days). The simplest way to **extend your stay** is to go to Hong Kong and re-enter Macau at a later date.

Airport departure tax

Airport **departure tax** in Macau is 80ptca for China and 130ptca for all other destinations.

Money and costs

The unit of **currency** in Macau is the pataca (abbreviated to ptca in this book; also sometimes seen as M$, MOP or MOP$), which is in turn broken down into 100 avos. **Notes** come in denominations of 20, 50, 100, 500 and 1000ptca; **coins** come as 10, 20 and 50 avos, and 1, 5 and 10ptca. The pataca is worth fractionally less than the HK dollar. At the time of writing, the **exchange rate** was £1 = 15ptca and US$1 = 7.7ptca. HK dollars are freely accepted as currency in Macau, and a lot of visitors from Hong Kong don't bother changing money at all. All the **major credit cards** are accepted in the larger hotels, but most guesthouses and restaurants want cash. If you need to get money, many ATMs in the centre of town will accept foreign credit cards. If you want to get money sent from overseas you'd be better off doing it in Hong Kong, where they are more efficient and experienced.

Costs

Food and accommodation are more expensive in Macau than most other Southeast Asian destinations, although they are cheaper than in Hong Kong. You may pay slightly more than in Hong Kong for the very cheapest beds, but will get much better value in the larger hotels – which drop their prices even further midweek. An excellent three-course Portuguese meal with wine and coffee can be had for as little as £12/$19. Buses and taxis are in any case extremely cheap. All in all, you could live on about £13/$21 a day if you took the cheapest accommodation and ate frugally. A more comfortable room and better meals will raise your **daily budget** to a more realistic £20–25/$31–38.

Information and maps

The **Macau Government Tourist Office** (MGTO; ⓦwww.macautourism.gov.mo) has offices in Hong Kong at the Macau Ferry Terminal, Room 1303, Shun Tak Centre (daily 9am–1pm & 2.15–5.30pm; ⓣ2857 2287); at the Visitor Information Centre at the Jetfoil Terminal in Macau (daily 9am–6pm; ⓣ726 416); and at Largo do Senado 9 in Macau (daily 9am–6pm; ⓣ315 566 or 397 1120). Look out for three useful, free news sheets, *Macau Travel Talk*, *Macau Where* and *Macau What's On*, all of which list forthcoming cultural events. The MGTO puts out a range of useful leaflets on all the enclave's sights, a good bilingual map and a leaflet explaining bus routes.

Accommodation

Accommodation is generally cheaper in Macau than in Hong Kong – at least midweek. For the same money that would get you a tiny box in Hong Kong's *Chungking Mansions*, you can find quite a spacious room with private shower and a window here. Be warned, however, that at weekends **prices** shoot up everywhere.

Food and drink

The territory's native cuisine, **Macanese food**, is a tempting blend of Portuguese and Asian. The Portuguese elements include fresh bread, cheap imported wine and good coffee, as well as an array of dishes ranging from *caldo verde* (vegetable soup) to *bacalhau* (dried salted cod). *Bacalhau* forms the base for several tasty dishes, which can come baked, grilled, casseroled or poached. There's also the Brazilian *feijoadas*, a heavy stew with beans, pork, sausages, cabbage and potatoes. One of Macau's most interesting Portuguese colonial dishes is **African chicken**, a concoction of Goan and east African influences, comprising chicken grilled with peppers and spices. Macau is also justly acknowledged for the exceptional quality of its sweet, flaky custard tarts or *natas*.

Straightforward **Cantonese restaurants**, often serving *dim sum* for breakfast and lunch, are also plentiful, though you'll find wine on the menus even here. Alongside the local dumplings and noodles, Macau's numerous snack bars often sell fresh-milk products, which is unusual for China.

The **water** meets European health stand-

Food and drink glossary

Basics and snacks

Arroz	Rice
Batatas fritas	French fries
Legumes	Vegetables
Manteiga	Butter
Ovos	Eggs
Pimenta	Pepper
Prego	Steak roll
Sal	Salt
Sandes	Sandwiches

Soups

Caldo verde	Green cabbage and potato soup
Sopa álentejana	Garlic and bread soup with a poached egg
Sopa de mariscos	Shellfish soup
Sopa de peixe	Fish soup

Meat

Almondegas	Meatballs
Bife	Steak
Chouriço	Spicy sausage
Coelho	Rabbit
Cordoniz	Quail
Costeleta	Chop
Dobrada	Tripe
Figado	Liver
Galinha	Chicken
Pombo	Pigeon
Porco	Pork
Salsicha	Sausage

Fish and seafood

Ameijoas	Clams
Bacalhau	Dried and salted cod
Camarões	Shrimps
Carangueijo	Crab
Gambas	Prawns
Linguado	Sole
Lulas	Squid
Meixilhões	Mussels

Specialities

Cataplana	Pressure-cooked seafood stew with bacon, sausage and peppers
Cozido á Portuguesa	Boiled casserole of mixed meats, eg pig's trotters, rice and vegetables
Galinha á Africana	Chicken rolled or marinated in a pepper and chilli paste
Galinha á Portuguesa	Chicken with eggs, potatoes, onion and saffron in a mild, creamy curry sauce
Feijoada	Brazilian bean, pork, sausage, cabbage and potato stew
Pasteis de bacalhau	Deep-fried cod fishcakes
Porco á álentejana	Pork and clam stew

Desserts

Arroz doce	Portuguese rice pudding
Nata	Egg tart
Pudim flán	Crème caramel

Drinks

Água mineral	Mineral water
Café	Coffee
Chá	Tea
Cerveja	Beer
Sumo de laranja	Orange juice
Vinho	Wine
Vinho do Porto	Port (both red and white)
Vinho verde	A slightly sparkling white wine

ards, though you may prefer bottled water. Restaurant **menus** are not always available in English – just Portuguese and Cantonese.

Communications

Airmail sent from Macau to Europe and North America takes between five days and a week. **Poste restante** is delivered to Macau's main post office (see "Listings", p.607). Local calls are free from **private phones**, 1ptca from payphones. Cardphones work with CTM cards, issued by the Macau State Telecommunication Company, on sale in hotels or at the back of the main post office in Largo do Senado (open 24hr), where you can also make direct calls. **Macau phone numbers**

have no area codes: just dial the five- or six-figure number given. Instructions on most phones are in English as well as Portuguese. For **calls to Hong Kong**, dial ⓣ01 followed by the eight-digit number.

You can make **international calls** from public phones or from the telephone office at the back of the main post office. Dial ⓣ00 + IDD country code (see p.64) + area code minus first 0 + subscriber number. There's also a **Home Direct** service (*Pais Directo*), which gives you access to an operator in the country you're calling, who can either charge calls collect or to your overseas phonecard (see "Basics", p.64). For international calls to Macau, the prefix is ⓣ853.

Most of the bigger hotels have business centres with **Internet access**. Alternatively, try the cybercafé in the UNESCO centre just off Avenida da Amizade, or those in the new Docks entertainment area, near the Kun Iam statue in the Porto Exterior (see p.602).

Opening hours and festivals

Government **offices** open Monday–Friday 9am–1pm and 3–5/5.30pm, Saturday 8.30/9am–1pm. **Shops** and businesses are usually open for longer and don't close for lunch. **Banks** generally open Monday to Friday from 9am until 4 or 4.30pm, but close by 12.30pm on Saturdays. All government offices close on public holidays and some religious festivals. As the Chinese use the **lunar calendar** and not the Gregorian calendar, many of the festivals fall on different days, even different months, from year to year; for exact details, contact MGTO (see p.591).

The normal Chinese **holidays** are celebrated in Macau, plus some Catholic **festivals** introduced from Portugal, such as the procession of Our Lady of Fatima from São Domingos Church annually on May 13 (although this is no longer a public holiday). Two of the most important Chinese festivals celebrated in Macau are **Chinese New Year** (Jan/Feb) and the **Mid-Autumn Festival** (Sept). Many of the festivals are highly symbolic and are often a mixture of secular and religious displays and devotions.

Time differences

Macau is in the same **time zone** as Hong Kong. That means it is eight hours ahead of the UK (GMT), thirteen hours ahead of New York, sixteen hours ahead of Los Angeles, two hours behind Sydney and four hours behind Auckland.

Public holidays

January 1: New Year
January/February: Chinese New Year (three days' holiday)
March/April: Easter (holidays on Good Friday and Easter Monday)
April: Ching Ming Festival
May: Buddha's Birthday
May 1: Labour Day
June: Tuen Ng (Dragon Boat) Festival; also Feast of St John the Baptist
September: Mid-Autumn Festival
October 1: Chinese National Day
October: Chung Yeung Festival
November 2: All Souls Day
December 8: Feast of Immaculate Conception
December 20: Macau SAR Establishment Day
December 22: Winter Solstice
December 25 and 26: Christmas and the next working day

Cultural hints

Macau shares many of the social taboos of other **Southeast Asian cultures**, described in "Basics" on p.68, though, as in Hong Kong, there is less emphasis on modest clothing. Topless bathing, however, is illegal.

Crime and safety

Macau is a **very safe place** for tourists. Although you may have read about some

Emergency phone numbers

Dial ☎999 for fire, police and ambulance.

dramatic crimes in the papers – shootings, robberies, arson – what crime there is is mostly Triad-organized, and hence not directed against foreigners. In addition, there has been a crackdown on the Triads since China took over, so generally things are very quiet. The main police station is listed on p.607. It is very unwise to have anything to do with **drugs** of any description.

Medical care and emergencies

Pharmacies (daily 9am–6pm) can help with minor injuries or ailments and will prescribe basic medicines: they're all registered, and may employ English speakers. For a **doctor**, contact the reception desk in the larger hotels or go straight to the 24-hour emergency department at the Centro Hospitalar Conde São Januário (see p.607). Casualty visits cost around 200ptca. You'll have to pay for a consultation and any medicines that are prescribed; be sure to get a receipt so that you can make an insurance claim when you get home.

History

For more than a thousand years, all trade between China and the West had been carried out by land along the Silk Road through Central Asia, but in the fifteenth century the growth in European seafaring, pioneered by the Portuguese, finally led to the demise of the land route. Henceforth, sea trade and control of sea ports were what the European powers looked for in Asia.

Having gained toeholds in India (Goa) and the Malay Peninsula (Malacca) in the early sixteenth century, the Portuguese finally managed to persuade local Chinese officials, in 1557, to rent them a strategically well-placed peninsula at the mouth of the Pearl River Delta with fine natural harbours, known as **Macao** (A-Ma-gao, or bay of A-Ma; A-Ma being the goddess of the sea). Owing to their important trade links with Japan, as well as with India and Malaya, the Portuguese soon found themselves in the delightful position of being sole agents for merchants across a whole swathe of east Asia. Given that the Chinese were forbidden from going abroad to trade themselves, and that other foreigners were not permitted to enter Chinese ports, their trade boomed and Macau grew immensely wealthy. With the traders came **Christianity**, and among the luxurious homes and churches built during Macau's brief half-century of prosperity was the Basilica of St Paul, whose facade can still be seen today.

By the beginning of the seventeenth century, however, Macau's fortunes were already on the wane, and a slow decline, which continued until very recently, set in. A combination of setbacks for the Portuguese, including defeats in war against the Spanish back home, the loss of trading relations with both Japan and China, and the rise of the Dutch as a trading power, saw Macau almost wiped off the map by mid-century.

In the eighteenth century, fortunes looked up somewhat, as more and more non-Portuguese European traders came looking for opportunities to prise open the locked door of China. For these people, Macau seemed a tempting base from which to operate, and eventually they were permitted to settle and build homes in the colony.

The British had greater ambitions than to remain forever as guests in someone else's colony and when they finally seized their own piece of the shore to the east in 1841, Macau's status – as a backwater – was definitively settled. Despite the introduction of **licensed gambling** in the 1850s, as a desperate means of securing some kind of income, virtually all trade was lost to Hong Kong.

During the twentieth century, Macau's population spiralled upwards to almost half a million, as repeated waves of **immigrants** flooded the territory, whether fleeing Japanese invaders or Chinese communists, but, unlike in Hong Kong, this growth was not accompanied by the same spectacular economic development. Indeed, in 1974, with the end of the fascist dictatorship in Portugal, the Portuguese attempted unilaterally to hand Macau back to China; the offer was refused. Only after the 1984 agreement with Britain over the future of Hong Kong did China agree to negotiate the formal return of Macau as well. In **1999**, the final piece of Asian soil still in European hands was surrendered. The Chinese mainland was united under a central government for the first time since the Ming dynasty, and Macau became, like Hong Kong, a semi-democratic capitalist enclave, subject to Beijing and classed as a "Special Administrative Region of the People's Republic of China". The new skyscrapers and giant casinos springing up across the territory are conspicuous proof of the spectacular, if rather indiscriminate, boom that has taken hold in Macau in the last couple of years as tycoon Stanley Ho's gambling monopoly was ended and mainlanders were given greater freedom to travel here.

Religion

The three main Chinese religions – Taoism, Confucianism and Buddhism – dominate in Macau (see "Religion", pp.69–71, for an introduction to all these religions), though there are dozens of Catholic churches here, too. The whole picture is further confused by the importance attached to superstition and ancestor worship.

Books

Austin Coates *City of Broken Promises* (OUP East Asia, UK). An entertaining novel that offers a colourful picture of eighteenth-century Macau, when the enclave was still a centre for China-related trade and intrigue. Coates was Assistant Colonial Secretary in Hong Kong in the 1950s.

Jill McGivering *Macau Remembers* (OUP). The reminiscences of some of Macau's most notable residents, offering a colourful insight into life in colonial Macau.

Language

The vast majority of people in Macau speak Cantonese (see "Language" in the Hong Kong chapter "Basics", p.197, for a pronunciation guide and some useful words and phrases) and many also speak Portuguese and English.

6.1

Macau

Macau comprises three distinct parts: the **peninsula**, which is linked by bridge to the island of **Taipa**, and beyond that the former island of **Coloane**, now joined to Taipa by an ever-widening strip of land reclamation. The peninsula of Macau, the location of the original old city and most of the historic sights (as well as the city amenities), is entirely developed right up to the border with China in the north, though the islands, Coloane in particular, contain a few quieter rural patches.

The peninsula is not large and it's possible to get around much of it on foot, though you'll need buses for the longer stretches. The most important road, **Avenida de Almeida Ribeiro**, cuts across from east (where it's known as Avenida do Infante d'Henrique) to west, taking in the *Hotel Lisboa*, one of Macau's most famous landmarks, and exits on its western end at the Porto Interior (Inner Harbour), near the old docking port (though foreigners can still depart here for the mainland city of Shenzhen in Guangdong). The western part of Almeida Ribeiro is also the budget-hotel area, albeit fairly sleazy.

Arrival

Access to Macau for many visitors is by **boat from Hong Kong**. Every day, large numbers of competing vessels make the one-hour journey between the Macau

Moving on from Macau

By plane

Planes fly from Taipa Island airport to Beijing (daily; 3hr), Shanghai (daily; 2hr), Xiamen (daily; 1hr), Taiwan (daily; 1hr 30min), Bangkok (daily; 2hr), Manila (2 weekly; 2hr), Kuala Lumpur (2 weekly), Seoul (4 weekly; 3hr) and as well as an increasing number of other Chinese cities.

By boat

Tickets for **boats to Hong Kong** (80–165pcta) are available in advance from the Jetfoil Terminal at the Porto Exterior. Otherwise, simply show up at the terminal, purchase a ticket for the next sailing, clear passport control and board.

By bus to China

You can **walk** across the border (daily 7.30am–midnight) at the Barrier Gate in the far north of the peninsula, into Zhuhai Special Economic Zone; buses #3, #5 and #9 connect the Barrier Gate with Avenida de Almeida Ribeiro and Rua da Praia Grande. Once in mainland China, you can easily pick up a bus to most destinations in Guangdong. Alternatively, cross via the Lotus Bridge at the Cotai Frontier Post on the block of reclaimed land joining Taipa and Coloane. The single-storey customs building is open from 9am to 8pm (take any Coloane-bound bus, including #26 or #21A, from *Hotel Lisboa*).

Ferry Terminal in Hong Kong and Macau's **Jetfoil Terminal** ("Nova Terminal" in Portuguese), in the southeast of town, at the Porto Exterior (Outer Harbour). The terminal is connected to the *Hotel Lisboa* and the budget-hotel area on Almeida Ribeiro by several buses, including #3A and #10. The boat services include a 24-hour turbojet route (every 15min from 5.50am until 1am, then every 30min), and catamarans (most of these depart from the China Ferry Terminal on Canton Road in Tsim Sha Tsui and leave roughly every hour between 8am and 9pm). **Ticket prices** vary; reckon on paying HK$80–165 each way. Simply show up at the terminal, purchase a ticket for the next sailing, clear passport control and board. **Planes** arrive at the **airport** on Taipa Island, connected by airport bus #AP1 to *Hotel Lisboa* and the Jetfoil Terminal.

City transport

Many, if not all, places in Macau can be reached on foot. **Taxis** are cheap (10ptca minimum charge), although don't expect the drivers to speak English. It's best to get someone to write your destination in Chinese characters first. There's a 2ptca surcharge if you're crossing to Taipa. Otherwise, hop onto one of the many very inexpensive **buses** (flat fare on the peninsula is 2.5ptca, the maximum you'll pay to Taipa is 5ptca; exact fare only). Some important bus interchanges include the Jetfoil Terminal (Nova Terminal), the *Hotel Lisboa*, Almeida Ribeiro, Praça Ponte e Horta (near the Porto Interior), Barra (near the Maritime Museum on the Porto Interior), the Barrier Gate (usually referred to by its Portuguese name, Portas do Cerco and the islands Taipa and Coloane. Useful routes include:

#3 and #3A from the Jetfoil Terminal to *Hotel Lisboa* and Almeida Ribeiro.

#5 and #10 from the Barra district in the southwest of the peninsula to Almeida Ribeiro and the Barrier Gate.

#21 and #21A from Almeida Ribeiro to Taipa Village and Coloane.

Cycling is also a possibility, on the islands at least, though note that you are not allowed to cycle over the causeway from the mainland to Taipa. For details on rental, see p.604. A fun way to cover a lot of ground is by **Mini Moke**, open-sided four-seaters that resemble slightly scaled-up golf carts. Avis, at the *Mandarin Oriental Hotel*, (☎336 789) rents them and prices start at 200ptca for a half day. You'll need a valid driving licence.

Accommodation

There are two main areas for hotels in Macau; three-star accommodation is located in the heart of casino-land just west of the *Hotel Lisboa*, while more downmarket guesthouses are at the western end of Almeida Ribeiro, spreading out from the Porto Interior, though one or two places can be found in remote, tranquil spots on Taipa and Coloane. Note that addresses are written with the number after the name of the street. Most hotels do cut-price deals if you stay during the week.

Hotel Central Ave de Almeida Ribeiro 264 ☎373 888. A great central location, and the array of serviceable (but slightly grubby) singles and doubles all have en-suite bathrooms, with TV, half-hearted a/c and hot water (though some don't have windows). No glamour here, but the staff are friendly. ⑥

East Asia Rua da Madeira 1A ☎922 433; Hong Kong reservations ☎2540 6333. In the heart of old Macau, off Rua de C de Outubro, the *East Asia* is the focus of the red-light district, its lobby often bustling with mainland prostitutes. The accommodation is more salubrious than this suggests, however. Singles, doubles and triples have a/c, en-suite bathroom and telephone, and are reasonably good value for money. ⑦

Hospedaria San Va Rua da Felicidade 67 ☎573 701. A very basic 42-room hostel with shared facilities. Recommended for a certain ramshackle charm, low rates and central location. Inspect a few rooms before you pay, some are distinctly gloomy while others (the rooms on the first floor facing the street, for instance) have fresh flowers and a small balcony. ❷

Hotel Lisboa Ave de Lisboa 2–4 ☎577 666, Hong Kong reservations ☎2546 6944. Macau's most famous hotel; luxurious quarters, four floors of in-house gambling, a 24hr coffee shop, a nightly strip show, owner Stanley Ho's priceless antique collection to gawp at in the lobbies, and lavish 1970s gold and marble chintz throughout. ❾

Mandarin Oriental 956–1110 Ave da Amizade ☎567 888, Hong Kong reservations ☎2881 1988. A plush spa and health facility (complete with enormous, landscaped swimming pool tucked, behind the Sands Casino) and sumptuous bedrooms make this an attractive choice if you want a bit of pampering (the Thai massage is superb). Good inclusive deals and mid-week discount rates available. ❾

Hotel Mondial Rua do Antonio Basto 8–10 ☎566 866. Perhaps the best-value hotel-style rooms on offer with fridge, a/c, video, TV and telephone. Rooms are light and clean. ❻

Pousada de São Tiago Ave da República ☎378 111; Hong Kong reservations ☎2739 1216. A tiny, fabulously romantic, old-fashioned, colonial hotel occupying an old fortress on the southern tip of the peninsula, with walled stairways lined with trickling streams, huge stone archways and traditionally furnished rooms. ❾

Hotel Sintra Ave de Joao IV ☎710 111. If your budget can't quite stretch to the *Lisboa*, the *Sintra*, with discounts of up to 50 percent in quieter times, is worth considering. It's central, and the rooms are huge, quiet and well equipped. ❾

Macau peninsula

The town of Macau was born in the south of the peninsula, around the bay-front road known as the **Praia Grande**, and grew out from there. Sadly, these days, a stroll on the seafront is not what it once was, with the bay now being enclosed, reclamation work underway and huge new buildings ceaselessly under construction. More rewarding is the main road that cuts the Praia from east to west, called **Avenida do Infante d'Henrique** to the east and **Avenida de Almeida Ribeiro** to the west. At the eastern end of the road rises the garish neon pineapple folly that is the *Hotel Lisboa*, though most of the interest lies in the section west of the Praia, particularly in the beautiful **Largo do Senado** (Senate Square), which marks the downtown area and bears the unmistakable influence of southern Europe, not only in its architecture but also in its role as a place for people to stroll, sit and chat.

At the northern end of Largo do Senado, away from the main road, is the handsome seventeenth-century Baroque church, **São Domingos** (daily 10am–6pm; free), while to the south, facing the square from across the main road, stands the **Leal Senado** (daily 9am–9pm; free), generally considered the finest Portuguese building in the city. Step into the interior courtyard here to see wonderful blue-and-white Portuguese tiles around the walls, while up the staircase from the courtyard, you reach first a formal garden and then the richly decorated **senate chamber** itself. In the late sixteenth century, all of the colony's citizens would cram into this hall to debate issues of importance. The senate's title *leal* (loyal) was earned during the period when Spain occupied the Portuguese throne and Macau became the final stronghold of those loyal to the true king. Today, the senate chamber is still used by the municipal government of Macau. Adjacent to the chamber is the wood-carved **public library**, whose collection includes many fifteenth- and sixteenth-century books which visitors are free to browse.

West from Largo do Senado, Almeida Ribeiro emerges on to the so-called **Porto Interior** (Inner Harbour), which overlooks the Chinese mainland just across the water. Some of the streets immediately inland from here are worth poking around; Rua da Felicidade, for example, has been nicely restored and is now full of small hotels, friendly restaurants and stalls selling a colourful array of egg rolls, peanut and sesame snacks and marinated meat. Be warned that at night the streets immediately north of Almeida Ribeiro become a red-light district, not unsafe so much as seedy.

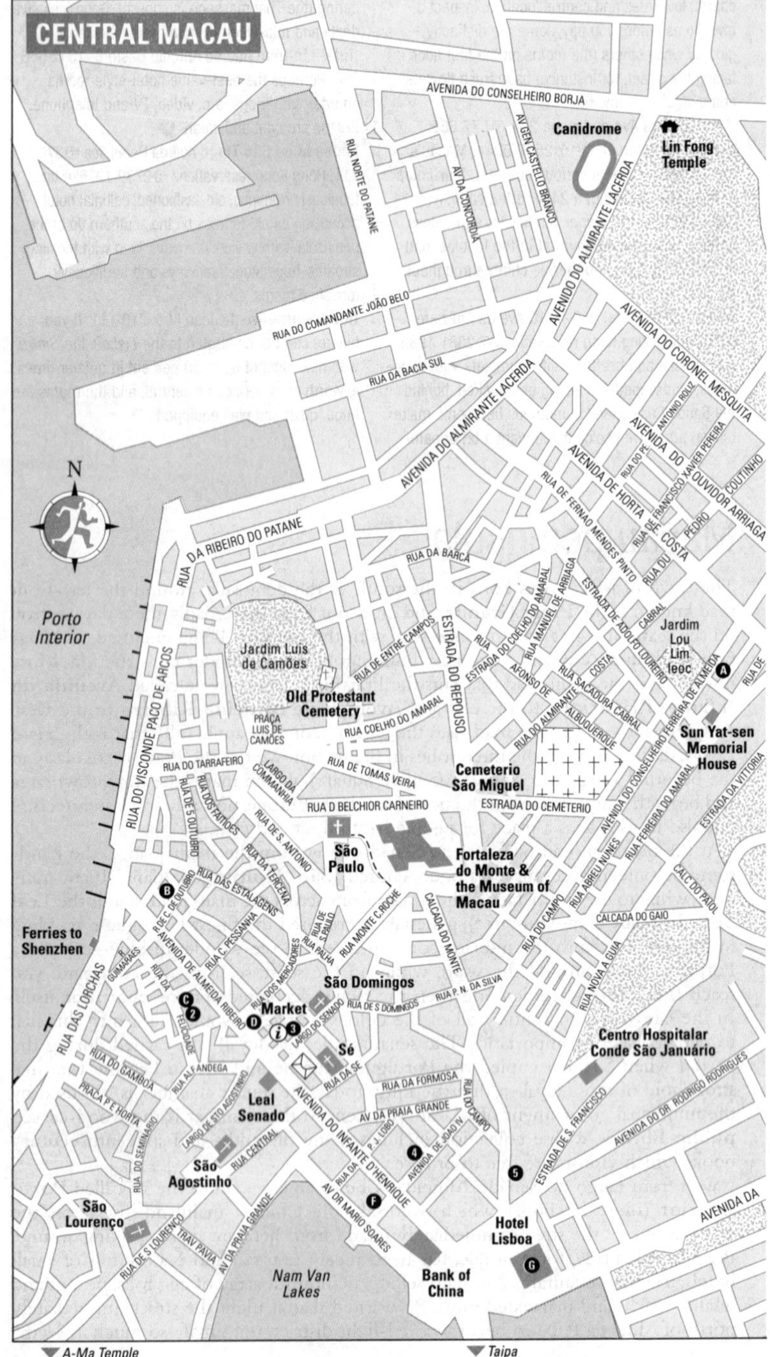
Portas do Cerco & Mainland China
CENTRAL MACAU
AVENIDA DO CONSELHEIRO BORJA
Canidrome
Lin Fong Temple
AV GEN CASTELLO BRANCO
AV DA CONCORDIA
RUA NORTE DO PATANE
AVENIDO DO ALMIRANTE LACERDA
RUA DO COMANDANTE JOÃO BELO
AVENIDA DO CORONEL MESQUITA
RUA DA BACIA SUL
AVENIDA DO ALMIRANTE LACERDA
AVENIDA DO OUVIDOR ARRIAGA
AVENIDA DE HORTA E COSTA
RUA DE FERNAO MENDES PINTO
RUA DO PE. ANTONIO ROLIZ
RUA DE FRANCISCO XAVIER PEREIRA
RUA DU PEDRO COUTINHO
N
RUA DA RIBEIRO DO PATANE
RUA DA BARCA
Porto Interior
Jardim Luis de Camões
Old Protestant Cemetery
RUA DE ENTRE CAMPOS
ESTRADA DO REPOUSO
ESTRADA DO COELHO DO AMARAL
RUA MANUEL DE ARRIAGA
ESTRADA DE ADOLFO LOUREIRO
CABRAL
Jardim Lou Lim Ieoc
RUA AFONSO DE ALBUQUERQUE
RUA SACADURA CABRAL
COSTA
RUA DO ALMIRANTE
RUA DE
RUA DO VISCONDE PACO DE ARCOS
PRACA LUIS DE CAMÕES
RUA COELHO DO AMARAL
AVENIDA DO CONSELHEIRO FERREIRA DE ALMEIDA
Sun Yat-sen Memorial House
RUA DO TARRAFEIRO
LARGO DA COMMANHIA
RUA DE TOMAS VEIRA
Cemeterio São Miguel
RUA FERREIRA DO AMARAL
ESTRADA DA VITORIA
RUA DE 5 OUTUBRO
RUA DOS FAITIOES
RUA D BELCHIOR CARNEIRO
ESTRADA DO CEMETERIO
RUA DE S. ANTONIO
RUA DA TERCENA
São Paulo
Fortaleza do Monte & the Museum of Macau
RUA ABREU NUNES
CALC DO PAIOL
RUA DAS ESTALAGENS
R. DE C. DE OUTUBRO
CALCADA DO MONTE
RUA DO CAMPO
CALCADA DO GAIO
Ferries to Shenzhen
R. GUIMARAES
AVENIDA DE ALMEIDA RIBEIRO
RUA C. PESSANHA
RUA DE S PAULO
RUA PALHA
RUA MONTE C.ROCHE
RUA NOVA A GUIA
RUA DA FELICIDADE
RUA DOS MERCADORES
São Domingos
RUA P. N. DA SILVA
RUA DAS LORCHAS
Market
LARGO DO SENADO
RUA DE S DOMINGOS
Centro Hospitalar Conde São Januário
Sé
RUA DO GAMBOA
RUA ALMANDEGA
RUA DA SE
RUA DA FORMOSA
AVENIDA DO DR. RODRIGO RODRIGUES
PRACA P E HORTA
LARGO DE STO AGOSTINHO
Leal Senado
AV DA PRAIA GRANDE
RUA DO CAMPO
ESTRADA DE S. FRANCISCO
RUA DO SEMINARIO
RUA CENTRAL
AVENIDA DO INFANTE D'HENRIQUE
P. J. LOBO
AVENIDA DE JOAO IV
São Agostinho
RUA DA
AVENIDA DA
São Lourenço
AV DR MARIO SOARES
Hotel Lisboa
RUA DE S LOURENCO
TRAV PAVIA
AV DA PRAIA GRANDE
Nam Van Lakes
Bank of China
A-Ma Temple
Taipa

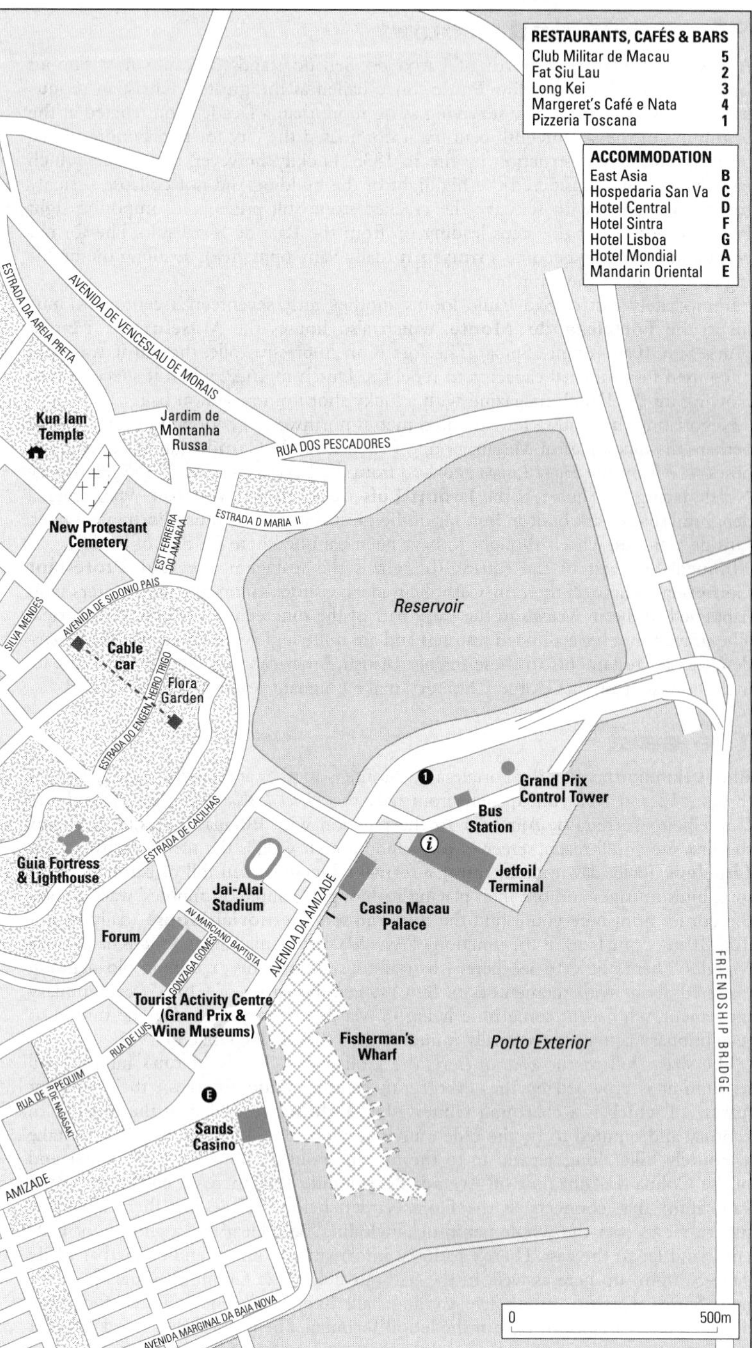
RESTAURANTS, CAFÉS & BARS
Club Militar de Macau 5
Fat Siu Lau 2
Long Kei 3
Margeret's Café e Nata 4
Pizzeria Toscana 1
ACCOMMODATION
East Asia B
Hospedaria San Va C
Hotel Central D
Hotel Sintra F
Hotel Lisboa G
Hotel Mondial A
Mandarin Oriental E
ESTRADA DA AREIA PRETA
AVENIDA DE VENCESLAU DE MORAIS
Kun Iam Temple
Jardim de Montanha Russa
RUA DOS PESCADORES
ESTRADA D MARIA II
New Protestant Cemetery
EST FERREIRA DO AMARAL
AVENIDA DE SIDONIO PAIS
SILVA MENDES
Cable car
Flora Garden
ESTRADA DO ENGEN. HEIRO TRIGO
Reservoir
Grand Prix Control Tower
Bus Station
ESTRADA DE CACILHAS
Guia Fortress & Lighthouse
Jai-Alai Stadium
Jetfoil Terminal
Casino Macau Palace
AVENIDA DA AMIZADE
AV MARCIANO BAPTISTA
GONZAGA GOMES
Forum
Tourist Activity Centre (Grand Prix & Wine Museums)
RUA DE LUIS
Fisherman's Wharf
Porto Exterior
FRIENDSHIP BRIDGE
RUA DE PEQUIM
R DE NAGASAKI
Sands Casino
AMIZADE
AVENIDA MARGINAL DA BAIA NOVA
0
500m
Airport & Taipa

São Paulo and around

A few hundred metres north of Largo do Senado stands Macau's most famous landmark, the church of **São Paulo**, once hailed as the greatest Christian monument in east Asia, but today surviving as no more than a facade. Constructed at the beginning of the seventeenth century, it dominated the city for two hundred years until its untimely destruction by fire in 1835. Luckily, however, the facade, which had always been considered the highlight of the building, did not collapse – richly carved and laden with statuary, the cracked stone still presents an imposing sight from the bottom of the steps leading up from the Rua de São Paulo. The former crypt and nave have become a **museum** (daily 9am–6pm; free), detailing the building and design of the church.

Immediately east of São Paulo looms another early seventeenth-century monument, the **Fortaleza do Monte**, which also houses the **Museum of Macau** (Tues–Sun 10am–6pm; 15ptca). The fort is an impressive pile, though it was only once used in a military capacity: to repel the Dutch in 1622, when it succeeded in blowing up the Dutch magazine with a lucky shot from a cannon ball.

Negotiating the roads a few hundred metres northwest of São Paulo brings you to perhaps the nicest part of Macau, around **Praça Luís de Camões** (also accessible on buses #17 from the *Hotel Lisboa* and #18 from the Barrier Gate and Inner Harbour). North, facing the square, is the **Jardim Luís de Camões** (daily 6am–9pm; free), a delightful shady park built in honour of the great sixteenth-century Portuguese poet, Luís de Camões, who is thought to have been banished here for part of his life.

Immediately east of the square, though, is the real gem, the **Old Protestant Cemetery**, where all the non-Catholic traders, visitors, sailors and adventurers who happened to die in Macau in the early part of the nineteenth century were buried. The gravestones have all been restored and are quite legible. In this quiet, shady garden, the last testaments to these mainly British, American and German individuals, including the painter George Chinnery, make poignant reading.

The east

About 1km northeast of the Fortaleza do Monte is another area worth walking around (buses #12 and #22 run up here from near the *Hotel Lisboa* along the Avenida do Conselheiro Ferreira de Almeida). At the junction with Estrada de Adolfo Loureiro, the first site you'll reach, screened off behind a high wall, is the scenic **Jardim Lou Lim Ieoc** (daily dawn–dusk; 1ptca), a formal Chinese garden full of bamboo, pavilions, birds in cages and old men playing mahjong. A couple of minutes' walk around the corner from here you'll find the **Sun Yat-sen Memorial House** (daily except Tues 10am–5pm; free), at the junction of Avenida de Sidonia Pais and the Rua de Silva Mendes. There's little to see here – basically, it's an attractive, rambling old mansion scattered about with mementoes of Sun Yat-sen, the father of China's revolutionary movement, who spent some time living in Macau in the years before he turned to revolutionary activities, eventually founding the Chinese Republic in 1911.

The sharp hill to the east of here, the Colina da Guia, is Macau's highest, and its summit is crowned by the seventeenth-century **Guia Fortress**, the dominant feature of which is a charming whitewashed **lighthouse**, added in the nineteenth century and reputed to be the oldest anywhere on the Chinese coast. You can take a leisurely hike along a path up to the fort in about an hour, or at the other end of the Colina da Guia, just off Avenida de Sidonido Pais, there's a **cable car** (daily 9am-5pm) that connects to the Flora Garden below. At the top there are some superb views over the whole peninsula, including, on a clear day, a glimpse of Lantau Island far to the east. There's a tourist information counter and coffee bar (daily 9am–5.30pm) up here as well. In the harbour below the Colina da Guia, the huge new **Sands Casino**, its massive gaming halls lined with one-hundred-foot-high plasma screens, lies south west of the Jetfoil Terminal. The inspiringly named **Tourist**

Activity Centre, containing the **Grand Prix Museum** (daily 10am–6pm; 10ptca), a collection of Formula 1 cars including one driven by racing legend Ayrton Senna, and the **Wine Museum** (daily 10am–6pm; 15ptca), which offers tastings, is also nearby. To the south, another feature of the Outer Harbour is the twenty-metre-high bronze statue of **Kun Iam**, the Goddess of Mercy. It stands on a small artificial island, linked to the seafront by a short causeway. The seafront area in front of the statue, along Avenida Marginal da Baia Nova, has become Macau's newest entertainment area, **The Nape**, with dozens of bars and restaurants open until the small hours.

The north

The northern part of the peninsula up to the border with China is largely residential, though it has a couple of points of interest. It's possible to walk the 3km from Almeida Ribeiro to the border, but the streets at this end of town are not particularly atmospheric, so it makes sense to resort to the local buses.

On Avenida do Coronel Mesquita, cutting the peninsula from east to west about 2km north of Almeida Ribeiro, is the enchanting **Kun Iam Temple** (daily 7am–6pm), accessible on bus #12 from the *Hotel Lisboa*. The complex of temples, dedicated to the Goddess of Mercy, is around four hundred years old. In 1844, the United States and China signed their first treaty of trade and co-operation here – you can still see the granite table they used. Around the central statue of Kun Iam, to the rear of the main temple, is a crowd of statues representing the eighteen wise men of China, among whom, curiously, is Marco Polo (on the far left), depicted with a curly beard and moustache. The temple is well used by locals who come here to divine their future by shaking a cylinder of bamboo fortune sticks.

You can catch bus #18 directly from the Kun Iam Temple to the **Portas do Cerco**, or Barrier Gate, the nineteenth-century stuccoed archway marking the border with China. These days, people actually cross the border through a customs and immigration complex to one side. A short walk to the west of the gate is **Sun Yat-sen Memorial Park**, which gives interesting views over Zhuhai in the People's Republic, immediately across a small canal. Buses #3 or #10 will get you back to Almeida Ribeiro and the *Hotel Lisboa* from the gate.

The south

The small but hilly tongue of land south of Almeida Ribeiro is dotted with colonial mansions and their gardens. The best way to start exploring this area is to walk up the steep Rua Central leading south from Almeida Ribeiro, just east of Largo do Senado. After five minutes you can detour off down a small road to your right, which contains the pastel-coloured early nineteenth-century church of **Santo Agostinho**. Back along Rua Central will lead you to another attractive church of the same era, the cream-and-white **São Lourenço**, standing amid palm trees.

Continuing several hundred metres further south, you'll reach the seafront on the southwestern side of the peninsula, which is known as the **Barra district**. As you face the sea, the celebrated **A-Ma Temple** is immediately to your right. Situated underneath Barra Hill overlooking the Inner Harbour, this temple may be as old as six hundred years in parts. Dedicated to the goddess A-Ma, a kind of merciful Virgin Mary figure whose identity blurs from Queen of Heaven into Goddess of the Sea (and who is known as Tin Hau in Hong Kong), the temple is an attractive jumble of altars among the rocks.

Immediately across the road from here, on the seafront, stands the **Maritime Museum** (daily except Tues 10am–5.30pm; 10ptca), a well-presented, if rather static, collection covering old explorers, seafaring techniques, equipment, models and boats. For an additional charge, you can join an English-language boat tour around the Inner Harbour (daily except Tues; 10ptca) on one of the junks moored just outside the museum.

A short walk south along the shore from the museum brings you to the very tip of the peninsula, which is today marked by the *Pousada de São Tiago*, an incredible hotel built into the remains of the seventeenth-century Portuguese fortress, the **Fortaleza de Barra**. Enter the hotel's front door and you find yourself walking up a stone tunnel running with water – it's well worth dropping into the *Pousada*'s veranda café for a drink overlooking the sea. Continuing the walk around the southern headland, and back to the north again, you'll pass a beautiful cream colonial-style building high up on the headland. This used to be the *Bella Vista*, the finest hotel in the territory, but at the handover it was given to Portugal's representative in Macau as a residence. The futuristic spike rising 338m on your right is the **Macau Tower**, which offers (the near-ubiquitous smog permitting) impressive views out to sea and over China. Adrenaline junkies can don a rope and helmet and clamber around the tower's exterior with bungy-jumping specialists AJ Hackett (☎933 339; 100-120ptca). For the less adventurous, there's also an observation deck, plus a revolving café and restaurant at the top.

The road north from here up to the *Praia Grande*, near the *Hotel Lisboa*, takes about another fifteen minutes on foot. The gracefully proportioned pink mansion on your left shortly before the *Praia Grande* is the nineteenth-century **Palácio do Governo**, (Government House) not open to visitors.

Taipa and Coloane

Taipa and **Coloane** are just dots of land that traditionally supported a few small fishing villages, though now, with the opening of the new airport on Taipa, a third bridge from the mainland and a huge reclamation and building programme, that old tranquillity has all but disappeared. Indeed, Taipa has become a rather drab, congested high-rise city suburb. Coloane, however, is still well worth a visit, either by bus or by rented bicycle. **Buses** #11 and #33 go to Taipa Village from different stops on Almeida Ribeiro, while buses #21, #21A, #26 and #26A stop outside the *Hyatt Regency* on Taipa before going on to Coloane.

Taipa

Until the eighteenth century, **Taipa** was two islands separated by a channel, the silting up of which subsequently caused the two to merge into one. The same fate has now befallen Taipa and Coloane, except that this time land reclamation is the culprit – the two islands have been fused into one, to make space for large-scale development.

Taipa Village on the southern shore, with its old colonial promenade, is worth a quick visit. There isn't much more than a few streets to the modern village, where the buses stop, though you'll find some great restaurants (see p.606) along the central north–south alley, Rua do Cunha, and, to the west – on the right as you face the shore – a couple of temples in the vicinity of a quiet old square. Next to the Pak Tai Temple you can **rent bicycles** for around 15ptca an hour.

The island's real interest lies a few minutes' walk to the east of Taipa Village, in the former waterfront area. Here, as though frozen in time, is a superb old colonial promenade, the **Avenida da Praia**, complete with its original pale-green houses, public benches and street lamps. The beautifully restored mansions overlook what was the sea – sadly, reclamation has pushed the shoreline almost out of sight. The mansions are now being opened to the public; one houses the **Taipa House Museum** (daily 10am–8pm; free), which gives you some idea of what bourgeois domestic life was like at the beginning of the twentieth century. Next door, the **House of the Islands** (10am-6pm; free) displays some interesting old photos of Taipa and Coloane, while the **House of the Portuguese Regions** (daily 10am–6pm; free), is a fairly dull celebration of pockets of pre-industrial Portuguese culture. The **Exhibition Gallery** next door hosts temporary art shows, while the final villa, the **House for Receptions**, is a piano bar and restaurant.

Coloane

Coloane is considerably bigger than Taipa, and, although it has no single outstanding attraction, it's a pleasant place to spend a few hours. After passing through Taipa, buses first pass the **Macau Motorsports Club** an open-air racing track that offers go-karting (Mon–Fri 10am–midnight, Sat & Sun 9am–midnight; $100 for 10min; ☎882 126) and the Macau Dome, the territory's massive new sports stadium. A few minutes further on is the **Parque de Seac Pai Van** (Tues–Sun 9am–5.45pm; free), a large park with pleasant walks. On top of the hill is a white marble statue of the goddess A-Ma, at almost twenty metres high the tallest in the world. Once past the park, the buses all stop at the roundabout in pretty **Coloane Village** on the western shore, overlooking mainland China just across the water. There's no beach, just mud, in which you'll see old men fishing with nets, but it's a pleasant spot for a coffee and a scrumptious Portuguese egg tart. To the north, you'll find a few junk-building sheds, while the street leading south from the village roundabout, one block back from the shore, contains a couple of interesting antique shops and the unexpected yellow-and-white **St Francis Xavier Chapel**, which is fronted by a couple of appealing al fresco restaurants. A few hundred metres beyond this is the **Tam Kong Temple**, housing a metre-long whale bone, carved into the shape of a dragon boat.

On the north side of the village roundabout there's a small shop where you can rent bicycles for 15ptca an hour. Cycling is a good way to travel the 3km farther round to **Hac Sa Beach** on the eastern shore (otherwise, take bus #21A, #25, #26 or #26A), perhaps dropping in on **Cheoc Van Beach** to the south on the way as well. The beach at Hac Sa, tree-lined and stretching far off round the bay, is without doubt the best in Macau, despite the black colour of its sand, and has good facilities including showers and toilets, as well as some decent restaurants nearby (see p.606). There's also a sports and swimming pool complex here (daily 8am–9pm, Sun until midnight; 15ptca).

Eating, drinking and entertainment

Most **restaurants** here don't open as late as they do in Hong Kong – although bars do. If you want to eat later than 10pm you'll probably end up either in a hotel (many of which have 24-hour coffee bars that also serve snacks) or in the new bar/restaurant area, The NAPE. Costs, however, are nearly always lower than across the water, with bills even in smart venues usually not exceeding 150–250ptca per head.

A cluster of new **bars** and **night-time cafés** lies in the stretch of reclaimed land just west of the Jetfoil Terminal and in front of the new Kun Iam statue (follow signs to NAPE or ZAPE reclamation). It's a pleasant place to down an evening beer, sitting outside and listening to live music, as long as the onshore winds aren't whipping up a storm. Fisherman's Wharf, a kind of dining theme park housing restaurants, bars and cafés, is scheduled to open on the waterfront by the new Sands Casino in mid-2005.

The **casinos** that draw gambling fanatics to Macau in their millions are dotted about the territory, but the majority of visitors tempted to try their luck head to one of the more famous (and accessible) casinos along the waterfront.

Restaurants and cafés

Macau

A Lorcha Rua do Almirante Sergio 289 ☎313 193. Often labelled the best Portuguese restaurant in Macau, with an extensive menu of wonderfully cooked dishes, including the heart-stopping *serradura*, a spectacular cream and biscuit dessert. Closed Tues.

Club Militar de Macau Ave da Praia Grande 795 ☎714 000. The starched linen, polished dark-wood floorboards and old-fashioned ceiling fans are authentic colonial Macau. Prices are modest, service is swift and the food terrific – traditional Portuguese fare, such as *bacalhau* (salt cod), wild boar ham or stewed pork cheek and trotter in red wine with cabbage.

Fat Siu Lau Rua da Felicidade 64 ☎573 585. A very popular, traditional old restaurant in a busy restaurant area. Pigeon is the speciality.
Long Kei Largo do Senado 7B ☎573 970. A 100-year-old traditional but inexpensive Cantonese restaurant, on the left as you face the square from Almeida Ribeiro. *Dim sum* available.
Margeret's Café e Nata Rua Comandante Mata e Oliveira. A Macau institution, with street-side benches where you can tuck into inexpensive chunky sandwiches, baguettes, home-baked quiches and muffins. Macau's creamy egg tarts, or *natas*, don't get any better than the delights served here.
Pizzeria Toscana Grand Prix Building, Ave da Amizade ☎726 637. Right by the Jetfoil Terminal. Genuine Italian food and not just pizzas – though these are superb, as is the coffee.
Praia Grande Praça Lobo D'Avila 10A, Ave da Praia Grande ☎973 022. One of Macau's best restaurants, just outside the city centre. Pleasant staff, excellent food, good value.

Taipa

Panda Rua Carlos Eugenio 4 ☎827 338. On a tiny alley leading east from the southern end of Rua da Cunha in Taipa Village. Reasonably priced Portuguese place, with outdoor tables in good weather.
Pinocchio Rua do Sol 33 ☎827 128. Good Macanese food, including fish cakes, crab, prawns and crispy roast duck. On the square opposite the fire station in Taipa Village.

Coloane

Restaurant Espaço Lisboa Rua das Gaivotas 8 ☎882 226. Off the main village square, this intimate little place serves honest, delicious, home-cooked Portuguese food. The daily specials are good value and the lemon tart is scrumptious.
Fernando's Hac Sa Beach ☎882 531. Not far from the bus stop. An institution amongst local expats, *Fernando's* has the casual, cheerful atmosphere of a Mediterranean bistro and great, reasonably priced Portuguese food. Advance booking recommended, especially at weekends.
La Gondola Cheoc Van Beach ☎882 534. Good Italian food, on the seafront, complete with a traditional wood-fired pizza oven.
Lord Stow's Bakery Coloane Town Square. A contender, with *Margaret's Café e Nata*, for Macau's best egg custard tart. You can sit and eat at the new *Lord Stow's Café* just around the corner. Alternatively, consume your treats on the benches overlooking the water.

Bars and nightlife

Casablanca Café Ave Dr Calos Assumpção, Ed Vista Magnifica ☎751 281. Overlooking the sea and the Kun Iam statue, this place has a 1930s Hollywood theme. A covered colonnade and wicker chairs outside mean it's protected from the weather, as well as being a good spot to watch the world go by. Things don't really get going until around midnight.
Macau Jazz Club The Glasshouse, Macau Waterfront ☎596 014. Very popular night spot on the harbourside near the Kun Iam statue. As you might expect, it hosts regular jazz festivals. Live music every Friday and Saturday. Wed–Sun from 9.30pm.
Signal Café Ave Marginal Da Baia Nova, Vista Magnifica Court ☎751 052. Hip-looking club/bar overlooking the harbour with comfy lounge chairs, nightly DJ at the bar and pool tables. Only gets moving after 1am.

Casinos

Hotel Lisboa Ave de Lisboa 2–4 ☎577 666. Old-school marble and gilt decor clash inside the *Lisboa*'s neon-lit 1970s facade, where a variety of high-end boutiques and restaurants are waiting to swallow up your winnings. *Lisboa*'s vaguely naughty "Crazy Paris" cabaret show – the closest you'll get to Las Vegas-style entertainment in the territory – features scantily clad Western girls high-kicking it for the punters.
Casino Macau Palace Avenida da Amizade ☎346 701. This giant floating pontoon – with what looks like a traditional Chinese temple plonked on top of it – is, inside, a rather dispiriting hall packed with hard-faced mainlanders gambling feverishly.
Sands Casino Avenida da Amizade ☎883 311. Modern, hi-tech and with something of the glitz of a Las Vegas casino (but none of its big-time entertainment), the huge new Sands Casino is likely to be the most familiar-looking and least intimidating venue for visitors wanting to try their luck at the tables or on the slot machines. There's also a food hall upstairs.

Listings

Airlines Air Macau is at Ave da Praia Grande 639 (☎396 555). Other airlines operating from Macau include Singapore Airlines (☎711 728); EVA Airways of Taiwan (☎726 866); and budget carrier AirAsia (☎3167 2299). At the time of writing, two other Asian budget carriers, ValuAir and Tiger Air, and two Australia-based budget carriers, Virgin Blue and JetStar, were negotiating to open routes to Macau. Call airport flight enquiries (☎861 111) or contact a travel agency for more information.

Banks and exchange In addition to the banks, there are also licensed moneychangers which exchange travellers' cheques (and which open seven days a week), including a 24hr one in the basement of the *Hotel Lisboa*, and one near the bottom of the steps leading up to São Paulo.

Hospitals There's a 24hr emergency department at the Centro Hospitalar Conde São Januário, Calçada Visconde São Januário (☎313 731; English spoken).

Pharmacy Several in Largo do Senado.

Police The main police station is at Ave do Dr Rodrigo Rodrigues (☎573 333). In an emergency, call ☎999.

Post office Macau's General Post Office is in Largo do Leal Senado, on the east side (Mon–Fri 9am–5.30pm, Sat 9am–12.30pm). Small red booths all over the territory also dispense stamps from machines.

Travel agencies CTS, Rua de Nagasaki (☎700 888), can sort out China visas and tickets, as can most other tour operators.

7

Malaysia

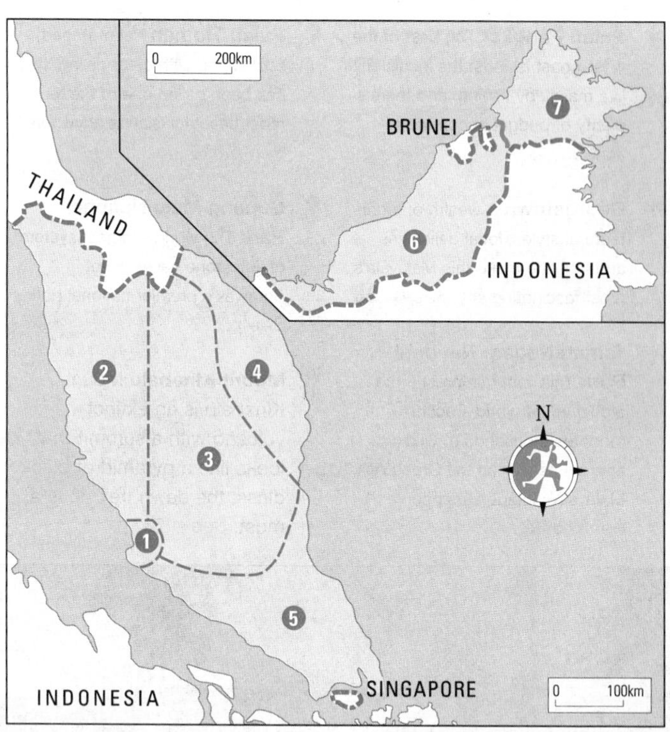
0 200km
BRUNEI
THAILAND
INDONESIA
SINGAPORE
INDONESIA
N
0 100km
1
2
3
4
5
6
7

Malaysia highlights

* **Cameron Highlands** Mercifully cool outposts typified by tea plantations, rolling green fields and country cottages. See p.650

* **Pulau Pangkor** The best of the west-coast islands: the locals still live mainly by fishing, and there's plenty of budget accommodation. See p.654

* **Georgetown** A wealth of architectural styles, local delicacies and nightlife make this Malaysia's most fascinating city. See p.656

* **Taman Negara National Park** This vast rainforest – the oldest in the world – accommodates thousands of wild animals as well as the Orang Asli, Malaysia's indigenous people. See p.670

* **Melaka** The historic heritage of Melaka is evident in its Portuguese, Dutch and British buildings and unique Peranakan ancestral homes. See p.689

* **Pulau Tioman** Palm-fringed, scenic and with great diving, this has been called one of the ten most beautiful islands anywhere. See p.696

* **Gunung Mulu National Park** The world's largest system of limestone caves is set in Sarawak's premier national park. See p.722

* **Mount Kinabalu** Mount Kinabalu is an extinct volcano with a summit that looks like a pyramid of black glass; the dawn trek up is a must. See p.737

△ Pulau Tioman

Introduction and basics

Malaysia does not have the grand, ancient ruins of neighbouring Thailand, but its rich cultural heritage is apparent, both in its traditional kampung (village) areas and in its commitment to religious plurality. The dominant cultural force has undoubtedly been Islam, but the country's diverse population of indigenous Malays, Chinese and Indians has spawned a fabulous juxtaposition of mosques, temples and churches, a panoply of festivals and a wonderful mixture of cuisines. In addition, Malaysia boasts fine beaches, as well as the world's oldest tropical rainforest and some spectacular cave systems.

Your first impressions of Malaysia's hi-tech, fast-growing west-coast capital, **Kuala Lumpur** (**KL**), are likely to be of a vibrant and colourful, if crowded, place. Traditionally, people have stayed just long enough to think about their next destination, but there are good reasons to linger a little longer: accommodation is plentiful and cheap, the food is excellent and its streets safe and friendly. Less than three hours' journey south lies the birthplace of Malay civilization, **Melaka**, a must on anybody's itinerary, while north up the coast is the first British settlement, the island of **Penang**, and its very appealing capital, Georgetown. For a taste of Old England and lots of walks, head for the hill station of the **Cameron Highlands**.

North of Penang, the premier tourist destination is **Pulau Langkawi**, a popular duty-free island. Routes down the Peninsula's east coast are more relaxing, with stops at the sleepy mainland kampung, such as Cherating, and the stunning islands of Pulau Perhentian and Pulau Tioman. The state capitals of **Kota Bharu**, near the northeastern Thai border, and **Kuala Terengganu**, further south, are showcases for the best of Malay crafts and performing arts, while the unsullied tropical rainforests of **Taman Negara National Park** offer trails, animal hides, a high canopy walkway and waterfalls.

Across the sea from the Peninsula, East Malaysia comprises the Bornean states of **Sarawak** and **Sabah**. For most travellers, their first taste of Sarawak is Kuching, the old colonial capital, and then the Iban longhouses of the Batang Ai and Batang Lupar river systems, or the Bidayuh communities closer to the Kalimantan border. The best time to visit is in late May to early June when the Iban and the Bidayuh celebrate their harvest festivals with ribald parties to which everyone is invited. Sibu, much further to the north, is another starting point for visits to other Iban longhouses and the idyllic Pelagus Rapids region. In the north of the state, **Gunung Mulu National Park** is the principal destination, its extraordinary razor-sharp limestone needles providing demanding climbing – its deep, cathedral-shaped caves are awe-inspiring.

The main reason for a trip to Sabah is to conquer the 4101-metre granite peak of **Mount Kinabalu**, though the lively modern capital **Kota Kinabalu** and its offshore islands have their moments, too. Beyond this, Sabah is worth a visit for its wildlife, including turtles, orang-utans, proboscis monkeys and hornbills, while oceanic **Pulau Sipadan** has a host of sharks, fish and turtles, as well as one of the world's top coral-reef dives.

Temperatures in Malaysia constantly hover around 30°C (22°C in highland areas), and humidity is high all year round. The major distinction in the seasons is marked by the arrival of the monsoon, which brings heavy and prolonged downpours to the east coast of Peninsular Malaysia, the northeastern part of Sabah, and the western end of Sarawak from November to February; boats to most of the islands do not run during the height of the monsoon. The Peninsula's west coast experiences fewer major thunderstorms during the months of April and May. The ideal time to visit is between April and October, avoiding the worst of the rains.

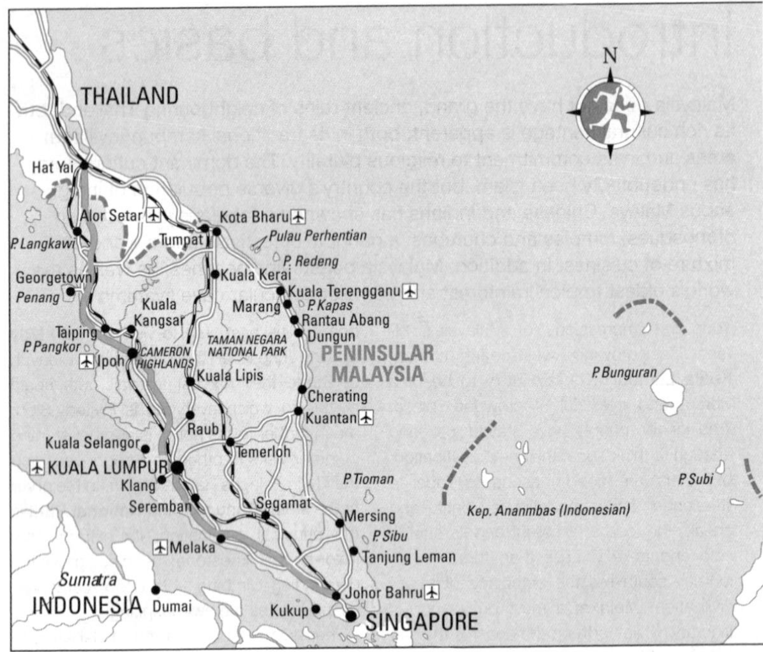

Overland and sea routes into Malaysia

Malaysia has land borders with Thailand, Singapore, Brunei and Indonesian Kalimantan. Aside from the options detailed below, there are regular boats from Bandar Seri Bagawan in **Brunei** to Lawas and Limbang in Sarawak and to Pulau Labuan in Sabah. Below is an outline of overland and sea routes: full details are given in the accounts of relevant departure points.

From Indonesia

A variety of ferries and speedboats depart **from Indonesia** to Malaysia. **Boats** run from Tanjung Balai (see p.346), in Sumatra, to **Port Klang**, just outside Kuala Lumpur; from Medan (see p.313), in north Sumatra, to **Penang**; from Dumai (see p.344), south of Medan, to **Melaka**; from Pulau Batam (see p.695), in the Riau archipelago, to **Johor Bahru**; from Pulau Nunukan and Tarakan (see p.465) in northeastern Kalimantan to **Tawau** in Sabah; and from Tanjung Balai (see p.346) to **Kukup**, 200km south of Melaka.

There is a **land border** at Entikong, 100km southwest of Kuching; buses run from Pontianak in southern Kalimantan through here to Kuching (see p.704).

From Thailand

Travelling **from Thailand** to Malaysia is straightforward and a very commonly used route. Most Western tourists can spend thirty days in Malaysia without having bought a visa beforehand, and the transport connections between the countries are excellent. This makes it an ideal route for tourists and expats needing to renew their Thai visas; there are Thai consulates in Kuala Lumpur, Georgetown (Penang) and Kota Bahru.

Most people choose to travel by long-distance **train** or bus to Malaysian cities such as KL or Butterworth, either from Bangkok, Krabi, Surat Thani or Hat Yai; see individual city accounts and "Travel details", p.743.

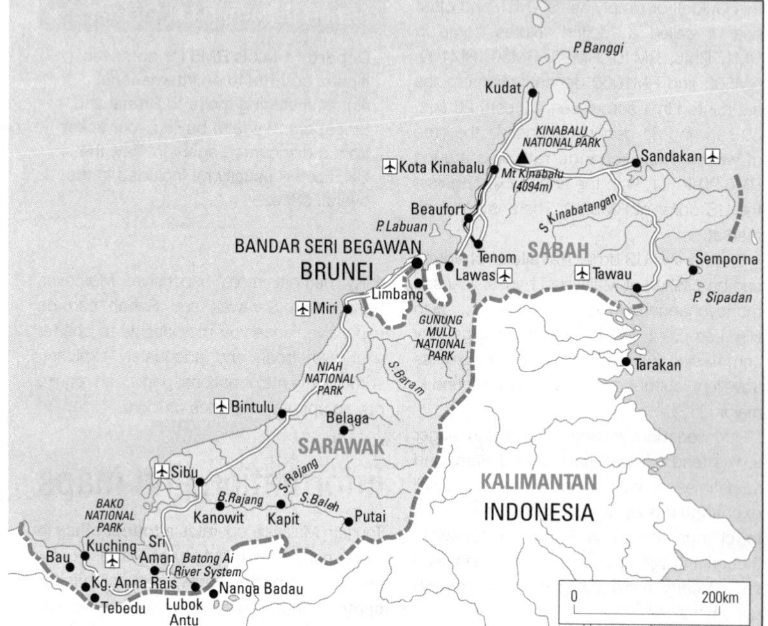

However, you can also travel by more local transport, as there are a number of border crossings between Thailand and Malaysia – from Satun (see p.1092) to Kuala Perlis and Pulau Langkawi; Dan Nok (see p.1094) to Alor Setar; Sungai Kolok (see p.1096) to Kota Bharu; Ban Taba (see p.1096) to Kota Bharu.

Plenty of **buses** also cross the Thai–Malaysian border every day. The southern Thai town of Hat Yai (see p.1093) is the major transport hub for international bus connections to Butterworth (5hr), Penang (6hr), Kuala Lumpur (12hr) and Singapore (18hr).

Entry requirements and visa extension

Most nationalities do not need a **visa** for stays of fewer than two months in Malaysia, but passports must be valid for three months beyond your date of departure, and for six months if you're going to Sabah or Sarawak. To **extend your visa**, go to an immigration department office (eg in KL, Penang or Johor Bahru), or simply cross into Singapore or Thailand and back. A one-month extension should be no problem, and a three-month extension may be possible.

Tourists travelling from the Peninsula to Sarawak and Sabah must be cleared again by immigration. Visitors **to Sabah** can remain as long as their original two-month stamp is valid. Visitors **to Sarawak** – whether from Sabah or the Peninsula – receive a new, one-month stamp that is rarely extendible. If you start your trip in Sarawak and then fly to the mainland, be sure to get your passport stamped by immigration with the usual two-month pass. If an officer isn't available to do this, then go to the Immigration Office in Kuching at the first opportunity to get it stamped there.

Money and costs

Malaysia's unit of **currency** is the Malaysian ringgit, divided into 100 sen. You'll see the ringgit written as "RM" (as it is throughout this Guide), or simply as "$" (M$), and often hear it called a "dollar". Notes come in RM1, RM5, RM10, RM20, RM50, RM100, RM500 and RM1000 denominations; coins are minted in 1 sen, 5 sen, 10 sen, 20 sen, 50 sen and $1 denominations. At the time of writing, the **exchange rate** was around RM6.90 to £1, with the ringgit fixed against the US dollar at RM3.80. There is no black market.

Sterling and US dollar **travellers' cheques** can be cashed at Malaysian banks, licensed moneychangers and some hotels. Ban Hin Lee Bank (BHL) doesn't charge any commission for changing American Express travellers' cheques, but can only be found in major cities.

Licensed moneychangers' kiosks in bigger towns tend to open until around 6pm, and sometimes at weekends; some hotels will **exchange** money at all hours. It's not difficult to change money in Sabah or Sarawak, though if travelling by river in the interior, you should carry a fair bit of cash, in smallish denominations.

Major **credit cards** are accepted in most hotels and large shops, but beware of illegal surcharges. Banks will advance cash against major credit cards, and with American Express, Visa and MasterCard as well as Cirrus, Plus and Maestrobank (debit) cards, you can withdraw money from automatic teller machines (ATMs) in big cities and many towns.

Wiring money to Malaysia is straightforward. In KL, the best bank to use is HSBC, 2 Lebuh Ampang, Little India (☎03/2070 0744). For more details on wiring money, see "Wiring money", p.60.

Costs

If entering Malaysia from Thailand, you will find your **daily budget** remains pretty much unchanged, but approaching from Indonesia, costs will take a step up. In **Peninsular Malaysia**, if you stay in basic accommodation, use local transport and eat at roadside stalls, you can manage on £10/US$15 a day. With air-con rooms, decent restaurants and the occasional beer, your daily budget becomes a more realistic £20/US$30.

You'll find living costs roughly similar in **East Malaysia**, though room rates are around thirty percent more expensive. Moreover, transport in Sarawak and Sabah can be expensive, since you may decide to charter your own boat, and adequately exploring some of the major national parks can require paying upfront for guides or tours.

Airport departure tax

Departure tax is RM5 for domestic flights, and RM40 on international flights, including those to Brunei and Singapore. If you're buying your ticket from a discounted agent in, say, the UK, tax will usually be included in the overall price.

Information and maps

Tourism Malaysia operates a **tourist office** in most major towns, but is not that useful for areas off the beaten track. Locally run **visitor centres**, found in most major towns, are more geared up to independent travellers' needs. You can also book permits and accommodation for the **national parks** at these centres.

The best general **maps** of Malaysia are Macmillan's 1:2,000,000 *Malaysia Traveller's Map* and the more detailed Nelles 1:650,000 *West Malaysia* (not including Sabah and Sarawak). The best detailed relief map of Sarawak is the Land and Survey Department's 1:500,000 issue, available in the bookshop at the Kuching *Holiday Inn*. The best coverage of Sabah is on maps produced by Nelles. **City maps** can usually be picked up in the visitor centres.

Getting around

Public **transport** in Malaysia is extremely reliable, though not as cheap as in other Southeast Asian countries. Buses and long-distance taxis are most useful on the Peninsula. Getting around in Sarawak has become easier with the sealing of the coast road, though you may still have to use boats and perhaps the odd plane. There is no boat service between Peninsular Malaysia and East Malaysia, so you'll have to fly. For a rough idea of frequency and duration of transport between major destinations, see "Travel details", p.743.

Buses

Inter-state destinations are covered by comfortable, air-con **express buses**, operated either by the government's Transnasional, or by state or private bus companies; each company has an office at the bus station, which is where you buy your ticket. Since prices are fairly similar on all routes, it matters little which company you opt for.

Buses for long-distance routes (over 3hr) typically leave in clusters in the early morning and late evening, while shorter routes are served throughout the day. In most cases, you can just turn up, though on popular routes like KL to Penang (8hr; RM22.50) you should reserve ahead. Local buses usually operate from a separate station, serve routes within the state, and are cheaper, but also slower, less comfortable and without air con; buy your ticket on the bus.

Several buses run across Sabah, but they're outnumbered by the more uncomfortable, and seldom faster, **minibuses** that leave when full, from the same terminals; Kota Kinabulu to Sandakan will cost RM15 by bus and RM20 by minibus. Landcruisers, outsized jeeps, are also common; they take eight passengers and cost less than a taxi but more than a bus. Modern air-con buses in Sarawak ply the trans-state coastal road between Kuching and the Brunei border, via Sibu (RM30), Bintulu and Miri (RM70).

Long-distance taxis

Most towns in Peninsular Malaysia have a **long-distance taxi** rank. The four-seater taxis are generally very reliable and a lot quicker than the buses; they charge fixed-price fares, which are 50–100 percent more than the regular bus fare (KL to Butterworth costs RM30, KL to Kota Bharu RM35). You have to wait until the car is full, but this is rarely long in big towns. As a foreigner, you may be pressured to charter the whole car (at four times the one-person fare).

Trains

The Peninsula's **train** service, operated by Keretapi Tanah Melayu (KTM), is limited, relatively expensive and very slow. However, it is the best way to reach some of the more interesting places in the interior. A free timetable for the whole country is available from major train stations.

There are only **two main lines** through Peninsular Malaysia, both originating in Thailand at the southern town of Hat Yai. The west coast route from Thailand via Padang Besar on the Malaysian border runs south through Butterworth (for Penang), Ipoh, Tapah Road (for the Cameron Highlands) and KL, where you usually have to change trains before continuing on to Singapore. The scenery along this route is rather monotonous: a highway parallels the rails for much of the journey and the landscape is more urban than rural, though there are stretches of rubber and palm oil plantations. However, serious fans of rail travel need not despair – between KL and Singapore the train route splits at Gemas, 58km northeast of Melaka, from where a second line runs north through the mountainous interior – a section known as the **Jungle Railway** – via Kuala Lipis and skirting Kota Bharu to the northeastern border town of Tumpat. Note that the train from Gemas going north is a night train, so if you've come to see the jungle views do this stretch from north to south. East Malaysia's only rail line is the bone-shaking 55-kilometre link between Kota Kinabalu and Tenom in Sabah; only the stretch between Beaufort and Tenom is worth considering (see pp.733–734).

Express trains run on the west coast line only and stop at principal stations; ordinary trains, labelled *M* on the timetables, run on both lines and stop at virtually every station. Both trains have three classes: second-class is fine for most journeys, and the only real advantage of first-class travel is the air con; third-class is more crowded. On overnight sleepers, there's only first- and second-class available, though you can opt for air con or not in second class. From KL to Butterworth costs RM67/59/17 for 1st/2nd/3rd class travel on an overnight express train. Seat reservations can be booked online at ⓦwww.ktmb.com.my.

Ferries and boats

Ferries sail to all the major islands off Malaysia's east and west coasts, but during the monsoon (Nov–Feb), east-coast services are vastly reduced. There are no ferry services from the Peninsula to East Malaysia, so you'll have to fly. Once you're **in Sarawak**, the most usual method of travel is by turbo-charged express boat along the river systems; they run to a fairly regular timetable. On the smaller tributaries, travel is by longboat, which you may have to charter. This mode of travel can get very expensive, as diesel prices multiply alarmingly the further into the interior you travel. Increasingly, however, longboat travel is becoming obsolete as isolated riverside longhouse communities are getting connected to the road network – mostly by way of logging tracks hacked out of the jungle by timber concessionaires. This makes them accessible by 4WD and trucks, if not yet by buses, taxis and cars. **Sabah** has no express boats, but regular ferries connect Pulau Labuan with its west-coast towns. Ferries **to Indonesia** from eastern Sabah ports are being increasingly used by travellers.

Planes

The Malaysian national airline, MAS, operates a wide range of **domestic flights**: from KL to Langkawi takes just 55 minutes, thus saving an eleven-hour bus journey followed by an hour's ferry ride. Night tourist flights can reduce the price of a flight significantly, as can special promotional fares. You can browse promotions and book online at Ⓦwww.malaysiaairlines.com.

If you buy an international MAS flight (excluding flights from Singapore or Brunei), you can get a **Discover Malaysia Pass**: US$199 for five flights within the country including one flight to Sabah or Sarawak. The passes are valid for 28 days; dates can be changed for free and you can alter the route for US$25. Flights to East Malaysia operate mainly out of Kuala Lumpur, with Johor Bahru providing additional services to Kuching and Kota Kinabalu. Within Sarawak and Sabah, there are numerous nineteen-seater Twin-Otter and Fokker flights from Miri to other towns in the state's northern interior, such as Lawas and Limbang. Small aircraft also fly from Kota Kinabalu to Kudat, Sandakan and Tuwau.

Vehicle rental

The condition of the roads in Peninsular Malaysia is generally excellent, making **driving** there a viable prospect for tourists, though not so in Sabah and Sarawak where the roads are rougher and susceptible to flash flooding.

Malaysians drive on the left, and wearing seat belts in the front is compulsory. Malaysian drivers flash their headlights when they are claiming the right of way, *not* the other way around, as is common practice in the West. The **speed limit** is 110km/hr on highways, 90km/hr on trunk roads, and 50km/hr in built-up areas; speed traps are common, and fines are up to RM300. The North–South Highway is the only toll road – you can reckon on paying approximately RM1 for every 7km travelled.

To rent a vehicle, you must be 23 or over and have held a clean driving licence for at least a year; a national driving licence should be sufficient. Avis, Budget, Hertz and National have offices in major towns and at the airports (book two days ahead). **Rates** start at RM120 (£23/US$32) per day or RM700 (£175/US$262) per week; local companies charge the same.

Motorbike rental is more informal, usually offered by guesthouses and shops in touristy areas (around RM30 per day). You may need to leave your passport as a deposit, but it's unlikely you'll have to show any proof of eligibility – officially, you must be over 21 and have an appropriate driving licence. Wearing helmets is compulsory and the laws are strictly enforced. **Bicycles** can be rented for about RM5 a day.

Accommodation

Accommodation in Malaysia is not the cheapest in Southeast Asia, but double rooms for under RM25 (£4.50/US$7) are common. East Malaysia is a little more expensive: Sabah is the pricier of the two states – you'll often have to pay RM40

(£7/US$11) for a very ordinary place there. Official **youth hostels** in Malaysia are often hopelessly far-flung and no cheaper than the guesthouses, and there are few official campsites. Malaysia may not be the cheapest, but it does have some of the most atmospheric accommodation in Southeast Asia. Fans of colonial-era architecture will find an abundance of options, and unlike in neighbouring countries, many of these are in the mid range – with all the amenities but without the shockingly high tariffs.

A single room usually contains one double bed, while a double has two double beds or two single beds. Room rates can rise dramatically during the major holiday periods – Christmas, Easter and Hari Raya Haji – but as a general rule it's always worth bargaining. At the budget end of the market, you'll have to share a bathroom. Older places sometimes have mandi (see "Bathrooms", p.62) instead of showers.

The mainstay of the travellers' scene in Malaysia are the **guesthouses**, now increasingly being called "backpackers", located in popular tourist areas and usually good places to meet other people and pick up information. They can range from simple beachside A-frame huts to modern multi-storey apartment buildings. Almost all offer dormitory beds (RM7) and basic double rooms (from RM15). Prices on the east coast can drop to as little as RM10 for a double room, but on the islands you'll get nothing for less than RM25.

The **cheapest hotels** in Malaysia are usually Chinese-run and cater for a predominantly local clientele. They're generally clean and there's never any need to book in advance, but they can be noisy and some of the cheapest ones double as brothels (especially those called *Rumah Persinggahan)*. Ordinary rooms start at RM20 and will have a washbasin, fan and a hard mattress; there's usually an air-con option, too. Bathrooms are shared.

Mid-range hotels have sprung mattresses, en-suite bathrooms, air-con and TV. Prices range from RM40 to RM100, but a genuine distinction is made between single rooms and doubles. Also in the mid-range category are the excellent-value Government Resthouses (*Rumah Rehat*): rooms are large, en suite and well equipped. In many towns they have been replaced by *Seri Malaysia* hotels (Ⓦwww.serimalaysia.com.my), which offer a uniformly good standard for RM100 per night.

High-class hotels are as comfortable as you might expect. Prices can be as reasonable as RM100 to RM150, but rates in popular destinations such as Penang can rocket to RM300. They're always cheaper if booked as part of a package. Prices often include an all-you-can eat buffet breakfast. Since the economic slump of the late 1990s many large hotels are finding it hard to reach capacity, so it's worth asking if any promotions are going – you can pick up a great room officially priced at around RM250 for as little as RM70.

The most atmospheric accommodation in Malaysia is in the stilted **longhouses**, found on the rivers of Sarawak and Sabah. These can house dozens of families, and usually consist of three elevated sections reached by a simple ladder. The snag is that it's getting increasingly hard to stay in them as an independent traveller – most tourists can only stay at longhouses as part of an organized tour. Also, the traditional, wooden longhouse design is fast disappearing and being replaced by more utilitarian concrete – although still long – structures.

Electricity in Malaysia is supplied at 220 volts, and plugs have three prongs like British ones.

Food and drink

Malaysian cuisine is inspired by the three main communities, Malay, Chinese and Indian. The standard of cooking is extremely high and food everywhere is remarkably good value. Basic noodle- or rice-based meals at a street stall will cost just a few dollars, and a full meal with drinks in a reputable restaurant will seldom cost more than RM40 a head.

The cuisines

Malay cuisine is based on rice, often enriched with *santan* (coconut milk), which is served with a dazzling variety of curries, vegetable stir-fries and sambals, a condiment of chillies and shrimp paste.

The most famous dish is **satay** – virtually Malaysia's national dish – which comprises skewers of barbecued meat dipped in spicy peanut sauce. The classic way to sample Malay curries is to eat **nasi campur**, a buffet (usually served at lunchtime) of steamed rice supplemented by any of up to two dozen accompanying dishes, including *lembu* (beef), *kangkong* (greens), fried chicken, fish steaks and curry sauce, and various vegetables. Another popular dish is **nasi goreng** (mixed fried rice with meat, seafood and vegetables). For breakfast, the most popular Malay dish is **nasi lemak**, rice cooked in coconut milk and served with *sambal ikan bilis* (tiny fried anchovies in hot chilli paste).

In Sabah, there's the Murut speciality of *jaruk* – raw wild boar fermented in a bamboo tube, but the most famous Sabah dish is *hinava*, or raw fish pickled in lime juice. **In Sarawak**, you're most likely to eat with the Iban, sampling wild boar with jungle ferns and sticky rice. A particular favourite in Kuching are bamboo clams, small pencil-shaped slivery delicacies that only grow in the wild in mangrove-dense riverine locations. These are called "monkey's penises" by the locals.

Typical **Nonya dishes** incorporate elements from Chinese, Indonesian and Thai cooking. Chicken, fish and seafood form the backbone of the cuisine, and unlike Malay

Food and drink glossary

General terms

Menu	*Menu*
Fork	*Garpu*
Knife	*Pisau*
How much is it?	*Berapa harga?*
Cold	*Sejuk*
Hot (temperature)	*Panas*
Hot (spicy)	*Pedas*
I don't eat meat or fish	*Saya tak makan daging*
I want to pay	*Saya nak bayar*

Noodles (*mee*) and noodle dishes

Bee hoon	Thin rice noodles, like vermicelli
Char kuey teow	Flat noodles with prawns, sausage, fishcake, egg, vegetables or chilli
Foochow noodles	Steamed and served in soy and oyster sauce
Hokkien fried mee	Yellow noodles fried with pork, prawn and vegetables
Kuey teow	Flat noodles, like tagliatelle
Laksa	Noodles, beansprouts, fish-cakes and prawns in a spicy coconut soup
Mee	Standard round yellow noodles made from wheat flour
Mee suah	Noodles served dry and crispy
Wan ton mee	Roast pork, noodles and vegetables served in a light soup containing dumplings

Rice (*nasi*) dishes

Claypot	Rice topped with meat, cooked in an earthen-ware pot over a fire
Daun pisang	Banana-leaf curry, a southern Indian meal with chutneys and curries
Nasi campur	Rice served with several meat, fish and vegetable dishes
Nasi goreng	Fried rice with diced meat and veg
Nasi lemak	A Malay classic: fried anchovies, cucumber, peanuts and fried or hard-boiled egg slices, served on coconut rice
Nasi puteh	Plain boiled rice

Meat, fish and basics

Ayam	Chicken
Babi	Pork
Daging	Beef
Garam	Salt
Goreng	Fried
Gula	Sugar
Ikan	Fish
Kambing	Mutton
Kepiting	Crab
Makan	Food

food, pork is used. Noodles (*mee*) flavoured with chillies, and rich curries made from rice flour and coconut cream, are common. A popular breakfast dish is *laksa*, noodles in spicy coconut soup served with seafood and beansprouts, lemon grass, pineapple, pepper, lime leaves and chilli. Other popular Nonya dishes include *ayam buah keluak*, chicken cooked with Indonesian "black" nuts; and *otak-otak*, fish mashed with coconut milk and chilli and steamed in a banana leaf.

Chinese food dominates in Malaysia – fish and seafood is nearly always outstanding, with prawns, crab, squid and a variety of fish on offer almost everywhere. Noodles, too, are ubiquitous, and come in wonderful variations – thin, flat, round, served in soup (wet) or fried (dry). Malaysians eat *mee* any time of the day or night, and a particular favourite is a dish called *hokkien mee*: fat, white noodles with *tempe* in a rich soy sauce whipped up in three minutes flat by a wok chef at the side of the road. The dominant style is Cantonese and the classic lunch is *dim sum*, a variety of steamed and fried dumplings served in bamboo baskets. Standard dishes include chicken in chilli or with cashew nuts; buttered prawns, or prawns served with a sweet and sour sauce; spare ribs; and mixed vegetables with tofu (beancurd) and beansprouts. For something a little more unusual, try a steamboat, a

Minum Drink
Sayur Vegetable
Sotong Squid
Sup Soup
Tahu Tofu (beancurd)
Telor Egg
Udang Prawn

Other specialities

Char siew pow Cantonese steamed bun stuffed with roast pork in a sweet sauce
Chay tow kueh An omelette made with white radish and spring onions
Gado gado Malay/Indonesian salad of lightly cooked vegetables, boiled egg, slices of rice cake and a crunchy peanut sauce
Murtabak Thick Indian pancake, stuffed with onion, egg and chicken or mutton
Otak-otak Fish mashed with coconut milk and chilli paste and steamed in a banana leaf
Popiah Chinese spring rolls; sometimes known as *lumpia*
Rendang Dry, highly spiced coconut curry with beef, chicken or mutton
Rojak Indian fritters dipped in chilli and peanut sauce
Roti canai Layered Indian pancake served with curry sauce or daal; also called *roti pratha*
Steamboat Raw vegetables, meat or fish dunked into a steaming broth

Desserts

Bubor cha cha Sweetened coconut milk with pieces of sweet potato, yam and tapioca balls
Cendol Coconut milk, palm syrup and pea-flour noodles poured over shaved ice
Es kachang Shaved ice with red beans, jelly, sweet corn, rose syrup and evaporated milk
Pisang goreng Fried banana fritters
Pisang murtabak Banana pancake

Drinks

Air minum Water
Bir Beer
Jus Fruit juice
Kopi Coffee
Kopi-o Black coffee
Kopi susu Coffee with milk
Lassi Sweet or sour yoghurt
Teh Tea
Teh-o Black tea
Teh susu Tea with milk
Teh tarik Sweet, frothy, milky tea

Chinese-style fondue filled with boiling stock in which you cook meat, fish, shellfish, eggs and vegetables; or a claypot – meat, fish or shellfish cooked over a fire in an earthenware pot.

North Indian food tends to rely more on meat, especially mutton and chicken, and breads – *naan*, *chapatis*, *parathas* and *rotis* – rather than rice. The most famous style of North Indian cooking is *tandoori* – named after the clay oven in which the food is cooked. A favourite breakfast is *roti canai* (pancake and *daal*) or *roti kaya* (pancake spread with egg and jam). **Southern Indian food** tends to be spicier and more reliant on vegetables. Its staple is the *dosai* (pancake), often served at breakfast time as a *masala dosai*, stuffed with onions, vegetables and chutney. Indian Muslims serve the similar *murtabak*, a grilled *roti* pancake with egg and minced meat. Many South Indian cafés serve *daun pisang* at lunchtime, usually a vegetarian meal where rice is served on banana leaves with vegetable curries. It's normal to eat a banana-leaf meal with your right hand, though restaurants will always have cutlery.

Where to eat

To eat inexpensively go to **hawker stalls**, traditionally simple wooden stalls on the roadside, with a few stools to sit at. They serve standard Malay noodle and rice dishes, satay, Indian fast food such as *roti canai*, plus more obscure regional delicacies. Most are scrupulously clean, with the food cooked in front of you. Avoid dishes that look as if they've been standing around, or have been reheated, and you should be fine. Hawker stalls don't have menus and you don't have to sit close to the stall you're patronizing: find a free table, and the vendor will track you down when your food is ready. You may find that the meal should be paid for when it reaches your table, but the usual form is to pay at the end. Most outdoor stalls open at around 11am, usually offering the day's nasi campur selection; prices are determined by the number of dishes you choose on top of your rice, usually about RM2–3 per portion. Hawker stalls generally close well before midnight.

Few streets exist without a *kedai kopi*, a **coffee house** or **café**, usually run by Chinese or Indians. Most open at 7am or 8am; closing times vary from 6pm to midnight. Basic Chinese coffee houses serve noodle and rice dishes all day, as well as cakes. The culinary standard might not be very high, but a filling one-plate meal only costs a couple of dollars. If available, full meals of meat, seafood and vegetables cost about RM5.

On the whole, proper **restaurants** are places to savour particular delicacies found nowhere else, like shark's-fin dishes, bird's-nest soup, and high-quality seafood. In many restaurants, the food is not necessarily superior to that served at a good café or hawker stall – you're just paying for air-con and tablecloths. Tipping is not expected and bills arrive complete with service charge and government tax. In the main, restaurants are open from 11.30am to 2.30pm and from 6 to 10.30pm.

Drinking

Tap water is said to be safe to drink in Malaysia, though it's wise to stick to bottled water (RM2 a litre). Using ice for drinks is generally fine, too, making the huge variety of seasonal fresh fruit drinks, available in hawker centres and street corners, even more pleasant. You'll often find that sweet condensed milk is added to tea and coffee unless you ask for it without. In city centres, look out for the sweetened soy milk and sugar-cane juice touted on street corners.

Only in certain places on the east coast of the Malaysian Peninsula is drinking alcohol outlawed. Elsewhere, despite the Muslim influence, alcohol is available in bars, restaurants, Chinese *kedai kopi*, supermarkets and sometimes at hawker's stalls. Anchor and Tiger **beer** (lager) are locally produced and are probably the best choices, although Carlsberg and Heineken are being marketed heavily. Locally produced whisky and rum are cheap enough, too, though pretty rough. The **brandy**, which is what some local Chinese drink, tends to be better. **Wine** is becoming more common and competitively priced, too. There is a thriving bar scene in KL, Kuching and Penang; less so in other towns. Fierce competition keeps happy hours a regular feature (usually 5–7pm), bringing the beer down to around RM5 a glass. Some bars open all day (11am–11pm), but most tend to double as clubs, opening in the evenings until 2 or 3am. All-night clubs are a relatively new development, and again liberal licensing seems to apply.

Communications

Malaysia's postal system was recently privatized, and while there were a lot of complaints at first, most of the bugs have been ironed out. Overseas **mail** takes four to seven days to reach its destination. Packages are expensive to send, with surface/sea mail taking two months to Europe, longer to the USA, and even air mail taking a few weeks. There's usually a shop near the post office that will wrap your parcel for RM5 or so. Each Malaysian town has a General Post Office (GPO), with a poste restante/general delivery section, where mail is held for two months. GPOs also forward mail (for one month), free of charge, if you fill in the right form. See "Poste restante" p.63 for advice on poste restante.

There are **public telephone boxes** in most towns in Malaysia; local calls cost 10 sen for an unlimited amount of time. For long-distance calls, it makes sense to use a **card phone**, either the ubiquitous Uniphone (yellow), the green Cityphone, or the widespread government Kadfon (blue). Cards of RM10, RM20, RM50 and RM100 are sold at Shell and Petronas stations, newsagents and most 7-Elevens. Note that the Uniphone only takes RM20 or RM50 cards. Check for an international logo on the phone booth before dialling overseas. To **call abroad** from Malaysia, dial ⓣ00 + IDD country code (see "IDD Codes" box, p.64) + area code minus first 0 + subscriber number.

You can also use your BT or AT&T chargecard in Malaysia. **Collect (reverse charge) calls** can be made from hotels or from a **Telekom** office (open office hours), though these are found only in larger towns. In KL, Penang and Kota Kinabalu there are also **Home Country Direct** phones – press the appropriate button and you'll be connected with your home operator, who can either arrange a collect call or debit you. Many businesses in Malaysia have mobile phone numbers; they are prefixed ⓣ011 or 010 and are expensive to call.

Internet cafés are plentiful and often found in smaller places, as well as major towns. Many small and remote hostels and guesthouses also provide Internet access, as do top-of-the-range hotels. Prices are very competitive, ranging between RM3 and RM10 per hour. Connections are usually pretty good.

Time differences

Malaysia is eight hours ahead of London (GMT), thirteen ahead of New York, sixteen hours ahead of Los Angeles, two hours behind Sydney and four hours behind Auckland.

Opening hours and festivals

Shops are open daily 9am to 7pm and shopping centres 10am to 11pm. **Government offices** work Monday to Thursday 8am to 12.45pm and 2pm to 4.15pm, Friday 8am to12.15pm and 2.45 to 4.15pm, Sat 8am to 12.45pm; however, in the states of Kedah, Kelantan and Terengannu, on Thursday the hours are 8am to 12.45pm, they're closed on Friday and open on Sunday. **Banking hours** are generally Monday to Friday 10am to 3pm and Saturday 9.30 to 11.30am. **Post offices** are open Monday to Saturday 8am to 6pm. During major holiday periods it can be difficult to get a seat on public transport or a room in a hotel, particularly over Ramadan and during Chinese New Year.

Festivals

Three great religions – Islam, Buddhism and Hinduism – are represented in Malaysia, and they play a vital role in the everyday lives of the population. Some **religious festivals** are celebrated at home or in the mosque or temple. During Ramadan, Muslims fast during the daytime for a whole month, while other festivals are marked with great spectacle. Most of the festivals have no fixed dates, but change annually according to the lunar calendar.

Festivals of interest to tourists include: **Chinese New Year**, when Chinese operas and lion and dragon dance troupes perform in the streets (Jan–Feb); **Thaipusam**, during which entranced Hindu penitents carry elaborate steel arches, attached to their skin by hooks and skewers (especially at KL's Batu Caves; Jan/Feb); **Gawai Dayak**, when Sarawak's Iban and Bidayuk people hold extravagant feasts to mark the end of the harvest, best experienced at the Iban longhouses on the Ai, Skrang and Lemanak rivers near Kuching (June) and in Bidayuh communities around Bau; the **Dragon Boat Festival** in Penang, Melaka and Kota Kinabalu (June/July); the **Festival of the Hungry Ghosts**, Yue Lan, when there are many free performances of Chinese opera and wayang, or puppet shows (late Aug); **Navarathiri**, when Hindu temples devote nine nights to classical dance and music in honour of the deities (Sept–Oct); and the **Kota Belud Tamu Besar**, Sabah's biggest annual market, which features cultural performances (Oct/Nov).

Cultural hints

Malaysia shares the same attitudes to dress and social taboos as other Southeast Asian cultures; see "Cultural hints", p.68 for details.

Diving and trekking

The crystal-clear waters of Malaysia and its abundance of tropical fish and coral make **snorkelling and diving** a must for any underwater enthusiast. This is particularly true of East Sabah's islands, which include Sipadan and Mabul, and the Peninsula's east-coast islands of Perhentian, Redang, Kapas and Tioman. Pulau Tioman offers the most choice for schools and dive sites. Make sure that the dive operator is registered with PADI (Professional Association of Diving Instructors) or equivalent; dive courses cost from RM750 for a four-day PADI Open Water course to RM1800 for a Divemaster course.

Public holidays

January 1: New Year's Day
January/February: Chinese New Year (2 days)
January/February: Thaipusam (depending on the full moon)
February/March: Hari Raya Haji
March/April: Maal Hijrah (the Muslim New Year)
May: Pesta Kaamatan (Sabah only)
May 1: Labour Day
May/June: Birthday of the Prophet Mohammed
June: Gawai Dayak (Sarawak only)
June 4: Yang di-Pertuan Agong's birthday
August 31: National Day
November: Deepavali
December: Hari Raya Puasa
December 25: Christmas Day

If you're already certified, it's possible to rent all the necessary equipment for a day's worth of diving for RM80–100.

The majority of **treks**, either on the Malaysian Peninsula or in Sarawak and Sabah, require some forethought and preparation, and you should be prepared for trails and rivers to become much more difficult to negotiate when it rains. That said, although the rainy season (Nov–Feb) undoubtedly slows your progress on some of the trails, conditions are less humid and the parks and adventure tours not oversubscribed. Most visitors trek in the large national parks to experience the remaining primary jungle and rainforest at first hand. For these, you often need to be accompanied by a guide, which can either be arranged through tour operators in KL, Kuching, Miri and Kota Kinabulu, or at the parks themselves. For inexperienced trekkers, Taman Negara National Park (see pp.670–675) is probably the best place to start, while Sarawak's Gunung Mulu National Park (see p.722) offers sufficient challenges for most tastes. Few people who make it across to Sabah forego the chance of climbing Mount Kinabalu (see pp.728–733) – not a task to be undertaken lightly, however. Details of essential trekking equipment are given in each relevant account.

Crime and safety

If you lose something in Malaysia, you're more likely to have someone running after you with it than running away. The most common crimes are perpetrated by pickpockets and snatch thieves. Take care if you rent a motorbike not to leave anything valuable in the basket on the handlebars. The ferry from Butterworth to Georgetown (Penang) is notorious for pickpockets who work in teams: a common tactic is for one to strike up a conversation to create a diversion, while the other works at your pack or pockets. **Theft** from dormitories by other tourists is also a common complaint. It's a good idea to keep one credit or debit card with you, and another in your room. In the more remote parts of Sarawak or Sabah there is little crime, and you needn't worry unduly about carrying more cash than usual. If you do need to report a crime in Malaysia, head for the nearest **police station**, where there'll be someone who speaks English – you'll need a copy of the police report for insurance purposes. In many major tourist spots, there are specific tourist police stations. It is very unwise to have anything to do with **drugs** of any description in Malaysia. The penalties for trafficking drugs in or out of either country are extreme – foreigners have been executed in the past.

Emergency phone numbers

Police/Ambulance ☎999
Fire Brigade ☎994

Medical care and emergencies

The levels of hygiene and **medical care** in Malaysia are higher than in much of the rest of Southeast Asia; staff almost everywhere speak good English and use up-to-date techniques. There's always a pharmacy in main towns, which is well stocked with brand-name drugs. They also sell oral contraceptives and condoms over the counter. Pharmacists can help with simple complaints, though if you're in any doubt get a proper diagnosis. Opening hours are usually Monday to Saturday 9.30am to 7pm; pharmacies in shopping malls stay open later. **Private clinics** are found even in the smallest towns; a visit costs around RM30, excluding medication. The **emergency department** of each town's General Hospital will see foreigners for the token fee of RM1, though costs rise rapidly if continued treatment or overnight stays are necessary. See the "Listings" sections at the end of major town accounts for addresses of pharmacies and hospitals.

History

Malaysia only gained full independence in 1957. Before that, its history was inextricably linked with events in the larger Malay archipelago, from Sumatra, across Borneo to the Philippines.

Srivijaya

The development of the Malay archipelago owed much to its location on the shipping route between India and China. The shipping trade flourished as early as the first century AD, introducing Hindu and Buddhist practices, along with wayang kulit (shadow plays), to the region.

The calm channel of the Straits of Malacca provided a refuge for ships that were forced to wait several months for a change in the monsoon winds, and from the fifth century onwards a succession of entrepôts (storage ports) was created to cater for the needs of passing vessels.

The mightiest of these entrepôts was **Srivijaya**, whose empire was eminent from the beginning of the seventh century until the end of the thirteenth, eventually encompassing all the shores and islands surrounding the Straits of Malacca. Srivijaya itself (Palembang, in Sumatra) became an important centre for Mahayana Buddhism.

The Melaka Sultanate

With the collapse of the Srivijayan Empire in the thirteenth century came the establishment of the **Melaka Sultanate** by a Palembang prince named Paramesvara.

Melaka was well endowed with a deep, sheltered harbour and grew into an international marketplace. The sultanate forged crucial trading and political agreements with China, Ayutthaya and Majapahit, and by the sixteenth century had expanded to include the west coast of the Peninsula as far as Perak, Pahang, Singapore and most of east-coast Sumatra.

Arab merchants brought Islam to the sultanate and this was adopted as the dominant religion. Meanwhile, the Melaka Sultanate refined Malay into a language of the elite, and it soon became the most widely used language in the archipelago.

The Portuguese conquest of Melaka

At the beginning of the sixteenth century, the **Portuguese** set about gaining control of crucial Eastern ports. They attacked Melaka in 1511; Sultan Mahmud Shah fled and was replaced by a colonial administration of eight hundred Portuguese officers. Despite frequent attacks from upriver Malays, the Portuguese controlled Melaka for the next 130 years, during which period they built numerous churches and converted many locals to Catholicism.

The kingdom of Johor

Fleeing Melaka, Sultan Mahmud Shah made for Pulau Bentan in the Riau archipelago, south of Singapore, where he established the first court of **Johor**. When, in 1526, the Portuguese attacked and razed the settlement, Mahmud fled once again, and it was left to his son, Alauddin Riayat Shah, to found a new court on the upper Johor river, though the capital of the kingdom then shifted repeatedly, during a century of assaults by Portugal and Aceh.

The arrival of the Dutch in Southeast Asia towards the end of the sixteenth century marked a distinct upturn in Johor's fortunes. The court aligned itself firmly with the new European arrivals, and was the supreme Malay kingdom for much of the seventeenth century. But by the 1690s, its empire was fraying under the irrational rule of another Sultan Mahmud, who was eventually murdered in 1699. This marked the end of the Melaka dynasty. In 1721, Bugis People from Sulawesi captured Johor – now based in Riau – installed a Malay puppet sultan, and ruled for over sixty years.

The Dutch in Melaka

Already the masters of Indonesia's valuable spice trade, the Vereenigde Oostindische Compagnie (VOC), or Dutch East India Company, successfully laid siege to **Melaka** in 1641. Instead of ruling from above as their predecessors had tried to do, the **Dutch** ensured that each racial group was represented by a Kapitan, a respected figure from the community who mediated between his own people and the new administrators.

The arrival of the British

At the end of the eighteenth century, Dutch control in Southeast Asia was more widespread than ever, but the VOC's coffers were empty and it faced the superior trading and maritime skills of the **British**. High taxes in Melaka were forcing traders to more economical locations such as the newly established British port of Penang, whose foundation in 1786 heralded the awakening of British interest in the Straits.

When the British East India Company (EIC) moved in on Melaka and the rest of the Dutch Asian domain in 1795, the VOC barely demurred. The British soon founded Singapore as their own regional entrepôt, signing an agreement with the Sultanate of Riau-Johor in 1819. The strategic position and free-trade policy of Singapore instantly threatened the viability of both Melaka and Penang, forcing the Dutch finally to relinquish their hold on the former to the British, and leaving the latter to decline.

The **Anglo-Dutch Treaty** of 1824, which divided territories between the two countries using the Straits of Malacca as the dividing line, split the Riau-Johor kingdom. This was followed in 1826 by the unification of Melaka, Penang and Singapore into one administration, known as the Straits Settlements, with Singapore replacing Penang as its capital in 1832.

The Anglo-Dutch Treaty did not include Borneo, however, and though the EIC discouraged official expansion, British explorer James Brooke (1803–68) managed to persuade the Sultan of Brunei to award him his own area – Sarawak – in 1841, becoming the first of a line of "White Rajahs" that ruled the state until the start of World War II.

The Pangkor Treaty

Although settlers had trickled into the Peninsula since the early days of Melaka, new plantations, and the rapidly expanding tin mines, attracted floods of willing **Chinese** workers eager to escape a life of poverty. By 1845, the Chinese formed over half of Singapore's population, while principal towns along the Peninsula's west coast as well as Sarawak's capital, Kuching, became predominantly Chinese.

Struggles between Chinese clan groups were rife, and Malay factions frequently became involved, too, causing a string of civil wars, often about control of the tin trade or tax claims. This was not good for trade, and finally the British intervened, at the request of a Perak Malay chief, Rajah Abdullah. On January 20, 1874, the Pangkor Treaty was signed between the British and Abdullah, formalizing British intervention in the political affairs of the Malay people.

British Malaya

By 1888, the name **British Malaya** had been brought into use. Over subsequent decades, the Malay sultans' powers were gradually eroded, while the introduction of rubber estates made British Malaya one of the most productive colonies in the world.

Each state soon saw the arrival of a Resident, a senior British civil servant whose main function was to act as advisor to the local sultan, but who also oversaw the collecting of local taxes. Agreements along the lines of the Pangkor Treaty were drawn up with Selangor, Negeri Sembilan and Pahang states in the 1880s, and in 1896 these three became bracketed together under the title of the Federated Malay States, with the increasingly important town of Kuala Lumpur made the regional capital.

By 1909, the northern Malay states of Kedah, Perlis, Kelantan and Terengganu – previously under Thai control – were brought into the colonial fold: along with Johor (which joined in 1914) they were grouped together as the Unfederated Malay States and by the outbreak of World War I, British political control was more or less complete. The seat of power was split between Singapore and Kuala Lumpur. Borneo, too, had been brought under British control: the three states of Sarawak, Sabah and Brunei had been transformed into protectorates in 1888.

Ethnic rivalries

In the first quarter of the twentieth century, hundreds of thousands of immigrants from China and India were encouraged by the British to emigrate to sites across Peninsular Malaysia, Sarawak, North Borneo and Singapore.

They came to work as tin miners or plantation labourers, and Malaya's population in this period doubled to four million.

This recruitment drive fuelled resentment among the Malays, who believed that they were being denied the economic opportunities advanced to others. A further deterioration in Malay–Chinese relations followed the success of the mainland Chinese revolutionary groups in Malaya. The educated Chinese, who joined the Malayan Communist Party (MCP) from 1930 onwards, formed the backbone of the politicized Chinese movements after World War II, which demanded an end to British rule and to what they perceived as special privileges extended to the Malays. In response, the Malays established the Singapore Malay Union, which gradually gained support in Straits Settlement areas where Malays were outnumbered by Chinese. It held its first conference in 1939 and advocated a Malay supremacist line.

Japanese occupation

By February 1942, the whole of Malaya and Singapore was in **Japanese** hands and most of the British were POWs. The Japanese regime brutalized the Chinese, largely because of Japan's history of conflict with China: up to fifty thousand people were tortured and killed in the two weeks immediately after the British surrender of Singapore. Allied POWs were rounded up into prison camps, and many were sent to build the infamous "Death Railway" in Burma and Thailand.

In Malaya, the occupiers ingratiated themselves with some of the Malay elite by suggesting that after the war the country would be given independence. Predictably, it was the Chinese activists in the MCP, more than the Malays, who organized resistance during wartime.

The Japanese invaded Sarawak in late 1941 and, once again, the Chinese were the main targets. In North Borneo, the Japanese invaded Pulau Labuan on New Year's Day, 1942, and over the next three years the main suburban areas were bombed by the Allies. By the time of the Japanese surrender in September 1945, most of Jesselton (modern-day Kota Kinabalu) and Sandakan had been destroyed.

The **Japanese surrender** on September 9, 1945 led to a power vacuum in the region, with the British initially left with no choice but to work with the Chinese activists, the **Malayan People's Anti-Japanese Army** (MPAJA), to exert political control. Violence occurred between the MPAJA and Malays, particularly towards those accused of collaborating with the Japanese.

The Federation of Malaya

Immediately after the war, the British updated the idea of a **Malayan union** – a position halfway towards full independence – which would make the Chinese and Indian inhabitants full citizens and give them equal rights with the Malays.

This quickly aroused **opposition** among the Malays, with Malayan nationalists forming the United Malays National Organization (UMNO) in 1946. Its main tenet was that Malays should retain their special privileges, largely because they were the region's first inhabitants.

The idea of union was subsequently replaced by the **Federation of Malaya**, established in 1948, which upheld the power of the sultans and brought all the regional groupings together under one government, with the exception of Chinese-dominated Singapore, whose inclusion would have led to the Malays being in a minority. Sarawak and North Borneo were made Crown Colonies of Britain.

The Emergency

In Peninsular Malaya, many **Chinese** were angered by the change of the status of the country from a colony to a federation, in which they effectively became second-class citizens. According to the new laws, non-Malays could only qualify as citizens if they had lived in the country for fifteen out of the last twenty-five years, and they also had to prove they spoke Malay or English.

More Chinese began to identify with the **MCP**, which under its new leader, **Chin Peng**, wanted to set up a Malayan republic. Peng established guerrilla cells deep in the jungle, and, from June 1948, launched sporadic attacks on rubber estates, killing planters and employees, and spreading fear among rural communities.

The period of unrest, which lasted from 1948 to 1960, was referred to as the **Emergency**, rather than a civil war, which it undoubtedly was. The British were slow to respond until Lieutenant-General Sir Harold Briggs enacted the resettlement of 400,000 rural Chinese – mostly squatters who had moved to the jungle borders to escape the Japanese – as well as thousands of Orang Asli seen as potential MCP sympathizers in four hundred "New Villages", scattered across the country. This made both Chinese and Orang Asli more sympathetic to the idea of a communist republic replacing British rule.

The **violence** peaked in 1950 with ambushes and attacks on plantations near Ipoh, Kuala Kangsar, Kuala Lipis and Raub, and the assassination of the British high commissioner to Malaya. In 1956, Peng and most of the remaining cell members fled over the border to Thailand where they received sanctuary; some still live there and only formally admitted defeat in 1989.

Towards independence

Although UMNO stuck to its "Malays first" policy, in 1955 the new leader, Tunku Abdul Rahman, forged a united position between UMNO, the moderate Malayan Chinese Association (MCA) and the Malayan Indian Association. This merger was called the Alliance, and it was to sweep into power under the rallying cry of **merdeka** (freedom) for **an independent Malaya**.

With British backing, Merdeka was promulgated on August 31, 1957. The first prime minister was Tunku Abdul Rahman. The **new constitution** allowed for the nine Malay sultans to alternate as king, and established a two-tier parliament – a house of elected representatives and a Senate with delegates from each of the states. Although the system was, in theory, a democracy, the Malay-dominated UMNO remained by far the most influential party. Rahman committed the country to economic expansion and full employment, and foreign investment was encouraged.

After full self-government was attained by **Singapore** in 1959, its leader Lee Kuan Yew wanted Singapore and Malaya to be joined administratively. Rahman initially agreed, although he feared the influence of pro-communist extremists in Singapore's ruling People's Action Party (PAP). He campaigned hard for the inclusion of Sarawak and North Borneo in a revised federation, to act as a demographic balance to the Chinese in Singapore.

Federation and the Konfrontasi

In September 1963, North Borneo (quickly renamed Sabah), Sarawak and Singapore joined Malaya in the **Federation of Malaysia**. Both Indonesia, which laid claim to Sarawak, and the Philippines, which argued it had jurisdiction over Sabah, reacted angrily. Although the Philippines backed down, Indonesia didn't, and border skirmishes known as the **Konfrontasi** ensued. Indonesian soldiers crossed the border, and only the arrival of British and Gurkha troops averted a wider war.

Differences soon developed between Lee Kuan Yew and the Malay-dominated Alliance party over the lack of egalitarian policies. Tensions rose in Singapore and ugly racial incidents developed into full-scale riots in 1964. Rahman decided it would be best if Singapore left the

Federation, and Singapore duly acquired full independence on August 9, 1965.

The **exclusion of Singapore** from the Malaysian Federation was not enough to quell the ethnic conflicts. Resentment built up among the Chinese over the principle that Malay be the main language taught in schools and over unfair job opportunities.

In 1969, the UMNO (Malay)-dominated Alliance lost regional power in parliamentary elections, and Malays in major cities reacted angrily to a perceived increase in power of the Chinese. Hundreds of people, mostly Chinese, were killed and injured in the **riots** that followed. Rahman kept the country under a state of emergency for nearly two years, using the draconian Internal Security Act (ISA) to arrest and imprison activists, as well as many writers and artists.

The New Economic Policy

Rahman resigned in 1971, handing over to the new prime minister, Tun Abdul Razak, also from UMNO, who took a less authoritarian stance – although still implementing the ISA. He brought the parties in Sarawak and Sabah into the political process and initiated a broad set of directives, called the **New Economic Policy** (NEP). This set out to restructure the management of the economy so that it would be less reliant on the Chinese. **Ethnic Malays** were classed as *bumiputras* (sons of the soil) and given favoured positions in business, commerce and other professions.

Contemporary Malaysia

For 22 years Malaysian politics was dominated by Prime Minister **Dr Mahathir Mohammed** who, like all previous PMs, led the **UMNO** party. He triumphed at every election after winning his party's nomination in 1981 until his resignation in 2003.

During Mahathir's rule many Malays got richer through the NEP's blatantly racist system of opportunities, such as tax, educational and financial breaks, but their share of the economy still stood at just twenty percent. In 1991, the supposedly less iniquitous **New Development Policy** succeeded the NEP, though it still favours *bumiputras*.

During this time, the main voice of opposition was (as it still continues to be) the **Islamic Fundamentalist Party**, PAS, which wants to bring strict Islamic law into force in **Kelantan**. In a Muslim country, Mahathir could not be seen to be too un-Islamic in opposing PAS outright. Instead, he did little to assist the economy of Kelantan, which to this day remains the poorest state in Malaysia. The **1999 general election** re-asserted the strong grip of the Barisan National (BN), an UMNO-dominated coalition, over the nation, but PAS made some significant gains, most notably taking Terengganu, a state that previously had been solidly behind the BN. The economic hardship that many Malaysians endured during the Southeast Asian **financial crisis** of 1997 is cited by some observers as the reason why voters turned away from the ruling party.

Mahathir may not have met with any substantial internal opposition, but some of Malaysia's **economic policies** were condemned internationally. **Logging** and development projects, such as the now-ditched Bakun Dam hydro-electric scheme, in particular, have brought severe criticism. Currently, logging is actually on the decrease, but critics say that within thirty years forests will cover less than twenty percent of the surface of the country, instead of the current sixty percent.

The issue that harmed Mahathir most, however, concerned his personal dealings with his former second-in-command, Deputy Prime Minister Anwar Ibrahim. Dr Mahathir began to see Anwar as a threat, and, in a manner that shocked many Malaysians and much of the democratic world, Anwar was imprisoned in 1998 on trumped-up charges of homosexual activity and corruption.

Amid increasing worries that Mahathir would go the way of other Asian autocrats such as Indonesia's Suharto, the prime minister engineered his own succession. In 2003, Mahathir stepped down after 22 years in power and handed over the reigns to **Abdullah Badawi**. The new prime minister inherited one of the healthiest economies in Southeast Asia, and early accounts indicated that his style would be vastly different from the caustic Mahathir. In a surprise move in 2004, Anwar Ibrahim was released from prison after serving six years of his fifteen-year sentence. These two events have resulted in a cautious optimism for the future of Malaysia, both at home and abroad.

Religion

The vast majority of Malaysians are Muslims, but there are also significant numbers of Hindus, Buddhists, Confucianists and animists among the population. For an introduction to all these faiths, see "Religion", pp.69–71.

Islam in Malaysia today is a mixture of Sufi and Wahabi elements and as such is relatively liberal. Although most Muslim women wear traditional costume, especially headscarves, very few adopt the veil, and some taboos, like not drinking alcohol, are ignored by a growing number of Malays. There are stricter, more fundamentalist Muslims – in Kelantan the local government is dominated by them – but in general, Islam here has a modern outlook, blending a vibrant, practising faith with a business-minded approach.

Hinduism arrived in Malaysia long before Islam, and Sufi Islam integrated some of its beliefs, including the tradition of pluralist deity worship, which accounts for the strong cultural importance of festivals like Deepavali and Thaipusam. Malaysian Chinese usually consider themselves either Buddhist, Taoist or Confucianist, although in practice they are often a mixture of all three.

Although many of Malaysia's ethnic groups are now nominally Christian or Muslim, many of their old **animist** beliefs and ceremonies still survive. Birds, especially the hornbill, are of particular significance to the Iban and the Kelabit peoples in Sarawak. Many Kelabit depend upon the arrival of migrating flocks to decide when to plant their rice crop, while Iban hunters still interpret sightings of the hornbill and other birds as good or bad omens. For the Orang Asli groups in the interior of the Peninsula, most of their remaining animist beliefs centre on healing and funeral ceremonies.

Peoples

Largely because of its pivotal position on the maritime trade routes between the Middle East, India and China, present-day Malaysia has always been a cultural melting-pot, attracting Malays from what is now Sumatra, Indians, and Chinese. But the region already contained many indigenous tribes, Orang Asli ("the first people"), thought to have migrated here around 50,000 years ago from the Philippines, which was then connected by a land bridge to Borneo and Southeast Asia.

On the Peninsula, the Malays still form just over fifty percent of the population, the Chinese number nearly 38 percent, Indians ten percent and the Orang Asli around one percent; in Sarawak and Sabah, on the other hand, the indigenous tribes account for around fifty percent of the population, the Chinese 28 percent, with the other 22 percent divided amongst Malays, Indians and Eurasians.

The Malays

The **Malays**, a Mongoloid people believed to have originated from the meeting of Central Asians with Pacific islanders, first moved to the west coast of the Malaysian Peninsula from Sumatra in early times. But it was the growth in power of the Malay sultanates from the fifteenth century onwards – coinciding with the arrival of Islam – that established Malays as a significant force. They developed an aristocratic tradition, courtly rituals and a social hierarchy that still have an influence today.

The main contemporary change for Malays in Malaysia was the introduction, some time after independence, of the bumiputra policy, which was designed to make it easier for the Malays, the Orang Asli of the Peninsula, and the Malay-related indigenous groups in Sarawak and Sabah, to compete in economic and educational fields against the high-achieving Chinese and Indians. But as the policy has developed, it's only really been the Malays who have gained, taking most of the top positions in government and in state companies.

The Chinese and Straits Chinese

It was in Melaka in the fifteenth century that the first significant **Chinese** community established itself. However, the ancestors of the majority of Chinese now living in Peninsular Malaysia emigrated from southern China in the nineteenth century to work in the burgeoning tin-mining industry. In Sarawak and Sabah, Chinese played an important part in opening up the interior. Chinatowns developed throughout the region, and Chinese traditions became an integral part of a wider Malayan culture. The Malaysian Chinese are well represented in parliament and occupy around a quarter of the current ministerial positions.

One of the few examples of regional intermarrying is displayed in the Peranakan or "Straits-born Chinese" heritage of Melaka and Penang. When male Chinese immigrants married local Malay women, their male offspring were termed "Baba" and the females "Nonya". Baba–Nonya society, as it became known, adapted elements from both cultures to create its own traditions: the descendants of these sixteenth-century liaisons have a unique culinary and architectural style. Most follow Chinese Confucianism and speak a distinct Malay dialect.

The Indians

The first large wave of **Tamil** labourers arrived in the nineteenth century to build the roads and railways and to work on the rubber estates. But an embryonic entrepreneurial class from **north India** soon followed and set up businesses in Penang; because most were Muslims, they found it easier to assimilate with the Malay community than the Hindu Tamils did. Although Indians comprise only ten percent of Malaysia's population, their impact is felt everywhere. The festival of Deepavali is a national holiday, and Indians dominate certain professional areas such as medicine and law. Despite this, in general Indians are second to bottom of the economic ladder, higher only than the Orang Asli.

The Orang Asli

The **Orang Asli** – the indigenous peoples of Peninsular Malaysia – mostly belong to three distinct groups, within which there are various tribes. Though most tribes retain some cultural traditions, government drives have encouraged many tribespeople to settle and work within the cash economy.

The largest of the groups is the **Senoi** (pop. 40,000), who live in the forested interior of Perak, Pahang and Kelantan states, and divide into two main tribes, the Semiar and the Temiar. They follow animist customs and practise shifting cultivation. The dark-skinned, curly haired **Semang** (or Negritos; pop. 2000) live in the northern areas of the Peninsula and share a traditional nomadic, hunter-gatherer culture. The so-called **Aboriginal Malays** live south of the Kuala Lumpur–Kuantan road. This group includes the Jakun, who live around Tasek Chini, and the Semelais of Tasek Bera, both of which have retained their animist religion and artistic traditions and are among the easiest of the Orang Asli to approach, since some work in the two lakes' tourist industries.

Sarawak's peoples

Nearly fifty percent of **Sarawak's population** is made up of various indigenous Dayak and Orang Ulu groups – including the Iban, Bidayuh, Kayan, Kenyah, Kelabit and Penan tribes, many of whom live in longhouses and maintain a rich cultural legacy.

The **Iban**, a stocky, rugged people, make up nearly one-third of Sarawak's population. They originated in the Kapuas Valley in Kalimantan, and migrated north in the sixteenth century. Nowadays, Iban longhouse communities are found in the Batang Ai river system in the southwest, and along the Rajang, Katibas and Baleh rivers. These communities are quite accessible, their inhabitants always hospitable and keen to show off their traditional dance, music, textile-weaving, blow-piping, fishing and game-playing. In their time, the Iban were infamous headhunters, but, these days, this tradition has been replaced by that of *berjelai*, or "journey", whereby a young man leaves the community to prove himself in the outside world – returning to his longhouse with television sets, generators and outboard motors, rather than heads.

The southernmost of Sarawak's indigenous groups are the **Bidayuh**, who traditionally lived away from the rivers, building their longhouses on the sides of hills. Culturally, they are similar to the Iban.

Most of the other groups in Sarawak are classed as **Orang Ulu** (people of the interior). They inhabit the more remote inland areas, on the upper Rajang, Balui, Baram and Linau rivers. The most numerous, the **Kayan** and the **Kenyah**, are longhouse-dwellers, animists and shifting cultivators. They are also considered to be the most artistic of Sarawak's people, with many excellent painters and musicians among them.

The **Kelabit** people live in longhouses on the highland plateau that separates north Sarawak from Kalimantan, and are Christian. The semi-nomadic **Penan** live in the upper Rajang and Limbang areas and rely on hunting and gathering. They are lighter skinned, largely because they live within the shade of the forest, rather than on the rivers and in clearings. The state government's resettlement programme – a controversial policy not entirely unconnected with the logging industry – is now largely complete, and few Penan still live their traditional lifestyle.

Sabah's peoples

The **Dusun**, or Kadazan/Dusun, account for around a third of Sabah's population. Traditionally agriculturists, they inhabit the western coastal plains and the interior. Although most Dusun are now Christians, remnants of their animist past are still evident, most obviously in the harvest festival. The mainly Muslim **Bajau** tribe drifted over from the southern Philippines some two hundred years ago, and now constitute ten percent of Sabah's population, living in the northwest. They are agriculturists and fishermen, noted for their horsemanship and their rearing of buffalo. The **Murut** inhabit the area between Keningau and the Sarawak border, in the southwest. They farm rice and cassava by a system of shifting cultivation and, at times, still hunt using blowpipes and poison darts.

Books

Malaysia has for over one hundred years offered a vivid subject for writers. Below is a selection of the most entertaining and informative works available. Publishers' details for books published in the UK and US are given in the form "UK publisher/US publisher" where they differ; if books are published in one of these countries only, this follows the publisher's name. "O/p" means "out of print".

Charles Allen *Tales from the South China Seas* (Futura/David Charles, o/p). Memoirs of the last generation of British colonists, in which predictable Raj attitudes prevail, though some of the drama of everyday lives is evinced with considerable pathos.

Barbara Watson Andaya and Leonard Andaya *The History of Malaysia* (Macmillan/St Martin's Press, o/p in UK). This standard text on the region takes a fairly even-handed view of Malaysia, and finds time for cultural coverage.

Noel Barber *War of the Running Dogs* (Arrow, UK, o/p). Illuminates the Malayan Emergency with a novelist's eye for mood.

Odoardo Beccari *Wanderings in the Great Forests of Borneo* (OUP, o/p in US). Vivid turn-of-the-century account of the natural and human environment of Sarawak.

Isabella Bird *The Golden Chersonese* (OUP/Century, o/p). Delightful epistolary romp through old Southeast Asia, penned by the intrepid Bird, whose adventures in the Malay states in 1879 included elephant-back rides and encounters with alligators.

Margaret Brooke *My Life in Sarawak* (OUP, UK, o/p). Engaging account of nineteenth-century Sarawak by White Rajah Charles Brooke's wife, which reveals a sympathetic attitude to her subjects and an unprejudiced colonial eye.

Anthony Burgess *The Long Day Wanes* (Minerva/Norton). Burgess's Malayan trilogy – *Time for a Tiger, The Enemy in the Blanket* and *Beds in the East* – published in one volume, provides a witty and acutely observed vision of 1950s Malaya, underscoring the racial prejudices of the period.

Iskandar Carey *The Orang Asli* (OUP, o/p). The only detailed anthropological work on the indigenes of Peninsular Malaysia.

Spencer Chapman *The Jungle is Neutral* (Mayflower/Royal Publications, o/p). This riveting, first-hand account of being lost, and surviving, in the Malay jungle during World War II reads like a breathless novel.

Mark Cleary & Peter Eaton *Borneo Change and Development* (Penerbit Fajar Bakti, Malaysia). A very readable composite of Bornean history, economy and society, that's rounded off by a section dealing with issues such as logging, conservation and the future of the Penan.

G.W.H. Davison & Chew Yen Fook *A Photographic Guide to Birds of Peninsular Malaysia and Singapore* (New Holland/ R. Curtis). Well keyed and user friendly, these slender volumes carry oodles of glossy plates that make positive identifying a breeze. The companion volume, *A Photographic Guide to Birds of Borneo*, is also excellent.

Peter Dickens *SAS The Jungle Frontier* (Lionel Leventhal). Gripping account of British special forces involvement in the Malayan Emergency.

C.S. Godshalk *Kalimantaan* (Abacus). Recent novel based around the life of James Brooke, the first White

Rajah. A brilliantly written story very faithful to the cultural facts of nineteenth-century Sarawak.

Eric Hansen *Stranger In The Forest* (Abacus/Houghton Mifflin o/p). A gripping book, the result of a seven-month tramp through the forests of Sarawak and Kalimantan in 1982, which almost saw the author killed by a poison dart.

Tom Harrisson *A World Within* (OUP, US, o/p). The only in-depth description of the Kelabit peoples of Sarawak, and a cracking good World War II tale courtesy of Harrisson, who parachuted into the Kelabit Highlands to organize resistance against the Japanese.

Victor T. King *The Best of Borneo Travel* (OUP Blackwell). Compendium of extracts from Bornean travel writing since the sixteenth century; an interesting travelling companion.

Dennis Lau Penans *The Vanishing Nomads of Borneo* (Lee Ming Press, Malaysia) and *Borneo – A Photographic Journey* (Travelcom Asia). Two brilliant photographic journeys with descriptive texts on Sarawak's indigenous peoples.

Andro Linklater *Wild People* (John Murray/Grove-Atlantic). As telling and as entertaining a glimpse into the lifestyle of the Iban as you could pack, depicting their age-old traditions surviving amidst the baseball caps and rock posters.

K.S. Maniam *The Return* (Skoob, UK); *In A Far Country* (Skoob, UK); *Haunting the Tiger*. The purgative writings of this Tamil-descended Malaysian author are strong, highly descriptive and humorous – essential reading.

W. Somerset Maugham *Short Stories Volume 4* (Mandarin/Penguin). Peopled by hoary sailors and colonials wearing mutton chop whiskers and topees, Maugham's short stories resuscitate turn-of-the-century Malaya; quintessential colonial literature graced by an easy style and a steady eye for a story.

Redmond O'Hanlon *Into The Heart of Borneo* (Picador/Vintage). A hugely entertaining yarn recounting O'Hanlon's refreshingly amateurish romp through the jungle to a remote summit on the Sarawak/Kalimantan border, partnered by the English poet James Fenton.

Ambrose B. Rathborne *Camping and Tramping in Malaya* (OUP, o/p). Lively nineteenth-century account with insights into the colonial personalities and working conditions of the leading figures of the day.

James Ritchie *Bruno Masser, The Inside Story* (Summer Times Publishing, Malaysia). Detailed account on the self-styled hero of the Penan in the early years of the 1990s when indigenous people manned barricades in a vain attempt to stop loggers ruining parts of Sarawak.

Spenser St John *Life in the Forests of the Far East* (OUP, UK). A description of an early ascent of Mount Kinabalu is a highlight of this animated nineteenth-century adventure, written by the personal secretary to White Rajah Charles Brooke.

Vinson H. Sutlive *The Iban of Sarawak* (Waveland Press, Malaysia). Academic work exploring the recent history of the largest and most influential of Malaysia's indigenous peoples, after the Malays themselves.

C. Mary Turnbull *A Short History of Malaysia, Singapore & Brunei* (Graham Brash, Singapore). Decent, informed introduction to the region.

Alfred Russell Wallace (see the Sarawak Museum, p.707) *The Malay Archipelago* (OUP/Dover, o/p). Wallace's peerless account of the flora and fauna of Borneo, based on travels made between 1854 and 1862 – during which time he collected over 100,000 specimens. Still required reading for nature lovers.

Language

The national language of Malaysia is Bahasa Malaysia. It's an old language, with early roots in the central and south Pacific, and simple enough to learn. In practice, you'll be able to get by with English in all but the most remote areas. As a general rule, older Malaysians speak better English than younger ones, as English used to be on the curriculum in schools, but is rarely these days.

Nouns have no genders and don't require an article, while the plural form is constructed just by saying the word twice; thus "child" is anak, while "children" is anak anak. Doubling a word can also indicate "doing"; for example, jalan jalan is used to mean "walking". Verbs have no tenses either. Sentence order is the same as in English, though adjectives usually follow the noun.

Pronunciation

The **pronunciation** of Bahasa Malaysia is broadly the same as the English reading of Roman script, with a few exceptions:

a as in c**u**p
c as in **ch**eap
e as in **e**nd
g as in **g**irl
i as in bout**i**que
j as in **j**oy
k hard, as in English, except at the end of the word, when you should stop just short of pronouncing it.
o as in g**o**t
u as in b**oo**t
ai as in f**i**ne
au as in h**ow**
sy as in **sh**ut

Greetings and basic phrases

Selamat is the all-purpose greeting derived from Arabic, which communicates general goodwill.

Good morning	Selamat pagi
Good afternoon	Selamat petang
Good evening	Selamat malam
Good night	Selamat tidur
Goodbye	Selamat tinggal
Bon Voyage	Selamat jalan
Welcome	Selamat datang
Bon Appetit	Selamat makan
How are you?	Apa kabar?
Fine/ok	Baik
See you later	Jumpa lagi
Please	Tolong
Thank you	Terima kasih
You're welcome	Sama sama
Sorry/excuse me	Maaf
No worries/never mind	Tidak apa-apa
Yes	Ya
No	Tidak
What is your name?	Siapa nama anda?
My name is...	Nama saya...
Where are you from?	Dari mana?
I come from...	Saya dari...
Do you speak English?	Bisa bercakap bahasa Inggris?
I don't understand	Saya tidak mengerti
What is this/that?	Apa ini/itu?
Can you help me?	Bolekah anda tolong saya?

Getting around

Where is the...?	Dimana...?
I want to go to...	Saya mahu naik ke...
How far?	Berapa jauh?
How long will it take?	Berapa lama?
When will the bus leave?	Bila bas berangkat?
What time does the train arrive?	Jam berapa keratapi ampai?
Stop	Berhenti
Right	Kanan
Left	Kiri
Straight	Terus
North	Utara
South	Selatan
East	Timur
West	Barat
Street	Jalan
Train station	Stesen keratapi
Bus station	Stesen bas
Airport	Lapangan terbang
Ticket	Tiket
Hotel	Hotel/rumah penginapan
Post office	Pejabat pos

Restaurant	Restoran
Shop	Kedai
Market	Pasar
Taxi	Teksi
Trishaw	Becak

Accommodation

How much is...?	Berapa...?
I need a room	Saya perlu satu bilik
Cheap/expensive	Murah/mahal
I'm staying for one night	Saya mahu tinggal satu hari
Can I store my luggage here?	Bisa titip barang?

General adjectives and nouns

Good	Bagus
A lot/very much	Banyak
A little	Sedikit
Hot	Panas
Sweet	Manis
Big	Besar
Small	Kecil
Closed	Tutup
Ill/sick	Sakit
Entrance	Masuk
Exit	Keluar
Toilet	Tandas
Man	Lelaki
Woman	Perempuan
Water	Air
Money	Wang/duit
Food	Makan
Drink	Minum
Boyfriend/girlfriend	Pacar
Husband	Suami
Wife	Istri
Friend	Kawan

Time and days of the week

What time is it?	Jam berapa?
It's...	
three o'clock	Jam tiga
ten past four	Jam empat lewat sepuluh
quarter to five	Jam lima kurang seperempat
six-thirty	Jam setengah tujuh (lit. "half to seven")
7am	Tujuh pagi
8pm	Lapan malam
Minute	Menit
Hour	Jam
Day	Hari
Week	Minggu
Month	Bulan
Year	Tahun
Today	Hari Ini
Tomorrow	Besok
Yesterday	Kemarin
Now	Sekarang
Not yet	Belum
Never	Tidak Perna
Monday	Hari Isnin
Tuesday	Hari Selasa
Wednesday	Hari Rabu
Thursday	Hari Kamis
Friday	Hari Jumaat
Saturday	Hari Sabtu
Sunday	Hari Ahad/minggu

Numbers

0	Nul
1	Satu
2	Dua
3	Tiga
4	Empat
5	Lima
6	Enam
7	Tujuh
8	Lapan
9	Sembilan
10	Sepuluh
11, 12, 13, etc	Sebelas, duabelas, tigabelas
20	Duapuluh
21, 22, 23, etc	Duapuluh satu, dua puluh dua, dua puluh tiga
30, 40, 50, etc	Tigapuluh, empatpuluh, limapuluh
100, 200, 300, etc	Seratus, duaratus, tigaratus, empatratus
1000	Seribu
1,000,000	Sejuta
A half	Setengah

7.1

Kuala Lumpur and around

Founded in the mid-nineteenth century, **KUALA LUMPUR**, or KL as it's popularly known, is the youngest Southeast Asian capital and the most economically successful after Singapore – and it's still growing: building sites abound and the city is awash with stunning examples of modern architecture, not least the famous Petronas Towers and the recently opened Museum of Islamic Arts. It's not one of Malaysia's most charming cities, perhaps: it doesn't have, for example, the narrow alleys, bicycles and mahjong games of Melaka or Kota Bharu or the atmospheric waterfront of Kuching. But it's safe and sociable, and with a population of nearly two million, it's usually exciting in the day and always buzzing with energy at night. From a cultural standpoint, it certainly has enough interesting monuments, galleries, markets and museums to keep visitors busy for at least a week.

KL began life as a swampy staging post for Chinese tin miners in 1857 – Kuala Lumpur means "muddy estuary" in Malay – and blossomed under the competitive rule of pioneering merchants. But as fights over tin concessions erupted across the country, the British used gunboat diplomacy to settle the Selangor Civil War and the British Resident, Frank Swettenham, took command of KL, making it the capital of the state and, in 1896, the capital of the Federated Malay States. Swettenham imported British architects from India to design suitably grand buildings, and thousands of Tamil labourers poured in to build them; development continued steadily through the first quarter of the twentieth century. The Japanese invaded in December 1941, but although they bombed the city, they missed their main targets. Following the Japanese surrender in September 1945, the British were once more in charge in the capital, but Nationalist demands had replaced the Malays' former acceptance of the colonizers, and Malaysian independence – Merdeka – finally came in 1957.

Arrival

KL is at the hub of Malaysia's **transport systems**. It has the country's main international airport, where you'll have to change if you're flying on to Sarawak or Sabah; buses from all over Peninsular Malaysia converge on one of four bus stations; the train station has connections with Thailand and Singapore; and there are ferries to Sumatra in Indonesia.

By air

The ultra-modern **Kuala Lumpur International Airport** (**KLIA**) at Sepang is 70km southwest of the centre. Getting into town has become much quicker and easier now that the **KLIA express trains** are in service. There are two classes of trains, "express" and "transit", but the latter are more for local commuters. The KLIA express trains (5am–midnight; every 15–20min; RM35) make the trip in half an hour and terminate at Kuala Lumpur's new transportation hub, KL Sentral, which conveniently interfaces inter-city trains with LRT and KL Monorail lines. This is by far the fastest and most efficient way into the city. **Airport coaches** (6.15am–midnight; every 30min; RM25) leave from the bus terminus at car park C and take an hour to get to the centre. Follow the clearly marked signs from the Arrivals area at Level 4 to the escalators down to the concourse. The coach will drop you directly at your accommodation.

Taxis into the centre cost around RM95-120, depending on the time of day – there's a surcharge from midnight until 6am. You'll need to buy a coupon at the taxi counter in the Arrivals hall; it's best to avoid the taxi touts, who may charge upwards of RM200, and have been known to demand payment in US, rather than Malaysian, dollars. All the major car rental companies have offices at the airport, and there are money exchange outlets here, too.

By train

Inter-city trains all stop at **KL Sentral station**, from where you can transfer to Kuala Lumpur's city rail systems: the LRT and KL Monorail.

Moving on from Kuala Lumpur

Journey times and frequency of boats and buses are given in "Travel details", p.743

By plane

For domestic and most international flights, check in is at KL Sentral, the city's new transportation hub. Check in at the KLIA counter one and a half hours before your flight and then take the new KLIA Express trains for the thirty-minute ride to the airport (RM35). The easiest way to get to the **airport** is to call a taxi from your hotel (RM70–80); taxis flagged down on the street tend not to want to go out that far. Most of the larger hostels can help arrange transport to the airport for around the same price. Otherwise, call the airport coach service (☎1800/880 737), preferably giving a day's notice, to ensure you're picked up from your hotel in good time.

By train

Kuala Lumpur's colonial-era Moorish railway station has been replaced by a new inter-city **train** station located at nearby KL Sentral. The station's information kiosk (daily during office hours; ☎03/2279 8888 for information and reservation) has up-to-date train timetables. You must book, preferably at least three days ahead, for the night sleeper to Singapore or Butterworth; most large hotels can do this for you.

By bus and long-distance taxi

Most long-distance **buses** leave from Pudu Raya bus station (☎03/2070 0145) on Jalan Pudu, just to the east of Chinatown. The buses leave from ground-floor bays, and ticket offices are on the floor above, along with a left-luggage office (daily 6am–midnight; RM2). Some buses also operate from outside the terminus – these are legitimate, but may only leave when full. **Long-distance taxis** also use Pudu Raya, arriving and departing from the second floor above the bus ticket offices.

For some destinations you'll need one of the other bus stations: Putra (☎03/4042 9530), near the Putra World Trade Centre, for the east coast; Klang (☎03/3344 8066) on Jalan Sultan Mohammed for Klang and Port Klang; and Pekeliling (☎03/4042 1256) at the northern end of Jalan Raja Laut, for Kuantan and the interior.

By ferry

Ferries to Tanjung Balai, in Sumatra, depart from Port Klang, 38km southwest of KL. Take the Komuter train or a bus from the Klang bus station on Jalan Sultan Mohammed to the port (see p.346).

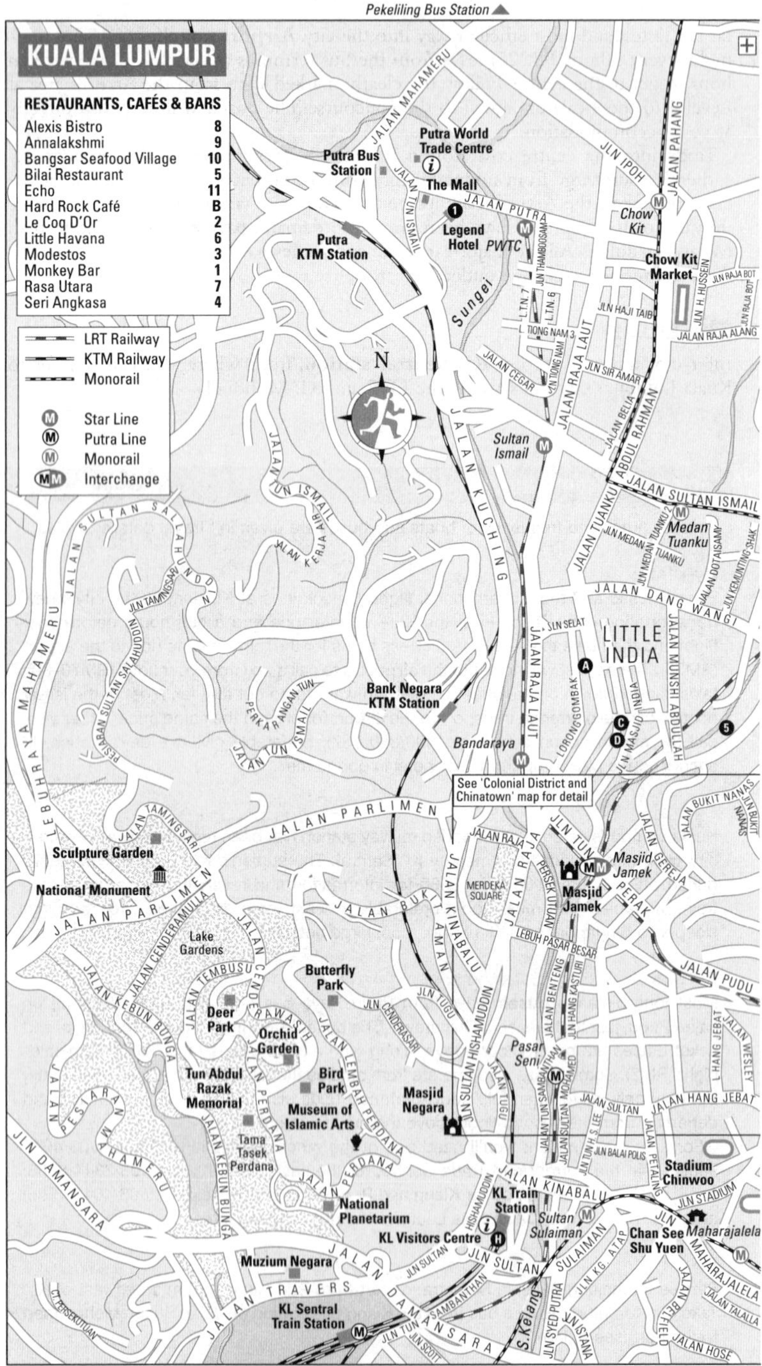
Pekeliling Bus Station
KUALA LUMPUR
RESTAURANTS, CAFÉS & BARS
Alexis Bistro 8
Annalakshmi 9
Bangsar Seafood Village 10
Bilai Restaurant 5
Echo 11
Hard Rock Café B
Le Coq D'Or 2
Little Havana 6
Modestos 3
Monkey Bar 1
Rasa Utara 7
Seri Angkasa 4
LRT Railway
KTM Railway
Monorail
Star Line
Putra Line
Monorail
Interchange
N
JALAN MAHAMERU
Putra World Trade Centre
Putra Bus Station
JALAN TUN ISMAIL
The Mall
JALAN PUTRA
Legend Hotel
PWTC
Putra KTM Station
JLN THAMBOOSAMY
Sungei
L.TN.7
L.TN.6
L.TIONG NAM 3
JLN TIONG NAM
JALAN CEGAR
JLN IPOH
JALAN PAHANG
Chow Kit
Chow Kit Market
JLN H. HUSSEIN
JLN RAJA BOT
JLN HAJI TAIB
JALAN RAJA ALANG
JLN SIR AMAR
JALAN RAJA LAUT
JALAN BELIA
JALAN TUANKU ABDUL RAHMAN
JALAN KUCHING
Sultan Ismail
JALAN SULTAN ISMAIL
Medan Tuanku
JLN MEDAN TUANKU
JALAN DOTAISAMY
JLN KEMUNTING SHAK
JALAN DANG WANGI
JALAN TUN ISMAIL
JALAN KERJA AIR
JALAN SULTAN SALAHUDDIN
JLN TAMINGSARI
PERSIARAN SULTAN SALAHUDDIN
LEBUHRAYA MAHAMERU
PERKARANGAN TUN ISMAIL
JALAN TUN ISMAIL
JLN SELAT
LITTLE INDIA
JALAN RAJA LAUT
LORONG GOMBAK
JLN MASJID INDIA
JALAN MUNSHI ABDULLAH
Bank Negara KTM Station
Bandaraya
See 'Colonial District and Chinatown' map for detail
JALAN PARLIMEN
JALAN TAMINGSARI
Sculpture Garden
National Monument
JALAN PARLIMEN
JALAN BUKIT AMAN
JALAN KINABALU
JALAN RAJA
MERDEKA SQUARE
PERSEK UTOAN
JLN TUN PERAK
Masjid Jamek
Masjid Jamek
JALAN GEREJA
JALAN BUKIT NANAS
JLN BUKIT NANAS
LEBUH PASAR BESAR
JALAN PUDU
Lake Gardens
JALAN CENDERAMULIA
JALAN KEBUN BUNGA
JALAN TEMBUSU
Deer Park
Orchid Garden
RAWASIH
Butterfly Park
JLN CENDERASARI
JLN TUGU
JALAN LEMBAH PERDANA
JALAN BENTENG
JLN HANG KASTURI
Pasar Seni
JALAN TUN SAMBANTHAN
JLN SULTAN MOHAMED
JLN SULTAN HISHAMUDDIN
JALAN HANG JEBAT
JALAN WESLEY
JALAN SULTAN
Tun Abdul Razak Memorial
Bird Park
Museum of Islamic Arts
Masjid Negara
JALAN PESIARAN MAHAMERU
JLN DAMANSARA
Tama Tasek Perdana
JALAN PERDANA
JALAN KEBUN BUNGA
JLN TUN H.S. LEE
JLN BALAI POLIS
JALAN PETALING
Stadium Chinwoo
JALAN KINABALU
KL Train Station
National Planetarium
Sultan Sulaiman
JLN STADIUM
Maharajalela
Chan See Shu Yuen
KL Visitors Centre
JLN SULTAN
Muzium Negara
JALAN SULAIMAN
JLN KG. ATAP
JALAN MAHARAJALELA
JALAN TRAVERS
JALAN DAMANSARA
KL Sentral Train Station
JLN TUN SAMBANTHAN
JLN SCOTT
S. Kelang
JLN SYED PUTRA
JLN ISTANA
JALAN BELFIELD
JALAN HOSE
JLN TALALLA
CT PERSEKUTUAN
Bangsar, 8, 9, 10, 11 & Airport (63km)

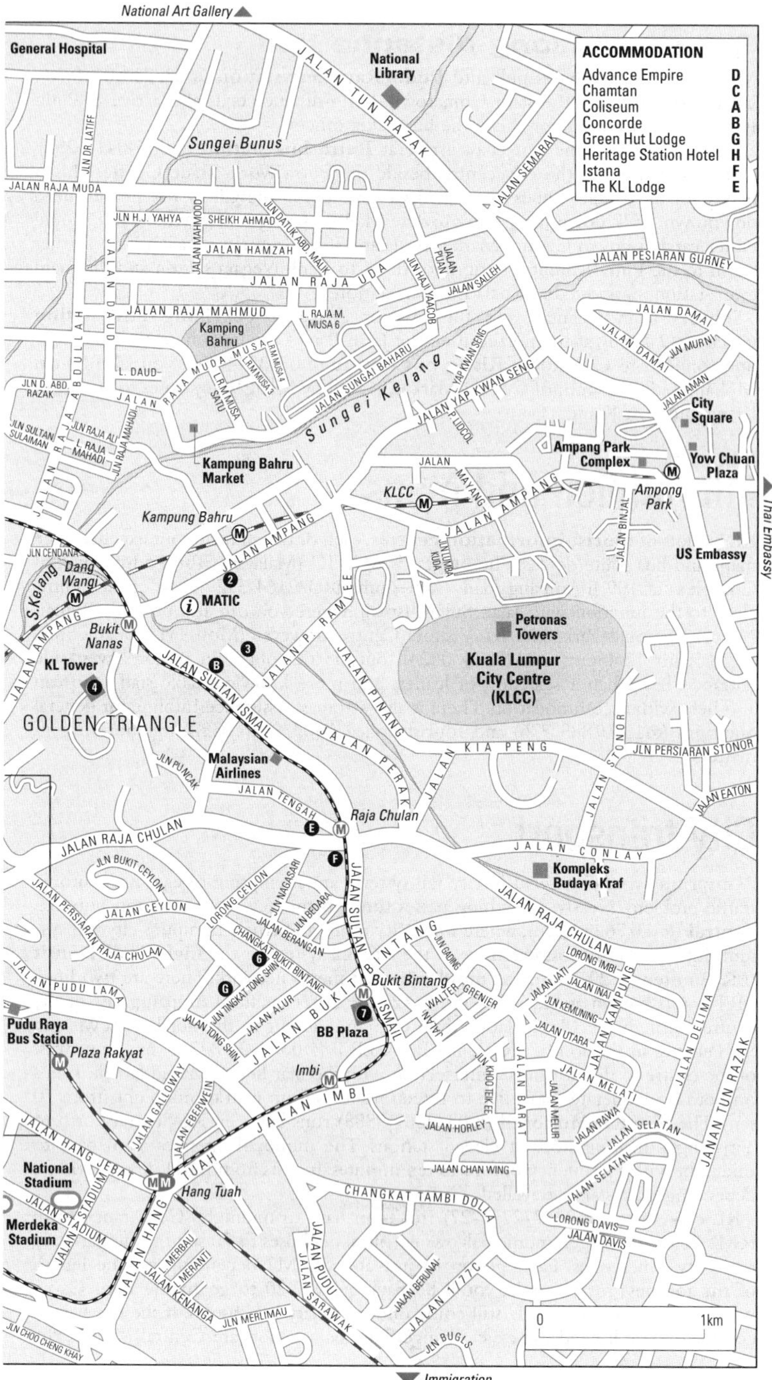
National Art Gallery
General Hospital
National Library
ACCOMMODATION
Advance Empire D
Chamtan C
Coliseum A
Concorde B
Green Hut Lodge G
Heritage Station Hotel H
Istana F
The KL Lodge E
JALAN TUN RAZAK
Sungei Bunus
JLN DR. LATIFF
JALAN RAJA MUDA
JALAN SEMARAK
JLN H.J. YAHYA
SHEIKH AHMAD
JALAN MAHMOOD
JLN DATUK ABD. MALIK
JALAN HAMZAH
JALAN RAJA UDA
JALAN PUAN
JLN HAJI YAACOB
JALAN SALLEH
JALAN PESIARAN GURNEY
JALAN DAUD
JALAN RAJA MAHMUD
L. RAJA M. MUSA 6
Kamping Bahru
JALAN ABDULLAH
JALAN DAMAI
JLN MURNI
JLN YAP KWAN SENG
L. DAUD
JLN D. ABD. RAZAK
JALAN RAJA MUDA MUSA
LRM MUSA 4
LRM MUSA 3
LRM MUSA SATU
JALAN SUNGAI BAHARU
Sungei Kelang
JALAN YAP KWAN SENG
JALAN AMAN
City Square
JLN SULTAN SULAIMAN
JLN RAJA ALI
L. RAJA MAHADI
JLN RAJA MAHADI
P. LIDCOL
Kampung Bahru Market
JALAN MAYANG
Ampang Park Complex
Yow Chuan Plaza
KLCC
Ampong Park
Thai Embassy
Kampung Bahru
JALAN AMPANG
JALAN BINJAI
US Embassy
JLN CENDANA
Dang Wangi
S. Kelang
JLN LIMBA KUDA
MATIC
Bukit Nanas
JALAN P. RAMLEE
Petronas Towers
KL Tower
JALAN SULTAN ISMAIL
Kuala Lumpur City Centre (KLCC)
JALAN PINANG
GOLDEN TRIANGLE
JALAN STONOR
JLN PERSIARAN STONOR
JALAN KIA PENG
Malaysian Airlines
JLN PUNCAK
JALAN PERAK
JALAN EATON
JALAN TENGAH
Raja Chulan
JALAN RAJA CHULAN
JALAN CONLAY
JLN BUKIT CEYLON
Kompleks Budaya Kraf
LORONG CEYLON
JLN NAGASARI
JALAN PERSIARAN RAJA CHULAN
JALAN CEYLON
JLN BEDARA
JALAN BERANGAN
CHANGKAT BUKIT BINTANG
JALAN BUKIT BINTANG
JLN GADING
LORONG IMBI
JALAN PUDU LAMA
JLN TINGKAT TONG SHIN
Bukit Bintang
JALAN JATI
JALAN INAI
JALAN WALTER GRENIER
JLN KEMUNING
JALAN ALUR
JALAN TONG SHIN
BB Plaza
JALAN KAMPUNG
JALAN DELIMA
Pudu Raya Bus Station
JALAN UTARA
JALAN TUN RAZAK
Plaza Rakyat
JLN KHOO TEIK EE
JALAN BARAT
Imbi
JALAN MELATI
JALAN MELUR
JALAN IMBI
JALAN GALLOWAY
JALAN EBERWEIN
JALAN RAWA
JALAN SELATAN
JALAN HORLEY
JALAN HANG JEBAT
JALAN TUAH
JALAN CHAN WING
National Stadium
JALAN STADIUM
Hang Tuah
CHANGKAT TAMBI DOLLA
JALAN SELATAN
Merdeka Stadium
LORONG DAVIS
JALAN DAVIS
JALAN HANG TUAH
L. MERBAU
L. MERANTI
JALAN KENANGA
JALAN PUDU
JALAN SARAWAK
JALAN BERUNAI
JALAN 1/77C
JLN MERLIMAU
JLN CHOO CHENG KHAY
JLN BUGIS
0
1km
Immigration

By bus and long-distance taxi

Most long-distance buses pull into **Pudu Raya bus station** (☎03/230 0145) on Jalan Pudu, just to the east of Chinatown. Long-distance taxis also arrive at Pudu Raya, on the second floor above the bus ticket offices.

Some buses from the east coast arrive at **Putra bus station** (☎03/4041 1295), to the northwest of the city centre, beside the Putra World Trade Centre. This is handy for the budget hotels on Jalan Raja Laut and in the Chow Kit area. To head downtown, walk down Jalan Putra to The Mall shopping centre, where you should either catch a bus to Central Market on Jalan Hang Kasturi or walk a little further south to the Putra Komuter station, for trains to Bank Negara station and the main train station, signposted as Kuala Lumpur station.

Services from Kuantan and the interior arrive at **Pekeliling bus station** (☎03/4042 7988), at the northern end of Jalan Raja Laut; from here, the Star LRT line connects to Chinatown. **Klang bus station** (☎03/3344 8066) on Jalan Sultan Mohammed, just south of Central Market, is used by Klang Valley buses to and from Klang and Port Klang.

Information and maps

KL has lots of **tourist information centres**, each of which hands out excellent free maps and bus route details. The biggest is MATIC (Malaysian Tourist Information Complex) at 109 Jl Ampang (daily 9am–6pm; ☎03/2164 3929), east of the centre, close to the junction with Jalan Sultan Ismail, where you can also book for Taman Negara National Park. The KL Visitors Centre, however (Mon–Fri 8.30am–5pm, Sat 8.30am–12.45pm; ☎03/2274 0624), outside the old train station's west-side entrance, has a better selection of leaflets and more knowledgeable staff who can also help with accommodation. There is also a Tourist Assistance Infoline for general questions (☎1300/885 776) and Tourist Police (☎03/2146 0522) for more urgent matters.

City transport

A surprisingly efficient grid of city rail systems are attempting to ease KL's chronic traffic problem. Nearly everything passes through the new transportation hub, **KL Sentral** (☎03/7625 8228), where inter-city trains and Kuala Lumpur's city rail systems interface. The most extensive of the city rail systems is the **Light Rail Transit** (LRT) system, a 29-kilometre, mostly elevated metro network. There are two lines. LRT1, also known as Star LRT (☎03/4294 2550), runs from Ampang, east of the centre, through the Masjid Jamek hub to Sentul Timur in the north of town and Sri Petaling in the south. LRT2, aka Putra LRT (☎03/7625 8228) runs from west of the centre to the northeast, intersecting with the Star line at Masjid Jamek. Trains on both lines operate every five to fifteen minutes from 6am to midnight (from 70 sen). The new **KL Monorail** (☎03/2267 9888) runs between KL Sentral north to Titiwangsa, making stops at eleven stations. The monorail operates from 6am to midnight with a frequency of four to ten minutes. It costs from RM1.20 to RM2.50 depending on distance travelled.

KL **city buses** (☎03/7727 2727) run from 6am to midnight. Costs range from RM1.20 on the larger, municipal-owned Intrakota buses to 70 sen on the privately run City Liner ones. Fares go up to just above RM2 depending on the length of the journey; for example, you'll be paying RM2.20 to go to the Batu Caves, which, although outside KL, still come under the city bus system. If the bus has no conductor, you'll need the exact change. The main depots are Central Market, the

Jalan Sultan Mohammed terminus (opposite Klang bus station), 100m south of the market, and Lebuh Ampang, on the northern edge of Chinatown.

If you're planning to stay in KL for more than a week, consider getting an **integrated bus and train card**, called Touch And Go, available from the main LRT stations and at KL Sentral. The minimum price is RM20; each fare is electronically deducted from the sum on your card when you go through the turnstiles. The downside is the RM15 deposit for the card, which you're unlikely to see again on account of the form-filling required for a refund.

Taxi fares start at RM2 and rise RM1 per kilometre; recommended cab companies are Mesra Taxis (☎03/4042 1019), City Line (☎03/9222 2828) and Sunlight Radio Teksi (☎03/9057 1111). Many taxi drivers can't speak English, and some don't know their way around the city, so it's best to carry a map.

The **Komuter train** (☎03/2267 1200) is of limited use in central KL, but is handy for sights outside the city. There are two lines – one from Rawang to Seremban (for Nilai), the other from Sentul to Port Klang (for Sumatra). Both connect at the central KL stations of Putra, Bank Negara and KL Sentral. Trains run at least every thirty minutes and tickets start at RM1; a RM5 day-ticket (valid Mon–Fri after 9.30am) allows unlimited travel.

Accommodation

Most travellers head for the **hotels** of Chinatown, though Little India has become a valid budget and mid-range alternative. There are a few inexpensive places close to the Pudu Raya bus station and around Jalan Pudu. Further east, the Golden Triangle – roughly the area inside Jalan Raja Chulan, Jalan Sultan Ismail and Jalan Ampang – is where the first-class hotels are situated. Many of these hotels offer excellent deals, and are worth checking out. West and north of Little India and Chinatown, the hotels along the two-kilometre stretch of Jalan Tuanku Abdul Rahman (often known as Jalan TAR) include some of the sleaziest and most infamous in town. Suffice to say, there's no need to book in advance. As with Singapore's crash pads, bedbugs can be a problem at some of KL's cheapest places.

Around Chinatown

Backpackers Travellers Inn 1st Floor, 60 Jl Sultan ☎03/2078 2473. Centrally located, with small, clean rooms – some a/c – and a dorm (RM10 per bed). Its rooftop bar is a highly convivial spot. The friendly staff go to great lengths to help guests, and provide numerous services. ❷

Backpackers Travellers Lodge 1st Floor, 158 Jl Tun HS Lee ☎03/2031 0889. Recommended sister operation, with a range of clean rooms – some a/c – and dorms (RM10). Also Internet access. Owner Stevie also runs excellent, inexpensive tours to Kuala Selangor Nature Park and the Kampung Kuantan fireflies in one trip (see p.649). ❸

Furama Kompleks Selangor, Jl Sultan ☎03/2070 1777. Modern a/c hotel with ambitions to join the top ranks – it comes close with comfortable and well-equipped rooms. ❻

Heritage Station Hotel Old KL train station, Jl Sultan Hishamuddin ☎03/2273 4522. Located within the old Moorish train station, this place has wonderful colonial atmosphere and is very central. Rumour has it that the hotel will be sold to an international chain, refurbished and upgraded, so enjoy it now while it's still reasonably priced. ❹

Leng Nam 165 Jl Tun HS Lee ☎03/2070 1489. In the heart of the quarter, this traditional Chinese hotel has small rooms with two large beds and shared facilities. A rather gothic air of decrepitude hangs over the place, and the staff are refreshingly indifferent. ❷

Lok Ann 113a Jl Petaling ☎03/2078 9544. Neat, reasonable-value hotel, with full facilities, though the rooms are rather charmless. ❹

Swiss Inn 62 Jl Sultan ☎03/2032 3333. Aptly named, this is a newish midrange place where everything works and the staff are efficient. ❻

Travellers Moon Lodge 36b Jl Silang ☎03/2070 6601. Just south of Jl Tun Perak, this popular lodge includes a dorm, small rooms and a roof terrace. Bring a sarong – the staff expect you to provide your own sheets. ❷

Wheelers Guest House 2nd Floor, 131–133 Jl Tun HS Lee ☎03/2070 1386. Owned by the same people that run the two Backpackers Travellers places, this hostel is clean, has new beds throughout, and provides a comprehensive range of useful services. A/c dorms (RM10). ❷

YWCA 12 Jl Hang Jebat ☎03/238 3225. Delightful, good-value, peaceful hostel that only rents its clean, comfortable singles and doubles to women, couples and families. ❸

Little India and Jalan TAR

Advance Empire 48b Jl Masjid India ☎03/2693 6890. A good deal, with en-suite rooms, and discounts for stays of over a month. ❸

Chamtan 62 Jl Masjid India ☎2693 0144. A good choice in the centre of Little India, with practical rooms boasting TVs and attached bathrooms. ❹

Coliseum 98 Jl TAR ☎03/2692 6270. They don't make them like KL's most famous old-style hotel any more. The lobby bar is deliciously seedy, oozes atmosphere and is full of exotic characters. ❸

Around Pudu Raya

Anuja Backpackers Inn 1st Floor, 28 Jl Pudu ☎03/2026 6479. Every service a backpacker could imagine has been anticipated at this tidy hostel with the full range of rooms, near Pudu Raya bus station. ❷

Kawana Tourist Inn 68 Jl Pudu Lama ☎03/2078 6714. Neat, small, very-good-value rooms in a modern place only two minutes' walk from Pudu Raya bus station. ❸

KL City Lodge 16 Jl Pudu ☎03/2070 5275. Convenient, but can be noisy. Dorms (RM12) and a/c rooms; laundry service and free lockers. ❷

The Golden Triangle

Concorde 2 Jl Sultan Ismail ☎03/2144 2200. The trendiest of the area's hotels, housing the *Hard Rock Café* and fashionable boutiques. Large rooms with full facilities. Price includes breakfast and airport pick-up. ❼

Green Hut Lodge 48 Jl Tingkat Tong Shin ☎03/2142 2112. Newly opened hostel-type place with common kitchen and lounge. Dorms RM8. ❷

Istana 73 Jl Raja Chulan ☎03/2141 9988. One of KL's best hotels. Palace-like decor, tropical plants, swimming pool and high-quality rooms. Ask about their promotions. ❾

The KL Lodge 2 Jl Tengah ☎03/2142 0122. One of the best-value deals in the Golden Triangle area, with motel-style rooms, its own restaurant, and a café by the swimming pool. ❻

The City

Despite much modernization, much of Kuala Lumpur's appeal – markets, temples and historic mosques – remains intact. The city centre is quite compact, with the **Colonial District** centred on Merdeka Square; close by, across the river and to the north, **Chinatown** and **Little India** are the two main traditional commercial districts. One of the most prominent (and busiest) of KL's central streets, Jalan Tunku Abdul Rahman, or **Jalan TAR**, as it's often known, runs due north from Merdeka Square for 2km to Chow Kit Market; closer in, west of the square, are the **Lake Gardens**, while to the south lie the **Masjid Negara** (National Mosque), the new **Islamic Arts Museum**, the landmark **Old KL train station** and the **Muzium Negara** (National Museum). From Merdeka Square, congested Jalan Tun Perak leads southeast to the Pudu Raya bus station, a kilometre further east of which is the fashionable consumer sector known as the **Golden Triangle**. Many of the city's expensive hotels, nightclubs and modern malls line the three main boulevards of Jalan Bukit Bintang, Jalan Imbi and Jalan Sultan Ismail. Its main landmarks are the lofty **KL** and **Petronas Towers**, which, at just over 490m high, were the tallest buildings in the world from 1996 until 2003. At the time of writing, there were no tours being given and only the first four floors, part of a shopping arcade, were open to the general public.

South and West of Merdeka Square

The small **Colonial District** is centred on the beautifully tended **Merdeka Square** on the west bank of the Klang: Malaysian Independence (merdeka, or freedom) was proclaimed here on August 31, 1957. Nearby, to the south, the **National Museum of History** (daily 9am–6pm; free), on the corner of Jalan Raja, provides an informative romp through the main points of the nation's history, from the geological formation of the Peninsula to former Prime Minister Mahathir's Vision 2020. South along Jalan Sultan Hishamuddin, the 35-storey Dayabumi Complex is home to the

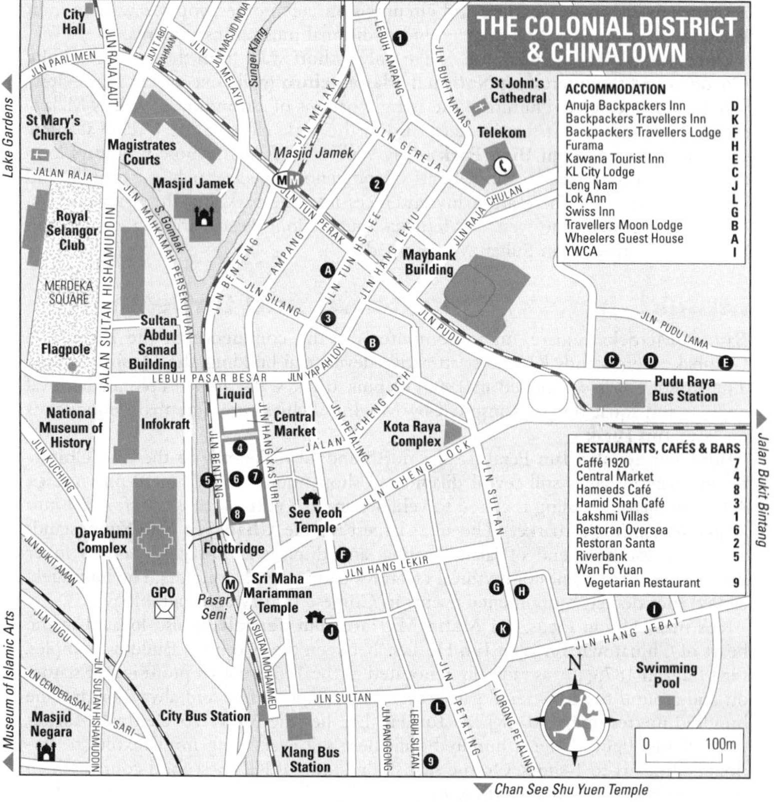

national oil company, Petronas, which maintains the excellent Galeri Petronas, on the ground floor, displaying contemporary Malaysian art.

Continuing south down Jalan Sultan Hishamuddin, you'll see the impressive seventy-metre-high minaret and geometric lattice work of the **Masjid Negara**, the National Mosque (daily 9am–noon, 3–4pm & 5.30–6.30pm; closed Fri mornings). To enter, you need to be properly dressed: robes can be borrowed from the desk at the entrance. Behind the mosque on Jalan Lembah Perdana is the ultra-modern **Museum of Islamic Arts** (Tues–Sun 10am–6pm; RM8). This fascinating collection of textiles, metalwork and ancient Korans is a must-see, as it's the first of its type in the world. Check out the calligraphic section, which includes hand-written sections of the Koran, some dating back a thousand years, and many of them intricate and beautiful.

A hundred metres south, the 1911 **Old KL train station** (the KTM Komuter Railway's Kuala Lumpur station), with its spires, minarets, domes and arches is probably the city's most famous building. Similar in concept to the British-era train station in Rangoon, Burma, Kuala Lumpur's old train station was a successful attempt at hybridizing European and culturally indigenous architectural motifs. Of all the European (and American) colonial-era structures in Southeast Asia, the old KL train station is quite possibly the most memorable. Ten minutes' walk west along Jalan Damansara brings you to the extensive ethnographic and archeological exhibits of the **Muzium Negara,** Malaysia's National Museum (daily 9am–6pm; RM1). Alongside dioramas of traditional Malaysian life, from simple kampung (village) activities to elaborate wedding and circumcision ceremonies, you see wayang kulit (shadow play) puppets, kris daggers, and traditional musical instruments.

Once at the National Museum you're only a short walk from the extensive **Lake Gardens** and the interesting **National Planetarium** (daily except Fri 10am–5pm; RM1), where displays illuminate the Islamic origins of astronomy as well as Malaysia's modern-day thrust for the stars. Also in the park, close to the Orchid Garden, you'll find the excellent **Bird Park** (daily 9am–6pm; RM8), whose walkways loop around streams to take in the habitats of indigenous species such as hornbills and the Brahminy Kite. There are many entrances into the park, but the main one is a thirty-minute walk due west of Merdeka Square along Jalan Parlimen, or you can take bus #21 from Jalan Sultan Mohammed.

Masjid Jamek, Chinatown and Little India

East of Merdeka Square, on a promontory at the confluence of the Klang and Gombak rivers, stands KL's most attractive devotional building, the **Masjid Jemek**. The mosque was completed in 1909, its pink brick walls, arched colonnades, oval cupolas and squat minarets inspired by Moghul architecture. The main entrance is on Jalan Tun Perak.

Bordered by Jalan Tun Perak to the north and Jalan Petaling to the east, **Chinatown**'s narrow lanes still reveal dilapidated shop-houses and Chinese pharmacies. After 6pm, Jalan Petaling is closed to vehicles and the entire area is transformed into a *pasar malam* (night market). The area's largest temple, **Chan See Shu Yuen**, stands at the far southern end of Jalan Petaling, and displays an ornately painted inner shrine covered in scenes of mythical creatures battling with warriors. The intricately carved roof depicts monumental events in Chinese history and mythology.

KL's main Hindu focus, **Sri Maha Mariamman Temple**, is also located in the heart of Chinatown, on Jalan Tun HS Lee, between the two main Buddhist temples. First built in 1873, it was radically renovated in the 1960s with a profusion of statues on and around the five-tiered gate tower. The temple is free and always open. One hundred metres due west of Jalan Tun HS Lee lies the Art Deco **Central Market** (daily 9am–10pm). Over a hundred stalls here sell everything from textiles to stationery, fine art to T-shirts. On the first floor is one of KL's best food courts, which serves excellent Indian and Malay food.

Just to the north of Chinatown, compact Little India is the commercial centre for KL's Indian community. Turning into Jalan Masjid India from Jalan Tun Perak, it's soon clear you've entered the Tamil part of the city, with *poori* and *samosa* vendors and cloth salesmen vying for positions on the crowded streets.

Chow Kit and the National Art Gallery

Two kilometres due north of Central Market along Jalan TAR lies **Chow Kit**, a daily market that sells anything and everything. There are excellent hawker stalls here, a great variety of textiles and clothes, as well as fish, meat and vegetables. Close by on the orbital highway, Jalan Tun Razak, you'll find the **National Art Gallery** (daily 10am–6pm; free), recently relocated here, which houses a disappointing permanent collection of Malaysian artists alongside temporary exhibitions of fine art and mixed media from a wider net of Southeast Asian artists.

Eating

All the **restaurants** listed here are open daily from 10am until midnight, unless otherwise stated. Phone numbers are given where you need to book ahead. Most **Malay** restaurants in KL serve a limited range of dishes, so for a wider selection you'll need to dine out at one of the big hotels, many of which offer special buffets.

Finding good **Chinese** or **Tamil** and **North Indian** food is much easier: it's served in cafés and restaurants in both Chinatown and Little India. In Little India especially, the cafés and hawker stalls do a manic trade at lunchtime in excellent banana-leaf curries, *murtabak*, *dosai* and *roti*. Thai restaurants are also popular and can be found all over the city. The trendiest area in KL to eat and drink in the evening is **Bangsar**, around 4km west of the centre (take any Bangsar bus from the Central Market), with over a dozen top-notch restaurants and two hawkers' areas – one inside a giant hangar, the other in the adjoining street.

Chinatown and Little India

Bilai Restaurant 33 Jl Ampang, Little India. At the city-centre end of Jl Ampang, this North Indian restaurant is particularly popular for its chicken and mutton curries. About RM15 for two people.

Caffé 1920 1st Floor, Central Market, Jl Hang Kasturi. Small and chic café serving authentic Italian specialities, including tiramisu and various gateaux, along with light pasta dishes. Excellent pasta, pastries and great coffee make this place perfect for brunch. Daily 10am-10pm.

Central Market 1st and 2nd Floors, Jl Hang Kasturi. Best are the superb Malay stalls on the top floor where plates of nasi campur cost just RM2.50.

Hameeds Café Ground Floor, Central Market, Jl Hang Kasturi. Superb, busy North Indian café serving tandoori chicken, curries and rice dishes.

Hamid Shah Café 30 Jl Silang, Chinatown. Excellent, busy café for Malay and North Indian curries and *roti*. Very good value at around RM10–12 for two. Open 6.30am–11pm.

Lakshmi Villas Lebuh Ampang, Little India. On the edge of Chinatown, this is the best South Indian café in KL. The ground floor serves various delicious *dosais*; the first floor specializes in banana-leaf curries, a bargain at around RM6 for two. Daily 7.30am–8.30pm.

Restoran Oversea Central Market, Jl Hang Kasturi ☎2274 6407. Clean and efficient Chinese restaurant aimed at the mainstream tourist market, where the dishes include baby king duck, and fried *meekon* with shredded cuttlefish. Around RM25 for two.

Restoran Santa 9 Jl Tun HS Lee (Little India end). Nicknamed the "chapati house", a lively place, best at midday to mid-afternoon, with delicious chapatis, and curries for around RM5.

Wan Fo Yuan Vegetarian Restaurant 8 Jl Panggong, Chinatown. The area's best-known vegetarian restaurant serving excellent tofu and vegetable dishes.

Golden Triangle

Le Coq D'Or 121 Jl Ampang ☎03/2142 9732. A corner of old colonial KL preserved in a converted tin tycoon's mansion. It's worth coming for a drink on the veranda, even if you don't want to sample the French, Malay and Chinese cuisine (RM40 a head). Dress smartish.

Modestos 94 Jl P Ramlee. Sprawling pizza and pasta joint with a lively bar.

Rasa Utara BB Plaza, Jl Bukit Bintang. This is a local chain with a moderately priced northern Malay menu: the *mee goreng istimewa* is an appetizing regional variation on a traditional dish.

Seri Angkasa KL Tower ☎03/2020 5057. Revolving restaurant that serves an excellent lunch, high tea and dinner buffets atop KL's landmark tower. Smart dress (no shorts and sandals) essential for dinner, which costs as little as RM100 for two.

Bangsar

Alexis Bistro 29 Jl Telawi Tiga ☎03/2284 2880. Big helpings of designer food, including Sarawak laksa, for KL's growing cappuccino class. Excellent pastries, too, at a buzzy hangout. Open noon–midnight.

Annalakshmi Mid Valley Megamall, Lingkaran Syed Putra ☎03/2282 3799. Sensational Indian restaurant adorned with antiques from the sub-continent, and boasting eighteen varieties of *dosai*. Closed Mon.

Bangsar Seafood Village Jl Telawi Empat. Busy Chinese favourite and an institution among *metsallehs* ("foreigners") and KL foodies. The chilli and cashew chicken dishes are a must. Plenty of outside seating.

Nightlife and entertainment

Most **bars** are open from noon until midnight. The music played at **clubs** is mostly US house and the lighter styles of techno. Entrance charges are around RM20 including a drink. The best place to see **traditional theatre** and **music** is at the

Malaysian Tourist Information Complex (MATIC), 109 Jl Ampang (☎03/2164 3929), which does costumed shows – call for show times.

Bars and live music

Echo Jl Telawi 2, Bangsar. Neon, quite minimal, but with comfortable sofas, this is a great bar for mid-evening through to the early hours. Local DJs provide a fine soundtrack with jazz earlier and house music later on.

Hard Rock Café *Concorde Hotel*, 2 Jl Sultan Ismail. Features well-known rock bands and gets packed on Friday and Saturday nights – there's a cover charge if you're not eating. Open 11am–2am.

Little Havana Changkat Bukit Bintang. Unpretentious cigar bar downstairs with a club upstairs featuring Friday night Salsa Night. Also serves salsa-style food.

Monkey Bar Jl Putra. Located in the *Legend Hotel*, on Fridays and Saturdays this place has a band with a very loyal following that does early 80s New Wave tunes.

Riverbank Central Market, Jl Benteng. Well-placed bar, opposite the river. Mostly a place to relax and have a break while exploring the Central Market.

Clubs

Beach Club Cafe 97 Jl P Ramlee. Every night is party night for a fun-loving crowd in a feelgood Club Tropicana atmosphere. Good food, unique spur-of-the-moment cocktails, and grass skirts abound. Daily noon–3am; happy hour 5–9pm.

Blue Moon Lounge *Hotel Equatorial*, Jl Sultan Ismail (opposite the MAS Building). Exclusive and crawling with lounge lizards, this is a nightclub in the old sense of the word. It's also the only place where you'll hear Malaysian golden oldies from the 1950s, French schmaltz and the golden-voiced P Ramlee. Open 7pm–midnight.

Flux 12 Jl Sultan Ismail. State of the art club with a capacity of 4000, catering to the thirty-something executive set. Open daily 6pm–3am; happy hour until 10pm.

Liquid Central Market annexe. With its young, gay and friendly weekend crowd, this superb, small atmospheric club is a must for house-music fans. Open Fri & Sat 10pm–3am.

Markets and shopping

Most of KL's malls are open daily from 10am to 10pm; elsewhere, shops are usually open daily from 9am to 6pm. However, most locals do their shopping at the **markets**. The Central Market is among the most popular (see p.644); the nearby Jalan Petaling market (daily 9am–10pm) is equally crowded and lively; and the sprawling Chow Kit market on Jalan Haji Hussein, off Jalan TAR (daily 9am–5pm), is quite an experience, with its warren of stalls selling everything from animals' brains to quality batik textiles. There's a good weekly night market at Pasar Minggu, Jalan Raja Muda Musa, Kampung Bharu (Sat 6pm–1am).

Recommended outlets for **handicrafts** and **batiks** include Aked Ibu Kota on Jalan TAR, opposite the Coliseum; Central Market on Jalan Hang Kasturi, where you can see the craftsmen at work; Infokraft, Jalan Sultan Hishamuddin, which deals in work by government-sponsored craftmakers; Kompleks Budaya Kraf, Jalan Conlay, which offers all of Malaysia's crafts under one roof, beside the MISC Museum; and Wisma Batek, Jalan Tun Perak, where shirts, sarongs, bags and paintings are inexpensive. More upmarket is Peter How, 2 Jl Hang Lekir, a stone's throw from Central Market, with beautiful bags, batik shirts and sarongs, as well as locally made and Indonesian crafts.

For English-language **books** try Berita Book Centre, BB Plaza; MPH, Jalan Telawi Lima, Bangsar; Times Books, Yow Chuan Plaza, Jalan Ampang; Minerva Book Store, 114 Jl TAR; and Yaohan Book Store, 2nd Floor, The Mall, Jalan Putra. KL is full of **shopping malls**, especially in the Golden Triangle, where you'll find BB Plaza on Jalan Bukit Bintang, which has excellent deals on cameras, electronic equipment, shoes and much else besides. Lot 10 Shopping Centre, junction of Jalan Bukit Bintang and Jalan Sultan Ismail, specializes in designer clothes, sportswear and music.

Listings

Airline offices Most airlines have offices in and around the Golden Triangle. Major airlines include: Aeroflot, Ground Floor, 1 Jl Perak ☎03/2161 0231; American Airlines, Angkasa Raya Building, 123 Jl Ampang ☎03/2078 1168; Bangladesh Airlines, Subang Airport ☎03/2148 3765; British Airways, 8 Jl Perak ☎1800/881 260; Cathay Pacific, UBN Tower, 10 Jl P Ramlee ☎03/2078 3377; China Airlines, Level 3, Amoda Building, 22 Jl Imbi ☎03/2142 7344; Delta Airlines, UBN Tower, 10 Jl P Ramlee ☎03/2691 5490; Garuda, 1st Floor, Angkasa Raya Building, 123 Jl Ampang ☎03/2162 2811; Japan Airlines, 20th Floor, Jl Ampang, Menara Lion ☎03/2161 1722; KLM, Shop 7, Ground Floor, President House, Jl Sultan Ismail ☎03/2711 9811; MAS, MAS Building, Jl Sultan Ismail ☎03/2161 0555; Pelangi Air, c/o MAS ☎03/262 4448; Qantas, 8 Jl Perak ☎1800/881 260; Royal Brunei, 1st Floor, Wisma Merlin, Jl Sultan Ismail ☎03/2070 7166; Singapore Airlines, Wisma SIA, 2 Jl Sang Wangi ☎03/2692 3122; Thai International, Wisma Goldhill Building, 67 Jl Raja Chulan ☎03/2031 2900; United Airlines, MAS Building, Jl Sultan Ismail ☎03/2161 1433.

Banks and exchange Main branches are: Bank Bumiputra, 6 Jl Tun Perak ☎03/2693 1722; HSBC, 2 Lebuh Ampang, Little India ☎03/2070 0744; Standard Chartered Bank, 2 Jl Ampang ☎03/2072 6555. Almost all of their branches change money (Mon–Fri 10am–4pm, Sat 9am–12.30pm), but you get better rates from official moneychangers, of which there are scores in the main city areas; the kiosk below the GPO, on Jl Sultan Hishamuddin, also gives good rates.

Car rental All main companies have offices at the airport; or contact Avis, 40 Jl Sultan Ismail ☎03/2141 7144; Budget, 29 Jl Yap Kwan Seng ☎03/2142 4693; Hertz, International Complex, Jl Sultan Ismail ☎03/2148 6433; National Car Rental, 9th Floor, Menara Bausted, 69 Jl Raja Chulan ☎03/2148 0522.

Embassies and consulates Australia, Jl Yap Kwan Seng ☎03/2146 5555; Brunei, 113 Jl U Thant ☎03/2161 2800; Cambodia, 83-JKR 2809 Lingkungan U Thant ☎03/4257 1150; Canada, 7th Floor, Osk Plaza, 172 Jl Ampang ☎03/2718 3333; China, 229 Jl Ampang ☎03/2142 8495; Indonesia, 233 Jl Tun Razak ☎03/2145 2011; Japan, 11 Persiaran Stonor ☎03/2142 7044; Laos, 108 Jl Damai ☎03/4251 1118; Netherlands, 4 Jl Mesra, off Jl Damai ☎03/2168 6200; New Zealand, Menara IMC ☎03/2078 2533; Philippines, 1 Jl Changkat Kia Peng ☎03/2848 9989; Thailand, 206 Jl Ampang ☎03/2148 8222; UK, 185 Jl Ampang ☎03/2148 2122; USA, 376 Jl Tun Razak ☎03/2168 5000; Vietnam, 4 Persiaran Stonor ☎03/2148 8060.

Emergencies Dial ☎999 for ambulance, police or fire. For the tourist police, call ☎03/2140 6590.

Hospitals and clinics General Hospital, Jl Pahang ☎03/2615 5555; Assunta Hospital, Petaling Jaya ☎03/7782 3433; Pantai, Jl Pantai, off Jl Bangsar, Bangsar ☎03/2282 5077; Tung Shin Hospital, Jl Pudu ☎03/2072 1655. There are 24hr casualty wards at all of the above.

Immigration Block 24G, Pusat Pentadbiran Kerajaan Persekutuan, Putrajaya (Mon–Fri 9am–4.30pm; ☎03/8880 1000). This is where you come for visa extensions.

Internet access Adamz Cyber Café, Lot 2, Annexe, Central Market; Dataran Cyber Café, Ground Floor, Medan Mara Building, Jl Raja Laut; Easy Access, 146a Jl Bukit Bintang (in front of *Planet Hollywood*); Golden Date Internet Zone, 1st Floor, City One Plaza, Jl Musha Abdullah; Hotspace Cyber Café, 354 Jl Raja Laut; Star Surf, 105 Jl Sultan (opp Rex Cinema). In Bangsar, 4km west of the city centre: Poem, 38a Jl Telawi 5; Surf, 54 Jl Maarof.

Pharmacy Kota Raya Pharmacy, 1st Floor, Kota Raya Plaza Complex Jl Cheng Lock, Chinatown.

Police The main tourist police station, where you must report stolen property and claim your insurance form, is 1PK, Jl Hang Tuah (☎03/2140 6590). It's opposite the old Pudu Jail.

Post office Poste restante at the GPO on Jl Sultan Hishamuddin, opposite Central Market (Mon–Fri 8am–4pm, Sat 8am–2pm).

Telephone services The cheapest places to make international calls are the Telekom Malaysia offices; the largest branch is in Wisma Jothi, Jl Gereja (daily Mon–Sun 8.30am–9pm).

Travel agencies Reliance Travel, 12 Jl Yap Kwen Seng ☎03/2162 8181; STA, 5th Floor, Magnum Plaza, 128 Jl Pudu ☎03/2148 9800; Tina Travel, 30 Jl Mamarda, Ampang Point ☎03/4257 8877.

Around KL

The biggest attractions **around KL** are north of the city, where limestone peaks rise up out of the forest and the roads narrow as you pass through small kampungs. There is dramatic scenery as close as 13km from the city, where the Hindu shrine at the **Batu Caves** attracts enough visitors to make it one of Malaysia's main tourist attractions. Further north, the **Orang Asli Museum** offers a fascinating insight into the Peninsula's native inhabitants, and the **Forestry Research Institute of Malaysia** (FRIM) encompasses the nearest portion of primary rainforest to the capital. Southwest of KL, the most alluring place is **Klang**, Selangor's first capital, location of a fascinating tin museum. **Ferries to Sumatra** leave from Port Klang, 8km southwest of Klang. A little further north along the coast, **Kuala Selangor Nature Park** and the fireflies at Kuala Kuantan are worth a visit.

The Batu Caves

Long before you reach the entrance to the **Batu Caves**, you can see them ahead: small, black holes in the vast limestone hills, 13km north of the city centre. Since 1891, the caves have sheltered Hindu shrines, and today they're surrounded by shops selling religious paraphernalia. The caves are always packed with visitors, never more so than during the three-day Thaipusam festival held at the beginning of every year. To the left of the staircase up to the main Temple Cave, a small path strikes off to the Art Gallery (daily 8.30am–7pm; RM1), which contains dozens of striking multi-coloured statues and murals, portraying scenes from the Hindu scriptures. At the top of the main staircase, Subramaniam Swamy Temple (daily 8am–7pm) is set deep in a huge cave, its walls lined with idols representing the six lives of Lord Subramaniam. The whole place is swarming with monkeys and they can turn vicious if you tease them with food. To get to the caves, catch bus #11d (30min) from the Bangkok Bank, outside Central Market.

The Orang Asli Museum

Located 24km north of the city, KL's **Orang Asli Museum** (Mon–Thurs & Sun 9am–5.30pm; free) provides a fine illustration of the cultural richness of the Orang Asli ("the first people"), Malaysia's indigenous inhabitants. Orang Asli groups are found in just about every part of the region, many of them maintaining a virtually pre-industrial lifestyle, and pursuing their traditional occupations in some isolation. Bus #174 leaves from Lebuh Ampang in Little India (every 30min; 50min); the museum stop is beside two rundown shops, but ask the driver to tell you when you've arrived.

The Forestry Research Institute of Malaysia

If you don't make it out to Taman Negara and its canopy walkway, you can stroll through the tree-tops at the **Forestry Research Institute of Malaysia**, or FRIM (walkway open Tues–Sat & second Sun of each month 8.30am–4.30pm; RM5; ☎03/6274 2633; prior booking required). The hourly bus #94 from next to the Bangkok Bank takes you there in about an hour (RM1.60). The canopy walkway, ten minutes' walk from the Institute's main building, takes about twenty minutes to cross and provides a unique view of KL's skyscrapers through the trees. As with all hikes into Malaysia's forests, bring plenty of drinking water, insect repellent and decent shoes. There are plenty of other treks within FRIM's fifteen square kilometres, as well as a museum (Mon–Thurs & Sat 8am–4.15pm).

Port Klang and on to Indonesia

You can catch a ferry to Tanjung Balai in Sumatra, Indonesia, from **PORT KLANG**, 38km southwest of KL in Selangor State. The six-times-weekly sailing is at 11am and takes three and a half hours (RM100 plus RM15 departure tax). Passport holders of all Western countries (except Peru) must purchase an Indonesian visa on arrival. The best way to get to Port Klang is on the Komuter train (every 30min; RM2.20) from KL's train station, which stops directly opposite the main jetty. Bus #58 from Klang bus station in KL (hourly; 1hr) stops 200m further along the road. The jetty complex has a small café and moneychanger.

Kuala Selangor Nature Park and the fireflies

North of Klang is the small **Kuala Selangor Nature Park** (☎03/889 1208), set in partial primary rainforest; the trails are short but lead to hides that make perfect bird-viewing spots. The park is accessible by bus #141 from KL's Pudu Raya bus station (hourly; RM3.90). Spartan but clean chalets in the park are available (RM25–45), and there is also accommodation in nearby Kuala Selangor town at *Hotel Kuala Selangor*, 88 Main St (☎03/3289 2709; ❷).

Ten kilometres away (no bus; RM20 return by taxi from Kuala Selangor) lies Kampung Kuantan, famous for its luminous **fireflies**. It costs RM10 to take a ride in a battery-powered sampan (small boat) along the river, Sungei Kuantan, at around 8pm, to see the thousands of flies glowing on the riverbank.

7.2

The west coast

The west coast of the Malaysian Peninsula, from Kuala Lumpur north to the Thai border, is the most industrialized and densely populated part of the country. Chinese towns punctuate the route north, many of them founded on the tin economy, and this is also the area in which the British held most sway, attracted by the political prestige of controlling such a strategic trading region. Most visitors are too intent on the beckoning delights of Thailand or the lure of the capital to bother stopping at anything other than the major destinations, and there are plenty of ways to **cross into Thailand**, by boat, bus or train (see p.612). You can get Thai visas in **Georgetown**, the vibrant and stimulating capital of the island of **Penang**, which rewards a few days' stay and is a magnet for travellers of all budgets. But before you leave Malaysia or strike on to KL, you can chill out happily at the **Cameron Highlands** hill station, or sun yourself on the pretty white-sand shores of popular **Pulau Langkawi**, a large and increasingly upmarket island.

Cameron Highlands

Amid the lofty peaks of Banjaran Titiwangsa, the various outposts of the **Cameron Highlands** (1524m) form Malaysia's most extensive hill station, and have been used as a weekend retreat since the 1920s. There are scads of hotels and luxury apartments, and on weekends and holidays it's absolutely packed with lowlanders seeking some altitude at which to cool off. The place tries hard to maintain something of a "Ye Olde English" atmosphere, and it does feel a bit contrived at times – multi-storey condos with mock-Tudor embellishments, etc. Still, it's a good place for long walks in the forest. The highlands encompass three small towns: **Ringlet**, site of the famous tea plantations; 13km beyond and 300m higher, **Tanah Rata**, the principal settlement of the highlands; and 5km further north, **Brinchang**, renowned for its farms. Tours of the whole region are organized by various hostels in Tanah Rata (3hr; RM25). Tanah Rata and Brinchang have the best accommodation, but prices shoot up at peak holiday times. Temperatures drop dramatically at night, so bring warm clothes.

The Cameron Highlands trails take in some of the most spectacular scenery in Malaysia. They are often badly signposted and maintained, though you can get sketch maps at some shops and hostels in Tanah Rata. The best is the black-and-white sketch map (free from any guesthouse), though some of its trails no longer exist. If you want to attempt any unofficial routes, you must go with a guide from the tourist office and you must get a permit from the District Office, just north of Tanah Rata (Mon–Fri 8am–1pm & 3pm–4.30pm, ☎05/491 1066). To get there, go north towards Brinchang, and take the first major right after about 1km. Always inform someone, preferably at your hotel, where you are going and what time you expect to be back. On longer trips, take warm clothing, water, a torch and a cigarette lighter or matches should you get lost. If someone else doesn't return as expected, inform the District Office.

Getting to the Cameron Highlands

The main access point for the Cameron Highlands is **TAPAH**, which has good **bus links** with major towns (see "Travel details", p.743). The **train station** is on Tapah Road, a few kilometres west of town and served by hourly local bus or by taxi (RM9) into Tapah. Tapah's **bus station** is on Jalan Raja, off the main street, and is the departure point for buses up to Tanah Rata in the Cameron Highlands (roughly hourly 8.30am–5.30pm; 2hr; RM5). Remember that if you're coming from KL, any backpacker hostel can arrange tickets for a direct coach to Tanah Rata (RM14). When leaving, you can buy long-distance bus tickets, including to Hat Yai in Thailand, from any express-bus agency in town, including Kah Mee, 10 Jl Raja (☎05/412 973), opposite the bus station. If you need a **hotel** in Tapah, try the clean *Hotel Bunga Raya*, 6 Jl Besar (☎05/401 1436; ❷) on the corner of the main street and Jalan Raja, or the good-value *Timuran*, 23 Jl Stesen (☎05/401 1092; ❷) where you'll pay an extra RM5 or so for a standard double, but will get hot water.

Ringlet

There's not much to **RINGLET**, the first settlement you come to in the Cameron Highlands. The best-known local attraction is the **Boh Tea Estate** (Tues–Sun 11am–3pm; free), 8km northeast of town, which has free tours. Here you can see the whole process, from the picking to the packing of the tea. There are eight daily buses from Ringlet to Habu – the junction for the Boh Tea Estate – daily between 6.30am and 6pm (buses start from Tapah, calling at Ringlet and Habu en route to Tanah Rata, where they turn and head back to Tapah along the same route).

Tanah Rata

Since many of the Cameron Highlands' **walks** start from nearby, the genteel town of **TANAH RATA**, the highlands' main development, is an ideal base. A couple of waterfalls and three reasonably high mountain peaks are all within hiking distance, and the town itself is festooned with white balustraded buildings, flowers and parks. It comprises little more than one street (officially called Jalan Pasar, but usually known as "Main Road"), the location of most hotels, banks and restaurants.

Buses from Tapah terminate at the **bus station** about halfway along the main road, where you'll have to change for local buses to Brinchang and Kampung Raja, the furthest point north. CS Travel, Main Road (☎05/491 1200), sells tickets for express buses from Tapah to all major destinations. For **tourist information**, head for Yam and Bob's Kiosk on Main Road, next to the *Kumar* restaurant. You can collect poste restante at the **post office** on Main Road; the **police station** (☎05/491 1222) is on Main Road, opposite the *New Garden Inn*; the **hospital** is at the north end of Main Road (☎05/491 1966), and there's a clinic at 48 Main Rd (8.30am–12.30pm & 2–4.30pm). There are a few **Internet** places around town; the best is Highlands Computer Centre (☎05/491 5678) at 39 Main Rd.

Accommodation

Cameronian Inn 16 Jl Mentigi ☎05/491 1327. Friendly, clean and well informed with Internet access and a library. There's a small dorm (RM8) and some double rooms. Trekkers set off from here at 9.30am most mornings, non-guests are welcome to join the treks at no charge. ❶

Cool Point Just off the main road behind the Shell station (☎05/491 4914). A newish hotel in a quiet location. It's well run and good value. ❺

Father's Guest House ☎05/491 2484. Three budget guesthouses set on a private hill in the outskirts of Tanah Rata. There are doubles in a stone house and dorm beds (RM8) in funky, tunnel-like aluminium outhouses. There's a large collection of books and films, a few Internet terminals and very friendly staff. ❶

Heritage Jl Gereja ☎05/491 3888. Set on a hill near the approach road from Ringlet, the most upmarket hotel in Tanah Rata is very comfortable and has several good restaurants. ❼

Orient 38 Main Rd ☎05/491 1633. Very good value with thoughtfully furnished, airy rooms, although it can be noisy during holiday periods. ❷
Seah Meng 39 Main Rd ☎05/491 1618. Clean, well-kept rooms, some with pleasant views. Very similar to the *Orient* next door. ❸

Twin Pines 2 Jl Mentigi ☎05/491 2169. Set back from the main road, this hippy hangout has small doubles, a garden and books full of travellers' tips. At night, the owner leads singalongs around the campfire. There are dorms (RM7), a café and Internet facilities. ❶

Eating

At night, **food stalls** set up on the main road. Many restaurants serve the local steamboat, which involves dipping raw fish, meat, noodles and vegetables in a steaming broth until cooked.

Bunga Suria Jl Perisan Camellia. The best South Indian restaurant in Tanah Rata and a haven for vegetarians as well as meat-eaters.
Excellent Food Centre On the main road opposite the post office. Lives up to its name with a large, inexpensive menu of Western and Asian dishes – it's great for breakfast, although the welcome can be less than ecstatic. Open 7am–noon and 7–10pm.
The Grasshopper 57b Persiran Camellia 3. On the second floor above the new shop-houses. Excellent-value steamboats, starting at just RM8, served by friendly staff in a tasteful setting. Also has traditional Chinese tea.
Jasmine Restoran 45 Main Rd. Popular with German and Dutch travellers for its *rijstafel* set meals. It has karaoke in the evenings, which can get a bit rowdy.

Orient Restoran 38 Main Rd. Standard Chinese food in the restaurant below the hotel. The set meals are reasonable value, as are the steamboats.
Restoran Kumar Main Rd. Along with *Thanam* next door, the *Kumar* specializes in clay-pot rice, and the chef knows his way around a *murtabak*.
Rich Bake Café Main Rd. Bright jazzy spot on the corner, which sometimes has live music; serves good pancakes.
Ye Olde Smokehouse Halfway to Brinchang from Tanah Rata, just south of the golf course ☎05/491 1215. The hotel opens its restaurant to non-residents, but enforces an absurd (given the decor) dress code. Unless you're absolutely dying for a traditional English dinner – and are ready to pay dearly for it – it's probably better to wait until you get home.

Brinchang and around

BRINCHANG, 5km north of Tanah Rata, is more tranquil and less touristy than its neighbour; some of the walks are easily approached from here, too, and it's closer to the farms and tea estates further north. You can also hike to the summit of Gunung Brinchang (2032m), a steep two- to three-hour climb along a sealed road, with wonderful views. To get to Brinchang, get a local bus from Tanah Rata (approximately hourly 6.30am–6.30pm) or a taxi (RM4).

The Sungai Palas Tea Estate (Tues–Sun 9am–4.30pm, tours every 10min; free) is set high in the hills and is refreshingly uncrowded. The tealeaves here are no longer hand-picked, but cut with shears, after which they go to the factory (which you'll be guided round) to be withered, sifted, rolled, fermented and then fired. Buses for the estate leave from Brinchang's bus station, just south of the square (8 daily, 6.45am–6.45pm; 25 min). You can also get back by making your own way to the main road (30min walk) and picking up one of the more regular Brinchang-bound buses from Kampung Raja. The last bus back from Sungai Palas leaves at 6pm.

Most of the **hotels** in Brinchang line the east and west sides of the central square. The only real budget accommodation is the *Silverstar*, 10 Main Rd (☎05/491 1387; ❸). It's one of the few places in Brinchang where you won't pay over the odds for clean sheets. The sumptuous *Rosa Passadena* (☎05/491 2288; ❻) dominates the village, and offers very reasonable deals on double rooms. Just opposite, *Pines and Roses* (☎05/491 2203; ❹) also offers comfortable, clean en-suite accommodation, all with TV. *Kowloon*, 34–35 Main Rd (☎05/491 1366; ❹) has small, comfortable rooms with TV and bathroom. The *Equatorial Hill Resort*, Kea Farm (☎05/496 1777; ❾), a luxury resort about 2km north of Brinchang, is the plushest place in the region, with lovely views and great-value rooms. As for **food**, *Restoran Sakaya* on Main Road is one of several good budget Chinese eating houses (along with *You Hoo* and *Kuan Kee*), doing cheap buffet lunches.

Ipoh

Eighty kilometres northwest of Tapah in the Kinta Valley, **IPOH** grew rich on the tin trade and is now the third biggest city in Malaysia. The muddy **Sungei Kinta** cuts the centre of Ipoh neatly in two; most of the hotels are situated east of the river, whilst the **old town** is on the opposite side between Jalan Sultan Idris Shah and Jalan Sultan Iskander. Some of Ipoh's old colonial street names have been changed in favour of something more Islamic, though the signs haven't always caught up; hence, Jalan CM Yusuf instead of Jalan Chamberlain, Jalan Mustapha Al-Bakri for Jalan Clare and Jalan Bandar Timar for Jalan Leech.

Many Ipoh buildings show the influence of colonial and Straits-Chinese architecture, the most impressive of which is the white stucco **Hong Kong Bank** north of the Birch Memorial Clocktower on Jalan Dato' Maharaja Lela. Turning right from the bank into Jalan Sultan Yusuf, you're on the outskirts of **Chinatown**, many of whose pastel-coloured, nineteenth-century shop-houses are now looking rather tatty. The **Perak Museum** (daily 9am–5pm; free) is housed in an elegant former tin miner's mansion, 400m north of the padang on Jalan Panglima Bukit Gantang Wahab, and displays photos of Ipoh's glory days during the tin boom.

The most prominent reminder of Ipoh's economic heyday, the **train station** was built in 1917, a typical example of the British conception of "East meets West", with its Moorish turrets and domes and a two-hundred-metre-long veranda. It's on Jalan Panglima Bukit Gantang Wahab, west of the old town, with the **GPO** practically next door. The **local bus station** is just south of the train station, at the junction with Jalan Tun Abdul Razak. Opposite, you'll find the taxi stand. **Express buses** operate from behind the ticket booths across the road. Local buses to **Lumut** (the departure point for Pulau Pangkor; see p.654) leave from a separate forecourt, beside a row of shops, a little further along Jalan Tun Abdul Razak; get a ticket from Perak Roadways under the bill hoardings. The **Sultan Azlan Shah Airport** is 5km from the city (☎05/312 2459). The **tourist office** is on Jalan Tun Sambanthan (Mon–Thurs 8am–1pm & 2pm–4.30pm, Fri 8am–12.15pm & 2.45–4.30pm; closed first & third Sat of every month; ☎05/241 2959). The main **banks** are on Jalan Sultan Idris Shah and Jalan Yang Kalsom, and there is **Internet** access at RND Café, 41 Jl CM Yusuf.

The best budget **accommodation** with private bathroom is the *Embassy*, Jalan CM Yusuf (☎05/254 9496; ❷); all rooms are clean and have air-con. The cheaper *West Pool Hotel*, 74 Clare St (☎05/254 5042; ❷), is also clean and has communal hot-water showers. The best mid-range choice is the *New Caspian*, 20–26 Jl Ali Pitchay (☎05/243 9254; ❸), where all the rooms have TV, fridge and bathrooms that you'd usually only see at twice the price. A close second is the *Ritz Garden*, CM Yusuf (☎05/254 7777; ❹). For a taste of the old colonial style, check into the *Majestic* (☎05/255 4217; ❻), on the third floor of the train station, off Jalan Panglima. You'll get a roomy en-suite opening onto a huge tiled veranda, where you'll be served afternoon tea on wicker chairs (RM10). Actually, a stay here alone almost warrants the stop – the days are probably numbered before the *Raffles* chain takes over this one and prices go sky high.

Many of Ipoh's **restaurants** close in the evenings, but there are excellent hawker stalls at the southern end of Jalan Greenhill, east of the Shanghai Hotel. Nearly a hundred stalls stay open well into the night, serving just about anything you care to name. Jalan CM Yusuf has the *Grand Cathay* restaurant, which is very popular with Chinese locals, and the *Rahman*, an extremely friendly Indian restaurant. Around Jalan Bandar Timar in the old town are several Chinese restaurants, the oldest and best known of which is the *Kedai Kopi Kong Heng* (lunchtime only) where you wander round the bustling stalls and pick your dish.

Pulau Pangkor

Pulau Pangkor is one of the west coast's more appealing islands, with some of the best beaches to be found on this side of the Malay Peninsula, and it's only a forty-minute ferry ride from the port of Lumut (85km southwest of Ipoh). The island is a mere 3km by 9km, but attracts a lot of weekenders, who have inevitably brought the odd concrete highrise with them, particularly in Pasir Bogak. There's already an airport here (flights from Singapore and KL) and several international-standard hotels, but the inhabitants still live largely by fishing rather than tourism. Most villages lie along the east coast, while tourist accommodation and the best beaches are on the west side of the island, at Pasir Bogak and Teluk Nipah.

Express ferries to Pulau Pangkor run from **LUMUT** approximately every half hour (daily 6.45am–9pm; RM3 one way), calling at Kampung Sungei Pinang Kecil before reaching the main jetty at Pangkor Town. You can also catch a catamaran from the same spot for RM5, which will get you to the island in half the time. **Buses** arrive at Lumut's bus station, a three-minute walk south of the jetty. There's a **Tourism Malaysia office** (Mon–Fri 9am–5pm, Sat 9am–1.45pm; ☎05/683 4057) just left, past the petrol pumps on Jalan Sultan Idris Shah itself. Should you have to spend the night, *Indah* at 208 Jl Iskandar Shah (☎05/683 5064; ❸), a little way northwest along the waterfront from the jetty, has comfortable en-suite rooms, as does the *Harbour View*, Jalan Titi Panjang (☎05/683 7888; ❸) which is visible from the bus station. To get there, walk to the service station and take a hairpin right onto the shore road. Just past the Harbour View is Lumut's least expensive option, the clean and basic *Phin Lum Hooi*, 93 Jl Panjang (☎05/683 5641; ❷).

The Lumut ferry docks at **Pangkor Town**, the island's principal settlement, from where buses and taxis will ferry you to the beaches. A sealed road runs right round the island, and across it from Pangkor Town to Pasir Bogak, 2km away on the west coast. The best way to explore is by motorbike (RM30) or bicycle (RM15), available from Pangkor Town and from guesthouses. Otherwise, there are **minibus taxis** charging RM5 to Pasir Bogak, RM10 to Teluk Nipah and RM40 for a round-island trip.

Pasir Bogak

PASIR BOGAK is the biggest and most upmarket beach on the island, but has a disappointingly narrow strip of grubby sand. Only a few of the chalets front the beach itself; most line the road that continues north along the west coast, but they're all reasonably close to the sea. *Pangkor Standard Camp* (☎05/685 1878; ❷) is the best deal for those on a budget, sleeping three at a squeeze and running courses in traditional Malay massage. A step up is *Beach Hut Hotel* (☎05/685 1159; ❹), with pleasant beachfront chalets and simple double rooms. *Khoo's Holiday Resort* (☎05/685 2190; ❹) is a large complex of tasteful doubles perched on the hillside. The views are fantastic, there are air-con options and the rate includes breakfast. *Sri Bayu Beach Resort* (☎05/685 1929; ❻) is by far the most characterful outfit on the beach. The carved wood and antique-strewn lobby leads onto a well-landscaped garden and some chalets, and there are 130 comfortable hotel rooms. The best value of the resort **restaurants** is *Ye Lin*, on the cross-island road, which offers huge plates of excellent Chinese food. The finest view belongs to the *Pangkor Paradise Resort* up a dirt track to the south of the main strip, whose beachfront restaurant – on stilts over the water – is great for a beer at sunset. Back in the thick of things, there are some stalls clustered around the inexpensive *Pantai Beach Seafood Restaurant* on the seafront just north of the *Pangkor Standard Camp*.

Teluk Ketapang and Teluk Nipah

Much better beaches than those at Pasir Bogak are to be found about 2km to the north at **TELUK KETAPANG**, whose broad, clean, white-sand shores are edged by palm trees, and at **TELUK NIPAH**, another few kilometres further on. The best beach at Teluk Nipah is Coral Beach, a perfect cove with crystal-clear sea and smooth white sand. The bay can be reached either by road, or on foot by climbing over the rocks at the northern end of Teluk Nipah's main beach (watch the tide).

Accommodation

Joe Fisherman Village ⓣ05/685 2389. One of the first set-ups and still the backpacker's spiritual home on Pangkor. With A-frames (RM20), chalets, and a communal eating area where Zura serves up fabulous "family dinners". ❷

Nazri Nipah Camp ⓣ05/685 2014. Laid-back traveller place with kitchen facilities, a dorm (RM10), some A-frames and chalets with shower. Jungle trekking tours also arranged. ❷

Nipah Bay Villa ⓣ05/685 2198. One of the best choices if you're going for a/c, satellite TV and hot water. Professionally run with an Internet terminal open to non-guests. ❻

Palma Beach Resort ⓣ05/685 3693. Well-designed, sturdy chalets with a/c, TVs and an efficient management. Rates are negotiable when things are quiet. ❻

Pangkor Bayview Resort ⓣ05/685 3540. Nicely designed, spacious chalets with all facilities. A good choice if you're spending a bit more than the average. ❻

Purnama Beach Resort ⓣ05/685 3530. Package-deal development with a good range of plush chalets, quickly snapped up by mainlanders on weekends. There's an Internet terminal open to non-guests. ❸

TJ Restoran and Bungalows ⓣ05/685 3477. The best-value accommodation along this stretch, boasting double chalets with shower at half the price you'll find elsewhere. The café is a good deal, too. ❷

Butterworth

The industrial town of **BUTTERWORTH** is the port for the island of Penang and its capital, Georgetown, and of no interest except as a transport hub. The **bus station**, port complex, taxi stand and **train station** (ⓣ04/323 7962) are all next door to each other on the quayside. All but one of the daily north–south trains stop here. The passenger and car **ferry service** (5am–11pm; 60 sen return) runs three times an hour from the port complex to Pengkalan Weld in Georgetown and takes twenty minutes. If necessary, you can **stay** near the port at *Sin Tong Ah* (ⓣ04/323 9679; ❸). To get there, walk northeast from the bus station along the main road for a minute or so and follow it left past a huge intersection; the hotel is on the other side of the road.

Penang

Penang, 370km from Kuala Lumpur on Malaysia's northwestern coast, is a confusing amalgam of state and island. Everything of interest in Penang State is on **Pulau Penang**, a large island of 285 square kilometres that is connected to the mainland by a bridge and by round-the-clock ferry services from Butterworth. Confusingly, the island's capital and Malaysia's second-largest city, **Georgetown**, is also often referred to as "Penang" (which is sometimes spelled "Pinang"). Most visitors make day-trips out from Georgetown to the island's north-coast beaches of **Batu Ferringhi** and **Tanjung Bungah**, though you can also stay in both these resorts.

Until the late eighteenth century, Pulau Penang was ruled by the sultans of Kedah. In 1771, Sultan Mohammed J'wa Mu'Azzam Shah II took a shine to Captain Francis Light, who worked for a European trading company, and thought it expedient to accept military protection in exchange for offering the British the use of densely forested Penang as a port. By 1791, the island, then inhabited by less than a hundred indigenous fishermen, had become the **first British settlement** in the Malay Peninsula and quickly evolved into a major colonial administrative centre. Francis Light was made superintendent and declared the island a free port, with Georgetown the capital of the newly established Straits Settlements (incorporating Melaka and

Singapore). But the founding of Singapore in 1819 was the beginning of the end for Georgetown, and Penang's fortunes rapidly began to wane. However, the strategic significance of Singapore proved to be Penang's saving grace, and there was little or no bomb damage to the island during World War II.

Georgetown

GEORGETOWN is Malaysia's most fascinating city and retains more of its cultural history than virtually anywhere else in the country. It's a magnet for budget travellers, a place not only to renew Thai visas, but to relax and observe street life in between trips to the beach. The most confusing thing about finding your way around Georetown is the fact that many **streets** have several names – Penang Road has become Jalan Penang, Penang Street is Lebuh Penang, Weld Quay has become Pengkalan Weld, and Beach Street is now Lebuh Pantai. Lebuh Cinta is almost uni-

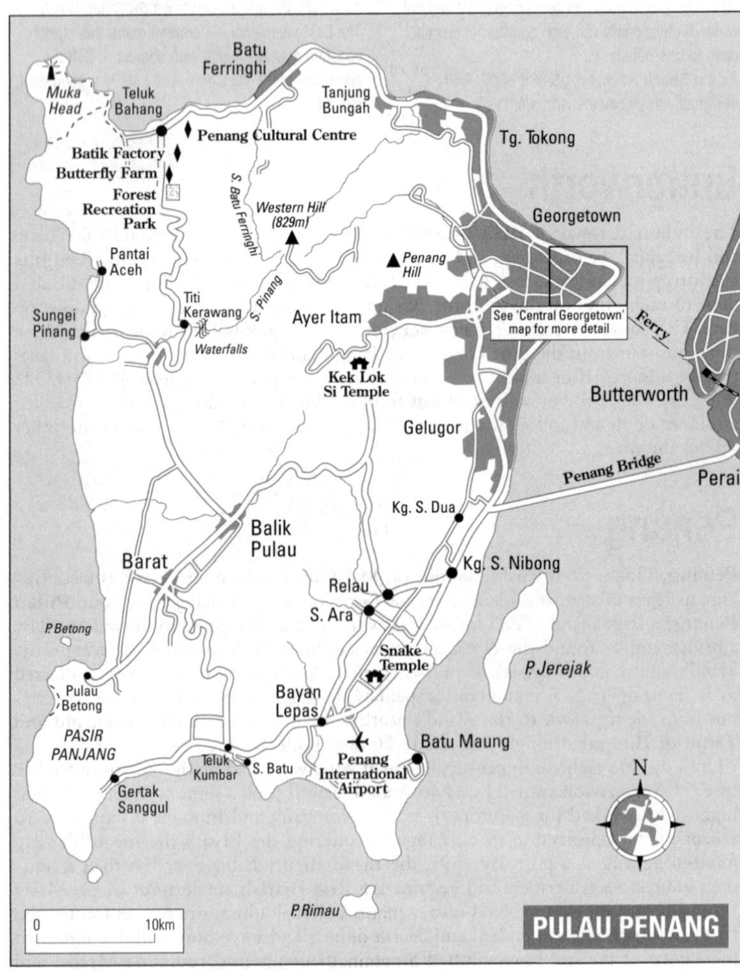

versally known as Love Lane, and Jalan Masjid Kapitan Kling is often referred to as Lebuh Pitt.

Arrival and information

The most convenient approach from the mainland is the passenger-and-car **ferry service from Butterworth**, which takes twenty minutes and docks at the centrally located terminal on Pengkalan Weld (60 sen return). The ferry runs from 5am until 11pm. **Long-distance taxis** from the Peninsula use the thirteen-kilometre-long Penang Bridge (RM7 toll), which crosses from just south of Butterworth at Perai to a point on Jalan Udini, 8km south of Georgetown on the east coast. **Penang International Airport** (☎04/643 0811) is on the southeastern tip of the island. Yellow bus #83 (hourly on the hour, 6am–10pm) takes about 45 minutes to get into Georgetown, dropping you next to the Pengkalan Weld ferry terminal. A taxi costs RM20 – buy a coupon inside the terminal building.

Arriving at either the bus station, taxi stand or ferry terminal on Pengkalan Weld or nearby Swettenham Pier puts you at the eastern edge of Georgetown, a twenty-minute walk from the hotels. On arrival, the most convenient tourist office is the **Penang Tourist Centre** (Mon–Fri 8.30am–1pm & 2–4.30pm, Sat 8.30am–1pm; ☎04/261 6663), on the ground floor of the Penang Port Commission building on Jalan Tun Syed Sheh Barakbah, which produces an excellent island and city **map** (RM1). Better, however, is the **Tourist Information Centre** (Mon–Sat 10am–6pm; t04/261 4461) on the third floor of the huge KOMTAR shopping complex in the centre of town, which is really clued up on local information and can also arrange half-day tours of the city (from RM30) – not a bad way to see Penang if your time is limited.

City transport

The city centre is small enough to get around on foot, but for longer journeys to the outskirts or to other parts of the island there is an excellent **bus service**. From the station next to the ferry terminal on Pengkalan Weld, blue buses serve the north of the island, and yellow buses the south and west, while red-and-white Transit Link buses – the most common of the lot – run on most routes through the island. A few buses are also run by the small Sri Negara company, and there are a number of minibuses. All buses stop at (and leave from) the station by the KOMTAR complex on Jalan Ria and most stop at the Pengkalan Weld station, too. **Fares** are rarely more than a Malaysian dollar, and are based on distance travelled, but you must have exact change in coins to board the bus – in other words, bring lots of coins. Services are frequent, though by 8pm in the evening they become more sporadic, and stop completely at 10pm.

A traditional way of seeing the city is by **pedicab**: drivers tout for custom outside the major hotels and all along Lebuh Chulia. Negotiate the price in advance and expect the opening price to be ridiculously high; a ride from the ferry terminal at Pengkalen Weld to the northern end of Lebuh Chulia costs around RM3. Otherwise, there are **taxi** stands by the ferry terminal and on Jalan Dr Lim Chwee Long, off Jalan Penang. Drivers rarely use their meters, so fix the fare in advance – a trip across town runs to about RM5, while a ride out to the airport or Batu Ferringhi costs RM20. To book a taxi in advance, call Jade Auto (☎04/226 3015), Sunshine Taxi (☎04/642 5961) or MCI Taxis (☎04/264 5534). For **bike or car rental** – useful if you plan to see the rest of the island – check the list of addresses in "Listings", p.663.

Accommodation

Georgetown is one of the few places in the country where you might experience difficulty in finding a **room**, so arrive early or book ahead. The budget places are mostly on and around **Lebuh Chulia**; most have dorm beds as well as rooms, and many will sell bus tickets to Thailand and obtain Thai visas. No. 1 Lebuh Chulia is at the southern end (nearest the ferry terminal).

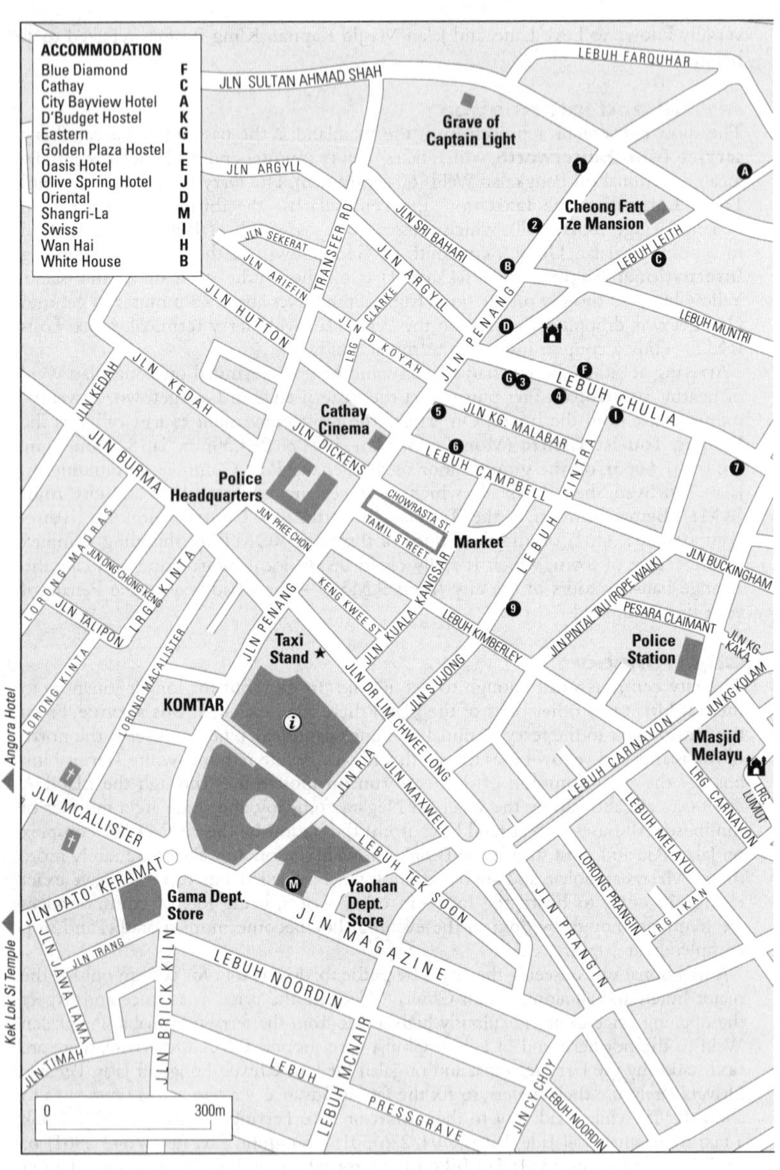

Blue Diamond 422 Lebuh Chulia ☎04/261 1089. Modern frontage but with an elaborate inner courtyard and a grand staircase. The large, high-ceilinged rooms with shower have luxurious sprung mattresses, there's a dorm (RM8) and the washing machine is free to guests. ❷

Cathay 15 Lebuh Leith ☎04/262 6271. Stylish colonial mansion dating from 1910. The cool greys of the decor, spacious rooms and courtyard fountain make for a tranquil environment. The hotel was used as a set for the film *Beyond Rangoon*. Not all rooms are alike in size or quality so have a look first. ❹

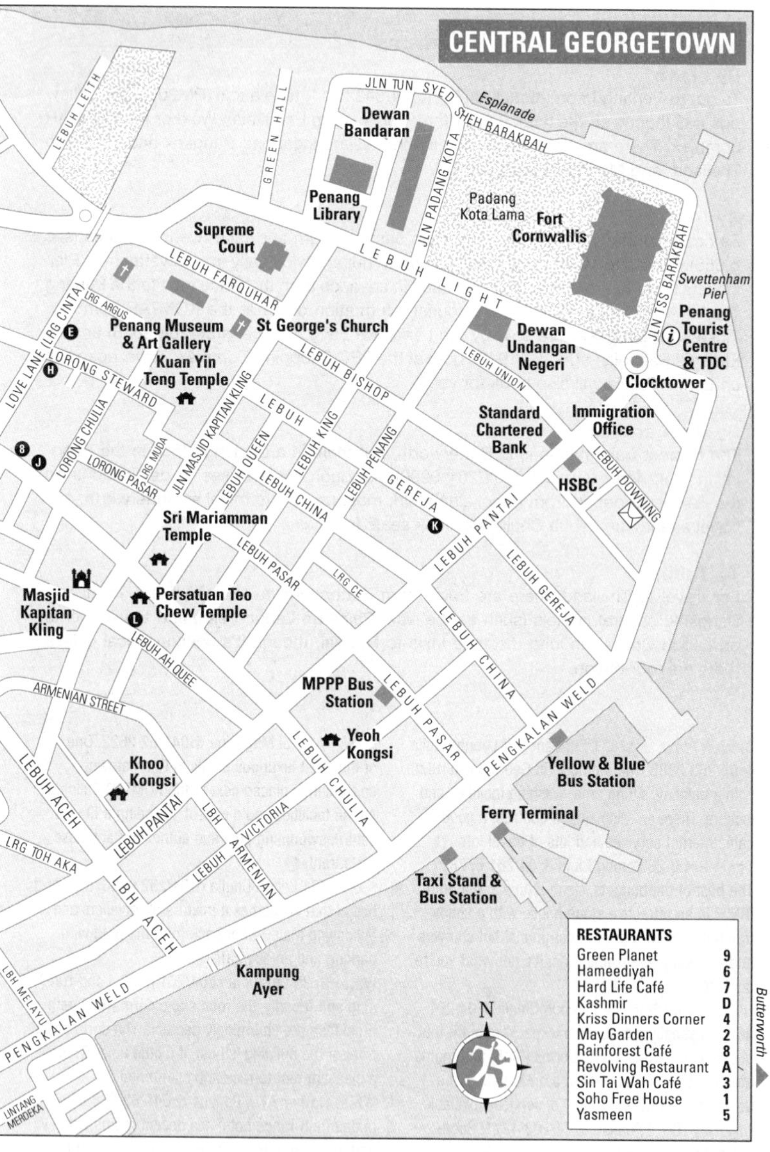

City Bayview Hotel 25a Lebuh Farquhar ☎04/263 3161. Modern four-star, with a pool and fantastic views over the bay from the rooftop revolving restaurant. ❽

D'Budget Hostel 9 Lebuh Gereja ☎04/263 4794. The long corridors are a bit claustrophobic, but the dorms (RM7) and rooms are very clean and secure. There are shared bathrooms with hot showers and Western-style toilets. ❷

Eastern 509 Lebuh Chulia ☎04/261 4597. Small, clean rooms with fan or a/c and saloon-style wooden doors. More solidly built than most. ❷

Moving on from Georgetown/Penang

By plane

To get to Penang International Airport (☎04/643 0811) take a taxi (RM20) or the yellow bus #83 (hourly on the hour, 6am–10pm; 45min) from Pengkalan Weld or the KOMTAR complex. There are flights to Medan in Indonesia; Singapore; Bangkok and Phuket in Thailand; and Madras in India (via KL).

By ferry

Ferries to Butterworth are frequent from 5am to 11pm and take twenty minutes (see p.655). Ferries to Medan and Pulau Langkawi depart twice daily from Swettenham Pier. Tickets for either route can be purchased in advance from the office next to the Penang Tourist Association and from the tourist information office at the KOMTAR complex. Tickets for Langkawi are sold by the Langkawi Ferry Service (☎04/264 2088) and by Ekspres Bahagia (☎04/263 1943), both at the PPC Shopping Complex. Travel agencies on Lebuh Chulia will also book for you.

By train and bus

The nearest train station is in Butterworth, but there is a booking office in the Pengkalan Weld ferry terminal (☎04/261 0290). Although some buses to destinations on the Peninsula depart from Pengkalan Weld, most use the terminal at Butterworth; any travel agency on Lebuh Chulia will book seats for you.

To Thailand

For travel to Thailand, there are trains from Butterworth to Hat Yai, Surat Thani and Bangkok; several hostels (such as the *New China* on Lebuh Leith) and travel agents on Lebuh Chulia run long-distance taxis to Hat Yai, though it's uneconomical unless there are four of you.

Golden Plaza Hostel 1 Pitt Lane, off Lebuh Chulia ☎04/263 2388. The top dorm in Georgetown (RM8) with a balcony, sitting area, washing facilities and lockers. There are also simple doubles, a good café, Internet services and lots of travel info. ❷

Oasis Hotel 23 Lorong Cinta ☎04/261 6778. The best of the budgets, clean rooms and a dorm (RM8) in an attractive stone house with a shady, tranquil garden. There are communal hot showers and a friendly atmosphere (no, it's not what you're thinking). ❷

Olive Spring Hotel 302 Lebuh Chulia ☎04/261 4641. Distinctly cut-above backpackers outfit that guests find hard to leave. Dorms (RM8) and rooms are bright and clean, there's a great café in the downstairs lobby and a host of services available.

Oriental 105 Jl Penang ☎04/263 4211. Good-value mid-range hotel with helpful, professional staff. ❺

Shangri-La Jl Magazine ☎04/262 2622. One of the most luxurious hotels in Georgetown, conveniently placed next to the KOMTAR Building. All the facilities you'd expect, including a fitness centre, swimming pool and authentic Cantonese restaurant. ❾

Swiss 431 Lebuh Chulia ☎04/262 0133. Standard hostel that welcomes a mixture of travellers and holidaying Malays. Set back from the road with parking and an airy café. ❷

Wan Hai 35 Lrg Cinta ☎04/261 6853. Long-running and friendly, the rooms and dorm (RM7 with breakfast) are charmingly decrepit. The dorm at the front of the building is best, if a little noisy. There's a pleasant roof terrace and bike rental. ❶–❷

White House 72 Jl Penang ☎04/263 2385. This budget mid-range hotel has decent rooms with TV and a/c for not much more than you'd spend for fan and shared bathrooms. ❸

The City

The site of **Fort Cornwallis** (daily 8.30am–7pm; RM1) on the northeastern tip of Pulau Penang marks the spot where the British fleet, under Captain Francis Light, disembarked on July 16, 1786. But for all its significance, it holds little of interest save a replica of a traditional Malay house and an underground bunker detailing the history of Penang. Southwest from the fort, **Lebuh Pantai** holds some fine colonial buildings,

△ Kek Lok Si Temple, Georgetown

including the Standard Chartered Bank and the HSBC Bank. West of Lebuh Pantai, on Jalan Masjid Kapitan Kling (or Lebuh Pitt), stands the Anglican **St George's Church** (Sunday services in English at 8.30am & 10.30am), one of the oldest buildings in Penang (1817–1819) and as simple and unpretentious as anything built in the Greek style in Asia can be. Next to the church on Lebuh Farquhar, **Penang Museum and Art Gallery** (daily 9am–5pm; RM1) has an excellent collection of rickshaws, press cuttings and black-and-white photographs. The area east of here, enclosed by parallel Lebuh King and Lebuh Queen, forms Georgetown's compact **Little India** district, full of sari and incense shops, banana-leaf curry houses, and the towering **Sri Mariamman Temple** (open early morning to late evening) on the corner of Lebuh Queen and Lebuh Chulia, a typical example of Hindu architecture.

To the south, in a secluded square at the end of an alleyway off Lebuh Aceh, stands the **Khoo Kongsi**, one of many *kongsi*, or traditional "clan-houses" in Penang where Chinese families gather to worship their ancestors. The original building was started in 1894 and meticulously crafted by experts from China. Its central hall is dark with heavy, intricately carved beams and pillars and bulky mother-of-pearl inlaid furniture. The hall on the left is a richly decorated shrine to Tua Peh Kong, the god of prosperity; the right-hand hall contains the gilded ancestral tablets. Connecting all three halls is a balcony minutely decorated in carvings of folk tales. Visitors are requested to ask permission and sign in at the adjacent office before entering.

On the western edge of Georgetown, on the corner of Lebuh Leith, is the stunning **Cheong Fatt Tze Mansion** (guided tours Mon, Wed, Fri & Sat 11am; RM10), whose outer walls are painted in a striking rich blue. It's the best example of nineteenth-century Chinese architecture in Penang, built by Thio Thiaw Siat, a Cantonese businessman. The elaborate halls of ceremony, bedrooms and libraries, separated by courtyards and gardens, have been restored and are privately owned. The mansion was used as a set for the film *Indochine* and is being turned into a boutique hotel.

Bedecked with flags, lanterns, statues and pagodas, the sprawling and exuberant **Kek Lok Si Temple** (open 9am–9pm; free) is supposedly the largest Buddhist temple complex in Malaysia and a major tourist spot. The "Million Buddhas Precious Pagoda" is the most prominent feature of the compound, with a tower of simple Chinese saddle-shaped eaves and more elaborate Thai arched windows, topped by a golden Burmese stupa. It costs RM2 to climb the 193 steps to the top, where there is a great view of Georgetown and the bay. Getting there involves a thirty-minute bus ride west on Transitlink #1, #101, #130, #351, #361, yellow bus #85 or minibus #21.

Eating

A local favourite is Penang *laksa*, noodles in thick fish soup, garnished with vegetables, pineapple and *belacan* (shrimp paste). The main travellers' hangouts around Lebuh Chulia serve Western **breakfasts**, banana pancakes and milkshakes for less than a couple of dollars each; they usually open from 9am to 5pm. There are also hawker stalls on Lebuh Kimberley and Lebuh Cintra.

Green Planet 63 Lebuh Cintra. This café serves international veggie food, chocolate cake to die for, homemade bread and even Baba-Nonya food. Also has a book exchange. Open 9.30am–3pm & 7pm–midnight.

Hameediyah 164 Lebuh Campbell. Great Indian food at reasonable prices in a century-old building; around RM4 a head for a full meal.

Hard Life Café 363 Lebuh Chulia. Bob Marley and co plastered across the walls and the sound system make this a laid-back spot for drinks, snacks and beers.

Kashmir Basement of *Oriental Hotel*, 105 Jl Penang. Very popular high-class North Indian restaurant; you'll need to book at weekends. Expensive but chic.

Kriss Dinners Corner 447 Lebuh Chulia. Tasty and surprisingly well-priced buffet of Chinese and Malay food. Shows films and football in the evenings.

May Garden 70 Jl Penang. Plush but affordable Cantonese restaurant serving excellent food.

Rainforest Café 300 Lebuh Chulia. Run by the friendly Mr Tan who also owns the *Green Planet*. Very welcoming, with good food and drinks, a book exchange system and Internet access.

Revolving Restaurant On the sixteenth floor of the *City Bayview Hotel*. Choose from Western and Oriental dishes during the 45-minute rotation. The buffet dinner from 6.30pm costs RM38.
Sin Tai Wah Café Lebuh Chulia. A good choice for a Western breakfast, this café is attractively festooned with greenery, and the owners know how to scramble an egg.
Soho Free House Jl Penang. A pub that might have been transported straight from England, with authentic fish and chips, pies and draught Guinness.
Yasmeen Jl Penang. Next to the *Ta*, the appeal of this Indian eatery is based on *roti* and tandoori chicken. Also, if you're going to have a banana pancake anywhere, have it here. Don't be taken in by the friendly English-speaking tout at the unspeakably filthy *Taj Mahal* restaurant next door – *Yasmeen* is the place for good, clean Indian food.

Drinking and nightlife

Most of Georgetown's **bars** are comfortable places to hang out, but when the fleet arrives, a good many turn into rowdy meat markets, so choose carefully. Usual opening hours are 6pm–2am. In Georgetown's **discos**, you're unlikely to hear the latest Western club sounds, and there's usually a cover charge of around RM10.

20 Leith Street. The most eclectic bar on the island is randomly adorned with film memorabilia, assorted antiques and rare LP covers; it also has a beer garden. Slightly pricey, but never dull.
Cheers Jl Peneng. Standout sports bar that emphasizes pitchers of beer and a generous happy hour (5-9pm). There's an adjacent wine bar if you prefer something more intimate.
Hong Kong Bar Lebuh Chulia. A classic liberty-port dive with command plaques and photos of warships adorning the walls – although if you happen to be here when the Australian fleet is in port, give this place a wide berth.
Old China Café Lebuh Pantai. Authentic colonial style of the 30s, packed with so much atmosphere you'll feel like you've got a part in a period movie.
Tai Wah Lebuh Chulia. This daytime café turns into a lively bar full of Indonesian guest workers in the evening, and has the cheapest beer in town. Whatever you do, don't let anyone lure you upstairs, though.

Listings

Airline offices Cathay Pacific, Menara PSCI, Jl Sultan Ahmed Shah ☎05/226 0411; Malaysia Airlines, Ground Floor, KOMTAR, Jl Penang ☎04/262 0011; Singapore Airlines, Wisma Penang Gardens, Jl Sultan Ahmed Shah ☎04/226 3201; Thai International, Wisma Central, Jl Macalister ☎04/226 6000.
American Express Care of Mayflower Acme Tours, MWE Plaza, 8 Lebuh Farquhar, (Mon–Fri 8.30am–5.30pm, Sat 8.30am–1pm; ☎04/262 8196). Credit-card and travellers' cheque-holders can use the office as a poste restante/general delivery address.
Banks and exchange Major banks (Mon–Fri 10am–3pm, Sat 9.30–11.30am) are along Lebuh Pantai, including Standard Chartered and the HSBC Bank, but since they charge a hefty commission, the licensed moneychangers on Lebuh Pantai, Lebuh Chulia and Jl Kapitan Kling (daily 8.30am–6pm) are preferable – they charge no commission and the rate is often better.
Bike rental Outlets on Lebuh Chulia rent out motorbikes and bicycles: RM20 a day for a motorbike (you need a valid driving licence – in practice, you'll rarely be asked to show it); RM8–10 for a bicycle.
Bookshops United Books Ltd, Jl Penang, has a large selection of English-language books, including travel books. There are several outlets in the KOMTAR building, including Popular Books on the 2nd Floor. Times Books in the main building also has a good selection. In addition, there are several secondhand bookshops on Lebuh Chulia.
Car rental Avis, at the airport (☎04/643 9633) and Batu Ferringhi (☎04/881 1522); Hertz, 38 Lebuh Farquhar (☎04/263 5914); ORIX at the City Bayview Hotel (☎04/261 8608) and at the airport (☎04/644 4772).
Consulates Australia, care of Denis Mark Lee, 1c Lorong Hutton ☎05/263 3320; Bangladesh, 15 Lebuh Bishop ☎04/261 1196; Canada, 1 Gat Lebuh Maccallum ☎04/262 4226; Denmark, Standard Chartered Bank Chambers, Lebuh Pantai ☎04/262 4886; France, care of Jumaboy and Sons, Wisma Rajab, 82 Lebuh Bishop ☎04/262 8816; Indonesia, 467 Jl Burma ☎04/227 4686; Japan, 2 Jl Biggs ☎04/226 8222; Netherlands, c/o Star Publications, 15 Jl Masjid Kapitan Keling ☎04/261 0891; Norway, Standard Chartered Bank Chambers, Lebuh Pantai ☎04/262 5333; Sweden, Standard Chartered Bank Chambers, Lebuh Pantai ☎04/262 5333; Thailand, 1 Jl Tunku Abdul Rah-

man ☎04/262 8029; UK, Standard Chartered Bank Chambers, Lebuh Pantai ☎04/262 5333. There is no representation for citizens of the USA, Ireland or New Zealand – KL has the nearest offices (see p.647).

Hospitals Adventist Hospital, Jl Burma ☎04/226 1133 – take blue bus #93, minibus #26, #31, #88 or Transitlink #202, #212; General Hospital, Jl Utama ☎04/229 3333 – take Sri Negara bus #136, #137.

Immigration office Pejabat Imigresen, Lebuh Pantai, on the corner of Lebuh Light ☎04/261 5122. For on-the-spot visa renewals.

Internet access As well as a few places in the KOMTAR building, you'll find no shortage of Internet terminals in Lebuh Chulia.

Pharmacy There are several pharmacies along Jl Penang (10am–6pm).

Police In emergencies, dial ☎999; the police headquarters is on Jl Penang.

Post office The GPO is on Lebuh Downing (Mon–Fri 8.30am–5pm, Sat 8.30am–4pm). The efficient poste restante/general delivery office is here, and parcel-wrapping is available from shops on Lebuh Chulia.

Sport You can play golf at Bukit Jambul Country Club, 2 Jl Bukit Jambul (☎04/644 2255; green fees RM74), or the Penang Turf Club Golf, Jl Batu Gantung (☎04/226 6701; green fees RM84, RM126 weekends); there's racing at the Penang Turf Club, Jl Batu Gantung (☎04/226 6701) – see the local paper for fixtures – and you can swim at the Pertama Sports Complex, Paya Terubong, near Ayer Itam (9–11am & 4–9pm; RM4).

Telephone services Calls within Penang made from public telephone booths cost a flat rate of 10 sen and can be dialled direct. For international calls, you can buy a phone card or use the Telekom office at the GPO on Lebuh Downing, open 24hr.

Travel agencies Try MSL Travel, *Angora Hotel*, 202 Jl McAllister, for student and youth travel. There are a large number of other agencies on Lebuh Chulia, including the reliable Happy Holidays at no. 442.

Batu Ferringhi

BATU FERRINGHI, a thirty-minute bus ride west of Georgetown on Transitlink #202 or Transitlink air-con #93 (but not the standard #93), has a decent beach and several guesthouses, albeit filthy sea. The road runs more or less straight along the coast for 3km, on which all the hotels and restaurants are lined up side by side. The bus stops in the centre, where you'll find the Telekom office, post office, police station and clinic.

Towards the western end of Batu Ferringhi there's a small enclave of similar-standard **budget guesthouses** facing the beach – take the road by the *Guan Guan Café*, and ignore taxi drivers quoting prices in excess of RM70 – they run a commission scam with some nameless budget hostels. Reliable deals include homely *Ah Beng* (☎04/881 1036; ❷), clean and cool *Ali's* (☎04/881 1316; ❷), with its relaxing open-air café and garden, and best of all, spotless *Baba's* (☎04/881 1686; ❷). Another excellent choice is *ET Budget Guest House*, which is as peaceful as any hostel you'll find (☎04/881 1553; ❷). The most popular of the expensive places is the grand *Park Royal* (☎04/881 1133; ❾), with lavish rooms and excellent restaurants.

Set just back from the main cluster of beachfront hotels, *Jewel of the North* serves very tasty North Indian **food** at around RM15 per dish, while *Indo Café*, on the main road, does Malay dishes from as little as RM3. On the beachfront, the *Sunset Café* has snacks and drinks, and in the middle of the beach you'll find *Eden Seafood Village*, a huge place whose boast is "Anything that swims, we cook it." At the western end of the main strip, *Happy Garden* is set just off the road in a colourful flower garden and serves cheapish Chinese and Western food.

Teluk Bahang

Five kilometres west of Batu Ferringhi, the small fishing kampung of **TELUK BAHANG** now shares this corner of the island with a **Butterfly Farm** (open 9am–6pm; RM10), which boasts over a hundred species of butterflies, but also has resident reptiles and amphibians. The newly built **Penang Cultural Centre** has daily "cultural tours" that include guided tours of examples of Malay architecture, as well as dancing and a mock Muslim wedding ceremony. Each tour lasts a couple of hours, and there's a nightly dinner show at 6pm. Reservations can be booked through major hotels or travel agencies along Lebuh Chulia in Georgetown. Nearby is a Batik Factory (9am–6pm; free), where you can watch Malaysian-style batik being made and buy the finished product. The beaches around the rocky headland of **Muka Head** are better than the ones at Teluk Bahang, and can be reached via a trail that runs west from Teluk Bahang.

Cheap **accommodation** is somewhat limited. The friendly *Rama's Guest House* (☎04/885 1179; ❶) is the cheapest place, a hippy homestay with basic dorm beds (RM8) and rooms; take the right (beachward) turn at the roundabout coming from Georgetown and it's about 20m down the road on the right. There's also *Miss Loh's* (❷), a longhouse and garden in the kampung a little back from the sea. To get there from the direction of Georgetown, turn left at the roundabout and carry on for 100m passing the batik factory and mosque. After the telecom tower, turn right, cross the bridge and you'll see the hostel on your left. You can book at the Kwong Tuck Hing shop on the main road. At the other end of the price scale is the beautifully decorated *Penang Mutiara* at the eastern end of the main road (☎04/886 8888; ❾). Teluk Bahang's real attraction is its plethora of inexpensive **places to eat** on the little stretch of main road. Excellent seafood restaurants include *End of the World I* (closed Tues) by the pier, and *Yellow Point Chinese* at 486 Mk2 (daily except Tues, 11am–3pm & 6–11pm).

Alor Setar

ALOR SETAR, the tiny state capital of Kedah, is the last major stop before the Thai border. It's a city that is keen to preserve its heritage – witness the many royal buildings and museums – and since Alor Setar has useful transport links to the east coast as well as to Thailand, you might as well spend at least a short time here. The main sights are located to the west of the town around the padang, whose west side is dominated by Masjid Zahir. Behind the elegant Istana Balai Besar (Royal Audience Hall) stands the old royal palace, now serving as the **Muzium Di Raja** (daily 9am–4.30pm; free), where some rooms have been kept exactly as they were when used by the sultan and his family. On the south side of the square, the grandiose, white stucco art gallery, **Balai Seni Negeri** (daily 9am–4pm; free), displays largely uninspiring works showing the influence of traditional Malay culture on contemporary artists.

South of the padang, across the Sungei Kedah, at 18 Lorong Kilang Ais, **Rumah Kelahiran Mahathir** (Tues–Sun 10am–5pm; Fri closed noon–3pm) is the birthplace of Dr Mahathir Mohammed; it's now a museum, documenting the life of the local doctor who became the most powerful Malaysian prime minister of modern times. The **Pekan Rabu** market, held every day from morning to midnight on Jalan Tunku Ibrahim, is a good place to buy handicrafts and sample local foods. North of the padang, beside the roundabout on Jalan Telok Wanjah, the **Nikhrodharam Buddhist Temple** is a glittering complex with numerous statues, mosaics and paintings, that shows the continuing influence of Thai culture.

Practicalities

Long-distance buses arrive at Alor Setar's huge **express bus station** (Shahab Perdana), 6km north of the centre, well connected to the city by municipal buses (60 sen) and taxis (RM7). The **local bus station** on Jalan Langgar runs services to the express terminal and is also the place to catch the #106 to Kuala Kedah for the Langkawi ferry. The **train station** is behind the Jalan Langar terminus, a five-minute walk east of the centre on Jalan Stesyen. The domestic **airport** (☎04/714 4021), 11km north of town, is served by the hourly "Kepala Batas" bus from the express bus station and by taxi (RM10).

It's worth seeking out the efficient **tourist office** (daily 9am–5pm; ☎04/922 2078) located on Jalan Bukit Kayuhitam. Most of the major **banks** are on Jalan Raja, and there are a few places in town where you can get **online** such as the cybercafés in the Citypoint shopping centre. Most budget **hotels** are in the vicinity of Jalan Langgar. Furthest away from the station, but by far the best value, is the *Lim Kung* (☎04/732 2459; ❶), with simple, clean and very inexpensive rooms. The *Sing Tak Sing Hotel* (☎04/732 5482; ❷) on Jalan Langgar is a slightly seedy, cavernous alternative at a higher price, while the best mid-range place is the *Hotel Regent*, 1536-G Jl Sultan Badlishah (☎04/731 1900; ❹), which looks a lot more expensive than it is, both inside and out. Alor Setar is known for its Thai **food** – try *Hajjah* opposite Citypoint on Jalan Tungku Ibrahim, for Thai seafood. Also good is *Seripab* on Jalan Langgar. For a variety of dishes under one roof, head for the Pekan Rabu market, also on Jalan Tungku Ibrahim.

Pulau Langkawi

Situated 30km off the coast at the very northwestern tip of the Peninsula is a cluster of 104 tropical islands, the largest of which is **Pulau Langkawi**. Pulau Langkawi has seen unparalleled development in recent years: some of the country's most luxurious hotels are here, and there's an international airport with flights from Japan, Taiwan and Singapore. The development is similar to Phuket in Thailand, yet the mountainous interior has remained relatively unspoiled. The principal town on Pulau Langkawi is **Kuah**, a boom town of hotels and shops in the southeast of the island. The main tourist development has taken place around two bays on the western side of the island, at **Pantai Tengah** and **Pantai Cenang**. Of these, Cenang is by far the most commercialized, but has some budget accommodation. The best beach on the island is at Pantai Kok in the west, though there is no budget accommodation here.

Arrival and information

All boat services to Langkawi dock at the jetty on the southeastern tip of the island, two minutes' taxi drive (RM5) from Kuah. The most common approach is by ferry **from Kuala Perlis**, adjacent to the Thai border (hourly; 45min; RM12 one way), but ferries also operate **from Kuala Kedah** (every 30min, 7.30am–7pm; 1hr 15min; RM15 one way), 8km from Alor Setar; **from Satun in Thailand** (4 daily; 1hr; RM18/weekends RM19); and **from Penang** (2 daily, 8am & 8.45am; 2hr 30min; RM35). The **airport** (☎04/955 1311) is 20km west of Kuah, near Pantai Cenang; a taxi is supposed to cost RM15 to Kuah, but drivers tend to ignore the posted fare; be sure to agree on a price before setting off. There's an MAS office (☎04/966 6622) on the ground floor of the Langkawi Fair Shopping Complex, 400m from the main jetty.

There is basically one circular road around the island, with the other main road connecting north and south, and some minor roads. There are no bus routes, so you'll have to get around by **taxi**: a journey to Pantai Cenang from the jetty will cost you RM15. Many of the chalets and motels offer **motorbike rental** (RM25 per day). The Langkawi **tourist office** (Sat–Thurs 9am–5pm; ☎04/966 7789), next to the mosque on the way into Kuah, is very helpful, and there's also an information booth at the airport, open daily.

Kuah

Lining a large sweep of bay in the southeastern corner of the island, **KUAH** is easily the largest town on Langkawi, and has a ferry terminal, hotels and shopping complexes. Beside the ferry terminal is Dataran Lang (Eagle Square) and **Lagenda**

Langkawi Dalan Taman (daily 9am–7pm; RM5), a landscaped "theme park" of giant sculptures based around the legends of the islands. Most of the hotels are further around the bay.

You'll find the post office (daily except Fri 9am–5pm) and police station (☎04/966 6222) on the main road, Jalan Kisap Kuah. The General Hospital is at Jalan Bukit Tekoh 07000, 7km from Kuah (☎04/966 3333). Behind the MAYA shopping complex, also on the main road, are three parallel streets with all the banks (virtually the only places to change money on the island) and the Telekom centre. You'll find plenty of cybercafés along Jalan Kisap Kuah. Kuah is not an unattractive place, but despite the multitude of hotels it's not somewhere you're likely to want to stay: *Hotel Langkawi*, 6–8 Pekan Kuah (☎04/966 6248; ④) and *JB Motel*, 19 Jl Pandak Maya 4 (☎04/966 8545; ③) near the banks, are the cheapest options; the huge *City Bayview* (☎04/966 1818; ⑥), on Jalan Pandak Mayah 1, is the luxury option. There are numerous places to eat, from the hawker stalls – past the post office heading towards the jetty – to the pricier seafood restaurants on the waterfront.

Pantai Tengah

A clearly signed junction 18km west from Kuah points you to the first of the western beaches, **PANTAI TENGAH**, 6km further on from the junction. It's a quiet beach and the sand isn't bad, but the water is murky. There are also jellyfish, so take local advice before you swim. **Accommodation** is limited to a couple of smart resorts and a handful of low-key chalet places. The budget places include *Tanjung Malie* (☎04/955 1891; ②) with comfortable fan or air-con chalets set in a garden, and next door the slightly superior *Sugary Sands Motel* (☎04/955 3473; ②) as well as the *Green Hills Resort* (☎04/955 1935; ②); all three are at the northern end of the beach. A good upmarket option is the *Sunset Beach Resort* (☎04/955 1751; ⑥), a cluster of luxury chalets set amongst shady trees, a little further south. For **eating**, the Chinese restaurants by the junction with Jalan Pantai Tengah have the best atmosphere. *Moody's*, on the junction, is a good place for Western breakfasts, though it's a little pricey and portions are small. Later in the day, *Charlie's* has beachfront barbecues, and next-door *Oasis* has the best bar. Further south, the *White Sands Restaurant* serves very good Malay seafood at around RM17 a dish.

Pantai Cenang

Five hundred metres north of Tengah, the development at **PANTAI CENANG** is the most extensive on the island, with cramped chalet sites side by side. The bay forms a large sweep of wide, white beach with crisp, sugary sand, but again the water here won't win any prizes for cleanliness. Plenty of places offer **watersports** and **boat rental**, where you can expect to pay RM50 for thirty minutes on a jet ski, the same for fifteen minutes' waterskiing, or RM200 for half a day's fishing (4-6 people). The main attraction on Pantai Cenang is the huge **Underwater World** (daily 10am–6pm; RM18), where the highlight is a walk-through aquarium.

Accommodation and eating

Delta Motel (☎04/955 1307; ③), just north of the Underwater World, has pleasant and inexpensive wooden chalets in a well-planned, shady garden; *Langkapuri Beach Resort* (☎04/955 1202; ④), next door, is plusher but overpriced with a range of sturdy brick chalets on a leafy patch of beach, and further north still, the *AB Motel* (☎04/955 1300; ③) is a good budget choice with hammocks and a terrace restaurant. A few steps along, *Amzar Beachview Chalets* (☎04/955 3596; ⑤) seems to have had a change in management and has recently gone upscale (and downhill), still not a bad choice, just not the great value it once was. Ten minutes' walk further, back from the road on the landward side, *Yahok Homestay* (☎04/955 8120; ②) features very simple, reasonably clean cabins and RM10 dorms, and is now the most popular budget option. Most of the resorts also have attached restaurants: the ones at *AB Motel* and *Delta* are good value, though the latter doesn't serve alcohol. The *Beach Garden Resort Bistro*, across from the track leading to the *Yeti*, is a pretty beachside operation serving up pizzas, pasta and beer, while opposite the *AB Motel*, the pricey *Champor Champor,* which combines Western and Oriental influence to successful effect in an enchanted grove atmosphere, is well worth the splurge. Just east of here there's another chance to blow a day's budget on some fine food at *Red Tomato,* with tasty breakfasts, pizzas and very cold beer.

Pantai Kok and Telaga Tujuh

PANTAI KOK lies on the far western stretch of Langkawi and is the best beach on the island, a large sweep of powdery white sand with relatively clear and shallow water – quieter and more secluded than Cenang and more intimate in feel. Accommodation, however, is limited to a few big resorts, only one of which – *Baru Bay* – is actually on the beach.

The road after the turn-off to the *Berjaya Langkawi Beach and Spa Resort* leads up to the island's most wonderful natural attraction, **Telaga Tujuh** or "Seven Wells", where the mossy rocks enable you to slide from one pool to another, before the fast-flowing water disappears over the cliff to form the ninety-metre waterfall. It's a steep two-hundred-metre climb to the pools from the base of the hill – in total, it's about a 45-minute walk from the road near the *Mutiara Burau Bay*.

Accommodation and eating

Heading north from Cenang, the first **accommodation** you'll come to is the Langkasuka Resort (☎04/955 6888; ⑦), a luxurious place on a lovely beach on the way to Pantai Kok that's very good value. Continue past Pantai Kok and you'll reach the *Mutiara Burau Bay* (☎04/959 1061; ⑨) at the western end of the beach where the facilities are up to scratch but the metallic and plastic chalets are a little tacky. Slightly further on is the *Berjaya Langkawi Beach and Spa Resort* (☎04/959 1888; ⑨), which is luxurious and a little kitsch, but the Japanese massages, facials and forest-spa are the real attraction. Last up, and least expensive by far, is the *Seven Wells Motel and Seafood Restaurant* (☎04/959 3842; ②), with a few double rooms with showers on a quiet spot west of the Berjaya.

The best **food** around also happens to be the cheapest, at the tiny *7 Wells Restoran*, just before you reach Telaga Tujuh, on the corner of the road to Datai, which has wonderful home cooking. Other than here, you're limited to the big resort restaurants.

Kuala Perlis and overland into Thailand

Boats to and from Pulau Langkawi (hourly; 45min; RM 12 one way) dock at the little town of **KUALA PERLIS**, 45km north of Alor Setar; although it's the second-largest settlement in the state, it only has two streets. Buses drop you next to the jetty, from where a wooden footbridge connects with the older, more interesting part of town, a ramshackle collection of buildings on stilts. Express buses to Padang Besar, Alor Setar and Butterworth are fairly frequent, but there are a couple of **hotels**, the cheapest of which is the *Asia*, 18 Taman Sentosa (☎04/985 5392; ②), a signposted right turn after a five-minute walk, keeping the water on your left, straight through town. There's also a restaurant downstairs.

You can reach Satun in Thailand directly from Kuala Perlis: small boats leave from the jetty en route from Langkawi as soon as they're full and charge RM4 for the thirty-minute journey. This is the quickest cross-border option if you're coming from Langkawi; otherwise, you have to cross by bus or train (see below). At weekends, you'll be charged an additional RM1 for the immigration officers' overtime payment.

The nearest train station is at **ARAU**, 16km east of Kuala Perlis, where you can catch the **daily train to Hat Yai and Bangkok** (though the train doesn't stop here on the return journey); there are also less convenient daily connections to Butterworth, Alor Setar, Taiping, Ipoh, Tapah Road and Kuala Lumpur. The northbound train comes to a halt at **PADANG BESAR**, where a very long platform connects the Malaysian service with its Thai counterpart. You don't change trains here, although you must get off and go through immigration and customs at the station. You can also do the journey by **bus**: there are frequent services from the local bus station (1km north of the express terminal) at **KANGAR**, 12km east of Kuala Perlis, to the border at Padang Besar. The crossing is open from 6am to 10pm. Buses also ply the North–South Highway, which runs to the Thai border at **BUKIT KAYU HITAM**, from where it's about a five-hundred-metre walk to Danok on the Thai side. Once you've passed through immigration, there are regular bus connections from both places with Hat Yai, 60km away – southern Thailand's transport hub (see p.1093).

7.3

The interior

Banjaran Titiwangsa (Main Range) forms the western boundary of the interior; to its east is an H-shaped range of steep, sandstone mountains and luxuriant valleys where small towns and kampung nestle. The rivers that flow from these mountains – Pahang, Tembeling, Lebir, Nenggiri and Galas – provide the northern interior's indigenous peoples, the Negritos and Senoi, with their main means of transport. Visitors, too, can travel by boat to perhaps the most stunning of all Peninsular Malaysia's delights, **Taman Negara National Park**. Bordering Taman Negara to the south, **Kenong Rimba** is a smaller, quieter, less visited national park, but none the worse for that. And what better way to get from the coasts to these wilderness places than by the **Jungle Railway**, which chugs leisurely through the scenic interior from **Gemas** in the south to **Kota Bharu** on the northwest coast.

The Jungle Railway

Unless you're in a real hurry to get to either coast, consider a trip on the **Jungle Railway**, which winds through the valleys and round the sandstone hills from Mentakab in southern Pahang to Kota Bharu, 500km to the northeast, with useful stops at Jerantut and Kuala Tembeling (see p.672), both access points for Taman Negara, and at Kuala Lipis (p.675), close to Kenong Rimba National Park. The line was completed in 1931 and runs at a snail's pace (it is seldom less than two hours behind schedule) along valley floors where trees and plants almost envelop the track. It's a great way to encounter rural life, as for the Malays, Tamils and Orang Asli who live in these remote areas, the railway is the only alternative to walking. Most people do this trip from south to north, but going in the opposite direction, from north to south, gives you many more hours of daylight in the jungle. The best is the "mail train" number 95, which departs Tumpat (Kota Bharu) at 5.45am and is scheduled to arrive at Gemas junction at 7.40pm.

Another approach to the Jungle Railway from KL is to take a bus to **MENTAKAB** (every 30min from Pekeliling; 2hr 30min), less than 100km east of KL. To reach the train station, walk from the bus station south onto the main road, Jalan Temerloh, and bear left for 50m to a big junction. Turn right, walk another 200m and watch for a narrow road on your right, marked to the train station – a fifteen-minute walk. There are numerous budget **hotels** on Jalan Temerloh that you'll reach if you carry on walking eastwards. The cleanest is the *London Café and Hotel*, 71 Jl Temerloh (☎09/277 1119; ❷), which features neat, basic doubles with attached bathrooms. A few doors away on a side street leading south is the *Hotel Hoover*, 25 Jl Moh Hee Kiang (☎09/277 1622; ❷), which has smaller and more expensive doubles than the London, but also offers single-room rates.

Taman Negara National Park

Peninsular Malaysia's largest and most popular national park is **Taman Negara**, 250km northeast of KL. Numerous rewarding trails snake through some of the oldest rainforest in the world and there are resorts, hides and campsites to stay in. To see any sizeable mammal, including the resident elephants, you really have to make a three- or four-day trek, or journey upriver to remote Kuala Keniam. Staying overnight in the hides (tree houses beside salt licks) might give you sightings of mouse deer, tapir and wild ox – and the park has over three hundred species of birds. The busiest place in the park is **Kuala Tahan**, where you'll find most of the accommodation and the park headquarters. For a quieter experience, there's the more basic **Nusa Camp**, 2km upstream, and the upriver camps at **Kuala Keniam** and **Kuala Trenggan**. The best time to **visit** the park is between February and October, during the "dry" season, although it still rains even then. In the wet season (mid-Oct to Feb), there may be restrictions on the trails and boat trips.

Access to the park

The usual approach to the park is by bus to **Tembeling jetty**, from where it's a three-hour boat trip (daily 9am & 2pm, except Fri 9am & 2.45pm; RM22) to the accommodation and park headquarters at **Kuala Tahan**. Tembeling jetty is 10km from the town of **Jerantut**, or thirty minutes' walk from the village of **Kuala Tembeling** – both these places are stops on the Jungle Railway. There's no accommodation at Kuala Tembeling, so many stay the night at Jerantut, from where you can also take a bus into the park. The return journey downriver is around an hour quicker;

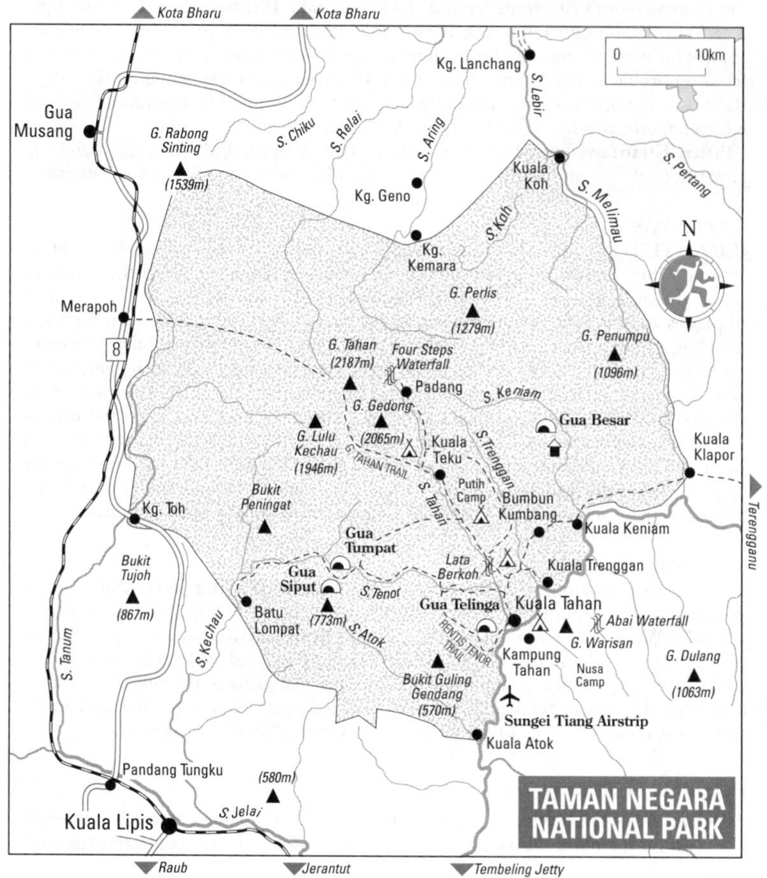

boats come back at the same times. Tickets for the return trip can be purchased at the resort and at some of the floating restaurants, but you must depart from the pier of the place where you bought the ticket.

From KL and the coasts

At the *Mandarin Pacific Hotel* (Jl Petaling ☎03/2072 0336) in KL's Chinatown, you can book accommodation for the *Taman Negara Resort* at Kuala Tahan and get a shuttle bus direct to Tembeling jetty (8am; RM30). If you're taking the shuttle it's a good idea to show up at least half an hour before departure – it leaves when full. By **public bus from KL**, first take the bus to Jerantut from Pekeliling station (4 daily; 3hr 30min; RM11), then either a **taxi** (RM16) or a **local bus** (8am, 11am & 1.30pm; 40min; RM1.20) to Tembeling jetty (the 1.30pm bus doesn't get to the jetty in time for the 2pm boat). Alternatively, join the *Hotel Sri Emas* **bus trip** that leaves Jerantut at 8.30am, stopping at cocoa, rubber and oil palm plantations before reaching Kuala Tahan at around 11am (RM25).

Air-con **express trains from KL** into the interior leave from Sentral station at 7am and 8pm. The earlier departure reaches **Jerantut** at 12.50pm and stops at **Kuala Lipis** an hour later. From **Wakaf Bharu** (7km from Kota Bharu), the 8.44am Kenali Express arrives at Kuala Lipis at 1.46pm, calling at Jerantut an hour later – there's also a 6.38pm service, which arrives at Kuala Lipis by 11.13pm. Local trains make the fifteen-minute run from Jerantut to tiny **Kuala Tembeling** at 11.10am, 6pm & 3.51am (Kampung Tembeling is an unscheduled stop, so you'll need to tell the guard you want to get off). From here, it's a two-kilometre walk west to the jetty. It's also possible to travel direct from Wakaf Bharu to Kuala Tembeling on the Jungle Railway – the 5.36am departure chugs into port at 3.24pm. The economy fare from KL to Jerantut is RM15 (RM18 from Wakaf Bharu).

From Kuantan, three daily buses (10am, 1pm & 3pm; RM10.50) go straight to Jerantut, or there's an hourly service to Temerloh, where you change for Jerantut.

Jerantut

JERANTUT is a small, busy town with only one major street, Jalan Besar. From Jerantut's **bus station** it's a five-minute walk south to Jalan Besar and the centre of town. The **train station** is off Jalan Besar, just behind *Hotel Sri Emas*. There are plenty of **places to stay**. One kilometre west of the train station on Jalan Benta is the large, rambling and good-value *Jerantut Resthouse* (☎09/266 6200; ❷), which offers free pick-up and has a dorm (RM8). The *Hotel Sri Emas* (☎09/266 4499; ❶), at the junction of Jalan Besar and the road that leads to the train station, has a dorm (RM7), inexpensive doubles and better air-con rooms, and offers a wealth of information on the park as well as fast Internet access. The friendliest place in town is the *Cheng Heng Hotel*, 24 Jl Besar (☎09/266 3693; ❶), run by a very helpful family. It's just south of the *Emas* on the opposite side of the road. Between the train and bus stations there are plenty of stalls and mini-restaurants serving Thai, Malay and Chinese **food**, usually open until 3am.

Tembeling jetty

Many motorized sampans depart for the park from **Tembeling jetty** (daily 9am & 2pm, except Fri 2.45pm; 3hr; RM22 one-way), and there are shops and cafés clustered around it. When here, you must buy a park entry **permit** (RM1) and a camera licence (RM5) at the nearby Taman Negara Resort ticket office. A fishing licence costs RM10. The Nusa Camp kiosk is to the left of the jetty. All boats leave at the same time, travelling along the Sungei Tembeling either to Taman Negara Resort and the park headquarters at Kuala Tahan, or to the private Nusa Camp, 2km further upriver.

Kuala Tahan

At **KUALA TAHAN**, visitors can stay either at the *Taman Negara Resort* or in the village itself on the other side of the river; the shuttle boat will ferry you across the river here for 50 sen. *Taman Negara Resort* office has an excellent free site and park **map**, and deals with all park queries, regardless of where you're staying. Behind the office is the official **Parks and Wildlife Department** headquarters where you can book sampans and hides. There's a minimart next door selling basic provisions. The nearby **camping shop** rents trekking and camping gear, including backpacks and lightweight jungle boots. You can also store your luggage at the camping shop (RM2 per day).

Accommodation at the *Taman Negara Resort* can be pre-booked in KL, either at MATIC (see p.640) or at the *Mandarin Pacific Hotel* (Jl Petaling ☎03/2072 0336). Alternatively, book with the Resort direct on ☎09/266 3500. Accommodation consists of twin-bed chalets (❽) and luxurious two-bedroom bungalows (RM700). You can also camp 300m from the resort office (RM2 per person), and tents can be rented for RM8 a night – the RM45 dorm isn't worth bothering with, as you can get the same standard at half the price across the river (although bear in mind that the village is prone to lengthy power cuts). The resort will also prepare good packed lunches.

Across the river **in Kuala Tahan** itself, the best place to stay if you don't want to spend too much is the *Tembeling Riverview Hostel and Chalets* (☎09/266 6766; ❸), an attractive complex of thatched, timber chalets and a café-garden. The doubles with shower are good value and the two dormitories (RM10) are the best around by a long shot. The *Liana* next door (☎03/266 9322) is a barracks-style corridor of four-bed dorms (RM10). Nearby *Agoh Chalets* (☎09/266 9570; ❸) is a better choice, offering RM15 dorms with attached bathroom and plain chalets in a good location. Behind the *Riverview*, *Ekotan Chalets* (☎09/266 9897; ❺) is the best mid-range option with slightly overpriced but comfortable air-con chalets. There's also a dorm (RM20) with air-con and shared bathroom.

Nusa Camp

Nusa Camp is 2km further upstream on Sungei Tembeling. Boats from Tembeling jetty will take you straight there, stopping briefly at Kuala Tahan first. Although accommodation and food is a little cheaper than at the resort, the disadvantage of staying here is that you are dependent on the sampans to ferry you around. For **accommodation**, it's best to book in advance at MATIC (☎03/2164 3929) in KL, or call SPKG Tours (☎09/266 2369) in Jerantut. They also have an office in Kuala Lumpur (☎03/230 5401) and another for Nusa Camp by the jetty at Kuala Tembeling (☎09/266 3043). The twin-bed "Malay Houses" (❻) are much more basic chalets than the ones at the resort, but have attached bathrooms. You can also stay in tiny tepee-like pyramid buildings for two people (❸), which have an external toilet and shower, or four-bed dorm rooms (RM15). Nusa Camp has one small cafeteria (daily 8am–10pm), which does cheap set meals.

The hides

Spending a night in one of the park's **hides** beside a salt lick doesn't guarantee sightings of large mammals, but it'll be a memorable experience, and you may catch sight of deer, tapir, elephant, leopard or wild ox. The hides offer very basic bunk accommodation for six to eight people and must be booked at the wildlife office in the resort (RM5 per person). They have no washing or cooking facilities, and no electricity, so bring a torch. Also take rain gear, hat and sleeping bag, and all the food and drink you will need – and bring all your rubbish back. It's best to go in a group and take turns keeping watch for animals. The closest hide to the resort is the **Bumbun Tahan**, just south of the junction with the Bukit Teresek trail. Much more promising are the **Bumbun Tabing**, on the east bank of Sungei Tahan, and the **Bumbun Cegar Anjing**, an hour from the Tabing, on the west bank of Sungei Tahan. The most distant hide to the north of the resort is the six-bed **Bumbun Kumbang**, an eleven-kilometre walk from Kuala Tahan, and the best place to catch sight of animals.

Exploring the park

There are numerous hiking possibilities in Taman Negara, the most popular of which are the day-treks out of Kuala Tahan, described here. For these, T-shirts, shorts and strong trainers are adequate, but always have a hat, mosquito repellent and water to hand. Binoculars are a good idea. Always **inform park staff** first, so they know where you are if you get into any difficulty. Although the trails are well marked, people do sometimes get lost.

Transport around the park is by sampan. Staff at the *Taman Negara Resort* office can arrange a trip for you, or you can speak to the boatmen at the jetty, and sort out a (cheaper) price with them. Always book your return trip at the same time, since the boatmen only operate out of Kuala Tahan and Nusa Camp. For trips to upriver sites or the falls at Lata Berkoh on Sungei Tahan, expect to spend at least RM80 a day per boat one-way.

Bukit Teresek

Although heavily used, the route to **Bukit Teresek** is an excellent starter. Follow the path between the chalets east of the resort office, beyond which a trail heads north-east away from the river. It's wide and easy to follow, hitting primary jungle almost immediately; after around twenty minutes, the trail divides, straight on to Bukit Teresek and left for the Tabing hide and Bukit Indah. The climb up 342-metre-high Bukit Teresek (1hr) offers marvellous views. Along the trail you might hear gibbons or hill squirrels in the trees. Back at the base of the hill, the canopy walkway (see below) is just 300m to the north along a clearly marked path.

The canopy walkway

About thirty minutes' walk east from Kuala Tahan along the riverside Bukit Indah trail is the **canopy walkway**. Only a small group of people can gain access to the walkway (daily 11am–2.45pm, except Fri 9am–noon; RM5) at any one time, so you may have to wait. The walkway is a swaying bridge made from aluminium ladders bound by rope and set 40m above the ground. At 450m, it's the longest walkway of its kind in the world. You reach it by climbing a sturdy wooden tower, and it takes thirty minutes to cross. Once you've got used to the swaying, it's a pleasurable experience taking in the fine views of Sungei Tembeling and observing the insect life and tree parasites that abound at that height. Other species usually visible include the grey-banded leaf monkey, and the white-eyed dusky leaf monkey.

The Bukit Indah trail

Past the canopy the route divides, north and slightly uphill to the Tabing hide, another 1km further on, or northeast along the lovely **Bukit Indah trail**, a three-hour round-trip from the resort office. Initially, this follows the riverbank, and you stand a chance of spotting monkeys, various birds, squirrels, shrews, a multitude of insects and perhaps tapir or wild ox. The path to Bukit Indah itself leaves the main riverside trail (which continues to Kuala Trenggan, 6km away) and climbs at a slight gradient for 200m to give a lovely view over Sungei Tembeling.

Gua Telinga and Kemah Keladong

Another major trail (the Rentis Tenor) leads south alongside the river, with branches to Gua Telinga and the campsite at Kemah Keladong. From the jetty by the KT Restoran, take a sampan across Sungei Tahan. On the other side, follow the trail through a small kampung into the trees. After 3km, follow the sign north for a further 200m to reach **Gua Telinga**, a small but deceptively deep limestone cave. In theory, it's possible to follow a guide rope through the eighty-metre cave, but you have to be pretty small to fit through the narrow cavities. Thousands of tiny round-leaf and fruit bats live in the cave, along with giant toads, black-striped frogs and whip spiders (which aren't poisonous). From Gua Telinga, it's another 500m to the noisy Belau hide, and another 1km to the one at Yong, where the trail divides, north to Kemah Rentis and left to the tranquil **Kemah Keladong** campsite, 1km further on. Given an early start, it's quite possible to reach this point, have a swim, and get back to the resort before dusk; bring at least a litre of water each and lunch.

Lata Berkoh

Most people visit the "roaring rapids" of **Lata Berkoh** by boat, but you could walk the trail there and arrange for a boat to pick you up for the return journey. **Sampans** from Kuala Tahan cost around RM80 for four people and take half an hour. The **trail** from the resort (8km; 3hr) starts at the campsite and leads through dense rainforest, passing Lubok Lesong campsite (3km), then crossing gullies and steep ridges, before reaching the river, which must be forded. The final part of the trail runs north along the west side of Sungei Tahan before reaching the falls. The **waterfall** itself is 50m north of Berkoh Lodge. There's a deep pool for swimming, and you may see kingfishers, large fish eagles, bulbul birds and monitor lizards.

Kuala Trenggan and Kuala Keniam

The upriver lodges are set in tranquil surroundings, and make excellent bases for exploring less-visited parts of the park. You should pre-book all lodges with the park wildlife office at the resort. *Trenggan Lodge* (10 beds; ❻) is the closest, and has polished wood chalets and a café. It's situated at **KUALA TRENGGAN**, 11km upstream from Taman Negara Resort, reached either by boat (30min; RM80 per boat), or by one of two trails (6–8hr). The shorter and more direct trail runs alongside Sungei Tembeling (9km), but can be quite hard going; the easier inland route (12km) runs north past the campsite at Lubok Lesong.

A further 20km north along Sungei Tembeling (2hr from the resort; RM140 per boat), *Keniam Lodge* (18 beds; ❻), at **KUALA KENIAM**, comprises several chalets and a small café. From here, the **Perkai trail** (3km; 2hr) is rich with banded and dusky leaf monkeys, long-tailed macaques and white-handed gibbons. The more popular hike from here is the **Keniam–Trenggan trail** (13km), a major highlight, combining the possibility of seeing elephants with visits to three caves. It's generally a tough, full day's hike, but can be done in around six hours; there are innumerable streams to wade through and hills to circumvent.

Kuala Lipis

KUALA LIPIS, 170km northeast of KL, was once a vibrant tin town and from 1898 to 1955 served as the state capital of Pahang, but today it's an inconsequential place, of interest to tourists mainly as a **transit point** en route to Kenong Rimba State Park. Both train and bus stations are very central, close to the town's inexpensive hotels. The jetty – from where boats leave on Saturdays for Kenong Rimba State Park – lies 50m northeast of the market on Jalan Jelai. There are two **tourist information offices**, both offering much the same services. One is a private concern (Mon–Fri 9am–5pm, Sat 9am–1pm; ☎09/312 3277, 24hr information on ☎09/312 2292), tucked away on the left of the train station exit, opposite the ticket booth; the other is just outside the station (Mon–Fri 9am–5pm, Sat 9am–1pm; ☎09/312 5032). The most atmospheric **place to stay** is the *Government Rest House*, on Jalan Bukit Residen (☎09/312 2600; ❸), which has twenty en-suite rooms with air-con or fan; the furniture is a bit old, but all the rooms are large and clean and the surrounds are stately. The budget options are in the town centre, mostly on Jalan Besar heading east from the bus station. Try *Gin Loke* at 64 Jl Besar (☎09/312 1388; ❶), or next-door *Hotel Lipis* (☎09/312 3142; ❶), run by Appu, a trekking guide; there's a spotless dorm (RM7), a range of rooms with shared showers, and Internet facilities.

Kenong Rimba State Park

Kenong Rimba State Park is one of the best reasons to travel the Jungle Railway into the interior and makes a good stop-off between KL and Kota Bharu. It offers a compact version of the Taman Negara experience – jungle trails, caves, riverside camping, mammal-spotting and excellent bird-watching – at much reduced prices and without the hype. No special equipment is needed, other than a tent and blanket for sleeping. Take lots of mosquito repellent and always carry at least one litre of water with you on the trails. You can organize a **tour** of the park from Kuala Lipis (4 days; RM180) at either of the tourist information offices (see above). The *Gin Loke* hotel and the *Hotel Lipis* also organize tours.

Practicalities

One way to get to the park is to travel **from Kuala Lipis** on Saturday, when a sampan (RM50) leaves the Jalan Jelai jetty at 9am, arriving at the Tanjung Kiara jetty around an hour and a half later. On other days of the week, you can charter a sampan directly from Kuala Lipis, at around RM160 per boat. However, it's cheaper to take the local train to **BATU SEMBILAN** (7.33am & 2.16pm; 30min; RM1), three stops to the south of Kuala Lipis, where you walk left (east) along a narrow road 50m to the jetty on Sungei Jelai. Here, sampans take you on the thirty-minute trip downstream (RM30 per person) to the **Tanjung Kiara jetty**. Alternatively, it's possible to charter a sampan from **Tembeling jetty** for around RM120. From the Tanjung Kiara jetty, it's then a thirty-minute walk along a road through Kampung Dusun, past a small store on your right to a bridge where the park proper begins. After a further hour along a forest path, you reach the **park headquarters** and chalets at **GUNUNG KESONG**.

The caves and trails

The first of the six **caves** in Rimba is outside the park proper, close to the Tanjung Kiara jetty. After about ten minutes' walk from the jetty along the road, look out for a path on your left (west), which leads to **Gua Batu Tinggi**. Inside, there's a surprising variety of plant life – including orchids and fig trees. **Gua Batu Tangga** can be reached direct from the camp at Gunung Kesong, though you can also get there from Tinggi by returning on the same trail and crossing the road, following the path to the left of a house – there's a sign pointing to the cave, another twenty minutes' walk further on. It has a wide, deep chamber, and in the northwest corner a row of rocks forms ledges or steps. Two smaller caves, **Gua Batu Tangkup** and **Gua Batu Telahup**, are just a few hundred metres beyond Tangga on the same trail. **Gua Hijau** is five minutes' walk from headquarters and home to thousands of bats.

The main trail in the park, the **Kesong trail**, leads to Seven Steps Waterfall (10km; 4hr one-way), which heads north from the headquarters along Sungei Kesong. Around 250m before the waterfall, you cross Sungei Kesong for the final time to reach the Kenong campsite. From here, the trail continues through high forest to a set of rapids, with jungle closing in all around. Returning on the southeastern loop of the trail takes longer – around twelve hours walking – and is harder going as it traverses small hills and follows a less well-defined path. You need at least a one-night stop. The first leg of the return trail is a six-hour walk to Gunung Putih (cave camp). After a further three hours or so, you pass close to a Batek village, where you can pitch a tent near the huts, if you ask. From here you could climb Bukit Agong (1800m; 2hr each way), a stiff ascent along an unmarked and overgrown track. Returning to headquarters from the village takes around another two hours on the main trail. Most people take four days to complete the circuit.

7.4

The east coast

The four-hundred-kilometre stretch from the northeastern corner of the Peninsula to Kuantan, roughly halfway down the east coast, is the most "Malay" region in Malaysia, with strong cultural traditions – particularly in **Kota Bharu**, the last major town before the Thai border, whose inhabitants still practise ancient Malay crafts such as kite-making and top-spinning. This region is also where Islam is most strictly adhered to in all of Malaysia – a siren signals the call to prayer and even hawkers stalls in the Kota Bharu's market must close for twenty minutes. There are some good beaches along the east coast, but women should keep in mind that beach attire will be frowned upon in urban areas. The casuarina-fringed beaches and coral reefs on two of the most beautiful islands in the South China Sea, **Pulau Perhentian** and **Pulau Kapas**, are the greatest attraction, but there are some appealing places on the mainland, too, not least the laid-back backpackers' resort of **Cherating**, and **Rantau Abang**, one of only five places in the world where giant leatherback turtles come to nest between May and September. Many of the east-coast islands are virtually out of bounds between November and February because of the annual monsoon.

Kota Bharu

At the very northeastern corner of the Peninsula, close to the Thai border, **KOTA BHARU** is the capital of Kelantan State and one of the most important cultural centres in Malaysia. The town is a showcase for skills and customs little practised elsewhere in Malaysia, with an impressive Cultural Centre and lots of craft workshops. It is also one of only three towns in Malaysia (together with Kuala Terengganu and Dungun) to have a Malay majority. Foreign women sometimes complain about feeling uncomfortable in Kota Bharu, but while it's not a place to sport beach wear, there's a relaxed air about the town that belies its political conservatism and mitigates its male-dominated outlook. During the month of **Ramadan**, late in the year, strongly Muslim Kota Bharu virtually shuts up shop.

Arrival and information

Long-distance **buses** arrive at one of the two **bus stations**, inconveniently situated on the southern outskirts of the town. The state bus company, SKMK, operates from the Langgar bus station on Jalan Pasir Puteh, as does the MARA company, which runs buses to KL and Singapore; other companies use the larger bus station on Jalan Hamzah, which also has a left-luggage facility. If you arrive at night, you're at the mercy of the unofficial taxis at the stations, whose drivers can charge up to RM15 for the two-kilometre drive to the centre: the daytime charge is around RM4. The **local bus station**, where buses from Kuala Terengganu arrive, is on Jalan Padong Garong; SKMK also operates some services from here and has an information counter (daily 7am–7pm; closed Fri 12.45–2pm). The **long-distance taxi** stand is behind the bus station on Jalan Doktor.

The nearest **train station** to Kota Bharu is 7km to the west at Wakaf Bharu, the penultimate stop on the Jungle Railway (see p.670). From here, it's a twenty-minute

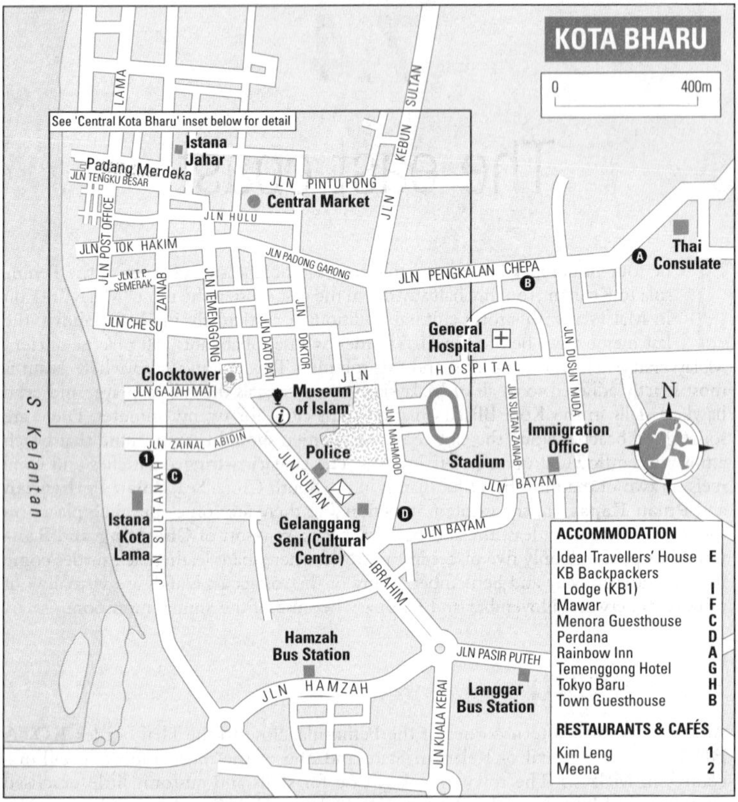

KOTA BHARU
0 400m
See 'Central Kota Bharu' inset below for detail
Airport & Pantai Dasar Sabak
Istana Jahar
Padang Merdeka
JLN TENGKU BESAR
Central Market
JLN PINTU PONG
JLN HULU
JLN POST OFFICE
JLN TOK HAKIM
JLN T.P. SEMERAK
ZAINAB
JLN TEMENGGONG
JLN DATO PATI
JLN DOKTOR
JLN PADONG GARONG
JLN PENGKALAN CHEPA
JLN KEBUN SULTAN
LAMA
JLN CHE SU
Clocktower
JLN GAJAH MATI
Museum of Islam
General Hospital
JLN HOSPITAL
JLN SULTAN ZAINAB
JLN DUSUN MUDA
Thai Consulate
Immigration Office
Stadium
JLN MAHMOOD
JLN BAYAM
JLN ZAINAL ABIDIN
Police
JLN SULTAN
JLN SULTANAH
Istana Kota Lama
Gelanggang Seni (Cultural Centre)
IBRAHIM
S. Kelantan
Hamzah Bus Station
JLN HAMZAH
JLN PASIR PUTEH
JLN KUALA KERAI
Langgar Bus Station
N
ACCOMMODATION
Ideal Travellers' House E
KB Backpackers Lodge (KB1) I
Mawar F
Menora Guesthouse C
Perdana D
Rainbow Inn A
Temenggong Hotel G
Tokyo Baru H
Town Guesthouse B
RESTAURANTS & CAFÉS
Kim Leng 1
Meena 2

0 100m
LAMA
Istana Batu
Kampung Kraftangan
Masjid Negeri
Istana Jahar
JLN HILIR KOTA
JALAN SULTAN
Foodstalls
Padang Merdeka
Istana Balai Besar
JLN TENGKU BESAR
JLN PINTU PONG
Sultan Ismail Petra Arch
JLN HULU KOTA
State Treasury Bank
Central Market
JLN KEBUN SULTAN
S. Kelantan
JLN TENGKU CHIK
JLN HULU
Bazaar Buluh Kubu
Nightmarket
JLN POST OFFICE
TOK HAKIM
JLN PADONG GARONG
Local Bus Station
JLN T.P. SEMERAK
JLN HILIR
Telekom
ZAINAB
JLN TEMENGGONG
JLN HULU PASAR
JLN SUARA MUDA
Taxi Stand
JLN CHE SU
JALAN ISMAIL
JLN DATO PATI
JLN DOKTOR
JLN MAHMOOD
N
JLN HOSPITAL
Clocktower
JLN GAJAH MATI
Museum of Islam
Stadium
CENTRAL KOTA BHARU

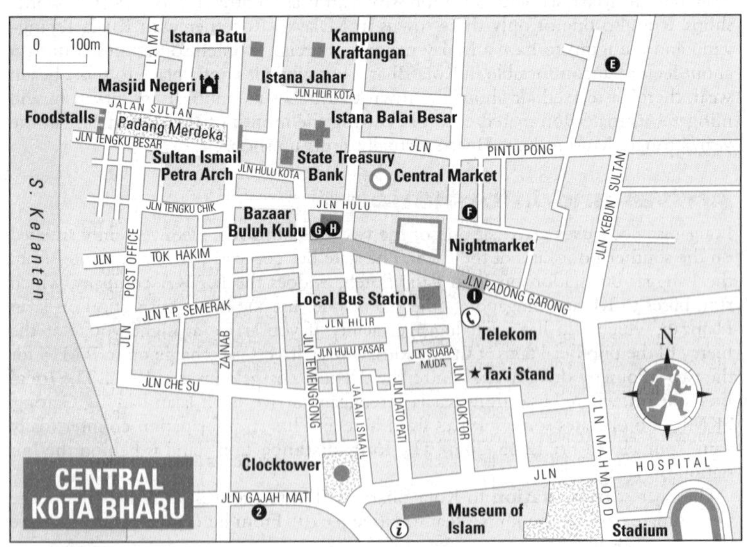

Crossing the border into Thailand

From Kota Bharu, you can cross the Thai border by river or land. If you're going to stay in Thailand for more than a month, you'll need a **visa**, easily obtainable from the town's consulate (see "Listings", p.681). Both **border posts** are open daily 6am–10pm; remember that Thai time is one hour behind Malaysian time.

The coastal access point is at **Pengkalan Kubor**, 20km northwest of Kota Bharu, which connects with the small town of Tak Bai on the Thai side. Take bus #27 or #43 from the local bus station for the thirty-minute journey (RM1.70), then the car ferry (50 sen).

More convenient, however, is the land crossing at **Rantau Panjang**, 30km southwest of Kota Bharu. Bus #29 departs from the local bus station in Kota Bharu every thirty minutes (6.45am–6.30pm) for the 45-minute trip (RM2.60), or you can take a share taxi from Kota Bharu for RM5 each; from Rantau Panjang, it's a short walk across the border to Sungai Kolok on the Thai side. Trains depart from here at 11am and 2.05pm for the 23-hour trip to Bangkok via Hat Yai and Surat Thani; if you want to be sure of a seat, tickets can be booked for around RM80 at the *Town Guesthouse* (see p.680). Buses to Bangkok leave at 8am, 11.30am and 12.30pm; buses to Hat Yai take four hours.

ride into town on bus #19 or #27. The **airport** is 9km northeast of the centre; a taxi into town costs RM15 – buy a coupon from the taxi counter in the airport. Tours to local craft workshops and homestays can be booked at the award-winning **Tourist Information Centre** (Mon–Wed & Sun 8am–1pm & 2–4.45pm, Thurs 8am–1pm & 2–4.30pm; ⓣ09/748 5534) on Jalan Sultan Ibrahim.

Accommodation

Kota Bharu has some of the cheapest **accommodation** in Malaysia; nearly all guesthouses have dorms as well as ordinary rooms, and the rates often include breakfast. There is a catch, however. If you're coming from Malaysia's west coast (or from Hat Yai, Thailand) you'll notice a drop in standards of cleanliness, although the price of the room doesn't necessarily have any bearing on the staff's lackadaisical attitude towards dirt and bugs – expensive rooms can be just as bad as cheap ones. An alternative option is the **homestay programme** run by the Tourist Information Centre (see above), which offers the chance to stay with a family, often expert in a particular craft (RM240 per person, minimum two people for three days, including all meals).

Ideal Travellers' House 3954f Jl Kebun Sultan ⓣ09/744 2246. Friendly and quiet – despite its very central location – this budget hostel with a peaceful beer garden and dorm (RM8) is the most pleasant retreat you'll find in Kota Bharu. ①

KB Backpackers Lodge (KB1) Jl Padang Garong ⓣ09/773 7707. Centrally located and cheap, the dorm accommodation (RM8) here is very popular. Rooms are cleaner than most of the competition, but that's not saying much.

Mawar Jl Parit Dalam ⓣ09/744 8888. A Baroque lobby and small but comfortable rooms. Breakfast is served in your room; for dinner, the hotel is situated right by the *pasar malam* (night market). ⑤

Menora Guesthouse 3338d Jl Sultanah Zainab ⓣ09/748 1669. Accommodation consists of a dorm (RM8) and large, brightly painted rooms with or without shower and toilet; there's also a lounge area, café, and roof garden with a river view. ①

Perdana Jl Mahmood ⓣ09/748 5000. A concrete monstrosity on the outside, but inside things improve: it's a good-value, upmarket hotel with swimming pool, squash courts, gym and its own shopping arcade. ⑥

Rainbow Inn 4423a Jl Pengkalan Chepa ⓣ09/743 4936. Clean rooms in a hundred-year-old wooden house east of the centre. Laid-back and friendly with a garden, dorms (RM8), and bikes for rent. ①

Temenggong Hotel Jl Tok Hakim 15000 ⓣ09/748 3481. A clean, mid-range choice in the centre. The modern rooms complete with bathtub, fridge, TV and a/c are excellent value, and the coffee house serves Thai food. ❹

Tokyo Baru 3945 Jl Tok Hakim ☎09/744 4511. Top-floor rooms have great balconies overlooking the town centre, and the simple, clean doubles with fan or a/c are good value. ❸

Town Guesthouse 286 Jl Pengkalan Chepa ☎09/748 5192. A warm and welcoming, family-run guesthouse with a communal lounge, café and Internet facilities. ❷

The Town

Small Padang Merdeka in the north part of town is Kota Bharu's historical heart. Near here, the **Istana Jahar** (daily except Fri 8.30am–4.45pm; RM3) houses the Royal Customs Museum whose ground floor is given over to a display of exquisite *ikat* and *songket* textiles and ornate gold jewellery; upstairs, you'll see life-size reconstructions of various traditional royal ceremonies, from weddings to circumcisions. Behind the istana, a **Weapon's Gallery** (RM2) displays an impressive collection of spears, daggers and kris.

As you leave the museum, turn the corner to your left and after a few metres you'll see the sky-blue **Istana Batu** (daily 8.30am–4.45pm, closed Fri; RM2), now the Kelantan Royal Museum, with the sultan's rooms left in their original state. Directly opposite, the **Kampung Kraftangan** (daily except Fri 8.30am–4.30pm), or "Handicraft Village", comprises gift shops, a café and a museum (RM1).

Situated on the corner of Jalan Hospital and Jalan Sultan Ibrahim, the **Museum of Islam** (daily except Fri 8.30am–4.45pm; RM1) features exhibits explaining the importance of Islam to the culture of Kelantan. The **Gelanggang Seni**, Kota Bharu's Cultural Centre, on Jalan Mahmood, has free performances (March–Oct Wed & Sat except during Ramadan) that feature many of the traditional pastimes of Kelantan, including the vigorous sport of top-spinning, and the playing of giant one-hundred-kilogram *rebana* drums. On Wednesday evenings, there are wayung kulit (shadow play) performances, which can last for two to three hours. On Saturday nights, shows combine singing, dancing and comedy, derived from nineteenth-century court entertainments.

For a chance to watch local crafts being made, and to buy them direct, visit the **workshops** (daily 10am–5pm) that line the road north from Kota Bharu to the coast. Kampung Penambang is particularly good for *songket* weaving and **batik** (many workshops here will allow you to create your own designs), while Kampung Kijang specializes in kite-making; both villages are barely beyond the town suburbs on the #10 bus, which leaves from beside the Central Market (pasar besar).

Eating

Easily the most exciting place to eat at is Kota Bharu's **night market** (daily 6.30pm–midnight; closes for evening prayers for 20min at around 7.30pm), with an amazing variety of food – although vegetarians could find themselves limited to vegetable *murtabaks*. Try the local speciality *ayam percik* (barbecued chicken with a creamy coconut sauce) or the delicious *nasi kerabu* (purple, green or blue rice with a dash of vegetables, seaweed and grated coconut), finish off with a filling *pisang murtabak* (banana pancake), and you won't have parted with much more than RM5. The town's **restaurants** are a letdown after the night market, but *Meena* on Jalan Gajah Mati does excellent, inexpensive banana-leaf curries and seafood specialities, and the unassuming *Kim Leng* on Jalan Sultanah Zainab serves quality Chinese food at RM3–5 per dish.

Listings

Airlines MAS, Kompleks Yakin, Jl Gajah Mati ☎09/744 7000.

Banks and exchange Bank Bumiputra, Jl Kebu Sultan; HSBC Bank, Jl Padong Garong; Standard Chartered Bank, Jl Tok Hakim.

Hospital The General Hospital is on Jl Hospital ☎09/748 5533.

Immigration On-the-spot visa renewals are available at the Immigration Office, 2nd Floor, Wisma Persekutuan, Jl Bayan (daily 8am–3.30pm except Thurs 8am–12.30pm; ☎09/748 2120).

Internet access It's not hard to find an Internet

café in Kota Bharu; most are clustered around the Central Market.

Police Headquarters on Jl Sultan Ibrahim ☎09/748 5522.

Post office The GPO is on Jl Sultan Ibrahim (daily except Fri 8.30am–5pm, closed first Sat of every month; ☎09/748 4033). Efficient poste restante/ general delivery at counter 20.

Telephone services The Telekom centre is on Jl Doktor (daily 8am–4.30pm).

Thai visas From the Royal Thai Consulate, 4426 Jl Pengkalan Chepa (☎09/748 2545; Mon–Thurs & Sun 9am–noon & 2–3.30pm, closed Fri & Sat). Two-month tourist visas (RM33) are issued within 24 hours.

Pulau Perhentian

Pulau Perhentian, just over 20km off the northeastern coast, is actually two islands – **Perhentian Kecil** (Small Island) and **Perhentian Besar** (Big Island). Both are textbook tropical paradises, neither more than 4km in length. Not surprisingly, they provide a popular getaway for KL and Singaporean weekenders (especially in August), and see a regular stream of backpackers. Neither island boasts a raging nightlife, as there's no alcohol in most places, but local people seem to have no objection to you bringing your own. Don't be tempted to bring drugs, though – there are frequent police road checks on the way to the islands. There's a good

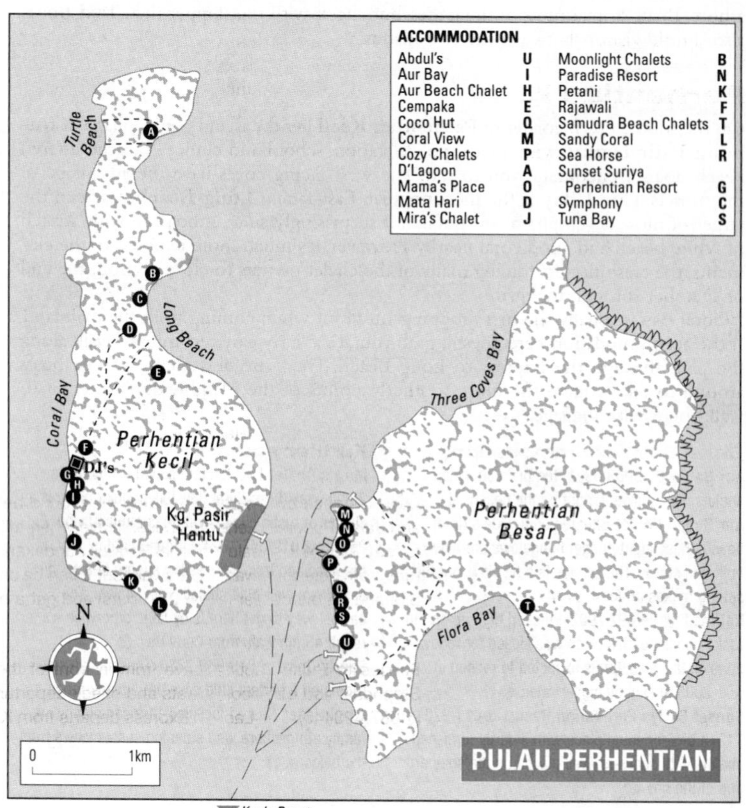

range of accommodation, but the places on the budget end of the spectrum all seem to suffer from a lack of bathing water. The electricity supply is also haphazard, with many places running generators from 7pm to10pm. Activities include snorkelling trips around the islands (RM25 – though you can rent your own gear for RM12 a day) and dive courses (RM750 for the four-day PADI Open Water course, fun dives RM70). The harsh east-coast **monsoon** means that the islands, reached by slow and unsophisticated fishing boats from Kuala Besut, are frequently inaccessible between November and February. There is a RM5 entrance fee to the islands that is supposed to go to the Department of Fisheries and is paid upon boarding the boat.

Getting there: Kuala Besut

The ragged little town of **KUALA BESUT**, 45km south of Kota Bharu, is the departure point for Pulau Perhentian. It's reached by taking bus #3 from Kota Bharu's local bus station to Pasir Puteh (every 15min; 1hr), and then bus #96 (every 30min; 30min) to Kuala Besut. Most guesthouses in Kota Bharu also organize share taxis (RM24) direct to Kuala Besut. There are no banks in Kuala Besut, or on the islands, so **change money** before you go. You have a choice here of **slow boats** (1hr 30min; RM20) or **fast boats** (20min; RM30), and there is a whole slew of companies to choose from. These will try to sell you a round-trip ticket, but it's best to pay for each way as you go. Boatmen act as touts for places of accommodation on the islands and will say anything to get you to stay where they'll get a commission – just sit back and enjoy the view. On arrival, you'll pay a further RM2 to be ferried ashore. Boats stop at most of the jetties, but check with the skipper first. **Taxi boats** also shuttle visitors between the two islands.

Perhentian Kecil

On the southeastern corner of **Perhentian Kecil** lies the island's only village, **Kampung Pasir Hantu**, with a jetty, police station, school and clinic – but the littered beach doesn't encourage you to stay. The west-facing coves have the advantage of the sunsets: **Coral Bay** is the most popular. East-facing **Long Beach** has been the target of most development on Kecil, not surprisingly, since it boasts a wide stretch of white beach and good coral nearby. However, it's much more exposed to the elements, the crashing surf forcing many of the chalet owners to close up from the end of October through to April.

Coral Bay is usually the first dropping-off point when coming from the mainland. If the accommodation here doesn't grab you, it's a fairly easy ten-minute walk along the path through the interior to Long Beach. There are also plenty of taxi boats around to take you to the more southerly points of the island – don't attempt to walk there with luggage.

Coral Bay accommodation

Aur Bay ⓣ019/963 0391. Ten plain but clean chalets with showers, right on the beach. ❸

Aur Beach Chalet Situated on a wide strip of beach, these eight budget bungalows are newly built and sturdy. The service is a bit slow, but the setting makes up for it. ❷–❸

Rajawali ⓣ09/697 7907. Perched high up on the rocky headland, this place was closed for renovations on last visit, but is expected to reopen in mid-2005 at slightly higher rates. ❸

Sunset Suriya Perhentian Resort ⓣ011/970 712. A dive-oriented place with smartly furnished chalets with showers, well placed on the southern end of the bay. ❻

Further south

Mira's Chalet Located on its own sandy bay a 25min walk from Coral Bay, this popular place is a cluster of rustic chalets with a communal vibe. ❷

Petani ⓣ019/957 1624. Fifteen minutes' around the headland from *Mira's* on a superb beach, this has clean, well-built chalets with shower. The easiest way to get here is by boat, otherwise it's a rough 45min walk from Coral Bay. ❹

Sandy Coral ⓣ019/969 2686. These longhouse rooms on a perfect little cove are already much sought-after. Shared facilities, hurricane lamps, a family atmosphere, and stunning sunset views from the balcony. ❷

Long Beach accommodation

Cempaka A mishmash of basic A-frames without electricity, and bungalows with shower. There are also some doubles in a longhouse with a generous veranda. ❷–❸

D'Lagoon ☎010/985 7089. Set in a tiny cove at the very northeast tip of the island 1km from Long Beach, with dorms and chalets. From here, you can clamber across the narrow neck of the island to the turtle-spotting beach on the other side. ❶–❷

Mata Hari Simple but well-designed chalets in a garden, complete with hammocks and a good restaurant. ❸

Moonlight Chalets ☎091/985 8222. Rustic chalets along with some upmarket units at the northern end of the beach; basic A-frames to doubles with attached bathrooms. This is the best place for food, and the upstairs restaurant has a good view across the beach. ❷

Symphony ☎019/910 4236. Some of the least-expensive accommodation on the island; leak-proof thatched roofs and very friendly staff. ❷

Perhentian Besar

The best place on the islands for turtle-watching is undoubtedly Three Coves Bay on the north coast of **Perhentian Besar**. A stunning conglomeration of three beaches, separated from the main area of accommodation by rocky outcrops and reached only by speedboat, it provides a secluded haven between May and September for green and hawksbill turtles to come ashore and lay their eggs. Most of the accommodation on Perhentian Besar is on the western half of the island and tends to be more upmarket than on Kecil. The beach improves as you go further south and the atmosphere is slightly more laid-back than at Long Beach. The best snorkelling beach (and it's not privately owned, despite signs up saying "only patrons can use our facilities") is just to the north in front of the *Perhentian Island Resort*. There is more accommodation on Flora Bay, the island's south beach, reached via a trail from *Abdul's*.

Abdul's ☎09/697 7058. Fronting one of the best strips of beach, all chalets are basic A-frames but have a small veranda. The generator runs until late evening (7–11pm) and then it gets very quiet here. One of the best places at the low end of the price spectrum. ❸

Coco Hut ☎019/910 5019. Yet another collection of A-frame bungalows with nothing to make it stand out except perhaps for the fine scenery and helpful staff. ❷

Coral View ☎010/903 0943. Located on a rocky outcrop, these tastefully designed and very well-furnished chalets are still the best accommodation on either island, ranging from well-designed doubles with shower to hotel-style en-suites with a/c, mini-bar and hot water. The restaurant is also worth the outlay. ❻–❼

Cozy Chalets Built on a headland that separates the beach north and south, this has smart chalets built two-by-two up on the rocks and family accommodation nearer the shore. There's also a scenic restaurant. ❸

Mama's Place With four rows of variously priced chalets, the most expensive nearest the beach. A licensed ferry service runs to surrounding islands, and the decent doubles are all en suite. ❹

Paradise Resort ☎010/981 0930. Next door to *Mama's*, with recently renovated chalets. The restaurant is also pricey, but the menu changes daily. ❻

Samudra Beach Chalets ☎010/983 4929. Pleasant bungalows and smaller, less-expensive A-frames set on the remote Flora Bay. Clean water supplied from an artificial well. ❸

Sea Horse ☎019/984 1181. True to the traveller spirit, this laid-back place on the south beach offers simple crashpad chalets without shower at the lowest rates on either island. The adjoining dive centre caters for all levels. Free pick-up service. ❶

Tuna Bay ☎09/699 1779. This new, upscale resort actually lives up to the touts' hype. The well-built bungalows are on a good stretch of beach along the south coast, and all the activities are lined up for you. ❽

Kuala Terengganu

The tiny Muslim metropolis, **KUALA TERENGGANU**, 160km south of Kota Bharu, is a traditional place set on an estuary, with dozens of craft workshops and an exceptional cultural museum complex, the new **Istana Tengku Long Museum** (daily except Fri 9am–5pm; RM5), which is set in landscaped gardens 3km west of the centre. The main building displays exquisite fabrics and crafts, and details the history of Terengganu. Elsewhere in the compound, you'll find a fine exhibit of Koranic calligraphy, two traditional sailing boats, a small Maritime Museum and some reconstructed ancient timber palaces. The supreme example of these is the Istana Tunku Long, originally built in 1888 with a high, pointed roof and wooden gables fitted with twenty gilded screens, intricately carved with Koranic verses. The museum is easily reached by the regular Losong minibus #7 (20min; 70 sen) from the local bus station.

At the west end of Kuala Terengganu, Jalan Bandar forms the centre of **Chinatown**, where you'll find the excellent Teratai, at no. 151, selling local arts and crafts. Kuala Terengganu's **Central Market** (daily 7am–6pm), a little further down on the right, close to the junction with Jalan Kota, also deals in batik, *songkets* and brassware. For other good craft buys, check out the small **brassware** workshop (daily 8.30am–6pm) on Jalan Ladang in the east of town. Ky Enterprises, about 3km due south of the centre on Jalan Panji Alam, is a good place to watch the *mengkuang* style of **weaving**, using pandanus leaves to make bags, floor mats and fans; take minibus #12, #15, #26 or #13c (70 sen) for the fifteen-minute ride from the local bus station. In neighbouring Pasir Panjang, about 500m west of Jalan Panji Alam, Abu Bakar bin Mohammed Amin on Lorong Saga, is a **kris** maker (call to make an appointment; ⓣ09/622 7968); take a minibus from the local bus station and get off at the sign marked "Sekolah Kebangsaan Psr. Panjang". You can catch **traditional dance** shows at the Gelanggang Seni cultural centre, a two-kilometre walk or trishaw ride southeast from the centre, facing the town's beach, Pantai Batu Buruk (pick up a timetable of events from the Tourist Information Centre).

Practicalities

The **local bus station** is opposite the taxi stand on Jalan Masjid Abidin, and the **express bus station** – where buses from Kota Bharu pull in – is across town on Jalan Sultan Zainal Abidin. **Sultan Mohammed Airport** lies 13km northeast of the centre (ⓣ09/666 3666), a RM20 taxi ride to the centre; the city bus marked "Kem Seberang Takir" picks up from the road directly outside and runs to the local bus station. The MAS office is at 13 Jl Sultan Omar (ⓣ09/622 1415).

There's a **Tourist Information Centre** (daily except Fri 9am–5pm; ⓣ09/622 1553) near the GPO on Jalan Sultan Zainal Abdin, and plenty of inexpensive **Internet** places on Jalan Tok Lam.

Accommmodation and eating

For a relaxing taste of rustic kampung life, the best **place to stay** is *Awi's Yellow House* (ⓣ09/624 5046; ❶), a rickety complex of stilted huts built over the water on the tiny island of Duyung; it has very basic cabins (with hole-in-the-floor toilets) with mosquito nets. If you arrive by boat, follow the river south as closely as possible – *Awi's* is known to all the locals. From the bus station, take minibus #16 or #20 (70 sen) or a taxi (RM5), and get off at the base of the Sultan Mahmud Bridge, from where *Awi's* is a short walk. Buses across the bridge are infrequent, and there are very few ferries after 6pm. Back in town, the *Ping Anchorage Travellers' Lodge*, 77a Jl Sultan Sulaiman (ⓣ09/626 2020; ❶) is a traveller-friendly hostel with spartan but clean rooms, a dorm (RM8) and a travel agency. The *KT Mutiara*, 67 Jl Sultan Ismail (ⓣ09/622 2655; ❸), has small, spotless rooms with air-con, but is a touch overpriced.

There are excellent **food stalls** behind the express bus station, serving the usual Malay dishes (11.30am–midnight). Otherwise, *MD Curry House*, 19c Jl Tok Lam, has some of the best South Indian thalis you'll find in Malaysia. *Restoran Golden Dragon*, Jalan Bandar, is the best Chinese, while *kedai kopi* and a wide range of dishes and Western fare – as well as beer – can be had at *Travellers Café* on Jalan Dato Isaac.

Marang

The small coastal town of **MARANG**, 17km south of Kuala Terengganu, attracts a steady trickle of foreign visitors, though most are simply en route to nearby Pulau Kapas, 6km offshore. There are a handful of guesthouses, banks and batik shops here, but nothing much else. Any Dungun- or Rhu Muda-bound **bus** (every 30min) from Kuala Terengganu, or Kuala Terengganu-bound bus from Cherating, will drop you on the main road at Marang, from where the centre is a short walk down one of the roads towards the sea. The **ferry companies** running boats over to Pulau Kapas (RM15 return) have their offices on the main road. Mid-morning is the usual departure time but there's no service during the monsoon (Nov–Feb). One of the best places to stay is the *Green Mango Inn* (➊), a travellers' hangout three minutes' walk from the main road (follow the sign for *Kapas Island Resort*). It has a dorm (RM7) and very basic A-frame doubles. The *Island View Resort* (☎09/618 2006; ➋) has a range of rooms, including air-con doubles, while the *Marang Guest House* up on the hill (☎09/618 1976; ➋) has nice cabins, and some A-frames with an excellent vantage point over the ocean.

Pulau Kapas

A thirty-minute ride by fishing boat from Marang takes you to **Pulau Kapas**, less than 2km in length and one of the nicest islands off the east coast. Coves on the western side are accessible only by sea or by clambering over rocks, but you'll be rewarded by sand and aquamarine water. Like many of its neighbours, Kapas is a designated marine park, the best snorkelling being around rocky Pulau Gemia, just off the northwestern shore, while the northernmost cove is good for turtle-spotting. However, the high number of visitors and a local lack of regard for the environment is causing some of the surrounding coral reef to die off. The only **accommodation** is at the two western coves that directly face the mainland. The best value is *Zaki Beach Chalet* (☎019/983 3435; ➋), which has comfortable A-frames, and its restaurant is definitely the place to be in the evenings. A wooden walkway over the rocks leads to the jetty in the next bay and to the *Kapas Island Resort* (☎09/623 6110; ➏), exclusive Malay-style chalets with a swimming pool and extensive watersports facilities. Next along is the lacklustre *Nyior Kapas Island* (☎09/624 5088; ➌). The *Tuty Puri Island Resort* (☎09/624 6090; ➌–➏) is a much better-value operation, whilst the most atmospheric place is the Malay longhouse-style *Lighthouse* (☎019/215 3558; ➋), which has dorm beds (RM10) and only a well shower.

Rantau Abang

The village of **RANTAU ABANG**, 43km from Marang, is no more than a dwindling collection of guesthouses strung out along two kilometres of dusty road, but it has made its name as one of a handful of places in the world where the increasingly rare **giant leatherback turtle** comes ashore to lay its eggs, returning year after year between May and September to the same beaches. Specific nesting areas and hatcheries have been established on the beach, fenced off from curious human beings. When the hatchlings have broken out of their shells, they are released at the top of the beach (4–6am), and their scurry to the sea is supervised to ensure their safe progress. When a female turtle does come ashore to lay eggs, visitors are asked to keep at least 5m away and not to use torches and camera flashes, although the guides are sometimes lax in enforcing these rules. The guesthouses will arrange for you to be woken during the night if one is sighted, for a fee of RM3. Actually, the chances of having your sleep interrupted and spotting a turtle are very small. The population of turtles in the area is said to be rapidly declining due to illegal fishing. The locals blame Chinese trawlers which ignore the law stating that turtles accidentally captured must be released. For interesting background, visit the **Turtle Information Centre** (May–Aug daily except Fri 8am–12.45pm & 2–4.15pm; Sept–April Mon–Wed & Sat 8am–12.45pm & 2–4pm, Thurs 8am–12.45pm; free), to the north of the central two-kilometre strip.

Local **buses** from Kuala Terengganu and Marang run every thirty minutes (7.30am–6pm; 1hr) to Rantau Abang. If you're coming by express bus from the south, you have to change at Dungun, 13km to the south, from where you can easily get a local bus for the remainder of the journey. Buses drop you on the main road, at the R&R Plaza, just a short walk from all the accommodation.

There are surprisingly few **accommodation** options, all of them close to the beach, and these are busiest when the turtles are in town (May–Sept). *Dahimah's Guest House* (☎09/845 2843; ❷), 1km south of the information centre, offers a range of rooms, from comfortable fan doubles to riverside air-con family rooms. *Awang's* (☎09/844 3500; ❶–❼), behind the information centre, is friendly and has a variety of simple rooms, but is a little rundown and the air-con chalets are overpriced. *Ismail's* (☎012/955 6495; ❷), next door, is very basic and not as clean. All guesthouses have their own **restaurants** (closed Nov–Jan). In addition, there are **food stalls** near *Awang's* – of these, the *Restoran Mikima* is a standout.

Cherating

The travellers' hangout of **CHERATING**, 47km north of Kuantan, hugs the northern end of a windswept bay, protected from the breeze by the shelter of a rocky cliff. Although most of the locals have long since moved to a small village further south, the settlement still tries to reflect kampung life. It's a good place in which to unwind, with a nightlife that comes as close as the east coast gets to raging. Cherating is ideal for **windsurfing**, and you can rent equipment for RM25 an hour. Clambering over the rocks at the eastern end of the bay brings you to a tiny secluded cove, though the beach isn't as good as that belonging to the exclusive *Club Med* over the next outcrop.

Any express or local **bus** between Kuala Terengganu and Kuantan will drop you off at Cherating – tell the driver beforehand. Two rough tracks lead from the road down into the main part of the village, about five minutes' away, although the one nearest the bridge is the most direct. The main drag is a tiny surfaced road that runs roughly parallel to the beach, and this is where you'll find most of the restaurants and bars, as well as provisions stores and art and craft shops selling batik, T-shirts and other trinkets. Limbong Art, in particular, has an excellent range of wood carvings upstairs. Travel Post (☎09/581 9825) acts as a travel agency where you can book bus tickets for destinations in Malaysia and to Singapore, as well as local river and snorkelling trips (RM35 including food). They also have **Internet** terminals, an international fax line, and money-changing services.

Accommodation

Cherating Cottage ☎09/581 9273. A sturdily built bar and restaurant surrounded by chalets catering for every budget. ❷

Coconut Inn ☎09/581 9299. On a quiet stretch of beach and fenced in, this place feels like it's miles away from the crowds. Chalets are small but clean and there is a decent restaurant. ❷

Mak Long Teh's ☎09/581 9290. Set back from the main road, this budget, ramshackle place offers chalets at dorm prices and home cooking in a warm family environment. ❶

Matahari ☎09/581 9835. Spacious, sturdy chalets without water but with a fridge and large veranda, as well as a separate communal area with a TV room, cooking facilities and a batik studio. ❷

Residence Inn ☎09/581 9333. The most upmarket place within the village, this hotel has large, well-equipped rooms arranged around a pleasant swimming pool and lobby area. ❻

Rhana Pippin A smallish collection of bungalows

around a big casuarinas tree, this place is quiet and feels more isolated than it really is. Some rooms have air-con, TV and fridge. ②–③

The Shadow of the Moon at Half-Past Four ☎09/581 9186. Well-designed timber chalets decorated with vintage film posters and tucked away in a beautiful wooded area. All have attached bathroom, hot water and hand-crafted furniture. There's also a dorm (RM12). ②

Tanjung Inn Villa ☎09/581 9081. An attractive range of excellent-value chalets and family rooms set in a scenic, landscaped garden with a lake. ②

Eating and drinking

Can't Forget Seafood Restaurant Despite the ambiguous name, this informal Chinese-owned eatery serves quality food. Strong points include sweet and sour fish and chicken with cashew nuts.

Deadly Nightshade At the *Shadow of the Moon at Half-Past Four*. One of the most imaginatively

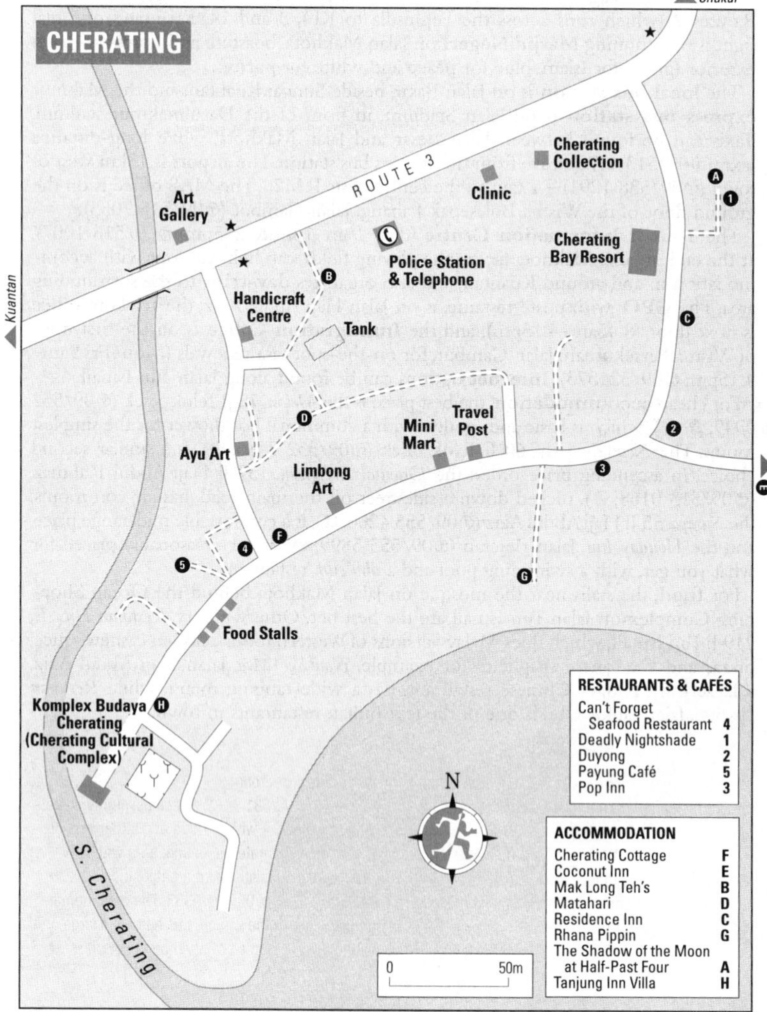

designed bars you'll come across in all of Malaysia. Fairy lights, piles of books, chess sets and home-made furniture add to the atmosphere. The menu embraces local, Western and Portuguese dishes for around RM12.

Duyong Good, inexpensive Chinese, Western and Thai food, with a beach view.

Payung Café Inexpensive meat dishes, in a riverside setting. Barbecue evenings are held frequently, and souvenir T-shirts are sold.

Pop Inn Pub-style steak house, also serving snacks by the beach. Stays open late and has the odd live band and DJ.

Kuantan

It's virtually inevitable that you'll pass through the dull, concrete town of **KUANTAN** at some stage, since it's the region's transport hub, lying at the junction of Routes 2 (which runs across the Peninsula to KL), 3 and 14. Kuantan's one real sight is the stunning **Masjid Negeri** on Jalan Makhota, boasting an impressive pastel exterior (green for Islam, blue for peace and white for purity).

The **local bus station** is on Jalan Basar, beside Sungai Kuantan, and the Makmur **express bus station** is on Jalan Stadium, in front of the Darulmakmur stadium. Taxis can be found between Jalan Besar and Jalan Makhota, while long-distance taxis (☎09/513 4478) leave from the express bus station. The airport is 15km west of town (☎09/538 1291) – a taxi to the centre costs RM20. The MAS office is on the ground floor of the Wisma Bolasepak Pahang, Jalan Gambut (☎09/515 7055).

The **Tourist Information Centre** (daily 9am–1pm & 2–5pm; ☎09/516 1007), at the end of Jalan Makhota facing the playing fields, can help you out with accommodation in and around Kuantan, and also organizes **day-trips** to the surrounding area. The **GPO**, with poste restante, is on Jalan Haji Abdul Aziz; the Telekom office is next door (8.45am–4.15pm); and the **Immigration Office** is on the first floor of Wisma Persekutuan, Jalan Gambut, for on-the-spot visa renewals (Mon–Fri 9am–4.15pm; ☎09/521373). **Internet** options can be found along Jalan Tun Ismail.

For cheap **accommodation**, the best place is the *Meian*, 78 Jl Teluk Sisek (☎09/552 0949; ❶–❷), which is basic and spotless with a communal hot shower for the simplest rooms. The *New Embassy*, 60 Jl Telok Sisek (☎09/552 7486; ❷), is a similar second choice. In ascending price order: the *Oriental Evergreen*, 157 Jl Haji Abdul Rahman (☎09/513 0168; ❷), tucked down a sidestreet off the main road, has air-con rooms; the *Suraya*, 55 Jl Haji Abdul Aziz (☎09/555 4266; ❹), is a comfortable mid-range place, and the *Holiday Inn*, Jalan Beserah (☎09/555 5899; ❽), is very reasonably priced for what you get, with a swimming pool and a *dim sum* restaurant.

For **food**, the stalls near the mosque on Jalan Makhota behind the Ocean Shopping Complex on Jalan Tun Ismail are the best bet. Otherwise, try *Restoran E & E*, 219 Jl Tun Ismail, which does Malay versions of Western food: steaks in cashew sauce, pizzas and Cantonese spaghetti, for example. *New Yee Mee*, Jalan Haji Abdul Aziz, a large busy, budget Chinese restaurant, has a wide-ranging menu, while *Restoran Beryani*, Jalan Bukit Ubi, is one of the few Indian restaurants in town.

7.5

The south

The south of the Malaysian Peninsula, below Kuala Lumpur and Kuantan, has some of the most historically and culturally significant towns in the country. The west-coast city of **Melaka**, two hours by bus south from KL, still displays an interesting heritage of cultures from its Portuguese, Dutch and British colonists, not to mention its unique Chinese–Malay community of Peranakans. There's plenty to see here, and the city is also just a short boat ride from **Sumatra**. There's little to recommend **Johor Bahru** (or JB) at the tip of the Peninsula, save for its speedy transport links into Singapore, just across the causeway. It's also handy for heading a little way up the east coast to **Pulau Tioman**, a large island with several nice beaches, good diving opportunities and plenty of budget accommodation.

Melaka

When Penang was known only for its oysters and Singapore was just a fishing village, **MELAKA** had already achieved worldwide fame. Under the auspices of the Melaka Sultanate, founded in the early fifteenth century, political and cultural life flourished, helping to define what it means to be Malay. The town grew rich by **trading spices** from the Moluccas in the Indonesian archipelago and textiles from Gujarat in northwest India. A levy on all imported goods made it one of the wealthiest kingdoms in the world, and it gradually expanded its territory to include Singapore and most of east-coast Sumatra. Yet, beginning in 1511, a series of takeovers and botched administrations by the Portuguese, Dutch and British caused the subjugation of the Malay people; Melaka's modern-day authorities are still working towards reversing the city's decline.

Legacies of all phases of Melaka's past remain in the city, constituting the main tourist sights. Of these, the most interesting are the ancestral homes of the **Baba-Nonya community**, a new racial mix also known as Peranakan that evolved from the sixteenth-century Chinese merchants who settled here and married Malay women. For a one-stop introduction to the city's history, watch the English-language **Sound and Light Show** on Padang Pahlawan Square (also known as Dutch Square; daily 9pm; 1hr; RM5).

Arrival

The daily ferry from Dumai in Sumatra docks at **Shah Bandar jetty** on Jalan Merdeka, close to the historical centre and the budget hostel area. There are two bus stations, both located on the northern outskirts of the city, off Jalan Hang Tuah. Buses from Singapore arrive at the **local bus station**. The chaotic **express bus station** is beyond the **taxi station**, a block to the south. From either, it's just a ten-minute walk over the bridge to the town centre. **Batu Berendam Airport** is 9km from the city centre (RM10 by taxi). There's no **train station** in Melaka itself, the nearest being at Tampin, 38km north; buses from Tampin drop you at the local bus station.

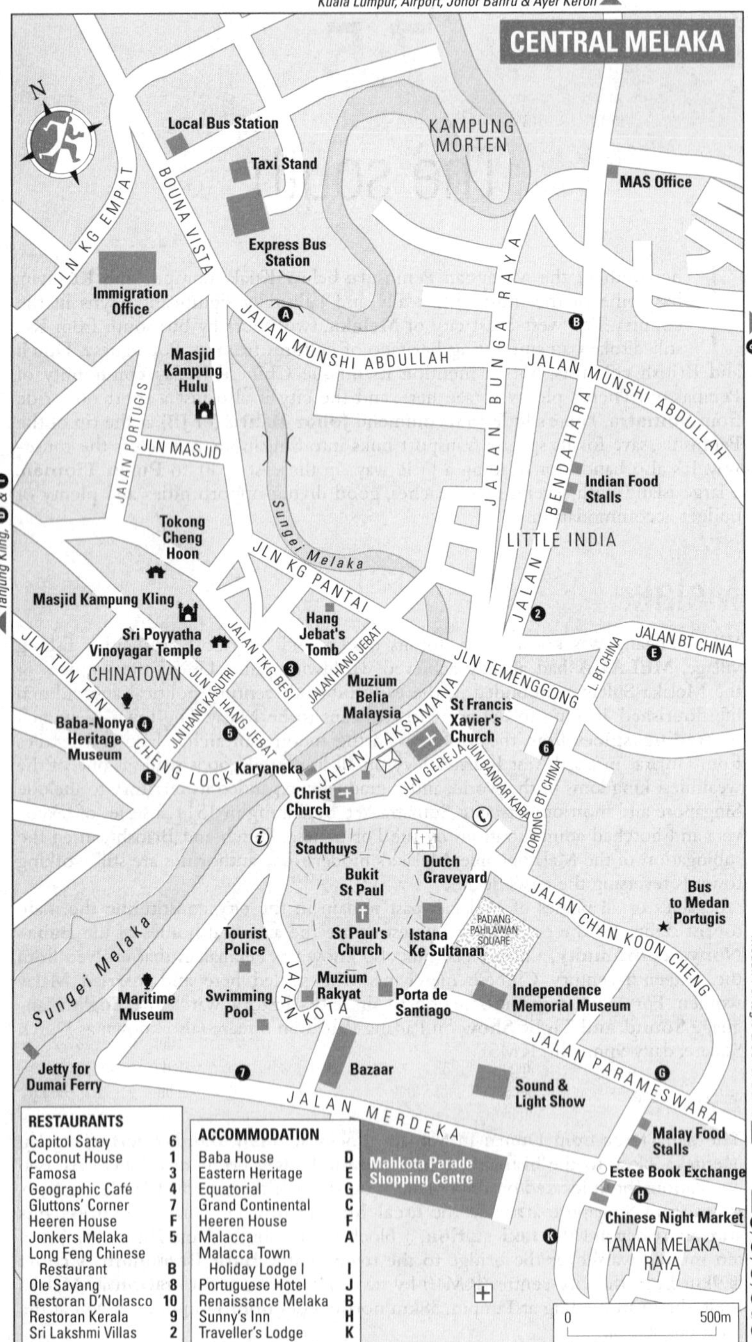
CENTRAL MELAKA
Kuala Lumpur, Airport, Johor Bahru & Ayer Keroh
Local Bus Station
Taxi Stand
Express Bus Station
KAMPUNG MORTEN
MAS Office
Immigration Office
JLN KG EMPAT
BOUNA VISTA
JALAN MUNSHI ABDULLAH
JALAN BUNGA RAYA
Masjid Kampung Hulu
JALAN PORTUGIS
JLN MASJID
JALAN BENDAHARA
Indian Food Stalls
LITTLE INDIA
Tokong Cheng Hoon
Sungei Melaka
JLN KG PANTAI
Masjid Kampung Kling
Hang Jebat's Tomb
Sri Poyyatha Vinoyagar Temple
JALAN TKG BESI
JALAN HANG JEBAT
JLN TEMENGGONG
JALAN BT CHINA
L BT CHINA
CHINATOWN
JLN TUN TAN CHENG LOCK
JLN HANG KASUTRI
JLN HANG JEBAT
Muzium Belia Malaysia
St Francis Xavier's Church
Baba-Nonya Heritage Museum
JALAN LAKSAMANA
Karyaneka
JLN GEREJA
JLN BANDAR KABA
LORONG BT CHINA
Christ Church
Stadthuys
Dutch Graveyard
Bukit St Paul
Bus to Medan Portugis
JALAN CHAN KOON CHENG
St Paul's Church
Istana Ke Sultanan
PADANG PAHLAWAN SQUARE
Tourist Police
Sungei Melaka
Muzium Rakyat
Porta de Santiago
Independence Memorial Museum
Maritime Museum
Swimming Pool
JALAN KOTA
JALAN PARAMESWARA
Jetty for Dumai Ferry
Bazaar
Sound & Light Show
JALAN MERDEKA
Malay Food Stalls
Mahkota Parade Shopping Centre
Estee Book Exchange
Chinese Night Market
TAMAN MELAKA RAYA
0
500m
Tanjung Kling, D & 1
Medan Portugis & Johor Bahru
C
I, J, 8, 9 & 10
RESTAURANTS
Capitol Satay 6
Coconut House 1
Famosa 3
Geographic Café 4
Gluttons' Corner 7
Heeren House F
Jonkers Melaka 5
Long Feng Chinese Restaurant B
Ole Sayang 8
Restoran D'Nolasco 10
Restoran Kerala 9
Sri Lakshmi Villas 2
ACCOMMODATION
Baba House D
Eastern Heritage E
Equatorial G
Grand Continental C
Heeren House F
Malacca A
Malacca Town Holiday Lodge I I
Portuguese Hotel J
Renaissance Melaka B
Sunny's Inn H
Traveller's Lodge K

Moving on from Melaka

By plane

Batu Berendam Airport, 9km from the city centre, caters only for small aircraft. Pelangi Air (☎06/317 4685) had ceased flights at the time of writing, though Ked-Air was rumoured to be negotiating for Pelangi Air's old routes. To get the current situation, ask at Atlas Travel (see "Listings, p.694) or any other travel agency.

By ferry

A daily **boat** leaves for Dumai, Sumatra (RM80) as well as Pekan Baru (RM120) three times weekly. Contact Indomal Express (☎06/283 2506), or call at the Tourist Information Centre, Jalan Kota (see below).

By bus

Melaka runs **buses** to all points on the Peninsula. There are frequent departures from the express bus station to KL, Ipoh, Butterworth and Alor Setar, while most express services to Singapore leave from the local bus station.

By train

Trains run to Singapore from the train station at Tampin, 38km north of Melaka (☎06/411 1034).

Information and city transport

You should be able to get a **trishaw** from the Padang Pahlawan Square and outside the Mahkota Parade Shopping Centre. A sightseeing tour costs RM25 for one hour. **Taxis** are quite hard to find on the street, but you can always get one from the taxi stand near the express bus station. The very helpful **Tourist Information Centre** is on Jalan Kota (Mon–Sat 9am–5pm, Sun 9am–4.30pm; ☎06/283 6538), 400m from the Shah Bandar jetty. The information board outside displays the times of the river trips to Kampung Morten (see p.740).

Accommodation

Hotel prices are a little higher than in other Malaysian towns, but so are standards. Most budget hostels are in the south of the city, in the Taman Melaka Raya area; take town bus #17 from the local bus station, or a taxi or trishaw (RM5).

Baba House 125 Jl Tun Tan Cheng Lock ☎06/281 1216. These beautifully restored Peranakan houses have been turned into an atmospheric hotel, though the rooms are a little on the small side. There is also a good café. ❺

Eastern Heritage 8 Jl Bukit China ☎06/283 3026. Set in an imaginatively decorated house that makes the best of its original architectural features. The dorms (RM10) and rooms are clean if a bit shabby. ❷

Equatorial Jl Bandar Hilir ☎06/282 8333. Has a wide range of restaurants and ranks alongside the *Renaissance* in terms of grandeur. ❾

Grand Continental 20 Jl Tun Sri Lanang ☎06/284 0088. Standard hotel that is very reasonably priced. Its facilities include a pool and coffee house. ❻

Heeren House 1 Jl Tun Tan Cheng Lock ☎06/281 4241. The tasteful rooms, some with four-poster beds, makes this the best choice for a small upmarket hotel. Reservations recommended. ❻

Malacca 27a Jl Munshi Abdullah ☎06/282 2252. Housed in a building of faded elegance, the large, well-furnished rooms are a little worn but good for the price. The drawback is the noisy road. ❷

Malacca Town Holiday Lodge I 148b Taman Melaka Raya, above the large *Kingdom* restaurant ☎06/284 8830. A guesthouse offering simple, clean rooms. ❶

Portuguese Hotel 12 Taman Melaka Raya ☎06/282 4100. Located on the waterfront, this old standby has a fair bit of atmosphere and a lobby full of shady characters. The a/c rooms are windowless, but the fan rooms are good value. ❷–❸

Renaissance Melaka Jl Bendahara ☎06/284 8888. The town's major luxury hotel, with an imposing lobby complete with huge chandeliers, and elegant, well-furnished rooms. ❼

Sunny's Inn 270a Taman Melaka Raya ☎06/227 5446. Traveller-oriented and homely family hostel, which has cable TV, a cosy communal lounge, a roof garden, bags of tourist information and RM9 dorms. ❶

Traveller's Lodge 214b Taman Melaka Raya ☎06/227 5708. As pleasant a hostel as you'll find in Malaysia, with Japanese-style sanded floorboards, downstairs cafeteria, roof terrace and a raised lounging area, complete with books and board games. There's home cooking, and the wide range of rooms – from dorms (RM11) to basic fan doubles to a/c en-suites – are all great value. ❷

The City

The centre of Melaka is split in two by the murky **Sungei Melaka**, the western bank of which is occupied by **Chinatown** and **Kampung Morten**, a small collection of stilted houses. On the eastern side of the river lies the colonial core with **Bukit St Paul** at its centre, encircled by Jalan Kota. Southeast of here, **Taman Melaka Raya** is a new town with a giant shopping centre and most of the budget hotels, restaurants and bars. A relaxing 45-minute **boat trip** up Sungei Melaka takes you past "Little Amsterdam", the old Dutch quarter of red-roofed *godowns*, which back directly onto the water. Boats leave from the jetty behind the Tourist Information Centre (hourly, depending on the tide, 10am–2pm; RM8).

Around Bukit St Paul

The imposing dark timber palace of **Istana Ke Sultanan** (daily 9am–6pm, closed Fri 12.15–2.45pm; RM1.50) on Jalan Kota is a reconstruction of the original fifteenth-century istana, complete with sharply sloping, multi-layered roofs. Inside, you'll find re-creations of scenes from Malay court life, as well as costumes and local crafts. East of here, the **Independence Memorial Museum** (daily 9am–6pm, closed Fri 12.15–2.45pm; free) charts the events surrounding the lead-up to independence in 1957, but relies rather too heavily on posters to impart its message.

The **Muzium Rakyat** (People's Museum) on Jalan Kota (Tues 9am–6pm, Fri closed 12.15–2.45pm; RM2) houses several displays, but its most interesting is the **Museum of Enduring Beauty** on the third floor, which shows the many ways in which people have sought to alter their appearance, including head deformation, dental mutilations, tattooing, scarification and foot-binding.

St Paul's Church – roofless, desolate and smothered in ferns – was constructed in 1521 by the Portuguese, and visited by the Jesuit missionary St Francis Xavier, whose body was brought here for burial; a brass plaque on the south wall of the chancel marks the spot. A winding path beside the church brings you to the sturdy **Stadthuys**, a collection of buildings that dates from 1660 and was used as a town hall during the Dutch and British administrations. It boasts typically Dutch interior staircases and high windows, and now houses the **Museum of Ethnography** (daily 9am–6pm, closed Fri 12.15–2.45pm; RM2), which displays Malay and Chinese ceramics and weaponry and a blow-by-blow account of Melakan history.

The **Maritime Museum** (daily except Tues 9am–6pm, closed Fri 12.15–2.45pm; RM2), on the quayside to the south of Stadthuys, is housed in a replica of a Portuguese cargo ship that sank here in the sixteenth century. Model ships and paintings chart Melaka's maritime history. Heading north of Stadthuys up Jalan Laksamana, skirting the busy junction with Jalan Temenggong and taking Jalan Bendahara directly ahead, you're in the centre of Melaka's tumbledown **Little India**, a rather desultory line of sari shops, interspersed with a few eating houses. East along Jalan Temenggong brings you to **Bukit China** (RM10 by taxi or trishaw), the ancestral burial ground of the town's Chinese community; it dates from around 1409 but is now used as a park.

Chinatown

Melaka owed a great deal of its nineteenth-century economic recovery to its Chinese community, many of whom settled in what became known as **Chinatown**, across Sungei Melaka from the colonial district. Today, the undeniable charm of these streets is marred only by the constantly churning traffic. Turn left after the bridge by the Tourist Information Centre, then first right, and you'll come to Jalan Tun Tan Cheng Lock, whose elegant townhouses are the ancestral homes of the Baba-Nonya community, descendants of the original Chinese pioneers who married local Malay women. The wealthiest and most successful built long, narrow-fronted houses, and minimized the "window tax" by incorporating several internal courtyards. At nos. 48–50, the **Baba-Nonya Heritage Museum** (daily 10am–12.30pm & 2–4.30pm; RM8) is an amalgam of three adjacent houses belonging to one family, and an excellent example of the Chinese Palladian style. Typically connected by a common covered footway, decorated with hand-painted tiles, each front entrance has an outer swing door of elaborately carved teak. Two red lanterns hang either side of the doorway, and a canopy of Chinese tiles frames the shuttered windows. Inside, the homes are filled with gold-leaf fittings, blackwood furniture inlaid with mother-of-pearl and delicately carved lacquer screens.

Seven hundred metres to the north of Chinatown, on the west bank of the Sungei Melaka, the village of **Kampung Morten** is a surprising find in the heart of the city. To get there, take the footbridge down a small path off Jalan Bunga Raya, one of the principal roads leading north out of town. The wooden stilted houses here are distinctively Melakan, with their long, rectangular living rooms and kitchens, and narrow verandas approached by ornamental steps. On the left as you cross the footbridge you'll find the **Villa Sentosa** (daily 9am–5pm; voluntary donation), whose welcoming family will gladly show you their artefacts and heirlooms.

Taman Mini Malaysia

Fourteen kilometres north of central Melaka, in the recreational park area of Ayer Keroh, **Taman Mini Malaysia** and mini **ASEAN** (daily 9am–6pm; RM5) holds full-sized reconstructions of typical houses from all thirteen Malay states and from Brunei, Indonesia, the Philippines, Singapore and Thailand. Cultural shows featuring traditional dance are regularly staged here, too. Town buses #19 and #105 run every thirty minutes to Ayer Keroh from the local bus station.

Eating

Sampling the spicy dishes of Nonya cuisine is a must in Melaka, with its emphasis on sour herbs like tamarind, tempered by creamy coconut milk. Usual opening hours are 9am–11pm unless otherwise stated.

Capitol Satay Jl Bukit China. Experience *satay celup*, where you take your pick of assorted fish, meat and vegetables skewered on sticks and cook them in a spicy peanut sauce at your table. Open 7pm–midnight.

Coconut House 128 Jl Tun Tan Cheng Lock. Effortlessly stylish restaurant, bookshop and art gallery housed in a restored shop-house with its own courtyard, where those in the know opt for the excellent woodfire pizzas. Daily 11am–midnight, closed Wed and Thurs am.

Famosa 28 Jl Hang Kasturi. Hole in the wall of an old shop-house, serving "chicken rice balls", a local favourite. The tables out front are a good place to have a beer or two.

Geographic Café Jl Hang Kasturi. Atmospheric little café in a corner shop-house complete with wicker chairs and lazy ceiling fans. Don't forget to wear your guayabera.

Gluttons' Corner Jl Merdeka. More a collection of permanent restaurants than food stalls, this is the city's highest-profile eating area. Prices are generally low, with RM5 guaranteeing a good feed at many stalls. One of the better restaurants is *Bunga Raya*, whose seafood is popular with the locals.

Heeren House 1 Jl Tun Tan Cheng Lock. This stylish, a/c café offers Nonya lunches at the weekends for RM15, and very reasonably priced local Portuguese food.

Jonkers Melaka 17 Jl Hang Jebat. In a beautiful

Peranakan house, this café is also a gift shop and art gallery. Good for vegetarians – set meals, including Nonya cuisine and desserts, start at RM16. Open 10am–5pm.
Long Feng Chinese Restaurant *Renaissance Melaka Hotel*, Jl Bendahara. Excellent Cantonese and Sichuan dishes in a classy setting. It's not cheap, though, at around RM25 per dish.
Ole Sayang 198–199 Taman Melaka Raya (☎06/283 4384). A moderately priced Nonya restaurant, with Peranakan decor. Daily specialities include *udang goreng asam* (deep-fried, tamarind-marinated prawns) and *ikan goreng cili* (deep-fried fish with fresh chillies); both cost around RM8. Daily except Wed 11.30am–2.30pm & 6–9.30pm.
Restoran D'Nolasco Medan Portugis. A Mediterranean atmosphere with oriental food such as crabs in tomato and chilli sauce with soy. Around RM20 a head.
Restoran Kerala 640 Taman Melaka Raya. Cheap and cheerful South Indian food in a sparkling clean establishment. Excellent banana-leaf curries, as well as tandoori set meals for about RM6. Breakfast is served from 8.30am.
Sri Lakshmi Villas 2 Jl Bendahara. A range of *dosais* and reliable South Indian thalis, with as many top-ups as you can eat. Good for vegetarians.

Shopping

Melaka is famed for its **antiques**, and there are many specialist outlets along Jalan Hang Jebat and Jalan Tun Tan Cheng Lock, though they are by no means cheap. If it's a genuine antique, check that it can be exported legally and fill in an official clearance form. Interesting places to browse on Jalan Hang Jebat include Dragon House at no. 65 for old coins and banknotes, and Wang Naga Antique Centre at no. 88, which specializes in artefacts salvaged from shipwrecks. Wah Aik at 103 Jalan Kubu sells silk shoes like the ones that used to be made to bind feet, whilst Gee's Original on Lorong Hang Kasturi has a shopful of handcrafted wooden articles behind the most attractive shop front in Melaka. For modern **crafts** and souvenirs, Tribal Arts Gallery at 27 Jl Hang Kasturi specializes in Sarawakian crafts, and Orang Utan, 59 Lorong Hang Jebat, is the outlet for local artist Charles Cham's witty cartoon T-shirts and paintings. Estee Book Exchange, Taman Melaka Raya, has a good selection of English-language **books**, as does MPH in the Mahkota Parade Shopping Centre.

Listings

Banks and exchange Hong Kong Bank, Jl Ongkimwee; Overseas Chinese Banking Corporation, Jl Hang Jebat. Moneychangers are often more convenient and offer as good rates as the banks: Malaccan Souvenir House and Trading, 22 Jl Tokong; SPAK, Jl Laksamana.
Car rental Avis, Equatorial Hotel, Jl Bandar Hilir ☎06/282 8333.
Hospital Sultan Hospital, Jl Bendahara ☎06/283 5888.
Immigration The Immigration Office is on the 2nd Floor, Bangunan Persekutuan, Jl Hang Tuah (☎06/282 4958) for on-the-spot visa renewals.
Internet access The east end of Jl Merdeka has a string of internet cafés.
Police The tourist police office (☎06/282 2222) is on Jl Kota and is open 24hr.
Post office The GPO is inconveniently situated on the way to Ayer Keroh on Jl Bukit Baru – take town bus #19. A minor branch on Jl Laksamana sells stamps and aerograms.
Telephone services The Telekom building is on Jl Chan Koon Cheng. (daily 8am–5pm).
Travel agents Try Atlas Travel at 5 Jl Hang Jebat (☎06/282 0777) for plane tickets.

Kukup: travel to Indonesia

About 200km south of Melaka and almost right at the tip of the Peninsula, the small fishing community of **KUKUP** is a little-known exit point from Malaysia to **Tanjung Balai in Indonesia** (see p.347), a 45-minute ferry ride leaving from the jetty (daily 8.30am, 10am, 3.30pm; info and tickets from Fast Ferry ☎07/696 0988). The problem with arriving in Kukup from Indonesia is that onward travel connections are sketchy – you'll have to catch a ferry or taxi ($6) to Pontian Kecil, 19km away, which has regular buses to Johor Bahru (the whole journey by taxi costs around RM15 per person). Kukup's main attraction is its **seafood**. The town's single tumbledown street is packed with restaurants, from the enormous *Makanan Laut,* closest to the jetty, where you can see the food being prepared in a vast array of woks, to the more modest *Restoran Zaiton Hussin* immediately opposite.

Johor Bahru

The southernmost Malaysian city of any size, **JOHOR BAHRU** – or simply **JB** – is the gateway into Singapore, linked to the city-state by a 1056-metre causeway, which is crossed by around 50,000 people a day. It also has good links to KL and Melaka, so there's little to detain you whichever direction you're travelling in. JB's one interesting attraction is the **Istana Besar**, the former residence of Johor's royal family. Surrounded by extensive gardens, it is a magnificent building set on a hillock overlooking the Johor Straits. To the right of the building is the ticket booth of the **Museum Di Raja Abu Bakar** (daily except Fri 9am–4pm; RM7), which displays gifts from foreign dignitaries, including stuffed tigers and daggers.

Larkin bus station is 3km away from the centre of JB on Jalan Geruda. Plenty of buses run from here to the causeway, or you can catch a taxi for around RM5. The **train station** is slightly east of the city centre, off Jalan Tun Abdul Razak. Flights to JB land at **Senai Airport**, 25km north of the city, from where a regular bus service (RM1.40) runs to the bus station. Heading out to the airport, MAS passengers can take the RM4 shuttle bus from outside the Tourist Information Centre. Alternatively, you can get a taxi to the airport for about RM25. The **MAS office** is at Level 1, Menara Pelangi, Jalan Kuning Taman Pelangi (☎07/334 1001). To **rent a car** (cheaper here than in Singapore) contact either Avis, at the Tropical Inn (☎07/223 7971), or Hertz, JOTIC building (☎07/223 7520).

Travel between JB and Singapore, and on to Indonesia

Two bus services run throughout the day between JB and **Singapore**. The air-con JB–Singapore Express (every 10min, 6.30am–11.30pm; RM2.40, or RM4.80 if you have luggage) is the most comfortable, though the #170 is cheaper (RM1.20). Confusingly, however, the #170 has two routes: every ten minutes (6am–11.30pm), it runs from Larkin bus station in JB either to the Queen Street terminal in central Singapore, or to Kranji MRT station. You can also catch a bus into Singapore from just outside the train station on the main road at the border. There's an MAS bus service (RM10) from JB's Senai Airport to Singapore's *Copthorne Orchid* hotel. Taxis between JB and Singapore departing from Pasar Bakti station, Jalan Trus, cost around RM10 per person, and leave only when they're full.

Whichever direction you're travelling, buses drop passengers outside the **immigration points** at either end of the causeway and immigration procedures take around ten minutes. If you want to stay in JB, don't get back on the bus, just take the short walk into town. Similarly, it's possible to board the buses to Singapore at the causeway terminal instead of trekking out to the bus station. The bus will drop you off at the border for the immigration procedures; they won't wait for you, but if you hold onto your ticket you can board any bus of the same number on the other side of the border. To avoid this hassle, you can make the journey by train, as the formalities are carried out on board, at RM2.90 for a second-class seat.

If you have a valid **Indonesian visa** you can also take a ferry to Tanjung Pinang and Pulau Batam from Sriwani Tours and Travel (☎07/221 1677) in the Bebas Cukai shopping centre, 2km east of the border crossing.

The main **Tourist Information Centre (JOTIC)** (Mon–Fri 9am–5pm, Sat 9am–1pm; ⓣ07/222 3591) is on Jalan Air Molek, and there is also an office on the causeway (Mon–Fri 9am–5pm, Sat & Sun 9am–4pm; ⓣ07/224 9485). There are **moneychangers** in the main shopping centres, or try Maybank, 11 Jl Selat Tebrau; Bank Bumiputra, 51 Jl Segget; or OCBC, Jalan Ibrahim. There is also a brace of cash-points on the south side of the Merlin Tower. **Internet cafés** are plentiful around City Square and the Komtar building.

JB attracts more businesspeople than tourists, but the best of the budget **accommodation** is *Footloose Homestay*, 4h Jl Ismail (ⓣ07/224 2881; ❶), where you'll find a basic dorm (RM15). If you can't get a bed here, try the grim but reasonably clean *Hawaii*, 21 Jl Meldrum (ⓣ07/224 0633; ❸). In the mid-range band, the *Rasa Sayang*, Jalan Datok Dalam (ⓣ07/224 8600; ❹), is comfortable enough, while the plushest place by far is the luxury *Puteri Pan Pacific*, Kotaraya, Jalan Trus (ⓣ07/223 3333; ❽) – ask about their promotions. The liveliest of the **places to eat** in JB is the large night market across the footbridge from the train station beside the Hindu Temple.

Mersing

The east-coast fishing port of **MERSING**, 130km north of Johor Bahru, is the main gateway to **Pulau Tioman** and the smaller islands of the Seribuat archipelago. The town is grouped around two main streets, Jalan Abu Bakar and Jalan Ismail, fanning out from a roundabout on Route 3.

Express buses drop you off just before the roundabout, and at the R&R Plaza near the jetty, from where they also depart. You can buy tickets from Restoran Malaysia and offices at R&R Plaza itself. The local bus station is on Jalan Sulaiman, close to the riverfront. The **Mersing Tourist Information Centre** (Mon–Sat, mornings at the ferry terminal 8am–1pm; afternoons at the office on Jalan Abu Bakar 2–4.30pm; ⓣ07/799 5212), is very helpful and offers impartial advice on the many different island deals.

The **jetty** is about ten minutes' walk from the roundabout along Jalan Abu Bakar. Inside the R&R Plaza near the jetty, a large signboard shows which of the thirteen companies' boats sail to Pulau Tioman and when (the last one is about 4.30pm; see p.698 for details). For the other islands, it's best to book ahead, either at the particular island office itself, around the jetty, or at one of the travel agencies on Jalan Abu Baker or Jalan Ismail. Make sure that you **change money** before you leave, as rates on the islands are lousy.

Omar's Backpackers' Hostel, Jalan Abu Bakar (ⓣ07/799 5096; ❷), is one of the cheapest **places to stay** in Mersing, with clean dorm beds (RM8) and excellent-value double rooms. A step up, the *Country*, 11 Jl Sulaimen (ⓣ07/799 1799; ❸), is more upmarket than its price suggests, while the spick-and-span *Embassy*, 2 Jl Ismail (ⓣ07/799 3545; ❷–❸), does the best-value budget doubles in town. If you're after real comfort, there's a *Seri Malaysia* on Jalan Ismail (ⓣ07/799 1876; ❻), opposite the hospital, a ten-minute walk from the jetty. The food stalls near the roundabout are particularly good, but there are plenty of great **restaurants**, too. In particular, *Al Arif* on Jalan Ismail, opposite the Parkson Ria supermarket, serves cheap, good-quality Indian food.

Pulau Tioman

Pulau Tioman, 30km east of Mersing, has long been one of Malaysia's most popular holiday islands. Thirty-eight kilometres long and nineteen kilometres at its widest point, it is the largest island in the Seribuat archipelago and has an inaccessible mountainous spine down its centre. Ever since the 1970s, when Tioman was voted one of the ten most beautiful islands in the world by *Time* magazine, crowds have been flocking to its palm-fringed shores. Now, noisy express boats travel here in less than two hours, and several daily flights arrive from Singapore and other parts of the Peninsula. Damage has been inflicted on the surrounding coral and marine life, but Pulau Tioman displays a remarkable resilience, and to avoid it is to miss out. Most of the habitation on Tioman is along the west coast, with the popular budget places

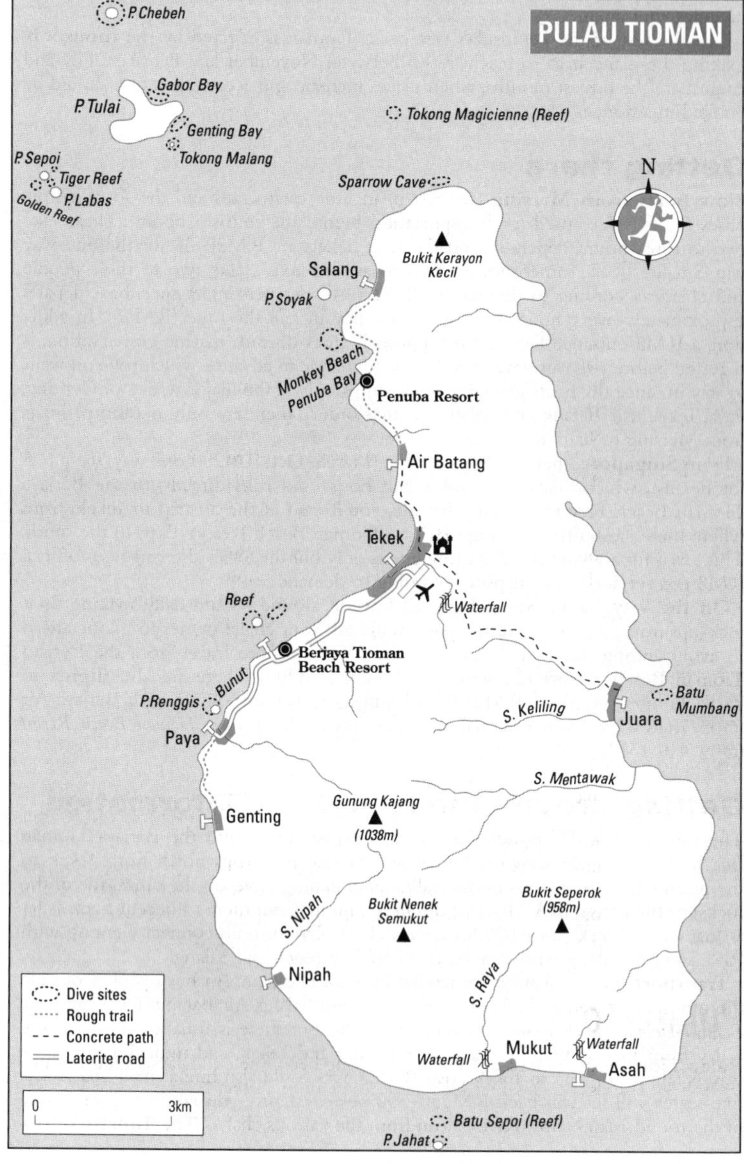

being in the main village of **Tekek** and the bay of **Air Batang**; the east coast's sole settlement, **Juara**, is less developed. **Salang** is a noisy, more upmarket resort, but **Nipah** and **Mukut** are just opening up to tourism.

Many of Tioman's nearby islets provide excellent opportunities for snorkelling, and most of the chalet operations offer day-trips (RM30) to nearby reefs. Many **dive centres** on Tioman offer the range of PADI certificates, from the four-day Open Water course (RM800) through to the fourteen-day Divemaster (RM1700); always check that qualified English-speaking instructors are employed, and that the cost includes equipment.

Like the rest of the Peninsula's east coast, Tioman is affected by the **monsoon**, making the island hard to reach by sea between November and February. July and August are the busiest months, when prices increase and accommodation should be booked in advance.

Getting there

Slow boats from Mersing (see p.696) include catamarans and the so-called sea buses (which were used for transportation before the tourism boom). These take two to three hours, depending on the tide; tickets are RM20–30 for the one-way trip. Smaller boats, sometimes referred to as "sea taxis", take two to three people and charge according to destination (RM20–40 per person). A speedboat departs approximately every hour, making the journey in half the time (RM35). In addition, a RM5 entrance fee, which supposedly goes towards marine conservation, is required before you can travel. You'll have to decide in advance which bay you want to stay in, since the boats generally make drops only at the major resorts of Genting, Paya, Tekek, Air Batang and Salang (in that order); there are only occasional boats from Mersing to Juara on the east coast.

From **Singapore**, there's a ferry service (March–Oct; RM200 one way; see p.695 for details), which takes four and a half hours and runs directly to the Berjaya Tioman Beach Resort. Arriving **by air**, you'll land at the airstrip in Tekek, from where there's a shuttle bus to the Berjaya Tioman Beach Resort, 2km to the south. This bus is for arriving and departing guests only, but the locals also run an unofficial RM3 taxi service to the airport according to demand.

On the way back, express boats all leave at around 8–9am daily, making their pick-ups from each jetty, though you should ask your chalet owner to phone ahead to avoid getting stranded. A fast catamaran to Singapore leaves from the Berjaya Tioman Beach Resort (2.30pm; 4hr 30min; RM200). There are also **flights** to Kuala Lumpur (1.10pm; RM214) and Singapore (11am; S$111) with Berjaya Air (☎03/7846 8228); you can make reservations at the *Berjaya Tioman Beach Resort* (☎09/419 1303).

Getting around the island and information

The only road wide enough for cars is between Tekek and the Berjaya Tioman Beach Resort, while a two-metre-wide concrete path runs north from Tekek to the promontory, a twenty-minute walk, commencing again on the other side of the rocks for the length of Air Batang. **Trails** are limited, but there's a decent track as far as Juara from Tekek (see p.699 for details). Less-obvious trails connect Genting with Paya, and Air Batang with Penuba Bay, Monkey beach and Salang.

Transport on the island is somewhat limited. The Juara sea bus operates outside the monsoon season and takes two hours to visit Salang, Air Batang, Tekek, and the *Berjaya Tioman Beach Resort*. It's very unreliable, but there is usually one departure a day from Juara calling at Salang, Air Batang and Tekek, and returning the same way. A fare from Juara to Tekek costs RM25. You could also hire a small boat, but a five-seater will set you back RM250–300 per day. Lastly, you could hop onto one of the round-island trips (RM55) run from the various chalets. The **Tourist Infor-**

mation Centre (daily 6.30am–1pm & 2–7pm), right beside the jetty at Air Batang, can help you with boat tickets and day-trips.

Tekek

The sprawling village of **TEKEK** is the main settlement on the island and the least inspiring part of Tioman. It has been overdeveloped and much of the seafront is now littered, rundown and fenced in, but it's the only place on the island where you'll find essential services: there are moneychangers and a post office in the new Terminal Complex next to the airstrip, and the police station is located a ten-minute walk south of the main jetty. You could distract yourself with the **Tioman Island Museum** (daily 9.30am–5pm; RM1), on the first floor of the Terminal Complex next to the airport. Displaying some twelfth- to fourteenth-century Chinese ceramics, which were lost overboard from early trading vessels, it also outlines facts and myths concerning the island. North of the main jetty, at the very end of the bay, it's hard to miss the large government-sponsored **Marine Centre** (daily 8.30am-4pm; free). Set up to protect the coral and marine life around the island, and to patrol the fishing taking place in its waters, it contains an aquarium and samples of coral.

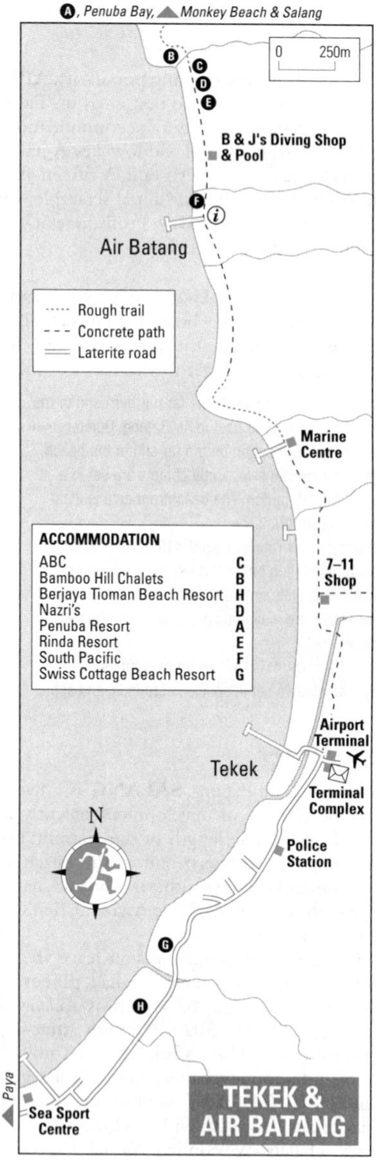

There are lots of **places to stay** in Tekek, though most of them are dilapidated and located next to piles of rubbish and ever-present building supplies. There are two exceptions, located a little way out of Tekek. Two kilometres to the south is the island's only international-standard place, the *Berjaya Tioman Beach Resort* (☎09/419 1000; ⑨), a village-sized complex with a nine-hole golf course and stables, offering everything from double rooms to deluxe apartments. Otherwise, try *Swiss Cottage Beach Resort* (☎09/419 1843; ②), the first place north of the resort, in a shady jungle setting, with a small restaurant. One of Tekek's nicest **restaurants**, *Liza*, is at the far southern end of the bay, with a wide-ranging menu specializing in Chinese food at RM20 a meal.

Air Batang

Despite its ever-increasing popularity, **AIR BATANG**, 2km north of Tekek (jetty to jetty), is still one of the best areas on Tioman, and gets most of the budget market. Although there's plenty of accommodation, it feels spacious, and development tends to be relatively tasteful and low-key. A jetty divides the bay roughly in half; the beach is better at the southern end. A fifteen-minute **trail** leads over the headland to the north, which – after an initial scramble – flattens out into an easy walk, ending up at secluded **Penuba Bay**. From here, it's an hour's walk to Monkey Beach, beyond which is Salang (see below).

Accommodation and eating

As you get off the boat, a signpost helpfully lists the direction of the numerous **places to stay** in the bay. Air Batang likes to keep its nightlife low-key, unlike Salang, which can get rowdy. Most of the chalets have **restaurants**.

ABC ⓣ09/419 1154. At the far northern end of the bay and among the best in Air Batang. Quieter than most with its location on the far end of the beach, the very inexpensive, pretty chalets are set in a well-tended garden. The beachfront café is ideal for a sunset drink. ❷

Bamboo Hill Chalets ⓣ09/419 1339. The best accommodation on Air Batang, these beautiful, wooden chalets on stilts, perched on the northern headland, are well equipped and enjoy stunning views. ❹

Nazri's ⓣ09/419 1375. A great outfit with large, air-con chalets set in spacious grounds, and some ordinary, cheaper ones. ❷–❹

Penuba Resort ⓣ013/772 0454. The only place to stay in Penuba Bay. Its stilted chalets, high up on the rocks, have fantastic views out to sea and a far better beach than Air Batang. ❷–❻

Rinda Resort ⓣ09/419 1157. Cheap accommodation in a good spot in a shaded setting at the northern end of Air Batang, perfect for watching the sun go down from one of the hammocks. ❶

South Pacific ⓣ09/419 1176). Close to the jetty. Clean chalets with bathrooms, some right on the beach. ❷

Salang

North of Air Batang, **SALANG** is a livelier option with a better beach, but there has been a lot of development recently and the string of hostels stretches pretty much the whole length of the seafront; prices tend to be a little higher than at Air Batang. The southern end of the beach is the most scenic, and Pulau Soyok, the small island off the southern headland, has a pretty reef for snorkelling. There are two good **dive schools**, Dive Asia and Ben's Diving Centre.

On the right (south) as you leave the jetty is a little cluster of budget **places to stay**, the best of which is *Salang Sayang* (ⓣ09/419 5020; ❹), with attractive hillside and beachfront chalets. You'll also find a moneychanger here. *Pak Long* (ⓣ09/419 5000; ❸), behind the little lagoon, is friendly, with well-kept en-suite chalets. Welcoming *Salang Pusaka* (ⓣ09/419 5317; ❸), is set back from the beach in landscaped gardens and has a range of rooms with private veranda, including some air-con. The largest outfit, towards the centre of the bay, is *Salang Indah* (ⓣ09/419 5015; ❷–❼), with a range of well-appointed chalets, from sea-facing boxes to double-storey family

chalets with air-con and hot shower; they also arrange snorkelling and sightseeing trips.

At the expensive **restaurants** of *Salang Dream* and *Salang Beach Resort* the emphasis is on Malay cuisine and seafood at around RM10 per dish, while the more informal *Salang Sayang* and *Pak Long* serve excellent Western and Malay dishes for no more than RM5. There's a wide range of choices for **nightlife**.

Juara

Life is simple at **Juara**. The locals speak less English and are much more conservative than elsewhere on the island: officially alcohol isn't served. There's only one sea bus a day to the kampung from the east coast of Tioman, so at any other time the journey to this isolated bay must be made **on foot** through the jungle, a steep trek that takes three hours from Tekek. The start of the trail (a five-minute walk from the airstrip) is easy enough to identify since it's the only concrete path that heads off in that direction, passing the local mosque before hitting virgin jungle after about fifteen minutes. There's no danger of losing your way: cement steps climb steeply through the greenery, tapering off into a smooth, downhill path once you're over the ridge. After 45 minutes, there is a **waterfall** – it's forbidden to bathe here, since it supplies Tekek with water. From the waterfall, it's another hour or so to Juara village. Juara is refreshingly free from the buzz of speedboats and motorbikes, while its lovely wide sweep of beach is far cleaner and less crowded than anywhere on the other side. The bay, however, facing out to the open sea, is the most susceptible on the island to bad weather.

Juara, in fact, consists of two bays – the northern has a jetty, opposite which the cross-island path emerges. Most of the accommodation and restaurants are here, too, although the southern bay does have a few chalets.

Accommodation and eating

Starting at the northern end, you'll find the best options are *Paradise Point* (☎09/419 3145; ❷), about 100m down the beach from the jetty, which has the cheapest **chalets** with shower, though the beach is not the cleanest. *Atan's* (❷), past the cross-island path, has double-storey guesthouses, rather like Swiss chalets, while the friendly *Juara Mutiara* (☎09/419 3161; ❶–❷) is the biggest operation, with a wide variety of room types and prices. These are also the people to see if you want to arrange a boat trip. A little further south, *Basir* (❶) has good sea-facing chalets, with some cheaper huts as well, while at the very end of the strip, *Rainbow* (☎09/419 3140; ❶) has characterful, painted A-frames right on the beach next to the comprehensive Sunrise dive shop. If you follow the path round to the even quieter southern bay you'll find several cheap places to stay, including *Mizanie Chalet* (☎09/547 8445; ❸), which has its own restaurant.

While there's less choice for **eating**, portions tend, on the whole, to be larger and the menus more imaginative than on the west coast. *Paradise Point* does good *rotis* and unusual dishes, such as fish with peanut sauce and fried rice with coconut. *Ali Putra* and *Beach Café*, by the jetty, both have a huge range of local and Western dishes. At night, try *Bushman's*, a shack next to *Sunrise*, and the only place serving alcohol at Juara.

Mukut

MUKUT, a tiny fishing village on the south coast, lies in the shadow of two granite outcrops known as the "dragon's horns". Shrouded by dense forest, and connected to the outside world by a solitary card phone, it's a wonderfully peaceful and friendly spot to unwind, though be warned that this is still a conservative place, unused to Western sunbathing habits; topless bathing is banned. The nicest position is occupied by *Chalets Park* (④), with secluded **chalets** shaded by trees. Those at *Sri Tanjung Chalets* (②) at the far western end of the cove overlook a patch of beach – ask at the house in the village where the name of the chalets is painted on a tyre. The **places to eat** are few and basic. The *Sri Sentosa* is a bit on the dingy side, though popular with the locals, while the views from *Mukut Coral Resort* and the *Harmony Coral* café just by the jetty make up for their lack of variety.

Nipah

For almost total isolation, head to **NIPAH** on Tioman's southwest coast. Comprising a clean, empty beach of coarse, yellow sand and a landlocked lagoon, there's no village to speak of here, but there is a dive centre and canoeing. You might be lucky enough to get a ferry from the mainland to drop you here since there is an adequate jetty, but it's more likely that you'll have to come by sea taxi from Genting; if so, the *Nipah Resort* operates a free service.

In fact, the *Nipah Resort* (☎09/799 4287; ③) is the only **place to stay**, offering basic chalets and more expensive A-frames, as well as a nicely designed restaurant; the food can get a little monotonous. The air-con longhouse, *Nipah Paradise*, at the far end, caters only for pre-booked packages from Singapore.

Pulau Sibu

Pulau Sibu is the most popular – if the least scenic – of the islands after Tioman, though the huge monitor lizards and the butterflies here make up for the lack of mountains and jungle. Like the rest of the east-coast islands, Sibu boasts fine beaches, though the sand is yellower and the current more turbulent than some. Shaped like a bone, the island's narrow waist can be crossed in only a few minutes, revealing a double bay known as Twin Beach. Many of the coves have offshore coral, though locals say that the reef is dying by inches. Most of the resorts on Sibu operate their own boats **from Tanjung Leman**, a tiny village about 30km down the coast from Mersing and an hour's boat ride from the island. It's not an established route, so you must ask the resort in advance to pick you up. On the way back, you'll almost certainly need to call a taxi from the jetty; cars take around twenty minutes to arrive.

Accommodation on the island has gone decidedly upmarket. The *Twin Beach Resort* (☎019/324 6464; ⑥), situated on a narrow strip of land with a beach on either side, has chalets that are set on nicely landscaped grounds. It's unique in that it is the only place with sunrise and sunset viewing. *Junansa Villa* (☎019/281 1994; ⑥) is a solid mid-range option, with snug chalets in a colourful garden. The friendly *Sea Gypsy Village Resort* (☎07/222 8642; ⑥–⑧) is easily the best-value resort on the island. Prices are similar to the competition, but the chalets and service are a cut above the rest. It's particularly good for families. There is an attached bar and restaurant.

Eating on Pulau Sibu is a pleasure. *Sea Gypsy* offers good food, whilst the restaurant at *Twin Beach* specializes in reasonably priced Malay food.

7.6

Sarawak

Six hundred kilometres across the South China Sea from Peninsular Malaysia, the two East Malaysian states of Sarawak and Sabah occupy the northwest flank of the island of Borneo (the rest of which, save the enclave of Brunei, is Indonesian Kalimantan). **Sarawak** is the larger of the two states, and though well developed, is a good deal wilder than Peninsular Malaysia. Clear rivers spill down the jungle-covered mountains, and the surviving rainforest, plateaux and river communities are inhabited by indigenous peoples – traditionally grouped as Land Dayaks, Sea Dayaks or Orang Ulu. They make up around half of the state's population and some still live in massive longhouses. A typical longhouse is made from brick or timber and might have one hundred doors – representing the number of families living there. Visits to these longhouses are one of the highlights of a trip to Sarawak. However, don't expect these longhouse communities to be living some kind of "primitive" lifestyle: almost all longhouses have electricity now and that of course means radio, televisions, if not yet computers. Few of the inhabitants wear traditional dress, but this takes nothing away from the enjoyment of being among these people; their warmth, hospitality and humour remain legendary, despite the passing of many traditions.

Most people start their exploration of Sarawak in the capital **Kuching**, from where you can visit **Iban longhouses** on the Batang Ai river system, **Bidayuh dwellings** near the Indonesian border, and **Bako National Park**. A four-hour boat ride north of Kuching, **Sibu** marks the start of the popular route along Batang Rajang, Sarawak's longest river. Most people stop at **Kapit** and from there visit longhouses on the Katibas and Baleh tributaries. North of Sibu, **Niah National Park** boasts a vast cave system and accessible forest hikes. On its way north to the Brunei border, the road goes to **Miri**, from where you either fly, or take a boat via Marudi, to the spectacular **Gunung Mulu National Park**, Sarawak's chief natural attraction, which features astonishing limestone pinnacles, some of the world's largest caves and a swathe of pristine rainforest.

Travelling in Sarawak can be expensive: flights from Peninsular Malaysia are costly, although flight deals around the state are an appealing option (see box below).

Getting to Sarawak

Most people fly to the Sarawak capital of **Kuching** on Malaysia Airlines, either from Kuala Lumpur (RM198 one-way), Kota Kinabalu (RM239), or Pontianak (RM340). There are also direct flights to Miri in the north from Kota Kinabalu (RM115). Air Asia has cheaper flights that can be booked online at ⓦwww.airasia.com.

Daily **boat** services run from Brunei (see p.81) to both Lawas and Limbang in north Sarawak. The main overland route into Sarawak is by bus from Kuala Belait in Brunei to Miri, a very straightforward crossing involving a ferry across the Belait River (see p.97). The other main crossing is via Sipitang in Sabah (see p.726) to Lawas, either by local bus or taxi or by the daily Lawas Express from Kota Kinabalu. From Indonesian Kalimantan, the easiest overland route is from Pontianak (see p.456) into southwest Sarawak, crossing via Entikong (Indonesia) to Tebedu (Malaysia), 100km south of Kuching.

Also, accommodation and internal travel – much of it by boat – are pricier than on the mainland.

Kuching and around

On the whole, **KUCHING** – the capital of Sarawak – is underrated by visitors. Most, unfortunately, only stay for a day or two to organize trips to Bako National Park, the longhouses and the interior. It may be long enough to pick up on Kuching's appeal but not to fall for its special magic. It is a highly attractive place: the courthouse and Astana (palace) still serve their original purpose, while the commercial district – in the heart of the old town – is a warren of crowded lanes and home to Kuching's Chinese community. Main Bazaar, the city's oldest street, sports the remains of its original godowns, now converted into shops but still overlooking

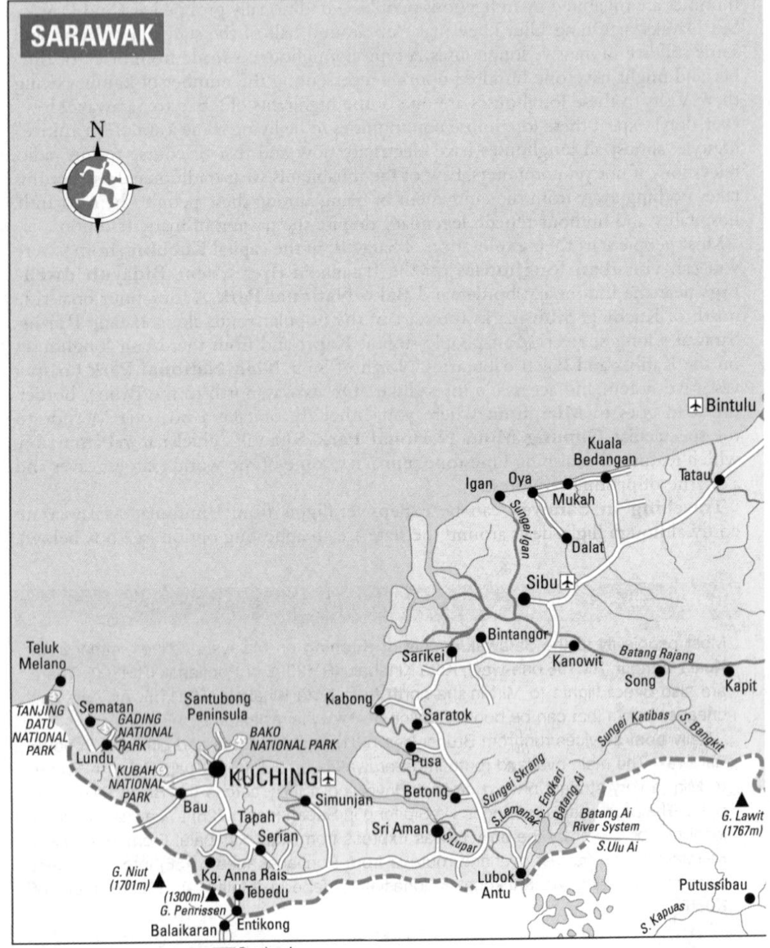

Sungei Sarawak, Kuching's main supply route since the city's earliest days when the Rajah Brookes ran the territory. The city is culturally as well as architecturally exciting – it has one of the finest museums in Southeast Asia – and keeps late hours, too: the eastern waterfront area around the *Hilton Hotel* and *Holiday Inn* is full of bars, pubs and plazas. But what's really unique about Kuching is its atmosphere. It is at once both buzzy and laid back, vibrant and mellow: a town where people are rarely too busy to introduce themselves and ask you where you're from. It's quite a unique place in fact, even for friendly Malaysia.

Arrival

Kuching Airport (☎082/457373) is 11km south of the city and has a good 24-hour information desk, currency exchange (daily 8am–9pm) and ATMs. From the airport, either take a taxi into the centre (RM17.50 coupons from a booth outside the arrivals hall; double price after midnight) or the #12a and 8a buses, which run

from a shelter 100m to your right (east) as you exit the terminal. They take thirty minutes (daily 7am–8.30pm; every 20min; RM1) and handily drop you off at the central STC and Chin Liang Long bus stations respectively.

All **express buses** from outside the immediate municipality arrive at the Third Mile (Jalan Penrissen) bus station, 5km (or three miles) south of downtown Kuching. Buses leave for Third Mile every few minutes from the STC station in town. To get back from Third Mile, walk to the main road where you'll see a bus shelter on your right. Opposite the shelter, Lorong Datuk Towi branches off west for 100m and ends at a T-junction. There are buses to central Kuching every few minutes from the stop over the road just outside the Esso petrol station. A taxi costs RM15.

Information and tours

The excellent **Sarawak Tourist Association** (STA) is next to the Sarawak Steamship Building on Main Bazaar, at the junction with Jalan Tun Haji Openg (Mon–Thurs 8am–12.45pm & 2–4.30pm, Fri 8–11.30am & 2.30–4.45pm, Sat 8am–12.45pm; ☎082/240620). **Sarawak Visitor Information Centre** (Mon–Fri 8am–6pm, Sat 8am–4pm, Sun & public holidays 9am–3pm; ☎082/410942), overlooking the padang at Jalan Masjid, has the booking desk of the National Parks and Wildlife Office, which issues permits for Semengoh, Bako, Gunung Gading and Kubah national parks (☎082/248088).

Many Kuching **tour operators** run tours to Iban longhouses on the Lupar, Lemanak and Skrang rivers, 200km east of Kuching, for around RM150 per person per day, although reductions are available, depending on the size of the group. They will also arrange trips in other parts of the state, including Gunung Mulu National Park. Recommended operators include Asian Overland, 286a 1st Floor, Westwood Park, Jalan Tubuan (☎082/251163); Tropical Adventure, 17 Main Bazaar (☎082/413088); and Borneo Adventure, 55 Main Bazaar (☎082/245175). All provide longhouse trips near Kuching and on the Batang Ai river system, as well as a range of treks both local and as far afield as Sabah. You might, however, prefer to organize your own, cheaper trip to a longhouse if you're willing to go it alone (see Batang Ai section, p.713).

Accommodation

On the whole, **accommodation** is more expensive than in Peninsular Malaysia; you'll pay around RM50 for a double room if the budget places are full.

Anglican Rest House (Diocesan Centre) Jl McDougall ☎082/414027. Still Kuching's best deal, it's set in the restful gardens of the Anglican Cathedral and has comfortable doubles with shared bathrooms. Often full, so book ahead. ❶

Arif Jl Haji Taha ☎082/241211. A friendly place, though it's located by a main intersection. There are a variety of rooms, from the very basic with fan to a/c en suites with bath. ❷

B&B Inn 1st Floor, 30–31 Jl Tabuan ☎082/237366. The city's bottom-dollar option has RM16 dorm beds and a handful of very bare private rooms. All facilities are shared. ❸

Borneo 30 Jl Tabuan ☎082/244122. A comfortable hotel – Kuching's oldest – whose lovely rooms have polished wooden floors, a/c, bath or shower, and TV. ❻

Fata Junction of Lebuh Temple and Jl MacDougall ☎082/248111. Pleasantly close to Reservoir Park; the rooms are smallish but have a/c, showers and TV. ❹

Green Mountain 1 Jl Green Hill ☎082/232828. Located next to the *Orchid Inn*, this place is cleaner and friendlier than its older neighbour. ❸

Kuching 6 Jl Temple ☎082/413985. About the best budget option after the *Anglican Rest House*. Clean, spartan and a bit gloomy, with one shower and toilet on each floor. ❷

Mandarin 6 Jl Green Hill ☎082/418269. One of the nicest places in Green Hill and on a par with the *Fata*. Full facilities – a/c, shower, toilet and TV – but most rooms are rather small. ❹

Merdeka Palace Jl Tun Haji Openg ☎082/258000. Top-of-the-range, palatial hotel overlooking the padang. Although expensive, it very often has a promotion on. ❽

Orchid Inn 2 Jl Green Hill ☎082/411417. This place has seen better days and the staff are less than helpful. Still, it's one of the more popular places in this area. ❸

Telang Usan Jl Ban Hok ☎082/415588. A real gem on a lane just north off Jalan Ban Hock itself (look for the "Penrisen Ban Hock" sign on your left when coming from the centre). With superb art by Tusan Padan adorning the walls, this is a meeting point for Kuching's cognoscenti and Orang Ulu. There's also an excellent restaurant and bar. 7

The City

The central area, sandwiched between Jalan Courthouse to the west, Jalan Temple to the east and Reservoir Park to the south, is usually referred to as colonial Kuching. Set just below the padang on Jalan Tun Haji Openg, is Kuching's prime tourist attraction, the Sarawak **Museum** (daily except Fri; free), whose main building dates from the 1890s and is set in lovely gardens. Part of the museum displays the diverse natural history collection of the nineteenth-century naturalist Alfred Russell Wallace, who spent two years in Sarawak in the 1850s. Upstairs, the excellent ethnographic section includes an authentic wooden Iban longhouse, a Penan hut, some fearsome Iban war totems, and woodcarvings from the Kayan and Kenyah ethnic groups. Across the road, in the new wing, there's an unparalleled collection of antique Chinese storage jars, brass kettles and cannons from Brunei, plus prehistoric relics and early trading goods. Behind the new wing, the **Islamic Museum** (daily except Fri 9am–6pm; free) exhibits diverse aspects of Islamic culture, from architecture to weaponry and textiles to prayer.

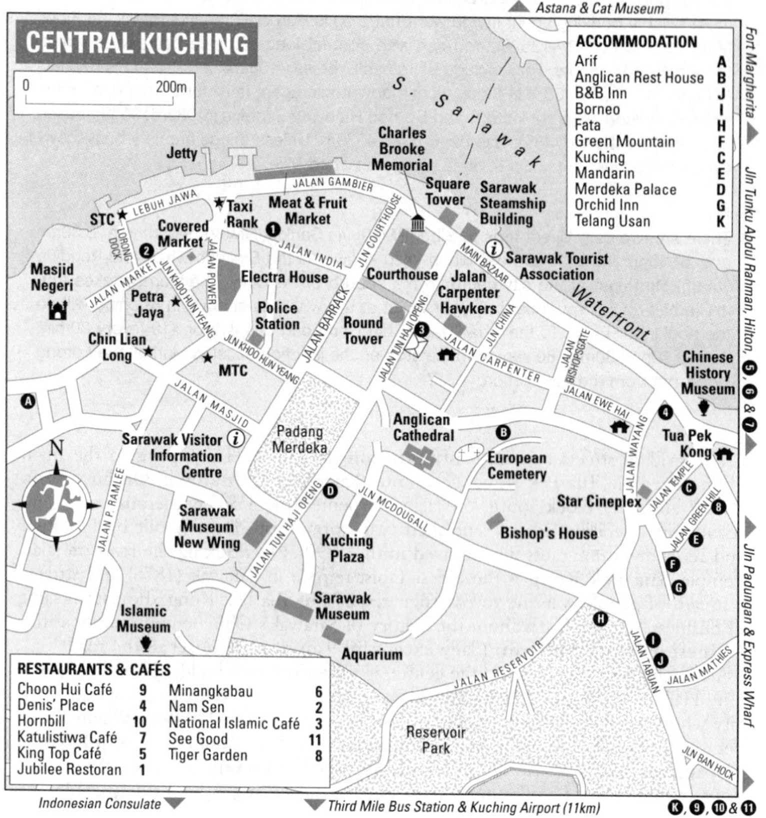

Moving on from Kuching

By plane

Take a taxi or the #12a bus from the STC station on Lebuh Jawa or the #8a from Chin Lian Long station (7am–8.30pm) out to the **airport** (flight enquiries ☎082/457 373). For flight routes, see "Travel details", p.743.

By bus

There are four **local bus companies**; the Sarawak Transport Company's (STC; ☎082/242966) green-and-yellow buses run from the western end of Lebuh Jawa to the airport, the Indonesian consulate, the immigration office and the express wharf (also known as the Bintawa wharf and Pending wharf). Chin Liang Long's blue-and-white buses run from Jalan Masjid towards the airport and express wharf. Petra Jaya Transport black-and-yellow buses run north from below the open-air market on Lebuh Market to Bako National Park. Matang Transport Company's orange-and-yellow buses (for Matang and Kubah) depart from the north end of Jalan P Ramlee. For Damai and the Sarawak Cultural Village, the only service is the shuttle from the *Holiday Inn*, Jalan Tunku Abdul Rahmen, on the waterfront just east of the centre (4 daily from 9am; 45min, RM10 one way; ☎082/423111).

All **express buses** to destinations in Sarawak outside the Kuching area and Pontianak in Indonesia, leave from Third Mile bus station (see p.706). STC provides the best general coverage of the local region; you're best off just turning up at Third Mile and buying a ticket. For long-distance companies operating out of Third Mile, the most reliable booking agent (if you want to book) is Borneo Interland Travel, 1st Floor, Main Bazaar, (☎082/413595). You can also contact long-distance companies direct, though it's no cheaper. They include Biaramas Express (☎082/452139) and PB Express (☎082/461277), No, 63, 1st Floor, whose downtown agent is Natural Colour in Lebuh Khoo Hun Yeng's Electra House; and Borneo Highway Express (☎082/619689), based at Yong Ngee Loong, 43 Jl Gambir (☎082/243794). Unless things are very busy, however, you can just buy a ticket once you get to Third Mile.

By boat

There are two daily direct trips to Sibu (RM40) via Sarikei (RM32) departing at 8.30am and 12.30pm from the express wharf (also known as the Bintawa wharf and Pending wharf), 5km east of the city centre in the suburb of Pending. The journey takes four and a half hours. You must buy your ticket at the wharf as nobody in Kuching will do the bookings. To get to the wharf, take Chin Lian Long bus #17 or #19 (every 30min, 6am–8.30pm; 30min; 80 sen) from the stop on the junction of Jalan Market and Lorong Dock, not from the bus station.

The grid of streets running eastwards from Jalan Tun Haji Openg to the main Chinese temple, Tua Pek Kong, constitutes Kuching's **Chinatown**. On busy Main Bazaar and, one block south, on Jalan Carpenter, there are numerous stores and restaurants operating out of renovated two-storey shop-houses, built by Hokkien and Teochew immigrants who arrived in the 1890s. Overlooking the river on Jalan Temple, **Tua Pek Kong** is the oldest Taoist temple in Sarawak (1876) and attracts a stream of people wanting to pay their respects to Tua Pek Kong, the patron saint of business. You can learn about the history of Sarawak's Chinese community at the **Chinese History Museum** (daily except Fri 9am–6pm; free) across the road.

Across the river and north of the centre, at a futuristic new building housing North City Hall, is Kuching's Cat Museum (daily except Fri; free). Wholly appropriate for a city whose name means "cat" in Malay, the museum features whimsical exhibits about pet cats through history, including a thousand-year-old mummified cat from Egypt.

Boats cross to the north side of Sungei Sarawak from several jetties on the waterfront, itself a pleasant esplanade, with cafés, bars and seating. A boat ride (RM25 per hour) is a great way to see the riverbanks and tranquil villages just outside town. To simply cross over, one boat leaves from opposite the courthouse on Main Bazaar every few minutes (6am–10pm; 50 sen) to Sapi jetty, close to the Astana – formerly the Brookes residence and now the home of the Head of State of Sarawak. Another route takes you closer to Fort Margherita, 1km east of the Astana; the only one of Sarawak's twenty historic river forts that's open to the public. It now houses a **Police Museum** (Tues–Sun 10am–6pm; free, but take your passport), which features old weapons and uniforms, and a reconstructed opium den complete with emaciated mannequins and winking opium lamps. From the fort, it's easy to thread your way eastwards and down to the atmospheric **Malay kampung** over which it stands guard: Kampung Boyan segues into Kampung Gersik, which in turn is assimilated by Kampung Sourabaya Ulu. From this side of the fort, boats will deposit you near the *Riverside Majestic Hotel* on the east side of the city centre.

The Sarawak Cultural Village

The **Sarawak Cultural Village** (9am–12.30am & 2pm–5.15pm, ⊕082/422411; RM45) is picturesquely located on the Santubong peninsula 35km north of Kuching, and provides a worthwhile day-trip from the city. It's very much a show for tourists, but nevertheless the Penan shelter and Iban, Melanau and Bidayuh houses are exact replicas of what you'd be lucky to find two weeks upriver in this day and age. Here you'll get a close-up of the fading traditions – dancing, top-spinning, weaving and carving – that you'll catch glimpses of in most longhouses. There's a traditional dance at 11.30am and 4.30pm and five minutes' walk away is a **beach** where you can swim. The SCV also hosts the annual Sarawak Rainforest World Music Festival, held during three days in July and featuring acts from around the globe. Information can be found online at ⊛www.rainforestmusic-borneo.com. To get to the Cultural Centre from Kuching, take the shuttle from the Holiday Inn, Jalan Tunku Abdul Rahmen (4 daily from 9am; 45min, RM10 one way; ⊕082/423111).

Eating and nightlife

Local **specialities** such as wild boar and deer sometimes crop up on Chinese menus; in addition, Kuching has its own *laksa*, a rich soup where rice vermicelli is combined with shredded chicken, prawns and beansprouts in a spicy coconut gravy. For **nightlife**, head for the area just east of the *Hilton*, most notably *De Tavern* bar, a Kayan-run watering-hole opposite the *Hilton* on Jalan Borneo (running south from the waterfront). Should you develop a taste for *tuak* (rice wine), try the range at the *Telang Usan Hotel*'s *Dulit Terrace* and *Tuak Bar*. Kuching's waterfront area, with its outdoor bars, cafés and eateries, is the place to go once the sun sets.

Choon Hui Café Jl Ban Hock. Spicy *laksa* and filling *kolok mee* (noodles, Kuching-style) make this a breakfast-time hit. Keep going along Jalan Ban Hock for five minutes; it's on your right, past the Hindu Temple.

Denis' Place 80 Main Bazaar. Expensive Western-style café-bar with great international cuisine, coffee and pastries.

Hornbill 85 Persiaran Ban Hock. Great steamboat and eat-as-much-as-you-like buffet place with a bizarre penalty system if you leave food on your plate. Opens 6pm.

Jubilee Restoran 49 Jl India. Excellent Malay restaurant serving tasty *kacang goreng* (peanuts in fish paste) and *sayur* (green beans in chilli and lemon). Full meals from RM10 for two.

Katulistiwa Café On the waterfront, this moderate restaurant has very good western breakfasts served round the clock, as well as a selection of Australian wines. Open until late.

King Top Café Turn left into a through-yard off Jalan Borneo, right opposite the *Hilton* foyer and 50m before *De Tavern* to find the city's best late-night cafés.

Minangkabau J 168 Jl Chan Chin Ann. Excellent Indonesian restaurant with a range of unusual dishes such as chilli-hot fish curries and beef rendang. RM20 for two.

Nam Sen 17 Jl Market. Lovely old coffee shop, complete with marble tables and "No spitting" signs. Handy for snatching an early-morning coffee or noodle soup before catching a bus.

National Islamic Café Jl Carpenter. Serves halal (Islamic) food, curries and *roti canai* from mid-morning until about 9pm. Very popular and inexpensive.

See Good Beside *Telang Usan Hotel*. Persiaran Ban Hock, a huddle of restaurants and bars just north of Jalan Ban Hock, has some great eating places and *See Good* is one of the best. Turn left at the sign a few minutes' walk past the *B&B Inn* heading out of the centre. The chilli crab is a house speciality.

Tiger Garden Jl Green Hill. One of the best *laksa* lounges in town, with a long Sunday brunch that will keep you full for the rest of the day.

Shopping

Kuching is the best place in Sarawak to buy just about anything, although it would be unwise to stock up on tribal textiles and handicrafts here before visiting Sibu or Kapit. Kuching's **Main Bazaar** has the bulk of the souvenir shops; check out Yeo Hing Chuan, 46 Main Bazaar, for interesting carvings and other handicrafts; Sarakraf in Sarawak Plaza (next to the Hilton) for baskets, textiles and ironwork; Sarawak Batik Art Shop, 1 Jl Temple, for fine Iban *pua kumbu* textiles; Tan and Son, Jalan Padungan, close to the junction with Jalan Mathies, for baskets, carvings and bags; and Talan Usan, Jalan Ban Hock, for superb Penan and Orang Ulu crafts. Adventure Images, 55 Main Bazaar, has the best postcards in Sarawak. Mohamad Yahiah & Sons, with branches in the *Holiday Inn*, and Bell Books in Sarawak Plaza, offer the biggest range of **books** in Sarawak, and also stock the best **maps** of the state. Sky Book Store, 57 Jl Padungan, and Star Books, 30 Main Bazaar, are good for geographical, cultural and anthropological material.

For a typical local shopping experience, head out to the weekend **market** at the Jalan Satok/Jalan Palm junction in the southwest of the city. Stalls here sell everything from rabbits to knives, and one alley is dedicated to Dayak produce and handicrafts. The market runs from Saturday afternoon until 2am, then from 6am to noon on Sunday; beware of pickpockets. Take bus #11 from the MTC bus station, or #6 or #2b from Petra Jaya station (5min).

Listings

Airline offices MAS, Lot 215, Jl Song Thian Cheok ☎082/246622; Merpati, c/o Sin Hwa Travel Service, 8 Lebuh Temple ☎082/246688; Royal Brunei Airlines, 1st Floor, Rugayah Bldg, Jl Song Thian Cheok ☎082/246288; Singapore Airlines, Wisma Bukit Maja Kuching, Jl Tunku Abdul Rahman ☎082/240266.

Banks and exchange Majid & Sons, 45 Jl India and Mohamad Yahia & Sons, in the basement of Jl Abell's Sarawak Plaza; both offer good rates. There's an office of Maybank with an ATM on Jalan Abell about 1km past the *Hilton*.

Hospitals Sarawak General Hospital, Jl Ong Kee Hui (☎082/257555), charges RM1 for A&E consultations; for private treatment, go to Norman Medical Centre, Jl Tun Datuk Patinggi (☎082/440055), or the Timberland Medical Centre, Jl Rock Road (☎082/234991). You can also try Dr Chan's Clinic, 98 Main Bazaar (☎082/240307).

Immigration 1st Floor, Bangunan Sultan Iskander, Jl Simpang Tiga (Mon–Fri 8am–noon & 2–4.30pm, closed every second Fri; ☎082/245661), for visa extensions; take Chin Lian Long bus #11, and get there by 3.30pm if you want service the same day. The Indonesian consulate is at 111 Jl Tun Haji Openg (Mon–Thurs 8.30am–noon & 2–4pm; ☎082/241734); take any STC bus from outside the post office. Visas cost RM10; allow at least two working days – EU, US, Canadian, Australian and New Zealand passport holders (among others) can be issued with visas at the Entikong border (see p.712).

Internet access Several shops with Internet access can be found on Jl Green Hill in the vicinity of the *Orchid Inn*.

Pharmacies There are a lot of pharmacies around the Electra House shopping centre on Jalan Power. Apex Phamacy, No 15, Ground Floor, Electra House (☎082/246011), inside the centre, is the most reputable.

Police Central Police Station on Jl Khoo Hun Yeang ☎082/241222.

Post office The GPO on Jl Tun Haji Openg (Mon–Sat 8am–6pm, closed Sun and first Sat of every month) keeps poste restante.

Telephone services International calls can be made from most public card phones, and from all major hotels. You can buy a Telekom card from camera shops and general stores.

Bako National Park

Bako National Park, a bus and boat journey (1hr 30min) northeast of Kuching, occupies the northern section of the Muara Tebas peninsula at the mouth of Sungei Bako. It's Sarawak's oldest national park (established in 1957) and the best place to see wildlife in the state. Many people come on a day-trip and then end up staying longer, taking picnics to one of the seven beaches, relaxing at the park headquarters area, or following the trails. You'll see plenty of flora and fauna, including the strange pitcher plants, whose deep, mouth-shaped lids open to trap water and insects, which are then digested in the soupy liquid. Watch out for these just on the verge of the path: most are small and green, some are pink. The best time to see wildlife on the trails is at night or in the early morning; you'll almost definitely catch sight of macaque monkeys and the bizarre bearded pigs at the HQ. Silver leaf monkeys, snakes, giant monitor lizards, squirrels, otters and mouse deer to name a few are plentiful in the park, and you'll probably see some of these if you walk (quietly) on any of the trails. Most famously, Bako is home to rare proboscis monkeys (known in Malay as the *orang belanda*, or Dutchman), found only in Borneo. The male has a distinctive pendulous nose, which he hoots through. The park headquarters and the open paths in the *kerangas* (sparse forest) are the best places for bird-watching: fifty species have been recorded in Bako, including two rare species of hornbills.

The park boasts some nineteen miles of trails, which all start from park headquarters and are colour-coded with paint splashes every twenty metres. Carry a litre of water per person (you can refill your bottle from the streams), a light rainproof jacket, mosquito repellent and sunscreen. Wear good shoes and a sunhat. Don't forget your swimming gear either, as cool streams cut across the trails, and beaches and waterfalls are never far away. Probably the most popular trail is the Lintang – a three-hour loop that takes in lowland jungle and *kerangas*. This is a good one for pitcher plants. Also popular is the hike to **Tajor Waterfall** (3.5km; about 2hr), which climbs up the forested cliff, through *kerangas* with plentiful pitcher plants, through peat bog and, eventually, to the waterfall itself, a lovely spot for swimming. Leaving the main trail at the wooden hut and viewpoint just after the *kerangas*, and turning west, a path descends to two beautiful beaches, **Telok Pandan Kecil** and **Telok Pandan Besar** (30min). The longest beach on the peninsula is **Telok Sibur beach**. To get there, continue past Tajor Waterfall, following the main trail for around forty minutes, before turning west on the black-and-red trail. The demanding descent to the beach takes anything from twenty minutes to an hour to accomplish. You'll have to drop down the cliff-face using creepers and roots to help you, and at the bottom you have to tread carefully through the mangrove swamp. After wading across a river, you reach the beach – not surprisingly, seldom visited. The best paths for spotting **proboscis monkeys** are Telok Paku and Telok Delima; be there for dawn or around dusk and listen for crashing and honking noises in the branches.

Practicalities

Before going to Bako you need to get a **permit** and reserve your accommodation at the visitor centre in Kuching (see p.706), though day-trippers can get their permits in Kampung Bako. Once at the park, you can extend your stay.

To get to the park, take Petra Jaya bus #6 (hourly 6.40am–4.40pm; 45min; RM2 one way) from Jalan Khoo Hun Yeang by the covered market beside Electra House to the jetty at Kampung Bako; the last bus back is at 5pm. From here, you can get a motorized boat to the park headquarters (RM30 per boat for up to seven people; 30min), which leaves when it's full or whenever a passenger or group of passengers is willing to pay RM30. Once at the park headquarters you need to pay the park fee (RM3 entry, plus RM5 camera and RM10 video camera), sign in and collect the informative map of the park.

At park headquarters, you can camp (RM4) or stay at the **hostel** (RM10.50) or one of the lodges (❹), all of which provide bed linen, fridge and cooking and washing facilities (there may be water shortages if it hasn't rained for a while). Some hikers prefer to camp on the trails, though there are no tents for rent. There's a simple café at headquarters and a provisions shop.

The Kalimantan border: Anna Rais and Bau

The mountains straddling the border with Kalimantan, 100km south of Kuching, are inhabited by Bidayuh, the only remaining Land Dayaks in Sarawak. Unlike other ethnic groups, the Bidayuh built their multi-levelled, elevated longhouses at the base of hills rather than on rivers, and, as a consequence, endured violent attacks during the nineteenth century from other more aggressive groups, especially the Iban. But the Bidayuh weren't exactly passive victims: traditional communities always had a head-house, where the heads of their enemies were kept and which served as a focus for male activities and rituals. Nowadays, only one traditional Bidayuh longhouse community remains – at Kampung **Anna Rais**. Local tour operators can arrange a visit. Independent visitors are charged a small fee for upkeep of the longhouse (RM5).

If you are in Sarawak during late May and early June it's well worth going to the **Bau** area, near Kuching, deep in Bidayuh country. Over this period the Bidayuhs celebrate **Gawai Padi**, a shamanistic ritual, in which people give thanks to the Rice Goddess for an abundant harvest. Each village has a slightly different kind of celebration, but it usually involves dancing and making offerings. Contact Diweng Bekir (☎082/492726) at the Ministry of Tourism for further details about Gawai Padi. **Buses** (#2, #2a and #2c of both STC and Bau Transport) leave from Jalan Masjid in Kuching for Bau every twenty minutes (6.30am–6pm).

Visiting the longhouses

From Kuching's Lebuh Jawa, STC bus #9 (6.40am–5.55pm; every 30min; 2hr) theoretically services **ANNA RAIS**, the largest Bidayuh settlement in the area, though in practice the return service is very unreliable and could leave you stranded. To be safe, visit through a tour operator (see p.706). The community is used to visitors, and everybody is greeted warmly. You'll be escorted around by a member of the community – which consists of two longhouses on either side of a river, Sungei Penrissen, and many separate dwellings. The best time to go is at the weekend, when the longhouse-based women are over with their farming duties, the children are in from school and the wage-earners back from work in the oil-palm plantations or in Kuching. As you wander around, you'll be offered food and drink, possibly even betel nut, and invited to watch and participate in craft demonstrations. Most visitors stay a couple of hours, returning to Kuching the same day, but you can stay the night. Alternatively, you can sleep in the community hall at **KAMPUNG ABANG** (RM20), a ten-minute drive beyond Anna Rais.

Serian and the border crossing

Some 20km southeast of Gunung Penrissen is the border crossing at **TEBEDU**. Buses to Tebedu leave from **SERIAN**, a workaday town on the main Kuching–Sri Aman road. You'll need to set off first thing, as local buses from Tebedu – which run south across the border to the Indonesian town of **ENTIKONG** and on to Pontianak – stop running in the early afternoon. The #3 and #3a from the STC station in Kuching go direct to Serian (2hr) and there are a number of services from Kuching's Third Mile. Tebedu is little more than an administrative centre, with a couple of dispiriting hotels.

You can also take a direct bus through Entikong to Pontianak from Third Mile (RM50). The border crossing at Entikong is open 6am–6pm. EU, US, Canadian, Australian and New Zealand passport holders (among others) can be stamped in at the border.

Batang Ai region

The **Batang Ai** river system lies 200km east of Kuching; this is where the Batang Ai and Engkari rivers flow into the Batang Ai Lake. The Skrang and Lemanak rivers are a little to the west. The area, designated a national park, is the most popular destination for longhouse visits from the capital. Many of the tour operators in Kuching have established good relations with the Iban communities here (roughly RM300 for a three-day, tour with a few extras such as jungle trekking thrown in; see p.706), but it's quite possible to travel here independently. One access point is via the sizeable town of **SRI AMAN**, which sits upriver on Sungei Lupar, 150km southeast of Kuching. It's reached from Kuching's Third Mile station by (among others) STC bus (four daily; 3hr; RM19). There are several hotels in town: the clean air-con *Champion Hotel*, 1248 Main Bazaar (☎083/320140; ❹), 100m northeast of the bus station on the riverside, is a little cramped; the *Hoover Hotel*, 139 Jl Club (☎083/321985; ❺), is the best in town and noticeably better.

From Sri Aman, you've got a few choices depending on which river you want to visit. To reach either the Engkari or the Batang Ai and its tributaries, you'll need to take an STC bus from Sri Aman southeast to **LUBOK ANTU**, 80km away. There is also one direct service there from Kuching's Third Mile station. If need be you can overnight at the *Kelingkang Inn* (☎083/584331; ❹), visible from the bus stop. The mega-basic *Mega Inn* (☎083/5841113; ❶) run by the friendly and informative Raymond Jee is another alternative 100m north along the main road. If you hang around the *Oriental Café* by the bus stop long enough, chances are you'll get invited upriver by someone for a lot less money than you'd have paid a tour operator in Kuching. If you don't get an invite, however, you've wasted your time – in either case, you'll end up visiting the same longhouses whether you take a guided tour or not. To reach the water from Lubok Antu, you'll need to take the local shuttle (RM1.80) down to the Batang Ai Lake jetty, about 15km to the northeast. Once there, you can take a boat across the lake and up the Enkari or the Batang Ai rivers.

The Skrang is reached by taking a Betong-bound bus from Sri Aman, and getting off just short of Entabau, at the **PAIS** jetty where you might get an invitation to a longhouse. Of all the tributaries in this region, the Skrang is the most touristy, and you may find that longhouses don't take you in unless you've booked through the operator which has "adopted" them.

Longhouse etiquette

Budget travellers abusing the traditional system of longhouse hospitality, in which any traveller could stay a night or two in exchange for a small gift, has caused the system to be scrapped in favour of one that operates on a fixed price per tourist per night – RM20. Do not show up unnanounced with a shiny new plastic bucket and expect the longhouse inhabitants to fall to their knees with gratitude. It's always wise to have an introduction: before you board a boat, ideally you'll have already been invited to a longhouse by someone you've met around town. Many of the Iban speak Malay but remember that you're unlikely to be able to communicate in English. Should you turn up on spec, ask to meet the *tuai rumah* (headman); under no circumstances should you waltz up the stairs and into a longhouse uninvited. The one time when the rules are relaxed is during the Gawai Padi (harvest) festival period in June when longhouses take turns to host a party for whoever turns up.

If the Lemanak River takes your fancy, take the STC bus from Sri Aman (every 2hr, 7am–3.15pm) to Lemanak Bridge, 50km to the east. From here, as at the Pais jetty, you might well meet up with an Iban boatman.

Visiting the longhouses

All the longhouses on the Skrang, Lemanak, Engkari and Batang Ai rivers are Iban and it is here that the Iban culture is most concentrated. It's especially visible during the **harvest festival**, or Gawai Padi, in early June, when traditional dress is encouraged and age-old rituals enacted, including wedding, christening and circumcision ceremonies. At other times of the year, it might be stretching the point to say that they still follow a traditional lifestyle (many have "good" jobs in Kuching, or live abroad, and televisions and music systems are in evidence). However, the gregarious, highly hospitable Iban will make a trip at any time of year an enjoyable one, and you'll find that just going fishing, eating delicious fish and jungle vegetables, and sitting on the longhouse veranda makes for a memorable experience. See the box on p.713 for longhouse etiquette.

Sibu

SIBU, 60km from the coast up Batang Rajang, is Sarawak's second-largest city and the state's biggest port. Most of the local population are Foochow Chinese (the town is known locally as New Foochow), and its remarkable modern growth is largely attributed to these enterprising immigrants. Most travellers treat Sibu as the first stage of an expedition upriver and, beyond simply soaking up the town's vibrant atmosphere, there's not much to do.

The town's most striking landmark is the towering, seven-storey **pagoda** at the back of Tua Pek Kong Temple beyond the western, waterfront end of Jalan Khoo Peng Loong. Two large concrete lions guard the entrance to the temple, to the left of which stands a statue of the deity, Tua Pek Kong, a prominent Confucian scholar and patron saint of business. The roof and columns are decorated with traditional dragon and holy bird statues, and murals depict the signs of the Chinese zodiac. Across the way, in the network of streets between Jalan Market, Jalan Channel and Jalan Central, is **Chinatown**, with its plethora of hardware shops, newspaper stalls, rowdy cafés, food vendors and hotels. The central artery, **Jalan Market**, runs from Jalan Pulau beside the temple, and forms the hub of possibly the most vibrant *pasar malam* (night market) in Sarawak. Beside Jalan Channel, the daily Lembangan Market opens before dawn and closes around 5pm; there are hundreds of stalls here, selling anything from edible delicacies such as flying fox, snake and jungle ferns, to rattan baskets, beadwork and charm bracelets.

Two kilometres north of the town centre, the modern Civic Centre contains in its **Cultural Exhibition Hall** (Tues–Sun 10.30am–5.30pm; free) a small but high-quality collection of photographs, artefacts and paraphernalia describing the varied peoples of the Rajang. These include costumes, backpacks, musical instruments, and a scale model of an Iban longhouse. To get there, take the Jalan Tun Abang Haji Openg bus from the bus terminal and ask for the Civic Centre.

Practicalities

Flights from Kuching, Bintulu and Miri use the **airport** (☎084/307770), 25km east of the city centre. Taxis cost RM22 into the centre, but the #3a bus (every 45min, daily 7am–6pm; RM2) stops on the main road outside the terminal, and runs to the **bus and taxi station** on Jalan Khoo Peng Loong, 200m west of Chinatown and close to many budget hotels. For onward journeys by bus, you can book seats here through bus company offices, though all express services are via the express bus terminal at the village of Sungai Antu. To get there, take the #2, #7 or #9 bus from the city bus station. MAS is at 61 Jl Tunku Osman (☎084/326166).

Boats dock at the **upriver boat wharf**, 100m northwest of the bus terminal. This is where you come to catch the express boat on to Kanowit (1hr; RM9), Song (2hr; RM10) and Kapit (3hr; RM15); they run more or less hourly from 5.30am until 2.30pm. From the **downriver wharf**, 100m further northwest, just beside the Chinese temple, Express Bahagia, 20a Jl Tukang Besi (☎084/319228), runs a daily service to Kuching at 11.30am, and Sejahtera Petrama Express, 2d Jalan Kampung Dato (☎084/321424), runs a similar service at 7am. The trip takes four and a half hours, costs RM40 and passes through Sarikei, one hour downriver.

You can pick up a good map of the town at Sibu's **visitor centre** (Mon–Fri 8am–5pm, Sat 8am–12.50pm, closed first and third Sat of the month; ☎084/340980), 32 Jl Cross off Jalan Lintang, at the back of the *Sarawak Hotel*. This really is the first place to go to ask about accessing the Rajang longhouses; head directly away from the water from the wharf to get there. Ibrahim Tourist Guide, 1 Lane One, Jalan Bengkel (Mon–Sat 9am–5.30pm; ☎084/318987), does an overnight **tour** to a nearby Iban longhouse (RM200 for two), and Frankie Ting at Sazhong Trading, 4 Jl Central (Mon–Sat 8am–4.40pm; ☎084/336017), runs a variety of tours upriver, mostly involving a stay at the Pelagus Resort and including jungle treks and longhouse visits. The prices are about RM250 per person per day; you might prefer to make your own way up the Rajang (see below). The **GPO** is on Jalan Kampung Nyabar (Mon–Fri 8am–6pm, Sat 8am–noon); the **police** are on Jalan Kampung Nyabor (☎084/336144); and the nearest **hospital** is 8km away on Old Oya Road (☎084/343333). **Internet** access is available at Superhighway on Level 4 of the giant Wisam Sayan tower in the west of the city, and at City.com, 1st Floor, Foo Chow Lane, behind the *Premier Hotel*.

Accommodation and eating

The best of the budget **accommodation** is the very clean *Hoover Lodging House*, close to the bus station on 34 Jl Tan Sri (☎084/334490; ❷); over in the west of town, *Hoover House Methodist Guesthouse* (☎084/332491; ❷) occupies a quiet spot on Jalan Pulau, with very pleasant double rooms (book ahead); *Miramar Hotel*, Jalan Channel Sibu (☎084/338009; ❸), is well run and friendly. Similar in price but a bit newer is the *Sentosa Hotel*, Jalan Pulau (☎084/349875; ❸). Otherwise, you should go for the quality *Zuhra*, Jalan Kampung Nyabor (☎084/310711; ❹), which has modern en-suite rooms with air-con and TV; or the *Premier* (☎084/323222; ❽), at the junction of Jalan Kampung Nyabor and Jalan Tinggi, a top-class hotel that occasionally does bargain promotions.

Throughout town there are Chinese **cafés** selling Sibu's most famous dish, foochow noodles – steamed and served in a soy and oyster sauce with spring onions and dried fish. Other local favourites include *kang puan mee* (noodles cooked in lard) and *kong bian* (oriental bagels, sprinkled with sesame seed). Hawker stalls at the Lembangan Market are the busiest place in the morning; in the evening, everyone congregates at the *pasar malam* in the town centre, though you can't sit down and eat here. For a good **restaurant** experience, try the well-known foochow restaurant *Hock Chu Leu Restoran*, 28 Jl Tukan Besi, which does great baked fish and fresh vegetables (RM25 for two, including beer); or the *Balkis Islamic Café*, near the post office at 69 Jl Osman, which serves good North Indian staples like *roti canai*, *murtabak* and curries. Top-of-the-league is The *New Capitol Restoran*, beside the *Premier Hotel*, the kind of Chinese restaurant where you can get shark's fin and other "delicacies" at around RM60 for two.

Up the Rajang: Kanowit to Putai

The 560-kilometre-long **Batang Rajang** – *batang* (big river) rather than sungei, because of its great width and length – lies at the very heart of Sarawak. This is the world of isolated colonial forts, logging wharves and boat trips to busy longhouses. The communities here are used to tourists, but not to the extent of those in the Kuching area. Express boats from Sibu (hourly 5.30am–2.30pm; RM15 economy class) take three hours to reach **Kapit**, stopping first at **Kanowit** and then at the little town of **Song**. Kapit, with its experienced tour operators, is the most popular springboard for the longhouses as well as trips much further inland. From Song, the Iban communities on the **Katibas** and **Baleh** tributaries are accessible.

Kanowit

An hour from Sibu, the boat reaches the attractive, sleepy settlement of **KANOWIT**. There are two well-kept hotels on waterfront Jalan Kubu, the *Kanowit Air Con Hotel* (☎084/725155; ③) and the *Harbour View Inn* (☎084/753188; ③), plus a few cafés. Fort Emma, which was built in 1859 of timber and bamboo, is just a couple of hundred metres to the north of the jetty but it's usually closed and pretty unimpressive.

Song and Sungei Katibas

The next stop is at **SONG**, another hour upstream at the head of one of the Rajang's major tributaries, Sungei Katibas, which winds and narrows as it runs south towards the mountainous border region with Kalimantan. The place is little more than a few blocks of waterfront shop-houses and cafés, a small Chinese temple and a few air-con hotels. The smart *Katibas Inn* (☎084/777323; ③) is the best in town and right on the riverfront; also very tidy are the *Mesra Inn* (☎084/777666; ②) and *Sukaramai Inn* (☎084/777686; ③), one block inland.

To explore **Sungei Katibas,** you need to catch the passenger longboat that leaves Song each morning; departure times change so ask at the canteen on the jetty. Private charters are a whopping RM300 or so. On the Katibas are several Iban longhouses worth visiting, including the large community at **Nanga Bangkit**, the junction of the Katibas and one of its own small tributaries, Sungei Bangkit. It takes between two and three hours to reach Nanga Bangkit, which comprises an impressive fifty-door longhouse and a dozen smaller dwellings on the opposite bank. You'll generally meet people and get invited to stay overnight, but if no offers are forthcoming you'll have to hope that the very basic *Rumah Tumai* public resthouse is open (RM2). The longhouse women are excellent weavers, and you can buy a wall-hanging here for around RM300, which sounds a lot, but you won't be able to find these *ikat* weavings anywhere else. There is also the possibility of chartering a boat from Nanga Bangkit to visit a longhouse even further up river (if you're invited to one). This should cost around RM50–100, but prices can vary enormously. The boat back to Song leaves at around 6am though – as ever – you could charter your own.

Kapit

KAPIT, around three hours east of Sibu by express boat, is a fast-growing timber town with a frontier atmosphere, where karaoke lounges and snooker halls are much in evidence. There are lots of good cafés and a decent museum, and this is the main place to organize trips to local Iban communities with one of the tour operators based in town.

Close to the jetty is Kapit's main landmark, **Fort Sylvia**. It was built in 1880 in an attempt to prevent the warring Iban attacking smaller groups such as the upriver Ukit and Bukitan. Kapit's main square, simply called **Kapit Square**, is surrounded by shops selling everything from noodles to rope. The walk west along Jalan Temenggong, which forms the square's northern edge, leads to the day market. Back from the jetty, near the pond, the **Civic Museum** (Mon–Fri 2–4.30pm; free) has a collection of interesting exhibits on the tribes in the Rajang basin, including a well-constructed longhouse and a mural painted by local Iban.

Express boats dock at the town jetty, close to the town centre. There is a Maybank with ATM and travellers' cheques facilities near the post office on Jalan Teo Chow Beng. Further east on the same road, **Internet** access is available at several places in the vicinity of the *Rejang* hotel.

You need a permit (free of charge) to **travel beyond Kapit**, available from the Resident's Office (Mon–Fri 8am–12.30pm & 2–5pm, Sat 8am–12.40pm) on the first floor of the State Government Complex, which is 100m north of the jetty on Jalan Selinik; take your passport with you.

There are two main **tour operators** in town, both offering a wide range of trips, including day visits to a local longhouse, overnight trips upriver and week-long trips to the remote Penan Highlands on the Kalimantan border. The Iban-run *New Rejang Inn* (ask for Joshua, ⓔjoana_37@hotmail.com) and Mr Tan Teck Chuan, Kapit Adventure Tours, 11 Jl Tan Sit Leong (ⓣ084/796352, ⓔtmembers.tripod.com/kapitadventure) will charge you in the region of RM70 for a day-trip and RM250 per person per night for overnight tours. The daily rate drops according to the numbers in the party and the length of the tour; get in touch at least a week in advance for long trips.

Accommodation and eating

The inexpensive *Rajang*, 28 Jl Temenggoh, New Bazaar (ⓣ084/796709; ❶), is one of Sarawak's best-known travellers' **hotels**, with clean fan rooms and large en suites overlooking the river. All eighteen rooms at *Fully Inn*, Jalan Temenggong (ⓣ084/797366; ❸), are inexpensive and appealing, and some have river views. Another decent budget option is the *Well Inn*, up a lane from the riverfront on Jalan Penghulu Geridang (ⓣ084/796009; ❸), while the *New Rajang Inn*, 104 Jl Teo Chow Beng (ⓣ084/796600; ❹), is a real bargain with plush, en-suite air-con rooms with TV and fridge.

The **food** from hawker stalls and markets is good, particularly at the covered market at Jalan Airport, where a dozen stalls serve Chinese, Malay and Dayak dishes, and at the day market on Jalan Teo Chow Beng. Of the proper restaurants, try *Hock Bing Seafood Café*, west of the temple, which serves the best prawn dishes in Kapit (RM20 for two, including beer), or the *Ah Kau Restoran*, Jalan Berjaya, which specializes in local recipes: wild boar, steamed fish and jungle vegetables (RM25 for two with beer). Beside the jetty, there's *Chuong Hin Café*, a must for breakfast, with a fine selection of sweet and savoury cakes.

Sungei Baleh and the Pelagus Rapids

Sungei Baleh branches off from the Rajang 10km east of Kapit. Several boats leave Kapit for Sungei Baleh between 7am and noon. Some ply only the 20km to **NANGA BALEH** (1hr 30min; RM8), a large, modern longhouse, where there is also a logging camp; some push on to the junction with the tributaries of Sungei Gaat and Sungei Merirai, two and a half hours from Kapit (RM10); while others follow the shorter stretch to the Sungei Mujong junction (1hr; RM6) – a large tributary closer to Kapit. The express boat ends its route at **PUTAI**, four hours from Kapit, where there's another logging camp.

There are Iban longhouses on the **Gaat and Merirai tributaries**, which can only be reached by renting a longboat (around RM80 one way). The longhouse wharves at the junctions of the Baleh and these smaller rivers are the places to ask for advice on how to travel further, and to find out which longhouses are good to visit. One place to make for on the upper Baleh is the river's only Kenyah longhouse, established by a group of Indonesian Kenyah, two hours beyond Putai by longboat. Although the longhouse is not a large wooden beauty, the people here are friendly and the location breathtaking. You're close here to the Kalimantan border and within sight of the remote peak, Batu Tiban.

Just beyond the Baleh turn on Batang Rajang (1hr from Kapit) are the **Pelagus Rapids**, an eight-hundred-metre stretch of rock-strewn shallow water that in dry season can be so dangerous the express boats are unable to operate. At the most attractive point of the rapids, as the river twists north, lies the *Regent Pelagus Resort* (☎084/799051), which can be reached by speedboat – or, if you have cash to burn, by helicopter from Kapit (Husqvarna Transport ☎084/799051). The resort is a beautiful longhouse-shaped hideaway tucked in between the rapids and the jungle-covered Bukit Pelagus behind. Exquisite rooms with attached bathroom and veranda begin at RM210 a night. The resort's resident guides lead excursions to an Iban longhouse nearby, as well as a fascinating two-hour boat trip to visit a Punan community where you can see rare Klirieng burial poles of elaborate design, with a dug-out chamber for storing the bones of aristocrats.

Bintulu

BINTULU, close to Niah National Park is a boom town, grown rich on offshore gas. The only sights worth visiting are the **markets**: the day market, housed in two large, open-sided circular buildings overlooking the river at the west end of Main Bazaar, the adjacent *pasar tamu* and, across town, the *pasar malam*, which starts up at around 6pm in the long-distance bus station. The town's compact rectangle of streets is bordered by the airfield to the east and Sungei Kemena to the west, with nothing much of interest in between.

Practicalities

The **airport** (☎086/331073) is, incredibly, right in the town centre, within 100m of most of the hotels and restaurants. MAS is at 129 Jl Masjid (☎086/331554). The long-distance **bus station** is 5km out of town at Medan Jaya and serves Batu Niah, Kuching, Sibu and Miri. Borneo Highway Express (☎086/339855) runs a daily (7pm) service to Pontianak (RM100). A taxi to the centre will cost RM10 or you can take any bus from the road behind the ticket booths to the local bus station on Lebuh Ray Abang Galau (60 sen), which becomes Jalan Sri Dagang as it enters town. Parallel and one block northeast (away from the river) is Jalan Keppel. The town's main **taxi rank** is just a few metres from the bus stop at the junction of Jalan Sri Dagang and Lebuh Queen. **Boats** up Sungei Kemena to Tubau, 60km east, dock at the jetty in the centre of town. The **GPO** is on Jalan Tun Razak, and the **Telekom** office is at the western end of Jalan Sommerville (Mon–Sat 8.30am–4.30pm). You'll find plenty of **Internet** facilities on Jalan Keppel. There are two **banks** on the western end of Jalan Keppel, the **police** are on Jalan Sommerville (☎086/331129), and the **hospital** is on Jalan Abang Galau (☎086/255899).

The most popular budget **accommodation** in Bintulu is the friendly *My House Inn* on Jalan Sri Dagang (☎086/336399; ❷). The slightly more upscale rooms at the friendly *Fata Inn*, 113 Jl Sri Dagang (☎086/332998; ❹), are en suite and have air-con, or you could try the similar *King's Inn*, 162 Jl Sri Dagang (☎086/337337; ❹). Best choice, however, is the friendly, helpful and spacious *Kemena Inn*, 78 Jl Keppel (☎086/331533; ❹).

For **eating**, there are hawker stalls at both the day market and the *pasar malam*, though this is take-away only. At *Popular Corner* on Lebuh Raya Abang Galau, several outlets under one roof sell claypots, seafood, chicken rice and juices. *Ama Restoran* on Jalan Keppel serves excellent curries, and *Sea View Restoran*, 254 Esplanade, is an atmospheric Chinese café, overlooking Sungei Kemena and serving quality food.

Niah National Park

Visiting **Niah National Park**, 131km north of Bintulu, is a highly rewarding experience – in less than a day you can see one of the largest caves in the world, as well as prehistoric rock graffiti in the remarkable Painted Cave, and hike along primary forest trails. In the outer area of the present park, deep excavations have revealed human remains, including skulls that date back forty thousand years, and artefacts such as flake stone tools, mortars and shell ornaments – the first evidence that people had lived in Southeast Asia that long ago.

The park is roughly halfway between Bintulu and Miri, 11km off the main road and close to the small town of Batu Niah, which you can reach by regular Syarikat Bus Suria services from either Bintulu or Miri; return services for both destinations begin at 6.30am. There are a few Chinese cafés here that serve breakfasts of porridge until noon, as well as one proper restaurant. The *Niah Cave Inn* (☎085/737332; ④) is the best accommodation option outside the park. The caves are 3km north of Batu Niah, and reached either by a half-hour walk, by longboat (around RM25) or taxi (RM10).

The path from Batu Niah leads straight to the **park headquarters** on the western bank of Sungei Niah. Here, you can sleep in the Asrama Agathis Hostels, which feature four-berth rooms (RM40), in the Jungle Lodge, which has two-berth rooms (RM60), or in chalets (④). There are also campsites if you have your own equipment. There's no need to book ahead, except at weekends. Contact the visitor centre in Miri (see p.720) to book or check availability of accommodation. There's a shop (daily 7am–10pm) that stocks basic foodstuffs, a canteen (daily 7.30am–10pm), and a small interpretation centre covering the geology of the caves and the economy of birds' nest collecting.

The caves and trails

From the park headquarters, it's a thirty-minute walk to the **caves**: take a sampan across the river and then follow a wooden walkway through dense rainforest where you're likely to see monkeys, hornbills, birdwing butterflies, tree squirrels and flying lizards. Some distance along the walkway, a clearly marked path branches off to an Iban longhouse, Rumah Chang, where you can buy drinks and snacks. The main walkway continues, heading up through the Trader's Cave (early nest-gatherers would congregate here to sell their harvests) to the mind-blowing, west mouth (60m by 250m) of the Great Cave. From within the immense, draughty darkness you can hear the voices of the bird's nest collectors who collect swiftlet nests for use in the famous bird's-nest soup; their thin beanstalk poles snake up from the cave floor. Once inside, the walkway continues, via Burnt Cave and Moon Cave, to the Painted Cave, thirty minutes' walk away. Here, early Sarawak communities buried their dead in boat-shaped coffins, arranged around the cave walls; dating of the contents has proved that the caves had been used as a cemetery for tens of thousands of years. One of these wooden coffins is still perched on an incline, its contents long since removed to the Sarawak Museum (see p.707). It's hard to distinguish the wall paintings behind the coffin – a thirty-metre-long tableau depicting boats on a journey, the figures apparently either jumping on and off, or dancing. This image fits various Borneo mythologies where the dead undergo challenges en route to the afterlife.

There are two other **trails** in the park. Jalan Madu splits off the main walkway around 800m from the park headquarters and cuts first east, then south, across a peat swamp forest, where you see wild orchids, mushrooms and pandanus. The trail crosses Sungei Subis and then follows its south bank to its confluence with Sungei Niah, from where you'll have to hail a passing boat to cross over to Batu Niah. The more spectacular trail to Bukit Kasut starts at the confluence of these two rivers. After crossing the river, the clearly marked trail winds through forest, round the foothills of Bukit Kasut and up to the summit – a hard one-hour slog, at the end of which there's a view both of the forest canopy and Batu Niah.

Miri

MIRI is another fast-growing town, with a significant expat community and a strong Chinese character. For tourists, it's the main departure point for independent and organized trips into Gunung Mulu National Park (see p.722) and the route north to Brunei and Sabah. Miri's old town around Jalan China in the west of town is the most enjoyable area to wander around. It's packed with cafés and shops, and there's a wet fish market and a Chinese temple at the top of Jalan China itself. The wide road running east from here and parallel to the river, Jalan Bendahara, is the simplest route into the new town area. The shopping centre Wisma Pelita, south of the old town on Jalan Padang, includes the Pelita Book Centre on the first floor, which has English-language books on Sarawak, and Longhouse Handicraft Centre on the top floor where you can buy rattan bags, *pua kumbu* (tie-died) textiles, and carvings. Directly south of the adjacent bus station is the padang, on whose border lies **Tamu Muhibbah** (daily 6am–4pm), the town's jungle produce market, where Orang Ulu come downriver to sell rattan mats, tropical fruits, rice wine and even jungle animals.

Practicalities

The **airport** (☎085/615433) is 8km west of the town centre: buses #28 and #30 (every 45min, daily 6.15am–8pm; RM1) run from outside the terminal to the **bus**

Moving on from Miri

By plane

This is the cheapest option for Gunung Mulu National Park; there are three or four daily **flights** to and from the airport (☎085/615433), but seats are limited so book ahead (RM153 return). Be sure to reconfirm your return flight upon arrival at Gunung Mulu. For other flights, see "Travel details", p.743. MAS is on Jalan South Yu Seng (☎085/414144). Vision Air (☎085/423221), based at the *Righa Hotel*, also runs a service to Mulu (RM98 one way) twice daily at 8.25am and 2.30pm. For those heading to **Sabah**, flying direct to Kota Kinabalu will save you two day's travel. There are four departures daily.

By bus

All **buses** towards Kuching leave from the Jalan Punjut express bus station 8km out of town; to get there, take the #33 from the local bus station. Syarikat Bus Suria (☎085/434317) operates services to Bintulu and other locations south, including Kuching and Pontianak. Miri Belait Transport Company (☎085/419129) runs five daily services (7am–3.30pm) to Kuala Belait in Brunei (RM12.50). Heading straight for Brunei from Miri, the trunk road north runs a few kilometres in from the coast to **Kuala Baram**, 30km away, a small town straddling the mouth of Batang Baram. After crossing the river by drive-on ferry (stay on the bus) you soon arrive at Malaysian immigration. Once through, the same bus will drop you off at Bruneian immigration where you and your luggage disembark (keep your ticket). After the formalities, board another waiting bus to the outskirts of the Bruneian town of Kuala Belait (see p.97), another 6km further on. At Kuala Belait, you hop on board a sampan to cross the Sungei Belait and get onto yet another bus that will drop you off at the Kuala Belait town centre bus station; your Miri Belait Transport Company ticket covers all transport up to this point. From here, buses run to Seria for connections to Bandar Seri Begawan. The last bus from Seria that will get you to the Bruneian capital the same day leaves at around 3.30pm (so set off early from Miri), and the first bus from there to the capital leaves at 7am, after which the service is very regular. You can also get to **Mulu** by bus and boat – this involves taking an early bus (every 15min; 45min; RM3) or taxi (RM20) from Miri to Kuala Baram; see p.723 for details of the various connections.

station on Jalan Padang, a five-minute walk from Jalan China and the old town.

Next to the bus station you'll find the **visitor information centre** (Mon–Fri 8am–5pm, Sat 8am–12.50pm; ⓣ085/434180), which handles all accommodation bookings for the local national parks. Pick up the excellent Sarawak Tourism Board **map** here. Several **tour operators** organize trips and treks to Gunung Mulu and other destinations. Seridan Mulu, 2km west of the centre (Lobby Arcade, *Park City Everly Hotel*, Jalan Temenggong; ⓣ085/414300, ⓔgracie@seridanmulu.com), is a very professional outfit run by Gracie Geikie, a mine of information on Mulu and other national parks. Also, there's Borneo Adventures, 9th Floor, Wisma Pelita ⓣ085/414935); Tropical Adventures, Ground Floor, Mega Hotel (ⓣ082/419337); and Borneo Overland (ⓣ085/430255 or 011/205162), beside the Standard Chartered Bank on Jalan Merpati.

There are **moneychangers** and ATMs along Jalan China. Internet access can also be found on Jalan China or at the Wisma Pelita shopping centre. The **post office** and **Telekom** office (daily 7.30am–10pm) are both on Jalan Post. The **immigration office** on Jalan Kipas (Room 3; Mon–Fri 8am–12.45 & 2–5pm, closed first & third Sat of every month, 8am–12.45 on second & third Sat) will only extend your Sarawak visa by a few days. Miri's General Hospital is on the airport road (ⓣ085/420033).

Accommodation and eating

Basic **lodging houses** with dorm beds offer the cheapest deal: bottom dollar are the men-only dorms (RM10) at the Tai Tong Lodging House, at the jetty end of Jalan China in the old part of town. There are a few private rooms (❷) as well. The simple and clean *Fairland Inn*, Jalan Raja, at Raja Square (ⓣ085/413981; ❷), has decent fan rooms as well as some air-con options. Best of the budgets, however, is the well-informed and well-maintained *Thai Foh Lodging House*, 19 Jl China (ⓣ085/418395; ❷). In the next category up, try the popular *Brooke Inn*, Jl 14 Brooke (ⓣ085/412881; ❹), where all rooms have TV, air-con and bathrooms.

As for **food**, the *Apollo Seafood Centre,* 4 Jl South Yu Seng, does exquisite grilled stingray and pineapple rice (RM45 for two, including beer); *Maxim Seafood Centre*, Lot 342, Blk 7, Jl Miri-Pujut, serves great grilled fish. There's *dim sim* for breakfast at the *Hock Guan Café* on Jalan Bendahara, and at night you can dine at the stalls in the market at the junction of Jalan Entiba and Jalan Begia. At the *Danish Hot Bread* bakery, next to the *Cosy Inn* on Jalan South Yu Seng, you can buy a cream cake to round off your meal.

Marudi

MARUDI, 80km southeast of Miri on Batang Baram, is the only sizeable town in the whole Baram watershed, and the jetty is the centre of the community. For travellers, there's a useful boat from here to Long Terawan, where there's a connection for Gunung Mulu National Park (RM25–50 per person, depending on number of passengers), and west to Kuala Baram, where numerous buses wait to take passengers to Miri or Brunei. There are daily flights to Mulu (RM40), which must be booked ahead. It only takes a few minutes to walk from the town to the airport.

If you have a few hours between boats, you can walk to **Fort Hose**, past the main Bazaar Square, west of the jetty, and along Jalan Fort to the top of the hill, which was built in 1901, and is still in good condition. The fort is now a government office, and also houses a Penan handicraft centre (Mon–Fri 9am–2pm).

The main **hotel**, the *Grand* (ⓣ085/755712; ❷), is just off the airport road, Jalan Cinema, and only five minutes' walk south of the jetty. It's a massive place, with clean, quiet rooms, and has information on Gunung Mulu National Park tours.

The *Alisan*, on Jalan Queen, off Jalan Cinema (☎085/755911; ③), is also a good deal. For **food**, try the Indian *Restoran Koperselara*, just past the *Alisan* hotel on Jalan Cinema, or *Boon Kee Restoran*, behind the main street on Jalan Newshop.

Gunung Mulu National Park

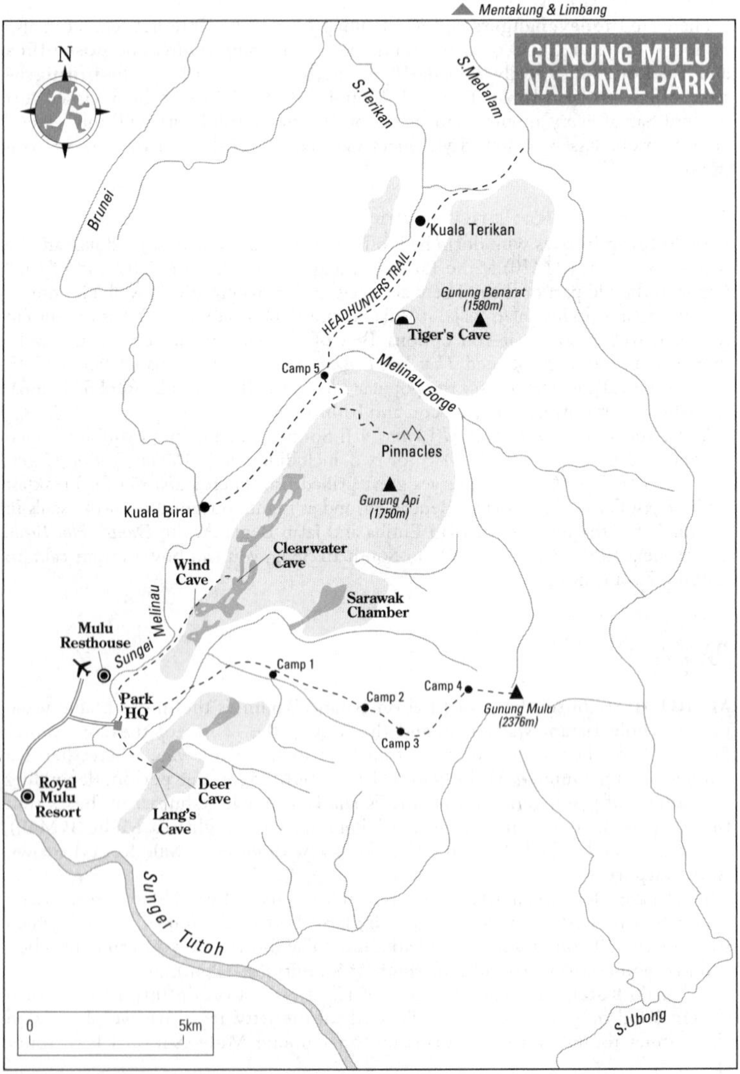

Gunung Mulu National Park is Sarawak's premier national park, located deep in the rainforest; at the last count, it featured over 300 animal species and nearly 3000

plant species. Quite apart from the park's primary rainforest, which is characterized by clear rivers and high-altitude vegetation, there are three dramatically eroded mountains, including fifty-metre-high limestone spikes known as the **Pinnacles**. The park also has the largest **limestone cave system** in the world, much of which is still being explored. The two major hikes, to the Pinnacles on **Gunung Api** and to the summit of **Gunung Mulu**, are daunting and involve camping out for at least two nights each, but you're rewarded with stupendous views of the rainforest, stretching as far as Brunei. The main caves are near the park headquarters and can be seen in a day.

If you're trekking **independently**, it makes sense to get a group together to spread the high cost of boat and guide fees in the park; post up a note on the board at headquarters and you should soon have a few replies. To give yourself time to get a group together, you'll probably spend the first day at the caves rather than hiking, even if you turn up early enough to set off on a trek same-day. **Register** at the park headquarters when you arrive or, if it's after 5.30pm, register the following day, and pay the RM3 park fee. Many visitors come to Mulu **as part of a tour group** from Kuching, Miri or Kuala Lumpur – a four-day trip to climb the Pinnacles and see the caves costs RM600 per person (three times what you'd pay with your own group of four), but covers all incidentals, including permits and guides.

Equipment you'll need for either hike includes a large water bottle, walking shoes, sun hat and swimming gear, a poncho/rain sheet, torch, mosquito repellent, ointment for bites, a basic first-aid kit and a thin mat. Mats and sleeping bags (should you want one) can usually be rented from the park headquarters. Wear shorts and T-shirts on the trails (it'll be easier to spot leeches), and bring long trousers and long-sleeved shirts for the dusk insect assault.

Practicalities

To **fly** to Mulu from Miri – which is usually the cheapest option – you must book ahead or go standby, as the small Twin-Otters only have nineteen seats. You touch down at the airport, 2km west of park headquarters where minibuses meet the planes to take you to the headquarters or accommodation. Return flights to Miri leave the park daily.

Reaching Mulu **by boat** from Miri involves four separate stages and takes all day. The first step is to take an early bus (every 15min; 45min; RM3) or taxi (RM20) to Kuala Baram (30min). From there, take the 7am or 8am express boat upriver to Marudi (2hr 30min; RM18) to connect with the noon express to Long Terawan (3hr; RM20). When the river is low, this boat may only go as far as Long Panai-Kuala Apoh (RM15–18), though you can then take a longboat (RM5) from there to Long Terawan. From Long Terawan, a longboat (RM25–50 per person, depending on numbers; 2hr) will take you to the park. For the return trip by boat, you have to arrange with the park headquarters for the longboat to pick you up at 6am. This connects with the early morning express or longboat at Long Terawan, which gets you to Marudi by late morning, in time to get the noon boat to Kuala Baram.

There's a range of **accommodation at the park**; the pleasant hostel has cooking facilities and dorm beds for RM10.50, and there are also four-person chalets in two price ranges (❹–❺). Near the hostel is a provisions shop and a good canteen (daily 8am–8pm). Across the bridge over Sungei Melinau is the alternative food option and main watering hole for those staying at the park: the Buyun Sipan Lounge. Further up the river, the very basic *Mulu Resthouse* (☎011/291641) has dorm beds for RM10. It's a short walk upstream from the park headquarters and friendly enough, but very dingy compared to the hostel. Further downstream is the park's last word in comfort, the *Royal Mulu Resort* (☎085/790100; ❾), which has a good restaurant.

The park

It is quite possible to see the main caves in a day, but if you're considering one of the treks as well you'll need to allow three or four days extra. If you're booking a flight back, bear in mind that you might have to wait a day or so to get a group together.

The show caves

Only five of the 25 caves so far explored in Mulu are open to visitors; they're known as "show caves" and can get quite crowded. Guide fees per group are RM18 for all caves, which includes the services of an amiable guide. From the headquarters, a well-marked three-kilometre plankway runs to the impressive **Deer Cave**, whose two-kilometre-long and 174-metre-high cave passage is believed to be the largest in the world. You follow the path through the cave for an hour to an incredible spot known as the Garden of Eden, where a large hole in the roof allows light to penetrate, feeding plants and attracting birds, insects and leaf monkeys. Nearby, **Lang's Cave** is small, but has fine curtain stalactites and coral-like growths – helictites – on its curved walls.

Probing some 107km through Mulu's substratum, **Clearwater Cave**, thought to be the longest in Southeast Asia, is reached by a fifteen-minute longboat journey (RM85 per boat) along Sungei Melinau from park headquarters, though you can walk the whole way if you wish (1hr) along a pleasant jungle boardwalk, which has the advantage of passing through **Moon Cave** (bring your torch). Visitors can only explore the small section close to the entrance, where a three-hundred-metre walkway leads to Young Lady's Cave, which ends abruptly in a fifty-metre-deep pothole. En route to Clearwater Cave, most visitors halt at the **Wind Cave**, which contains a great variety of stalactites and stalagmites and the surreal King's Chamber. If you're reasonably fit and in no way claustrophobic, you have the further option of **adventure caving** (RM85 guide fees per group plus RM40 equipment rental per person): an awesome eight-kilometre journey to the subterranean Clearwater River, which flows through passages reaching heights and widths of as much as 90m. Wear shorts, take lunch and be prepared for some tricky balancing on rock ledges.

The Pinnacles

Five million years ago, a constant splatter of raindrops dissolved Gunung Api's limestone and carved out the razor-sharp fifty-metre-high pinnacles from a solid block of rock. The first part of the **Pinnacles** trek from park headquarters is by longboat along Sungei Melinau to Kuala Birar (RM350 per boat, guide fees RM100 per group). When the river's low you'll have to get out every five minutes to push the boat, so bring some wet-shoes. From here, it's a three-hour walk to Camp 5, which nestles under Gunung Api (1750m) and Gunung Benarat (1580m). Most climbers spend two nights at Camp 5, where there's a large hostel-like sleeping hut and cooking facilities. You'll probably be able to get food cooked for you here and rent mattresses and blankets, but ask first at park headquarters. A bridge straddles the river, and the path on the other side is the Headhunter's Trail (see opposite). It's a beautiful spot with a swimming hole, which, despite the number of hikers passing through, still retains a wild, elemental edge.

It's quite a taxing ascent up the south face of Gunung Api to get a good view of the Pinnacles (7hr there and back), but the incredible views are worth it. Bring at least two litres of water and a bite for lunch, but otherwise travel light. After two hours' climb, a striking vista opens up over the rainforest. The climb gets tougher as you scramble between the rocks, and the high trees give way to moss forest, full of pitcher plants. The last thirty minutes is almost a sheer vertical manoeuvre up ladders, thick pegs and ropes. At the top of the ridge there's a stunning view of the dozens of fifty-metre-high grey limestone pinnacles, jutting out from their perch in an unreachable hollow on the side of the mountain. The return slog takes two to three hours.

Walks from Camp 5

Once back at the camp, most people rest, swim, eat and sleep, preferring to start the return trip to park headquarters the following day. There are some other interesting walks from here, however. A path from the camp follows the river further upstream and ends at a beautiful spot below the **Melinau Gorge** (2hr return), where a vertical wall of rock rises 100m above the vanishing river. A much longer option from Camp 5 is to follow the so-called **Headhunter's Trail**, a route once traced by Kayan war parties. Cross the bridge, turn left and walk along a wide trail passing a large rock (around 4km). From here, a clearly marked flat trail to **Kuala Terikan**, a small Berawan settlement on the banks of Sungei Terikan, takes four hours (11km). You can stay at basic hut accommodation. From here, the trail continues for two hours to Sungei Medalam, where you can take a longboat (RM200–300 per boat) to the Iban longhouse at Bala. It's best to stay here and then continue next day down Sungei Medalam in a longboat into Sungei Limbang and on up to **Limbang,** an all-day trip. This is a good way of getting to Brunei from Mulu, as boats run frequently from Limbang to Bandar Seri Begawan (hourly until 6pm; RM15). In Limbang, the best place to stay is the *Muhibbah Inn* (☎085/212488; ❹) on Jalan Banking, although the *Royal Hotel* (☎085/215690; ❷), on Jalan Tarap, is cheaper.

Gunung Mulu

The route to the summit of **Gunung Mulu** (2376m) is a straightforward climb, though very steep, and any reasonably fit person can complete it. Park regulations require that you hire a guide (RM250 per group). The first stage is from park headquarters to Camp 3, an easy three-hour walk on a flat trail. The first night is at the open hut at Camp 3, which has cooking facilities. Day two comprises a hard, ten-hour, uphill slog, some of it along the southwest ridge, a series of small hills negotiated by a narrow, twisting path. The hut at Camp 4 is at 1800m; it can be cool here, so bring a sleeping bag. Most climbers set off well before dawn for the hard ninety-minute trek to the summit, to arrive at sunrise. Near the top you have to haul yourself up by ropes onto the cold, windswept, craggy peak. From here, the view is exhilarating, looking down on Gunung Api. It's just about possible to do the whole return trip from the summit to park headquarters in one day. This takes around twelve hours and cuts out the last night at Camp 4. The red-and-white trail marks are easy to see, so you shouldn't lose your way.

Lawas

Boxed in between Sabah and Brunei, **LAWAS** town sits on Sungei Lawas. There's little to see, but it's an important transit point. Daily **boats** arrive here from Muara in Brunei, Sabah's Pulau Labuan, and Limbang. There are also daily departures for these places (see "Travel details", p.743); tickets cost RM20. The jetty is beside the old mosque, 400m east of the town. A daily **express bus** from Kota Kinabalu (RM30) calls in here via the Sabah border town of Sipitang and then goes on through Brunei's little-known Temburong district before terminating in Limbang. There's also a bus going the other way to Kota Kinabalu at 7.30am and 1.30pm. Lawas **airport** is around 3km south of town – a bus usually meets the daily flights from Kota Kinabalu, Limbang, Miri, Bario and Ba Kelalan. The MAS agent is Eng Huat Travel Agency, 455 Jl Law Siew Ann (☎085/285570). The *Southern Comfort Lodge* (☎085/493523; ❷) offers comfortable **accommodation** or you can go more upmarket and make for the *Federal Hotel* (☎085/284115; ❹) on Jalan Punang. For inexpensive **food**, try the upper floor of the market, where you can get delicious nasi campur (daily 9am–4pm). Otherwise, most of the best eating places cluster around the *Mee Yan Hotel*. Lawas is online too: Jalan Punang has three Internet cafés.

7.7

Sabah

Bordering Sarawak on the northeastern flank of Borneo, **Sabah**'s beauty lies in its natural resources, wildlife and intriguing mix of ethnic peoples. The peoples of the Kadazan/Dusun tribes constitute the largest indigenous racial group, along with the Murut of the southwest, and Sabah's so-called "sea gypsies", the Bajau. Latterly, many economic migrants from the southern part of the Philippines and from neighbouring Kalimantan in Indonesia have made Sabah their home, further contributing to the state's rich ethnic mix.

Until European powers began to gain a foothold here in the nineteenth century, the northern tip of this remote landmass was inhabited by tribal groups who had only minimal contact with the outside world, so that their costumes, traditions and languages were quite unique to the region. Sabah was once ruled by the Sultan of Sulu, but by signing a deceitful lease to the British North Borneo Company the area eventually became a British protectorate, while the Sultan of Sulu lost much of his power during the American colonization of the Philippines. To this day, the government of the Philippines maintains claims to Sabah.

Since joining the Malaysian Federation in 1963, Sabah has undergone rapid, if patchy modernization, not least because of the logging industry and oil palm plantation expansion, which together are substantially eating away at the remaining forests in the state. But environmentalists are optimistic, as plans are on the drawing board to protect a larger proportion of Sabah's remaining forests. The two most ecologically important areas that will gain from this policy are the Maliau Basin in the south of the state and much of the Kinabatangan River catchment to the east.

This is good news, as Sabah's swampy coasts, rainforests and spectacular high mountains host an astounding range of **wildlife**, the region's chief draw. Here, you can watch turtles hatch in **Turtle Islands National Park**, see baby orang-utans at the **Sepilok Orang-utan Rehabilitation Centre**, and marvel at forest-dwelling proboscis monkeys along the lower reaches of the Kinabatangan. And then there are the turtles, sharks, barracuda and reefs of **Pulau Sipadan**, which is rated as one of the top diving destinations in the world. Sabah's other huge attraction is the climb up the awesome granite shelves of 4101-metre-high **Mount Kinabalu**, its challenging but manageable slopes seemingly tailor-made for amateur climbers.

Getting to Sabah

There are frequent **flights** to Kota Kinabalu (KK) from Kuala Lumpur (8 daily; RM345), Johor Bahru (2 daily; RM352), Kuching (6 daily; RM233), Bandar Seri Begawan (6 weekly; RM123), Manila (2 weekly; US$219), and Sydney (daily; US$425). You can also fly to Tawau from Tarakan in Kalimantan (2 weekly; RM322).

Daily **boats** from Brunei (1–2 daily; 1hr 30min), and from Lawas and Limbang in northern Sarawak, run to Pulau Labuan, which has good connections to KK. There's also a ferry from Tarakan and Nunukan in Kalimantan to Tawau (one or two daily). The only overland route is from Lawas, which is a short bus ride away from the border at Merapok.

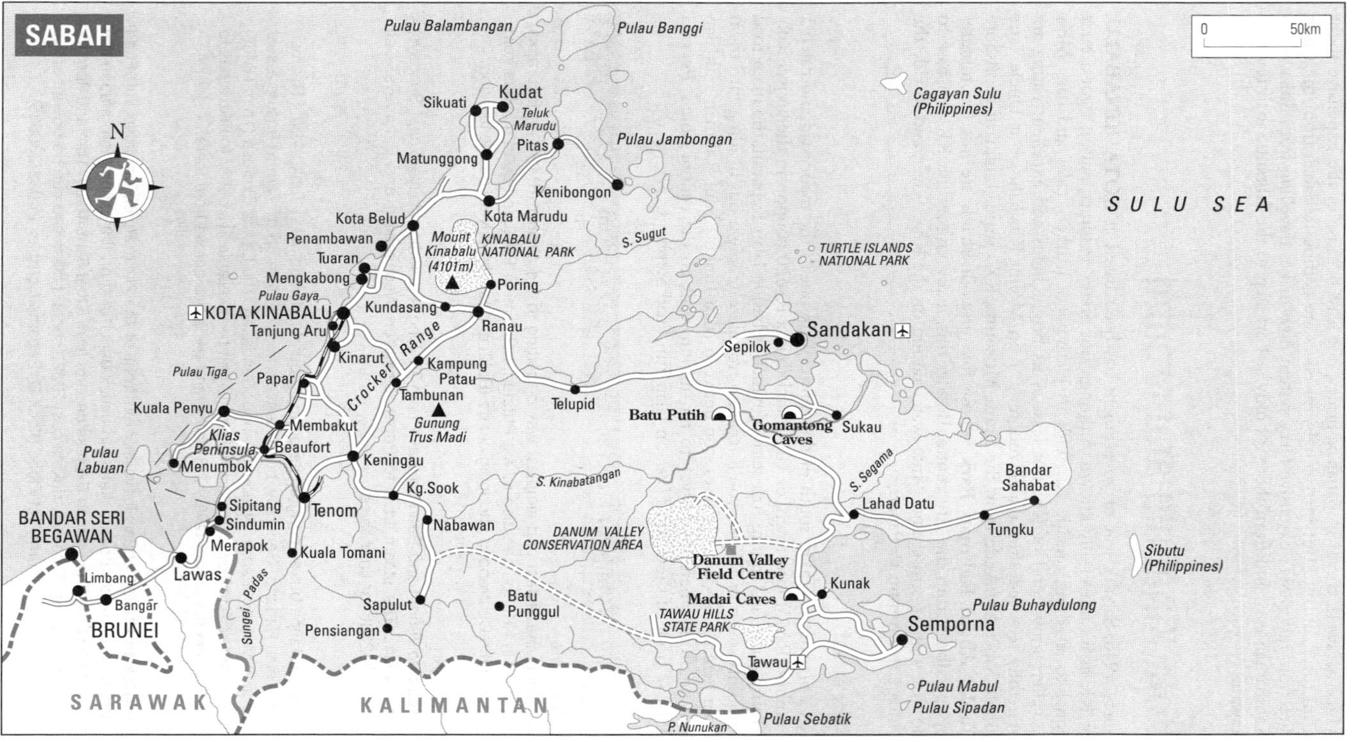

SABAH
N
0 50km
SULU SEA
Pulau Balambangan
Pulau Banggi
Cagayan Sulu (Philippines)
Kudat
Sikuati
Teluk Marudu
Pitas
Pulau Jambongan
Matunggong
Kenibongon
Kota Marudu
Kota Belud
Penambawan
Tuaran
Mengkabong
Pulau Gaya
Mount Kinabalu (4101m)
KINABALU NATIONAL PARK
Poring
S. Sugut
TURTLE ISLANDS NATIONAL PARK
KOTA KINABALU
Tanjung Aru
Kundasang
Ranau
Sandakan
Sepilok
Kinarut
Crocker Range
Kampung Patau
Tambunan
Pulau Tiga
Papar
Telupid
Kuala Penyu
Membakut
Gunung Trus Madi
Batu Putih
Gomantong Caves
Sukau
Klias Peninsula
Beaufort
Pulau Labuan
Menumbok
Keningau
S. Segama
Bandar Sahabat
Kg.Sook
S. Kinabatangan
Sipitang
Tenom
Lahad Datu
BANDAR SERI BEGAWAN
Sindumin
Nabawan
DANUM VALLEY CONSERVATION AREA
Tungku
Merapok
Danum Valley Field Centre
Sibutu (Philippines)
Kuala Tomani
Lawas
Limbang
Sungei Padas
Kunak
Bangar
Sapulut
Batu Punggul
Madai Caves
Pulau Buhaydulong
TAWAU HILLS STATE PARK
Semporna
BRUNEI
Pensiangan
Tawau
Pulau Mabul
SARAWAK
KALIMANTAN
Pulau Sipadan
P. Nunukan
Pulau Sebatik

Like Sarawak, **travel** in Sabah is pricey, not least because of the expensive flight from the mainland. But increasingly, travellers are getting to Sabah from the other direction. Indonesia's extensive ferry system now makes travelling from Sulawesi to Kalimantan easy, and from there it's only a short step to the vibrant Sabah town of Tawau.

Kota Kinabalu and around

Since 1946, Sabah's seat of government has been based at **KOTA KINABALU**, or KK as it's universally known. Although not pretty architecturally, it's got a buzz equal to anything outside KL with its plethora of markets, cafés and bars. Most travellers grow fond of KK, not least as its bright lights and excellent eating are gratefully received after a spell roughing it on Mount Kinabalu or at Uncle Tan's Jungle Sanctuary. Aside from the **State Museum**, KK's major highlight is offshore **Tunku Abdul Rahman Park**, whose five unspoilt islands are just ten minutes by speedboat from the city centre. Besides this, many visitors use KK as a base to do firefly night cruises and white-water rafting on the Klias River, and to ride the vintage steam train to Papar.

Arrival

KK's **airport** is 6.5km south of the centre. Walk out to the main road and catch a minibus (RM3) into town; or take a taxi (buy a RM20 coupon in the arrival hall). **Trains** arrive at Tanjung Aru station, which is beside Jalan Kepayan, the main road to points south of KK, so you'll have no trouble catching a bus heading into town from here. Long-distance buses stop between Jalan Tunku Abdul Rahman and Jalan Padang, from where it's a five- to ten-minute walk to the central hotels. **Ferries** dock in front of the *Hyatt Hotel*, on Jalan Tun Fuad Stephens.

Moving on from Kota Kinabalu

By plane

A taxi is the fastest and simplest way of getting to the **airport** (RM10) as taxi ranks abound in KK. You can also take a Putatan, Lokkami or Petagas-bound minibus from behind the Centrepoint shopping centre (RM2) and tell the driver your destination.

By train

Trains to Tenom and Beaufort leave from Tanjung Aru station daily (except Sundays) at 7.45am. The steam train to Papar leaves on Wednesdays and Saturdays. Call ☎088/252536 for timetables.

By bus

Long-distance **buses** congregate on the ground between Jalan Tunku Abdul Rahman and Jalan Padang. Generally, buses leave when full; turn up by 7am to ensure a seat to, say, Mount Kinabalu National Park or Sandakan. The Lawas Express (1pm; RM30) runs from here to Lawas in Sarawak, but it can be unreliable. It's better to take a bus to Sipitang on the border (every 2/3 hours) and get a bus across from there.

By ferry

Ferries to Pulau Labuan leave from in front of the *Hyatt Hotel*, on Jalan Tun Fuad Stephens; you can book tickets and check departures on the Labuan information line (☎087/423445). The Labuan Express departs from KK at 8am, 10am, 1pm and 3pm for the one-hour trip. One-way tickets cost RM28 second class and can be bought at the jetty or at Rezeki Murni, 1st Floor, Block D, Segama Complex (☎088/236835).

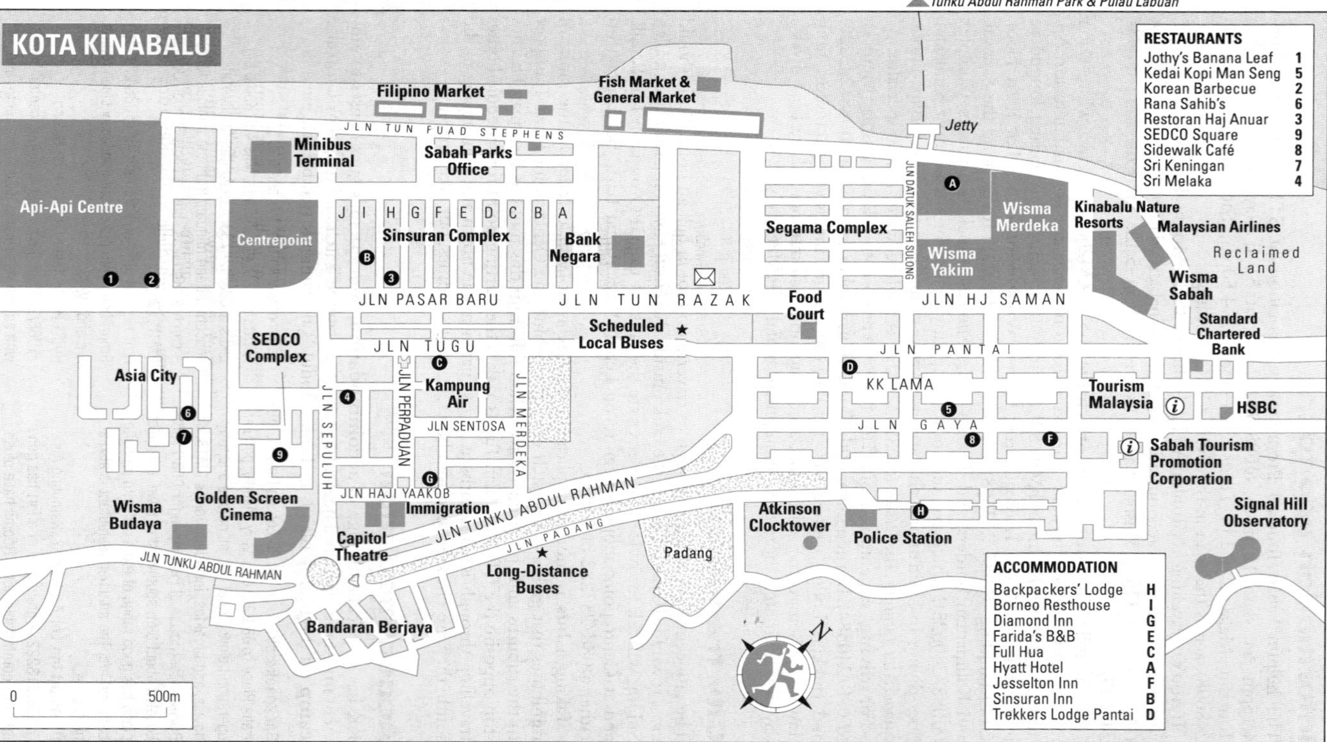

KOTA KINABALU
Tunku Abdul Rahman Park & Pulau Labuan
E
1, Sabah State Museum, Tanjung Aru Train Station & Airport
RESTAURANTS
Jothy's Banana Leaf 1
Kedai Kopi Man Seng 5
Korean Barbecue 2
Rana Sahib's 6
Restoran Haj Anuar 3
SEDCO Square 9
Sidewalk Café 8
Sri Keningan 7
Sri Melaka 4
ACCOMMODATION
Backpackers' Lodge H
Borneo Resthouse I
Diamond Inn G
Farida's B&B E
Full Hua C
Hyatt Hotel A
Jesselton Inn F
Sinsuran Inn B
Trekkers Lodge Pantai D
Filipino Market
Fish Market & General Market
Jetty
Minibus Terminal
Sabah Parks Office
Api-Api Centre
Centrepoint
Sinsuran Complex
Bank Negara
Segama Complex
Wisma Merdeka
Wisma Yakim
Kinabalu Nature Resorts
Malaysian Airlines
Reclaimed Land
Wisma Sabah
Standard Chartered Bank
Tourism Malaysia
HSBC
Sabah Tourism Promotion Corporation
Signal Hill Observatory
JLN TUN FUAD STEPHENS
JLN DATUK SALLEH SULONG
JLN PASAR BARU
JLN TUN RAZAK
JLN HJ SAMAN
Food Court
Scheduled Local Buses
JLN PANTAI
KK LAMA
JLN GAYA
SEDCO Complex
Asia City
JLN TUGU
JLN SEPULUH
JLN PERPADUAN
Kampung Air
JLN SENTOSA
JLN MERDEKA
JLN HAJI YAAKOB
Immigration
JLN TUNKU ABDUL RAHMAN
JLN PADANG
Atkinson Clocktower
Police Station
Padang
Long-Distance Buses
Wisma Budaya
Golden Screen Cinema
Capitol Theatre
Bandaran Berjaya
N
0 500m

Information and tours

The helpful Sabah Tourism Promotion Corporation or STPC (Mon–Fri 8am–4.15pm, Sat 8am–12.45pm; ⓣ088/212121) is at 51 Jl Gaya. Far less useful is Tourism Malaysia (Mon–Thurs 8am–noon, 2–4.50pm, Sat 8am–2pm; ⓣ088/248698), across the road in the EON CMG Building.

If you're travelling to Tunku Abdul Rahman Park, Mount Kinabalu or Poring, you must book your accommodation at the Kinabalu Nature Resorts office, Lot G15, Ground Floor, Wisma Sabah (Mon–Fri 8am–5am, Sat 8am–2am; ⓣ088/243629).

All the following **tour operators** charge about RM200 for a day's white-water rafting, and RM600 upwards for extended tours into the forested interior: Api Tours, 13 Jl Punai Kedut and Mile 5 Jl Tuaran (ⓣ088/421963), for rafting, longhouse tours and the Mount Trusmadi trek; Borneo Wildlife Adventure, Lot F, 1st Floor, GPO building (ⓣ088/213668), for tailor-made adventure tours along the Sarawak and Kalimantan borders; and *Trekkers Lodge Sinsuran*, Block L, Sinsuran Complex (ⓣ088/240625), which has the most competitive rates for trips out of Sandakan, does diving in Sipidan and also arranges white-water rafting. Borneo Expeditions, *Shangri-La Tanjung Aru Resort* (ⓣ088/222721), is a white-water rafting specialist.

For **diving** expeditions, Sipadan Dive Centre, 10th Floor, Wisma Merdeka (ⓣ088/240584), Borneo Divers, 9th Floor, Menara Jubili, Jalan Gaya (ⓣ088/222226) and Trekkers Lodge arrange trips for RM400 a night inclusive of transport from Tawau (or Semporna), with food, accommodation, all transport, three boat dives a day plus unlimited shore dives. Equipment rental is RM80 daily.

City transport

The city centre is compact enough to traverse on foot in half an hour. **Taxis** should cross town for RM8, although the rank outside the *Hyatt Hotel* on Jalan Datuk Salleh Sulong will ask for twice that. Better are the ranks at the GPO on Jalan Tun Razak, and at Centrepoint shopping centre on Lebuh Raya Pantai Baru. Book a taxi on either ⓣ088/253282 or 51863.

Taking a **bus** is more complicated, as there is no visible order in the ranks of minibuses that gather on a patch of gravel behind the Centrepoint Plaza. Transport to the suburbs and the airport leave when full from this minibus terminal. The bus stop opposite the GPO on Jalan Tun Razak is the starting point for scheduled buses travelling through KK's suburbs as far as Tuaran in the north and Penampang in the south; they are cheaper than minibuses, leave at set times, but take longer.

Accommodation

KK has an excellent range of **accommodation**, from spacious guesthouses to efficient mid-range inns and beyond to top-of-the-range hotels and resorts. You can also **camp** on the nearby islands in Tunku Abdul Rahman Park (see p.732).

Backpackers' Lodge Lot 25 Lorong Dewan, Australia Place ⓣ088/261495. Very friendly, popular operation below Signal Hill; all guitars and tatty novels, and breakfast included. Dorms RM18. ➊

Borneo Resthouse Jl Penampang ⓣ088/718856. Located about 3km southwest of town, this quiet place has good range of rooms all with en-suite bath and a/c. The attached restaurant is also a plus. ➍–➏

Diamond Inn Lot 7, Block 37, Kampung Air ⓣ088/213222. A great deal of effort has gone into this comfortable hotel. Rooms have plush bathrooms with tub, TVs and a/c. ➍

Farida's B&B 413 Jl Saga, Mile 4.5, Kampung Likas ⓣ088/428733. A delightful family-run concern, fifteen minutes from the minibus terminal – catch a "Kg Likas" bus to Likas School. Dorms RM18. ➌

Full Hua 14 Jl Tugu, Kampung Air ⓣ088/234950. Smart hotel with pokey but spotlessly clean rooms, a/c and TV. ➍

Hyatt Hotel Jalan Datuk Salleh Sulong ⓣ088/221234. KK's most luxurious central hotel, with sumptuous rooms, a business centre and

Japanese restaurant. ❽

Jesselton Inn 69 Jl Gaya ☎088/223333. This well-run mid-range has just what you'd expect, including a/c and satellite TV. ❻

Sinsuran Inn Lot 1, Block I, Sinsuran Complex ☎088/215799. Spartan rooms are capacious and clean, and have TV, bathroom and a/c. ❹

Trekkers Lodge Pantai Pantai 4th Floor, 46 Jalan Pantai ☎088/213888. The identical sister of the *Trekkers Lodge Sinsuran* – equally good, entrance round the back. Dorms RM17. ❸

The City

Downtown KK was almost obliterated by World War II bombs, and only in the northeastern corner of the city centre – an area known as KK Lama, or old KK – are there even the faintest remains of its colonial past. Jalan Gaya in particular is an attractive street lined with colourful and popular Chinese *kedai kopis*.

The most diverting of the waterfront markets is the **Filipino Market**, opposite blocks K and M of the Sinsuran Complex, which sells Sabahan ethnic wares as well as Filipino baskets, shells and trinkets. Next door is the dark and labyrinthine General Market and, behind that, the manic waterfront fish market.

KK's most rewarding cultural experience, though, is the **Sabah State Museum** (daily except Fri 9am–5pm; RM5), twenty minutes' walk west of the town centre along Jalan Tunkul Abdul Rahman (or take a bus from opposite the GPO), and housed in Murut- and Rungus-style longhouses. Its highlight is the ethnographic collection, which includes human skulls from Sabah's head-hunting days, and totems. Photographs trace the development of Kota Kinabalu, and there's also a natural history section, an archeology gallery and an Islamic civilization gallery. Fronting the museum is an **Ethnobotanic Garden** (daily except Fri 9am–5pm), whose huge range of tropical plants is best experienced on one of the free, guided tours (9am & 2pm except Fri). Exquisitely crafted traditional houses representing all Sabah's major tribes border the garden, in the Kampung Warisan.

Eating and drinking

KK is known for its ultra fresh seafood and there are many **restaurants** where the offerings are swimming in tanks waiting for you to pick them out. If you're a sensitive soul, simply order from the menu and let someone else pass the death sentence. There's a line of these restaurants at the SEDCO Complex. You'll find good **hawker stalls** on the upper floor of the General Market, Jalan Tun Fuad Stephens, and at the night market, behind the Filipino Market, Jalan Tun Fuad Stephens. For night-time **drinking**, check out the popular but expensive *Shenanigans* at the *Hyatt Hotel*. Actually, it's better to slam a few beers at the bars across the street before going into *Shenanigans* – it lessens the shock of the prices and the RM15 cover charge. *Razzmatazz* and *Yaaha Cowboy Lounge* at the Asia City Complex are also popular. The latter has a superb bar with a food court alongside. A picturesque bar full of interesting characters is the no-frills Chinese and Filipino café/drinking hole, *Fun Sen*, a few doors down from the *Diamond Inn*. Solo women might want to avoid this place, however.

Jothy's Banana Leaf Gang 9, Api Api Centre ☎088/261595. Mountainous *daun pisang* (banana leaf) meals, biriyanis and curries – good for vegetarians. Daily 10am–10pm.

Kedai Kopi Man Seng 86 Jalan Gaya. Busy Chinese eatery with outdoor tables – popular with the local crowd.

Korean Barbecue Api Api Centre. Popular with locals, this DIY Korean barbecue is best if you're in a party of two or more.

Rana Sahib's Block G, Asia City Complex ☎088/231354. Tasty North Indian food experience marred by high prices and over-fussy owner. However, its *sag gost* and chicken kashmir are wonderful. Daily 11.30am–2.30pm & 6.30–10.30pm.

Restoran Haj Anuar Block H, Sinsuran Complex. Cosy, open-fronted place with a Malay menu including *soto*, *nasi lemak* and nasi campur. Daily 7am–7pm.

SEDCO Square SEDCO Complex. Restaurant-lined square, with outdoor tables; a fine place for barbecued meat and fish.

Sidewalk Café 85 Jl Gaya. Pleasant café that opens late and has decent Western as well as

local fare served outdoors under the parasols.
Sri Keningan Block G, Asia City Complex. Simple but lively café with a large variety of rice and noodle dishes.
Sri Melaka 9 Jl Laiman Diki, Kampung Air. Exquisite Malay and Nonya food at one of KK's best and most fashionable places; try the excellent assam fishhead (RM12 portion feeds two). Open 11am–10.30pm.

Listings

Airline offices Dragon Air, Ground Floor, Block C, Kuwasa Complex, Jl Karamunsing ☎088/254733; MAS, 11th Floor, Gaya Centre, Jalan Tun Fuad Stephen ☎088/290600; Philippine Air, Karamunsing Complex, Jl Tuaran ☎088/239600; Royal Brunei, Ground Floor, Block C, Kuwasa Complex, Jl Karamunsing ☎088/242193; Singapore Airlines, Ground Floor, Block C, Kuwasa Complex, Jl Karamunsing ☎088/255444; Thai Airways, Ground Floor, Block C, Kuwasa Complex, Jl Karamunsing ☎088/232896.
American Express Lot 3.50 & 3.51, 3rd Floor, Karamunsing Complex (Mon–Fri 8.30am–5.30pm; ☎088/241200). Credit card- and travellers' cheque-holders can use the office as a poste restante/general delivery address.
Banks and exchange Moneychangers (Mon–Sat 10am–7pm) in Wisma Merdeka include Ban Loong Money Changer and Travellers' Money Changer, both on the ground floor; there's also an office in the Taiping Goldsmith, Block A, Sinsuran Complex.
Books For an unparalleled array of books on Southeast Asia, head for Borneo Crafts (Wisma Merdeka), or to their branch at the Sabah State Museum.
Hospital Queen Elizabeth Hospital is beyond the Sabah State Museum, on Jl Penampang (☎088/218166). In an emergency, dial ☎999.
Immigration office 4th Floor, Wisma Dang Bandang, Jl Hj Yaakob (Mon–Fri 8am–12.30pm & 2–4.15pm, Sat 8am–12.45pm; ☎088/216711).
Internet access A handful of Internet cafés can be found in the vicinity of *Trekkers Lodge Pantai* on Jalan Pantai, as well as at the Centrepoint shopping centre.
Pharmacy Apex Pharmacy, 2 Jalan Pantai ☎088/255100; UMH Pharmacy, 80 Jalan Gaya ☎088/215312.
Police Balai Polis KK (☎088/258191 or 258111) is below Atkinson Clocktower on Jl Padang.
Post office The GPO (Mon–Sat 8am–5pm, Sun 10am–1pm) is on Jl Tun Razak keeps poste restante.
Shopping Borneo Handicraft (1st Floor, Wisma Merdeka) has a good choice of woodwork, basketry and gongs; Borneo Handicraft & Ceramic Shop (Ground Floor, Centrepoint) stocks ceramics, antiques and primitive sculptures.
Telephone services There are IDD facilities at Kedai Telekom (daily 8am–10pm), in the Sadong Jaya Complex. Phonecards, available at the GPO, can be used for international calls in orange, but not yellow, public phone booths – there are some in Centrepoint.

Tunku Abdul Rahman Park

Situated within an eight-kilometre radius of downtown KK, the five islands of Tunku Abdul Rahman Park (TAR Park) represent the most westerly ripples of the undulating Crocker mountain range. Largest of the park's islands is Pulau Gaya, where a twenty-kilometre system of trails snakes across the lowland rainforest. Most of these trails start on the southern side of the island at Camp Bay, which also offers pleasant enough swimming, but a more alluring alternative is Police Beach, on the north coast. Boatmen demand extra for circling round to this side of Gaya (RM20 return), but it's money well spent: the dazzling white-sand bay is idyllic. Wildlife on Gaya includes hornbills, wild pigs, lizards, snakes and macaques – which have been known to swim over to nearby Pulau Sapi, a 25-acre islet off the northwestern coast of Gaya that's popular with swimmers, snorkellers and picnickers. Though far smaller than Gaya, Sapi too is ringed by trails.

The park's three other islands cluster together 2.5km west of Gaya. The park headquarters is situated on crescent-shaped Pulau Manukan, the most developed of all the park's islands, but boasting fine beaches and coral. Across a narrow channel is tiny Pulau Mamutik, which can be crossed on foot in fifteen minutes and has excellent sands on either side of its jetty. Pulau Sulug is the most remote of the islands and consequently the quietest. Its good coral makes it popular with divers.

Practicalities

The Sabah Parks boat service leaves KK at 8am, 9am, 10am, 11am, noon, 2pm and 4.30pm, returning at 7.30am, 9.30am, 10.30am, 11.30am, 3pm and 4pm (RM10 return); it calls at all five islands. Chartering a boat to go island-hopping costs RM20 a head (minimum six people). Contact Sabah Parks (☎088/211585) at Block K, Sinsuran Complex, for details, or make directly for the waterfront behind the *Hyatt*. The best private company is the dependable Sutima, which offers a similar service and will arrange to pick you up at a mutually agreed time. Otherwise, numerous speedboats gather daily behind the *Hyatt* – they won't leave for less than RM40–50, but you should only pay when you're safely back in KK. The boatmen rent snorkelling gear for RM5 a day.

A RM5 entry fee is charged on landing at Sapi, Manukan and Mamutik. Accommodation is available in the park at attractive chalets on Pulau Manukan (RM8 for a four-person unit), which must be booked through Kinabalu Nature Resorts (see p.730). The Manukan resort also has the only place to eat on the islands. Sabah Parks (see above) can rent you a tent for RM35 should you want to camp on any of the other islands; snorkelling gear (RM10) can be rented from Sutima, or the *Trekkers Lodge*.

The Rafflesia Reserve

Heading southeast from Kota Kinabalu, paddy-fields give way to the rolling foothills of the Crocker mountain range, and once through, Tembunan-bound buses (11 daily from the long-distance bus station; 2hr) start the long haul up to the 1649-metre-high Sinsuron Pass and on to the Rafflesia Reserve, 58km from KK. You'll have views of Mount Kinabalu, weather permitting. Should you wish to dally for a little longer in the bracing chill of the Sinsuron Pass, you can stay at the *Gunung Emas Highlands Resort* (☎011/811562; ②–③), which has dorms (RM16), rooms (RM32), treetop cabins and suites at the 52-kilometre mark of the KK–Tambunan road.

A few kilometres beyond the pass, the Rafflesia Reserve (Mon–Fri 8am–12.30pm & 2–4.30pm, Sat & Sun 8am–5pm; free) houses examples of the rafflesia flower, a parasitic plant whose rubbery, liver-spotted blooms can reach up to one metre in diameter – making it the world's largest flower. It was first catalogued in Sumatra in 1818, by Sir Stamford Raffles and the naturalist Dr Joseph Arnold. There's no need to hire one of the guides from the visitor centre, as the park's paths are simple to follow; someone at the centre should be able to direct you to a plant that's in bloom, though you could phone the visitor centre's hotline (☎011/861499) before leaving KK as each flower only lasts a few days before dying. There are sometimes rafflesia flowers blooming nearer to KK. Ask at the *Jesselton Inn* (see p.731) for information on where the latest bloom is located, and be prepared to hire a guide if it is on private property.

Tenom

The small town of **TENOM** was once the bustling headquarters of the Interior District of British North Borneo, but today it's a peaceful backwater that's best known for the impressive train journey to Beaufort (2hr 30min). **Three types of train** ply the Tenom–Beaufort route daily – diesel locomotive (Mon–Sat 8am & 2.50pm, Sun 8am, 12.10pm & 2.30pm; RM2.75); cargo (Mon–Sat 10.15am; RM2.75); and railcar (Mon–Sat 6.40am, Sun 7.25am; RM8.35). The fastest and most comfortable of these is the railcar, but you must book ahead for this on ☎087/735514 or at the station. Tenom station is on the southern edge of the padang. There is talk of having the old steam train do this stretch of tracks, too, though at the time of writing it only ran from KK to Papar and back.

Buses circle around Tenom all day long: north to Keningau (RM5), from where you can continue on to KK, and south to Kuala Tomani (RM5); you can catch the bus on the main street, at the western edge of the padang. A **taxi** to KK (RM25), however, should work out about the same cost as the multi-stage bus journey. Share taxis to Keningau cost RM5 and leave from the main street. Walk straight ahead out of the train station (northwest) and you'll reach the high street, Jalan Tun Mustapha, where you'll find **accommodation** at the friendly and helpful *Hotel Sri Perdana* (☎087/734001; ❸), and the slightly scruffier *Sri Jaya* hotel (☎087/735077; ❸). The pick of the bunch on Jalan Tun Mustapha is the *Hotel Orchid* (☎087/737600; ❸), which was recently refurbished and offers TV and air-con along with their spotless rooms. **Places to eat** are plentiful in the area around the market, southwest along Jalan Tun Mustafa, where you'll also find the Netcafé Internet shop. Not far off is a Standard Chartered Bank.

Beaufort

BEAUFORT is an uneventful town, normally only used by tourists on their way to the white-water rafting on nearby Sungei Padas (try Traverse Tours (☎088/729500) or those doing the spectacular train ride from Beaufort to Tenom. Although the line runs all the way from KK to Tenom, it's only the two-and-a-quarter-hour journey through dramatic jungle from Beaufort to Tenom that's really worth making. Three types of train run from Beaufort – diesel locomotive (Mon–Sat 10am & 4.50pm; Sun 7am, 10am & 4.20pm; RM2.75); cargo (Mon–Sat 1.30; RM2.75); and railcar (Mon–Sat 8.30am, Sun noon; RM8.35). The fastest and most comfortable of these is the railcar, but you must book ahead on ☎087/221518. The **train station** is next to Sungei Padas at the southern side of town, from where it's a minute's walk up the road opposite the station forecourt into the town centre.

Night cruises on the nearby Sungei Klias to spot fireflies are easiest arranged in KK (ask at the *Jesselton Inn*). The insects congregate on trees along the river and the spectacular displays of bioluminescence are magical to witness – thousands of fireflies often gather in one tree.

Buses stop in the centre itself, beside the market, while taxis congregate outside the train station. Beaufort's two **hotels** are the *Beaufort* (☎087/211911; ❹), east of the market, and the similar *Mandarin Inn* (☎087/212800; ❹), five minutes' walk across the river, first turning on the left. The excellent *Christopher's Corner Parking*, across from the train station, will rustle you up a really good Western breakfast with rambutan juice or you could try the *Rahmat* **restaurant** behind the *Beaufort Hotel*. Across the street is the LA Internet Café, and there's a branch of HSBC next to the market.

Pulau Labuan

The small island of **Pulau Labuan**, around 10km west of the Klias peninsula, is a duty-free port, used mainly by Bruneians and Sabahans in search of prostitutes and cheap beer. For travellers, it's most useful as a transit point between KK and Brunei, though the offshore shipwrecks are popular dive spots – Borneo Divers on Jalan Tun Mustapha in Labuan Town (☎087/415867) charges RM185 for two wreck dives. Also in town, you'll find a Hong Kong Bank and the **tourist information office** (☎087/423445) on Jalan Merdeka, the main street along the seafront. Running north from the middle of Jalan Merdeka, and effectively splitting the town in two, is Jalan Tun Mustapha.

Ferries to Kota Kinabalu (RM30), Limbang (RM20), Lawas (RM20) and Bandar Seri Begawan (RM24) dock at the ferry terminal, below Jalan Merdeka. Plenty of speedboats also run from here to Menumbok (RM10), from where it's a two-hour bus ride to Kota Kinabalu. Tickets can be bought from Duta Muhibbah Agency (☎087/413827). Labuan's **airport** is 3km north of town and served by minibuses, which run from the eastern end of Jalan Bunga Melati; there's a MAS office in the *Federal Hotel*, on Jalan Bunga Kesuma (☎087/412263).

The best **accommodation** deal in town is a room with a fan in the Indian-run *Pantai View Hotel*, Jalan Bunga Tanjung (☎087/411339; ❷), or try *Melati Inn* (☎087/416307; ❷), right opposite the ferry terminal, which has en-suite rooms with TV and air-con. On Jalan Merdeka and Jalan OKK Awang Besar you'll find a number of no-frills Chinese and Indian **restaurants**: particularly good for *rotis*, *murtabaks* and curries is *Restoran Farizah*, next to the *Pantai View*. At night, make a beeline for the stalls west of the town cinema, above Jalan Muhibbah.

Sipitang and on to Sarawak

On the bumpy gravel road 47km southwest of Beaufort, **SIPITANG** is a sleepy seafront town worth bearing in mind if you need a place to stay en route to Sarawak. Approaching from the north, a bridge marks the start of town, and there's a jetty here from where a boat leaves for Pulau Labuan (daily 7am; RM20); 250m beyond that, you're in the town centre. Buses for Beaufort, KK and Lawas congregate in the centre of town; the taxi stand is next door. There's nothing much to do here except eat – try the *Kami* and the *Rina*, which occupy pretty west-facing positions on Brunei Bay or, across the main road, *Restoran Bismillah*, which does good curries. Of the hotels on the main road, the *Hotel Asanol* (☎087/821506; ❷) is the friendliest and most affordable.

The easiest way to travel **from Sipitang to Lawas in Sarawak** is to take a minibus or taxi from the centre of town (both RM10; 1hr). The Lawas Express (RM6) passes through Sipitang (on its way from KK) at around 4pm and gets to Lawas after 5pm; or you can catch a RM2 minibus to Sindumin, on the Sabah side of the border, and then connect with a Sarawak bus. Whichever you choose, the driver will wait while you pass through the passport controls flanking the border – one in Sindumin, the other a couple of hundred metres away at Merapok in Sarawak.

Kota Belud Sunday market

KOTA BELUD, 75km northeast of KK on the road to Kudat, springs to life each Sunday, as hordes of villagers from the surrounding countryside congregate at its weekly market, said to be the biggest in Sabah, ten minutes' walk out of town along Jalan Hasbollah. Tribes represented include the Rungus, Kadazan/Dusun and Bajau, though it is very rare for them to wear anything traditional these days – unless you can differentiate the languages, it's impossible to tell them apart. Kota Belud's popularity among KK's tour operators means it always has tourists, but you're far more likely to see dried fish, chains of yeast beads (used to make rice wine), buffalo and betel nut for sale, than souvenirs. The annual *tamu besar*, or "big market", usually takes place in November and also features cultural performances such as traditional dance on a stage set up for the purpose.

To catch the weekly *tamu* at its best, plan to leave KK around 7am. Buses leave from the far side of the Shell garage near the GPO (RM5), or catch a Kudat-bound bus (RM5) from the long-distance bus station; it's a scenic ninety-minute trip. Buses stop beside the district office in the centre of Kota Belud, and with onward connections so good, it's a fine jumping-off spot for Kinabalu National Park (see below), which can be reached via Tamparuli.

Kinabalu National Park

There's no more astounding sight in Borneo than the cloud-encased summit of **Mount Kinabalu** – at 4101m, half the height of Everest – shooting skywards from the 750 square kilometres of **Kinabalu National Park**. Plainly visible from Sabah's west coast and 85km northeast of KK, Kinabalu's jagged peaks look impossibly daunting, but in fact, the mountain is a relatively easy, if exhausting, climb. The well-defined, 8.5-kilometre path weaves up the mountain's southern side to the bare granite of the summit where a mile-deep gully known as Low's Gully cleaves the peak in two. Limbs that are weary from the climb will welcome the sulphurous waters of the **Poring Hot Springs**, 43km away and reached via **Ranau**.

You'll need at least two days to climb Mount Kinabalu, though you'll be glad of a spare day or two, in case cloud cover spoils the view from the summit. It's quite possible to get an early bus from KK, climb up to the accommodation huts at base camp and summit the next morning, and return to park headquarters by midday. This, however, is more than a three-kilometre altitude change on the first day, so you might want to acclimatize by spending the first night at headquarters. Midweek, you should have no problem getting a dorm bed in one of the park's hostels, but it's a good idea to book a few days in advance if you're going on a weekend or want some more luxurious accommodation. Bookings can be made at the Kinabalu Nature Resorts office in KK (see p.730); you can make a telephone booking first and pay when you arrive. Upon arrival, you'll need to pay park entry (RM3 per person), get a climbing permit (RM50 per person) from the park headquarters, and pay for an obligatory guide (RM80 for up to ten people including insurance). It's usually easy enough to meet up with a few others to share the guide fee with at reception. The guides do not try to keep everyone walking at the same pace, so it is OK if you strike out on your own as long as you stay on the trail.

Most people spend their first night at the **accommodation** in the park headquarters area, either at the basic *Old* or *New Fellowship* hostels (❶), or in nearby cabins (❻), four-person annexe rooms (RM184 per room), or at the swish *Kinabalu* or *Rajah Lodges* (RM340–980). Prices are forty percent higher on weekends or during holidays. You can eat at *Kinabalu Balsam* (daily 6am–10pm, Sat until 11pm), near reception, which also has a provisions shop, and at *Liwagu Restaurant* (daily 6am–10pm, Sat until 11pm). Alternatively, you can base yourself in another part of the park, the much quieter, higher altitude, *Mesilau Nature Resort*, 27km northeast of the park headquarters. Again contact Kinabalu Nature Resorts for accommodation details (dorm RM40; four-bed chalet units RM350; eight-bed lodge RM480). There is no public transport to *Mesilau*, though Kinabalu Nature Resorts will take you there from KK (RM50) or provide minibus transport (RM110 for the vehicle) from the park headquarters.

Scaling the mountain from either location gets you on the second night to the basic huts at *Gunting Lagadan*, *Panar Laban* or *Waras* (all RM17), which have electricity and cooking facilities, or at the more comfortable *Laban Rata Rest House* (RM34 per person), which has central heating, hot water and a restaurant (daily 7am–8pm). *Sayat-Sayat Hut* (RM10) is an hour further up the mountain, but has no electricity. The advantage of making it as far as this camp on the first day, however, is that you won't need to get up so early the following morning to reach the summit by sunrise.

A bus leaves KK's long-distance station for the park daily at 7.15am (2hr), after which minibuses depart when they're full; both cost RM20. Buses stop about 50m from the park reception office (daily 7am–7.30pm), which is the check-in point for accommodation near the park headquarters. Staff here will provide you with useful maps and can also arrange charter buses (RM40) to Poring, though it's cheaper, if more time consuming, to make your own way if you're alone (see opposite).

Climbing Mount Kinabalu

You should aim to be at the park reception by 7am. (Note, however, that hikers staying at the *Mesilau Nature Resort* meet their guides at the Resort Office and strike off from there.) You can hire a porter at the park reception (RM60 a day for loads of up to 24lb), though the lockers and saferoom at reception (RM1) make this an unnecessary expense. Useful things to take with you include a torch, suntan lotion, strong shoes, warm clothes for the summit, and raincoats (sold at the park's souvenir shop). It's over an hour's walk from the reception to the Timpohon Gate at the start of the mountain trail, so many people prefer to take the shuttle bus (RM10). Should you at any time experience a bad headache and nausea, descend immediately as you might be experiencing altitude sickness, which is potentially fatal.

△ Mount Kinabalu, Sabah

Climbing to your first night's accommodation, at around 3350m, takes three to six hours, depending on your fitness. Two or three hours into the climb, incredible views of the hills, sea and clouds below you start to unfold. The end of your first day's climbing is heralded by the appearance of the mighty granite slopes of the Panar Laban rock face. You'll spend the night at one of the resthouses at the foot of Panar Laban, from where views of the sun setting over the South China Sea are exquisite. Plan to get up at 2.30am the next morning to join the procession to the top for sunrise. Although ropes have been strung up, none of the climbing is really hairy. After sunrise on the peak, it's back down to Panar Laban for a hearty breakfast before the two- to three-hour descent to park headquarters.

Ranau and Poring Hot Springs

The small town of **RANAU** sits on the south side of the main KK–Sandakan road, 20km from Kinabalu National Park. As there's no bus service to Poring, you'll have to come here to get a minibus for the extra 19km to Poring. There are two obvious accommodation options should you need to stay the night. Best is the *Rafflesia Inn*, Lot 2, Block N (☎088/879359; ❹); if it's full, try the *Hotel Kinabalu* next door in Lot 3 (☎088/876028; ❹). There's Internet access at Cyber Station, Ground Floor, Block B, Jalan Taman Ranau, near *KFC*.

The hot (48–60°C) sulphurous waters of **Poring Hot Springs** (RM5), situated on the park's southeastern border, are a great place to soak your hiking pains away. The 24-hour open-air hot baths are close to the main park gates – choose your own and turn on the tap. There's also a cold plunge pool and two enclosed baths (RM20 an hour). Go on a weekday, otherwise there's not enough hot water for everyone and you'll get a lukewarm trickle instead. A fifteen-minute walk beyond the baths brings you to Poring's canopy walk (daily 6.30am–5.30pm; RM5; RM35 with camera), where five tree huts connected by suspended walkways 40m above ground afford you a monkey's-eye view of the surrounding lowland rainforest. A trail strikes off to the right of the baths, reaching 150-metre-high Langanan Waterfall about ninety minutes later. On its way, the trail passes smaller Kepungit Waterfall – whose icy pool is ideal for swimming. If it's been raining, there'll be leeches on the trail and even dropping from the trees – they'll drop off if you squirt them with some mosquito repellant. If that doesn't work, try burning them with a cigarette. (If you think that sounds cruel, you'll change your mind as soon as you discover one sucking your blood.)

If you're in a group, it's best to charter a minibus to take you from Kinabalu park headquarters to Poring (1hr). Otherwise, just walk out of the main gate and hail any passing Sandakan-bound bus. They'll drop you off at Ranau (RM5), from where you can take a minibus (RM5) to the springs. There's a café at the springs, and two restaurants just outside the gates. No permit is needed to visit Poring, though you'll have to book your accommodation at Kinabalu Nature Resorts office in KK (see p.730) or at the park headquarters. Accommodation in Poring is backpacker-oriented. Camping is RM6 per person and the dorm beds in the hostels RM12. Cabin units are RM80 for four people, and chalet units RM120 for six people.

Sandakan and around

Sandwiched between sea and cliffs on the northern lip of Sandakan Bay, **SANDAKAN** isn't an appealing city, but it does make a good base for day-trips to the **Sepilok Orang-utan Rehabilitation Centre**, wildlife-spotting river trips on the Sungei Kinabatangan, **Turtle Islands Park**, and the **Gomantong Caves**. Fifteen minutes' walk west of the dense downtown area along Jalan Leila are the blocks of shops that make up Bandar Ramai Ramai, while to the east, running up round the bay, is Jalan Buli Sim-Sim. The heart of the town is the colourful market along the harbour's edge: here, stalls sell baskets, fruits, scaly fish, clothing and much else besides. A fifteen-minute walk east of the town centre, along Jalan Buli Sim-Sim, brings you to Sandakan's modern mosque. Beyond this is Kampung Buli Sim-Sim, the water village around which Sandakan expanded in the nineteenth century, its countless photogenic shacks spread like lilies out into the bay. Sandakan's less central addresses are pinpointed according to their distances out of the downtown area, hence "Mile 1 1/2", "Mile 3", and so on.

Practicalities

The long-distance **bus station** is just north of Tun Razak Park. There are buses to and from KK (frequently from 6.30am–10am then at 2pm and 8pm; 6hr; RM29), Ranau and Tawau (RM25). Long-distance taxis also operate from this area. Sandakan's two local bus stations are within a couple of minutes' walk of each other, in the centre of town. The scheduled services of the Labuk Road Bus Company leave from the waterfront Labuk Road station – blue-and-white buses travel up Labuk Road itself, while those with red, yellow and green stripes go west, along Jalan Leila. A short walk west along Jalan Pryer brings you to the minibus area. The two stations have many destinations in common, so it's worth checking both to find the earliest departure. The airport (☎089/273966) serving KK is 11km north of town and connected by minibuses (RM3) to the southern end of Jalan Pelabuhan, and by taxis (RM15). MAS is in the Sabah Building, Jalan Pelabuhan (☎089/273966).

To get to Turtle Islands Park by early evening – the best time to watch the turtles – you'll need to be on an official tour run by Crystal Quest (☎089/212711), 12th Floor, Wisma Khoo Siak Chiew, Sandakan. This tour company is the only one actually allowed to stay overnight in the park. *Uncle Tan's* (see below) also runs trips to the islands, but these independent outfits aren't permitted to stay overnight within the park.

Sandakan's main post office is five minutes' walk west of town, on Jalan Leila (Mon–Fri 8am–5pm, Sat 10am–1pm). There's a Telekom office on the 6th Floor, Wisma Khoo (daily 8.30am–4.45pm) and an HSBC bank at the junction of Lebuh Tiga and Jalan Pelabuhan. The main police station is on Jalan Sim Sim (☎089/211222). Internet access can be found along Lebuh Tiga and Lebuh Empat.

Accommodation and eating

As Sandakan is mainly used as a base from which to explore the Orang-utan centre and Turtle Islands, many travellers choose to bypass the town altogether and stay instead at *Uncle Tan's* excellent **guesthouse** (☎089/531639), around 28km west of Sandakan and quite near the Orang-utan Centre (coming from KK by bus, ask to be dropped outside *Uncle Tan's*). The guesthouse is actually in Gum Gum village at Mile 16 Labuk Road, a thirty-minute bus ride from town. They charge RM20 for a bed in a basic hut, and the price includes three good meals. The guesthouse also arranges wildlife-spotting trips to its jungle camp on Sungei Kinabatangan (see p.741). If you want to stay in Sandakan itself, there are a handful of budget and mid-range hotel options, none of them standouts. Better than most are the clean and newly renovated rooms at *New Sabah Hotel*, 18 Jl Singapura (☎089/218711; ❹), or mid-range *Ramai*, Mile 1 1/2 Jl Leila (☎089/273222; ❺), whose en-suite rooms all have TV and air-con.

For hawker stalls, the market on Jalan Pryer is fantastic but don't miss the utterly wonderful *Supreme Garden Vegetarian Restaurant*, Block 30, Bandar Ramai-Ramai, Jalan Leila (10am–2pm & 5.30–9pm). Otherwise, try the popular but hard-to-spot Muslim Indian restaurant *Haji*, on Second Avenue (Lebuh Dua), south of the padang (8.30am–9.30pm) or *SRC Happy Seafood Restaurant* (11.30am–2pm & 5–10pm), at the Sandakan Recreation Club, Jalan Singapore, which serves good Cantonese dishes.

Sepilok Orang-utan Rehabilitation Centre

One of only three orang-utan sanctuaries in the world, the **Sepilok Orang-utan Rehabilitation Centre** (daily 9–11am & 2–3.30pm; feeding times 10am & 3pm;

RM10; ☎089/531180), 25km west of Sandakan, trains orphaned and domesticated orang-utans to fend for themselves. Close to feeding time, a warden leads you to feeding Station A, where you'll be able to see the apes spectacularly competing for bananas with the local troop of pig-tailed Macaque monkeys. You can get close to the orang-utans, but give them a little room, don't touch them (you might transmit a virus) and keep quiet. There's a better chance of seeing semi-mature and more independent orangs a thirty-minute hike from the visitor centre at Station B. Other hikes in the park are described at reception but you'll have to register there before you set off. Beware of hungry Macaques on the trail – they will grab at anything that catches their eye and then run into the jungle with it. They will also bite if you're foolish enough to use food to lure them into the range of your camera lens. On the popular Mangrove trail (4hr return) you'll have a chance of seeing proboscis monkeys and you can even stay overnight at *Sepilok Laut Cabins* (RM80 per person) at the trail's end. Contact the forestry department (☎089/213135) two days in advance to book. Red, yellow and green striped "Batu 14" buses leave for the centre (roughly hourly 7.30am–4.30pm) from the central bus station in Sandakan or from just outside Bandar Ramai Ramai on Jalan Leila. The same bus can drop you off at the express ("Mile Three") bus station which is en route, should you want to move onto Semporna, KK or Tawau. The Centre's *Rest House* has pleasant rooms (☎089/534900; RM45), is only a few yards from the centre itself and offers guided night walks at 6pm (RM18), but most people stay at *Uncle Tan's* (see p.739) or in Sandakan. There are two other excellent options: *Sepilok B&B* (☎089/532288; dorms RM20; ④) is 1km before the Centre's entrance, and *Labuk B&B* (☎089/533190; ③), 2km further back on the KK–Sandakan road.

Turtle Islands National Park

Peeping out of the Sulu Sea some 40km north of Sandakan, three tiny islands comprise Sabah's **Turtle Islands National Park**, the favoured egg-laying sites of the green and hawksbill turtles, varying numbers of which haul themselves laboriously above the high-tide mark to bury their clutches of eggs. All three of the park's islands (Pulau Selingaan, Pulau Bakkungan Kechil and Pulau Gulisaan) have a hatchery – though only Selingaan has amenities for tourists. Flash photography of the turtles is prohibited (the turtles are frightened by the light).

Turtles visit the park every day of the year, but the peak nesting time falls between July and October. They begin to come ashore around 7.30pm, then dig a nesting pit and lay upwards of a hundred eggs. With hatchings a nightly event, you're almost guaranteed the stirring sight of scores of determined little turtles wriggling up through the sand. In the meantime, Selingaan's quiet beaches are good for swimming and sunbathing, or you can go snorkelling off nearby Bakkungan Kechil (RM15 per person, minimum four people; details from park headquarters).

As mentioned above, the only way to stay overnight on Selingaan is to come on a tour with Crystal Quest (see p.739). Sabah Parks allows no more than twenty visitors a night onto Selingaan, all of whom are put up in the island's four comfortable chalets. *Uncle Tan's* and the *Travellers' Rest Hostel* visit Selingaan during the day and then take you to other islands, which are not in the park, for the night. *Roses' Café* inside the visitor centre provides meals for the limited number of people in the evening and for extra visitors during the day.

Gomantong Caves

Further afield, the **Gomantong Caves**, south of Sandakan Bay, are inspiring enough at any time of the year, though you'll get most out of the trip when the edible nests of their resident swiftlets are being harvested (Feb–April & July–Sept). Bird's-nest soup has long been a Chinese culinary speciality and Chinese merchants have been coming to Borneo to trade for birds' nests for at least twelve centuries.

Of the two major caves, Simud Hitam is easiest to visit: follow the trail from behind the staff quarters to the right of the reception building, taking a right fork after five minutes, and continue for a further ten minutes. Simud Hitam supports a colony of black-nest swiftlets, whose nests – a mixture of saliva and feathers – sell for US$40 a kilogram. Above Simud Hitam, the larger but less accessible Simud Putih is home to the white-nest swiftlet, whose nests are of pure, dried saliva and can fetch prices of over US$500 a kilogram. To reach Simud Putih, take the left fork, five minutes along the trail behind reception, and start climbing.

It's easiest to go with a tour agency (from RM80 per person from *Uncle Tan's* – see p.739), but under your own steam, regular minibuses leave daily from Jalan Pryer in Sandakan for Sukau (6am onwards), 20km beyond the turning to Gomantong. This drops you 5km from the caves on a former logging road. Be sure to bring a torch.

Sungei Kinabatangan

East of the entrance to Sandakan Bay, Sabah's longest river, the 560-kilometre **Kinabatangan**, ends its northeasterly path from the interior to the Sulu Sea. Though elephants are rare, you're quite likely to spot proboscis monkeys, orang-utans, gibbons, macaques, wild boar, huge water monitors and crocodiles in the forest flanking the river, making this one of the best spots in Sabah to see wildlife. The resident bird life – hornbills, Brahming kites, crested serpent eagles, egrets, exquisite stork-billed kingfishers and oriental darters – is equally impressive. The best way to appreciate the river is to stay in one of the several jungle camps or lodges on its banks. The camps, run by *Uncle Tan's* in Sandakan (see p.739), charge RM145 and RM150 respectively for the car and riverboat ride to camp, plus two safari boat trips a day. Meals and accommodation are an extra RM15 a day. About two hours downstream from the camps, in Sukau, *Sukau Rainforest Lodge* (❽) is more upmarket, but well worth the extra cost, as its location is breathtaking and the chalets lovely. The *Lodge* is run by Borneo Eco Tours in KK, at Lot 12a, 3 Lorong Bernam, Taman Soon Kiong (☎088/234009), who will get you from Sandakan to Sukau free of charge.

Semporna

The Bajau fishing town of **SEMPORNA**, 108km east of Tawau, is the departure point for Pulau Sipadan. The only feature of note in Semporna itself is the huge water village stretching southwards along the coast from the centre, which incorporates mosques, shops and hundreds of dwellings. Chances are that the company taking you to Sipadan will have booked you in at the Minangkabau-style *Dragon Inn Hotel*, actually part of the wharf on Jalan Custom (☎089/781088; ❺) where you can get a dorm for RM20 if you're diving. If not, the *Hotel Damai Traveller's Lodge*, Jalan Jakarulla (☎089/782011; ❸), sits right in the centre of town at the minibus stand and has a range of very good-value, spacious and clean rooms. There's also a Maybank, Internet cafés and restaurants on Jalan Jakarulla itself. Borneo Divers, Sipadan Dive Centre and Borneo Sea Adventures all have offices at the Semporna Ocean Tourism Centre (SOTC) on the waterfront causeway, as does Today Travel Service, Semporna's MAS agent.

Pulau Sipadan

The waters around tiny **Pulau Sipadan**, 30km south of Semporna in the Celebes Sea, literally teem with giant hawksbill turtles, white-tip sharks, barracuda, vast schools of tropical fish, and a huge diversity of coral; unsurprisingly, Sipadan is listed as one of the top dive sites in the world. Twenty metres from the shore, the bottom plunges to over 600 feet, which means you can shore-dive a limitless wall of coral as often as you like from right outside your room. As most companies offer "unlimited shore dives" along with the boat dives in the package, you can dive five times a day (self-navigation is easy), making the RM400 a night charge easier to swallow. You'll get three boat dives if you only stay one night (and have time for about 5 extra shore dives if you're really keen). The diving highlights include a network of marine caves, White-tip Avenue, Barracuda Point, and the Hanging Gardens (soft coral). Snorkellers accompanying divers to the island can expect to see reef sharks and white-tips, lion fish, barracudas and scores of turtles, without having to leave the surface. The island itself is carpeted by lush forest, and fringed by white-sand beaches, used by green turtles to lay their eggs; you can see this happen if you register for a nightly "turtle walk" at Borneo Divers.

The only way to stay on Pulau Sipadan is by booking through a tour operator – all but one of the companies selling diving trips operate out of Kota Kinabalu (see p.739), the exception being *Sipadan Island Resort*, which is based in Tawau (see belows). A package will cost you about RM1200 including equipment rental and meals. It's possible to make independent day-trips to the island: locals with boats (and snorkelling equipment) for rent are plentiful on the SOTC causeway in Semporna. Expect to pay around RM100 for the boat and RM50 for snorkelling equipment or RM100 for diving equipment.

Tawau and on to Indonesia

TAWAU, Sabah's southernmost town of any size, is a major departure point for Indonesian Kalimantan. There's not a great deal to see or do here, though the market beside *Soon Yee* hotel is worthy of a browse if you happen to be there before noon. Long-distance **buses** terminate at Sabindu bus station on the eastern end of Jalan Dunlop (which runs parallel to the shore) with landcruisers to Keningau leaving from the same site. There's a bus to Sandakan (6hr) and KK (12hr) at around 7am and another at 6pm. The local bus and minibus station, serving the airport, is on Jalan Stephen Tan (west and one block inland of Sabindu). The new **airport** (☎089/775819) is 28km outside of town and can be reached by minibus (RM10, 45min). The sole Pulau Sipadan dive operator not based in KK is here: *Sipadan Island Resort*, Block P, Bandar Sabindo (☎089/765200). As well as several banks, the commercial estate known as the Fajar Centre, east of Jalan Masjid, houses both the Telekom building in Block 35, and the MAS office in Wisma Sasco; you'll find the post office across the southern side of Jalan Dunlop.

The best bargain **accommodation** in town is the friendly Chinese hotel *Soon Yee*, on Jalan Stephen Tan (☎089/772447; ❶), which has fan or air-con rooms, while the *Belmost Marco Polo* on Jalan Clinic is the top hotel in town (☎089/777988; ❼). Two blocks below Jalan Dunlop in the Sabindo Complex, the two-hundred-metre stretch of open-air **restaurants** and stalls collectively known as Taman Selera sets up daily. You'll find lots more hawkers, and along the waterfront there are several excellent seafood restaurants. Internet access is available at several outlets on Jalan Chester.

Transport into Indonesia

Tawau is the main stepping-stone for onward travel to Kalimantan. **Ferries to Indonesia** depart from Customs Wharf, 150m south of Jalan Dunlop's Shell station. There are four departures a day – at 7am and noon for the Indonesian islands of Tarakan (RM75) and 2pm and 4pm for Nunukan (RM25). There is no service on Sundays. Check at Sasaran (☎089/772441) and Perkhidmatan Pelayaran Bumiputra (☎019/8415618) ticket booths north of the jetty by the fish market (Pasar Ikan) on Jalan Pelabuhan. Nunukan is an hour from Tawau, after which it's a further two hours to Tarakan. There are also **flights** on MAS from Tawau to Tarakan in Indonesia.

Travel details

Buses

Alor Setar to: Butterworth (every 45min; 30min); Hat Yai, Thailand (hourly; 3hr); Ipoh (3 daily; 3hr); Johor Bahru (2 daily; 16hr); Kota Bharu (2 daily; 8–9hr); Kuala Lumpur (2 daily; 5hr); Kuala Perlis (hourly; 1hr 30min); Kuala Terrenganu (2 daily; 8hr); Kuantan (2 daily; 9hr 30min).
Bintulu to: Batu Niah (8 daily; 2hr); Kuching (6 daily; 11hr); Miri (every 30min; 3hr); Sibu (8 daily; 4hr).
Butterworth to: Alor Setar (every 30min–1hr; 2hr 30min); Bangkok, Thailand (2 daily; 18hr); Hat Yai, Thailand (2 daily; 5hr 30min); Ipoh (hourly; 3hr); Kota Bharu (2 daily; 6hr); Kuala Lumpur (at least 15 daily; 7hr); Kuala Perlis (5 daily; 3hr 45min); Kuala Terengganu (2 daily; 8hr); Kuantan (3 daily; 12hr); Lumut (4 daily; 4hr); Melaka (1 daily; 6–10hr); Padang Besar (5 daily; 4hr); Singapore (at least 2 daily; 16hr); Surat Thani, Thailand (2 daily; 10hr 30min); Tapah (2 daily; 4hr 30min).
Ipoh to: Butterworth (hourly; 3hr); Kuala Kangsar (every 45min; 3hr); Kuala Lumpur (hourly; 4hr); Lumut (hourly; 90min); Penang (hourly; 3hr); Singapore (4 daily; 10–11hr); Tapah (hourly; 1hr).
Johor Bahru to: Alor Setar (2 daily; 16hr); Butterworth (at least 2 daily; 14hr); Ipoh (4 daily; 9hr); Kota Bharu (2 daily; 12hr); Kuala Lumpur (every 30min; 7hr); Kuala Terengganu (2 daily; 10hr); Kuantan (6 daily; 6hr); Melaka (5 daily; 4hr); Mersing (at least 2 daily; 2hr 30min); Singapore (every 30min; 1hr).
Kota Bharu to: Kuala Lumpur (2 daily; 7hr).
Kota Kinabalu to: Beaufort (15 daily; 2hr); Kinabalu National Park (8 daily; 1hr 45min); Kota Belud (16 daily; 2hr 10min); Lawas (1 daily; 4hr); Menumbok (6 daily; 2hr 30min); Ranau (10 daily; 2hr); Sandakan (12 daily; 5hr 30min); Tawau (2 daily; 9hr).
Kuala Lumpur (Pekeliling station) to: Jerantut (4 daily; 3hr 30min); Kuala Lipis (4 daily; 4hr); Mentakab (hourly; 1hr 15min).
Kuala Lumpur (Pudu Raya station) to: Alor Setar (9 daily; 9hr); Butterworth (every 30min; 7hr); Cameron Highlands (hourly; 4hr 30min); Ipoh (every 30min; 4hr); Johor Bahru (5 daily; 6hr); Kuala Perlis (6 daily; 9hr); Lumut (8 daily; 5hr 30min); Melaka (every 30min; 2hr); Mersing (1 daily; 7hr); Penang (every 30min; 8hr); Singapore (7 daily; 7hr).
Kuala Lumpur (Putra station) to: Kota Bharu (8 daily; 10hr); Kuala Terengganu (3 daily; 7hr); Kuantan (every 30min; 5hr); Temerloh (hourly; 3hr).
Kuala Terengganu to: Alor Setar (2 daily; 9hr 30min); Butterworth (2 daily; 9–10hr); Ipoh (1 daily; 11hr); Johor Bahru (2 daily; 10hr); Kota Bharu (5 daily; 4hr); Kuala Lumpur (2 daily; 8–9hr); Kuantan (6 daily; 4hr); Marang (every 30min; 30min); Melaka (3 daily; 7hr); Mersing (2 daily; 6hr); Rantau Abang (every 30 min; 1hr).
Kuantan to: Butterworth (3 daily; 10hr); Jerantut, for Taman Negara National Park (4 daily); Kota Bharu (5 daily; 6hr); Kuala Lipis (2 daily; 6hr); Kuala Lumpur (6 daily; 5hr); Kuala Terengganu (6 daily; 4hr); Melaka (2 daily; 5hr); Mersing (6 daily; 3hr 30min); Singapore (3 daily; 7hr).
Kuching to: Anna Rais (4 daily; 2hr); Bako (12 daily; 1hr); Pontianak, Indonesia (6 daily; 8–10hr); Serian (8 daily; 1hr); Sibu (6 daily; 7hr); Sri Aman (6 daily; 3hr).
Lawas to: Kota Kinabalu (1 daily; 4hr).
Lumut to: Tanah Rata (1 daily; 5hr); Tapah (1 daily; 2hr).
Melaka to: Alor Setar (11 daily; 8hr); Butterworth (11 daily; 6hr); Ipoh (11 daily; 4hr); Johor Bahru (5 daily; 4hr); Kota Bharu (1 daily; 11hr); Kuala Lumpur (14 daily; 2hr); Kuala Terengganu (1 daily; 8hr); Kuantan (1 daily; 6hr); Mersing (2 daily; 5hr); Singapore (9 daily; 5hr); Tapah (1 daily; 3hr 30min).
Mersing to: Singapore (4 daily; 3hr 30min); Johor Bahru (2 daily; 2hr 30min); Kuala Lumpur (2 daily; 7hr); Kuantan (3 daily; 3hr 30min); Melaka (2 daily; 5hr).
Miri to: Batu Niah (8 daily; 2hr); Kuala Belait (5 daily; 2hr 30min); Kuching (2 daily; 15hr).
Ranau to: Sandakan (8 daily; 3hr 30min).
Sri Aman: to Lubok Antu (4 daily; 1hr).
Tapah to: Butterworth (3 daily; 4hr 30min); Hat Yai, Thailand (daily; 10hr); Kuala Lumpur (10 daily; 2hr 30min); Lumut (2 daily; 2hr); Melaka (2 daily; 3hr 30min).
Tawau to: Sandakan (6 daily; 4hr 30min).

Trains

Alor Setar to: Bangkok, Thailand (1 daily; 21hr 30min); Butterworth (2 daily; 1hr 45–2hr 45min); Hat Yai, Thailand (2 daily; 2hr 35–4hr 10min); Kuala Lumpur (1 daily; 13hr 10min); Tapah Road (1 daily; 9hr 25min).
Butterworth to: Alor Setar (2 daily; 2hr); Bangkok, Thailand (1 daily; 23hr 30min); Hat Yai, Thailand (2 daily; 4hr 45–6hr); Ipoh (1 daily; 5hr); Kuala Kangsar (1 daily; 3hr 30min); Kuala Lumpur (1 daily; 10hr 25min); Tapah Road (1 daily; 6hr 30min).
Gemas to: Jerantut (3 daily; 4hr); Kuala Lipis (3 daily; 4hr–6hr 30min); Mentakab (3 daily; 3hr);

Tumpat (2 daily; 9hr–15hr); Wakaf Bharu (2 daily; 8hr 50–9hr 45min).
Ipoh to: Tapah Road (1 daily; 1hr 25min).
Johor Bahru to: Gemas (5 daily; 3–4hr); Kuala Lipis (2 daily; 7hr); Kuala Lumpur (4 daily; 5hr 30min–7hr 10min); Singapore (6 daily; 1hr); Tumpat (1 daily; 12hr 30min).
Kuala Kangsar to: Tapah Road (1 daily; 3hr).
Kuala Lumpur to: Alor Setar (1 daily; 13hr 10min); Butterworth (1 daily; 10hr 40min); Gemas (6 daily; 2hr 40–4hr 10min); Ipoh (1 daily; 5hr 30min); Johor Bahru (4 daily; 5hr 30–8hr); Singapore (4 daily; 7–9hr); Tapah Road (1 daily; 4hr).
Padang Besar to: Alor Setar (2 daily; 1hr 15min); Bangkok, Thailand (1 daily; 19hr 50min); Butterworth (2 daily; 3–4hr); Hat Yai (2 daily; 50min–2hr 25min); Ipoh (1 daily; 9hr 15min); Kuala Lumpur (1 daily; 14hr 30min); Tapah Road (1 daily; 10hr 45min).

Boats

Bintulu to: Tubau (5 daily; 3hr).
Kapit to: Nanga Baleh (4 daily; 2hr); Sungei Gaat (2 daily; 2hr 30min).
Kota Kinabalu to: Labuan (5 daily; 2hr).
Kuching to: Sarikei (1 daily; 2hr); Sibu (1 daily; 4hr).
Kukup to: Tanjung Balai, Indonesia (4 daily; 45min).
Lawas to: Muara, Brunei (1 daily at 7am); Limbang (1 daily at 9am; 30min); Pulau Labuan (1 daily at 7.30am; 1hr).
Melaka to: Dumai, Indonesia (1 daily; 2hr).
Marudi to: Kuala Baram (7 daily; 3hr); Long Terawan (1 daily; 3hr).
Nanga Baleh to: Kapit (2 daily; 1–2hr).
Penang to: Butterworth (every 20min–1hr, 24hr service; 20min); Medan, Indonesia (2 daily; 4hr); Pulau Langkawi (2 daily; 2hr).
Port Klang to: Tanjung Balai, Sumatra (6 weekly; 3hr 30min).
Pulau Labuan to: Bandar Seri Begawan, Brunei (4 daily; 1hr 30min); Kota Kinabalu (5 daily; 3hr); Lawas (daily at 1pm; 1hr); Limbang (daily at 12.30pm; 1hr); Menumbok (3 daily; 1–2hr).
Sibu to: Kanowit (9 daily; 1hr); Kapit (9 daily; 3hr); Kuching (1 daily; 4hr); Song (6 daily; 2hr).
Tawau to: Nunukan (2 daily; 1hr).

Flights

Bintulu to: Kota Kinabalu (5 weekly; 1hr 15min); Kuching (2 daily; 1hr); Miri (2 daily; 35min); Sibu (3 daily; 35min).
Johor Bahru to: Kota Kinabalu (1 daily; 2hr 15min); Kuching (3 daily; 1hr 25min).
Kota Kinabalu to: Bintulu (5 weekly; 1hr 15min); Kuching (5 daily; 2hr 15min); Johor Bahru (1 daily; 2hr 15min); Pulau Labuan (5 daily; 30min); Miri (4 daily; 40min); Sandakan (7 daily; 50min); Sibu (2 daily; 1hr 35min); Tawau (5 daily; 45min).
Kuala Lumpur to: Alor Setar (2 daily; 50min); Bandar Seri Begawan, Brunei (1 daily; 2hr 20min); Ipoh (2 daily; 35min); Johor Bahru (4 daily; 45min); Kota Bharu (4 daily; 50min); Kota Kinabalu (10 daily; 1hr 45 min); Kuala Terengganu (3 daily; 45min); Kuantan (4 daily; 40min); Kuching (10 daily; 1hr 45 min); Miri (4 daily; 2hr 15min); Penang (11 daily; 45min); Pulau Langkawi (4 daily; 55min); Pulau Tioman (2 daily; 45min); Sibu (1 daily; 2hr); Singapore (10 daily; 55min).
Kuching to: Bandar Seri Begawan, Brunei (3 weekly; 1hr 40min); Bintulu (9 daily; 1hr); Johor Bahru (3 daily; 1hr 25min); Kota Kinabalu (6 daily; 2hr 15min); Kuala Lumpur (9 daily; 1hr 40min); Miri (7 daily; 1hr); Penang (1 daily; 2hr); Pontianak, Indonesia (5 weekly; 1hr); Sibu (9 daily; 40min); Singapore (2 daily; 1hr 20min).
Miri to: Bintulu (3 daily; 35min); Kota Kinabalu (5 daily; 40min); Kuala Lumpur (3 daily; 2hr 15min); Kuching (5 daily; 1hr); Pontianak, Indonesia (5 weekly; 2hr 35min); Sibu (4 daily; 1hr).
Penang to: Bangkok, Thailand (3 daily; 1hr 40min); Johor Bahru (at least 3 daily via KL; 1hr 5min–3hr 45min); Kota Bharu (at least 3 daily via KL; 3hr 15min–4hr); Kuala Lumpur (at least 14 daily; 45min); Kuching (1 daily; 2hr); Medan, Indonesia (1 daily; 20min); Phuket, Thailand (3 weekly; 30min); Pulau Langkawi (2 daily; 30min); Singapore (at least 8 daily via KL; 1hr 10min–3hr 55min).
Pulau Langkawi to: Kuala Lumpur (5 daily; 55min); Penang (2 daily; 30min); Phuket, Thailand (1 daily; 40min); Singapore (1 daily; 1hr 25min).
Pulau Tioman to: Kuala Lumpur (2 daily; 45min); Singapore (1 daily; 30min).
Sandakan to: Kota Kinabalu (7 daily; 50min).
Sibu to: Bintulu (3 daily; 35min); Kota Kinabalu (2 daily; 1hr 35min); Kuala Lumpur (1 daily; 2hr); Kuching (9 daily; 40min); Miri (4 daily; 1hr).

8

The Philippines

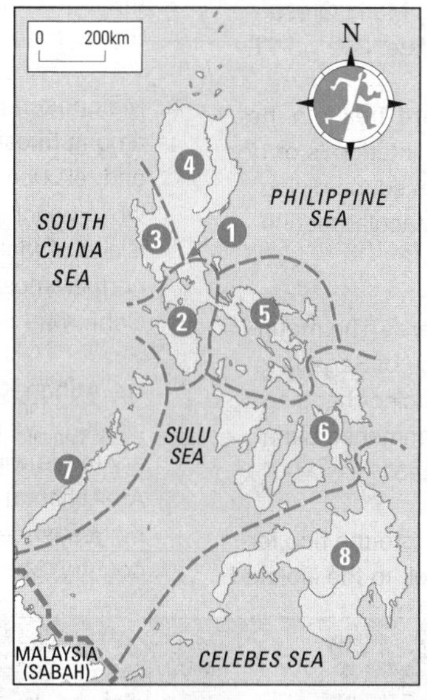

Philippines highlights

* **Manila nightlife** For a flamboyant night on the town, look no further than the old part of Malate; around Remedios Circle, with its fashionable clubs and bohemian cafes; JM Nakpil Street and neighbouring Maria Orosa Street in Malate. See p.791

* **Puerto Galera** Trek into the jungle-clad hinterlands or do some serious scuba diving among spectacular marine life. See p.803

* **The Cordilleras** The mountaintop village of Sagada is the site of ancient hanging coffins and immense burial caves. See p.817

* **Banaue** Explore the rice terraces and trek to the isolated tribal barrio of Batad. See p.825

* **Boracay** First stop for most sun-worshippers is the dumbell-shaped island of Boracay in the Visayas and the famous White Beach. See p.856

* **Malapascua Island** Dive among thresher sharks and relax on the blindingly white beaches of the tiny island of Malapascua, off the northernmost tip of mainland Cebu. See p.848

* **Ati-Atihan** Kalibo on Panay Island plays host every January to the wild and wonderful Ati-Atihan, undoubtedly the biggest street festival in the country. See p.855

△ Celebrating Ati-Atihan

Introduction and basics

The Philippines has suffered in the tourism stakes because of its position on the map. The flamboyant former First Lady Imelda Marcos once said it was "hamburgered" geographically. What she meant was that the Philippines receives fewer visitors than other Southeast Asian countries – about two million a year compared to Thailand's six million – because it is not part of the Southeast Asian mainland. Travellers on the traditional Asian trails tend to get as far as Thailand or Hong Kong, but ignore the Philippines because it often involves an extra flight, albeit a short one, across the South China Sea.

Perversely, it is this very lack of mass tourism that makes the Philippines such an attractive destination. If you want to explore, and if you are ready to cope with some eccentric infrastructure and a distinctly laid-back attitude towards the passage of time, the Philippines has more to offer than many of its neighbours.

A big country in a small package, the Philippines is the second-largest archipelago in the world (after Indonesia), with **7107 islands** – sixty percent of them uninhabited – and 58,390km of coastline – all in a land mass no bigger than Arizona. Filipinos refer to it as their string of pearls. Your biggest problem is likely to be deciding which of the pearls to see first.

Most flights from outside the country land in the capital, **Manila**, which is choked with traffic and dilapidated, but also has some of the ritziest shopping malls and most spectacular nightlife in Asia. JM Nakpil Street in Malate on a Friday night (although it actually doesn't begin to warm up until midnight) is a sight to behold. Beatnik poets mingle with film stars, models, swaggering transvestites and a smattering of expats to create a good-natured outdoor rave that makes all other raves look tame by comparison.

For beach connoisseurs, the central **Visayan region** is an island-hopper's paradise, with white sand everywhere and unspoiled fishing barrios where there's nothing to do at night except watch the fireflies, listen to the geckos, and perhaps share a bottle of local rum. Travellers are discovering quiet islands around Cebu and Bohol in the Visayas; if you're willing to leave the beaten track, it's not hard to find your own deserted tropical beach. **Palawan**, one hour to the southwest of Manila by plane or an overnight journey by ferry, is an unforgettable wilderness of diamond-blue lagoons, volcanic lakes and first-rate scuba diving. In the **Cordillera Mountains** of northern Luzon live tribes who make propitiatory offerings to rice gods, and whose way of life has barely changed since they first settled there around 500 BC. One of the few concessions they have made to modernity is to give up headhunting.

The Philippines will turn every notion you ever had of Asia on its head. Centuries of **colonial rule** have resulted in a delightfully schizophrenic country of potent but conflicting influences. When Magellan placed a sovereign hand on the Philippines on behalf of King Philip of Spain in 1521, he brought with him Catholicism, European architecture and the *mañana* ethic. When monsoon rains swamp the streets, or when volcanoes erupt, Filipinos remain stoically fatalistic, their usual reaction is to smile, throw up their hands, and say *bahala-na* – "what will be will be".

Three centuries after Magellan, in 1898, there was another bizarre twist in the country's colonial history when **America** bought the Philippines from Spain for US$20 million, part of the booty from a war the two powers had fought over Cuba. It was from America that the Philippines got its town planning, its constitution, and its passion for basketball, beauty pageants and pizza. Independence was finally granted on July 4, 1946, making the Philippines Asia's first real democracy, a fact most Filipinos remain fiercely proud of.

But it was the events of the 1980s that brought the Philippines to the general attention of the rest of the world. In 1972, **President Ferdinand Marcos** decided to

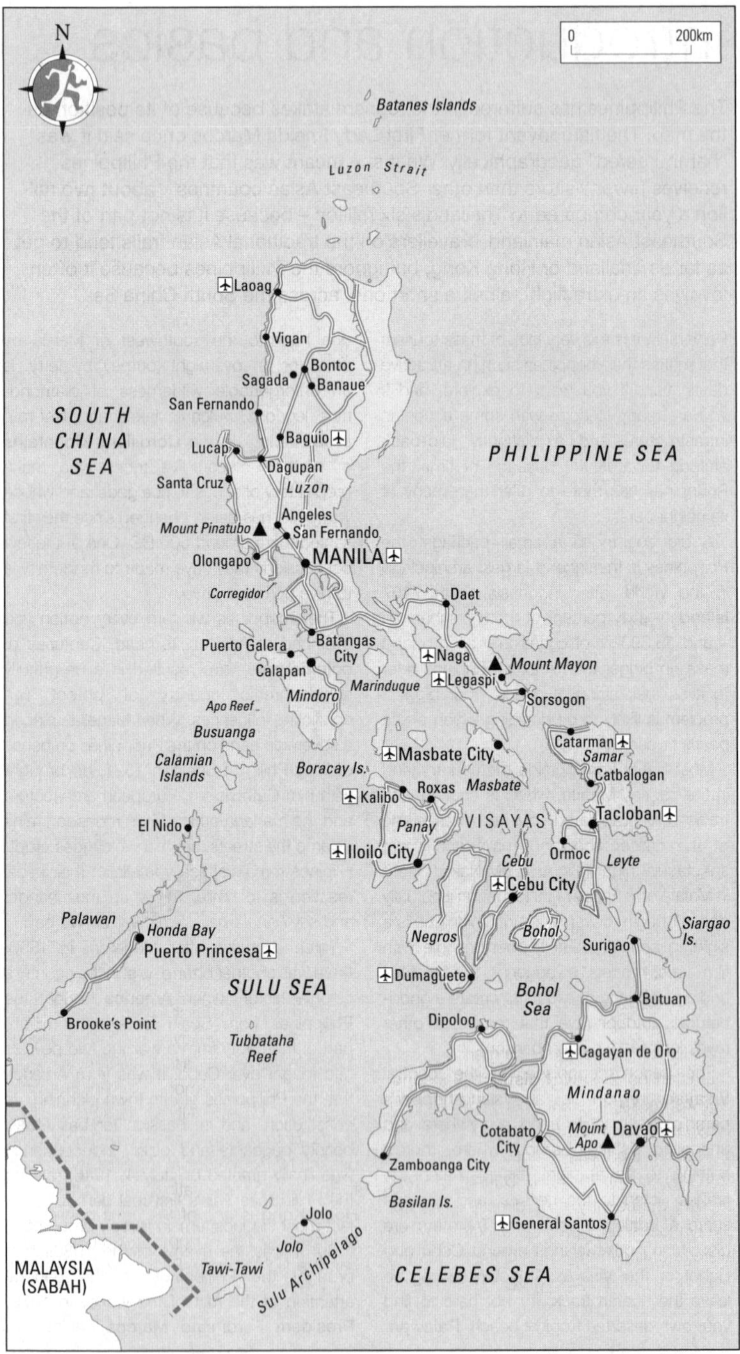
N
0 200km
Batanes Islands
Luzon Strait
Laoag
Vigan
Bontoc
Sagada
Banaue
San Fernando
SOUTH CHINA SEA
Baguio
Lucap
Dagupan
PHILIPPINE SEA
Santa Cruz
Luzon
Angeles
Mount Pinatubo
San Fernando
Olongapo
MANILA
Corregidor
Daet
Batangas City
Puerto Galera
Naga
Mount Mayon
Calapan
Legaspi
Mindoro
Marinduque
Sorsogon
Apo Reef
Busuanga
Catarman
Masbate City
Samar
Calamian Islands
Boracay Is.
Catbalogan
Kalibo
Roxas
Masbate
VISAYAS
Tacloban
El Nido
Panay
Ormoc
Iloilo City
Cebu
Leyte
Cebu City
Palawan
Siargao Is.
Honda Bay
Bohol
Puerto Princesa
Negros
Surigao
SULU SEA
Dumaguete
Bohol Sea
Butuan
Brooke's Point
Dipolog
Tubbataha Reef
Cagayan de Oro
Mindanao
Cotabato City
Mount Apo
Davao
Zamboanga City
Basilan Is.
Jolo
General Santos
Jolo
Sulu Archipelago
MALAYSIA (SABAH)
Tawi-Tawi
CELEBES SEA

cling on to power by declaring martial law. When Marcos's lifelong political rival, **Ninoy Aquino**, was assassinated at Manila Airport in August 1983, patience with the dictator ran out. What followed was nothing short of momentous: a "people power" revolution to kick out Marcos and his ambitious wife Imelda. In February 1986, they fled to Hawaii, where Ferdinand died in exile. Imelda's famous shoe collection was turned into a museum exhibit, but has since been boxed up and put into storage. People power re-emerged in January 2001, when anger over the alleged corruption and incompetence of President Joseph Estrada, a former tough-guy movie star, led thousands to gather in the streets to demand his resignation. He was driven from Malacañang Palace and is now under arrest, facing a charge of plunder.

Despite the political intrigues and the poverty, **Filipinos** themselves remain enviably optimistic and gregarious. It has become hackneyed to describe the Philippines as the land where Asia wears a smile, but there's no denying it's true. Filipinos are an accommodating lot. Graciousness and warmth seem to be built into their genes. English is widely spoken, even in the provinces, and everywhere you go you will be greeted with the honorific "ma'am" or "sir".

Filipinos are also passionate, sometimes hot-headedly so. They love food, they love life and they love romance. The Philippines is a passion play writ large and nowhere is this more evident than in the hundreds of **fiestas** and religious ceremonies that are held every year. Some are theatrical, like the **Ati-Atihan** in Kalibo and the **Lanzones** in Camiguin. Others have their origins in the Scriptures and are solemn.

The Philippines has a tropical marine climate characterized by **two distinct seasons**: the wet season (southwest monsoon, or *habagat*) from May to October and the dry season (northeast monsoon, or *amihan*) from November to April. During the wet season, the country is hit directly by five or six typhoons and partially affected by an average of fifteen that pass close by, leaving wind and rain in their wake. This doesn't necessarily mean the wet season is a bad time to travel. Cyclonic storms are more of an inconvenience than a serious threat, with flights cancelled and roads made impassable by floodwaters, even in the capital. But they only last a few days. The first typhoon can hit as early as May, although typically it is June or July before the rains really start, with August the wettest month. The southern Visayas and Palawan are less prone to typhoons; Mindanao is below the typhoon belt and sees heavy rain during the wet season but no typhoons.

Weather bulletins are issued by the Philippine Atmospheric, Geophysical and Astronomical Service in Quezon City (☎929 6010–19), known by the abbreviation PAGASA, which also means "hope". Storm warnings range from one to four, with four being the highest. Even when storm warning one is issued, many schools and offices shut down and ferries stop sailing. Temperatures are fairly constant throughout the year. November and December are the coolest months, with daytime highs of around 28°C and pre-dawn lows of 17°C in the lowlands and a chilly 9°C in Baguio and the Cordillera. March, April and May are very hot: expect temperatures to peak at 36°C.

At Christmas and Easter, the whole of the Philippines hits the road and getting a seat on a bus or plane can be difficult. If you have to travel on public holidays, time your trip so you can leave a day before and return a day after.

Air and sea routes into the Philippines

Most major Southeast Asian airlines have regular **flights** to Ninoy Aquino International Airport in Manila, with a few also flying to Cebu City and the recently modernized international airport in Davao. All Philippines Airlines flights, both domestic and international, now use the NAIA Centennial Terminal Two, close to the existing international airport terminal. **Hong Kong** is one of the most convenient gateways to the Philippines: Cathay Pacific has five flights a day, Philippine Airlines has three and Cebu Pacific two.

Elsewhere in **Asia** and the **Pacific Rim**, there are regular flights from many major cities, including Bangkok, Tokyo, Seoul, Shanghai, Beijing, Taipei, Singapore, Kuala Lumpur, Darwin, Sydney, Melbourne and Auckland. Most major European airlines have flights to Manila; flying via the Middle East **from Europe** is also a good option, with Qatar Airways flying via Doha, Gulf Air via Bahrain and Emirates via Dubai. **From the US**, there are regular Philippine Airlines, Northwest, Continental and Continental Micronesia flights to Manila.

Five passenger **ferries** sail from Bitung in northern **Sulawesi**, Indonesia to Davao via General Santos. Many unlicensed **boats** ply back and forth between the Malaysian state of Sabah and the southern Philippines, but note that these craft are often overloaded and poorly maintained.

Entry requirements and visa extension

Most tourists do not need a visa to enter the Philippines for up to **21 days**, though a passport valid for at least six months and an onward ticket to another country are required.

You can apply for a **59-day** visa-in-advance from a Philippine embassy or consulate before you travel. A single-entry visa, valid for three months from the date of issue, costs around $35, and a multiple-entry visa, valid for one year from the date of issue, around $100. Apart from a valid passport and a completed application form (downloadable from some Philippine embassy websites, such as ⓦwww.philemb.org.uk), you will have to present proof that you have enough money for the duration of your stay in the Philippines.

Without a visa-in-advance, the 21-day stay you're granted on arrival can be extended by 38 days (giving a total stay of 59 days) at immigration offices in major cities and some key tourist destinations, or through many travel agents. The extension fee is P2200, which includes a P500 Express Lane fee, guaranteeing you get your visa within 24 hours (otherwise expect it to take at least one week, possibly longer). A subsequent extension of **three or four months** is possible at the immigration office in Manila or Cebu City. There's nothing to stop you from applying for additional extensions, though once you've stayed more than six months the bureaucracy becomes an obstacle: besides a police clearance certificate from the National Bureau of Investigation in Ermita, Manila (for which you'll be photographed and fingerprinted), you'll have to secure a Certificate of Temporary Residence (P710) and pay a legal search fee (another P710).

Airport departure tax

For international flights, Philippine airport **departure tax** is P550. There is a P100 departure tax at the domestic airport in Manila and for domestic flights leaving from Philippine Airlines' NAIA Centennial Terminal Two. Many provincial domestic airports have a nominal departure tax or "terminal fee", usually from P10 to P40.

Money and costs

The Philippine **currency** is the piso (P), although it is almost always spelt "**peso**". It is divided into 100 centavos, with bills in denominations of P10, P20, P50, P100, P200, P500 and P1000. Coins come in 25 centavos, P1, P5 and P10. The P10 and P20 notes are being phased out and replaced by coins. Most banks will not change sterling, euros or anything other than **US dollars**, although at private moneychangers in tourist areas you should be able to change major foreign currencies. Changing **travellers' cheques** can also be problematic at banks although, again, you can change them at moneychangers in major resort areas. However, if you're likely to be going off the beaten track, you should always have a ready supply of cash, in dollars and pesos; and make sure you keep small denominations of pesos handy for transport and tips. Political and economic uncertainty have combined to see the peso devalue dramatically in recent years, but the **exchange rate** has now settled at around P56 to US$1 and P100 to £1.

Visa, MasterCard and, to a lesser extent, American Express are widely accepted throughout Manila and other major cities, and also in popular tourist destinations such as Boracay. You can withdraw cash from 24-hour ATMs (in the Visa, Plus, Mastercard and Cirrus networks) in all cities and even many smaller towns. Most banks will advance cash against cards (generally Visa and MasterCard) for a commission. If you use credit cards to pay for airline tickets and hotels, there is sometimes an extra charge of around 2.5 percent. Some shops impose a credit-card supplement of six percent, so always check first.

Having money wired from home is never cheap and should be considered as a last resort. Moneygram has a few hundred agents throughout the country, usually local banks such as Bank of Commerce and Equitable PCI, while Western Union has its own branches in all major locations and many local agents, such as Allied Bank, Metrobank, Banco de Oro, and the M. Lhuillier chain of pawnshops.

It's also possible to have **money wired** directly from a bank in your home country to a bank in the Philippines, although this is somewhat less reliable because it involves two separate institutions. If you go down this route, your home bank will need the address of the bank where you want to pick up the money, and the address and telex number of the Manila head office, which will act as the clearing house. The local bank will ask you to open an account, which can be done over the counter in a matter of minutes, as long as you have two forms of identification, each bearing your picture. Money wired this way normally takes at least five working days to arrive, and the transaction costs around £25/$40. Some **banks**, such as Equitable PCI, will let you open an account and give you an ATM card for a minimum deposit of P2000.

Costs

The Philippines is about the same price as Thailand for travel. Getting around by bus is cheap, with the longest bone-crunching journeys costing less than P200, and an air ticket from Manila to Davao and back costing less than P5000, depending on who you fly with and how far in advance you book. You should be able to **get by on £8/$12 a day** if you're willing to shop around and bargain hard. In out-of-the-way places, you can live like a king for well under P1000 a day, eating fresh fish and washing it down with San Miguel beer bought from a local *sari-sari* store for P12 a bottle. When it comes to accommodation, it's always worth haggling. If a beach hut is P300 a night, ask if you can book it for five days for P200 a night. Accommodation in the provinces can still be had for as little as P100 a night, although this will invariably mean a lack of creature comforts, infrequent electricity and no hot water.

Information and maps

The Philippine **Department of Tourism** (DoT) has a small number of overseas offices, where you can pick up glossy brochures and get answers to general pre-trip questions about destinations, major hotels and domestic travel. These offices aren't so helpful, however, when it comes to information about off-the-beaten-track places. It's not their fault: there simply isn't much information about less well-known destinations in the first place. The DoT has offices throughout the Philippines, but most of them have small budgets, poorly trained staff, and very little in the way of reliable information or brochures. The best sources of up-to-date information on travelling in the Philippines are guesthouses and hotels that cater to backpackers, most of which have notice boards where travellers can swap tips and ideas. At the DoT Head Office (☎02/524 1703 or 524 2384; 24 hours, seven days a week) in Room 106 of the Department of Tourism Building, TM Kalaw Street, Ermita (on the eastern edge of Rizal Park, Manila), you can claim your free copy of the *Tourist Map of the Philippines*. This useful folding map also includes a street map of Manila, contact numbers for all overseas and domestic DoT offices, and listings of hotels, embassies and bus companies. United Tourist Promotions (☎045/322 8767) publishes a range of maps called E-Z Map, covering Manila and other destinations, such as Boracay, Baguio, Batangas, Palawan, Angeles and Davao. These are sold in many bookshops and branches of Mercury drug store for P80. The *E-Z Map Philippines Travel Atlas* is a convenient book-style atlas with various city maps, regional maps, island maps and listings, covering most of the archipelago. Road maps and country maps can be bought at National Book Store branches throughout Manila and in most provincial cities. One of the best is the *National Auto Club Street Map of Manila* (P180). You can also find them in hotel gift shops, but they sometimes cost more. Nelles Verlag publishes two good maps – a country map and a Manila map – which you can buy at home before you travel. For a good selection of detailed maps and sea charts of the Philippines, take a taxi to the National Mapping & Resources Information Authority (☎02/810 4867, 810 4831 ext 238) in Fort Bonifacio, ten minutes' from the centre of Makati, Manila.

Getting around

The number of **flights** and **ferry services** between major destinations makes it easy to cover the archipelago, even when you're on a budget. Local road transport is mostly limited to buses and jeepneys, although in cities such as Manila, Cebu City and Davao it's still relatively cheap to get around by taxi.

For an idea of journey times between major destinations, see "**Travel details**", p.883".

Planes

Air travel is a godsend for island-hoppers in the Philippines, with a number of airlines both large and small linking Manila to most of the country's major destinations. Philippines Airlines has a comprehensive domestic schedule, with all flights leaving from the new NAIA Centennial Terminal Two. Air Philippines and Cebu Pacific are newer airlines, but both have comprehensive schedules and offer slightly cheaper fares than Philippine Airlines. Asian Spirit and Southeast Asian Airlines (SEAIR) are excellent small airlines offering regular flights to major resort areas and also to interesting destinations often not served by larger airlines. Air Philippines, Cebu Pacific, Asian Spirit and SEAIR all operate out of the old domestic airport terminal.

To give you some idea of **prices**, Philippine Airlines charges US$66 one-way from Manila to Kalibo (for Boracay) if the ticket is purchased outside the Philippines. If you book the same ticket more than three days in advance, it costs $59. A ticket for the same trip booked within the Philippines costs P2908 (P5816 return). Manila to Kalibo with Cebu Pacific is P2309, and Cebu City to Davao P2039. Philippine Airlines has a Jetsetter Pass, which is a book of twelve one-way tickets between Manila and destinations in the Visayas (P26,400), or Manila and destinations in Mindanao (P31,800). The pass is valid for one year. On the Manila–Caticlan route (for Boracay), not served by the big three, the return fare with both SEAIR and Asia Spirit is P5580; Cebu City to Caticlan costs P5400, also with both SEAIR and Asian Spirit.

Buses

For Filipinos, the journey is as much a part of the experience as the destination. Nowhere is this truer than on the **buses**. Dilapidated contraptions with no air-conditioning compete with bigger bus lines with all mod cons on hundreds of routes that span out from Manila. Fares are cheap, but journeys can be long. Manila to Baguio, for instance, costs P120 on an air-conditioned bus, but takes anything up to nine hours. You might want to make this type of trip overnight, when traffic is lighter and delays less likely. The longest of long bus trips is Philtranco's Manila to Davao service. It leaves the Pasay City terminal every day at 6pm and snakes ponderously through the Bicol region, Samar, Leyte and eastern Mindanao, arriving in Davao two days later. A one-way ticket costs P1341.

Ferries

Boats are the bread and butter of Philippine travel, with wooden outrigger boats – known as bancas – and luxury ferries ready to take you from one destination to the next in varying degrees of comfort and safety. Remember that even in the dry season, the open ocean can get rough, so think carefully about using small boats that look ill-equipped or overcrowded.

Ferry disasters are not unknown, often with great loss of life. Major lines include **WG&A** and **Negros Navigation**, which have daily sailings throughout the country from Manila's North Harbour, but even these have not been accident-free. On less popular routes you might have to take your chances with smaller lines. Ferries are cheap but often crowded, although on overnight journeys you can always keep away from the dormitory crowds by sleeping on the deck. WG&A has cabins for those who want privacy and comfort. **One-way fares** on WG&A from Manila to Cebu City in tourist class are P1460, without meals. A cabin costs P1650, and a suite room P4440.

Taxis

The flag-down rate for **taxis** is P30 and P2.50 per 200m. Before you get in a taxi make sure the driver will use his meter or that you have negotiated a reasonable fare. From the Manila Bay area to the business district of Makati, the metered fare will be P100–120. Never use a taxi if the driver has companions and never use one that isn't clearly marked as a taxi. All taxi registration plates have black letters on a yellow background. Private cars and vans have white letters on a green background, so it's easy to tell the difference. You stand more chance of getting a taxi if you use them at off-peak times. Few taxi drivers will jump at the chance to take you to the airport at five o'clock on a Friday afternoon in a monsoon downpour, so you'll need to be flexible and allow yourself time. Major hotels have their own taxi services, but guests take preference and rates are higher; it's usually about P350 from the Manila Bay area to the airport.

Local transport

The stalwart of the transport system is the fabled **jeepney**, a legacy of World War II, when American soldiers left behind army jeeps; these were converted by ingenious locals into factotum vehicles, carrying everything from produce to livestock and people. Over the years, they evolved into today's colourful workhorses of the road, with their fairy lights, boomboxes and cheesy decor. In some cities, Cebu City in particular, old jeepneys are now being replaced with modern Isuzu vans, although they are still decorated in the same ostentatious manner. Jeepneys ply particular routes, indicated on the side of the vehicle. Provincial jeepneys charge as little as P2.50 a ride, while in Manila, prices range from P5 for a short hop to P20 for longer distances. Jeepneys stop anywhere, so simply flag one down and hop on. When you want to get off, bang on the roof or shout "para!"

In Manila and other cities, **Toyota FX Tamaraws** are a popular way to get around. Owners of these functional air-conditioned vehicles, which can seat up to ten passengers at a squeeze, hang signs in their windows with the name of the destination. FXs, as they are affectionately known, have become a common sight, with many office workers using them because they are cheaper than taxis and more comfortable than jeepneys or buses. The fare is set by the driver – usually P10 for a short trip and anything up to P100 on longer routes.

Tricycles are the Filipino equivalent of the Thai tuk-tuk, and while they are not allowed on major roads they can be useful for getting from a bus station to a beach and back again. Most tricycles carry four passengers, and fares tend to increase dramatically when a tourist approaches, so always reach agreement beforehand. Fares are lower, often as little as a few pesos per person, if you are willing to share the tricycle with anyone else who flags it down and can fit on board. To hire the tricycle exclusively for yourself – or for a small group of you – P50 is a reasonable fare for a ten-minute journey.

Vehicle rental

It's easy and relatively cheap to **rent a self-drive car** in the Philippines. The question is whether or not you would want to. Most Filipino drivers seem to have a very relaxed attitude towards the rules of the road. Swerving is common, as is changing lanes suddenly and driving with one hand permanently on the horn, particularly for bus and jeepney drivers. The demands of time and traffic make many drivers belligerent and aggressive, so if you do rent a car you'll require nerve and patience. If you need to get somewhere quickly and have money to spare, you can always hire a **car with a**

Addresses

It's common in the Philippines for buildings to give an **address** as 122 Legaspi cor. Velasco Streets. This means the place you are looking for is at the junction of Legaspi Street and Velasco Street. Streets are sometimes renamed in honour of new heroes or because old heroes have been discredited or boundaries moved. Pasay Road in Makati is now Arnaiz Avenue, but confusingly everyone still calls it Pasay Road. The ground floor of multi-storey buildings is referred to as the first floor and the first floor as the second. Buildings do not have a 13th floor; it is considered unlucky.

driver for about P2000 a day, depending on distance (plus a tip for the driver if he gets you there in one piece). Major car rental firms are listed in the *Yellow Pages* under "Automobile Renting and Leasing". They include Avis (Ⓣ02/525 2206), Budget (Ⓣ02/831 8256) and Filcar (Ⓣ02/843 3530). In Malate, try Kei Transport Corporation in the lobby of the *Palm Plaza Hotel* at the junction of Pedro Gil and Adriatico (Ⓣ02/524 6834, fax 526 1210). Self-driven cars start from P1400 a day. Hiring a small van for day trips is also possible for small groups. A van big enough for around eight people will cost about P4000 a day.

Accommodation

There is **accommodation** for all budgets in the Philippines, from swanky private resorts where Hollywood stars chill out, to humble huts on a stretch of deserted beach. On the outlying islands you can find nipa huts, made from indigenous palms, ranging in price from P250 for a simple room with a shower to P1000 for something a bit more refined with air-con or fan. The top-end luxury resorts charge up to US$350 a night.

In the poorer areas of the country there is no running **water**. Even in the rich enclaves of Manila you'll find that water can be a problem. The water authorities pump water only twice a day into residential areas – many households save it in a purpose-built tank with a small electric pump attached so they can use it when they need it. Households without tanks often keep water in a large plastic dustbin and shower by scooping it over their heads with a plastic scoop known as a *tabo*. In the provinces, this is the normal way to bathe.

Electricity is usually supplied at 220 volts, although you may come across 110 volts. Plugs are two pins, with the pins flat and rectangular, as opposed to round. Power cuts ("brownouts") are common, especially in the more rural areas. If you use valuable electrical appliances in the Philippines – a laptop computer, for instance – always use an automatic voltage regulator (AVR). This is a small appliance, available in all department stores, that ensures the voltage to your computer remains constant even if there is a sudden fluctuation or surge in power. Without one, your hard disk could be irreparably damaged. AVRs cost around P2000 and are heavy, so it's probably not worth buying; ask your hotel if you can borrow one.

Food and drink

The high esteem in which Filipinos hold their **food** is encapsulated by the common greeting "Let's eat!", Filipino cuisine has not been accepted worldwide as Indian or Thai food have, perhaps because it has an unwarranted reputation for being one of Asia's less adventurous cuisines, offering a relatively bland meat and rice diet with little variety or spice. But those willing to experiment will find even the most simple rural dishes can offer an intriguing blend of the familiar and the exotic. Trying the local fare is also a good way for travellers to be inducted into the culture: visitors who are willing to eat *balut* (an allegedly aphrodisiac duck embryo) or *bagoong* (a smelly, salty fish paste) gain instant admiration. Food is something of a comfort blanket for Filipinos and to be without it is cause for panic. Any Filipino who eats only three meals a day is usually considered unwell because that's simply not considered enough. A healthy appetite is seen as a sign of a robust constitution and sundry smaller meals and snacks – *merienda* – are eaten in between every meal. Not to partake when offered can be considered rude.

Filipino food is undergoing something of a nationalist revival, with intellectuals and cookery writers espousing the virtues of traditional home-and-hearth dishes. The cuisine is an intriguing mixture of the familiar and the exotic. Coconut, soy sauce, vinegar and *patis* (a brown fish sauce, more watery than *bagoong*) are widely used to add flavour. Colonization and migration have resulted in touches of Malay, Chinese, Spanish and, more recently, American culinary influence, sometimes all within the same meal.

Meat dishes, notably of chicken and pork (both cheap and easily available), form the bulk of the Filipino diet. The **national dish**, if there is one, is *adobo*, which is chicken or pork (or both) cooked in soy sauce and vinegar, with pepper and garlic. *Baboy* (pig) is the basis of many coveted dishes such as *pata* (pig's knuckle) and *sisig*. At special celebrations, Filipinos are passionate about their *lechon*, roasted pig stuffed with pandan (screwpine) leaves and cooked so the skin turns to crackling. *Lechon de leche* is roasted suckling pig. Pork is also the basis of Bicol Express (the most well known of the very few spicy local dishes), consisting of pork ribs cooked in coconut milk, soy sauce and vinegar, with hot chillies (a vegetable version is also available).

The **beer** of choice in the Philippines is San Miguel, but with meals many Filipinos tend to stick to soft drinks such as iced tea. Fresh *buko* (coconut) juice is a refreshing alternative on a hot day. If you fancy something stronger, there are plenty of cheap Philippine-made spirits such as Tanduay rum and San Miguel *ginebra* (gin). For something authentically native, try the strong and pungent *tapuy* (rice wine). *Lambanog* is another potent spirit, made by gathering sap from coconut trees and fermenting it with fruit in a hole in the ground.

Communications

Letters from the Philippines take at least five days to reach other countries by air, sometimes significantly longer. If you have to post anything valuable, use registered mail or pay the extra for a reliable courier. Letters sent in the general post are sometimes rifled and the contents stolen. For incoming mail, major post offices in Manila have a counter for **poste restante**. See "Basics" p.63 for general advice on poste restante.

The country's **telephone** system has made great advances, although outside urban centres it can still be temperamental. Public **payphones** are not common outside big cities; the best place to find them is in malls (where there are often long queues to use them) and hotel lobbies. They either take P1 and P5 coins or, in the case of Philippine Long-Distance Telephone (PLDT) payphones, PLDT cards, known as **Fonkards**. These are available in P100, P200, P300 and P500 denominations and can be bought from hotels or convenience stores such as 7/11. A typical **long-distance domestic call** costs P4 from a payphone during the off-peak hours of 7pm–7am and all day Sunday, or P5 a minute at other times.

Rates for **International domestic calls** (IDD) are fixed and charged in US dollars by the "pulse", equivalent to six seconds. As an indication of charges from a landline or payphone, the first minute of a call to Australia or the UK costs around 19 cents, while each subsequent pulse costs around 15 cents. Calls are twenty percent cheaper 9pm–8am and all day Sunday. Accommodation in rural areas may allow only local calls to be dialled from the premises. If you want to make other calls, you'll have to ask the operator to connect you and reverse the charges. To **call abroad** from the Philippines, dial ☎00 + IDD country code + area code (minus the first 0) + number. The international operator is ☎108. PLDT also has a service for making overseas collect calls. If you dial ☎105 plus the country access code, you'll be connected to the operator of the country you are calling. These calls can be billed to your credit card.

The Philippines has embraced the **mobile-phone** age with vigour, partly because sending text messages is cheap and because mobile networks provide coverage in areas where landlines are limited. If you want to use a cellular phone bought abroad

Food and drink glossary

General terms and requests

Rice — *Bigas* (the uncooked grain) or *kanin* (cooked)

I'm vegetarian — *Vegetarian ako* or *gulay lang ang kinakain ko* (literally, "I only eat vegetables")

Can I see the menu? — *Patingin ng menu*?

I would like... — *Gusto ko*...

With/without — *Meron/wala*

Delicious — *Sarap*

Hot (spicy) — *Maanghang*

Can I have the bill please? — *Puwede kunin ang check?*

To split the cost — *KKB* (from *kanya-kanyang bayad*; literally, "each his own pays")

Main dishes

Adobo — Chicken and/or pork simmered in soy sauce and vinegar, with pepper and garlic

Beef tapa — Beef marinated in vinegar, sugar and garlic, then dried in the sun and fried

Bicol Express — Fiery dish of pork ribs cooked in coconut milk, soy sauce, vinegar, *bagoong* and hot chillies

Bistek tagalog — Beef tenderloin with *calamansi* and onion

Bulalo — Beef shank in onion broth

Daing na bangus — *Bangus* marinated in vinegar and spices, then fried

Diniguan — Pork cubes simmered in pig's blood, with garlic, onion and laurel leaves

Gambas — Shrimps sautéed in chilli and garlic sauce

Kare-kare — Rich oxtail stew with aubergine, peanut and banana heart

Lechon (de leche) — Roast whole (suckling) pig, dipped in a liver-paste sauce

Longganisa/longganiza — Small beef or pork sausages, with lots of garlic

Longsilog — *Longganisa* with garlic rice and fried egg

Pinakbet — Vegetable stew with *bagoong*, cooked in broth, often with small pieces of meat added

Sisig — Fried chopped pork, liver and onions

Tapsilog — Beef *tapa* with garlic rice and fried egg

Tinola — Tangy soup with chicken, papaya and ginger

Tocino — Marinated fried pork

Tosilog — Marinated fried pork with garlic rice and fried egg

Vegetables (*gulay*)

Adobong kang kong — *Kangkong* cooked *adobo*-style, in vinegar and soy sauce, with lots of garlic

Bicol Express — Vegetables cooked with coconut milk, soy sauce, vinegar, hot chillies and a dash of *bagoong*

Laing — Taro leaves cooked in coconut milk

Pechay — Chinese cabbage, sometimes spelled *petsay* or *pitsay*; also known as *bok choi* or *pak choi*

Noodles and egg-roll dishes

Lumpia — Egg rolls, filled with vegetables and sometimes meat

Lumpia ubod — Egg rolls filled with palm hearts

Mami — Noodle soup

Pancit — Noodles

Pancit bihon — Thin vermicelli rice noodles with shrimp and vegetable

Pancit canton — Thick rice noodles with shrimp and vegetable

Snacks (*merienda*) and street food

Adidas — Chicken's feet; named after the sports-shoe manufacturer, they're served on a stick with a choice of sauces for dipping

Arroz caldo Rice porridge with chicken
Balut Raw, half-formed duck embryo
Camote Sweet potato fried with brown sugar, or boiled and served with a pat of butter
Chicheron Fried pork skin, served with a vinegar dip
Dilis Dried anchovies, eaten whole and dipped in vinegar as a bar snack, or added to vegetable stews
Ensaimada Sweet cheese rolls
Fish balls, squid balls Mashed fish or squid, blended with wheat flour and deep fried; served on a stick with a sweet sauce
Taho Mushy confection of mashed bean curd, caramel and tapioca; a popular breakfast on-the-move, it's sold by vendors who carry it in canisters over their shoulders
Tokneneng Hard-boiled *balut* covered in orange dough and deep-fried while you wait

Fruit (*fruitas*)

Atis Custard apple
Balimbin Starfruit (aka *carambola*)
Buko Coconut
Calamansi Lime
Guayabano Soursop (large, oval fruit with knobbly spines outside and fragrant flesh inside)
Kaimito Star apple (plum-coloured and round, about the size of a tennis ball, with leathery skin and soft white pulp inside)
Langka Jackfruit
Lanzones Outside, the size and colour of a small potato; inside, sweet, translucent flesh with a bitter seed
Mangga Mango (available in sweet and sour varieties)
Pakwan Watermelon
Papaya Papaya
Piña Pineapple

Desserts

Bibingka Cake made of ground rice, sugar and coconut milk, baked in a clay stove and served hot with fresh, salted duck's eggs on top
Halo-halo Sweet concoction made from ice cream, crushed ice, jelly, beans and tinned milk; the name literally means "mix-mix"
Leche flan Caramel custard
Puto bumbong Glutinous rice steamed in a bamboo tube, infusing it with a delicate, woody taste; lilac colouring gives it a distinctive purple sheen
Saging Banana (dozens of varieties, from the cooking banana *sabo* to finger-like *senoritas* and red-skinned *morado*)
Sago at nata de coco Blend of sago and coconut served cold in a glass
Suman Sweet and sticky rice cake served inside a banana leaf

Drinks (*inumin*)

Alak Wine (though in practice, everyone just says "wine")
Beer Beer
Buko juice Coconut water
Calamansi juice/soda *Calamansi* juice taken either cold – by adding soda – or hot – by adding boiled water and a touch of honey
Chocolate-eh Thick hot chocolate
Gatas Milk
Ginebra Gin
Juice Juice
Kape Coffee
Rum Rum; the cheap, popular Tanduay has become almost synonymous with rum, so you could just ask for Tanduay and coke
Tapuy Rice wine
Tsa Tea
Tubig Water

Useful numbers

☎ **108** International operator
☎ **109** Assistance with long-distance domestic calls
☎ **112** Check an area code within the Philippines
☎ **114** Nationwide directory assistance

in the Philippines, you'll need a GSM/Triband phone and before you leave home you'll need to make sure the global roaming service is activated as well as checking charges for making and receiving calls. Another way of getting mobile access in the Philippines is to buy a local SIM (subscriber identity module) card, available at dozens of mobile-phone outlets in malls for any of the country's three mobile networks: Smart, Globe and Sun Cellular. Costing just P150–170, the card makes your home mobile a member of a local network, but you'll need to make sure before you travel that your phone isn't locked to you local network and have it unlocked if needed. Once you've inserted your local SIM card, you can buy prepaid cards, which come in units of P300 and P500, to make calls. Standard-rate domestic calls from mobiles cost from P6 a minute; there are no charges for receiving calls. There are card outlets and dispensing machines in malls and convenience stores, and at airports.

Basic mobiles in the Philippines are inexpensive, starting at less than P3000, so it can be worth buying one if you plan to stay for any length of time and need to keep in touch. Unless you have a permanent address in the country for home billing, you'll be funding your calls with prepaid cards.

Internet cafés are springing up all over Manila, and an increasing number of the more popular resorts and dive centres have email facilities you can use for a small charge.

Time differences

The Philippines is eight hours ahead of London (GMT), twelve hours ahead of New York, sixteen hours ahead of Los Angeles, two hours behind Sydney and four hours behind Auckland.

Opening hours and festivals

Most **government offices** are open Monday to Friday 8.30am–5.30pm. Businesses generally keep the same hours, with some also open for half a day on Saturday from 9am until noon. **Post offices** in major cities are open Monday to Friday 8.30am–5.30pm. Off the beaten track, the hours are less regular. **Banks** open Monday to Friday 9am–3pm, while **shops** in major shopping centres are generally open 10am–8pm, seven days a week.

Festivals

Every year, hundreds of **fiestas** are celebrated in the Philippines, and it's worth timing your journey to see one of the major ones. It's at these festivals that you get a chance to see legendary Filipino hospitality at its best. The beer flows, pigs are roasted and there's dancing in the streets for days on end. More solemn fiestas, usually religious in nature, are a mixture of devotion, drama, passion and reaffirmation of faith. The **crucifixions** held every Good Friday in Pampanga draw tourists who come to see penitents being flogged then nailed to a cross. Other major festivals include the **Ati-Atihan** (every third week of January in Kalibo), the **Flores de Mayo** (held throughout May in honour of the Virgin Mary), and the **Lanzones** festival

Public holidays

January 1 New Year's Day
February 25 Anniversary of the Overthrow of Marcos
April 9 Bataan Day
Maundy Thursday
Good Friday
May 1 Labour Day
June 12 Independence Day
November 1 All Saints' Day
November 30 Bonifacio Day
Mid-December (moveable) Aidilfitri, end of Ramadan
December 25 Christmas Day
December 26 Public Holiday
December 30 Rizal Day

(every October in Camiguin, celebrating the island's favourite fruit).

Entertainment and sport

Entertainment in the Philippines is synonymous with **live music**. Everyone is a singer or a musician, from the humblest farmer to the richest politician. Bands play in the seediest bars and the ritziest hotels, while popular local groups like The Mongols and Barbie's Cradle grace MTV Asia and give regular concerts in clubs and malls. Filipinos are Asia's troubadours, so you won't have to go far to find live entertainment, whether your taste is for sultry lounge singers or hard rock.

Filipinos are enamoured of America and love the **cinema**. Standard fare in the Philippines is either the Hollywood blockbuster or the Pinoy (slang for "Filipino") blockbuster. You won't find much in the way of alternative cinema. Pinoy films usually have plots revolving around love, violence, sex or all three. Seeing a film in the Philippines isn't always a memorable experience because of the bizarre ticket system. You can't usually book a specific seat in advance, so you have to turn up and take potluck. Limitless tickets are sold, so you might end up standing at the back or sitting in an aisle. To make matters worse, films are screened continuously and you can enter the cinema at any time. All this makes for an endless number of disturbances that can drive even the most patient film lover to distraction. If you want to see a film in Manila, try the cinemas at Greenbelt and Rockwell, both in Makati. For certain showings they offer guaranteed seats, which means you can watch in peace. Tickets cost P120. For more on the cinema industry in the Philippines, see p.768.

By far the number one sport – again thanks to America – is **basketball**, with two hugely popular leagues playing games throughout the country. Matches in Manila are played at the Cuneta Astrodome on Roxas Boulevard.

Cockfighting might not be everyone's idea of fun, but there's no denying its part of the Filipino psyche. National hero Jose Rizal said Filipino men love their roosters more than their children, and sometimes it seems he wasn't far wrong. Cockfights take place every Sunday in barangays (villages) throughout the archipelago, with farmers winning (or losing) the equivalent of a week's wages in what amounts to a two-minute explosion of feathers and blood. In Manila, there are highly publicized "cock derbies" on which thousands, sometimes millions, of pesos are wagered. The capital also sees regular cockfights at the Roligon cockpit in Pasay and occasional "mega-derbies" at the Araneta Coliseum in Cubao, also known as the Big Dome.

Outdoor activities

The Philippines' third-world status has limited most people's exposure to the kind of leisure activities that are taken for granted in the West. Facilities are poor, and for rural families there are more important considerations than sporting excellence. That said, even the most isolated barangay has some sort of rudimentary basketball court where villagers gather to play in the cool of the late afternoon. **Trekking** is becoming popular among young professionals, with a number of clubs organizing regular trips up famous peaks such as Mount Apo, Mount Pulag and Mayon Volcano. Among the more active ones are Ayala Mountaineers, the Association of Philippine Mountaineers (☎02/922 5760), the Metropolitan Mountaineers Society (☎02/850 3337) and Tropang Kubaw (☎02/800 4062). These clubs organize regular trips and may be willing to take you along. Caving, rock climbing, kayaking and mountain biking are all developing a respectable following. Surfing is also taking off, with major international competitions held regularly in Siargao, northeast Mindanao.

Scuba diving

Of the two million tourists who visit the Philippines every year, many come for the **scuba diving**. It's hardly surprising that in a nation made up of 7107 islands there are dive sites all over the place, with the exception perhaps of the far north. Two hours from Manila by road, you can dive on the reefs of **Anilao** in the province of Batangas. An hour

Major festivals

January to February

Feast of the Black Nazarene (Jan 9) Quiapo, Manila. Devotees gather in the plaza outside Quiapo Church to touch a miraculous image of Christ.

Coconut Festival (Jan 11–15) San Pablo, Laguna. Grand mardi-gras procession to pay homage to the area's most ubiquitous crop.

Sinulog (Third Sun in Jan) Cebu City. The second city's biggest annual event, in honour of its patron saint, Santo Niño. Huge street parade, live music and plenty of food and drink.

Ati-Atihan (Third week of Jan) Kalibo, Aklan province. Street dancing and wild costumes at arguably the biggest festival in the country, held to celebrate an ancient land pact between settlers and indigenous Atis.

Dinagyang (Fourth week of Jan) Iloilo City, Panay Island. Relatively modern festival based on the Ati-Atihan and including a parade on the Iloilo River.

Pamulinawen (First two weeks in Feb) Laoag. City-wide fiesta in honour of St William the Hermit. Events include street parties, beauty pageants, concerts and religious parades.

Baguio Flower Festival (Third week in Feb) Baguio. The summer capital's largest annual event includes parades of floats beautifully decorated with flowers from the Cordillera region. There are also flower-related lectures and exhibitions.

March to May

Moriones (Easter weekend) Marinduque. A celebration of the life of the Roman centurion Longinus, who was blind in one eye. Legend says that when he pierced Christ's side with his spear, blood spurted into his eye and cured him.

Pasayaw Festival (Third week of March) Canlaon, Negros. Thanksgiving festival to God and St Joseph, with twelve barangays competing for honours in an outdoor dancing competition. The final "dance-off" is held in the city gym.

Allaw Ta Apo Sandawa (Second week of April) Kidapawan, North Cotabato. Gathering of highland tribes to pay respects to the sacred Mount Apo.

Flores de Mayo (Throughout May) Countrywide. Religious procession celebrating the coming of the rains, with girls dressed as the various "Accolades of our Lady", including Faith, Hope and Charity. Processions are sometimes held after dark and lit by candles, a lovely sight.

from Batangas City by ferry is the hugely popular area around **Puerto Galera**, home to many dive schools and fine beaches. Around the **Visayas** in the central Philippines are Boracay, Apo Island (near Dumaguete), Cebu and Bohol. A one-hour flight or twelve-hour ferry journey from the capital takes you to the "last frontier" of **Palawan**, where you can dive at World War II Japanese wrecks in the company of dolphins and manta rays. On the southernmost island of Mindanao, there is excellent diving around **Davao** and on the northeast coast at laid-back **Siargao Island**. **Tubbataha Reef** in the Sulu Sea offers some of the best diving in the world, but the only way you can reach it is by live-aboard from Puerto Princesa. In short, you can slip into a wet suit just about anywhere.

The Professional Association of Dive Instructors, better known as **PADI**, organizes most scuba tuition in the Philippines. Always pick a PADI dive centre and ask to see their certification. If you haven't been diving before, you can start with a "Discovery Dive" to see if you like it. The full PADI Open Water Diver course takes around four days and costs around US$300. You might want to consider doing a referral course with PADI at home, which involves doing the pool sessions and written tests before you travel, then doing the final checkout dives with a PADI resort in the Philippines. It saves time and means you don't have to slave over homework in the tropical heat. You'll need to bring your PADI referral documents with you, as your instructor in the Philippines will want to see them.

Carabao Carroza (May 3–4) Iloilo City, Panay Island. Races held to celebrate the humble *carabao* (water buffalo), beast of burden for many a provincial farmer.
Carabao Festival (May 14–15) Pulilian, Bulacan Province and Angono, Rizal Province. Thanksgiving for a good harvest, with *carabao* parades and races.
Pahiyas (May 15) Lucban, Quezon; also celebrated in the nearby towns of Candelaria, Tayabas, Sariaya, Tiaong and Lucena. Colourful harvest festival that sees houses gaily decorated with fruit and vegetables. It's held in honour of San Isidro Labrador, the patron saint of farmers.
Obando Fertility Rites (May 17–19) Obando Bulacan. On the feast day of San Pascual, women gather in the churchyard to chant prayers asking for children.

June to September

Kadayawan sa Davao (Third week of Aug) Davao. Week-long harvest festival with civic parades, military parades, street dances and horsefighting.
Peñafrancia Fluvial Festival (Third Sat in Sept) Naga, Camarines Sur. A sacred statue of Our Lady of Peñafrancia, the patron saint of the Bicol region, is paraded through the streets, then taken on board a candlelit pagoda and sailed down the Bicol River back to its shrine.

October to December

Ibalong (Third week of Oct) Legaspi City and throughout the Bicol region. Epic dances and street presentations portraying Bicol's mythical superheroes and gods.
Kansilay (October 19 or closest weekend) Silay City. Modern festival commemorating Silay's charter day. Eating and drinking contests, beauty pageants and an elaborate street parade.
Lanzones festival (Third week of Oct) Lambajao, Camiguin. Vibrant and good-natured outdoor party giving thanks for the island's lanzone crop.
Masskara (Third week of Oct) Bacolod, Negros Occidental. Modern festival conceived in 1980 to promote the city. Festivities kick off with food fairs, mask-making contests, brass-band competitions, beauty and talent pageants, a windsurfing regatta and so forth. The climax is a mardi-gras-style parade, where revellers don elaborate mask and costumes and dance to Latin rhythms Rio de Janeiro-style.

Cultural hints

Filipinos are outgoing people who are not afraid to ask **personal questions** and certainly don't consider it rude. Prepare to be interrogated by everyone you meet. Filipinos will want to know where you are from; why you are in the Philippines; how old you are; whether you are married; if not, why not; and so on and so forth. They pride themselves on their hospitality and are always ready to share a meal or a few drinks. Don't offend them by refusing outright.

A sense of *delicadeza* is also important to Filipinos. This is what you might refer to as propriety, a simple sense of good behaviour, particularly in the presence of elders or women. Filipinos who don't speak good English will often answer any question you ask them with a smile and a nod. Be careful: a smile and a nod doesn't always mean "yes". It can also mean "no", "maybe" or "I have no idea what you are talking about". Colonization by America left its mark on the national psyche, so don't be offended if everyone in the provinces thinks you are a *kano*. Protestations that you are from Britain, France or Australia will often be greeted with the response, "Is that in America?"

It's not advisable to **lose your temper** in the Philippines. Filipinos hate to be embarrassed in front of others and the culture of revenge is strong, so you might end up being the one that is sorry. The general rule is to behave in a manner conducive to what the locals refer to as "SID", or smooth interpersonal relationships.

Filipinos share the same attitudes to **dress** as other Southeast Asian countries; see "Cultural hints", p.68 for details.

Crime and safety

The Philippines is a **safe** place to travel as long as you exercise discretion and common sense. There are a number of insurgent groups in the Philippines fighting for causes that range from an independent Muslim homeland in Mindanao to communist rule, and there have been isolated cases of tourists being kidnapped in the west and far southwest areas of Mindanao, sometimes with tragic consequences. For updates on the situation, you can check foreign ministry, state department and embassy websites.

You'll find the same con artists and hustlers here that you'll find anywhere else, but most Filipinos are friendly and helpful. One of the most common scams is for foreigners to be approached by well-dressed young men or women who offer to buy you a coffee or a beer. The next day you wake up from a deep drug-induced sleep to find you have been relieved of your personal belongings. In the Malate area of Manila there is a gang known as the Ativan Gang, who use Ativan – the brand name for the drug Lorazepam – to make their victims drowsy or put them to sleep. In most tourist areas it is best to be suspicious of well turned-out people who offer to buy you drinks. There have also been cases reported in Intramuros and Baguio.

Another gang at work in the Malate area is the Kotong Gang (*kotong* is street slang for "rip-off") whose apparently friendly members approach you on the street and offer high exchange rates for changing money before short changing you and disappearing. Never change money in this manner, however tempting the exchange rate and friendly the person who approaches you.

Snatching mobile telephones – often while the owner is making a call – has become a problem, so try to make calls in safe places such as shops and restaurants, not on dark street corners. A number of Western men have also fallen into the so-called "honey-trap", finding themselves charged with serious crimes such as rape by local "girlfriends". Needless to say, the charges are quickly dropped once a substantial amount of money is handed over, but not before the victim has languished for a while in some grim local jail.

Police in the Philippines are not Asia's finest. Successive governments have made some headway in cleaning up the force, but it is still plagued by accusations of corruption, collusion and an alleged willingness to shoot first and ask questions later. Part of the problem is the low pay police officers receive. New recruits receive the equivalent of US$140 a month, considerably less than the $310 the government says is needed to feed a family of six. This makes some of them – a tiny minority, according to senior officers – willing to supplement their income with payoffs from anyone from the humblest motorist to the most notorious drug king.

Medical care and emergencies

There are **pharmacies** everywhere in the Philippines, so if you have a minor ailment and need to buy medicine over the counter, finding one should not be a problem. The biggest chain is Mercury, which has branches all over the place, but even the smallest village tends to have some sort of store where you can buy the basics.

Emergency phone numbers

The 24-hour number for **emergency services** (police, fire and ambulance) throughout the Philippines is ☎166, but it doesn't always work in the provinces, where ambulances and fire stations are few and far between. Even in Manila the emergency services are not known for their efficiency. In Manila, a ☎117 hotline is open for all emergencies, staffed 24 hours a day. Other emergency numbers include police and fire (☎757) and 24-hour tourist police (☎116).

In Manila and other major tourist centres, **hospitals** are reasonably well equipped and staffed by English-speaking doctors. Hotels and resorts sometimes have their own doctor on duty, or can at least point you in the direction of a local clinic. In case of serious illness you will need to be evacuated, either to Manila or your home country, so make sure you have arranged health insurance before you leave home (see p.50). Remember that if you are hospitalized in the Philippines, you won't be allowed to leave the hospital until the bill is settled.

History

Filipinos have often been accused of not having a sense of history and even of not knowing who they really are, a result perhaps of the many diverse influences – Malay, Chinese, European, American – that have collided randomly down the centuries.

In reality, human fossil remains found in Palawan suggest the country's "modern" history goes back nearly 50,000 years, when humans first migrated across land bridges formed to mainland Asia and Borneo during the Ice Age. The islands were eventually inhabited by different groups, the first of which was the Aeta or **Negritos**, a tribe that arrived around 25,000 years ago from the Asian continent. Many historians believe the Negritos are the true aboriginal inhabitants of the Philippines.

Archeological evidence, such as that discovered at Tabon Caves in Palawan, shows a rich **pre-colonial culture** that included skills in weaving, shipbuilding, mining and goldsmithing. Contact with Asian neighbours dates back to at least 500 BC, in the form of trade with the powerful Hindu empires in Java and Sumatra. Trade ties with China were extensive by the tenth century, while commerce with Arab traders reached its peak in the twelfth century. In 1380, the Arab scholar Makdam arrived in the Sulu Islands, and in 1475, the Muslim leader Sharif Mohammed Kabungsuwan, from Johore, married a native princess and declared himself the first sultan of Mindanao. By the time the Spaniards arrived, Islam was well established in Mindanao, and had started to influence groups as far north as Luzon.

Spanish rule

The country's turbulent modern history began on April 24, 1521, when Ferdinand Magellan, a Portuguese seafarer in the service of Spain, arrived in Cebu and claimed the islands for **Spain**. Days later he waded ashore on nearby Mactan Island with 48 men in full armour and was promptly killed in a skirmish with warriors led by chief Lapu-Lapu.

It wasn't until 1565 that serious Spanish colonization of the archipelago began. **Miguel Lopez de Legaspi** left Spain with orders from King Philip II to conquer the islands. He duly did so, establishing a colony in Bohol and then moving on to Cebu, where he erected the first Spanish fort in the Philippines. The conquest moved further north in 1571, when Legaspi conquered Manila and a year later the whole country. He never managed to bring the Islamic Sulu Islands and Mindanao under Spanish control, but felt nevertheless that he had done his job well and left for home with a cargo of cinnamon.

In his absence, the Spanish conquistadors and friars zealously set about building churches and propagating Catholicism. The British managed to occupy Manila for a few months in 1762, but handed it back to Spain under the conditions of the Treaty of Paris, signed in 1763.

With the opening of the Suez Canal in 1869, young Filipinos left their country to study in Europe and returned with liberal ideas and talk of freedom. A small revolt in Cavite in 1872 was quickly put down, but the anger and frustration Filipinos felt about colonial rule would not go away. Intellectuals such as Marcelo H del Pilar and Juan Luna were the spiritual founders of the burgeoning independence movement, but it was the critical writings of a diminutive young doctor from Laguna province, **Jose Rizal**, that provided the spark. His novel *Noli Me Tangere* (Touch Me Not) was written while he was studying in Spain, and portrayed colonial rule as a cancer and the Spanish friars as unscrupulous and depraved. It was promptly banned by the Spanish, but distributed underground along with other inflammatory essays by Rizal and, later, his second novel, *El Filibusterismo*.

In 1892, Rizal returned to Manila and founded the reform movement **Liga Filipina**. He was arrested four days later and exiled to Mindanao. Andres Bonifacio took over the reins by establishing the secret society known as the Katipunan, or KKK. In August, 1896, the armed struggle for independence broke out, and Rizal was arrested as he tried to escape to Cuba and accused of masterminding it. He was found guilty at a sham trial and executed by firing squad in what is now known as Rizal Park on December 30, 1896. The night before he died he wrote *Mi Ultimo Adios*, a valedictory poem to the country he loved.

The US

News of Rizal's martyrdom inflamed the uprising ignited by Bonifacio. Spanish officials deluded themselves, blaming it on a few troublemakers, but by now Bonifacio had decided violence was the only option and, with the young firebrand general, Emilio Aguinaldo, he called openly for a government "like that of the United States". In 1897, when it became clear they were facing all-out insurrection, the Spanish negotiated a truce with Aguinaldo, who had by now declared himself generalissimo, fallen out with Bonifacio, and had a kangaroo court condemn him to death.

In 1898, as a result of a dispute over Cuba, war broke out between the **US** and Spain, and as an extension of it the US decided to expel Spain from the Philippines. The Spanish fleet was soundly beaten in Manila Bay. The Filipinos fought on the side of the US, and when the battle was over General Aguinaldo declared the Philippines independent. The US, however, had other ideas and paid Spain US$20 million for its former possession. Having got rid of one colonizing power, Filipinos were now answering to another.

The **Filipino–American War** that followed lasted for more than ten years, resulting in the death of more than 600,000 Filipinos. This little-known war has been described as the "first Vietnam". US troops used tactics they would later employ in Vietnam, such as strategic hamleting and a scorched-earth policy, to pacify locals. The war officially ended on July 4, 1902, but it wasn't until 1935 that a bill was passed in Washington allowing President Roosevelt to recognize a new Philippine constitution, making the Philippines a commonwealth of the US. Presidential Elections were held in September of that year and won by **Manuel Quezon**, who became the first president of the Commonwealth of the Philippines.

World War II

The Philippines, especially Manila, underwent heavy bombardment during **World War II** and casualties were high. Japanese troops landed on Luzon and conquered Manila on January 2, 1942. MacArthur and Quezon abandoned Corregidor, the tiny island in the heart of Manila Bay that had been used as the American base, when it became clear the situation was hopeless, but after arriving in Darwin, Australia, MacArthur promised Filipinos "I have come through and

I shall return". Presidential advisers later suggested he revise the wording of his famous statement to "We shall return", so the rest of the army and the White House could bathe in his reflected glory. He refused. MacArthur later said of Corregidor: "It needs no epitaph from me. It has sounded its own story at the mouth of its guns."

When he fled, MacArthur left behind soldiers engaged in a protracted and bloody struggle for Bataan, west of Manila. When the peninsula inevitably fell to Japanese forces, Corregidor was next. The Japanese launched an all-out assault on May 5, 1942, and the island, defended by starving and demoralized troops huddled in damp tunnels, capitulated within days. During the notorious Bataan Death March that followed, as many as 10,000 Americans and Filipinos died from disease, malnutrition and wanton brutality.

MacArthur duly kept his promise, wading ashore at Leyte and recapturing the archipelago from retreating Japanese forces. The Philippines was granted full **independence** from the US on July 4, 1946, when Manuel Roxas was sworn in as the first president of the republic.

The Marcos years

Ferdinand Edralin Marcos (1917–1989) was born in Sarrat, Ilocos Norte. A brilliant young lawyer who had successfully defended himself against a murder charge, he was elected to the Philippine House of Representatives in 1949 and to the Senate in 1959. Promoting himself as a force for unification and reform amidst the corruption that had defined Philippines politics during the postwar period, Marcos was elected president in 1965. His first term was innovative and inspirational. He invigorated both populace and bureaucracy, embarking on a huge infrastructure programme and unifying scattered islands with a network of roads, bridges, railways and ports.

Marcos was the first Filipino President to be re-elected for a **second term**. The country's problems, however, were grave. Poverty, social inequality and rural stagnation were rife. The country, chiefly Manila, was roiled by student, labour and peasant unrest, much of it stoked by communists. Marcos used the protests, and the excuse of several spurious attempts to liquidate him, to perpetuate his hold on power. On September 21, 1972, he declared **martial law**, arresting Senator Ninoy Aquino and other opposition leaders.

By the spring of 1980, **Aquino** had been languishing in jail for seven years, but was released on condition he went into exile in the US. In 1983, he decided to return, and when he emerged from his plane at Manila Airport on August 21, 1983, was assassinated. The country was outraged. At a snap election called in panic by Marcos on February 7, 1986, the opposition united behind Aquino's widow, Cory. On February 25, both Marcos and Cory claimed victory and were sworn in at separate ceremonies. Cory became a rallying point for change and was backed by the Catholic Church, in the form of Archbishop Jaime Cardinal Sin, who urged the people to take to the streets. Ferdinand and Imelda fled from Malacañang Palace to Clark Air Base in helicopters provided by the CIA, and from there into exile in Hawaii, where Ferdinand died in 1989. Conservative estimates of their plunder put the figure at $10 billion, $600 million of it spirited away into Swiss bank accounts.

The return of democracy

The presidency of **Cory Aquino** was plagued by problems because she never managed to bring the powerful feudal families or the armed forces under her control. **Land reform** was eagerly awaited by the country's landless masses, but when Aquino realized this would also include her own family's haciendas in Tarlac, she quietly shelved the idea. She survived seven coup attempts and made little headway in improving life for the majority of Filipinos who were – and still are – living below the poverty line. The communist **New People's Army** (NPA) emerged once again as a threat, as it had during the excesses of the later Marcos years, and human rights abuses continued.

Aquino's only legacy was that she maintained some semblance of a democracy, which was something for her successor, Fidel Ramos, to build on. **Ramos** took office on July 1, 1992 and announced plans to create jobs, revitalize the economy, and reduce the burdensome foreign debt of US$32 billion. But the first thing he had to do was establish a **reliable electricity supply**. The country was being paralysed for hours every day by power cuts, and no multinational companies wanted to invest their money under such difficult conditions. Ramos's success in revitalizing the ailing energy sector laid the foundations for a moderate influx of **foreign investment**, for industrial parks and new manufacturing facilities.

His successor, former vice-president **Joseph Estrada** (universally known as Erap), was a former tough-guy film actor with pomaded hair and a cowboy swagger. He had a folksy, macho charm that appealed to the masses, but he got off to a troubled start in Malacañang, plagued by accusations of a lack of direction and a return to the cronyism of the Marcos years. Erap bumbled his way from one disaster to the next, including accidentally signing papers that secured the release from prison of a notorious cannibal who had killed and eaten a priest.

On 24 July 2000, reports surfaced in the media detailing vast discrepancies between Estrada's declared assets and his actual assets. The reports listed seventeen pieces of real estate worth P2 billion that had been acquired by Estrada and his various family members since 1998. Some, it was alleged, were for his favourite mistress, former actress Laarni Enriquez.

In October 2000, Luis Singson, a member of the "midnight cabinet" – consisting largely of Estrada's drinking friends and governor of Ilocos Sur – alleged that Estrada had received P500 million in gambling payoffs from an illegal numbers game known as jueteng (pronounced wet-eng). As a result, Estrada became the first President of the Philippines to be impeached, but the trial fell apart when pro-Erap senators voted against allowing new evidence into court. Filipinos felt robbed of a real chance for truth and justice: the influential Catholic Church and its leader, Cardinal Jaime Sin, demanded Estrada step down; half a million people gathered in scenes reminiscent of those before the downfall of Marcos; and fifty thousand militants massed near Malacañang, preparing to kick out the President by force if necessary, but the decisive blow only came when the military announced it had withdrawn its support for Estrada. The next morning he was ushered ignominiously from Malacañang, and on 20 January, 2001, vice-president Gloria Macapagal-Arroyo was promptly sworn in as the fourteenth President of the Republic of the Philippines.

Gloria Macapagal-Arroyo

In 2002, claiming she was sick of the bickering and self-aggrandizing of the politicians, **Macapagal-Arroyo** announced that she would free herself of political patronage by not running in the next election in May 2004. In relieving herself of the duty of pandering to vested interests for votes, she said she would be able to push ahead with her reform agenda unencumbered. In reality, she still needed opposition support to push through key legislation, and this support was rarely forthcoming. The opposition greeted Macapagal-Arroyo's withdrawl with cynicism – and justifiably so, for one year later, she decided to run after all. In the 2004 elections, Macapagal-Arroyo was pitched against four main rivals for the Presidency in a race that had a familiar look to it. The main opposition candidate was Fernando Poe Jr., a swarthy action-movie star and close friend of Joseph Estrada's. The elite and the middle classes groaned.

Macapagal-Arroyo, however, had the advantage of the incumbency and a vast political machine that gave her access to the kind of funds needed for a Presidential campaign. Poe's campaign was run badly and even his supporters wondered if he had the nouse needed for public office. When the final count was in – and it took weeks – Macapagal-Arroyo had won, offering hope of political stability and modest economic growth.

The opposition and the masses that supported it believed Poe's narrow defeat was down to election fraud by the administration. After Estrada's eviction from Malacañang, Macapagal-Arroyo's victory was seen as another galling example of how an inbred elite pulls all the strings in the Philippines. Estrada may have made things incalculably worse during his two-and-a-half years of misrule, but the country's woes go back a long way — and down a long way too, to the core of political and economic life. Corruption runs unchecked, and the gap between the impoverished masses and the thin layer of super-wealthy grows ever wider – just sixty of the Philippines' estimated 15 million families control virtually all the nation's wealth, and about 200 run its political life. At the bottom of the pile, the dirt-poor grow in numbers and wretchedness, accounting for about sixty percent of the population of 76 million.

Religion

The Philippines is the only predominantly Catholic nation in Asia. Ninety-five percent of the population is Catholic, with the rest either Protestant or animist. Indigenous tribes have beliefs that combine elements from a number of religions with the worship of their own gods such as the Bulul, or rice god.

Over the past decade, a number of charismatic religions have been born, the largest of which is **El Shaddai**, headed by lay preacher Mike Velarde, a real-estate developer who found God when his business failed. Velarde is known to his followers as Brother Mike and has captured the imagination of the country's poor Catholics, many of whom feel isolated from the mainstream church, apart from at life's three critical moments: baptism, marriage and death. To make the polarization worse, priests preach in English, a language most barrio folk only have a rudimentary knowledge of. Velarde has bridged this gap by preaching in colloquial and heavily accented Tagalog at huge open-air gatherings every weekend near the Center for International Trade Exhibitions and Missions on Roxas Boulevard, overlooking Manila Bay. He wears screamingly loud made-to-measure suits and outrageous bow ties, but his message is straightforward: give to the Lord and He will return it to you tenfold. He now has eight million followers, most of whom suffer from *sakit sa bulsa*, or "ailment of the pocket", but are nevertheless happy to pay ten percent of their income to become card-carrying members of Brother Mike's flock. Brother Mike's relationship with the mainstream Catholic Church, headed by Manila Archbishop Jaime Cardinal Sin, is uneasy. His relationship with politicians is not. With eight million followers hanging on his every word, Brother Mike is a potent political ally and few candidates for high office are willing to upset him. In the 1998 elections, Brother Mike backed Joseph Estrada, a significant factor in the former movie actor's success.

The film industry

You can't miss them in the Philippines: iconoclastic hand-painted billboards advertising so-called bomba movies, made in a couple of days on the kind of budget that wouldn't buy a Caesar salad in Hollywood.

Bombas are cheap, histrionic and full of wonderfully crass Taglish dialogue ("You're nothing but a second-rate, trying hard to copycat"). They endure because they espouse the kind of escapist hopes that preoccupy the country's masses: a bashful barrio hunk takes on witless thugs who victimize a beautiful girl. The endings are frothy. The hunk whips the thugs, the girl falls for the hunk, and then becomes a famous actress in Manila, city of dreams.

The proliferation of Tagalog bodice-busters (many of them shown on the popular cable channel Pinoy Blockbusters) worries academics and intellectuals, but their hold over the public shows no sign of slackening. While "Pinoywood" is nowhere near as productive or prodigious as Bombay's Bollywood, it is still a potent popular force. Around two hundred bombas are made every year, and stars with unlikely names like Ronnie Ricketts, Tipso Cruz III and Boy Chico are known in every barrio.

But not everybody's a fan. Former president Fidel Ramos got so tired of the interminable diet of guns, goons and breathless maidens that he once summoned Manila's top producers to Malacañang Palace to give them a dressing-down. He told them to start making serious films that showed the Philippines in a positive light. His plea fell on deaf ears, however, and the deluge of bombas continued unabated, as it does today.

The main reason the industry thrives is money. **Prestige films** are a rarity because of the financial problems associated with producing high-class cinematic art in a developing country where quality education is available only to a few. The margin of profit is shrinking and few producers are willing to take a chance on films that have little chance of a paying audience outside arthouse cinemas in Manila.

One true story illustrates the problem. In 1984, Regal Films produced *Sister Stella L*, a reflective biopic about a Catholic nun working with trade unions. It swept the local awards, but losses were so huge that Regal producer Lily Monteverde was too traumatized to make another socially relevant film. The bomba bandwagon rolled on.

The **first filmmakers** came to the Philippines from America at the beginning of the twentieth century, using the islands as a bulk-standard Asian backdrop for any film that required palm trees and heat. The end of World War II, followed by Filipino independence from the US, saw a cinematic blossoming dominated by four studios modelled after the Hollywood majors. Most of the films followed reliable genre formats, but the **post-war period** also brought more artistically ambitious works by the likes of Gerardo de Leon, who later tried to break into Hollywood using an unlikely vehicle, *The Mad Doctor of Blood Island*, about an unscrupulous scientist who turns his lab assistant into a green-blooded plant monster.

In the **1960s**, as the country descended into political turmoil, things went belly up. The industry collapsed and all the major studios stopped production, with dozens of smaller independents appearing on the scene. Under-capitalized and lacking the clout of the now-defunct majors, the independents turned to sensational projects for quick profit, and the bomba was born. Guns were drawn and cleavages exposed, although most bombas are in fact rather tame, with the artless cliché of surf crashing on a sandy shore still used regularly as a symbol for sexual gratification.

Serious cinema in the Philippines has flapped but never taken off, handicapped by pitiful budgets and the lack of a moneyed audience. But in the **1970s**, things began to change, with a new generation of filmmakers galvanizing themselves in opposition to the Marcos dictatorship.

This age of censorship was also, ironically, the **golden age** of Philippine cinema, with the late Ishmael Bernal and others like him showing their work at European and American festivals. One of Bernal's most striking films is the noirish *City After Dark*, originally known as *Manila by Night* until Imelda Marcos took exception to the unflattering depictions of life in "her city".

One of the strangest martial law stories concerned director Mike de Leon, scion of one of the oligarch families who bitterly opposed Marcos. He directed *Batch 81*, a thinly disguised allegory about the Marcos dictatorship graphically dramatizing fraternity violence at universities. A brave piece of casting saw the fraternity's sadistic Grand Vizier and chief torturer played by Chito Ponce Enrile, brother of Marcos's defence minister Juan Ponce Enrile. The film ran to packed houses and Marcos made no attempt to ban it.

Philippine cinema today is still in a quandary, torn between the easy profits of bankable bombas and the creeping need to give the country's emerging middle class something more than heaving chests and testosterone. So, worthy productions come and go, but the bombas roll on. The Philippines wouldn't be the Philippines without them, and without the peculiar brand of risqué dialogue they perpetrate. Who could fail to snigger at a line as memorable as: "You're young, fresh and beautiful. What could you possibly want from a poor farmer like me? Eggplant?"

Books

Alfonso Aluit *By Sword and Fire: The Destruction of Manila in World War II* (Bookmark). A comprehensive and brutally dispassionate chronological account of man's capacity for pain, revealed not only in the narrative but also in the many black and white photographs. The scale of destruction in Manila is horrifying to see, but it's the stories of individuals that are weaved through the text that really make you understand how grisly this period of history was and how much ordinary Filipinos endured and suffered during the Japanese occupation.

Alan Berlow *Dead Season: A Story of Murder and Revenge* (Vintage UK & US). Prepare to be depressed. This brilliantly atmospheric work of reportage is the story of three murders that took place on the Philippine sugar-producing island of Negros. Impossible to read without feeling intense despair for a country where humble and peaceful people have too often become the tragic pawns in the depraved game of power and money that is played out around them. Even Cory Aquino comes out of it badly. The Church asked her to investigate the murders but she refused, fearful that she might be treading on too many toes.

Alex Garland *The Tesseract* (Penguin/ Riverhead). Alex Garland, author of *The Beach*, has made no secret of his love for the Philippines. Hardly surprising then that his second novel, a sinister and ingenious exploration of fate and chance, is based there. The prose is devilishly taut and brought more comparisons by critics to Graham Greene. The story? Well, it involves a foreigner abroad, a villainous tycoon called Don Pepe, some urchins and a beautiful girl. The characters are straight from Cliché Street, but Garland's plot is so intriguing and his observational powers so keen that it's impossible not to be swept along by the bravado of it all.

Jessica Tarahata Hagedorn *Dogeaters* (Penguin UK & US). Filipino-American Jessica Tarahata Hagedorn assembles a cast of diverse and dubious characters that comes close to encapsulating the mania and surrealism of life in Manila. Urchins, pimps, seedy tycoons and druggie movie queens are brought together in a brutal but beautiful narrative that serves as a jolting reminder of all the country's frailties and woes.

James Hamilton-Paterson *Ghosts of Manila* (Vintage/Farrar Straus & Giroux). Hamilton-Paterson's excoriating novel is haunting, powerful and for the most part alarmingly accurate. Much of it is taken from real life: the extra-judicial salvagings, the corruption, the abhorrent saga of Imelda Marcos's infamous film centre. Here is a writer who not only sees the city, but *knows* it. A lucid story that is thriller, morality play and documentary in one. Pretty it's not, but if you want Manila dissected, look no further.

James Hamilton-Paterson *Playing With Water: Passion and Solitude on a Philippine Island* (Granta/New Amsterdam). "No money, no honey," says one of the (real-life) characters in Hamilton-Paterson's lyrical account of several seasons spent among the impoverished fishermen of a small barrio on the island of Marinduque. It's the kind of refrain you hear time and again in the Philippines, and one that leads large numbers of young men to turn their backs on provincial life to seek their fortune in Manila, where they usually end up hawking newspapers, living in shanties and wondering what went wrong. A rich and original travel book, which by turns warms and disturbs you.

James Hamilton-Paterson *America's Boy: The Rise and Fall of Ferdinand Marcos and Other Misadventures of US Colonialism in the Philippines* (Granta/Henry Holt). A controversial narrative history of the US-supported dictatorship that came to define the Philippines. Hackles were raised by the book's claim that the Marcoses were merely the latest in a long line of corrupt Filipino leaders in a country that had historically been ruled by oligarchies. Ferdinand, do not forget, was welcomed at the White House by Lyndon Johnson, Nixon and Reagan. In the end, a "democratic revolution" replaced him with Corazon Aquino, who came from another great political and landowning dynasty. She, in turn, was followed by Fidel Ramos, Imelda's cousin. Hamilton-Paterson has gathered astonishing information from senators, cronies, rivals, and Marcos family members, including Imelda. If you buy one book about recent history in the Philippines, buy this one.

Nick Joaquin *Manila, My Manila* (Bookmark, Philippines). Veteran Filipino poet and novelist Nick Joaquin was asked to write this accessible history by a former mayor of Manila, who wanted a school textbook that would ignite young people's interest in their roots and culture. The result is straightforwardly readable odyssey through the centuries from the day the diminutive Kingdom of Namayan was established on the banks of the Pasig River to the tumultuous post-war period and the arrival of the Marcoses. Joaquin never quite gets round to saying precisely what he thinks of contemporary Manila, but reading between the lines it's not hard to feel his dismay, leaving you with the sense that this is a tribute to the city that was, not the city that exists today.

F. Sionil Jose *Dusk* (Modern Library, US). National Artist Jose's acclaimed Rosales saga chronicles Filipino struggles and triumphs during the last century. *Dusk*, the fifth book in the saga, takes place at the end of the nineteenth century as the Filipinos, with the aid of the Americans, finally expelled the Spanish after three centuries of often brutal rule. Of course, it wouldn't be a quintessential Filipino novel if it didn't touch on the themes of poverty, corruption, tyranny and love. *Dusk* was only recently released in America in paperback, but you can always buy it from the bookshop owned by Jose himself, in Padre Faura Street, Ermita.

Stanley Karnow *In Our Image: America's Empire in the Philippines* (Ballantine UK & US). *In Our Image*, which won the Pulitzer Prize, focuses on the relationship that has existed between the Philippines and the United States since 1898, examining how America has sought to remake the archipelago as a clone of itself, an experiment marked from the outset by blundering, ignorance and mutual misunderstanding. But more than being a book about the deficiencies of colonialism, this is also a lucid and comprehensive exposition of general Philippine history and perhaps the best non-fiction book ever written about the country.

Jose Rizal *Noli Me Tangere – Touch Me Not* (Bookmark, Philippines). "The book that sparked a revolution" (see p.766) is still required reading for every Filipino schoolchild. It's hard to find outside the Philippines, but worth picking up a copy when you get there. The *Noli*, a passionate exposure of the evils of the friar's rule, was published in 1886 and promptly banned by the Spanish colonial government. It tells the story of barrio boy Crisostomo Ibarra's love for the beautiful Maria Clara, but infuses it with tragedy and significance of almost Shakespearian proportions, documenting the religious fanaticism, double standards and rank injustice of colonial rule.

Language

There are more than 150 languages and dialects in the Philippines, nine of which are spoken by almost ninety percent of the population. Tagalog, also known as Filipino or Pilipino, is spoken as a first language by 17 million people – mostly on Luzon, and also in some parts of the Visayas – and was made the national language by the government in 1947.Many English words have been cleverly adopted by Filipinos, giving rise to a small canon of slang patois known affectionately as Taglish. Why ask someone to take a photograph when you can ask them to do some "kodaking"?

Tagalog

The structure of **Tagalog** is simple, though the **word order** is different from English – as an example, take "*kumain ng mangga ang bata*", which literally translates as "ate a mango the child". Another key difference between the two languages is the lack of the verb "to be" in Tagalog, which means a simple sentence such as "the woman is kind" is rendered "*mabait ang babae*", literally "kind the woman". For **plurals**, the word *mga* is used – hence *bahay/mga bahay* for house/houses – although in many cases Filipinos simply state the actual number of objects or use *marami* (several) before the noun. Tagalog sounds staccato to the foreign ear, with clipped vowels and consonants.

Stresses

Unlike some other Southeast Asian languages, Tagalog has no tones, and most words are spoken as they are written, though working out which syllable to **stress** is tricky. In words of two syllables, the first syllable tends to be stressed, while in words of three or more syllables the stress is almost always on the final or penultimate syllable; thus Boracay is pronounced Bo-**ra**-kay or sometimes Bo-ra-**kay**, but never **Bo**-ra-kay. Sometimes a change in the stress can drastically alter the meaning: *lalake*, for instance, can mean "man" if the stress falls on the second syllable, or "to grow big" if the stress falls on the first.

Vowels that fall consecutively in a word are always pronounced individually, as is every syllable, adding to the choppy nature of the language; for example, *tao* meaning person or people is pronounced ta-o, while *oo* for yes is pronounced o-o (with each vowel closer to the "o" in "show" than in "bore").

Key to pronunciation

Vowels

a is pronounced as in "**a**pple"
e as in "m**e**ss"
i as in "d**i**tto", though a little more elongated than in English
o as in "b**o**re"
u as in "p**u**t"
ay as in "b**uy**"
aw in "m**ou**nt"
iw is the sound **ee** continued into the **u** sound of "put"
oy as in "n**oi**se"
uw as in "**qua**rter"
uy produced making the sound **oo** and continuing it to the **i** sound in "d**i**tto"

Consonants

c as in "s**k**in"
g as in "**g**et"
k as in "s**k**in" (unaspirated)
mga is pronounced as "mang"
ng as in si**nging**
p as in "s**p**eak" (unaspirated)
t as in "s**t**op" (unaspirated)

Words and phrases

Greetings and basic phrases

Hello	Kamusta (There's no word for hello in Filipino. People usually use Kamusta, which means "how are you?")
How are you?	Kamusta ka or kamusta?
Fine, thanks	Mabuti, salamat
Pleased to meet you	Ikinalulugod kitang makilala (formal) Masaya akong makilala ka (colloquial)
Goodbye	Bye
Good evening	Magandang gabi
Excuse me (to say sorry)	Ipagpaumanhin mo ako
Excuse me (to get past)	Makikiraan lang po
Please	No direct equivalent. Instead use the word paki before a verb. For example, upo means sit, so "please sit" is paki-upo
Thank you	Salamat
What's your name?	Anong pangalan mo?
My name is…	Ang pangalan ko ay…
Do you speak English?	Marunong ka bang mag-Ingles?
Yes	oo
No	hindi
I don't understand	Hindi ko naiintindihan
Could you repeat that?	Paki-ulit?

Getting around

Where is the... ?	Saan ang... ?
How many kilometres is it to... ?	Ilang kilometro papunta sa...?
We'd like to go to the airport please	Gusto naming pumunta sa airport
Where do I catch the bus to... ?	Saan puwedeng kumuha ng bus papuntang... ?
When does the bus for Manila leave?	Kailan aalis ang bus papuntang Manila?
Can I book a seat?	Puwedeng bumili kaagad ng ticket para I-reser ba ang upuan?
How long does it take?	Gaano katagal?
Ticket	Tiket
Aeroplane	Eroplano
Airport	Airport
Bus	Bus (pronounced boos)
Bus station	Istasyon ng bus
Train station	Istasyon ng tren
Boat	Banca (small boat or canoe or boat with outriggers)
Ship	Barco
Taxi	Taxi
Car	Kotse
Filling station	Gasolinahan
Bicycle	Bisikleta
Bank	Banko
Post office	Koreo
Passport	Pasaporte
Hotel	Hotel
Restaurant	Restoran
Please stop here	Paki-tigil dito
Left	Kaliwa
Right	Kanan
North	Hilaga
South	Timog
East	Silangan
West	Kanluran

Accommodation

Do you have any rooms?	Maroon pa kayong kuwarto?
How much is it?	Magkano?
Do you have... ?	Meron kang... ?
Could I have the bill please?	Puwedeng kunin ang bill?
Room with a private bathroom	Kuwarto na may sariling banyo
Cheap/expensive	Mura/mahal
Single room	Kuwarto para sa isa
Double room	Kuwarto para sa dalawang tao
Air conditioning	Aircon
Fan	Elektrik fan
Mosquito net	Kulambo
Telephone	Telepono
Laundry	Labahan

Shopping

Money	Pera
How much?	Magkano?
It's too expensive	Masyadong mahal
I'll take this one	Kukunin ko ito
Cigarettes	Sigarilyo
Matches	Posporo
Soap	Sabon
Toilet paper	Tisyu

Days of the week and time

(Note that when telling the time, Filipinos often resort to Spanish numbers. Likewise, days of the week and months of the year are mostly derived from Spanish.)

Monday	Lunes
Tuesday	Martes
Wednesday	Miyerkoles
Thursday	Huwebes
Friday	Biyernes
Saturday	Sabado
Sunday	Linggo
What's the time?	Anong oras na?
9 o'clock	alas nuwebe
10.30	alas diyes y media
Noon	Tanghali
Midnight	Hatinggabi
Minute	Minuto
Hour	Oras
Day	Araw
Week	Linggo
Month	Buwan
Year	Taon
Today	Ngayong araw
Tomorrow	Bukas
Yesterday	Kahapon
Now	Ngayon
Morning	Umaga
Afternoon	Hapon
Evening	Gabi
Night	Gabi

Numbers

0	zero
1	Isa
2	Dalawa
3	Tatlo
4	Apat
5	Lima
6	Anim
7	Pito
8	Walo
9	Siyam
10	Sampu
11, 12, 13, etc	Labing-isa, labing-dalawa, labing-tatlo
20	Dalawampu or beinte
21, 22, 23, etc	Dalawampu't isa or beinte isa, dalawampu't dalawa or beintedos, dalawampu't tatlo or beintetatlo
30, 40, 50, etc	Tatlumpu or trienta, apat napu or kwarenta, limampu or singkwenta
100	Isang daan
200	Dalawang daan
1000	Isang libo
2000	Dalawang libo
10,000	Sampu libo

Emergencies

Can you help me?	Puwede mo akong tulungan?
There's been an accident	May aksidente
Please call a doctor	Paki-tawag ng duktor
Hospital	Ospital
Police station	Istasyon ng pulis

8.1

Manila

The capital of the Philippines, a grouping of six cities and eighteen municipalities, is technically known as Metro Manila but usually referred to simply as **MANILA**, home to 10 million people. Manila will never be a serious tourist destination until the authorities deal with the evils of traffic and pollution; most tourists are in the capital because they have a day or two to kill either at the beginning or the end of a trip to the rest of the country. In its favour, Manila has friendly people, some excellent nightlife, a few historical sights that are worth the effort, plus some of the most cavernous shopping malls in Asia. At first sight, the city may seem clamorous, unkempt and rough around the edges, but what it lacks in architectural sophistication it makes up for with an accessible chaotic charm. The way to enjoy it is to step into the fray and go with the flow, which is exactly what Manileños have learned to do.

Manila started life as a tiny settlement around the banks of the Pasig River. The name comes from the words *may* ("there is") and *nilad* (a type of plant that grew near the Pasig). With Spanish colonization, it grew into an important port. King Philip II of Spain called Manila "Insigne y Siempre Leal Ciudad" ("Distinguished and Ever Loyal City"). Images of the city in the eighteenth century show grand merchants' houses and schooners moored in the Pasig. The area around Binondo, later to become Chinatown, was alive with mercantile activity. Nineteenth-century travellers arriving in Manila were enchanted. Manila's population was 150,000 and there had been one murder in five years.

But this Manila was a doomed city. At 7pm on June 3, 1863, an earthquake struck and Manila crumbled. The new Manila that grew in its stead was thoroughly modern, with streetcars, steam trains and American-style public architecture. This was one of the most elegant and cosmopolitan cities in the Orient, but when the smoke cleared at the end of Japanese occupation in March 1945, it was once again in ruins, having undergone relentless shelling from American howitzers and been set alight by retreating Japanese troops. The Battle of Manila lasted 29 days and claimed 100,000 civilian lives. Rebuilding was slow and plagued by corruption and government inertia. As a consequence, the city that greets visitors today is one of emotional counterpoints, with areas of extreme poverty encroaching on frothy mansions and soaring glass skyscrapers.

Arrival

Ninoy Aquino International Airport, also known by the acronym NAIA, is in Parañaque, on the southern fringes of the city. In the arrivals hall there's a small 24-hour **Department of Tourism** (DoT) reception desk, where you can get maps. There are two **banks**, but their opening hours are erratic. US dollars are not always accepted as currency, so make sure you have some pesos with you when you arrive.

Getting from the airport to the city can be a headache. The Manila Bay area is only 7km away, but there are no airport shuttle buses. The best thing is to take an official a**irport taxi**; they charge around P350 to the main tourist areas. You pay in advance at a small booth in the arrivals hall, then present your receipt to the driver. Taking a non-official taxi from the airport is a risk, with many tourists being conned into paying much more than the metered rate. You should never get into a taxi that

Moving on from Manila

Journey times and frequency of planes, ferries, buses and trains are given in "Travel details", p.883.

By plane

International **flights** leave from Ninoy Aquino International Airport (☎02/877 1109) in Parañaque. Other domestic flights go from the nearby Manila Domestic Airport (☎02/832 3566) on Domestic Road, while all PAL fights use NAIA Centennial Terminal Two (☎02/877 1109). Domestic departure tax from Manila is P100; international is P550. Security has been tightened recently, and you now need identification to check in. The airport management has embraced the texting mania that has swept the Philippines. For flight inquiries, complaints and suggestions, you can send a text message, 24 hours a day, to ☎0917 839 6242.

By ferry

Nearly all inter-island **ferry** departures sail from the North Harbor, a few kilometres north of Intramuros, beyond the *Manila Hotel*. A taxi from Ermita to the North Harbor will cost about P80. WG&A Superferry (hotline ☎02/528 7000) now uses the Eva Macapagal Terminal at Pier 15, close to the *Manila Hotel*, for many of its departures. WG&A has sailings to Bacolod, Cagayan de Oro, Cebu City, Coron Town, Davao, Dumaguete, Dumaguit, General Santos, Iloilo City, Masbate, Puerto Princesa, Roxas, Surigao and Tagbilaran. There are ticket offices at Pier 4 and Pier 14, plus various outlets around the capital, including one in Malate at 1105 A Francisco St, on the corner of Singalong Street. You can also buy tickets in the Park Square II shopping mall near the *Hotel Inter-Continental* in Makati, and there's an office at the Manila Domestic Airport (Door 1, Ding Velayo Building, Domestic Road). Negros Navigation (hotline ☎02/245 5588) has sailings to most of the archipelago's major destinations, including Cebu City, Davao, Dumeguete, Puerto Princesa, Tagbilaran and Surigao. Booking offices are at 849 Pasay Rd, Makati (☎02/818 4102) and at Pier 2, North Harbor (☎02/245 5588). Other ferry companies include Sulpicio Lines (☎02/241 9701) and Aleson Shipping Lines (☎02/712 0507), which sail from Manila to Boracay. For an idea of fares, WG&A charges P760 (tourist class) or P1100 (cabin for four people) from Manila to Coron Town in Palawan. Latest rates for Negros Navigation from Manila to Davao are P1425 (tourist class, with meals), P1580 (business class, with meals), P1790 (deluxe cabin, with meals) or P2265 (en-suite cabin, with meals). Without meals, the fare is about ten percent cheaper, but remember that some of the journeys last two or three days, depending on stops, so you'll have to pack a lot of food.

is unmarked or has other people in it. All international and domestic Philippine Airlines (PAL) flights now arrive next door at NAIA Centennial Terminal Two, which is cleaner, better lit and more salubrious than its neighbour. There is no public transport here, so go to the taxi booths outside the arrivals hall and buy a ticket to your destination. The fare to Makati and Manila Bay is P350.

An enormous new terminal for international arrivals has been built at the northern end of the airport, about 11km from Makati and 9km from Manila Bay, but its opening has been delayed by allegations of corruption.

Orientation and information

The great urban sprawl of Metro Manila covers 636 square kilometres, stretching from Caloocan (sometimes spelled Kaloocan) and Quezon City in the north,

By bus

There is no single unifying **bus station** for Manila. Instead, a number of competing bus companies have terminals either in the Pasay area of EDSA, in the south, or at the northern end of EDSA in Cubao. Buses from Pasay terminals usually go south, and from Cubao they usually go north. One of the city's major terminals is behind Araneta Coliseum in Cubao, on the eastern side of EDSA, where various bus companies have departures heading south to Batangas and the Bicol region. This is the terminal used by BLTB buses going south to Nasugbu, Calamba, Batangas, Santa Cruz, Lucena, Naga and Legaspi. BLTB also does epic 28-hour journeys to towns in the Visayas and to Sorsogon in southern Luzon from here. Nearby on EDSA in Cubao is the terminal for Victory Liner (☎02/727 4534) going north to various destinations, including Dau (for Clark), Olongapo and Baguio. Victory has a second terminal at Caloocan, which can be reached from the Malate area by LRT, and a third, in Pasay, which serves Cubao. Also in Cubao are terminals for Five Star (south to Batangas and the Bicol region), Baliwag Transit (north to Bulacan province) and Dagupan (north to Lingayen and Baguio). Philippine Rabbit (☎02/364 3477) has a terminal at 1240 EDSA, Quezon City, and is popular for destinations in the north such as Angeles, Baguio, Vigan, Laoag, San Fernando (La Union) and Tarlac. There's another Philippine Rabbit terminal in Taft Avenue, easily reached from Don Jose LRT station.

In Pasay, there's a JAM Transit (☎02/831 0465) terminal on Taft Avenue servng various destinations in Batangas and Laguna. Philtranco (☎02/833 5061) is on EDSA at the corner of Apelo Cruz Street, Pasay, and does daily runs as far afield as Quezon, Bicol, Masbate, Leyte, Samar and even Davao. A popular bus line for the long trips to Baguio and Banue is Dangwa, which has overnight services leaving at 7pm from its terminal in Dimasalang Street, Sampaloc, Manila. For the 10-hour trip to Tuguegarao in the far north, you can take Victory Liner or Dangwa.

By train

The government-funded Philippine National Railways (PNR) has been racked by debt and bad management and only has one line running from Manila to the Bicol region. **Trains** are slow, uncomfortable and occasionally involved in fatal accidents. At peak times, passengers cling perilously to the carriage roofs, which are sloped to prevent trackside squatters throwing their rubbish on top. Buses are more frequent, marginally safer and generally faster. The main station in Manila, Tutuban PNR Station, is on Dagupan Street, Manila, a twenty-minute walk west of Tayuman LRT station. There's another station on the southern edge of Makati, Buendia, at the junction of Senator Gil Puyat and the South Superhighway (also known as President Osmena Boulevard).

southwards through Makati, Manila and Pasay to Muntinlupa in the south. The key **tourist district** is Manila, fronting Manila Bay along Roxas Boulevard, taking in the neighbourhoods of Ermita and Malate, and stretching north to the old walled city of Intramuros and over the Pasig River to Chinatown, also known as Binondo. On Manila Bay are landmarks such as the **Cultural Center of the Philippines** and, at the north end of the bay, Rizal Park and the Manila Hotel. Makati is the **Central Business District** (CBD), built around the main thoroughfare of Ayala Avenue, and home to banks, insurance companies, five-star hotels and all the other paraphernalia of modern life. A short taxi ride north of Makati is the new shopping area of **Rockwell**, built on the site of an old power plant. Beyond it, heading north through the heaving traffic on Epifano de los Santos Avenue (commonly referred to as EDSA) is the commercial district of **Ortigas**, which is trying to out-Makati Makati with its hotels, malls and air-con themed-restaurants. Beyond Ortigas is **Quezon City**, which is off the map for most visitors but has some lively nightlife catering to the nearby University of the Philippines.

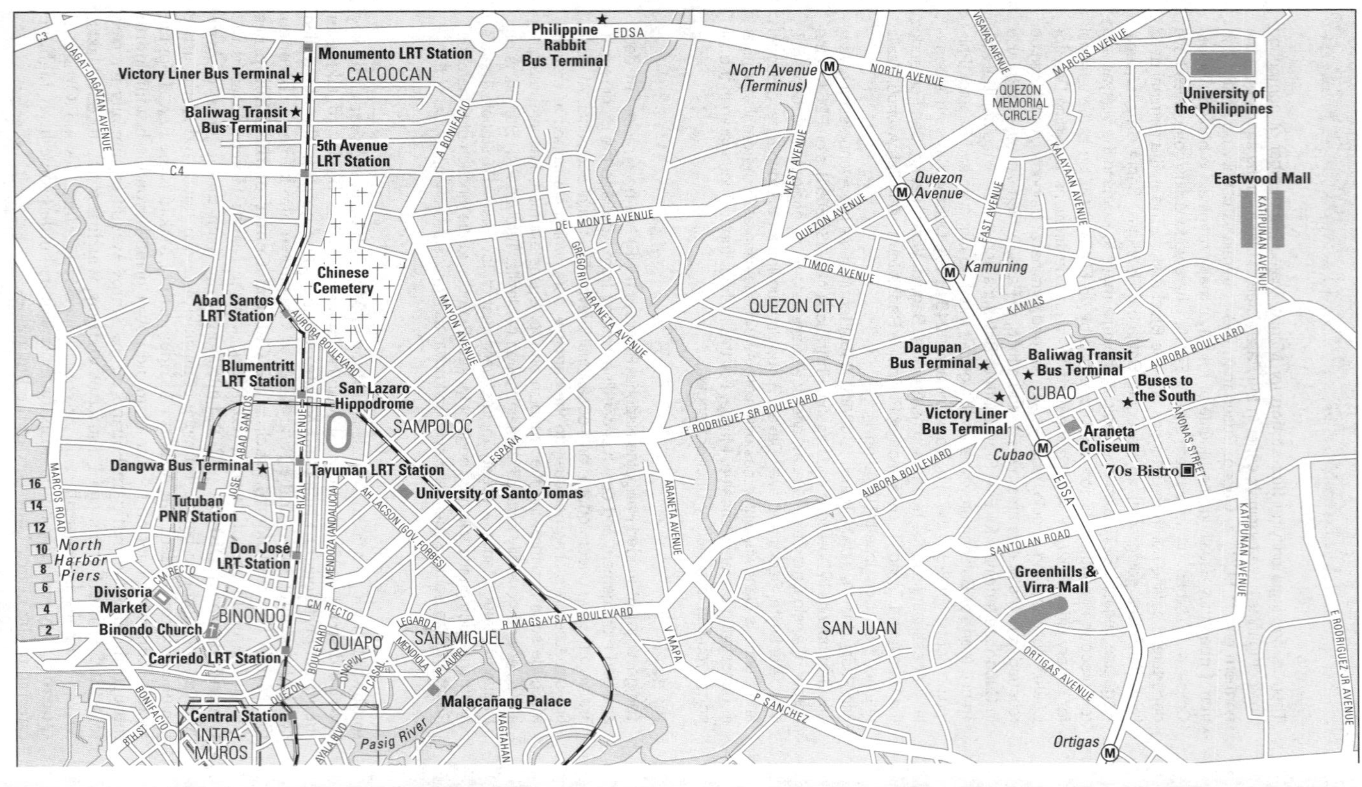
Monumento LRT Station
CALOOCAN
Victory Liner Bus Terminal
Baliwag Transit Bus Terminal
5th Avenue LRT Station
Philippine Rabbit Bus Terminal
EDSA
C3
C4
DAGAT-DAGATAN AVENUE
A BONIFACIO
North Avenue (Terminus)
NORTH AVENUE
VISAYAS AVENUE
MARCOS AVENUE
QUEZON MEMORIAL CIRCLE
University of the Philippines
Eastwood Mall
KATIPUNAN AVENUE
WEST AVENUE
Quezon Avenue
QUEZON AVENUE
EAST AVENUE
KALAYAAN AVENUE
DEL MONTE AVENUE
Chinese Cemetery
GREGORIO ARANETA AVENUE
TIMOG AVENUE
Kamuning
KAMIAS
QUEZON CITY
MAYON AVENUE
Abad Santos LRT Station
AURORA BOULEVARD
Blumentritt LRT Station
Dagupan Bus Terminal
Baliwag Transit Bus Terminal
CUBAO
Buses to the South
San Lazaro Hippodrome
SAMPOLOC
E RODRIGUEZ SR BOULEVARD
Victory Liner Bus Terminal
Araneta Coliseum
Cubao
ANONAS STREET
70s Bistro
ESPAÑA
ABAD SANTOS
AVENUE
Dangwa Bus Terminal
Tayuman LRT Station
University of Santo Tomas
ARANETA AVENUE
MARCOS ROAD
16
14
12
10
8
6
4
2
North Harbor Piers
Tutuban PNR Station
JOSE
RIZAL
A MENDOZA (ANDALUCIA)
AH LACSON (GOV. FORBES)
SANTOLAN ROAD
Don José LRT Station
CM RECTO
Divisoria Market
Greenhills & Virra Mall
Binondo Church
BINONDO
R MAGSAYSAY BOULEVARD
V MAPA
SAN JUAN
QUIAPO
SAN MIGUEL
LEGARDA
MENDIOLA
JP LAUREL
OINGPIN
P CASAL
BOULEVARD
Carriedo LRT Station
QUEZON
ORTIGAS AVENUE
E RODRIGUEZ JR AVENUE
BONIFACIO
Malacañang Palace
P SANCHEZ
Central Station
8TH ST
INTRA-MUROS
AYALA BLVD
Pasig River
NAGTAHAN
Ortigas

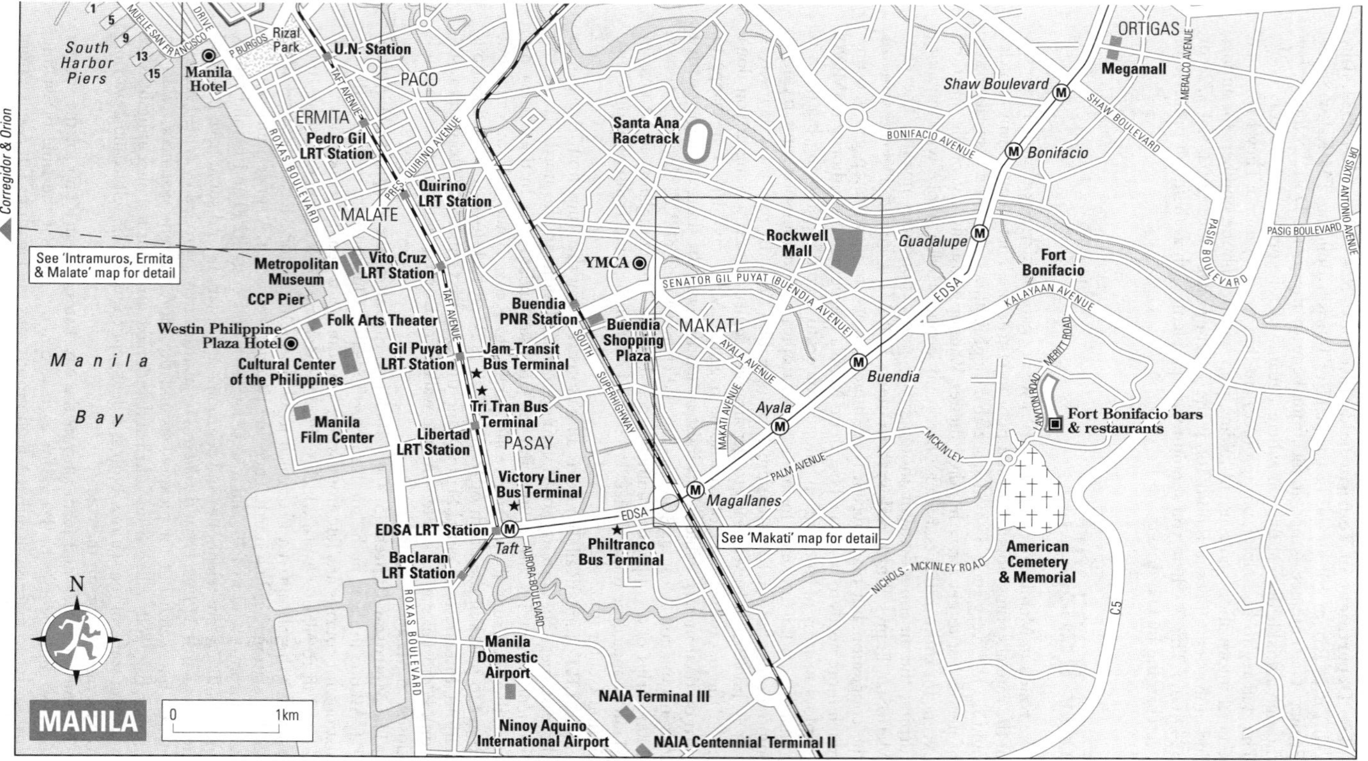
MANILA
0
1km
N
Corregidor & Orion
South Harbor Piers
1
5
9
13
15
MUELLE SAN FRANCISCO
DRIVE
P BURGOS
Rizal Park
Manila Hotel
U.N. Station
TAFT AVENUE
PACO
ERMITA
Pedro Gil LRT Station
ROXAS BOULEVARD
PRES. QUIRINO AVENUE
Quirino LRT Station
MALATE
See 'Intramuros, Ermita & Malate' map for detail
Metropolitan Museum
Vito Cruz LRT Station
CCP Pier
Folk Arts Theater
Westin Philippine Plaza Hotel
Manila Bay
Cultural Center of the Philippines
Gil Puyat LRT Station
Jam Transit Bus Terminal
Tri Tran Bus Terminal
Manila Film Center
Libertad LRT Station
PASAY
Victory Liner Bus Terminal
EDSA LRT Station
Taft
Baclaran LRT Station
AURORA BOULEVARD
Philtranco Bus Terminal
EDSA
Manila Domestic Airport
Ninoy Aquino International Airport
NAIA Terminal III
NAIA Centennial Terminal II
Santa Ana Racetrack
YMCA
Buendia PNR Station
Buendia Shopping Plaza
SOUTH SUPERHIGHWAY
SENATOR GIL PUYAT (BUENDIA AVENUE)
MAKATI
Rockwell Mall
AYALA AVENUE
MAKATI AVENUE
Ayala
Buendia
PALM AVENUE
Magallanes
See 'Makati' map for detail
Guadalupe
Fort Bonifacio
KALAYAAN AVENUE
MERITT ROAD
LAWTON ROAD
Fort Bonifacio bars & restaurants
MCKINLEY
American Cemetery & Memorial
NICHOLS - MCKINLEY ROAD
C5
Shaw Boulevard
BONIFACIO AVENUE
Bonifacio
SHAW BOULEVARD
ORTIGAS
Megamall
MERALCO AVENUE
PASIG BOULEVARD
DR SIXTO ANTONIO AVENUE

The **Department of Tourism** head office (☎02/524 1703 or 524 2384; daily 24hr) is in Room 106 of the Department of Tourism Building, TM Kalaw Street, Ermita. The entrance is not at the front beneath the grand Doric columns, but through a double door at the rear, where a guard will ask you to sign a visitors' book. The staff try to be helpful, but resources are thin on the ground. They have some general information and a useful folding map with telephone numbers for airlines and embassies. Opposite Room 106 is the Tourist Police office (☎02/524 1728 or 524 1660). This is where you should report problems such as theft, lost property, or overcharging by taxi drivers.

City transport

The **roads** in Manila are in a perpetual state of chaos bordering on anarchy, a result of the capital's rising population and poor infrastructure. There are so many vehicles fighting for every inch of road space that at peak times it can be a sweaty battle of nerves just to get a few hundred metres. Walking is usually out of the question, except for short distances, because buses and jeepneys belch smoke with impunity, turning the air around major thoroughfares into a poisonous miasma. The new MetroStar Express **light rail system** along EDSA has helped alleviate some of the congestion, but many recent road improvements are merely stop-gap measures much more needs to be done. The Metro Manila Development Authority (MMDA) employs an army of blue-shirted traffic enforcers to keep things moving, but theirs is a thankless task. They stand for hours under tropical sun or monsoon rains, trying to impose order but rarely getting much co-operation from the road users themselves.

It is, however, relatively easy to get around Manila by **taxi** as long as you don't mind the occasional bout of wearisome haggling. Many taxi drivers are happy to turn on their meters, while others insist on starting even the shortest journey with a long negotiation. Most taxis are air-con and charge an initial P25, plus P2 for every 200m. Trips of a couple of kilometres cost P40–50. For complaints about taxis in Manila, contact the traffic police (☎02/877 1791) or the Land Transportation Office Action Center (☎02/926 5024).

The **LRT** (Light Rail Transit) is an elevated railway that runs from Baclaran in the east (near the airport) to Monumento in Caloocan in the north. Trains run frequently from 5.30am to 9pm and the fare is a standard P10. In the Manila Bay area, the LRT runs above Taft Avenue, parallel to Roxas Boulevard. You can use it to get to places in the north of Manila, such as Rizal Park (exit at United Nations station), Intramuros (Central Station), and the Chinese Cemetery (Abad Santos station). Pedro Gil station is a ten-minute walk from Ermita, while Quirino station is closest to Malate.

The **Metrostar Express** (5.30am–10.30pm) runs along the length of EDSA from Taft Avenue in Pasay in the south to North Avenue, Quezon City in the north. Key stations for tourists are Taft, from where you can get a taxi, a jeepney or the LRT along Taft to Malate; Ayala, which is close to Makati's malls and hotels; Shaw Boulevard for the Shangri-La Plaza mall in Ortigas; Ortigas for Megamall; and Cubao for bus stations heading north. There are two types of ticket. A single-journey ticket ranges from P9.50 to P15, and a stored-value ticket costs P200 and is valid for six months. There are telephones and restrooms at all stations and some have fast-food outlets such as *McDonald's* and *Jollibee*. The platforms are patrolled by armed security guards, but watch out for pickpockets and the more brazen "snatchers", who rip phones, bags and wallets from your hand and make a run for it. Police mugshots are posted at some of the stations, both as a deterrent to would-be felons and a warning to passengers to be on their guard.

Jeepneys go back and forth all over the city. Fares start at P2.50 for the shorter journeys and increase by P0.50 for each kilometre after (at the time of writing, this was set to increase slightly). A useful route runs the length of Taft Avenue from

Baclaran in the south to Bindondo in the north. From Baclaran, you can get jeepneys to the bus terminals in Pasay. Jeepneys heading to Cubao will take you past a number of bus terminals at the northern end of EDSA, where you can get buses to destinations in the north, such as Baguio and Vigan.

Local **buses** in Manila bump and grind their way along all major thoroughfares (Taft Avenue, EDSA, Senator Gil Puyat Avenue). The destination is written on a sign in the front window, and fares start at P8. These "rolling coffins", most of them hand-me-downs from Japan and Taiwan, are in cut-throat competition for your trade because drivers get paid by the number of passengers they carry. Some of the drivers are extraordinarily reckless, swerving from lane to lane and blocking busy junctions while they pick up passengers. The drivers also work long hours and the MMDA has become worried that some are resorting to drugs to stay awake. Needless to say, alternative modes of city transport are generally a better bet.

Accommodation

Most of Manila's budget **accommodation** is in the Manila Bay area, specifically in the enclaves of **Ermita** and **Malate**, which also have a high density of restaurants, bars and tourist services. Ermita was once a notorious red-light district, but former mayor Alfredo Lim drove out all the "girlie bars" and they have now set up shop in Pasay where the authorities are more tolerant. In **Makati**, there is some reasonably priced accommodation in and around P Burgos Street at the northern end of Makati Avenue.

Intramuros, Ermita and Malate

Aloha Hotel 2150 Roxas Blvd, Malate ⓣ02/526 8088. The *Aloha* is a Manila Bay stalwart and was a bit rough around the edges until it got a lick of pink paint recently. The rooms have also been refurbished. Make sure you pay a little extra for a room at the front, with views of the sea and the sunset. ❻

Best Western Hotel La Corona 1166 MH Del Pilar cnr Arquiza St, Ermita ⓣ02/524 2631-38. Smart and friendly little hotel with double rooms, including buffet breakfast for two. ❺–❻

City Garden Hotel 1158 A Mabini St, Ermita ⓣ02/536 1541. Bog standard mid-range hotel with a/c throughout and a coffee shop in the lobby. Ten percent discount if you stay fourteen days or longer. ❻

Citystate Tower Hotel 1315 A Mabini St, Ermita ⓣ400 7351-61. With its chandeliers and gold trimmings the lobby deserves some sort of award for extremely bad taste, but the rooms are good value. The travel agent near the reception desk can arrange flights, visas and tours. ❹

Ermita Tourist Inn 1549 A Mabini St, Ermita ⓣ02/521 8770-71. Another good budget choice. Clean and relatively spacious tiled a/c doubles with private bath. The staff are friendly and helpful, and there's a travel agent downstairs for flights and visas. ❸

Garden Plaza Hotel 1030 Belen St ⓣ02/522 4835. Congenial and well managed, the *Garden Plaza* is right next to Paco Park and has a/c rooms, a lovely little swimming pool on the roof and an excellent Swiss restaurant. ❹

Hotel Intramuros de Manila Plaza San Luis Complex, cnr Urdaneta and Cabildo sts, Intramuros ⓣ524 6730-32. Powder-pink Spanish colonial structure with arched windows and a wraparound first-floor balcony. The hotel is used as a training hotel for hospitality staff and is the only accommodation within the walls of Intramuros. *Café Luna* in the lobby serves Filipino and continental cuisine. ❺–❻

Iseya Hotel 1241 MH Del Pilar St, Ermita ⓣ02/523 8166-68. Dusty old pension house close to the noisy junction with Padre Faura and surrounded by moneychangers and *halal carinderias* (canteens). ❷–❸

Mabini Pension 1337 A Mabini St, Ermita ⓣ02/523 3930. Convenient, friendly and well established. A basic fan room with bath costs P550 and an a/c double with bath P900. Tourist information, visa extensions and flight reservations. ❷–❺

Malate Pensionne 1771 M Adriatico St, Malate ⓣ02/523 8304. A popular place furnished in Spanish colonial style and in a good position, a stone's throw from Remedios Circle, next to *Sidebar* and *Portico*. Rooms have varying facilities. Reservations recommended. ❸–❻

Palm Plaza Hotel Pedro Gil cnr M Adriatico St, Malate ⓣ02/522 1000. New hotel with 120 a/c rooms, some with views of Manila Bay. There's a travel agent and a car rental office in the lobby

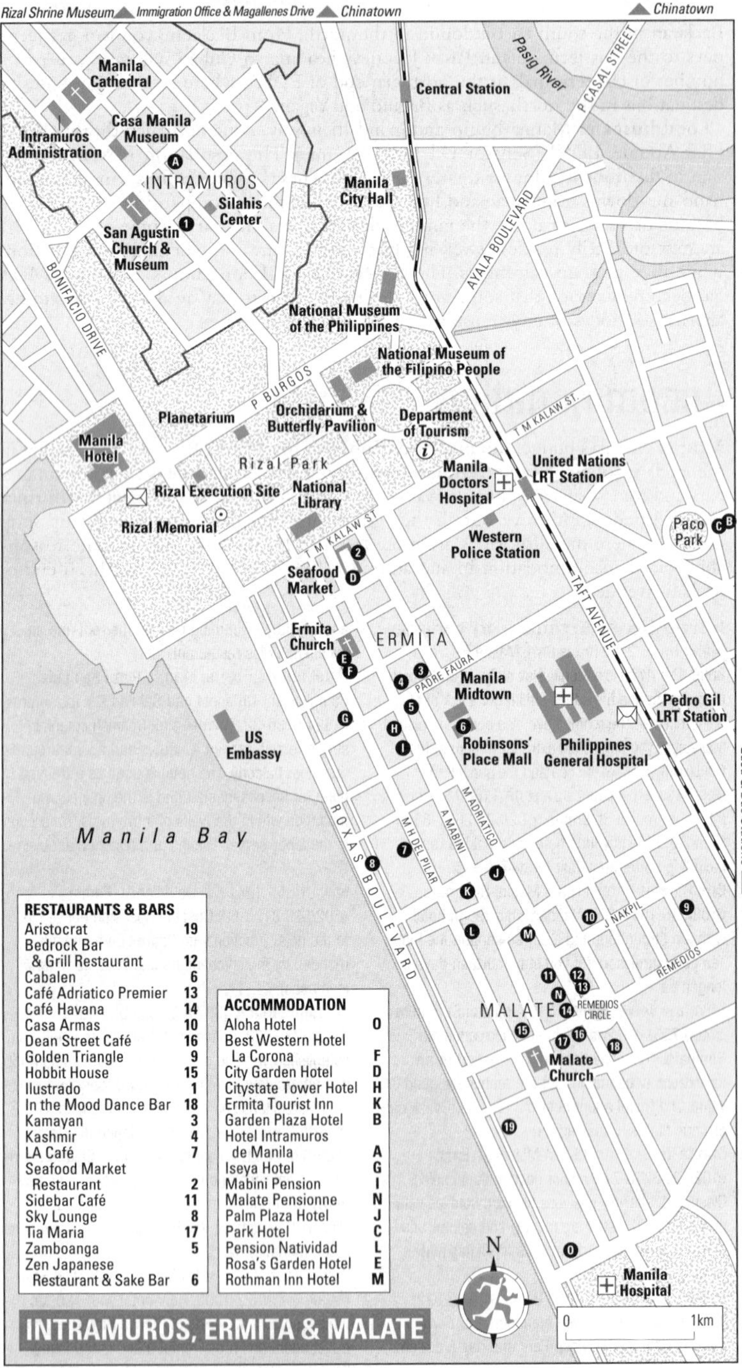
Rizal Shrine Museum
Immigration Office & Magallenes Drive
Chinatown
Chinatown
Ferry Piers (North Harbour)
Fort Santiago (200m) &
Manila Cathedral
Casa Manila Museum
Intramuros Administration
INTRAMUROS
Silahis Center
San Agustin Church & Museum
Central Station
Pasig River
P CASAL STREET
Manila City Hall
AYALA BOULEVARD
BONIFACIO DRIVE
National Museum of the Philippines
National Museum of the Filipino People
P BURGOS
Planetarium
Orchidarium & Butterfly Pavilion
Department of Tourism
T M KALAW ST.
Manila Hotel
Rizal Park
Manila Doctors' Hospital
United Nations LRT Station
Rizal Execution Site
National Library
Rizal Memorial
Paco Park
T M KALAW ST
Western Police Station
Seafood Market
TAFT AVENUE
Ermita Church
ERMITA
PADRE FAURA
Manila Midtown
Pedro Gil LRT Station
US Embassy
Robinsons' Place Mall
Philippines General Hospital
Edsa & Bus Stations
M ADRIATICO
A MABINI
M H DEL PILAR
ROXAS BOULEVARD
Manila Bay
J NAKPIL
REMEDIOS
MALATE
REMEDIOS CIRCLE
Malate Church
Manila Hospital
N
0
1km
RESTAURANTS & BARS
Aristocrat 19
Bedrock Bar & Grill Restaurant 12
Cabalen 6
Café Adriatico Premier 13
Café Havana 14
Casa Armas 10
Dean Street Café 16
Golden Triangle 9
Hobbit House 15
Ilustrado 1
In the Mood Dance Bar 18
Kamayan 3
Kashmir 4
LA Café 7
Seafood Market Restaurant 2
Sidebar Café 11
Sky Lounge 8
Tia Maria 17
Zamboanga 5
Zen Japanese Restaurant & Sake Bar 6
ACCOMMODATION
Aloha Hotel O
Best Western Hotel La Corona F
City Garden Hotel D
Citystate Tower Hotel H
Ermita Tourist Inn K
Garden Plaza Hotel B
Hotel Intramuros de Manila A
Iseya Hotel G
Mabini Pension I
Malate Pensionne N
Palm Plaza Hotel J
Park Hotel C
Pension Natividad L
Rosa's Garden Hotel E
Rothman Inn Hotel M
INTRAMUROS, ERMITA & MALATE

(self-drive cars cost P1400 a day or P1200 for at least 3 days). ④–⑥

Park Hotel 1032 Belen St ☏02/521 2371 to 2375. Next door to the *Garden Plaza*, outside the walls of Paco Park. Standard, deluxe and superior rooms, some with four-poster bed and whirlpool bath. Not as plush as its neighbour, but rooms are slightly cheaper and good value. Swimming pool, 24hr restaurant, and a travel agency in the lobby. ④

Pension Natividad 1690 MH del Pilar St, Malate ☏02/521 0524. Choice of forty rooms in an old family house that was built before the war and partially destroyed by bombing. Dorm beds are P200, fan rooms with bath P650 and double a/c rooms with bath P800. The pleasant terrace café serves a small but reasonably priced range of drinks and snacks, including coffee (P10), homemade yoghurt (P50), breakfast (from P50) and sandwiches (from P50). Luggage storage is P5 per bag per day. Along with the *Malate Pensionne* this is the best budget accommodation in the area. ④

Rosa's Garden Hotel 1140 MH del Pilar St, Ermita ☏02/404 1621 or 404 1622. New establishment with institutional but clean a/c rooms with private shower. Only the larger rooms have a refrigerator. Cable TV, telephones and coffee shop. Close to *Pizza Hut*. ⑤

Rothman Inn Hotel 1633 M Adriatico St, Malate ☏02/523 4501-10. A grim concrete edifice with lugubrious interiors. The literature ambitiously boasts that the hotel overlooks "the sunset of Manila Bay": some rooms do, but not many. However, it's a good location close to nightlife. ④–⑤

Makati

Citadel Inn Makati 5007 P Burgos St, Bel-Air ☏02/897 2370. Coffee shop, swimming pool and email and Internet access. Rooms are ordinary, but comfortable and clean, and all with a/c and shower. ④–⑥

City Garden Hotel Makati 7870 Makati Ave cnr Kalayaan Ave ☏02/899 1111. Comfortable boutique hotel with a/c rooms, tiny swimming pool and, should you need it, a helipad. Good location though, and off-season discounts mean you can negotiate a deal. ⑤–⑥

El Cielito Inn 804 Pasay Rd ☏02/815 8951. A small but clean "businessman's hotel" close to Makati's malls. Best to book in advance. ⑥

Fersal Apartelle Tourist Inn 107 Neptune St ☏02/911 2161 or 897 9123. Clean and functional hotel in a relatively quiet sidestreet off Makati Ave. A simple but clean a/c double comes with refrigerator. ④–⑤

Oxford Suites P Burgos corner Durban St ☏02/899 7988. The grandest hotel on the P Burgos strip, with 223 rooms and suites, gymnasium, 24hr coffee shop and fourth-floor restaurant. Some rooms have kitchenette, living room and terrace. Buffet breakfast included. ⑥

Pensionne Virginia 816 Pasay Rd ☏02/844 5228 or 843 2546. In a convenient location at the business end of Makati, close to malls and offices. Clean rooms, all with a/c, cable TV, telephone and mini-bar. Situated between ACA Video and a branch of the popular bakery, Goldilocks. One of a number of mid-range hotels in this area of Pasay Rd (also known as Arnaiz Ave). ⑥

Robelle House 4402 B Valdez St, Makati ☏02/899 8209-13. This rambling family-run pension, behind the International School at the P Burgos end of Makati Ave, has been in business for years and is still the most atmospheric Filipino budget accommodation in the business district. The floors are polished tile and the wooden staircases are authentically creaky, although the rooms, for the price, are no more than serviceable. Ask for one on the first floor overlooking the small pool. ⑤–⑥

Tower Inn 1002 Arnaiz Ave (also known as Pasay Rd), San Lorenzo Village, Makati ☏02/888 5170. Modern, clean business hotel with 48 rooms, coffee shop and small Mediterranean restaurant. Walking distance to Makati's shops and restaurants. ⑥

YMCA 7 Dao St ☏02/899 6380 to 6382. Clean budget accommodation in a residential area close to the big Makati Cemetery, 5min by taxi from Makati's malls and 20min from Manila Bay. Beds in the fan-cooled dorm are cheapest (P200), but there are also good rooms with fan or a/c, all with private bathrooms, for anything from two to six people. The food in the canteen is average, but very cheap. ③

The City

Manila's reputation as a forbidding city for visitors stems partly from its size and apparent disorder. The relentless growth of the conurbation has not been helped by unchecked urban development and an influx of *provincianos* looking for work, most of whom live in shanties on the periphery, continually encroaching on rainforest and paddy-field. To see the major sights you'll have to sweat it out in heavy traffic and be

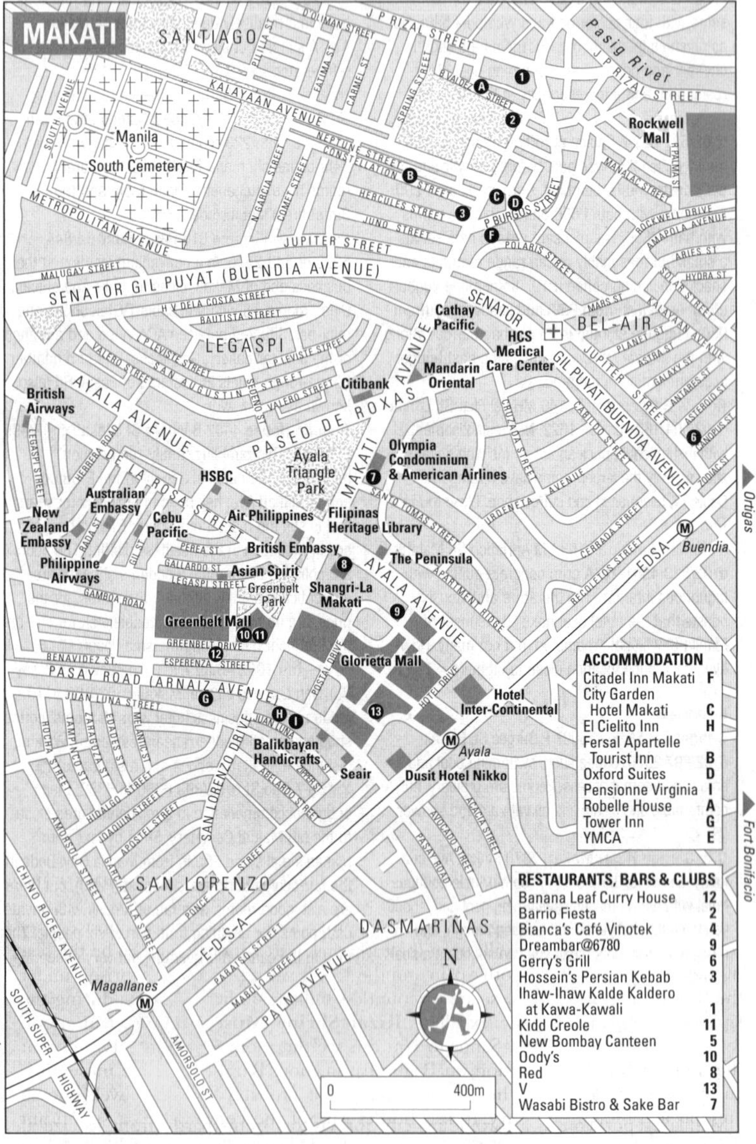
Quezon City
MAKATI
SANTIAGO
Manila South Cemetery
LEGASPI
BEL-AIR
SAN LORENZO
DASMARIÑAS
Pasig River
Rockwell Mall
Cathay Pacific
HCS Medical Care Center
Mandarin Oriental
Citibank
British Airways
Ayala Triangle Park
Olympia Condominium & American Airlines
HSBC
Australian Embassy
New Zealand Embassy
Cebu Pacific
Air Philippines
Filipinas Heritage Library
British Embassy
The Peninsula
Philippine Airways
Asian Spirit
Greenbelt Park
Shangri-La Makati
Greenbelt Mall
Glorietta Mall
Hotel Inter-Continental
Balikbayan Handicrafts
Seair
Dusit Hotel Nikko
Ayala
Buendia
Magallanes
Ortigas
Fort Bonifacio
Pasay and Roxas Boulevard
E & 4
5
SENATOR GIL PUYAT (BUENDIA AVENUE)
AYALA AVENUE
PASEO DE ROXAS
MAKATI AVENUE
PASAY ROAD (ARNAIZ AVENUE)
KALAYAAN AVENUE
METROPOLITAN AVENUE
JUPITER STREET
J P RIZAL STREET
EDSA
SAN LORENZO DRIVE
CHINO ROCES AVENUE
SOUTH SUPER-HIGHWAY
PALM AVENUE
0 400m
ACCOMMODATION
Citadel Inn Makati F
City Garden Hotel Makati C
El Cielito Inn H
Fersal Apartelle Tourist Inn B
Oxford Suites D
Pensionne Virginia I
Robelle House A
Tower Inn G
YMCA E
RESTAURANTS, BARS & CLUBS
Banana Leaf Curry House 12
Barrio Fiesta 2
Bianca's Café Vinotek 4
Dreambar@6780 9
Gerry's Grill 6
Hossein's Persian Kebab 3
Ihaw-Ihaw Kalde Kaldero at Kawa-Kawali 1
Kidd Creole 11
New Bombay Canteen 5
Oody's 10
Red 8
V 13
Wasabi Bistro & Sake Bar 7

prepared for delays, but at least the main attractions are close to one another, grouped mostly along the crescent sweep of Manila Bay and Roxas Boulevard. Budget visitors usually base themselves in the enclave of **Malate**, from where it's a relatively short hop to **Rizal Park** and the old town of **Intramuros**. Beyond **Chinatown** (Binondo), the gargantuan **Chinese Cemetery** is morbidly interesting, while the rather sterile business districts of **Makati** and **Ortigas** are best known for their malls and restaurants.

Intramuros

Don't miss **Intramuros**, the old Spanish capital of Manila. It's the one part of the metropolis where you get a real sense of history. It was built in 1571 and remains a monumental, if ruined, relic of the Spanish occupation: it's a city within a city, separated from the rest of Manila by its crumbling walls. This ancient capital featured well-planned streets, plazas, the Governor's Palace, fifteen churches and six monasteries. It also had dozens of cannon that were used to keep the natives in their place. Many buildings were reduced to rubble in World War II, but Intramuros still lays claim to most of Manila's top tourist sights. **Manila Cathedral** (daily 9am-7pm; free), originally built in 1581, has been destroyed several times down the centuries by a combination of fire, typhoon, earthquake and war. It was last rebuilt between 1954 and 1958.

A few hundreds yards beyond the cathedral on the right is **San Agustin Church** (daily 9am–noon & 1–5pm; P25, which includes admission to the monastery), with its magnificent Baroque interiors and trompe l'oeil murals, which dates back to 1599 and is the oldest stone church in the Philippines. Over four hundred years, San Agustin has withstood fire, typhoons, earthquakes, the heavy bombings of the British Invasion of 1762 and World War II. Next door, built around a quiet plaza, is the old Augustinian monastery (same hours as church), which houses a **museum** of icons and artefacts along with an eighteenth-century Spanish pipe organ that was recently restored. The monastery complex accommodated the Augustinians and illustrious guests such as the Governor General and religious dignitaries from Europe, as well as being a centre of learning for artists and theologians, with its own printing press.

Opposite San Agustin on General Luna Street in the Plaza San Luis Complex is the splendid **Casa Manila Museum**, a sympathetically restored colonial-era house (Tues–Sun 9am–6pm; P50). Redolent of a grander age, the house contains an impressive *sala* (living room) where *tertulias* (soirees) and *bailes* (dances) were held. The family latrine is a two-seater, allowing husband and wife to gossip out of earshot of the servants while simultaneously going about their business. Beyond Casa Manila Museum, at 744 Calle Real del Palacio, is the **Silahis Center**, an emporium selling arts, artefacts, antiques and cultural publications. Through a pretty courtyard at the rear is the elegant *Ilustrado* restaurant and the atmospheric *Kuatro Kantos Bar* (see "Eating"), which is open all week for breakfast, lunch, *merienda* (snacks) and cocktails.

The ruins of **Fort Santiago** (daily 8am–9pm) stand at the northernmost end of Intramuros, a five-minute walk from the cathedral. Fort Santiago used to be the seat of the colonial powers of both Spain and the US. It was also a dreaded prison under the Spanish regime and the scene of countless military-police atrocities during the Japanese occupation. In the excellent **Rizal Shrine Museum** (daily 8am–noon & 1–5pm; P15) inside Fort Santiago you can see the room where Jose Rizal spent the hours before his execution on Bagumbayan (now Rizal Park). The museum is an atmospheric and thoughtful representation of probably the most well-known episode in Philippine history. It also houses one of the country's most significant historical documents – the original copy of his valedictory poem, Mi Ultimo Adios, which was secreted in an oil lamp and smuggled to his family.

For details of all the attractions in Intramuros, and to arrange walking tours with a guide, call the Intramuros Administration, 5/F Palacio del Gobernador, Intramuros

(☎02/527 3138 or 527 3141) or the Intramuros Visitor Center (☎02/527 2961), which has a small office in the grounds of Fort Santiago.

Rizal Park

In a city notoriously short of greenery, **Rizal Park** (also known as the Luneta) was where the colonial-era glitterati used to promenade after church every Sunday. These days, the park is an early-morning jogging circuit, a weekend repository for children and a refuge for couples and families trying to escape the clamour of the city. People take picnics and lie in the shade, or sit in a shady area known as Chess Plaza, gambling a few centavos on the outcome of a game. Hawkers sell everything from balloons and mangoes to plastic bags full of *chicheron*, a local version of pork scratchings served with a little container of vinegar and chilli for dipping. Few visitors to the park report any problems with hustlers or what Filipinos refer to as "scalawags", but if you do need assistance you can call the park hotline on ☎117.

The park's sundry attractions include a rundown **planetarium** (P50), an amphitheatre where open-air concerts are held every Sunday at 5pm, a giant relief map of the Philippines, and Chinese and Japanese gardens. At the bay end of the park, close to the *Manila Hotel*, is the **Rizal Memorial** and the flagpole where Manuel Roxas, first President of the Republic, was sworn in on July 4, 1946. Rizal's execution site is near here, close to a memorial marking the execution site of three priests garrotted by the Spanish for alleged complicity in the Cavite uprising in 1872. One of the park's newest features is the **Orchidarium & Butterfly Pavilion**, designed and operated by the Clean & Green Foundation.

Beyond the Orchidarium lie the country's two major museums, both under the auspices of the National Museum and both worth a visit. The **National Museum of the Philippines** (Tues–Sun 10am–4.30pm; free) is in what used to be the old Congress Building and houses Filipino masters' paintings and clearly labelled displays of geology, zoology, botany, crafts and weapons. There are plans to turn the nearby Department of Tourism building into the third wing of the National Museum. Directly opposite, the **National Museum of the Filipino People** (Tues–Sun 10am–4.30pm; P100) is in what used to be the Government Finance Building and includes treasures from the San Diego, which sank off the coast of Fortune Island in Batangas in 1600. Not all the artefacts recovered from the wreck were intrinsically valuable; you'll see chicken bones and hazelnuts from the ship's store, as well as porcelain, rosaries and silver goblets. The anthropology section upstairs is equally enthralling, with reburial jars that date back to 5 BC. These jars were used to hold the bones of ancestors, who were buried and then exhumed and stored for safekeeping.

Makati

Makati was a vast expanse of malarial swampland until the Ayala family, one of the country's most influential business dynasties, started developing it at the turn of the century. It is now Manila's business district and is chock-full of plush hotels, international restaurant chains, expensive condominiums and monolithic air-con malls containing everything from cinemas and bowling alleys to cacophonous food courts. The main triangle of Makati is bordered by Ayala Avenue, Paseo de Roxas and Makati Avenue, and is where most of the banks, insurance companies and multinational corporations are sited. For sightseers, Makati is something of a wasteland, but for shoppers and eaters it's nirvana. The biggest mall by far is **Glorietta**, opposite the *Shangri-La Makati*, which heaves with people seeking refuge from the traffic and the heat. The central area of the mall is reserved for concerts, promotions, events and small-scale shows, each with a sound system competing for dominance over its neighbour. Glorietta has a modern cinema complex (☎02/729 7777) with seven cinemas, including the Art Film cinema, one of only a handful in the country that shows anything other than blockbusters.

On the other side of Makati Avenue from Glorietta is **Greenbelt Park** with its pleasant white-domed church. Makati's other main mall is **Greenbelt Mall**, which has recently undergone major redevelopment and has numerous shops, bars, restaurants and cinemas. The new **Ayala Museum** (Tues–Sat 8am–6pm; free) is also now housed in the Greenbelt Mall complex. It's a vast improvement on the old museum and not to be missed, with original works by Filipino master painters such as Fernando Amorsolo, Juan Luna and Damian Domingo; a multimedia "People Power" room that documents the turmoil of the Marcos years and the restoration of democracy; and a talking museum for children. There's also a terrific café and gift shop on site.

The **Filipinas Heritage Library** on Makati Avenue, opposite *The Peninsula Hotel*, is an interesting little piece of history: it was Manila's first airport, and Paseo de Roxas is now where the runway used to be. The library is privately owned (by the Ayala family) but has a bookshop selling books about the Philippines and a quiet café with Internet access. On the edge of Makati in McKinley Avenue is the **American Cemetery and Memorial** (daily 6.30am–4.30pm; free). The cemetery covers a wide area and contains the largest number of graves of American military dead of World War II, a total of 17,206. A short taxi ride north of Makati is **Rockwell**, the city's newest mall, built on the site of an old power plant. The basement level contains dozens of small restaurants and on the top floor is Power Plant Cinema (☎02/898 1440 or 1441), Manila's newest and best. The choice of films is limited to big-name thrillers and melodramas, but unlike many other cinemas in the Philippines you can at least reserve a ticket in advance (P120). On the ground floor, look out for Page One bookstore, which has a good travel-guide section.

Manila Bay

When Manila was in its heyday, **Manila Bay** must have been a sight to behold, with its sweeping panorama across the South China Sea and dreamy sunsets. Manileños still watch sunsets from the harbour wall or the outside bar at the *Westin Philippine Plaza Hotel*, but much of Manila Bay is trading on its romantic past. Its buildings were bombed flat during the war and have been replaced with boxes made of poured concrete. Horse-drawn carriages (*calesas*) still tout for business, but the horses look exhausted and even the palm trees that line Roxas Boulevard are drooping from pollution. A trip along the boulevard heading north from its southern end in Pasay takes you past the *Heritage Hotel* and on towards reclaimed land jutting out into the bay. This is the site of the *Westin Philippine Plaza Hotel*, the Cultural Center of the Philippines and the ruins of Imelda Marcos's infamous Manila Film Center, which she hoped would turn Manila into the Cannes of the East. Construction was rushed to beat tight deadlines and as a result the building collapsed, trapping an unknown number of workers inside. The Marcos government covered up the disaster and continued with the work. Some say bodies are still trapped inside today.

While you're in the area, make a beeline for the **Metropolitan Museum**, usually known as the Met, at the Bangko Sentral ng Pilipinas Complex, Roxas Boulevard (Mon–Sat 10am–6pm; P50). This fine-arts museum, a Filipino mini-Guggenheim, also houses the Central Bank's collection of prehistoric jewellery and coins. Roxas Boulevard ends at the Manila Hotel, home from home in Manila for the likes of General Douglas MacArthur (who has a suite named after him), Michael Jackson and Bill Clinton. The hotel has a small but fascinating historical archive, with signed photographs of famous guests and unique images from World War II. It's not open to the public, but if you want to see it you can call the concierge in advance (☎02/527 0011).

Ermita and Malate

Two of the city's oldest neighbourhoods, **Ermita** and **Malate**, nestle behind Roxas Boulevard within ten minutes' walk of Manila Bay. Ermita was infamous up until the late 1980s for its go-go bars and massage parlours until tough-guy mayor Alfredo Lim came along and shut them all down. New bars opened, but the bulk of the tourist trade had moved on and many promptly closed. Ermita is now a ragbag of budget hotels, choked streets and fast-food outlets. A good place to stay it may be, but for anything to see and do you'll have to walk north to Intramuros or east along M Adriatico Street to **J Nakpil Street** in Malate, where a lively café society thrives. Modish restaurants and bars have spread like a rash along Nakpil and neighbouring **Maria Orosa Street**, and on Friday and Saturday nights this is the place to be seen. Don't lose credibility by getting there early: at weekends, things rarely get going before 10pm and the pavements are still bustling at dawn. There are more cafés and bars in nearby Remedios Circle. A five-minute walk towards the sea from Remedios brings you to **Malate Church**, on MH del Pilar Street. British soldiers took refuge inside during Britain's brief occupation of the Philippines from 1762 to 1763. Major malls in the area include Robinson's Place, next to the *Manila Midtown Hotel*, and Harrison Plaza, across A Mabini Street from the Metropolitan Museum.

Chinatown

The Chinese and their Chinese-Filipino descendants (known as Chinoys) have found a niche in Philippine society and nowhere is this more apparent than in **Chinatown**, also known as Binondo. It's interesting to wander through the mercantile hubbub of Ongpin Street, past the gold shops and the apothecaries. Urban legend speaks of a special soup you can buy here, enigmatically called Soup Number Five. It is sold in most of the Chinese restaurants in the area and is said to cure everything from colds to impotence, but its contents are a mystery. For something rather more conventional, try the *mongo hopia* (sweet bean cake) from Eng Bee Tin bakery and deli at 628 Ongpin St. **Binondo Church**, at the west end of Ongpin, is where the first Filipino saint, Lorenzo Ruiz, served as a sacristan. Built in 1614 by Dominicans, it quickly became the hub of the Catholic Chinese community. At the far eastern end of Chinatown, across Rizal Street, you reach the **Quiapo area** and Quiapo Church. Every year on January 9, the plaza in front of the church is the venue for the Feast of the Black Nazarene, when 200,000 barefooted Catholic faithful come together to worship a revered crucifix bearing a black figure of Christ. The crowd is dense and fervent, and traffic around the plaza is solid. Quiapo is a good area for bargain-hunters; several stores that sell handicrafts at local prices are squeezed under Quiapo Bridge, a place known as Sa Ilalim ng Tulay ("Under the Bridge"). Outside, the church vendors sell *anting-antings* (amulets). Two kilometres north of Chinatown, a short walk from the Abad Santos LRT station, is the impressive **Chinese Cemetery**, established by merchants because the Spanish would not allow foreigners to be buried in Spanish cemeteries. Many of the tombs resemble houses, with fountains, balconies and, in at least one case, a small swimming pool. It has become a sobering joke in the Philippines that this "accommodation" is among the best in the city.

Malacañang Palace

The shoes are gone, but you can still take a tour of the place the president of the Philippines calls home. The area open to the public is kown as the **Malacañang Museum** (Mon–Fri 9am–3pm; P20) and the entrance is in JP Laurel Street, San Miguel, Manila; use the entrance at Gate Six. There are no guides; if you want to arrange a guided tour of the museum you'll have to write to the museum's managing director, May Tapud.

Malacañang was once a stone house, bought by Colonel Luis Miguel Formento in 1802 for the grand sum of P1100. In 1825, the Spanish government bought it for P5100, and, in 1849, made it the summer residence of the Governor General in the Philippines. In the great tremor of 1863, the Governor General's palace in Intramuros was destroyed, so he moved to Malacañang permanently. Rooms were added and renovations made, but on a number of occasions the building was damaged either by earthquake or typhoon. During the last major renovation in 1978, it underwent extensive interior and exterior changes, and was expanded to its present size – only a portion of the basement remains from the original structure. Malacañang will forever be associated with the excesses of the **Marcoses**. When Cory Aquino became president she didn't want to associate herself with her profligate predecessors and refused to use the palace as a home, keeping it only for official functions. She opened the Malacañang Museum of Marcos Memorabilia, but when Fidel Ramos took over he severed the Marcos connection and asked that the museum focus only on Philippine presidential history, although the Marcos Room does contain some of the late dictator's personal belongings. Current president Gloria Macapagal-Arroyo uses about two thirds of the palace for her official functions and duties, while the museum takes up about one third.

Corregidor

The small tadpole-shaped island of **Corregidor**, which lies in the mouth of Manila Bay and was fought over bitterly during World War II, makes a fascinating side trip from Manila. Sun Cruises (℡02/813 8140, 524 8140 or 524 0333) organizes day-trips and overnight trips from the Cultural Center of the Philippines pier every morning. Accommodation for the overnight trips is in the *Corregidor Inn*, formerly owned by the Marcos family as a weekend retreat and guesthouse. It has an airy restaurant and views towards the Bataan peninsula. A day-trip package usually costs P1500 per person although to drum up trade during lean periods tickets are sometimes reduced to P500. Overnight packages start at P1745. It's worth making time for a visit to the Malinta tunnels, where General Douglas MacArthur set up temporary headquarters and where vicious hand-to-hand combat took place, a ghostly reminder of the horrors of the war. You can walk on the island's trails, rent mountain bikes or explore the gun batteries. There is also a Japanese cemetery, a museum and a memorial to the thousands who died here.

Eating

Intramuros, Ermita and Malate

Aristocrat 432 San Andres St, Malate. Plastic seats and linoleum floors, but *Aristocrat* is an institution among Filipinos looking for comfort food such as *arroz con callo* (rice porridge with entrails; P58) and *dinuguan* (blood stew; P75). The less adventurous can settle for barbecue chicken or pork, noodles, sandwiches or adobo. Opposite Malate Church, close to the seafront.

Cabalen Robinson's Place Manila 2/L Padre Faura Wing. Hugely popular chain of restaurants serving traditional dishes from the province of Pampanga, including *camaru* (rice field crickets), *batute* (fried pig's feet), *kilawing puso ng saging*, *kuhol* (snails), *asadong dila ng baka*, *kare-kare*, *sinigang tiyan ng bangus* (milkfish belly) and desserts such as *tibok-tibok*, *tibok-mais* and *halayang ube*, all made from root crops. If you're daunted by the menu, try the buffet. Seven branches include one in Glorietta, Makati, near Tower Records.

Casa Armas 573 J Nakpil St, Malate. Paella, cochinillo, fiery shrimp gambas, tapas and other Spansh specialities. This is the original and best *Casa Armas*. It has been replicated in Jupiter St, Makati, where the service is amateurish and the vegetables come from a tin.

Dean Street Café 612 Remedios St, Malate. Choose from thirty blends of coffee (P50-100) while using the off-track betting room to wager a few pesos on the nags at Santa Ana or San Lazaro. You can claim your winnings on-site.

Golden Triangle 1806 Maria Orosa St, Malate. Unpretentious and quiet little restaurant specializing in cuisine from northern Thailand. Indigenous decor and reasonably priced food. For dessert, try the mango with black sticky rice.

Ilustrado 744 Calle Real, Intramuros ℡02/527 3674. Nothing compares to *Ilustrado* if you're looking for the ambience of colonial Manila. The floors are polished wood, the tables are set with starched linen, ceiling fans whirr quietly, and the cuisine is rich and grand. Signature dishes include paella, *kaldereta* (Filpino beef stew), venison adobo and a three-course set dinner with steak (P1000) or fish (P800) as the main course. Reservations recommended.

Kamayan 532 Padre Faura cnr M Adriatico St, Ermita & 47 Pasay Rd, Makati. The word *kamayan* means "with your hands", which is how you eat, without knife and fork. The staff are dressed in great Filipino costumes and the dudes in shades work the tables doing requests. If you want a whole roast suckling pig, order it a day ahead. There is also a branch in Glorietta, close to Tower Records.

Kashmir Merchants Center Building, Padre Faura St, Ermita. Curry, chicken tikka, a mouthwatering selection of breads, and wonderfully cheesy ersatz Raj decor. Be warned, the *Kashmir* chefs can be liberal with the spices, so think twice before you ask for anything very hot. There's another branch at Fastejo Building, 816 Pasay Rd.

Kuatro Kantos In the same old building as *Ilustrado.* Charming little bar and café, which opens for breakfast and stays open until 10pm – perfect for a good cup of coffee or a bite to eat while you're wandering around Intramuros. The hot *pan de sal* with corned beef or carabao cheese makes an excellent and very affordable snack. The pesto in the pesto pasta is homemade and organic.

Seafood Market Restaurant J Bocobo St, Malate. Typical of the many seafood restaurants in the Malate area where the day's catch is laid out on ice and you pick from whatever the boat brought in. The choice normally includes giant prawns, lapu-lapu, lobster, fish lips and sea slug, all cooked as you watch by wok chefs in a glass-fronted kitchen.

Sidebar Café 1771 M Adriatico St, Malate. Agreeable little bar on the ground floor of the *Malate Pensionne.* What makes it so pleasant is that it has no themes and no affectations, just some good music, reasonably priced drinks, and a menu whose most adventurous dish is Pinoy corned beef and cabbage, served in tamarind broth. The clientele is a happy mix of expats, travellers, young Filipinos and a few executive folk. Next door is the popular *Portico* bistro and restaurant.

Zamboanga 1619 M Adriatico St, Ermita. Fresh seafood from the deep south, a trio of crooning guitarists, and nightly cultural shows at 8pm. This is the restaurant that features on many travel agents' night-time city tours.

Zen Japanese Restaurant and Sake Bar Level 2, Robinson's Place. Unfussy and affordable Japanese restaurant with a big menu that includes sushi, tempura and inexpensive noodle dishes such as ramen noodles with beef soup and cold udon noodles with raw egg and seaweed.

Makati

Banana Leaf Curry House Greenbelt Mall, Greenbelt. Kitsch interior with plastic plants and tinkling waterfalls, but some of the best Asian cuisine in an area otherwise dominated by franchized Western restaurants and fast food. Something for everyone on a menu that includes Thai, Malaysian, Indonesian and Indian grub. Crab curry starts from P168 depending on the size of the crab, black lamb curry is P368, *tom yam gung* P148 and gado-gado salad P88. Next to *KFC.*

Barrio Fiesta Makati Ave. There are various branches of this popular and colourful Filipino restaurant dotted around the metropolis, all serving indigenous food such as adobo and lechon with hefty portions of rice. Buffet lunch and dinner. In Ermita, there's a branch in United Nations Ave.

Bianca's Café Vinotek 7431 Yakal St. A lovely, comfortable European café. The menu du jour (from P290) is excellent value: a typical meal is a salad starter followed by a pasta dish. Wine is P90 a glass and San Miguel P70.

Gerry's Grill Jupiter St, Makati. This is where Filipinos go for native cuisine, and it's so popular that on Friday nights you'll have to queue to get in. A big, noisy, nipa restaurant at the EDSA end of Jupiter, a right turn off Makati Ave.

Hossein's Persian Kebab 7857 LKV Building, Makati Ave. The unpretentious old *Hossein's* was closed in 1999 to make way for this glitzy new version with frou-frou decor and increased prices to match. If you're not in the mood for a brain sandwich, there are dozens of curry and kebab dishes. Almost opposite is another Middle Eastern restaurant, *Jerusalem*, where the staff are so bad at explaining the dishes they show you photographs instead. The hummus, however, is excellent. *Jerusalem* can also be found at 1533 MH del Pilar St, Malate.

Ihaw-Ihaw Kalde Kaldero at Kawa-Kawali Makati Ave cnr JP Rizal St. Raucous but friendly seafood and grilled meat restaurant where the waiters and waitresses sing as they work. Also a branch on the 4th floor of Megamall in Ortigas.

New Bombay Canteen G/F Sagittarius Building III, HV de la Costa St. This newer branch of the original Buendia *New Bombay* serves the same food at the same low prices. Opposite the *Grand Stamford Hotel*, a few minutes' walk from the *Mandarin Oriental.* Open daily 9.30am–10pm.

Oody's Level Two, Greenbelt 3, Makati Ave. There are dozens of good-value restaurants serving all sorts of cuisine on the second level of this new mall. *Oody's* specializes in noodle and rice dishes, including Thai, Chinese and even some Italian. There's also a reasonable choice for vegetarians, including Thai green curry vegetable rice.

Wasabi Bistro & Sake Bar Olympia Building, 7912 Makati Ave. Minimalist, trendy Japanese restaurant with a relaxed ambience. Clientele runs the gamut from office workers and politicians to diplomats and travelling Japanese executives. Excellent set lunch for P250. A short walk from the *Mandarin Hotel*.

Nightlife and entertainment

Bedrock Bar & Grill Restaurant 1782 M Adriatico St, Malate. Two live bands plays three sets each every night until 4am, and there's no entrance fee. Stone-grilled food includes a hunk of premium Kobe beef for P850. Open Mon–Wed & Sun 6pm–4am, Thurs–Sat 6pm–5am.

Café Adriatico Premier 1900 M Adriatico St, Malate. This chic and casual stalwart of the Malate nightlife scene has benefited from recent renovation.

Café Havana 1903 M Adriatico St, Malate. Uncomfortably busy on Friday and Saturday nights, but evidently the place to see and be seen. The modus operandi is to get drunk and dance to the live samba music. Also features the Ernest Hemingway cigar room. There's another *Café Havana*, a newer one, at the Greenbelt mall on Makati Avenue in Makati. Daily 11am–2am.

Dreambar@6780 Ground Floor, 6780 Ayala Ave, Makati. When the popular *Giraffe* bar and restaurant closed in 2000, Makati's after-midnight ravers went into a decline. Now they have this, an "adult amusement park" that has opened on the same site and is once again home to the drinkers, dancers and cross-dressers that gave *Giraffe* its wild reputation. Beer is P95, a glass of average wine P120 and Scotch P170.

Hobbit House 1801 A Mabini St, Ermita. Twenty years ago, a young Manila entrepreneur decided to open a bar that would pay homage to his favourite book, *The Lord of the Rings*. As a tribute to Bilbo Baggins he staffed it with twenty dwarves, and a legend was born. *Hobbit House* has somehow endured and transmogrified into a middle-class live-music venue, still employing short people, with nightly appearances at 9pm by popular groups such as the bluesy rock band Color It Red. Menu includes Filipino, international and grilled food.

In the Mood Dance Bar 1900 M Adriatico St, Malate. Ballroom dancing is a craze in the Philippines, and this is where you can learn. If you've got two left feet, DIs (dance instructors) are available for a price. Daily 11am–1am.

Kidd Creole Level 3, Greenbelt 3, Makati Ave, Makati. It's the music that draws the crowds on Friday and Saturday nights – some of the most accomplished blues and jazz bands in Manila performing "outdoors" on a balcony overlooking the traffic jams on Makati Avenue. These "Jazz on the Deck" concerts feature luminaries of the local scene, such as the quintet Affinity, whose mellifluous brand of "adobo jazz" – smooth and creamy, like the dish – has secured them high profile gigs at the Blue Note in New York. Flip-flops and vests are out, but pretty much anything else goes. Music starts at 9pm, but aficionados show their practised cool by never turning up before 10pm.

LA Café 1429 MH del Pilar St, Ermita. Manila veterans will notice the familiar doors as they enter *LA Café*; the originals from the infamous *Rosie's Diner* pick-up joint, which once stood on this site. *LA Café* has its share of single customers on the make, but is generally more wholesome than *Rosie's* despite its sepulchral interior. The waitresses are friendly, the San Miguel is on draught, and there are live bands upstairs at 9pm most evenings. The menu includes all the staples of global cuisine: pasta, steak, pizza, Mexican and Indian, with most main dishes costing P150–200. Every Friday from noon until 3pm there is an Indian curry buffet.

Red *Shangri-La Makati*, Makati Ave, Makati. The most popular happy hour in Makati, with all-you-can-drink San Miguel for P180 between 6pm and 9pm and some good live music from 11.30am to 1am.

Sky Lounge *Manila Diamond Hotel*, Boulevard cnr Dr J Quintos St, Ermita. The view across Manila Bay is memorable, and so is the *Sky Lounge*'s hypnotic fibre-optic ceiling, a representation of the galaxy with shooting stars. Romantic cover versions every night from various sultry dames. Get there for cocktails and grab a table by the window. Happy hour 5pm–9pm; open daily 5pm–2am.

Tia Maria's 532 Remedios St, Malate. Branch of a popular Mexican restaurant chain that has become known less for its food, which is average, and more for its cheap drinks (a pitcher of San Miguel costs P138) and live bands. The music starts at 9pm every night and goes on until the small hours, by which time most of the audience have abandoned their seats and taken enthusiastically to the dance floor. The bands are a walking Filipino cliché: four-piece combos with two pretty girls sharing lead vocals on a standard selection of smoochy ballads and groovy pop.

V Glorietta 2, Ayala Center. Posh bistro and club that for years has been packing in a flaky crowd of execs, expats, socialites, models and personalities. Look out for the kitsch blue doors at street level at the back end of Ayala Center, facing Pasay Rd.

Shopping

There are **shopping malls** everywhere in Metro Manila and hardly anything you can buy in London or New York that you can't buy here, at least as far as chic designer labels and trinkets are concerned. However, the first stop for tourists looking for indigenous gifts and **handicrafts** is usually Balikbayan Handicrafts, which has five branches and sells an inspiring range of products. Native **jewellery**, ethnic carvings and household decor are a bargain. The biggest branch is at 290–298 C Palanca St, Quiapo, with others in Pasay Road, Makati and A Mabini Street, Ermita. There are plenty of other antique and handicraft shops along A Mabini Street, while opposite San Agustin Church in Intramuros is a complex of small art and tribal shops, selling everything from carved rice gods and oil paintings to native basketware and jewellery. For a range of bargain goods from fabric and Christmas decorations to clothes, candles, bags and hair accessories, try fighting your way through the crowds at the immense Divisoria Market in CM Recto Street, Binondo, open every day from 10am. The pretty lanterns (*parols*) made from capiz seashells that you see all over the country at Christmas cost P750, half what you would pay in a mall. Divisoria is very busy sometimes and while it's not notorious for pickpockets and snatchers, it's best to dress down and leave valuables at your hotel, just in case. You also stand a better chance of picking up a bargain if you don't look too well off.

You can hunt down **woodcarvings**, capiz-shell items, buri bags and embroidery under Quezon Bridge in Quiapo. In Baclaran, at the southern tip of Roxas Boulevard, is a flea market selling clothes. Haggling is the order of the day in these places. For a small but interesting range of Filipino **books** and environmental videos, go to the Filipino Bookstore at G-72, Ground Floor, Glorietta 1, Ayala Center, Makati. Solidaridad Bookshop, owned by Filipino novelist F. Sionil Jose, is at 531 Padre Faura.

Malls are generally open from 10am until 8pm, although in some cases it's 9am to 10pm. For the cheapest and most mind-boggling choice of fruit in the archipelago, take a wander through the labyrinth San Andres Market in San Andres Street, Manila, close to Quirino Avenue LRT station. Twenty-four hours a day, seven days a week, hundreds of stalls groan under the weight of mango, pomelo, jackfruit, cantaloupe, watermelon, mangosteen, rambutan and durian.

Listings

Airline offices Air Canada, 21st Floor, Tower 2, The Enterprise Center, 6766 Ayala Ave, Makati ⓣ02/884 8294 or 884/8995; Air India, Gammon Center Building, Makati ⓣ02/815 1280 or 817 5865; Air Philippines, 15th Floor, Multinational Bankcorporation Center, 6805 Ayala Ave, Makati ⓣ02/855 9000; American Airlines, Olympia Condominium, Makati ⓣ02/817 8675; Asian Spirit, LPL Towers, 112 Legaspi St, Makati ⓣ02/851 8888 or 853 1957; British Airways, De La Rosa cnr Legaspi St, Legaspi Village, Makati ⓣ02/817 0361; Cathay Pacific, 22nd Floor, LKG Tower, 6801 Ayala Ave ⓣ02/757 0888; Cebu Pacific, Express Ticket Office, Beside Gate 1, Terminal Building 1, Manila Domestic Airport ⓣ02/636 4938, or general sales agent Supersonic Services Inc at G/F Colonnade Residence, Carlos Palanca St, Legaspi Village, Makati ⓣ02/840 4587, 819 5546 or 816 6485; China Airlines, Ground Floor, Midtown Arcade, M Adriatico St, Ermita ⓣ02/523 8021-24; Corporate Air, Old Domestic Passenger Terminal, Manila Domestic Airport ⓣ02/852 5504; or 852 5505; Emirates, Pacific Star Building, Makati Ave cnr Senator Gil Puyat Ave, Makati ⓣ02/811 5278-80;

Japan Airlines, *Dusit Hotel Nikko*, Makati ☎02/886 6868; KLM Royal Dutch Airlines, 160 Alfaro St, Makati ☎02/815 4790-92; Lufthansa, 134 Legaspi St, Makati ☎02/810 4596; Northwest, Ground Floor, Gedisco Building, 1148 Roxas Blvd ☎02/521 1928 or 819 7341; Mexicana Airlines, G/F Colonnade Residence, Carlos Palanca St, Legaspi Village, Makati ☎02/840 4587, 819 5546 or 816 6485; Pakistan International Airlines, G/F Colonnade Residence, Carlos Palanca St, Legaspi Village, Makati ☎02 840 4587, 819 5546 or 816 6485; PAL, G/F Legaspi Street, Legaspi Village, Makati, 24hr reservations ☎02/855 8888; Singapore Airlines, 138 HV De la Costa St, Salcedo Village, Makati ☎02/810 4951–59; Qatar Airways ☎02/232 1000, G/F The Collonade, Legaspi Village, Makati; South East Asian Airlines (SEAIR), 2/F Dona Concepcion Building, 1020 Pasay Rd, Makati (☎02/851 5555); Swissair, Zuellig Building, Makati ☎02/818 8351; Thai Airways, Country Space 1 Building, Senator Gil Puyat Ave, Makati ☎02/817 4044; Qantas, Filipino Merchants Building, De la Rosa cnr Legaspi St, Makati ☎02/812 0607; Varig Brazilian Airlines, G/F Colonnade Residence, Carlos Palanca St, Legaspi Village, Makati ☎02/840 4587, 819 5546 or 816 6485; Vietnam Airlines, general sales agent Imex Travel, Ground Floor, Colonnade Building, 132 Carlos Pelanca St, Makati ☎02/810 3406, 810 3653 or 893 2083.

Banks and exchange American Express, Manila Branch, 1810 A Mabini St, Malate ☎02/524 8681 or 526 8406; Bank of the Philippine Islands (BPI; ☎02/818 5541 for details of all branches); Citibank, 8741 Paseo de Roxas, Makati ☎02/813 9101; Hong Kong & Shanghai Banking Corp, Ayala Ave, Makati ☎02/635 1000; Solidbank, 777 Paseo De Roxas, Makati ☎02/811 4769; Standard Chartered Bank, 6756 Ayala Ave, Makati ☎02/892 0961. Most major bank branches have 24hr ATMs for Visa and MasterCard cash advances.

Embassies and consulates Australia, 1st–5th Floor, Ty Tower, 104 Paseo de Roxas, Makati ☎02/728 1860; Brunei, 11th Floor, BPI Building, 104 Paseo de Roxas, Makati ☎02/816 2836; Canada, 9–11th Floor, Allied Bank Center, 6754 Ayala Ave, Makati ☎02/867 0001; France, 16/F Pacific Star Building, Makati Ave, Makati ☎02/810 1981; Germany, 6/F Global bank Center, 777 Paseo de Roxas, Makati ☎02/892 4906; Indonesia, 185 Salcedo Street, Legaspi Village, Makati ☎02/892 5061; Ireland, Third Floor, 70 Jupiter St, Bel-Air 1, Makati ☎02/896 4668; Malaysia, 107 Tordesillas St, Salcedo Village, Makati ☎02/817 4581; Japan, 2627 Roxas Boulevard ☎02/551 5710; the Netherlands, 9th Floor, King's Court Building, 2129 Pasong Tamo, Makati ☎02/812 5981; New Zealand, 23rd Floor, Far East Bank Center, Sen Gil Puyat Ave, Makati ☎02/891 5358; Singapore, 6th Floor, ODC International Plaza, 219 Salcedo St, Legaspi Village, Makati ☎02/816 1764; Spain, 5/F ACT Tower, 135 Gil Puyat Ave, Makati ☎/02/818 5526; Sweden, PCI Bank Tower II, Makati Ave cnr De la Rosa St, Makati ☎02/819 1951; Switzerland, Solid Bank Building, 777 Paseo de Roxas, Makati ☎02/892 2051; Thailand, Royal Thai Embassy Building, 107 Rada St, Legaspi Village, Makati ☎02/815 4219; UK, 15th–17th Floor, LV Locsin Building 6752 Ayala Ave cnr Makati Ave, Makati ☎02/816 7116; US, 1201 Roxas Blvd ☎02/523 1001; Vietnam, 554 Vito Cruz St, Malate ☎02/524 0354.

Emergencies The Department of Tourism has two assistance lines (☎02/524 1703 or 524 2384) and two Tourist Hotlines (☎02/524 1728 or 524 1660).

Hospitals and clinics Makati Medical Center, 2 Amorsolo St, Makati (☎02/815 9911), is the largest and one of the most modern hospitals in Manila. It has an emergency department and dozens of specialist clinics. You can't make an appointment for the clinics – you just have to turn up and join the queue. Opening times are 10am–noon and 2–4pm. An initial consultation costs around P350. The HCS Medical Care Center, also in Makati at 3rd Floor, Equitable Bank Building, Senator Gil Puyat Ave (☎02/897 9111-20), has a rotating team of doctors who deal with ambulant cases. It's a good place to go for basic care and prescriptions, but there are no emergency facilities. A consultation costs P350. In the Manila Bay area, Manila Doctors' Hospital (☎02/524 3011) is at 667 United Nations Ave, and the Medical Center Manila (☎02/523 8131) is at 1122 General Luna St, Ermita.

Immigration Bureau of Immigration and Deportation, Magellanes Drive, Intramuros (☎02/527 3257 or 527 3280). Open 8am–noon & 1–5pm. There is a new Immigration Office in Makati where queues are often shorter. It's at 4th Floor, Gotiaco Building, MC Briones St, opposite Makati City Hall.

Internet access Internet access is very easy to find in all tourist areas. Global Café (☎02/536 8023) is at 3rd Floor, Pedro Gil Wing, Robinson's Place, Ermita. In Makati, the Filipinas Heritage Library in Makati Ave (☎02/892 1801) charges P100 an hour. Mailstation at 30-A Park Square 1, Ayala Center, Makati (☎02/817 8134 or 817 3135) charges P30 an hour, as do a number of email stations nearby, in the area opposite the *Dusit Hotel Nikko*.

Pharmacies You're never far from a Mercury Drug outlet in Metro Manila. At the last count, there were two hundred of them. In Ermita, there's one at 444 TM Kalaw St and another at Robinson's Place in M Adriatico. In Makati, there's a big branch in the Glorietta mall on the ground floor near Tower Records.

Police Tourist Police, Room 112, Department of Tourism Building, Teodoro Valencia Circle, TM Kalaw St, Ermita (☎02/524 1660 or 524 1728); Western District Police, United Nations Ave, Ermita.

Post office Never post anything valuable to or from the Philippines because there's a chance it will be pilfered. If you want to be sure, use a courier company such as DHL or Federal Express. A document couriered from Manila to the UK will cost about P1600. In the Manila Bay area there's a small post office opposite the *Manila Hotel* and a general post office at Liwasang Bonifacio, Intramuros, near MacArthur Bridge on the Pasig River. The closest LRT station is Central. In Makati, there is a post office at the junction of Gil Puyat and Ayala Aves, next to Makati Fire Station. Look out also for the numerous Mailstation outlets, where you can post letters, make telephone calls and often find email services.

Telephone services Pre-paid PLDT Fonkards are available from 7–11 stores and allow you to make local or international (IDD) calls from PLDT cardphones.

Travel agents Adventure International Tours, 1810 A. Mabini St, Malate (☎02/524 8681); Bridges Travel, Unit B, Acosta Building, Senator Gil Puyat Ave, Pasay (☎02/867 1186); Century Travel & Tours, 1991 A. Mabini St, Malate (☎02/526 6180); Danfil Express, 1780 A. Mabini St, Malate (☎02/524 8703); Filipino Travel Center, G/F Ramona Apartments, 1555 M. Adriatico St, Malate (☎02/528 4507).

8.2

South of Manila and Mindoro

Leaving the sprawl of Manila behind and heading south takes you along the South Luzon Expressway, known to Filipinos as the South Luzon Distressway, and into the provinces of Cavite, Laguna and Batangas. Traffic heading south can be grim, particularly on weekends and holidays, so try to time your journey for a weekday. **Laguna**, known for hot springs and mountain pools, is the first province south of the capital. It was named after Laguna de Bay, the lake that forms its northern boundary, and is a major source of sampaguita flowers, orchids, coconuts, rice, sugar, citrus fruits and lanzones. **Cavite** is being touted as a new industrial zone, but will forever be associated with the revolution. In 1872, three Filipino priests – Jose Burgos, Mariano Gomez and Jacinto Zamora – were implicated in the Cavite Revolt, in which two hundred Filipinos rose up in arms against the Spanish forces in the garrisons. They were garrotted by the Spanish in what is now Rizal Park, where a memorial stands at the execution site. The so-called Phoney Revolution was soon cut down, but when the real thing broke out on August 28, 1896, Cavite became a bloody theatre of war, as Emilio Aguinaldo led Caviteños in a series of daring surprise attacks on Spanish headquarters, soon liberating the whole province. Aguinaldo directed the revolution to its end and the proclamation of the first republic in Asia, the Republic of the Philippines, was made on June 12, 1898 in the small town of Kawit. The town hall where the proclamation was made from a balcony still stands and has become the focus of commemorations every June 12. The province of **Batangas** is Manila's weekend playground, with tropical-style beach resorts and **Taal Volcano**. The provincial capital, **Batangas City**, is a polluted port town with little to recommend it except its ferry pier, from where you can escape to the island of **Mindoro** and the beach resorts of **Puerto Galera**.

Bus departures start early, at around 4am and continue at regular intervals, usually every hour, until the middle of the evening, with the final departure at around 8pm. BLTB (behind Areneta Colisum in Cubao) and Jam Liner (on Taft Avenue) are two of the most popular services.

Laguna province

The largely agricultural province of **Laguna** follows the south and southeastern coast of Laguna de Bay, its topography dominated by the massive hulk of **Mount Makiling**. On the province's western edge is the town of **Calamba**, birthplace of national hero José Rizal, and on its eastern edge the town of **Pagsanjan** and nearby **Pagsanjan Falls** and **Lake Caliraya**. The area around **Los Baños** has a number of resorts with bathing pools fed by **hot springs** on the slopes of Mount Makiling, while the challenging **Mount Banahaw**, on the border with Quezon province, is reached from the provincial capital of **San Pablo**.

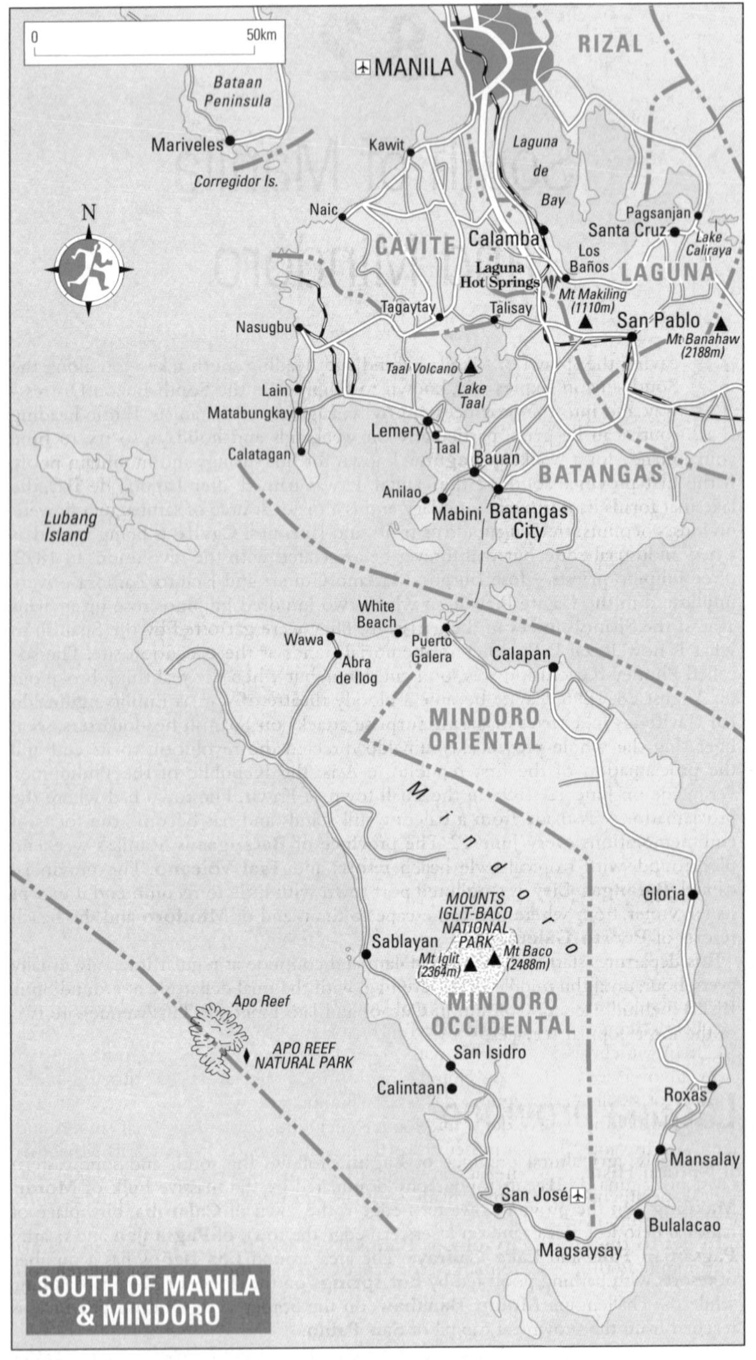
0
50km
MANILA
RIZAL
Bataan Peninsula
Mariveles
Corregidor Is.
Kawit
Laguna de Bay
Naic
CAVITE
Calamba
Pagsanjan
Santa Cruz
Lake Caliraya
Los Baños
LAGUNA
Laguna Hot Springs
Mt Makiling (1110m)
Tagaytay
Talisay
Nasugbu
San Pablo
Mt Banahaw (2188m)
Taal Volcano
Lake Taal
Lain
Matabungkay
Lemery
Taal
Calatagan
Bauan
BATANGAS
Anilao
Mabini
Batangas City
Lubang Island
White Beach
Wawa
Abra de Ilog
Puerto Galera
Calapan
MINDORO ORIENTAL
Mindoro
Gloria
MOUNTS IGLIT-BACO NATIONAL PARK
Sablayan
Mt Iglit (2364m)
Mt Baco (2488m)
Apo Reef
MINDORO OCCIDENTAL
APO REEF NATURAL PARK
San Isidro
Calintaan
Roxas
Mansalay
San José
Bulalacao
Magsaysay
SOUTH OF MANILA & MINDORO

Jac Liner, Tritran, JAM Transit and BLTB buses all operate at least hourly from the Pasay terminals to Calamba, Los Baños (and Mount Makiling), San Pablo and **Santa Cruz** (for Pagsanjan), and there are some Calamba services from the Taft Avenue end of Rizal Park. The **rail** line from Manila runs through Calamba and San Pablo. From Batangas City, it's straightforward to get buses to all these destinations.

Calamba

The town of **CALAMBA** – once a rural backwater, now a choked and noisy extension of Manila – hugs the coast of the southern tip of Laguna de Bay at the foot of Mount Makiling, just 54km from the capital. You can reach Calamba on numerous **buses** heading south from Pasay or Cubao. Tri Tran, Jam Transit and BLTB all have hourly departures, sometimes more. There's nothing to see in the new part of Calamba, just the usual malls, fast-food outlets and hundreds of din-making tricycles. The old town, however, was built in Spanish colonial style, with a shady plaza in front of a town hall and a church, San Juan Bautista. A marker inside the church indicates that national hero and revolutionary **José Rizal** was baptized here by Fray Rufino Collantes on June 22, 1861. Rizal's stature in the Philippines, a country notoriously short of heroes, is such that a number of religious cults have sprung up in his honour, most of them professing that Rizal is the Son of God and will one day return to lead his disciples to salvation. One such group has its headquarters near the church, on Lecheria Hill.

Opposite the church is the house where Rizal was born on June 19, 1861. Now a **museum** (Tues–Sun 8am–noon & 1–5pm; free), it's a typical nineteenth-century Philippine *bahay-na-bato*, with lower walls of stone and upper walls of wood, plus *narra* wood floors and windows made from capiz shell. The house, which was restored in 1996 for the Centennial of the Philippine Revolution, also has a small stable for horses and storage for carriages on the ground floor, while the upper floor marks the living area. All the rooms feature period furniture and there are displays of Rizal's belongings, including the clothes he was christened in and a suit he wore as a young man. In the garden is a *bahay kubo* (wooden) playhouse, a replica of the one Rizal used to spend his days in as a child.

Los Baños and around

LOS BAÑOS, just south of Calamba on the South Luzon Expressway, is home to the University of the Philippines Los Baños (UPLB; ⓦwww.uplb.edu.ph), the forestry campus of the Manila-based university. The campus lies at the foot of **Mount Makiling**; the **rainforest** in this area is unspoiled and there are some nice walking trails. There are a number of other attractions on the campus, including the International Rice Research Institute (IRRI), which was established to help farmers in developing countries grow more rice on limited land with less water and labour, fewer chemicals, and with less harm to the environment. The IRRI is home to the excellent **Riceworld Museum** (Mon–Fri 8am–noon & 1–5pm; ⓦwww.riceworld.org; free), which opened in 1994 with grants from the German government. Apart from an overview of the developing world's food shortages, the museum has a number of small but intriguing displays, including one where visitors can inspect live paddy-field insects under a microscope, including damselflies, wolf spiders and aggressive fire ants. Another museum worth making time for is the **UPLB Museum of Natural History** (Mon–Sat 8am–5pm; P10), which has more than 200,000 biological specimens of Philippine plants, animals and micro-organisms. Sunday visits are possible if you call first.

To get to the University of Los Baños take a BLTB bus from Pasay in Manila (1hr 30min; P60). Buses are marked for Santa Cruz and the conductor will tell you where to get off. From Calamba, take a jeepney from the main square (P15). From Pagsanjan, buses to Manila go through Los Baños (1hr).

The Laguna hot springs

The area of **Laguna** around Los Baños trades heavily for its tourist custom on the health properties of its **hot springs**, which bubble from the lower slopes of Mount Makiling. There are dozens of resorts of varying quality, all using the springs to fill swimming pools that become wallowing holes for visitors from Manila, especially at the weekend. Many of these resorts are big and also cater to company outings, day-trippers and business conferences, so don't expect rural peace and quiet. Most of the resorts are on the main road between Calamba and Los Baños. The biggest concentration starts around the fifty-kilometre marker south of Manila. The standard of **accommodation** at the resorts is generally disappointing – pretty nipa huts been replaced by concrete air-con boxes with tatty furniture and no views. *Crystal Springs* (☎02/895 9423; ⑥) is on the slopes of Mount Makiling at the 57-kilometre marker – on the right as you leave Los Baños – and has a variety of water rides, though the place feels a little down at heel. The pools close at 5pm, and the restaurant is hot and grubby. The rooms, though faded, are spacious, with double bed, plastic sofa and a deep bath that can be filled with hot springwater. One of the biggest resorts in the area is the *Monte Vista Hot Springs and Conference Resort* (☎049/545 1259, ⑤), on the right if you're heading south from Calamba. It has eighteen hot mineral pools, assorted giant slides, and enough room for 1500 day visitors. Rooms have air-con and en-suite tiled bathrooms. **To reach the resorts** from Calamba, you can take a southbound jeepney. BLTB buses heading from Cubao in Manila to Santa Cruz also pass this way.

Mount Makiling

The dormant volcano of **Mount Makiling** (1110m) is in Laguna province, half an hour south of Calamba by jeepney or bus, and is identifiable by its unusual shape, rather like a reclining woman. The mountain is named after Mariang Makiling (Mary of Makiling), a young woman whose spirit is said to protect the mountain – on quiet nights, she is said to play the harp. Tribespeople say they rarely hear the music any more and believe it is because Makiling is angry about the scant regard paid to the environment by the authorities.

Mount Makiling is the source of the famous Laguna hot springs. There is a well-established and strenuous trail to the summit starting at UPLB, but climbing it alone is not recommended. Enquire at the university's administration building, on the left just inside the main gate, about hiring a **guide**, which will cost at least P1000 excluding provisions for the guide. You'll need to bring all your own gear though, including tent, food and enough water for 48 hours. Alternatively, contact AMCI Mountaineers (Ⓦwww.amci.org.ph) about joining an organized trek. Most climbers camp below the summit for the night and then walk the remaining distance to the top early the following day to watch the sunrise. To **get to Makiling** from Calamba, take a bus or jeepney from the main square heading south (P15). From the university campus, take a jeepney marked for the Scout Jamboree Park.

Pagsanjan Falls and Lake Caliraya

Francis Ford Coppola chose **PAGSANJAN**, 80km southeast of Manila, as the location for the final scenes in *Apocalypse Now*. Most tourists come here not for its Hollywood memorabilia value, however, but to shoot the fourteen rapids down the Bombongan River from the **Pagsanjan Falls**. The local *bangkeros* have become adept at manoeuvring their canoes between the boulders, but have also gained a reputation for being hard-nosed when the time comes to demand a tip. Prices are already rather steep for the seven-kilometre thrill ride, starting at more than P1000 for a single passenger or P580 per person if there are two or three of you. Bear in mind that the official Department of Tourism (DoT) rate is pegged at P580 per person, so you shouldn't pay more. Many tour operators in Manila offer day tours that you can book in the capital (see p.794). Bridges Travel (☎02/867 1186) has a tour for US$55 per person for a minimum of two people, including transport and lunch at the *Riverside Hotel*. It's best to get to the falls early before the hordes arrive, and to avoid weekends if possible. The last rapids trip is usually a couple of hours before sundown, at around 4pm. The rapids are at their most thrilling in the wet season, while during the dry season the ride is much more sedate.

Practicalities

The falls are best reached through the small town of **Santa Cruz**, two hours southeast of Manila on the southern shore of Laguna de Bay. Santa Cruz is served by regular **BLTB and Jam Liner buses** from Manila. From Santa Cruz, it's an easy ten-minute jeepney ride to the river, but watch out for touts who will intercept you as you get off the bus and try to guide you towards their boat. Others will offer "special rides" to the falls, but there's no need as Jeepneys run regularly from the little square in the centre of Santa Cruz and cost P10.

There's no shortage of **accommodation** in and around Pagsanjan. The *Pagsanjan Youth Hostel* (☎049/645 2347; ❷) at 237 General Luna St, has basic dorm beds with fan for P150 and singles/doubles with fan. Guesthouses include the simple but clean *Willy Flores Guesthouse*, 821 Garcia St (❹), offering singles and doubles with fan and bath. More expensive is *La Corona de Pagsanjan* (☎049/808 1753, 808 1793, or the Manila reservations office ☎02/564 2631–38; ❼), on the road from Pagsanjan towards Cavinti. There are standard doubles and deluxe doubles, with breakfast included. You can get discounts if you book through Asia Travel (☎02/747 1270). The resort has a nice pool and a campsite at the rear where you can pitch a tent. It's close to the falls and also to other attractions such as the village of Paete, known for the quality of its woodcarvings, and the underground cemetery at Nagcarlan. This cemetery, built in 1851, takes its name from an underground crypt beneath a pretty old Spanish chapel where a number of Nagcarlan's luminaries are buried. *Pagsanjan Falls Lodge and Summer Resort* (☎02/632 7834 in Manila; ❼), in Barangay Pinagsanjan (take a jeepney from General Luna Street), has thirteen air-con doubles and fifteen fan rooms (❻), both for a maximum of three people. The resort charges P650 per person for the boat ride, made up of P580 DoT fee, P20 for a cushion and P50 for a lifejacket. Their set lunch is P242.

Lake Caliraya

The impressive man-made **Lake Caliraya** is 3050m above sea level and cooler year round than Manila by about eight degrees. The area affords impressive views of **Laguna de Bay** and nearby **Mount Banahaw**, while on the lake you can hire jet-skis, water skis, kayaks and windsurfers. **Pagsanjan Falls** are only a few minutes away, and the neighbouring town of **Lumban** is famous for its beautiful embroidered barongs, the traditional Filipino dress shirt. The villagers of Paete sell intricate woodcarvings and colourful papier-mâché masks and sculptures.

Jeepneys from Pagsanjan go to Caliraya every half hour or when they are full (P20), travelling along the lakeshore to all the accommodation. The most popular **place to stay** at Lake Caliraya is the *Lagos Del Sol Resort* (☎02/526 8088 or 523 1835, or c/o the *Aloha Hotel* in Malate; ❺), set in immense tropical gardens where you can walk and jog, and offering water skiing, windsurfing, tennis, and a swimming pool. Accommodation here comprises spacious, comfortable lakeside cottages for up to four, or a choice of rooms in the main building. The native-style restaurant is rundown and the food isn't very good for the price, so people spending the weekend here tend to bring their own sandwiches and snacks.

Mount Banahaw

About 130km southeast of Manila, near Dolores in Quezon province, is 2188-metre **Mount Banahaw**. Considered a sacred mountain by seventeen religious sects with different beliefs and rituals, Banahaw has spawned a vast number of legends and superstitions: one says that every time a foreigner sets foot on the mountain it will rain. Every year at Easter, thousands of pilgrims flock to the mountain. Banahaw is a challenging but rewarding climb, its slopes thick with jungle and with panoramic views of the surrounding country from the crater rim. To get to the start of the trail, take a **jeepney** from **SAN PABLO** to the barangay of **Kinabuyahan**. Treat this mountain seriously because although the early part of the trail looks wide and well-trodden it soon peters out into inhospitable rainforest – even experienced climbers allow three days to reach the summit and get back down safely, and a crater descent should only be attempted by expert climbers. You will need to hire a **guide** at the barangay hall in Kinabuyahan and sign a logbook before you are allowed to proceed. If you haven't got time to reach the summit you can trek to **Kristalino Falls** ("Crystalline Falls") and back in a day. One-and-a-half hours' further is a second waterfall, whose surroundings are ideal for a **campsite**.

Tagaytay and Taal Volcano

TAGAYTAY, 70km south of Manila, perches on a 600-metre-high ridge overlooking Taal Volcano, and because of its cool climate – on some days it even gets foggy – is a popular weekend retreat from the heat of the nearby capital. Unfortunately, rash development and abuse of building restrictions have rather turned Tagaytay into the tourist town from hell, with congested roads and menacing shoals of tricycles. Thankfully, you don't actually have to go as far as Tagaytay itself to enjoy spectacular views of the volcano. The views are best if you get off the bus near the *Taal Vista Lodge Hotel*, where you can visit the gardens (free admission) and get a good Filipino buffet lunch. **Taal Volcano** is still active, and there are occasional rumblings that force the authorities to issue evacuation warnings to local inhabitants. The volcano last erupted in 1965, without causing major damage, but when it blew its top in 1754, thousands died and the town of Taal was destroyed and had to be rebuilt in a new location on safer ground. If you want to climb it, the jumping-off point is the small town of **Talisay** on the shores of Lake Taal, hiring a boat and guide in Talisay for around P1000. If you make an early start, you can climb to either the new crater or the old crater (both are active) and be back in Talisay in time for a good fish lunch at one of the many native-cuisine restaurants along the shore. There is not much shade on the volcano and it can get hot, so don't go without sunblock, a good hat and plenty of water. You can find out more about Taal Volcano and other volcanoes at the **Taal Volcano Science House**, 5km west of Talisay in **Buco**, next to the *Buco Resort*.

Practicalities

From Manila, several BLTB **buses** run daily from Cubao to Tagaytay (2hr, P70), but it's usually quicker to miss out Tagaytay altogether: take a BLTB bus from Pasay marked for Lemery and get off in **Tanauan**, where you can catch a jeepney at the public market for the thirty-minute bumpy trip to Talisay (P18). Another option is to get off the bus from Manila at Tagaytay Rotunda, the big roundabout at the approach to the volcano's ridge, from where you can also take a jeepney to Talisay. There are regular jeepneys running all day from Tagaytay to Talisay and back (40min). You can also use these jeepneys to take you back and forth along the ridge, which is about 4kms long. **From Batangas City**, some buses bound for Pasay in Manila pass through Tanuaun and others take a route through Tagaytay. Make sure you ask the driver before you get on.

Views from the ridge overlooking the lake make it more expensive **to stay** here than in one of the barangays by the lake around Talisay, a more convenient area if you intend to climb the volcano – your accommodation will arrange the boat across to the volcano for you. Less than 1km west of Talisay on the road to Leynes and close to the lakeshore is *San Roque Beach Resort* (☎043/773 0271 or 0919/310 7976; ❹), a warm and welcoming place right on the lake – there's even a small grey-sand beach with deckchairs – with magnificent views across to the volcano. Accommodation is in pretty whiteshed huts with thatched roofs, and boats to the volcano cost P1000. *Taal Lake Yacht Club*, about 1km east of Talisay on the shore (☎02/811 3183 or 811 3283; ❹) is a popular and well-run sailing club with private huts and sailing boats available for rent (respectively P400 and P3800 per day). There's also a pleasant and secure campsite, and air-con cabins with a kitchen at the resort next door if you want to stay overnight. Their bancas to the volcano are among the safest on the lake, with mobile phones, lifejackets and fire extinguishers, and the price of P1400 includes admission to the club (normally P100 per person), a guide, and a hut with hot showers where you can change. Up on the ridge, *Taal Vista Lodge Hotel* (☎046/413 1223; ❼) is a rambling hotel above the lake, on the left if you approach Tagaytay from Manila. Rooms are spacious, and off-season discounts are available. Resorts and hotels around Tagaytay all have simple **restaurants** and near the *Taal Vista Lodge Hotel* are a number of fast-food places. Also on the ridge, a little past the *Taal Vista Lodge Hotel* heading south, is *Josephine's*, a popular Filipino restaurant with a huge menu of affordable dishes. On Aguinaldo Highway, the main road from Manila to Tagaytay, is *Gourmet Café*, a quaint, rustic restaurant that serves organic produce grown on its own farm. It's a few kilometres north of the lake ridge and a little tricky to reach by public transport. The best way is to take a northbound jeepney from Tagaytay Rotunda.

Taal Town

The name Taal is usually associated with the brooding volcano. Most visitors overlook the town of **TAAL** itself, which is a shame because it offers a blast from a glorious past, with faded Spanish colonial architecture, the house where the first Philippine flag was sewn, and the magnificent **Basilica of St Martin de Tours**, said to be the biggest church in Southeast Asia. The original church was completed in 1575 but destroyed by volcanic eruption in 1754. The present church was built in 1856 and inaugurated by Augustinian friars in 1865 and has been made a national shrine by presidential decree. The town's *bahay-na-bato* (stone houses) are being preserved by the Taal Heritage Foundation, and there's a **Lourdes grotto** with water that is believed to have healing powers. The **market** in Taal is a good place to look for local embroidery. The area is also well known for the manufacture of deadly fan knives, which have a hidden blade that flicks out from the handle.

If you want to **stay** overnight, try *Casa Punzalan* (❺), a pretty colonial-era guesthouse overlooking the town square, with simple, comfortable rooms furnished in reproduction Batangas antiques. The Taal Heritage Foundation (☎043/421 1053 or 421 3034) can put you in touch with local homestays. From Manila, a number of **buses** (BLTB, Tri Tran and Jam) ply the Manila-Taal-Lemery route (P80). From Tagaytay, you can either catch a bus marked for Lemery and get off in Taal, or take a jeepney (P15). From Batangas City, buses to Manila sometimes pass through Taal, but check with the driver first.

Batangas beach resorts

For many hardworking city-dwellers, the first stop at the weekend is one of the many **beach resorts in Batangas**. In truth, the beaches are nothing to write home about, but they are at least relatively close to Manila. Three hours after leaving the smoke you can be breaking out the suntan oil. When travelling to the beach resorts of Batangas there are two areas to choose from. You can take a bus (BLTB, hourly departures from Pasay terminal; P100, 2–3hr) to **NASUGBU**, **LIAN** or **CALATAGAN** on the west coast. The road that runs north and south from Nasugbu to Calatagan passes through Matabungkay and is lined with resorts; the best thing to do is take a tricycle from wherever you get off the bus.

The other area of Batangas province with sea and sand is **ANILAO**, further south, which you reach by taking a bus (BLTB) from Cubao in Manila (P120, 3hr) for Batangas City but asking to be let off in Bauan. From here you can take a jeepney to the pier at Anilao, then a tricycle along the coastal road to the resort of your choice. Another option from Batangas City is to take one of the regular Batangas–Anilao or Batangas–Mabini jeepneys from outside *McDonald's* on P Burgos Street. Hiring a small van for the trip to Anilao in Batangas costs around P4000, which makes it worth considering if there are enough passengers with whom to split the costs.

Nasugbu area accommodation

Coral Beach Club On the beach near Lian, south of Nasugbu ☎0912/318 4868. A quiet, attractive place with a beachside pool and standard or deluxe a/c rooms. It claims its white beach is the closest to Manila. 6–7

Lago de Oro Beach Club Balibago, Calatican ☎0917/504 3719 or 504 2685. Modern hacienda-style resort well run by friendly Germans. Good food in the European-style restaurant and a lake for water skiing. Overlooking the beach south of Matabungkay. 6–7

Matabungkay Beach Resort & Hotel ☎043/750 1459. Basic but clean rooms, some big enough for families, with large balconies. There's a pleasant restaurant and a swimming pool, although the beach is not great. Take a jeepney from Nasugbu, heading south (20min; P20). 6

Punta Buluarte Resort Balitoc, Calatagan ☎02/892 4202. Sprawling development with upmarket pretensions and a wide range of rooms, from a double with a sunrise view, to your own native-style Bicol house for four. Two swimming pools, and buffet meals in the seashore restaurant. The beach is not good for swimming. 7

White Sands Beach Resort Muntingbuhangin Cove ☎02/833 5608. 4km north of Nasugbu by boat or tricycle. Shady cottages with showers, perched on a hillside overlooking a peaceful sand beach. Some huts sleep up to six people, and are ideal for families. 5

Anilao area accommodation

Anilao Seasport Center ☎043/807 4570 or 807 4574. Good range of rooms, from standard doubles to spacious rooms opening onto a veranda and family rooms for five people. 4

Aquaventure Reef Club ☎02/899 2831. Comfortable, unpretentious resort 3km along the coastal road beyond Anilao. Operated by Manila-based dive outfit Aquaventure, it's primarily a scuba resort, though it also offers island-hopping and snorkelling trips in rented bancas. Double rooms come with fan and bath; buffet-style meals are served in a nice open restaurant overlooking the sea. 3

Dive Solana ☎02/721 2089. Along the coastal road beyond the *Aquaventure Reef Club*, this is a charming and slightly bohemian little retreat owned by Filipina filmmaker Marilou Diaz-Abaya. There are a/c and fan rooms, some right on the beach, with an ethnic touch, and the rate includes three buffet meals a day. Always full at weekends, so book in advance. Prices fall ten percent during the week. 4

Planet Dive The last of the resorts along the Anilao strip ☎02/410 6193. Native-style cottages opposite the Twin Rocks dive site, where the bay is sheltered enough for good snorkelling. You can have candlelight dinners on the shore, and there's a viewing deck from which to take in Anilao's wonderful sunsets. 3

Villa Ligaya ☎02/896 6016. Well-run resort that's geared up for divers, but homey and friendly enough for non-divers too. There's a choice of fan or a/c rooms, all simple but chic, with wooden floors and dazzling white linen on the beds. All meals are buffet style and there's a shady terrace and a nipa hut where you can relax and admire the sea views. 4

Batangas City

BATANGAS CITY (as opposed to Batangas province) is a transit point for tourists on their way to Puerto Galera. As a destination in its own right, it has nothing to offer; as an industrial city, there are signs that it is springing into life, with a new pier and talk of numerous industrial zones. But for most visitors, the only sight they see in Batangas City is the ferry terminal (for all ferry schedules call ☎043/723 8245).

If you get stuck overnight in Batangas City you can take your pick from a number of poorly maintained flophouses or try the relatively superior **Avenue Pension House** (☎043/725 3720; ❸) at 30 JP Rizal Ave. If you have cash to spare there's a new **Days Inn** (☎043/723 6931–36; ❼) on the outskirts of the city, fifteen minutes from the pier. BLTB **buses** to Batangas City leave from Pasay in Manila starting at 5.30am (3hr; P75). They go first to the ferry pier (for Puerto Galera) and then to the terminal in JP Rizal Avenue, near the cathedral. On the way back from Puerto Galera, numerous buses wait at the pier for the trip to Manila. Try to take a direct bus marked for Pasay – some buses go through the barrios, making it a long journey.

Puerto Galera

It may be touristy and the importunate hawkers can frazzle your nerves, but **PUERTO GALERA** on the northern coast of **Mindoro**, 80km south of Manila, has become one of the Philippines' most popular tourist attractions, and rightly so. It has a stunning natural harbour, countless coves and beaches, a good range of affordable accommodation and excellent scuba diving, with around thirty listed **dive sites**. There are dozens of accredited dive operators in the area, making it a good place to strike a deal and get yourself a discount on the going rates. Puerto Galera is actually the name of a small town here but is generally used to refer to the area between Sabang, 5km to the east, and White Beach, 8km to the west.

Puerto Galera's extensive and diverse coral reefs have been declared a UNESCO Man and the Biosphere Marine Reserve – a marine environment of global importance. The direct protection that comes from such a declaration is minimal, but the reefs remain intact thanks to the efforts of local people, hotel owners and dive operators, who all co-operate to ensure the undersea riches are not frittered away.

Even arriving at Puerto Galera is memorable, the ferry from Batangas City slipping gently through aquamarine waters past a series of headlands fringed with haloes of

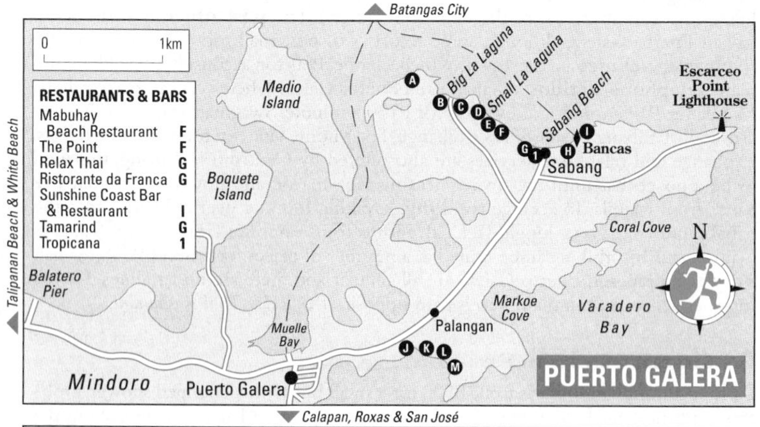

ACCOMMODATION

Angelyn Beach Resort	G	Cataquis Lodge	C	Kalaw Place	J	Sabang Inn Beach & Dive Resort	I
At-Cans Inn	H	Club Mabuhay Dive Resort	F	La Laguna Beach Club & Dive Center	C	Seashore Lodge	I
Atlantis Dive Resort	G	Coco Beach Island Resort	A	Nick and Sonia's Cottages	E	Tanawin Bay Resort	L
Big Apple Dive Resort	G	Deep Blue Sea Inn	D	Paradise Lodge	B	Villa Estelita Beach Resort	C
Blue Crystal Beach Resort	M	El Galleon Beach Resort	F	Portofino Beach Resort	D	Villa Sabang	I
Captain Gregg's Divers Resort	G	El Oro	C	Roelyn's Inn	F		
Carlo's Inn	D	Franklyn Highland Beach Resort	K				

sand and coconut trees. Brilliant white yachts lie at anchor in Muelle Bay, and in the background looms the brooding hulk of **Mount Malasimbo**, invariably crowned with a ring of cumulus. There's plenty on offer in addition to diving, including excellent snorkelling, trekking into the mountains and beach-hopping by banca, perhaps with a packed lunch so you can picnic in the deserted cove of your choice.

Sabang is the busiest beach, with a mind-boggling variety of accommodation dotted haphazardly along the shoreline, some above-average restaurants and a couple of go-go bars. Neighbouring **Small La Laguna** and **Big La Laguna** are rather more laid-back and family-oriented. Twenty minutes by jeepney the other side of Puerto Galera town is **White Beach**. Accommodation here is strictly of the bamboo-hut variety, and for meals you'll have to eat what you are given: it might be catch of the day or a tin of sardines. Five minutes beyond White Beach by jeepney is **Talipanan Beach**. Both are good bases for **trekking** in the mountains.

Access to Puerto Galera is from **Batangas Pier** on the outskirts of Batangas City. BLTB, Jam and Tritran **buses** run regularly from Pasay in Manila to Batangas Pier (3hr; P80). Once you get to Batangas Pier there are numerous **ferry** options, with regular departures for Puerto Galera town (Muelle Pier), Sabang and even a few direct sailings to White Beach. Fares are around P110 plus P10 terminal fee. A bus-and-ferry service with an all-in-one ticket for P600 one-way departs at 9am sharp from the *City State Tower Hotel* at 1315 A Mabini St, Ermita. There's a similar service from the *Swagman Hotel* in Malate in Manila (☎02/523 8541). Travel time from Manila to Batangas Pier is about three hours, from where it's another ninety minutes by boat.

Most travellers chose to take a ferry either directly to Sabang or White Beach. For Sabang, there are daily direct departures at 9.30am, 10.30am, 11.30am, noon, 1.30pm and 2.30pm. If you arrive at Muelle Pier, you can hop on a jeepney or a small banca to one of the beaches. Jeepneys charge P10 to Sabang and P30 to White Beach, but only leave when they are full, meaning packed to the gills with people, baggage, produce and farm animals. It's not unusual on these routes for passengers to be hanging from the sides or sitting on the roof. For the jeepney to Sabang you have to walk up the hill to the left for about 150m. All boats are met by a welcoming committee of touts offering "special rides" for P200. A banca to Sabang will cost around P150 depending on your negotiating skills. White Beach is further and will cost around P200 (you can always share the boat with others). The **post office** is at the town hall in Puerto Galera, although some resorts will post mail for a charge. There are rudimentary **clinics** in the town, which charge P80 for a consultation. There are many **telephone stations** in Sabang and Puerto Galera where you can make calls to Manila for P12 a minute or overseas for P130 a minute. Swagman Travel at the western end of Sabang beach offers exchange, fax, phone, visa extension and air tickets. Exchange and telephone services are also offered by Centrum in Sabang; this used to be a go-go bar until the owner became vice-mayor, and now hosts regular live bands from Manila. To arrange **trekking**, kayaking tours or overnight trips into the tribal hinterland, go to Jungle Trek Adventure Tours opposite Tropicana on Sabang's main drag. Motorbikes can be rented at a number of places for around P500 for half a day. Telephones in Puerto Galera are all cellular and there are no landlines. There's Internet access on the main beach path opposite the *Relax Thai Restaurant*.

Accommodation

Basic accommodation starts from P300 for a small hut with a cramped shower, probably with not much of a view. For a decent room with a balcony overlooking the sea, you'll pay from P400 upwards.

Sabang

Angelyn Beach Resort ☎0912/306 5332 or 043/442 0038. Good location right on the beach and only a short walk from dive operators, bars and restaurants. Choice of spacious double cottages with fan and shower or a/c cottages with comfy sofas on the balcony. There's a small open-air restaurant and a beauty parlour where you can get a haircut for P70 and a pedicure for P50. ❸

At-Cans Inn ☎0917/463 8233. Good budget option at the quieter end of the beach, a short distance before *Seashore Lodge*. Plain rooms but they have big balconies right on the shore. ❹

Atlantis Dive Resort ☎0917/562 0294. At the far western edge of the beach (turn left at the T-junction) near Swagman Travel. Luxurious a/c rooms in a whitewashed Mediterranean-style building overlooking the sea. All mod cons, scuba facilities, well-trained and knowledgeable staff, and a good outdoor restaurant. ❼

Big Apple Dive Resort ☎043/287 3134. Set back from the shore on the main footpath (turn left at the T-junction where the jeepneys stop). Five fan cottages, eight family cottages and fourteen a/c cottages, all in a quiet garden surrounding a swimming pool. *Big Apple* is one of Sabang's best-known resorts, with a dive centre. You can book in Makati (☎02/899 6854) or Ermita (☎02/526 7592) in Manila.

Captain Gregg's Divers Resort ☎0917/540 4570. Turn left at the end of the road in Sabang and *Captain Gregg's* is a 5min walk along the beach. Popular, well-established resort catering mainly to divers. Acceptable rooms, decent grub in the restaurant, and good advice from the resident divers in the dive shop, many of whom have lived in Sabang for years. ❸

Sabang Inn Beach & Dive Resort At the quieter eastern end of the beach ☎0912/311 4335. New rooms with tiled floors, refrigerator, a/c or fan, many with pleasant balconies. Dive centre, small swimming pool, travel desk, pub and breakfast bar on the beach that also serves lunch. From the main junction in Sabang, face the sea and walk to your right. ❹

Seashore Lodge Almost at the far eastern end of the beach, a 5min walk from the main road, but still an easy stroll from shops and nightlife. Pleasant, quiet, friendly resort with large, airy bamboo huts on the beach, most with balconies, and a restaurant in the centre of a grass courtyard. ❸

Villa Sabang ☎0917/562 0214. Modern, whitewashed concrete rooms with a/c, reliable hot water from the resort's own water system, and balconies. Large suites have a kitchen and mini-bar. Ideal for longer stays and the location is great – turn right in Sabang and it's along the beach in a quiet area right on the shore. Swimming pool, billiards, bar and fast food. Part of Octopus Divers. ❹

Small La Laguna

Carlo's Inn ☎0912/301 0717. Quiet location at the far end of the beach. Laid-back, friendly little family-run resort with various rooms and cottages built into the hillside and wonderful views of the sea. Good budget choice, close to the scuba operators, but with no clubs or bars to disturb the peace. ❸

Club Mabuhay Dive Resort ☎043/ 287 3097. Completed in 2002, this big resort set in expansive tropical gardens is one of the newest in Puerto Galera. All 34 rooms have a/c and are finished to a high standard, with balconies overlooking the central swimming pool. The stylish *Mabuhay Beach Restaurant* is right on the shore, and there's a silent 24hr generator should the power fail. ❼

Deep Blue Sea Inn On the west end of Small La Laguna Beach, 30m from Action Divers. Simple but very comfortable apartments, private cottages and a/c doubles with private bathrooms, and a restaurant on the first floor that has fine views across the sea towards Verde Island. An excellent budget choice in a quiet location. ❹

El Galleon Beach Resort From the main road in Sabang (Manila office ☎02/834 2974). *El Galleon* is a 10min walk along the beach to the west. Professionally run tropical-style hotel with airy bamboo rooms for two, many with a balcony. Try to get one of the rooms on the first floor at the front, right on the beach. The pleasant seaside restaurant serves breakfast (P65–135) and a good range of lunch and dinner dishes, including pasta, chicken, salads and seafood, produced by a resident French chef. The fresh *lapu-lapu* is P130 per 250g. There's a computer in the lobby with Internet for P50 per half hour. Next door is Asia Divers, where you can arrange scuba diving (from $22 a dive) and above it a popular bar called *The Point*, which is open until midnight and offers a choice of over 200 cocktails and 15 special shooters. ❹

Nick and Sonia's Cottages At the centre of Small La Laguna. Simple nipa huts with their own cooking facilities and a fridge. ❸

Portofino Beach Resort ☎639/7377 6704. A Mediterranean-style complex with 25 units, ranging from a studio to a two-bedroom apartment overlooking the beach. Polished tiles or wooden floors throughout and a lovely swimming pool with an al fresco bar and restaurant. ❻

Roelyn's Inn Just past *El Galleon*. Simple place with a selection of concrete huts, including doubles with private showers. Set back from the beach with a small restaurant, which is open until 2am. ❸

Big La Laguna

Cataquis Lodge The first accommodation you reach on Big La Laguna Beach as you walk down the path from Small La Laguna. Very simple bamboo huts, but they're clean and cheap and the location is exceptional. ❷

Coco Beach Island Resort ☎02/521 5260. Not strictly in Big La Laguna, but a little further along the coast to the west and reachable only by private banca from the sea. Secluded, private and idyllic, with a full range of facilities, including day-trips, diving and tennis. The 89 rooms are built using indigenous materials – the Super Banana hut (a small native house with a private veranda and enormous bed) is particularly impressive. The only problem with *Coco Beach* is that there's no public transport so you'll have to depend on the resort's private bancas to take you anywhere, even out for dinner at night, and the extra charges can add up. The resort does, however, have four restaurants of its own. ❺

El Oro About half way along the beach ☎0912/306 6642. Offers the usual range of clean but basic nipa huts, either with or without a veranda. The restaurant has a pool table and is open till 11pm. ❸

La Laguna Beach Club & Dive Center ☎043/287 3181 or 0973/855545. Big resort with various palm-roofed rooms and cottages surrounding a beautiful swimming pool. All rooms have a/c, private bathrooms and hot water. Reputable diving school, first-class restaurant and a relaxing upstairs bar with large balcony for sunset-watching. ❻

Paradise Lodge Clean, spacious standard doubles, and like most places, offers discounts for longer stays. ❹

Villa Estelita Beach Resort ☎0917/459 5485. Big, quiet rooms in a charming tropical garden with an agreeable al fresco bar and restaurant on the sand. ❹

Palangan

There are some quiet and respectable places to stay in this small barrio, on the road from Puerto Galera town to Sabang. Most are on the ridge, with marvellous views across Puerto's bays and islets.

Blue Crystal Beach Resort ☎0917/562 0129. A little pricey, but has its own secluded beach. There are six double rooms and one family suite. ❹–❺

Franklyn Highland Beach Resort On the ridge above the road ☎0912/314 8133. Has cheap cottages but no beach. The restaurant and pool, however, have great views. ❸–❹

Kalaw Place On a promontory 2km from Puerto Galera on the road to Sabang ☎0917/532 2617. This gracious and relaxed family-run resort is really something special. The rooms are beautifully furnished in native style with expansive bamboo balconies and unforgettable views. There's a *bahay kubo* (wooden house) for six and a little wooden house for three with its own kitchenette. The restaurant serves food prepared by the owners, including vegetarian dishes. ❹–❺

Tanawin Bay Resort ☎0973/859821. A range of atmospheric native huts including the *Snail House*, which stands alone and has picture windows and a large bamboo terrace. *Tanawin* is a 5min walk to the sea. ❸–❻

White Beach

White Beach has no girlie bars and fewer boorish scuba divers than Sabang. It gets busy at peak times, especially Easter, when backpackers from Manila hold all-night raves on the sand. Don't let the touts tie you down. They will try to lead you to their own accommodation, but take time to wander up and down the beach to find the cleanest rooms at the best price. White Beach is a beautiful spot for extended R&R, so for longer stays negotiate a discount. Most of the accommodation is little above adequate though, with dozens of "resorts" offering ragtag cottages with cold showers.

Cherry's Inn ☎0917/788 8239. Flimsy wooden cottages that have become a little careworn over the years, but are nevertheless in a good spot approximately half way along the beach. "Fixers" from *Cherry's* are always waiting to greet the ferry in an effort to corral visitors. ❸

Mylah's Nipa Hut and Restaurant Amiable place with a pleasant restaurant at the quieter eastern end of the beach. Standard wooden cottages big enough for two, and right on the sand. ❸

Summer Connection ☎0912/316 5910. Simple lodge and restaurant with nipa huts at the western edge of the beach in a fine location on the sand. Friendly, laid-back and humble, but comfortable enough with reasonable private bathrooms. ❸

White Beach Lodge ⓣ0917/732 7674. At the west end of the beach near *Cherry's Inn*. Large wooden huts and cottages, some with balconies and all with their own bathrooms. ❸

White Beach Nipa Hut ⓣ0912/272 0774. Near *Cherry's Inn*. A slightly larger resort than most, with a choice of concrete cottages good for two, or fan rooms on the first floor of the main building. ❹

Eating

If you're not sure what to eat in Puerto Galera, eat fish: it comes straight from the sea and is guaranteed fresh. The *Relax Thai Restaurant* in Sabang does brisk business with its P145 Thai curries and joss-stick atmosphere. The *Galley* at *El Galleon Beach Resort* serves Filipino and foreign dishes and bakes its own bread. For tropical charm right on the water, try *Tamarind Restaurant* in Sabang, where the food fluctuates in quality but the view is wonderful. Opposite *Tamarind* is *Ristorante da Franca*, which is part of the *Atlantis Resort Hotel* and does brisk business. On the main road as you come into Sabang sits *Tropicana*, a two-storey bamboo edifice that has an eclectic menu but is particularly known for its pizzas. For something exceedingly different, the *Sunshine Coast Bar and Restaurant* (turn right at the main junction and walk for two minutes) has a "Feeling Shitty Breakfast" (P100) consisting of coffee, Coke, two cigarettes, cornflakes and fresh fruit.

Sablayan and around

The little fishing and trading town of **SABLAYAN** on Mindoro's west coast is a convenient jumping off point for a number of excellent trips. From here, you can travel inland to the Mounts Iglit-Baco National Park or by sea to the picturesque *Pandan Island Resort* and further afield to Apo reef, which offers some superb diving. From Batangas City, the Montenegro ferry sails twice a week straight to Sablayan; five daily ferries serve **Abra de Ilog**, from where you can catch a bus south along the scenic coastal road to Sablayan (3hr). If coming from from Puerto Galera, you'll need to hire a banca (P1500) to take you west along the coast of Mindoro to the barrio of Wawa before tracking a few kilometres inland by jeepney to Abra de Ilog. You can also reach Sablayan by taking a bus or jeepney north from San José.

To the southeast of Sablayan, **Mounts Iglit-Baco National Park** is dominated by the twin peaks of Mount Iglit (2364m) and Mount Baco (2488m), which offer some challenging trekking and climbing through a wilderness landscape inhabited only by occasional Mangyan tribespeople. There are also some leisurely treks through the park's foothills, where you may be lucky enough to glimpse the endangered **tamaraw**, of which fewer than 200 are said to exist. The park is also the habitat of the Philippine deer, wild pigs and other endemic species such as the Mindoro scops owl and Mindoro imperial pigeon. To visit the park you first have to secure a **permit** at the Pandan Eco-Tourism Office (daily 8am-5pm) on the pier in Sablayan. Buses run regularly along the copast to Popoy, from where you can take a jeepney or walk into the park.

From Sabalyan's pier, you can take a twenty-minute water-taxi ride (P100) to the solar-powered *Pandan Island Resort* (ⓣ02/523 7007; ❺) on North Pandan Island. This is a marvellous place on an idyllic tropical island, with a blinding white beach on one side and dense jungle behind. Accommodation is in pretty little native cottages and the crab and *lapu-lapu* they dish up are straight from the sea. In 1994, a sanctuary was established around the eastern half of the island, so the marine life is remarkable; a small dive shop at the resort organizes overnight safaris southwards to **Apo Reef Natural Park** and Coron in northern Palawan. The diving at Apo reef, about 30km off the west coast of Mindoro, is tremendous. The reef stretches 26km from north to south and 20km east to west, and teems with a dazzling variety of reef fish, occasional sharks, barracuda, tuna and most of the Philippines' 450 species of coral.

San José and on to Boracay

Forty kilometres down the coast from Sublayan is the town of **SAN JOSÉ**, which also acts as a staging post for ferries to Boracay. The San José bus terminal is in Rizal Street, and ferries for Boracay (6am and 8am daily, 4hr, P60) leave from the North Pier, a short jeepney ride across the Pandururan River. Note: these ferries do not follow a strict timetable and may only leave if and when they're full. Air Philippines has **flights** three times a week (Tues, Fri & Sun; P2741 return) from Manila Domestic Airport at 5.45am, returning at 7am on the same days. It's possible to get to San José from Puerto Galera by taking a series of jeepneys clockwise around the coast of Mindoro via Calapan and the uninspiring town of Roxas, but the journey is rough, dusty and rarely travelled by tourists.

The best **place to stay** in San José is *Sikatuna Beach Hotel* (☎043/491 2182; ❷) on Airport Road, just north of San José, while the *Sikana Town Hotel* (☎043/491 1274; ❷) on Sikatuna Street is decent enough.

8.3

Northwest of Manila

The provinces of Luzon that lie immediately **northwest of Manila** are so diverse in geographical character that you can go in a day from the volcanic landscape of **Zambales** to the tropical beaches and islands of the **Lingayen Gulf**. The spurs of the **Caraballo Mountains** lie in the east, in Bulacan, the first province you reach travelling north from the capital; in the west lie the fertile lowlands of **Pampanga**, where much of the country's rice and mangoes are produced. Life in this area is far from sophisticated, and the kind of upmarket resorts found in the Visayas are conspicuous by their absence. Major attractions include **Mount Pinatubo**, **One Hundred Islands**, and the unspoiled **beaches** of La Union, where breakers roll in from the South China Sea and surfing has become popular.

There's only one way to get out of Manila heading north and that's on the **North Luzon Expressway**, which runs north from Manila through the provinces of Bulacan, Pampanga, Tarlac and Pangasinan. Victory Liner and Philippine Rabbit have dozens of departures daily for all points north of Manila, including Angeles, Dau (for Clark) and Lingayen (for One Hundred Islands National Park).

San Fernando

SAN FERNANDO, 50km northwest of Manila and the capital of Pampanga province, is best known for its controversial **crucifixion of flagellants**. Every year on Good Friday a dozen or so penitents – mostly men but with the occasional woman and sometimes even the odd foreigner – are taken to a rice field in the barrio of San Pedro Cutud, 3km from San Fernando, and nailed to a cross using two-inch stainless steel nails that have been soaked in alcohol to disinfect them. The penitents are taken down seconds later. Other penitents flagellate themselves using bamboo sticks tied to a rope. The blood is real, but the motivation is questionable. The Catholic Church does not approve of the crucifixions and does not endorse them. The media has also turned against the rites, calling them pagan and barbaric but generally admitting they are still a good show.

Bus terminals in Manila are closed on Good Friday, so you'll have to travel to San Fernando the night before. Victory Liner buses leave every hour from Cubao. Make sure you don't confuse San Fernando in Pampanga with San Fernando in La Union, further north. Most buses travel up the North Luzon Expressway and exit at Paskuhan, a tourist village that sells native handicrafts: ask the bus driver to let you get off here. Paskuhan is also the site of a **tourist office** (☎045/961 2665). San Fernando proper lies five minutes away by road – you can reach it by jeepney from Paskuhan. Regular jeepneys connect San Fernando with its northern neighbours of Angeles and Clark (15-20 mins, P6-8).

There are few good **places to stay** in San Fernando, the best option being *Hotel Grace Lane* (☎045/860 1234; ❶), just off the MacArthur Highway, which has simple air-con doubles. Most travellers opt to spend the night in nearby Clark, where there's a much wider choice of rooms. San Fernando's main drag – actually the road to Subic Bay and Olongapo – is lined with fast-food restaurants.

JARIN
SHEIK
REYNALD
FIREBIRD
FIREBIRD
LADY TINA
Sarao
DDR·462
PILIPINAS.
'83

△ Jeepney

Clark and around

Some 70km north of Manila, **CLARK**, formerly the site of an American air base, is popular with visitors for its proximity to the volcanic mountains of **Pinatubo and Arayat**. In 1991, **Clark Air Base** became the subject of one of the hottest political debates ever to rage in the Philippines. Many Filipinos, enjoying an era of new nationalism in the wake of the downfall of the Marcos regime, saw no reason for the Philippines, however poor, to depend on the world's greatest superpower for its defence. Senators agreed and voted to end the US Air Force's lease on Clark Air Base. America's undignified departure from the Philippines was hastened somewhat by the catastrophic eruption of Mount Pinatubo (see p.813), which showered the base in ash. The greatest concern over the withdrawal of 20,000 US air force personnel from the area was the potentially devastating effect it might have on the economy. A decision was taken to turn the base – which is roughly as big as Singapore – into a special economic zone with incentives for companies setting up shop there. Plans to convert the existing airport into an alternative to the Ninoy Aquino International Airport with a high-speed railway link to Manila are, however, like many things in the Philippines, taking a long time to come to fruition

Inside the former base, there are a number of golf courses, one hotel and a few mediocre restaurants. The area alongside the base, including Fields Avenue and Don Juico Avenue, is famous for another legacy of the American tenancy, go-go bars. Prostitution is rife in these bars, with many male visitors flying in from Europe for one thing only.

But, besides climbing mounts Pinatubo and Arayat, there are an increasing number of other activities in and around Clark, including mountain biking, trekking, microlight flying and parachuting. The Tropical Asia Parachute Center at 940 Fields Ave has been operating at Clark since 1996 and does courses for US$240. At the Angeles City Flying Club (Ⓣ0918/920 3039 or 0917/335 5073; Ⓦwww.angelescityflying-club.com), about forty-five minutes' east of Clark by road in Sitio Talimundok. Magalang, you can have a thirty-minute introductory **microlight** flight along the Pampanga River and over the lower slopes of Mount Arayat for around P1000. If you prefer to keep your feet closer to the ground, for P500 a half-day, you can rent a Yamaha motorcycle from Trent Transport at 222 Fields Ave, Clark (Ⓣ045/332 1712) that will take you through the fields of lahar, a mass of volcanic debris and water that has solidified into gargantuan cliffs and spires. If you're in the market for something even more memorable, for US$85 per person (minimum two people) you can take an early morning crater flight in a small aircraft from Clark. Contact Swagman Travel for details (see above). Also from Clark, SEAIR offers forty-minute flights over the crater in a small plane or a helicopter.

Practicalities

The nearest **bus station** is at Dau, served by hourly Victory Liner buses from Manila. From there you can take a tricycle for the short ride to Fields Avenue or Don Juico Avenue, with most drivers charging P50. The main **jeepney station** in Clark is at the MacArthur Highway end of Fields Avenue. You can catch jeepneys from here to the air base and also to Angeles, Pinatubo, Arayat and San Fernando. Jeepneys up and down Fields Avenue cost P5, no matter where you get on and off. SEAIR **flies** from Manila to Clark at 6pm Mondays to Saturdays for around P900 one-way. From Clark to Manila, the flight is at 8.15am (also Mon–Sat). There's a free shuttle bus that takes passengers between the airport and a number of hotels on Fields Avenue, a trip of about fifteen minutes. SEAIR's Clark office (Ⓣ045/892 4767 or 323 6712) is in the *Sub Delicious* sandwich bar on Fields Avenue at the junction with Raymond Street. For car rental in Clark, try Daxis (Ⓣ045/625 6422) or Zaiwin (Ⓣ045/892 6428).

Most of the bars, restaurants and tourist facilities in Clark are on Fields Avenue, which at some unidentifiable point becomes Don Juico Avenue (which, to add to the confusion, is also known as Perimiter Road). There are dozens of moneychangers on Fields Avenue and **banks** on the nearby MacArthur Highway. At the City Airport Terminal (which is no longer an airport terminal), on Fields Avenue, you'll find convenience stores, ticketing offices and tour operators. Swagman Travel (☎045/322 2890) in the City Airport Terminal building near the bars on Don Juico Avenue is the best place for tour bookings, airline bookings and visa-extension services. There is an immigration office on 7th Street in Dau where you can get your visa extended, although it's easier to ask a hotel or travel agent to do it for you, for a fee.

Accommodation

America Hotel Don Juico Ave ☎045/332 1023. Big, carpeted establishment with enormous rooms ranging from deluxe doubles to a suite with its own whirlpool bath. There's a pool and a restaurant. ④

Clarkton Hotel ☎045/322 3424. On Don Juico Ave, away from the hustle and bustle, with a well-kept swimming pool and a popular bar. ⑥

Holiday Inn Resort Clark Field ☎045/599 8000. Five-star hotel inside the former US base with swimming pool, restaurants and bars. Rooms have all the usual five-star facilities, but are functional rather than comfortable. At weekends, the restaurant is packed, making a relaxed lunch impossible. ⑨

La Casa Pension 511 Tamarind St, Clarkview Subdivision ☎045/322 7984. Quiet rooms with bath or shower in a family home. Food is served at the next door *Blue Boar Inn*, which is owned by the same couple, a former US Air Force officer and his wife. To get there, take a jeepney (P5) to the far end of Don Juico Ave. ②

Orchid Inn ☎045/332 0370. In the busy bar area at the northern end of Don Juico Ave, so it can be noisy. It does though have modern, clean, a/c rooms, with tiled bathrooms. ④

Phoenix Hotel ☎045/8882195. Rambling place a little to the west of the *America Hotel* in a quiet area of Fields Avenue. The huge a/c rooms smelling of disinfectant, and the bathrooms are only average, but staff are reasonably friendly and there's a pleasant bar serving good western-style food. ⑤

Woodland Park Resort Kilometer 87, MacArthur Highway, Dau ☎045/892 1002. Peaceful and secluded garden-resort 5min from the bus station by tricycle. Clean rooms, large swimming pool, restaurant and bar. ⑤

Eating

American Legion Don Juico Ave. Excellent low-cost food including Salisbury steak and spaghetti with meatballs. The hash browns for breakfast are excellent. Just past the *Phoenix Hotel*.

Cottage Kitchen Café 352 Don Juico Ave, Clark View. Modest but wonderful Cajun-Creole restaurant owned and lovingly overseen by a retired US Air Force Major who even chooses the music from his extensive blues and jazz collection. Eveything is delicious, from the grilled seafood, Angus steak, and spicy burgers to the mouthwatering pork loin dinner that includes refried beans, homemade corn bread and perfect French fries.

Krung Thai Restaurant Fields Ave. Simple and affordable family-run Thai restaurant at the eastern end of Fields Avenue close to the bars. The menu is vast and includes spring rolls, spicy Thai soups, a range of curries, and fried rice dishes that are a meal in themselves.

Margarita Station Fields Ave. A Fields Avenue institution. The windows are made of chicken wire and the doors of plywood, but *Margarita Station* serves some of the most consistently reliable and reasonably priced food in Clark, including Western, Filipino and a tempting range of Thai dishes. The Mexican soft-shell tacos stuffed with scrambled egg and sausage are good for breakfast, and the chicken teriyaki sandwiches make a great light lunch. The clientele is mostly single, white and male, but the atmosphere's friendly and the staff helpful.

Salvatore's Field Ave. Popular Italian restaurant on the first floor above a bar called *Illusions*. The bulk of the menu consists of pizza, but there are also some good pasta dishes and the honey-roast chicken is tangy and delicious.

Zapata's 480 Don Juico Ave. Good-value and popular Mexican restaurant with tacos, burritos, enchiladas and tortillas, along with a number of vegetarian dishes.

Mount Pinatubo

On April 2, 1991, people from the village of Patal Pinto on the lower slopes of **Mount Pinatubo** (1780m) saw small explosions followed by steaming and the smell of rotten eggs coming from the upper slopes of the supposedly dormant volcano, whose last known eruption was six hundred years ago. The Philippine Institute of Volcanology and Seismology (PHIVOLCS) immediately installed portable seismometers near the mountain and began recording several hundred earthquakes a day. US Geological Survey personnel arrived in the area on April 23. All signals indicated that magma was rising within the volcano and that an eruption was likely, but no one knew quite how big it would be. On June 12, the first of several major explosions took place. The eruption was so violent that shockwaves could be felt in the Visayas. Nearly twenty million tonnes of sulphur dioxide gas were blasted into the atmosphere, causing red skies to appear for months after the eruption. A giant ash cloud rose 35km into the sky and red-hot blasts seared the countryside. Ash paralysed Manila, closing the airport for days and turning the capital's streets into an eerie grey post-apocalyptic landscape. Particles from the eruption landed as far away as the United States. By June 16, when the dust had settled, the top of the volcano was gone, replaced by a two-kilometre-wide caldera containing a lake. Lava deposits had filled valleys, buildings had collapsed and 350 people were dead.

Pinatubo is quiet once again, except for tourist activity. Regulations require all trekkers to be accompanied by a **guide**; the usual tourist crater trek begins at your hotel at 5am, when a car picks you up for the drive north to the jump-off point in Santa Juliana, where you must register with the Barangay office. You then transfer to a 4x4 jeep that takes you another forty minutes to the start of the climb proper in Crow Valley. It takes three hours of strenuous walking to get to the crater and the same to get back down. Overnight treks can also be arranged. Tour companies such as Trent Transport (see p.811), charge P3000 per person for the day package and around P3500 for an overnight trip that includes tents, food, guides and transport. Trekking the lower slopes – without reaching the crater – costs P650 for six hours with a guide. You can book similar tours at Swagman Travel & Tours (see p.811), or try one of the local trekking companies: R&J Pinatubo Trek (ⓣ045/602 5231) and Dream Treks (ⓣ0917 955 3409).

Mount Arayat

Mount Arayat, a 1030-metre extinct volcano in Arayat, rises from the lowlands of Pampanga in solitary and dramatic fashion, the only mountain for miles around. It's said to be inhabited by Mariang Sinukuan (Maria the Abandoned), the sister of Mariang Makiling (Maria of Makiling). When Mariang Sinukuan comes down from the mountain and visits the lowlands her presence can be felt because the air turns fragrant. Some say there is a place on Arayat's wooded slopes where there are many types of fruit, all of which belong to Maria. You can eat as much fruit as you want, but don't take any away from the mountain because an angry Maria will cause you to lose your way.

It takes between seven and nine hours to reach the top of Arayat, making an even more strenuous climb than nearby Pinatubo. One of the adventure-tour companies in Clark will arrange a guide and transport for you; see p.811 for details. At the foot of the mountain, Arayat National Park features picnic sheds and swimming pools. To **get to Mount Arayat** from Clark, take a jeepney (45min; P30) from the terminal in Fields Avenue. A taxi will cost about P100.

Olongapo and Subic Bay

Another US base, another US withdrawal. **Subic Bay Naval Base**, 12km north of **OLONGAPO** and two hours southeast of Clark, in Zambales province, closed down when US forces left in 1992 and is slowly being turned into a playground for the relatively rich, with a yacht club and the usual golf courses and five-star hotels. These days the base is known by the acronym **SBMA**, for Subic Bay Metropolitan Authority. The former base area is immense, and to get around inside it you'll either have to depend on the regular shuttle buses or rent a car for a day. Avis (☎047/223 3256) has an office in the Subic Sports Plaza on Perimeter Road, as does Dollar (☎047/223 2394).

There are plenty of small barrios and beaches outside the base, however, where native life goes on. **Barrio Barretto**, north of the naval base, fronts onto Baloy Beach, which is one of the best in Luzon. The barrio was another infamous R&R centre for excitable sailors (it featured briefly in the film *An Officer and a Gentleman*), but many of the bars have closed down. The area is popular with budget tourists, and you'll find plenty of accommodation of varying degrees of quality and cleanliness.

There are some good **adventure activities** at Subic. Inside the base, near the airport, you can visit the Jungle Environmental Survival Training Camp (JEST; ☎047/252 4123) and take tours into the area's impressive rainforest with members of the Aeta tribe who trained US marines here for service in Vietnam. Short trips include lectures and demonstrations on basic jungle survival. Overnight trips cost from P2000 and involve finding your own potable water and setting traps for food: bat barbecue is a speciality. For diving on wrecks (planes as well as ships), try *Johan's Adventure & Wreck Dive Center* (☎047/224 8915) on Baloy beach or Masterdive (☎047 252 5987) at Magellan's Point, a ten-minute drive south of the Subic Bay Yacht Club inside the base. At Ocean Adventure (☎047 252 9000) inside SBMA at Camayan Wharf you can swim with dolphins and whales for P2600.

Practicalities

Victory Liner runs hourly **buses** to Olongapo (P110) from the terminal at Caloocan in Manila. From Dau and Angeles, regular buses start in the early morning. When you get to Olongapo you can take a blue jeepney (P3) for the five-kilometre journey to Barrio Barretto. The naval base is served by jeepneys and taxis from Olongapo. Subic has an impressive airport but, while Air Philippines flew there briefly from Manila in 2000, flights have now stopped. The only arrivals are international charters and cargo aircraft. There is a **tourist information office** just north of *Palladium Beach Resort* in Barrio Barretto, and another one in Building 662, Taft Street (☎047/252 4154), inside the base itself.

Dozens of **banks** are scattered in and around Subic and most have ATMs where you can get a cash advance on your Visa card. There's a hospital, the Subic Legend Health and Medical Center (☎047/252 9280–88), inside the naval base at Cubi Point.

Accommodation and eating

Inside the base, the most welcoming **accommodation** is at the dive outfit Masterdive (☎047 252 5987; ❹) at Magellan's Point, which has simple rooms on the water. Otherwise, it's all boxy hotels; *Legenda Hotel* (☎047/252 1888; ❼), *Grand Seasons Hotel* (☎047/252 2888; ❼–❽) and *Subic International Hotel* (☎047/252 2222; ❻) are similar establishments, all charging from around US$65 for a double including buffet breakfast. None has much to offer in the way of tropical ambience, but all are comfortable and quiet. The *Legenda* is the most luxurious and has an outdoor pool.

Most travellers head for one of the laid-back resorts outside the base on Baloy Beach in Barrio Barretto, a twenty-minute jeepney ride from Olongapo. *Barts Resort Hotel* at 117C National Highway (☎047/223 4148; ❸) has comfortable doubles in a grey motel-style building around a small garden and swimming pool, but is close to the beach. *By The Sea* at 99 National Highway (☎047/222 2718; ❹) has forty comfortable air-con rooms either right on the beach or set back around a quiet garden, while nearby *Playa Papagayo* at 43 National Highway (☎047/222 3825; ❷) is a hacienda-style development with a choice of new air-con double rooms either on the beach or around a quiet courtyard. *Sheavens* on Baloy Beach (☎047/223 9430; ❺) is a quaint and clean resort in an unbeatable location right on the bay; *Johan's Adventure & Wreck Dive Center* (☎047/224 8915; ❺) has five big air-con rooms and a restaurant and bar open 24 hours; and the *Mangrove Hotel & Restaurant* (☎047/222 7909; ❻) is the newest and most modern hotel on the beach, with seventeen very comfortable rooms, those at the front having large balconies and sea views. All of these resorts have decent **restaurants**, but another popular hangout on Baloy Beach for good food and drink is *Beachside Café*.

The Zambales coast

Zambales is a mountainous province that borders the South China Sea to the west, and the coastal road that runs north from Olangapo to Santa Cruz and into the neighbouring province of Pangasinan gives you direct access to a number of sweeping beaches that tourists are only just beginning to discover. First stop on the journey is the small town of **SAN ANTONIO**, one hour by road north of Olangapo, from where you can catch a jeepney at the market square to the fishing village of **PANDAQUIT**, 5km south, which has a nice long beach. In Pandaquit, you can hire bancas for P500 for half a day and explore Camera and Capones islands. By far the best place to stay is the splendid little *Capones Beach Resort* (☎0918/816 4816; ❸), which is on the sand at Pandaquit and has clean rooms with fan and shower.

Continuing north, you come to the provincial capital, **IBA** (birthplace in 1907 of popular former President Ramon Magsaysay, who was known as "The Guy"). There are a number of reasonable resorts on the beach at Iba, the best of which is the *Ocean View Beach House* (book in Manila ☎02/895 3560; ❸) in Balintabog, Amungan, a few kilometres north of Iba at the centre of a gentle crescent beach protected by reefs at both ends. It's a typical concrete barangay home with two bedrooms, a living room and a gate to the beach that you can rent by the day for P3500 at weekends and P1800 during the week. *Palmera Garden Beach Resort* (☎047/811 2109; ❸) in Bantangalinga is a more established resort with rustic cottages with fan or air-con. The beach cottages are best.

Next are the small towns of Palauig and Masinioc and **SANTA CRUZ**, with its expansive saltworks. This also marks the southern end of Dasol Bay, where a handful of resorts have sprung up along beautiful beaches, such as **Tambobong**. To get to Tambobong beach, take a jeepney (10min; P4) from the plaza in Santa Cruz. There are two islands in **Dasol Bay** that you can reach by hired banca from the small wharf in Santa Cruz. **Hermana Mayor Island** is also known as Miss Universe Island because it was where candidates for the Miss Universe title in 1979 had their photographs taken. **Hermana Menor Island** is smaller and unspoiled by development. There is no accommodation on either island, but both have some lovely coves of fine white sand and good snorkelling.

Victory Liner **buses** run regularly from Olongapo to Iba, a distance of about 85km or two hours, and then on to Alaminos, which takes about another two hours. Jeepneys run from town to town along the Zambales coast, but it can be a slow journey.

One Hundred Islands National Park

It's actually 123, but who's counting? These emerald-like tiny islands are part of a **national park** covering almost twenty square kilometres, nestling in the Lingayen

Gulf. The park is accessible year-round and there are no opening hours: the only restriction is that you have to register and pay a fee of P50 at the Philippine Tourist Authority **office** in Lucap on the mainland. Some islands have beaches, but many are no more than coral outcrops crowned by scrub. Sadly, much of the underwater coral in the park has been damaged by a devastating combination of cyanide and dynamite fishing, typhoons and the El Niño weather phenomenon. On a positive note, the authorities are going all out to protect what coral is left and help it regenerate, meaning you can only snorkel in approved areas. Marine biologists from the University of the Philippines have been at the forefront of the protection movement, replanting hundreds of *taklobos* (giant clams). There's an area of the park known as Taklobos Reef, where many of the clams have been planted and where the snorkelling is better than anywhere else because of the marine life they have attracted.

The best place to base yourself for exploring the islands is **Lucap**, which is right on the shore and from where you can island-hop by day (you'll need to take your own food and water), returning to a shower and a comfy bed in the evening. Don't expect Robinson Crusoe solitude, especially at weekends when many of the islands are overrun by day-trippers. You can find your own piece of paradise here (try Marta, Marcos or Cuenco islands), but you'll have to make it clear to the boatman that you're not interested in the bigger islands.

From where the buses arrive in Lingayen, there are plenty of tricycles, jeepneys and FX taxis for the fifteen-minute ride to Lucap. If you hire your own tricycle, you'll pay from P50 upwards, depending on your bargaining skills; the jeepney fare is P10 and FX's charge around P15. You can pay your park entrance fee and arrange camping permits at the small Philippine Tourist Authority office (daily 8am–5pm) at the pier in Lucap. From the pier, you can also arrange a boatman and a boat (P300 for 5hr, P40 every additional hour).

The only three islands with any form of development are Governor's Island, Children's Island and Quezon Island, where there's basic accommodation. You can **camp** overnight at any of these for a small fee, usually P150. On **Governor's Island** there's a **guesthouse** ideal for a family (❷). It has two bedrooms, a living room, dining room, water (four drums), generator lighting and cooking facilities. *Bahay kubos* (wooden houses; ❶) on **Children's Island** are for budget travellers and have screened bedrooms with kerosene lighting and one drum of fresh water. Common areas are provided for dining and cooking as well as for toilet and bath. On **Quezon Island**, thirty minutes from Lucap at the northern edge of the park, there's a concrete motel-type structure where plain rooms range from doubles to family rooms for up to eight people (❶).

Some of the accommodation in **Lucap** itself (see below) features good waterfront restaurants that dish up fresh seafood.

Barny's Lodge & Restaurant ☎075/551 6148 or 0919/430 6589. British-owned and one of the best places near the pier. It's cosy, clean and has a/c rooms with bamboo double beds, private bathrooms and cable TV. Also features a charming native-style restaurant. ❹

Gloria's Cottages ☎075/551 2388. Good location for island-hopping with plain, orderly fan doubles right over the water near the pier. Rooms are basic but good value and all have clean private bathrooms. ❸

Maxine by the Sea ☎075/551 2537. Right on the pier. Plain but clean and adequate doubles with either a/c or fan and private bathrooms. The seafood restaurant here is popular. ❸

Ocean View Lodge ☎075/551 2537. Small home-style guesthouse opposite the pier. Doubles are spacious and come with a choice of a/c or fan, but some of them are windowless and dim. The little restaurant does average local cuisine, but their fish is always fresh. ❸

Vista del Mar ☎075/551 2492. New hotel with a whitewashed exterior and a pleasant coffee shop in the garden. A/c rooms with mod cons such as refrigerator and cable TV for P1500. Set back from the waterfront about 500m from the pier. ❸

8.4

The Cordilleras and the far north

To Filipino lowlanders, brought up on sunshine and beaches, the mountainous north is still seen as a mysterious Shangri-La full of enigmatic tribes and their unfamiliar gods. **Baguio**, the traditional mountain retreat for Manileños during the fierce heat of Easter week, is about as far north as many southerners get. But it's not until you get beyond Baguio that the adventure really starts. The Benguet, Ifugao and Mountain provinces are the **tribal heartlands** of the northern Philippines, settled first by indigenous Negritos and then during the Spanish regime by hunter-gatherers from neighbouring areas who were on the move looking for food and water. Life for many of these tribal people has changed little in hundreds of years, with traditional ways and values still very much in evidence. However, an

Tribes of the Cordilleras

There are **tribes** throughout the Philippines, but those of the Central Cordillera are the best known. The Cordilleras are home to six main indigenous Filipino tribes: the Ibaloi, the Kankanay, the Ifugao, the Kalinga, the Apayao and the Bontoc, collectively known as **Igorots**. There are also sub-tribes among these tribes. The Ibaloi, a large ethnic group of around 85,000, comprises Ibaloy, Ibadoy, Igodot, Benguet and Nabaloi. Then there are dozens of smaller family tribes, including the **Dalicans** and the **Fidelisans**. Tribal conflict is less common that it used to be but by no means unknown. Disputes arise over land and water resources and often end in death. The Dalicans and the Fidelisans once came to blows over water rights and the Dalican tribal elders magnanimously proposed a truce, but only because they had run out of bullets. Tribal spats are rarely resolved these days through headhunting, as they were up until the turn of the twentieth century; the usual method is for all tribes from the mountains to be present and help mediate between the two factions. After reaching an agreement for a peace pact, the tribes celebrate by having a huge party, known as a *canao*, a ritual feast during which food, rice wine and blood flow freely. A typical *canao* will involve the slaughter of a carabao, a pig and half a dozen chickens, whose bladders are "read" for signs of good fortune, in much the same way other cultures read tea leaves. A tribe that breaks a peace pact is obliged to pay compensation in the form of livestock or rice.

Tribes began to gather in small, isolated communities in the Philippines during pre-Spanish times when lowland Filipinos, both Muslim and Christian, expanded into the interiors of Luzon, isolating upland tribes into pockets in which they still exist today. Like other Filipinos, **upland tribes** were a blend of various ethnic origins. Technologically, they ranged from the highly skilled Bontoc and Ifugao to the more primitive groups. Some have intermarried with lowlanders for more than a century, but others, like the **Kalinga**, remain isolated from lowland influences and are happy to remain so. The tribe most visitors to the north are likely to come into contact with is the **Ifugao**, who live in and around Banaue and who built the famous rice terraces.

increasing number of tribal folk are making more from the sale of handicrafts than they do from the production of rice. One of the challenges faced by the government is to make the highlands accessible to travellers, without causing the breakup of a social and economic structure that is unique to the region.

North of Baguio, the Ibaloi village of **Kabayan** is where a group of mummies, possibly dating as far back as 2000 BC, were discovered in caves in the early twentieth century. You can trek up to the caves and use Kabayan as a base for scaling **Mount Pulag**, the highest mountain in Luzon. A swing through the north should also include visits to the the mountain village of **Sagada**, with its caves and hanging coffins; the riverside town of **Bontoc**, capital of Mountain province; and the huge **rice terraces at Banaue**. The bucolic **Batanes Islands** off the northern tip of the Philippines are a challenge to reach, but rewarding if you make the effort. And it isn't all mountains and tribes. To the west of Baguio, on the western seaboard, are the provinces of **Ilocos Sur** and **Ilocos Norte**, with miles of beautiful coastline and old Spanish colonial outposts such as **Vigan**.

You can **fly** from Manila to Baguio and Laoag. Otherwise, you'll have to take the **bus**: Victory Liner and Philippine Rabbit are two of the most popular services, travelling to most towns in the north from their terminals in Manila. The journey to Baguio takes around seven hours. You can change buses in Baguio to continue north towards Sagada and Bontoc.

Baguio and around

BAGUIO, also known as City of Pines or City of Flowers, lies on a plateau 1400m above sea level. It was built by the colonizing Americans as a recreational and administrative centre, from where they could preside over their precious tropical colony without working up too much of a sweat. Baguio is also etched on the Filipino consciousness as the site of one of the country's worst natural disasters, the earthquake of July 16, 1990, in which hundreds died. Most of the damage was to shanty towns, which have either been cleared or rebuilt.

Although for many visitors it's little more than a stopping-off point en route to Sagada and the mountain provinces, Baguio, with its pine trees and rolling hills, has a few secrets worth discovering, such as its parks and bohemian cafés, and the climate is a pleasant respite from the searing heat of the south.

Arrival and information

Loakan Airport is 7km south of the city beyond Camp John Hay. Asian Spirit (☎074/447 3912) flies daily from Manila to Baguio at 8.30am. Jeepneys run regularly from the airport to Burnham Park and Session Road. **Buses** from Manila, including Victory Liner, Dangwa, Dagupan and Philippine Rabbit, drop passengers on the eastern edge of the city, around the Supreme Court Compound in Session Road 2. You can also get to Baguio by bus from most other towns in the north, including San Fernando (La Union), Dau (Clark), Angeles and Vigan. These buses also arrive at terminals on Governor Pack Road.

The **tourist information office** (daily 9am–noon & 1–7pm; ☎074/442 6708 or 442 7014) is in the DoT Complex on Governor Pack Road, a ten-minute walk south from Session Road. They have maps of Baguio, but not much else, and even the maps aren't great. A good place to go for general advice, guided tours and visa extensions is the ubiquitous Swagman Travel at 92 Upper General Luna St, Corfu Village, just off Leonard Wood Road (☎074/442 9859). There's a **post office** with a poste restante service at the junction of Session and Governor Pack roads. **Internet cafés** are becoming more common, one of the most popular being Cyberspace, at the *Mount Crest Hotel* in Legarda Road. In the centre of Baguio, try IWC Inc Internet, on the 4th Floor of La Azotea Building on Session Road, which is open 24

❶, Slaughter Bus Station, Sagada, St Louis Museum, Easter School of Weaving, ▲ Dangwa Bus Terminal (500m) & Tam-awan Village

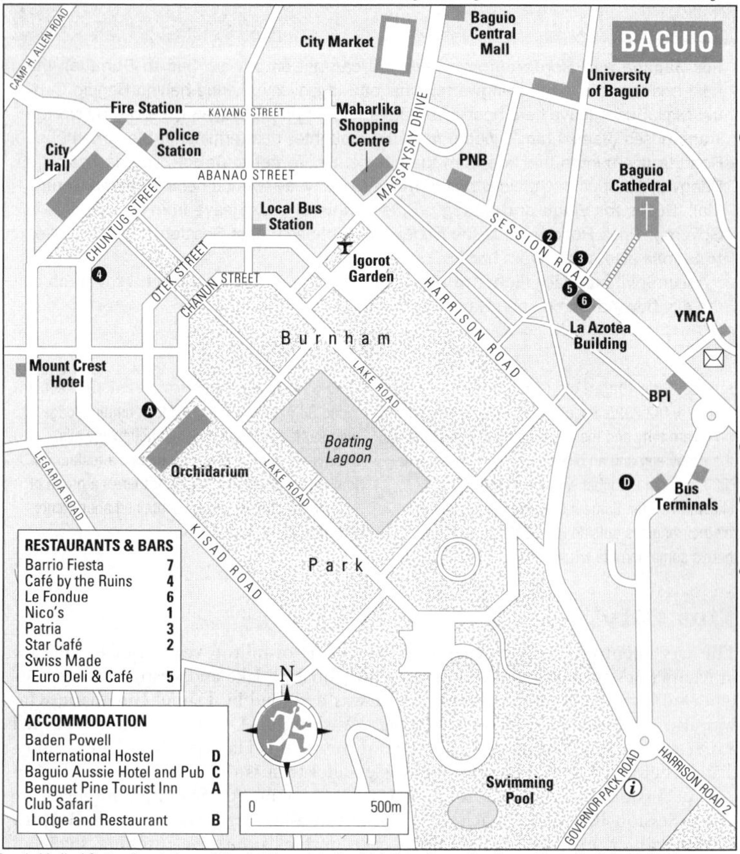

BAGUIO

RESTAURANTS & BARS

Barrio Fiesta	7
Café by the Ruins	4
Le Fondue	6
Nico's	1
Patria	3
Star Café	2
Swiss Made Euro Deli & Café	5

ACCOMMODATION

Baden Powell International Hostel	D
Baguio Aussie Hotel and Pub	C
Benguet Pine Tourist Inn	A
Club Safari Lodge and Restaurant	B

❼ (50m) & Botanical Gardens (4km) ▶

▶ Ⓑ (1km), Ⓒ (2km), Wright Park & Mines View Park

Baguio Medical Centre, Baguio General Hospital, Camp John Hay Main Gate, Airport, San Fernando ▼ (La Union) & Manila

hours. You can **change money** at the PNB at the northern end of Session Road, while PCI on Magsaysay Avenue will give cash advances on MasterCard or Visa. BPI has a number of branches, including one in Session Road close to the Baden Powell hostel. The **police** station is located near City Hall, next to the fire station off Abanao Street. **Baguio Medical Center** (☎074/442 4216) lies on Governor Pack Road and Baguio General Hospital is at the city end of the Marcos Highway; you pass it as you approach Baguio by bus from the south.

Accommodation

Baden Powell International Hostel 26 Governor Pack Rd ☎074/442 5836 or ☎02/721 7818. Atmospheric old building visible from the bus station end of Session Road. The lovely sitting room has a fireplace and a piano, but the quality of the rooms varies widely, so look first. Dorm beds cost P280. ❷

Baguio Aussie Hotel and Pub 92 General Luna St, Corfu Village ☎074/442 5139. Latest addition to the Swagman chain in a quiet area on the eastern edge of the city. Twelve deluxe rooms and two family rooms, all with fan, hot water and electric blanket should the nights get chilly. The Swiss chalet-style restaurant has a cosy atmosphere and fine food, there's a friendly little bar called *Frank's* and staff can arrange tours, vehicle rental and plane tickets. ❺

Moving on from Baguio

For Sagada and Bontoc (from where you can get an onward bus **to Banaue**), the best bus terminal is the Dangwa terminal off Magsaysay Avenue behind Baguio Central Mall. Buses leave here hourly for Sagada from 6am. **Kabayan** is served by Norton Trans buses (9am, 11am & noon) from the Slaughter bus terminal in Slaughterhouse Road, a five-minute taxi ride from the city centre. To get **to Tabuk**, you can catch a Dangwa, Autobus or GL Lines bus from the Magsaysay Avenue behind Baguio Central Mall. Buses **for Vigan and Laoag** on the northwest coast leave from the terminal in Governor Pack Road outside the *Baden Powell* hostel, near Session Road; all buses **to Manila** also depart from here.

Asian Spirit has daily **flights to Manila** (9.45am) from Loakan Airport, 7km south of the city beyond Camp John Hay.

Benguet Pine Tourist Inn Chanum St corner Otek St ⓣ074/442 7325. Popular with travellers, but the rooms are tatty and the inclusive breakfast consists of a runny egg and an oily slice of sweet ham. For P800, you get a double with small shower and lukewarm water. Some rooms are noisy: jeepneys rev their engines outside from before dawn and there's some horrible karaoke. ❸

Club Safari Lodge and Restaurant 191 Leonard Wood Rd ⓣ074/442 2419. Mock hunting lodge with stuffed animal heads on the lobby walls. Rooms are comfortable, and there's a restaurant that serves European dishes. If there's a group of you, go for one of the self-contained apartments, which have log fires. ❺

The City

The city's centrepiece is **Burnham Park**, a sort of hilltop version of Rizal Park in Manila. It's a nice place for a stroll, with a boating lake and strange little three-wheeled bicycles for rent. The park area was designed by Daniel Burnham, who was also responsible for parts of Chicago, Washington DC and much of colonial American Manila. On the eastern edge of the park is Harrison Road and immediately behind that and running almost parallel to it is the city's congested main artery, Session Road, lined with shops and restaurants. Standing imperiously above Session Road, and reached by a flight of a hundred steep steps, is **Baguio Cathedral**, an example of "wedding cake gothic" in an eye-catching shade of rose pink.

The northern end of Session Road leads to Magsaysay Drive and the City Market, one of the liveliest and most colourful in the country and selling produce from the Cordilleras, such as strawberries, peanut brittle, sweet wine, honey, textiles, handicrafts and jewellery. The best museum in Baguio is the **St Louis University Museum of Arts and Culture** (Mon–Sat 9am–4.30pm), near St Louis Hospital on Bonifacio Street, a fifteen-minute walk north of Session Road; it displays hundreds of artefacts from the Cordilleras such as tribal houses, weapons and costumes. Travelling out of the city eastwards on Leonard Wood Road for 4km brings you to the **Botanical Gardens** (daily 7am–8pm; P5), also known as the Igorot Village because it contains replica native huts typical of Igorot dwellings in the Cordilleras, and then to **Wright Park**, where you can hire horses for riding, and a little further to **Mines View Park**, where there are souvenir stalls, antique shops and some restaurants. Jeepneys to Wright Park and Mine's View leave from the northern end of Session Road. For some ethnic shopping, try the **Easter School of Weaving**, Easter Road, on the northwestern outskirts of the city. Weavers produce everything from clothing to tablecloths and you can to watch them at work. You can get there by jeepney from Kayang Street, at the northern end of Burnham Park.

Eating

Barrio Fiesta 113 Session Rd. At the eastern end of Session Road where it becomes Session Road 2, this is a big, brash branch of the popular Manila restaurant chain that offers big portions of Filipino home-cooking at very affordable prices. Popular dishes include *kare-kare*, sizzling beef, sour soup and adobo.

Café by the Ruins 25 Chuntug St. Try not to leave Baguio without eating here. It's far and away one of the city's culinary highlights, with excellent organic food prepared with home-grown herbs. There are good vegetarian dishes on the menu, alongside *pinikpikan*, a tribal chicken delicacy that's also known as "killing me softly" because the chicken is beaten slowly to death with a hammer to make the meat bloody and tender. Tofu vegeburger is P110 and native rice wine (*tapuey*) P25 a glass or P90 a bottle.

Le Fondue 4th Floor, La Azotea Building, Session Rd. Folksy live music and Swiss fondue at P190 for two. San Miguel is P36 and cocktails P55–105. Try for a table on the small balcony overlooking Session Rd. Opposite *Don Henrico's* pizza restaurant.

Nico's Slaughterhouse Compound, Barangay Santo Nino. One of half a dozen cult canteens, close to the slaughter house and the Slaughter bus station, where you can test your bravery with a bowl of Soup No. 5. It contains, according to the waitress, "the balls of the cow" and is cheap, too, at P45. Other dishes include what could be the world's cheapest T-bone steak (also P45).

Patria 181 Session Rd ☎074/442 4963. Baguio has a number of good Chinese restaurants, but this is a classic. It's old and dusty, but always busy because the food is excellent and there's a great deal of it. Soup and noodle dishes start from P65, while an enormous mound of fried rice with vegetables is P70.

Star Café 39 Session Rd. "Famous since 1940" for its Chinese cuisine. The portions are immense, and it's cheap. A "small" order of Shanghai fried rice and chicken corn soup will set you back P200 and feed three.

Swiss Made Euro Deli & Café 46 Session Rd. Cosy little bistro with eye-catching blue floors and red walls. Gourmet sandwiches, homemade chilli con carne and Swiss lime tart. On a cool evening, have a rich hot chocolate (P27). Next to La Azotea Building.

Tam-awan Village

On the northwest outskirts of Baguio, **TAM-AWAN VILLAGE** (Pinsao Proper, off Tacay Road; ☎074/446 2949) is a replica Ifugao tribal village where you can stay in wooden tribal huts and drink rice wine around a traditional Ifugao *dap-ay*, an outdoor meeting place with a fire at its centre. Food is available from a small kitchen, work by local artists is on sale in the shop and staff will often perform impromptu ceremonies, songs and dances. There are eight Ifugao houses and one Kalinga hut. One particular hut, built on stilts like all the rest, is a fertility hut, its walls adorned with carvings of men with impressive sex organs. Tam-awan is hardly the height of luxury, but well worth an overnight stay for the experience. Small huts for two people are P550 a night and family huts are P800, but toilets and showers are shared. Take a jacket because it can get surprisingly cold. You can reach Tan-awan Village by taxi for less than P100; it's past the Easter School of Weaving on the road to la Trinidad.

Kabayan

The road north from Baguio, known as the Halsema Highway, affords breathtaking views as it snakes up to Sagada. Be prepared for a long – six or seven hours – uncomfortable journey, though, as the road is little more than a single lane of rocks and rubble in many places. The isolated mountain village of **KABAYAN**, 50km or five hours by bus north of Baguio, gained some notoriety in the early twentieth century when a group of mummies was discovered in surrounding caves. The mummies are believed by some scientists to date back as far as 2000 BC. When the Spanish arrived, mummification was discouraged and the practice died out. Controversy still surrounds the Kabayan mummies, some of which have "disappeared" to overseas collectors, sold for a quick buck by unscrupulous middlemen. One was said to have been stolen by a Christian pastor in 1920 and wound up as a sideshow in a Manila circus. Some mummies remain, however, and you can see them in their mountaintop caves and also in the small Kabayan branch of the National Museum, which displays the so-called Smiling Mummy and the Laughing Mummy. The museum doesn't keep regular opening hours, although the curator is usually around during business hours and will let you in. Admission is free, but leave a donation. Officials know of dozens of other mummies in the area, but will not give their locations for fear of desecration.

You can hire a guide to trek up to some of the mummy caves: ask at the museum or at **Brookside Café**. **Timbak Cave** is one of the best, but it's high on a mountaintop and a strenuous four- to five-hour climb.

Practicalities

Kabayan is best reached from Baguio, a journey along narrow dirt roads that takes about five hours and is terrifying.

There are two **places to stay** in the village. The *Kabayan Coop Lodge* (❶) has rooms with bunk beds for two people with a shared bath and toilet. It's a clean and friendly place, built mostly of pine. If the *Lodge* is full, which is unlikely, the municipal building up the road has a hall with bunk beds. There are half a dozen *sari-sari* stores in Kabayan where you can get snacks, but the only **place to** eat is the *Brookside Café*, next to the *Kabayan Coop Lodge*, where the owner can rustle up pork soup and rice (P45), or eggs and bread (P35). The sugary Benguet coffee (P10) is just the tonic on a cold Cordilleran morning. Kabayan is dry: local officials have banned the sale of alcohol, so if you're likely to want a quick restorative after a long day's hiking, bring your own from Baguio.

Mount Pulag

Standing 2992m above sea level, **Mount Pulag** is the highest mountain in Luzon and classified by the Metropolitan Mountaineering Society of the Philippines as a Level III strenuous climb. Which means unless you're experienced, don't try it alone. Villagers in Kabayan, where many climbers spend a night before setting off, will tell you it's possible to go without a guide and to get up and down in a day. But their familiarity with these mountains means they tend to overestimate the skill and stamina of city dwellers. Pulag is a challenge: the terrain is steep, there are gorges and ravines and, in the heat of the valleys below, it's easy to forget it's bitterly cold on top.

The two best **trails** for first-timers are those that start from Ambangeg and Kabayan. Both are accessible from Baguio on the Norton Trans bus. In Ambangeg, the trail begins near the police sub-station in **Bokod**: ask the bus driver to let you off in Ambangeg itself, which is a regular stop on the route. The main ranger station and the Department of Environment and Natural Sources (DENR) office are both a short way along this trail, close to the gate that marks the entrance to Mount Pulag National Park. You must **register** here and it's a good place to get a guide. There are no lodgings in Bokod, but if you need to rest up for a night the staff at the municipal building will find you a room in the school or a private home. The Kabayan trail, known as the Akiki or Killer Trail, starts 2km south of Kabayan on the Baguio–Kabayan road. Most climbers on this route rest up for a night in Kabayan beforehand. Whichever way you choose to climb Pulag, take a tent and expect to spend the night on top. The next morning wake early to watch the sun rise and to marvel at the whole of Luzon at your feet.

San Fernando (La Union) and around

SAN FERNANDO is the capital of La Union province and a good place to rest up for a night during a tour of the north. The city itself comprises the usual jumble of jeepneys and fast-food restaurants, but nearby, especially to the north, there are some nice little resorts on the beach. The main road is Quezon Avenue, which runs through the city from south to north. Outside the city limits, Quezon Avenue becomes the National Highway.

Buses from Manila heading north stop at one of a number of terminals. The Philippine Rabbit terminal lies a few kilometres south of the city, while Dominion stops near *McDonald's* just before the city centre, and Partas terminates on the northern fringe of the city in Quezon Avenue beyond the Town Plaza. The closest **airport** served by regular tourist flights is Baguio, from where you can take a bus (2–3hr) to San Fernando. The **tourist information office** (☎072/888 2411) is in the *Oasis Country Resort*, a few kilometres south of the city. Swagman Travel has an office on the main road from Bauang to San Fernando, opposite the entrance to *Cabana Beach Resort*.

The best **accommodation** in the city is the *Sea and Sky Hotel* (☎072/242 0465; ❸–❺) at the northern end of town on Quezon Avenue. The rooms at the back look out onto the sea, while the rooms at the front face the road, which is always busy. Centrally located near the noisy Town Plaza is the dingy *Plaza Hotel* (☎072/888 2996; ❸), offering singles and doubles with air-con and shower. *Hotel Mikka* (☎072/242 5737; ❸) is just beyond the Partas bus terminal on Quezon Avenue. It has 43 modern rooms, a restaurant and a bar.

For beach accommodation around San Fernando, there are two options: **BAUANG** and **SAN JUAN**. Bauang is a few kilometres south of San Fernando and has a number of resorts spread out along an average beach. San Juan, 7km north of San Fernando is superior in every respect, with a marvellous crescent of a beach, pounding surf and some quant, quiet resorts.

Bauang

Many of the resorts – though not all – are engaged in sex tourism and have "nightclubs" attached. The following are among the more wholesome establishments, where families, children and single women travellers are welcome.

Bali Hai Beach Resort ☎072/242 5679. A well-managed place at the southern end of the beach with a large pool, a restaurant and big, clean double rooms. If things are quiet you can get a twenty-percent discount. ❺–❼

China Sea ☎072/242 6101. A relaxing and quiet resort on the beach close to *Bali Hai* offering spacious, clean cottages on the beach, a well-kept swimming pool, a bar and a restaurant. ❺–❻

Coconut Grove Beach Resort ☎072/ 888 4276. A favourite resort among retired expats who meet here regularly to play bowls. *Coconut Grove*, which is one of the first resorts at the southern end of the beach, also has a large swimming pool and a shady restaurant. ❻

San Juan

Buses northbound for Loaog, Vigan or Abra pass through **San Juan**; ask the driver to let you off at one of the resorts, which are all signposted along the road. You can also catch a jeepney, marked for Bacnotan, to San Juan from the junction of P Burgos Street and Quezon Avenue in San Fernando.

La Union Surf Resort ☎072/242 4544. The first resort on your left as you leave the neat little town of San Juan, with its gothic Spanish church and tree-lined plaza. This is where most of the die-hard surfers stay. It's on the beach and has a bar and restaurant. ❸

Las Villas ☎072/242 3770. It's worth looking out for this lovely hacienda-style house when you get off the bus. It's down a little dirt road close to the beach and has a rambling tropical garden and a selection of rooms, each with terracotta floors and unique little decorative touches. Homey, comfortable and well run, with a shady bar and restaurant and a small pool. ❹

Scenic View Tourist Inn ⓣ072/242 2906. Slightly set back from the shore at the northern end of the beach, close to *Sunset German Beach Resort*. Features an impressive marbled lobby, a pool, and a choice of average rooms. ❸

Se-Bay Surf Resort & Entertainment Centre ⓣ072/242 5484. Beachside resort with ten pleasant native-style rooms and a restaurant that serves a good range of meals and snacks. Next to *La Union Surf Resort*. ❹

Sunset German Beach Resort ⓣ0917/921 2420. Pleasant little rustic resort right on the beach, with a touch of European efficiency courtesy of the friendly German owner. Rooms are spotless, the food is consistently good and there are surfboards and body boards for rent. Also a dorm where budget surfers can stay for P80 a night. Next to *Scenic View Tourist Inn* at the northern end of the beach. ❶

Sagada

The village of **SAGADA**, 160km north of Baguio, has oodles of charm and mystery, much of it connected with the hanging coffins that can be seen perched high in the limestone cliffs. Some of these ancient traditions survive; the dead are still sometimes positioned outside their house in a chair known as the death chair. This is believed to give the soul a chance to escape before the remains are disposed of. Sagada began to open up as a destination when it got electricity in the early 1970s, and intellectuals – internal refugees from the Marcos dictatorship – flocked here to write and paint. They didn't produce anything of note, perhaps because they are said to have spent much of their time drinking the local rice wine, known as *tapuy*. European hippies followed and so did the military, who thought the *turistas* were supplying funds for an insurgency. Indeed, a 9pm curfew remains in place today. But the artistic influence has left its mark in the form of quaint little cafés and inns and a distinctly bohemian feel. Most of the village's restaurants and guesthouses are located on the nameless main street, which runs through the town centre past the little market area, the town hall, the police station and the post office. About 500m from the centre of the village heading towards Bontoc is the **Eduardo Masferre Studio** (Mon–Fri 10am–4pm; free), where you can see fascinating old photographs of tribal life in the early twentieth century, while at nearby **Sagada Weaving**, fabrics are produced using traditional tribal designs.

Sagada's forest paths and numerous caves provide some excellent **trekking**, although you must register first with the Sagada Environmental Guides Association (SEGA) at the town hall; the tourist information office and police outpost are here, too. A typical five-hour trek for one to four people costs P300 for the group. One of the most popular day-hikes, taking about five hours in all, is to the **hanging coffins** in **Echo Valley**, high on the surrounding limestone cliffs. There are dozens of little paths leading off through deep foliage in this area, so a guide from SEGA is essential.

Caving in Sagada's labyrinth network of channels and caverns is an exhilarating but potentially risky activity. A small number of tourists have died in these caves, so don't go alone. The best is Sumaging Cave, a forty-five-minute walk south of town, an old burial cave whose chambers and rock formations are an immense and eerie sight.

Dangwa **buses** from Baguio to Sagada terminate close to the town hall on the main street. These buses are rudimentary to say the least, often with uncomfortable seats and no glass in the windows. Jeepneys leave Sagada for Bontoc from near the town hall.

Guesthouses in Sagada are extremely cheap. One of the quietest places to stay is the rustic *Masferré Country Inn and Restaurant* (❷), at the far end of Sagada's main street, beyond the town hall; they also do a good chicken curry. *Sagada Igorot Inn* (ⓣ0919/809 2448; ❷) is the most comfortable hotel in Sagada, a three-storey white building with bright and neat rooms overlooking a green valley.

Up the hill in the village centre past the *Sagada Guest House*, is the *Log Cabin Café*, which does some of the best food in town. *The Shamrock Café* and the *Shamrock II Yoghurt House*, on the main street past the town hall heading west, are legendary for their pancakes and homemade yoghurt.

Bontoc and around

The capital of Mountain province, **BONTOC** is the first major town in the north beyond Baguio. It lies on the banks of the Chico River, about an hour east of Sagada by jeepney. Jeepneys and buses arrive at the terminal opposite the town plaza, close to the market.

Bontoc is primarily a commercial town used by tourists as a rest-stop on the circuit to Banaue. It is, however, gaining a reputation as a good place for **trekking;** contact the Bontoc Ecological Tour Guides Association at the *Pines Kitchenette and Inn*, behind the market in Rizal Plaza (guides charge P300–500 per day). Don't miss the small but well-run **Bontoc Museum** (Mon–Sat 9.30am–noon & 1–5pm; P20), next to the post office, close to the town plaza. It contains photographs of headhunting victims and of zealous American missionaries trying to persuade incredulous warriors to choose the path of righteousness. *Pines Kitchenette and Inn* (☎074/602 1509; ❷) is one of the few places to stay in Bontoc, with big doubles and private shower or cheaper rooms with shared facilities. *Ridge Brook* (☎0919/675 5252; ❷) a three-storey hotel on the southern edge of Bontoc near the bridge, has twelve simply furnished but well-kept rooms, but only one has its own bathrooms; the rest share.

Leaving Bontoc, buses and jeepneys go back to Sagada and Baguio, and onwards to Banaue. From the market, you can get jeepneys (P38) north to **Tinglayan** (3hr) and from there to **Tabuk** – both towns are in the province of Kalinga, home to the Kalinga tribespeople who were once fierce headhunters and are still called the Peacocks of the North because of their indomitable, fiery spirit and refusal to ever be colonized. Tabuk is the place to sign up for white-water rafting trips on the Chico River – Chico River Quest, a well-run company that has high standards of safety, has an office in Callagdao, Tabuk (☎0912/840 1202). To **get to Tabuk** from Baguio, you can catch a Dangwa, Autobus or GL Lines bus (6-7hr). **From Manila,** Victory Liner and Dangwa make the epic ten-hour trip, though a quicker and more comfortable option is to fly with Philippines Airlines to Tuguegarao (Mon, Wed & Sat), where a representative from Chico River Quest can pick you up.

Banaue and around

It's a rugged but spectacular four-hour trip south from Bontoc to **BANAUE** in Ifugao province along a winding road that leads up into the misty Cordilleras, across a mountaintop pass, then down precipitous mountainside. It may only be 300km north of Manila, but Banaue is a world away, 1300m above sea level and far removed in spirit and topography from the beaches and palm trees of the south. This is the heart of **rice-terrace** country: the terraces in Banaue itself are some of the most impressive and well known, although there are hundreds of others in the area, some of the best of which are at nearby **BATAD**, where there is also rustic accommodation so you can stay overnight and hike back the next morning.

Banaue itself is a small town centred on a marketplace, where there are a few guesthouses and some souvenir shops. Two kilometres up the road from the marketplace is the main **lookout point** for the rice terraces. Ifugao in traditional costume will ask for a small fee if you want to take their photograph. A handful of souvenir

The Stairways to Heaven

The **rice terraces** at Banaue are one of the great icons of the Philippines. They were hewn from the land 2000 years ago by Ifugao tribespeople using primitive tools, an achievement in engineering terms that ranks alongside the building of the pyramids. Called the "Stairways to Heaven" by the Ifugaos, the terraces would stretch 20,000km if laid out end to end.

The future of the terraces, recently added to the United Nations' **World Heritage list**, is closely tied to the future of the tribespeople themselves. Part of the problem, it must be said, is tourism. People who would otherwise have been working on the terraces are now making a much easier buck selling reproduction tribal artefacts or rare orchids from the surrounding forests. What's more, rice farming has little allure for the young tribespeople of the Cordilleras. They are tired of the subsistence livelihood that their parents eked out from the land, and are packing their bags for Manila. The resulting labour shortage means the terraces are producing a mere 35 percent of the area's rice needs when they should be producing a hundred percent.

stalls surrounding the lookout sell carved wooden bowls and woven blankets at bargain prices. Don't miss the remarkable little **museum** (daily 8am–5pm; free) at the *Banaue View Inn* (see below), which documents the extraordinary life of Henry Otley Beyer, an American anthropologist who came to study Ifugao tribes at the beginning of the twentieth century and, after marrying an Ifugao woman, settled and died in the region. His remains, shrouded in accordance with Ifugao tradition, are also on view.

Buses and jeepneys terminate at the marketplace near the town hall and close to the **tourist information office** (Mon–Sat 3–6pm), where you can get maps of the area for trekking. They'll also help you find a **guide** for half-day treks to local Ifugao communities or longer treks through the rice terraces to isolated communities, such as Batad. There are no banks in Banaue, but most hotels **change** money. The **post office** has poste restante, but it's a ten-minute jeepney ride from the marketplace near the *Banaue Hotel & Youth Hostel.* You can also make **telephone calls** from the post office.

Accommodation and eating

Accommodation in Banaue is generally basic but clean and friendly, and many places have restaurants attached. There are nineteen hotels or lodging houses so finding somewhere without a reservation is not a problem, except at Christmas and Easter. The best and most expensive place to stay is *Banaue Hotel and Youth Hostel* (☎074/386 4087 or 386 4088; dorm beds P75; rooms ❼), a ten-minute journey from the marketplace by jeepney. It stands on the edge of a ledge with nice grounds, a swimming pool and views across the valley to the terraces. Steep steps lead down from the hotel to Tam-An Village, where you can meet Ifugao people and buy handicrafts. If you decide to stay at the *Banaue Hotel and Youth Hostel,* it's best to book in advance from Manila (☎02/752 0307 or 752 0308). Ask for a room with a view across the terraces: rooms have big balconies and sunrise over the valley is magical. Next best option is the *Banaue View Inn* (☎02/729 3448 or 074/386 4078; ❷), a few minutes south of town in a pretty flower garden. Amenities are simple, but rooms are spick and span; you can also arrange a guide here.

Batad

The fifteen-kilometre trek from Banaue to the remote little village of **BATAD** has become something of a pilgrimage for visitors looking for rural isolation and unforgettable rice-terrace scenery. You'll need to take a jeepney from the market in

Banaue for the first 12km before starting a tiring walk up a steep trail. Batad nestles in a natural amphitheatre, close to the glorious **Tappia Waterfall**, which is 21m high and has a deep, bracing pool for swimming. Village life in Batad has remained virtually unchanged for centuries, although the development of tourism has seen half a dozen primitive **guesthouses** spring up to cater for the influx. Rooms in Batad must be among the cheapest on the planet: P35–50 per head. Choose from the *Foreigner's Inn*, which has a nice balcony restaurant, the wonderful *Hillside Inn*, with its majestic views, and *Simon's Inn*, which has a good cosy café, serving, of all things, pizza.

Vigan

About 135km north of San Fernando in La Union lies the old Spanish town of **VIGAN**, an obligatory stop on any trip through the northern provinces. It has become a bit of a cliché to describe Vigan as a living museum, but it does do some justice to the tag. One of the oldest towns in the Philippines, it was called Nueva Segovia in Spanish times and was an important political, military, cultural and religious centre. It still has pavements of cobbled stones and some of the finest **Spanish colonial architecture** in the country, including impressive homes that once belonged to friars, merchants and colonial officials. Vigan can thank Juan de Salcedo for its glorious architecture. The grandson of conquistador Miguel de Legaspi, he was made ruler of Ilocos province in the late sixteenth century and immediately set about replicating his grandfather's design of Intramuros. Vigan's time-capsule ambience is aided by the decision to close some of the streets to traffic and allow only pedestrians and **carretelas,** one-pony, two-seat traps – a ride in one of these makes for a romantic way to tour the town. Various governmental and non-governmental organizations have joined forces to preserve the old buildings; many are still lived in, others are used as curio shops and a few have been converted into museums.

Vigan is one of the easier Philippine towns to negotiate because its streets follow a fairly regular grid. Mena Crisolog Street runs south from Plaza Burgos and is lined with quaint old antique shops and cafés. Running parallel to it is the main thoroughfare, Governor A. Reyes Street. Between Plaza P. Burgos and Plaza Salcedo stands **St Paul's Metropolitan Cathedral** (daily 6am–9pm), dating back to 1641 – one of the oldest cathedrals in the country. Next to the cathedral, the **Ayala Museum** (Mon–Fri 8.30–11am & 1.30–4.30pm; P10) is a captivating old colonial house that was once home to one of the town's most famous residents, Padre José Burgos, whose martyrdom in 1872 galvanized the revolutionary movement. It houses Burgos memorabilia, as well as fourteen paintings by the artist Villanueva, depicting the violent 1807 Basi Revolt, prompted by a Spanish effort to control the production of *basi* (sugar-cane wine).

Souvenir-hunters after something more than the usual bulk-produced tourist knick-knacks should head for **Rowilda's Hand Loom**, on Mena Crisologo Street near the Cordillera Inn, which offers the kind of old-style textiles that used to be traded during colonial times. Vigan is also known for its **pottery**. The massive wood-fired kilns at the Pagburnayan Potteries in Rizal Street, at the junction with Liberation Boulevard, turn out huge jars, known as *burnay*, in which northerners store everything from vinegar to fish paste. Carabao (water buffalo) are used to squash the clay under hoof.

Practicalities

From Manila, a limited number of **bus** companies make the eight-hour trip north: Philippine Rabbit buses pull in at their terminal on General Luna Street, one of the town's major east–west thoroughfares, a short walk or tricycle ride from the hotels and attractions. Partas buses arrive at the Partas terminal near the Vigan Public Market in Alcantara Street at the southern end of town, while there's a third terminal, for Dominion buses arriving from Laoag and San Fernando, at the southern end of Quezon Avenue, the main street running south to north.

The **tourist information office** (Mon–Sat 8am–5pm; ☎077/732 5705) is in Leona Florentina House, near *Café Leona* in Plaza Burgos. You can also get information at the nearby Provincial Capitol Building. There are branches of Allied Bank, Metro bank, BPI, Far East Bank and PCI Bank all pretty close to each other on Quezon Avenue. The **post office** is at the junction of Governor A. Reyes and Bonifacio streets. Also on Governor A. Reyes Street is Powernet, where you can send and receive **emails** for P50 an hour. Vigan's main **hospital** is the Gabriela Silang General Hospital (☎077/722 2722) on Quirino Boulevard, and the **police station** is at the eastern end of Florentino Street.

Accommodation

Cordillera Inn Crisologo St, a 5min walk east of the Philippine Rabbit bus terminal ☎077/722 2727. Ordinary doubles with fan and shared bath, or slightly more comfortable doubles with a/c and cramped shower. ❶

El Juliana Hotel Quirino Blvd cnr Liberation Blvd ☎077/722 2994. Small a/c or fan rooms come with a toilet and shower. There's a swimming pool, also open to the public. ❷

Grandpa's Inn 1 Bonifacio St ☎077/722 2118. Rather tired old place on the eastern edge of Bonifacio Street near the river. It's full of curios and has cell-like fan singles and slightly seedy doubles with a/c and bath. Inspect the rooms before you commit yourself because some are better than others. ❶

Vigan Hotel Burgos St ☎077/722 1906. Good location a short walk to the east of Plaza Burgos. Dignified colonial building offering rooms with a/c, cable TV and fridge. ❸

Villa Angela Heritage House Quirino Blvd, a 20min walk south from Plaza Burgos. ☎077/722 2914. The most colonial of all the colonial hotels, this beautiful old museum of a place is the billet of choice if you want to wallow in history and don't mind paying a little extra for the privilege. You can ask for the room Tom Cruise slept in: he stayed here for a few weeks when *Born on the Fourth of July* was being filmed on the sand dunes near Laoag. Even the dorm (P150) has Spanish-style wooden bunkbeds and billowing mosquito nets and curtains. ❺

Eating and drinking

At *Café Leona* in Plaza Burgos you can order **native Ilocano dishes**, all for less than P150; try the Special Vigan Sinanglaw, a dish of pork entrails sautéed with ginger, vinegar, fish sauce, onion and pepper. *The Cool Spot Restaurant* at the back of the *Vigan Hotel* has also acquired a good reputation for its Ilocano cooking. At the pleasant olde worlde *Café Floresita* near the Ancieto Mansion, opposite Plaza P. Burgos, native *longganiza* (sausage) features in many dishes. Another of Vigan's specialities is *empanada*, a type of tortilla that you can pick up for a few pesos from one of the many street stalls and small bakeries, where they are freshly baked. For **drinks** in a convivial puib-like atmosphere, try *Halftime Sports Bar* at the junction of Reyes and General Luna Streets.

Moving on from Vigan

Philippine Rabbit **buses** leave every hour from the main terminal on the National Highway, a short walk north of Plaza Salcedo, for destinations including Manila and Laoag. Dominion buses leave throughout the day from the terminal at the junction of Quezon Boulevard and Liberation Avenue for Laoag, with a limited number going all the way to Manila. Florida buses go north to Pagudpud, leaving from the Caltex Bantay bus terminal, a P10 tricycle ride south from the city centre. There are two buses a day, one at 6am and the other at 4pm. Opposite the market in Alcantara Street is a Partas bus terminal for trips north and south. From the minibus and jeepney terminal, also close to the market, you can catch air-con **minibuses** north to Laoag.

Laoag and around

In 1818, the province of Ilocos was divided into two and the city of **LAOAG**, two hours' drive north from Vigan, became the capital of Ilocos Norte. In more recent years, Ilocos Norte has become associated in most Filipino minds with former president Ferdinand Marcos. This was very much his patch, and his son, Bong-Bong, and daughter, Imee, both of whom have entered politics, are still popular in these parts. Marcos was born south of Laoag in Sarrat, while the family seat was 15km southeast of the city, in **Batac**, where the dictator's frozen body rests today (see p.829). There's little to see in Laoag itself, though it's worth making time for **St William's Cathedral**, on FR Castro Avenue, which dates back to 1650. Further east along FR Castro is Ermita Hill, which has nice **views** across Laoag and out to the South China Sea. It's a thirty-minute walk, or you can take a jeepney from outside the cathedral.

Practicalities

Air Philippines has a daily flight from Manila to Laoag. From the **airport**, it's only 3km into town: a tricycle will cost P10 or you can negotiate for a private ride in a jeepney or van (about P150). Philippine Rabbit, Partas and Farinas **buses** all make the long trip north from Manila, each arriving at a different terminal. The Philippine Rabbit terminal is at the west end of General Antonio Luna Street close to the *Starlight Lodging House*, the Farinas terminal is in E. Bonifacio Avenue a short walk from Aurora Park and Partas is on the northern edge of the city in Paco Roman Street. From all these terminals you can easily walk to the city centre or hop on a tricycle. Laoag City **Tourism Council** (☎077/772 0001) is in the City Hall of Laoag, on the south side of Aurora Park in the city centre, as is the Department of Tourism Tourist Information and Assistance Office (☎077/772 0467). There are plenty of banks, convenience stores and pharmacies at the eastern end of Rizal Avenue around the Odeon Cinema. The Philippine National Police Station is on the east side of Aurora Park.

Accommodation and eating

Laoag isn't a major tourist destination and **hotels** are few and far between, but the new *Hotel Tiffany* (☎077/770 3550; ❶), on General Fidel Segundo Avenue, has small, clean doubles with private shower and a good diner on the ground floor serving burgers, rice dishes and pizza. The *Texicano Hotel* (☎077/722 0290; ❷), on Rizal Avenue, has bog-standard air-con double rooms with cable TV. *Starlight Lodging House* (❶) near the Philippine Rabbit bus terminal features a choice of uninspiring but reasonably clean fan or air-con budget doubles with private showers, while one block to the south is *La Elliana* (❷), which has modern, clean doubles with air-con and cable TV. The most upmarket and ostentatious hotel in the area, perhaps in the country, is *Fort Ilocandia Resort Hotel* (☎077/772 116; ❽) on the seafront in barangay Calayab, 3km south of the airport. It was built in 1973 and hastily completed for the wedding reception of Ferdinand and Imelda Marcos's youngest daughter, Irene. Amenities include a government-run casino, a golf course and half a dozen restaurants.

For wholesome Filipino **food**, *Barrio Fiesta* on Manuel Nolasco Street is good value. *La Preciosa Restaurant* on Rizal Avenue opposite the *Texicano Hotel* and *Nereo's Dagupan House* on Governor Primo Lazaro Avenue both specialize in Ilocano dishes such as *pinakbet* (vegetables sautéed in fish paste) and *kare-kare*, and neither costs more than P150 per person, including a couple of San Miguels.

Batac

In **BATAC**, a thirty-minute jeepney ride southeast of Laoag (P12), you can visit the **Marcos Mansion** (Mon–Sat 9am–4pm; P25), which is full of the dictator's old belongings; you can even see his refrigerated corpse, although many believe it's nothing more than a wax model. Impressive Batac Church, opposite the mansion, is where Imee was married with the kind of pomp and ceremony rarely seen outside royal families. A few kilometres southwest of Batac is the World-Heritage-listed iconic **Paoay Church**, built in a style known as "earthquake baroque", with immense side supports for its walls.

Pagudpud

From Laoag, it's only another couple of hours by bus to the crashing surf and sweeping white beach of **PAGUDPUD**, backdrop for many a Filipino bodice-buster movie. Pagudpud is deservedly becoming known as a destination that has all the beauty of Boracay, but without the tourists and the nightlife. It's not a place for ravers, just somewhere to grab yourself a cottage on the shore and relax for a few days.

Florida, Autobus and RJC **buses** from Laoag to Tuguegarao will let you off on the highway, from where you can catch a tricycle to the best-known local beach, **Saud Beach**. Resorts on Saud Beach are a little pricier than similar resorts elsewhere, simply because there are so few of them that there's little competition. All the following **resorts** are near the centre of Saud Beach, close to the narrow road leading from Pagudpud town. The best and most expensive is *Saud Beach Resort* (☎077/764 1005; ❼). Amenities include a karaoke bar, outdoor sports, a restaurant and boats for hire; rooms are spacious and comfortable with air-con and private showers, and there's good food in the restaurant, including fresh fish every day and big Filpino-style breakfasts. *Arinaya White Resort* (☎077/764 1079; ❻) has a range of ordinary doubles and family rooms set back from the beach in a neat garden. At their little wooden restaurant, they grill the catch of the day, as long as you give advanced notice. *Villa del Mar* (☎077/764 1084; ❺) has less well-maintained doubles, but is worth considering if you're on a budget – you can rent a two-man tent (P700) and camp in the garden. *Terra Rika Beach Resort* (☎077/764 1009; ❻) is a family-run place with a choice of concrete cottages and double rooms. The restaurant serves breakfast (two eggs with garlic rice and spicy native sausage), lunch and dinner.

Batanes Islands

About 100km off the northern coast of Luzon, **Batanes** is the smallest, most isolated province in the country: the land that time forgot. There are no cinemas, hotels, shops or newspapers and hardly any tourists. Cable television arrived a few years ago, causing great excitement, but on some of the ten small islands that make up Batanes electricity is still limited to three or four hours a day. To say the islands are different from the rest of the country is an understatement. At times, with its limestone houses and restless seas, Batanes is more reminiscent of the Scottish Highlands than the sunny Philippines. The people are different, the language is different, even the weather is different. Winter (Dec–Feb) can get quite cold with temperatures as low as 7°C, while the summer (April–June) is searing during the day, but cooler at night. Remember that the weather changes quickly, often stranding tourists for days.

The most economically important islands in the Batanes group are **Batan** – the location of the capital **BASCO** – **Sabtang** and **Itbayat**. The other islands are Dequey, Siayan, Mabudis, Ibuhos, Diago, North Island and Y'Ami, which is closer to Taiwan than it is to the Philippines. The native inhabitants of Batanes, the Ivatan, trace their roots to prehistoric Formosan immigrants and latter-day Spanish conquistadors. Most still make a living from the cultivation of yam and garlic or the raising of goats and cows. Many still wear the *soot*, a raincape made from the stripped leaves of the *vuyavuy* vine. The main dialect, Ivatan, includes some pidgin Spanish: "thank you" is *dios mamajes* and "goodbye" is *dios mavidin*, said only by the person leaving. The person staying behind says *dios machivan*.

The Batanes landscape is rugged and makes for some great trekking and exploring. The climb to the abandoned radar station on the hill behind Basco is not too strenuous and gives remarkable 360-degree views of the islands. From Ivana in Batan, you can take a ferry (P30) at 6.30am to Sabtang Island, 5km to the south. **Sabtang** has no telephones, limited electricity and only two vehicles to service the whole island. To make the most of your visit, stay overnight; locals will be happy to accommodate you, but show your appreciation by bringing some gifts such as sweets, matches, lighters and snacks. **Itbayat**, 40km north of Batan, criss-crossed with trails, one of which leads to the summit of Mount Riposed (231m). The only way to get to the island is on the daily ferry from Bosco on Batan, which leaves at either 5am or 6am (4hr; P200) – it won't run if the weather is anything less than perfect – and the only **place to stay** is the mayor's guesthouse (P100 a night). You can contact him as soon as you arrive at the town hall in Mayen.

Practicalities

The quickest way **to get to Batanes** from Manila is on the Asian Spirit **flight** to Basco on Mondays, Thursdays and Saturdays. Make sure you book your tickets well in advance because the chances of getting a peak-season seat at short notice are slim. Flights around Easter are usually fully booked, with a long waiting list of hopefuls.

Two **cargo ships** owned by the Batanes Multi-Purpose Cooperative regularly ply the Manila–Basco sea route, bringing in supplies. The *M/V Queen of Fatima* and the *M/V Don Rudito* both accept passengers, but are not equipped as passenger ships.

The **best time** to strike out for Batanes is between December and May – at any other time, your chances of getting there are slimmer because strong winds and typhoons result in the cancellation or lengthy delay of flights.

Accommodation

Batanes Resort. A government-owned resort with gentle, well-intentioned staff and an absolutely unbeatable location. The six tidy, little stone duplex cottages sit on a breezy hillside a couple of kilometres south of Basco, with steps leading down to a marvellous crescent black-sand cove. The food (breakfast P80, lunch P150, dinner P150) is undistinguished, but you don't have to eat at the resort. A jeepney into town for dinner costs P5 and a tricycle back to the resort at night P30. ❸

Batanes Seaside Lodge and Restaurant 400m along the National Road from Basco towards *Batanes Resort*. *Seaside Lodge* may be new, tiled and clean, but the fan and a/c rooms (single, double, family) are relatively expensive and the food and service in the dreary restaurant dismal. There is, however, a pleasant terrace at the rear with sea views, and the upper floors have a wraparound seaview balcony shared by all the guests. ❷

Ivatan Lodge Faded yellow building that represents last chance saloon in terms of accommodation in Basco. On the ground floor are various small offices and storerooms, while on the first floor are seven dusty, dilapidated rooms with shared facilities. *Ivatan Lodge* is on the seafront side of the National Road, 200m beyond *Shanedel's* towards the town plaza. ❶

Shanedel's Inn and Café 0669 Kaychanarianan cnr National Rd and Abad St. This congenial little guesthouse has six rooms with a shared bathroom and offers the best budget accommodation – and the best food – in Basco itself by some way. Grab yourself a cold beer in the terrace restaurant at the rear and watch the sun set over Basco harbour while the owners rustle you up a dinner of sizzling beef and grilled flying fish. Four people can eat and drink here for less than P500. ❶

8.5

South Luzon (the Bicol region)

The region south of Batangas and Quezon is technically known as Region V, but commonly known to Filipinos as **South Luzon** or **Bicol**. The northernmost province of the Bicol region is Camarines Norte. The National Highway meanders south from here to Camarines Sur through the towns of **Daet**, **Naga** and **Legaspi**, which are typically provincial, with their jumbled traffic, concrete malls and occasional Spanish-era relics. Legaspi is the jumping-off point for the active volcano **Mount Mayon**. Continuing further south still, you reach the coastal town of Sorsogon, from where it's a fifty-kilometre ride to the bucolic backwater of **Donsol**. Donsol has seen an increase in tourism recently because of the number of plankton-eating whale sharks that congregate here. From **Matnog** in **Sorsogon** province, you can take a ferry across the Bernardino Strait to Samar, the gateway to the rest of the Visayas. Two of the archipelago's lesser-known islands, **Masbate** and **Marinduque**, are off the west coast of the Bicol mainland and well worth exploring if you're looking for an unspoiled taste of Philippine provincial life, well away from the tourist trail.

The Bicol region is easily accessible **by air** from Manila. BLTB also has **buses** that run up and down the National Highway daily, taking you to most major jumping-off points in the area. BLTB even has services that run all the way to Sorsogon, but the journey is a long one – be prepared to sweat it out for the best part of twenty hours. Many choose to take a bus that leaves Manila in the evening and travels overnight, when the roads are quiet, arriving early the next day. Philtranco has a new service that goes all the way from Manila to Davao, using ferries where it has to: it stops at Daet, Naga and Legaspi, before heading on to the port of **Matnog** at the southernmost tip of South Luzon for the **Samar** ferry.

Daet and around

DAET, 200km from Manila, is an unassuming town with little to detain you, but it's a good place to bed down for the night before setting out to explore the rest of the province of Camarines Norte. It's an area that has been largely overlooked as a tourist destination, but undeservedly so. If it's unspoiled beaches you're after, the coastline to the east of Daet has more than its fair share.

Buses arriving in Daet stop on the edge of the city on the National Highway, from where it's less than 2km into town; plenty of tricycles ply the route. In Daet itself there are a number of simple **guesthouses**, including the *Dolor Hotel* (❸), on Vinzons Avenue, and the *Karilagan Hotel* (❷) on Morena Street, in the centre of town.

One of the most pleasant surprises around Daet is **Bagasbas beach**, 4km from Daet and accessible by jeepney and bus from the station on Pimentel Avenue, near the Shell petrol station in Daet. The waves crash in from the Pacific and are

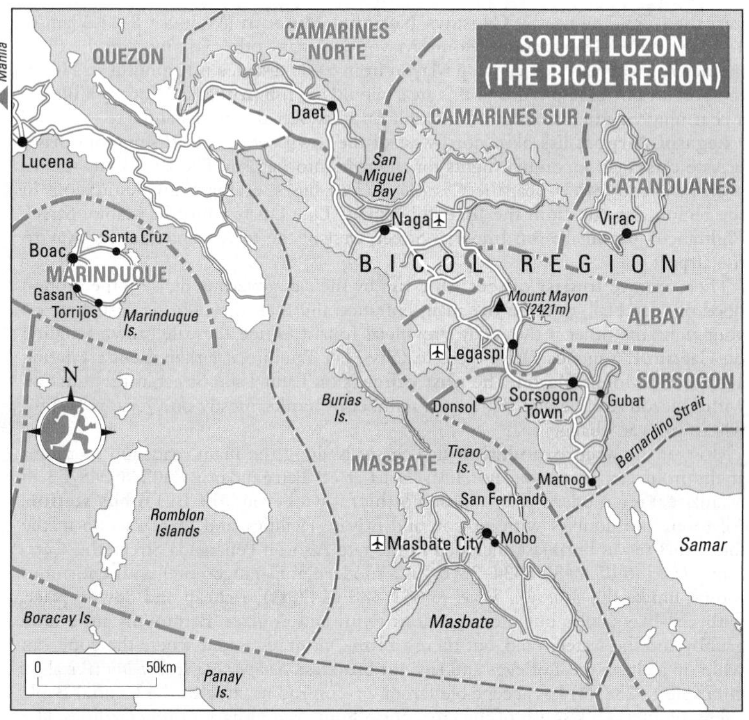

sometimes big enough for surfing. In fact, the whole area of coast east of Daet has become something of a surfer's hangout in the making: the best person to see is Alvin Obsuan, owner of *Alvinos' Pizza and Surf Camp* (❷), a small guesthouse with dorm rooms for P125 and a couple of private rooms, at the back of Bagasbas beach on a road known simply as The Boulevard.

Other attractions in the Daet area include **Mananap Falls,** 18km west of Daet. Catch a bus or jeepney from Pimentel Avenue in Daet. The last stretch of the journey consists of a bracing three-kilometre hike, but you can have a refreshing swim in the falls' deep pools when you arrive.

Legaspi

The port city of **LEGASPI** (also spelt Legazpi), four hours south of Naga, is the place to base yourself if you fancy climbing **Mount Mayon**. Legaspi is a bustling place, with one main thoroughfare, Peñaranda Street, that connects the port area with the district of Albay, where most of the accommodation and restaurants are. The town itself has little in the way of tourist attractions, but one sight worth seeing are the **Cagsawa Ruins**, the eerie remains of a church that was buried in the devastating eruption of Mayon in 1814. The best time to see the ruins is at dawn before the vendors and hawkers stake a claim to it and the clouds roll in and obscure the view of the volcano. The ruins are located fifteen minutes' drive west of Legaspi – take a jeepney from Rizal Street bound for Guinobatan and ask the driver to let you off near the ruins. The nearby **Cagsawa National Museum** (Mon–Sat 8–11.30am & 1–4.30pm) has exhibits about Mount Mayon and many other volcanoes in the Philippines. A good place for viewing Mayon from a safe distance is Kupuntukan Hill in the port area of Legaspi. Also in this area, behind the fish market, is **Victory Village,** a charmingly rustic bamboo village built on stilts over the black-sand bay.

Legaspi Airport lies 3km northwest of the town centre, off Washington Drive; private cars meet incoming flights for the ride into Legaspi. The BLTB bus station is on Peñaranda Street near the *Casablanca Hotel*; buses serving many destinations in the region also run from the JB Bicol Express Line bus terminal in Mabini Street. Philtranco's terminal is on Imperial Street, west of the town centre on the way to the airport.

There are two **tourist offices**. One, run by the city government, is on the ground floor of City Hall, through the main entrance and then through the first door on your right; the other is the Albay Provincial Tourist Office, the pale brown building on Captain F. Aquenda Drive close to City Hall. Enquire at either about arranging a guide for Mount Mayon. The **post office** is on Lapu-Lapu Street at the junction with Quezon Avenue, and there are a number of **banks**, mostly on Quezon Avenue, where you can change cash.

Most of the **accommodation** in Legaspi is along the main road, and so rooms at the front can be noisy. The *Albay Hotel* at 88 Peñaranda St (☎02/893 5733 in Manila; ❹) is a modern place a little north of town beyond the BLTB **bus station**. All rooms are doubles with air-con and private facilities, and there's a café in the lobby that serves breakfast, included in the rate. Also on Peñaranda Street, the *Casablanca Hotel* (☎052/480 8334–36; ❹) is a modern, mid-range hotel with enormous rooms, unlike the *Magayon Hotel* (☎052/480 6147; ❶), a cheap and dowdy place, with cell-like singles but more spacious twins and doubles. Bathrooms are a little grubby and the water's cold, but there's a large, clean restaurant where the cook can whip up a cheap meal of eggs and rice for breakfast. *Sampaguita Tourist Inn* (Rizal St; ☎052/480 6258; ❸) has acceptable fan or air-con rooms close to the Central Bank, a few minutes' walk south of the city centre. Some rooms have private facilities. The little coffee shop is dark and stuffy, but does adequate snacks. At the time of writing, a new *Sampaguita Tourist Inn* was opening. It's next door, behind the Petron petrol station and looks grander and more spacious than its ageing predecessor. The *Alicia Hotel* on F. Aquende Drive (☎052/481 0801; ❹) has good, clean air-con doubles in a quiet location very close to the airport.

The population of Legaspi seems to subsist almost entirely on **fast food**. In Pacific Mall, the brown and green building a short walk west from the market in Imperial Street, there are branches of *Jollibee*, *McDonald's* and *Chow King*. There's also a branch of *Graceland*, a local fast-food restaurant that serves dishes such as barbecue pork, barbecue chicken and adobo with rice, all for around P80. Another *Graceland* can be found opposite Rizal Park and a third on the main road at the Albay end of the city.

The best **restaurant** in Legaspi is the *Legaspi Four Seasons* at 205 Magallanes St, up a concrete staircase, close to Rizal Park. It's a simple, clean Chinese place: portions are freshly cooked and huge, so choose a few different dishes and share them around. For native **Bicol cuisine**, try the *Waway* restaurant in Peñaranda Street, a ten-minute walk north beyond the *Albay Hotel*. Most of the hotels above have **cafés**, but they're often empty.

Mount Mayon

The perfectly smooth cone of **Mount Mayon** (2421m) in Albay province makes it look benign from a distance, but don't be deceived. Mayon is a devil in disguise and has claimed the lives of a number of climbers in rock avalanches in recent years. It is the most active volcano in the country and has erupted more than thirty times since

1616, the date of its first recorded eruption. Recent eruptions occurred in 1984 and 1993, and as recently as the beginning of 2002 it was blowing steam from its crater and forcing authorities to evacuate farmers from its lower slopes. It's no wonder the locals spin fearful stories around it. The most popular legend says Mayon was formed when a beautiful native princess eloped with a brave warrior. Her uncle, Magayon, was so possessive of his niece that he chased the young couple, who prayed to the gods for help. A landslide buried the raging uncle alive, but he is said to still be inside the volcano, his anger sometimes bursting forth in the form of eruptions.

The presence of Mayon has an adverse effect on Legaspi's weather conditions; the only window of opportunity for an ascent is **March to May**, and even then you should be prepared for cold nights at altitude and the possibility of showers. At other times of the year, you could be hanging around for days waiting for a break in the weather. Furthermore, the slopes of Mayon are not as silky smooth as they look from a few miles away. It takes at least two days to reach the summit, working your way through forest, grassland and deserts of rock-sand boulders, and another day to descend.

The **safest approach** is from the northwestern slope, which starts at 762m above sea level on a ledge where the Philippine Institute of Volcanology and Seismology (PHIVOLCS) research station and the derelict remains of the *Mayon Skyline Hotel* are located: you'll need to register at PHIVOLCS. *Mayon Resthouse* is a simple place with dorm beds for P200–300 a night and some rudimentary cooking facilities; make sure you bring your own food, as the menu is limited. To get there, take a public bus or jeepney from Rizal Street in Legaspi and ask to get off near the *Resthouse*. You might have to walk the last few kilometres if the narrow road leading uphill to the guesthouse and PHIVOLCS is impassable.

From PHIVOLCS, the trail creeps upwards through a tropical secondary forest, then cuts across a wilderness of razor-sharp *talahib* (grass) before turning sharply at approximately 1220m towards Buang Gully, a ravine formed by ancient molten lava flow. On the gully's floor are enormous depressions containing rainwater. At slightly above 1524m, Buang Gully branches out into two canals. This spot is ideal for a campsite since it's near enough to the summit, yet far enough away from the poisonous fumes that can blow down from the crater with a sudden shift in wind direction. Most climbers make camp here the first night and rise before dawn to continue the next morning, which is when the trail gets really hard. After scrambling over rocks and boulders, you reach a cliff system at 2195m. A forty-degree ascent on loose volcanic cinder and lava sand follows, before finally – the summit. You should reach the summit at around 11am, allowing time to descend to the same overnight camp before dark. On the third day, continue your descent to PHIVOLCS, where you must report your arrival.

You can approach the volcano by taking a jeepney or bus from Legaspi to **Tabaco**, 26km north of Legaspi, then another heading west to **Buang**, where the narrow concrete road up to the deserted and half-ruined *Mayon Skyline Hotel* is on the left just before you reach Buang itself, marked by a green signpost. It's just over 8km from the turn-off to the ruins, so if you don't fancy the walk, catch one of the tricycles that hang around at the turn-off. A quicker and more comfortable way to get there is to rent a vehicle in Legaspi. Whatever you do, don't go without a **guide**. You can arrange one at the tourist offices in Legaspi or through Mayon Mountaineers Club (ask the tourist office to put you in touch). You can also arrange for a tent and sleeping bag; it can be chilly on the higher slopes, so don't bank on sleeping outside. You'll have to bring all your food with you from Legaspi; there are sources of water on the volcano, but you'll need purifying tablets.

Sorsogon Town and Gubat

On the southeastern tip of the Bicol peninsula, **SORSOGON TOWN**, capital of the same-name province, makes a good base for visiting Donsol and exploring the beaches of the eastern seaboard, where waves hammer in from the Pacific and surfing is a growing industry. One of the nicest beaches is **Rizal Beach**, in the barrio of **GUBAT**, a twenty-minute jeepney ride from Sorsogon, where you can get an ageing but adequate room at the *Rizal Beach Resort Hotel* (☎056/211 1056; ❸). In Sorsogon itself, by far the most attractive accommodation is *Fernandos Hotel* (☎056/211 1357; ❹) in Pareja Street. The owner, Gina Duran, is a mine of information about the area. The hotel has a quaint, antique ambience and sixteen air-con rooms, plus a small patio restaurant.

Donsol

The peaceful fishing community of **DONSOL** lies almost equidistant between Legaspi and Sorsogon Town; you can get there by frequent bus from either in less than two hours. The area around Donsol is best known for one of the greatest concentrations of **whale sharks** in the world, and your first stop in town should be the **Visitor Centre** (daily 7am–4pm) next to the town hall, where you can complete all the formalities of hiring a boat for a whale shark-watching trip. The number of sightings varies: during peak season (Dec–Jan), there's a good chance of seeing ten or fifteen whale sharks – known locally as *butanding* – a day, but on some days you might strike out and see none.

Tourists intent on seeing the sharks are not allowed to board a boat without first being briefed by a **Butanding Interaction Officer** (BIO), who explains how to behave in the water near one of these huge creatures. The number of snorkellers around any one whale shark is limited to six; flash photography is not permitted, nor is scuba gear, and don't get anywhere near the animal's tail because it's powerful enough to do you some serious damage. Take plenty of protection against the sun and a good book. Once a whale shark has been sighted you'll need to get your mask, snorkel and flippers on and get in the water before it dives too deep to be seen.

Boats **cost** P2200 for up to six people, and there's also a registration fee of P300 for foreigners and P100 for Filipinos. Each boat has a crew of three, the captain, the BIO and the spotter, each of whom will expect a token of your appreciation (at least P100 to each person) at the end of a successful day (and even an unsuccessful one). All this makes it an expensive day out by Philippine standards, but take heart from the fact that your money is helping the conservation effort.

Masbate

The province of **Masbate** lies in the centre of the archipelago, bounded in the north by the Bicol peninsula, in the south by the Visayan Sea, in the west by the Sibuyan Sea, and in the east by the Samar Sea. It includes the main island of **Masbate** and a number of smaller islands, including the **Burias Islands** and the large island of **Ticao**, off the northeastern coast. Masbate is the Philippines' wild east. It ranks second only to Bukidnon in Mindanao in cattle production and plays host to a number of rodeos, which are being touted by the local government as a new tourist attraction. Otherwise, Masbate is off the main tourist trail. There are some excellent beaches, including **Dacu beach** in Mobo town, a fifteen-minute jeepney ride from the capital **MASBATE CITY**, on the northeast coast of Masbate Island. **Talisay beach**, famous for its rock formations, on Ticao Island, is situated 13km south of San Fernando or 30km from Masbate. **Deagan Island** was once famous for being the favourite hideaway of former First Lady Imelda Marcos. Most of Masbate's beaches have small resorts, all of them simple, rustic places that offer little in the way of food or amenities. In Masbate itself, *Saint Anthony Hotel* (❷), on Quezon Street, is one of only a few options.

Masbate **airstrip** is just a five-minute jeepney ride (P10) from Masbate City: Asian Spirit flies direct from Manila four times a week. Sulpicio Lines and WG&A both have ferry services from Manila leaving once or twice a week and ferries also connect Masbate to Cebu and Leyte. **Buses** and jeepneys link Masbate City with other places on the island, leaving from the main square, opposite the Provincial Capitol Building.

Marinduque

The heart-shaped island of **Marinduque**, 170km southeast of Manila, is a quiet backwater, chiefly known for its **Moriones Festival**, a unique and animated Easter tradition featuring masked men dressed like Roman soldiers. This week-long celebration starts on Holy Monday and culminates on Easter Sunday, when the story of the centurion Longinus and his links to Christ are re-enacted in pantomime. Celebrated in the capital **Boac**, on the island's west coast, and also in the nearby villages of Mogpog and Gasan, the festival starts with masked men roaming the streets playing pranks on the residents (and tourists), serenading ladies, frightening children and engaging in mock swordfights.

Aside from the festival, you can explore the immense **Bathala Caves** in barangay Ipil, on the north coast, thirty minutes' from Boac by tricycle. One of the four accessible caves contains human bones believed to be the remains of World War II soldiers. You've a good chance of seeing pythons here, along with the thousands of bats that call the caves home. The caves are privately owned and you have to pay the caretaker P100 for a guided tour. **Tres Reyes Islands**, off the coast of the town of Gasan in the southwest, have some marvellous beaches and coral reefs. To get to Tres Reyes, take a jeepney south to Gasan, where you can hire a boat (30min). Off the small town of Santa Cruz on the northeast coast, 35 minutes from Boac pier by boat, are the islets of **Polo**, **Mompong** and **Maniuaya**, with powdery sand beaches that rival Boracay. There is no accommodation on these tiny islands, so you should take drinking water, food and tents if you plan to stay. The waters around Marinduque offer excellent diving, with 83 chartered dive sites.

Practicalities

Asian Spirit **flies** to Marinduque on Monday, Wednesday and Friday. When the plane lands at Marinduque Airport, twenty minutes south of Boac, there's a van waiting to take tourists into Boac (P20). The Asian Spirit office (☎042/332 2065) is on the ground floor of the *Boac Hotel*.

The long journey from Manila to Marinduque by **bus** and **ferry** starts at the BLTB terminal in Pasay, where buses depart hourly for the port of Dalahican on the outskirts of Lucena (3hr). The ferry leaves Dalahican for the small port of Balanacan on the north coast of Marinduque at 8.30am, 9am, 2pm and 2.30pm, but be prepared to wait in Dalahican because departure times do change, particularly in inclement weather. From Balanacan, it's easy to get a jeepney (P10) to Boac. The return ferry leaves Balanacan for Dalahican at 7am, 9am, 2.45pm and 4pm (2hr; P120). There is also a Viva Shipping Lines "roll-on, roll-off" vessel that leaves Dalahican at 10am and arrives at Balanacan at 2.30pm, returning the following morning at 6am. Balanacan is half an hour north of Boac and all arriving ferries are met by various tricycles and jeepneys, so getting into town is not difficult. There are no taxis on Marinduque, which means transport is limited to jeepneys, tricycles for shorter distances, and small boats.

The best **accommodation** in the provincial capital is the *Tahanan sa Isok* (☎042/332 1231; ④), a white building in Canovas Street on the eastern edge of town. It has twelve air-con rooms with en-suite bathrooms. If you are willing to unplug the air-con and make do with a fan the price goes down. The hotel is used as a training hotel for hospitality industry students and has a café, a lovely garden restaurant, and is about the only good place to get transport details and general advice on what to see and do on the island. The estimable *Boac Hotel* (☎042/332 2065; ❷) in the shadow of the cathedral has boxy singles and doubles with fan, toilet and shower. The advantage of staying at the *Boac Hotel* is that it's easy to get to the airport for the early morning flight back to Manila. Asian Spirit staff are based at the hotel and allow passengers to hitch a lift in their van, which leaves at 5.30am on flight days. On the south side of town, in an area known as Mercado, is the splendidly named *Happy Bunny's Lodging House* (☎042/332 2040; ❷), where there are three double rooms with toilet and shower.

Dozens of small resorts are scattered round the island. Take a jeepney south to Torrijos and spend a few quiet nights at *Poctoy White Beach* (❶), a few kilometres outside town, which has basic wooden huts in a garden set back from the shore. The owner cooks simple dishes and serves cold beer at her nearby house, and also has a small store where you can buy bare essentials.

8.6

The Visayas

Rightly or wrongly, the **Visayas** are considered the cradle of the Philippines. It was here that Ferdinand Magellan laid a sovereign hand on the islands for Spain. The islands were also the scene of some of the bloodiest battles fought against the Japanese during World War II and where General Douglas MacArthur waded ashore to liberate the country after his famous promise, "I shall return". No one seems entirely sure how many islands there are in the Visayas, but the number certainly runs into the thousands. Everywhere you turn there's a patch of tropical sand or coral reef awaiting your attention, usually with a ferry or banca to take you there. There are nine major islands – Cebu, Bohol, Guimaras, Samar, Leyte, Panay, Negros, Romblon and Siquijor – but it's the hundreds of others in between that make this part of the archipelago so irresistible. A short journey by banca can take you from air-conditioned ritziness to bucolic nirvana.

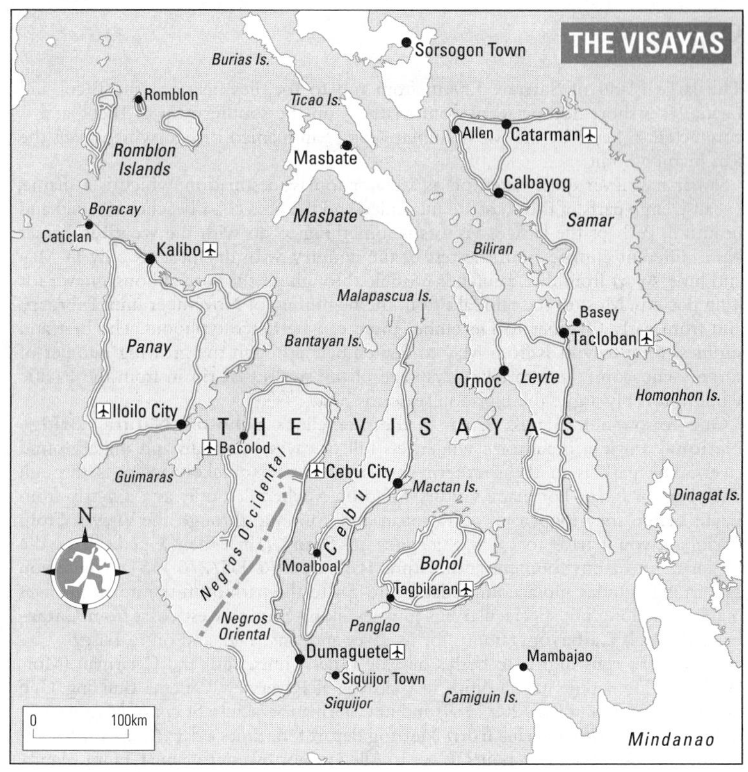

Despite recent efforts to turn Cebu into a major international freeport, most of the islands remain lost in their own little world. Vast areas of **Bohol**, **Leyte**, **Panay** and **Samar** and the sugar plantation island of **Negros** are relatively undiscovered, while the island of **Siquijor** is said to be home to witches and faith healers. **Romblon** can still only be reached by boat and offers some of the country's most pristine wilderness areas, while sleepy **Guimaras**, known for the sweetness of its mangoes, has marvellous beaches that few tourists make the effort to see. Of the smaller islands, some are famous for their beaches (nowhere else in the country will you find the same kind of proliferation of bars and resorts as on Boracay, off the northern tip of Panay), some for their fiestas, some for sugar and some for their folklore. No one can accuse the Visayas, and the Visayans who live here, of being a uniform lot. In some areas they speak Cebuana, while in others it's Ilonggo, Waray Waray or Aklan. Bigger islands have the kind of glitzy shopping malls and hotels that can do serious damage to the most liberal travel budget, while others are enchantingly rustic, the sort of places where even the grasshoppers are slow.

Getting around the Visayas is fairly easy. Boracay, Cebu, Panay, Bohol, Negros, Leyte and Samar are all accessible by air, with **flights** daily or every few days from Manila. Within the Visayas, the **ferry network** is so extensive that it doesn't really matter if you can't get a flight. Ferries link almost every city and town in the Visayas with neighbouring islands. Cebu, for example, has dozens of ferry departures every day to the rest of the Visayas, Manila and Mindanao. But the beauty of the Visayas is that there's no need to make formal plans. There's always another island, another beach, another place to stay.

Samar

The large island of **Samar**, 320km from top to toe, lies between the Bicol and Leyte. It's a short hop by ferry from Matnog, on the southern tip of Bicol, and is connected to Leyte by the two-kilometre-long San Juanico Bridge, which spans the San Juanico Strait.

Samar has never quite taken off as a major tourist destination, which is a shame, because large parts of the coast are unspoiled and the east-coast beaches are wild and beautiful. Perhaps the lack of visitors is something to do with the **weather**. Samar has a different climate from the rest of the country, with dry periods only in May and June. Apart from that, rainfall is possible throughout the year, although never for long periods. Most of the rain falls from the beginning of November until February, and from early October to December there can be fierce typhoons. The best and sunniest time to visit is from May to September, although the growing number of surfers who come here to take advantage of the swells that rip in from the Pacific would probably argue the typhoon season is best.

One reason not to miss Samar is the marvellous **Sohoton Natural Bridge National Park**, a prehistoric wilderness full of caves, waterfalls and underground rivers. The park is in the southern part of Samar, so quickest access is through Tacloban on Leyte. For many visitors, Sohoton is scheduled only as a day-trip from Leyte before they loop back to Tacloban and continue through the Visayas. From Tacloban, you'll have to catch a jeepney to **Basey** (1hr), then a pedicab to the Department of Environment and Natural Resources (☎055/276 1151), where you can arrange guides and accommodation. To get to the park from the north involves making the long but spectacular bus journey along Samar's west coast from **Catarman** through **Calbayog**, famous for its caves and waterfalls, and on to Basey.

Asian Spirit runs **flights** to both Calbayog (Tues, Thurs, Sun) and Catarman (Mon, Wed, Fri). The airline has an office in Calbayog at Riverview Cinema Building, G/F Gomez Extension (☎055/209 1189) and in Catarman at Jacinto St cnr of Magsaysay St (☎05540/354 1378). **Ferries from Matnog** depart four times a day (6am, 7am, 9am & 10am) and take about two hours to get to Allen in northwestern Samar. From Manila,

BLTB has a service that crosses on the Matnog-Allen ferry and runs down the coastal road to Calbayog, taking about twelve hours from the capital. The daily Philtranco service between Manila and Davao passes through Allen, Calbayog and Catbalogan.

Leyte

In the sixteenth century, Magellan passed through Leyte on his way to Cebu, making a blood compact with the local chieftain as he did so. But it was **World War II** that really brought Leyte fame, when its jungle hinterlands were the scene of brutal fighting. On October 20, 1944, General Douglas MacArthur landed at Leyte, fulfilling the famous promise he had made to Filipinos, "I shall return." He brought with him the first President of the Commonwealth, Sergio Osmeña.

On the northeast coast, the capital of Leyte, **TACLOBAN**, the usual arrival point, is associated with that tireless collector of shoes, Imelda Marcos, who was born here to a humble family called Romualdez. The airport has been renamed Daniel Z. Romualdez Airport and numerous streets and buildings bear the same name. In her youth, Imelda was a local beauty queen, and referred to herself in later life as "the rose of Tacloban". There's little to see in the town itself. A climb up to the town hall atop Kanhuraw Hill in front of Santo Niño Church rewards you with **panoramic views** of Cancabato Bay, San Pedro Bay, San Juanico Strait, Cataisan Point and Samar Island. The **Tacloban Festival** in the last week of June kicks off with the Subiran Regatta, an annual boat race held at the eastern entrance of the San Juanico Strait.

Around Tacloban there are a number of sights associated with the war, including the Leyte Landing Memorial, marking the spot where General MacArthur waded ashore on Red beach, Palo, south of Tacloban; you can reach it by jeepney. Just outside Palo, on Hill 522, foxholes still remain.

From Tacloban, buses travel through the rugged hinterland to the port town of **ORMOC**, where ferries set sail for Cebu. Ormoc is also the starting point for the **Leyte Mountain Trail**, a beautiful but gruelling forty-kilometre trek that winds through jungle and over mountains to serene Lake Mahagnao, from where you can catch a jeepney or bus back to Ormoc; the town hall can provide details.

Practicalities

Leyte's only major airport is at Tacloban, served by **flights** from Manila with PAL and Cebu Pacific. Good **ferry** connections link and other ports on Leyte's west coast with Manila and ports in Luzon, Cebu, Bohol and Mindanao. There are also sailings between Samar and Tacloban. **Buses** to Leyte operate from Manila (a long haul through Bicol and Samar) and from Mindanao, arriving at a terminal at the junctions of Quezon Boulevard and Rizal Avenue, on the northeastern edge of the city, close to the coast; there are also regular daily services from Samar via either the San Juanico Bridge or the car ferry from Basey. **Moving on from Tacloban**, buses leave the terminal daily for Calbayog, Basey, and even Davao and Manila. Note that Philtranco buses, which serve most major destinations on Leyte and also go north to Manila and south to Davao, have their own terminal south of the city. Negros Navigation and Cebu Ferries sail between Tacloban and Manila, but WG&A only operates between Manila and Ormoc.

The **tourist information office** (☎053/321 2048 or 321 4333) is near Children's Park off Magsaysay Avenue. There's a **post office** near the harbour on Bonifacio Street; the **Philippine National Bank**, and a number of others, are on J Romualdez Street. The Net Surf Café at 170 Veteranos St has **Internet** access for P60 an hour.

Accommodation and eating

Cecilia's Lodge at 178 Paterno St (☎053/321 2815; ❷) is the place many travellers head for. It has singles and doubles with fan. Also on Paterno Street is *LNU House* (☎053/321 3175 or 321 2170; ❸), which has functional but bright accommodation, popular with local students. The *Asia Stars Hotel* (☎053/321 4942; ❺) on Zamora Street is quiet and clean and has mid-range air-con doubles. *Hotel Alejandro* on P. Paterno St (☎053/321 7033; ❺) is a well-managed, bright hotel two blocks from Santo Niño Park. Rooms are spacious and feature air-con and hot shower. There's also a good restaurant and coffee shop. The most prestigious place to lay your head in Tacloban is at the *Leyte Park Hotel* (☎053/325 6000; ❼–❽) on Magsaysay Avenue, a sprawling resort-style development that sits on top of a hill overlooking San Juanico Strait and San Pedro Bay.

The best place to try Tacloban's seafood is at *San Pedro Bay Seafood*, a large, popular **restaurant** that's part of the *Leyte Park Resort* complex, with beautiful views out to sea. It's not the cheapest place in town; P300 or so per person pays for a good meal from a menu that includes fresh tuna steaks, blue marlin, lobster, giant crabs and clams. *Giuseppi's* is a long-standing Italian favourite in the Anover Building on Veteranos Avenue, while the newer *Bistro Uno* at 41 Juan Luna St has sandwiches, burgers and traditional Filipino dishes such as pancit and adobo. The local delicacy *binagul*, a hot sticky concoction made of coconut and nuts, can be bought freshly made every morning from hawkers around town. In the evening, *Kyle's Wine Bar* on P. Gomez Street has live music and serves a menu of pasta, salads and Philippine favourites.

Cebu

The island of **Cebu** is the ninth largest in the Philippines and site of the second largest city, **Cebu City**, an important transport hub. The closest beaches to Cebu City are on **Mactan Island** just to the southeast, although they're by no means the best. Head north instead to the marvellous island of **Malapascua**, where the sand is as fine as Boracay's, or to tranquil **Bantayan** off the northwest coast. South of Cebu City, on the opposite coast, lies the diving haven of **Moalboal** and its nearby beaches.

Cebu City and around

Like many Philippine cities, **CEBU CITY**, nicknamed the "Queen City of the South", has become something of an urban nightmare in recent decades, with jeepneys taking over the inadequate road network. There's history and architecture in there somewhere, but you have to look hard for it among the clutter, the exhaust fumes and the nondescript concrete malls. The good news is that it's not half as chaotic as some parts of Manila; it's possible to get from one side of the city to the other in less than thirty minutes. The big annual attraction in Cebu City is the **Sinulog Festival**, which culminates on the third Sunday of January with a wild mardi-gras-style street parade and an outdoor concert at Fuente Osmeña. The festival, in honour of Cebu's patron saint the Santo Niño, is almost as popular as Kalibo's Ati-Atihan and hotels are usually full, particularly for the climax of the festivities. For information, call the Sinulog Foundation (☎032/253 3700).

Arrival, orientation and information

Planes land at Mactan Cebu International Airport (MCIA). There's a tourist information counter (daily 6am–midnight) in the arrivals hall; outside, airport taxis (around P180, depending on your destination) take you to Cebu City itself, 8km away across the suspension bridge that links Mactan Island to the main island of Cebu. You can also cross the road to the departures area and pick up a metered taxi, which will cost no more than P100 into the city. The arrival point for **ferries** is the harbour area beyond Fort San Pedro. Jeepneys and buses line up along Quezon Boulevard for the short journey into the city. Look for one

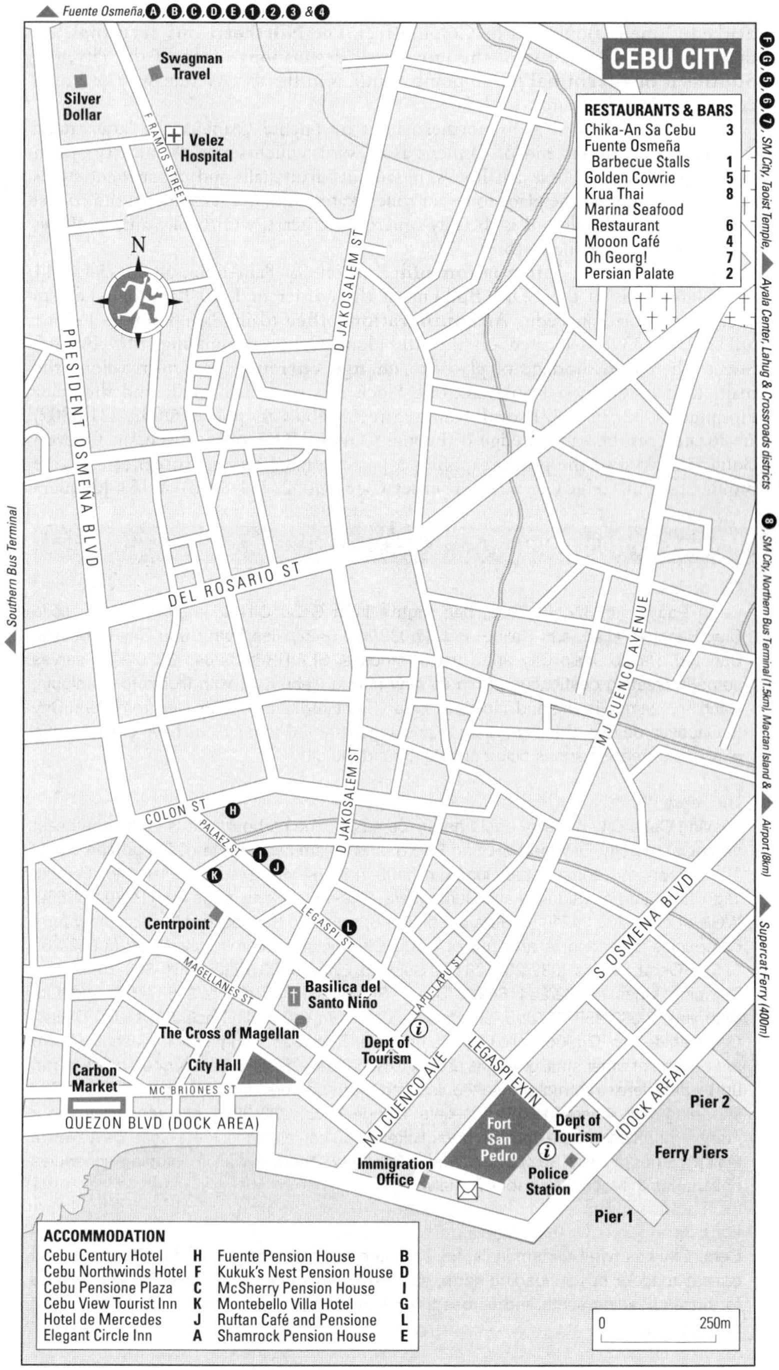

Fuente Osmeña, A, B, C, D, E, 1, 2, 3 & 4

CEBU CITY

RESTAURANTS & BARS

Chika-An Sa Cebu	3
Fuente Osmeña Barbecue Stalls	1
Golden Cowrie	5
Krua Thai	8
Marina Seafood Restaurant	6
Mooon Café	4
Oh Georg!	7
Persian Palate	2

F, G, 5, 6, 7, SM City, Taoist Temple, Ayala Center, Lahug & Crossroads districts

8, SM City, Northern Bus Terminal (1.5km), Mactan Island & Airport (8km)

Supercat Ferry (400m)

Southern Bus Terminal

Swagman Travel
Silver Dollar
Velez Hospital
F RAMOS STREET
N
D JAKOSALEM ST
PRESIDENT OSMEÑA BLVD
DEL ROSARIO ST
MJ CUENCO AVENUE
COLON ST
PALAEZ ST
H
I
J
K
L
Centrpoint
LEGASPI ST
MAGELLANES ST
LAPU-LAPU ST
Basilica del Santo Niño
The Cross of Magellan
Dept of Tourism
City Hall
Carbon Market
MC BRIONES ST
QUEZON BLVD (DOCK AREA)
MJ CUENCO AVE
LEGASPI EXTN
S OSMENA BLVD
(DOCK AREA)
Fort San Pedro
Dept of Tourism
Police Station
Immigration Office
Pier 2
Ferry Piers
Pier 1

ACCOMMODATION

Cebu Century Hotel	H	Fuente Pension House	B
Cebu Northwinds Hotel	F	Kukuk's Nest Pension House	D
Cebu Pensione Plaza	C	McSherry Pension House	I
Cebu View Tourist Inn	K	Montebello Villa Hotel	G
Hotel de Mercedes	J	Ruftan Café and Pensione	L
Elegant Circle Inn	A	Shamrock Pension House	E

0 250m

marked Osmeña Boulevard or Colon Street. The **Northern bus terminal**, on the coastal road, just east of the city, serves destinations north of the city; the **Southern bus terminal** for all points south, is in Bacalso Avenue, west of President Osmeña Boulevard.

Cebu City is defined at its northern limit by Fuente Osmeña, the large traffic roundabout at the far end of Osmeña Boulevard, which serves as the city's main north–south artery. There are hotels, restaurants, fruit stalls and department stores here, and at night it's the place to be for roller skaters and promenaders. At the coastal end of Osmeña Boulevard is the city's mercantile heart, with banks, airline offices and yet more department stores.

The **main tourist information office** (Mon–Sat 8am–6pm; ⓣ032/254 2811 or 254 6007) is in the LDM Building at the corner of Lapu-Lapu and Legaspi streets near Fort San Pedro. An **immigration office** (daily 8am–noon & 1–5pm; ⓣ032/253 4339) is located on the 4th Floor, Ceutiaco Building, MC Briones Street. There's no shortage of places to **change currency**, particularly along the main drag of Osmeña Boulevard, one block east of which you'll find the Velez Hospital (ⓣ032/253 1871) on F. Ramos Street. Cebu City police (ⓣ032/231 5802) are located on the eastern edge of Fuente Osmeña. **The post office**, on Quezon Boulevard close to the port area, offers a poste restante service. **Internet** cafés are proliferating in Cebu City: try Cybernet Café (ⓣ032/254 8533) at 151 Junquera

Moving on from Cebu City

By plane

Cebu Pacific (ⓣ032/340 7980) has **flights** from Cebu City to Manila, Davao, Iloilo City, Bacolod, Clark and Kalibo. PAL (ⓣ032/340 0422) flies from Cebu City to Manila, Bacolod, Davao, Iloilo City and Puerto Princesa. SEAIR (ⓣ032/341 30201–22) serves some interesting destinations from its new hub in Cebu City, with flights to Camiguin, Caticlan, Siargao Island and Tacloban. Asian Spirit (ⓣ032/341 2555) flies from Cebu City to Cagayan de Oro, Caticlan, Siargao and Tagbilaran. All four airlines have offices at the airport, as well as various ticket outlets around the city.

By ferry

Leaving Cebu City by **ferry** could hardly be easier. The harbour area is in the southeast corner of the city, beyond Fort San Pedro, and is jammed with ferries large and small. The air-con and comfortable Supercat (ⓣ032/231 9494) leave from Pier 4 for Ormoc, Tagbilaran, Larena (Siquijor) and Dumaguete. One-way tickets range from P220 to P660. WG&A (ⓣ032/232 0421–29) pulls out of Pier 6, sailing to Surigao and Manila. Other ferry companies operating in and out of Cebu City include Negros Navigation (ⓣ032/232 6255), Cebu Ferries (032/232 2611), Sulpicio Lines (ⓣ032/232 5361–80), Trans-Asia Shipping Lines (ⓣ032/254 6491), Socor Shipping Lines (ⓣ032/255 7767) and Lite Shipping (ⓣ032/253 7776). Main destinations from Cebu City include Manila, Davao, Cagayan de Oro, Ormoc, Iloilo City, Dumaguete, Tagblaran, Surigao, and Masbate. There are dozens of other smaller ferries sailing to secondary destinations. A good place to get up-to-date ferry information (schedules and pier numbers often change) is at SM City shopping mall, where the SM travellers' lounge (ⓣ032/232 0291) has schedules and a number of offices where you can book tickets. You can also check the *Cebu Daily News*, which carries a daily *Shipping Guide & Directory*. There's even a shipping schedules channel on the local Sky cable TV network.

By bus

Cebu City has two **bus** terminals, the Northern bus terminal just outside the city on the coastal road for buses heading north, and the Southern bus terminal in Bacalso Avenue for buses heading south and across the island to destinations on the west coast such as Moalboal.

St next to the *Elicon Hotel Café* or *Ruftan Internet Café & Pensione* on Legaspi Street. Both charge P50 an hour.

Accommodation

Cebu Century Hotel Colon St cnr. Pelaez St ☎032/255 1341-47. Faded, airless rooms in a hotel that has seen better days, redeemed by its location in the old area of the city and its low prices. Some rooms have cable TV and there are a number of family deluxe rooms with two double beds. 3

Cebu Northwinds Hotel Salinas Drive, Lahug ☎032/233 0311-13. Close to Lahug's bars and restaurants, next door to the *Golden Cowrie* (see p.846). Clean and bright, modern, mid-range hotel with standard doubles, coffee shop, restaurant and bar. 5

Cebu Pensione Plaza North Escario St ☎032/254 6300. Large, clean deluxe rooms, with more than enough room for two. Top-of-the-range suites also available. 4

Cebu View Tourist Inn 200 Sanciangko St ☎032/254 8333. Impressive new budget hotel in a quiet road close to Colon St. Clean, comfortable and secure, with a little café downstairs. The cheapest room is a deluxe double, which has a/c and cable TV. 3

Hotel de Mercedes 7 Pelaez St ☎032/253 1105-10. Close to the bustle of Colon St. Choices include a standard single, a standard double or the presidential suite. All rooms have a/c, but ask to see a selection first because some have been refurbished and are much more attractive than those that haven't. 5

Elegant Circle Inn Fuente Osmeña ☎032/254 1601. Glass edifice benefiting from a good location right on Fuente Osmeña. All rooms have a/c, and there's a coffee shop. 3

Fuente Pension House 0175 Don Julio Llorente St ☎032/253 6789. Well-run place behind Fuente Osmeña, in a quiet road. The location is excellent and the rooms clean. A/c singles are a good deal and have cable TV. 4

Kukuk's Nest Pension House 157 Gorordo Ave ☎032/412 2026. A hangout for artists and beatniks, offering quaintly furnished rooms, some with a/c, bath and cable TV. Also has a garden restaurant. 2

McSherry Pension House In an alley off Pelaez St, behind the *Hotel de Mercedes* (no phone). *McSherry* has been around for years. Not great, but cheap. Single fan P250, single a/c P350. 2

Montebello Villa Hotel Banilad, Cebu City ☎032/231 3681-89, ⓦwww.montebellovillahotel.com. Rambling and atmospheric hotel set among a profusion of greenery. It's a rather eccentric place, with noisy air-cons and dodgy plumbing, but it remains a great choice because of its gardens, its shady outdoor café and its swimming pools. Rates include breakfast. 6

Ruftan Café and Pensione 61 Legaspi St ☎032/256 2613. Cebu's ultimate budget accommodation, near the Basilica del Santo Niño. The rooms are very average, but there's Internet access and a host of travel information from staff and other guests. In the red-tiled café downstairs, you can get a bacon sandwich for P30 and a cup of coffee for P20. 2

Shamrock Pension House Fuente Osmeña ☎032/255 2999. Budget accommodation in the hubbub of Fuente Osmeña, so close to the barbecue stalls that you can smell grilled meat from the lobby. All rooms are a/c and there's a choice of standard, deluxe or studio. 3

The City

The old part of Cebu City is a seething cobweb of sunless streets between Carbon Market and **Colon Street**, the latter said to be the oldest mercantile thoroughfare in the country. About ten minutes' walk south of Colon Street, Carbon Market is an area of covered stalls where the range of goods on offer, edible and otherwise, will leave you reeling.

The city's spiritual heart is a small crypt opposite the town hall that houses the **Cross of Magellan**. It's actually a modern hollow cross that is said to contain fragments of the original brought by the famous conquistador in 1521 and used in the first conversions of locals to Christianity. Next to the cross on Osmeña Boulevard is the dusty and towering **Basilica del Santo Niño**, where vendors with tawdry religious icons and amulets offer cures for everything from poverty to infertility. Inside the basilica, built 1735–37, is probably the most famous religious icon in the Philippines, a statue of the Santo Niño (child Christ), said to have been presented to Queen Juana of Cebu by Magellan after her baptism in 1521. The next conquistador, Miguel Lopez de Legaspi, arrived in 1565 and built **Fort San Pedro**, near the port area at the end of Quezon Boulevard, whose shaded garden is today one of the quietest spots in Cebu, away from the choking din of the city centre.

Eating

Chika-An Sa Cebu Century Plaza Complex, Juan Osmeña St. A Cebu institution that serves popular rustic fare such as chicken, pork barbecue, *lechon kawali*, sizzling *bangus* and *bulalo* (beef bone stew). Close to Fuente Osmeña and probably your first stop for affordable native Cebuano cuisine.

Fuente Osmeña Barbecue Stalls Even the smoke from these stalls, all gathered in a cluster on Fuente Osmeña, smells good. Cooking tends to start with vengeance at dusk. Cheap and tasty, but only for carnivores.

Golden Cowrie Salinas Dr, Lahug. The interior is Philippine Zen with white walls and bamboo furniture; the food is chic traditional. Lots of seafood dishes such as tuna jaw and grilled *lapu-lapu*. The Bicol Express-style vegetables are very spicy. Busy, especially at weekends.

Krua Thai Crossroads Mall, Banilad. On the main road close to the airport, this popular Thai restaurant has an ample menu of authentic Thai cuisine, including spicy soups, curries, spring rolls and desserts.

Marina Seafood Restaurant Nivel Hills, Lahug. Laid-back native-style al fresco restaurant on a hill above the city. Two people can feast on tuna belly, grilled marlin, and shrimps with chilli and coconut for about P200 a head.

Mooon Café S Osmeña cnr J Diaz St. *Mooon*, with three Os, is a small café and art gallery with a nouveau Mexican menu that includes nachos and chimichangas.

Oh Georg! Coffee and Dessert Bar Level 1, Ayala Center. The Ayala Center is chock full of fast-food restaurants and coffee shops, but this one deserves special mention. The Batangas coffee is rich and strong and the menu full of real homemade dishes such as bean and vegetable soup, Greek salad and an enormous Mexican salad that's big enough to share.

Persian Palate Mango Square, Maxilom Ave. Spicy – very spicy – Singaporean, Malaysian, Indian, Middle Eastern and halal dishes. Good vegetarian choices.

Nightlife and entertainment

Cebu City, like its big brother Manila, is a city that never – or rarely – sleeps. There's sassy nightlife at Crossroads, a strip of bistros, bars and clubs in Lahug, in Archbishop Reyes Avenue close to the *Waterfront Cebu City Hotel*. If you need a karaoke fix there are *Juke Box* (Cebu Grand Convention Center, Archbishop Reyes Avenue), *Vudu* (at Crossroads) and *Arena* (11th Avenue, North reclamation Area). Something of a Cebu institution, *Silver Dollar* on Osmeña Boulevard is a dark and boozy go-go bar where hustlers monopolize the pool table and cockroaches make occasional guest appearances on the sticky counter top. *Our Place* in Pelaez Street, right on the junction with Sanciangko Street, is another Cebu stalwart, straight from the pages of Graham Greene. It's a small upstairs bar cooled by ceiling fans, where expat men swill San Miguel into the early hours and complain about the hardships of life in the tropics.

Around Cebu City

A twenty-minute taxi ride from the city takes you to the hills above the city where the **Taoist Temple** and immense houses are testament to the influence and wealth of the Cebuano Chinese, whose forefathers arrived from eastern China as early as the sixteenth century to trade in silks, porcelain and spices.

The closest beaches to Cebu City are on Mactan Island, linked to the main island of Cebu by Mandaue–Mactan Bridge and the New Mandaue–Mactan bridge.

Moalboal

Three hours by road and almost 100km from Cebu City on the southwestern flank of Cebu Island, lies the sleepy coastal village of **Moalboal**, a favourite hangout of travellers and scuba divers. Most of the activity in Moalboal is in fact centred around **diving** and it's hardly surprising: the sea is crystal clear, and, while many reefs along the mainland coast were damaged by a typhoon more than ten years ago, the enigmatic Pescador Island survived, an alluring site a few miles offshore (30min by banca). Divers return from here every day with stories of sharks, mantas and moray eels. Sun-worshippers looking for a Boracay-style sandy beach will be disappointed, though – there isn't one. Moalboal makes up for this in other ways, with a great range of cheap accommodation, a marvellous view of the sunset over distant Negros, and some good discounts on diving and rooms if you hang around long enough.

Ceres Liner runs regular **bus** services from Cebu City's Southern bus terminal. You'll be dropped off on the main road, from where a tricycle will take you down the dusty track to **Panagsama Beach**, where all the resorts are. There's a wide range of **accommodation** and it's all huddled in more or less the same area. Towards the southern end of the beach is *Pacitas Beach Resort* (☎0918/770 9982; ❸), which has a range of bungalows set back from the seafront in a quiet garden. In the middle of the beach, the popular *Savedra Beach Resort* (☎032/474 0014; ❹) has functional, clean rooms, all with large balconies overlooking Pescador Island. The popular *Hannah's Place* (☎032/474 0091 or 0918/771 3439; ❹) is a large home with two family rooms and three standard rooms, all with air-con and marble bathroom. The terrace is beautiful, alive with hibiscus and orchids, and Hannah herself, the owner, is attentive and helpful.

Opposite the *Savedra Beach Resort*, there's excellent Indian food at the British-owned *Moti's*, while a short walk north along the path at the back of the beach will bring you to *The Last Filling Station*, which is little more than a few chairs and tables perched on a veranda above the beach. This quaint little European-owned restaurant does everything from homemade pizza to spicy Thai curry and crepes.

For non-diving adventure, visit Planet Action (☎032/474 0068), a short walk south of *Savedra Beach Resort*, where you can arrange climbing, trekking and mountain biking trips. Planet Action has the only reliable **Internet** connection in the area.

Bantayan Island

Bantayan Island, just off the northwest coast of Cebu, is quiet and bucolic, a flat arable island, without the moody mountains of mainland Cebu. It's a great place to explore, though divers will be disappointed that there seems to be little coral left along the shore. Most of the island's resorts and beaches are around the attractive little town of **SANTA FE** on Bantayan's southeast coast. The beach at Santa Fe has had rave reviews, but it's not a patch on Bounty Beach at Malapascua.

The quickest way to reach Bantayan is to **fly**; Pacific Air can arrange a flight for a minimum of three passengers at P1050 a head one way (Cebu ☎032/340 5000 or Bantayan ☎0917/549 6293). As for **ferries**, you could hop on a bus from Cebu City's Northern bus terminal to the northern port town of Hagnaya (P72). It will take you to Hagnaya's pier, where you pay a P2 pier fee and P55 for the one-hour ferry (7.30am, 9.30am, 12.30pm & 6.30pm) crossing to Santa Fe. The overnight option is to take Palacio Shipping's rusty old Don Martin ferry, which leaves Pier One at Cebu port on Tuesday, Thursday and Saturday at 9pm arriving in Santa Fe at 6am (P175–275 depending on the class of accommodation). It returns from Santa Fe at 9pm on Wednesday, Friday and Sunday. From further afield, there are big banca to **Bantayan**, a port town on the west coast, from Bacolod or Cadiz on Negros, and from Iloilo City on Panay, departures depending on the tide. The only local transport is the trusty tricycle, known on Bantayan as a *tricikad*. It's fun to rent a motorbike or moped and tour the island by the coastal road, but be careful: some of the bike owners are hustlers and will try to charge you for scratches that were already there. Inspect the bike thoroughly beforehand and get the renter to sign an agreement that details all existing damage, however insignificant.

Among the **accommodation** options on Bantayan are the *Santa Fe Beach Club* and *Ogtong Cave* (☎032/438 0031; ❸) both owned by the same family. *Santa Fe* is on the beach close to the pier where the ferry arrives: the breezy and spacious beach cottages are best, sleeping up to three, but avoid the rooms in the main building, which are airless and have poor views. *Ogtong* is about fifteen minutes away by tricycle and has modern cottages with verandas set in pleasant gardens with a swimming pool fed by spring water. A short walk takes you down to the beach, where you can arrange fishing expeditions with the locals – ask the *Ogtong* chef to cook whatever you catch. Ten minutes beyond Ogtong by road is the friendly and neat *Maia's Beach Resort* (☎032/438 0077; ③), which has simple cottages on the shore. A short ride west of Santa Fe, *Kota Beach Resort* (③) features basic fan rooms and cottages with fan and bath. It's expensive for what you get, but the restaurant serves up excellent seafood and has memorable views. A few minutes past *Santa Fe Beach Club* on Alice beach, five minutes by tricycle from the pier, is St Bernard's Resort (☎0917/963 6162; ③) offering quaint little circular cottages right on the beach and a good restaurant and bar. *Marlin Beach Resort* (☎032/438 9393; ④) is an attractive two-storey resort on the beach on the southern outskirts of Santa Fe, where staff will arrange boat trips, windsurfing and golf.

Malapascua Island

Eight kilometres off the northern tip of Cebu, the island of **Malapascua**, is one of Southeast Asia's finest scuba-diving destinations. Anyone staying more than a few days is almost guaranteed a sighting of manta rays and thresher sharks. Nearby **Gato Island** is a marine sanctuary and a breeding place for black-and-white banded sea snakes, which are potentially deadly but do not attack divers, and overnight trips can be arranged to the tiny volcanic island of **Maripipi**, where reef sharks and dolphins are common. At 2.5km long and about 1km wide, Malapascua has been touted as the next, albeit smaller, Boracay, largely because of **Bounty Beach**, a blindingly white stretch of sand on the island's south coast that's home to a dozen simple resorts, including *BB's Lodging House* (②), which has basic doubles, and the more upmarket *Cocobana Beach Resort* (⑥), comprising spacious cottages. One of the most popular places on Bounty Beach, especially for divers, is *Malapascua Exotic Island Dive and Beach Resort* (☎0918/774 0484; ③) where you can get full board in a comfortable beachside cottage. The resort has a small restaurant and 24-hour electricity from its own generator, something of a luxury in these parts.

You can **get to Malapascua** direct from Cebu City. From the Northern bus terminal, take a Rough Riders or Cebu Autobus bus to Maya Bagay. Buses run every hour from 4am and it's best to set off early to avoid traffic and the heat. The ferry from Maya Bagay to Malapascua takes around thirty minutes and costs P50. You can rent your own banca for P350–500, but don't expect to have it exclusively to yourself; locals will take advantage of your generosity to avail themselves of a free ride. The trip is shorter and more comfortable if you charter a taxi to take you from Cebu City to Maya Bagay; the going rate is P1500, and you shouldn't pay more than P2000. Coming from Bantayan, you can rent a banca (P1500). On Malapascua itself, tricycles are the only form of transport.

Bohol

It's hard to imagine that idyllic, sleepy **Bohol**, a two-hour hop south of Cebu by fast ferry, has a bloody past. The only reminder of the unpleasantness is a memorial stone in the barrio of **Bool**, denoting the spot where Rajah Sikatuna and Miguel Lopez de Legaspi concluded hostilities in 1565 by signing a compact in blood. Even before Legaspi arrived and brought Catholicism with him from Spain, members of the indigenous Bool tribe were using the coves around Panglao and Tagbilaran to hide from vicious Muslim marauders who swept north through the Visayan Islands from their bases in Mindanao. These days, however, apart from some mercantile activity in the capital, **TAGBILARAN**, Bohol is a dozy sort of place. The only serious activity is on the beautiful beaches of **Panglao Island**, connected to the mainland by a bridge from the capital and another from Bool, where scuba divers gather. Everywhere else, Bohol is on Filipino time and runs at Filipino pace. Even the carabao chew slowly.

For most visitors, the only obligatory sortie away from Panglao's beaches is into Bohol's hinterland to see the island's most iconic tourist attraction, the **Chocolate Hills**. Some geologists believe that these unique forty-metre mounds were formed from deposits of coral and limestone sculpted by centuries of erosion. The locals, however, will tell you the hills are the calcified tears of a giant, whose heart was broken by the death of a mortal lover. The best time to see the Chocolate Hills – there are allegedly 1268 of them – is at dawn, when the rising sun plays spectacular tricks with light, shadow and colour. Aficionados recommend the end of the dry season (April or May), when the grass has turned brown, and with a short stretch of the imagination, the hills really do resemble chocolate drops.

More and more people are visiting Bohol for its world-class **scuba diving** – not only at Panglao, but at the lesser-known islands of Cabilao, Ajo, Mahanay and Lapinin, all off the northern coast. There's also excellent diving around the exquisite little island of **Balicasag**, southwest of Panglao, which you can reach by renting a banca on Panglao; the only place to stay is *Balicasag Dive Resort* (Manila ⓣ02/812 1984), which has ten duplex cottages for around $30 a night, depending on the season. Experienced divers should not miss a trip to **Pamilacan Island**, where it's possible to see short-finned pilot whales, long-snouted spinner dolphins, spotted dolphins, bottlenose dolphins and melon-headed dolphins. You can organize a day-trip to Pamilacan Island from any resort, or rent your own banca.

Practicalities

Tagbilaran Airport is less than 2km outside the city of Tagbilaran. Asian Spirit and PAL both have flights from Manila. The Asian Spirit office in Tagbilaran (ⓣ038/411 2353 or 235 4154) is at the airport, while PAL has three ticket outlets on Bohol, one at the airport (ⓣ038/411 2232), one at the *Metro Centre Hotel* in Carlos P Garcia Avenue (ⓣ038/411 3552) and another nearby at 38 Carlos P Garcia Avenue (ⓣ038/411 3102). The **ferry pier** in Tagbilaran is in the northwest of the city off Gallares Street. Getting around **Bohol** by bus, all journeys start at the Dao integrated bus terminal in E Butalid Street, ten minutes north of Tagbilaran along Clarin Avenue by tricycle. Buses and jeepneys heading **for Panglao** are marked for Alona.

The **tourist information office** (Mon–Sat 9am–5pm; ⓣ038/411 3059) is rather inconveniently situated in the Governor's Mansion, ten minutes by tricycle outside Tagbilaran on the road towards the airport. However, most resorts are well geared up for tourists and can offer better information. PNB is on the junction of CPG Avenue and Clarin Street, while there's a BPI with an ATM in Carlos Garcia Avenue. The **police station** is near City Hall, behind St Joseph's Cathedral. The **post office** is also near here, at the end of the City Hall car park. There are a number of cheap cyber cafés near the market in Grupo Street and many resorts also offer **Internet.**

Accommodation and eating

There's not much notable accommodation in **Tagbilaran** itself. The best hotel is the *Metrocentre Hotel and Convention Centre* (ⓣ038/411 2599; ❻), a short walk north of the Caltex petrol station on Carlos Garcia Avenue. *Nisa Traveller's Inn* on Carlos P. Garcia Avenue is the best budget place in town (ⓣ038/411 3731; ❶), featuring good doubles with fan and clean bathroom, as well as more expensive air-con rooms. Out of town, not far from the pier, the *Hotel La Roca* in Graham Avenue (ⓣ038/411 3796; ❸) has a choice of rooms ranging from standard doubles to a penthouse, and benefits from a homely atmosphere.

Most of the budget beach accommodation on **Panglao Island** is at Alona Beach. *Alona Kew White Beach Resort* (ⓣ038/502 9042; ❹) at the eastern end of the beach is a chic place standing in lush grounds, with a stylish restaurant and comfortable suites with air-con and bath. *Alona Palm Beach Resort and Restaurant* (☎038/502 9141; ⑧) is one of the most luxurious resorts here, with accommodation in stylish double cottages set back from the beach around a beautiful swimming pool. *Bohol Divers Resort* (☎038/411 4983; ③), a French-run place with double cottages with fan or air-con, sits right on the beach and has a good restaurant and bar. *Flower Garden Resort* (☎038/502 9012; ②) and *Swiss Bamboo House* (☎038/502 9070 or 0918/600 0245; ②) are both homey, Swiss-run establishments with basic but spotless rooms, restaurants and scuba diving facilities.

Negros

The island of **Negros** lies at the heart of the Visayas, between Panay to the west and Cebu to the east. Shaped like a boot, it is split diagonally into the northwestern province of Negros Occidental and the southeastern province of Negros Oriental. The demarcation came when early missionaries decided the central mountain range was too formidable to cross, even in the name of God. It's an island many tourists miss out and as a result is largely unspoilt: it has miles of untouched coastline, some pleasant towns – **Dumaguete**, the capital of Negros Oriental is one of the stateliest towns in the Philippines – and dormant **volcanoes**. Negros is also "Sugarlandia", producing fifty percent of the country's **sugar**. Around **Bacolod**, the capital of Negros Occidental, authentic 1912 steam locomotives and well-preserved Spanish ancestral homes serve as reminders of the rich sugar barons and Spanish families of the past.

Bacolod and around

The city of **BACOLOD** on the northern coast of Negros is another testament to the wonders you can perform with concrete. It's big, it's hot, it's noisy and there's not much to see or do. The Old Capitol Building is one of the few architectural highlights and houses the excellent **Negros Museum** (Mon–Sat 9am–6pm; P20), which details 5000 years of local history. During the third week of October everybody who is anybody attends the flamboyant **Masskara Festival**, a mardi-gras-style jamboree of street dancing and beauty pageants. The street-dancing participants wear masks, hence the festival's name.

Practicalities

Bacolod's **airport** is 5km south of the city off Araneta Street; turn left outside the airport to pick up a jeepney going to the city. PAL, which operates four flights a day from Manila, has an office at the airport (☎034/434 7878). Cebu Pacific, who have an office at the airport (☎034/707 3933 to 3935) and another in Victoria Arcade, Rizal Street (☎034/434 2020 to 2023), fly from Manila and Cebu City. Air Philippines has an airport ticket office (☎034/433 9211).

Ticket offices for major ferry companies operating out of Bacolod are at **Palanca port**, on reclaimed land 500m west of the plaza. This is the arrival and departure point for most major ferries (including WG&A; ☎034/435 4965), with the exception of Negros Navigation services, which uses the old **Banago wharf** 8km north of Bacolod and has its ticket office there (although there are many outlets in the city itself).

There are two **bus terminals** of the Ceres Liner bus company, next to each other on Lopez Jaena Street on the eastern edge of the city. One, the Ceres North Terminal, is for buses heading north along the coastal road to Silay and Cadiz. Some of these buses continue from Cadiz to San Carlos and round on to Dumaguete, 313km away (P150; 8hr). There's also a Ceres service from Bacolod that boards a ferry in San Carlos for Toledo, on the western coast of Cebu, where it continues on to Cebu City. Buses heading south along the coast road leave from the Ceres South terminal. The old **northern bus station** on Lopez Jaena Street is used by Royal

Express Transport and by express air-con buses leaving for Dumaguete (P120; 6hr), heading south and cutting cross-country through Kabankalaan. From the **Murcia bus terminal** off Libertad Street near the market, you can catch slow, non-air-con buses to Silay and Victorias.

The **tourist information office** (Mon–Sat 8.30am–5.30pm; ☎034/433 2515 or 435 1001) is in the administrative building of the provincial government complex in City Plaza, San Juan Street. **Immigration** (☎034/708 9502) is on Gatuslao Street and can arrange visa extensions. The **post office** is also on Gatuslao Street, near the junction with Burgos Street. Most of Bacolod's **banks**, including PCI and PNB, are near the city plaza in Araneta and Gonzaga streets. The trendy Cyberheads Café (☎033/434 1604) on the junction of Lacson and 7th Street offers **Internet** access for P60 an hour.

On relatively peaceful 10th Street is *Bacolod Pension House* (❸), which has bare but clean rooms and a decent restaurant. Also at the budget end of the price range is the *Star Plus Pension House* (❸), on Lacson Street, with small but clean rooms with air-con. *L'Fisher Hotel* (☎034/433 3730 to 433 3739; ❼), further west on Lacson Street, is a modern glass-fronted building with one hundred rooms. One of the better **restaurants** in Bacolod is the Austrian-owned *Vienna Kaffeehaus* on Lacson Street, where a good Teutonic breakfast, lunch or dinner will cost P120–200 a head. Next door is an affordable little Japanese place, *Kaisai*, which does noodles, tempura and some excellent sushi. Don't miss the barbecue chicken at *Chicken House*, Araneta Street, at the corner of Rodriguez Street. Otherwise, you can nibble on sweet delicacies such as *piyaya* (a hardened pancake with sugar melted inside) and *bay ibayi* (sugar and coconut served in a coconut shell), sold all over the city from street stalls and hole-in-the-wall canteens.

Mount Kanlaon National Park

Mount Kanlaon – sometimes spelled Canlaon - two hours from Bacolod by jeepney, is the tallest peak in the central Philippines. Climbers have died scaling it, so don't underestimate its fury – this is still one of the thirteen most active volcanoes in the country (locals believe it is home to many spirits). The surrounding forest contains all manner of wonderful fauna, including pythons, monitor lizards, tube-nosed bats and the *dahoy pulay*, a poisonous green tree snake, and it was here that President Manuel Quezon hid from invading Japanese forces during World War II. There are several routes up the volcano, most involving three tough days of walking and two nights of camping. One of the best is from the village of **Guintubdan** on the western slopes, where you can arrange park permits (P300). The best way to get here is by jeepney in two stages, via Murcia, southeast of Bacolod. For up-to-date information about the safety of climbing Kanlaon, contact the City Tourism Office in Bacolod (☎034/435 1001 or 433 2517).

Silay and Victorias

North of Bacolod, **SILAY**, a 45-minute ride by bus or jeepney, is one of the historic centres of the sugar industry. The few tourists that come here do so for the sugar trains and the marvellous ancestral houses. The most interesting aspect of the trains – iron dinosaurs, as they are known – is that they are fuelled by bagasse, a by-product of sugar production. Silay offers a first-rate impression of what life was like in the heyday of the plantations. It's worth making time to spend a few hours at the **Balay Negrense Museum**, 5 Novembre St (Tues-Sat 10am–6pm; P25), a lifestyle museum and formerly one of the grandest plantation homes in the area. In neighbouring **VICTORIAS**, at the Vicmico Public Relations Office on Ossario Avenue, is the Church of St Joseph the Worker, built 1948–50. The church is home to the controversial icon called the Angry Christ, which depicts Jesus sitting in front of the hands of God, straddling a serpent-spewing skull.

Dumaguete and around

"The City of Gentle People" lives up to its name. **DUMAGUETE**, capital of Negros Oriental, lies on the southeast coast of Negros, within sight of the most southerly tip of Cebu Island. It's a perfect jumping-off point for the beach resorts of nearby Dauin and the marine sanctuary of Apo Island, where the scuba diving is superlative.

The small **airport** is a few kilometres northwest of the city centre on the far bank of the Bona River. Tricycles make the trip to the city for about P50. The **ferry pier** is near the northern end of Rizal Boulevard, within easy walking distance of the centre. WG&A sails to Manila, Tagbilaran and Cagayan de Oro, Negros Navigation serves Manila and Tagbilaran, and Supercat has two daily sailings to Cebu City via Tagbilaran and one to Larena on Siquijor. From Siquijor, local **bancas** arrive several times a week at Silliman Beach, 1km north of Dumaguete along Flores Avenue and easy to reach on foot, by tricycle or jeepney.

Ceres Liner **buses** arrive and depart at the Ceres terminal in Governor Perdices Street, on the southern side of the Banica River. A jeepney into the city costs P10, but if you haven't got much luggage you can walk it almost as fast. For bus departures to the north of the island, it's worth making sure you get on an express bus, shaving a few painful hours from journey times. There's a **tourist office** (Mon–Sat 8.30am–6pm; ⓣ035/225 0549) in the City Hall complex on Colon Street, near Quezon Park. For **Internet** access, the cafés around the Silliman University complex, at the northern end of Hibbard Street, are a good bet; try Surf Station Internet Café on Katada corner Hibbard Avenue. The *Music Box* on Rizal Avenue is Dumaguete's premier expat hangout and a good place to find out what's going on locally. It offers Internet access and transport to local beach resorts.

There is plenty of affordable **accommodation** in Dumaguete. *Bethel Guest House* (ⓣ035/225 2009; ❹) on Rizal Boulevard is in an excellent location on the seafront, with clean studio rooms and doubles, some with a sea view, although you'll pay extra for that. Rooms at the front are big and bright, with picture windows. A few blocks away is the lovely *La Residencia al Mar* (ⓣ035/225 7100 or 225 7101; ❺), an elegant old house that was once the home of the governor of Negros Occiental and is now a quaint hotel with sixteen charming air-con rooms, some with balconies overlooking the sea. In the city centre, *Dumaguete Pension* (ⓣ035/225 4631; ❷) on Taft Avenue is a long-established, friendly place on the west side of the market, with small rooms and a coffee shop.

South of Dumaguete is beach-resort country, with a good range of clean and affordable accommodation close to the sea, often with dive schools attached. **DAUIN**, a popular port of call, lies twenty minutes' journey by bus or jeepney from Dumaguete. *El Dorado Beach Resort* (ⓣ035/425 2274; ❺) is a casual and friendly native-style resort on a black-sand beach. It offers standard and family rooms, standalone family cottages and a dormitory. The resort's dive operation, Sea Explorers, specializes in trips to Apo Island. On **APO ISLAND** itself – accessible by banca from Damaguete (45min; P50) – you can stay at *Apo Island Beach Resort* (035/422 9663 or 035/422 9663; ❷), which stands on an isolated sandy cove hemmed in by rocks. You can choose from simple bamboo cottages, either on the beach or elevated on the hill behind it. This is the simple life: there's no electricity and the bathrooms often lack running water, so buckets of water are distributed daily.

Siquijor

Siquijor, a laid-back little island where life is simple and tourists are made very welcome, lies slightly apart from the rest of the Visayas off the southern tip of Cebu and about 22km east of Negros. Very little is known about Siquijor and its inhabitants before the arrival of the Spaniards in the sixteenth century. The Spanish sailors nicknamed Siquijor the Isla del Fuego ("Island of Fire") because of eerie luminescence generated by swarms of fireflies at night. This sense of mystery still persists today, with many Filipinos believing Siquijor to be a centre of witchcraft and black magic. It's a view that's enforced by the annual staging of the Conference of Sorcerers and Healers in the mountain village of San Antonio every Easter. You can circumnavigate Siquijor by bus and jeepney along the coastal road. **SIQUIJOR TOWN**, the capital, lies twenty minutes by jeepney southwest of Larena, the main port.

The most popular beaches on Siquijor are Sandugan, half an hour by jeepney north of Larena, and Paliton on the west coast, which you can reach easily by jeepney from Siquijor Town and most places along the coastal road. There is plenty of nipa-type rustic beach **accommodation** in these areas. In Sandugan, try *Islanders Paradise Beach Resort* (☎035/481 5002; ❷), where rustic doubles on a beautiful beach with excellent snorkelling start from just P200. *Coral Cay Resort* (☎035/481 5024; ❸) on the beach in San Juan, is a relaxed but well-managed place with budget rooms at the back and beach cottages right on the sand.

There are no flights to Siquijor, but there is an excellent fast **ferry** connection with Supercat, which has one trip daily from Cebu City to Larena (P420), via Tagbilaran on Bohol and Dumaguete on Negros. Other options for getting to Siquijor include a Palacio Shipping ferry that sails to Larena from Tagbilaran. There's also a wharf in Siquijor Town where local bancas from Dumaguete dock; the trip can be very rough and wet. Irregular ferries, most of them rusty old tubs, from Plaridel in Mindanao arrive in Lazi, a small port town on Siquijor's southeast coast.

Panay

The big heart-shaped island of **Panay** has been largely bypassed by tourism, perhaps because everyone seems to get sucked towards Boracay off its northern tip instead. Panay comprises four provinces: Antique on the west coast, Aklan in the north, Capiz in the northeast and Iloilo running along the east coast to the capital of Iloilo province, **Iloilo City** in the south. The province that interests most tourists is Aklan, whose capital **Kalibo** is the site of the big and brash **Ati-Atihan Festival**, held every second week of January. The northeast coast from Concepcion to Estancia offers access by banca to a number of unspoilt islands, the largest of which is Sicogon, eleven square kilometres, fringed by white sandy beaches and home to monkeys, wild pigs and eagles. Most of these islands have few places to stay, so if you want to spend the night take a sleeping bag, water and food. On the other side of Panay, Antique is a poor, bucolic province of beaches and precipitous cordillera mountains.

Iloilo City

ILOILO CITY is a useful transit point for Guimares Island (see p.840) and other Visayan islands, but otherwise of little interest. There's something drearily homogenous about the ramshackle nature of Philippine port cities and, apart from some graceful old houses in its sidestreets and a handful of interesting churches, Iloilo City has little to distinguish it from other horrors of urban planning perpetrated throughout the archipelago. You can't help but wonder where all the nice buildings are. The city's handful of sights includes the rather threadbare **Museo Iloilo and Antique Collection**, behind the Provincial Capitol Building on Bonifacio Drive (Mon–Sat 9am–5pm; P10), which documents the history and traditions of the Western Visayas (Negros and Panay). West of the city in Molo district is **Molo Church**, a splendid nineteenth-century Gothic Renaissance church made of coral. If you're visiting in January, the Dinagyang Festival adds some extra frenzy to the city during the fourth weekend.

Iloilo Mandurriao Airport is about 8km north of the city; a taxi to the centre will cost about P100. A cheaper option is to take a jeepney marked "Iloilo–Mandurriao". Ferries arrive at the **wharf** at the eastern end of the city, off San Pedro Drive. Air Philippines (☎033/320 8048), Cebu Pacific (☎033/320 6889) and PAL (☎033/321 0260) all have small ticket offices at the airport itself.

The **city's tourist information office** (Mon–Sat 9.30am–5.30pm; ☎033/337 5411) is on Bonifacio Drive and the Bureau of Immigration is at the Old Customs House on Aduana Street, although visa extensions arranged here take time because they go through Manila. The **post office** is in the same building and has poste restante.

Accommodation

Amigo Terrace Hotel Iznart St cnr Delgado St ☎033/335 0908. Upmarket, marbled, a/c sanctuary in the throbbing heart of the city, with its own bistro, restaurant, disco and big outdoor swimming pool. Standard doubles have all mod cons, including cable TV and refrigerator. ❻

Chito Hotel 180 Jalandoni St cnr de Leon St ☎033/337 6415. Very pleasant accommodation in a/c en-suite rooms with cable TV. The outdoor *Lobby Café*, surrounded by greenery and overlooking a small swimming pool, is a civilized place to eat. ❸

Hotel del Rio M.H. Del Pilar St, Molo ☎033/335 1171. Comfortable, modern hotel with views of the river from some rooms. Standard doubles have a/c, cable TV and hot water. ❹

Family Pension House General Luna St ☎033/335 0070. One of the city's few good budget options, boasting a helpful travel office with good local information, a pleasant restaurant and simple singles and doubles with private shower. ❶

Four-Season Hotel Fuentes St cnr Delgado St ☎033/336 1070. Reliable establishment with unfussy but comfortable and well-maintained a/c rooms, all with piping hot showers, starched bed linen and cable TV. The lobby has a good restaurant and coffee shop. ❺

Iloilo Midtown Hotel Yulo St ☎033/336 6688. Ordinary rooms, though all are well kept and have quiet a/c and hot shower. ❹

Eating

Iloilo City is known for a number of delicacies, including **pancit Molo soup** a garlicky concoction with pork dumplings and noodles in rich broth. It is named after the Molo area of the city and is sold at numerous street stalls. **Batchoy**, an artery-hardening combination of liver, pork and beef with thin noodles, is also available everywhere you look. For an authentic helping, try *Ted's Batchoy* on Solis Street near the river.

Tatoy's Manukan and Seafoods is a favourite with locals for fresh oysters and other seafood, and should be your first stop if you're looking for something with an authentic Visayan flavour. It's at Villa Beach in the area of Arevalo, ten minutes west of the city by taxi. Another good source of native-style fare is a group of restaurants called *Marina* on Diversion Road, north of the river. The menu here includes lobster, *lapu-lapu*, all sorts of grilled meat and fish, and some non-Visayan Filipino specials such as *kare-kare* and Bicol Express. Two can eat here and have a few drinks for around P500, with live music thrown in on Friday and Saturday nights. For reliable European food, head straight for the *Bavaria Restauraant and Bar* at the *Nagarao City Inn*, 113 Seminario Street, Jaro, where pork knuckle, schnitzel and roast chicken start at P120.

Moving on from Iloilo City

Buses connect Iloilo City to other towns in Panay. The Ceres bus terminal on Tanza Street is the departure point for Caticlan (for Boracay) and Kalibo, via Concepcion and Roxas.

Iloilo City is a busy port with numerous **ferry** services to Manila and other places throughout the Visayas. WG&A (☎033/ 337 7151) and Negros Navigation sail to Manila and other destinations, such as Cebu City, Cagayan de Oro, Davao, and General Santos. On the river, near City Hall, you can catch Sea Angels fast ferries (☎033/336 1316) to Bacolod, the capital of Negros Occidental.

Ati-Atihan festival

Every January, the Filipino town of Kalibo on the island of Panay erupts into Southeast Asia's biggest street party, the **Ati-Atihan**. Thousands of revellers dress up in outrageous outfits, blacken their faces with soot (in honour of the aboriginal **Ati**, whose descendants still live on Panay), and salsa through the streets. It is said that the festival originated when ten Malay chieftains chanced upon the island and persuaded the Ati to sell it to them; the deal was naturally sealed with a party, and the Malays darkened their faces to emulate their new neighbours. Centuries later, the Spanish incorporated Catholic elements into Ati-Atihan and the modern festival is now dedicated to the **Santo Niño** (**Holy Infant Jesus**). The event comes to a climax with a huge Mass in the cathedral, and the three-day party ends with a masquerade ball and prizes for the best dressed.

Kalibo

KALIBO lies on the well-trodden path to Boracay and for most of the year is an uninteresting town, but every third Sunday of January it hosts what is probably the biggest street party in the country, the **Ati-Atihan** (@www.atihan.net; see box). This exuberant festival celebrates the original inhabitants of the area, the Atis, and culminates with choreographed dances through the streets by locals daubed in black paint (Ati-Atihan means "to make like the Atis"). Revellers blacken their faces in imitation of their aboriginal forefathers and stage a shuffling dance in the streets amid cries of "*hala bira, puera pasma*" ("keep on going, no tiring"). Good accommodation can be hard to find during the Ati-Atihan and prices increase by up to a hundred percent. Direct flights to Kalibo from Manila are often fully booked.

Kalibo is a compact place with most city destinations within walking distance. The

Moving on from Kalibo

For **Caticlan** (the jumping-off point for Boracay), buses leave the terminal on Roxas Avenue every hour (2hr 30min; P100; also served by FX vans); jeepneys, also from this terminal, leave when they are full, often taking as much as four hours to complete the journey as they stop dozens of times along the way. Air-con vans and FX taxis also leave from the Ceres Liner bus terminal, one kilometre south of Kalibo on Laserna Street. From the airport, a more convenient way to make the trip to Caticlan wharf is to take one of the FX taxis or L300 vans that meet incoming flights (2hr; P150). Every flight landing at Kalibo is also met by drivers with private vehicles; you can usually find someone with a van to take you to Caticlan for around P1500, divided among as many as nine passengers. If you're arriving in Kalibo by ferry, you can get a bus or jeepney from Dumaguit, a fifteen-minute jeepney ride outside Kalibo, to Caticlan.

From the Ceres Liner bus terminal, there are **buses** south to Iloilo City.

From Dumaguit, there are Negros Navigation **ferries** on Wednesday to Cebu City and twice a week to Manila, one going via Roxas on Mindoro. The Negros Navigation office is in Laserna Street (☎036/262 4943), south of the market. WG&A sails to Manila on Tuesday, Thursday and Sunday at 3.30pm; tickets can be obtained from the WG&A office in Archbishop Reyes Street at the junction with Acevedo Street (☎036/268 4391). Moreta Shipping (☎036/262 3003) at the northern end of Roxas Avenue, opposite Metrobank, has one boat a week to Manila. All these ferry operators also have ticket outlets at the pier in Dumaguit. For tickets, there's also a convenient Aboitiz outlet right in Kalibo town centre at the junction of Burgos Street and Luis Barrios Street.

There are several **flights** to and from Manila daily. PAL (☎036/262 3260), Air Philippines (☎036/262 4444), and Cebu Pacific (☎036/262 5406) all have ticket offices at the airport; Cebu Pacific also has an office in Legaspi Street, behind Kalibo Cathedral.

major thoroughfare is Roxas Avenue, which runs into town from the **airport** in the southeast, with most streets leading off it to the southwest. The ten-minute tricycle ride into town from the airport costs around P10. **Banks**, including BPI and PNB, are on Martyr's Street, which runs along the southern edge of Pastrana Park, close to Kalibo Cathedral. The **post office** is in the Provincial Capitol Building, in Mabini Street, off Roxas Avenue. There are three or four **Internet cafés**, the most popular of which is Webquest on Roxas Avenue (P90 per hour). The Kalibo provincial **hospital** is on Mabini Street.

Apartelle Marietta (ⓣ036/262 3353; ②) on Roxas Avenue features fan rooms with balconies and shower. Two of the better budget deals in town are *Glowmoon Hotel & Restaurant* (ⓣ036/262 2373; ②) on Martelino Street and *Garcia Legaspi Mansion* (ⓣ036/262 5588; ③) on the town's main street, Roxas Avenue, both with monastic but clean rooms. *Gervy's Gourmet & Lodge* (ⓣ036/262 4190; ②) features quiet rooms with fan and bath on R. Pastrada Street, while *Casa Felicidad* (ⓣ036/268 4320; ④), on Archbishop Reyes Street near the plaza, has an aura of faded luxury. Note that the price of accommodation increases drastically during Ati-Atihan, and air-con doubles can cost up to P800–1000. The *Glowmoon Hotel* features a nice restaurant with a surprisingly good range of local and continental dishes. *Peking House Restaurant*, on Martyr's Street, is an ever-popular place for cheap Chinese food, while the newer *Willhelm Tell Deli & Restaurant*, on Roxas Avenue, dishes up European steaks and pastas from P120.

Guimaras

The small island of **Guimaras** lies a short ferry ride away from Iloilo City and is famous for its mangoes, which not only grow in profusion, but are said to be among the sweetest in the Philippines. It's more than just a day-trip destination: from the ferry pier in the capital, **Jordan**, you can catch a jeepney to the south side of the island around **Cabalagnan** and **San Isidro**, where there are some wonderful, quiet beaches (except at weekends, when the locals converge) and a handful of cheap nipa resorts. The spacious *Raymen Resort* (②), in Alubihod, Nueva Valencia, on the island's southwest coast, are built on a perfect white-sand beach and have large balconies. There's no restaurant or menu, but the owners will make sure there's always a supply of fresh fish, which they will cook for you in their small kitchen and serve under the stars. More upmarket resorts include *Nagarao Island Resort* (ⓣ033/320 6290, ⓦwww.nagarao.com ⑥), 22 native-style bungalows on the tiny island of Nagarao, off the southeast coast of Guimaras. Meals are available, too, though as there are no other restaurants on Nagarao, you're a captive audience. You can make bookings direct or at *Nagarao Pension House* in Iloilo City (113 Seminario St, Jaro).

Several small **ferries** leave Iloilo daily for the short crossing to Jordan, starting at 5am. The best place to catch them is the wharf near the post office, although some also depart from Ortiz wharf at the southern end of Ortiz Street near the market. Ferries arriving in Jordan are greeted by jeepneys serving the beaches on the south side of the island.

Boracay

BORACAY, off the northeastern tip of Panay 350km south of Manila, is not the dozy tropical backwater it used to be. That's the bad news. The good news is that Boracay is still an exceptional destination. It may be only 7km long and 1km wide at its narrowest point, but it's a big tropical island in a small package, with thirty beaches and coves and sunsets that are worth the journey on their own. The most famous is **White Beach** on the island's western shore: 4km of the kind of powder-

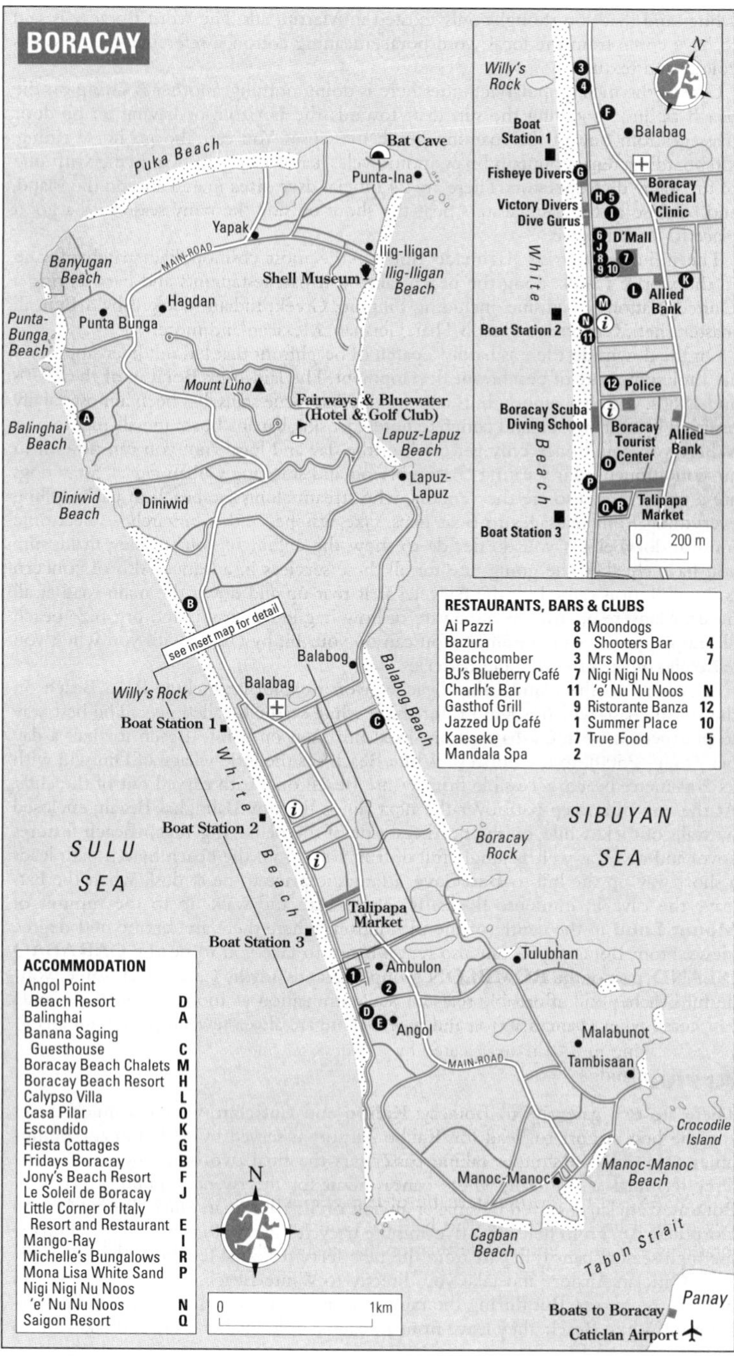
BORACAY
Puka Beach
Bat Cave
Punta-Ina
Yapak
Ilig-Iligan
Ilig-Iligan Beach
Shell Museum
MAIN-ROAD
Banyugan Beach
Hagdan
Punta Bunga
Punta-Bunga Beach
Mount Luho
Fairways & Bluewater (Hotel & Golf Club)
Balinghai Beach
Lapuz-Lapuz Beach
Lapuz-Lapuz
Diniwid Beach
Diniwid
see inset map for detail
Balabog
Balabog Beach
Willy's Rock
Balabag
Boat Station 1
Boat Station 2
Boat Station 3
White Beach
Talipapa Market
SULU SEA
SIBUYAN SEA
Boracay Rock
Tulubhan
Ambulon
Angol
Malabunot
Tambisaan
Crocodile Island
Manoc-Manoc
Manoc-Manoc Beach
Cagban Beach
Tabon Strait
Panay
Boats to Boracay
Caticlan Airport
N
0 1km
Willy's Rock
Balabag
Boracay Medical Clinic
Fisheye Divers
Victory Divers
Dive Gurus
D'Mall
Allied Bank
Police
Boracay Scuba Diving School
Boracay Tourist Center
Talipapa Market
0 200 m
ACCOMMODATION
Angol Point Beach Resort D
Balinghai A
Banana Saging Guesthouse C
Boracay Beach Chalets M
Boracay Beach Resort H
Calypso Villa L
Casa Pilar O
Escondido K
Fiesta Cottages G
Fridays Boracay B
Jony's Beach Resort F
Le Soleil de Boracay J
Little Corner of Italy Resort and Restaurant E
Mango-Ray I
Michelle's Bungalows R
Mona Lisa White Sand P
Nigi Nigi Nu Noos 'e' Nu Nu Noos N
Saigon Resort Q
RESTAURANTS, BARS & CLUBS
Ai Pazzi 8
Bazura 6
Beachcomber 3
BJ's Blueberry Café 7
Charlh's Bar 11
Gasthof Grill 9
Jazzed Up Café 1
Kaeseke 7
Mandala Spa 2
Moondogs
Shooters Bar 4
Mrs Moon 7
Nigi Nigi Nu Noos 'e' Nu Nu Noos N
Ristorante Banza 12
Summer Place 10
True Food 5

white sand that you thought only existed in Martini ads. The word Boracay is said to have come from the local word borac, meaning cotton, a reference to the sand's colour and texture.

One of the most popular activities here is doing nothing: another is sitting on the beach at dusk watching the sun drift towards the horizon, or having an outdoor massage from one of the roaming beach masseuses. You can also go horse riding, kiteboarding, rent mountain bikes, motorcycles, kayaks, or go scuba diving with one of the many dive operators. There are 24 official **dive sites** in and around the island, and because of the calm waters near the shore outside the rainy season it's a good place to learn to dive.

The influx of tourists has made Boracay the most cosmopolitan patch of sand in the world: a walk along the beach takes you past restaurants and bars serving a United Nations of cuisine, including Filipino, Greek, Indian (cooked by a Bengali master chef), Caribbean, French Thai, German, Mexican and more.

On the downside, there is hardly a patch of beachfront that has not been appropriated for some sort of beachfront development. The laid-back Boracay of the 1970s and 1980s, with its bamboo huts and wobbly barbecue stalls, has been almost totally usurped by a string of bland concrete hotels, jet skis, banana boats and all-night raves. Where you could once only get catch of the day and local rum you can now sit in air-conditioned luxury eating chateaubriand and smoking Cuban cigars. Stray dogs are a problem and so are the vendors, who stream along the beach in packs selling everything from massages to boat trips, fake watches and – bizzarely – electronic musical doorbells. If you do decide to show the colour of your money, make sure you have checked the going rate for all these services in advance. Also of concern is the pollution caused by the tricycles that roar up and down the main road at all hours. Many resort owners are aware of how fragile Boracay is and organize beach cleanups and recycling seminars. You can do your bit by taking with you when you leave all your plastic bags and batteries.

Elsewhere on the island, other beaches worth exploring include Puka Beach on the north coast, which is famous for shiny white seashells called *puka*. The best way to get there is to hire a banca from local boatmen on White Beach for half a day per group (P500). To the north of White Beach sits the little village of Diniwid with its 200-metre beach, accessible from White Beach on a path carved out of the cliffs. At the end of a steep path over the next hill is the tiny Balinghai Beach, enclosed by walls of rock, while, on the northeast side of the island, Ilig-Iligan Beach features coves and caves, as well as jungle full of fruit bats. From the beach here, a path leads a short way up the hill to **Bat Cave**, a fantastic place to be at dusk when the bats leave the cave in immense flocks. It's also worth the walk up to the summit of **Mount Luho** in the centre of the island, from where there are terrific 360-degree views. From Boracay you can also rent a banca to take you to nearby **CARABAO ISLAND**, part of the **ROMBLON** group of islands. Idyllic Carabao has some wonderful beaches and affordable seafront accommodation at Inobahan on the island's east coast, where bancas arrive, and where there are also a few simple restaurants.

Arrival

There are two gateways to Boracay: **Kalibo** and **Caticlan**, which is much closer and the best airport to head for. Kalibo Airport is served by PAL and Air Philippines, with air-con shuttles taking passengers the final two hours by road to the ferry terminal at Caticlan, where bancas await for the twenty-minute journey to Boracay. Caticlan is served by smaller aircraft of SEAIR, Asian Spirit, Pacific Air and Corporate Air. From here, it's a five-minute tricycle ride (P50) to the bancas. During the high season, bancas depart from the new ferry terminal less than one kilometre from Caticlan Airport and take you directly to White Beach, from where you can walk to the resorts. But during the rainy season, when the waves make landing difficult on White Beach, they leave from a beach a little further away and take you to the southern end of Boracay. From this arrivals point there are plenty of tricycles to take you to your accommodation. If you've booked a resort in advance, someone will meet you at the airport. If you're travelling independently to Caticlan, take a tricycle to the banca departure point and then a public banca to Boracay. You can buy a ticket where the bancas leave from; one-way tickets are P16.30 for Filipinos and P19.60 for tourists, plus a P2 terminal fee. Try to get a banca going to Boat Station 3, which is in front of the *Swiss Inn Restaurant* and the *Queen's Beach Resort*, close to most of the budget accommodation.

WG&A has departures every Tuesday, Thursday and Sunday from Manila to Dumaguit in Aklan, from where you can travel by bus to Caticlan. Negros Navigation also serves Dumaguit, with a weekly sailing from Manila on Tuesdays at 4pm. From Iloilo City, catch a Ceres Liner bus or air-con van from their terminal on Rizal Street to Caticlan (4hr).

Orientation, information and transport

Main Road runs the western length of Boracay, from Yapak in the north, through White Beach and down to Banca Dock on its southern tip. Not surprisingly, most of the development on the island centres along **White Beach**. The northern end of the beach, beyond Boat Station 1, is the quietest and home to the more expensive resorts. Roughly in the middle of the beach is Boat Station 2, which is where most of the restaurants and nightlife can be found, and at the southern end Boat Station 3. Talipapa Market is between stations 2 and 3, while D'Mall, a busy little area of shops and restaurants, is a little south of station 1.

The **Boracay Tourist Center** (daily 8am–8pm; ☎036/288 3704) about halfway along White Beach is the best place for general information and travel assistance; staff will help you arrange visas and make long-distance telephone calls. The boom in tourism on Boracay means Visa, MasterCard and American Express are widely accepted, although sometimes with a small surcharge.

Fares for the tricycles that run along the length of the Main Road are P10 per person for a trip, if you're willing to share the tricycle with others, which means it will pick up passengers along the way. For most foreigners, the flat rate for a private trip is P50 per tricycle, not per person. Make sure you agree the fare in advance.

Accommodation

Boracay boasts about two hundred resorts, and this proliferation of accommodation, from the monastic to the luxurious, means that except at peak times (Christmas, New Year and Easter) you should be able to find something simply by taking a stroll down White Beach from south to north. Prices rise sharply at peak times and it's always worth negotiating for a discount, especially if you plan to stay a while. Huts and cottages are usually good for two people.

Angol Point Beach Resort ☎036/288 3107 or 032/522 0012. At the south end of the beach. It's a little more pricey than many resorts of its ilk because the conservationist owner, Francis, has built only one cottage where most developers would have put three or four – which means you get expansive rooms, huge verandas and the benefit of acres of space in the peaceful coconut grove where the resort stands. It's a short walk from bars and restaurants and very quiet. Good choice for families. ❻

Balinghai ☎036 288 3646. If you're looking for desert-island solitude and don't mind being a few minutes' tricycle ride from the buzz of White Beach, *Balinghai* fits the bill. On a small, secluded cove surrounded by cliffs on the northern part of Boracay, it's set into a steep slope with lots of steps, and boasts a handful of private bungalows and houses built from local materials, with consideration for the environment. One house has a tree in the kitchen and another is carved from the rockface, with a balcony facing the sunset. There's a small restaurant serving excellent vegetarian fare. ❺

Banana Saging Guesthouse ☎036/288 6121. Atmospheric, rambling, native-style guesthouse on Balabog Beach, a 10min walk across the island from White Beach. There's a choice of rooms, all built from bamboo and wood, with slatted floors and, in some cases, shady balconies. No restaurant, but there's a shared kitchen where you can cook. ❸

Boracay Beach Chalets ☎036/288 3993. 50m north of the Tourist Center, roughly in the middle of the beach. Standard rooms good for one or two people, and family rooms for five, though the "rooms" are actually big, pleasant cottages standing in a quiet, tropical garden. Perks include cable TV, fridge, free tea or coffee and free mineral water. ❺

Boracay Beach Resort ☎036/288 3208. Big choice of pleasant bungalows in an excellent location, right on the beach between Boat Station 1 and D'Mall. There's also a lovely suite room that has a living area and a patio with ocean views. Tasty breakfast included. ❸

Calypso Villa ☎036/288 3206. Walk down the footpath at the back of the Tourist Center and they're on the left. Worth the effort to find if you're looking for good-value, comfortable accommodation close to the beach but away from the noise of the bars and clubs. In a new, whitewashed house standing in peaceful gardens, the downstairs rooms have French windows that open onto a patio area, while the upstairs rooms have large balconies. Simple, charming and immaculately clean. ❺

Casa Pilar ☎036/288 3073. On the beach near Boat Station 3. Clean and comfortable wooden huts with breezy balconies overlooking quiet gardens. All rooms have either fan or a/c and private shower. ❹

Escondido ☎036/288 5575 Spacious, modern a/c concrete rooms a 10min walk inland from Boat Station 2. The off-beach location makes this place a little cheaper than others like it. The restaurant specializes in seafood, especially crab and prawns. ❸

Fiesta Cottages ☎036/288 3818. In an unbeatable location at the northern end of the beach near Boat Station 1 and Fisheye Divers. There's peace and quiet at night in simple nipa and bamboo rooms, and it's only a 10min walk from other resorts and from bars and nightlife. ❹

Fridays Boracay ☎036/288 6200 in Boracay, 02/892 9283 or 810 1027 in Manila. One of the most expensive resorts on Boracay, but you get a splendidly peaceful location at the northern end of White Beach and five-star service right down to your own pair of handmade hemp slippers. The beach bar is ideal for an aperitif before you dine al fresco under the stars. The food is pricey by local standards, but if money is no object you can at least wash it down with a bottle of vintage Louis Roederer champagne for P14,000 before retiring to your balcony with a Filipino-made Fighting Cock Flyboy cigar (P350). ❾

Jony's Beach Resort ☎036/288 6119. Friendly and conveniently situated family resort with a convivial beach ambience and a good beachfront restaurant specializing in Mexican food. Rooms are in a building less than 100m from the beach across the road and all are spotless, with a/c and private bathrooms. ❹

Le Soleil de Boracay ☎036/288 6209-12 in Boracay, 02/895 1182 in Manila. Small but spick and span a/c rooms in a newish concrete hotel a short walk south of D'Mall. Great location, comfortable little restaurant (breakfast included) and Internet. ❼

Little Corner of Italy Resort and Restaurant ☎036/288 5078. At the southern end of the beach. Besides dorm beds (P100), there are a/c doubles and group rooms for twelve. Slightly faded but very friendly, and the Italian owner, Mario, cooks some mean pasta. ❶

Mango-Ray ☎036 288 3301. Near Sea World Dive Center, roughly in the centre of the beach. Four large a/c furnished rooms (each more like a small apartment) with shower, fridge, TV, telephone and spacious porch. If you plan to hang around for a while, they're worth considering at P40,000 a month. Floors are tiled, the whitewashed walls are decorated with tasteful Filipino art and the surrounding gardens are lush and peaceful. ❾

Michelle's Bungalows ☎036/288 8086. Near the action just north of Boat Station 3, but cheaper than many resorts because it's set back from the bustle of White Beach in a pleasant courtyard. Quiet, homey and with a small native bar and restaurant, this place is understandably popular. ❸

Mona Lisa White Sand ☎036/288 3012. A relatively new addition to the beachfront skyline with charming gardens and comfortable cottages. At the southern end of White Beach near Talipapa Market. ❸

Nigi Nigi Nu Noos 'e' Nu Nu Noos ☎036/288 3101. Long-standing and popular resident of White Beach between the Tourist Center and Boat Station 2. The Indonesian-style cottages are almost as impressive as the name. The restaurant is popular and very affordable, plus there's a good cybercafé. ❺

Saigon Resort ☎036/288 3203. Next to Western Union and near Talipapa Market, *Saigon* is so ordinary that it's easy to miss. The half-dozen cottages are, however, clean and sturdy, and have balconies where you can swing in the complimentary hammock. Friendly staff, reasonable rates and right on the beach. An excellent budget option. ❸

Eating and drinking

Restaurants and bars come and go in Boracay, but there are so many you can eat and drink your way up and down White Beach almost 24 hours a day.

Ai Pazzi Fashionable Italian restaurant near the entrance to D'Mall offering pasta, pizza and homemade gelato. A perfect place to grab a table overlooking the beach and watch the world go by.
BJ's Blueberry Café Shady and modest little straw-hut hideaway towards the back of D'Mall; decorated with ethnic regalia and serving excellent cheap rice dishes and herbal teas.
Gasthof Grill One of Boracay's most enduring restaurants, on the beach path near the entrance to D'Mall. Food is mostly straightforward and tasty Bavarian fare, but also with a good selection of fresh seafood that you can choose yourself and have cooked any way you want.
Kaeseke Cheap and tasty Japanese noodles, sashimi and sushi. Inside D'Mall.
Mandala Spa The vegetarian restaurant at this upmarket spa offers the best vegetarian cuisine on the island, all homemade or using ingredients flown in every day from Manila. Choose from aubergine and feta, pan-friend tofu and Thai noodles. There are also excellent fruit and vegetable shakes. It's a little more expensive than other places listed here, but worth the extra. Open 10am-10pm.
Mrs Moon Budget Chinese food such as noodles and stir-friend rice. Convenient location inside D'Mall and a smattering of vegetarian choices such as bak choi and dumplings.
Nigi Nigi Nu Noos 'e' Nu Nu Noos Popular resort restaurant with an excellent "eat all you can" English breakfast for P165, as well as affordable lunches and dinners, with tables set on the beach in the evening.
Ristorante Banza The owner and chef worked as a lawyer in Macau, but gave it all up to start this excellent little Portuguese restaurant. The food is marvellous, simply cooked but delicious. The chicken piri-piri is wonderfully tangy and fresh seafood is available every day. On the main beach path near the Boracay Tourist Center.
Summer Place Best known as a rowdy all-night bar and disco, but from 8pm-11pm does a tasty Mongolian Grill.
True Food Sit on cushions at low tables at Boracay's most authentic Indian restaurant. Perfect setting overlooking the beach and a mouthwatering choice of curries, including many vegetarian options.

Nightlife

Nightlife on Boracay starts with drinks at sunset and continues all night, and ranges from the convivial to the downright raucous.

Bazura Hugely popular disco, part open air and part covered by a flimsy bamboo roof. Like all of Boracay's discos you don't have to dress up for this place. Music is loud and goes on all night.
Beachcomber One of Boracay's most longstanding and well-known discos. The kind of place that doesn't get going until after midnight and doesn't cool down until sunrise.
Charlh's Bar Small outdoor place near Nigi's with live acoustic music on the beach from dusk and a popular happy hour.
Jazzed Up Café Convivial little beach bar a few minutes' walk south of Boat Station 3, with live jazz and Latin music every evening.
Moondogs Shooters Bar Very lively bar at the back of the *Cocomangas Beach Resort* at Balabag (northern end of White Beach) is famous – infamous – for its drinking games involving potent cocktails.
Summer Place Big nipa establishment on the beach path where dancing and drinking go on all night.

Listings

Airlines Inside the Boracay Tourist Center is a branch of Filipino Travel Center where you can book tickets for PAL, Air Philippines, Seair, Asian Spirit, Cebu Pacific and WG&A.
Banks and exchange There are two branches of Allied Bank on the island where you can change travellers' cheques, although many resorts also act as de facto currency changers. In D'Mall, there's a small branch of BPI with an ATM.
Dive operators These firms are all on White Beach: Aquarius Diving ⓣ036/288 3132; Boracay Safari Divers ⓣ036/288 3260; Boracay Scuba Diving School ⓣ036/288 3327; Calypso Diving Resort ⓣ036/288 3206, ⓦwww.calypso.ph; Dive Gurus ⓣ036/288 5486, ⓦwww.divegurus.com; Fisheye Divers ⓣ036/288 6090, ⓦwww.fisheyedivers.com; Lapu-Lapu Diving Centre ⓣ036/288 3302, ⓦwww.lapulapu.com; Safari Divers ⓣ036/288

3260; Victory Divers ⓣ036/288 3209, ⓦwww.victorydivers.com.

Hospitals and clinics The main hospital is the Don Ciriaco Senares Tirol Senior Memorial Hospital (ⓣ036/288 3041) off Main Rd by the *Aloja Delicatessen.* There are also a number of clinics: the Metropolitan Doctors Medical Clinic is on Main Rd (ⓣ036/288 6357), by the market. It can provide first aid or deal with emergencies and will send a doctor to your hotel. The Boracay Medical Clinic is at the northern end of Main Rd (ⓣ036/288 3141) 200m past *Pink Patio.* There's also a small clinic in D'Mall called Bysshe Medical Clinic and a pharmacy next door.

Internet access There are now dozens of cybercafés on Boracay, most with reasonably fast dedicated connections – among the most popular are Boracay Tourist Center, *Nigi Nigi's*, Rubicano's Internet Café (on the beach near *Sandcastle's Resort*) and *Boracay Beach Cottages*, close to *Nigi Nigi's.* The usual charge is P50 an hour.

Post The post office in Balabag, the small community halfway along White Beach, is open Mon–Fri 9am–5pm. The Boracay Tourist Centre on White Beach has poste restante costing P5 per letter, and there's a FedEx office in Mail and More in D'Mall.

Pharmacies There are pharmacies selling most necessities in D'Mall, Boracay Tourist Center and Talipapa Market.

Police The Philippine National Police have a small station a short walk inland between Boat Stations 2 and 3, immediately behind the Boracay Tourist Centre.

Shopping Dozens of small *sari-sari* stores line White Beach selling beachwear, T-shirts and souvenirs, and at Talipapa Market you can buy fruit and fish. D'Mall has expanded rapidly in recent years and now has dozens of small shops selling clothes, souvenirs and handicrafts.

8.7

Palawan

If you believe the travel agent clichés, **Palawan** is the Philippine's last frontier. For once, it's almost true. Tourism has yet to penetrate much of this long, sword-shaped island to the southwest of Luzon, and travellers willing to take the rough with the smooth will find a Jurassic landscape of coves, beaches, lagoons and razor-sharp limestone cliffs that rise from crystal-clear water. Palawan province encompasses 1780 islands and islets, most of which have irregular coastlines that make excellent harbours. Thick forests covering these steeply sloped mountains assure adequate watersheds for rivers and streams. Many of the islands are surrounded by a coral shelf that acts as an enormous feeding ground and nursery for marine life; it is sometimes said that Palawan's **Tubbataha** Reef is so ecologically important that if it dies, the Philippines will also die.

Palawan's **history** can be traced back 47,000 years, as confirmed by the discovery of caveman remains in Quezon, southwest Palawan. Anthropologists believe these early inhabitants came from Borneo across a land bridge that connected the two. There are several stories regarding the origin of the name Palawan. Some contend that it was derived from the Chinese words *pa lao yu* meaning "Land of the Beautiful Harbours". Popular belief, however, is that "Palawan" is a corrupted form of the Spanish word *paragua*, because the main island is shaped like a closed umbrella.

The capital of Palawan, **Puerto Princesa** makes a good starting point for exploring the province. A typical journey through Palawan might take you from Puerto Princesa, north to **Honda Bay** and the **Underground River**, then onwards up the coast to **Port Barton**, San Vicente and El Nido. From El Nido you can take a ferry north to **Busuanga** (Coron), and from there you can fly or take a ferry back to Manila. The southern half of Palawan, from Puerto Princesa downwards, is relatively unexplored.

The main gateway **to Palawan** is Puerto Princesa, served by daily flights from Manila with PAL, Air Philippines and SEAIR. Asian Spirit and SEAIR fly to Sandoval near Taytay in North Palawan, and to Busuanga, off the island's northern tip. WG&A and Sulpicio Lines ferries sail regularly from Manila to Busuanga and Puerto Princesa, while Negros Navigation operates from Manila to Puerto Princesa and Bacolod to Puerto Princesa, via Iloilo City. SEAIR has a particularly good network of flights **within Palawan** itself.

Puerto Princesa and around

The provincial capital **PUERTO PRINCESA** is the only major urban sprawl in Palawan, with 120,000 residents. It's been touted in the media as one of the country's cleanest and greenest cities, but the reality is different. The main drag, three-kilometre-long Rizal Avenue, is a deafening jumble of tricycles spewing noxious fumes. There are a few sights around Puerto Princesa, but hardly any in the city itself, which is why most visitors treat it as a one-night stop on the way to or from Palawan's beaches, islands and coral reefs.

The **Palawan Museum** (Mon, Tues, Thurs & Fri 9am–noon & 2–5pm; P12) in Mendoza Park on Rizal Avenue, offers an overview of the history, art and culture of

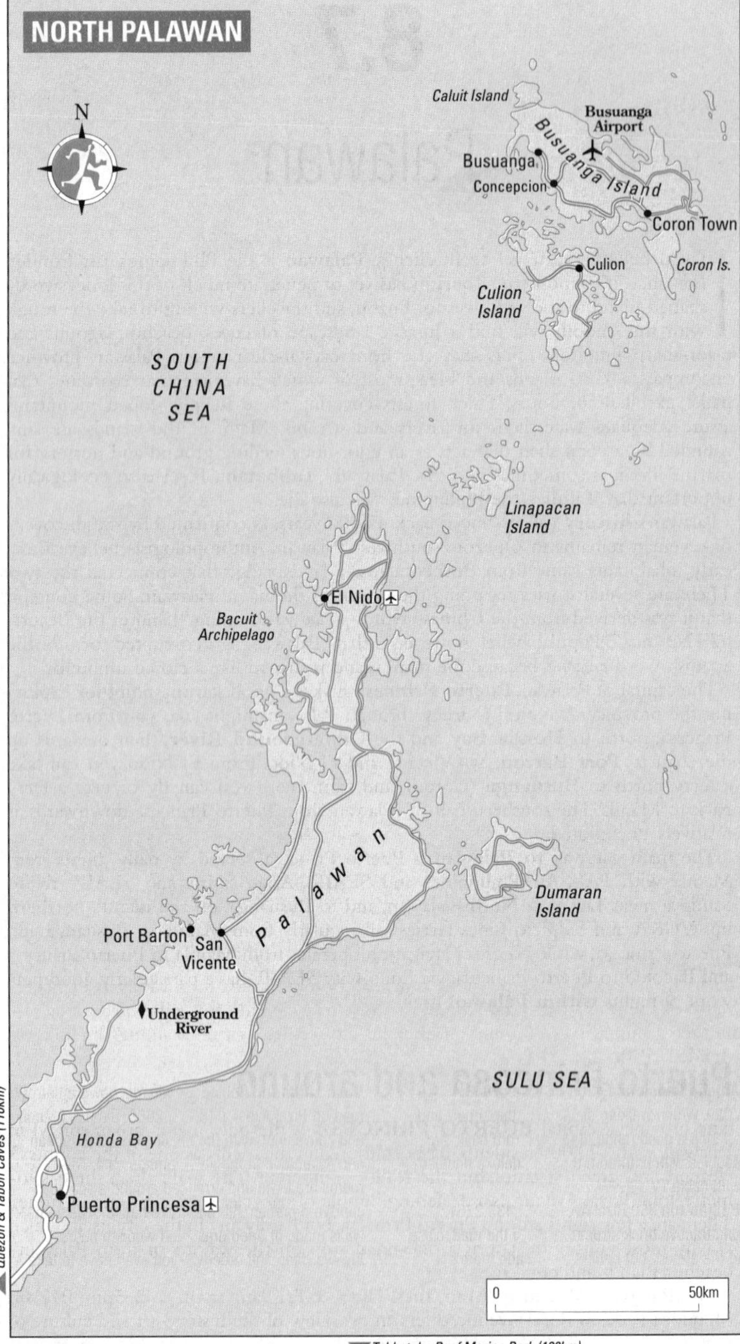
NORTH PALAWAN
N
Caluit Island
Busuanga Airport
Busuanga Island
Busuanga
Concepcion
Coron Town
Culion
Coron Is.
Culion Island
SOUTH CHINA SEA
Linapacan Island
El Nido
Bacuit Archipelago
Palawan
Dumaran Island
Port Barton
San Vicente
Underground River
SULU SEA
Honda Bay
Puerto Princesa
Quezon & Tabon Caves (110km)
0
50km
Tubbataha Reef Marine Park (130km)

Palawan, but is only worth the effort if you're really at a loose end. The **Immaculate Concepcion Cathedral** at the west end of Rizal Avenue is a pretty, angular structure with sharp turrets and spires, but it's not historically significant.

In Iwahig, 23km to the northwest of Puerto Princesa, is the **Iwahig Penal Colony**. Jeepneys leave Mavlar Street every day at 9.30am (P35), for the colony, also known as the Prison Without Bars (daily 8am–7pm; free). Prisoners live here as if in a normal village, fishing and cultivating rice and root crops. The "inmates" are identifiable by their prison T-shirts and ID badges, returning to the prison halls only for meals and sleep. Some long-term residents – those deemed least likely to make a run for it – are allowed to stay in small nipa huts with their families. Tourists are also welcome at the souvenir shop that sells handicrafts made by the prisoners. Prison officials say the rate of repeat offending among those released from Iwahig is significantly lower than among those incarcerated in the country's traditional jails.

Practicalities

There are a number of direct daily **flights** to Puerto Princesa from Manila with PAL, Air Philippines and Cebu Pacific, which also has flights from Cebu City. SEAIR flies here from Manila via Busuanga and El Nido. Negros Navigation runs ferries direct to Puerto Princesa from Manila every Thursday at 2pm (22hr); it returns on Fridays at 7pm. Their service from Bacolod leaves every Wednesday at 10am and sails to Puerto Princesa via Iloilo City (22hr), which makes it possible to reach Palawan from the Visayas without backtracking to Manila. WG&A has a service that leaves Manila North Harbour every Friday at 4pm for Coron Town in Busuanga (arriving 6am Saturday) before sailing on to Puerto Princesa. **Buses** and jeepneys depart for Honda Bay, Quezon and other parts of the island from the chaotic market area in Malvar Street.

The **tourist office** (Mon–Sat 9am–5pm; ⓣ048/433 2968) is in the Provincial Capitol Building on Rizal Avenue, but it only has a handful of old maps and brochures. The small tourist information centre at the airport itself is also not of much use, but a good place to plug into the travellers' grapevine is *Casa Linda Inn*, where the staff are knowledgeable and helpful.

The **post office** is on Burgos Street at its junction with Rizal Avenue. Almost next door is the Hexagon Café, one of a growing number of cybercafes in town that offers access for P45 an hour. Rizal Avenue is also the best place to look for **banks** and moneychangers; PNB lies at the western end, just beyond Mendoza Park. There are two good **hospitals**, the Palawan Adventist Hospital on the National Highway, ten minutes' north of the city centre, and the Provincial Hospital on Malvar Street, opposite Jeshiela Pension.

Accommodation

There are more than fifty pensions and small hotels dotted around Puerto Princesa. Many of them are on Rizal Avenue, a short tricycle ride from the airport, while another group is based in and around the city centre, within walking distance of Mendoza Park.

Amelia Pensionne 420 Rizal Ave ⓣ048/433 7029. Within walking distance of the airport and offering a good range of rooms, from basic a/c doubles with bathroom to larger deluxe doubles with cable TV. ❸

Badjao Inn 350 Rizal Ave ⓣ048 433 2761. Unattractive brick structure facing the road, close to the airport, but behind the facade there's a lovely garden and a good choice of spacious rooms overlooking the greenery. The efficient travel desk can book transport for you. Dorm beds $6. ❺

Casa Linda Inn Behind *Badjao Inn*, down a narrow road off Rizal Ave ⓣ048/433 2606. Simple, friendly and convenient, with the bonus of good European and Asian food in the little bamboo café. The rooms are large and arranged around a spacious courtyard garden. All rooms are native-style with walls made of dried grass and wooden floors. Always clean and orderly – you even have to take you shoes off before you enter. ❶

Hotel Fleuris Lacao St ⓣ048/434 4338, ⓦwww.fleuris.com. Modest, well-maintained modern establishment, where all rooms have a/c, private bathroom and cable TV. The rate includes a decent breakfast in the small poolside restaurant. 7

Legend Hotel Northeastern end of Malvar St ☎048/433 9076. Upmarket option with spacious a/c rooms and big, tiled bathrooms. The rate includes a buffet breakfast. 8

Moana Hotel Rizal Ave Extn ☎048/434 5272 Simple, affordable but spacious rooms right next to the airport. There's a small restaurant serving Italian food, and you can arrange scuba diving trips here.

Puerto Pension 35 Malvar St, close to the ferry port ☎048/433 2969 or 4149. Cool, clean and quiet, with native ambience and an al fresco top-floor restaurant that has views across the bay. Fan or a/c rooms, all with private bathroom. 2

Eating and nightlife

There are a handful of exceptionally good **restaurants** in Puerto Princesa. *Ka Lui Restaurant*, at 369 Rizal Ave almost opposite the *Badjao Inn*, is a pretty bamboo restaurant where you take your shoes off before you step inside. The daily set meals are built around either seafood or meat, and most come with a good salad and a small portion of fresh, raw seaweed. There's also an à la carte menu featuring sweet-and-sour *mameng* (wrasse) or spicy squid and grilled prawns. The *Badjao Inn Seafront Restaurant* is a classy but informal native-style restaurant on the shore about 5km south of Rizal Avenue off Abueg Road, reached on foot across a short, dainty bamboo bridge through mangroves. It's a little more expensive than *Ka Lui's*; expect to pay about P500 a head for fresh, wonderfully tasty grilled seafood. If you're here in the evening, getting transport back to the centre can be tricky, so you might want to arrive by tricycle and pay the driver P100 to take you out there, wait while you eat and then take you back.

The area has a community of Vietnamese refugees, and a few 24-hour Vietnamese noodle shops, known locally as *chaolaongan*, operate near the market. If you'd prefer to eat at a restaurant, try the *Pho Vietnamese* on Rizal Avenue, opposite the airport, for cheap baguette sandwiches, vegetarian dishes and seafood. There's another excellent Vietnamese restaurant twenty minutes north of town by tricycle in barangay Santa Lpourdes; *Vietville Restaurant* serves authentic Vietnamese cuisine prepared by expat Vietnamese who live in nearby Vietville, a community established by the Philippine authorities for boat people who fled the communist government in Hanoi during the 1970s.

Nightlife in Puerto Princesa is limited to a few convivial and quiet bars at places such as *Ka Lui's*, *Casa Linda Inn* and *Badjao Inn*. *Kinabuchs Grill and Bar* at 348 Rizal Ave is a large bamboo place with pool tables, a lively bar and loud music.

Honda Bay

Picturesque **Honda Bay** sits 10km north of Puerto Princesa by road and makes a good day-trip, though there's the option to stay overnight. There are seven islands in the bay, including **Snake Island**, with a good reef for snorkelling, and **Starfish Island**, which has a rustic restaurant where the seafood, when it's still available, is as fresh as it comes. Look out for **Bat Island**: in the late afternoon, scores of bats leave here on their nocturnal hunting trips.

Any jeepney or bus going north from Puerto Princesa will take you to Honda Bay. You'll need to get off at **Santa Lourdes wharf** (this may involve a tricycle ride from where the bus or jeepney leaves you) and sign in at the little tourist office and book a banca. A boat will cost anything from P200 to P500 depending on which island you plan to visit and for how long. Some islands ask visitors to pay a fee (P20). On Starfish Island, the **Starfish Sandbar Resort** has rustic huts that sleep four (P500–800), but remember to bring your own tinned food because the small restaurant often runs out. On nearby Meara Marina Island is a small resort that claims to be the only island resort in Honda Bay without entrance fees. There are cottages (3) on the beach, and you can book in Puerto Princesa at **Trattoria Inn**, on Rizal Avenue.

The Underground River

The **Underground River**, or to give it its proper name, St Paul's Subterranean National Park, is the sight most visitors to Palawan want to see. The longest underground river in the world, it meanders for more than 8km beneath the surface, passing a bewildering array of stalactites, stalagmites, caverns, chambers and pools, the formations made even more eerie on your ride through by the shadows cast by the boatman's kerosene lamp (trips daily 7am–5pm).

The park is some way north of Puerto Princesa – more than two hours by road and another twenty minutes by banca. Buses and jeepneys going north from Puerto Princesa pass through Sabang, the jumping-off point for the Underground River. You can also club together and hire your own jeepney for the three-hour trip (about P1000) and then catch a private banca or wait until 1pm for the daily resort boat that leaves from Sabang's pier. At the Visitors Assistance Centre in Sabang, close to the pier, you pay a P150 per person to enter the cave, plus another P400–500 for four passengers in the boat. While you're at the visitors' centre, look out for the famous resident monitor lizards (bayawak) that are tame enough to take food from your hand. Sabang has beaches stretching either side where there are a few simple **places to stay**. The best of these is the quiet, idyllic **Mary's Beach Resort** (❷–❸) a ten-minute walk north of the pier along Sabang Beach,with no-frills cottages right on the sand.

Port Barton

On the northwest coast of Palawan, roughly halfway between Puerto Princesa and El Nido, **Port Barton** has become something of a travellers' rest stop. There are several white-sand islands in the bay and Port Barton itself has a short stretch of beach that is home to half-a-dozen resorts. **Buses** and **jeepneys** from Puerto Princesa arrive on Rizal Street, very close to the beach and the town centre. **Bancas** from destinations along the coast, including Sabang, Taytay, El Nido and San Vicente, arrive right on the main beach.

The best-value **accommodation** is *Swissippini Lodge and Resort* (☎02/365 2344; ❷), right on the beach, a short walk from Rizal Street. The resort has big A-frame cottages, all with balconies and private bathrooms, and also offers Internet access. Close by, *Princesa Michaella's* (❷) offers basic, fan-cooled huts on the beach. Also on the beach, *Greenview Resort* (❷) and *El Dorado Sunset Resort* (❸) both have fan cottages on the shore, all with private bathrooms and verandas.

San Vicente

About 15km north along a rough coastal road from Port Barton is the sleepy fishing village of **SAN VICENTE**, which has a market and a pier where bancas can be chartered. San Vicente isn't a tourist destination in itself, but around it there are some marvellous beaches, including, about 5km south of the village, **Long Beach**, an undeveloped fourteen-kilometre stretch of sand that ranks as one of the most extraordinary beaches in the country – it's so long you can see both ends only on a brilliantly clear day. A few kilometres north of San Vicente, a quiet and charming resort right on a dazzling white crescent of sand, *Caparii Dive Camp* (☎0916/824 1252; ❻) is an idyllic, laid-back sort of place, with few visitors except those who know it and return regularly. To get to *Caparii* or Long Beach, take a motorcycle ride there from San Vicente's market, near the pier (P50).

Bacuit archipelago and El Nido

In the far northwest of Palawan is the small coastal town of **EL NIDO**, departure point for trips to the many islands of the **BACUIT ARCHIPELAGO**. This is limestone-island country, with spectacular formations rising from the sea everywhere you look. These iconic karst cliffs with their fearsomely jagged rocky outcrops are believed to have been formed sixty million years ago, emerging from the sea as a result of India colliding with mainland Asia. As soon as the cliffs emerged, weathering and erosion started working on them to form deep crevices, caves, underground rivers and sinkholes. The area's beauty has not gone unnoticed by developers, who have established a number of exclusive and expensive resorts on some of the islands. If US$200 a night for a taste of corporate-style paradise is too much for you, then you can stay in rustic El Nido itself – where electricity cuts off at midnight – and island-hop by day.

Buses and jeepneys from Port Barton arrive in El Nido along Rizal Street the town's main thoroughfare. The closest **airport** is El Nido, served by three flights a week by SEAIR from Manila via Busuanga. From here it's a straightforward jeepney or tricycle ride into town.

The **tourist office** on Calle Real Street (daily 8am–6pm), near the town hall one block inland from the beach, is one of the best in the country, with useful hand-drawn maps of the area, a list of accommodation and information on trips and activities. Another good place to get up-to-date local information is the El Nido Boutique & Art Shop in Palmera Street.

It's easy to walk from Rizal Street to all the town's **accommodation**, of which there's no shortage, most of it budget. Options on the beach include *New Bayview Inn* (❶), which has simple fan cottages with bathroom and veranda, and *Tandikan Cottages* (❶) with fan cottages in a pretty garden leading back from the beach and a quaint little restaurant offering simple food. Roughly in the middle of the beach, *Marina Garden Beach Resort* (❷) has spacious, neatly furnished cottages with balcony and private bathroom. At the northern end of town on the shore is *Lally and Abett Beach Cottages* (❸), where the cottages, many of which face the sea, have balconies where you can sit and watch the world go by. There's also a good restaurant.

The Calamian Islands

A great area for island-hopping and diving, the beautiful **Calamian Islands** off the northern edge of mainland Palawan number a few hundred, the largest of which is **Busuanga**, followed in size by **Culion** and **Coron** islands.

Access to the Calamian Islands is through the rickety little fishing community of **CORON TOWN**, which confusingly is on Busuanga, not Coron. The presence of several Japanese World War II wrecks in the bays near Coron Town has led to an increase in the number of scuba divers making a pilgrimage to the area. There is no beach in the town and most accommodation is geared towards divers. To find your own patch of sand you can hire a banca and nip off for a day, or longer, to the island of your choice.

The precipitous limestone cliffs of **Coron Island**, twenty minutes by boat from Coron Town, are spectacular. It's only when you get close to them in a banca that they reveal dozens of perfect little coves, hidden in the folds of the mountains. Tribes, including the Tagbanua, still live in the interior, where a short, steep climb takes you to the island's volcanic **Cayangan Lake**, a great place to swim and one of the area's favourite dive sites. You could spend a lifetime on Coron and still not get to see every hot spring, hidden lake or pristine cove. South of Coron Town is the large island of **Culion**, home to a former leper colony and a fascinating **museum** (Mon–Sat 10am–5pm; P25) detailing the colony's history.

From Coron Town, you can also catch a bus or jeepney to take you west along the **south Busuanga coast** to the villages of Concepcion, Salvacion and Old Busuanga, where there are a number of resorts, and piers with bancas for hire.

Practicalities

SEAIR and Asian Spirit both have regular **flights** to Busuanga. The airport is half an hour by jeepney (P100) from Coron Town. WG&A and Sulpicio Lines have a weekly sailing from Manila to Coron Town, and a third ferry, the smaller MV Salve Juliana makes the trip twice a week; both **ferries** arrive at the pier east of Coron Town, from where it's a short tricycle ride into town. The WG&A ticket office (☎0919/540 1695) is a one-kilometre tricycle ride along the National Highway east out of town. The ticket office for the MV Salve Juliana is also near here.

The centre of Coron Town is huddled around the town pier, where you can hire bancas for island trips; most of the other tourist facilities are no more than a short walk or tricycle ride away. Overlooking the pier is Bayside Divers Lodge, a good place to get advice from staff on where to go and what to see. On the ground floor of Bayside you'll find ABC Divers, one of a dozen or so dive outfits in town. Dive Right is near L&M Pe Lodge and Discovery Divers lies a short walk out of town heading back towards the airport. West of Bayside (a left turn at the junction) are more dive shops and, at the next junction, Swagman Travel. Next to that is a Western Union office and adjacent to that, Pascual Video, which has **Internet** access.

Accommodation and eating

Most of the **accommodation** on Busuanga is around the pier in Coron Town and can be noisy. The locals perform some terrible karaoke at night and the cockerels start their dawn chorus well before dawn. If you want quieter accommodation you'll have to stay out of town, which means taking a tricycle back and forth to the pier when you dive or go island hopping. Around Busuanga there are a number of pricey resorts, most of them on their own private island. There's no regular transport to most of these places, so you'll generally need to book in advance and arrange to be met at the airport.

Food in Coron Town is largely limited to whatever happens to be available at the market that day. *Bayside Divers Lodge* serves various noodle dishes and sandwiches and *L&M Pe Lodge* has grilled fish, fried chicken and some good curries. **Nightlife** is limited to tall stories among divers in a few bars. The bar at *L&M Pe Lodge* is a popular hangout after a day's diving, as is the bar at *Bayside*.

Coron Town

Bayside Divers Lodge ☎02/371 9928 or 02/372 6031. A good landmark, right on the water's edge overlooking the pier. It has spartan but clean doubles and upstairs there's a comfortable restaurant with marvellous views across the bay to the jungle-covered pinnacles of Coron Island. ❸–❹

Coral Lodge An old house on the western edge of town offering the cheapest accommodation in the area, with shared facilities. Rooms are basic, but good value for the low price. ❶

Darayonan Lodge ☎02/821 0637 or 02/823 2752. Rambling bamboo house that has seven twin rooms nicely furnished in native style. On the eastern edge of town, 10 minutes on foot from the pier. ❸–❹

Kalamayan Inn☎02/633 4701 in Manila. Two deluxe rooms downstairs and four standard rooms upstairs (US$20 for two) with shared bath. Prices include breakfast. Try to choose an inside room away from the road, because the tricycles start revving their engines early. A little beyond the pier on the left. ❸–❺

KokusNuss resort The first accommodation as you approach Coron Town from the airport, on the left-hand side about 1km before the town. *KokosNuss* has simple but comfortable and quiet bungalows built around a pleasant garden and a native-style restaurant. ❸–❺

L&M Pe Lodge Simple, small rooms and a popular bar and restaurant where divers gather in the evening to swap stories. Also right on the pier. ❸–❹

Sea Breeze Lodging House Quiet location down a track leading off the main road to the right. These concrete huts are basic but clean and have two double beds and private shower and toilet. This area is also relatively quiet because it is away from the activity of the main road and the pier. ③

Village Lodge The cleanest and quietest rooms in Coron. There are three double rooms with private bathroom and two double rooms sharing a common bathroom. Breakfast in the pleasant restaurant is included. On the eastern edge of town, a 10min walk from the pier. ③–⑤

Elsewhere in the Calamians

Club Paradise ⓣ02/838 4956 to 4960, ⓦwww.clubparadisepalawan.com. Rather upmarket resort on Dimakya Island, a fifteen-minute banca ride off the northern coast of Busuanga. It's a slick, German-owned place with a/c cottages a stone's throw from the sea, various water sports and diving. ⑨

Coral Bay Marine Reserve ⓣ02/371 9928 or 02/372 6031, ⓦwww.coralbay.com.ph. Marvelously rustic getaway on Popototan Island, one hour by banca from Coron Town at the western end of Coron Bay. There are rarely more than a few guests on Popototan and the owners deliberately keep it that way so tranquillity is guaranteed. The coral reef offshore is breathtaking: snorkel the length of it and you'll come face to face with puffer fish, batfish and giant grouper. ⑥

Dive Link ⓣ02/371 9928 or 02/372 6031, ⓦwww.divelink.com.ph. A quiet resort ten minutes from Coron Town by banca on Uson Island, owned by the same people who own *Bayside Divers Lodge* and *Coral Bay Marine Reserve*. Accommodation is in quaint little wooden cottages, each with private shower a balcony. ⑧

Southern Palawan

A journey through **southern Palawan** represents one of the last great travel challenges in the Philippines. Much of the area is sparsely populated, with limited accommodation and nothing in the way of dependable transport, communications or electricity. About the only noted tourist attraction in the southern half of Palawan are the **Tabon Caves**, 100km southwest of Puerto Princesa in **Quezon** and one of the country's most significant archeological sites. A number of hotels and travel agents in Puerto Princesa organize day-trips to the caves for about US$40 per person. Alternatively, you can catch a bus or jeepney from Puerto Princesa to Quezon wharf (5hr), where you can hire a banca for P500 for the thirty-minute ride to the caves and back. There are actually more than two hundred caves in the area, but only three are open to visitors. (daily 9am–4pm; P15). The main entrance to the caves, measuring 18m high and 16m wide, overlooks a beautiful bay studded with white-sand beach islands. It was inside these caves during the 1960s that archeologists discovered a fragment of the skull of **"Tabon Man"**, dated to 47,000 years ago. Crude tools dating back some 22,000 years were unearthed, along with fossils and a large quantity of Chinese pottery. Most of these items have been transferred to the National Museum in Manila for preservation, though some artefacts are on display in the caves. The best **place to stay** close to the caves is the *Tabon Village Resort* (①) in the village of **Tabon**, which as simple cottage-style accommodation with fan and private bathrooms, plus a good restaurant.

Continuing south down the west coast by bus or jeepney brings you to the village of **Rizal**, from where the road crosses the island west to east, to **Batarza**, one of the few places with recognized accommodation in the form of the *Bonbon Lodging House* (③). The journey north takes you back to Puerto Princesa via **Brooke's Point**, a trading post, 25km from Mount Matalingahan, Palawan's highest peak at 2086m. Further north between Narra and Aborlan there are some quiet resorts on **Tigman Beach**. From Aborlan, it's 69km back to Puerto Princesa.

One of the area's greatest treasures is in the Central Sulu Sea far offshore: **Tubbataha Reef Marine Park** is the country's largest coral reef, offering some of the most thrilling scuba diving in the world.

Tubbataha Reef Marine Park

Located in the middle of the Central Sulu Sea, 181km southeast of Puerto Princesa, **Tubbataha Reef Marine Park** was inscribed on the World Heritage List in

1993. It has become a magnet for **scuba divers**, who sail to it every year during high season (March to June) on liveaboard dive boats operating mostly out of Puerto Princesa. Dive operators in Manila can arrange packages, which cost around US$1200 for one week, including flights to Puerto, all food and up to five dives a day. The reef is one of the best in the world, with sightings of sharks and manta rays a daily occurrence. But the visits of around two thousand divers annually, and the trade in coral handicrafts has taken its toll. Sixty percent of Filipinos' animal protein comes from fish, and fishermen rely on reefs such as this for their livelihood and as nurseries that regenerate stocks, but overfishing continues. Repeated anchoring on the fragile coral, and dynamite fishing – which literally blasts fish in the water – have both added to the damage at Tubbataha, which is why the government is zealously protecting it, albeit with a meagre budget and only a small number of overworked rangers.

Independent travel to Tubbataha is impossible and even licensed dive boats need a permit. For details of liveaboards visiting the reef, try ABC Divers in Coron Town, or any of the big dive outfits in Manila, including Asia Divers (☎02/834 2974); Aquaventure (☎02/899 2831); Dive Buddies (☎02/899 7388); Ocean Colors (☎02/890 4142); and Scuba World (☎02/895 3551).

8.8

Mindanao

The signals **Mindanao** sends to the rest of the Philippines and the rest of the world, are nothing if not mixed. This massive island at the foot of the archipelago is in many ways the cultural and artistic heart of the country, a place where tribalism and capitalism clash head on, and where refugees from Manila's pollution have fled in search of cleaner air and greener pastures. This has led to something of a cultural and economic boom in cities such as **Davao**, Mindanao's de facto capital and gateway to the region.

Mindanao is also a troubled island, with various indigenous Islamic or Moro groups agitating, sometimes violently, for autonomy (see box below). Some parts of the island are considered unsafe for tourists (Cotabato City and the region west of Marawi, and the far southwest, including Zamboanga City and the Sulu Archipelago) and are not covered here. The northern half of Mindanao, however, remains peaceful and includes terrific destinations such as **Siargao Island** and the volcanic island of **Camiguin**, which can also be easily reached by bus and ferry from the busy city of **Cagayan de Oro** on Mindanao's north coast.

Getting **to Mindanao** is easy: PAL has daily **flights** from Manila to Davao, Cagayan de Oro and General Santos and from Cebu City to Davao. Cebu Pacific also flies from Manila to Davao and Cagayan de Oro, while SEAIR and Asian Spirit fly Cebu City to Siargao Island. WG&A and Negros Navigation **ferries** ply the long route from Manila (at least 36hr), serving Davao, Cagayan de Oro, General Santos and Surigao.

The Mindanao problem

Mindanao has been a nagging thorn in the side of successive governments, with repeated attempts by the island's Muslims to break away from the governance of Manila and establish their own autonomous regions on the island. Mindanao's Muslims (or Moro) are seeking self-determination from majority Christian Filipinos, while the indigenous Lumad peoples assert rights to their traditional lands.

The **Moro National Liberation Front** (MNLF) resorted to a war for independence in the 1970s. Meanwhile, a communist-led rebellion spread from the northern Philippines to Mindanao, drawing many majority Filipinos, particularly among the rural poor, and some Lumads into the New People's Army (NPA). In the early 1990s, one disaffected group of flighters left the MNLF and formed **Abu Sayyaf** ("Bearer of the Sword"), whose centre of operations is largely Basilan Island, part of the Sulu Archipelago off Mindanao's south coast. The group is said to have ties to a number of Islamic fundamentalist organizations around the world, inclduding al-Qaeda.

In 1996, the Philippine Government signed a peace pact with the MNLF granting a certain degree of autonomy to four provinces on condition of a plebiscite. But this peace is by no means final or universal, and splinter groups are still engaged in conflict.

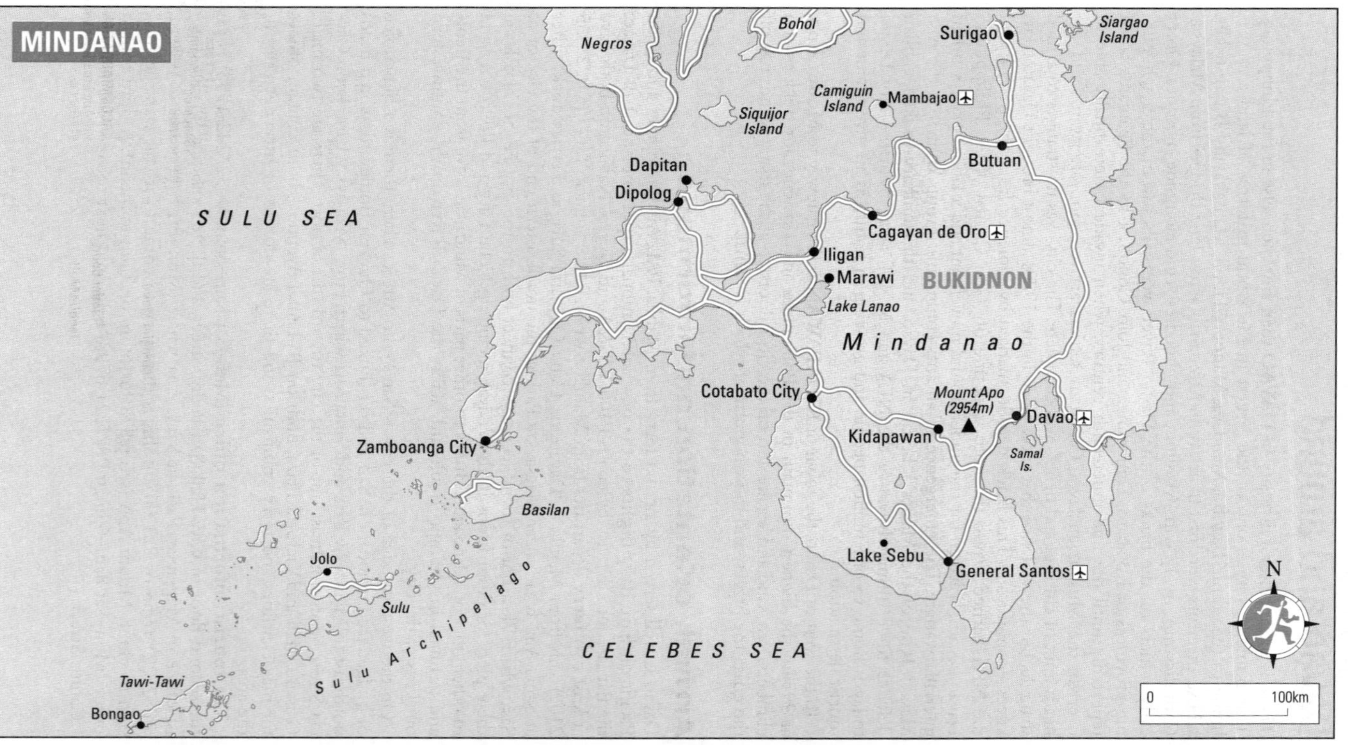
MINDANAO
SULU SEA
CELEBES SEA
Negros
Bohol
Siquijor Island
Camiguin Island
Mambajao
Siargao Island
Surigao
Butuan
Dapitan
Dipolog
Cagayan de Oro
Iligan
Marawi
Lake Lanao
BUKIDNON
Mindanao
Cotabato City
Mount Apo (2954m)
Kidapawan
Davao
Samal Is.
Lake Sebu
General Santos
Zamboanga City
Basilan
Jolo
Sulu
Sulu Archipelago
Tawi-Tawi
Bongao
N
0
100km

Davao and around

There is more cultural diversity in **DAVAO** than anywhere else in the Philippines. This immense city – one of the largest in the world in terms of land area – is home to the ethnic Bagobo, Mandaya, Manobo, Tiboli, Mansaka and B'laan tribes, whose ancestors were first to arrive in Mindanao across land bridges from Malaysia. Catholics mix freely with Muslims, and churches stand alongside mosques. Other early settlers on the banks of the Davao River were tribes from the neighbouring provinces of Kotabato, Zamboanga and Jolo. Conquest by the Spaniards failed repeatedly until the mid-nineteenth century, when invaders were finally able to overrun the Muslim enclaves. Christian settlers arrived soon afterwards and the heady mix of cultures and beliefs was complete. The city was no stranger to armed struggle, but the violence that took place in the 1980s almost brought Davao to its knees economically. This black decade, marked by violence from the MNLF and the NPA, earned Davao the notorious title of "Gun Capital of the Philippines." Davao became a haven for the underground movement and a laboratory for urban guerrilla warfare. The emergence of an anti-communist group known as the Alsa Masa ("Rise of the Masses") began in Davao, and this military-backed civilian defence force ultimately drove the NPA and MNLF away from the city. Davao today is home to one million people and growing in stature as an investment and tourist destination.

To the west of Davao, the town of **KIDAPAWAN** is the gateway to **Mount Apo**, at 2954m the highest mountain in the Philippines and a magnet for trekkers and climbers. Sun, sand and sea are also on the city's doorstep at the many islands just off the coast, the biggest and most popular of which is Samal.

Arrival, orientation and information

Davao is well served by air and ferry from Manila. PAL, Air Philippines and Cebu Pacific all have daily **flights** to the new international airport, northeast of Davao; the flat fare into the city by taxi is P100. WG&A and Negros Navigation both have at least two **ferry** departures from Manila a week, while Sulpicio Lines (☎082/235 2107) sails from Manila to Davao via Cebu City and Surigao. Ferries dock either at Santa Ana wharf, near Magsaysay Park at the northeastern end of the city, or at Sasa wharf, 7km out of town. Jeepneys connect both to the city. Ferries also leave these piers for destinations in the Visayas, including Cebu City and Iloilo City, and to other cities on Mindanao. **Buses** to other parts of Mindanao leave from the Ecoland terminal in Quimpo Boulevard, across the Davao River on the southwestern outskirts of the city.

On the western edge of the city is San Pedro Street, where there is a big choice of budget accommodation. San Pedro is linked to Quezon Boulevard, which heads northeast to Magsaysay Park and Santa Ana wharf. From Magsaysay Park, Leon Garcia Street heads northeast out of the city towards the airport. There are two malls, Gaisano Mall and Victoria Plaza, both on JP Laurel Avenue – both contain offices for major airlines and ferry companies, and there are dozens of **Internet** cafés in the area.

The **tourist information office** (Mon–Sat 8am–6pm; ☎082/222 1956) is on the second floor of City Hall, San Pedro Street, and there's another, smaller tourist office in Magsaysay Park, at Santa Ana wharf (Mon–Fri 8am–noon & 1–5pm; ☎082/221 6955 or 221 0070); this is the office to come to if you want permission to climb Mount Apo (see p.878 for more on the mountain). A third tourist office (Mon–Sat 8am–6pm; ☎082/221 6798) is located next to *Apo View Hotel* in J Camus Street.

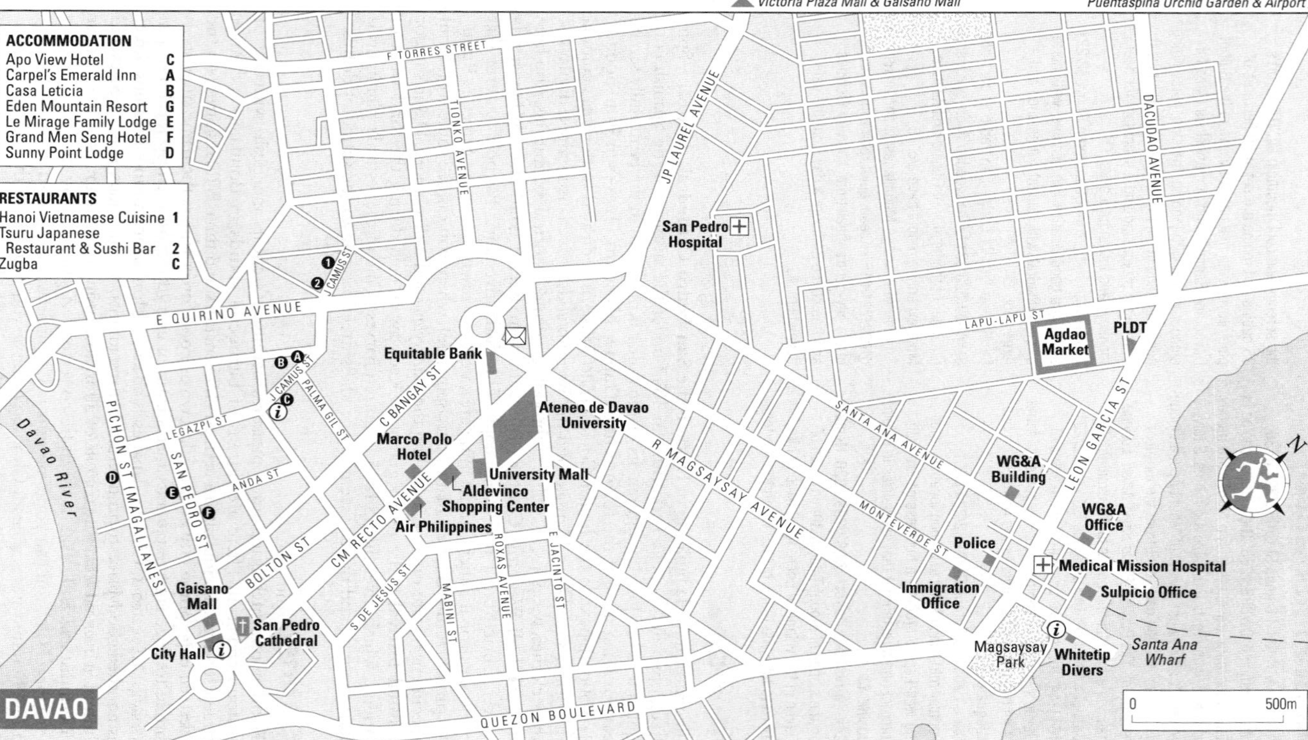
Victoria Plaza Mall & Gaisano Mall
Puentaspina Orchid Garden & Airport
Sasa Wharf, Dabaw Museum & T'Boli Weaving Center
Samal
G & Ecoland Bus Terminal
ACCOMMODATION
Apo View Hotel C
Carpel's Emerald Inn A
Casa Leticia B
Eden Mountain Resort G
Le Mirage Family Lodge E
Grand Men Seng Hotel F
Sunny Point Lodge D
RESTAURANTS
Hanoi Vietnamese Cuisine 1
Tsuru Japanese Restaurant & Sushi Bar 2
Zugba C
F TORRES STREET
TIONKO AVENUE
JP LAUREL AVENUE
DACUDAO AVENUE
San Pedro Hospital
J CAMUS ST
E QUIRINO AVENUE
LAPU-LAPU ST
Agdao Market
PLDT
Equitable Bank
PALMA GIL ST
C BANGAY ST
Ateneo de Davao University
LEGAZPI ST
SANTA ANA AVENUE
LEON GARCIA ST
Davao River
PICHON ST (MAGALLANES)
SAN PEDRO ST
ANDA ST
Marco Polo Hotel
University Mall
Aldevinco Shopping Center
Air Philippines
R MAGSAYSAY AVENUE
WG&A Building
WG&A Office
MONTEVERDE ST
Police
Medical Mission Hospital
Sulpicio Office
Immigration Office
BOLTON ST
CM RECTO AVENUE
S DE JESUS ST
MABINI ST
ROXAS AVENUE
E JACINTO ST
Gaisano Mall
San Pedro Cathedral
City Hall
Magsaysay Park
Whitetip Divers
Santa Ana Wharf
N
0
500m
DAVAO
QUEZON BOULEVARD

Accommodation

Apo View Hotel J Camus St ☎082/221 6430; Manila office ☎02/893 1288. The hotel of choice in Davao for many travellers with a bit of extra money to spend, with big, comfortable a/c rooms. Sadly, you don't always get a view of Mount Apo, although on a clear day you can see it from the top-floor restaurant. The Pagasa *Piano Bar & Music Lounge* has some entertaining bands in the evening. ❻

Carpel's Emerald Inn J Camus Extn ☎082/221 1641-44. This hotel's position close to some of Davao's biggest shopping malls accounts for some of its popularity. The facilities are rudimentary but adequate. ❹

Casa Leticia J Camus St ☎082/224 0501. Popular mid-range hotel in a good location, offering well-kept a/c rooms, a business centre with Internet and a restaurant that specializes in Filipino cusine. ❹

Eden Mountain Resort ☎082/299 1020. Nestled on the slopes of Mount Talamo 30min south of Davao in the village of Eden. You'll have to hire a taxi to take you there, but it's worth the trip for the serenity and cool mountain air. The resort's 35 cabins and rooms are set in 80 hectares of pine groves with magnificent views of the Gulf of Davao and Samal Island. A marvellous place for outdoor lovers, with jogging, trekking, horse riding, and swimming in cool waterfalls. Kids will love it – there's a playground and a sanctuary for deer, monkeys and Indian peacocks. ❹

Grand Men Seng Hotel San Pedro St ☎082/221 9040. In a good location five minutes' walk north of the cathedral, with decent coffee shop and a large pool. ❷

Le Mirage Family Lodge San Pedro St cnr Anda St ☎082/226 3811. The wooden floors are a small reminder of the heyday of Filipino architecture. More expensive rooms have a/c. ❶

Sunny Point Lodge Magallanes St cnr Legaspi St ☎082/221 0155. Clean, quiet rooms in the thick of the city-centre maelstrom. Laundry facilities and free coffee 24 hours a day from the café downstairs. ❷

The City

The most notable building in Davao is the **San Pedro Cathedral** (daily 6am–8pm; free), opposite Osmeña Park. Built in 1847 under the auspices of the Spanish conquistador Don José Uyanguren, its original altar is preserved in the beautifully serene eastern wing. East of the town centre, **Dabaw Museum** (Tues–Sun 9am–noon & 1–5.30pm), next to the *Insular Century Hotel Davao*, is dedicated to the area's cultural minorities such as the Mansaka and the Bogobo and has well-maintained displays of their clothes, weapons, as well as anthropological and historical exhibitions. Also here is the **T'boli Weaving Center** (daily 9am-6pm; free), a good place to buy handwoven fabric from T'boli tribespeople. This distinctive fabric has bold patterns that symbolize tribal beliefs. In the same area, north of town on Bolcan Street, is **Puentaspina Orchid Garden** (daily 9am–8pm; free), where you can see some wonderful specimens of rare orchids, including the *ylang-ylang* and *waling-waling*. Davao's major **annual festival** is the mardi gras-style Kadayawan, held during the third week of August, which gives thanks for a bountiful harvest. One of the festival's highlights is horsefighting and there is seemingly endless street dancing to the sound of drums.

Eating

Food is one of Davao's great pleasures because it's cheap and fresh, with lots of seafood and fruit. There are dozens of **barbecue stands** in Bonifacio and Anda streets serving delicious flame-cooked chicken, pork and tuna. F Torres Street on the western edge of the city centre is known as Food Street and, as the name suggests, is home to dozens of restaurants specializing in everything from cheap local *merienda* (snacks) to seafood, Chinese, Japanese and even Mongolian cuisine. J Camus Street is another good place to find affordable restaurants; try the crabs, eels, noodles and hotpot at *Hanoi Vietnamese Cuisine* or affordable sushi and tempura at *Tsuru Japanese Restaurant and Sushi Bar*. In the al fresco seafood *Zugba restaurant* (5–11pm only) at *Apo View Hotel*, you can gorge on tuna jaw, king prawn and grilled *lapu-lapu* for only a few hundred pesos a head. Choose whatever you fancy from the display and the waiter will give you options on how it can be cooked.

Davao is the **durian** capital of the Philippines. The bright green fruit has a pungent smell that has been described as a combination of old cheese, turpentine and onion, but don't let the slightly noxious perfume put you off – aficionados say the durian's tender white flesh has a taste suggestive of almonds, sherry, custard and ice cream. Durian (along with other cheap fresh fruit) can be found at the roadside stands on Anda and Rizal streets. In Davao, it's also used in durian shakes, durian pie and durian ice cream, and, at the *Blugre Cafe*, which has branches in most malls, including Victoria Plaza on JP Laureal Avenue, you can even sample a durian frappuccino.

Listings

Airlines Air Philippines has a ticket office on CM Recto St, opposite the *Marco Polo Hotel* (☎082/224 6977); Cebu Pacific has one at Summit World on the second floor of Victoria Plaza Mall at the northern end of JP Laurel Ave (☎082/224 0960).
Banks and exchange Many are gathered in the area around University Mall, Roxas Ave. Equitable Bank is near the post office at the northern end of Roxas Ave.
Diving Whitetip Divers has a shop at PPA Building, Santa Ana wharf (☎082/227 0234), a good place to stop for information about scuba diving in the area.
Ferry offices The main WG&A ticket office is at the eastern end of Santa Ana Ave (☎ 082/221 1390); the Sulpicio Lines office is 125m directly south.
Hospitals The city's major hospital is the Davao Doctors' Hospital (☎ 082/224 0616) on the southwest edge of the city on E Quirino Ave. In Guerrero St in the city centre, you'll find San Pedro Hospital (☎082/224 0616).
Immigration office On the third floor of the CAM Building on Monteverde Ave (☎082/227 4783).
Internet access There are dozens of Internet cafés on the main road outside Victoria Plaza Mall.
Phones PLDT has an office on CM Recto Ave where you can place long-distance calls.
Police The main Philippine National Police office is known as Camp Catitipan and is on Santa Ana Ave (☎082/232 5215).
Post The main post office is on Roxas Ave, close to the junction with Magsaysay Ave.
Shopping For souvenirs and handicrafts, go to the Aldevinco Shopping Center opposite the *Marco Polo Hotel* on CM Recto Street. It's a maze of small shops selling tribal artefacts and cheap batik clothes from the Philippines, Indonesia and Thailand. With a little hard bargaining, you can grab a sarong for P100.

Samal Island and Talikud Island

Samal Island and the smaller island of **Talikud**, lie a stone's throw southeast of Davao in the Gulf of Davao, across the narrow Pakiputan Strait. You can get to Samal Island by hopping on a public banca from Sasa wharf (1hr; P20). Jeepneys marked "Sasa" will take you to within spitting distance of the boat station. You can also get a more expensive ferry (P150) from the pier at the *Insular Century Hotel Davao*, just off JP Cabaguio Avenue, on the road to the airport. Boats for Talikud leave every morning at 6am, 7am and 9am (P30) from Santa Ana wharf in Davao.

Pearl farms once dotted Samal, but these days the main temptation for wealthy tourists are the classy resorts on the west coast. On the northwestern coast, facing Davao, there are some very average beaches and half a dozen resorts, all along the same stretch of sand, offering acceptable rooms and simple food. *Paradise Island Resort* (❸) can get busy at weekends, but has good clean doubles with private shower. Next door are *Costa Marina* (❹) and *Blue Waters* (❸). Off the southwest coast of Samal Island across the Talikud Strait, Talikud has a quieter selection of resorts, including the rural but wonderful little *Pacific Little Secret Resort* (☎082/235 1325 or 0917/ 747 7637; ❷), where, presuming you want electricity, you'll have to pay a few hundred pesos on top of the room rate to buy petrol for the generator.

Kidapawan and Mount Apo

About two hours' drive west of Davao, **Kidapawan** sits on the lower slopes of Mount Apo, and is the best starting point for treks to the summit. If you haven't already hired a guide through one of the tourist offices in Davao, you can arrange one here at the City Hall, next to the police station on the north side of the main plaza. All buses arrive at the terminal on the National Highway, opposite the mosque, near to which are a couple of cheap lodgings: the *Highlander* (❶) is behind the mosque, and *Supercool Inn* (❶), is south of the National Highway, in Roxas Street.

Climbing Mount Apo

Mount Apo (2954m) overlooks Davao and lords it over the Philippines as the highest mountain in the country. No wonder it was called Apo, which means "Grandfather of all Mountains." Apo is actually a volcano, but is certified "inactive" and has no recorded eruptions. What it does have is enough flora and fauna to make your head spin: thundering waterfalls, rapids, lakes, geysers, sulphur pillars, primeval trees, endangered plant and animal species and a steaming blue lake. It is the home of the Philippine Eagle, the tiny falconet and the Mount Apo mynah. Then there are exotic ferns, carnivorous pitcher plants and the queen of Philippine orchids, the *waling-waling*. The local tribes, the Bagobos, believe the gods Apo and Mandaragan inhabit its upper slopes; they revere it as a sacred mountain, call it Sandawa or "Mountain of Sulphur".

Recently, however, Mount Apo has become something of an environmental hot potato and the government is trying to dissuade people from climbing it because of the **damage** they have done to trails and the litter they have left behind. Small groups of climbers with special interests, such as botany or photography, will still be allowed, but large groups could find they get turned back. The situation is uncertain, but the best advice is that visitors go to the tourist information centre in Magsaysay Park (see p.874) to plead their case. Senior Davao tourism officials are based at this office and if anyone can help, they can. If you have a well-prepared case and some documentation to back it up (a letter from your university or employer explaining why you would like to climb Apo, for instance), there's a good chance you'll get **permission**.

Don't attempt Mount Apo alone: hire a guide from one of the tourist offices in Davao or from the City Hall in Kidapawan. Experienced Apo climbers advise allowing four or five days for the climb, averaging four hours of trekking a day, with an average load of forty pounds to supply you with food and shelter for four days in extreme weather. Towards the peak, temperatures are as low as 5°C, so don't go without a good sleeping bag, warm clothes and a tent. It's a tough trek, but well worth it. The trail is lined with flowers, and on the first day you should reach **Mainit Hot Spring**, where you can take a refreshing dip. Day two brings you to the dramatic **Lake Venado**, which looks like a scene from the Jurassic Age, with giant trees, vines and a fine fog floating above the lake itself. At the end of the third day you can make camp below the summit and rise at 5am to get to the top in time for sunrise. The views are nothing short of spectacular. This is the highest point in the Philippines, with the whole of Mindanao spread out before you.

Philippine Eagle Foundation

The **Philippine Eagle Foundation** (daily 8am–5pm; P12; ☎082/224 3021), just outside Davao in Malagos, is known for its excellent work breeding the Philippine Eagle, or monkey-eating eagle, a majestic beast with a fearsome beak and two-metre wingspan. The Philippine Eagle (*Pithecophaga jeffryi*) is extremely elusive and its existence was documented only in 1896, a century after most other bird species. That first known sighting was by the intrepid British bird collector John Whitehead in Samar, who gave the eagle its Latin name jeffryi after his father, Jeffrey, who financed his expedition. Sadly, the eagle is now officially on the endangered species list, with only one hundred to three hundred believed to be living in the wilds of Mindanao, Samar and Leyte. But there is hope: the Foundation has a captive breeding programme that focuses on developing a viable gene pool for the species by propagating the eagles in captivity. The goal is to reintroduce the eagles back into their natural habitat. Two eagles, named Pag-Asa (Hope) and Pagkakaisa (Unity) were bred in 1992.

To get to the Foundation, take a **bus** to Calinan (45min) from the Annil transport terminal next to Ateneo de Davao University, from where it's a short tricycle ride.

General Santos and Lake Sebu

Southwest of Davao on Sarangani Bay, **GENERAL SANTOS** – or "Gensan" – has the distinction of being the Philippines' southernmost city, which for many travellers means it's one bus journey too far. You can reach General Santos by air from Manila and Cebu City or by bus on the Davao–Gensan Highway (3hr). Accommodation in the town is nothing to write home about. Decent budget options include *Pension Eleona* (❷) at the junction of Quirino Avenue and Lapu-Lapu Street, and *Anahaw Village Inn* (❷) on Laurel Avenue, which also has a coffee shop.

It's possible to continue westwards by bus from General Santos to the isolated and beautiful **Lake Sebu** (3hr), on the shores of **T'BOLI**, in an area inhabited by the T'Boli tribe. There's some reasonably good accommodation around Lake Sebu and it's a great place to see T'Boli culture at first hand. The best place to stay is *Punta Isla Lake Resort* (ⓣ083/238 8503; ❸), which sites on a hill with views of the lake and can be reached by tricycle in fifteen minutes from where the buses stop. The choice of rooms includes dorm beds for P100; singles; doubles; and one stand-alone cottage for two people, prettier than the rest and with a lovely veranda. There's a **restaurant** that specializes in *tilapia*, a fish that is caught in the lake.

Cagayan de Oro

CAGAYAN DE ORO on the north coast of Mindanao is the starting point for many travellers for trips to Camiguin, a dazzling little volcanic island off Mindanao's north coast. Cagayan de Oro itself is generally unimpressive, a noisy mish-mash of busy streets and fast-food restaurants, hardly enough to tempt you to stay longer than a day or night before moving on to greener pastures. You'll find few memorable sights, apart from the eighteenth-century **San Augustine Cathedral**, a pretty, off-white stone edifice just south of Gaston Park, with a gold-plated altar and immense stained-glass windows. The **Xavier Museo de Oro** (Tues–Sun 9am–5pm; P20 minimum donation) at Xavier University on Corrales Avenue gives an interesting overview of local culture stretching back thousands of years; there are evocative dioramas of the Spanish period, when gold was discovered in the Cagayan River (hence the "Oro" in Cagayan's name).

If you pass through the eastern suburbs of the city (on the road to Balingoan, for instance), you'll notice the sweet smell of the source of much of Cagayan de Oro's income today: pineapples from enormous plantations inland, mostly owned by Del Monte, which are brought to the suburbs for canning.

Practicalities

Cagayan de Oro is served by daily **flights** from Manila and Cebu City on Air Philippines, PAL, Cebu Pacific and SEAIR, who also fly here from Davao. The airport is 10km outside the city – a taxi ride into Cagayan de Oro will cost about P80. WG&A and Negros Navigation both run regular **ferries** from Manila, Bacolod and Iloilo City, docking at Macabalan Wharf, 5km north of the centre, with regular jeepneys back and forth; a taxi from here into the city costs about P50. All **buses** arrive at the Integrated Bus Terminal on the northeastern outskirts next to Agora Market, from where it's an easy tricycle or jeepney ride into town.

The regional **tourism office** (Mon–Sat 8am–noon & 1–5pm; ☎088/22 727275) is on A Velez Street, a short walk north of the city centre close to the library, and has maps, details of guided tours and lists of accommodation in and around the city, including on Camiguin. There's also a tourism information centre in a more convenient location, close to the *Grand City Hotel* on RN Abejuela Street.

Accommodation and eating

The area around T Neri Street in the south of the city, near Gaston Park, is home to most of the town's budget **accommodation**. *Parkview Hotel* (☎08822/723 223; ③), in a quiet area right next to the park on T Neri Street, is one of the better options, with adequate rooms with air-con or fan. *Sampaguita Inn* (☎08822/722 640; ③) on Borja Street has average rooms with fan and shower, while the *Philtown Hotel* (☎08822/726 295; ⑤) on Velez Street is very clean and in a great location. The best hotel in town, though it's not cheap, is the *Pryce Plaza Hotel* (☎08822/726685–6; ⑧) west of town, at Carmen Hill on the road from the airport.

One of the liveliest places for **food** and drink is *Padi's Point* at the southern end of A Velez Street: it's open until late and fills up with students after 9pm. A short walk south is *Paolo's*, a convivial bistro that offers an incredible range of pasta, pizza and Asian dishes. The most authentic Filipino restaurant is *Bulaluhan sa Cagayan*, across the river, which specializes in grilled seafood served with a steaming hot portion of rice.

Camiguin Island

Sitting in the Mindanao Sea about 20km off the north coast of mainland Mindanao, the pint-sized island of **Camiguin** is one of the country's most appealing tourist spots, offering ivory beaches, iridescent lagoons and undulating scenery. There's no shortage of adventure here either, with reasonable scuba diving and some tremendous trekking and climbing in the rugged interior, especially on volcanic **Mount Hibok-Hibok**. Camiguin also features six other volcanoes, a multitude of hot springs, a submerged cemetery for divers to explore near the coastal town of **Bonbon**, a spring that gushes natural soda water, and 35 resorts, most in the northern half of the island but some on the southwest coast near **Catarman**. Another major tourist draw is the annual **Lanzones Festival**, held in the fourth week of October. Revellers stomp and dance in the streets as a tribute to the humble fruit, one of the island's major sources of income. The festival is one of the liveliest and most welcoming in the country, and this on an island already renowned for the friendliness of its people. It's also a peaceful, almost spiritual island, where residents are proud of their faith. Old Spanish documents indicate that Ferdinand Magellan and Miguel Lopez de Legazpi passed this way in 1521 and 1565 respectively, but it wasn't until 1598 when the first Spanish settlement was established here and the natives – mostly from nearby Surigao – converted to Catholicism.

The beauty of Camiguin is that it doesn't really matter where you stay because you can see all the sights easily from anywhere. The **coastal road** is almost 70km long, making it feasible to circle the island in a day. If you don't want to depend on public transport, consider hiring your own private jeepney or tricycle for the trip. Many resorts also offer motorcycle rental.

Practicalities

Ferries from Balingoan, about 80km northeast of Cagayan de Oro (reached by bus from Cagayan's Integrated Bus Terminal), arrive at Benoni on Camiguin's southeast coast: the Camiguin authorized ticket agent (☎08822/387 4000) in the Negros Navigation Office in Benoni will help you arrange tours, make long-distance telephone calls and book ferry tickets. From here, several jeepneys run every day to **Mambajao**, the bustling little capital on the north coast. If you know where you're going to be staying you can take a tricycle straight to your resort; in many cases, the resort will send a vehicle to meet you.

The other way to get to Camiguin is on the twice-weekly SEAIR **flight** from Cebu City, which lands at the airstrip a few kilometres to the west of Mambajao, from where it's an easy tricycle ride into town or to your resort. The Philippine Rural Reconstruction Movement in Manila (☎02/372 3931, Ⓦwww.prrm.org) runs **homestay tours** to Camiguin: guests stay with locals in old wooden houses and tour the island with their own guide and driver.

Accommodation

Most of the best beach **accommodation** in Camiguin is west of Mambajao on the beaches between the small towns of **Bug-ong** and **Naasag**. The resorts in this area are well prepared for foreign tourists and have lots of information about diving and trekking; resorts near the town of Agoho, a little west of Bug-ong, are popular because it gives quickest access to White Island, a dazzling serpentine ribbon of sand only visible at low tide.

One of the closest resorts to Mambajao is *Jasmine by the Sea* (☎088/387 9015; ❷) in Bug-ong. *Jasmine* is excellent value, with spacious fan cottages on the shore and a restaurant that serves some organic dishes. Next door is *Morning Glory Cottages* (☎088/387 9017; ❷) where the cottages are equally homey, but there's no restaurant. Instead, you can order simple meals from the staff to eat on your veranda. *Paras Beach Resort* (☎088/387 9008 or 387 9081; ❻), 4km beyond Bug-ong in Yumbing, was a private beach house belonging to the Paras family until they decided to add eighteen air-con rooms and open it to the public. It's in a spectacular position on the shore and the staff are efficient organizers of tours. A short walk south along the beach from *Paras* is *Camiguin Beach Club* (☎088/387 9028; ❹), a well-run establishment with solid twin and double beach cottages, most with spacious, shady balconies. There's also a restaurant and a swimming pool.

Siargao Island

Off the northeastern tip of Mindanao lies the little island of **Siargao**, an undeveloped backwater with Boracay-type beaches and dramatic coves and lagoons. It's off the tourist trail and few venture this way, but it won't be long before they do. Siargao has got everything, with a typically tropical coastal landscape of palms trees and dazzling seas, and a verdant hinterland of rustic little barrios and coconut groves. Some of the first tourists here were **surfers**, who discovered a break at Tuason Point that was so good they called it Cloud 9. Kayaking is a great way to explore the area, paddling through mangrove swamps or into hidden coral bays. You can also hire a banca to do some serious **island-hopping**, or rent a motorcycle for the day and tootle up the dusty coastal road to Alegria and Burgos at the island's northernmost tip, visiting beaches that few tourists see.

There are some modest but comfortable seaside resorts around the island's friendly little capital of **GENERAL LUNA**, known as GL. You can base yourself here to tour Siargao itself or grab a boat and head out to Dacas Island, East Bucas Island and Bucas Grande Island, all with superb snorkelling in palm-fringed coves. Bucas Grande is especially striking, with mushroom-shaped limestone rocks, green with foliage, sprouting from its shimmering waters. There's a cove here that leads to a stunning lagoon – and you can swim through a short tunnel into a hidden cave where there are bats, strange fishes, stalactites, rock oysters, corals, cycads and wild orchids. You can organize this **trip** at any resort or simply by asking around to rent a banca for half a day. It will cost around P500 per person, but is well worth it.

Another good day-trip from Siargao is to the **Twin Islands**, La Janoza and Mamon, said to be the easternmost islands in the archipelago. There's a powdery white-sand beach and a quaint fishing village on La Janoza, and between the two islands is a pellucid lagoon that's wonderful for swimming and snorkelling.

For **surfers**, the main area is Tuason Point, less than 2km north of GL. Waves here include Cloud 9, Jacking Horse, Tuason Left and Cemetery. You can rent equipment from the resorts, and lessons cost about P300 an hour.

Practicalities

Getting to Siargao has become much easier recently with regular SEAIR and Asian Spirit flights from Cebu City. From Surigao, there are daily fast ferries, which arrive on the southwest coast at **Dapa**. From the Intergrated Bus Terminal in Cagayan de Oro, take a bus to Surigao (4hr) and then take the ferry. It's very easy to hop on a tricycle or jeepney from here to GL. In the town hall here there's a **tourist office** – although information from the many resort and bar owners is more reliable and up-to-date – and a public telephone office. There are no banks and credit cards aren't accepted, so bring **cash**. If you want to see the island by motorcycle, you can rent one for about P500 a day from many resorts, including those at Cloud 9 and Jadestar Lodge on the seafront in General Luna.

On the main road in GL you can get cheap beer, Filipino **food**, and watch the world go by at *Maridyl's* or *Lalay's*. Both are fairly primitive *carinderias*, but the food is good and the service very friendly. Next door to *Lalay's* is *Ruth's*, where the chicken and pork barbecue is said to be the best in Mindanao. For a really good quality feed at reasonable prices – prawns, fish steaks, banana leaves, curry, spaghetti, fish soup and salad – head for the *Pub*, down by the sea in GL itself. Go down the main street to the school, turn left, right at the end of this road and straight on to the shore. The breakfasts here are also excellent: try the Surfer's Superfry.

Accommodation

Accommodation in Siargao covers the whole range, from modest lodges aimed at backpackers and low-budget surfers, to upmarket tropical resorts where you can be pampered. Most accommodation is a short distance from GL.

Cabuntog Lodge and Cottages Takbo, General Luna. Near GL proper, this is a popular lodge thanks to its low prices; it comprises three stand-alone deluxe rooms with a/,c and fourteen rooms in a motel-style concrete building. ❶

Cheri Nicole Beach Resort A short tricycle ride north of GL. Modest, friendly place with only three cottages, all on the beach. There's no shower, so the owner provides buckets of water for you to tip over your head. Small restaurant, and bancas for rent. ❶

Drop In Resort Cloud 9. Five simple double cottages in a fine location on the beach. Each has a private bathroom with the luxury of a hot shower, and there's a restaurant where specialities include chop suey and fried chicken. ❷

Jungle Reef Surf Resort Cloud 9. Choice of three fan cottages, all with private bathrooms and fine views. Most of the Cloud 9 resorts have laid-back seafront restaurants and this is no exception. ❷

Pansukian Tropical Resort ⓣ032/234 1282 or 0918/903 9055, ⓦwww.pansukian.com. You can't get any swankier than this on Siargao. Accommodation is of two types: the Tropical Pagoda and the Garden Cottage. Excellent location south of GL, attentive service and good food. ❾

Sagana Resort Cloud 9 ⓣ0919 809 5769. The newest resort at Cloud 9, Sagana has six cottages in a landscaped garden with coconut trees and large, leafy plants. Cottages are beautifully made following a Laotian motif. Some cottages have fans, others are a/c and all have hot water. ❹

Marawi and Lake Lanao

MARAWI, on the shores of Lake Lanao, was renamed the Islamic City of Marawi on April 15, 1980. The city is the centre of the Islamic religion in the Philippines:

92 percent of the population is Muslim. Marawi's greatest attraction is placid **Lake Lanao**, which sits in a green bowl circled by distant mountains. It's the second largest lake in the Philippines and easy to explore now that authorities have finally completed a circumferential road; you can set out from Marawi early, travel around the shore and return to town in the early evening. The best way to do this is to hire a vehicle and driver for the day (about P1000).

Marawi is also a terrific place to **shop**. The Palitan (barter centre) is a two-storey building in the heart of the city where you can find virtually any type of clothing, from jeans to traditional tribal garments. Colourful raw cloth and batik products are sold in seemingly endless rows of shops, while other stores stock gold jewellery, exquisite wooden chests and brassware, made from raw materials from the province's own mines and manufactured in the nearby barangay of Tugaya – items include serving trays, chests and ceremonial *bolos* (swords). Near the Palitan is the **market** where you can buy local delicacies such as *dudul*, a snack made from coconut milk, ground rice, sugar and durian. There's also *amik*, a native cake made with ground rice, brown sugar and fermented cassava starch.

Marawi has no permanent **tourist office**, but Raifa Raki-in Adiong, chairwoman of the Committee on Provincial Tourism, Culture and Arts (☎063/352 0549) is unfailingly helpful and will make sure you're well looked after; she can find guides, transport and accommodation. The best **place to stay** is the *Marawi Resort Hotel* (☎063/520 981; ❸) on the Mindanao State University campus. It's a quiet establishment surrounded by greenery and has a good choice of well-maintained rooms. Also on the campus is the **Aga Kahn Museum** (Mon-Fri 9am-12 noon, 2pm-4pm; P15), which has an interesting collection of indigenous art from Mindanao, Sulu and Palawan.

There are daily **buses** from Cagayan de Oro west along the coast to Iligan (1hr 30min; P70), where you change for a bus south to Marawi (1hr; P65); the bus station in Iligan is on the junction of Roxas Avenue and Zamora Street.

The Philippines travel details

Buses

Baguio to: Kabayan (3 daily; 5hr); Sagada (6–7 daily; 4–8hr); San Fernando (La Union; 4–5 daily; 3–4hr).
Cebu City (Southern bus terminal) to: Moalboal (5–6 daily; 3–4 hr).
Cebu City (Northern bus terminal) to: Hagnaya (2–3 daily; 3–4hr); Maya Bagay (2–3 daily; 4hr).
Daet to: Naga (daily; 1–2hr).
Dau (Clark) to: Baguio (5–6 daily; 5–6hr); Olongapo (frequent; 2hr).
Davao to: Cagayan de Oro (2–3 daily; 5hr); Cebu City (1 daily; 39 hr); General Santos (2–3 daily; 3hr); Kidapawan (hourly; 2–3hr); Manila (1 weekly; 36hr); Surigao (1 daily; 8hr).
Iloilo City to: Caticlan (2–3 daily; 5hr); Kalibo (2–3 daily; 4hr).
Kalibo to: Caticlan (5–6 daily; 2hr); Iloilo City (several daily; 6hr).
Legaspi to: Donsol (2–3 daily; 3hr); Naga (daily; 2hr); Sorsogon (2–3 daily; 3–4 hr).
Manila to: Baguio (12–15 daily; 6–8hr); Banaue (5–6 daily; 7–9hr); Batangas City (18–20 daily; 3hr); Calamba (1–12 daily; 2hr); Dau (frequent; 2hr); Daet (6–8 daily; 7–8hr); Iba (3–4 daily; 6hr); Laoag (6–8 daily; 8–10hr); Lingayen (8–10 daily; 6–7hr); Legaspi (8–10 daily; 8–10hr); Lucena (1–12 daily; 3hr); Naga (6–8 daily; 6–8hr); Nasugbu (6–8 daily; 3hr); Olongapo (8–10 daily; 4–5hr); San Fernando (La Union; 4–6 daily; 6–8hr); San Fernando (Pampanga; 8–10 daily; 2–3hr); San Pablo (10–12 daily; 3hr); Santa Cruz (6–8 daily; 2–3hr); Pagsanjan (10–12 daily; 3hr); Sorsogon Town (2–3 daily; 24hr); Taal (10–12 daily; 2–3hr); Tagaytay (10–12 daily; 2–3hr); Vigan (6–8 daily; 8–10hr).
Olongapo to: Alaminos (frequent; 4hr); Barrio Barretto (frequent; 30min); Iba (frequent; 2hr).
San Fernando (La Union) to: Baguio (4–5 daily; 3–4hr); Laoag (hourly; 5hr); Vigan (5–6 daily; 3–4 hr).
Sorsogon Town to: Donsol (3–4 daily; 1hr).
Tacloban to: Calbayog (hourly; 4hr); Davao (1 weekly; 22hr); Manila (1 weekly; 28hr); Ormoc (1 daily; 5hr).
Vigan to: Laoag (3–4 daily; 3hr).

Trains

Manila to: Naga (2 daily; 5hr); Legaspi (2 daily; 8hr).

Ferries

It's not uncommon for ferry schedules to change, so it's always best to check in advance with the ferry companies that services are running.

Bacolod to: Cagayan de Oro (1 daily; 7hr); Cebu City (1 daily; 5hr); Iloilo City (2 daily; 2hr).
Cagayan de Oro to: Bacolod (1 daily; 7hr); Dumaguete (3 weekly; 6hr).
Caticlan to: Carabao Island (daily; 2hr); Manila (several weekly; 12hr).
Cebu City to: Bantayan Island (3 weekly; 9hr); Cagayan de Oro (3 weekly; 8hr); Davao (daily; 18hr); Dumaguete (4 daily; 4–6hr); Dumaguit (daily; 14hr); Iloilo City (2 daily; 8hr); Larena (daily; 4hr 15min); Manila (1-2 daily; 21hr); Masbate (3 weekly; 8hr); Ormoc (5 weekly; 5hr); Sandakan (Malaysia; weekly; 55hr); Surigao (3 weekly; 7hr); Tagbilaran (3 daily; 1hr 30min); Talibon (5 daily; 3hr).
Dumaguete to: Cagayan de Oro (several weekly; 6hr 30min); Cebu City (2 daily; 3hr); Larena (1 daily; 30min); Manila (4 weekly; 22–25hr); Tagbilaran (2 daily; 1hr 30min); Siquijor Town (daily; 4hr).
Hagnaya to: Santa Fe (2–3 daily; 1hr).
Iloilo City to: Bacolod (4 daily; 1hr); Cebu City (2 daily; 8hr); Davao (weekly; 34hr); General Santos (weekly; 24hr); Jordan (Guimaras; 24 daily; 1hr).
Manila (North Harbour) to: Bacolod (3–4 week; 19hr); Bohol (1–2 daily; 28–36hr); Cagayan de Oro (1–2 daily; 36hr); Catbalogan (4–5 weekly; 24hr); Cebu City (1–2 daily; 21hr); Coron Town (2–3 weekly; 14hr); Dumaguit (3–4 weekly; 17hr); Davao (1–2 daily; 52hr); Dumaguete (5–6 weekly; 22hr); General Santos (2 weekly; 43hr) Iloilo City (1–2 daily; 18–25hr); Masbate (weekly; 7hr); Ormoc (2 weekly; 18hr); Puerto Princesa (1–2 daily; 28hr); Roxas (Panay; 1–2 daily; 16hr); San Carlos (1 weekly; 28hr); Surigao (2–3 weekly; 26–53hr); Tacloban (2 weekly; 26 hr); Tagbilaran (3–4 weekly; 28hr).
Surigao to: Manila (2 weekly; 36hr).
Tagbilaran to: Cagayan de Oro (3 weekly; 6hr); Cebu City (3 daily; 1hr 30min); Dumaguete (2 daily; 3hr); Larena (1 daily; 2hr 15min).

Flights

Bacolod to: Cebu City (daily; 30min); Manila (several daily; 1hr 20min).
Baguio to: Manila (daily; 1hr 10min).
Cagayan de Oro to: Cebu City (4 weekly; 1hr); Davao (2 weekly; 50min); Manila (8 daily; 1hr 30min).
Calbayog to: Manila (3 weekly; 1hr 15min).
Camiguin Island to: Cebu City (2 weekly; 35min).
Catarman to: Manila (3 weekly; 1hr 15min).
Caticlan to: Manila (several daily; 1hr); Cebu City (daily; 1hr).
Cebu City to: Bacolod (daily; 35min); Bantayan Island (2 weekly; 30min); Cagayan de Oro (3 weekly; 1hr); Camiguin Island (2 weekly; 35m); Caticlan (1 daily; 1hr); Davao (several daily; 50min); General Santos (daily; 1hr 15min); Iloilo City (daily; 40 min); Manila (16 daily; 1hr 10min); Siargao Island (2 weekly; 50min).
Davao to: Cagayan de Oro (2 weekly; 50min); Cebu City (2 daily; 1hr); Manila (8 daily; 1hr 45min).
Dumaguete to: Manila (2–3 daily; 1hr 10min).
General Santos to: Cebu City (2 daily; 1hr 5min); Manila (2 daily; 1hr 45min).
Iloilo City to: Cebu City (daily; 40min); Davao (daily; 2hr 5min); Manila (8 daily; 1hr 15min).
Kalibo to: Manila (5 daily; 55min).
Laoag to Manila: (daily; 50min).
Legaspi to Manila: (3–4 daily; 1hr 10min).
Manila to: Bacolod (up to 9 daily; 1hr 10min); Baguio (daily; 1hr 10min); Busuanga (daily; 1hr); Basco (Batanes islands; 3 weekly; 2hr); Cagayan de Oro (8 daily; 1hr 25min); Calbayog (4 weekly; 1hr 30min); Catarman (5 weekly; 1hr 30min); Caticlan (5 daily; 1hr); Cebu City (up to 21 daily; 1hr 10min); Clark (6 weekly; 30min); Davao (up to 10 daily; 1hr 40min); Dumaguete (up to 3 daily; 1hr 10min); General Santos (2 daily; 1hr 40min); Iloilo City (10 daily; 1hr); Kalibo (7–8 daily; 50min); Laoag (daily; 50min); Legaspi (3–4 daily; 1hr 10min); Marinduque (5 weekly; 40min); Masbate City (2 daily; 1hr 20min); Naga (2–3 daily; 1hr); Puerto Princesa (2–3 daily; 1hr 10min); San José (1–2 daily; 1hr); Tacloban (6–7daily; 1hr 10min); Tagbilaran (daily; 2hr); Virac (2 daily; 1hr 20min).
Marinduque to Manila: (5 weekly; 40min).
Masbate City to Manila: (2 daily; 1hr 20min).
Naga to Manila: (2–3 daily; 1hr).
Puerto Princesa to Manila: (2–3 daily; 1hr 10min).
San José to Manila: (1–2 daily; 1hr).
Siargao Island to: Cebu City (2 weekly; 50min).
Tacloban to: Manila (several daily; 1hr 10min).
Tagbilaran to: Manila (1 or 2 daily; 1hr 15min).

9

Singapore

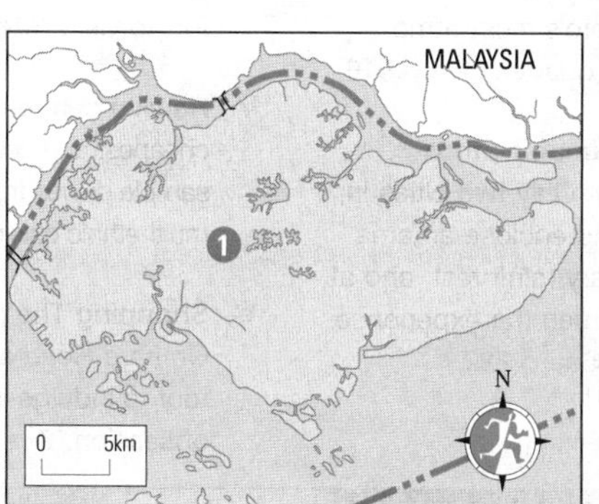

Singapore highlights

* **Chinatown** Terraces of traditional shop-houses, impressive Hokkien architecture, fiery red temples and venerable restaurants proliferate this district. See p.912

* **Little India** Ornate temples, manic markets and fine restaurants characterize Singapore's most atmospheric quarter. See p.916

* **Bukit Timah Nature Reserve** Only two cities in the world enclose an area of primary rainforest, and at Bukit Timah the experience is free. See p.922

* **Singapore Zoological Gardens** More than two thousand animals are housed here in a humane environment, where moats are preferred to cages. See p.923

* **Sentosa** A theme-park island where there's also a choice of beaches and an historic fort to visit. See p.924

* **Hawker centres** By far the cheapest and best places to sample dishes from the island's multi-ethnic cuisine. See p.926

* **Shopping** The glitzy malls of Orchard Road are prime territory to indulge in the national obsession. See p.929

△ Orchard Road

Introduction and basics

Conveniently linked by a kilometre-long causeway to the southern tip of Malaysia, the tiny city-state of Singapore makes a gentle gateway for many first-time travellers to Asia, providing Western standards of comfort and hygiene alongside traditional Chinese, Malay and Indian enclaves. Its downtown areas are dense with towering skyscrapers and gleaming shopping malls, yet the island retains an abundance of nature reserves and lush, tropical greenery.

Singapore is a wealthy nation compared to the rest of Southeast Asia, with an average per capita income of over US$15,000. At the core of this success story is an unwritten bargain between Singapore's paternalistic **government** and acquiescent population, which stipulates the loss of a certain amount of personal freedom, in return for levels of affluence and comfort that would have seemed unimaginable at independence in the 1960s. Outsiders often bridle at this, and it's true that some of the **regulations** can seem extreme: neglecting to flush a public toilet, jaywalking, chewing gum and eating on the subway all carry sizeable fines. Yet the upshot is that Singapore is a clean, safe place to visit, its amenities are second to none and its public places are smoke-free and hygienic. Of more relevance to the millions of visitors Singapore receives each year is the fact that improvements in living conditions have been shadowed by a steady loss of the state's **heritage**, though thankfully historic buildings and streets are no longer being bulldozed to make way for shopping centres.

Singapore undoubtedly lacks the personality of some Southeast Asian cities, but its reputation for being sterile and sanitized is unfair. Much of the country's fascination springs from its **multicultural population**: of the 3.3 million inhabitants, 77 percent are Chinese (a figure reflected in the predominance of Chinese shops, restaurants and temples across the island), 14 percent are Malay, and 8 percent are Indian, the remaining 1 percent being comprised of other ethnic groups.

The entire state is compact enough to be explored exhaustively in just a few days. Forming the core of downtown Singapore is the **Colonial District**, around whose public buildings and lofty cathedral the island's British residents used to promenade. Each surrounding enclave has its own distinct flavour, from the aromatic spice stores of **Little India** to the tumbledown backstreets of **Chinatown**, where it's still possible to find calligraphers and fortune-tellers, or the **Arab Quarter**, whose cluttered shops sell fine cloths and silks.

Beyond the city, is the **Bukit Timah Nature Reserve**, the splendid **Singapore Zoological Gardens**, complete with night safari tours, and the oriental Disneyworld attractions of **Haw Par Villa**. Offshore, you'll find **Sentosa**, the island amusement arcade, which is linked to the south coast by a short causeway (and cable car), and **Pulau Ubin**, off the east coast, where the inhabitants continue to live a traditional kampung (village) life.

Singapore is just 136km north of the equator, which means that you should be prepared for a hot and sticky time whenever you go; **temperatures** hover around 30°C throughout the year. November, December and January are usually the coolest and wettest months, but rain can fall all year round. July usually records the lowest annual rainfall.

Overland routes into Singapore

Singapore is connected by a causeway to Johor Bahru at the southern tip of Peninsular Malaysia, and a second crossing connects the island to southwestern Johor state. There are excellent road and rail connections with numerous **Malaysian cities**, as well as even longer-distance connections by road and

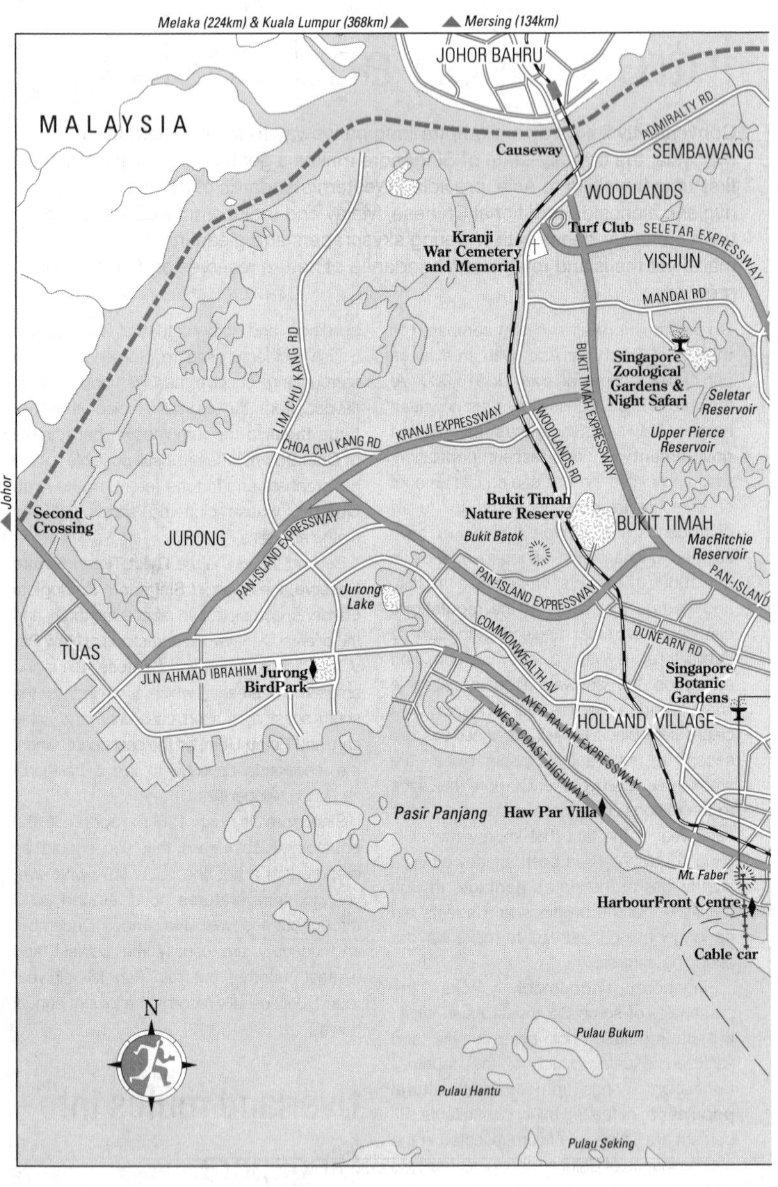

rail to **Thailand**. In addition, there are daily ferries from Malaysia to Singapore, and from **Indonesia**. Details of all these options are given in the box on pp.902–903 and in 'Travel details" at the end of this chapter.

Entry requirements and visa extension

Citizens of Western Europe, the USA and Commonwealth countries don't need a visa

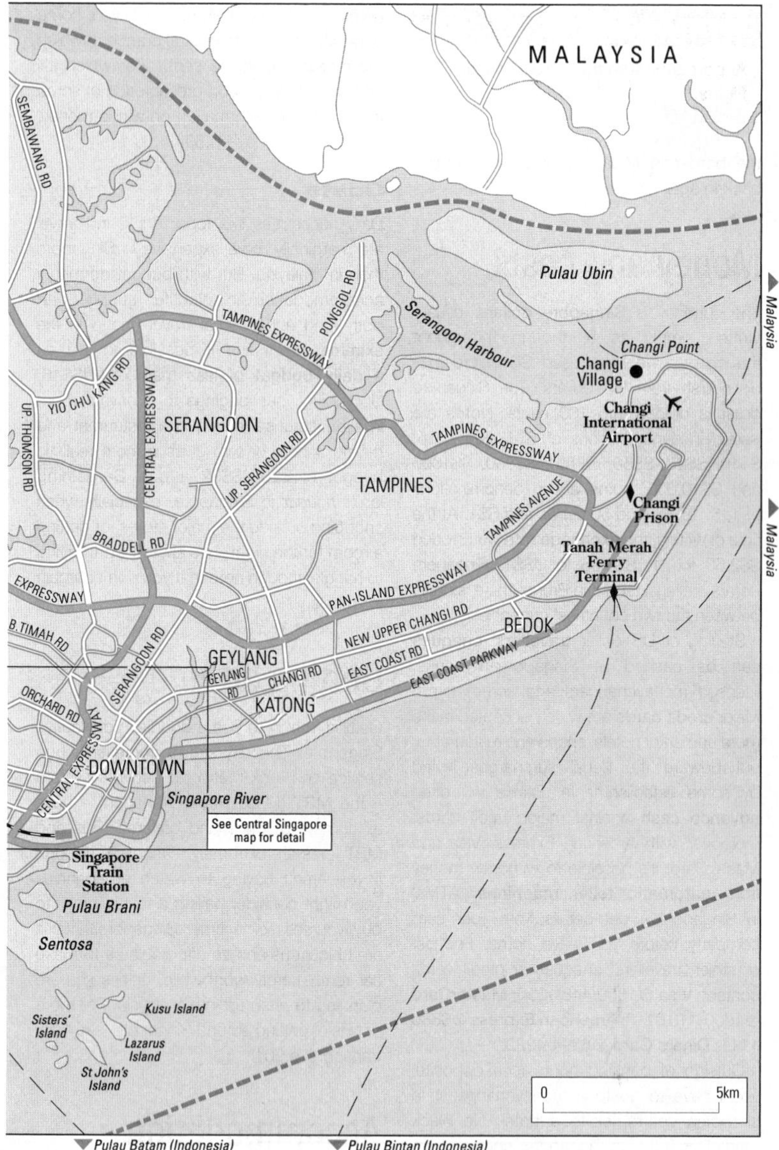

to enter Singapore; check with the relevant embassy before departure (see "Red tape and visas", p.44). Unless you specify how long you intend staying, you'll normally be stamped in for **fourteen days**.

It's possible to **extend your visa** for up to three months, at the discretion of the Singapore Immigration and Registration Department (Mon–Fri 9am–5pm; ⓣ6391 6100). Extensions beyond three months are less common, but there's always the option of taking a bus up to Johor Bahru, across

Airport departure tax

Airport departure tax is S$15 on all flights.

the border in Malaysia, and then coming back in again.

Money and costs

The currency is **Singapore dollars**, usually written simply as $, though throughout the chapter we have used S$ in order to distinguish from US dollars. The Singapore dollar is divided into 100 cents. **Notes** are issued in denominations of S$1, S$2, S$5, S$10, S$20, S$50, S$100, S$500, S$1000 and S$10,000; **coins** are in denominations of 1, 5, 10, 20 and 50 cents, and S$1. At the time of writing, the **exchange rate** was around S$2.50 to £1, S$1.65 to US$1. Singapore dollars are legal tender in Brunei (there is parity between the two countries' currencies).

Sterling or US dollar **travellers' cheques** can be cashed at Singaporean banks, licensed moneychangers and some hotels. Major **credit cards** are widely accepted in the more upmarket hotels, shops and restaurants, but beware the illegal surcharges levied by some establishments. Banks will often **advance cash** against major credit cards; moreover, with American Express, Visa and MasterCard, it's possible to withdraw money from **automatic teller machines** (ATMs) in Singapore – get details from your card company before you leave home. For lost or stolen travellers' cheques or credit cards contact: **Visa** ⓣ1800/448 1250; **MasterCard** ⓣ1800/110 0113; **American Express** ⓣ6880 1111; **Diners Card** ⓣ6294 4222.

Outside of banking hours (see opposite) you'll have to go to a moneychanger in a shopping centre, or to a hotel. No black market operates in Singapore, nor are there any restrictions on carrying currency in or out of the state. This means that rates at moneychangers are as good as you'll find at the banks.

Wiring money – which can take anything from two to seven working days – incurs a small fee in Singapore and a larger one back home. You'll need, first, to supply your home bank with details of the local branch to which the money should be sent, after which it'll be issued to you upon presentation of some form of ID. For information on wiring money, see "Wiring money", p.60.

Costs

Daily necessities like food, drink and travel are marginally more expensive in Singapore than in Malaysia. But with budget dormitory accommodation in plentiful supply, and both food and internal travel cheap in the extreme, you'll find it possible to live on a **daily budget** of less than £10/US$16. Upgrading your lodgings to a private room in a guesthouse, eating in a restaurant and having a beer or two gives a more realistic budget of £20/US$32 a day. **Bargaining** is *de rigueur* in Singapore, especially when shopping outside the major stores, or getting a room for the night – it's always worth trying to haggle, though note that you don't bargain for meals.

Getting around

Getting from A to B is a doddle in diminutive Singapore. The city-state's impressive **bus** service and slick metro rail network system – the **MRT** (Mass Rapid Transport) – have all corners of the island covered. Bus and MRT fares are extremely reasonable, though if you aren't having to watch the pennies you might consider hailing a taxi in order to buy yourself some time. Singaporean taxis are ubiquitous and so affordable as to make car rental hardly worthwhile, unless you are planning to push up into Malaysia. For more details of getting around Singapore, see "City transport" p.901.

Accommodation

The **accommodation** scene in Singapore satisfies all tastes and all pockets. Downtown guesthouses cater for travellers on tight budgets, and in these you can get a simple but secure room with access to shared facilities for as little as S$20 a night – or you can crash in a dormitory for around S$10 a night. Another S$10–20 will buy you air-con and a private bathroom. In Singapore's mid-range hotels, you can expect to pay S$60–90 a night for a double room with all mod cons, while at the upper end of the accommodation scale, you'll find that Singapore has an enormous range of hotels of varying levels of splendour. **Electricity** is supplied at 220 volts.

Food and drink

Eating is the most profound pleasure that Singapore affords its visitors. The mass of establishments serving **Chinese** food reflects the fact that Chinese residents account for more than three quarters of the population. **North and South Indian** cuisines give a good account of themselves too, as do restaurants serving **Malay**, **Indonesian**, **Korean**, **Japanese** and **Vietnamese** food. The closest Singapore comes to an indigenous cuisine is **Nonya**, a hybrid of Chinese and Malay food developed by the Peranakan community, formed as a result of the intermarrying of nineteenth-century Chinese immigrants and Malay women. For a guide to local cuisine, see the Food and Drink section in the Malaysia chapter, p.617. Note that **tap water** is drinkable throughout Singapore.

Communications

Singapore's **postal system** is predictably efficient, with letters and cards often reaching their destination within three days. You can receive **poste restante** beside Paya Lebar MRT (see p.931); for general advice on poste restante, see "Poste restante", p.63. There are other post offices across the state, with usual hours of Monday to Friday 8.30am–5pm and Saturday 8.30am–1pm, though postal services are available until 9pm at the Comcentre on Killiney Road.

Local calls from public phones cost 10¢ for three minutes, with the exception of Changi Airport's free courtesy phones. Singapore has **no area codes** – the only time you'll punch more than eight digits for a local number is if you're dialling a toll-free (☎1800-) number. Many businesses have **mobile phone numbers** – usually prefixed ☎011 or 010 – these are very expensive to call. **Card phones** are taking over from payphones in Singapore: cards, available from the **Comcentre** and post offices, as well as 7-11s, stationers and bookshops, come in denominations of S$2 upwards.

International calls (IDD) can be made from all public card-phones. Otherwise, use a credit-card phone. IDD calls made from hotel rooms in Singapore carry no surcharge. To call abroad, dial ☎001 + IDD country code (see "IDD codes" box, p.64) + area code minus first 0 + subscriber number. Some booths are equipped with **Home Country Direct** phones – see "Phones", p.64 for the procedure – or you can use your BT or AT&T **chargecard**.

Getting **online** is no problem in Singapore, which prides itself on being among the most wired-up of societies. Cybercafés can be found across the island – see p.931 for a selection of the most central ones.

Time differences

Singapore is eight hours ahead of London (GMT), thirteen ahead of New York, sixteen hours ahead of San Francisco, two hours behind Sydney and four hours behind Auckland.

Opening hours and festivals

Shopping centres open daily 10am–7.30pm; **banks** open at least Monday to Friday 10am–3pm, Saturday 9.30am–1pm; while **offices** generally work Monday to Friday 8.30am–5pm and sometimes on Saturday mornings. In general, **Chinese temples** open daily from 7am to around 6pm, **Hindu temples** from 6am to noon and 5 to 9pm and **mosques** from 8.30am to noon and 2.30pm to 4pm.

Festivals

With so many ethnic groups and religions represented in Singapore, you'll be unlucky if your trip doesn't coincide with some

Public holidays

January 1: New Year's Day
January/February: Chinese New Year (two days)
February/March: Hari Raya Haji
March/April: Good Friday
May 1: Labour Day
May: Vesak Day
August 9: National Day
November: Deepavali
December: Hari Raya Puasa
December 25: Christmas Day

sort of **festival**, secular or religious. Most of the festivals have **no fixed dates**, but change annually according to the lunar calendar; check with the tourist office (see p.899). Bear in mind that the major festival periods may play havoc with even the best-planned travel itineraries. Over the month of Ramadan in particular, transport networks and hotel capacity are stretched to their limits, as countless Muslims return to their family homes; throughout **Ramadan**, Muslims fast during the daytime. Many hotels and restaurants shut for up to a week over Chinese New Year (late Jan or early Feb). Some festivals are also public holidays (when everything closes); check the list above.

Not all religious festivals are celebrated in public, but some are marked with truly spectacular parades and street performances. During **Chinese New Year**, Chinese operas and lion and dragon dances are performed in the streets, and colourful parades march along Orchard Road. And at **Thaipusam**, entranced Hindu penitents pierce their own flesh with elaborate steel arches, and process from the Sri Srinivasa Perumal Temple to the Chettiar Hindu Temple. Similar feats are executed by mediums on the occasion of the **Birthday of the Monkey God** (Sept), best witnessed at the Monkey God Temple on Seng Poh Road. Every year, the whole island goes into an eating frenzy for the month-long **Singapore Food Festival** (July), with almost every food outlet staging events, tastings and special menus. The **Festival of the Hungry Ghosts** (July) is a good time to catch a free performance of a Chinese opera, or *wayang*, in which characters act out classic Chinese legends, accompanied by cymbals, gongs and singing; a few weeks later, the **Moon Cake Festival**, or Mid-Autumn Festival, is celebrated with children's lantern parades after dark in the Chinese Gardens. For the nine nights of **Navarathiri** (Oct), Chettiar Hindu Temple stages classical dance and music, and at the Sri Mariamman Temple, the Hindu firewalking ceremony of **Thimithi** (Oct) is marked by devotees running across a pit of hot coals. **Diwali** (Oct/Nov), the Hindu festival celebrating the victory of Light over Dark, is marked by the lighting of oil lamps outside homes.

Cultural hints

Though relatively liberal in outlook, Singapore shares the same basic attitudes to dress and social taboos as other Southeast Asian cultures; see "Cultural hints", p.68.

Crime and safety

Singapore is a **very safe place** for travellers, though you shouldn't become complacent – muggings have been known to occur and theft from dormitories by other tourists is a common complaint.

It's with some irony that Singaporeans refer to the place as a **"fine city"**. There's a fine of S$500 for smoking in public places such as cinemas, trains, lifts, air-conditioned restaurants and shopping malls, and one of S$50 for jaywalking – here defined as crossing a main road within 50m of a pedestrian crossing or bridge. Littering carries a S$1000 fine, with offenders forced to do litter-picking duty, while eating or drinking on the MRT could cost you S$500. Other fines include

Emergency phone numbers

Police ⓣ999
24-hour Tourist Assistance ⓣ1800/736 2000
Ambulance and Fire Brigade ⓣ995

those for urinating in lifts (some lifts are supposedly fitted with urine detectors), not flushing a public toilet and chewing gum (which is outlawed in Singapore). It's worth bearing all these offences in mind, since foreigners are not exempt from the various Singaporean punishments – as American Michael Fay discovered in 1994, when he was given four strokes of the cane for vandalism.

In Singapore, the possession of **drugs** – hard or soft – carries a hefty prison sentence and trafficking is punishable by the death penalty. If you are caught smuggling drugs into or out of the country, at the very best you are facing a long stretch in a foreign prison; at worst, you could be hanged.

Singapore's **police**, who wear dark blue, keep a fairly low profile, but are polite and helpful when approached. For details of the main police station, see "Listings", p.931.

Medical care and emergencies

Medical services in Singapore are excellent, with staff almost everywhere speaking good English and using up-to-date techniques and facilities. **Pharmacies** (Mon–Sat 9am–6pm) are well stocked with familiar brand-name drugs, and pharmacists can recommend products for skin complaints or simple stomach problems, though if you're in any doubt, it always pays to get a proper diagnosis. Pharmacists also stock oral contraceptives, spermicidal gels and condoms.

Larger hotels have **doctors** on call at all times. **Dentists** are listed in the *Singapore Buying Guide* (equivalent to the *Yellow Pages*) under "Dental Surgeons", and "Dentist Emergency Service". For details of **hospital casualty departments**, see "Listings", p.931.

History

What little is known of Singapore's ancient history relies heavily upon legend and supposition. In the late thirteenth century, Marco Polo reported seeing a place called Chiamassie, which could have been Singapore: by then the island was known locally as Temasek – "sea town" – and was a minor trading outpost of the Sumatran Srivijaya Empire. The island's present name – from the Sanskrit Singapura, meaning "Lion City" – was first recorded in the sixteenth century.

Throughout the fourteenth century, Singapore felt the squeeze as the Ayutthaya and Majapahit empires of Thailand and Java struggled for control of the Malay Peninsula. Around 1390, a Sumatran prince called **Paramesvara** threw off his allegiance to the Javanese Majapahit Empire and fled from Palembang to present-day Singapore. There, he murdered his host and ruled the island until a Javanese offensive forced him to flee north, up the Peninsula, where he and his son, Iskandar Shah, subsequently founded the Melaka Sultanate.

With the rise of the **Melaka Sultanate**, Singapore evolved into an inconsequential fishing settlement; a century or so later, the arrival of the Portuguese in Melaka forced Malay leaders to flee southwards to modern-day Johor Bahru for sanctuary. A Portuguese account of 1613 described the razing of an unnamed Malay outpost at the mouth of Sungei Johor to the ground, an event that marked the beginning of two centuries of historical limbo for Singapore.

Raffles and the British

By the late eighteenth century, with China opening up for trade with the West, the British East India Company felt the need to establish outposts along the Straits of Melaka to protect its interests. Penang was secured in 1786, but with the Dutch expanding their rule in the East Indies (Indonesia), a port was needed further south. Enter **Thomas Stamford Raffles** who, as lieutenant-governor of Bencoolen (in Sumatra), was authorized in 1818 by the governor-general of India to establish a **British colony** at the southern tip of the Malay Peninsula; early the following year, he stepped ashore on the northern bank of the Singapore River accompanied by Colonel William Farquhar, former Resident of Melaka and fluent in Malay. Despite living and working in a period of imperial arrogance, Raffles maintained an unfailing concern for the welfare of the people under his governorship, and a conviction that British colonial expansion was for the general good. Today he is the man whom history remembers as the founder of modern Singapore.

At the time of his first landing there, inhospitable swampland and tiger-infested jungle covered Singapore, and its population is generally thought to have numbered around 150, although some historians suggest it could have been as high as a thousand. Raffles recognized the island's potential for providing a deep-water harbour, and immediately struck a treaty with **Abdul Rahman**, *temenggong* (chieftain) of Singapore, establishing a British trading station there. The Dutch were furious at this British incursion into what they considered their territory, but Raffles – who still needed the approval of the Sultan of Johor for his outpost, as Abdul Rahman was only an underling – disregarded Dutch sensibilities. He approached the sultan's brother, Hussein, recognized him as the true sultan, and concluded a second treaty with both the *temenggong* and **His Highness the Sultan Hussein Mohammed Shah**. The Union Jack was raised, and Singapore's future as a free trading post was set.

With its strategic position at the foot of the Straits of Melaka, and with no customs duties levied on imported or exported goods, Singapore's expansion was meteoric. The population had reached ten thousand by the time of the first census in 1824, with Malays, Chinese, Indians and Europeans arriving in search of work as coolies and merchants. In 1822, Raffles set about drawing up the **demarcation lines** that divide present-day Singapore. The area south of the Singapore River was earmarked for the Chinese; a swamp at the mouth of the river was filled and the commercial district established there. Muslims were settled around the Sultan's Palace in today's Arab Quarter.

Nineteenth-century boom

In 1824, Sultan Hussein and the *temenggong* were bought out, and Singapore ceded outright to the British. Three years later, the fledgling state united with Penang and Melaka (now under British rule) to form the **Straits Settlements**, which became a British crown colony in 1867. For forty years the island's *laissez-faire* economy boomed, though life was chaotic, and disease rife. More and more immigrants poured in; by 1860 the population had reached eighty thousand, with each ethnic community bringing its attendant cuisines, languages and architecture. Arabs, Indians, Javanese and Bugis all came, but most populous of all were the **Chinese** from the southern provinces of China, who settled quickly, helped by the clan societies (*kongsis*) already establishing footholds on the island. The British, as was their custom in their Asian colonies, used convict labour to erect impressive public buildings. In 1887, the Armenian Sarkies brothers opened the *Raffles Hotel*, three years after opening their *Eastern & Oriental Hotel* in Penang. *The Raffles* quickly became the social hub of a booming and cosmopolitan Singapore.

By the end of the nineteenth century, the opening of the Suez Canal and the advent of the steamship had consolidated Singapore's position at the hub of international trade in the region, the port becoming a major staging post on the Europe–East Asia route. In 1877, Henry Ridley began his one-man crusade to introduce the **rubber plant** into Southeast Asia, a move that further bolstered Singapore's importance, as the island soon became the world centre of rubber exporting. This status was further enhanced by the slow but steady drawing of the Malay Peninsula under British control – a process begun with the Treaty of Pangkor in 1874 and completed in 1914 – which meant that Singapore gained further from the mainland's tin- and rubber-based economy. Between 1873 and 1913 trade increased eightfold, a trend that continued well into the twentieth century.

Singapore's Asian communities found their **political voice** in the 1920s. In 1926, the Singapore Malay Union was established, and four years later, the Chinese-supported Malayan Communist Party (MCP). But grumblings of independence had got no further than a faint whisper before an altogether more immediate problem reared its head.

World War II

The bubble burst in 1942. In December 1941, the Japanese bombed Pearl Harbor and invaded the Malay Peninsula; less than two months later they were at the top of the causeway, safe from the guns of "Fortress Singapore", which pointed south from what is now Sentosa Island. The inhabitants of Singapore had not been prepared for an attack from this direction and on February 15, 1942, the **fall of Singapore** (which the Japanese then renamed Syonan, or "Light of the South") was complete. Winston Churchill called the British surrender "the worst disaster and the largest capitulation in British history"; cruelly, it later transpired that the Japanese forces had been outnumbered and their supplies hopelessly stretched immediately prior to the surrender.

Three and a half years of brutal **Japanese** rule ensued, during which thousands of civilians were executed in vicious anti-Chinese purges and Europeans were either herded into **Changi Prison**, or marched up the Peninsula to work on Thailand's infamous "Death Railway". Less well-known is the vicious campaign, dubbed Operation Sook Ching, mounted by the military police force, or Kempeitai, during which upwards of 25,000 Chinese males between 18 and 50 years of age were shot dead at Punggol and Changi beaches as enemies of the Japanese.

Towards independence

Following the atomic bombing of Hiroshima and Nagasaki in 1945, Singapore was passed back into British hands, but things were never to be the same. Singaporeans now wanted a say in the government of the island, and in 1957 the British government agreed to the establishment of an elected, 51-member legislative assembly. Full internal **self-government** was achieved in May 1959, when the **People's Action Party** (PAP), led by Cambridge law graduate **Lee Kuan Yew**, won 43 of the 51 seats. Lee became Singapore's first prime minister, and quickly looked for the security of a merger with neighbouring Malaya. For its part (despite reservations about aligning with Singapore's predominantly Chinese population), anti-communist Malaya feared that extremists within the PAP would turn Singapore into a communist base, and accordingly preferred to have the state under its wing.

In 1963, Singapore combined with Malaya, Sarawak and British North Borneo (modern-day Sabah) to form the **Federation of Malaysia**. The alliance, though, was an uneasy one, and within two years Singapore was asked to leave the federation, in the face of outrage in Kuala Lumpur at the PAP's attempts to break into Peninsular politics in 1964. Hours after announcing Singapore's **full independence**, on August 9, 1965, a tearful Lee Kuan Yew went on national TV and described the event as "a moment of anguish". One hundred and forty-six years after Sir Stamford Raffles had set Singapore on the world map, the tiny island, with no natural resources of its own, faced the prospect of being consigned to history's bottom drawer of crumbling colonial ports.

Contemporary Singapore

Instead, Lee's personal vision and drive transformed Singapore into an Asian economic heavyweight, a position achieved at a price. Heavy-handed **censorship** of the media was introduced, and even more disturbing was the government's attitude towards **political opposition**. When the opposition Worker's Party won a by-election in 1981, for example, the candidate, JB Jeyaretham, found himself charged with several criminal offences, and chased through the Singaporean law courts for the next decade.

The archaic **Internal Security Act** still grants the power to detain without trial anyone the government deems a threat to the nation, which kept political prisoner Chia Thye Poh under lock and key for a full 23 years for allegedly advocating violence. Population policies, too, have brought criticism from abroad. These began in the early 1970s, with a birth control campaign that proved so successful that it had to be reversed.

At other times, Singapore tries so hard to reshape itself that it falls into self-parody. "We have to pursue this subject of fun very seriously if we want to stay competitive in the twenty-first century", was the reaction of former Minister of State George Yeo, when confronted with the fact that some foreigners find Singapore dull. The government's annual **courtesy campaign**, which in 1996 urged the population to hold lift doors open for neighbours and prevent their washing from dripping onto passers-by below, appears equally risible to outsiders.

However, adults beyond a certain age remember how things were before independence and, more importantly, before the existence of the Mass Rapid Transit (MRT) system, housing projects and saving schemes. But their children and grandchildren have no such perspective, and telltale signs – presently nothing more extreme than feet up on MRT seats and jaywalking – suggest that the government can expect more **dissent** in future years. Already a substantial brain drain is afflicting the country, as skilled Singaporeans choose to move abroad in the pursuit of heightened civil liberties. Furthermore, the trade-off between freedoms and economic efficiency has been shown to be no surefire bet; recent years have seen the island buffeted first by the Asian financial crisis of 1997 and then, in 2001, by the worst recession since independence, the economy shrinking by a couple of percentage points thanks to a global downturn in the IT and electronics sectors.

The man charged with leading Singapore into the new millennium is **Goh Chok Tong**, who became prime minister upon Lee's retirement in 1990. Goh has made it clear that he favours a more open form of government. He has the mandate to make whatever changes he wishes, and many agree that restrictions have loosened up somewhat over the past few years. Singapore certainly no longer deserves the "nanny state" reputation that it has for so long been saddled with – as the current arts, culture and nightlife scenes attest.

Religion

Buddhism is the main religion in Singapore, though many Singaporean Chinese consider themselves specifically **Taoist** or **Confucianist**. There's also a smaller, but significant, **Hindu** Indian presence, as well a **Muslim** community, mostly comprised of the island's Malays. Buddhism, Hinduism and Islam all play a vital role in the everyday lives of the population. Indeed, some religious festivals, like Muslim Hari Raya and Hindu Thaipusam, have been elevated to such stature that they are among the main cultural events in the calendar. For an introduction to all these faiths, see "Religion", pp.69–71.

Books

In the selection of books below, where a book is published in the UK and the US, the UK publisher is given first, followed by the US one; the abbreviation o/p means out of print.

Noel Barber *Sinister Twilight* (Arrow, UK). Documents the fall of Singapore to the Japanese by re-imagining the crucial events of the period.

James Clavell *King Rat* (Hodder/Dell). Set in Japanese-occupied Singapore, a gripping novel of survival in the notorious Changi Prison.

Maurice Collis *Raffles* (Century, o/p). The most accessible and enjoyable biography of Sir Stamford Raffles – very readable.

Harry Foster *A Beachcomber in the Orient* (Dodd, Mead & Company, o/p). An hilarious first-person account of a proto-backpacker who travelled the region in the 1920s. Well worth the effort to find a copy – online sources are your best bet.

Maya Jayapal *Images of Asia: Old Singapore* (OUP). Concise volume that charts the growth of the city-state, drawing on contemporary maps, sketches and photographs to engrossing effect.

Tan Kok Seng *Son Of Singapore* (Heinemann, o/p). Tan Kok Seng's candid and sobering autobiography on the underside of the Singaporean success story, telling of hard times spent as a coolie.

C. Mary Turnbull *A Short History of Malaysia, Singapore & Brunei* (Graham Brash, Singapore). Decent, informed introduction to the region.

Michael Wise (ed), *Travellers' Tales of Old Singapore* (In Print Publishing, UK). A catholic and engrossing collection of vignettes.

Language

English, Mandarin, Malay (for more on which, see p.634) and Tamil all have the status of official languages, and you should have no problem getting by in English. One intriguing by-product of Singapore's ethnic melting pot is Singlish, or Singaporean English, a patois that blends English with the speech patterns, exclamations and vocabulary of Chinese and Malay.

9.1

Singapore

The diamond-shap island of Singapore is 40km from east to west at its widest points, and 23km from north to south. The **downtown** city areas huddle at the southern tip of the diamond, radiating out from the mouth of the **Singapore River**. Two northeast–southwest roads form a dual spine to the central area, both of them traversing the river: one starts out as **North Bridge Road**, crosses the river and becomes **South Bridge Road**; the other begins as **Victoria Street**, becomes Hill Street and skirts Chinatown as **New Bridge Road**.

At the very heart of the city, on the north bank, the **Colonial District** is home to a cluster of buildings that recall the days of early British rule – Parliament House, the cathedral, the Supreme Court, the Cricket Club and, most famously, *Raffles Hotel*. To the west, the fringes of **Fort Canning Park** contain several attractions, including Singapore's History Museum. From here, it's a five-minute stroll to the eastern end of **Orchard Road**, the main shopping area in the city. North from Fort Canning Park you soon enter **Little India**, whose main drag – Serangoon Road – is around fifteen minutes' walk from *Raffles Hotel*. Ten minutes southeast from Little India, Singapore's traditional **Arab Quarter** squats at the intersection of North Bridge Road and Arab Street.

South, across the river, the monolithic towers of the **Central Business District** (CBD) cast long shadows over **Chinatown**, whose row of shop-houses stretches for around one kilometre, as far as Cantonment Road. Singapore's **HarbourFront Centre** is a fifteen-minute walk southwest of the outskirts of Chinatown, and from there cable cars run across to **Sentosa**.

Arrival and information

A 1056-metre-long **causeway** links Johor Bahru (JB) in Malaysia with Woodlands, and is used by all buses and trains from Malaysia; the so-called Second Crossing connects the southwest of Johor state with Tuas in the west of the island.

By air

Changi International Airport (Ⓣ1800/542 4422) is at the far eastern end of Singapore, 16km from the city centre. Facilities there include duty-free shops, moneychanging and left-luggage services, hotel reservations counters and, in Terminal One's basement, a cheap food centre. Now that the eastern arm of the **MRT** underground system (see p.902) has been extended to the airport, it's possible to reach central areas of the city in around half an hour. Alternatively, the **bus** departure points in the basements of both terminals are well signposted: get hold of the exact fare before you leave the terminal. Take the **#36** (every 10min, 6am–midnight; S$1.70), which heads west to Stamford Road (ask the driver to give you a shout at Stamford Road's Capitol Building for Beach Road, and at the YMCA stop if you're planning on staying at one of the guesthouses on Bencoolen Street, across Bras Basah Park) before skirting the southern side of Orchard Road. Another option is to take a MaxiCab shuttle into town. These six-seater taxis depart every fifteen minutes, or when full, and will take you to any hotel in the city for a flat fare of S$7 each, or S$5 for children under 12. MaxiCabs are equipped to take wheelchairs. **Taxis** from the airport cost around S$20 into downtown Singapore (20min); pick-up points are well signposted.

By bus

Singapore has three bus terminals. The Singapore-KL Express and local buses **from Johor Bahru** and arrive at **Ban San terminal** at the junction of Queen and Arab streets, from where a two-minute walk up Queen Street, followed by a left along Rochor Road takes you to Bugis MRT station. Buses from elsewhere in **Malaysia** and **from Thailand** terminate at one of two sites, **Lavender Street terminal** and the **Golden Mile Complex**. Lavender Street terminal is at the corner of Lavender Street and Kallang Bahru, five minutes' walk from Lavender MRT. Alternatively, walk a short way in the other direction to the end of Jalan Besar and hop on bus #139, if you're heading for the guesthouses of Bencoolen Street. Bus #145 passes the Lavender Street terminal on its way down North Bridge and South Bridge roads. From outside the Golden Mile Complex, buses run up Beach Road towards City Hall MRT.

By train

Trains to and from Malaysia use the **Singapore train station** on Keppel Road, southwest of Chinatown. From Keppel Road, bus #97 travels past Tanjong Pagar MRT and on to Selegie and Serangoon roads. If you want to avoid taking the train down to its terminus in the south of the island, get off in Johor Bahru, clear Malaysian immigration and buy a ticket on bus #160 or #170. The buses pause at the **Woodlands checkpoint** where you clear Singapore immigration; thereafter you can get on another #160 or #170 bus (your original ticket will be honoured) at several convenient transfer points, including Newton MRT.

By boat

Boats to and from the Indonesian Riau archipelago dock at two different piers. Boats from Pulau Batam arrive at the **HarbourFront Centre**, near the MRT of the same name. Boats from Pulau Bintan use the **Tanah Merah ferry terminal**. This ferry terminal is connected to Bedok MRT station by bus #35.

Bumboats (traditional cargo boats) from Kampung Pengerang on the southeastern coast of Johor Bahru (daily when full, 7am–4pm; 45min; S$5 one-way) moor at **Changi Village**, beyond the airport. Bus #2 travels from Changi Village (see p.905) into the centre, via Geylang, Victoria and New Bridge roads. Newer, more reliable Ferrylink ferries from Tanjung Belungkor, also in Johor, dock at the **Changi ferry terminal**, a little way east of Changi Village, from where a taxi ride is necessary to get to the nearest #2 bus stop.

Information

The Singapore Tourism Board (STB) maintains five **Tourist Information (Visitors) Centres**, including one in the arrivals area of each terminal at Changi Airport. In town, you'll find one at the intersection of Orchard and Cairnhill roads (daily 8am–10pm; ⓣ1-800/736 2000); another at Liang Court Shopping Centre, Level 1, 177 River Valley Road (daily 10.30am–9.30pm; ⓣ6336 2888); and the third at Plaza Singapura Mall, 68 Orchard Road (daily 10am–10pm; ⓣ6332 9298). The most useful of their free hand-outs is the *Uniquely Singapore Guide*. The best **what's on** listings publications are the weekly *8 Days magazine* ($1.50), and the newer *I-S*, a free paper published weekly. The best map also happens to be free, STB's Official Map of Singapore.

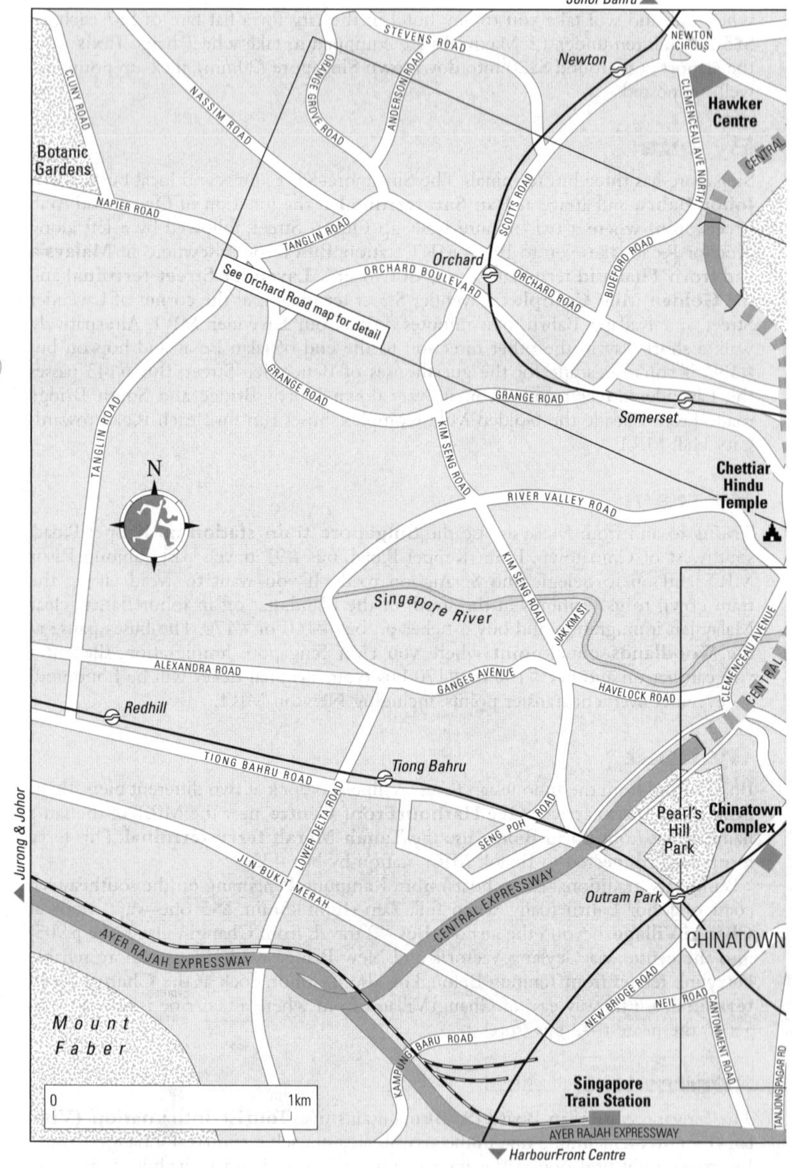

With so many of Singapore's shops, restaurants and offices located in vast high-rise buildings and shopping centres, deciphering **addresses** can sometimes be tricky; an address containing #10-08 refers to room number 8 on the tenth floor (ground level is denoted #01).

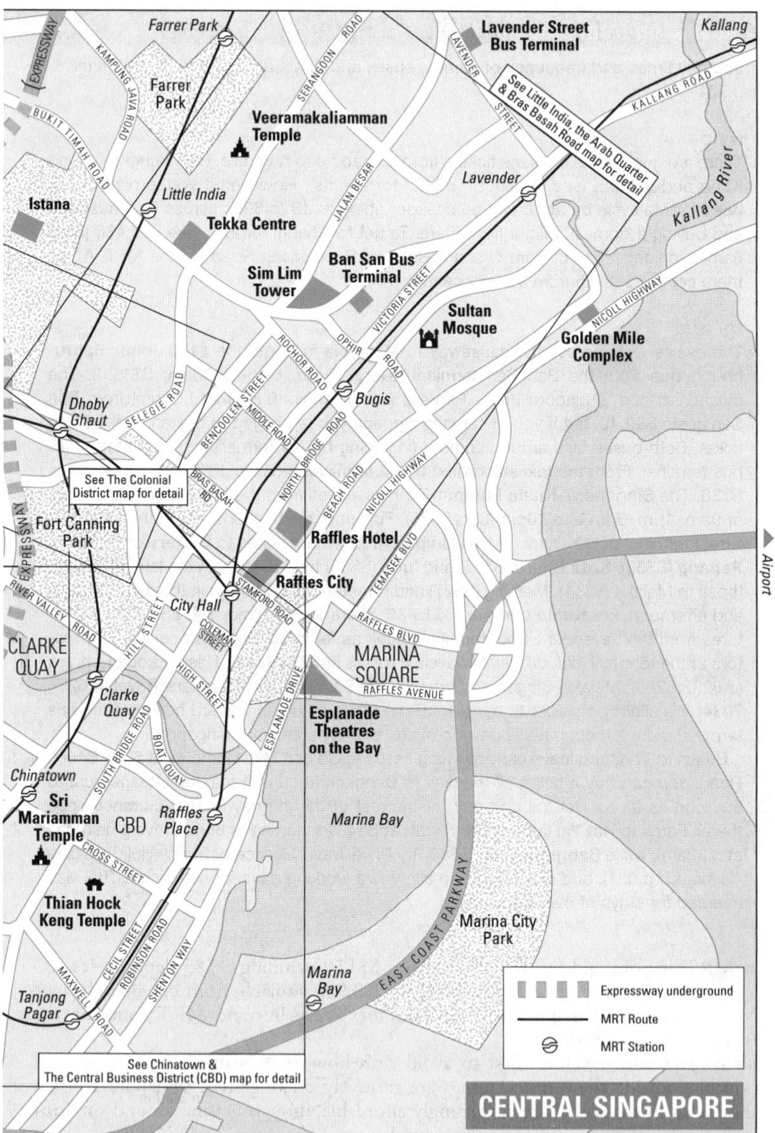

City transport

All parts of the island are accessible by **bus** or **MRT** – the metro rail network – and fares are reasonable; consequently, there's little to be gained by renting a car. If you're going to be making a number of journeys, it's worth buying an **ez-link card**, a stored-value card valid on all MRT and bus journeys in Singapore; and sold

Moving on from Singapore

Journey times and frequency of planes, buses and boats are given in "Travel details", p.931

By plane

There are good deals on plane tickets from Singapore to Australia, Bali, Bangkok, Hong Kong and Jakarta (see "Listings", p.930, for agents). However, if you're planning to head for Malaysia **by air**, it can be cheaper going to JB (p.695), across the causeway and buying a domestic flight from there. To get to Changi Airport, take bus #36 (daily 6am–midnight; S$1.70) from Orchard Road or Bras Basah Road, or the MRT. A taxi there costs S$12–15 from the city centre.

By bus

The easiest way across the causeway to **Malaysia** is to get the #170 **Johor Bahru**-bound **bus** from the Ban San terminal (every 15min, 6am–12.30am; S$1.20). The plusher air-con Singapore–Johor Express (every 10min, 6.30am–11.30pm) from Ban San costs S$2.40, but if you're carrying luggage you're obliged to buy another S$2.40 ticket. Both buses take around an hour (including border formalities); both stop at JB bus terminal. From the taxi stand next to the terminal, a car to JB (seating four) costs S$30. The **Singapore–Kuala Lumpur** Express leaves from the Ban San terminal daily at 9am, 1pm, 5pm and 10pm (6hr; S$25). For other destinations, go to the Lavender Street terminal or the Golden Mile Complex, from where buses to **Butterworth** (S$37), **Penang** (S$38), **Kota Bharu** (S$35) and **Ipoh** (S$33) tend to leave in the late afternoon; those to Melaka (S$11), Mersing (S$27) and Kuantan (S$17) depart in the early morning and afternoon. For **Kuala Lumpur** (S$15-30), there are both morning and night departures from the Lavender Street terminal. Book as far in advance as possible – operators at the terminal include Pan Malaysia Express (☎6294 7034), Hasry Ekoba Express (☎6292 6243), Melaka–Singapore Express (☎6293 5915) and Masmara Travel (☎6294 7034). It's slightly cheaper to travel to JB and then catch an onward bus from the bus terminal there – though it still pays to make an early start from Singapore.

Buses to **Thailand** leave early morning from the Golden Mile Complex at 5001 Beach Road. You can buy a ticket all the way to Bangkok (though it may be cheaper just to buy one as far as Hat Yai and pay for the rest of the journey in Thai currency once there). Fares to **Hat Yai** (around 14hr) start at S$40 (departing at 6pm, arriving next day at 6.30am), while **Bangkok** costs S$80. Try Phya Travel Service or Sunny Holidays (see "Listings", p.931), and don't forget to allow two working days for securing a Thai visa (needed for stays of over thirty days).

at MRT stations and bus interchanges for S$15 (including a S$5 deposit). It's also a good idea to pick up a *Transitlink Guide* ($3.90), available from bus interchanges, MRT stations and major bookshops, outlines every bus and MRT route on the island in exhaustive detail.

However you travel, it's best to avoid rush hour (8–9.30am & 5–7pm) if at all possible; outside these times, things are relatively uncongested. Singapore also has thousands of **taxis** that are surprisingly affordable, though getting around **on foot** is the best way to do justice to the central areas.

The MRT (Mass Rapid Transit) System

Singapore's clean, efficient and good-value **MRT** system (Transitlink Hotline ☎1-800/767 4333) has three main lines: the north–south line, which runs from Marina Bay up to the north of the island and then southwest to Jurong; the north-east line, which runs from the HarbourFront Centre up to Punggol; the east–west line, connecting Boon Lay to Pasir Ris and branching off to Changi Airport; see the MRT map on p.950 for details. Trains run about every five minutes, daily from 6am until

By train

Trains from the Singapore Train Station on Keppel Road run either to Kuala Lumpur or up through the interior of Malaysia to Tumpat in the northeast, near Kota Bharu; for more on the Malaysian train system, see p.614. You can make free seat **reservations** up to one month in advance of departure at the information kiosk (daily 8.30am–7pm; ☎6221 3390) in the station. The 10pm Express Senandung Malam gets into **Kuala Lumpur** early the next morning; the 8.30am Express Rakyat arrives in the early afternoon. Unfortunately, none of the trains to Kuala Lumpur connects conveniently with northbound services up the west coast, including the **international express to Bangkok**. The morning Express Rakyat will put you in Kuala Lumpur with about five hours to kill, though some people find it a convenient way to see a bit of Malaysia's capital before moving on. Singapore to Bangkok is a tiring journey done in one go, particularly if you don't book a berth on the overnight leg between Butterworth and Bangkok, but it is the quickest way (other than flying) to travel right through Malaysia, should you wish to do so.

By boat

Boats to **Pulau Batam** in **Indonesia**'s Riau archipelago depart throughout the day from the HarbourFront Centre (7.30am–7pm; S$35 one-way), docking at Sekupang, from where you take a taxi to Hangnadim Airport for internal Indonesian flights. There are also four boats a day (S$45 one-way) from the Tanah Merah ferry terminal (bus #35 from Bedok MRT) to Tanjung Pinang on **Pulau Bintan**, also in the Riau archipelago; info and tickets from Dino Shipping (☎6276 9722), or Bintan Resort Ferries (☎6542 4369). From Kijang Port, south of Tanjung Pinang, there are boat services to **Jakarta**.

It's also possible to travel between Singapore and **Malaysia** by boat. Bumboats to **Kampung Pengerang** on the southeastern coast of Johor Bahru (daily when full, 7am–4pm; 45min; S$5 one-way) leave from Changi Village, beyond the airport. Newer, more reliable Ferrylink ferries depart from Changi ferry terminal for **Tanjung Belungkor**, in Johor, a little way east of Changi Village, leaving daily at 7.30am, 11.30am, 4pm and 8pm (45min; S$32 return; ☎6545 3600); check in one hour before departure. Ferries to **Pulau Tioman** run from the **Tanah Merah ferry terminal** (March–Oct daily at 8.35am; around S$160 return). Information and tickets from Auto Batam (☎6271 4866); check-in is one hour beforehand. Most travellers to Tioman find it much easier and cheaper to simply take the bus to Mersing in Malaysia, and then a ferry from there (see p.696).

midnight, and cost S$0.80–1.80 one-way. A **no-smoking** rule applies on all trains, and eating and drinking are also prohibited.

Buses

Far more comprehensive than the MRT, Singapore's **bus** network is operated by the **Singapore Bus Service** (SBS) and **Trans-Island Bus Services** (TIBS). Information about fares and routes can be had by calling the Transitlink Hotline (see opposite). Most buses charge distance-related fares, ranging from S$0.70 to S$1.40 (S$0.80–1.70 for air-con buses); others charge a flat fare, displayed on the front of the bus. If you don't have an ez-link card (see p.901), tell the driver where you want to go, and he'll tell you how much money to drop into the metal chute. Change isn't given, so make sure you have enough coins.

Taxis

Taxis are all metered, the fare starting at S$2.40 for the first kilometre, then rising

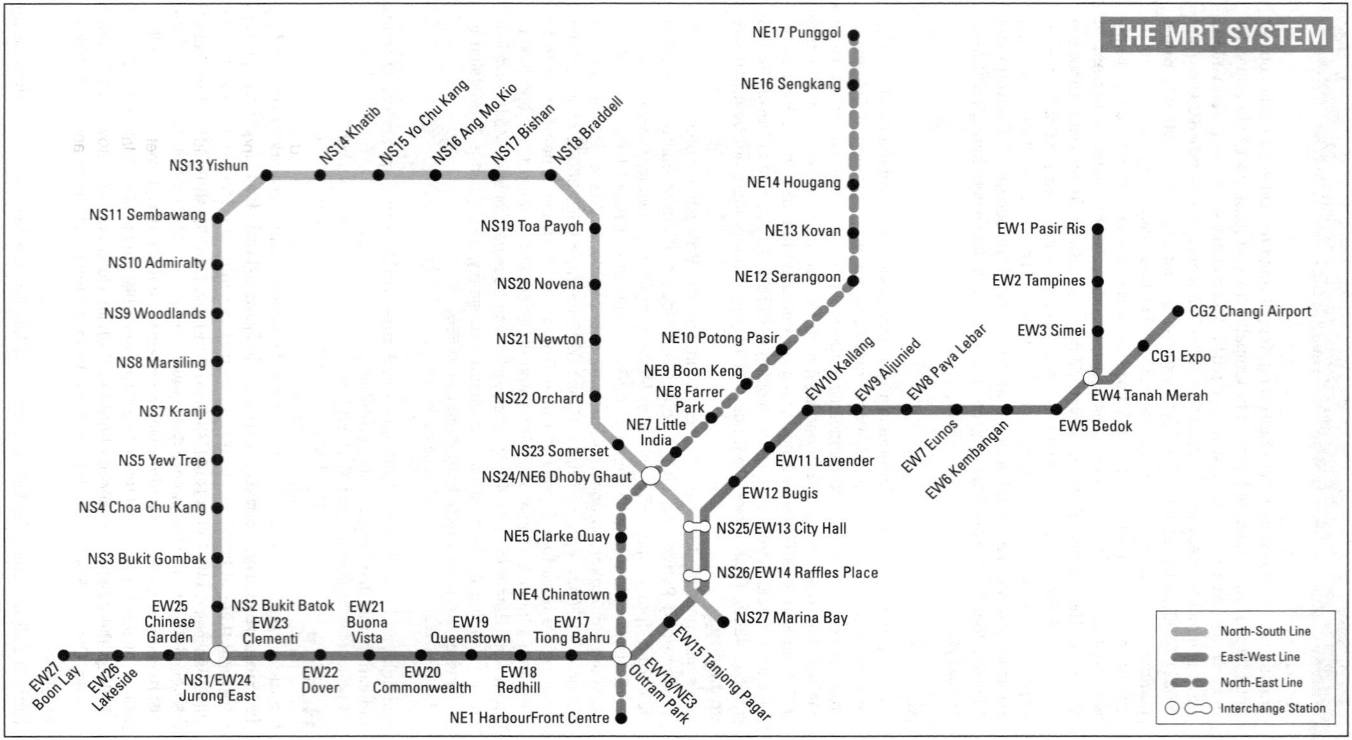

THE MRT SYSTEM

NE17 Punggol
NE16 Sengkang
NE14 Hougang
NE13 Kovan
NE12 Serangoon
NE10 Potong Pasir
NE9 Boon Keng
NE8 Farrer Park
NE7 Little India
NS24/NE6 Dhoby Ghaut
NE5 Clarke Quay
NE4 Chinatown
EW16/NE3 Outram Park
NE1 HarbourFront Centre

NS1/EW24 Jurong East
NS2 Bukit Batok
NS3 Bukit Gombak
NS4 Choa Chu Kang
NS5 Yew Tree
NS7 Kranji
NS8 Marsiling
NS9 Woodlands
NS10 Admiralty
NS11 Sembawang
NS13 Yishun
NS14 Khatib
NS15 Yo Chu Kang
NS16 Ang Mo Kio
NS17 Bishan
NS18 Braddell
NS19 Toa Payoh
NS20 Novena
NS21 Newton
NS22 Orchard
NS23 Somerset
NS25/EW13 City Hall
NS26/EW14 Raffles Place
NS27 Marina Bay

CG2 Changi Airport
CG1 Expo
EW1 Pasir Ris
EW2 Tampines
EW3 Simei
EW4 Tanah Merah
EW5 Bedok
EW6 Kembangan
EW7 Eunos
EW8 Paya Lebar
EW9 Aljunied
EW10 Kallang
EW11 Lavender
EW12 Bugis
EW15 Tanjong Pagar
EW17 Tiong Bahru
EW18 Redhill
EW19 Queenstown
EW20 Commonwealth
EW21 Buona Vista
EW22 Dover
EW23 Clementi
EW25 Chinese Garden
EW26 Lakeside
EW27 Boon Lay

North-South Line
East-West Line
North-East Line
Interchange Station

10cents for every 225m thereafter. However, there are a host of **surcharges**, including surcharges on journeys between midnight and 6am, a S$3-5 surcharge from Changi Airport, and a S$3 surcharge for taxis booked over the phone. The Singaporean government has introduced an Electronic Road Pricing programme (ERP) in order to relieve congestion within the city's **Central Business District** (CBD) at peak times, and these electronic tolls will be reflected in your bill, depending upon the time of day. Singaporean taxi drivers don't always speak good English, so it's a good idea to have in mind the name of a nearby landmark or major road. If a taxi displays a red destination sign on its dashboard, it means the driver is changing shift and will accept customers only if they are going in his direction. TIBS Taxis (☎6555 8888) have ten **wheelchair**-accessible cabs.

Renting cars and bikes

The Singapore government has introduced huge disincentives to driving in order to combat traffic congestion, making it expensive and tiresome to **rent a car**. Rates begin at around S$200 per day, but if you want to take the car into Malaysia the insurance surcharge bumps up the price still further. Either way, a valid national driving licence is sufficient. **Bicycle rental** (S$4–8 an hour, with ID) is possible along the East Coast Parkway, where a cycle track skirts the seashore. The dirt tracks on Pulau Ubin, off Changi Point (see p.923), are ideal for biking, and there's a range of bikes available for rent next to the ferry terminal on Sentosa Island (S$3–8 an hour), providing by far the best way to see the island.

Useful bus routes

Note that many of the services heading out of the centre from the Orchard Road area actually leave from Penang Road or Somerset Road.

#2 passes along Eu Tong Sen Street (in Chinatown) and Victoria Street (past the Arab Quarter) en route to Changi Prison and Changi Village.

#7 runs along Orchard Road, Bras Basah Road and Victoria Street; its return journey takes in North Bridge Road, Stamford Road, Penang Road and Somerset Road en route to Holland Village.

#36 loops between Orchard Road and Changi Airport.

#65 terminates at the HarbourFront Centre, after passing down Jalan Besar, Bencoolen Street, Penang Road and Somerset Road.

#97 runs along Stamford Road to Little India, then on to Upper Serangoon Road; returns via Bencoolen Street and Collyer Quay.

#103 runs between New Bridge Road terminal (Chinatown) and Serangoon Road (Little India).

#124 connects Scotts Road, Orchard Road and North Bridge Road with South Bridge Road, Upper Cross Street and New Bridge Road in Chinatown; in the opposite direction, travels along Eu Tong Sen Street, Hill Street, Stamford Road and Somerset Road.

#139 heads past Tai Gin Road, via Dhoby Ghaut, Selegie Road, Serangoon Road and Balestier Road.

#167 passes down Scotts Road, Orchard Road and Bras Basah Road, Collyer Quay, Shenton Way and Neil Road (for Chinatown).

#170 starts at the Ban San terminal at the northern end of Queen Street, passing Bukit Timah Nature Reserve and Kranji War Cemetery on its way to JB in Malaysia.

#190 is the most direct service between Orchard Road and Chinatown, via Scotts Road, Orchard Road, Bras Basah Road, Victoria Street, Hill Street and New Bridge Road; returns via Eu Tong Sen Street, Hill Street, Stamford Road, Penang Road, Somerset Road and Scotts Road.

Accommodation

Room rates take a noticeable leap when you cross the causeway from Malaysia into Singapore, but good deals still abound if your expectations aren't too high or, at the budget end of the scale, if you don't mind sharing. Advance booking is only necessary at Chinese New Year and the two Hari Raya festivals. The **Singapore Hotel Association** has booking counters at Changi Airport, though they only represent Singapore's official hotels. Touts at the airport also hand out flyers advertising rooms, but things can get embarrassing if you get a lift with them and then turn down the place they represent.

The cheapest beds are in the communal **dormitories** of many resthouses, where you'll pay S$10 or less a night. Have a good look before parting with your cash though, as some of these places are simply flats whose inner walls have been knocked down and every available space crammed with bunk beds. Bedbugs can be a problem and the lights are left burning all night. These crashpads serve as cheap accommodation for many of Singapore's guest workers, so if you want to practise your Thai or Tagalog, you'll have ample opportunity. The next best deals are at **guesthouses**, most of which are situated along Bencoolen Street, with an increasing number in nearby Little India and some also south of the river, in Chinatown. Guesthouses aren't nearly as cosy as their name suggests: costing S$20–30, the rooms are tiny, bare, and divided by paper-thin partitions, toilets are shared, and showers are cold. However, another S$10–20 secures a bigger, air-con room, and often TV, laundry and cooking facilities, lockers and breakfast are included. Always check that the room is clean and secure, and that the shower and air-con work before you hand over any money. It's always worth asking for a discount, too. Finally, since guesthouses aren't subject to the same safety checks as official hotels, without sounding alarmist, it's a good idea to check for a fire escape. The appeal of Singapore's **Chinese-owned hotels**, similar in price to guesthouses, is their air of faded grandeur, but sadly only a few of these now remain. In more modern, **mid-range hotels**, an en-suite room for two with air-con and TV will cost around S$60–90.

Between Bras Basah Road and Rochor Road

Rochor Road and the western part of the Rochor canal broadly divide Little India and the Arab Quarter from the old-time backpacker centres of Bencoolen Street and the southern part of Beach Road. There are still some good options to be had in **Bencoolen Street**, while **Beach Road** boasts a mixture of charismatic old Chinese hotels and smart new guesthouses. The establishments listed below are marked on the map on pp.918–919.

Ah Chew Hotel 496 North Bridge Rd ⓣ6837 0356. Simple and a bit grubby but functional enough rooms in a good location. Despite its address, it's just around the corner from North Bridge Road, on Liang Seah Street. ❸

City Bayview 30 Bencoolen St ⓣ6337 2882. One of Bencoolen Street's posher hotels, with very comfortable rooms, a compact rooftop swimming pool and a friendly, modern café. ❻

Hawaii Hostel 2nd Floor, 171b Bencoolen St ⓣ6338 4187. Welcoming staff here maintain small, tidy, a/c rooms. Dorms S$12. ❺

Metropole Hotel 41 Seah St ⓣ6336 3611. Friendly, great-value establishment just across the road from *Raffles*, with roomy lodgings served by the intriguing *Imperial Herbal Restaurant*. ❼

New 7th Storey Hotel 229 Rochor Rd ⓣ6337 0251. Classy, tastefully furnished rooms at a fraction of what you'd pay elsewhere: spotless dorms have a/c and TV, and even a deluxe double won't break the bank. Dorms S$15. ❸

Peony Mansions Travellers' Lodge 2nd Floor, 131a Bencoolen St ⓣ6334 8697. Singapore's classic guesthouse address, a cluster of establishments shoehorned into several floors of a decrepit apartment building. Lots of clean, featureless rooms (some en-suite) and one five-bed dorm. ❹

Raffles Hotel 1 Beach Rd ⓣ6337 1886, ⓦwww.raffleshotel.com. The flagship of Singapore's tourism industry, *Raffles* takes shameless advantage of its reputation but is still a beautiful place, dotted with frangipani trees and palms, and the suites are as tasteful as you would expect at these prices. 9

South East Asia Hotel 190 Waterloo St ☎6338 2394. Spotless doubles with a/c, TV and phone. Downstairs is a vegetarian restaurant serving Western breakfasts. 7

Strand Hotel 25 Bencoolen St ☎6338 1866. An excellent-value hotel with clean, welcoming rooms and a variety of services. 7

Sun Sun Hotel 260–262 Middle Rd ☎6338 4911. Housed in a splendid 1928 building, with decent rooms, some a/c, and plenty of communal bathrooms. 6

Waffles Home Stay 3rd Floor, 490 North Bridge Rd ☎6338 8826. Recommended crashpad. Breakfast included, and discounts if you introduce new guests. Good noticeboards. Dorms S$10. 3

Little India

Little India's hotels and guesthouses are attracting an increasing number of backpackers. Buses along Jalan Besar connect Little India with the rest of central Singapore. For the locations of the establishments listed below, see the map on pp.918–919.

Fortuna City Hotel 2 Owen Rd ☎6295 3577. Mid-range hotel offering brilliant value for money; facilities include an Indian restaurant and a health centre. 8

Goh's Homestay 40–43 Upper Weld Rd ☎6339 6561. Established guesthouse where cleanliness comes as standard in all rooms, including the three-bed dorms; facilities include a cosy canteen area, laundry service and bike rental at S$10 per day. Dorm beds S$20. 6

InnCrowd Hostel I 35 Campbell Ln ☎6296 9169. In a renovated century-old shop-house, this hostel goes way above and beyond as far as amenities, comfort and cleanliness is concerned. Exceptionally friendly and helpful staff, too. The S$18 dorm beds include breakfast and free Internet access. ~~The hostel is~~ Very popular so advanced booking is a good idea. 4–7

InnCrowd Hostel II 73 Dunlop St ☎6296 9169. Just around the corner from the original, this place is just as well run with spotless common areas and comfortable dorm beds. 4–7

Kerbau Hotel 54–62 Kerbau Rd ☎6297 6668. Friendly hotel, if starting to show its age a little. The spruce and welcoming rooms all have TV. 6

Little India Guest House 3 Veerasamy Rd ☎6294 2866. A smart guesthouse with excellent, fresh-looking rooms and spotless toilets. 5

Perak Lodge 12 Perak Rd ☎6299 7733. One of the new breed of upper-bracket guesthouses, in a back street behind the Little India arcade. The rooms are secure, well-appointed and welcoming, and the price includes breakfast. Internet access available. Ask for the S$65 twin-share deal, or the reduced monthly rate. 7

Chinatown and around

Despite being such a big tourist draw, **Chinatown** isn't very well furnished with budget accommodation. The places listed below are marked on the map on pp.914–915.

Dragon Inn 18 Mosque St ☎6222 7227. Sizeable, comfortable double rooms in the middle of Chinatown, all with a/c, TV, fridge and bathroom, and set in attractive shop-houses. 6

Majestic Hotel 31–37 Bukit Pasoh Rd ☎6222 3377. Scrupulously clean and enormously friendly hotel. All rooms have a/c and private bathrooms, while those at the front boast little balconies. Room rate includes American-style breakfast. 7

Orchard Road and around

Sumptuous hotels abound in the **Orchard Road** area (see map on pp.920–921), with most double rooms here costing at least S$80.

Holiday Inn Park View 11 Cavenagh Rd ☎6733 8333. Smart hotel with all the trimmings, across the road from Singapore's presidential residence. 9

Lloyd's Inn 2 Lloyd Rd ☎6737 7309. Motel-style building boasting attractive rooms and a fine location, just 5min from Orchard Road. 7

Mitre Hotel 145 Killiney Rd ☎6737 3811. Ramshackle old Chinese hotel, set amid overgrown grounds, and with an endearingly shabby air about it; there's a great lobby bar downstairs. 3

YMCA International House 1 Orchard Rd ☎6336 6000. Plush but overpriced rooms and dorms, with a rooftop pool and a branch of *McDonald's* linked to the lobby. There's a first-day charge of S$5 for non-members. Bus #36 from the airport stops right outside. Dorms S$25. 8

Downtown Singapore

Ever since Sir Stamford Raffles first landed on its northern bank, in 1819, the area around the Singapore River, which strikes into the heart of the island from the south coast, has formed the hub of Singapore. All the city's central districts lie within a three-kilometre radius of the mouth of the river – which makes **Downtown Singapore** an extremely convenient place to tour.

The Colonial District

As the colony's trade grew in the last century, the **Singapore River** became its main artery, clogged with traditional cargo boats (known as "bumboats"), which ferried coffee, sugar and rice to the godowns. A recent campaign to clean up the river relocated the bumboats to the west coast, though a handful still remain, offering trips downriver and around Marina Bay. From Raffles Place MRT it's just a couple of minutes' walk past the former General Post Office – now a swish hotel – to the elegant suspension struts of **Cavenagh Bridge** – a good place to start a tour of Singapore's colonial centre. Stepping off the bridge, you're just a stone's throw away from the **landing site** where, in January 1819, Sir Stamford Raffles, the man who is credited as the founder of Singapore, apparently took his first steps on Singaporean soil. Now the lower end of North Boat Quay, the site is marked with a statue of Raffles. Singapore River cruise boats (see box below) depart from a tiny jetty a few steps along from Raffles' statue. North of the statue up Parliament Lane, the dignified white Victorian building on the left ringed by fencing is **Parliament House**, built as a private dwelling for a rich merchant in 1833. Today, it is being converted into a centre for the arts.

Asian Civilisations Museums

Between Cavenagh Bridge and Raffles Landing Site, sits the **Empress Place Building**, a robust Neoclassical structure named for Queen Victoria and constructed with Indian convict labour in 1864. After a recent renovation, it now houses the main collection of the **Asian Civilisations Museum** (Tues–Sun 9am–6pm; S$3, free on Fri 6–9pm), featuring insightful exhibits highlighting the principal cultures of Asia and how they interface with each other. Each of the museum's ten galleries is devoted to the art and culture of a particular region of Asia, including China, India and Southeast Asia.

The smaller, original Asian Civilisations Museum (same times and entrance fee as the flagship ACM), at 39 Armenian St, features exhibits given over to understanding the hybrid nature of Peranakan culture, detailling how Singaporean, Malay and Indonesian influences took their place alongside the traditional beliefs and practices of the Peranakan Chinese. If you intend to visit both museums, a joint S$5 ticket can be purchased at either museum.

Singapore river, island and harbour cruises

Fleets of cruise boats ply Singapore's southern waters every day and night. The best of these, the Singapore River cruises (☎6336 6111), cast off from North Boat Quay, Raffles' Landing Site, Riverside Point Landing Steps and Clarke Quay (daily 9am–11pm; every 10min) for a S$10 cruise on traditional bumboats, passing the old godowns (warehouses) upriver where traders once stored their merchandise. Several cruise companies also operate out of Clifford Pier and the HarbourFront Centre, offering everything from luxury catamaran trips around Singapore's southern isles to dinner on a Chinese sailing boat. A straightforward cruise costs about S$25, a dinner special S$35–50.

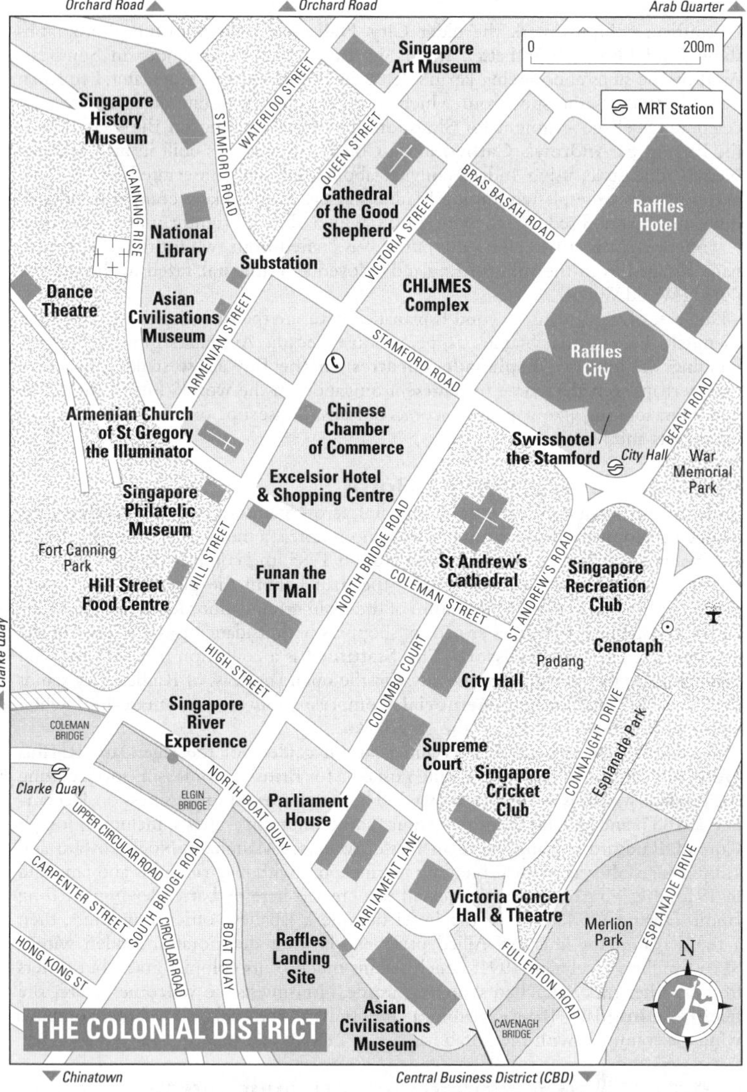

The Padang and Esplanade

The very essence of colonial Singapore, the **Padang** was earmarked by Raffles as a recreation ground shortly after his arrival. At the southwestern end, the **Singapore Cricket Club**, founded in the 1850s, was the hub of colonial British society and still operates a "members-only" rule; its brown-tiled roof, whitewashed walls and dark green blinds have a certain nostalgic charm. Just to the west, Singapore's Neo-classical **Supreme Court** was built between 1937 and 1939, and sports a domed roof of green lead and a splendid, wood-panelled entrance hall. It was here that the British formally surrendered to the Japanese in 1942. Uniform rows of grandiose

Corinthian columns mark the older **City Hall**, next door. Wartime photographs show Lord Louis Mountbatten (then Supreme Allied Commander in Southeast Asia) on the steps announcing Japan's defeat in 1945. Fourteen years later, Lee Kuan Yew chose the same spot from which to address his electorate at a victory rally celebrating self-government for Singapore. The final building on the west side of the Padang, **St Andrew's Cathedral** on Coleman Street, was built in high-vaulted, Neo-Gothic style, using Indian convict labour, and was consecrated in 1862. Its exterior walls were plastered using Madras *chunam* – an unlikely composite of eggs, lime, sugar and shredded coconut husks which shines brightly when smoothed – while the small cross behind the pulpit was crafted from two fourteenth-century nails salvaged from the ruins of England's Coventry Cathedral, razed to the ground during World War II.

Due east of the Padang, beyond Esplanade Drive, are the twin Esplanade buildings. In much the way that Sydney's Opera House became Australia's most recognized building, the futuristic **Esplanade Theatres on the Bay** are so striking that they may perhaps someday come to represent Singapore in the world's imagination. The buildings, looking like a pair of iconic durians, house not only theatres but also restaurants and boutiques.

Raffles City and Raffles Hotel

Immediately north of St Andrew's Cathedral, across Stamford Road, is **Raffles City**, a huge development comprising two enormous hotels, a multi-level shopping centre and floor upon floor of offices. Completed in 1985, the complex was designed by Chinese–American architect IM Pei – the man behind the glass pyramid which fronts the Louvre in Paris. One feature of the main ground-floor lobby is a spectacular fountain, which transfixes crowds of shoppers with its dancing water jets. On the top three floors of the **Swissotel The Stamford** is a collection of restaurants and bars with spectacular views of the city. On the open land east of Raffles City stands the imposing **Civilian War Memorial**. Comprising four seventy-metre-high white columns, it's known locally as "the chopsticks".

The lofty halls, restaurants, bars and peaceful gardens of the legendary **Raffles Hotel** all conspire to evoke an aching nostalgia for British colonialism (sorry, cuffing the punkah wallah is no longer allowed). The hotel opened for business on December 1, 1887, and quickly began to attract some impressive guests, including Joseph Conrad, Rudyard Kipling, Herman Hesse, Somerset Maugham, Noël Coward and Günter Grass. It was the first building in Singapore with electric lights and fans, and in 1915, the "Singapore Sling" cocktail was created here by bartender Ngiam Tong Boon. During World War II, the hotel became a Japanese officers' quarters, then a transit camp for liberated Allied prisoners. Postwar deterioration ended with a S$160-million facelift in 1991, which retains much of its colonial grace, but suffers from a rather tacky attached shopping arcade. Non-guests are welcome to visit the free **museum** (daily 10am–7pm) located upstairs, at the back of the hotel complex, which is crammed with memorabilia.

CHIJMES, the Singapore Art Museum and the History Museum

Bras Basah Road cuts west from Raffles, crossing North Bridge Road and then passing Singapore's newest and most aesthetically pleasing eating place, the **CHIJMES** complex. Based around the Neo-Gothic husk of the former Convent of the Holy Infant Jesus (from whose name the complex's acronymic title is derived), CHIJMES is a rustic version of London's Covent Garden, with lawns, courtyards, waterfalls, fountains and sunken forecourt; the shops here open from 9am to 10pm, most restaurants and bars from 11am to 1am. Northwest of CHIJMES, at 71 Bras Basah, the new **Singapore Art Museum** (Mon–Sun 10am–7pm; S$3, free on Fri 6–9pm) is housed in the venerable St Joseph's Institution, Singapore's first Catholic school, many of whose original rooms survive. SAM's strength lies in its contemporary regional and pan-Asian exhibitions, mapping the modern Asian experience by drawing on a permanent collection of 5500 artworks. Touring exhibitions typically remain on display for around four months. The museum's new Cyber Gallery incorporates experimental forms that are pushing the boundaries of what most Singaporeans have come to expect from an art museum. Guides conduct free **tours** (Tues–Fri 11am & 2pm, Sat & Sun 11am, 2pm & 3.30pm) around the museum's major works.

The **Singapore History Museum** on Stamford Road was undergoing extensive renovations at the time of writing and is expected to be closed to the public until 2006. In the meantime, the museum is being temporarily housed at 30 Merchant Road, near Riverside Point. Sensibly, the ongoing exhibition focuses on the Singapore River and its role in the history of the settlement. The **Rivertales Exhibition** (Tues–Thurs and Sun 9am–7pm; Mon 1pm–7pm; Fri 9am–9pm; S$2, free on Fri 7–9pm) includes short documentaries screened throughout the day.

Bugis Village

One block east of Waterloo Street's shops and temples, at the junction of Rochor Road and Victoria Street sits **Bugis Village** – a rather tame manifestation of infamous Bugis Street. Until the area was remodelled to make way for an MRT station, Bugis Street embodied old Singapore: after dark it was a chaotic place, crawling with rowdy sailors (who euphorically referred to it as "Boogie Street"), transvestites and prostitutes – anathema to a Singapore government keen to clean up its country's reputation. Singaporean public opinion demanded a replacement, and Bugis Village duly opened in 1991. However, with its beer gardens, seafood restaurants and pubs, it is a sad shadow of its former self, though the covered and air-conditioned "streets" of nearby PARCO Bugis Junction Shopping Centre are a welcome escape from the heat.

Fort Canning Park and Clarke Quay

When Raffles first caught sight of Singapore, **Fort Canning Park** was known locally as Bukit Larangan (Forbidden Hill). The five kings of Singapura were said to have ruled the island from here six hundred years ago, and archeological digs have proved it was inhabited as early as the fourteenth century. The last of the kings, Sultan Iskandar Shah, reputedly lies here, and a *keramat*, or auspicious place, on the eastern slope of the hill marks the supposed site of his grave. When the British arrived, Singapore's first British Resident (a political officer appointed by London), William Farquhar, displayed typical colonial tact by promptly having the hill cleared and building a bungalow on the summit. The bungalow was replaced in 1859 by a fort, but of this only a gateway, guardhouse and adjoining wall remain. An early European **cemetery** survives, however, upon whose stones are engraved intriguing epitaphs to nineteenth-century sailors, traders and residents.

There's a "back entrance" to the park that involves climbing the exhausting flight of steps that runs between the Hill Street Food Centre, on Hill Street. Once you reach the top, you're greeted by a brilliant view along High Street towards the Merlion monument at the mouth of the Singapore River. The hill, which houses two theatres, is ringed by two walks, signs along which illuminate aspects of the park's fourteenth- and nineteenth-century history. What's more, the underground operations complex, from which the Allied war effort in Singapore was masterminded, has recently been opened to the public. Known as the **Battle Box** (daily 10am–5pm; S$8), the complex uses audio and video effects and animations to bring to life the last hours before the Japanese occupation began in February, 1942.

On the other side of River Valley Road, which skirts the southwestern slope of Fort Canning Park, a chain of nineteenth-century godowns has been renovated into the attractive **Clarke Quay** shopping and eating complex. There's also an interesting flea market held here every Sunday. A river taxi for Clarke Quay (daily 11am–11pm; S$2 return) departs every five minutes from the quayside above the Standard Chartered Bank, two minutes' walk from Raffles Place MRT.

Chinatown

The two square kilometres of **Chinatown**, bounded by New Bridge Road to the west, Neil and Maxwell roads to the south, Cecil Street to the east and the Singapore River to the north, once constituted the focal point of Chinese life and culture in Singapore. Nowadays, the area is on its last traditional legs, scarred by the wounds of demolition and dwarfed by the Central Business District. Even so, a wander through the surviving nineteenth-century streets unearths aged craft shops and provision stores, and restaurants unchanged in forty years.

The area was first earmarked for settlement by the Chinese community by Sir Stamford Raffles himself, who decided on his second visit to the island in June 1819 that the ethnic communities should live separately. As increasing numbers of immigrants poured into Singapore, Chinatown became just that – a Chinese town, where new arrivals from the mainland, mostly from the Guangdong (Canton) and Fujian provinces, would have been pleased to find temples, shops and, most importantly, *kongsi* (clan associations), which helped them to find food and lodgings and work, mainly as small traders and coolies. By the mid-twentieth century, the area was rich with the imported cultural heritage of China, but the government regarded the tumbledown slums of Chinatown as an eyesore and embarked upon a catastrophic **redevelopment campaign** that saw whole roads bulldozed to make way for new shopping centres, and street traders relocated into organized complexes. Only recently did public opinion finally convince the Singaporean authorities to restore the area.

The **Chinatown Heritage Centre** (daily 10am–7pm; S$8) at 48 Pagoda Street, is housed in a row of traditional shop-houses that have been restored to give visitors an idea of what the whole neighbourhood once looked like.

Along Telok Ayer Street

Follow the signs for Maxwell Road out of Tanjong Pagar MRT and you'll surface on the southern edge of Chinatown. Take the left-hand path in front of the station and cross Maxwell Road; after about 50m you'll hit **Telok Ayer Street**, and the square Chinese Methodist Church. Further up, shortly beyond McCallum Street, the enormous **Thian Hock Keng Temple** (the "Temple of Heavenly Happiness") is a hugely impressive Hokkien building. Built on the site of a small joss house where immigrants made offerings to Ma Chu Por (or Tian Hou), the Queen of Heaven, the temple was started in 1839 using materials imported from China. A statue of the goddess stands in the centre of the temple's main hall, flanked by the God of War on the right and the Protector of Life on the left. From the street, the temple looks spectacular: dragons stalk its broad roofs, while the entrance to the temple compound bristles with ceramic flowers, foliage and figures. Two stone lions stand guard at the entrance, and door gods, painted on the front doors, prevent evil spirits from entering. Look out, too, for the huge ovens, always lit, in which offerings to either gods or ancestors are burnt.

Telok Ayer Street continues north beyond Cross Street to **Far East Square**, a new shopping-cum-dining centre that taps Chinatown's heritage for its inspiration. It also boasts the Fuk Tak Ch'i Street Museum (daily 10am–10pm; free), housed in one of Singapore's oldest Chinese temples, and displaying paraphernalia such as opium pipes, Peranakan jewellery and a model junk perched atop what was once the main altar.

A block west of Telok Ayer Street, **Amoy Street** (along with China and Telok Ayer streets) was also designated a Hokkien enclave in the colony's early days. Long terraces of shop-houses flank the street, all featuring characteristic **five-foot ways**, simply covered verandas that were so-called because they jut five feet out from the house. Some of the shop-houses are in a ramshackle state, while others have been marvellously renovated, only to be bought by companies in need of some fancy office space. It's worth walking down to the **Sian Chai Kang Temple**, at 66 Amoy St, its eaves painted a shade of red every bit as fiery as the dragons on its roof.

Along South Bridge Road

Turn right out of Ann Siang Hill and you'll see **Eu Yan Sang Medical Hall** (Mon–Sat 8.30am–6pm) at 267–271 South Bridge Road, first opened in 1910 and geared up, to an extent, for the tourist trade – some of the staff speak good English. The shop has been beautifully renovated and sells a weird assortment of ingredients, from herbs and roots to various dubious remedies derived from exotic and endangered species. The ground-up gall bladders of snakes or bears apparently work wonders on pimples; monkey's gallstones aid asthmatics; while deer penis is supposed to provide a lift to any sexual problem. Antlers, sea horses, scorpions and turtle shells also feature regularly in Chinese prescriptions, though the greatest cure-all of Oriental medicine is said to be ginseng, a clever little root that will combat anything from weakness of the heart to acne and jet lag; if you need a pick-me-up, the shop administers free glasses of ginseng tea.

Across the road from the front doors of Eu Yan Sang, the compound of the **Sri Mariamman Hindu Temple** bursts with wild-looking statues of deities and animals in primary colours, and there's always some ritual or other being attended to by one of the temple's priests. The present temple was completed in around 1843 and boasts a superb gopura over the front entrance. Once inside, you'll see splendidly vivid friezes on the roof depicting a host of Hindu deities, including the three manifestations of the Supreme Being: Brahma the Creator (with three of his four heads showing), Vishnu the Preserver, and Shiva the Destroyer (holding one of his sons). The main sanctum, facing you as you walk inside, is devoted to Goddess Mariamman, who's worshipped for her power to cure disease. To the left of the main sanctum there's a patch of sand; once a year during the festival of Thimithi, it is covered in red-hot coals, which male Hindus run across to prove the strength of their faith.

Chinatown Complex and beyond

After crumbling Telok Ayer and Amoy streets, much of the section of Chinatown west of South Bridge Road seems far less authentic. This is tour-bus Chinatown, heaving with gangs of holidaymakers plundering souvenir shops. The hideous concrete exterior of the **Chinatown Complex**, at the end of Sago Street, belies the charm of the teeming market it houses. Walk up the front steps, past the fruit and nut hawkers, and once you're inside, the market's many twists and turns reveal stalls selling silk, kimonos, rattan, leather and clothes. Prices aren't fixed, so you'll need to haggle.

Sago Street skirts to the right of the Chinatown Complex, and turns into **Trengganu Street**, packed with shops selling Singapore Airlines uniforms, presentation chopstick sets, and silk hats with false pony tails – plus a few relics of Chinatown's old trades and industries.

The Central Business District (CBD)

Raffles Place forms the nucleus of the **Central Business District** (commonly referred to as the CBD) – the commercial heart of the state, home to many of its 140 banks and financial institutions – and is ringed by buildings so tall that pedestrians crossing the square feel like ants in a canyon. The most striking way to experience the giddy heights of the CBD is by surfacing from Raffles Place MRT – follow the signs for Cecil Street out of the station. To your left is the soaring metallic triangle of the OUB Centre (Overseas Union Bank), and, right of that, the rocket-shaped UOB Plaza 2 (United Overseas Bank); in front of you are the rich brown walls of the Standard Chartered Bank, and to your right rise sturdy Singapore Land Tower and the almost Art Deco Caltex House. The three roads that run southwest from Raffles Place – Cecil Street, Robinson Road and Shenton Way – are all choc-a-bloc with more high-rise banks and financial houses. Just north of Raffles Place, and beneath the "elephant's trunk" curve of the Singapore River, the pedestrianized row of shop-houses known as **Boat Quay** is Singapore's most fashionable hangout, sporting a huge collection of restaurants and bars.

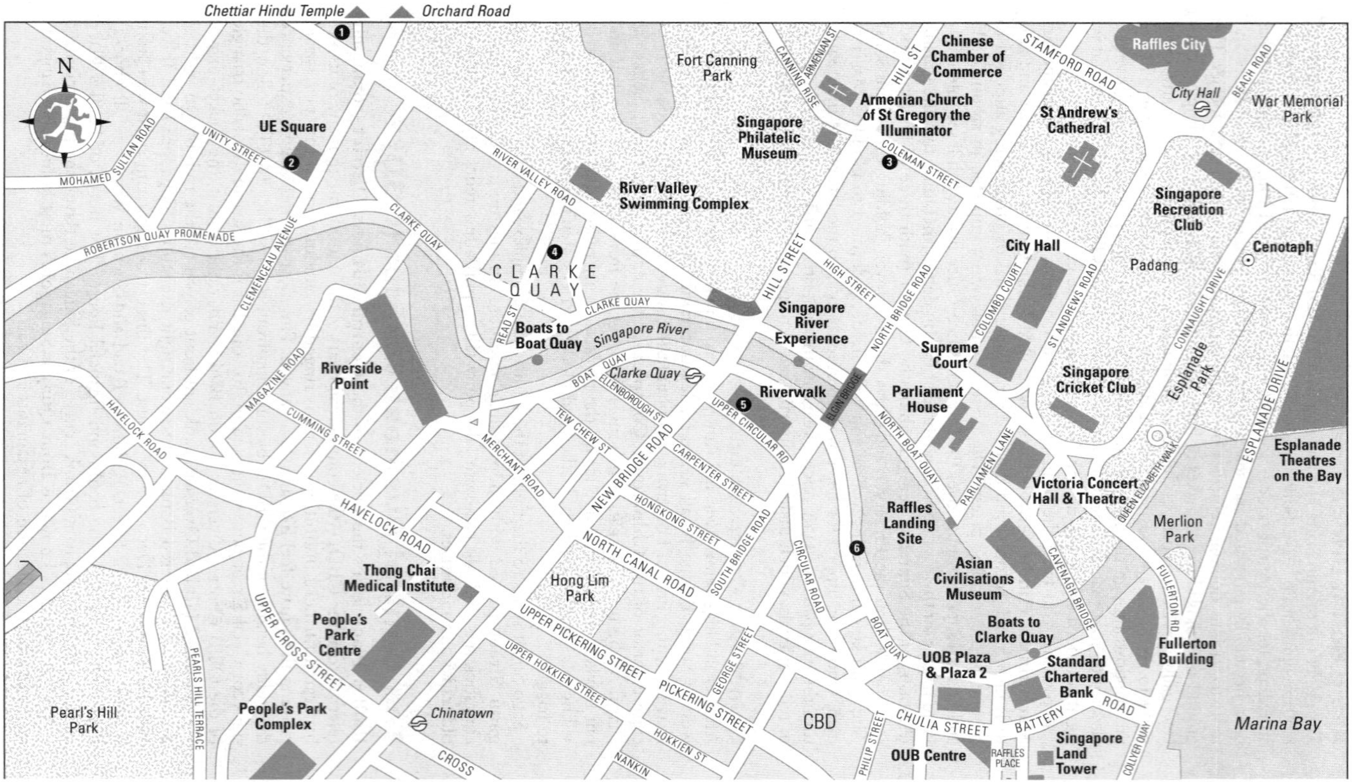

Chettiar Hindu Temple
Orchard Road
N
UE Square
Fort Canning Park
Chinese Chamber of Commerce
Armenian Church of St Gregory the Illuminator
Singapore Philatelic Museum
River Valley Swimming Complex
St Andrew's Cathedral
Raffles City
City Hall
War Memorial Park
Singapore Recreation Club
Cenotaph
Padang
City Hall
Supreme Court
Singapore Cricket Club
Esplanade Park
Esplanade Theatres on the Bay
CLARKE QUAY
Boats to Boat Quay
Singapore River
Singapore River Experience
Clarke Quay
Riverwalk
Parliament House
Victoria Concert Hall & Theatre
Merlion Park
Riverside Point
Raffles Landing Site
Asian Civilisations Museum
Boats to Clarke Quay
Fullerton Building
Standard Chartered Bank
UOB Plaza & Plaza 2
Thong Chai Medical Institute
Hong Lim Park
People's Park Centre
People's Park Complex
Chinatown
CBD
OUB Centre
Singapore Land Tower
Raffles Place
Marina Bay
Pearl's Hill Park
STAMFORD ROAD
BEACH ROAD
HILL ST
ARMENIAN ST
CANNING RISE
COLEMAN STREET
RIVER VALLEY ROAD
HILL STREET
HIGH STREET
NORTH BRIDGE ROAD
COLOMBO COURT
ST ANDREWS ROAD
CONNAUGHT DRIVE
ESPLANADE DRIVE
QUEEN ELIZABETH WALK
PARLIAMENT LANE
NORTH BOAT QUAY
ELGIN BRIDGE
CAVENAGH BRIDGE
FULLERTON RD
COLLYER QUAY
BATTERY ROAD
CHULIA STREET
PHILIP STREET
BOAT QUAY
CIRCULAR ROAD
SOUTH BRIDGE ROAD
GEORGE STREET
PICKERING STREET
HOKKIEN ST
NANKIN
CROSS
UPPER CIRCULAR RD
CARPENTER STREET
HONGKONG STREET
NORTH CANAL ROAD
UPPER PICKERING STREET
UPPER HOKKIEN STREET
NEW BRIDGE ROAD
ELLENBOROUGH ST
TEW CHEW ST
MERCHANT ROAD
BOAT QUAY
CLARKE QUAY
READ ST
CUMMING STREET
MAGAZINE ROAD
HAVELOCK ROAD
UPPER CROSS STREET
PEARLS HILL TERRACE
CLEMENCEAU AVENUE
ROBERTSON QUAY PROMENADE
UNITY STREET
SULTAN ROAD
MOHAMED

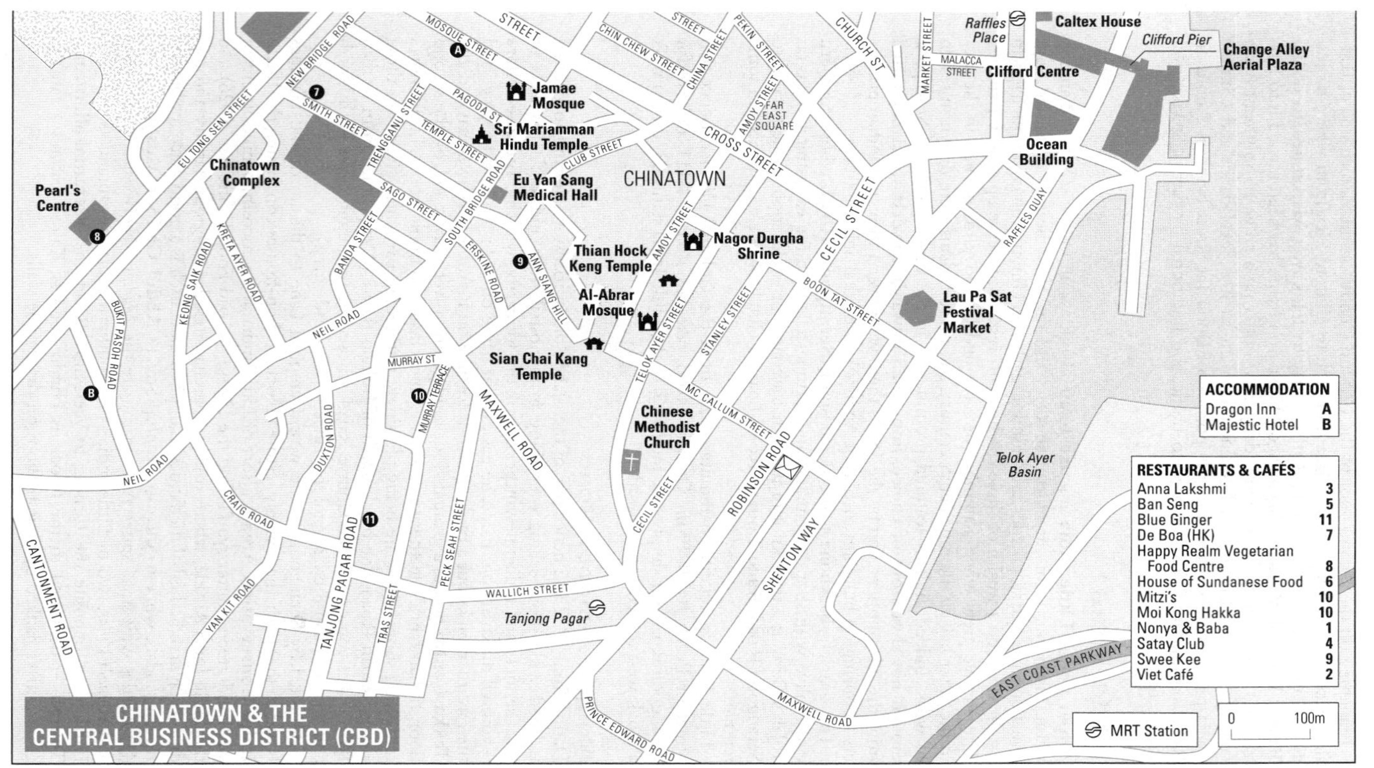
CHINATOWN & THE
CENTRAL BUSINESS DISTRICT (CBD)
ACCOMMODATION
Dragon Inn A
Majestic Hotel B
RESTAURANTS & CAFÉS
Anna Lakshmi 3
Ban Seng 5
Blue Ginger 11
De Boa (HK) 7
Happy Realm Vegetarian Food Centre 8
House of Sundanese Food 6
Mitzi's 10
Moi Kong Hakka 10
Nonya & Baba 1
Satay Club 4
Swee Kee 9
Viet Café 2
MRT Station
0 100m
Raffles Place
Caltex House
Clifford Pier
Change Alley Aerial Plaza
MALACCA STREET
MARKET STREET
Clifford Centre
Ocean Building
CHURCH ST
PEKIN STREET
STREET
CHINA STREET
CHIN CHEW STREET
STREET
MOSQUE STREET
NEW BRIDGE ROAD
Jamae Mosque
PAGODA ST
Sri Mariamman Hindu Temple
SMITH STREET
TRENGGANU STREET
TEMPLE STREET
AMOY STREET
FAR EAST SQUARE
CROSS STREET
CLUB STREET
EU TONG SEN STREET
Chinatown Complex
Pearl's Centre
Eu Yan Sang Medical Hall
CHINATOWN
SAGO STREET
SOUTH BRIDGE ROAD
RAFFLES QUAY
CECIL STREET
AMOY STREET
Nagor Durgha Shrine
Thian Hock Keng Temple
BANDA STREET
ERSKINE ROAD
ANN SIANG HILL
KRETA AYER ROAD
KEONG SAIK ROAD
BOON TAT STREET
Lau Pa Sat Festival Market
Al-Abrar Mosque
TELOK AYER STREET
STANLEY STREET
NEIL ROAD
BUKIT PASOH ROAD
MURRAY ST
Sian Chai Kang Temple
MURRAY TERRACE
MC CALLUM STREET
Chinese Methodist Church
MAXWELL ROAD
DUXTON ROAD
ROBINSON ROAD
Telok Ayer Basin
NEIL ROAD
CRAIG ROAD
CECIL STREET
TANJONG PAGAR ROAD
PECK SEAH STREET
SHENTON WAY
CANTONMENT ROAD
YAN KIT ROAD
WALLICH STREET
Tanjong Pagar
TRAS STREET
EAST COAST PARKWAY
MAXWELL ROAD
PRINCE EDWARD ROAD

Branching off the second floor of the Clifford Centre, on the eastern side of Raffles Place, Change Alley Aerial Plaza leads you to Clifford Pier, from where it's just a short walk to the south along Raffles Quay to Telok Ayer Market, renamed **Lau Pa Sat Festival Market**. This octagonal cast-iron frame has been turned into Singapore's most tasteful food centre (daily 24hr), offering a range of Southeast Asian cuisines as well as laying on free entertainment such as local bands and Chinese opera performances. After 7pm, the portion of Boon Tat Street between Robinson Road and Shenton Way is closed to traffic, and traditional hawker stalls take over the street.

Little India

A tour around **Little India** amounts to an all-out assault on the senses. Indian pop music blares out from gargantuan speakers and the air is heavily perfumed with sweet incense, curry powder and jasmine garlands; Hindu women promenade in bright saris; and a wealth of "hole-in-the-wall" restaurants serve up superior curries. The enclave grew when a number of cattle and buffalo yards opened in the area in the latter half of the nineteenth century, and more Indians were drawn in search of work. Indeed, Indians featured prominently in the development of Singapore, though not always out of choice: from 1825 onwards, convicts were transported from the subcontinent, and by the 1840s there were over a thousand Indian prisoners labouring on buildings such as St Andrew's Cathedral and the Istana.

The district's backbone is the north–south **Serangoon Road**, whose southern end is alive with shops, restaurants and fortune-tellers. To the east, stretching as far as Jalan Besar, is a tight knot of roads that are ripe for exploration; while parallel to Serangoon Road, **Race Course Road** boasts a clutch of fine restaurants and some temples.

Little India is just fifteen minutes' walk from the Colonial District, Bencoolen Street or Beach Road. From Orchard Road, take bus #65 or #111 and ask for Serangoon Road. Or simply take the MRT to the Little India station, and then walk a block west to Serangoon Road.

Along Serangoon Road

Dating from 1822 and hence one of the island's oldest roadways, **Serangoon Road** is lined with shops selling everything from nostril studs and ankle bracelets to incense sticks and Indian newspapers. Look out for parrot-wielding **fortune-tellers** – you tell the man your name, he passes your name on to his feathered partner, and the bird then picks out a card with your fortune on it. At the southwestern end, the **Tekka Centre** houses a ground-floor food centre, a wet market and, on the second floor, Indian fabrics, leatherware, watches and cheap electronic goods. Little India's remaining shop-houses are being pleasingly restored; in particular, check out those along Kerbau Road, one block north of Buffalo Road. (A right turn from Kerbau Road takes you onto Race Course Road, whose fine restaurants serve both North and South Indian food; several specialize in fish-head curry.)

Bounded by Serangoon to the west, Campbell Lane to the north and Hastings Road to the south, the lovingly restored block of shop-houses comprising the **Little India Conservation Area** is a sort of Little India in microcosm: behind its cream walls and green shutters you'll find the Hastings Road Food Court (see p.926) and the Little India Arcade, where you can purchase textiles, religious statuary and traditional ayurvedic herbal medicines. Campbell Lane itself is a good place for buying Indian sandals, while to the east, Dunlop Street's **Abdul Gaffoor Mosque** (at no. 41) bristles with small spires. Also nearby are the *Madras New Woodlands Restaurant* and *Komala Villas*, two of Little India's best southern Indian restaurants (see p.927). Further up, opposite the turning to Veerasamy Road, the **Veeramakaliamman Temple** – dedicated to the ferocious Hindu goddess, Kali – features a fanciful gopura that's flanked by majestic lions on the temple walls.

You won't find **Pink Street** – one of the most incongruous and sordid spots in the whole of clean, shiny Singapore – on any city map. The entire length of the "street" (in fact, it's merely an alley between the backs of Rowell and Desker roads) is punctuated by open doorways, inside which gaggles of bored-looking prostitutes sit knitting or watching TV. Stalls along the alley sell sex toys, blue videos and potency pills, while con-men work the "three cups and a ball" routine on unwary passers-by.

North of Desker Road

Each year, on the day of the Thaipusam festival (Jan/Feb), inside the courtyard of the **Sri Srinivasa Perumal Temple**, at 397 Serangoon Road, Hindu devotees don huge metal frames topped with peacock feathers, which are fastened to their flesh with hooks and prongs. The devotees then parade all the way to the Chettiar Hindu Temple on Tank Road, off Orchard Road. Even if you miss the festival, it's worth a trip here to see the five-tiered gopura with its sculptures of the manifestations of Lord Vishnu the Preserver. On the wall to the right of the front gate, a sculpted elephant, its leg caught in a crocodile's mouth, trumpets silently.

Just beyond the Sri Srinivasa Perumal temple complex, a small path leads northwest to Race Course Road, where the slightly kitsch **Sakaya Muni Buddha Gaya Temple** (or the "Temple of the Thousand Lights"), built entirely by a Thai monk, is on the right at no. 366. On the left as you enter is a huge replica of Buddha's footprint, inlaid with mother-of-pearl; beyond sits a enormous Buddha ringed by the thousand electric lights from which the temple takes its alternative name, and 25 scenes from the Buddha's life decorate the pedestal on which he sits. It is possible to walk inside the Buddha itself, through a door in his back; inside is a smaller representation, this time of Buddha reclining.

Double back onto Serangoon Road and a five-minute walk southeast along Petain Road leads to Jalan Besar, a route which takes in some immaculate examples of **Peranakan shop-houses**, their facades covered with elegant ceramic tiles; there's more Peranakan architecture on Jalan Besar itself (turn right at the end of Petain Road).

The Arab Quarter

Before the arrival of Raffles, the area of Singapore southwest of the Rochor Canal housed a Malay village known as Kampung Glam, after the Gelam tribe of sea gypsies who lived there (an alternative explanation is that *glam* is the name of a particular type of tree that grew in the area). Raffles allotted the area to the newly installed Sultan Hussein Mohammed Shah and designated the land around it as a Muslim settlement. Soon the zone was attracting Arab traders, as the road names in today's **Arab Quarter** – Baghdad Street, Muscat Street and Haji Lane – suggest. The Arab Quarter is no more than a ten-minute walk from Bencoolen Street; to get there from Orchard Road, take **bus** #7 to Victoria Street and get off when you spot the *Golden Landmark Hotel* on your right; alternatively, head for Bugis MRT.

The pavements of **Arab Street** are an obstacle course of carpets, cloths, baskets and bags. Most of the shops have been renovated, though one or two still retain their original dark-wood and glass cabinets. Textile stores are most prominent, along with shops dealing in leather, basketware, gold, gemstones and jewellery. The quarter's most evocative patch is the stretch of **North Bridge Road** between Arab Street and Jalan Sultan. Here, the men sport long sarongs and Abe Lincoln beards, the women fantastically colourful shawls and robes, while the shops and restaurants are geared more towards locals than tourists.

Squatting between Kandahar and Aliwal streets, the **Istana Kampong Glam** was built as the royal palace of Sultan Ali Iskandar Shah, son of Sultan Hussein who negotiated with Raffles to hand over Singapore to the British. Generations of the sultan's descendants lived here until recently when, amid some controversy, the government took possession of the building, which has been slated to become a Malay heritage museum. A few steps further on, Baghdad Street crosses pedestrianized Bus-

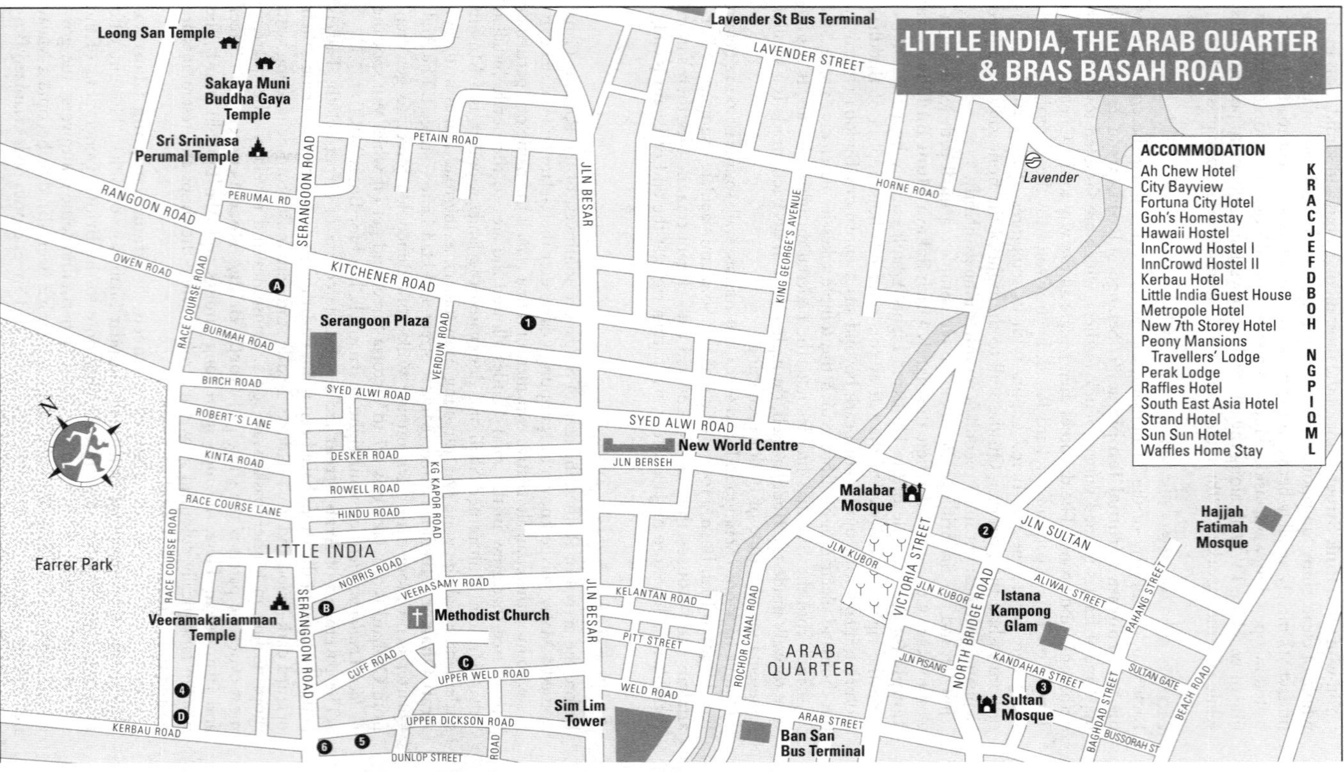
LITTLE INDIA, THE ARAB QUARTER & BRAS BASAH ROAD
ACCOMMODATION
Ah Chew Hotel K
City Bayview R
Fortuna City Hotel A
Goh's Homestay C
Hawaii Hostel J
InnCrowd Hostel I E
InnCrowd Hostel II F
Kerbau Hotel D
Little India Guest House B
Metropole Hotel O
New 7th Storey Hotel H
Peony Mansions Travellers' Lodge N
Perak Lodge G
Raffles Hotel P
South East Asia Hotel I
Strand Hotel Q
Sun Sun Hotel M
Waffles Home Stay L
Lavender St Bus Terminal
Lavender Street
Lavender
Horne Road
King George's Avenue
Jln Besar
Petain Road
Serangoon Road
Leong San Temple
Sakaya Muni Buddha Gaya Temple
Sri Srinivasa Perumal Temple
Perumal Rd
Rangoon Road
Owen Road
Race Course Road
Kitchener Road
Burmah Road
Birch Road
Robert's Lane
Kinta Road
Race Course Lane
Serangoon Plaza
Verdun Road
Syed Alwi Road
Desker Road
Rowell Road
Hindu Road
KG Kapor Road
New World Centre
Jln Berseh
Malabar Mosque
Jln Sultan
Hajjah Fatimah Mosque
Little India
Farrer Park
Norris Road
Veerasamy Road
Methodist Church
Veeramakaliamman Temple
Cuff Road
Upper Weld Road
Upper Dickson Road
Dunlop Street
Kerbau Road
Kelantan Road
Pitt Street
Weld Road
Sim Lim Tower
Rochor Canal Road
Arab Street
Ban San Bus Terminal
Arab Quarter
Jln Kubor
Victoria Street
Jln Pisang
North Bridge Road
Istana Kampong Glam
Aliwal Street
Kandahar Street
Sultan Mosque
Baghdad Street
Bussorah St
Sultan Gate
Pahang Street
Beach Road

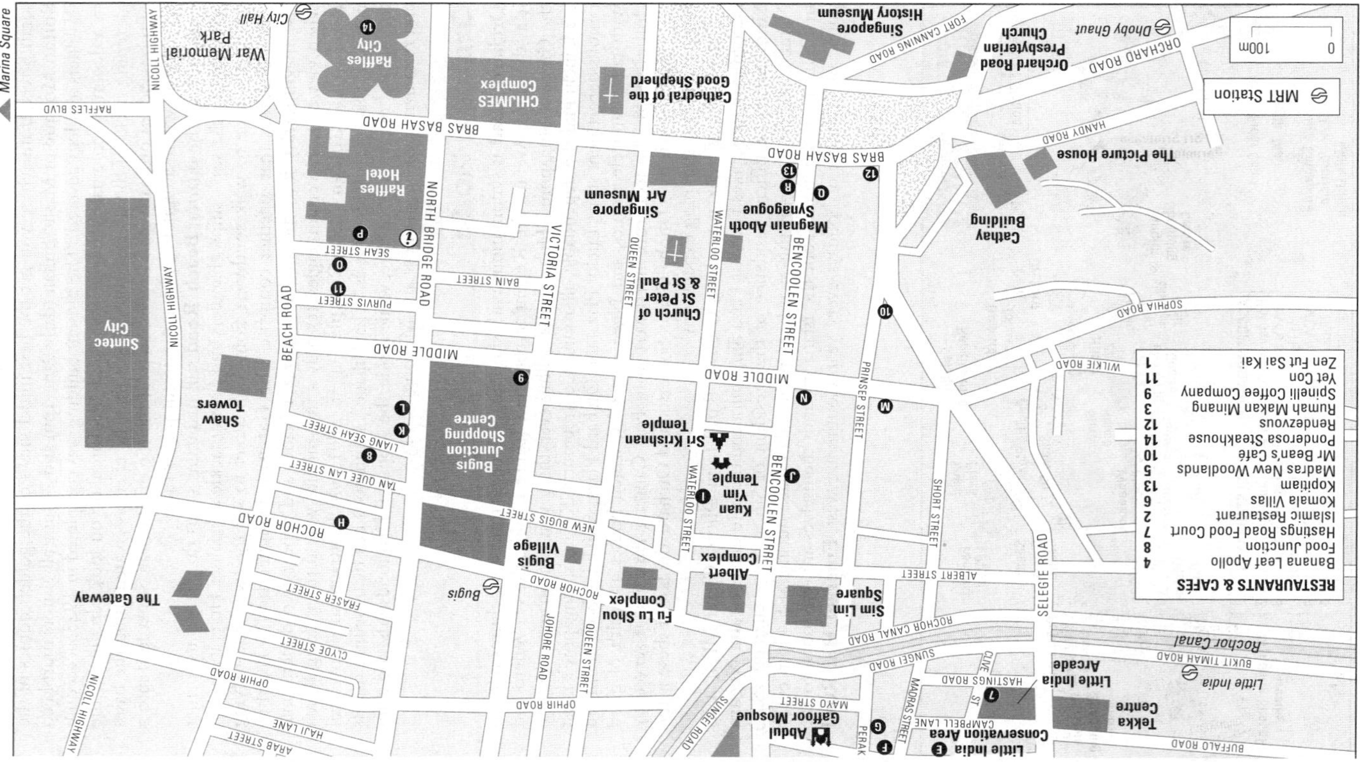
RESTAURANTS & CAFÉS
Banana Leaf Apollo 4
Food Junction 8
Hastings Road Food Court 7
Islamic Restaurant 2
Komala Villas 6
Kopitiam 13
Madras New Woodlands 5
Mr Bean's Café 10
Ponderosa Steakhouse 14
Rendezvous 12
Rumah Makan Minang 3
Spinelli Coffee Company 9
Yet Con 11
Zen Fut Sai Kai 1
MRT Station
0 100m
Marina Square
Suntec City
The Gateway
Shaw Towers
War Memorial Park
City Hall
Raffles City
Raffles Hotel
CHIJMES Complex
Bugis Junction Shopping Centre
Bugis
Bugis Village
Fu Lu Shou Complex
Albert Complex
Kuan Yim Temple
Sri Krishnan Temple
Church of St Peter & St Paul
Singapore Art Museum
Cathedral of the Good Shepherd
Magnain Aboth Synagogue
Singapore History Museum
Sim Lim Square
Abdul Gaffoor Mosque
Little India Conservation Area
Little India Arcade
Tekka Centre
Little India
Rochor Canal
Cathay Building
The Picture House
Orchard Road Presbyterian Church
Dhoby Ghaut
NICOLL HIGHWAY
RAFFLES BLVD
BEACH ROAD
NORTH BRIDGE ROAD
VICTORIA STREET
QUEEN STREET
WATERLOO STREET
BENCOOLEN STREET
PRINSEP STREET
SELEGIE ROAD
BRAS BASAH ROAD
MIDDLE ROAD
ROCHOR ROAD
OPHIR ROAD
ARAB STREET
HAJI LANE
CLYDE STREET
FRASER STREET
TAN QUEE LAN STREET
LIANG SEAH STREET
PURVIS STREET
SEAH STREET
BAIN STREET
NEW BUGIS STREET
JOHORE ROAD
SUNGEI ROAD
MAYO STREET
PERAK
MADRAS STREET
CAMPBELL LANE
HASTINGS ROAD
CLIVE ST
ROCHOR CANAL ROAD
ALBERT STREET
SHORT STREET
WILKIE ROAD
SOPHIA ROAD
HANDY ROAD
ORCHARD ROAD
FORT CANNING ROAD
BUFFALO ROAD
BUKIT TIMAH ROAD

sorah Street, from where you get the best initial views of the golden domes of the **Sultan Mosque** or Masjid Sultan (daily 9am–1pm and 2–4pm; all visitors must keep shoulders and legs covered). The present building was completed in 1925, according to a design by colonial architects Swan and MacLaren: if you look carefully at the glistening necks of the domes, you can see that the effect is created using the bases of thousands of ordinary glass bottles. Steps at the top of Bussorah Street lead into a wide lobby, where a digital display lists current prayer times.

Just outside the quarter, **Beach Road** still maintains shops that betray its former proximity to the sea – ships' chandlers and fishing tackle specialists. Here, it's worth taking the time to walk southwest from Arab Street to see the two logic-defying office buildings that together comprise **The Gateway**. Designed by IM Pei, they rise magnificently into the air like vast razor blades and appear two-dimensional when viewed from certain angles. It's only a five-minute walk further along Beach Road to the **Golden Mile Complex** at no. 5001, which attracts so many Thai nationals that locals refer to it as "Thai Village". Numerous bus firms selling tickets to Thailand operate out of here, while inside, the shops sell Thai foodstuffs, and cafés and restaurants sell Singha beer and Mekong whisky.

Orchard Road

Orchard Road is synonymous with shopping – indeed, tourist brochures refer to it as the "Fifth Avenue, the Regent Street, the Champs Elysées, the Via Veneto and the Ginza of Singapore". Huge **malls**, selling everything you can imagine, line the road, including the dependable, all-round Centrepoint; CK Tang's, Singapore's most famous department store; Lucky Plaza and Orchard Plaza, which are both crammed with tailors and electronics; and Ngee Ann City, which houses a wealth of good clothes shops. The road runs northwest from Fort Canning Park and is served by three **MRT stations** – Dhoby Ghaut, Somerset and Orchard; the last of these is the most central for shopping expeditions.

Three minutes' walk west along Orchard Road from Dhoby Ghaut MRT, at its eastern extremity, takes you past Plaza Singapura and the gate of the **Istana Negara Singapura**, the official residence of the president of Singapore – currently S.R. Nathan. The changing-of-the-guard ceremony takes place outside at 5.45pm every first Sunday of the month, but the Istana grounds themselves are only open to the public on a couple of holidays every year. Continuing west, **Emerald Hill Road**

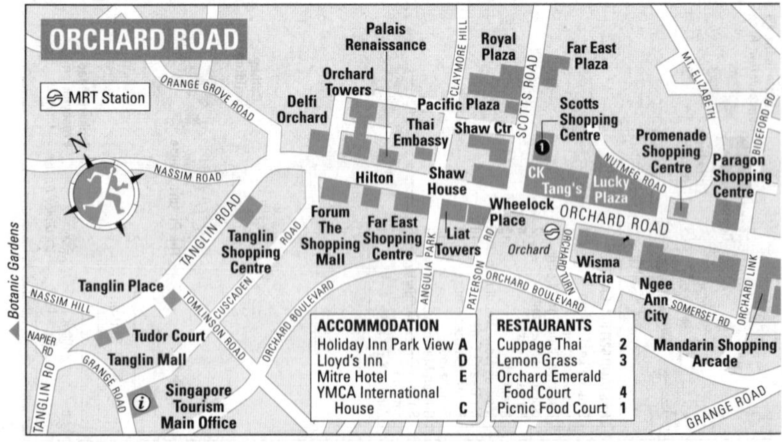

holds a number of exquisitely crafted houses built in the late nineteenth century by members of the Peranakan community, which evolved in Malaya as a result of the intermarriage between early Chinese settlers and Malay women. Built in a decorative architectural style known as Chinese Baroque, the houses are typified by highly coloured ceramic tiles, carved swing doors, shuttered windows and pastel-shaded walls with fine plaster mouldings.

By the time you reach the western end of Orchard Road, you'll be glad of the open space afforded by the **Singapore Botanic Gardens** (daily 5am–midnight; free) on Cluny Road. Founded in 1859, it was here, in 1877, that the Brazilian seeds from which grew the great rubber plantations of Malaysia were first nurtured. The fifty-odd hectares of land feature a mini-jungle, rose garden, topiary, fernery, palm valley and lakes. There's also the **National Orchid Garden** (daily 8.30am–7pm; S$2) containing sixty thousand plants, and orchid jewellery, made by plating real flowers with gold (S$100 per piece). You can pick up a free **map** of the grounds at the ranger's office, to the right of the main gate. The Botanic Gardens are a ten-minute walk from the western end of Orchard Road, or you can catch **bus** #7, #106 or #174 from Orchard Boulevard, one block south. The #106 passes down Bencoolen Street before heading on towards the gardens, while the #174 originates in New Bridge Road in Chinatown.

Around the island

Beyond the downtown area, Singapore still retains pockets of greenery in between its sprawling new towns. Most rewarding are the **Bukit Timah Nature Reserve**, and the excellent **Singapore Zoological Gardens**, both in the north of the island. Dominating the eastern tip of the island is Changi Airport and, beyond that, **Changi Village**, in whose prison the Japanese interned Allied troops and civilians during World War II. From Changi Point, it's possible to take a boat to picturesque **Pulau Ubin**, a small island with echoes of pre-development Singapore. Although western Singapore has developed into the manufacturing heart of the state, it remains remarkably verdant, and is the location of fascinating **Jurong BirdPark** and the garish **Haw Par Villa** theme park. There are theme rides aplenty on the island of **Sentosa**, just off southern Singapore, as well as some nice beaches.

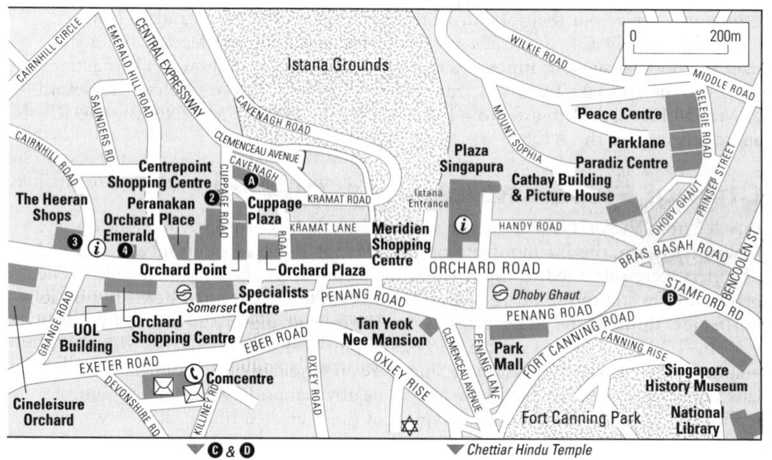

Bukit Timah Nature Reserve

Bukit Timah Road shoots northwest from the junction of Selegie and Serangoon roads, arriving 8km later at the faceless town of **BUKIT TIMAH**, and then on to Singapore's last remaining pocket of primary rainforest, which now comprises **Bukit Timah Nature Reserve** (daily 7am–7pm; free). Tigers roamed the area in the mid-eighteenth century, but now the 81-hectare reserve provides a refuge for the dwindling numbers of species still extant in Singapore – only 25 types of mammal now inhabit the island. Creatures you're most likely to see here are long-tailed macaques, butterflies, insects, and birds like the dark-necked tailorbird, which builds its nest by sewing together leaves. Scorpions, snakes, flying lemurs and pangolins (anteaters) can be found here, too. Four well-signposted, colour-coded **paths** lead out from the informative **Visitor Centre** (daily 8.30am–6pm) to the top of Bukit Timah Hill. **Bus** #171 passes down Somerset and Scotts roads en route to Bukit Timah Reserve, while the #961 can be picked up on North Bridge Road, South Bridge Road or New Bridge Road; a third option is to take the #170 from the Ban San terminal on Queen Street.

Singapore Zoological Gardens and Night Safari

The **Singapore Zoological Gardens** (daily 8.30am–6pm; S$12; ⓦwww.zoo.com.sg) on Mandai Lake Road is one of the world's few open zoos, where moats are preferred to cages. Though leopards, pumas and jaguars still have to be kept behind bars, this is a thoughtful, humane place, which manages to approximate the natural habitats of the animals it holds. There are over two thousand animals here, representing more than 240 species, so it's best to allow a whole day for your visit. A **tram** (S$2.50) circles the grounds on a one-way circuit. Highlights include the Komodo dragons, the polar bears (which you view underwater from a gallery) and the primate kingdom. You can take your pick of **animal shows**, especially enjoyable for children, four during weekdays, with additional performances on weekends and holidays. Naturally enough, kids also take to the **Children's World** section of the zoo. Supposedly the largest colony of **orang-utans** from Borneo and Sumatra are here, as well as a new exhibit called Elephants of Asia, which explains the habits and history of what was once one of Asia's most important beasts of burden. It's also possible to go on a **Night Safari** here (daily 7.30pm–midnight; S$18; ⓦwww.nightsafari.com.sg), which means you watch as over a hundred species of animals – among them elephants, rhinos, giraffes, leopards, hyenas, otters, and incredibly cute (but shy) fishing cats – play out their nocturnal routines under a forest of standard lamps.

Buy the S$1 *Guide to S'pore Zoo* on arrival: besides riding and feeding times and a map, the booklet suggests itineraries that take in all the major shows and attractions. To get to the zoo, take **bus** #171 from either Stamford Road or Orchard Boulevard to Mandai Road, then transfer to #138. Alternatively, take the MRT to Ang Mo Kio and connect with the #138.

Changi Prison Museum & Chapel

Bus #2 from Victoria Street, or from Tanah Merah MRT, drops you right outside **Changi Prison**, the infamous site of a World War II POW camp in which Allied prisoners were subjected to the harshest of treatment by their Japanese jailers. The prison itself is still in use (drug offenders are periodically executed here), but on its north side, through the outer gates, is the hugely moving prison **museum** (daily 9.30am–4.30pm, religious service Sun 5.30–7pm; free), where sketches and photographs plot the Japanese invasion of Singapore and the fate of the soldiers and civilians subsequently incarcerated here and in nearby camps. Beyond the museum is a replica of a simple wooden chapel, typical of those erected in Singapore's wartime prisons; its brass cross was crafted from spent ammunition casings, while the north wall carries poignant messages, penned by former POWs and relatives.

Journey's end for bus #2 is at the terminal at **CHANGI VILLAGE**, ten minutes further on from the prison. There's little to bring you out here, save to catch a boat from **Changi Point**, behind the bus terminal, for Pulau Ubin, or to the coast of Johor in Malaysia (see box on pp.902–903). The left-hand jetty is for Ubin, the right-hand one for bumboats to Johor.

Pulau Ubin

With the recent shelving of a plan to reclaim land on **Pulau Ubin** for military use, this lazy backwater situated 2km offshore in the Straits of Johor is suddenly a fashionable destination for Singaporeans wishing to discover what their island would have been like fifty years ago. It's a great place to head for when you get tired of shops, high-rises and traffic, and it's almost worth coming for the boat trip alone, made in an old, oil-stained bumboat, which departs from Changi Point throughout the day, leaving when full (10min; S$2). The last boat back to Changi may leave as late as 11pm, but plan to be at the jetty by 8.30pm at the latest, just in case. The boats dock at **Ubin Village**, where Malay stilt houses teeter over the sludgy, mangrove beach.

The best, and most enjoyable, way to explore the dirt tracks of Ubin is by **mountain bike**, which can be rented for S$5–15/day from Universal Adventure on the left-hand side of the road leading west from the jetty. You'll be given a baffling map of the island's labyrinthine network of tracks, though it's more fun to strike off and see where you end up – Ubin is only a small island (just 7km by 2km) so you won't get lost. Ride through the village until you come to a basketball court, where a **right turn** takes you past raised kampung houses and rubber trees to the eastern side of the island. Turning left instead takes you to the centre of the island, past a quarry, to a rather incongruous **Thai Buddhist Temple**, complete with portraits of the King and Queen of Thailand, and murals telling the story of the life of Buddha. If you follow the **left track** out of Ubin Village for twenty or thirty minutes you'll come to a steep slope: a right turn at the top takes you straight to the temple, just beyond which is another quarry, where you can swim. Ignoring the right turn to the temple at the top of the steep slope and continuing straight ahead takes you towards the *Ubin Restaurant*, the island's best; it's a bit tricky to find, though – you'll have to look out for a taxi taking Singaporean diners there, to discover which track to turn down.

Telok Blangah, the HarbourFront Centre and Mount Faber

A twenty-minute walk west of Chinatown is the area known as **Telok Blangah**, in which stands Singapore's **HarbourFront Centre**, itself a splendid shopping centre-cum-marine terminal, where boats depart Singapore for Indonesia's Riau archipelago. Lots of buses come this way: #97 and #166 travel down Bencoolen Street; from Scotts and Orchard roads, take bus #143. You'll know when to get off, because you'll see cable cars rocking across the skyline in front of you, on their way to and from Mount Faber.

Mount Faber – 600m north of the HarbourFront Centre – was named in 1845 after Government Engineer Captain Charles Edward Faber; the top of the "mount" (hillock would be a better word) commands fine views of Keppel Harbour and, to the northeast, central Singapore – views that are even more impressive at night, when the city is lit up. It's a long, steep walk from Telok Blangah Road up to the top of Mount Faber – it's better to take the **cable car** from the HarbourFront Centre complex (daily 8.30am–9pm; S$8.90 return).

Haw Par Villa

A monument to whimsy, **Haw Par Villa** is a time capsule of Old Singapore – grotesque and tacky, yet with enough unintentional surrealism to make it hip. Tellingly, you won't find it in any of the glossy tourist brochures: one gets the feeling that this oldest of Singapore tourist attractions no longer fits the Tourism Board's idea of what should be officially touted. Located 7km west of downtown, at 262 Pasir Panjang Rd (daily 9am–7pm; free), it's a gaudy parade of over a thousand statues inspired by Chinese legends and mythologies. Previously known as **Tiger Balm Gardens**, the park now takes its name from its original owners, the Aw brothers, Boon Haw and Boon Par, who made a fortune early in the last century selling Tiger Balm – a cure-all unction created by their father. When the British government introduced licensing requirements for the possession of large animals, the private zoo that the brothers maintained on their estate here was closed down and replaced by statues. To get there, take the **MRT** to Buona Vista and change on to a #200 **bus** to Pasir Panjang Road. Bus #51 trundles down North Bridge Road on its way to the park, while the #143 can be picked up on Scotts, Orchard and New Bridge roads.

Jurong BirdPark

The twenty hectares of land that comprise the **Jurong BirdPark** (daily 9am–5pm; S$12.25), on Jalan Ahmad Ibrahim in the Jurong Lake area, has more than eight thousand birds from over six hundred species, ranging from Antarctic penguins to New Zealand kiwis. This makes it one of the world's largest bird collections, and the biggest in Southeast Asia. A ride on its **Panorail** (S$3) is a good way to get your bearings, the running commentary pointing out the attractions. Be sure at least to catch the **Waterfall Walk-in Aviary**, which allows visitors to walk among 1500 free-flying birds in a specially created patch of simulated rainforest, dominated by a thirty-metre-high waterfall. Other exhibits to seek out are the colourful **Southeast Asian Birds**, where a tropical thunderstorm is simulated daily at noon; the **Penguin Parade** (feeding times 10.30am & 3.30pm); and the **World of Darkness**, a fascinating exhibit that simulates night for its nocturnal residents. The best of the **bird shows** is undoubtedly the "Kings of the Skies" (4pm) – a tour de force of speed-flying by a band of trained eagles, hawks and falcons. Entrance to this, and to the similar "World of Hawks" show (10am) and "JBP All Stars Bird Show" (11am & 3pm), is included with your ticket. To get to the BirdPark, take either **bus** #194 or #251 from the bus interchange outside Boon Lay MRT station, a ten-minute ride.

Sentosa

Heavily promoted for its beaches, sports facilities, hotels and attractions, and ringed by a speeding monorail, the theme-park island of **Sentosa**, 3km by 1km in size, is a contrived but enjoyable place. It's linked to the southern shore of downtown Singapore by a five-hundred-metre causeway and by a necklace of cable cars. Avoid coming at the weekend, and don't even think about visiting on public holidays.

Two nature-oriented attractions outshine all others on Sentosa. At the **Underwater World and Dolphin Lagoon** (daily 10.30am–6pm; S$17) near monorail station 2, a moving walkway carries you along a tunnel between two large tanks: sharks lurk menacingly on all sides, huge stingrays drape themselves languidly above you, and immense shoals of gaily coloured fish dart to and fro. This may not sound all that exciting, but the sensation of being engulfed by sea life is breathtaking. Equally fascinating is the nearby **Butterfly Park and Insect Kingdom** (daily 9am–6.30pm; S$10) where you can wander through a virtual blizzard of tropical butterflies, or witness the magical twinkling of thousands of fireflies. Another major-league attraction is the **Images of Singapore Exhibition** (daily 9am–7pm; S$8), near monorail station 2. Here, life-sized dioramas present the history and heritage of Singapore from the fourteenth century through to the surrender of the Japanese in

1945. The highlight is the Surrender Chambers, where audio-visuals and dioramas recount the events of World War II.

A trip up to **Fort Siloso** (monorail station 3), on the far western tip of the island, ties in nicely with a visit to the Surrender Chambers. The fort – actually a cluster of buildings and gun emplacements above a series of tunnels bored into the island – guarded Singapore's western approaches from the 1880s until 1956, but was rendered obsolete in 1942, when the Japanese invaded Singapore from the north. Today, the recorded voice of Battery Sergeant Major Cooper talks you through a mock-up of a nineteenth-century barracks, complete with living quarters, laundry and assault course. The rest of Sentosa is crammed with less interesting options, and it's probably best to head for the three **beaches** (monorail station 2 or 5, or take bus A or bus M) on its southwestern coast. Created with thousands of cubic metres of imported white sand and scores of coconut palms, they offer canoes, surfboards and aqua bikes for rent. The water here is great for swimming, and Singapore doesn't demand the same modesty on its beaches as some parts of Malaysia, although topless and nude bathing are out.

Practicalities

Basic **admission** to Sentosa costs S$3, which includes transport to the island on the Sentosa bus that departs frequently from the **HarbourFront Centre** in Telok Blangah. You can save a buck by walking across the bridge; if you drive yourself, admission is S$2 per person plus an additional S$2 entrance fee for the car. The most spectacular way there, however, is by one of the **cable cars** (daily 8.30am–9pm) that travel between mainland Mount Faber and Sentosa, via the HarbourFront Centre. Tickets cost S$8.90 to S$15 per person, depending on what kind of cable car you take – the higher fare will get you a glass-bottomed car and a vertigo-inducing view. The cable car fare doesn't include the basic admission fee to the island. Free maps showing the various attractions and transport routes can be picked up at the main entry gate.

Sentosa's basic admission fee gives unlimited rides on the island's **monorail and bus systems** – there's a colour-coded system of four bus lines that link the island's attractions, while the monorail runs from 9am until 10pm. But the best way to get about is to **rent a bike** for the day (S$3–8 an hour, S$50 deposit) from the kiosk beside the old ferry terminal. There are lots of options for **eats** on Sentosa, including *Warung Pantai*, serving local cuisine as fast food, and even a *Burger King*.

Eating

Along with shopping, **eating** ranks as the Singaporean national pastime. An enormous number of food outlets cater for this obsession, and strict government regulations ensure that they are consistently hygienic. By far the cheapest and most fun place to dine in Singapore is in a **hawker centre** or **food court**, where scores of stalls let you mix and match Asian dishes, fast-food style, at really low prices; it's possible to eat like a king for S$5. Otherwise, there's a whole range of **restaurants** to visit, ranging from no-frills, open-fronted eating-houses and coffee shops to sumptuously decorated establishments. Even in restaurants, you'll be hard-pressed to spend more than S$30–40 a head, including drinks, unless you opt for one of the island's more exclusive addresses.

Several specialist Chinese restaurants, a number of Indian restaurants and a few stalls at hawker centres serve **vegetarian food**, but otherwise vegetarians need to tread very carefully: chicken and seafood will appear in a whole host of dishes unless you make it perfectly clear that you don't want them.

Breakfast, brunch and snacks

Western breakfasts are available, at a price, at all bigger hotels, most famously at the *Hilton* or *Raffles*. For a really cheap fry-up, you can't beat a Western food stall in a hawker centre, where S$8 buys steak, chops and sausage. The classic **Chinese breakfast** is *congee*, a watery rice porridge augmented with strips of meat, though *dim sum* tend to be more palatable to Western tastes.

Champagne Brunch At The Hilton *Hilton Hotel*, 581 Orchard Rd ☎6737 2233. Around S$65 buys a superb free flow of delicacies – oysters, salmon, curry and cakes – washed down with litres of champagne and orange juice at the Hilton's *Checkers Brasserie*. Reservations are essential. Sun 11.30am–2.30pm only.

De Boa (HK) Restaurant 42 Smith St, Chinatown. Right opposite the Chinatown Complex, this smashing little coffee shop offers *dim sum*, *pow* and Chinese tea. Daily 7.30am–5pm.

Mr Bean's Café 30 Selegie Rd, Colonial District. Based in the same wedge-shaped colonial building as the Selegie Arts Centre, *Mr Bean's Café* draws a crowd with its muffins, croissants, toast and coffee.

Spinelli Coffee Company #01–15 Bugis Junction Shopping Centre, 230 Victoria St, Colonial District. San Francisco-based franchise riding on the local mania for fresh coffee; the narrow bar is ideal for a quick espresso.

Tiffin Rooms *Raffles Hotel*, 1 Beach Rd, Colonial District ☎6337 1886. Have your buffet breakfast here and you won't eat again until dinner; S$35 per adult, children S$20. Daily 7–10am.

Yasinn Restaurant 127 Bencoolen St, Colonial District. Does a roaring trade in *roti pratha* each morning; the *murtabak* also has plenty of devotees.

Hawker centres and food courts

The unprepossessing, functional buildings that house most **hawker centres** tend to get extremely hot, so an increasing number of smaller, air-con **food courts** are popping up, where eating is a slightly more civilized, if less atmospheric affair. Hawker centres and food courts are open from lunchtime through to dinner-time and sometimes beyond. Avoid the peak lunching (12.30–1.30pm) and dining (6–7pm) periods, and you should have no problems in finding a seat.

Chinatown Complex Smith St, off New Bridge Rd. A huge range of dishes with a predictably Chinese bias.

Food Junction B1, Seiyu Department Store, Bugis Junction Shopping Centre, 200 Victoria St, Colonial District. Buzzing, newly renovated food court where Thai and Japanese cuisines are represented, as are *nasi padang* (highly spice Sumatran cuisine) and claypot options.

Hastings Road Food Court Little India Arcade, Serangoon Rd. Diminutive food court whose handful of stalls are labelled by region – Keralan, Mughlai, Sri Lankan and so on.

Kopitiam Corner of Bencoolen St & Bras Basah Rd, Colonial District. Glitzy hawker centre gleaming with chrome and neon, where the food is as colourful and varied as the furniture.

Lau Pa Sat Festival Market 18 Raffles Quay. The smartest hawker stalls in Singapore, and now open round the clock.

Orchard Emerald Food Court Basement, Orchard Emerald, 218 Orchard Rd. Smart food court where the Taiwanese counter is the pick of a varied bunch.

Picnic Food Court Scotts Shopping Centre, 6 Scotts Rd, off Orchard Rd. Squeaky clean, and with lots of choice.

Satay Club Clarke Quay, Singapore River. A Singapore institution not to be missed, serving inexpensive chicken and mutton satay. Open evenings only, from around 7pm.

Restaurants

Most restaurants are open daily between 11.30am and 2.30pm and 6–10.30pm at least, though cheaper places tend to open longer hours.

Chinese

The majority of the **Chinese** restaurants in Singapore are Cantonese, from Guangdong in southern China, though you'll also come across northern Beijing (or Peking) and western Szechuan cuisines, as well as the Hokkien specialities of the southeastern province of Fujian, and Teochew dishes from the area east of Canton. Whatever the region, it's undoubtedly the real thing – Chinese food as eaten by the Chinese – which means it won't always sound particularly appealing to foreigners: the Chinese eat all parts of an animal, from its lips to its undercarriage. Fish and seafood is nearly always outstanding, but for something a little more unusual, try a **steamboat**, a Chinese-style fondue filled with boiling stock in which you cook meat, fish, shellfish, eggs and vegetables; or a **claypot** – meat, fish or shellfish cooked over a fire in an earthenware pot. The other thing to note is that in many Cantonese restaurants (and in other regional restaurants, too), lunch consists of **dim sum** – steamed and fried dumplings served in little bamboo baskets.

Ban Seng B1–44 The Riverwalk, 20 Upper Circular Rd, Chinatown ☎6533 1471. Traditionally prepared Teochew dishes, including steamed crayfish, braised goose and stuffed sea cucumber; mid-priced. Daily 12–2.30pm & 6–10pm.

Happy Realm Vegetarian Food Centre #03-16 Pearls Centre, 100 Eu Tong Sen St, Chinatown ☎6222 6141. "No meat or alcoholics" declares a helpful sign at this cheerful restaurant, serving tasty and reasonably priced vegetarian dishes. Daily 11am–8.30pm.

Kwan Yim Vegetarian Restaurant 190 Waterloo St, near Bencoolen Street, Colonial District ☎6338 2394. A huge display of sweet and savoury *pow* is the highlight of this unfussy veggie establishment. Daily 8.30am–9pm.

Mitzi's 24–26 Murray Terrace, Chinatown ☎6222 0929. The cracking Cantonese food in this simple place, situated in a row of restaurants known as "Food Alley", draws the crowds, so be prepared to wait in line. Two can eat for S$30, drinks extra. Daily 11.30am–3pm & 5.30–10pm.

Moi Kong Hakka 22 Murray Terrace, Chinatown ☎6221 7758. Hakka food relies heavily on salted and preserved ingredients, and here, at the best outlet of its kind in Singapore, you'll have the chance to sample stewed pork belly with preserved vegetables or the incredibly named abacus yam starch beads. Daily 10.30am–2.30pm & 6–10pm.

Swee Kee *Damenlou Hotel*, 12 Ann Siang Hill, Chinatown ☎6221 1900. A Cantonese restaurant that's been serving *ka shou* fish-head noodles for over sixty years. Daily 11am–2.30pm & 5.30–11pm.

Yet Con Chicken Rice Restaurant 25 Purvis St, off Beach Rd ☎6337 6819. Cheap and cheerful, old-time Hainanese restaurant: try "crunchy, crispy" roast pork with pickled cabbage and radish, or S$10 buys classic chicken rice, washed down with barley water, to feed two. Daily 10.30am–9.30pm.

Zen Fut Sai Kai 147 Kitchener Rd, Little India ☎6291 2350. Old-fashioned vegetarian Cantonese restaurant, where beancurd is shaped and textured to resemble meat or fish. S$15 is sufficient for two. Tues–Sun 10am–9pm.

Indian

Anna Lakshmi *Excelsior Hotel* & Shopping Centre, 5 Coleman St, Colonial District ☎6339 9993. Terrific North and South Indian vegetarian food, all the profits from which go to an Indian cultural association. Many of the staff are volunteers from the Hindu community, so your waiter might just be a doctor or a lawyer. Dishes from S$10. Mon–Sat 11.30am–3pm & 6–9.30pm.

Banana Leaf Apollo 54–58 Race Course Rd, Little India ☎6293 8682. Pioneering fish-head-curry restaurant where South Indian dishes are all served on banana leaves. Reckon on S$30 for two people. Daily 10.30am–10pm.

Islamic Restaurant 791–797 North Bridge Rd, Arab Quarter ☎6298 7563. Muslim restaurant serving the best traditional chicken biriyani in Singapore. S$10 for two. Daily 10am–10pm.

Komala Villas 76–78 Serangoon Rd, Little India ☎6293 6980. A cramped, inexpensive and popular vegetarian establishment specializing in fifteen varieties of *dosai*. The vegetarian *thali* is justifiably popular, featuring various curries, pickles and condiments spread across a huge banana leaf, and served with rice. Daily 7am–10pm.

Madras New Woodlands 12–14 Upper Dickson Rd, Little India ☎6297 1594. Recommended, canteen-style place serving up decent vegetarian food at bargain prices (there's an upmarket sister operation in nearby Belilios Lane). *Thali* set meals from around S$5. Daily 8am–11pm.

Southeast Asian

Blue Ginger 97 Tanjong Pagar Rd, Chinatown ☎6222 3925. Trendy Peranakan restaurant offering *ikan masal assam gulai* (mackerel simmered in a tamarind and lemongrass gravy), and *ayam buah keluak* – braised chicken with Indonesian black nuts. Daily noon–2.30pm & 6.30–10.30pm.

Cuppage Thai Food Restaurant 49 Cuppage Terrace, behind Centrepoint Shopping Centre, off Orchard Rd ☎6734 1116. Cheap and cheerful restaurant serving quality Thai dishes at around the S$8 mark. Daily 6pm–11pm.

House of Sundanese Food 75 Boat Quay, Singapore River ☎6534 3775; and Suntec City Mall ☎6345 5020. Spicy salads and barbecued seafood characterize the cuisine of Sunda (West Java). Try the tasty *ikan sunda* (grilled fish) – an S$18 fish serves two to three people. Mon–Fri 11am–2pm & daily 6–10pm.

Lemon Grass The Hereen Bldg, 260 Orchard Rd ☎6736 1998. Thai cuisine that tends to be on the sweet side, but nice ambience and snappy service. Daily 3pm-11pm.

Nonya & Baba 262 River Valley Rd, Clarke Quay ☎6734 1382. Respected Nonya restaurant where the *otak otak* (fish steamed in a banana leaf wrapper) and *ayam buah keluak* are both terrific; other dishes cost around S$7. Daily 11.30am–10pm.

Rendezvous Restaurant #02-02 Hotel Rendezvous, 9 Bras Basah Rd ☎6339 7508. Revered *nasi padang* joint that still turns out lip-smacking curries, *rendangs* and *sambals*. Daily 11am–11pm.

Rumah Makan Minang 18a Kandahar St, Arab Quarter. Fiery *nasi padang* in the heart of the Arab Quarter; S$4 ensures a good feed. Daily 8am–10.30pm.

Viet Café #01-57 UE Square, Unity Street, west of Fort Canning Park ☎6333 6453. The heady mint, basil and citrus aromas of *pho* – Vietnamese soup – hang heavy in the air at this sleek café. Daily noon–2.30am.

US and international

Don Noodle Bistro #01-16 Tanglin Mall, Tanglin Rd, on the way out to the Botanic Gardens ☎6738 3188. Something of a paradox: a Western-style take on the noodle bar, imported back to the East with a non-country-specific menu. Daily 11.30am–10.30pm.

Ponderosa Steakhouse #02-20 Raffles City, 252 North Bridge Rd ☎6334 4926. Chicken, steak and fish set meals come with baked potato, sundae, and as much salad as you can eat, at a reasonable S$20. Daily 11.30am–9.30pm.

Seah Street Deli *Raffles Hotel*, 1 Beach Rd ☎6337 1886. New York-style deli boasting some of the most mountainous sandwiches in Asia, at around S$10 each. Daily 11am–10pm, Fri & Sat until 11pm.

Drinking, nightlife and entertainment

Singapore's burgeoning **bar and pub** scene means there's a wide range of drinking holes to choose from, with the Colonial District, Boat Quay and Orchard Road areas offering particularly good pub-crawl potential. With competition hotting up, more and more bars are turning to **live music** to woo punters, though this is usually no more than cover versions performed by local bands. **Clubs** also do brisk business; glitzy yet unpretentious, they feature the latest imported pop, rock and dance music, though don't expect anything like a rave scene – Ecstasy isn't in the Singaporean dictionary.

Bars and pubs

It's possible to buy a small glass of beer in most **bars and pubs** for around S$5, but prices can be double or treble that, especially in the Orchard Road area. During happy hour in the early evening, bars offer local beers and house wine either at half price, or "one for one" – you get two of whatever you order, but one is held back for later. Most places close around midnight (a bit later Fri & Sat).

Anywhere #04-08/09 Tanglin Shopping Centre, 19 Tanglin Rd, near Orchard Rd. Tania, Singapore's most famous covers band, plays nightly to a boozy roomful of expats that are at their rowdiest on Friday nights. Mon–Fri 6pm–3am, Sat 8–3am; happy hour Mon–Fri 6–10pm.

Balaclava Suntec City Covention Centre. ☎6533 9160. Don't be put off by the location, this stylish place is worth seeking out for its unique ambience. Can get very crowded on weekends. Daily noon-2am.

Bar and Billiards Room *Raffles Hotel*, 1 Beach Rd. A Singapore Sling (S$14), in the colonial elegance of the hotel where it was invented in 1915, is required drinking on a visit to Singapore. Daily 11.30am–midnight.

Bar None 320 Orchard Rd ☎6831 4656. Under the *Singapore Marriott*, one of the city's better jazz venues. If it gets too crowded on the floor, there's a mezzanine level that's a great place to lounge. Daily 11am-3am.

Bernie Goes to Town 82a/b Boat Quay ☎6536 3533. Sixties and Seventies classics vie with special-guest bands at this laid-back, roadhouse-style joint. Mon–Thurs & Sun noon–2am, Fri & Sat noon–3am.

Crazy Elephant #01-07 Trader's Market, Clarke Quay. Clarke Quay's best bar, playing decent rock music on the turntable between live sessions by various bands. Try to nab a table out by the water's edge. Mon–Thurs & Sun 5pm–1am, Fri & Sat 5pm–2am; happy hour daily until 9pm.

Harry's Quayside 28 Boat Quay ☎6538 3029. Live jazz Tues–Sat, with an all-day happy hour on Mon, when a fifteen-piece swing band adds to the fun.

Ice Cold Beer 9 Emerald Hill, off Orchard Road. Noisy, hectic and happening place, very popular with expats – and the beer really is ice cold. Daily 5pm–2am; happy hour daily until 9pm.

Muddy Mirphy's Orchard Hotel Arcade, Orchard Rd ☎6735 0400. One of those prefab Irish pubs that gets better with each pint of Guinness. Very friendly staff and a good mix of both expats and locals. Daily 5pm–2am; happy hour until 9pm.

Clubs

Singaporean **clubs** have become increasingly sophisticated over recent years: European and American dance music dominates, and many feature live cover bands. Clubs tend to open around 9pm, and most have a **cover charge** of S$10–30, at least on weekends. Singapore also has a plethora of extremely seedy, extortionately priced hostess clubs, worked by aged Chinese hostesses.

Amoeba #01-59/60 UE Square, 207 River Valley Rd ☎6735 6193. This decidedly swish night spot, where local celebs pose in the velvet booths lining the walls, is owned by a former MTV host. The music ranges from soul to acid jazz and salsa, after which you'll be ready to recuperate at the bar with a Bellini cocktail. Mon–Sat 7pm–3am.

Centro 1 Fullerton Rd ☎6220 2288. Vast house/garage club with a bar marooned in the middle. Things are more relaxed upstairs, where the seating area offers wonderful views over Marina Bay. Tues–Sun 9pm–3am.

Double O 11 Unity St, Robertson Walk, ☎6735 2008. Packed to the rafters with Singapore's beautiful crowd, though not as pretentious as it sounds. "Retro Saturday" seems to be the most popular night. Wed-Sun 9pm–3am.

Liquid Room #01-05 *Gallery Evason Hotel*, 76 Robertson Quay, west of Clarke Quay ☎6333 8117. Highly rated among club-goers, this venue is laid out along simple lines: dance upstairs, chill out downstairs. The bar area features an aquarium built into the wall. Daily 10.30pm–3am.

Zouk 17–21 Jiak Kim St ☎6738 2988. Still one of Singapore's trendiest venues, with different-themed sub-clubs within the club to keep things interesting. DJs from Europe and the US often guest here. There is a S$20 cover charge to keep out the riff raff. Happy hour 11pm–midnight; open Tue–Sat 9pm–3am.

Traditional entertainment

If you walk around Singapore's streets for long enough, you're likely to come across some sort of streetside **cultural event**, most usually a **wayang**, or Chinese opera, played out on tumbledown outdoor stages that spring up overnight next to temples and markets, or just at the side of the road. Wayangs are highly dramatic and stylized affairs, in which garishly made-up and costumed characters enact popular Chinese legends to the accompaniment of the crashes of cymbals and gongs. Wayangs take place throughout the year, but the best time to catch one is during the Festival of the Hungry Ghosts (see p.891), when they are held to entertain passing spooks. Also, look out for the Festival of the Nine Emperor Gods in October, during which the nine-day sojourn of the deities on earth is celebrated in Upper Serangoon Road with Chinese operas, and mediums cavorting in the streets. The Singapore Tourist Board (STB) may also be able to help you track down a wayang, and as usual the local press is worth checking, or you could pop along to the Chinese Opera Teahouse, 5 Smith Street, near the Chinatown Complex (☎6323 4862), where S$20 buys you Chinese tea and an opera performance with English subtitles. Another fascinating traditional performance, **lion dancing**, takes to the streets during Chinese New Year (see p.891), as do **puppet theatres**.

Shopping

For many stopover visitors, Singapore is synonymous with **shopping**, though prices aren't rock bottom across the board. Good deals can be found on watches, cameras, electrical and computer equipment, and fabrics and antiques, and cut-price imitations – Rolexes, Lacoste polo shirts and so on – are rife, but many other articles offer no substantial saving. Choice and convenience though, make the Singapore shopping experience a rewarding one. What's more, come during the **Great Singapore Sale** (usually in June or July), and you'll find seriously marked-down prices in many outlets across the island. The free monthly, *Where Singapore*, has plenty of suggestions as to what you can buy and where, and the STB publishes a *Merchants of the Gold Circle* brochure, which lists those shops deemed courteous and reliable enough to display the "Gold Circle Promise of Excellence" logo in their windows.

Usual **shopping hours** are daily 10am–9pm, though some shopping centres, especially those along Orchard Road, stay open until 10pm (except the Christian-owned CK Tang's, which closes on Sunday). Note that there is a goods and services **tax** (GST) of three percent, but tourists can claim a refund on purchases of S$300 or over at retailers displaying a blue and grey **Tax-Free Shopping** sticker. Ask retailers to draft you a Tax-Free Shopping Cheque, which you can then redeem subsequently at the airport.

For designer clothes, tailor-made suits, sports equipment, electronic goods or antiques, head for the shopping malls of **Orchard Road** (see p.920). On **Arab Street** (p.917), you'll find exquisite textiles and batiks, and some good deals on jewellery. From here, make a beeline for the silk stores and goldsmiths of **Little India** (see p.916), via the intersection of **Bencoolen Street and Rochor Road**, known for their electrical goods. As well as its souvenir shops, **Chinatown** (see p.912) boasts some more traditional outlets.

Books Books Kinokuniya, #03-10/15 Ngee Ann City, 391 Orchard Rd, is the island's biggest bookshop. MPH shops are also well stocked, especially the flagship store on #73 Stamford Rd, as are Times bookshops, at #04-08/15 Centrepoint Shopping Centre, 175 Orchard Rd; and #02-24/25 Raffles City, 252 North Bridge Rd. Select Books, #03-15 Tanglin Shopping Centre, 19 Tanglin Rd, has a huge array of books on Southeast Asia.
Camping equipment Campers' Corner, 11 Stamford Rd.
Computers and software Funan the IT Mall, 109 North Bridge Rd. Square, 1 Rocher Canal Rd.
Electronic equipment Sim Lim Square, 1 Rocher Canal Rd.
Fabrics and silk Jim Thompson Silk Shop, #01-07 Raffles Hotel Arcade, 328 North Bridge Rd; Aljunied Brothers, 91 Arab St. Dakshaini Silks, 87 Serangoon Rd.
Music Beethoven Record House, #03-41 Centrepoint Shopping Centre, 176 Orchard Rd, for classical sounds; Lata Music Centre, 18 Buffalo Rd, for Indian music on tape; Roxy Records, #03-36 Funan the IT Mall, 109 North Bridge Rd, for new releases; Supreme Record Centre, #03-28 Centrepoint Shopping Centre, 175 Orchard Rd; Tower Records, 9 Suntec City Mall, for a wide choice of music on CD.
Souvenirs Eng Tiang Huat, 284 River Valley Rd, for Oriental musical instruments, wayang costumes and props; Funan Stamp and Coin Agency, #03-03 Funan the IT Mall, 109 North Bridge Rd; Sai Artefacts, 18 Kerbau Rd, for ethnic furniture and Indian curios; Selangor Pewter, #02-38 Raffles City, 252 North Bridge Rd, for fine pewterwork; Singapore Handicraft Centre, Chinatown Point, 133 New Bridge Rd, with around fifty souvenir shops under one roof; Zhen Lacquer Gallery, 1 Trengganu St.

Listings

Airline offices Aeroflot, #01-02/02-00 Tan Chong Tower, 15 Queen St ☎6336 1757; Air Canada, #02-43/46 Meridien Shopping Centre, 100 Orchard Rd ☎6256 1198; Air India, #17-01 UIC Building, 5 Shenton Way ☎6225 9411; Air New Zealand, #24-08 Ocean Building, 10 Collyer Quay ☎6535 8266; American Airlines, #15 Cairnhill Rd ☎1800/616 2113; Cathay Pacific, #16-01 Ocean Building, 10 Collyer Quay ☎6533 1333; Garuda, #01-68 United Sq, 101 Thomson Rd ☎6250 5666; KLM, #12-06 Ngee Ann City Tower A, 391a Orchard Road ☎6737 7622; Lufthansa, #05-07 Palais Renaissance, 390 Orchard Rd ☎6835 5912; Malaysia Airlines, #02-09 Singapore Shopping Centre, 190 Clemenceau Ave ☎6336 6777; Philippine Airlines, #01-10 Parklane Shopping Mall, 35 Selegie Rd ☎6336 1611; Qantas British Airways, #15 Cairnhill Rd ☎6589 7000; Royal Brunei, #03-11/12 UE Square, 81 Clemenceau Ave ☎6235 4672; Royal Nepal Airlines, #03-09 Peninsula Shopping Centre, 3 Coleman St ☎6339

5535; Scandinavian Airways, #2108/10 Shaw House, 350 Orchard Rd ☎6235 8211; Silkair, see Singapore Airlines; Singapore Airlines, #08-02 Temasek Tower, 8 Shenton Way ☎6223 6666, and also at #02-26/28 The Paragon, 290 Orchard Rd ☎6224 4122; Sri Lankan Airlines, #13-01a/b, 133 Cecil St ☎6225 7233; Thai Airways, #02-00 The Globe, 100 Cecil St ☎1800/224 9977; United Airlines, #01-03 Hong Leong Building, 16 Raffles Quay ☎6873 3533.

American Express #18-01 The Concourse, 300 Beach Rd ☎1800/732 2244.

Banks and exchange All Singapore's banks change travellers' cheques. Licensed moneychangers abound on Arab Street, at the Serangoon Road's Mustafa Centre, and in Orchard Road's shopping centres.

Embassies and consulates Australia, 25 Napier Rd ☎6836 4100; Brunei, 235 Tanglin Hill ☎6733 9055; Canada, #14-00 IBM Towers, 80 Anson Rd ☎6325 3240; India, 31 Grange Rd ☎6737 6777; Indonesia, 7 Chatsworth Rd ☎6737 7422; Ireland, Liat Towers ☎6238 7616; Laos, #05-03A, United Sq, 101 Thomson Rd ☎6250 6044; Malaysia, 301 Jervois Rd ☎6235 0111; New Zealand, #15-06, Ngee Ann City Tower A, 391a Orchard Rd ☎6235 9966; Philippines, 20 Nassim Rd ☎6737 3977; Sri Lanka, #13-07/13 Goldhill Plaza, 51 Newton Rd ☎6254 4595; Thailand, 370 Orchard Rd ☎6737 2644; UK, Tanglin Rd ☎6473 9333; USA, Napier Road ☎6476 9100; Vietnam, 10 Leedon Park ☎6462 5938.

Hospitals Singapore General, Outram Road ☎6222 3322; Alexandra Hospital, Alexandra Rd ☎6473 5222; and National University Hospital, Kent Ridge ☎6779 5555.

Internet access Cyberian City, #01-01 *Hotel Rendezvous*, 9 Bras Basah Rd ☎6883 2383; DotCom Online Services, 53 Dunlop St, Little India ☎6296 0760; Travel Café, 50 Prinsep St ☎6338 9001.

Laundry Washington Dry Cleaning, 2 Bukit Batok St (Mon–Sat 9am–7.45pm); Washy Washy, #01-18 Cuppage Plaza, 5 Koek Rd, off Orchard Rd (Mon–Sat 10am–7pm).

Mail Poste restante c/o the GPO, beside Paya Lebar MRT (Mon–Fri 8am–6pm, Sat 8am–2pm).

Pharmacy Guardian Pharmacy has over forty outlets, including ones at Centrepoint Shopping Centre, 176 Orchard Rd, and Raffles City, 252 North Bridge Rd.

Police Report theft at Tanglin Police Station, 17 Napier Rd, off Orchard Road (☎6733 0000); in an emergency, dial ☎999.

Telephone services IDD calls can be made from any public cardphone or credit-card phone; see p.891.

Travel agents The following agents are good for discounted air fares and buying bus tickets to Malaysia and Thailand: Airpower Travel, 131a Bencoolen St ☎6334 6571; Phya Travel Service, Golden Mile Complex, 5001 Beach Rd, ☎6294 5415; STA Travel, Cuppage Terrace ☎6737 7188; Sunny Holidays, Bugis Junction, 200 Victoria St, ☎6292 7927.

Singapore travel details

Buses

Ban San terminal to: Kuala Lumpur, Malaysia (Pudu Raya station; 7 daily; 6hr).

Golden Mile Complex to: Hat Yai, Thailand (several daily; 14hr).

Lavender Street terminal to: Butterworth, Malaysia (at least 2 daily; 16hr); Ipoh, Malaysia (4 daily; 10–11hr); Johor Bahru, Malaysia (every 30min; 1hr); Kota Bharu, Malaysia (at least 1 daily; 10hr); Kuala Lumpur, Malaysia (7 daily; 7hr); Kuantan, Malaysia (3 daily; 7hr); Melaka, Malaysia (9 daily; 5hr); Mersing, Malaysia (4 daily; 3hr 30min).

Trains

Singapore to: Johor Bahru (6 daily; 1hr); Kuala Lumpur (4 daily; 7–9hr); Wakaf Bharu (for Kota Bharu; 1 daily; 13hr).

Ferries

Changi ferry terminal to: Tanjung Belungkor (Johor Bahru), Malaysia (4 daily; 45min).

Changi Point to: Kampung Pengerang (Johor Bahru), Malaysia (hourly; 45min).

HarbourFront Centre to: Pulau Batam, Indonesia (every 30min; 40min).

Tanah Merah ferry terminal to: Pulau Bintan, Indonesia (4 daily; 1hr) Pulau Tioman, Malaysia (March–Oct 1 daily; 4hr 30min).

Flights

Singapore to: Kota Kinabalu, Sabah (1 daily; 2hr 30min); Kuala Lumpur, Malaysia (10 daily; 55min); Kuching, Sarawak (2 daily; 1hr 20min); Langkawi, Malaysia (3 weekly; 1hr 25min); Penang, Malaysia (at least 5 daily; 1hr 10min); Pulau Tioman, Malaysia (1 daily; 30min).

10

Thailand

BURMA (MYANMAR)
LAOS
CAMBODIA
VIETNAM
ANDAMAN SEA
GULF OF THAILAND
MALAYSIA
N
0
250km

Thailand highlights

* **The Grand Palace, Bangkok** The country's unmissable sight, incorporating its holiest and most dazzling temple, Wat Phra Kaeo. See p.974

* **Kanchanaburi** Sleep in a rafthouse on the River Kwai, ride the historic Death Railway, and explore cave temples by bicycle. See p.988

* **Chiang Mai** Old-town temples, fine crafts, great restaurants and the widest choice of hilltribe treks. See p.1010

* **Nan** An under-rated all-rounder, offering beautiful temple murals and handicrafts, and scenic mountain-trekking. See p.1018

* **Wat Phu Tok** A uniquely atmospheric meditation temple on a steep sandstone outcrop. See p.1052

* **Ko Tao** Take a dive course, or just explore this remote island's contours by boat or on foot. See p.1067

* **Khao Sok National Park** Tree-houses, mist-clad cliffs and whooping gibbons make for a memorable stay. See p.1073

* **Sea-kayaking in the Krabi region** A great way to explore the extraordinary Andaman coast. See p.1082

* **Ko Lanta** Choose from several fine beaches on this long, laid-back island. See p.1086

△ Ko Lanta

Introduction and basics

With nearly eleven million foreigners flying into the country each year, is Asia's primary holiday destination and a useful and popular first stop on any overland journey through Southeast Asia. The influx of tourist cash has played a significant part in the country's recent development, yet Thailand's cultural integrity remains largely undamaged. In this country of sixty-three million people, some ninety percent are practising Theravada Buddhists, and King Bhumibol is a revered figure across his nation. Tiered temple rooftops and saffron-robed monks dominate every vista, and, though some cities and beach resorts are characterized by high-rises and neon lights, the typical Thai community is the traditional farming village: almost fifty percent of Thais still earn their living from the land.

Most journeys start in **Bangkok**. Thailand's huge, noisy, polluted capital can be an overwhelming introduction to Southeast Asia, but there are traveller-oriented guesthouses aplenty here, and heaps of spectacular temples to visit. It's also the best place for arranging onward travel and visas for neighbouring countries. A popular side-trip from the city takes in the rafthouses of **Kanchanaburi**, the infamous site of the Bridge over the River Kwai. After Bangkok, most travellers head north, sometimes via the ancient capitals of **Ayutthaya** and **Sukhothai**, to the enjoyably laid-back city of **Chiang Mai**, where they organize treks to nearby hilltribe villages. There's tranquil countryside by the bucketload up in the northern highlands around **Mae Hong Son** and **Pai**, and along the **Mekong River** in Thailand's northeast (Isaan), where you can stay in village guesthouses and hop across the border into Laos. The northeast is the least visited area of Thailand, but holds two fine ancient Khmer ruins at **Phimai** and **Phanom Rung**, and the country's most accessible national park, **Khao Yai**.

After trekking and rural relaxation, most visitors want to head for the **beach** – and Thailand's eastern and southern coasts are lined with gorgeous white-sand shores, aquamarine seas and kaleidoscopic reefs. The most popular of these are the east-coast backpacker resorts of Ko Samet and Ko Chang, the Gulf coast islands of Ko Samui, Ko Pha Ngan and Ko Tao, and the Andaman coast idylls of Ao Nang, Laem Phra Nang, Ko Lanta, Ko Tarutao and Ko Lipe. The southern island of Phuket and the east-coast resort of Pattaya are more expensive, package-tour-oriented spots. In the deep south, Thailand merges relatively seamlessly with Malaysia, and there are plenty of border crossing points here; the city of **Hat Yai** in particular offers convenient long-distance bus and rail links to many Malaysian towns. Getting into Cambodia overland is more tortuous, but the most straightforward crossings are at Aranyaprathet and Hat Lek.

Parts of the Andaman coast were very badly damaged by the December 2004 **tsunami** and there was great loss of life in this area. By May 2005, however, when this book went to press, most of the affected tourist resorts had been reconstructed and reopened: for more details, see box on p.1071.

The **climate** of most of Thailand is governed by three seasons: rainy (roughly June–Oct), caused by the southwest monsoon; cool (Nov–Feb); and hot (March–May). The cool season is the pleasantest time to visit and the most popular. Christmas is peak season, when accommodation gets booked way ahead and prices rise significantly. In the hot season, temperatures can rise to 40°C. The rainy season hits the Andaman coast (Phuket, Krabi, Phi Phi) harder than anywhere else in the country – heavy rainfall usually starts in May and persists until November. The Gulf coast (Ko Samui, Ko Pha Ngan and Ko Tao) gets much less rain from the southwest monsoon, but is also hit by the northeast monsoon, which brings rain between October and January.

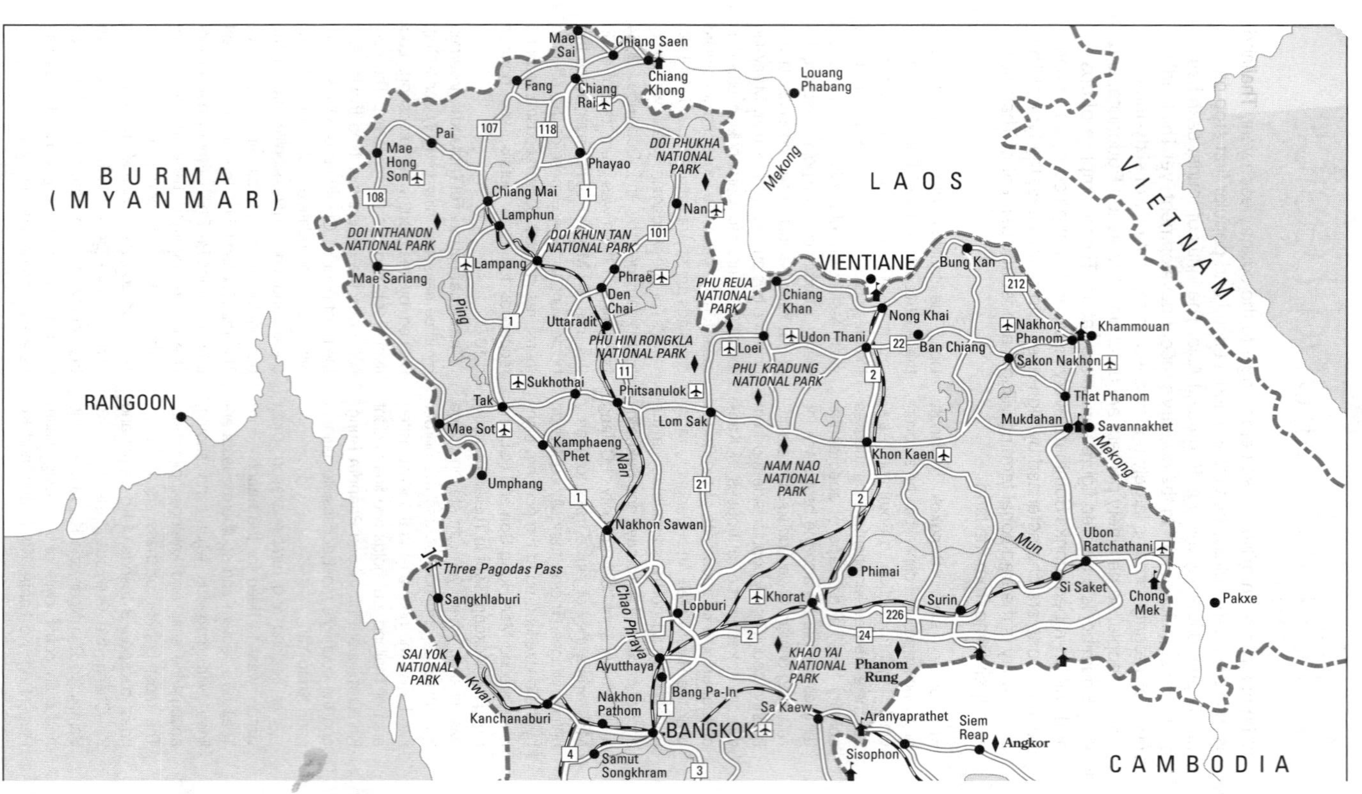
BURMA
(MYANMAR)
LAOS
VIETNAM
CAMBODIA
RANGOON
VIENTIANE
BANGKOK
Louang Phabang
Mekong
Mae Sai
Chiang Saen
Chiang Khong
Fang
Chiang Rai
Pai
Mae Hong Son
Phayao
DOI PHUKHA NATIONAL PARK
Chiang Mai
Lamphun
Nan
DOI INTHANON NATIONAL PARK
DOI KHUN TAN NATIONAL PARK
Lampang
Mae Sariang
Phrae
Den Chai
Ping
Uttaradit
PHU REUA NATIONAL PARK
Chiang Khan
Bung Kan
Nong Khai
Nakhon Phanom
Khammouan
Loei
Udon Thani
Ban Chiang
Sakon Nakhon
PHU HIN RONGKLA NATIONAL PARK
PHU KRADUNG NATIONAL PARK
Sukhothai
Phitsanulok
That Phanom
Tak
Lom Sak
Mukdahan
Savannakhet
Mae Sot
Kamphaeng Phet
Nan
NAM NAO NATIONAL PARK
Khon Kaen
Umphang
Nakhon Sawan
Mun
Ubon Ratchathani
Three Pagodas Pass
Phimai
Sangkhlaburi
Chao Phraya
Lopburi
Khorat
Surin
Si Saket
Chong Mek
Pakxe
SAI YOK NATIONAL PARK
Kwai
Ayutthaya
KHAO YAI NATIONAL PARK
Phanom Rung
Nakhon Pathom
Bang Pa-In
Sa Kaew
Aranyaprathet
Siem Reap
Angkor
Kanchanaburi
Sisophon
Samut Songkhram
107
118
108
1
101
212
22
2
11
21
226
24
4
3

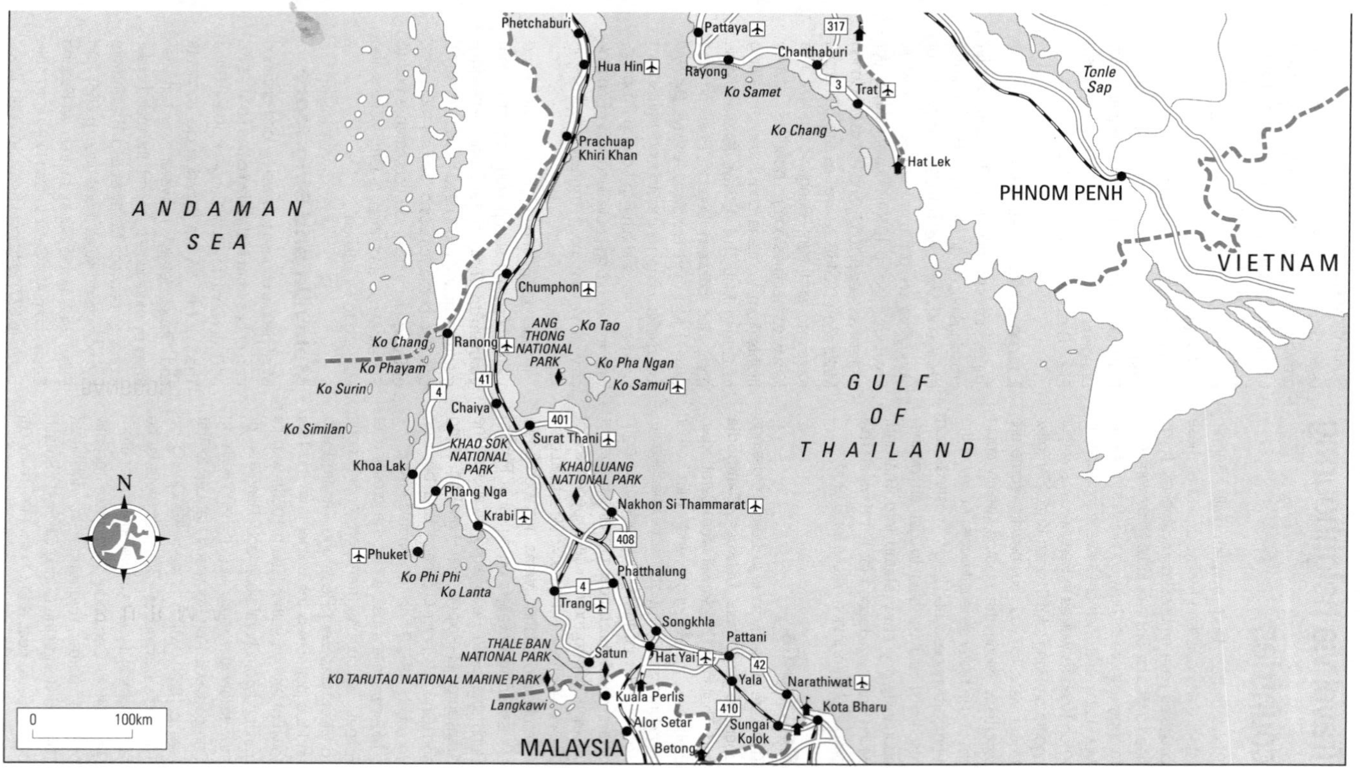

ANDAMAN SEA
GULF OF THAILAND
PHNOM PENH
VIETNAM
MALAYSIA
Tonle Sap
Phetchaburi
Hua Hin
Pattaya
Rayong
Chanthaburi
Ko Samet
317
3
Trat
Ko Chang
Hat Lek
Prachuap Khiri Khan
Chumphon
ANG THONG NATIONAL PARK
Ko Tao
Ko Pha Ngan
Ko Samui
Ko Chang
Ranong
Ko Phayam
Ko Surin
41
4
Chaiya
401
Surat Thani
Ko Similan
KHAO SOK NATIONAL PARK
KHAO LUANG NATIONAL PARK
Khoa Lak
Phang Nga
Nakhon Si Thammarat
Krabi
408
Phuket
Ko Phi Phi
Ko Lanta
Phatthalung
4
Trang
Songkhla
Pattani
THALE BAN NATIONAL PARK
Satun
Hat Yai
42
KO TARUTAO NATIONAL MARINE PARK
Yala
Narathiwat
Kuala Perlis
Langkawi
410
Kota Bharu
Alor Setar
Sungai Kolok
Betong
N
0
100km

Travel via neighbouring countries

Thailand has land borders with Burma, Laos, Cambodia and Malaysia, and all these countries have embassies in Bangkok. If you need a visa for China or India, you might want to apply at their less busy consulates in Chiang Mai. Laos and Vietnam have consulates in Khon Kaen as well as in Bangkok. Many tour agents on Bangkok's Thanon Khao San offer to get visas for you, but beware: some are reportedly faking the stamps, which could get you in pretty serious trouble. At any of the land borders described below, most passport holders should be able to get an on-the-spot thirty-day **entry stamp into Thailand**, which can be extended for ten days at Thai provincial immigration offices for B1900.

Cambodia

There are currently six legal border crossings open to non-Thais between **Cambodia** and Thailand. Check with the Cambodian Embassy in Bangkok and with other travellers first, as regulations are changeable. See the relevant town accounts for specific details on all the border crossings, and for travellers' up-to-the-minute experiences of the same, check out ⓦwww.talesofasia.com/cambodia-overland. **Visas** for Cambodia are issued to travellers on arrival at Phnom Penh and Siem Reap airports, and at the Aranyaprathet–Poipet, Hat Lek–Koh Kong and Chong Chom–O'Smach land borders; you need US$20 and two photos for this.

Most travellers use either the crossing at Poipet, which has transport connections to Sisophon, Siem Reap and Phnom Penh and lies just across the border from the Thai town of Aranyaprathet (see p.1053), with its transport to Chanthaburi and Bangkok; or they follow the route from Sihanoukville in Cambodia via Koh Kong and Hat Lek to Trat (see p.1034), which is near Ko Chang on Thailand's east coast – the Trat route is the fastest option if you're travelling nonstop from Bangkok to Cambodia. The more recently opened border crossings in northeast Thailand include the Chong Chom–O'Smach border pass, near Kap Choeng in Thailand's Surin province (see p.1045), and the little-used Sa Ngam–Choam border in Si Saket province – from both these borders there's transport to Anlong Veng and Siem Reap. There are also two crossings in Chanthaburi province (see p.1034), with transport to and from Pailin in Cambodia.

The speedier alternative to the above overland routes is to make use of the Bangkok Airways **flights** that connect both Bangkok and Phuket with Phnom Penh and Siem Reap (ⓦwww.bangkokair.com).

Laos and Vietnam

There are currently five Thai-**Lao border** crossings open to tourists: Houayxai (for Chiang Khong; see p.1029); Vientiane (for Nong Khai; see p.1051); Thakhek (for Nakhon Phanom; see p.1053); Savannakhet (for Mukdahan; see p.1053); and Pakxe (for Chong Mek; see p.1046). As well as the numerous routes to and from Bangkok, Lao Airlines (ⓦwww.laoairlines.com) operates handy **flights** from Vientiane and Louang Phabang to Chiang Mai, Thai Airways (ⓦwww.thaiair.com) flies between Louang Phabang and Chiang Mai, and Bangkok Airways (ⓦwww.bangkokair.com) runs outbound flights from Bangkok and Sukhothai to Louang Phabang, with the incoming route landing in Bangkok only (there are no immigration facilities in Sukhothai).

If you have the right Lao visa and Vietnamese exit stamp, you can travel from **Vietnam** to Thailand via Savannakhet in a matter of hours; you'll need to use Vietnam's Lao Bao border crossing (see p.1196), west of Dong Ha, where you can catch a bus to Savannakhet and then a ferry across the Mekong to Mukdahan.

Malaysia and Singapore

Most people choose to travel by long-distance train or bus **from Malaysian cities** such as KL or Butterworth to either Bangkok, Krabi, Surat Thani or Hat Yai; see individual city accounts and "Travel details". However, you can also travel by more local transport: the main border crossings between Malaysia and Thailand are by boat from Kuala Perlis (see p.668) and Pulau Langkawi to Satun; by train via Padang Besar; from Alor Setar to Dan Nok; from Kota Bahru (p.677) to Sungai Kolok and Ban Taba.

The nearly-two-thousand-kilometre-long train journey **from Singapore** to Bangkok via Malaysia involves several changes, but can be done in around 48 hours and for as little as £33/US$50; **trains** leave at least once a day from both ends. The most straightforward route is along the west-coast line, via KL and Butterworth. The east-coast route involves a short taxi ride across the actual border, as the lines don't quite connect. For a comprehensive guide to the routes, and advice on how to save money on your tickets, see ⓦwww.seat61.com/Malaysia.htm; for the current timetable and ticket prices, visit the Malaysian Railways website (ⓦwww.ktmb.com.my).

Plenty of **buses** also cross the Thai–Malaysian border every day. Hat Yai is the major transport hub for international bus connections, and there are regular buses here from Singapore (around £12/US$18; 18hr) and KL (£9/US$13; 12hr), as well as air-con minibuses and share taxis from Penang (£9/US$13; 5hr). You'll also find long-distance buses and minibuses to Bangkok, Krabi, Phuket and Surat Thani from Kuala Lumpur, Penang and Singapore, as well as in the reverse direction.

In addition to the numerous daily **flights** on any number of international airlines from Malaysia and Singapore to Bangkok, Bangkok Airways (ⓦwww.bangkokair.com) operates daily flights between Singapore and Ko Samui, while Phuket is served by flights from KL with Malaysia Airlines (ⓦwww.malaysia-airlines.com) and Singapore with Silk Air (ⓦwww.silkair.com). There are also regular flights from Singapore to Hat Yai (Singapore Airlines; ⓦwww.singaporeair.com) and Chiang Mai (Silk Air).

Entry requirements and visa extension

Most foreign passport holders are allowed to enter the country for **stays of up to thirty days** without having to apply for a visa, but may have to show proof of means of living while in the country. It's easy enough to get a new thirty-day stay by hopping across the border into a neighbouring country, especially Malaysia, or by taking a day-trip into Burma at Kaw Thaung (see p.1072), Mae Sot (see p.1003) or Thakhilek (see p.1027).

If you're fairly certain you want to stay longer than thirty days, then from the outset you should apply for a **sixty-day tourist visa** from a Thai embassy instead (see p.45 for a list of Thai embassies abroad), accompanying your application – which generally takes several days to process – with your passport and two photos. The sixty-day visa currently costs B1000 per entry – multiple-entry versions are available, which are handy if you're going to be leaving and re-entering Thailand.

It's not a good idea to **overstay** your visa limits. Once you're at the airport or the border, you generally pay a fine (one-day overstay free, two days B400, thereafter B200 per day) before you leave. However, if you're in the country with an expired visa and get involved with police or immigration officials for any reason whatsoever, they're obliged to take you to court, possibly imprison you, and deport you.

Thirty-day stays can be **extended** in Thailand for a further ten days, sixty-day tourist visas for thirty days, at the discretion of officials; extensions cost B1900 and are issued over the counter at immigration offices (*kaan khao muang*) in nearly every provincial capital – most offices ask for one or two photos as well, plus two photocopies of the main pages of your passport, including your Thai arrival card, arrival stamp and visa. Many Khao San tour agents offer to get your visa extension for you, but beware that some are reportedly faking the stamps.

For the latest information, see the Thai Ministry of Foreign Affairs' **website** at ⓦwww.mfa.go.th/web/12.php; for further, unofficial details, such as the perils of overstaying your visa, see ⓦwww.thaivisa.com.

Airport departure tax

Airport **departure tax** on international flights is B500.

Money and costs

Thailand's unit of **currency** is the baht (abbreviated to "B"), which is divided into 100 satang. Notes come in B10, B20, B50, B100, B500 and B1000 denominations. At the time of writing, the **exchange rate** was averaging B68 to £1 and B40 to US$1. The Don Muang Airport exchange counters operate 24 hours, so there's little point arranging to buy baht before you arrive. If you have a PIN number for your credit/debit card, you should also be able to withdraw cash from hundreds of 24-hour **ATMs**.

Costs

In a country where the daily minimum wage is B170 a day or under, it's hardly surprising that Western tourists find Thailand an extremely cheap place to travel. At the bottom of the scale, you could manage on a **daily budget** of about B400 (£6/$10) if you're willing to opt for basic accommodation and eat, drink and travel as the locals do, spending B80–150 for a bed (less if you share a room), around B150–200 on three meals, and the rest on travel and incidentals. With extras like air conditioning in rooms and on buses, taking tuk-tuks rather than buses for cross-town journeys, and a meal and a couple of beers in a more touristy restaurant, a day's outlay will rise to a minimum of B600. Staying in expensive hotels and eating in the more exclusive restaurants, you should be able to live in extreme comfort for around B2000 a day. It's usual to **tip** hotel bellboys and porters B10–20, and to round up taxi fares to the nearest B10.

Information and maps

For impartial **information** on local attractions and transport, call in at the efficient **Tourism Authority of Thailand** (TAT; ⓦwww.tourismthailand.org), which has offices in Bangkok and 23 regional towns, all open daily 8.30am–4.30pm. You can also contact the TAT Call Centre from anywhere in the country on ⓣ1672 (daily 8am–8pm). For a decent **map** of the country, try either Rough Guides' 1:1,200,000 rip-proof map of Thailand or the 1:1,500,000 maps produced by Nelles and Bartholomew.

Getting around

The wide range of efficient **transport** options makes travelling around Thailand easier than elsewhere in Southeast Asia, and usually just as inexpensive. For a rough idea of frequency and duration of transport between major towns, see "Travel details", p.1096. Nearly all tourist centres rent **cars** (around B1200 per day) and **motorbikes** (from B150 per day), for which a national driver's licence is usually acceptable; helmets are obligatory on bikes. Thais drive on the left, and the speed limit is 60km/hr within built-up areas and 90km/hr outside them; a major road doesn't necessarily have right of way over a minor, but the bigger vehicle *always* has right of way. Avoid driving at night, which can be very dangerous.

Buses

Orange-coloured **ordinary buses** (*rot thammadaa*) are state-run, incredibly inexpensive and cover most short-range routes between main towns (up to 150km) very frequently during daylight hours. They can get packed and are usually quite slow because they stop frequently and often wait until they have enough passengers to make the journey worthwhile. The state-run blue **air-con buses** (*rot air*) are faster and more comfortable, but cost up to twice as much, depart less frequently, and don't cover nearly as many routes. In a lot of cases they're indistinguishable from privately owned, air-con buses (often known as *rot tua*), which ply the most popular long-distance routes and often operate out of government bus terminals. On some longer routes, there are also more expensive VIP buses, with fewer seats and more legroom. Major private companies, such as Nakorn Chai and Win Tour, are generally reliable, but many smaller companies on the main travellers' routes, especially from Thanon Khao San to Chiang Mai and Surat Thani, have a poor reputation for service and comfort, attracting customers with bargain fares and convenient timetables. Travellers have reported a frightening lack of safety awareness and frequent thefts from luggage on these routes, too. **Tickets** for all buses can be bought from the departure terminals, but for ordinary buses it's normal to buy them onboard. Air-con buses may operate from a separate station, and tickets for the more popular routes should be booked a day in advance. As a rough indication of prices, a trip from Bangkok to Chiang Mai costs B625 VIP, B403/314 by air-con bus (first/second class), and B215 by ordinary bus.

In rural areas, the bus network is supplemented or replaced by **songthaews**, open-ended vans with two facing benches for passengers. In most towns, you'll find the songthaew "terminal" near the market; to pick one up between destinations, just flag it down, and to indicate to the driver that you want to get out, press the bell, shout, or rap hard with a coin on the ceiling. In the deep south, **share taxis**, often clapped-out old limos, connect all the major towns. They're gradually being replaced by more comfortable **air-con minibuses**, which also now feature on popular routes in the central plains and elsewhere.

Trains

Managed by the State Railway of Thailand (SRT), the **rail network** consists of four main lines and a few branch lines. Fares depend on the class of seat, whether or not you want air conditioning, and on the speed of the train. Hard, wooden, third-class seats are very cheap (Bangkok–Chiang Mai B161); in second class, you can often choose between reclining seats or berths, with or without air-con, on long journeys (Bangkok–Chiang Mai B321–761); and in first class (B1233) you get a private two-person air-con compartment. Nearly all long-distance trains have dining cars. The speed supplements are as follows: Special Express (B120), Express (B80) and Rapid (B60). **Advance booking** of at least one day is strongly recommended for first- and second-class seats on all lengthy journeys, and for sleepers needs to be done as far in advance as possible. It should be possible to make bookings at the station in any major town, or by fax to Bangkok's Hualamphong Station on ⓕ02 226 6068. The SRT has a 24-hour hotline (ⓣ1690) and publishes clear and fairly accurate free **timetables** with fare information in English; the best place to get hold of them is over the counter at Hualamphong, or from their website at ⓦwww.railway.co.th.

Planes

Thai Airways (ⓦwww. thaiair.com) still dominates the internal **flight** network, which extends to all parts of the country, using some two-dozen airports. Bangkok Airways (ⓦwww. bangkokair.com), Air Andaman (ⓦwww. airandaman.com), PB Air (ⓦwww.pbair.com), Phuket Airlines (ⓦwww.phuketairlines.com) and One-Two-Go (ⓦwww.onetwo-go.com) provide useful additional services often at cheaper rates than Thai Airways, with more smaller airlines apparently on their way. Book early if possible – you can reserve online with Thai Airways, Bangkok Airways and One-Two-Go. To give an idea of **fares**, Bangkok to Chiang Mai costs B2275 with Thai Airways, B1350 with One-Two-Go. If you're planning to make lots of domestic flights, consider buying Thai's or Bangkok Airway's **airpass** – their complex conditions and prices are posted on their websites.

Local transport and taxis

Most sizeable towns have some fixed-fare transport network of local buses, songthaews or even longtail boats, often with set routes, but never with rigid timetabling; within some towns, songthaews act like communal taxis, picking up a number of people who are going in roughly the same direction and taking each of them right to their destination.

Named after the noise of its excruciatingly un-silenced engine, the three-wheeled open-sided **tuk-tuk** is the classic Thai vehicle and is basically a cheap taxi. They are fast, fun and inexpensive: fares start at around B20 (B30 in Bangkok) regardless of the number of passengers. With all types of taxi, bar Bangkok's metered taxis, always establish the fare before you get in. Tuk-tuks are also sometimes known as samlors (literally "three wheels"), but the real **samlors** are tricycle rickshaws propelled by pedal power alone. Samlors still operate in many towns, though not in Bangkok, and drivers usually charge a minimum fee of around B10, adding B10 per kilometre, possibly more for a heavy load. Even faster and more precarious than tuk-tuks, **motorbike taxis** feature both in big towns and out-of-the-way places.

Accommodation

Thailand is stuffed full of traveller-oriented **guesthouses** (see "Accommodation", pp.61–63), offering simple double rooms with shared bathrooms for B100–250. If you're travelling on your own, expect to pay anything between sixty and one hundred percent of the double-room price. You'll find these guesthouses in their dozens in Bangkok, Chiang Mai and all the main backpacker beach resorts – where they're also called bungalows – and even in the most unlikely back-country spots. Check-out time is usually noon, so during high season (roughly Nov–Feb & July–Aug) you should arrive to check in at about 11.30am: few places will draw up a "waiting list" and they rarely take advance bookings.

With just twenty officially registered **youth hostels** in the whole country (ⓦwww.tyha.org), it's not worth becoming a YHA member just for your trip to Thailand. There's little point in lugging a tent around Thailand either, unless you're planning an extensive tour of national parks: accommodation everywhere else is too inexpensive to make **camping** a necessity, and anyway there are no campsite inside town perimeters; camping is allowed on nearly all islands and beaches, but few people bother. Many **national parks** offer basic hut accommodation where advance booking is unnecessary except on weekends and holidays; the easiest option is to do it online at ⓦwww.thaiforestbooking.com/nationalpark-eng.htm. The alternatives are to pay on the spot in Bangkok at the Forestry Department offices near Kasetsart University on Thanon Phaholyothin, about 4km north of the Mo Chit Skytrain terminus (Mon–Fri 8.30am–4.30pm, ⓣ02 579 5734 or 02 579 7223); to book on the phone (not much English spoken), then send a baht money order and wait for confirmation; or to pay through a bank and take the receipt with you when checking in. A few national parks accept phone bookings themselves (these are highlighted in the Guide).

Few Thais use guesthouses, opting instead for Chinese–Thai-run **budget hotels**, often located near the bus station, with rooms in the B100–600 range. They're generally clean and en suite, but usually lack any communal area. Beds in these places are large enough for a couple, and it's quite acceptable for two people to ask and pay for a single room (*hong diaw*). **Mid-range hotels** – priced between B600 and B1200 – can sometimes work out to be good value, with TV, fridge, air con and pool. Many of Thailand's **upmarket hotels** belong to international chains such as *Holiday Inn*, *Marriott* and *Sheraton*, maintaining top-quality standards in Bangkok and major resorts at prices of B2500 (£40/US$60) and upward for a double; some of the best upmarket Thai hotels are up to B1000 cheaper. Many upmarket hotels quote rates in US dollars, but will accept baht; they all add ten percent tax and a ten percent service charge. Try ⓦwww.asia-hotels.com for discount rates.

Electricity is supplied at 220 volts AC and available at all but the most remote villages and basic beach huts. Several **plug** types are commonly in use, most usually with two round pins, but also with two flat-blade pins, and sometimes with both options.

Food and drink

Thai **food** is renowned for its fiery but fragrant dishes spiced with lemon grass, basil and chilli, and you can eat well and cheaply even in the smallest provincial towns. Hygiene is a consideration when eating anywhere in Thailand, but there's no need to be too cautious: wean your stomach gently by avoiding excessive amounts of chillies and too much fresh fruit in the first few days and always drink either bottled or boiled water. You can be pretty sure that any noodle stall or curry shop that's permanently packed with customers is a safe bet. At a cheap stall or café, you'll get a main course for under B60, while upmarket, expensive restaurants can charge over B130.

Throughout the country most inexpensive Thai restaurants specialize in one general food type or preparation method – a "noodle shop", for example, might do fried noodles and noodle soups plus a basic fried rice, but nothing else; a restaurant displaying whole roast chickens and ducks will offer these sliced or with chillies and sauces served over rice; and "curry shops" serve just that. As often as not, the best and most entertaining places to eat are the local

Food and drink glossary

General terms and requests

I am vegetarian/vegan	*Phõm* (male) /*diichãn* (female) *kin ahãan mangsàwirát/jeh*
Can I see the menu?	*Khãw duù menu?*
I would like...	*Khãw...*
With/without	*Sai/mâi saì*
Can I have the bill please?	*Khãw check bin?*

Noodles

Ba mii	Egg noodles
Ba mii kràwp	Crisp fried egg noodles
Kwáy tiãw	White rice noodles
Kwáy tiãw/ba mii haêng	Rice noodles/egg noodles fried with egg, meat and vegetables
Kwáy tiãw/ba mii nám (mũu)	Rice noodle/egg noodle soup, made with chicken broth (and pork balls)
Kwáy tiãw/ba mii rât nâ (mũu)	Rice noodles/egg noodles fried in gravy-like sauce with vegetables (and pork)
Pàt thai	Thin noodles fried with egg and beansprouts, topped with ground peanuts
Pàt siyú	Wide or thin noodles fried with soy sauce, egg and meat

Rice (khâo)

Khâo man kài	Chicken served over marinated rice
Khâo nâ kài/pèt	Chicken/duck with sauce over rice
Khâo niãw	Sticky rice
Khâo pàt kài/ mũu/kûng/ néua/phàk	Fried rice with chicken/pork/shrimp/ beef/vegetables
Khâo rât kaeng	Curry over rice
Khâo tôm	Rice soup

Curries, soups and other dishes

Kaeng phèt	Hot, red curry
Kaeng phánaeng	Thick, savoury curry
Kaeng khiãw wan	Green curry
Kài pàt nàw mái	Chicken with bamboo shoots
Kài pàt mét mámûang	Chicken with cashew nuts
Kài pàt khĩng	Chicken with ginger
Mũu prîaw wãan	Sweet and sour pork
Néua pàt krathiam phrík thai	Beef fried with garlic and pepper
Néua pàt nám man hõy	Beef in oyster sauce
Pàt phàk bûng	Morning glory fried in garlic and bean sauce
Pàt phàk lãi yàng	Stir-fried vegetables
Plaa rât phrík	Whole fish cooked with chillies
Plaa thâwt	Fried whole fish
Sôm tam	Spicy papaya salad
Tôm khàa kài	Chicken coconut soup
Tôm yam kûng	Hot and sour prawn soup
Yam néua	Spicy beef salad

Drinks (khreûang deùm)

Bia	Beer
Chaa ráwn	Hot tea
Chaa yen	Iced tea
Kaafae ráwn	Hot coffee
Nám klûay	Banana shake
Nám mánao/sôm	Fresh, bottled or fizzy lemon/ orange juice
Nám plaò	Drinking water (boiled or filtered)
Nom jeùd	Milk
Sohdaa	Soda water

night markets (*talaat yen*), where "specialist" pushcart kitchens congregate from about 6pm to 6am on permanent patches in most towns, often close to the fruit and vegetable market or the bus station. Each stall is fronted by tables and stools, and you can choose your food from wherever you like.

What to eat and drink

Thais eat **noodles** (*kway tiaw* or *ba mii*) when Westerners would dig into a sandwich – for lunch, as a late-night snack or just to pass the time – and at B20–30 they're the cheapest hot meal you'll find anywhere. They come in assorted varieties (wide and flat, thin and transparent, made with eggs, soy-bean flour or rice flour) and get boiled up as soups (*kway tiaw nam*), doused in sauces (*kway tiaw rat na*), or stir-fried (*kway tiaw haeng* or *kway tiaw pat*). The usual practice is to order the dish with extra chicken, beef, pork or shrimps. The most popular noodle dish is *kway tiaw pat thai*, usually abbreviated to *pat thai*, a delicious combination of fried noodles, beansprouts and egg, sprinkled with ground peanuts and lime juice, and often spiked with dried shrimps. Fried **rice** (*khao pat*) is the other faithful standby. Although very few Thais are **vegetarian** (*mangsawirat)*, you can nearly always ask for a vegetable-only fried rice or noodle dish – though in rural spots this is often your only option unless you eat fish. All traveller-oriented restaurants are veggie-friendly.

Aside from fiery **curries** (*kaeng*) and **stir-fries**, restaurant menus often include spicy Thai **soup**, which is eaten with other dishes, not as a starter. Two favourites are *tom kha kai*, a creamy coconut chicken soup, and *tom yam kung*, a prawn soup without coconut milk. Food from the northeastern **Isaan** region is popular throughout the country, particularly sticky rice (*khao niaw*), which is rolled up into balls and dipped into chilli sauces and other side dishes, such as the local dish *som tam*, a spicy green-papaya salad with garlic, raw chillies, green beans, tomatoes, peanuts and dried shrimps. Barbecued chicken on a stick (*kai yaang*) is the classic accompaniment. Raw minced pork is the basis of another popular Isaan and northern dish called *larb*, subtly flavoured with mint and served with vegetables.

Sweets (*khanom*) don't really figure on most restaurant menus, but a few places offer bowls of *luk taan cheum*, a jellied concoction of lotus seeds floating in a syrup, and coconut custard (*sangkaya*) cooked inside a small pumpkin. Cakes are sold on the street and tend to be heavy, sticky affairs made from glutinous rice and coconut cream pressed into squares and wrapped in banana leaves.

Thais don't drink **water** straight from the tap, and nor should you: plastic bottles of drinking water (*nam plao*) are sold countrywide, even in the smallest villages. Night markets, guesthouses and restaurants do a good line in freshly squeezed **fruit juices** and shakes, as well as fresh coconut milk (*nam maprao*) and freshly squeezed sugar-cane juice (*nam awy*), which is sickeningly sweet.

Beer (*bia*) is comparatively expensive at around B60 for a 330ml bottle; the most famous beer is the slightly acrid locally brewed Singha, but Kloster, Carlsberg and Heineken, which are also brewed locally, are more palatable. At about B60 for a 375ml bottle, the local **whisky** is a lot better value and Thais think nothing of consuming a bottle a night. The most drinkable and widely available of these is the 35 percent proof Mekhong. Sang Thip is an even stronger **rum**. Bars aren't an indigenous feature, as Thais rarely drink out without eating, but you'll find a fair number in Bangkok and the tourist centres.

Communications

Mail takes around a week to get from Bangkok to Europe or North America, longer from more isolated areas. Almost all main post offices across the country operate a **poste restante** service and will hold letters for two to three months (see "Poste restante", p.63). All parcels must be officially boxed and sealed at main post offices – you can't just turn up with a package and buy stamps for it. Surface packages take three months, airmail parcels take about ten days.

Payphones come in several colours. Red and pale-blue phones are for local calls and take one-baht coins. Dark-blue and stainless steel ones are for any calls within Thailand, but they gobble up B1, B5 and B10 coins over long distances, so you're better off buying a TOT phonecard for domestic calls (B25–240) available from hotels and many shops); it comes with a PIN number and can be used in designated orange cardphones or the stainless-steel payphones. Thai area codes have recently been incorporated into the subscriber number so even when phoning from the same city, you must dial the entire number as shown in the Guide. For directory enquiries within Thailand, call ⓣ1133.

For **international** direct-dial (IDD) phone calls, the most expensive time is Monday to Saturday 7am to 9pm. You can benefit from government IDD rates with a Thaicard, the **international phonecard** issued by the Communications Authority of Thailand (CAT). Found in B50–3000 denominations at post offices and many shops, Thaicards can be used in designated purple cardphones and at government telephone centres, which are usually located within or adjacent to the town's main post office. On the same phones, you can also use CAT's Internet-based Phone Net cards (B300, B500 or B1000, from the same outlets), with far cheaper tariffs. The private international cardphone system, Lenso, operates in Bangkok and the biggest resorts. To use Lenso's yellow phones, buy a Lenso phonecard (B300 or B500 from shops near the phones) or use a credit card. Rates are ten percent higher than government IDD rates. Private call offices are more expensive again; cheapest of all is to call via the Internet, and you'll find that many Internet cafés in touristy areas deeply undercut government phone rates. Collect or **reverse-charge** calls can be made free of charge at government phone centres, or from many guesthouses and private phone offices, usually for a fee of B100. From the government phonecentres, as well as from some payphones and fixed telephones, you can make "Home Country Direct" calls to your own international operator, who will arrange for you to make a credit-card or reverse-charge call. For international directory enquiries, call ⓣ100. See "IDD Code" box, p.64, for how to call abroad from Thailand.

An increasing number of tourists take their **mobile phones** to Thailand, but not all foreign networks have links with Thai networks so you should verify this before you leave home. Visitors from the US may well need to have a dual- or tri-band phone, but GSM 900Hz and 1800Hz, the systems most commonly found in other parts of the world, are available in Thailand; for a full list of network types and providers in Thailand, go to ⓦwww.teletechnics.com/reference/telecom/cellular.html.

Internet access is available at private outlets almost everywhere in Thailand, averaging B1 per minute in tourist centres, as little as B20 per hour upcountry. There's also a public Internet service, Catnet, at most government telephone offices; you need to buy a B100 card with a Catnet PIN, which gives you about three hours of Internet time.

Time differences

Bangkok is seven hours ahead of GMT, twelve hours ahead of Eastern Standard Time, fifteen hours ahead of Pacific Standard Time and three hours behind Australian Eastern Standard Time. Thailand has no daylight saving timetable.

Opening hours and festivals

Most **shops** open at least Monday to Saturday from about 8am to 8pm, while **department stores** operate daily from around 10am to 9pm. **Banking hours** are Monday to Friday 8.30am to 3.30 or 4.30pm, but exchange kiosks in the main tourist centres are often open till 10pm, and upmarket hotels change money 24 hours a day. **Post offices** are generally open Monday to Friday 8.30am to 4.30pm, Saturday 9am to noon. **Private office** hours are generally Monday to Friday 8am to 5pm and Saturday 8am to noon, though in tourist areas these hours are longer, with weekends worked like any other day. **Government offices** work Monday to Friday 8.30am to noon and 1 to 4.30pm, and national museums tend to stick to these hours, too, but some close on Mondays and Tuesdays rather than at weekends. Most shops and tourist-oriented businesses, including TAT, stay open on national holidays. The only time an inconvenient number of shops, restaurants and hotels do close is during **Chinese New Year**, which, though not marked as an official national holiday, brings many businesses to a standstill for several days in late January or early February.

Public holidays

January 1 Western New Year's Day
February (day of full moon) Maha Puja. Commemorates the Buddha preaching to a spontaneously assembled crowd of 1250
April 6 Chakri Day. The founding of the Chakri dynasty
April (usually 13–15) *Songkhran*. Thai New Year
May 5 Coronation Day
May (early) Royal Ploughing Ceremony. Marks start of rice-planting season
May (day of full moon) Visakha Puja. The holiest of all Buddhist holidays, celebrating the birth, enlightenment and death of the Buddha
July (day of full moon) Asanha Puja. Commemorates the Buddha's first sermon
July (the day after Asanha Puja) Khao Pansa. The start of the annual three-month Buddhist rains retreat, when new monks are ordained
August 12 Queen's Birthday
October 23 Chulalongkorn Day. The anniversary of Rama V's death
December 5 King's Birthday
December 10 Constitution Day
December 31 Western New Year's Eve

Festivals

Thais use both the Western Gregorian **calendar** and a Buddhist calendar – the Buddha is said to have died (or entered Nirvana) in the year 543 BC, so Thai dates start from that point: thus 2006 AD becomes 2549 BE (Buddhist Era). Dates for religious festivals are often set by the lunar calendar, so check specifics with TAT or consult ⓦwww.thailandgrandfestival.com.

The most spectacular religious **festivals** include **Songkhran** (usually April 13–15), when the Thai New Year is welcomed in with massive public waterfights in the street (most exuberant in Chiang Mai and on Bangkok's Thanon Khao San); the **Candle Festival** in Ubon Ratchathani (July, three days around the full moon), when enormous wax sculptures are paraded to mark the beginning of the annual Buddhist retreat period; the **Vegetarian Festival** in Phuket and Trang (Oct), when Chinese devotees become vegetarian for a nine-day period and then parade through town performing acts of self-mortification; and **Loy Krathong** (late Oct or early Nov), when baskets of flowers and lighted candles are floated on rivers, canals and ponds nationwide (best in Sukhothai and Chiang Mai) to celebrate the end of the rainy season. The main tourist-oriented festival is the Surin **Elephant Roundup** (third weekend of Nov), when two hundred elephants play team games, and parade in battle dress.

Cultural hints

Tourist literature has so successfully marketed Thailand as the "Land of Smiles" that a lot of tourists arrive in the country expecting to be forgiven any outrageous behaviour. This is just not the case: there are some things so universally sacred in Thailand that even a hint of disrespect will cause deep offence. The worst thing you can possibly do is to bad-mouth the universally revered **royal family**. The king's anthem is always played before every film-screening in the cinema, during which the audience is expected to stand up.

Thais very rarely shake hands, using the **wai**, a prayer-like gesture made with raised hands, to greet and say goodbye and to acknowledge respect, gratitude or apology. The *wai* changes according to the relative status of the two people involved: as a farang (foreigner) your safest bet is to go for the "stranger's" *wai*, raising your hands close to your chest and placing your fingertips just below your chin. Although all Thais have a first name and a family name, everyone is addressed by their first name – even when meeting strangers – prefixed by the title "**Khun**" (Mr/Ms).

Thailand shares the same attitudes to dress and social taboos, described in "Cultural hints", p.68, as other Southeast Asian cultures.

Traditional drama and sport

Drama pretty much equals dance in Thai theatre, and many of the traditional dance-dramas are based on the Hindu epic the Ramayana (in Thai, Ramakien), a classic adventure tale of good versus evil that is known across Southeast Asia. The most spectacular form of traditional Thai theatre is **khon**, a stylized drama performed in masks and elaborate costumes by a troupe of highly trained classical dancers whose every graceful, angular gesture depicts a precise event, action or emotion that will be familiar to educated *khon* audiences. The story is chanted and sung by a chorus, accompanied by a classical *phipat* orchestra.

Serious and refined, **lakhon** is derived from *khon*, but is used to dramatize a greater range of stories, including Buddhist Jataka tales, local folk dramas and the Ramayana. The form you're most likely to come across is *lakhon chatri*, which is performed at shrines such as Bangkok's Erawan and Lak Muang as entertainment for the spirits and as a token of gratitude from worshippers. Dancers wear decorative costumes but no masks, and dance to the music of a *phipat* orchestra.

Likay is a much more popular derivative of *khon*, with lots of comic interludes, bawdy jokes and over-the-top acting. Most *likay* troupes adapt pot-boiler romances or write their own, and travel around the country doing shows on makeshift outdoor stages and at temple fairs.

Thai boxing (*muay Thai*) enjoys a following similar to football in Europe: every province has a stadium, and whenever it's shown on TV you can be sure that large noisy crowds will gather round the sets in streetside restaurants and noodle shops. The best place to see live Thai boxing is at one of Bangkok's two stadiums (see ⓦwww.tat.or.th/do/muay.htm). There's a strong spiritual and ritualistic dimension to *muay Thai*, adding grace to an otherwise brutal sport. Any part of the body except the head may be used as an offensive weapon in *muay Thai*, and all parts except the groin are fair targets. Kicks to the head are the blows that cause most knockouts. As the action hots up, so the orchestra speeds up its tempo and the betting in the audience becomes more frenetic.

Meditation centres and retreats

Of the hundreds of **meditation** temples in Thailand, a few cater specifically for foreigners by holding meditation sessions and retreats in English. The meditation taught is mostly Vipassana or "insight", which emphasizes the minute observation of internal physical sensation. Novices and practised meditators alike are welcome. To join a session in Bangkok, drop in at Wat Mahathat (see p.976). Longer retreats are for the serious-minded only. Days are dominated by meditation; there's generally no talking, and no eating after midday; tobacco, alcohol, drugs and sex are forbidden; and conditions are spartan. The most popular foreigner-oriented retreat takes place the first ten days of every month at Wat Suan Mokkh near Surat Thani (see p.1056). Frequent ten-day retreats led by foreign teachers are also held at Wat Khao Tham on Ko Pha Ngan (see p.1065). For further pointers, try ⓦwww.dharmanet.org/thai_94.html, though it's a little out of date.

Trekking and diving

The vast majority of travellers' itineraries take in a few days' trekking in the north and a stint of snorkelling or diving off the beaches of the south. **Trekking** is concentrated in the north and is described on pp.1050–1054, but there are smaller, less touristy trekking operations in Kanchanaburi (see p.990), Sangkhlaburi (p.992) and Umphang (p.1004), all of which are worth considering. Some **national parks**, such as Khao Yai (see p.992) and Khao Sok (p.1073), offer shorter trails for unguided walks; most national parks charge a B200 entrance fee.

You can **dive** all year round in Thailand, as the coasts are subject to different monsoon seasons: the diving seasons are from November to April along the Andaman coast, from January to October on the Gulf coast, and all year round on the east coast. See ⓦwww.divethailand.net/ontheweb.html for dive reports and links. The major dive centres are Pattaya and Ko Chang on the east coast; Phuket, Ao Nang and Ko Lanta on the Andaman coast; and Ko Tao, Ko Samui and Ko Pha Ngan on the Gulf coast. You can organize dive expeditions (B1800–4500 plus equipment) and do a certificated diving course (B6000–13,000 for a four-day PADI Open Water course) at all these places; Ko Tao dive centres offer the cheapest courses. Always verify the dive instructors' Professional Association of Diving Instructors (PADI) or equivalent accreditation and check ⓦwww.padi.com to see if the dive shop is a member of PADI's International Resorts and Retailers Association (IRRA) as this guarantees a certain level of professionalism. There are currently six **recompression chambers** in Thailand, in Sattahip near Pattaya (see p.1030), on Ko Samui (p.1057), on Ko Tao (see p.1067) and on Phuket (p.1076).

Crime and safety

As long as you keep your wits about you and follow the precautions outlined in "Crime and safety" on p.66, you shouldn't encounter much trouble in Thailand. **Theft** and **pickpocketing** are two of the main problems, but the most common cause for concern are the **con-artists** who dupe gullible tourists into parting with their cash: be suspicious of anyone who makes an unnatural effort to befriend you, never buy anything from a tout, and heed specific warnings given throughout the Guide. The most notorious scam entails flogging low-grade **gems** at vastly inflated prices: read ⓦwww.2bangkok.com/2bangkok/Scams/Sapphire.shtml before you shell out any cash at all. Theft from some long-distance, **overnight buses** is also a problem, with the majority of reported incidents taking place on the temptingly cheap buses run by private companies direct from Bangkok's Thanon Khao San (as opposed to those that depart from the government bus stations) to destinations such as Chiang Mai and the southern beach resorts. The best solution is to go direct from the bus stations. On any bus or train, be wary of accepting food or drink from strangers, especially on long overnight journeys: it may be drugged so as to knock you out while your bags are stolen. Violent crime against tourists is not common but it does occur. There have been several serious attacks on **women travellers** in the last few years, but bearing in mind the millions of tourists visiting the country every year, the statistical likelihood of becoming a victim is extremely small. Unfortunately, it's also necessary for female tourists to think twice about spending time alone with a monk, as there have been rapes and murders committed by men wearing the saffron robes of the monkhood.

Drug-smuggling carries a maximum penalty of death in Thailand, dealing will get you anything from four years to life in a Thai prison, and possession of Category 1 drugs (heroin, amphetamines, LSD and ecstasy) for personal use can result in a life sentence; travellers caught with even the smallest amount of drugs at airports and international borders are prosecuted for trafficking.

Emergency phone numbers

In any emergency, contact the English-speaking **tourist police** who maintain a 24-hour toll-free nationwide line (ⓣ1155) and have offices within many regional TAT offices. TAT has a special department for tourist-related crimes and complaints called the **Tourist Assistance Center (TAC)**, which is based in the TAT headquarters on Thanon Rajdamnoen Nok, Bangkok (daily 8.30am–4.30pm; ⓣ02 281 5051).

Medical care and emergencies

Thai **pharmacies** (*raan khai yaa*; typically daily 8.30am–8pm) are well stocked with local and international branded medicaments, and most pharmacists speak English. All provincial capitals have at least one **hospital** (*rong phayaabahn*). Cleanliness and efficiency vary, but generally hygiene and healthcare standards are good; most doctors speak English. In the event of a major health crisis, get someone to contact your embassy (see p.984) or insurance company – it may be best to get yourself flown to Bangkok or even home.

History

The region's first distinctive civilization, Dvaravati, was established around two thousand years ago by an Austroasiatic-speaking people known as the Mon. One of its mainstays was Theravada Buddhism, which had been introduced to Thailand during the second or third century BC by Indian missionaries. In the eighth century, peninsular Thailand to the south of Dvaravati came under the control of the Srivijaya Empire, a Mahayana Buddhist state centred on Sumatra that had strong ties with India.

From the ninth century onwards, however, both Dvaravati and Srivijaya Thailand succumbed to invading **Khmers** from Cambodia, who took control of northeastern, central and peninsular Thailand. They ruled from Angkor and left dozens of spectacular temple complexes throughout the region. By the thirteenth century, however, the Khmers had overreached themselves and were in no position to resist the onslaught of a vibrant new force in Southeast Asia, the Thais.

The earliest Thais

The earliest traceable history of the **Thai people** picks them up in southern China around the fifth century AD, when they were squeezed by Chinese and Vietnamese expansionism into sparsely inhabited northeastern Laos. Their first significant entry into what is now Thailand seems to have happened in the north, where, some time after the seventh century, the Thais formed a state known as Yonok. Theravada Buddhism spread to Yonok via Dvaravati around the end of the tenth century, which served not only to unify the Thais themselves, but also to link them to the wider community of Buddhists.

By the end of the twelfth century, they formed the majority of the population in Thailand, then under the control of the Khmer Empire. The Khmers' main outpost, at Lopburi, was by this time regarded as the administrative capital of a land called "Syam".

Sukhothai

Some time around 1238, Thais in the upper Chao Phraya Valley captured the main Khmer outpost in the region at **Sukhothai** and established a kingdom there. When the young Ramkhamhaeng came to the throne around 1278, he seized control of much of the Chao Phraya Valley, and over the next twenty years gained the submission of most of Thailand under a complex tribute system.

Although the empire of Sukhothai extended Thai control over a vast area, its greatest contribution to the Thais' development was at home, in cultural and political matters. A famous inscription by Ramkham-haeng, now housed in the Bangkok National Museum, describes a prosperous era of benevolent rule, and it is generally agreed that Ramkhamhaeng ruled justly according to Theravada Buddhist doctrine. A further sign of the Thais' growing self-confidence was the invention of a new script to make their tonal language understood by the non-Thai inhabitants of the land.

The growth of Ayutthaya

After the death of Ramkhamhaeng around 1299, his empire quickly fell apart, and **Ayutthaya** became the Thai capital. Soon after founding the city in 1351, the ambitious king Ramathibodi united the principalities of the lower Chao Phraya Valley, which had formed the western provinces of the Khmer

Empire. When he recruited his bureaucracy from the urban elite of Lopburi, Ramathibodi set the style of government at Ayutthaya, elements of which persist to the present day. The elaborate etiquette, language and rituals of Angkor were adopted and, most importantly, the concept of the ruler as devaraja (divine king): when the king processed through the town, ordinary people were forbidden to look at him and had to be silent while he passed.

The site chosen by Ramathibodi for an international port was the best in the region, and so began Ayutthaya's rise to prosperity, based on exploiting the upswing in trade in the middle of the fourteenth century along the routes between India and China. By 1540, the Kingdom of Ayutthaya had grown to cover most of the area of modern-day Thailand. Despite a 1568 invasion by the Burmese, which led to twenty years of foreign rule, Ayutthaya made a spectacular comeback, and in the seventeenth century its foreign trade boomed. In 1511, the Portuguese had become the first Western power to trade with Ayutthaya, and a treaty with Spain was concluded in 1598; relations with Holland and England were initiated in 1608 and 1612 respectively. European merchants flocked to Thailand, not only to buy Thai products, but also for the Chinese and Japanese goods on sale there.

In the mid-eighteenth century, however, the rumbling in the Burmese jungle to the north began to make itself heard again. After an unsuccessful siege in 1760, the **Burmese** descended upon the city in February 1766 for the last time. The Thais held out for over a year, but finally, in April 1767, the city was taken. The Burmese savagely razed everything to the ground, led off tens of thousands of prisoners to Burma and abandoned the city to the jungle.

Taksin and Thonburi

Out of this lawless mess emerged **Phraya Taksin**, a charismatic general, who was crowned king in December 1768 at his new capital of **Thonburi**, on the opposite bank of the river from modern-day Bangkok. Within two years, he had restored all of Ayutthaya's territories and, by the end of the next decade, had brought Cambodia and much of Laos into a huge new empire.

However, by 1779 all was not well with the king. Taksin was becoming increasingly irrational and sadistic, and in March 1782 he was ousted in a coup. Chao Phraya Chakri, Taksin's military commander, was invited to take power and had Taksin executed.

The early Bangkok Empire: Rama I

With the support of the Ayutthayan aristocracy, Chakri – reigning as **Rama I** (1782–1809) – set about consolidating the Thai kingdom. His first act was to move the capital across the river to what we know as Bangkok, on the more defensible east bank. Borrowing from the layout of Ayutthaya, he built a new royal palace and impressive monasteries in the area of Ratanakosin – which remains the city's spiritual heart – within a defensive ring of two (later expanded to three) canals. In the palace temple, Wat Phra Kaeo, he enshrined the talismanic Emerald Buddha, which he had snatched during his campaigns in Laos. Trade with China revived, and the style of government was put on a more modern footing: while retaining many of the features of a devaraja, he shared more responsibility with his courtiers, as a first among equals.

Rama II and Rama III

The peaceful accession of Rama I's son as **Rama II** (1809–24) signalled the establishment of the Chakri dynasty, which is still in place today. This Second Reign is best remembered as a fertile period for Thai literature; indeed, Rama II himself is renowned as one of the great Thai poets.

By the reign of Rama III (1824–51), the Thais were starting to get alarmed by British colonialism in the region. In

1826, Rama III was obliged to sign the Burney Treaty, a limited trade agreement with the British, by which the Thais won some political security in return for reducing their taxes on goods passing through Bangkok.

Mongkut

Rama IV, more commonly known as **Mongkut** (1851–68), had been a Buddhist monk for 27 years when he succeeded his brother. But far from leading a cloistered life, Mongkut had travelled widely throughout Thailand, and had taken an interest in Western learning, studying English, Latin and the sciences.

Realizing that Thailand would be unable to resist the military might of the British, the king reduced import and export taxes, allowed British subjects to live and own land in Thailand and granted them freedom of trade under the Bowring Treaty. Within a decade, similar agreements had been signed with France, the United States and a score of other nations. Thus, by skilful diplomacy the king avoided a close relationship with just one power, which could easily have led to Thailand's annexation.

Chulalongkorn

Mongkut's son, **Chulalongkorn**, took the throne as Rama V (1868–1910) at the age of only 15, but he was well prepared by an excellent education that mixed traditional Thai and modern Western elements – provided by Mrs Anna Leonowens, subject of *The King and I*. One of his first acts was to scrap the custom by which subjects were required to prostrate themselves in the presence of the king. In the 1880s, he began to restructure the government to meet the country's needs, setting up a host of departments – for education, public health, the army and the like – and bringing in scores of foreign advisors to help with everything from foreign affairs to rail lines.

Throughout this period, however, the Western powers maintained their pressure on the region. The most serious threat to Thai sovereignty was the Franco–Siamese Crisis of 1893, which culminated in the French sending gunboats up the Chao Phraya River to Bangkok. Flouting numerous international laws, France claimed control over Laos and made other outrageous demands, which Chulalongkorn had no option but to agree to. During the course of his reign, the country was obliged to cede almost half of its territory, and forewent huge sums of tax revenue in order to preserve its independence; but by Chulalongkorn's death in 1910, the frontiers were fixed as they are today.

The end of absolute monarchy

Chulalongkorn was succeeded by a flamboyant, British-educated prince, Vajiravudh (Rama VI, 1910–25). His extravagance left severe financial problems for his successor, the young and inexperienced Prajadhipok, seventy-sixth child of Chulalongkorn (Rama VII, 1925–35).

On June 24, 1932, a small group of middle-ranking officials, led by a lawyer, Pridi Phanomyong, and an army major, Luang Phibunsongkhram (Phibun), staged a coup with only a handful of troops. Prajadhipok weakly submitted to the conspirators, and a hundred and fifty years of **absolute monarchy** in Bangkok came to a sudden end. The king was sidelined to a position of symbolic significance, and in 1935 he abdicated in favour of his ten-year-old nephew, Ananda, then a schoolboy living in Switzerland.

Up to World War II

Phibun emerged as prime minister after the decisive elections of 1938, and a year later officially renamed the country Thailand ("Land of the Free") – Siam, it was argued, was a name bestowed by external forces, and the new title made it clear that the country belonged to the Thais rather than the economically dominant Chinese.

The Thais were dragged into **World War II** on December 8, 1941, when, almost at the same time as the assault on Pearl Harbour, the Japanese invaded the east coast of peninsular Thailand, with their sights set on Singapore to the south. The Thais at first resisted fiercely, but realizing that the position was hopeless, Phibun quickly ordered a ceasefire.

The Thai government concluded a military alliance with Japan and declared war against the United States and Great Britain in January 1942, probably in the belief that the Japanese would win. However, the Thai minister in Washington, Seni Pramoj, refused to deliver the declaration of war against the US, and, in co-operation with the Americans, began organizing a resistance movement called Seri Thai. Pridi Phanomyong, now acting as regent to the young king, secretly co-ordinated the movement, smuggling in American agents and housing them in Bangkok. By 1944, Japan's defeat looked likely, and in July, Phibun, who had been most closely associated with them, was forced to resign by the National Assembly.

Postwar upheavals

With the fading of the military, the election of January 1946 was for the first time contested by organized political parties, resulting in Pridi becoming prime minister. A new constitution was drafted, and the outlook for democratic, civilian government seemed bright. Hopes were shattered, however, on June 9, 1946, when King Ananda was found dead in his bed, with a bullet wound in his forehead. Three palace servants were hurriedly tried and executed, but the murder has never been satisfactorily explained. Pridi resigned as prime minister, and in April 1948, Phibun, playing on the threat of communism, took over the premiership.

As **communism** developed its hold in the region with the takeover of China in 1949 and the French defeat in Indochina in 1954, the US increasingly viewed Thailand as a bulwark against the red menace. Between 1951 and 1957, when its annual state budget was only about $200 million a year, Thailand received a total of $149 million in American economic aid and $222 million in military aid.

Phibun narrowly won a general election in 1957, but only by blatant vote-rigging and coercion. After vehement public outcry, General Sarit, the commander-in-chief of the army, overthrew the new government in September 1957. Believing that Thailand would prosper best under a unifying authority, Sarit set about re-establishing the monarchy as the head of the social hierarchy and the source of legitimacy for the government. Ananda's successor, Bhumibol (Rama IX), was pushed into an active role, while Sarit ruthlessly silenced critics and pressed ahead with a plan for economic development.

The Vietnam (American) War

Sarit died in 1963, whereupon the military succession passed to General Thanom. His most pressing problem was the **Vietnam War**. The Thais, with the backing of the US, quietly began to conduct military operations in Laos, to which North Vietnam and China responded by supporting anti-government insurgency in Thailand. By 1968, around 45,000 US military personnel were on Thai soil, which became the base for US bombing raids against North Vietnam and Laos. The effects of the American presence were profound. The economy swelled with dollars, and hundreds of thousands of Thais became reliant on the Americans for a living, with a consequent proliferation of prostitution – centred on Bangkok's infamous Patpong district – and corruption. Moreover, the sudden exposure to Western culture led many to question traditional Thai values and the political status quo.

The democracy movement and civil unrest

Poor farmers in particular were becoming increasingly disillusioned with their lot, and many turned against the Bangkok government. At the end of 1964, the Communist Party of Thailand and other groups formed a broad left coalition, which soon had the support of several thousand insurgents in remote areas of the northeast and the north. By 1967, a separate threat had arisen in southern Thailand, involving Muslim dissidents and the Chinese-dominated Communist Party of Malaysia.

Thanom was now facing a major security crisis, and in November, 1971, he imposed repressive **military rule**. In response, student demonstrations began in June 1973, and in October as many as 500,000 people turned out at Thammasat University in Bangkok to demand a new constitution. Clashes with the police ensued but elements in the army, backed by King Bhumibol, prevented Thanom from crushing the protest with troops. On October 14, 1973, Thanom was forced to resign.

In a new climate of openness, Kukrit Pramoj formed a coalition of seventeen elected parties and secured a promise of US withdrawal from Thailand, but his government was riven with feuding. In October 1976, the students demonstrated again, protesting against the return of Thanom to Bangkok. This time there was no restraint: supported by elements of the military and the government, the police and reactionary students launched a massive assault on Thammasat University. On October 6, hundreds of students were brutally beaten, scores were lynched and some even burnt alive; the military took control and suspended the constitution.

Premocracy

Soon after, the military-appointed prime minister, Thanin Kraivichien, forced dissidents to undergo anti-communist indoctrination, but his measures seem to have been too repressive even for the military, who forced him to resign in October 1977. General Kriangsak Chomanand took over, and began to break up the insurgency with shrewd offers of amnesty. He in turn was displaced in February 1980 by General Prem Tinsulanonda, backed by a broad parliamentary coalition.

Untainted by corruption, Prem achieved widespread support, including that of the monarchy. Overseeing a period of rapid economic growth, Prem maintained the premiership until 1988, with a unique mixture of dictatorship and democracy sometimes called **Premocracy**: although never standing for parliament himself, Prem was asked by the legislature after every election to become prime minister. He eventually stepped down because, he said, it was time for the country's leader to be chosen from among its elected representatives.

The 1992 demonstrations

The new prime minister was indeed an elected MP, Chatichai Choonhavan. He pursued a vigorous policy of economic development, but this fostered widespread corruption. Following an economic downturn and Chatichai's attempts to downgrade the political role of the military, the armed forces staged a bloodless coup on February 23, 1991, led by Supreme Commander Sunthorn and General Suchinda, the army commander-in-chief, who became premier. When Suchinda reneged on promises to make democratic amendments to the constitution, hundreds of thousands of ordinary Thais poured onto the streets around Bangkok's Democracy Monument in mass **demonstrations** between May 17 and 20, 1992. Suchinda brutally crushed the protests, leaving hundreds dead or injured, but was then forced to resign when King Bhumibol expressed his disapproval in a ticking-off that was broadcast on world television. In the ensuing elections, the Democrat Party, led by Chuan Leekpai, a noted upholder of democracy and the rule of law, came to power, where it remained until 1995.

The economic crisis

After the short premiership of the "walking ATM", Banharn Silpa-archa, in 1996 General Chavalit Yongchaiyudh, leader of the New Aspiration Party (NAP), won what was dubbed the most corrupt election in Thai history, with an estimated 25 million baht spent on vote-buying in rural areas. At the start of Chavalit's premiership, the Thai **economy** was already on shaky ground. In February 1997, foreign-exchange dealers began to mount speculative attacks on the baht, alarmed at the size of Thailand's private foreign debt – 250 billion baht in the unproductive property sector alone, much of it accrued through the proliferation of prestigious skyscrapers in Bangkok. The government defended the pegged exchange rate, spending $23 billion of the country's foreign-exchange reserves, but at the beginning of July was forced to give up the ghost – the baht was floated and soon went into free-fall.

In August, the International Monetary Fund (IMF) put together a rescue package for Thailand of $17 billion. Among the conditions, the government was to slash the national budget, control inflation and open up financial institutions to foreign ownership. Chavalit's performance in the face of the crisis was viewed as inept, and in November, he was succeeded by Chuan Leekpai, who took up what was widely seen as a poisoned chalice for his second term.

Chuan immediately took a hard line to restore confidence, following the IMF's advice, which involved maintaining cripplingly high interest rates to protect the baht. Although this played well abroad, at home the government encountered increasing hostility. Unemployment had doubled to 2 million by mid-1998, and there were frequent public protests against the IMF. By the end of 1998, however, the baht stabilized at just under 40 to the US dollar, and interest rates and inflation were starting to fall. Foreign investors slowly began returning to Thailand, and by October 1999 Chuan was confident enough to forgo almost $4 billion of the IMF's planned $17 billion rescue package.

Thaksin

The 2001 election was the first under the 1997 constitution, which was intended to take the traditionally crucial role of money, especially for vote-buying, out of politics. However, this election coincided with the emergence of a major new party, Thai Rak Thai (Thai Loves Thai), formed by one of Thailand's wealthiest men, telecoms tycoon **Thaksin Shinawatra**. Shrugging off serious corruption charges, Thaksin achieved a sweeping victory. In government, Thaksin carried through the nationalistic rhetoric of his election campaign with protectionist policies to discourage foreign investment, while attempting to muzzle the press and water down the constitution. Among populist reforms, however, he issued a three-year loan moratorium for perennially indebted farmers and set up a one-million-baht development fund for each of the country's seventy thousand villages. To improve public health access, a standard charge of B30 per hospital visit was introduced.

As part of a wider social order campaign, Thaksin also waged war on drugs. An estimated one billion tablets of *ya baa* (methamphetamines) are smuggled into Thailand from Burmese laboratories each year, aimed at three million users, many of them in schools and colleges. In a brutal clampdown in the first half of 2003, there were 51,000 arrests and over 2000 extra-judicial killings, much to the consternation of human rights watchers. Thaksin proclaimed a resounding victory, which brought an indirect admonition from King Bhumibol in his birthday speech, when he pointed out that the war on drugs was far from over and requested a full explanation of all the deaths.

In early 2004, violence in the **Islamic southern provinces** escalated sharply. This has included the killings of more than sixty police, soldiers and even Buddhist monks, and the bombing of a bar area in Sungai Kolok frequented by Malaysian tourists, injuring thirty people. The troubles reached new heights in April when security forces brutally fought off fifteen or so co-ordinated attacks, killing over a hundred assailants. At the time of writing, the Thai authorities seem unsure how to handle the problem. Some officials have described the attackers as Muslim separatists and hinted at links with Al-Qaeda and Jemaah Islamiyah, but Thaksin dismissed them as bandits, bent on stealing and smuggling arms. Nor does the government seem to have made up its mind about whether to get tough, which would appear to be Thaksin's natural instinct, or to adopt a more softly-softly approach towards defusing tensions, which has worked in the past.

Religion

Some ninety percent of Thais practise Theravada Buddhism, one of the two main schools of Buddhism in Asia. The other ten percent are Mahayana Buddhists, Muslims, Hindus, Sikhs and Christians; see "Religion", pp.69–71, for an introduction to all these faiths.

While regular Buddhist merit-making insures a Thai for the next life, there are certain **Hindu gods** and animist spirits that most Thais also cultivate for help with more immediate problems, such as passing an exam, becoming pregnant or winning the lottery. Even the Buddhist King Bhumibol employs Brahmin priests to officiate at certain royal ceremonies, and, like his royal predecessors of the Chakri dynasty, he also associates himself with the Hindu god Vishnu by assuming the title Rama IX – Rama, hero of the Hindu epic the Ramayana, having been Vishnu's seventh manifestation.

Whereas Hindu deities tend to be benevolent, **animist spirits** (or *phi*) are not nearly as reliable and need to be mollified more frequently. So that these *phi* don't pester human inhabitants, each building has a special **spirit house** in its vicinity, as a dwelling for spirits ousted by the building's construction. Usually raised on a short column and designed to look like a temple or a traditional Thai house, these spirit houses are generally about the size of a dolls' house, but their ornamentation is supposed to reflect the status of the humans' building – thus, if that building is enlarged or refurbished, then the spirit house should be improved accordingly.

Traditional art and architecture

Aside from pockets of Hindu-inspired statuary and architecture, the vast majority of Thailand's cultural monuments take their inspiration from Theravada Buddhism, and so it is temples and religious images that constitute the kingdom's main sights.

The **wat** or Buddhist temple complex serves both as a community centre and a shrine for holy images. The most important wat building is the bot, or "ordination hall", which is only open to monks, and often only recognizable by the eight *sema* (boundary stones) surrounding it. Often almost identical to the bot, the viharn (assembly hall) is for the lay congregation, and usually contains the wat's principal Buddha image. Thirdly, there's the chedi, a stupa that was originally conceived to enshrine relics of the Buddha, but has since become a place to contain the ashes of royalty – and anyone else who can afford it.

In the early days of Buddhism, image-making was considered inadequate to convey the faith's abstract philosophies, but gradually images of the Buddha were created, construed chiefly as physical embodiments of his teachings rather than as portraits of the man. Of the four postures in which the Buddha is always depicted, the seated Buddha, which represents him in meditation, is the most common in Thailand. The reclining pose symbolizes the Buddha entering Nirvana at his death, while the standing and walking images both represent his descent from Tavatimsa heaven. Hindu images tend to be a lot livelier than Buddhist ones: the most commonly seen in Thailand are Vishnu, the "Preserver" who often appears in his manifestation of Rama, the epitome of ideal manhood. Shiva (the Destroyer) is commonly represented by a lingam or phallic pillar; he is the father of the elephant-headed boy Ganesh.

In the 1920s, art historians compiled a classification system for Thai art and architecture that was modelled along the lines of the country's historical periods. The first really significant period is known as the **Khmer and Lopburi** era (tenth to fourteenth centuries), when the Hindu Khmers of Angkor built hundreds of imposing stone castle-temples, or *prasat*, across their newly acquired "Thai" territory – blueprints for the even more magnificent Angkor Wat. Almost every surface of these sanctuaries was adorned with intricate carvings of Hindu deities, incarnations and stories. The very finest of the remaining *prasat* are at Phimai and Phanom Rung in Thailand's northeast. During the Khmer period the former Theravada Buddhist principality of Lopburi produced a distinctive style of broad-faced, muscular Buddha statue, wearing an ornamental headband – a nod to the Khmers' ideological fusion of earthly and heavenly power.

The **Sukhothai period** (thirteenth to fifteenth centuries) is considered the acme of Thai artistic endeavour, and is particularly famous for its elegantly sinuous Buddha sculptures, instantly recognizable by their slim oval faces and slender curvaceous bodies. Sukhothai-era architects also devised the equally graceful lotus-bud chedi, a slender tower topped with a tapered finial that was to become a hallmark of the era. Examples of Sukhothai art and architecture can be seen across the country, but the finest are found in the old city of Sukhothai itself.

Though essentially Theravada Buddhists, the **Ayutthayan kings** (fourteenth to eighteenth centuries) also adopted some Hindu and Brahmin beliefs from the Khmers. Their architects retained the concentric layout of Khmer temples, elongated the prang – central tower – into a corncob-shaped tower, and adapted the Sukhothai-style chedi. Like the Lopburi images, early Ayutthayan Buddha statues wear crowns to associate kingship with Buddhahood; as the court became ever more lavish, so these figures became increasingly adorned, with earrings, armlets, anklets and coronets. When Bangkok emerged as Ayutthaya's successor, the new capital's founder was determined to revive the old city's grandeur, and the **Ratanakosin** (or Bangkok) period (eighteenth century to present) began by aping what the Ayutthayans had done. Since then, neither wat architecture nor religious sculpture has evolved much further.

Books

We have included publishers' details for books that may be hard to find outside Thailand; other titles should be available worldwide.

Steve van Beek *The Arts of Thailand* (Periplus, Singapore). Lavishly produced introduction to the history of Thai architecture, sculpture and painting, with fine photographs by Luca Invernizzi Tettoni.

Vatcharin Bhumichitr *The Taste of Thailand*. The author runs a Thai restaurant in London and provides about 150 recipes adapted for Western kitchens, plus plenty of background detail.

Ashley J. Boyd and Collin Piprell *Diving in Thailand*. A thorough guide to 84 dive sites, detailing access, visibility, and marine life for each.

Karen Connelly *Touch the Dragon* (Silkworm Books, Chiang Mai). The humorous journal of an impressionable Canadian teenager, sent on an exchange programme to Den Chai in northern Thailand for a year.

James Eckardt *Bangkok People* (Asia Books, Bangkok). A renowned expat journalist's entertaining encounters with a gallery of Bangkokians, from construction workers and street vendors to boxers and politicians.

Alex Garland, *The Beach*. Gripping cult thriller (made into a film in 1999) that uses a Thai setting to explore the way in which travellers' ceaseless quest for "undiscovered" utopias inevitably leads to them despoiling the idyll.

Sandra Gregory with Michael Tierney *Forget You Had A Daughter: Doing Time in the "Bangkok Hilton" – Sandra Gregory's Story*. The frank and shocking account of a young British drug-smuggler's stay in Bangkok's notorious Lard Yao prison.

Thom Henley *Krabi: Caught in the Spell – A Guide to Thailand's Enchanted Province* (Thai Nature Education, Phuket). Highly readable features on the attractions and people of south Thailand's most beautiful region.

Michel Houellebecq *Platform*. Sex tourism in Thailand provides the nucleus of this brilliantly provocative (some would say offensive) novel, in which Houellebecq presents a ferocious critique of Western decadence and cultural colonialism, and of radical Islam, too.

Sumet Jumsai *Naga: Cultural Origins in Siam and the West Pacific*. Wide-ranging discussion of water symbols, offering a stimulating mix of art, architecture, mythology and cosmology.

Khammaan Khonkhai *The Teachers of Mad Dog Swamp* (Silkworm Books, Chiang Mai). The engaging story of a progressive young teacher who is posted to a remote village school.

Chart Korpjitti *The Judgement* (Thai Modern Classics). Sobering modern-day tragedy about a good-hearted Thai villager who is ostracized by his hypocritical neighbours.

Elaine and Paul Lewis *Peoples of the Golden Triangle*. Hefty, exhaustive work describing every aspect of hilltribe life.

Nitaya Masavisut (ed) *The SEA Write Anthology of Thai Short Stories and Poems* (Silkworm Books, Chiang Mai). Interesting contemporary short stories and poems by eleven Thai writers who have won Southeast Asian Writers' Awards.

Christopher G Moore *God Of Darkness* (Asia Books, Bangkok). A cracking thriller by Thailand's best-selling expat novelist, set during the economic crisis of 1997.

Cleo Odzer *Patpong Sisters*. An

American anthropologist's funny and touching account of her life with the bar girls of Bangkok's notorious red light district.

James O'Reilly and Larry Habegger (eds.) *Travelers' Tales: Thailand.* An absorbing anthology of contemporary writings about Thailand, by Thailand experts, social commentators, travel writers and first-time visitors.

Phra Peter Pannapadipo *Little Angels: The Real-Life Stories of Twelve Thai Novice Monks.* A dozen young novice monks, many of them from desperate backgrounds, tell their tales.

Pasuk Phongpaichit and Sungsidh Piriyarangsan *Corruption and Democracy in Thailand.* Fascinating study, revealing the nuts and bolts of corruption in Thailand. Their sequel, a study of Thailand's illegal economy, *Guns, Girls, Gambling*, Ganja, co-written with Nualnoi Treerat, makes equally eye-opening reading.

Denis Segaller *Thai Ways and More Thai Ways* (Post Books, Bangkok). Fascinating collections of short pieces on Thai customs.

Khamsing Srinawk *The Politician and Other Stories* (Silkworm Books, Chiang Mai). Anthology of brilliantly satiric short stories that capture the vulnerability of peasant farmers in the modern world.

William Stevenson *The Revolutionary King.* Fascinating biography of the normally secretive King Bhumibol, by a British journalist who was given unprecedented access.

Pira Sudham *People of Esarn* (Shire Books, Bangkok). Wry and touching real-life stories of villagers from the poverty-stricken northeast.

William Warren *Jim Thompson: the Legendary American of Thailand.* The engrossing biography of the ex-OSS agent, art collector and Thai silk magnate whose disappearance in Malaysia in 1967 has never been satisfactorily resolved.

David K Wyatt *Thailand: A Short History.* An excellent treatment, scholarly but highly readable, with a good eye for witty details.

Language

Most Thais who deal with tourists speak some English, but off the beaten track you'll probably need at least a few words of Thai. Being tonal, Thai is extremely difficult for Westerners to master. Five different tones are used – low (syllables marked `), middle (unmarked), high (marked ´), falling (marked ^), and rising (marked ˇ) – by which the meaning of a single syllable can be altered in five different ways. Thus, using four of the five tones, you can make a sentence from just one syllable: mái mài mâi mãi – "New wood burns, doesn't it?"

Thai script has 44 consonants to represent 21 consonant sounds, and 32 vowels to deal with 48 different vowel sounds. However, street signs in touristed areas are nearly always written in Roman script as well as Thai. Because there's no standard system of transliteration of Thai script into Roman, the Thai words and proper names in this book will not always match the versions written elsewhere. A town such as Ubon Ratchathani, for example, could come out as Ubol Rajatani, while Ayutthaya is synonymous with Ayudhia.

A few essential phrases are given below; for more help, try *Thai: A Rough Guide Phrasebook*.

Pronunciation

Vowels

a as in dad.
aa is pronounced as it looks, with the vowel elongated.
ae as in there.
ai as in buy.
ao as in now.
aw as in awe.
e as in pen.
eu as in sir, but heavily nasalized.
i as in tip.
ii as in feet.
o as in knock.
oe as in hurt, but more closed.
oh as in toe.
u as in loot.
uay "*u*" plus "*ay*" as in pay.
uu as in pool.

Consonants

r as in rip; in everyday speech, it's often pronounced like "l".
kh as in keep.
ph as in put.
th as in time.
k is unaspirated and unvoiced, and closer to "g".
p is also unaspirated and unvoiced, and closer to "b".
t is also unaspirated and unvoiced, and closer to "d".

Greetings and basic phrases

Whenever you speak to a stranger in Thailand, it's polite to end your sentence in *khráp* if you're a man, *khâ* if you're a woman – especially after *sawàt dii* (hello/goodbye) and *khàwp khun* (thank you). *Khráp* and *khâ* are also often used to answer "yes" to a question, though the most common way is to repeat the verb of the question (preceded by *mâi* for "no").

Hello	sawàt dii
Where are you	pai nãi? (not always meant literally, but used as a general greeting)
I'm out having fun/ I'm travelling	pai thîaw (answer to pai nãi, almost untranslatable pleasantry)
Goodbye	sawàt dii/la kàwn
Good luck/cheers	chôk dii
Excuse me	khãw thâwt
Thank you	khàwp khun
How are you?	sabai dii reũ?
I'm fine	sabai dii
What's your name?	khun chêu arai?
My name is...	phõm (men)/diichãn (women) chêu...
I come from...	phõm/diichãn maa jàak...
I don't understand	mâi khâo jai
Do you speak English?	khun phûut phasãa angkrìt dâi mãi?
Do you have... ?	mii... mãi?
Is... possible?	...dâi mãi?
Can you help me?	chûay phõm/diichãn dâi mãi?
(I) want...	ao...
(I) would like to...	yàak jà...
(I) like...	châwp...

Getting around

Where is the... ?	...yùu thîi nãi?
How far?	klai thâo rai?
I would like to go to...	yàak jà pai...
Where is this bus going?	rót níi pai nãi?
When will the bus leave?	rót jà àwk mêua rai?
Stop here	jàwt thîi nîi
Here	thîi nîi
There/over there	thîi nâan /thîi nôhn
Right	khwãa
Left	sái
Straight	trong
Street	thanõn
Train station	sathàanii rót fai
Bus station	sathàanii rót meh
Airport	sanãam bin
Ticket	tũa
Hotel	rohng raem
Post office	praisanii
Restaurant	raan ahãan
Shop	raan
Market	talàat
Hospital	rohng pha-yaabaan
Motorbike	rót mohtoesai
Taxi	rót táksîi
Boat	reua

Accommodation

How much is... ?	...thâo rai/kìi bàat?

How much is a room here per night?	hâwng thîi nîi kheun lá thâo rai?
Do you have a cheaper room?	mii hâwng thùuk kwàa mãi?
Can I/we look at the room?	duu hâwng dâi mãi?
I/We'll stay two nights	jà yùu sãwng kheun
Can I store my bag here?	fàak krapão wái thîi nîi dâi mãi?
Cheap/expensive	thùuk/phaeng
Air-con room	hãwng ae
Bathroom/toilet	hãwng nám
Telephone	thohrásàp
Fan	phát lom

General adjectives and nouns

Bad, no good	mâi dii
Big	yài
Closed	pìt
Delicious	aròi
Dirty	sokaprok
Food	ahãan
Foreigner	fàràng
Friend	phêuan
Fun	sanùk
Hot (spicy)	phèt
Unwell	mâi sabai
Open	pòet
Very	mâak

Time and days of the week

The commonest system for telling the time, as outlined below, is actually a confusing mix of several different systems. The State Railway and government officials use the 24-hour clock (9am is *kâo naalikaa,* 10am *sìp naalikaa*, and so on), which is easier.

1–5am	tii nèung–tii hâa
6–11am	hòk mohng cháo–sìp èt mohng cháo
Noon	thîang
1pm	bài mohng
2–4pm	bài sãwng mohng–bài sìi mohng
5–6pm	hâa mohng yen–hòk mohng yen
7–11pm	nèung thûm–hâa thûm
Midnight	thîang kheun
What time is it?	kìi mohng láew?
Minute	naathii
Hour	chûa mohng
Day	waan
Week	aathít
Month	deuan
Year	pii
Today	wan níi
Tomorrow	phrûng níi
Yesterday	mêua wan
Now	diãw níi
Next week	aathít nâa
Morning	cháo
Afternoon	bài
Evening	yen
Night	kheun
Monday	wan jan
Tuesday	wan angkhaan
Wednesday	wan phút
Thursday	wan pháréuhàt
Friday	wan sùk
Saturday	wan são
Sunday	wan aathít

Numbers

0	sũun
1	nèung
2	sãwng
3	sãam
4	sìi
5	hâa
6	hòk
7	jèt
8	pàet
9	kâo
10	sìp
11	sìp èt
12, 13, etc	sìp sãwng, sìp sãam…
20	yîi sìp/yiip
21	yîi sìp èt
22, 23, etc	yîi sìp sãwng, yîi sìp sãam…
30, 40, etc	sãam sìp, sìi sìp…
100, 200, etc	nèung rói, sãwng rói…
1000	nèung phan
10,000	nèung mèun

10.1

Bangkok

The headlong pace and flawed modernity of **BANGKOK** (called "Krung Thep" in Thai) match few people's visions of the capital of exotic Siam. Spiked with scores of highrise buildings of concrete and glass, it's a vast flatness that holds a population of at least nine million, and feels even bigger. But under the shadow of the skyscrapers, you'll find a heady mix of frenetic markets and hushed golden temples, of glossy cutting-edge clubs and early-morning alms-giving ceremonies. Most budget travellers head for the **Banglamphu** district, which is just a short walk from the dazzling **Grand Palace** and **Wat Pho** and the very worthwhile **National Museum**. For livelier scenes, explore the dark alleys of **Chinatown's bazaars** or head for the water: the great **Chao Phraya River** is the backbone of a network of canals and a useful way of crossing the city.

Bangkok is a relatively young capital, established in 1782 after the Burmese sacked Ayutthaya, the former capital. A temporary base was set up on the western bank of the Chao Phraya, in what is now Thonburi, before work started on the more defensible east bank. The first king of the new dynasty, Rama I, built his palace at **Ratanakosin** and this remains the city's spiritual heart. Initially, the city was largely amphibious: only the temples and royal palaces were built on dry land, while ordinary residences floated on thick bamboo rafts on the river and canals, and even shops and warehouses were moored to the river bank. In the late nineteenth century, Rama IV and Rama V modernized their capital along European lines, building roads and constructing a new royal residence in Dusit, north of Ratanakosin.

Since World War II, and especially from the mid-1960s onwards, Bangkok has seen an explosion of modernization, leaving the city without an obvious centre. Most of the canals have been filled in, to be replaced by endless rows of concrete shop-houses, sprawling over a built-up area of 330 square kilometres. The benefits of the economic boom of the 1980s and early 1990s were concentrated in Bangkok, as were the calamitous effects of the late-1990s economic crisis, both of which attracted mass migration from all over Thailand and made the capital ever more dominant: the population, over half of which is under 30 years of age, is now forty times that of the second city, Chiang Mai, and Bangkokians own eighty percent of the nation's cars.

Arrival and information

Once you're through immigration at **Don Muang Airport**, 25km north of the city, you'll find 24-hour exchange booths, ATMs, two TAT information desks (daily 9am–midnight; ⓣ02 523 8973), an accommodation booking desk (24hr) and several left-luggage offices (B90 per day). The domestic terminal is 500m from Terminal 2, connected by a walkway and a free shuttle bus (daily 5am–midnight; every 20min). (At the time of writing, the new Suvarnabhumi Airport, ⓦwww.bangkokairport.org, is under construction 30km east of Bangkok. All international flights are slated to arrive here, with Don Muang becoming the domestic airport. It's officially set to open in September 2005, but may well be delayed.)

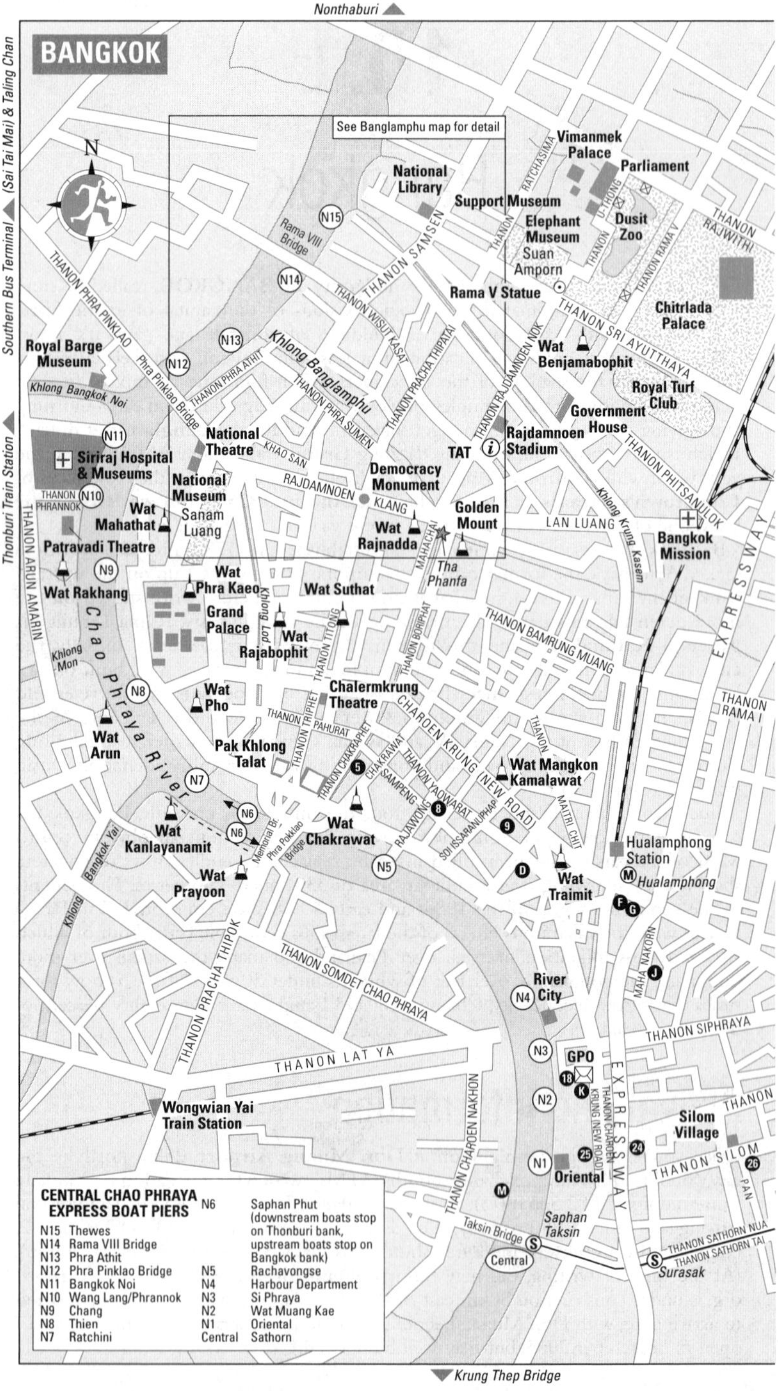

BANGKOK

Nonthaburi

See Banglamphu map for detail

National Library
Vimanmek Palace
Parliament
Support Museum
Elephant Museum
Suan Amporn
Dusit Zoo
Thanon Rajwithi
Chitrlada Palace
Rama V Statue
Thanon Sri Ayutthaya
Wat Benjamabophit
Royal Turf Club
Government House
Thanon Phitsanulok
Rajdamnoen Stadium
TAT
Democracy Monument
Golden Mount
Wat Rajnadda
Tha Phanfa
Lan Luang
Bangkok Mission
Khlong Krung Kasem
Expressway
Thanon Samsen
Thanon Ratchasima
Thanon U-Thong
Thanon Rama V
Thanon Wisut Kasat
Thanon Pracha Thipatai
Thanon Rajdamnoen Nok
Rama VIII Bridge
Khlong Banglamphu
Thanon Phra Athit
Thanon Phra Sumen
Khao San
Rajdamnoen Klang
Mahachai
Thanon Phra Pinklao
Phra Pinklao Bridge
Royal Barge Museum
Khlong Bangkok Noi
Siriraj Hospital & Museums
Thanon Phrannok
National Theatre
National Museum
Sanam Luang
Wat Mahathat
Patravadi Theatre
Wat Rakhang
Thanon Arun Amarin
Wat Phra Kaeo
Grand Palace
Wat Suthat
Wat Rajabophit
Khlong Lod
Thanon Titong
Thanon Boriphat
Thanon Bamrung Muang
Khlong Mon
Chao Phraya River
Wat Pho
Wat Arun
Chalermkrung Theatre
Thanon Triphet
Thanon Pahurat
Thanon Rama I
Charoen Krung (New Road)
Pak Khlong Talat
Thanon Chakraphet
Chakrawat
Sampeng
Thanon Yaowarat
Wat Mangkon Kamalawat
Maitri Chit
Rajawong
Soi Issaranuphap
Wat Chakrawat
Memorial Br.
Phra Pokklao Bridge
Wat Kanlayanamit
Wat Prayoon
Bangkok Yai
Khlong
Wat Traimit
Hualamphong Station
Hualamphong
Maha Nakorn
Thanon Pracha Thipok
Thanon Somdet Chao Phraya
River City
Thanon Siphraya
Thanon Lat Ya
GPO
Thanon Charoen Nakhon
Krung (New Road)
Thanon Charoen
Wongwian Yai Train Station
Silom Village
Thanon Silom
Pan
Oriental
Saphan Taksin
Taksin Bridge
Central
Thanon Sathorn Nua
Thanon Sathorn Tai
Surasak

CENTRAL CHAO PHRAYA EXPRESS BOAT PIERS

N15	Thewes	N6	Saphan Phut (downstream boats stop on Thonburi bank, upstream boats stop on Bangkok bank)
N14	Rama VIII Bridge		
N13	Phra Athit		
N12	Phra Pinklao Bridge	N5	Rachavongse
N11	Bangkok Noi	N4	Harbour Department
N10	Wang Lang/Phrannok	N3	Si Phraya
N9	Chang	N2	Wat Muang Kae
N8	Thien	N1	Oriental
N7	Ratchini	Central	Sathorn

Krung Thep Bridge

Southern Bus Terminal (Sai Tai Mai) & Taling Chan

Thonburi Train Station

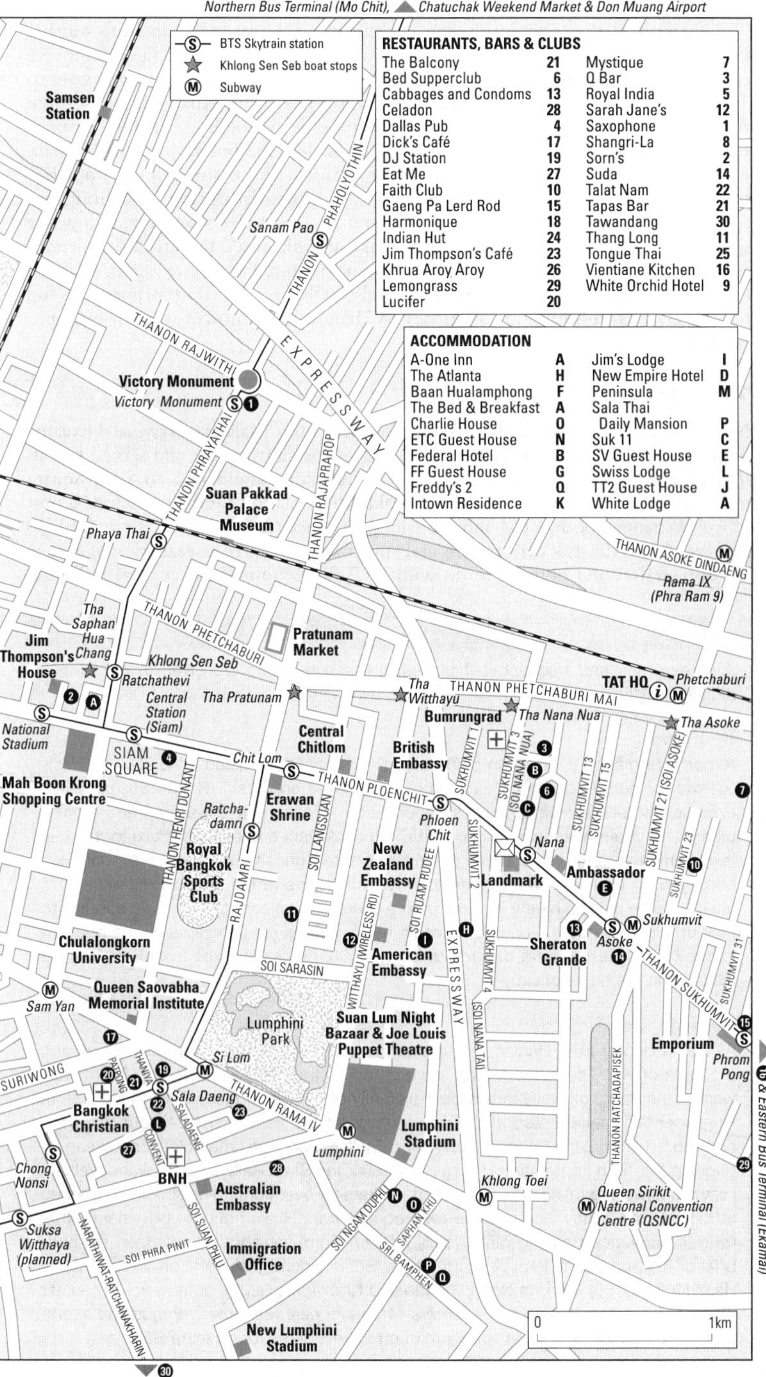
Northern Bus Terminal (Mo Chit), Chatuchak Weekend Market & Don Muang Airport
BTS Skytrain station
Khlong Sen Seb boat stops
Subway
RESTAURANTS, BARS & CLUBS
The Balcony 21
Bed Supperclub 6
Cabbages and Condoms 13
Celadon 28
Dallas Pub 4
Dick's Café 17
DJ Station 19
Eat Me 27
Faith Club 10
Gaeng Pa Lerd Rod 15
Harmonique 18
Indian Hut 24
Jim Thompson's Café 23
Khrua Aroy Aroy 26
Lemongrass 29
Lucifer 20
Mystique 7
Q Bar 3
Royal India 5
Sarah Jane's 12
Saxophone 1
Shangri-La 8
Sorn's 2
Suda 14
Talat Nam 22
Tapas Bar 21
Tawandang 30
Thang Long 11
Tongue Thai 25
Vientiane Kitchen 16
White Orchid Hotel 9
ACCOMMODATION
A-One Inn A
The Atlanta H
Baan Hualamphong F
The Bed & Breakfast A
Charlie House O
ETC Guest House N
Federal Hotel B
FF Guest House G
Freddy's 2 Q
Intown Residence K
Jim's Lodge I
New Empire Hotel D
Peninsula M
Sala Thai Daily Mansion P
Suk 11 C
SV Guest House E
Swiss Lodge L
TT2 Guest House J
White Lodge A
Samsen Station
Sanam Pao
Thanon Phaholyothin
Thanon Rajwithi
Expressway
Victory Monument
Thanon Phrayathai
Thanon Rajaprarop
Suan Pakkad Palace Museum
Phaya Thai
Thanon Asoke Dindaeng
Rama IX (Phra Ram 9)
Thanon Phetchaburi
Pratunam Market
Tha Saphan Hua Chang
Jim Thompson's House
Khlong Sen Seb
Ratchathevi
Central Station (Siam)
Tha Pratunam
Tha Witthayu
Thanon Phetchaburi Mai
TAT HQ
Phetchaburi
Bumrungrad
Tha Nana Nua
Tha Asoke
National Stadium
Siam Square
Chit Lom
Central Chitlom
British Embassy
Mah Boon Krong Shopping Centre
Thanon Henri Dunant
Erawan Shrine
Thanon Ploenchit
Sukhumvit 1
Sukhumvit 3 (Soi Nana Nua)
Sukhumvit 13
Sukhumvit 15
Sukhumvit 21 (Soi Asoke)
Ratchadamri
Soi Langsuan
Phloen Chit
Nana
Sukhumvit 23
Royal Bangkok Sports Club
Rajdamri
New Zealand Embassy
Soi Ruam Rudee
Sukhumvit 2
Landmark
Ambassador
Sukhumvit
Witthayu (Wireless Rd)
Expressway
Sukhumvit 4 (Soi Nana Tai)
Sheraton Grande
Asoke
Chulalongkorn University
American Embassy
Soi Sarasin
Thanon Sukhumvit
Sukhumvit 31
Queen Saovabha Memorial Institute
Sam Yan
Lumphini Park
Suan Lum Night Bazaar & Joe Louis Puppet Theatre
Emporium
Phrom Pong
Si Lom
Suriwong
Patpong
Thaniya
Sala Daeng
Thanon Rama IV
Thanon Ratchadapisek
Bangkok Christian
Saladaeng
Convent
Lumphini Stadium
Lumphini
Chong Nonsi
BNH
Australian Embassy
Khlong Toei
Queen Sirikit National Convention Centre (QSNCC)
Soi Ngam Duphli
Saphan Khu
Suksa Witthaya (planned)
Soi Phra Pinit
Soi Suan Phlu
Immigration Office
Sri Bamphen
Narathiwat-Ratchanakharin
New Lumphini Stadium
16 & Eastern Bus Terminal (Ekamai)
0
1km
30

The **airport bus** (5am–midnight; every 30min; B100) picks up from outside each terminal and takes about ninety minutes to the end of each line. Route A1 runs to the west end of Thanon Silom, via Thanon Rajdamri; route A2 goes to Thanon Phra Athit in Banglamphu, via Thanon Tanao (for Khao San); and route A3 runs along Thanon Sukhumvit to Soi Thonglor via the Eastern Bus Terminal. **Public buses** are cheaper, but slower and crowded; the bus stop is on the main highway just outside the northern end of Arrivals. The **train** (50min; from B5) to Hualamphong station is the quickest way into town during rush hour, but services are irregular; trains to the north and northeast also stop here; follow the signs from Arrivals in Terminal 1. Never take an unlicensed taxi from the airport, as robberies are not unknown. Licensed and metered taxis are operated from clearly signposted counters outside Arrivals: including the B50 airport pick-up fee and B70 expressway tolls, a journey to Thanon Silom downtown, for example, costs around B300.

Trains

Nearly all **trains** to Bangkok, including services from Malaysia, arrive at Hualamphong station, which is at the southern end of the subway line and served by bus #53 to Banglamphu (from the east side of the station), and #25 to Siam Square (for Skytrain connections) and Thanon Sukhumvit. Station **facilities** include a post office, exchange booth, ATM and a left-luggage office (daily 4am–10.30pm; B10–30 per day). Avoid tuk-tuk drivers here, and any itinerant "tourist assistance" staff as they are **con-artists** and nothing to do with TAT. Trains from Kanchanaburi pull in at

Moving on from Bangkok

Journey times and frequency of planes, trains and buses are given in the "Travel details", p.1096.

By plane

Airport information is given on p.961 and airline offices are listed on p.984. The fastest way of getting to Don Muang Airport is by **metered taxi** (B120–350, plus B70 expressway toll); set off at least an hour before check-in. To save time and money, take the Skytrain or subway to Mo Chit/Chatuchak Park and pick up a taxi for the last few kilometres to the airport from there. Nearly every guesthouse and travel agent can book you on to one of the frequent **private minibuses** to the airport (B60–80); you'll need to leave at least ninety minutes before check-in as it can take up to 45 minutes to pick up all passengers. The B100 **airport bus services** are unreliable on the outward journey. The **international departure tax** is B500; domestic taxes from Bangkok are included in the ticket price.

By train

All **trains** depart from Hualamphong station except the service to Kanchanaburi and a couple of Hua Hin trains, which leave from Thonburi station, about an 850m walk west of the Bangkok Noi express-boat pier. All north- and northeast-bound trains from Hualamphong make a stop at the Don Muang Airport station. The 24-hour "Information" booth at Hualamphong Station keeps English-language timetables, or you can try phoning the Train Information Hotline on ⓣ1690; the State Railway of Thailand website (ⓦwww.railway.co.th) carries a fare chart. Tickets for overnight trains should be booked at least a day in advance and are best bought from Hualamphong; buy them either from the advance booking office (daily 8.30am–4pm), which also sells joint rail-and-boat or rail-and-bus tickets via Surat Thani (B650 second-class air-con sleeper) to Ko Samui (plus B150), Ko Pha Ngan, Ko Tao and Krabi (plus B200), or from ticket counter #2 (daily 5–8.30am & 4–10pm); counters #1 and #2 deal with ticket refunds and alterations. You can also buy train tickets through travel agents for an extra B50.

Thonburi station, which is near the express-boat line (see box below), just across the Chao Phraya River from Banglamphu and Ratanakosin.

Buses

Bangkok has three main long-distance **bus** terminals, each in a different corner of the city; see box below for details of city bus routes to these terminals. Services from Malaysia and the south come in at the **Southern Bus Terminal** (*sathaanii sai tai mai*), at the junction of Thanon Borom Ratchonni and the Nakhon Chaisri Highway in Thonburi; air-con city buses #507/#7 and #511/#11 run from the main road into Banglamphu. Services from the north and northeast use the **Northern Bus Terminal** (*sathaanii mo chit*), on Thanon Kamphaeng Phet 2, near Chatuchak Weekend Market in the far north of the city; easiest access into town is by Skytrain from the Mo Chit BTS station (or the subway at the adjacent Chatuchak Park Station) fifteen minutes' walk away. Buses from the east coast pull into the **Eastern Bus Terminal** (*sathaanii ekamai*), at Soi 40, Thanon Sukhumvit (a few east-coast services also use the Northern Bus Terminal); the Ekamai BTS Skytrain station is right next door.

Information and maps

The Bangkok Tourist Bureau (BTB) provides a decent information service both from its headquarters, the **Bangkok Information Centre**, located next to Phra Pinklao Bridge at 17/1 Thanon Phra Athit in Banglamphu (daily 9am–7pm; ⓣ02

By bus

Seats on long-distance air-con **bus** services to Chiang Mai, Krabi, Phuket and Surat Thani should be reserved ahead either at the relevant bus station or through guesthouses; see "Getting around", p.940 for a guide to the different services and relevant fares. From Banglamphu, you'll need at least ninety minutes (outside rush hour) to get to the Eastern Bus Terminal, and a good hour to reach the Northern or Southern terminals. For transport to the bus terminals, see "Buses", above.

The **Southern Bus Terminal** (*sathaanii sai tai mai*), at the junction of Thanon Borom Ratchonni and the Nakhon Chaisri Highway, handles services to all points south of the capital, including Chumphon, Surat Thani, Phuket and Krabi, as well as destinations west of Bangkok, such as Kanchanaburi. Services to the north and northeast – including Chiang Mai, Chiang Rai, Nong Khai and Aranyaprathet – as well as services to Ayutthaya and Sukhothai, and a few to Pattaya, Chanthaburi and Trat on the east coast, use the **Northern Bus Terminal** (*sathaanii mo chit*), on Thanon Kamphaeng Phet 2, near Chatuchak Weekend Market. The **Eastern Bus Terminal** (*sathaanii ekamai*), at Soi 40, Thanon Sukhumvit, serves east-coast destinations such as Pattaya, Ban Phe and Trat.

Budget transport

Many Bangkok outfits offer **budget transport** on small and large buses to Chiang Mai, Surat Thani, Krabi, Ko Samet and Ko Chang. This often works out cheaper than a public air-con bus, and departures are usually from Thanon Khao San, but many of the buses are cramped and airless, drivers often race, and drop-off points can be miles from the town centre, despite adverts to the contrary. Security on large buses is also a big problem, so keep everything of value on your person at all times and lock other luggage. If you're heading for an island, check whether your bus ticket covers the ferry ride. Consult other travellers before booking any budget transport and consider taking the train or a public air-con bus instead.

225 7612–4, ⓦbangkoktourist.bma.go.th/english/index.php), and from its twenty or so booths around the capital. For destinations further afield, visit the **Tourism Authority of Thailand** (**TAT**), which has an office at 4 Rajdamnoen Nok (daily 8.30am–4.30pm; ⓣ02 282 9773, 24hr freephone tourist assistance ⓣ1672, ⓦwww.tat.or.th), a twenty-minute stroll from Thanon Khao San or a short ride in air-con bus #503/#3; TAT headquarters is at 1600 Thanon Phetchaburi Mai (daily 8.30am–4.30pm; ⓣ02 250 5500), near the junction with Sukhumvit Soi 21 and close to the Phetchaburi subway stop and the Khlong Sen Seb canal boat pier at Tha Asoke. The most useful listings magazines are the expat-oriented *Metro*, available in bookstores across the city (monthly; B100), and the backpackers' publication *Farang* (monthly; B100), which is mainly sold in Banglamphu.

Of the several **bus maps** sold at bookshops and hotels, the best and most useful is Bangkok Guide's *Bus Routes & Map*, while the idiosyncratic, heavily annotated Nancy Chandler's *Map of Bangkok* (ⓦwww.nancychandler.net) is great for shopping.

City transport

The main form of transport in the city are **buses**, but where possible it's nearly always faster to opt for boats, the subway or the Skytrain instead. Bangkok Tourist Bureau runs **tours**, including a night-time bicycle tour of Ratanakosin (every Sat 7–9.30pm; B390 including bicycle), weekend walking tours (B100), and a highly

Useful bus routes

#3 (ordinary and air-con, 24hr): Northern Bus Terminal–Chatuchak Weekend Market–Th Samsen–Th Phra Athit (for Banglamphu guesthouses)–Th Sanam Chai–Th Triphet–Memorial Bridge–Wat Suwan.

#16 (ordinary and air-con): Th Srinarong–Th Samsen–Thewes (for guesthouses)–Th Phitsanulok–Siam Square–Th Suriwong–GPO–Tha Si Phraya.

#25 (ordinary and air-con, 24hr): Eastern Bus Terminal–Th Sukhumvit–Siam Square–Hualamphong Station–Th Yaowarat (for Chinatown and Wat Traimit)–Wat Pho–Tha Chang (for the Grand Palace).

#29 (ordinary and air-con, 24hr): Don Muang Airport–Chatuchak Weekend Market–Victory Monument–Siam Square–Th Rama 1V–Hualamphong Station.

#38 (ordinary): Chatuchak Weekend Market–Victory Monument–Th Phetchaburi–Soi Asoke–Th Sukhumvit–Eastern Bus Terminal.

#39 (ordinary and air-con): Chatuchak Weekend Market–Victory Monument–Th Sri Ayutthaya–Th Lan Luang–Democracy Monument–Rajdamnoen Klang (for Th Khao San guesthouses)–Sanam Luang.

#53 circular (also anti-clockwise; ordinary): Thewes–Th Krung Kasem–Hualamphong Station–Th Yaowarat–Th Maharat (for Wat Pho and the Grand Palace)–Sanam Luang–Th Phra Athit and Th Samsen (for Banglamphu guesthouses)–Thewes.

#56 circular (also clockwise; ordinary): Th Phra Sumen–Wat Bowoniwes–Th Pracha Thipatai–Th Ratchasima (for Vimanmek Palace)–Th Rajwithi–Krung Thon Bridge–Thonburi–Memorial Bridge–Th Chakraphet (for Chinatown)–Th Mahachai–Democracy Monument–Th Tanao (for Khao San guesthouses)–Th Phra Sumen.

#59 (ordinary and air-con, 24hr): Don Muang Airport–Chatuchak Weekend Market–Victory Monument–Th Phetchaburi–Phanfa (for Khlong Sen Seb and Golden Mount)–Democracy Monument (for Banglamphu guesthouses)–Grand Palace–Sanam Luang.

#124 (ordinary): Southern Bus Terminal–Phra Pinklao Bridge (for Banglamphu guesthouses)–Sanam Luang–Wat Pho.

#159 (ordinary): Southern Bus Terminal–Phra Pinklao Bridge–Democracy Monument–Hualamphong Station–MBK Shopping Centre–Th Ratchaprarop–Victory Monument–Chatuchak Weekend Market–Northern Bus Terminal.

recommended bike ride along the canal towpaths of Thonburi (first Sun of month; B650 including bike).

Buses

There are three types of **bus** services in the city: ordinary (non-air-con; B3.50–5.50), which come in various colours and run either from around 4am to 10pm or 24hr (noted in the box below); the blue, white or orange air-con buses (B8–24), most of which stop at around 8.30pm; and the pink, daytime-only air-con microbuses (B10/20). Note that an attempt to clarify the numbering of the main air-con buses by adding a "5" on the front has so far not been fully enforced – you're likely to find, for example, both air-con #11 and air-con #511 plying the same route between the Southern Bus Terminal and Thanon Sukhumvit.

Boats

Bangkok was built around the Chao Phraya River, and its network of canals (khlongs) and **boats** are still one of the fastest ways of getting around the city. The **Chao Phraya Express** runs large water buses between Krung Thep Bridge in the south and Nonthaburi in the north, stopping at numbered piers (*tha*) all along its course; "standard" boats (roughly 6am–7pm; every 15min; B6–10) do not necessarily stop at every landing, but will pull in if people want to get on or off. During busy periods (roughly Mon–Fri 6–9am & 3–7pm, "orange flag" also

#502 or **#2** (air-con): Loetsin Hospital–Th Silom–Th Rama IV–MBK Shopping Centre (for Siam Square)– Victory Monument–Chatuchak Weekend Market–Suwinthawong.
#503 or **#3** (air-con): Southern Bus Terminal–Phra Pinklao Bridge (for Banglamphu guesthouses)–Democracy Monument–Rajdamnoen Nok (for TAT and boxing stadium)–Wat Benjamabophit–Th Sri Ayutthaya (for Thewes guesthouses)–Victory Monument–Chatuchak Weekend Market–Rangsit.
#504 or **#4** (air-con): Don Muang Airport–Th Rajaprarop–Th Silom–Th Charoen Krung–Krungthep Bridge–Thonburi.
#507 or **#7** (air-con): Southern Bus Terminal–Phra Pinklao Bridge (for Banglamphu guesthouses)–Sanam Luang–Th Charoen Krung–Th Chakraphet–Th Yaowarat (for Chinatown and Wat Traimit)–Hualamphong Station–Th Rama IV (for Soi Ngam Duphli guesthouses)–Pak Nam (for Ancient City buses).
#508 or **#8** (air-con): Wat Pho–Grand Palace–Th Charoen Krung–Th Krung Kasem–Siam Square–Th Sukhumvit–Eastern Bus Terminal–Pak Nam (for Ancient City buses).
#509 or **#9** (air-con): Nonthaburi Pier–Chatuchak Weekend Market–Victory Monument–Th Rajwithi–Th Sawankhalok–Th Phitsanulok–Th Rajdamnoen Nok–Democracy Monument–Rajdamnoen Klang (for Banglamphu guesthouses)–Phra Pinklao Bridge–Thonburi.
#510 or **#10** (air-con): Don Muang Airport–Chatuchak Weekend Market–Victory Monument–Dusit Zoo–Th Rajwithi–Krung Thon Bridge (for Thewes guesthouses)–Thonburi.
#511 or **#11** (air-con): Southern Bus Terminal–Phra Pinklao Bridge–Rajdamnoen Klang–Wat Bowoniwes (for Banglamphu guesthouses)–Democracy Monument–Th Lan Luang–Th Phetchaburi–Th Sukhumvit–Eastern Bus Terminal–Pak Nam (for Ancient City buses).
#512 or **#12** (air-con): Northern Bus Terminal–Chatuchak Weekend Market–Th Phetchaburi–Th Lan Luang–Democracy Monument (for Banglamphu guesthouses)–Sanam Luang–Tha Chang (for Grand Palace)–Pak Khlong Talat.
#513 or **#13** (air-con): Don Muang Airport–Chatuchak Weekend Market–Victory Monument–Th Sri Ayutthaya–Th Rajaprarop–Th Sukhumvit–Eastern Bus Terminal–Sukhumvit Soi 62.

Central stops for the Chao Phraya Express Boat

Piers are marked on the map on pp.1010–1011.

N15	Thewes (all boats) – for Thewes guesthouses.
N14	Rama VIII Bridge (standard and orange flag) – for Samsen Soi 5.
N13	Phra Athit (standard) – for Th Phra Athit, Th Khao San and Banglamphu guesthouses.
N12	Phra Pinklao Bridge (all boats) – for Royal Barge Museum.
N11	Bangkok Noi (or Thonburi Railway Station; standard) – for trains to Kanchanaburi.
N10	Wang Lang (or Prannok; all boats) – for Siriraj Hospital.
N9	Chang (standard and orange flag) – for the Grand Palace.
N8	Thien (standard) – for Wat Pho, and the cross-river ferry to Wat Arun.
N7	Ratchini (standard).
N6	Saphan Phut (Memorial Bridge; standard and orange flag) – for Pahurat. Boats going downstream stop on the Thonburi bank, upstream boats on the Bangkok side; cross-river ferries connect the two.
N5	Rachavongse (all boats) – for Chinatown.
N4	Harbour Department (standard).
N3	Si Phraya (all boats) – for River City shopping complex.
N2	Wat Muang Kae (standard) – for GPO.
N1	Oriental (standard and orange flag) – for Th Silom.
Central	Sathorn (all boats) – for the Skytrain and Th Sathorn.

Sat 7–9am & 4–6pm), there are extra limited-stop "special express" services, flying either a yellow (B15) or orange (B10) flag; a sign on each pier shows which service stops there. The important central Chao Phraya Express stops are outlined in the box above and marked on our city map (see pp.1010–1011). Chao Phraya Express tourist boats, distinguished by light-blue flags, with on-board guides, run between Banglamphu (every 30min 10am–3.30pm) and Sathorn, stopping at Wang Lang, Maharaj (near Wat Mahathat, with free connecting boats across to the Royal Barge Museum), Thien, the Princess Mother Memorial Park in Thonburi, Rachawongse, Si Phraya and Oriental. A one-day ticket for unlimited trips, which allows you to use other express boats within the same route between 9am and 7.30pm, costs B75.

Longtail boats (*reua hang yao*) run every fifteen minutes during daylight hours along **Khlong Sen Seb** canal from the Phanfa pier (Tha Phanfa) near Democracy Monument (handy for Banglamphu, Ratanakosin and Chinatown), and head way out east, with useful stops at Thanon Phrayathai, aka Saphan Hua Chang (for Jim Thompson's House and Ratchathevi Skytrain stop), Pratunam (for the Erawan Shrine), Thanon Witthayu (Wireless Rd), and Soi Nana Nua (Soi 3), Soi Asoke (Soi 21, for TAT headquarters and Phetchaburi subway stop), Soi Thonglo (Soi 55) and Soi Ekamai (Soi 63), all off Thanon Sukhumvit. This is your quickest and most interesting way of getting across town, if you can stand the stench of the canal; fares cost B7–15.

The Skytrain and subway

Although their networks are limited, the BTS Skytrain and the subway provide much faster alternatives to the bus. There are two **Skytrain** lines (ⓦwww.bts.co.th), both running daily every few minutes from 6am to midnight, with fares of B10–40 per trip depending on distance travelled. The **Sukhumvit Line** runs from Mo Chit (stop N8, right next to Chatuchak Weekend Market and near the Northern Bus Terminal) in the northern part of the city to the interchange, **Central Station** (CS), at Siam Square, and then east along Ploenchit and Sukhumvit roads, via Ekamai (E7, a couple of minutes' walk from the Eastern Bus Terminal) to Soi On Nut (E9). The **Silom Line** runs from the National Stadium (W1) through Siam Square Central station, and then south and west along Rajdamri, Silom and Sathorn roads, via Sala Daeng near Patpong (S2), to Saphan Taksin (Taksin Bridge; S6) to link up with express boats on the Chao Phraya River.

The **subway** runs a frequent service (up to every 2min in rush hour) from Hualamphong train station, first heading east along Thanon Rama IV, with useful stops at Silom (near the Sala Daeng Skytrain station) and Lumphini (near Thanon Sathorn). The line then turns north up Soi Asoke/Thanon Ratchadapisek via Sukhumvit Station (near Asoke Skytrain station) and the Thailand Cultural Centre, before looping around via Chatuchak Park (near Mo Chit Skytrain station) and Kampaeng Phet (best stop for the Chatuchak Weekend Market) to terminate at Bang Sue train station in the north of the city. Fares are B14–36, and trains run from 6am to midnight.

Taxis

Fares in Bangkok's metered, air-con **taxi cabs** start at B35 (look out for the "TAXI METER" sign on the roof, and a red light in the windscreen by the passenger seat, which means the cab is free). Try to have change with you as cabs tend not to carry a lot of money; tipping of up to ten percent is common, though occasionally a cabbie will round down the fare on the meter. The noisy, three-wheeled, open-sided, unmetered buggies known as **tuk-tuks** are nippier than cabs and can be an exhilarating way to get around, but be warned that there have been cases of robberies and attacks on solo women in tuk-tuks late at night, and see p.948 about cons. Faster still are **motorbike taxis**, which can only carry one passenger and generally do shortish local journeys. The riders wear numbered, coloured vests; crash helmets are now compulsory on all main thoroughfares in the capital.

Accommodation

If your time in Bangkok is limited, you should think carefully about what you want to do in the city before deciding which part of town to stay in. The capital's traffic jams are so appalling that you may find yourself not wanting to explore too far from your hotel. Unless you pay a cash deposit in advance, bookings of any kind are rarely accepted by budget guesthouses; from November to February, you may have difficulty getting a room after noon.

Thanon Khao San and Banglamphu

Nearly all backpackers head straight for the legendary **Thanon Khao San** in **Banglamphu**, Bangkok's long-established travellers' ghetto and location of the cheapest accommodation and some of the best nightlife in the city. Banglamphu is within easy reach of the Grand Palace and is served by plenty of public transport. All the guesthouses listed lie close to one of three Chao Phraya Express boat stops, and public longtail boats also ply one of the khlongs in the area (see p.967). Useful bus routes in and out of Banglamphu include air-con #511/#11 from both the Eastern and the Southern bus terminals; #3 (ordinary and air-con) and air-con #512/#12 to and from the Northern Bus Terminal; and #53 (ordinary) to Hualamphong Station. Bus route details are given in the box on pp.966–697. Airport bus A2 has several stops in Banglamphu, though for the cheapest route from Don Muang to Banglamphu (B7, about 1hr 30min) take ordinary bus #29 from the road 100m right of International Terminal 1 as far as Mo Chit Skytrain station and change onto ordinary bus #3 to Thanon Phra Athit.

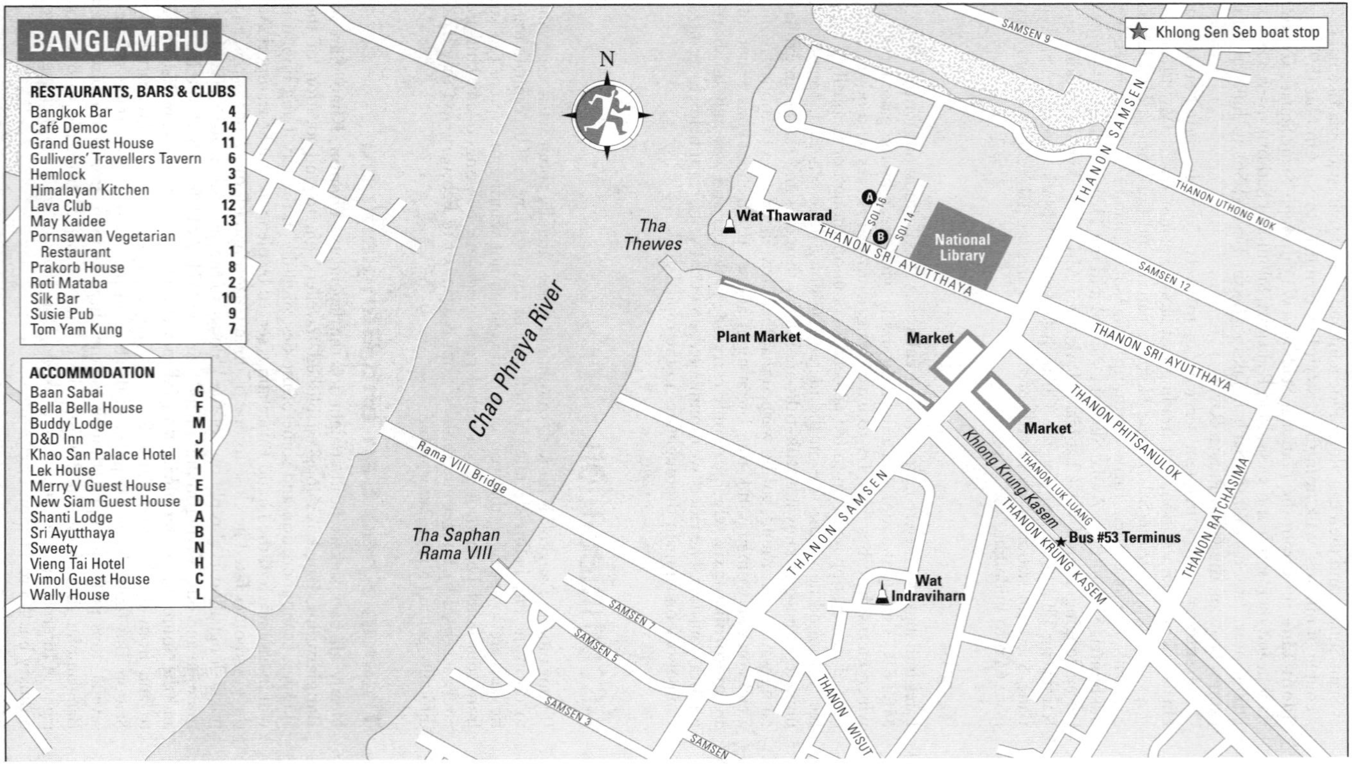

BANGLAMPHU

RESTAURANTS, BARS & CLUBS	
Bangkok Bar	4
Café Democ	14
Grand Guest House	11
Gullivers' Travellers Tavern	6
Hemlock	3
Himalayan Kitchen	5
Lava Club	12
May Kaidee	13
Pornsawan Vegetarian Restaurant	1
Prakorb House	8
Roti Mataba	2
Silk Bar	10
Susie Pub	9
Tom Yam Kung	7

ACCOMMODATION	
Baan Sabai	G
Bella Bella House	F
Buddy Lodge	M
D&D Inn	J
Khao San Palace Hotel	K
Lek House	I
Merry V Guest House	E
New Siam Guest House	D
Shanti Lodge	A
Sri Ayutthaya	B
Sweety	N
Vieng Tai Hotel	H
Vimol Guest House	C
Wally House	L

★ Khlong Sen Seb boat stop

N
Chao Phraya River
Tha Thewes
Tha Saphan Rama VIII
Rama VIII Bridge
Wat Thawarad
National Library
Plant Market
Market
Market
Wat Indraviharn
Bus #53 Terminus
Khlong Krung Kasem
THANON SAMSEN
THANON SRI AYUTTHAYA
THANON PHITSANULOK
THANON RATCHASIMA
THANON UTHONG NOK
THANON LUK LUANG
THANON KRUNG KASEM
THANON WISUT
SOI 16
SOI 14
SAMSEN 9
SAMSEN 12
SAMSEN 7
SAMSEN 5
SAMSEN 3
SAMSEN

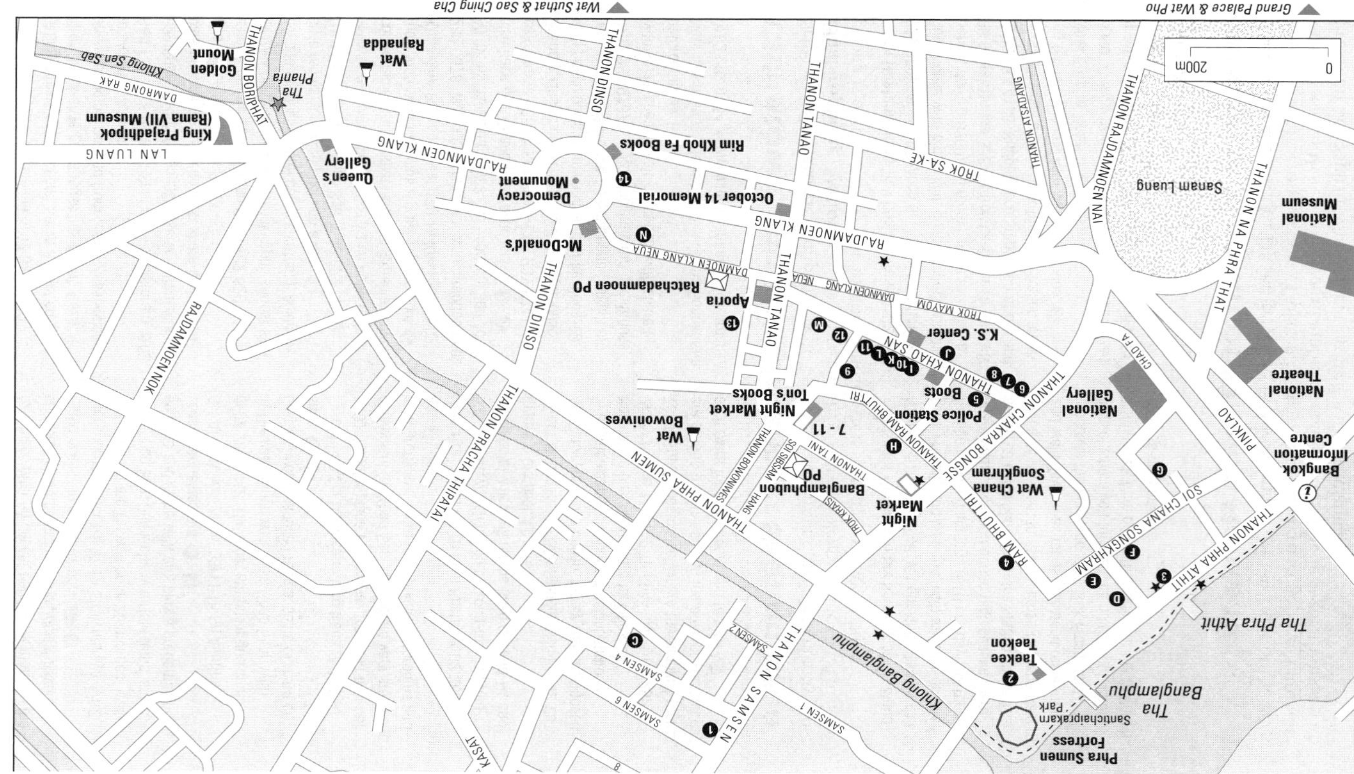
Royal Barge Museum
Grand Palace & Wat Pho
Wat Suthat & Sao Ching Cha
Phra Sumen Fortress
Santichaiprakarn Park
Tha Banglamphu
Tha Phra Athit
Bangkok Information Centre
National Theatre
National Museum
National Gallery
Wat Chana Songkhram
Taekee Taekon
Khlong Banglamphu
Night Market
Banglamphubon PO
Police Station
Boots
K.S. Center
7 - 11
Night Market
Ton's Books
Wat Bowoniwes
Aporia
Ratchadamnoen PO
McDonald's
October 14 Memorial
Rim Khob Fa Books
Democracy Monument
Queen's Gallery
Wat Rajnadda
Tha Phanfa
Golden Mount
King Prajadhipok (Rama VII) Museum
Khlong Sen Seb
Sanam Luang
THANON SAMSEN
SAMSEN 1
SAMSEN 2
SAMSEN 4
SAMSEN 6
KASAT
THANON PHRA SUMEN
THANON PRACHA THIPATAI
RAJDAMNOEN NOK
LAN LUANG
DAMRONG RAK
THANON BORIPHAT
RAJDAMNOEN KLANG
THANON DINSO
THANON TANAO
DAMNOEN KLANG NEUA
TROK SA-KE
THANON ATSADANG
THANON RAJDAMNOEN NAI
THANON NA PHRA THAT
PINKLAO
THANON PHRA ATHIT
SOI CHANA SONGKHRAM
CHAD FA
THANON CHAKRA BONGSE
RAM BHUTTRI
THANON RAM BHUTTRI
THANON KHAO SAN
TROK MAYOM
THANON TANI
TROK KRAIS
SOI SIBSAM HANG
THANON BOWONNIWES
200m

Baan Sabai 12 Soi Rongmai ⓣ02 629 1599, ⓔbaansabai@hotmail.com. Set in a quiet soi, this large, hotel-style guesthouse has bright, fresh, en-suite rooms, ranging from windowless versions to a/c ones. ❷–❸

Bella Bella House 74 Soi Chana Songkhram ⓣ02 629 3090. Delightful guesthouse with immaculate pale-pink rooms; the cheapest share bathrooms, and the priciest have a/c. ❷–❸

Buddy Lodge 265 Th Khao San ⓣ02 629 4477, ⓦwww.buddylodge.com. Banglamphu's most stylish and expensive hotel offers charming, colonial-style rooms, a rooftop pool and a spa. ❼

D&D Inn 68–70 Th Khao San ⓣ02 629 0526, ⓦwww.khaosanby.com. Good-value hotel with comfortable if not immaculate a/c, en-suite rooms, most with windows, plus a great rooftop pool. ❸

Khao San Palace Hotel 139 Th Khao San ⓣ02 282 0578. Well-appointed hotel with a rooftop pool. All rooms have bathrooms and windows and some also have a/c, TV and panoramic views. ❷–❹

Lek House 125 Th Khao San ⓣ02 281 8441. Friendly, classic old-style Khao San guesthouse, with small, basic rooms and shared facilities. ❷

Merry V Guest House 35 Soi Chana Songkhram ⓣ02 282 9267. Large, efficiently run guesthouse, with small, cheap, basic rooms, all with shared bathrooms. ❶

New Siam Guest House 21 Soi Chana Songkhram ⓣ02 282 4554, ⓦwww.newsiam.net. Well-organized place offering decent hotel-style rooms – the cheapest share bathrooms, the priciest have a/c – and access to a nearby pool. ❷–❸

Shanti Lodge Soi 16, 37 Th Sri Ayutthaya ⓣ02 281 2497. In the Thewes area, 25 minutes' walk from Khao San. Quiet, characterful rooms, some en suite and some with a/c, plus a predominantly vegetarian restaurant. ❷–❸

Sri Ayutthaya Soi 14, 23/11 Th Sri Ayutthaya ⓣ02 282 5942. The most attractive guesthouse in Thewes (25min walk from Khao San), with elegant, wood-panelled rooms, some of them en suite. ❷–❸

Sweety 49 Soi Damnoen Klang Neua ⓣ02 280 2191. Popular place that's away from the fray but convenient for Khao San. Rooms are very small and a bit grotty: pay extra for a private bathrooms and a/c. ❶–❷

Vieng Tai Hotel 42 Th Ram Bhuttri ⓣ02 280 5392, ⓦwww.viengtai.co.th. Long-running mid-range hotel where all rooms have a/c and TV, and there's a big pool. ❼

Vimol Guest House 358 Samsen Soi 4 ⓣ02 281 4615. Exceptionally cheap, family-run guesthouse in an interesting, untouristed neighbourhood. Rooms are basic and share facilities. ❶

Wally House 189/1–2 Th Khao San ⓣ02 282 7067. Small guesthouse, where the simplest rooms are among the cheapest in the area, or you can pay a bit extra for a bathroom and fan. ❶–❷

Chinatown and Hualamphong Station area

Staying in **Chinatown** (Sampeng), or in one of the sois around the conveniently close **Hualamphong Station**, can be noisy, but there's always plenty to look at. Hualamphong is on the subway system, and Chinatown is served by plenty of buses.

Baan Hualamphong Trok Chalongkrung ⓣ02 637 8095, ⓔsriyot@yahoo.de. Stylish, modern guesthouse with big, bright, double rooms and five-person dorms (B200); all rooms share facilities. ❸

FF Guest House 338/10 Trok La-O, off Th Rama IV ⓣ02 233 4168. Budget accommodation at the end of an alley just a 5min walk from the station, offering ten basic rooms with shared facilities. ❶

New Empire Hotel 572 Th Yaowarat ⓣ02 234 6990, ⓦwww.newempirehotel.com. Medium-sized hotel in the thick of the Chinatown bustle, offering exceptionally good-value superior rooms with a/c, TV and panoramic views. ❹

TT2 Guest House 516 Soi Sawang, off Th Maha Nakorn ⓣ02 236 2946, ⓔttguesthouse@hotmail.com. Friendly and well-run, with traveller-oriented facilities and left luggage (B10 per day). All rooms share bathrooms, and during high season there are B100 dorm beds. From the station, cross Th Rama IV, walk left for 250m, cross Th Maha Nakorn and walk down it as far as a seafood restaurant (opposite the lane signed as Trok Fraser and Neave),where you turn left, then first right. About 15min walk from either the station or the Si Phraya express-boat stop. ❷

Downtown: south of Thanon Rama IV

South of Thanon Rama IV and traversed by the Skytrain, the left bank of the river contains a full cross-section of places to stay. At the eastern edge near Lumphini subway station there's Soi Ngam Duphli, a small ghetto of budget guesthouses with prices on Soi Saphan Khu comparing well with Banglamphu.

Charlie House 1034/36–37 Soi Saphan Khu ⓣ02 679 8330–1, ⓦwww.charliehousethailand.com. Good mid-range alternative to the crash pads of Soi Ngam Duphli: carpeted bedrooms with hot-water bathrooms, a/c and TV, close to Th Rama IV. ❸
ETC Guest House 5/3 Soi Ngam Duphli ⓣ02 287 1477–8, ⓔetc@mozart.inet.co.th. Above a branch of the recommended, eponymous travel agent, near Th Rama IV. Friendly and very clean, catering mainly to Japanese travellers. Rooms can be dingy, and come with fan or a/c, shared or en-suite hot-water bathrooms. ❶–❷
Freddy's 2 27/40 Soi Sri Bamphen ⓣ02 286 7826, ⓔfreddyguesthouse2@hotmail.com. Popular, clean, well-organized, though rather noisy, guest-house with shared bathrooms, and a small café at the rear. ❶
Intown Residence 1086/6 Th Charoen Krung ⓣ02 639 0960–2, ⓔintownbkk@hotmail.com. Clean, welcoming hotel on the main road, where large, chintzy rooms come with a/c, hot water and satellite TV. ❹
Peninsula 333 Th Charoennakorn ⓣ02 861 2888, ⓦwww.peninsula.com. Superbly stylish top-class hotel with flawless service. Although it's on the Thonburi bank of the river, the hotel operates a shuttle boat across to the *Shangri-La Hotel*. ❾
Sala Thai Daily Mansion 15 Soi Saphan Khu ⓣ02 287 1436. The pick of the area. A clean and efficiently run place at the end of this quiet alley, with shared hot-water bathrooms and a roof terrace. ❷–❸
Swiss Lodge 3 Th Convent ⓣ02 233 5345, ⓦwww.swisslodge.com. Swish, friendly, good-value boutique hotel, just off Th Silom, with a terrace swimming pool. ❽

Downtown: around Siam Square and Thanon Ploenchit

Siam Square and nearby Thanon Ploenchit are handy for all kinds of shopping and the Skytrain. There's no budget accommodation here, but a few guesthouses have sprung up in their own "ghetto" on Soi Kasemsan 1 (offThanon Rama I, to the west of Siam Square and Thanon Phrayathai), all of them offering air-con and en-suite hot-water bathrooms.

A-One Inn 25/13 Soi Kasemsan 1, Th Rama I ⓣ02 215 3029, ⓦwww.aoneinn.com. The original upscale guesthouse and still justifiably popular, with helpful staff and en-suite satellite TV. ❸
The Bed & Breakfast 36/42 Soi Kasemsan 1, Th Rama I ⓣ02 215 3004. Bright, clean, family-run and friendly, though the rooms are a bit cramped. Breakfast is included. ❸
Jim's Lodge 125/7 Soi Ruam Rudee, Th Ploenchit ⓣ02 255 3100–3, ⓔanant@asiaaccess.net.th. In a residential area, international standards at bargain prices; rooftop Jacuzzi. ❻
White Lodge 36/8 Soi Kasemsan 1, Th Rama I ⓣ02 216 8867. Well-maintained, shining-white cubicles and a welcoming atmosphere. ❸

Thanon Sukhumvit

Thanon Sukhumvit is not the place to come if you're on a tight budget, but it's handy for restaurants, nightlife (some of it seedy) and shops. Although a long way from the main sights, it's well served by the Skytrain, the subway and the Khlong Sen Seb canal boats.

The Atlanta At the far southern end of Soi 2 ⓣ02 252 1650, ⓦwww.theatlantahotel.bizland.com. Classic colonial-era hotel with lots of character. Rooms are simple and a bit scruffy, but all are en suite and some have a/c. Has two pools and a good Thai restaurant. ❸
Federal Hotel 27 Soi 11 ⓣ02 253 0175, ⓔfederalhotel@hotmail.com. Efficiently run mid-sized hotel, with a pool. All rooms have a/c and TV; the upstairs ones are worth paying extra for. ❹–❻
Suk 11 Behind the 7/11 store at 1/3 Soi 11 ⓣ02 253 5927, ⓦwww.suk11.com. Inviting, characterful little hotel that's got excellent traveller-oriented facilities and a nice roof terrace. All rooms have a/c, some are en suite, and in high season there are B250 dorm beds available. ❸
SV Guest House Soi 19 ⓣ02 253 1747. Some of the least expensive rooms in the area: all share bathrooms, but some have a/c. ❷–❸

The City

Bangkok is sprawling, chaotic and exhausting: to do it justice and to keep your sanity, you need time, boundless patience and a bus map. The place to start is **Ratanakosin**, the royal island on the east bank of the Chao Phraya and location of the **Grand Palace**, **Wat Pho** and the **National Museum**. The other main areas of interest are **Chinatown** for its markets, **Thonburi** for its traditional canalside life and boat rides; and several impressive historical residences in downtown Bangkok, including **Jim Thompson's House** and **Suan Pakkad Palace Museum**. If you're here at a weekend, you shouldn't miss the enormous **Chatuchak Weekend Market**.

A **word of warning**: if you're heading for sights such as the Grand Palace, Wat Pho or Jim Thompson's House, you may come across tuk-tuk drivers or people pretending to be students or officials, who'll tell you that the sight is closed when it's not, because they want to lead you on a shopping trip (for which they'll receive a hefty commission). It's rare for these places to be closed for national holidays or state occasions, and far better to put in the legwork to check it out for yourself.

Wat Phra Kaeo and the Grand Palace

Built as the private royal temple, **Wat Phra Kaeo** (®www.palaces.thai.net) is the holiest site in the country and houses the most important image, the Emerald Buddha. The temple occupies the northeast corner of the huge Grand Palace, which dates back to 1785, but is now only used for state functions, as the king resides in Chitrlada Palace in Dusit. The only entrance to the complex is on Thanon Na Phra Lan, within easy walking distance of Banglamphu, and close to the Tha Chang express-boat pier. Admission to Wat Phra Kaeo and the palace is B200 (daily 8.30am–3.30pm, palace halls closed Sat & Sun; free tours in English at 10am & 1.30pm, plus 10.30am & 2pm most days), and includes entry to Vimanmek Palace (see p.978). As it's Thailand's most sacred site, there's a dress code (legs and shoulders must be covered; no see-through clothes, sarongs, fisherman's trousers, slip-on sandals or flip-flops), but you can borrow suitable garments and shoes at an office just inside the entrance if you leave some ID as surety or a deposit of B100.

The turnstiles in the west wall of the temple open onto the back of the bot (main sanctuary), which contains the **Emerald Buddha**. Inside, a pedestal supports the tiny jadeite Buddha image, a hugely sacred figure renowned for its miraculous powers. The king ceremonially changes the statue's costumes according to the season: the crown and ornaments of an Ayutthayan king for the hot season; a gilt monastic robe for the rainy season retreat; and a full-length gold shawl to wrap up in for the cool season. (The two costumes not in use are on display in the Royal Decorations and Coins Pavilion near the temple entrance, and an old set of three costumes is in the Wat Phra Kaeo Museum, opposite the Dusit Maha Prasat – see below.)

On the terrace to the north of the bot is the splendid **Prasat Phra Thep Bidorn**, which contains precisely life-size bronze and gold statues of all the Bangkok-era kings, and the **Phra Mondop**, housing the *Tripitaka* or Buddhist scriptures, but both are normally closed to the public. At the western end of the terrace, dazzlingly gold **Phra Si Ratana Chedi** enshrines a piece of the Buddha's breastbone. Extending for over a kilometre in the arcades that run inside the wat walls, the surreal murals of the *Ramayana* depict every blow of this ancient Hindu story of the triumph of good over evil. The story is told in 178 panels, labelled and numbered in Thai only, starting in the middle of the northern side. Panel 109 shows the climax of the story, when Rama, the hero, kills the ten-headed demon Totsagan (Ravana).

Coming out of the exit in the southwest corner of Wat Phra Kaeo you'll reach the grand residential complex of the palace, most of which is closed to the public. The first building you can enter is the former supreme court, **Phra Thinang Amarin Winichai**, which centres on an open-sided throne with a spired roof, floating on a boat-shaped base. Next door you can admire the exterior of the main palace build-

△Guardian statue at the Grand Palace, Bangkok

ing, the **Chakri Maha Prasat**, nicknamed "the farang (foreigner) with a Thai hat" because its English-designed Neoclassical facade is topped with three Thai spires. On the western side of the courtyard, the delicately proportioned **Dusit Maha Prasat**, another audience hall, epitomizes traditional Thai architecture with the soaring tiers of its red, gold and green roof culminating in a gilded spire. Inside, you can still see the original throne, a masterpiece of mother-of-pearl inlaid work.

Wat Pho

Bangkok's oldest temple, the seventeenth-century **Wat Pho** (daily 8am–6pm; B20; ⓦwww.watpho.com), is most famous for housing the enormous statue of a reclining Buddha. It lies south of the Grand Palace, close to the Tha Thien express-boat pier. In 1832, Rama turned the temple into "Thailand's first university" by decorating the walls with diagrams on subjects such as history, literature and animal husbandry. The wat is still a centre for traditional medicine, notably Thai massage: a massage on the compound's east side costs B300 per hour. The elegant bot at the centre of the compound has beautiful teak doors decorated with mother-of-pearl, showing stories from the *Ramayana*, but it is the chapel of the Reclining Buddha, in the northwest corner of the courtyard, that draws the crowds. The image in question is a 45-metre-long gilded statue of plaster-covered brick, depicting the Buddha entering Nirvana. The beaming smile is five metres wide, and the vast black feet are beautifully inlaid with mother-of-pearl showing the 108 lakshanas or auspicious signs that distinguish the true Buddha.

Wat Mahathat

On the western side of the huge grassy area of Sanam Luang, with its main entrance on Thanon Maharat, **Wat Mahathat** (daily 9am–5pm; free) houses the Mahachulalongkorn Buddhist University. Situated in Section Five of the wat is its Vipassana Meditation Centre, where meditation practice is available in English (daily 7–10am, 1–4pm & 6–8pm; ⓣ02 222 6011 or 623 5685 for further information). Talks in English on meditation and Buddhism are held here every evening (8–10pm), as well as at the International Buddhist Meditation Centre (Room 105 or 209) in the Mahachulalongkorn Buddhist University building on the second and fourth Saturdays of every month (3–5pm). Outside, along the pavements of Maharat and surrounding roads, vendors set up stalls to sell some of the city's most reasonably priced amulets.

The National Museum

The **National Museum** (Wed–Sun 9am–4pm; B40), at the northwestern corner of Sanam Luang, houses a colossal hoard of Thailand's chief artistic riches, and offers worthwhile free guided tours in English (Wed & Thurs 9.30am). Among its numerous attractions are King Ramkhamhaeng's stele, a black stone inscription from Sukhothai that dates back to the thirteenth century and is thought to be the earliest record of the Thai alphabet. The main collection boasts a fine chronological survey of the developing styles of religious sculpture in Thailand, from Dvaravati-era (sixth to eleventh centuries) stone and terracotta Buddhas through to the more naturalist style of the modern Bangkok era.

Elsewhere in the museum compound, **Wang Na**, a former palace, contains a fascinating array of Thai objets d'art, including an intricately carved ivory howdah, some fine theatrical masks, and a collection of traditional musical instruments. The Phra Sihing Buddha, the second holiest image in Thailand after the Emerald Buddha, is housed in the beautifully ornate **Buddhaisawan Chapel**, the vast, muralled hall in front of the entrance to the Wang Na. In a large garage behind the chapel, near the restaurant, the fantastically elaborate, teak funeral chariots of the royal family are stored.

Chinatown and the Golden Buddha

The sprawl of narrow alleyways, temples and shop-houses packed between Charoen Krung (New Road) and the river is Bangkok's **Chinatown** (Sampeng). Easiest access is by Chao Phraya Express boat to Tha Rajavongse (Rajawong) at the southern end of Thanon Rajawong, by subway to Hualamphong Station, or by any Hualamphong-bound bus (see box on pp.960–967).

About 250m west of Hualamphong Station on Thanon Tri Mit, Wat Traimit (daily 9am–5pm; B20) boasts the world's largest solid-gold Buddha. Over 3m tall and weighing five and a half tons, the **Golden Buddha** gleams as if coated in liquid metal and is a fine example of the curvaceous grace of Sukhothai art. Cast in the thirteenth century, the image was completely encased in stucco for several hundred years, probably to protect it from the marauding Burmese. No one realized what was underneath until 1955 when the image was accidentally knocked in the process of being moved to Wat Traimit; it's now valued, by weight alone, at $14 million. Sections of the stucco casing are displayed alongside the Golden Buddha.

Leaving Wat Traimit by the Charoen Krung/Yaowarat exit (at the back of the temple compound), walk northwest along Thanon Yaowarat and make a left turn onto Thanon Songsawat to reach **Sampeng Lane** (also signposted as Soi Wanit 1), a kilometre-long alleway that's packed full of tiny, bargain-basement shops grouped together according to their merchandise. About halfway down Sampeng Lane, take a right into **Soi Issaranuphap** (also signed in places as Soi 16) for more unusual fare such as ginseng roots, fish heads and cockroach-killer chalk. Soi Issaranuphap finally ends at the Thanon Plaplachai intersection with a knot of shops specializing in paper funeral art: Chinese people buy miniature paper replicas of necessities (like houses, cars, suits and money) to be burned with the body. **Wat Mangkon Kamalawat**, 10m up Thanon Charoen Krung from the Soi Issaranuphap junction, is a lovely example of a much-used Mahayana Buddhist Chinese temple. It's dotted with undulating Chinese dragons, statues of bearded sages and saffron-clad Buddha images, and centres on an open-sided room of gold paintwork, red-lacquered wood, and panels inlaid with mother-of-pearl.

Wat Arun, the Royal Barge Museum and Thonburi canal tours

Almost directly across the river from Wat Pho, in the Thonburi district, rises the enormous five-pranged **Wat Arun** (daily 7am–5pm; B20), the Temple of Dawn, Bangkok's most distinctive landmark. To get there, just take a cross-river ferry (B2) from Tha Thien. The temple has been reconstructed numerous times, but the Wat Arun you see today is a classic prang (tower) structure of Ayutthayan style, built as a representation of Mount Meru, the home of the gods in Khmer mythology. The prangs are decorated with polychromatic flowers made from bits of broken porcelain donated by local people. Statues of mythical figures support the different levels, and on the first terrace there are statues of the Buddha at the four most important stages of his life: at birth (north), in meditation (east), preaching his first sermon (south) and entering Nirvana (west). In January and February, Wat Arun hosts a free son-et-lumière show every night at 7, 8 and 9pm: see ⓦwww.thailandgrandefestival.com for details.

Until 1967, the king would make an annual procession down the Chao Phraya River to Wat Arun in a flotilla of 51 ornate royal barges, but this now only happens on very special occasions – the last full royal procession was in 1999, to mark the king's 72nd birthday, and a version for heads of state was held in 2003. The eight intricately lacquered and gilded vessels at the heart of the ceremony are moored in the **Royal Barge Museum** on the north bank of Khlong Bangkok Noi (daily 9am–5pm; B30). To get there, cross the river, either by ferry to Tha Bangkok Noi or by bus across Phra Pinklao Bridge, and then take the first left along Soi Wat Dusitaram, which leads, via winding alleys, to the museum, about ten-minutes' walk away.

One of the most popular ways of seeing Wat Arun and the traditional riverine neighbourhoods of Thonburi is to embark on a **canal tour** in a longtail boat. Fixed-priced trips with The Boat Tour Centre (☎02 235 3108) at Tha Si Phraya cost B500 per boat for one hour, B800 for two hours, while Mitchaopaya Travel Service (☎02 623 5340), operating out of Tha Chang, offers a one-hour trip for B600 per boat, or two hours with an orchid farm thrown in for B1200. It's also possible to organize your own boat trip around Thonburi from other piers, including Tha Oriental (at the *Oriental Hotel*), and Tha Wang Nah, next to the Bangkok Information Centre on Thanon Phra Athit in Banglamphu.

Vimanmek Palace and Wat Benjamabophit

Vimanmek Palace (daily 9.30am–4pm; compulsory free guided tours every 30min, last tour 3.15pm; B100, or free if you have a Grand Palace ticket, which remains valid for one month; Grand Palace dress rules apply, see p.974) stands at the heart of the leafy royal district of Dusit, to the northeast of Banglamphu and Ratanakosin. It was built for Rama V and is constructed entirely of golden teak, without a single nail; gardens and lotus ponds encircle it. On display inside is Rama V's collection of artefacts from all over the world, including bencharong ceramics, European furniture and bejewelled Thai betel-nut sets. Considered progressive in his day, Rama V introduced many newfangled ideas to Thailand: the country's first indoor bathroom is here, as is the earliest Thai typewriter. All visitors are treated to a free Thai dance show daily at 10.30am & 2pm, and the ticket price also covers entry to half a dozen other small museums in the palace grounds, including the **Support Museum**, filled with exquisite traditional crafts, and the **Elephant Museum**. The main entrance to the Vimanmek compound is on Thanon Rajwithi, but there are also ticket gates on Thanon Ratchasima, and opposite Dusit Zoo on Thanon U-Thong. From Banglamphu, the #70 bus runs from Rajdamnoen Klang to Thanon U-Thong, or take the express boat to Tha Thewes and then walk. From downtown Bangkok, easiest access is by bus from the Skytrain and subway stops at Victory Monument: both air-con #510/10 and #16 go via Thanon Rajwithi.

Located on Thanon Sri Ayutthaya, about 600m southeast from Vimanmek's U-Thong gate, or 200m south of the zoo's Thanon Rama V entrance, **Wat Benjamabophit** (daily 7am–5pm; B20) was commissioned by Rama V in the early 1900s and is the last major temple to have been built in Bangkok. It's an interesting fusion of classical Thai and nineteenth-century European design, with its Carrara marble walls – hence the tourist tag "The Marble Temple" – complemented by unusual stained-glass windows. The courtyard behind the bot houses a gallery of Buddha images from all over Asia. This is also a very good place to see the daily early-morning ritual alms-giving ceremony when, between about 6 and 7.30am, Wat Benjamabophit's monks line up with their bowls on Thanon Nakhon Pathom, awaiting donations from local citizens.

Jim Thompson's House

Even now over thirty years after his death, the legendary American Jim Thompson remains Thailand's most famous farang (foreigner). A former agent of the OSS (later to become the CIA), Thompson was involved in clandestine operations in the Far East, before settling in Bangkok at the end of World War II and eventually disappearing mysteriously in Malaysia's Cameron Highlands in 1967. But he is most famous for introducing Thai silk to the world and for his collection of traditional art, much of which is now displayed in his home at **Jim Thompson's House** (daily from 9am, last tour 5pm; B100, under-25s B50; National Stadium or Central Skytrain stations; ⓦwww.jimthompson.com), near Siam Square at 6 Soi Kasemsan 2, Thanon Rama I. The grand, rambling house is a kind of Ideal Home in elegant

Thai style, constructed – without nails – from six two-hundred-year-old teak houses that Thompson shipped to Bangkok from around the kingdom. The tasteful interior has been left as it was during Thompson's life and displays dozens of fine Southeast Asian artefacts.

The Erawan Shrine

Marking the horribly congested corner of Ploenchit and Rajdamri roads, the luridly ornate **Erawan Shrine** is essentially a huge spirit house for the neighbouring hotel, now the *Grand Hyatt Erawan*, but also serves any Bangkokian who feels the need to pray – or offer thanks – for good luck. The shrine is dedicated to Brahma, the Hindu creation god, and Erawan, his elephant, and is always garlanded in offertory flowers and incense. The shrine's group of classical dancers are frequently hired by devotees to perform thanks-giving routines here.

Suan Pakkad Palace Museum

The **Suan Pakkad Palace Museum** (daily 9am–4pm; B100; Ⓦwww.suanpakkad.com), five minutes' walk from Phaya Thai Skytrain station at 352–4 Thanon Sri Ayutthaya, comprises a private collection of beautiful Thai artefacts, displayed in four groups of traditional wooden houses in a fine garden. The highlight is the Lacquer Pavilion, an amalgam of two temple buildings set on stilts whose interior is beautifully decorated with *Ramayana* panels in gilt on black lacquer. Divided between House no.8 and the Ban Chiang Gallery is a fine collection of pottery and jewellery from the tombs at the Bronze Age settlement in Ban Chiang, and elsewhere you'll find Thai and Khmer sculptures, ceramics and some fine theatrical khon masks. The attached **Marsi Gallery** displays interesting temporary exhibitions of contemporary art (Ⓣ02 246 1775–6 for details).

Chatuchak Weekend Market

With eight thousand open-air stalls to peruse, the enormous **Chatuchak Weekend Market** (Sat & Sun 7am–6pm) is Bangkok's most enjoyable shopping experience. Best buys here include lacquerware, northern crafts, jeans, musical instruments, jewellery and basketware. The market occupies a huge patch of ground between the Northern Bus Terminal and Mo Chit Skytrain and subway stations, and can also be reached by air-con buses #503/#3 or #509/#9 from Rajdamnoen Klang in Banglamphu (1hr). Nancy Chandler's *Map of Bangkok* shows the location of all the specialist sections within the market. TAT also hands out a free map of Chatuchak from their counter in the market building on the southwest edge of the market, across the car park. You can change money (7am–7pm) in the market building, and there's an ATM here, too.

Muang Boran Ancient City

A day-trip out to the **Muang Boran Ancient City** open-air museum (daily 8am–5pm; B100), 33km southeast of Bangkok, is a great way to enjoy the best of Thailand's architectural heritage, especially if you rent a bike (B50; B150 for a tandem) to explore the 115 traditional Thai buildings scattered around the pleasantly landscaped grounds. Many of the buildings are copies of the country's most famous monuments, while others are the original structures, reassembled on site. To get there, take air-con bus #511/11 from Banglamphu/Thanon Rama I/Thanon Sukhumvit to Samut Prakan on the edge of Greater Bangkok, then change onto songthaew (pick-up) #36 for Muang Boran. A faster alternative is to take a Chao Phraya Express boat down to Tha Sathorn, change on to the Skytrain as far as Ekamai and then pick up the #511/11 from there.

Eating

Bangkok boasts an astonishing fifty thousand **places to eat** – that's almost one for every hundred citizens. The best gourmet Thai restaurants operate from the downtown districts around Thanon Sukhumvit and Thanon Silom, while over in Banglamphu, Thanon Phra Athit has become famous for its trendy little restaurant-bars.

Banglamphu

Hemlock 56 Th Phra Athit ☎02 282 7507. Small, stylish, highly recommended restaurant that offers a long, mid-priced menu of unusual Thai dishes and a good veggie selection. Mon–Sat 5pm–midnight; worth reserving on Friday and Saturday nights.

Himalayan Kitchen 1 Th Khao San. Specializes in mid-priced Nepalese veg and non-veg thalis.

May Kaidee 123–125 Th Tanao, though actually on the parallel soi to the east; easiest access is to take first left on Soi Damnoen Klang Neua. Simple, soi-side foodstall serving the best, and cheapest, vegetarian food in Banglamphu. Try the very cheap tasty green curry with coconut or the sticky black-rice pudding. May Kaidee herself also runs veggie cookery classes. Shuts about 9pm.

Pornsawan Vegetarian Restaurant 80 Th Samsen, between sois 4 and 6. Cheap Thai veggie café that uses soya products instead of meat in its curries and stir-fries. Daily 7am–6.30pm.

Prakorb House Th Khao San. Archetypal and inexpensive travellers' haven, with an emphasis on wholesome ingredients. Herbal teas, mango shakes, delicious pumpkin curry, and lots more besides.

Roti Mataba 136 Th Phra Athit. Famous outlet for very cheap fried Indian breads, or *rotis*, served here in lots of sweet and savoury varieties, including with vegetable and meat curries, and with bananas and condensed milk. Closed Sun.

Tom Yam Kung Th Khao San. Delicious, fairly expensive, authentic Thai food, such as spicy fried catfish and coconut-palm curry with tofu, served in a beautiful early twentieth-century villa that's hidden behind Khao San's modern clutter. Open 24hr.

Chinatown and Pahurat

Royal India Just off Th Chakraphet at 392/1. Famously good mid-priced curries served in the heart of Pahurat, Bangkok's most Indian of neighbourhoods, to an almost exclusively South Asian clientele.

Shangri-La 306 Th Yaowarat (cnr of Th Rajawong). Cavernous place serving mid-priced Chinese classics, including lots of seafood, and lunchtime dim sum. Very popular.

White Orchid Hotel 409–421 Th Yaowarat. Recommended for its fairly expensive dim sum, served 11am–2pm & 5–10pm.

Downtown: south of Thanon Rama IV

Celadon *Sukhothai Hotel*, 13/3 Th Sathorn Tai ☎02 287 0222. Consistently rated as the best Thai hotel restaurant in Bangkok, in an elegant setting among lotus ponds; well worth a splurge.

Eat Me 1/6 Soi Phiphat 2, Th Convent ☎02 238 0931. Striking art gallery and expensive restaurant with a very good international menu.

Harmonique 22 Soi 34, Th Charoen Krung, on the lane between Wat Muang Kae express-boat pier and the GPO ☎02 237 8175. Relaxing, moderately priced restaurant, where tables are scattered throughout several old houses and a leafy court-yard, and the Thai food is varied and delicious.

Indian Hut 311/2–5 Th Suriwong ☎02 635 7876–7. Bright, moderately expensive, north Indian restaurant, with plenty of veggie options, that's justly popular with local Indians.

Jim Thompson's Café 120/1 Soi 1, Th Saladaeng ☎02 266 9167–8. A civilized, moderately priced haven with delicious Thai daily specials and desserts, pasta, cakes and other Western food.

Khrua Aroy Aroy 3/1 Th Pan. In a fruitful area for cheap food (including a night market across Th Silom on Soi 20), this simple shop-house stands out for its choice of tasty dishes from around the kingdom. Roughly Mon–Fri 8am–6pm, Sat & Sun 8am–4pm.

Talat Nam Th Silom opposite Thaniya Plaza. Popular street stall, surrounded by similar competitors, with tables in the adjoining alley and fresh seafood temptingly displayed on ice. Evenings only.

Tongue Thai 18–20 Soi 38, Th Charoen Krung, in front of Oriental Place shopping mall ☎02 630 9918–9. Very high standards of food in an elegant one-hundred-year-old shop-house. Veggies are amply catered for, while carnivores should try the fantastic beef curry.

Downtown: Siam Square and Thanon Ploenchit

Mah Boon Krong Food Centre Floor 6, MBK shopping centre, corner of Rama I and Phrayathai roads. Inexpensive dishes from all over the country served at specialist stalls.

Sarah Jane's Ground Floor, Sindhorn Tower 1, 130–132 Th Witthayu ☎02 650 9992–3. Long-standing restaurant serving excellent, simple, moderately priced northeastern food.

Sorn's 36/8 Soi Kasemsan 1, Th Rama I. A laid-back hangout offering delicious, moderately priced Thai and Western dishes, varied breakfasts and good coffee.

Thang Long 82/5 Soi Lang Suan ☎02 251 3504. Excellent, moderately expensive Vietnamese food in this stylish, minimalist restaurant.

Thanon Sukhumvit

Cabbages and Condoms 6–8 Soi 12. Run by the Population and Community Development Association of Thailand: diners are treated to authentic moderately priced Thai food in the Condom Room, and barbecued seafood in the beer garden. Try the fried cottonfish with mango and chilli, or the marinated chicken baked in pandanus leaves. All proceeds go to the PDA.

Gaeng Pa Lerd Rod Soi 33/1; no English sign but it's just before the *Bull's Head*. Hugely popular outdoor restaurant where the inexpensive dishes range from conventional catfish and beef curries to more adventurous fried cobra with chilli, and curried frog.

Lemongrass Soi 24 ☎02 258 8637. Delicious and fairly pricey Thai nouvelle cuisine – including a particularly good minced chicken with ginger – served in a converted traditional house. A vegetarian menu is available on request. Reservations advisable.

Suda Soi 14. Unpretentious shop-house restaurant serving a good, long menu of cheap Thai favourites, including deep-fried chicken in banana leaves, and fried tuna with cashews and chilli.

Vientiane Kitchen (Khrua Vientiane) 8 Soi 36, about 50m south off Th Sukhumvit: a 3min walk west then south from Thong Lo Skytrain station. This little corner of Isaan serves a menu full of mid-priced northeastern delicacies – vegetable curry with ants' eggs, spicy-fried frog, jackfruit curry – while a live band croons heart-felt folk songs.

Nightlife and entertainment

More than a thousand sex-related businesses operate in Bangkok: they dominate Thanon Sukhumvit's Soi Cowboy (between sois 21 and 23), Clinton Entertainment Plaza (between sois 13 and 15) and Nana Plaza (Soi 4), but the city's most notorious zone is **Patpong**, between the eastern ends of thanons Silom and Suriwong. Here, girls cajole passers-by in front of lines of go-go bars, with names like *French Kiss* and *Love Nest*, while insistent touts proffer printed menus detailing the degradations of the sex shows upstairs. If you do end up at a sex show, be warned that you'll be charged exorbitant prices for drinks, and will have to face a menacing bouncer if you refuse to pay. In amongst the bars there's a night market, which mainly sells fake designer clothes – and attracts all sorts to the strip after dark, including demure tourists of both sexes.

Fortunately, Bangkok's nightlife has become more sophisticated and stylish in the last few years. Silom 4 (ie Soi 4, Thanon Silom), just east of Patpong, is one of Bangkok's most happening after-dark haunts, along with the high-concept clubs and bars of Sukhumvit, studenty Siam Square and the lively, teeming venues of Banglamphu. Though Silom 4 started out as a purely gay area, it now offers a mixed range of styles, while the city's other main gay area is the more exclusive Silom 2 (towards Thanon Rama IV). Note that the current government's Social Order Policy has involved clampdowns on illegal drugs, including urine testing of bar customers, and ID checks to curb under-age drinking – you're supposed to be over 21 in bars and clubs, though Thais seem to be more rigorously checked than foreigners.

Bars and clubs

Though **Banglamphu** bars tend to be more backpacker-oriented than the **downtown** places, the majority of venues attract a good mix of local and foreign drinkers.

Banglamphu

Bangkok Bar 149 Soi Ram Bhuttri. Not to be confused with the restaurant of the same name on Th Phra Sumen, this small, narrow dance bar is fronted by a different DJ every night and draws capacity crowds of drinkers and clubbers.

Café Democ 78 Th Rajdamnoen Klang. Fashionable, dark and dinky bar offering lots of cocktails and nightly sessions from up-and-coming Thai DJs. Closed Mon.

Grand Guest House Middle of Th Khao San. Cavernous place lacking in character, but popular because it stays open 24hr. Videos are shown non-stop.

Gullivers' Travellers Tavern Th Khao San. Backpacker-oriented a/c sports pub with two pool tables, sixteen TV screens, masses of sports memorabilia and reasonably priced beer. Daily 11am–2am.

Lava Club Bayon Building, 209 Th Khao San. Self-consciously sophisticated basement lounge bar done out in "volcanic" red and black with laser displays to enhance the look. DJs play mainly house and rave from 8pm.

Silk Bar 129–131 Th Khao San. The two-tiered outdoor decks are a popular spot for sipping cocktails while watching the nightly Khao San fashion parade; inside, there's a pool table and a DJ. Daily 6am–2am.

Susie Pub Next to *Marco Polo Guest House* on the soi between Th Khao San and Th Ram Bhuttri. Big, dark, phenomenally popular pub with a pool table, decent music, resident DJs and cheapish beer. Sometimes asks farangs to show ID (passports) at the door. Daily 11am–2am.

Downtown

The Balcony Soi 4, Th Silom. Cheery gay bar with a large, popular terrace, cheap drinks and karaoke.

Bed Supperclub 26 Soi 11 ⓣ02 651 3537. Seductively curvaceous spacepod bar whose futuristic all-white interior is furnished with bed-style couches. DJs, cocktails and a surprisingly cosy atmosphere. Daily 8pm–2am.

Dallas Pub Soi 6, Siam Square. Typical dark, noisy "songs for life" (Thai folk-rock) hangout – buffalo skulls, American flags – but a lot of fun: singalongs to decent live bands, dancing, and friendly staff.

Dick's Café Duangthawee Plaza, 894/7–8 Soi Pratuchai, Th Suriwong. Stylish, gay café-gallery, opposite Wall St Tower, ideal for eating good Thai and Western food or just drinking. Daily 11am–2am.

DJ Station Soi 2, Th Silom. Highly fashionable but unpretentious gay disco, packed at weekends, attracting a mix of Thais and farangs; cabaret show at 11.30pm. B100 including one drink (B200 including two drinks Fri & Sat).

Faith Club Soi 23, Th Sukhumvit. Highly rated little club with a vaguely industrial but intimate feel and weekly hip-hop, techno and chillout evenings: check *Metro* or *Farang* magazines for schedules. Daily 8pm–2am.

Lucifer 76/1–3 Patpong 1. Popular dance club in the dark heart of Patpong, done out with mosaics and stalactites like a satanic grotto; no admission charge. *Radio City*, the bar downstairs, features famous Elvis and Tom Jones impersonators.

Mystique 71/8 Soi 31, Th Sukhumvit. Very fashionable three-floored mega club with a state of the art dancefloor, an ultra-gothic purple ballroom, and a chill-out Moroccan-style rooftop terrace. Tues–Sun 8pm–2am. Entry costs B650 Fri & Sat, including two drinks; free Mon & Tues–Thurs.

Q Bar 34 Soi 11, Th Sukhumvit. Very dark, very trendy, New York-style bar that attracts a mixed, fashionable crowd. DJs on Fri and Sat nights when there's a B600 cover charge after 10pm that includes two free drinks. Daily 8pm–2am.

Saxophone 3/8 Victory Monument (southeast corner), Th Phrayathai ⓣ02 246 5472. Lively bar that hosts nightly jazz, blues, folk and rock bands and attracts a relaxed mix of Thais and farangs.

Tapas Bar Soi 4, Th Silom. Cool, long-standing bar with tables on the soi and main dance floor upstairs (B200 to go up).

Tawandang German Brewery 462/61 Th Rama III ⓣ02 678 1114–6. A taxi-ride south of Th Sathorn down Th Narathiwat Ratchanakharin – and best to book a table in advance – this vast all-rounder is well worth the effort: good food, micro-brewed beer, and mercurial cabaret (Mon–Sat from 8.30pm) led by Bruce Gaston, blending Thai classical and popular with Western music styles.

Culture shows and Thai boxing

Many tourist restaurants stage nightly **culture shows**, usually a hotchpotch of Thai dancing and classical music, to accompany a set dinner. Worth checking out are *Baan Thai* restaurant (ⓣ02 258 5403), on Soi 32, Thanon Sukhumvit (performances at 8.30pm; B550), the outdoor restaurant in Silom Village (ⓣ02 234 4581) on Thanon Silom (8.30pm; B550), and *Supatra River House* in Thonburi (ⓣ02 411 0305; Fri & Sat only at 8.30pm; B650–850; free shuttle boat transport from Tha Maharaj in front of Wat Mahathat). The Joe Louis Puppet Theatre (ⓣ02 252 9683–4, ⓦwww.

joelouis-theater.com) stages enjoyable tourist-oriented traditional puppet dramas at Suan Lum Night Bazaar on Thanon Rama IV (Mon–Fri 7.30pm; Sat & Sun 5pm & 7.30pm; arrive 30min early for mask-making demonstration; B600, kids B300). **Thai boxing matches** (*muay Thai*) can be very violent, but are also very entertaining (see p.947). Sessions usually feature ten bouts of five three-minute rounds and are held in the capital every night of the week at either the Rajdamnoen Stadium, next to the TAT office on Rajdamnoen Nok (Ⓣ02 281 4205; Mon, Wed & Thurs 6pm, Sun 5pm), and at Lumphini Stadium on Thanon Rama IV (Ⓣ02 252 8765; Tues & Fri 6.30pm, Sat 5pm & 8.30pm); a new Lumphini Stadium is due to open on Thanon Nang Linchee, off Soi Ngam Duphli, in late 2005Tickets go on sale one hour beforehand and start at B220 (B50 on Sun).

Shopping

Department stores and tourist-oriented shops in the city open at 10 or 11am and close at about 9pm. The Central Chidlom department store on Thanon Ploenchit is probably the city's best, but Robinson's (on Sukhumvit Soi 19 and at the Silom/Rama IV junction) and Big C (on Thanon Charoen Krung near Thanon Sathorn) are also good. The best place to buy anything to do with mobile phones is the Mah Boon Krong (MBK) shopping centre, Floor 3, at the Rama I/Phrayathai intersection. The massive Chatuchak Weekend Market is a marvellous **shopping** experience (see p.979), as is Thanon Khao San in Banglamphu. Suan Lum Night Bazaar, corner of Rama IV and Witthayu roads (daily 3pm–midnight; Ⓦwww.thainightbazaar.com), is aiming to become a night-time Chatuchak, with some interesting clothes and handicrafts stalls, as well as an open-air food and beer garden, with nightly live music. For contemporary interior design, fusing minimalist Western ideals with traditional Thai and other Asian elements, head for the third floor of Gaysorn Plaza on Thanon Ploenchit or the fourth floor of Siam Discovery Centre and this on Thanon Rama I. The Patpong night market (daily 5pm until late) is the place to stock up on fake designer goods, from pseudo-Rolex watches to Burberry shirts. Bangkok is a good place to buy cut and uncut rubies, blue sapphires and diamonds, but never accompany touts, "guides" or tuk-tuk drivers to the shops they recommend (there are no TAT-endorsed jewellery shops): many a gullible traveller has wasted thousands of dollars on worthless stones; see Ⓦwww.2bangkok.com/2bangkok/Scams/Sapphire.shtml for a detailed description of the typical scam and advice on what to do if you get done. Tailored suits are another excellent buy, but avoid the tailors offering $99 deals, which are likely to churn out shoddy work, and aim to spend about B12,000 for a well-made two-piece.

A Song Tailor 8 Trok Chartered Bank, off Th Charoen Krung, near the *Oriental Hotel* Ⓣ02 630 9708, Ⓔasongtailor@yahoo.com. Friendly, helpful tailoring service that's a good first port of call if you're on a tight budget.

Aporia Th Tanao, Banglamphu. One of Banglamphu's main outlets for new books. Also sells secondhand books.

Asia Books Branches on Th Sukhumvit between sois 15 and 19, in Landmark Plaza between sois 4 and 6, in Times Square between sois 12 and 14, and in Emporium between sois 22 and 24; in Peninsula Plaza on Th Rajdamri; in Siam Discovery Centre on Th Rama I; and in Thaniya Plaza near Patpong off Th Silom. English-language bookstore that's recommended for its books on Asia.

Bookazine Branches on Th Silom in the CP Tower (Patpong) and in the Silom Complex; in Siam Square; in the Amarin Plaza on Th Ploenchit; in All Seasons Place on Th Witthayu; and at the mouth of Sukhumvit Soi 5. Huge range of foreign newspapers and magazines plus a decent selection of English-language books.

Come Thai 2nd Floor, Amarin Plaza, Th Ploenchit. No English sign, but easily spotted by its carved wooden doorframe. Impressive range of unusual handwoven silk and cotton fabrics, much of it made up into traditional-style clothes.

Golden Wool 1340–1342 Th Charoen Krung Ⓣ02 233 0149, Ⓔgoldenwool@hotmail.com; and **World Group** 1302–1304 Th Charoen Krung, Ⓣ02 234 1527, Ⓔworldgroupbkk@hotmail.com. Part of the

same company, they can turn around decent work in a couple of days. One of the tailors here has made suits for the king.
Jim Thompson's Thai Silk Company Main shop at 9 Th Suriwong, plus branches at Jim Thompson's House (see p.978), Central Chidlom department store on Th Ploenchit, at Emporium on Th Sukhumvit, and at many hotels around the city, and a factory sales outlet at 149/4–6 Th Suriwong. Stocks silk and cotton by the yard and ready-made items from dresses to cushion covers, which are well designed and of good quality, but pricey. Also home furnishings and a good tailoring service.
Johnny's Gems 199 Th Fuang Nakhon, near Wat Rajabophit in Ratanakosin. Reputable gem and jewellery shop.
The Legend Floor 3, Amarin Plaza, Th Ploenchit, and Floor 3, Thaniya Plaza, Th Silom. Well-made Thai handicrafts at reasonable prices. Subsidiary Tamnan Mingmuang, Floor 3, Thaniya Plaza, concentrates on unusual basketry from all over the country.
Mah Boon Krong (MBK) Rama I/Phrayathai intersection. Labyrinthine shopping centre that houses hundreds of small, mostly inexpensive outlets, including plenty of high-street fashion shops.
Shaman Books Two branches on Th Khao San. The best-stocked and most efficient secondhand bookshop in the city. Don't expect bargains, though.
Siam Centre Th Rama I. Good for trendy local labels.
Siam Square Worth poking around the alleys here, especially near what's styled as the area's "Centerpoint" between sois 3 and 4. All manner of inexpensive boutiques selling colourful street gear.
Ton's Bookseller 327/5 Th Ram Bhuttri. One of Banglamphu's best-stocked outlets for books about Thailand and Southeast Asia; also sells the best Bangkok map, Bangkok Guide's *Bus Routes & Map*, and some English-language fiction.

Listings

Airlines, domestic Air Andaman, 3388/56 16th Floor, Sirinrat Bldg, Th Rama IV, ☎02 229 9555; Bangkok Airways, 1111 Th Ploenchit ☎02 254 2903; PB Air, UBC 2 Bldg, 591 Sukhumvit Soi 33 ☎02 2610220–5; Phuket Airlines, 1168/102 34th Floor Lumpini Tower Bldg, Th Rama IV ☎02 679 8999; Thai Airways, 485 Th Silom ☎02 232 8000, and 6 Th Lan Luang near Democracy Monument ☎02 280 0060, 24hr reservations ☎02 628 2000.
Airlines, international Aeroflot ☎02 254 1180–2; Air Canada ☎02 670 0400; Air France ☎02 635 1186–7; Air India ☎02 235 0557–8; Air New Zealand ☎02 254 8440; Biman Bangladesh Airlines ☎02 233 3640; British Airways ☎02 636 1747 or ☎02 236 2800; Cathay Pacific ☎02 263 0616; China Airlines ☎02 253 4242–3; Druk Air ☎02 535 1960; Egyptair ☎02 231 0505–8; Emirates ☎02 664 1040; Eva Air ☎02 240 0890; Finnair ☎02 635 1234; Garuda ☎02 679 7371–2; Gulf Air ☎02 254 7931–4; Japan Airlines ☎02 234 9114–5; KLM ☎02 679 1100; Korean Air ☎02 635 0465; Lao Airlines ☎02 237 6982; Lauda Air ☎02 267 0873; Lufthansa ☎02 264 2400; Malaysia Airlines ☎02 263 0565–71; Olympic Airways ☎02 237 6141; Pakistan International (PIA) ☎02 234 2961–5; Philippine Airlines ☎02 633 5713; Qantas Airways ☎02 636 1747; Royal Brunei ☎02 637 5151; Singapore Airlines ☎02 236 0440; Sri Lankan Airlines ☎02 236 4981; Swiss ☎02 636 2150; Thai Airways ☎02 280 0060, 24hr reservations ☎02 628 2000; United Airlines ☎02 253 0558; Vietnam Airlines ☎02 655 4137–40.
Airport enquiries General enquiries ☎02 535 1111; international departures ☎02 535 1386; international arrivals ☎02 535 1149; domestic departures ☎02 535 1277; domestic arrivals ☎02 535 1305.
Embassies and consulates Australia, 37 Th Sathorn Tai ☎02 287 2680; Burma (Myanmar), 132 Th Sathorn Nua ☎02 234 0278; Cambodia, 185 Th Rajdamri (enter via Th Sarasin) ☎02 254 6630; Canada, 15th floor, Abdulrahim Place, 990 Th Rama IV ☎02 636 0560; China, 57 Th Rajadapisek ☎02 245 7030–45; Germany, 9 Th Sathorn Tai (☎02 213 2331–6); India, 46 Soi Prasarnmitr, Soi 23, Th Sukhumvit ☎02 258 0300; Indonesia, 600–602 Th Phetchaburi ☎02 252 3135–40; Ireland, 12th Floor, TISCO Tower, 48/20 Th Sathorn Nua ☎02 638 0303; Laos, 520 Ramkhamhaeng Soi 39 ☎02 539 6667–8, ext 1053; Malaysia, 35 Th Sathorn Tai ☎02 679 2190–9; Nepal, 189 Sukhumvit Soi 71 ☎02 391 7240; Netherlands, 106 Th Witthayu (Wireless Road) ☎02 253 8693; New Zealand, 93 Th Witthayu ☎02 254 3856, 253 5363 or 253 0429; Pakistan, 31 Sukhumvit Soi 3 ☎02 253 5325; Philippines, 760 Th Sukhumvit, opposite Soi 47 ☎02 259 0139–40; Singapore, 129 Th Sathorn Tai ☎02 286 2111; Sri Lanka, 89 Sukhumvit Soi 15 ☎02 251 2788–9; Vietnam, 83/1 Th Witthayu ☎02 251 7201–3; UK, 1031 Th Witthayu, embassy ☎02 305 8333, consulate ☎02 305 8318; US, 120 Th Witthayu ☎02 205 4000.

Emergencies For all emergencies, either call the tourist police (free 24hr phoneline ☎1155), who also maintain a 24hr booth in the Suan Lum Night Bazaar on Th Rama IV; visit the Banglamphu Police Station at the west end of Th Khao San; or contact the Tourist Police Headquarters, CMIC Tower, 209/1 Soi 21 (Asoke), Th Sukhumvit ☎02 664 0222–6.

Hospitals, clinics and dentists Most expats rate the private Bumrungrad Hospital, 33 Sukhumvit Soi 3 ☎02 667 1000, emergency ☎02 667 2999, as the best and most comfortable in the city, followed by the Bangkok Nursing Home (BNH) Hospital, 9 Th Convent ☎02 632 0550; the Bangkok General Hospital, 2 Soi Soonvijai 7, Th Phetchaburi Mai, ☎02 310 3102; and the Samitivej Sukhumvit Hospital, 133 Sukhumvit Soi 49 ☎02 392 0011. You can get vaccinations and malaria advice, as well as rabies advice and treatment, at the Thai Red Cross Society's Queen Saovabha Memorial Institute (QSMI) and Snake Farm on the corner of Th Rama IV and Th Henri Dunant (Mon–Fri 8.30–noon & 1–4.30pm; ☎02 252 0161–4 or 0167, ⓦwww.redcross.or.th). Among general clinics, the Australian-run Travmin Bangkok Medical Centre, 8th Floor, Alma Link Building, next to the Central Chidlom department store at 25 Soi Chitlom, Th Ploenchit (☎02 655 1024–5; B650 per consultation), is recommended. For dental problems, try the Bumrungrad Hospital's dental department on ☎02 667 2300, or the following dental clinics (not 24hr): Dental Hospital 88/88 Sukhumvit Soi 49 ☎02 260 5000–15, Glas Haus Dental Centre, mouth of Sukhumvit Soi 25, ☎02 260 6120–2, Siam Family Dental Clinic 292/6 Siam Square Soi 4 ☎02/255 6664–5.

Immigration office About 1km down Soi Suan Phlu, off Th Sathorn Tai (Mon–Fri 8.30am–4.30pm, plus Sat 8.30am–noon for visa extensions only; ☎02 287 3101–10); visa extensions take about an hour. They also send a weekly mobile office to the *Emerald Hotel*, Th Ratchadaphisek near the Huay Khwang intersection, in the northeast of the city (Wed 9am–noon; ☎02 693 9333–8). Be very wary of any Khao San tour agents who offer to organize a visa extension for you: some are reportedly faking the relevant stamps, which has caused problems at immigration.

Internet access Banglamphu is packed with places offering Internet access, in particular along Th Khao San. The Ratchadamnoen Post Office on Banglamphu's Soi Damnoen Klang Neua (daily 8am–7pm) also has very cheap public Catnet Internet booths (see p.945). Th Sukhumvit has a number of clued-up Internet cafés, including Login, Ground Floor, Ploenchit Center, Sukhumvit Soi 2 (daily 10am–7pm), and Time Internet Centre on the second floor of Times Square, between sois 12 and 14 (Mon–Sat 9am–midnight, Sun 10am–midnight); the Soi Nana Post Office between sois 4 and 6 also has some Catnet Internet terminals. In the Silom area, head for Patpong Internet on Patpong 2 (daily noon–10pm). There are Catnet centres in the 24hr public telephone office adjacent to the GPO on Th Charoen Krung, and at Don Muang Airport.

Left luggage At Don Muang Airport (international and domestic; B90 per day); Don Muang train station (B15 per day); Eastern Bus Terminal (B30 per day), Hualamphong Station (B10–30 per day), and at most hotels and guesthouses (B10–20 per day).

Mail The GPO is at 1160 Th Charoen Krung, a few hundred metres left of the exit for Wat Muang Kae express-boat pier. Poste restante can be collected here Mon–Fri 8am–8pm, Sat, Sun & holidays 8am–1pm; letters are kept for three months. The parcel-packing service at the GPO operates Mon–Fri 8am–4.30pm, Sat 9am–noon. If you're staying in Banglamphu, it's more convenient to use the poste restante service at one of the two local post offices: the one closest to Khao San is Ratchadamnoen Post Office on Soi Damnoen Klang Neua (Mon–Fri 8am–5pm, Sat 9am–noon); letters are kept for two months and should be addressed to you c/o Poste Restante, Ratchadamnoen PO, Bangkok 10200. Banglamphu's other post office is on Soi Sibsam Hang, just west of Wat Bowoniwes (Mon–Fri 8.30am–5.30pm, Sat 9am–noon); its poste restante address is Banglamphubon PO, Bangkok 10203. You can also send and receive faxes there on ☎02 281 1579. In the Th Sukhumvit vicinity, poste restante can be sent to the Th Sukhumvit post office between sois 4 and 6, c/o Nana PO, Th Sukhumvit, Bangkok 10112 (daily 8am–7pm).

Pharmacies There are English-speaking staff at most of the capital's pharmacies, including the city-wide branches of Boots the Chemist (most usefully on Th Khao San, in the Siam Centre on Th Rama I and inside the Emporium on Th Sukhumvit), which are also the easiest places to buy tampons.

Telephones International cardphones are dotted all over the city, and there are public telephone offices in or adjacent to major post offices (see above for addresses), including the GPO on Th Charoen Krung (24hr), which also offers a free collect-call service, and the post offices (all 8am–7pm) at Hualamphong Station, on Th Sukhumvit, and in Banglamphu.

Travel agents Th Khao San is a notorious centre of fly-by-night operations, some of which have been known to flee with travellers' money overnight, so check that the travel agent belongs to the Association of Thai Travel Agents (ATTA; ☎02 237 6046–8, ⓦwww.atta.or.th). Recommended travel agents include Diethelm Travel, which is especially good for travel to Cambodia, Laos and Vietnam: 12th Floor, Kian Gwan Building II, 140/1 Th Witthayu (Wireless Road) ⓣ02 255 9200, wwww.diethelm-travel.com; Educational Travel Centre (ETC), inside the *Royal Hotel*, Room 318, 2 Th Rajdamnoen Klang, Banglamphu ⓣ02 224 0043, ⓦwww.etc.co.th, at 180 Th Khao San, Banglamphu ⓣ02 282 2958, and at 5/3 Soi Ngam Duphli ⓣ02 286 9424; NS Tours, inside the *Vieng Tai Hotel*, Th Ram Bhuttri, Banglamphu ⓣ02 629 0509, ⓔnstravel@hotmail.com, and at 46/1 Th Khao San ⓣ02 282 1900; Royal Exclusive, 21 Th Silom ⓣ02 267 1536, ⓦwww.royalexclusive.com; and the Bangkok branch of the worldwide STA Travel, 14th Floor, Wall Street Tower, 33 Th Suriwong ⓣ02 236 0262, ⓦwww.statravel.co.th. Many travel agents can also arrange visas for neighbouring countries.

10.2

The central plains

North and west of the capital, the unwieldy urban mass of Greater Bangkok peters out into the vast, well-watered **central plains**, a region that for centuries has grown the bulk of the nation's food and been a tantalizing temptation for neighbouring power-mongers. The riverside town of **Kanchanaburi** has long attracted visitors to the notorious Bridge over the River Kwai and is now well established as a budget-travellers' hangout. Few tourists venture further west except to travel on the Death Railway, but the tiny hilltop town of **Sangkhlaburi** is worth the trip. On the plains north of Bangkok, the historic heartland of the country, the major sites are the ruined ancient cities of **Ayutthaya**, **Lopburi** and **Sukhothai**. **Mae Sot** makes a therapeutic change from old monuments and is the departure point for **Umphang**, a remote border region that's becoming increasingly popular for trekking and rafting.

Nakhon Pathom

NAKHON PATHOM, 56km west of Bangkok, is probably Thailand's oldest town and is thought to be the point at which Buddhism first entered the region, when, over two thousand years ago, it was visited by two Indian missionaries. Legend has it that the Buddha rested in Nakhon Pathom, and the original Indian-style **Phra Pathom Chedi** may have been erected to commemorate this. The chedi (stupa) was rebuilt with a Khmer prang (tower) between the eighth and twelfth centuries, which was later encased in the enormous 120-metre-high plunger-shaped chedi that exists today. The inner and outer chambers at the cardinal points each contain a tableau of the life of the Buddha. There are two **museums** within the chedi compound: Phra Pathom Chedi National Museum (Wed–Sun 9am–noon & 1–4pm; B30), which is clearly signposted from the bottom of the chedi's south staircase, displays historical artefacts excavated nearby, while the Phra Pathom Chedi Museum (same hours; free), halfway up the steps near the east viharn, contains curios.

Arriving at Nakhon Pathom's **train station**, a two-hundred-metre walk south across the khlong and through the market will get you to the chedi's north gate. Buses from Bangkok, Damnoen Saduak and Kanchanaburi terminate 1km east of the town centre, but most circle the chedi first, dropping you near its southern gate. The most traveller-friendly **accommodation** is at *Mitpaisal Hotel* (Ⓣ034 242422, Ⓔmitpaisal@hotmail.com; ❶–❷), which offers fan and air-con rooms at 120/30 Thanon Sukhaphiban Phaya Pan: it has one entrance a few metres to the right of the station exit, and another across from the north bank of the khlong (near the stop for buses to Bangkok). For inexpensive Thai and Chinese food, head for any of the **restaurants** along the eastern arm of Thanon Phraya Gong, which runs along the south (chedi) side of the canal. You can change money at the exchange booth (banking hours) between the train station and the chedi, and you can store luggage in the controller's office at the train station or at the ticket booth inside the chedi's southern entrance.

Damnoen Saduak floating markets

To get an idea of what shopping in Bangkok used to be like before all the canals were tarmacked over, many people take an early-morning trip to the floating markets of **DAMNOEN SADUAK**, 60km south of Nakhon Pathom. Vineyards and orchards here back onto a labyrinth of narrow canals, thick with paddle boats selling fresh fruit and vegetables every morning between 6 and 11am. It's a big draw for tour groups and some visitors have complained of seeing more tourists than vendors – but you can avoid the worst of the crowds if you arrive before 9am. The target for most groups is the main **Talat Khlong Ton Kem**, 2km west of the tiny town centre at the intersection of Khlong Damnoen Saduak and Khlong Thong Lang. Touts congregate at the Ton Kem pier to sell boat trips (hourly rates from B150 per person); a quieter alternative is to explore on foot along the canalside walkways.

Damnoen Saduak is a 109-kilometre **bus** journey from Bangkok's Southern Bus Terminal (from 6am; 2hr 30min). Buses and songthaews from Nakhon Pathom leave every twenty minutes from 6am and take an hour, picking up passengers outside the chedi's southern gate. From Kanchanaburi, take bus #461 to Ban Phe (every 15min from 5.25am; 1hr 15min), then change to bus #78. The bus terminal is just north of Thanarat Bridge and Khlong Damnoen Saduak. Songthaews cover the 2km to Ton Kem, but a walkway follows the canal from Thanarat Bridge, or you can cross the bridge and take the road to the right, Thanon Sukhaphiban 1, through the orchards. The best **place to stay** in town is *Little Bird Hotel*, also known as *Noknoi* (☎032 254382; ❶–❷), visible from the main road and Thanarat Bridge.

Kanchanaburi and around

Set in a fine landscape of limestone hills 65km northwest of Nakhon Pathom, the peaceful riverside rafthouses of **KANCHANABURI** make this a popular and very pleasant travellers' hangout. Aside from the town's main sights – the Bridge over the River Kwai and several moving memorials to the town's role in World War II – there are caves, waterfalls and historical sites to explore. A very popular commemorative son et lumière River Kwai Bridge Festival is held here for ten days every November.

Arrival and information

Trains connect Kanchanaburi with Bangkok's Thonburi station via Nakhon Pathom. Coming from Hua Hin and points further south, take the train to Ban Pong and change on to a Kanchanaburi-bound train (or bus). Kanchanaburi train station is about 2km north of the town centre, so some guesthouses send free transport. **Buses** run from Bangkok's Southern Bus Terminal via Nakhon Pathom to the bus station, which is a five-minute walk from the **TAT office** (daily 8.30am–4.30pm; ☎034 511200, ⓔtatkan@tat.or.th) and a ten-minute samlor ride (B50) from the Soi Rongheabaow and Maenam Kwai guesthouses. From Bangkok, the speediest journey is by **tourist minibus** from Thanon Khao San (2hr). For transport between the bus station, Maenam Kwai guesthouses and the Bridge, use the **songthaews** that run along Thanon Saeng Chuto via the Kanchanaburi War Cemetery (Don Rak) and then up Thanon Maenam Kwai to the Bridge (every 15min; 15min; B5). They start from outside the Bata shoe shop on Thanon Saeng Chuto, one block north of the bus station. The best way to explore Kanchanaburi and its countryside is by renting a **bicycle** from one of the many outlets along Thanon Maenam Kwai.

There are several **banks** with ATMs and moneychanging facilities on the main Thanon Saeng Chuto. The **tourist police** (☎034 512795) have booths right beside the Bridge, near *Beer Barrel* on Thanon Maenam Kwai, and on Thanon Song Kwai.

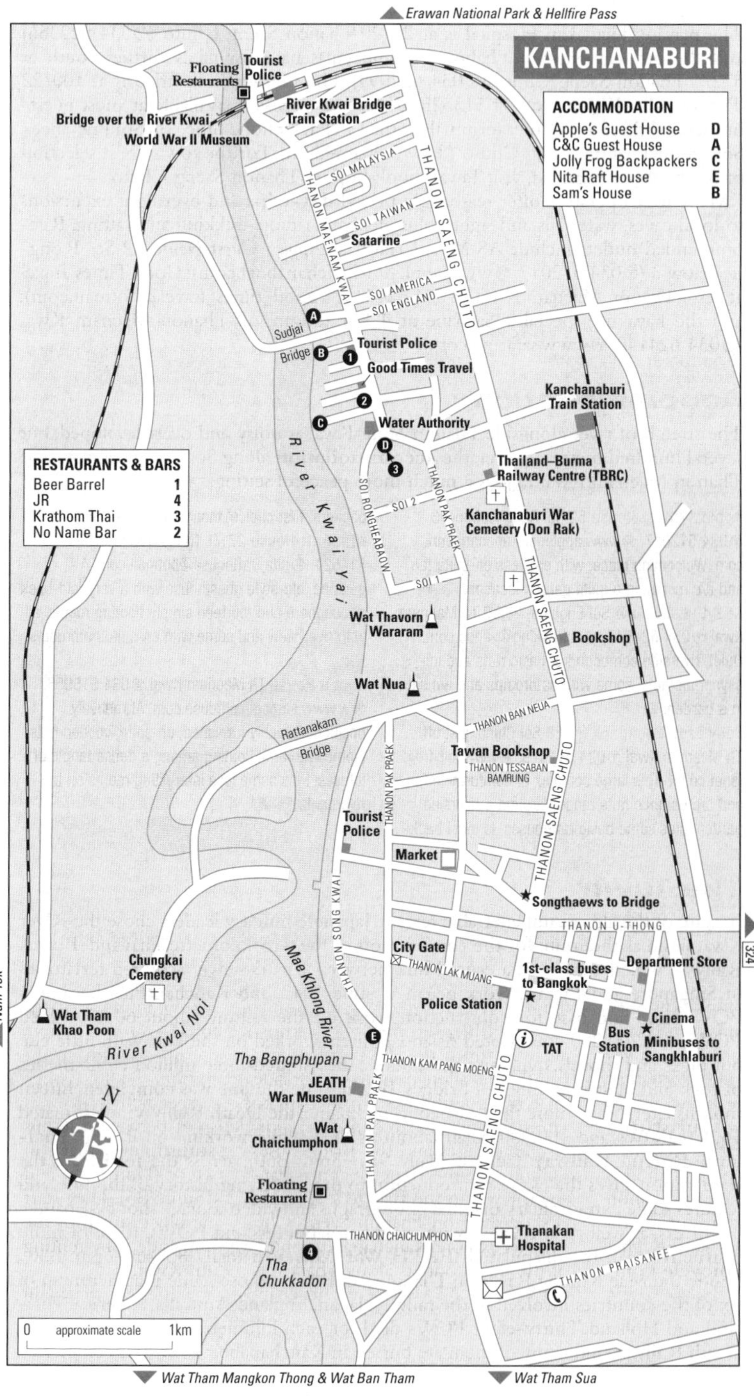

Erawan National Park & Hellfire Pass
KANCHANABURI
ACCOMMODATION
Apple's Guest House D
C&C Guest House A
Jolly Frog Backpackers C
Nita Raft House E
Sam's House B
RESTAURANTS & BARS
Beer Barrel 1
JR 4
Krathom Thai 3
No Name Bar 2
Floating Restaurants
Tourist Police
River Kwai Bridge Train Station
Bridge over the River Kwai
World War II Museum
SOI MALAYSIA
SOI TAIWAN
SOI AMERICA
SOI ENGLAND
THANON MAENAM KWAI
THANON SAENG CHUTO
Satarine
Sudjai Bridge
Tourist Police
Good Times Travel
Water Authority
Kanchanaburi Train Station
Thailand–Burma Railway Centre (TBRC)
Kanchanaburi War Cemetery (Don Rak)
River Kwai Yai
SOI RONGHEABAOW
THANON PAK PRAEK
SOI 2
SOI 1
Wat Thavorn Wararam
Bookshop
Wat Nua
Rattanakarn Bridge
THANON BAN NEUA
Tawan Bookshop
THANON TESSABAN BAMRUNG
Tourist Police
Market
Songthaews to Bridge
THANON U-THONG
THANON SONG KWAI
City Gate
THANON LAK MUANG
1st-class buses to Bangkok
Department Store
Police Station
Cinema
Bus Station
Minibuses to Sangkhlaburi
TAT
Chungkai Cemetery
Wat Tham Khao Poon
River Kwai Noi
Mae Khlong River
Tha Bangphupan
THANON KAM PANG MOENG
JEATH War Museum
Wat Chaichumphon
Floating Restaurant
THANON CHAICHUMPHON
Thanakan Hospital
THANON PRAISANEE
Tha Chukkadon
Nam Tok
324
0 approximate scale 1km
Wat Tham Mangkon Thong & Wat Ban Tham
Wat Tham Sua

The private Thanakan Hospital is at 20/20 Thanon Saeng Chuto (☎034 622366) and the government-run Phahon Phonphayulasena Hospital is further south at 572/1 Thanon Saeng Chuto (☎034 622999). The immigration office is at 100/22 Thanon Mae Khlong (☎034 513325). **Internet access** is available at most guest-houses and there are Catnet terminals at the CAT telephone office on Soi Praisanee/Soi 38 off Thanon Saeng Chuto (daily 8.30am–8pm). For the town's best selection of books about Thailand, visit Tawan bookshop on Thanon Saeng Chuto.

Many tour operators offer reasonably priced **day-trips** and overnight excursions to local caves, waterfalls and sights, plus elephant-riding, trekking and rafting. Recommended outlets include AS Mixed Travel at *Apple's Guest House*, 52 Soi Rongheabaow 3 (☎034 512017, Ⓦwww.applenoi-kanchanaburi.com); Good Times Travel at 63/1 Thanon Maenam Kwai (☎034 624441, Ⓔgood_times_travel@hotmail.com); and the kayaking specialist Safarine at 4 Soi Taiwan, off Thanon Maenam Kwai (☎034 624140, Ⓦwww.safarine.com).

Accommodation

The stretch of river alongside Thanon Song Kwai is noisy and over-developed, but several hundred metres upriver, the **accommodation** along Soi Rongheabaow and Thanon Maenam Kwai enjoys a much more peaceful setting.

Apple's Guest House 52 Soi Rongheabaow 3 ☎034 512017, Ⓦwww.applenoi-kanchanaburi.com. Welcoming place, with spotless en-suite fan and a/c rooms, in a quiet garden location. ❶–❸

C&C Guest House Soi England, 265/2 Th Maenam Kwai ☎034 624547, Ⓔcctrekking@yahoo.com. Quiet, riverside compound of basic rafts and idiosyncratic huts, some with bathrooms and a/c set in a garden. ❶–❷

Jolly Frog Backpackers 28 Soi China, just off Th Maenam Kwai ☎034 514579, Ⓦwww.jollyfrog.fsnet.co.uk. This large complex of comfortable fan and a/c bamboo huts ranged around a riverside garden, plus some basic rafthouses, is most backpackers' first choice, though it can be noisy. ❶–❷

Nita Raft House 271/1 Th Pak Praek ☎034 514521, Ⓔnita_rafthouse@hotmail.com. A genuine, old-style guesthouse with a very laid-back atmosphere and fourteen simple floating rooms, all with river view and some with en-suite bathrooms. ❶

Sam's House Th Maenam Kwai ☎034 515956, Ⓦwwww.samsguesthouse.com. Attractively positioned, nicely furnished, en-suite wooden huts (some with a/c), floating among a dense tangle of lotuses. Plus some less interesting rooms on the riverbank. ❷–❸

The Town

In spite of the almost impenetrable terrain, Japanese military leaders chose the River Kwai basin as the route for the construction of the 415-kilometre Thailand–Burma Railway, which was to be a crucial link between Japan's newly acquired territories in Singapore and Burma. Work began in June 1942, and Kanchanaburi became a POW camp and base for construction work on the railway. About 60,000 Allied POWs and 200,000 conscripted Asian labourers worked on the line. With little else but picks and shovels, dynamite and pulleys, they shifted three million cubic metres of rock and built nine miles of bridges. By the time the line was completed, fifteen months later, it had more than earned its nickname, the Death Railway: an estimated 16,000 POWs and 100,000 Asian labourers died while working on it. The **Thailand–Burma Railway Centre** (daily 9am–5pm; B60), across the road from the train station, gives the clearest introduction to the horrifying history of this line, and features some extraordinary original photographs and video footage shot by Japanese engineers, as well as interviews with surviving labourers and POWs. It's a lot more instructive than the dilapidated **JEATH War Museum** (daily 8.30am–6pm; B30), beside the Mae Khlong River on Thanon Pak Praek, whose name is an acronym of six of the countries involved in the railway: Japan, England, Australia, America, Thailand and Holland. Thirty-eight POWs died for each kilometre of track laid on the Death Railway, and many of them are buried in Kanchanaburi's two war cemeteries:

next to the Thailand–Burma Railway Centre, the **Kanchanaburi War Cemetery**, also known as Don Rak (daily 8am–4pm; free), is the bigger of the two, with 6982 POW graves laid out in straight lines amidst immaculately kept lawns.

For most people the plain steel arches of the **Bridge over the River Kwai** come as a disappointment: it's commercialized and looks nothing like as awesome as it appears in David Lean's famous 1957 film of the same name. The Bridge was severely damaged by Allied bombers in 1944 and 1945, but has since been repaired and is still in use today. In fact, the best way to see the Bridge is by taking the train over it: the Kanchanaburi–Nam Tok train crosses it three times a day in each direction (see p.988), stopping briefly at the River Kwai Bridge station on the east bank of the river. Otherwise, take any songthaew heading north up Thanon Saeng Chuto, hire a samlor, or cycle – it's 5km from the bus station. Whilst at the Bridge, you can't fail to see the signs for the nearby **World War II Museum** (daily 8am–6pm; B30), 30m south along Thanon Maenam Kwai, a privately owned collection of bizarre curios that has little to do with the war.

Sights across the river

Several of Kanchanaburi's other sights lie some way **across the river**, and are best reached by bike. For Chungkai Cemetery and Wat Tham Khao Poon, both on the west bank of the Kwai Noi, either take the two-minute ferry ride (for pedestrians and bikes) from the pier at the confluence of the two rivers on Thanon Song Kwai, or cycle over Rattanakarn Bridge 1km north of the pier. After about 2km you'll reach **Chungkai Cemetery**, built on the banks of the Kwai Noi at the site of a former POW camp, and final resting place for some 1750 POWs. One kilometre on from Chungkai Cemetery, at the top of the road's only hill, sits the cave temple **Wat Tham Khao Poon** (daily 8am–6pm; donation), a labyrinthine grotto presided over by a medley of religious icons.

The impressive scenery across on the east bank of the River Kwai Noi makes for an equally worthwhile bike trip, but the cave temple on this side – **Wat Tham Mangkon Thong**, otherwise known as the "**Floating Nun Temple**" – is fairly tacky. The attraction here is a Thai nun who will get into the temple pond and float there, meditating – if tourists give her enough money to make it worth her while. Behind the pond, an enormous naga staircase leads up to a cave temple behind. To get there by bicycle or motorbike, take the ferry across the Mae Khlong River at Tha Chukkadon and then follow the road on the other side for about 4km. Alternatively, take **bus** #8191 (every 30min; 20 min) from Kanchanaburi bus station (the last return bus passes the temple at about 4.15pm).

Eating and drinking

At dusk, the ever-reliable **night market** sets up alongside Thanon Saeng Chuto on the edge of the bus station.

Beer Barrel Th Maenam Kwai. Rustic-styled outdoor beer garden where you sit amid a jungle of low-lit trees. Serves some snacks to accompany the ice-cold draught beer.

JR South of Tha Chukkadon. Floating restaurant that affords especially pretty river views and serves good, mid-priced Thai-Chinese dishes.

Krathom Thai At *Apple's Guest House*, 52 Soi Rongheabaow 3. Exceptionally delicious, traditional, mid-priced Thai food, including mouthwatering curries and huge set dinners. Cookery classes available on request.

No Name Bar Th Maenam Kwai. Popular farang-run travellers' hangout, with international sport on the satellite TV, a pool table and well-priced beer. Open till the early hours.

Around Kanchanaburi

The two-hour rail journey from Kanchanaburi to Nam Tok (three trains daily in both directions) travels the POW-built **Death Railway** and is very scenic. Highlights include crossing the Bridge over the River Kwai, squeezing through ninety-foot solid rock cuttings at Wang Sing (Arrow Hill), and the Wang Po viaduct, where a three hundred-metre trestle bridge clings to the cliff face as it curves with the Kwai Noi.

At Konyu, 18km beyond Nam Tok, seven separate cuttings were dug over a three-kilometre stretch. The longest and most brutal of these was **Hellfire Pass**, which got its name from the hellish lights of the fires the POWs used when working at night. Hellfire Pass has now been turned into a circular, ninety-minute memorial **walk** (4km), which follows the old rail route through the eighteen-metre-deep cutting and on to Hin Tok creek, and at the trailhead the beautifully designed **Hellfire Pass Memorial Museum** (daily 9am–4pm; donation), the best and most informative of all Kanchanaburi's World War ll museums, movingly documents the POWs' story. Most Kanchanaburi tour operators feature visits to Hellfire Pass, or any **bus** from Kanchanburi (1hr 5min) or Nam Tok (20min) that's bound for Thong Pha Phum will drop you outside; the last bus back to Kanchanaburi passes the museum at about 4.45pm.

Chances are that when you see a poster of a waterfall in Thailand, you'll be looking at a picture of the seven-tiered falls in **Erawan National Park** (daily 8am–4pm; B200), 65km northwest of Kanchanaburi. The falls are a popular day-trippers' destination, and there's a fairly easy trail up to the fifth tier (2km), beyond which you have to scramble (wear strong shoes); the best pools for swimming are on levels two and seven. Most Kanchanaburi guesthouses arrange songthaew transport to the falls for B80 per person, or take a bus to Srinakarind market (#8170; every 50min, 8am–5.20pm; 2hr), then walk 1km to the national park headquarters, food stalls and trailhead; the last bus home leaves at 4pm.

Sangkhlaburi and Three Pagodas Pass

Located right at the northernmost tip of the 73-kilometre-long Khao Laem Reservoir, the tiny hilltop town of **SANGKHLABURI**, 220km north of Kanchanaburi, is a charming if uneventful hangout. You can boat across the reservoir in search of the sunken temple Wat Sam Phrasop in canoes (B25 per hour) rented from *P Guest House*, or join a sunset longtail boat trip (B350–500 per boat). Across the reservoir stands the Mon village of **Ban Waeng Ka**, which grew up in the late 1940s after the outbreak of civil war in Burma forced the country's ethnic minorities to flee across the border. To reach it, walk across the lake via the spider's web of a wooden bridge, said to be the longest hand-made wooden bridge in the world: the easiest approach is from beside *Burmese Inn*. You'll need a motorbike taxi to get to Wat Wang Wiwekaram, however, which stands 2km away at the edge of the village, its massive, golden chedi modelled on the centrepiece of India's Bodh Gaya, the sacred site of the Buddha's enlightenment. There's a good tourist market in the chedi compound.

Three Pagodas Pass (Ban Chedi Sam Ong)

The Burmese border is marked by the 1400-metre-high **Three Pagodas Pass**, 18km from Sangkhlaburi and easily reached by songthaew (every 40min; 40min). All border trade for hundreds of kilometres has to come through here, and over the last half-century it has been fought over by several Burmese factions; it's currently controlled by the Burmese government. The pagodas themselves are tiny, whitewashed stupas on the edge of Ban Chedi Sam Ong, a small village comprising just a Thai market and a wat. Burmese land starts 50m away, at the village of Payathonzu. At the time of writing, foreign nationals are only allowed to get 1km **across the border** here (daily 6am–6pm), to the far edge of the Burmese border market. Even to make this rather pathetic trip you need to arrive at the border with a permit from the immigration office in Sangkhlaburi (see p.992), whereupon you have to pay US$10 to enter Burma. All of which means it's hardly worth the effort, especially as the **market** on the Thai side of the border post is full of interesting Burmese goods, though there is a magnificent teakwood temple, Wat Sao Roi Ton, ten minutes' walk inside Burma from the border.

Practicalities

Minibuses depart from Kanchanaburi bus station and terminate behind Sangkhlaburi's market near Pornpailin Hotel (daily at 7.30am, 11.30am & 4.30pm; 3hr; reserve ahead). Air-con buses (#8203; 3 daily; 3hr) and regular buses (4 daily; 5–6hr) stop on the western edge of Sangkhlaburi at the top of the town's most useful thoroughfare, which leads south, downhill, to the **post office** (with Catnet terminal), *Burmese Inn*, *Bakery* and *P Guest House*. The market is the focus of the tiny grid of streets that runs east of the bus station and post office, and here you'll find the **bank** (with exchange but no ATM) and immigration office (daily 6am–6pm), where you need to get your permit for crossing into Burma at Three Pagodas. The town is small enough to walk round in an hour, but there are plenty of motorbike taxis and *P Guest House* rents out motorbikes. Sangkhlaburi has two prettily sited waterside **guesthouses,** both of which run day-trips in the area: *Burmese Inn* (Ⓣ06 168 1801, Ⓦwww.sangkhlaburi.com; ❶–❹), 700m down the hill from the bus station then right down Soi 1, has fan and air-con bungalows, while *P Guest House* (Ⓣ034 595061, Ⓦwww.pguesthouse.com; ❷–❹), 1.3km down the hill from the bus station, offers fan rooms with shared facilities and air-con en suites. The cheapest places to **eat** are around the market in the town centre; elsewhere, the chilled-out *Bakery* (daytime only), 900m south down the hill from the post office, serves brown-bread sandwiches and banana cake and is staffed by the nearby Baan Unrak orphans' home (Ⓦwww.geocities.com/baanunrak). Another community project that's worth supporting is Women for Weaving, set up by a group of Karen refugees from Burma, whose shop is about 450m down the hill from the post office.

Ayutthaya

The city of **AYUTTHAYA**, 80km north of Bangkok, was founded in 1351, and by the mid-fifteenth century had wrested power from the kingdom of Sukhothai to become the capital of an empire covering most of the area of modern-day Thailand. Ayutthaya grew into an enormous amphibious city, which by 1685 had one million people – roughly double the population of London at the same time – living largely on houseboats in a 140-kilometre network of waterways. In 1767, this golden age of prosperity came to an abrupt end when the Burmese captured and ravaged Ayutthaya, and the city was abandoned to the jungle.

The core of the former capital was a four-kilometre-wide river island; the hub of the small, modern town rests on its northeast bank, while the majority of the ancient remains are spread out across the western half of the island in a patchwork of parkland. Distances are deceptively large, but guesthouses rent out **bicycles** (B30–50 per day) and **motorbikes** (B250 per day) and there are plenty of tuk-tuks and motorbike taxis around.

The City

One kilometre west out of the new town centre along Thanon Chao Phrom (which becomes Thanon Naresuan), the overgrown **Wat Phra Mahathat**, on the left (daily 8am–6pm; B30), is the epitome of Ayutthaya's atmospheric decay. Across the road, towering **Wat Ratburana** (daily 8am–6pm; B30) retains some original stucco work, including fine statues of garudas swooping down on nagas. It's possible to go down steep steps inside the prang to the crypt, where you can make out fragmentary murals of the early Ayutthaya period.

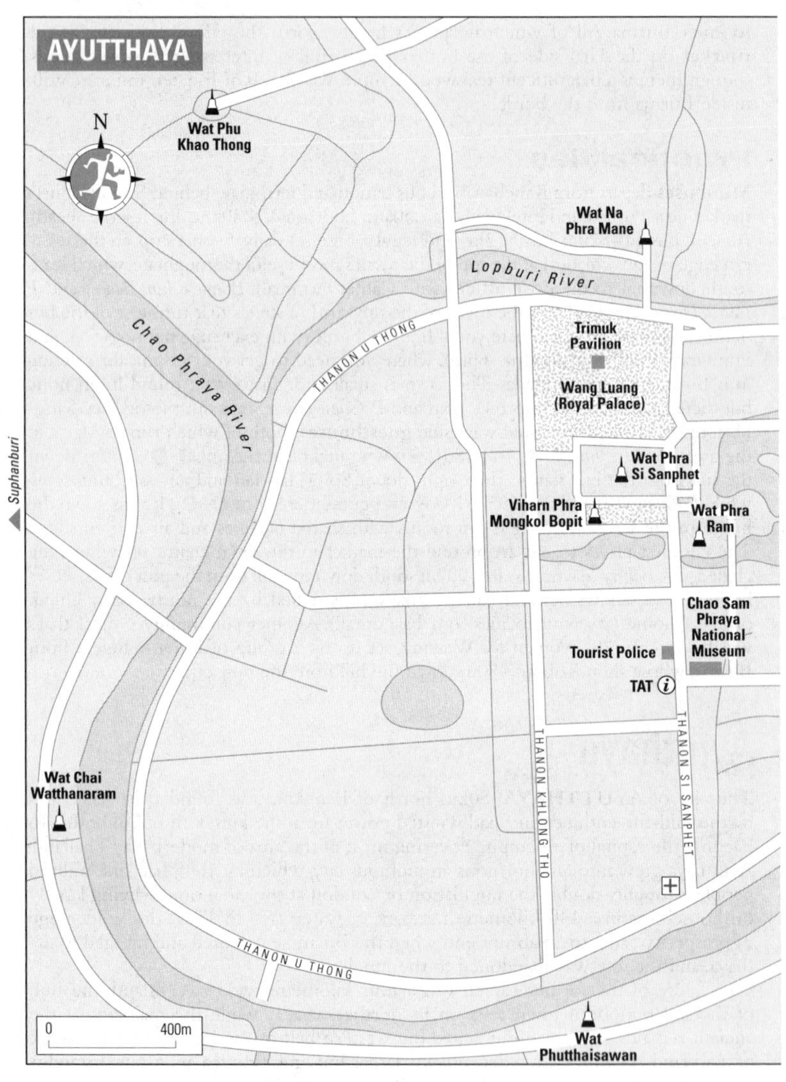

Further west, the grand, well-preserved **Wat Phra Si Sanphet** (daily 8am–6pm; B30) was built in 1448 as a private royal chapel, and its three grey chedis have become the most hackneyed image of Ayutthaya. Save for a few bricks in the grass, the wat is all that remains of the huge walled complex of royal pavilions that extended north as far as the Lopburi River.

Viharn Phra Mongkol Bopit (Mon–Fri 8.30am–4.30pm, Sat & Sun 8.30–5.30pm), on the south side of Wat Phra Si Sanphet, boasts a pristine replica of a typical Ayutthayan viharn (assembly hall), complete with characteristic chunky lotus-capped columns. It was built in 1956, with help from the Burmese to atone for their flattening of the city two centuries earlier, in order to shelter

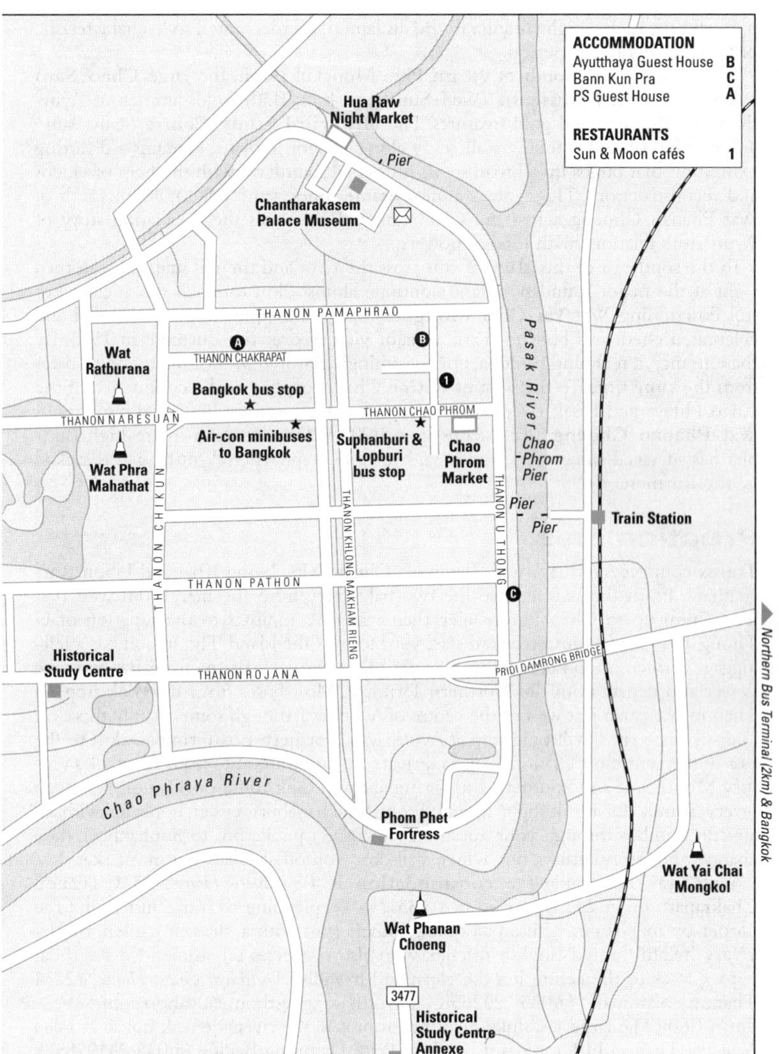

the revered Phra Mongkol Bopit. This powerfully austere bronze statue, with its flashing mother-of-pearl eyes, was cast in the fifteenth century, then sat exposed to the elements from the time of the Burmese invasion until its new home was built.

Across on the north bank of the Lopburi River, **Wat Na Phra Mane** (daily 8am–5pm; B20 donation) is Ayutthaya's most rewarding temple, as it's the only one from the town's golden age that survived the ravages of the Burmese. The main bot, built in 1503, shows the distinctive outside columns topped with lotus cups, and slits in the walls instead of windows to let the wind pass through. Inside, underneath a rich red-and-gold coffered ceiling representing the stars around the moon, sits a powerful six-metre-high Buddha in the disdainful, overdecorated style characteristic of the later Ayutthaya period.

Ten minutes' walk south of Viharn Phra Mongkol Bopit, the large **Chao Sam Phraya National Museum** (Wed–Sun 9am–4pm; B30) holds numerous Ayutthaya-era Buddhas and gold treasures. The **Historical Study Centre** (daily 9am–4.30pm; B100), five minutes' walk away along Thanon Rojana, contains a diverting exhibition that builds up a broad social history of Ayutthaya with the help of videos and reconstructions. The centre's annexe (same times, same ticket), 500m south of Wat Phanan Choeng across the Chao Phraya River, tells the fascinating story of Ayutthaya's relations with foreign powers.

To the southeast of the island, if you cross the river and the rail line, you can turn right at the major roundabout, and continue almost 2km to reach the ancient but still functioning **Wat Yai Chai Mongkol** (daily 8am–5pm; B20). Its colossal and celebrated chedi was built to mark a major victory over the Burmese in 1593. By the entrance, a reclining Buddha, now gleamingly restored in toothpaste white, dates from the same time. To the west of Wat Yai Chai Mongkol, at the confluence of the Chao Phraya and Pasak rivers, stands the city's oldest and liveliest working temple, **Wat Phanan Choeng** (daily 8am–5pm; B20), whose nineteen-metre-high Buddha has survived since 1324, and is said to have wept when Ayutthaya was sacked by the Burmese.

Practicalities

Trains connect Ayutthaya with Bangkok, Chiang Mai, Nong Khai and Ubon Ratchathani. From the station, take the two-baht ferry from the pier 100m west (last ferry 7pm) up to Chao Phrom pier, then walk five minutes to the junction of U Thong and Chao Phrom roads to start your tour of the island. The station has a left-luggage service (supposedly 24hr; B10 per piece per day). **Buses** from Bangkok are slower and depart from the Northern Terminal. Most buses from Bangkok stop on Thanon Naresuan just west of the centre of Ayutthaya, though some, mainly those on long-distance runs, will only stop at Ayutthaya's Northern Bus Terminal, 2km to the east of the centre on Thanon Rojana. Private air-con minibuses from Bangkok's Victory Monument and Southern Bus Terminal finish their route on Thanon Naresuan (every 30min during daylight hours). From Kanchanaburi, either hook up with an air-con minibus through your guesthouse or take a public bus to Suphanburi, then change onto an Ayutthaya bus, which will drop you off at Chao Phrom market.

Ayutthaya's best budget **accommodation** is *PS Guest House*, 23/1 Thanon Chakrapat (ⓣ035 242394 or 06 644 6331; ❶–❷; planning to move just round the corner on to Thanon Chikun), a quiet, homely spot with a pleasant garden, run by a very helpful retired English teacher, who also organizes recommended riverboat trips. Closer to the centre lies the clean and friendly *Ayutthaya Guest House*, 12/34 Thanon Naresuan (ⓣ035 232658, ⓔayutthaya_guesthouse@yahoo.com; ❶–❷, dorm B80). The large, tastefully furnished rooms in the riverside teak house at *Bann Kun Pra*, Thanon U Thong, just north of Pridi Damrong Bridge (ⓣ035 241978; ❷, dorm B150) are also a good option. The main travellers' hangouts are the laid-back, adjacent *Sun* and *Moon* cafés, on the same lane as the *Ayutthaya Guest House*, which serve good Western and Thai **food**. The **TAT** office (ⓣ035 246076–7) and **tourist police** are opposite the Chao Sam Phraya National Museum on Thanon Si Sanphet; at the former, it's well worth heading upstairs to their smartly presented multimedia exhibition on Ayutthaya (daily except Wed 9am–5pm).

Lopburi

LOPBURI, 150km due north of Bangkok, is famous for its historically important but rather unimpressive Khmer ruins, and for the large pack of tourist-baiting monkeys that swarm all over them. The ruins date from around the eleventh century, when Lopburi served for two hundred years as the local capital for the extensive Khmer Empire. The town was later used as a second capital both by King Narai of Ayutthaya and Rama IV of Bangkok because its remoteness from the sea made it less vulnerable to European expansionists.

The centre of Lopburi sits on an egg-shaped island between canals and the Lopburi River, with the rail line running across it from north to south. Most of the hotels and just about everything of interest lie to the west of the line, within walking distance of the train station.

Coming out of the train station, the first thing you'll see are the sprawled grassy ruins of **Wat Phra Si Ratana Mahathat** (daily 6am–6pm; B30), where the impressive centrepiece is a laterite prang in the Khmer style of the twelfth century, decorated with finely detailed stucco work and surrounded by a ruined cloister.

The heavily fortified palace of **Phra Narai Ratchanivet** (grounds open daily 7am–5.30pm), a short walk northwest of Wat Mahathat, was built by King Narai in 1666 and lavishly restored by Rama IV in 1856. The grounds house ruined elephant stables, throne halls and treasure warehouses, but the best feature is the **Narai National Museum** (Wed–Sun 8.30am–4.30pm; B30), in the central courtyard. The museum contains fine thirteenth- and fourteenth-century examples of Lopburi-style Buddha images, which mix traditional Khmer elements – such as the conical ushnisha or flame on the Buddha's head – with new features such as a more oval face and slender body. Next door, the typically Ayutthayan Chanthara Phisan Pavilion contains a fascinating exhibition on Narai's reign.

About 200m north of the palace complex along rue de France is **Ban Vichayen** (daily 7am–6pm; B30), built by Narai as a residence for foreign ambassadors, complete with a Christian chapel incongruously stuccoed with Buddhist motifs. East of here along Thanon Vichayen, **Phra Prang Sam Yod** (daily 7am–6pm; B30) seems to have been a Hindu temple, later converted to Buddhism under the Khmers. The three chunky prangs, made of dark laterite with some restored stucco work, are Lopburi's most photographed sight, and a favourite haunt of Lopburi's monkeys. Across the rail line at San Phra Karn, there's even a monkey's adventure playground for the benefit of tourists, beside the ruins of a huge Khmer prang.

Practicalities

Lopburi is on the main **train** line from Bangkok via Ayutthaya to Chiang Mai and works best as a half-day stop-off. **Buses** from Bangkok's Northern terminal also go via Ayutthaya. The long-distance bus terminal is 2km east of the town centre: a blue city bus or red songthaew will save you the walk. **TAT**'s office (Ⓣ036 422768–9) is on Thanon Wat Phra That, on the north side of Wat Phra Si Ratana Mahathat. Running north from the train station, Thanon Na Phra Karn is a minefield of seedy **hotels**, but a far better option is the clean and friendly *Nett Hotel*, over towards Phra Narai Ratchanivet at 17/1–2 Soi 2, Thanon Ratchadamnern (Ⓣ036 411738; ❷-❸).

Phitsanulok

Pleasantly located on the east bank of the Nan River, **PHITSANULOK** makes a handy base for exploring the Sukhothai area, but only holds a couple of significant sights itself. The fourteenth-century **Wat Phra Si Ratana Mahathat** (aka Wat Mahathat or Wat Yai) is home to the country's second most important Buddha image and stands at the northern limit of town (local buses #1, #5, #8 and #11 from the city bus centre); because the image is so sacred, shorts and skimpy clothing are forbidden, and there's an entrance fee of B10. The holy statue itself, Phra Buddha Chinnarat, is a lovely example of late-Sukhothai style, with a distinctive halo; it is said to have wept tears of blood during a thirteenth-century war.

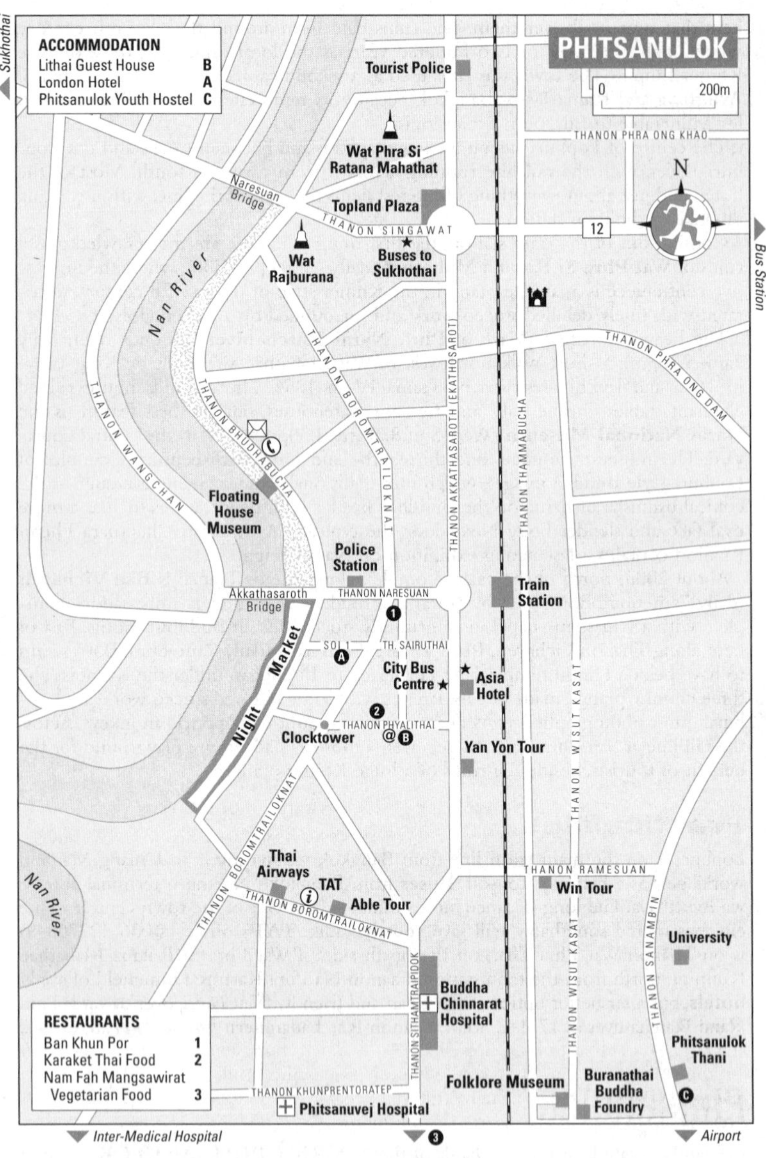

Across town on Thanon Wisut Kasat, southeast of the train station, the **Sergeant Major Thawee Folklore Museum** (Tues–Sun 8.30am–4.30pm; B50) is one of the best ethnology museums in the country and includes a reconstruction of a typical village house and traditional musical instruments. Local bus #8 from the train station will drop you close by. Cross the road from the museum and walk south about 50m a rare chance to see Buddha images being forged at the **Buranathai Buddha Bronze-Casting Foundry**, located behind a big green metal gate at 26/43

Thanon Wisut Kasat. The foundry, which also belongs to Sergeant Major Thawee, is open during working hours and anyone can drop in to watch the stages involved in moulding and casting a Buddha image.

Practicalities

All Bangkok–Chiang Mai **trains** stop at Phitsanulok. **Buses** are more frequent, but you'll need to catch local bus #1, #2 or #8 into town from the regional (government) bus station, 2km east on Highway 12. The private air-con buses operated by Win Tour, who are based on Thanon Ramesun, and Yan Yon Tour (Thanon Akkathasaroth) drop off and pick up passengers at their offices. If you've arrived at Phitsanulok train station and want to make an immediate bus connection **to Sukhothai**, either pick up a Sukhothai-bound bus (daily 5.30am–6pm; every 30min; 1hr) as it passes near the Topland Plaza shopping centre on Thanon Singawat (northbound local buses #5, #8 and #11 run past the Topland Plaza roundabout), or take local bus #1, #2 or #8 to the regional bus station. The **airport** is on the southern edge of town; Thai Airways share-taxis charge B50 per person to any Phitsanulok accommodation, or you can walk 100m north from the airport gates and take city bus #4 into town from Thanon Sanambin.

In the town centre, most **city buses** (B5 or B7 air-con) run via Thanon Akkathasaroth, 150m south of the train station, where southbound buses pick up outside the *Asia Hotel*, and northbound ones from across the road. Useful routes include: #1, from the regional bus station to the train station and Wat Mahathat; #4, from the train station to *Phitsanulok Youth Hostel* and the airport; #5 and #11, from the train station to Topland Plaza and Wat Mahathat; #6, from the regional bus station to the train station; and #8, from the regional bus station to the Folklore Museum, train station, Topland Plaza and Wat Mahathat.

On the eastern arm of Thanon Boromtrailoknat (known to local taxi drivers as Surasi Trade Centre) you'll find a **TAT** office (daily 8.30am–4.30pm; Ⓣ055 252742, Ⓔtatphs@loxinfo.co.th); Able Tour and Travel (Ⓣ055 242206, Ⓔabletour_phs@yahoo.com), which rents cars with driver (B1200 a day); and Thai Airways (Ⓣ055 258020). There's **Internet access** at various locations across town (including just to the west of *Lithai Guest House*), as well as Catnet inside the telephone office on Thanon Bhudhabucha (daily 8am–6pm). The **tourist police** are based north of Wat Mahathat on Thanon Akkathasaroth (Ⓣ055 245358) and the main private hospital is Inter Medical Hospital on Thanon Boromtrailokanat (Ⓣ055 284228–32).

Accommodation and eating

The most traveller-oriented **place to stay** is the *Phitsanulok Youth Hostel*, 38 Thanon Sanambin (Ⓣ055 242060, Ⓦwww.tyha.org; ❷), offering characterful, wood-panelled en-suite rooms in a delightful, shady compound, bicycles for rent, and a B120 dorm. Unfortunately, it's a 1.5-kilometre walk from the centre: take city bus #4 from the train station to the *Phitsanulok Thani Hotel* next door. *Lithai Guest House* at 73/1–5 Thanon Phayalithai (Ⓣ055 219629; ❷–❸) is much more central and has big, clean, bright rooms with fan or air-con, while the funky and similarly well-placed *London Hotel* at 21–22 Soi Buddhabucha (Phuttabucha) 1 (Ⓣ055 225145; ❶–❷) offers very cheap, basic rooms in a converted family home.

For **food**, try the lively night market, which sets up along the east bank of the river at about 6pm: several stall-holders serve "flying vegetables", a strong-tasting morning-glory (*phak bung*), which is stir-fried before being tossed flamboyantly in the air. *Karaket Thai Food* on Thanon Phaylithai is a popular, cheap Thai curry shop (shuts around 8.30pm); *Nam Fah Mangsawirat Vegetarian Food* on Thanon Sithamtraipidok, about 150m south of the Thanon Khunprentoratep junction, or 100m north of the *Indra Hotel*, dishes out simple Thai veggie fare at B15 per plate (Sat–Thurs 6am–2pm); while *Ban Khun Por* on Thanon Chao Phraya is a cosy, parlour-style dining room serving an authentic, mid-priced Thai menu.

Sukhothai and around

For a brief but brilliant hundred and fifty years (1238–1376), the walled city of **SUKHOTHAI** presided as the capital of Thailand. Now an impressive assembly of elegant ruins, Muang Kao Sukhothai (Old Sukhothai), 58km northwest of Phitsanulok, has been designated a historical park and is the most famous place in Thailand to celebrate the Loy Krathong Festival (Ⓦwww.grandfestivalthailand) in October/November. Most travellers stay in "New" Sukhothai, 12km to the east, which has good travel links and is better for accommodation.

New Sukhothai

Straddling the River Yom, **NEW SUKHOTHAI** is a small, friendly town with good guesthouses. All buses use the Sukhothai **bus terminal**, located about 3km west of New Sukhothai's town centre, just off the bypass; purple #1 songthaew (about every 20min from 6am–6pm; B5) runs from the bus terminal into town – depending on where you're staying, either get off at the bus stop for Old Sukhothai, just before crossing the river, or in front of Wat Ratchathani, just after crossing the river. None of the New Sukhothai guesthouses are more than ten minutes' walk from the river. Tiny Sukhothai **airport** is about 15km north of town; flights are met by shuttle buses (B80). The local Bangkok Airways office (Ⓣ055 647224) is located here, though you can also buy air tickets from the more central Sukhothai Travel Agency at 10–12 Thanon Singhawat (Ⓣ055 613075, Ⓔsukhothaitravelservice@yahoo.com). Frequent songthaews (every 15min; 15min) run between New Sukhothai and the historical park; they leave from behind the police box on Thanon Charodvithitong. Most guesthouses organize local tours (the cycle trips from *Ban Thai* are recommended), and rent motorbikes and bicycles. There are about a dozen private **Internet centres** in central Sukhothai, plus Catnet at the CAT phone office on Thanon Nikhon Kasem (Mon–Fri 8.30am–4.30pm, Sat 8.30am–noon). Sukhothai Hospital (Ⓣ055 611782) is west of New Sukhothai on the road to Old Sukhothai; there's a more central 24-hour clinic on Thanon Singhawat.

Old Sukhothai (Muang Kao Sukhothai)

Prior to the thirteenth century, the land now known as Thailand was divided into a collection of petty principalities, most of which owed their allegiance to the Khmer Empire and its administrative centre Angkor (in present-day Cambodia). In 1238, two Thai generals ousted the Khmers and founded the kingdom of **Sukhothai**, with General Intradit as king; soon after, they took control of much of present-day Thailand. The third and most important of Sukhothai's eight kings, Intradit's youngest son Ramkhamhaeng (c.1278–1299), turned the city of Sukhothai into a vibrant spiritual and commercial centre, establishing Theravada Buddhism as the common faith and introducing a Thai alphabet. But his successors lacked his kingly qualities and, by the second half of the fourteenth century, Sukhothai had become a vassal state of Ayutthaya.

In its prime, **Old Sukhothai** boasted some forty separate temple complexes and covered an area of about seventy square kilometres. At its heart stood the walled royal city, protected by a series of moats and ramparts. **Sukhothai Historical Park** (daily 6am–6pm) covers all this area and is divided into five zones: entry to the central zone is B40, plus B10–50 per vehicle; all other zones cost B30 each, inclusive. Songthaews from New Sukhothai stop about 300m east of the museum and central zone entrance point, close to several bicycle rental outlets (the best way to explore the ruins). You can also cycle here from New Sukhothai: ask guesthouses about the fourteen-kilometre back-road route. There's a currency exchange booth (daily 8.30am–12.30pm) next to the museum and several restaurants near the songthaew drop.

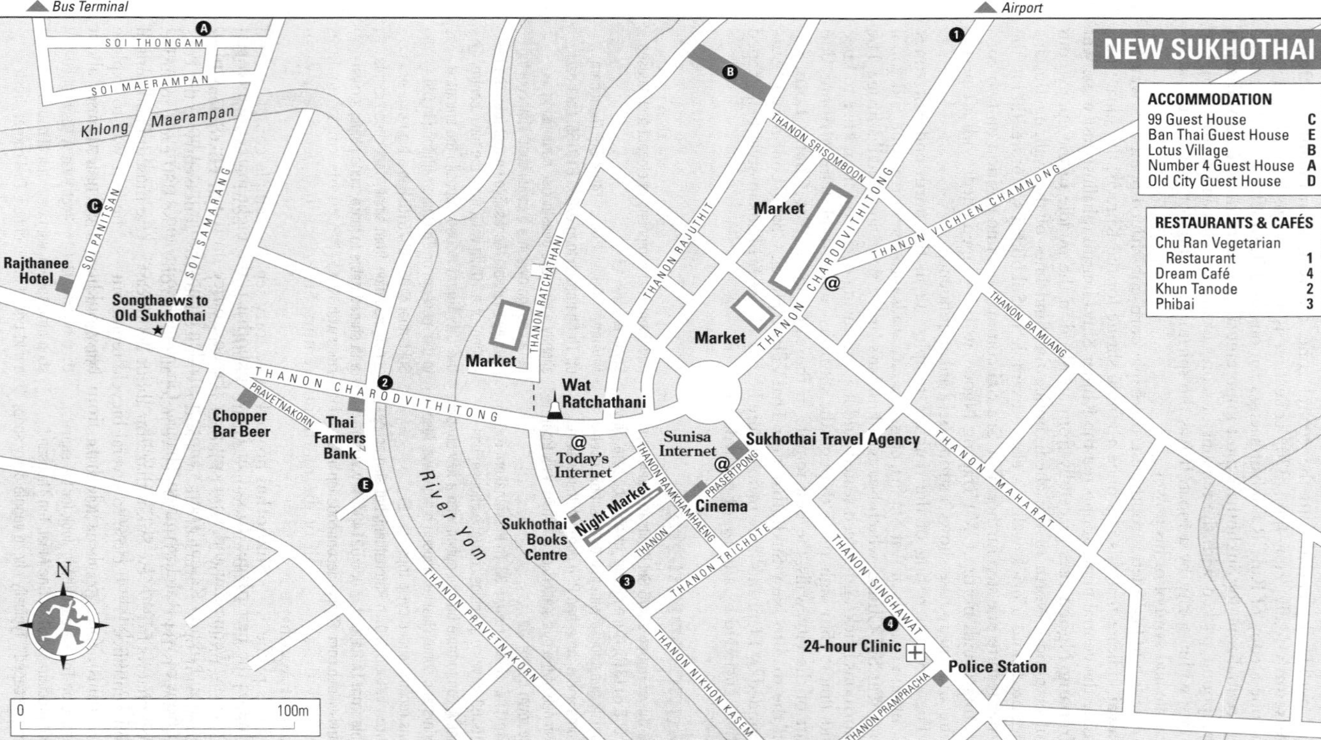
NEW SUKHOTHAI
ACCOMMODATION
99 Guest House C
Ban Thai Guest House E
Lotus Village B
Number 4 Guest House A
Old City Guest House D
RESTAURANTS & CAFÉS
Chu Ran Vegetarian Restaurant 1
Dream Café 4
Khun Tanode 2
Phibai 3
Bus Terminal
Airport
Phitsanulok
Bus Terminal, Old Sukhothai & D
, CAT (200m) & Night Market
SOI THONGAM
SOI MAERAMPAN
Khlong Maerampan
SOI PANITSAN
SOI SAMARANG
Rajthanee Hotel
Songthaews to Old Sukhothai
THANON CHARODVITHITONG
PRAVETNAKORN
Chopper Bar Beer
Thai Farmers Bank
River Yom
THANON PRAVETNAKORN
THANON RATCHATHANI
Market
Wat Ratchathani
Today's Internet
Sukhothai Books Centre
Night Market
THANON RAMKHAMHAENG
THANON
THANON NIKHON KASEM
THANON TRICHOTE
Sunisa Internet
PRASERTPONG
Cinema
Sukhothai Travel Agency
THANON RAJUTHIT
THANON SRISOMBOON
Market
Market
THANON CHARODVITHITONG
THANON VICHIEN CHAMNONG
THANON BAMUANG
THANON MAHARAT
THANON SINGHAWAT
24-hour Clinic
Police Station
THANON PRAMPRACHA
N
0
100m

The ruins

Just outside the entrance to the central zone, the **Ramkhamhaeng National Museum's** (daily 9am–4pm; B30) collection is not very inspiring, but it does include a copy of King Ramkhamhaeng's famous stele. Turn left inside the gate to the central zone for Sukhothai's most important site, the enormous **Wat Mahathat** compound, packed with the remains of scores of monuments and surrounded, like a city within a city, by a moat. It was the spiritual epicentre of the city, the king's temple and symbol of his power.

A few hundred metres southwest, the triple corn-cob-shaped prangs of **Wat Sri Sawai** indicate that this was once a Hindu shrine for the Khmers; the square base inside the central prang supported the Khmer Shiva lingam (phallus). Just west, **Wat Trapang Ngoen** rises gracefully from an island in the middle of the eponymous "silver pond". North of the chedi, notice the fluid lines of the walking Buddha mounted onto a brick wall – a classic example of Sukhothai sculpture. Taking the water feature one step further, **Wat Sra Sri** commands a fine position on two connecting islands north of Wat Trapang Ngoen; its bell-shaped chedi with a tapering spire and square base shows a strong Sri Lankan influence.

The most interesting of the outlying temples are in the north and east zones. Continuing north of Wat Sra Sri, cross the city walls into the north zone and you'll find **Wat Sri Chum**, which boasts Sukhothai's largest surviving Buddha image. The enormous brick-and-stucco seated Buddha, measuring over 11m from knee to knee and almost 15m high, peers through the slit in its custom-built temple. About 1km east of the city walls, the best temple in the east zone is **Wat Chang Lom**, just off the road to New Sukhothai, near Thai Village Hotel. Chang Lom means "Surrounded by Elephants": the main feature here is a large, Sri Lankan-style, bell-shaped chedi encircled by a frieze of pachyderm.

Accommodation

99 Guest House 234/6 Soi Panitsan (Panichsan) ⓣ055 611315, ⓔninetynine_gh@yahoo.com. Tiny, homely guesthouse with just three simple double rooms and a three-bed B80 dorm. Within walking distance of the bus station, or a 10min walk from the town centre. ❶

Ban Thai Guest House 38 Th Pravetnakorn ⓣ055 610163, ⓦwww.geocities.com/guesthouse_banthai. A comfortable budget option with a few simple rooms and some classier wooden bungalows. Also runs recommended cycle trips. ❶–❷

Lotus Village 170 Th Ratchathani, but also accessible from Th Rajuthit ⓣ055 621484, ⓦwww.lotus-village.com. Stylish accommodation in a traditional Thai compound of elegant teak houses. Some a/c. ❸–❺

Number 4 Guest House 140/4 Soi Thongham, off Th Charodvithitong ⓣ055 610165. Laid-back, slightly alternative guesthouse comprising ten rattan bungalows in a tranquil spot. Thai cooking courses available. Accessible on foot from the bus station, or a 10min walk from the town centre. ❶

Old City Guest House Opposite the entrance to the museum on Th Charodvithitong in Old Sukhothai ⓣ055 697515. Has a big range of accommodation, from small, dark cheap rooms with shared baths to large, quite plush, a/c versions with TV. ❶–❷

Eating

One of the best **places to eat** in New Sukhothai is the night market, which sets up every Wednesday and Thursday near the post office on the southeastern end of Thanon Nikhon Kasem. There's another smaller, nightly, gathering of hot-food stalls in front of Wat Ratchathani on Thanon Charodvithitong, and a permanent covered area for night market-style restaurants on the soi between Thanon Ramkhamhaeng and Thanon Nikhon Kasem.

Chu Ran Vegetarian Restaurant Next to the temple on Th Charodvithitong; look for the sign that proclaims "Eat 'J' One Meal, Ten Thousand Lives Escaped". Typically cheap veggie curry shop, with dishes priced at B20. Daily 7am–3pm.

Dream Café 88/1 Th Singhawat. A cosy coffee-shop atmosphere, with walls full of curios and a mid-priced menu of fiery Thai curries, fresh

Vietnamese-style spring rolls, deep-fried banana-flower fritters – and gin-and-tonics.
Khun Tanode Th Charodvithitong. A breezy river-side location and cheap food, including crispy-fried chicken drumsticks in Sukhothai sauce.

Phibai Corner of Th Prasertpong and Th Nikhon Kasem. Popular DIY barbecue restaurant where B100 gets you six different kinds of meat and fish to cook in a steamboat at your own table.

Tak

The provincial capital of **TAK**, 79km west of Sukhothai, is of little interest to tourists except as a place to change buses for continuing north to Lampang and Chiang Mai, south to Ayutthaya and Bangkok, or west to Mae Sot and Umphang. The **bus terminal** is about 3km east of the town centre. **TAT** has an office in the town centre at 193 Thanon Taksin (8.30am–4.30pm; ⓣ055 514341, ⓔtattak@tat.or.th). If you need a **hotel**, try the slightly faded *Mae Ping*, across the road from the market at 231 Thanon Mahattai Bamroong (ⓣ055 511807; ❶–❷).

Mae Sot

Located 100km west of Tak and only 6km from the Burmese border, **MAE SOT** boasts a thriving trade in gems and teak and a rich ethnic mix of Burmese, Karen, Hmong and Thai, plus a lively injection of committed NGO expats working with the thousands of refugees from Burma. There's little to see in the small town apart from several glittering Burmese-style temples, but it's a relaxed place to hang out before heading down to Umphang for some trekking (see p.1004). There are no exchange facilities in Umphang, so change money in one of the booths on Mae Sot's Thanon Prasat Vithi (Mon–Fri 8.30am–3.30pm), where there are also ATMs.

Frequent songthaews run from just west of the market on Thanon Prasat Vithi to the Burmese border at **Rim Moei**, 6km from Mae Sot, where a large, slightly tacky market for Burmese handicrafts and other goods crowds the banks of the River Moei. At the time of writing, access to the Burmese village of Myawaddy on the opposite bank of the River Moei is only open to farangs for a day's shopping (B500 entry); visitors are allowed no further into Burma. When coming back through Thai customs (daily 6am–6pm) you will automatically be given a new one-month Thai visa.

Practicalities

There are several different **bus** and **songthaew** terminals across town. Government minivans to and from Tak, and songthaews to and from Mae Sariang, use a depot north off Thanon Indharakhiri, about 200m behind the police station. Buses to and from Chiang Mai, Chiang Rai, Mae Sai and Lampang use the stand on Thanon Indharakhiri, about 150m east of the police station, while buses to and from Bangkok use the bus station east of town near the Highway 105/1090 intersection. Songthaews and minivans to and from Phitsanulok and Sukhothai arrive at a terminus on Thanon Banthung on the southern edge of town. You can also **fly** into Mae Sot from Bangkok; the airport is 3km west of town and the Thai Airways office (ⓣ055 531730) is at 76/1 Thanon Prasat Vithi. There is no TAT office here, but both *Bai Fern* and *Khrua Canadian* restaurants are good sources of local **information. Internet** access is available at Southeast Tours on Thanon Indharakiri, the post office is further east along the same road, and the government telephone office is at the far west end of Thanon Indharakiri, about 800m from the town centre. You can **rent motorbikes** from a bike-repair shop near the Bangkok Bank on Thanon Prasat Vithi as well as from *Bai Fern*. Donations of clothes and medicines for the refugees living at the nine camps along the nearby Burmese border can be left at *Krua Canadian* and *Bai Fern* restaurants.

The most popular **place to stay** in the centre of town is the welcoming *Bai Fern Guest House* (Ⓣ055 533343, Ⓔrungrapee@hotmail.com; ❶), at 660/2 Thanon Indharakiri, which offers noisy, basic rooms but a great restaurant. About 100m further east along Thanon Indharakiri, behind the posh *Salakthai* restaurant, *Mate's Place* (❶) has nice, simple rooms with shared bath in a big, old wooden house, while *Green Guest House*, across the stream from the Tak/Mae Sariang bus station at 406/8 Thanon Indharakiri, offers good, clean, en-suite rooms set round a yard (Ⓣ055 533207; ❶).

For classy and unusual **food** visit *Bai Fern* (see above), nearby *Khun's*, or *Krua Canadian Restaurant*, diagonally across from the police station, just off Thanon Indharakiri, all of which are highly recommended.

Umphang

Even if you don't fancy joining a trek, it's worth considering making the spectacular 164-kilometre trip south from Mae Sot to the village of **UMPHANG**, both for

Trekking around Umphang

The focus of most Umphang treks is the three-tiered **Tee Lor Su Waterfall**, which is at its most thunderous just after the rainy season in November, when you can also swim in the beautifully blue lower pool, though trails can still be muddy at this time. During the dry season (Dec–April), you can get close to the falls by road and it's usually possible to climb up to one of the upper tiers. At other times, the falls are reached by a combination of rafting and walking. It's possible to arrange your trek in Mae Sot, but the best place to set up a trip is in Umphang itself. A **typical trek** lasts three days and features rafting, hot springs, three or four hours' walking per day, a night in a Karen village, and an elephant ride. Guides should provide tents, bedrolls, mosquito nets and sleeping bags, plus food and drinking water; trekkers may be asked to help carry some of the gear. Bring a fleece as nights can get pretty chilly. Costs range from B3500 for a three-day trek to U$400 for seven days. From June through October, other trips feature whitewater rafting from the Karen village of Umphang Khi via the forty-plus rapids of the Umphang River, as well as one- and two-day rafting outings to Thi Lor Leh Falls.

Mae Sot trekking operators

Khun Om c/o *Number 4 Guest House*, 736 Th Indharakiri Ⓣ055 544976, Ⓦwww.geocities.com/no4guesthouse. The treks run by the taciturn Khun Om get rave reviews, particularly his seven-day expedition. Book ahead by email if possible.

Max One Tour In the *DK Hotel* plaza at 296/1 Th Indharakiri Ⓣ055 542942, Ⓦwww.maxonetour.com. A Mae Sot outlet for the Umphang-based Umphang Hill trek operator (see below).

Umphang trekking operators

BL Tour West of the wat at 1/438 Th Umphang-Palata Ⓣ055 561021. Enthusiastic and well-informed guides earn this outfit lots of good reviews. Has accommodation (❷) in a glorious rural spot 2km east of town.

Trekker Hill 700m northeast of the wat, off Thanon Pravitpaiwan Ⓣ055 561090. Mr Tee and his "jungle team" of five guides get good reviews. Offers accommodation for trekkers in en-suite double bungalows at B200

Umphang Hill At *Umphang Hill Resort* on Th Umphang-Palata, but can also be booked through Max One Tour in Mae Sot Ⓣ055 561063, Ⓦwww.umphanghill.com. Very efficiently run, this reputable place often undercuts rival outfits and has English-speaking staff at the office throughout the day.

the fine mountain scenery and for the buzz of being in such an isolated part of Thailand. Songthaews leave Mae Sot from a spot two blocks south of Thanon Prasat Vithi (hourly 7.30am–3.30pm). The drive takes about four hours and the road – dubbed the "Sky Highway" – careers round the edges of endless steep-sided valleys. Umphang is effectively a dead end, so you need to return to Mae Sot to continue anywhere else; return songthaews leave hourly throughout the day.

Surrounded by mountains and sited at the confluence of the Mae Khlong and Umphang rivers, Umphang itself is small and quiet. It has few signed roads, but the two main points of **orientation** are the river at the far western end of the village, and the wat – about 500m east of the river – that marks its centre. Most of the shops and restaurants are clustered along the two roads that run parallel to the wat; there is an **Internet** centre (daily 8am–8pm) to the south of the temple on Thanon Pravitpaiwan, and a pharmacy close by the temple on the same road. Mountain **bikes** can be rented from Tu Ka Su.

In the heart of the village, about 500m northeast of the wat at 106 Thanon Umphang-Palata, *Phu Doi Campsite* (ⓣ055 561049, ⓦwww.phudoi.com; ❷) offers decent en-suite **rooms** in two wooden houses overlooking a pond. Most of Umphang's other accommodation is down by the river, to the west of the wat, along Thanon Umphang–Palata: *Boonyaporn Garden Huts* on the east bank (ⓣ055 561093; ❶–❷) has simple rattan huts in a garden, plus some more comfortable en-suite wooden huts. Across on the west bank, *Tu Ka Su* (ⓣ055 561295; ❸) has pricier but nicely designed en-suite wooden cabins in a pretty garden. For **meals**, try *Phu Doi Restaurant* (closed Sundays), on Thanon Pravitpaiwan just north of the temple, or the inexpensive nearby noodle shop *Noong Koong*.

10.3

The north

Beyond the northern plains, the climate becomes more temperate, nurturing the fertile land that gave the old kingdom of the **north** the name of **Lanna**, "the land of a million rice fields". Until the beginning of the last century, Lanna was a largely independent region, with its own styles of art and architecture. Its capital, the cool, pleasant city of **Chiang Mai**, is now a major travellers' centre and the most popular base from which to organize treks to nearby hilltribe villages. Another great way of exploring the scenic countryside up here is to rent a jeep or motorbike and make the six hundred-kilometre loop over the forested western mountains, via the backpackers' honeypot of **Pai**, to **Mae Hong Son** and back. **Nan**, to the east of Chiang Mai, is largely untouristy, but combines rich mountain scenery with eclectic temple art. Heading north from Chiang Mai towards the Burmese border brings you to the increasingly upmarket town of **Chiang Rai**, and then on to the frontier settlement of **Mae Sai**, the so-called "**Golden Triangle**" at Sop Ruak, and the ruined temples of **Chiang Saen**. **Chiang Khong**, on the Mekong River, is an important crossing point to Laos.

The best **map** of the area is *Thailand North* (Berndtson & Berndtson; 1:750,000), which shows accurately the crisscross of dirt tracks and minor roads, and also contains a 1:500,000 inset of the Golden Triangle and a 1:300,000 inset of the Chiang Mai area.

Hilltribe treks

Trekking in the mountains of northern Thailand – which is what brings most travellers here – differs from trekking in most other parts of the world, in that the emphasis is not primarily on the scenery but on the region's inhabitants. Northern Thailand's **hilltribes**, now numbering over 800,000 people living in around 3500 villages, have so far preserved their way of life with little change over thousands of years (you'll increasingly hear the more politically correct term "mountain people" used to describe them).Visiting their settlements on a trek entails walking for several hours between villages, and over a hundred thousand travellers now go trekking each year, the majority heading to certain well-trodden areas such as the Mae Tang Valley, 40km northwest of Chiang Mai, and the hills around the Kok River west of Chiang Rai. Beyond the basic level of disturbance caused by any tourism, this steady flow of trekkers creates pressures for the traditionally insular hilltribes. Foreigners unfamiliar with hilltribe customs can easily cause grave offence, especially those who go looking for drugs. Most tribespeople are genuinely welcoming to foreigners, appreciating the contact with Westerners. Nonetheless, it is important to take a responsible attitude when trekking.

The hilltribes are big business in northern Thailand: in **Chiang Mai**, there are over two hundred agencies that between them cover just about all the trekkable areas in the north. **Chiang Rai** is the second-biggest trekking centre, and agencies can also be found in **Mae Hong Son**, **Pai** and **Nan**, although these usually arrange treks only to the villages in their immediate area. Guided trekking on a much smaller scale than in the north is available in Umphang (see p.1004), Kanchanaburi (see p.988) and Sangkhlaburi (see p.992).

Trekking etiquette

As guests, it's up to farangs to adapt to the customs of the hilltribes and not to make a nuisance of themselves.

• Dress modestly, avoiding skimpy shorts and vests.

• Before entering a hilltribe village, look out for taboo signs of woven bamboo strips on the ground outside the village entrance, which mean a special ceremony is taking place and that you should not enter. Be careful about what you touch. In Akha villages, keep your hands off cult structures such as the entrance gates and the giant swing. Do not touch or photograph any shrines, or sit underneath them. You'll have to pay a fine for any violation of local customs.

• Most villagers do not like to be photographed. Be particularly careful with pregnant women and babies – most tribes believe cameras affect the soul of the foetus or newborn. Always ask first.

• Taking gifts is dubious practice: writing materials for children and clothing are welcome, as are sewing needles, but sweets and cigarettes may encourage begging.

The basics

On any trek, you'll need walking boots or training shoes, long trousers (against thorns and wet-season leeches), a hat, a sarong or towel, a sweater or fleece, plus insect repellent and, if possible, a mosquito net. On an organized trek, water, blankets or a sleeping bag, and possibly a small backpack, should be supplied. It's wise not to take anything valuable with you; most guesthouses in Chiang Mai have safes, but check their reputation with other travellers, and sign an inventory – theft and credit-card abuse are not uncommon.

Organized treks

Organized treks usually last for three days, have six to twelve people in the group, and follow a route regularly used by the agency. There will be a few hours' walking every day, plus the possibility of an elephant ride and a trip on a bamboo raft. The group usually sleeps on the floor of the village headman's hut, and the guide cooks communal meals. A typical three-day trek costs B1800–2000 in Chiang Mai, sometimes less in other towns, and much less without rafting and elephant rides.

Word of mouth is often the best yardstick when choosing a trekking agency. If you want to trek with a small group, get an assurance from your agency that you won't be tagged onto a larger group. Meet the guides, who should speak reasonable English, know about hilltribe culture and have a certificate from the Tourism Authority of Thailand (TAT). Check how much walking is involved per day, and ask about the menu. Also enquire about transport from base at the beginning and end of the trek, which sometimes entails a long public bus ride. Before setting off, each trek should be registered with the tourist police in case of any trouble.

Independent trekking

The options for **independent trekking** are limited, chiefly by the poor mapping of the area – there are Royal Thai Survey Department 1:50,000 maps but each covers a very limited area, For most independent travellers, the only feasible approach is to use as a base one of the guesthouses set deep in the countryside, within walking range of hilltribe villages. These include *Wilderness Lodge* near Mae Suya (see p.1022), *Cave Lodge* at Ban Tum and *Lisu Lodge* near Soppong (see p.1022).

The hilltribes

Within the small geographical area of northern Thailand there are at least ten different **hilltribes**, many of them divided into distinct subgroups. Originating in various parts of China and Southeast Asia, the tribes are often termed Fourth World people, in that they migrate without regard for established national boundaries. Most arrived in Thailand in the twentieth century, and many have tribal relatives in other parts of Southeast Asia. (Note that the Thai Yai – or Shan – are not a hilltribe, but a subgroup of Thais.)

The tribes are mostly pre-literate societies, with sophisticated systems of customs, laws and beliefs. They are predominantly animists, believing all natural objects to be inhabited by spirits, which must be propitiated to prevent harm to the family or village. The base of their economy is swidden agriculture, a crude form of shifting cultivation, but many villages have in the past taken up large-scale opium production. In recent years, however, the Thai government has largely eradicated the production of opium on Thai soil, although the cash crops introduced in its place have often led to environmental damage in the form of pollution and deforestation. The most conspicuous characteristics of the hilltribes are their exquisitely crafted costumes, though many men and children now adopt Western clothes for everyday wear. To learn more about the tribes, visit the Tribal Museum in Chiang Mai (see p.1013) or the Hilltribe Museum in Chiang Rai (see p.1025).

Karen

The **Karen** form by far the largest hilltribe group in Thailand (pop. 500,000), and began to arrive here in the seventeenth century, though many are recent refugees from Burma. Most of them live in a broad tract of land west of Chiang Mai, stretching all the way down to Kanchanaburi. Karen do not live in extended family groups, so their wooden stilt houses are small. Unmarried Karen women wear loose V-necked shift dresses, often decorated with grass seeds at the seams; some subgroups decorate them more elaborately, Sgaw girls with a woven red or pink band above the waist, and Pwo girls with woven red patterns at the hem. Married women wear blouses and skirts in bold red or blue. Men wear blue, baggy trousers, also with red or blue shirts.

Hmong

The **Hmong** (or Meo; pop. 110,000) originated in central China or Mongolia and are now found widely in northern Thailand; they are still the most widespread minority group in south China. There are two subgroups: the Blue Hmong, who live to the west of Chiang Mai; and the White Hmong, who are found to the east. Hmong villages are usually built at high altitudes, and most Hmong live in extended families in traditional houses with dirt floors and a roof descending almost to ground level. Blue Hmong women wear intricately embroidered pleated skirts decorated with parallel horizontal bands of red, pink, blue and white; their jackets are of black satin, with wide orange and yellow embroidered cuffs and lapels. White Hmong women wear white skirts for special occasions, black baggy trousers for everyday use and simple jackets with blue cuffs. Men of both groups generally wear baggy black pants with colourful sashes and embroidered jackets. All the Hmong are famous for their chunky silver jewellery.

Lahu

The **Lahu** (pop. 80,000) originated in the Tibetan highlands and centuries ago migrated to southern China, Burma and Laos; only since the end of the nineteenth century did they begin to come into Thailand from northern Burma. Their settlements are concentrated close to the Burmese border, in Chiang Rai, northern Chiang Mai and Mae Hong Son provinces. The Lahu language has become the lingua franca of the hilltribes, since the Lahu often hire out their labour. About one-third of Lahu have been converted to Christianity (through exposure in colonial Burma), and many have abandoned their traditional way of life as a result. The remaining animist Lahu believe in a village guardian spirit, who is often worshipped at a central temple that is surrounded by banners and streamers of white and yellow flags. Ordinary houses are built on high stilts and thatched with grass. Some Lahu women wear a distinctive black cloak with diagonal white stripes, decorated in bold red and yellow at the top of the sleeve, but many groups now wear Thai dress. The tribe is famous for its richly embroidered shoulder bags.

Akha

The poorest of the hilltribes, the **Akha** (pop. 50,000) migrated from Tibet over two thousand years ago to Yunnan in China, where many still live. From around 1910, the tribe began to settle in Thailand and are now found in Chiang Rai, Chiang Mai, Lampang and Phrae provinces. Every Akha village is entered through ceremonial gates decorated with carvings of human attributes – even cars and aeroplanes – to indicate to the spirit world that beyond here only humans should pass. To touch or disrespect any of these carvings is punishable by fines or sacrifices. Akha houses are recognizable by their low stilts and steeply pitched roofs. Women wear elaborate headgear consisting of a conical wedge of white beads interspersed with silver coins, topped with plumes of red taffeta and framed by dangling silver balls. They also sport decorated tube-shaped ankle-to-knee leggings, an above-the-knee black skirt with a white beaded centrepiece, and a loose-fitting black jacket with heavily embroidered cuffs and lapels.

Mien

The **Mien** (or Yao; pop. 42,000) consider themselves the aristocrats of the hilltribes. Originating in central China, they began migrating more than two thousand years ago southwards to southern China, Vietnam, Laos and Thailand. They are now widely scattered throughout the north, especially around Nan, Phayao and Chiang Rai. They are the only people to have a written language, and a codified religion based on medieval Chinese Taoism, although in recent years many have converted to Christianity and Buddhism. Mien women wear long black jackets with lapels of bright scarlet wool, and heavily embroidered loose trousers and turbans. Babies wear embroidered caps with red or pink pom-poms.

Lisu

The **Lisu** (pop. 30,000), who originated in eastern Tibet, first arrived in Thailand in 1921 and are found mostly in the west, particularly between Chiang Mai and Mae Hong Son. They are organized into patriarchal clans that have authority over many villages, and their strong sense of clan rivalry often results in public violence. The Lisu live in extended families at moderate to high altitudes, in bamboo houses built on the ground. The women wear a blue or green parti-coloured knee-length tunic, split up the sides to the waist, with a wide black belt and blue or green pants. Men wear green, pink or yellow baggy pants and a blue jacket.

Lawa

The **Lawa** people (pop. 17,000) have inhabited Thailand since at least the eighth century and they were certainly here when the first Thais arrived eight hundred years ago. As a result, most Lawa villages look no different from Thai settlements and most Lawa speak Thai as their first language. But between Hot, Mae Sariang and Mae Hong Son, the Lawa still live a largely traditional life. Unmarried Lawa women wear strings of orange and yellow beads, white blouses edged with pink, and tight skirts in parallel bands of blue, black, yellow and pink. After marriage, they don a long fawn dress, but still wear the beads. All the women wear their hair tied in a turban, and some men wear light-coloured baggy pants and tunics.

Chiang Mai

Despite recent and rapid economic progress, **CHIANG MAI** – Thailand's second city – manages to preserve a little of the atmosphere of an overgrown village alongside its modern urban sophistication. The old quarter, set within a two-kilometre-square moat, has retained many of its traditional wooden houses, and inviting guesthouses, good markets, a broad range of courses – from cookery and massage to meditation, yoga and t'ai chi – and plenty of sights make it a hugely appealing place to many travellers. Plus, of course, Chiang Mai is the main centre for **hilltribe trekking**.

Arrival and information

Most people arrive at the **train station** on Thanon Charoen Muang, just over 2km from the landmark Tha Pae Gate on the eastern side of town, or at the long-distance **Arcade bus station** on Thanon Kaeo Nawarat, 3km out to the northeast. Getting from either of these to the centre is easy by songthaew or tuk-tuk. Beware that many of the low-cost private buses from Bangkok's Thanon Khao San stop on a remote part of the Superhighway, where they "sell" their passengers to various guesthouse touts. Arriving at the **airport**, 3km southwest of the centre, you'll find banks, a post office, and taxis (around B150 to the city centre). **TAT** have an office (daily 8.30am–4.30pm; ⓣ053 248607) at 105/1 Thanon Chiang Mai–Lamphun, on the east bank of the river. Nancy Chandler's **map** of Chiang Mai (B140) is very handy for a detailed exploration.

City transport

Although you can comfortably walk between the most central temples, **bicycles** are handy and can be rented for B30–50 a day at places around Tha Pae Gate. Many

Trekking and other outdoor activities around Chiang Mai

Eagle House (see p.1011) is a reliable **trekking** operator, and passes on a proportion of costs towards funding projects in hilltribe villages. As well as treks, Chiangmai Green Alternative Tours, 31 Th Chiangmai–Lamphun (ⓣ053 247374, ⓔcmgreent@cmnet.co.th), offers nature field trips, birdwatching and **mountain-biking**. The last-mentioned is the speciality of Northern Trails (ⓦwww.northerntrails.com), who organize one-day rides near Chiang Dao, as well as multiple-day trips and customized itineraries in Thailand, Laos or Cambodia. Northern Trails are represented by adventure tourism agency Contact Travel, 73/7 Thanon Charoen Prathet (ⓣ053 277178, ⓦwww.activethailand.com), who also offer treks, lake- and river-kayaking and Thai Adventure Rafting's **whitewater rafting** trips on the Pai River (see p.1025). For a one-day rafting trip closer to Chiang Mai, on the Mae Tang River, Wild Rivers, in the Peak Plaza on Thanon Chang Klan (ⓣ053 818244), are recommended. There's a fifteen-metre **rock-climbing** wall at The Peak on Thanon Chang Klan (ⓣ053 820777 or 01 716 4032, ⓦwww.thepeakthailand.com), where you can take three-day courses and arrange out-of-town climbing trips. Chiang Mai Rock Climbing Adventures, 55/3 Thanon Ratchaphakinai (ⓣ06 911 1470, ⓦwww.thailandclimbing.com), also lead climbing and caving trips and a wide range of courses, and offer equipment rental, crag info and a partner-finding service. A trip that's more difficult to categorize is to the **Elephant Nature Park**, about an hour north of Chiang Mai. It's essentially a hospital for sick elephants, but hands-on educational – and recreational – visits by the public are encouraged, including signing up as a paying volunteer for a week or two. Have a look at their detailed website (ⓦwww.thaifocus.com/elephant) or contact the park's Chiang Mai office at Gem Travel, Soi 6, Thanon Charoen Prathet (ⓣ053 272855).

places in the same area rent out **motorbikes** (from around B100 per day); the reliable Queen Bee Travel Service, just south of Tha Pae Gate at 5 Thanon Moonmuang (☎053 275525), can also offer limited insurance. Red **songthaews** (other colours serve outlying villages) act as shared taxis within the city, picking up people headed in roughly the same direction and taking each to their specific destination; expect to pay around B10 from Wat Phra Singh to Tha Pae Gate. The city is also stuffed with **tuk-tuks** (around B50 from the train station to Tha Pae Gate) and **samlors**.

Accommodation

The main concentration of **guesthouses** is on the surprisingly quiet sois around the eastern side of the old moat and Tha Pae Gate. This puts you between the old town and the new town, in the middle of a larder of Thai and travellers' restaurants. Many of the least expensive guesthouses make their money from hilltribe trekking, which can be convenient, as a trek often needs a lot of organizing beforehand, but some put pressure on guests to trek; most of the places listed below can arrange trekking, but at none of them should you get this kind of undue hassle.

Eagle House 1 16 Soi 3, Th Chang Moi Kao ☎053 235387 and *Eagle House 2*, 26 Soi 2, Th Ratchawithi ☎053 210620; Ⓦwww.eaglehouse.com. Two friendly guesthouses with garden cafés and en-suite rooms (more comfortable at *Eagle House 2*), plus dorms (B80); well-organized treks and cookery courses on offer, plus free pick-ups from train, bus or airport. ❶–❷

Galare Guest House 7 Soi 2, Th Charoen Prathet ☎053 818887 or 053 821011, Ⓦwww.galare.com. Well-run, popular, upmarket guesthouse with a shady riverside lawn; a/c and hot water. ❺

Julie Guest House 7/1 Soi 5, Th Phra Pokklao ☎053 274355, Ⓦwww.julieguesthouse.com. Laid-back place in a concrete block, with shared or en-suite hot showers, a roof terrace with hammocks, and a shady garden café. Dorm B60, ❶

Kavil Guest House 10/1 Soi 5, Th Ratchdamnoen ☎053 224740. Smallish, friendly, well-run place in a quiet soi with fan and a/c rooms; all have hot-water bathrooms. ❶–❷

Lek House 22 Th Chaiyapoom near Somphet Market ☎053 252686. Central and set back from the road, with clean, en-suite rooms around a garden. ❶

Libra House 28 Soi 9, Th Moonmuang ☎053 210687, Ⓔlibra_guesthouse@hotmail.com. Excellent, modern trekking-oriented guesthouse. All rooms en suite, some with hot water, some a/c. ❶–❷

River View Lodge 25 Soi 2, Th Charoen Prathet ☎053 271109–10, Ⓦwww.riverviewlodgch.com. Tasteful, quiet and well-run alternative to international-class hotels, with a beautiful riverside garden and a swimming pool. ❻

Sarah Guest House 20 Soi 4, Th Tha Pae ☎053 208271, Ⓦwww.sarahguesthouse.com. A very clean, peaceful, central establishment with a courtyard café and en-suite rooms, some with hot water, some a/c. ❶–❷

Supreme Guest House 44/1 Soi 9, Th Moonmuang ☎053 222480. Friendly German-run guesthouse in a modern concrete block with en-suite hot showers, a pleasant roof veranda and a useful library/secondhand bookshop. ❷

Your House 8 Soi 2, Th Ratchawithi ☎053 217492, Ⓦwww.yourhouseguesthouse.com. Welcoming old-town teak house. Big rooms with shared hot-water bathrooms, plus some smaller en-suite ones in a modern annexe, some a/c. Good French food and free pick-ups from train, bus or airport. ❶–❸

The City

If you see only one temple in Chiang Mai it should be **Wat Phra Singh**, at the far western end of Thanon Ratchdamnoen in the old town. Its largest structure, a colourful modern viharn fronted by naga balustrades, hides from view the beautiful Viharn Lai Kam, a wooden gem of early nineteenth-century Lanna architecture, with its squat, multi-tiered roof and exquisitely carved and gilded pediment. Inside sits a portly, radiant and much-revered bronze Buddha in fifteenth-century Lanna style. The walls are enlivened by murals depicting daily life in the north a hundred years ago.

A ten-minute walk east along Thanon Ratchadamnoen brings you to **Wat Chedi Luang** on Thanon Phra Pokklao, where an enormous crumbling pink-brick chedi,

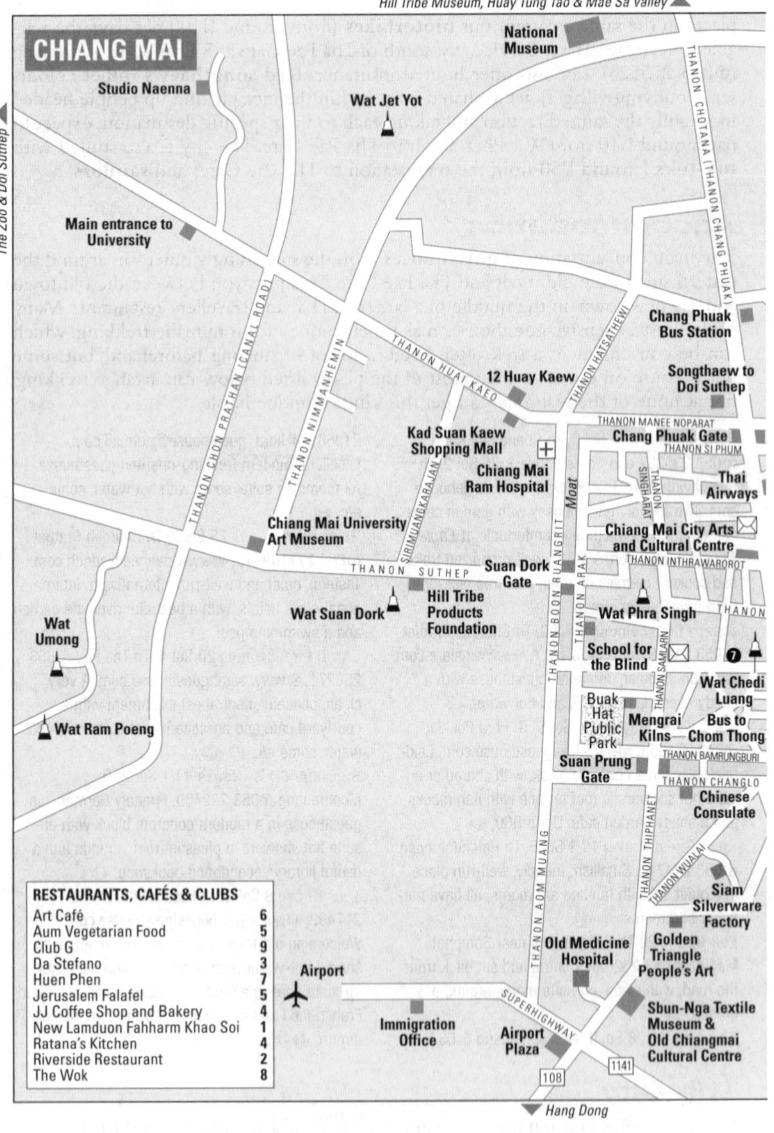

which once housed the Emerald Buddha but was toppled by an earthquake in 1545, presents an intriguing spectacle – especially in the early evening when the resident bats flit around. On the north side of the chedi, "Monk Chat" is advertised (Mon–Sat noon–6.30pm), giving you a chance to meet and talk to the monks in English. Five minutes' walk north on Phra Pokklao, in the elegant 1920s former provincial office, the **Chiang Mai City Arts and Cultural Centre** (Tues–Sun 8.30am–5pm; free) is an informative museum of the history, customs and culture of the city and the region that's well worth a visit. The oldest temple in Chiang Mai, **Wat Chiang**

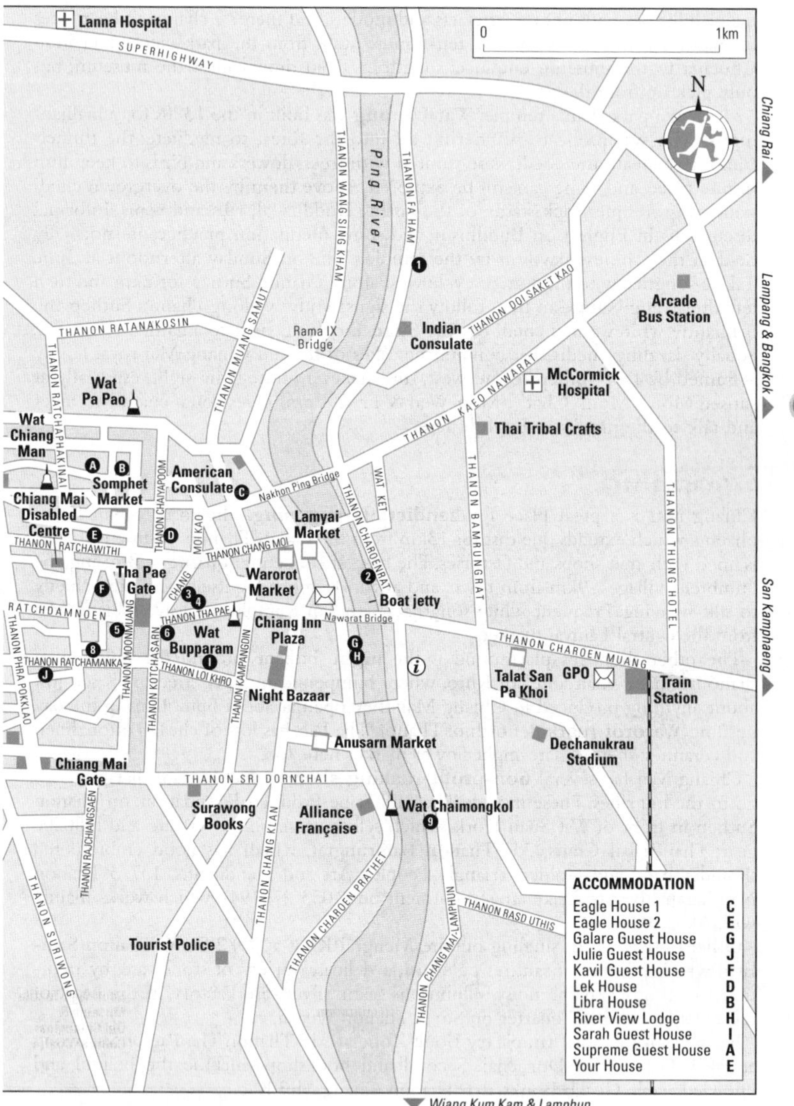

Man, is ten minutes' walk away on Thanon Ratchaphakinai and houses two graceful and very holy Buddha images.

For a fuller picture of Lanna art, head for the **National Museum**, on the northwestern outskirts of Chiang Mai (Wed–Sun 9am–4pm; B30), which houses a wealth of Buddha images and a fine collection of ceramics. To get there, charter a tuk-tuk or songthaew from the centre of town. One kilometre north of the Superhighway off Thanon Chotana, the very worthwhile **Tribal Museum** (daily 9am–4pm; free) stands in the artfully landscaped Ratchamangkla Park. The exhibition introduces the major hilltribes with photos, artefacts and models, and there's a chance to hear tapes of traditional music. It's about a ten-minute walk from the park gate on Thanon Chotana to the museum entrance; songthaews can drop you at the museum, but only pick up from the gate.

More of a park than a temple, **Wat Umong** was built in the 1380s for a brilliant monk who was prone to wandering off into the forest to meditate; the tunnels (umong) beneath the chedi were painted with trees, flowers and birds to keep him in one place, and some can still be explored. Above them by the overgrown chedi stands a grotesque black statue of the fasting Buddha, all ribs and veins. Informal discussions in English on Buddhism, and some meditation practice, are normally held in the Chinese pavilion by the temple's lake on Sunday afternoons at 3pm. Take a songthaew to the wat, or cycle west along Thanon Suthep for 2km and turn left after Wang Nam Gan then follow the signs. Midway along Thanon Suthep, the brilliantly whitewashed chedi of **Wat Suan Dork** sits next to a garden of smaller, equally dazzling chedis that contain the ashes of the old Chiang Mai royal family – framed by Doi Suthep to the west, this makes a photogenic sight, especially at sunset. More "Monk Chat" (Mon, Wed & Fri 5–7pm) gives you a chance to meet and talk to the monks in English here.

Shopping

Chiang Mai is a great place for **handicrafts shopping**. The road to San Kamphaeng, which extends due east for 13km from the end of Thanon Charoen Muang, is lined with craft shops and factories. The biggest concentrations are at Bo Sang, the "umbrella village", 9km from town, and at San Kamphaeng itself, dedicated chiefly to silk-weaving. Frequent white songthaews to San Kamphaeng leave Chiang Mai from the central Lamyai market.

The other shopper's playground is the **night bazaar**, around the junction of thanons Chang Klan and Loi Khro, where bumper-to-bumper street stalls sell just about anything produced in Chiang Mai; they open at about 5pm. During the day, bustling **Warorot market**, north of Thanon Tha Pae, has lots of cheap cotton, linen and ceramics; there's a late-night flower market here, too.

Chiang Mai has several **non-profit-making shops**, which ensure that proceeds go to the hilltribes. These include The Hill Tribe Products Foundation, on Thanon Suthep in front of Wat Suan Dork, which sells cotton, silk, silverware and hilltribe gear; Thai Tribal Crafts, 204 Thanon Bamrungrat, which has good embroidered shoulder bags; and Golden Triangle People's Art and Handicrafts, 137/3 Thanon Nantharam (best to make an appointment on ⓣ053 276194), which works mainly with Akha women.

Other outlets worth singling out are Mengrai Kilns at 79/2 Soi 6, Thanon Samlarn, which produces beautiful **celadon**, a delicate variety of stoneware, by traditional methods; and the noisy, sulphurous Siam Silverware Factory, in the heart of the old **silversmiths'** quarter on Soi 3, Thanon Wualai.

For new **books and maps**, try Book Zone at 318 Thanon Tha Pae or Surawong at 54/1 Thanon Sri Dornchai. Secondhand bookshops include the helpful and knowledgeable Gecko Books, 2/6 Thanon Chang Moi Kao.

Eating and drinking

Northern **food** has been strongly influenced by Burmese cuisine, especially in curries such as the spicy *kaeng hang lay*, made with pork, ginger and tamarind. Another favourite local dish, especially for lunch, is *khao soi*, a thick broth of curry and coconut cream, with egg noodles and meat. There are several good **night markets**: Anusarn, off Thanon Chang Klan; along Thanon Bamrungburi by Chiang Mai Gate; and at Talat San Pa Khoi, out towards the train station on the south side of Thanon Charoen Muang.

Art Café 263/1 Th Tha Pae. Popular, reasonably priced farang hangout with all the café favourites and a big veggie menu.

Aum Vegetarian Food On the corner of thanons Ratchdamnoen and Moonmuang. Small and relaxing long-time favourite, serving cheap and interesting veggie dishes, Thai desserts and organic hilltribe coffee.

Club G 68/2 Th Chiang Mai–Lamphun, 500m south of TAT. Fun, full-on, sweaty club, packed with young Thais dancing to techno on tables and around their bar stools. No admission charge but pricey drinks.

Da Stefano 2/1–2 Th Chiang Moi Kao. Just round the corner from Tha Pae Gate, Chiang Mai's most popular Italian restaurant, with a winning combination of tasteful ambience, efficient service and delicious food.

Huen Phen 112 Th Ratchamanka. Probably Chiang Mai's most authentic northern restaurant – try the selection of local appetizers – with bags of ambience.

Jerusalem Falafel 35/3 Th Moonmuang. Small and simple a/c café serving pitta bread, home-made cheeses and yoghurts, and inexpensive Israeli food right near Tha Pae Gate.

JJ Coffee Shop and Bakery Th Tha Pae. In bustling, a/c surroundings, all kinds of very popular Thai, Western and veggie food, but best for breakfast, with home-baked croissants, and great homemade muesli and yoghurt.

New Lamduon Fahharm Khao Soi 352/22 Th Charoenrat. Excellent, inexpensive *khao soi* prepared to a secret recipe. Also satay and *som tam*. Daily 9am–3pm.

Ratana's Kitchen 320–322 Th Tha Pae. A favourite among locals both for northern specialities such as *kaeng hang lay* and *khao soi* and for tasty Western breakfasts, sandwiches and steaks.

Riverside Restaurant 9 Th Charoenrat ⓣ053 243239. Archetypal farang bolthole: candlelit terraces by the water, mid-priced Western and Thai food, live bands and reasonable draught beer. Dinner cruises on the river nightly at 8pm.

The Wok 44 Th Ratchamanka. Moderately priced Thai restaurant, with a relaxing ambience, and quality guaranteed as it's run by the Chiang Mai Cookery School.

Listings

Boat trips Converted rice barges leave the jetty beside the *Riverside Restaurant* every couple of hours or so between 10am and 5.30pm and cruise up the Ping River through lush countryside (1hr 40min; B150; ⓣ01 885 0663 or 01 884 4621).

Consulates China, 111 Th Changlo ⓣ053 276125; India, 344 Th Charoenrat ⓣ053 243066; US, 387 Th Witchayanon ⓣ053 252629–31.

Cookery lessons Many guesthouses now offer lessons, but the original – and still the best – courses are run by the Chiang Mai Thai Cookery School, 1–3 Th Moonmuang ⓣ053 206388, ⓦwww.thaicookeryschool.com. One to five days (B900–4200), covering common Thai and traditional Lanna dishes; book ahead. Sign up with the Chiang Mai Thai Farm Cooking School, at 10/1 Soi 5, Thanon Ratchadamnoen (ⓣ053 224740, ⓔthaifarmcooking@hotmail.com), and you can pick your own organic vegetables, herbs and fruits for cooking on their farm thirty minutes' drive from town (B800 per day).

Hospitals 24hr emergency service (and dentistry) at Lanna Hospital, 103 Superhighway (ⓣ053/357234–53), east of Th Chotana; McCormick Hospital on Th Kaeo Nawarat (ⓣ053/241010) and Chiang Mai Ram Hospital at 8 Th Boon Ruangrit (ⓣ053/224851–81) also have good reputations.

Immigration office 300m east of the airport ⓣ053 277510.

Internet access At the Chiang Mai Disabled Centre, 133/1 Thanon Ratchaphakinai (ⓣ053 213941, ⓦwww.infothai.com/disabled), cheap Internet access, among many other services, helps to support the Foundation to Encourage the Potential of Disabled Persons. Click'n'Drink, 147 Thanon Chang Klan near the corner of Thanon Loi Khro stays open until 1am and offers a range of coffees.

Massage Highly respected massages and courses at Old Medicine Hospital, 78/1 Soi Mo Shivagakomarpaj, off Th Wualai ⓣ053 275085, ⓦwww.thaimassageschool.ac.th; shorter courses at the Thai Massage School of Chiang Mai (ⓦwww.1thaimassage.com), which has two locations: TMC1 to the northeast of town on the Mae Jo road, 2km beyond the Superhighway (ⓣ053 854330), and TMC2 on Thanon Nimmanhemin next to Chiang Mai University's Contemporary Museum (ⓣ053 907193). Massages by extremely competent blind masseurs at the School for the Blind, 41 Th Arak ⓣ053 278009, and by disabled masseurs at the Chiang Mai Disabled Centre (see "Internet access" above), and at the well-run and reliable Let's Relax, with two convenient locations on Thanon Chang Klan, in the Chiang Inn Plaza (ⓣ053 818198) and in the Chiangmai Pavilion opposite the *Royal Princess Hotel* (ⓣ053 818498).

Meditation Northern Insight Meditation Centre, at Wat Ram Poeng (aka Wat Tapotaram) on Th Canal near Wat Umong (☎053 278620 extension 13, ⓦwww.watrampoeng.cjb.net), holds disciplined Vipassana courses; the minimum stay is ten days, with a basic course lasting 26 days. The other respected monastery for meditation retreats in the area is Wat Phra That Chom Thong, in Chom Thong 60km southwest of Chiang Mai, where a basic course lasts around 21 days; call as far as possible in advance to book a place (☎053 826869, ⓦwww.sirimangalo.org). For an introduction to meditation and Buddhist culture, sign up for one of the free overnight courses run by Mahachulalongkorn Buddhist University, based at Wat Suan Dork. As places are limited you should make contact in advance (☎09 855 5446 or 053 278967 ext. 200, ⓦwww.cmbu.net).

Post office The GPO is near the train station on Th Charoen Muang (Mon–Fri 8.30am–4.30pm, Sat & Sun 9am–noon). Poste restante should be addressed to: your name, Chiang Mai Post Office, Th Charoen Muang, Chiang Mai 50000.

Telephone services International phones at the Chiang Mai Telecommunication Center (open 24hr) on the Superhighway, just south of the east end of Th Charoen Muang, and at the GPO.

Thai language courses AUA, 24 Th Ratchadamnoen (☎053 211377 or 053 278407, ⓦwww.auathailand.org/chiangmai), for classes and individual tuition.

Tourist police Down a soi behind the *Lanna Palace Hotel*, off Thanon Chang Klan ☎053 278559 or nationwide helpline ☎1155.

Doi Suthep

A jaunt up **Doi Suthep**, the mountain that rises steeply at Chiang Mai's western edge, is the most satisfying short outing you can make from the city, chiefly on account of beautiful **Wat Phra That Doi Suthep**, which dominates the hillside, and, because of a magic relic enshrined in its chedi, is the north's holiest shrine. Its upper terrace is a breathtaking combination of carved wood, filigree and gleaming metal, whose altars and ceremonial umbrellas surround the dazzling gold-plated chedi. Frequent **songthaews** leave the corner of thanons Manee Noparat and Chotana for the sixteen-kilometre trip up the mountain (B40 to the wat, B70 return). The road, although steep in places, is paved all the way and well suited for motorbikes.

Lampang and the Thai Elephant Conservation Centre

The north's second-largest town and an important transport hub, **LAMPANG**, 100km southeast of Chiang Mai, boasts a sedate, traditional charm and a few low-key attractions, notably the imposing, Burmese-influenced **Wat Phra Kaeo Don Tao** on Thanon Phra Kaeo. It's also well worth heading 15km southwest of town to **Wat Phra That Lampang Luang**, a grand and well-preserved capsule of beautiful Lanna art and architecture; take a songthaew from outside the Thai Farmers Bank on Thanon Robwiang.

The **Thai Elephant Conservation Centre** (shows daily 10am & 11am plus Sat & Sun 1.30pm; bathing at 9.45am and 1.15pm; B50; ☎054 229042 or 228034; ⓦwww.changthai.com), 37km northwest of Lampang on Highway 11 towards Chiang Mai, is the most authentic place to see elephants displaying their skills; it also cares for abandoned and sick elephants in its elephant hospital. An interpretive centre has exhibits on the history of the elephant in Thailand, cheap elephant rides (B100–400) are available, and there is a homestay programme, on which you spend usually three days learning how to care for and control elephants for around B1500 a day. It's best visited en route between Chiang Mai and Lampang; if coming by bus, allow for the two-kilometre walk from the entrance gates to the centre.

Practicalities

From Chiang Mai, you can catch **buses** to Lampang from Thanon Chiang Mai–Lamphun just south of Nawarat Bridge, or from the Arcade station. Seven **trains** a

△ Elephant trainer, Chiang Mai

day, in each direction on the Bangkok–Chiang Mai line, also stop in Lampang. The train and bus stations lie less than 1km to the southwest of town, but many buses also stop on Thanon Phaholyothin in the centre. The **airport** is just to the south of the centre, and there's a small **tourist information** centre (Mon–Fri 8.30am–noon & 1–4.30pm), just east of the clocktower and next to the fire station on Thanon Takrao Noi. *Boonma Guest House*, 256 Thanon Talat Kao (☎054 322653; ❶) occupies a gorgeous, stilted wooden building, while a little further east, the delightful *Riverside Guest House*, 286 Thanon Talat Khao (☎054 227005, ©riversidefamily@yahoo.com; ❷), is a traditional compound of elegant, mostly en-suite **rooms**, whose helpful owner rents out motorbikes, and also owns the excellent *Riverside* **restaurant** at 328 Thanon Tipchang. Another highly recommended place to eat is *Huen Chom Wang*, 276 Thanon Talat Kao, which features many northern specialities.

Nan and around

Ringed by high mountains, the sleepy provincial capital of **NAN**, 225km northeast of Lampang, rests on the west bank of the Nan River and comprises a disorientating grid of crooked streets, around a small core of shops, where thanons Mahawong and Anantaworarichides meet Thanon Sumondhevaraj. The best place to start an exploration is to the southwest at the **National Museum** (daily 9am–4pm; B30), housed in a converted palace on Thanon Phakwang, where informative displays introduce the history and peoples of Nan. Located 150m south along Thanon Phakwang, **Wat Phumin** will grab even the most over-templed traveller. Its five-hundred-year-old centrepiece is an unusual cruciform building, combining both the bot and the viharn, its doors beautifully carved with animals and flowers. Inside, the restored 1857 murals take you on a whirlwind tour of heaven, hell, the Buddha's previous incarnations and incidents from Nan's history and legends, in vivacious, sometimes bawdy, detail.

Wat Phra That Chae Haeng, on the opposite side of the river 2km southeast of town, is another must, not least for its setting on a hill overlooking the Nan Valley. The wide driveway is flanked by monumental serpents gliding down the slope, and inside the walls stand a slender, 55-metre-high golden chedi, and a viharn whose roof has no less than fifteen Lao-style tiers, stacked up like a house of cards.

Shops and tours

There are several good **handicrafts shops** in Nan, notably Pha Nan at 21/2 Thanon Sumondhevaraj for superb local cotton, and Hattasin off Thanon Sumondhevaraj at 50/10 Thanon Norkham, run by the Thai-Payap Development Association to bring surplus income to local hilltribes through craft production.

When you tire of the town, consider heading into the remote, mountainous countryside around Nan, which runs a close second to the headlong scenery of Mae Hong Son province. Fhu Travel at 453/4 Thanon Sumondhevaraj (☎054 710636, ©fhutravel@hotmail.com) organizes **tours** to Wat Nong Bua (see opposite) (B600), whitewater-rafting trips (around B1000 per day), homestays and treks of two days (B1200) or three days (B1500) through thick jungle and high mountains to villages of Hmong and Mien, as well as the lesser-known Htin and Phi Tong Luang.

Practicalities

From Chiang Mai, it's a six-hour bus journey to Nan. The main **bus station** is on Thanon Anantaworarichides on the west side of town, but Bangkok and Phitsanulok services use a smaller station to the east of the centre on Thanon Kha Luang; both are a manageable walk from the centre. The **airport** lies a short way northwest of town. Oversea, at 488 Thanon Sumondhevaraj, rents out **bicycles** (B30–50) and

motorbikes (B150). Nan boasts one very good **guesthouse**, out on the north side of town. *Doi Phukha Guest House*, 94/5 Soi 1, Thanon Sumondhevaraj (☎054 751517; ❶), occupies a beautiful wooden house, with simple rooms sharing hot showers and an informative noticeboard. If *Doi Phukha* is full, head for *Amazing Guest House*, 25/7 Thanon Rat Amnuay (☎054 710893; ❶), which runs west off Thanon Sumondhevaraj, not far north of Doi Phukha. The night market and several good, small Thai **restaurants** line Thanon Anantaworarichides, notably *Poom Sam*, just next to the *Sukkasem Hotel*, which prepares excellent Thai and Chinese food with great service at rock-bottom prices, and next door, *Tanaya Kitchen*, a homely café that serves good vegetarian food.

Ban Nong Bua

The most popular day-trip out of Nan is to the village of **BAN NONG BUA** and its eponymous temple. If you're on a bike, ride 40km north up Highway 1080 to the southern outskirts of the town of Tha Wang Pha, where signs point to **Wat Nong Bua**, 3km away; buses and songthaews from Nan's Thanon Anantaworarichides go to Tha Wang Pha (roughly hourly; 1hr), from where you can take a motorbike taxi, or walk the last 3km. The wat's beautifully gnarled viharn was built in 1862 in typical Lanna style, with low, drooping roof tiers, but its most outstanding features are the remarkably intact late-nineteenth-century murals that depict, with much humour and vivid detail, scenes from the Chanthakhat Jataka, the story of one of the Buddha's previous incarnations as a hero called Chanthakhat. High-quality cotton in richly coloured geometric patterns is produced and sold in Ban Nong Bua by **Thai Lue weavers**, distant cousins of the Thais who've migrated from China in the past 150 years.

Doi Inthanon National Park

Covering a huge area to the southwest of Chiang Mai, **Doi Inthanon National Park** (B200 entrance fee per person, plus B20–30 per vehicle), with its hilltribe villages, dramatic waterfalls and fine panoramas, is a popular destination for naturalists and hikers. The park supports about 380 bird species and, near the summit, the only red rhododendrons in Thailand (in bloom Dec–Feb). Night-time temperatures can drop below freezing, so bring warm clothing. Both the **visitor centre**, 9km up the main park road from **Chom Thong**, and the **park headquarters**, a further 22km on, have park **maps**. Three sets of waterfalls provide the main roadside attractions on the way to the park headquarters: overrated and overcrowded **Mae Klang Falls**, 8km in; **Vachiratharn Falls**, a long misty drop 11km beyond; and the twin cascades of **Siriphum Falls**, behind the park headquarters. The more beautiful **Mae Ya**, believed to be the highest in Thailand, are accessed by a paved fourteen-kilometre track that heads west off the main park road 3km north of Chom Thong. For the most spectacular views in the park, head for the twin chedis on the summit road. Near the chedis, lies the trailhead of **Kew Mae Pan Trail**, an easy two-hour circular walk through forest and savannah – home of the red rhododendrons – around the steep, western edge of Doi Inthanon; you need to hire a **guide** from headquarters to walk the trail (B200 per group). Doi Inthanon's **summit** (2565m), 6km beyond the chedis, is a disappointment. The paved Mae Chaem road skirts yet more waterfalls: 7km after the turn-off, look for a steep, unpaved road to the right, leading down to a ranger station and, just to the east, the dramatic long drop of **Huai Sai Luaeng Falls**. A circular two-hour trail from the ranger station takes in small waterfalls, such as **Mae Pan Falls**.

Practicalities

By **motorbike** or jeep, you could do the park justice in a day-trip from Chiang Mai, or treat it as the first stage of a longer trip to Mae Hong Son. The gateway to the park is **Chom Thong**, 58km southwest of Chiang Mai on Highway 108; the main road through the park leaves Highway 108 1km north of here, winding northwestwards for 48km to the top of Doi Inthanon; a second paved road forks left 10km before the summit, reaching the riverside market of Mae Chaem, southwest of the park, after 20km, and Highway 108 towards Mae Hong Son after a further 45km. **Buses** run from the bottom of Thanon Phra Pokklao in Chiang Mai (Chiang Mai Gate) to Chom Thong (every 30min; 1hr); from here, you can catch a songthaew through the park towards Mae Chaem, leaving you to hitch the last 10km to the summit, or you can charter a whole songthaew from Chom Thong's temple (from B700 round trip).

You can **stay** in the national park bungalows (B800–3000; bookings at the park on ⓣ053 268550) near the headquarters, or camp near the headquarters and at Huai Sai Luaeng Falls (B30 per person per night). Fully equipped two-person tents (B250) can be rented at the headquarters. **Food** stalls operate at Mae Klang, Vachiratharn and Mae Ya Falls (daytime only) and at the park headquarters and Mae Pan Falls, and there's a daytime canteen by the twin chedis.

Mae Sariang

Apart from admiring the town's Burmese-style wats, there's nothing pressing to do in the outpost of **MAE SARIANG**, 183km from Chiang Mai, but many visitors make a day-trip to the trading post of **Mae Sam Laeb**, 46km to the southwest on the Salween River, on the border with Burma. Highly recommended **boat trips** are organized by *See View Guest House* (see below), including transport out to Mae Sam Laeb. The boat cruises down the Salween through idyllic countryside to the small, unspoilt Karen village of Sop Moei and back (B600–1000 per person).

Buses from Chiang Mai's Arcade station enter Mae Sariang from the east along its main street, Thanon Wiang Mai, terminating on Thanon Mae Sariang, one of two north–south streets; the other, Thanon Laeng Phanit, parallels the Yuam River to the west. The bone-rattling 230km south **to Mae Sot** is covered by songthaews (7 daily; 6hr), which makes a scenic link between the north and the central plains. The best **place to stay** in town is the very helpful *See View Guest House* (ⓣ053 681556 or 09552 7616, ⓦwww.thai.net/seeviewguesthouse.com; ❷), which has nice rooms and bungalows across the river from the town centre; they also rent bicycles (B50). The *River Side Guest House* occupies a choice position above the curving river at 85 Thanon Laeng Phanit (ⓣ053/681188; ❷). Don't be put off by the basic appearance of the *Inthira Restaurant* on Thanon Wiang Mai – it's the locals' favourite, and serves excellent Thai food. **Motorbikes** (B200) can be rented from Pratin Kolakan, opposite the bus terminal, or from the guesthouses.

Mae Hong Son and around

Set deep in a mountain valley, **MAE HONG SON** is often billed as the "Switzerland of Thailand" and has become one of the fastest-developing tourist centres in the country. Most travellers come here for trekking in the beautiful countryside and cool climate, but crowds are also drawn here every April for the spectacular parades of the Poy Sang Long Festival, which celebrates local Thai Yai/Shan boys' temporary ordination into the monkhood. **Trekking** up and down Mae Hong Son's steep inclines is tough, but the hilltribe villages are generally unspoilt and the scenery is magnificent. To the west, trekking routes tend to snake along the Burmese border and can sometimes get a little crowded; the villages to the east are more traditional. Many guesthouses and travel agencies run treks out of Mae Hong Son: the *Mae Hong Son Guest House* is reliable (from B1500 per person for 3 days).

Mae Hong Son's main Thanon Khunlumprapas, lined with shops and businesses, runs north to south and is intersected by Singhanat Bamrung at the traffic lights in the centre of town. To the southeast of this junction, the town's classic picture-postcard view is of its twin nineteenth-century Burmese-style temples, **Wat Chong Kham** and **Wat Chong Klang**, from the opposite bank of Jong Kham Lake. The latter temple is famous for its paintings on glass, depicting stories from the lives of the Buddha. It also houses a fabulous collection of humorous and characterful Burmese teak statues. The town's vibrant, smelly **morning market** is a magnet for hilltribe traders and worth getting up at dawn for; next door, the many-gabled viharn of **Wat Hua Wiang** shelters the beautiful bronze Burmese-style Buddha image, Chao Palakeng. For a godlike overview of the area, especially at sunset, climb up to **Wat Doi Kong Mu** on the steep hill to the west.

Practicalities

Buses to Mae Hong Son, whether along the southern route via Mae Sariang or the northern route via Pai (both 8hr), depart from Chiang Mai's Arcade bus station and arrive at the northern end of Thanon Khunlumprapas, close to the guesthouses; air-con minibuses cover the ground via Pai four times a day in about six hours. Surprisingly inexpensive **flights** from Chiang Mai arrive at the airport on the east side of town. **TAT** have a helpful office (Mon–Fri 8.30am–4.30pm, plus Sat & Sun same times in high season; ⓣ053 612982–3, ⓦwww.travelmaehongson.org) opposite the post office on Khunlumprapas. Thai Yai, at 20 Singhanat Bamrung (ⓣ053 620105), rents out **motorbikes** (B180) and **bicycles** (B100). The most reliable place to rent a **four-wheel drive** is Avis at the airport (ⓣ053 611367; B1200 per day). For organized **tours**, including boating and rafting on the Pai River and elephant rides, Sunflower, 2/1 Soi 3, Thanon Khunlumprapas (ⓣ053 620549) is the best fixer.

Mae Hong Son has many peaceful, scenic **guesthouses** (all those described below have hot showers), of which the smart, lakeside *Friend House*, at 21 Thanon Pradit Jongkham (ⓣ053 620119; ❶), is one of the best. Further east along the lake shore, on Thanon U-domchaonitesh, *Johnnie House* (ⓣ053 611667; ❶) is a clean, friendly place with nice, airy rooms. Out on the west side of town, the relaxing, long-established *Mae Hong Son Guest House*, 295 Thanon Makkasandi (ⓣ053 612510; ❷-❸), offers a choice between en-suite rooms and large, attractive bungalows, while the mid-priced *Sang Tong Huts*, down a small lane off Thanon Makkasandi (ⓣ053 620680, ⓦwww.sangtonghuts.com; ❹), does tasteful rustic chic on a steep, jungly slope on the edge of town.

For Thai **food**, try the very popular *Kai Muk* on Thanon U-Domchaonitesh, the upmarket, tourist-oriented *Fern* at 87 Thanon Khunlumprapas, or *Lakeside*, which offers live bands and views of Jong Kham Lake.

Nai Soi and the long-neck women

The most famous – and notorious – sight in the Mae Hong Son area is its contingent of **"long-neck" women**, members of the Padaung tribe of Burma who have fled to Thailand to escape repression. Though the women's necks appear to be stretched to 30cm and more by a column of brass rings, the pressure of eleven pounds of brass actually squashes the collarbones and ribs; to remove a full stack would cause the collapse of the neck and suffocation. Girls of the tribe start wearing the rings from about the age of 6, adding one or two each year until they are 16. Only half of the Padaung women now lengthen their necks; left to its own course, the custom would probably die out, but the influence of tourism may well keep it alive for some time yet.

The original village of long-neck Padaung women in the Mae Hong Son area, **NAI SOI**, 28km northwest of town, has effectively been turned into a human zoo for snap-happy tourists, with an entrance fee of B250 per person. At least much of the entrance fee is used to support the Karenni National People's Party in their fight for the independence of Burma's Kayah state (where the Padaung come from), and the "long necks" themselves get paid a living wage. Without your own transport, you'll have to join a **tour** (about B800, including the entrance fee) from town. By motorbike, head north along Highway 1095 for 2km and turn left after the police box; cross the bridge over the Pai River, turn left at the next village and continue for another 10km.

Pha Sua Falls and Mae Aw

North of Mae Hong Son, a trip to **Pha Sua Falls** and the border village of Mae Aw takes in some spectacular and varied countryside, best visited by motorbike or on a tour (around B600). Head north for 17km on Highway 1095 (ignore the first signpost for Pha Sua, after 10km) and then, after a long, steep descent, turn left onto a side road, paved at first, which passes through the village of Ban Bok Shampae. About 9km from the turn-off, you'll reach the wild, untidy Pha Sua Falls; take care when swimming, as several people have been swept to their deaths here.

Above the falls, the paved road climbs 11km to the village of Naphapak, from where it's another 7km to **MAE AW** (aka Ban Ruk Thai), a settlement of Kuomintang (anti-communist Chinese) refugees. It's the highest point on the Burmese border that visitors can reach, and provides a fascinating window on Kuomintang life. Bright-green tea bushes line the slopes, and Chinese ponies wander the streets of long bamboo houses. In the marketplace on the north side of the village reservoir, shops sell Oolong and Chian Chian tea, and dried mushrooms.

Around Soppong and Tham Lot

Set in wild countryside 3km east of the Thai Yai/Kuomintang village of **MAE SUYA** (which is 40km northeast of Mae Hong Son on Highway 1095 to Pai), *Wilderness Lodge* (❶, dorm B70) is a great place to base yourself for hikes through the mountains to hilltribe villages. It's also within easy reach of two significant caves (accessible Nov–May only), the 1600-metre-long Tham Nam Pha Daeng, and the dramatic Tham Nam Lang, one of the biggest caves in the world, which has a towering entrance chamber and a spectacular, nine-kilometre, full-on caving route beyond. To get to *Wilderness Lodge*, take the left turning by the police box 3km east of Mae Suya, then continue on a dirt road for 1km.

The small market town of **SOPPONG**, 28km from Mae Suya, gives access to the area's most famous cave, **Tham Lot**, 9km north in **BAN TUM** (or Ban Tham). There's no public transport along the paved road to the village, so without your own wheels you'll have to hitch, walk or rent a motorbike taxi (B60) or songthaew (B200). Turn right in the village for the entrance to the Tham Lot Nature Education Station, where you have to hire a **guide** for B100. A short walk through the forest brings you to the entrance of Tham Lot, where the Lang River begins a six-hundred-metre subterranean journey through the cave, for most of the year requiring you to hire a bamboo raft (B100 per group of one to four). Two hours should allow you enough time for travelling through the broad, airy tunnel, and for climbing up to see the enormous stalagmites and other weird formations in the sweaty caverns in the roof.

The hillside **bungalows** at *Cave Lodge* (Ⓣ053 617203, Ⓦwww.cavelodge.com; ❶–❷, dorm B60), on the other side of Ban Tum from the cave, make an excellent base for exploring the area, either with local trekking guides or with maps for self-guided walks. The owners also organize kayak tours through Tham Lot and occasional guided trips through other caves; bamboo rafting and elephant riding can also be arranged nearby. On the main road at the western end of Soppong, *Jungle Guest House* (Ⓣ053 617099; ❶–❷) is the most popular accommodation in town and can give advice on local hikes.

About 9km east of Soppong on Highway 1095, the Lisu village of **BAN NAM RIN** is home to the easy-going *Lisu Lodge* (☎09 953 4243; ❶–❷). On a pretty slope at the west end of the village stand A-frame huts with shared hot showers and smart, en-suite cottages. The owners can advise on trekking, either on your own or with a guide from the village, with the possibility of staying over at other hilltribe villages.

Pai

Once just a stopover on the tiring journey to Mae Hong Son, **PAI**, 43km from Soppong, is now a destination in its own right, and travellers settle into the town's laid-back, New-Agey feel for weeks. There's all manner of outdoor activities, courses and therapies – including retail therapy at the art studios, leather and jewellery shops.

It's a good place for undemanding valley walks and for **trekking** (around B500 per day, plus B250 each for rafting and elephant-riding) through varied terrain to Karen, Lisu and Lahu villages, which can be arranged through guesthouses or Back Trax at 17 Thanon Chaisongkhram (☎053 699739, ©backtraxinpai@yahoo.com). Among several **elephant camps** around town, Joy, with an office on Chaisongkhram opposite the bus station (☎01 881 3923, ©cchiamchit@hotmail.com), offers something slightly different: you can opt for a ride (from B250 per hour), which includes going into the river and feeding, or you can volunteer to stay and earn your keep at the camp. From July to January, you can take an impressive two-day **rubber-raft trip** down the Pai River to Mae Hong Son (B2000) with the reliable Thai Adventure Rafting, based on Thanon Rungsiyanon (☎053 699111, ⓦwww.activethailand.com/rafting). Back Trax can also arrange a two-and-a-half-hour **bamboo-rafting** trip down the Pai River for around B500 per person.

On the east side of town is a large open-air **swimming pool** (daily 10.30am–8.30pm; B50). About 7km down the same minor road, the **hot springs** aren't up to much, but nearby **spas** put the piped hot water to much better use. *Thapai Spa*

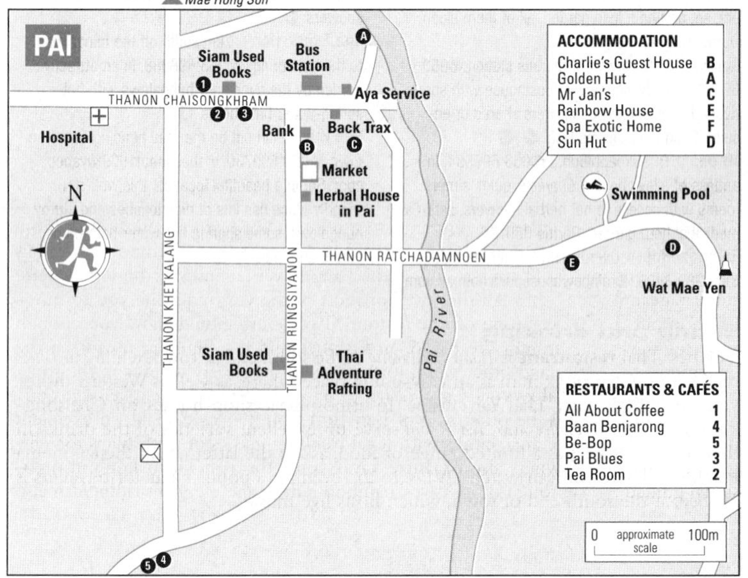

Camping (☎09 557 6079), down a side road about 1km north of the springs, has a large pool (B50) and offers massages and other treatments. They also have rooms and tents, but for accommodation you're better off going to *Spa Exotic Home* nearby (see below); the latter also has spa tubs (B40) for non-guests.

Mr Jan's is famous for its Thai and Burmese/Shan **massages** (B150 per hour) and saunas (B50), while Herbal House in Pai, near the market on Rungsiyanon (☎053 699964, ©tiger_healing@hotmail.com), offers massages for B180 an hour and other treatments. A government-certified training centre, Herbal House also lays on **massage courses** (B800 per day), as well as live-in courses (B2000 per day) at a retreat outside town, which feature meditation and yoga practice. Bebe's Wok'n'Roll, based near the tourist police (☎1155) at the south end of town (☎09 953 0205, ©thom_bebe@yahoo.com), holds Thai **cooking courses** of one (B750) or two (B1350) days.

Practicalities

Buses and faster air-con minibuses from Mae Hong Son and Chiang Mai stop at the **bus station** near the junction of Thanon Rungsiyanon and Thanon Chaisongkhram; motorbike **taxis** are available on the junction itself, air-con minibus taxis on the east side of the bus station. The most reliable place to rent **motorbikes** is Aya Service, a travel agency on Chaisongkhram (☎053 699940), which charges from B80 a day, including insurance; Pai Mountain Bike Tours, a couple of doors away on the same street, and *Duang Guest House* opposite rent **mountain bikes** (B80), the former providing a simple map for touring. At the **post office** at the southern end of Thanon Khetkalang, you can make international calls. Among several **bookshops** in Pai, Siam Used Books has a good selection across two branches, one on Rungsiyanon, the other on Chaisongkhram, while the choice at The Bookshop at *Mr Jan's* is more eclectic.

Accommodation

Charlie's Guest House 9 Th Rungsiyanon ☎053 699039. Rooms with en-suite or shared hot showers, set around a lush garden, all of them clean. Dorms B60. ❶–❷

Golden Hut Northeast of the bus station ☎053 699949. Shady, congenial guesthouse with some riverside balconies; hot showers shared or en-suite. Good food. Dorms B50. ❶–❸

Mr Jan's Th Sukhaphibun 3 ☎053 699554. In a mess of alleys behind *Charlie's*, quiet, simple rooms with access to hot herbal showers, set in a medicinal herb garden. Dorms B60, ❶

Rainbow House Over the bridge, on the right ☎01 289 8409, ©rainbowhousepai@hotmail.com. Welcoming, family-run place with lots of local info; very clean bungalows, with en-suite or shared hot showers. ❶–❷

Spa Exotic Home 7km south off the minor road to the hot springs ☎053 698088. In an attractive garden by the river, cosy bungalows with hot-spring-water bathrooms. ❹

Sun Hut 10min out on the road heading east from town ☎053 699730, ©thesunhut1999@yahoo.com. Set in a beautiful location, this well-run, friendly place has lots of nice touches and sturdy bungalows, some sharing hot-water bathrooms, others en-suite. ❶–❸

Eating and drinking

The best Thai **restaurant** is *Baan Benjarong* at the south end of town, while *Pai Blues* on Thanon Chaisongkhram is an easy-going place where, as well as Western dishes, you can sample tasty Thai Yai cuisine. In atmospheric shop-houses on Chaisongkhram, *All About Coffee* and *Tea Room* serve up excellent varieties of the drinks in their names, as well as a limited range of food; ask at the latter about their Cinema Pairadiso, where you can watch DVDs. In the evening, a popular **bar** for travellers is *Be-Bop*, at the south end of town, which hosts live music.

Tha Ton and the Kok River

Leafy **THA TON**, 176km north of Chiang Mai, huddles each side of a bridge over the Kok River, which flows out of Burma 4km upstream. The main attractions here are boat and raft rides, but if you've got a morning to kill visit the over-the-top ornamental gardens of **Wat Tha Ton** on the south side of the bridge.

Travelling down the hundred-kilometre stretch of the Kok River to Chiang Rai gives you a chance to soak up a rich diversity of typical northern landscapes, through rice-fields and orchards, past riverside wats and over rapids. Noisy, canopied longtail boats leave from the south side of the bridge in Tha Ton every day at 12.30pm for the four-hour trip to Chiang Rai (B250, plus B300 for motorbikes). Boats from Chiang Rai leave at 10.30am. If you have more time, choose the peaceful bamboo rafts, which glide downriver to Chiang Rai in two days. They leave at about 8–9am, generally take four people and the price includes sleeping bags, mosquito nets, soft drinks and food. *Thip's Traveller House* (see below) organizes such raft trips (B1500), with a night spent at some hot springs and an elephant ride.

Buses between Chiang Mai's Chang Phuak bus station and Tha Ton take about four hours. *Thip's Traveller House* (Ⓣ053 459312, Ⓦwww.thiptravel.com; ❶), on the south side of the bridge, is a convenient **place to stay**, with decent en-suite rooms and good food. On the north side of the river, *Garden Home Nature Resort* (Ⓣ053 373015; ❶–❻), has very attractive en-suite bungalows in an orchard, some with hot water and air con, and rents bikes. Back on the south bank, *Mae Kok River Village Resort* (Ⓣ053 459355–6, Ⓦwww.track-of-the-tiger.com; ❼) is an outstanding upmarket choice and organizes an imaginative variety of courses and soft adventure tours (around B1500 per day).

Chiang Rai

The long arm of the package-tour industry has reached **CHIANG RAI**, now a predominantly upmarket resort town of well over two thousand hotel rooms, but also known for its trekking. A walk up to **Doi Tong**, the hummock to the northwest of the centre, offers a fine view up the Kok River. On the highest part of the hill stands a kind of phallic Stonehenge centred on the town's new lak muang, representing the Buddhist layout of the universe. The old wooden lak muang can be seen in the viharn of **Wat Phra That Doi Tong**, the city's first temple, which sprawls shambolically over the eastern side of the hill. Carved in China from 300kg of milky green jade, a beautiful replica of the Emerald Buddha (see p.974), Thailand's most important image, can be seen at **Wat Phra Kaeo** on Thanon Trairat.

There are plenty of handicraft shops in the town, with the most authentic selection at the non-profit-making **Hilltribe Museum and Shop** at 620/25 Thanon Tanalai, run by the Population and Community Development Association (PDA). The upstairs museum (Mon–Fri 9am–6pm, Sat & Sun 10am–6pm; B50) is a good place to find out about the local hilltribes before going on a trek. A **night bazaar** sells handicrafts off Thanon Phaholyothin next to the bus station.

The Chiang Rai region offers a range of **treks**, from gentle walking trails near the Kok River to tough mountain slopes further north towards the Burmese border. Among trekking guesthouses in Chiang Rai, *Chat House*, *Chian House* and *Mae Hong Son* are responsible and reliable. An average three-day trek, with an elephant ride, costs B2500–3000. The PDA (Ⓣ053 740088, Ⓦwww.pda.or.th/chiangrai; see above) also offers treks and tours, as well as one-day **mountain-biking trips** up the Kok River (B2200). *Mae Hong Son Guest House* and *Chian House* also offer motorbike trekking, and the latter can lay on horse riding. With Lost Valley on Thanon Jet Yot (Ⓣ053 752252, Ⓦwww.lostvalleyadventure.com), you can paddle a **rubber raft** down the Kok River to the west of town, typically paying B1800 for a two-day trip.

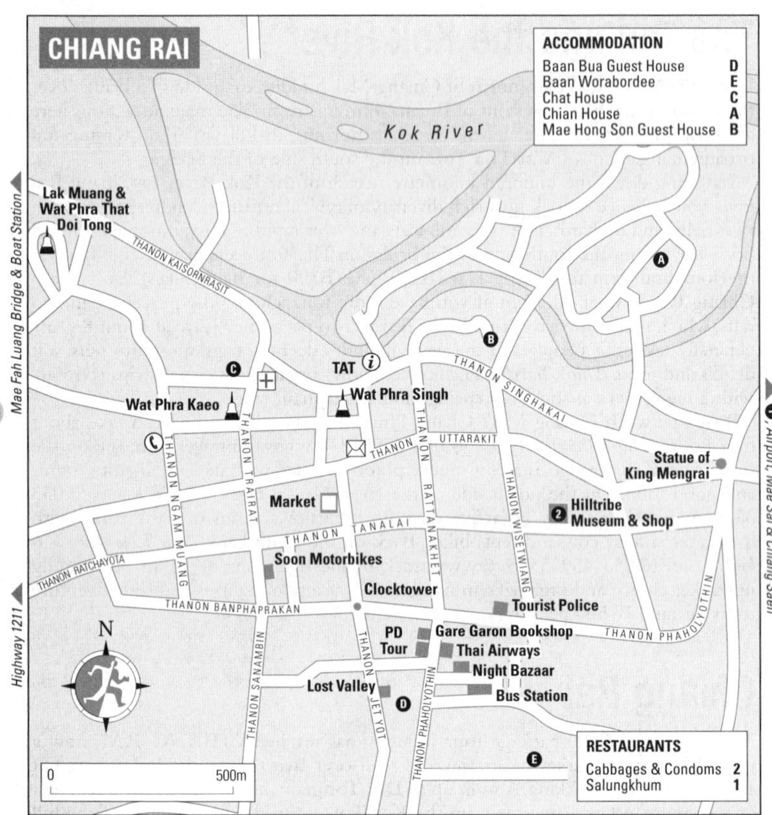

Arrival and information

Buses arrive at the **bus station** just off Thanon Phaholyothin, a long walk to most guesthouses, but served by tuk-tuks (B30–50) and songthaews. The latter have no set routes, but cost B10–20 for short hops. **Longtails** from Tha Ton dock at the boat station on the north side of the Mae Fah Luang Bridge. The **airport**, 8km northeast of town, is served by taxis (B200). Soon Motorbikes, at 197/2 Thanon Trairat (☎053 714068), has the best choice of **motorbikes** (from B150) and **mountain bikes** (B100), and PD Tour at 869/108 Thanon Pemavipat, near the *Wangcome Hotel* (☎053 712829), rents out **jeeps** (around B800). **TAT** is at 448/16 Thanon Singhakai near Wat Phra Singh (daily 8.30am–4.30pm; ☎053 717433); the **tourist police** (☎1155) are on Thanon Phaholyothin next to the *Golden Triangle Inn*. Gare Garon, 869/18 Thanon Phaholyothin, has a small range of new and used **books**.

Accommodation

Most of Chiang Rai's **guesthouses** are scattered along the south bank of the river; those reviewed below have hot-water showers.

Baan Bua Guest House 879/2 Th Jet Yot ☎053 718880, ⓔ baanbua@yahoo.com. Well-run establishment around a surprisingly large, quiet garden. Some of the very clean concrete rooms have a/c. ❷

Baan Woraborde 59/1 Moo 18, Th Sanpanard ☎053 754488, ✉baan_waraborde@hotmail.com. Well-appointed place down a quiet lane off the main street. Comfortable rooms with small balconies, cable TV and fan or a/c. ❷–❸

Chat House 3/2 Soi Sangkaew, Th Trairat ☎053 711481. Chiang Rai's longest-running travellers' hangout has a laid-back atmosphere and en-suite rooms. ❶

Chian House 172 Th Koh Loy ☎053 713388. Pleasant en-suite rooms, some with a/c, and bungalows in a lively compound around a small pool. Internet access. ❶–❷

Mae Hong Son Guest House 126 Th Singhakai ☎053 715367. Friendly courtyard establishment with bar and café in a quiet street. Good rooms, some en suite. ❶

Eating and drinking

Salungkhum, at 843 Thanon Phaholyothin (across from the Cosmo petrol station, between King Mengrai's statue and the river), serves the best **Thai food** in town, with a garden for evening dining. Another excellent mid-priced option is *Cabbages and Condoms*, on the ground floor of the Hilltribe Museum, which is run by the family planning and HIV/AIDS prevention organization, and does some traditional northern and veggie dishes. For cheaper Thai food, there's a food centre in the night bazaar with a **beer garden** and cabaret.

Mae Sai

MAE SAI, with its bustling border crossing, is Thailand's northernmost town, 61km from Chiang Rai. Thanon Phaholyothin is the town's single north–south street, which ends at the bridge over the Mae Sai River, the frontier with Burma. Farangs can make a day-trip across to **Thakhilek** (6.30am–5.30pm), though the frontier is sporadically closed during international disputes between the two countries – and note that visa regulations change frequently. If you want a new thirty-day entry stamp for Thailand, first get stamped out at the main immigration office (daily 8am–5pm; ☎053 731008), 2km south of the bridge on Thanon Phaholyothin; on the other side of the bridge, you pay B250 to Burmese immigration for a one-day stay; on your return, you'll be given your new thirty-day stamp at the Thai immigration office by the bridge. If, however, you don't want to affect your existing visa, photocopy the relevant pages of your passport at one of the handy copying booths by the frontier, leave your passport at Thai immigration at the bridge, and pay the Burmese B250 for a one-day stamp on the photocopies.

Shopping is the main interest in Thakhilek: the huge market on the right after the bridge is an entrepôt for everything from Jacob's Cream Crackers to tigers' intestines, but the Burmese handicrafts are disappointing. You'll probably have better luck craft shopping back in Mae Sai: try Village Product, 51/24 Moo 10, Thanon Muang Daeng (about 500m south of the border, turn left near the 7–11, then 200m on your right). For a good view over Mae Sai and the border, climb up to the chedi of **Wat Phra That Doi Wao** (behind the *Top North Hotel*); there's a daytime market of Burmese and Chinese stuff in the temple grounds.

Buses stop 4km south of the frontier at the bus station, from where frequent songthaews shuttle into town. There's a **tourist police** booth (☎1155) hard by the frontier bridge. You can rent **motorbikes** from Pon Chai, opposite the Bangkok Bank (B150). A handful of mostly ropey **guesthouses** are strung out along the riverbank west of the bridge. By far the best of these is *Mae Sai* (☎053 732021; ❷–❸), a prettily located set of bungalows with en-suite hot-water bathrooms, wedged between a steep hill and the river, fifteen minutes from the main road. About 1km south of the bridge off Thanon Phaholyothin, the welcoming and informative *Chad Guest House* on Soi Wiangpan is the classic travellers' rest, and serves good food (☎053 732054; ❶). A popular **eating** place is *Rabieng Kaew*, opposite the Krung Thai Bank, which serves excellent Thai cuisine.

Sop Ruak

Opium growing has been illegal in Thailand since 1959, but during the 1960s and 70s, rampant production and refining of the crop in the lawless region on the borders of Thailand, Burma and Laos earned the area the nickname "the **Golden Triangle**". Two "armies" have traditionally operated most of the trade within this area: the Shan United Army from Burma, led by the notorious warlord Khun Sa, and the Kuomintang (KMT) refugees from communist China. The Thai government's concerted attempt to eliminate opium growing within its borders has been successful, but Thailand still has a vital role to play as a conduit for heroin; most of the production and refinement of opium has simply moved over the borders into Burma and Laos. More worryingly for the Thai authorities, factories just across the Burmese border are now also producing vast quantities of *ya baa*, or methamphetamines, destined for consumption in Thailand itself.

For the benefit of tourists, "the Golden Triangle" has now been artificially concentrated into the precise spot where the borders meet, at the confluence of the Ruak and Mekong rivers, 70km northeast of Chiang Rai: **SOP RUAK**. Don't expect to run into sinister drug-runners, addicts or even poppy-fields here – instead, you'll find souvenir stalls and huge, much-photographed "Golden Triangle" signs. The ambitious **Hall of Opium** at the Mae Sai end of the village (Tues–Sun 10am–3.30pm; B300) gives an imaginatively presented, balanced picture, in Thai and English, of the use and abuse of opium, and its history over five thousand years. For uninterrupted views of the meeting of the rivers and the lands of Burma and Laos beyond, climb up to **Wat Phra That Phu Khao**, a 1200-year-old temple perched on a small hill above the village. For B400, you can take a longtail **boat** from the pier in the centre of the village for a whistle-stop tour of the "Golden Triangle", which takes in a market on the Laos side (B20 admission).

To **get to Sop Ruak** you'll have to go via Chiang Saen or Mae Sai first. From Chiang Saen, you can go by regular songthaew, rented bicycle (an easy 10km ride on a paved road) or longtail boat tour up the Mekong (B300 per person). From Mae Sai, songthaews make the 45-minute trip from the side of the *Sri Wattana Hotel* on Thanon Phaholyothin.

Chiang Saen

Combining tumbledown ruins with sweeping Mekong River scenery, **CHIANG SAEN**, 60km northeast of Chiang Rai, makes a good base camp for the border region east of Mae Sai. Coveted for its strategic location, guarding the Mekong, Chiang Saen was passed back and forth between the kings of Burma and Thailand for nearly three hundred years until Rama I razed the place to the ground in 1804. The present town was resettled in 1881. The **National Museum** (Wed–Sun 8.30am–4.30pm; B30) makes an informative starting point, housing some impressive locally cast Buddha images and architectural features rescued from the ruins, as well as rural artefacts. **Wat Phra That Chedi Luang**, originally the city's main temple, is worth looking in on next door for its imposing, overgrown octagonal chedi. Beyond the ramparts to the west, laterite columns and restored brick buildings make **Wat Pa Sak** (B30) the most impressive of Chiang Saen's many temples. The central chedi owes its eclectic shape largely to the grand temples of Pagan in Burma and displays some beautiful carved stucco decoration.

Practicalities

Buses from Chiang Rai and **songthaews** from Sop Ruak stop just west of the T-junction of the main Thanon Phaholyothin and the river road; songthaews from

Chiang Khong stop on the river road to the south of the T-junction. **Bicycles** (B70), **motorbikes** (B180) and **four-wheel drives** (B900) can be rented at *Gin's Guest House*.

The best guesthouse is *Gin's Guest House* (☎053 650847; ❶–❸), outside the ramparts, 2km north of the T-junction, which offers large A-frame bungalows in a lychee orchard, or pricier rooms in the main house. The **night market** sets up along the riverfront by the cargo pier.

As well as trekking and tours, *Gin's* can also arrange two-day, one-night passage on **cargo boats to Jing Hong** in China for B2700 per person; the period after the rainy season (Oct–Jan) is the most reliable time. It's best to get your Chinese visa yourself in Bangkok or Chiang Mai, but *Gin's* can arrange this if necessary in five days (B1800).

Chiang Khong and the Laos border

CHIANG KHONG, 70km downriver from Chiang Saen, is the only crossing point into Laos in this part of Thailand. Fifteen-day **visas for Laos** are available on arrival across the river at **Houayxai** (US$30 or B1500); note, however, that visa regulations change frequently. Frequent boats to Houayxai (B20, plus B20 "overtime" at lunchtime and after 4pm) depart from Chiang Khong's main pier, Hua Wiang, at the north end of town, and from Houayxai (see p.561) you can get boats down the Mekong to Louang Phabang. There are plenty of songthaews from Chiang Saen to Chiang Khong, but a more scenic way is by motorbike, following minor roads along the riverbank via the Thai Lue weaving village of Ban Hat Bai; an exciting alternative is to run the rapids on a hired longtail boat (B1300; 3hr). Regular buses also run to Chiang Khong from Chiang Rai, and there are direct air-con minibuses from Chiang Mai, available through travel agents (see p.1010).

Chiang Khong's best **guesthouse** is the helpful, easy-going *Ban Tam-Mi-La*, down a riverside lane off the main street at 113 Thanon Sai Klang (☎053 791234, Ⓔbaantammila@hotmail.com; ❶-❷), which has tasteful, en-suite wooden bungalows and rooms, an excellent daytime restaurant, and bike and motorbike rental. Among the twenty or so other guesthouses in town, *Ban Fai* to the south at 27 Thanon Sai Klang (☎053 791394; ❶) offers clean rooms with shared bath in a family-style wooden house. On a jungly slope on the north side of town, the congenial *Bamboo Riverside Guest House* (☎053 791621, Ⓦwww.arriveat.com/bamboo; ❶–❷) offers attractive bungalows with shared or en-suite bathrooms, as well as dorm beds (B70) and a popular **restaurant**.

10.4

The east coast

Thailand's **east coast** is a five-hundred-kilometre string of fairly dull beaches and over-packaged family resorts, the largest and most notorious of which is **Pattaya**. Offshore, however, the tiny island of **Ko Samet** attracts backpackers and Bangkokians to its pretty white-sand beaches, while further east the much larger, forested island of **Ko Chang** is developing into quite a mainstream destination, leaving budget travellers to explore the quieter islands of **Ko Whai** and **Ko Mak**. East of Ko Chang lies the Cambodian border post of Hat Lek, one of two points in this region – the other being Aranyaprathet, a little way north – where it is currently legal to **cross overland into Cambodia** (see p.1035).

Pattaya

With its murky sea, streets packed with high-rise hotels, and touts on every corner, **PATTAYA** is the epitome of exploitative tourism gone mad. The town swarms with male and female prostitutes, and plane-loads of Western men flock here to enjoy their services in the rash of go-go bars for which "Patpong-on-Sea" is notorious. Yet watersports facilities here are among the best in the country, and it's not a bad place to learn to **dive**, though the reefs off the Andaman Coast are more spectacular. Reputable dive shops that run four-day PADI Open Water courses (B12,000) and diving expeditions include Aquanauts on Soi Yodsak, Central Pattaya (Ⓣ038 361724, Ⓦwww.aquanautsdive.com) and Pattayaland Soi 1, South Pattaya (Ⓣ038 710727); and Mermaid's Dive Centre between sois 10 and 11 on Th Beach, Central Pattaya (Ⓣ038 232219, Ⓦwww.mermaiddive.com). Be wary of unqualified instructors and dodgy equipment when signing up at any dive centre; the nearest divers' recompression chamber is at the Apakorn Kiatiwong Naval Hospital (Ⓣ038 601185) in Sattahip, 26km south of Pattaya.

Air-con **buses** to and from Bangkok's Eastern and Northern bus terminals use the bus station on Thanon North Pattaya, from where share taxis to hotels cost B40 per person. Non-air-con buses use the government bus station on Thanon Chaiyapruk in Jomtien, south of Pattaya. Buses from Rayong and Trat generally drop passengers on Thanon Sukhumvit, from where songthaews will ferry you into town. Pattaya's **U-Tapao Airport** is 25km south of the resort and runs flights to Ko Samui and Phuket; the Bangkok Airways office is at 75/8 Thanon Pattaya 2, Central Pattaya (Ⓣ038 412382). Taxis from Pattaya to Bangkok's Don Muang Airport cost about B800. Public **songthaews** in Pattaya follow a standard anticlockwise route up Thanon Pattaya 2 as far as Thanon North Pattaya and back down Thanon Pattaya Beach (B10). Songthaews to Jomtien leave from the junction of Thanon Pattaya 2 and Thanon South Pattaya (B10–20).

The **TAT** office is at 609 Thanon Pratamnak (Cliff Road), between South Pattaya and Jomtien (daily 8.30am–4.30pm; Ⓣ038 428750, Ⓔtatpty@chonburi.ksc.co.th). There are dozens of **Internet** centres throughout the resort – including the efficient 24hr Explorer Internet Café between Sois 9 and 10 on Thanon Pattaya Beach, Central Pattaya – and there's Catnet at the small public CAT phone office on Soi 13/2. The main CAT international **telephone** office is on Thanon South Pattaya, just east of the junction with Thanon Pattaya 3. The best-equipped **hospital** is the Bangkok-Pattaya Hospital (☎038 427777) on Thanon Sukhumvit, about 400m north of the intersection with Thanon North Pattaya. There are police stations on Thanon Pattaya 2, just south of Soi 6 (☎038 429371) and on Thanon Beach, just south of Soi 9. DK Books on Soi 13/2, Central Pattaya stocks an excellent range of new **books**.

Accommodation, eating and nightlife

Really cheap **hotels** are almost impossible to find in Pattaya, but prices in all categories plummet when demand is slack. The best of the **Pattaya** cheapies is *Sawasdee Guest House* at 502/1 Soi Saisong II (aka Soi Honey Inn), off Thanon Pattaya 2 in Central Pattaya (☎038 425360, Ⓦwww.sawasdee-hotels.com; ❷), which has decent if spartan fan and air-con rooms. The enormous fan and air-con rooms at *Diana Dragon Apartment*, 198/16 Soi Diana Inn, off Thanon Pattaya 2 in Central Pattaya (☎038 423928; ❷-❸) are good value, and guests have use of the pool at *Diana Inn*, 100m away. Another good deal are the smart, peaceful garden bungalows of *The Cottage*, off Thanon Pattaya 2, North Pattaya (☎038 425660, Ⓔthe_cottage2002@yahoo.com; ❹), which has two small pools.

PIC Kitchen on Soi 5, North Pattaya is a fine traditional Thai **restaurant**, with an elegantly presented mid-priced menu. Alternatively, check out the tiger prawns and giant lobsters at *Lobster Pot*, opposite Soi 14 on Walking Street in South Pattaya. Of the four hundred-odd **bars** in Pattaya, the majority are open-air "bar beers" staffed by hostesses, but not too seedy. Alternatives include The *Hopf Brew House,* between sois 13/1 and 13/2 on Thanon Pattaya Beach, Central Pattaya, which simulates a German beer hall; the Irish-style joint *Shenanigans*, next to the *Royal Garden Plaza* on Thanon Pattaya 2, Central Pattaya; and the Thai country-and-western bar, *Kum Pun*, on Soi 2, North Pattaya. Drinks are a lot more expensive in the bouncer-guarded go-go and live-sex bars on Walking Street in South Pattaya. Go-go dancers and shower shows are also the mainstays of the gay scene, centred on Pattayaland Soi 3, South Pattaya. Tour groups constitute the main audience at the family-oriented **transvestite cabarets** (B500), which are performed three times a night at *Alcazar*, opposite Soi 4 on Thanon Pattaya 2; *Tiffany's*, north of Soi 1 on Thanon Pattaya 2 (both in North Pattaya); and *Simon Cabaret* on Walking Street in South Pattaya.

Ko Samet

The dazzling white-sand beaches of pretty little **Ko Samet**, 80km southeast of Pattaya, draw big crowds of backpackers, package tourists and Bangkokians (especially on weekends and national holidays, when listed accommodation rates rise by up to sixty percent), but the diminutive national park island is only six kilometres long and is suffering under a glut of poorly landscaped bungalows and innumerable piles of rotting rubbish, so not everyone is a fan. There's a B200 national park entrance fee on arrival, payable at the checkpoint near Hat Sai Kaew or at Ao Wong Duan pier.

A rough track connects the east-coast bays, or you can walk along the beach at low tide; there are also motorbikes for rent on every beach, and a sporadic **songthaew** service starts at Na Dan pier and continues down the track as far as Wong Duan (B10–50). There are international **phone** services and **Internet** access at *Naga Bungalows* on Ao Hin Kok, and at the bigger bungalow operations on every main beach. Ko Samet **post office** is also run out of *Naga Bungalows*: poste restante letters are kept here for three months and should be addressed c/o Poste Restante, Ko Samet Post Office, Naga Bungalows, Ko Samet. The biggest bungalows will change money, and there are small shops on the main beaches. CP Travel (☎038 644208) on Hat Sai Kaew, beside the main track on the edge of the *White Sand* complex, sells **air tickets**. You can organize **dive** trips through Ploy Scuba (☎06 143 9318) on Hat Sai Kaew. Ko Samet's **health centre** and **police** station are in Na Dan.

Transport to and from Ko Samet

The mainland departure point for Ko Samet is the fishing port of **BAN PHE**, about 200km from Bangkok. **Buses** from Bangkok's Eastern Bus Terminal run hourly to Ban Phe pier (B100), or you can take a bus to Rayong instead (every 15min) and then change onto a songthaew to Ban Phe pier (30min). Tourist **minibuses** run direct from Thanon Khao San to Ban Phe (about B230). Buses from Chanthaburi

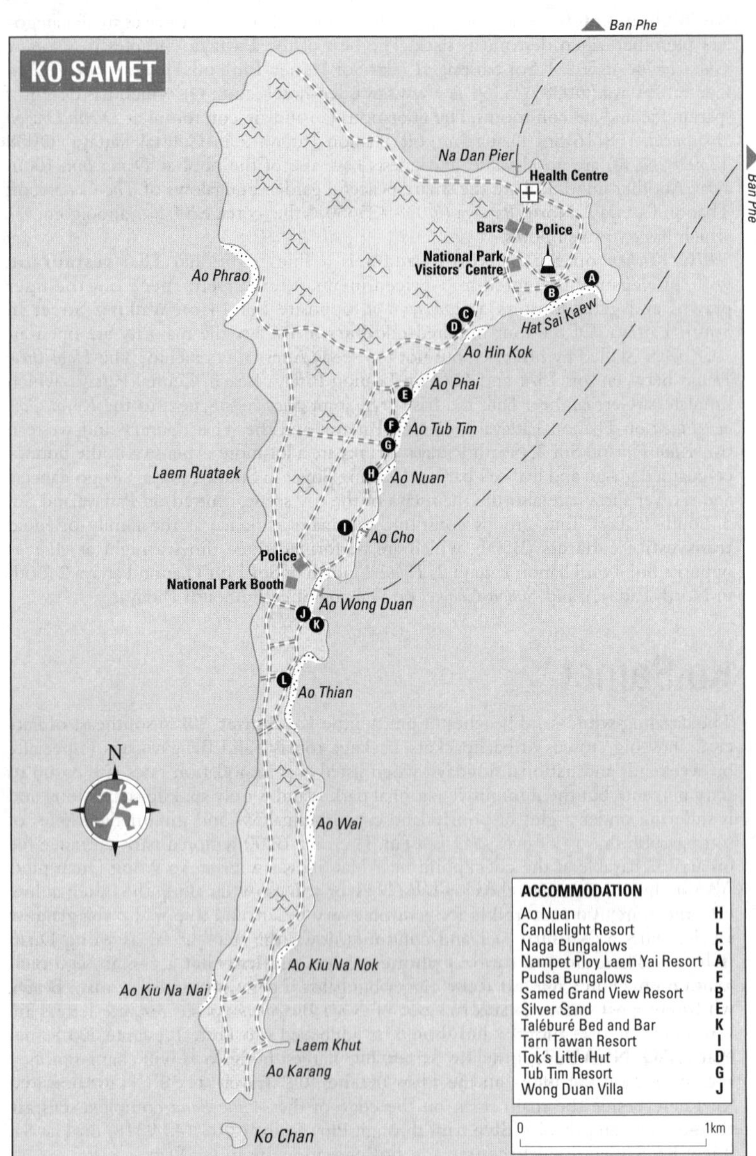

and Trat drop you on Thanon Sukhumvit, 5km by songthaew or motorbike taxi from the pier. There are email centres on the road by the pier in Ban Phe, as well as the traveller-oriented hotel TN Place (ⓣ038 651824; ❷).

From November to February, up to nine **boats** a day make the trip from Ban Phe to Ko Samet (approximately hourly 8am–5pm; 30min; B50). Most go to **Na Dan pier**, but if you're headed for Ao Wong Duan, Ao Cho or Ao Thian, it's more convenient to take the boat to **Ao Wong Duan** (approximately hourly 8am–5pm; 40min; B60). Boats for both destinations leave from Ban Phe's Saphaan Nuan Tip pier, opposite the 7–11 shop. Outside high season, there should be up to four boats daily to both piers. On the **return** leg, four scheduled boats (daily 7am–5pm) leave Na Dan pier for Ban Phe, and five run from Ao Wong Duan (daily every two hours from 8.30am–4.30pm); tourist minibuses do Ban Phe–Thanon Khao San (Bangkok) and Ban Phe–Laem Ngop (for Ko Chang); otherwise, take a songthaew from Ban Phe to Rayong bus station and make onward connections there.

Hat Sai Kaew

HAT SAI KAEW, or Diamond Beach, named for its beautiful long stretch of luxuriant sand, lies ten minutes' walk south from Na Dan. It's the most popular – and congested – beach on Samet, packed with bungalows, restaurants and beachwear stalls. The cheapest accommodation is at *Samed Grand View Resort* (ⓣ09 244 1382; ❸–❻), where the fan and air-con bungalows are unimaginatively designed but widely spaced around a garden. The comfortable wooden bungalows at *Nampet Ploy Laem Yai Resort* (ⓣ038 644077; ❻–❽) occupy the prettiest spot on the beach, under the headland at the far northern end.

Ao Hin Kok and Ao Phai

Separated from Hat Sai Kaew by a low promontory on which sits a mermaid statue, **AO HIN KOK** is much smaller and more traveller-oriented; you can walk here from Na Dan in about fifteen minutes. The popular *Naga Bungalows* (ⓣ038 644167; ❶–❸) has the cheapest accommodation on Ko Samet, in the shape of simple plank huts with shared facilities, as well as pricier en-suite ones; it also has a pool table and bakes its own bread and cakes. Next door, the unusual blue-painted en-suite bungalows at *Tok's Little Hut* (ⓣ038 644072; ❷–❹) are built high on stilts and all have views from their verandas. *Jep's* is deservedly the most popular **restaurant** here, serving up a great menu of travellers' fare at its tables on the beach, under trees prettily decorated with fairylights.

Past the next rocky divide, reasonably attractive **AO PHAI** is one of the livelier places to stay on the island, mainly because of the frequent parties held on the beach here at *Silver Sand* (ⓣ01 996 5720; ❸–❻), which has decent, well-maintained bungalows with nice bathrooms.

Ao Tub Tim and Ao Nuan

Also known as Ao Pudsa, **AO TUB TIM** is a small white-sand bay sandwiched between rocky points. It feels secluded, but is only a short stroll from Ao Phai or a half-hour's walk from Na Dan. *Pudsa Bungalows* (ⓣ038 644030; ❸) is small and welcoming and offers a range of pretty nice, large and sturdy huts; it shares the beach with the sprawling *Tub Tim Resort* (ⓣ038 644025, ⓦwww.tubtimresort.com; ❸–❼), which comprises around sixty bungalows of various sizes and comfort.

Clamber up over the next headland to reach Samet's smallest and least commercial beach, **AO NUAN**. The mellow restaurant of the *Ao Nuan* has some of the best veggie food on the island and its idiosyncratic huts (❷–❹) are simple, with shared facilities, but unusual, and a few are built right over the beach. The rocky beach is not great for swimming, but Ao Tub Tim is only five minutes' walk away.

Ao Cho, Ao Wong Duan and Ao Thian (Candlelight Beach)

A five-minute walk south along the track from Ao Nuan brings you to **AO CHO**, a wide stretch of beach that seems to be less popular than the others and has just a handful of bungalow outfits, the most interesting of which is *Tarn Tawan Resort* (ⓣ038 644070; ⓔislandtour1999@hotmail.com; ④), whose characterful, white-washed bungalows are set around a peaceful lawn and decorated with shell mobiles and pale-blue-and-pink paintwork.

The horseshoe bay of **AO WONG DUAN**, round the next headland, is dominated by pricey bungalow resorts and lined with stalls. If you're staying here, you may as well splash out, either on *Wong Duan Villa* (ⓣ038 652300; ④–⑥), whose characterful fan and air-con white-plank huts are built on stilts and have picture windows and decks; or on the super-sleek *Talébure Bed and Bar* (ⓣ01 862 9402, ⓔtalebure@hotmail.com; ⑥–⑦), where the minimalist whitewashed timber bungalows have dark-wood floors and great views, and the restaurant deck juts out over the water.

AO THIAN (also known as **Candlelight Beach**) has none of the commerce of Wong Duan, a couple of minutes' walk over the hill, though its lovely, scenic shorefront is fronted by an unbroken line of bungalows and little restaurants. *Candlelight Resort* (ⓣ01 153 3813; ③–④) makes the most of the views: its plain but decent fan huts are strung out in a long line, with each one facing the water.

Chanthaburi

Though there's not much to see in the provincial capital of **CHANTHABURI**, 80km east of Ban Phe, you may find yourself stranded here between **buses**, as this is a transit point for most Rayong–Trat buses and a handy terminus for buses to and from the northeast. Eight daily buses make the scenic six-hour Chanthaburi–Sa Kaew–Khorat journey in both directions, with Sa Kaew (3hr) being a useful interchange for buses to Aranyaprathet and **the Cambodian border** (see box on opposite for details). Buses to and from all these places, as well as Bangkok's Eastern and Northern bus terminals, use the Chanthaburi bus station on Thanon Saritidet, about 750m northwest of the town centre and less than ten minutes' walk west of *Kasemsan 1* hotel (ⓣ039 312340; ②), at 98/1 Thanon Benchama-Rachutit, which has sizeable fan and air-con rooms.

Trat

The small, engaging market town of **TRAT,** 68km east of Chanthaburi, is the perfect place to stock up on essentials before heading out to Ko Chang and the outer islands, via the port at Laem Ngop (see p.1036), or on to **Cambodia**, via the border at Hat Lek (see p.1036). Private and government air-con **buses** from Bangkok's Eastern and Northern bus terminals, Ban Phe and Chanthaburi all drop their passengers along the central four-hundred-metre stretch of the main Thanon Sukhumvit, within a few hundred metres of the departure points for Laem Ngop and Hat Lek. Tiny **Trat Airport** is served by flights to and from Bangkok, and taxis ferry air-passengers the 16km on to Laem Ngop; the Bangkok Airways office (ⓣ039 525299) is on the northern edge of town, just beyond the Highway 317 turn-off to Khlong Yai. There's **Internet** access at many guesthouses, at Cybercafé on Thanon Sukhumvit, and at the CAT overseas telephone office on Thanon Vivatthana on the eastern edge of town (daily 7am–4.30pm). The best sources of local **information** are the Tratosphere bookshop, 200m east

Overland into Cambodia via Aranyaprathet-Poipet and Chanthaburi province

The most commonly used **overland crossing into Cambodia** is at **Poipet**, which lies just across the border from the Thai town of **Aranyaprathet**. The border here is open daily from 7am to 8pm and officials will issue thirty-day Cambodian **visas on arrival** (see p.984 for details, and ⓦwww.talesofasia.com/cambodia-overland-bkksr-self.htm for a description of the crossing). Once through the border, you face a gruelling eight- to twelve-hour journey in the back of a pick-up to cover the 150km of potholed road between Poipet and Siem Reap. If you need a **hotel** in Aranyaprathet, try either the comfortable fan and air-con rooms at *Inter Hotel* on Thanon Chatasingh (ⓣ037 231291; ❷–❺), or the cheaper *Aran Garden II* at 110 Thanon Rat Uthit (❶–❸).

Travelling to Poipet from east-coast towns, the easiest route is to take a bus **from Chanthaburi** to the town of **Sa Kaew**, 130km to the northeast, and then change to one of the frequent buses for the 55-kilometre ride east to Aranyaprathet. **From Bangkok**, the easiest way to get to Aranyaprathet is by **train** (2 daily; 6hr): you'll need to catch the one at 5.55am to ensure reaching the border before 5pm; the other leaves at 1.05pm. Return trains depart Aranyaprathet at 6.35am and 1.35pm. Tuk-tuks will take you the 4km from the train station to the border post. Alternatively, take a **bus** from Bangkok's Northern Bus Terminal to Aranyaprathet (4 daily until 5.30pm; 4hr 30min), then a tuk-tuk to the border. The last Aranyaprathet–Bangkok bus leaves at 5pm. It's also possible to buy a **through ticket to Siem Reap** from Bangkok from almost any travel agent in Banglamphu for about B1600; transport is by minibus to the border and then by pick-up to Siem Reap. There are also two less-used crossings in **Chanthaburi province**, giving access to the Cambodian town of **Pailin**, just east of the border: Daung Lem Border Crossing at **Ban Laem** is 88km northeast of Chanthaburi and the Phsa Prom border crossing is at **Ban Pakkard** (aka Chong Phakkat), 72km northeast of Chanthaburi. Both border points are accessible by chartered songthaew from the town of **Pong Nam Ron**, 42km north of Chanthaburi on Highway 317. Songthaews from Chanthaburi to Pong Nam Ron take about ninety minutes. The borders are open daily from 7am to 8pm, but at the time of writing do not issue **visas** on arrival.

along Thanon Lak Muang from Thanon Sukhumvit, at 23 Soi Kluarimklong, and *Cool Corner* restaurant (see below). The best **hospital** is the Bangkok-Trat Hospital ⓣ039 532735, on the Sukhumvit Highway, 1km north of Trat Department Store.

Recommended **guesthouses** include *Jame*, 200m walk south along Thanon Sukhumvit from the bus drops, then 50m east down Thanon Lak Muang (ⓣ039 530458; ❶), which has just eleven rooms, all with shared bath, split between two houses (one of which has cooking facilities) on opposite sides of the road; *Ban Jaidee*, 200m walk east across from Thanon Sukhumvit's Trat Department Store, then a few metres' walk north up Thanon Chaimongkon (ⓣ039 520678; ❶), a calm, inviting and rather stylish guesthouse with a pleasant seating area downstairs and just seven simple bedrooms upstairs; and *Guy Guest House*, 300m walk south down Thanon Sukhumvit from the bus stops then 200m walk east along Thanon Thoncharoen (ⓣ039 524556, ⓔguy_gh2001@hotmail.com; ❶), a popular, commercial guesthouse with well-priced if thin-walled rooms, some of them en suite.

The day market, on the ground floor of the Thanon Sukhumvit shopping centre, and the night market, between Soi Vichidanya and Soi Kasemsan, east of Thanon Sukhumvit, are both great **places to eat**, while *Cool Corner*, west of *Guy's Guest House*, on the corner of Soi Yai Onn and Thanon Thoncharoen, is an enjoyably arty spot to chill-out over homemade bread, real coffee and veggie specials, and keeps excellent travellers' comment books on Ko Chang and Cambodia.

Laem Ngop

The piers for Ko Chang, Ko Mak and Ko Whai are at **LAEM NGOP**, 17km southwest of Trat and served by songthaews from Thanon Sukhumvit (every 30min; 20–40min); details of boat services are given in the relevant accounts. **Tourist minibus** services also run direct to Laem Ngop from Bangkok's Thanon Khao San, Pattaya, and Ban Phe (near Ko Samet). You can buy ferry tickets and reserve island accommodation (definitely worthwhile in peak season) at the old pier-head near the **TAT office** (daily 8.30am–4.30pm; ⓣ039 597259, ⓔtatrat@ksc.th.com). The passenger-ferry pier (for foot-passengers), which is known as Laem Ngop Monument Pier, or Tha Kromaluang Chumphorn, is a fifteen-minute walk from here. The Immigration Office is 3km northeast of Laem Ngop pier, on the road to Trat pier (Mon–Fri 8.30am–4.30pm; ⓣ039 597261).

Ko Chang

The focal point of a national marine park archipelago of 52 islands, **KO CHANG** is Thailand's second-largest island (after Phuket) and an increasingly popular destination. During peak season, accommodation on the west coast fills up very fast, but it gets quieter (and cheaper) from May to October, when fierce storms can make the sea too rough to swim in. Though mosquitoes are not much in evidence, Ko Chang is one of the few areas of Thailand still considered to be **malarial**, so you may want to start taking prophylactics before you arrive; for on-the-spot advice contact Ko Chang International Clinic on Hat Sai Khao (daily 9am–8pm, ⓣ039 551151; 24hr ⓣ01 863 3609).

Overland into Cambodia via Hat Lek–Koh Kong

Many travellers use the **Hat Lek–Koh Kong border crossing** (daily 7am–8pm) for overland travel into Cambodia, not least because thirty-day **visas on arrival** are issued here and Koh Kong has reasonable transport connections to Sihanoukville and, via Sre Ambel, Phnom Penh. For a comprehensive guide to the crossing, see ⓦwww.talesofasia.com/cambodia-overland-bkkpp.htm, and check the travellers' comment books at *Cool Corner* restaurant in Trat (see p.1035).

The only way to get to **Hat Lek** is by minibus from Trat, 91km northwest. **Minibuses** leave Trat approximately every 45 minutes between 6am and 5pm (1hr–1hr 30min; B100) from near the market on Thanon Sukhumvit. In the reverse direction, the timetable is almost the same.

Hat Lek (on the Thai side) and Koh Kong (in Cambodia) are on opposite sides of the Dong Tong River estuary, but a bridge connects the two banks. If you want to reach **Sihanoukville** in one day, you'll need to catch the 6am minibus from Trat, which should give you just enough time to connect with the daily 8am **boat** to Sihanoukville from **Koh Kong** (sometimes referred to as Krong Koh Kong) across on the eastern bank of the estuary. To reach Koh Kong pier, you need to take a motorcycle or car taxi from the Hat Lek immigration post, across the bridge, to Koh Kong on the east bank of the estuary. Shortly after leaving Koh Kong, the Sihanoukville boat makes a brief stop at **Pak Khlong** (aka Bak Kleng) at the (western) mouth of the estuary, which you can reach by boat from the immigration post without having to go via Koh Kong, though the boats are old and reportedly not very safe.

If you leave Trat later in the day and need to overnight in Koh Kong, simply follow the route described above to Koh Kong pier. For a thorough guide to Koh Kong and how to reach it from both sides of the border, visit ⓦwww.kohkong.com/kohkong/overland.html.

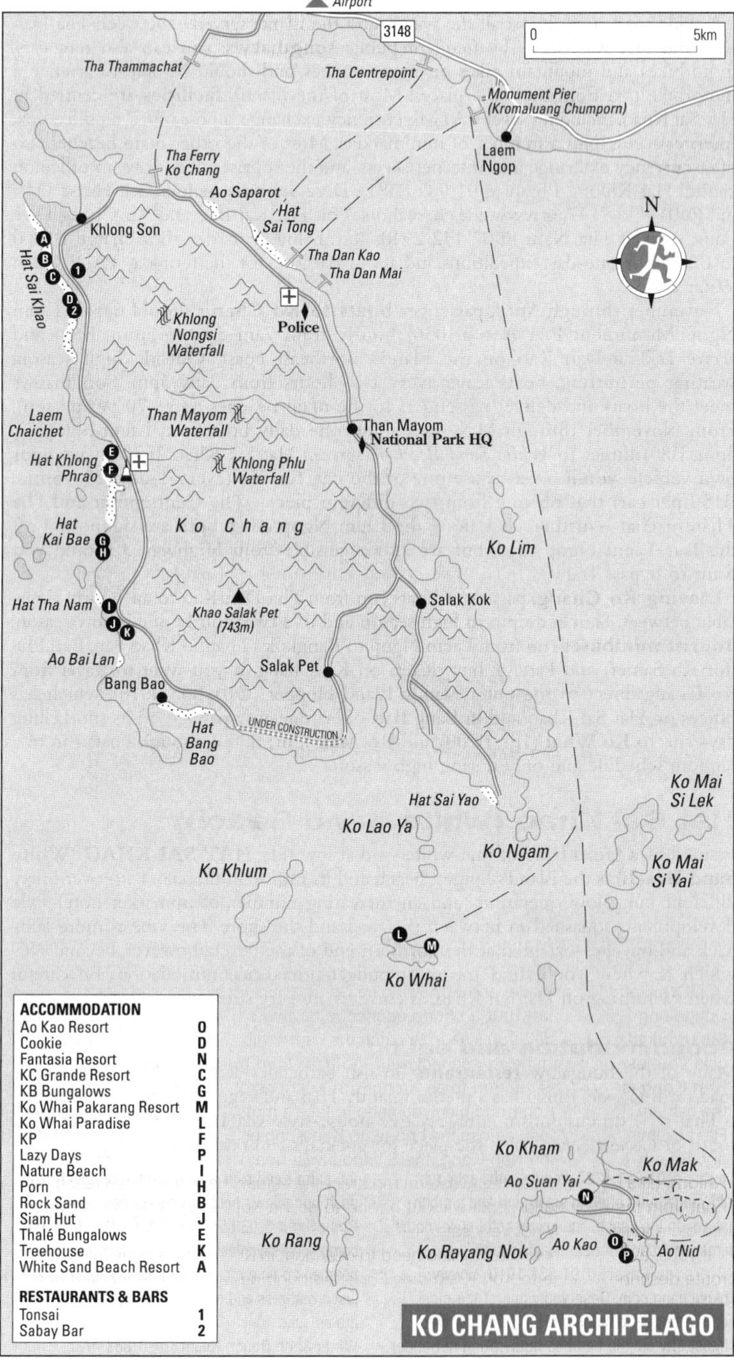

KO CHANG ARCHIPELAGO

A wide road runs almost all the way round the island, served – between Tha Dan Kao and Hat Kai Bae – by frequent public **songthaews**; you can also rent cars, motorbikes and mountain bikes on most beaches, and should be able to arrange a motorbike taxi from the same places. Most of the island's **facilities** are centred in Hat Sai Khao, including several ATMs, currency exchange, a post office, a police box, Internet access, plus a number of minimarkets. Most of the other main beaches also offer currency exchange and Internet access, and the tourist police have an office on central Hat Khlong Phrao (ⓣ01 982 8381). **Dive schools** include Sea Horse Diving (ⓣ01 996 7147, ⓦwww.ede.ch/seahorse) on Hat Kai Bae, and Ko Chang Dive Point on Hat Tha Nam (ⓣ07 142 2948, ⓔarnhelm@gmx.de); they charge B1800 to B2700 for one-day expeditions and about B10,000 for the four-day PADI Open Water course.

November through April, passenger **boats to Ko Chang** should depart Laem Ngop Monument Pier (see p.1036) hourly from 7am–5pm (45min; B50) and arrive at Tha Dan Kao on the island's northeast coast. Outside high season, weather permitting, boats leave every two hours from 9am–5pm. Songthaews meet the boats and deliver passengers to the main beaches (B30–70 per person). From November through May, there's also one daily boat from Laem Ngop (at 3pm; B80) direct to *White Sand Beach Resort* on Hat Sai Khao. If you have your own vehicle, you'll need to use one of the **car ferries** (every 1-2hr; 25–45min; B150 per car) that operate from two different piers – Tha Centrepoint and Tha Thammachat – further west along the Laem Ngop coast; both are signposted off the Trat–Laem Ngop road, but are also accessible from Highway 3 should you want to bypass Trat.

Leaving Ko Chang, passenger boats run from Tha Dan Kao to an hourly timetable between 8am and 6pm in high season and to a two-hourly one in low season. **Tourist minibuses** run from Laem Ngop to Bangkok's Thanon Khao San, Ban Phe (for Ko Samet) and Pattaya: buy tickets on Ko Chang. If you want to travel from Ko Chang direct to the outer islands, Island Hopper (ⓣ01 865 0610), which has offices on Hat Sai Khao and in Bang Bao, offers one-way passage on its snorkelling day-trips to **Ko Whai** (1hr; B200) and **Ko Mak** (2hr; B300), though boats run to a random schedule and only during high season.

Hat Sai Khao (White Sand Beach)

Framed by a broad band of fine white sand at low tide, **HAT SAI KHAO (White Sand Beach)** is the island's longest beach and its most commercial, with over thirty different bungalow operations and an increasing number of upmarket hotel-style developments squashed in between the road and the shore. The vibe is more laid-back and traveller-oriented at the northern end of the beach, however, beyond *KC*, which is where you'll find the most budget-priced accommodation. Be careful when swimming off Hat Sai Khao, as currents are very strong here.

Accommodation and eating

Many of the bungalow **restaurants** do fish barbecues at night. North across the road from *Cookie*, Tonsai has a predominantly Thai and vegetarian menu and seating is Thai-style on cushions in a breezy tree-house-style sala. Down on the beach, just south of *Cookie*, *Sabay Bar* is the place for cocktails and rave music.

Cookie ⓣ01 861 4227. Popular, efficiently run mid-range outfit offering smart, fan and a/c bungalows on the beach, and luxury hotel-style rooms across the road from the beach. ❹–❽

KC Grande Resort ⓣ01 833 1010, ⓦwww.kckohchang.com. Deservedly one of the most popular budget options on Hat Sai Khao, with almost fifty simple bamboo huts strung out under the palm trees over a long stretch of beach. The posh bungalows here are overpriced. ❷–❾

Rock Sand ⓣ039 551165. A travellers' favourite, comprising seventeen simple, idiosyncratic huts perched up on a rocky ledge; the cheapest have just a mattress and a mosquito net, the better ones are en suite. ❷

White Sand Beach Resort ⓣ01 863 7737,

ⓦwww.whitesandbeachresort.com. Located in a secluded, very attractive spot at the far north end of the beach (about 10min walk along the sand from *Rock Sand*), *White Sand Beach Resort* offers a range of nicely spaced huts, many of them quite basic, but most with uninterrupted sea views. ❷–❺

Hat Khlong Phrao and Hat Kai Bae

Just south of the khlong fed by **Khlong Phu Waterfall** (B200 entry fee), the long sandy beach of central **HAT KHLONG PHRAO** is partially shaded by casuarinas and backed by a huge coconut grove. Its northerly end is occupied by the primitive wooden-plank **huts** of one of the cheapest places to stay on Ko Chang, *Thalé Bungalows* (ⓣ01 926 3843; ❶–❷), whose land runs right up to the khlong. Less basic but still very much traveller-oriented, the popular *KP* (ⓣ01 863 7262; ❷–❸) has fifty fairly simple wooden huts, some of them designed for families, attractively scattered through a coconut grove just a few steps from the beach. The management rents out mountain bikes and kayaks, and organizes snorkelling and fishing day-trips.

About 5km further south, the narrow, once beautiful beach at **HAT KAI BAE** has been almost ruined by breakneck development. The nicest remaining stretch of beach is in front of *KB Bungalows* (ⓣ01 862 8103; ❹–❻) whose attractive fan and air-con bungalows have huge glass windows and comfy interiors. The laid-back travellers' hangout *Porn* (ⓣ09 099 8757; ❷), a few hundred metres south down the beach, is the only cheap place to stay here now and offers both bamboo huts with shared facilities and en-suite wooden bungalows, as well as an appealing shoreside deck.

Hat Tha Nam (Lonely Beach)

Around the southern headland from Hat Kai Bae, the long curve of white sand bay at **HAT THA NAM** – dubbed **Lonely Beach** before it became the backpackers' mecca – is one of the nicest beaches on the island. It's also got cheapish accommodation and is Ko Chang's main party beach. Be extremely careful when swimming here, however, especially around *Siam Beach* at the far northern end, as the steep shelf and dangerous current result in a sobering number of **drownings** every year – twenty in 2003; do your swimming further south and don't go out at all when the waves are high.

In the central beach area, *Nature Beach* (ⓣ01 803 8933; ❷–❸) is a friendly, popular place with simple, en-suite huts, plus pricier, attractively furnished options. Close by, *Siam Hut* (ⓣ09 833 4747; ❷) has rows and rows of primitive, split-bamboo huts, all of them en suite. Set on the rocky headland at the southern end of the bay, the German-Thai-managed *Treehouse* (ⓣ01 847 8215; ❶–❷) is the place that put this beach on the map and is the most chilled spot on Hat Tha Nam. Its forty cute, shaggy-thatched huts all contain just a mattress, a mosquito net and a paraffin lamp (there's no electricity in the huts) and all of them share bathrooms; there's also an inviting seaside deck area with hammocks and floor cushions.

Ko Whai

Lovely, peaceful little **KO WHAI** (or Ko Wai), which lies about 10km off Ko Chang's southeastern headland, is the perfect place to escape the commercial chaos of Ko Chang. It's only about 3km long and 1.5km wide and has no facilities at all except for a couple of **places to stay** (Nov–April): basic bamboo huts at the inviting, laid-back *Ko Whai Paradise* (ⓣ039 597031; ❶–❷) on the western end of the island; and the more comfortable bungalows of *Ko Whai Pakarang Resort* (ⓣ01 945 4383; ❷–❸) towards the eastern headland. **Boats** to Ko Whai depart Laem Ngop's Monument Pier once a day at 3pm (Nov–April; 2hr 30min; B150), and Island Hopper boats (Ⓣ01 865 0610) run several times a week during high season from Ko Chang (1hr; B200) and Ko Mak (1hr; B200).

Ko Mak

KO MAK (sometimes spelt "Maak"), 20km southeast of Ko Chang, fosters an equally seductive atmosphere but is a little larger and more developed than Ko Whai, with at least a dozen places to stay scattered along its two finest white-sand beaches. The island is traversed by a couple of narrow concrete roads, but most people get about by bicycle or on foot via the network of sandy tracks that cuts through the coconut and rubber plantations.

The nicest beach is palm-fringed **Ao Kao** on the southwest coast, where the British-run *Lazy Days* sits at the far southern end (Ⓣ09 099 7819, Ⓔblacktip24@hotmail.com; closed June–Sept; ❶–❷), a deservedly popular, traveller-oriented spot where you can choose between thatched tepees and huts with or without private bathrooms. Neighbouring *Ao Kao Resort* (Ⓣ039 501001, Ⓔkhunrano@yahoo.com; ❷–❹) drops down to the prettiest part of the beach and has a big range of accommodation, from rattan huts with shared facilities to large, en-suite timber bungalows. Long, curvy **Ao Suan Yai** on the northwest coast is home to the inviting *Fantasia Resort* (Ⓣ039 501013, Ⓦwww.kohmakresort.com; closed June–Sept; ❶–❺), with huge, very comfortable en-suite octagonal bungalows built alongside a small lagoon, and some simpler A-frame huts among the palm trees. The **food** at *Fantasia* is particularly good, with specialities including homemade bread, pastas and pizzas.

There is no bank on the island but bungalows will change money; there's **Internet** access at *Ao Kao Resort* and at *Koh Mak Resort* on Ao Suan Yai, a post office at *Koh Mak Resort*, and a small clinic on the cross-island road. From November to April, there's one **boat** a day from Laem Ngop's Monument Pier to Ao Nid on Ko Mak's southeastern coast (departs 3pm; 3hr 30min; B210); the return boat leaves Ao Nid daily at 8am. During the rest of the year, the boat runs only if the weather permits. Bungalow staff meet the boats. Travelling to or from Ko Chang (2hr; B300) or Ko Whai (1hr; B200) you can make use of the Island Hopper boats (Ⓣ01 865 0610), which run several times a week during high season to *Ko Mak Resort* on the northwest coast.

10.5

The northeast: Isaan

Bordered by Laos and Cambodia on three sides, the tableland of **northeast** Thailand, known as **Isaan**, is the least-visited region of the kingdom and the poorest, but also its most traditional. Most northeasterners speak a dialect that's more comprehensible to residents of Vientiane than Bangkok, and Isaan's historic allegiances have tied it more closely to Laos and Cambodia than to Thailand. Between the eleventh and thirteenth centuries, the all-powerful Khmers covered the northeast in magnificent stone temple complexes, which can still be admired at **Phimai** and **Phanom Rung**. The mighty **Mekong River** forms 750km of the border between Isaan and Laos, and there are four points along it in this region where foreigners are allowed to cross the border (there's also a little-used border crossing into Cambodia from Isaan, described on p.1041). The river makes a popular backpackers' trail, not least because of its laid-back waterfront guesthouses in **Chiang Khan**, **Sang Khom**, **Nong Khai** and **That Phanom**. Inland scenery is rewarding too, with good hiking trails at the national parks of **Khao Yai** and **Phu Kradung** and an extraordinary hilltop meditation retreat at **Wat Phu Tok**.

Khao Yai National Park

Khao Yai National Park offers a realistic chance of seeing white-handed (lar) gibbons, pig-tailed macaques, hornbills, civets and barking deer, plus the possibility of sighting an elephant or a tiger. The park has lots of waterfalls and several undemanding walking trails; it's only 120km northeast of Bangkok, and is Thailand's most popular national park. The best way to see Khao Yai is to stay either in the park itself, just outside it, or in the nearby town of Pak Chong; you have the choice of exploring the trails yourself or joining a backpackers' tour. Bring warm clothes as it gets cool at night.

Fifteen well-worn **trails** radiate from the area around the park's visitor centre and headquarters (at kilometre stone 37), and a few more branch off from the roads that cross the park. The main trails are numbered and should be easy to follow; sketch maps are available at the visitor centre. The most popular include Trail 5 to Nong Pak Chee observation tower (4.5km one-way; 2hr 30min) and Trail 1 to Haew Suwat Falls (8.3km one-way; 3–4hr), which featured in the 1999 film *The Beach*.

Practicalities

To get to the park, first take a **bus** or **train** to **PAK CHONG**, which is 37km north of Khao Yai's visitor centre and major trailheads. The cheapest way to get from Pak Chong to Khao Yai is to take a songthaew (every 30min 6.30am–5pm; 30min) from outside the 7–11 shop, 200m west of the footbridge on the north (railway) side of Pak Chong's main road, to the park checkpoint, which is about 14km short of the Khao Yai visitor centre and main trailheads. Public songthaews aren't allowed beyond here, so at the checkpoint (where you pay the B200 entrance fee), park rangers will get passing cars to give you a ride up to the visitor centre. Alternatively, charter a songthaew from Pak Chong to the park instead (B1200 for the day) – charters are allowed into the park like any private vehicle. Coming back from the park, hitch back to the checkpoint then take a songthaew (last one about 5pm).

To stay at the **national park lodges** (❹) in the heart of Khao Yai, you need to reserve ahead through the Royal Forestry Department office in Bangkok (see "Accommodation", p.942), but if you want to camp you can just turn up at the park headquarters (Ⓣ09 424 7698) and arrange to rent a **tent**, bedding and cooking equipment (B250 inclusive) there; avoid weekends, which get booked out well in advance. There's a cafeteria complex opposite the HQ and visitor centre.

Alternatively, you could base yourself in Pak Chong, at the spartan *Phubade Hotel* (Ⓣ044 314964; ❶–❷), located just 50m south of the train station on Tesaban Soi 15. If you're doing a tour, you'll stay at the tour operators' accommodation (see below). Pak Chong's exceptionally good **night market** sets up on the edge of the main road, between Tesaban sois 17 and 19.

Tours and night safaris

The good thing about joining a **tour** of Khao Yai is that you're accompanied by an expert wildlife-spotter, and you have transport between the major sights of the park; book ahead if possible. As Khao Yai has recently been plagued with unscrupulous, fly-by-night tour operators, we are recommending only three companies, all of which run budget tours lasting for a day and a half (B950), with the middle night spent outside the park: accommodation and the B200 park entrance fee are extra. Wildlife Safari (Ⓣ09 628 8224, Ⓔwildlifesafari@bigfoot.com) is at 39 Thanon Pak Chong Subsanun, Nong Kaja, about 2km north of Pak Chong train station; call for free transport from Pak Chong. Accommodation is at the pleasant lodgings (❷) behind their office. *Khao Yai Garden Lodge* (Ⓣ044 365178, Ⓦwww.khaoyai-garden-lodge.com) is based outside Pak Chong at kilometre-stone marker 7 on the road into the park, and offers a range of accommodation in a beautifully landscaped garden, and a pool (❷–❺). Family-run *Green Leaf Guest House and Tour* (Ⓣ044 365073, Ⓔbirdman_nine@hotmail.com), not to be confused with Green Leaf Travel Service at the station, is at kilometre-stone 7.5 on the park road, 12.5km out of Pak Chong, and offers simple en-suite rooms (❶) and a good, cheap restaurant.

A much-touted park attraction are the hour-long **night safaris** ("night lightings") that take truckloads of tourists round Khao Yai's main roads in the hope of sighting deer and civets, or even elephants and tigers. Most tours include a night safari, but if you're on your own, book a place on one of the trucks at the national park headquarters; they leave from there every night at 7pm and 8pm and cost B330 for up to eight people.

Khorat (Nakhon Ratchasima)

Ninety kilometres from Pak Chong, **KHORAT** (officially known as Nakhon Ratchasima) has nothing of interest in itself but can be used as a base for exploring Phimai and Phanom Rung. If you're looking for something to do, take local bus #1307 from Bus Terminal 2 or Khorat's southern city gate to the interesting little pottery village of **DAN KWIAN**, 15km south of Khorat on Route 224.

There are two long-distance **bus terminals** in Khorat, of which Bus Terminal 2, situated on the far northern edge of the city on Highway 2, is the more useful, used by regular and air-con buses to most places, including Phimai, Pak Chong, Ban Tako, Bangkok, Chiang Mai, Surin, Khon Kaen and Nong Khai. The easiest way to get to and from Bus Terminal 2 is by tuk-tuk. Bus Terminal 1 is just off Thanon Suranari, close to the town centre and most hotels, and runs a few buses to Bangkok. Arriving at the **train station** on Thanon Mukkhamontri, you're midway between the commercial centre to the east (1km) and the TAT office to the west (1km). The **airport** is 20km east of town on Highway 226.

Local buses (B7) and songthaews (B5) travel most of Khorat's main roads: yellow #1 heads west along Thanon Chumphon, past the train station, returning east via Thanon Yommarat; #2 runs between the main TAT office in the west, via the train station, and Suranari and Assadang roads, to the east; and #3 also runs right across the city, via Mahathai and Jomsurangyat roads, past the train station, to the **TAT** office (daily 8.30am–4.30pm; ⓣ044 213666, ⓔtatsima@tat.or.th), on the western edge of town, which has free city bus maps.

The best budget **accommodation** in Khorat are the quiet, simple fan and air-con rooms at *Siri Hotel*, 688 Thanon Pho Klang, ten minutes' walk east from the train station (ⓣ044 242831; ❶-❷); the hotel runs minibus trips to Phimai. The more luxurious *Chomsurang Hotel* at 2701/2 Thanon Mahathai (ⓣ044 257088, ⓦwww.chomsurang.com; ❺) has a pool and is good value.

The night bazaar on Thanon Manat includes a few hot-food stalls, but there's a bigger selection of night-market-style **food** stalls about 800m further east near the *Iyara* hotel on Thanon Chumphon. *Bibi's*, 300m east of *Sri Hotel* at 520 Thanon Pho Klang (closes about 6pm), is a very cheap Muslim foodshop serving halal curries and standard one-dish Thai meals; while *Thai Phochana* at 142 Thanon Jomsurangyat is known for its mid-priced duck curries and Khorat-style noodles cooked with coconut cream.

There is **Internet** access opposite the *Sripatana Hotel* on Thanon Suranari, and a few hundred metres west of the train station on Thanon Mukhamontri; the CAT overseas telephone office is inside the city walls on Thanon Sanpasit. Nanta Travel Service, just east of the *Sripatana Hotel* on Thanon Suranari (ⓣ044 251339, ⓦwww.nantatravel.com), sells bus and air tickets, rents out motorbikes and cars, and runs day-trips to local sights. The private St Mary's Hospital is at 307 Thanon Mittraphap (Highway 2), near Bus Terminal 2 (ⓣ044 261261), and the main **police** station is opposite Bus Terminal 2 on Highway 2 (ⓣ044 341777–9).

Phimai

The tiny modern town of **PHIMAI**, 60km northeast of Khorat, is dominated by the exquisitely restored eleventh-century Khmer temple complex of **Prasat Hin Phimai** (daily 7.30am–6pm; B40). Built mainly of dusky pink and greyish-white sandstone, it was connected by a direct road to the Khmer capital Angkor and follows the classic precepts of Khmer temple design: a series of walls or galleries punctuated by false balustraded windows, surrounding an inner sanctuary containing several prangs (corn-cob-shaped tower), which house important religious images. Phimai's magnificent main prang has been restored to its original cruciform ground-plan, complete with an almost full set of carvings. Those around the outside of the prang depict predominantly Hindu themes: Shiva – the Destroyer – dances above the main entrance to the southeast antechamber, his destruction dance heralding the end of the world and the creation of a new order. Most of the other external carvings pick out episodes from the *Ramayana*. By the early thirteenth century, Phimai had been turned into a Buddhist temple, and the main prang now houses Phimai's most important image, the Buddha sheltered by a seven-headed naga (snake). Many other stonecarvings can be seen at the well-presented **Phimai National Museum** (daily 8.30am–4pm; B30) northeast of the ruins, just inside the old city walls.

Regular **bus** #1305 runs from Khorat's Bus Terminal 2 (every 30min; 90min) to Phimai and stops near the ruins; the last return bus departs Phimai at 7pm. Phimai makes a much more appealing **overnight** stop than Khorat: *Old Phimai Guest House* (ⓣ044 471918; ❶–❷) is a lovely old wooden house with a roof garden and B80 dorms, just off Thanon Chomsudasadet near the ruins; it also runs day-trips to Phanom Rung (B380). *Bai Teiy* on Thanon Chomsudasadet serves tasty Thai dishes, including fresh fish, and rents bicycles. There is **Internet** access at the Agfa photo shop on Thanon Chomsudasadet.

Prasat Hin Khao Phanom Rung and Prasat Muang Tam

Built during the same period as Phimai, the temple complexes of **Prasat Hin Khao Phanom Rung** (often shortened to just Phanom Rung) and **Prasat Muang Tam** form two more links in the chain that once connected the Khmer capital with the limits of its empire. To get to the ruins, you first need to take a bus to the small town of **BAN TAKO**, located on Highway 24, 115km southeast of Khorat or 83km southwest of Surin; bus #274 travels between the two provincial capitals (every 30min). From Ban Tako, it's 12km south to Phanom Rung and another 8km south to Muang Tham, so you'll either have to hitch or rent a motorbike taxi (B300 per person for the round trip). Most people do the ruins as a day-trip from Khorat, Phimai (67km to the north) or Surin, but there's a welcoming guesthouse, *Honey Inn* (ⓣ044 622825, ⓦhoneyinn.com; ❷) in the town of **NANG RONG**, 14km west of Ban Tako on Highway 24; call for availability and directions.

PRASAT HIN KHAO PHANOM RUNG (daily 6am–6pm; B40) dates back to the tenth century and stands as the finest example of Khmer architecture in Thailand, its every surface ornamented with exquisite carvings and its buildings so perfectly aligned that on the morning of April's full-moon day you can stand at the westernmost gateway and see the rising sun through all fifteen doors. This day marks Songkhran, the Thai New Year, which is celebrated here with a day-long festival of huge parades. Before entering the temple, it's well worth visiting the excellent, museum-like **Phanom Rung Tourist Information Centre** (daily 9am–4pm; free) inside the Gate 1 car park to bone up on symbolism and background. You approach the temple compound along a dramatic two-hundred-metre-long avenue flanked with lotus-bud pillars, going over the first of three naga (snake) bridges, and past four small purification ponds. This constitutes the symbolic crossing of the abyss between earth and heaven. Part of the gallery that runs right round the inner compound has been restored to its original covered design, with arched roofs, small chambers inside and false windows. Above the entrance to the main prang (corn-cob shaped tower), are carvings of a dancing ten-armed Shiva, and of a reclining Vishnu, who is dreaming up a new universe.

Down on the well-watered plains 8km to the southeast of Phanom Rung, and accessed via a scenic minor road that cuts through a swathe of rice-fields, the small but elegant temple complex of **PRASAT MUANG TAM** (daily 7.30am–6pm; B30) is sited behind a huge kilometre-long *baray* (Khmer reservoir), which was probably constructed at the same time as the main part of the temple, in the early eleventh century. Like Phanom Rung, Muang Tam is based on the classic Khmer design of a central prang, flanked by minor prangs and encircled by a gallery punctuated with gateways. The four stone-rimmed L-shaped ponds between the gallery and the outer wall may have been used to purify worshippers as they entered the complex.

Surin and around

Best known for the much-hyped elephant round-up held here every year on the third weekend of November (details and bookings through Saren Travel, ⓣ044 513599, ⓔsarentour@yahoo.com), **SURIN**, 197km east of Khorat, is an otherwise typical northeastern town but makes a good base for Phanom Rung and has a fine guesthouse. It's also an excellent place to buy silk, either from the women who sell their cloth around the Tannasarn–Krungsrinai intersection, or from the Ruen Mai Silk Shop at 52 Thanon Chitramboong.

One of the best reasons for coming to Surin is to take one of the outstanding local **tours** organized from *Pirom's Guest House* (see below). Pirom is a very knowledgeable former social worker whose day-trips (from B550 per person) give tourists an unusual

Overland into Cambodia via Chong Chom–O'Smach

Buses leave Surin approximately once an hour from dawn until 4.30pm for the ninety-minute journey via Prasat to Kap Choeng's **Chong Chom** border pass. Cambodian **visas** are issued on arrival at the Chong Chom–O'Smach checkpoint (daily 7am–8pm; $20 or B1000), from where you can get transport to Anlong Veng. Arriving from Cambodia, songthaews and motorbike taxis ferry travellers from the border checkpoint to the bus stop for Prasat and Surin. For travellers' accounts of the border crossing, see ⓦtalesofasia.com/cambodia-overland-osm-reports.htm; for details on other overland routes into Cambodia, see p.1036.

glimpse into rural northeastern life; some itineraries also feature the Ban Ta Klang elephant trainers' village. The **Surin National Museum** (Wed–Sun 8.30am–4.30pm; B30), about 5km south of town on Highway 214 (any Khorat-bound bus will drop you outside), is the place to get a handle on the province's diverse cultural roots.

Surin **train station** is on the northern edge of town, ten minutes' walk from the central market area on Thanon Krungsrinai. The **bus terminal** is one block east of the train station. *Pirom's Guest House*, one block west of the market at Thanon 242 Krungsrinai (ⓣ044 515140 or 09 355 4140; ❶), is one of the friendliest in Isaan; **rooms** have shared facilities, and there's a B70 dorm. Pirom has an overspill guesthouse amidst the rice-fields: phone for details. The best of the budget hotels is the friendly *Nit Diew Sangthong Hotel*, across from the post office and CAT overseas telephone office at 155 Thanon Tannasarn (ⓣ044 512099; ❶–❷), where all fan and air-con rooms are en suite. For fiery Isaan **food**, you can't beat Surin's lively night market, which occupies the eastern end of Thanon Krungsrinai. There is **Internet** access next to Surin Plaza off the north end of Thanon Thetsabarn, and opposite the market on Thanon Krungsrinai.

Ubon Ratchathani

Almost always referred to simply as Ubon – not to be confused with Udon (Udon Thani) to the north – **UBON RATCHATHANI**, east of Surin, is Thailand's fifth-largest city, but only really worth stopping at en route to the Lao border. If you're here in early July though, drop by for the Ubon Candle Festival, when huge beeswax sculptures are paraded through the streets. Central Ubon, between Thanon Sumpasit in the north and the Mun River in the south, is easy enough to negotiate, with Thung Si Muang Park making a useful landmark. Of the city's eight main wats, **Wat Thung Si Muang,** 300m east of the park along Thanon Sri Narong, is noteworthy for its well-preserved teak library – raised on stilts over an artificial pond to keep book-devouring insects at bay – and its murals in the bot, to the left of the library, which display lively scenes of nineteenth-century life. The **Ubon Ratchathani National Museum** (Wed–Sun 9am–4pm; B30), south from the park across Thanon Sri Narong, has decent displays on the region's geology, history and folk crafts. To buy current northeastern **crafts** such as triangular pillows and silk, visit Punchard, at 128 Thanon Ratchabut (50m east of the museum, off Thanon Khuenthani).

Practicalities

Ubon Airport is just north of the town centre, and the **train station** is in the suburb of Warinchamrab, south across the Mun River. White **city bus** #2 runs from the train station across the river into central Ubon, passing along Thanon Khuenthani, location of the TAT office. City buses #1, #3 and #6 also cross the river into Ubon. TYTS Travel Agent on Thanon Chayangkun, near the Sumpasit junction in the city centre (ⓣ045 243601), sells flights and train tickets. Nearly all long-distance buses pass through the main Ubon **bus terminal** on Thanon Chayangkun, on the northwest edge of town, which is served by city buses #2 and #3, but private air-con buses operated by Nakorn Chai use the terminal just south of the River Mun, on the road to Warinchamrab (served by city buses #1, #2, #3 and #6); the **TAT office** on Thanon Khuenthani (daily 8.30am–4.30pm; ⓣ045 243770) keeps details of which company serves what destination. Regular **local buses** and songthaews to and from Phibun Mangsahan (for connections to Chong Mek) use the terminal near the Talat Kao market place in **Warinchamrab** (served by city bus #3), but there's also a Phibun-bound service out of Ubon's main bus terminal. You can rent **motorbikes** and **cars** from Chow Wattana (ⓣ045 242202) at 39/8 Thanon Suriyat, opposite Nikko Massage. There's **Internet** access at the CAT telephone office, next to the main post office on the Thanon Srinarong/Luang intersection. Rom Kao Hospital, near the museum on Thanon Upparat (ⓣ045 244658), is well regarded and has English-speaking staff; the **police** station is on Thanon Suriyat (ⓣ045 244941).

The best and friendliest of Ubon's budget **hotels** is *Tokyo Hotel*, about a five-minute walk north of the museum at 178 Thanon Auparat (ⓣ045 241739; ❷–❸); all rooms have showers, some have air-con. Handy for the train station and connections to Chong Mek and the Lao border, but way out of central Ubon, traveller-friendly *River Moon Guest House* at 21 Thanon Si Saket 2, Warinchamrab (ⓣ045 286093, ⓔPhanth_Boonjob@yahoo.com; ❶) comprises a group of five old houses, each with a couple of basic fan rooms upstairs and shared bathrooms downstairs; from the train station, walk straight ahead for 200m, turn left down Thanon Si Saket 2, and it's 200m further, opposite the fire station; from the main bus terminal in Ubon, take city bus #2 across the Mun River to the guesthouse or train station. For inexpensive Thai and Western **food**, try *Chiokee*, across from the museum on Thanon Khuenthani; the much posher *Sakhon*, at 66 Thanon Pha Daeng, is one of Ubon's best northeastern restaurants, but moderately priced; and Ubon's main night market sets up on the north bank of the River Mun.

East to Chong Mek and into Laos

Ninety-nine kilometres east of Ubon, Highway 217 hits the **Lao border** at **Chong Mek**, site of a busy Thai-Lao market, and one of the five legal border crossings for foreigners. The border **market** here is well worth a browse, especially at weekends when it's at its liveliest. Among the stalls are traditional herbalists, lots of basketware sellers and vendors of cheap jeans, combat gear and sarongs; foreign shoppers can cross over to the Lao-side market in Vangtao simply by paying B5 at the checkpoint.

To get to Chong Mek from Ubon involves a convoluted journey via Warinchamrab (see above) and the town of **Phibun Mangsahan** (known locally as Phibun). From Ubon, take city bus #3 across the river to the Warinchamrab bus station near the Talat Kao market, and change onto a local bus to Phibun market (every 30min until 4.30pm), where you can catch a Chong Mek songthaew (hourly between 7am and 3.30pm; 1hr 30min). It's possible to get a Lao **visa** on arrival at Vangtao, the Lao side of the Chong Mek **border crossing** (official hours: Mon–Fri 8am–4pm; US$1 "surcharge" hours, Mon–Fri 4–6pm, Sat, Sun & hols 8.30am–6pm), but you'll be charged $30 and will only receive a fifteen-day visa – half the time-period of the cheaper visas issued at the Lao consulates in Bangkok and Khon Kaen; you'll also need two passport photos. Whichever option you choose, on reaching Chong Mek you first need to get the Thai exit stamp from the office hidden behind the market on the Thai side (daily 8.30am–noon & 1–4.30pm). Once through the Lao border, there's a songthaew service from Vangtao to Pakxe, 40km away (until about 5pm). Arriving at Chong Mek **from Laos**, you simply pay the Lao exit tax (B20, or B50 during "surcharge" hours) and get your Thai visa-on-arrival for free; there are two daily air-con buses from the market (4 and 5pm) to Bangkok's Northern Bus Terminal (12hr), or you can catch songthaews into Ubon.

Khon Kaen

The lively city of **KHON KAEN**, 188km northeast of Khorat makes a decent resting point on the Bangkok–Nong Khai rail line and, crucially, it also has both a Lao and a Vietnamese consulate, the only ones outside Bangkok. In keeping with its status as a university town, Khon Kaen boasts several fine collections in its **museum** on Thanon Lung Soon Rachakarn (daily 9am–4pm; B30), including Bronze Age pots from Ban Chiang, Buddha sculptures, and local folk art. The striking, modern, nine-tiered, red, white and gold pagoda at **Wat Nongwang** is also well worth a visit; it's at the far southern end of Thanon Klang Muang and served by city songthaews #8 (light blue) from the central stretch of Thanon Klang Muang and #14 (blue) from the train station, Thanon Si Chan and south-central Thanon Klang Muang. The cavernous **Prathamakant Local Goods Centre** (daily 9am–8.30pm) at 81 Thanon Ruen Rom stocks hundreds of gorgeous cotton and silk weaves, as well as triangular pillows, khaen pipes and jewellery; take almost any local bus down Thanon Na Muang to the Ruen Rom junction.

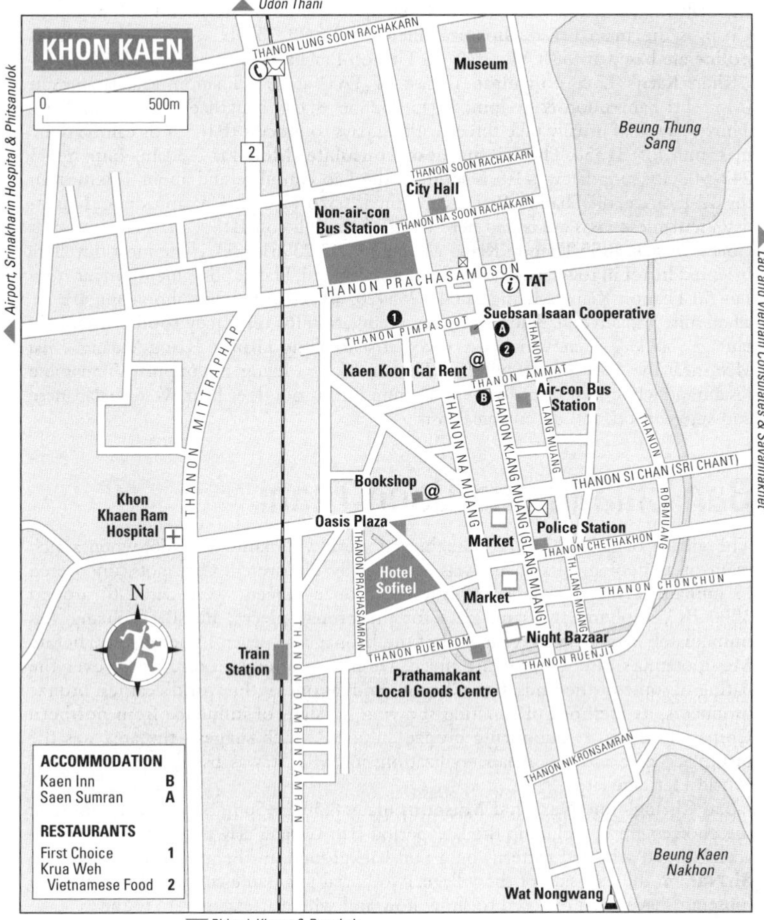

Practicalities

Khon Kaen **train station** is about fifteen minutes' walk from the main hotel area; the non-air-con **bus station** is a five-minute walk northwest of the Thanon Klang Muang hotels; the air-con bus station is right in the town centre; and the **airport** is 10km west of the city centre. The Thai Airways office is inside the *Hotel Sofitel* on Thanon Prachasumran (⊕043 227701). The most useful of the **city buses and songthaews** (B5; B6 air-con) are: #3 (yellow; train station–non-air-con bus station); #8 and #9 (both light blue; regular bus terminal–air-con-bus station–Thanon Klang Muang); #10 (blue; non-air-con bus station–TAT–Lao consulate–Vietnamese consulate–air-con-bus station– Thanon Klang Muang); #11 (red; train station–Thanon Si Chan–air-con-bus station–TAT–Lao consulate); and #15 (yellow) and #21 (brown), which both run up and down Thanon Klang Muang at least as far as Thanon Chonchun. The **TAT office** (8.30am–4.30pm; ⊕043 244498) on Thanon Prachasamoson publishes a handy **map** showing the colour-coded routes.

There's **Internet** access next to the *Roma Hotel* on Thanon Klang Muang and opposite the *Charoen Thani* hotel Thanon Si Chan. Kaen Koon Car Rent at 54/1–2 Thanon Klang Muang (⊕043 239458, ⊜kaenkoontravel@yahoo.co.uk) rents cars and sells flights. Khon Kaen Ram Hospital, on the far western end of Thanon Si Chan, is the main private **hospital** in town (⊕043 333900–3), and the **tourist police** are based at the TAT office on Thanon Prachasamoson (⊕043 236937).

Khon Kaen's **Lao consulate** is east of TAT at 171 Thanon Prachasamoson (Mon–Fri 8am–noon & 1–4pm; ⊕043 242856–8; city songthaews #11 and #10). Thirty-day visas usually take three working days to process (B1050) or can be done in 15min for B1350. The **Vietnamese consulate** (Mon–Fri 8.30am–4pm; ⊕043 242190; city songthaew #10) is south of the Lao consulate and about 1.5km from the TAT office, off Thanon Prachasamoson at 65/6 Thanon Chaiaphadung. Thirty-day Vietnamese visas are issued here within 24hr and cost B1800.

Saen Sumran, at 55 Thanon Klang Muang (⊕043 239611; ❶), is the most traveller-oriented **hotel** in town, and has a useful noticeboard. The good-value rooms at *Kaen Inn*, 56 Thanon Klang Muang (⊕043 245420, ⊜kaeninnhotel@yahoo.com; ❹), are all en suite and air-con. Khon Kaen has a reputation for very spicy **food**, particularly sausages, *sai krog isaan*, which are served at stalls along Thanon Klang Muang. *Krua Weh*, near the *Saen Sumran* hotel on Thanon Klang Muang, is a popular Vietnamese restaurant, while *First Choice* at 18/8 Thanon Pimpasoot does Thai, Western, Japanese and veggie food, and decent breakfasts.

Ban Chiang and Udon Thani

The village of **BAN CHIANG** achieved worldwide fame in 1966, when a rich seam of archeological remains was accidentally discovered. Clay pots, uncovered in human graves alongside sophisticated bronze objects, were dated to around 3000 BC, implying the same date for the bronze pieces, and Ban Chiang was immediately hailed as the vanguard of the Bronze Age, seven hundred years before Mesopotamia's discovery of the metal. Despite continuing controversy over the dating of some of the finds, Ban Chiang stands as one of the world's earliest bronze producers, its methods of smelting showing no signs of influence from northern China and other neighbouring bronze cultures, which suggests the area was the birthplace of Southeast Asian civilization; in 1992, it was listed as a UNESCO World Heritage site.

Ban Chiang's fine **National Museum** (daily 8.30am–5pm; B30) displays some of the choicest finds, including the late-period Ban Chiang clay pots, with their characteristic red whorled patterns on a buff background. In the grounds of **Wat Pho Si Nai**, on the east side of the village, two burial pits (same times and ticket as the museum) have been exposed to show how and where artefacts were found.

To get to Ban Chiang from Khon Kaen or Nong Khai, you have to go via the charmless grey city of **UDON THANI**. The **train station** is on the east side of the centre, off Thanon Prajak. **Buses** pull into Udon Thani at a variety of locations: Loei, Phitsanulok and Chiang Mai services use the terminal on the town's western bypass; Nong Khai and Ban Phu buses terminate at Talat Rungsina market on the north side of town; Bangkok, Khorat, Khon Kaen, Nakhon Phanom, Sakhon Nakhon and Ubon Ratchathani services use the other main terminal on Thanon Sai Uthit. Numbered songthaews, such as #15 between the Thanon Sai Uthit and western bypass bus terminals, ply set routes around town (B5 per person; map from TAT), and there are plenty of "skylabs", local versions of tuk-tuks, for charter (from B20).

Direct **songthaews** run between Udon's morning market, Talat Thai Isaan, on the east side of the centre, and Ban Chiang, 50km east (Mon–Sat every 30min; from Udon until about 1.30pm, from Ban Chiang until 9am; 1hr 30min), or you could catch a Sakhon Nakhon-bound bus (every 20min) to Ban Palu and then a motorized samlor (B30 per person) for the last 5km from the main road to the village.

Udon's **TAT office** (ⓣ042 325406–7) and adjoining tourist police office are north-west of the town centre on Thanon Mukmontri, and if you need to **stay** in Udon the central *Queen Hotel* at 6–8 Thanon Udon–Dussadi (ⓣ042 221451; ❶) is your best budget bet. However, the excellent *Lakeside Sunrise Guest House* (ⓣ042 208167, ⓔalexovenden696@hotmail.com; ❶) in Ban Chiang itself is a much more appealing option, with bikes available for exploring the surrounding countryside. Walk beyond the museum, then turn right at the first intersection; it's just a few minutes' stroll.

Loei

LOEI, 147km west of Udon Thani, is really only useful as a transport hub – or as a base for the famous, bawdy festival of Phi Ta Kon, held over three days at the end of June or beginning of July in Dan Sai, 80km southwest. Buses run to Loei from Udon, Khon Kaen, Phitsanulok and Bangkok, while frequent songthaews and buses link the town to Chiang Khan, an hour to the north; other buses, bypassing Chiang Khan, run to Pak Chom, Sang Khom and Nong Khai. They all use the bus terminal on Highway 201, the main north–south road, about 2.5km south of the centre. The **TAT office** (ⓣ042 812812) is in the old district office on Thanon Charoenrat on the south side of the centre. The town boasts an outstanding guest house, five minutes' walk from the top of Thanon Charoenrat on the north side of the centre, *Sugar Guest House*, 4/1 Soi 4, Thanon Wisuttitep (ⓣ042 812982, ⓔsugarnamtan@hotmail.com; ❷). Bicycles and motorbikes can be rented here, and the friendly, informative owners can arrange day-trips by car. The central **night market** is on the east side of Thanon Charoenrat.

Phu Kradung National Park

The most accessible and popular of the parks in Loei province, **Phu Kradung National Park**, about 80km south of Loei, protects a grassy 1300-metre plateau, whose temperate climate supports plant and bird species not normally found in tropical Thailand. Walking trails crisscross much of the plateau and take three days to explore fully; the trip from Loei to the top of the plateau and back can't be done in a day. The park is closed during the rainy season (June–Sept), and October is muddy, though the waterfalls are in full cascade; December brings out the maple leaves, and April is good for the rhododendrons and wild roses. Elephants, sambar deer and gibbons can be seen very occasionally.

Most hikers take at least three hours to do the main trail from the Sri Taan visitor centre at the base of the plateau up the eastern side of Phu Kradung (5km). It gets steep and rocky at the end, but the view from the rim is well worth the slog. Several feeder trails fan out from here, including a ten-kilometre path along the precipitous southern edge and a three-kilometre trail to the Wang Kwang visitor centre.

To **get to the park**, take any bus between Loei and Khon Kaen and get off at the village of Phu Kradung (1hr 30min), then hop on a B20 songthaew for the remaining 7km to the Sri Taan visitor centre (Oct–May daily 7am–2pm), where you can pick up a trail map and pay the B200 admission fee. You can leave your gear here, or hire a porter to tote it to the top for B10 per kilo. At the Wang Kwang visitor centre (ⓣ042 871333), up on the plateau, there are ten national park **bungalows** sleeping from eight people upwards (B200 per person); you can also rent tents for B200 per day (or pitch your own for B30), and blankets for B10; there are food stalls here and at the rim of the plateau.

Chiang Khan

The Mekong route starts promisingly at relaxing **CHIANG KHAN**, whose rows of wooden shop-houses stretch out in a two-kilometre-long ribbon parallel to the river. The town has only two streets – Highway 211, also known as Thanon Sri Chiang Khan, and the quieter Thanon Chai Khong on the waterfront – with a line of sois connecting them numbered from west to east. Arguably the most enjoyable thing you can do here is to join other travellers for a **boat trip** on the river, organized through one of the guesthouses. Upstream trips (around B250 per person; 3hr) head west to the mouth of the Heuang River; downstream trips go to Pak Chom (B1500 per boat; 6hr round trip) through some of the most beautiful scenery on the Thai Mekong.

Songthaews from Loei and Pak Chom and **buses** from Loei stop at the west end of town near the junction of Highway 201 (the road from Loei) and Highway 211. Among several good **guesthouses** strung out along the riverside Thanon Chai Khong, two stand out, both of which can arrange boat trips, massages and motorbike rental. The welcoming *Ton Kong Guest House* at no. 299/3, between sois 9 and 10 (ⓣ042 821547, ⓔtonkhong@hotmail.com; ❶–❷), has some en-suite and air-con rooms, a good restaurant and a first-floor terrace overlooking the river, perfect for lounging. Extras on offer include cookery courses and Internet access. A little further west at no. 294, opposite Soi 8, the *Rimkong Pub and Restaurant* (ⓣ042 821125; ❶–❷) is run by a helpful couple who are a great source of information on the area and can organize a huge range of tours and bicycle rental; a variety of rooms share bathrooms, and there's a small terrace on the top floor. For **food**, try the market, on the south side of Thanon Sri Chiang Khan between sois 9 and 10, which opens in the early morning and from 4.30 to 8pm.

Pak Chom and Sang Khom

Songthaews from Chiang Khan (hourly in the morning, twice only in the afternoon) cover the beautiful, winding route to **PAK CHOM**, 41km downriver, where you can pick up a bus from Loei to continue your journey towards Nong Khai via Sang Khom. *Pak Chom Guest House* (ⓣ042 881332; ❶–❷), on Soi 1 at the west end of town, is set in leafy grounds with peerless views of the Mekong, and offers boat trips, massages and a communal Thai-Lao dinner.

Staying in quiet, tree-shaded **SANG KHOM**, 63km east of Pak Chom, puts you in the heart of an especially lush stretch of the river within easy biking distance of several villages, secluded Than Tip Falls, 16km west, and the meditation temple of Wat Hin Maak Peng, 19km east. Best of several **guesthouses** here, in a particularly choice riverside location with good food, is *Bouy* (ⓣ042 441065; ❶). The obliging owners can arrange day-trips to Ban Phu, for instance (see p.1052), and boat trips, while massages, Internet access and bicycle rental are also available.

Nong Khai and into Laos

The major border town in these parts is **NONG KHAI**, the terminus of the rail line from Bangkok and the easiest place for overland travel to Laos, whose capital Vientiane is just 24km away. The town is still a backwater, but has been developing fast since the construction of the huge Thai–Australian Friendship Bridge over the Mekong on the west side of town. As with most of the towns along this part of the Mekong, the thing to do in Nong Khai is just to take it easy, enjoying the peaceful settings of the guesthouses.

The town stretches four kilometres along the south bank of the Mekong. Running from east to west, Thanon Meechai dominates activity, with the main shops and businesses plumb in the middle around the post office and the main pier, Tha Sadet. To catch the best of life on the river, take the ninety-minute boat trip (B30), which sets out from the *Ruenpae Haisoke* floating restaurant at the top of Thanon Haisoke every evening at 5.30pm. On the south side of the centre at 1151 Soi Chitapanya, Thanon Prajak, Village Weaver Handicrafts (Ⓣ042 411236, Ⓦwww.thaivillageweaver.com), with a branch at 1020 Thanon Prajak, on the corner of Thanon Haisoke, sells *mut mee* cotton, silk and axe pillows made under a local self-help project.

Practicalities

From Bangkok, you'll most likely be coming to Nong Khai by night **train**, arriving at the station 3km west of the centre. The **bus terminal** is on the east side of town off Thanon Prajak. **Motorbikes** (from B200) and **bicycles** (B30) can be rented on Thanon Keawworut opposite *Mut Mee Guest House*, while Village Weaver Handicrafts rents four-wheel drives (B1000 including insurance).

There's a **TAT** information booth on the road leading up to the Friendship Bridge (Ⓣ042 467844). Hornbill Bookshop, near *Mut Mee Guest House*, stocks new and secondhand books and offers **Internet** access, plus a phone and fax service.

Across the Friendship Bridge to Laos

The **border crossing** at Nong Khai is the **Friendship Bridge** (open daily 6am–10pm), and you get a fifteen-day **visa** on arrival here (US$30 or B1500). To cross the border from downtown Nong Khai, take a tuk-tuk to the foot of the Bridge (about B45–50), then a minibus (B10) across the span itself, before catching a bus (B10), a tuk-tuk (about B100) or a taxi (about B200) to Vientiane, 24km away (see p.523).

Accommodation and eating

The attractive riverside *Mut Mee Guest House* on the west side of town at 1111 Thanon Keawworut (Ⓔmutmee@nk.ksc.co.th; ①–③) is a magnet for travellers, offering well-kept **rooms** and B80 dorm beds, plus yoga, mountain bikes and a recommended restaurant. Near Tha Sadet at 1126 Thanon Rimkhong, *Ruan Thai Guest House* (Ⓣ042 412519; ①–③) occupies a quiet garden compound of attractive wooden houses, with a smart outdoor café. *Sawasdee Guest House*, east of the centre at 402 Thanon Meechai (Ⓣ042 412502; ①–②), is a well-restored, grand old shop-house, set round a pleasant courtyard, with helpful management and some air-con. Just round the corner at 538 Soi Srikunmuang, you'll find *Esan Guest House* (Ⓣ01 262 6996, Ⓔguyfernback@hotmail.com; ②), a welcoming, traditional wooden house looking onto a neat ornamental garden.

Don't miss the delicious Vietnamese **food** at *Daeng Naem-Nuang*, near Tha Sadet at 1062/1–2 Thanon Banterngjit (closes 7pm), particularly the *nam nueng* – make-it-yourself fresh spring rolls with barbecued pork. *Udomrod*, nearby on Thanon Rimkhong, is a riverside terrace restaurant that also does Vietnamese spring rolls as well as northeastern Thai specialities. For honest, inexpensive Thai food you won't do better than *Thai Thai Restaurant*, Thanon Prajak (daily 3pm–2am).

Sala Kaeo Kou (Wat Khaek)

Just off the main highway, 5km east of Nong Khai and served by frequent songthaews, **SALA KAEO KOU** (daily 7am–6pm; B10) is best known for its bizarre sculpture garden, which looks like the work of a giant artist on acid. The temple was founded by the unconventional and charismatic holy man, Luang Phu Boonlua Surirat, who died in 1996. The garden bristles with Buddhist, Hindu and secular figures, all executed in concrete with imaginative abandon by unskilled followers under Luang Phu's direction. The religious statues, in particular, are radically modern while others illustrate Thai proverbs. Luang Phu established a similarly weird "Buddha Park" (Xiang Khouan) across the Mekong near Vientiane in Laos (see p.532).

Ban Phu

Deep in the countryside, 61km southwest of Nong Khai, the wooded slopes around **BAN PHU** are dotted with strangely eroded sandstone formations that have long exerted a mystical hold over local people. Many of the outcrops, which were probably caused by glacial erosion, were converted into small temples from around the ninth century onwards. Together with a stupa enshrining a Buddha footprint, the rock formations fall under the **Phu Phra Bat Historical Park** (daily dawn–dusk; B30), with a visitor centre (daily 8am–4.30pm) and a well-signposted network of paths. Among the most interesting are Tham Wua and Tham Khon, two natural shelters whose paintings of oxen and human figures suggest that the area was first settled two to three thousand years ago. The spectacular Hor Nang Ussa, a mushroom formed by a flat slab capping a five-metre-high rock pillar, is thought to be a Dvaravati shrine from the ninth to eleventh centuries.

Coming by **public transport**, it's best to take the 7.15am bus from Nong Khai to Ban Phu; the last bus back to Nong Khai leaves at around 3.30pm. From Ban Phu, it's another 14km west to the historical park; take a songthaew for the first 10km to the Ban Tiu intersection; from here a motorbike taxi will bring you the final 4km to the visitor centre.

Wat Phu Tok

The astonishing hilltop retreat of **Wat Phu Tok**, founded by famous meditation master Phra Ajaan Juen in 1968, occupies a sandstone outcrop deep in the countryside to the east of Nong Khai, its fifty or so monks living in huts perched high above breathtaking red cliffs. As you get closer, the horizontal white lines across the cliffs reveal themselves to be painted wooden walkways, built to give the temple seven levels to represent the seven stages of enlightenment. Long wooden staircases take you to the third level, where you fork left for the fifth level and the Sala Yai, which houses the temple's main Buddha image in a dimly lit cavern. From here you can walk along to the dramatic northwest tip on the same level: on the other side of a deep crevice spanned by a wooden bridge, the monks have built an open-sided Buddha viharn under a huge anvil rock. The flat top of the hill forms the seventh level, where you can wander along overgrown paths through thick forest.

Wat Phu Tok is best reached with your own **transport** from Nong Khai, but can be done by bus if you leave early. From Nong Khai, take a bus to Bung Kan (2hr), then a Pang Khon-bound bus (every 30min; about 30min) to Ban Siwilai (which has very basic hotels); from here songthaews make the hour-long, twenty-kilometre trip east to Phu Tok (services are more frequent in the morning). There are **food** stalls just outside the wat, but no accommodation.

Nakhon Phanom and That Phanom

NAKHON PHANOM, 313km from Nong Khai, affords stunning views of the Mekong and the mountains behind but is chiefly of interest for access to Laos, via the town of Thakhek across the river. The ferry pier is in the centre of town opposite the market: boats cross to **Thakhek** (see p.565) usually every half-hour or so (B50), and fifteen-day Lao **visas** can be bought on arrival for US$30. There's a **TAT office** 500m north of the ferry pier in Nakhon Phanom at 184/1 Thanon Sunthon Vichit, corner of Thanon Salaklang (ⓣ042 513490–1). The bus terminal is about 2km west of the centre, and the best **place to stay** is *Grand Hotel*, at 210 Thanon Sri Thep (ⓣ042 511526; ①–②), a block back from the river just south of the passenger ferry and market.

Around 50km south of Nakhon Phanom, the riverside village of **THAT PHANOM** sprawls around **Wat Phra That Phanom**, one of the four sacred pillars of Thai religion, which reputedly dates back to the eighth year after the death of the Buddha (535 BC), when local princes built a simple chedi to house bits of his breastbone. It's a fascinating place of pilgrimage that used to serve both Thais and the Lao, but since 1975, the Lao have only been allowed to cross the river for the annual Phra That Phanom festival (usually Feb) and the Monday- and Thursday-morning waterfront markets. The white-and-gold chedi, modelled on That Louang in Vientiane, looks like a giant upturned table leg. From each of the four sides, an eye stares down, and the whole thing is surmounted by an umbrella made of 16kg of gold. Look out for the brick reliefs above three of the doorways in the base: the northern side shows Vishnu mounted on a garuda; on the western side, the four guardians of the earth are shown putting offerings in the Buddha's alms bowl; and above the south door, there's a carving of the Buddha entering Nirvana.

Frequent **buses** connect That Phanom with Nakhon Phanom (also served by songthaews), Mukdahan and Ubon Ratachathani, and stop near the wat. The centre of the village is 200m due east of here, around the pier on the Mekong. That Phanom's outstanding **accommodation** choice is the welcoming *Niyana Guest House*, two blocks north of the pier at 110 Moo 14, Thanon Rimkhong (ⓣ042 541450; ①). The owner is a fund of local information, and rustles up excellent Thai and Western vegetarian and meaty food (breakfast and dinner only), as well as renting out bicycles.

Mukdahan and into Laos

Fifty kilometres downriver of That Phanom, **MUKDAHAN** is the last stop on the Mekong trail before Highway 212 heads off inland to Ubon Ratchathani, 170km to the south. You may feel as if you're in the Wild East out here, but this is one of Thailand's fastest-developing provinces, owing to increasing friendship with Laos and the proximity of Savannakhet (see pp.567–570), the second-biggest Lao city, just across the water; a bridge across the Mekong is planned. You can cross the **Lao border** here on the ferry (7 daily Mon–Fri, 4 on Sat & 2 on Sun; B50), and fifteen-day **visas** are available on arrival (US$30).

Half-hourly **buses** from That Phanom and Ubon Ratchathani stop at the bus terminal, about 2km northwest of the centre on Highway 212. The daily **market** at the main river pier is good for local fabrics and Chinese ceramics. At the southern edge of town rises the 65-metre-high **Mukdahan Tower** (daily 8am–6pm; B20), which has an interesting array of historic artefacts from the area and expansive views over the Mekong into Laos. The best budget **accommodation** is *Ban Thom Kasem*, a four-storey hotel centrally located at 25–25/2 Thanon Samut Sakdarak (ⓣ042 611235 or 612223; ①–②).

10.6

Southern Thailand: the Gulf coast

Southern Thailand's Gulf coast is famous chiefly for its three fine islands of the Samui archipelago: the large and increasingly upmarket **Ko Samui**, the laid-back **Ko Pha Ngan**, site of monthly full-moon parties at **Hat Rin**, and the tiny **Ko Tao**, which is encircled by some of Thailand's best dive sites. Other attractions seem minor by comparison, but the historic town of **Phetchaburi** has a certain charm, and the grand old temples in **Nakhon Si Thammarat** are worth a detour.

Phetchaburi

Straddling the River Phet about 120km south of Bangkok, the provincial capital of **PHETCHABURI** flourished as a seventeenth-century trading post and retains many fine old historical wats, which make an interesting day-trip from Bangkok or Hua Hin. The main non-air-con **bus station** is on the southwest edge of Khao Wang, about thirty minutes' walk or a ten-minute songthaew ride from the town centre, but non-air-con buses to and from Hua Hin terminate just east of the market in the town centre. From the air-con bus terminal just off Thanon Rajwithi, it's about ten minutes' walk south to Chomrut Bridge; the **train station** is about 500m northwest of the air-con bus terminal. The most traveller-oriented **hotel** is *Rabieng Rimnum (Rim Nam) Guest House*, beside Chomrut Bridge at 1 Thanon Chisa-in (☎032 425707; ❷), which has simple rooms in an old house, a great restaurant, and bicycle and motorbike rental. There's **Internet** access at the CAT phone office (daily 8.30am–4.30pm), which is next to the main post office on Thanon Rajwithi.

The town's central sight district clusters around Chomrut Bridge (*saphaan Chomrut*) and the River Phet. About 700m east of the bridge, the still-functioning seventeenth-century **Wat Yai Suwannaram** contains a remarkable set of murals, depicting divinities ranged in rows of ascending importance, and a well-preserved scripture library built on stilts over a pond. The five tumbledown Khmer-style prangs of **Wat Kamphaeng Laeng**, fifteen minutes' walk east and then south from Wat Yai Suwannaram, were built to enshrine Hindu deities, but were later adapted for Buddhist use. Turning west across the river, you reach Phetchaburi's most fully restored and important temple, **Wat Mahathat**, which was probably founded in the fourteenth century. The five landmark prangs at its heart are adorned with stucco figures of mythical creatures, while miniature angels and gods embellish the roofs of the main viharn and the bot.

Dominating the western outskirts, about thirty minutes' walk from Wat Mahathat, Rama IV's hilltop palace is a stew of mid-nineteenth-century Thai and European styles known as **Khao Wang**; it's reached on foot from near the western end of Thanon Rajwithi or by cable car from the western base of the hill off Highway 4 (daily 8.15am–5.15pm; B50); white songthaews from Chomrut Bridge should drop you close to either access point. The wooded, monkey-infested hill is littered with wats, chedis and gazebos, as well as the king's summer house and observatory, **Phra Nakhon Khiri** (daily 9am–4pm; B40), now a moderately interesting museum.

Hua Hin

The country's oldest beach resort, **HUA HIN** is popular with Thai families, but the beach is nowhere near as attractive as those of Ko Samui, and the shorefront is packed with hotels. Hua Hin **train station** is at the west end of Thanon Damnern Kasem, about ten minutes' walk from the seafront; the main bus depot is off the western end of Thanon Chomsin, five minutes' walk from the main through-road, Thanon Phetkasem. There's a **tourist information** desk (daily Dec–Feb 8.30am–4.30pm, Mon–Fri only March–Nov; ⓣ032 532433) on the corner of Thanon Damnern Kasem and Thanon Phetkasem (about 50m east of the train station) and an overseas CAT international phone office, with **Internet** access, just south across Thanon Phetkasem (daily 8am–11pm). The best private hospital in Hua Hin is the San Paulo, 222 Thanon Phetkasem (ⓣ032 532576–8), south of the tourist information office; there's a police box opposite the *Sofitel* at the beachfront end of Thanon Damnern Kasem (ⓣ032 515995).

The most atmospheric **places to stay** in Hua Hin are the budget guesthouses built on converted squid piers, with rooms strung out along wooden jetties right over the waves: *Mod Guest House*, 116 Thanon Naretdamri (ⓣ032 512296; ❷–❸) has both basic and comfortable rooms (some air-con) and a seafront seating area, and nearby *Bird*, 31/2 Thanon Naretdamri (ⓣ032 511630; ❸), is similar. Inland, *Pattana Guest Home*, 52 Thanon Naretdamri ⓣ032 513393, ⓔhuahinpattana@hotmail.com; ❷–❸), has cosy rooms (some en suite) in an appealingly traditional teak-wood house, quietly located at the end of a small soi.

Hua Hin is famous for its seafood, and the jetty **restaurant** *Chao Lay* on Thanon Naretdamri is a good source. The excellent and very cheap seafood at *Som Moo Joom*, 51/6 Thanon Dechanuchit (corner of Thanon Naebkehat; no English sign) is a big hit with Thai holidaymakers, and fish also features heavily at the night market, which sets up at sunset along the western end of Thanon Dechanuchit. Nightlife in Hua Hin is becoming increasingly dominated by hostess **bars**, many of them on Soi Bintaban.

Chumphon

CHUMPHON is a useful departure point for Ko Tao, but of little other interest. The main **bus terminal** is on Thanon Tha Tapao, one block west of Chumphon's main thoroughfare, Thanon Sala Daeng; the **train station** is about 500m further north. The **airport** (ⓣ077 591068), 35km north of town, runs flights to Bangkok. Most guesthouses sell tickets for **boats to Ko Tao**; otherwise, try Songserm Travel (24hr; ⓣ077 506205), Infinity Travel (daily 6am–11pm; ⓣ077 501937) or Ban's Diving Pub (daily 8am–10pm; ⓣ077 570751), all on Thanon Tha Tapao – Infinity and Ban's offer free showers and video shows to travellers awaiting onward connections. The main departure points for Ko Tao boats are in the port area at Pak Nam, 14km southeast of Chumphon; passengers get free transport from Chumphon for the early-morning boats, but for the slow, midnight boat you'll need to take the taxi vans offered by guesthouses, which leave town at about 10pm (B50). Full details on getting to Ko Tao from Chumphon are given on pp.1060–1061.

Chumphon's **guesthouses** are used to accommodating Ko Tao-bound travellers, so it's generally no problem to check into a room for half a day before catching the night boat. Most places will also store luggage. The central *Mayaze's Resthouse*, off Thanon Sala Daeng at 111/35 Soi 3 (aka Soi Bangkok Bank; ⓣ077 504452, ⓔmayazes@hotmail.com; ❷) is friendly and comfortable; *Sooksamer Guest House* at 118/4 Thanon Suksamer Soi 8 (ⓣ077 502430, ⓔsooksamerguesthouse@hotmail.com; ❶) is a simpler, old-style guesthouse in a traditional wooden house; and *Suriwong Chumphon*, 125/27–29 Thanon Sala Daeng (ⓣ077 511397; ❷), is a large, clean budget hotel with fan and air-con. The **night market** sets up along both sides of Thanon Komluang Chumphon.

The main CAT overseas **phone** centre is on the far southeastern edge of town, about 600m east of the main post office on Thanon Paramin Manka: any Paramin Manka songthaew will drop you outside. The more central *Fame* restaurant, opposite the *Jansom Thara* hotel, also offers overseas phone, fax and **Internet** services. The private Virasin Hospital (ⓣ077 503238–40) is off the southern end of Thanon Tha Tapao; the **police** station is on the north end of Thanon Sala Daeng (ⓣ077 511505).

Wat Suan Mokkh

The forest temple of **Wat Suan Mokkh** is internationally renowned as a place of meditation. Popular anapanasati **meditation retreats** are led by Thai and Western teachers over the first ten days of every month at the International Dharma Heritage, 1km from the main temple. These retreats are serious undertakings, intended as a challenging exercise in mental development for both novices and experienced meditators: conditions are spartan, there is a rule of silence, and the day begins before dawn. Sleeping quarters are segregated and meditators help with chores. The B1200 fee includes two vegetarian meals a day and accommodation; bring a flashlight. Each course has space for about 100 people – enrol at the information desk in Wat Suan Mokkh (ⓣ077 431661–2, ⓦwww.suanmokkh.org) by 4pm on the last day of the month. Wat Suan Mokkh is on the Chumphon–Surat Thani **bus** route (hourly). **Trains** pull into Chaiya train station, 6km north of the wat; songthaews and motorbike taxis run from the station to the wat.

Surat Thani

Uninspiring **SURAT THANI**, 60km south of Wat Suan Mokkh, is of use only as the main jumping-off point for trips to Ko Samui and Ko Pha Ngan; for details on island boats, see the box on pp.1060–1061. Most **buses** to Surat Thani arrive at Thanon Taladmai in the centre of town, either at Talat Kaset I on the north side of the road (local buses) or opposite at Talat Kaset II (long-distance, including Phuket and Hat Yai). The new bus terminal 2km southwest of the centre mostly handles buses from Bangkok. The **train station** is at Phunphin, 13km to the west, from where buses run into town every ten minutes between 6am and 8pm; many long-distance buses heading west out of Surat also make a stop here. You can buy boat tickets to Ko Samui and Ko Pha Ngan from the train station, including a connecting bus to the relevant pier. A minibus (B70) connects **Surat Thani Airport** with the town centre, or you can buy a combination ticket to Ko Samui (B280) or Ko Pha Ngan (B420); minibuses to the airport leave from Phantip Travel, in front of Talat Kaset I at 293/6–8 Thanon Taladmai (ⓣ077 272230 or 077 272906). Small **share-songthaews** buzz around town, charging around B10 per person.

Boat tickets are available from Seatran, on Thanon Ban Don near the night-boat pier (ⓣ077 275060–2; ⓦwww.seatranferry.com), which has fast boats to Samui and Pha Ngan and vehicle ferries to Samui (with connecting buses), both sailing from Don Sak, 68km east of Surat; Samui Tour, 326/12 Thanon Taladmai (ⓣ077 282352), which handles buses to Ko Samui via the Raja vehicle ferries from Don

Sak; Phangan Tour, also on Thanon Taladmai (☎077 205799), which handles buses to Ko Pha Ngan via the Raja vehicle ferries from Don Sak; and ADV on Thanon Namuang (☎077 205418–9 or 077 287124) for Songserm Express Boats to Samui, Pha Ngan and Tao (and from there to Chumphon) from the pier at Pak Nam Tapi, on the east side of Surat town.

Train **tickets** can be booked in central Surat through Phantip Travel (see above). Private, long-distance air-con minibuses congregate around Talat Kaset II; beware, however, that there have been many reports of scams on the more tourist-oriented routes, notably to Khao Sok and Malaysia.

TAT (☎077 288817–9) is at the western end of town at 5 Thanon Taladmai, with the tourist police adjacent (☎1155 or 077 421281). If you get stuck in Surat and need a **hotel**, try the clean en-suite rooms at *Ban Don Hotel*, above a decent restaurant at 268/2 Thanon Namuang (☎077 272167; ❶), or splash out on the *Wangtai Hotel*, 1 Thanon Taladmai at the western end of town (☎077 283020–39, ⓔwangtai@loxinfo.co.th; ❹), which is great value with good restaurants and large, smart rooms around a swimming pool. The **night market** sets up between Si Chaiya and Ban Don roads and at Ban Don pier.

Ko Samui

An ever-widening cross-section of visitors, from globetrotting backpackers to suitcase-toting fortnighters, come to southern Thailand just for the beautiful beaches of **Ko Samui**, 80km from Surat Thani – and at 15km across and down, Samui is generally large enough to cope with this diversity, except during the rush at Christmas and New Year. The paradisal sands and clear blue seas are fringed by palm trees, but development behind the beaches is extensive and often thoughtless. The island is served by frequent ferries: for details, see the box on pp.1060–1061.

The northeast monsoon blows heaviest here in November, but can bring rain at any time between October and January; January is often breezy, March and April are very hot, and between May and October the southwest monsoon blows mildly onto Samui's west coast and causes a little rain. There are few **bungalows** left on the island for under B250, but nearly all now have en-suite bathrooms and constant electricity. All the accommodation prices given below are for high season, but they plummet out of season (roughly April–June, Oct and Nov). A fifty-kilometre road encircles the island and is served by **songthaews**, which set off from between the two piers in Na Thon and run along set routes to all the beaches (destinations marked in English; B30–50 per person, though in the evenings you may have to charter the vehicle), and motorbike and air-con taxis. You can rent motorbikes at all main beaches, though note that dozens are killed on Samui's roads each year, so proceed with caution.

TAT runs a small but helpful office (daily 8.30am–noon & 1–4.30pm; ☎077 420504), tucked away on an unnamed side road in Na Thon (north of the pier and inland from the post office).

Another useful source of **information** is ⓦwww.samui.sawadee.com, which allows, among other things, direct bookings at a range of hotels on the island.

Ko Samui has a recompression chamber at Bangrak, and a dozen **dive operators**, offering day-trips to Ko Tao reefs (B3000) and PADI courses throughout the year. Reliable operators include Samui International Diving School (ⓦwww.planet-scuba.net), which has its head office at the *Malibu Resort* towards the north end of Central Chaweng (☎077 422386); and Easy Divers (ⓦwww.thaidive.com), with its head office at the north end of Lamai (☎077 231190).

Na Thon

The island capital, **NA THON** is a frenetic half-built town that most travellers use only for stocking up with supplies en route to the beaches. The two piers come

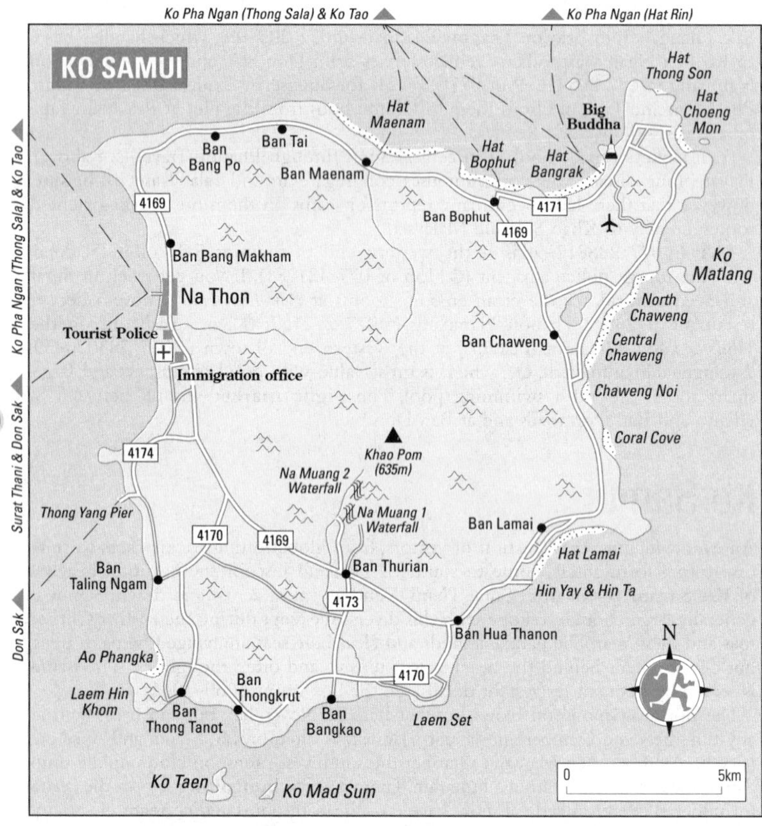

to land at the promenade, Thanon Chonvithi, which is paralleled first by narrow Thanon Ang Thong, then by Thanon Taweeratpakdee, aka Route 4169, the round-island road; the main cross-street is Thanon Na Amphoe, by the more northerly of the piers.

At the northern end of the promenade, the **post office** (Mon–Fri 8.30am–4.30pm, Sat & Sun 9am–noon) has an international phone service and Catnet **Internet** access upstairs (7am–10pm). Nathon Book Store, on Thanon Na Amphoe, is a good secondhand **bookshop**. The **tourist police** are based 1km south of town on Route 4169 (☎1155 or 077 421281), and the island's main **hospital** (☎077 421230–2) is a further 2km south off the same road. Tourist visas may be extended at the **immigration office**, 2km down Route 4169 (☎077 421069). If you really need a **place to stay** in Na Thon, head for *Jinta Residence* towards the south end of Thanon Chonvithi (☎077 420630-1, Ⓦwww.tapee.com; ③), with smart, bright bungalows (some with en-suite hot-water bathrooms and air-con) and its own Internet café. The Garden Home Health Center, 2km north along Route 4169 in Ban Bang Makham, dispenses some of the best **massages** on the island (B250 per hr), along with herbal **saunas** (B300).

Ang Thong National Marine Park

All main beaches sell tickets for boat trips to **Ang Thong National Marine Park** (B750 including entry to the national park, B850 with pick-up from your accommodation, or B1800 all-in by speedboat), a gorgeous group of 42 small islands, 30km west of Samui. Boats generally leave Na Thon or Bophut at 8.30am and return at 5.30pm. First stop on any boat tour is usually Ko Wua Talab, site of the park headquarters, from where it's a steep 430-metre climb (about 1hr return; bring walking sandals or shoes) to the island's peak and fine panoramic views. The feature that gives the park the name Ang Thong, meaning "Golden Bowl", and that was the inspiration for the setting of Alex Garland's cult bestseller, *The Beach*, is a landlocked lake, 250m in diameter, on Ko Mae Ko to the north of Ko Wua Talab. A well-made path (30min return) leads from the beach through natural rock tunnels to the rim of the cliff wall encircling the lake, which is connected to the sea by an underground tunnel. Most day-trip boats now carry a few desultory kayaks on board, but if you're interested in **kayaking**, it's best to go to one of the two dedicated operators, Sea Canoe (see p.1082) or Blue Stars. The latter is based at Gallery Lafayette near the *Full Circle* nightclub on Chaweng (Ⓣ077 413231, Ⓦwww.bluestars.info), and charges B1990 for a day, B4750 for a two-day trip.

Maenam

The four-kilometre bay at **MAENAM**, 13km from Na Thon, is not the island's prettiest, but it's quiet and offers cheap accommodation, which makes it Samui's most popular destination for shoestring travellers. *Angela's Bakery*, opposite the **police station** on the main through-road to the east of the pier, offers excellent Western **food**, including cakes, pies and deli goods during the daytime, and further east is a **post office**.

Accommodation

The far eastern end of the bay, though it has the poorest stretch of beach, offers the best choice of budget **accommodation**.

Friendly About 1.5km east of the village Ⓣ077 425484. Easy-going place. All the bungalows are very clean and have their own bathrooms. ❶–❷

Moonhut Near the village, just east of the pier Ⓣ077 425247, Ⓦkohsamui.com/moonhut. Quiet, welcoming place on a large, sandy plot, with substantial, clean bungalows; all en suite, some with hot water and a/c. ❷–❹

Morning Glory Next door to *Friendly* at the eastern end of the bay. Laid-back old-timer (formerly *Rose*), with basic thatched huts in a shady compound. No fans, and electricity stops at 11.30pm. ❶–❷

Naplarn Villa At the far western end, off the access road to *Home Bay* Ⓣ077 247047. Good value if you don't mind a 5min walk to the beach: excellent food and clean, well-furnished, en-suite bungalows round a garden. ❶–❸

Shangrilah About 500m west of the village Ⓣ077 425189, Ⓦwww.geocities.com/pk_shangrilah. Friendly place in a flower-strewn compound on the nicest stretch of sand along Maenam. Smart, en-suite bungalows, some with a/c and hot water. ❷–❹

SR At the far eastern end of the bay Ⓣ077 427529–31. A quiet, welcoming place with a very good restaurant. Accommodation is in en-suite beachfront huts. ❷

Bophut, Bangrak (Big Buddha Beach) and Choeng Mon

The next beach east of Maenam, quiet, 2km-long **BOPHUT**, has a similar look, and attracts a mix of young and old travellers, as well as families. Ban Bophut (aka "Fisherman's Village") is well geared to travellers' needs, including a branch of *Angela's Bakery* (see above). The best low-priced **accommodation** here is *Smile House* at the western end of the village (Ⓣ077 425361, Ⓦwww.smilehouse-samui.com; ❸–❻), a reliable set of chalets, some with hot water and air-con, grouped around a

Getting to Ko Samui, Ko Pha Ngan and Ko Tao

Ferry services to these islands have fluctuated considerably over the last few years, and you can also expect variations according to demand, the time of year and the weather.

Getting to Ko Samui

The most obvious way of getting to Ko Samui is on a **boat** from the **Surat Thani** area. Of these, the longest-established is the night boat, which leaves Ban Don pier in Surat Thani itself for Na Thon – the main port on Samui – at 11pm daily (7hr); tickets (B120) are sold at the pier on the day of departure.

From **Pak Nam Tapi** pier, on the east side of Surat, one Songserm Express Boat a day (on Samui ⓣ077 421316–9) runs to Na Thon (2hr 30min; B150 including transport from Surat or Phunphin train station to the pier). Seatran vehicle ferries run every two hours from **Don Sak** pier, 68km east of Surat, to Na Thon (1hr 30min; B80, or B150 including bus from Surat or Phunphin; on Samui ⓣ077 426000–2). Twice a day, the Seatran Express (passengers only) covers the same route in 45 minutes (B200 including bus from Surat or Phunphin). Raja vehicle ferries run hourly between Don Sak and **Thong Yang**, 8km south of Na Thon (1hr 30min; B69; on Samui ⓣ077 415230–3); every two hours to coincide with alternate boats, Samui Tour (see p.1056) runs buses from Surat or Phunphin to Don Sak, and from Thong Yang to Na Thon, charging B150 total. Note that the total journey time from Surat using the vehicle ferries from Don Sak is much the same as with Songserm from Pak Nam Tapi; only the Seatran Express will save time significantly.

From Bangkok, the State Railway does train/bus/boat packages through to Samui that cost a little less than if you organized the parts independently – about B550 in a second-class bunk. Overnight bus–boat packages from the government-run Southern Terminal cost around B450 air-con, B650 VIP, and are far preferable to the deals offered by unreliable companies on Thanon Khao San (around B370).

You can get to Samui direct **by air** on Bangkok Airways (in Bangkok ⓣ02 265 5555; at Samui Airport ⓣ077 245601–8; ⓦwww.bangkokair.com); around fifteen flights a day leave Bangkok (from B2000), and there are daily flights from Phuket, Krabi, Pattaya and Singapore, with routes from Trat and Kuala Lumpur planned. Air-con minibuses from the **airport** in the northeastern tip of the island charge B100 to Chaweng, for example. The terminal has currency-exchange facilities and an ATM, a post office with international telephones (daily 8am–noon & 1–7pm), a tourist police booth (ⓣ1155 or 077 425611) and Budget car rental (ⓣ077 427188; ⓦwww.budget.co.th).

For information about boats from Ko Samui to **Ko Pha Ngan** and **Ko Tao**, see below; all offer the same service in the return direction.

Getting to Ko Pha Ngan

The slowest **ferry** from the mainland leaves Ban Don pier in **Surat Thani** at 11pm every night for Thong Sala (7hr; B200); tickets are available from the pier on the day of departure. From Don Sak to Thong Sala, there are four Raja vehicle ferries a day

small swimming pool. The stylish rooms at *Eddy's*, on the main road at the far west end of Bophut (ⓣ077 245221, ⓔ**ed_samui@ksc.th.com**; ⑤), offer good value for the facilities, and downstairs is an excellent restaurant.

BANGRAK is also known as Big Buddha Beach, after the huge but not all that comely **Big Buddha** statue that gazes down at sunbathers from its island in the bay. A short causeway at the eastern end of the bay leads across to a clump of souvenir shops and food stalls in front of the temple, and ceremonial dragon-steps lead to the terrace around the statue, from where there's a fine view of the sweeping north coast.

(2hr 30min; B240; on Ko Pha Ngan ☎077 377452–3) and two Seatran Express Boats (1hr 30min; B320; on Ko Pha Ngan ☎077 238130); from Pak Nam Tapi, there's one Songserm Express Boat a day (4hr; B250; on Pha Ngan ☎077 377046); all the above include bus transport to the pier from Surat Thani.

Two Songserm Express Boats a day do the 45-minute trip from Na Thon on **Ko Samui** to Thong Sala (B115), while Seatran does the same voyage twice a day in thirty minutes (B120). Speedboats from Bangrak, Bophut and Maenam on Samui (at least twice a day) and the Lomprayah catamaran from Maenam (twice a day; Ko Samui head office ☎077 247401–2) call in at Thong Sala after thirty minutes (B250), on their way to Ko Tao. From Bangrak, three passenger boats a day take an hour to cross to Hat Rin (B100). If the weather's good enough – generally reliable between January and October – one longtail boat a day crosses from Maenam to Hat Rin (B100), before sailing up Ko Pha Ngan's east coast to Thong Nai Pan (B200).

Four kinds of vessel currently run between Ko Pha Ngan and **Ko Tao**: one slow boat a day (3hr; B180); one Songserm Express Boat a day (2hr; B250); the Lomprayah catamaran twice a day (1hr; B350); and at least two speedboats a day (50min–1hr; B350). **From Bangkok**, bus and train packages similar to those for getting to Ko Samui are available.

Getting to Ko Tao

All services to and from Ko Tao are at the mercy of the weather, especially between June and November when travellers can get stranded for several days.

There are five different **boat** services from **Chumphon** on the mainland (see p.1055) to Ko Tao. The fastest is Lomlahk Speedboat (daily at 7am; 1hr 30min; B400; ☎077558212) from Ao Thung Makkham Noi, 25km south of Chumphon, which cannot run in windy weather. Three other services also depart at 7am, from Pak Nam port, 14km southeast of Chumphon: Songserm Express Boats (Jan–Oct; 3hr; B400, also through-tickets to Ko Pha Ngan; ☎077 506205); Ko Tao Cruiser (2hr 30min; B400; ☎09 587 4107); and Ekawin Speed Ferry (2hr 30min; B400; ☎077 501821). The slow boat (daily at midnight; 6hr; B200; ☎077 521615) departs from Pak Nam in all but the very worst weather. Companies such as Ekawin, which also has an office in Banglamphu at 42 Thanon Tanao (☎02 629 4598), organize VIP bus-and-boat packages from Bangkok via Chumphon.

Four kinds of vessel currently run between Thong Sala on **Ko Pha Ngan** and Ko Tao: one slow boat a day (3hr; B180); one Songserm Express Boat a day (2hr; B250; on Ko Tao ☎077 456274); the Lomprayah catamaran twice a day (1hr; B350; on Ko Tao ☎077 456176); and at least two speedboats a day (50min–1hr; B350). The speedboats originate at Bangrak, Bophut and Maenam, the Lomprayah catamaran at Maenam, on **Ko Samui** (total journey time to Ko Tao on either 1hr 30min; B550), while the Songserm Express Boat originates at Na Thon (total journey time to Ko Tao 3hr 30min; B345). There's also a night boat from **Surat Thani**, departing at 11pm (9hr; B500).

After Bangrak comes the high-kicking boot of the northeastern cape and beautiful **CHOENG MON**, whose white sandy beach is lined with casuarina trees and served by songthaews. *Ô Soleil* (☎077 425232, ⓔosoleil@loxinfo.co.th; ❷–❻) is a lovely place in a pretty garden here, with sturdy, wooden, en-suite bungalows, some with hot water and air-con. The bay also shelters the best place to splurge on the island, *Tongsai Bay Cottages and Hotel* (☎077 425015–28, ⓦwww.tongsaibay.co.th; ❾), an easy-going establishment with luxurious cottages, picturesque grounds, a private beach and swimming pools, very fine restaurants and a health spa.

Chaweng

For sheer natural beauty, none of the other beaches can match **CHAWENG**, with its gently sloping six-kilometre strip of white sand framed between the small island of Ko Matlang at the north end and the headland above Coral Cove in the south. Such beauty has not escaped attention, of course, in the shape of the island's heaviest development and highest accommodation prices, as well as thumping nightlife and diverse watersports. An ugly village of amenities stretches for two kilometres behind the central section and has banks with ATMs, supermarkets, Internet outlets, clinics, motorbike rental (from B150) and four-wheel drives (from B800). Running from north to south on Central Chaweng, Travel Solutions is a good travel agent (Ⓣ077 230203, Ⓦwww.travelsolutions.co.th); there's a tourist police booth near *Chawengburi Resort* (Ⓣ1155); while Boots pharmacy is a few doors away from Bookazine, selling books, newspapers and magazines. The original village of **Ban Chaweng**, 1km inland of Central Chaweng beach on the round-island road, has a police station, a post office with poste restante, a Budget car-rental outlet (Ⓣ077 413384, Ⓦwww.budget.co.th), and a branch of Bangkok Airways (Ⓣ077 422512–9).

Accommodation

Over fifty bungalow resorts and hotels at Chaweng are squeezed into thin strips running back from the beachfront.

Charlie's Huts In the heart of Central Chaweng Ⓣ077 422343 or 077 230285. Cheap wooden huts with shared bathrooms and mosquito nets in a grassy compound; en-suite and a/c bungalows also available, but no hot water. ❷–❹

Four Seasons At the top end of Central Chaweng Ⓣ077 422238. Secluded among dense trees in what used to be *Dew Drop Huts*, large, en-suite bungalows on high stilts, now joined by some upgraded pads with hot water and a/c on the beach. ❸–❼

IKK Around the point at the far north end of North Chaweng Ⓣ077 413281. Comfortable en-suite bungalows in an immaculately kept flower garden on a peaceful stretch of sand. ❸

Long Beach Lodge Towards the north end of Central Chaweng Ⓣ077 422372. Unusually spacious and shady sandy compound of decent-sized en-suite bungalows, some with hot water and a/c. ❹–❼

Marine Towards the north end of North Chaweng Ⓣ077 422416. Plenty of diversity and value here, with en-suite, fan-cooled bungalows of various sizes and shapes as well as reasonably priced a/c ones. ❷–❹

Eating, drinking and nightlife

For cheap Thai **food**, join local workers at the night-time food stalls of Laem Din market, on the road between the heart of Central Chaweng and Ban Chaweng, or head for *Ninja*, a basic, 24-hour restaurant near *Charlie's Huts*, which also serves crepes and other Western dishes. At the top end of the price range, *Betelnut* (Ⓣ077 413370), on Soi Colibri at the south end of Central Chaweng opposite Central Samui Beach Resort, is Samui's best restaurant, serving exceptional Californian-Thai fusion food; the same owners run *Andaluz*, an elegant tapas bar opposite. Also on Soi Colibri, you can eat some of the best Thai food on the island (evenings only), or take a highly recommended **Thai cookery course,** at the Samui Institute of Thai Culinary Arts (SITCA; Ⓣ077 413172, Ⓦwww.sitca.net).

Avoiding the raucous hostess bars and English theme pubs on the main through-road, the best place to **drink** is at the candlelit tables that materialize on the beach after dark, especially towards the north end of Chaweng. Bang in the heart of Central Chaweng, back from the beach, The *Reggae Pub* is Samui's oldest **night-club**, an unpretentious good-time venue that's similar in outlook to Chaweng's other long-standing megaclub, *Green Mango*, at the north end of Central Chaweng. More sophisticated fare, including plenty of visiting DJ talent, are on offer at *Full Circle*, on North Chaweng, and the chic, new *Mint Bar* on the alley leading to *Green Mango*.

Lamai and around

Although **LAMAI** is less heavily developed than Chaweng, its nightlife is if anything tawdrier, with planeloads of European tourists sinking buckets of booze at women's Thai boxing and mud-wrestling shows and hostess bars. Running roughly north to south for 4km, the white palm-fringed beach is, fortunately, still a picture, and it's possible to avoid the mayhem by staying at the quiet extremities of the bay, where the backpackers' resorts have a definite edge over Chaweng's. The action is concentrated behind the centre of the beach, where you'll also find supermarkets, banks, ATMs, clinics, Internet outlets, motorbike rental (from B150) and four-wheel drives (from B800). There's a police box, set back from the beach in the original village of Ban Lamai, and the post office is on the way out south on Highway 4169. The small rock formations nearby on the bay's southern promontory, Hin Yay (Grandmother Rock) and Hin Ta (Grandfather Rock), never fail to raise a giggle with their resemblance to the male and female sexual organs. Sea Canoe (ⓣ077 230484 or 01 893 1220), on Highway 4169 opposite *Weekender Villa*, run kayaking trips to Ang Thong National Marine Park (see p.1059; B2300 for a day, B5500 for a two-day trip), and to the islands off Samui's south coast (B1500), as well as offering kayak rental (B150 per hr).

Accommodation

Lamai's budget accommodation is concentrated around the far southern end of the bay towards the Grandparent Rocks.

Long Island Resort At the far north end of the beach ⓣ077 424202 or 418456, ⓦwww.sawadee.com/samui/longisland. A "boutique resort" with stylish but cosy bungalows (some with a/c), an attractive pool, a spa and a good restaurant. ❹–❾

Noi Just beyond the headland, at the far southern end of the bay ⓣ077 424562, ⓔgaborwan@hotmail.com. Cramped compound, but tidy and well run, right on the beach and with a mellow atmosphere. Clean bungalows range from shared bathrooms to a/c with hot water. ❷–❹

The Spa Resort At the far north end of the beach ⓣ077 230855, ⓦwww.spasamui.com. One of Samui's oldest and best spas, offering all manner of treatments from massages, yoga and meditation to week-long cleansing programmes. Cosy, well-constructed rooms – the cheapest with mosquito nets and cold-water bathrooms, the priciest with a/c. A more upmarket branch with a swimming pool, *Village Spa*, has opened in the hills above, linked by regular shuttle buses. ❷–❾

Wanchai Villa On the access road to *White Sand*, at the far southern end of the bay ⓣ077 424296, ⓔwanchai_villa@hotmail.com. Quiet, spacious, family-run operation set back from the beach, offering a range of very clean bungalows, and excellent, cheap food. ❷–❺

Weekender Villa At the far north end of the beach ⓣ077 424116, ⓔweekendervilla@samui2002.com. Very well-maintained, friendly establishment, with large, en-suite wooden bungalows (some with hot water) and an attractive beachside bar-restaurant in a smart, spacious compound. ❸–❹

White Sand At the far southern end of the bay ⓣ077 424298. Long-established and laid-back budget place with simple beachside huts; popular with long-term travellers. ❶

Eating and drinking

The varied beachside **restaurant** at *The Spa Resort* is excellent, and there are several decent Italian places a short way north of the tourist village's main crossroads. Just west of the crossroads, *Eldorado*, a good-value Swedish restaurant, comes highly recommended, while *Ninja* dishes up basic, cheap Thai faves, crepes and other Western dishes on Highway 4169, on the north side of the tourist village. *Bauhaus*, a barn-like entertainment complex by the main crossroads, is the main **nightlife** draw.

Na Muang Falls

About 10km inland of Lamai, off the round-island road, lie **Na Muang Falls**. Each of the two main falls has its own kilometre-long paved access road off Route 4169: the lower falls splash down a twenty-metre wall of rock into a large pool, while Na

Muang 2, upstream, is a more spectacular cascade that requires a bit of foot-slogging from the car park (about 15min uphill); alternatively, you can walk up there from Na Muang 1, by taking the 1500-metre trail that begins 300m back along the access road from the lower fall. From Na Muang 1 entrance, you can take forty-minute elephant rides, including Na Muang 2 Falls (B700 per person).

Ko Pha Ngan

In recent years, backpackers have tended to move over to Ko Samui's little sibling, **Ko Pha Ngan**, 20km to the north, but the island still has a simple atmosphere, mostly because the lousy road system is an impediment to the developers. With dense jungle covering its inland mountains and rugged granite outcrops along the coast, Pha Ngan lacks sweeping beaches, but it does have some coral and a few beautiful, sheltered bays, including **Hat Rin**, a pilgrimage site for ravers. For exploring, it's well worth picking up from supermarkets on the island Visid Hongsombud's regularly updated map of Ko Pha Ngan and Ko Tao (B70). Full details on getting to Ko Pha Ngan are given on pp.1060–1061.

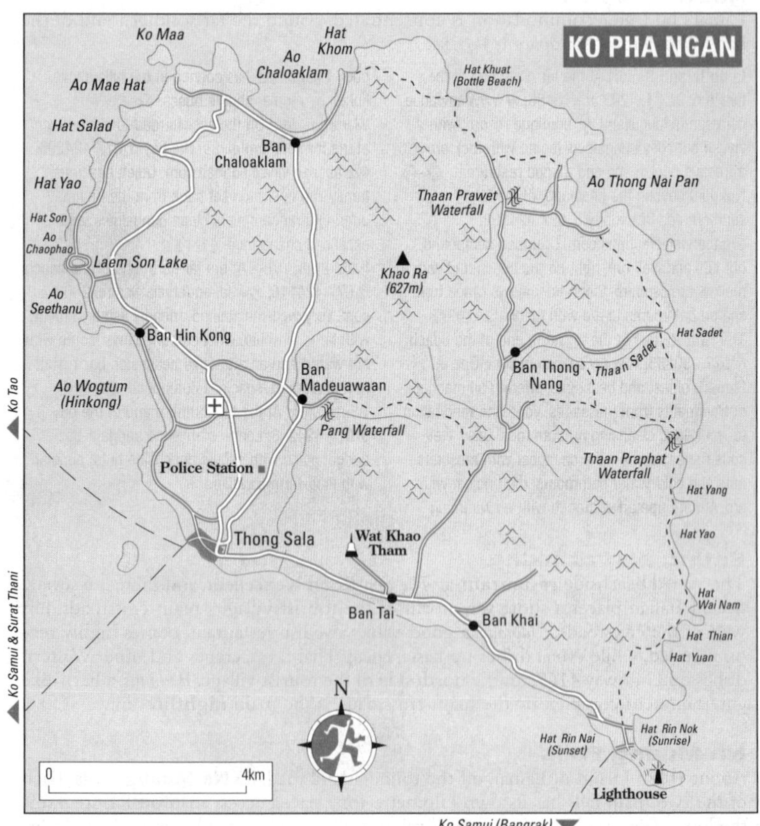

Thong Sala and Wat Khao Tham

THONG SALA is a port of entrance and little more. In front of the piers, transport to the rest of the island (songthaews, jeeps and motorbike taxis) congregates by a dusty row of banks, travellers' restaurants, supermarkets, dive centres and motorbike and jeep rental places. If you go straight ahead from the pier, you can turn right onto the town's old high street, where you'll find on the right the multi-talented Phangan Batik, which besides selling batiks offers cheap **Internet** access; they also maintain a useful **website** on the island (Ⓦwww.kohphangan.com). Further on, about 500m from the pier, is the **post office** (Mon–Fri 8.30am–noon & 1–4.30pm, Sat 9am–noon). The island's **hospital** (Ⓣ077 377034) lies 3km north of town, on the road towards Mae Hat, while the **police station** (Ⓣ077 377114) is nearly 2km up the Ban Chaloaklam road – though there's a tourist police booth (Ⓣ1155) by the main pier in Thong Sala.

Ko Pha Ngan's south coast is lined with bungalows, but it's hard to recommend staying here, as the beaches are mediocre by Thai standards. On a quiet hillside above Ban Tai, 4km east of Thong Sala, **Wat Khao Tham** holds ten-day meditation retreats with farang teachers most months of the year (B3500 per person to cover food; minimum age 20). Space is limited, so it's best to pre-register either in person or by writing to Wat Khao Tham, PO Box 18, Ko Pha Ngan, Surat Thani 84280. For further information, go to Ⓦwww.watkowtahm.org.

Hat Rin

The monthly full-moon parties on **HAT RIN** are famous around the world, attracting up to ten thousand revellers to the beach – something like *Apocalypse Now* without the war – but there's a more sedate side to Hat Rin's alternative scene, too, with old and new-age hippies packing out the t'ai chi, yoga and meditation classes, and helping consume the drugs that are readily available here. It's not all so chilled-out unfortunately, as dodgy pills and mushroom teas send an average of two farangs a month into psychiatric care. The local authorities have set up a permanent police box at Hat Rin, as well as instigating regular bungalow searches and roadblocks, and draft in scores of police, both uniformed and plain-clothes, on full-moon nights.

Hat Rin comprises two back-to-back beaches, joined by transverse roads at the north and south ends. The main, eastern beach, usually referred to as **Sunrise** or Hat Rin Nok and lined with bars, restaurants and bungalows, is a classic curve of fine sand between two rocky slopes, though with so much boat traffic these days its waters are far from limpid. **Sunset** beach (Hat Rin Nai) is usually littered with flotsam, but has plenty of quieter accommodation. Unfortunately, the ugly, cramped and chaotic development between the beaches does no justice to the setting. Here – especially around what's known as Chicken Corner, where the southern transverse road meets the road along the back of Sunrise – you'll find clinics, supermarkets, travel agents, motorbike rental places (from B150 per day), overseas phone facilities, dozens of Internet outlets, plenty of ATMs and bank currency-exchange booths, two bookshops (north of Chicken Corner near the school) and a post office (near the pier on Sunset). Plenty of places on Hat Rin organize day-long boat-trips up the east coast, typically charging B300 per person. Arriving from Thong Sala, you can take songthaews or motorbike taxis along the steep rollercoaster road that follows the south coast, but from Ko Samui, or even Surat Thani, it's best take one of the direct boats from Samui to Hat Rin; see pp.1060–1061 for details.

As there are only around three thousand rooms on the whole island, for the **full-moon party** you should either arrive a day or more early, forget about sleep altogether, or join one of the many **party boats from Ko Samui** (about B400 per person), which usually leave between 9pm and midnight and return around dawn. On the night, *Paradise* styles itself as the party host, but the mayhem spreads along most of Sunrise, fuelled by hastily erected drinks stalls and sound systems. For somewhere to chill, head for *Mellow Mountain Bar*, which occupies a great position up in the rocks on the north side of Sunrise; the *Back Yard* club, up the hill behind the southern end of Sunrise, hosts the morning-after.

Accommodation

On the west side of the headland, white-sand, palm-fringed Leela Beach, a twenty-minute walk along a well-signposted route from Chicken Corner, is a good **accommodation** alternative to Sunset and Sunrise.

Leela Beach Bungalows Leela Beach ⓣ077 375094, ⓦwww.leelabeach.com. With plenty of space under the palm trees and half of the white-sand beach to themselves, these sturdy, no-frills bungalows have mosquito nets and en-suite bathrooms. ❶–❷

Neptune's Villa Near the small promontory at the centre of Sunset ⓣ077 375251, ⓔneptune1@thaimail.com. Laid-back place in grassy, shady grounds. Simple, clapboard huts with or without their own bathrooms, or rooms with hot water, some with a/c. ❷–❻

Palita At the northern end of Sunrise ⓣ077 375170, ⓔpalitas9@hotmail.com. Smart, clean bungalows (some a/c) give onto the beach, and large, simple, en-suite huts stand among the palms behind. The food gets rave reviews. ❷–❺

Paradise Spread over the far southern end of Sunrise ⓣ077 375244–5. Well-established place, with two good restaurants. All rooms and bungalows are en suite and some of the hillside options offer fine views. ❷

Sarikantang (*Bumble Bee Lodge*) Leela Beach ⓣ077 375055–6, ⓦwww.sarikantang.com. Stylish boutique resort: plain rooms or wooden bungalows with cold-water bathrooms or chic "superior" rooms with a/c, hot-water showers and outdoor sunken baths. ❸–❻

Sun Cliff High up on the tree-lined slope above the south end of Sunset ⓣ077 375134. Friendly place with great views and a range of well-maintained bungalows, some with hot water and a/c. ❷–❻

The east coast

North of Hat Rin, no roads run along the rocky, exposed **east coast**, only a rough, steep, fifteen-kilometre trail, which starts from Hat Rin's northern transverse road (signposted). About ninety minutes up the trail (or accessible by boat from Hat Rin Sunrise), the small, sandy bays of Hat Yuan and **HAT THIAN** make a quiet alternative to Hat Rin. Good accommodation options on Hat Thian include *Haad Tien Resort* (ⓣ01 229 3919; ❷), with en-suite wooden bungalows on the slope above the beach; and *The Sanctuary* (ⓣ01 271 3614, ⓦwww.thesanctuary-kpg.com; ❷–❼), which offers a huge range of basic and luxury en-suite bungalows, as well as dorm accommodation (B60), and good food. It also hosts courses in yoga, meditation and the like, and has a massage and beauty spa as well as a fasting and cleansing centre.

AO THONG NAI PAN is a beautiful, sandy, W-shaped bay, good for swimming and backed by steep, green hills, which supports a few shops, dive outfits and restaurants. A bumpy dirt road winds the 12km from Ban Tai on the south coast. Jeeps connect with boats at Thong Sala every day, though not if there's very heavy rain. A dozen resorts line the southern half of the bay, where friendly *Pingjun* (ⓣ077 299004; ❶–❷) has a range of large, en-suite bungalows. The clean, well-maintained bungalows at *Star Huts* (ⓣ077 299005, ⓔstar_hut@hotmail.com; ❶–❸) are the best budget choice on the northern beach; the friendly owners dish up good food and provide information about local walks.

The north coast

AO CHALOAKLAM, the largest bay on the **north coast**, is an R&R stop for fishing trawlers and a low-key tourist destination, which can easily be reached by songthaew or motorbike taxi from Thong Sala, 10km away. Best bet here is friendly *Coral Bay* (ⓣ077 374245; ❶–❸) on the grassy promontory that divides Chaloaklam from the tiny, sandy cove of Hat Khom (good for snorkelling). If the sea is not too rough, longtail boats run three times a day for most of the year from Ban Chaloaklam to the lovely, secluded **HAT KHUAT** (Bottle Beach); you could also walk there in about ninety minutes along a testing trail from Hat Khom. On a pretty flower-strewn hillside, *Smile Resort* (❷) is the best, though not the cheapest, of the four resorts here.

The west coast

Pha Ngan's **west coast** has almost as much development as the forgettable south coast, but the landscape here is more attractive, with good sunset views over the islands to the west; most of the bays, however, are enclosed by reefs, which keep the sea too shallow for a decent swim, especially between May and October. All the places mentioned below are accessible by songthaew or motorbike taxi. On the southern cape of nondescript **AO SEETHANU,** the excellent *Loy Fah* (ⓣ077 377319; ❶–❸) is a well-run place, commanding fine views and offering good snorkelling and swimming from the rocks. Round the next headland on **AO CHAOPHAO**, *Seaflower* (ⓣ077 349090; ❷–❸) is quiet and congenial, with great food; ask about their three-day snorkelling treks (B2200) to Ang Thong National Marine Park (see p.1059).

Beyond Chaophao, the long, gently curved beach of **HAT YAO** is justifiably becoming more popular, with several bars and restaurants, diving outfits, supermarkets and jeep (about B1000 per day) and bike (B150 per day) rental. Good bets here are *Ibiza* (ⓣ077 349121; ❷–❻), with smart, en-suite bungalows in a spacious garden, some with hot water and air-con, and kayaks for rent; and the friendly *Bay View* (ⓣ077 349235; ❶–❸), which offers good food and views from the quiet northern headland.

Ko Tao

Forty kilometres north of Ko Pha Ngan, small, forested **Ko Tao** is the last and most remote island of the archipelago, with a long curve of classic beach on its west side and secluded rocky coves along its east coast. Famed for its excellent diving and low-key bungalows, it's a popular travellers' destination, especially from December to March. Ko Tao feels the southwest monsoon more than Samui and Pha Ngan, so June to October can have strong winds and rain; some of its hundred or so bungalow operations close from June to August. The regularly updated and widely available free booklet, *Ko Tao Info*, is a useful source of information, along with its associated website, ⓦwww.kohtaoonline.com. Ko Tao's all-purpose fixer is Mr J, with a supermarket and travel agency five minutes' walk north of Ban Mae Hat opposite the school (ⓣ077 456066–7), and branches in Mae Hat and Ao Chaloke Ban Kao. Here you can do everything from renting motorbikes to selling unwanted air tickets, from organizing visa extensions to borrowing money. Full details on getting to Ko Tao are given on pp.1060–1061.

Blessed with clear seas (visibility up to 35m), a wide range of coral species and other marine life, and deep water relatively close to shore, Ko Tao is one of Thailand's premier **diving** locations. Diving is possible year-round, but visibility is best from April to July, in September (usually best of all) and October; November is the worst time. There's a one-person recompression chamber and diving medicine centre, Badalveda in Mae Hat (ⓣ077 456664, ⓦwww.badalveda.com). Ko Tao has forty or so dive companies, making this the largest training centre in Southeast Asia. PADI's four-day Open Water course costs anything from B6000 to B9000; at a reliable company such as Easy Divers, you can expect to pay around B7400, including accommodation and insurance. For qualified divers, one dive typically costs B800, a ten-dive package B5500. PADI Five-Star Dive Centres, all of which are committed to looking after the environment, include Big Blue at Mae Hat ⓣ077 456050 and on Hat Sai Ree ⓣ077 456415, ⓦwww.bigbluediving.com; Easy Divers at Mae

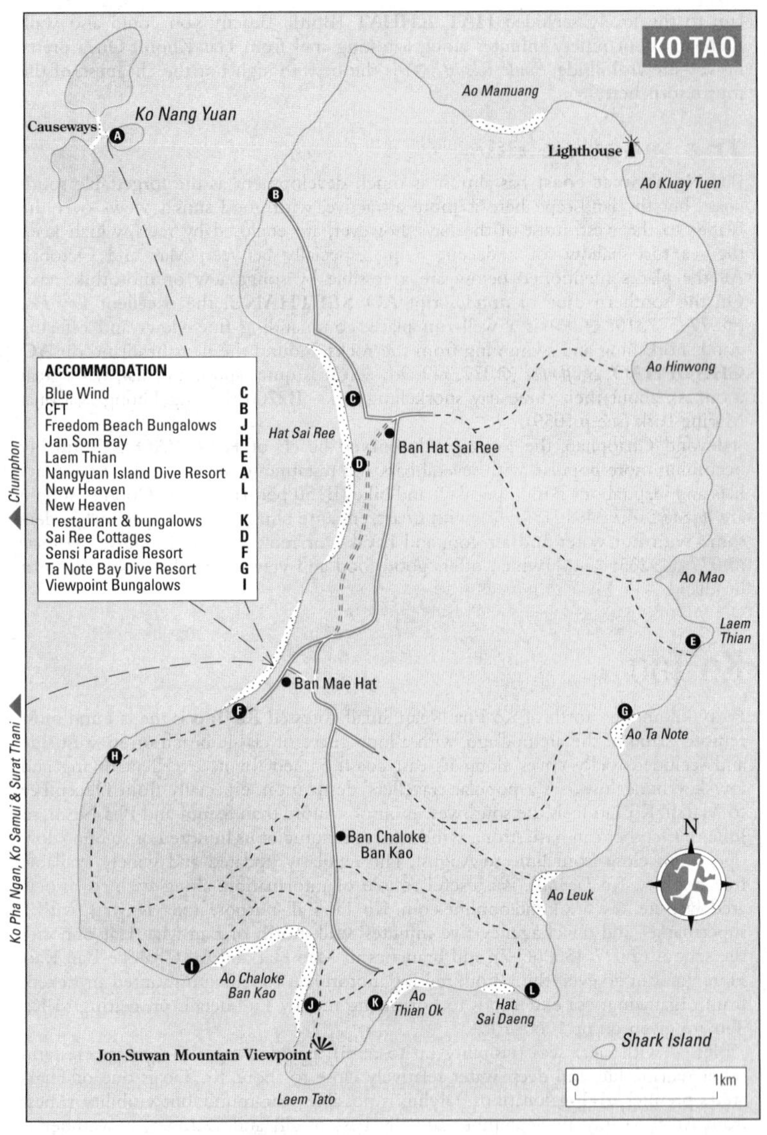

Hat ⓣ077 456010, ⓦwww.thaidive.com; Planet Scuba at Mae Hat ⓣ077 456110–1, ⓦwww.planet-scuba.net; and Scuba Junction on Hat Sai Ree ⓣ077 456164 or 077 456013, ⓦwww.scuba-junction.com.

You can **get around** easily enough on foot, but there are roads of sorts now to most of the resorts, though some are still four-wheel-drive only; motorbike taxis and pickups (B30–80 per person, more late at night), rental mopeds (B150 per day) and even a few jeeps (B1000 per day) are available in Mae Hat. Longtail-boat taxis are also available, as well as round-island boat tours, either on charter (B1000–1500 per boat for the day) or with a group tour (about B450 per person).

Ban Mae Hat, Sai Ree and Ko Nang Yuan

All boats to the island dock at **BAN MAE HAT**, a small, lively village with restaurants, bars, Internet outlets, travel agents, clinics, a bookshop, a currency exchange booth as well as a bank with ATM and Western Union facilities (both open daily), and a post office (Mon–Fri 8.30am–4pm, Sat 8.30am–noon) with telephone and poste restante facilities.

For somewhere to stay, try *Sensi Paradise Resort* (ⓣ077 456244, ⓦwww.kohtaoparadise.com; ❸–❼), which sprawls over the lower slopes of the headland to the south of the village. It offers some of the best upmarket accommodation on the island, in well-designed, wooden cottages, some with air-con. In this direction, also handy for the village (15min walk) is *Jan Som Bay* (ⓣ09 031 5324; ❸), a characterful place overlooking a rocky beach.

To the north of Mae Hat, **Hat Sai Ree**'s two-kilometre strip of white sand is Ko Tao's only long beach. Over twenty bungalow resorts have set up shop here, and a small village, **BAN HAT SAI REE**, with bars, restaurants, Internet outlets, clinics, supermarkets and a bank with ATM, has evolved at its northern end. Towards the midpoint of the beach, twenty minutes' walk from Mae Hat, *Sai Ree Cottages* (ⓣ077 456126; ❷–❸) has well-maintained, en-suite huts and bungalows in a flower-strewn garden by the beach and serves excellent grub. *Blue Wind* (ⓣ077 456116; ❷) near the village offers smart bungalows in a shady compound, a very good beachside restaurant and yoga courses. The track north of the village ends at secluded *CFT* (ⓣ077 456730; ❶–❹) on the rocky northwest flank of the island, which offers cheap shacks or en-suite bungalows and good food; there's no beach here, but great views and you can swim, snorkel or kayak off the rocks. Based at *CFT* is Here and Now (ⓦwww.hereandnow.be), a respected centre for massages, as well as t'ai chi and massage courses.

One kilometre off the northwest of Ko Tao, the three tiny islands of **KO NANG YUAN** are encircled by a ring of coral, and joined by a causeway of fine white sand. Boats from Mae Hat run back and forth three times a day (B60 return); day-trippers are charged B100 to land on the island, and cans and plastic bottles are banned. The *Nangyuan Island Dive Resort* (ⓣ077 456088–93, ⓦwww.nangyuan.com; ❻–❾) makes the most of its beautiful location, its swanky fan and air-con bungalows spreading over all three islands.

The east and south coasts

The sheltered inlets of the **east coast**, most of them containing one or two sets of bungalows, can be reached by boat, pick-up or four-wheel-drive. In the middle of the coast, the dramatic tiered promontory of **Laem Thian** shelters a tiny beach and a reef on its south side. With the headland to itself, *Laem Thian* (ⓣ077 456477, ⓔpingpong_laemthian@hotmail.com; ❷–❹) offers comfy bungalows and hotel-style rooms, decent food and a remote, castaway feel. Laem Thian's coral reef stretches down towards **Ao Ta Note**, a horseshoe inlet, with the best snorkelling just north of the bay's mouth. The pick of the resorts here is *Ta Note Bay Dive Resort* (ⓣ077 456757–9; ❷–❹), which has plenty of well-designed, en-suite wooden bungalows set among thick bougainvillaea.

The **southeast corner** of the island sticks out in a long, thin mole of land, which shelters sandy **Hat Sai Daeng** on its west side. Straddling the headland is *New Heaven* (ⓣ077 456462, ⓦwww.newheavenresort.com; ❷), a laid-back place with a good kitchen, a dive school and kayaks and snorkelling equipment; its pleasantly idiosyncratic en-suite bungalows enjoy good views. Overlooking **Ao Thian Ok**, the next bay along on the **south coast**, *New Heaven* also own a scenic restaurant with bungalows (same phone number and website; ❸). The remote hills between Hat Sai Daeng and Ao Thian Ok provide the spectacular location for Ko Tao's first **spa**, *Jamahkiri* (call ⓣ077 456400–1 for reservation and pick-up; ⓦwww.jamahkiri.com). This coast is sheltered from the worst of both monsoons, and consequently the main bay, **Ao Chaloke Ban Kao**, has seen a fair amount of development. Run by a friendly, young bunch and home to Big Bubble Diving, *Viewpoint Bungalows* (ⓣ077 456666, ⓔviewpointresort@hotmail.com; ❷–❻) offers well-built, en-suite bungalows, some with air-con, along the western side of the bay and its headland. On the east side of the bay, resolutely old-style *Freedom Beach Bungalows* (ⓣ077 456593; ❶–❸) come with or without bathrooms; they dot a spacious slope that leads down to the idyllic, palm-lined white sand of Freedom Beach.

Nakhon Si Thammarat

NAKHON SI THAMMARAT, the south's religious capital, is an absorbing place, well known for traditional handicrafts, shadow plays and especially its festivals. The biggest of these is Tamboon Deuan Sip every September/October, which is marked by a ten-day fair at Sri Nakharin park, processions, shadow plays and other theatrical shows. The town runs 7km from north to south, to either side of Thanon Ratchadamnoen, which is served by frequent blue songthaews. The south's most important temple, **Wat Mahathat**, is on this road, about 2km south of the town centre. Its courtyard is dominated by the huge Sri Lankan-style chedi enshrining relics of the Buddha, around which are arrayed row upon row of smaller chedis, an Aladdin's cave of a temple museum, and local handicraft stalls. A few minutes' walk south of Wat Mahathat, the **National Museum** (Wed–Sun 9am–4pm; B30) houses a small but diverse collection covering prehistoric finds, Buddha images and ceramics. The best possible introduction to southern Thailand's **shadow puppet theatre** is to head for 110/18 Soi 3, Thanon Si Thammasok, ten minutes' walk east of Wat Mahathat (ⓣ075 346394): here, Suchart Subsin, one of the south's leading exponents of nang thalung, and his son have opened their workshop to the public and, for a small fee (around B100), will show you scenes from a shadow play. You can also buy puppets here and see them being made.

Nakhon's **bus terminal** and **train station** are both centrally placed, while most **air-con minibuses** congregate on Thanon Chamroenwithi near the train station. The **TAT office** is on Sanam Na Muang park (ⓣ075 346515–6). For ultra-cheap **accommodation**, *Thai Lee Hotel* at 1130 Thanon Ratchadamnoen (ⓣ075 356948; ❶) is the best deal; moving up the scale, the central *Nakorn Garden Inn*, 1/4 Thanon Pak Nakhon (ⓣ075 313333; ❸), offers air-con, hot water and excellent value. Nakhon is a great place for **food**. *Khanom Jiin Muangkorn*, on Thanon Panyom near Wat Mahathat, is famous for lunchtime *khanom jiin*, noodles topped with hot, sweet or fishy sauce. *Khanom jiin* and other good local lunch dishes are served at *Krua Nakhon*, in the Bovorn Bazaar on Thanon Ratchadamnoen in the city centre, a complex that also houses a traditional coffee shop, a popular bar and an Internet café. The best of Nakhon's evening restaurants is *Hua Thale*, opposite the Nakorn Garden Inn (daily 4–10pm), renowned among locals for its excellent, inexpensive seafood. The night market is on Thanon Chamroenwithi.

10.7

Southern Thailand: the Andaman coast

The landscape along the Andaman coast is lushly tropical and spiked with dramatic limestone crags, best appreciated by staying in **Khao Sok National Park** or taking a boat trip around the bizarre **Ao Phang Nga Bay**. Most people, however, come here for the beaches and the coral reefs: **Phuket** is Thailand's largest island and the best place to learn to dive, but it's package-tour-oriented, so backpackers usually head straight for the beaches around **Krabi**, or to the island of **Ko Lanta**. Unlike the Gulf coast, the Andaman coast is hit by the southwest monsoon from May to October, when the rain and high seas render some of the outer islands inaccessible and litter many beaches with debris; prices drop significantly during this period.

Ranong and around

The multi-ethnic provincial capital of **RANONG,** which thrives on its proximity to Burma, is chiefly of interest for the boats to Ko Chang and Ko Phayam, and to Kaw Thaung in Burma, which leave from the harbour at **Saphan Pla**, 5km southwest of the town centre and served by regular songthaews from Thanon Ruangrat.

All west-coast buses from Bangkok to Phuket or Krabi pass through Ranong, stopping at the **bus terminal** on Highway 4 (Thanon Phetkasem), 1.5km southeast of the centre; songthaews ferry passengers on to Thanon Ruangrat in the town centre or to the port at Saphan Pla. **Ranong Airport** is 20km south of town on Highway 4, served by share taxis charging up to B100 per person.

The most popular budget **hotel** is the *Asia Hotel*, 39/9 Thanon Ruangrat (Ⓣ077 811113; ❶–❷), about 70m south of the market, which has scruffy but decent fan

After the tsunami

The Andaman Coast was severely battered by the devastating **tsunami** of December 26 2004. Many coastal communities and beach resorts suffered extensive loss of life and massive damage to homes and businesses. Among the worst-hit tourist resorts were Khao Lak and parts of Ko Phi Phi. At the time of going to press, in May 2005, reconstruction in these two resorts was still in its early stages, so we have printed only skeletal information on those places; to supplement this, regularly updated information will be posted on Ⓦwww.roughguides.com/tsunami/thailand. Though many other areas of the Andaman Coast were affected to varying degrees by the tidal waves, nearly all the tourist destinations managed to rebuild within just a few months.

and air-con en-suite rooms; the New Zealand-run *Kiwi Orchid Guest House*, in the bus station compound on Thanon Phetkasem, 1.5km from the town centre (☎078 890473, ©erl@Thailand.com; ❷) is more traveller-oriented, though rooms all share facilities. Both *Kiwi Orchid* and *Pon's Place* restaurant, 300m north of the *Asia Hotel* on Thanon Ruangrat, are good sources of **info** on the islands. *Chaong Thong*, across from the *Asia Hotel* and south a bit, next to the Bangkok Bank at 8–10 Thanon Ruangrat has a cheap and varied farang-friendly **food** menu, and *Coffee House*, 173 Thanon Ruangrat, is great for filled baguettes, pancakes – and coffee. North of *Pon's Place*, Thanon Ruangrat has half a dozen places offering **Internet** access, and the CAT international **phone** office (Mon–Fri 8.30am–4.30pm) on Thanon Tha Muang also has Catnet Internet terminals.

Kaw Thaung (Ko Song) and into Burma

The southernmost tip of **Burma** – known as **Kaw Thaung** in Burmese, **Ko Song** in Thai, and **Victoria Point** when it was a British colony – is currently accessible to foreigners entering from the Thai side of the border, and can be done as a day-trip (getting a new thirty-day Thai visa on re-entry), though there's nothing much to do in Kaw Thaung itself, except browse the markets around the port. Longtail **boats** to Kaw Thaung (30min; B50) leave throughout the day from the PTT quay in Saphan Pla, but before boarding you must get a Thai exit stamp from the Thai immigration office (daily 8.30am–4.30pm) on the outskirts of Saphan Pla, opposite the Thai Farmers Bank. Just before docking at Kaw Thaung, all boats stop at Burmese immigration, where you buy your Burmese visa: US$5 (or B300) for a one- to three-day pass into Burma, or US$36 for a thirty-day pass. For stays of over a day, you also need to change US dollars into Foreign Exchange Certificates (FECs): $50 for two to three days, or $300 for a month's stay. Legally, you are not allowed to travel beyond Kaw Thaung unless you have already bought a proper visa from a Burmese embassy to supplement the Kaw Thaung passes. There's an airport 7km north of Kaw Thaung, which has flights to Rangoon.

Ko Chang

Not to be confused with the much larger island of Ko Chang on Thailand's east coast (see pp.1036–1039), Ranong's **Ko Chang** is a forested little island about 5km offshore, with a charmingly low-key atmosphere. The beaches are connected by tracks through the trees; there are no cars and only sporadic electricity. To date, there is barely any commercial activity on Ko Chang, save for a couple of local minimarkets, a dive operator, and foreign exchange and an overseas phone service at *Cashew Resort*. The dozen or so family-run **bungalow** operations are mostly scattered along the west coast, many of them hidden amongst the shorefront trees of the longest and prettiest beach, Ao Yai; they nearly all close from June through October. *Cashew Resort*, north of the lagoon on central Ao Yai (☎077 820116; ❶–❷) is the largest outfit, comprising both simple and more comfortable wooden huts. Towards the far north end of Ao Yai, *Sunset Bungalows* (☎077 820171; ❶–❷) is a popular outfit of decent huts (some en suite) set in a grove of cashew-nut trees. Just south of the lagoon, the welcoming and exuberantly run *Golden Bee* (☎077 820129; ❶) has cheap, simple huts and is open all year. Further south, many of the en-suite bungalows at *Ko Chang Resort* (☎077 820176, ©sound_of_sea@lycos.com; ❶–❷) occupy a fabulous spot high on the rocks.

Longtail **boats** to Ko Chang leave from Saphan Pla. Frequent songthaews run from Ranong's Thanon Ruangrat and bus station to Saphan Pla (20min; B7 to the main road or B10–15 to the pier); if you're dropped on the main road, follow signs to the pier, about 500m away. At the time of writing, there was one scheduled daily boat departure (1hr; B100) at 9am, and usually another one at noon (ask in Ranong); the boatman will drop you as close as possible to your chosen Ko Chang bungalow.

Rainy-season boats only go to the east coast, from where it's a three-kilometre walk to Ao Yai. The return boat leaves Ko Chang between about 7 and 9am.

Ko Phayam

Diminutive **KO PHAYAM** measures just 4km by 7km, offers fine white-sand beaches and is also very peaceful. Slightly more developed than Ko Chang, it has a network of concrete roads, a fledgling though still very low-key bar scene, and a **village** at the port comprising several small shops and restaurants – including *Oscar's*, a favourite expat watering hole and excellent source of island **info** – Internet access and a dive shop. Most bungalows close down during the wet season (June–Oct).

Ko Phayam's nicest beach is the three-kilometre-long **Ao Yai** on the southwest coast, a beautiful sweep of soft white sand that gets pounded by quite big waves. Here you'll find *Aow Yai Bungalow Gilles and Phatchara*, at the southern end (ⓣ077 821753, ⓦwww.r24.org/travelsmart.net/nst/aowyai; ❶–❸), which has a good travellers' vibe and offers all sorts of bungalows, mostly en suite, in a garden; contact them about rainy-season opening. The characterful *Bamboo Bungalows*, in the centre of the bay (ⓣ077 820012; ❶–❸), have been built with imaginative use of local materials and all have bathrooms and mosquito nets; they stay open all year round. Nearby *Coconut Bungalow* (ⓣ077 820011; ❶–❸) has both small bamboo en-suite huts as well as concrete bungalows. Across on the northwest coast, on the prettiest, northern stretch of **Ao Kao Kwai** (also known as Ao Kao Fai, or Buffalo Bay), *Mr Gao* (ⓣ077 823995; ❶–❸) comprises just seven exceptionally well-designed bungalows and runs snorkelling expeditions to Ko Surin.

From November to May, there's at least one **boat** a day from Ranong's port area, Saphan Pla, to Ko Phayam, departing at 9am and taking two to three hours to reach the village pier on the east coast (B100); there should also be another boat at about 2pm, but check in Ranong. (See "Ko Chang", opposite, for details of how to get to the Saphan Pla pier from Ranong.) Motorbike taxis meet incoming boats at the pier in Ko Phayam village and charge B50 to most bungalows. The boat returns from Ko Phayam to Saphan Pla at about 8am, and there is sometimes another departure at 3pm. Boats are less regular during the rainy season.

Khao Sok National Park

Whether you're heading down the Andaman or the Gulf coast, the stunning jungle-clad karsts of **KHAO SOK NATIONAL PARK** (B200 entry, valid for three days) are well worth veering inland for. Much of the park is carpeted in impenetrable rainforest – home to gibbons, gaurs, leopard cats, tigers and up to 155 species of bird – but nine fairly easy **trails** radiate from the visitor centre (daily 8am–6pm), which hands out sketch maps showing their routes and sells a good guidebook to the park, *Waterfalls and Gibbon Calls* (B470). The most popular trails run to **Ton Gloy Waterfall** (7km from the centre; 3hr each way) and to the eleven-tiered **Sip-et Chan Waterfall**, which can be tricky to reach and involves some climbing plus half a dozen river crossings (4km; 3hr each way). Take plenty of water, as Khao Sok is notoriously humid. Longer **guided treks** into the jungle can be arranged through most guesthouses (B300–550), but the most popular outings are the Cheow Lan lake trips (B1200), which include a boat ride and a swim/hike through the Nam Talu river-cave. Most guesthouses also lead **night safaris** along the main park trails, at around B300 for two hours, and many also do tubing and canoeing trips B300/B600.

Most Surat Thani-bound **buses** from Khao Lak pass the park entrance, which is located at kilometre-stone marker 109 on Highway 401 – less than an hour by bus from **TAKUA PA**, ninety minutes from Khao Lak, or two hours from Surat Thani. Buses run at least every ninety minutes in both directions; at the park entrance, you'll

△ Khao Sok National Park

be met by guesthouse staff offering free lifts to their accommodation, the furthest of which is 3km away. Coming by bus from Bangkok or Chumphon, take a Surat Thani-bound bus, but ask to be dropped off at the junction with the Takua Pa road, about 20km before Surat Thani, and then change onto a Takua Pa bus. If coming direct from Surat Thani, think twice about using the tourist **minibus** services to Khao Sok that leave at or after 3pm as they have a reputation for dumping passengers at the wrong guesthouse.

A tourist village has grown up along the north-south access road to the national park visitor centre and trailheads, and along the main east-west track that bisects it. As well as around twenty sets of **bungalows**, all of which serve **food**, you'll find minimarkets and Internet centres, currency exchange (but no ATM), and motorbike rental. Set well off the main access road, about 900m north of the highway, *Garden Huts* (ⓣ07 282 8223; ❷) comprises simple, en-suite, bamboo huts in a karst-view flower garden. Three hundred metres along the quieter east–west sidetrack, *Bamboo House 1* (ⓣ01 787 7484, ⓦwww.krabidir.com/bamboo/index; ❶–❸) has en-suite huts, treehouses, and a swimming platform in the river. Next door, the friendly *Nung House* (ⓣ077 359024, ⓦwww.nunghouse.com; ❶–❸) also has huts, bungalows and treehouses and serves good food. About fifteen minutes' walk further east (or an hour from the highway), *Our Jungle House* (ⓕ09 909 6814, ⓦwww.losthorizonsasia.com; ❸) is the most romantically located of them all, offering elegant, beautifully situated treehouses and cabins by the river.

Khao Lak

Thirty kilometres south of Takua Pa and ninety minutes by bus from Khao Sok National Park, the calm, family-oriented, mid-priced resort of **KHAO LAK** became headline news in December 2004, after suffering horrendous damage from the tsunami. The waves destroyed nearly all its seafront hotels and there was massive loss of life. Inland shops, businesses and guesthouses were also affected, but most were repairable and those listed here are all operational. Reconstruction will take a long time and was in its very earliest stages as this book went to press, in May 2005. The information printed here is therefore minimal, but we are posting ongoing updates on the rebuilding of Khao Lak at ⓦwww.roughguides.com/tsunami/thailand.

The area usually referred to as Khao Lak is in fact three separate beaches: Nang Thong is the business centre, with banks, ATMs, dive shops and Internet access. Bang Niang, 45 minutes' walk north along the sand, has the best beach; and Khao Lak proper, about 5km to the south, is quiet. All **buses** running from Phuket to Takua Pa and Ranong (and vice versa), as well as some of the Phuket–Surat Thani services, pass through Khao Lak; if you're coming from Krabi or Phang Nga, take a Phuket-bound bus to Khokkloi and change. Most bus drivers will drop you near your chosen accommodation; if not, get off at Nang Thong supermarket and walk.

The cheapest **places to stay** are on the roadside in central Nang Thong, about 600m from the beach, and include the good bungalows at the friendly *Jai* (ⓣ076 420390; ❷–❸), north of Nang Thong supermarket; and the spotlessly clean, concrete bungalows at *Phu Khao Lak Resort* (ⓣ076 420141, ⓔphukhaolak@hotmail.com; ❷–❸), south of the supermarket. Seven kilometres south of central Nang Thong, on a rocky shore in Khao Lak proper, stands *Poseidon Bungalows* (ⓣ076 443258, ⓦwww.similantour.com; ❷–❹; closed May–Oct), a lovely place to hang out for a few days and also a long-established organizer of snorkelling expeditions to the Similan Islands (see below). To reach *Poseidon*, either get off the bus at the village of Laem Kaen (between kms 51 and 52) and take a motorbike taxi, or get off at the turn-off between km 53 and km 54 and walk the 1km to the bungalows. Recommended **restaurants** in Nang Thong, all just north of Nang Thong supermarket, include the well-priced curries and seafood at *Jai*; the very popular *Khao Lak Seafood*; and the chilled-out cocktail bar and upstairs dining area at *Happy Snapper*.

Khao Lak is renowned for the live-aboard **snorkelling and diving trips** to the spectacular, world-famous reefs off **Ko Similan** and **Ko Surin** (chiefly Nov through April). Prices start at B11,000 for two-night trips, with about thirty per-cent off for snorkellers. Some operators also do Similan day-trips in speedboats for B4000, and they all do dive courses (B8000 for the four-day PADI Open Water). The longest-running Khao Lak dive operator is the highly regarded Sea Dragon Dive Center (☎076 420420, Ⓦwww.seadragondivecenter.com), across from Nang Thong supermarket. *Poseidon Bungalows* (see above) also runs recommended three-day trips to the Similans; these are for snorkellers only, cost B6300 and depart twice weekly (Tues and Fri), so book ahead.

Phuket

Thailand's largest island and a province in its own right, **Phuket** (pronounced "Poo-ket") ranks second in tourist popularity only to Pattaya. Thoughtless developments have scarred much of the island, particularly along the central west coast, and the trend on all the beaches is upmarket, with very few budget possibilities. Parts of the island were extremely badly damaged by the December 2004 tsunami and there was significant loss of life and property. Many beaches escaped almost unscathed, however, and elsewhere reconstruction has, for the most, part been rapid. Phuket is Thailand's most important **diving** centre, offering easy access to some of the most spectacular reefs and islands in the world, and the country's best-value dive shops (see Ⓦphuket.com/diving/guide.htm for links), all of which offer day-trips (B2000–3500) and diving courses (from B8400–9900 for a four-day PADI Open Water). Always check the equipment and staff credentials carefully and ask whether the dive centre has membership for one of Phuket's three recompression chambers: at Hyperbaric Services Thailand (HST), 233 Thanon Raja Uthit Song Roi Phi on Ao Patong (☎076 342518, Ⓦwww.sssnetwork.com); Badalveda Diving Medicine Centre at Bangkok Phuket Hospital, 2/1 Thanon Hongyok Utis, on the outskirts of Phuket Town, (☎076 254425, Ⓦwww.badalveda.com); and at Wachira Hospital, Soi Wachira, Thanon Yaowarat, Phuket Town (☎076 211114). The sea gets quite rough from May to October, when diving is less rewarding and swimming can be dangerous. Aside from the beaches and the reefs, the island's main attractions include the dramatic headland of **Laem Promthep** at Phuket's southernmost tip – a popular coach-tour stop for sunset – and the **Gibbon Rehabilitation Centre** (daily 10am–4pm, last tour at 3.15pm; donation; Ⓦwww.warthai.org), which is near Bang Pae in Phra Taew National Park, 10km northeast of the Heroines' Monument, off Route 4027, and accessible by songthaew from Phuket Town (most frequent in the mornings; 40min) then a 1km walk.

Phuket is served by dozens of government and private **bus** services to and from Bangkok, southern Thai destinations and Malaysia (see "Travel details", p.1096). Nearly all buses terminate at the bus station at the eastern end of Thanon Phang Nga in Phuket Town (none serve the beaches), from where it's a fifteen-minute walk to the Thanon Ranong songthaew stop for the beaches. Some travellers prefer to take the overnight train from Bangkok to Surat Thani (about B650), about 290km east of Phuket, and then a bus. A private minibus service also runs from Phuket Town's *Montri Hotel* on Thanon Montri to Surat Thani. **Ferries** connect Phuket with Ko Phi Phi, Ko Lanta and Ao Nang, usually docking at Rassada Port; minibuses meet the ferries and charge B100 for transfers to Phuket Town and the west-coast beaches, or B150 to the airport. **Phuket International Airport** is about 32km northwest of Phuket Town; the airport limousine bus will drop you at your hotel (B100 per person into town, B150 to Ao Patong and B180 to Ao Karon), or taxis charge about three times that.

Although Phuket's west-coast beaches are connected by road, to get from one beach to another by public transport you generally have to go back into Phuket

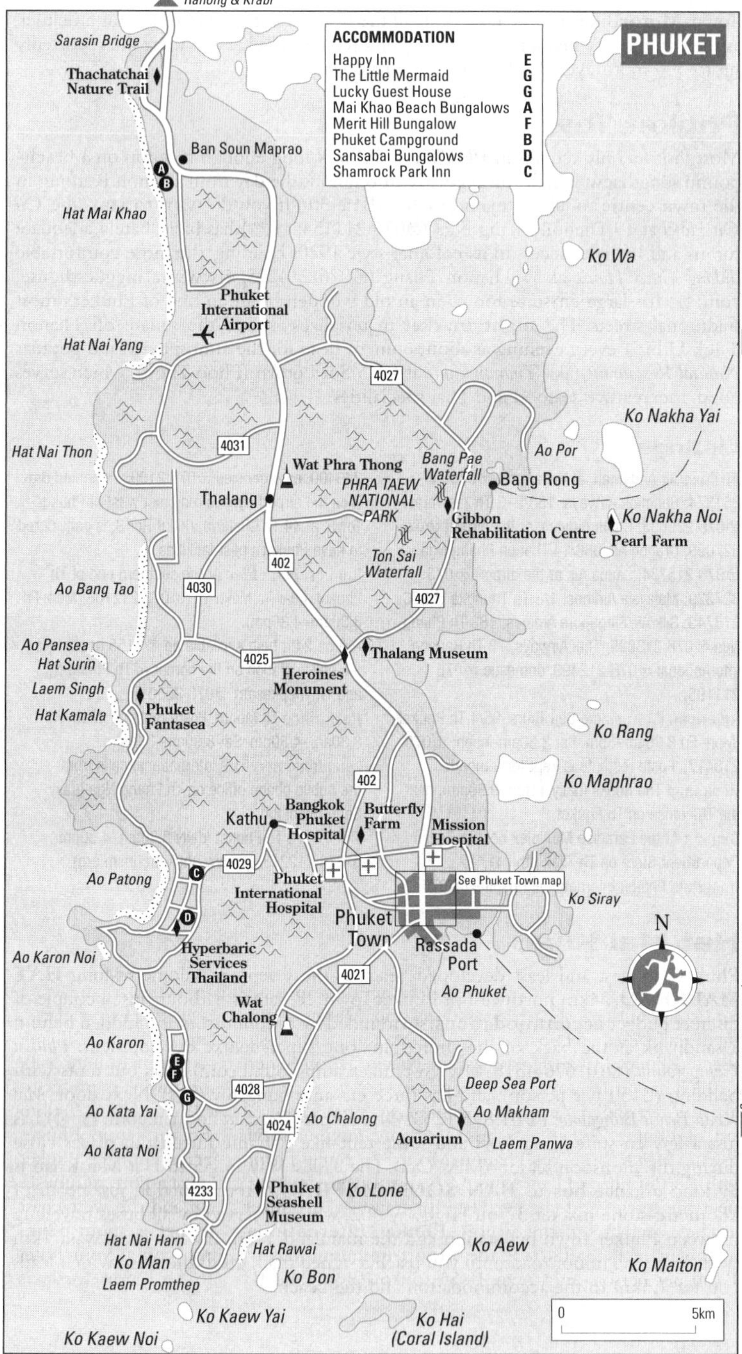
PHUKET
ACCOMMODATION
Happy Inn E
The Little Mermaid G
Lucky Guest House G
Mai Khao Beach Bungalows A
Merit Hill Bungalow F
Phuket Campground B
Sansabai Bungalows D
Shamrock Park Inn C
Ranong & Krabi
Sarasin Bridge
Thachatchai Nature Trail
Ban Soun Maprao
Hat Mai Khao
Phuket International Airport
Hat Nai Yang
Hat Nai Thon
Ko Wa
Ko Yao Yai and Ko Yao Noi
Ko Nakha Yai
Ao Por
Bang Pae Waterfall
Bang Rong
Wat Phra Thong
Thalang
PHRA TAEW NATIONAL PARK
Gibbon Rehabilitation Centre
Ko Nakha Noi
Pearl Farm
Ton Sai Waterfall
Ao Bang Tao
Ao Pansea
Hat Surin
Laem Singh
Hat Kamala
Thalang Museum
Heroines' Monument
Phuket Fantasea
Ko Rang
Ko Maphrao
Kathu
Bangkok Phuket Hospital
Butterfly Farm
Mission Hospital
Ao Patong
Phuket International Hospital
See Phuket Town map
Ko Siray
Phuket Town
Rassada Port
Ao Karon Noi
Hyperbaric Services Thailand
Ao Phuket
Wat Chalong
Ao Karon
Deep Sea Port
Ao Makham
Ao Kata Yai
Ao Chalong
Aquarium
Laem Panwa
Ao Kata Noi
Phuket Seashell Museum
Ko Lone
Ko Phi Phi, Ko Lanta & Ao Nang
Hat Nai Harn
Hat Rawai
Ko Aew
Ko Maiton
Ko Man
Laem Promthep
Ko Bon
Ko Kaew Yai
Ko Hai (Coral Island)
Ko Kaew Noi
Ko Racha Yai
0
5km
N
4027
4031
402
4030
4025
4029
4021
4028
4024
4233

Town. **Motorbikes** can be rented on all the beaches but be sure to ask for a helmet, as the compulsory helmet law is strictly enforced on Phuket and there are reportedly up to 300 motorcycle fatalities on the island every year.

Phuket Town

Most visitors only remain in **PHUKET TOWN** long enough to jump on a beach-bound songthaew, which run regularly throughout the day from Thanon Ranong in the town centre to all the main beaches (B15–30). If you do want **to stay**, the *On On Hotel* at 19 Thanon Phang Nga (☎076 211154; ❶-❷) has basic, barely adequate rooms and Internet access in its colonial-style 1920s building; the more comfortable *Talang Guest House* at 37 Thanon Talang (☎076 214225, Ⓦwww.talangguesthouse.com; ❷) has large en-suite rooms in an old wooden house in one of Phuket's most traditional streets. The **night market** materializes around the square off Thanon Tilok Uthit 1 every evening at about 6pm, or head for the atmospheric and popular *Natural Restaurant* (aka *Thammachat*) at 62/5 Soi Putorn (Phoo Thon), which serves good, inexpensive seafood and Thai specialities.

Listings

Airlines Air Andaman, at the airport ☎076 351374; Bangkok Airways, 158/2–3 Th Yaowarat ☎076 225033; China Airlines, at the airport ☎076 327099; Dragon Air, 956/14 Thanon Phang Nga ☎076 215734; Lauda Air, at the airport ☎076 327329; Malaysia Airlines, 1/8 Th Thungka ☎076 213749; Silk Air/Singapore Airlines, 183 Th Phang Nga ☎076 213895; Thai Airways, 78 Th Ranong, international ☎076 212499, domestic ☎076 211195.

American Express c/o Sea Tours, 95/4 Th Phuket (Mon–Fri 8.30am–5pm, Sat 8.30am–noon; ☎076 218417). Poste restante is kept for a month.

Bookshop The Books (daily 11am–9.30pm), near the TAT office on Th Phuket.

Cinema At the Paradise Multiplex next to Ocean Department Store on Th Tilok Uthit 1.

Hospitals Phuket International Hospital (☎076 249400, emergencies ☎076 210935), behind Big C on the airport bypass road just west of Phuket Town, at 44 Th Chalermprakiat Ror 9, is considered to have Phuket's best facilities.

Immigration office At the southern end of Th Phuket, near Ao Makham (☎076 212108; Mon–Fri 8.30am–4.30pm).

Police 24hr help available on ☎1155 or contact the police station on the corner of Th Phang Nga and Th Thepkasatri ☎076 355015.

Post office Th Montri. Poste restante: Mon–Fri 8.30am–4.30pm, Sat 8.30am–3.30pm.

Telephone services International calls from the public phone office on Th Phang Nga (daily 8am–midnight).

TAT 73–75 Th Phuket (daily 8.30am–4.30pm ☎076 212213, Ⓦwww.phukettourism.org).

Hat Mai Khao

Phuket's longest and least developed beach is the seventeen-kilometre-long **HAT MAI KHAO**, 34km northwest of Phuket Town. To date, it harbours just a couple of discreet budget **accommodations**, surrounded by coconut trees and hidden behind a sandbank at the back of the shore, plus one super-deluxe development. *Phuket Campground* (☎01 676 4318, Ⓦwww.phuketcampground.com) rents out tents with bedding (B150 per person), and has three en-suite bungalows (❸). Next door, *Mai Khao Beach Bungalows* (☎01 895 1233, Ⓔbmaikhao_beach@hotmail.com; ❷–❸) has just a few en-suite bungalows and some tent-like A-frame huts. Both places close during the monsoon season (May–Oct). The easiest way to get to Hat Mai Khao is by long-distance **bus** to **BAN SOUN MAPRAO**, a road junction just north of kilometre-stone marker 37 on Highway 402, which is served by all buses travelling between Phuket Town bus station and the mainland. From the bus drop, walk 1km west down the minor road until you reach a signed track off to the west, which leads you for 1.5km to the accommodation and the beach.

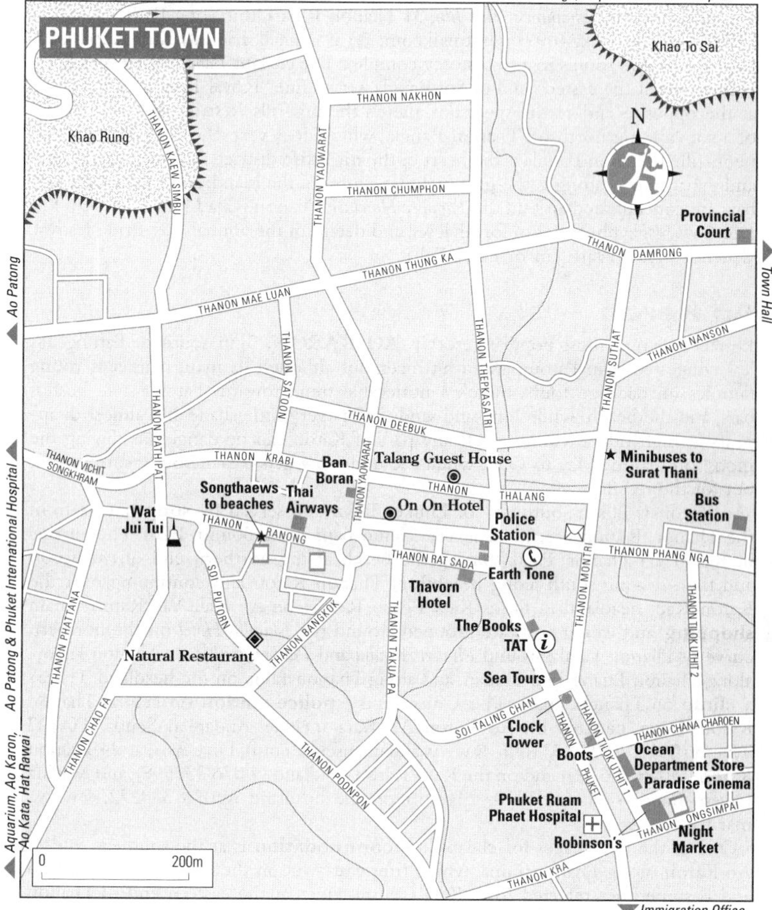

Ao Patong

Packed with high-rise hotels, hostess bars and touts, **AO PATONG** – 15km west of Phuket Town – is the busiest and ugliest of all Phuket's beaches and hard to recommend. However, its broad, three-kilometre beach does have good sand and plenty of shade, and offers the island's biggest choice of watersports and **dive centres**, including Santana at 222 Thanon Thavee Wong (ⓣ076 294220, ⓦwww.santanaphuket.com); and Scuba Cat at 94 Thanon Thavee Wong (ⓣ076 345246, ⓦwww.scubacat.com). The beachfront strip was badly smashed by the tsunami of December 2004, but reconstruction was swift and there was no damage inland of Thanon Thavee Wong. **Songthaews** from Phuket Town's Thanon Ranong (every 15min 6am–6pm; 20min; B15) approach Patong from the northeast, driving south along beachfront Thanon Thavee Wong before turning round at the Patong Merlin.

Sansabai Bungalows, about 500m from the beach off the eastern end of Thanon Bangla at 17/21 Soi Saen Sabai (ⓣ076 342948, ⓦwww.phuket-sansabai.com; ❸–❺), has plain but comfortable **bungalows** in a peaceful garden, while at the northern end of the resort, *Shamrock Park Inn*, 31 Thanon Raja Uthit Song Roi Phi (ⓣ076 342275, ⓔshamrock340991@hotmail.com; ❹) is a small, friendly little hotel with pleasant air-con rooms in a two-storey complex. The elegant *Baan Sukhothai*, a hotel **restaurant** at the eastern end of Soi Bangla, serves fine "Royal Thai" cuisine, while at the opposite end of the spectrum, there's the no-frills *Restaurant 4* at the back of a soi running north off Thanon Bangla, which does very cheap seafood. Sleazy, neon-filled Thanon Bangla is the heart of the **nightlife** district, filled with girlie bars and expat pubs. Patong is the **gay** nightlife centre of the island, and most of the gay bars are concentrated around the *Paradise Hotel* on Thanon Raja Uthit Song Roi Phi (see ⓦwww.gayphuket.com for reviews, and details of the annual Gay Pride festival, which is held in late Jan or early Feb).

Ao Karon

Phuket's second most popular resort is **AO KARON,** 5km south of Patong. It's less congested than Patong and a bit nicer, but although its main market is young families on package tours, there's a noticeable trend towards Patong-style hostess bars, and the beach, while long and sandy, offers very little shade and almost disappears at high tide. Swimming off any part of Karon can be dangerous during the monsoon season (May to Oct), when the undertow gets treacherously strong: look out for the red flags.

Ao Karon is 20km southwest of Phuket Town and served by **songthaews** from the Thanon Ranong terminal (every 20min 6am–6pm; 30min; B20). They arrive in Karon via Thanon Patak, hitting the beach at the northern end of Ao Karon and then driving south along beachfront Thanon Karon and continuing over the Karon/Kata headland as far as Kata Beach Resort on Ao Kata Yai. Karon's main **shopping** and eating areas are grouped around the *Islandia Hotel* on the northern curve of Thanon Patak, around *Phuket Arcadia* and *Phuket Orchid* on Thanon Karon, along Thanon Luang Pho Chuan, and along Thanon Taina on the headland. There's a **clinic** on Thanon Luang Pho Chuan and a **police station** on central Thanon Karon. **Dive centres** on Ao Karon/Ao Kata include: Andaman Scuba, 111/22 Thanon Taina (ⓣ076 331006, ⓦwww.andamanscuba.com); Dive Asia, at 24 Thanon Karon (ⓣ076 396199) and on the Kata/Karon headland (ⓣ076 330598); and Marina Divers, next to Marina Phuket Resort on the headland (ⓣ076 330272; ⓦwww.marinadivers.com).

One of the best places for cheapish **accommodation** is at the southern end of Ao Karon, along Thanon Taina, which runs east-west on the Karon/Kata headland and is sometimes referred to as Kata Centre. Here, at the eastern end of Thanon Taina, you'll find *The Little Mermaid* at 94/25 (ⓣ076 330730, ⓔmermaid@phuket.ksc.co.th; advance booking essential; ❷–❺), which offers good air-con bungalow rooms set round a pool, plus some city-style fan rooms; further west at 110/44–45, *Lucky Guest House* (ⓣ076 330572, ⓔluckyguesthousekata@hotmail.com; ❸–❺) has large, bright rooms in a block and some bungalows. The other budget accommodation hub is off the central stretch of Thanon Karon, on Thanon Luang Pho Chuan's Soi 1. Here, the smart fan and air-con bungalows at *Happy Inn* (ⓣ076 396260; ❸) sit in a surprisingly peaceful garden, while 300m further south, at 28 Soi 2, *Merit Hill Bungalow* (ⓣ076 333300; ❸–❺) has apartment-style bungalows and fan-cooled chalets overlooking a palm grove up a slope across the road from the beach, plus some cheapish rooms. Many of Karon's best **restaurants** and bars are on Thanon Taina, including *Kwong Seafood Shop*, for mid-priced barbecued fish and *Kampong-Kata Hill Restaurant*, which serves classy Thai dishes and enjoys commanding views. The string of five open-fronted streetside restaurants just north of the Ruam Thep Inn on Thanon Karon serve a decent spread of cheapish food. Most of the Thanon Taina **bars** are small, genial places: *Café del Mar* and *Blue Fin* are both recommended.

Ao Phang Nga

Covering some four hundred square kilometres of coast between Phuket and Krabi, the mangrove-lined bay of **AO PHANG NGA** is littered with dramatic limestone karst formations of up to 300m in height. The most affordable way of seeing the bay is to join one of the longtail **boat trips** arranged from the nearby town of **Phang Nga**: Triple Friends Tour (ⓣ076 430195), Sayan Tour (ⓣ076 430348, ⓦwww.sayantour.com) and Mr Kean Tour (ⓣ076 430619) all have offices inside the bus station and offer similar itineraries; all prices exclude the B200 national park entry fee. Half-day tours (B200) depart every day at 8am and 2pm and last about three hours; full-day tours (8am; B500) last until 4pm. Overnight trips with a stay on the Muslim stilt village of Ko Panyi cost an extra B250. All tours include a chance to swim in the bay, and most offer the option of a canoeing session as well, for an extra B300 per hour. The standard itinerary follows a circular or figure-of-eight route around the bay, passing weirdly shaped karst silhouettes including "James Bond Island" which was Scaramanga's hideaway in *The Man With the Golden Gun*. Most boats return to the mainland via Ko Panyi. Kayaking tours of the bay are more rewarding but a lot more expensive and should be arranged from Khao Lak, Phuket, Krabi or Ao Nang.

Phang Nga town has frequent **bus** connections with Phuket and Krabi, and some to Surat Thani. The bus station is on Thanon Phetkasem, a few minutes' walk from the hotels, banks (with ATMs and exchange) and restaurants along the same road. The bus station boat-tour operators will store your baggage for a few hours; they also sell bus and boat tickets to Krabi, Ko Phi Phi, Ko Lanta and Ko Samui. Phang Nga's main budget **hotel** is *Thawisuk Hotel* at 77 Thanon Phetkasem (ⓣ076 412100; ❶). The *Phing Kan Restaurant* under the similar, nearby *Ratanapong Hotel* at no. 111 (ⓣ076 411247; ❶-❷) serves decent noodle and rice standards.

Krabi

The small estuary town of **KRABI** is the transport hub for the islands of Ko Phi Phi and Ko Lanta and makes a nice spot for a couple of nights. Although the town has no beaches of its own, it's only a 45-minute boat ride to the stunning bays of Laem Phra Nang and about the same time in a songthaew to Ao Nang. Every Krabi travel agent sells **sea-kayaking** expeditions and snorkelling trips, and many also offer tours of Krabi's mangrove swamps.

Krabi Airport is 18km east of town, just off Highway 4; flights are met by Thai Airways minibuses (B60 per person) and taxis (B300 to Krabi or B500 to Ao Nang). Airline offices in Krabi include Bangkok Airways on Thanon Maharat (ⓣ075 622955); PB Air (ⓣ075 692143) and Phuket Airlines (ⓣ075 636393), both at the airport; Silk Air on Soi 4, Thanon Maharat (ⓣ075 623370); and Thai Airways, beside *Maritime Park Resort Krabi*, 2km north of TAT on Thanon Utrakit (ⓣ075 622440). Krabi runs government **buses** and private minibuses to and from numerous southern Thai destinations, Malaysia, and Bangkok (see "Travel details" on p.1096). Some travellers take the overnight train from Bangkok to Surat Thani (about B650) and then pick up a Krabi bus. Nearly all buses terminate at the Krabi bus station 5km north of town at Talat Kao, from where there's a frequent songthaew service to Thanon Maharat in the town centre. **Ferries** to and from Ko Phi Phi (B200–250; see p.1085) and Ko Lanta (B200; see p.1086) use the Krabi Passenger Port outside Krabi town, 2km to the southwest. Ferry tickets bought from tour operators in town should include a free transfer from central Krabi, though any Ao Nang-bound songthaew will also go via the port if requested (a ride of about 10min). **Longtail boats** for East Railay on Laem Phra Nang (45min; B70) leave on demand from the town-centre piers at Tha Chao

Fa on Thanon Kong Ka and nearby on Thanon Utrakit. Public **songthaews** to Ao Nang, via Krabi Passenger Port (5.30am–10.30pm; every 30min) depart from outside the Vogue Department Store on Thanon Maharat.

The **TAT** office (daily 8.30am–4.30pm; ⓣ075 622163) is beside the estuary on Thanon Utrakit at the northern edge of the town centre. The CAT international **phone** office is 2km further north on Thanon Utrakit (Mon–Fri 8am–8pm, Sat & Sun 8.30am–4.30pm), reached on any songthaew heading up that road. The main post office is south of *Cha Guest House* on Thanon Utrakit; the immigration office is about 150m further south (Mon–Fri 8.30am–4.30pm; ⓣ075 611097); and the police station is another 200m further south still (ⓣ075 611222). Krabi Hospital is about 1km north of the town centre at 325 Thanon Utrakit (ⓣ075 611202) and also has dental facilities, but the better hospital is considered to be the private Muslim hospital, Jariyatham Ruampat Hospital (ⓣ075 611223), which is about 3km north of town and has English-speaking staff.

For **accommodation**, the traveller-oriented *Cha Guest House* (ⓣ075 621125, ⓔchaguesthouse@hotmail.com; ❶-❷) has a range of good rooms near the post office at 45 Thanon Utrakit. Nearby, blue-and white-themed *Chan-Cha-Lay*, at 55 Thanon Utrakit (ⓣ075 620952, ⓦwww.geocities.com/chan_cha_lay; ❷–❹), is stylish and funky, while *Lipstic* at 20 Soi 2, off Thanon Maharat (ⓣ075 612392, ⓔkayanchalee@hotmail.com; ❶) makes a good cheap choice. Krabi has plenty of traveller-oriented **restaurants**, or try either the riverside night market near the longtail-boat pier on Thanon Kong Ka or the inland night market on Soi 10, Thanon Maharat. *Raan Ahaan Jeh (Vegetarian Café)* at the north end of Thanon Pruksa Uthit, one block west of Thanon Maharat, is a cheap Thai veggie café (daily 6.30am–2pm), while *Muslim Restaurant,* across the road, does inexpensive filling *rotis* with curry sauces.

Sea-kayaking in the Krabi area

By far the most rewarding way of exploring the glories of the Krabi coastline is by **sea kayak**. Paddling silently and stealthily into the eerie mangrove swamps and secret tidal lagoons, or *hongs*, hidden inside the limestone karsts is an awesome experience and gives you close-up views of birds, animals and plants that would be impossible from a roaring longtail.

Hongs can only be accessed at certain tides in canoes small enough to travel along the narrow tunnels that lead into the karst's central pool. Once inside a *hong* you are enclosed by a ring of cliff faces hung with strange plants that nourish a local population of flying foxes and monkeys and support an ecosystem that has remained unchanged for millennia.

The most popular kayaking destination is **Ao Thalen** (aka Ao Talin or Talane), about 25km northwest of Krabi town, where you paddle out to the *hongs* and beaches of **Ko Hong** and **Ko Bileh**. This is the best area for wildlife and general wilderness, but is quite often inaccessible. Another 25km north up the Krabi coast, the **Ban Bor Tor** (aka Ban Bho Tho) area of **Ao Luk** bay is famous for its caves, in particular **Tham Lod**, which has a long tunnel hung with stalagmites and stalactites, and **Tham Phi Hua Toe**, whose walls display around a hundred prehistoric cave-paintings.

Kayaking **trips** to any of the above destinations usually cost about B1700 for a full day or B900 for half a day; the better companies will take groups of two and limit their numbers to fourteen. Trips can be arranged through any tour operator in Krabi town, Laem Phra Nang or Ao Nang, or directly with reputable kayaking operators such as John Gray Sea Canoe (ⓣ076 254505, ⓦwww.johngray-seacanoe.com) and Sea Canoe (ⓣ075 637170, ⓦwww.seacanoe.net). Tour leaders should give you full kayaking instruction; if asked, most tour operators can arrange for someone else to paddle you around for an extra B300.

Laem Phra Nang (Railay)

The stunning headland of **Laem Phra Nang** is accessible only b from Krabi (45min) or Ao Nang (10min), so staying on one of its fou like being on an island. The sheer limestone cliffs, pure white san waters make it a spectacular spot, but bungalows have now been b every inch of available land and the whole place feels congested. Lae four beaches are all within ten minutes' walk of each other: **Ao Phra Nang** is the prettiest, with luxuriously soft sand, reefs close to shore, and just one discreet super-luxury hotel. Ao Phra Nang is flanked by **Hat Railay**, technically one bay, but in fact composed of distinct east and west beaches. **East Railay** is not suitable for swimming because of its fairly dense mangrove growth and a tide that goes out for miles, but accommodation here is cheaper. **West Railay**, on the other hand, enjoys impressive karst scenery, crystal-clear water and a much longer stretch of good sand. On the other side of a rocky promontory from West Railay, the beach at **Ao Ton Sai** is scruffy and littered with rocks that make it impossible to swim at low tide, but this is the travellers' beach, with scores of budget bungalows set amongst the palms several hundred metres back from the shore, and regular all-night beach parties at the beachfront *Freedom Bar* and *Chillout Bar*.

Laem Phra Nang is Thailand's premier **rock-climbing** centre, with six hundred bolted sport-climbing routes on the cape alone (see ⓦwww.simonfoley.com/climbing), and no shortage of places where you can rent equipment and hire guides and instructors. Check with other tourists before choosing a climbing guide, as operators' safety standards vary. A typical half-day introduction costs B800.

Longtail boats to the cape depart from various spots along the Krabi riverfront (see p.1081) and dock at East Railay, from where it's easy to cut across to West Railay along any of the through-tracks. Krabi boats do run during the rainy season, but it's safer to go via Ao Nang instead (see p.1084). Ao Nang is much closer to Laem Phra Nang, and longtails run from the beachfront here to West Railay and Ao Ton Sai (10min) year-round. During high season, there's one direct boat a day between Laem Phra Nang and Ko Phi Phi. Several bungalows change money and offer Internet access and overseas phone services but prices are higher than in Krabi. There is a clinic in the Railay Bay compound.

Accommodation

During high season, from November to February, it's essential to arrive on the beaches as early in the morning as possible.

Coco Central East Railay ⓣ01 228 4258. Basic but decent enough huts in a small garden compound. ❷

Dream Valley Resort Ao Ton Sai ⓣ075 622583, ⓦwww.krabidir.com/dreamvalresort/index.htm. Nearly eighty bamboo huts and a/c cabins set discreetly amongst the trees. ❷–❺

Railay Village West Railay ⓣ075 622578, ⓦwww.railay.com/railay/accommodation/railay_village.shtml. Attractive fan and a/c bungalows occupying landscaped grounds – with pool – in between the two beaches. ❺–❽

Rapala Rock Wood Resort Northern end of East Railay ⓣ075 622586, ⓔrapala@loxinfo.co.th. The most traveller-friendly option on Railay has nice wooden huts with mattress-beds set around a garden high up above the beach. ❸

Tonsai Bungalow Ao Ton Sai ⓣ075 622584. Popular place with simple huts 200m back from the shore, plus more upmarket concrete versions close to the seafront. ❷–❸

Ya Ya Bungalows Central East Railay ⓣ075 622593. Dozens of huts and three-storey wooden towers claustrophobically jammed into a small area. Some a/c. ❸–❺

ᴊ Nang and Hat Nopparat Thara

Though it lacks the cape's fine beaches, lively **AO NANG** (sometimes confusingly referred to as Ao Phra Nang), 45 minutes by road from Krabi or a ten-minute boat ride from Laem Phra Nang, is a less claustrophobic if rather faceless mainland resort. A road runs right alongside a big chunk of Ao Nang's narrow shore, with the resort area stretching back over 1km along both arms of Highway 4203, meeting Hat Nopparat Thara at the northwestern limit. But 1km east down the track beside *Phra Nang Inn* lies a much prettier part of the beach, and beyond that sits Ao Phai Plong, another bay of fine gold sand. Ao Nang is full of **sea-kayaking** outlets, such as the reputable Sea Canoe (Ⓣ075 637170, Ⓦwww.seacanoe.net; day-trips for B1700), and dive shops, including Ao Nang Divers at *Krabi Seaview Resort* (Ⓣ075 637242, Ⓦwww.aonang-divers.com) on Route 4203, whose one-day trips average B2500, and four-day PADI Open Water courses cost B11,9000. The local **tourist police** are based next to the *Ao Nang Pakasai Resort* (Ⓣ075 637208), and there's a **clinic** at Bibi's (daily 9am–4pm). **Songthaews** run to and from Krabi (every 10min from 6am–6.30pm, every 30min from 6.30pm–10.30pm; 45min), frequent longtail **boats** travel to and from Laem Phra Nang (10min), and from November to May daily boats connect Ao Nang with Ko Phi Phi Don (2hr; B250), Ko Lanta (2hr 30min; B250) and Phuket (2hr; B400).

Follow the road northwest of Ao Nang, past Krabi Resort, for about 1km and you come to the eastern end of two-kilometre-long **HAT NOPPARAT THARA**, a national park beach whose visitors' centre is another kilometre further on, beyond the T-junction. The **western** stretch of Hat Nopparat Thara (aka Hat Ton Son) is separated from the visitors' centre and eastern beach by a khlong, which must be crossed by longtail. Here, just a few inexpensive bungalows share the long swathe of peaceful shoreline, with no shops or hassle. From 6am–6.30pm, all Krabi–Ao Nang **songthaews** go via the national park visitors' centre (night-time ones take a different route), from where **longtails** cross the khlong to the western beach when full.

Accommodation and eating

Seafood is Ao Nang's strong suit, best enjoyed on so-called Soi Seafood, a cluster of little **restaurants** off the western end of the beachfront road. *Tanta's Restaurant*, just north of *Phra Nang Inn* on Route 4203, is another very popular spot, serving exceptionally tasty, Thai and seafood dishes.

Accommodation

Ao Nang and eastern Hat Nopparat Thara

Bream Guest House 75m up Route 4203 Ⓣ075 637555. Urban-style guesthouse offering some of the cheapest rooms in the resort, all with shared bathroom. ❷

Green Park Bungalow 200m up Route 4203 Ⓣ075 637300. Recommended, friendly, family-run place; en-suite bamboo and concrete huts set among shady trees. ❷–❹

Laughing Gecko 200m down a track from eastern Hat Nopparat Thara's main beachfront road, about 1.5km from Ao Nang Ⓣ075 695115. An exceptionally welcoming and traveller-friendly haven offering dorms (B100) and a range of simple bamboo huts. ❶–❷

Sea World 75m up Route 4203 Ⓣ075 637388, Ⓔseaworld_aonang@hotmail.com. Popular, well-priced rooms (some with a/c) with bathroom, balcony and good views. ❷–❻

Western Hat Nopparat Thara

Andaman Inn 100m west of the khlong Ⓣ01 956 1173. The most commercial and popular option, with a huge range of huts, from very simple to very comfortable. Closes May to early Sept. ❶–❸

Long Beach Bungalow and Camp 500m west of the khlong Ⓣ09 885 5559, Ⓔlongbeachfishcamp@yahoo.com. Laid-back outfit with simple bamboo huts, some en suite. Runs fishing expeditions. Should be open all year. ❷

Ko Phi Phi

One of southern Thailand's most famous destinations, the two spectacular **Ko Phi Phi** islands, 40km south of Krabi and 48km east of southern Phuket, leapt to international notoriety as the location for the 1999 film *The Beach*. Then, in December 2004, they became headline news again as the tsunami wreaked inconceivable destruction on the two main beaches of the larger island, **Ko Phi Phi Don,** and on the densely packed tourist village connecting them. Many people in this part of the island lost their lives and hundreds of bungalows were pulverized. As this book went to press, in May 2005, the rebuilding process was in its early stages so we have been able to print only minimal information on the worst-affected beaches of Ao Ton Sai and Ao Loh Dalum; we are, however, posting ongoing updates on Ko Phi Phi at Ⓦwww.roughguides.com/tsunami/thailand. Some of Phi Phi Don's other beaches were less badly damaged. Phi Phi Don's sister island, **Ko Phi Phi Leh**, is an uninhabited national marine park and can only be visited on day-trips; it escaped the tidal waves relatively unscathed.

Scheduled **ferries** connect Ko Phi Phi Don with Krabi (1hr 30min–2hr; B200–250) and Phuket (1hr 30min–2hr 30min; B350–500) at least once a day year-round. From November to May, there are also daily boats from Ao Nang (2hr; B250) and Ko Lanta Yai (1hr 30min; B200). All boats dock at Ao Ton Sai. From here, you can catch a **longtail** to any of the other beaches or walk – there are no roads or vehicle tracks on Phi Phi Don, just a series of paths across the steep and at times rugged interior. **Diving** and snorkelling around Ko Phi Phi is exceptionally good, and you can arrange day-dives (from B1800) and four-day PADI courses (B10,000) through Moskito (Ⓣ076 283208, Ⓦwww.moskitodiving.com).

Ao Ton Sai, Laem Hin and Ao Loh Dalum

Ko Phi Phi Don would itself be two islands were it not for the narrow isthmus that connects the hilly expanses to the east and west, separating the stunningly symmetrical double bays of **AO TON SAI** to the south and Ao Loh Dalum to the north. The land between the two bays is occupied by a tourist village, crammed with guesthouses, tour operators, restaurants, bars, Internet cafés and dive centres.

East along the coast from the pier, about ten minutes' walk down the main track, the **LAEM HIN** promontory overlooks a quieter patch of swimmable beach. Here, *PP Don Chukit Resort* (Ⓣ075 618126; ❺–❼) offers mid-range air-con bungalows in a garden, and similar but pricier versions beside the seafront walkway. Just inland, *Gypsy* (Ⓣ01 894 5658; ❸) has reasonable, en-suite concrete bungalows set round an unusually spacious lawn.

Just a few minutes' walk north through Ton Sai village, seductively curvaceous **AO LOH DALUM** is much better for swimming and sunbathing, though the tide here goes out for miles. The viewpoint that overlooks the far eastern edge of the beach affords a magnificent wraparound panorama of both Ao Loh Dalum and Ao Ton Sai; it's accessible via a steepish track.

Hat Yao

With its deluxe luxurious white sand and large reefs just 20m offshore, **HAT YAO (Long Beach)** is the best of Phi Phi's main beaches. Longtail boats do the ten-minute shuttle between Ao Ton Sai and Hat Yao from about 8am to 8pm, but it's also possible to walk between the two in half an hour. At low tide you can get to Hat Yao along the rocky shore; otherwise, take the path via *Bay View Resort* on Laem Hin.

The most attractive of Hat Yao's **accommodation** is the welcoming *Ma Prao* (Ⓣ075 622486, Ⓦwww.maprao.com; call ahead to book; ❷–❺), whose simple but characterful bungalows, some of them en suite, overlook a little cove west of Hat Yao itself, with easy access via a rocky path. Of the two bungalow operations on Hat Yao itself, *Long*

Beach Bungalows (☎075 612217; ❷–❸) has a range of cheap huts, some of them right on the beachfront. The bungalows at the efficient and well-equipped *Paradise Pearl* (☎075 622100, ⓦwww.ppparadise.com; ❸–❼) are larger and more sophisticated.

Ko Lanta Yai

Appealing, forested, 25-kilometre long **Ko Lanta Yai** offers plenty of fine sandy beaches along its west coast and is a deservedly popular destination. It's also within easy day-tripping distance of the stunning beaches and reefs of Ko Rok Nai and Ko Rok Nok, 47km south (B1300 through any tour agent). Accommodation prices listed here are for high season, but expect them to at least double during the over-subscribed months of December and January; in the rainy season (May–Oct) rates are vastly discounted, some bungalows close down, and the seas become too rough for boats to get here from Krabi.

From mid-October to mid-May there are **ferries** to Ko Lanta Yai's commercial centre and port, **BAN SALA DAN**, from **Krabi** (departing Krabi at 10.30am and 1.30pm; returning at 8am & 1pm), and from November to May ferries also run to Sala Dan from Rassada Port on **Phuket** (departing Phuket at 8.30am; returning at 1.30pm), and from Tha Hat Nopparat Thara near **Ao Nang** via West Railay on Laem Phra Nang (departing Ao Nang at 11am; returning at 1.30pm); there may also be services from **Ko Phi Phi**. Bungalow touts always meet the boats, and transport you to the beach of your choice. During the rainy season, you'll need to arrange **minivan** transport from Krabi with one of the tour agencies (2 daily). Minivans also run year-round to Ko Lanta Yai from Trang (4 daily).

A road runs the entire length of Ko Lanta Yai's west coast, but there's no regular songthaew service on the island, so many bungalows rent out **motorbikes**, and there is a motorbike taxi service from Ban Sala Dan. Most bungalows change money (there's an ATM in Ban Sala Dan), many offer international phone services, and Internet centres are popping up everywhere. Ban Sala Dan has a health centre and several **dive shops**, including Ko Lanta Diving Centre (☎075 684065, ⓦwww.kohlantadivingcenter.com) and Lanta Diver (☎075 684208, ⓦwww.lantadiver.com), which do day-trips (from B2500) and four-day PADI Open Water courses (B10,500). The diving season only runs from November to April.

Hat Khlong Dao

Lanta Yai's longest and most popular beach is beautiful, broad, gold-sand **HAT KHLONG DAO**, in the northwest, about half an hour's walk from Ban Sala Dan, or 2–3km by road. **Accommodation** on Khlong Dao is almost entirely mid-market, but room standards are high and nothing's more than 100m from the beach. *Laguna Beach Club* (☎075 684172, ⓦwww.laguna-beach-club.com; closed June–Sept; ❹–❺) offers half a dozen different types of thoughtfully designed accommodation – and a swimming pool. The fifteen brightly painted fan and air-con bungalows at *Cha-Ba Bungalows and Art Gallery* (☎075 684118, ⓦwww.krabidir.com/chababungalows/index.htm; ❸) are cute and full of character, matched only by the chic whitewashed interiors furnished with local fabrics at tiny *Time for Lime* (☎075 684590, ⓦwww.timeforlime.net; closed mid-June–early Nov; ❸), which is attached to a cooking school at the rocky, far southern end of the beach. As for **food**, the seafood barbecues at *Lanta Villa* are popular and *Banana Beach* serves very good curries, as well as cocktails and ice creams. The most chilled out **bar** is *Bomp Bar*, with cushions, deckchairs and low tables spread out on the sand, a campfire, and decent music.

Ao Phra-Ae (Long Beach)

A couple of kilometres south of Khlong Dao, **AO PHRA-AE** (also known as **Long Beach**) boasts a beautiful long strip of white sand and an enjoyably youthful,

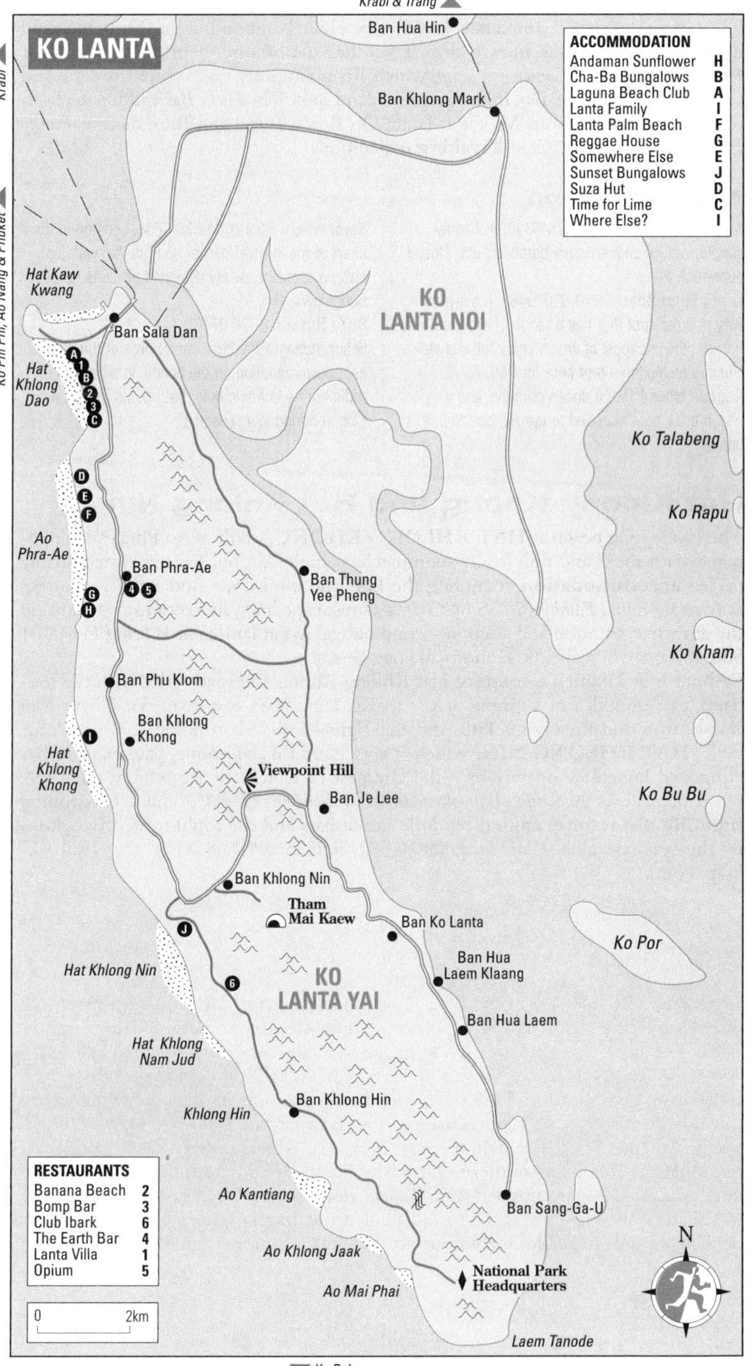
KO LANTA
Krabi & Trang
Krabi
Ko Phi Phi, Ao Nang & Phuket
Ko Rok
ACCOMMODATION
Andaman Sunflower H
Cha-Ba Bungalows B
Laguna Beach Club A
Lanta Family I
Lanta Palm Beach F
Reggae House G
Somewhere Else E
Sunset Bungalows J
Suza Hut D
Time for Lime C
Where Else? I
RESTAURANTS
Banana Beach 2
Bomp Bar 3
Club Ibark 6
The Earth Bar 4
Lanta Villa 1
Opium 5
0 2km
Ban Hua Hin
Ban Khlong Mark
KO LANTA NOI
Hat Kaw Kwang
Ban Sala Dan
Hat Khlong Dao
Ao Phra-Ae
Ban Phra-Ae
Ban Thung Yee Pheng
Ko Talabeng
Ko Rapu
Ko Kham
Ban Phu Klom
Ban Khlong Khong
Hat Khlong Khong
Viewpoint Hill
Ban Je Lee
Ko Bu Bu
Ban Khlong Nin
Tham Mai Kaew
Ban Ko Lanta
Ko Por
Hat Khlong Nin
KO LANTA YAI
Ban Hua Laem Klaang
Ban Hua Laem
Hat Khlong Nam Jud
Ban Khlong Hin
Khlong Hin
Ao Kantiang
Ban Sang-Ga-U
Ao Khlong Jaak
National Park Headquarters
Ao Mai Phai
Laem Tanode
N

if not exactly peaceful, ambience. Traveller-oriented bamboo huts are fairly plentiful here, as are beach-shack **bars** with mats on the sand, among them the very popular *Funky Fish*, next to *Somewhere Else*, which has a famously good sound system, and the nearby *The Ozone Bar*. Inland, on the island road, *The Earth Bar* and *Opium* both play mainly dance music. Mr Yat at Lanta On Beach Travel and Tour, next to *Funky Fish*, organizes boating and **kayaking** expeditions.

Accommodation

Andaman Sunflower ⓣ075 684023. Twenty simple, well-priced, en-suite bamboo huts. Closed June–Oct. ❷

Lanta Palm Beach ⓣ01 787 9483. A busy and very popular spot that has a range of different bungalows, the cheapest of which enjoy full sea views. You can also pitch a tent here for B50. ❸–❺

Reggae House Half a dozen primitive and very cheap brick huts attached to the *Reggae House* bar. ❶

Somewhere Else ⓣ01 536 0858. Located in the heart of the liveliest part of Ao Phra-Ae, with just sixteen spacious, nicely designed en-suite bamboo bungalows. ❷

Suza Hut ⓣ01 370 9710, ⓔsuzahutlanta@hotmail.com. Some of the cheapest accommodation on the beach, in a handful of rudimentary bamboo huts; bathrooms are shared. Closed during low season. ❶

Hat Khlong Khong and Hat Khlong Nin

The lovely long beach at **HAT KHLONG KHONG**, south of Ao Phra-Ae, is peppered with rocks and only really swimmable at high tide, but has lots of reasonably priced **accommodation**, including the huts and bungalows under the palm trees at friendly *Lanta Family* (ⓣ075 648310, ⓔdumsupaporn@yahoo.com.sg; ❷–❺); and the attractive bamboo and coconut-wood bungalows at laid-back *Where Else?* (ⓣ01 536 4870, ⓔwhereelse2004@hotmail.com; ❷–❸).

About four kilometres south of Hat Khlong Khong, the road forks, with the left-hand, east-bound arm running across to Ko Lanta Yai's east coast, via Tham Mai Kaew caves and Viewpoint Hill, and the right-hand fork running south to long, sandy **HAT KHLONG NIN**, which is very good for swimming, has several rather congested bungalow operations – the cheapest of which are the whitewashed terraced bungalows at *Sunset Bungalows* (ⓣ01 535 6288; ❷–❹) – and a burgeoning **nightlife** that revolves around ten little beach bars and the sophisticated Bangkok-by-the-sea-style club, *Club Ibark* (ⓣ01 582 2625 or 09 668 4104, ⓦwww.ibark-krabi.com).

10.8

The deep south

As Thailand drops down to meet Malaysia, the cultures of the two countries begin to merge. Many inhabitants of the **deep south** are ethnically more akin to the Malaysians, and a significant proportion of the 1,500,000 followers of Islam here speak Yawi, an old Malay dialect. Some also yearn for secession from Thailand, and in 2004 there was an escalation in violent militancy, leading the Thai government to introduce special security measures in certain parts of Pattani, Yala and Narathiwat provinces – for up-to-the-minute advice, consult your government travel advisory. The most popular **border crossings to Malaysia** are detailed below, with the most efficient transport connections to Malaysia starting at the ugly, modern city of **Hat Yai**. The nearby old town of **Songkhla** is a more sympathetic spot for sightseeing, and other attractions include the uncrowded beaches of the **Trang coast** and the spectacular islands around **Ko Tarutao**.

Trang and around

TRANG holds an eye-catching **Vegetarian Festival** every October (see p.946), but is chiefly of interest for the string of gorgeous beaches and islands nearby. Most **buses** arrive at the terminal on Thanon Huay Yod, to the north of the centre; buses from Satun stop on Thanon Ratsada, which runs south from the eastern end of the main street, Thanon Rama VI. The **train station** is at the western end of Thanon Rama VI.

TAT has a small **tourist office** on Thanon Ruenrom, around the back of the city hall off Thanon Rama VI, 100m east of the clocktower (daily 8.30am–4.30pm; ⓣ075 215867); further information on the town is available at ⓦwww.trangonline.com. The town's outstanding budget **hotel** is to the north of the clocktower, the *Yamawa Bed and Breakfast* at 94 Thanon Wisetkul (ⓣ075 216617; ❷-❸), a beautifully decorated, partly air-conditioned guesthouse with shared bathrooms; the friendly owners also organize treks (Jan–May) and tours in the Trang area. If you can't get a room here, a good second best is the en-suite *Ko Teng Hotel* at 77–79 Thanon Rama VI (ⓣ075 218622; ❷). The **night market** is on Thanon Ruenrom, while *Meeting Point* (with Internet access) and *Wunderbar* near the station both cater well to travellers. The well-informed owners of the excellent **bookshop**, Ani's, near the Yamawa B&B at 285 Thanon Ratchadamnoen, have **motorbikes** to rent.

Near the station at 22 Thanon Sathanee, staff at Sukorn Beach Bungalows and Tours (ⓣ075 211457, ⓦwww.sukorn-island-trang.com) are also a good source of **information** on the Trang area, and arrange local transport (including air-con minibuses to Hat Yai, Nakhon, Ko Lanta and Pak Bara), in addition to running a resort on Ko Sukorn (see p.1090); they can arrange **car hire**, with driver, make reservations at any of the island resorts, and organize day-trips to the islands, as well as **trekking**, **white-water rafting** and **canoeing** excursions inland. For self-drive car hire, contact Avis (ⓣ075 691941) at Trang Airport.

The Trang coast

From Pak Meng, 40km due west of Trang town, to the mouth of the Trang River runs a thirty-kilometre stretch of beautiful beaches, dotted with dramatic limestone outcrops and one or two bungalow resorts. You'll need a car or motorbike to fully explore the coast, but there are **air-con minibuses** from Trang to the mediocre beach at Pak Meng and to Ban Chao Mai via Hat Yao (both roughly half-hourly; 1hr; B50). **Hat Yao** runs in a broad five-kilometre, white-sand strip, backed by casuarina trees; just beyond its southern end, friendly *Sinchai's Chaomai Resort* (Ⓣ01 396 4838; ❶–❹) offers ramshackle huts and rooms, tasty meals and boat tours. A short walk away lies the Muslim fishing village of **BAN CHAO MAI**, which shelters *Had Yao Nature Resort* (Ⓣ075 203012, Ⓔnatureresorts@hotmail.com; ❷–❹), an efficiently run hostel, with excellent food and accommodation ranging from dorm beds (B150) to self-contained bungalows; bikes, boat trips and kayaks are available, and the owners also run a very good resort (❹) on (and boat trips to) **Ko Libong**, the large island opposite Ban Chao Mai famous for its dugongs and migratory birds. Also based in Ban Chao Mai are X-Site (Ⓣ075 207518, Ⓦwww.laoliangisland.com), who run all-in, three-day scuba-diving, snorkelling or rock-climbing trips from here to **Ko Lao Lieng**, twin desert islands to the south near Ko Sukorn (B4500–5600).

The Trang islands

Of all the Trang islands, **Ko Hai** (aka **Ko Ngai**), 16km southwest of Pak Meng, offers the best combination of accommodation and scenery. Boats leave Pak Meng daily at 10.30am (1hr; B150), though in low season (June to Oct) the sea is often too rough. The cheapest of the island's four resorts, *Ko Ngai Villa* (Ⓣ075 203263; Trang office at 112 Th Rama VI Ⓣ075 210496; ❷–❹, tents B200), overlooks the long white-sand beach on the east coast. There's a well-organized scuba-diving outfit (Nov–April; Ⓦwww.rainbow-diver.com) at the more upmarket *Ko Ngai Resort* (Ⓣ075 206924–6; Trang office at 66/4 Thanon Sathanee, Ⓣ075 210317; Ⓦwww.kohngai.com; ❺–❼), which occupies a sandy cove by the island's jetty and runs great snorkelling trips.

Ko Mook, about 8km southeast of Ko Hai, is known for Tham Morakhot, the beautiful "Emerald Cave" on the west coast, which can only be reached by boat (whether from Mook itself, Ko Hai or the mainland). After a short swim through the cave, you'll emerge at an inland beach at the base of a natural chimney whose walls are coated with dripping vegetation. Hat Farang to the south of Tham Morakhot is the best strip of sand, good for swimming and snorkelling. The nicest of the bungalow outfits on Hat Farang is *Charlie's* (Ⓣ075 203281–2; Trang office at 17 Th Sathanee, Ⓣ075 217671–2; Ⓦwww.kohmook.com; ❹–❼), with an excellent restaurant and all manner of facilities, including kayaks and a dive shop; a longtail charter to the Emerald Cave will set you back B300 per person. On the shady slope behind the beach, friendly *Hat Farang* (Ⓣ07 884 4785; ❶–❷) offers simple huts and rooms, as well as good food. To get to Hat Farang from the mainland, it's best to book a minibus-and-boat package through one of the resort offices or travel agents in Trang (B200 per person).

A good way south of the other Trang islands, **Ko Sukorn** lacks the white sand and coral of its neighbours, but makes up for it with one excellent resort and the chance to glimpse how island fishermen and rubber farmers live. On the island's main beach – 500m of gently shelving brown sand along the southwestern shore – you'll find the congenial *Sukorn Beach Bungalows* (Ⓣ075 207707; Trang office at 22 Th Sathanee, Ⓣ075 211457, Ⓦwww.sukorn-island-trang.com; ❸–❻). Nicely decorated bungalows and rooms – all spotlessly clean and with en-suite bathrooms – are set around a lush garden, and there's an excellent well-priced restaurant. Fishing and snorkelling trips are available, as well as kayaks, rental motorbikes and mountain bikes. A songthaew-and-boat transfer to the island (B90 per person) leaves the resort's office in Trang daily at 11.30am and takes a couple of hours.

Ko Tarutao National Marine Park

The unspoilt **Ko Tarutao National Marine Park** is probably the most beautiful of all Thailand's accessible beach destinations. The park covers 51 mostly uninhabited islands, of which three – Tarutao, Adang and Lipe – are easy to reach and offer accommodation. The park's forests and seas support a fascinating array of wildlife, including turtles, which lay their eggs on Ko Tarutao between September and April. Snorkelling gear can be rented at Pak Bara visitor centre or on Ko Adang for B50 per day, and is widely available from the private bungalow outfits or dive shops on Ko Lipe. The park amenities on Tarutao and Adang are closed to tourists from mid-May to mid-November, while the private concerns on Lipe claim to stay open year-round, though getting there at the height of the monsoon in September and early October is an unlikely – or at the very least unappealing – proposition.

In season, **ferries** currently leave **PAK BARA** at 10.30am and 3pm daily for the roughly ninety-minute voyage to Ao Pante on Ko Tarutao (B200 one way); the 10.30am boat then continues on to Ko Adang (B450 from Pak Bara), about two hours west of Ko Tarutao, from where it's a short longtail hop (B30) to any of the beaches on Ko Lipe. There's also a 1.30pm ferry via Ko Bulon Lae (see p.1092) to Ko Adang (about 3hr in total; B450). At busy times, there may be additional ferries and speedboats. Call the Pak Bara National Park Visitor Centre (☎074 783485 or 074 783597) for up-to-date information. From **Thammalang** pier near Satun town, the 11am boat calls in at Ao Taloh Wow on the east side of Ko Tarutao (1hr; B250 one way; car to Ao Pante B40 per person), before continuing to Ko Lipe (roughly 2hr; B500).

To **get to Pak Bara** from Trang, either take the direct high-season minibus run by Sukorn Beach Bungalows and Tours (see p.1089), or catch a Satun-bound bus (2hr 30min) or share taxi (1hr 30min) to Langu and change to a red songthaew for the ten-kilometre hop to the port. From Satun, frequent buses and taxis travel the 50km to Langu. From Hat Yai, catch a bus from the terminal or the clocktower all the way through to Pak Bara (6 daily; 2hr 30min), a direct air-con minibus from an office just up from the train station off Thanon Rattakan. If you miss the boat, you can **stay** in Pak Bara at the friendly *Bara Guesthouse* (☎09 654 2801; ❷), 500m before the pier.

Ko Tarutao

Hilly **Ko Tarutao**, the largest of the islands, is covered in rainforest and has perfect beaches all along its 26-kilometre west coast. Boats dock at **Ao Pante**, on the north-western side, where the admission fee (B200) is collected; here you'll find the park headquarters (☎074 729002–3) and a visitor centre, restaurants and a small shop. You can stay here in national park bungalows (❹), longhouses (❸), or tents (B100–200), or pitch your own tent (B20 per person per night). Behind the settlement, the steep, half-hour climb to To-Boo Cliff is a must, especially at sunset, for its fine views. Boat trips from the visitor centre (1hr; B40 per person) venture up a bird-filled, mangrove-lined canal to Crocodile Cave. A half-hour walk south from Ao Pante brings you to the quiet, white-sand bays of **Ao Jak** and **Ao Molae**, the latter with bungalows (❺) and a restaurant; beyond (2hr from Ao Pante; look out for the road behind the house at the south end of Ao Molae) lies **Ao Sone**, whose freshwater stream makes it a good spot for camping – you can rent a tent (B100) and eat at the simple restaurant. More adventurous campers can set out for **Ao Taloh Wow**, a rocky bay with a ranger station, restaurant and campsite on the east side of the island (12km by road from Ao Pante, B40 per person in a car), and on, along an overgrown

5hr trail, to **Ao Taloh Udang**, a sandy bay on the south side with the remains of a penal colony for political prisoners.

Ko Adang and Ko Lipe

At **Ko Adang**, a wild island covered in rainforest, the park station is at Laem Sone on the southern beach. There are rooms in bungalows (B400, sleeping four), longhouses (B300, sleeping three), tents (B100–200 for 2–4 people; pitch your own for B20 per person per night) and a restaurant here. About 2km west along the coast, there's a small beach lined with coconut palms, and behind an abandoned customs house a trail leads to the small Pirate Waterfall (20min). You can rent longtail boats through the rangers for excellent snorkelling trips to nearby islands (B1000 for 6–8 people).

Covered in coconut plantations and home to seven hundred *chao ley* or sea gypsies (a traditionally nomadic group scattered around the west coast of the Malay peninsula, who speak their own language and follow animistic beliefs), **Ko Lipe** is something of a frontier maverick, attracting ever more backpackers with one dazzling beach, a dozen private bungalow resorts and a rough-and-ready atmosphere. In addition, it supports two reliable **dive shops**, which both offer day-trips and PADI courses: Sabye Sports at *Porn Resort* (Ⓣ074 728026, Ⓦwww.sabye-sports.com); and the slightly cheaper Starfish Scuba at *Lee Pae Resort* on Hat Pattaya (Ⓣ074 728089 or 01 896 9319; Ⓦwww.starfishscuba.com), who also have a yacht for liveaboards.

Hat Pattaya is a beautiful crescent of squeaky-soft white sand on the south side of the island, with a good offshore reef to explore. At its far west end, *Pattaya Song* (Ⓣ074 728034, Ⓦwww.pattayasongresort.com; ❷–❸) is a good bungalow choice in a lovely location; fishing and snorkelling trips can be arranged, and sea-kayaks rented. On the path that connects the eastern end of Hat Pattaya to the island village is *Pooh's*, a popular bar-restaurant-travel agent, providing Internet access. On the northwest side of the island, Sunset Beach is not as postcard-perfect as Hat Pattaya, but *Porn* here is a very attractive, well-kept resort (❷).

Ko Bulon Lae

Tiny **Ko Bulon Lae** is actually just outside Ko Tarutao National Park, but is also reached from Pak Bara, 20km to the east. In high season, ferries leave Pak Bara daily at about 1.30pm and 3pm (1hr–1hr 30min; B200 one way, B300 return); the former continues to Ko Adang (2hr; B300 one way). Services are reduced, sometimes to nothing, during the monsoon season; contact *Pansand Resort* or their agent in Trang, First Andaman Travel, 82–84 Thanon Wisetkul (Ⓣ075 218035), for the latest information. A two-kilometre strip of fine white sand runs the length of Ko Bulon Lae's east coast and there are good reefs off the east and south shores. Snorkelling gear and boats can be rented at *Pansand*, the island's largest and best resort (Ⓣ01 397 0802, Ⓔpansand@cscoms.com; ❻–❼). The best of several budget resorts is friendly *Bulone* (Ⓣ01 897 9084; ❶–❹), with a good restaurant at the north end of the main beach.

Satun and boats to Malaysia

Remote **SATUN** nestles in the last wedge of Thailand's west coast and is chiefly of interest for its **boat services to Malaysia** and **Ko Tarutao**. However, if you find yourself with time on your hands, it's worth seeking out the **National Museum** (Wed–Sun 9am–4pm; free), in a graceful colonial-style mansion on Soi 5, Thanon Satun Thani, on the north side of the centre. The bus terminal is at the north end of town on Thanon Satun Thani, but many buses also make a detour through the town centre; share taxis and air-con minibuses are based in the centre around the junction of Thanon Saman Pradit (the main east–west thoroughfare) and Thanon Buriwanit, which runs parallel to Thanon Satun Thani. There's Internet access at Andaman Trips and Services, 148 Thanon Satun Thani (☎074 725148, ©andamantrips@hotmail.com), where friendly fixer Bon can organize motorbike and minivan rental, sea-kayaking trips, cooking classes and ferry tickets. *Rian Thong* (☎074 711036; ❶), by the town pier at 4 Thanon Saman Pradit, is the best budget **hotel**.

From Thammalang pier, 10km south of Satun, longtail **boats** run to Kuala Perlis (30min; B100 per person) on the northwest tip of **Malaysia**, from where there are plentiful transport connections down the west coast. Six ferry boats a day cross to the Malaysian island of Langkawi from Thammalang (see p.1091; 50min; B220); you can get information in town from Satun Travel and Ferry Service, opposite the *Pinnacle Wangmai Hotel* at 45/16 Thanon Satun Thani (☎074 711453), or from Thai Ferry Centre at the pier (☎074 730511–2), who both also handle ferries from Thammalang to Tarutao and Lipe (see p.1091). Frequent songthaews and motorbike taxis run to Thammalang from near the junction of Thanon Saman Pradit and Thanon Buriwanit, taking around fifteen minutes.

Hat Yai and transport to Malaysia

HAT YAI, the transport axis of the region, is a concrete mess, but attracts a million tourists a year, nearly all of them Malaysians who nip across the border – just 50km away – to shop and get laid. The **TAT office** is at 1/1 Soi 2, Thanon Niphat Uthit 3 (☎074 243747) and the **tourist police** are based at Thanon Sripoovanart on the south side of town (☎074 246733 or 1155). Arriving at the **airport**, 12km west

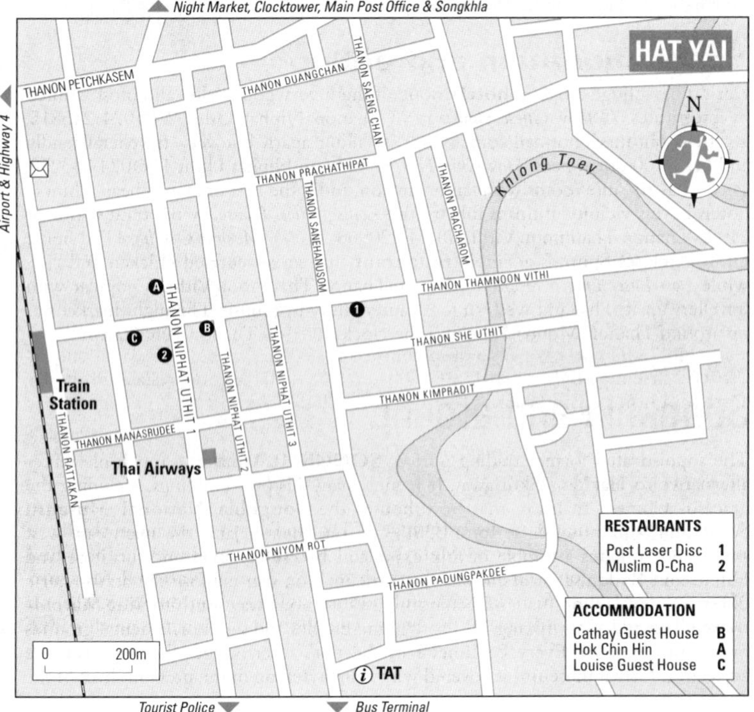

of town, you'll be shuttled into the centre by shared minibus (B60) or taxi (B240); there are regular minibuses back to the airport from the **Thai Airways office** at 180 Thanon Niphat Uthit 1 (☎074 230445–6). The **train station**, on the west side of the centre at the end of Thanon Thamnoon Vithi, has a useful left-luggage office (daily 5.30am–6pm; from B10 per piece per day); the **bus terminal** is to the far southeast of town on Thanon Kanchanawanit, but most buses make a stop at the clocktower (the old Plaza Cinema) on Thanon Petchkasem, on the north side of the centre. **Share-taxis** and **air-con minibuses** should drop you off at your destination. For departure, they have dozens of different ranks around town according to where you want to go, but these stands tend to move frequently for bureaucratic reasons, and the local authorities are trying to group them all together near the bus terminal – ask at your accommodation or TAT for the latest information. You'll certainly find vehicles to Songkhla, and perhaps other destinations, outside the train station. The helpful Cathay Tour, at the guesthouse of the same name, can **book** flight and bus tickets, and also handles air-con minibuses to many destinations. For **car rental**, Avis has a desk at the airport (☎074 250321).

Into Malaysia

Share taxis depart Hat Yai every morning for Penang, **Malaysia** (4–5hr; B250). Air-con **minibuses** charge slightly less to do the same run, as well as serving Sungai Kolok (3hr) and Butterworth (4hr); **VIP buses** head off to Kuala Lumpur (12hr) and Singapore (18hr). Seven **trains** make the daily run to Sungai Kolok (see p.1096), and one a day heads via the frontier at Padang Besar to Butterworth (for the ferry to Penang or trains on to Kuala Lumpur). The least expensive but most time-consuming method is to catch a **bus** straight down Highway 4 to Dan Nok (1hr 30min), walk 500m across the frontier to Bukit Kayu Hitam, and take a bus down Malaysia's North–South Highway to Alor Setar (about 1hr) and beyond.

Accommodation and eating

Hat Yai has a huge range of **hotels**, none of them very good value and most worked by prostitutes. *Cathay Guest House* at 93 Thanon Niphat Uthit 2 (☎074 243815, Ⓔcathay_ontours@hotmail.com; ❶–❷) is falling apart, but very traveller-friendly and has B100 dorm beds. *Hok Chin Hin*, 87 Thanon Niphat Uthit 1 (☎074 243258; ❶–❷), has en-suite rooms with fan or air-con, and is the best of many cheap Chinese hotels in this vicinity; if this is full, try the *Louise Guest House*, by the train station at 21–23 Thanon Thamnoon Vithi (☎074 220966; ❷–❸). *Muslim O-Cha*, 117 Niphat Uthit 1 (closes 8pm), is a simple **restaurant** that serves curried chicken and rice, while *Post Laser Disc*, a restaurant-bar on Thanon Thamnoon Vithi, is popular with travellers for its Thai and Western food, and nightly live music. The night market sets up around Thanon Montri 2, behind the clocktower on Thanon Petchkasem.

Songkhla and around

The sophisticated former trading port of **SONGKHLA** makes a much pleasanter alternative to Hat Yai, 25km away. It retains many historic buildings, including the graceful Chinese mansion that now houses the **Songkhla National Museum** (Wed–Sun 9am–noon & 1–4pm; B30) – it's on Thanon Jana, the main east–west street, and contains a jumble of folk exhibits, Chinese ceramics and furniture, and Hindu and Buddhist statues. From the museum, you can explore the atmospheric old streets of Nakhon Nai and Nakhon Nawk on your way south to **Wat Matchimawat**, a grand affair mixing Thai and Chinese styles and set in ornamental grounds on Thanon Saiburi. Every centimetre of the bot's interior (get the key from the adjacent informal museum) is covered with murals, telling of the previous lives of the

Buddha, mixed in with vivacious tableaux of nineteenth-century Songkhla life. Sitting on the fringe of town at the southern end of **Hat Samila** – the 8km of beach along the eastern shore – **Khao Saen** is an impoverished but vibrant fishing village, whose multicoloured boats provide Songkhla's most hackneyed postcard image.

Buses from Hat Yai and other main towns arrive at the major junction of Thanon Ramwithi with thanons Jana and Platha. Share taxis congregate on the south side of the main bus stop, just off Thanon Ramwithi. *Abritus* is a welcoming **guesthouse** at 28/16 Thanon Ramwithi (☎074/326047, ⓔabritus_th@yahoo.com; ❷), with large, clean rooms, and great breakfasts and other Western food; you can access the Internet and rent mountain bikes and motorbikes here. Also excellent value is the clean and homely *Amsterdam Guest House*, at 15/3 Thanon Rong Muang on the north side of the museum (☎074/314890; ❷). Songkhla's most famous **restaurant**, *Raan Tae*, at 85 Thanon Nang Ngarm, is justly popular, serving especially good seafood – but it closes between 2 and 5pm and after 8pm. The night market sets up south of the post office on Thanon Nakhon Nai. A sprinkling of Westernized bar-restaurants such as *Auntie* at 62/1 Thanon Sisuda cater to workers from the offshore oil rigs.

Ko Yo

Ko Yo, the small island in the Thale Sap to the west of Songkhla, has long been a destination for day-trippers, and the road link with the land on both sides of the lagoon has accelerated the transformation of **Ban Nok** – the island's main settlement – into a souvenir market, especially for high-quality, locally woven fabrics. *Pa Nu*, a food stall just off the main road in the centre of the village, is justly famous for its delicious southern Thai speciality, *khao yam*, a salad-like dish of marinated rice, coconut, shrimp paste and vegetables. The chief appeal of Ko Yo is the **Thaksin Folklore Museum** (daily 8.30am–5pm; B60), which sprawls over a hillside on the northern tip of Ko Yo, with stunning panoramas, especially from its viewing tower and café. The park is strewn with all kinds of boats and wooden reproductions of traditional southern houses, in which the collections are neatly set out. The exhibits inside, such as the shadow-puppet paraphernalia and the kris – long knives with intricately carved handles and sheaths – show the strong influences of Malaysia and Indonesia on southern Thailand. Also on show are elaborate dance costumes and carved wooden coconut-scrapers. To **get to Ko Yo** from Songkhla, take one of the frequent songthaews from Thanon Jana (30min). From Hat Yai, take a Songkhla-bound bus or minibus, but get off at the junction with Highway 408, and catch a songthaew across the bridge to Ko Yo.

Into Malaysia from Narathiwat and Sungai Kolok

NARATHIWAT (often shortened to Nara) is the most attractively sited of the Muslim towns in southern Thailand, and offers the opportunity of a good day at the beach, at gently curving **Ao Manao**, 6km south of town and dotted with seafood restaurants. Nara also boasts an outstanding **place to stay**, *Baan Burong Riverside Guest House* at 399 Thanon Puphapugdee (☎073 511027, ⓔnatini@chaiyo.com; ❷–❸). In a centrally located old Sino-Portugese house overlooking the river, the welcoming guesthouse has attractive rooms sharing hot-water bathrooms; guests have free use of bicycles and kayaks, and motorbike rental and car hire with driver can be arranged, as well as activities such as batik-making and goat-milking. Nara's **TAT** office is 2km south of town on the Tak Bai road (☎073 516144). Note that trains on the Bangkok–Sungai Kolok line stop at Tangyongmat, a half-hour songthaew ride from the centre.

At the riverside frontier post of **BAN TABA**, southeast of Narathiwat, boats (B7) shuttle across to the Malaysian town of Pengkalan Kubor, which has frequent buses to Kota Bharu, 20km southeast (see p.677). There are frequent buses and songthaews from Nara to Ban Taba (1hr 30min).

The seedy brothel town of **SUNGAI KOLOK** is at the end of the rail line from Bangkok, and right on the Malay border. The **train station** is in the northern part of town, and from here you can walk 800m or take a motorbike taxi to the border. Hat Yai and Narathiwat air-con minibuses are based opposite the station, and most buses stop there, too. From Rantau Panjang on the other side of the border, frequent taxis and buses head for Kota Bharu, 30km northeast (see p.677).

Thailand travel details

Buses

Ayutthaya to: Chiang Mai (12 daily; 8hr); Lopburi (every 20min; 2hr); Phitsanulok (9daily; 5hr).

Bangkok (Eastern Bus Terminal) to: Ban Phe (12 daily; 3hr); Pattaya (every 30min; 2hr–3hr 30min); Rayong (every 15min; 2hr 30min); Trat (at least hourly; 5–6hr).

Bangkok (Northern Bus Terminal) to: Aranyaprathet (10 daily; 4hr 30min); Ayutthaya (every 15min; 2hr); Ban Phe (12 daily; 3hr); Chiang Khong (10 daily; 13–14hr); Chiang Mai (19 daily; 10–11hr); Chiang Rai (16 daily; 12hr); Chong Mek (2 daily; 12hr); Khon Kaen (23 daily; 6–7hr); Khorat (every 20min; 4–5hr); Lampang (10 daily; 8hr); Loei (18 daily; 10hr); Lopburi (every 20min; 3hr); Mae Hong Son (2 daily; 18hr); Mae Sai (8 daily; 13hr); Mae Sot (10 daily; 8hr 30min); Mukdahan (13 daily; 11hr); Nakhon Phanom (17 daily; 12hr); Nan (13 daily; 13hr); Nong Khai (17 daily; 10hr); Pak Chong (every 15min; 3hr); Pattaya (every 30min; 2–3hr); Phitsanulok (up to 19 daily; 5–6hr); Sukhothai (17 daily; 6–7hr); Surin (up to 20 daily; 8–9hr); Trat (5 daily; 4–5hr); Ubon Ratchathani (19 daily; 10–12hr); Udon Thani (every 15min; 9hr).

Bangkok (Southern Bus Terminal) to: Chumphon (12 daily; 6hr 30min–9hr); Damnoen Saduak (every 20min; 2hr); Hat Yai (21 daily; 12–15hr); Hua Hin (every 40min; 3hr 30min); Kanchanaburi (every 15min; 2–3hr); Ko Samui (5 daily; 15hr); Krabi (9 daily; 12–14hr); Nakhon Pathom (every 10min; 40min–1hr 20min); Nakhon Si Thammarat (11 daily; 12hr); Narathiwat (4 daily; 17–19hr); Phang Nga (4 daily; 11hr–12hr 30min); Phetchaburi (every 30min; 2hr); Phuket (at least 10 daily; 14–16hr); Ranong (7 daily; 9–10hr); Satun (2 daily; 16hr); Sungai Kolok (3 daily; 18–20hr); Surat Thani (7 daily; 10–11hr); Trang (8 daily; 12–14hr).

Chiang Mai to: Bangkok (19 daily; 10–11hr); Chiang Khong (3 daily; 6hr); Chiang Rai (every 30min; 3–6hr); Chiang Saen (2 daily; 5hr); Chom Thong (every 30min; 1hr); Khon Kaen (10 daily; 12hr); Lampang (every 20min; 2hr); Mae Hong Son (10 daily; 8hr); Mae Sariang (6 daily; 4–5hr); Mae Sai (12 daily; 5hr); Mae Sot (2 daily; 6–7hr); Nan (11 daily; 7hr); Pai (4 daily; 4hr); Phitsanulok (5 daily; 5–6hr); Rayong (7 daily; 15hr); Sukhothai (11 daily; 5hr); Tha Ton (6 daily; 4hr); Ubon Ratchathani (6 daily; 17hr); Udon Thani (5 daily; 12hr).

Chiang Rai to: Chiang Khong (hourly; 2–3hr); Chiang Mai (every 30min; 3–6hr); Chiang Saen (every 15min; 1hr 30min); Lampang (every 20min; 5hr); Mae Sai (every 15min; 1hr 30min); Nan (daily; 6–7hr); Phitsanulok (4 daily; 7hr).

Damnoen Saduak to: Nakhon Pathom (every 20min; 1hr).

Hat Yai to: Chumphon (6 daily; 9hr); Ko Samui (daily; 7hr); Krabi (14 daily; 4–5hr); Nakhon Si Thammarat (every 30min; 3–4hr); Narathiwat (3 daily; 3–4hr); Padang Besar (every 10min; 1hr 40min); Pak Bara (6 daily; 2hr 30min); Phuket (13 daily; 7–9hr); Satun (every 15min; 1hr 30min); Songkhla (every 10min; 30min); Sungai Kolok (daily; 4hr); Surat Thani (10 daily; 5hr–6hr 30min); Trang (every 30min; 3–4hr).

Hua Hin to: Chumphon (daily every 40min; 3hr 30min–4hr 30min).

Kanchanaburi to: Nakhon Pathom (every 10min; 1hr 20min); Sangkhlaburi (11 daily; 3–6hr); Suphanburi (every 20min; 2hr).

Khao Lak to: Khao Sok (every 90min; 1hr 30min); Phuket (11 daily; 2hr 30min); Ranong (8 daily; 2hr 30min–3hr); Surat Thani (every 90min; 3hr 30min); Takua Pa (every 40min; 30min).

Khon Kaen to: Bangkok (23 daily; 6–7hr); Chiang

Rai (5 daily; 12hr); Khorat (hourly; 2hr 30min–3hr); Loei (every 30min; 4hr); Nakhon Phanom (12 daily; 5hr); Nong Khai (10 daily; 2–3hr); Phitsanulok (6 daily; 5–6hr); Sri Chiangmai (6 daily; 3hr); Surin (hourly; 4hr 30min–6hr); Ubon Ratchathani (15 daily; 6hr); Udon Thani (every 30min; 2hr).

Khorat to: Chiang Mai (7 daily; 12–14hr); Chiang Rai (5 daily; 14–16hr); Lopburi (11 daily; 3hr 30min); Nong Khai (7 daily; 6–8hr); Pak Chong (for Khao Yai) (every 20min; 1hr 30min); Pattaya (7 daily; 6–8hr); Phitsanulok (7 daily; 7–9hr); Rayong (18 daily; 4hr); Sri Chiangmai (6 daily; 6hr 30min); Surin (every 30min; 4–5hr); Ubon Ratchathani (7 daily; 5–7hr); Udon Thani (every 45min; 3hr 30min–5hr).

Krabi to: Hat Yai (14 daily; 4–5hr); Phang Nga (hourly; 1hr 30min–2hr); Phuket (every 30min; 3–5hr); Ranong (5 daily; 6–7hr); Surat Thani (hourly; 4hr); Takua Pa (5 daily; 3hr 30min–4hr 30min); Trang (at least hourly; 2–3hr).

Mae Sot to: Chiang Rai (2 daily; 11hr); Mae Sai (2 daily; 12hr); Mae Sariang (hourly 6am–midday; 5hr); Phitsanulok (7 daily; 3hr 15min–5hr); Sukhothai (6 daily; 3hr); Tak (every 30min; 1hr 30min–3hr); Umphang (hourly 7.30am–3.30pm; 4hr).

Mukdahan to: Nakhon Phanom (hourly; 2hr); That Phanom (every 30min; 1hr 20min); Ubon Ratchathani (every 30min; 2–3hr).

Nakhon Phanom to: Bung Kan (6 daily; 4hr); That Phanom (hourly; 1hr); Ubon Ratchathani (7 daily; 4hr); Udon Thani (9 daily; 6hr).

Nong Khai to: Bung Kan (14 daily; 2hr); Loei (hourly via Pak Chom; 6–7hr); Nakhon Phanom (5 daily; 6hr).

Phetchaburi to: Chumphon (every 2hr; 5–6hr).

Phitsanulok to: Ayutthaya (9 daily; 5hr); Chiang Rai (17 daily; 6–7hr); Loei (5 daily; 4hr); Sukhothai (every 30min; 1hr); Ubon Ratchathani (7 daily; 12hr); Udon Thani (5 daily; 7hr).

Phuket to: Hat Yai (16 daily; 6–8hr); Khao Lak (11 daily; 2hr 30min); Khao Sok (at least 2 daily; 3–4hr); Krabi (22 daily; 3–5hr); Phang Nga (30 daily; 1hr 30min–2hr 30min); Ranong (8 daily; 5–6hr); Surat Thani (20 daily; 4hr 30min–6hr); Takua Pa (17 daily; 3hr); Trang (22 daily; 5–6hr).

Ranong to: Chumphon (every 90min; 2hr); Krabi (3 daily; 4hr).

Rayong to: Bangkok's Eastern Terminal (every 15min; 2 hr 30min); Ban Phe (for Ko Samet; every 30min; 30 min); Chanthaburi (8 daily; 2hr); Trat (6 daily; 3hr 30min); Ubon Ratchathani (9 daily; 9hr).

Sukhothai to: Ayutthaya (6 daily; 6hr); Chiang Rai (4 daily; 8–9hr); Khon Kaen (7 daily; 6–7hr); Tak (every 90min; 2hr).

Surat Thani to: Chaiya (hourly; 1hr); Chumphon (every 30min; 3hr); Hat Yai (11 daily; 4–5hr); Nakhon Si Thammarat (13 daily; 3hr); Phuket (20 daily; 4hr 30min–6hr); Ranong (7 daily; 4hr); Trang (2 daily; 3hr).

Trang to: Krabi (hourly; 2–3hr); Nakhon Si Thammarat (3 daily; 2–3hr); Satun (every 30min; 3hr).

Trat to: Ban Phe (6 daily; 3hr); Hat Lek (every 45min; 1hr–1hr 30min); Chanthaburi (hourly; 1hr 30min); Pattaya (6 daily; 4hr 30min).

Ubon Ratchathani to: Pattaya (7 daily; 10 hr); Surin (12 daily; 2hr 30min); That Phanom (9 daily; 4hr).

Udon Thani to: Khon Kaen (every 30min; 2hr); Loei (every 20min; 3hr); Mukdahan (5 daily; 4hr); Nong Khai (every 20min; 1hr); That Phanom (4 daily; 4hr); Ubon Ratchathani (7 daily; 5–7hr).

Trains

Ayutthaya to: Bangkok Hualamphong (20 daily; 1hr 30min); Chiang Mai (6 daily; 12hr); Lopburi (15 daily; 1hr 30min); Nong Khai (3 daily; 9hr 30min); Ubon Ratchathani (7 daily; 8hr 30min–10hr).

Bangkok (Hualamphong Station) to: Aranyaprathet (2 daily; 5hr 30min); Ayutthaya (20 daily; 1hr 30min); Butterworth, Malaysia (daily; 23hr); Chiang Mai (7 daily; 12–14hr); Chumphon (12 daily; 7hr–9hr 30min); Don Muang Airport (30 daily; 50min); Hat Yai (5 daily; 14–16hr); Hua Hin (9 daily; 3hr 35min–4hr 35min); Khon Kaen (5 daily; 7hr 30min–10hr 20min); Khorat (9 daily; 4–5hr); Lampang (7 daily; 11hr); Lopburi (15 daily; 2hr 30min–3hr); Nakhon Pathom (10 daily; 1hr 20min); Nakhon Si Thammarat (2 daily; 15hr); Nong Khai (4 daily; 11–12hr); Pak Chong (11 daily; 3hr 30min–4hr 45min); Phetchaburi (8 daily; 2hr 45min–3hr 45min); Phitsanulok (10 daily; 5hr 40min–8hr); Sungai Kolok (2 daily; 20hr); Surat Thani (11 daily; 9hr–11hr 30min); Surin (10 daily; 7–10hr); Trang (2 daily; 16hr); Ubon Ratchathani (7 daily; 8hr 30min–14hr); Udon Thani (5 daily; 9hr–12hr 30min).

Bangkok (Thonburi Station) to: Hua Hin (2 daily; 4hr 30min); Kanchanaburi (2 daily; 3hr); Nakhon Pathom (3 daily; 1hr 10min); Nam Tok (2 daily; 5hr).

Chiang Mai to: Ayutthaya (6 daily; 12hr); Bangkok (7 daily; 12–14hr); Lampang (7 daily; 2hr); Lopburi (6 daily; 11hr); Phitsanulok (6 daily; 5hr 50min–7hr 40min).

Hat Yai to: Butterworth, Malaysia (daily; 5hr 30min); Padang Besar (daily; 1hr); Sungai Kolok (7 daily; 3hr 30min–5hr); Surat Thani (7 daily; 4hr–6hr 30min).

Khorat (Nakhon Ratchasima) to: Ayutthaya (7 daily; 3hr 30min); Khon Kaen (daily; 2hr 30min); Pak Chong (11 daily; 1hr 30min–2hr); Surin (7 daily; 2hr 30min–3hr 40min); Ubon Ratchathani (7 daily; 5hr–6hr 40min); Udon Thani (daily; 4hr 45min).

Nong Khai to: Bangkok (4 daily; 11–12hr), via Udon Thani (1hr), Khon Kaen (3hr) and Ayutthaya (10hr).

Surat Thani (Phunphin) to: Butterworth, Malaysia (daily; 11hr); Hat Yai (5 daily; 4–5hr); Nakhon Si Thammarat (2 daily; 3hr 30min); Sungai Kolok (2 daily; 9hr); Trang (2 daily; 4hr).

Boats

Ban Phe to: Ko Samet (4–18 daily; 30min).

Chumphon to: Ko Tao (5 daily; 1hr 30min–6hr).

Don Sak to: Ko Samui (at least hourly; 45min–1hr 30min); Ko Pha Ngan (6 daily; 1hr 30min–2hr 30min).

Ko Pha Ngan to: Ko Samui (at least 9 daily; 30min–1hr); Ko Tao (at least 6 daily; 50min–3hr).

Ko Phi Phi to: Ao Nang and Laem Phra Nang (Nov–May daily; 2hr); Ko Lanta Yai (Nov–May 2 daily; 1hr 30min); Krabi (2–5 daily; 1hr 30min–2hr); Phuket (2–3 daily; 1hr 30min–2hr 30min).

Ko Lanta Yai to: Ao Nang (Nov–May daily; 2hr 30min); Ko Phi Phi Don (Nov–May 2 daily; 1hr 30min); Krabi (mid-Oct to mid-May 2 daily; 2hr 30min); Phuket (Nov–May daily; 4hr 30min).

Ko Samui to: Ko Tao (at least 5 daily; 1hr 30min–3hr 30min).

Krabi to: Ko Lanta Yai (mid-Oct to mid-May 2 daily; 2hr 30min); Ko Phi Phi Don (2–5 daily; 1hr 30min–2hr).

Laem Ngop to: Ko Chang (hourly; 25min–1hr); Ko Mak (Nov–April daily; 3hr 30min); Ko Whai (Nov–April daily; 2hr 30min).

Surat Thani to: Ko Pha Ngan (2 daily; 4–7hr); Ko Samui (2 daily; 2hr 30min–7hr); Ko Tao (daily; 9hr).

Flights

Bangkok to: Chiang Mai (14–17 daily; 1hr); Chiang Rai (5 daily; 1hr 20min); Hat Yai (7 daily; 1hr 25min); Khon Kaen (5 daily; 55min); Khorat (2 daily; 50min); Ko Samui (15 daily; 1hr 20min); Krabi (4 daily; 1hr 20min); Lampang (1–2 daily; 1hr); Loei (4 weekly; 1hr 20min); Mae Sot (8 weekly; 1hr 25min–2hr 25min); Nakhon Phanom (daily; 1hr 5min); Nakhon Si Thammarat (2–3 daily; 1hr 15min); Nan (daily; 1hr 40min); Narathiwat (1–2 daily; 2hr); Phitsanulok (3 daily; 45min); Phuket (20 daily; 1hr 25min); Ranong (daily; 1hr 20min); Sukhothai (daily; 1hr 10min); Surat Thani (2 daily; 1hr 10min); Trang (1–2 daily; 1hr 30min); Trat (2 daily; 50min); Ubon Ratchathani (2 daily; 1hr 5min); Udon Thani (3 daily; 1hr).

Chiang Mai to: Bangkok (14–17 daily; 1hr); Jinghong, China (3 weekly; 2hr 30min); Kunming, China (2 weekly; 2hr 30min); Louang Phabang, Laos (6 weekly; 1hr); Mae Hong Son (5 daily; 35min); Mandalay, Burma (1 weekly; 50min); Phuket (daily; 2hr); Rangoon, Burma (3–5 weekly; 40min); Sukhothai (daily; 40min); Vientiane, Laos (3 weekly; 2hr 10min); Xi'an, China (3 weekly; 4hr).

Hat Yai to: Phuket (daily; 45min); Singapore (daily; 1hr 35min).

Ko Samui to: Krabi (daily; 50min); Phuket (2 daily; 50 min); Singapore (daily; 1hr 40min); U-Tapao (Pattaya; daily; 1hr).

Phuket to: Chiang Mai (daily; 1hr 55min); Hat Yai (daily; 45min); Ko Samui (2 daily; 50min); U-Tapao, Pattaya (daily; 2hr 20min).

11

Vietnam

CHINA
BURMA (MYANMAR)
LAOS
THAILAND
CAMBODIA
South China Sea
N
0
400km
1
2
3
4
5
6
7
8

Vietnam highlights

* **Cu Chi tunnels** Crawl through the original underground tunnel system, home to the Vietcong during the Vietnam War. See p.1141
* **Mekong Delta** A network of slender, shaded canals harbouring secluded floating markets, fruit orchards and coconut plantations. See p.1143
* **Hoi An** Have a new silk wardrobe run up at dirt-cheap prices in this charming ancient port town. See p.1182
* **Cham Towers, My Son** These awesome brick sanctuaries are relics of Vietnam's ancient kingdom of Champa. See p.1183
* **Royal City of Hue** The hillside mausoleums of former emperors can be reached by slow boat along Hue's Perfume River. See p.1187
* **Old Quarter, Hanoi** Spend hours wandering through the narrow, fascinating streets of Hanoi's ancient merchant quarter. See p.1204
* **Ha Long Bay** Sail through this spectacular World Heritage Site – crammed with grottoes, islands and jagged limestone outcrops jutting out of the sea. See p.1217
* **Sa Pa** The perfect mountain base for trekking through the paddy-fields and villages of the Dao and Hmong minority peoples. See p.1233

△ Ha Long Bay

Introduction and basics

History weighs heavily on Vietnam. For more than a decade, reportage of the infamous war that racked the country portrayed it as a savage netherworld, yet, nearly thirty years after the war's end, this incredibly resilient nation is beginning to emerge from the shadows.

As the number of tourists finding their way here soars, the word is out that this is a land not of bomb craters and army ordnance, but of shimmering paddy-fields and sugar-white beaches, full-tilt cities and venerable pagodas. The speed with which Vietnam's population of 79 million has been able to transcend the recent past comes as a surprise to visitors who are generally met with warmth and curiosity rather than shell-shocked resentment and war fatigue.

Inevitably, that's not the whole story. The adoption of a **market economy** has polarized the gap between rich and poor: average monthly incomes remain at about $50 for city dwellers, but drop to $15 in the poorest provinces.

For the majority of visitors, the furiously commercial southern city of **Ho Chi Minh City** (HCMC) provides a head-spinning introduction to Vietnam, so a trip out into the rice fields and orchards of the nearby **Mekong Delta** makes a welcome next stop – best explored by boat from **My Tho**, **Vinh Long** or **Can Tho**. Heading north, the quaint hill-station of **Da Lat** provides a good place to cool down, but some travellers eschew this for the **beaches** of **Vung Tau** and **Mui Ne**. A few hours' ride further up the coast, the city of **Nha Trang** has become a crucial stepping stone on the HCMC–Hanoi run. Next up comes the enticing little town of **Hoi An**, full of wooden shop-houses and close to Vietnam's greatest Cham temple ruins at **My Son**. The temples, palaces and imperial mausoleums of aristocratic **Hue** should also not be missed. One hundred kilometres north, war sites litter the **Demilitarized Zone** (**DMZ**), which cleaved the country in two from 1954 to 1975.

Hanoi has served as Vietnam's capital for close on a thousand years and is a rapidly developing, but absorbing, city of pagodas and dynastic temples, where life proceeds – for now – at a relatively gentler pace than in Ho Chi Minh. From here, most visitors strike out east to the labyrinth of limestone outcrops in **Ha Long Bay**, usually visited either from the resort town of **Bai Chay** or, more interestingly, from tiny **Cat Ba Island**. The market town of **Sa Pa**, set in spectacular uplands close to the Chinese border in the far northwest, makes a good base for exploring nearby ethnic minority villages.

Vietnam has a tropical monsoon **climate**, dominated by the south or southwesterly monsoon from May to September and the northeast monsoon from October to April. Overall, late September to December and March and April are the **best times** if you're covering the whole country, but there are distinct regional variations. In **southern Vietnam and the central highlands** the dry season lasts from December through April, and daytime temperatures rarely drop below 20°C in the lowlands, averaging 30°C during March, April and May. Along the **central coast** the wet season runs from September through February, though even the dry season brings a fair quantity of rain; temperatures average 30°C from June to August. Typhoons can hit the coast around Hue in April and May and the northern coast from July to November, when flooding is a regular occurrence. **Hanoi and northern Vietnam** are generally hot (30°C) and very wet during the summer, warm and sunny from October to December, then cold and misty until March.

Overland routes into Vietnam

It's possible to cross **overland** from Cambodia, Laos and China into Vietnam.

From Cambodia

You can go by bus from Phnom Penh to **HCMC**, via the Moc Bai border crossing.

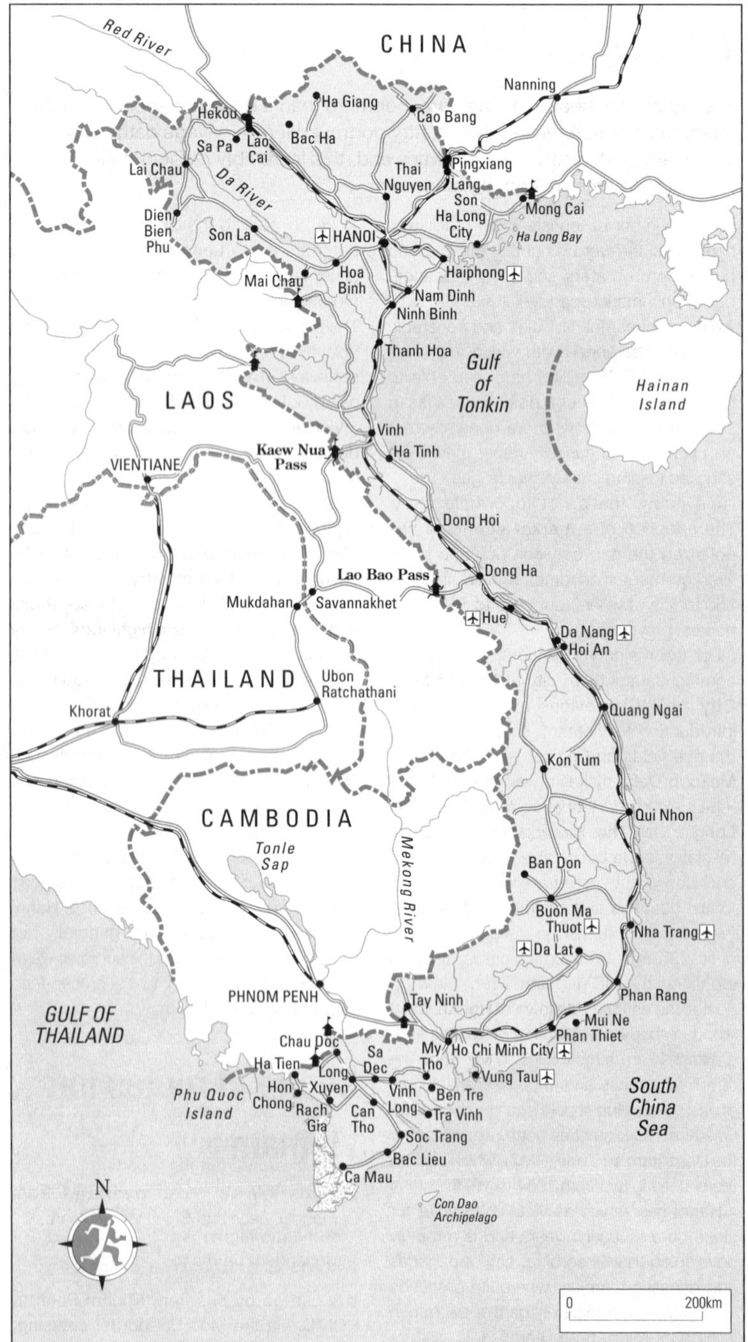
CHINA
Red River
Nanning
Ha Giang
Cao Bang
Hekou
Bac Ha
Sa Pa
Lao Cai
Pingxiang
Lai Chau
Da River
Thai Nguyen
Lang Son
Mong Cai
Dien Bien Phu
Ha Long City
Son La
HANOI
Ha Long Bay
Haiphong
Mai Chau
Hoa Binh
Nam Dinh
Ninh Binh
Thanh Hoa
Gulf of Tonkin
Hainan Island
LAOS
Vinh
Kaew Nua Pass
Ha Tinh
VIENTIANE
Dong Hoi
Lao Bao Pass
Dong Ha
Mukdahan
Savannakhet
Hue
Da Nang
Hoi An
THAILAND
Ubon Ratchathani
Quang Ngai
Khorat
Kon Tum
Qui Nhon
CAMBODIA
Tonle Sap
Mekong River
Ban Don
Buon Ma Thuot
Nha Trang
Da Lat
Phan Rang
PHNOM PENH
Tay Ninh
GULF OF THAILAND
Mui Ne
Phan Thiet
Chau Doc
Sa Dec
My Tho
Ho Chi Minh City
Ha Tien
Long Xuyen
Vung Tau
Hon Chong
Vinh Long
Ben Tre
South China Sea
Phu Quoc Island
Rach Gia
Can Tho
Tra Vinh
Soc Trang
Bac Lieu
Ca Mau
Con Dao Archipelago
N
0
200km

Alternatively, take a local bus from Phnom Penh to the border, then continue by share taxi to HCMC; see p.127 for details. A second, more difficult, border crossing at Vinh Xuong, near Chau Doc in the Mekong Delta, has recently opened up to foreigners; some tour operators run boats from Phnom Penh down the Mekong River through to **Chau Doc** in Vietnam (see p.1153 for details). There is also a third border checkpoint at Tinh Bien, near Chau Doc. See box on p.1153 for details of all three border crossings.

From Laos

There are four border points between **Laos** and Vietnam where tourists can cross overland. The **Lao Bao Pass** (see p.1196), roughly 240km from Savannakhet, is the most popular and gives you access to Dong Ha, 80km away. There's also an international bus link between Savannakhet and Da Nang (which can take up to 24hr), although it's cheaper to travel by local buses. There are border points at **Nong Het** (east of Phonsavan), and at **Nameo** (east of Xam Nua), while the crossing from Lak Xao to the Vietnamese town of Vinh, via the Kaew Nua Pass (usually referred to as Nam Phao in Lao) and **Cau Treo**, can be more difficult; see p.1196.

It's worth noting that there have been several complaints from travellers using buses coming from Laos to the Vietnam border. Due care should be taken with operators; try and ask fellow travellers about the more reliable ones.

From China

At the time of writing, the Chinese border was open to foreigners at three points: at Lao Cai (from Kunming on the Chinese side; see p.1222), Mong Cai (from Guangzhou; see p.1221) and, busiest of all, at Huu Nghi (from Pinxiang; see p.1228). There is one **direct train service** between China and Vietnam: from Beijing to Hanoi. The Kunming–Hanoi service was suspended in 2004; you can take the bus to Lao Cai, and then take the train from there to Hanoi. See p.1200 for more details.

Entry requirements and visa extension

All foreign nationals need a visa to enter Vietnam. **Tourist visas** are generally valid for thirty days and cost $80. **Three-month visas** are also available for $130; both types take seven to ten days to process. See p.45 for a list of Vietnamese embassies abroad. In Southeast Asia, Bangkok is the most popular place to apply for a Vietnamese visa (4 to 5 working days).

On arrival, you'll need to hand over a completed **Arrival and Departure Card**. Note that if you're arriving with more than $3000, you'll need to declare it on this form. Customs keep the top white copy and you keep the yellow copy; you'll need to hand this yellow form in when you leave the country, and it is also used, along with your passport, for registering at hotels.

There are now a few authorized agents in Vietnam – including Ann Tours and Exotissimo Travel in HCMC (see p.1141) – who can issue **visas on arrival** (contact the agent five days before to secure paperwork; costs start at $40 plus $25 "stamp fee"); this is especially helpful for people with no Vietnamese consulate in their home country, or simply those strapped for time. The agent will give you a special clearance fax to show upon arrival in Vietnam and will inform the relevant airline for boarding clearance; they will then meet you off your flight and hand over the official documents at immigration.

At the time of writing, thirty-day **visa extensions** were being issued through tour agents and travellers' cafés in HCMC, Nha Trang, Hoi An, Hue, Da Nang and Hanoi (around $25; 2–5 days), but the situation

Airport departure tax

Airport departure tax is $12 for **international flights** departing HCMC and $14 for Hanoi departures – payable in dong or dollars. Tax for **domestic flights** is 10,000–25,000d (dependent on the individual airports), payable in dong. Some airline tickets include domestic tax in the price.

changes frequently, so check with the embassy before you leave. The **fine** for overstaying your visa can also vary, ranging from no charge for up to a week's overstay, to a maximum of $50 for longer.

Money and costs

Vietnam's unit of **currency** is the dong, usually abbreviated as "d" (occasionally "VND"). Notes come in denominations of 200d, 500d, 1000d, 2000d, 5000d, 10,000d, 20,000d, 50,000d and 100,000d; coins – the first in Vietnam for 25 years – were issued in 2003 in denominations of 200d, 500d, 1000d, 2000d and 5000d. The US **dollar** operates in parallel to the dong as unofficial tender, and most travellers carry some dollars as backup for when banks won't change travellers' cheques. At the end of your trip, you can change leftover dong back into dollar bills. At the time of writing, the **exchange rate** was 28,700d to £1 and 15,700d to $1.

US dollar travellers' cheques are the safest method of carrying money around in Vietnam. They can be cashed at major banks (Vietcombank usually charges the lowest rates), but often not at banks in smaller towns. Dong are not available outside the country at present, though if you take in some small-denomination US dollars you'll have no problems getting by until you reach a bank. A black market of sorts exists in Vietnam, but is best avoided, especially as the mark-up is tiny.

Major **credit cards** – Visa, MasterCard and, to a lesser extent, American Express – are becoming more acceptable in Vietnam. You can withdraw cash from a growing network of 24-hour ATMs (in the Visa, Plus, MasterCard and Cirrus networks) in all main tourist centres (dong only). Even outside the major cities, banks and some travellers' cafés can now advance cash against cards (generally Visa and MasterCard) for a small commission, which is more convenient than carrying around wads of travellers' cheques.

If you need to have **money wired**, contact the Vietcombank in Hanoi or HCMC, though some provincial branches can also now handle telegraphic transfers. Vietcombank has arrangements with selected banks across the world, including Lloyd's Bank in London; the Commonwealth Bank in Sydney; the Royal Bank of Canada; and the Chase Manhattan Bank and Citibank in New York (Vietcombank has a full list). Payment can be made to you in dong or dollars, but hefty charges are levied at both ends. Vietcombank and major post offices also accept the faster, but even more expensive, Moneygram. Again, this has to come from a designated bank; contact any branch of Vietcombank for details. Charges are levied at the sender's end, and to collect the money all you need is the sender's eight-digit reference number.

Costs

Despite what you might have heard, travelling in Vietnam needn't be much more expensive than in its Southeast Asian neighbours; if anything, the cost of travelling here has fallen in recent years. By eating and sleeping at the simplest places and travelling on local buses, you should be able to manage on a **daily budget** of £6-8/US$10–15. Upgrading to more salubrious lodgings, eating good food followed by a couple of beers in a bar, and signing up for the odd minibus tour would bring it to around £18/$30.

Vietnam still maintains a **two-tier pricing system**, with foreigners paying more than locals for some modes of transport and accommodation. The system is now being officially phased out, with most hotels and buses now operating standardized prices, and the national train system recently implementing a one-price policy. However, this is a long, slow process and it will probably be a while before two-tier pricing disappears completely. For the moment, it

In Vietnam, most of the larger costs (eg accommodation and transport) are almost always paid for in US **dollars**; smaller amounts (eg for a street meal or a museum entrance ticket) change hands in **dong**. Prices are given throughout the chapter to reflect this variation.

remains something of a grey area and the amount you pay may well depend on the person you happen to be dealing with.

Information and maps

Your best bet for information are the multitude of **travellers' cafés** and tour operators across the country, but especially in Hanoi and HCMC. The Vietnamese government maintains a handful of **tourist promotion offices** around the globe, but state-owned tourist offices in Vietnam itself are profit-making concerns and not information bureaux. The biggest of these is Vietnamtourism (ⓦ www.vietnamtourism.com), with offices in Hanoi, HCMC and other major tourist centres. There's also a general **information telephone number**, government-run and in English – dial ⓣ1080 (free).

The best **maps** of Vietnam are the International 1:1,000,000 *Travel Map of Vietnam* (available in paperback online) and the Nelles 1:1,500,000 map of Vietnam, Laos and Cambodia. The 1:2,000,000 *Vietnam, Cambodia & Laos World Travel Map* from Bartholomew isn't bad either. All but the Nelles map feature plans of HCMC and Hanoi.

Getting around

Vietnam's main thoroughfare is Highway 1, which runs from Hanoi to HCMC, passing through Hue, Da Nang and Nha Trang en route, and is ghosted by the country's main rail line. **Public transport** has improved considerably in the last few years, with many upgraded trains and state-run buses, fleets of "open-tour" buses run by travellers' cafés, and an increasing amount of high-quality, privately owned minibuses. Having said that, there's still much room for improvement: local bus timetables are for the most part redundant and some travellers find themselves overcharged for tickets, or forced to change buses mid-route and pay a second time. Many tourists opt for internal flights or private tours in order to escape the unreliable buses and relatively slow trains.

For an idea of journey times between major destinations, see "Travel details" on p.1229.

Planes

Vietnam Airlines operates a reasonably cheap, efficient and comprehensive network of **domestic flights** and has branch offices in many towns. The two-hour journey between Hanoi and HCMC ($110), for instance, compares favourably with the thirty or more hours you might spend on the train. Book as far ahead as you can.

Buses and minibuses

Vietnam's national **bus network** offers daily services between all major towns. The government is slowly introducing a national upgrading of state buses, but for now many remain unbearably cramped with hard seats, breakdowns are frequent and progress slow. All towns have a bus station, and larger places have both a local and a long-distance station. Most buses depart early, from 5am through to mid-morning, waiting only as long as it takes to get enough passengers. For longer journeys, tickets are best bought a day in advance, since many routes are heavily over-subscribed. Prices at certain tourist hot spots can be over the odds; always try to ascertain the correct price and obtain a ticket before boarding.

Privately owned **minibuses** compete with public buses on most routes; they sometimes share the local bus station, or simply congregate in the centre of a town; you can also flag them down along the major highways. Though generally even more cramped than ordinary buses, they do at least run throughout the day. There are also an increasing number of privately owned "high-quality" **air-con minibuses** – particularly in the south – that operate from their own offices as opposed to bus stations; these usually stick to a timetable, don't pick up passengers en route, and provide complimentary bottled water and airplane-style refreshing tissues.

Special **"open-tour" buses** shuttling between major tourist destinations are the most popular way for foreigners to travel in Vietnam. Competition is fierce, so prices are coming down, though they are still more expensive than local buses. The best thing to do is buy a one-way through-ticket, for example from HCMC to Hue ($16) or Hanoi ($23), which enables you to stop off at specified destinations en route: heading north, the main stops are Da Lat, Nha Trang, Phan Thiet/Mui Ne, Hoi An, Da Nang and Hue. You can either make firm bookings at the outset or, for around $3 more, opt for an open-dated ticket. You can also buy separate sector tickets between certain destinations. Tickets and onward reservations are available from agents in each town.

Trains

Though Vietnamese **trains** (Ⓦ www.vr.com.vn) can be slow on some services, travelling on them can be a pleasant experience if you splash out on a soft-class berth or seat – though this can work out quite expensive.

The country's main line shadows Highway 1 on its way **from HCMC to Hanoi** (1726km), passing through Nha Trang, Da Nang and Hue en route. **From Hanoi**, one branch goes northwest to Lao Cai; another runs north to Dong Dang, and is the route taken by the two weekly trains from **Hanoi to Beijing**; and the third goes to **Hai Phong**.

The most popular lines with tourists are the shuttle from Da Nang to Hue, and the overnighters from Hue to Hanoi and from Hanoi up to Lao Cai, for Sa Pa. Four "**Reunification Express**" trains depart each day from Hanoi to HCMC and vice versa. They are labelled S1 to S8; odd-numbered trains travel south, even ones north, hence the S2 (34hr), S4, S6 and S8 (all 40hr) depart daily from HCMC, and the S1 to S7 (same times) make the trip in the opposite direction.

When it comes to choosing which **class** to travel in, it's essential to aim high. Hard seats are bearable for short journeys, but even soft seats are grim for long hauls. On overnight journeys, you should go for a **berth**: cramped hard-sleeper berth compartments have six bunks (cheapest at the top) and soft-sleeper berths have only four bunks. S3–S8 trains have a choice of soft-sleeper berths and soft seats with air-con or fan; hard-sleeper berths and hard seats have fan only. On the modern S1 and S2 (faster) trains, all compartments, even hard-sleeper, have air-con, and reclining soft seats are located in brand new double-decker carriages. Simple meals are included in the price of the ticket on overnight journeys.

The train reservation system has become computerized in major train stations, such as Nha Trang, HCMC, Hanoi, Hue and Danang, which has made life easier when reserving tickets; more stations nationwide are implementing the same system. Booking ahead is essential; you may need your passport when you buy a ticket.

Fares vary according to the class and the speed of the train. On the slowest services from HCMC to Hanoi (S4, S6 & S8), HCMC to Nha Trang costs around $6 for a hard seat, $12 for a soft berth; from HCMC to Da Nang, the same classes cost $14 and $28; and from HCMC to Hanoi they cost $24 and $49. On S1 and S2 express trains, soft seats from HCMC to Hanoi cost $35 and soft-sleepers $58.

Vehicle rental

Self-drive in Vietnam is reserved for foreign officials, or those with special permits; for most foreign visitors to Vietnam, this is still not an option. However, it's easy to hire a **car, jeep or minibus with driver** from tour agencies and tourist offices ($20–60 per day). Check who pays for the driver's accommodation and meals, fuel, tolls, parking fees and repairs, and what happens in the case of a major breakdown. Sign a contract showing this and the agreed itinerary, and arrange to pay half before and the balance at the end. Note that right-hand-drive vehicles are still prohibited in Vietnam.

Bicycles are available from hotels and tour agencies in most towns; main tourist spots usually charge under $1 per day. **Motorbike** ($6–10 per day) and/or **moped** ($4–7) rental is possible in most major towns, but the appalling road discipline of most Vietnamese drivers means that the risk of an accident is very real. Check everything carefully, especially brakes, lights and horn. From 1st June 2001, wearing a **helmet** became a legal requirement on all of Vietnam's roads; at the time of writing, fines for non-wearers were only being levied on national and provincial roads, but expect this to gradually include all routes. Helmets can be bought in Hanoi and HCMC for $20–35. Also check the small print on your **insurance** policy, and consider taking out local accident insurance anyway. The biggest local insurer is Bao Viet, with offices in HCMC and Hanoi; their policies cost $14 for the basic three-month cover and are easy to obtain. **Repair shops** are fairly ubiquitous – look for a Honda sign or ask for *sua chua xe may* (motorbike repairs) – but you should still carry at least a puncture-repair kit, pump and spare spark plug. Fuel (*xang*) is around $0.45 per litre and widely available; many roadside vendors keep a few bottles handy. Always leave your bike in a parking compound (*gui xe*) or pay someone a dollar or two to keep an eye on it.

The theory is that you **drive on the right**, though in practice motorists and cyclists swerve and dodge wherever they want, using no signals and their **horn** as a surrogate brake. **Right of way** invariably goes to the biggest vehicle on the road; note that overtaking vehicles assume you'll pull over onto the hard shoulder to avoid them. It's best to avoid driving after dark, since many vehicles don't use headlights. If you are involved in an **accident** and it was deemed to be your fault, the penalties can involve fairly major fines.

Local transport

Taxis are becoming increasingly common in big cities, and there are also some city **bus** services. Elsewhere, you'll have to rely upon a host of two- and three-wheeled vehicles. Cheap, ubiquitous and fun, **cyclos** – three-wheeled bicycle rickshaws – can carry one person (two at a push) and cost a dollar or less for a five- to ten-minute hop, depending on your bargaining prowess. However, there's a growing problem with hiring cyclos and taxis across the country, particularly in cities. As a general guideline, when using cyclos, avoid travelling after dark and always secure a price before setting off, ensuring you know which currency you are dealing in (five fingers could mean 5000d or $5), and whether you're negotiating for one passenger or two; it's best to write the fare down before you start your journey. When hiring a taxi, if you don't agree the fare upfront, make sure that the meter is on before you start your journey. Be wary of some meters that suddenly race ahead with the fare, or taxis insisting that your hotel is "closed" or "full," and taking you to another one; this is usually part of a commission scam – always be firm with your directions. It's best to try and get your hotel to recommend you a taxi or cyclo.

The motorized version of the cyclo, found in the south, is known as the **cyclo mai**. In the Mekong Delta, the **xe dap loi** is also a variation on the cyclo theme, and the motorized version is known as a **Honda loi**. **Honda oms** or motorbike taxis, known in the north as a **xe oms**, are becoming more common in the main cities; prices are a shade cheaper than a cyclo.

Xe lams (also known as **Lambros**) are three-wheeled, motorized buggies whose drivers squeeze in more passengers than you'd believe possible. These act as a local bus service outside Hanoi and HCMC, and rows of them are usually found either at the local bus station, or outside the local market. A typical xe lam ride of a few kilometres costs around $0.35.

Accommodation

Compared to other Southeast Asian countries, **accommodation** in Vietnam can be poor quality and/or pricey, though standards and prices are generally good in the main tourist spots. Expect to pay from around $5 for the most basic double room with fan and attached bathroom; it's always worth bargaining. Some places add a government **tax** and service charge of fifteen percent.

A "**single**" room could have a single or twin beds in it, while a "double" room could have two, three or four single beds, a single and a twin, and so on. In the cheapest places, rooms are cleaned irregularly and may have cockroaches and even rats roaming free; you can minimize health risks by not bringing foodstuffs or sugary drinks into your room.

Hotel **security** can be a big problem, so never leave valuables in your room, and use your own padlock on the door if possible. **Prostitution** is rife in Vietnam, and in less reputable budget hotels it's not unknown for Western men to be hassled at night.

Addresses

Where two numbers are separated by a slash, such as 110/5, you simply make for no. 110, where an alley will lead off to a further batch of buildings – you want the fifth one. Where a number is followed by a letter, as in 117a, you're looking for a single block encompassing several addresses, of which one will be 117a.

Not all places are permitted to take foreigners: if the staff merely smile and shake their heads, chances are this is the case. On the whole there's no need to book ahead, except during the festival of Tet (early spring).

Types of accommodation

There are no youth hostels in Vietnam; however, some destinations such as Nha Trang and Mui Ne offer **camping** facilities, around $3 per tent. Camping aside, the cheapest form of accommodation is a bed in a dormitory; an increasing number of budget **guesthouses** (*nha khach*) and **rooms for rent** in Hanoi, HCMC, plus some other tourist hot spots, offer dorms at around $2–3 per bed per night. Otherwise, you'll need to upgrade to a simple fan room with shared washing facilities, in either a room for rent or a state-run **hotel** (*k hach san*) or guesthouse; this should cost $4–6. In the main tourist destinations, rooms for rent, **mini-hotels** (a modest, privately owned hotel) and hotels now offer fairly decent rooms with fan, private bathroom, hot water and phone, for around $6–10; add air-con and satellite TV and they can cost anything from $10 to $30. Elsewhere, you'll probably have to upgrade to the local state-run hotel. Paying $35–75 will get you a room in a mid-range hotel of some repute, with in-house restaurant, bar and room service; while at the top of the range you're likely to spend $90–150 a night in international-class hotels.

Electricity is usually supplied at 220 volts, though you may come across 110 volts; plugs are two-pinned, with the pins rounded.

Food and drink

Though closely related to Chinese cuisine, **Vietnamese food** is quite distinct, using herbs and seasoning rather than sauces, and favouring boiled or steamed dishes over stir-fries. The usual basic **health** precautions apply when eating out in Vietnam; see "Food and water", p.53, for advice.

Where to eat

The cheapest and most fun places to eat are the **street kitchens**, which range from makeshift food stalls set up on the street, to open-fronted eating houses. They are permanent, with an address if not a name, and most specialize in one type of food, generally indicated on a signboard, or offer the ubiquitous *com pho* rice dishes and noodle soups. **Com binh dan**, "people's meals", comprise an array of prepared dishes like stuffed tomatoes, fried fish, tofu, pickles and eggs, plus rice; expect to pay from around $1 for a good plateful. Outside the major cities, street kitchens rarely stay open beyond 8pm.

Western-style **Vietnamese restaurants** (*nha hang*) have chairs and menus and usually serve a wide range of meat and fish dishes. Menus often don't show prices and overcharging is a regular problem. Peanuts, hot towels and tissues on the table will be added to the bill even if untouched; ask for them to be taken away if you don't want them. A modest meal for two will cost roughly $8–10. The more expensive restaurants tend to stay open until 9.30 or 10.30pm, have menus priced in dollars and, in some cases, accept credit cards; a meal for two will cost around $10 and up.

Catering primarily to budget travellers, **travellers' cafés** tend to serve mediocre Western and Vietnamese dishes, from banana pancakes to steak and chips or fried noodles – and usually open from 7am to 11pm. They're mainly found in Hanoi, HCMC, Hoi An, Hue, Nha Trang and Da Lat.

A glossary of food and drink

Some names differ between north (N) and south (S).

General terms and requests

how much is it?	*bao nhieu tien?*
cheers!	*can chen* (N); *can ly* (S)
delicious	*rat ngon*
vegetarian	*nguoi an chay*
I don't eat meat or fish	*toi khong an thit*

Rice and noodles

bun	round rice noodles
bun bo	beef with bun noodles
bun ga	chicken with bun noodles
com	cooked rice
com rang; com chien	fried rice
com trang	steamed or boiled rice
chao	rice porridge
mi xao	fried noodles
pho	flat rice noodles, usually in soup
pho bo tai	noodle soup with rare beef
pho bo chin	with medium done-beef
pho co trung	with eggs

Fish, meat and vegetables

ca	fish
ca ran (N); *ca chien* (S)	fried fish
cua	crab
luon	eel
muc	squid
tom	shrimp or prawn
tom hum	lobster
thit	meat
bo	beef
ga	chicken
lon (N); *heo* (S)	pork
vit	duck
rau co or *rau cac loai*	vegetables
ca chua	tomato
ca tim	aubergine
dau	beans
khoai tay	potato
mang	bamboo shoots
ngo (N); *bap* (S)	sweetcorn
rau xao cac loai	stir-fried vegetables

Miscellaneous

banh	cake
banh mi	bread
bo	butter
duong	sugar
pho mat, fo mat	cheese
lac (N); …*dau phong* (S)	peanuts
muoi	salt
mut	jam
ot	chilli
tao pho (N); *dau hu* (S)	tofu
trai cay	fruit
trung	egg
trung om let or *op lep*	omelette
trung ran or *trung op la*	fried eggs

Drinks

bia	beer
ca phé den	black coffee
ca phé sua	coffee with milk
tra	tea
khong da	no ice
nuoc	water
nuoc khoang	mineral water
nuoc cam	orange juice
nuoc chanh	lime juice
nuoc dua	coconut milk
or choum	rice alcohol
so da cam	orange soda
sua tuoi	fresh milk

Vietnamese food

The staple of Vietnamese meals is **rice** (*com*), with noodles a popular alternative. Typically, rice will be accompanied by a fish or meat dish, a vegetable dish and soup. Even in the south, Vietnamese food tends not to be overly spicy, as chilli sauces are served separately. Vietnam's most popular seasoning is *nuoc mam*, a fermented fish sauce. The use of monosodium glutamate (**MSG**) can be excessive, and what looks like salt on the table may be MSG, so taste it first. You can try asking for no MSG in your food: "*khong co my chinh*".

The most famous Vietnamese dish has to be **spring rolls**, known as *cha gio, cha*

nem, nem ran or just plain *nem*. Various combinations of minced pork, shrimp or crab, rice vermicelli, onions and beansprouts are rolled in rice-paper wrappers, and then eaten fresh or deep-fried, usually dipped in the ubiquitous chilli sauce. The other great staple is **pho** (pronounced "fur"), a noodle soup eaten at any time of day but primarily at breakfast. The basic bowl of *pho* consists of a light beef broth flavoured with ginger and coriander, to which are added broad, flat rice-noodles, spring onions and slivers of chicken, pork or beef. *Lau* is more of a main meal than a soup, where the vegetable broth arrives at the table in a **steamboat** (a ring-shaped dish on live coals or, nowadays, often electrically heated) and you cook slivers of beef or prawns in it, and then afterwards drink the flavourful liquid that's left in the pot.

Most restaurants offer a few meat-free dishes, ranging from stewed spinach or similar greens, to a mix of onion, tomato, bean sprouts, various mushrooms and peppers; places used to foreigners may be able to do **vegetarian** spring rolls (*nem an chay*, or *nem khong co thit*). At street kitchens you're likely to find tofu and one or two dishes of pickled vegetables. However, soups are usually made with beef stock, morsels of pork fat sneak into many dishes and animal fat tends to be used for frying. The phrase to remember is *nguoi an chay* (vegetarian), or seek out a vegetarian rice shop (*tiem com chay*). On the 1st and 14th/15th days of every lunar month, many Vietnamese spurn meat, so you'll find more veggie options on these days.

Vietnam is blessed with dozens of tropical and temperate **fruits**. Pineapple, coconut, papaya, mangoes, longan and mangosteen flourish in the south. Da Lat is famous for its strawberries, but a fruit you might want to give a miss is the durian, a spiky, yellow-green football-sized fruit with an unmistakably pungent odour reminiscent of mature cheese and caramel, but tasting like an onion-laced custard.

Drinks

Giai khat means "quench your thirst", and you'll see the signs everywhere. The simple rule is don't drink the **water** in Vietnam, but **ice** is frequently added to drinks; avoid this by using the phrase *"dung bo da, cam on"* ("no ice, thanks"). Contaminated water causes diarrhoea, gastroenteritis, typhoid, cholera, dysentery, poliomyelitis, hepatitis A and giardia. Particular care should be taken anywhere where there is flooding, as raw sewage may be washed into the water system. However, most guesthouses and hotels provide thermos flasks of boiled water, hot tea is always on offer, and cheap, **bottled water** ($1 or less per litre) and carbonated drinks are widely available. When buying bottled water check the seal is unbroken.

Other good thirst-quenchers include fresh coconut milk, orange and lime **juices**, and sugar-cane juice (*mia da*). Somewhere between a drink and a snack is **chè**, sold in glasses at the markets. It's made from taro flour and green bean, and served over ice with chunks of fruit, coloured jellies and even sweetcorn or potato. Small cups of refreshing, strong green **tea** are presented to all guests or visitors in Vietnam: the well-boiled water is safe to drink. The Vietnamese drink **coffee** very strong and in small quantities, with a large dollop of condensed milk at the bottom of the cup.

Several foreign **beers** are brewed under licence in Vietnam, but good local brews include 333 (Ba Ba Ba) and Bivina. **Bia hoi** ("fresh" or draught beer) is served warm from the keg and then poured over ice. Its quality varies, but it's unadulterated by chemicals. *Bia hoi* has a 24-hour shelf life, which means the better places sell out by early evening. There are dozens of *bia hoi* outlets in Hanoi and HCMC, ranging from a few ankle-high stools gathered round a barrel on the pavement to beer gardens; most offer snacks of some sort. The stronger, pricier **bia tuoi** comes in a light or dark brew and is served from pressurized barrels. The most common local wine is rice alcohol; the ethnic minorities drink stem alcohol (*ruou can*).

Communications

Mail can take anywhere from four days to four weeks in or out of Vietnam; from major towns, eight to ten days is the norm. Rates

countries in which to travel. That said, there are a few things to be wary of. Some tourist destinations, such as HCMC and Nha Trang, now have a fairly bad reputation for thieves, pickpockets and con-artists. In recent years, Nha Trang, but especially HCMC, has seen an escalation in **bag snatching** – day or night – that has led in some cases to serious injuries. Always take care when carrying valuables and money around with you; wherever possible leave them behind in a secure place at your hotel. You should also be careful with taxis and cyclos (see "Local Transport", p.1107). At night, there is a fair amount of **drug selling** on the streets of HCMC, Hanoi, Nha Trang and even Sa Pa. In some places, cyclo drivers can sell you **drugs** and then turn you in to the police. A substantial bribe might persuade them to drop the matter; otherwise, you're looking at fines and jail sentences for lesser offences, or the death penalty for smuggling large quantities.

Vietnam is generally a safe country for **women** to travel around alone; most Vietnamese will simply be curious as to why you are on your own. That said, it pays to take the normal precautions, especially late at night, when you should avoid taking a cyclo by yourself; it's wise to use a taxi instead. Asian women travelling with a white man have reported cases of harassment – attributed to the fact that some Vietnamese men automatically label all such women as prostitutes.

If you have anything stolen, you'll need to go to the **police** station nearest to the scene of the crime and get the police to write up a report for your insurance company; try to recruit an English-speaker to come with you – and be prepared to pay a few dollars as a "fee". Corruption among police and other officials can be a problem: very occasionally, trumped-up fines are imposed on bus, cyclo or other drivers seen carrying a Westerner – fines *you'll* often be expected to pay. But with patience, plus a few cigarettes to hand round, you should be able to bargain fines down considerably.

Not surprisingly, the Vietnamese authorities are sensitive about **military installations**, border regions, military camps, bridges, airports and train stations. Anyone taking photographs near such sites risks having the film removed from their camera, or the ubiquitous "fine". **Unexploded mines** still pose a serious threat: the problem is most acute in the Demilitarized Zone, where each year a few local farmers are killed or injured. Always stick to well-trodden paths and never touch any shells or half-buried chunks of metal.

Medical care and emergencies

Pharmacies can generally help with minor injuries or ailments, and in major towns you may well find a pharmacist who speaks French or even English. Both HCMC and Hanoi now have reasonably well-stocked pharmacies. That said, drugs past their shelf life and even counterfeit medicines are rife, so inspect packaging carefully, check use-by dates – and bring anything you know you're likely to need from home. Condoms (*bao cao su*) are sold in Hanoi and HCMC – reliable imported brands to look out for are OK and Trust.

Tampons are still hard to come by outside HCMC and Hanoi; wherever possible, stock up with supplies before entering Vietnam. Local **hospitals** will treat minor problems, but in a real emergency your best bet is to head for Hanoi or HCMC, where excellent international medical centres can provide diagnosis and treatment. Hospitals expect immediate cash payment for health services rendered; you will then have to seek reimbursement from your insurance company (hang on to receipts).

Emergency phone numbers

Try to get a Vietnamese-speaker to phone for you.
Police ☎113
Fire ☎114
Ambulance ☎115

History

Vietnam as a unified state within its present geographical boundaries has only existed since the early nineteenth century. The national history, however, stretches back thousands of years to a kingdom in the Red River Delta.

The beginnings

The most significant period in Vietnam's early history began in about 2000 BC with the emergence of a highly organized society of rice-farmers, the Lac Viet. Held to be the original Vietnamese nation, this embryonic kingdom, Van Lang, evolved into a sophisticated Bronze Age culture whose greatest creations were the ritualistic **bronze drums**, found near Dong Son.

Chinese rule

In 111 BC, the Han emperors annexed the whole Red River Delta, and so began a thousand years of Chinese domination. They introduced **Confucianism** and with it a rigid, feudalistic hierarchy dominated by a mandarin class. Mahayana Buddhism first entered Vietnam from China during the second century AD.

The local aristocracy increasingly resented their Chinese rulers and engaged in various insurrections, culminating in the battle of the Bach Dang River in 938 AD, a famous victory for Ngo Quyen, leader of the Vietnamese forces, who subsequently declared himself ruler of **Nam Viet**, heralding what was to be nearly ten centuries of Vietnamese independence.

Champa

Meanwhile, in the south of Vietnam it was the Indianized kingdom of **Champa** that dominated the region until the late tenth century. Ruled over by divine kings who worshipped first Shiva and later embraced Buddhism, the Champa people built temples all along the coast of south-central Vietnam, including the magnificent My Son.

By the end of the eleventh century, Champa had lost its territory north of Hue to the Viets, and four centuries later the whole kingdom became a vassal state under Viet hegemony.

Independent Vietnam

Back in the Red River Delta, the period immediately following independence from Chinese rule in 939 AD was marked by factional infighting until Dinh Bo Linh finally united the country in 968, securing its future by paying tribute to the Chinese emperor, a system that continued until the nineteenth century.

For the next ten centuries, Dai Viet (Great Viet) was ruled by a sequence of dynasties (see box opposite), the most important of which were the **Ly dynasty**, who founded the city of Thang Long, the precursor of modern Hanoi; the **Tran dynasty**, who repelled three successive Mongol invasions; and the **Later Le dynasty** who reconstructed the nation after a brief relapse into Chinese rule from 1407 to 1428.

As the Later Le declined in the sixteenth century, two powerful clans took over, splitting the country in two at the Gianh River, near Dong Hoi. The **Trinh** lords held sway in Hanoi and the north, while the **Nguyen** set up court at Hue. The Nguyen lords conquered the Mekong Delta, and by the mid-eighteenth century Viet people occupied the whole peninsula down to Ca Mau.

The Nguyen dynasty

In 1771, three disgruntled brothers raised their standard in Tay Son village, west of Qui Nhon, and ended up ruling the whole country. Their **Tay Son rebellion** gained broad support for

The Vietnamese dynasties	
Ngo	939–965 AD
Dinh	968–980
Early Le	980–1009
Ly	1009–1225
Tran	1225–1400
Ho	1400–1407
(Ming Chinese	1407–1428)
Later Le	1428–1789
Nguyen and Trinh lords	1592–1788
Tay Son	1788–1802
Nguyen	1802–1945

its message of equal rights, justice and liberty, and by the middle of 1788 had overthrown both the Trinh and Nguyen lords.

One of the few Nguyen lords to survive the Tay Son rebellion was Prince Nguyen Anh who, with the help of a French bishop, Pigneau de Béhaine, raised an army and regained the throne in 1802 as **Emperor Gia Long**.

For the first time **Vietnam**, as the country was now called, fell under a single authority from the northern border all the way down to the point of Ca Mau. Gia Long established his capital at Hue, where he built a magnificent citadel in imitation of the Chinese emperor's Forbidden City. Gia Long and the **Nguyen dynasty** he founded were resolutely Confucian. He immediately abolished the Tay Son reforms, re-imposing the old feudal order, and gradually closed the country to the outside world.

French rule

In the nineteenth century, French governments began to see Vietnam as a potential route into the resource-rich provinces of southern China, and in 1858 an armada of fourteen French ships captured Da Nang. By 1862, they controlled the whole Mekong Delta, and by 1887 had power over the whole country, which they combined with Cambodia and, later, Laos to form the **Union of Indochina**. For the next seventy years, Vietnam was once again under foreign occupation.

Paul Doumer, governor-general from 1897 to 1902, launched a massive programme of **infrastructural development**, which was funded by punitive taxes. There was a shift to large-scale rice production for export, which eroded traditional social systems and forced peasants off the land to work as indentured labour.

Up until the mid-1920s, Vietnam's various anti-colonial movements tended to be fragmented. But, over the border in southern China, Vietnam's first Marxist–Leninist organization, the Revolutionary Youth League, was founded in 1925 by **Ho Chi Minh**. Born in 1890, "Uncle" Ho left Vietnam in 1911, became a founding member of the French Communist Party and, by 1923, was in Moscow, training as a communist agent.

In 1930, Ho persuaded the various rival anti-colonial movements to unite into one **Indochinese Communist Party** whose main goal was an independent Vietnam governed by workers, peasants and soldiers. In preparation for the revolution, cadres went into rural areas and among urban workers to set up party cells.

World War II

The German occupation of France in 1940 overturned the established order in Vietnam, and by mid-1941 the region's coal mines, rice fields and military installations were all under Japanese control.

In February 1941, Ho returned to Vietnam after thirty years in exile, joining other resistance leaders at Pac Bo cave, near Cao Bang, where they forged a nationalist coalition, known as the **Viet Minh**. The organization was specifically designed to win broad popular support for independence, followed by moderate social and democratic reforms.

Over the next few years, Viet Minh recruits received military training in southern China and the **Vietnamese Liberation Army** was formed. Gradually, the Viet Minh established liberated zones in the northern mountains to provide bases for future guerrilla operations.

Meanwhile, Japanese forces seized full control of the country in March 1945. They declared a nominally independent state under Bao Dai, the last Nguyen emperor, and imprisoned most of the French Army. The Viet Minh quickly moved onto the offensive.

The August revolution

The Japanese surrender on August 14 left a power vacuum and Ho Chi Minh immediately called for a national uprising. On September 2, 1945, he proclaimed the establishment of the **Democratic Republic of Vietnam**.

The **Potsdam Agreement**, which marked the end of World War II, failed to recognize the new Republic of Vietnam. Instead, Japanese troops south of the Sixteenth Parallel were to surrender to British authority, while those in the north would defer to the Kuomintang Chinese nationalists. In the south, the British commander proclaimed martial law and Saigon was soon back in French hands.

The French War

In the north, the 200,000 Chinese soldiers on Vietnamese soil acted increasingly like an army of occupation, obliging Ho Chi Minh to sign a treaty allowing a limited French force to replace them. In return, France recognized the Democratic Republic as a "free state" within the proposed French Union. However, it soon became apparent that the French were not going to abide by the treaty, and skirmishes between Vietnamese and French troops escalated into an all-out conflict.

For the first years of the **war against the French** (also known as the First Indochina War) the Viet Minh kept largely to their mountain bases in northern and central Vietnam, where they could simply melt away into the jungle whenever threatened.

The communist victory in China in 1949 proved to be a turning point. Almost immediately, both China and Russia recognized the Democratic Republic of Vietnam and military aid started to flow across the border. Suddenly, Bao Dai's shaky government in the south was seen as the last bastion of the free world, and America was drawn into the war, funding the French military with at least $3 billion by 1954.

But by 1953, France was tiring of the war and both sides agreed to peace discussions at the Geneva Conference, due to take place in May the following year. Meanwhile, a crucial battle was unfolding near **Dien Bien Phu**, where French battalions established a massive camp, deliberately trying to tempt the Viet Minh into the open. After 59 days of bitter fighting, the Viet Minh forced the French to surrender, on May 7, 1954, the eve of the Geneva Conference.

The Geneva Conference

The nine delegations attending the **Geneva Conference** succeeded only in reaching a stopgap solution, dividing Vietnam at the Seventeenth Parallel, along the Ben Hai River, pending nationwide free elections to be held by July 1956; a demilitarized buffer zone was established on either side of this military front. France and the Viet

Minh agreed to an immediate ceasefire, but crucially neither the United States nor Bao Dai's government endorsed the Accords, fearing that they heralded a reunited, communist-ruled Vietnam.

Diem and the South

On July 7, Emperor Bao Dai named himself president, and the vehemently anti-communist **Ngo Dinh Diem** prime minister, of South Vietnam. Diem promptly ousted Bao Dai, declared himself President of the Republic of Vietnam, and began silencing his enemies, chiefly members of the Hoa Hao and Cao Dai religious sects and Viet Minh dissidents in the South. Over 50,000 citizens died in his pogrom.

Back in Hanoi...

In **Hanoi** meanwhile, Ho Chi Minh's government set about constructing a socialist society. Years of warring with France had profoundly damaged the country's infrastructure, and now it found itself deprived of the South's plentiful rice stocks. Worse still, the **land reforms** of the mid-1950s saw many thousands of innocents "tried" as landlords by ad hoc People's Agricultural Reform Tribunals, tortured, and then executed or sent to labour camps.

Conscription was introduced in April 1960, cadres and hardware began to creep down the Ho Chi Minh Trail (see box on p.570), and Hanoi orchestrated the creation of the **National Liberation Front** (NLF), which drew together all opposition forces in the South. Diem dubbed its guerrilla fighters **Vietcong**, or VC, Vietnamese Communists, though in reality the NLF represented a united front of Catholic, Buddhist, communist and non-communist nationalists.

America enters the fray

In early 1955, the White House began to bankroll Diem's government and the training of his army, the **ARVN** (Army of the Republic of Vietnam). Behind these policies lay the fear of the chain reaction that could follow in Southeast Asia were South Vietnam to be overrun by communism – the so-called **Domino Effect**.

Diem's brutally repressive government was losing ground to the VC in the battle for the hearts and minds of the population. Buddhists celebrating Buddha's birthday were fired upon by ARVN soldiers in Hue, sparking off riots against religious repression, and provoking **Thich Quang Duc**'s infamous self-immolation in Saigon. America tacitly sanctioned a coup in 1963 that ousted Diem, who was shot.

In August 1964, when two American ships were subjected to allegedly unprovoked attacks from North Vietnamese craft, reprisals followed in the form of 64 **bombing** sorties against northern coastal bases. US senators empowered Johnson to deploy regular American troops in Vietnam, "to prevent further aggression".

The escalation of the American War

Early 1965 saw the start of **Operation Rolling Thunder**, a sustained carpet-bombing campaign, which lasted three and a half years and saw twice the tonnage of bombs dropped (around 800 daily) as had fallen on all World War II's theatres of war. Despite this, Rolling Thunder failed either to break the North's sources or their lines of supply. North Vietnamese Army (NVA) troops continued to infiltrate the South in increasing numbers, so that by 1967 over 100,000 a year were making the trek south along the Ho Chi Minh Trail.

By the end of 1965, there were 200,000 GIs in Vietnam – a figure that was to approach half a million by the winter of 1967. Their mission was largely confined to keeping the NVA at bay in the central highlands and neutralizing the guerrilla threat in the Viet Cong power-bases of the South. They

The Ho Chi Minh Trail

The **Ho Chi Minh Trail** was conceived in early 1959 as a safe route by which to direct men and equipment down the length of Vietnam in support of communist groups in the South. By the end of its "working" life, the Ho Chi Minh Trail had grown from a rough assemblage of jungle paths to become a highly effective **logistical network** stretching from near Vinh, north of the Seventeenth Parallel, to Tay Ninh province on the edge of the Mekong Delta. For much of its southerly route the Trail ran through **Laos** and **Cambodia**, always through the most difficult, mountainous terrain.

Initially, it took up to six months to walk the Trail from north to south, most of the time travelling at night, but by 1975, the Trail – comprising at least three main arteries plus several feeder roads and totalling over **15,000km** – was wide enough to take tanks and heavy trucks, and could be driven in just one week. It was protected by anti-aircraft emplacements and supported by fuel depots, ammunition dumps, food stores and hospitals, often located underground.

By early 1965, **aerial bombardment** of the Trail had begun in earnest, using napalm and defoliants as well as conventional bombs. In eight years the US Air Force dropped over two million tonnes of bombs, mostly over Laos, in an effort to cut the flow. But the Trail was never completely severed.

also flushed active Viet Cong soldiers out of villages, most infamously at **My Lai** (see p.1176).

The Tet Offensive

On January 21, 1968, around 40,000 NVA troops laid siege to a remote American military base at **Khe Sanh**, near the Lao border. They were met with a carpet-bombing campaign that claimed over 10,000 victims. However, Khe Sanh was primarily a decoy to steer US troops and attention away from the **Tet Offensive** that exploded a week later. In the early hours of January 31, a combined force of 70,000 communists violated a New Year truce to launch offensives on over a hundred urban centres across the South. But the campaign failed to spark a hoped-for revolt against the Saigon regime and the VC was left permanently lamed.

However, success *did* register across the Pacific, where the assault on the **US Embassy in Saigon**, during which five Americans died, caused a sea change in popular US perceptions of the war. On March 31, President Johnson announced a virtual cessation of bombing, and peace talks began a month later.

The fall of the South

In 1969, Richard Nixon's presidency introduced the strategy of "**Vietnamization**", a gradual US withdrawal coupled with a stiffening of ARVN forces and hardware and a dramatic increase in the scale of bombing. By the end of 1970, only 280,000 US troops remained, while ARVN numbers topped a million.

Under the terms of the **Paris Accords**, signed on January 27, 1973 by the United States, the North, the South and the Viet Cong, a ceasefire was established, and all remaining American troops were repatriated. But the agreements allowed the NVA and ARVN troops to retain whatever positions they held and **renewed aggression** soon erupted. Thieu's ARVN soon set about retaking territory lost to the North and then, over Christmas 1974, an **NVA drive** overran the area north of Saigon now called Song Be province. Towns in the South fell like ninepins, President Thieu fled to Taiwan, and Saigon fell to the North on April 30.

The **toll** of the American War, in human terms, was staggering. Of the 3.3 million Americans who served in Vietnam between 1965 and 1973, over 57,600 died, and more than 150,000 received wounds that required hospitalization. The ARVN lost 250,000 troops. Hanoi declared that over two million Vietnamese civilians, and one million communist troops, died during the war.

Post-reunification Vietnam

Vietnam was once again a unified nation, and in July 1976 the **Socialist Republic of Vietnam** was officially born. However, the North had no industry, a co-operative system of agriculture, and much of its land had been bombed on a massive scale. In stark contrast, American involvement in the South had underwritten what John Pilger describes as "an 'economy' based upon the services of maids, pimps, whores, beggars and black-marketeers", which dried up when the last helicopter left Saigon.

Hanoi was intent on ushering in a rigid socialist state. Privately owned land was confiscated, collectivization of agriculture was introduced, and as the state took control of industry and trade, output dwindled. Vietnam was, until 1993, unable to look to the IMF, World Bank or Asian Development Bank for **development loans**.

Anyone with remote connections with America was interned in a "**re-education camp**", along with Buddhist monks, priests and intellectuals. Hundreds of thousands of southerners were sent to these camps, and some remained for over a decade. Discrimination against those on the "wrong side" in the war continues today, in areas as diverse as healthcare and job opportunities.

The quagmire Vietnam found itself in after reunification prompted many of its citizens to flee across the oceans; from 1979 until the early 90s alone, an estimated 840,000 of these "**boat people**" arrived safely in "ports of first asylum" (Hong Kong was the prime destination), of whom more than 750,000 were eventually resettled overseas.

A return to war

Three weeks before the fall of Saigon in 1975, **Pol Pot**'s genocidal regime had seized power in Cambodia; within a year his troops were making cross-border forays into regions of Vietnam around the Mekong Delta and north of Ho Chi Minh City (as Saigon had been renamed). Finally, on Christmas Day 1978, 120,000 **Vietnamese troops invaded Cambodia** and ousted Pol Pot. They remained there until September 1989.

Doi moi... and the future

By the early 1980s, the only thing keeping Vietnam afloat was Soviet aid. Finally, in 1986, Nguyen Van Linh introduced sweeping economic reforms, known as **doi moi** or "renovation". Collectivization and central planning were abandoned, a market economy was embraced, agriculture and retail businesses were privatized, and attempts were made to attract foreign capital.

In 1993, the Americans lifted their veto on aid, and Western cash began to flow in to Vietnam. By year's end, inflation was down to five percent. Vietnam was admitted into **ASEAN** (the Association of Southeast Asian Nations) in July 1995, and full diplomatic relations with the US were restored.

Revenues from oil, manufacturing and tourism took off and everyone was forecasting Vietnam as the next **Asian tiger**. But by 1997 the honeymoon period was well and truly over. Economic growth flagged as foreign companies scaled back, or pulled out altogether, frustrated by an overblown bureaucracy and regulations in a constant state of flux. As the economic crisis in Southeast Asia took hold, Vietnam's state-run industries became increasingly uncompetitive, and smuggling grew at an alarming rate.

National elections in July 1997 ushered in the popular new prime minister, **Phan Van Khai** (still in power at the time of writing), who has forged ahead with economic reforms. One of the government's immediate problems was how to speed up the restructuring and privatization of debt-ridden state enterprises. Entering the new millennium, the Communist Party showed further signs of flexibility, with increasingly progressive policy makers and the appointment of General Secretary **Nong Duc Manh.** Still bound by "market economy under socialist directions", the 2001 Ninth National Congress unveiled its long-term plan to turn Vietnam into a major industrial power by 2010. Furthermore, the National Constitution has been amended, state-owned enterprises – the grass-roots of the economy – have been heavily reformed and the private sector is accelerating dramatically. On the corruption front, a recent crack-down by Van Khai led to a number of senior government officials and police officers facing trial in February 2003. The trial, which concerned the alleged bribing of public officials by a shadowy underworld figure called Nam Cam, was something of a test case in the continuing battle against political sleaze. In June of the same year, Nam Cam was sentenced to death, but many senior government officials received relatively lenient sentences.

Vietnam now enjoys an optimistic position, with positive steps achieved in a comparatively short time. With its GDP increasing by seven percent in 2004, the country is now ranked second to China in Asian economic growth. *Doi moi* reached further heights with the ratification in 2001 of the **Bi-lateral Trade Agreement** between Vietnam and the USA. This not only brings the two countries closer together, but is a huge step forward in economic reform, opening the door for Vietnam to fully enter the world economy.

Religion

The moral and religious life of most Vietnamese people is governed by a mixture of Confucian, Mahayana Buddhist and Taoist teachings interwoven with ancestor worship and ancient, animistic practices. Vietnam also has small Hindu, Muslim and Theravada Buddhist communities, as well as the second-largest Catholic congregation in Southeast Asia, after the Philippines. For an introduction to all these faiths, see "Religion", pp.69–71.

After 1975, the Marxist–Leninist government of reunified Vietnam declared the state atheist: churches and pagodas were closed down and religious leaders sent for re-education. Since 1986, the situation has eased, and many Vietnamese are once again openly practising their faith.

No matter what their religion, virtually every Vietnamese household will maintain an ancestral altar for rituals associated with **ancestor worship**, which is based on the principles of filial piety and obligation to the past, present and future generations. Residual **animism** plus a whole host of spirits borrowed from other religions further complicate Vietnam's mystical world, in which the universe is divided into three realms – the sky, earth and man – under the overall guardianship of Ong Troi, Lord of Heaven.

Up to two-thirds of the Vietnamese population consider themselves **Mahayana Buddhists**, while at the same time adhering to a **Confucian** philosophy, whose emphasis on conformity and duty has played an essential role in Vietnam's political, social and educational systems. Many **Taoist** deities have been absorbed into other more mainstream cults, in particular Mahayana Buddhism.

Vietnam in the movies

The embroilment of the US in Vietnam and its conflicts has spawned hundreds of movies, ranging from fond soft-focused colonial reminiscences, to blood-and-guts depictions of the horrors of war.

Even by the mid-1950s, the country was often treated less as a nation with its own unique set of political issues, and more as a generic Asian theatre of war, in which the righteous battle against communism could be played out. **China Gate** (1957) is an early example of this trend. Rather more depth of thought went into the making of **The Quiet American** (1958, remade 2002), in which Michael Redgrave played the British journalist and cynic, Fowler, while Audie Murphy played Pyle, the eponymous "hero" of Graham Greene's novel. To Greene's chagrin, Pyle was depicted not as a representative of the American government, but of a private aid organization – something which the author felt blunted his anti-American message.

With American troops duly deployed by 1965, it was only a matter of time before John Wayne produced his patriotic and monumentally bad **The Green Berets** (1968), which depicts American soldiers in spotless uniforms fighting against no less a threat than total "communist domination of the world". But the war was a much dirtier affair than *The Green Berets* made it seem and, as popular support for the conflict soured, a raft of exploitation movies was churned out, in which the mental scars of Vietnam provided topical window-dressing to improbable tales of martial arts, motorbikes and mayhem. At best, vets were treated as dysfunctional vigilantes acting beyond the pale of society – most famously in **Taxi Driver** (1976), which has Robert De Niro's disturbed insomniac returnee, Travis Bickle, embarking on a one-man moral crusade to purge the streets of a hellish New York.

Only in 1978 did Hollywood finally pluck up courage enough to confront the war head-on, and so aid the nation's healing process. Movies no longer sought to make sense of past events, but to highlight their futility, and audiences were confronted by disaffected troops seeking comfort in prostitution and drug abuse, along with far more shocking examples of soldiers' fraying moral fibre. **Coming Home** (1978), which cast Jane Fonda as a military careerman's wife who falls in love with a wheelchair-bound veteran (Jon Voight), was significant for its sensitive consideration of the emotional and physical tolls exacted by the war. Similarly concerned was **The Deer Hunter** (1978), in which the conscription of three friends fractures their Russian orthodox community in Pennsylvania. The friends' "one-shot" code of honour, espoused on a last pre-Vietnam hunting trip, contrasts wildly with the moral vacuum of the war, whose random brutality is embodied in the movie's central scenes of Russian roulette. But for all its power, *The Deer Hunter* is marred by overt racist stereotyping of the Vietnamese. Francis Ford Coppola's hugely indulgent but visually magnificent **Apocalypse Now** (1979) rounded off the vanguard of postwar Vietnam combat movies. It was described by one critic as "Film as opera... it turns Vietnam into a vast trip, into a War of the Imagination". Coppola totally mythologizes the conflict, rendering it not so much futile as insane.

The precedent set by *Coming Home* of sympathetic consideration for returning veterans' mindsets spurred many movies along similar lines in subsequent years. These focused on the disillusionment and disorientation felt by soldiers coming back, not to heroes' welcomes, but to indifference and even disdain. One of the first was **First Blood** (1982), which introduced audiences to Sly Stallone's muscle-bound super-vet, John Rambo.

Alan Parker's **Birdy** (1984) and Oliver Stone's **Born on the 4th of July** (1989) reiterated the message of stolen youth.

During the 1980s, Hollywood attempted, bizarrely, to rewrite the script, in a series of revisionist movies. Richard Gere had made the armed forces hip again in 1982's weepie **An Officer and a Gentleman**; and a year later the first of an intriguing sub-genre of films hit cinemas, in which Americans returned to Vietnam, invariably to rescue MIAs, and "won". **Uncommon Valor** (1983), a rather silly piece about an MIA rescue starring Gene Hackman, kicked things off, closely followed by **Missing in Action** (1983), in which Chuck Norris karate-kicks his way towards the same resolution. The mother of them all, though, was **Rambo: First Blood, Part II** (1985), in which the hero of *First Blood* gets to settle some old scores.

The backlash to the patent nonsense of the revisionist films came in a series of shockingly realistic movies that attempted to reveal the real Vietnam, routine atrocities, indiscipline and all. There are no heroes in these GI's-view movies, only fragile, confused-looking young men in fatigues. In **Platoon** (1986), Oliver Stone, himself a foot-soldier in Vietnam, shows the circumstances under which young American boys became murderers of civilians. It powerfully conjures the paranoiac near-hysteria spawned by fear, confusion, loss of motivation and inability to discriminate between friend and foe. In **Hamburger Hill** (1987), the image of an entire generation stumbling towards the maws of death is strengthened by the fact that the cast includes no big-name actors – the men who fall are neighbours, sons or brothers, not film stars. Stanley Kubrick's **Full Metal Jacket** (1987) picks up this theme of the war's theft of American youth with a brutal drill-sergeant who sets about expunging the soldiers' humanity.

Vietnamese people have mostly been noticeable by their absence from Hollywood films, or have been viewable only through the filter of blatant stereotyping. **Heaven and Earth** (1993), the final part of Oliver Stone's Vietnam trilogy, went some way towards rectifying this imbalance. Its depiction of a Vietnamese girl's odyssey from idyllic early childhood to the traumas of life as a wife in San Diego acts as a timely reminder that not only Americans suffered during the struggle.

Meanwhile, Tran Anh Hung has emerged as Vietnam's pre-eminent domestic film director. **Cyclo** (1996), his grisly tale of murder and prostitution on Vietnam's mean streets, contrasted hugely with **Scent of Green Papaya** (1993), the nostalgic colonial period piece that made his name. Tran Anh Hung's latest film is the critically acclaimed **At the Height of Summer** (2001), set in Hanoi.

Books

Mark Baker *Nam* (Abacus, UK; Berkley, US). Unflinching first-hand accounts of the GI's descent from boot camp into the morass of death, paranoia, exhaustion and tedium.

John Balaban and Nguyen Qui Duc (eds.) *Vietnam: A Traveller's Literary Companion* (Whereabouts Press, UK/US). Entertaining volume of short stories, written by Vietnamese writers based both at home and abroad.

Bao Ninh *The Sorrow of War* (Minerva, UK; Berkley, US). This is a ground-breaking novel, largely due to its portrayal of communist soldiers suffering the same traumas, fear and lost innocence as their American counterparts.

Maria Coffey *Three Moons in Vietnam* (Abacus, UK). Delightfully jolly jaunt around Vietnam by boat, bus and bicycle, in which Coffey conspires to meet more locals in one day than most travellers do in a month.

Duong Thu Huong *Novel Without a Name* (Picador, UK; Penguin, US). A tale of young Vietnamese men seeking glory but finding only loneliness, disillusionment and death, as war abridges youth and curtails loves.

Duong Van Mai Elliot *The Sacred Willow* (OUP). Mai Elliot brings Vietnamese history to life in this compelling account of her family through four generations.

Marguerite Duras *The Lover* (Flamingo, UK; HarperCollins, US). The story of a young French girl's affair with a wealthy Chinese from Cholon depicts a dysfunctional French family in Vietnam and provides an interesting slant on expat life.

Bernard Fall *Hell in a Very Small Place* (Da Capo, UK/US). The classic account of the siege of Dien Bien Phu.

Graham Greene *The Quiet American* (Penguin, UK/US). Greene's prescient and cautionary tale of the dangers of innocence in uncertain times, which second-guessed America's boorish manhandling of Vietnam's political situation, is still the best single account of wartime Vietnam.

Graham Greene *Ways of Escape* (Penguin, UK; Pocket Books, US). Greene's global travels in the 1950s took him to Vietnam for four consecutive winters; the coverage of Vietnam in this slim autobiographical volume is intriguing, but tantalizingly short.

Anthony Grey *Saigon* (Pan, UK; Dell o/p, US). A rip-roaring narrative, whose Vietnamese, French and American protagonists conspire to be present at all defining moments in recent Vietnamese history, from French plantation riots to the fall of Saigon.

Michael Herr *Dispatches* (Pan, UK; Random House, US). Infuriatingly narcissistic at times, Herr's spaced-out narrative still conveys the mud, blood and guts of the American war effort in Vietnam.

Henry Kamm *Dragon Ascending.* Pulitzer prize-winning correspondent Kamm lets the Vietnamese – art dealers, ex-colonels, academics, doctors, authors – speak for themselves in this convincing portrait of contemporary Vietnam.

Stanley Karnow *Vietnam: A History* (Pimlico, UK; Penguin, US). Weighty, august tome that elucidates the entire span of Vietnamese history.

Gabriel Kolko *Vietnam: Anatomy of a Peace* (Routledge, UK). No other recent account of contemporary Vietnam has done a better job of describing the social, political and economic upheavals that the country has suffered over the past few years.

Le Ly Hayslip *When Heaven and Earth Changed Places* (Pan, UK; NAL-Dutton, US). This heart-rending tale of villagers trying to survive in a climate of hatred and distrust is perhaps more valuable than any history book.

Norman Lewis *A Dragon Apparent* (Eland, UK; Hippocrene, US). When in 1950 Lewis made the journey that would inspire his seminal Indochina travelogue, the Vietnam he saw was still a land of longhouses and imperial hunts, though poised for renewed conflict.

Michael Maclear *Vietnam: The Ten Thousand Day War* (Mandarin OP, UK; Avon, US). A detailed yet accessible account of the French and American wars.

Nguyen Du *The Tale of Kieu* (Yale University Press, UK/US). Vietnamese literature reached its zenith with this tale of ill-starred love.

Nguyen Huy Thiep *The General Retires and Other Stories* (Oxford University Press, UK/US). These short stories by Vietnam's pre-eminent writer articulate the lives of ordinary Vietnamese.

Tim O'Brien *The Things They Carried* (Flamingo, UK; Penguin, US). Through a mix of autobiography and fiction O'Brien lays to rest the ghosts of the past in a brutally honest reappraisal of the war.

Robert Olen Butler *A Good Scent from a Strange Mountain* (Minerva, UK; Penguin, US). Pulitzer prize-winning collection of short stories that ponder the struggles of Vietnamese in America to maintain the cultural ley lines linking them with their mother country, and the gulf between them and their Americanized offspring.

John Pilger *Heroes* (Pan, UK). Pilger's systematic dismantling of the myth that America's role was in any way a justifiable "crusade" makes his Vietnam reportage required reading.

Neil Sheehan *A Bright Shining Lie* (Pan, UK; Random House, US). This monumental account of the war, hung around the life of the soldier John Paul Vann, won the Pulitzer Prize for Sheehan; one of the true classics of Vietnam-inspired literature.

Robert Templer *Shadows and Wind* (Little, Brown & Co). This hard-hitting book casts a critical eye over Vietnam's decade of reform, from corruption and censorship to the emergence of a consumer-oriented youth culture.

Justin Wintle *Romancing Vietnam* (Penguin, UK; Pantheon OP, US). Wintle's genial but lightweight yomp upcountry was one of the first of its kind, post-*doi moi*.

Gavin Young *A Wavering Grace* (Penguin, UK). The poignant tale of a Vietnamese family torn apart by the war and its aftermath, as witnessed by this veteran adventurer.

Language

Linguists are uncertain as to the exact roots of Vietnamese, though it betrays Thai, Khmer and Chinese influences. It's tonal, and extremely tricky for Westerners to master – luckily, English has now superseded Russian as the language to learn in Vietnam. The script is Romanized. Vietnam's minority peoples have their own languages, and may not understand standard Vietnamese. For further phrases, try *Vietnamese: A Rough Guide Phrasebook*.

Pronunciation

The Vietnamese language is tonal, that is, one in which a word's meaning is determined by the pitch at which you deliver it. Six tones are used – the mid-level tone (syllables with no marker), the low falling tone (syllables marked `), the low rising tone (syllables marked g), the high broken tone (syllables marked ˜), the high rising tone (syllables marked ´) and the low broken tone (syllables marked.). Depending upon its tone, the word *ba*, for instance, can mean three, grandmother, poisoned food, waste, aunt or any.

Vowels

a	'a' as in father
ă	'u' as in hut (slight 'u' as in unstressed English 'a')
â	'uh' sound as above only longer
e	'e' as in bed
ê	'ay' as in pay
i	'i' as in -ing
o	'o' as in hot
ô	'aw' as in awe
ơ	'ur' as in fur
u	'oo' as in boo
ư	'oo' closest to French 'u'
y	'i' as in -ing

Vowel combinations

ai	'ai' as in Thai
ao	'ao' as in Mao
au	'a-oo'
âu	'oh' as in oh!
ay	'ay' as in hay
ây	'ay-i' (as in 'ay' above but longer)
eo	'eh-ao'
êu	'ay-oo'
iu	'ew' as in few
iêu	'i-yoh'
oa	'wa'
oe	'weh'
ôi	'oy'
ới	'uh-i'
ua	'waw'
uê	'weh'
uô	'waw'
uy	'wee'
ưa	'oo-a'
u.u	'er-oo'
ướí	'oo-uh-i'

Consonants

c	'g'
ch	'j' as in jar
d	'y' as in young
v	'd' as in day
g	'g' as in goat
gh	'g' as in goat
gi	'y' as in young
k	'g' as in goat
kh	'k' as in keep
ng/ngh	'ng' as in sing
nh	'n-y' as in canyon
ph	'f'
q	'g' as in goat
t	'd' as in day
th	't'
tr	'j' as in jar
x	's'

Greetings and basic phrases

How you speak to somebody in Vietnam depends on their sex, and on their age and social standing, relative to your own. As a rule, if you address a man as *ông*, and a woman as *bà*, you are being polite. With someone of about your age, you can use *anh* (for a man) and *chi* (for a woman).

Hello	chào ông/bà
How are you?	ông/bà có khie không?
Fine, thanks	tôi khỏe cám ơn
Pleased to meet you	hân hạnh gặp ông/bà
Goodbye	chào, tạm biệt
Goodnight	chúc ngủ ngon
Excuse me (to say sorry)	xin lỗi
Excuse me (to get past)	xin ông/bà thứ' lỗi
Please	làm ơn
Thank you	cám ơn ông/bà
What's your name?	ông/bà tên gì?
My name is...	tên tôi là...
Do you speak English?	ông/bà biwt nói tiếng Anh không?
I don't understand	tôi không hiểu
Could you repeat that?	xin ông/bà lập lại?
Yes	vâng (north); dH (south)
No	không

Emergencies

Can you help me?	ông/bà có th giúp tôi không?
There's been an accident	có một vụ tai nạn
Please call a doctor	làm ơn gui bác se
hospital	bệnh viện
police station	don cong an

Getting around

Where is the...?	....ở đâu?
How many kilometres is it to...?	bao nhiêu câysố thì đến...?
We'd like to go to...	chúng tôi muốn đi...
To the airport, please	làm ơn vda tôi đi sân bay
Where do we catch the bus to...?	ở vâu vón xe đi...?
When does the bus for Hoi An leave?	khi nào xe Hoi An chạy?
Can I book a seat?	tôi có thể đặt ghw trướ'c không?
How long does it take?	phải tốn bao lâu?
Please stop here	xin dừng lại đây
ticket	vé

aeroplane	máy bay
airport	sân bay
boat	tàu bè
bus	xe buxt
bus station	bwn xe buxt
train station	bwn xe lửa
taxi	tắc xi
car	xe hơi
filling station	trạm xăng
bicycle	xe đạp
bank	nhà băng
post office	sổ bưu đi-n
passport	hộ chiếu
hotel	khách sạn
restaurant	nhà hàng
left/right	bên trái/bên phải
north	phía bắc
south	phía nam
east	phía vông
west	phía tây

Accommodation

Do you have any rooms?	ông/bà có phòng không?
How much is it?	bao nhiêu tiền?
Can I have a look?	xem có được không?
I'd like...	cho tôi xin mot...
Could I have the bill please?	làm ơn tính tiền?
room with a private bathroom	một phòng tắm riêng
cheap/expensive	rẻ/đắt
single room	phòng một ngưai
double room	phòng hai ngưai
air conditioner	máy lạnh
fan (electric)	quạt máy
mosquito net	cái màn
toilet paper	giấy v- sinh
telephone	viện thoại
laundry	quần ào dơ
blanket	chăn (north) mWn (south)
open/closed	mở cửa/vóng cửa

Numbers

For numbers ending in 5, from 15 onwards, *lăm* is used in northern Vietnam and *nhăm* in the south, rather than the written form of *năm*. Also, an alternative for numbers that are multiples of ten is *chục* —-so, ten can be *một chục*, twenty can be *hai chục*, etc.

0	không
1	một
2	hai
3	ba
4	bốn
5	năm
6	sáu
7	bảy
8	tám
9	chín
10	mười
11, 12, 13 etc	mười một, mười hai, mười ba
20	hai mười
21, 22, 23, etc	hai mười một, hai mười hai, hai mười ba
30, 40, 50, etc	ba mười, bốn mười, năm mười
100	mot trăm
200, 300, 400, etc	hai trăm, ba trăm, bốn trăm
1000	mot ngàn
2000	mười ngàn

Time

What's the time?	mấy giờ rời?
noon	buổi trưa
midnight	nửa đêm
minute	phút
hour	giờ
day	ngày
week	tuần
month	tháng
year	năm
today	hôm nay
tomorrow	mai
yesterday	hôm qua
now	bây giờ
morning	buổi sáng
afternoon	buổi chiều
evening	buổi tối
night	ban đêm

11.1

Ho Chi Minh City and around

Washed ashore above the Mekong Delta, some 40km north of the South China Sea, **HO CHI MINH CITY** (HCMC) is a city on the march, a boomtown where the rule of the dollar is absolute. Fuelled by the sweeping economic changes wrought by *doi moi*, this effervescent city, perched on the west bank of the Saigon River, now boasts fine restaurants, immaculate hotels, and glitzy bars among its colonial villas, venerable pagodas and austere, Soviet-style housing blocks. Sadly, HCMC is also full to bursting with people for whom progress hasn't yet translated into food, lodgings and employment, so begging, stealing and prostitution are all facts of life here. **Petty crime** has increased dramatically in the last few years, particularly bag snatching, and care should be taken at all times with personal belongings whilst walking the streets, or travelling on cyclos and motorbikes – especially after dark and around tourist nightspots.

HCMC started life as a fishing village known as Prei Nokor and, during the Angkor period (until the fifteenth century), it flourished as an entrepôt for Cambodian boats pushing down the Mekong River. By the seventeenth century, it boasted a Khmer garrison and a community of Malay, Indian and Chinese traders. During the eighteenth century, Hue's Nguyen dynasty ousted the Khmers, renamed Prei Nokor **Saigon**, and established a temporary capital here between 1772 and 1802, after which the Emperor Gia Long used it as his regional administrative centre. The French seized Saigon in 1861, and a year later the Treaty of Saigon declared the city the capital of French Cochinchina. They set about a huge public works programme, building roads and draining marshlands, but ruled harshly. After a thirty-year war against the French, Saigon was finally designated the capital of the **Republic of South Vietnam** by President Diem in 1955, soon becoming both the nerve-centre of the American war effort, and its R&R capital, with a slough of sleazy bars catering to GIs on leave of duty. The American troops withdrew in 1973, and two years later the Ho Chi Minh Campaign rolled through the gates of the presidential palace and the communists were in control. Within a year, Saigon had been renamed HCMC. Happily, however, the evocative old name lives on: the city's central Distict 1 is invariably referred to as Saigon, and the name is also listed in railway timetables.

Arrival, information and city transport

Tan Son Nhat Airport (☎08/844 3179) is 7km northwest of the city centre. The excellent SASCO Visitors Information and Services Centre near the exit of the international arrivals terminal (daily 6.30am–11.30pm; ☎08/848 6711) stocks free maps and brochures and can assist with information, car rental and hotel reservations. The adjacent currency exchange counter (daily 7am–midnight) can exchange travellers' cheques and arrange cash advances on Visa and MasterCard. ATM machines are

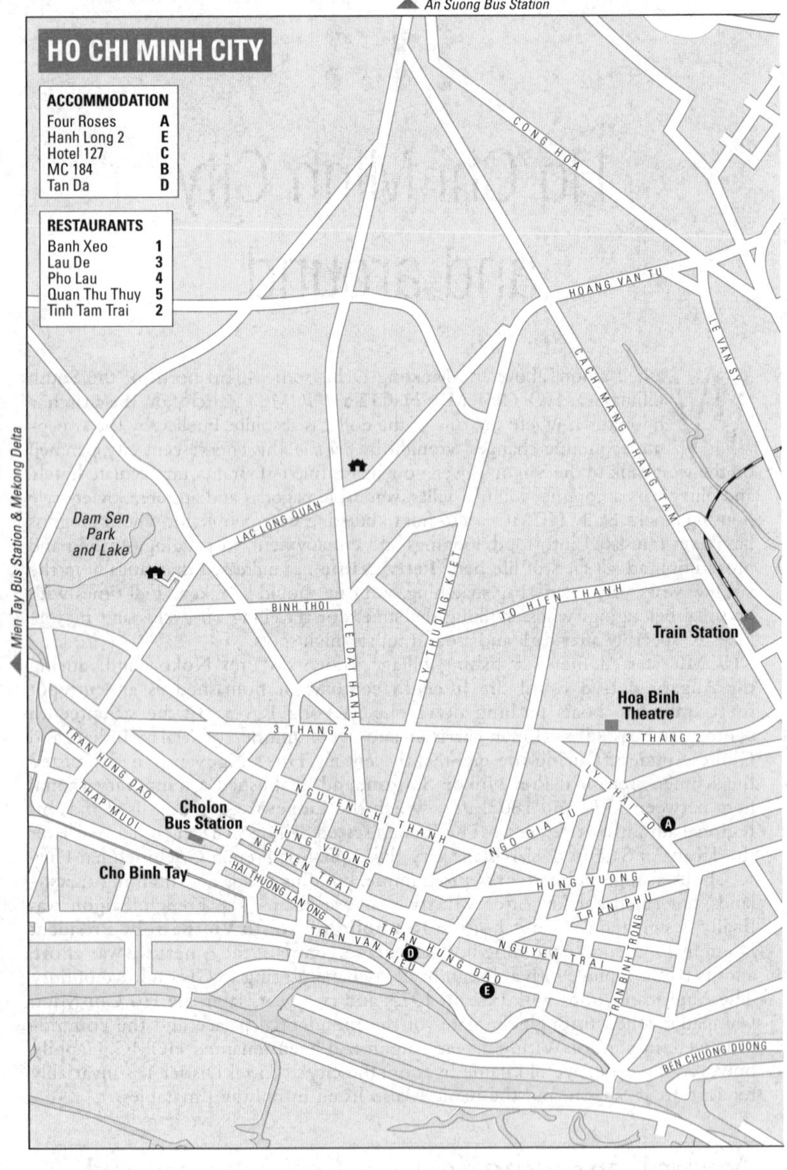

located next to the baggage carousels and inside the domestic terminal. There's also a post office outside the international departures terminal (daily 7.30am–10pm).

Metered Airport and Saigon Taxi **taxis** wait outside both the domestic and international terminals and charge \$4–8 for the journey into the city. Make sure that the meter is on and that the driver is wearing an official name badge, and always insist on being taken to the hotel you've requested; very often, taxis will claim that a hotel

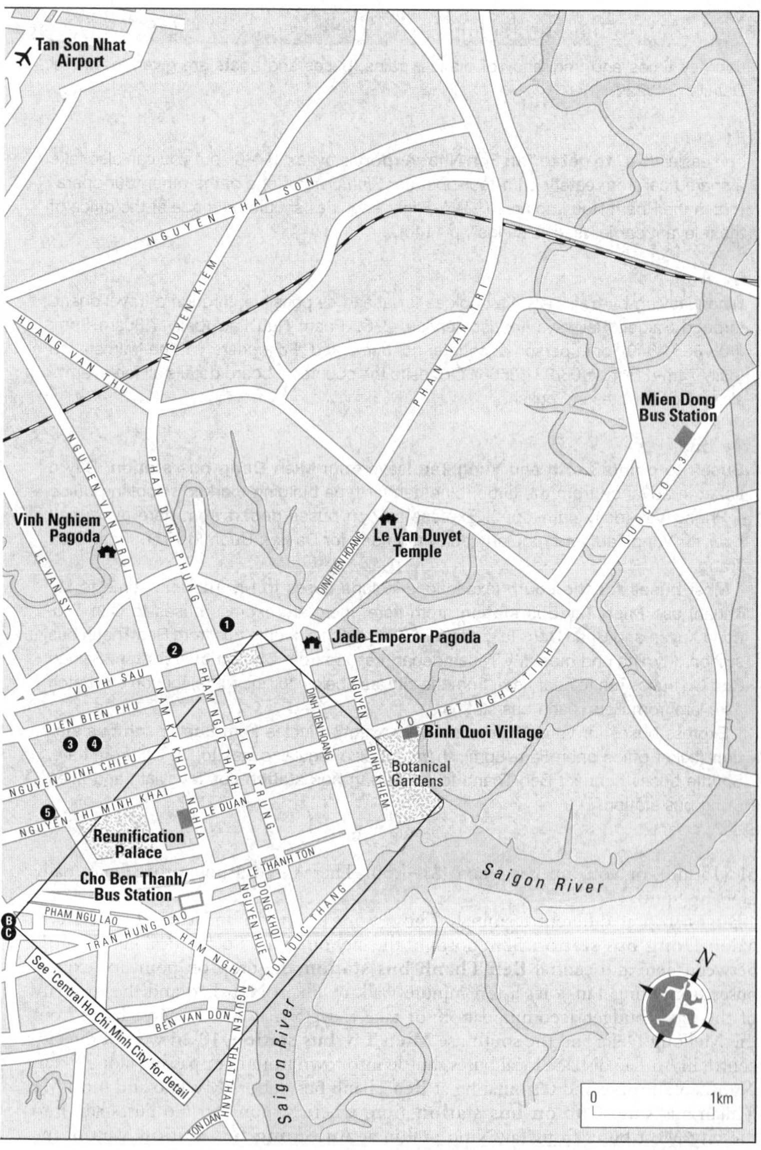

is full or closed and take you to an alternative one for their own commission gain. A cheaper option is to try and gather enough passengers (normally six to eight) to fill a minibus taxi ($2 per person), or you could get a Honda om or cyclo ($2) from outside the airport gates.

Trains from the north pull in at the **train station**, or Ga Saigon, 3km north-west of town at 1 Nguyen Thong. Cyclos will take you to the centre for less than

Moving on from Ho Chi Minh City

Journey times and frequency of planes, trains, buses and boats are given in "Travel Details", p.1229.

By plane

The easiest way **to get to Tan Son Nhat Airport** is by taxi ($4–6), but you can also take a shared car from eatery-cum-tour-operator *Sinh Café* or one of the other tour operators in the Pham Ngu Lao area ($2–5). Flight enquiries should be made at the office of the relevant carrier (see "Listings", p.1140).

By train

When leaving by **train**, always book as far ahead as possible, through a travel agent, through Saigon Railways Tourist Service, 275c Pham Ngu Lao (daily 7.30am–8pm; ⓣ08/836 7640), or in person at counter no. 5 (marked "Foreigners") at the train station (daily 7am–11pm; ⓣ08/931 0666). Opposite the counter, a board details all fares, arrivals and departures in English.

By bus

Buses to points north and **Vung Tau** leave from **Mien Dong bus station**. Buy a ticket in advance from the large, blue hangar-type building marked "Booking office – Phong Ve" (daily 4am–6pm). Express air-con buses depart from here every half hour for Vung Tau, and regularly during the day for Da Lat, Buon Me Thuot and Nha Trang.

Most **buses for the south** (exceptions include buses to My Tho and some to My Thuan) use **Mien Tay bus station**; from here, there are express buses to Can Tho, Long Xuyen and Chau Doc. To get to Mien Tay, catch a shuttle bus from Ben Thanh bus station. My Tho and most My Thuan departures are from **Cholon bus station**. Saigon Star Co buses run to near here, from the city (see below for the route), or you can catch a xe lam from Ben Thanh bus station.

Express buses for Vung Tau depart every twenty minutes from **Ben Thanh bus station** (ticket office open 5am–6pm); there are also regular buses to Cu Chi from here. Shuttle buses connect Ben Thanh to **An Suong bus station** (for Tay Ninh) and Mien Dong bus station.

$1 (15min), or you can get a taxi ($1–1.50). There's also a post office here (daily 6.30am–9pm).

Buses stop at different terminals. Those from the north and Vung Tau arrive at **Mien Dong bus station**, 5km north of the city on Quoc Lo 13; local buses shuttle between here and central **Ben Thanh bus station**, the drop-off point for express buses from Vung Tau – it's a ten-minute walk to Pham Ngu Lao and the majority of the city's budget accommodation; or take a cyclo mai ($2–3). Most buses from the Mekong Delta and the south use **Mien Tay bus station**, 10km west of the city centre in An Lac district; local buses shuttle into town from here, passing along Pham Ngu Lao en route and terminating at Ben Thanh bus station. My Tho and most My Thuan buses use **Cholon bus station**, from where Saigon Star Co buses run into the city. Most buses from Tay Ninh pull in at **An Suong bus station**, west of the airport on Highway 22, and linked by shuttle bus with Ben Thanh bus station; some arrivals from Cu Chi town also end their journeys here, though most continue on to Ben Thanh.

Hydrofoils from Vung Tau dock at the **Passengers Quay of HCMC**, opposite the end of Ham Nghi. Boats from My Tho and Ben Tre generally moor 1.5km south of the Ho Chi Minh Museum, on the corner of **Den Van** and **Ton That Thuyet**; while those from further afield terminate near Cholon's Cho Binh Tay (Binh Tay market), at the junction of Chu Van An and Tran Van Kieu.

Open-tour buses mainly depart from Kim Travel and *Sinh Café* in De Tham (see p.1141) and run to the main tourist destinations such as Da Lat, Nha Trang, Mui Ne, Hoi An, Da Nang, Hue and Hanoi.

By boat

Hydrofoils to Vung Tau (11 daily; 1hr 30min; $10) leave from the **Passengers Quay of HCMC** opposite the end of Ham Nghi. Tickets can be purchased here. Boats for My Tho and Ben Tre generally leave from the mooring on the corner of Den Van and Ton That Thuyet, 1.5km south of the Ho Chi Minh Museum.

Overland travel to Cambodia

At present, the main **overland** entry and exit point between Cambodia and Vietnam for foreigners is at **Moc Bai**, which is northwest of HCMC, the usual overland departure point for this crossing. The **Moc Bai** border is open daily 7am–5pm. *Sinh Café* and Kim Travel (see p.1141) both run daily air-con buses ($6) **to Phnom Penh** from their respective offices in De Tham, departing at 8.45am and arriving at around 5pm. For a higher price but with no change of bus at the border, direct state-run buses for Phnom Penh depart from Saigon Passenger Transport Company, 309 Pham Ngu Lao (daily 8am–5pm; ⓣ08/920 3623), on Tuesdays, Thursdays and Saturdays at 6am, arriving around 2pm in Phnom Penh; tickets ($12) can be purchased here. All bus tickets mentioned can be bought in advance or on the day. Another option is to sign up with a tour operator for a **share taxi** in Pham Ngu Lao ($15–25 for a full car); this will take you as far as the **Moc Bai border crossing**, from where you can walk over the border and negotiate onward transport to Phnom Penh. You'll need a **Cambodian visa** from the consulate at 41 Phung Khac Khoan (ⓣ08/829 2751; $26; 1 days' processing).

There's a second Cambodian border crossing for foreigners at **Vinh Xuong**, 30km north of Chau Doc. Land access is still relatively difficult; however, Saigontourist Travel Service (Delta Adventure Tours), 267 De Tham, HCMC (ⓣ08/920 2110), and the *Victoria Chau Doc Hotel*, 32 Le Loi, Chau Doc (ⓣ076/865010), both operate **boat transfers** from Chau Doc up the Mekong River to Phnom Penh, crossing at the new riverside border point (see pp.126–127 for more details). There's also a third border crossing at **Tinh Bien**, close to Chau Doc.

Information

As with the rest of Vietnam, there is no efficient and impartial tourist information office in HCMC. Your best sources of **information** are the tour agencies and travellers' cafés. They also offer open-tour buses, motorbike and car rental, guide services and day-trips; some also do longer tours and visa services. Popular jaunts include a one-day trip to Tay Ninh's Cao Dai Temple and the Cu Chi tunnels ($5, plus $4 entrance) and one- to five-day tours of the Mekong Delta. For a list of recommended agencies, see "Listings" on p.1141.

Three publications carry **listings** information in and around HCMC; the *Vietnam Economic Times*' ($4.50 monthly) supplement *The Guide*, which can also be purchased separately ($1); the weekly *Vietnam Investment Review's* ($2) *Time Out*, and the monthly *Vietnam Discovery* magazine ($1). A fairly detailed city **map** is available from street hawkers, the post office or from Vietnamtourism and Saigontourist (see p.1105). There's also an English-speaking, state-run information telephone service; dial ⓣ1080 (free).

City transport

With over fifty thousand **cyclos** (three-wheeled cycle-rickshaws) operating in HCMC, hailing one is easy and rates are pretty consistent throughout the city, though you should always agree a price before setting off. Avoid taking cyclos after dark, and take care of your belongings – bag snatchings are common. **Taxis** gather outside the *Rex Hotel* (see p.1134); you can also phone for one of the white Airport Taxis (☎08/844 6666) or yellow Vinataxis (☎08/811 1111). A trip within the city centre will cost around $1; make sure the meter is on when you start your journey. Cheaper colonial-era Peugeots also operate around the city; you can track them down below Cho Ben Thanh, on Pham Ngu Lao and outside the Rex. The two-wheeled motorbike taxis or **Honda om** cost about the same as a cyclo but are faster; again, agree the price first and keep a close grip on your bag during the journey. With all of the above means of transport, the best way to ensure a hassle-free ride is to ask your hotel to recommend a reliable taxi service, cyclo or motorbike driver.

The only time you might use a **city bus** is to get to one of the long-distance bus terminals (see box on pp.1130–1131) or to go to Cholon. Saigon Star Co runs buses to Cholon (daily 5am–10pm), looping between the south side of Mei Linh Square and Huynh Thoai Yen, below Cho Binh Tay. From Pham Ngu Lao, head south to where Bui Vien meets Tran Hung Dao to pick up the service to Cholon; on the return journey, you'll be dropped at the far side of Tran Hung Dao. A small number of **xe lams** – three-wheeler buggies – function as buses around the city. They're slightly less expensive than buses, but crowded. They gather at Ben Thanh bus station, and at the corner of Pham Ngu Lao and Nguyen Thai Hoc.

Most **bike, moped and motorbike rental** operations are around Pham Ngu Lao; average daily costs are under $1 for a bicycle and $5–10 for a moped or medium-sized motorbike. Try the kiosk outside the *Que Huong-Liberty 3 Hotel*, at 187 Pham Ngu Lao; *Hotel 265*, 265 De Tham; or *Huong Mini-Hotel*, 40/19 Bui Vien. Discounts for long-term motorbike rental are offered by *Hotel 211*, 211 Pham Ngu Lao. In the centre, Getrantours, 24 Hai Ba Trung (☎08/829 2366), rents out a wide selection of cars with drivers, motorbikes and mopeds, as does Tuan-Thuat Tourism Service at 23 Ngo Duc Ke (☎0903709589; ask for Mr Tuan); the latter is one of the few operators that rents out larger motorbikes, including 125cc. Bao Viet at 23–25 Thai Van Lung (☎08/825 1500) offers motorbike **insurance**. Pretty much every one of the city's tour operators (see p.1141) can arrange **car rental** plus driver ($20–60 per day); self-drive is not as yet an option for tourists.

Accommodation

HCMC's budget enclave centres on **Pham Ngu Lao**, **Bui Vien** and **De Tham**, 1km west of the city centre, where you'll also find travel agencies, restaurants, bars and Internet cafés. Competition is fierce in this area, and room rates start from $4 for a clean fan room with en-suite bathroom and hot water; for a few dollars more, you can get a bright, air-con room, usually with fridge and satellite TV. The most pleasant and convenient area in which to stay is the region around **Dong Khoi**, which has mid-range as well as top hotels. Staying in **Cholon** leaves you marooned in the bustle of the city's Chinatown, but there are a few bargains and you're away from the travellers' enclave. There shouldn't be any need to book in advance unless you're hitting town around Tet (usually late Jan/mid-Feb).

Pham Ngu Lao and Cho Ben Thanh

Anh Quang 217/12 De Tham ☎08/836 9906. One of several private homes down a Dickensian alleyway between 217 and 219 De Tham, offering a handful of bargain rooms reached via a perilously steep staircase: similar options in nearby alleys include *Beba* (☎08/837 9658) and *Kim Anh* (☎08/836 7375). ❶–❷

Bach Cung 170–172 Nguyen Thai Binh ☎08/821 2777. Gaudy – there's a Christmas tree permanently in the lobby – but comfortable, with negotiable room rates and good facilities, including hot water, fridge and satellite TV. ❹

Hong Kong 22 Bui Vien ☎08/836 4904. Popular and nicely furnished mini-hotel, offering clean, modern rooms, with either fan or a/c; staff will also help with tour bookings. ❸

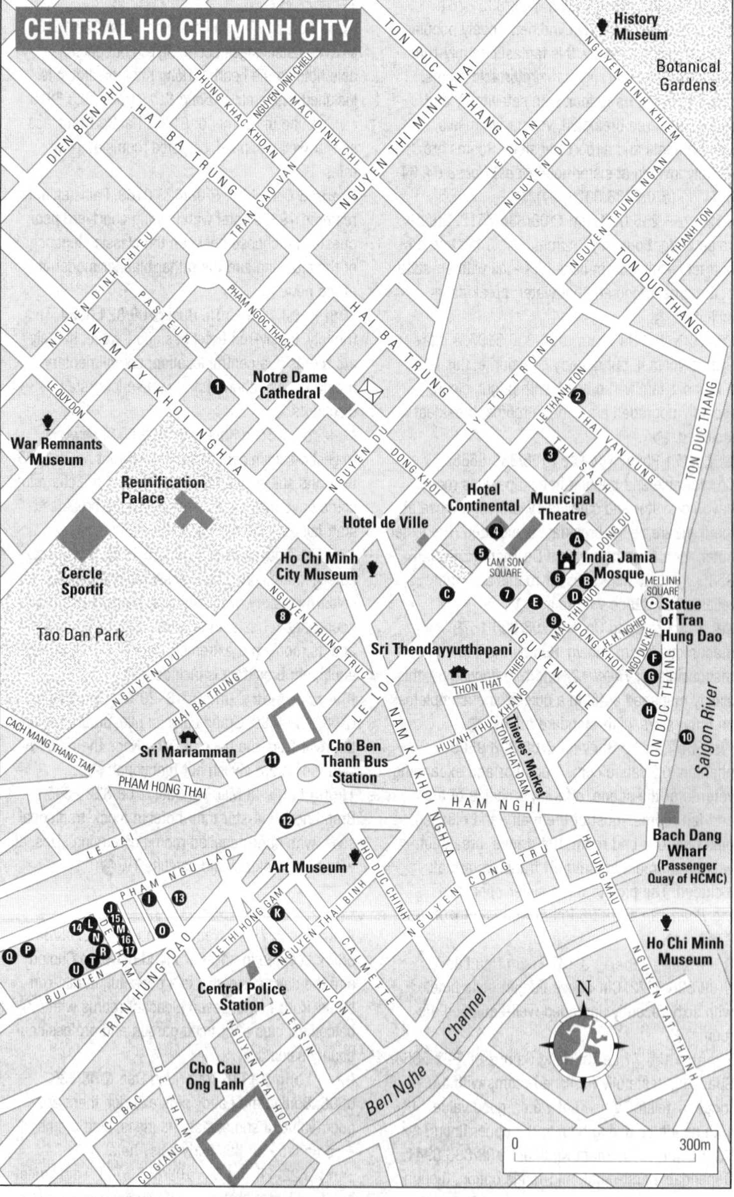

ACCOMMODATION

Anh Quang	R	Hotel 265	N	Que Huong-Liberty 3	J
Bach Cung	S	Lan Anh	M	Rex	C
Bong Sen I	E	Le Le	I	Riverside Hotel Saigon	F
Bong Sen II	A	Linh Hotel	B	Thang Long	D
Guesthouse 64	T	Majestic	H	Thanh Thao	K
Grand	G	Phan Lan	Q	Vien Dong	P
Hong Kong	O	Phuong Lan	U	Vinh Guesthouse	L

RESTAURANTS

Ashoka	2	Lemon Grass	7	Saigon Xua & Nay	8
Bao	13	Pho 2000	11	Sinh Café	17
Cay Xoai	3	Pho Hoa	1	Tan Nam	6
Continental Palace Restaurant	4	Saigon Café	14	Tin Nghia	12
Givral	5	Saigon Floating Restaurant	10	Vietnam House	9
Kim Café	16			Zen	15

Hotel 127 127 Cong Quynh ☎08/836 8761 ⓔguesthouse127@bdvn.vnd.net. Hugely popular and unfailingly friendly, this fantastic family-run guesthouse has a range of comfortable rooms, some sleeping up to four, with satellite TV and fridge, plus free breakfast, vegetarian meals, refreshments and airport transfers. Rooms are equally inviting at sister hotel *Guest House 64*, 64 Bui Vien (☎08/836 5073; ❷). ❸

Hotel 265 265 De Tham ☎08/836 7512. Great-value budget option with immaculate fan and a/c quarters – plus dorm beds ($3) – all with en-suite bathrooms, fridge and hot water; breakfast is included. ❷

Lan Anh 252 De Tham ☎08/836 5197. A relative newcomer, but already a favourite, this is a friendly, family-run hotel, with bright, clean, recently upgraded a/c and fan rooms; breakfast is included. ❷

Le Le 171 Pham Ngu Lao ☎08/836 8686. Comfortable and popular hotel. Spacious rooms have hot water and satellite TV, although those at the front are noisy; breakfast is included. The sister hotel, *Vinh Guesthouse*, 269 De Tham (☎08/836 8585; ❷), has nine cheaper rooms and offers reliable assistance with tours. ❸

MC 184 184 Cong Quynh ☎08/836 1679 madamcuc@hcm.vnn.vn. Run by the same people responsible for *Hotel 127* and *Guesthouse 64*, this slickly managed outfit in a quieter spot completes an impressive, high-standard trilogy. ❹

Phuong Lan 70 Bui Vien ☎08/836 9569 phanlan36@yahoo.com. A popular and expanding veteran of the scene, offering a choice of a/c and fan rooms, most of them airy and pleasant, plus one four-bed room. Hot drinks, breakfast, vegetarian meal and airport transfers are all included. The pick of three sister operations is the *Phan Lan* at 283/6 Pham Ngu Lao (☎08/837 8749; ❷). ❷

Que Huong-Liberty 3 187 Pham Ngu Lao ☎08/836 9522. Cut-above budget-style hotel with sixty recently upgraded well-equipped a/c rooms. ❻

Thanh Thao 71 Le Thi Hong Gam ☎08/822 5664. Sparkling, tastefully furnished rooms with a/c, fridge, satellite TV and hot water; good value, but with no lift it's a long haul to the upper floors. ❹

Vien Dong 275a Pham Ngu Lao ☎08/836 8941. Dependable first-night, mid-range option, though rates are negotiable; all rooms have a/c, fridge, satellite TV and complimentary buffet breakfast. ❻

Dong Khoi and around

Bong Sen I 117–123 Dong Khoi ☎08/829 1516 ⓦwww.hotelbongsen.com. Stylish but personable hotel in the heart of Dong Khoi; breakfast is included. The smaller *Bong Sen II* (☎08/823 5818; ❻), around the corner at 61–63 Hai Ba Trung, has similar well-equipped, carpeted rooms at lower rates. ❼

Grand 8 Dong Khoi ☎08/823 0163. Painstakingly restored 1930s hotel with inviting courtyard pool; guests can choose between the classic elegance of the old wing and the rather blander modernity of the new. ❼

Linh Hotel 16 Mac Thi Buoi ☎08/824 3954. This friendly, family-run hotel has good-value, homely a/c rooms in a central location; complimentary breakfast. Ask about the attractive long-stay discounts. ❹

Majestic 1 Dong Khoi ☎08/829 5514 ⓦwww majestic-saigon.com. Historic riverfront hotel, 1925-built and still oozing character. Rooms are charming, some have river views, and all include breakfast; staff fall over themselves to be helpful. ❾

Rex 141 Nguyen Hue ☎08/829 2185 ⓦwww.rex-hotelvietnam.com. The *Rex* shamelessly milks its colourful history, with ashtrays, slippers and other keepsakes for sale, but the main lobby is stunning and its rooms are extremely comfortable and well equipped; breakfast is included. ❽

Riverside Hotel Saigon 18–20 Ton Duc Thang ☎08/822 4038. Grand colonial pile, proudly eyeing the river from the base of Dong Khoi; the modernized rooms are stylish but functional. ❼

Thang Long 48 Mac Thi Buoi ☎08/822 2595. Brand new one-star mini-hotel in mock-traditional style, with dark-panelled rooms of varying sizes, all with a/c, breakfast and satellite TV. ❹

Cholon and around

Four Roses 790/5 Nguyen Dinh Chieu ☎08/832 5895. Located in no-man's land between Cholon and the city centre, this is a peaceful, family-run home-from-home: seven pleasant rooms with balconies, plus a terraced garden and professional beauty salon. ❸

Hanh Long 2 1115 Tran Hung Dao ☎08/838 0806. Behind the gaudy pink exterior, there are good-value, if somewhat cheerless, tiled rooms – some a/c – in this fairly noisy hotel. ❷

Tan Da 22–24 Tan Da ☎08/855 5711. Fairly quiet hotel, with straightforward if slightly overpriced no-frills fan and a/c rooms. ❷

The City

Ho Chi Minh City is divided into eighteen districts, though tourists rarely travel beyond districts One, Three and Five, unless it's to visit the tunnels at Cu Chi (see p.1141). The city proper hugs the west bank of the Saigon River, and its central area, District One, nestles in the hinge formed by the confluence of the river with the silty Ben Nghe Channel; traditionally the French Quarter of the city, this area is still widely known as **Saigon**. Dong Khoi is its backbone, and around the T-shape it forms along with Le Duan are scattered most of the city's museums and colonial remnants, including the late-nineteenth-century Notre Dame Cathedral, the *Hotel Continental*, once a bastion of French high society, and the ostentatious former Hotel de Ville, which now houses the People's Committee. But, except for **Cholon**, HCMC's frenetic Chinatown, the city doesn't carve up into homogeneous districts, so visitors have to do a dot-to-dot between sights. These are almost invariably places that relate to the American War, such as the **War Remnants Museum**, the **Ho Chi Minh City Museum** and the **Reunification Palace**. But there are many religious sights too, most notably the **Jade Emperor Pagoda**.

The Ho Chi Minh City Museum

Of all the stones of empire thrown up in Vietnam by the French, few are more eye-catching than the former **Gia Long Palace** at 65 Ly Tu Trong, built in 1886 for the governor of Cochinchina. Diem decamped here in 1962, and it was in the tunnels under the building that he spent his last hours of office, before fleeing to the church in Cholon, near which he met his death. Nowadays, it houses the recently overhauled **Ho Chi Minh City Museum** (daily 8am–4pm; 10,000d; ⓦwww.hcmc-museum.edu.vn), one of the city's more user-friendly museums, clearly labelled with English-language signs. The ground floor focuses on archeology and the environment, with exhibits including a thousand-year-old stone *pesari* and various local insect species. There's also a gallery dedicated to the history of HCMC and its ethnic communities, with some interesting photos of early twentieth-century Saigon. Upstairs, the focus turns predictably to anti-French and anti-American resistance in the twentieth century, depicted through photographs, artefacts and displays; there's also a model of the Cu Chi tunnels.

The Reunification Palace

Five minutes' stroll through the parkland northwest of the Ho Chi Minh City Museum, a red flag billows proudly above the **Reunification Palace** (entrance at 135 Nam Ky Khoi Nghia; daily 7.30–11am & 1–4pm; $1 including guided tour), which occupies the site of a colonial mansion erected in 1871 to house the governor-general of Indochina. With the French departure in 1954, Ngo Dinh Diem commandeered this extravagant monument as his presidential palace, but after the February 1962 assassination attempt, the place had to be pulled down. The present building was labelled the Independence Palace in 1966, only to be re-titled the Reunification Hall when the South fell in 1975. Spookily unchanged from its working days, much of the building's interior is a veritable time-capsule of 1960s and 1970s kitsch: pacing its airy rooms, it's as if you've strayed into the arch-criminal's lair in a James Bond movie. Most interesting is the third floor, with its presidential library, projection room and entertainment lounge complete. The basement served as the former command centre and displays archaic radio equipment and vast wall maps.

The War Remnants Museum

One block northwest of the palace, at 28 Vo Van Tan, the **War Remnants Museum** (daily 7.30–11.45am & 1.30–5.15pm; 10,000d; main building under renovation at time of writing) is probably the city's most popular attraction. Its exhibits speak for themselves, a distressing compendium of the horrors of modern warfare. Some of the perpetrators of these horrors are on display in the courtyard outside, including a 28-tonne howitzer, a ghoulish collection of bomb parts, and a renovated Douglas Sky raider plane. A series of halls present a grisly portfolio of photographs of mutilation, napalm burns and torture. One gallery details the effects of the 75 million litres of defoliant sprays dumped across the country, including hideously malformed foetuses preserved in pickling jars; another looks at international opposition to the war as well as the American peace movement. There's also an excellent photographic display entitled "Requiem", which presents war photographs from the countless photojournalists who lost their lives working amidst the French and American wars. The museum rounds off with a grisly mock-up of the tiger cages, the prison cells of Con Son Island.

The History Museum

A pleasing, pagoda-style roof crowns the city's **History Museum** (Mon–Sat 8–11.30am & 1.30–4.30pm, Sun 8.30am–4.30pm; 10,000d), whose main entrance is tucked just inside the gateway to the Botanical Gardens. If you want to visit the museum only, use the side entrance on Nguyen Binh Khiem to avoid paying the extra 8000d for the gardens. The museum houses a train of galleries illuminating Vietnam's past from primitive times to the end of French rule by means of a decent if predictable array of artefacts and pictures. There's also a **water puppetry theatre** ($1), with six shows a day.

Jade Emperor Pagoda

After ten minutes' walk northwest from the Botanical Gardens up Nguyen Binh Khiem, you'll reach the spectacular **Jade Emperor Pagoda** (daily 6am–6pm) on Mai Thi Luu, built by the city's Cantonese community around 1900, and still its most captivating pagoda. If you visit just one temple in town, make it this one, with its exquisite panels of carved gilt woodwork, and its panoply of Taoist and Buddhist deities beneath a roof that groans under the weight of dragons, birds and animals. A statue of the Jade Emperor lords it over the main hall's central altar, sporting impressive moustaches. The Jade Emperor monitors entry into Heaven, and his two keepers – one holding a lamp to light the way for the virtuous, the other wielding an ominous-looking axe – are on hand to aid him. A rickety flight of steps in the chamber to the right of the main hall runs up to a balcony, behind which is set a neon-haloed statue of Quan Am, a female saint in Buddhist tradition, known as Quan Yin in Chinese. Left out of the main hall stands Kim Hua, to whom women pray for children, and in the larger chamber behind you'll find the Chief of Hell alongside ten dark-wood reliefs depicting all sorts of punishments.

Cholon

The dense cluster of streets comprising the Chinese ghetto of **Cholon** is linked to the city centre by five-kilometre-long Tran Hung Dao and best reached by Saigon Star Co bus to Huynh Thoai Yen, on Cholon's western border. The full-tilt mercantile mania here is breathtaking, and from its beehive of stores, goods spill exuberantly out onto the pavements. The ethnic Chinese, or Hoa, first began to settle here around the turn of the nineteenth century and Cholon is now the biggest Hoa community in the country. Residents tended to gravitate towards others from their region of China, and each congregation built its own places of worship and clawed out its own commercial niche – thus the Cantonese handled retailing and groceries, the Teochew dealt in tea and fish, the Fukien were in charge of rice, and so on. By the 1950s, Cholon was also thriving with vice industries, including numerous opium dens or fumeries.

If any one place epitomizes Cholon's vibrant commercialism, it's **Cho Binh Tay** on Thap Muoi Binh Tay, near the bus terminus. The market's corridors are abuzz with stalls offering everything from dried fish and chilli paste to pottery and bonnets. To the north, Tran Chanh Chieu is given over to a poultry market, with cereals and pulses at its eastern end, where you'll also see the slender pink spire of **Cha Tam Church**, though its entrance is on Hoc Lac. It was in this unprepossessing little church that President Ngo Dinh Diem and his brother Ngo Dinh Nhu holed up on November 1, 1963, during the coup that had chased them out of the Gia Long Palace; as they drove into town next morning to surrender, they were both shot dead by ARVN soldiers.

Northeast of the church on tiny Lao Tu, **Quan Am Pagoda** has ridged roofs encrusted with "glove-puppet" figurines and gilt panels at the doorway depicting scenes from traditional Chinese court life. A Pho, the Queen of Heaven, stands in the centre of the main hall, and in the courtyard behind her are two statues of Quan Am. Nearby at 184 Hung Vuong, **Phuoc An Hoi Quan Temple** displays menacing dragons and sea monsters on its roof, and a superb wood carving of jousters and minstrels over the entrance. In the sanctuary sits a blood-red-faced Quan Cong and two attendant storks.

Eating

HCMC offers an extensive scope of culinary options, ranging from streetside stalls to cafés and sophisticated restaurants. Expats, tourists and foreign influences have somewhat fuelled the global choices now available, with a mushrooming number of international establishments; however, flavoursome, good-value Vietnamese cuisine can be found almost everywhere. Where phone numbers are given, it's advisable to book ahead.

Around Pham Ngu Lao

Bao 132 Nguyen Thai Hoc. Popular with locals tucking into grilled goat, rabbit, bird, boar and kangaroo at red-clothed trestle tables. 6am–3am.

Kim Café 268 De Tham. Besides breakfasts, fresh juices and veggie meals galore, there's guacamole, garlic bread, mashed potatoes and a fantastic Malay-style chicken curry (around $2). 7am–2am.

Pho 2000 1–3 Phan Chu Trinh. Next to Ben Cho Thanh. Tuck into big bowls of delicious noodle soup for around $1 at gleaming aluminium tables; there's another branch at 1 Phan Van Dat, near Mei Linh Square. 6am–2am.

Quan Thu Thuy 26 Cach Mang Thang Tam. Banana-leaf parcels of cured pork hang along the frontage of this excellent *nem* specialist, a short walk north of Pham Ngu Lao. 6.30am–10pm.

Saigon Café 195 Pham Ngu Lao. No-nonsense expat hangout with commanding streetside position, good music, beer and excellent menu that runs to Western, Indian and Thai dishes, all at reasonable prices. 6.30am–3am.

Sinh Café 246–248 De Tham. The big daddy of the traveller scene, doling out average but affordable meals in bright surroundings. 6am–11pm.

Tin Nghia 9 Tran Hung Dao. Mushrooms, tofu and homemade soups provide the backbone to the inventive menu in this genial "pure vegetarian" restaurant, established 80 years ago. 7am–2pm & 4–9pm.

Zen 185/30 Pham Ngu Lao. One of the few really authentic eating options along Pham Ngu Lao. Bargain-priced, imaginative veggie dishes including a great Indian and southern Vietnamese range. 6.30am–11pm.

Around Dong Khoi and Thi Sach

Ashoka 17a/10 Le Thanh Ton. Smart Indian restaurant with authentic moghul Indian dishes like *cho cho tikka* (chicken marinated in yoghurt); daily buffet lunches ($6), and free home delivery service (☎08/823 1372). 11am–2pm & 5–10.30pm.

Cay Xoai 15a Thi Sach. One of several charismatic restaurants along this strip, which gets lively by evening; popular with locals, good-value seafood is guaranteed. 10am–10pm.

Continental Palace Restaurant At the *Hotel Continental*, 132–134 Dong Khoi (☎08/825 7679). Stylish restaurant in the hotel's charming courtyard. Imaginative dishes such as braised mudfish in clay pot or deep-fried sweet and sour tiger shrimps, shouldn't cost more than $4; the authentic Italian-cuisine menu groans with lavish pizzas. 6.30am–10.30pm.

Givral 169 Dong Khoi. A HCMC institution, facing the *Hotel Continental*, now restored to its original 1950s style. There's an extensive Western menu and own-recipe cocktails, as well as an adjoining patisserie. 6.30am–11pm.

Lemon Grass 4 Nguyen Thiep (☎08/822 0496). Located off Dong Khoi, this stylish 100-seater restaurant, complete with Mediterranean-style decor, serves highly rated Vietnamese food to the strains of nightly traditional music recitals. Main courses are priced around $3. 11am–2pm & 5–10pm.

Saigon Floating Restaurant Ton Duc Thang. One of four boats offering two-hour dinner cruises along the Saigon River, though these tend to be overrun with tour-groups. Choose between set meals (from $7 a head) or the à la carte menu; departures 6–8.30pm.

Saigon Xua & Nay 33 Nguyen Trung Truc. Welcoming new place serving mid-priced traditional Vietnamese fare, already established as the eatery of choice amongst the local artistic community. 6am–midnight.

Tan Nam 60–62 Dong Du (☎08/829 8634). Top-notch Vietnamese meat dishes and sumptuous seafood hotpots, plus veggie alternatives and set menus ($6–10) in traditional, open-fronted surroundings. 7am–10.30pm.

Vietnam House 93–95 Dong Khoi (☎08/829 1623). Occupying a splendid colonial building, this is a cracking introduction to Vietnamese food, with a pianist on the ground floor or traditional folk music upstairs each night. Set lunches start at $10; otherwise, opt for the $3 "sampler" taken from 100 dishes. 10am–10pm.

Around Dien Bien Phu

Banh Xeo 46a Dinh Cong Trang. Cheap, filling Vietnamese pancakes, stuffed with shrimps, pork, beans and egg at around $1, are the speciality at this streetside place off Hai Ba Trung. 10am–10.30pm.

Lau De 45 Ngo Thoi Nhiem. Goat meat – boiled, fried or barbecued at your table – is the order of the day at this cavernous, dimly lit local restaurant. 8am–10pm.

Pho Hoa 260c Pasteur. Heaving with locals and decorated with striking bamboo murals, this restaurant serves up generous portions of *pho* with big chunks of beef or chicken and piles of fresh greens. 5am–midnight.

Pho Lau Bo Minh 107/P Truong Dinh. *Lau* (steamboat) and *pho* are the staples at this streetside, no-frills restaurant. 6am–11pm.

Tinh Tam Trai 170a Vo Thi Sau. Friendly restaurant dishing up flavoursome, if unidentifiable, vegetables in imaginative combinations. 6am–1pm & 3–9pm.

Nightlife and entertainment

HCMC's **nightlife** is developing rapidly in direct proportion to the number of foreigners hitting town and the growth of a new generation of increasingly affluent and somewhat Westernized Vietnamese youth. The main listings supplements, *Time Out*, *Vietnam Discovery* and *The Guide* (see p.1131), catalogue new venues.

Bars and clubs

The Dong Khoi area is predictably well endowed with **bars** and pubs, while another boozy enclave has developed around Le Thanh Ton, Hai Ba Trung and Thi Sach. Most places shut in the early hours of the morning; take care of your bag when leaving the premises, and be aware, too, that quite a few bars in the centre of town and in the Pham Ngu Lao area have upfront prostitution. A Vietnamese beer at a streetside café won't come to more than 10,000d, but you can multiply that by four in a more upmarket bar. If you can't afford a labelled brew, try a **bia hoi bar**, spit-and-sawdust roadside set-ups where locals glug cheap local beer over ice by the jug-full. Some **clubs** and discos levy a cover charge (normally $2–4) entitling you to your first drink free.

Allez-Boo 187 Pham Ngu Lao. Pham Ngu Lao's largest bar, busy most nights and popular for its good music, award-winning reasonably priced menu (including excellent Thai food) and good selection of cocktails, in traditional bamboo surroundings. 6.30am–midnight.

Apocalypse Now 2c Thi Sach. One of the original Saigon nightspots, attracting travellers, locals and expats with its party atmosphere and eclectic mix of danceable music. Always heaving and sweaty at weekends, though it can be dull during the week. No cover charge. 7pm–late.

GO2 187 De Tham. Fabulously cheesy fifties throwback that's big on rippling neon and dry ice. Vietnamese and Western snacks are served to a soundtrack of forgotten classics. 7pm–midnight.
Long Phi Café 325 Pham Ngu Lao. Stylish, slightly more expensive bar than its neighbours, but relaxing and popular, with Italian food and table footie. 10am–late.
Lost in Saigon 169 Pham Ngu Lao. A long-established faithful, attracting a decent mix of drinkers well into the early hours; pool table and good music. 4pm–late.
O'Briens 74 A2 Hai Ba Trung. Not a world away from an intimate London Irish pub. Deservedly popular with expats and travellers alike, for its cool music, good bar food and pool room.
Saigon–Saigon Bar At the *Caravelle Hotel*, 19 Lam Son Square. Voted the city's best bar by the *Vietnam News*, the stunning views of the city plus nightly live music (8.30–11.30pm) in this elegant and lofty hotel bar compensate for the pricey drinks list. Daily 11am–2am.
Underground Basement, Lucky Plaza, 69 Dong Khoi. A winning blend of international food, live sports coverage, weekly live bands, lunch buffets, Sunday barbeques and an extended daily happy hour (10am–9pm) has made this new bar-restaurant a hit with expats and tourists alike. Open 10am–midnight.
Vasco's 16 Cao Ba Quat. Set in the terraced garden of *Camargue Restaurant*, this stylish bar is quiet during the week, but comes alive on Friday and Saturday nights, when live rock music plays. 6pm–midnight, closed Sun.
Volcano 148 Cong Quynh. For something well out of the ordinary, this cabaret-style nightclub offers plush seating, Vietnamese crooners and a rare chance to glimpse the city's youth at play.

Traditional entertainment

There are regular performances of modern and traditional **Vietnamese music** at 3 Thang 2's Hoa Binh Theatre (☎08/865 5199), as well as traditional theatre and dance. Festivals held at the Le Van Duyet Temple, at the northern end of Dinh Tien Hoang, on the first and eighth days of every lunar month include performances of **Vietnamese opera**. The only real tourist-oriented venue in the city is Binh Quoi Village I & II, (a large riverside resort 2km northwest of the centre at 1147 Xo Viet Nghe Tinh ☎08/899 4104); traditional Vietnamese **cuisine fairs**, with a chance to sample 52 dishes, are held in the lush, coconut-tree gardens of Binh Quoi I (Sat 5–8pm, Sun 11am–2pm & 5–8pm; ☎08/888 3018; $4.70), while Binh Quoi II hosts three weekly open-air **traditional wedding show** performances, plus dinner, combined with a boat cruise from the centre ($30; minimum two persons), organized by Saigontourist (☎08/829 8914). The History Museum on Le Duan, hosts **water puppetry**, with six shows daily (see p.1136).

Shopping

Generally speaking, **shops** open daily 10am to dusk, with some larger stores staying open beyond 8pm. For lacquerware, ceramics and other **handicraft souvenirs**, try Art Arcade at 151 Dong Khoi, Precious Qui at 27–29a Dong Khoi, Bich Lien at 125a Dong Khoi, or Butterfly 26, 26b Le Thanh Ton. Kim Phuong at 77 Le Thanh Ton and 110 Nguyen Hue, Minh Huong at 85 Mac Thi Buoi, or Authentique Boutique at 6 Dong Khoi are all good for **hand-embroidered** household wares and clothes. For **tailoring**, try Albert at 22 Vo Van Tan or Zakka at 134 Pasteur, while for **ao dais** head to Bich Son, 135 Dong Khoi. **Paintings on silk** and **rice paper** can be found at Workshop Hai, 239 and 241 De Tham. Recommended picture galleries are Gallerie Lotus, 55 Dong Khoi, and Vietnam Oil Painting at 158a Dong Khoi. For traditional **musical instruments**, try the shops along Nguyen Thien Thuat. Check out the booths inside the main post office and on Dong Khoi itself for old **coins, stamps**, notes and greetings cards featuring typical Vietnamese scenes. HCMC's best **bookshops** are found on Dong Khoi: seek out Xuan Thu at no. 185 or Bookazine at no. 28 for a large second-hand range; Lao Dong, opposite the Rex at 104 Nguyen Hue, stocks a wide range of magazines and newspapers. Some of the country's best-value **electronics** outlets jostle for attention along Huynh

Thuc Khang. Not far from here, the city's biggest **market** is Cho Ben Thanh, at the junction of Tran Hung Dao, Le Loi and Ham Nghi, where you can find everything from conical hats, basketware bags, Da Lat coffee and Vietnam T-shirts to buckets of eels and heaps of pigs' ears and snouts. Cholon's equivalent is Cho Binh Tay (see p.1134), below Thap Muoi. If you're looking for American and Vietnamese army surplus, try Dan Sinh Market at 336 Nguyen Cong Tru. The spacious courtyard of Vinh Nghiem Pagoda, at 339 Nam Ky Khoi Nghia, turns into a bustling market on religious holidays (see p.1112).

Listings

Airline offices Air France, 130 Dong Khoi ☎08/829 0981; British Airways, 1st Floor, 114a Nguyen Hue ☎08/822 4141; Cathay Pacific, Jardine House, 58 Dong Khoi ☎08/822 3203; China Airlines, 132–134 Dong Khoi ☎08/825 1388; China Southern Airlines, Somerset Chancellor House, 1st Floor, 21–23 Nguyen Thi Minh Khai ☎08/823 5588; Emirates, 1st Floor, 114a Nguyen Hue ☎08/825 6576; Japan Airlines, Sun Wah Tower, Ground Floor, 115 Nguyen Hue ☎08/821 9099; KLM, Saigon Riverside, 2A–4A Ton Duc Thang ☎08/823 1990; Lao Aviation, 93 Pasteur ☎08/822 6990; Lufthansa, 132–134 Dong Khoi ☎08/829 8529; Malaysia Airlines, 132–134 Dong Khoi ☎08/829 2529; Pacific Airlines, 177 Vo Thi Sau ☎08/932 5978; Philippine Airlines, 229 Dong Khoi ☎08/822 2241; Qantas, 1st Floor, 114a Nguyen Hue ☎08/823 8844; Siem Reap Airways, 132–134 Dong Khoi ☎08/823 9288; Singapore Airlines, Saigon Tower, 29 Le Duan ☎08/823 1588; Thai Airways, 65 Nguyen Du ☎08/829 2809; United Airlines, 7th Floor, Jardine House, 58 Dong Khoi ☎08/823 4755; Vietnam Airlines, 116 Nguyen Hue (☎08/832 0320).

Banks and exchange Most banks and exchanges can arrange cash advances on Visa and MasterCard, some on JCB (usual fee is 3–4 percent) and electronic money transfers from abroad. 24hr ATMs can be found at HSBC and ANZ; both accept Cirrus, Plus, Visa and MasterCard and dispense dong only with no charge. HSBC, 235 Dong Khoi, changes cash and travellers' cheques (waiving the fee for HSBC account holders), and there's an adjoining ATM annexe and service desk, which can arrange Visa and MasterCard cash advances (daily 8.30am–noon & 1–4.30pm). Vietcombank's main branch at 29 Chuong Duong (for Visa and MasterCard cash advances) and a second branch at 17 Chuong Duong (for telegraphic transfers) offer good rates for travellers' cheques and cash (Mon–Fri 7.30–11.30am & 1–4pm), as does Vietincombank, 1st Floor, 79a Ham Nghi (Mon–Fri 7.30–11.30am & 1–4.30pm). ANZ, 11 Me Linh Square (Mon–Fri 8.30am–4pm), charges slightly higher rates for travellers' cheques and cash advance. Outside normal banking hours, try the Vietcombank bureaux either inside the *Rex Hotel* lobby (daily 8.30am–7.30pm) or at Fiditourist, 187a Pham Ngu Lao (Mon–Sat 7.30am–8.30pm); the airport exchanges (daily 7am–midnight); or Sacombanks' foreign exchange annexe on the corner of Pham Ngu Lao at 211 Nguyen Thai Hoc (Mon–Fri 7.30–11.30am & 1–4.30pm, Sat 7.30–11.30am; closed Sun).

Embassies and consulates Australia, Landmark Building, 5b Ton Duc Thanh ☎08/829 6035; Cambodia, 41 Phung Khac Khoan ☎08/829 2751; Canada, 235 Dong Khoi ☎08/827 9899; China, 39 Nguyen Thi Minh Khai ☎08/829 2457; India, 49 Tran Quoc Thao ☎08/930 4387; Indonesia, 18 Phung Khac Khoan ☎08/825 1888; Laos, 93 Pasteur ☎08/829 7667; Malaysia, Room 1208, Mei Linh Point Tower, 2 Ngo Duc Ke ☎08/829 9023; New Zealand, 5th Floor, 41 Nguyen Thi Minh Khai ☎08/822 6907; Singapore, Saigon Centre, 65 Le Loi ☎08/822 5173; Thailand, 77 Tran Quoc Thao ☎08/932 7637; UK (and British Council), 25 Le Duan ☎08/823 2604; USA, 4 Le Duan ☎08/822 9433.

Emergencies Dial ☎113 for the police, ☎114 in case of fire or ☎115 for an ambulance; it's advisable to get a Vietnamese-speaker to call on your behalf.

Hospitals and clinics International SOS Clinic, 65 Nguyen Du (☎08/829 8424), has international doctors with consultation fees starting at $80; they also have a dental clinic, can arrange emergency evacuation and have a 24hr emergency service (☎08/829 8520). Columbia Asia, Saigon International Clinic, 8 Alexandre De Rhodes (☎08/823 8455) and 1 No Trang Long, Binh Thanh (☎08/803 0678), have multinational doctors with a 24hr A&E unit, emergency cover and evacuation, charging from $43 for consultations. HCM City Family Medical Practice, Diamond Plaza, 34 Le Duan (☎08/822 7848), is an international clinic with multinational doctors, a dental surgery and a specialist knowledge in vaccinations, as well as 24hr emergency cover and evacuation (☎091234911); consultations start at $50 ($85 after office hours). International Medical Centre, 1 Han Thuyen (☎08/827 2366), is a French-run, non-profit 24hr hospitalization centre with inpatient wards, intensive care and emergency surgery; general consultations start at $40, with profits subsidizing heart operations for underprivileged children. Cholon's Cho Ray Hospital, at 201 Nguyen Chi Thanh (☎08/855 8074), has an outpatients' room for foreigners ($3.60 per consultation) and a foreigners' ward ($27 per night). Grand Dentistry, Ground Floor, Sun Wah Tower, 115 Nguyen Hue (☎08/821 9446), is an international-standard dental clinic; basic check-ups start from $30; 24hr emergency line ☎090 364 7156.

Immigration For re-entry visas: the Ministry of the Interior, 254 Nguyen Trai, at the junction with Nguyen Cu Trinh. For extension visas: Immigration of HCMC, 161 Nguyen Du.

Internet and computer access Many hotels have business centres, and there are countless Internet outlets around De Tham and Pham Ngu Lao; Internet rates are currently 100–300d per minute. Try Dai Ly Internet at 177 & 220 De Tham (email rate 150d/min, use of printer 1000d/page, use of scanner 2000d/page), or FPT Internet, 239 Pham Ngu Lao (email 100d/min, printer and scanner 1000 and 3000d/page respectively). CyberCafe Saigon, 232 De Tham, charges 100d per minute and has Internet phone to all countries. Cheapest Internet access in the area is downstairs at the *Phi Long Hotel*, 38 Bui Vien (4000d/hr). Downtown, try CyberCafe, 48 Dong Du, an a/c business centre; email is 300d per minute and hourly computer rates are 9000d, including use of colour printer, fax and scanner.

Pharmacies There are several around Pham Ngu Lao area, including 214 De Tham and 81 Bui Vien. Downtown, there are pharmacies at 197–199 Dong Khoi, 199 and 205 Hai Ba Trung and 14a Nguyen Dinh Chieu.

Post offices The main post office (daily 6.30am–9.30pm) is beside the cathedral at the head of Dong Khoi. Poste restante is held here, and incoming faxes are accepted both here (☎08/822 5662) and at nearby 230 Hai Ba Trung (☎08/829 8540); there's a 2200d pick-up fee for first page, 1100d for each remaining page. International parcel dispatch is located behind the main post office at 117 Hai Ba Trung; parcels are received next door at no. 119 – bring your passport and 3000d for the customs fee (Mon–Fri 7am–7pm; Sat & Sun 7.30am–4.30pm). There are also post offices at 303 Pham Ngu Lao, at 156 Cong Quynh (with poste restante), and at Ga Saigon train station.

Telephone services There are IDD, fax and telex facilities at the post office and numerous IDD telephone kiosks around De Tham and Pham Ngu Lao, plus IDD facilities at most hotels.

Travel agencies Ann Tours, 58 Ton That Tung ☎08/833 4356; Cam On Tours, Unit 63, 6th Floor, 7 Phung Khac Khoan ☎08/825 6074; Fiditourist, 195 Pham Ngu Lao ☎08/836 1922; Kim Travel, 270 De Tham ☎08/836 9859; New Indochina (STA Travel branch), 4/F Yoco Building, 41 Nguyen Thi Minh Khai ☎08/822 7904; Saigontourist Travel Service (Delta Adventure Tours), 267 De Tham ☎08/920 2110; *Sinh Café*, 246–248 De Tham ☎08/836 7338; Sinhbalo, 43 Bui Vien ☎08/836 7682. Larger, more upmarket outfits include Exotissimo Travel, Saigon Trade Centre, 37 Ton Duc Thang ☎08/825 1723; Saigontourist, 49 Le Thanh Ton ☎08/829 8914; and Vietnamtourism, Room 303, Mondial Centre, 203 Dong Khoi (☎08/824 2000) & 234 Nam Ky Khoi Nghia (☎08/829 2442).

Around Ho Chi Minh City

The single most popular trip out of the city takes in two ofVietnam's most memorable sights: the **Cu Chi tunnels**, for twenty years a bolt hole, first for Viet Minh agents, and later for Vietcong cadres; and the weird and wonderful **Cao Dai Holy See** at Tay Ninh, the fulcrum of the country's most charismatic indigenous religion. Most HCMC travel agents combine these two sights, with tours costing $5 (not including entrance to the tunnels).

The Cu Chi tunnels

During the American War, the villages around the district of Cu Chi supported a substantial Vietcong (VC) presence. Faced with American attempts to neutralize them, they quite literally dug themselves out of harm's way, and the legendary **Cu**

Chi tunnels were the result. Today, the tunnels have been widened to allow passage for Western tourists, but it's still a dark, sweaty, claustrophobic experience. The most popular site is **Ben Dinh** (daily 7.30am–5pm; $4), 40km from HCMC and best visited on a tour, but also accessible by bus from **Ben Thanh bus station** in HCMC. Buses stop in **CU CHI**, from where you'll need to take a Honda om for the final 10km to the site ($1.50); on a motorbike, turn right off the highway when you reach Cu Chi post office.

Anti-colonial Viet Minh dug the first **tunnels** here in the late 1940s, and over a decade later VC activists controlling this staunchly anti-government area went to ground. By 1965, 250km of tunnels crisscrossed Cu Chi and surrounding areas. Tunnels could be as small as 80cm wide and 80cm high, and were sometimes four levels deep; there were latrines, wells, meeting rooms and dorms here, as well as rudimentary hospitals, where operations were carried out by torchlight using instruments fashioned from shards of ordnance. At times it was necessary to stay below ground for weeks on end: inhabitants often had to lie on the floor in order to get enough oxygen to breathe. American attempts to flush out the tunnels proved ineffective. They evacuated villagers into strategic hamlets and then used defoliant sprays and bulldozers to rob the VC of cover, in "scorched earth" operations. GIs known as tunnel rats would go down themselves, but faced booby traps and bombs. Finally, they sent in the B52s to level the district with carpet-bombing.

The Cao Dai Holy See at Tay Ninh

Northwest of Cu Chi, signed 10km off Highway 22 at **Tay Ninh**, a grand gateway marks the entrance to the grounds of the fantastical confection of styles that is **Cao Dai Cathedral**; buses to Tay Ninh depart from HCMC's An Suong bus station, but tours are preferable. The cathedral is the Holy See of the Cao Dai religion, a faith that was founded in October 1926 as a fusion of oriental and occidental religions, propounding the concept of a universal god. Cao Daism borrowed the structure and terminology of the Catholic Church, but is primarily entrenched in Buddhism, Taoism and Confucianism. By following its five commandments, Cao Daists look to hasten the evolution of the soul through reincarnation. Tay Ninh became the Cao Daists' Holy See in 1927, and the first pope was Le Van Trung, a reformed mandarin from Cholon.

The cathedral's central portico is topped by a bowed, first-floor balcony and a Divine Eye, the most recurrent motif in the building. A figure in semi-relief emerges from the towers to either side: on the left is Cao Daism's first female cardinal, Lam Huong Thanh, and on the right, Le Van Trung. Men enter the cathedral through an entrance in the right wall, women by a door to the left, and all must take off their shoes. The eclectic ideology of Cao Daism is mirrored in the **interior**, and tourists are welcome to wander through the nave, as long as they remain in the aisles, and don't stray between the rows of pink pillars, entwined by green dragons, that march up the chamber. The papal chair stands at the head of the chamber, its arms carved into dragons. Dominating the chamber, though, and guarded by eight scary silver dragons, a vast, duck-egg-blue sphere, speckled with stars, rests on a polished, eight-sided dais. The ubiquitous Divine Eye peers through clouds painted on the front. **Services** are held daily at 6am, noon, 6pm and midnight and are well worth attending. A traditional band plays as robed worshippers chant, pray and sing.

11.2

The Mekong Delta

The orchards, paddy-fields and swamplands of the **Mekong Delta** stretch from Ho Chi Minh's city limits southwest to the Gulf of Thailand, criss-crossed by nine tributaries of the Mekong River. By the time it reaches Vietnam, the mighty Mekong has already covered more than 4000km from its source high up on the Tibetan Plateau, via southern China, Burma, Laos, Thailand and Cambodia – a journey that ranks it as Asia's third-longest river, after the Yangtse and Yellow rivers. Here at its delta, not only does it water "Vietnam's rice bowl", but it also serves as a crucial transportation artery, teeming with rowing boats, sampans, ferries and floating markets. In fact, the most enjoyable way to experience delta life is by boat: most people hire boats in **My Tho**, but from here a ferry traverses the uppermost strand of the Tien Giang to laid-back **Ben Tre**. You can cross the main body of the Tien Giang on the spectacular My Thuan Bridge, convenient for visiting the flower markets of **Sa Dec** and bustling **Vinh Long**, which are situated on the "island" between Tien Giang and Hau Giang. **Can Tho**, on the west bank of the Hau Giang, holds the delta's most famous floating markets; access to the city is by ferry until the much-anticipated Can Tho Bridge is finally completed. From here, a road runs via **Long Xuyen** to the Cambodian border towns of **Chau Doc** and **Ha Tien**. It's now possible for foreigners to cross into Cambodia near Chau Doc at **Vinh Xuong**, most conveniently by organized boat transfer (see p.1131); another border crossing is also open at nearby **Tinh Bien**.

My Tho

Seventy kilometres southwest of HCMC, **MY THO** sits on the north bank of Tien Giang, the Mekong River's northernmost strand, and attracts crowds of tourists because of its boat trips. The city is ringed by waterways, and the main tourist-oriented hotels, businesses and restaurants can be found on the waterfront streets of **30 Thang 4**, which runs east–west along the town's southern edge, and **Trung Trac**, running northeast–southwest, round the corner from 30 Thang 4, along the west bank of Bao Dinh canal. Most restaurants are located along Trung Trac, which has recently benefited from extensive waterside renovations, and **Tet Mau Than**, which runs northwards alongside a redeveloped canal off Le Thi Hong Gam west of town. The lower of the two bridges spanning Bao Dinh canal deposits you at the start of waterfront Phan Thanh Gian, home to My Tho's modest **Chinese quarter**, where shop fronts are piled to the rafters with sugarcane poles, watermelons and fish awaiting transportation up to HCMC. A cyclo journey east of Phan Thanh Gian, Nguyen Trung Truc's attractive **Vinh Trang Pagoda** (daily 7am–noon & 2–5pm), with its Rajah's palace-style front facade, has become rather a tourist trap. It's said that VC soldiers hid here in the 1960s, but today it's home only to monks. The main chamber has formidable dark-wood pillars and tons of gilt woodwork, and the pagoda boasts classical pillars, Grecian-style mouldings and glazed tiles.

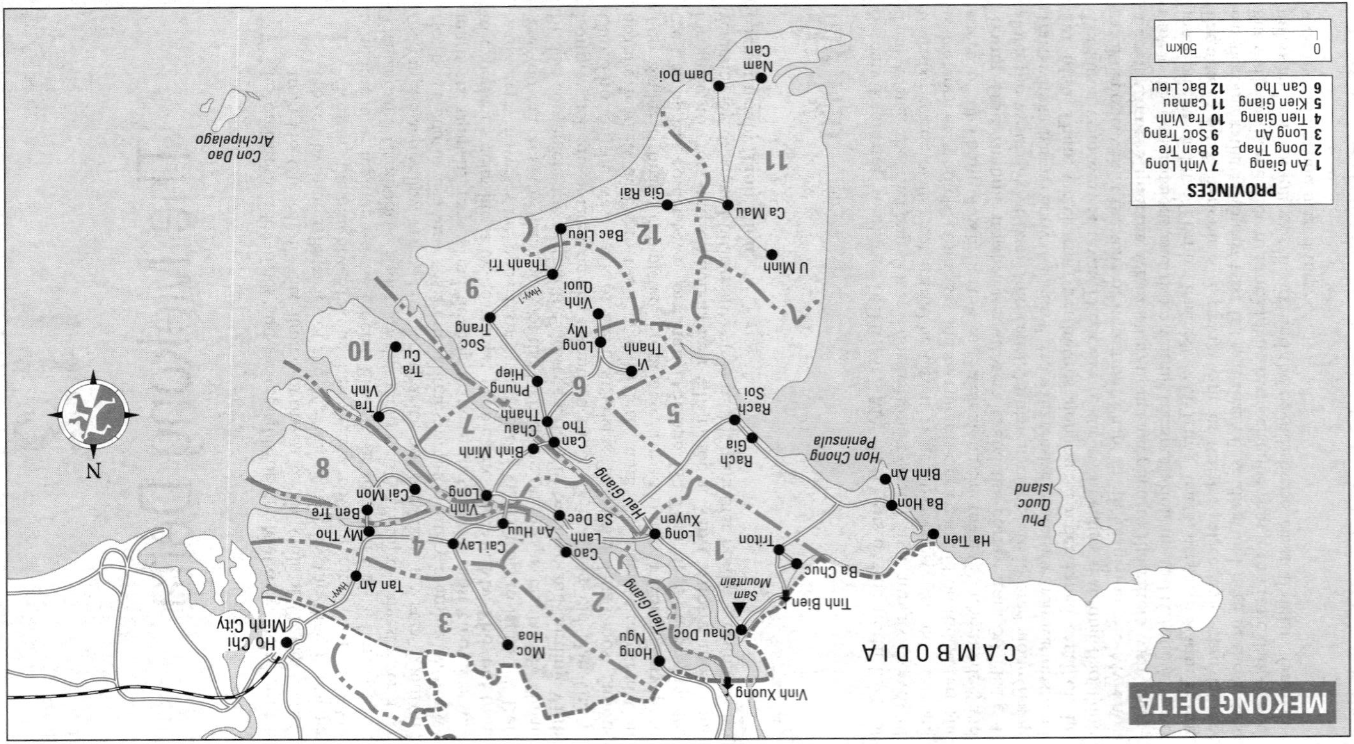

MEKONG DELTA

CAMBODIA
Vinh Xuong
Chau Doc
Hong Ngu
Moc Hoa
Ho Chi Minh City
Tinh Bien
Sam Mountain
Tien Giang
Ba Chuc
Triton
Ha Tien
Phu Quoc Island
Ba Hon
Binh An
Hon Chong Peninsula
Long Xuyen
Cao Lanh
Sa Dec
An Huu
Cai Lay
Tan An
Hwy-1
My Tho
Ben Tre
Cai Mon
Vinh Long
Hau Giang
Rach Gia
Rach Soi
Can Tho
Binh Minh
Chau Thanh
Phung Hiep
Tra Vinh
Tra Cu
Vi Thanh
Long My
Vinh Quoi
Soc Trang
Thanh Tri
Bac Lieu
U Minh
Ca Mau
Gia Rai
Nam Can
Dam Doi
Con Dao Archipelago
N

PROVINCES

1 An Giang
2 Dong Thap
3 Long An
4 Tien Giang
5 Kien Giang
6 Can Tho
7 Vinh Long
8 Ben Tre
9 Soc Trang
10 Tra Vinh
11 Camau
12 Bac Lieu

0 50km

Boat trips on the delta

Taking a **boat trip** on the Mekong is the undoubted highlight of a stay in My Tho. Of the four nearby islands, Tan Long, Phung Island and Thoi Son are all regularly visited by tourist boats, though you'll get more time on the water if you ask to explore the labyrinthine north coastline of Ben Tre province, or just to idle along the river – in which case the **Dong Tam snake farm** (daily 7am–4.45pm; $1) provides an interesting enough focus. Whatever you do, it's worth making an early start to catch the river at its mistiest. Beyond its chaotic shoreline of stilthouses and boat-yards, **Tan Long** ("Dragon Island") boasts bounteous sapodilla, coconut and banana plantations. **Phung Island** (daily 7am–5pm) is famed as the home of an offbeat religious sect set up three decades ago by the eccentric Coconut Monk, Ong Dao Dua, but only the skeleton of the open-air complex he established remains. Beyond the compound stretch acres of orchards, whose fruits can be sampled at the several cafés dotted around the island. **Thoi Son** ("Unicorn Island") is the largest of the four islands and most tours out of HCMC stop here for lunch. Slender canals, their banks shaded by water coconut trees, allow boats to weave through its interior.

The cheapest way of getting onto the water is to take a **public ferry** to one of the islands. For Phung Island, you'll need to get across to Ben Tre by public ferry from the **Ben Tre ferry terminal** (Ben Pha Rach Mieu; 24hr), 300m west of Cho Vong Nho, and from there take another boat to the island. Ferries to Tan Long depart from Trung Trac; Thoi Son ferries leave from either Vong Nho or Binh Duc markets.

However, for a full-on tropical river experience, you should **charter** a boat. Tien Giang Tourist Company, at no. 8, 30 Thang 4 (☎073/873184), and Ben Tre Tourist Company, 2km west of the centre at 4/1 Le Thi Hong Gam (☎073/879103), both offer boat trips to the islands, but touts for private companies will undercut them, offering three-hour trips for $5–10.

Practicalities

Buses terminate at Tien Giang bus station, 3km northwest of town, from where cyclos shuttle into the centre. For onward travel to HCMC or Vinh Long, make your way to Nga Ba Trung Luong roundabout a few kilometres out of town, where you can easily flag down buses passing in either direction along the highway. The local bus to Vinh Long, for example, takes two hours and costs $3. Tourist boats for the islands leave either from the small jetty at the corner of the southern end of Le Loi and 30 Thang 4, or at Tien Giang Tourist (see above). Cargo/passenger **boats** heading to Tan Chau (for Chau Doc), stopping en route at My Thuan (for Vinh Long) use the jetty below Cho Vong Nho, 200m west of the foot of Tran Hung Dao (1 daily, between 11am and noon). Vietnam Airlines (☎073/872006) can organize flights out of HCMC; there's a branch next to Tien Giang Tourist.

Cyclos are plentiful, and Honda oms await custom at the junction of Trung Trac and Thu Khoa Huan. **Bicycles** can be rented (20,000d) from the *Rang Dong Hotel*, and a car plus driver is available from either Tien Giang Tourist or the *Cong Duan Hotel* along the waterfront on 30 Thang 4. The **State Bank**, 15b Nam Ky Khoi Nghia, at Thu Khoa Huan's western end, changes travellers' cheques and advances cash against Visa and MasterCard; the Agribank on the corner of Le Loi and Thu Khoa Huan changes dollars. **Internet** facilities are found at Vinh Tan Computer, 203 Le Dai Hanh.

The best budget **accommodation** options are the *Cong Doan Hotel*, beside the post office on the waterfront on 30 Thang 4 (☎073/874324; ❷), which has spartan but light double rooms with both fan and air-con, and the *Rang Dong*, 300m west along the street at no. 25 (☎073/874400; ❷), with slightly smarter rooms, all with air-con. The *Song Tien*, conveniently located by the river at 101 Trung Trac, (☎073/872009; ❷), is another sound budget choice with 36 clean, unfussy rooms. The smartest place in town, boasting an impressive riverside location, is the relatively new *Chuong Duong* on 30 Thang 4, opposite the post office at no. 10 (☎073/870875; ❹).

The best **eating** option in My Tho is the *Chi Thanh*, 279 Tet Mau Than, where the well-cooked Vietnamese **food** and bright, clean surroundings draw nightly crowds. Further along at no. 141b, *Quan Bia Hai Xuan* serves reasonable dishes and *bia tuoi* in a pleasant, leafy courtyard area. Along the riverfront, the tourist restaurant at no. 8 30 Thang 4 has decent Vietnamese fare, while the more formal restaurant at the *Chuong Duong Hotel* has a reasonably priced, extensive menu specializing in seafood; unfortunately, the riverside open-air dining terrace is now encased in glass.

Ben Tre and Cai Mon

The few travellers who push on beyond My Tho into riverlocked **Ben Tre province** – nearly all of whom do so as part of organized tours – are rewarded with breathtaking scenery of fruit orchards and coconut groves. Ben Tre town itself is a pleasant place, a world away from touristy My Tho. **Ferries** from My Tho disgorge their passengers at Ben Tre's Hongvan port, 1km north of the town centre, following the forty-minute trip; a Honda loi or Honda om will take you into town in around ten minutes. Buses either terminate at the bus station 2km out of town, or nearer the centre at Truc Giang Lake. Near here, at 65 Dong Khoi, Ben Tre Tourism (ⓣ075/829618) can help with **tours**.

Once you've scanned Ben Tre's buzzing **market** in the centre of town, you'll want to pass over the quaint bridge leading to Ben Tre River's more rustic south bank, where scores of boats moor in front of thatch houses. With a bicycle (bring one from My Tho, or ask at your hotel), you can explore the maze of dirt tracks and visit the riverside **wine factory**, 450m west of the bridge, where *ruou trang* (rice wine) fizzes away in earthenware jars.

Honda oms congregate outside the post office in the centre of Ben Tre, and for $5 they'll whisk you off on a three-hour round-trip to the fruit orchards of **CAI MON**. Ten minutes' ride west of town you cross a river on the Ham Luong ferry, then head off into waxy green paddy-fields to the coconut village of Ba Vat (20min). Twenty-five minutes later, the road reaches Cai Mon, a sleepy community whose residents make a living by cultivating fruit in the vast plain of orchards, veined by miles of canals and paths.

The all-new riverside *Hung Vuong* (ⓣ075/822408; ❸) has spotlessly clean rooms, all with satellite TV, bathtub and hot water, and the best location of Ben Tre's **hotels**; *Ben Tre* (ⓣ075/822223; ❺) has a dozen slightly overpriced air-con rooms and is at the wrong end of town, at 8/2 Tran Quoc Tuan. The *Thao Nhi Guest House*, located north of town near the Tien Giang River (ⓣ075/860009; ❷), has six basic fan and air-con rooms set amongst quiet fruit gardens; to get there, turn left immediately after leaving the ferry terminal and continue parallel to the river for about 500m until you see a sign for the guesthouse on the right. The *Ben Tre Floating Restaurant*, near the bridge, is unmissable, painted in shocking pink; it's a good spot for a sunset drink, with a reasonably priced menu, and is more enticing than the hotel restaurants.

Vinh Long

Ringed by water and besieged by boats and tumbledown stilthouses, the island that forms the heart of **VINH LONG** has the feel of a medieval fortress. Waterfront hotels, restaurants and cafés conjure up a riviera atmosphere far quainter and more genuine than My Tho's, and make a great spot to idly watch life on the Co Chien River roll by. There's not much else to see in town, aside from a few war relics and a handful of colonial buildings, but the chief attraction is the trip to An Binh Island.

An Binh Island

A five-minute ferry ride across the Co Chien River from the top of town accesses a patch of the delta's most breathtaking scenery. Known by locals as **An Binh Island**, it is in fact a jigsaw of bite-sized pockets of land, skeined by a fine web of channels and criss-crossed by dirt paths, making it ideal for a morning's rambling; a sealed road now dissects the island. A grove of longan trees a few paces north of the jetty shades sandy, century-old **Tien Chau Pagoda**. Inside, monks sup tea against the ghoulish backdrop of a mural depicting sinners being trampled by horses and devoured by snakes in the ten Buddhist hells. As an alternative to following the island's narrow tracks and single-log bridges, you could rent a **boat** out of Vinh Long. Cuu Long Tourist (daily 7am–5pm; ⓣ070/823616) at the top of 1 Thang 5 can arrange home-stays on the island as well as leisurely **boat trips** on the Co Chien River costing upwards of $10. The boat-owners themselves charge less and can be contacted on the waterfront; theoretically, they're not supposed to take tourists, but their boats usually set off from the back of the market on 1 Thang 5. With a vessel at your disposal, it's also possible to tootle along the river or, provided you set out early enough, head upriver to the floating market at Cai Be (5am–2pm).

Practicalities

Long-distance **buses**, including those from My Tho, pull in to the provincial bus station, 2km southwest of Vinh Long on Nguyen Hue; from here, take a xe om into the centre of town. If you're coming from Can Tho, buses can drop you off near the three-way roundabout at the northern end of Nguyen Hue, about 800m west of the centre, as they pass through here en route. Buses from Sa Dec and Long Xuyen bypass Vinh Long completely, crossing over the My Thuan Bridge, 7km west of Vinh Long, so you'll need to arrange with your driver a convenient point from where Honda oms can take you into town. If you're coming from Ben Tre, you'll need to take a ferry from An Binh Island, which will drop you 3km east of central Vinh Long.

Moving on, you'll need to head for the bus station, or you can flag down buses bound for Can Tho or HCMC at the three-way roundabout. Alternatively, express minibuses run to HCMC ($2.50) from 166a Nguyen Hue, near the bus station (ⓣ070/824634), or Phu Vinh Long Bus Company (ⓣ070/824634) can arrange hotel pick-ups. If you're heading for My Tho, take a HCMC-bound bus and ask the driver to drop you off at the Nga Ba Trung Luong roundabout, a few kilometres out of My Tho.

Most of Vinh Long's **accommodation** options are near the waterfront 1 Thang 5: the riverside *Cuu Long 'A' Hotel* (ⓣ070/822494; ❹) has overpriced but homely rooms, some with balcony overlooking the river, whilst opposite the *Phuong Thuy Floating Restaurant*, the smart *Cuu Long 'B'* (ⓣ070/823656; ❻) has well-appointed rooms, also with fine views of the Vinh Long Riviera. The best deal in town, however, is the *Phuong Hoang Mini-hotel*, behind the market on Hung Vuong (ⓣ070/825185; ❷), which boasts immaculate, sparkling rooms all with air-con, fridge and hot water. For **food**, head east of the market along 30 Thang 4 to 2 Thang 9, which has plenty of eating options, including the *Lan Que* and the *Tiem Com Tu Hai* across the road, both serving a good range of Vietnamese dishes. The *com* restaurant by the three-way roundabout at 210 Le Thai To, serves cheap and tasty rice, noodles and *bun bo Hue* dishes. Directly opposite, the Incombank changes travellers' cheques and can arrange cash advances against Visa and MasterCard; for straight US **currency** transactions, its Hoang Thai Hieu branch is more central. There's **Internet** access for 500d per minute at the Mekong Queen Bar, next to the *Cuu Long 'B'*; DELTA Internet next to the Phuong Hoang has a much cheaper hourly rate of 3000d.

Sa Dec

A cluster of brick and tile kilns announces your arrival in the charming town of **SA DEC**, 20km upriver of Vinh Long. French novelist Marguerite Duras lived here as a child, and the town's stuccoed shop-houses, riverside mansions and remarkably busy stretch of the Mekong provided the backdrop for the movie adaptation of her novel *The Lover*.

Buses terminate 300m southeast of the town centre: turn left out of the station and continue westwards along Nguyen Sinh Sac. Just across the bridge, the town's three main arteries – Nguyen Hue, Tran Hung Dao and Hung Vuong – branch off to your right, along Nguyen Sinh Sac. Duck straight down into Nguyen Hue to find Sa Dec's extensive riverside market. Halfway up the street, behind the market stalls, ferries cross to the childhood **home of Marguerite Duras**, a crumbling old colonial villa (now a police station) that's the nearest of the two villas to the place where boats drop you.

Across the metal bridge that runs above the top of Nguyen Hue and over the river, climb down the steps to your left and follow the river road west and past Sa Dec's Cao Dai temple: after 25 minutes, a gaggle of cafés tells you that you've hit **Qui Dong**, Sa Dec's famed flower village (especially crowded on Sundays), where over a hundred farms cultivate ferns, fruit trees, shrubs and flowers.

The only tourist **hotel** in town at present is the somewhat neglected and state-run *Sa Dec* at 108/5A Hung Vuong (☎067/861430; ❸). When it's time for **eating**, the family-run *Chanh Ky* on Nguyen Sinh Sac, opposite the new covered market, serves Chinese rice and noodle staples; otherwise, the *Quan Com Cay Sung*, just near the crossroads down from the Sa Dec on Hung Vuong, is a popular local *com* shop with an extensive menu. The hole-in-the-wall *Hu Tieu Chay My Phoc* on 37 Phan Boi Chau, between Hung Vuong and Tran Hung Dao, serves good vegetarian dishes.

Can Tho

Sited at the confluence of the Can Tho and Hau Giang rivers, **CAN THO** is the delta's biggest city (pop. 1,900,000), a major trading centre and transport interchange. However, abundant rice fields are never far away, and boat trips along the canals and rivers, through memorable floating markets, are undoubtedly Can Tho's star attraction. Broad Hoa Binh is the city's backbone, and the site of the **Ho Chi Minh Museum** (Mon–Fri 8am–4pm), where yet more photographs and army ordnance are displayed. Can Tho was the last city to succumb to the North Vietnamese Army, a day after the fall of Saigon, on May 1, 1975 – the date that has come to represent the absolute reunification of the country. The impressive **Can Tho Museum**, 1 Hoa Binh (Tues, Wed & Thurs 8–11am & 2–5pm, Sat & Sun 8–11am & 6.30–9pm), presents "the history of the resistance against foreign aggression of Can Tho people", as well as local economic and social achievements.

The city's **central market** swallows up the entire central segment of waterfront Hai Ba Trung. North of the market, **Ong Pagoda** is a prosperous place financed and built in the late nineteenth century by a wealthy Chinese townsman, Huynh An Thai. Inside, a ruddy-faced Quan Cong presides, flaunting Rio Carnival-style headgear. On his right is Than Tai, to whom a string of families come on the first day of every month, asking, not unreasonably, for money and good fortune.

Boat trips and floating markets

Every morning an armada of boats takes to the web of waterways spun across Can Tho province, and makes for one of its **floating markets**. Lacking the almost staged beauty and charm of Bangkok's riverine markets, as snapshots of Mekong life these

△ Navigating the Mekong River

tableaux are still unbeatable. Everything your average villager could ever need is on sale, from haircuts to coffins, though predictably fruit and vegetables make up the lion's share of the wares on offer. Each boat's produce is identifiable by a sample hanging off a bamboo mast in its bow.

Of the three major markets in the province, two are west of the city. First up, 7km out of Can Tho, is the busiest and largest of the three, **Cai Rang**, sited under Cai Rang Bridge, where dozens of boats jostle and bump along the water's edge, whilst their owners shout out to advertise their wares. Another 10km west and you're at the more modest, but still interesting **Phong Dien**. Although tour groups frequent both markets, they are still relatively friendly and uncommercialized. **Phung Hiep**, however, 32km south of Can Tho on the road to Soc Trang, is a shadow of its former self; its floating market is dispersed amongst different parts of the river, although some activity can be viewed from Phung Hiep Bridge, carrying the main road across the river. It's possible to visit Cai Rang, Phong Dien and Phung Hiep by boat, but with the round-trip to Phong Dien (passing Cai Rang) taking around five hours, and getting to Phung Hiep and back more like eight, you'd be wiser to go by **road** for these two, and rent a sampan (approximately $2–3 an hour) on arrival. A Honda om ($3–4 return) is the safer bet for Phong Dien, while Phung Hiep is served by xe lams from Ly Tu Trong. However you travel, you'll need a really **early start**: any boat-owner who tells you the spectacle is just as impressive throughout the day is lying. Most organized tours take in one of the above markets and return to Can Tho via the maze of surrounding canals; otherwise, you can negotiate your own itinerary with any of the numerous touts along the waterfront for a maximum of $10.

Practicalities

Long-distance buses take you across the Hau Giang estuary and into the Mekong's transportation hub, Can Tho's **bus station**, 1200m northwest of town at the junction of Nguyen Trai and Hung Vuong. Most buses terminate here, though some local services from Vinh Long dump you on the north bank of the Hau Giang River at Binh Minh, from where you'll have to take a short ferry ride. **Moving on**, express high-quality minibuses to Chau Doc and HCMC depart from 75a Tran Phu (or arrange a hotel pick-up on ⓣ071/761761); ask the driver to stop en route for Vinh Long or My Tho. Can Tho Tourist, 20 Hai Ba Trung (ⓣ071/821853), has a Vietnam Airlines branch and can help with **car rental** and **boat tours**, though for the latter, you'll do better to book an unofficial boat ($2–3 per hour) through a tout on Hai Ba Trung.

Most **hotels** are on Hai Ba Trung and Chau Van Liem. Delightful, cottagey little *Tay Ho*, 36 Hai Ba Trung (ⓣ071/823392; ❶), sits in an aged row of shop-houses and is currently in the process of upgrading its rooms. The genial but jaded *Hau Giang 'B'*, 27 Chau Van Liem (ⓣ071/821950; ❷), has no-frills quarters that are cleaner inside than out and some four-bed rooms, and *Huy Hoang*, 35 Ngo Duc Ke (ⓣ071/825833; ❷), is also well maintained, with fair-value, pleasant rooms; both are popular with tour groups. For more upmarket accommodation, try the smart *Quoc Te International Hotel*, 12 Hai Ba Trung (ⓣ071/822080; ❹) where it's worth paying the extra for unsurpassable river views, or the attractive and well-appointed *Ninh Kieu*, 2 Hai Ba Trung (ⓣ071/821171; ❻), next to the boat jetty; a new sixty-room annexe is currently nearing completion. Rates at both of these hotels include breakfast. Back in the town centre, the brand new *Xuan Mai* 17 at 94 Nguyen An Minh (ⓣ071/815217; ❸) has risen the bar significantly with its scrupulously clean, businesslike rooms at rock-bottom rates.

Hai Ba Trung also serves up the best variety of **eating** options. The 24-hour *Mekong Restaurant* at no. 38 is hard to top for cheap, flavoursome Vietnamese and Chinese meals – fried fish in sweet and sour sauce (around $1.50) comes highly recommended. *Ninh Kieu*, in the hotel of the same name, is conveniently set on a riverside terrace and serves steamboat for two at around $6, whilst the popular

Nambo Café at no. 50 (9am–2pm & 5–11pm), serves French-influenced dishes in colonial-style elegance and has a pleasant balcony overlooking the riverfront. Next door at no. 48, the *Phuong Nam* offers quality cooking at more than reasonable rates; house specialities include fried squid in tamarind sauce for around $1.50. For simpler, less expensive fare, head for the *Thien Hoa* at no. 26 (9am–2pm & 5–11pm), where you get large portions of sour soups and other local and Chinese food, or the highly-regarded *Quan Com* 31 at 31 Ngo Duc Ke for wholesome home cooking – the beef steaks are particularly recommended.

Vietcombank at 7 Hoa Binh will **change** cash and travellers' cheques and arrange cash advances against Visa and MasterCard, while further along, the **post office** has IDD, fax and poste restante services. **Internet** facilities can be found at Phuc Thai, 161 Ly Tu Trong, and there's a **pharmacy** further down at no. 88–90.

Long Xuyen

The traffic-choked city of **LONG XUYEN**, 60km northwest of Can Tho, at the junction of the two main routes to the delta's northwestern corner, is of interest mainly as a transport hub. If you do need to while away a few hours, however, the delightfully tranquil **My Hoa Hung Island** lies just across the river, its unspoilt and friendly villages easily explored on rented bicycle. The island also happens to be the birthplace of Ton Duc Thang, successor to Ho Chi Minh as president of the Democratic Republic of Vietnam. An impressive museum dedicated to him, the **Ton Duc Thang Exhibition House** (daily 7–11am & 1–5pm; free), set in three hectares of pleasant grounds, displays well-presented photos and memorabilia. To get to My Hoa Hung Island, take a local ferryboat from the jetty at the end of Nguyen Hue.

Buses from Can Tho stop a few hundred metres south of town at Long Xuyen bus station, opposite 96 Tran Hung Dao – yell for the driver to stop as you pass the central cathedral. Some local buses from Chau Doc and Rach Gia terminate at a second bus station, Binh Khanh, to the north of town, also on Tran Hung Dao. Travelling to and from Cao Lanh, you'll come via Choi Moi Isle – to the east – and the **An Hoa ferry**, at the end of Ly Thai To in the centre of town. Transportation services from HCMC come either through Can Tho, to the south, or via Sa Dec, across Choi Moi and the An Hoa ferry. The main and largest ferry terminal, **Van Long**, 7km south of the city, links back up with the main highway to HCMC, via Sa Dec. If you are heading for HCMC or Sa Dec, high-quality minibuses operate from 58 Nguyen Trai (☎076/840950); alternatively, you can catch onward buses at the intersection of Tran Hung Dao and Hung Vuong – express buses to Chau Doc also pass through here – or at the Van Long and An Hoa ferry terminals. Passenger/cargo **boats** for Sa Dec, Tan Chau (for Chau Doc) and Rach Gia depart from sporadically Long Xuyen's local ferry terminal in the centre of town, at the corner of Pham Hong Thai and Le Thi Nhieu – enquire locally for times and costs.

Vietcombank at 1 Hung Vuong can arrange **cash advances** against Visa and MasterCard and change travellers' cheques – something none of Chau Doc's banks do yet. **Internet** access is available at Lan Vy Internet, 48 Nguyen Thi Minh Khai.

The best place to **stay** is the family-run *Thoai Chau* 2, 283a Tran Hung Dao (☎076/843882; ❷), which has well-kept, conventional rooms. If full, its neighbour, the *An Long*, 281 Tran Hung Dao (☎076/843298; ❸), is a similarly good-value bet. The cheapest deal in town is the *Xuan Phuong*, 68 Nguyen Trai (☎076/841041; ❶), although the rooms are well past their prime; moving up the scale, the *Long Xuyen* at 19 Nguyen Van Cung (☎076/841927; ❷) has mid-market aspirations and smarter rooms. When it's time to **eat**, the genial *Tiem Com Huynh Loi*, at 252/1 Nguyen Trai, serves decent rice, noodles and *bun bo hue*; round the corner on Luong Van Cu, the two-storey *Hong Phat Restaurant* has tasty Chinese and Vietnamese fish and meat dishes.

Chau Doc

Snuggled against the west bank of the Hau Giang River, next to the Cambodian border, **CHAU DOC** was under Cambodian rule until the mid-eighteenth century and still sustains a large Khmer community. Forays by Pol Pot's genocidal Khmer Rouge into this corner of the delta led to the Vietnamese invasion of Cambodia in 1978, but today Chau Doc is a bustling, friendly town that's well worth a visit. First stop should be the town's **market**, located roughly between Quang Trung, Doc Phu Thu, Tran Hung Dao and Nguyen Van Thoi. One or two colonial relics are on parade in nearby Doc Phu Thu, some of whose grand shop-house terraces flaunt arched upper-floor windows and decorous wrought-iron struts. A grand, four-tiered gateway deep in the belly of the market announces **Quan Cong Temple**, ornamented with two rooftop dragons and some vivid murals.

Northwest up Tran Hung Dao, long boardwalks lead to sizeable stilthouse communities, and from here, at the junction with Thuong Dang Le, you can get a ferry across the Hau Giang River to the stilthouses of **Con Tien Island**. Downriver from the first jetty, opposite the post office on the corner of Tran Hung Dao and Nguyen Van Thoai, a second jetty runs boats out to Cham-dominated **Chau Giang district**. Turn right when you dock, and you'll discover kampung-style wooden houses, sarongs and white prayer caps that betray the influence of Islam, as do the twin domes and minaret of the Mubarak Mosque. Just beyond the mosque, another ferry delivers you back to the west bank and town, setting you down just below the *Victoria Chau Doc Hotel*, or at another jetty further down, opposite 364 Le Loi, heading towards the bus station.

Sam Mountain

Arid, brooding **Sam Mountain** rises dramatically from an ocean of paddy-fields 5km southwest of Chau Doc, and Vietnamese tourists flock here to worship at its clutch of pagodas and shrines. From town, a road runs straight to the foot of the mountain, covered by xe dap lois and xe lams, or easily done by a rented bicycle. As you approach from Chau Doc, you'll see the kitsch, 1847-built **Tay An Pagoda**, its frontage awash with portrait photographers, beggars, joss stick vendors and bird-sellers. Inside, there are over two hundred gaudy statues of deities and Buddhas. A track leads **up the mountain** from beyond a large, mustard-coloured school, 1km around Sam in a clockwise direction. After fifteen minutes, an observatory affords fine views of the patchwork of fields below. However, if you carry on for another twenty minutes to the top, there are spectacular 360-degree views from the summit; here "military zone no picture" is daubed in red on a boulder at the peak and Vietnamese soldiers keep a sharp eye on the Cambodian border.

Practicalities

Buses offload 2km southeast of town, on Le Loi, from where xe dap lois run into town; some minibuses also offload in the centre on Thu Khoa Nghia. If you're heading onward to HCMC, express buses depart hourly for Cholon from the kiosk at 62 Nguyen Huu Canh (☎076/867786); regular express minibuses to Long Xuyen operate from offices at 37 Nguyen Van Thoai (☎076/866221).

The Vietcombank branch opposite the bus station changes travellers' cheques. There's **Internet** access at Quoc Thai, 16/2 Nui Sam, and at numerous other outlets. Around 400m up Tran Hung Dao, heading north from the Con Tien jetty, a narrow concrete path marked "Ben Tau Ha Tien, Kien Luong" at 86a Tran Hung Dao signals the departure point for passenger/cargo boats along the Vinh Te Canal, which defines the border with Cambodia, to **Ha Tien** (depart 4am subject to availability; $4.50). Bear in mind that with the recent proliferation of private operators throughout the Mekong Delta competition is forcing boat prices down. With your

Into Cambodia

With the opening of the **Vinh Xuong border crossing** (daily 8am–5pm), 30km north of Chau Doc, it's now possible to cross into Cambodia from Chau Doc. The **overland route** to the border is still fairly difficult: by motorbike, cross over the Hau Giang and then follow a precarious track along the river to the border crossing (avoid this route after heavy rains); from here, your best bet is a local taxi-boat for onward travel into Cambodia. Much easier than slogging it out overland is to take a **boat** from Chau Doc. *Victoria Chau Doc Hotel* (see below) operates direct taxi-service speedboats – subject to availability – up the Mekong River to Phnom Penh (daily at 7am; 4hr; minimum 2 people; $35). A cheaper option is offered by Saigontourist Travel Service (Delta Adventure Tours), 267 De Tham, HCMC (Ⓣ08/920 2110), who operate daily motorboat departures (2hr) from Chau Doc to Vinh Xuong, linking up with a boat/bus connection to central Phnom Penh. This all-in transfer costs $18 from HCMC and includes one night's accommodation in Chau Doc. Both *Victoria Chau Doc* and Saigontourist provide guides that will assist with paperwork at the border; however, you'll still need to have a valid Cambodian visa (see p.103).

Another border crossing near Chau Doc, at **Tinh Bien**, 25km west of Sam Mountain, has also recently opened. The road from Chau Doc to Tinh Bien is poor; covering the 30km takes an hour by car ($40) or one hour thirty minutes by motorbike ($10) or local bus ($1.30). The Chau Doc office of Delta Adventure Tours at Khom 8, Phuong A, Thi Xa (Ⓣ076/861249) can arrange car and motorbike transport to the border. For onward travel into Cambodia, the same office operates a daily bus leaving at 8am and arriving in Phnom Penh at around 5pm ($5). Again, you'll need to arrange a Cambodian **visa** in advance (see p.103).

own motorbike, or on a Honda om, you could negotiate the Chau Doc–Ha Tien road, which runs more or less parallel to the Vinh Te Canal. It's a very rough and tiring ride, but the stunning scenery more than compensates. Several buses a day ply this route, although they may re-route during some months of the wet season when the road gets impassable with rising floodwater.

For somewhere to **stay**, easily the best deal in town is the waterfront *Thuan Loi Hotel*, 18 Tran Hung Dao (Ⓣ076/866134; ❷). The choice of comfortable, clean rooms includes bargain fan quarters, some of which have absorbing views of river life drifting by; there's also a stilt restaurant. Alternatively, the recently renovated *Ngoc Phu*, centrally located near the market at 17 Doc Phu Thu (Ⓣ076/866484; ❷), has a range of good-value, clean and quiet quarters boasting frilly bed linen, or there's the *Thanh Tra*, 77 Thu Khoa Nghia (Ⓣ076/866788; ❷), which gets a steady flow of tour groups and is of a fair standard for the price. The cheapest fan and air-con rooms in town can be found at the somewhat jaded *My Loc*, 51b Nguyen Van Thoai (Ⓣ076/866455; ❶). Moving upmarket, the smart *Nui Sam Hotel* (Ⓣ076/861999; ❸) is clinically clean and characterless, but ideally situated at the base of Sam Mountain, while the colonial-style, international-standard *Victoria Chau Doc Hotel*, 32 Le Loi (Ⓣ076/865010 Ⓦwww.victoriahotels-asia.com/txt/hotels/chaudoc.php; ❾), has a first-class position along the riverfront, and four "junior suites" amongst its 92 pristine rooms. The hotel also changes travellers' cheques.

For **food**, *Lam Hung Ky*, 71 Chi Lang, serves the town's most imaginative menu, featuring dishes like beef with bitter melon and black beans, whilst the *Thanh* and its near neighbour *Truong Van*, on Quang Trung, serve tasty, inexpensive Vietnamese dishes and are popular with both tourists and locals. **Internet** cafés are scattered liberally around town, with most located on Nguyen Van Thoai.

Rach Gia

Teetering precariously over the Gulf ofThailand, **RACH GIA** is home to a farming and fishing community of almost 150,000 people. A small islet in the mouth of the Cai Lon River forms the hub of town, its central area shoehorned tightly between Le Loi and Tran Phu, but the urban sprawl spills over bridges to the north and south of it and onto the mainland. Once you've seen the wartime souvenirs and Oc Eo relics – shards of pottery, coins and bones – of the pedestrian **museum** at 27 Nguyen Van Troi (Mon–Fri 7–11am & 1–5pm; free) and dived through the lively markets, you've pretty much bled Rach Gia town dry of sights.

Practicalities

Buses from points north pull up 500m above town, at Nguyen Binh Khiem's station, next to the new covered market. Arrivals from Long Xuyen and beyond hit the coast at Rach Soi, 7km southeast of Rach Gia. Some, including those from Can Tho, continue into town, dropping you along central Tran Phu; others terminate at Rach Soi bus station, from where a shuttle minibus, xe lam or Honda om will get you to the centre. Arriving at the **airport** (flights from HCMC), you'll need to catch a xe lam to Rach Soi and then a minibus, xe om or Hondo om direct to Rach Gia.

When you're ready to **move on**, xe lams and shuttle minibuses heading back to Rach Soi can be picked up on Tran Phu; if you're heading for Ha Tien or the Hon Chong Peninsula, you'll leave from Nguyen Binh Khiem's bus station. Local services rattle their way to Ha Tien ($1.50) in around three hours, departing as demand dictates. If you're taking one of the three nightly express buses to HCMC, you'll board in town: tickets cost $4 and should be bought in advance from the booth marked "Toc Hanh" in front of the Vietcombank on Mac Cuu. From the "Ben Tau Rach Meo" terminal, 5km south of town on Ngo Quyen, passenger/cargo boats leave for destinations in the delta.

Kien Giang Tourism at 12 Ly Tu Trong (Ⓣ077/862081) can arrange **tours** and car hire around Rach Gia. Vietcombank exchanges travellers' cheques and **cash** and can advance cash against Visa and MasterCard – a priority if you're pushing on to Ha Tien or the Hon Chong peninsula owing to the lack of facilities there; the bank at 44 Pham Hong Thai can also exchange cash. Vietnam Airlines has a branch at 180 Nguyen Trung Truc (Ⓣ077/861 8480), and there's **Internet** access at the Information Room, inside the "Children's House" at 4 Nguyen Cong Tru.

As far as **accommodation** goes, if you're on a strict budget, head for the *Thanh Binh I Hotel* (Ⓣ077/863053; ❶), opposite Kien Giang Tourism, which has very basic fan rooms, some with inside bathrooms; a similar set-up can be found at the crumbling *Thanh Binh II Hotel*, 37 Hung Vuong (Ⓣ077/861921; ❶). Otherwise, the *To Chau*, 16 Le Loi (Ⓣ077/863718; ❸), has a range of good-value, comfortable rooms, all with hot water. Finally, the smart *Palace Hotel*, 243 Tran Phu (Ⓣ077/863049; ❹), has a range of refurbished, spacious and smartly tiled air-con doubles, some of which get cheaper the higher you climb. For **food**, the *Tay Ho* on Nguyen Du enjoys a good reputation, as does the *Vinh Hong 1* by the river at 39b Tran Hung Dao, where the ingredients of its seafood dishes eye you warily from tanks mounted on the walls. Otherwise, the *Thien Nga*, next to the *To Chau* hotel, serves tasty Vietnamese and Chinese home cooking. For a fast fill-up, you can't go far wrong with the *Ao Dai Moi* at 26 Ly Tu Trong, which offers cheap local fare in a warm family atmosphere.

Hon Chong peninsula

The calm waters and palm-fringed beaches of **Hon Chong peninsula** are best reached by taking a bus from Rach Gia's bus station at 2 Tran Phu to **BINH AN** (daily at 10am; return bus from Binh An at 4am). The bulk of the area's **accom-**

modation lies a couple of kilometres south of Binh An, and buses can drop you off here along the main drag: *Binh An Hotel* (☎077/854332; ❸) has accommodation to suit all pockets, including five-bed rooms; the *Hon Trem Hotel* (☎077/854331; ❸) is currently relocating to Ving Luong, where its all-new incarnation will include a pool and tennis court; while the 24-room motel-style *My Lan* (☎077/759044; ❸) has excellent-value, sparkling rooms, all with air-con and satellite TV. The **beach** in front of the main drag is relatively undeveloped for now and is fine for sunbathing and swimming. About 1.5km further south, after passing cacti, tamarind and thot not trees, the coastal track peters out at a towering cliff, into which the Hai Son Tu ("Sea and Mountain Pagoda") has been hewn: a low doorway leads from its outer chamber to a grotto with statues of Quan Am and several Buddhas. The cramped stone corridor that runs on from here makes a romantic approach to a small beach. As you hit the sand, the twin peaks of Hon Phu Thu ("Father and Son Isle") rear up in front of you. The beach itself is a little gem, although sadly it's now completely overrun with souvenir stalls and restaurants, many of which run right down to the waters edge.

Ha Tien

Many visitors find **HA TIEN**, with its shuttered terraces, crumbling colonial buildings and seafood drying in the sun, the quaintest and most beautiful town in the delta. Lapped by the Gulf of Thailand, 93km northwest of Rach Gia and only a few kilometres from the Cambodian border, the town has a real end-of-the-line feel. Ha Tien is big on atmosphere, if a little short on sights beyond the lively waterfront **market** on Tran Hau and fishing boats unloading below the common land to the west of it. Walk up Mac Thien Tich and west along Mac Cuu, though, and a temple dedicated to **Mac Cuu**, the 17th-century feudal lord who founded Ha Tien, stands at the foot of the hill. He and his relatives lie buried here in semicircular Chinese graves. Mac Cuu's grave is uppermost on the hill, daubed with a yin and yang symbol, and guarded by two swordsmen, a white tiger and a blue dragon. From this vantage point, there are good views down to the river. Further up Mac Thien Tich, **Tam Bao Pagoda** is set in tree-lined grounds dominated by a huge statue of Quan Am.

Biking around Ha Tien

A full day can be spent **biking** through the countryside around Ha Tien, and a convenient circular sealed route northwest of town means you won't need to backtrack; bikes can be rented at the *Dong Ho* and *To Chau* hotels (see p.1156). Strike off west along Lam Son, through rice fields, coconut groves and water palm, past a war cemetery (2.5km from town) – from where it's 1.5km to the first of three marked turnings, all with toll gates (1500d) – to **Mui Nai** peninsula, a relatively peaceful, dark-sand cove, somewhat marred, however, by ongoing development. A large gateway announces the second Mui Nai turning, several hundred metres further on, which leads to the largest stretch of the beach, a 400-metre curve of sand, shaded by coconut palms and backed by lush green hills. The third turning, just a little further on, brings you to a similar but more picturesque part of the beach; both stretches have numerous cafés and restaurants running alongside a promenade, so it's feasible to spend a full day here.

You'll see the 48-metre-high granite outcrop housing **Thach Dong** cave long before you reach it; 3–4km past Mui Nai, a right turn deposits you at its base. A monument shaped like a clenched fist and commemorating the 130 people killed by the Khmer Rouge near here in 1978 marks the entrance (daily 7am–5pm) to Thach Dong, beyond which steps lead up to a cave-pagoda that's home to a colony of bats. To your right is Cambodia. From here, another 3km brings you back to Ha Tien.

Practicalities

Local services shudder to a halt 1km north of the town centre, whilst **long-distance minibuses** terminate at a tiny enclosure next to the *Dong Ho* hotel; the seven-hour ride to HCMC costs $4.50. From here, it's a short walk up to town. The most important street is waterfront Tran Hau, from where passenger and cargo **boats** – some alarmingly small and decrepit – depart for Chau Doc (6am subject to availability). Kien Giang Tourist Company is located inside the Kim Du hotel at 14 Phuong Thanh; the local Vietcombank on the corner of Chi Lang and Tuan Phu Dat has the best rates for exchanging dollars; and **Internet** outlets are cropping up around town, with two on Tran Hau, at nos. 54 and 72.

Accommodation

Dong Ho 2 Tran Hau ⓣ077/852141. Near to the *To Chau Hotel*, this is another reliable and inexpensive option that even provides minibar and TV. ❷
Du Hung 17a Tran Hau ⓣ077/951555. Swankiest option of the bunch with pristine, modern rooms overlooking the sea. ❸
Hai Van 55 Lam Son ⓣ077/852872. Another good, convivial choice offering immaculate, spacious rooms with satellite TV; superior doubles are available in a new mid-range annexe (ⓣ077/852001; ❹). ❶
Hoa Mai 1-3 Tran Hau ⓣ077/852670. Family-run guesthouse offering comfortable rooms, all with en-suite bathrooms. ❷
Phao Dai Hotel 1 Mac Thien Tich ⓣ077/851849. Spectacular location overlooking the bay, and its upper fan rooms with communal balcony are a bargain. ❷
To Chau Hotel 56 Dong Ho ⓣ077/852148. Adjacent to the pontoon bridge at the southern end of To Chau, this hotel offers spartan, though clean, fan and a/c rooms. ❷
Viet Toan 74 Chi Lang ⓣ077/850109. Best bet in value terms, with restful lilac rooms and spotless bathrooms. ❷

Eating

The cheery *Xuan Thanh* on the waterfront is the best option for **eating**, serving cheap Western, Chinese and Vietnamese dishes and making good use of fresh local seafoods, while the *Huong Bien* round the corner on To Chau has a wide range of reliable staples averaging around $1.50.

11.3

The southern and central highlands

After a hot and sticky stint labouring across the coastal plains, the little-visited **southern and central highlands**, with their host of ethnic minorities, mist-laden mountains and crashing waterfalls, can provide an enjoyable contrast - though the region is not as spectacular nor ethnically diverse as the far north. Many of the highlands' 2.5 million inhabitants are *montagnards* ("mountain folk") from Bah Nar, E De, Jarai, Sedang, Koho and Mnong **ethnic minorities**, but visiting their villages independently can be difficult and is best done by basing yourself at the highland towns of **Buon Ma Thuot** and **Kon Tum**, from where you can either book a tour or take a Honda om with a local guide. For most tourists up here, the main target is **Da Lat**, a former French mountain retreat that, with its dreary tourist trappings, is not as idyllic as it sounds, though it does have its charms, among them some beguiling colonial buildings, picturesque bike rides and a market overflowing with fruit and vegetables.

Da Lat and around

Nestled at an elevation of around 1500m among the hills of the Lang Bian Plateau, the city of **DA LAT** is Vietnam's premier hill station, an amalgam of mazy streets and picturesque churches, spliced unfortunately with ugly new constructions and touristic kitsch. In 1897, the Governor-General of Indochina ordered the founding of a convalescent hill station here, where Saigon's hot-under-the-collar *colons* could recharge their batteries, enjoy the bracing alpine chill, and even partake in a day's game-hunting. By tacit agreement during the American War, both Hanoi and Saigon refrained from bombing the city and it remains much as it was half a century ago, a great place to chill out, literally and metaphorically.

Arrival, information and city transport

Buses from HCMC, Nha Trang and elsewhere arrive south of the centre at Da Lat **bus station** but may drop you off at the western end of Xuan Hong Lake. **Lien Khuong Airport** (Ⓣ63/843373) is 29km south of the city, off the road to HCMC: Vietnam Airlines buses ($3) depart from here to their offices at 40 Ho Tung Mau (Ⓣ63/822895), while a taxi or xe om will cost about $10 or $3 respectively.

Open-tour buses usually drop you off at the hotel of your choice, or will let you see a few options. Tickets for daily departures to HCMC ($7), Mui Ne ($7) and Nha Trang ($6) are on sale at most hotels; otherwise, contact the operators: *Sinh Café* inside the *Trung Cang Hotel* at 4a Bui Thi Xuan (Ⓣ63/822663, Ⓦwww.sinhcafevn.com); Dalat Tourist Transportation Service (Kim Travel), 9 Le Dai Hanh (Ⓣ063/822479, dltoseco@hcm.vnn.vn); and TM Brothers at 7/2 Hai Thuong (Ⓣ63/823631).

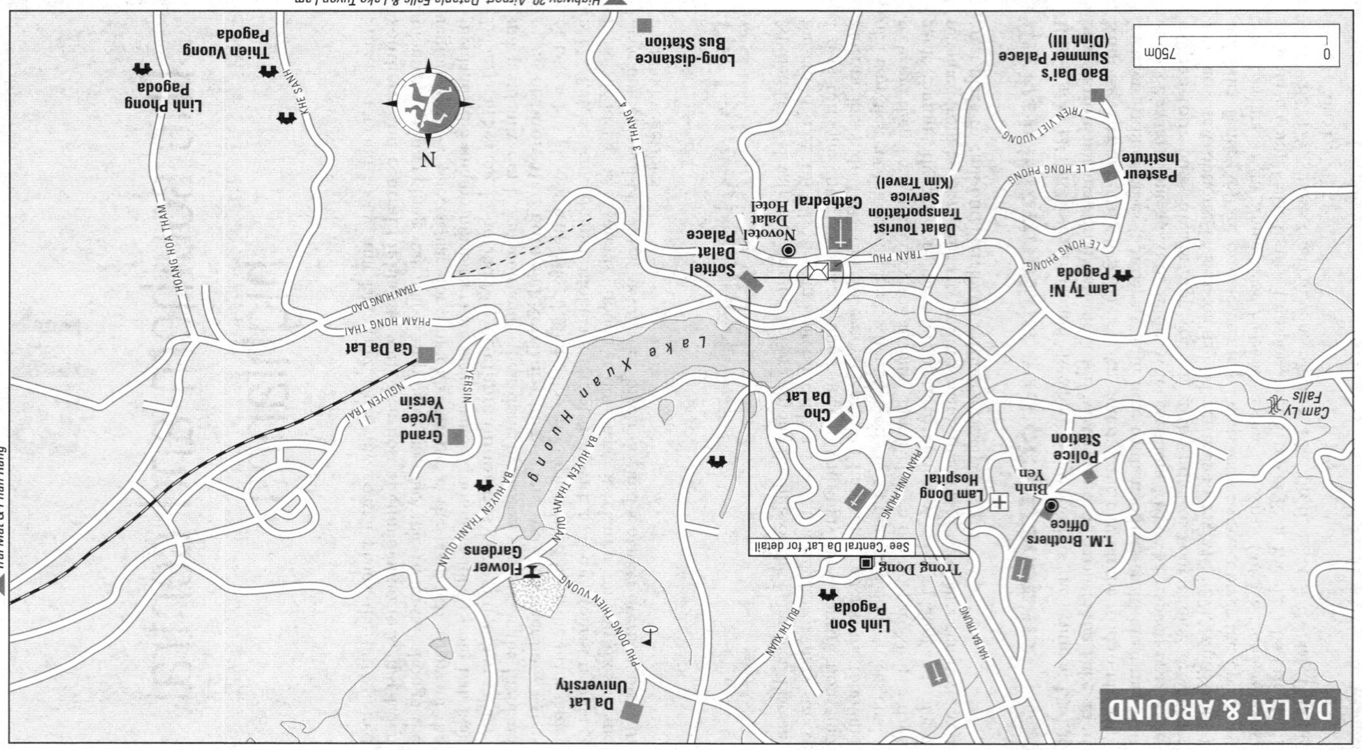
DA LAT & AROUND
Trai Mat & Phan Rang
Highway 20, Airport, Datanla Falls & Lake Tuyen Lam
HOANG HOA THAM
Linh Phong Pagoda
Thien Vuong Pagoda
KHE SANH
NGUYEN TRAI
Ga Da Lat
Grand Lycée Yersin
PHAM HONG THAI
TRAN HUNG DAO
YERSIN
BA HUYEN THANH QUAN
Flower Gardens
Lake Xuan Huong
Da Lat University
PHU DONG THIEN VUONG
3 THANG 4
Long-distance Bus Station
Sofitel Dalat Palace
Novotel Dalat Hotel
Cho Da Lat
BUI THI XUAN
Linh Son Pagoda
Trong Dong
See 'Central Da Lat' for detail
PHAN DINH PHUNG
Cathedral
Dalat Tourist Transportation Service (Kim Travel)
TRAN PHU
HAI BA TRUNG
Lam Dong Hospital
Binh Yen
T.M. Brothers Office
Police Station
Lam Ty Ni Pagoda
LE HONG PHONG
TRIEN VIET VUONG
Bao Dai's Summer Palace (Dinh III)
Pasteur Institute
0
750m
Cam Ly Falls
N

Hotels and tourist offices rent **bicycles** and mountain bikes ($2-3). **Honda om** drivers charge $8–10 for a day-long tour to local pagodas, waterfalls and ethnic villages; if they don't find you first, ask for the Easy Riders, who speak English and come highly recommended. **Taxis** charge $12 upwards for a day-long tour; they congregate beside the food stalls on Le Dai Hanh and two blocks above the cinema. Several **tourist offices** can organize tours, guides and cars with drivers ($25–30); try the bus operators listed above or Dalat Travel Service, at *Thuy Tien Hotel*, 7 3 Thang 2 (Ⓣ63/822125), or Dalat Travel Bureau at 1 Nguyen Thi Minh Khai (Ⓣ063/510104, dalattravelbureau@pmail.vnn.vn). For something more energetic, Phat Tire Ventures at 73 Truong Cong Dinh (Ⓣ063/829422, Ⓦwww.phattireventures.com) can organize **adventure trips** including hiking, mountain biking, climbing and canyoning; prices start at $14 for a day's hike to $75 for a two-day all-included off-road mountain bike trip.

The **post office** at 14 Tran Phu (daily 6.30am–9pm) has poste restante, IDD, fax and DHL courier services. Vietincombank, 46–48 Khu Hoa Binh, and Agribank at 36 Hoa Binh, can both **change** travellers' cheques and cash, as well as arrange Visa and MasterCard advance payments; Vietcombank ATMs can be found just south of the market, Cho Da Lat, at the post office and in the *Novotel Hotel*. **Pharmacies** can be found at 131 Phan Dinh Phung and 34 Khu Hoa Binh. Lam Dong **hospital** is at 4 Pham Ngoc Thach (Ⓣ63/827529), and the **police** are at 9 Tran Binh Trong (Ⓣ63/822460). **Internet** access is available at Viet Hung Internet Café, 7 Nguyen Chi Thanh, and in the *Dreams* and *Chau Au (Europa)* hotels; rates are around $0.25-0.40 per hour.

Accommodation

The densest concentrations of **budget hotels** lie on the web of roads around the cinema and along Phan Dinh Phung, and there's also a run of mini-hotels along Bui Thi Xuan – check that prices include hot water and heating in winter, necessities in Da Lat.

Binh Yen 7/2 Hai Thuong Ⓣ63/823631. Nicely tucked away at the top of Hai Thuong, offering functional rooms, all with hot water, TV and breakfast; three-bed rooms cost $20. TM Brothers are based here, and mountain bikes available for rent. ❷–❹

Chau Au (Europa) 76 Nguyen Chi Tanh Ⓣ63/822870, Ⓔeuropa@hcm.vnn.vn. Popular, well-run mid-range hotel; rooms are homely and dazzlingly clean, some with balcony; breakfast is included, staff are helpful and there's Internet access. ❷–❹

Dreams 151 Phan Dinh Phung Ⓣ63/833748, Ⓔdreams@hcm.vnn.vn. Mini-hotel with well-equipped and spotlessly clean en-suite rooms. Generous free breakfasts, friendly staff and free Internet access have made this a hit with travellers. ❸

Golf 3 4 Nguyen Thi Minh Khai, Ⓣ063/830396, golf3hotel@hcm.vnn.vn. On the main drag between the market and the lake, the *Golf 3* has standard doubles, comfy suites, and loud karaoke parties on weekend nights. ❹

Hoa Binh I 64 Truong Cong Dinh Ⓣ63/822787. Friendly, budget hotel popular with backpackers. Basic but great-value rooms have hot water and private facilities; there's also the adjoining *Peace Café* serving above-average travellers' fare; and mountain bikes for rent. An identical set-up is found at *Hoa Binh II* (Ⓣ63/822982), at no. 67. Both ❷

Hoang Hau 8a Ho Tung Mau Ⓣ63/821431. Just below the post office. An appealing hotel in a villa, with homely, well-appointed rooms, some overlooking the city gardens. Breakfast included. ❸–❹

Sofitel Dalat Palace 12 Tran Phu, Ⓣ063/825444, Ⓦwww.sofitel.com. Overlooking the lake, this beautiful upmarket colonial hotel has reassuringly old-fashioned rooms that are updated with the latest gadgets. Across the street, the sister *Novotel Dalat Hotel* (7 Tran Phu, Ⓣ063/825777; ❼) occupies another grand building with less pretentious rooms and lower rates. ❾

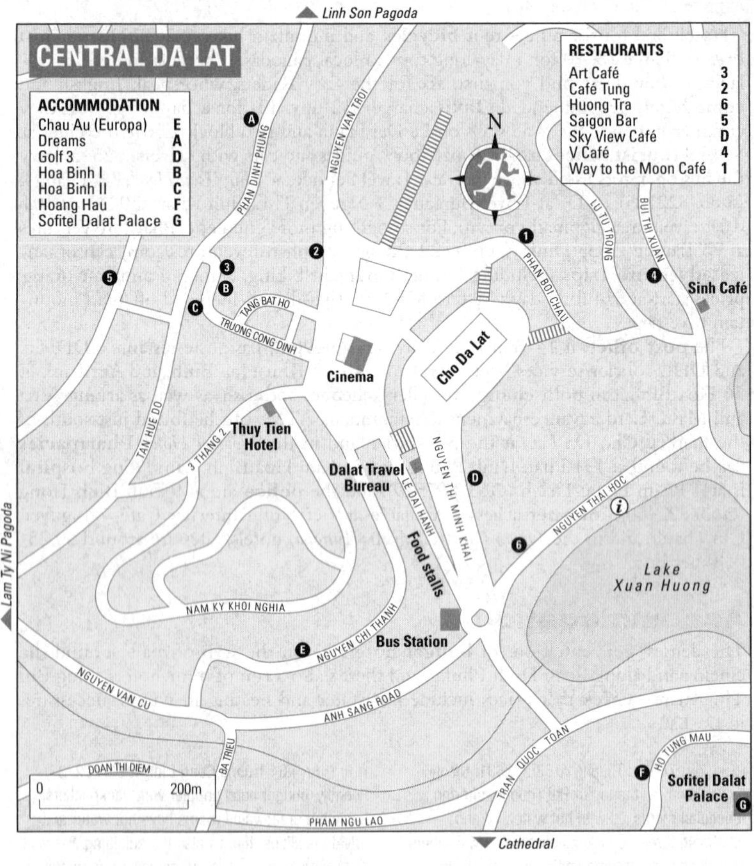

The City

Cho Da Lat is housed in a charmless reinforced concrete structure, but offers the usual entertainment in its staggering range of fruit and vegetables, as well as some interesting souvenirs such as watergourds, lacquerware, and hilltribe backpacks and fabrics on its upper level, linked by a raised walkway to the top of Le Dai Hanh. The centre is traffic-free on weekend evenings, offering a very rare opportunity to walk across a Vietnamese street without being run down by a motorbike.

Cycling or walking round glassy, man-made **Lake Xuan Huong** is a pleasant pastime and takes in Da Lat's **flower gardens** (daily 6am–6pm; $0.25) at its north-eastern corner, from where you continue south down Ba Huyen Thanh Quan, with the option of striking east up Nguyen Trai to **Ga Da Lat**, the city's Art Deco train station, built in 1938. Only one tourist train is operational, running a shuttle service (departures on demand; $5 return) through market gardens to the village of **Trai Mat**, a few kilometres away; the train idles for thirty minutes – time enough to take a look at **Linh Phuoc Pagoda** – before returning to Da Lat. Back at the southwest corner of the lake, the splendidly restored **Dalat Palace Hotel** is back in French hands again as part of the Sofitel Hotel empire; the original was the social heart of colonial-era Da Lat. Across the road, Da Lat's pink Venetian-style **cathedral**, completed in 1942, is dedicated to Saint Nicholas, protector of the poor; its seventy stained-glass windows were mostly crafted in Grenoble.

The nautical portholes punched into its walls, and the mast-like pole sprouting from its roof give **Dinh III** (daily 7.30-11am & 1.30-5pm; $0.30), erstwhile summer palace of Emperor Bao Dai, the distinct look of a ship's bridge. Reached by bearing left onto Le Hong Phong 500m west of the cathedral, and then left again when you see the wide mansion housing the Pasteur Institute to your right, the palace was erected between 1933 and 1938 to provide Bao Dai with a bolthole between elephant-slaughtering sessions. Once inside, you have the chance to nose into his working room, festivities room and imperial bedrooms.

One of the most popular attractions in Da Lat is dropping in at **Lam Ty Ni Pagoda** at the western edge of town, north of Le Hong Phong on Thien My. The pagoda is home to Vien Thuc, the so-called "mad monk" of Da Lat, who is also a poet, gardener, builder, sculptor, artist and somewhat astute businessman. His studio is stacked with over 100,000 abstract watercolours, all for sale, and Vien Thuc relishes visitors, for whom he gives a full conducted tour in English.

Eating and drinking

Most of Da Lat's **restaurants** are on Phan Dinh Phung and near the cinema. *Pho* and *com* are bashed out at the covered food market at the base of Le Dai Hanh, where there are also one or two vegetarian stalls, signposted as *com chay*. The city has a few **bars**, but it's Da Lat's **cafés** that are far more prevalent.

Art Café 70 Truong Cong Dinh. A stylish, bamboo-clad restaurant serving delicious Vietnamese dishes, as well as some Western options and cocktails.

Café Tung 6 Khu Hoa Binh. A dimly lit, low-key café, with a somewhat bohemian ambience and decor truly lost in time; local paintings adorn the walls.

Huong Tra 1 Nguyen Thai Hoc. Popular lakeside restaurant, sometimes deluged with tour groups. Rice dishes cooked in a clay pot are a speciality, and the menu also runs to rabbit and frog.

Saigon Bar 11a/1 Hai Ba Trung. A reassuringly dark and shabby Western-style bar, with friendly staff, pool, darts and sports on TV.

Sky View Café At the *Golf 3 Hotel*, 4 Nguyen Thi Minh Khai. Perched on the hotel's top floor, this bar is a fine venue for relaxing over a beer and watching the city unfurl below.

Trong Dong 220 Phan Dinh Phung. Impressive service and menu, with tasty sugarcane prawns and special salads (shrimps, peanuts, lotus gourd, pork and herbs) in a refined setting.

V Café 1/1 Bui Thi Xuan. A few minutes' walk east of the market, this American-run restaurant near the lake has good food, pastries and a relaxed atmosphere.

Way to the Moon Café 57 Phan Boi Chau. Giving new meaning to the term "concrete jungle", this café/restaurant is a maze of fake tree trunks, plants and twisting staircases leading to ever more mezzanine floors, with plenty of romantic nooks and crannies to sit and sip coffee.

Around Da Lat

Five kilometres south of Da Lat, halfway down the Prenn Pass, are the **Datanla Falls** (7am–5pm; $0.30), signposted on the right of the road as "Thac Datanla". The falls are unthrilling, but a popular photo opportunity; there are also some good walking opportunities here. A couple of hundred metres before Datanla is the right turn to **Lake Tuyen Lam** (daily 7am–5pm); boats can be rented on the lake's north shore, and on the summit behind is a meditation pagoda, home to over one hundred monks and nuns. See p.1159 for transportation options.

Buon Ma Thuot and around

A beautiful 200km drive west from Nha Trang and a similar distance north of Da Lat, **BUON MA THUOT** is chiefly of interest for its outlying minority E De village of **Ban Don**. The town itself is the western highlands' unofficial capital and, during French colonial times, developed on the back of the coffee, tea, rubber and hardwood crops that grew so successfully in its fertile red soil; coffee is still the backbone of the visibly wealthy local economy. If you need to while away a few hours in town, try the **History Museum** (daily 7.30–10.30am & 2–4.30pm) on Le Duan, chronicling the struggles against both the French and the Americans, and the more interesting **Ethnographic Museum**, a little further down the road on the opposite side (entrance on Nguyen Du; same times), with its display of exhibits pertaining to local minority peoples, among them a scale model of an E De longhouse, rice-wine jars and instruments for taming elephants.

Buon Ma Thuot practicalities

Buon Ma Thuot's **bus station** (Ⓣ50/876833) is 4km north of town; several air-con buses depart daily to Nha Trang ($2) and to HCMC ($5). Note that Buon Ma Thuot is often indicated as "Dak Lak" on buses. The **airport** is a few kilometres down the road towards Nha Trang; Vietnam Airlines (67 Nguyen Tat Thanh, Ⓣ50/954442) has a shuttle bus running to its office ($1.50); otherwise, a taxi into town costs around $3.50. The helpful **Dak Lak Tourist** occupies a wooden building at 3 Phan Chu Trinh (Ⓣ50/852108, Ⓦwww.daklaktourist.com) while **Highland Travel** is a new travel agent based at 24 Ly Thuong Kiet (Ⓣ050/855009, Ⓦwww.vietnamhighland-travel.com.vn); both can arrange tours and treks in the surrounding hills and jungles, such as a three-day trek in Yok Don National Park ($70) with nights spent in traditional villages, and the permits you need for visiting the villages.

Vietcombank, at 121 Y-Jut, can **change** travellers' cheques, foreign currencies and advance cash on Visa, MasterCard and JCB cards; it has an ATM outside the *Thang Loi Hotel*. The **post office** overlooks the victory monument at 6 Le Duan; for **Internet** access, head to Ba Trieu, just north of the park along Nguyen Tat Thanh.

The best **accommodation** in town is the *Damsan Hotel*, a kilometre out of town at 212 Nguyen Cong Tru (Ⓣ050/851234, damsantour@dng.vnn.vn ❺), which has comfortable rooms (some overlooking a green valley), a tennis court and pool. The smart *Thang Loi* opposite the victory monument at 1 Phan Chu Trinh (Ⓣ50/857615, Ⓦwww.daklaktourist.com; ❻) is the central upmarket option, with well-equipped rooms and complimentary breakfast. Just north of the town centre, the *White Horse Hotel* (Bach Ma) at 9 Nguyen Duc Canh (Ⓣ050/815656, Ⓦwww.bachma.com.vn; ❻) is an elegant Chinese-style business hotel with spacious rooms, sauna and Jacuzzi. Cheaper alternatives include the *Thanh Phat*, 41 Ly Thuong Kiet (Ⓣ50/854857, thanhphat@pmail.vnn.vn; ❷-❸), with good-value clean rooms, some of the more spacious ones with balcony, and the *Anh Vu*, 7 Hai Ba Trung (Ⓣ50/814045; ❷), which has a range of cheap, clean fan and air-con rooms.

When it's time to **eat**, the friendly *Thanh Hung*, 14 Ly Thuong Kiet, has excellent *nem* (spring rolls) in spotless, bright surroundings. Try *bon me* (sizzling beef and egg) at *Bon Trieu*, 33 Hai Ba Trung. In the evenings, locals converge on *Nguyen Duc Canh* to consume platefuls of seafood and vast quantities of Tiger beer. Most of the restaurants along here are simply called *Bia Lanh* (cold beer), followed by the street number.

The Dray Sap and Trinh Nu Falls

The splendid crescent-shaped **Dray Sap Falls** (7am–5pm; $0.50), 20km from Buon Ma Thuot, are accessed by heading southwest out of town along Doc Lap. A Honda om return trip will cost around $6. Almost 15m high and over 100m wide, the "waterfall of smoke" can be reached by clambering through bamboo groves and over rocks to the right of the pool formed by the falls. A few kilometres south of here, **Trinh Nu Falls** (7am–5pm; $0.40) are not as spectacular as Dray Sap, though you can **stay** nearby: Dak Lak Tourist runs the low-key Trinh Nu Falls Resort

(☎50/882587), dramatically perched above the Serepok River, with a bamboo bar-restaurant, good-value, well-equipped bungalows (❷), and basic longhouse accommodation (❶). Trekking, elephant riding, fishing and abseiling can also be arranged from here. To get there, turn left off the road to Dray Sap at the sign for "Trinh Nu" and continue along a dirt track for about 2km.

Yok Don National Park and Ban Don

The entrance to Vietnam's largest wildlife reserve lies 45km west of Buan Ma Thuot. Here, the 58,000-hectare **Yok Don National Park** lies nestled into the hinge of the Cambodian border and the Serepok River. Over sixty species of animals, including tigers, leopards and bears, and around two hundred types of birds, from peacocks to hornbills, populate Yok Don Park, but **elephant rides** are the park's main attraction ($30 for 90min). There are also one-day walking tours and overnight safaris ($40 for two) available, the latter best in the dry season when wildlife is more visible. Longer tours penetrating deeper into the forest where animals still preside are also available. For enquiries and bookings, phone the park HQ (☎050/783020).

The three sub-hamlets that comprise the well-touristed village of **BAN DON** lie 2km beyond Yok Don's Park HQ on the bank of the crocodile-infested Serepok River. Khmer, Thai, Lao, Jarai and Mnong live in the vicinity, though it's the **E De** who are in the majority. They adhere to a matriarchal social system, and build their houses on stilts. As you explore, you may be welcomed in somewhere to share tea or rice wine ($5 a jar). Ban Don Tourist Centre (☎50/783019), in the centre of the village, can organize elephant rides ($20 per hour). The two Buon Ma Thuot travel agents (see opposite) arrange tours here, but you could just as well hire a Honda om ($10 return).

Both the Ban Don Tourist Centre and the Yok Don park HQ can organize **cultural programmes** of E De dance, music and wine (about $65 and $55, respectively) with the option of spending the night in a nearby longhouse ($5 extra); there's also a range of basic **accommodation** available at both the park HQ (❶) and the Ban Don Tourist Centre (❷).

Dak Lake and Jun Village

About 60km south of Buon Ma Thuot, Highway 27 passes **Dak Lake**, a beautiful and peaceful spot that's one of the top tourist attractions in Vietnam. Along the lake's shoreline, the unsightly ruined remains of Emperor Bao Dai's palace enjoy a prime spot, although development is earmarked for this area. Beyond this sits **JUN VILLAGE**, a thriving Mnong community, whose impressive longhouses have remained little changed.

Dak Lak Tourist has a branch office here (☎050/586184) and a couple of longhouses where it's possible to overnight (❷); there is also a simple stilt restaurant built out on the lake, which offers magnificent views. Through the tourist office, you can arrange to stay with a family at one of the Jun longhouses in the village ($5), partake in organized rice wine feasts ($60 per group), guided treks or elephant rides around the lake ($30 for two for 90 min); there are also dug-out canoe excursions ($10 per hour for two). Although Dak Lake is mostly geared towards organized tour groups – it gets very busy at weekends – it's possible to arrive here independently, either by Honda om, or by one of three morning buses from Buon Ma Thuot; you should ring ahead and book accommodation first though.

Kon Tum and the Bah Nar villages

Some 250km north of Buon Ma Thuot, northbound Highway 14 crosses the Dakbla River and runs into the southern limits of diminutive **KON TUM**, a sleepy, friendly town that serves as a springboard for jaunts to its outlying **Bah Nar villages**. Phan Dinh Phung forms the western edge of town; running east above the river is Nguyen Hue, and between these two axes lies the town centre. Kon Tum had a hard time of it during the American War, and yet a stroll along Nguyen Hue still reveals some red-tile terraces of shop-houses left over from the French era. At the base of Tran Phu stands the grand, whitewashed bulk ofTan Huong Church. Further east is the so-called **Wooden Church**, built by the French in 1913. In the grounds, there's a scale model of a communal house.

Practicalities

Buses approaching Kon Tum from the south pass over the main bridge, which signals the start of town, before terminating at Kon Tum's **bus station**, 3km north of the bridge along Phan Dinh Phung. Alighting at the bridge, it's a 250-metre walk east along riverside Nguyen Hue to the foot of Le Hong Phong, and another 150m to Tran Phu; both run up into the town centre. Travelling to or from the north or the coast is much easier now that highways 14 and 24 have been resurfaced; there's a daily bus service to Quang Ngai (foreigners $6).

Kon Tum's selection of **hotels** is steadily improving. The two "upmarket" tour group hotels, the large riverside *Dakbla* at 2 Phan Dinh Phung (ⓣ60/863333; ❻), and the *Quang Trung* (ⓣ60/862762; ❹–❻), north of the centre at 168 Ba Trieu, are overpriced; you're better off in one of the new hotels. The *Bi Bi Hotel*, just off Phan Dinh Phung, at 274 Tran Hung Dao (ⓣ060/862777; ❷), has good-value, clean rooms. A short walk east, the friendly *Family Hotel* at 55 Tran Hung Dao (ⓣ060/862448, phongminhkt@yahoo.com; ❷–❸) also offers motorbike rental. The reception of the *Tay Nguyen*, next door at no. 53 (ⓣ060/869484, kstaynguyen@yahoo.com; ❸–❺), may look like a garage, but there are comfortable rooms upstairs.

Kon Tum Tourist (ⓣ60/861626, ⓦwww.kontumtourist.com.vn), located in the *Dakbla Hotel* and with a branch office in the *Quang Trung Hotel*, can offer tailor-made **tours**; ask for Mr Huynh, who is a mine of information on the area. A popular two-day tour combines a jungle trek with a night in a Bah Nar village stilt house and a riverboat trip; expect to pay about $40 for two. Agribank on Tran Phu does **currency exchange**.

The top choice for **food** is *Dakbla's* at 168 Nguyen Hue (temporarily located at no. 107 at the time of writing), which serves surprisingly sophisticated local and Western dishes, and sells local handicrafts. The *Hiep Thanh* further east at 129 Nguyen Hue is a reliable alternative for simple food. The *Dakbla Hotel Restaurant* enjoys idyllic river views from its terrace and the extensive menu is reasonably priced.

Kon Ko Tu

There are dozens of Bah Nar villages encircling Kon Tum, but one of the most accessible is **KON KO TU**, a relatively timeless community only 5km east of Kon Tum. Follow Tran Hung Dao east, crossing Duong Dao Duy Tu and passing an impressive high-roofed *rong* (communal house) just before you cross Dakbla River over the suspension bridge. Turn left at the first crossing after the bridge and continue for 3–4km to reach the village. Although there has been some outside influence here, many of the dwellings in Kon Ko Tu are still made of bamboo and secured with rattan string. It's the village's immaculate *rong*, with its impossibly tall thatch roof, that commands the most attention. Constructed with wood and bamboo, and without the use of any nails, the *rong* is used as a venue for festivals and village meetings, and as a village court at which anyone found guilty of a tribal offence has to ritually kill a pig and a chicken, and must apologize in front of the village. Just 2km beyond, the asphalt stops at another, more traditional, settlement of Kon Ko Tu. The village *rong* (on the left, below the road) is in need of repair but is original; delicate patterns feature on the roof and on the bamboo floor.

11.4

The south-central coast

Extending from the wetlands of the Mekong Delta right the way up to the central provinces, Vietnam's south-central coast was, from the seventh to the twelfth century, the domain of the Indianized trading empire of Champa. A few communities of Cham people still live in the area, around Phan Thiet and Phan Rang, and there are some fine relics of their ancestors' temple complexes near **Nha Trang**, which also boasts an attractive municipal beach and some good snorkelling trips to nearby islands. The **Vung Tau** peninsula offers a couple of fairly decent beaches, though nothing compared to the high dunes and aquamarine waters of **Mui Ne**, a short hop from the fishing town of **Phan Thiet**. The scars of war tend not to intrude too much along this stretch of the country, except at the village of Son My near Quang Ngai, sombre site of the notorious **My Lai massacre**.

Vung Tau

With every passing day, a little more of the charm ebbs from **VUNG TAU**, "The Bay of Boats", located some 125km southeast of HCMC on a hammerheaded spit of land jutting into the mouth of the Saigon River. Once a thriving, riviera-style beach resort, the city is now a shadow of its former, quaint self. Today, Western oil-workers nurturing the city's burgeoning oil industry are a common sight around town, and a slather of bars and massage parlours have sprung up to cater for them. That said, as a retreat from the frenzy of Ho Chi Minh, Vung Tau is worth considering.

Downtown Vung Tau nestles between two diminutive peaks, Nui Lon ("Big Mountain") to the north, and Nui Nho ("Small Mountain") to the south. Roads loop around both, and these circuits take in all of the city's **beaches** – quiet, northerly Bai Dau ("Mulberry Beach"), blustery Bai Dua ("Pineapple Beach"), and Bai Sau ("Back Beach"), which has the city's best sands. Between them runs Bai Truoc ("Front Beach"), Vung Tau's skinny municipal beach.

Arrival and information

Public **buses** terminate at Vung Tau bus station, at the northeastern end of Nam Ky Khoi Nghia. **Moving on**, frequent express **minibuses** ($2) run from here to Ben Thanh and Mien Dong bus stations in HCMC; private, high-quality minibuses to Cholon ($2) operate from next door at no. 190 (☎064/522696). **Hydrofoils** from Ham Nghi (HCMC) use the jetty opposite Hai Au Hotel, just south of the city centre on Ha Long, or during the rainy season, the PTSC terminal, 12km northeast of the city; free shuttle buses to and from the jetty are provided. Two companies run hydrofoils to HCMC: Vina Express/Greenlines has a ticket office next to the Hai Au Hotel (11 daily; $10; ☎064/810202); whilst Petro Express has their office opposite, at the jetty (10 daily; $10; ☎064/810625).

Cyclos and Honda om are ubiquitous, and there are taxis in the central areas. The Song Hong and Thang Muoi hotels rent bikes for $1 per day, and most hotels can arrange motorbike hire ($5–7 per day). **Car rental** plus driver can be arranged at Vicarrent, 9 Le Loi (☎064/856875). Vietcombank, 27 Tran Hung Dao (Mon–Fri

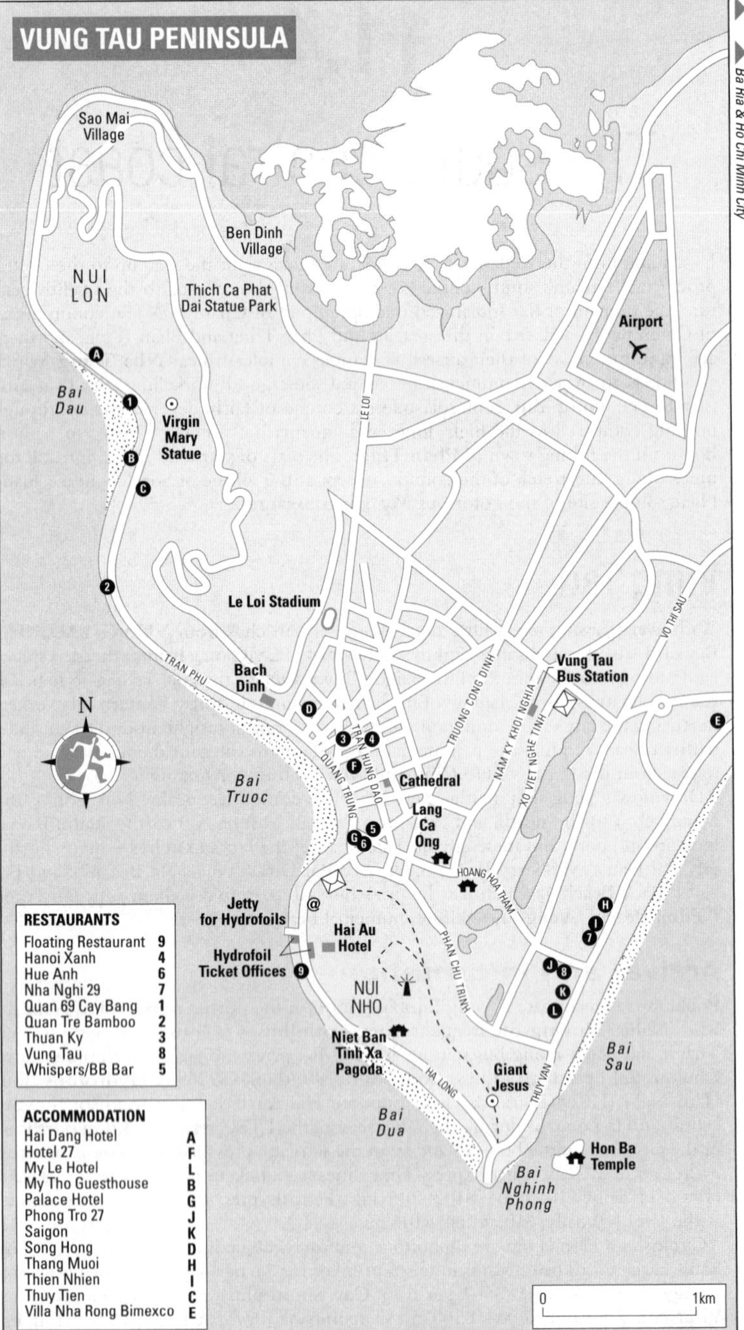
PTSC Port for Hydrofoils & Jetty for Con Dao boats
VUNG TAU PENINSULA
Ba Ria & Ho Chi Minh City
Sao Mai Village
Ben Dinh Village
NUI LON
Thich Ca Phat Dai Statue Park
Airport
Bai Dau
Virgin Mary Statue
LE LOI
Le Loi Stadium
TRAN PHU
Bach Dinh
N
TRAN HUNG DAO
QUANG TRUNG
Bai Truoc
Cathedral
Lang Ca Ong
TRUONG CONG DINH
NAM KY KHOI NGHIA
XO VIET NGHE TINH
VO THI SAU
Vung Tau Bus Station
HOANG HOA THAM
Jetty for Hydrofoils
Hydrofoil Ticket Offices
Hai Au Hotel
PHAN CHU TRINH
NUI NHO
Niet Ban Tinh Xa Pagoda
HA LONG
Giant Jesus
THUY VAN
Bai Sau
Bai Dua
Hon Ba Temple
Bai Nghinh Phong
0
1km
RESTAURANTS
Floating Restaurant 9
Hanoi Xanh 4
Hue Anh 6
Nha Nghi 29 7
Quan 69 Cay Bang 1
Quan Tre Bamboo 2
Thuan Ky 3
Vung Tau 8
Whispers/BB Bar 5
ACCOMMODATION
Hai Dang Hotel A
Hotel 27 F
My Le Hotel L
My Tho Guesthouse B
Palace Hotel G
Phong Tro 27 J
Saigon K
Song Hong D
Thang Muoi H
Thien Nhien I
Thuy Tien C
Villa Nha Rong Bimexco E

7.30–11.30am & 1.30–4pm), changes travellers' cheques and **advances cash** on Visa and MasterCard. Travellers' cheques can also be cashed at the *Hai Au Hotel*; there's an ATM here too, and another in the lobby of the *Grand Hotel* at 2 Nguyen Du. The **post office** at 408 Le Hong Phong has IDD and fax (24hr), poste restante and DHL services; there's also a sub-post office at 156 Ha Long. Vietnam Airlines is at 21 Tran Hung Dao (☎064/856099). A few steps along at no. 29 is Vung Tau Tourist (☎064/857527), which can arrange **tours** and car rental, as can OSC Vietnam Tours, at 9 Le Loi (☎064/852008). **Internet** access is available for 4000d per hour at Johnny Pham Internet, 22 Tran Hung Dao. There's a **pharmacy** at 70 Tran Hung Dao; Le Loi Hospital, 22 Le Loi (☎064/832667), has an outpatients' **clinic** for foreigners, while the International SOS Clinic at 1 Le Ngoc Han (☎064/858776) is a 24-hour international medical centre with expat doctors.

Accommodation

Bai Sau offers the biggest range of lodgings and the best beach, but Bai Dau is more peaceful. Rooms get snapped up quickly at weekends, when rates can also increase sharply.

Bai Sau (Back Beach)

My Le Hotel 57–59 Thuy Van ☎064/852177. Friendly place with brand new swimming pool and appealingly bright, modern rooms with IDD and satellite TV; includes breakfast. ❻

Phong Tro 27 170a Hoang Hoa Tham ☎064/858124. Good-value, friendly, motel-style guesthouse, set back from the beach; rooms are spacious, though spartan, and some have a/c. ❷

Saigon 85 Thuy Van ☎064/852317. Not blessed with Bai Sau's best strip of beach but still good value given the quality of the rooms; cheapest rooms are found at ground level and on the higher floors. ❸

Thang Muoi 151 Thuy Van ☎064/852665. Motel-style with a wide range of good-value clean and capacious rooms, with garden restaurant featuring "dishes winning medals". ❹

Thien Nhien 145a Thuy Van ☎064/525427. New mini-hotel, with spotless, great-value rooms, some with balcony; neglected but acceptable beachside fan rooms (❶) also available across the road. The owners are friendly and helpful to a fault. ❹

Villa Nha Rong Bimexco Thuy Van ☎064/859916. Peacefully sited in pine groves up at the far northeastern end of Thuy Van, where obliging English-speaking staff help you choose from a range of woodenstilt beach huts, some with a/c, or more modern rooms in a new block set back from the beach. ❷

Bai Truoc (Front Beach) and the city centre

Hotel 27 46 Trung Trac ☎064/850087 yen-tk@yahoo.com. Small but perfectly formed town centre gem with a handful of superb rooms at the price. Owners can also arrange motorbike rental. ❷

Palace Hotel 1 Nguyen Trai ☎064/856411 ⓦwww.palace.oscvn.com. Longer-stay discounts make this mid-standard option surprisingly affordable; guests can choose from 120 individually styled rooms and have access to quality sports facilities. ❻

Song Hong 3 Hoang Dieu ☎064/852137. Competitively priced, set back from the beach; the comfortable rooms all boast a/c, bathtubs and satellite TV. ❺

Bai Dau (Mulberry Beach)

Hai Dang Hotel 164 Tran Phu ☎064/838536. Out on a limb, but peaceful and friendly, with good-size, light a/c rooms, six of which gaze out to sea. ❹

My Tho Guesthouse 43 Tran Phu ☎064/832035. A gem of a place run by a charming couple. Big fan rooms looking onto the beach, or smaller, internal rooms with a/c; plus there's a sun terrace. Several more tranquil rooms are available nearby at no. 39. At both locations, laundry service and bicycle rental are free. ❷

Thuy Tien Hotel 84 Tran Phu ☎064/835220. The immaculate rooms in this villa-style hotel, set in pleasant gardens, all have balconies, a/c and hot water; there's also a gym, sun terrace and pool room. ❸

Around the peninsula

The skinny strip of litter- and rubble-strewn town beach, **Bai Truoc** or **Front beach**, is ribbed by souvenir shops, bars and restaurants and is of most interest at dawn and dusk, when fishermen dredge its shallows. Imposing late-nineteenth century **Bach Dinh** (daily 7am–5pm; 5000d), on the southern slope of Nui Lon above the northern extent of Quang Trung, has long served as a holiday home to Vietnam's political players and now exhibits "valuable antique items" excavated from a seventeenth-century shipwreck, and an imposing Cambodian Buddhist statuary.

The foot of Quang Trung is the starting block for the six-kilometre circuit of **Nui Nho**. From there, the exposed coastal road, Ha Long, loops around the south side of the mountain. Not far past the former post office, a pretty pink villa marked "53/2 Ha Long" signposts the left turn up to Vung Tau's **lighthouse**, which affords panoramic views of the peninsula. The most noteworthy of several pagodas strung along this stretch of coastline is **Niet Ban Tinh Xa Pagoda** (daily 7am–5pm), a modern and multi-level complex fronted by a structure resembling a high-rise dovecote. **Bai Dua**, or **Pineapple Beach**, south of the pagoda, is a composite of shingle, dark sand and rocks, so if you want a swim or a sunbathe, hold on until you round the promontory. Meanwhile, a gruelling fifteen-minute hike from the southwestern tip of Nui Nho brings you to Vung Tau's own little touch of Rio, its 33-metre-high **Giant Jesus** (daily 7.30–11.30am & 1.30–5pm). Climb the steps inside the statue and you'll enjoy giddying views. Immediately around the headland is the sweet, sandy cove of **Bai Nghinh Phong**, and beyond that, **Hon Ba Temple** marooned a little way out to sea on a tiny islet, accessible only at low tide.

Despite its ugly block-buildings and ongoing development, **Bai Sau**, or **Back Beach**, is far and away Vung Tau's widest, longest (8km) and best beach. A new municipal beach development, **Ocean Park**, at 8 Thuy Van, incorporates restaurants, cafés, watersports facilities and swimming pools; it also happens to be sited on the cleanest stretch of beach. Hoang Hoa Tham cuts around the north side of Nui Nho to reach the city centre.

North of Bach Dinh, sleepy **Bai Dau**, or **Mulberry Beach**, is the most hassle-free of all Vung Tau's beaches. Barring the odd restaurant, there's very little action here, but heavy stone walls and blue-shuttered buildings lend it a Mediterranean ambience. The actual beach is short, dark and slightly pebbly, but still suitable for swimming. With a bicycle, you could continue north from Bai Dau to the leaf-roofed stilthouses of the delightful fishing village of **Sao Mai**. Further clockwise, Sao Mai blends into the busy quayside of bigger **Ben Dinh**.

Eating, drinking and entertainment

Vung Tau's community of expat workers (and its close proximity to HCMC) have ensured a certain amount of Western influence, and the city boasts numerous restaurants and bars. For something a little different, there's **greyhound racing** every Saturday night (7–10pm) at the Le Loi Stadium, 15 Le Loi (☎064/807309); tickets cost 20,000d and are available from most tourist outlets in town as well as the stadium itself.

Bai Sau (Back Beach)

Nha Nghi 29 29 Thuy Van. Attached to the *Thien Nhien* beachside rooms, this is an unpretentious restaurant that does the simple things well using traditional Mekong methods. 6am–10pm.

Vung Tau 170a Hoang Hoa Tham. Attached to the Phong Tro 27 guesthouse, this is a good-value and friendly restaurant, serving tasty Vietnamese home cooking. 6am–10pm.

Bai Truoc (Front Beach) and the city centre

Floating Restaurant 150 Ha Long ☎064/856320. The emphasis is squarely on seafood in this upmarket Vietnamese/Chinese restaurant housed right on the sea, though the menu still yields many affordable dishes. 9am–9.30pm.

Hanoi Xanh 20 Tran Hung Dao. Frog, squid, eel, tortoise: few creatures that hop, swim or crawl escape the frying pan at this popular and central eatery.

Hue Anh 15a Truong Cong Dinh. The menu in this popular Chinese/Vietnamese restaurant is extensive; all dishes are well presented, with chicken in plum sauce or French-style diced beef both highly recommended; garden terrace available. 9.30am–9.30pm.

Thuan Ky 23–25 Trung Nhi. Huge and hugely popular *com* and *pho* shop, slap-bang in the centre of the city. 5am–10pm.

Whispers/BB Bar 13–15 Nguyen Trai. The two main expat hangouts in Vung Tau. *Whispers*, the more refined, has a restaurant-cum-bar serving traditional roasts and good-quality Western fare; the adjoining *BB Bar* shares the same menu but resembles a fun-pub. Daily 11am–2pm & 5pm–midnight.

Bai Dau (Mulberry Beach)

Quan 69 Cay Bang 93 Tran Phu. A little pricey, but popular with locals who come out of town for reputable seafood overlooking the beach at sunset. Weekends are busy, though restaurants either side cater for the overspill. 10am–9pm.

Quan Tre Bamboo 7 Tran Phu. The glorious setting of the candlelit, open-air terraced dining area beside the sea could have been lifted straight from the south of France; the reasonably priced extensive menu ranges from grilled chicken with soya cheese to red clam salad. 10am–9pm.

Phan Thiet

The friendly fishing port of **PHAN THIET** is one of the stepping-stones between HCMC and Hanoi, not least because of its proximity to wonderful **Mui Ne**, a 21-kilometre-long arc of fine sand (see p.1170). Though Mui Ne is undoubtedly the main draw of the area, Phan Thiet does have some hidden charms of its own and makes a good break from the beach. Quaint colonial villas season Phan Thiet's main streets, some decorated with glazed ceramic tiles, most with louvred windows and colonnaded facades. Turn left off the southwestern end of Tran Hung Dao Bridge and stroll along Trung Trac, and you'll soon plunge into the wharfside **fish market**. Back in the other direction, Trung Trac skirts the city centre en route to the riverside **Ho Chi Minh Museum** (Tues–Sun 7.30–11.30am & 1.30–4.30pm; $0.30), rather a flat museum, but with some nicely quaint memorabilia. A couple of hundred metres south on Tran Phu, **Ong Pagoda** also merits a browse. Over Tran Hung Dao Bridge, Vo Thi Sau strikes off to the right and to the city **beach**, which, 700m northeast, opens out into a more pleasant pine-shaded spot.

Practicalities

Buses terminate at the **bus station** a couple of kilometres north of Phan Thiet. Coming from HCMC, you can save yourself a cyclo fare by getting off as the bus passes through the city centre. **Open-tour buses** can drop you off near the centre, though all of them continue to Mui Ne.

Sinh Café's Tour Service Office is at Thon 3 Ham Thien (☎62/8473997); onward tickets for Nha Trang or HCMC can be bought here (both $6), or in Mui Ne. The nearest **train station** is Muong Man, 10km from Phan Thiet; to get to town, take a Honda om or arrange a taxi in advance with Binh Thuan Tourist. If you're staying in Mui Ne, some of the resorts can arrange shuttle transfers in advance. Binh Thuan Tourist at 82 Trung Trac (☎62/816821, ⓔbinhthuantourist@hcm.vnn) has a 24-hr taxi service (☎062/814814) and houses the **Vietnam Airlines** office. You can change dollars at the Agribank on the main square; for travellers' cheques and cash advances on Visa, MasterCard and JCB, you'll need to go to the Vietcombank office on Tran Hung Dao. There's **Internet** access at 70 Trung Trac.

Of the relatively few budget **places to stay** in Phan Thiet, your best bet in the centre of town is the friendly *Phan Thiet Hotel*, 276 Tran Hung Dao (☎62/819907; ❸), which offers comfortable and spacious rooms, with TV, bathtub and air-con; prices lower the higher you climb, and breakfast is included. If you want to be near the sea, the huge *Novotel Ocean Dunes Resort* (☎062/822393, ⓔnovpht@hcm.vnn.vn; ❾) has a golf course and two swimming pools. For **eating**, head for the southwest side of the main square below the city's suspension bridge, where the bright *Nam Thanh Lau* restaurant serves good seafood and generous portions of a variety of dishes.

Mui Ne

In the space of just a few years, **MUI NE** has established itself as a major tourist and beach destination – unsurprising given the laid-back, low-key atmosphere and its endless palm-shaded, golden sands, lapped by clear waters. Mui Ne is also recognized on the wind- and kitesurfing circuit, forming part of the annual Asian Windsurf Tour (Feb–March). Mui Ne beach commences soon after you've crossed Ke Bridge and passed the Phu Hai Cham towers, but the best stretch starts around 12km out of Phan Thiet, after which the coconut trees give way to Mui Ne village and the impressive red dunes for which this area is famous. From here onwards, a large cluster of guesthouses and hotels has sprung up along Nguyen Dinh Chieu, the main drag. Only low-rise development is allowed, and Mui Ne is still very much a quiet, relaxing place; if you want to party, you're better off in Nha Trang.

Practicalities

Every day around noon, **open-tour buses** run through Mui Ne en route to Nha Trang and HCMC (both $6); most of them will allow you to view a few hotels until you find something suitable. Kim Travel buses end up at the *Hanh Café 2* (Ⓣ62/847347), near the *Full Moon Beach* resort. The TM Brothers' base is the *Coco Café* (Ⓣ062/847359), a few metres further along the main drag. If you're coming from Phan Thiet, a Honda om should cost around $1.50, a taxi $5. Blue Ocean Resort at km12 (Ⓣ62/847322) runs a daily **express minibus** service to central HCMC at 2pm ($6). There are no shuttle buses along the main drag, so your best option is to use the ever-present Honda oms.

Most hotels can arrange motorbike and bike rental; the *Seabreeze Resort* has **mountain bikes** for rent ($3 per day). The Hot Rock Information Centre opposite the *Sun Sea Resort* at Km12 (Ⓣ062/847608) offers the usual ticketing and watersport rental services, as well as sunrise and sunset tours ($2) and jeep or motorbike day-trips to attractions including the red and white dunes ($28 per jeep). At the time of writing, it was preparing a Cham pottery course centre. For watersports, wind- and kitesurfing, contact *Jibe's Beach Club* (90 Nguyen Dinh Chieu, km13.5, Ⓣ062/847405, Ⓦwww.windsurf-vietnam.com) or one of the upmarket resorts.

Coco Café has the cheapest **Internet** access in Mui Ne (150d/min), but Hot Rock's (250d/min) is more central. The **bank** next to the *Swiss Village Resort* (Mon-Fri 7.30am–noon & 1-4.30pm) can change cash and travellers' cheques and give advances against Visa and MasterCard at better rates than the hotels.

Accommodation

There's a good mix of luxury and mid-range accommodation along the beach, but few budget options. Satellite TV, air-con, en-suite bathrooms with hot water, and sun chairs on a guarded and cleaned stretch of beach are standard in most resorts. In low season (May–Nov), rates can drop by $10 to $20. Addresses in Mui Ne are usually denoted by distance from Phan Thiet.

Bamboo Village Seaside Resort 38 Nguyen Dinh Chieu, km11.8, Ⓣ62/847007, Ⓦwww.bamboovillageresort.com. Attractive bamboo bungalows and lodges ranging from standard to luxurious, with all mod cons, set in coconut and banana gardens. Pool, Jacuzzi and watersports centre. ⑧–⑨

Coco Beach (Hai Duong Resort) 58 Nguyen Dinh Chieu, km12.5, Ⓣ62/84711, Ⓦwww.cocobeach.net. This long–established French-run resort has well-equipped, wooden, thatched stilt bungalows set in spacious manicured gardens; pool, library, watersports centre and complimentary breakfast. ⑨

Full Moon Beach 84 Nguyen Dinh Chieu, km14, ⓣ62/847008. Run by the Jibe's people, this relaxed resort has a choice of well-appointed, tasteful stone quarters, some with kitchens, or bamboo bungalows with fabulous bathtubs. There's an atmospheric beach bar, and a pool. ❼–❽

Hiep Hoa 80 Nguyen Dinh Chieu, km13.3, ⓣ062/847262, hiephoatourism@yahoo.com. A friendly, family-run resort with good-value rooms in bungalows surrounding a garden. ❸–❹

Indochina Dreams 74 Nguyen Dinh Chieu, km13, ⓣ062/847271. High-ceilinged stone a/c chalets line a lane leading down to the beach. There's a good restaurant here and roadside pool table, too. ❻

Mui Ne Sailing Club 24 Nguyen Dinh Chieu, km11, ⓣ062/847440, ⓦwww.sailingclubvietnam.com. Mui Ne's best resort, with deluxe bungalows, a swimming pool and restaurant set in a lush garden. Activities on offer including wind- and kitesurfing and sailing. ❻–❾

Small Garden 48 Nguyen Dinh Chieu, km12.5, ⓣ062/847012, smallgarden@hcm.vnn.vn. The budget travellers' resort – a relaxed Swiss-run place in a coconut grove with access to the beach. The six basic bamboo bungalows (from $10) have en-suite cold showers and fans. ❽–❾

Sun Sea Resort 50 Nguyen Dinh Chieu, km12.5, ⓣ062/847700, ⓦwww.sunsearesort-muine.com. A new boutique resort with rooms facing the pool, and round thatched cottages facing the sea. Breakfast included. Located next to the spot where local fishermen picturesquely drag their coracles and catch ashore. ❼

Vietnam-Austria 88 Nguyen Dinh Chieu, km 13.5, ⓣ062/847047. Budget guesthouse with decent rooms, some with seaview, a bungalow ($12) and, sadly, a monkey on a leash. ❸

Eating and drinking

There are numerous excellent local **eateries** along Nguyen Dinh Chieu. Most hotels and guesthouses have pleasant, albeit pricey, beachside restaurants: *Bamboo Village*, *Full Moon Beach* and *Chez Nina* (at *Paradise Huts*, km14) are recommended for their outstanding fish dishes and beachside seating. The Australian-run *Hot Rock* bar-restaurant at km12.5 has excellent seafood (try the table barbeque) as well as steaks and local dishes. *Good Morning Vietnam* at km11.8 (ⓣ062/847585) can deliver authentic Italian food to your hotel, or alternatively, can come pick you up. There's not much **nightlife** in Mui Ne apart from crabs scurrying around on the beach, though the windsurfers' favourite bar, *Jibe's Beach Club* (see opposite) occasionally hosts parties, and also serves good food.

Nha Trang and around

Nestled below the bottom lip of the Cai River, some 260km north of Phan Thiet, **NHA TRANG** has earned its place on Vietnam's tourist conveyor belt partly on merit and partly owing to its location. By the time the Nguyen lords wrested this patch of the country from Champa in the mid-seventeenth century, the intriguing **Po Nagar Cham towers** had already stood, stacked impressively on a hillside above the Cai River, for over seven hundred years. They remain Nha Trang's most famous image, yet it's the coastline that brings tourists flocking: the town boasts the finest municipal beach in Vietnam, scuba-diving courses are available here, and there are plenty of day-trips to outlying islands too. It's worth bearing in mind, however, that the Nha Trang region has a **rainy season** lasting from November through to early January, and that for relaxing, Mui Ne has a much better and cleaner beach.

Most new arrivals in the city make a beeline for the **municipal beach**, a grand six-kilometre scythe of soft yellow sand that's only five minutes' stroll east of Cho Dam. The Pasteur Institute at the top of Tran Phu Boulevard, the main drag running parallel to the beach, houses the **Alexandre Yersin Museum** (Mon–Sat 8–11am & 2–4.30pm, closed Sat afternoon; $1.65), which profiles the life of the Swiss-French scientist who settled in Nha Trang in 1893 and became a local hero, thanks not to his greatest achievement – the discovery of a plague bacillus – but rather because of his educational work in sanitation and agriculture, and his ability to predict typhoons and thus save the lives of fishermen. Yersin's desk is here, with his own French translations of Horace still slotted under its glass top; so, too, are the barometers and telescope he used to forecast the weather, and his phenomenal library. The huge **White Buddha** seated on a hillside above Long Son Pagoda in the northwest of town is Nha Trang's major landmark. It was crafted in 1963 to symbolize the Buddhist struggle against the repressive Diem regime, and around its lotus-shaped pedestal are carved images of the monks and nuns that set fire to themselves in protest. You can soak yourself in mud and mineral water baths at the **Thap Ba Hot Springs** (from $3.20; ⓣ058/830090, ⓦwww.thapbahotspring.com.vn), 4km north of town. Phone ahead or ask your hotel for their $0.60 pickup service.

Arrival and information

Nha Trang's **train station** (ticket office daily 6.30–11.30am & 1.30–10pm; ⓣ58/822113) is just west of the centre along Thai Nguyen. The **long-distance bus station** is 500m further west on the same street. There are several morning minibus departures for Buon Ma Thuot (4hr; $3) and HCMC (9hr; $5.50). **Open-tour buses** will usually stop at a selection of hotels in town, before terminating at their respective offices. The new **Cam Ranh Airport**, a former US Air Force base 30km south of town, is linked to Nha Trang by a new coastal road; Vietnam Airlines (ⓣ58/826768) runs buses to and from its office at 91 Nguyen Thien Thuat ($2); a taxi to town will cost about $9.

Bicycles can be rented from most hotels ($1 and under) and there are plentiful **cyclos** and **Honda oms** – these have a reputation for overcharging and taking you to the wrong hotel or restaurant, so be firm. Various **tour operators** can arrange car rental ($30–35 per day), open-tour buses to HCMC ($7), Da Lat ($5), Hoi An ($8), Mui Ne ($7), and Da Nang ($9), and tours of the region and further afield, as well as **boat trips** to nearby islands ($6 a head). Operators include *Hanh Café*, 22 Tran Hung Dao (ⓣ58/827814, haphuongnt1@dng.vnn.vn); Khanh Hoa Tourism, 1 Tran Hung Dao (ⓣ58/822753); Nhi Phi (*Sinh Café*), 10 Biet Thu (ⓣ58/811981, ⓦwww.sinhcafevn.com); and *TM Brothers Café*, 22b Tran Hung Dao (ⓣ58/814556, huuhanhnguyen@yahoo.com); M. Linh (boat trips only), 2a Hung Vuong (ⓣ58/826693). With its outlying islands and plentiful marine life, Nha Trang is among the best places to **dive** in Vietnam. Expect to pay $35 for a day at sea with two "try dives" - accompanied dives for beginners - and lunch. The most reliable operators are Octopus Diving Club, 62 Tran Phu Boulevard (ⓣ58/810629, ⓦwww.octopusdiving-vn.com), and Rainbow Divers, 90a Hung Vuong (ⓣ58/829946, ⓦwww.divevietnam.com).

Vietcombank ATMs can be found outside the upmarket hotels along Tran Phu Boulevard; the Vietcombank office at 17 Quang Trung changes **cash** and travellers' cheques, and can also advance cash against Visa, MasterCard and JCB cards; Nhi Phi, also offers these services at slightly higher rates. The main **post office**, 4 Le Loi (daily 6.30am–10pm), has fax, poste restante, DHL courier and IDD phone facilities; IDD is also available at the smaller post offices at 50 Le Thanh Ton (6.30am–midnight), and at 23c Biet Thu (6.30am–9.30pm). Find **Internet** access in hotels and in several cafés around Biet Thu – rates start at $0.20 per hour. The main **police** station is at 2 Le Thanh Ton (ⓣ058/510144). Nha Trang's **hospital** is at 19 Yersin (ⓣ 58/822168); there's also a resident French GP, Dr Catherine Bonnotte, who has a small surgery at 37b Dong Da (ⓣ58/512308; $15 per consultation). There's a **pharmacy** at 23d Biet Thu.

Nha Trang seems to have more petty **crime** than elsewhere, so take care of your possessions (particularly after dark) in bars and on cyclos. Dial ⓣ113 for an emergency police unit. Leave all valuables in the hotel safe when heading for the beach; the *La Louisiane* café and *Sailing Club* beaches have security guards who usually keep beach-sellers away.

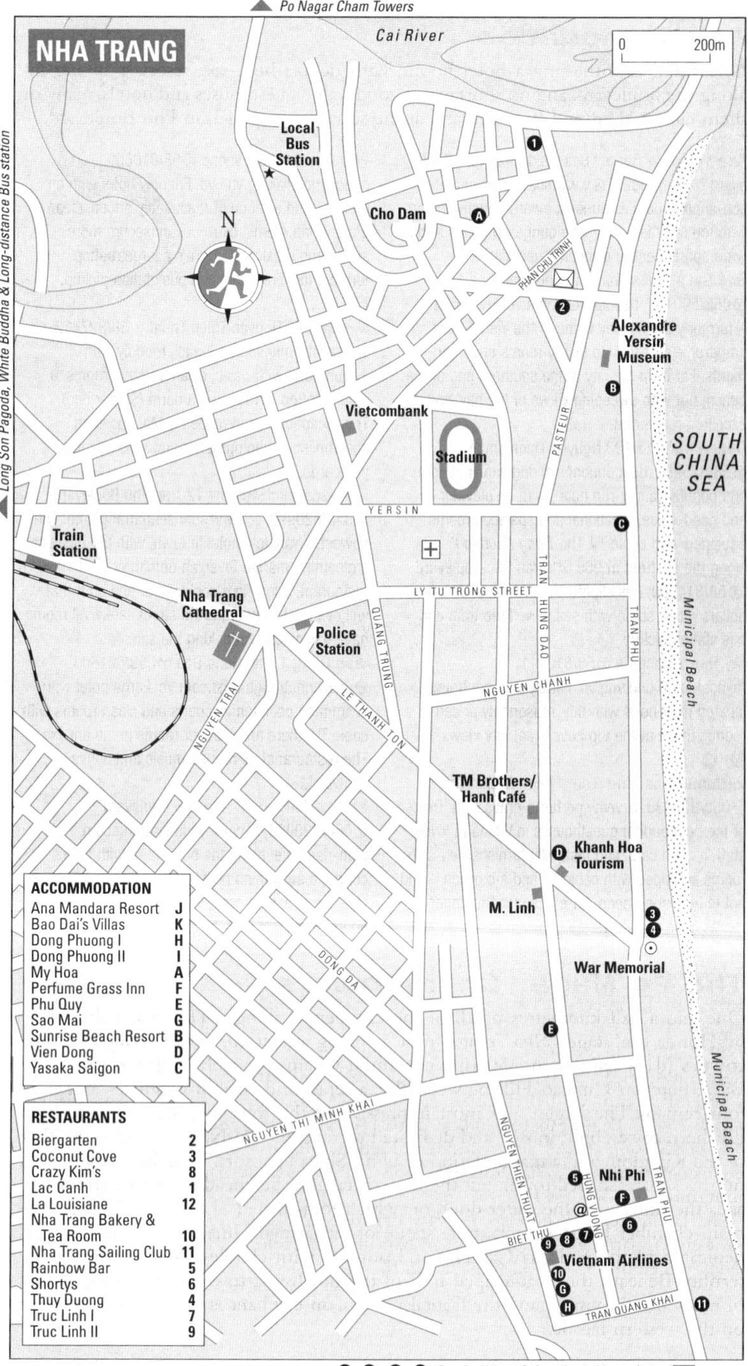
NHA TRANG
Po Nagar Cham Towers
Cai River
0 200m
Long Son Pagoda, White Buddha & Long-distance Bus station
Local Bus Station
Cho Dam
N
Phan Chu Trinh
Alexandre Yersin Museum
Vietcombank
Stadium
Pasteur
SOUTH CHINA SEA
Yersin
Train Station
Ly Tu Trong Street
Tran Hung Dao
Tran Phu
Municipal Beach
Nha Trang Cathedral
Police Station
Quang Trung
Le Thanh Ton
Nguyen Chanh
Nguyen Trai
TM Brothers/ Hanh Café
Khanh Hoa Tourism
M. Linh
War Memorial
Dong Da
Nguyen Thi Minh Khai
Nguyen Thien Thuat
Hung Vuong
Nhi Phi
Biet Thu
Vietnam Airlines
Tran Quang Khai
ACCOMMODATION
Ana Mandara Resort J
Bao Dai's Villas K
Dong Phuong I H
Dong Phuong II I
My Hoa A
Perfume Grass Inn F
Phu Quy E
Sao Mai G
Sunrise Beach Resort B
Vien Dong D
Yasaka Saigon C
RESTAURANTS
Biergarten 2
Coconut Cove 3
Crazy Kim's 8
Lac Canh 1
La Louisiane 12
Nha Trang Bakery & Tea Room 10
Nha Trang Sailing Club 11
Rainbow Bar 5
Shortys 6
Thuy Duong 4
Truc Linh I 7
Truc Linh II 9
12, I, J, K, Cau Da Wharf & Cam Ranh Airport (30km)

Accommodation

Nha Trang is witnessing a hotel boom, with deluxe high-rise resorts popping up along the boulevard, and no shortage of good-value guesthouses and hotels, many of them clustered around Biet Thu and at the southern end of Tran Phu Boulevard.

Ana Mandara Resort Beachside Tran Phu Boulevard ⓣ58/829829, ⓦwww.six-senses.com/evason-anamandara. Luxurious, award-winning resort with top facilities, attractive bungalow suites and a watersports centre; discounts negotiable. ❾
Bao Dai's Villas Tran Phu Boulevard ⓣ058/590147, baodai@dng.vnn.vn. Five villas – formerly the holiday home of the Vietnamese emperor – split up into luxury rooms and apartments. Far from the city at the southern end of the beach, but with sweeping views of the bay, and an excellent restaurant. ❻–❽
Dong Phuong I 103 Nguyen Thien Thuat ⓣ58/825986, dongphuongnt@dng.vnn.vn. Large and popular family-run hotel, with an elevator and good-value, functional and spacious rooms equipped with cable TV. The *Dong Phuong II*, along the seafront at 96a 6/1 Tran Phu Boulevard (ⓣ58/814580) has slightly larger rooms for a few dollars more, some with sea view. Free train and bus station pickup. ❶–❹
My Hoa 7 Hang Ca ⓣ58/810111, myhoahotel@dng.vnn.vn. Family-run, centrally located mini-hotel with tidy, reasonably priced rooms; those at the top have great city views. ❶–❹
Perfume Grass Inn (Que Thao) 4a Biet Thu ⓣ058/822433, ⓦwww.perfume-grass.com. One of the best budget guesthouses in Vietnam; lovely staff, a good café, and tastefully furnished en-suite rooms equipped with cable TV and a/c or fan – and not lit by glaring neon, for a change. The upper rooms have sea views. ❷
Phu Quy 54 Hung Vuong ⓣ58/810609, phuquyhotel@dng.vnn.vn. Friendly hotel with an elevator and a range of reasonably priced, clean a/c and fan rooms; extra dollars secure more space and a balcony. There's a large rooftop terrace, too. Free train and bus station pickup. ❷–❹
Sao Mai 99 Nguyen Thien Thuat ⓣ58/827412, saomaiht@dng.vnn.vn. Small, friendly, family-run hotel with basic, clean en-suite rooms, a small rooftop terrace and a dorm ($3 per bed). The receptionist and guide Mr Mai Loc is an accomplished photographer and sells beautiful postcards. ❷
Sunrise Beach Resort 12 Tran Phu Boulevard ⓣ058/820999, ⓦwww.sunrisenhatrang.com. The newest, swankiest hotel in town, with top facilities, a gleaming marble foyer, an upmarket Cantonese restaurant, a top-floor cocktail bar and staff that will even help you cross the street safely. All rooms have balconies overlooking the sea. ❾
Vien Dong 1 Tran Hung Dao ⓣ058/821606, ⓦwww.nhatrangtourist.com.vn. Large hotel with swimming pool, tennis courts and clean rooms with cable TV; there are cheaper rooms in the annexe. The restaurant has regular music and dance shows. ❺–❼
Yasaka Saigon 18 Tran Phu Boulevard ⓣ058/820090, ⓦwww.yasanhatrang.com. Deluxe high-rise hotel along the boulevard, with tennis courts, a swimming pool and restaurant. All rooms face the sea, with great views from the higher floors. Breakfast is included. ❾

The Po Nagar Cham towers

One and a half kilometres north of the city centre along 2 Thang 4, a short ride by Honda om, stands Nha Trang's most gripping attraction, the **Po Nagar Cham towers** (daily 6am–6pm; 4500d). The Hindu Chams probably built ten towers, or *kalan*, here on Cu Lao Hill between the seventh and twelfth centuries, but only four remain. The largest and most impressive of the towers is the 23-metre-high northern tower, built in 817 and dedicated to Yang Ino Po Nagar, Goddess Mother of the Kingdom and a manifestation of Uma, Shiva's consort. Time has taken its toll on this square-shaped tower, but the lotus-petal and spearhead motifs are still intact, as is the lintel over the outer door, on which four-armed Shiva dances. Inside, the main chamber holds a black stone statue of ten-armed Uma. The central tower is dedicated to the god Cri Cambhu and popular with childless couples praying for fertility. Beneath the boat-shaped roof of the northwest tower, half-formed statues in relief are still visible, and the frontal view of an elephant is just about discernible on the western facade.

The islands

Perhaps the single greatest pleasure of a stay in Nha Trang is an excursion to one of the nearby **islands**, best reached on one of the popular day-trips ($6 per person) organized by the tour operators listed on p.1172. It's also possible, but pricey, to charter your own boat from Cau Da Wharf, 6km south of Nha Trang; prices start at $50 per boat per day.

The closest of the islands to Cau Da, **Hon Mieu**, is also served by a local ferry departing from Cau Da Wharf (15min; $1 return), which docks at Tri Nguyen, a fishing village. From here it's a few minutes' walk to Tri Nguyen Aquarium, a series of saltwater ponds constructed for breeding and research purposes and a small indoor aquarium. Southeast of the aquarium there's a shingly beach at the fishing village at Bai Soai, with some basic accommodation and camping facilities (❸; contact Khanh Hoa Tourism – see p.1172 – for details). The shallows that ring **Hon Tam**, 2km southeast of Mieu, are good for snorkelling; Hon Tam Resort has a range of accommodation (❸–❻), as well as watersports facilities; for further information, contact Hon Tam Resort Office, 72 Tran Phu Boulevard (☎58/829100, Ⓦwww.hontamresort.com.vn). **Hon Tre**'s cliffs lend a welcome dash of drama to this, the largest of Nha Trang's islands, and offset the fine white sand of its beach, Bai Tru, perhaps the best beach in the area. Two smaller isles hover off Hon Tre's southern coast: **Hon Mot** has a stony beach but good snorkelling; **Hon Mun** harbours caves where sea swifts' nests are harvested and sold at thousands of dollars per kilo for use in birds' nest soups. There's no beach to speak of on Mun, but some great coral for snorkelling.

Pricier boat excursions ($20 per person) run by Con Se Tre Tour Office, 100/16 Tran Phu Boulevard (☎58/811163), take in some of the above islands, before arriving at the resort area of **Con Se Tre** on Hon Tre Island. The resort attempts to recreate the atmosphere of a Vietnamese village, with its thatched huts, bamboo bridges, traditional local games and restaurant, where lunch is hosted. Con Se Tre Tours also has a range of other tour options available, such as evening excursions, and boat taxis across to Con Se Tre Resort ($5 return). *Nha Trang Sailing Club*, 72 Tran Phu Boulevard (☎58/826528), also runs full-day motorized boat trips ($6), taking in Hin Bmun, Hon Mot, Hon Tam and Mieu village.

Eating and drinking

Nha Trang wins over Mui Ne when it comes to food and nightlife; there are enough street stalls and good local and international restaurants here to keep you happy for days, as well as a couple of buzzing bars. Mind your belongings when you go out - it's best to leave all valuables in your hotel.

Biergarten 7c Le Loi. German-run beergarden with a breakfast menu, German and international dishes, and San Miguel draught beer for under $1. 9am-late.

Coconut Cove Tran Phu Beach. The most pleasant place in the cluster of restaurants north of the war memorial, shaded by large palm trees and serving good seafood. 7am-midnight.

Crazy Kim's 19 Biet Thu. Recently expanded bar run by a wacky local. Enjoy the huge cocktails during the 10am to 10pm happy "hour", or drop by for a hangover breakfast. The party's either here or at the *Sailing Club*. 10am-2am.

Lac Canh 44 Nguyen Binh Khiem. Set in the quiet streets east of Cho Dam *Lac Canh* is renowned for its mouth- and eye-watering cooked-at-table barbecues. 9am–9.30pm.

La Louisiane Tran Phu Beach. Good, inexpensive beach club with a free pool, patrolled beach (sun chairs $0.60), restaurant and pastry bar. Also has a watersports centre and travel agent. Open from 7.30am.

Nha Trang Bakery & Tea Room 99b Nguyen Thien Thuat. The best place in backpackersville to stock up on pastries or have a decent breakfast before a long bus ride. Open from 5.30 am.

Nha Trang Sailing Club 7 Tran Phu. Draws a well-heeled expat crowd and hordes of tourists to its refined beachfront bar and dancefloor, which gets less refined as the night wears on; happy hour 8.30–10.30pm. As well as bar food, there's a decent Italian and Japanese restaurant, plus an excellent "Seafood Corner" in the club compound. Noon–3am.

Rainbow Bar 90a Hung Vuong, ⓣ058/524351. An excellent travellers' café with foreign beers, Western and local food and early breakfasts at higher than average prices, plus a welcoming atmosphere. Also Rainbow Divers' main office. 7am–3am.
Shortys 1 Biet Thu. Excellent home-style chips, hamburgers and full English breakfast at this pub-style place, plus pool, happy hour (6–10.30pm) and book exchange. 8am–late.

Thuy Duong Tran Phu Beach. Near the memorial, this popular beachside restaurant serves excellent and well-priced fish, fresh from the tank.
Truc Linh I & II 11 & 21 Biet Thu. Great Vietnamese food at two locations; a simple corner restaurant at no. 11 and a more upmarket seafood restaurant at no. 21. Daily 6am–10pm and 5–11pm respectively.

Quang Ngai and Son My Village

The area around **QUANG NGAI**, 130km south of Da Nang, had a long tradition of resistance against the French, which found further focus during American involvement. In response, this region suffered some of the most extensive bombing meted out during the war: by 1967, seventy percent of villages in the town's surrounding area had been destroyed. A year later, the Americans turned their sights on Son My Village, site of the infamous **My Lai massacre**, which is now remembered in a moving memorial garden and museum.

Quang Ngai practicalities

From the north, Highway 1 enters Quang Ngai over the new Tra Khuc Bridge. Near here, Quang Trung leads 300m east to the centre of town, at the junction with Hung Vuong. **Trains** arrive 2km west of town along Hung Vuong. **Buses** terminate at the bus station 500m south of the centre, and 50m east of Quang Trung on Le Thanh Ton. You can request **open-tour buses** en route to Nha Trang and Hoi An to set you down at the southern end of the new Tra Khuc Bridge (for the town centre) or 500m east of the bus station, where Highway 1 meets Le Than Ton (look for the large "Central Hotel" sign); onward open-tour bus travel should be arranged before arrival as there are no scheduled stops here.

The **post office** is 100m west of the main crossing on Hung Vuong. At the far western end of Hung Vuong, at no. 345, Vietcombank **exchanges** travellers' cheques, dollars and can arrange cash advances on Visa, MasterCard and JCB cards; the same services can be found at the more central Vietincombank at 89 Hung Vuong. There's **Internet** access at 415 Quang Trung and, closer to the bus station, at no. 611.

Good-value fan and air-con **accommodation** can be found at the genial and central *Kim Thanh Hotel*, near the post office at 19 Hung Vuong (ⓣ55/823471; ❷), and at the *Hung Ha Hotel*, 495 Quang Trung (ⓣ55/815772; ❷). The more upmarket *My Tra Hotel*, on the north side of the old Tra Khuc Bridge along Quang Trung (ⓣ55/842985; ❸–❻), enjoys a prime riverside location – its well-appointed rooms all have balconies. Near the bus station, the large, new *Central Hotel*, at 784 Quang Trung (ⓣ055/829999, central@dng.vnn.vn; ❺–❽), has good modern rooms. On lengthy **My Khe beach**, 3km east of Son My, Quang Ngai Tourist (office at 310 *Quang Trung*, ⓣ55/843316) has decent beach huts (❷); the *My Tra Hotel* will open a resort hotel here in 2005. The *My Tra*'s terrace **restaurant** looks out across the river and its selection of local dishes are reasonable; otherwise, head for two decent *com* shops – the *Mimosa* and the *Bac Son* – next door to the *Kim Thanh* in town.

Son My Village

The massacre of civilians in the hamlets of **Son My Village**, the single most shameful chapter of America's involvement in Vietnam, began at dawn on March 16, 1968. US Intelligence suggested that the 48th Local Forces Battalion of the North Vietnamese Army (NVA) was holed up in Son My, and the task force assembled to flush them out included the 20th Infantry's Charlie Company, whose First Platoon was assigned to sweep through My Lai 4 (Tu Cung). Charlie Company had suffered casualties and losses from snipers and booby traps and had come to feel frustrated and impotent, so Son My offered the chance to settle some old scores. At a briefing, GIs were glibly told that all civilians would be at the market by 7am and that anyone remaining was bound to be an active VC sympathizer. A massacre ensued. Five hundred Son My villagers were killed, 347 of them from Tu Cung. Not one shot was fired at a GI in response. The My Lai massacre is remembered at the **Son My Memorial Park** (daily 7am–5pm; $0.60), 12km east of Quang Ngai in Son My's sub-hamlet of Tu Cung. The garden retains its scars – bullet holes in trees; foundations of homes burnt down, each with a stone tablet recording its family's losses. Inside the two buildings on its western flank (to be replaced by a new museum in 2005) there's a memorial plaque recording the names of the dead, and a grisly photograph gallery documenting the events of that tragic day.

Buses for Son My leave occasionally from the bus station in Quang Ngai, but the most efficient means of reaching the village is by Honda om ($2-3 return).

11.5

The central provinces

Vietnam's narrow waist comprises a string of provinces squeezed between the long, sandy coastline and the formidable barrier of the Truong Son Mountains, which mark the border between Vietnam and Laos. For foreigners, there are four **overland crossings into Laos** here: the straightforward and accessible Lao Bao, along Highway 9 from Dong Ha (see p.1193), the more remote Cau Treo, on Highway 8 from Vinh (see p.1196), Nam Can along the road to Phonsavan and Nameo along the route to Xam Nua. Laos visas can be obtained in the city of **Da Nang**, a useful transport hub but not much more. Just south of Da Nang, the much visited riverside town of **Hoi An** is renowned for its crafts, traditional Chinese merchants' houses and temples, and also makes a good base for visiting the beach and exploring the fine ruins of the Cham temple complex at nearby **My Son**. The former Vietnamese capital of **Hue** is equally impressive, and its nineteenth-century palaces, temples and royal mausoleums constitute one of Vietnam's highlights. In 1954, Vietnam was divided at the Seventeenth Parallel, only 100km north of Hue, where the **Demilitarized Zone** (**DMZ**) marked the border between North and South Vietnam until reunification in 1975. The desolate battlefields of the DMZ and the extraordinary complex of residential tunnels at nearby **Vinh Moc** are a poignant memorial to those, on both sides, who fought here and to the civilians who lost their lives in the bitter conflict.

Hoi An

The ancient core of seductive, charming **HOI AN** – recognized as a UNESCO World Cultural Heritage Site – is a rich architectural fusion of Chinese, Japanese, Vietnamese and European influences dating back to the sixteenth century. In its heyday the port town attracted vessels from the world's great trading nations, and many Chinese merchants stayed on. Somehow the town escaped damage during both the French and American wars and its charming two-hundred-year-old wooden-fronted shop-houses are among its chief attractions. Combined with excellent shopping opportunities and an attractive beach, Hoi An is one of Vietnam's most pleasant towns.

> There have been a number of changes in **street names** between the bus station and the town centre, but the locals continue to use the old names on signs and business cards. Nhi Trung is now called Hai Ba Trung, and the road looping west of it is now Ba Trieu; Le Hong Phong is now Nguyen Tat Thanh, but is called Ly Thuong Kiet east of the crossing with Hai Ba Trung.

Arrival and information

People generally arrive in Hoi An by car, by Honda om from Da Nang Airport or train station (30km), or on an **open-tour bus**, which may drop you off at central hotels. Local **buses** drop you at the corner of Nhi Trung and Le Hong Phong. Bicycles ($0.40) and motorbikes ($4–6 per day) are available for rent from guesthouses and the stall opposite 6 Le Loi.

The friendly, new state-run **Tourist Information Office** at 45 Le Loi (daily 7am-7pm, ⓣ0510/910919, ⓦwww.hoianworldheritage.org) sells maps and books and can help with information about sights, tours and hotels, though you can't book here. Hoi An has plenty of **tour agencies** offering tours, visas, rail and air tickets: try Camel Travel at 23 Phan Dinh Phung (ⓣ0510/861203), *Hoi An Hotel* at 6 Tran Hung Dao (ⓣ0510/861373, ⓦwww.hoiantourist.com), Seventeen's, 17 Tran Hung Dao (ⓣ0510/861947, ⓔseventeenstours@yahoo.com), An Phu Travel, 29 Phan Dinh Phung (ⓣ0510/862643, ⓦwww.anphutouristhoian.com), or *Sinh Café*, 11 Le Loi, (ⓣ0510/863948, ⓦwww.sinhcafevn.com). They can all arrange car hire, as well as book open-tour buses to Hue ($3) and Nha Trang ($8). For transport **to Da Nang**, hire a car ($7–10) or Honda om ($3), or arrange to be dropped off in town on an open-tour bus ($2), as local buses (every 30min until 5pm; $0.60) are slow, and happy to overcharge.

Vietcombank at 35 Tran Hung Dao has an ATM and can change cash and travellers' cheques, and arrange cash advances against Visa and MasterCard. The **post office** at 4b Tran Hung Dao also has a Vietcombank ATM. For a selection of **Internet cafés**, head to Hai Ba Trung, Phan Dinh Phung or Nguyen Duy Hieu. You'll find the **police** watching Chinese soaps on TV all day at 8 Hoang Dieu, and there's an English-speaking **pharmacy**, Bac Ali, at 68 Nguyen Thai Hoc.

Accommodation

Several high-standard hotels have popped up just north of the historic core on Hai Ba Trung and Ba Trieu over the last few years. Prices have subsequently fallen and, outside of high season, you should be able to negotiate the room rate down by 10-20 percent.

Hoi An 6 Tran Hung Dao ⓣ510/861373, ⓦwww.hoiantourist.com. Colonial-style hotel, with a range of well-appointed rooms, plus tennis courts, pool, money exchange, bike rental and tour desk. Its sister hotel, *Hoi An Beach Resort* (ⓣ510/927011; ➒), is a more upmarket, large-scale resort, themed in traditional style and situated right on Cua Dai beach, with free shuttle buses to Hoi An. ➐–➒

Hoi An Riverside Resort Cua Dai ⓣ510/864800, ⓦwww.hoianriverresort.com. Beautiful riverside resort, 2km out of town and 1km from the beach. Well-equipped villa rooms are in Vietnamese or Japanese style; some have river balcony. Facilities include pool and gym; room rates are sometimes negotiable. ➒

Thanh Binh III Ba Trieu ⓣ0510/916777. One of several similar and similarly priced hotels in the Hai Ba Trung cluster, with spacious a/c rooms and a small swimming pool. ➍–➏

Thien Thanh 34 Ba Trieu ⓣ0510/916545, ⓦwww.hoianthienthanhhotel.com. Quiet, good-value rooms, friendly staff and a small swimming pool just north of the centre. ➌–➎

Thuy Duong I 11 Le Loi ⓣ510/861574, ⓦwww.thuyduonghotel-hoian.com. The central location and cheap rooms, plus the in-house *Sinh Café* tour and Internet centre, make this a popular choice. The *Thuy Duong III*, on Ba Trieu (ⓣ510/916565; ➎–➏), has well-equipped rooms and a courtyard swimming pool. ➋

Vinh Hung I 143 Tran Phu ⓣ510/861621, ⓦwww.vinhhunghotels.com. Accommodation in this well-restored, central Chinese merchant house consists of superb wood-panelled rooms, complete with all mod cons. The elegant *Vinh Hung II*, on Ba Trieu (ⓣ0510/863717; ➎–➏) has large rooms around a courtyard pool. ➍–➐

The Town

The **historic core** of Hoi An consists of just three short parallel-running streets: Tran Phu is the oldest and, even today, the principal commercial street, with plenty of crafts shops and galleries; one block south, Nguyen Thai Hoc has many wooden townhouses and some galleries; while riverfront Bach Dang holds the market and several waterside cafés.

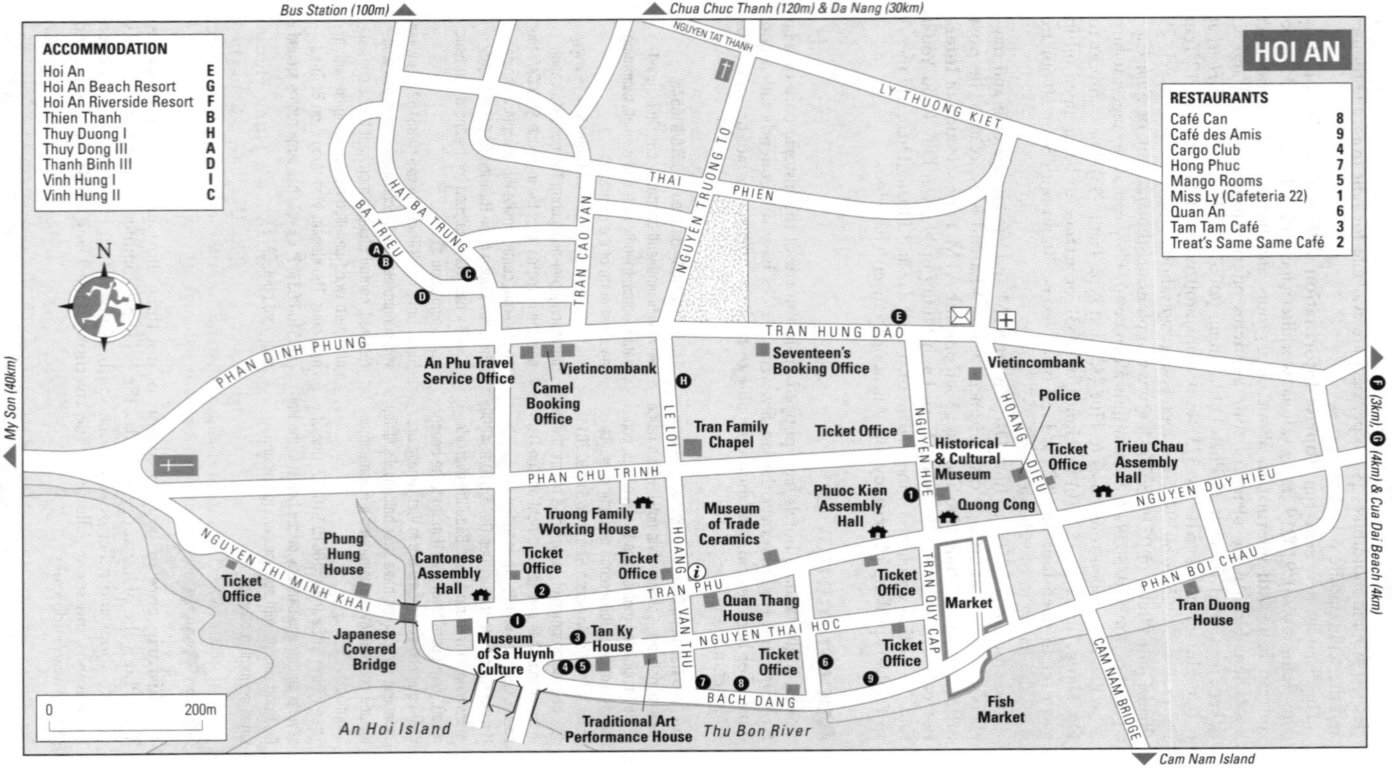

HOI AN

ACCOMMODATION

Hoi An	E
Hoi An Beach Resort	G
Hoi An Riverside Resort	F
Thien Thanh	B
Thuy Duong I	H
Thuy Dong III	A
Thanh Binh III	D
Vinh Hung I	I
Vinh Hung II	C

RESTAURANTS

Café Can	8
Café des Amis	9
Cargo Club	4
Hong Phuc	7
Mango Rooms	5
Miss Ly (Cafeteria 22)	1
Quan An	6
Tam Tam Café	3
Treat's Same Same Café	2

Bus Station (100m)
Chua Chuc Thanh (120m) & Da Nang (30km)
F (3km), G (4km) & Cua Dai Beach (4km)
Cam Nam Island
My Son (40km)
NGUYEN TAT THANH
LY THUONG KIET
THAI PHIEN
NGUYEN TRUONG TO
TRAN CAO VAN
HAI BA TRUNG
BA TRIEU
TRAN HUNG DAO
PHAN DINH PHUNG
LE LOI
PHAN CHU TRINH
NGUYEN HUE
HOANG DIEU
NGUYEN DUY HIEU
PHAN BOI CHAU
CAM NAM BRIDGE
TRAN PHU
HOANG VAN THU
NGUYEN THAI HOC
TRAN QUY CAP
BACH DANG
NGUYEN THI MINH KHAI
An Phu Travel Service Office
Vietincombank
Camel Booking Office
Seventeen's Booking Office
Vietincombank
Police
Tran Family Chapel
Ticket Office
Historical & Cultural Museum
Ticket Office
Trieu Chau Assembly Hall
Phuoc Kien Assembly Hall
Quong Cong
Museum of Trade Ceramics
Truong Family Working House
Ticket Office
Ticket Office
Cantonese Assembly Hall
Phung Hung House
Ticket Office
Japanese Covered Bridge
Museum of Sa Huynh Culture
Tan Ky House
Quan Thang House
Ticket Office
Ticket Office
Ticket Office
Market
Fish Market
Tran Duong House
Traditional Art Performance House
Thu Bon River
An Hoi Island
0 200m

Visiting Hoi An's sights

A **combined ticket** ($5) covers Hoi An's more famous sights and allows access to five sights, one from each of the following groups: one of the three museums (Trade Ceramics, Sa Huynh Culture or Historical and Cultural); one of the four participating merchants' houses; one of the three participating Chinese assembly halls; a traditional music concert or a handicraft workshop; the temple on the Japanese Covered Bridge or Quang Cong Temple. Tickets are valid for two days and can be purchased at seven clearly marked **outlets** in and around the historic centre. All offices and relevant sights are open daily from 6.30am to 6pm; a **guide** for groups of more than eight is free.

Japanese Covered Bridge

The western end of Tran Phu is marked by a small bridge known as the **Japanese Covered Bridge**, which has been adopted as Hoi An's emblem. It has been reconstructed several times since the mid-sixteenth century to the same simple design. Inside the bridge's narrow span are a collection of stelae and four statues, two dogs and two monkeys, usually said to record that work began in the year of the monkey and ended in that of the dog. Motorized traffic can't use the bridge, and pedal bikes must be pushed across.

The Chinese Assembly Halls

Historically, Hoi An's ethnic Chinese population organized themselves according to their place of origin (Fujian, Guangdong, Chaozhou or Hainan), and each group maintained its own assembly hall as both community centre and house of worship. The most populous group hails from Fujian, and their **Phuoc Kien Assembly Hall**, at 46 Tran Phu, is an imposing edifice with an ostentatious, triple-arched gateway. The hall is dedicated to Thien Hau, Goddess of the Sea and protector of sailors. She stands, fashioned in 200-year-old papier mâché, on the main altar flanked by her green- and red-faced assistants, who between them can see or hear any boat in distress over a range of a thousand miles.

Trieu Chau Assembly Hall, on the far eastern edge of town at 157 Nguyen Duy Hieu, was built in 1776 by Chinese from Chaozhou and has a remarkable display of woodcarving. In the altar-niche sits Ong Bon, a general in the Chinese Navy, surrounded by a frieze teeming with bird, animal and insect life; the altar table also depicts life on land and in the ocean.

The merchants' houses

Most of Hoi An's original wooden buildings are on Tran Phu and south towards the river, which is where you'll see the best-known merchants' house, at 101 Nguyen Thai Hoc. The **Tan Ky House** is a beautifully preserved example of a two-storey, late eighteenth-century shop-house, with shop space at the front, a tiny central courtyard, and access to the river at the back. It is wonderfully cluttered with the property of seven generations grown wealthy from trading silk, tea and rice and boasts two exceptionally fine hanging poem-boards. The house gets very crowded and is best visited early or late in the day.

Just up from the covered bridge, at 4 Nguyen Minh Khai, **Phung Hung House** has been home to the same family for eight generations since they moved from **Hue** in about 1780 to trade cinnamon and hardwoods from the central highlands. The large two-storey house is Vietnamese in style although its eighty ironwood columns and small glass skylights denote Japanese influence. An upstairs living area features a shrine to the ancestors as well as a large shrine to the protector deity Thien Hau, suspended from the ceiling.

Phan Chu Trinh, one block north of Tran Phu, hides two captivating "family chapels" or "worship houses". On Phan Chu Trinh itself is the 200-year-old **Tran Family Chapel** within a walled compound on the junction with Le Loi. Over homemade lotus flower tea you learn about the family, going back thirteen generations (300 years) to when the first ancestor settled in Hanoi. Family portraits are displayed in the reception room, and oblong wooden funerary boxes contain a name-tablet and biographical details of deceased family leaders. The smaller but more elaborate **Truong Family Working House** is hidden down an alley beside *Pho Hoi Restaurant* at 69 Phan Chu Trinh (not covered by ticket scheme; 7.30am–noon & 2–5pm; small donation expected). The Truong ancestors fled China in the early eighteenth century following the collapse of the Ming dynasty. The four finely carved wooden partitions in the sanctuary room come from Fujian and gifts from the Hue court are on display.

Museums and markets

Housed in a traditional timber residence-cum-warehouse, the **Museum of Trade Ceramics** at 80 Tran Phu showcases the history of Hoi An's ceramics trade, which peaked in the fifteenth and sixteenth centuries. The smaller **Museum of Sa Huynh Culture** at 149 Tran Phu displays artefacts found in Sa Huynh, 130km south of Hoi An, which flourished between the second century BC and the second century AD, while the **History and Cultural Museum**, behind the seventeenth-century Quang Cong temple at 7 Nguyen Hue, has a small overview of historical artefacts and documents relating to Hoi An's industrious past. The **market** at the east end of Tran Phu retains the atmosphere of a typical, traditional country market despite the number of tourists. This is a good place to buy **silk** (which is generally cheaper than in Hanoi or HCMC, but not as good as Thai silk).

The bustling riverside **fish market** (6–7am), opposite the southern end of the market, is worth setting the alarm clock for; it's a hive of early-morning activity, as dozens of fishwives sell the catch of the night.

Shopping

Many visitors extend their stay in Hoi An after discovering the delights of shopping for **tailor-made** clothes, shoes and bags; the number of places selling extra suitcases to overburdened travellers is an indication of the volume of their business. Lining the streets are scores of tailors that can knock up beautiful garments in a matter of hours and at minimal cost. They can make (or copy) just about any item of clothing. Ask around to find out price levels and reliable companies, and try having one item made before you order a complete wardrobe. Recommended addresses include: the shop at 36 Le Loi and Bi Bi Silk at 13 Phan Chu Trinh for women; and flamboyant Mr. Xe's shop at 71 Nguyen Thai Hoc for men. You can buy your own materials locally, or choose from the **silk** and **cotton** the tailor has in stock; take examples or photos of clothes if you have something specific in mind. There are also dozens of **workshops** that can make shoes and bags to your specifications.

Eating, drinking and entertainment

Hoi An has excellent food of all kinds, including local **specialities** such as *cao lau* ('white rose'), thick rice-flour noodles, beansprouts and pork-rind croutons in a light soup topped with thin slices of pork. Also look out for the steamed manioc-flour parcels of finely diced crab or shrimp called *banh bao* (or *banh vac*), and fried wanton (*hoanh thanh chien*). Hoi An shuts down early, though on Nguyen Thai Hoc **drinking** goes on until midnight. try *Tam Tam*, *Mango Rooms*, the *Lounge Bar* (at no. 102) or *Yellow Star Café* (at no. 73).

Café Can 74 Bach Dang. A welcoming restaurant offering Hoi An specialities and an excellent-value three-course set menu.

Café des Amis 52 Bach Dang. Renowned for its "Vietnamese cuisine plus imagination" and charismatic host, there's no menu, just four dishes for just over $3. The veggie and seafood specialities are all great. Try the Vietnamese set menu to sample a bit of everything.

Cargo Club 107 Nguyen Thai Hoc. A colonial-style, Vietnamese and international restaurant with speciality tea and coffee, cooking classes and rooftop dining. Also famed for its excellent breakfasts, with homemade cakes and pastries.

Hong Phuc 86 Bach Dang. A friendly, good-value eatery in a great waterside location, run by two multilingual female cousins who niftily fillet your fish at the table. The fish in banana leaf with lemon sauce is highly recommended. Happy hour 5–7pm.

Mango Rooms 111 Nguyen Thai Hoc. Delicious and imaginative Vietnamese dishes are cooked up in the open kitchen by the young owner, Duc. The elegant restaurant has two terraces, facing the river or the street.

Miss Ly (Cafeteria 22) 22 Nguyen Hue. This well-established restaurant, run by a delightful family, serves great Hoi An specialities; try the *cau lau*.

Quan An 19 Hoang Van Thu. A budget travellers' favourite, with outside seating, friendly service, cold draught beer for just $0.18, and a range of tasty set meals.

Tam Tam Café 110 Nguyen Thai Hoc. Stylish French-run bar-restaurant open late, with music, pool and upscale international cuisine served on balconies overlooking the street – safe from the postcard hawkers.

Treat's Same Same Café 158 Tran Phu. Popular bar-restaurant with traveller-friendly fare, and pool; a second outlet at 31 Phan Dinh Phung enigmatically promises to be "same same, not different".

Entertainment

There are one-hour evening performances of **traditional folk music** and dance (Mon–Sat 9pm; $2.50) at the Performance House of Traditional Arts, 75 Nguyen Thai Hoc. On the eve of the full moon every lunar calendar month, the centre of Hoi An celebrates a **Full-Moon Festival**; vehicles are banned, the streets are taken over by traditional entertainment and performances, and the only lights allowed are a mass of coloured silk lanterns.

My Son

The mouldering, overgrown World Heritage-listed ruins of Vietnam's most evocative Cham site, **MY SON** (daily 6.30am–5pm; $3, includes transport 2km from the ticket office to the ruins), lie 40km southwest of Hoi An, in a bowl of lushly wooded hills. The track out to the site strikes west from Highway 1 at Duy Xuyen and is quite treacherous, so most visitors come on a tour bus from Hoi An ($2), rather than on a rented motorbike. Many tour companies in Hoi An now arrange tours to My Son returning part of the way by boat, taking in traditional villages along the river ($5).

Excavations at My Son show that Cham kings were buried here as early as the fourth century, but the ruined sanctuaries you see today were erected between the seventh and thirteenth centuries. My Son was considered the domain of gods and god-kings, and in its prime, comprised some seventy buildings. The sanctuaries weathered well until the 1960s when the Vietcong based themselves here and were pounded by American B52s. There are **unexploded mines** in the area, so don't stray from main paths.

Group B is regarded by archeologists as the spiritual epicentre of My Son. Of the central *kalan* (sanctuary), **B1**, only the base remains; but stone epitaphs reveal that it was dedicated to the god-king Bhadresvara, a hybrid of Shiva and King Bhadravarman, and erected in the eleventh century. **B5**, the impressive **repository room**, boasts a bowed, boat-shaped roof still in reasonably good shape. The outer walls support ornate columns and statues of deities, and, on the western side, a bas-relief depicting two elephants with their trunks entwined around a coconut tree. Next door in **Group C**, the central *kalan*, **C1**, is fairly well preserved; statues of gods stand around the walls and a carved lintel runs across the entrance.

East of B and C, the two long, windowed meditation halls that comprise **Group D** have now both been converted into modest galleries. **D1** contains a lingam, the remains of a carving of Shiva, and a statue of Nandi, Shiva's Bull; while in **D2** you'll see a fine frieze depicting many-armed Shiva dancing, and, below the steps up to its eastern entrance, a statue of Garuda. Bomb damage was particularly cruel in the

△ Cham Tower, My Son

vicinity of **Group A**, reducing the once-spectacular *kalan*, **A1**, to a heap of toppled columns and lintels. Within, a huge lingam base is ringed by a number of detailed, fifteen-centimetre-high figures at prayer.

Da Nang

Central Vietnam's dominant port and its fourth largest city, **DA NANG** harbours few sights beyond the exceptional Cham Museum, but is a major transport hub with air connections as well as road and rail links. In the American War it served as a massive South Vietnamese airbase and played host to thousands of US troops as well as refugees searching for work. But walking around today, it's the earlier, French presence that is more apparent in the leafy boulevards and colonial-style houses.

Two blocks south of **Cho Han**, past the salmon-pink cathedral, colonial Da Nang is represented by a few wooden and stucco houses at the eastern end of Tran Quoc Toan. From here, turn right along the river for 750m to reach the **Cham Museum**, at the southern end of Bach Dang (daily 7am–5.30pm; $1.30), the most comprehensive display of Cham art in the world. Its display of graceful, sometimes severe, terracotta and sandstone figures gives a tantalizing glimpse of an artistically inspired culture that ruled most of southern Vietnam for a thousand years. Exhibits are grouped according to their place of origin: My Son (4–11C), Tra Kieu (Simhapura; 4–10C), Dong Duong (Indrapura; 8–10C), and Binh Dinh (11–15C).

Da Nang's **Cao Dai Temple**, on Hai Phong opposite the hospital, was built in 1956 and is Vietnam's second most important after Tay Ninh (see p.1142). An elderly archbishop, assisted by seventeen priests, ministers to a congregation here said to number 50,000. The temple is a smaller, simpler version of Tay Ninh, dominated inside by the all-seeing eye of the Supreme Being and paintings of Cao Dai's principal saints, Lao-tzu, Confucius, Jesus Christ and Buddha. You can watch adherents worshipping four times a day (6am, noon, 6pm & midnight).

Practicalities

Da Nang's **airport** is 3km southwest of the city centre and served by taxis ($2.60–3.30) and Honda om ($1.30). The **train station** lies 1,5km west of town at 128 Hai Phong. Long-distance **buses** arrive 1km further out at Lien Tinh bus station. To get into town from either of these take a cyclo or a xe om (less than $1). **Open-tour buses** generally drop off and pick up passengers at the Cham Museum on Bach Dang. Some hotels and tour agents offer **bicycle** rental ($0.65–1.30 per day), **car** rental ($15–30) and self-drive **motorbikes** ($5–7). For tours, car rental, tickets and **information**, An Phu Tourist, 82 Dong Da (☎511/818366) with another branch near the train station at 4 Hoang Hoa Tham (☎511/750195), is the best budget option; some open-tour buses depart from here, and they sell tickets for the **bus to Laos**. Others include *Hanh Café* at 161 Le Loi (☎0511/828205, ⓔhuusoncop@dng.vnn.vn), Dana Tours at 25 Hoang Dieu (☎0511/825653, ⓦwww.vietnamwelcomes.com), and Vietnamtourism at 83 Nguyen Thi Minh Khai (☎511/823660, vitourdad@dng.vnn.vn). Vietnam Airlines is at 39 Tran Phu (☎511/821130).

Exchange facilities, including an ATM, credit-card transactions and travellers' cheques, are available at Vietcombank, 147 Le Loi; the bank also has ATMs inside the *Bamboo Green Riverside* hotel and at the crossing of Le Loi and Tran Quoc Toan. The main **post office** is at 60 Bach Dang, but the poste restante is across the street at no. 64. **Internet** access can be found in several places along Tran Quoc Toan, and at Club Internet, 90 Hai Phong.

The **immigration police** are at 1 Nguyen Thi Minh Khai, there's a **pharmacy** at 5 Le Duan and the city **hospital** is at Benh Vien Da Khoa, 124 Hai Phong (☎511/821118), opposite the Cao Dai Temple. You can get **tourist visas for Laos** at the Lao Consulate, 16 Tran Quy Cap (Mon–Fri 8–11am & 2–4pm;

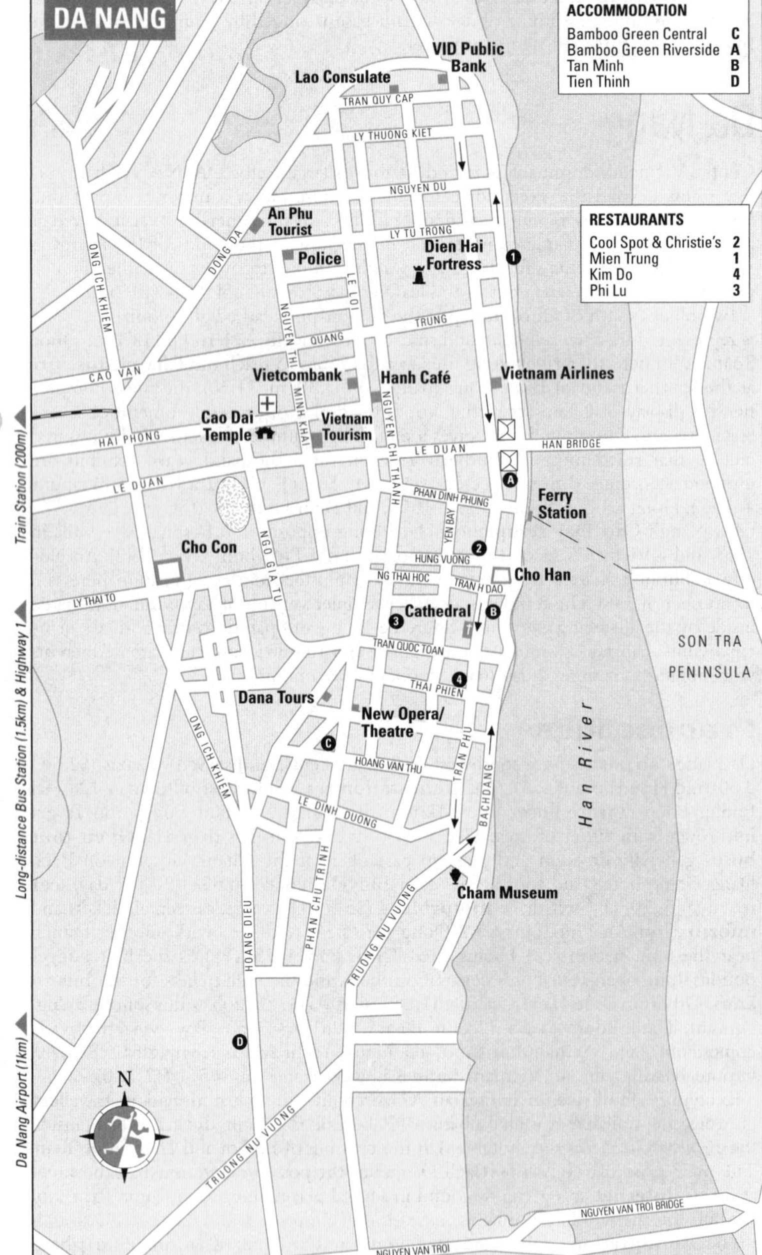
DA NANG
ACCOMMODATION
Bamboo Green Central C
Bamboo Green Riverside A
Tan Minh B
Tien Thinh D
RESTAURANTS
Cool Spot & Christie's 2
Mien Trung 1
Kim Do 4
Phi Lu 3
VID Public Bank
Lao Consulate
TRAN QUY CAP
LY THUONG KIET
NGUYEN DU
An Phu Tourist
LY TU TRONG
Police
Dien Hai Fortress
DONG DA
ONG ICH KHIEM
LE LOI
NGUYEN THI MINH KHAI
TRUNG
QUANG
CAO VAN
Vietcombank
Hanh Café
Vietnam Airlines
Cao Dai Temple
Vietnam Tourism
NGUYEN CHI THANH
HAI PHONG
LE DUAN
HAN BRIDGE
Ferry Station
PHAN DINH PHUNG
YEN BAY
NGO GIA TU
Cho Con
HUNG VUONG
Cho Han
NG THAI HOC
TRAN H DAO
LY THAI TO
Cathedral
TRAN QUOC TOAN
THAI PHIEN
SON TRA
PENINSULA
Dana Tours
New Opera/ Theatre
HOANG VAN THU
TRAN PHU
BACHDANG
Han River
LE DINH DUONG
Cham Museum
PHAN CHU TRINH
HOANG DIEU
TRUONG NU VUONG
N
NGUYEN VAN TROI BRIDGE
NGUYEN VAN TROI
0
500m
Train Station (200m)
Long-distance Bus Station (1.5km) & Highway 1
Da Nang Airport (1km)
My Khe Beach (2km)
My Khe Beach (3km) & Monkey Mountain (11km)
Marble Mountains (15km), Non Nuoc Beach & Hoi An (32km)

☎511/821208); see below for details on Lao border crossings. Da Nang has plenty of **hotels**, but you'll still find better value and choice in Hoi An. On the riverfront, *Tan Minh*, at 142 Bach Dang (☎511/827456, ⓔtanminhhotel@dgn.vnn.vn; ③), has good budget rooms. The *Tien Thinh*, 448 Hoang Dieu (☎511/834566; ④), is a good-value hotel with twenty clean rooms offering satellite TV and air-con; the rate includes breakfast. Transport and ticketing can be arranged via the reception. *Bamboo Green Riverside*, 68 Bach Dang (☎0511/832591; ⑥) is a more upmarket choice, with plush rooms overlooking the river. Finally, the *Bamboo Green Central*, just south of the centre at 158 Phan Chau Trinh (☎511/822996; ⑦), caters mainly to businesspeople and groups, but has well-equipped, comfortable rooms.

Fruitful hunting grounds for local **restaurants** and foodstalls are around the market, the southern end of Nguyen Chi Thanh, and streets around the Le Loi-Tran Quoc Toan crossroads. Meet Da Nang's expats at the Japanese/Australian-run *Cool Spot & Christie's*, 112 Tran Phu, where the upstairs restaurant serves spicy curries from across Asia, as well as pizzas, burgers and Japanese dishes; the ground-floor bar shows sports on TV. *Mien Trung*, overlooking the river at 9 Bach Dang, won't win any prizes for decor, but does serve excellent regional food to a mostly local clientele. For Chinese food, *Kim Do*, at 180 Tran Phu, is a popular and upmarket place, while *Phi Lu*, at 225 Nguyen Chi Thanh, is a cheaper option.

Moving on from Da Nang

Heading **to Hue**, you can take the train, the bus or a hire car ($20–30). Frequent local buses for Hue leave from the main Lien Tinh bus station; there are also convenient open-tour buses ($3) leaving daily. Bikes wait outside Da Nang train station to whisk you off **to Hoi An** (45min; $4–5); by taxi or hire car, it's about $10–15. Local buses run to Hoi An from Lien Tinh bus station (every 30mins; 1hr–1hr 30min; $0.65), though it's quicker to flag one down at Nguyen Van Troi bridge instead of waiting endlessly for it to fill up at the bus station. A more expediant option is the open-tour buses, with daily departures to Hoi An ($3), as well as Nha Trang ($7) and Hue ($3). An Phu Tourist (see p.1185), can organize tickets; alternatively, wait outside the Cham Museum for *Sinh Café* open-tour buses passing through en route to Hue, usually around 8am. Daily air-con buses run from Da Nang via the Lao Bao border crossing **to Savannakhet** on the **Laos/Thai border** (3.30pm; 24hr); tickets ($21) are available at An Phu Tourist.

Hue

Unlike Hanoi, HCMC and most other Vietnamese cities, **HUE** somehow seems to have stood aside from the current economic frenzy and, despite its calamitous history, has retained a unique cultural identity. It's a small, peaceful city, full of lakes, canals and lush vegetation, and some magnificent historical sights – including the nineteenth-century walled citadel, the remnants of its once-magnificent Imperial City and seven palatial Royal Mausoleums. With all this to offer, Hue is inevitably one of Vietnam's pre-eminent tourist destinations. It's also the main jumping-off point for day-tours of the DMZ (see p.1194), as well as a springboard for buses to Savannakhet and Laos, via the Lao Bao border (see p.1196).

In 1802, Emperor Gia Long, founder of the **Nguyen dynasty**, moved the capital from Hanoi and built his Imperial City in Hue. From then on, the Nguyen dynasty ruled Vietnam from Hue until the abdication of Emperor Bao Dai in 1945, though the French seized the city in 1885, leaving them as nominal rulers only. During the 1968 **Tet Offensive**, the North Vietnamese Army (NVA) held the city for 25 days, and in the ensuing counter-assault the city was all but levelled. Seven years later, on

March 26, 1975, the NVA were back to liberate Hue, the first big town south of the Seventeenth Parallel. The huge task of rebuilding received a boost in 1993 when UNESCO listed Hue as a World Heritage Site.

Arrival, information and city transport

Flights into Hue's **Phu Bai Airport**, 15km southeast of the city, are met by an airport bus ($1.60), which goes to central hotels, and by metered taxis (about $7). Heading back to the airport, the airport bus departs from the Vietnam Airlines branch office at 12 Ha Noi (☎54/823 249), or you can arrange a pick-up from your hotel reception. The main Vietnam Airlines office can be found in the Thuan Hoa Hotel at 7 Nguyen Tri Phuong (☎54/824709). The **train station** lies about 1.5km from the centre of town at the far western end of Le Loi, a boulevard running along the south bank of the Perfume River. Note that trains out of Hue get booked up quickly, so make onward travel arrangements as early as possible.

Hue has two long-distance **bus stations**: services from the south pull into An Cuu station, 3km southeast of the centre along Highway 1; while buses from Hanoi and the north dump you at An Hoa station, 4km northwest on Highway 1: cyclos and xe om are on hand to take you into the centre.

Bicycles ($0.40–0.60 per day), **motorbikes** ($4–5) and **cars** ($20–30) can be rented from hotels, guesthouses and cafés, all of which can help arrange onward transport by bus or hired car to Hoi An, Da Nang and Hanoi.

The helpful *Sinh Café* at 12 Hung Vuong (☎054/845022, ⓦwww.sinhcafevn.com), on the corner with Nguyen Tri Phuong, arranges Perfume River boat trips and DMZ tours, tickets for buses to Laos and Thailand, and rents out quality bicycles. Kim Travel open-tour buses operate from 10 Hung Vuong (☎54/822825). Both the *Café on Thu Wheels* (see p.1193) and the *Stop & Go* café at 10 Ben Nghe (☎054/827051) are recommended for their **motorcycle tours** around town ($6) or of the DMZ ($13).

The main **post office** is at 14b Ly Thuong Kiet and offers the usual poste restante facilities. Vietcombank is at 78 Hung Vuong; more convenient is its **exchange** office outside the *Saigon Morin Hotel* (Mon-Sat 7am-10pm), which also has an ATM and can deal with travellers' cheques and Visa and MasterCard cash advances (as can *Sinh Café*). **Internet** access is available in the main tourist enclaves along Hung Vuong and at the northern end of Le Loi. Hue Central **Hospital** is at 16 Le Loi (☎54/822325) and the **immigration police** are at 77 Ben Nghe. There are **pharmacies** at nos. 33 and 36 Hung Vuong.

Moving on from Hue

Open-tour buses to and from Hanoi (12hrs, $9) and Hoi An (4-6hrs, $2) stop at the cluster of travel agent offices and hotels along Hung Vuong or the northern end of Le Loi. The public bus **to Savannakhet in Laos** via the Lao Bao border departs daily at 5.30pm, arriving at around 5pm after a night in Dong Ha (tickets $13, including hotel); there's a connecting bus to Vientiane ($9 extra), arriving there in the early morning. A quicker and more comfortable option is the air-con tourist bus ($16), leaving at 6am on odd days with a change of bus in Dong Ha at 8am, and arrival in Savannakhet around 4pm; in Hue, you can buy tickets through **to Vientiane** ($26, arrival around 3pm the following day, includes a night in a hotel in Savannakhet) or for the connecting night bus **to Bangkok** ($55 including the Thai border ferry; arrival at 6am the following day). In both cases, you could combine the DMZ bus tour with a next-day departure from Dong Ha.

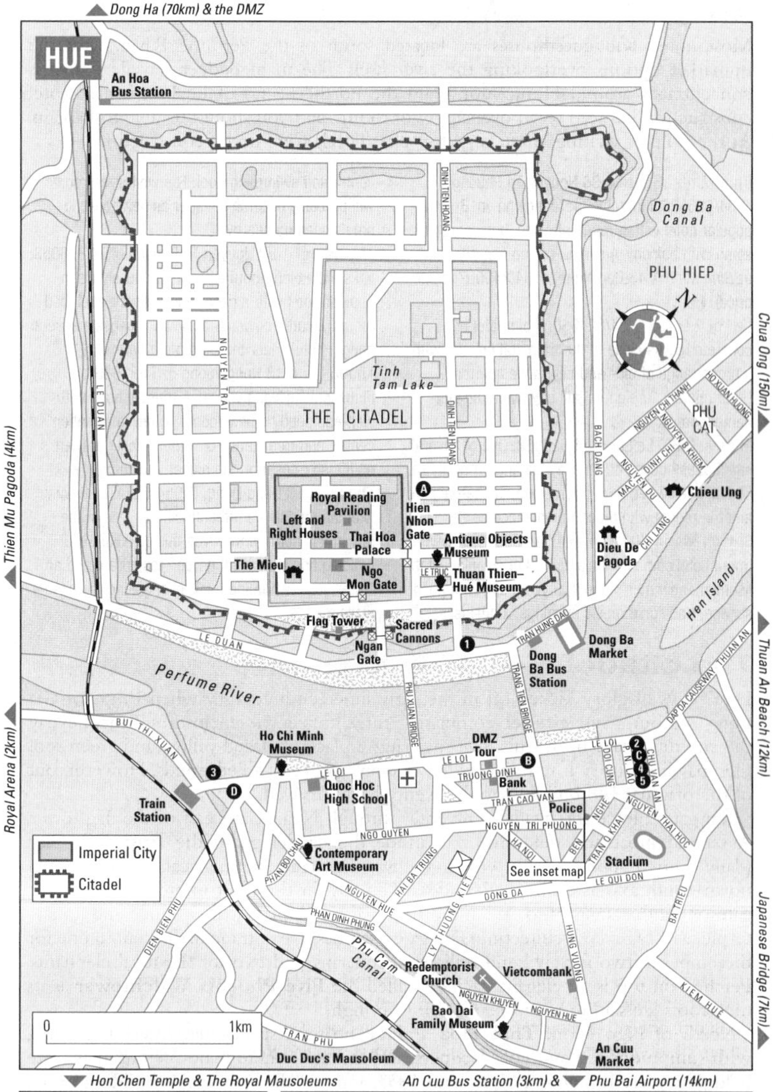
HUE
Dong Ha (70km) & the DMZ
An Hoa Bus Station
Dong Ba Canal
PHU HIEP
N
Chua Ong (150m)
DINH TIEN HOANG
NGUYEN TRAI
LE DUAN
Tinh Tam Lake
THE CITADEL
PHU CAT
BACH DANG
HO XUAN HUONG
NGUYEN CHI THANH
NGUYEN B KHIEM
NGUYEN DINH CHI
MAC DINH CHI
NGUYEN DU
CHI LANG
Chieu Ung
Thien Mu Pagoda (4km)
Royal Reading Pavilion
Left and Right Houses
Thai Hoa Palace
Hien Nhon Gate
Antique Objects Museum
The Mieu
Ngo Mon Gate
LE TRUC
Thuan Thien–Hué Museum
Dieu De Pagoda
Hen Island
Flag Tower
Sacred Cannons
Ngan Gate
TRAN HUNG DAO
Dong Ba Market
Dong Ba Bus Station
Thuan An Beach (12km)
THUAN AN
DAP DA CAUSEWAY
Perfume River
PHU XUAN BRIDGE
TRANG TIEN BRIDGE
BUI THI XUAN
Royal Arena (2km)
Ho Chi Minh Museum
DMZ Tour
LE LOI
DOI CUNG
P.N. LAO
CHU VAN AN
TRUONG DINH
Bank
Quoc Hoc High School
Train Station
TRAN CAO VAN
Police
NGHE
NGUYEN THAI HOC
NGO QUYEN
NGUYEN TRI PHUONG
HA NOI
BEN
TRAN Q KHAI
Stadium
Imperial City
Citadel
Contemporary Art Museum
PHAN BOI CHAU
HAI BA TRUNG
See inset map
LE QUI DON
DONG DA
NGUYEN HUE
LY THUONG KIET
BA TRIEU
DIEN BIEN PHU
PHAN DINH PHUNG
HUNG VUONG
Japanese Bridge (7km)
Phu Cam Canal
Redemptorist Church
Vietcombank
NGUYEN KHUYEN
NGUYEN HUE
KIEM HUE
Bao Dai Family Museum
0
1km
TRAN PHU
Duc Duc's Mausoleum
An Cuu Market
Hon Chen Temple & The Royal Mausoleums
An Cuu Bus Station (3km) & Phu Bai Airport (14km)

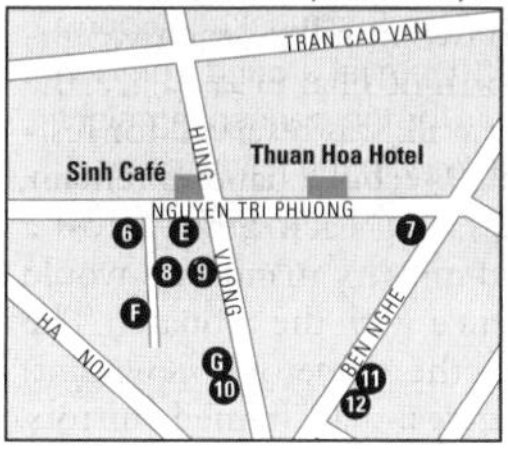
TRAN CAO VAN
Sinh Café
Thuan Hoa Hotel
HUNG
NGUYEN TRI PHUONG
VUONG
HA NOI
BEN NGHE

ACCOMMODATION	
Binh Minh I Sunrise	E
Le Loi	D
Mimosa	C
Saigon Morin	B
Thai Binh I	F
Thang Long	G
Thanh Noi	A

RESTAURANTS & BARS			
B4 Bar	12	La Boulangerie Française	10
Café 3	3	La Carambole	5
Café on Thu Wheels	8	Lac Thien	1
Co Do	7	Omar Khayyam's Tandoori	6
DMZ Bar	2	Violon Bar	11
Dong Tam	4	Xuan Trang	9

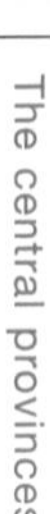

Accommodation

Most hotels and guesthouses are located south of the Perfume River, with the upmarket options overlooking the river itself. The main budget travellers' area is concentrated around Hung Vuong and the northern end of Le Loi; frantic hotel construction has lead to an oversupply of rooms, and you should be able to bargain. At the time of writing, three large top-class hotels were under construction.

Binh Minh I Sunrise 36 Nguyen Tri Phuong ⓣ54/825526, binhminhhue@dng.vnn.vn. Bright, popular hotel with a range of clean, homely rooms, some with balcony. A similar set-up can be found at *Binh Minh II*, 45 Ben Nghe (ⓣ54/849007; same price). ❷–❹

Le Loi 2 Le Loi ⓣ54/824668. A big hotel of concrete blocks close to the train station, and with a broad range of old- and new-style quarters. Unfortunately, foreigners still pay twice the Vietnamese rates. ❷–❺

Mimosa 46/6 Le Loi ⓣ54/828068. One of several small guesthouses on an alley leading off northern Le Loi, this sweet, family-run place has bargain a/c and fan rooms with a communal balcony. ❷

Saigon Morin 30 Le Loi, ⓣ054/826526, ⓦwww.morinhotel.com.vn. Hue's upmarket colonial establishment, now more than 100 years old, with good service, traditional music evenings, a business centre and swimming pool. The well-sized rooms will probably become cheaper as new top-end hotels open up nearby. ❾

Thai Binh I 10/9 Nguyen Tri Phuong ⓣ54/828058, ⓔksanthaibinh@hotmail.com. Spotlessly clean, popular hotel with a good range of well-equipped rooms, located down an alleyway alongside several budget hotels near the *Binh Minh Sunrise*. ❷–❻

Thang Long 18 Hung Vuong ⓣ54/826462, dinhxuanlong@dng.vnn.vn. A friendly hotel with well-equipped homely rooms, a tour information centre, and free station or airport pickups. There's no lift, so rates drop the higher you climb. ❷–❸

Thanh Noi 3 Dang Dung, ⓣ054/522478, ⓦwww.vietnamtourism.com/thanhnoihotel. One of the few hotels north of the river, this colonial-style building has a pleasant garden restaurant and an "intelligent swimming pool" overlooking the citadel walls. ❺–❻

The citadel

Hue's days of glory kicked off in the early nineteenth century when Emperor Gia Long laid out a vast **citadel**, comprising three concentric enclosures. In its heyday, the city must have been truly awe-inspiring, a place of glazed yellow and green roof tiles, pavilions of rich red and gilded lacquer, and lotus-filled ponds. However, out of the original 148 buildings, only twenty have survived.

Ten gates pierce the citadel wall: enter through Ngan Gate, east of the flag tower. A second moat and defensive wall inside the citadel guard the **Imperial City** (daily 6am–5.30pm; $3.50), which follows the same symmetrical layout along a north–south axis as Beijing's Forbidden City. By far the most impressive of its four gates is south-facing **Ngo Mon**, the Imperial City's principal entrance and a masterpiece of Nguyen architecture. The gate itself has five entrances: the central one for the emperor; two for civil and military mandarins, and two for the royal elephants. Perched on top is an elegant pavilion called the **Five Phoenix Watchtower** as its nine roofs are said to resemble five birds in flight.

North of Ngo Mon, **Thai Hoa Palace** boasts a spectacular interior glowing with sumptuous red and gold lacquers, and this was where major ceremonies were held. The present building dates from 1833, and was the only major building in the Imperial City to escape bomb damage. Eighty ornate ironwood pillars, each weighing two tonnes, hold up the roof of the throne room. North of Thai Hoa Palace, the ten-hectare **Forbidden Purple City**, enclosed by a low wall, was reserved for residential palaces, many of which were destroyed in a fire in 1947, but a handful remain, including the restored **Left House** and **Right House** facing each other across a courtyard immediately behind Thai Hoa Palace. Civil and military mandarins would spruce themselves up here before proceeding to an audience with the monarch. The Right House (actually to your left – the names refer to the emperor's viewpoint) is the more complete with its ornate murals and two gargantuan framed mirrors. Northeast from here, the **Royal Reading Pavilion** is an appealing, two-tier structure surrounded by bonsai; the nearby Royal Theatre holds daily court music and theatre performances (9am, 10am, 2.30pm, 3.30pm; $1.30). To the southwest, **The Mieu** dynastic temple, a decorous low, red-lacquerwork building, has a row of thirteen altar tables dedicated to the Nguyen Royal Emperors.

Boat trips on the Perfume River

A boat trip on the **Perfume River** is one of the city's highlights, puttering in front of the citadel, past row-boats heading for Dong Ba market. The standard **boat trip** takes you to Thien Mu Pagoda, Hon Chen Temple and the most rewarding royal mausoleums, and it's usually possible to take a bicycle on the boat and cycle back to **Hue**. Most tour agents and hotels offer river tours starting at $2 per person (though this does not include entrance to the tombs or Hon Chen Temple). The same agents can arrange charter boats at $20–25 for the day; alternatively, go direct to the wharf east of the Trang Tien Bridge, where the going rate should be $2–3 per hour.

Founded in 1601 by Nguyen Hoang, **Thien Mu Pagoda** (free) is the oldest in **Hue** and has long been a focus for Buddhist protest against repression. In 1963, it hit international headlines when one of its monks, Thich Quang Duc, burned himself to death in Saigon, in protest at the excesses of President Diem's regime. The monk's powder-blue Austin car is now on display here, with a copy of the famous photograph that shocked the world. The seven tiers of the octagonal, brick stupa each represent one of Buddha's incarnations on earth. Thien Mu Pagoda is also within **cycling** distance of Hue (6km; 30min). Follow Le Duan (Highway 1) south from the citadel as far as the train tracks and then just keep heading west along the river.

Hon Chen Temple, ($1.40) is most memorable for its scenery of russet temple roofs among towering trees. Of several shrines and temples that populate the hillside, the most interesting is the main sanctuary, Hue Nam, up from the landing stage and to the right, with its unique nine-tier altar table and small, upper sanctuary room accessible via two steep staircases. The temple is 9km from Hue and is only accessible from the river. If you don't want to take a **tour**, hire a sampan either from the ferry station (accessible from the riverside road, near Thieu Tri Mausoleum; $0.30 per person return), from Minh Mang pier (around $2 per person return) or from boat stations off Le Loi in Hue ($5 per boat return).

A more unusual way to enjoy the Perfume River is to attend a traditional **folk-song performance** on its waters. Under the Nguyen emperors Hue was the cultural as well as political capital of Vietnam, and artists would entertain the gentry with poetry and music from sampans on the river. Tourist offices and hotels can sell you tickets for nightly performances on the river ($3–5). Minh-Hai Boat Company (☎54/845060) can also organize dinner cruises with traditional music for $22, which includes a boat for up to six people and the musicians; food is another $3 per person.

The Royal Mausoleums

The Nguyens built themselves magnificent **Royal Mausoleums** in the valley of the Perfume River among low, forested hills to the south of Hue. Each one is a unique expression of the monarch's personality, usually planned in detail during his lifetime to serve as his palace in death. Once an auspicious site was found, artificial lakes, waterfalls, hills and garden settings were added. Though the details vary, all the mausoleums consist of three elements: the main **temple** is dedicated to the worship of the deceased emperor and his queen, and houses their funeral tablets and possessions; a large, stone **stele** records details of his reign, in front of which spreads a paved courtyard, where ranks of stone mandarins line up to honour their emperor; and the royal **tomb** itself is enclosed within a wall.

The contrasting mausoleums of Tu Duc, Khai Dinh and Minh Mang are the most attractive and well preserved, as well as being easily accessible. These are also the three covered by the boat trips, so they can get crowded; everywhere gets packed at weekends. **Entry** to the mausoleums (daily 7am–5.30pm) is $3.50 each for the main three, $1.40 for the majority of the others. To **get to the mausoleums** you can either rent a bicycle or motorbike, or take a Perfume River boat trip (see p.1190), which entails a couple of longish walks that may induce you to hire one of the awaiting Honda oms, at a further cost of about $1.30 for a return trip. A good compromise is to take a bike on board a tour boat and cycle back to Hue from the last stop.

The Mausoleum of Tu Duc

Emperor Tu Duc was a romantic poet and a weak king, who ruled Vietnam from 1847 to 1883. The **Mausoleum of Tu Duc** is the most harmonious of all the mausoleums, with elegant pavilions and pines reflected in serene lakes. It took only three years to complete (1864–67), allowing Tu Duc a full sixteen years here for boating and fishing, meditation, and composing some of the 4000 poems he is said to have written. Entering by the southern gate, brick paths lead beside a lake and a couple of waterside pavilions, from where steps head up through a triple-arched gateway to a second enclosure containing the **main temple**, Hoa Khiem, which Tu Duc used as a palace before his death. Behind the temple stands the colourful royal theatre. The second group of buildings, to the north, is centred on the **emperor's tomb**, preceded by the salutation court and stele-house. Tu Duc's Mausoleum is 7km from central Hue by road. From the boat jetty, it's a two-kilometre walk from the river, or take one of the Honda oms waiting on the river bank.

The Mausoleum of Khai Dinh

By way of a complete contrast the **Mausoleum of Khai Dinh** is a monumental confection of European Baroque and ornamental Sino-Vietnamese style, set high up on a wooded hill. Khai Dinh was the penultimate Nguyen emperor and his mausoleum has neither gardens nor living quarters. Though he only reigned for nine years (1916–25) it took eleven (1920–31) to complete his mausoleum. The approach is via a series of dragon-ornamented stairways leading first to the salutation courtyard and the stele-house. Climbing up a further four terraces brings you to the **principal temple**, built of concrete with slate roofing imported from France, whose walls, ceiling, furniture, everything is decorated to the hilt in glass and porcelain mosaic that writhes with dragons and is peppered with symbolic references and classic imagery. A life-size statue of the emperor holding his sceptre sits under the canopy. Khai Dinh's Mausoleum is 10km from Hue by road. Arriving by boat, it's a 1.5-kilometre walk or Honda om ride on a paved road, heading eastwards with a giant Quan Am statue on your right until you see the mausoleum on the opposite hillside.

The Mausoleum of Minh Mang

Court officials took fourteen years to find the location for the **Mausoleum of Minh Mang** and then only three years to build it (1841–43), using 10,000 workmen. Minh Mang, the second Nguyen emperor (1820–41), was a capable, authoritarian monarch who was passionate about architecture, and he designed his mausoleum along traditional Chinese lines, with fifteen hectares of superb landscaped gardens and plentiful lakes to reflect the red-roofed pavilions. Inside the mausoleum a processional way links the series of low mounds bearing all the main buildings. After the salutation courtyard and stele-house comes the crumbling principal temple where Minh Mang and his queen are worshipped. Continuing west you reach **Minh Lau**, the elegant, two-storey "Pavilion of Pure Light" standing among frangipani trees, symbols of longevity.

Until the new road bridge is completed, you can reach Minh Mang's Mausoleum from Khai Dinh's by following the **road** west until you hit the Perfume River (1.5km); turn left along the bank and you'll find sampans to take you across the river ($0.65 return). The entrance is then 200m walk away on the other side. This is also where you pick up sampans for Hon Chen Temple (see p.1191).

Eating and nightlife

The most famous **Hue dish** is *banh khoai*, a small, crispy yellow pancake, fried up with shrimp, pork and bean sprouts, and served with peanut and sesame sauce, star-fruit, green banana, lettuce and mint. For that early open-tour bus departure, fresh croissants, brown bread, pastries and cakes can be purchased at the La Boulangerie Francaise outlet at 20 Hung Vuong; profits go to local charities. Hue's main **night-spots** include the *DMZ Bar* at 44 Le Loi, popular for its pool tables and dancing, and *Café on Thu Wheels* at 10/2 Nguyen Tri Phuong. This tiny bar-café, run by the charmingly nutty Mrs. Thu, has loud music, good food and friendly staff that run excellent motorbike tours - attested by the recommendations scribbled on the walls. Popular with locals and romantics, the *Violon Bar* at 65 Ben Nghe is one of the few candlelit places in the country, with upmarket drinks and nightly live music under a thatched roof. Just down the street at no. 75, the relaxed *B4 Bar* has pool, local Huda beer on tap and bottled Belgian beers; Bruno, the congenial Flemish owner, is a good source of travel tips.

Café 3 3 Le Loi. A cheap and cheerful streetside café opposite the *Le Loi Hotel*, serving the standard range of Western and Vietnamese dishes. They also have a variety of tours on offer.

Co Do 22 Ben Nghe. A small, no-frills corner restaurant using predominantly lemongrass and chilli to flavour its cheap and tasty squid, chicken or shrimp dishes.

Dong Tam 48/7 Le Loi. A vegetarian restaurant with a garden courtyard down an alley off Le Loi, run by a Buddhist family who offer a short business-card menu, including vegetarian *banh khoai* and a good-value set menu.

La Carambole 19 Pham Ngu Lao, ⓣ054/810491. Excellent international and local dishes are served at this chic French-run restaurant. Try one of the set menus. Reservations recommended.

Lac Thien 6 Dinh Tien Hoang. Probably Hue's friendliest and most interesting eatery, located on the citadel side. Run by a deaf-mute family, who communicate by a highly developed sign language, the food is excellent, taking in the Hue staples. Not to be confused with similarly named restaurants along this street.

Omar Khayyam's Tandoori 10 Nguyen Tri Phuong. A good-value Indian restaurant, deservedly popular for its reasonably priced North Indian fare, which includes a good vegetarian and thali selection. Open for breakfast from 8am.

Xuan Trang 14a Hung Vuong. An ugly but above-average backpackers' eatery with an extensive and reasonably priced menu; its ice creams and Hue speciality dishes are recommended. Also doubles as a tour agency.

Dong Ha

As a former US Marine Command Post and then ARVN base, **DONG HA** was obliterated in 1972, but it has bounced back, thanks largely to its administrative status and location at the eastern end of Highway 9, which leads through Laos to Savannakhet on the Mekong River. As the closest town to the DMZ, Dong Ha also attracts a lot of tourist traffic, though most people choose to stay in nearby Hue.

Dong Ha is a two-street town: Highway 1, known here as Le Duan Avenue, forms the north-south artery, while Highway 9 takes off inland at a central T-junction. The town's **bus station** is located on this junction, and its **train station** lies 1km south towards Hue, just west of the highway. The market and bridge over the Cua Viet River, 1km beyond the bus station, mark Dong Ha's northern extremity, where a road branches left to the **post office** (easily recognizable by the tall radio mast) and the remains of three US tanks.

For **information**, car rental, guides and DMZ motorbike tours ($14), contact Sepon Travel, behind the petrol station at 198 Le Duan (ⓣ053/855289, ⓔtmqttour@dng.vnn.vn). They also sell tickets for the DMZ tour bus originating in Hue ($8), and open-tour buses both within Vietnam and to Laos and Thailand. The **bank** at 1a Le Quy Don – walk left out of the bus station onto Le Duan for about 400m and take the first left – can do Visa and MasterCard cash advances and change dollars, but not travellers' cheques. There's an **Internet café** at 88 Le Duan ($0.40/hr), and another one 500m west of here.

The best **accommodation** can be found at the *Phung Hoang 2 Hotel*, 146 Le Duan (☎53/854567, ©victoryqt@dng.vnn.vn; ❸–❹), 500m south of the bus station on the Hue highway, which has a range of clean, good-value, air-con and fan rooms. A cheaper alternative a little closer to the bus station is *Trung Tam Quan* at 201 Le Duan (☎53/852972; ❶), offering just two rooms with clean shared facilities. Dong Ha's best **restaurants** are *Tan Chau II*, at 222 Le Duan near the *Phung Hoang 2 Hotel*, and *Hiep Loi* on the intersection of Highways 1 and 9.

Moving on from Dong Ha

Dong Ha is a convenient place to catch the bus **to Laos**, as passengers from Hue and Da Nang need to change buses or stop for the night here. Sepon Travel (see above) can arrange tickets. The public bus **to Savannakhet** ($10) leaves Dong Ha at 5am, arriving at around 5pm, and the air-con tourist bus ($14) leaves at 8am on odd days, arriving in Savannakhet around 4pm. See p.567 for connections to Vientiane and Bangkok.

The DMZ and across to Laos

Under the terms of the 1954 Geneva Accords, Vietnam was split in two along the Seventeenth Parallel, pending elections intended to reunite the country in 1956. The demarcation line ran along the Ben Hai River and was sealed by a strip of no man's land 5km wide on each side known as the **Demilitarized Zone**, or DMZ. All communist troops were supposed to regroup north in the Democratic Republic of Vietnam, leaving the southern Republic of Vietnam to non-communists. When the elections failed to take place, the Ben Hai River became the de facto border until 1975. In reality, both sides of the DMZ were anything but demilitarized after 1965, and anyway the border was easily circumvented – by the Ho Chi Minh Trail to the west and sea routes to the east – enabling the North Vietnamese to bypass a string of American firebases overlooking the river. The North Vietnamese Army (NVA) finally stormed the DMZ in 1972 and pushed the border 20km further south. The two provinces either side of the DMZ were the most heavily bombed and saw the highest casualties, civilian and military, American and Vietnamese, during the American War. So much firepower was unleashed over this area, including napalm and herbicides, that for years nothing would grow in the chemical-laden soil, but the region's low, rolling hills are now mostly reforested and green. Note that there's not that much see here nowadays, except for the occasional bunker or rusting tank, though just visiting such infamous sites is worth the trip for most.

You can explore the DMZ independently, but it's highly recommended to take a local **guide**, who will be able to show you the unmarked sites and will know which paths are free from **unexploded mines**. The daily **DMZ bus** day-trip starting in Hue (from 6am–6pm, $8) is the easiest way to see the most important places, and can be booked at most travel agents; arriving on an open-tour night-bus from Hanoi, you can also join it in Dong Ha at around 8am. As well as the sights detailed below, the day-trip takes in the Rockpile, a 230m-high hill used by the US as an artellery base, the Ho Chi Minh Trail and the touristy Van Kieu Bru minority village. Keep in mind this tour is very long when done from Hue, with short stops for photographs, and your understanding of the area depends a lot on how good the guide is. For an in-depth tour of the area, it's better to spend a few dollars more and hire a car or motorbike and guide from Hue or, for more time at the sites, Dong Ha (see pp.1185 and 1188).

North to the Vinh Moc tunnels

The American front line comprised a string of firebases set up on a long, low ridge of hills looking north across the DMZ and the featureless plain of the Ben Hai River. The most accessible of these, **Doc Mieu Firebase**, sits at the top of a hill along Highway 1, 14km north of Dong Ha. A track, marked by a concrete sign and a rusting American tank, leads a few hundred metres to where a number of NVA-built bunkers still stand amid a landscape pocked with craters. Before the NVA overran Doc Mieu in 1972, the base played a pivotal role in the South's defence, and for a while, this was the command post for calling in airstrikes along the Ho Chi Minh Trail. Just beyond Doc Mieu, Highway 1 drops down into the DMZ, running between paddy-fields to **Hien Luong Bridge** and the Ben Hai River, which lies virtually on the Seventeenth Parallel. It was destroyed in 1967, and reopened in 1975 as a symbol of reunification.

One kilometre north, 22km from Dong Ha, a signpost indicates a right turn to an amazing complex of tunnels where over a thousand people sheltered, sometimes for weeks on end, during the worst American bombardments. A section of the **Vinh Moc tunnels** has been restored and opened to visitors, with a small museum at the entrance (daily 7am–5pm; $1.60 including guide and flashlight); the tour through cramped passageways takes fifteen minutes. From 1966, villagers spent two years digging more than fifty tunnels here, which were constructed on three levels at 10, 15 and 20–23m deep with freshwater wells and a generator and lights. The underground village had a school, clinics, and a maternity room where seventeen children were born. Each family was allocated a tiny cavern, and were only able to emerge at night; the lack of fresh air and sunlight was a major problem, especially for young children. In 1972, the villagers were finally able to abandon their tunnels and rebuild their homes above ground. Vinh Moc is 16km from Highway 1 on a twisting, unmarked route that takes you north beside the coast.

Con Thien Firebase and the Truong Son Cemetery

The largest American installation along the DMZ was **Con Thien Firebase**, which, in the lead-up to the 1968 Tet Offensive, became the target of prolonged shelling. The Americans replied with everything in their arsenal, but the NVA finally overran the base in the summer of 1972. In the last twenty years, the pulverized land has struggled back to life and now has a veneer of green. From the US-built bunker in the ruined lookout post on Con Thien's highest point you get a great view over the DMZ and directly north to former enemy positions on the opposite bank of the Ben Hai River. To get there, drive west on Highway 9 from Dong Ha as far as Cam Lo town (11km) and then turn north on Highway QL15, following signs to the Truong Son Cemetery. The base is roughly 12km out of Cam Lo and 1km east of the road on an unmarked, winding path, which is best travelled with a guide.

Eight kilometres further along the same road, you come to the **Truong Son War Martyr Cemetery**, dedicated to the estimated 25,000 men, women and children – some soldiers were as young as 12 - who died on the Truong Son Trail, better known in the west as the Ho Chi Minh Trail. Many bodies were never recovered, but a total of 10,036 graves lie in the fourteen-hectare cemetery. Graves are arranged in five geographical regions, and each headstone announces *liet si* ("martyr").

Khe Sanh

The **battle of Khe Sanh** attracted worldwide media attention and, along with the simultaneous Tet Offensive, demonstrated the futility of America's efforts to contain their enemy. In late 1967, skirmishes around Khe Sanh increased as intelligence reports indicated a massive build-up of NVA troops, possibly as many as 40,000, facing 6000 Marines together with a few hundred South Vietnamese. Both the Western media and American generals were soon presenting the confrontation as a crucial test of America's credibility in South Vietnam – President Nixon famously remarked that he didn't want "any damn Dinbinfoo". The NVA's attack on the US base at Khe Sanh began in the early hours of January 21, 1968, and the battle lasted nine weeks, during which time the US pounded the area with nearly 100,000 tonnes of bombs, averaging one airstrike every five minutes, backed up by napalm and defoliants. The NVA were so well dug in that they continued to return fire, despite horrendous casualties. By the middle of March, the NVA had all but gone, having successfully diverted American resources away from southern cities prior to the Tet Offensive. Three months later, the Americans also withdrew, leaving a plateau that resembled a lunar landscape, contaminated for years to come with chemicals and explosives, although that's hard to imagine now, with widespread greenery and coffee and rubber plantations.

The town of **KHE SANH** (now officially rechristened **Huang Hoa**) is a bleak, one-street settlement, its frontier atmosphere reinforced by the smugglers' trail across the border to Laos, only 19km away. To find **Khe Sahn base**, fork right beside a three-legged monument on the town's eastern outskirts, follow the road for 2km and then turn right beside a house onto an unmarked path. There are two very basic **guesthouses** on Khe Sanh's dusty main street (Highway 9): *Khe Sahn Hotel* (☎53/880740; ❶), in the centre of town under the radio mast, has bigger rooms; 1km further west is the slightly cheaper but more run-down *Huong Hoa Guest House* (☎53/880563; ❶). Opposite the *Khe Sahn Hotel*, and about 20m west, are a few wooden shacks, which serve as pretty good **restaurants**. There is no bus station in Khe Sanh, but along Highway 9 you can flag down frequent **buses** en route to Lao Bao and the **Lao border**, and Dong Ha in the opposite direction; change in Dong Ha for Hue.

The Lao Bao border crossing to Laos

Twenty kilometres from Khe Sanh, the **Lao Bao border crossing** (daily 7am–5pm), is the most popular of Vietnam's four overland routes into Laos. To reach the border gate, take a local bus from Dong Ha or Khe Sanh as far as Lao Bao village, where you can pick up a Honda om for the final 3km. At the crossing you just walk 50m between inspection posts. Some tourist offices in Hue and Da Nang sell tickets for buses to Laos and Savannakhet, which pass through this border enroute (see p.1188 & p.1185). On the Lao side of the border, you can stay at **Daen Sawan**, 2km away (see p.571), or catch a bus for the transport hub of Savannakhet (see pp.567–570), which is also on the Thai border. Four buses to Savannakhet leave from Daen Sawan in the morning, the last at 2pm.

Vinh and the Cau Treo border crossing to Laos

Although Lao Bao is by far the most popular land crossing into Laos, it is also possible to cross the border at **CAU TREO** (daily 7.30am–5pm), 105km west of the city of **VINH** on Highway 8. From Vinh's provincial bus station (Ben Xe Cho Vinh), about 500m from Vinh's market, several morning buses depart for Trung Tram (formerly known as Huong Son), the last settlement of any size before the border. From here, you'll either have to pick up a motorbike taxi for the last 35km to Cau Treo, or catch one of the regular shuttle buses that ferry locals to the border. Alternatively, hotels in Vinh can arrange a share taxi all the way to the border (105km) for around $28, or a xe om for $15. An easier option are the Laos-bound buses, booked in Hanoi, that trundle through this border en route to Vientiane. Facilities at Cau Treo amount to about half a dozen pho stalls, so sort out money and anything else you need before leaving.

In **VINH**, you can **stay** at the ostentatious *Hong Ngoc I*, just north of the bus station at 99 Le Loi (☎38/841314; ❷). The *Railway Station Guest House* (☎38/853754; ❶–❷), a basic guesthouse above a café in the northeast corner of the station forecourt, has slightly cheaper rooms. The *Saigon Kim Lien Hotel*, 25 Quang Trung (☎ 38/838899; ❻–❼), can assist with transport arrangements and general information, and the Vietcombank at 9 Nguyen Sy Sach can arrange Visa and MasterCard **cash advances**, as well as change cash and travellers' cheques. **Open-tour buses** can set down passengers in Vinh en route; however, make sure you reconfirm onward travel with the relevant office before arrival.h1/11.6

11.6

Hanoi and around

The Vietnamese nation was born among the lagoons and marshes of the Red River Delta around 4000 years ago and for most of its independent existence has been ruled from **HANOI**, Vietnam's small, elegant capital lying in the heart of the northern delta. Given the political and historical importance of Hanoi and its burgeoning population of three million, it's a surprisingly low-key city, with the character of a provincial town – though with a dramatic rise in motorbike ownership, increased traffic and Western-style retail outlets, it's catching up fast with the brash, young HCMC. For the time being, however, it remains relatively laid-back. It still retains buildings from the eleventh-century court of its founding father King Ly Thai To, most notably the **Temple of Literature**, and some of the streets in the **Old Quarter** still trade in the same speciality goods they dealt in 500 years ago. In 1887, the French turned Hanoi into the centre of government for the entire Union of Indochina, replacing ancient monuments with grand colonial residences, many of which survive today. Hanoi finally became the capital of independent Vietnam in 1954, with Ho Chi Minh its first president: **Ho Chi Minh's Mausoleum** is now the city's biggest crowd-puller. The city sustained serious damage in the American War, particularly the infamous Christmas Bombing campaign of 1972, much of it lucidly chronicled in the **Army Museum**. Until recently, political isolation together with lack of resources preserved what was essentially the city of the 1950s. However, since the advent of tourism in 1993, the city has seen an explosion in travellers' cafés, mini-hotels and cybercafés. Indeed, Hang Bac, one of the Old Quarter's main drags, which is home to a large number of traveller hangouts, is starting to resemble a little piece of Bangkok's Khao San Road in Hanoi. The big question now is how much of central Hanoi will survive the onslaught of modernization.

Arrival and information

It's a 45-minute ride into central Hanoi from **Noi Bai Airport** (Ⓣ4/584 4427), 35km away. Just outside the international and domestic arrival terminals, you'll find Noi Bai Transport (Ⓣ4/886 5615) airport minibuses ($2) and taxis ($8-9) waiting. These operate from the first to the last flight, and maintain a well-organized service and standardized prices, dropping off in the centre of Hanoi. The minibuses will bring you to the Vietnam Airlines office at 1 Quang Trung. If taking a taxi, always insist on the hotel you wish to be taken to, as many will try to take you to alternative hotels in order to gain commission. In the arrivals hall, there's a tourist information office booth (daily 8am-7pm) that can help you find a hotel, a Vietcombank ATM that accepts Visa and MasterCard, and a few exchange bureaus that offer reasonable rates.

Arriving by **train** from HCMC, all points south and from China, you'll exit the main station onto Le Duan. However, trains from the east and north (Hai Phong, Lang Son and Lao Cai) pull into platforms at the rear of the main station, bringing you out onto Tran Quy Cap. There are a few hotels nearby that are useful if you arrive late or have an early start; otherwise, pick up a cyclo or xe om (motorbike taxi) to the Old Quarter for less than $1.

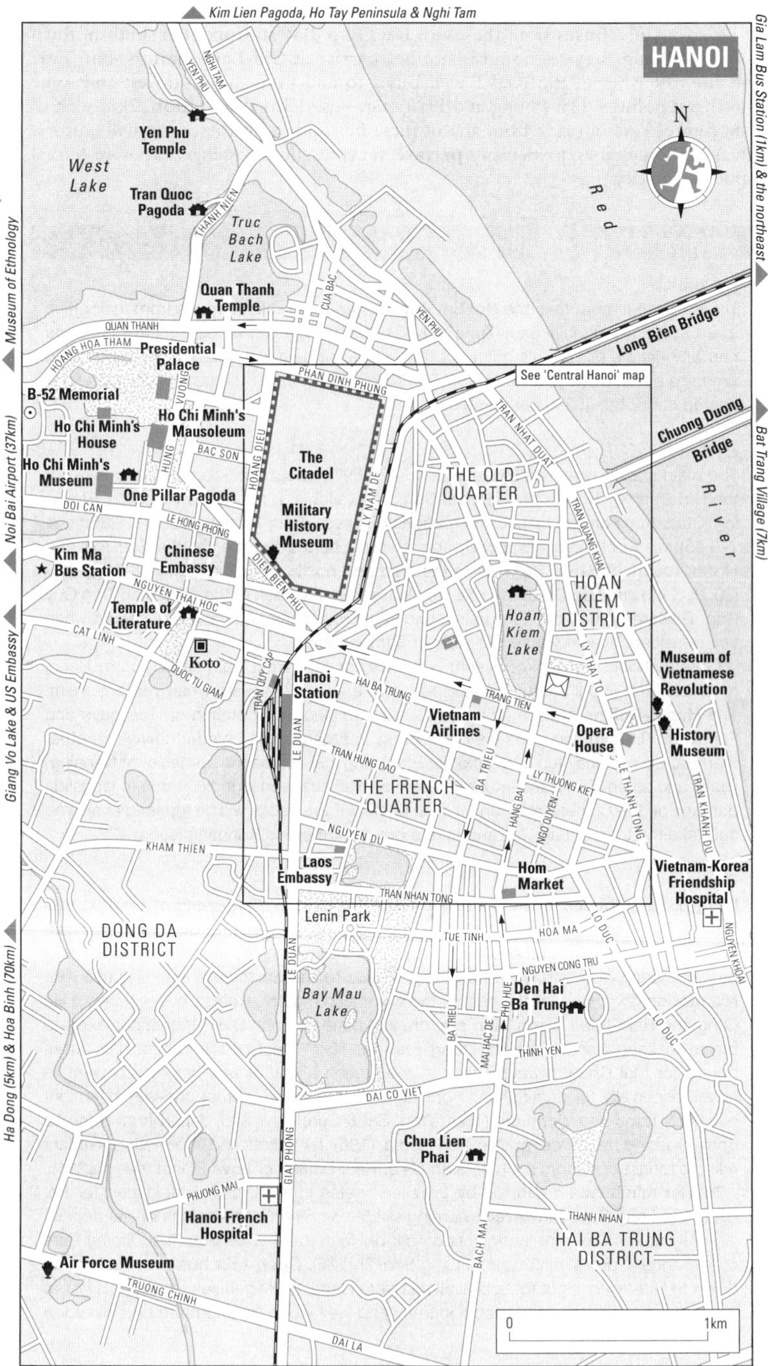

HANOI
Kim Lien Pagoda, Ho Tay Peninsula & Nghi Tam
Gia Lam Bus Station (1km) & the northeast
Bat Trang Village (7km)
Museum of Ethnology
Noi Bai Airport (37km)
Giang Vo Lake & US Embassy
Ha Dong (5km) & Hoa Binh (70km)
Giap Bat Bus Station (1.5km), Perfume Pagoda (60km) & Ninh Binh (90km)
N
West Lake
Yen Phu Temple
Tran Quoc Pagoda
Truc Bach Lake
Quan Thanh Temple
Presidential Palace
B-52 Memorial
Ho Chi Minh's House
Ho Chi Minh's Mausoleum
Ho Chi Minh's Museum
One Pillar Pagoda
The Citadel
Military History Museum
Kim Ma Bus Station
Chinese Embassy
Temple of Literature
Koto
Hanoi Station
Vietnam Airlines
Opera House
Museum of Vietnamese Revolution
History Museum
Laos Embassy
Hom Market
Vietnam-Korea Friendship Hospital
Lenin Park
Bay Mau Lake
Den Hai Ba Trung
Chua Lien Phai
Hanoi French Hospital
Air Force Museum
Hoan Kiem Lake
THE OLD QUARTER
HOAN KIEM DISTRICT
THE FRENCH QUARTER
DONG DA DISTRICT
HAI BA TRUNG DISTRICT
Red River
Long Bien Bridge
Chuong Duong Bridge
See 'Central Hanoi' map
YEN PHU
NGHI TAM
THANH NIEN
CUA BAC
QUAN THANH
HOANG HOA THAM
PHAN DINH PHUNG
VUONG
HUNG
BAC SON
HOANG DIEU
LY NAM DE
TRAN NHAT DUAT
DOI CAN
LE HONG PHONG
DIEN BIEN PHU
NGUYEN THAI HOC
CAT LINH
QUOC TU GIAM
TRAN QUY CAP
TRAN QUANG KHAI
LY THAI TO
HAI BA TRUNG
TRANG TIEN
LE DUAN
TRAN HUNG DAO
BA TRIEU
LY THUONG KIET
HANG BAI
NGO QUYEN
LE THANH TONG
TRAN KHANH DU
NGUYEN DU
KHAM THIEN
TRAN NHAN TONG
TUE TINH
HOA MA
LO DUC
NGUYEN KHOAI
NGUYEN CONG TRU
PHO HUE
MAI HAC DE
THINH YEN
DAI CO VIET
GIAI PHONG
PHUONG MAI
THANH NHAN
BACH MAI
TRUONG CHINH
DAI LA
0
1km

Long-distance **buses** from the south use **Giap Bat station**, 6km south of town on Giai Phong. Services from the northeast arrive at **Gia Lam station**, 4km away on the east bank of the Red River. Buses to and from the northwest and some northeast points – Hai Phong and Ha Long – use **Kim Ma station**, 2km west of the centre. A xe om ride from any of these bus stations to the centre will cost less than $1. Some buses, particularly **private services**, drop passengers at more central spots in the city.

Moving on from Hanoi

By plane

To get to the airport, take the **Noi Bai Airport minibus**, which departs from their office at 2 Quang Trung (daily 5am–7pm; ⓣ4/934 4070) every half an hour (5am–6pm); you can buy tickets ($2) at this office, or from the minibus driver. Alternatively, you could organize a **taxi from your hotel** ($8–9), or sign up at one of the travellers' cafés for a shared car or bus ($3–5 per person).

By train

The main station is at 120 Le Duan (ⓣ4/942 3697), about one kilometre southwest of the Old Quarter. Tickets and **information** are available at the window marked "Booking Office for Foreigners and International Express Train" (daily 7.30am–12.30pm & 1–8.45pm). Book early, especially for sleeping berths to Hue (berths $12–27) and HCMC (berths $28–63). Services **to the east and north**, including trains for Hai Phong ($0.75-1.40) and Lao Cai (berths $6–13), leave from the back of the station on Tran Quy Cap. Beware of theft on night trains, and keep your bags and valuables secure when you're asleep, even if you're in a sleeper compartment.

Tickets should be booked well in advance for the direct train service from Hanoi to **China**, and you'll need your passport with a valid China visa when you buy them. The **Hanoi–Beijing** service (45hr; $126) leaves Hanoi main station on Tuesdays and Fridays at 6.30pm and goes via Dong Dang, but cannot be boarded anywhere other than Hanoi; in China, you can get off at Pingxiang just across the border, or at Nanning, Guilin and so on. The Hanoi–Kunming service was suspended in 2004 due to landslide damage on the Chinese side, and it's yet unclear if the tracks will be repaired at all; you can take the train to Lao Cai, and take a bus from there to Kunming (see p.1222).

By bus

Long-distance **buses** to the south use **Giap Bat station**, 6km south of town on Giai Phong. Services **to the northeast** (Hai Phong, Bai Chay/Ha Long Bay and Cao Bang) depart from **Gia Lam station**, 4km away on the east bank of the Red River; express buses to Lang Son also leave from here. Buses **to the northwest** (Lao Cai) use **Kim Ma station**, 2km west of the centre; there are also regular express buses here for Ha Long and Hai Phong. **Long Bien station**, just beneath Long Bien Bridge, has express buses to Lang Son; whilst **Ha Dong station**, 10km west of the centre, has buses bound for Mai Chau. Always check at the station a day or two before you want to travel, especially for destinations north and west of Hanoi. Direct one-way overnight buses for **Laos** and **Vientiane** (Tues, Wed, Sat & Sun; 24hr; $25) depart from Hanoi at 6pm, crossing the border at Cau Treo (see p.1196); for tickets and information, contact reliable tourist operators such as *Sinh Café*, Real Darling or Love Planet (see p.1211).

Tourist minibuses organized by travellers' cafés in the Old Quarter depart for Bai Chay (Ha Long Bay) early every morning ($2.50–5); *Sinh Café* also has buses departing daily at 7am from the northwest corner of Hoan Kiem Lake ($5). *Real Darling Café* can arrange express minibuses to Lang Son (3hr; $6). **Open-tour buses** make the trek down to Hue every night (details available from Hanoi tour agencies – see p.1211), but it's a long and very uncomfortable journey and well worth forking out a bit extra for a sleeper on the train.

State-run **tourist offices** such as Vietnamtourism and Vinatour are unreliable, as too are the batch of duplicate-name travel agencies, such as the plethora of "Sinh" and "Kim" cafés in the Old Quarter, trading on the reputation of the originals. It's best go to one of the reliable travellers' cafés, such as *Love Planet* or *Kangaroo Café* (see "Listings" on p.1211) for information on visas, tours and transport. Many cafés can also arrange day tours of the city ($8–20, including lunch). Hidden Hanoi ⓣ091/225 4045, ⓦwww.hiddenhanoi.com) organizes several excellent **walking tours** ($10 per hr), among others in the French Quarter and Kim Lien district, as well as Vietnamese language and cooking lessons.

A number of publications carry **listings information** and maps for Hanoi and the surrounding area, best of which is the monthly *Vietnam Pathfinder*, which has restaurant and bar reviews. Others include the monthly *Vietnam Economic Times*' supplement *The Guide*; the weekly *Vietnam Investment Review*'s *Time Out*; and the monthly tourist magazine, *Vietnam Discovery*. They can be picked up for free in hotel lobbies or at travellers' cafés. For an English-language, state-run telephone information service, dial ⓣ1080.

City transport

Cyclos are banned from some roads in central Hanoi, notably around Hoan Kiem Lake (Dinh Tien Hoang and Le Thai To) and in some parts of the Old Quarter, so don't be surprised if you seem to be taking a circuitous route. Always insist on a price in advance, take great care with your possessions and try to avoid using cyclos at night; it's a good idea to get your hotel to recommend a cyclo for you. **Taxis** wait outside the more upmarket hotels and at the north end of Hoan Kiem Lake and cost just over $1 per 2km; make sure the meter is running when you start your journey.

Bicycles can be rented for around $0.40-0.65 a day from many hotels and travellers' cafés in the Old Quarter. It's best to pay the minuscule charge at a supervised bike park (gui xe dap), rather than run the risk of a stolen bike. Parking is banned on Trang Tien and Hang Khay; elsewhere, it's only allowed within designated areas.

Motorbikes are available from guesthouses and small tour agencies (see p.1211), and also from the *Meeting Café*, 59b Ba Trieu, and *Memory Café*, 33b Tran Hung Dao. Prices start from $3 per day, including use of a helmet. You'll be required to leave your passport, departure card or cash as a deposit. Park in supervised motorbike parks (gui xe may). Bao Viet at 15c Tran Khanh Du (ⓣ4/8267 664) can arrange motorbike insurance. For motorbike repairs, try the workshops at the eastern end of Luong Ngoc Quyen, or along Thinh Yen at the south end of Pho Hue. Any tour agency will rent you a **car** with **driver** ($25–35 per day).

Hanoi's new air-con **city buses** are mainly useful for transport between the long-distance bus stations (every 15min, 5am–5.30pm; flat fare of $0.10), though it's just as easy to either hire a taxi or motorbike to travel across the city.

Accommodation

Most of the budget **hotels** are found in the Old Quarter, and there are now some excellent bargains to be had, though generally rooms are more expensive than in HCMC. Several hotels adopt the same name, so you'll need an exact address if arriving by cyclo or taxi. Again, beware of being dropped off at the wrong hotel; insist on being taken to the hotel of your choice.

The Old Quarter and west of Hoan Kiem Lake

Anh Dao 37 Ma May ⓣ4/826 7151, ⓦwww.camellia-hotels.com. Friendly and good-value budget hotel on one of the Old Quarter's quieter streets. Rooms are bright and clean and include breakfast and satellite TV; some have balcony and bathtub. ❸–❺

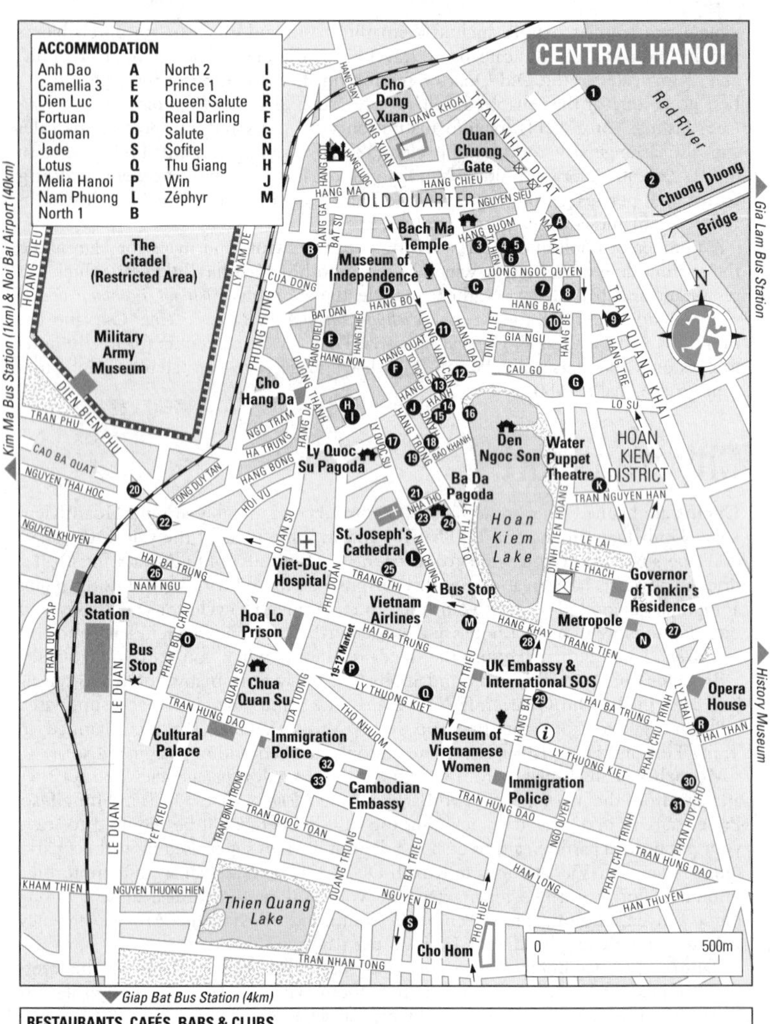

RESTAURANTS, CAFÉS, BARS & CLUBS

Al Fresco's	29	Com Chay Nang Tam	32	Jazz Club	11	Luna d'autunno	20	Red Beer	8
Au Lac	27	Funky Monkey	14	Kinh Do Café	22	Moca Café	21	Rendez-Vous Café	24
Bittet	3	Half Man, Half Noodle	5	La Salsa	23	New Century	25	Stop Café	15
Café Giang	13	Highway 4	9	Le Maquis	4	Pepperonis	17	Tamarind	7
Café Pho	31	Hoa Sua	33	Little Hanoi	6	Pepperonis II	18	Tandoor	10
Café Puku	19	Indochine	26	Little Hanoi (Hoan Kiem)	12	Phuc Tan	1	Thuy Ta	16
Ciao Café	28					Quan Hue	30	Titanic	2

Camellia 3 31 Hang Dieu ⓣ4/828 5704, ⓦwww.camellia-hotels.com. Plush rooms with satellite TV and fridges, all with phone, a/c and generous bathrooms with bathtub at a reasonable price. Staff are extremely friendly. Rates include breakfast and free Internet access. ③–④

Fortuan 68 Hang Bo ⓣ4/828 1324. A good-value mini-hotel with comfortable rooms, some with rattan furniture and dwarf-sized bathtubs. Well-located in the heart of the Old Quarter. ④–⑤

Nam Phuong 26 Nha Chung ⓣ4/824 6894. This friendly, small hotel located in the cathedral area, has good-value bright and airy rooms facing a busy street, some with a/c and balcony. ❷–❹

North 2 5 Tam Thuong ⓣ4/828 5030, northhotel@fpt.vn. One of two family-run mini-hotels, offering basic accommodation located down a quiet alleyway. Rooms have satellite TV, fridge and phone as standard, but can be very small. Similar rooms can be found at the larger *North 1* at 15 Hang Ga (ⓣ4/826 7242; ❷). ❷–❸

Prince 1 51 Luong Ngoc Quyen ⓣ4/828 0155, ⓦwww.hanoiprincehotel.com. A smart hotel with spotlessly clean rooms, located in the heart of the Old Quarter. The pricier rooms are beautiful, but some cheap ones have no windows. Rates include breakfast and Internet access. ❸–❺

Queen Salute 50 Hang Be ⓣ4/826 7356, ⓦwww.salutehotels.com. Large guesthouse bustling with backpackers, boasting clean no-frills rooms and dorms ($3), all with en-suite bathroom. At ground level, there's a travellers' café, tour booking, bar and restaurant, as well as cheap Internet access ($0.18/hr). ❷

Real Darling 33 Hang Quat ⓣ4/826 9386, darling_cafe@hotmail.com. Friendly travellers' café with Internet access and a range of budget rooms, all equipped with private bathroom and a/c (charged extra). A dormitory ($3) is also available. ❷

Salute 7 Hang Dau ⓣ4/825 8003, ⓦwww.salutehotels.com. A smart, modern hotel in the Old Quarter, one of the few in this area with a lift. Rooms are comfortable and well equipped, with chic marble-effect bathrooms. Prices include breakfast served at the downstairs café. ❺–❻

Thu Giang 5a Tam Thuong ⓣ4/828 5734, thugiangn@hotmail.com. A peaceful, welcoming family guesthouse near *North 2*. The no-frills, basic rooms can be very small but all have private bathroom and balcony. Not to be confused with the inferior *Thu Giang* guesthouse on Thuoc Bac. ❶–❷

Win 34 Hang Hanh ⓣ4/828 7371. Not the cheapest, but one of the best mini-hotels, situated on the Hang Hanh café strip. Rooms are spotless, large and airy, have all mod cons and breakfast is included. ❺–❻

The French Quarter and east of Hoan Kiem Lake

Dien Luc 30 Ly Thai To ⓣ4/825 3167. A bland-looking hotel, but in a good central location. Built around a pleasant tree-filled courtyard, with cheaper rooms at the back. ❹–❻

Guoman 83a Ly Thuong Kiet ⓣ4/822 2800, ⓦwww.guomanhotels.com. A smart boutique hotel in neo-colonial style near the train station. Rooms are tastefully decorated, breakfast is included in the price, and there are upscale facilities. ❾

Jade Hotel 73 Ba Trieu ⓣ4/943 5669. A quiet location south along of Ba Trieu and a friendly welcome from the French-speaking owner makes this mini-hotel worth seeking out. The comfortable rooms have decent facilities, some with balconies. ❹

Lotus 42v Ly Thuong Kiet ⓣ4/826 8642, ⓦwww.lotus-guesthouse.com. Entered through the funky *Safari* bar, the *Lotus* guesthouse has cheap dorm beds ($3), small rooms with private bathroom, and apartments for longer stays. Popular for its prime location in the quieter French Quarter and friendly staff; it's best to book ahead. ❷–❹

Melia Hanoi 44b Ly Thuong Kiet ⓣ4/934 3343, ⓦmeliahanoi.com. A gleaming skyscraper in the French Quarter offering international-class accommodation. Luxurious rooms, a swimming pool and Jacuzzi, as well as a gym and business centre make this a good option for the business traveller. ❾

Sofitel 15 Ngo Quyen ⓣ04/826 6919, ⓦwww.sofitel.com. Luxurious accommodation in Hanoi's most famous hotel, which has hosted kings, presidents, journalists and spies for over a century. Includes some excellent restaurants and a swimming pool. ❾

Zéphyr 4 Ba Trieu ⓣ4/934 1256, ⓦwww.zephyrhotel.com.vn. A very smart French-run hotel in a great location near Hoan Kiem Lake. The tastefully decorated rooms don't come cheap, but rates include breakfast, fruit and admission to a nearby gym. ❾

The City

At the heart of Hanoi lies **Hoan Kiem Lake**, around which you'll find the banks, airlines and main post office, plus many hotels, restaurants, shopping streets and markets. The lake lies between the cramped but endlessly diverting **Old Quarter** in the north, and the tree-lined boulevards of the **French Quarter** to the south. West of this central district, across the rail tracks, some of Hanoi's most impressive monuments occupy the wide, open spaces of the former **Imperial City**, grouped around Ho Chi Minh's Mausoleum on Ba Dinh Square and extending south to the ancient, walled gardens of the Temple of Literature. The large **West Lake** sits north of the city, harbouring a number of interesting temples and pagodas.

Around Hoan Kiem Lake

Hoan Kiem Lake itself is small – you can walk round it in thirty minutes – but to Hanoians this is the soul of their city. A squat, three-tiered pavilion known as the **Tortoise Tower** ornaments a tiny island in the middle of Hoan Kiem, "Lake of the Restored Sword". The names refer to a legend of the great fifteenth-century Vietnamese hero, Le Loi, whose miraculous sword was swallowed by a golden turtle/tortoise in this lake. Cross the red-lacquered Huc Bridge to a second island on which stands **Den Ngoc Son** temple (daily 8am–6pm; $0.18), founded in the fourteenth century and rebuilt in the 1800s in typical Nguyen dynasty style. National hero General Tran Hung Dao, who defeated the Mongols in 1288, is depicted on the principal altar, while a giant stuffed turtle, found in the lake, sits in an air-con glass box in a side room.

The neo-Gothic **St Joseph's Cathedral** at the far end of Nha Tho Street, west of the lake, was constructed in the early 1880s, and boasts an impressive interior featuring an ornate altar and French stained-glass windows. Enter the cathedral through a small door on the south side; if it's closed, ring the bell. North of the cathedral on Ly Quoc Su, the small thirteenth-century **Ly Quoc Su Pagoda** houses a statue of the Buddhist teacher and healer Ly Quoc Su, the man credited with curing the hallucinating King Ly Than Tong from believing he was a tiger.

The Old Quarter

The northern end of Hoan Kiem Lake is dominated by a terraced modern building in the shape of a ship's aft. Walk behind this onto Cau Go and suddenly you're in the congested square kilometre known as the **Old Quarter**. Hanoi is the only city in Vietnam to retain its ancient merchants' quarter, and its street names date back five centuries to when the area was divided among 36 artisans' guilds, each gathered around a temple or a *dinh* (communal house) dedicated to the guild's patron spirit. Even today, a surprising number of streets are still dedicated to the original craft or its modern equivalent: Hang Quat remains full of bright red banners and lacquerware for funerals and festivals, and at Hang Ma, paper votive objects have been made for at least five hundred years.

The aptly named fifteenth-century **tube-houses** evolved from market stalls into narrow shops of a single storey. Some are just 2m wide, the result of taxes levied on street-frontages and of subdivision for inheritance, while behind stretches a succession of storerooms, living quarters and courtyards up to 60m in length. The range of building styles along Hang Bac and Ma May are typical, and Ma May even retains its own **dinh**, or communal house (no. 64), which served as both meeting hall and shrine to the neighbourhood's particular patron spirit. From here, walk north and along Hang Buom, past an attractive row of tube-houses at nos. 10–14, to reach the quarter's oldest and most revered place of worship, **Bach Ma** ("White Horse") **Temple** (daily 7.30–11.30am & 1.30–6pm). The present structure dates from the eighteenth century and features an ornate wooden chariot carved with dragons.

The city's largest covered market, **Cho Dong Xuan**, occupies a whole block behind its original, 1889 facade, and is packed with stalls selling fresh and dried food. One block east, two ramps take bikes and pedestrians up onto **Long Bien Bridge** which, until the 1980s, was the Red River's only bridge and therefore of immense strategic significance. During the American War, this was one of Vietnam's most heavily defended spots. Cutting back southwards, it was at 48 Hang Ngang that Ho Chi Minh drafted the Declaration of Independence for the Democratic Republic of Vietnam in 1945. The house where he lived for those heady months is now the

Museum of Independence (Mon–Sat 8am–4.30pm; free), and upstairs you can see where he slept, wrote and debated.

The French Quarter

The first French concession was granted in 1874, and gradually elegant villas filled plots along the grid of tree-lined avenues to the south and east of Hoan Kiem Lake. The jewel in the crown was the stately **Opera House** (now known as the Municipal Theatre), at the eastern end of Trang Tien, which was based on the Neo-Baroque Paris Opéra, complete with Ionic columns and tiles imported from France. After ten years in the making, it was finally opened in 1911; in 1945, the Viet Minh proclaimed the August Revolution from its balcony. One block east of the Opera House, Hanoi's **History Museum**, at 1 Pham Ngu Lao (Tues–Sun 8–11.30am & 1.30–4.30pm; $1) is a fanciful blend of Vietnamese palace and French villa, which came to be called "Neo-Vietnamese" style. Inside, exhibits include arrowheads and ceremonial bronze drums from the Dong Son culture, a sophisticated Bronze Age civilization that flourished in the Red River Delta from 1200 to 200 BC. Upstairs, there are eye-catching ink-washes depicting Hue's Imperial Court in the 1890s, along with sobering evidence of royal decadence and French brutality. The story continues at the **Museum of Vietnamese Revolution**, just opposite at 25 Ton Dan (Tues–Sun 8–11.30am & 1.30–4pm; $0.65), which catalogues the "Vietnamese people's patriotic and revolutionary struggle" from the first anti-French movements of the late nineteenth century to post-1975 reconstruction.

South of **Trang Tien**, the main artery of the French Quarter, you enter French Hanoi's principal residential district, whose distinguished villas run the gamut of styles from elegant Neoclassical through to 1930s Modernism and Art Deco. To take a swing through the area, drop down Hang Bai onto Ly Thuong Kiet and start heading west. Just around the corner, the **Museum of Vietnamese Women**, at 36 Ly Thuong Kiet (Tues–Sun 8am–4pm; $0.65), puts a different perspective on national history. Further west, at 1 Hoa Lo, the French-built **Hoa Lo Prison** (Tues–Sun 8–11.30am & 1.30–5pm; $0.30) only deals with the pre-1954 period when the French incarcerated many nationalist leaders here. As yet, there's little to see beyond a few, grim cells, which were still in use up to 1994. At the next junction west, turn left down Quan Su to find the arched entrance of **Chua Quan Su**, or the Ambassadors' Pagoda (daily: summer 5.30am–9.30pm; winter 6am–9.30pm), one of Hanoi's most active pagodas. A magnificent iron lamp hangs over the crowded prayer-floor and ranks of crimson-lacquered Buddhas glow through a haze of incense.

Ho Chi Minh's Mausoleum and around

The wide, open spaces of **Ba Dinh Square**, 2km west of Hoan Kiem Lake, are the nation's ceremonial epicentre. It was here that Ho Chi Minh read out the Declaration of Independence to half a million people on September 2, 1945, and here that Independence is commemorated each National Day with military parades. Cyclos and xe om will bring you to Ba Dinh Square from the centre for less than $1. The square's west side is dominated by **Ho Chi Minh's Mausoleum** (April-Sept Tues–Thurs 7.30–10.30am, Sat & Sun 7.30–11am; Dec-March Tues–Thurs 8–11am, Sat & Sun 8–11.30am; free), where, in the tradition of great communist leaders, Ho Chi Minh's embalmed body is displayed under glass in a cold, dark room. Huge crowds come here to pay their respects to "Uncle Ho", especially at weekends: sober behaviour and appropriate dress is required (no shorts or vests). Every year, the mausoleum closes for two months while Ho undergoes maintenance, usually in October and November.

Follow the crowd on leaving Ho's mausoleum and you pass the grand Presidential Palace, constructed in 1901 for the governor-general of Indochina, en route to **Ho Chi Minh's house** at 3 Ngoc Ha (Tues–Thurs, Sat & Sun 7.30–11am & 2–4pm;

$0.30). After Independence in 1954, President Ho Chi Minh built a modest house for himself behind the palace, modelling it on an ethnic minority stilt house. The ground-level meeting area was used by Ho and the politburo; upstairs, his study and bedroom are sparsely furnished and unostentatious.

Close by the mausoleum, the tiny **One Pillar Pagoda** rivals the Tortoise Tower as a symbol of Hanoi and represents a flowering of Vietnamese art. Founded in the eleventh century (and reconstructed in 1954), it is supported on a single column rising from the middle of a lake, the whole structure designed to resemble a lotus blossom, the Buddhist symbol of enlightenment. **Ho Chi Minh's Museum** (Tues–Thurs, Sat & Sun 8–11am & 2–6pm; $0.30), the gleaming white building just 200m west of the One Pillar Pagoda, celebrates Ho Chi Minh's life and the pivotal role he played in the nation's history.

Around 500m southeast from Ba Dinh Square, Lenin's statue still stands opposite a white, arcaded building housing the **Military History Museum** at 28 Dien Bien Phu (Tues–Thurs, Sat & Sun 8–11.30am & 1–4.30pm; $0.65). The museum chronicles military history from the 1930s to the present day, a period dominated by the French and American wars, well documented in two separate halls. Unlike HCMC's revamped War Remnants Museum, the captions here are still clogged with outdated communist rhetoric – "spies", "bandits" and "puppet-regime soldiers" are everywhere.

Across busy Nguyen Thai Hoc and entered from Quoc Tu Giam is the **Temple of Literature** or **Van Mieu**, Vietnam's principal Confucian sanctuary and its historical centre of learning (daily: summer 7.30am–5.30pm; winter 7.30am–5pm; $0.30; optional guide $3.15). The temple is one of the few remnants of Thang Long, the Ly kings' original eleventh-century city, and consists of five walled courtyards, modelled on that of Confucius's birthplace in Qufu, China. Entering the third courtyard, via an imposing double-roofed gateway, you'll see the central Well of Heavenly Clarity (a walled pond), flanked by the temple's most valuable relics: 82 stone **stelae** mounted on tortoises. Each stele records the results of a state examination held at the National Academy between 1442 and 1779, and gives biographical details of successful candidates. Passing into the fourth courtyard brings you to the **ceremonial hall**, a long, low building whose sweeping, tiled roof is crowned by two lithe dragons bracketing a full moon. Here, the king and his mandarins would make sacrifices before the altar of Confucius. Directly behind the ceremonial hall lies the temple sanctuary, where Confucius sits with his four principal disciples. The fifth courtyard was formerly the site of the National Academy, Vietnam's first university, but was destroyed by French bombs in 1947. However, a reconstructed ceremonial hall hosts traditional music performances on request.

Around West Lake

North of the city, cool breezes drift off **West Lake**, a shallow lagoon left behind as the Red River shifted course eastward to leave a narrow strip of land. In the seventeenth century, villagers built a causeway across the lake's southeast corner, creating a small fishing lake, still in use today and now called **Truc Bach**. The eleventh-century **Quan Thanh Temple** (daily 8am–4.30pm, $0.10) still stands on the lake's southeast bank, and is dedicated to the Guardian of the North, Tran Vo, whose statue, cast in black bronze in 1677, is nearly 4m high and weighs 4 tonnes. The shrine room also boasts a valuable collection of seventeenth- and eighteenth-century poems and parallel sentences (boards inscribed with wise maxims and hung in pairs). The gate of Quan Thanh is just a few paces south of the causeway, Thanh Nien Street, which leads to Hanoi's oldest religious foundation, **Tran Quoc Pagoda**, occupying a tiny island in West Lake (daily 7–11.30am & 1.30–6pm; no shorts allowed). The pagoda probably dates back to the sixth century, and the sanctuary's restrained interior is typical of northern Vietnamese pagodas but contains nothing of particular importance. West of Quan Thanh, down the alley next to 55 Hoang Hoa Tham, lies the **B-52 Memorial**. The remains of the downed bomber, half-submerged in a lake, form a poignant memorial tribute to the victims of the 1972 "Christmas Bombing" raids.

Museum of Ethnology

The **Museum of Ethnology**, or Bao Tang Toc Hoc Viet Nam, situated on the western outskirts of Hanoi in the Cau Giay district along Nguyen Van Huyen (Tues–Sun 8.30am–5.30pm; $0.65), is a bit of a trek out of town, but worth the effort, offering a significant amount of information on all the country's major ethnic groups. Musical instruments, games, traditional dress and other items of daily life fill the showcases, alongside excellent life-size displays on, amongst other things, funerary ceremonies, conical-hat production and traditional sacrificial spears. Outside in the museum grounds, there are detailed replicas of various ethnic dwellings and burial statues. The museum is 6km from the centre, signposted left off Hoang Quoc Viet Street (also known as Nghia Do). A taxi from the Old Quarter will cost around $4, or hop on city bus no. 14 to the Hoang Quoc Viet stop, from where it's a 500m walk.

Eating

For sheer value for money and atmosphere, it's hard to beat the rock-bottom, stove-and-stools **food stalls** or the slightly more upmarket street kitchens; try streets such as Mai Hac De, Hang Dieu and Duong Thanh. At conventional restaurants you'll need to **get there early**: local places stop serving around 8pm, while Western-style restaurants and top hotels tend to allow an extra hour or two. Most restaurants open up early to serve breakfast. Phone numbers are given where it's advisable to make reservations. Look out for two Hanoi **specialities**: the ubiquitous *pho* noodle soup, and *bun cha*, small barbecued pork burgers served with a bowl of rice noodles.

The Old Quarter and west of Hoan Kiem Lake

Bittet 51 Hang Buom. Hidden down a long, dark passage, this small and bustling restaurant probably represents the best bargain in the Old Quarter. Around $2 will buy you a plate of *bittet* – a Vietnamese corruption of traditional French biftec and chips served with lashings of garlic, a salad, crusty bread and beer. 5am–9pm.

Café Giang 7 Hang Gai. A café famous for its Vietnamese take on cappuccino, café trung – delicious and extremely rich coffee frothed up with whipped egg. Alternatively, this little hole-in-the-wall café offers cacao trung or even bia trung for a few thousand dong.

Highway 4 5 Hang Tre. The Old Quarter's most atmospheric restaurant/bar, with a warren of rooms on three floors culminating in a great rooftop terrace. Known for its excellent Vietnamese dishes and traditional medicinal liquors. 9am–2am; food served until 9pm.

Koto 61 Van Mieu. The deli-style "Know One Teach One" restaurant overlooking the Temple of Literature, serves good breakfasts, as well as reasonably priced lunch. The staff are disadvantaged children and former streetkids, being trained to work in restaurants by an Australian-run charity. 7am–4pm.

La Salsa 25 Nha Tho. One of the smartest eateries in town, in the heart of the trendy cathedral area. Seasonal Western menu, great wines and authentic tapas and ambience have made this an expat favourite. Free deliveries available (☎4/828 9052). 10am - midnight.

Little Hanoi 25 Ta Hien ☎4/926 0168. Small, friendly and great-value restaurant on a quiet sidestreet, serving traditional Vietnamese fare. Try the fried tofu in tomato sauce and pork with lemon and chilli. Usually busy with tourists, so book ahead. Not to be confused with the other *Little Hanoi*. 7am–11pm.

Little Hanoi 21 Hang Gai ☎4/828 8333. Just off Hoan Kiem Lake, this intimate bar-café, decked in bamboo and wood decor, serves good-value, decent light dishes, such as pasta, quiches and soups, a baguette sandwich selection, plus an extensive range of bar drinks. The takeaway and delivery menu is cheaper. 7.30am–11pm.

Luna d'autunno 11b Dien Bien Phu. Excellent pizzas and fresh pasta at reasonable prices make this Italian restaurant a good-value option, despite the trek from the Old Quarter. There's a garden courtyard plus a/c dining room, serving fine Italian wines and cuisine. Delivery service available (☎4/823 7338). 11am–11.30pm.

Moca Café 14–16 Nha Tho. Located in the hippest part of town near the cathedral, this lofty bar-café is something of a favourite with expats, with its colonial-style decor and Western-friendly dishes. The menu includes good coffee and a great Indian and breakfast selection. 8am–11pm.

Pepperonis 29 Ly Quoc Su. This good-value Western-style pizza chain has excellent pasta, salads and vegetarian specials for those craving a break from noodles. Buffet lunches ($1.80) and evening salad buffets ($1.30) are available on weekdays. Free pizza delivery service (☎4/928 5246). Another outlet, *Pepperonis II*, can be found at 31 Bao Khanh.

Rendez-Vous Café 136 Hang Trong. Bright and airy, this café-bistro next to the lake is best at lunchtimes, when set lunches cost $3-4.50. Nightly live classical music. 7am–midnight.

Stop Café 11B Ngo Bao Khanh. An elegant French-run restaurant serving terrific Vietnamese dishes, as well as Western breakfasts and desserts. Upstairs, the more upmarket *Café des Arts*, with its comfy seating and rooftop terrace, is a great place to splash out. 9.30am–11pm.

Tamarind 80 Ma May. A cut above most vegetarian restaurants, serving innovative, delicious food with a Japanese-Vietnamese slant, amongst traditional decor; head for the back, where there are Asian-style wooden dining platforms. 6am–11pm.

Tandoor 24 Hang Be. A well-established Indian restaurant, popular with tourists. Traditional decor and great curries: fish tikka, tandoori chicken and plenty of vegetarian dishes, plus set meals for $2.50-4. Tandoor's sister Indian restaurant *Dakshin* (94 Hang Trong, same hours) serves excellent vegetarian dishes. 11.30am–2.30pm & 6–10.30pm.

Thuy Ta 1 Le Thai To. With its prime position right on Hoan Kiem Lake, it's worth paying a little extra for the extensive range of light Western and Vietnamese dishes, ice creams, drinks and pastries. Choice of a waterfront terrace or an adjacent a/c dining room. 8am–11pm.

The French Quarter and east of Hoan Kiem Lake

Al Fresco's 23L Hai Ba Trung ☎4/826 7782. A relaxed, expat-run place, with a pleasant balcony on the first floor. Café, bar and grill in one, the menu includes good-quality American and international fare (ribs, salads, Australian steaks and pizzas), all served in hefty portions. 9am–10.30pm.

Au Lac 57 Ly Thai To. Located opposite the *Sofitel*, this popular and upmarket garden café has a strong reputation and some of Hanoi's best, and priciest, coffee. It's a lovely spot to sup your cappuccino and snack on a sandwich. Live jazz sessions on winter evenings. 8am–10.30pm.

Café Pho 15 Ly Thuong Kiet. A delightful garden café similar in layout to Au Lac, but with more locals, fewer hawkers and lower prices. Serves possibly the best cup of tea in Hanoi using fresh milk, not the sickly condensed gloop prevalent around town. 8am–10pm.

Ciao Café 2 Hang Bai. A Western-style menu including sandwiches and pasta makes this another favourite for travellers and expats seeking tastes from home and prepared to pay a little extra. Try the ice creams. 9am–11pm.

Com Chay Nang Tam 79a Tran Hung Dao (☎4/942 9184). Small, elegant vegetarian restaurant down a quiet alleyway off Tran Hung Dao, and named after a Vietnamese Cinderella character. *Goi bo*, a main-course salad of banana flower, star fruit and pineapple, is recommended, or try one of the well-priced set menus. No MSG is used. 11am–1.30pm & 5–10pm.

Hoa Sua 28A Ha Hoi, ☎4/942 4448. Excellently presented food and superb desserts with a heavy French influence, served inside or on the garden terrace. Hoa Sua is part of a non-profit vocational training school giving disadvantaged children a start in the restaurant trade. Find the restaurant by walking down Xom Ha Hoi alley from Tran Hung Dao and turning right. 7am–10.30pm.

Indochine 16 Nam Ngu, ☎04/942 4097. Near the train station, this old villa with a lush garden terrace is famous for its delicious and well-priced Vietnamese dishes. Popular with groups, so book ahead. 11am–2pm & 5.30–10pm.

Kinh Do Café 252 Hang Bong. "Café 252" became famous after Catherine Deneuve complimented the patron on his yoghurts, which are indeed good, as are the delicious fresh salad rolls, and patisserie. 7am–10pm.

Quan Hue 6 Ly Thuong Kiet. Serving authentic Hue cuisine at reasonable prices, *Quan Hue* is a simple restaurant with open-air seating. Don't miss the banana-flower salad, and pep it up with eel fried in chilli and lemongrass. 8am–10pm.

Nightlife and entertainment

For a capital city, Hanoi doesn't have a wide choice of bars, and venues open and close quickly, so check the English-language press such as *Vietnam Pathfinder* for the latest listings information. **Pool halls** are more numerous and popular with young Vietnamese, although they tend to be a male preserve. The best are found in-between the cafés on Hang Hanh, or try *Sao Bang* at 46 Hang Giay (24hr), or *Dong Khoi*, 7 Bao Kanh.

Bars and clubs

For **drinking**, there's the happening *Funky Monkey* bar, 15b Hang Hanh, very popular for its loud music, extended happy hours and live sports coverage. *Red Beer*, 97 Ma May, is a microbrewery serving home-brewed beers in a high-ceilinged space. Walk down the hall at 2f/60 Hang Trong to find *Café Puku*, a trendy first-floor café with balcony seating, good food and music. The brilliantly named *Half Man, Half Noodle*, at 52 Dao Duy Tu, has a quirky atmosphere, but for a spot of intimacy, try the tiny *Le Maquis*, 2a Ta Hien, or *Highway 4* (see p.1207). Summertime riverside drinking is possible at *Phuc Tan*, found by crossing Tran Nhat Duat and going down Bao Linh to the very end, where a yellow sign points you towards the terrace. The *Jazz Club*, 31 Luong Van Can, has live jazz music every night led by the charismatic Mr Quyen Van Minh. For **clubbing**, try the brash *New Century*, 10 Trang Thi; admission is $1.30–2.70, with live music, laser show and disco, and drinks average around $2.70. Another popular party option is the *Titanic* club, on a boat moored on the Red River along Chuong Duong Do; your xe om driver should know where it is, otherwise cross Tran Nhat Duat and go down Bao Linh, turn right at the end and continue until you see the boat's brightly lit pier.

Bia hoi

Serious beer drinking tends to be an all-male preserve in Vietnam, but don't be put off as the local **bia hoi** outlets are fun, friendly and extremely cheap. The best-known and popular with locals is at 59 Ly Thuong Kiet. Right in the heart of backpackersville, the large *bia hoi* at 27 Hang Be serves the more alcoholic, pressurized beer, *bia tuoi*, and a variety of more sophisticated dishes, such as pan-fried prawns in coconut milk and honey ginger chicken, all at bargain prices. Also good for food is the *bia hoi* at 72 Ma May, where you choose from the range of dishes displayed in a large case, or the one north of the cathedral at 8 Chan Cam.

Traditional entertainment

Most people don't leave Hanoi without seeing a performance by the traditional **water puppets**, *mua roi nuoc* – literally, puppets that dance on the water – a uniquely Vietnamese art form that originated in the Red River Delta. Traditional performances consist of short scenes depicting rural life or historic events accompanied by musical narration. Puppeteers stand waist-deep in water, manipulating the heavy wooden puppets attached to long underwater poles. The Thang Long Water Puppet Troupe gives nightly tourist-oriented performances of their updated repertoire at Kim Dong Theatre, 57b Dinh Tien Hoang (daily 6.30pm, 7.15pm & 8pm; ☎4/824 9494). Tickets cost $1.30-2.60; the view from the pricier front seats isn't that much better, but you get a free cassette of traditional music.

Ballroom dancing is still popular with the Vietnamese. You can take a turn or two at the Hotel Chessboard, 87 Nguyen Thai Hoc (daily 9.30am–noon, 3.30–6pm & 8.30–10.30pm), or the Dong Do Dancing Club, 18 Luong Ngoc Quyen (9.30am–noon, 3.30–6pm & 8.30–10.30pm).

Shopping and markets

Hanoi has perhaps the best value, quality and choice when shopping for traditional silk clothes, accessories and souvenirs in Vietnam, something to bear in mind when planning your shopping itineraries as you travel through the country. The best areas to browse are Hang Gai in the Old Quarter, and around the southeastern edge of Hoan Kiem Lake. Compared with Thailand, Vietnamese **silk** is slightly inferior quality, but prices are lower and the tailoring is great value. So many silk shops are concentrated on Hang Gai, at the southern edge of the Old Quarter, that it's now known as "Silk Street". The best known is Khai Silk at 96 Hang Gai, but try also Thanh Ha at no. 114, and Kenly Silk at no. 108. For a large selection of exquisite silk bags and shoes, go to Ha Dong Silk at 102 Hang Gai. The Tailoring Shop Co, 18 Nha Tho, and Song – probably Hanoi's most famous shop – opposite at 5 Nha Tho, have the best handmade clothes in town. **Embroideries** and drawn threadwork can be found at Song, Hoa Sua at 63 Trang Thi, and Tan My at 66 Hang Gai – the last of which has a three-level showhouse shop packed with handmade bed-linens, tablecloths and quilts.

The non-profit Craft Link, at 43–45 Van Mieu, sells traditional **crafts** made by ethnic minorities, including lacquerware, paper goods, baskets and clothes. Most ordinary souvenir shops also stock ethnic minority crafts, particularly the Hmong and Dao bags, coats and jewellery that are so popular in Sa Pa, though many are actually factory-made. For high-quality **lacquerware**, head for Minh Tam at 2 Hang Bong, which sells handmade masks, plates and boxes, created from egg-shells. For more unusual mementoes, have a look at the traditional Vietnamese **musical instruments** on sale at 11 Hang Non, or 1a and 1c Hang Hanh. Several small shops on Hang Bong supply Communist Party **banners and badges** and Vietnamese flags, while the gallery at 17 Nha Chung sells pricey old propaganda posters. Hanoi also has a flourishing **art** scene and any exploration should start with the Apricot Gallery, 40b Hang Bong, a well-established gallery with a range of works by local artists.

Hanoi has over fifty **markets**, selling predominantly foodstuffs: Cho Dong Xuan on Dong Xuan Street is a good place to buy cheap bags, shoes, hats and materials; also try Cho Hom, at 81 Pho Hue, which has clothing upstairs. All around Cho Hom are specialist shopping streets: Tran Nhan Tong focuses on shirts and jackets, while Phung Khac Khoan, off Tran Xuan Soan, is a riot of colourful fabrics. Hanoi's wholesale flower market is held each dawn beside Nghi Tam Avenue at its most northerly junction with Yen Phu; the action starts around 5am (6am in winter), and lasts an hour.

Listings

Airline offices Aeroflot, *Daewoo Hotel*, 360n Kim Ma ☎4/771 8742; Air France, 1 Ba Trieu ☎4/824 7066; Cathay Pacific, 49 Hai Ba Trung ☎4/826 7290; China Airlines, 18 Tran Hung Dao ☎4/824 2688; China Southern Airlines, Ground Floor, Dae Ha Business Centre, 360 Kim Ma ☎4/771 6611; Emirates, 25 Ly Thuong Kiet ☎4/934 7240; Japan Airlines, 63 Ly Thai To ☎4/826 6693; Lao Aviation, 40 Quang Trung ☎04/942 5362; Malaysia Airlines, 49 Hai Ba Trung ☎4/826 8820; Pacific Airlines, 36 Dien Bien Phu ☎4/733 2162; Qantas, 25 Ly Thuong Kiet ☎4/934 7238; Scandinavian Airlines System (SAS), 49 Hai Ba Trung ☎4/934 2626; Singapore Airlines, 17 Ngo Quyen ☎4/826 8888; Thai International, 44b Ly Thuong Kiet ☎4/826 6893; Vietnam Airlines, 1 Quang Trung (☎4/832 0320) for domestic and international services; sales agents at 112 Cau Go (☎4/934 3144) and 46 Ly Thuong Kiet (☎4/824 3606).

Banks and exchange Vietcombank's main branch is at 198 Tran Quang Khai, and contains all services including cash withdrawals on credit cards, telegraphic transfers and Visa and MasterCard cash advances; there's another branch at 78 Nguyen Du, and agents all over town. There's a 24hr Vietcombank ATM, which accepts Visa and

MasterCard, outside the main post office. ANZ Bank, 14 Le Thai To, has a 24hr ATM for Visa, Visa Plus and MasterCard holders. VID Public Bank at 2 Ngo Quyen will also change travellers' cheques and cash. Money-changers in and around the main post office offer higher rates than banks, but will try to befuddle you with stacks of small denominations – watch out for notes folded to count twice. You can also change money in some gold shops.

Books and bookshops Apart from small outlets in top-class hotels, the expat-run Bookworm, at 15a Ngo Van So (closed Mon), and *Love Planet* (see below) are the best places to pick up English-language books; the latter has an extensive library and book exchange. Trang Tien is the main area for local books; try the stalls along the pavement, the Foreign Language Bookshop at 61 Trang Tien, the Hanoi Bookshop at no. 34 or Thang Long at no. 53.

Embassies and consulates Australia, 8 Dao Tan, Van Phuc ☎4/831 7755; Burma, 298a Kim Ma ☎4/845 3369; Cambodia, 71 Tran Hung Dao ☎4/942 4788; Canada, 31 Hung Vuong ☎4/823 5500; China, 46 Hoang Dieu ☎4/845 3736; India, 58–60 Tran Hung Dao ☎ 4/824 4990; Indonesia, 50 Ngo Quyen ☎4/825 3353; Japan, 27 Lieu Giai ☎4/846 3000; Lao PDR, 22 Tran Binh Trong ☎4/942 4576; Malaysia, Fortuna Hotel, 6b Lang Ha ☎4/831 3400; New Zealand, 63 Ly Thai To ☎4/824 1481; Philippines, 27b Tran Hung Dao ☎4/943 7948; Singapore, 41-43 Tran Phu ☎4/823 3965; Thailand, 63–65 Hoang Dieu ☎4/823 5092; UK, 5th Floor, 31 Hai Ba Trung ☎4/936 0500; USA, 7 Lang Ha ☎4/772 1500.

Emergencies Dial ☎113 for police, ☎114 for fire service and ☎115 for an ambulance.

Hospitals and clinics Hanoi French Hospital, 1 Phuong Mai, offers international-class doctors and facilities at their outpatients clinic (daily 8am–7pm for GP consultations; $55 consultation fee; ☎4/574 0740), plus surgery and a 24hr emergency and ambulance service (☎4/574 1111). Hanoi Family Medical Practice in Van Phuc, Building A1, 109–112 Kim Ma (Mon–Fri 8.30am–5.30pm, Sat 8.30am–12.30pm; ☎4/843 0748), has multinational doctors and an outpatients clinic ($50 standard consultation fee), plus intensive care and 24hr emergency service and evacuation (☎90401919); they also have an international-standard dental surgery in Building A2 (☎4/823 0281). The emergency assistance company, International SOS, at Central Building, 31 Hai Ba Trung, provides routine care to travellers (Mon–Fri 8am–7pm, Sat 8am–2pm; $59 consultation fee, $10 more for a foreign doctor; ☎4/934 0666), and 24hr emergency care and evacuation (☎4/934 0555.) Of the local hospitals, your best bet is the Vietnam-Korea Friendship Hospital at 12 Chu Van An (☎4/843 7231), which has some English-speaking doctors and charges around $5 initial consultation fee. The Institute of Acupuncture is at H3, Vinh Ho, Thai Thinh (☎4/853 3881).

Immigration office 40 Hang Bai, with a branch office at 89 Tran Hung Dao.

Internet access Numerous outlets in the travellers' enclaves come and go; best of the bunch at the time of writing are *Queen Salute* at 50 Hang Be; and *Song Pho Bar and Internet* at 52 Ly Thuong Kiet; rates are around 50–100d per minute.

Pharmacies At 119 Hang Gai, and near Hoan Kiem Lake at 29 Dinh Tien Hoang and 3 Trang Tri. The latter stocks a good range of US and French supplies.

Police At 89 Tran Hung Dao and 40b Hang Bai; police reports should be made at the nearest station to the scene of the crime.

Post offices The main post office occupies a whole block at 75 Dinh Tien Hoang (6.30am–9.30pm). International postal services, including parcel dispatch and poste restante are located in the southernmost hall (Mon–Fri 7.30–11.30am & 1–4.30pm). The next entrance up is for telephone and fax services; call between 10pm–7am or on Sunday for lower rates; dial prefix ☎171 for substantial savings (see p.1111). Useful sub-post offices are at 66 Trang Tien, 66 Luong Van Can, 20 Bat Dan and at Hanoi train station.

Travel agencies Many travellers' cafés organize similar bargain-basement tours to the Perfume Pagoda ($9–16), Ha Long Bay/Cat Ba Island (3 days; $25–55) and Sa Pa (3–4 days; $25–95). They also do car rental, visa services and airport transport. Recommended reliable agencies include: Ann Tours, 18 Duong Thanh (☎4/923 1366, Ⓦwww.anntours.com); Handspan, 80 Ma May (☎4/933 2377, wwww.handspan.com); Hanoi Toserco, 18 Luong Van Can (☎4/928 6631, Ⓦwww.tosercohanoi.com); *Kangaroo Café*, 18 Bao Khanh (☎4/828 9931); *Love Planet*, 25 Hang Bac (☎4/828 4864, Ⓔloveplanet8@hotmail.com); *Real Darling*, 33 Hang Quat (☎4/826 9386, darling_cafe@hotmail.com); *Sinh Café*, 52 Luong Ngoc Quyen (☎04/926 1568, Ⓦwww.sinhcafevn.com).

Around Hanoi

The fertile and densely populated landscape of the Red River Delta that surrounds Hanoi is crisscrossed by massive ancient dykes and studded with temples, pagodas, family graves, communal houses and all the other leftovers of successive generations. It's worth venturing into by motorbike or car, or with a tour from Hanoi, for the chance to visit the Perfume Pagoda, and a couple of other, more tranquil religious sites.

The Perfume Pagoda

Sixty kilometres southwest of Hanoi, a forested spur shelters north Vietnam's most famous pilgrimage site, the **Perfume Pagoda**, Chua Huong, said to be named after spring blossoms that scent the air. The pagoda is the most popular day-trip out of Hanoi, though be warned that many travellers are disappointed by the low-key nature of the grotto, combined with the long walk and the barrage of hawkers en route; if you're seeing temples further afield in Vietnam, it's probably best skipped. The easiest way to visit the pagoda is on an all-included day tour out of Hanoi ($10–30) or in a rental car. Alternatively, it's a two- to three-hour motorbike ride: follow Highway 6 through Ha Dong as far as the fourteen-kilometre marker where the highway crosses the rail tracks, then turn left on the D426 heading due south, through Thanh Oai and Van Dinh, to Duc Khe village and the Suoi Yen (Yen River) boat station. There's a sightseeing **fee** of $3.20 to visit the pagoda, though this does include the return boat trip; tickets are sold at the entrance to the village beside the post office (*buu dien*). There are some overpriced **food stalls** at the boat station and at the start of the walk to Chua Thien Chu.

The Perfume Pagoda occupies a grotto over 50m high; the journey there begins with an appealing, half-hour sampan ride up a flooded valley among karst hills, then a path brings you to the seventeenth-century Chua Thien Chu ("Pagoda Leading to Heaven"), in front of which stands a magnificent, triple-roofed bell pavilion. Quan Am, Goddess of Mercy, takes pride of place on the pagoda's main altar. To the right of the pagoda, a three-kilometre path leads steeply uphill (1–2hr) to the Perfume Pagoda, also dedicated to Quan Am. The walk is rewarded when the gaping cavern is revealed beneath the inscription "supreme cave under the southern sky". A flight of 120 steps descends into the dragon's mouth-like entrance, where gilded Buddhas emerge from dark recesses wreathed in clouds of incense (bring a torch). Note that long trousers and long-sleeve shirts are required for entry to Chua Thien Chu, and that shoes with good grip are highly recommended.

Thay Pagoda

Thay Pagoda (Chua Thay) or the **Master's Pagoda** was founded in the reign of King Ly Nhan Tong (1072–1127) and is an unusually large complex overlooking a lake in the lee of a limestone crag. The Master was the ascetic monk and healer Tu Dao Hanh, an accomplished water puppeteer – hence the lake's dainty theatre-pavilion – and the pagoda is dedicated to the cult of Tu Dao Hanh in his three incarnations as monk (the Master), Buddha and king. Nearly a hundred statues fill the atmospheric prayer halls, including two seventeenth-century giant guardians made of clay and papier mâché, which weigh a thousand kilos apiece. The highest altar holds a Buddha trinity, dating from the 1500s, and a thirteenth-century wooden statue of the Master as a bodhisattva, dressed in yellow and perched on a lotus throne. On a separate altar to the left, he appears again as King Ly Than Tong, also in yellow, with two giggling Cambodian slaves. In front of the pagoda are two covered bridges with arched roofs, built in 1602 and dedicated to the sun and moon: one leads to an islet where spirits of the earth, water and sky are worshipped in a tiny Taoist temple; the second takes you to a flight of steps up the limestone hill. Thay

Pagoda lies 30km from Hanoi in Sai Son village, between Ha Dong and Son Tay, and is best visited by car, motorbike or xe om. The easiest route is to head along the Hanoi-Hoa Lac highway, turning right to Sai Son immediately after passing the tollgate near Quoc Oai. The entry fee ($0.18) includes an English-speaking guide; Sundays are very crowded.

Tay Phuong Pagoda

Six kilometres west of the Thay Pagoda, the smaller **Tay Phuong Pagoda** perches atop a fifty-metre-high limestone hillock and was one of the first pagodas built in Vietnam. It's renowned for its fine collection of jackfruit-wood **statues**, particularly the eighteen *arhats*, disturbingly life-like representations of Buddhist ascetics, grouped around the main altar. As Tay Phuong is also an important Confucian sanctuary, disciples of the sage are included on the altar, each carrying a gift to their master, some precious object, a book or a symbol of longevity, alongside the expected Buddha effigies. To get there from the Thay Pagoda, backtrack to the main road, turn right, and right again at the roundabout onto the TL80 towards Son Tay through Thach Tat. In the village after the 11km marker, 18km before Son Tay, take the first road left across the paddy-field towards the hills to find the pagoda entry gate ($0.18).

11.7

Ha Long Bay and the northern seaboard

The mystical scenery of **Ha Long Bay**, peppered with thousands of evocatively craggy limestone outcrops, is what draws people to the northeast coast of Vietnam, and there are plenty of tourist boats and accommodation in nearby **Ha Long City** to facilitate your visit. **Cat Ba Island**, accessible from Ha Long City and the port city of **Hai Phong**, makes a slightly less touristy base for bay trips. There's more magnificent karst scenery inland at **Tam Coc**, a rewarding day-trip from Ninh Binh, south of Hanoi. Vietnam borders China 150km up the coast from Ha Long Bay, and you can **enter China** at Mong Cai.

Ninh Binh and around

The dusty provincial capital of **NINH BINH**, 90km south of Hanoi, has little to detain you, but the surrounding hills shelter **Tam Coc**, where sampans slither through the limestone tunnels of "Ha Long Bay on land", and dynastic temples from the ancient capital, **Hoa Lu**. Two radio masts provide convenient landmarks in town: the taller stands over the post office in the south, while the shorter signals the northern extremity 2km away up Highway 1 (Tran Hung Dao). Exactly halfway between the two, Le Hong Phong shoots off east at a major junction, taking traffic to join the Nam Dinh road. To the east, a dismembered church spire bears witness to American bombing raids of the late 1960s.

Ninh Binh's **bus and train stations** lie east of the Van River, less than a kilometre by xe om from Tran Hung Dao, or an easy walk east along Van Giang, turning right onto Le Dai Hanh after crossing the bridge; turn left onto Hoang Hoa Tham to reach the train station after 200m, or continue south for another 200m for the bus station. Open-tour buses en route to and from Hanoi pick up and drop off at their associated hotels along Tran Hung Dao. The Vietincombank, located on the main strip on Tran Hung Dao, does not have an ATM, but can **exchange** cash and travellers' cheques, and arrange Visa and MasterCard cash advances.

The best **place to stay and eat** is the dazzlingly clean *Thuy Anh Hotel* at 55a Truong Han Sieu (ⓣ30/871602, ⓦwww.thuyanhhotel.com; ③–⑥), which has a range of quiet, well-equipped rooms and a good restaurant. A cheaper central option is *Than Thuy's Guesthouse* at 128 Le Hong Phong (ⓣ030/871811, ⓔtuc@hn.vnn.vn; ①–③) with decent rooms, some with balcony. Otherwise, there are two friendly budget hotels near the train station; the *Queen* at 21 Hoang Hoa Tham (ⓣ30/871874, luongvn2001@yahoo.com; ①–③), and the *New Guesthouse* at 3 Hoang Hoa Tham (dorm $2; ⓣ30/871874; ①), both of which have excellent bargain-priced rooms. All the above hotels can assist with tours, car and motorbike rental, as well as onward open-tour buses. For **Internet** access, visit one of the e-gaming places along Luong Van Thuy.

Tam Coc and Bich Dong Pagoda

The film *Indochine* put the **Tam Coc region**, 9km southwest of Ninh Binh, firmly on the map for French tour groups, and it's hard not to be won over by the mystical, watery beauty of the area, which is a miniature, landlocked version of Ha Long Bay. The three-hour sampan-ride through the flooded landscape is a definite highlight, and journey's end is **Tam Coc**, three long, dark tunnel-caves eroded through the limestone hills with barely sufficient clearance for the sampan in places. **Boats** leave the dock in Van Lam village – the starting point for all boat trips to Tam Coc – between 6.30am and 5pm (go early or late to avoid the crowds), and cost $3.50 per person, which includes entry to Bich Dong Pagoda.

Follow the road another 2km beyond the boat dock to visit the cave-pagoda of **Bich Dong**, where stone-cut steps, entangled by the thick roots of banyan trees, lead up a cliff face peppered with shrines to the cave entrance. Three Buddhas sit unperturbed on their lotus thrones beside a head-shaped rock, which bestows longevity if touched. Exit the cave higher up the cliff to climb the steps to a viewpoint and a small shrine. From here, you can scramble up a jungle path to the top of the hill for excellent views of the surrounding landscape.

The easiest and most enjoyable way to reach Tam Coc is to rent a **bicycle** ($0.50–0.65 per day) or **motorbike** ($5–6) from a Ninh Binh guesthouse, which should also be able to provide a photocopied map. The turning, marked by four large pillars, is 4km south of the town centre on Highway 1. A **xe om** from Ninh Binh will cost about $4–7 all-in. If your next stop is Hoa Lu (see p.1215), you can take a back road for a spectacular ten-kilometre ride through rice fields, karst scenery and villages full of waving children; the thirty-kilometre round trip is easily done in a day. This back road starts in the village halfway down the road between Highway 1 and the boat landing; follow the signs for Troung Yen village to reach Hoa Lua.

Hoa Lu

Thirteen kilometres northwest of Ninh Binh stands **Hoa Lu** (entrance $0.65), site of the tenth-century capital of an early, independent Vietnamese kingdom called Dai Co Viet. The fortified royal palaces of the Dinh and Le kings are now in ruins, but their dynastic temples, seventeenth-century copies of eleventh-century originals, still rest quietly in a narrow valley surrounded by hills. First stop at the site should be the more imposing **Den Dinh Tien Hoang**, dedicated to King Dinh Tien Hoang who seized power in 968 AD and moved the capital south from Co Loa in the Red River Delta to this secure valley far from the threat of Chinese intervention. Dinh Tien Hoang's gilded effigy can be seen in the temple's second sanctuary room, flanked by his three sons. The second temple, **Den Le Dai Hanh**, is dedicated to the army commander who succeeded Dinh Tien Hoang in 980. He is enshrined in the temple's rear sanctuary with his eldest son and queen. Opposite the temples, steps lead up "Saddle Mountain" for a panoramic view of Hoa Lu. It's also possible to take a **boat trip** (2–3hr; $3.20 per person) along the Sao Khe River.

The quickest way out to Hoa Lu is by xe om ($5–8 round trip), but going by **bicycle** is more fun. After the first five unnerving kilometres on Highway 1, it's a pleasant ride on paved back roads west of the highway, following signs to Truong Yen village and Hoa Lu (13km in total). You can then cycle back along the Sao Khe River: take the paved road heading east directly in front of the temples, turn right over the bridge and follow the dirt track for about 4km to the first village. Here, a left turn leading to a concrete bridge will take you back to Ninh Binh, while the road straight ahead continues for another 6km to Tam Coc.

Hai Phong

Located 100km east of Hanoi on the Cua Cam River, one of the main channels of the Red River Estuary, **HAI PHONG** has long been North Vietnam's principal port, and its history runs the gamut from major seventeenth-century trading centre through bombardment by both the French and the Americans. Today, it's a small, orderly city of broad avenues and subtle, cosmopolitan charms, with good hydrofoil and ferry links to Cat Ba Island, Mong Cai and Hong Gai (for Ha Long Bay), but not much else of interest. The city's crescent-shaped nineteenth-century core lies between the curve of the Tam Bac River and the loop of the train tracks. To the north of the main artery, **Dien Bien Phu**, you'll find broad avenues and colonial architecture. To the south is the merchants' quarter, these days a dilapidated area of street markets between Tran Trinh Street and the market, Cho Sat; immediately below here is Tam Bac Lake. A ten-minute walk eastwards along the south bank will bring you to the **Den Nghe Temple on** Me Linh, noted for its carvings, particularly on the massive stone table in the first courtyard.

Practicalities

Hai Phong **train station** is on the southeast side of town, close to the centre. Next to the train ticket counters, the station has a desk where you can buy ferry tickets for Cat Ba Island, Bai Chay and Mong Cai. The **ferry station** is on the Cua Cam River about 500m north of the city centre along Ben Binh. Ferry services to Cat Ba (3 daily; 1-2hr; $4.50) and Bai Chay (Ha Long; 1 daily; 1hr; $6), and **hydrofoil** services to Cat Ba (3 daily; 45min–1hr; $6) and Mong Cai (1 daily; 4hr; $16) depart from here; the main ticket office for ferries can be found at the front of the ferry terminal, while hydrofoil tickets can be purchased from four different boat companies on Ben Binh.

Hai Phong's **Cat Bi Airport** (flights to and from HCMC only; ⓣ31/921137) is 7km southeast of the city, around $4 by taxi. Vietnam Airlines is at 30 Tran Phu (ⓣ31/921242), next to the Cat Bi Hotel. **Buses** from the south and west usually pitch up at Niem Nghia bus station, about 3km from the centre. Some Hanoi services use Tam Bac bus station, near the west end of Tam Bac Lake and Cho Sat. Buses from Bai Chay and the northeast arrive at Binh bus station on the north bank of the Cua Cam River, 300m from the cross-river ferry, but if you're coming from this direction the Bai Chay ferry is a more scenic alternative. **Leaving Hai Phong**, Hanoi-bound minibuses hang around the ferry station and Tam Bac bus station, where you'll also find public buses to Hanoi; all other buses to the south and west depart from Niem Nghia bus station, whilst northeast and Bai Chay buses depart from Binh station. **Information** about tours, car rental and air tickets can be had from Vietnamtourism at 15 Le Dai Hanh (ⓣ31/822516, vntourism.hp@bdvn.vnmail.vnd.net) and Hang Khong Tourism at 62 Dien Bien Phu (ⓣ031/822777, hktourism_hp@yahoo.com).

Various **banks** change currency and travellers' cheques, amongst them Techcombank at 16 Tran Hung Dao and VID Bank at 56 Dien Bien Phu, whilst Vietcombank at 11 Hoang Dieu can also arrange Visa and MasterCard cash advances and has an ATM. The main **post office** is at the junction of Nguyen Tri Phuong and Hoang Van Thu, with a sub-post office at 36 Quang Trung. Ben Vien Viet-Tiep **hospital** is at 1 Nha Thuong (ⓣ31/700570), and there's a **pharmacy** at 61 Dien Bien Phu. **Internet access** can be found at 133 Dien Bien Phu or nearer to the train station at 36 Minh Khai (both $0.18/hr).

Budget **accommodation** is in short supply, the best bargain in town being the elegant colonial-style *Hotel du Commerce* at 62 Dien Bien Phu (ⓣ030/842790, ❸-❹), with shabby, cheap rooms and acceptable mid-range doubles. Right in the station courtyard, the *Station Guest House* (ⓣ31/855391; ❸-❹) at 75 Luong Khanh Thien has dingy air-con rooms. More upmarket are the spacious rooms of the *Ben*

Binh hotel (☎031/842260, ⑤-⑥), next to the ferry station at 6 Ben Binh. The new *Monaco* (☎031/746468, monacohotel@hn.vnn.vn; ⑤-⑦) at 103 Dien Bien Phu has a warped Egyptian theme and large, luxurious rooms, windowless downstairs.

For **eating**, try the group of restaurants from nos. 22–26 along Tran Hung Dao – Quang Minh at no. 26 is recommended. Both the *Saigon Café* at 107 Dien Bien Phu and the cosier *Maxim's* further down the road at no. 31 are bar-restaurants with Western menus and nightly live music. For nightlife, look no further than the space-themed *Bien Goi* disco, on Dien Bien Phu near *Maxim's*, which looks like a set from *Star Trek*.

Ha Long Bay

Nearly 2000 bizarrely shaped limestone outcrops jut out of the emerald **Ha Long Bay**, its hidden bays, echoing caves and needle-sharp ridges providing the inspiration for dozens of local legends and poems. Navigating the silent channels and scrambling through caves is a hugely popular activity, but with so much hyperbole, some find Ha Long disappointing: this stretch of coast is an industrialized region, and views in February and March can be poor. Most travellers visit Ha Long Bay on an organized tour from Hanoi; otherwise, the epicentre of tourism in Ha Long Bay itself is **Bai Chay**, a resort on the north shore, which offers rather mediocre accommodation and overpriced restaurants plus hordes of boatmen. It also tends to be overrun with domestic and Asian tourists, especially in the summer months. A more low-key base is **Hong Gai**, a short hop away by ferry across a narrow channel east of Bai Chay (soon to be linked by a suspension bridge). The other option is to base yourself on the slightly quieter Cat Ba Island (see p.1220).

Bai Chay and Hong Gai (Ha Long City)

In 1994, Hong Gai and Bai Chay were amalgamated into **Ha Long City**, but locals still stick to the old names – as do ferry services and minibuses – since this is a useful way to distinguish between the two towns, which lie on either side of the narrow Cua Luc channel. Neon signs blaze out at night along the **BAI CHAY** waterfront, advertising north Vietnam's most developed resort, whose main business is boat tours around the bay. **HONG GAI**, on the other hand, is a bustling working harbour.

The **accommodation** in Hong Gai may be basic, but the atmosphere of the town has a certain charm and the welcoming, family-run *Hien Cat* guesthouse, conveniently located right by the ferry pier, at 252 Ben Tau (☎33/827417; ②), has the most scenic bathrooms in Ha Long City. **Bai Chay** has a bigger choice of hotels, most located along the two main drags, Ha Long Avenue and Vuon Dao, but quality is variable. The friendly *Hoa Binh* (☎33/846009; ②) is one of the better mini-hotels on Vuon Dao, with some of its rooms affording sea views. The *Than An*, a steep climb further up the hill at 100 Vuon Dao (☎033/846959; ③), has large clean rooms offering sweeping bay views from the balconies. All three hotels can arrange boats for hire. Located on quiet, leafy Ho Xuan Huong near the bus station and ferry jetty, the family-run *Minh Tuan* (☎33/846200; ②) and the new *Huyen Long* (☎33/845777; ②), both have cheap, quiet rooms.

Bai Chay's Vietcombank on Ha Long Avenue can **change cash** and travellers' cheques, and also has ATMs both here and opposite Hong Gai post office. The larger hotels in Bai Chay and both post offices will also be able to change money. Fresh seafood is the natural speciality of Ha Long Bay, with excellent lobster, crab and fish on offer at the **restaurants**. The restaurants on Ha Long Avenue in Bai Chay tend to cater for tourist groups, but the *Van Song* and *Thuy Hien* restaurants are worth a try. Alternatively, the *Quang Vinh* restaurant at 24 Vuon Dao serves decent, cheap Vietnamese and Western food; the German-speaking owner can help with boat tours. Over in Hong Gai, the best eating is found at the market food stalls. There's

Internet access in Bai Chay at the Emotion Cybercafé on Ha Long Avenue, and in several places near the post office. Bai Chay has a **pharmacy** at 59 Vuon Dao. The frequent **buses** between Hanoi, Hai Phong and Bai Chay use the Western bus station, at the far end of Ha Long Avenue; you can also flag down buses during the day on Ha Long Avenue around the main post office – negotiating direct with the driver can secure you a seat on an air-con Hanoi-bound bus for around $2.20. Alternatively, tour buses returning to Hanoi leave from Bai Chay's Tourist Wharf, between noon and 1pm; bus prices are negiotiable, but usually average around $3. Buses from Mong Cai and the north use the Eastern bus station; from here, Hong Gai centre is 1km back down Le Thanh Tong, or you can cross over to Bai Chay on the passenger ferry that shuttles between the two bus stations. A slower and more expensive, but far more scenic approach, is to take the **train** from Hanoi to Hai Phong and then the public **ferry** to Hong Gai (2 daily; 2hr). There are no public ferries to Cat Ba Island, but there is one connection per day from Hong Gai to Cat Hai, an adjacent island, from where a ferry to Phu Long village and a thirty-kilometre bus or xe om ride will get you to Cat Ba Town. **Hydrofoil** services to Mong Cai (2 daily; 3hr; $6) depart from the hydrofoil jetty near Bai Chay bus station.

Boat trips

The vast majority of visitors to Ha Long Bay come on organized tours from Hanoi, with most overnighting in Cat Ba. For the best experience, choose an operator offering one or two nights sleeping on the boat (with the chance of a midnight dip in the phosphorous waters) and a guided hike though Cat Ba National Park. You could try and **charter a boat** locally, though it's a hassle and usually works out more

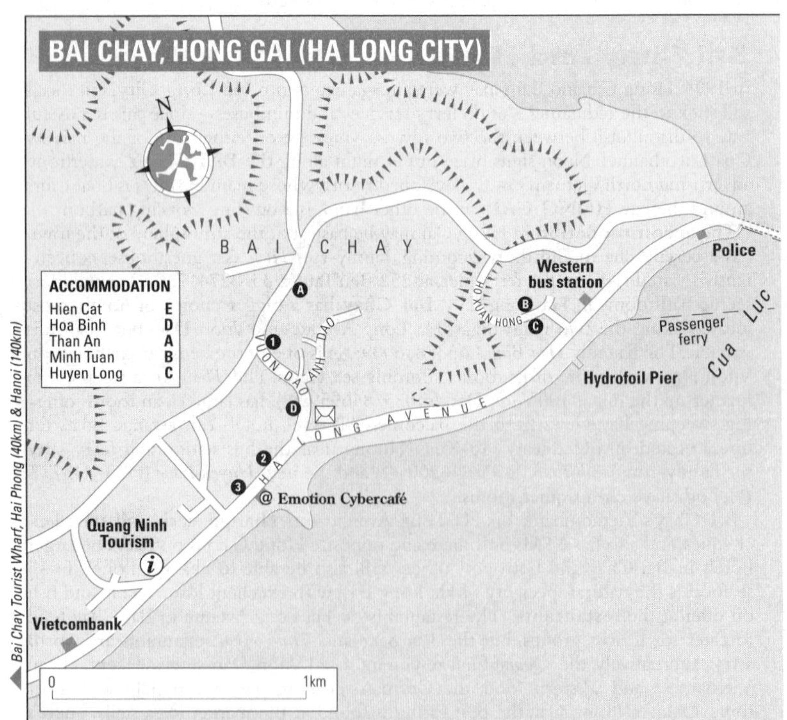

expensive than a tour. Most hotels in Bai Chay can help with boat hire, as can the information office at Bai Chay **Tourist Wharf**, 2km west of town; they have several itineraries, including a rushed standard four-hour tour ($3.15).

The caves and islands

Ha Long Bay is split in two by a wide channel running north–south: the larger, western portion contains the most dramatic scenery and best caves, while to the east lies an attractive area of smaller islands, known as Bai Tu Long. Note that independent visitors to the bay need to buy a $2 **excursion ticket** at the tourist wharf, which includes insurance and entrance to the caves along your route. The bay's most famous cave is the closest to Bai Chay: **Hang Dau Go** ("Grotto of the Wooden Stakes"). In 1288, General Tran Hung Dao amassed hundreds of wooden stakes here; these were driven into the Bach Dang River estuary mud, skewering the boats of Kublai Khan's Mongol army as the tide went out. The same island also boasts the beautiful **Hang Thien Cung** cave, whose rectangular chamber, 250m long and 20m high, holds a textbook display of sparkling stalactites and stalagmites. Continuing south, you should single out Ho Dong Tien ("Grotto of the Fairy Lake") and the enchanting Dong Me Cung ("Grotto of the Labyrinth").

Of the far-flung sights, **Hang Hanh** is one of the more adventurous day-trips from Bai Chay: the tide must be exactly right (at half-tide) to allow a coracle ($10 extra) access to the two-kilometre-long tunnel-cave; a powerful torch is very useful. Dau Bo Island, on the southeastern edge of Ha Long Bay, encloses **Ho Ba Ham** ("Three Tunnel Lake"), a shallow lagoon wrapped round with limestone walls and connected to the sea by three low-ceilinged tunnels that are only navigable by sam-

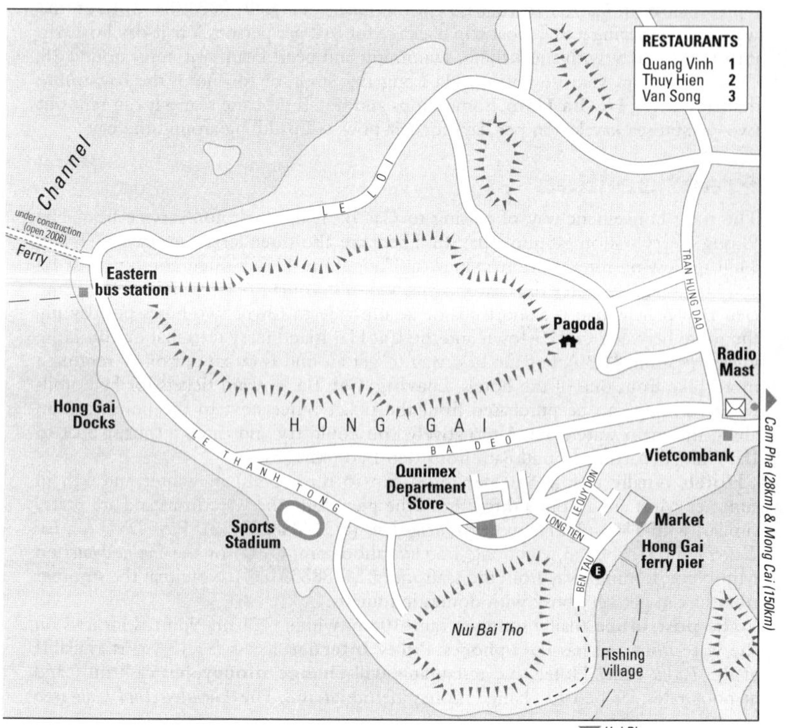

pan at low tide. This cave can be included in a one- or two-day excursion out of Bai Chay and can also be arranged from Cat Ba Island.

Cat Ba Island

Dragon-back mountain ranges mass on the horizon 20km out of Hai Phong as boats approach **Cat Ba Island**, the largest member of an archipelago sitting on the west of Ha Long Bay. The island's main settlement is Cat Ba Town, from where it's 30km across a landscape of forested peaks or along the coast to tiny Phu Long village. **Cat Ba Town** consists of a much depleted original fishing village and market and, 800m to the east across a small headland, the main ferry pier, Ben Ca. A steep road just east of the waterfront leads to a small, sandy **beach**; from here, a ten-minute walk further along a cliff-hugging boardwalk leads you to a second, quieter and more secluded beach. Both have beach facilities, including toilets, sun-loungers and lockers, as well as restaurants selling snacks and drinks.

In 1986, almost half the island and adjacent waters were declared a **national park** (entrance fee $1), the entrance to which is 16km along the road from Cat Ba Town. It's worth hiring an experienced and English-speaking guide to explore the UNESCO-listed park (around $5–7 for up to one day), as people have got seriously lost on the unmarked paths. You'll need good boots, lots of water, mosquito repellent and a compass. The going can be quite tough and paths slippery in wet weather; after heavy rains, trekking in the park should be avoided due to treacherous conditions.

Most Cat Ba hotels can help arrange **boat tours** and treks in the national park. The most popular option is a full-day trip with a trek through the national park, lunch in a village, and a boat trip back to Cat Ba town via Lan Ha Bay, with a swimming stop and a visit to a pearl farm. Hanoi's Handspan travel company has a representative in Cat Ba Town, based at the *Giang Son Hotel* (☎31/888214), on the waterfront, offering a trek/boat trip package for $12 per person. A half-day boat trip into Lan Ha Bay with snorkelling, swimming and pearl farm visit costs around $8. Other boat trips venture up into Ha Long Bay itself, or to one of the bay's more dramatic caves, **Ho Ba Ham**. Some shops and hotels near the seafront can rent out two-person sea kayaks ($6 per day) for self-powered paddling around the bay.

Practicalities

The most convenient way of getting to Cat Ba is the hydrofoil service from Hai Phong's ferry station (45min–1hr; $6). There are also three ferries every day (1-2hr; $4.40), allowing for a more relaxing trip. Tours from Hanoi often combine Cat Ba and Ha Long Bay (three days/two nights; $25–55). Tourist boats will drop you at the Ben Beo pier, which is a short bus or xe om ride to town. Two buses per day ply the route between Cat Ba Town and the Cat Hai Island ferry terminal in Phu Long village (45min; $1.30), but the best way to get around is by xe om or by renting a motorbike from one of the hotels. **Leaving Cat Ba**, onward tickets for hydrofoils to Hai Phong can be purchased from the ticket office next to the police station along the main waterfront. Alternatively, you could try and catch a tourist boat to Bai Chay, departing around 8am from Ben Bao (4hr; $5).

Hotels usually charge $10 per room (up to three beds) in winter and $15 in summer. Most are a stone's throw from the pier along the waterfront and are pretty similar, with TV and air-con: try *Quang Duc* (☎31/888231; ❷), *Vien Dong* (or *Far Eastern*; ☎031/888555, viendong_hotel@yahoo.com; ❷–❸) or the *Pacific Hotel* on Mui Ngoc, leading away from the seafront (☎31/888331; ❷). Note that the summer months can get very busy with domestic tourists.

The **post office** (daily: summer 7am–10pm; winter 7.30am–9pm) is located on the waterfront and has IDD phones. Pricey **Internet** access ($1.15/hr) is available at the *Pacific Hotel*. Hotels and restaurants will **change money**, but cash only and at poor rates; it's best to change money before arrival. The *Flightless Bird Café* (see below) can also change cash and travellers' cheques, and organizes boat trips.

Most of Cat Ba's **restaurants** are located along the waterfront. Commission-grabbing guides often lead tour groups into the mediocre *Dolphin* restaurant, but there's much better seafood to be had at the popular *Huu Dung*, just up the road from the *Hoang Huang* hotel, whilst the trendy *Green Mango*, east along the seafront, serves more innovative dishes at slightly higher prices. The latter is also the only cocktail bar in town, with relaxed music and soft couches to lounge on. The friendly *Flightless Bird Café*, west towards the market, is run by a New Zealander and serves a good range of international drinks, and has book exchange, darts and pool.

Mong Cai and the Chinese border

Since the border reopened for trade in 1992, **MONG CAI** has been booming, and its markets are stuffed with Chinese goods. **Hydrofoils** from Ha Long and Hai Phong arrive 16km outside town, from where a complimentary shuttle bus brings you to the centre. Highway 18 enters the town from the west across a bridge and then peters out in a large roundabout, with the public **minibus station** to the east and the post office on the south side. The blue, space-age building northwest of the roundabout identifies Mong Cai's focal point, the covered market. The **Chinese border** is just 1km away; walk north along Tran Phu and turn left at the end of the road to reach the border gate (daily: summer 7am–4.30pm; winter 7.30am–4pm).

Mong Cai's **hotels** are located around the covered market area, and all offer air-con, hot water and TV. The *Tuan Thanh* mini-hotel, near the post office at 4 Nguyen Du (Ⓣ33/881481; ❷), is the best central option, with clean, comfortable rooms, some with balcony, and English-speaking staff. The new *Cuu Long* (Ⓣ033/770666; ❸-❹), east of the roundabout, on Hung Vuong, is a good alternative. Hidden north of the market, off Van Don, the *Bien Hoa* at 63 Thuong Mai (Ⓣ033/882135; ❷) is a cheap option, while *Thang Loi* at 61 Tran Phu (Ⓣ033/881002; ❷) has similar budget rooms but a messy lobby.

Streets near the market turn into open-air **food** stalls in the evening. For **money exchange**, Vietcombank has a branch with a 24hr ATM north of the market, on Van Don, and another ATM inside the post office. Several **Internet cafés** can be found around the post office.

Hydrofoil tickets to Bai Chay (2 daily; 3hr including shuttle bus; $6.30) can be purchased from the Mui Ngoc office at 1 Tran Phu (Ⓣ33/883988), opposite the post office. Hydrofoil tickets for Hai Phong (1 daily; 4hr including shuttle bus; $15) are available from the Greenlines office, 43 Tran Phu (Ⓣ33/881214). The ticket price includes a shuttle bus to the boat terminal (16km) and, at low tide, a small boat that ferries passengers out mid-bay, transferring over to the awaiting hydrofoil. During bad weather, this operation for arriving and departing boats can be exciting, to say the least.

11.8

The far north

Vietnam fans out above Hanoi, the majority of it a mountainous zone wrapped around the Red River Delta. Two arteries carry road and rail links north from the capital towards the **Chinese border crossings of Lao Cai and Dong Dang** (Lang Son), and the rest of the region is mostly wild and inaccessible, sparsely populated by a fascinating mosaic of **ethnic minorities**, whose presence is the chief tourist attraction around here. The hill station of **Sa Pa** has become famous for its weekend market, when minority villagers trek in to buy, sell and gossip, and is also the main departure point for treks to their settlements. **Mai Chau** and **Bac Ha** are less visited centres for walks to minority villages. Note that finding ATMs and changing travellers' cheques north of Hanoi can be problematic, and cash exchanges garner poor rates, so make sure you have all the **cash** (in dong) you need before you leave the capital.

Lao Cai and the Chinese border

Follow the Red River Valley northwest from Hanoi and after 300km, pushing ever deeper into the mountains, you eventually reach the border town of **LAO CAI**, of little interest in itself except as the railhead for Sa Pa and, since the discontinuation of trains further north from here, as the place to catch the bus **into China** for travellers heading to Kunming. Most people arrive on the night train from Hanoi at Lao Cai **train station** on the east bank of the Red River, just 3km due south of the Chinese border. Follow the road north from the station towards the border and, after 2km, you reach Coc Leu Bridge, spanning the river to link up with the bulk of Lao Cai town over on the opposite bank. Immediately across the bridge, turn left for the **bus station** and market.

Note that several travel agents and hotels hook their own air-con, soft-berth carriages up to the three nightly trains between Hanoi and Lao Cai ($16/berth). However, these are no different from the Vietnam Railways (VR) carriages, and you're better off buying a VR ticket (hard air-con sleeper $6-10, soft air-con sleeper $9-13) in Hanoi, purchasing the return ticket at Sa Pa's VR office.

Tourist buses **to Sa Pa** ($1.60; 1hr) meet the morning Hanoi trains, as do minibuses ($0.65), which also depart regularly for Sa Pa from the bus station. If you've booked a room in Sa Pa, your hotel may include a pick-up. Otherwise, your options are to take a jeep or a xe om ($4–5 per person) all the way from the train or bus station. The Tulico Tourist Company, based at the *Darling Hotel* on Thac Bac in Sa Pa (Ⓣ20/871961), has a desk (Ⓣ020/835463) inside the train station complex which can arrange transport and trips to Sa Pa and Bac Ha. If you're an experienced rider, rent a Minsk motorbike ($5-6 per day) from one of the cafés on the station square; bring warm clothing, check the bike carefully and demand to have spare parts, as roads can be bad and some bikes have taken a battering.

Lao Cai's tourism boom has led to a plethora of new **hotels**. Near the station, try the *Gia Nga Gueshouse* (020/830459; ❶), or splash out at the glam *Lao Cai International Hotel*, in the town centre at 88 Thuy Hoa (Ⓣ020/826668, Ⓦwww.laocaihotel.com; ❾), which is popular with Chinese tourists for its casino. East of the border gate and just across the railway line is the basic *Song Hong Guest House* (Ⓣ20/830004;

❷). The road outside the train station is lined with food stalls, and there are several **restaurants**, crammed with foreigners waiting for their return trains on Sunday evenings; the *Nhat Linh* and the *Thai Du* are good.

Into China: Hekou border crossing

The border crossing from Lao Cai **into China** is via the **Hekou border gate** (7am–5pm), on the east bank of the Red River. Queues at immigration are longest in the early morning. Inside the Vietnamese border post building, you'll find an exchange desk that deals in dong, dollars and yuan, but not travellers' cheques. There's a bank across the street, and plenty of women hanging around who are eager to change cash. Travellers **entering Vietnam** at Lao Cai may have to pay a small "fee" for paperwork. Across on the Chinese side, several high-quality air-con **buses depart for Kunming**, 520km away, from Hekou bus station, 100m from the border crossing (four in the morning, five sleeper services in the evening; 12hr; $10). Friendly Travel (inside Sa Pa's *Royal Hotel*, ⓣ20/832759, or in Hanoi at 33 Hang Giay, ⓣ04/926 2098) runs three daily air-con buses to Kunming from Lao Cai's bus station (10hrs, $16), leaving at 10am & 2pm (seats) and 7pm (sleeper).

Sa Pa and around

Forty kilometres from Lao Cai, the small market town of **SA PA** perches dramatically on the western edge of a high plateau and enjoys a refreshing climate set in magnificent scenery, with plenty of walks out to **minority villages** of Hmong, Dao and Giay peoples. Sa Pa itself is ethnically Vietnamese, but the **weekend market**, which runs from noon on Saturday to noon on Sunday, draws in minority villagers from all around and has become a major tourist attraction, not least for the chance to see minority women clad in their colourful finery. In peak season, however, tourists can outnumber locals and some visitors may find the market slightly disappointing. Accommodation and restaurants get rather overrun at weekends throughout the year as tour groups head in; if you have the chance to visit during the week, you'll find Sa Pa a lot quieter and more interesting. Before you set off on a trek, visit the free exhibition inside Sa Pa's **Tourism Information and Service Centre** (see below) for a taster of life in the minority villages; the wonderful "Through H'mong eyes"exhibition upstairs has photos taken by young minority girls, complete with comments about their daily lives.

Practicalities

The most popular routing is a **train** to Lao Cai (see p.1222) and a connecting **bus** ($1.60) up to Sa Pa, which drops you at various hotels or along the main street, Cau May. Heading **back to Lao Cai**, local buses leave all day from near the church on the main square and will tout for business up and down Cau May. The **Lao Cai Railway Station Office** at 24 Cau May (daily 7.30–11am & 1.30–4pm; ⓣ20/871480) is the main ticket office for buses and trains. Tourist buses for Lao Cai station depart from here at 7.30am, 4.30pm and 6.30pm ($1.60; 1hr). Tickets for the night trains are in short supply at Lao Cai station, so book as far ahead as possible in Sa Pa, either at the Lao Cai Railway Station Office, or (more expensively) through your guesthouse. The latter can also organize jeeps back to Lao Cai for $10 per vehicle, as well as arrange **motorbike taxis**. Motorbike rental can be found at several shops near the *Auberge Guesthouse*.

Sa Pa's **Tourism Information and Service Centre** at 28 Cau May (daily 8-11.30am & 1.30-5.30pm, ⓣ020/871975, ⓦwww.sapatourism.info) provides information, publishes a good hiking map, organizes tours and guides, and has a shop selling village handicrafts. Most guesthouses can also help with booking tours, guides and transportation; of these, the *Auberge Guesthouse* and *Cat Cat Guesthouse* are the best choices. Responsible travel agents who include insurance in their tour fees and who pay their guides decently include **Handspan** at 17 Cau Mai (ⓣ020/872110, ⓦhandspan.com), who also have guided mountainbike tours, and **Topas** at 20 Cau May (ⓣ020/871331, ⓦwww.topas-adventure-vietnam.com) offering quality tailor-made trips, treks to Fan Si Pan and accommodation at the new *Ecolodge* in the Muong Hoa valley (see below). All the above can arrange jeeps ($25–35 per day) and provide information on walks to minority villages; guides are available for around $10–15 per day.

The **bank** near the market and some hotels and guesthouses can change money, and the *Auberge* can arrange cash advances against Visa and MasterCard, but rates are better in Hanoi. **Internet access** is available below the *Auberge* for $0.60/hr, and at double that rate in a few other places.

Accommodation

Sa Pa is generally busy all year round, especially at weekends, but at quieter times, rates can be discounted by a few dollars. In high season and at weekends, rooms in Sa Pa can be in short supply.

Auberge Guesthouse Cau May ⓣ20/871243, auberge@fpt.com.vn. The most popular of the cluster of hotels at the bottom end of Cau May, offering views from the higher rooms, tours and good food. ②–⑥

Baguette & Chocolat Thac Bac ⓣ020/871766, ⓦwww.hoasuaschool.com. At the top end of Cau May. Elegant guest rooms with a delicious bakery breakfast included in the price. ③

Bamboo Hotel Cau May ⓣ20/871075, ⓦwww.sapatravel.com. More upmarket accommodation in an old French villa and its new extension. ③–⑦

Cat Cat ⓣ20/871946, catcatht@hn.vnn.vn. A popular terraced guesthouse just below the market, boasting budget rooms with fireplaces and good views of Mt Fan Si Pan. ②–③

Gecko Ham Rong (ⓣ020/871504, ⓦwww.geckohotel.com. Next to the post office. Sleep in proximity to good food in *Gecko*'s oven-heated guest rooms. ③

Queen Hotel Cau May ⓣ20/871301. Good-value budget accommodation next door to the *Auberge*. ①–②

Royal Cau May ⓣ20/871313, ⓦwww.royalhotelsapa.com. A decent option with good views over the valley, and blocking those of the *Auberge* across the street. ②–④

Topas Ecolodge Muong Hoa valley ⓣ020/872404, ⓦwww.topas-eco-lodge.com. A new deluxe bungalow complex offering great views. Advance bookings only. ⑨

Victoria Hotel ⓣ20/871522, ⓦwww.victoriahotels-asia.com. Splash out at Sa Pa's best hotel, which boasts an à la carte restaurant, pool, tennis courts and gym. ⑨

Eating and drinking

A good place for **eating** is the *Mimosa* restaurant, set in a small garden villa off Cau May; its great-value, tasty Vietnamese and European dishes are hard to beat. The more upmarket *Gecko* (see above) serves excellent French and Vietnamese food. For delicious bakery snacks, look no further than *Baguette & Chocolat* (see above); they also sell lunch packets for gourmet hikers. The *Victoria Hotel* has a decent **bar**, complete with pool table and satellite sports coverage, Hmong girls practise their pool skills in the Tau Bar beneath the *Hoang Mai Hotel* on Cau May, but the best place to hang out at night is the British-run *Red Dragon Pub*, south of the *Auberge* at 23 Muong Hoa, where you can wash down a shepherd's pie with a pint.

Walks to surrounding villages

In a move to protect Sa Pa's vulnerable minority areas, tourists are only allowed to visit the area around Sa Pa (including Ta Phin, Hoang Lien valley and Fan Si Pan) with a **permit and guide**; some villages are out of bounds altogether.

Cat Cat village and the Silver Waterfall can be explored without a guide but you still need a permit. Permits are free of charge and can be arranged quickly by licensed tour agents (see p.1223).

There are several Hmong villages within easy walking distance of town, of which the most popular is **CAT CAT** village, roughly 3km away ($0.30 entrance fee). Follow the track west from the market square, past the steeple-shaped building, then turn left onto a path that drops steeply down to the river. Cat Cat, a huddle of wooden houses, hides among fruit trees and bamboo. Look out for tubs of indigo dye, used to colour the hemp cloth typical of Hmong dress. Cat Cat waterfall is just below the village. For a longer (and guided) walk, instead of cutting down to Cat Cat, continue on the main track, turning right at the last bend before a river to follow a footpath up the valley. After 4km you'll reach **SIN CHAI** village, a much larger Hmong settlement.

The ethnic minorities

Historically, all the peoples of northern Vietnam migrated from southern China at various times throughout history: those who arrived first, notably the Tay and Thai, settled in the fertile valleys, where they now lead a relatively prosperous existence, whereas late arrivals, such as groups of Hmong and Dao, were left to eke out a living on the inhospitable higher slopes. Around five million minority people (nearly two-thirds of Vietnam's total) now live in the northern uplands, mostly in isolated villages. The largest ethnic groups are **Thai** and **Muong** in the northwest, **Tay** and **Nung** in the northeast, and **Hmong** and **Dao** dispersed throughout the region. Despite government efforts to integrate them into the Vietnamese community, many of the minorities in these remote areas continue to follow a way of life little changed over the centuries. For an insight into their cultures, visit the exhibition in Sa Pa's tourism office (see p.1223) and Hanoi's Museum of Ethnology (see p.1207).

Visiting minority villages

For many people, one of the highlights of travelling in Vietnam is the experience of visiting the minority villages in the north. This is easiest with your own transport. If you're reliant on public services, you'll need to allow more time but, basing yourself in the main towns, it's still possible to get out to traditional villages – notably around Sa Pa, Son La, Mai Chau and Cao Bang. A popular, hassle-free alternative is to join an **organized trip** from a Hanoi tour agency, whose usual destinations are Sa Pa for the weekly market (4 days; from $25 per person), and Mai Chau (2 days; from $20). The standard package includes guided walks to at least two different minority villages – with Sa Pa tours, the Sunday market at Bac Ha is included – and in the case of Mai Chau, a night in a stilt house. You'll need strong boots or training shoes, socks and long trousers (against thorns and leeches), a hat, sunblock and warm clothing; take plenty of water. You might also want a sleeping bag, mosquito net and food – though these may be provided. Otherwise, you could try and arrange an individual programme through a Hanoi tour agent or provincial tourist offices, but English-speaking guides who know the area may be hard to find; the guesthouses in Sa Pa are probably your best source. Don't turn up at a village and expect to find accommodation, as your hosts may get in trouble with the authorities and crime is becoming a problem.

It's preferable to visit the minority villages as part of a **small group**, ideally four people or fewer, as this causes least disruption and allows for greater communication. There's a whole debate about the ethics of cultural tourism and its negative impact on traditional ways of life. Most villagers are genuinely welcoming, appreciating contact with Westerners and the material benefits which they bring; tourism may also help to protect the minorities against enforced Vietnamization, at least in the short term, by encouraging greater respect for cultural diversity. Nonetheless, it's important to take a responsible attitude, and try not to cause offence. Dress modestly (no shorts or vests), never take photographs without asking and only enter a house when invited, removing your shoes first. Small gifts, such as fresh fruit, are always welcome. However, there is a view that even this can foster begging, and that you should only ever give in return for some service or hospitality. A compromise is to buy craftwork produced by the villagers. Take litter back to the towns and be frugal if burning local wood.

One of the most enjoyable guided treks is along the newly resurfaced road from the *Auberge* south down the Muong Hoa valley for 12km to a wooden suspension bridge and **TA VAN** village, on the opposite side of the river. Ta Van actually consists of two villages: immediately across the bridge is a Giay community, while further uphill to the left is a Dao village. From here, it's possible to walk back towards Sa Pa on the west side of the river, as far as another Hmong village, **LAO CHAI**, before rejoining the main track.

Further along the main road, a track leads to the Dao settlement of **GIANG TA CHAI**, or **CHAI MAN**. After crossing a suspension bridge it's 1km to the village, with unprepossessing **SU PAN** village another 6km along the track. From here, 4km straight down into the valley brings you to the Tay village of **BAN HO**, which straddles the river at a suspension bridge. Ban Ho is the staging point for longer treks in the next valley. Of the more remote villages, **BANG KHOANG** and **TA GANG PHINH** can be explored by jeep in a day-trip from Sa Pa. Other worthwhile trips include a Sunday day-trip to the Muong Hum market ($50 per jeep), and the challenging three-day trek scaling Mount Fan Si Pan, Vietnam's highest mountain at 3143m, from about $50 per person.

Bac Ha and around

The small town of **BAC HA**, nestling in a high valley 40km northeast of Highway 7, makes a long but popular day excursion from Sa Pa on Sundays, when villagers of the Tay, Dao, Nung, Giay and above all Flower Hmong ethnic minorities trek in for the **market** (8am–2pm). Some travellers feel that an extra day spent hiking around Sa Pa is preferable to the tiring day-trip to Bac Ha, but if you have time, the town is much less touristy than Sa Pa and worth lingering in. If you're here on a Saturday, you could take in the livestock market at Can Cau (see p.1227) as well.

The road that leads in from Pho Lu forms the **main street** of Bac Ha, and a bend in the road outside the main post office marks the centre of town, before continuing through Bac Ha for another 2km and then onwards in the direction of Can Cau. A road branching off to the right immediately beside the post office leads to the market and a couple of guesthouses.

Practicalities

Coming **from Hanoi**, get off the bus or train at Pho Lu, from where there are two buses a day to Bac Ha (5.30am & 6.30am; 1hr 20min; $1) from the bus station on the highway, just across from the railway station. Coming **from Lao Cai**, there are two daily buses direct to Bac Ha, at 6am and 10am (2hr 30min; $1.5). Buses return to Pho Lu at 7am and 11am, and to Lao Cai at noon and 2pm. Local buses terminate at Bac Ha's bus station, near the town market's south entrance; to get to the bus station, come up the hill from the post office, turn off the main road into the first street on the right, and then continue 200m down. Coming **from Sa Pa**, it's easier and quicker to join a tour ($7), which will include the market and a short trek. A motorbike from Sa Pa takes three hours and costs about $8–10. Returning from Bac Ha, buses for Lao Cai (sometimes via Pho Lu) depart at 5am, 7am, 11am and 1pm, while those direct to Pho Lu leave at 7am and 11am; pick up the bus either from the bus station, or along the main street. A jeep or motorbike to Lao Cai takes two hours.

Places to stay in Bac Ha are basic, and prices usually lower during the week. The friendly *Hoang Vu Hotel* (☎20/880264; ❷) has ten basic en-suite rooms, and can arrange tours and transport. To find it, go past the post office on your right along the main street and walk up the hill until you come to a road leading left at a hammer and sickle sign – the hotel is immediately on your left. Further down the same street, the imposing *Sao Mai Hotel* (☎20/880288; ❹–❺), frequented by

tour groups, has somewhat overpriced rooms in a new wooden stilt-
cheaper, smaller rooms in the old quarter. Alternatively, the *Dang K*
on the main street near the post office (☎20/880290; ③), has clea
with balcony in a newer block.

For **eating**, the *Tran Sin Hotel* (☎20/880240), located next to the n
and the genial *Cong Fu Restaurant*, just off the main road along the sa
bus station, are both popular with the Sunday tourists and serve go
and noodle dishes; the former also has dark but adequate double r
Sao Mai Hotel restaurant has a more sophisticated menu, serving decent European dishes at reasonable prices.

Trips to surrounding villages

Recently, Bac Ha has attempted to emulate Sa Pa's success by developing its own trekking business focused around the nearby rural markets. The picturesque Hmong hamlet of **BAN PHO**, 3km from town, makes a pleasant stroll. Take the road half left at the hammer and sickle sign and head down past the *Sao Mai Hotel*, turning left immediately after the next big building, which is the local hospital. The road continues up the hill for 2km after the village, and affords good views of the valley.

The village of **CAN CAU**, 18km north of Bac Ha, hosts a market each Saturday, which is well worth the effort if you can organize transport out there from one of the Sa Pa hotels. The market has an emphasis on livestock, especially buffalo, with traders trekking in from as far afield as China in search of bargains. Relatively few visitors get there, and the fair retains much of its authenticity. Other than this, there's nothing at all to see in Can Cau, but the ride, across a high, empty range with panoramic views on either side, is glorious: simply follow the main road north out of town. You can book a day-trip to Can Cau in Sa Pa for about $12 per person; or slightly cheaper from hotels in Bac Ha.

Mai Chau and around

The minority villages of the fertile **Mai Chau Valley**, inhabited mainly by Thai people, are close enough to Hanoi (150km) to make this a popular destination, particularly at weekends. The valley itself, however, is still largely unspoilt, a peaceful scene of rice fields and jagged mountains. **MAI CHAU** is the valley's main village, a friendly, quiet place that suddenly bursts into life for its Sunday **market**, when minority people trek in to haggle over buffalo meat, starfruit, sacks of tea or groundnuts. Unlike in Sa Pa, the minorities here have largely forsaken their traditional dress, but there's plenty of colour on the road outside the market where freshly dyed yarn hangs up to dry. You can overnight in Mai Chau, but it's more interesting to head for the outlying villages; at the southern end of the village, across the street from the *Mai Chau Guesthouse* (☎18/867262; ②; undergoing renovation at time of writing), a thatched stilt house offers basic accommodation ① and good food.

The most accessible village in the Mai Chau Valley is **BAN LAC**, a White Thai settlement of seventy houses where you can buy hand-woven textiles, watch performances of traditional dancing and sleep overnight in a stilt house. The village receives a fair number of tourists and can feel overly organized. To reach Ban Lac, turn right 500m south of the *Mai Chau Guesthouse*. Houses displaying cloth outside are most likely to offer accommodation; expect to pay around $3 per person per night, plus around $1 per meal. For a less touristy stilt-house village, head for pretty **POM COONG**, marooned on a small hill in a sea of rice paddies, and reached by turning right immediately before the *Mai Chau Guesthouse*. Of several stilt houses offering accommodation, the large one in the northwest corner of the (past the volleyball court to the right) is the most authentic. **BAN VAN** ...ge, signposted to the east from the middle of Mai Chau, is a less-visited village ...emmed in by the hills; the first house you see is the friendly *Ban Van Guesthouse* (☎018/867182, ❶).

Most people visit the Mai Chau Valley on an organized tour out of Hanoi, though the newly widened road has lead to faster public transport connections, with three direct buses leaving Hanoi daily at 6am, 10am and 2pm (4hrs; $1-2).

Lang Son and the Chinese border

For most people, **LANG SON** is merely an overnight stop on the journey through the northeast or en route **to China**, only 18km away to the north. The Ky Cung River splits the town in two, leaving the main bulk on the north side of the Ky Lua Bridge and provincial offices to the south. Highway 1, the town's main north–south artery – also known as Tran Dang Ninh – runs between the bridge and **Cho Ky Lua**, which is well worth investigating in the early morning, when Tay, Nung and Dao women come to trade. Chinese imports dominate alongside an amazing array of local produce, from freshwater fish to silkworm larvae. The post office lies near the Ky Lua Bridge, 200m east of the highway down Le Loi. Next door, at 51 Le Loi, the Vietincombank changes US dollars and yuan, as can some hotels. Ngo Quyen Street branches off to the right from Le Loi, where about 100m along you'll find the provincial **bus station**, though most long-distance buses will drop off and pick up along Le Loi and Tran Dang Ninh. If you're coming from Hanoi, minibuses depart regularly from Hanoi's Gia Lam station; alternatively, private air-con minibuses ($6) can be arranged through the *Real Darling Café* (see p.1203).

When it comes to **accommodation**, budget travellers should head for *Hoa Phuong Guest House*, 92 Tran Dang Ninh (☎25/871233; ❷), where there are basic air-con or fan rooms. However, it's worth paying a little more for the spacious and friendly accommodation a few hundred metres north at the *Hoa Binh Guest House*, opposite the market entrance at 127 Tran Dang Ninh (☎25/870127; ❸). Rooms at the top afford great views over a nearby lake, and there's a rooftop terrace. For **food**, try the street kitchens on Tran Dang Ninh – no. 28 is recommended, opposite the junction with Tam Thanh – or head for *Binh Dan* restaurant, opposite the bus station at 13 Ngo Quyen, which serves tasty and cheap rice dishes.

The Chinese border: Huu Nghi and on to Nanning

The road crossing known as the **Huu Nghi ("Friendship") border gate** is 18km north of Lang Son and 4km from Dong Dang at the end of Highway 1. If you're travelling by local bus, spend the night in Lang Son and then take a motorbike to the border gate (about $2). Otherwise, **minibuses** shuttle between Lang Son's Le Loi and Dong Dang town (look for those marked "Tam Thanh" at the front), but you'll then have to hop on a motorbike for the last leg (less than $1). Local **trains** from Hanoi (hard seat only) terminate at Dong Dang station, 800m south of the main town, from where you can take a xe om up to the border (less than $1). Dong Dang train station is also the border checkpoint for international trains entering China; note that although the international train stops here for Vietnamese customs, you cannot board it here, only in Hanoi (see p.1200). The Huu Nghi **border gate** (daily 7am–6pm) is just a small road checkpoint and has no exchange facilities; there's a walk of less than 1km between the two checkpoints. On the Chinese side, taxis and rickshaws (from ¥15–30 yuan) will take you to **Pingxiang**, 15km away, for the nearest accommodation and the 2.40pm train to Nanning.

Vietnam travel details

Buses

It's almost impossible to give the frequency with which buses run, though scheduled, long-distance public buses won't depart if empty. Moreover, some private services, often minibuses or pick-ups, ply more popular routes, and depart only when they have enough passengers to make the journey worthwhile. Highway 1 sees a near-constant stream of buses passing through to various destinations, and it's possible to flag something down at virtually any time of the day. Off the highway, to be sure of a catching a bus, it's advisable to start your journey early – most long-distance departures leave between 5 and 9am, and very few run after midday. On several main routes, there is now an increasing number of high-quality air-con buses operating from private addresses. They usually depart on time whether full or not, don't pick up extra passengers en route, and provide complimentary bottled water; some hotels can book these for you. Journey times for buses can vary; figures below show the approximate normal length of time you can expect the journey to take.

Buon Ma Thuot to: Da Nang (15hr); HCMC (7–8hr); Nha Trang (4hr).

Can Tho to: Chau Doc (2hr 30min); Ha Tien (7hr); HCMC (4hr); Long Xuyen (1hr 30min); My Tho (2hr–2hr 30min).

Chau Doc to: Can Tho (2hr 30min); HCMC (5–6hr); Long Xuyen (1hr 15min).

Da Lat to: Buon Ma Thuot (5–6hr); Da Nang (14–17hr); HCMC (5–7hr); Nha Trang (5–6hr).

Da Nang to: Da Lat (14–17hr); Dong Ha (4hr); Hoi An (45min–1hr); Hue (3hr); Nha Trang (12hr); Quang Ngai (3hr–3hr 30min).

Dong Ha to: Hue (2hr 30min); Khe Sanh (3hr).

Hai Phong to: Bai Chay (2hr); Hanoi (2hr); Ninh Binh (3hr).

Hanoi to: Bai Chay (3hr–3hr 30min); Hai Phong (2hr); Hue (16–17hr); Lang Son (3hr); Mai Chau (4hr); Ninh Binh (2hr); Son La (7–10hr).

Ha Tien to: Can Tho (5–6hr); HCMC (8hr); Long Xuyen (4hr); Rach Gia (3hr).

Ho Chi Minh City to: Buon Ma Thuot (7–8hr); Can Tho (4hr); Chau Doc (6hr); Da Lat (5–7hr); Da Nang (21hr); Hanoi (42hr); Ha Tien (8hr); Hue (27hr); Mui Ne (4hr); My Tho (1hr 30min); Nha Trang (9hr); Rach Gia (5–6hr); Vung Tau (2hr).

Hoi An to: Da Nang (45min–1hr); Quang Ngai (3hr).

Hue to: Da Nang (3hr); Dong Ha (2hr); Hanoi (16–17hr).

Khe Sanh to: Dong Ha (3hr); Lao Bao (40min).

Lao Cai to: Sa Pa (1hr–1hr 30min).

Long Xuyen to: Chau Doc (1hr 15min); Ha Tien (4hr); HCMC (5hr); Rach Gia (2hr).

Mong Cai to: Hanoi (5hr 30min–6hr); Hong Gai (5–6hr).

Mui Ne to: HCMC (4hr); Nha Trang (6hr).

My Tho to: Can Tho (2hr–2hr 30min); Cholon, HCMC (1hr 30min); My Thuan Bridge (1hr–1hr 30min).

Nha Trang to: Buon Ma Thuot (4hr); Da Lat (5–6hr); Da Nang (12hr); Hanoi (32hr); HCMC (9hr); Hue (17hr).

Ninh Binh to: Hai Phong (3hr); Hanoi (2hr).

Quang Ngai to: Da Nang (3hr–3hr 30min); Nha Trang (8hr).

Vinh to: Dong Ha (5hr 30min–7hr); Dong Hoi (4hr); Hue (11–12hr); Ninh Binh (4hr); Thanh Hoa (3hr).

Vinh Long to: Sa Dec (40min).

Vung Tau to: Ba Ria (40min); Da Lat (7–8hr); HCMC (2hr); Hue (25–26hr); Nha Trang (10–11hr).

Trains

Da Nang to: Hanoi (6 daily; 12–19hr); HCMC (6 daily; 15hr–23hr); Hue (7 daily; 2hr 30min–4hr 40min); Nha Trang (6 daily; 9hr–12hr).

Dong Ha to: Hanoi (6 daily; 11–14hr); Hue (7 daily; 1hr–1hr 20min).

Hanoi to: Beijing, China (2 weekly; 45hrs); Da Nang (6 daily; 12–19hr); Dong Dang (3 daily; 4–6hr); Dong Ha (6 daily; 11–14hr); Hai Phong (3 daily; 1hr 40min–2hr 50min); HCMC (6 daily; 30–41hr); Hue (7 daily; 11hr–16hr); Lao Cai (4 daily; 7hr 30min–10hr 15min); Nha Trang (6 daily; 23hr–34hr); Ninh Binh (6 daily; 2hr 15min–4hr); Vinh (6 daily; 5hr–6hr 40min).

Ho Chi Minh City to: Da Nang (6 daily; 15hr–23hr); Hanoi (6 daily; 30–41hr); Hue (6 daily; 17hr 40min–24hr 30min); Nha Trang (7 daily; 6hr 20min–10hr); Ninh Binh (4 daily; 34hr 40min–36hr); Quang Ngai (5 daily; 14hr–18hr 30min); Vinh (6 daily; 24hr 30min–35hr 30min).

Hue to: Da Nang (7 daily; 2hr 30min–4hr 40min); Dong Ha (7 daily; 1hr–1hr 20min); Hanoi (4 daily; 12hr 30min–16hr 30min); HCMC (6 daily; 17hr 40min–24hr 30min); Nha Trang (6 daily; 11hr 30min–26hr 20min); Ninh Binh (4 daily; 13hr).

Lao Cai to: Hanoi (4 daily; 7hr 30min–10hr 15min).

Nha Trang to: Da Nang (6 daily; 8hr 30min–13hr); Hanoi (6 daily; 23hr–34hr); HCMC (7 daily; 6hr 20min–10hr); Hue (6 daily; 11hr 30min–26hr 20min).

Ninh Binh to: Hanoi (6 daily; 2hr 15min–4hr); Hue (4 daily; 13hr).

Hydrofoils

Hai Phong to: Cat Ba Island (3–6 daily; 45min–1hr); Mong Cai (1 daily; 4hr).
Ha Long (Bai Chay) to: Mong Cai (2 daily; 3hr).
Ho Chi Minh City to: Vung Tau (9 daily; 1hr 15min).
Mong Cai to: Ha Long (Bai Chay; 2 daily; 3hr); Hai Phong (1 daily; 4hr).
Vung Tau to: HCMC (9 daily; 1hr 15min).

Ferries

Cat Ba to: Hai Phong (2 daily; 2hr 30min).
Hai Phong to: Ha Long (Hong Gai; 2 daily; 2hr); Cat Ba (2 daily; 2hr 30min).
Ha Long (Ba Chay) to: Hai Phong (1 daily, 1hr).
Rach Gia to: Phu Quoc Island (1 daily; 7–8hr).

Flights

Buon Ma Thuot to: Da Nang (7 weekly; 1hr 10min); Hanoi (3 weekly via Da Lat; 6hr); HCMC (7 weekly; 55min).
Da Lat to: Hanoi (7 weekly; 1hr 40min); HCMC (7 daily; 40min).
Da Nang to: Buon Ma Thuot (6 weekly; 1hr 10min); Hanoi (3 daily; 1hr 10min); HCMC (1–2 daily; 1hr 10min); Nha Trang (3 weekly; 1hr 20min).
Hanoi to: Da Nang (3 daily; 1hr 15min–1 hr 45min); Dien Bien Phu (1 daily; 1hr); HCMC (10 daily; 1hr 45min); Hue (2-3 daily; 1hr 10min); Nha Trang (1 daily; 1hr 40min).
Ho Chi Minh City to: Buon Ma Thuot (1 daily; 1hr); Da Lat (1 daily; 40min); Da Nang (1 daily; 45min); Hai Phong (5 weekly; 2hr–3hr 20min); Hanoi (10 weekly; 1hr 45min); Hue (1 daily; 1hr 20min); Nha Trang (1 daily; 1hr 5min).
Hue to: HCMC (1 daily; 1hr 20min).
Nha Trang to: Da Nang (1 daily; 1hr 15min); Hanoi (1 daily; 1hr 40min); HCMC (1 daily;1hr 5min).
Rach Gia to: HCMC (5 weekly; 2hr 40min).

Rough Guides advertiser

STA TRAVEL

small print and Index

A Rough Guide to Rough Guides

In the summer of 1981, Mark Ellingham, a recent graduate from Bristol University, was travelling round Greece and couldn't find a guidebook that really met his needs. On the one hand there were the student guides, insistent on saving every last cent, and on the other the heavyweight cultural tomes whose authors seemed to have spent more time in a research library than lounging away the afternoon at a taverna or on the beach.

In a bid to avoid getting a job, Mark and a small group of writers set about creating their own guidebook. It was a guide to Greece that aimed to combine a journalistic approach to description with a thoroughly practical approach to travellers' needs – a guide that would incorporate culture, history and contemporary insights with a critical edge, together with up-to-date, value-for-money listings. Back in London, Mark and the team finished their Rough Guide, as they called it, and talked Routledge into publishing the book.

That first *Rough Guide to Greece*, published in 1982, was a student scheme that became a publishing phenomenon. The immediate success of the book – with numerous reprints and a Thomas Cook prize shortlisting – spawned a series that rapidly covered dozens of destinations. Rough Guides had a ready market among low-budget backpackers, but soon also acquired a much broader and older readership that relished Rough Guides' wit and inquisitiveness as much as their enthusiastic, critical approach. Everyone wants value for money, but not at any price.

Rough Guides soon began supplementing the "rougher" information about hostels and low-budget listings with the kind of detail on restaurants and quality hotels that independent-minded visitors on any budget might expect, whether on business in New York or trekking in Thailand.

These days the guides – distributed worldwide by the Penguin Group – offer recommendations from shoestring to luxury and cover more than 200 destinations around the globe, including almost every country in the Americas and Europe, more than half of Africa and most of Asia and Australasia. Our ever-growing team of authors and photographers is spread all over the world, particularly in Europe, the USA and Australia.

In 1994, we published the *Rough Guide to World Music* and *Rough Guide to Classical Music*; and a year later the *Rough Guide to the Internet*. All three books have become benchmark titles in their fields – which encouraged us to expand into other areas of publishing, mainly around popular culture. Rough Guides now publish:

- Travel guides to more than 200 worldwide destinations
- Dictionary phrasebooks to 22 major languages
- History guides ranging from Ireland to Islam
- Maps printed on rip-proof and waterproof Polyart™ paper
- Music guides running the gamut from Opera to Elvis
- Restaurant guides to London, New York and San Francisco
- Reference books on topics as diverse as the Weather and Shakespeare
- Sports guides from Formula 1 to Man Utd
- Pop culture books from *Lord of the Rings* to Cult TV
- World Music CDs in association with World Music Network

Visit **www.roughguides.com** to see our latest publications.

Rough Guide credits

Text editor: Keith Drew
Layout: Dan May
Cartography: Katie Lloyd-Jones
Picture editor: Jj Luck
Production: Katherine Owers
Proofreader: Amanda Jones
Cover design: Chloë Roberts

Editorial: London Kate Berens, Claire Saunders, Geoff Howard, Ruth Blackmore, Gavin Thomas, Polly Thomas, Richard Lim, Clifton Wilkinson, Alison Murchie, Sally Schafer, Karoline Densley, Andy Turner, Ella O'Donnell, Keith Drew, Edward Aves, Nikki Birrell, Helen Marsden, Joe Staines, Duncan Clark, Peter Buckley, Matthew Milton, Daniel Crewe; **New York** Andrew Rosenberg, Richard Koss, Steven Horak, AnneLise Sorensen, Amy Hegarty, Hunter Slaton
Design & Pictures: **London** Simon Bracken, Dan May, Diana Jarvis, Mark Thomas, Jj Luck, Harriet Mills, Chloë Roberts; **Delhi** Madhulita Mohapatra, Umesh Aggarwal, Ajay Verma, Jessica Subramanian, Amit Verma, Ankur Guha
Production: Julia Bovis, Sophie Hewat, Katherine Owers
Cartography: **London** Maxine Repath, Ed Wright, Katie Lloyd-Jones; **Delhi** Manish Chandra, Rajesh Chhibber, Jai Prakash Mishra, Ashutosh Bharti, Rajesh Mishra, Animesh Pathak, Jasbir Sandhu, Karobi Gogoi
Online: **New York** Jennifer Gold, Suzanne Welles, Kristin Mingrone; **Delhi** Manik Chauhan, Narender Kumar, Shekhar Jha, Rakesh Kumar
Marketing & Publicity: **London** Richard Trillo, Niki Hanmer, David Wearn, Demelza Dallow, Louise Maher; **New York** Geoff Colquitt, Megan Kennedy, Milena Perez; **Delhi** Reem Khokhar
Custom publishing and foreign rights: Philippa Hopkins
Manager India: Punita Singh
Series editor: Mark Ellingham
Reference Director: Andrew Lockett
PA to Managing and Publishing Directors: Megan McIntyre
Publishing Director: Martin Dunford
Managing Director: Kevin Fitzgerald

Publishing information

This third edition published August 2005 by
Rough Guides Ltd,
80 Strand, London WC2R 0RL
345 Hudson St, 4th Floor,
New York, NY 10014, USA
Distributed by the Penguin Group
Penguin Books Ltd,
80 Strand, London WC2R 0RL
Penguin Putnam, Inc.
375 Hudson Street, NY 10014, USA
Penguin Group (Australia)
250 Camberwell Road, Camberwell
Victoria 3124, Australia
Penguin Books Canada Ltd,
10 Alcorn Avenue, Toronto, Ontario,
Canada M4V 1E4
Penguin Group (New Zealand)
Cnr Rosedale and Airborne Roads
Albany, Auckland, New Zealand

Typeset in Bembo and Helvetica to an original design by Henry Iles.
Printed in Italy by Legoprint

1256pp includes index
A catalogue record for this book is available from the British Library

ISBN 1-84353-437-1

1 3 5 7 9 8 6 4 2

Help us update

We've gone to a lot of effort to ensure that the third edition of **The Rough Guide to South East Asia** is accurate and up to date. However, things change – places get "discovered", opening hours are notoriously fickle, restaurants and rooms raise prices or lower standards. If you feel we've got it wrong or left something out, we'd like to know, and if you can remember the address, the price, the time, the phone number, so much the better.

We'll credit all contributions, and send a copy of the next edition (or any other Rough Guide if you prefer) for the best letters. Everyone who writes to us and isn't already a subscriber will receive a copy of our full-colour thrice-yearly newsletter. Please mark letters: "**Rough Guide South East Asia Update**" and send to: Rough Guides, 80 Strand, London WC2R 0RL, or Rough Guides, 4th Floor, 345 Hudson St, New York, NY 10014. Or send an email to **mail@roughguides.com**

Have your questions answered and tell others about your trip at **www.roughguides.atinfopop.com**

Acknowledgements

The authors would like to thank the following:

Russell Briggs Thanks go to the following people for help and advice during my travels around the Nusa Tenggara, Kalimantan and Sulawesi: Gunawan on Sumbawa, for his motorbike; Mr Ali on Sumba, for his warm hospitality; Monal in Sulawesi, for some great practical information; and Steve, for his excellent reading tips.

David Dalton Thanks and love as always to Giselle and Bridget. Flying around the Philippines was hassle-free thanks to the sterling work of all the people at SEAIR. Others who have contributed in one way or another and to whom I am grateful include: John Walsh of Press Association, Bettina Walsh of Qatar Airways, Lynne Palma of *Philippine Tatler*, and John Shepherd in Switzerland.

Ron Emmons First and foremost, special thanks to Doss Saroun and Chap Chamroeun from Siem Reap for their tireless efforts. Also, thanks to Jim Heston, Matt Jacobson (both in Phnom Penh) and Gordon Sharpless (in Siem Reap); Joe Putek in Kompong Cham and Mr T in Stung Treng; and in Banlung, Mr Leng and Si Savet. Finally, in the south, thanks to Moung Vivath in Kampot, and Bert and Leon Wigchert in Sihanoukville.

Paul Gray Thanks to Joe De Souza for his invaluable help and comradeship.

Steve Martin Special thanks go to Benjamin Sirirat, Linda McIntosh, Angeline Thangaperakasam, John & Narisa Murray, Liz Younn, Alex Tan, Jack Barton, Karishma Vyas and Richard Lim.

Lesley Reader Enormous thanks to all the following for expertise, calmness and patience beyond measure; Hasan Nur, Ketut Lagun, Made Wijana, Wayan Artana and Yopi.

Lucy Ridout Thanks to Tom Vater and Ferenc Fulmer for their updates.

Andrew Stone Thanks to Joanne Hodson from the HKTB and Ed Peters.

Carl Thompson In Saigon: Steven Dang and Kim Tran at Delta Adventure Tours; Linh Huynh; Mr Duong Nghiep Khanh at Sinh Café; Tung Nguyen at Threeland Travel; and the staff at Sinhbalo Adventures. In Can Tho: Mr Duc at the Xuan Mai.

Jeroen van Marle Thanks to Hahn An Tran, Claire Sutherland, Hans Christian, and the guy who patched up my Minsk motorbike after it exploded.

Readers' letters

Thanks to all the readers who have taken the time to write in with comments and suggestions (and apologies if we've inadvertently omitted or misspelt anyone's name):

Allen Ackerman, Esmé Allen & Stuart Foulkes, Martin Allen, Kiersten Aschauer, Ed Ashby, Karen Aslett, Tony Awerner, K Babu, Robert Bachweizen, Jatinder Bahia, Lisa Barley, David Barnes, Maarten Bax, Julie Baxter, Jane Bell, Alison Berry, Graham Biles, Barrie Lie-Birchall, Rubert Blum, Sharon Bolton, Julia Bonn, John Boutell, Alex Borione, Chuck Bradley, Norbert Braun, H van den Broek, Adrian R Brown, Thomas Brown, Nicholas Bull, Anna Burgess, Steve Burroughs, Hans Buyl, Fionnuala Callaghan, Denise Callahan, Leanna Cashen & Gareth Evans, Steve Chapman, Julia Charles, Vanessa Cheeseham & Gilbert Dedominicis, Chris, Chuanhui, James Clarke, Yoav Cohen, Gwyn Cole, Katie Collins, Karin Conroy, Joseph Copeland, Frances Cornford, Paolo Cortini, Paul Costa, Brian Cox, Holly Crofton & Jamie Dixon, Peter Cunningham, Justin Dane, Lorraine Davies, Debbie, Alex Diez, Matthew Dillon, Bob Dixon, Mark J Dodds, Ron Doering, Barry Doherty, Don Dunlop, Sean Dwyer, Kristin Eichhorn, Ursula Esser, Kate Fewins, Sophy Fisher, D Fletcher, Leanne Fogarty, Jim Fogden, John & Marilyn Francis, Mark French, Tim Frier, Jelle de Gee, Bart van Geleuken & Sakia Ligthart, Maggy Goossens, Quinton & Irene Gradwell, David Granger, Gerald Haberfellner, Gary & Luke Hampson, Marcus Hans, Tony Harrould, Bettina Hartas, Linda Hartley, Kevin Harvey, Noel Hathorn, Christian Hawkins, John Heebink, Anne Held, Alex Herrmann & Isabelle Rzehulka, Alan Hickey, George van der Hilst. Gerard Holohan, Emma Hooijberg & Flo Herold, Anne and Kenneth Hoy, Atle Ingebrigtsen, William Ingram, Michelle Jarman, Dorothy Jekill, Sarah Jhirad, Miriam Jones, Jennifer Jordan, Mark Kater & Esther Wolfs, Peter Kempinsky & Katarina Ulfstdotter, Jason Kennedy, Jim Kennedy & Julie Swettenham, Paul D Kester, David Kitching, Kornelis Klevering, Eric Kloor, E Knott, Ian Knowlson & Ragnhild P. Sandvik, Jesse Koche, Anne Krawic, Wenche Kristoffersen, Andrew Ktoris, Kajanga Kulatunga, Julien Lake, Sander Lommertzen, S Laurence, Ann Marie Lee, Paul J Lee, Howell Lewis, Willem Lindeijer, Josephine Lindop, N Lipp, Arjen van Loenen and Edith Beerdsen, Iris Lohrengel, Fatima

Lopes & Vasco Silva, Hien Luong, Matt and Donna Maciejewski, Sarah Martinsson, Gavin Mason & Stephen Penning, Rod McCormick, Lyn McCoy, Chris McCullough, Larry McGuirk, Penny McKenzie, Donald Mcvean, Matt Mecke, Tony Messenger, Dafydd Meurig, Robin Miles, Ron Morris, Fred Moss, Michael Mueller, Keith Mundy, Jane Murphy, KP Narayan, Sheila Nelson, Neil Noe & Sara Ladewig, Therese Nordenskar, Tessa Lyander Nordsten, Heidi Nunn & Darren Hern, Maureen O'Keefe, P John O'Neill, Thomas Ormes, Peter Peirson, Timothy Pike, Felix Preston, Alexandra Pitman, N Platt, Sara Platt, Jan Plihal, Rowena Poston, Elsie Rasmussen, Helen Read, Heather Rhodes, Andreas Rieck, Anna Ritchie & Sean Quigley, Christine Ross, Bill Ryan, HH Saffery, Jackie & Pete Sanders, Vivian Schatz, Peter Schubert, Marc Schneider, Steve Scott, Matt Sheriff, Debbie Slonowsky, Kate Smith, Maya Smith, Michael Smith, Jonny Söderström, Thomas Sourmail, Ruud Spek, Kerry Start & Tony Shilling, Rachel Stevens, Hoe Yen Tam, Anna Taylor, Dawn & Neil Taylor, Stephen Taylor, Les Thompson, Tony, Filip Vandamme, Laura Vella, Pete & Nikki Vesey, Clive Walker, Colin Waller, Bjorn & Karen Weynants, Alex White, Lennart Widell, Melanie Wielens, Maja Wildisen, Joe Willard & Ginette Morley, Helen Williams, Jody Williams, Michael Williams, Simon Williams, Timmy Williams, MT Willis, Jenny Wilson, Brendt Wohlberg, Matthias Zehner.

Photo credits

Cover

Main front picture: Monks collecting Lotus flowers, Thailand © Lawrenceworcester.com
Small front top picture: Elephant, Phuket, Thailand © Getty
Small front lower picture: Cebu, The Philippines © Alamy
Back top picture: Limestone tower, Ha Long Bay, Vietnam © Getty
Back lower picture: Orang-utan, Malaysia © Getty

Title page

Borocay, The Philippines © Robert Francis/Robert Harding

Full page

Angkor Wat, Siem Reap, Cambodia © Jon Arnold Images/Alamy

Introduction

Sing monks' robes drying, Wat Phra, Chiang Mai, Thailand © David Sanger photography/Alamy
Gunung Batukau, Bali © Lucy Ridout
Woman snorkelling underwater near Pulau Bunaken, Sulawesi, Indonesia © Mark Lewis/Alamy
Rickshaw, Thailand © Wilmar Photography.com/Alamy
Ancient Buddhist temple of Borobudur, Indonesia © Petr Svarc / Alamy
Thanon Khao San, Bangkok © Neil Setchfield

Things not to miss

1 Sunset on the Mekong © Beverley Palmer
2 Rice terraces, Banaue © John S. Callahan/Photo Resource Hawaii
3 Walkway at Taman Negara © Nigel Bowen Morras/Travel Ink
4 The south peak of Mount Kinabalu, Sabah © Tourism Malaysia
5 Hong Kong City skyline from Kowloon © Kevin Wilkinson/Alamy
6 Casino Lisboa, Macau © Jeroen van Marle
7 Painter, Ubud © Rofl Rumarson/Robert Harding
8 Surfing at G-Land, Indonesia © John Helper
9 Orangutans eating bananas at Bukit Lawang © Khaled Kassem/Alamy
10 Silks © Ron Emmons
11 Ko Nang Yuan islets, Ko Tao © John S. Callahan/Alamy
12 Torajan funeral effigy © Trip
13 Monks at Angkor Wat © Chris Lisle/Corbis
14 Hawker stalls in the Lau Pa Sat building, Chinatown, Singapore © Johan Furusjö/Alamy
15 Diver and turtle © Lawson Wood/Ocean Eye Films
16 Ao Phra Nang, Krabi, Thailand © Nicholas Pitt/Alamy
17 Dim Sum, Hong Kong © Tim Hall/Axiom
18 Air Batang Bay, Pulau Tioman, Malaysia © Robert Harding Picture Library Ltd/Alamy
19 Gunung Rinjani, Indonesia © Lesley Reader
20 Ha Long Bay, Vietnam © Jim Holmes/Axiom
21 Plain of Jars, Laos © Steve Davey/La BelleAurore
22 Glass mosaics at Wat Xiang Thong, Luang Phabang, Laos © Nevada Wier/Corbis
23 Women from the Red Dao Dzao hilltribe, Sapa, Vietnam © Hugh Sitton Photography/Alamy
24 Old Quarter, Hanoi, Vietnam © Michael S. Yamashita/Corbis
25 Gili Islands © Sang Man
26 Hue railway station © Mark Henley/IMPACT
27 White Beach, Boracay, Visayas, Philippines © Nick Hanna/Alamy
28 Tea plantation, Cameron Highlands, Malaysia © Crazy Zky/Alamy
29 Forbidden Purple City, Hue, Vietnam © Tibor Bognar/Alamy
30 Relief carving, Prambanan, Java, Indonesia © Robert Harding Picture Library Ltd/Alamy
31 Khao Sok National Park © Craig Lovell/Eagle Visions Photography/Alamy
32 Limestone karst cliffs, Nam Xong River, Vang Viang, Laos © La Belle Aurore/Alamy
33 Wat Phra Keo in The Grand Palace, Bangkok, Thailand © Steve Allen/Alamy
34 Mekong River © Rolf Richardson/Robert Harding
35 River Kwai, Thailand © Nik Wheeler/Corbis

Black and whites

Omar Ali Saifuddien Mosque, Brunei © Jeremy Horner/Alamy (p.80)
Sihanoukville, Cambodia © Jeroen Krol / Alamy (p.100)
South Gate leading to Angkor Thom, Cambodia © Alison Wright/Corbis (p.151)
Trolley of buns © Robert Harding (p.184)
Tian Tan Buddha, Lantau Island, Hong Kong © Hing-Keung So/Corbis (p.225)
Komodo Dragon, Komodo, Indonesia © Stuart Westmorland/Corbis (p.232)
Prambanan © T. Bognar/Trip (p.296)
Bromo-Tengger-Semeru National Park, Java, Indonesia © Albrecht G. Schaefer/Corbis (p.309)
Farmers working terraced fields, near Ubud, Indonesia © Wolfgang Kaehler/Corbis (p.383)
Buddha statues in the Pak Ou Caves, with the Mekong River behind, near Luang Prabang, Laos © La Belle Aurore/Alamy (p.496)
Macau © Jeroen van Marle (p.588)
Pulau Tioman © Abbie Ennock/Travel Ink (p.610)
Georgetown temple, Malaysia © R. Nichols/Trip (p.661)
Mount Kinabalu, Malaysia © imageshop – zefa visual media uk ltd/Alamy (p.737)
Dancers perform at the Ati-Atihan Festival in downtown Kalibo, Philippines © Paul A. Souders/Corbis (p.746)
The front bonnet of a jeepney, Manila, Philippines © Albrecht G. Schaefer/Corbis (p.810)
Shopping along Orchard Road, Singapore © Henry Westheim/Alamy (p.886)
Ao Phra Ae beach, Ko Lanta, Thailand © Nicholas Pitt/Alamy (p.934)
Detail of Colossi of Suriyaphop, Bangkok © Macduff Everton/Corbis (p.975)
Elephant and mahout near Chiang Mai, Thailand © D. Maybury/Trip (p.1017)
Limestone cliffs, Khao Sok National Park © Craig Lovell/Eagle Visions Photography/Alamy (p.1074)
Ha Long Bay, Vietnam © Ron Emmons (p.1100)
Mekong River during the monsoon, Can Tho, Vietnam © Tim Page/Corbis (p.1151)
Cham tower © Ron Emmons (p.1186)

Index

Map entries are in colour.

Abbreviations		
Brunei (B)	Macau (Ma)	Thailand (T)
Cambodia (C)	Malaysia (M)	Vietnam (V)
Hong Kong (H)	Philippines (P)	
Indonesia (I)	Singapore (S)	

A

B

C

D

E

F

G

H

INDEX

I

J

K

L

INDEX

M

N

O

P

Q

R

Q

R

INDEX

X

Y

Z

INDEX

Map symbols

maps are listed in the full index using coloured text

International boundary
State boundary
Chapter boundary
Motorway/expressway
Main road
Minor road
Unpaved road
Pedestrianized road
One-way street
Steps
Path
Track
Railway
Ferry route
Waterway
Wall
Airport
Point of interest
Temple
Khmer temple
Chinese pagoda
Mosque
Wat
Synagogue
Monument
Museum
Statue
Fort
Ruins
Border crossing point
Cave

Peak
Mountains
Volcano
Spring
Waterfall
Surfing beach
Snorkelling
Lighthouse
Gardens/fountain
Golf course
Petrol station
Transport stop
Metro station
Accommodation
Restaurant/bar
Campsite
Information office
Telephone office
Internet access
Hospital
Post office
Building
Church
Market
Stadium
Park
Beach
Forest
Swamp
Christian cemetery
Muslim cemetery